BROMLEY'S FAMILY LAW

LNM — Standard.
FMLY
BRO

BROMLEY'S
FAMILY LAW

Birmingham ∣ Bristol ∣ Chester ∣ Guildford ∣ London ∣ Manchester ∣ Leeds

OXFORD

OXFORD
UNIVERSITY PRESS

Great Clarendon Street, Oxford, OX2 6DP
United Kingdom

Oxford University Press is a department of the University of Oxford.
It furthers the University's objective of excellence in research, scholarship,
and education by publishing worldwide. Oxford is a registered trade mark of
Oxford University Press in the UK and in certain other countries

Eighth edition 1992
Ninth edition 1998
Tenth edition 2007

Impression: 1

Published in the United States of America by Oxford University Press
198 Madison Avenue, New York, NY 10016, United States of America

British Library Cataloguing in Publication Data
Data available

Library of Congress Control Number: 2014940645

ISBN 978-0-19-958040-8

Printed in Great Britain by
Ashford Colour Press Ltd, Gosport, Hampshire

PREFACE

We begin our preface to this, the eleventh edition of *Bromley's Family Law,* by recording with great sadness that Professor Peter Bromley passed away in 2013. As respectively a former co-author, and a former student, of Peter's, we know how much our insights into family law were enriched and expanded by his immense learning and his rigorously high standards, which were always coupled with good humour and kindness. We shall miss him enormously, and both the discipline of family law and the United Kingdom academic community have lost a towering and inspiring figure.

There has never been a period in the book's history since Peter published his first edition in 1957 during which the pace of developments in family law has been other than relentless, both through significant legislation and a seemingly never-ending cascade of judicial decisions, often at the highest level. This edition reflects the most recent changes, through a fundamental re-organisation of the structure of the book, involving in particular a division of the chapters into more manageable and discrete topic areas, especially in relation to parental responsibility, which is now discussed in Chapters 10 and 11; public child law, which now forms Chapters 15 to 18; and financial remedies after divorce, in Chapters 22 and 23. We have also introduced new chapters focused on cohabitation, the legal position of children and international child law and ensured that appropriate attention is paid to the growing significance of human rights jurisprudence throughout.

Our last edition in 2007 marked what we fairly confidently thought would represent a long-standing landmark in family law reform, the enactment of the Civil Partnership Act 2004. It seems astonishing that this has now been largely superseded by the Marriage (Same Sex Couples) Act 2013, which went through Parliament with remarkably little real opposition. While the 2004 Act involved an extensive and laborious trawl through the statute book to capture and amend every mention of 'spouse', 'husband' and 'wife', the 2013 Act takes an admirably concise and efficient approach to ensuring that those terms now include, as appropriate, married partners of the same sex. There is clearly scope for further reform, either by extending civil partnership to heterosexual couples or abolishing it entirely, while the protection of those religious groups opposed to same-sex marriage from being required to permit gay and lesbian couples to marry according to their rites may be challenged in the future, but no one can under-estimate the significance of the change to the social understanding of 'marriage' in this jurisdiction wrought by the 2013 Act. We discuss the changes brought about by the 2013 Act in Chapter 2 and throughout the book.

Only slightly less ground breaking are the further changes made by the Human Fertilisation and Embryology Act 2008 to the attribution of parenthood to those who have used assisted reproduction to create a child. The extension of parental status to same-sex couples marks another fundamental shift in the conception (so to speak) of parenthood. While the legislation might be regarded as still promoting a two-parent norm and perpetuating the law's problematic course between genetic and social parenthood, it nonetheless betokens the same liberal tolerance of alternative family forms as the 2013 Act which is a world away from the regime which Peter set out in his first edition over half a century ago. We consider the amendments in Chapter 8.

The Children Act 1989 has been the subject of further reform, possibly of a more far-reaching nature than previous amendments which focused on re-structuring and minor changes to particular provisions and Parts of the statute. The Children and Families Act 2014 could be said to mark a more fundamental 're-set' of the legal approach to parenting, driven by the recommendations of the Family Justice Review chaired by David Norgrove and published in 2011, particularly in the context of family breakdown. The new Act makes the first legislative inroad into the 'welfare principle' since 1989 by introducing a presumption that involvement of each parent in the life of the child concerned will further that child's welfare. It also attempts, yet again, to reduce the 'win/lose' character of parenting disputes by abolishing 'residence' and 'contact' orders and instead providing for 'child arrangements orders' which will 'regulate' the arrangements relating to with whom a child is to live, spend time or otherwise have contact. Given that in popular culture, orders making such arrangements stubbornly continue to be known as 'custody' and 'access', it will be interesting to see whether these attempts to mould social attitudes and beliefs about the appropriate way to bring up a child when parents have separated are any more successful than previous reform efforts. We explore how the law has been amended and consider its implications in particular in Chapters 12 and 14.

Legislative amendments in other parts of the subject, ranging from the introduction of forced marriage protection orders and, recently, the criminalisation of breach of such orders, to yet another attempt to make the child support system effective—largely by abandoning most parents to making their own arrangements and dissuading them from actually resorting to the child support scheme itself—represent two polarised ways of regulating family ties. On the one hand, legitimate concern for vulnerable members of particular minority communities appears to have produced a firm assertion of the prerogative of the state to control and deter families from dictating marital choices against the wishes of the child and contrary to the mores of the majority community. We examine these and other attempts to deter and reduce domestic abuse in Chapter 6. On the other hand, the message that 'family based arrangements' are the correct way of handling the financial support of children when parents do not live together reflects a laissez faire orientation towards the benefit of private ordering and the withdrawal of state coercion from enforcing family obligations. We discuss the attempts to reformulate child support and the wider duty to maintain in Chapter 21.

That withdrawal of interest in, and support for, the assertion of legal rights and duties through the family justice system probably reflects the other most significant development since the last edition of this work. Ironically, it comes despite the final creation, forty years after its most developed exposition by the Finer Committee on One Parent Families in 1974, of a unified 'family court'. This has been achieved in a remarkably short space of time after the enactment of the Crime and Courts Act 2013 through the flexible joining up of the family proceedings, county court and High Court jurisdictions in family matters. While one might have thought the establishment of the family court meant that at last, there is a developed family justice system available for those facing family disputes, it coincides with the dismantling of the legal aid system which had survived, albeit in steadily more attenuated form, since 1949 and the loss of legal aid for most private family law proceedings. The consequential increase in the number of litigants in person appearing in the family courts may be a temporary phenomenon pending the message finally sinking in that those family courts are not intended as a routine first port of call for the resolution of family disputes. Rather, they are for those in such urgent and serious need of legal redress that they can demonstrate either satisfaction of the criteria based on being at risk of violence and continue to receive some public funding for their case, or a determination to go through the stress and difficulty of representing themselves in court or to incur heavy expenses in order to obtain legal representation. Additionally, of course, the courts remain available to those who can afford to spend sometimes eye-watering amounts of money on litigation, usually over post-divorce financial arrangements. We highlight the changes to legal aid and other procedural changes (including the introduction of stronger 'case management' mechanisms, most notably through the imposition of a 26 week limit on the duration of care proceedings) in Chapter 1, and consider their ramifications throughout the book.

The law on what used to be called 'ancillary relief' on divorce and is now referred to as 'financial remedies', together with the law governing the rights of cohabiting couples, now represent the last major areas of family law which await thoroughgoing reform. The Law Commission's major reports setting out detailed proposals for a new scheme for dealing with property and finance when cohabiting couples separate (and their work on inheritance and intestacy when a spouse or cohabiting partner dies), and on the enforceability of marital property agreements (popularly known as 'pre-nups'), are discussed in depth in Chapters 23, 24 and 25.

The 'internationalisation' of family law continues to have major effects on the shape of the law, particularly in relation to jurisdiction, recognition and enforcement. The European Union now impacts increasingly directly on the content of the rules to be applied, most notably through the Brussels II Revised Regulation, and is to a considerable extent dwarfing the effects of other international instruments emanating from either The Hague, such as the International Child Abduction Convention, or the United Nations. The growing volume of case-law interpreting the extent and effects of the new rules, emanating from both the Court of Justice of the European Union and the domestic courts, including the House of Lords and Supreme Court, is considered in detail in Chapter 26.

The important case-law developments which either resolve problems, or underscore the urgency of reform of the law, are considered throughout the work. We devote particular attention to the decisions of the House of Lords and later the Supreme Court in *Stack v Dowden* and *Jones v Kernott* in Chapter 5, and to the Supreme Court's decision in *Granatino v Radmacher* in Chapters 21 and 22. The developing jurisprudence on the difficult issue of family relocation, particularly across international borders, is explored in Chapter 14. Public child law decisions, especially those concerning the vexed interpretation of the 'threshold criteria' for obtaining a care or supervision order under the Children Act 1989 s 31(2), including *Re B* and *Re S-B*, and (and not to confuse) *Re B-S* concerning the approach to be taken when considering whether to grant an adoption order, are considered in Chapters 17 and 19. The continuing relevance of wardship and the inherent jurisdiction generally is discussed in Chapter 20.

We have, as always, benefited from discussion of many of the issues covered in this edition with our colleagues at Cardiff Law School, including Cathy Cobley, Julie Doughty, Mervyn Murch, Anne Nutter and Leanne Smith. We are also fortunate members of the 'family' of family law scholars both in this country, particularly our colleagues on the editorial team of the *Child and Family Law Quarterly* and *Family Law* and members of the SLS and SLSA, and further afield, through the Commission on European Family Law and the International Society of Family Law. We are enormously grateful to the staff at Oxford University Press for their unflagging patience, support and understanding. We have also been greatly helped by two exceptional students from Cardiff Law School, Adele Cameron and Ella Carroll, who kindly assisted with, respectively, some of the early identification of necessary updates and amendments, and tracking down citations and references at the proof stage. We thank Cardiff Law School for providing funding assistance for their involvement.

We have sought to take account of developments in the law up to 1 June 2014. Fortunately for us, both the Children and Families Act 2014 and the Inheritance and Trustees' Powers Act 2014 made it onto the statute book in time to be fully included. We have also sought to include later developments where possible.

We are absolutely delighted to dedicate this edition to our respective grandchildren—Madoc Vaughan Lowe John and Benjamin Rhys Chick.

Nigel Lowe
Gillian Douglas
St Swithin's Day, 2014

CONTENTS

Table of statutes   xxiv

Table of cases   lxi

1   INTRODUCTION   1

2   FORMATION OF MARRIAGE AND CIVIL PARTNERSHIP   30

3   DETERMINING THE VALIDITY OF A MARRIAGE OR
    CIVIL PARTNERSHIP   62

4   THE PERSONAL AND PROPERTY CONSEQUENCES OF
    MARRIAGE AND CIVIL PARTNERSHIP   89

5   THE FAMILY HOME   122

6   DOMESTIC VIOLENCE AND ABUSE   164

7   DIVORCE AND DISSOLUTION   211

8   PARENTS AND GUARDIANS   244

9   THE LEGAL POSITION OF CHILDREN   296

10 WHAT IS PARENTAL RESPONSIBILITY?   330

11 WHO HAS PARENTAL RESPONSIBILITY?   368

12 THE WELFARE PRINCIPLE   397

13 THE VOICE OF THE CHILD   445

14 THE COURT'S POWERS TO MAKE ORDERS UNDER PART II
    OF THE CHILDREN ACT 1989   479

15 CHILDREN AND LOCAL AUTHORITIES   552

16 CHILDREN AND LOCAL AUTHORITIES: INVESTIGATION
    OF CHILD ABUSE   579

17 CHILDREN AND LOCAL AUTHORITIES: CARE AND
    SUPERVISION PROCEEDINGS   594

18 CHILDREN AND LOCAL AUTHORITIES: THE POSITION
    OF CHILDREN IN CARE   654

19 ADOPTION AND SPECIAL GUARDIANSHIP   682

20 THE HIGH COURT'S INHERENT POWERS IN RESPECT
    OF CHILDREN   741

21 FINANCIAL OBLIGATIONS TO MEMBERS OF THE FAMILY   773

22 FINANCIAL REMEDIES ON DIVORCE, DISSOLUTION,
    NULLITY AND SEPARATION: THE COURT'S POWERS   826

23 FINANCIAL REMEDIES: PRINCIPLES AND ASSESSMENT 867

24 COHABITATION 934

25 INHERITANCE AND INTESTACY 959

26 INTERNATIONAL ASPECTS OF CHILD LAW 994

Index 1101

DETAILED CONTENTS

Table of statutes   xxiv

Table of cases   lxi

1 INTRODUCTION   1

A. The nature and scope of family life   1
  1. The meaning of 'family'   1
  2. The functions of family law   3

B. Trends in family law   4
  1. Equalisation of legal position of men and women   4
  2. Shift in emphasis from past fault to future needs   5
  3. Shift of attention from adults to children   6
  4. Growing recognition of cohabitation outside marriage   6
  5. Greater recognition of same sex relationships   8
  6. Greater focus on autonomy   9
  7. Private ordering and the withdrawal of legal aid   10
  8. Multi-disciplinary and specialist approaches to family problems   14

C. The family justice system   15
  1. The development of the family court 'system'   15
  2. Pressure for a family court and the *Family Justice Review*   17
  3. The single Family Court   18
  4. Governance and professionalism   19

D. The internationalisation of family law   21
  1. United Nations Convention on the Rights of the Child   22
  2. European Convention on Human Rights   23
  3. Other conventions and international instruments of influence   25

2 FORMATION OF MARRIAGE AND CIVIL PARTNERSHIP   30

A. Introduction   30
  1. Marriage   30
  2. The introduction of civil partnerships   31
  3. The Marriage (Same Sex Couples) Act 2013   33

B. The right to marry   35

C. The nature of marriage   37
  1. Marriage as a contract   37
  2. Marriage as creating status   37
  3. Definition of marriage   38

D. Agreements to marry or form a civil partnership   39
  1. Agreements to marry   39
  2. Civil partnership agreements   40

E. Entry into marriage   40
    1. Capacity to marry   40
    2. Formalities of marriage   47

F. Presumption of marriage   56

G. Entry into a civil partnership   58
    1. Capacity   59
    2. Formalities   60
    3. Conversion of civil partnership into marriage   61

**3 DETERMINING THE VALIDITY OF A MARRIAGE OR CIVIL
PARTNERSHIP**   **62**

A. Introduction   62

B. Declaration as to marital status   62

C. Decree of nullity   63
    1. Historical background   64
    2. The current distinction between void and voidable marriages 66
    3. A void marriage—or no marriage at all?   67

D. Grounds on which a marriage will be void   70
    1. Lack of capacity   71
    2. Formal defects   71
    3. Proposals for reform   73

E. Voidable marriages   73
    1. The unconsummated marriage   73
    2. Lack of consent   76
    3. Mental disorder   82
    4. Venereal disease and pregnancy by another   83
    5. Gender reassignment   83
    6. Bars to relief   84

F. Effect of decree on voidable marriage   85

G. Is there a continuing need for nullity?   86

H. Establishing the validity of a civil partnership   87
    1. Declaration   87
    2. Annulment of a civil partnership   87
    3. Void civil partnerships   87
    4. Voidable civil partnerships   88

**4 THE PERSONAL AND PROPERTY CONSEQUENCES OF
MARRIAGE AND CIVIL PARTNERSHIP**   **89**

A. Introduction   89
    1. The doctrine of unity   90
    2. Consortium   92

B. Personal consequences   94
    1. Use of surname   94
    2. Sexual intercourse   95
    3. Evidence in legal proceedings   96
    4. Contracts   98

        5. Torts   99
        6. Criminal law   100
        7. Citizenship and right to live in the United Kingdom   101
    C. Property consequences of marriage and civil partnership   104
        1. Historical introduction   104
        2. The modern law   108
        3. Reform proposals   119

5   THE FAMILY HOME   122

    A. Introduction   122
    B. Ownership   123
        1. The background to the current law   123
        2. The current law   125
        3. Enforcing the trust   144
        4. Protection of beneficial interests   147
    C. Occupation   151
        1. 'Home rights'   152
        2. Other forms of protected occupation   156
    D. Insolvency and the family home   158
        1. Mortgages and charges   158
        2. Bankruptcy   159
    E. Reform   162

6   DOMESTIC VIOLENCE AND ABUSE   164

    A. Introduction   164
        1. The definition of domestic violence and abuse   164
        2. The scale of domestic abuse   165
        3. Historical developments   166
        4. Government strategy   167
        5. Gender-based abuse as a breach of human rights   168
    B. Protection afforded by the criminal law   169
        1. The criminal justice system   169
        2. The Protection from Harassment Act 1997   173
    C. Civil law remedies   178
        1. The Family Law Act 1996 Part IV   179
        2. Protection from Harassment Act 1997   195
        3. Injunctions in other civil proceedings   196
        4. Forced marriage protection orders   197
        5. Domestic violence protection notices and orders   201
    D. Remedies through housing law   203
        1. Actions in relation to rented properties   203
        2. Seeking help under the homelessness legislation   205
    E. A criminal or civil matter?   209

7   DIVORCE AND DISSOLUTION   211

    A. Introduction   211
        1. Divorce before 1857   212

   2. The Matrimonial Causes Act 1857 212
   3. Extension of the grounds for divorce 212
   4. The Divorce Reform Act 1969 213

B. The Matrimonial Causes Act 1973 214
   1. The substantive law 214
   2. The procedure for obtaining the divorce 226
   3. Reconciliation 229

C. Proposals for reform 230
   1. The Booth Committee on Matrimonial Causes Procedure .. 230
   2. The Law Commission's proposals 231
   3. Divorce under the Family Law Act 1996 234

D. The future of divorce reform 238

E. Dissolution of civil partnership 240

F. Judicial separation and separation orders 241
   1. Judicial separation in marriage 241
   2. Separation in civil partnership 243

8 PARENTS AND GUARDIANS 244

A. Introduction 244

B. Legal parentage 244
   1. Who are the legal parents of a child? 245
   2. Who is the legal mother? 246
   3. Who is the legal father? 248
   4. Female parenthood 256
   5. Overall summary and commentary 257
   6. Establishing or contesting parentage 260
   7. Declarations of parentage 270
   8. Registration of births 271
   9. Discovering genetic parentage 272
  10. The legal significance of parentage 274
  11. Surrogacy agreements 274
  12. Parental orders 277

C. Guardianship 284
   1. The position before the Children Act 1989 284
   2. The current law 286
   3. Distinguishing guardianship from other relationships 293

9 THE LEGAL POSITION OF CHILDREN 296

A. Introduction 296

B. The meaning of 'child' 296

C. The meaning of 'child of the family' 296

D. The child's status 298
   1. Introduction 298
   2. The concept of legitimacy 299
   3. Declarations of status 303
   4. The significance of the child's status 304
   5. Should reference be made to legitimacy and illegitimacy? . 305

E. The changing nature of the parent–child relationship   307
    1. Introduction   307
    2. The initial strength of the father's position   308
    3. The strengthening of the mother's position   311
    4. The increasing recognition of the child's position   312

10 WHAT IS PARENTAL RESPONSIBILITY?   330

    A. Introduction   330
       1. International acceptance of the concept of parental responsibility   330
       2. Contexts in which parental responsibility is relevant   331
    B. The meaning and function of 'parental responsibility'   333
       1. The need to define parental responsibility   333
       2. Can there be a meaningful general definition?   334
       3. Further preliminary observations   336
       4. What parental responsibility comprises   337
       5. Liability for children's acts   363
       6. Liability for interference with parents' and children's rights   366

11 WHO HAS PARENTAL RESPONSIBILITY?   368

    A. Introduction   368
    B. The allocation of parental responsibility at the child's birth   368
       1. The position at the child's birth   368
    C. Acquisition of parental responsibility subsequent to the child's birth   370
       1. Acquisition of parental responsibility by unmarried fathers   370
       2. Acquisition of parental responsibility by female parents who are
          neither married to nor in civil partnership with the mother   385
       3. Acquisition of parental responsibility by step-parents 386
       4. Acquisition of parental responsibility by other individuals   389
       5. Acquisition of parental responsibility by local authorities   390
    D. In respect of whom is there responsibility?   390
    E. Duration of parental responsibility   391
    F. Sharing parental responsibility for a child   392
    G. Effect of third parties acquiring parental responsibility 394
    H. Delegation of parental responsibility   395
    I. Caring for a child without having parental responsibility 395

12 THE WELFARE PRINCIPLE   397

    A. Introduction   397
    B. The paramountcy of the child's welfare   397
       1. The meaning of 'welfare'   398
       2. The meaning of 'paramount'   414
    C. Criticisms of the welfare principle   430
    D. The importance of an ongoing relationship with both parents
       after family separation   432
       1. Background to reform   432
       2. The section 1(2A) presumption   433

E. Delay prima facie prejudicial to the child's welfare   436

F. Orders to be made only where better than no order   438
   1. Introduction and background   438
   2. When section 1(5) applies   439
   3. Applying section 1(5)   440
   4. Form of order   443
   5. The interrelationship of the paramountcy principle and section 1(5) 443
   6. The interrelationship of human rights and section 1(5)   444

13 THE VOICE OF THE CHILD   445

A. Introduction   445

B. The obligation to have regard to the child's views   446
   1. Domestic law   446
   2. International obligations   448

C. How children's views are investigated   451
   1. Cafcass   452
   2. Welfare reports   455
   3. The role of the children's guardian   459

D. The child's direct participation in proceedings   465
   1. Private law proceedings   465
   2. Public law proceedings   470

E. Children as litigants   470
   1. The substantive law   470
   2. The procedure   471

F. The needs for and requirements of a child-friendly family justice system 472
   1. Messages from research   472
   2. Moves to improve the family justice system   474

G. Looking after children's wider interests—the Commissioners for Children 475
   1. Background   475
   2. Overview of the English Commissioner's role   476

14 THE COURT'S POWERS TO MAKE ORDERS UNDER PART II
   OF THE CHILDREN ACT 1989   479

A. Introduction   479
   1. The original scheme of Part II   479
   2. Changes made by the Children and Adoption Act 2006   480
   3. Changes made by the Children and Families Act 2014   481

B. Section 8 orders   485
   1. The powers   485
   2. General restrictions on making section 8 orders   510
   3. Who may apply for section 8 orders?   513
   4. Effect of child arrangements orders   520
   5. When section 8 orders can be made   535
   6. Enforcing section 8 orders   537
   7. Varying and discharging orders   543
   8. Appeals   543

C. Other powers 546
  1. Family assistance orders 546
  2. Section 37 directions 550
D. Some final remarks 551

15 CHILDREN AND LOCAL AUTHORITIES 552

A. Introduction 552
  1. Some basic dilemmas 552
  2. The general role of the courts and local authorities 553
  3. An overview of the development of local authority powers 553
  4. The current law: some key underlying principles 557
B. Local authority support for children and families 559
  1. General duty to children in need 560
  2. Specific duties and powers 562
  3. Accommodating children in need 564
  4. Secure accommodation 572

**16 CHILDREN AND LOCAL AUTHORITIES: INVESTIGATION
OF CHILD ABUSE** 579

A. General duty of investigation under s 47 579
B. Co-operating with other agencies to discharge investigative duties 580
C. Short-term protection 582
  1. Introduction 582
  2. Emergency protection orders 583
  3. Child assessment orders 589
  4. Police protection 592

**17 CHILDREN AND LOCAL AUTHORITIES: CARE AND
SUPERVISION PROCEEDINGS** 594

A. Introduction 594
B. Initiating proceedings 596
  1. Applicants 596
  2. In respect of whom applications may be made 596
  3. Parties 596
C. The threshold criteria 597
  1. Some preliminary observations 597
  2. The criteria 599
D. The welfare stage 625
E. Tackling delay in care proceedings 628
F. Court orders 629
G. Appeals 650
H. Discharge of care orders and discharge and variation of
supervision orders 651

**18 CHILDREN AND LOCAL AUTHORITIES: THE POSITION
OF CHILDREN IN CARE** 654

A. Introduction 654

B. Contact with children in care   654
   1. Introduction   654
   2. The scheme under section 34   655

C. Local authority duties towards 'looked after children'   660

D. Disputing local authority decisions   662
   1. Introduction   662
   2. The complaints procedure   663
   3. Applying to the 'local government ombudsman'   666
   4. Children's Commissioners   666
   5. Wardship and the inherent jurisdiction   667
   6. Seeking leave to apply for a child arrangements order   668
   7. Judicial review   669
   8. Suing the local authority for negligence   673
   9. Suing the local authority for breach of human rights   677

E. Some concluding remarks   680

19 ADOPTION AND SPECIAL GUARDIANSHIP   682

A. Introduction   682
   1. The nature of adoption and background to the legislation 682
   2. A comparison of adoption with other legal relationships and orders 684
   3. Adoption and human rights   684
   4. The changing pattern of adoption   687
   5. Responsibility for placing children for adoption   692

B. General principles when reaching decisions about adoption   694
   1. The weighting of the child's welfare   694

C. Adoption service   696
   1. The development of an adoption service   696
   2. The current position   697

D. Placement for adoption   698
   1. Introduction   698
   2. The placement scheme under the 2002 Act   699

E. The making of adoption orders   704
   1. Who may be adopted   704
   2. Who may apply for adoption   705
   3. Consent to the making of an order   709
   4. Dispensing with consent   713

F. Procedure for the making of adoption orders   718
   1. The child must live with the applicants before the making of an order 718
   2. Notice to local authority must be given in non-agency placements 719

G. Contact considerations   719
   1. Section 46(6)   719
   2. Section 51A orders   720

H. Registration of adoption and the adoption contact register   721
   1. The adopted children register   721
   2. The adoption contact register   722

I. The effects of an adoption order   722
  1. Complete and permanent transfer of legal parentage   722
  2. The child's change of status   725
  3. Consequences of the change of status and transfer of parentage   725

J. Offences   728
  1. Illegal placements   728
  2. Illegal payments   729
  3. Advertisements   729

K. Special guardianship   730
  1. Introduction   730
  2. The power to make special guardianship orders   731
  3. Principles upon which orders are made   733
  4. Powers when making a special guardianship order   733
  5. The effects of special guardianship orders   735
  6. Variation and discharge   736
  7. Duration of order   737
  8. Special guardianship support services   737
  9. The use made of special guardianship   739

20 THE HIGH COURT'S INHERENT POWERS IN
RESPECT OF CHILDREN   741

A. Introduction   741

B. Wardship   742
  1. Historical development   742
  2. Characteristics of the wardship jurisdiction   743
  3. Who can be warded   746
  4. The discretion to exercise jurisdiction   748
  5. Who can apply to ward a child?   749
  6. Respondents   749
  7. Duration of wardship   750
  8. The court's powers   751
  9. The principles on which the court acts   752
  10. The use of the jurisdiction   753

C. The inherent jurisdiction   762
  1. Jurisdiction and procedure   762
  2. The effect of invoking the inherent jurisdiction   763
  3. The court's powers   763
  4. Local authority use of the jurisdiction   768
  5. Private law use of the jurisdiction   771

D. Commentary   772

21 FINANCIAL OBLIGATIONS TO MEMBERS OF THE FAMILY   773

A. Introduction   773
  1. The duty to maintain a spouse or civil partner   774
  2. Parents' duty to maintain children   775
  3. Support obligations outside marriage or civil partnership   775

B. State support   776
    1. Tax allowances and credits   776
    2. Welfare benefits   777
    3. Child benefit   779

C. Private agreements   779
    1. Between spouses and civil partners   779
    2. Between parents   784

D. The courts' jurisdiction to make orders for financial support   786
    1. Orders for spouses or civil partners   786
    2. Obtaining financial relief for children   791

E. Maintenance under the Child Support Act 1991   800
    1. Background   800
    2. The key features of the child support scheme   804
    3. The residual role of the courts   820

F. Evaluation   823

22 FINANCIAL REMEDIES ON DIVORCE, DISSOLUTION,
    NULLITY AND SEPARATION: THE COURT'S POWERS   826

A. Introduction   826
    1. The settlement culture   827
    2. Development of the court's powers   828
    3. Powers of the court   830
    4. Application for orders   831
    5. Financial remedies procedure   832

B. Orders that may be made   836
    1. Maintenance pending suit and legal services orders   836
    2. Periodical payments   839
    3. Lump sum payments   840
    4. Orders in relation to pensions   842
    5. Transfer and settlement of property   845
    6. Variation of marriage or relevant settlements   848
    7. Orders for the sale of property   848
    8. Consent orders   849
    9. Costs and the legal aid statutory charge   862
    10. The limits of the court's powers   864

C. Financial provision after divorce etc or dissolution: Comparable
    provisions under the Matrimonial Causes Act 1973 and Civil
    Partnership Act 2004   865

23 FINANCIAL REMEDIES: PRINCIPLES AND ASSESSMENT   867

A. Introduction   867

B. General principles   867
    1. The objective of the jurisdiction   867
    2. Fairness   869
    3. Treating the welfare of any child of the family as the first consideration   874
    4. Placing greater emphasis on the parties becoming self-sufficient   876
    5. The current approach   880

C. Factors to be taken into account when assessing what orders
should be made for a spouse 882
1. Income, earning capacity, property and resources 882
2. Needs, obligations and responsibilities 888
3. Standard of living 891
4. Age and duration of marriage 892
5. Disability 896
6. Contribution 896
7. Conduct 899
8. Loss of benefit 903

D. The matrimonial home 903

E. Appeals 908
1. Appeal 908
2. Appeal out of time 909

F. Variation of orders 912
1. Orders that may be varied 912
2. Factors to be taken into consideration 914
3. Variation of consent orders 915

G. Enforcement of orders 916
1. Methods of enforcement 916
2. Attempts to defeat claims for financial relief 918

H. Financial relief after foreign divorce, dissolution, annulment or
legal separation 920
1. Background to the legislation 920
2. When relief may be sought 920
3. Applicants are required to obtain leave 921
4. Applying for an order 923
5. Orders that may be made 923

I. Reform 925

24 COHABITATION 934

A. Introduction 934

B. The extent of cohabitation 935
1. Incidence 935
2. Duration and stability 936
3. Attitudes to cohabitation 937

C. Defining cohabitation 939
1. 'Are living with each other' 939
2. 'In the same household' 940
3. 'A man and a woman' 941
4. 'As husband and wife' 942
5. A general definition? 944

D. Legal provision for separating cohabitants 945
1. Cohabitants' property arrangements 946
2. Cohabitants' knowledge of their legal position 947
3. Contracts 948
4. Transfer of tenancies 950

E. Reform of the law   951
    1. Cohabitants' separation arrangements   951
    2. Reform proposals by the Law Commission   952
    3. Status or function?   957

25 INHERITANCE AND INTESTACY   959

A. Presumption of death   959

B. Succession   960
    1. Testate succession   961
    2. Intestate succession   967

C. Provision for members of the family and other dependants   974
    1. Who may apply for an order   976
    2. Reasonable provision   983
    3. Factors to be taken into account   984
    4. Property available for financial provision   989
    5. Orders that may be made   989
    6. Relationship to existing agreements and orders   992

D. Conclusion   993

26 INTERNATIONAL ASPECTS OF CHILD LAW   994

A. Introduction   994

B. The revised Brussels II Regulation   994
    1. Background   994
    2. The general scope of BIIR   995
    3. The jurisdictional rules   996
    4. Recognition and enforcement   1004
    5. Central authorities   1007

C. International aspects of adoption   1008
    1. Introduction   1008
    2. The 1993 Hague Convention on Intercountry Adoption   1009
    3. Overseas adoptions   1012
    4. Domestic adoptions of foreign children   1014
    5. Restrictions on bringing children into the UK for adoption   1014
    6. Removing a child from the British Islands for adoption   1015

D. International parental child abduction   1016
    1. Introduction   1016
    2. Preventing children from being abducted out of the United Kingdom 1017
    3. Dealing with children taken to or brought from another part of the
        United Kingdom and Isle of Man   1021
    4. Dealing with children abducted to or brought from a 'non-Convention
        country' outside the United Kingdom   1024

E. Dealing with children abducted to or brought from a 'Convention
    country'   1031
    1. The relevant international instruments   1031
    2. The strategy and aims of the international instruments   1032

3. Central authorities 1032
4. How abduction applications are handled 1033
5. The 1980 Hague Abduction Convention 1034
6. The 1980 European Custody Convention 1083
7. Evaluating the use and effect of the 1980 Conventions 1088

F. International protection of children: the 1996 Hague Convention
on the Protection of Children 1091
1. Introduction 1091
2. Scope of the Convention 1092
3. The jurisdictional rules 1093
4. Applicable law 1096
5. Recognition and enforcement 1097
6. Co-operation 1098
7. Commentary 1099

Index 1101

TABLE OF STATUTES

UK PRIMARY LEGISLATION

Abortion Act 1967 . . . 391
Access to Health Records Act 1990 . . . 361, 381
Access to Justice Act 1999 . . . 234
   s 8(3) . . . 12
Access to Personal Files Act 1987 . . . 361
Administration of Estates Act 1925 . . . 967
   s 41 . . . 966
   s 42(1) . . . 360
   Pt IV (ss 45–52) . . . 360
   s 46 . . . 969, 970
   s 46(1) . . . 972
   s 46(1)(vi) . . . 973
   s 46(2A) . . . 968
   s 46A . . . 972
   s 47(1) . . . 972
   s 47(1)(i) . . . 972
   s 47A . . . 970
   s 55(1)(x) . . . 969
   Sch 1A
      para 4 . . . 970
Administration of Justice Act 1960
   s 12 . . . 745
Administration of Justice Act 1970
   s 1 . . . 15
   s 1(2) . . . 743
   s 28 . . . 191
   Sch 1 . . . 743
   Sch 8 . . . 191
   Sch 11 . . . 365
Administration of Justice Act 1973
   s 8 . . . 159
Administration of Justice Act 1982 . . . 7, 304
   s 2(b) . . . 360, 366
   s 3(1) . . . 367
   s 18 . . . 962
   s 18(2) . . . 963
   s 21 . . . 963
   s 22 . . . 965
   s 73(7) . . . 962
   s 76(11) . . . 962
Adoption Act 1926 . . . 727
   s 2 . . . 705
   s 3(b) . . . 401
Adoption Act 1949 . . . 727
Adoption Act 1950
   s 5(1)(b) . . . 401
Adoption Act 1958 . . . 683
   s 7(2) . . . 401
Adoption Act 1976 . . . 179, 683, 712, 713
   s 1 . . . 697

s 6 . . . 280, 401, 427, 694
.s 7 . . . 696
s 14(1) . . . 705
s 14(3) . . . 708
s 15(1) . . . 705
s 15(4) . . . 708
s 18(6) . . . 701
s 24(2) . . . 729
s 51A . . . 690, 722
s 56(4)–(7) . . . 692
s 57(3) . . . 729
s 57A . . . 692
s 72(1A) . . . 718
Adoption of Children Act 1926 . . . 683, 692
   s 3(b) . . . 446
Adoption of Children Act 1949 . . . 683, 966
Adoption and Children Act 2002 . . . 16, 179,
   182, 287, 295, 355, 383, 412, 418, 427, 460, 461,
   480, 503, 536, 640, 683, 689, 692, 697, 739, 907,
   1009
   s 1 . . . 280, 281, 686, 695, 702, 704, 715, 721
   s 1(1) . . . 446, 694
   s 1(2) . . . 280, 694, 696, 710, 714
   s 1(3) . . . 436, 696
   s 1(4) . . . 281, 695, 696, 714, 715, 716, 717, 733
   s 1(4)(a) . . . 401, 446, 712
   s 1(4)(c) . . . 695, 716
   s 1(4)(f) . . . 695, 711, 716
   s 1(5) . . . 350, 696, 713
   s 1(6) . . . 281, 439, 696, 716
   s 1(7) . . . 703, 704, 721
   s 1(8) . . . 711
   s 1(8)(a) . . . 695
   s 1(8)(b) . . . 695
   s 2 . . . 715
   s 2(1) . . . 693, 699
   s 2(2) . . . 693
   s 2(6) . . . 697
   s 3 . . . 697
   s 3(2) . . . 697
   s 3(4) . . . 697
   s 4 . . . 692, 697
   s 4A . . . 692, 698
   s 4B . . . 698
   s 5 . . . 697
   s 18 . . . 699
   s 18(1) . . . 699, 700
   s 18(2) . . . 699
   s 18(3) . . . 700
   s 19 . . . 700, 703, 704, 713
   s 19(2) . . . 700
   s 19(3) . . . 700

s 20 . . . 700, 704, 709, 710, 713
s 20(3) . . . 700
s 20(4) . . . 701
s 21 . . . 381
s 21(1) . . . 701
s 21(3) . . . 702
s 21(4) . . . 703
s 22 . . . 701
s 22(1) . . . 700
s 24 . . . 703
s 24(2) . . . 710, 729
s 24(3) . . . 703, 737
s 24(5) . . . 703
s 25 . . . 700, 703
s 25(4) . . . 736
s 26 . . . 704, 1093
s 26(1) . . . 704
s 26(2)(a) . . . 704
s 27(2) . . . 704
s 28(1) . . . 704
s 28(2) . . . 358, 704, 1015
s 28(3) . . . 704
s 28(3)(a) . . . 358
s 28(4) . . . 704
s 29 . . . 704
s 29(1) . . . 651
s 29(2) . . . 639
s 29(4) . . . 704
s 29(5) . . . 704, 734
s 29(6) . . . 732
s 29(7)(a) . . . 736
s 29(7)(b) . . . 735
s 31 . . . 700
s 32 . . . 700
s 34 . . . 703
s 35(2) . . . 718
s 36(1) . . . 281
s 42 . . . 718
s 42(4) . . . 719
s 42(5) . . . 719
s 42(6) . . . 718, 719
s 42(7) . . . 718
s 43 . . . 719
s 44 . . . 719
s 44(3) . . . 710
s 44(4) . . . 719
s 44(7) . . . 710
s 45 . . . 727
s 46 . . . 281, 391, 684
s 46(1) . . . 722, 723
s 46(2) . . . 722, 730
s 46(2)(a) . . . 393
s 46(2)(b) . . . 639, 723
s 46(2)(d) . . . 281, 726
s 46(3)(a) . . . 723
s 46(3)(b) . . . 707, 723
s 46(4) . . . 726
s 46(5) . . . 705, 724
s 46(6) . . . 719, 720
s 47(2) . . . 381, 390, 393, 709, 736

s 47(2)(b) . . . 704
s 47(3) . . . 704
s 47(4) . . . 704
s 47(4)(b)(i) . . . 700
s 47(5) . . . 704, 710
s 47(7) . . . 704, 710
s 47(8)(8A) . . . 705
s 47(9) . . . 705
s 49 . . . 1013
s 49(1) . . . 705
s 49(2) . . . 705
s 49(3) . . . 705
s 49(4) . . . 704
s 50 . . . 387, 705
s 51 . . . 705
s 51(2) . . . 707, 725
s 51(2)(b) . . . 716, 718
s 51(3)(3A) . . . 706
s 51(4) . . . 706
s 51A . . . 720–1, 1093
s 51A(2) . . . 720
s 51A(3) . . . 720
s 51A(4) . . . 721
s 51A(5) . . . 721
s 51A(6) . . . 720
s 51A(7) . . . 720
s 51A(8) . . . 721
s 51B(1) . . . 721
s 51B(2) . . . 721
s 51B(7) . . . 721
s 52 . . . 700, 713
s 52(1)(a) . . . 714, 717
s 52(1)(b) . . . 715, 716, 717
s 52(2)(b) . . . 716
s 52(3) . . . 700, 713
s 52(4) . . . 700
s 52(5) . . . 712
s 52(6) . . . 381, 700, 709, 710
s 52(8) . . . 700
s 52(9) . . . 700, 709
s 52(10) . . . 700, 709
s 55 . . . 723
s 55(1) . . . 303
s 60 . . . 722
s 60(2) . . . 722
s 63 . . . 722
Chp 4 (ss 66–76) . . . 1015
s 66(1)(c) . . . 1011
s 66(1)(d) . . . 1013
s 67 . . . 281, 725, 966, 980
s 67(1) . . . 281, 725, 973
s 67(2) . . . 281, 725
s 67(3) . . . 725
s 67(3)(a) . . . 725
s 67(4) . . . 725, 973
s 69 . . . 281, 966
s 69(2)(a) . . . 727
s 69(4) . . . 727, 966
s 69(5) . . . 727
s 70 . . . 281, 727

s 71 . . . 281
s 71(1) . . . 725
s 71(2) . . . 725
s 71(3) . . . 725
s 72 . . . 281
s 73 . . . 281
s 73(2) . . . 727
s 74(1) . . . 281, 726
s 74(1)(a) . . . 726
s 74(1)(b) . . . 726
s 74(1)(c) . . . 726
s 74(2) . . . 281, 725
s 75 . . . 726
s 76 . . . 727
s 77 . . . 282
s 77(1) . . . 721
s 77(2) . . . 721
s 78 . . . 282
s 78(1) . . . 721
s 78(2) . . . 721
s 78(3) . . . 721
s 79 . . . 721, 722
s 79(7) . . . 282
s 80 . . . 690, 722
s 80(2) . . . 722
s 80(5) . . . 722
s 83 . . . 1014
s 83(1) . . . 1014
s 83(1)(b) . . . 1014
s 83(2) . . . 1014
s 83(3) . . . 1015
s 83(4) . . . 1015
s 83(7) . . . 1015
s 83(8) . . . 1015
s 84 . . . 280, 1010, 1015
s 85(1) . . . 1015
s 85(4) . . . 1015
s 85(6) . . . 1015
s 87 . . . 1013
s 88 . . . 1011
s 89(1) . . . 1011
s 89(2) . . . 1013
s 89(4) . . . 1011, 1013
s 91A . . . 1015
s 92 . . . 283, 693, 728, 729
s 92(3) . . . 728
s 92(4) . . . 728
s 93(5) . . . 728
s 94 . . . 729
s 95 . . . 276, 729
s 95(3)(b) . . . 729
s 95(4) . . . 729
s 96 . . . 729
s 97(b) . . . 729
s 109 . . . 20, 437, 696
s 111 . . . 371
s 111(7) . . . 371
s 112 . . . 386
s 113 . . . 515
s 115 . . . 730

s 115(3) . . . 401, 733
s 115(4) . . . 290
s 115(4)(b) . . . 390, 735
s 116 . . . 561
s 117 . . . 664
s 118 . . . 642
s 119 . . . 663
s 120 . . . 412, 600
s 121 . . . 627
s 122(1)(b) . . . 451, 461
s 123 . . . 729, 730
s 123(4)(a) . . . 729
s 124 . . . 730
s 124(3) . . . 730
s 125 . . . 689
s 125A . . . 689
s 138 . . . 728
s 139(1) . . . 569
s 144(1) . . . 390, 699, 700, 719, 728, 736, 1011
s 144(1)(a) . . . 387
s 144(1)(b) . . . 387
s 144(4) . . . 705, 706, 707, 710
Sch 1 . . . 272
Sch 2 . . . 722
Sch 3 . . . 51, 736
    para 56(d) . . . 736
    para 63 . . . 390
    para 63(a)(i) . . . 736
    para 68(b) . . . 389
    para 68(c) . . . 389
Sch 4 . . . 463
Adoption of Children (Regulation)
    Act 1939 . . . 683, 696
    s 1 . . . 692
Adoption (Intercountry Aspects)
    Act 1999 . . . 683, 1009
    s 2(1) . . . 1010
    s 2(2A) . . . 1010
    Sch 1 . . . 1009
Affiliation Proceedings Act 1957 . . . 776
Age of Majority 1967 . . . 44, 49
Age of Marriage Act 1929 . . . 66
    s 1 . . . 44
Aliens Act 1844
    s 16 . . . 102
Anti-Social Behaviour Act 2003 . . . 365
    s 25 . . . 365
Anti-Social Behaviour, Crime and Policing
    Act 2014
    Pt 10 . . . 199
    s 109(5) . . . 201
    s 110 . . . 201
    s 120 . . . 199
    s 121 . . . 200
    s 121(1) . . . 200
    s 121(2) . . . 201
    s 121(3) . . . 201
    s 121(4) . . . 201
Asylum and Immigration (Treatment of
    Claimants, etc) Act 2004

s 19 ... 49
s 19(3) ... 55
Attachment of Earnings Act 1971 ... 917
  Sch 1 ... 191

Bastardy Laws Amendment Act 1872 ... 776
Births and Deaths Registration Act 1836 ... 49
Births and Deaths Registration Act 1953 ... 356
  s 2 ... 271, 356
  s 3A ... 356
  s 10 ... 271, 356
  s 10(1) ... 272
  s 10(1)(a)–(c) ... 371
  s 10A ... 272
  s 10A(1) ... 272, 371
  s 10A(1)(a)–(c) ... 371
  s 10ZA ... 271
  s 14 ... 272
  s 14A ... 371
  s 34(2) ... 262
Borders, Citizenship and Immigration
  Act 2009
  s 40 ... 102
British Nationality Act 1948 ... 102
British Nationality Act 1981 ... 102
  s 1(5) ... 281, 725, 1012
  s 1(6) ... 725
  s 3(1) ... 1013
  s 4 ... 102
  s 6(2) ... 102
  s 47(1) ... 305
  Sch 1
    para 3, 4 ... 102
British Nationality and Status of Aliens Act 1918
  s 2(5) ... 102
British Nationality and Status of Aliens
  Act 1933
  s 1(1) ... 102

Care Standards Act 2000
  s 74 ... 666
Carers and Disabled Children Act 2000
  s 17(1) ... 561
Child Abduction Act 1984 ... 441, 499, 526, 527,
  1018–19
  s 1 ... 339, 366, 382, 393
  s 1(1) ... 355, 1018
  s 1(2) ... 366
  s 1(3) ... 1018
  s 1(3)(a)(ii) ... 381
  s 1(4) ... 1018
  s 1(4)(b) ... 355
  s 1(4A) ... 1018
  s 1(5) ... 339, 355
  s 1(5)(c) ... 355
  s 1(5A) ... 355
  s 1(6) ... 355
  s 2 ... 339, 366
  s 2(3)(a) ... 366
  s 2(3)(b) ... 366

s 3(a) ... 366
s 3(c) ... 366
s 4 ... 366
Child Abduction and Custody Act 1985 ... 1031,
  1062
  s 3 ... 1033
  s 4 ... 16, 1038
  s 5 ... 1038
  s 8 ... 1052, 1053
  s 9 ... 1038
  s 14 ... 1033
  s 16 ... 16, 1085
  s 16(4)(c) ... 1032
  s 18 ... 1085
  s 23(2) ... 1084
  s 25 ... 1054
  s 27 ... 1038
  s 27(4) ... 1082
  Sch 3 ... 1054, 1084
Child Benefit Act 1975 ... 779
Child Benefit Act 2005
  s 1(1) ... 779
Child Care Act 1980 ... 553, 655
  ss 12A–12F ... 655
  s 21A ... 572, 573
Child Maintenance and Other Payments Act
  2008 ... 803, 817
  s 1 ... 805
  s 22 ... 817
  s 42 ... 806
  s 45 ... 778
Child Support Act 1991 ... 13, 66, 265, 274, 304,
  380, 427, 752, 775, 776, 778, 787, 791, 792, 793,
  798, 799, 800–23, 840, 911, 917
  s 1 ... 726
  s 1(1) ... 806
  s 2 ... 415, 805
  s 3 ... 293
  s 3(1) ... 806, 821
  s 3(2) ... 806
  s 3(3) ... 487, 806
  s 3(4) ... 806
  s 3(5) ... 806
  s 4 ... 817
  s 4(1) ... 807
  s 4(2A) ... 817
  s 4(4) ... 808
  s 4(5) ... 816
  s 4(10) ... 807
  s 4(10)(aa) ... 822
  s 6 ... 808
  s 8 ... 785
  s 8(1) ... 821
  s 8(3) ... 821
  s 8(3A) ... 821
  s 8(4) ... 822
  s 8(5) ... 821
  s 8(10) ... 821
  s 8(11) ... 822
  s 9(1) ... 784

s 9(2) . . . 785
s 9(2A) . . . 785, 804
s 9(3)–(4) . . . 785
s 9(5) . . . 785
s 9A . . . 785
s 10 . . . 821
s 12 . . . 808, 813
s 14A . . . 808
s 14A(4) . . . 808
s 15 . . . 808
s 15(1) . . . 810
s 16 . . . 816
s 17 . . . 816
s 20 . . . 816
s 24 . . . 816
s 26 . . . 809
s 27 . . . 264, 270, 271, 809, 810
s 27A . . . 809, 810
s 28A(1) . . . 813
s 28D(1)(b) . . . 813
s 28E . . . 815
s 28F . . . 813, 815
s 29 . . . 817
s 30 . . . 817
s 31 . . . 817
s 32(5) . . . 817
ss 32A–32K . . . 817
s 32L . . . 818
s 32M . . . 818
s 33 . . . 818
s 33(4) . . . 819
s 33D . . . 817
s 35 . . . 818
s 36 . . . 818
s 39A . . . 818
s 39H . . . 818
s 39I . . . 818
s 40 . . . 818
s 43A . . . 817
s 44 . . . 821
s 44(2A) . . . 821
s 45 . . . 816
s 46(5) . . . 808
s 49D . . . 818
s 54 . . . 726, 806
s 55 . . . 806
Sch 1 . . . 810, 813
    para 1 . . . 810
    para 2(1) . . . 810
    para 2(2) . . . 810
    para 3 . . . 811
    para 4 . . . 811
    para 5 . . . 811
    para 5A . . . 811
    para 7 . . . 807
    para 8 . . . 807
    para 10(3) . . . 812
    para 10C(2) . . . 810
    para 16 . . . 816

Sch 4B . . . 813, 815
    para 2 . . . 813
    para 2(3)(e) . . . 814
Child Support Act 1995 . . . 802, 813
Child Support (Assessment) Act 1989
    s 98C(1)(b)(ii) . . . 815
    s 117(1)(b)(ii) . . . 815
Child Support, Pensions and Social Security
    Act 2000 . . . 270, 303, 802
    s 15(1) . . . 810
    s 82 . . . 268, 765
    s 83(5) . . . 272
Childcare Act 2006 . . . 556
    Pt 1 (England) (ss 1–21) . . . 556, 559
    s 16 . . . 556
    Pt 2 (Wales) (ss 22–30) . . . 556, 559
Children Act 1948 . . . 554
Children Act 1975 . . . 554, 555, 683, 694, 707,
    708, 966
    s 28 . . . 693
    s 32 . . . 692
    s 85(1) . . . 284
    Sch 1
        Pt III . . . 966
Children Act 1989 . . . 5, 11, 15, 16, 19, 20, 23, 50,
    94, 179, 182, 225, 226, 233, 281, 284, 285, 289,
    308, 330, 336, 341, 359, 360, 385, 386, 400, 414,
    425, 438, 446, 465, 470, 481, 484, 528, 551, 555,
    557, 558, 566, 569, 573, 592, 594, 598, 600, 608,
    628, 639, 641, 650, 654, 668, 683, 692, 694,
    716, 720, 723, 741, 754, 755, 768, 776, 801, 907,
    1024, 1039, 1047, 1080
    Pt I (ss 1–7) . . . 535
    s 1 . . . 291, 318, 374, 397, 413, 426, 434, 533,
        599, 625, 627, 704, 805, 1026, 1034
    s 1(1) . . . 276, 292, 312, 318, 325, 337, 340, 383,
        397, 414, 415, 418, 419, 421, 423, 424, 427, 429,
        433, 439, 443, 488, 498, 508, 516, 519, 520, 575,
        576, 586, 590, 625, 629, 652, 733, 753
    s 1(1)(e) . . . 397
    s 1(2) . . . 436, 437, 439, 459, 489, 642, 644,
        733, 753
    s 1(2A) . . . 339, 376, 397, 417, 433, 488, 492,
        532, 533
    s 1(2B) . . . 339, 433, 488
    s 1(3) . . . 291, 292, 375, 389, 400, 401, 517, 523,
        531, 547, 548, 590, 598, 625, 629, 652, 695,
        733, 753
    s 1(3)(a) . . . 326, 400, 402, 403, 446, 448
    s 1(3)(c) . . . 409, 410
    s 1(3)(e) . . . 412, 413, 627, 652
    s 1(3)(g) . . . 400, 439, 629
    s 1(4) . . . 292, 401
    s 1(4)(a) . . . 446
    s 1(4)(b) . . . 401, 448, 625, 733
    s 1(5) . . . 289, 292, 326, 332, 375, 378, 383,
        438, 439, 440, 441, 442, 443, 444, 490, 557,
        576, 586, 590, 598, 625, 627, 629, 635, 649,
        733, 753

s 1(6) . . . 433
s 1(7) . . . 376, 433
s 2 . . . 332
s 2(1) . . . 274, 307, 311, 368, 370, 382
s 2(1A) . . . 369
s 2(2) . . . 274, 307, 311, 369
s 2(2)(b) . . . 370
s 2(2A) . . . 369, 385
s 2(3) . . . 368, 370, 385, 386
s 2(4) . . . 286, 312
s 2(5) . . . 333, 392
s 2(6) . . . 333, 392, 393, 394, 638
s 2(7) . . . 333, 358, 381, 393, 394, 730, 735
s 2(8) . . . 333, 393
s 2(9) . . . 333, 395
s 2(10) . . . 395
s 2(11) . . . 395
s 3(1) . . . 334, 336
s 3(3) . . . 360
s 3(4)(b) . . . 360
s 3(5) . . . 294, 395, 567, 569
s 3(5)(b) . . . 333
s 4 . . . 5, 373, 374, 375, 376, 378, 380, 381, 382,
　　401, 420, 470, 520, 651, 809
s 4(1)(a) . . . 3
s 4(1)(b) . . . 372, 401
s 4(1)(c) . . . 373
s 4(1A) . . . 272
s 4(1B) . . . 371
s 4(2) . . . 372
s 4(2A) . . . 371, 383
s 4(3) . . . 371, 383, 392
s 4(3)(b) . . . 375, 470
s 4(4) . . . 375, 383
s 4A . . . 387, 470, 513, 638, 651, 655, 737
s 4A(1) . . . 387
s 4A(1)(b) . . . 388
s 4A(2) . . . 388
s 4A(3) . . . 389
s 4A(3)(b) . . . 470
s 4A(4) . . . 389
s 4ZA . . . 386, 470, 520
s 4ZA(1) . . . 385
s 4ZA(5) . . . 386
s 4ZA(6)(b) . . . 470
s 5 . . . 286, 291, 293, 371, 386, 401, 710, 730, 731
s 5(1) . . . 290
s 5(3) . . . 287, 381
s 5(4) . . . 287, 390, 735
s 5(5) . . . 287
s 5(5)(a) . . . 287
s 5(5)(b) . . . 287
s 5(6) . . . 286, 291, 389
s 5(7) . . . 382
s 5(7)(a) . . . 288
s 5(7)(b) . . . 288
s 5(8) . . . 288
s 5(9) . . . 290
s 5(10) . . . 287

s 5(11)(12) . . . 286
s 6 . . . 286
s 6(1) . . . 287
s 6(2) . . . 287
s 6(3) . . . 288
s 6(3A) . . . 288, 964
s 6(3B) . . . 288, 964
s 6(3B)(b) . . . 288
s 6(4) . . . 288
s 6(5) . . . 289
s 6(6) . . . 289
s 6(7) . . . 288, 289, 291
s 6(7)(b) . . . 470
s 7 . . . 400, 451, 453, 455, 456, 459
s 7(1) . . . 455
s 7(1)(b) . . . 456
s 7(3) . . . 458
s 7(4) . . . 458
s 7(5) . . . 455
s 7A . . . 513
Pt II (ss 8–16A) . . . 412, 479, 480, 512, 535, 733
s 8 . . . 181, 274, 276, 288, 291, 292, 326, 348,
　　375, 376, 380, 381, 400, 401, 420, 423, 430,
　　433, 440, 446, 461, 470, 479, 480, 481, 483,
　　485, 486, 503, 504, 505, 507, 510, 511, 513,
　　521, 527, 535, 537, 538, 543, 548, 570, 586,
　　590, 597, 629, 630, 631, 632, 649, 651, 658,
　　659, 684, 704, 734, 735, 746, 749, 752, 756,
　　768, 769, 770, 806, 1020, 1022, 1054, 1082,
　　1084, 1093
s 8(1) . . . 334, 485
s 8(2) . . . 485, 543
s 8(3) . . . 535, 586, 590, 629, 731, 742, 751
s 8(3)(a) . . . 754, 763
s 8(4) . . . 535, 586, 629, 731
s 8(4)(d) . . . 696
s 8(5) . . . 447
s 9 . . . 515, 537, 632, 756
s 9(1) . . . 511, 658, 668, 763, 768
s 9(2) . . . 487, 511, 520, 757, 763, 768
s 9(3) . . . 515, 731
s 9(5) . . . 503, 504, 511
s 9(5)(a) . . . 503
s 9(5)(b) . . . 503, 504, 569
s 9(6) . . . 291, 375, 510, 537, 734
s 9(7) . . . 510
s 10 . . . 480, 513, 519, 668, 771
s 10(1) . . . 291, 535, 536, 537
s 10(1)(a)(ii) . . . 470, 515
s 10(1)(b) . . . 537, 629, 696, 746
s 10(2)(b) . . . 326
s 10(3) . . . 537
s 10(4) . . . 380, 442, 513
s 10(5) . . . 514
s 10(5)(aa) . . . 514
s 10(5)(b)(c) . . . 731
s 10(5)(d) . . . 514
s 10(5A)–(5C) . . . 515
s 10(6) . . . 442, 515

s 10(7A) . . . 736
s 10(8) . . . 181, 383, 470, 515, 516, 518, 519, 731
s 10(9) . . . 428, 440, 515, 516, 517, 519, 657,
    731, 737, 771
s 10(9)(a) . . . 517
s 10(9)(b) . . . 516
s 10(9)(c) . . . 440, 517, 518
s 10(9)(d)(i) . . . 517, 668
s 10(10) . . . 514, 731
s 11 . . . 20
s 11(1) . . . 437
s 11(3) . . . 488, 490, 504, 649
s 11(4) . . . 383
s 11(5) . . . 487
s 11(6) . . . 490
s 11(7) . . . 485, 486, 490, 501, 502, 503, 504,
    505, 506, 507, 508, 525, 526, 541, 544, 549,
    649, 652, 735
s 11(7)(a) . . . 504
s 11(7)(b) . . . 498, 505, 541, 543
s 11(7)(c) . . . 488, 504, 735
s 11(7)(d) . . . 505, 506
s 11A(3) . . . 496
s 11A(4) . . . 497
s 11A(6) . . . 497
s 11A(7) . . . 496
s 11B(2) . . . 497
s 11B(3) . . . 497
s 11B(7) . . . 497
s 11B(9) . . . 497
s 11C . . . 497
s 11C(5) . . . 497
s 11D . . . 497
s 11E . . . 497
s 11E(5) . . . 497, 498
s 11E(6) . . . 497, 498
s 11E(7) . . . 497
s 11F . . . 497
s 11G . . . 496, 498
s 11H . . . 498
s 11H(3)(c) . . . 498
s 11H(3)(za) . . . 498
s 11H(6) . . . 498
s 11J . . . 541
s 11J(4) . . . 541
s 11J(5) . . . 541, 542
s 11J(9) . . . 541
s 11J(10) . . . 542
s 11K . . . 541
s 11L . . . 540, 541, 542
s 11L(7) . . . 423, 542
s 11M . . . 541
s 11M(1) . . . 542
s 11N . . . 541, 542
s 11O . . . 542
s 11O(5) . . . 543
s 11O(6) . . . 542, 543
s 11O(14) . . . 423
s 12(1) . . . 374, 379, 388, 392
s 12(1A) . . . 380, 386, 520

s 12(2) . . . 389, 392, 486, 488, 520
s 12(2A) . . . 389, 488, 515, 520
s 12(3) . . . 294, 488, 520, 709
s 12(3)(b) . . . 389
s 12(3)(c) . . . 389
s 12A . . . 514
s 13 . . . 401, 420, 499, 521, 525, 526, 527
s 13(1) . . . 355, 401
s 13(1)(a) . . . 357, 358, 520, 521
s 13(1)(b) . . . 486, 499, 525, 529, 1020
s 13(2) . . . 355, 483, 484, 487, 489, 499, 526,
    1020
s 13(3) . . . 526
s 13(4) . . . 525, 526
ss 14A–14G . . . 294, 730
s 14A . . . 684
s 14A(1) . . . 731
s 14A(2)(a) . . . 731
s 14A(2)(b) . . . 731
s 14A(3)(b) . . . 731
s 14A(4) . . . 731
s 14A(5) . . . 731
s 14A(5)(c) . . . 731
s 14A(6) . . . 696
s 14A(6)(b) . . . 731, 733
s 14A(7) . . . 732
s 14A(8) . . . 732, 733
s 14A(9) . . . 732, 733
s 14A(10) . . . 732
s 14A(11) . . . 732
s 14A(12) . . . 731
s 14B(1)(a) . . . 733
s 14B(1)(b) . . . 734
s 14B(1A) . . . 733
s 14B(2)(a) . . . 357, 734
s 14B(2)(b) . . . 735
s 14C(1) . . . 390, 735
s 14C(1)(b) . . . 394, 730
s 14C(2)(a) . . . 735
s 14C(2)(b) . . . 390, 710, 736
s 14C(3) . . . 358, 735
s 14C(4) . . . 735
s 14C(5) . . . 736
s 14D . . . 736
s 14D(1) . . . 736
s 14D(1)(c) . . . 734, 736
s 14D(1)(e) . . . 470
s 14D(2) . . . 736
s 14D(3) . . . 470, 731, 737
s 14D(4) . . . 470, 737
s 14D(5) . . . 731, 737
s 14E . . . 733
s 14E(4) . . . 735
s 14E(5) . . . 735
s 14F . . . 737
s 14F(3) . . . 738
s 14F(4) . . . 738
s 14F(6) . . . 738
s 14G . . . 738
s 15 . . . 145, 293, 479, 793

s 16 . . . 480, 546, 547, 548, 549, 550, 632
s 16(1) . . . 546, 547
s 16(2) . . . 547
s 16(3)(b) . . . 547
s 16(4) . . . 548
s 16(4A) . . . 548
s 16(5) . . . 548
s 16(6) . . . 548
s 16(7) . . . 546, 548
s 16A . . . 412, 480
Pt III (ss 17–30) . . . 349, 421, 558, 559, 561,
    562, 563, 564, 570, 630, 635, 637, 663, 664
s 17 . . . 325, 421, 561, 565, 570, 571, 671
s 17(1) . . . 421, 560, 631, 638
s 17(1)(b) . . . 558
s 17(3) . . . 561
s 17(4A) . . . 561
s 17(5) . . . 562, 563
s 17(6) . . . 561
s 17(7) . . . 561
s 17(8) . . . 562
s 17(9) . . . 562
s 17(10) . . . 560, 561, 631
s 17(11) . . . 560, 561
s 17A . . . 561
s 18 . . . 563
s 18(1) . . . 563
s 18(2) . . . 563
s 18(4) . . . 563
s 19 . . . 563
s 20 . . . 332, 511, 565, 566, 567, 568, 571, 572,
    606, 671, 756
s 20(1) . . . 564, 565, 570
s 20(1)(a) . . . 566
s 20(1)(b) . . . 566
s 20(1)(c) . . . 566
s 20(3) . . . 566, 570
s 20(4) . . . 567
s 20(5) . . . 567, 574
s 20(6) . . . 564, 567, 568
s 20(7) . . . 381, 504, 564, 568
s 20(8) . . . 381, 564, 568
s 20(9) . . . 569
s 20(11) . . . 564, 569
s 22 . . . 325, 421, 561, 633, 634, 635, 636
s 22(1) . . . 660
s 22(2) . . . 574, 660
s 22(3) . . . 421, 515, 569, 576, 607, 638, 661,
    668
s 22(3A) . . . 556, 661
s 22(3B) . . . 556
s 22(3C) . . . 556
s 22(4) . . . 661
s 22(5) . . . 661
s 22(5)(c) . . . 411
s 22(6) . . . 421, 576
s 22A . . . 661
s 22B . . . 661
s 22C . . . 564, 661
s 22C(3) . . . 661

s 22C(6) . . . 661
s 22C(7)(a) . . . 661
s 22C(8) . . . 661
s 23(1) . . . 607
s 23C . . . 662
s 23ZA . . . 662
s 23ZB . . . 662
s 24 . . . 607
s 24D . . . 662, 663, 664
s 25 . . . 439, 574, 575, 576, 577, 578
s 25(1) . . . 573, 574, 576
s 25(1)(a) . . . 574, 575
s 25(1)(a)(i) . . . 574, 575
s 25(1)(a)(ii) . . . 575
s 25(1)(b) . . . 427, 574
s 25(3) . . . 573, 575
s 25(4) . . . 575, 576
s 25(5) . . . 575
s 25(6) . . . 575
s 25(9) . . . 577
ss 25A–25C . . . 642
s 26 . . . 570, 642, 663, 665, 669
s 26(3) . . . 663, 664
s 26(3)(b) . . . 596
s 26(3A) . . . 664
s 26(3B) . . . 664
s 26(4) . . . 663
s 26(7) . . . 664
s 26(8) . . . 663
s 26A . . . 663
s 26A(1) . . . 663
s 26A(2) . . . 663
s 26A(4) . . . 663
s 26A(5) . . . 663
s 29(4) . . . 293
Pt IV (ss 31–42) . . . 428, 437, 448, 453, 512,
    520, 535, 536, 629, 664
s 31 . . . 185, 336, 349, 412, 420, 426, 443, 511,
    512, 549, 575, 581, 595, 600, 605, 624, 627,
    632, 639, 642, 652, 653, 733, 754, 764, 769
s 31(1) . . . 553, 596
s 31(1)(b) . . . 633
s 31(2) . . . 597, 599, 620, 632, 642, 652, 701
s 31(2)(a) . . . 263, 413, 605, 607, 608, 609, 610
s 31(2)(b) . . . 613
s 31(2)(b)(i) . . . 615, 617
s 31(3) . . . 596, 758
s 31(3A) . . . 627
s 31(3B) . . . 628
s 31(5) . . . 629
s 31(5)(a) . . . 632
s 31(6) . . . 596
s 31(7) . . . 596
s 31(9) . . . 210, 412, 435, 560, 585, 590, 596,
    600, 601
s 31(10) . . . 600, 603
s 31A . . . 627, 628
s 31A(2) . . . 627
s 31A(5) . . . 627
s 32 . . . 438, 629

s 32(1) ... 437
s 33(1) ... 636
s 33(3) ... 392
s 33(3)(a) ... 390, 636
s 33(3)(b) ... 390, 638, 704, 736
s 33(4) ... 390
s 33(5) ... 638
s 33(6) ... 390
s 33(6)(a) ... 350, 638
s 33(6)(b) ... 638, 709
s 33(7) ... 358, 420, 521, 525, 639
s 33(7)(b) ... 355
s 33(8) ... 525
s 33(8)(a) ... 356, 639
s 33(8)(b) ... 356
s 33(9) ... 638
s 33(11) ... 656
s 34 ... 274, 318, 380, 417, 420, 428, 429, 460,
    508, 510, 516, 558, 640, 652, 655, 656, 657,
    658, 659, 660, 662, 680, 704, 736
s 34(1) ... 339, 654, 655, 657, 659
s 34(2) ... 656, 657, 658
s 34(3) ... 657
s 34(3)(b) ... 657
s 34(4) ... 656, 657, 658, 659, 660
s 34(5) ... 657
s 34(6) ... 656
s 34(6A) ... 656
s 34(7) ... 657
s 34(9) ... 659
s 34(11) ... 656, 657, 660
s 35 ... 1093
s 35(1) ... 633
s 36 ... 349, 596, 600, 996
s 36(3)–(4) ... 349
s 36(5) ... 349
s 36(8)–(9) ... 349
s 37 ... 455, 460, 463, 480, 512, 550, 579, 642,
    754, 758
s 37(3) ... 550
s 37(4) ... 550
s 38 ... 642, 643, 754
s 38(1) ... 642
s 38(1)(b) ... 550
s 38(2) ... 642
s 38(3) ... 632, 649
s 38(4) ... 649
s 38(6) ... 423, 587, 634, 645, 646, 647, 648,
    650, 765
s 38(7) ... 646
s 38A ... 563, 648
s 38A(1) ... 648
s 38A(2) ... 648
s 38A(3) ... 648
s 38A(4) ... 649
s 38A(5) ... 649
s 38A(8) ... 649
s 38A(10) ... 649
s 38B ... 649
s 38B(2) ... 649
s 39 ... 420, 471, 511, 640, 651, 652, 662

s 39(1) ... 639, 651
s 39(1)(b) ... 651
s 39(2) ... 653
s 39(3) ... 653
s 39(4) ... 652
s 39(5) ... 652, 653
s 40(3) ... 652
s 41 ... 460, 575
s 41(2)(b) ... 461
s 41(3)(4) ... 462
s 41(6) ... 460, 467
s 41(6)(hh) ... 460
s 41(6A) ... 451, 461
s 42 ... 463, 464
s 42(1) ... 463
Pt V (ss 43–52) ... 428, 448, 460, 536, 582,
    583, 664
s 43 ... 592
s 43(1) ... 590
s 43(3) ... 590
s 43(4) ... 590
s 43(5) ... 591
s 43(6) ... 591
s 43(7) ... 591
s 43(8) ... 591, 634, 765
s 43(9) ... 591
s 43(10) ... 591
s 43(11) ... 590
s 43(12) ... 471
s 43(13) ... 590
s 44 ... 182
s 44(1) ... 584, 585, 586
s 44(1)(b) ... 584, 585
s 44(1)(c) ... 585
s 44(4)(a) ... 586
s 44(4)(b) ... 586
s 44(4)(c) ... 390, 392, 586
s 44(5)(a) ... 587
s 44(5)(b) ... 352, 390, 587
s 44(6) ... 586, 587
s 44(6)(b) ... 587
s 44(7) ... 587, 591, 634, 765
s 44(8) ... 587
s 44(10) ... 587
s 44(13) ... 340, 587
s 44A ... 563, 587
s 44A(3) ... 587
s 44A(4) ... 588
s 44A(5) ... 588
s 44A(10) ... 588
s 44B ... 588
s 44B(2) ... 588
s 45(1) ... 588
s 45(4) ... 588
s 45(5) ... 588
s 45(6) ... 588
s 45(7) ... 586
s 45(8) ... 471, 588
s 45(9) ... 588
s 45(10) ... 588
s 45(11) ... 588

s 46 . . . 592, 593
s 46(1) . . . 592
s 46(4) . . . 593
s 46(5) . . . 593
s 46(6) . . . 592
s 46(7) . . . 593
s 46(8) . . . 593
s 46(9) . . . 593
s 47 . . . 579, 580, 582, 585
s 47(1) . . . 579, 584
s 47(1)(b) . . . 584
s 48(3)(4) . . . 586
s 48(9) . . . 586
s 50 . . . 199
s 51A . . . 503
s 51B(7) . . . 503
s 63 . . . 539
Pt IX (ss 66–70) . . . 295
s 66 . . . 295
s 67(1) . . . 295
s 78(6) . . . 293
s 84 . . . 663
s 91 . . . 632
s 91(1) . . . 489, 511, 639, 651, 659
s 91(1A) . . . 489
s 91(2) . . . 636, 651
s 91(3) . . . 636
s 91(4) . . . 636, 668, 750, 754
s 91(5) . . . 636
s 91(5A) . . . 651, 736
s 91(7)–(8) . . . 291, 382, 389
s 91(10) . . . 510
s 91(11) . . . 510
s 91(12) . . . 639
s 91(14) . . . 504, 508, 509, 510, 549, 660,
    735, 736
s 91(15) . . . 508, 653
s 91(17) . . . 423, 508, 659, 660
s 92(2) . . . 535
s 92(7) . . . 373
s 94(1) . . . 577, 650
s 96(2) . . . 470
s 100 . . . 742, 756, 758, 764, 766, 771
s 100(1) . . . 754
s 100(2) . . . 503, 756, 757, 758, 764, 768
s 100(2)(a) . . . 596, 754, 765
s 100(2)(b) . . . 504, 756
s 100(2)(c) . . . 668, 754, 755
s 100(2)(d) . . . 756, 764
s 100(3) . . . 756, 763, 768
s 100(4) . . . 756
s 100(4)(a) . . . 768, 769
s 100(4)(b) . . . 769
s 100(5) . . . 757
s 100(5)(b) . . . 769
s 101 . . . 525
s 105(1) . . . 287, 291, 295, 296, 297, 359, 372,
    374, 390, 412, 427, 435, 436, 560, 566, 633,
    737, 796
s 105(3) . . . 293
s 108(11) . . . 525

s 108(12) . . . 525
s 120 . . . 412
s 321 . . . 20
Sch A1
    Pt 2 (paras 4–10) . . . 542
    para 4 . . . 541
Sch 1 . . . 125, 145, 189, 203, 293, 304, 427, 439,
    479, 512, 752, 773, 775, 776, 793–800, 806,
    807, 823, 837, 841, 852, 955
    para 1(1) . . . 793
    para 1(1)(a) . . . 794, 795
    para 1(1)(b) . . . 794
    para 1(2)(a) . . . 794
    para 1(2)(b) . . . 795
    para 1(2)(c) . . . 794
    para 1(2)(d)(e) . . . 795
    para 1(5) . . . 795
    para 1(5)(a) . . . 794, 799
    para 1(5)(b) . . . 795
    para 1(6) . . . 793
    para 1(7) . . . 793
    para 2 . . . 799
    para 3(1) . . . 799
    para 3(2) . . . 799, 822
    para 3(3) . . . 799
    para 3(4) . . . 799
    para 4(1) . . . 796
    para 4(2) . . . 799
    para 4(3) . . . 799
    para 4(4) . . . 796
    para 5 . . . 798
    para 5(2) . . . 794
    para 5(5) . . . 794
    para 10 . . . 784, 785
    para 10(3) . . . 785
    para 10(5) . . . 785
    para 11 . . . 784, 785
    para 14 . . . 795
    para 15 . . . 562, 794
    para 16(2) . . . 794
Sch 2
    Pt I (paras 1–11) . . . 562
    para 1 . . . 562
    para 1(2)(a) . . . 562
    para 1(2)(b) . . . 562
    para 2 . . . 561
    para 4 . . . 563
    para 5 . . . 563, 649
    para 6 . . . 561, 563
    para 7(c) . . . 573
    para 8 . . . 562
    para 9 . . . 562
    para 11 . . . 563
    para 15 . . . 558, 562
    para 16 . . . 562, 654
    para 19 . . . 356, 769
    para 19(1) . . . 639
    para 19(2) . . . 639
    para 20 . . . 359
    Pt III (paras 21–25) . . . 669
    para 21(3) . . . 293

Sch 3 ... 633, 653
  para 1 ... 634
  para 2 ... 633
  para 2(2) ... 634
  para 2(3) ... 634
  para 3 ... 634
  para 4 ... 634
  para 4(1) ... 634
  para 4(4)(a) ... 634
  para 5 ... 634
  para 5(5)(a) ... 634
  para 6(1) ... 633
  para 6(3) ... 633
  para 9 ... 633
  para 12(1)(a) ... 349
  para 12(1)(b) ... 349
  para 15(1)–(5) ... 349
  para 15(6) ... 350
  para 17 ... 350, 579
  para 18 ... 349
  para 19 ... 349
Sch 8
  para 5 ... 283, 295
  para 9 ... 295
Sch 10 ... 683
  para 21 ... 722
Sch 12 ... 51, 341
  para 6 ... 271
  para 33 ... 297
  para 43 ... 297
Sch 13 ... 341
  para 45(2) ... 750
  para 56 ... 274
Sch 15 ... 51, 286, 708
Children Act 2004 ... 347, 553, 555, 556, 559
  Pt 1 (ss 1–9) ... 476, 666
  s 2 ... 477
  s 2(1) ... 476, 477
  s 2(2) ... 476, 477
  s 2(3) ... 477
  s 2(3)(i) ... 478
  s 2(5) ... 478
  s 2(7) ... 477
  s 2A ... 478
  s 2B ... 478
  s 2D ... 478
  s 3 ... 477, 478
  s 3(3) ... 477
  s 4 ... 477, 478
  s 5 ... 476
  s 6 ... 476
  s 7 ... 476
  s 8A ... 478
  s 10(2) ... 559
  s 10(4) ... 559
  s 11 ... 418
  s 13 ... 581
  s 14 ... 581
  s 14(2) ... 553
  s 25(2) ... 559

s 25(4) ... 559
s 34 ... 14
s 52 ... 556
s 53 ... 561
s 53(2) ... 567
s 58 ... 341, 347
s 58(1) ... 347
s 58(3) ... 347
s 58(5) ... 347
Children and Adoption Act 2006 ... 423, 432,
  480, 496, 540, 541, 542, 547
  s 6(3) ... 548
  s 6(5) ... 548
  s 9 ... 1012
  s 13 ... 1015
  s 14 ... 1014
  Sch 1 ... 541
Children and Families Act 2014 ... 225, 238,
  240, 242, 339, 389, 476, 477, 481, 496, 514, 533,
  540, 551, 651, 683, 697, 823
  Pt 1 (ss 1–9) ... 689, 721
  s 3 ... 696, 713
  s 4 ... 689
  s 5 ... 692, 698
  s 6 ... 689, 698
  s 7 ... 689
  s 8 ... 656
  s 8(2) ... 655
  s 8(5) ... 656, 657, 660
  s 9 ... 503, 556
  s 10 ... 12, 447, 485
  s 10(3) ... 447
  s 11 ... 376, 397, 433
  s 11(2) ... 339, 417
  s 11(3) ... 433
  s 12 ... 485
  s 14 ... 20, 438, 629
  s 14(4) ... 649
  s 15 ... 627
  s 17 ... 221, 226, 241, 304, 446
  s 17(1)(a) ... 444
  s 18 ... 235, 447
  s 52 ... 661
  s 107 ... 477, 478
  s 108 ... 478
  s 114 ... 478
  Pt 5 (ss 90–106) ... 476
  Sch 2
    para 2 ... 382
    para 2(2) ... 290
    para 2(3) ... 288
    para 2(4) ... 290
    para 4 ... 503
    para 4(3) ... 487, 511
    para 4(5) ... 510
    para 4(6) ... 510
    para 5 ... 631
    para 5(3) ... 514
    Para 5(4) ... 515
    Para 5(5) ... 515

Para 5(6) ... 515
para 5(7) ... 513
para 6 ... 487
para 6(4) ... 490
paras 7–13 ... 496
para 7(2) ... 496
para 8(3) ... 497
para 14(4)(b) ... 498
paras 16–19 ... 541
para 19(5) ... 543
para 20 ... 541
para 21(2) ... 380, 386, 520
para 21(3) ... 389, 489, 520
para 21(4) ... 389, 488, 520
para 22 ... 520, 525, 1020
para 22(3) ... 355, 489, 526
para 22(5) ... 525
para 24 ... 730
para 25 ... 730, 733
para 25(3) ... 733
para 26 ... 730, 734, 736
para 27 ... 548
para 28 ... 569
para 29 ... 564, 661
para 31 ... 655
para 35 ... 587
para 37 ... 489, 511, 651
para 47(2) ... 366
para 47(3) ... 1018
para 48 ... 1084
para 60(2) ... 704
para 60(3) ... 704
para 61 ... 704
para 62 ... 704
Sch 4
para 21(2) ... 386
Children and Families (Wales) Measure
   2010 ... 556
Children (Leaving Care) Act 2000 ... 664
   s 2 ... 662
Children (Protection From Offenders)
   (Miscellaneous Amendments) Regulations
   1997 (SI 1997/2308) ... 757
Children (Scotland) Act 1995 ... 331, 346, 385
   s 1(1) ... 335
   s 1(1)(d) ... 340
   s 2(1) ... 335
   s 2(1)(d) ... 359
   s 7 ... 289
   s 11(2)(a) ... 392
Children and Young Persons Act 1933 ... 294,
   341
   s 1 ... 294, 345, 347, 351, 396
   s 1(1) ... 341
   s 1(2)(a) ... 293, 342, 351
   s 1(2)(b) ... 342
   s 1(7) ... 341, 345, 347
   s 4 ... 342
   s 11 ... 342
   s 17 ... 294, 341, 395

s 23 ... 342
s 24 ... 342
s 25 ... 342
s 55 ... 365, 571
s 55(5) ... 365, 571
Children and Young Persons Act 1963 ... 341,
   554
   s 3 ... 596
   ss 37–40 ... 342
   s 41 ... 342
   s 42 ... 342
   Sch 3 ... 342
   Sch 5 ... 342
Children and Young Persons Act 1969 ... 16,
   341, 553, 554, 572
   s 3(6) ... 365
   s 70(1) ... 359, 391
   Sch 5 ... 365
   Sch 6 ... 365
Children and Young Persons Act 1993
   s 55 ... 365
Children and Young Persons Act
   2008 ... 556, 564
   s 7 ... 556
   s 8 ... 661
   s 10 ... 642
   s 15 ... 662
   s 21 ... 662
   s 24 ... 561
   s 30 ... 588
Children and Young Persons (Amendment)
   Act 1952 ... 341
   s 8 ... 342
Children's Commissioner for Wales Act
   2001 ... 475, 556, 666
Civil Evidence Act 1968
   s 12 ... 809
Civil Jurisdiction and Judgments Act
   1982 ... 28
Civil Partnership Act 2004 ... 1, 3, 9, 36, 58, 88,
   90, 102, 112, 144, 153, 187, 203, 211, 240, 241,
   293, 387, 791, 944, 977, 980, 992
   s 1 ... 32
   s 1(1) ... 32
   s 1(3) ... 32
   s 2(1) ... 61
   s 2(5) ... 61
   s 3 ... 87
   s 3(1) ... 59
   s 4 ... 60
   s 4(4) ... 744
   s 5(1) ... 60
   s 6 ... 60
   s 6A(3A) ... 59
   s 7(1) ... 61
   s 8(1) ... 989
   s 9(1) ... 61
   s 9(5)(c) ... 61
   s 9(6) ... 61
   s 16 ... 959

s 29(1) . . . 61
Pt 2, Chp 2 (ss 37–64) . . . 240
s 37 . . . 87
s 37(1)(a) . . . 241
s 37(1)(d) . . . 243
s 37(2) . . . 241
s 38 . . . 241
s 39 . . . 241
s 41 . . . 241
s 42 . . . 241
s 44 . . . 241
s 44(5) . . . 152
s 45 . . . 241
s 47 . . . 241
s 48 . . . 241
s 49(b) . . . 87
s 50 . . . 88
s 51 . . . 88
s 55 . . . 959
s 56 . . . 152, 243
s 57 . . . 152, 971
s 58 . . . 87
s 63 . . . 304
s 65 . . . 143
s 66 . . . 117, 118, 145
s 66(2) . . . 118
s 67 . . . 117
s 68 . . . 118
s 69 . . . 100
s 70 . . . 92
s 70A . . . 112
s 71 . . . 962, 964, 967, 976
s 72 . . . 144, 203, 786
s 72(1) . . . 830
s 72(4) . . . 920
s 73 . . . 40, 180
s 73(3) . . . 109
s 74 . . . 118
s 74(4) . . . 118
s 74(5) . . . 109
s 75(2) . . . 386
s 75(3) . . . 297
s 76 . . . 288, 964
s 77 . . . 514
s 79 . . . 706
s 79(3) . . . 705
s 79(4) . . . 706
s 82 . . . 152, 153
s 84 . . . 97
s 181 . . . 16
s 188 . . . 16
s 210 . . . 60
s 211 . . . 60
Pt 5, Chp 2 (ss 212–218) . . . 32, 70
ss 212–17 . . . 87
Pt 5, Chp 3 (ss 219–238) . . . 288
s 222 . . . 959
Sch 1 . . . 726
Sch 2 . . . 60
    para 6 . . . 87
    para 12 . . . 87

Sch 3
    paras 1–4 . . . 83
Sch 4
    para 2 . . . 83, 962, 964
    para 5 . . . 965
    paras 7–12 . . . 967, 968, 972
    para 7 . . . 968, 972
    para 8 . . . 972
    para 9 . . . 970
    para 13 . . . 971
    para 14(6) . . . 983
    paras 15–27 . . . 976
    para 15(5) . . . 978
    para 16 . . . 989, 991
    para 17 . . . 986
    para 17(5) . . . 986
    para 18 . . . 987
    para 21 . . . 992
    para 22 . . . 993
    para 25 . . . 992
    para 26 . . . 990
Sch 5 . . . 144, 203, 536, 830, 881
    Pt 1 (paras 1–5) . . . 865
    Pt 2 (paras 6–9) . . . 118
        para 6 . . . 865
        para 7 . . . 865
        para 7(3) . . . 848
        paras 8–9 . . . 865
    Pt 3 (paras 10–14) . . . 865
    Pt 4 (paras 15–19) . . . 865
        para 19(1) . . . 865
    Pt 5 (paras 20–23) . . . 865, 867
    Pt 6 (paras 24–29) . . . 866
    Pt 7 (paras 30–37) . . . 866
    Pt 8 (para 38) . . . 865
        para 38A . . . 865
    Pt 9 (paras 39–45) . . . 775, 786, 790, 866
        para 39(b) . . . 793
        para 40 . . . 790
        para 41 . . . 790
        para 42(1) . . . 791
        para 43(4) . . . 790
    Pt 10 (paras 46–49)
        para 46 . . . 866
        para 47 . . . 866
        para 47(5) . . . 866
        para 48 . . . 866
        para 49 . . . 866
        para 49(6) . . . 793
    Pt 11 (paras 50–62)
        paras 50–52 . . . 866
        paras 53–54 . . . 866
        para 55 . . . 793, 866
        paras 56–62 . . . 866
    Pt 12 (paras 63–65) . . . 866
    Pt 13 (paras 66–73) . . . 866
        para 67 . . . 781, 992
        para 67(2) . . . 782
        para 68 . . . 781
        paras 69–73 . . . 783
    Pt 14 (paras 74–80) . . . 866

Sch 6 . . . 536, 775, 786, 787, 793
  para 1 . . . 152
  para 3 . . . 789
  Pt 3 (paras 15–19) . . . 789
  para 15(1) . . . 789
  para 18 . . . 789
  para 26(1)(b) . . . 788
  para 26(2) . . . 788
  para 27(6) . . . 793
  para 29(2) . . . 788
Sch 7
  Pt I (paras 1–16) . . . 920
Sch 9 . . . 153, 907
  para 1 . . . 152
  para 5 . . . 187, 189
  para 6 . . . 187
  para 8 . . . 190
  para 13 . . . 180, 942, 950
  para 17 . . . 907
  para 18 . . . 907
Sch 27
  para 17 . . . 45
  para 40 . . . 71
  para 56 . . . 101
  para 57 . . . 788
  para 92 . . . 16
  para 97 . . . 97
Commissioner for Children and Young People
  (Scotland) Act 2003 . . . 476
Congenital Disabilities (Civil Liability)
  Act 1976
  s 2 . . . 343
  s 4(2)(a) . . . 343
Contempt of Court Act 1981
  s 14(1) . . . 193, 538
County Courts Act 1984
  s 38 . . . 196
Court and Crimes Act 2013
  Sch 10 . . . 303
Courts and Legal Services Act 1990
  Sch 16
    para 18 . . . 463
  Sch 20 . . . 752
Crime and Courts Act 2013 . . . 15, 18
  s 17 . . . 786, 787
  s 17(3) . . . 15
  Sch 10 . . . 485, 786, 787
    para 31H . . . 538
  Sch 11 . . . 916
Crime and Disorder Act 1998 . . . 579
  s 8 . . . 349, 365
  s 9 . . . 349, 365
  s 9(1)(b) . . . 365
  s 11 . . . 536
  s 12 . . . 536
Crime and Security Act 2010 . . . 202
  s 24 . . . 202
  s 24(3) . . . 202
  s 24(6) . . . 202
  s 24(8) . . . 202
  s 24(9) . . . 202

s 25(1)(b) . . . 202
s 25(1)(c) . . . 202
s 25(2) . . . 202
s 26 . . . 202
s 27 . . . 202
s 28 . . . 203
s 28(2)(3) . . . 203
s 28(4)(5) . . . 203
s 28(9) . . . 203
s 28(10) . . . 203
Criminal Evidence Act 1898 . . . 97
Criminal Justice Act 1925
  s 47 . . . 100
Criminal Justice Act 1972
  Sch 5 . . . 365
Criminal Justice Act 1988 . . . 846
  s 23 . . . 171
Criminal Justice Act 1991
  s 57(2) . . . 365, 571
  s 70 . . . 16
Criminal Justice Act 2003 . . . 349
  Sch 37
    Pt 9 . . . 778
Criminal Justice and Court Services Act
  2000 . . . 14, 452, 453
  s 12(1) . . . 453
  s 12(5)(b) . . . 461, 463
Criminal Justice and Public Order Act 1994
  s 142 . . . 95
Criminal Justice (Scotland) Act 2003
  s 51 . . . 346
Criminal Law Act 1977
  s 2(2)(a) . . . 101
  s 36 . . . 365
Custody of Children Act 1891 . . . 313
Custody of Infants Act 1873 . . . 311, 313

Data Protection Act 1998 . . . 361
Debtors Act 1869
  s 4 . . . 191
  s 5 . . . 191, 917
Diplomatic Privileges Act 1964 . . . 428
Divorce Reform Act 1969 . . . 214, 219, 232, 233,
  242, 316, 787, 828–9
  s 2 . . . 242
Divorce (Religious Marriages) Act 2002 . . . 225
Domestic Proceedings and Magistrates' Courts Act
  1978 . . . 94, 166, 536, 775, 786, 787–90, 791, 920
  s 1 . . . 152, 787, 788, 790
  s 1(b) . . . 787
  s 2 . . . 788
  s 2(1)(a)(c) . . . 788
  s 3(1) . . . 789
  s 3(3) . . . 791
  s 3(4) . . . 791
  s 4(1) . . . 788
  s 4(2) . . . 788
  s 5(1) . . . 792
  s 5(2) . . . 788, 792
  s 5(3) . . . 792
  s 5(4) . . . 793

s 6 ... 788
s 6(1)(b) ... 789
s 6(2) ... 788
s 6(4) ... 788
s 6(5) ... 789
s 6(7) ... 792, 793
s 7 ... 789
s 7(1) ... 789
s 7(4) ... 789
s 7(5) ... 791
s 7(7) ... 792, 793
ss 16–18 ... 166
s 19 ... 788
s 20 ... 788
s 20(12)(b) ... 793
s 20A(1) ... 793
s 22 ... 788
s 25(1) ... 788, 793
s 25(2) ... 793
s 26 ... 788
s 38 ... 297
s 88(2) ... 788
Domestic Violence, Crime and Victims Act
  2004 ... 180, 192
s 2 ... 938
s 2(2) ... 189, 943
s 3 ... 180, 941, 950
s 4 ... 180
s 5 ... 342
s 9 ... 168
s 10 ... 170
s 12 ... 176
s 12(5) ... 177
Sch 10
  para 34 ... 187
  para 34(3) ... 189
  para 36 ... 182
  para 37 ... 195
  para 38 ... 193
  para 38(4) ... 194
Domestic Violence, Crime and Victims
  (Amendment) Act 2012
s 1 ... 342
Domestic Violence and Matrimonial
  Proceedings Act 1976 ... 167, 187, 939, 941
s 1(2) ... 939
Domicile and Matrimonial Proceedings
  Act 1973
Sch 1
  para 8(1) ... 428
Dower Act 1833 ... 974
Drug Trafficking Act 1994 ... 846

Education Act 1996
  ss 7, 8 ... 293, 294, 347
s 9 ... 348
Pt IV (ss 312–349) ... 381
s 408 ... 348
s 437(1) ... 349
s 437(3) ... 349

s 443 ... 349
s 444 ... 349
s 444(8A) ... 349
s 447 ... 349
s 447(2) ... 349
s 548 ... 346
s 550A ... 346
s 562 ... 578
s 576(1) ... 293, 294, 348
Education and Skills Act 2008
  Pt 1 (ss 1–67) ... 348
  Pt 4 (ss 92–148) ... 348, 349
Equality Act 2010 ... 50, 112
s 110 ... 50
s 198 ... 775
s 199 ... 111, 128
s 200 ... 112
s 200(2) ... 111
s 201 ... 112
s 202 ... 59
Sch 3
  para 25A ... 50
Estates of Deceased Persons (Forfeiture Rule
  and Law of Succession) Act 2011 ... 972
European Communities Act 1972
s 1(2) ... 1091
s 2(2) ... 995, 1091
Evidence Amendment Act 1853 ... 97

Family Allowance Act 1945 ... 779
Family Law Act 1986 ... 62, 374, 441, 489, 536,
  747, 996, 1017, 1021–3, 1041, 1092
s 1 ... 1024
s 1(1)(a) ... 1022
s 1(1)(d) ... 1022
s 2 ... 1022, 1024
s 2A ... 1022
s 3 ... 1022, 1024
s 5 ... 749
s 14A ... 272
s 25 ... 1023
s 25(3) ... 1023
s 27(1) ... 1023
s 27(3) ... 1023
s 29(1) ... 1023
s 29(2) ... 1023
s 30 ... 1023
s 31 ... 1023
s 32(1) ... 1023
s 33 ... 538, 1019
s 34 ... 538
s 36 ... 1023
s 37 ... 1019
s 38 ... 744, 1020
s 41 ... 1022, 1023
s 41(1) ... 1022
s 41(2) ... 1022
s 41(3) ... 1022
s 42 ... 1021
Pt II (ss 44–54) ... 288

Pt III (ss 55–63) . . . 15
s 55 . . . 16, 62
s 55(2) . . . 63
s 55(3) . . . 63
s 55A . . . 16, 270, 272, 809, 810
s 55A(2) . . . 270
s 55A(3) . . . 271
s 55A(4) . . . 271
s 55A(5) . . . 271
s 55A(6) . . . 271
s 55A(7) . . . 271
s 56 . . . 272, 303, 809
s 56(4) . . . 304
s 58(1) . . . 63, 271, 303
s 58(2) . . . 63, 271, 304
s 58(3) . . . 271, 304
s 58(4) . . . 62
s 58(5)(a) . . . 62
s 59 . . . 63
s 59(1) . . . 303
s 59(2) . . . 303
s 60(2)(b) . . . 63
s 60(2)(c) . . . 63
s 60(3) . . . 63
s 61 . . . 62
s 63 . . . 303
Family Law Act 1996 . . . 117, 152, 158, 160, 178,
    179, 181, 183, 230, 234–8, 242, 536, 563, 587,
    648, 903, 907, 943
    Pt I (s 1) . . . 234
s 1 . . . 235
s 1(a) . . . 235
s 1(b) . . . 235
s 1(c) . . . 235
s 1(d) . . . 235
    Pt II (ss 2–25) . . . 234, 235, 903
s 6 . . . 236
s 7(3) . . . 237
s 7(6) . . . 237
s 7(12)(b) . . . 238
s 8(2) . . . 235
s 11 . . . 447
s 11(4) . . . 432
s 16 . . . 843
    Pt III (ss 26–29) . . . 234, 235
    Pt IV (ss 30–63) . . . 7, 15, 16, 40, 153, 160, 167,
    173, 174, 178, 179, 180, 201, 202, 204, 205,
    207, 210, 502, 505, 536, 631
s 30 . . . 153, 154
s 30(1) . . . 153
s 30(1)(a) . . . 190
s 30(2) . . . 153, 184
s 30(3) . . . 154, 159
s 30(4) . . . 154
s 30(5) . . . 154
s 30(6) . . . 154
s 30(7) . . . 154
s 30(9) . . . 154
s 31 . . . 154, 155
s 31(2) . . . 155

s 31(3) . . . 155
s 31(10) . . . 148, 155
s 31(10)(b) . . . 155
ss 33–41 . . . 179
s 33 . . . 154, 184, 191
s 33(1)(a) . . . 184
s 33(1)(a)(i) . . . 184
s 33(1)(b) . . . 184
s 33(2) . . . 184
s 33(3) . . . 184, 186
s 33(4) . . . 184
s 33(5) . . . 156, 184
s 33(6) . . . 186
s 33(6)(a)–(c) . . . 907
s 33(7) . . . 185
s 33(8) . . . 185
s 33(9)(a) . . . 184
s 33(10) . . . 187
s 35 . . . 191
s 35(1)(c) . . . 187
s 35(3) . . . 188
s 35(4) . . . 188
s 35(5) . . . 188, 189
s 35(6) . . . 188, 189
s 35(6)(g) . . . 189
s 35(7)–(8) . . . 189
s 35(10) . . . 190
s 36 . . . 187, 191
s 36(3) . . . 188
s 36(4) . . . 188
s 36(5) . . . 189
s 36(6) . . . 189
s 36(6)(e) . . . 938, 943, 950
s 36(6)(f) . . . 950
s 36(6)(h) . . . 950
s 36(7)–(8) . . . 190
s 36(10) . . . 190
s 37 . . . 191
s 37(1) . . . 187
s 37(1A) . . . 187
s 37(3) . . . 190
s 37(4) . . . 191
s 37(5) . . . 191
s 38 . . . 191
s 38(1) . . . 187
s 38(3) . . . 190
s 38(4) . . . 191
s 38(5) . . . 191
s 38(6) . . . 191
s 39(2) . . . 183
s 40 . . . 191
s 41 . . . 189
s 41(2) . . . 938
s 42 . . . 179, 196, 198
s 42(1) . . . 179
s 42(2)(a) . . . 182
s 42(2)(b) . . . 182
s 42(3) . . . 182
s 42(4) . . . 180
s 42(4A) . . . 182

s 42(4B) . . . 182
s 42(5) . . . 182
s 42(6) . . . 183
s 42A . . . 192, 193, 195
s 42A(1) . . . 192
s 42A(3)(4) . . . 193
s 42A(5)(a) . . . 193
s 43 . . . 181
s 44 . . . 40, 180
s 44(2)(b) . . . 40
s 45 . . . 194
s 45(2) . . . 194
s 45(3)(4) . . . 194
s 46 . . . 195
s 46(2) . . . 195
s 46(3) . . . 195
s 46(3A) . . . 195
s 47 . . . 192, 193
s 47(2) . . . 182, 192
s 47(3) . . . 194
s 47(6) . . . 193
s 47(7) . . . 194
s 47(8) . . . 193
s 49 . . . 187, 190
s 49(1)(2) . . . 183
s 53 . . . 203, 907
s 54(1)(2) . . . 153
s 55 . . . 159
s 55A(7) . . . 371
s 56 . . . 159
s 56(4) . . . 371
s 60 . . . 201
s 62 . . . 181, 941
s 62(1) . . . 204, 941, 950
s 62(1)(a) . . . 180
s 62(2) . . . 179, 182
s 62(3) . . . 180, 184
s 62(4) . . . 181
s 62(5) . . . 181
s 63 . . . 154
s 63(1) . . . 180, 181, 182, 184
s 63(2) . . . 181, 182, 907
s 63(3) . . . 185
s 63(4) . . . 154
s 63(5) . . . 153, 180
Pt 4A (ss 63A–63S) . . . 197, 199, 200
s 63A . . . 78, 198
s 63A(2) . . . 198
s 63A(3) . . . 198
s 63A(4) . . . 198
s 63A(6) . . . 198
s 63C . . . 199
s 63C(4) . . . 199
s 63C(7) . . . 199
s 63CA . . . 199
s 63D . . . 198
s 63E . . . 198
ss 63F–63G . . . 198
s 63H(1) . . . 199
s 63H(2) . . . 199

s 63H(4) . . . 199
s 63J . . . 199
s 66(1) . . . 900
Sch 4
    para 2 . . . 155
Sch 6 . . . 197
Sch 7 . . . 203, 204, 907, 924
    para 1 . . . 950
    para 3(2) . . . 950
    para 4(b) . . . 950
    para 5 . . . 907
    para 5(c) . . . 907
    para 7(1)–(2) . . . 907
    para 8(1)–(2) . . . 907
    para 10(4) . . . 907
    para 11 . . . 907
    para 12(a) . . . 907
    para 12(b) . . . 907
    para 13 . . . 907
    para 14(1) . . . 907
Sch 8
    para 9(2) . . . 900
    para 16 . . . 914, 915
    para 53 . . . 159
    para 59 . . . 159
Family Law Reform Act 1969 . . . 49, 304
s 1 . . . 746
s 1(1) . . . 296
s 3(1)(b) . . . 360
s 3(2) . . . 972
s 6 . . . 752
s 8 . . . 320, 323, 353, 648, 712
s 8(2) . . . 352
s 14 . . . 972
s 15 . . . 966
Pt III (ss 20–25) . . . 269
s 20 . . . 264, 265
s 21 . . . 267, 268, 765
s 21(3) . . . 267, 268, 271, 352
s 21(3)(b) . . . 268
s 21(4) . . . 268
s 23(1) . . . 268
s 23(2) . . . 269
s 26 . . . 262, 263
Sch 3
    para 3 . . . 750
Family Law Reform Act 1987 . . . 251,
254, 257, 258, 259, 304, 305, 306, 307,
776, 972
s 1 . . . 306, 368, 386, 972
s 1(1) . . . 306
s 1(2) . . . 306, 368
s 1(3) . . . 306, 368, 369, 385, 386
s 1(3)(b) . . . 370
s 1(4) . . . 306, 368
s 4 . . . 372
s 17 . . . 773
s 18 . . . 972
s 18(2) . . . 360, 973
s 18(2A) . . . 973

s 18(3) . . . 972
s 19(2) . . . 304, 305
s 19(4) . . . 304
s 22 . . . 303
s 24 . . . 271
s 27 . . . 252, 272
s 27(1) . . . 251
s 27(2) . . . 251
s 28(1) . . . 300
s 28(2) . . . 301
Family Law (Scotland) Act 1985
s 9 . . . 868
s 9(1) . . . 831
s 10 . . . 868
s 10(1) . . . 831
s 25 . . . 120
Family Law (Scotland) Act 2006 . . . 387, 952
s 2 . . . 76
s 3 . . . 56, 116
s 21 . . . 299
s 23 . . . 371, 385
s 25 . . . 945
s 25(2) . . . 942
Fatal Accidents Act 1846 . . . 93
Fatal Accidents Act 1976 . . . 7, 94, 304, 367, 726,
940, 945, 979
s 1 . . . 367
Finance Act 1988 . . . 777
Finance Act 2012
s 8 . . . 779
Sch 1 . . . 779
Forced Marriage (Civil Protection) Act
2007 . . . 78, 86, 197
Forced Marriage etc. (Protection and
Jurisdiction)(Scotland) Act 2011 . . . 198

Gender Recognition Act 2004 . . . 43, 52, 66, 83, 248
s 1 . . . 43
s 2 . . . 43
s 3 . . . 43
s 4 . . . 43
s 5B . . . 44
s 11A . . . 43
s 12 . . . 248, 369
s 25 . . . 43
Sch 1(1) . . . 43
Sch 2
para 2 . . . 83
para 3 . . . 83
para 5 . . . 83
Sch 4
para 3 . . . 52
Guardianship Act 1973 . . . 312
s 1 . . . 5
Guardianship of Infants Act 1886 . . . 285, 312,
313, 314
s 5 . . . 313
Guardianship of Infants Act 1925 . . . 94, 284,
285, 312, 316
s 1 . . . 5, 314, 315, 316, 350, 397, 414

Guardianship of Minors Act 1971 . . . 285, 318,
795
s 1 . . . 312, 316, 397, 414
s 1(b) . . . 422
s 3 . . . 286
s 14 . . . 384

Homelessness Act 2002 . . . 205
s 10(1)(a) . . . 206
Housing Act 1985 . . . 7, 907
s 75 . . . 391
Sch 2
Pt 1, ground 2A . . . 204
Housing Act 1988 . . . 7, 943
Sch 2
Pt 2, ground 14A . . . 204
Housing Act 1996 . . . 404
Pt VII (ss 175–218) . . . 205
s 175(1) . . . 205
s 175(2)(a) . . . 206
s 175(3) . . . 206
s 176 . . . 205
s 177 . . . 205, 206
s 179 . . . 205
s 184 . . . 205
s 185 . . . 205
s 186 . . . 205
s 188 . . . 205
s 189(1) . . . 207
s 190 . . . 208
s 191(1) . . . 208
s 193 . . . 205
s 193(2) . . . 208
s 198 . . . 209
s 198(2)(3) . . . 209
Human Fertilisation and Embryology Act
1990 . . . 245, 247, 250, 251, 258, 300, 489,
806, 809
s 2(1) . . . 252, 253
s 13(5) . . . 258
s 24(4) . . . 249
s 27 . . . 248, 251, 254, 273
s 28 . . . 251, 252, 254, 273
s 28(2) . . . 252, 254, 278
s 28(3) . . . 249, 252, 254, 278
s 28(4) . . . 252
s 28(5)(a) . . . 252
s 28(5A)–(5C) . . . 250
s 28(5D) . . . 250, 255
s 28(5E)–(5I) . . . 250
s 28(6) . . . 248, 252
s 28(7)(a) . . . 252
s 28(7)(b) . . . 252
s 28(8) . . . 254
s 29 . . . 251, 273
s 29(3A) . . . 250
s 29(3B) . . . 250
s 30 . . . 247, 277, 282
s 30(7) . . . 280
s 31 . . . 273

s 31(3) . . . 273
s 31ZA . . . 273
s 31ZA(2)(a) . . . 273
s 31ZA(4) . . . 273
s 31ZA(6) . . . 273
s 34 . . . 273
s 49(3) . . . 248
Sch 2 . . . 248, 251
Sch 3
    para 1 . . . 249
    para 5 . . . 248, 249
Human Fertilisation and Embryology Act
    2008 . . . 244, 245, 249, 251, 254–6, 258, 517,
    706, 794, 806, 809, 979–80
s 14(1) . . . 258
s 14(2) . . . 258
s 24 . . . 273
Pt 2 (ss 33–58) . . . 302, 369
ss 33–47 . . . 273
s 33 . . . 248, 276, 307
s 33(1) . . . 247
s 33(3) . . . 248
s 34 . . . 307
s 35 . . . 254, 256, 276, 278, 307
s 35(2) . . . 254
s 36 . . . 254, 256, 278
s 36(1) . . . 276
s 37 . . . 90, 254, 256
s 37(1)(c) . . . 255
s 37(1)(d) . . . 255
s 37(2) . . . 255
s 37(3) . . . 255
s 39 . . . 250
s 39(2) . . . 250
s 39(3) . . . 250
s 40(1) . . . 255
s 40(2) . . . 255
s 40(3) . . . 255
s 40(4) . . . 255, 256
s 41 . . . 248
s 42 . . . 256, 257, 271, 278, 297, 302, 369
s 43 . . . 256, 257, 271, 272, 278, 297, 302, 303,
    369, 385, 386, 520, 709, 784, 973
s 44 . . . 90, 256
s 45 . . . 256
s 46 . . . 257
s 46(1) . . . 256
s 46(2) . . . 256
s 46(3)(4) . . . 256
s 47 . . . 248, 257
s 48(3) . . . 250, 255, 256
s 48(6) . . . 302
s 48(7) . . . 302
s 54 . . . 247, 272, 276, 277, 278, 280, 282, 369,
    370, 391, 682, 729, 761, 973, 980
s 54(1) . . . 281
s 54(2) . . . 278, 281
s 54(2)(c) . . . 278
s 54(3) . . . 278, 281
s 54(4) . . . 281

s 54(4)(a) . . . 278
s 54(4)(b) . . . 278
s 54(5) . . . 278, 281
s 54(6) . . . 279, 281
s 54(7) . . . 279, 281
s 54(8) . . . 279, 280, 281
s 54(10) . . . 277
s 56 . . . 973
s 57(1) . . . 248, 369
s 57(4) . . . 277
s 58(2) . . . 254, 255, 278
s 59 . . . 275
s 59(7) . . . 275
Sch 1
    para 10(8) . . . 784
Sch 2
    para 26(3) . . . 385
Sch 6
    para 6 . . . 271, 371
    para 16 . . . 303, 386
    para 17 . . . 303
    para 19 . . . 386
    para 25(1) . . . 973
    para 25(2) . . . 973
    para 26(1) . . . 369
    para 26(2) . . . 369
    para 26(3) . . . 369
    para 27 . . . 385, 386
    para 29 . . . 386
Human Fertilisation and Embryology
    (Deceased Fathers) Act 2003 . . . 250, 255
Human Rights Act 1998 . . . 9, 23, 24, 28, 32, 161,
    318, 322, 332, 397, 415, 416, 424, 509, 529, 675,
    676, 677, 678, 941, 1039
s 2 . . . 24
s 2(1)(a)–(d) . . . 24
s 3 . . . 24, 347, 641
s 4 . . . 24, 25, 577
s 4(5) . . . 24
s 6 . . . 25, 577, 650
s 6(3) . . . 25, 678
s 7 . . . 25, 577, 641, 678, 679
s 7(7) . . . 679
s 8 . . . 25, 678, 679
s 8(4) . . . 679
s 10 . . . 25

Immigration Act 1971
s 5 . . . 104
Immigration and Asylum Act 1999 . . . 49
s 15 . . . 1029
s 24 . . . 82
s 24(5) . . . 81
Income Tax Act 2007
s 45 . . . 92
Income Tax (Earnings and Pensions)
    Act 2003
s 681B . . . 779
Infant Life (Preservation) Act 1929
s 1 . . . 391

Inheritance (Family Provision) Act
 1938 ... 975
Inheritance (Provision for Family and
 Dependants) Act 1975 ... 7, 15, 223, 251, 304,
 726, 832, 895, 940, 945, 954, 961, 963, 968, 971,
 974, 975, 978
 s 1(1) ... 976, 983
 s 1(1)(d) ... 298
 s 1(1)(e) ... 978, 979
 s 1(1ZA) ... 976
 s 1(2) ... 983
 s 1(2A) ... 977
 s 1(3) ... 980, 982
 s 2(1) ... 983, 989, 990
 s 2(1)(f) ... 991
 s 2(1)(g) ... 991
 s 2(1)(h) ... 992
 s 2(2)(3) ... 990
 s 3 ... 984
 s 3(1) ... 984, 990
 s 3(2) ... 986, 987
 s 3(2A) ... 987
 s 3(3) ... 988
 s 3(4) ... 981, 988
 s 4 ... 976
 s 5 ... 990
 s 6 ... 990
 s 7 ... 991
 s 9 ... 989
 s 9(3) ... 989
 s 10 ... 989, 992
 s 11 ... 989, 992
 s 15 ... 877, 977, 992
 s 15A ... 993
 s 15B ... 993
 s 15ZA ... 992
 s 17(4) ... 992
 s 18 ... 992
 s 18A ... 992
 s 19(2) ... 990
 s 20(1) ... 976
 s 20(2) ... 990
 s 23 ... 976
 s 25(1) ... 977, 980, 984, 989
 s 25(2) ... 989
 s 25(4) ... 977
 s 25(4A) ... 977
 s 25(5) ... 977
 s 25(5A) ... 977
Inheritance Taxes Act 1984
 s 18 ... 92
Inheritance and Trustees' Powers Act
 2014 ... 968, 969
 s 1(2) ... 970, 972
 s 3(1) ... 969
 s 4(1) ... 966
 s 5 ... 973
 Sch 1 ... 970
 Sch 2
  para 2 ... 976, 977, 980

 para 2(2)(b) ... 976
 para 2(3) ... 976, 977
 para 3 ... 980, 982
 para 4 ... 992
 para 5(2) ... 987
 para 5(3) ... 988
 para 5(4) ... 981, 988
 para 7 ... 976
 para 7(2) ... 989
 Sch 4
  para 1(2) ... 969
  para 2 ... 971
Insolvency Act 1986 ... 116
 s 282(1)(a) ... 919
 s 283A ... 161
 s 329 ... 117
 s 335A ... 160, 161
 s 335A(3) ... 161
 s 336 ... 160
 s 336(1)–(2) ... 160
 s 336(4) ... 160
 s 336(5) ... 161
 s 337 ... 160
 s 337(1)–(4) ... 160
 s 337(5) ... 160
 s 337(6) ... 161
 s 338 ... 160
 s 339 ... 116, 159
 s 341(1)(a) ... 116
 s 341(2) ... 116
 s 342(2) ... 116
 s 342(4) ... 116
 s 385(1) ... 160
 s 423 ... 116, 159, 918, 989
 s 425(2)–(3) ... 116
 s 435 ... 116
 s 436 ... 116
Insolvency Act 1996
 s 335A ... 145
Interpretation Act 1978
 s 5 ... 525
 s 6(c) ... 287, 290
 Sch 1 ... 355, 525, 920, 977
Intestates' Estates Act 1890 ... 967
Intestates' Estates Act 1952 ... 971, 975
 s 5 ... 971
 Sch 2 ... 971
  para 1(1) ... 971
  para 1(2) ... 971
  para 1(4)–(5) ... 971
  para 2 ... 971
  para 3 ... 971
  para 3(1)(b) ... 971
  para 4 ... 971
  para 4(5) ... 971
  para 5(2) ... 971

Jobseekers Act 1995
 Sch 2
  para 19(2) ... 562

Judicature Act 1873 ... 64, 212, 309, 310
  s 25(10) ... 310
Judicature Act 1875 ... 212, 309

Land Charges Act 1972 ... 150, 155
  s 2(4) ... 150
  s 2(7) ... 150, 155
  s 4(8) ... 155
Land Registration Act 1925
  s 20(1) ... 148
Land Registration Act 2002 ... 148
  s 42 ... 148
  s 46 ... 148
  s 116 ... 158
  Sch 1
    para 2 ... 155
  Sch 3
    para 2 ... 149, 155
    para 2(b) ... 149, 150
    para 2(c) ... 149, 150
Law of Property Act 1925 ... 145
  s 27(1) ... 147
  s 30 ... 144, 145
  s 37 ... 107
  s 53(1)(b) ... 127
  s 53(2) ... 127
  s 177 ... 962
Law of Property (Miscellaneous Provisions)
  Act 1989
  s 1 ... 780
  s 2(5) ... 140
Law Reform (Husband and Wife) Act
  1962 ... 117
  s 1 ... 99
  s 3(3) ... 99
Law Reform (Married Women
  and Tortfeasors) Act 1935 ... 91, 99, 107, 962
  s 1 ... 99
  s 1(c) ... 99
Law Reform (Miscellaneous Provisions) Act
  1949 ... 743
  s 4(1) ... 65, 301
Law Reform (Miscellaneous Provisions) Act
  1970 ... 109
  s 1 ... 39, 40
  s 1(2) ... 40
  s 2 ... 39
  s 2(1) ... 118, 124, 143
  s 2(2) ... 118
  s 3(1) ... 109
  s 3(2) ... 109
Law Reform (Miscellaneous Provisions)
  Act 1989
  s 1(3) ... 929
Law Reform (Parent and Child) (Scotland) Act
  1986 ... 306
  s 5 ... 261
Law Reform (Succession) Act 1995 ... 288, 964,
  967, 968, 980
  s 1(1) ... 968
  s 2 ... 7, 976, 978

s 3 ... 963
s 4 ... 964
Legal Aid, Sentencing and Punishment of
  Offenders Act 2012 ... 13, 210, 838, 863
  s 8(1) ... 863
  s 25(1) ... 863
  s 51 ... 849
  Sch 1 ... 13
    para 1 ... 210
    para 12(9) ... 13, 210
    para 13(3) ... 13
    para 14 ... 13
    para 18(3) ... 1033
Legitimacy Act 1926 ... 302, 966, 972
  s 1(1) ... 302
  s 1(2) ... 302
Legitimacy Act 1959 ... 300
  s 1 ... 302
  s 1(2) ... 302
  s 3 ... 384
Legitimacy Act 1976 ... 386
  s 1 ... 301, 306, 368
  s 1(1) ... 300, 302
  s 1(2) ... 300
  s 1(3) ... 301
  s 1(4) ... 301
  s 2 ... 302
  s 2A ... 303, 386
  s 3(2) ... 303
  s 4 ... 303, 725
  s 4(2) ... 727
  s 5 ... 305, 972
  s 5(3) ... 966
  s 5(6) ... 727
  s 6(2) ... 727
  s 8 ... 305
  s 10 ... 368, 386
  Sch 1
    para 1 ... 302
    para 4(2) ... 305
Legitimacy Declaration Act 1858 ... 62, 303
Life Assurance Act 1774 ... 92
Limitation Act 1980
  s 9 ... 819
Local Authority Social Services Act 1970 ... 554
  s 7 ... 561
Local Government Act 1974
  s 26(4) ... 666
  s 26(5) ... 666
Lord Campbell's Act *see* Fatal Accidents
  Act 1846
Lord Hardwicke's Act 1753 ... 48, 49, 55

Magistrates Courts Act 1980 ... 539
  s 75 ... 788
  s 76 ... 917
  s 93 ... 917
  s 127(1) ... 728
Maintenance Enforcement Act 1991
  s 1 ... 917
Maintenance Orders Act 1958 ... 916

Maintenance Orders (Reciprocal Enforcement)
   Act 1972 . . . 916
Marriage Act 1823 . . . 48
Marriage Act 1836 . . . 49, 55
Marriage Act 1949 . . . 49, 57, 68, 69,
   70, 71, 72
   s 1(1) . . . 46
   s 1(2) . . . 46
   s 1(3) . . . 46, 297
   s 2 . . . 44
   s 2(1) . . . 49
   s 3(1) . . . 51
   s 3(1)(b) . . . 51
   s 3(1A)(a)(i) . . . 381
   s 3(3) . . . 51
   s 3(5) . . . 51
   s 3(6) . . . 51, 744
   s 4 . . . 52
   Pt II (ss 5–25) . . . 51
   s 5 . . . 51
   s 5A . . . 52
   s 12(2) . . . 52
   s 16(3) . . . 52
   s 17 . . . 55
   s 22 . . . 52
   s 24 . . . 72
   s 25 . . . 52, 72
   s 25(2) . . . 72
   s 26(1) . . . 52
   s 26(1)(bb) . . . 54
   s 26(1)(d) . . . 53
   s 26B . . . 53
   s 33 . . . 52
   s 34 . . . 53
   s 35 . . . 53
   s 36 . . . 53
   s 41 . . . 53
   s 42 . . . 53
   s 44(2) . . . 52, 53
   s 44(3) . . . 53
   s 45(1) . . . 53
   s 45(2) . . . 54
   s 45A . . . 55
   s 45A(2) . . . 52
   s 45A(3) . . . 52
   s 46 . . . 54
   s 46A . . . 54
   s 46B . . . 54
   s 47 . . . 53
   s 47(3) . . . 72
   s 48 . . . 72
   s 49 . . . 72
   s 49A . . . 72
   s 52 . . . 53
   Pt IV (ss 53–67) . . . 49
   s 55 . . . 69
   s 71 . . . 72
   s 72 . . . 72
   s 75 . . . 71

s 75(1)(a) . . . 52
s 75(2)(a) . . . 68
s 78 . . . 46
s 78(1) . . . 46, 297
s 78(2) . . . 51
Sch . . . 1
   Pt I . . . 45, 726
   para 1(2) . . . 45
   Pt II . . . 45, 46
Marriage Act 1949 (Amendment) Act
   1954 . . . 49
Marriage Act 1961
   s 12 . . . 44
Marriage Act 1983 . . . 49, 55
   s 1(6) . . . 55
   Sch 1 . . . 52, 72
Marriage Act 1994 . . . 49, 54
   s 1(1) . . . 52
   s 26A . . . 53
   s 44(1) . . . 53
   s 44(2) . . . 53
   s 44(3) . . . 53
Marriage Acts Amendment Act 1958 . . . 49
   s 1(1) . . . 53
Marriage Ceremony (Prescribed Words) Act
   1996 . . . 49
Marriage and Civil Partnership (Scotland) Act
   2014 . . . 9, 33
Marriage (Enabling) Act 1960 . . . 49
Marriage (Prohibited Degrees of Relationship)
   Act 1986 . . . 46, 49, 52
   s 1(1) . . . 46
   s 1(5) . . . 46
   s 3 . . . 52
Marriage (Registrar General's Licence) Act
   1970 . . . 49, 54
   s 1 . . . 55
   s 12 . . . 72
   s 13A . . . 72
   s 15 . . . 49
   s 16 . . . 71
Marriage (Registration of Buildings)
   Act 1990
   s 1(1) . . . 53
Marriage (Same Sex Couples) Act 2013 . . . 3, 9,
   33–4, 36, 41, 50, 56, 61, 65, 73, 189, 218, 251,
   256, 744, 944
   s 1(1) . . . 34
   s 1(3) . . . 50, 52
   s 1(4) . . . 50, 52
   s 2 . . . 50
   s 2(5) . . . 50
   s 2(6) . . . 50
   s 4 . . . 50, 53
   s 5 . . . 50, 53
   s 7 . . . 55
   s 8 . . . 52
   s 9 . . . 44
   s 9(1) . . . 44

s 9(2) . . . 44
s 11(1) . . . 90
s 11(2) . . . 90
s 12 . . . 44
s 14 . . . 56
s 15 . . . 34, 61, 88, 241
Sch 1
   para 1 . . . 34
   para 5 . . . 34
Sch 3
   para 1 . . . 90, 143
   para 2 . . . 944
   para 5(2) . . . 90
   para 5(2)(b) . . . 258
Sch 4
   Pt 2 (para 2) . . . 262
   para 3 . . . 215, 241
   para 4 . . . 73, 74, 95
Sch 5
   para 3 . . . 43
   para 5 . . . 44
   para 10 . . . 43
Sch 7
   para 4 . . . 72
   para 15 . . . 72
   para 25 . . . 72
   para 27 . . . 42, 71
   paras 37–41 . . . 256
Marriage (Scotland) Act 1977
   s 20A . . . 76
Marriage (Society of Friends) Act 1860 . . . 53
Marriage (Wales) Act 1986 . . . 49
Marriage (Wales and Monmouthshire) Act
   1962 . . . 49
Married Women (Restraint upon Anticipation)
   Act 1949 . . . 107
Married Women's Property Act 1870 . . . 91, 106, 107
   s 11 . . . 99
Married Women's Property Act 1882 . . . 99, 101,
   106, 107, 774, 961–2
   s 1(1) . . . 106
   s 2 . . . 106
   s 5 . . . 106
   s 11 . . . 92
   s 17 . . . 100, 107, 117, 118, 124, 127, 145, 829,
      832
Married Women's Property Act 1964 . . . 111
   s 1 . . . 111
Matrimonial Causes Act 1857 . . . 63–4, 93, 212
   s 27 . . . 212
Matrimonial Causes Act 1878 . . . 166, 786
   s 4 . . . 166
Matrimonial Causes Act 1923 . . . 94, 212
   s 1 . . . 212
Matrimonial Causes Act 1937 . . . 66, 74, 83, 212,
   301, 959
   s 7(2) . . . 301
Matrimonial Causes Act 1965
   s 8(2) . . . 52
   ss 26–28 . . . 975

Matrimonial Causes Act 1973 . . . 46, 65, 66, 144,
   189, 203, 214–30, 241, 293, 535, 791, 828–9,
   831, 832, 837, 846, 848, 864, 920, 925, 928, 929,
   953, 977, 980, 991, 992
   s 1(1) . . . 214
   s 1(2) . . . 152, 214
   s 1(2)(a) . . . 214, 216
   s 1(2)(b) . . . 215
   s 1(2)(c) . . . 218
   s 1(2)(d) . . . 219
   s 1(2)(e) . . . 221
   s 1(3) . . . 214
   s 1(5) . . . 228
   s 1(6) . . . 215, 241
   s 2(1) . . . 215
   s 2(2) . . . 215
   s 2(3) . . . 217
   s 2(5) . . . 218, 219, 221
   s 2(6) . . . 220
   s 2(7) . . . 220
   s 3 . . . 214
   s 4(1) . . . 242
   s 4(2) . . . 242
   s 5 . . . 219, 222, 224, 238, 242
   s 5(3) . . . 223
   s 6(1) . . . 229
   s 9(2) . . . 228
   s 10 . . . 219, 222, 224, 228, 242
   s 10(1) . . . 221
   s 10(2) . . . 224
   s 10(3) . . . 224
   s 10(4) . . . 224
   s 10A . . . 225, 241
   s 10A(3) . . . 225
   s 11 . . . 43, 70
   s 11(a)(i) . . . 71
   s 11(a)(ii) . . . 71
   s 11(a)(iii) . . . 68, 71
   s 11(b) . . . 71
   s 11(c) . . . 25, 42, 71
   s 11(d) . . . 71
   s 12 . . . 73, 83, 95
   s 12(1)(a) . . . 74, 75
   s 12(1)(b) . . . 74, 75
   s 12(1)(c) . . . 76, 84
   s 12(1)(d) . . . 82
   s 12(1)(e) . . . 83
   s 12(1)(f) . . . 83
   s 12(1)(g) . . . 83, 85
   s 12(1)(h) . . . 83
   s 12(2) . . . 74
   s 13 . . . 75
   s 13(1) . . . 84
   s 13(2) . . . 85
   s 13(2A) . . . 83
   s 13(3) . . . 85
   s 13(4) . . . 85
   s 14(1) . . . 71
   s 15 . . . 67
   s 16 . . . 65, 67, 86, 301, 302

s 17 . . . 242
s 18(1) . . . 152, 242
s 18(2) . . . 971
s 19 . . . 959, 960
s 19(3) . . . 960
Pt II (ss 21–40) . . . 829, 844, 865, 906, 924
s 21 . . . 830, 866
s 21A . . . 223, 830, 865
s 21A(1) . . . 844
s 21A(1)(b) . . . 844
s 22 . . . 787, 837, 838, 865
ss 22A–24 . . . 849
s 22ZA . . . 849, 865
s 22ZA(1) . . . 838
s 22ZA(2) . . . 838
s 22ZA(3) . . . 839
s 22ZA(4) . . . 839
s 22ZA(10) . . . 839
s 23 . . . 830, 842, 843, 865
s 23(1) . . . 831
s 23(1)(a) . . . 839
s 23(1)(b) . . . 839
s 23(1)(c) . . . 840, 913
s 23(1)(d) . . . 840
s 23(3) . . . 841
s 23(3)(c) . . . 841, 913
s 23(5) . . . 831
s 24 . . . 108, 118, 125, 203, 830, 847, 865, 907
s 24(1) . . . 831
s 24(1)(a) . . . 845
s 24(1)(b) . . . 845
s 24(1)(c) . . . 848
s 24(1)(d) . . . 848
s 24(3) . . . 831
s 24A . . . 223, 829, 830, 849, 865, 906, 914
s 24A(6) . . . 849
s 24B . . . 223, 830, 842, 865
s 24B(1) . . . 831, 843
s 24B(2) . . . 831
s 24B(3) . . . 844
s 24B(5) . . . 844
s 24C . . . 223, 830, 865
s 24D . . . 223, 830, 844, 865
s 25 . . . 837, 849, 850, 854, 856, 857, 858, 865,
    867, 870, 890, 891, 896, 900, 901, 930
s 25(1) . . . 427, 805, 829, 874, 895
s 25(1)(c) . . . 789
s 25(1)(f) . . . 900
s 25(2) . . . 790, 874, 875, 882, 895, 909
s 25(2)(a) . . . 877
s 25(2)(b) . . . 889, 891
s 25(2)(d) . . . 871
s 25(2)(e) . . . 871, 886
s 25(2)(f) . . . 125, 895, 899
s 25(2)(g) . . . 854, 895, 898, 899, 901, 902
s 25(3) . . . 791
s 25(4) . . . 791, 875
s 25A . . . 865
s 25A(1) . . . 830, 876
s 25A(2) . . . 830, 876, 879

s 25A(3) . . . 829, 876
s 25B . . . 223, 830, 866
s 25B(1) . . . 842
s 25B(4) . . . 842
s 25B(5) . . . 842
s 25B(7) . . . 843
s 25C . . . 223, 830, 866
s 25C(2)(a) . . . 842
s 25C(2)(b) . . . 843
s 25D . . . 223, 830, 865, 866
s 25D(3) . . . 842
s 25D(4) . . . 842
s 25E . . . 842, 866
s 26 . . . 866
s 27 . . . 536, 775, 786, 790–1, 866, 920
s 27(3) . . . 790
s 27(3A) . . . 791
s 27(3B) . . . 790
s 27(5) . . . 790
s 27(6) . . . 790
s 27(6A) . . . 866
s 27(6B) . . . 793, 866
s 27(7) . . . 791
s 28 . . . 866
s 28(1)(a)(b) . . . 839
s 28(1A) . . . 866, 877, 878, 879, 880, 913
s 28(3) . . . 832
s 29 . . . 792, 866, 876
s 29(1)–(3) . . . 845
s 29(4) . . . 793, 840
s 30 . . . 866
s 31 . . . 782, 866, 913
s 31(1) . . . 912
s 31(2) . . . 912
s 31(3) . . . 912
s 31(7) . . . 866
s 31(7)(a) . . . 914
s 31(7A) . . . 866, 877, 915
s 31(7B) . . . 866, 877, 915
s 31(7B)(a) . . . 914
s 31(7B)(b) . . . 914
s 31(7B)(ba) . . . 915
s 31(7B)(c) . . . 915
s 31(7C) . . . 866, 877, 915
s 31(7D) . . . 866, 877
s 31(7E) . . . 866, 877, 915
s 31(7F) . . . 866, 877
s 31(7G) . . . 866, 877
s 31(10) . . . 915
s 32 . . . 866, 916, 918
s 33 . . . 866, 916
s 33A . . . 850, 866
s 34 . . . 38, 781, 782, 783, 784, 855, 856, 859,
    866, 992
s 34(2) . . . 782
s 35 . . . 782, 783, 784, 855, 857, 859, 866, 928
s 36 . . . 782, 866
s 37 . . . 866, 918, 919
s 37(4) . . . 919
s 38 . . . 866, 916

s 39 . . . 866
s 40 . . . 866
s 40A . . . 866
s 41 . . . 225, 226, 228, 230, 238, 242, 304,
　　444, 446, 447
s 45 . . . 303
s 52 . . . 297, 866
s 52(3) . . . 832, 839
Sch 4 . . . 830
Matrimonial Causes (Property and
　Maintenance) Act 1958 . . . 975
s 7 . . . 117
s 7(7) . . . 118
Matrimonial and Family Proceedings Act
　1984 . . . 16, 214, 829, 830, 868, 877, 880, 882,
　924
s 2 . . . 85
s 3 . . . 829, 874, 876, 901
s 3(4) . . . 829, 830
s 7 . . . 850
Pt III (ss 12–27) . . . 58, 536, 920, 921, 922,
　　923, 924, 925
s 12(1) . . . 920
s 12(2) . . . 921
s 12(3) . . . 921
s 13(1) . . . 921
s 13(2) . . . 921
s 14 . . . 923
s 15 . . . 921
s 15(1) . . . 922
s 16 . . . 924
s 16(1) . . . 923
s 16(2) . . . 921, 923
s 17 . . . 924
s 18 . . . 924
s 18(1)–(5) . . . 924
s 18(6) . . . 924
s 19 . . . 924
s 20 . . . 922, 924
s 21 . . . 924
s 23 . . . 924
s 25(3) . . . 993
s 27 . . . 920, 922
s 31A . . . 15
s 31E . . . 303
s 33(3) . . . 16
s 36A(6) . . . 16
s 38(2)(b) . . . 743, 762
s 38(5) . . . 762
s 39 . . . 16
Sch 1
　　para 11 . . . 849
Matrimonial Homes Act 1967 . . . 94, 153,
　155, 167
Matrimonial Homes Act 1983 . . . 153, 167, 505
Matrimonial Homes and Property
　Act 1981
s 7 . . . 829, 830, 849
Matrimonial Proceedings (Children)
　Act 1958
s 2(1) . . . 226

Matrimonial Proceedings and Property Act
　1970 . . . 124, 143, 214, 775, 829
s 4 . . . 108
s 5 . . . 867
s 37 . . . 133, 143, 144
s 39 . . . 117
s 41 . . . 99, 775
Matrimonial Property Act 1964 . . . 111
Mental Capacity Act 2005 . . . 320, 714, 715, 743
s 1(4) . . . 80
s 27(1)(a) . . . 80
s 67 . . . 714
Sch 6 . . . 714
Mental Health Act 1983 . . . 82, 85, 743, 758
s 1(2) . . . 82
s 33 . . . 745
Mental Health Act 2007 . . . 743

National Assistance Act 1948 . . . 777
Nationality, Immigration and Asylum
　Act 2002
s 1 . . . 102
Naturalisation Act 1870
s 10(1) . . . 102
Nullity of Marriage Act 1971 . . . 65, 70
s 1 . . . 43
s 2 . . . 73
s 5 . . . 86

Offences Against the Person Act 1828
　(9 Geo 4, c31)
s.2 . . . 92
Offences Against the Person Act 1861
s 18 . . . 347
s 20 . . . 347
s 27 . . . 341
s 47 . . . 347

Pension Schemes Act 1993
s 101B . . . 844
s 101C(1) . . . 844
Pensions Act 1995
s 166 . . . 223
s 166(1) . . . 830
s 166(2) . . . 903
s 166(3)(a) . . . 912
Pensions Act 2004
　Pt 2, Chp 3 (ss 120-181) . . . 842
　Sch 12
　　para 3 . . . 842
Perjury Act 1911
s 3 . . . 71
s 4 . . . 250
Places of Worship Registration Act
　1855 . . . 53
Police and Criminal Evidence Act 1984 . . . 97,
　170
s 17(1)(e) . . . 592
s 48 . . . 592
s 80 . . . 97, 171
s 80(7) . . . 97

s 80A . . . 98
Sch 1A
    para 14A . . . 170
Poor Law Amendment Act 1844 . . . 776
Poor Relief Act 1601 . . . 2, 777
   s 6 . . . 773
Powers of Criminal Courts (Sentencing)
   Act 2000
   ss 90–91 . . . 573
   s 150(1) . . . 365
   s 150(1)(a) . . . 365
   s 150(1)(b) . . . 365
   s 150(2) . . . 365
Presumption of Death Act
   2013 . . . 959, 960
   s 1 . . . 959
   s 1(3) . . . 959
   s 1(4) . . . 959
   s 2 . . . 959
   s 3 . . . 960
   s 4 . . . 960
   s 5 . . . 960
   s 15 . . . 960
   Sch 2
      para 3 . . . 959
Proceeds of Crime Act 2002 . . . 835–6
   s 328(1) . . . 835
Property (Relationships) Act 1976 . . . 831
Protection of Freedoms Act 2012 . . . 173
   s 111 . . . 175
   s 114(1) . . . 52
Protection from Harassment Act
   1997 . . . 173–8, 180, 193, 195–6
   s 1 . . . 174, 175, 180
   s 1(1) . . . 174, 175
   s 1(1)(a) . . . 174
   s 1(2) . . . 174
   s 2 . . . 174, 176
   s 2(2) . . . 174
   s 2A . . . 175
   s 3(1) . . . 196
   s 3(2) . . . 196
   s 3(6)–(8) . . . 196
   s 3(9) . . . 196
   s 4 . . . 175, 176
   s 4(1) . . . 176
   s 4(4) . . . 176
   s 4(5) . . . 176
   s 4A . . . 176
   s 4A(1) . . . 176
   s 5 . . . 176
   s 5(3)(b) . . . 177
   s 5(4) . . . 177
   s 5(5) . . . 177
   s 5A . . . 177
   s 5A(3) . . . 177
   s 7(2) . . . 174
   s 7(3) . . . 174
Public Order Act 1986
   s 4A . . . 174

Registration of Births, Deaths and Marriages
   (Scotland) Act 1965
   s 2(6) . . . 371
   s 18(1)(a)–(c) . . . 371
   s 20(1)(a) . . . 371
Rent Act 1977 . . . 7, 941
   Sch 1
      para 2(2) . . . 941
Rights of Children and Young Persons (Wales)
   Measure 2011 . . . 418
   s 1 . . . 22
Royal Marriages Act 1772 . . . 41

School Standards and Framework Act 1998
   s 71 . . . 350, 381
   s 86 . . . 348, 381
   s 92 . . . 348
   s 131 . . . 346
Senior Courts Act 1981
   s 37 . . . 196, 768, 769
   s 41(1) . . . 750
   s 41(2) . . . 750
   s 41(2A) . . . 750, 754
   s 41(3) . . . 750
   s 49 . . . 310
   s 116(1) . . . 360
   Sch 1 . . . 15
Serious Crime Act 2007
   Pt 2 (ss 44–67) . . . 97
Serious Organised Crime and Police
   Act 2005
   s 110 . . . 170
Sex Disqualification (Removal) Act
   1919 . . . 315
Sexual Offences Act 2003
   s 64 . . . 46, 726
   s 65 . . . 726
Sexual Offences (Amendment) Act 1976
   s 1 . . . 96
Social Security Administration Act
   1992 . . . 293
   s 78(6) . . . 726
   s 105 . . . 778
   s 105(3) . . . 726
   s 106 . . . 778
Social Security Contributions and Benefits Act
   1992 . . . 7
   s 141 . . . 779
   s 142 . . . 779
   s 143 . . . 779
   Sch 9 . . . 571
   Sch 10
      para 5 . . . 779
Status of Aliens Act 1914
   s 10 . . . 102
Statute of Distribution of 1670 . . . 967
Statute of Distribution of 1685 . . . 967
Statute of Merton 1235 . . . 302
Succession to the Crown Act 2013
   s 3 . . . 41

Supreme Court Act 1981 *see* Senior Courts
  Act 1981
Surrogacy Arrangements Act 1985 . . . 274, 276
  s 1(2) . . . 246, 274
  s 1A . . . 276
  s 2 . . . 761
  s 2(1) . . . 275
  s 2(2A)–(2C) . . . 275
  s 3 . . . 275
  s 3(1A) . . . 275

Talfourd's Act 1839 . . . 311
Tenures Abolition Act 1660 . . . 309, 743
Theft Act 1968
  s 30(1) . . . 101
  s 30(4) . . . 101
Theft Act 1978
  s 5(2) . . . 101
Tribunals, Courts and Enforcement Act
  2007 . . . 917
  s 13 . . . 816
Trusts of Land and Appointment of Trustees
  Act 1996 . . . 147, 796
  s 4 . . . 144
  s 5 . . . 144
  s 11 . . . 147
  s 12(1) . . . 146
  s 12(2) . . . 146
  s 13 . . . 146
  s 14 . . . 118, 119, 144, 145, 146, 158, 160, 907
  s 15 . . . 145, 146, 907
  s 15(1) . . . 145
  s 15(3) . . . 145
  s 15(4) . . . 145
  Sch 3
    para 4(8) . . . 147
    para 23 . . . 160

Visiting Forces Act 1952 . . . 768

Welfare Reform Act 2009
  Sch 6 . . . 272, 385
  Sch 7
    Pt 1 . . . 778
Welfare Reform Act 2012
  Pt 1 (ss 1–43) . . . 778
  s 33 . . . 778
  s 69 . . . 778
  s 136 . . . 804
  s 136(1) . . . 785
  s 137 . . . 817
  s 138 . . . 785
Welfare Reform and Pensions Act
  1999 . . . 843–4, 882
  s 19 . . . 829
  s 21 . . . 830
  s 29 . . . 844
  s 34(1) . . . 844
  s 47(2) . . . 844
  Sch 3 . . . 223, 830
    para 1 . . . 829, 850

  para 3 . . . 848
  para 5 . . . 874
  para 6 . . . 829, 876
  para 7(2) . . . 912
  para 7(5) . . . 915
  para 8 . . . 850
  Sch 4 . . . 830
Wills Act 1837 . . . 962
  s 9 . . . 287
  s 18 . . . 962
  s 18(2) . . . 962
  s 18(3) . . . 962
  s 18(4) . . . 962
  s 18A . . . 963
  s 18B . . . 962
  s 18C . . . 964
Wills (Soldiers and Sailors) Act 1918
  s 1 . . . 360

Youth Justice and Criminal Evidence Act
  1999 . . . 97
  Part II
    Chp 1 . . . 171
  s 23 . . . 172
  s 24 . . . 172
  s 25(4)(b) . . . 172
  s 27 . . . 172
  s 28 . . . 172
  s 53 . . . 97

BILLS

Child Abduction and Custody Bill . . . 1039
Children and Families Bill . . . 625
  cl 18(2) . . . 900
Civil Partnership Bill 2002 . . . 32
Cohabitation Bill 2013 . . . 974
Cohabitation Rights Bill 2013 . . . 945, 957
Family Law Bill 1996 . . . 902
Housing (Wales) Bill 2013 . . . 205, 207
Human Fertilisation and Embryology Bill
  1990 . . . 283
Nuptial Agreements Bill . . . 929, 987
Relationships (Civil Registration) Bill
  2001 . . . 32
Social Services and Well-being (Wales) Bill
  2014 . . . 559
Surrogacy Arrangements (Amendment) Bill
  1986 . . . 276

AUSTRALIA LEGISLATION

Family Law Act 1975
  s 21 . . . 17
  s 60(CC)(2)(a)–(b) . . . 435
Family Law (Child Abduction Conventions)
  Regulations 1986 . . . 1083
Family Law Reform Act 1995 (Cth) . . . 331
  s 61B . . . 334

IRELAND LEGISLATION

Civil Partnership and Certain Rights and
  Obligations of Cohabitants Act 2010 . . . 952

ISLE OF MAN LEGISLATION

Family Law Act 1991 . . . 331

NETHERLANDS LEGISLATION

Civil Code . . . 61

NEW ZEALAND LEGISLATION

Care of Children Act 2004
  Pt 2 . . . 331, 1083
  Pt 4 . . . 299
Family Courts Act 1980
  s 4 . . . 17
Property (Relationships) Act 1976 . . . 945
Status of Children Act 1969
  s 3(1) . . . 299

NORWAY LEGISLATION

Children Act 1981 . . . 331

UK SECONDARY LEGISLATION

Access to Personal Files (Social
  Services) Regulations 1989
  (SI 1989/206) . . . 361
Adopted Children and Adoption Contact
  Registers Regulations 2005
  (SI 2005/924) . . . 722
  regs 3–5 . . . 1012
  reg 10 . . . 721
Adoption Agencies Regulations 2005
  (SI 2005/389) . . . 693
  regs 3–5 . . . 693
  reg 13 . . . 693
  reg 14 . . . 693
  reg 17 . . . 693
  reg 18 . . . 693
  reg 20 . . . 713
  reg 22 . . . 693
  reg 25(3)(a) . . . 705
  reg 26 . . . 693
  reg 35(4) . . . 700
  reg 46 . . . 704
Adoption Agencies (Wales) Regulations 2005
  (SI 2005/1313)(W.95)
  reg 3 . . . 693
  reg 13 . . . 693
  reg 14 . . . 693
  reg 17 . . . 693
  reg 18 . . . 693
  reg 20 . . . 713
  reg 21 . . . 693
  reg 25 . . . 693
  reg 26(3)(a) . . . 705
  reg 36(7) . . . 700
  reg 47 . . . 704
Adoption and Children Act 2002
  (Commencement No 4) Order 2003
  (SI 2003/3079) . . . 371, 461
Adoption and Children Act 2002
  (Commencement No 7) Order 2004
  (SI 2004/3203) . . . 412
Adoption and Children Act 2002
  (Commencement No 9) Order 2005
  (SI 2005/2213) . . . 386
Adoption (Designation of Overseas Adoptions)
  Order 1973 (SI 1973/19) . . . 1013
Adoption (Designation of Overseas
  Adoptions) (Variation) Order 1993
  (SI 1993/690) . . . 1013
Adoption Support Services (England)
  Regulations and Adoption Agencies
  (Miscellaneous Amendments) Regulations
  2005 (SI 2005/2720)
  reg 3 . . . 697
  reg 6 . . . 697
Adoption Support Services Regulations 2005
  (SI 2005/691) . . . 692
Adoption Support Services (Wales) Regulations
  2005 (SI 2005/1514)
  reg 2 . . . 697
  reg 4 . . . 697
Adoptions with a Foreign Element Regulations
  2005 (SI 2005/392) . . . 1009, 1013, 1015
  reg 9 . . . 1015
Arrangements for Placement of Children
  Regulations 1991 (SI 1991/890) . . . 570
  reg 3 . . . 570
Asylum and Immigration (Treatment of
  Claimants, etc) Act 2004 (Remedial) Order
  2001 (SI 2011/1158) . . . 55

Births and Deaths Registration (Northern
  Ireland) Order 1976 (SI 1976/1041)
  Art 14(3)(a)–(c) . . . 371

Care Planning, Placement and Case Review
  (England) Regulations 2010 (SI 2010/959)
  reg 8(2) . . . 656
  reg 8(4) . . . 660
  Pt 3 (regs 9–14) . . . 661
  Pt 6 (regs 32–38) . . . 662
  Pt 8 (regs 45–47) . . . 662
Child Maintenance and Other Payments
  Act 2008 (Commencement No 11 and
  Transitional Provisions) Order 2013
  (SI 2013/1860) . . . 804
Child Support Fees Regulations 2014
  (SI 2014/612) . . . 804

Child Support (Maintenance Calculation
    Procedure) Regulations 2001 (SI 2001/157)
    reg 7 . . . 809
Child Support Maintenance Calculation
    Regulations 2012 (SI 2012/2677) . . . 815
    reg 4 . . . 812
    reg 14 . . . 816
    reg 17 . . . 816
    regs 19–22 . . . 816
    reg 23 . . . 816
    Pt 4 (regs 34–55) . . . 808
    regs 34–42 . . . 812
    reg 43 . . . 811
    reg 44 . . . 811
    reg 45 . . . 811
    reg 46 . . . 807
    reg 46(5) . . . 807
    reg 47 . . . 807
    reg 49 . . . 809
    reg 50 . . . 807
    reg 52 . . . 813
    reg 57 . . . 815
    reg 60 . . . 815
    reg 65 . . . 814
    reg 66 . . . 814
    reg 68 . . . 813
    reg 68(4) . . . 814
    regs 69–71 . . . 814
    reg 72 . . . 815
    reg 73 . . . 815
Child Support (Meaning of Child and New
    Calculation Rules) (Consequential and
    Miscellaneous Amendment) Regulations
    2012 (SI 2012/2785) . . . 806
Children Act 1989 Representation Procedure
    (England) Regulations 2006
    (SI 2006/1738) . . . 663, 664
    reg 13 . . . 665
    reg 18 . . . 664
    reg 19 . . . 664
Children (Admissibility of Hearsay Evidence)
    Order 1993 (SI 1993/621) . . . 470, 746
Children (Allocation of Proceedings) Order
    1991 (SI 1991/1677) . . . 17
    Art 3 . . . 16
    Art 3(1) . . . 16
    Art 5 . . . 16
Children and Families Act 2014 (Transitional
    Provisions) Order 2014 (SI 2014/1042)
    Art 6 . . . 485
Children (Northern Ireland) Order 1995
    (SI 1995/755) . . . 331
Children (Prescribed Orders—Northern
    Ireland, Guernsey and Isle of Man)
    Regulations 1991 (SI 1991/2032) . . . 525
Children (Private Arrangements for
    Fostering) Regulations 2005 (SI
    2055/1533) . . . 295
Children (Protection From Offenders)
    Miscellaneous Amendments Regulations
    1997 (SI 1997/2308) . . . 766

Children (Secure Accommodation) Regulations
    1991 (SI 1991/1505) . . . 573
    reg 3 . . . 573
    reg 4 . . . 574
    regs 5(2)(a)(b) . . . 574
    reg 10(1) . . . 573
    reg 11 . . . 576
    reg 12 . . . 576
    reg 16 . . . 576
    reg 17 . . . 576
Children's Commissioner for Wales Regulations
    2001 (SI 2001/2787) (W 237)
    reg 5 . . . 667
    reg 6 . . . 667
    reg 22 . . . 478
Children's Homes (England) Regulations 2001
    (SI 2001/3967)
    reg 17(5)(a) . . . 346
Children's Homes (Wales) Regulations 2002
    (SI 2002/327)
    reg 17(5)(a) . . . 346
Civil Jurisdiction and Judgments (Maintenance)
    Regulations 2011 (SI 2011/1484)
    Sch 6 . . . 916, 923
Civil Legal Aid (Financial Resources and
    Payments of Services) Regulations 2013
    (SI 2013/480)
    reg 5(1)(h) . . . 1033
Civil Legal Aid (Statutory Charge) Regulations
    2013 (SI 2013/503)
    reg 4 . . . 863
    reg 5 . . . 864
    reg 22 . . . 864
Civil Procedure Rules 1998 (SI 1998/3132)
    r 8.2 . . . 670
    Pt 21 . . . 471
    r 21.2(2) . . . 358
    r 22.12(1) . . . 286
    r 22.12(2) . . . 286
    Pt 25 . . . 670
    r 25.1(9) . . . 762
    r 40.20 . . . 762
    Pt 52 . . . 544
    r 52.3 . . . 650
    r 52.3(1) . . . 577
    r 52.3(2)(3) . . . 544
    r 52.3(6) . . . 544
    r 52.10(2) . . . 544
    r 52.11(1) . . . 545
    r 52.11(3) . . . 545, 650
    r 52.13 . . . 544
    r 52.13(2) . . . 544
    PD 52A
        para 4.6 . . . 544
        para 4.7 . . . 544
        para 4.9 . . . 544
    r 54.1(2)(a) . . . 669
    r 54.2 . . . 670
    r 54.3 . . . 669
    r 54.3(2) . . . 670
    r 54.4 . . . 670

r 54.5 . . . 670
r 54.12(3) . . . 670
r 54.19 . . . 669
PD Judicial Review
   para 5.1 . . . 670
   para 5.6 . . . 670
   para 5.7 . . . 670
   para 8.4 . . . 670
Commissioner for Children and Young People
   (Northern Ireland) Order 2003 (SI 2003/439)
   (NI 11) . . . 476
Contact with Children Regulations 1991
   (SI 1991/891)
   reg 2 (which now only applies in
      Wales) . . . 656
   reg 3 (which now only applies in
      Wales) . . . 660

Data Protection (Subject to Access Modification)
   (Education) Order 2000 (SI 2000/414)
   reg 5 . . . 362
Data Protection (Subject to Access Modification)
   (Health) Order 2000 (SI 2000/413)
   reg 5(1) . . . 361
   reg 5(3) . . . 362
Day Care and Child Minding (National
   Standards) (England) Regulations 2003
   (SI 2003/1996)
   reg 3 . . . 345
   reg 5 . . . 346

Emergency Protection Order (Transfer
   of Responsibilities) Regulations 1991
   (SI 1991/1414) . . . 584
Enrolment of Deeds (Change of Name)
   Regulations 1994 (SI 1994/604) . . . 357
European Communities (Definition of
   Treaties) (1996 Hague Convention on
   Protection of Children etc) Order 2010
   (SI 2010/232) . . . 1091
European Communities (Jurisdiction and
   Judgments in Matrimonial and Parental
   Responsibility) Regulations 2005
   (SI 2005/265) . . . 995

Family Court (Composition and Distribution
   of Business) Rules 2014 (SI 2014/840) . . . 575
Family Court (Contempt of Court) (Powers)
   Regulations 2014 (SI 2014/883) . . . 538
Family Law Act 1986 (Dependent Territories)
   Order 1991 (SI 1991/1773)
   Sch 3 . . . 1021
Family Procedure (Amendment No 3) Rules
   2012 (SI 2012/2046) . . . 1007
Family Procedure Rules 2010 (SI 2010/2955) . . . 12,
   20, 214, 229, 437, 447, 763, 833
   r 1.4 . . . 437
   r 2.3 . . . 742
   r 2.27(1)(a) . . . 575
   PD 3A . . . 12
   r 5 . . . 749

PD 5A . . . 701, 749, 850
PD 6C . . . 1019
Pt 7 . . . 226, 241
r 7.12 . . . 220
r 7.12(8) . . . 226
r 7.32(3) . . . 228
rr 8.18–8.20 . . . 303
r 8.22 . . . 271
rr 8.24–8.25 . . . 921
r 9.26 . . . 850
r 12.2(a) . . . 521
r 12.2(c) . . . 521
r 12.3 . . . 381, 521, 749
r 12.3(1) . . . 596
r 12.14 . . . 470
r 12.14(4) . . . 652
r 12.16(1)(a) . . . 500
r 12.27 . . . 460, 467
r 12.28(1)(2) . . . 587
r 12.29 . . . 648, 649
r 12.29(1)(b) . . . 588
r 12.36 . . . 743
r 12.36(1) . . . 763
r 12.37(1) . . . 750
r 12.38 . . . 749
r 12.39 . . . 1019
r 12.39(2) . . . 745
r 12.41(1) . . . 750
r 12.42 . . . 744
rr 12.44–12.57 . . . 1085
r 12.45(a) . . . 16
r 12.48(1)(c) . . . 1073
r 12.58 . . . 1033
r 12.58(1)(a) . . . 1007
r 12.58(1)(b) . . . 1033
r 12.58(1)(c) . . . 1033
r 12.68 . . . 1003
PD 12A . . . 438, 461
PD 12B . . . 1, 20, 21
PD 12D . . . 742, 744, 763
   para 1.1 . . . 763
   para 1.3 . . . 741, 742, 763
   para 1.3(a) . . . 744
   para 3.1.I . . . 750
   para 5.1 . . . 745
PD 12F . . . 355, 1018
   para 2.11(b) . . . 1075
   para 3.5 . . . 1030
   para 4.4 . . . 1018
   para 4.5 . . . 1018
   para 4.6 . . . 1018
   para 4.7 . . . 1019
   para 4.8 . . . 1019
   para 4.10 . . . 1019
   para 4.15 . . . 1019
   Pt 5 . . . 742
   Pt 6 . . . 1030
PD 12K . . . 649
PD 12M . . . 547
Pt 13 . . . 281
r 13.5 . . . 281

r 13.11 ... 279
r 13.12 ... 281
r 13.20(1) ... 282
r 13.20(2) ... 282
r 13.21(1) ... 282
r 13.21(2)(b) ... 282
r 13.21(c) ... 282
Pt 14 ... 467
r 14.3(1) ... 711
r 14.3(3)(a) ... 711
r 14.9(4) ... 715
r 14.10 ... 701
r 14.21 ... 711
Pt 16 ... 471
r 16.1 ... 467
r 16.2 ... 451, 467, 468
r 16.3(1) ... 575
r 16.3(4) ... 460
r 16.4 ... 469
r 16.4(c) ... 468
r 16.5 ... 471
r 16.6 ... 326, 359, 470, 471, 472, 755
r 16.6(3) ... 468, 471
r 16.6(8) ... 472
r 16.19 ... 461
r 16.20 ... 461
r 16.24 ... 468
r 16.24(2) ... 469
r 16.24(4) ... 469
r 16.25 ... 461, 469
r 16.27 ... 469
r 16.28 ... 469
r 16.29 ... 462
r 16.30 ... 713
r 16.33 ... 458
r 16.33(1) ... 457
r 16.33(2) ... 455
r 16.33(4) ... 402, 458
r 16.33(5) ... 459
PD 16A ... 461, 467, 469
   para 5 ... 463
   para 6.1 ... 462
   para 6.2 ... 457, 462
   para 6.2(c) ... 464
   para 6.3 ... 462
   para 6.6 ... 462
   para 6.11 ... 464
   para 9.3 ... 458
   para 9.4 ... 458
   para 9.4(a) ... 459
   para 9.4(c) ... 469
r 28 ... 863
r 29.4 ... 750
r 29.4(2) ... 595
Pt 30 ... 723, 908
r 30 ... 544
r 30.2(b) ... 577
r 30.3 ... 650
r 30.3(1) ... 543
r 30.3(2) ... 543

r 30.3(7) ... 544, 908
r 30.4 ... 544
r 30.11 ... 544
r 30.12(1) ... 545
r 30.12(3) ... 545, 650, 908, 909
PD 30A ... 544
   para 2(1) ... 543
   para 4.2 ... 544
Pt 31 ... 1005
PD 31A ... 1005
Pt 32 ... 800
   Chp 4 (r 32.23–32.32) ... 1023
r 32.23 ... 1023
r 32.26 ... 1023
Pt 33 ... 800
r 33.16(1) ... 917
PD 36C ... 20, 438
Sch 4
   para 12 ... 283
Family Proceedings (Amendment No 2) Rules
   1999 (SI 1999/3491) ... 20, 833
Family Proceedings (Amendment) Rules 2006
   (SI 2006/352) ... 863
   Practice Direction (Ancillary
      Relief: Costs) ... 863
Family Proceedings Courts (Children Act
   1989) Rules ... 1991
   r 21(5)–(6) ... 20
Family Proceedings Rules 1991
   (SI 1991/1247)
   r 9.2A ... 471, 755
   r 9.5 ... 467
Family Provision (Intestate Succession) Order
   (SI 1993/2906) ... 969
Fostering Services (England) Regulations 2011
   (SI 2011/581) ... 295, 758
   reg 32 ... 670
   Sch ... 5
      para 2(c) ... 346
Fostering Services Regulations 2002 (SI
   2002/57) ... 758
Fostering Services (Wales) Regulations 2003
   (SI 2003/237) (W 35) ... 295, 758
   reg 32 ... 670
   Sch 5 ... 346

Homeless Persons (Priority Need) (Wales)
   Order 2001 (SI 2001/607) ... 208
Homelessness (Priority Need for
   Accommodation) (England) Order 2002 (SI
   2002/2051) ... 207
Housing Benefit (Amendment) Regulations 2012
   (SI 2012/3040) ... 778
Human Fertilisation and Embryology Act
   2008 (Commencement No 1 and
   Transitional Provisions) Order 2009 (SI
   2009/479) ... 369
Human Fertilisation and Embryology
   Authority (Disclosure of Donor Information)
   Regulations 2004 (SI 2004/1511)

reg 2(3) . . . 249
Human Fertilisation and Embryology
(Parental Orders) Regulations 2010
(SI 2010/985) . . . 272, 280
reg 2 . . . 280
Sch 1 . . . 280
Sch 4
   para 12 . . . 295

Immigration (European Economic Area)
Regulations 2006 (SI 2006/1003) . . . 102
Immigration Rules (HC 395) . . . 102, 682
para 5 . . . 103, 104
para 277 . . . 51, 102
paras 278–280 . . . 103
para 281 . . . 103
para 290 . . . 103
para 295A . . . 942
para 365 . . . 104
para 389 . . . 104
Insolvency Rules 1986 (SI 1986/1925)
r 12.3 . . . 917

Legal Aid, Sentencing and Punishment of
Offenders Act 2012 (Amendment of
Schedule 1) Order 2013
(SI 2013/748) . . . 13, 210
Local Safeguarding Children
Boards Regulations 2006
(SI 2006/90) . . . 581

Marriage Act 1949 (Remedial Order) 2007
(SI 2007/438) . . . 47
Marriages (Approved Premises) Regulations
1995 (SI 1995/510)
s 2(1) . . . 54
Marriages and Civil Partnerships (Approved
Premises) (Amendment) Regulations 2011
(SI 2011/2661) . . . 59

Non-Contentious Probate Rules 1987
(SI 1987/2024) . . . 359

Parental Orders (Human Fertilisation and
Embryology) Regulations 1994
(SI 1994/2767) . . . 280
Parental Responsibility Agreement
(Amendment) Regulations 1994
(SI 1994/3157) . . . 372
Art 3(1) . . . 372
Art 3(2) . . . 373
Art 3(3) . . . 373
Parental Responsibility Agreement
(Amendment) Regulations 2005
(SI 2005/2808) . . . 372
Parental Responsibility Agreement
(Amendment) Regulations 2009
(SI 2009/2026) . . . 372, 385, 388
Parental Responsibility Agreement
Regulations 1991 (SI 1991/1478) . . . 372, 388

Parental Responsibility and Measures for
the Protection of Children (International
Obligations) (England and Wales and
Northern Ireland) Regulations 2010
(SI 2010/1898) . . . 1092
reg 5 . . . 1096
reg 12 . . . 1099
Parental Responsibility and Measures for
the Protection of Children (International
Obligations) (Scotland) Regulations 2010
(SI 2010/213) . . . 1092
Public Bodies (Child Maintenance and
Enforcement Commission: Abolition and
Transfer of Functions) Order 2012
(SI 2012/2007) . . . 805

Registration of Births and Deaths (Amendment)
(England and Wales) Regulations 2009
(SI 2009/2165) . . . 385
Registration of Births and Deaths
(Amendment) Regulations 1994
(SI 1994/1948) . . . 356
Registration of Births and Deaths Regulations
1987 (SI 1987/2088) . . . 356
Art 2(b) . . . 286
Art 21 . . . 286
reg 9(3)(a) . . . 357
reg 9(3)(b) . . . 356
Sch 1 . . . 272
Representation Procedure (Children) (Wales)
Regulations 2005 (SI 2005/3365)
(W. 262) . . . 663, 664
reg 19 . . . 665
Restriction on the Preparation of Adoption
Reports Regulations 2005
(SI 2005/1711) . . . 729
Review of Children's Cases (Amendment)
(England) Regulations 2004
(SI 2004/1419) . . . 642
Review of Children's Cases Regulations 1991
(SI 1991/895) . . . 651, 661
reg 2A (which now only applies in
   Wales) . . . 662
reg 7 (which now only applies in
   Wales) . . . 662
Sch 2
   para 1 . . . 651
   para 5 . . . 651

Special Guardianship Regulations 2005
(SI 2005/1109) . . . 737, 738
reg 2(1) . . . 738
reg 3(1)(a)–(d) . . . 738
reg 3(2) . . . 738
reg 6 . . . 738
reg 7 . . . 738
reg 8 . . . 739
reg 9 . . . 737, 739
reg 10 . . . 739
reg 11(1) . . . 738

reg 11(2) . . . 738
reg 11(3) . . . 738
reg 14 . . . 738
Chp 4 (reg 17–18) . . . 738
reg 18 . . . 739
Sch . . . 732
Special Guardianship (Wales)
    Regulations 2005
    (SI 2005/1513) . . . 732, 737, 738
    reg 1(3) . . . 738
    reg 3 . . . 738
    reg 4 . . . 738
    reg 4(2) . . . 739
    reg 5 . . . 738
    reg 12 . . . 738
    reg 12(2) . . . 739
Suitability of Adopters Regulations 2005
    (SI 2005/1712) . . . 706
Supreme Court Rules 2009 (SI
    2009/1603) . . . 544
    r 10 . . . 544

CIRCULARS

Home Office Circular 63/1968 . . . 351
Home Office Circular 395 see Immigration Rules
    (HC 395)
Home Office Circular 60/1990 . . . 170
Home Office Circular 19/2000 . . . 170
Home Office Circular 316/2013 Queries about
    Employment and Support
    Allowance . . . 549
Ministry of Health Circular
    F/19/113 1967 . . . 351

EUROPEAN PRIMARY LEGISLATION

Charter of Fundamental Rights of the European
    Union . . . 325, 328–9
    Art 9 . . . 35, 36
    Art 24 . . . 328
EC Treaty
    Art 10 . . . 1076
    Art 226 . . . 1076
Treaty of Amsterdam . . . 28
Treaty on European Union
    Art 6 . . . 328
Treaty on the Functioning of the European
    Union
    Art 56 . . . 254
    Art 267 . . . 995
Treaty of Lisbon (2009) . . . 328
    Protocol 30 . . . 328, 329
Treaty of Nice . . . 328
Treaty of Rome
    Art 59 . . . 254

EUROPEAN SECONDARY
LEGISLATION

Directive 2004/38/EC Free Movement of
    Persons Directive . . . 102
Recommendation No 1121 (1990) on the Rights
    of Children . . . 328
Recommendation No 1286 (1990) on a European
    Strategy for Children . . . 328
Recommendation No R84(4) on Parental
    Responsibility . . . 330, 331
    Principle 9 . . . 288
Recommendation No R85(4) on Violence in the
    Family (1985) . . . 26, 328
    para 12 . . . 346
Regulation (EC) No 1347/2000 (Brussels
    II) . . . 16, 28, 331, 410, 831, 994, 995, 1071, 1072
    Art 4 . . . 1071
    Art 12 . . . 837
    Art 15(a) . . . 1004
Regulation (EC) No 44/2001 (Brussels I) . . . 28,
    1072
    Art 15(2) . . . 1004
Regulation (EC) No 1206/2001 . . . 1074, 1081
    Art 2 . . . 1074
    Art 5 . . . 1074
Regulation (EC) No 2201/2003 (revised Brussels
    II/BIIR) . . . 16, 28, 29, 286, 331, 334, 335, 374,
    441, 744, 747, 763, 771, 922, 994–1008, 1017,
    1020, 1024, 1030, 1032, 1033, 1038, 1041, 1042,
    1061, 1070, 1072, 1088, 1089
    Recital (5) . . . 374, 995
    Recital (13) . . . 1001
    Recital (19) . . . 1073
    Recital (20) . . . 1081
    Recital (21) . . . 1004
    Art 1(1)(a) . . . 995
    Art 1(1)(b) . . . 374, 995
    Art 1(2)(3) . . . 335, 995
    Art 2 . . . 1074
    Art 2(3) . . . 995, 996, 1071
    Art 2(7) . . . 335, 995
    Art 2(10) . . . 1006
    Art 2(11) . . . 998
    Art 2(11)(b) . . . 1073
    Art 7(1) . . . 1000
    Arts 8–13 . . . 1000, 1043
    Art 8 . . . 374, 747, 997
    Art 8(1) . . . 996
    Art 9 . . . 997
    Art 10 . . . 997, 998, 1080, 1093
    Art 10(b)(iv) . . . 998
    Art 11 . . . 1052, 1072
    Art 11(1) . . . 1072
    Art 11(2) . . . 1073, 1074
    Art 11(3) . . . 1038, 1076–7, 1080
    Art 11(4) . . . 1061, 1075, 1092
    Art 11(5) . . . 1074
    Art 11(6)–(8) . . . 998, 1006, 1037, 1038, 1054,
        1077–81

Art 11(6) ... 1037, 1038, 1077
Art 11(7) ... 998, 1037, 1038, 1078, 1079, 1080
Art 11(8) ... 1005, 1006, 1007, 1037, 1038,
    1075, 1078, 1079, 1080
Art 12 ... 999, 1000
Art 12(1) ... 998, 999
Art 12(2) ... 999
Art 12(3) ... 999, 1000
Art 12(4) ... 999, 1000
Art 13 ... 374
Art 13(1)(2) ... 1000
Art 14 ... 374, 747, 1000, 1043
Art 15 ... 999, 1001, 1022
Art 15(1) ... 1000, 1001
Art 15(3) ... 1001, 1002
Art 16 ... 1003
Art 17 ... 1003
Art 19 ... 1003
Art 19(2) ... 1003
Art 19(3) ... 1003
Art 20 ... 1002, 1003, 1095
Art 20(1) ... 1002
Art 20(2) ... 1002
Art 21(1) ... 1004
Art 21(3) ... 1004
Art 23 ... 1004, 1005
Art 24 ... 1004
Art 26 ... 1004
Art 27 ... 1004
Art 28(1) ... 1005
Art 28(2) ... 1005
Art 30 ... 1005
Art 31(1) ... 1005
Art 31(2) ... 1005
Art 31(3) ... 1005
Art 33 ... 1006
Art 36 ... 1006
Art 36(1) ... 1006
Art 36(2) ... 1006
Art 40(1)(b) ... 1078
Art 41(1) ... 1006
Art 41(2) ... 1007
Art 41(3) ... 1007
Art 42 ... 1078, 1079
Art 42(1) ... 1080
Art 42(2) ... 1080
Art 43 ... 1007
Art 45 ... 1007
Art 46 ... 995, 997, 1004, 1032
Art 47 ... 1007
Art 47(1) ... 1005
Art 48 ... 1007
Art 50 ... 1005
Art 53 ... 1007, 1033
Art 55 ... 1007, 1033
Art 55(b) ... 1005
Art 57 ... 1033
Art 57(1) ... 1007
Art 57(3) ... 1008
Art 57(4) ... 1008

Art 60(a) ... 1032
Art 60(e) ... 1032, 1071, 1100
Art 61 ... 1032
Annex III ... 1007
Annex IV ... 1007
Regulation (EC) No 4/2009 ... 28, 916, 923

INTERNATIONAL LEGISLATION

African Charter on Human and People's Rights
    (1981) ... 23
American Convention on Human Rights
    (1969) ... 23
    Art 17 ... 21
Brussels Convention on Jurisdiction and
    Enforcement of Judgments in Civil and
    Commercial Matters (1968) ... 28
    see also Regulation (EC) No 44/2201 (Brussels
       I); Regulation (EC) No 1347/2000 (Brussels
       II); Regulation (EC) No 2201/2003 (revised
       Brussels II/BIIR)
Convention on Preventing and Combating
    Violence against Women and Domestic
    Violence (Istanbul Convention) ... 169
European Abduction Convention
    (1980) ... 1031, 1032–4
    Art 5 ... 1033
European Convention on the Adoption of
    Children (1967) ... 26
European Convention on the Adoption of
    Children (Revised) 2008
    Art 5 ... 712
    Art 5(1)(b) ... 712
    Art 27(1) ... 712
European Convention on Contact Concerning
    Children (2003) ... 26, 328, 1090
    Art 4 ... 327, 432
European Convention on the Exercise of
    Children's Rights (1996) ... 26, 328, 451
    Art 3 ... 451
    Art 4 ... 451
European Convention on Human Rights ... 2,
    22, 23–5, 35, 100, 161, 248, 317, 327–8, 345,
    397, 415, 417, 448, 529, 577, 655, 663, 745, 767,
    768, 770, 994, 996, 1062
    Art 2 ... 169, 171, 327, 354
    Art 3 ... 23, 24, 169, 171, 197, 327, 345, 347,
       354, 597, 624, 677
    Art 5 ... 23, 322, 769
    Art 5(1) ... 577
    Art 5(1)(d) ... 577
    Art 5(4) ... 572
    Art 6 ... 24, 269, 416, 436, 438, 448, 461, 469,
       470, 510, 567, 578, 588, 596, 641, 674, 677,
       724, 820, 824, 835, 838, 917, 1029, 1053
    Art 6(1) ... 509, 578
    Art 6(3)(c) ... 578
    Art 8 ... 1, 4, 23, 25, 36, 42, 51, 95, 103, 104,
       122, 161, 171, 197, 204, 246, 249, 250, 254,

268, 269, 273, 318, 321, 322, 327, 337, 339,
340, 351, 367, 383, 411, 414, 416, 418, 424,
425, 434, 448, 461, 466, 469, 492, 495, 498,
522, 583, 588, 594, 597, 602, 603, 610, 624,
641, 647, 673, 676, 677, 678, 679, 684, 685,
686, 695, 706, 707, 710, 711, 724, 768, 818,
820, 836, 941, 1029, 1035, 1036, 1037, 1053,
1077, 1079, 1080
Art 8(1) . . . 1, 122, 492
Art 8(2) . . . 415, 416, 676, 685
Art 9 . . . 327, 346, 350, 411
Art 10 . . . 327, 424, 425, 768
Art 11 . . . 327
Art 12 . . . 1, 23, 25, 31, 35, 36, 42, 47, 49, 54, 55
Art 13 . . . 340, 641, 666, 677, 678, 679
Art 14 . . . 4, 23, 49, 95, 169, 383, 411, 469, 685,
706, 941, 966, 1029
Art 25 . . . 24
Art 34 . . . 679
Art 41 . . . 679
Art 53 . . . 25
Protocol 1
　Art 1 . . . 122, 818
　Art 2 . . . 327, 346, 348
European Convention on the Legal Status of
Children Born Out of Wedlock (1975) . . . 26, 328
Art 9 . . . 328
European Convention on the Protection of
Children Against Sexual Exploitation and
Sexual Abuse (2007) . . . 328
European Convention on Recognition and
Enforcement of Decisions Concerning
Custody of Children and on Restoration of
Custody of Children (1980) . . . 26, 410, 419,
1007, 1017, 1020, 1024, 1083–8
Art 1(c) . . . 1084
Art 1(d) . . . 1084
Art 4(2) . . . 1084
Art 5 . . . 1085
Art 7 . . . 1084, 1085
Art 8 . . . 1085
Art 9 . . . 1085, 1087
Art 9(3) . . . 1085, 1088
Art 10 . . . 1085, 1086, 1087
Art 10(1) . . . 1087
Art 10(1)(a) . . . 1086
Art 10(1)(b) . . . 1086, 1087
Art 10(1)(c)(d) . . . 1086
Art 10(2) . . . 1087
Art 11(1) . . . 1087
Art 11(2) . . . 1007, 1087, 1088
Art 12 . . . 1084
Art 15 . . . 1086
Art 17 . . . 1085
Art 17(2) . . . 1085
European Custody Convention see European
Convention on Recognition and Enforcement
of Decisions Concerning Custody of Children
and on Restoration of Custody of Children
(1980)

Hague Abduction Convention see Hague
Convention on the Civil Aspects of
International Child Abduction (1980)
Hague Convention on the Celebration and
Recognition of the Validity of Marriages
(1973) . . . 27
Hague Convention on the Civil Aspects of
International Child Abduction (1980) . . . 26,
27, 332, 381, 410, 417, 419, 423, 428, 441, 749,
759, 760, 770, 771, 772, 1004, 1005, 1006,
1007, 1016, 1017, 1024, 1025, 1026, 1030, 1031,
1032–83, 1084, 1088, 1093, 1100
Preamble . . . 1034
Art 1 . . . 1034
Art 1(b) . . . 1081
Art 3 . . . 1040, 1045, 1046, 1047, 1048, 1050,
1051, 1052, 1054, 1073, 1077, 1093
Art 3(b) . . . 1051
Art 4 . . . 1039, 1040, 1082
Art 5 . . . 1048, 1050, 1077, 1092
Art 5(a) . . . 1047
Art 7 . . . 1033, 1081
Art 8 . . . 1054
Art 9 . . . 1038
Art 11 . . . 1038, 1076
Art 11(3) . . . 1036
Art 12 . . . 1037, 1039, 1046, 1054, 1055, 1056,
1067, 1068, 1069, 1071, 1073
Art 12(2) . . . 998, 1054, 1064, 1068, 1069,
1074, 1077
Art 13 . . . 1025, 1037, 1038, 1039, 1051, 1052,
1054, 1056, 1058, 1061, 1062, 1066, 1067,
1068, 1069, 1072, 1073, 1077
Art 13(a) . . . 998, 1051, 1052, 1056, 1061
Art 13(b) . . . 1061–6, 1070, 1071, 1075, 1079,
1080, 1092
Art 15 . . . 1047, 1052, 1053, 1054
Art 16 . . . 1034, 1038, 1054
Art 18 . . . 1039, 1069
Art 19 . . . 1034, 1038
Art 20 . . . 1029, 1037, 1039, 1077, 1096
Art 21 . . . 1082, 1083
Art 27 . . . 1038
Art 29 . . . 1038
Art 35 . . . 1035
Hague Convention on Jurisdiction, Applicable
Law and Recognition of Decrees Relating to
Adoptions (1965) . . . 1008
Hague Convention on Jurisdiction, Applicable
Law, Recognition, Enforcement and
Co-operation in Respect of Parental
Responsibility and Measures for the
Protection of Children (1996) . . . 27, 533, 994,
996, 999, 1000, 1017, 1020, 1021, 1024, 1031,
1032, 1033, 1038, 1047, 1088–100
Art 1 . . . 1091
Art 2 . . . 1092
Art 3 . . . 27, 1092, 1093, 1095
Art 3(b) . . . 1092
Art 4 . . . 27, 1093, 1096

Art 4(d) . . . 1092
Arts 5–10 . . . 1095
Art 5 . . . 1093, 1094
Art 5(2) . . . 1093
Art 6 . . . 1094
Art 7 . . . 998, 1093, 1094
Art 7(2) . . . 1093
Art 7(3) . . . 1095
Art 8 . . . 1094, 1099
Art 9 . . . 1094, 1099
Art 10 . . . 1094
Art 11 . . . 1066, 1094, 1095, 1096, 1100
Art 12 . . . 1066, 1094, 1095
Art 13 . . . 1094
Art 13(2) . . . 1094
Art 14 . . . 1096
Art 15 . . . 1096, 1097
Art 15(1) . . . 1096
Art 15(3) . . . 1096
Art 16 . . . 27, 1096, 1097
Art 16(1)(2) . . . 1096
Art 16(3)(4) . . . 27, 1097
Art 17 . . . 27, 1096, 1097
Art 18 . . . 1096, 1097
Art 19 . . . 1096
Art 20 . . . 1097
Art 22 . . . 1096, 1097
Chp IV (Arts 23–28) . . . 1097
Art 23(1) . . . 1097
Art 23(2) . . . 1097, 1098
Art 24 . . . 1097, 1098
Art 26(1) . . . 1097
Art 26(2) . . . 1098
Art 26(3) . . . 1098
Art 27 . . . 1098
Art 28 . . . 1098
Art 29 . . . 1033, 1098
Art 30 . . . 1033, 1098
Art 31 . . . 1033, 1099
Art 32 . . . 1099
Art 33 . . . 1098
Art 35 . . . 28, 1099
Art 35(1)–(3) . . . 1099
Art 36 . . . 1099
Art 37 . . . 1099
Art 55 . . . 27
Art 60(1) . . . 1096
Art 61(1) . . . 1091
Hague Convention on Protection of Children
  (1902) . . . 27
Hague Convention on Protection of Children
  (1961) . . . 27
Hague Convention on Protection of Children
  (1996) see Hague Convention on Jurisdiction,
  Applicable Law, Recognition, Enforcement
  and Co-operation in Respect of Parental
  Responsibility and Measures for the
  Protection of Children (1996)
Hague Convention on Protection of Children
  and Co-operation in Respect of Intercountry

Adoption (1993) . . . 27, 28, 284, 683, 994,
  1008, 1009–12, 1014, 1092
Art 1 . . . 1009
Art 2 . . . 1012
Art 4(a)(b) . . . 1009
Art 4(c)(d) . . . 1009, 1012
Art 5 . . . 1010
Art 6 . . . 1010
Art 7(1)(2) . . . 1010
Art 8 . . . 1010
Art 9 . . . 1010
Arts 10, 11 . . . 1010
Arts 14, 15, 16 . . . 1010
Art 17 . . . 1010
Art 21(1)(b) . . . 331
Chp V (Arts 23–27) . . . 1010
Art 23 . . . 1010
Art 24 . . . 1011
Art 26(1) . . . 1011
Art 26(2) . . . 1011
Art 27 . . . 1011
Hague Convention on Recognition of Divorce
  and Legal Separation (1970) . . . 27
Hague Convention on Recognition and
  Enforcement of Decisions Relating to
  Maintenance Obligations (1973) . . . 27
Hague Intercountry Adoption Convention
  1993 see Hague Convention on Protection
  of Children and Co-operation in Respect of
  Intercountry Adoption (1993)
Luxembourg Convention see European
  Abduction Convention
UK-Pakistan Protocol . . . 1024, 1030, 1031
  paras 1, 2 . . . 1030
  para 3 . . . 1030
United Nations Convention on the Elimination
  of All Forms of Discrimination Against
  Women (1979) (CEDAW) . . . 168
Art 1 . . . 168
Art 16 . . . 91
United Nations Convention on the Rights of the
  Child (1989) . . . 6, 22–3, 26, 325–7, 331, 346,
  417, 418, 431, 444, 447, 448–51, 452, 475, 478,
  994, 1012, 1037
Art 1 . . . 296
Art 3 . . . 325, 418, 419, 1035
Art 3(1) . . . 325, 398, 399, 416, 418, 419, 421,
  430
Art 5 . . . 331
Art 6 . . . 326
Art 7 . . . 266, 326, 327, 356, 522
Art 8 . . . 326, 327, 522
Art 9 . . . 326, 331, 419, 451
Art 9(1) . . . 326
Art 9(2) . . . 449
Art 9(3) . . . 326, 340, 492
Art 11 . . . 1035
Art 12 . . . 325, 326, 402, 443, 448, 449, 450,
  451, 1004
Art 12(1) . . . 325, 326, 402

Art 13 . . . 327
Art 14 . . . 327
Art 15 . . . 327
Art 16 . . . 327
Art 18(1) . . . 331
Art 19 . . . 346
Art 21 . . . 419
Art 27(4) . . . 327
Art 28 . . . 327
Art 37 . . . 345

Universal Declaration on Human Rights
     (1948) . . . 22
     Art 16(3) . . . 21
Vienna Convention on the Law of Treaties
     (1969)
     Art 31(3)(b) . . . 1082
'Washington Declaration' [2010] IFL
     211 . . . 534, 535

TABLE OF CASES

Entries of the form R (on the application of X) are alphabetised as R (X)

A v A [2007] 2 FLR 467 847

A v A [2013] EWHC 3554 (Fam) [2014] Fam Law 157 . . . 748

A v A; B v B [2000] 1 FLR 701 . . . 834

A v A (A Minor: Financial Provision) [1994] 1 FLR 657 . . . 795, 796, 798, 875

A v A (Attorney General Intervening) [2012] EWHC 2219 (Fam) [2013] Fam 51 . . . 58, 63, 69, 71, 72

A v A (Children: Habitual Residence) (Reunite International Child Abduction Centre intervening) [2013] UKSC 60 [2014] AC 1 . . . 374, 744, 747, 748, 763, 996, 1000, 1040, 1041, 1042, 1043, 1044, 1093

A v A (Custody Appeal: Role of Appellate Court) [1988] 1 FLR 193, CA . . . 544

A v A (Family: Unborn Child) [1974] Fam 6 . . . 298

A v A (Financial Provision: Conduct) [1995] 1 FLR 345 . . . 901

A v A (Financial Provision) [1998] 2 FLR 180 . . . 892

A v A (Maintenance Pending Suit: Provision of Legal Fees) [2001] 1 FLR 377 . . . 838

A v A (Return Order on the Basis of British Nationality) [2013] EWHC 3298 (Fam) [2014] Fam Law 157 . . . 748, 760

A v A (Shared Residence) [2004] EWHC 142 (Fam) [2004] 1 FLR 1195 . . . 482, 486, 488, 510, 550

A v B (Abduction: Declaration) [2008] EWHC 2524 (Fam) [2009] 1 FLR 1253 . . . 1053

A v B (Jurisdiction) [2011] EWHC 2752 (Fam) [2012] 1 FLR 768 . . . 374, 996

A v B and C (Lesbian Co-Parents: Role of Father) [2012] EWCA Civ 785 [2012] 2 FLR 607 . . . 509

A v B and Hereford and Worcester County Council [1986] 1 FLR 289 . . . 668

A v B and Newport City Council: Re K [2007] 1 FLR 1116 . . . 739

A v C [1985] FLR 445, CA . . . 275, 276

A v East Sussex County Council and Chief Constable of Sussex Police [2010] EWCA Civ 743 [2010] 2 FLR 1596 . . . 583, 593

A v Essex County Council [2003] EWCA Civ 1848 [2004] 1 FLR 749, CA . . . 675

A v J [1989] 1 FLR 110 . . . 75

A v L (Contact) [1998] 1 FLR 361 . . . 489, 493

A v L (Departure from Equality: Needs) [2011] EWHC 3150 (Fam) [2012] 1 FLR 985 . . . 888

A v L (Overseas Divorce) [2010] EWHC 460 (Fam) [2010] 2 FLR 1418 (Egypt) . . . 921

A v Liverpool City Council [1982] AC 363, HL . . . 316, 428, 510, 667, 668, 748, 765, 766, 767, 771

A v N (Committal: Refusal of Contact) [1997] 1 FLR 533, CA . . . 423, 538, 539

A v P [2011] EWHC 1738 (Fam) [2012] Fam 188 . . . 270, 278, 281

A v S (Financial Relief after Overseas US Divorce) [2002] EWHC 1157 (Fam) [2003] 1 FLR 431 . . . 924

A v SM and HB (Forced Marriage Protection Orders) [2012] EWHC 435 (Fam) [2012] 2 FLR 1077 . . . 198

A v United Kingdom (Human Rights: Punishment of Child) [1998] 2 FLR 959 . . . 327, 346, 347

A v Y (Child's Surname) [1999] 2 FLR 5 . . . 524

A, Re (1940) 164 LT 230 . . . 284

A (A Child) v Chief Constable of Dorset Police [2010] EWHC 1748 (Admin) [2011] 1 FLR 11 . . . 593, 671

A (A Child) (Adoption: Placement outside Jurisdiction), Re [2013] EWHC 578 (Fam) [2013] 3 WLR 1454 . . . 1015

A (A Minor) (Abduction), Re [1988] 1 FLR 365, CA . . . 1054, 1061

A (A Minor) (Custody), Re [1991] 2 FLR 394, CA . . . 404

A (a minor) (parental responsibility), Re [1996] 1 FCR 562 . . . 380

A (A Minor) (Paternity: Refusal of Blood Test), Re [1994] 2 FLR 463, CA . . . 269

A (A Minor) (Residence Order: Leave To Apply), Re [1993] 1 FLR 425 . . . 517

A (A Minor) (Wardship: Immigration), Re [1992] 1 FLR 427, CA . . . 767

A (A Minor) (Wardship: Police Caution), Re [1989] Fam 103 . . . 745

A (Abduction: Habitual Residence), Re [1998] 1 FLR 497 . . . 1044

A (Abduction: Habitual Residence), Re [2007] EWHC 779 (Fam) [2007] 2 FLR 129 . . . 1044

A (Abduction: Rights of
Custody: Imprisonment), Re [2004]
1 FLR 1 . . . 1051, 1056
A (Adoption: Agreement: Procedure), Re
[2001] 2 FLR 455 . . . 712
A (Adoption: Removal), Re [2009] EWCA
Civ 141 [2009] 2 FLR 597 . . . 718
A (Adoption of a Russian Child), Re [2000]
1 FLR 539 . . . 710, 715
A (Area of Freedom, Security and Justice),
Re (C-523/07) [2009] 2 FLR 1, ECJ . . . 996,
1002, 1003, 1095
A (Care: Discharge: Application by Child),
Re [1995] 1 FLR 599 . . . 651, 653, 656
A (Care Proceedings: Asylum Seekers), Re
[2003] EWHC 1086 (Fam) [2003] 2 FLR
921 . . . 260
A (Child of the Family), Re [1998] 1 FLR 347,
CA . . . 297, 514, 794
A (Children) (Abduction: Interim Powers),
Re [2010] EWCA Civ 586 [2011] Fam
179 . . . 1039
A (Children) (Conjoined Twins: Surgical
Separation), Re [2001] Fam 147, CA . . . 351,
353, 397, 419, 430
A (children) (fact-finding appeal), Re [2013]
EWCA Civ 1026 [2014] 1 FCR 24 . . . 546
A (children) (placement orders: conditions),
Re [2013] EWCA Civ 1611 [2014] 2 FCR
123 . . . 666, 702
A (Children) (Specific Issue Order: Parental
Dispute), Re [2001] 1 FLR 121, CA . . . 500–1
A (Contact: Separate Representation), Re [2000]
1 FLR 663 . . . 468
A (Contact: Witness Protection Scheme), Re
[2005] EWHC 2189 (Fam), [2006] 2 FLR
551 . . . 489
A (Contact), Re [1998] 2 FLR 171 . . . 494
A (Custody Decision after Maltese Non-Return
Order), Re [2006] EWHC 3397 (Fam) [2007] 1
FLR 1923 . . . 749, 1079
A (Fact-finding Hearing: Judge Meeting With
Child), Re [2012] EWCA Civ 185 [2012] 2 FLR
369 . . . 467
A (Family Proceedings: Electronic Tagging),
Re [2009] EWHC 210 (Fam) [2009] 2 FLR
891 . . . 1039
A (Father: Knowledge of Child's Birth),
Re [2011] EWCA Civ 273 [2011] 2 FLR
123 . . . 711
A (Foreign Access Order: Enforcement),
Re [1996] 1 FLR 561, CA . . . 1085, 1086,
1087, 1088
A (Intractable Contact Dispute: Human Rights
Violations), Re [2013] EWCA Civ 1104 [2014]
1 FLR 1185 . . . 482, 492, 494, 545
A (Male Sterilisation), Re [2000]
1 FLR 549 . . . 398
A (Minors) (Abduction: Custody Rights), Re
[1992] Fam 106, CA . . . 1056, 1058, 1059, 1061

A (Minors) Abduction, Re [1991] 2 FLR 241,
CA . . . 1059
A (minors) (child abuse: guidelines), Re [1992] 1
All ER 153 . . . 584, 585
A (Minors) (Residence Orders: Leave to Apply),
Re [1992] Fam 182, CA . . . 423, 428, 440,
516, 519, 668
A (Placement of Child in Contravention of the
Adoption Act 1976, s 11), Re [2005] 2 FLR
727 . . . 728
A (Section 8 Order: Grandparents' Application),
Re [1995] 2 FLR 153, CA . . . 517
A (Security For Return To Jurisdiction) (Note),
Re [1999] 2 FLR 1 . . . 533
A (Supervision Order: Extension), Re [1995] 1
FLR 335, CA . . . 633
A (Temporary Removal From Jurisdiction),
Re [2004] EWCA Civ 1587 [2005] 1 FLR
639 . . . 488, 489, 531
A (Wardship: Jurisdiction), Re [1995] 1 FLR
767 . . . 393
A and B v Essex County Council [2002] EWHC
2707 (QB) [2003] 1 FLR 615 . . . 675
A and B v P Council and M (A Child by his
Children's Guardian) [2014] EWHC 1128
(Fam) [2014] All ER (D) 181 (Apr) . . . 711
A and B v United Kingdom [1998]
1 EHRLR 82 . . . 679
A and B (Infants), Re [1897] 1 Ch 786 . . . 313
A and B (Minors) (No 2), Re [1995]
1 FLR 351 . . . 437, 455
A and B (Parental Order: Domicile),
Re [2013] EWHC 426 (Fam) [2014] 1 FLR
169 . . . 278, 279, 387
A and C (Equality and Human Rights
Commission Intervening), Re [2010] EWHC
978 (Fam) [2010] 2 FLR 1363 . . . 769
A City Council v C [2013] EWHC 8 (Fam) [2013]
1 WLR 3009 . . . 699, 762
A City Council v T, J and K [2011] EWHC 1082
(Fam) [2011] 2 FLR 803 . . . 470, 575
A County Council v K, CJ and T [2011] EWHC
1672 (Fam) [2011] 2 FLR 817 . . . 460, 461
A County Council v M and Others (No
4) (Foreign Adoption: Refusal of Recognition)
[2013] EWHC 151 (Fam) [2014] 1 FLR
881 . . . 1013
A and D (Local Authority: Religious
Upbringing), Re [2010] EWHC 2503 (Fam)
[2011] 1 FLR 615 . . . 509, 638, 658, 679
A Local Authority v D [2006] EWHC 295 (Fam)
[2006] All ER (D) 392 (Feb) . . . 750
A Local Authority v DL [2011] EWHC 1022
(Fam) [2012] 1 FLR 1119 . . . 197
A Local Authority v GC [2008] EWHC 2555
(Fam) [2009] 1 FLR 299 . . . 700
A Local Authority v Mrs A (Test For Capacity
As To Contraception) [2010] EWHC 1549
(COP) [2011] 1 FLR 26 . . . 321

A Local Authority v S and Others [2012] EWHC
3764 (Fam) [2014] 1 FLR 1313 . . . 260
A Local Authority v SB, AB and MB
[2010] EWHC 1744 (Fam) [2010] 2 FLR
1203 . . . 757, 769
A Local Authority v W, L, W, T and R (By the
Children's Guardian) [2005] EWHC 1564
(Fam) [2006] 1 FLR 1 . . . 424, 425
A Local Authority v X and A (Child)
[2013] EWHC 3274 (Fam) [2014] 2 FLR
123 . . . 62, 71, 79
A Local Authority v Y, Z and Others [2006] 2
FLR 41 . . . 732, 733
A Metropolitan Borough Council v DB [1997] 1
FLR 767 . . . 351, 573
A National Health Service Trust v D [2000] 2
FLR 677 . . . 354
A and S v Lancashire County Council [2012]
EWHC 1689 (Fam) [2013] 2 FLR 803 . . . 678
A Subpoena (Adoption: Comr for Local
Administration), Re [1996] 2 FLR 629 . . . 666
A, HA v MB (Brussels II Revised: Article 11(7)
Application) [2007] EWHC 2016 (Fam) [2008]
1 FLR 289 . . . 998, 1080
A, J and J (minors) (Residence and
Guardianship Orders), Re [1993] Fam Law
568 . . . 287, 289, 290
AA v BB (2007) 83 OR (3d) 561 . . . 259
AB v CD and Z (Fertility Clinic) [2013]
EWHC 1418 (Fam) [2013] 2 FLR 1357 . . . 255,
272, 274
AB v JLB (Brussels II Revised: Article 15) [2008]
EWHC 2965 (Fam) [2009] 1 FLR 517 . . . 1001
AB (Adoption: Joint Residence), Re [1996] 1 FLR
27 . . . 487, 706
ABB, BBB, CBB and DBB v Milton Keynes
Council [2011] EWHC 2745 (QB) [2012]1 FLR
1157 . . . 579
Abbey National Building Society v Cann [1991]
1 AC 56, HL . . . 149, 151
Abbey National plc v Moss [1994] 1 FLR 307,
CA . . . 146
Abbott v Abbott 560 US (2010) (No
08-65) . . . 1050
Abbott v Abbott [2007] UKPC 53 [2008] 1 FLR
1451 . . . 129
Abdullah v Westminster City Council [2011]
EWCA Civ 1171 . . . 153
Abdureman v Abdureman (1978) 122 *Sol Jo*
663 . . . 892
Abram (Deceased), Re [1996] 2 FLR 379 . . . 983,
988
AC v DC and Others (Financial Remedy: Effect
of s 37 Avoidance Order) [2012] EWHC 2032
(Fam) [2013] 2 FLR 1483 . . . 919
AC v DC and Others (No 2) [2012] EWHC 2420
(Fam) [2013] 2 FLR 1499 . . . 887
Adam v Germany [2009] 1 FLR, ECtHR . . . 436
Adams v Adams [1984] FLR 768, CA . . . 405
Adams, Re [1951] Ch 716 . . . 301

Adeoso v Adeoso [1980] 1 WLR 1535, CA . . . 940
Adoption Application (Payment for Adoption),
Re [1987] Fam 81 . . . 278, 729
AF v T and Another (Brussels II revised: Art
11(7) Application) [2011] EWHC 1315 (Fam)
[2011] 2 FLR 891 . . . 1080
A-G v Prince Ernest Augustus of Hanover [1957]
AC 436 . . . 315
A-G (*ex rel* Tilley) v London Borough of
Wandsworth [1981] 1 All ER 1162 . . . 560
A-G of Hong Kong v Humphreys Estate
(Queen's Gardens) Ltd [1987] AC 114,
PC . . . 141
Agar-Ellis, Re (1883) 24 ChD 317, CA . . . 308,
309, 311, 338
Agbaje v Agbaje [2010] UKSC 13 [2010] 1 AC
628 . . . 921, 922, 923, 924
AGN (Adoption: Foreign Adoption), Re [2000] 2
FLR 431 . . . 710
Agricultural Mortgage plc v Woodward [1996] 1
FLR 226, CA . . . 116
Aguirre Zarraga, Re (Case C-491/10 PPU)
unreported . . . 1006, 1079
A-H (Infants), Re [1963] Ch 232 . . . 768
Ahmed v Kendrick [1988] 2 FLR 22, CA . . . 151
Ahrens v Germany (App No 45071/09) [2012] 2
FLR 483 . . . 270
Aintree University Hospitals NHS Foundation
Trust v James [2013] UKSC 67 [2014] AC
591 . . . 408
Airey v Ireland (1979) 2 EHRR 305 . . . 838
AJ (Adoption Order or Special Guardianship
Order), Re [2007] EWCA Civ 55 [2007] 1 FLR
507 . . . 709, 730, 740
AJ (Brussels II Revised), Re [2011] EWHC 3450
(Fam) [2012] 2 FLR 689 . . . 998, 1080
AJ (Contact: Brussels II Revised), Re [2012]
EWHC 931 (Fam) [2012] 2 FLR 1065 . . . 998
A-K (Foreign Passport: Jurisdiction), Re [1997] 2
FLR 569, CA . . . 1019
Akhtar v Rafiq [2006] 1 FLR 27 . . . 227
Al Habtoor v Fotheringham [2001] EWCA Civ
186 [2001] 1 FLR 951 . . . 747
Al-Kandari v JR Brown & Co [1988] QB 665,
CA . . . 1019
Al-Khatib v Masry [2002] EWHC 108 (Fam)
[2002] 1 FLR 1053 . . . 902, 916
Al-Khatib v Masry [2004] EWCA Civ 1353
[2005] 1 FLR 381 . . . 834
Al-Saedy v Musawi (Presumption of Marriage)
[2010] EWHC 3293 (Fam) [2011] 2 FLR 287 . . . 58
Aldrich v A-G [1968] P 281 . . . 303
Alfonso-Brown v Milwood [2006] EWHC 642
(Fam) [2006] 2 FLR 265 . . . 79
Alhaji Mohamed v Knott [1969] 1 QB 1 . . . 596,
601
Allan v Allan (1973) 4 Fam Law 83 . . . 224
Allen v Wood (1834) 1 Bing NC 8 . . . 67
Allington v Allington [1985] FLR 586,
CA . . . 409

A-M v A-M (Divorce: Jurisdiction: Validity of
    Marriage) [2001] 2 FLR 6 . . . 57, 68
Ampthill Peerage case [1977] AC 547 . . . 246,
    260, 261
AMR (Adoption: Procedure), Re [1999] 2 FLR
    807 . . . 391
AMS v Child Support Officer [1998] 1 FLR
    955 . . . 840
An Adoption Application, Re [1992] 1 FLR
    341 . . . 712
An NHS Trust v R [2013] EWHC 2340 [2014]
    Fam Law 294 . . . 408
An NHS Trust v SR (Radiotherapy and
    Chemotherapy) [2012] EWHC 3842 (Fam)
    [2013] 1 FLR 1297 . . . 353, 499
An Unborn Child, High Court, Re Hamilton
    M171/02, 11 October 2002 . . . 746
Andrews v Salt (1873) 8 Ch App 622 . . . 292, 310,
    348, 350
Andrews, Re (1873) LR 8, QB 153 . . . 308
Annulment Funding Company Ltd v Cowey
    [2010] EWCA Civ 711 . . . 151
Anon v Anon (1856) 23 Beav 273 . . . 261
Ansah v Ansah [1977] Fam 138, CA . . . 194, 539
Ansari v Ansari (Miah intervening) [2008]
    EWCA Civ 1456 [2010] Fam 1 . . . 919
Anthony v Anthony [1986] 2 FLR 353,
    CA . . . 864, 874, 901
Anthony and Another v Donges and Another
    [1998] 2 FLR 775 . . . 963
Anufrijeva v Southwark London Borough
    Council [2003] EWCA Civ 1406 [2004] QB
    124 . . . 679
AP v TD (Relocation: Retention of Jurisdiction)
    [2010] EWHC 2040 (Fam) [2011] 1 FLR
    1851 . . . 1000
AP v Vale of Glamorgan [2007] EWCA Civ 1265,
    sub nom Re P (Split Hearing) [2007] All ER
    (D) 475 (Nov) . . . 613
AR v AR (Treatment of Inherited Wealth)
    [2011] EWHC 2717 (Fam) [2012]
    2 FLR 1 . . . 884, 891
AR (A Child: Relocation), Re [2010] EWHC 1346
    (Fam) [2010] 2 FLR 1577 . . . 530, 531, 534
Archer v Archer [1999] 1 FLR 327, CA . . . 223
Armitage v Nanchen (1983) 4 FLR 293 . . . 264
Armstrong v Armstrong (1974) 4 Fam Law 156,
    CA . . . 901
AS (Secure Accommodation Order), Re [1999] 1
    FLR 103 . . . 575
Asaad v Kurter [2013] EWHC 3852 (Fam) [2014]
    Fam Law 459 . . . 58, 69, 70
ASB v MQS (Secretary of State for the Home
    Department) [2009] EWHC 2491 (Fam)
    [2010] 1 FLR 748 . . . 695
Ash v Ash [1972] Fam 135 . . . 216
Ashburn Anstalt v Arnold [1989] Ch 1,
    CA . . . 157
Ashley v Blackman [1988] Fam 85 . . . 5

Askew-Page v Page [2001] Fam Law 794 . . . 841
Aspden v Elvy [2012] EWHC 1387 (Ch) [2012] 2
    FLR 807 . . . 133
Associated Provincial Picture Houses Ltd v
    Wednesday Corporation [1948] 1 KB 223,
    CA . . . 670
Atkinson v Atkinson [1988] Fam 93 [1988] 2
    FLR 353, CA . . . 888, 942
Atkinson v Atkinson [1995] 2 FLR 356 . . . 888
Attwood v Attwood [1968] P 591 . . . 892
AV v RM [2012] EWHC 1173 (Fam) [2012] 2 FLR
    709 . . . 908
AW (Adoption Application), Re [1993] 1 FLR
    62 . . . 749
Aylesford Peerage Case (1885) 11 App Cas 1,
    HL . . . 263
AZ (A Minor) (Abduction: Acquiescence),
    Re [1993] 1 FLR 682, CA . . . 1046, 1051,
    1058, 1059, 1060

B v A and B [2005] EWHC 1291 (Fam) . . . 760
B v A (Wasted Costs Order) [2012] EWHC
    3217(Fam) [2013] 2 FLR 958 . . . 500
B v A-G [1966] 2 All ER 145n . . . 303
B v B 1998 SLT 1245 . . . 427
B v B (A Minor) (Residence Order) [1992] 2 FLR
    327 . . . 395, 442
B v B (Abduction: Child With Learning
    Difficulties) [2011] EWHC 2909 (Fam) [2012]
    1 FLR 881 . . . 1068
B v B (Adult Student: Liability to Support) [1998]
    1 FLR 373, CA . . . 792, 840, 875
B v B (Ancillary Relief) [2008] EWCA Civ 284
    [2008] 2 FLR 1627 . . . 896
B v B (Assessment of Assets: Pre-Marital
    Property) [2012] EWHC 314 (Fam) [2012] 2
    FLR 22 . . . 884
B v B (Brussels II Revised: Jurisdiction)
    [2010] EWHC 1989 (Fam) [2011]
    1 FLR 54 . . . 997, 999
B v B (Child Abuse: Contact) [1994] 2 FLR
    713 . . . 437, 549
B v B (Consent Order: Variation) [1995] 1 FLR
    9 . . . 851
B v B (Custody of Children) [1985] FLR 166,
    CA . . . 404
B v B (Financial Orders: Proportionality)
    [2013] EWHC 1232 (Fam) [2013] Fam Law
    1374 . . . 833
B v B (Financial Provision: Welfare of Child and
    Conduct) [2002] 1 FLR 555 . . . 875, 880
B v B (Financial Provision: Welfare of Child and
    Conduct) [2002] 1 FLR 555 . . . 902
B v B (Mesher Order) [2002] EWHC 3106 (Fam)
    [2003] 2 FLR 285 . . . 894, 905
B v B (Minors) (Interviews and Listing
    Arrangements) [1994] 2 FLR 489, CA . . . 437
B v B (Occupation Order) [1999] 1 FLR 715,
    CA . . . 185

B v B (Residence: Condition Limiting Geographic Area) [2004] 2 FLR 979 . . . 505, 507, 751

B v B (Residence Order: Reasons for Decision) [1997] 2 FLR 602, CA . . . 402

B v B (Residence Order: Restricting Applications) [1997] 1 FLR 139, CA . . . 405

B v B (Transfer of Tenancy) [1994] Fam Law 250 . . . 793

B v B and E (B intervening) [1969] 3 All ER 1106, CA . . . 269

B v D (Abduction: Inherent Jurisdiction) [2008] EWHC 1246 (Fam) [2009] 1 FLR 1015 . . . 772

B v H (Habitual Residence: Wardship) [2002] 1 FLR 388 . . . 996, 1043, 1044

B v I [2010] 1 FLR 1721 . . . 79

B v IB (Order to set aside disposition under Insolvency Act) [2013] EWHC 3755 (Fam) [2014] Fam Law 287 . . . 989

B v K (child abduction) [1993] 1 FCR 382 . . . 1054, 1065, 1067, 1068

B v Lewisham Borough Council [2008] EWHC 738 (Admin) [2008] 2 FLR 523 . . . 672, 739

B v M (Child Support: Revocation of Order) [1994] 1 FLR 342 . . . 814, 822

B v P (Adoption by Unmarried Father) [2000] 2 FLR 717 . . . 707

B v Reading Borough Council and Another [2007] EWCA Civ 1313 [2008] 1 FLR 797 . . . 676

B v S (Contempt: Imprisonment Of Mother) [2009] EWCA Civ 548 [2009] 2 FLR 1005 . . . 539

B v S (Financial Remedy: Marital Property Regime) [2012] EWHC 265 (Fam) [2012] 2 FLR 502 . . . 860, 879

B v UK [2000] 1 FLR 1, ECtHR . . . 369, 655

B v W (wardship: appeal) [1979] 3 All ER 83, HL . . . 544

B, Re (2009) 72 MLR 463 . . . 413

B, Re; RB v FB and MA (Forced Marriage: Wardship Jurisdiction) [2008] EWHC 1436 (Fam) [2008] 2 FLR 1624 . . . 747, 748, 760

B (A Child) (Care Proceedings: Threshold Criteria), Re [2013] UKSC 33 [2013] 1 WLR 1911 . . . 407, 418, 426, 428, 444, 545, 546, 576, 600, 601, 602, 625, 630, 635, 650, 666, 685, 686, 702, 716, 717

B (A Child) (Residence: Biological Parent), Re [2009] UKSC 5 [2009] 1 WLR 2496 . . . 407

B (A Minor) (Abduction), Re [1994] 2 FLR 249, CA . . . 1048, 1057

B (A Minor) (Adoption: Natural Parent), Re [2001] UKHL 70 [2002] 1 WLR 258 . . . 546

B (A Minor) (Care Order: Criteria), Re [1993] 1 FLR 815 . . . 443, 568, 642

B (A Minor) (Care Order: Review), Re [1993] 1 FLR 421 . . . 639, 640

B (A Minor) (Child in Care: Blood Test), Re [1992] Fam Law 533 . . . 638

B (A Minor) (Contact: Interim Order), Re [1994] 2 FLR 269 . . . 436, 504

B (A Minor) (Secure Accommodation), Re [1995] 1 WLR 232 . . . 576

B (A Minor) (Wardship: Child in Care), Re [1975] Fam 36 . . . 770

B (A Minor) (Wardship: Medical Treatment), Re [1981] 1 WLR 1421, CA . . . 353, 750, 759

B (A Minor) (Wardship: Sterilisation), Re [1988] AC 199, HL . . . 317, 352, 354, 398, 500, 745

B (Abduction: Acquiescence), Re [1999] 2 FLR 818 . . . 1060

B (abduction: views of children), Re [1998] 3 FCR 260 . . . 1068

B (Adoption: Jurisdiction To Set Aside), Re [1995] Fam 239, CA . . . 724

B (Adoption: Natural Parent), Re [2001] UKHL 70 [2002] 1 WLR 258 . . . 686, 707

B (Adoption By One Natural Parent to Exclusion Of Other), Re [2001] 1 FLR 589, CA . . . 685, 707

B (Adoption Order: Nationality), Re [1999] 2 AC 136, HL . . . 694, 695, 1014

B (Care: Expert Witness), Re [1996] 1 FLR 667, CA . . . 633

B (Care: Interference With Family Life), Re [2003] EWCA Civ 876 [2003] 2 FLR 813 . . . 597

B (Care Proceedings: Appeal), Re [2013] UKSC 33 [2013] 2 FLR 1075 . . . 908

B (Care Proceedings: Expert Witness), Re [2007] EWCA Civ 556 [2007] 2 FLR 979 . . . 647

B (Care Proceedings: Interim Care Order), Re [2009] EWCA Civ 1254 [2010] 1 FLR 1211 . . . 643

B (Care Proceedings: Notification of Father Without Parental Responsibility), Re [1999] 2 FLR 408 . . . 401–2, 596

B (Care or Supervision Order), Re [1996] 2 FLR 693 . . . 636

B (Change of Surname), Re [1996] 1 FLR 791, CA . . . 401, 403, 420, 499, 521, 523, 527

B (Child: Property Transfer), Re [1999] 2 FLR 418, CA . . . 796

B (Child Abduction: Wardship: Power to Detain), Re [1994] 2 FLR 479, CA . . . 765, 766

B (children) (abduction: new evidence), Re [2001] EWCA Civ 625 [2001] 2 FCR 531 . . . 1064

B (Children) (Care Proceedings: Standard of Proof) (Cafcass intervening), Re [2008] UKHL 35 [2009] 1 AC 11 . . . 262, 413, 599, 610, 611, 616, 617, 619, 625, 626, 1057

B (Court's Jurisdiction) [2004] EWCA Civ 681 [2004] 2 FLR 741 . . . 1022

B (GC) v B (BA) [1970] 1 All ER 913 . . . 915

B (Grandmother: Joinder as Party), Re [2012]
EWCA Civ 737 [2012] 2 FLR 1358 . . . 517, 518
B (Infants), Re [1962] Ch 201, CA . . . 667
B (Interim Care Order: Directions), Re [2002]
EWCA Civ 25 [2002] 1 FLR 547 . . . 646
B (Interim Care Order), Re [2009] EWCA Civ
324 [2010] 2 FLR 283 . . . 643
B (JA) (An Infant), Re [1965] Ch
1112 . . . 744, 745
B (Leave To Remove: Impact Of Refusal),
Re [2004] EWCA Civ 956 [2005] 2 FLR
239 . . . 530
B (MAL) v B (NE) [1968] 1 WLR 1109 . . . 914
B (Medical Treatment), Re [2008] EWHC 1996
(Fam) [2009] 1 FLR 1264 . . . 352, 390
B (Minor) (Disclosure of Evidence), Re [1993]
Fam 142, CA . . . 458
B (Minors) (Abduction) (No 1), Re [1993] 1 FLR
988 . . . 1039
B (Minors) (Abduction) (No 2), Re [1993] 1 FLR
993 . . . 1046, 1059
B (Minors) (Application for Contact), Re [1994]
2 FLR 1 . . . 510
B (Minors) (Care Proceedings: Practice), Re
[1999] 1 WLR 238 . . . 618
B (Minors) (Residence Order), Re [1992] Fam
162, CA . . . 503
B (Minors) (Termination of Contact: Paramount
Consideration), Re [1993] Fam 301,
CA . . . 420, 639, 659, 746, 771
B (Non Accidental Injury), Re [2002] EWCA Civ
752 [2002] 2 FLR 1133 . . . 611
B (Parentage), Re [1996] 2 FLR 15 . . . 248, 253
B (Prohibited Steps Order), Re [2007] EWCA Civ
1055 [2008] 1 FLR 613 . . . 499
B (Removal From Jurisdiction), Re; Re S
(Removal From Jurisdiction) [2003] EWCA
Civ 1149 [2003] 1 FLR 1043 . . . 530
B (Residence: Second Appeal), Re [2009] EWCA
Civ 548 [2009] 2 FLR 632, CA . . . 407
B (Residence Order: Status Quo), Re [1998] 1
FLR 368, CA . . . 409, 459
B (Role of Biological Father), Re [2007] EWHC
1952 (Fam) [2008] 1 FLR 1015 . . . 375, 378,
379
B (S) (Infant), Re [1968] Ch 201 . . . 705
B (Supervision Order: Parental Undertaking),
Re [1996] 1 FLR 676, CA . . . 634
B (T) (a minor) (residence order), Re [1995] 2
FCR 240, CA . . . 405, 409
B (Wardship: Abortion), Re [1991] 2 FLR
426 . . . 353
B (Wardship: Place of Safety Order), Re (1979) 2
FLR 307 . . . 745
B and G (Minors) (Custody), Re [1985] FLR 493,
CA . . . 411
B and L v United Kingdom (Application No
36546/02) [2006] 1 FLR 35 . . . 47
B and T (Care Proceedings: Legal Representation),
Re [2001] 1 FLR 485, CA . . . 437

BA (Wardship and Adoption), [1985] FLR
1008 . . . 666
Babington v Babington 1955 SC 115 . . . 1021, 1024
Baby, Re M 537 A 2d 1227 (1988) . . . 276
'Baby Cotton' case see C (A Minor)
(Wardship: Surrogacy), Re [1985] FLR 846
Bailey v Bailey (1884) 13 QBD 855, CA . . . 916
Balfour v Balfour [1919] 2 KB 571, CA . . . 98,
780
Balraj v Balraj (1980) 11 Fam Law 110,
CA . . . 222, 224
Banbury Peerage Case (1811) 1 Sim & St 153,
HL . . . 263
Banik v Banik [1973] 3 All ER 45, CA . . . 223
Bank of Credit and Commerce International SA
v Aboody [1990] 1 QB 923, CA . . . 114
Bank of Ireland Home Mortgages Ltd v Bell and
Bell [2001] 2 FLR 809, CA . . . 158
Bank of Montreal v Stuart [1911] AC 120,
PC . . . 114
Banks v Banks [1999] 1 FLR 726 . . . 183, 186
Bannister v Bannister (1980) 10 Fam Law 240,
CA . . . 215
Barber v Barber [1993] 1 FLR 476, CA . . . 865
Barca v Mears [2004] EWHC 2170 (Ch) [2005] 2
FLR 1 . . . 161
Barclays Bank plc v Hendricks; Re Turner [1975]
1 All ER 5 . . . 161
Barclays Bank plc v O'Brien [1994] 1 AC 180,
HL . . . 114
Barclays Bank plc v Rivett [1999] 1 FLR 730,
CA . . . 114
Barder v Caluori [1988] AC 20, HL . . . 909, 910
Barnardo v McHugh [1891] AC 388, HL . . . 311
Barnes v Barnes [1972] 3 All ER 872, CA . . . 889
Barnett v Hassett [1981] 1 WLR 1385 . . . 156
Barrack v M'Culloch (1856) 3 K & J 110 . . . 110
Barrett v Enfield London Borough Council
[1995] 2 AC 633 . . . 674
Barrett v Enfield London Borough Council
[2001] 2 AC 550, HL . . . 343
Barron v Woodhead [2008] EWHC 810 (Ch)
[2009] 1 FLR 747 . . . 984
Bashall v Bashall (1894) 11 TLR 152, CA . . . 115,
116
Basham (decd), Re [1986] 1 WLR 1489 . . . 141
Bateman v Bateman [1979] Fam 25 . . . 901
Baxter v Baxter [1948] AC 274, HL . . . 74, 75
Baynes v Hedger [2008] EWHC 1587 (Ch) [2008]
3 FCR 151 . . . 978
Baynes v Hedger [2009] EWCA Civ 374 [2009] 2
FLR 767 . . . 981
Bazeley v Forder (1868) LR 3 QB 559 . . . 775
Beamish v Beamish (1861) 9 HL Cas 274,
HL . . . 47
Beaufort v Berty (1721) 1 P Wms 703 . . . 292
Beaumont, Re [1980] Ch 444 . . . 981, 982
Bebee v Sales (1916) 32 TLR 413 . . . 364
Bedfordshire Police v U and another [2013]
EWHC 2350 (Fam) [2014] Fam 69 . . . 199, 200

Bedson v Bedson [1965] 2 QB 666, CA . . . 146

Beeken v Beeken [1948] P 302, CA . . . 219

Belcher v Belcher [1995] 1 FLR 916 . . . 853

Bellenden (formerly Satterthwaite) v Satterthwaite [1948] 1 All ER 343 . . . 908

Bellinger v Bellinger [2003] UKHL 21 [2003] 2 AC 467 . . . 25, 41, 42

Ben Hashem v Al Shayif [2009] 1 FLR 115 . . . 847

Bendall v McWhirter [1952] 2 QB 466 . . . 152

Bennett v Bennett [1969] 1 All ER 539 . . . 82

Benson v Benson [1996] 1 FLR 692 . . . 910

Berkshire County Council v B [1997] 1 FLR 171 . . . 659

Bernard v Josephs [1982] Ch 391 . . . 134, 146

Berrehab v Netherlands (1988) 11 EHRR 322 . . . 1

Besant, Re (1879) 11 Ch D 508, CA . . . 405

Best v Samuel Fox & Co Ltd [1952] AC 716, HL . . . 93

Besterman, Re [1984] Ch 458, CA . . . 984, 990

Besterman, Re; Re Bunning; Jessop v Jessop [1992] 1 FLR 591, CA . . . 986

Bettinson's Question, Re [1956] Ch 67 . . . 118

B-G v B-G [2008] EWHC 688 (Fam) [2008] 2 FLR 965 . . . 1059

Bhaiji v Chauhan, Queen's Proctor Intervening (Divorce: Marriages Used for Immigration Purposes) [2003] 2 FLR 485 . . . 82, 103, 227, 229

Bheekhun v Williams [1999] 2 FLR 229 . . . 989

Bhura v Bhura [2012] EWHC 3633 (Fam) [2013] 2 FLR 44 . . . 917

Biggs v Biggs and Wheatley [1977] Fam 1 . . . 217

Binions v Evans [1972] Ch 359, CA . . . 158

Birch v Curtis [2002] EWHC 1158 (Ch) [2002] 2 FLR 847 . . . 964

Bird v Secretary of State for Work and Pensions [2008] EWHC 3159 [2009] 2 FLR 660 . . . 819

Birmingham v Renfrew (1936) 57 CLR 666 (Aust) . . . 964

Birmingham City Council v AG and A [2009] EWHC 3720 (Fam) [2010] 2 FLR 580 . . . 580

Birmingham City Council v D; Birmingham City Council v M [1994] 2 FLR 502 . . . 290, 513, 567, 607, 608

Birmingham City Council v H [1992] 2 FLR 323 . . . 631

Birmingham City Council v H (A Minor) [1994] 2 AC 212, HL . . . 12, 46, 428, 429, 430, 516, 658, 659

Birmingham City Council v M [2008] EWHC 1085 (Fam) [2008] 2 FLR 542 . . . 575

Birmingham City Council v R [2006] EWCA Civ 1748 [2007] Fam 41 . . . 732

Bishop v Plumley [1991] 1 All ER 236, CA . . . 980, 982

Bishop, Re [1965] Ch 450 . . . 111

B-J (Power of Arrest), Re [2000] 2 FLR 443, CA . . . 183, 193

BJ v MJ (Financial Order: Overseas Trust) [2011] EWHC 2708 (Fam) [2012] 1 FLR 667 . . . 846, 848

Blackwell v Blackwell [1943] 2 All ER 579, CA . . . 111

Blood and Tarbuck v Secretary of State for Health (unreported 28 February 2003) . . . 250

Blower v Blower [1986] 1 FLR 292 . . . 889

Blunkett v Quinn [2004] EWHC 2816 (Fam) [2005] 1 FLR 648 . . . 437

BN v MA [2013] EWHC 4250 (Fam) [2014] Fam Law 443 . . . 837, 838, 839

Bond v Leicester City Council [2001] EWCA Civ 1544 [2002] 1 FCR 566 . . . 206

Bothe v Amos [1976] Fam 46, CA . . . 118

Bouette v Rose [2000] 1 FLR 363, CA . . . 982

Boultif v Switzerland [2001] 2 FLR 1228 . . . 104

Bowlas v Bowlas [1965] P 450, CA . . . 792

Bowman v Fels [2005] EWCA Civ 226 [2005] 2 FLR 247 . . . 835

Boylan v Boylan [1988] 1 FLR 282 . . . 782

Bradford case see R v Local Commissioner for the North and East Area of England, ex parte Bradford [1979] QB . . . 287

Bradley v Bradley [1973] 3 All ER 750, CA . . . 217

Bramblevale Ltd, Re [1970] Ch 128, CA . . . 539

Brasserie du Pécheur SA v Germany; R v Secretary of State for Transport, ex parte Factortame Ltd and others (cases C-46, 48/93) [1996] ECR I-I1029 [1996] 1 CMLR 889 . . . 1077

Bremner (A Bankrupt), Re [1999] 1 FLR 912 . . . 161

Brett v Brett [1969] 1 All ER 1007, CA . . . 841, 886

Brickell v Brickell [1974] Fam 31, CA . . . 224

Bridgend County Council v GM and Another [2012] EWHC 3118 (Fam) [2013] 1 FLR 987 . . . 996, 1000

Brierley v Brierley [1918] P 257 . . . 262

Brinnand v Ewens (1987) 19 HLR 415, CA . . . 142

Bristol and West Building Society v Henning [1985] 2 All ER 606, CA . . . 151

British Airways v Laker Airways [1985] AC 58, HL . . . 418

Brixey v Lynas 1996 SLT 908 [1996] 2 FLR 499 . . . 403

Brockwell v Brockwell (1975) 6 Fam Law 46, CA . . . 850

Brodie v Brodie [1917] P 271 . . . 854

Bromage, Re [1935] Ch 605 . . . 261

Bromley v Bromley 30 F Supp 2d 857 (ED Pa 1998) . . . 1083

Brookes v Secretary of State for Work and Pensions [2010] EWCA Civ 420 [2010] 2 FLR 1038 . . . 805, 819

Brooks v Blount [1923] 1 KB 257 . . . 341, 682

Brooks v Brooks [1986] AC 375, HL . . . 848

Brough v Law [2011] EWCA Civ 1183 [2012] 1 FLR 375 . . . 816

Brown v Brown (1981) 3 FLR 161 . . . 864, 888

Brown, Re (1910) 26 TLR 257 . . . 966

Browne v Browne [1989] 1 FLR 291, CA . . . 846

Browne v Pritchard [1975] 3 All ER 721, CA . . . 892, 904, 906

Bryant v Bryant (1976) 6 Fam Law 108, CA . . . 904

B's Settlement, Re [1940] Ch 54 . . . 1024, 1026

B-S (Children) (Adoption Order: Leave to Oppose), Re [2013] EWCA Civ 1146 [2014] 1 WLR 563 . . . 399, 400, 439, 546, 685, 686, 696, 702, 703, 709, 710, 711, 713, 716–17, 718, 739

Buchanan v Milton [1999] 2 FLR 844 . . . 359, 423

Buchanan-Wollaston's Conveyance, Re [1939] Ch 738 [1939] 2 All ER 302, CA . . . 146

Buckinghamshire County Council v M [1994] 2 FLR 506, CA . . . 463

Buckland v Buckland [1968] P 296 . . . 77

Buffery v Buffery [1988] 2 FLR 365, CA . . . 216

Bullock v Bullock [1960] 2 All ER 307 . . . 960

Bunning, Re [1984] Ch 480 . . . 984, 990

Bunning, Re [1992] 1 FLR 591, CA . . . 986

Bunting v Lepingwell (1585) 4 Co Rep 29a . . . 48

Burden v United Kingdom (Application No 13378/05) [2008] 2 FLR 787 . . . 59, 60, 218

Burgess v Burgess [1996] 2 FLR 34, CA . . . 842

Burghardz v Switzerland [1995] Fam Law 71 (ECtHR) . . . 95

Burnett v George [1992] 1 FLR 525, CA . . . 196

Burns v Burns [1984] Ch 317, CA . . . 133, 163

Burris v Azadani [1995] 1 WLR 1372, CA . . . 183, 185

Burrows v HM Coroner for Preston [2008] EWHC 1387 (QB) [2008] 2 FLR 1225 . . . 359, 772

Burton v Burton [1986] 2 FLR 419 . . . 865

Burton v Camden London Borough Council [1998] 1 FLR 681, CA . . . 154

Bush v Bush [2008] EWCA Civ 865 [2008] 2 FLR 1437 . . . 999

Butler v Butler (Queen's Proctor Intervening) [1990] 1 FLR 114 . . . 47

Butterworth v Supplementary Benefits Commission (1981) FLR 264 . . . 942

C v C [1942] NZLR 356 . . . 79

C v C (A Minor) (Child Abuse: Evidence) [1988] 1 FLR 462 . . . 412

C v C (Child Abuse: Evidence) [1988] 1 FLR 462 . . . 494

C v C (Financial Provision: Personal Damages) [1995] 2 FLR 171 . . . 5, 886, 896

C v C (Financial Relief: Short Marriage) [1997] 2 FLR 26, CA . . . 834, 892

C v C (Minor: Abduction: Rights of Custody Abroad) [1989] 1 WLR 645 . . . 1062

C v C (Minors: Custody) [1988] 2 FLR 291, CA . . . 405

C v C (Minors) (Child Abduction) [1992] 1 FLR 163 . . . 1051

C v C (Non-Molestation Order: Jurisdiction) [1998] Fam 70 . . . 174, 179–80

C v C (Variation of Post-Nuptial Settlement: Company Shares) [2003] EWHC 1222 (Fam) [2003] 2 FLR 493 . . . 848, 898

C v C and C (legitimacy: photographic evidence) [1972] 3 All ER 577 . . . 263

C v D (Abduction: Grave Risk of Harm) [2014] Fam Law 404 . . . 1092

C v F (Disabled Child: Maintenance Order) [1998] 2 FLR 1, CA . . . 799, 822

C v Flintshire County Council [2001] 2 FLR 33, CA . . . 675

C v H (Abduction: Consent) [2009] EWHC 2660 (Fam) [2010] 1 FLR 225 . . . 1057

C v Humberside County Council [1994] 2 FLR 759 . . . 576

C v K (Inherent Powers: Exclusion Order) [1996] 2 FLR 506 . . . 197, 366, 766

C v S [1988] QB 135, CA . . . 312, 391, 996

C v Salford City Council [1994] 2 FLR 926 . . . 536

C v Secretary of State for Work and Pensions [2002] EWCA Civ 1854 [2003] 1 FLR 829 . . . 807

C v Solihull Metropolitan Borough Council [1993] 1 FLR 290 . . . 436, 631, 644

C v XYZ County Council [2007] EWCA Civ 1206 [2008] Fam 54 . . . 711

C, Re (Case C-435/06) [2008] 1 FLR 490, ECJ . . . 996

C (A Baby), Re [1996] 2 FLR 43 . . . 354, 762, 770

C (A Child) (Adoption: Duty of Local Authority), Re [2007] EWCA Civ 1206 [2008] Fam 54 . . . 694

C (a child) (adoption: leave to oppose), Re [2013] EWCA Civ 431 [2014] 1 FCR 50 . . . 686, 695, 723

C (A Minor) (Abduction), Re [1989] 1 FLR 403, CA . . . 1051

C (A Minor) (Adopted Child: Contact), Re [1993] Fam 210 . . . 724

C (A Minor) (Adoption: Freeing Orders), Re [1999] Fam 43 . . . 766

C (A Minor) (Adoption: Parental Agreement: Contact), Re [1993] 2 FLR 260, Re CA . . . 714

C (A Minor) (Adoption Order: Conditions), Re [1989] AC 1, HL . . . 691, 708, 719

C (A Minor) (Care: Child's Wishes), Re [1993] 1 FLR 832 . . . 470

C (A Minor) (Interim Care Order: Residential Assessment), Re [1997] AC 489 . . . 646

C (A Minor) (Leave to Seek Section 8 Orders), Re [1994] 1 FLR 26 . . . 423, 519

C (A Minor) (Residence Order: Lesbian Co-parents), Re [1994] Fam Law 468 . . . 487

C (A Minor) (Wardship: Jurisdiction), Re [1991] 2 FLR 168, CA . . . 767

C (A Minor) (Wardship: Medical Treatment), Re [1990] Fam 26, CA . . . 354

C (A Minor) (Wardship: Surrogacy), Re [1985] FLR 846 . . . 275, 754

C (A Minor) (Wardship Proceedings), Re [1984] FLR 419, CA . . . 545

C (Abduction: Application to Set Aside Return Order: Remission), Re [2012] EWCA Civ 1144 [2013] 1 FLR 403 . . . 1054

C (Abduction: Consent), Re [1995] 1 FLR 878 . . . 1057

C (Abduction: Grave Risk of Physical or Psychological Harm), Re [1999] Fam 478 . . . 1063, 1076

C (Abduction: Grave Risk of Psychological Harm), Re [1999] 1 FLR 1145, CA . . . 1062, 1063

C (Abduction: Separate Representation of Children), Re [2008] EWHC 517 (Fam) [2008] 2 FLR 6 . . . 771, 1040, 1074

C (Abduction: Settlement) (No 2), Re [2005] 1 FLR 938 . . . 1055

C (Abduction Consent), Re [1996] 1 FLR 414 . . . 1052

C (Adoption: Notice), Re [1999] 1 FLR 384 . . . 515

C (Adoption: Parties), Re [1995] 2 FLR 483, CA . . . 709

C (Adoption: Religious Observance), Re [2002] 1 FLR 1119 . . . 670

C (An Infant), Re (1956) The Times, 14 December . . . 746

C (An Infant), Re [1959] Ch 363 . . . 747

C (Appeal From Care and Placement Order), Re [2013] EWCA Civ 1257 . . . 413

C (Breach of Human Rights: Damages), Re [2007] EWCA Civ 2 [2007] 1 FLR 1957 . . . 679, 680

C (Care: Consultation with Father not in Child's Best Interests), Re [2005] EWHC 3390 (Fam) [2006] 2 FLR 787 . . . 361

C (Care: Discharge Of Care Order), Re [2009] EWCA Civ 955 [2010] 1 FLR 774 . . . 652

C (Care or Supervision Order), Re [1999] 2 FLR 621 . . . 637

C (Change of Surname), Re [1998] 1 FLR 549, CA . . . 525

C (Change of Surname), Re [1998] 2 FLR 656, CA . . . 523, 525

C (Child Abduction: Settlement), Re [2006] EWHC 1229 (Fam) [2006] 2 FLR 797 . . . 1055

C (Child Abduction) (Unmarried Father: Rights of Custody), Re [2002] EWHC 2219 (Fam) [2003] 1 FLR 252 . . . 1048

C (Contact: Jurisdiction), Re [1995] 1 FLR 777, CA . . . 511

C (Contact: No Order for Contact), Re [2000] 2 FLR 723 . . . 494

C (Detention: Medical Treatment), Re [1997] 2 FLR 180 . . . 323, 573, 770

C (Direct Contact: Suspension), Re [2011] EWCA Civ 521 [2011] 2 FLR 912 . . . 493

C (Disclosure), Re [1996] 1 FLR 797 . . . 361

C (Family Assistance Order), Re [1996] 1 FLR 424 . . . 548

C (Guardian ad Litem: Disclosure of Report), Re [1996] 1 FLR 61 . . . 463

C (HIV Test), Re [1999] 2 FLR 1004, CA . . . 353, 408, 500, 513, 769

C (Jurisdiction and Enforcement Of Orders Relating To Child), Re [2012] EWHC 907 [2012] 2 FLR 1191 . . . 455

C (MA) (an infant), Re [1966] 1 All ER 838, CA . . . 410

C (Medical Treatment), Re [1998] 1 FLR 384 . . . 354, 768, 770

C (Minors) [1992] 2 All ER 86 . . . 377

C (Minors) (Access), Re [1985] FLR 804, CA . . . 494

C (Minors) (Adoption: Residence Order), Re [1994] Fam 1 . . . 513

C (minors) (adoption by relatives), Re [1989] 1 All ER 395, CA . . . 291

C (Minors) (Parental Rights), Re [1992] 1 FLR 1 . . . 380

C (minors) (wardship: adoption), Re [1989] 1 All ER 395, CA . . . 728

C (Minors) (Wardship: Adoption), Re [1989] 1 WLR 61 . . . 752

C (Minors) (Wardship: Jurisdiction), Re [1978] Fam 105, CA . . . 411

C (Prohibition on Further Applications), Re [2002] EWCA Civ 292 [2002] 1 FLR 1136 . . . 468

C (Residence: Child's Application for Leave), Re [1995] 1 FLR 927 . . . 423, 519

C (Section 8 Order: Court Welfare Officer), Re [1995] 1 FLR 617, CA . . . 437, 459

C (Secure Accommodation Order: Representation), Re [2001] EWCA Civ 458 [2001] 2 FLR 169, CA . . . 574, 575, 578

C (Wardship and Adoption), Re (1979) 2 FLR 177, CA . . . 17

C (Welfare of Child: Immunisation), Re [2003] EWCA Civ 1148 [2003] 2 FLR 1095 . . . 333, 353, 354, 382, 388, 394, 500, 735

C (Welfare of Child: Immunisation), Re [2003] EWHC 1376 (Fam), [2003] 2 FLR 1054 . . . 500

C and B (Care Order: Future Harm), Re [2001] 1 FLR 611 . . . 584, 685, 716

C and C (Petitioners and Respondents to Adopt X) [1997] Fam Law 226 . . . 277

C and V (Contact and Parental Responsibility), Re [1996] 1 FLR 484 . . . 378

C and V (Contact and Parental Responsibility), Re [1998] 1 FLR 392, CA . . . 336, 377, 494

Cackett v Cackett [1950] P 253 . . . 75

Cadogan v Cadogan [1977] 3 All ER 831, CA . . . 989

Calder v Calder (1975) 6 Fam Law 242, CA . . . 887

Calderbank v Calderbank [1976] Fam 93, CA . . . 862, 888, 891

Calderdale Borough Council v H and P [1991] 1 FLR 461 . . . 766

Callaghan v Hanson-Fox [1992] Fam 1 . . . 227

Callaghan, Re [1985] Fam 1 . . . 971, 980, 985

Cameron v Treasury Solicitor [1996] 2 FLR 716, CA . . . 877, 993

Camm v Camm (1982) 4 FLR 577, CA . . . 851

Campbell v Campbell [1976] Fam 347 . . . 894

Campbell v Corley (1856) 28 LTOS 109 . . . 72

Campbell and Cosans v United Kingdom (1982) 4 EHRR 293 . . . 345

Cannon v Cannon [2004] EWCA Civ 1330 [2005] 1 WLR 32 . . . 1054, 1055, 1068, 1069

Carlton v Goodman [2002] EWCA Civ 545 [2002] 2 FLR 259 . . . 128

Carmarthenshire County Council v Lewis [1955] AC 549, HL . . . 364

Carp v Bryon [2005] EWCA Civ 1035 [2006] 1 FCR 1 . . . 494

Carr v Carr [1974] 1 WLR 1534, CA . . . 215

Carroll, Re [1931] 1 KB 317 . . . 315, 316

Carron v Carron [1984] FLR 805, CA . . . 297

Carson v Carson [1983] 1 All ER 478, CA . . . 905, 914

Cartwright v Cartwright (1853) 3 De GM & G 982 . . . 854

Cartwright v Cartwright (No 2) [2002] EWCA Civ 931 [2002] 1 FLR 919 . . . 916

Cattle v Evans [2011] EWHC 945 (Ch) [2011] 2 FLR 843 . . . 987

CB v CB (Abduction: Child's Objections) [2013] EWHC 2092 (Fam) [2014] 1 FLR 663 . . . 1068

CB (A Minor) (Blood Tests), Re [1994] 2 FLR 762 . . . 266

CB (A Minor) (Parental Responsibility Order), Re [1993] 1 FLR 920 . . . 374

CB (a minor) (wardship: local authority), Re [1981] 1 All ER 16, CA . . . 745

CB (Access: Court Welfare Reports), Re [1995] 1 FLR 622, CA . . . 459

CE (Section 37 Direction), Re [1995] 1 FLR 26 . . . 463, 550

CF v Secretary Of State For The Home Department [2004] EWHC 111 (Fam) [2004] 2 FLR 517 . . . 398, 416, 767

CG v IF (Inter-Relationship of Part III Matrimonial and Family Proceedings Act 1984 and Lugano Convention) [2010] EWHC 1062 (Fam) [2010] 2 FLR 1790 . . . 923

CH (Care or Interim Care Order), Re [1998] 1 FLR 402, Re CA . . . 628

CH (Contact: Parentage), Re [1996] 1 FLR 569 . . . 252

Chalmers v Johns [1999] 1 FLR 392 . . . 186

Chamberlain v Chamberlain [1974] 1 All ER 33, CA . . . 795, 845, 875

Chan Pui Chun v Leung Kam Ho [2002] EWCA Civ 1075 [2003] 1 FLR 23 . . . 131, 146

Chandler v Kerley [1978] 2 All ER 942, CA . . . 157

Chaplin, Re [1950] Ch 507 . . . 969

Chapman v Jaume [2012] EWCA Civ 476 [2012] 2 FLR 830 . . . 128, 129

Chapman v Secretary of State for Work and Pensions [2007] EWCA Civ 1211 [2008] 1 FLR 638 . . . 812

Chapman v United Kingdom (2001) 33 EHRR 399 . . . 122

Chard v Chard [1956] P 259 . . . 960

Charman v Charman [2005] EWCA Civ 1606 [2006] 2 FLR 422 . . . 846

Charman v Charman (No 4) [2007] EWCA Civ 503 [2007] 1 FLR 1246 . . . 831, 870, 873, 884, 888, 898, 926

Chartier v Chartier [1999] 1 SCR 242 . . . 794

Chaudhury v Chaudhury [2013] EWCA Civ 758 [2013] 2 FLR 1526 . . . 129

Chechi v Bashier [1999] 2 FLR 489, CA . . . 181, 193

Chester v Afshar [2004] UKHL 1 AC 134 [2005] 1 AC 134 . . . 320

Chhokar v Chhokar [1984] FLR 313 . . . 146

Chief Adjudication Officer v Bath [2000] 1 FLR 8, CA . . . 57

Chief Constable of Greater Manchester v KI and KW (by Their Children's Guardian, CAFCASS Legal) and NP [2007] EWHC 1837 (Fam) [2008] 1 FLR 504 . . . 501, 771

Child Support Agency v Learad; Child Support Agency v Buddles [2008] EWHC 2193 (Admin) [2009] 1 FLR 31 . . . 819

Chilton v Chilton [1952] P 196 . . . 774

Chopra v Bindra [2009] EWCA Civ 203 [2009] 2 FLR 786 . . . 129

Christie, Re [1979] Ch 168 . . . 983

Churchill v Roach [2004] 2 FLR 989 . . . 982

Ciliz v The Netherlands [2000] 2 FLR 469, ECtHR . . . 340

City of London Building Society v Flegg [1988] AC 54, HL . . . 148, 150

Clark v Clark [1999] 2 FLR 498, CA . . . 902

Clark v London General Omnibus Co Ltd [1906] 2 KB 648, CA . . . 359

Clarke v Clarke [1943] 2 All ER 540 . . . 74, 301

Clarke, Re (1857) 7 E & B 186 . . . 309

Clarke-Hunt v Newcombe (1983) 4 FLR 482, CA . . . 399, 405, 430, 546

Clarkson v Clarkson (1930) 143 LT 775 . . . 215

Claughton v Charalambous [1999] 1 FLR 740 . . . 161

Cleary v Booth [1893] 1 QB 465 . . . 345

Cleary v Cleary [1974] 1 All ER 498, CA . . . 215

Cleaver, Re [1981] 2 All ER 1018 . . . 964

Cleveland County Council v F [1995] 2 All ER 236 . . . 462

Clibbery v Allan and Another [2002] EWCA Civ 45 [2002] Fam 261 . . . 833

Clifton-Brown v Clifton-Brown (orse CB v CB) [1988] Fam Law 471 . . . 878

The Clitheroe Case see R v Jackson [1891] 1 QB 671, CA

Close Invoice Finance Ltd v Pile [2008] EWHC 1580 (Ch) [2009] 1 FLR 873 . . . 160

Clutton v Clutton [1991] 1 All ER 340, CA . . . 906

CMEC v Beesley and Whyman [2010] EWCA Civ 1344 [2011] 1 FLR 1547 . . . 818

CMEC v Forrest [2010] EWHC 264 (Admin) [2010] 2 FLR 1805 . . . 808

CMEC v Mitchell [2010] EWCA Civ 333 [2010] 2 FLR 622 . . . 819

CMEC v NC [2009] UKUT 106 (AAC) [2010] 2 FLR 1812 . . . 813

Co v Co (Ancillary Relief: Pre-marital Cohabitation) [2004] EWHC 287 (Fam) [2004] 1 FLR 1095 . . . 895

Cobb v Cobb [1955] 2 All ER 696 . . . 117

Cobbe v Yeoman's Row Management Ltd [2008] UKHL 55 [2008] 1 WLR 1752 . . . 141

Cochrane, Re (1840) 8 Dowl 630 . . . 93

Cocksedge v Cocksedge (1844) 14 Sim 244 . . . 780, 854

Cohen v Sellar [1926] 1 KB 536 . . . 109

Cole, Re [1964] Ch 175, CA . . . 116

Coleman v Coleman [1973] Fam 10 . . . 840, 841

Coleman, Re [1976] Ch 1 . . . 962

Collins v Collins (1973) 4 Fam Law 133, CA . . . 154

Collins v Collins [1987] 1 FLR 226, CA . . . 864

Collins, Re [1990] Fam 56 . . . 726

Collins (Deceased), Re [1990] Fam 56 . . . 980, 991

Compton v Compton [1960] P 201 . . . 845

Conran v Conran [1997] 2 FLR 615 . . . 890, 896, 898

Constantinides v Constantinides [2013] EWHC 3688 (Fam) [2014] Fam Law 440 . . . 917

Cook v Blackley 1997 SLT 853 . . . 1023

Cooke v Head [1972] 2 All ER 38, CA . . . 7

Coombes v Smith [1986] 1 WLR 808 . . . 142, 157

Corbett v Corbett [1971] P 83 . . . 41, 42, 43

Cornick v Cornick [1994] 2 FLR 530 . . . 911

Cornick v Cornick (No 2) [1995] 2 FLR 490, CA . . . 914

Cossey v United Kingdom [1991] 2 FLR 492 . . . 42

Costello-Roberts v United Kingdom (1996) 19 EHRR 293 . . . 345

Council of Civil Service Unions v Minister for the Civil Service [1985] AC 374, HL . . . 670

Court and Others v Despallieres [2009] EWHC 3340 (Ch) [2011] 2 All ER 451 . . . 963

Couvaras v Wolf [2002] 2 FLR 107 . . . 919

Coventry, Re [1980] Ch 461 . . . 983, 985, 986, 988

Coventry City Council v C, B, CA and CH [2012] EWHC 2190 (Fam) [2013] 2 FLR 987 . . . 564, 568

Coventry City Council v O (Adoption) [2011] EWCA Civ 729 [2011] 2 FLR 936 . . . 703

Cowan v Cowan [2001] EWCA Civ 679 [2002] Fam 97 . . . 897

Cowcher v Cowcher [1972] 1 All ER 943 . . . 126, 135

Cowen v Cowen [1946] P 36, CA . . . 74

Cowley v Cowley [1900] P 305, CA; affd [1901] AC 450, HL . . . 95

Cox v Jones [2004] EWHC 1486 (Ch) [2004] 2 FLR 1010 . . . 109, 115, 131

CR v SR (Financial Remedies: Permission to Appeal) [2013] EWHC 1155 (Fam) [2014] 1 FLR 186 . . . 908

CR v United Kingdom; SW v United Kingdom [1996] 1 FLR 434 . . . 96

Crake v Supplementary Benefits Commission; Butterworth v Supplementary Benefits Commission (1981) FLR 264 . . . 942

Crawford, Re (1982) 4 FLR 273 . . . 977

Crawley Borough Council v Ure [1996] QB 13, CA . . . 204

Crispin's Will Trusts, Re [1975] Ch 245, CA . . . 969

Crittenden v Crittenden [1990] 2 FLR 361, CA . . . 918

Crossley v Crossley [2007] EWCA Civ 1491 [2008] 1 FLR 1467 . . . 854

Croydon London Borough Council v A [1992] Fam 169 . . . 501, 537, 630

Crozier v Crozier [1994] 1 FLR 126 . . . 877, 910

Currey v Currey (No 2) [2006] EWCA Civ 1338 [2007] 1 FLR 946 . . . 838

Cuzner v Underdown [1974] 2 All ER 351, CA . . . 901

Cyganik v Agulian [2006] EWCA Civ 129 [2006] 1 FCR 406 . . . 976

D v B [1979] Fam 38, CA . . . 521

D v B (Surname: Birth Registration) [1979] Fam 38, CA . . . 356

D v Bury Metropolitan Borough Council [2006] EWCA Civ 1 [2006] 1 WLR 917 . . . 676

D v D (application for contact) [1994] 1 FCR 694 . . . 441

D v D (Child of the Family) (1981) 2 FLR 93, CA . . . 297

D v D (County Court Jurisdiction: Injunctions) [1993] 2 FLR 802, CA . . . 762

D v D (Custody: Jurisdiction) [1996] 1 FLR 574 . . . 1022

D v D (Custody of Child) (1981) 2 FLR 74 . . . 467

D v D (Financial Provision: Periodical Payments) [2004] EWHC 445 (Fam) [2004] 1 FLR 988 . . . 880

D v D (Lump Sum Order: Adjournment of
    Application) [2001] 1 FLR 633 . . . 842
D v D (Nullity: Statutory Bar) [1979] Fam
    70 . . . 84
D v D (Shared Residence Order) [2001] 1 FLR
    495, CA . . . 488
D v East Berkshire Community Health NHS
    Trust [2005] UK HL 23 [2005] 2 WLR
    993 . . . 343, 675–6
D v Hereford and Worcester County Council
    [1991] Fam 14 . . . 377
D v L (Surrogacy) [2012] EWHC 2631 (Fam)
    [2013] 2 FLR 275 . . . 280
D v M (A Minor: Custody Appeal) [1983] Fam
    33 . . . 409
D v N (Contact Order: Conditions) [1997] 2 FLR
    797, CA . . . 501, 507
D v N and D (by the Guardian Ad Litem)
    (Brussels II Revised: Art 11 (7)) [2011] EWHC
    471 (Fam) [2011] 2 FLR 464 . . . 1080
D v S (Abduction: Acquiescence) [2008] EWHC
    363 (Fam) [2008] 2 FLR 293 . . . 771, 772,
    1051, 1057, 1059
D v United Kingdom (1997) 24
    EHRR 423 . . . 354
D, Re [1943] Ch 305 . . . 743
D (A Child) (Abduction: Rights of Custody),
    Re [2006] UKHL 51 [2007]
    1 AC 619 . . . 1050, 1053, 1054, 1070
D (A Minor) v Berkshire County Council [1987]
    AC 317 . . . 296, 537
D (a minor) v DPP [1995] 2 FLR 502 . . . 365
D (A Minor), Re (1978) 76 LGR 653 . . . 751
D (A Minor), Re [1987] AC 317, HL . . . 359, 391
D (a minor), Re [1992] 1 All ER 892, CA . . . 500
D (A Minor) (Abduction: Rights of Custody), Re
    [2006] UKHL 51 [2007]
    1 AC 619 . . . 1073, 1075
D (A Minor) (Adoption Order: Validity), Re
    [1991] Fam 137, CA . . . 694
D (A Minor) (Child: Removal From
    Jurisdiction), Re [1992] 1 WLR 667,
    CA . . . 500, 503
D (A Minor) (Child Removal From Jurisdiction),
    Re [1992] 1 WLR 315, CA . . . 1020
D (A Minor) (Justices' Decision: Review) [1977]
    Fam 158 . . . 752
D (A Minor) (Wardship: Sterilisation), Re [1976]
    Fam 185, *The Times*, 21 May 1985 . . . 317, 353,
    354, 749
D (Abduction: Acquiescence), Re [1998] 2 FLR
    335, CA . . . 1059
D (Abduction: Discretionary Return), Re [2000]
    1 FLR 24 . . . 1070
D (Abduction: Rights of Custody), Re [2006]
    UKHL 51 [2007] 1 AC 619 . . . 1036
D (Adoption: Foreign Guardianship), Re [1999]
    2 FLR 865 . . . 710
D (Article 13B: Non-Return), Re [2006]
    EWCA Civ 146 . . . 1064

D (Brussels II Revised: Contact), Re [2007]
    EWHC 822 (Fam) [2008] 1 FLR 516 . . . 1006
D (Care: Natural Parent Presumption), Re [1999]
    1 FLR 134, CA . . . 405
D (Care: Threshold Criteria: Significant Harm),
    Re [1998] Fam Law 656 . . . 603
D (Care Proceedings: Preliminary hearings),
    Re [2009] EWCA Civ 472 [2009] 2 FLR
    668 . . . 616
D (Children) (Parental Order: Foreign
    Surrogacy) (Practice Note), Re [2012] EWHC
    2631 (Fam) [2013] 1 WLR 3135 . . . 279
D (Contact: Interim Orders), Re [1995] 1 FLR
    495 . . . 490
D (Contact: Reasons for Refusal), Re [1997] 2
    FLR 48, CA . . . 494
D (contact and parental responsibility: lesbian
    mothers and known fathers), Re [2006]
    EWHC 2 (Fam) [2006] 1 FCR 556 . . . 259,
    378, 384
D (Intractable Contact Dispute: Publicity),
    Re [2004] EWHC 727 (Fam) [2004] 1 FLR
    1226 . . . 482
D (Leave to Remove: Appeal), Re [2010] EWCA
    Civ 50 [2010] 2 FLR 1605 . . . 530
D (Local Authority Responsibility), Re [2012]
    EWCA Civ 627 [2013] 2 FLR 673 . . . 337
D (Minors) (Adoption Reports: Confidentiality),
    Re [1996] AC 593, HL . . . 425, 458, 462
D (Nigerian Fertility Clinic: Fact Finding),
    Re [2012] EWHC 4231 (Fam) [2013] 2 FLR
    1417 . . . 260
D (Parental Responsibility), Re [2001] EWCA
    Civ 230 [2001] 1 FLR 971 . . . 378
D (Parental Responsibility: IVF Baby), Re [2001]
    1 FLR 972, CA . . . 489
D (Paternity), Re [2006] EWHC 3565 (Fam)
    [2007] 2 FLR 26 . . . 267
D (Prohibited Steps Order), Re [1996] 2 FLR
    273 . . . 502, 505
D (Residence: Imposition of Conditions), Re
    [1996] 2 FLR 281, CA . . . 502, 631
D (Secure Accommodation Order) (No 1), Re
    [1997] 1 FLR 197 . . . 574
D (Stay of Children Act Proceedings), Re [2003]
    EWHC 565 (Fam) [2003] 2 FLR 1159 . . . 427
D (Unborn Baby), Re [2009] EWHC 2811 (Fam)
    [2009] 2 FLR 313 . . . 746
D (Withdrawal of Parental Responsibility)
    [2014] EWCA Civ 315 [2014] Fam Law
    971 . . . 383, 501
D Borough Council v AB [2011] EWHC 101
    (COP) [2011] 2 FLR 72 . . . 320
D and H (Termination of Contact), Re [1997] 1
    FLR 841, CA . . . 659
D, L and LA (Care: Change of Forename), Re
    [2003] 1 FLR 339 . . . 357, 358, 396, 571
Dailey v Dailey [2003] UKPC 65 [2003] 3 FCR
    369, PC . . . 114
Dale, Re [1994] Ch 31 . . . 964

Dalrymple v Dalrymple (1811) 2 Hag Con
54 . . . 47, 48

Dart v Dart [1996] 2 FLR 286, CA . . . 890, 891

Daubney v Daubney [1976] Fam 267, CA . . . 885

Davies v Davies [1986] 1 FLR 497, CA . . . 842

Davis v Johnson [1979] AC 264, HL . . . 179, 187,
191

Dawson v Jay (1854) 3 De G, M & G 764 . . . 1024

Dawson v Wearmouth [1999] 2 AC 308,
HL . . . 357, 440, 499, 501, 521, 522, 524

DB v CMEC [2011] UKUT 202 (AAC) . . . 812

D-E v A-G (1845) 1 Rob Eccl 279 . . . 74

De Falco v Crawley Borough Council [1980] QB
460, CA . . . 207

de Lasala v de Lasala [1980] AC 546, PC . . . 850,
853

De Reneville v De Reneville [1948]
P 100, CA. . . . 65

DE v AB (Financial Provision for Child) [2011]
EWHC 3792 (Fam) [2012] 2 FLR 1396 . . . 798

Deacock v Deacock [1958] P 230, CA . . . 959

Deak v Romania and the United Kingdom
[2008] 2 FLR 994 . . . 1053

Dean v Dean [1978] Fam 161 . . . 850

Dean v Dean [1987] 1 FLR 517, CA . . . 539

Debenham, Re [1986] 1 FLR 404 . . . 991

Delaney v Delaney [1990] 2 FLR 457, CA . . . 790

Dennis v Dennis [1955] P 153 . . . 215, 241

Dennis v Dennis [2000] 2 FLR 231 . . . 228, 229

Dennis v McDonald [1982] Fam 63,
CA . . . 146, 147

Dennis (deceased), Re [1981] 2 All ER
140 . . . 983

Densham, Re [1975] 3 All ER 726, CA . . . 135

Department of Health v JWB and SMB (1992)
66 ALJR 300 . . . 352

Department of Health and Community Services
v JWB and SMB (1992) 66 ALJR 300 . . . 765

Detiček v Sgueglia (Case C-403/09 PPU) [2010]
1 FLR 1381, ECJ . . . 1003

Devon County Council v B [1997] 1 FLR 591,
CA . . . 762, 768

Devon County Council v S [1992] Fam
176 . . . 537

Devon County Council v S [1994] Fam
169 . . . 196, 764, 770

DH (A Minor) (Child Abuse), Re [1994] 1 FLR
679 . . . 505, 547, 549, 632, 633

Dharamshi v Dharamshi [2001] 1 FLR
736 . . . 897

Dibble v Pfluger [2010] EWCA Civ 1005 [2011] 1
FLR 664 . . . 143, 144

Dickinson v Jones Alexander & Co [1993] 2 FLR
521 (decided in 1989) . . . 853

Din v Wandsworth London Borough Council
[1983] 1 AC 657, HL . . . 208

Dinch v Dinch [1987] 1 All ER 818, HL . . . 905

Dingmar v Dingmar [2006] EWCA Civ 942
[2007] Ch 109 . . . 989

Dipper v Dipper [1981] Fam 31, CA . . . 394

Dipple v Dipple [1942] P 65 . . . 832

Diwell v Farnes [1959] 2 All ER 379 . . . 7

Dixon v Dixon (1878) 9 Ch D 587 . . . 110

Dixon v Marchant [2008] EWCA Civ 11 [2008] 1
FLR 655 . . . 910

DL v EL (Hague Abduction Convention: Effect
of Reversal of Return Order on Appeal) [2013]
EWHC 49 (Fam) [2013] 2 FLR 163 . . . 1042

DL v EL (Reunite International Child Abduction
Centre intervening) [2013] EWCA Civ 865
[2013] 3 FCR 69 . . . 1042, 1046

DL v Local Authority [2012] EWCA Civ
253 . . . 743

DM (A Minor) (Wardship: Jurisdiction), Re
[1986] 2 FLR 122, CA . . . 667

DN v MD and AR (Contact) [2011] EWHC 2290
(Fam) [2012] Fam Law 127 . . . 370

Dolan v Corby [2011] EWCA Civ 1664 [2012] 2
FLR 1031 . . . 186

Dombo Beheer BV v Netherlands (1993) 18
EHRR 213 . . . 838

Donaldson v McNiven [1952] 2 All ER 691,
CA . . . 364

Donnelly v Joyce [1974] QB 454, CA . . . 366

Donofrio v Burrell 2000 SLT 1051 . . . 1083

Dorney-Kingdom v Dorney-Kingdom [2000] 2
FLR 855, CA . . . 822, 905

Down Lisburn Health and Social Services
Trust v H [2006] UKHL (NI) 36 [2007] 1 FLR
121 . . . 713, 719

DP v Commonwealth Central Authority [2001]
HCA 39 (Australia) . . . 1035

DP v Community Central Authority; JLM
v Director-General NSW Department
of Community Services (2001) 180 ALR
402 . . . 1061

Drake v Whipp [1996] 1 FLR 826, CA . . . 131

Draper v United Kingdom (1980) 24 D & R
72 . . . 54

Draskovic v Draskovic (1980) 11 Fam Law 87 . . . 795

Dredge v Dredge [1947] 1 All ER 29 . . . 74, 301

Dryden v Dryden [1973] Fam 217 . . . 70

Du Boulay v Du Boulay (1869) LR
2 PC 430, PC . . . 95

Dufour v Pereira (1769) 1 Dick 419 . . . 965

Dukali v Lamrani (Attorney-General
Intervening) [2012] EWHC 1748 (Fam) [2012]
2 FLR 1099 . . . 58, 69

Dunhill, Re (1967) 111 Sol Jo 113 . . . 749

Dunn v Dunn [1949] P 98 . . . 152

Duranceau, Re [1952] 3 DLR 714
(Canada) . . . 983

Durham v Durham (1885) 10 PD 80 . . . 80, 92

Duxbury v Duxbury [1992] Fam 62n,
CA . . . 888, 890, 897, 901

DWS (Deceased), [2001] Ch 568, CA . . . 972

DX (An Infant), Re [1949] Ch 320 . . . 708

Dyer v Dyer [1775-1802] All ER Rep 205 . . . 110

Dyson Holdings Ltd v Fox [1976] QB 503,
CA . . . 7

E v C (Child Maintenance) [1996] 1 FLR
    472 . . . 792, 796
E v E [2008] 1 FLR 220 . . . 832
E v E (Child Abduction: Intolerable Situation)
    [1998] 2 FLR 980 . . . 1061
E v E (Financial Provision) [1990] 2 FLR
    233 . . . 899
E v London Borough of X [2005] EWHC 811
    (Fam) [2006] 1 FLR 731 . . . 758
E (A Minor), Re (1990) 9 BMLR 1 . . . 324
E (A Minor) (Care Order: Contact), Re [1994]
    1 FLR 146, CA . . . 640, 659
E (A Minor) (Child Support Act: Blood Test),
    Re [1994] 2 FLR 548 . . . 264
E (A Minor) (Medical Treatment), Re [1991]
    2 FLR 585 . . . 745
E (Abduction: Rights of Custody), Re [2005]
    EWHC 848 (Fam) [2005] 2 FLR 759 . . . 1047
E (an infant), Re [1963] 3 All ER 874 . . . 411
E (an infant), Re (1990) 9 BMLR 1 . . . 403
E (By Her Litigation Friend, PW) v London
    Borough of X [2005] EWHC 2811 (Fam)
    [2006] 1 FLR 730 . . . 746, 749, 754, 767
E (By Her Litigation Friend The Official
    Solicitor) v Channel Four and St Helens
    Borough Council [2005] EWHC 1144 (Fam)
    [2005] 2 FLR 913 . . . 325
E (Children) (Abduction: Custody Appeal),
    Re [2011] UKSC 27 [2012] 1 AC 144 . . . 424,
    1034, 1035, 1036, 1037, 1061, 1062, 1075
E (D) (An Infant), Re [1967] Ch 287, CA . . . 1025
E (Family Assistance Order), Re [1999] 2 FLR
    512 . . . 548, 549
E (Minors) (Residence: Condition), Re [1997]
    2 FLR 638 . . . 506
E (minors) (wardship: jurisdiction), Re [1984]
    1 All ER 21, CA . . . 667, 668
E (Parental Responsibility: Blood Tests),
    Re [1995] 1 FLR 392 . . . 265
E (Parental Responsibility), Re [1994] 2 FLR
    709 . . . 420
E (Residence: Imposition of Conditions), Re
    [1997] 2 FLR 638, CA . . . 505
E (SA) (a minor) (wardship), Re [1984] 1 All ER
    289, HL . . . 743, 745, 746
E (Wardship Order: Child In Voluntary
    Accommodation), Re [2011] EWCA Civ 1173
    [2013] 2 FLR 63 . . . 756, 757, 764
Eaves, Re [1940] Ch 109, CA . . . 65
EB v France [2008] 1 FLR 850, ECtHR (Grand
    Chamber) . . . 2, 684
EC (Child Abduction) (Stayed Proceedings),
    Re [2006] EWCA Civ 1115 [2007]
    1 FLR 57 . . . 1003
Edgar v Edgar [1980] 3 All ER 887; [1980] 1 WLR
    1410, CA . . . 781, 851, 880
Edwards v Edwards [1986] 1 FLR 187; affd [1986]
    1 FLR 205, CA . . . 410, 458
EF v MGS [2011] EWHC 3139 (Fam) [2012]
    2 FCR 65 . . . 1044

El Gamal v Al Maktoum [2011] EWHC 3763
    (Fam) [2012] 2 FLR 387 . . . 69
Elliot v Joicey [1935] AC 209, HL . . . 291, 296,
    359, 372, 391, 537, 560
Elwes (No 2), Re, The Times, 30 July 1958 . . . 746
Emery's Investments' Trusts, Re [1959]
    Ch 410 . . . 113
EO and VP v Slovakia [2004] 2 FCR 242,
    ECtHR . . . 436
Equity and Law Home Loans Ltd v Prestidge
    [1992] 1 All ER 909, CA . . . 151
Erskine Trust, Re [2012] EWHC 732 (Ch) [2012]
    2 FLR 725 . . . 966
Eshak v Nowojewski (1980) 11 Fam Law 115,
    CA . . . 906
Espinosa v Bourke [1999] 1 FLR 747 . . . 985, 988
Essex County Council v F [1993]
    1 FLR 847 . . . 588
Essex County Council v Mirror Group
    Newspapers Ltd [1996] 1 FLR 585 . . . 769, 771
Ettenfield v Ettenfield [1940] P 96 . . . 261
Evans v Amicus Healthcare Ltd [2004] EWCA
    Civ 727 [2005] Fam 1 . . . 249, 253, 254, 255
Evans v Evans [1989] 1 FLR 351, CA . . . 901
Evans v Evans [1990] 2 All ER 147 . . . 832
Evans v Hayward [1995] 2 FLR 511, CA . . . 128
Evans v United Kingdom [2007] 1 FLR 1990
    (ECtHR (Grand Chamber)) . . . 249, 254
Eve, Re (1986) 31 DLR (4th) 1, Canadian
    Supreme Court . . . 317, 742
Evelyn, Re [1998] Fam 55, CA . . . 406
Evers' Trust, Re [1980] 3 All ER 399, CA . . . 146
Eves v Eves [1975] 3 All ER 768, CA . . . 130, 131,
    132, 137
Ezair v Ezair [2012] EWCA Civ 893 [2013]
    1 FLR 281 . . . 863

F v Cambridge County Council [1995]
    1 FLR 516 . . . 512
F v Child Support Agency [1999] 2 FLR
    244 . . . 269
F v F [1902] 1 Ch 688 . . . 292
F v F (Ancillary Relief: Substantial Assets) [1995]
    2 FLR 45 . . . 837, 849, 854
F v F (Divorce: Insolvency: Annulment
    of Bankruptcy Order) [1994] 1 FLR
    359 . . . 919
F v F (Financial Remedies: Premarital Wealth)
    [2012] EWHC 438 (Fam) [2012] 2 FLR
    1212 . . . 782
F v F (Minors) (Custody: Custody Order) [1989]
    Fam 1 . . . 1086
F v F (MMR: Vaccine) [2013] EWHC 2683 (Fam)
    [2014] 1 FLR 1328 . . . 353, 382
F v F (MMR: Vaccine) [2013] EWHC 2769 (Fam)
    [2014] 1 FLR 1328 . . . 500
F v F (S Intervening) (Financial
    Provision: Bankruptcy: Reviewable
    Disposition) [2002] EWHC 2814 (Fam) [2003]
    1 FLR 911 . . . 146

F v G (Child: Financial Provision) [2004] EWHC 1848 (Fam) [2005] 1 FLR 261 . . . 797

F v Leeds City Council [1994] 2 FLR 60, CA . . . 429

F v M (Abduction: Grave Risk of Harm) [2008] 1467 (Fam) [2008] 2 FLR 1263 . . . 1075

F v M and N (Abduction: Acquiescence: Settlement) [2008] EWHC 1525 (Fam) [2008] 2 FLR 1270 . . . 1055, 1071

F v R (Contact: Justices' Reasons) [1995] 1 FLR 227 . . . 507

F v R (Contact) [1995] 1 FLR 227 . . . 501

F v Suffolk County Council (1981) 2 FLR 208 . . . 601

F v Wirral Metropolitan Borough Council [1991] Fam 69, CA . . . 360, 366

F (a child) (contact order), Re [2001] 1 FCR 422 . . . 494

F (a child) (placement order best interests), Re [2013] EWCA Civ 1277 [2014] 1 FCR 415 . . . 702

F (A Minor) (Abduction: Custody Rights Abroad), Re [1995] Fam 224, CA . . . 1048, 1064

F (A Minor) (Abduction: Jurisdiction), Re [1991] Fam 25, CA . . . 1025, 1026

F (A Minor) (Blood Tests: Parental Rights), Re [1993] Fam 314, CA . . . 265, 266, 373

F (A Minor) (Care Order: Withdrawal of Application), Re [1993] 2 FLR 9 . . . 595–6

F (A Minor) (Child Abduction), Re [1992] 1 FLR 548, CA . . . 1040, 1044, 1059

F (A Minor) (Immigration: Wardship), Re [1990] Fam 125, CA . . . 748, 767

F (A Minor) (Wardship: Appeal), Re [1976] Fam 238, CA . . . 546

F (Abduction: Child's Right to Family Life), Re [1999] Fam Law 806 . . . 1035

F (Abduction: Child's Wishes), Re [2006] EWCA Civ 468 [2007] 2 FLR 697 . . . 1073

F (Abduction: Refusal To Return), Re [2009] EWCA Civ 416 [2009] 2 FLR 1023 . . . 1079

F (Abduction: Unborn Child), Re [2006] EWHC 2199 (Fam) [2007] 1 FLR 626 . . . 1040, 1043

F (Abduction: Unmarried Father: Sole Carer), Re [2002] EWHC 2896 (Fam) [2003] 1 FLR 839 . . . 1048

F (An Infant), Re [1969] 2 Ch 238 . . . 404

F (care: termination of contact), Re [2000] 2 FCR 481 . . . 655

F (Care Proceedings: Interim Care Order), Re [2010] EWCA Civ 826 [2010] 2 FLR 1455 . . . 643

F (Child: Surname), Re [1993] 2 FLR 837n . . . 523

F (Children) (Abduction: Rights of Custody), Re [2008] EWHC 272 (Fam) [2008] 3 WLR 527 . . . 1050, 1068, 1070, 1075

F (children) (restriction on applications), Re [2005] EWCA Civ 499 [2005] 2 FLR 950 . . . 510

F (Contact), Re [2007] EWHC 2543 (Fam) [2008] 1 FLR 1163 . . . 524

F (Contact: Child in Care), Re [1995] 1 FLR 510 . . . 429, 510, 657, 658

F (Contact: Enforcement: Representation of Child), Re [1998] 1 FLR 691, CA . . . 539

F (Contact Restraint Order), Re [1995] 1 FLR 956, CA . . . 468

F (Family Proceedings: Section 37 Investigation), Re [2005] EWHC 2935 (Fam) [2006] 1 FLR 1122 . . . 550

F (In Utero), Re [1988] Fam 122, CA . . . 746

F (Indirect Contact), Re [2006] EWCA Civ 1426 [2007] 1 FLR 1015 . . . 383, 489

F (Infants) (Adoption Order: Validity), Re [1977] Fam 165, CA . . . 705

F (Interim Care Order), Re [2011] EWCA Civ 258 [2011] 2 FLR 856 . . . 624

F (Internal Relocation), Re [2010] EWCA Civ 1428 [2011] 1 FLR 1382 . . . 499, 501, 507

F (Mental Health Act: Guardianship), Re [2000] 1 FLR 192 . . . 758

F (Mental Patient: Sterilisation), Re [1990] 2 AC 1, HL . . . 351, 743

F (minors) (contact: appeal), Re [1997] 1 FCR 523, CA . . . 459

F (Minors) (Denial of Contact), Re [1993] 2 FLR 677, CA . . . 403, 494, 537, 547

F (Minors) (Wardship: Jurisdiction), Re [1988] 2 FLR 123, CA . . . 751

F (Otherwise A) (A Minor), Re [1977] Fam 58 . . . 745

F (Paternity: Jurisdiction), Re [2007] EWCA Civ 873 [2008] 1 FLR 225 . . . 273, 501

F (Paternity: Registration), Re [2011] EWCA Civ 1765 [2013] 2 FLR 1036 . . . 271

F (Placement Order), Re [2008] EWCA Civ 339 [2008] 2 FLR 550 . . . 546, 703

F (R) (An Infant), Re [1970] 1 QB 385, CA . . . 714

F (Relocation), Re [2012] EWCA Civ 1364 [2013] 1 FLR 645 . . . 531, 532

F (Shared Residence Order), Re [2003] EWCA Civ 592 [2003] 2 FLR 397 . . . 488

F (Shared Residence Orders), Re [2009] EWCA Civ 313 [2010] 1 FLR 354 . . . 409

F (Specific Issue: Child Interview), Re [1995] 1 FLR 819, CA . . . 340, 363, 427, 501

Fairpo v Humberside County Council [1997] 1 FLR 339 . . . 348

Falconer v Falconer [1970] 3 All ER 449, CA . . . 124

Farley v Secretary of State for Work and Pensions [2006] UKHL 31 [2006] 3 All ER 935 . . . 819

Fender v St John Mildmay [1938] AC 1 . . . 949

Ferguson and Others v United Kingdom (Application lodged 2 February 2011) ECtHR . . . 37, 60, 61

Fessi v Whitmore [1999] 1 FLR 167 . . . 359

FG v MBW (Financial Remedy for Child) [2011] EWHC 1729 (Fam) [2012] 1 FLR 152 . . . 798

Field v Field [2003] 1 FLR 376 . . . 918

Fielden v Cunliffe [2005] EWCA Civ 1508 [2006] Ch 361 . . . 986, 990

Fielden and Another v Cunliffe [2005] EWCA Civ 1508 [2006] Ch 361 . . . 986

First National Bank plc v Achampong [2003] EWCA Civ 487 [2004] 1 FCR 18 . . . 158

Fisher v Fisher [1989] 1 FLR 423, CA . . . 875, 887, 889

Fitzpatrick v Sterling Housing Association Ltd [2001] 1 AC 27, HL . . . 9, 24, 32, 941, 943, 993

Flavell v Flavell [1997] 1 FLR 353, CA . . . 879, 914

Fleming v Fleming [2003] EWCA Civ 1841 [2004] 1 FLR 667 . . . 878, 888, 914

Fleming v Pratt (1823) 1 LJOS 194 . . . 339

Foley v Foley [1981] Fam 160 . . . 894

Ford v Ford [1987] Fam Law 232 . . . 76

Ford v Stier [1896] P 1 . . . 79

Foster v Foster [2003] EWCA Civ 565 [2003] 2 FLR 299 . . . 893

Fournier v Fournier [1998] 2 FLR 990, CA . . . 878

Fowler v Barron [2008] EWCA Civ 377 [2008] 2 FLR 831 . . . 137

Foyle v Turner [2007] BPIR 43 . . . 161

Francis v Francis [1960] P 17 . . . 263

Freckleton v Freckleton [1966] CLY 3938 . . . 840

Fretté v France [2003] 2 FLR 9 . . . 684

Fribance v Fribance [1957] 1 All ER 357 . . . 124

Fullard, Re [1982] Fam 42, CA . . . 977, 985

Fuller v Fuller [1973] 2 All ER 650, CA . . . 220

Furneaux v Furneaux (1973) 118 *Sol Jo* 204 . . . 782

Fynn, Re (1848) 2 De G & Sm 457 . . . 310

FZ v SZ and Others (Ancillary Relief: Conduct: Valuations) [2010] EWHC 1630 (Fam) [2011] 1 FLR 64 . . . 902

G v A (children: surname) [1995] 2 FCR 223n . . . 523

G v B (Financial Remedies: Asset Beneficiaries) [2013] EWHC 3414 (Fam) [2014] Fam Law 290 . . . 883

G v C (Residence Order: Committal) [1998] 1 FLR 43 CA . . . 540

G v G (1908) 25 TLR 328 . . . 75

G v G [1964] P 133 . . . 219

G v G [1985] 1 WLR 647, HL . . . 908

G v G [2007] EWCA Civ 680 [2007] 2 FLR 1127 . . . 539

G v G (Custody: Appeal) [1985] 1 WLR 647, HL . . . 545, 546

G v G (Financial Provision: Equal Division) [2002] EWHC 1339 (Fam) [2002] 2 FLR 1143 . . . 897

G v G (Financial Provision: Separation Agreement) [2004] 1 FLR 1011 . . . 903

G v G (Matrimonial Property: Rights of Extended Family) [2005] EWHC 1560 (Admin) [2006] 1 FLR 62 . . . 131, 882

G v G (Minors: Custody Appeal) [1985] 1 WLR 647, HL . . . 426, 427, 650

G v G (Minors) (Abduction) [1991] 2 FLR 506, CA . . . 1025

G v G (Non-molestation Order: Jurisdiction) [2000] 2 FLR 532 . . . 181

G v G (Occupation Order: Conduct) [2000] 2 FLR 36, CA . . . 186

G v G (Ouster: *Ex parte* Application) [1990] 1 FLR 395, CA . . . 194

G v G (Parental Order: Revocation) [2012] EWHC 1979 (Fam) [2013] 1 FLR 286 . . . 281, 282

G v G (Periodical Payments: Jurisdiction) [1997] 1 FLR 368, CA . . . 792, 913

G v M (1885) 10 App Cas 171, HL . . . 73, 84

G v Netherlands (1993) 16 EHRR CD 38 . . . 2

G, Re: Re Z (Children: Sperm Donors: Leave To Apply For Children Act Orders) [2013] EWHC 134 (Fam) [2013] 1 FLR 1334 . . . 256, 517

G, Re [2005] UKHL 68 [2005] 3 WLR 1166 . . . 645, 647

G, Re [2012] EWCA Civ 1233 [2013] 1 FLR 677 . . . 399

G (a child) (domestic violence: direct contact), Re [2001] 2 FCR 134, CA . . . 378

G (A Child) (Parental Responsibility Order), Re [2006] EWCA Civ 745 [2006] 2 FLR 1093 . . . 378

G (A Minor) (Abduction: Enforcement), Re [1990] 2 FLR 325 . . . 1086

G (A Minor) (Care Order: Threshold Condition), Re [1995] Fam 16 . . . 443

G (A Minor) (Care Proceedings), Re [1995] Fam 16 . . . 599

G (A Minor) (Child Abduction: Enforcement), Re [1990] 2 FLR 325 . . . 1086

G (A Minor) (Enforcement of Access Abroad), Re [1993] Fam 216, CA . . . 1039, 1082, 1083

G (A Minor) (Interim Care Order: Residential Assessment), Re [2005] UKHL 68 [2005] 3 WLR 1166 . . . 20, 438, 640, 645, 646

G (A Minor) (Parental Responsibility Order), Re [1994] 1 FLR 504 . . . 375, 378, 420

G (a minor) (social worker: disclosure), Re [1996] 2 All ER 65, CA . . . 463

G (a minor) (ward: criminal injuries compensation), Re [1990] 3 All ER 102, CA . . . 745

G (A Minor) (Witness Summons), Re [1988] 2 FLR 396 . . . 768

G (Abduction: Children's Objections), Re [2010] EWCA Civ 1232 [2011] 1 FLR 1645 . . . 450

G (Abduction: Custody), Re [2010] EWCA Civ 1232 [2011] 1FLR 1645 . . . 450, 466

G (Abduction: Psychological Harm), Re [1995] 1 FLR 64 . . . 1065

G (Abduction: Rights of Custody), Re [2002] 2 FLR 703 . . . 1048

G (Abduction: Striking Out Application), Re [1995] 2 FLR 410 . . . 1056

G (Abduction: Withdrawal of Proceedings, Acquiescence, Habitual Residence), Re [2007] EWHC 1837 (Fam) [2008] 2 FLR 351 . . . 772

G (Adoption: Contact), Re [2002] EWCA Civ 761 [2003] 1 FLR 270 . . . 719

G (Adoption: Illegal Placement), Re [1995] 1 FLR 403, CA . . . 728, 729

G (Adoption: Placement Outside the Jurisdiction) (No 2), Re [2008] EWCA Civ 1052 [2008] 1 FLR 1497 . . . 1015

G (Adoption: Placement Outside the Jurisdiction), Re [2008] EWCA Civ 105 [2008] 1 FLR 1484 . . . 1015

G (Adoption: Unmarried Couple), Re [2008] UKHL 38 [2009] AC 173 . . . 706

G (Adoption Order), Re [1999] 1 FLR 400, CA . . . 711

G (Care Proceedings: Threshold Conditions), Re [2001] EWCA Civ 968 [2001] 2 FLR 1111 . . . 604

G (Care Proceedings: Welfare Evaluation), Re [2013] EWCA Civ 965 [2014] 1 FLR 670 . . . 414, 545, 625, 630, 702

G (Child Case: Parental Involvement), Re [1996] 1 FLR 857, CA . . . 384

G (Children), Re [2005] EWCA Civ 1283 [2006] 1 FLR 771 . . . 440

G (Children) (Residence: Same Sex Partner), Re [2006] UKHL 43 [2006] 1 WLR 2305 . . . 244, 274, 318, 402, 403, 406, 407, 419, 442, 549

G (Decree Absolute: Prejudice), Re [2002] EWHC 2834 (Fam) [2003] 1 FLR 870 . . . 228

G (Direct Contact: Domestic Violence), Re [2000] 2 FLR 865 . . . 495

G (Education: Religious Upbringing), Re [2012] EWCA Civ 1233 [2013] 1 FLR 677 . . . 309, 312, 325, 350, 398, 404, 408, 410, 420, 432, 501

G (Financial Provision: Liberty to Restore Application for Lump Sum), Re [2004] EWHC 88 (Fam) [2004] 1 FLR 997 . . . 887, 894

G (Foreign Adoption: Consent), Re [1995] 2 FLR 534 . . . 710

G (Foreign Contact Order: Enforcement), Re [2003] EWCA Civ 1607 [2004] 1 WLR 521 . . . 1007, 1082, 1087, 1088

G (Interim Care Order), Re [2011] EWCA Civ 745 [2011] 2 FLR 955 . . . 643

G (Maintenance Pending Suit), Re [2006] EWHC 1834 (Fam) [2007] 1 FLR 1674 . . . 837

G (minor) (social worker: disclosure), Re [1996] 2 All ER 65 . . . 463

G (Minors) (Interim Care Order), Re [1993] 2 FLR 839, Re CA . . . 569, 643

G (Minors) (Welfare Report: Disclosure), Re [1993] 2 FLR 293, CA . . . 458, 462

G (Parentage: Blood Sample), Re [1997] 1 FLR 360, CA . . . 269

G (Parental Responsibility: Education), Re [1994] 2 FLR 964, CA . . . 333, 382, 388, 393, 394, 491, 735

G (Removal From Jurisdiction), Re [2005] EWCA Civ 170 [2005] 2 FLR 166 . . . 530

G (Residence: Same-Sex Partners), Re [2005] EWCA Civ 462 [2005] 2 FLR 957; affd [2006] UKHL 43 [2006] 1 WLR 2305 . . . 488

G (Secure Accommodation), Re [2000] 2 FLR 259, CA . . . 574

G (Secure Accommodation Order), Re [2001] 1 FLR 884 . . . 574

G (Special Guardianship Order), Re [2010] EWCA Civ [2010] 2 FLR 696 . . . 737

G (Surrogacy: Foreign Domicile), Re [2007] EWHC 2814 (Fam) [2008] 1 FLR 1047 . . . 280, 1015

G (Wardship) (Jurisdiction: Power of Arrest), Re (1982) 4 FLR 538 . . . 766

G and G v Decision of OLG Hamm January 18 1995, 35 ILM 529 (1996) (Germany) . . . 1035

Galan v Galan [1985] FLR 905, CA . . . 187

Gallarotti v Sebastianelli [2012] EWCA Civ 865 [2012] 2 FLR 1232 . . . 137

Galloway v Goldstein [2012] EWHC 60 (Fam) [2012] 1 FLR 1254 . . . 63, 69

Gammans v Ekins [1950] 2 KB 328, CA . . . 7

Gandhi v Patel [2002] 1 FLR 603 . . . 68

Gandolfo v Gandolfo [1981] QB 359, CA . . . 917

Gardner v Gardner (1877) 2 App Cas 723, HL . . . 261, 263

Garland v Morris [2007] EWHC 2 (Ch) [2007] 2 FLR 528 . . . 985, 988

Garner v Garner [1992] 1 FLR 573, CA . . . 909, 914

Gas and Dubois v France (App No 25951/07, 15 March 2012) . . . 684

The Gaskin Case [1990] 1 FLR 167, ECtHR . . . 268, 273, 327, 677

Gatehouse v Robinson [1986] 1 WLR 18 . . . 728

Gay v Sheeran [1999] 2 FLR 519, CA . . . 950

Geapin v Geapin (1974) 4 Fam Law 188, CA . . . 494

Geary v Rankine [2012] EWCA Civ 555 [2012] 2 FLR 1409 . . . 129

George v George [2003] EWCA Civ 202 [2004] 1 FLR 421 . . . 846

Gereis v Yagoub [1997] 1 FLR 854 . . . 68, 72

Ghaidan v Godin-Mendoza [2004] UKHL 30 [2004] 2 AC 557 . . . 9, 24, 25, 32, 250, 941, 943

Gibson v Revenue and Customs Prosecution Office [2008] EWCA Civ 645 [2009] QB 348 . . . 128

Gillett v Holt [2001] Ch 210 [2000] 2 FLR 266, CA . . . 141, 142

Gillick v West Norfolk and Wisbech Area Health Authority [1984] QB 581 . . . 308

Gillick v West Norfolk and Wisbech Area Health Authority [1986] AC 112, HL . . . 319, 320, 321, 322, 323, 332, 337, 351, 352, 392

In the Goods of Gilligan [1950] P 32 . . . 962
Gillow v United Kingdom (1986) Series A, No
    109; 11 EHRR 335 . . . 122
Gissing v Gissing [1971] AC 886, HL . . . 124,
    125, 127, 129, 133, 134, 829
Glaser v U K [2001] 1 FLR 148 . . . 492
Gloucester City Council v Miles [1985] FLR
    1043, CA . . . 208
Gloucestershire County Council v P [2000]
    Fam 1, CA . . . 537
Gogay v Hertfordshire County Council [2001]
    1 FLR 280 . . . 580
Gojkovic v Gojkovic (No 2) [1992] Fam 40,
    CA . . . 841, 862, 889, 891, 895, 896
Golubovich v Golubovich [2011] EWCA
    Civ 479 [2011] 2 FLR 1193 . . . 922
Goodchild, Re [1997] 1 WLR 1216 . . . 988
Goodchild (Deceased), Re [1996] 1 FLR 591
    [1996] 1 All ER 670 affd [1997] 1 WLR 1216,
    CA . . . 964, 965, 984
Goodman v Gallant [1986] Fam 106, CA . . . 125,
    126, 135
Goodrich v Goodrich [1971] 2 All ER 1340 . . . 215
Goodwin v United Kingdom [2002] 2 FLR
    487 . . . 35, 42, 84
Gordon v Douce [1983] 2 All ER 228 . . . 133
Gordon v Goertz [1996] 2 SCR 27 . . . 533, 534
Gorely v Codd [1966] 3 All ER 891 . . . 364
Görgülü v Germany [2004] 1 FLR 894 . . . 724
Gorman, Re [1990] 1 All ER 717 . . . 125
Gorman (A Bankrupt), Re ex parte The Trustee
    of the Bankrupt v The Bankrupt and Another
    [1990] 2 FLR 284 . . . 161
Gould v Gould [1970] 1 QB 275, CA . . . 98, 780
Gouriet v Union of Post Office Workers [1978]
    AC 435, HL . . . 391
Governor & Co of the Bank of Scotland v
    Grimes [1985] 2 All ER 254, CA . . . 158
Gowers v Gowers [2011] EWHC 3485 (Fam)
    [2012] 1 FLR 1040 . . . 864
GR v CMEC (CSM) [2011] UKUT 101 (AAC)
    [2011] 2 FLR 962 . . . 806
GR (Care Order), Re [2010] EWCA Civ 871
    [2011] 1 FLR 669 . . . 643
Graham v Murphy [1997] 1 FLR 860 . . . 981,
    988, 991
Granatino v Radmacher (Formerly Granatino)
    [2010] UKSC 42 [2011] 1 AC 534 . . . 10, 94,
    779–80, 781, 782, 783, 785, 787, 856–9, 860,
    861, 926, 928, 950, 993
Grant v Edwards [1986] Ch 638, CA . . . 130, 131,
    132, 137, 140
Graves v Graves (1864) 3 Sw & Tr 350 . . . 219
In the Estate of Gray (1963) 107 Sol Jo
    156 . . . 962
Gray v Gee (1923) 39 TLR 429 . . . 93
Gray v Perpetual Trustee Co Ltd [1928] AC 391,
    PC . . . 964, 965
Gray v Secretary of State for Work and Pensions
    [2012] EWCA Civ 1412 [2013] 2 FLR 424 . . . 812

Greasley v Cook [1980] 3 All ER 710, CA . . . 142,
    157
Greaves v Greaves (1872) LR 2 P & D 423 . . . 72
Green v Green [1993] 1 FLR 326 . . . 847
Grenfell v Grenfell [1978] Fam 128, CA . . . 222
Griffiths v Dawson & Co [1993] 2 FLR 315 . . . 224
Griffiths v Fleming [1909] 1 KB 805, CA . . . 92
Griffiths v Griffiths [1974] 1 All ER 932,
    CA . . . 841, 900
Griffiths v Griffiths [1984] Fam 70, CA . . . 875
Grimes v Grimes [1948] P 323 . . . 75
GS v L (Financial Remedies: Pre-Acquired
    Assets: Needs) [2011] EWHC 1759 (Fam)
    [2013] 1 FLR 300 . . . 860
G-U (A Minor) (Wardship), Re [1984] FLR
    811 . . . 745
Gubisch Maschinenfabrik v Palumbo (Case
    144/86) [1987] ECR 4861 . . . 1003
Gully v Dix [2004] EWCA Civ 139 [2004] 1 WLR
    1399 . . . 979
Gumbrell v Jones [2001] NZFLR 593 . . . 1083
GW v RW (Financial Provision: Departure from
    Equality) [2003] EWHC 611 (Fam) [2003] 2
    FLR 108 . . . 884, 892, 893, 894, 933

H v Austria (App No 57813/00) [2012] 2 FCR
    291 . . . 245
H v C [2009] 2 FLR 1540 . . . 794
H v F (Refusal of leave to remove a child from
    the jurisdiction) [2005] EWHC 2705 (Fam)
    [2006] 1 FLR 776 . . . 529
H v H [1954] P 258 . . . 76
H v H [1975] Fam 9 . . . 899
H v H [1984] Fam Law 112, CA . . . 459
H v H [2007] EWHC 459 (Fam) [2007] 2 FLR
    548 . . . 872
H v H (A Minor); K v K (minors) [1990] Fam 86,
    CA . . . 458
H v H (Child Abduction: Stay of Domestic
    Proceedings) [1994] 1 FLR 530 . . . 1051
H v H (Child Abuse: Access) [1989] 1 FLR 212,
    CA . . . 412, 494
H v H (Financial Provision: Conduct) [1994]
    2 FLR 801 . . . 901
H v H (Financial Provision: Conduct) [1998]
    1 FLR 971 . . . 845, 891
H v H (Financial Provision) [1988] 2 FLR
    114 . . . 877
H v H (Financial Relief: Attempted Murder as
    Conduct) [2005] EWHC 2911 (Fam) [2006]
    1 FLR 990 . . . 901
H v H (Financial Relief: Costs) [1997] 2 FLR
    57 . . . 862
H v H (Jurisdiction To Grant Wardship) [2011]
    EWCA Civ 796 [2012] 1 FLR 23 . . . 747
H v H (Minors) (Forum Conveniens) [1995]
    1 FLR 314 . . . 427
H v H (Pension Sharing: Rescission of Decree
    Nisi) [2002] EWHC 767 (Fam) [2002] 2 FLR
    116 . . . 228

H v P (Illegitimate Child: Capital Provision) [1993] Fam Law 515 . . . 796

H v S (Recognition of Overseas Divorce) [2012] 2 FLR 157 (Saudi Arabia) . . . 921

H v W (1857) 3 K & J 382 . . . 780, 854

H v W (Cap on Wife's Share of Bonus Payments) [2013] EWHC 4105 (Fam) [2014] Fam Law 445 . . . 887

H, Re; Re G (Adoption: Consultation of Unmarried Fathers) [2001] 1 FLR 646 . . . 711

H, Re; Re S (Abduction: Custody Rights) [1991] 2 AC 476 . . . 1051

H (a child: residence), Re [2002] 3 FCR 277, CA . . . 405

H (A Child: Summary Return: Child's Objections), Re [2012] EWHC B32 (Fam) [2013] 2 FLR 1163 . . . 1071

H (A Child) (Abduction: Habitual Residence: Agreement), Re [2012] EWCA Civ 148 [2013] 2 FLR 1426 . . . 1044

H (a child) (interim care order), Re [2002] EWCA Civ 1932 [2003] 1 FCR 350 . . . 643

H (A Minor) (Abduction: Rights of Custody), Re [2000] 1 FLR 201, CA . . . 1050

H (A Minor) (Abduction: Rights of Custody), Re [2000] 2 AC 291, HL . . . 1050

H (A Minor) (Abduction), Re [1990] 2 FLR 439 . . . 1051

H (a minor) (blood tests: parental rights), Re [1997] Fam 89 [1996] 4 All ER 28, CA . . . 264, 266, 423

H (A Minor) (Care Proceedings: Child's Wishes), Re [1993] 1 FLR 440 . . . 462, 471

H (A Minor) (Care or Residence Order), Re [1994] 2 FLR 80 . . . 632

H (A Minor) (Contact and Parental Responsibility), Re [1993] 1 FLR 484, CA . . . 377–8

H (A Minor) (Custody: Religious Upbringing), Re (1980) 2 FLR 253 . . . 411

H (A Minor) (Foreign Custody Order: Enforcement), Re [1994] Fam 105, CA . . . 1085, 1086

H (A Minor) (Section 37 Direction), Re [1993] 2 FLR 541 . . . 550

H (A Minor) (Shared Residence), Re [1994] 1 FLR 717, CA . . . 381

H (Abduction: Child of 16), Re [2000] 2 FLR 51 . . . 771, 1040, 1084

H (Abduction: Grave Risk), Re [2003] EWCA Civ 355 [2003] 2 FLR 141 . . . 455, 1063

H (Abduction: Habitual Residence: Agreement), Re [2013] EWCA Civ 148 [2013] 2 FLR 1426 . . . 760

H (Abduction: Jurisdiction), Re [2009] EWHC 2280 (Fam) [2010] 1 FLR 598 . . . 1080

H (An Infant), Re [1959] 1 WLR 1163 . . . 291

H (Application To Remove From Jurisdiction) [1998] 1 FLR 848 . . . 528

H (Care: Change in Care Plan), Re [1998] 1 FLR 193, Re CA . . . 628

H (Care Plan: Human Rights), Re [2011] EWCA Civ 1009 [2012] 1 FLR 191 . . . 678

H (Child Abduction: Mother's Asylum), Re [2003] EWHC 1820 (Fam) [2003] 2 FLR 1105 . . . 1029, 1030

H (Child Abduction) (Unmarried Father: Rights of Custody), Re [2003] EWHC 492 (Fam) [2003] 2 FLR 153 . . . 1048

H (Children) (Residence Order: Condition), Re [2001] EWCA Civ 1338 [2001] 2 FLR 1277 . . . 440, 441, 486, 499, 507, 525, 530, 535

H (Child's Name: First Name), Re [2002] EWCA Civ 190 [2002] 1 FLR 973, CA . . . 357, 358, 524

H (Conciliation: Welfare Reports), Re [1986] 1 FLR 476 . . . 457

H (Contact: Domestic Violence), Re [1998] 2 FLR 42, CA . . . 489, 494

H (Contact Order) (No 2), Re [2002] 1 FLR 22 . . . 468

H (Contact Order), Re [2010] EWCA Civ 448 [2010] 2 FLR 866 . . . 402

H (Contact With Biological Father), Re [2012] EWCA Civ 281 [2012] 2 FLR 627 . . . 402

H (Father) v B (Mother) [2013] EWHC 2950 (Fam) . . . 748

H (infants), Re [1966] 1 All ER 886, CA . . . 1025

H (Leave To Remove), Re [2010] EWCA Civ 915 [2010] 2 FLR 1875 . . . 530, 534

H (Minors) (Abduction: Acquiescence), Re [1998] AC 72, HL . . . 1058, 1059, 1060, 1061

H (Minors) (Abduction: Custody Rights), Re; Re S (Minors) (Abduction: Custody Rights) [1991] 2 AC 476, HL . . . 1040, 1046

H (Minors) (Local Authority: Parental Rights) (No 3), Re [1991] Fam 151, CA . . . 375, 376

H (Minors) (Prohibited Steps Order), Re [1995] 1 WLR 667, CA . . . 491, 499, 503

H (Minors) (Sexual Abuse: Standard of Proof), Re [1996] AC 563, HL . . . 262, 412, 598, 609, 610, 611, 612, 618, 620, 621, 623, 626

H (Minors) (Wardship: Surety), Re [1991] 1 FLR 40, CA . . . 1020

H (Parental Responsibility), Re [1998] 1 FLR 855, CA . . . 374, 376, 378, 420

H (Parental Responsibility: Maintenance), Re [1996] 1 FLR 867, CA . . . 378

H (Residence Order: Child's Application For Leave), Re [2000] 1 FLR 780 . . . 519

H (Shared Residence: Parental Responsibility), Re [1995] 2 FLR 883, CA . . . 487

H (Shared Residence: Parental Responsibility), Re [2005] EWCA Civ 642 [2005] 2 FLR 957 . . . 488

H and A (Paternity: Blood Tests), Re [2002] EWCA Civ 383 [2002] 1 FLR 1145 . . . 263, 267

H and Others (Minors) (Prohibited Steps Order), Re [1995] 1 WLR 667 . . . 506

Haase v Germany [2004] 2 FLR 39, ECtHR . . . 492, 716

Hadak, Newman and Hadak, Re (1993) FLC
92-421 (Australia) . . . 406

Hadjimilitis (Tsavliris) v Tsavliris
(Divorce: Irretrievable Breakdown) [2003]
FLR 81 . . . 216, 222

Hagger, Re [1930] 2 Ch 190 . . . 965

Hagger, Re; Re Green [1951] Ch 148 . . . 965

Haghighat (A Bankrupt), Re [2009] EWHC 90
(Ch) [2009] 1 FLR 1271 . . . 162

Hains v Jeffell (1696) 1 Ld Raym 68 . . . 46

Halden v Halden [1966] 1 WLR 1481, CA . . . 118

Hale v Hale [1975] 2 All ER 1090, CA . . . 846

Hale v Tanner [2000] 1 WLR 2377,
CA . . . 194, 539

Halifax Building Society v Clark [1973] 2 All ER
33, CA . . . 159

Hall v Hall [1911] 1 Ch 487 . . . 116

Hall v Hall (1914) 111 LT 403, CA . . . 914

Hall v Hall [1962] 3 All ER 518, CA . . . 219

Hamer v United Kingdom (1982)
24 D & R 5 . . . 54

Hamilton v Hamilton [2013] EWCA Civ 13
[2014] 1 FLR 55 . . . 840, 841, 913

Hamlin v Hamlin [1986] Fam 11,
CA . . . 845, 918

Hammersmith and Fulham London
Borough Council v Monk [1992] 1 AC 478,
HL . . . 155, 204

Hammerton v Hammerton [2007] EWCA Civ
248 [2007] 2 FLR 1133 . . . 539

Hammond v Mitchell [1992] 2 All ER
109 . . . 130, 132

Hammond, Re [1911] 2 Ch 342 . . . 966

Hampshire County Council v S [1993] Fam
158 . . . 644

Hanbury v Hanbury [1999] 2 FLR 255 . . . 983,
985, 989

Hancock (Deceased), Re [1998] 2 FLR 346,
CA . . . 985, 988

Hanlon v Hanlon [1978] 2 All ER 889,
CA . . . 864, 904, 905

Harben v Harben [1957] 1 All ER 379 . . . 746

Haringey London Borough Council v MA, JN
and IA [2008] EWHC 722 (Fam) [2008] 2 FLR
1857 . . . 1010

Harman v Glencross [1986] 1 All ER 545,
CA . . . 905

Harnett v Harnett [1973] Fam 156 . . . 143, 792,
868

Harnett v Harnett [1974] 1 All ER 764,
CA . . . 143, 841, 900

Haroutunian v Jennings (1980) 1 FLR 62 . . . 796,
798

Harrington v Gill (1983) 4 FLR 265, CA . . . 991

Harris v Goddard [1983] 3 All ER 242,
CA . . . 126

Harris v Manahan [1997] 1 FLR 205, CA . . . 850,
851, 915

Harrison v Lewis [1988] 2 FLR 339, CA . . . 187,
188, 940

Harrison (Deceased), Re [2005] EWHC 2957
(Ch) [2006] 1 WLR 1212 . . . 965

Harrod v Harrod (1854) 1 K & J 4 . . . 53, 67, 79

Harrow London Borough Council v Johnstone
[1997] 1 WLR 459, HL . . . 204

Harrow London Borough Council v Qazi [2003]
UKHL 43 [2004] 1 AC 983 . . . 122

Harthan v Harthan [1949] P 115, CA . . . 75

Hartshorne v Gardner [2008] EWHC B3 (Ch)
[2008] 2 FLR 1681 . . . 360, 772

Harvey v Harvey [1987] 1 FLR 67 . . . 905

Harwood v Harwood [1991] 2 FLR 274,
CA . . . 143, 845

Haskins v Haskins [2003] EWCA Civ 1084
[2003] 2 FLR 1124 . . . 862

Hawkins v A-G [1966] 1 All ER 392 . . . 301

Hawksworth v Hawksworth (1871) LR Ch App
539 . . . 350

HB (Abduction: Children's Objections), Re
[1998] 1 FLR 422 . . . 1068

Healey v Healey [1984] Fam 111 . . . 298

Health Service Executive v SC and AC
(Case C-29/12 PPU) [2012] 2 FLR 1040,
CJEU . . . 1003, 1006, 1079

Heath, Re [1945] Ch 417 . . . 261

Hellyer v Hellyer [1996] 2 FLR 579, CA . . . 917

Henderson, Re (1888) 20 QBD 509, CA . . . 917

Hendricks v Netherlands (1982) 5 EHRR
223 . . . 416, 417

Hereford and Worcester County Council v EH
[1985] FLR 975 . . . 544

Heseltine v Heseltine [1971] 1 All ER
952 . . . 110

Hetherington v Hetherington (1887) 12 PD
112 . . . 261

Hewer v Bryant [1970] 1 QB 357, CA . . . 337, 339,
392, 746

Hewitson v Hewitson [1995] Fam 100 [1995] 1
FLR 241, CA . . . 910, 922

HG (Specific Issue Order: Sterilisation), Re
[1993] 1 FLR 587 . . . 352, 500, 519

Hildebrand v Hildebrand [1992] 1 FLR
244 . . . 836

Hill v Hill [1998] 1 FLR 198, CA . . . 896, 910

Hinde v Hinde [1953] 1 All ER 171, CA . . . 916

Hine v Hine [1962] 1 WLR 1124, CA . . . 124

Hipgrave and Hipgrave v Jones [2004] EWHC
2901 (QB) [2005] 2 FLR 174 . . . 175

Hirani v Hirani (1983) 4 FLR 232, CA . . . 77

H-J v H-J (Financial Provision: Equality) [2002]
1 FLR 415 . . . 889, 897

HJ (Transfer of Proceedings) [2013] EWHC 1867
(Fam) [2014] 1 FLR 430 . . . 1002

H-K (Habitual Residence), Re [2011] EWCA Civ
1100 [2012] 1 FLR 436 . . . 1044

HK v Finland [2007] 1 FLR 632, ECtHR (Grand
Chamber) . . . 655

H-L (A Child) (Expert Evidence: Test for
Permission), Re [2013] EWCA Civ 655 [2013]
2 FLR 1434 . . . 14

HMRC v Charman and Charman [2012] EWHC
    1448 (Fam) [2012] 2 FLR 1119 . . . 834
Hobhouse v Hobhouse [1999] 1 FLR 961 . . . 892
Hobley, Re [2006] WTLR 467 . . . 964
Hoddinott v Hoddinott [1949] 2 KB 406,
    CA . . . 111
Hodges v Hodges (1796) Peake Add Cas
    79 . . . 348
Hodgkiss v Hodgkiss [1984] FLR 563,
    CA . . . 265
Hoffmann v Austria (1993) 17 EHRR 293 [1994]
    1 FCR 193, ECtHR . . . 350, 411
Hokkanen v Finland [1995] 2 FCR 320 [1996] 1
    FLR 289, ECtHR . . . 340, 492
Holliday v Musa [2010] EWCA Civ 335 [2010] 2
    FLR 702 . . . 976
Holliday, Re [1981] Ch 405, CA . . . 162
Holliday (a bankrupt), Re [1980] 3 All ER 385,
    CA . . . 146
Holmes v Holmes [1989] Fam 47 . . . 922
Holmes-Moorhouse v Richmond-upon-Thames
    London Borough Council [2009] UKHL 7
    [2009] 1 WLR 413 . . . 208, 413
Hope v Hope (1854) 4 De GM & G 328 . . . 743
Hope v Krejci and Others [2012] EWHC 1780
    (Fam) [2013] 1 FLR 182 . . . 848
Hope-Smith v Hope-Smith [1989] 2 FLR 56,
    CA . . . 911
Hopes v Hopes [1949] P 227 . . . 218, 220
Hoppe v Germany [2003] 1 FLR 384 . . . 417
Horner v Horner [1982] Fam 90 at 93 . . . 179
Horrocks v Forray [1976] 1 All ER 737,
    CA . . . 156, 157, 948, 949
Horton v Horton [1947] 2 All ER 871, HL . . . 75
Hoskyn v Metropolitan Police Comr [1979]
    AC 474, HL . . . 96
Hounslow London Borough Council v A [1993]
    1 WLR 291 [1993] 1 FLR 702 . . . 511, 636, 644
Howes v Bishop [1909] 2 KB 390, CA . . . 114
Hoy v Hoy 1968 SLT 413 . . . 1021
HSE Ireland v SF [2012] EWHC 1640 (Fam)
    [2012] 2 FLR 1131 . . . 1003
Hudson v Leigh [2009] EWHC 1306 (Fam)
    [2013] Fam 77 . . . 63, 68, 69, 70, 301
Humberside County Council v B [1993] 1 FLR
    257 . . . 600, 602
Humphreys v Humphreys [2004] EWHC 2201
    (Ch) [2005] 1 FCR 712 . . . 115
Humphreys v Revenue and Customs
    Commissioners [2012] UKSC 18 [2012] 4 All
    ER 27 . . . 778, 779
Humphrys v Polak [1901] 2 KB 385,
    CA . . . 682
Hunt v Severs [1994] 2 AC 350, HL . . . 93, 366
Hunter v Edney (1881) 10 PD 93 . . . 80
Hunter v Murrow (Abduction: Rights of
    Custody) [2005] EWCA Civ 976 [2005] 2 FLR
    1119 . . . 1047, 1050, 1053, 1054, 1082
Huntingford v Hobbs [1993] 1 FLR 736,
    CA . . . 128, 135

Hyde v Hyde (1866) LR 1 P & D 130 . . . 38
Hyett v Stanley [2003] EWCA Civ 942 [2004] 1
    FLR 394 . . . 131
Hyman v Hyman [1929] AC 601, HL . . . 98, 780,
    782, 785, 928

I v United Kingdom [2002] 2 FLR 518 . . . 42
I (A Child) (Contact Application: Jurisdiction)
    (Centre for Family Law and Practice
    Intervening), Re [2009] UKSC 10 [2010]
    1 AC 319 . . . 999, 1000
Ignaccolo-Zenide v Romania (Application No
    31679/96) (2001) 31 EHRR 7, ECtHR . . . 1036
IH (A Child) (Permission to Apply for
    Adoption), Re [2013] EWHC 1235 (Fam)
    [2014] 1 FLR 70 . . . 695, 1014
IJ (Foreign Surrogacy Agreement; Parental
    Order), Re [2011] EWHC 921 (Fam) [2011] 2
    FLR 646 . . . 279, 281
Ilott v Mitson and Others [2011] EWCA Civ 346
    [2012] 2 FLR 172 . . . 985
Imerman v Tchenguiz and Others [2010] EWCA
    Civ 908 [2010] 2 FLR 814 . . . 836
Iosub Caras v Romania [2007] 1 FLR 66 . . . 1036
Iqbal v Ahmed [2011] EWCA Civ 900 [2012] 1
    FLR 31 . . . 985, 987, 991
Islington London Borough Council v E
    [2010] EWHC 3240 (Fam) [2011] 1 FLR
    1681 . . . 759, 769
Ismailova v Russia (App No 37614/02) [2008] 1
    FLR 533 . . . 411

J v C [1969] 1 All ER 788 . . . 350
J v C [1970] AC 668, HL . . . 309, 313, 314, 315,
    316, 317, 318, 406, 411, 414, 419, 1025, 1026
J v C (Child: Financial Provision) [1999] 1 FLR
    152 . . . 796, 799
J v C (Void Marriage: Status of Children) [2006]
    EWCA Civ 551 [2007] Fam 1 . . . 251
J v G (Parental Orders) [2013] EWHC 1432
    (Fam) [2014] 1 FLR 297 . . . 276, 280
J v J [1947] P 158 . . . 75
J v J (A Minor: Property Transfer) [1993] 2 FLR
    56 . . . 794
J v J (Financial Orders: Wife's Long-term Needs)
    [2011] EWHC 1010 (Fam) [2011] 2 FLR
    1280 . . . 884
J v J (Relinquishment of Jurisdiction)
    [2011] EWHC 3255 (Fam) [2012] 1 FLR
    1259 . . . 1001
J v S-T (Formerly J) (Transsexual:
    Ancillary Relief) [1997] 1 FLR 402,
    CA . . . 66, 67, 71, 831
J v V (Disclosure: Offshore Corporations) [2003]
    EWHC 3110 (Fam) [2004] 1 FLR 1042 . . . 833
J (A Child), Re [2013] EWHC 2694 (Fam) . . . 363
J (A Child) (Custody Rights: Jurisdiction), Re
    [2005] UKHL 40 [2006] 1 AC 80 . . . 312, 412,
    419, 501, 749, 1024, 1026, 1027, 1028, 1029,
    1031, 1039

J (A Minor) (Abduction: Custody Rights), Re [1990] 2 AC 562 . . . 1042, 1048

J (A Minor) (Adoption Order: Conditions), Re [1973] Fam 106 . . . 691

J (A Minor) (Change of Name), Re [1993] 1 FLR 699 . . . 639

J (A Minor) (Child in Care: Medical Treatment), Re [1993] Fam 15, CA . . . 351, 768

J (A Minor) (Contact), Re [1998] 1 FLR 392, CA . . . 494

J (A Minor) (Interim Custody: Appeal), Re [1989] 2 FLR 304, CA . . . 410

J (A Minor) (Residence), Re [1994] 1 FLR 369 . . . 504

J (A Minor) (Wardship), Re [1988] 1 FLR 65 . . . 264, 752

J (A Minor) (Wardship: Jurisdiction), Re [1984] 1 WLR 81 . . . 766

J (Abduction: Acquiring Custody Rights By Caring For Child), Re [2005] 2 FLR 791 . . . 1049

J (Abduction: Children's Objections), Re [2011] EWCA Civ 1448 [2012] 1 FLR 457 . . . 450, 467

J (Abduction: Child's Objections To Return), Re [2004] EWCA Civ 428 [2004] 2 FLR 64 . . . 1068

J (Abduction: Declaration of Wrongful Removal), Re [1999] 2 FLR 653 . . . 1053

J (Adoption: Consent of Foreign Public Authority), Re [2002] EWHC 766 (Fam) [2002] 2 FLR 618 . . . 710, 715

J (Child Returned Abroad: Human Rights), Re [2004] 2 FLR 85 . . . 1029

J (Children: ex parte Order), Re [1997] 1 FLR 606 . . . 409

J (Children) (Care Proceedings: Threshold Criteria), Re [2013] UKSC 9 [2013] 1 AC 680 . . . 597, 620, 622–3, 624, 625, 628

J (Fostering: Wardship), Re [1999] 1 FLR 618 . . . 757

J (Income Support: Cohabitation), Re [1995] 1 FLR 660 . . . 942

J (Leave to Issue Application for Residence Order), Re [2002] EWCA Civ 1364 [2003] 1 FLR 114 . . . 517, 518, 657

J (Minors) (Care: Care Plan), Re [1994] 1 FLR 253 . . . 645

J (Parental Responsibility), Re [1999] 1 FLR 784 . . . 379

J (Paternity: Welfare of Child), Re [2006] EWHC 2837 (Fam) [2007] 1 FLR 1064 . . . 273, 501

J (Recognition of Foreign Adoption Orders), Re [2012] EWHC 3353 (Fam) [2013] 2 FLR 298 . . . 762

J (Residence and Contact Dispute), Re [2012] EWCA Civ 1231 [2013] 1 FLR 716 . . . 455

J (Residential Assessment: Rights Of Audience), Re [2009] EWCA Civ 1210 [2010] 1 FLR 1290 . . . 647

J (Specific Issue Order: Leave To Apply), Re [1995] 1 FLR 669 . . . 502, 570, 631

J (Specific Issue Orders: Muslim Upbringing and Circumcision), Re [1999] 2 FLR 678; affd [2000] 1 FLR 571, CA . . . 350, 352, 382, 394, 408, 410, 420, 499, 501, 735

J (Wardship: Medical Treatment), Re [1991] Fam 33 . . . 408

J and K (Abduction: Objections of Child), Re [2004] EWHC 1985 (Fam) [2005] 1 FLR 273 . . . 1068

JA (Abduction: Non-Convention Country), Re [1998] 1 FLR 231 . . . 1026

JA (Child Abduction: Non Convention Country), Re [1998] 1 FLR 231 . . . 1025

Jackson v Jackson [1973] Fam 99 . . . 832

Jacobs v Davis [1917] 2 KB 532 . . . 109

James v Thomas [2007] EWCA Civ 1212 [2008] 1 FLR 1598 . . . 134, 139

Jane v Jane (1983) 4 FLR 712, CA . . . 505

Jane (Publicity), Re [2010] EWHC 3221 (Fam) [2011] 1 FLR 1261 . . . 770

Janvier v Sweeney [1919] 2 KB 316, CA . . . 195

Janzik v Shand No. 99C 6515, 2000 WL 1745203 (DN111. Nov 27, 2000) . . . 1083

Jauffir v Akhbar, The Times, 10 February 1984 . . . 364

JB (Child Abduction) (Rights of Custody: Spain), Re [2003] EWHC 2130 (Fam) [2004] 1 FLR 796 . . . 1047

Jeffreys v Luck (1922) 153 LT Jo 139 . . . 109

Jelley v Iliffe [1981] Fam 128, CA . . . 980, 981, 982

Jennifer L Schultz v Jodilynn and Carol Frampton 2007 PA Super 118 . . . 259

Jennings v Brown (1842) 9 M & W 496 . . . 784

Jennings v Rice [2002] EWCA Civ 159 [2003] 1 FCR 501 . . . 141, 142

Jennings (Deceased), Re [1994] Ch 286, CA . . . 984

Jessop v Jessop [1992] 1 FLR 591, CA . . . 986, 989

Jevremovic v Serbia [2008] 1 FLR 550, ECtHR . . . 436

Jodla v Jodla [1960] 1 All ER 625 . . . 75

Johansen v Norway (1996) 23 EHRR 33, ECtHR . . . 416

Johns' Assignment Trusts, Re [1970] 2 All ER 210n . . . 112

Johnson v Calvert 5 Cal 4th 84 (1993) . . . 246, 247

Johnson v Walton [1990] 1 FLR 350, CA . . . 174

Johnston v Ireland (1986) 9 EHRR 203 . . . 1

Johnston v Johnston (1976) 6 Fam Law 17, CA . . . 831

Johnstone v Beattie (1843) 10 Cl & Fin 42 . . . 310, 743

Jones v Challenger [1961] 1 QB 176, CA . . . 146

Jones v Jones [1976] Fam 8, CA . . . 885, 900

Jones v Jones [1993] 2 FLR 377, CA . . . 539

Jones v Jones [1997] 1 FLR 27, CA . . . 907

Jones v Jones [2000] 2 FLR 307 . . . 878

Jones v Jones [2011] EWCA Civ 41 [2011] 1 FLR 1723 . . . 884, 931

Jones v Kernott [2011] UKSC 53 [2012] 1 AC 776 . . . 127, 128, 129, 137, 138, 139, 147, 163

Jones v Maynard [1951] Ch 572 . . . 110, 111

Jones v Newtown and Llanidloes Guardians [1920] 3 KB 381 . . . 774

Jordan v Jordan [1999] 2 FLR 1069 . . . 922

Joseph v Joseph [1953] 2 All ER 710, CA . . . 219

JP v LP and Others (Surrogacy Arrangements: Wardship) [2014] EWHC 595 (Fam) [2014] Fam Law 813 . . . 280, 761

J-PC v J-AF [1955] P 215, CA . . . 886

JPC v SLW and SMW (Abduction) [2007] EWHC 1349 (Fam) [2007] 2 FLR 900 . . . 1057

JS v SS 2003 SLT 344 . . . 1051, 1056

JS (A Minor), Re [1981] Fam 22, CA . . . 766

JS (A Minor) (Declaration of Paternity), Re [1981] Fam 22, CA . . . 303

JS (A Minor) (Wardship: Boy Soldier), Re [1990] Fam 182 . . . 748, 768

JS (Private International Adoption), Re [2000] 2 FLR 638 . . . 1050

JT (A Minor) (Wardship: Committal to Care), Re [1986] 2 FLR 107 . . . 770

Judd v Brown [1999] 1 FLR 1191, CA . . . 161

Judd v Brown, Bankrupts (Nos 9587 and 9588 of 1994) [1998] 2 FLR 360 . . . 161

K v H (Child Maintenance) [1993] 2 FLR 61 . . . 427, 439, 796

K v K [2006] EWHC 2685 (Fam) [2007] 1 FCR 355 . . . 1073

K v K (Children: Permanent Removal from Jurisdiction) [2011] EWCA Civ 793 [2012] 2 WLR 941 . . . 531, 532

K v K (Financial Relief: Management of Difficult Cases) [2005] EWHC 1070 (Fam) [2005] 2 FLR 1137 . . . 833

K v K (minors: property transfer) [1992] 2 All ER 727, CA . . . 795

K v K (Relocation: Shared Care Arrangement) [2011] EWCA Civ 793 . . . 527

K v L (Child Abduction) [2012] EWHC 1234 (Fam) [2013] 1 FLR 998 . . . 1052

K v L (Non-Matrimonial Property: Special Contribution) [2011] EWCA Civ 550 [2011] 2 FLR 980 . . . 884, 885, 892, 896, 899

K v M (Paternity: Contact) [1996] 1 FLR 312 . . . 267

K, Re; A Local Authority v N [2005] EWHC 2956 (Fam) [2007] 1 FLR 399 . . . 444, 603, 615

K (A Child) (Reunite International Child Abduction Centre intervening), Re [2014] UKSC 29 [2014] 2 WLR 1304 . . . 1016, 1046–7, 1049

K (A Child) (Secure Accommodation Order: Right To Liberty), Re [2001] Fam 377, CA . . . 574, 575, 576, 577, 578

K (A Minor) (Adoption Order: Nationality), Re [1995] Fam 38, CA . . . 725

K (Abduction: Case Management), Re [2010] EWCA Civ 1546 [2011] 1 FLR 1268 . . . 1067

K (Abduction: Child's Objections), Re [1995] 1 FLR 977 . . . 1066

K (Abduction: Consent), Re [1996] 1 FLR 414 . . . 1057

K (Abduction: Consent), Re [1997] 2 FLR 212 . . . 1058

K (Abduction: Psychological Harm), Re [1995] 2 FLR 550, CA . . . 1062

K (Adoption) (Permission To Advertise), Re [2007] EWHC 544 (Fam) [2007] 2 FLR 326 . . . 729

K (Adoption and Wardship), Re [1997] 2 FLR 221, CA . . . 723, 761

K (Appeal: Contact), Re [2010] EWCA Civ 1365 [2011] 1 FLR 1592 . . . 493, 510

K (Care: Threshold Criteria), Re [2005] EWCA Civ 1226 [2006] 2 FLR 868 . . . 613

K (Care Order), Re [2007] EWCA Civ 697 [2007] 2 FLR 1066 . . . 647

K (Care Order or Residence Order), Re [1995] 1 FLR 675 . . . 537, 630, 632, 637

K (Care Proceedings: Care Plan), Re [2007] EWHC 393 (Fam) [2008] 1 FLR 1 . . . 656

K (children) (care orders: jurisdiction to renew interim care orders), Re [2012] EWCA Civ 1549 [2013] 1 FCR 87 . . . 550

K (Children With Disabilities: Wardship), Re [2011] EWHC 4031 (Fam) [2012] 2 FLR 745 . . . 596, 749, 757

K (Contact), Re [2008] EWHC 540 (Fam) [2008] 2 FLR 581 . . . 657

K (Contact: Committal Order), Re [2002] EWCA Civ 1559 [2003] 1 FLR 377 . . . 539

K (Contact: Psychiatric Report), Re [1995] 2 FLR 432, CA . . . 456, 512

K (Contact Order: Condition Ousting Parent From Family Home), Re [2011] EWCA Civ 1075 [2012] 2 FLR 635 . . . 502, 505

K (Foreign Surrogacy), Re [2010] EWHC 1180 (Fam) [2011] 1 FLR 533 . . . 278

K (KJS) (an infant), Re [1966] 3 All ER 154 . . . 768

K (Minors) (Children: Care and Control), Re [1977] Fam 179, CA . . . 316, 404

K (Minors) (Incitement to Breach Contact Order), Re [1992] 2 FLR 108 . . . 539

K (Minors) (Wardship: Criminal Proceedings), Re [1988] Fam 1 . . . 745, 748, 768

K (Non-Accidental Injuries: Perpetrator: New Evidence), Re [2004] EWCA Civ 1181 [2005] 1 FLR 285 . . . 437, 616

K (Removal From Jurisdiction: Practice), Re [1999] 2 FLR 1084 . . . 526

K (Shared Residence Order), Re [2008] EWCA Civ 526 [2008] 2 FLR 380 . . . 487

K (Specific Issue Order), Re [1999] 2 FLR 280 . . . 273, 501

K (Supervision Orders), Re [1999] 2 FLR 303 . . . 635

K (Wardship: Jurisdiction: Interim Order), Re
    [1991] 2 FLR 104, CA . . . 1023
K and A (Local Authority: Child Maintenance),
    Re [1995] 1 FLR 688 . . . 794
K and H, Re [2006] EWCA Civ 1898 [2007] 1
    FLR 2043 . . . 644
K and S (Minors) (Wardship: Immigration), Re
    [1992] 1 FLR 432 . . . 767
K and T v Finland [2001] 2 FLR 707 (2001) 31
    EHRR 18 . . . 583, 610
Kacem v Bashir [2011] 2 NZLR 1 . . . 426, 533
Kalsi v Kalsi [1992] 1 FLR 511, CA . . . 184
Karcheva v Bulgaria [2006] 3 FCR 434,
    ECtHR . . . 436
Karner v Austria [2003] 2 FLR 623 . . . 941
Karoonian v CMEC; Gibbons v CMEC
    [2012] EWCA Civ 1379 [2013] 1 FLR
    1121 . . . 818, 917
Kassim v Kassim [1962] P 224 . . . 79
Katz v Katz [1972] 3 All ER 219 . . . 217
Kaur v Singh [1972] 1 All ER 292, CA . . . 75
Kautzor v Germany (App No 23338/09) [2012] 2
    FLR 396 . . . 270
KD, Re [1988] AC 806, HL . . . 340
KD (A Minor) (Ward: Termination of Access),
    Re [1988] AC 806, HL . . . 317, 339, 340, 415
Keegan v Ireland (1994) 18 EHRR 342 . . . 2
Kehoe v United Kingdom (Application
    no 2010/06) [2008] 2 FLR 1014,
    ECtHR . . . 820, 824
Kelly v BBC [2001] Fam 59 . . . 502
Kelly v Kelly (1932) 49 TLR 99 . . . 79
Kelly v Monklands District Council 1986 SLT
    169, Ct of Sess . . . 207
Kelner v Kelner [1939] P 411 . . . 114
Kemmis v Kemmis (Welland Intervening)
    [1988] 1 WLR 1307, CA . . . 919, 920
Kent County Council v C [1993] Fam 57 . . . 463,
    639, 640, 658, 660
Kenward v Kenward [1950] P 71; revsd [1951]
    P 124 . . . 79
Kiely v Kiely [1988] 1 FLR 248, CA . . . 792, 840,
    845, 875
Kilgour v Kilgour 1987 SLT 568 . . . 1040
Kilpin v Ratley [1892] 1 QB 582 . . . 115
Kim v Morris [2012] EWHC 1103 (Fam)
    [2013] 2 FLR 1197 . . . 217, 228
Kimber v Brookman Solicitors [2004] 2 FLR
    221 . . . 833
Kimber v Kimber [2000] 1 FLR 383 . . . 181,
    942, 944
Kinch v Bullard [1999] 1 WLR 423 . . . 126
King v King [1942] P 1 . . . 152
Kinzler v Kinzler [1985] Fam Law 26, CA . . . 154
Kisala v Kisala (1973) 117 Sol Jo 664 . . . 216
Klucinski v Klucinski [1953] 1 All ER
    683 . . . 886
Knowles v Knowles [1962] P 161 . . . 261, 300
Kokosinski v Kokosinski [1980] Fam 72 . . . 894,
    895, 901, 903

Koniarska v United Kingdom Application No.
    33670/96 (12 October 2000) . . . 577
Kopf and Liberda v Austria [2012] 1 FLR 1199,
    ECtHR . . . 492, 494
Kosmopoulou v Greece [2004] 1 FLR 800,
    ECtHR . . . 340, 492, 655
Kotke v Saffarini [2005] EWCA Civ 221
    [2005] 2 FLR 517 . . . 940, 979
Kourkgy v Lusher (1981) 4 FLR 65 . . . 982, 985
KR (Abduction: Forcible Removal By Parents),
    Re [1999] 2 FLR 542 . . . 760
Kremen v Agrest [2010] EWHC 2571 [2011]
    2 FLR 478 . . . 919
Kremen v Agrest [2013] EWCA Civ 41 [2013]
    2 FLR 187 . . . 918
Kremen v Agrest (Committal Under
    Debtors Act) [2011] EWCA Civ 1482 [2012]
    1 FLR 894 . . . 918
Kremen v Agrest (Financial
    Remedy: Non-Disclosure: Post-Nuptial
    Agreement) [2012] EWHC 45 (Fam) [2012]
    2 FLR 414 . . . 859
Kremen v Agrest (No 2) [2011] 2 FLR
    v490 . . . 847
Kroon v The Netherlands (1995) 19 EHRR
    263 . . . 270
Krubert (decd), Re [1997] Ch 97 . . . 983
Krystman v Krystman [1973] 3 All ER
    247, CA . . . 894
KT (A Minor: Adoption), Re [1993] Fam
    Law 567 . . . 719
Kusminow v Barclays Bank Trust Co Ltd [1989]
    Fam Law 66 . . . 991
Kutzner v Germany (2002) 35 EHRR
    25 . . . 270, 610
KW v Lancaster City Council and Secretary of
    State for Work and Pensions [2011] UKUT
    266 (AAC) [2012] 1 FLR 282 . . . 818
KY v DD (Injunctions) [2011] EWHC 1277
    (Fam) [2012] 2 FLR 200 . . . 500
Kyte v Kyte [1985] FLR 789 . . . 901

L v Finland [2000] 2 FLR 118 . . . 518
L v Human Fertilisation and Embryology
    Authority and the Secretary of State for
    Health [2008] EWHC 2149 (Fam) [2008]
    2 FLR 1999 . . . 249
L v L (1882) 7 PD 16 . . . 75
L v L [1949] P 211 . . . 74
L v L (Child Abuse: Access) [1989] 2 FLR 16,
    CA . . . 412
L v L (Financial Provision: Contributions)
    [2002] 1 FLR 642 . . . 897, 898
L v L (Financial Remedies: Deferred Clean
    Break) [2011] EWHC 2207 (Fam) [2012] 1
    FLR 898 . . . 880
L v L (Minors) (Separate Representation) [1994]
    1 FLR 156, CA . . . 460
L v London Borough of Bexley [1996] 2 FLR
    595 . . . 627

L v London Borough of Bromley [1998]
1 FLR 709 . . . 628, 656
L v P (Paternity Test: Child's Objection) [2010]
EWCA Civ 1145 [2011] 1 FLR 708 . . . 810
L v P (Paternity Test: Child's Objection)
[2011] EWHC 3399 (Fam) [2013] 1 FLR
578 . . . 267, 324
L v Tower Hamlets London Borough Council
[2000] 1 FLR 825, CA . . . 674, 675
L (A Child) (Contact: Domestic Violence),
Re; Re V (A Child) (Contact: Domestic
Violence); Re M (A Child) (Contact:
Domestic Violence); Re H (Children)
(Contact: Domestic Violence) [2001] Fam
260 . . . 378, 415, 495
L (A Child) (Custody: Habitual Residence)
(Reunite International Child Abduction
Centre intervening), Re [2013] UKSC 75
[2013] 3 WLR 1597 . . . 1041, 1042, 1046, 1069
L (A Child), Re [2005] EWHC 1237 (Fam) [2006]
1 FLR 843 . . . 1051, 1056
L (A Child) (Parental Order: Foreign Surrogacy),
Re [2010] EWHC 3146 (Fam) [2011] Fam
106 . . . 280, 281
L (A Child) (Recognition of Foreign Order),
Re [2012] EWCA Civ 1157 [2013] Fam
94 . . . 1005, 1006
L (a minor: freedom of publication), Re [1988] 1
All ER 418 . . . 745
L (A Minor) (Police Investigation: Privilege), Re
[1997] AC 16 . . . 425, 426
L (Abduction: Child's Objections To Return),
Re [2002] EWHC 1864 (Fam) [2002] 2 FLR
1042 . . . 1068
L (Abduction: European Convention: Access),
Re [1999] 2 FLR 1089 . . . 1087
L (Abduction: Future Consent), Re [2007]
EWHC 2181 (Fam) [2008] 1 FLR 914 . . . 1057
L (Abduction: Pending Criminal Proceedings),
Re [1999] 1 FLR 433 . . . 1062, 1084
L (Adoption: Contacting Natural Father), Re
[2007] EWHC 1771 (Fam) [2008] 1 FLR
1079 . . . 711
L (An Infant), Re [1968] P 119, CA . . . 741
L (Care: Chronic Neglect), Re [2009] EWCA Civ
822 [2010] 1 FLR 80 . . . 644
L (Care: Threshold Criteria), Re [2007] 1 FLR
2050 . . . 602
L (Care Order: Immigration Powers To
Remove), Re [2007] EWHC 158 (Fam) [2007]
2 FLR 789 . . . 639
L (Child Abduction: European Conventions),
Re [1992] 2 FLR 178 . . . 1086
L (children) (abduction: declaration), Re [2001]
2 FCR 1 . . . 1053
L (Contact: Transsexual Applicant), Re [1995]
2 FLR 438 . . . 378, 489, 494
L (Family Proceedings Court)
(Appeal: Jurisdiction), Re [2003] EWHC
1682 (Fam) [2005] 1 FLR 210 . . . 810

L (Identity of Birth Father), Re [2008] EWCA
Civ 1338 [2009] 1 FLR 1152 . . . 273, 501
L (Interim Care Order: Extended Family),
Re [2012] EWCA Civ 179 [2013]
2 FLR 302 . . . 455
L (Medical Treatment: Gillick Competence), Re
[1998] 2 FLR 810 . . . 323
L (Minors) (Separate Representation), Re [1994]
1 FLR 156 . . . 468
L (Minors) (Wardship: Jurisdiction), Re [1974] 1
WLR 250, CA . . . 1025, 1027
L (Occupation Order), Re [2012] EWCA Civ 721
[2012] 2 FLR 1417 . . . 186
L (Recognition of Foreign Order), Re [2012]
EWCA Civ 1157 [2013] Fam 94 . . . 1040
L (Removal From Jurisdiction: Holiday), Re
[2001] 1 FLR 241 . . . 533
L (Residence: Justices' Reasons), Re [1995] 2 FLR
445 . . . 409, 412, 413
L (Section 37 Direction), Re [1999] 1 FLR 984,
CA . . . 550
L (Sexual Abuse: Standard of Proof), Re [1996] 1
FLR 116 . . . 644
L (Shared Residence Order), Re [2009] EWCA
Civ 20 [2009] 1 FLR 1157 . . . 499
L (Special Guardianship: Surname), Re
[2007] EWCA Civ 196 [2007] 2 FLR
50 . . . 732, 733, 734
L (Vulnerable Adults with Capacity: Court's
Jurisdiction) (No 2), Re [2010] EWHC 2675;
(Fam) [2011] Fam 189 . . . 197
L (Vulnerable Adults with Capacity: Court's
Jurisdiction) (No 2), Re [2013] Fam 1 . . . 197
L (Vulnerable Adults with Capacity: Court's
Jurisdiction) (No 2), Re (sub nom A Local
Authority v DL) [2011] EWHC 1022 (Fam)
[2012] 1 FLR 1119 . . . 197
L and H (Residential Assessment), Re [2007]
EWCA Civ 213 [2007] 1 FLR 1370 . . . 647
LA (Care: Chronic Neglect), Re [2009] EWCA
Civ 822 [2010] 1 FLR 80 . . . 643
LAB v KB (Abduction: Brussels II Revised)
[2009] 2243 (Fam) [2010] 2 FLR
1664 . . . 1005, 1006
Ladd v Marshall [1954] 3 All ER 745 . . . 545
Laird v Laird [1999] 1 FLR 791 . . . 146
Lake v Lake [2006] EWCA Civ 1250 [2007] 1
FLR 427 . . . 907
Lamagni v Lamagni [1995] 2 FLR 452,
CA . . . 920
Lambert v Lambert [2002] EWCA Civ 1685
[2003] 1 FLR 139 . . . 898, 899, 932
LaMusga v LaMusga 32 Cal 4th 25
(2004) . . . 534
Lancashire County Council v B [2000] 2 AC
147 . . . 594, 614, 615, 617, 618, 622, 623, 625
Lancashire County Council v B [2002] 2 WLR
346, CA . . . 611, 623
Langley v Liverpool City Council [2005] EWCA
Civ 1173 [2006] 2 WLR 375 . . . 512, 592

Langley v Liverpool City Council [2005] EWCA
　Civ 1181 [2005] 3 FCR 303 . . . 769
In the Estate of Langston [1953] P 100 . . . 962
Laskar v Laskar [2008] EWCA Civ 347 [2008] 2
　FLR 589 . . . 110, 129
Lau v DPP [2000] 1 FLR 799 . . . 174
Lauder v Lauder [2007] EWHC 1227 (Fam)
　[2007] 2 FLR 802 . . . 872
Lavelle v Lavelle [2004] EWCA Civ 223 [2004] 2
　FCR 418 . . . 127
Law v Inostroza Ahumuda and Others [2010]
　EWCA Civ 1145 [2011] 1 FLR 708 . . . 270, 810
Lawrence v Gallagher [2012] EWCA Civ 394
　[2012] 2 FLR 643 . . . 867
Lawrence v Pembrokeshire County Council
　[2007] EWCA Civ 446 [2007] 1 WLR
　2991 . . . 676
Layton v Martin [1986] 2 FLR 227 . . . 141, 948
LC (Children) (Reunite International Child
　Abduction Centre intervening), Re [2014]
　UKSC 1 [2014] 2 WLR 124 . . . 445, 450, 472,
　1042, 1045, 1074
LCG v RL (Abduction: Habitual Residence and
　Child's Objections) [2013] EWHC 1383 (Fam)
　[2014] 1 FLR 307 . . . 1065, 1071
Le Foe v Le Foe and Woolwich plc [2001] 2 FLR
　970 . . . 134
Le Marchant v Le Marchant [1977] 3 All ER 610,
　CA . . . 223
Leach, Re [1986] Ch 226, CA . . . 298, 980, 983
Leadbeater v Leadbeater [1985] FLR 789 . . . 875,
　887, 889, 893, 901
Leake v Bruzzi [1974] 2 All ER 1196, CA . . . 147
Lebbink v Netherlands [2004] 2 FLR 463,
　ECtHR . . . 2, 492
Lee v Lee [1952] 2 QB 489n, CA . . . 118
Lee v Lee (1973) 117 Sol Jo 616 . . . 223
Leeds City Council v C [1993] 1 FLR
　269 . . . 505, 549
Leeds City Council v West Yorkshire
　Metropolitan Police [1983] 1 AC 29,
　HL . . . 365
Leeds County Council v C [1993] 1 FLR
　269 . . . 548
Leeds Teaching Hospitals NHS Trust v A [2003]
　EWHC 259 (QB) [2003] 1 FLR 1091 . . . 249,
　252, 253, 254
Leete v Leete and Stevens [1984] Fam Law
　21 . . . 459
Legey v O'Brien (1834) Milw 325 . . . 81
Leman's Will Trusts, Re (1945) 115 LJ Ch
　89 . . . 261
Lewis v Lewis [1977] 3 All ER 992, CA . . . 914
Lewis v Lewis [1978] Fam 60 . . . 192
Lewisham London Borough v Lewisham
　Juvenile Court Justice [1980] AC 273 . . . 569
Lightbody (or Jacques) v Jacques 1997
　SC (HL) 20 . . . 831
Lilford v Glynn [1979] 1 All ER 441, CA . . . 792,
　845, 875

Lilleyman v Lilleyman [2012] EWHC 821 (Ch)
　[2013] 1 FLR 47 . . . 976, 986, 987, 991
Lincolnshire County Council v RJ, X
　Intervening [1998] 2 FLR 110 . . . 757
Lindop v Agus, Bass and Hedley [2009] EWHC
　1795 (Ch) [2010] 1 FLR 631 . . . 979
Linton v Linton (1885) 15 QBD 239 . . . 916
Lissimore v Downing [2003] 2 FLR 308 . . . 141
Livesey (formerly Jenkins) v Jenkins [1985] AC
　424, HL . . . 833, 850, 853, 865, 906
Livingstone-Stallard v Livingstone-Stallard
　[1974] Fam 47 . . . 216
L-K v K (Brussels II Revised: Maintenance
　Pending Suit) [2006] EWHC 153 (Fam) [2006]
　2 FLR 1113 . . . 1003
Lloyds Bank plc v Rosset [1989] Ch 350,
　CA . . . 149
Lloyds Bank plc v Rosset [1991] 1 AC 107,
　HL . . . 130, 131, 132, 133, 139, 149
L-M (Transfer of Irish Proceedings), Re [2013]
　EWHC 646 (Fam) [2013] 2 FLR 708 . . . 1002
LM v Essex County Council [1999]
　1 FLR 988 . . . 576, 577
Lock v Heath (1892) 8 TLR 295 . . . 115
Lockwood, Re [1958] Ch 231 . . . 973
Lomas v Parle [2003] EWCA Civ 1804 [2004]
　1 All ER 1173 . . . 209
London Borough of Islington v TM [2004]
　EWHC 2050 (Fam) . . . 767
London Borough of Redbridge v B, C and A
　(A Child) [2011] EWHC 517 (Fam) [2011]
　2 FLR 117 . . . 420
London Borough of Southwark v B [1993] 2 FLR
　559, CA . . . 595
Lopez v Lizazo (Case C-68/07) [2008] 3 WLR
　338, CJEU . . . 374
Loraine v Loraine [1912] P 222, CA . . . 846
Lord Audley's Case (1631) 3 State Tr 401,
　HL . . . 95
Lord Leigh's Case (1674) 3 Keb 433 . . . 166
Lorraine Share, Re [2002] 2 FLR 88 . . . 130
Lough v Ward [1945] 2 All ER 338 . . . 392
Lowe, Re [1929] 2 Ch 210 . . . 302
Lowrie, Re [1981] 3 All ER 353 . . . 161
Luckwell v Limata [2014] EWHC 502 (Fam)
　[2014] 2 FLR 168 . . . 861
LW (children) (contact order: committal),
　Re [2010] EWCA Civ 1253 [2011] 1 FLR
　1095 . . . 1006
LW (Enforcement and Committal: Contact),
　Re; CPL v CH-W and Others [2010] EWCA
　Civ 1253 [2011] 1 FLR 1095 . . . 423, 539, 541,
　542, 543
Lynch v Knight (1861) 9 HL Cas 577 . . . 92
Lynch, Re [1943] 1 All ER 168 . . . 966
Lyus v Prowsa Developments Ltd [1982] 2 All ER
　953 . . . 158

M v A (Wardship: Removal From Jurisdiction)
　[1993] 2 FLR 715 . . . 529

M v B (Ancillary Proceedings: Lump Sum)
[1998] 1 FLR 53 . . . 888

M v B, A, S (By her Litigation Friend, the Official
Solicitor) [2005] EWHC 1681 (Fam) [2006] 1
FLR 117 . . . 80

M v Birmingham City Council [1994] 2 FLR
141 . . . 414, 577, 616

M v C (Children Orders: Reasons) [1993] 2 FLR
584 . . . 503

M v F and H (Legal Paternity) [2014] 1 FLR
352 . . . 249, 254, 272, 278, 371

M v M [1957] P 139 . . . 75

M v M [2007] EWHC 1404 (Fam) [2007] 2 FLR
1010 . . . 1070

M v M (Abduction: England and Wales) [1997] 2
FLR 263 . . . 428

M v M (Abduction: Settlement) [2008] EWHC
2049 (Fam) [2008] 2 FLR 1884 . . . 997, 1055

M v M (child: access) [1973] 2 All ER
81 . . . 339, 340

M v M (Child of the Family) (1980) 2 FLR 39,
CA . . . 298

M v M (Financial Provision) [2010] EWHC 2817
(Fam) [2011] 1 FLR 1773 . . . 923

M v M (Financial Relief: Substantial Earning
Capacity) [2004] EWHC 688 (Fam) [2004] 2
FLR 236 . . . 895

M v M (Maintenance Pending Suit) [2002]
EWHC 317 (Fam) [2002] 2 FLR 123 . . . 837

M v M (Minor: Custody Appeal) [1987] 1 WLR
404, CA . . . 402, 545

M v M (Parental Responsibility) [1999] 2 FLR
737 . . . 379

M v M (Property Adjustment: Impaired
Life Expectancy) [1993] 2 FLR 723,
CA . . . 865

M v M (Residence Order: Ancillary Injunction)
[1994] Fam Law 440 . . . 501, 502

M v M (Specific Issue: Choice of School) . . . 501

M v M (Stay of Proceedings: Return of Children)
[2005] EWHC 1159 (Fam) [2006] 1 FLR
138 . . . 427, 1001

M v M (Welfare Report) [1989] 2 FLR 354,
CA . . . 545

M v M and Others [2013] EWHC 2534 (Fam)
[2014] 1 FLR 439 . . . 127, 847

M v Newham London Borough Council [1995] 2
AC 633, HL . . . 673, 677

M v T (Abduction) [2008] EWHC 1383 (Fam)
[2009] 1 FLR 1309 . . . 1075

M v T (Abduction: Brussels II Revised, Art 11
(7)) [2010] EWHC 1479 (Fam) [2010] 2 FLR
1685 . . . 1080

M v W (Declaration of Parentage) [2006] EWHC
2341 (Fam) [2007] 2 FLR 270 . . . 270

M v Warwickshire County Council [1994] 2 FLR
593 . . . 633

M v Warwickshire County Council (M
intervening) [2007] EWCA Civ 1084 [2008] 1
WLR 991 . . . 703, 710

M v Wigan Metropolitan Borough Council
[1979] Fam 36 . . . 614

M, Re (1989) *The Times*, 29 December,
CA . . . 438, 507

M, Re; J (Wardship: Supervision and
Residence Orders), Re [2003] EWHC 1585
(Fam) [2003] 2 FLR 541 . . . 511, 630–1, 751,
758, 764

M (A Child), Re [2006] EWCA Civ 360 . . . 1077

M (A Child), Re [2013] EWCA Civ 969 [2013] All
ER (D) 12 (Aug) . . . 374

M (A Child) (Adoption: Placement outside
Jurisdiction), Re [2010] EWHC 1694 (Fam)
[2011] Fam 110 . . . 1015

M (A Minor) (Abduction: Child's Objections),
Re [1994] 2 FLR 126, CA . . . 1024, 1068

M (A Minor) (Abduction: Child's Objections),
Re [2007] EWCA Civ 260 [2007] 2 FLR
72 . . . 1068

M (A Minor) (Abduction), Re [1996] 1 FLR
315 . . . 1045

M (A Minor) (Care Order: Threshold
Conditions), Re [1994] 2 AC 424 [1994] Fam
95, HL . . . 595, 601, 604, 605, 606, 607, 608,
630, 632

M (A Minor) (Child Abduction), Re [1994] 1
FLR 390, CA . . . 1067

M (A Minor) (Contact: Conditions), Re [1994]
1 FLR 272 . . . 489

M (A Minor) (Justices' Discretion), Re [1993]
2 FLR 706 . . . 465

M (A Minor) (Secure Accommodation Order),
Re [1995] Fam 108, CA . . . 421, 427, 574, 575,
576

M (Abduction: Child's Objections), Re [2007]
EWCA Civ 260 [2007] 2 FLR 72 . . . 1068

M (Abduction: Habitual Residence), Re [1996]
1 FLR 887 . . . 1044, 1045

M (Abduction: Intolerable Situation), Re [2000]
1 FLR 930 . . . 1062

M (Abduction: Non-Convention Country), Re
[1995] 1 FLR 89, CA . . . 1026, 1029

M (Abduction: Paternity: DNA Testing),
Re [2013] EWCA Civ 1131 [2014] 1 FLR
695 . . . 1048

M (Abduction) (Consent: Acquiescence), Re
[1999] 1 FLR 171 . . . 1057, 1058

M (Adoption or Residence Order), Re [1998]
1 FLR 570, CA . . . 487, 712

M (An Infant), Re [1955] 2 QB 479, CA . . . 709

M (An Infant), Re [1961] Ch 328, CA . . . 667, 765

M (application for stay of order), Re [1996] 3
FCR 185, CA . . . 420

M (Care: Challenging Decisions By Local
Authority), Re [2001] 2 FLR 1300 . . . 679

M (Care: Contact: Grandmother's Application
For Leave), Re [1995] 2 FLR 86, CA . . . 517,
518, 657

M (Care: Leave To Interview Child), Re [1995]
1 FLR 825 . . . 340, 363, 427, 501, 764, 770

M (Care Order: Parental Responsibility),
  Re [1996] 2 FLR 84 . . . 290, 567, 606, 608
M (Care Proceedings: Judicial Review), Re
  [2003] EWHC 850 (Admin) [2003] 2 FLR
  171 . . . 583, 586, 669, 670
M (Child: Refusal of Medical Treatment),
  Re [1999] 2 FLR 1097 . . . 403
M (Child Abduction: European Convention),
  Re [1994] 1 FLR 551 . . . 1086
M (Child Support Act: Parentage), Re [1997] 2
  FLR 90 . . . 248, 251
M (children: evidence), Re [2007] EWCA Civ
  1150 [2008] 1 FCR 787 . . . 771
M (Children) (Abduction: Rights of Custody),
  Re [2007] UKHL 55 [2008] AC 1288 . . . 1064,
  1069, 1070, 1071, 1073–4
M (Child's Upbringing), Re 'the Zulu boy case'
  [1996] 2 FLR 441, CA . . . 403, 408, 412, 437,
  751, 761
M (Contact: Long-Term Interests), Re [2005]
  EWCA Civ 1090 [2006] 1 FLR 627 . . . 493
M (Contact: Violent Parent), Re [1999] 2 FLR
  321 . . . 494
M (Contact: Welfare Test), Re [1995] 1 FLR 274,
  CA . . . 493
M (Contact Family Assistance Order), Re [1999]
  1 FLR 75, CA . . . 549
M (Contact Refusal: Appeal), Re [2014] Fam Law
  148 . . . 546
M (D) v M (S) and G (M (DA) Intervening)
  [1969] 1 WLR 843 . . . 267
M (Deceased), Re [1968] P 174 . . . 993
M (Disclosure: Children and Family Reporter),
  Re [2002] EWCA Civ 1199 [2002] 2 FLR
  893 . . . 456, 459
M (Family Proceedings: Affidavits), Re [1995]
  2 FLR 100, CA . . . 403
M (handicapped child: parental responsibility),
  Re [2001] 3 FCR 454 . . . 376, 378
M (infants), Re [1967] 3 All ER 1071,
  CA . . . 410
M (Interim Care Order: Removal), Re [2005]
  EWCA Civ 1594 [2006] 1 FLR 1043 . . . 642
M (Interim Contact: Domestic Violence), Re
  [2000] 2 FLR 377, CA . . . 491
M (Intractable Contact Dispute: Interim Care
  Order), Re [2003] EWHC 1024 (Fam) [2003]
  2 FLR 636 . . . 455, 550
M (Jurisdiction: Forum Conveniens), Re [1995]
  1 FLR 224 . . . 1026
M (Leave To Remove Child From Jurisdiction),
  Re [1999] 2 FLR 334 . . . 521, 527
M (Medical Treatment: Consent), Re [1999]
  2 FLR 1097 . . . 323
M (Minors) (Abduction: Peremptory Return),
  Re [1996] 1 FLR 478 . . . 1026
M (minors) (abduction: psychological harm),
  Re [1998] 2 FCR 488, CA . . . 1064
M (Minors) (Abduction: Undertakings), Re
  [1995] 1 FLR 1021, CA . . . 1066

M (Minors) (Adoption), Re [1991] 1 FLR 458,
  CA . . . 712, 723
M (Minors) (Custody: Jurisdiction), Re [1992]
  2 FLR 382 . . . 1023
M (Minors) (Disclosure of Evidence), Re [1994]
  1 FLR 760, CA . . . 458, 502
M (Minors) (Residence Order: Jurisdiction),
  Re [1993] 1 FLR 495, CA . . . 1022
M (Minors) (Sexual Abuse: Evidence), Re [1993]
  1 FLR 822 . . . 518
M (Official Solicitor's Role), Re [1998] 2 FLR 815,
  CA . . . 550
M (Parental Responsibility Order), Re [2013]
  EWCA Civ 969 [2014] 1 FLR 339 . . . 375, 379
M (Residence), Re [2004] EWCA Civ 1574 [2005]
  1 FLR 656 . . . 459
M (Residential Assessment Directions),
  Re [1998] 2 FLR 371 . . . 423, 646
M (Section 91 (14) Order), Re [2012] EWCA
  Civ 446 [2012] 2 FLR 758 . . . 509
M (Section 94 Appeals), Re [1995] 1 FLR 546,
  CA . . . 412
M (Secure Accommodation Order), Re [1995]
  1 FLR 418, CA . . . 439
M (Sexual Abuse Allegations: Interviewing
  Techniques), Re [1999] 2 FLR 92 . . . 489
M (Sperm Donor Father), Re [2003] Fam Law
  94 . . . 249
M and B (children) (contact: domestic violence),
  Re [2001] 1 FCR 116, CA . . . 495
M and H (Minors) (Local Authorities: Parental
  Rights), Re [1990] 1 AC 686, HL . . . 667
M and N (Minors) (Wardship: Publication
  of Information), Re [1990] Fam 211,
  CA . . . 362, 753
M and R (Child Abuse: Evidence), Re [1996]
  2 FLR 195 . . . 412, 413, 435, 625, 627
MA v DB (Inherent Jurisdiction) [2010] EWHC
  1697 (Fam) [2011] 1 FLR 724 . . . 741, 763
MA (Care Threshold), Re [2009] EWCA Civ 853
  [2010] 1 FLR 431 . . . 601, 602, 612, 764
Mabon v Mabon [2005] EWCA Civ 634 [2005]
  Fam 366 . . . 326, 450, 460, 464, 465, 469, 471,
  472
McBroom, Re [1992] 2 FLR 49 . . . 976
McCallion v Dodd [1966] NZLR 710 . . . 343
McCarthy, Re [1975] 2 All ER 857 . . . 161
McCartney v Mills McCartney [2008] EWHC
  401 (Fam) [2008] 1 FLR 1508 . . . 884, 890, 894
MacDonald v MacDonald [1964] P 1CA . . . 916
McEwan v McEwan [1972] 2 All ER 708 . . . 886
Macey v Macey (1981) 3 FLR 7 . . . 864, 888
McFarlane v McFarlane; Parlour v Parlour
  [2004] EWCA (Civ) 872 [2005] Fam
  171 . . . 833, 878, 891, 894
McFarlane v McFarlane [2009] EWHC 891
  (Fam) [2009] 2 FLR 1322 . . . 879
McG v R [1972] 1 All ER 362 . . . 220
McGladdery v McGladdery [1999] 2 FLR
  1102 . . . 911

McGrath v Wallis [1995] 2 FLR 114, CA . . . 111, 128

McGrath (Infants), Re [1893] 1 Ch 143 . . . 398

McHardy & Sons (A Firm) v Warren and Hutton [1994] 2 FLR 338, CA . . . 135

McKee v McKee [1951] AC 352, PC . . . 1024, 1026

Mackenzie v Royal Bank of Canada [1934] AC 468, PC . . . 114

McL v Security of State for Social Security [1996] 2 FLR 748 . . . 571

McLean v Nugent (1980) 1 FLR 26, CA . . . 187

Maclennan v Maclennan 1958 SLT 12 . . . 215

MacLeod v MacLeod [2008] UKPC 64 [2010] 1 AC 298 . . . 94, 242, 780, 782, 783, 855, 856, 858, 859, 929

McMinn v McMinn (Ancillary Relief: Death of Party to Proceedings) [2002] EWHC 1194 (Fam) [2003] 2 FLR 823 . . . 832

Mahadervan v Mahadervan [1964] P 233 . . . 56, 58

Mahmood v Mahmood 1993 SLT 589 . . . 77

Mahmud v Mahmud 1994 SLT 599 . . . 77

Maire v Portugal (Application No. 48206/99) [2004] 2 FLR 653, ECtHR . . . 1036

MAK and RK v United Kingdom (App Nos 45901/05 and 40146/06) [2010] 2 FLR 451, ECtHR . . . 351, 678

Malialis v Malialis [2012] EWCA Civ 1748 [2013] 2 FLR 1216 . . . 863

Malone v Harrison [1979] 1 WLR 1353 . . . 981

Manchanda v Manchanda [1995] 2 FLR 590, CA . . . 47, 228, 229

Manchester City Council v B [1996] 1 FLR 324 . . . 637

Manser v Manser [1940] P 224 . . . 959

Mansey v Mansey [1940] P 139 . . . 152

Mansfield v Mansfield [2011] EWCA Civ 1056 [2012] 1 FLR 117 . . . 886, 896

Marckx v Belgium (1979) 2 EHRR 330, ECtHR . . . 1, 327, 684

Mark v Mark [2005] UKHL 42 [2006] 1 AC 98 . . . 1044

Marquis of Westmeath v Marchioness of Westmeath (1830) 1 Dow & Cl 519 . . . 854

Marriage of Burgess, Re 13 Cal 4th 25 (1996) . . . 533

Marsh v Von Sternberg [1986] 1 FLR 526 . . . 118, 135

Marsland, Re [1939] Ch 820, CA . . . 965

Martin v Martin [1978] Fam 12, CA . . . 906

Masefield v Alexander [1995] 1 FLR 100, CA . . . 853

Maskell v Maskell [2001] EWCA Civ 858 [2003] 1 FLR 1138 . . . 912

Mason v Mason (1980) 11 Fam Law 143 . . . 218

Masson, Templier & Co v De Fries [1909] 2 KB 831, CA . . . 112

Mata Estevez v Spain Application No 56501/00, 10 May 2001 . . . 36

Mathias v Mathias [1972] Fam 287 . . . 222, 224

Matthews v Matthews [2013] EWCA Civ 1874 [2014] Fam Law 962 . . . 877

Maumousseau and Washington v France [2007] 51 EHRR 822 . . . 1036

May v May [1986] 1 FLR 325, CA . . . 408, 413

Mazurek v France (2006) 42 EHRR 9 . . . 302

MB v KB [2007] EWHC 789 (Fam) [2007] 2 FLR 586 . . . 799

MCA, Re: HM Customs and Excise Commissioners and Long v A and A; A v A (Long Intervening) [2002] EWCA Civ 1039 [2003] 1 FLR 164 . . . 846

McFarlane v McFarlane; Parlour v Parlour [2004] EWCA (Civ) 872 [2005] Fam 171, see also Miller v Miller: McFarlane v McFarlane [2006] UKHL 24 [2006] 2 AC . . . 618

Medway Council v BBC [2001] 1 FLR 104 . . . 502

Mehta v Mehta [1945] 2 All ER 690 . . . 79

Mendes v Mendes (1747) 1 Ves Sen 89 . . . 746

Mercier v Mercier [1903] 2 Ch 98, CA . . . 113

Mercredi v Chaffe [2011] EWCA Civ 272 [2011] 3 WLR 1229 . . . 1042

Mercredi v Chaffe (Case C-497/10 PPU) [2012] Fam 27, CJEU . . . 995, 996, 1003, 1042, 1044, 1093

Merritt v Merritt [1970] 2 All ER 760, CA . . . 780

Merthyr Tydfil Borough Council v C [2010] EWHC 62 (QB) [2010] 1 FLR 1640 . . . 676

Mesher v Mesher and Hall (1973) [1980] 1 All ER 126n, CA . . . 886, 904, 905

MET v HAT (Interim Maintenance) [2013] EWHC 4247 (Fam) [2014] Fam Law 447 . . . 837, 921

MET v HAT (Interim Maintenance) (No 2) [2014] EWHC 717 (Fam) . . . 921

Mette v Mette (1859) 1 Sw & Tr 416 . . . 962

MH v GP (Child: Emigration) [1995] 2 FLR 106 . . . 526

MH (A Child), Re; Re SB and MB (Children) [2004] 2 FLR 1334 . . . 463

Michael v Michael [1986] 2 FLR 389, CA . . . 842, 887

Middleton v Middleton [1998] 2 FLR 821, CA . . . 911

Midland Bank plc v Cooke [1995] 4 All ER 562, CA . . . 114, 130, 133

Midland Bank plc v Dobson [1986] 1 FLR 171, CA . . . 131

Midland Bank plc v Massey [1994] 2 FLR 342, CA . . . 114

Midland Bank Trust Co Ltd v Green (No 3) [1979] Ch 496 . . . 91

Midland Bank Trust Co Ltd v Green (No 3) [1982] Ch 529, CA . . . 91

Mikulić v Croatia [2002] 1 FCR 720, ECtHR . . . 268, 269, 270, 320

Miller v Miller: McFarlane v McFarlane [2006] UKHL 24 [2006] 2 AC 618 . . . 839, 859, 870, 871, 872, 873, 874, 879, 881, 882, 883, 884, 885, 893, 895, 898, 903, 926, 927, 932, 933, 955, 986

Miller v Miller [2005] EWCA Civ 984 [2006] 1
    FLR 151 . . . 879, 894, 895, 903
Mills v Mills [1940] P 124, CA . . . 914, 916
Milne v Milne (1871) LR 2 P & D 295 . . . 846
Milne v Milne (1981) 2 FLR 296, CA . . . 864
Minister for Immigration and Ethnic Affairs v
    Teoh (1995) 183 CLR 273 . . . 419
Minton v Minton [1979] AC 593, HL . . . 5, 849,
    853, 876
Mir v Mir [1992] Fam 79 . . . 538, 1021
Missi v Malta (2008) 46 EHRR 27 . . . 270
Mitchell v Mitchell [1984] FLR 387, CA . . . 887
M-J (Adoption Order or Special Guardianship
    Order), Re [2007] EWCA Civ 56 [2007]
    1 FLR 691 . . . 444, 709, 740
Mohamed Arif (An Infant), Re; Re Nirbhai
    Singh (An Infant) [1968] Ch 643,
    CA . . . 428, 748, 767
Moore v Holdsworth [2010] EWHC 683 (Ch)
    [2010] 2 FLR 1501 . . . 985
Moore v Moore [2004] EWCA Civ 1243 [2005]
    1 FLR 666 . . . 154, 155, 156, 184
Morris v Davies (1837) 5 CL & Fin 163,
    HL . . . 263
Morris v Morris [1985] FLR 1176, CA . . . 879
Morris v Morris [2008] EWCA Civ 257 [2008]
    Fam Law 521 . . . 139
Mortgage Corporation v Shaire [2001]
    4 All ER 364 . . . 145
Mortimer v Mortimer-Griffin [1986]
    2 FLR 315, CA . . . 904, 905
Mortimore v Wright (1840) 6 M & W
    482 . . . 363, 775
Moschetta v Moschetta (1994) 25 Cal App 4th
    1218 . . . 246
Moses-Taiga v Taiga [2005] EWCA Civ 1013
    [2006] 1 FLR 1074 . . . 837
Moss v Moss [1897] P 263 . . . 79
Mossop v Mossop [1989] Fam 77 . . . 118
Mouncer v Mouncer [1972] 1 All ER 289 . . . 220,
    789
Mountney v Treharne [2002] EWCA Civ 1174
    [2002] 2 FLR 930 . . . 845, 918
Moynihan v Moynihan (Nos 1 and 2) [1997]
    1 FLR 59 . . . 227
Moynihan, Re [2000] 1 FLR 113 . . . 262
MT v MT (Financial Provision: Lump Sum)
    [1992] 1 FLR 362 . . . 842, 887
M-T v T [2006] EWHC 2494 (Fam) [2007]
    2 FLR 925 . . . 795
Mubarak v Mubarak [2001] 1 FLR 673 . . . 847
Muema v Muema [2013] EWHC 3864
    (Fam) . . . 204, 919
Mullard v Mullard (1981) 3 FLR 330 . . . 865
In the Marriage of Murray and Tam (1993)
    16 Fam LR 982 . . . 1035
Musa v Holliday [2012] EWCA Civ 1268
    [2013] 1 FLR 806 . . . 991
MW (Adoption: Surrogacy), Re [1995] 2 FLR
    759 . . . 728

Myerson v Myerson (No 2) [2009] EWCA Civ
    282 [2009] 2 FLR 147 . . . 912

N v B and Others (Adoption by Grandmother)
    [2013] EWHC 820 (Fam) [2014] 1 FLR
    369 . . . 709, 740
N v C (Financial Provision: Schedule 1 Claims
    Dismissed) [2013] EWHC 399 (Fam) [2013]
    Fam Law 799 . . . 795
N v D [2008] 1 FLR 1629 . . . 797
N v F (Financial Orders: Pre-Acquired Wealth)
    [2011] EWHC 586 (Fam) [2011] 2 FLR
    533 . . . 884
N v N [1992] 1 FLR 266 . . . 227
N v N (Abduction: Article 13 Defence) [1995]
    1 FLR 107 . . . 1062
N v N (Consent Order: Variation) [1993] 2 FLR
    868, CA . . . 427, 880
N v N (Financial Provision: Sale of Company)
    [2001] 2 FLR 69 . . . 887
N v N (Foreign Divorce: Financial Relief) [1997]
    1 FLR 900 . . . 854
N (A Child: Religion: Jehovah's Witness),
    Re [2011] EWHC 3737 (Fam) [2012] 2 FLR
    917 . . . 411
N (Abduction: Brussels II Revised)) [2014]
    EWHC 749 (Fam) [2014] Fam Law
    947 . . . 1005
N (A Minor) (Access: Penal Notices), Re
    [1992] 1 FLR 134, CA . . . 494
N (Abduction: Appeal), Re [2012] EWCA Civ
    1086 [2013] 1 FLR 57 . . . 747, 748
N (Child Abduction: Jurisdiction), Re [1995]
    Fam 95 . . . 1039
N (Infants), Re [1967] Ch 512 . . . 741
N (Leave to Withdraw Care Proceedings),
    Re [2000] 1 FLR 134 . . . 596
N (Minors) (Abduction), Re [1991]
    1 FLR 413 . . . 1055
N (Payments for Benefit of Child), Re
    [2009] EWHC 11 (Fam) [2009] 1 FLR
    1442 . . . 799, 800
N (Recognition of Foreign Adoption Order),
    Re [2009] EWHC 29 (Fam) [2010] 1 FLR
    1102 . . . 725
NA v MA [2006] EWHC 1227 (Fam) [2007]
    1 FLR 1760 . . . 780
Nachimson v Nachimson [1930] P 217,
    CA . . . 38
Napier v Napier [1915] P 184, CA . . . 73
Nash v Nash [1940] P 60 . . . 75
National Provincial Bank Ltd v Ainsworth
    [1965] AC 1175, HL . . . 152, 153
National Provincial Bank Ltd v Hastings Car
    Mart Ltd (No 3) [1964] Ch 665, CA . . . 919
National Westminster Bank plc v Morgan [1985]
    AC 686 . . . 114
Naylor v Naylor [1962] P 253 . . . 218
Negus v Bahouse [2007] EWHC 2628
    (Ch) [2008] 1 FCR 768 . . . 987

Nessa v Chief Adjudication Officer [1999] 2 FLR
　1116, HL . . . 1044
Neulinger and Shuruk v Switzerland (2010)
　(App No 41615/07) [2011] 1 FLR 122 . . . 417,
　1036, 1037, 1062
Newham London Borough v AG [1993] 1 FLR
　281 . . . 600, 623
Newton v Edgerley [1959] 3 All ER 337 . . . 364
Newton v Newton [1990] 1 FLR 33, CA . . . 886
NG v SG (Appeal: Non-Disclosure)
　[2011] EWHC 3270 (Fam) [2012]
　1 FLR 1211 . . . 834
Ng (A Bankrupt), Re, Trustee of the Estate of Ng
　v Ng [1998] 2 FLR 386 . . . 145, 161
Nicholson, Re [1974] 2 All ER 386 . . . 143
Nielsen v Denmark (1989) 11 EHRR
　175 . . . 322, 577
NL (Appeal: Interim Care Order: Facts and
　Reasons), Re [2014] EWHC 270 (Fam) [2014]
　1 FLR 1384 . . . 643
NLW v ARC [2012] EWHC 55 (Fam) [2012] 2
　FLR 129 . . . 908
Norman v Norman [1983] 1 All ER 486 . . . 914
Norris v Norris [2002] EWHC 2996 (Fam)
　[2003] 1 FLR 1142 . . . 889, 897, 898
Norris v Norris; C v C (Variation of Post-Nuptial
　Settlement: Company Shares) [2003] EWHC
　1222 (Fam) [2003] 2 FLR 493 . . . 898
Norris v Norris; Haskins v Haskins [2003]
　EWCA Civ 1084 [2003] 2 FLR 1124 . . . 862
North Yorkshire County Council v G [1993] 2
　FLR 732 . . . 519
North Yorkshire County Council v SA [2003]
　EWCA Civ 839 [2003] 2 FLR
　849 . . . 617, 620, 626
Northamptonshire County Council v S [1993]
　Fam 136 . . . 606
Nottingham County Council v H [1995] 1 FLR
　115 . . . 463
Nottingham County Council v P [1994]
　Fam 18, CA . . . 340, 491, 502, 503, 511, 512,
　520, 550, 595, 769
Nottinghamshire County Council v J (26
　November 1993, unreported) . . . 569
Nottinghamshire County Council v October
　Films Ltd [1999] 2 FCR 529 . . . 761
NP v KRP (Recognition of Foreign Divorce)
　[2013] EWHC 694 (Fam) [2013] Fam Law
　1385 . . . 921
NP v South Gloucestershire County Council
　(2005) 7 November, CA . . . 652
NS v MI [2006] EWHC 1646 (Fam) [2007] 1 FLR
　444 . . . 77, 78
NS-H v Kingston Upon Hull City Council and
　MC [2008] EWCA Civ 493 [2008] 2 FLR
　918 . . . 702, 703
Nugent v Vetzera (1866) LR 2 Eq 704 . . . 1024
Nutting v Southern Housing Group Ltd [2004]
　EWHC 2982 (Ch) [2005] 1 FLR 1066 . . . 943
Nwogbe v Nwogbe [2000] 2 FLR 744, CA . . . 191

NXS v Camden London Borough Council
　[2009] EWHC 1786 (QB) [2010]
　1 FLR 100 . . . 675

O v L (Blood Tests) [1995] 2 FLR 930, CA . . . 267
O v United Kingdom (1987) 10 EHRR 82,
　ECtHR . . . 655, 677
O (A Minor) (Blood Tests: Constraint), Re
　[2000] Fam 139 . . . 268, 269, 765
O (A Minor) (Care
　Order: Education: Procedure), Re [1992] 1
　WLR 912 . . . 616
O (A Minor) (Care Proceedings: Education), Re
　[1992] 1 WLR 912 . . . 349, 601, 603
O (A Minor) (Contact: Indirect Contact), Re
　[1995] 2 FLR 124 . . . 399
O (A Minor) (Medical Treatment), Re [1993] 2
　FLR 149 . . . 759, 769, 770
O (a minor) (wardship: adopted child), Re [1978]
　2 All ER 27, CA . . . 724
O (Abduction: Consent and Acquiescence), Re
　[1997] 1 FLR 924 . . . 1052
O (Abduction: Custody Rights), Re [1997] 2 FLR
　70 . . . 1048
O (Care or Supervision Order), Re [1996] 2 FLR
　755 . . . 630, 635, 716
O (Child Abduction: Re-Abduction), Re [1997]
　2 FLR 712 . . . 1039
O (Child Abduction: Undertakings), Re [1994]
　2 FLR 349 . . . 1065, 1066
O (Contact: Imposition of Conditions), Re
　[1995] 2 FLR 124 . . . 493
O (Contact: Withdrawal of Application), Re
　[2003] EWHC 3031 (Fam) [2004] 1 FLR
　1258 . . . 482, 491, 496
O (Family Appeals: Management), Re [1998]
　1 FLR 431 . . . 408
O (Imposition of Conditions), Re [1995]
　2 FLR 124, CA . . . 507
O (infants), Re [1962] 2 All ER 10, CA . . . 405
O (Minors) (Care: Preliminary Hearing), Re
　[2003] UKHL 18 [2004] 1 AC . . . 413
O (Minors) (Leave To Seek Residence Order),
　Re [1994] 1 FLR 172 . . . 489
O (Minors) (Medical Examination), Re [1993]
　1 FLR 860 . . . 650
O (Supervision Order), Re [2001] EWCA
　Civ 16 [2001] 1 FLR 923 . . . 576, 636
O and Another (Minors) (Care: Preliminary
　Hearing), Re; Re B (A Minor) [2003]
　UKHL 18 [2004] 1 AC 523 . . . 218, 414,
　420, 580, 597, 611, 615, 618, 619, 620, 621,
　624, 625, 626, 627
Oakey v Jackson [1914] 1 KB 216 . . . 342
O'D v O'D [1976] Fam 83 . . . 890
Odièvre v France [2003] 1 FCR 621,
　ECtHR . . . 246, 269
Official Receiver for Northern Ireland v Rooney
　and Paulson [2008] NI Ch 22 [2009] 2 FLR
　1437 . . . 161

Official Solicitor v K [1965] AC 201, HL . . . 310, 361, 425

Official Solicitor to the Senior Courts v Yemoh and Others [2010] EWHC 3727 (Ch) [2011] 4 All ER 200 . . . 969, 970

Ogilby, Re [1942] Ch 288 . . . 969

O'Hara, Re [1900] 2 IR 232, CA . . . 310

Oldham, Re [1925] Ch 75 . . . 964

Oldham Metropolitan Borough Council v E [1994] 1 FLR 568, CA . . . 402, 511

Oliver v Birmingham and Midland Omnibus Co Ltd [1933] 1 KB 35 . . . 344

Omielan v Omielan [1996] 2 FLR 306, CA . . . 830, 849, 914

O'Neill v O'Neill [1975] 1 WLR 1118, CA . . . 216

O'Neill v Williams [1984] FLR 1, CA . . . 940

Ontario Court v M and M (Abduction: Children's Objections) [1997] 1 FLR 475 . . . 1065, 1067, 1068

O v O (Child Abduction: Return to Third Country) [2013] EWHC 2970 (Fam) [2014] 2 WLR 1213 . . . 1054

Opuz v Turkey App no 33401/02 (2009) 50 EHRR 695 . . . 169, 171

OS v DS (Oral Disclosure: Preliminary Hearing) [2004] EWHC 2376 (Fam) [2005] 1 FLR 675 . . . 834

Osman v Elasha [2000] Fam 62 . . . 1026

Osman v United Kingdom (1999) 29 EHRR 345, ECtHR . . . 674

Overbury, Re [1955] Ch 122 . . . 261

Oxfordshire County Council v L (Care or Supervision Order) [1998] 1 FLR 70 . . . 630, 636, 637

Oxfordshire County Council v L and F [1997] 1 FLR 235 . . . 463

Oxfordshire County Council v P [1995] Fam 161 . . . 462, 463

Oxfordshire County Council v X, Y and J [2011] EWCA Civ 581 [2011] 1 FLR 272 . . . 720

Oxley v Hiscock [2004] EWCA Civ 546 [2005] Fam 211 . . . 130, 138, 140

P v G, P and P (Family Provision: Relevance of Divorce Provision) [2004] EWHC 2944 (Fam) [2006] 1 FLR 431 . . . 987

P v P [1978] 3 All ER 70, CA . . . 896

P v P [2006] EWHC 2410 (Fam) [2007] 2 FLR 439 . . . 760

P v P (Abduction: Acquiescence) [1998] 2 FLR 835, CA . . . 1060

P v P (Ancillary Relief: Proceeds of Crime) [2003] EWHC Fam 2260 [2004] 1 FLR 193 . . . 835

P v P (Contempt of Court: Mental Capacity) [1999] 2 FLR 897, CA . . . 183

P v P (Financial Relief: Non Disclosure) [1994] 2 FLR 381 . . . 862

P v R (Forced Marriage: Annulment: Procedure) [2003] 1 FLR 661 . . . 77, 79

P, Re [2008] EWCA Civ 535 [2008] 2 FLR 625 . . . 695

P (A Child) (Abduction: Custody Rights), Re [2004] EWCA Civ 971 [2005] Fam 293 . . . 1050, 1052

P (A Child) (Adoption Proceedings), Re [2007] EWCA Civ 616 [2007] 1 WLR 2556 . . . 703, 710

P (A Minor) (Care: Evidence), Re [1994] 2 FLR 751 . . . 611

P (A Minor) (Education), Re [1992] 1 FLR 316 . . . 446

P (a minor) (inadequate welfare report), Re [1996] 2 FCR 285 . . . 457, 459

P (A Minor) (Parental Responsibility Order), Re [1994] 1 FLR 578 . . . 378, 380, 441

P (A Minor) (Residence Order: Child's Welfare), Re [2000] Fam 15, CA . . . 22, 350, 412, 508, 509, 632

P (Abduction: Declaration), Re [1995] 1 FLR 831, CA . . . 487, 1053

P (Care Orders: Injunctive Relief), Re [2000] 2 FLR 385 . . . 638, 768, 769

P (Care Proceedings: Father's Application To Be Joined As Party), Re [2001] 1 FLR 781 . . . 596

P (Child: Financial Provision), Re [2003] EWCA Civ 837 [2003] 2 FLR 865 . . . 796, 797, 798

P (Children Act: Diplomatic Immunity), Re [1998] 1 FLR 624 . . . 428, 747

P (Children Act 1989, ss 22 and 26: Local Authority Compliance), Re [2000] 2 FLR 910 . . . 421, 423, 508, 638

P (Contact: Supervision), Re [1996] 2 FLR 314, CA . . . 493, 494

P (Diplomatic Immunity: Jurisdiction), Re [1998] 1 FLR 1026 . . . 1052, 1053

P (Emergency Protection Order), Re [1996] 1 FLR 482 . . . 588, 611

P (Enforced Caesarean: Reporting Restrictions), Re [2013] EWHC 4048 (Fam) [2014] Fam Law 949 . . . 363

P (Forced Marriage), Re [2011] EWHC 3467 (Fam) [2011] 1 FLR 2060 . . . 78

P (GE) (An Infant), Re [1965] Ch 568 . . . 746

P (Identity of Mother), Re [2011] EWCA Civ 79 [2012] 1 FLR 351 . . . 260

P (Medical Treatment: Best Interests), Re [2003] EWHC 2327 (Fam) [2004] 2 FLR 1117 . . . 323, 403

P (Minors) (Contact with Children in Care), Re [1993] 2 FLR 156 . . . 656

P (Minors) (Custody order: Penal Notice), Re [1990] 1 WLR 61,, CA . . . 521

P (Minors) (Interim Care), Re [1993] 2 FLR 742, CA . . . 645

P (minors) (wardship: care and control), Re [1992] 2 FCR 681 . . . 402

P (Minors) (Wardship: Surrogacy), Re [1987] 2 FLR 421 . . . 276

P (Parental Responsibility), Re [1997] 2 FLR 722, CA . . . 357, 379, 525

P (Parental Responsibility), Re [1998] 2 FLR 96, CA . . . 378, 380

P (Placement Orders: Parental Consent), Re [2008] EWCA Civ 535 [2008] 2 FLR 625 . . . 694, 702, 704, 715, 716, 718

P (Residence: Appeal), Re [2007] EWCA Civ 1053 [2008] 1 FLR 198 . . . 276

P (Sexual Abuse: Standard of Proof), Re [1996] 2 FLR 333, CA . . . 412

P (Split Hearing), Re [2007] All ER (D) 475 (Nov) . . . 613

P (Surrogacy: Residence), Re [2008] 1 FLR 177 . . . 751, 761

P (Terminating Parental Responsibility), Re [1995] 1 FLR 1048 . . . 383

P (Witness Summons), Re [1997] 2 FLR 447, CA . . . 423

P, C and S v United Kingdom (2002) 35 EHRR 546 [2002] 2 FLR 631 . . . 583, 597

Pace v Doe [1977] Fam 18 . . . 782

Paddington Building Society v Mendelsohn (1985) 50 P & CR 244, CA . . . 151

Page v Page (1981) 2 FLR 198 . . . 890

Paget v Paget [1898] 1 Ch 470, CA . . . 116

Palau-Martinez v France [2004] 2 FLR 810, ECtHR . . . 350, 411

Pardy v Pardy [1939] P 288 . . . 219

Parghi v Parghi (1973) 117 Sol Jo 582 . . . 224

In the Estate of Park [1954] P 112 . . . 80

Parkes v Legal Aid Board [1997] 1 FLR 77, CA . . . 863

Parkinson v Parkinson [1939] P 346 . . . 960

Park's Estate, Re [1954] P 89 . . . 67

Parlour v Parlour [2004] 2 FLR 904 . . . 878, 898 see also McFarlane v McFarlane; Parlour v Parlour [2004] EWCA (Civ) 872 [2005] Fam . . . 171

Parojcic v Parojcic [1959] 1 All ER 1 . . . 76

Parra v Parra [2002] EWCA Civ 1886 [2003] 1 FLR 942 . . . 887

Parrucker v Vallés Pérez (Case C-256/09) [2011] Fam 254, CJEU . . . 1002, 1095

Parrucker v Vallés Pérez (No 2) (Case C-296/10) [2012] 1 FLR 925, CJEU . . . 1003

Parry v Parry [1986] 2 FLR 96, CA . . . 864

Pascoe v Turner [1979] 2 All ER 945 [1979] 1 WLR 431, CA . . . 142

Patel v Patel' [1988] Fam Law 395 [1988] FLR 179, CA . . . 179, 195

Paton v British Pregnancy Advisory Service Trustees [1979] QB 276 . . . 312, 391

Paton v United Kingdom (1980) 3 EHRR 408 . . . 391

Paul v Constance [1977] 1 All ER 195, CA . . . 110, 127

Paulík v Slovakia (2009) 46 EHRR 1 . . . 270

Payne v Payne [2001] EWCA Civ 166 [2001] 1 FLR 1052 [2001] Fam 473 . . . 401, 416, 418, 420, 527, 528, 529, 530, 531, 532

Pazpena de Vire v Pazpena de Vire [2001] 1 FLR 460 . . . 57, 58

P-B (Contact: Committal), Re [2009] EWCA Civ 143 [2009] 2 FLR 6 . . . 658

PB v CMEC [2009] UKUT 262 (AAC) [2010] 2 FLR 956 . . . 814

PC (Change of Surname), Re [1997] 2 FLR 730 . . . 333, 357, 358, 382, 394, 521

PC, YC and KM (Brussels IIR: Jurisdiction Within the United Kingdom), Re [2013] EWHC 2336 (Fam) [2014] 1 FLR 605 . . . 1001, 1022

P(D) v P(J) [1965] 2 All ER 456 . . . 218

Peacock v Peacock [1984] 1 All ER 1069 . . . 837

Peacock v Peacock [1991] 1 FLR 324 . . . 915

Pearce v Pearce [2003] EWCA Civ 1054 [2004] 1 WLR 68 . . . 914, 915

Pearce (Deceased), Re [1998] 2 FLR 705, CA . . . 985, 988, 991

Pearson v Franklin [1994] 1 WLR 370 . . . 502, 766, 795–6

Peete, Re [1952] 2 All ER 599 . . . 67

Penrose v Penrose [1994] 2 FLR 621, CA . . . 913

Pereira v Keleman [1995] 1 FLR 428 . . . 342

Pettitt v Pettitt [1970] AC 777, HL . . . 117, 118, 124, 125, 127, 133, 138, 143, 829

PG v TW (No 2) (Child: Financial Provision) [2014] 1 FLR 940 . . . 797

Pheasant v Pheasant [1972] Fam 202 . . . 215, 216

Phelps, Re [1980] Ch 275, CA . . . 971

Phillips v Peace [1996] 2 FLR 230 . . . 798, 815, 841

Phillips v Peace [2004] EWHC 3180 (Fam) [2005] 2 FLR 1212 . . . 795, 798

Phippen v Palmers (a firm) [2002] 2 FLR 415 . . . 877

Pickering v Wells [2002] 2 FLR 797 . . . 160

Piglowska v Piglowski [1999] 1 WLR 1360, HL . . . 832, 849, 882, 888, 908

Pilot v Gainfort [1931] P 10 . . . 962

Pini and Bertani; Manera and Atripaldi v Romania [2005] 2 FLR 596 . . . 724

P-J (Children) (Abduction: Consent), Re [2009] EWCA 588 [2010] 1 WLR 1237 . . . 1044, 1056, 1057

PJ (Adoption: Practice on Appeal) [1998] 2 FLR 252, CA . . . 723

PJ (An Infant), Re [1968] 1 WLR 1976 . . . 768

PK v BC (Financial Remedies: Schedule 1) [2012] EWHC 1382 (Fam) [2012] 2 FLR 1426 . . . 799, 821, 823

Place v Searle [1932] 2 KB 497 . . . 94

Plunkett v Alker [1954] 1 QB 420 . . . 348

PM (Parental Orders: Payments To Surrogacy Agency), Re [2013] EWHC 2328 (Fam) [2014] 1 FLR 725 . . . 279, 280

Poel v Poel [1970] 1 WLR 1469 . . . 528, 529

Porcelli v Strathclyde Regional Council [1986] ICR 564, Court of Session . . . 174

Portsmouth NHS Trust v Wyatt [2005] EWHC
    2293 (Fam) [2006] 1 FLR 652 . . . 351
Potter v Potter (1975) 5 Fam Law 161, CA . . . 75
Pounds v Pounds [1994] 1 FLR 775, CA . . . 781,
    850, 853
Povse v Alpago (Case C-211/10 PPU) [2011] Fam
    199 . . . 998, 1079
Povse v Austria [2014] 1 FLR 944,
    ECtHR . . . 998, 1036, 1079
Practice Direction [1977] 2 All ER 714 . . . 228
Practice Direction [1986] 1 All ER 983 . . . 355
Practice Direction [1988] 1 All ER 182 . . . 745
Practice Direction [1995] 1 All ER 832 . . . 358
Practice Direction Interim Guidance to Assist
    Cafcass [2009] 2 FLR 1407 . . . 454
Practice Direction (Justices: Clerk to Court)
    [2000] 1 WLR 1886 . . . 15
Practice Direction (Residence and Contact
    Orders: Domestic Violence) (No 2) [2009] 1
    WLR 251 . . . 206
Practice Note [1978] 1 WLR 1123 . . . 187
Practice Note [1978] 2 All ER 919 . . . 194
Practice Note [1993] 1 FLR 804 . . . 1082
Practice Note [1993] 3 All ER 222 . . . 352, 500
Practice Note (Minor: Removal from
    Jurisdiction) [1984] 1 WLR 1216 . . . 1024
Pre-Action Protocol [2000] 1 FLR 997 . . . 833
President's Direction: Family Law Act 1996 Part
    IV [1998] 1 FLR 496 . . . 195
Prest v Petrodel Resources Ltd and
    Others [2013] UKSC 34 [2013] 2 AC
    415 . . . 847, 918
Preston v Preston [1982] Fam 17 . . . 889
Preston-Jones v Preston-Jones [1951] AC 391,
    HL . . . 261, 263
Pretty v United Kingdom [2002] 2 FLR
    45 . . . 327
Price v Price [1951] P 413, CA . . . 152, 774
Priest v Priest [1987] 1 FLR 189, CA . . . 887
Prinsep v Prinsep [1929] P 225 . . . 848
Proceedings brought by A (Case C-523/07)
    [2010] Fam 42 . . . 1040, 1041, 1042
P-S (Children) (Family Proceedings: Evidence),
    Re [2013] EWCA Civ 223 [2013] 1 WLR
    3831 . . . 326, 403, 448, 449, 450, 465
PS (Incapacitated or Vulnerable Adult), Re
    [2007] EWHC 2689 (Fam) [2009] 1 FLR
    487 . . . 743
Pugh v Pugh [1951] P 482 . . . 44
Purba v Purba [2000] 1 FLR 444, CA . . . 919
Putnam & Sons v Taylor [2009] EWHC 317 (Ch)
    [2009] BPIR 769 . . . 158
Puttick v A-G [1980] Fam 1 . . . 303

Q v Q [2008] EWHC 1874 (Fam) [2009] 1 FLR
    935 . . . 141
Q v Q (Costs: Summary Assessment) [2002] 2
    FLR 668 . . . 423
Q (Adoption) [2011] EWCA Civ 1610 [2012] 1
    FLR 1228 . . . 694

Q (Contact: Natural Father), Re (2001,
    unreported) . . . 495
Q (Parental Order), Re [1996] 1 FLR
    369 . . . 253, 278
Quazi v Quazi [1980] AC 744, HL . . . 920
Queskey, Re [1946] Ch 250 . . . 51
Quoraishi v Quoraishi [1985] FLR 780,
    CA . . . 219

R v A [2012] EWCA Crim 434 [2012] 2 Cr App
    Rep 80 . . . 171
R v Algar [1954] 1 QB 279 . . . 65
R v Avon County Council, ex parte Crabtree
    [1996] 1 FLR 502, CA . . . 672
R v Avon County Council, ex parte M [1994] 2
    FCR 259 . . . 665
R v Barnardo, Jones's Case [1891] 1 QB
    194 . . . 310
R v Barnet London Borough Council, ex parte
    Shah [1983] 2 AC 309 . . . 1041
R v Bedfordshire County Council, ex parte C
    [1987] 1 FLR 239 . . . 671, 672
R v Berry [1996] 2 Cr App R 226, CA . . . 366
R v Bham [1966] 1 QB 159, CCA . . . 68
R v Birmingham City Council, ex parte A [1997]
    2 FLR 841 . . . 570, 665, 670, 672
R v Birmingham Inhabitants (1828) 8 B & C
    29 . . . 72
R v Brent London Borough Council, ex parte
    Awua [1996] AC 55 . . . 207
R v Brighton Inhabitants (1861) 1 B & S
    447 . . . 46
R v Bubb (1850) 4 Cox CC 455 . . . 340
R v Calder Justices, ex parte C (4 May 1993,
    unreported) . . . 574
R v Central Independent Television plc [1994]
    Fam 192, CA . . . 362, 424, 768
R v Chapman [1959] 1 QB 100, CCA . . . 96
R v Chattaway (1922) 17 Cr App Rep 7,
    CCA . . . 341
R v Chief Constable of Cheshire, ex parte K
    [1990] 1 FLR 70 . . . 538
R v Chief Constable of North Wales Police ex
    parte Thorpe [1998] 2 FLR 571 . . . 168
R v Children and Family Court Advisory and
    Support Service [2003] EWHC 235 (Admin)
    [2003] 1 FLR 953 . . . 437, 461
R v Chrastny [1992] 1 All ER 189, CA . . . 101
R v Clarence (1888) 22 QBD 23 . . . 95
R v Clarke [1949] 2 All ER 448 . . . 95
R v Colohan [2001] EWCA Crim 1251 [2001] 2
    FLR 757 . . . 174
R v Cornwall County Council, ex parte
    Cornwall and Isles of Scilly Guardians ad
    Litem and Reporting Officers Panel [1992] 2
    All ER 471 . . . 452
R v Cornwall County Council, ex parte LH
    [2000] 1 FLR 236 . . . 669, 672
R v Court (1912) 7 Cr App Rep 127,
    CCA . . . 100

R v D [1984] AC 778, HL . . . 308, 319, 339, 366, 1018
R v Darwin [2009] EWCA Crim 860 . . . 100
R v De Manneville (1804) 5 East 221 . . . 309
R v Derby Magistrates' Court, *ex parte* B [1996] AC 487 . . . 425
R v Derriviere (1969) 53 Cr App Rep 637, CA . . . 345
R v Devon County Council, *ex parte* L [1991] 2 FLR 541 . . . 671, 673
R v Devon County Council, *ex parte* O (Adoption) [1997] 2 FLR 388 . . . 672
R v Ditta, Hussain and Kara [1988] Crim LR 42, CA . . . 100
R v E and F (Female Parents: Known Father) [2010] EWHC 417 (Fam) [2010] 2 FLR 383 . . . 374, 379
R v Ealing London Borough Council, *ex parte* Sidhu (1982) 3 FLR 438 . . . 207, 208
R v East Sussex County Council, *ex parte* R; R v Devon County Council, *ex parte* L; R v Lewisham Borough Council, *ex parte* P . . . 673
R v East Sussex County Council, *ex parte* W [1998] 2 FLR 1082 . . . 665
R v Gibbins and Proctor (1918) 13 Cr App Rep 134, CCA . . . 340
R v Gibson and Gibson [1984] Crim LR 615, CA . . . 341
R v Greenhill (1836) 4 Ad & El 624 . . . 309
R v Griffin [1993] Crim LR 515, CA . . . 1018
R v Gwynedd County Council, *ex parte* B [1992] 3 All ER 317, CA . . . 291, 359, 391
R v Gyngall [1893] 2 QB 232, CA . . . 310, 743
R v H (Assault of Child: Reasonable Chastisement) [2001] EWCA Crim 1024, [2001] 2 FLR 431 . . . 345
R v Hale [1974] QB 819 . . . 366
R v Harrow London Borough Council, *ex parte* D [1990] Fam 133, CA . . . 669, 672, 673
R v Hatton [1925] 2 KB 322, CCA . . . 341
R v Hereford and Worcester County Council, *ex parte* D [1992] 1 FLR 448 . . . 669, 671, 672
R v Hertfordshire County Council, *ex parte* B [1987] 1 FLR 239 . . . 672, 673
R v High Peak Magistrates' Court, *ex parte* [1995] 1 FLR 568 . . . 670
R v Highbury Corner Magistrates Court, *ex parte* Deering [1997] 1 FLR 683 . . . 423
R v Hills [2001] 1 FLR 580, CA . . . 174
R v Hopley (1860) 2 F & F 202 . . . 344
R v Human Fertilisation and Embryology Authority, *ex parte* Blood [1999] Fam 151, CA . . . 248, 253
R v Immigration Appeal Tribunal, *ex parte* Tohur Ali [1988] 2 FLR 523, CA . . . 682
R v Ireland; R v Burstow [1998] AC 147, HL . . . 173, 176
R v Isley (1836) 5 Ad & El 441 . . . 311
R v Jackson [1891] 1 QB 671, CA . . . 93

R v Kayani; R v Solliman [2011] EWCA Crim 2871 [2012] 1 WLR 1927 . . . 1018
R v Kensington and Chelsea London Borough Council, *ex parte* Kihara (1996) 29 HLR 147, CA . . . 207
R v Kirklees Metropolitan Borough Council, *ex parte* C (A Minor) [1992] 2 FLR 117 . . . 351
R v Kowalski [1988] 1 FLR 447, CA . . . 95
R v Lancashire County Council, *ex parte* M [1992] 1 FLR 109, CA . . . 670, 671
R v Leak [1976] QB 217, CA . . . 95
R v Leather [1993] 2 FLR 770, CA . . . 366
R v Lewisham London Borough Council, *ex parte* P [1991] 1 WLR 308 . . . 671
R v Lister (1721) 1 Stra 478 . . . 93
R v Local Authority and Police Authority in the Midlands *ex parte* LM [2000] 1 FLR 612 . . . 168
R v London Borough of Barnet, *ex parte* B [1994] 1 FLR 592 . . . 663, 669
R v London Borough of Brent, *ex parte* S [1994] 1 FLR 203 . . . 664
R v London Borough of Lambeth, *ex parte* Vagliviello (1990) 22 HLR 392, CA . . . 208
R v London Borough of Wandsworth, *ex parte* P [1989] 1 FLR 387 . . . 671, 672
R v Luffe (1807) 8 East 193 . . . 261
R v McNaughten [2003] 2 Cr App R (S) 142 . . . 172
R v Miller [1954] 2 QB 282 . . . 95
R v Millis (1844) 10 Cl & Fin 534, HL . . . 47
R v Mohamed (Ali) (1943) [1964] 2 QB 350n . . . 68
R v Mousir [1987] Crim LR 561, CA . . . 366
R v New (1904) 20 TLR 583 . . . 311
R v Newham London Borough Council, *ex parte* Dada [1996] QB 507, CA . . . 205, 296, 359, 372, 391, 537, 560
R v Norfolk County Council, *ex parte* M [1989] QB 619 . . . 672
R v Northampton Juvenile Court, *ex parte* London Borough of Hammersmith and Fulham [1985] 1 FLR 193 . . . 573
R v Northavon District Council, *ex parte* Smith [1994] 2 AC 402 . . . 565
R v O'Brien [1974] 3 All ER 663 . . . 95
R v Oxfordshire County Council (Secure Accommodation Order) [1992] Fam 150 . . . 535, 576
R v Patel [2004] EWCA Crim 3284 [2005] 1 FLR 803 . . . 174, 176
R v R [1952] 1 All ER 1194 . . . 75
R v R [1992] 1 AC 599, HL . . . 5, 95
R v R (Financial Orders: Contributions) [2013] Fam Law 28 . . . 896
R v R (Financial Remedies: Needs and Practicalities) [2011] EWHC 3093 (Fam) [2013] 1 FLR 120 . . . 874
R v R (Inland Revenue: Tax Evasion) [1998] 1 FLR 922 . . . 834

R v R (Lump Sum Repayments) [2003] EWHC
    3197 (Fam) [2004] 1 FLR 928 . . . 878
R v R (Private Law Proceedings: Residential
    Assessment) [2002] 2 FLR 953 . . . 456, 752
R v Rahman (1985) 81 Cr App Rep 349,
    CA . . . 339, 344, 345, 366, 1018
R v R(AJ) [2013] EWCA Crim 591 [2013] 2 Cr
    App Rep 128 . . . 177
R v Registrar-General, ex parte Smith [1991] 2
    QB 393, CA . . . 722
R v Reid [1973] QB 299, CA . . . 93
R v Roberts [1986] Crim LR 188, CA . . . 95
R v Rotherfield Greys Inhabitants (1823) 1 B & C
    345 . . . 392
R v Royal Borough of Kingston-upon-Thames,
    ex parte T [1994] 1 FLR 798 . . . 570, 664, 665
R v Secretary of State for Social Security, ex parte
    Biggin [1995] 1 FLR 851 . . . 805, 819
R v Secretary of State for Social Security, ex parte
    W [1999] 2 FLR 604 . . . 373, 809
R v Secretary of State for Social Security, ex parte
    West [1999] 1 FLR 1233, CA . . . 809
R v Senior [1899] 1 QB 283 . . . 342
R v Shepherd (1862) Le & Ca 147 . . . 341
R v Sheppard [1981] AC 394, HL . . . 341, 342
R v Shortland [1996] 1 Cr App Rep 116 . . . 100
R v Smith (1916) 12 Cr App Rep 42
    CCA . . . 100
R v Smith (Mark John) [2012] EWCA Crim
    2566; noted in [2013] Crim LR 250 . . . 177
R v Soper (1793) 5 Term Rep 278 . . . 311
R v Steele (1976) 65 Cr App Rep 22, CA . . . 95
R v Tameside Metropolitan Borough Council, ex
    parte J [2000] 1 FLR 942 . . . 396, 569, 571
R v Torpey (1871) 12 Cox CC 45 . . . 100
R v UK; O v UK; W v United Kingdom [1988] 2
    FLR 445 . . . 340
R v United Kingdom (1988) 10 EHRR 74 [1988] 2
    FLR 445 . . . 318, 367, 492, 655, 677
R v Vann (1851) 2 Den 325; 15 JP 802 . . . 359
R v Waveney DC, ex parte Bowers [1983] QB
    238 . . . 208
R v Willis [1990] Crim LR 714 . . . 341
R v Wilmington Inhabitants (1822) 5 B & Ald
    525 . . . 392, 746
R v Woods (1921) 85 JP 272 . . . 344, 345
R, Re; Re G (minors) [1990] 2 All ER 633 . . . 745
R, Re [2005] EWCA Civ 1128 [2006] 1 FLR
    373 . . . 720
R, Re and H v United Kingdom [2011] 2 FLR
    1236 . . . 686
R (A) v Coventry City Council [2009] EWHC 34
    (Admin) [2009] 1 FLR 1202 . . . 564, 565, 671
R (A) v Croydon London Borough Council;
    R (M) v Lambeth Borough Council [2008]
    EWCA Civ 1445 [2009] 1 FLR 1324 . . . 565
R (A) v Croydon London Borough Council;
    R (M) v Lambeth Borough Council [2009]
    UKSC 8 [2009] 1 WLR 2557 . . . 560, 564, 565,
    566, 567, 671

R (A Child) (IVF: Paternity of Child), Re [2003]
    EWCA Civ 182 [2003] Fam 129 . . . 252
see also R (IVF: Paternity of Child), Re [2005]
    UKHL 33 [2005] 2 FLR . . . 843
R (a child) (prohibited steps order), Re [2013]
    EWCA Civ 1115 [2014] 1 FCR 113 . . . 499, 526
R (A Minor: Abduction), Re [1992] 1 FLR
    105 . . . 1068
R (A Minor) (Access), Re [1988] 1 FLR 206,
    CA . . . 412
R (A Minor) (Blood Tests: Constraint), Re [1998]
    Fam 66 . . . 264, 267, 762
R (A Minor) (Blood Transfusion), Re [1993] 2
    FLR 757 . . . 353, 500, 513, 752, 759, 763, 769
R (A Minor) (Child Abuse), Re [1988] Fam Law
    129 . . . 494
R (A Minor) (Contact), Re [1993] 2 FLR 762,
    CA . . . 492, 493
R (A Minor) (Contempt), Re [1994] 2 FLR
    185 . . . 759
R (A Minor) (Residence: Religion), Re (1975) 2
    FLR 239, CA . . . 410
R (A Minor) (Residence: Religion), Re [1993] 2
    FLR 163, CA . . . 403, 410, 411, 467, 504, 549
R (A Minor) (Wardship: Consent to Medical
    Treatment), Re [1992] Fam 11, CA . . . 322,
    323, 326, 351, 354, 392, 744, 765
R (A Minor) (Wardship: Restrictions on
    Publication), Re [1994] Fam 254 . . . 764, 768
R (AB) v SSHD [2013] EWHC 3453
    (Fam) . . . 329
R (Abduction: European and Hague
    Conventions), Re [1997] 1 FLR 663,
    CA . . . 1086
R (Adoption: Contact), Re [2005] EWCA Civ
    1128 [2006] 1 FLR 373 . . . 720
R (adoption), Re [1966] 3 All ER 613 . . . 715
R (Aguilar Quila); R (Bibi) v Secretary of State
    for the Home Department [2011] UKSC 45
    [2012] 1 AC 621 . . . 102
R (Anton) v Secretary of State For The Home
    Department; Re Anton [2004] EWHC
    2730/2731 (Admin/Fam) [2005] 2 FLR 818,
    CA . . . 748, 767
R (Axon) v Secretary of State For Health
    and the Family Planning Association
    [2006] EWHC 37 (Admin) [2006] 2 FLR
    206 . . . 321, 322, 353
R (B) v Merton London Borough Council
    [2003] EWHC 1689 (Admin) [2003] 2 FLR
    888 . . . 560, 665
R (Baiai and others) v Secretary of State for the
    Home Department [2008] UKHL 53 [2009]
    AC 287 . . . 49, 55, 82
R (Berhe) v Hillingdon London Borough
    Council [2003] EWHC 2075 (Admin) [2004] 1
    FLR 439 . . . 571
R (BG) v Medway Council [2005] EWHC 1932
    (Admin) [2006] 1 FLR 663 . . . 561, 665
R (BM) v R (DN) [1978] 2 All ER 33, CA . . . 521

R (Care: Disclosure: Nature of Proceedings),
Re [2002] 1 FLR 755 . . . 611, 626, 627

R (Care Proceedings: Adjournment), Re [1998] 2
FLR 390, CA . . . 644

R (CD) v Isle of Anglesey County Council
[2004] EWHC 1635 (Admin) [2005] 1 FLR
59 . . . 402, 671, 672

R (Charlton Thomson and Others) v Secretary of
State for Education and Skills [2005] EWHC
1378 (Admin) at [2005] Fam Law 861 . . . 1012

R (Child Abduction: Acquiescence), Re [1995] 1
FLR 716 . . . 1059, 1067, 1071

R (Costs: Contact Enforcement), Re [2011]
EWHC 2777 (Fam) [2012] 1 FLR 445 . . . 541

R (D) v Secretary of State for the Home
Department [2003] EWHC 155 (Admin)
[2003] 1 FLR 979 . . . 560

R (Denson) v Child Support Agency [2002]
EWHC 154 (Admin) [2002] 1 FLR 938 . . . 818

R (ET) v Islington Borough Council
[2012] EWHC 3228 (Admin) [2013]
2 FLR 347 . . . 671

R (G) v Barnet London Borough Council; R
(W) v Lambeth London Borough Council;
R (A) v Lambeth London Borough Council
[2003] UKHL 57 [2004] 2 AC 208 . . . 560, 561,
565, 566

R (G) v Nottingham City Council [2008] EWHC
152 (Admin) [2008] 1 FLR 1660 . . . 583

R (G) v Southwark London Borough Council
[2009] UKHL 26 [2009] 2 FLR 380 . . . 565,
566, 568

R (Green) v Secretary of State for the
Department for Work and Pensions [2010]
EWHC 1278 (Admin) . . . 819

R (H) v Essex County Council [2009] EWCA Civ
1504 [2010] 1 FLR 1781 . . . 670

R (on the application of Hodkin and another)
v Registrar General of Births, Deaths and
Marriages [2013] UKSC 77 [2014] 1 All ER
737 . . . 53, 411

R (Howard League for Penal Reform) v
Secretary of State for the Home Department
[2002] EWHC 2497 (Admin) [2003] 1 FLR
484 . . . 421, 560, 669, 767

R (Inter-Country Adoption), Re [1999] 1 FLR
1014 . . . 761

R (Intercountry Adoptions: Practice), Re [1999]
1 FLR 1042 . . . 1014

R (IVF: Paternity of Child), Re [2005] UKHL 33
[2005] 2 FLR 843 . . . 252, 253

R (JL) v Islington Borough Council [2009]
EWHC 458 (Admin) [2009] 2 FLR 515 . . . 565

R (Johns and another) v Derby City Council
(Equality and Human Rights Commission
Intervening) [2011] EWHC 375 (Admin)
[2011] 1 FLR 2094 . . . 421

R (Joplin) v Child Maintenance and
Enforcement Commission [2010] EWHC
1623 (Admin) [2010] 2 FLR 1510 . . . 805, 819

R (K) v London Borough of Lambeth
[2003] EWHC 871 (Admin) [2003]
2 FLR 439 . . . 82

R (Kehoe) v Secretary of State for Work and
Pensions [2005] UKHL 48 [2006] 1 AC
42 . . . 775, 820

R (Kimani) v Lambeth London Borough
Council [2003] EWCA Civ 1150 [2004] 1
WLR 272 . . . 103

R (L) v Merton London Borough Council
[2008] EWHC 1628 (Admin) [2008] 2 FLR
1481 . . . 671

R (on the application of L) and Others v
Manchester City Council; R (on the
Application of R) v Manchester City Council
[2002] EWHC Admin 707 [2002] 1 FLR
43 . . . 671

R (Liverpool City Council) v Hillingdon
Borough Council [2009] EWCA Civ 43
[2009] 1 FLR 1536 . . . 568

R (M) v Hammersmith and Fulham London
Borough Council [2008] UKHL 14 [2008] 1
WLR 1384 . . . 565, 566, 568

R (M) v London Borough of Bromley [2002]
EWCA Civ 1113 [2002] 2 FLR 802 . . . 671

R (Minors) (Abduction), Re [1994] 1 FLR
190 . . . 1059

R (Minors) (Wardship: Criminal Proceedings),
Re [1991] Fam 56, CA . . . 745

R (Minors) (Wardship: Jurisdiction), Re (1981)
2 FLR 416 . . . 316

R (on the application of the National Association
of Guardians ad Litem and Reporting
Officers) v Children and Family Court
Advisory and Support Service [2001] EWHC
693 (Admin) [2002] 1 FLR 255 . . . 454

R (Nicolaou) v Redbridge Magistrates'
Court [2012] EWHC 1647 (Admin) [2012]
2 Cr App R 23 . . . 1018

R (O) v East Riding of Yorkshire Council
(Secretary of State for Education Intervening)
[2011] EWCA Civ 196 [2011] 2 FLR
207 . . . 564, 567

R (on the application of O) v Hammersmith
and Fulham London Borough Council
[2011] EWCA Civ 925 [2012] 1 WLR
1057 . . . 421, 424, 669, 671, 673

R (P) v Secretary of State for the Home
Department; R (Q) v Secretary of State for
Home Department [2001] EWCA Civ 1151
[2001] 1 WLR 2002 . . . 421, 423, 671

R (Parental Responsibility), Re [2011]
EWHC 1535 (Fam) [2011] 2 FLR
1132 . . . 271, 388

R (Quila); R (Bibi) v Secretary of State for the
Home Department [2011] UKSC 45 [2012] 1
FLR 788 . . . 51

R (Recognition of Indian Adoption), Re
[2012] EWHC 2956 (Fam) [2013] 1 FLR
1487 . . . 1013

R (Recovery Orders), Re [1998] 2 FLR
  401 ... 590
R (Residence: Contact: Restricting
  Applications), Re [1998] 1 FLR 749,
  CA ... 509, 660
R (Residence Order: Finance), Re [1995] 2 FLR
  612, CA ... 400
R (Rowley) v Secretary of State for Work and
  Pensions [2007] EWCA Civ 598 [2007] 2 FLR
  945 ... 820
R (on the application of S) v London Borough
  of Wandsworth, London Borough of
  Hammersmith and Fulham, London Borough
  of Lambeth [2001] EWHC Admin 709 [2002]
  1 FLR 469 ... 669
R (S) v Sutton London Borough Council
  [2007] EWHC 1196 (Admin) [2007] 2 FLR
  849 ... 566, 568
R (Smith) v Secretary of State for Defence and
  Secretary of State for Work and Pensions
  [2004] EWHC 1797 (Admin) [2005] 1 FLR
  97 ... 843, 844
R (Surname: Using Both Parents), Re
  [2001] EWCA Civ 1344 [2001] 2 FLR
  1358 ... 522, 524
R (T) and Legal Aid Agency v London Borough
  of Ealing [2013] EWHC 960 (Admin) ... 759
R (TG) v Lambeth London Borough Council
  (Shelter Intervening) [2011] EWCA Civ 526
  [2011] 2 FLR 1007 ... 565, 679
R (TT) v London Borough of Merton [2012]
  EWHC 2055 (Admin) [2013] 2 FLR
  773 ... 739
R (Ullah) v Special Adjudicator; Do v
  Immigration Appeal Tribunal [2004] UKHL
  26 [2004] 2 AC 323 ... 1029
R v Local Commissioner for the North and East
  Area of England, ex parte Bradford [1979] QB
  287 ... 666
R (W) v Leicestershire County Council [2003]
  EWHC 704 (Admin) [2003] 2 FLR 185 ... 673
R (W) v North Lincolnshire Council [2008]
  EWHC 2299 (Admin) [2008] 2 FLR
  2150 ... 565, 568
R (on the application of Williamson) v
  Secretary of State for Education and
  Employment [2001] EWHC Admin 960
  [2002] 1 FLR 493 ... 345, 346
R (on the application of Williamson) v Secretary
  of State for Education and Employment
  [2005] UKHL 15 [2005] 2 AC 246 ... 345,
  346, 350
R (X) v London Borough of Tower Hamlets
  [2013] EWHC 480 (Admin) [2013]
  2 FLR 199 ... 671
R and another v A (Costs in Children
  Proceedings) [2011] EWHC 1158 (Fam) [2011]
  2 FLR 672 ... 750
R and Others v Cafcass [2012] EWCA Civ 853
  [2012] 2 FLR 1432 ... 461, 464, 671

RA, Re (1974) 4 Fam Law 182 ... 705
Raban v Israel [2010] ECHR 1625 ... 1037
Radmacher case see Granatino v Radmacher
  (Formerly Granatino)
Radwan v Radwan (No 2) [1973] Fam 35 ... 71
Rampal v Rampal (No 2) [2001] EWCA Civ 989
  [2001] 2 FLR 1179 ... 831
Ramsamy v Babar [2003] EWCA Civ 1253 [2005]
  1 FLR 113 ... 153
Ramussen v Denmark (1985) 7 EHRR 371,
  ECtHR ... 269
RB v FB & MA [2008] EWHC 1669 (Fam) [2008]
  2 FLR 1588 ... 760
RB, Re [2009] EWHC 3269 (Fam) [2010] 1 FLR
  946 ... 352
RC and BC (Child abduction) (Brussels II
  Revised: Article 11(7)), Re [2009] 1 FLR
  574 ... 1077
RD (Child Abduction) (Brussels II
  Revised: Articles 11(7) and (19)), Re [2009]
  1 FLR 586 ... 1077
Redbridge London Borough Council v B and
  C and A (Through His Children's Guardian)
  [2011] EWHC 517 (Fam) [2011] 2 FLR
  117 ... 596
Reed v Royal Exchange Assurance Co (1795)
  Peake Add Cas 70 ... 92
Rees v Newbery and the Institute of Cancer
  Research [1998] 1 FLR 1041 ... 981, 984,
  988, 991
Rees v United Kingdom (1986) 9 EHRR
  56 ... 42
Reid v Reid [2003] EWHC 2878 (Fam) [2004]
  1 FLR 736 ... 910
Reiterbund v Reiterbund [1975]
  Fam 99, CA ... 223
REL v EL [1949] P 211 ... 301
Reynold's Will Trusts, Re [1965] 3 All ER
  686 ... 969
Rice v Miller (1993) FLC 92-415
  (Australia) ... 406
Richards v Richards [1972] 3 All ER 695 ... 214
Richards v Richards [1984] AC 174, HL ... 167,
  197, 316, 422, 766
Richardson v Richardson [1989] Fam 95 ... 538,
  1021
Richardson v Richardson [1994] 1 FLR
  286 ... 878, 913
Richardson v Richardson (No 2) [1996] 2 FLR
  617, CA ... 875
Rimmer v Rimmer [1953] 1 QB 63, CA ... 111
Rinau, Re (Case C-195/08 PPU) [2008] 2 FLR
  1495 ... 1078
Risch v McFee [1991] 1 FLR 105, CA ... 133
R-J (Minors) (Fostering: Person disqualified),
  Re [1999] 2 FLR 60 ... 751
RJ (Foster Placement), Re [1998] 2 FLR
  110 ... 766
RJ (Fostering: Person Disqualified), Re [1999] 1
  WLR 581 [1999] 1 FLR 605 ... 420, 752, 757

RJ (Wardship), Re [1999] 1 FLR 618 . . . 512, 630, 764

RK v RK (Financial Resources: Trust Assets) [2011] EWHC 3910 (Fam) [2013] 1 FLR 329 . . . 846

Roberts v Roberts [1962] P 212 . . . 792

Roberts v Roberts [1970] P 1 . . . 889

Roberts, Re [1978] 3 All ER 225, CA . . . 66, 962

Robertson v Robertson (1982) 4 FLR 387 . . . 893

Robins v Robins [1907] 2 KB 13 . . . 916

Robinson v Collins [1975] 1 All ER 321 . . . 971

Robinson v Murray [2005] EWCA Civ 935 [2005] 3 FCR 504 . . . 178

Robson v Robson [2010] EWCA Civ 1171 [2011] 1 FLR 751 . . . 884

Rochdale Borough Council v A [1991] 2 FLR 192 . . . 552, 584

Roddy (A Child) (Identification: Restriction on Publication), Re [2003] EWHC 2927 (Fam) [2004] 2 FLR 949 . . . 325

Rogers' Question, Re [1948] 1 All ER 328, CA . . . 117

Rondeau, Le Grand & Co v Marks [1918] 1 KB 75, CA . . . 112

Rooker v Rooker [1988] 1 FLR 219, CA . . . 911

Rose v Secretary of State for Health and Human Fertilisation and Embryology Authority [2002] EWHA 1593 (Admin) [2002] 2 FLR 962 . . . 273

Rowe v Prance [1999] 2 FLR 787 . . . 113, 127

Rowe v Rowe [1980] Fam 47, CA . . . 298

Rowlands, Re [1984] FLR 813, CA . . . 986

Royal Bank of Scotland plc v Etridge (No 2) [2001] UKHL 44 [2002] 2 AC 773 . . . 114, 115, 151

Różański v Poland (2007) 45 EHRR 26 . . . 270

RP v Nottingham City Council and the Official Solicitor (Mental Capacity of Parent) [2008] EWCA Civ 462, [2008] 2 FLR 1516 . . . 715

RP v RP [2006] EWHC 3409 (Fam) [2007] 1 FLR 2105 . . . 872, 874

RP v United Kingdom [2013] 1 FLR 774 . . . 686

RP and Others v United Kingdom [2013] 1 FLR 744, ECtHR 715 270w . . . 270

RS v KS (Abduction: Wrongful Retention) [2009] EWHC 1494 (Fam) [2009] 2 FLR 1231 . . . 1051

Rukat v Rukat [1975] Fam 63 . . . 222, 224

In the Goods of Russell (1890) 15 PD 111 . . . 962

Russell v Russell [1956] P 283, CA . . . 916

Ruttinger v Temple (1863) 4 B & S 491 . . . 776

Ryan v Fildes and Others [1938] 3 All ER 517 . . . 345

Rye v Rye [2002] EWHC 956 (Fam) [2002] 2 FLR 981 . . . 228, 846

S v AG (Financial Orders: Lottery Prize) [2011] EWHC 2637 (Fam) [2012] 1 FLR 651 . . . 886

S v B (Abduction: Human Rights) [2005] EWHC 733 (Fam) [2005] 2 FLR 878 . . . 1036, 1062, 1063

S v B (Ancillary Relief: Costs) [2004] EWHC 2089 (Fam) [2005] 1 FLR 474 . . . 905

S v B and Newport City Council; Re K [2007] 1 FLR 1116 . . . 734, 735

S v Gloucestershire County Council; L v Tower Hamlets London Borough Council [2000] 1 FLR 825, CA . . . 674–5

S v H (Abduction: Access Rights) [1998] Fam 49 [1997] 3 WLR 1086 . . . 1049

S v Knowsley Borough Council [2004] EWHC 491 (Fam) [2004] 2 FLR 716 . . . 575, 576, 577

S v M (Access Order) [1997] 1 FLR 980 . . . 440

S v M (Maintenance Pending Suit) [2012] EWHC 4109 (Fam) [2013] 1 FLR 1173 . . . 837

S v McC; W v W [1972] AC 24 . . . 741

S v P (Contact Application: Family Assistance Order) [1997] 2 FLR 277 . . . 548

S v R (parental responsibility) [1993] 1 FCR 331 . . . 443

S v S [1976] Fam 18n . . . 888, 904

S v S [1977] Fam 127, CA . . . 841

S v S [1988] Fam Law 128, CA . . . 493

S v S [2008] EWHC 2288 (Fam) [2009] 1 FLR 241 . . . 760

S v S (Ancillary Relief: Consent Order) [2002] EWHC 223 (Fam) [2003] Fam 1 . . . 911

S v S (Divorce: Staying Proceedings) [1997] 2 FLR 100 . . . 854

S v S (Financial Provision: Departing from Equality) [2001] 2 FLR 246 . . . 889

S v S (Financial Provision) (Post Divorce Cohabitation) [1994] 2 FLR 228 . . . 910

S v S (Financial Remedies: Arbitral Award) [2014] EWHC 7 (Fam) [2014] 1 FLR 1257 . . . 12, 852

S v S (Inland Revenue: Tax Evasion) [1997] 2 FLR 774 . . . 834

S v S (No 2) (Ancillary Relief: Application to Set Aside Order) [2009] EWHC 2377 (Fam) [2010] 1 FLR 993 . . . 912

S v S (otherwise C) [1956] P 1 . . . 75, 76

S v S (otherwise W) [1963] P 162, CA . . . 73

S v S (Rescission of Decree Nisi: Pension Sharing Provision) [2002] 1 FLR 457 . . . 228, 229

S v S, W v Official Solicitor (or W) [1972] AC 24 [1970] 3 All ER 107, HL . . . 263, 265, 268, 422

S v W (1980) 11 Fam Law 81 . . . 409

S v Walsall Metropolitan Borough Council [1986] 1 FLR 397, CA . . . 343

S v X and X (Interveners) [1990] 2 FLR 187 . . . 794

S (A Child: Abduction), Re [2002] EWCA Civ 1941 [2003] 1 FLR 1008 . . . 1023

S (A Child) (Abduction: Rights of Custody), Re [2012] UKSC 10 [2012] 2 AC 257 . . . 1036, 1037, 1056, 1062, 1064

S (a child) (care and placement orders; proportionality), Re [2013] EWCA Civ 1073 [2014] 2 FCR 139 . . . 702

S (a child) (declaration of parentage), Re [2012] EWCA Civ 1160 [2012] All ER (D) 140 (Aug) ... 271, 303

S (A Child) (Identification: Restrictions on Publication), Re [2004] UKHL 47 [2005] 1 AC 593 ... 424, 425, 502, 745, 767, 768, 770

S (a child) (residence order: condition), Re [2001] EWCA Civ 847 [2001] 3 FCR 154 ... 505, 506, 527

S (a child) (residence order: condition) (No 2), Re [2002] EWCA Civ 1795 [2003] 1 FCR 138 ... 505, 507

S (A Minor) (Abduction: Custody Rights), Re [1993] Fam 242, CA ... 1067, 1068

S (A Minor) (Abduction), Re [1991] 2 FLR 1, CA ... 1040

S (a minor) (abduction), Re [1993] 2 All ER 683, CA ... 1067

S (A Minor) (Adopted Child: Contact), Re [1999] Fam 283 ... 516, 517, 519

S (A Minor) (Adoption by Step-parents), Re [1988] 1 FLR 418, CA ... 690

S (A Minor) (Care: Contact Order), Re [1994] 2 FLR 222, CA ... 639, 640, 658

S (A Minor) (Custody), Re [1991] 2 FLR 388, CA ... 404

S (a minor) (custody: habitual residence), Re [1998] AC 750 ... 395, 1046, 1047, 1084

S (A Minor) (Guardian Ad Litem/Welfare Officer), Re [1993] 1 FLR 110, CA ... 460

S (A Minor) (Independent Representation), Re [1993] Fam 263 ... 519

S (A Minor) (Medical Treatment), Re [1993] 1 FLR 376 ... 769

S (a minor) (parental responsibility), Re [1995] 3 FCR 564 ... 336, 380, 382

S (A Minor) (Parental Responsibility; Jurisdiction), Re [1998] 2 FLR 921 CA ... 374

S (A Minor) (Parental Rights), Re [1993] Fam Law 572 ... 360, 367

S (Abduction: Acquiescence), Re [1998] 2 FLR 115, CA ... 1059, 1061

S (Abduction: Custody Rights), Re [2002] EWCA Civ 908 [2002] 2 FLR 815 ... 1061, 1064

S (Abduction: Hague and European Convention), Re [1997] 1 FLR 958 ... 395

S (Abduction: Intolerable Situation: Beth Din), Re [2000] 1 FLR 454 ... 1063

S (Abduction: Return into Care), Re [1999] 1 FLR 843 ... 1062

S (Abduction: Sequestration), Re [1995] 1 FLR 858 ... 539

S (Adoption), Re [1999] 2 FLR 374, Ct of Session ... 714

S (Adoption Order or Special Guardianship Order), Re [2007] EWCA Civ 54 [2007] 1 FLR 819 ... 513, 708, 715, 730, 732, 733, 734, 735, 736, 740

S (Adoption Order or Special Guardianship Order) (No 2), Re [2007] EWCA Civ 90 [2007] 1 FLR 853 ... 732

S (Application for Judicial Review), Re [1998] 1 FLR 790, CA ... 670

S (Arrangements for Adoption), Re [1985] FLR 579, CA ... 728

S (BD) v S (DJ) (Children: Care and Control) [1977] Fam 109, CA ... 316, 404

S (Brussels II: Recognition: Best Interests of Child) (No 1), Re [2003] EWHC 2115 (Fam) [2004] 1 FLR 571 ... 1004

S (Brussels II: Recognition: Best Interests of Child) (No 2), Re [2003] EWHC 2974 (Fam) [2004] 1 FLR 582 ... 1005

S (Brussels II Revised: Enforcement of Contact Order), Re [2008] 2 FLR 1358 ... 749, 1006

S (Brussels IIR: Prorogation), Re [2013] EWHC 647 (Fam) [2013] 2 FLR 1584 ... 999

S (Care: Jurisdiction), Re [2008] EWHC 3013 (Fam) [2009] 2 FLR 550 ... 1002, 1096

S (Care: Residence: Intervener), Re [1997] 1 FLR 497, CA ... 515

S (Care Order: Criminal Proceedings), Re [1995] 1 FLR 151, CA ... 642

S (Change of Names: Cultural Factors), Re [2001] EWCA Civ 1344 [2001] 2 FLR 1358 ... 524

S (Change of Surname), Re [1999] 1 FLR 672 ... 420

S (Child: Financial Provision), Re [2004] EWCA Civ 1685 [2005] 2 FLR 94 ... 793, 794, 795

S (Child Abduction: Asylum Appeal), Re [2002] EWCA Civ 843 [2002] 2 FLR 465 ... 1029

S (Child Abduction: Delay), Re [1998] 1 FLR 651 ... 1046, 1055, 1068

S (Children), Re [2002] EWCA Civ 583 ... 404

S (Appeal from Care and Placement orders), Re [2014] EWCA Civ 135 [2014] Fam Law 774 ... 702

S (Contact: Application By Sibling), Re [1998] 2 FLR 897 ... 423, 659

S (Contact: Grandparents), Re [1996] 1 FLR 158, CA ... 420, 442, 463, 494

S (Contact: Intractable Dispute), Re [2010] EWCA Civ 447 [2010] 2 FLR 1517 ... 482, 494

S (Contact: Prohibition of Applications), Re [1994] 2 FLR 1057 ... 510

S (Contact: Promoting Relationship With Absent Parent), Re [2004] EWCA Civ 18 [2004] 1 FLR 1279 ... 492, 493, 538, 540

S (Contact Dispute: Committal), Re [2004] EWCA Civ 1790 [2005] 1 FLR 812 ... 539

S (Contact Order), Re [2010] EWCA Civ 705 [2011] 1 FLR 183 ... 503

S (Discharge of Care Order), Re [1995] 2 FLR 639, CA ... 652

S (Habitual Residence), [2009] EWCA Civ 1021 [2010] 1 FLR 1146 ... 1044

S (Infants), Re [1967] 1 WLR 396 ... 744

S (J) (A Minor) (Care or Supervision Order), Re [1993] 2 FLR 919 . . . 634, 636

S (Leave To Remove From Jurisdiction: Securing Return From Holiday), Re [2001] 2 FLR 507 . . . 760

S (Minors) (Abduction: Acquiescence), Re [1994] 1 FLR 819, CA . . . 1058, 1059, 1067

S (Minors) (Abduction: Wrongful Retention), Re [1994] Fam 70 . . . 1046, 1051

S (Minors) (Access: Religious Upbringing), Re [1992] 2 FLR 313, CA . . . 350

S (Minors) (Care Order: Implementation of Care Plan), Re; Re W (Minors: Care Order: Adequacy of Care Plan) [2002] UKHL 10 [2002] 2 AC 291 . . . 24, 25, 639, 641, 643, 645, 647, 678, 679

S (Minors) (Child Abduction: Wrongful Retention), Re [1994] 1 FLR 82 . . . 393

S (minors) (custody), Re [1992] 1 FCR 158, CA . . . 437

S (Minors) (Inherent Jurisdiction: Ouster), Re [1994] 1 FLR 623 . . . 196, 766

S (Parental Order), Re [2009] EWHC 2977 (Jud) [2010] 1 FLR 1156 . . . 279

S (Parental Responsibility), Re [1995] 2 FLR 648 . . . 334, 336, 375, 376, 377, 379, 381, 382

S (Parenting Skills: Personality Tests), [2004] EWCA Civ 1029 [2005] 2 FLR 658 . . . 632

S (Permission to Seek Relief), Re [2006] EWCA Civ 1190 [2007] 1 FLR 482 . . . 490, 504, 509

S (Placement Order: Revocation), Re [2008] EWCA Civ 1333 [2009] 1 FLR 503 . . . 703

S (Relocation: Parental Responsibility), Re [2013] EWHC 1295 (Fam) [2013] 2 FLR 1453 . . . 371

S (Removal From Jurisdiction), Re [1999] 1 FLR 850, CA . . . 533

S (Residence Order: Forum Conveniens), Re [1995] 1 FLR 314 . . . 427

S (Sexual Abuse Allegations: Local Authority Response), Re [2001] EWHC Admin 334 [2001] 2 FLR 776 . . . 579, 580, 671

S (Specific Issue Order: Religion: Circumcision), Re [2004] EWHC 1282 (Fam) [2005] 1 FLR 236 . . . 410, 499, 501

S (Unco-operative Mother), Re [2004] EWCA Civ 597 [2004] 2 FLR 710 . . . 493

S (Violent Parent: Indirect Contact), Re [2000] 1 FLR 481 . . . 489

S (Wardship), Re Guidance in cases of Stranded Spouses [2011] 1 FLR 319 . . . 761

S (Wardship: Peremptory Return), Re [2010] EWCA Civ 465 [2010] 2 FLR 1960 . . . 749, 759, 770

S (Wardship: Stranded Spouses), Re [2010] EWHC 1669 (Fam) [2011] 1 FLR 305 . . . 760

S and D (Children: Powers of Court), Re [1995] 2 FLR 456, CA . . . 504, 569, 762

S and J (Adoption: Non-Patrials), Re [1994] 2 FLR 111 . . . 695

S and P (Discharge of Care Order), Re [1995] 2 FLR 782 . . . 652

S and W (Care Proceedings), Re [2007] EWCA Civ 232 [2007] 2 FLR 275 . . . 670

SA, Re [2005] EWHC 2942 (Fam) [2006] I FLR 867 . . . 80

SA v PA (Pre-Marital Agreement: Compensation) [2014] EWHC 392 (Fam) [2014] Fam Law 799 . . . 860, 872

SA (Vulnerable Adult with Capacity: Marriage), Re [2006] 1 FLR 867 . . . 197

Sahin v Germany; Sommerfeld v Germany [2003] 2 FLR 671 [2003] 2 FCR 619, ECtHR . . . 337, 448, 466, 469, 492

Sahin v Germany; Sommerfeld v Germany; Hoffman v Germany [2002] 1 FLR 119 . . . 469

Salgueiro da Silva Mouta v Portugal [2001] 1 FCR 653 . . . 2, 4

Samson v Samson [1960] 1 All ER 653, CA . . . 113

Sanctuary Housing Association v Campbell [1999] 2 FLR 383, CA . . . 155

Sandwell Metropolitan Borough Council v RG and Others [2013] EWHC 2373 (COP) [2013] COPLR 643 . . . 81

Santos v Santos [1972] Fam 247, CA . . . 220

Saunders v Garett (2005) NLJ 1486 . . . 978

Saunders v Saunders [1965] P 499 . . . 219

Saunders v Vautier (1841) Cr & Ph 240 . . . 968

S-B (Children) (Care Proceedings: Standard of Proof), Re [2009] UKSC 17 [2010] 1 AC 678 . . . 611, 613, 614, 616, 617, 618, 619, 620, 621, 622, 623, 624, 625

SB v RB (Residence: Forced Marriage: Child's Best Interests) [2008] EWHC 938 (Fam) [2008] 2 FLR 1588 . . . 760

SB and MB (Children), Re [2001] 2 FLR 1334 . . . 461

SC (A Minor) (Leave to Seek Residence Order), Re [1994] 1 FLR 96 . . . 423, 513, 519

Scallon v Scallon [1990] 1 FLR 194, CA . . . 864

Schaefer v Schuhmann [1972] AC 572, PC . . . 975

Schalk and Kopf v Austria [2011] 2 FCR 650 . . . 1, 36

Scheeres v Scheeres [1999] 1 FLR 241 . . . 846

Schofield v Schofield [2011] EWCA Civ 174 [2011] 1 FLR 2129 . . . 923

Schuller v Schuller [1990] 2 FLR 193, CA . . . 886, 906

Scott v Combined Property Services Ltd (1996) EAT/757/96 . . . 174

Scott v Scott [1913] AC 417 . . . 313, 745

Scott v Scott [1978] 3 All ER 65, CA . . . 904

Scott v Scott [1986] 2 FLR 320, CA . . . 414, 457

Scott v Sebright (1886) 12 PD 21 . . . 78

Scott v UK [2000] 1 FLR 958, ECtHR . . . 417, 655, 686

Scozzari and Giunta v Italy (2002) 35 EHRR 12 . . . 610

Sears Tooth (a firm) v Payne Hicks Beach
    (a firm) [1997] 2 FLR 116 . . . 838
Seaton v Seaton [1986] 2 FLR 398, CA . . . 877
Secretary for Justice v Sigg (1992) 10 FRNZ
    164 . . . 1083
Secretary of State for Social Security v Shotton
    [1996] 2 FLR 241 . . . 819
Secretary of State for Social Services v S [1983] 3
    All ER 173, CA . . . 723
Secretary of State for Work and Pensions v
    Jones [2003] EWHC 2163 (Fam) [2004]
    1 FLR 282 . . . 263, 269
Secretary of State for Work and Pensions v
    Wincott [2009] EWCA Civ 113 [2009] 1 FLR
    1222 . . . 814–15
Sehota, Re [1978] 3 All ER 385 . . . 977
Sekhi v Ray [2013] EWHC 2290 (Fam) [2014]
    1 FLR 612 . . . 832
Serio v Serio (1983) 4 FLR 756 . . . 262
SH v MM and RM (Prohibited Steps
    Order: Abduction) [2011] EWHC 3314 (Fam)
    [2012] 1 FLR 837 . . . 500, 998
SH v NB (Marriage: Consent) [2009] EWHC
    3274 (Fam) [2010] 1 FLR 1927 . . . 63, 79
SH (Care Order: Orphan), Re [1995] 1 FLR
    746 . . . 289, 290, 567, 606, 607, 608, 731
Shagroon v Sharbatly [2012] EWCA Civ 1507
    [2013] Fam 67 . . . 40, 69
Sharland v Sharland [2014] EWCA Civ 95 [2014]
    Fam Law 449 . . . 850
Shaw v Fitzgerald [1992] 1 FLR 357 . . . 39, 119
Shaw v Hungary [2012] 2 FLR 1314 . . . 1036,
    1076–7
Shaw v Shaw [2002] EWCA Civ 1298 [2002] 2
    FLR 1204 . . . 909
Sheffield and Horsham v United Kingdom [1998]
    2 FLR 928 (1999) 27 EHRR 163 . . . 35, 42
Sheffield City Council v E and S [2004] EWHC
    2808 (Fam) [2005] 1 FLR 965 . . . 37, 79, 80, 94
Shelley v Westbrooke (1817) Jac 266n . . . 410
Shipman v Shipman [1924] 2 Ch 140, CA . . . 152
Shirt v Shirt [2012] EWCA Civ 1029 [2013] 1
    FLR 232 . . . 141
Shoffmann v Russia (2007) 44 EHRR
    35 . . . 270
Sidaway v Board of Governors of the Bethlem
    Royal Hospital and the Maudsley Hospital
    [1985] AC 871, HL . . . 320
Silver v Silver [1958] 1 All ER 523, CA . . . 113
Simpson v Simpson [1992] 1 FLR 601 . . . 114
Sims v Dacorum Borough Council [2013]
    EWCA Civ 12 [2013] 1 EGLR 52 . . . 204
Sinclair, Re [1985] Ch 446 . . . 963
Singh v Kaur (1981) 11 Fam Law 152, CA . . . 77
Singh v Singh [1971] P 226, CA . . . 75, 77
Singla v Browne [2007] EWHC 405 (Ch) [2008]
    2 FLR 125 . . . 125
SJ (a child) (Habitual Residence: Application
    to Set Aside), Re [2014] EWHC 58
    (Fam) . . . 1077

SK (an adult) (forced marriage: appropriate
    relief), Re [2004] EWHC 3202 (Fam) [2005] 3
    ALL ER 421 . . . 771
SL (Adult Patient) (Medical Treatment), Re
    [2001] Fam 15 . . . 399
Slingsby v A-G (1916) 33 TLR 120, HL . . . 260,
    263
Smalley, Re [1929] 2 Ch 112, CA . . . 966
Smallwood v United Kingdom (App No
    29779/96); (1999) 27 EHRR 155 . . . 383
Smethurst v Smethurst [1978] Fam 52 . . . 915
SMH and RAH, [1990] FCR 966n . . . 666
Smith v Bottomley [2013] EWCA Civ 953 [2014]
    1 FLR 626 . . . 848
Smith v Clerical Medical and General Life
    Assurance Society [1993] 1 FLR 47 . . . 46
Smith v Secretary of State for Work and
    Pensions [2006] UKHL 35 [2006] 1 WLR
    2024 . . . 418, 812
Smith v Smith [1990] 1 FLR 438 . . . 228
Smith v Smith [2011] EWHC 2133 (Ch) [2012]
    2 FLR 230 . . . 989
Smith v Smith (Smith Intervening) [1992]
    Fam 69, CA . . . 909, 910
Šneersone and Kampanella v Italy [2011]
    2 FLR 1232, ECtHR . . . 1037
Snoek, Re (1983) 13 Fam Law 18 . . . 985
Snow v Snow [1972] Fam 74, CA . . . 792
Societé d'Information Service Realisation v
    Ampersand Software BV, The Times, 29 July
    1993, CA . . . 1004
Sorrell v Sorrell [2005] EWHC 1717 (Fam)
    [2006] 1 FLR 497 . . . 899
South Glamorgan County Council v W and B
    [1993] 1 FLR 574 . . . 587, 591, 634, 648, 765
Southern Housing Group Ltd v Nutting
    [2004] EWHC 2982 (Ch) [2005] 1 FLR
    1066 . . . 978
Southern Housing Group Ltd v Nutting [2009]
    EWCA Civ 374 [2009] 2 FLR 767, CA . . . 978
Southwark London Borough v B [1993] 2 FLR
    559, CA . . . 401, 420, 764, 770
Southwark London Borough v B [1998] 2 FLR
    1095 . . . 606
Spellman v Spellman [1961] 2 All ER 498,
    CA . . . 98
Spence, Re (1847) 2 Ph 247 . . . 196, 743
Spence, Re [1990] Ch 652, CA . . . 56, 67, 300,
    302
Spencer v Camacho (1983) 4 FLR 662,
    CA . . . 187
Springette v Defoe [1992] 2 FLR 388,
    CA . . . 126, 128, 130, 135
S-R (Jurisdiction: Contact), Re [2008] 2 FLR
    1741 . . . 999
SRJ v DWJ (Financial Provision) [1999] 2 FLR
    176, CA . . . 877
Stack v Dowden [2007] UKHL 17 [2007]
    2 AC 432 . . . 126, 128, 129, 134, 135, 136,
    137, 138, 140, 146, 163

Staffordshire County Council v B [1998]
1 FLR 261 . . . 966

Stallion v Albert Stallion Holdings (Great
Britain) Ltd [2009] EWHC 1950 (Ch) [2010]
2 FLR 78 . . . 141

Stead v Stead [1985] FLR 16, CA . . . 991

Stephenson v Stephenson [1985] FLR 1140,
CA . . . 404

Stevens v Stevens [1979] 1 WLR 885 . . . 217

Stewart v Law Society [1987] 1 FLR 223 . . . 864

Stewart v Stewart [1973] Fam 21 . . . 196

Stodgell v Stodgell [2009] 2 FLR 244 . . . 846

Stone v Hoskins [1905] P 194 . . . 964

Stuart v Marquis of Bute (1861) 9 HL Cas
440 . . . 310

Style v Style [1954] P 209, CA . . . 845

Suggitt v Suggitt [2011] EWHC 903 (Ch) [2011] 2
FLR 875 . . . 141

Sullivan v Sullivan (1818) 2 Hag Con 238 . . . 81

Sundelind Lopez v Lopez Lizazo (Case C-68/07)
[2008] Fam 21, CJEU . . . 1000

Surrey County Council v Al Hilli and Others
[2013] EWHC 3404 (Fam) [2014] 2 FLR
217 . . . 740

Surrey County Council v Battersby [1965] 2 QB
194 . . . 295

Surrey County Council v M and others [2013]
EWHC 2400 (Fam) [2014] 1 FCR 429 . . . 568

Surtees v Kingston-upon-Thames Borough
Council [1991] 2 FLR 559, CA . . . 343

Süss v Germany [2006] 1 FLR 522,
ECtHR . . . 436

Suter v Suter and Jones [1987] Fam 111,
CA . . . 427, 874, 877, 901

Sutton v Mishcon De Reya and Gawor and
Co [2003] EWHC 3166 (Ch) [2004] 1 FLR
837 . . . 949

Sutton v Sutton [1984] Ch 184 . . . 98, 783

Sutton London Borough Council v Davis [1994]
1 FLR 737 . . . 345

SW (A Minor) (Wardship: Jurisdiction), Re
[1986] 1 FLR 24 . . . 510, 596

SY v SY (otherwise W) [1963] P 37, CA . . . 75

Sylvester v Austria (Application Nos
36812/97 and 40104/98) [2003] 2 FLR 211,
ECtHR . . . 1036

Szechter v Szechter [1971] P 286 . . . 76, 81

T v Child Support Agency [1997] 2 FLR
875 . . . 766

T v R (Abduction: Forum Conveniens) [2002] 2
FLR 544 . . . 1086, 1087

T v S (Financial Provision for Children) [1994] 2
FLR 883 . . . 795, 798, 799

T v S (Wardship) [2011] EWHC 1608
(Fam) [2012] 1 FLR 230 . . . 509, 549,
744, 752, 761

T v T (Agreement not Embodied in Consent
Order) [2013] EWHC B3 (Fam) [2013] Fam
Law 801 . . . 781, 851

T v T (Child Abduction: Non Convention
Country) [1998] 2 FLR 1110 . . . 752

T v T (Financial Provision) [1988] 1 FLR
480 . . . 913

T v T (Financial Relief: Pensions) [1998] 1 FLR
1072 . . . 843, 844, 993

T v W (Contact: Reasons for Refusing Leave)
[1996] 2 FLR 473 . . . 517

T (A Child: Art 15 BIIR), Re [2013] EWCA Civ
895 [2014] 1 FLR 749, CA . . . 1000, 1001

T (A Child: Art 15 BIIR), Re [2013] EWHC 521
(Fam) [2013] 2 FLR 909 . . . 996, 1000, 1001

T (A Child: One Parent Killed By Other Parent),
Re [2012] 1 FLR 472 . . . 494

T (A Minor) (Care Order: Conditions), Re [1994]
2 FLR 423, CA . . . 511, 628, 639

T (A Minor) (Care or Supervision Order), Re
[1994] 1 FLR 103, CA . . . 635, 636, 637

T (A Minor) (Child: Representation), Re [1994]
Fam 49, CA . . . 359, 471, 536, 755, 759, 763

T (A Minor) (Guardian ad Litem: Case Record),
Re [1994] 1 FLR 632, CA . . . 463

T (A Minor) (Parental Responsibility: Contact),
Re [1993] 2 FLR 450, CA . . . 378, 494

T (a minor) (wardship: medical treatment), Re
[1997] 1 All ER 906, CA . . . 354, 419, 770

T (A Minor) (Wardship: Representation), Re
[1994] Fam 49, CA . . . 751

T (A Minor) (Welfare Report Recommendation),
Re (1977) 1 FLR 59 . . . 465

T (Abduction: Child's Objections to Return), Re
[2000] 2 FLR 192, CA . . . 1065, 1067

T (Accommodation by Local Authority), Re
[1995] 1 FLR 159 . . . 570, 665, 669

T (Adoption: Consent), Re [1995] 2 FLR
251 . . . 713, 719

T (Adoption: Contact), Re [2010] EWCA Civ
1527 [2011] 1FLR 1805 . . . 720

T (An Infant), Re (1974) 4 Fam Law 48 . . . 465

T (Care Order), Re [2009] EWCA Civ 121 [2009]
2 FLR 574 . . . 630, 632, 635, 652

T (Change of Name), Re [1998] 2 FLR 620,
CA . . . 523, 524

T (Contact: Parental Alienation: Permission to
Appeal), Re [2002] EWCA Civ 1736 [2003] 1
FLR 531 . . . 496

T (Judicial Review: Local Authority Decisions
Concerning Child In Need), Re [2003] EWHC
2515 (Admin) [2004] 1 FLR 601 . . . 671

T (minor) (termination of contact: discharge of
order), Re [1997] 1 All ER 65, CA . . . 423

T (Minors) (Custody: Religious Upbringing), Re
(1981) 2 FLR 239 . . . 411

T (Minors) (Hague Convention: Access), Re
[1993] 2 FLR 617 . . . 1082

T (minors) (international child abduction:
access), Re [1993] 3 All ER 127n . . . 1082

T (minors) (termination of contact: discharge
of order), Re [1997] 1 All ER 65, CA . . . 420,
659, 660

T (otherwise H) (an infant), Re [1963] Ch 238 [1962] 3 All ER 970 . . . 358

T (Paternity: Ordering Blood Tests), Re [2001] 2 FLR 1190 . . . 267, 268

T (Placement Order), Re [2008] EWCA Civ 248 [2008] 1 FLR 1721 . . . 702

T (Removal From Jurisdiction), Re [1996] 2 FLR 352, CA . . . 530

T (Residential Parenting Assessment), Re [2011] EWCA Civ 812 [2012] 2 FLR 308 . . . 648

T (Wardship: Review of Police Protection Decision) (No 1), Re [2010] 1 FLR 1017 . . . 761

T and E (Proceedings: Conflicting Interests), Re [1995] 1 FLR 581 . . . 420, 430, 460

T and J (Abduction: Recognition of Foreign Judgment), Re [2006] EWHC 1472 (Fam) [2006] 2 FLR 1290 . . . 1004

TA v DPP [1997] 2 FLR 887, CA . . . 571

Talbot v Talbot (1971) 115 Sol Jo 870 . . . 222

Tanfern Limited v Cameron MacDonald and Another [2000] 1 WLR 1311 . . . 908

Tanner v Tanner [1975] 3 All ER 776, CA . . . 7, 156, 784, 948

Tattersall v Tattersall [2013] EWCA Civ 774 [2014] 1 FLR 997 . . . 905

Tavoulareas v Tavoulareas [1998] 2 FLR 418, CA . . . 845, 902

Taylor's Application, Re [1972] 2 QB 369 . . . 359

T-B (Care Proceedings: Criminal Trial), Re [1995] 2 FLR 801, CA . . . 437

TB v JB (Abduction: Grave Risk of Harm) [2001] 2 FLR 515, CA . . . 1063, 1065

TB (Care Proceedings: Criminal Trial), Re [1995] 2 FLR 801, CA . . . 642

TC and JC (Children: Relocation), Re [2013] EWHC 292 (Fam) [2013] 2 FLR 484 . . . 532

Tchenguiz-Imerman v Imerman [2013] EWHC 3627 (Fam) [2014] Fam Law 451 . . . 834, 836, 848

Tee v Tee and Hillman [1999] 2 FLR 613, CA . . . 144

Teeling v Teeling [1984] FLR 808, CA . . . 297, 298

Tejeiro Fernandez v Yeagar 121 F Supp 2d 1118 (WD Mich 2000) . . . 1083

TG (Care Proceedings: Case Management: Expert Evidence), Re [2013] EWCA Civ 5 [2013] 1 FLR 1250 . . . 14

Thain, Re [1926] Ch 676 . . . 315, 409

Thames Guaranty Ltd v Campbell [1985] QB 210, CA . . . 126

Thomas v Fuller-Brown [1988] 1 FLR 237, CA . . . 143

Thomas v Thomas [1995] 2 FLR 668, CA . . . 831, 846

Thomasset v Thomasset [1894] P 295, CA . . . 308

Thompson v Hurst [2012] EWCA Civ 1752 [2013] 1 FCR 522 . . . 137

Thompson v Thompson [1956] P 414 . . . 960

Thompson v Thompson [1986] 1 FLR 212n, CA . . . 458

Thompson v Thompson [1986] Fam 38, CA . . . 914

Thompson v Thompson [1987] Fam 89, CA . . . 399

Thompson v Thompson [1993] 2 FLR 464, CA . . . 862, 907

Thomson v Thomson [1994] 3 SCR 551, Can Sup Ct . . . 1034

Thorner v Major(s) [2009] UKHL 18 [2009] 2 FLR 405 . . . 140, 141

Thurlow v Thurlow [1976] Fam 32 . . . 217

Thyssen-Bornemisza v Thyssen-Bornemisza (No 2) [1985] FLR 1069, CA . . . 833

Tiemann BVerfGE 99, 145 (FRG) . . . 1016

Tinker v Tinker [1970] P 136, CA . . . 113

Tinsley v Milligan [1994] 1 AC 340, HL . . . 128

TL v ML and Others (Ancillary Relief: Claim against Assets of Extended Family) [2006] 1 FLR 1263 . . . 837, 846

Torok v Torok [1973] 3 All ER 101 . . . 920

Tower Hamlets London Borough Council v MK and Others [2012] EWHC 426 (Fam) [2012] 2 FLR 762 . . . 657

TP and KM v United Kingdom [2001] 2 FLR 549, ECtHR . . . 339, 448, 677, 678

Traversa v Freddi [2011] EWCA Civ 81 [2011] 2 FLR 272 . . . 922

Treharne v Secretary of State for Work and Pensions [2008] EWHC 3222 (QB) [2009] 1 FLR 853 . . . 820

Tremain's Case (1719) 1 Stra 167 . . . 348

Tribe v Tribe [1995] 2 FLR 966, CA . . . 113

Trimingham v Associated Newspapers Ltd [2012] EWHC 1296 (QB) [2012] 4 All ER 717 . . . 174

Trippas v Trippas [1973] Fam 134, CA . . . 900, 903

Trowbridge v Trowbridge [2003] 2 FLR 231 . . . 918

Trustee of the Estate of Eric Bowe (A Bankrupt) v Bowe [1998] 2 FLR 439 . . . 161

Trustor AB v Smallbone (No 2) [2001] 1 WLR 1177 . . . 847

TSB Bank plc v Marshall, Marshall and Rodgers [1998] 2 FLR 769 . . . 145

TT (Surrogacy), Re [2011] EWHC 33 (Fam) [2011] 2 FLR 392 . . . 277

Turner v Avis and Avis [2009] 1 FLR 74 . . . 161

Turner v Meyers (1808) 1 Hag Con 414 . . . 79

Turner, Re (1872) 41 LJQB 142 . . . 308

Turner, Re [1975] 1 All ER 5 . . . 161

Turnock v Turnock (1867) 36 LJP & M 85 . . . 261

TW v PL (Agreement) [2013] EWHC 3078 (Fam) [2014] 2 FLR 106 . . . 852, 853

Tweney v Tweney [1946] P 180 . . . 960

Tyler v Tyler [1989] 2 FLR 158 . . . 529

Tymoszczuk v Tymoszczuk (1964) 108 Sol Jo 676 . . . 112

Tyrer v United Kingdom (1979–80) 2 EHRR 1 . . . 345

U v W (A-G Intervening) [1998] Fam 29 . . . 253, 254

U (Application to Free for Adoption), Re [1993] 2 FLR 992, CA . . . 549

UL v BK (Freezing Orders: Safeguards: Standard Examples) [2013] EWHC 1735 (Fam) [2013] Fam Law 1379 . . . 836, 918

The 'Up Yaws' [2007] EWHC 210 (Admlty) [2007] 2 FLR 444 . . . 113

Ussher v Ussher [1912] 2 IR 445 . . . 79

V v V (Child Maintenance) [2001] 2 FLR 799 . . . 786, 822, 840, 841

V v V (Contact: Implacable Hostility) [2004] EWHC 1215 (Fam) [2004] 2 FLR 851 . . . 403, 540, 549

V v V (Prenuptial Agreement) [2011] EWHC 3230 (Fam) [2012] 1 FLR 1315 . . . 860, 861

V (A Minor) (Wardship), Re (1979) 123 Sol Jo 201 . . . 765

V (Abduction: Habitual Residence), Re [1995] 2 FLR 992 . . . 1040, 1046

V (Care or Supervision Order), Re [1996] 1 FLR 776, CA . . . 601, 634

V (Care or Supervision), Re [1996] 1 FLR 776, CA . . . 616

V (Forum Conveniens), Re [2004] EWHC 2663 (Fam) [2005] 1 FLR 718 . . . 427

V (Jurisdiction: Habitual Residence), Re [2001] 1 FLR 253 . . . 747

V (Residence: Review), Re [1995] 2 FLR 1010, CA . . . 402, 459

Valentine's Settlement, Re [1965] Ch 831 . . . 1013

Valier v Valier (1925) 133 LT 830 . . . 79

Valier v Wright & Bull Ltd (1917) 33 TLR 366 . . . 116

Van Den Boogaard v Laumen [1997] QB 759 . . . 916

Van Laethem v Brooker [2005] EWHC 1478 (Ch) [2006] 2 FLR 495 . . . 141

Vansittart v Vansittart (1858) 2 De G & J 249 . . . 682

Vaughan v Vaughan [1973] 3 All ER 449 . . . 179

Vaughan v Vaughan [2007] EWCA Civ 1085 [2008] 1 FLR 1108 . . . 887

Vaughan v Vaughan [2010] EWCA Civ 349 [2010] 2 FLR 242 . . . 915

V-B (Abduction: Custody Rights), Re [1999] 2 FLR 192, CA . . . 1050

VB v JP [2008] EWHC 112 (Fam) [2008] 1 FLR 742 . . . 872, 874

Vervaeke v Smith [1983] 1 AC 145 . . . 81

Vicary v Vicary [1992] 2 FLR 271, CA . . . 889, 897

Vigreux v Michel [2006] EWCA Civ 630 [2006] 2 FLR 1181 . . . 1075

Vince v Wyatt [2013] EWCA Civ 495 [2014] 1 FLR 246 . . . 832

VK v JV (Abduction: Consent) [2012] EWHC 403 (Fam) [2013] 2 FLR 237 . . . 1058

Vojnity v Hungary (App No 29617/07) [2013] 2 FCR 495, ECtHR . . . 411

Von Colson and Kamann v Land Nordrhein-Westfalen [1984] ECR 1891, [1986] 4 CMLR 430 . . . 1076

W v A (Minor: Surname) [1981] Fam 14, CA . . . 521, 523

W v Avon County Council (1979) 9 Fam Law 33 . . . 766

W v Ealing London Borough Council [1993] 2 FLR 788, CA . . . 377

W v Essex County Council [1999] Fam 90, CA . . . 675, 679

W v Essex County Council [2001] 2 AC 592, HL . . . 343, 675, 679

W v Federal Republic of Germany (1985) 50 D & R 219 . . . 417

W v Hertfordshire County Council [1993] 1 FLR 118 . . . 20

W v Nottingham County Council [1986] 1 FLR 565, CA . . . 667

W v O, 14 June 1995 (INCADAT cite: HC/E/AR 362) (Argentina) . . . 1035

W v Shropshire County Council [1986] 1 FLR 359, CA . . . 667

W v United Kingdom (1987) 10 EHRR 29, ECtHR . . . 655

W v W (1981) 2 FLR 291 . . . 888

W v W [2001] Fam Law 656 . . . 899

W v W (Ancillary Relief: Procedure) [2000] Fam Law 473 . . . 834

W v W (Child Abduction: Acquiescence) [1993] 2 FLR 211 . . . 1051, 1059

W v W (Child of the Family) [1984] FLR 796, CA . . . 298, 875

W v W (Joinder of Trusts of Land Act and Children Act Applications) [2003] EWCA Civ 924 [2004] 2 FLR 321 . . . 145, 146, 796

W v W (No 3) [1962] P 124 . . . 886

W v W (Nullity) [2001] FAM 110 . . . 42

W v Wakefield City Council [1995] 1 FLR 170 . . . 455, 461, 517

W, Re; Re B (Abduction: Father's Rights) [1999] Fam 1 . . . 1018

W, Re; Re B (Child Abduction: Unmarried Father) [1998] 2 FLR 146 . . . 1048

W (A Child) (Adoption Order: Leave to Oppose) (Practice Note), Re [2013] EWCA Civ 1177 [2014] 1 WLR 1993 . . . 710

W (A Child) (Illegitimate Child: Change of Surname), Re [2001] Fam 1, CA . . . 356, 501, 521, 522, 524

W (a child) (revocation of adoption: inherent jurisdiction), Re [2013] EWHC 1957 (Fam) [2013] 3 FCR 336 . . . 724, 762

W (A Minor) (Adoption by Grandparents), Re (1980) 2 FLR 161, CA . . . 708

W (A Minor) (Contact), Re [1994] 1 FLR
   843 . . . 20
W (A Minor) (Contact), Re [1994] 2 FLR 441,
   CA . . . 441
W (A Minor) (Custody), Re (1983) 4 FLR 492,
   CA . . . 404, 457, 459
W (a minor) (HIV test), Re [1995] 2 FCR
   184 . . . 408
W (a minor) (medical treatment: court's
   jurisdiction), Re [1993] Fam 64 [1992] 4 All
   ER 627, CA . . . 322, 323, 324, 326, 351, 352,
   353, 392, 401, 403, 419, 648, 741, 742, 744, 763,
   764, 765, 770
W (A Minor) (Residence Order), Re [1992] 2 FLR
   332, CA . . . 373, 404
W (A Minor) (Residence Order), Re [1993] 2 FLR
   625, CA . . . 402, 487
W (A Minor) (Secure Accommodation Order),
   Re [1993] 1 FLR 692 . . . 463, 576, 578
W (A Minor) (Wardship: Jurisdiction), Re [1985]
   AC 791, HL . . . 667
W (Abduction: Acquiescence: Children's
   Objections), Re [201] EWHC 332 (Fam) [2010]
   2 FLR 1150 . . . 1067
W (Abduction: Appeal) (Minors), Re [2010]
   EWCA 520 [2010] 2 FLR 1165 . . . 1067
W (Abduction: Domestic Violence), Re [2004]
   EWCA Civ 1366 [2005] 1 FLR 727 . . . 1065
W (Abduction: Domestic Violence), Re [2004]
   EWHC 1247 (Fam) [2004] 2 FLR 499 . . . 1065
W (Abduction: Procedure), Re [1995] 1 FLR
   878 . . . 1057
W (Adoption: Homosexual Partner), Re [1997]
   2 FLR 406 . . . 706
W (An Infant), Re [1971] AC 682 . . . 714
W (application for leave: whether necessary),
   Re [1996] 3 FCR 337n . . . 510, 515
W (Arrangements to Place for Adoption),
   Re [1995] 1 FLR 163 . . . 389
W (Change of Name), Re [2013] EWCA Civ 1488
   [2014] Fam Law 147 . . . 522
W (Contact: Application by Grandparent),
   Re [1997] 1 FLR 793 . . . 517
W (Contact: Joining Child As Party), Re
   [2001] EWCA Civ 1830 [2003] 1 FLR
   681 . . . 468, 490
W (Contact Application: Procedure), Re [2000]
   1 FLR 263 . . . 517, 518
W (Cross-Examination), Re [2010] EWCA Civ
   1449 [2011] 1 FLR 1979 . . . 463
W (Direct Contact) [2012] EWCA Civ 999 [2013]
   1 FLR 494 . . . 377, 493
W (Discharge of Party to Proceedings), Re
   [1997] 1 FLR 128 . . . 420, 423
W (Exclusion: Statement of Evidence), Re [2000]
   2 FLR 666 . . . 587, 649
W (Family Proceedings: Applications), Re [2011]
   EWHC 76 (Fam) [2011] 1 FLR 2163 . . . 494
W (Leave To Remove), Re [2008] EWCA Civ 538
   [2008] 2 FLR 1170 . . . 466

W (Minors), Re (1980) 10 Fam Law 120 . . . 465
W (minors) (removal from jurisdiction), Re
   [1994] 1 FCR 842 . . . 371
W (minors) (residence order), Re [1992] 2 FCR
   461, CA . . . 402
W (minors) (residence order), Re [1998] 1 FCR
   75, CA . . . 601
W (Minors) (Surrogacy), Re [1991] 1 FLR
   385 . . . 246, 247, 283
W (Minors) (Wardship: Contempt), Re [1989]
   1 FLR 246 . . . 745
W (Minors) (Wardship: Evidence), Re [1990]
   1 FLR 203, CA . . . 746
W (otherwise K) v W [1967] 3 All ER 178n . . . 75
W (Parental Responsibility
   Order: Inter-Relationship with Direct
   Contact), Re [2013] EWCA Civ 335 [2013]
   2 FLR 1337 . . . 378, 492
W (Relocation: Removal Outside Jurisdiction),
   Re [2011] EWCA Civ 345 . . . 527
W (Residence), Re [1999] 2 FLR 390, CA . . . 459
W (Residence Order), Re [1999] 1 FLR
   869, CA . . . 412
W (RJ) v W(SJ) [1972] Fam 152 . . . 298
W (Section 34(2) Orders), Re [2000] 1 FLR 502,
   CA . . . 658, 660
W (Shared Residence Order), Re [2009] EWCA
   Civ 592 [2009] 2 FLR 436 . . . 488
W (Staying Contact), Re [1998] 2 FLR 450,
   CA . . . 491
W (Wardship: Discharge: Publicity), Re [1995] 2
   FLR 466, CA . . . 363, 502, 751, 761
W (Welfare Reports), Re [1995] 2 FLR 142,
   CA . . . 456
W and B, Re; Re W (Care Plan), Re [2001]
   EWCA Civ 757 [2001] 2 FLR 582 . . . 24, 25,
   640, 645
W and Others v Legal Services Commission
   [2000] 2 FLR 821 . . . 462
W and W v H (Child Abduction: Surrogacy)
   (No 2) [2002] 2 FLR 252 . . . 772
W and X (Wardship: Relatives Rejected As
   Foster Carers), Re [2003] EWHC 2206 (Fam)
   [2004] 1 FLR 415 . . . 512, 631, 757, 764, 766
Wachtel v Wachtel [1973] Fam 72, CA . . . 841,
   900, 904
Wachtel v Wachtel (No 1) Times, 1 August
   1972 . . . 216
Wagstaff v Wagstaff [1992] 1 All ER 275,
   CA . . . 885
Wagstaff, Re [1908] 1 Ch 162, CA . . . 966
Wakefield v Mackay (1807) 1 Hag
   Con 394 . . . 79
Wakefield Metropolitan District Council
   v T [2008] EWCA Civ 199 [2008] 1 FLR
   1569 . . . 633
Wales v Wadham [1977] 2 All ER 125 . . . 850
Walker v Hall [1984] FLR 126 . . . 128
Walker v Walker and Harrison [1981] NZ Recent
   Law 257 . . . 398

Wallbank v Price [2007] EWHC 3001 (Ch) [2008] 2 FLR 501 . . . 114

Walrond v Walrond (1858) John 18 . . . 682

Walsall Metropolitan Borough Council v K [2013] EWHC 3192 (Fam) [2014] 2 FLR 227 . . . 1002

Walsh v Singh [2009] EWHC 3219 (Ch) [2010] 1 FLR 1658 . . . 134

Ward v Laverty [1925] AC 101 . . . 313, 314

Warr v Warr [1975] Fam 25 . . . 218

Warren v CARE and HFEA [2014] EWHC 602 (Fam) [2014] Fam Law 803 . . . 249

Watkins, Re [1953] 2 All ER 1113 . . . 960

Watkinson v Legal Aid Board [1991] 2 All ER 953, CA . . . 864

Watson v Nikolaisen [1955] 2 QB 286 . . . 566

Watson v Watson [1954] P 48 . . . 262

Watson v Willmot [1991] 1 QB 140 . . . 726

Watson (Deceased), Re [1999] 1 FLR 878 . . . 942, 978, 979

Watts v Waller [1973] QB 153, CA . . . 155

Wayling v Jones [1995] 2 FLR 1029, CA . . . 131, 142

W-B (Family Proceedings: Appropriate Jurisdiction Within UK), Re [2012] EWCA Civ 592 [2013] 1 FLR 677 . . . 1022

WB (Residence Orders), Re [1995] 2 FLR 1023 . . . 389, 488

Webb v Webb [1986] 1 FLR 462, CA . . . 458

Webster v Norfolk County Council and the Children (By Their Children's Guardian) [2009] EWCA Civ 59 [2009] 1 FLR 1378 . . . 724

Webster v Webster [2008] EWHC 31 (Ch) [2009] 1 FLR 1240 . . . 987

Wellesley v Duke of Beaufort (1827) 2 Russ 1 . . . 311

Wells v Wells [1992] 2 FLR 66, CA (decided in 1980) . . . 910

Wermuth v Wermuth (No 2) [2002] EWCA Civ 50 [2003] 1 WLR 942 . . . 837

West v West [1978] Fam 1, CA . . . 899

West Glamorgan County Council v P [1992] 2 FLR 369 . . . 657

Westbury v Sampson [2001] EWCA Civ 407 [2002] 1 FLR 166 . . . 913

Westminster City Council v C and Others [2008] EWCA Civ 198 [2009] Fam 11 . . . 41, 63, 80

WF v FJ, BF and RF (Abduction: Child's Objections) [2010] EWHC 2909 (Fam) [2011] 1 FLR 1153 . . . 1062, 1067, 1068, 1074

Whaley v Whaley [2011] EWCA Civ 617 [2012] 1 FLR 735 . . . 846, 888

Whiston v Whiston [1995] Fam 198, CA . . . 66, 67, 71, 831

Whitby, Re [1944] Ch 210, CA . . . 969

White v White [1948] P 330 . . . 75

White v White [2001] 1 AC 596 . . . 832, 853, 859, 869–70, 873, 879, 881, 882, 884, 890, 891, 892, 896, 897, 898, 905, 911, 926, 932, 986, 991

White v Withers LLP and Dearle [2009] EWCA Civ 1122 [2010] 1 FLR 859 . . . 836

Whiting v Whiting [1988] 2 All ER 275, CA . . . 877

Whittaker, Re (1882) 21 Ch D 657 . . . 113

Whyte-Smith v Whyte-Smith (1974) 5 Fam Law 20 . . . 892

Wickler v Wickler [1998] 2 FLR 326 . . . 228

Wicks v Wicks [1998] 1 FLR 470, CA . . . 837

Widdowson v Widdowson (1982) 4 FLR 121 . . . 192

Wiggins v United Kingdom (1978) 13 DR 40 . . . 122

Wilde v Wilde [1988] 2 FLR 83, CA . . . 196

Wilkins v Wilkins [1969] 2 All ER 463 . . . 915

Wilkinson v Downton [1897] 2 QB 57 . . . 195

Wilkinson v Kitzinger (No 2) [2006] EWHC 2022 (Fam) [2007] 1 FLR 295 . . . 32, 36, 87

Wilkinson v Payne (1791) 4 Term Rep 468 . . . 57

Williams v Doulton [1948] 1 All ER 603 . . . 360

Williams v Johns [1988] 2 FLR 475 . . . 985, 986

Williams v Lindley [2005] EWCA Civ 103 [2005] 2 FLR 710 . . . 910

Williams v Thompson Leatherdale and Francis [2008] EWHC 2574 (QB) [2009] 2 FLR 730 . . . 911

Williams v Williams [1976] Ch 278 [1977] 1 All ER 28, CA . . . 108, 146

Williams v Williams [1985] FLR 509, CA . . . 494

Williams and Glyn's Bank Ltd v Boland [1981] AC 487, HL . . . 148, 149, 150

Wilson v First County Trust Ltd (No 2) [2003] UKHL 40 [2004] 1 AC 816 . . . 24

Windeler v Whitehall [1990] 2 FLR 505 . . . 113

Windle, Re [1975] 3 All ER 987 . . . 780

Wing v Taylor (1861) 2 Sw & Tr 278 . . . 72

Winnipeg Child and Family Services (Northwest Area) v G (1997) 152 DLR (4th) 193, Can Sup Ct . . . 746

Witkowska v Kaminski [2006] EWHC 1940 (Ch) [2006] 3 FCR 250 . . . 982

WM (Adoption: Non-Patrial), Re [1997] 1 FLR 132 . . . 706, 729, 1014

Woodley v Woodley [1992] 2 FLR 417, CA . . . 917, 919

Woodley v Woodley (No 2) [1993] 2 FLR 477, CA . . . 917

Woolf v Pemberton (1877) 6 Ch D 19 . . . 359

Wright v Wright (1980) 2 FLR 276, CA . . . 494

Wroth v Tyler [1974] Ch 30 . . . 154, 156

WSCC v M, F, W, X Y and Z [2010] EWHC 1914 (Fam) [2011] 1 FLR 188 . . . 401, 420

Wyatt v Portsmouth Hospital NHS Trust [2005] EWCA Civ 1181 [2005] 1 WLR 399 . . . 408

Wynne v Wynne and Jeffers [1980] 3 All ER 659, CA . . . 888

X v Bedfordshire County Council [1995] 2 AC 633, HL . . . 665

X v Belgium and Netherlands (1975) D & R 75 . . . 684

X v Latvia [2012] 1 FLR 860 . . . 1037
X v Latvia [2014] 1 FLR 1135 . . . 1037, 1049
X v United Kingdom (1981) 4 EHRR 181 . . . 572
X v X (Crown Prosecution Service
    Intervening) [2005] EWHC 296 (Fam)
    [2005] 2 FLR 487 . . . 846
X v Y and Z Police Force, A, B and C (By Their
    Children's Guardian) [2012] EWHC 2838
    (Fam) [2013] 1 FLR 1277 . . . 1064
X, Re [1899] 1 Ch 526 . . . 292
X (A Minor) (Adoption Details: Disclosure), Re
    [1994] Fam 174 . . . 762
X (A Minor) (Wardship: Jurisdiction), Re [1975]
    Fam 47, CA . . . 422, 765, 766
X (Care: Notice of Proceedings), Re [1996] 1 FLR
    186 . . . 423
X (Children) (Parental Order: Surrogacy), Re
    [2008] EWHC 3030 (Fam) [2009] 2 WLR
    1274 . . . 254, 278, 279
X (Emergency Protection Orders), Re [2006]
    EWHC 510 (Fam) [2006] 2 FLR 701 . . . 583,
    585, 586, 590
X (Minors) v Bedfordshire County Council
    [1995] 2 AC 633, HL . . . 343, 673–4, 677
X (Minors) (Care Proceedings: Parental
    Responsibility), Re [2000] Fam 156 . . . 372
X (Parental Responsibility Agreement: Children
    in Care), Re [2000] 1 FLR 517 . . . 638
X Council v B (Emergency Protection
    Orders) [2004] EWHC 2015 (Fam) [2005]
    1 FLR 341 . . . 461, 583, 585, 586, 588,
    590, 592, 596
X County Council v A [1985] 1 All ER 53 . . . 767
X and Y (Leave To Remove From
    Jurisdiction: No Order Principle), Re [2001] 2
    FLR 118 . . . 440
X and Y (Parental Order: Retrospective
    Authorisation of Payments), Re [2011] EWHC
    3147 (Fam) [2012] 1 FLR 1347 . . . 279
X, Y and Z v United Kingdom [1997] 2 FLR 892
    (1997) 24 EHRR 143 . . . 2, 42
X's Settlement, Re [1945] Ch 44 . . . 743
Xydhias v Xydhias [1999] 1 FLR 683, CA . . . 781,
    852, 854

Y v Y (child: surname) [1973] Fam 147 [1973] 2
    All ER 574 . . . 358
Y v Y (Financial Orders: Inherited Wealth)
    [2012] EWHC 2063 (Fam) [2013] 2 FLR
    924 . . . 884
Y (a minor) (ex parte interim orders), Re [1993] 2
    FCR 422 . . . 489
Y (Abduction: Undertakings Given for Return
    of Child), Re [2013] EWCA Civ 129 [2013] 2
    FLR 649 . . . 1021, 1066, 1092
Y (Leave To Remove From Jurisdiction), Re
    [2004] 2 FLR 330 . . . 531, 532
Y (Minors) (Adoption: Jurisdiction), Re [1985]
    Fam 136 . . . 719
Yates v Yates [2012] EWCA Civ 532 [2013] 2 FLR
    1070 . . . 878, 889, 914
Yaxley v Gotts [2000] Ch 162 . . . 140

YC v United Kingdom [2012] 2 FLR 332 . . . 686,
    695
Yemshaw v Hounslow London Borough Council
    [2011] UKSC 3 [2011] 1 WLR 433 . . . 206
Young v Young [1962] P 27, CA . . . 848
Young v Young [1998] 2 FLR 1131, CA . . . 902
Young v Young [2012] EWHC 138 (Fam) [2012]
    2 FLR 470 . . . 918
Young v Young [2013] EWHC 3637 (Fam) [2014]
    Fam Law 291 . . . 834, 838, 849
Yousef v Netherlands (2003) 36 EHRR 20 [2003]
    1 FLR 210 . . . 416

Z v A (Financial Remedies: Overseas Divorce)
    [2012] EWHC 467 (Fam) [2012] 2 FLR
    667 . . . 922
Z v A (Financial Remedy after Overseas Divorce)
    [2012] EWHC 1434 (Fam) [2013] Fam Law
    393 . . . 925
Z v UK [2001] 2 FLR 612 . . . 327, 677, 678
Z v Z [1992] 2 FLR 291 . . . 837
Z v Z (No 2) (Financial Remedy: Marriage
    Contract) [2011] EWHC 2878 (Fam) [2012] 1
    FLR 1100 . . . 860, 861
Z v Z (Removal of Child: Consent) [2012]
    EWHC 3954 (Fam) [2013] 2 FLR 500 . . . 1031
Z (A Child), Re [2006] EWCA Civ 1219 . . . 1031
Z (A Minor) (Identification: Restrictions on
    Publication), Re [1997] Fam 1, CA . . . 347,
    362, 363, 424, 425, 502, 742, 765, 767, 768
Z (Abduction), Re [2008] EWHC 3473 (Fam)
    [2009] 2 FLR 298 . . . 1058
Z (Minors) (Child Abuse: Evidence), Re [1989] 2
    FLR 3 . . . 751
Z and B v C (Parental Order: Domicile) [2011]
    EWHC 3181 (Fam) [2012] 2 FLR 797 . . . 278
Z and others v United Kingdom [2001] 2 FLR
    612, ECtHR . . . 666
Zaffino v Zaffino (Abduction: Child'sView)
    [2005] EWCA 1012 [2006] 1 FLR 410 . . . 1071
Zamet v Hyman [1961] 3 All ER 933, CA . . . 114
Zennel v Haddow 1993 SLT 975 . . . 1057
ZH (Tanzania) v Secretary of State for the Home
    Department [2011] UKSC 4 [2011] 2 AC
    166 . . . 418, 419, 420, 423, 428, 449, 1035
Znameskaya v Russia (2007) 44 EHRR
    15 . . . 270
Zoumbas v Secretary of State for the Home
    Department [2014] UKSC 74 [2014] 1 FCR
    141 . . . 418
Zuk v Zuk [2012] EWCA Civ 1871 [2013] 2 FLR
    1466 . . . 917

1

INTRODUCTION

A. THE NATURE AND SCOPE OF FAMILY LAW

1. THE MEANING OF 'FAMILY'

The word 'family' is one which it is difficult, if not impossible to define.[1] In one sense it can mean all persons related by blood or marriage (including, since 2014, same sex marriage) or, since 2005, civil partners;[2] in another it may include all the members of a household, including parents and children with perhaps other relations, lodgers and even servants. But these definitions are unsatisfactory for our purposes. The fact that two persons can claim descent from a common ancestor may not, of itself, affect their legal relations at all. Similarly, the legal relationship between the head of a household and lodgers and servants is contractual and therefore lies outside the scope of this book. Moreover, intimate or caring relationships may be regarded as constituting a 'family' even though there are no blood or status ties between the parties.

Some elucidation of the concept of 'family', at least within European society, can be gleaned from the jurisprudence derived from the European Convention on Human Rights. Article 8(1) of the Convention guarantees to everyone 'the right to respect for his private and family life, his home and his correspondence' and Art 12 provides that 'Men and women of marriageable age have the right to marry and to found a family . . .'. The position is slightly complicated because Art 8 refers to 'family life' rather than 'the family' per se, but case law of the European Commission and European Court of Human Rights establishes that, for the purposes of the Convention, the relationship between spouses will always create a 'family life',[3] although it is only recently that cohabitation between unmarried partners has been held to do so.[4] It is clear that the relationship between a mother and her child will always be regarded under the Convention as constituting a 'family' even if the child is born outside wedlock.[5] However, the Court has distinguished between married and unmarried fathers, and between unmarried mothers and unmarried fathers, holding that family life arises between a married father and his child automatically,[6] but that unmarried fathers must show

---

[1] See further A Diduck *Law's Families* (2003); B Hale, D Pearl, E Cooke and D Monk *The Family, Law and Society: Cases and Materials* (2008, 6th edn) ch 1; A Diduck and F Kaganas *Family Law, Gender and the State: Text Cases and Materials* (2012, 3rd edn) ch 1.

[2] The Marriage (Same Sex Couples) Act 2013. The Civil Partnership Act 2004, creates a legal status broadly equivalent to marriage, for same sex partners; see further Ch 2. Unless otherwise stated, references to spouses or marriage include civil partners and civil partnership.

[3] *Berrehab v Netherlands* (1988) 11 EHRR 322.

[4] *Schalk and Kopf v Austria* [2011] 2 FCR 650: in fact a case concerning a same sex couple.

[5] *Marckx v Belgium* (1979) 2 EHRR 330 on which see W Pintens and J Scherpe 'The *Marckx* case: A "whole code of family law"?' in S Gilmore, J Herring and R Probert (eds) *Landmark Cases in Family Law* (2011).

[6] *Johnston v Ireland* (1986) 9 EHRR 203.

more than the blood tie to establish a family life with their child.[7] Cohabitation outside marriage with the mother, even if it terminates before the child is born, may suffice[8] and the father need not cohabit with the mother at all, provided that he can demonstrate a sufficient interest in and commitment to the child.[9] Once such a relationship is shown, it will not matter that the parent is homosexual or trans-gender.[10] Moreover, the Court has held that states may not use sexual orientation alone as a basis for restricting who may adopt.[11] Nonetheless, the Court still lags behind many European states, including the United Kingdom, in its treatment of relationships outside marriage and its concept of the family, although, as we will see, the incorporation of the European Convention on Human Rights into domestic law has done much to spur both judicial and legislative reform in widening legal recognition of what constitutes a family.

For our purposes, we regard the family as a basic social unit constituted by at least two people, whose relationship may fall into one of three categories. Most families will consist of three or more members falling into at least two different categories.

First, the relationship may be that of two persons in a marital relationship (including civil partners), or who are living together in a manner similar to spouses.[12] 'In 2012, there were 5.9 million people cohabiting in the United Kingdom, double the 1996 figure. Over the same period, the percentage of people aged 16 or over who were cohabiting increased from 6.5% to 11.7%.'[13] This growth has forced the law to adapt to this change in social behaviour.[14] If an extra-marital union—between either heterosexual or same sex partners—comes to an end by separation or death, the parties and their children may need the same protection as spouses and their children, and consequently the legal position of cohabitants has to a certain extent been assimilated to that of married persons. Secondly, a family may be constituted by a parent living with one or more children. Thirdly, brothers and sisters or other persons related by blood or marriage may be regarded as forming a family. The relationship, however, has only very limited effects on their legal position, and these arise principally on the death of another member of the family.[15]

Whilst the relationship between parents and their children forms much of the content of family law, as we will see, it is conceived as applying usually only whilst the child is a minor, and it is a relationship in which obligations are imposed only upon the parents towards their child, not vice versa. The proportion of the population which is surviving into old—and extreme—old age, is growing rapidly, with the number of people aged 65 or over in the United Kingdom increasing by 20% between 1985 and 2010, to 10.3 million, representing 17% of the total population and expected to account for nearly a quarter by 2035. Moreover, the number of people aged 85 and over doubled over the same period, to 1.4 million and is projected to constitute 5% of the total population by 2035.[16] There has been no legal duty cast upon children to support, or indeed care for in any way, their parents since the abolition of the Poor Law in the 1940s, yet many elderly people lack adequate pension provision, and may also lack physical care and emotional support. The question of whether what is recognised as a *moral* obligation of care felt by adult children

---

[7] *G v Netherlands* (1993) 16 EHRR CD38.   [8] *Keegan v Ireland* (1994) 18 EHRR 342.
[9] *Lebbink v Netherlands* [2004] 2 FLR 463 (father regularly visited the child and baby-sat).
[10] *Salgueiro da Silva Mouta v Portugal* [2001] 1 FCR 653; *X, Y and Z v United Kingdom* (1997) 24 EHRR 143.   [11] *EB v France* [2008] 1 FLR 850.
[12] Whether the basic conjugal model should continue to shape our definition of the family, and its legal recognition, is a matter open to debate and is discussed later.
[13] ONS *Short Report: Cohabitation in the UK, 2012* (2012) p 1.   [14] See further Ch 24.
[15] See Ch 25.
[16] ONS, http://www.statistics.gov.uk/hub/population/ageing/older-people [online] accessed 16 August 2013.

towards their parents should be once again translated into a legal responsibility to provide financial and caring support to them is one which is sometimes raised,[17] but almost never answered, in debates on the family, with the consequence that this book, which is concerned with family policy and regulation as it is currently elaborated in the law, does not discuss it in any detail either.[18]

2. THE FUNCTIONS OF FAMILY LAW

In this context the law has three distinct but related functions.

(a) Definition and alteration of status

Historically this was the law's main role because it was concerned primarily with the rights which one member of the family could claim over another or over the latter's property. In the case of a man and woman living together, these arose only if they were married, and their legal relationship still depends largely on their status. Similarly, there were virtually no rights and duties with respect to children unless they were legitimate (which in turn depended on whether their parents were married). Questions of status are also important in public law, for on these may turn such matters as a person's nationality and right to live in the United Kingdom and claims to contributory social security benefits.

Akin to the courts' power to define status is their power to alter it. Among the most important aspects of this is their jurisdiction to grant divorces and make adoption orders, because a marriage can be dissolved and a child can be legally adopted only by judicial process.

It might have been argued at one time that the law was moving away from a focus on determining people's rights by virtue of their status, and that greater freedom was being given to them to shape and agree the legal consequences of their personal relationships for themselves.[19] We will see below that this is still an important trend in how family law is developing. But the extension of marriage to same sex couples[20] following swiftly on the introduction of a new legal status of 'civil partnership' for such couples,[21] the automatic acquisition of parental responsibility by unmarried fathers so long as they are named on the child's birth certificate[22] and the fact that extra-marital cohabitation already attracts certain legal consequences suggests that relationship status is still an important source of legal rights.

(b) Normative role

Linked to status is the question of normativity. The types of relationship which attract legal recognition are not selected at random but as a policy choice.[23] The grant of rights and duties marks out both the nature and the functions of the relationship which the state approves

---

[17] See J Millar and A Warman, *Family Obligations in Europe* (1996); S Frank Edelstone 'Filial Responsibility: Can the Legal Duty to Support Our Parents Be Effectively Enforced?' (2002) 36(3) *Family Law Quarterly* 501.

[18] For full consideration of the issues raised, see J Herring *Older People in Law and Society* (2009).

[19] As Sir Henry Maine famously put it: 'the movement of the progressive societies has hitherto been a movement from Status to Contract', *Ancient Law* (1931), at 141.

[20] Marriage (Same Sex Couples) Act 2013.   [21] Civil Partnership Act 2004.

[22] Children Act 1989 s 4(1)(a), discussed in Ch 11, Acquisition of parental responsibility by unmarried fathers, p 371.

[23] See A Diduck 'Shifting Familiarity' (2005) *Current Legal Problems* 235; L Glennon 'Displacing the "conjugal family" in legal policy—a progressive move?' [2005] CFLQ 141 and discussion in Ch 24.

and promotes. The legal recognition of marriage, and the lack of equivalent recognition for cohabitation, for example, should be seen as a deliberate decision to encourage intimate relationships to be fitted within the framework of marriage (or civil partnership) law. The extension of marriage to same sex couples represents a decision to indicate that their relationships are also approved and regarded as acceptable by the state. Usually, legal recognition will follow social acceptance, but in the case of same sex relationships, part of the impetus for reform has been based on the view that human rights law requires an end to the discrimination previously suffered by gay and lesbian people. Article 14 of the European Convention on Human Rights, although not a free-standing right, does require that the enjoyment of the rights and freedoms set out in the Convention are secured 'without discrimination on any ground such as sex, race' etc. The European Court of Human Rights has held that discrimination based on sexual orientation may be a breach of this Article taken with Art 8.[24]

(c) Remedial role

The courts may be required to resolve disputes between members of the family, to provide protection for weaker members, and to manage the consequences of the termination of the family unit, for example, on a divorce.

The protection of the weaker members of the family has two aspects: physical and economic. The former usually raises the more urgent problems and the courts can give protection to the victims of domestic violence by making non-molestation orders and orders excluding a party from the family home. As a last resort they may order a child to be taken into the care of a local authority. The economic protection of a member of the family usually assumes importance when the family unit ceases to exist, and the courts have extensive powers to make orders for financial provision on divorce.

Even though the termination of the family unit may leave the members adequately provided for, justice may nonetheless require the redistribution of their capital assets, and the courts have power to make orders for this purpose on the breakdown of a marriage and, to a more limited extent, on the death of a member of the family. Similarly, if a person dies intestate, his property will have to be distributed, and the law of intestate succession is essentially a part of family law because it provides for the division of a deceased person's property amongst members of his family.

During the past century English family law has shown a steady movement away from the former of these functions to the latter, and today its remedial role is of much greater importance than that of conferring rights. The result has been to give individual judges much greater discretion, for while Parliament and appellate courts can lay down general principles for, say, the resolution of disputes relating to children or the award of financial relief, their application will vary enormously according to the circumstances of each family.

B. TRENDS IN FAMILY LAW

1. EQUALISATION OF LEGAL POSITION OF MEN AND WOMEN

As family law developed during the nineteenth and especially the twentieth century, certain major trends became apparent.[25] The first of these was an equalisation in the

---

[24] *Salgueiro da Silva Mouta v Portugal* [2001] 1 FCR 653.
[25] See generally G Douglas and N Lowe 'The Continuing Evolution of Family Law' in G Douglas and N Lowe (eds) *The Continuing Evolution of Family Law* (2009) ch 1.

positions of men and women. The abolition of the position of the husband as possessor of his wife (and owner of her property) was addressed in the nineteenth century as a major element in the move to women's emancipation which culminated in their obtaining the franchise.[26] (Although the last vestige of this common law favouring of men was removed only in 1991 by the House of Lords when they held that a husband may be convicted for rape of his wife.)[27] Accompanying the recognition of the position of the woman as *wife* was a corresponding move to give the woman as *mother* the same rights over her legitimate[28] children as the father had traditionally possessed. One of the most significant steps in this development was the enactment of s 1 of the Guardianship of Infants Act 1925, which provided that in proceedings before a court, neither the father nor the mother should be regarded as having a claim superior to the other in respect of the custody or upbringing of the child.[29] But again, the process was a lengthy one; it was not until 1973 that parents were given equal rights to determine their children's upbringing, by s 1 of the Guardianship Act 1973; and only under the Children Act 1989 was the rule abolished that a father is sole guardian of his legitimate children during his lifetime.

This recognition of equality has had further consequences for women which they may not have found so palatable. There has been an increasing view that women, who, after all, now expect to work in paid employment throughout most of their lives, rather than remain at home as housewives and child-carers, should be financially independent of their former partners. A 'clean break' between ex-spouses, whereby the man is no longer expected to support his former wife, has become the favoured disposition of finance and property on a divorce, justified further by a view that those who no longer share married status with each other should not be 'shackled' together by economic bonds either.[30]

2. SHIFT IN EMPHASIS FROM PAST FAULT TO FUTURE NEEDS

Another crucial trend has been the extent to which the law has withdrawn from seeking to pass judgment on the misconduct of family members towards each other, as a justification for making an order to settle their future legal positions and relationships.[31] Instead, increasing attention has been focused upon the likely needs of the parties in the aftermath of the breakdown of their relationship. This trend has been fostered by recognition of the difficulty for a court in ascribing blame when it is dependent upon the evidence which a party chooses to place before it. The whole story may never be brought out which would, in theory at least, enable the court to form a valid judgment as to fault. This has been particularly true of divorces, where virtually all suits are undefended. Facts may be

---

[26] L Holcombe *Wives and Property* (1983); D Stetson *A Woman's Issue: the Politics of Family Law Reform in England* (1982).

[27] *R v R* [1992] 1 AC 599, HL on which see J Herring 'No More Having and Holding: The Abolition of the Marital Rape Exemption' in S Gilmore, J Herring and R Probert (eds) *Landmark Cases in Family Law* (2011).

[28] The mother of a child born outside marriage was, and remains, solely entitled automatically to exercise parental responsibility for that child; the father may now acquire shared parental responsibility with her under s 4 of the Children Act 1989.

[29] See S Cretney '"What Will the Women Want Next?" The Struggle for Power Within the Family 1925–1975' (1996) 112 LQR 110, for a description of the political lobbying and history which lay behind its enactment.

[30] *Minton v Minton* [1979] AC 593, HL; *Ashley v Blackman* [1988] Fam 85; *C v C (Financial Provision: Personal Damages)* [1995] 2 FLR 171.

[31] K O'Donovan 'Love's Law: Moral Reasoning in Family Law' in D Morgan and G Douglas (eds) *Constituting Families: A Study in Governance* (1994) p 40.

highlighted in a party's case in order to fit the constraints of the law, but may bear little relation to their true significance in leading to the breakdown as far as the parties themselves are concerned.[32]

The futility of ascribing blame has also been recognised. A decision that a spouse is responsible for the failure of the marriage does not contribute positively to arriving at a settlement of the financial position where, for example, the 'guilty' spouse is going to continue to care for the couple's children, and hence will need to remain in the former matrimonial home, with the former husband correspondingly being kept out of his share of this capital asset.

3. SHIFT OF ATTENTION FROM ADULTS TO CHILDREN

There has been a significant shift in the attention of law makers and the courts away from the adults to the children in the family. This seems to be a counterpart to the other trends we have discussed. Adults are presumed capable of looking after themselves and therefore not to require the same degree of protection from the law and the courts that those who are vulnerable may need. The most vulnerable family members are, of course, the children. As divorce has become more common, the economic, psychological, health and educational consequences of the marriage break-up for the children have been more closely researched and the findings, although not clear-cut, have been sufficiently worrying to prompt greater concern that the law and legal processes at least should not add to any deficit which might be suffered.[33] Changes in the thinking about how children develop psychologically have also fed through into legal proceedings, so that adoption and child care proceedings, as well as disputes between parents when their relationship breaks up, have become informed and infused by the desire to ensure that legal outcomes are the best available for the child. At the same time, a growing willingness to recognise children's developing right to autonomy has resulted in a concern to provide mechanisms to enable them to express their wishes and feelings about what should happen to them, both within legal proceedings and more generally when decisions about their future are being taken. The desire to place children at the centre of legal attention has not been confined to this country, but is a worldwide phenomenon, culminating in the drafting and opening for signature of the United Nations Convention on the Rights of the Child in 1989.[34]

4. GROWING RECOGNITION OF COHABITATION OUTSIDE MARRIAGE

The large increase in the number of couples living together outside marriage has already been noted. There are various reasons for this development. Some couples cannot marry, because one of them is in the process of obtaining a divorce (or, occasionally, is unable to do so). Some wish to avoid the financial responsibilities attached to marriage. Others wish to postpone the assumption of the legal incidents of marriage and regard cohabitation as a form of trial marriage or merely 'a pre-marital experience'. Some drift into cohabitation

---

[32] L Stone has shown how, even in the days of Parliamentary divorce, evidence was concocted and colluded in: see *Road to Divorce: England 1530–1987* (1990) Part X.

[33] See eg B Rodgers and J Pryor *Divorce and Separation: The Outcomes for Children* (1998); R Emery 'Inter-parental conflict and the children of discord and divorce' (1982) 92 *Psychological Bulletin* 310; K Rhoades 'Children's responses to interparental conflict: A meta-analysis of their associations with child adjustment' (2008) 79 *Child Development* 1942.   [34] See p 22 and Ch 13.

as their relationship becomes more intimate. Some regard marriage as irrelevant and may cohabit because they reject 'the traditional marriage contract and the assumption of the roles which necessarily seem to go with it'.[35]

Until comparatively recently, cohabitation outside marriage gave the parties no rights over and above those possessed by, say, a brother and sister living together. Indeed, they might have found themselves, legally speaking, in a worse position because their relationship, involving, as it did, 'fornication',[36] might deprive them of rights which they might otherwise have. If, for example, a woman contributed a sum towards the purchase of a house in which she was to live with her brother in consideration of his undertaking to have it conveyed into their joint names, she could enforce the contract; if, however, she entered into a similar agreement with a man with whom she was going to cohabit, the illicit purpose of the transaction probably made it unenforceable. Extra-marital sexual intercourse was regarded as immoral, and consequently any agreement entered into with this object in view was liable to be struck down as contrary to public policy. For example, in *Diwell v Farnes*[37] the Court of Appeal expressed the view that any attempt by a woman to claim an interest in a house bought by the man with whom she had been living by spelling out an agreement that they should buy it as a joint venture was doomed to failure, because such a contract would be unenforceable as founded on an immoral consideration.

A complete change in the courts' attitude came a decade or so later. In 1972 the Court of Appeal held that the property rights of cohabitants who intended to marry as soon as they were free to do so should be determined in the same way as the rights of spouses.[38] Three years later they held that a cohabitant could rely on a contractual licence to give her a right to occupy a house bought by her former partner.[39] In the same year they reached the more controversial decision that a cohabitant could claim the transmission of a statutory tenancy under the Rent Act as a member of the deceased tenant's family.[40]

At the same time Parliament started to give claims to cohabitants which could scarcely have been imagined even 25 years before. By enabling a de facto dependant to apply for an order, the Inheritance (Provision for Family and Dependants) Act 1975 gave a cohabitant the right to claim provision after her (or his) partner's death which she did not have during his lifetime.[41] The Administration of Justice Act 1982 amended the Fatal Accidents Act 1976 so as to enable a cohabitant to maintain an action under that Act for the death of her (or his) partner. The Housing Acts 1985 and 1988 include persons who were living together 'as husband and wife' among those who can claim a tenancy on the tenant's death. Part IV of the Family Law Act 1996 enables a court to grant an occupation or non-molestation order to cohabitants who are defined as 'two persons who are neither married to each other nor civil partners of each other but are living together as husband and wife or as if they were civil partners'. Similarly, the Social Security Contributions and Benefits Act 1992 defines a 'couple' as, inter alia, 'a man and woman who are not married to each other but are living together as husband and wife' for the purpose of establishing entitlement to certain social security benefits.[42]

---

[35] A Barlow et al *Cohabitation, Marriage and the Law: social change and legal reform in the 21st century* (2005).

[36] R Probert *The Changing Legal Regulation of Cohabitation: From Fornicators to Family 1600–2010* (2012).

[37] [1959] 2 All ER 379 at 384 (per Ormerod LJ) and 388 (per Willmer LJ) CA: see also *Gammans v Ekins* [1950] 2 KB 328, CA.　　　　　　　　　　　　　　　　[38] *Cooke v Head* [1972] 2 All ER 38, CA.

[39] *Tanner v Tanner* [1975] 3 All ER 776, CA: see Ch 24.

[40] *Dyson Holdings Ltd v Fox* [1976] QB 503, CA.

[41] Express recognition of cohabitation was made by the Law Reform (Succession) Act 1995 s 2: see Ch 25.

[42] Equivalent provisions apply to same sex cohabitants.

The judicial and parliamentary attitude towards extra-marital cohabitation merely reflects the attitude of society generally. But it is not without its critics.[43] Convincing arguments can be put forward on both sides. The strongest reason for giving rights to cohabitants is that, as many unmarried couples are virtually indistinguishable from married ones, the parties (or the survivor) and their children may be as much in need of legal protection as spouses if the union breaks down as a result of separation or is brought to an end by death. This argument, taking a 'functional' approach to family regulation which focuses on what the parties do for each other and their children (caring, support, etc)[44] rather than a 'formal' one focused on status, is particularly strong if the parties were unable to marry each other for some reason. Against this can be raised a number of counter-arguments. The first is a purely moral one and reflects the old common law position: extra-marital cohabitation is wrong and consequently no legal rights should be granted to those who engage in it. The second reason for not according rights to cohabitants rests on the premise that it is in the interests of society generally that the relationship that a couple enter into should be as stable as possible, particularly if they have children. As marriage implies an emotional and legal commitment, marital relationships, it is argued, should be more stable than extra-marital ones. Consequently, by giving to the unmarried rights previously possessed only by the married, the law is weakening the institution of marriage and thus undermining the family. The force of this argument depends on whether the assumption about the comparative stability of marriage is correct, and evidence is beginning to be produced which does lend it some support.[45] Finally, it is argued that the law should respect 'autonomy' and not force the parties to accept the obligations of marriage they have consciously chosen to reject, or confer on them the attendant rights, particularly when it is possible for them, in part at least, to regulate their own legal relationship by contract. These arguments ultimately take two contrasting positions—one emphasises the vulnerability of the weaker party and children of the relationship; the other focuses on the autonomy of the parties to choose how to shape their relationship and to opt out from the burdens of marriage.

English law has adopted a typical compromise and has assimilated the legal position of cohabitants to that of spouses only in isolated fields. This inconsistency no doubt reflects the ambivalence of society generally to the question of cohabitation, as well as the number of different reasons that couples have for living together outside marriage. As the number of cohabiting couples increases, the problems resulting from the breakdown of their relationship and the attendant loss of home and support will become more common and more acute. Whatever the difficulties, the introduction of a coherent policy is essential.

5. GREATER RECOGNITION OF SAME SEX RELATIONSHIPS

The position has become even more acute because there has been a major shift in the attitude towards same sex partnerships in the past decade. The trend began with the courts

---

[43] See particularly R Deech 'The Case against Legal Recognition of Cohabitation' in J Eekelaar and S Katz (eds) *Marriage and Cohabitation in Contemporary Societies: Areas of Legal, Social and Ethical Change* (1980). Cf. C Barton *Cohabitation Contracts: Extra Marital Partnerships and Law Reform* (1985) pp 73–5; Baroness Hale of Richmond 'Unmarried Couples in Family Law' [2004] Fam Law 419.

[44] For consideration of how families are constituted by what they 'do' rather than how they are structured, see D Morgan *Rethinking Family Practices* (2011) and for caring as the essence of family bonds, see J Herring *Caring and the Law* (2013).

[45] E Beaujouan and M Ni Bhrolcháin 'Cohabitation and Marriage in Britain since the 1970's' *Population Trends No 145* (2011) p 19. See also M Maclean and J Eekelaar *The Parental Obligation* (1997) pp 19–21.

seeking to assimilate the position of homosexual partners with that of heterosexuals in the realm of tenancy law, holding first that such a partner could succeed to a tenancy held by his or her deceased partner as a member of the deceased tenant's family,[46] and then, after the Human Rights Act 1998 came into force, that the legislation should be construed so that such a person could succeed as if he or she were the spouse of the deceased.[47] Meanwhile, after two private member's bills were introduced into Parliament and withdrawn on the Government undertaking to bring forward its own legislation, the Civil Partnership Act was eventually passed in 2004, enabling same sex couples to achieve a recognised legal status with virtually all the same rights and duties as spouses.[48]

Finally, in 2013, the Marriage (Same Sex Couples) Act was passed to enable gay and lesbian couples to marry. It is striking that both pieces of legislation passed comparatively easily through Parliament, notwithstanding the opposition of many (though by no means all) organised religions. Perhaps the legislative strategy of creating a separate legal status of civil partnership, akin to but not identical with marriage, and of (initially at least) providing that this status could not be acquired through a religious ceremony, enabled the public to become comfortable with the idea of same sex couples having legal rights which put them on a par with married couples. It then perhaps seemed natural, or at least, not a major extension, to open up marriage to such couples. Perhaps too, the fact that many other jurisdictions, including individual states within the USA, many European countries, including France, Belgium and Spain, and other countries including Argentina, South Africa and New Zealand, had all opened up marriage to same sex couples, made the idea seem to be an ordinary aspect of law in a liberal democracy. The first same sex weddings in England and Wales[49] were performed in March 2014.

Paradoxically, while one might have thought it would become harder to argue that heterosexual cohabitants should be denied additional rights and protection in the light of such a profound change in social and legal attitudes, the grant of marital *status* to same sex partners has enabled Government to resist this by arguing that there is now no barrier to any couple obtaining the legal benefits of marriage if they wish, and thus that those who decline to do so cannot complain if they are denied them.

6. GREATER FOCUS ON AUTONOMY

Resistance to claims from cohabitants, and acceptance of the desirability of financial independence when a relationship ends, highlight a trend towards regarding adults as entitled to shape the terms of their relationship without state interference, which fits with a general cultural emphasis on liberalism and individuality in British society. Some sociologists have argued that adult intimate relationships are increasingly 'negotiated' and 'contingent', underpinned by the freedom to walk away without continuing ties when the relationship no longer provides emotional fulfilment.[50] Such views may be overstated, particularly when the parent–child relationship is included in the picture,[51] but they may

---

[46] *Fitzpatrick v Sterling Housing Association Ltd* [2001] 1 AC 27, HL. See A Diduck 'A Family by any other Name . . . Or Starbucks Comes to England' (2001) 28 *Journal of Law and Society* 290.

[47] *Ghaidan v Godin-Mendoza* [2004] UKHL 30, [2004] 2 AC 557. Lord Millett dissented. See R Probert 'Same sex Couples and the Marriage Model' (2005) 13 *Feminist Legal Studies* 135. See further Ch 24, 'As husband and wife', pp 942–943.   [48] See Ch 2.

[49] For Scotland, see the Marriage and Civil Partnership (Scotland) Act 2014. The Northern Ireland Assembly voted against equivalent legislation in 2013.

[50] U Beck and E Beck-Gernsheim *The Normal Chaos of Love* (1995); A Giddens *Modernity and Self-Identity* (1991).   [51] C Smart *Personal Life: New Directions in Sociological Thinking* (2007).

influence the climate in which arguments over how to balance competing claims take place. Thus, whereas family law has traditionally been characterised as a discretionary exercise of judgment by courts adopting an 'inquisitorial' approach designed to facilitate decisions which are in the best interests of the family members, married couples (and cohabitants) who separate are increasingly encouraged to settle their financial affairs without recourse to the courts. Indeed, they may, if they so wish, sort these out in advance of any break-up by making a 'pre-nup' (marital property agreement), provided that the result is not 'unfair',[52] even if this leaves the more vulnerable partner worse off than they would have been had the court determined the outcome. This new emphasis on the parties' right to 'contract' into, and about, the terms of their relationship sits uneasily with the renewed significance of 'status' reflected in the extension of marriage to same sex couples, for it raises the question of what the status brings by way of content, as opposed to the mere title itself. It also runs the risk of conceptualising legal family ties as a form of dry contract which sits even more uneasily with emotional bonds of love and caring. Finally, it reinforces arguments over gender—for as long as the majority of 'vulnerable' partners in a relationship are women, formal equality rules which fail to take into consideration the economic and social realities may simply brush over the hardship and substantive unfairness that is produced. The problem was elegantly summed up by Baroness Hale, in the context of discussing the validity of 'pre-nups':

> Some may regard freedom of contract as the prevailing principle in all circumstances; others may regard that as a 19th century concept which has since been severely modified, particularly in the case of continuing relationships typically (though not invariably) characterised by imbalance of bargaining power (such as landlord and tenant, employer and employee). Some may regard people who are about to marry as in all respects fully autonomous beings; others may wonder whether people who are typically (although not invariably) in love can be expected to make rational choices in the same way that businessmen can. Some may regard the recognition of these factual differences as patronising or paternalistic; others may regard them as sensible and realistic. Some may think that to accord a greater legal status to these agreements will produce greater certainty and lesser costs should the couple divorce; others may question whether this will in fact be achieved, save at the price of inflexibility and injustice. Some may believe that giving greater force to marital agreements will encourage more people to marry; others may wonder whether they will encourage more people to divorce. Perhaps above all, some may think it permissible to contract out of the guiding principles of equality and non-discrimination within marriage; others may think this a retrograde step likely only to benefit the strong at the expense of the weak.[53]

7. PRIVATE ORDERING AND THE WITHDRAWAL OF LEGAL AID

This new emphasis on autonomy has accompanied the withdrawal of the law from attempting to pass judgment on the moral failings of those in family relationships, and has led to an equally strong drive to discourage the use of legal proceedings to 'resolve' family disputes, by promoting a 'settlement culture'.[54] There are several reasons for this. Historically, couples and their families may have sought to avoid legal proceedings because

---

[52] *Granatino v Radmacher (Formerly Granatino)* [2010] UKSC 42 [2011] 1 AC 534.
[53] *Granatino v Radmacher (Formerly Granatino)* at [135].
[54] S Cretney, G Davis and J Collins *Simple Quarrels* (1994) p 211.

of the scandal and stigma attached to them, and to seek to arrive at compromises satisfactory to all concerned without attracting the attention of the hoi polloi in open court hearings. The extent to which this could be done depended upon the outcome sought: clearly, a quiet separation, with financial support for the wife privately agreed between two families, was more easily achieved than a divorce, which could not be obtained without the glare of publicity, until the 1970s. Yet private negotiations ran the risk that, if discovered, any change in legal status being sought would be denied, on the basis that the parties had acted 'collusively' to conceal relevant matters from the court, and it remains the case that the parties cannot 'oust the jurisdiction of the court' by striking a financial bargain which prohibits them from later asking a court to produce a different outcome. The modern purpose of retaining this state scrutiny over family relationships is to ensure that the 'burden' of support is not thrown onto the public purse.[55]

Nonetheless, the desirability of arriving, in private, at a solution agreeable to both sides came to be recognised by courts, lawyers and finally the Government. Legal costs can be reduced by avoiding trial (since it is the actual hearing which is the most expensive part of litigation), and this may in turn reduce public expenditure on courts and legal aid and save court time. The 'win–lose' essence of adversarial legal proceedings may antagonise and add to the general unhappiness and bitterness associated with the breakdown of a relationship, and this may be emotionally and psychologically damaging to any children affected.[56] Court orders and legal rules are blunt instruments for dealing with complex human problems, and the legal process is ill-equipped to provide the full range of support needed by family members going through crises and change. They may be particularly inappropriate where there is a need to preserve and foster a relationship notwithstanding a change in legal status. For example, a court may be able to determine the legal parentage of a child, or who should inherit under a will or intestacy, but may be less competent to assess whether children will benefit from continued contact with their absent parent after a divorce, and still less be able to ensure that such contact takes place. Recognition of this legal impotence has coincided with a political preference for less state intervention in the privacy of the family, manifested in an emphasis, in the Children Act 1989, upon parents having responsibility for their children, and consequently being trusted to take decisions for and about them without undue scrutiny by a court. Finally, the breadth of discretion, which, of necessity, is entrusted to courts to determine issues which turn on a myriad of individual facts, makes it hard to predict the outcome of litigation, and acts as an incentive to parties to try to minimise uncertainty by arriving at their own agreement. Ironically, at the same time this broad discretion forces legal advisers to attempt to second-guess what courts may do, by relying on either reported precedents, or practice within their local area, and to use such knowledge to persuade clients that a particular outcome is the most likely to be obtained, and hence may as well be agreed without waiting for the court to produce a ruling.[57]

For all these reasons, the law now offers firm encouragement to families in dispute to resort to means other than the courts to arrive at settlements. Lawyer-led negotiations

---

[55] See Chs 21, 22.

[56] Law Com No 192, *The Ground for Divorce* (1990) paras 2.16, 2.19–2.20; Lord Chancellor's Department *Looking to the Future: Mediation and the Ground for Divorce* Cm 2424 (1993) paras 5.11–5.15 and Cm 2799 (1995) paras 2.22–2.25. For empirical research, see in particular J Pryor and B Rodgers *Children in Changing Families: Life after Parental Separation* (2001); L Trinder et al *Making Contact: How Parents and Children Negotiate and Experience Contact after Divorce* (2002).

[57] R Mnookin and L Kornhauser 'Bargaining in the Shadow of the Law: The Case of Divorce' (1979) 88 Yale LJ 950.

remain the prevailing device for achieving these.[58] Many family lawyers developed a more 'conciliatory', non-adversarial approach to their clients' problems in the 1970s and 1980s, to a great extent through the establishment of what was then called the Solicitors Family Law Association, now known as 'Resolution'[59] which has a code of practice for its members which emphasises the need to minimise conflict between family members during legal processes. Some lawyers have also begun to practise 'collaborative law', whereby the lawyers for both sides undertake not to act for their clients if the case proceeds to court, thus encouraging them to work with the clients to achieve a settlement. And most recently, in a bid to secure privacy for clients from an increasingly intrusive media, as well as the benefits of potentially cheaper and speedier resolution, the Institute of Family Law Arbitrators (IFLA) has been established to train and disseminate guidance to legal experts offering arbitration to those with financial disputes.[60]

Alongside this trend, 'alternative dispute resolution' through mediation or conciliation has been introduced both as a part of the legal process, and as an adjunct to it.[61] Mediation and conciliation may be defined as processes whereby a neutral third party acts as a facilitator of discussion between the parties in dispute, helping them to arrive at their own agreed resolution. Many schemes offering these services are focused particularly on disputes relating to children, and in these, the facilitator is most likely to have social work training. But many lawyers are also trained mediators and they offer the service as another aspect of their provision for family clients. Mediation has developed both outside of the courts, so that it is available to couples who may not have begun any legal proceedings as well as those who are engaged in them, and within the courts as an essential step in the legal procedure. Such 'in court' processes may be moderated by either a Cafcass officer,[62] if the dispute concerns children (when it tends to be referred to as conciliation), or a district judge, in the case of financial and property disputes.[63]

It had long been the case that an applicant for legal aid in a family dispute would not be permitted to receive it until the suitability of the case for mediation had first been established. If the case was deemed suitable, a refusal to engage in mediation could result in the litigant being denied legal aid.[64] The Family Procedure Rules 2010[65] expanded this approach by laying down an 'expectation' that any applicant[66] taking proceedings for financial relief or orders relating to their children would first have attended a meeting to determine if the dispute could be resolved by mediation, known as a 'MIAM'—'mediation information and assessment meeting'. However, attendance was not compulsory—and particularly not where there were safety issues affecting the applicant or a child—and varied across the country, depending upon how far lawyers and judges in the locality regarded it as effectively mandatory.[67] The Children and Families Act 2014 s 10 makes

---

[58] See especially, S Cretney et al *Simple Quarrels* (1994) and J Eekelaar, M Maclean and S Beinart *Family Lawyers: The Divorce Work of Solicitors* (2000).

[59] For its code of practice, see http://www.resolution.org.uk/editorial.asp?page_id=26 accessed 16 August 2013.

[60] http://ifla.org.uk/ accessed 16 August 2013. The IFLA scheme was endorsed by the President of the Family Division in *S v S Financial Remedies: Arbitral Award* [2014] EWHC 7 (Fam) [2014] 1 FLR 1257.

[61] For discussion of these see Ch 7, Proposals for reform, pp 230–238 and Ch 22, Financial remedies procedure, pp 832–834.

[62] See Ch 1, Multi-disciplinary and specialist approaches to family problems and Ch 13, Cafcass, p 14 and p 452.   [63] See Ch 22, Financial remedies procedure, p 832.

[64] Access to Justice Act 1999 s 8(3); Community Legal Service *Funding Code Part II Procedures* (2005), Section 7—Referral for Family Mediation.

[65] *Practice Direction 3A—Pre-application protocol for mediation and assessment.*

[66] Respondents would be expected to attend 'if invited'.

[67] See Sir N Wall 'The President's Resolution Address 2012' [2012] Fam Law 817 at 820.

attendance compulsory (subject to victims of violence or abuse being exempted) in a further attempt to divert litigants away from court.

However, the Government went still further by withdrawing all legal aid from family litigation other than where there is a risk of violence to the applicant or a relevant child. The Legal Aid, Sentencing and Punishment of Offenders Act 2012 (LASPO 2012) provides that civil legal services are only available in certain types of legal proceedings. Schedule 1 to the Act specifies that, as far as family disputes are concerned, these are limited to the care, supervision and protection of children (which means cases of child abuse and neglect), child abduction and domestic violence. Other family proceedings may be covered provided that there has been, or is a risk of, domestic violence between the applicant and respondent. Domestic violence is defined as 'any incident, or pattern of incidents, of controlling, coercive or threatening behaviour, violence or abuse (whether psychological, physical, sexual, financial or emotional) between individuals who are associated with each other'.[68] If the proceedings relate to a child, then (unless—which is rare—the child is made a party, in which case he or she will receive legal aid to be represented in the case) legal aid is also available if there has been, or is a risk of, abuse of the child. Abuse is defined as 'physical or mental abuse, including (a) sexual abuse, and (b) abuse in the form of violence, neglect, maltreatment and exploitation'.[69]

Legal aid is still available to those who are financially eligible, for mediation and for legal assistance to support that mediation, such as the drawing up of an agreement to embody the terms of the settlement reached in the mediation, and having this endorsed by the court as a consent order.[70]

The *intended* impact of these measures is to encourage those in dispute to reach settlements out of court. The *potential* impact is to increase the number of litigants in person who feel they have no alternative but to take the case to court, with the consequential difficulties, for themselves in terms of trying to conduct a legal case and examine witnesses; for their family members in the hostility and distress this may engender; and for the courts in having to assist such litigants so that they can receive justice.[71]

The motivation for the withdrawal of legal aid was the need to reduce public expenditure, both directly through legal aid and through the use of the courts. A similar motivation to save money, compounded by the dreadful political fallout from the failings of the child support scheme, has resulted in the promotion of private settlement to resolve the level of child maintenance to be paid by a non-resident parent when parents separate, rather than use of the Child Support Agency.[72] This represents a major reversal of policy driven by the dire performance of the Agency due to the complexity of the

---

[68] LASPO 2012 Sch 1 para 12(9) as amended by SI 2013/748. There may be difficulties in producing the required evidence of such abuse—see Rights of Women, *Evidencing domestic violence: a barrier to family law legal aid* (2013) [online] http://www.rightsofwomen.org.uk/pdfs/Policy/Evidencing_domestic_violence_ II.pdf (accessed 8 April 2014) which found that of 377 cases collected in two surveys of women experiencing domestic violence, almost half (49.5%) did not have any of the prescribed forms of evidence and thus could not apply for legal aid. Of 38 respondents who provided further information, 60.5% of these took no further action; 23.7% paid for a solicitor to represent them and 15.8% represented themselves at court.

[69] LASPO 2012 Sch 1 para 13(3).   [70] LASPO 2012 Sch 1 para 14.

[71] See Civil Justice Council, *Access to Justice for Litigants in Person (or self-represented litigants)* (2011); R Moorhead and M Sefton (2005) *Litigants in person: Unrepresented litigants in first instance proceedings* Department for Constitutional Affairs Research Series 2/05 (2005); K Williams *Litigants in person: a literature review*, Ministry of Justice Research Summary 2/11 (2011); Rights of Women, *Evidencing domestic violence: a barrier to family law legal aid* (2013) [online] http://www.rightsofwomen.org.uk/pdfs/Policy/ Evidencing_domestic_violence_II.pdf (accessed 8 April 2014).

[72] See Ch 21, Maintenance under the Child Support Act 1991, p 800.

scheme it had to administer. It can also be seen as representing a further withdrawal of the state from family regulation in favour of the 'autonomy' of parents to sort things out for themselves. The problem is that the person who will potentially lose by the change is not an autonomous adult, but the child whose parent fails adequately to support them.

8. MULTI-DISCIPLINARY AND SPECIALIST APPROACHES TO FAMILY PROBLEMS

As the law and legal process have become increasingly regarded as inappropriate to respond to and deal with family problems, attention has turned to other disciplines and other mechanisms outside or alongside law to fill the gap.[73] A key feature of family law today is the extent to which non-legal professionals are involved in its practice and administration. This operates in several different ways. It is perhaps traditional for accountants and tax advisers to be involved in the provision of financial advice and assistance to wealthy divorcees. Social work professionals, working both within the courts and in local authority social services departments, are largely responsible for the handling of child protection, albeit with some court control. The creation of a unified service, Cafcass (Children and Family Court Advisory and Support Service), in 2001[74] brought together court welfare officers, who had been trained as probation officers, guardians ad litem, social workers who usually had local authority child care experience, and lawyers and social workers who had previously been attached to the Official Solicitor's office, to provide advice to the family courts, and to represent the interests, and sometimes the voices, of children who are the subjects of litigation.

Paediatricians, psychologists, psychoanalysts and psychiatrists play an important role in the diagnosis and treatment of child abuse and neglect, and in the provision of support for children facing trauma during and after family breakdown. The legal process makes use of their expertise as expert witnesses to help determine both the occurrence or likelihood of abusive acts and the best mode of dealing with their aftermath for the child,[75] although recent moves to reduce cost and delay in the courts have led to a restriction on their use, from appointment where this was considered 'reasonably required to resolve the proceedings', to having to be 'necessary'—a significantly more stringent test.[76] The rise of mediation and attempts to provide support for adults undergoing relationship breakdown[77] are further instances of non-legal approaches to what was once regarded as a strictly legal subject.

[73] For opposing views on the interaction of different disciplines within the legal process, see M Murch and D Hooper *The Family Justice System* (1992); M Murch 'The cross-disciplinary approach to family law—are we trying to mix oil with water?' in D Pearl (ed) *Frontiers of Family Law* (1995); M King and C Piper *How the Law Thinks About Children* (2nd edn, 1995); and M King and J Trowell *Children's Welfare and the Law: The Limits of Legal Intervention* (1992), drawing upon Teubner's theory of 'autopoeisis'.

[74] Under the Criminal Justice and Court Services Act 2000. Note that the Children Act 2004 s 34 devolved Cafcass functions relating to Wales to the National Assembly for Wales and these functions are carried out by 'Welsh family proceedings officers' rather than 'Cafcass officers'. For details, see O Rees 'Devolution and the Development of Family Law in Wales' [2008] CFLQ 45 and 'Devolution and Family Law in Wales: A Potential for Doing Things Differently?' (2012) 33(3) *Statute Law Review* 192.

[75] Mr Justice Wall (ed) *Rooted Sorrows: Psychoanalytic Perspectives on Child Protection, Assessment, Therapy and Treatment* (1997).

[76] *Re TG (Care Proceedings: Case Management: Expert Evidence)* [2013] EWCA Civ 5 [2013] 1 FLR 1250; *Re H-L (A Child) (Expert Evidence: Test for Permission)* [2013] EWCA Civ 655 [2013] 2 FLR 1434.

[77] See Private ordering and the withdrawal of legal aid, pp 10–14.

C. THE FAMILY JUSTICE SYSTEM

Sometimes a question of family law arises in a case of contract or tort or in a criminal prosecution. For example, it may be necessary to determine whether a woman can claim damages in respect of her husband's death or whether the accused's spouse is a compellable witness. Each of these cases will, of course, be tried in the ordinary civil or criminal courts and no special problem arises. What we are concerned with here are the courts which hear and determine cases raising issues solely of family law, for example the annulment or dissolution of marriage, settling with whom a child is to live, and the making of financial provision. Together with the professionals and agencies noted earlier in this chapter, these form the 'family justice system' which deals with families in dispute.[78]

There has been a gradual grafting onto the basic court hierarchy of a system of linked courts, exercising the same or similar jurisdiction, staffed by judges and magistrates specially trained to deal with family matters, resulting in a family court 'system', if not a 'single Family Court'. The latter has now been introduced by the Crime and Courts Act 2013.[79]

1. THE DEVELOPMENT OF THE FAMILY COURT 'SYSTEM'

Until the implementation of the new 'single Family Court', there were three levels of courts with original jurisdiction to hear family cases. In order of superiority, they were the High Court, county court and magistrates' court (known as 'family proceedings courts'). The former two were entirely staffed by professional judges. The latter were mainly staffed by unpaid 'lay' persons known as magistrates or justices with a tribunal consisting of three magistrates. There have also been full-time professional judges known as district judges (magistrates' courts) (formerly known as 'stipendiary magistrates'). All lay magistrates' courts have had the services of a justices' clerk, who is a trained lawyer[80] and whose function, inter alia, is to advise the bench on matters of law.[81]

In the High Court, family law disputes were handled by the Family Division[82] which continues to deal with cases under the Court's 'inherent jurisdiction' and cases with an international dimension. Judges sitting in the Family Division are mainly, but not exclusively, drawn from the specialist Family Law Bar and spend a substantial part of their judicial time sitting in family law cases.

County courts handled the vast majority of family business, including all divorce and civil partnership suits; claims for declarations of status under the Family Law Act 1986, Part III; property claims and claims under the Inheritance (Provision for Family and Dependants) Act 1975; applications concerning children under the Children Act 1989 and for adoption orders; and domestic violence applications made under the Family Law Act 1996, Part IV.

Originally resulting from their jurisdiction to administer criminal law, magistrates acquired expanding jurisdiction to make maintenance orders between spouses and for children and, following the creation of the juvenile court in 1908 (renamed the 'youth

---

[78] M Murch and D Hooper *The Family Justice System* (1992).
[79] Section 17(3) inserting s 31A into the Matrimonial and Family Proceedings Act 1984.
[80] A clerk must be a barrister or solicitor of at least seven years' standing.
[81] See *Practice Direction (Justices: Clerk to Court)* [2000] 1 WLR 1886.
[82] Created by the Administration of Justice Act 1970, s 1. Work assigned by the Senior Courts Act 1981, Sch 1.

court' in 1991),[83] had important jurisdiction over both child offenders and children at risk of abuse.[84] They were empowered to hear private law applications concerning children (that is, applications between private individuals, usually the parents) under the Children Act 1989 and declarations of parentage under the Family Law Act 1986, s 55A. They could also hear adoption applications under the Adoption and Children Act 2002 and domestic violence cases under the Family Law Act 1996 Part IV. They did not, however, have jurisdiction to hear divorce or other matrimonial causes nor applications to dissolve civil partnerships or other civil partnership causes nor did they have jurisdiction over property matters.

Unless specifically prescribed, parties were free to choose in which court to make an application. Accordingly, actions for protection against domestic violence,[85] free-standing private law applications concerning children[86] and adoption applications[87] could be brought at any level of first instance court. However, all matrimonial causes (that is, applications for divorce, nullity and judicial separation and the equivalent actions in relation to civil partnerships) together with all the ancillary issues relating to children, property (including the matrimonial or family home) and money had to be brought in the county court.[88] Magistrates had no jurisdiction to deal with property issues or declarations of marital or partnership status.[89] Conversely, all public law applications involving children had to be commenced in the magistrates' court.[90] In certain other areas, such as international child abduction or actions for recognition and enforcement under Council Regulation (EC) No 2201/2003,[91] jurisdiction was confined to the High Court.[92] The High Court also has special power to deal with children under its wardship and inherent jurisdictions.[93]

To ensure efficiency, the Matrimonial and Family Proceedings Act 1984 provided that certain proceedings might be transferred from the High Court to the county court and vice versa, where the complexity (or otherwise) of the case, or the convenience for witnesses of holding the trial in a particular venue, made this suitable.[94] The transfer of cases dealing with children was subject to different rules. Certain 'specified proceedings'[95] had to be commenced in the magistrates' court, while others were 'self-regulating' in the sense that, if other proceedings, such as divorce, were already pending in a particular court,

---

[83] Criminal Justice Act 1991, s 70.

[84] Views on the appropriate treatment of juvenile offenders have vacillated (see G Douglas 'The Child's Right to Make Mistakes: Criminal Responsibility and the Immature Minor' in G Douglas and L Sebba (eds) *Children's Rights and Traditional Values* (1998) 264 at pp 270–6). At one time the Children and Young Persons Act 1969 gave magistrates the option of dealing with young offenders through care proceedings alongside child victims of abuse but this option was abolished by the Children Act 1989.

[85] See the Family Law Act 1996, Part IV.

[86] Viz. those not related to any other proceedings, such as divorce. Applications are made under the Children Act 1989.   [87] See the Adoption and Children Act 2002.

[88] See the Matrimonial and Family Proceedings Act 1984, s 33(3) (Matrimonial Causes), s 36A(6) (added by the Civil Partnership Act 2004, Sch 27, para 92) (civil partnership causes).

[89] Family Law Act 1986, s 55 (marital status); Civil Partnership Act 2004, ss 181 and 188 (civil partnership status).   [90] Children (Allocation of Proceedings) Order 1991, Art 3(1).

[91] Regulation concerning jurisdiction and the recognition and enforcement of judgments in matrimonial matters and the matters of parental responsibility repealing Regulation (EC) No 1347/2000—the so-called revised Brussels II Regulation. See Ch 26.

[92] See the Child Abduction and Custody Act 1985 ss 4 and 16 and the Family Procedure Rules 2010 (SI 2010/2955) r 12.45(a).

[93] See Ch 20.

[94] Matrimonial and Family Proceedings Act 1984 s 39; Children (Allocation of Proceedings) Order 1991 Art 5.

[95] Those concerning care proceedings, principally care and related proceedings: see Children (Allocation of Proceedings) Order 1991, Art 3.

actions concerning the children of the family had to be dealt with in the same court. To speed up the hearing of cases and to match the appropriate degree of judicial expertise to the complexity of the case, there was provision for proceedings to be transferred from one court level to another, and also *between* courts of the same level.[96]

2. PRESSURE FOR A FAMILY COURT AND THE *FAMILY JUSTICE REVIEW*

Even with these developments, proceedings relating to members of the same family might take place in a number of courts simultaneously. For example, a wife, having sought a non-molestation order in the family proceedings court, might then seek a divorce in a divorce county court; at the same time a child of the family might have been made a ward in the High Court.[97] This fragmented and overlapping jurisdiction causes confusion, complicates proceedings, and it has long been recognised that it leads to inconvenience, unnecessary cost and unreasonable delay.[98] While it could be said that England and Wales had a family court 'system' of sorts, it did not fully address the long-standing debate concerning the desirability of establishing a discrete Family Court to deal with all aspects of family litigation. Family Courts have existed in the United States for some time and have been introduced in Australia and New Zealand.[99] Impetus for their introduction in this country was provided by the Report of the Committee on One-parent Families (the Finer Report) in 1974.[100] In 1983 the Lord Chancellor's Department issued a consultation paper, which was in turn overtaken by the establishment of a review committee which published its own consultation paper in 1986.[101] After nearly two decades of inactivity, interest in a Family Court was renewed with the publication by the Department of Constitutional Affairs (DCA) in February 2005 of a Consultation Paper 'A Single Civil Court?' and a further paper in response to the consultation in October 2005.[102]

But it was the *Family Justice Review*[103] in 2011 which finally led to firm proposals and legislative change. The Review was set up under the Labour Government to respond to mounting criticism that the family justice system, comprising the courts *and* the agencies and professionals involved in working with families in dispute (including Cafcass and local authority social workers engaged in child protection proceedings), was failing to deliver fair outcomes and was working in an inefficient and opaque way. Extensive delays in court proceedings (particularly care proceedings which took on average, a year to complete),[104] alleged bias by the courts against fathers seeking greater involvement with their children after separation from the mother,[105] and mounting costs both of the courts themselves and

---

[96] See generally the Children (Allocation of Proceedings) Order 1991.

[97] As occurred in *Re C (Wardship and Adoption)* (1979) 2 FLR 177, CA. See also B Hoggett 'Family Courts or Family Law Reform?' (1986) 6 *Legal Studies* 1, pp 3–5.

[98] See the Lord Chancellor's Department's Consultation Paper (1986). B Hoggett, 'Family Courts or Family Law Reform?' (1986) 6 *Legal Studies* 1, p 5; M Murch et al *The Overlapping Family Jurisdictions of Magistrates Courts and County Courts—Research Report* (1987).

[99] See LN Brown 'The Legal Background to the Family Court' [1966] BJ Crim 139 (USA); the Family Law Act 1975, s 21 (Australia); the Family Courts Act 1980, s 4 (New Zealand).

[100] Cmnd 5629, Pt 4, s 13 and s 14 on which see S Cretney *Family Law in the Twentieth Century—A History* 746 ff. [101] A useful summary of the contents of the paper is to be found in [1986] Fam Law 247.

[102] DCA *Focusing Judicial Resources Appropriately* (2005).

[103] D Norgrove, *Family Justice Review: Interim Report* (2011) and *Final Report* (2011).

[104] *Final Report* para 2.10.

[105] *Interim Report* paras 5.33–5.36. Research has found no evidence of such bias: see *Final Report* para 4.21.

of legal representation,[106] were all seen as indicating the need for fundamental change. The Review panel, chaired by David Norgrove, was accordingly charged with considering, amongst other things, the extent to which the adversarial nature of the court system could promote solutions and good quality family relationships; what options there might be for making the system more inquisitorial; whether areas of work could be dealt with more efficiently via an administrative, rather than court-based process; and how the different agencies and professionals engaged in the family justice system fulfil their different roles and how they can work effectively together.[107]

The Review recommended that a unified Family Court would be able to provide:

> clarity for court users in providing a single point of entry when applications are made to court;
>   opportunities to use the court estate more flexibly as between different tiers of the family court;
>   opportunities for greater efficiency in tying the work of the different court jurisdictions more closely together; and
>   consistency in case allocation through agreed initial assessment standards.[108]

In the light of this view (and other criticisms discussed in this chapter), the judiciary led a programme of 'modernisation of family justice'[109] and worked with the Court Service (HMCTS) to help shape the single family court created by the Crime and Courts Act 2013.

3. THE SINGLE FAMILY COURT

The President of the Family Division, Sir James Munby, announced the structure of the new Family Court in 2013.[110] The term, 'single Family Court' has two meanings: the first is as a unified court for the whole of England and Wales, and the second is as an organisational unit within a local court area.

(a) The Unified Family Court

The Family Court is to deal with all family cases, except cases invoking the inherent jurisdiction of the High Court and international cases concerning applications relating to child abduction and matters of jurisdiction, recognition and enforcement under certain EU Regulations.[111] The judiciary of the Family Court includes High Court judges, circuit judges and Recorders, district judges and magistrates, and legal advisers (justices' clerks). The family proceedings court of the magistrates has ceased to exist and all family work other than the reserved matters noted is now handled in the Family Court. Instead of referring cases up to the High Court due to complexity, judges of the High Court may hear them in the Family Court itself and only the President of the Family Division or a High Court judge is able to transfer a case to the High Court.

---

[106] *Final Report* para 2.12.
[107] *Interim Report* para 1.2.
[108] *Interim Report* para 3.155.
[109] http://www.judiciary.gov.uk/publications-and-reports/reports/family/the-family-justice-modernisation-programme (accessed 8 April 2014).
[110] Sir James Munby P and K Sadler, HMCTS, 'The Single Family Court: a Joint Statement' [2013] Fam Law 600.   [111] See Ch 26.

(b) The Local Family Court

In each court area, there is a Designated Family Centre, headed by a Designated Family Judge, which serves as the point of entry for all proceedings. Thus, it is no longer possible to choose which level of court to bring an application for, say, a non-molestation order. Every new application is allocated by a 'gate-keeping' team consisting of a district judge and legal adviser, to the appropriate level of judge (including magistrates) and to the appropriate Hearing Centre within that court area.

4. GOVERNANCE AND PROFESSIONALISM

(a) The Family Justice Board

Efforts to promote greater consistency across different courts via dissemination of 'best practice' guidance and training, and greater collaboration between the different professional agencies, were made through the establishment of various local and national bodies during the 1990s and the first decade of the new century. In particular, the Family Justice Council, set up in 2002[112] sought to promote an inter-disciplinary approach to the needs of family justice and through consultation and research to monitor the effectiveness of the system and advise on reforms necessary for continuous improvement. Local family justice councils, chaired by designated Family Judges and made of up representatives of all the various professionals and agencies involved in family justice, fed local information up to the national Council and received guidance in return. The Norgrove Review panel considered that family justice extends beyond the court system to embrace other forms of dispute resolution such as mediation, and that all such aspects need to be brought within a Family Justice *Service* co-ordinated by a new body, the Family Justice Board, established in 2012.[113] However, concerns about preserving the independence of the courts and the judiciary led to a clarification that, in effect, the Service would consist of Cafcass[114] but that the Board would lead the monitoring of performance and promotion of best practice. The national Board is served by local family justice boards which have replaced the local councils[115] but which are not chaired by the judiciary, as they now feed into Government rather than the courts.[116]

(b) A more managerial approach

Attempts to streamline court processes in order to reduce delays and control costs have been a key feature of the court system for well over a decade. Along with a greater emphasis on training of the judiciary and magistracy in handling family matters, greater demands were made on the magistrates' courts in particular, in order to bring them into conformity with the higher courts, so that they could exercise the common jurisdiction introduced by the Children Act 1989. For the first time, a requirement of advance disclosure of written evidence was imposed, with an expectation that magistrates will have read

---

[112] On which see 'The Work of the Family Justice Council' [2005] Fam Law 65.

[113] *Final Report* paras 2.38–2.86.

[114] Whether this could operate in Wales, given that Cafcass Cymru falls within the purview of the Welsh Government, was left open.

[115] But the national Family Justice Council has been retained as a multi-disciplinary expert advisory group.

[116] See J Doughty and M Murch 'Judicial independence and the restructuring of family courts and their support services' [2012] CFLQ 333.

the papers in advance of the hearing. Magistrates, as well as judges, must give reasons for their decisions, and a failure to provide adequate reasons is a ground for appeal.[117]

The judiciary and practitioners sought over several years to streamline court procedure, resulting in a revised system introduced in 2000,[118] and subsequently updated by the more comprehensive Family Procedure Rules 2010[119] and accompanying Practice Directions. The overriding objective of these Rules is to enable the court to deal with cases justly, having regard to any welfare issues involved, and this includes,

> so far as is practicable—
>
> (a) ensuring that it is dealt with expeditiously and fairly;
> (b) dealing with the case in ways which are proportionate to the nature, importance and complexity of the issues;
> (c) ensuring that the parties are on an equal footing;
> (d) saving expense; and
> (e) allotting to it an appropriate share of the court's resources, while taking into account the need to allot resources to other cases.

The Children Act 1989 also introduced elements of greater 'court control' over the process of family litigation, by requiring courts to set timetables for the determination of the litigation, and emphasising the importance of judicial directions to the parties in the collection and sharing of written evidence and instruction of expert witnesses.[120] However, the early expectations at the time of the 1989 Act that private law cases would generally be disposed of in 16 weeks and public law cases within 12 weeks proved wildly optimistic.[121] Consequently new initiatives to control public law Children Act cases were introduced and a 40-week target was fixed for the completion of such cases. In particular, the 2010 'Public Law Outline' (as it is known) set out in detail the stages in the court process at which different aspects of the management of the case must be completed (such as the clarification of issues, the commissioning of expert evidence and the resolution of factual disputes). But despite these endeavours, cases continued to last for a year or more,[122] and the *Family Justice Review* recommended a *statutory* 26 week limit to force the courts to deal with proceedings more quickly.[123] This was enacted in the Children and Families Act 2014[124] and meanwhile, the modernisation of family justice programme, led by Ryder LJ, produced a revised Public Law Outline in 2013 geared to the 26 week limit.[125]

While concern at delay has been greatest in the public law field, because of the risk to a child who has been subject to abuse or neglect of continuing failure to provide a long-term safe and secure placement, there is also concern that private law cases can drift and the courts therefore also worked subject to a complementary, albeit less detailed, Direction issued by the then President of the Family Division, Dame Elizabeth Butler-Sloss, known as the Private Law Programme.[126] With the introduction of the

---

[117] *W v Hertfordshire County Council* [1993] 1 FLR 118 and *Re W (A Minor) (Contact)* [1994] 1 FLR 843.
[118] Family Proceedings (Amendment No 2) Rules 1999, SI 1999/3491.   [119] SI 2010/2955 (L17).
[120] See, eg, Children Act 1989 ss 11 and 32l and Adoption and Children Act 2002 s 109.
[121] See the comments by Baroness Hale in *Re G (A Minor) (Interim Care Order: Residential Assessment)* [2005] UKHL 68, [2005] 3 WLR 1166 at [58].
[122] D Norgrove, *Family Justice Review Final Report* (2011) para 3.55.
[123] Norgrove, *Family Justice Review Final Report* para 3.71.
[124] Section 14.   [125] *Practice Direction 36C* (2013).
[126] *Practice Direction 12B—The Revised Private Law Programme* (2010).

Family Court, this has been replaced by the Child Arrangements Programme (CAP) which seeks to respond to the general trend towards diversion of proceedings to alternative dispute resolution services, recognition of the need to hear the voice of the child, and the ability to deal with greater numbers of litigants in person after the withdrawal of legal aid.[127] Similar efforts to manage the conduct of financial and property cases on divorce have also been put in place.[128]

D. THE INTERNATIONALISATION OF FAMILY LAW

A final important feature to note at this stage is the increasing significance of international law in the shaping of new thinking about families, and in new legislation regulating them.[129] In part this is because there are many more cases involving an international element, be it the involvement of spouses or partners of different nationalities or the ownership of property abroad, or of foreign families living here.[130] One result of the growing phenomenon of cross-border families has been increasing international attempts both to create basic rights regulating the family and to provide international solutions to common problems. This has meant that the UK's legal systems have become subject to international pressure both to conform to global or European norms and to co-operate in transnational ventures to control worldwide problems. Furthermore, familiarity with different legal systems has given new opportunities for rethinking domestic law.

Beginning with the Universal Declaration of Human Rights (1948), which, in Article 16(3), provides that the family 'is the natural and fundamental group unit of society and is entitled to protection by society and the State' there has been increasing attention paid to mechanisms for enhancing the position of the family.[131] In some ways this might be regarded as strange, given that the difficulty of defining the family, alluded to at the start of this chapter, is even greater in a global context where many different family forms are to be found. There is also a tension, increasingly recognised, between laying down norms for 'family' rights, and providing rights for individual members of families. There may be conflicts of interest between the two. For example, how far should the importance of recognising the family as an entity entitled to protection take priority over the potential need to protect individuals from abuse or exploitation by other family members? The American Convention on Human Rights (1969) attempts, perhaps not wholly successfully, to deal with this problem by heading its Art 17 'Rights of the Family' and then including within that Article the rights of individuals within the family. Nonetheless, international efforts to support families, and to protect family members, have grown

---

[127] *Report to the President of the Family Division of the Private Law Working Group* [2013] Fam Law 1594.

[128] See Ch 22 Financial remedies procedure p 832.

[129] See generally N Lowe 'Where in the World is International Family Law Going Next?' in G Douglas and N Lowe (eds) *The Continuing Evolution of Family Law* (2009) ch 12, particularly pp 261–271.

[130] According to statistics produced by Eurostat (ed) *People in Europe* (2002) p 12, 15% of those entering into marriage within Europe are of different nationalities, often of different European States, and the same is true of other relationships, be they same sex or heterosexual. Within the EU (that is, before its enlargement) more than 5% of citizens, about 9 million people, did not have citizenship of the State in which they lived, and of these, almost 6 million citizens of the Union lived in another Member State.

[131] H Sokalski 'The International Year of the Family: New Frontiers for Families' in N Lowe and G Douglas (eds) *Families across Frontiers* (1996) 1; G Douglas 'The Significance of International Law for the Development of Family Law in England and Wales' in C Bridge (ed) *Towards the Millennium: Essays for P M Bromley* (1997) 85.

apace. These have manifested themselves in a variety of international instruments. Some of these can be seen as 'norm-setting', such as the Universal Declaration itself or the European Convention on Human Rights, and the United Nations Convention on the Rights of the Child (UNCRC), which sets out an extensive list of the rights, both civil and political, and social and economic, which a child should enjoy.[132]

1. UNITED NATIONS CONVENTION ON THE RIGHTS OF THE CHILD

At the global level, the most important of the international instruments may be seen as the UNCRC of 1989,[133] now signed by over 200 states, including the United Kingdom in 1991. This Convention sets out a variety of rights which must be safeguarded by signatory States through their internal laws. While focusing upon the rights of the child, both within the family, and in relation to the State, it marks an important stage in the international recognition of the family as a distinct unit. Its preamble, for example, states that signatories are:

> *Convinced* that the family . . . [is] the fundamental group of society and the natural environment for the growth and well-being of all its members and particularly children . . . [and] should be afforded the necessary protection and assistance so that it can fully assume its responsibilities within the community . . .

Although the United Kingdom is bound internationally by the Convention, because it has not been internally incorporated, it is not binding domestically.[134] Even so, it is increasingly referred to in domestic case law[135] and a duty to pay due regard to the UN Convention has been imposed on Welsh ministers.[136] While it might not be directly binding upon the courts, like all signatories, the United Kingdom is required to submit reports (within two years of ratification) to a Committee on the Rights of the Child on their progress in implementing the terms of the Convention, and is thus subject to some degree of scrutiny by the international community.[137] Signing the

---

[132] For discussion, see P Newell *The UN Convention and Children's Rights in the UK* (1991); D Fottrell *Revisiting Children's Rights: 10 Years of the UN Convention on the Rights of the Child* (2000); A Parkes *Children and International Human Rights Law: The Right of the Child to be Heard* (2013). A duty to pay due regard to the UN Convention has been imposed on Welsh ministers by the Rights of Children and Young Persons (Wales) Measure 2011 s 1. A duty to consider the UN Convention also lies on both the English and Welsh Commissioners for Children, see Ch 13.

[133] For definitive studies of the international rights of the child, see G Van Bueren *The International Law on the Rights of the Child* (1995) and T Buck, *International Child Law* (2010, 2nd edn). For further assessments see M Freeman 'The End of the Century of the Child' (2000) 53 *Current Legal Problems* 505 and D Fottrell *Revisiting Children's Rights: 10 years of the UN Convention on the Rights of the Child* (2000).

[134] Though as Ward LJ said in *Re P (A Minor) (Residence Order: Child's Welfare)* [2000] Fam 15 at 42, the Convention commands and receives respect.

[135] It was, for example, referred to in 26 cases reported in Family Law Reports between 1999 and 2005 but in only five cases reported before 1999.

[136] Rights of Children and Young Persons (Wales) Measure 2011 s 1. See also Ch 13, Looking after children's wider interests—the Commissioners for Children, p 475.

[137] See United Nations Concluding Observations of the Committee on the Rights of the Child: United Kingdom of Great Britain and Northern Ireland CRC/C/GBR/CO/4 20 October 2008. The Committee has continued to repeat criticisms made of the UK's observation of the UNCRC since its first report in 1995 (see CRC/C/15Add34 (1995)), particularly in relation to the continuing legality of physical punishment of children and the low age of criminal responsibility (10 in England and Wales and N Ireland, and 8 in Scotland).

Convention also leaves governments open to both internal and international criticism should they be seen to be failing in fulfilling their international obligations. For some[138] this scrutiny is simply not good enough. The Committee charged with overseeing compliance with the Convention is, it is argued, under-resourced and overstretched and in any event many countries are slow to produce their initial reports and their periodic reports. Nevertheless, notwithstanding this perhaps justifiable criticism the Convention should not be written off simply as an international gesture of no significance. One often overlooked effect is its influence in shaping subsequent international instruments, some of which have very much greater bite.

Obtaining worldwide agreement to a set of wide-ranging norms which can be implemented nationally is obviously a difficult task, and runs the risk that such norms will be pitched at a fairly minimal or very general level to attract maximum adherence. It may be more fruitful to develop agreed standards at a regional level where there is greater cultural, economic and political similarity between States. There are several Conventions operating at this level,[139] and the one of greatest significance to the United Kingdom is the European Convention on Human Rights particularly since its incorporation into domestic law by the Human Rights Act 1998.

2. EUROPEAN CONVENTION ON HUMAN RIGHTS

Although the United Kingdom was one of the original signatories to the European Convention for the Protection of Human Rights and Fundamental Freedoms (having ratified it in 1951) and, since 1966, has allowed individuals to take their complaints to the European Court of Human Rights in Strasbourg, the Convention remained solely an international obligation until its incorporation by the Human Rights Act 1998 which came into force in October 2000.[140] Nevertheless even before this it played an increasingly significant part in the legislative development of English domestic law.[141] That significance has accelerated after the implementation of the 1998 Act, though perhaps not as much as some anticipated.[142]

So far as family law is concerned, the two key Articles of substantive relevance are Art 8, which provides that everyone has the right to respect for his private and family life, his home and his correspondence, and Art 12, which provides that men and women of marriageable age have the right to marry and to found a family according to the national laws governing the exercise of this right. Four other Articles of substantive relevance are Art 3 relating to the right not to be tortured or be subject to inhuman and degrading treatment or punishment, Art 5 which provides for the right to liberty and security of person, Art 14 which provides that the enjoyment of the rights prescribed by the Convention shall be

[138] See M Freeman 'The End of the Century of the Child' (2000) 53 *Current Legal Problems* 505.

[139] See, for example, the American Convention on Human Rights referred to earlier (although one might query how far the two American continents can be regarded as sharing cultural and economic standards) and the African Charter on Human and People's Rights (1981).

[140] See generally, S Choudhry and J Herring, *European Human Rights and Family Law* (2010).

[141] It was certainly influential, for example in the drafting of the new Children Act 1989, see eg G Douglas 'The Family and the State under the European Convention on Human Rights' (1988) 2 Int J Law and Fam 76 and, more generally, P Duffy 'English Law and the European Convention on Human Rights' (1980) 29 ICLQ 585.

[142] There was, for example, speculation as to the compatibility of the paramountcy of the child's welfare principle and the status of unmarried fathers; the lawfulness of secure accommodation orders and about the inability of the courts to oversee local authority care plans, all of which survived human rights challenges (although in fact in some respects the law has since been changed).

secured without discrimination, and, of major procedural relevance, Art 6, under which
in the determination of civil rights everyone is entitled to a fair and public hearing within
a reasonable time.

We consider the impact of these provisions throughout the book, but at this introductory stage it will be helpful to outline the basic scheme of the Human Rights Act 1998.
What this Act does in general, apart from incorporating into domestic law the terms of
the Convention, is to:

(a) oblige all domestic courts at all levels to take Convention case law into account
when deciding a question relating to a Convention right;

(b) provide that, so far as it is possible to do so, primary and subordinate legislation
must be read and given effect to in a way that is compatible with Convention rights;

(c) empower the higher courts to make declarations of incompatibility if satisfied that
a statutory provision is incompatible with a Convention right;

(d) make it unlawful for public authorities to act in a way that is incompatible with a
Convention right save where the authorities are obliged to do so by primary legislation;

(e) permit persons to bring proceedings against a public authority acting or proposing
to act in a way made unlawful by the 1998 Act;

(f) empower the courts to give an appropriate remedy, including damages in respect of
any act (or proposed act) of a public authority which is (or would be) found to be
unlawful.

The 1998 Act is without prejudice to the right of any individual alleging a violation of a
Convention right to apply to the European Court of Human Rights in Strasbourg after
exhausting local remedies.[143]

So far as (a) is concerned, s 2 only requires case-law[144] to be taken into account but the
jurisprudence is not binding in any strict sense of precedent, and indeed it is open to the
English courts to go further than the European Court of Human Rights.[145]

The requirement to construe, so far as practicable, legislation in a manner that is
compatible with the Convention is provided by s 3. As Hale LJ said,[146] 'the 1998 Act was
carefully designed to promote the search for compatibility rather than incompatibility'.
However, while s 3 entitles the courts to depart from earlier domestic precedents insofar
as they are thought to be incompatible with Convention rights, there are limits to this
power; in particular it does not entitle the courts to legislate. As Lord Nicholls stressed
in Re S (Minors) (Care Order: Implementation of Care Plan), Re W (Minors) (Care Order:
Adequacy of Care Plan),[147] 'Interpretation of statutes is a matter for the courts, the enactment of statutes and the amendment of statutes, are matters for Parliament'.

Once it has been concluded that it is not possible to read and give effect to legislation in a way that is compatible with the Conventions, then, but only then,[148] under s 4
is it open to the High Court and the appellate courts[149] to make a formal declaration of

---

[143] See Art 25.
[144] Ie judgments of the European Court of Human Rights and opinions of the former Commission
including decisions on admissibility: s 2(1)(a)–(d).
[145] See eg Fitzpatrick v Sterling Housing Association Ltd [2001] 1 AC 27, HL, and Ghaidan v Godin-Mendoza [2004] UKHL 30, [2004] 2 AC 557, HL, discussed at Ch 24, 'A Man and a Woman', p 941.
[146] Re W and B, Re W (Care Plan) [2001] EWCA Civ 757 [2001] 2 FLR 582 at [50].
[147] [2002] UKHL 10 [2002] 2 AC 291 at [39].
[148] See Wilson v First County Trust Ltd (No 2) [2003] UKHL 40 [2004] 1 AC 816.
[149] Human Rights Act 1998 s 4(5).

incompatibility. Such declarations do not in themselves affect the validity of the legislation in question but the expectation is that the offending provision(s) will consequently be amended.[150] This sanction is slightly weaker than if the Strasbourg court holds the State to have violated the Convention, which obligates that State to remedy its offending domestic law.[151] Section 4 declarations have been relatively rarely made but one example is *Bellinger v Bellinger*[152] in which the House of Lords declared s 11(c) of the Matrimonial Causes Act 1973 (which required the parties to the marriage to be respectively male and female) to be incompatible with Arts 8 and 12.It seems that declarations can only be made in respect of specific provisions; it is not therefore possible to make a declaration of incompatibility against the scheme of a whole Act.[153]

Another significant function of the Act is that of enabling individuals to enforce their Convention rights against a public authority, which for these purposes includes local authorities and the courts.[154] The scheme of the Act in this respect was well described by Lord Nicholls in *Re S*:[155]

> Sections 7 and 8 of the Human Rights Act 1998 have conferred extended powers on the courts. Section 6 makes it unlawful for a public authority to act in a way which is incompatible with a Convention right. Section 7 enables victims of conduct made unlawful by section 6 to bring court proceedings against the public authority in question. Section 8 spells out, in wide terms, the relief a court may grant in those proceedings. The court may grant such relief or remedy, or make such order, within its powers as it considers just and appropriate. Thus, if a local authority conducts itself in a manner which infringes the Article 8 rights of a parent or child, the court may grant appropriate relief on the application of a victim of the unlawful act.

3. OTHER CONVENTIONS AND INTERNATIONAL INSTRUMENTS OF INFLUENCE

The Conventions so far discussed may be seen as operating inter alia at the political level, the intention being to educate States to improve their human rights records. But other international instruments are more focused on specific family law issues and problems of common concern. Some aim to harmonise laws in particular areas while others provide a mechanism for handling or control of inter-state family problems. Until recently, there have been two main sources of these types of instruments, namely, the Council of Europe and the Hague Conference on International Private Law, but another institution has now come into play, namely, the European Union. We end this chapter with a brief introductory resumé of the contributions in the family law field of each of these institutions.

---

[150] Human Rights Act 1998 s 10.

[151] See Art 53 of the Convention.

[152] [2003] UKHL 21 [2003] 2 AC 467, see Ch 2, Capacity to marry, p 42. For a general list of cases in which declarations of incompatibility have been made, see the Appendix to Lord Steyn's judgment in *Ghaidan v Godin-Mendoza*.

[153] *Re W and B, Re W (Care Plan)* [2001] EWCA Civ 757 [2001] 2 FLR 582 at [50], per Hale LJ impliedly upheld by the House of Lords on appeal in *Re S* [2002] UKHL 10 [2002] 2 AC 291 at [41] per Lord Nicholls.

[154] Human Rights Act 1998 s 6(3) which states that a 'public authority' includes (a) a court or tribunal, and (b) any person certain of whose functions are functions of a public nature.

[155] In *Re S* [2002] UKHL 10 [2002] 2 AC 291 at [45]. For further discussion of ss 7 and 8 see Ch 18, Suing the local authority for negligence, p 673.

(a) The Council of Europe

Apart from its key role in relation to the maintenance of the European Court of Human Rights, the Council of Europe[156] has pursued an active programme of work in the family law field principally aimed at harmonising laws and practices at the European level.[157]

Through its Parliamentary Assembly, Committee of Ministers and Conferences, the Council has produced a number of Recommendations (which are best described as statements of international aspirations, such as the Recommendation on Violence in the Family (1985)[158] that legislation on corporal punishment of children be reviewed) and Conventions intended to promote common policy among its member states. Some of the earlier Conventions, such as the 1967 European Convention on the adoption of children, which aimed to provide a uniform approach to certain aspects of adoption, and the 1975 European Convention on the Legal Status of Children Born out of Wedlock, which aimed to reduce discrimination against children whose parents are not married have become dated and have been the subject of internal review by the Council culminating in its 2002 publication of a 'White Paper' on Principles Concerning the Establishment and Legal Consequences of Parentage.[159] Of more lasting consequence (though somewhat overshadowed by the 1980 Hague Abduction Convention) is the 1980 European Convention on Recognition and Enforcement of Decisions Concerning Custody of Children and on Restoration of Custody of Children, the prime role of which is to provide a uniform approach to international child abduction.

Two more recent Conventions are the 1996 European Convention on the Exercise of Children's Rights, which is intended to complement the UN Convention on the Rights of the Child by providing more detailed provisions concerning procedures for enabling children to exercise the rights guaranteed in the UN Convention and the 2003 European Convention on Contact Concerning Children which aims to provide both harmonising general principles to be applied to contact orders and a scheme to deal with trans-frontier contact issues. We discuss these last three Conventions in greater detail in later chapters.

(b) The Hague Conference

Like the Council of Europe, the Hague Conference[160] has pursued an active programme of work in the family law field. Traditionally, it has been associated with private international law, promoting internationally agreed rules of jurisdiction and consequent recognition and enforcement. But increasingly its instruments have become very much relevant to the mainstream family lawyer. Although of principal concern in this work is

---

[156] The Council of Europe is not to be confused with the European Union. It is a larger body comprising in excess of 40 Member States drawn from the whole continent of Europe and includes Russia and Turkey. It was founded in 1949.

[157] For a general discussion of the Council's work see eg M Killerby 'The Council of Europe's Contribution to Family Law (Past, Present and Future)' in N Lowe and G Douglas (eds) *Families Across Frontiers* (1996) 13. See also 'Achievements and documents in Family Law', available on the Council of Europe's website.

[158] Recommendation No R 85(4). Other Recommendations of note include that relating to parental responsibilities (1984) and on mediation (1998).   [159] CJ-FA (2001) 16 Rev.

[160] The Conference has a long history, formally beginning with an international conference called by the Dutch Government in 1893. For its work generally see K Lipstein 'One Hundred Years of Hague Conference on Private International Law' (1993) 42 ICLQ 553. Unlike the Council of Europe, membership of the Hague Conference is global. As of July 2014 there were 75 Member States.

a trilogy of Conventions dealing with different aspects of child law, its work in the field of maintenance[161] and marriage and divorce[162] should not be overlooked.

The three Conventions affecting children are, in chronological order, the 1980 Hague Convention on the Civil Aspects of International Child Abduction, the 1993 Hague Convention on Protection of Children and Co-operation in Respect of Intercountry Adoption and the 1996 Hague Convention on Jurisdiction, Applicable Law, Recognition, Enforcement and Co-operation in Respect of Parental Responsibility and Measures for the Protection of Children. The Abduction Convention, to which there are, at the time of writing, 92 Contracting States, provides rules governing the return of and access to children wrongfully removed to or retained in another Contracting State. The Intercountry Adoption Convention, to which there are, at the time of writing, 93 Contracting States, provides an international regulatory framework governing the adoption of a child from one country by adopters of another. These latter highly successful instruments are discussed in Chapter 26.

The 1996 Child Protection Convention,[163] which came into force for the United Kingdom in 2012,[164] in broad terms provides for common jurisdictional rules and consequent provisions for the recognition and enforcement of judgments concerned with child protection. 'Protection' for these purposes is a wide term referring to both private and public law measures taken by judicial and administrative bodies to safeguard children. In particular it governs[165] the attribution, exercise, termination and delegation of parental responsibility,[166] rights of custody and access, guardianship, curatorship and analogous institutions, the designation and functions of any person or body having charge of the child's person or property, representing or assisting the child; placing the child in foster or institutional care or the provision of care by *Kafala*[167] or an analogous institution; public authority supervision of the care of a child and the administrative conservation or disposal of the child's property.[168] It specifically does not include[169] establishing or contesting a parent–child relationship, adoption, names, emancipation, maintenance, trusts or succession, social security, general public measures on health or education, measures taken as a result of penal offences committed by children; and the right of asylum and immigration decisions.

---

[161] Ie the 1973 Conventions on the Law Applicable to Maintenance Obligations and the Recognition and Enforcement of Decisions Relating to Maintenance Obligations.

[162] On which note the 1970 Convention on Recognition of Divorce and Legal Separation and 1973 Convention on the Celebration and Recognition of the Validity of Marriages.

[163] This in fact is the third Convention on the Protection of Children; the first was drawn up and signed in 1902 and the second in 1961. That latter Convention will be superseded by the 1996 Convention. For detailed discussion of the 1996 Convention see N Lowe, M Everall and M Nicholls *International Movement of Children: Law, Practice and Procedure* (2004) ch 24.

[164] The Convention itself has been in force since 2002 and at the time of writing there are 40 Contracting States.

[165] See Art 3 which provides illustrative but not definitive examples.

[166] On which there are detailed provisions (see Arts 16 and 17) including the provisions (see Art 16(3) and (4)) that where parental responsibility exists under the law of the State of the child's habitual residence it will continue to exist notwithstanding a change of that residence to another State but where the law of the State of the child's new habitual residence automatically confers responsibility on a person who does not already have it, the latter law will prevail. The net effect of these provisions therefore is that they affect *domestic* substantive law on the allocation of parental responsibility.

[167] *Kafala* is an Islamic concept akin to fostering but short of adoption.

[168] Though note under Art 55, reservations may be entered with respect to measures directed at protecting the child's property.   [169] Art 4 which provides a definitive list of exclusions.

Notwithstanding these exemptions, the importance of the 1996 Convention lies in part on the width of its application. For example, it plugs a gap in the 1993 Intercountry Adoption Convention by applying both to *Kafala* (which is important to Islamic states) and to fostering. It also has the potential advantage of its practical global reach. As well as providing jurisdictional rules, etc the Convention contains important provisions with regard to co-operation and the exchange of information and has some particularly useful provisions for safeguarding rights of access.[170]

One disadvantage of the Convention is that it is one of a number concerning custody and particularly access which add to the complexity concerning the interrelationship between the international instruments.[171]

(c) The European Union and the Brussels Regulations

As significant a development as the Human Rights Act was the entry into family law of the European Union (EU).[172] Although the EU had long had some potential to impact upon family law issues, until March 2001 it did so only peripherally as, for example, through the provisions governing free movement rights and, the then 1968 Brussels Convention on Jurisdiction and Enforcement of Judgments in Civil and Commercial Matters which had been incorporated into UK domestic law by the Civil Jurisdiction and Judgments Act 1982.[173] In fact the Brussels Convention (which subsequently became a Regulation)[174] only impacted upon maintenance. It expressly excluded matters of status and rights of property arising from marriage because it was considered too difficult to unify the applicable jurisdiction rules of even the then six Member States.[175] But this 'hands off' family law approach radically changed with the conclusion of Council Regulation (EC) No 1347/2000 of 29 May 2000 on jurisdiction and the recognition and enforcement of civil and commercial judgments in matrimonial matters and matters of parental responsibility for children of both spouses—the so-called 'Brussels II' which came into force on 1 March 2001.[176] The 2000 Regulation was soon revised by Council Regulation (EC) No 2201/2003 of 27 November 2003 concerning jurisdiction and the recognition and enforcement of judgments in matrimonial matters and in matters of parental responsibility, repealing Regulation (EC) No 1347/2000, 'the revised Brussels II' or 'BIIR', which came into force

---

[170] Under Art 35, discussed in Ch 26, Co-operation, p 1099.

[171] On which see the concerns expressed by N Lowe 'New International Conventions Affecting the Law Relating to Children—A Cause for Concern?' [2001] IFL 171.

[172] See, for example, the full treatment of the treatment of children under EU Law by H Stalford *Children and the European Union: Rights, Welfare and Accountability* (2012).

[173] See, for example, the discussion in C Hamilton and K Standley *Family Law in Europe* (1995, 1st edn) at 580–597.

[174] Viz. Council Regulation (EC) No 44/2201 of 22 December 2000 on Jurisdiction and the Recognition and Enforcement of Judgments in Civil and Commercial Matters. Although this is commonly known as 'Brussels I', it came into force one year *after* 'Brussels II'. From 2011 maintenance has been regulated by Council Regulation (EC) No 4/2009 on jurisdiction, applicable law, recognition and enforcement of decisions and co-operation in matters relating to maintenance obligations which replaced the maintenance provisions in Brussels I.

[175] See the Jenard Report (the Explanatory Report on the Convention) [1979] OJ C59, which specifically singled out divorce as 'a problem which is complicated by the extreme divergences between the various systems of law'.

[176] This instrument also began life as a Convention—in fact building upon the earlier Civil and Commercial Matters Convention, which is why it became known as 'Brussels II'. It was transformed into a Regulation following the Treaty of Amsterdam.

on 1 March 2005. BIIR provides binding exclusive and separate rules of jurisdiction in relation to matrimonial proceedings and in matters of parental responsibility for children and for a consequent scheme of recognition and enforcement. The EU dimension has become a common feature of international family law work at any rate in London. The final arbiter on the application of BIIR is the Court of Justice of the European Union (CJEU), which sits in Luxembourg, and which adds yet another foreign dimension to family law. BIIR will be examined in greater detail in Chapter 26.

2

FORMATION OF MARRIAGE
AND CIVIL PARTNERSHIP

A. INTRODUCTION

This chapter examines how the law on entry into marriage has developed and what are the current requirements for a valid marriage. It then considers the equivalent rules enacted for couples (at present only same sex couples) entering into a 'civil partnership'. In Chapter 3, we discuss the law and procedures for annulling these unions.

1. MARRIAGE

While traditionally and historically, marriage was the only acceptable form in which an intimate adult relationship could be given legal recognition, the latter part of the twentieth century saw a fracturing of social mores and an increased willingness amongst people living in the United Kingdom both to enter into more diverse forms of relationship and to attach legally enforceable consequences to these. Today, perhaps the major debate in family policy concerns how far such diversity should be accepted and embraced or, by contrast, rejected and controlled. The current focus of attention is upon the extent to which relationships other than heterosexual, state-sanctioned marriage should be recognised. But it would be wrong to imagine that this kind of debate is new. The legal recognition of adult relationships has always occupied the minds of policy-makers, from the concerns of the medieval Catholic church over the extent of the prohibitions on marriage between those who might be very distantly related, either by blood or marriage, to each other, to the worries of the English upper classes in the eighteenth century over the problem of 'clandestine marriage' and the loss thereby of their landed estates to the rogue seducers of their daughters.[1] A bar on remarriage of the divorced, still a moral issue for the Anglican church in the matter of the marriage of the Prince of Wales in 2005,[2] and uncertainty over how far to recognise polygamous unions sanctioned by other religions, were continuing subjects of debate over the past one hundred years.[3] All such issues show how the question of legal recognition of relationships marks out the very foundation of state control over family life and serves to set the boundaries for what forms of intimate behaviour will be tolerated or facilitated by society. The power of the State in this issue may be controlled by

---

[1] See C Brooke *The Medieval Idea of Marriage* (1989) ch 6; L Stone *Uncertain Unions, Marriage in England 1660–1753* (1992); S Cretney *Family Law in the Twentieth Century: A History* (2003) Part 1.

[2] See R Probert 'The wedding of the Prince of Wales: royal privileges and human rights' [2005] CFLQ 363.

[3] See A Campbell *How have policy approaches to polygamy responded to women's experiences and rights? An international and comparative analysis: final report status of Women Canada* (2005) [online] http://papers.ssrn.com/sol3/papers.cfm?abstract_id=1360230 (accessed 20 April 2014).

the recognition in human rights law of the right to 'marry and found a family', contained, inter alia, in Article 12 of the European Convention on Human Rights, and the ambit of this right needs to be discussed.

Marriage is declining in popularity, although it is still likely that the majority of the population will marry at some point in their lives.[4] In 2010, the provisional number of marriages registered in England and Wales was 243,808, a slight rise on the previous year, but not much more than half of the number recorded in 1972, the peak year for marriages in the post-war era, when the total reached 426,421. In 2010, 161,028 were first marriages for both parties, while 34% of the total were remarriages. Meanwhile, the age at which people marry is rising, with an average (mean) age at first marriage for men of 36.2 years, and for women of 33.6 years.[5]

One of the reasons for the decline in marriage has been the growth in cohabitation outside marriage, which we discuss in depth in Chapter 24. There has also been increasing acceptance of same sex partnerships. This increasing diversity of family forms suggests that the 'norm' of the married couple, whilst still reflecting the majority of 'family' modes, no longer encompasses the majority of the population, and the law will increasingly have to cater for relationships which do not fit neatly within the traditional model of family building within marriage. Nonetheless, the law of marriage will remain important for a sizeable number of people for some time to come and, as we will see, it continues to provide the benchmark against which other relationships are measured and (to a greater or lesser extent) accommodated in the law.

2. THE INTRODUCTION OF CIVIL PARTNERSHIPS

One of the most significant recent legal innovations in the United Kingdom was the enactment of a civil partnership law[6] to provide a legal status, comparable to marriage, for same sex couples to enter into through a registration process. But there are few estimates of the size of the lesbian, gay or bisexual population for whom this measure is intended. The Government used a figure of 5% of the population of Great Britain in seeking to determine the possible take-up of the registration procedure.[7] Alternatively, the General Household Survey found 2% of households to consist of two or more unrelated adults, and 8% cohabiting, of whom an unknown proportion may be same sex couples, compared with 47% made up of married couples, 31% single people, 10% lone parents and 2% consisting of two or more families together.[8] In fact, by the end of 2011 53,417 civil partnerships had been entered into since the Act came into force in December 2005.[9]

---

[4] ONS, *Marital Status population projections, 2008-based* (2010) [online] http://www.ons.gov.uk/ons/rel/npp/marital-status-population-projections-for-england-wales/2008-based-marital-status-projections/index.html, p 1 (accessed 20 April 2014).

[5] All data are taken from ONS, *Marriages in England and Wales (Provisional) 2011* (2013).

[6] See M Harper et al *Civil Partnership: The New Law* (2005) chs 1–3 for background, and DTI Women and Equality Unit *Civil Partnership: A framework for the recognition of same sex couples* (2003).

[7] DTI Women and Equality Unit, *Civil Partnership: a framework for the recognition of same sex couples* (2003) Annex A(1) p 76.

[8] ONS, *Living in Britain: General Household Survey 2002* (2004) Table 3.5.

[9] ONS, *Civil Partnerships in the UK, 2011,* (2012) Table 2. For a full survey of developments across Europe, see I Curry-Sumner *All's well that ends registered? The substantive and private international law aspects of non-marital registered relationships in Europe* (2005) and K Boele-Woelki and A Fuchs (eds) *Legal Recognition of Same-Sex Relationships in Europe: National, cross-border and European perspectives* (2nd edn, 2012).

Section 1 of the Civil Partnership Act 2004 provides that:

> (1) A civil partnership is a relationship between two people of the same sex ('civil partners')—
>   (a) which is formed when they register as civil partners of each other— . . . or
>   (b) which they are treated . . . as having formed . . . by virtue of having registered an overseas relationship[10]. . .
> (3) A civil partnership ends only on death, dissolution or annulment.

The model of creating a broadly equivalent but separate legal status, rather than extending marriage to same sex couples, originated in Denmark[11] and was rapidly adopted in many other, mainly European, jurisdictions.[12] It enables governments to avoid the charge that they are 'weakening' the institution of marriage and allows them to present the measure as an anti-discrimination device and even as a 'pro-family' policy. The UK Government summarised the advantages of civil partnership registration as:

> an important equality measure for same sex couples . . . who are unable to marry each other. It would provide for the legal recognition of same sex partners and give legitimacy to those in, or wishing to enter into, interdependent, same sex couple relationships that are intended to be permanent. Registration would provide a framework whereby same sex couples could acknowledge their mutual responsibilities, manage their financial arrangements and achieve recognition as each other's partner. Committed same sex relationships would be recognised and registered partners would gain rights and responsibilities which would reflect the significance of the roles they play in each other's lives. This in turn would encourage more stable family life.[13]

The Civil Partnership Act 2004 was introduced in response to two private member's bills which had earlier been presented to Parliament.[14] It was enacted against a backdrop of developing judicial activism concerning the rights of gays and lesbians, in particular based on the view that continuing discrimination could no longer be upheld since the Human Rights Act 1998 had incorporated the European Convention into domestic law.[15] Although attempts were made to wreck the Bill by extending its ambit to, for example, two elderly sisters living together, a general party political consensus ensured its successful passage and it entered into force on 5 December 2005, enabling the first registrations to take place on 21 December 2005.

We explore throughout this book how far civil partners in fact have the same rights and obligations as spouses under the 2004 Act. It may suffice here to note that the approach of

---

[10] In accordance with Part 5 Ch 2 of the Act. Note the unsuccessful challenge to this provision in *Wilkinson v Kitzinger (No 2)* [2006] EWHC 2022 (Fam) [2007] 1 FLR 295. See further later, The right to marry, p 36.

[11] See L Nielsen 'Family rights and the "registered partnership" in Denmark' (1990) IJLF 297.

[12] See DTI Women and Equality Unit *Civil Partnership: a framework for the recognition of same sex couples* (2003) Tables 1, 2.

[13] DTI Women and Equality Unit, *Civil Partnership: a framework for the recognition of same sex couples* (2003) paras 1.2, 1.3.

[14] See the Relationships (Civil Registration) Bill 2001, presented to the House of Commons by Jane Griffith MP, which would simply have extended the rights of marriage to any couple (hetero- or homosexual) who registered their relationship, and the Civil Partnerships Bill 2002, presented to the House of Lords by Lord Lester of Herne Hill, also open to both hetero- and homosexual couples, but which was a much more ambitious scheme which sought to move the law forward from that applicable to existing marriages.

[15] See *Fitzpatrick v Sterling Housing Association Ltd* [2001] 1 AC 27, HL; *Ghaidan v Godin-Mendoza* [2004] UKHL 30, [2004] 2 AC 557, discussed at Ch 24 'A Man and a Woman' at p 941.

the legislation is almost entirely to equate both institutions.[16] In other states which have enacted civil partnership laws, the extent to which the registered partnership resembles marriage in its legal consequences varies according to national preference; so too does the question of whether it is a status open to heterosexual as well as same sex couples,[17] and this is discussed further later.[18] A variant on the model is to view it primarily as registration of a *contract* between the parties, rather than as registration of their *relationship*, as in France, where the *pacte civil de solidarité* (PACS) leaves it primarily to the parties to shape the terms and conditions of their union, although certain additional rights and obligations are attached. The French *pacte* may be entered into by both heterosexual and same sex partners, and is avowedly intended to be different and not equivalent to marriage.[19] It may thereby have some attraction for those couples, be they heterosexual or same sex, who reject the traditional values attached to marriage.

3. THE MARRIAGE (SAME SEX COUPLES) ACT 2013

By contrast, many same sex lobby groups have sought the opening up of marriage to same sex couples, arguing that only this approach is compatible with constitutional or human rights requirements. An increasing number of jurisdictions have adopted this view; the Netherlands introduced same sex marriage in 2001, with several other countries, including Belgium, Spain and France enacting similar laws subsequently. Outside Europe, Argentina, New Zealand and South Africa have all legislated to permit same sex marriage. Constitutional challenges to a bar on same sex marriage have been brought across Canada and the USA,[20] and in the United Kingdom, both the Scottish Government and the United Kingdom Coalition Government (in respect of England and Wales) proposed opening up marriage to same sex couples in 2012.[21] Initially, the Coalition Government proposed in their public consultation on the issue that this would be limited to civil marriage ceremonies,[22] but in their response to the consultation, they announced that new legislation would permit (but not require) religious organisations to marry same sex couples, although this right would not be extended to the Church of England.[23] The

---

[16] For a critical analysis, see L Glennon 'Strategizing for the Future through the Civil Partnership Act' (2006) 33 *Journal of Law and Society* 244.

[17] As in the Netherlands, for example. See A Barlow 'Regulation of Cohabitation, Changing Family Policies and Social Attitudes: A Discussion of Britain Within Europe' (2004) *Law and Policy* 57 especially pp 61–7.   [18] See later, Conversion of civil partnership into marriage p 61.

[19] But see E Steiner 'The spirit of the new French registered partnership law—promoting autonomy and pluralism or weakening marriage?' [2000] CFLQ 1, who describes it as 'ersatz marriage' at p 8. See also R Probert 'From lack of status to contract: assessing the French *Pacte Civil de Solidarité*' (2001) 23 JSWFL 257.

[20] See L Glennon 'Displacing the "conjugal family" in legal policy—a progressive move?' [2005] CFLQ 141; S Katz, *Family Law in America* (2003) pp 53–8. For the view that the goal of those seeking equality for homosexuals should not be assimilation with marriage, see K Norrie 'Marriage is for heterosexuals—may the rest of us be saved from it' [2000] CFLQ 363.

[21] The Act only applies to England and Wales; Scotland and Northern Ireland have their own jurisdiction to determine whether same sex marriages are to be permitted. Scotland has enacted the Marriage and Civil Partnership (Scotland) Act 2014 but the Northern Ireland Assembly rejected a motion to introduce same sex marriage for the third time in April 2014: see [online] http://www.bbc.co.uk/news/uk-northern-ireland-27201120 (accessed 7 May 2014).

[22] Government Equalities Office, *Equal civil marriage: a consultation* (2012).

[23] HM Government, *Equal marriage: The Government's response* (2012). The restriction would also have applied to the Church in Wales, but the subsequent legislation does not apply the same prohibition. See later, Formalities of marriage, Marriage (Same Sex Couples) Act 2013, p 50.

legislation was duly enacted in 2013, with the first same sex couples being able to marry from March 2014.[24]

Section 1(1) of the Act states that 'Marriage of same sex couples is lawful'. The Act then goes on to make provision for how such marriages are to be performed, the consequences for other areas of the law and for the interpretation of existing legislation and legal documents of the extension of marriage to same sex couples, how civil partnerships may be converted into marriages, the implications for trans-gender people, and for a review of civil partnership[25] (in particular to consider the question whether the status is still necessary and if so, whether it should be opened up to heterosexual couples). Schedule 3 para 1 provides that:

> In existing England and Wales legislation—
>
> (a) a reference to marriage is to be read as including a reference to marriage of a same sex couple;
> (b) a reference to a married couple is to be read as including a reference to a married same sex couple; and
> (c) a reference to a person who is married is to be read as including a reference to a person who is married to a person of the same sex.
> (2) Where sub-paragraph (1) requires a reference to be read in a particular way, any related reference (such as a reference to a marriage that has ended, or a reference to a person whose marriage has ended) is to be read accordingly.

Para 5 also states that

> (2) The following expressions have the meanings given—
>
> (a) "husband" includes a man who is married to another man;
> (b) "wife" includes a woman who is married to another woman;
> (c) "widower" includes a man whose marriage to another man ended with the other man's death;
> (d) "widow" includes a woman whose marriage to another woman ended with the other woman's death;
> and related expressions are to be construed accordingly.
> (3) A reference to marriage of same sex couples is a reference to—
> (a) marriage between two men, and
> (b) marriage between two women.
> (4) A reference to a marriage of a same sex couple is a reference to—
> (a) a marriage between two men, or
> (b) a marriage between two women.

It follows that in the discussion in this chapter, we use the term spouses to refer to both heterosexual and same sex couples unless the context requires otherwise. It will be noted that the legislation assumes that the parties to a same sex marriage between two men are to be referred to as 'husbands' and parties to a same sex marriage between two women are 'wives', but where we refer to 'husband and wife' below, we include two men or two women in a same sex marriage unless, once more, the context otherwise requires.

---

[24] DCMS 'First Same Sex weddings to happen from 29 March 2014' [online] https://www.gov.uk/government/news/first-same-sex-weddings-to-happen-from-29-march-2014 (accessed 20 April 2014).

[25] Marriage (Same Sex Couples) Act 2013 s 15.

B. THE RIGHT TO MARRY

The right to marry is enshrined in human rights law, and may be seen as a fundamental part of the freedom of the individual to form personal relationships according to his or her own inclination. The focus of the European Convention on Human Rights was on the risk of totalitarian state control and the aim was to carve out an area of personal liberty beyond the interference of the state. Modern concerns may now extend to how far the state should *enable* the formation and recognition of relationships, either where these may be opposed by other family members (such as in the case of some cultures where the tradition of arranged marriages may tip over into the abuse of forced marriage)[26] or by sections of the community (such as opposition to same sex or polygamous marriages).

Article 12 of the European Convention provides that:

> Men and women of marriageable age have the right to marry and to found a family according to the national laws governing the exercise of this right.

This Article has been interpreted by the European Court of Human Rights as being 'mainly concerned to protect marriage as the basis of the family' and thus establishing only one right—the right to marry and found a family.[27] In other words, there is no right, as so far understood, to found a family *outside* marriage. By contrast, Art 9 of the Charter of Fundamental Rights of the European Union asserts 'The right to marry *and* the right to found a family shall be guaranteed in accordance with the national laws governing the exercise of these rights',[28] implying the recognition of two separate rights.

Notwithstanding the linkage of the right to marry with that of founding a family, the Court held in *Goodwin v United Kingdom*[29] that marriage no longer implies a procreative purpose:

> Article 12 secures the fundamental right of a man and woman to marry and to found a family. The second aspect is not however a condition of the first and the inability of any couple to conceive or parent a child cannot be regarded as *per se* removing their right to enjoy the first limb of this provision.

It went on to assert that whilst the right is 'subject to the national laws of the Contracting States . . . the limitations thereby introduced must not restrict or reduce the right in such a way or to such an extent that the very essence of the right is impaired.' It added that the margin of appreciation left to states in translating the rights in the Convention into national law cannot be so broad as to amount to an effective bar on the individual's right to marry. In *Goodwin* the issue was whether a transsexual could be prevented from marrying a person of her choice because her legal gender, fixed at birth, no longer reflected her identity. The Court found:

> that it is artificial to assert that post-operative transsexuals have not been deprived of the right to marry as, according to law, they remain able to marry a person of their former opposite sex. The applicant in this case lives as a woman, is in a relationship with a man and would only wish to marry a man. She has no possibility of doing so. In the Court's view, she may therefore claim that the very essence of her right to marry has been infringed.

---

[26] Discussed in Ch 3, Duress, at p 76 and Ch 6, Forced marriage protection orders, p 197.
[27] *Sheffield and Horsham v United Kingdom* (1999) 27 EHRR 163.   [28] Emphasis added to text.
[29] [2002] 2 FLR 487 at paras 98–9.

By the same reasoning, it would not be a valid argument to assert that a lesbian or gay person could still marry a person of the opposite sex, if the only person she or he would ever contemplate marrying was of the same sex—the very right to marry would be rendered nugatory.

The question of whether same sex couples have the right to marry under Art 12 was considered in *Wilkinson v Kitzinger (No 2)*.[30] The petitioner and her lesbian partner, both domiciled in England, went through a legally recognised marriage ceremony in British Columbia. On their return to the United Kingdom, they sought a declaration that their marriage was valid in English law. However, Potter P held that there was no breach of either Art 12 or the right to respect for family life under Art 8 of the European Convention on Human Rights, since there was, as yet, no consensus across Europe as to how same sex relationships should be treated and the existing European jurisprudence had not interpreted either Article as extending to such couples. The issue was raised again a few years later in Strasbourg in *Schalk and Kopf v Austria*.[31] Once more, the European Court found there was insufficient consensus across Europe to impose an obligation on states to permit this. However, it noted the different wording of Art 9 of the Charter. From this it reasoned that it:

> would no longer consider that the right to marry enshrined in Article 12 must in all circumstances be limited to marriage between two persons of the opposite sex. Consequently, it cannot be said that Article 12 is inapplicable to the applicants' complaint. However, as matters stand, the question whether or not to allow same sex marriage is left to regulation by the national law of the Contracting State.[32]

It added that 'marriage has deep-rooted social and cultural connotations which may differ largely from one society to another. The Court reiterates that it must not rush to substitute its own judgment in place of that of the national authorities, who are best placed to assess and respond to the needs of society.'[33]

It did go on, however, to rule that same sex relationships can be protected by the right to respect for family life enshrined in Art 8 of the Convention (having previously held only that they were covered by the right to respect for one's *private* life).[34] It relied upon the rapid evolution of social attitudes towards same sex relationships over the past decade and concluded that it would be 'artificial to maintain the view that, in contrast to a different-sex couple, a same sex couple cannot enjoy "family life" for the purposes of Article 8.'[35] However, the Court did not hold that every Member State is required to provide a similar kind of status for same sex couples, since the position across Europe is still evolving.[36] Satisfaction of this right in this jurisdiction was in any case provided by the availability of the Civil Partnership Act 2004, but is now clearly guaranteed by the Marriage (Same Sex Couples) Act 2013, which has, in part, pre-empted challenges to the United Kingdom's position brought to the European Court by homosexuals wishing to

---

[30] [2006] EWHC 2022 (Fam) [2007] 1 FLR 295. For discussion, see R Harding 'Sir Mark Potter and the Protection of the Traditional Family: Why Same Sex Marriage is Still a Feminist Issue' (2007) 15 *Feminist Legal Studies* 223.

[31] Application No 30141/04, [2011] 2 FCR 650. See L Hodson 'A Marriage by Any Other Name? *Schalk and Kopf v Austria*' (2011) 11 *Human Rights Law Review* 170.

[32] *Schalk and Kopf v Austria* [2011] 2 FCR 650 at para 58.

[33] *Schalk and Kopf v Austria* [2011] 2 FCR 650 paras 61, 62.

[34] *Mata Estevez v Spain* Application No. 56501/00, 10 May 2001.

[35] *Schalk and Kopf v Austria* [2011] 2 FCR 650 at para 94.

[36] *Schalk and Kopf v Austria* [2011] 2 FCR 650 para 105.

marry. However, similar challenges disputing the UK's limitation of civil partnership to same sex couples are also pending, and may result in yet further change to the scope of the law.[37]

C. THE NATURE OF MARRIAGE

Quite apart from its abstract meaning as the social institution of marriage, 'marriage' has two distinct meanings: the ceremony by which a couple become spouses, or the *act of marrying*; and the relationship existing between spouses, or the *state of being married*.[38] This distinction largely corresponds with its dual aspect of contract and status and it applies equally to civil partnerships.

1. MARRIAGE AS A CONTRACT

Marriage, whether civil or religious, is a contract, formally entered into. It confers on the parties the status of husband and wife, the essence of the contract being an agreement between a man and a woman to live together, and to love one another as husband and wife, to the exclusion of all others. It creates a relationship of mutual and reciprocal obligations, typically involving the sharing of a common home and a common domestic life and the right to enjoy each other's society, comfort and assistance.[39]

In English law, marriage is an agreement by which two people enter into a certain legal relationship with each other and which creates and imposes mutual rights and duties. Looked at from this point of view, marriage is clearly a contract. It presents similar problems to other contracts—for example, of form and capacity; and like other contracts it may be void or voidable. But it is, of course, quite unlike any commercial contract, and consequently it is *sui generis* in many respects. In particular we may note the following distinctive characteristics:

(1) The law relating to the capacity to marry is different from that of any other contract.

(2) A marriage may only be contracted if special formalities are observed.

(3) The grounds on which a marriage may be void or voidable are for the most part completely different from those on which other contracts may be void or voidable.

(4) Unlike other voidable contracts, a voidable marriage cannot be declared void *ab initio* by rescission by one of the parties, but may be set aside only by a decree of nullity pronounced by a court of competent jurisdiction.

(5) A contract of marriage cannot be discharged by agreement, frustration or breach. Apart from death, it can be terminated only by a formal legal act, pronounced by a court of competent jurisdiction.

2. MARRIAGE AS CREATING STATUS

Marriage additionally creates a status, that is, 'the condition of belonging to a particular class of persons [ie married persons] to whom the law assigns certain peculiar legal

---

[37] See *Ferguson and Others v United Kingdom* http://equallove.org.uk/wp-content/uploads/2011/02/equalloveapplicationtoechr.pdf (accessed 20 April 2014). See later, Conversion of Civil Partnership into Marriage, p. 61. [38] R Graveson *Status in the Common Law* (1982) pp 80–1.
[39] Per Munby J in *Re Sheffield City Council v E and S* [2004] EWHC 2808 (Fam); [2005] 1 FLR 965.

capacities or incapacities.'[40] It is the *status* of marriage that those lobbying for the extension of marriage to same sex couples have been seeking, on the basis that, notwithstanding that the same rights and obligations that spouses have may be bestowed on civil partners, they do not enjoy true equality with those who are married since they are subject to a different legal status.[41] This may have more to do with subjective perception than legal reality, but it is an important *political* argument, since it stems from the principle of non-discrimination and substantive equality of treatment.

The effect of marital status is manifested in two ways. In the first place, whereas the parties to a commercial agreement may make such terms as they think fit (provided that they do not offend against rules of public policy or statutory prohibition), the spouses' mutual rights and duties[42] are largely fixed by law and not by agreement. An increasing number of these may be varied by consent: for example, the spouses may agree not to live together. But many may still not be altered: thus, notwithstanding the existence of a marital property agreement between them, neither may contract completely out of his or her power to apply to the court for financial relief in the event of divorce.[43]

Secondly, unlike a commercial contract, which cannot affect the legal position of anyone who is not a party to it, marriage may also affect the rights and duties of third persons and the relationship of the individual with Government bodies. So, for example, private or state pensions may be payable to a person by virtue of their status as a surviving spouse.

3. DEFINITION OF MARRIAGE

The classic definition of marriage in English law is that of Lord Penzance in *Hyde v Hyde*:[44]

> I conceive that marriage, as understood in Christendom, may . . . be defined as the voluntary union for life of one man and one woman to the exclusion of all others.

It will be seen that this definition involves four conditions.

First, the marriage must be *voluntary*. Thus, as we shall see,[45] it can be annulled if there was no true consent on the part of one of the parties.

Secondly, it must be *for life*. If by marriage 'as understood in Christendom' Lord Penzance was referring to the view traditionally taken in Western Europe by the Roman Catholic Church and some other denominations, his statement is of course unexceptional. But it does not mean that by English law marriage is indissoluble: divorce by judicial process had been possible in England for over eight years when *Hyde v Hyde* was decided. The only interpretation that can be put on Lord Penzance's statement is that the marriage must last for life unless it is previously determined by a decree or some other act of dissolution.[46]

Thirdly, it must be *monogamous*. Neither spouse may contract another marriage so long as the original union subsists.

---

[40] C Allen 'Status and Capacity' (1930) 46 LQR 277, 288. In this article the author critically discusses a number of other definitions of status and analyses this elusive legal concept. See also Graveson, op cit.

[41] See R Wintermute, http://equallove.org.uk/the-legal-case/ (accessed 20 April 2014).

[42] Although for the view that there are virtually no duties attached to marriage any more, see R Deech 'Divorce Law and Empirical Studies' (1990) 106 LQR 229 at pp 243–4.

[43] Matrimonial Causes Act 1973 s 34. See below Ch 21, Private agreements, Between spouses and civil partners, p 780.   [44] (1866) LR 1 P & D 130, 133.   [45] Ch 3, Lack of consent, pp 76 *et seq.*

[46] *Nachimson v Nachimson* [1930] P 217, CA at 225, 227 (per Lord Hanworth MR), 235 (per Lawrence LJ), 243–4 (per Romer LJ).

The fourth requirement, that the union must be *heterosexual,* has, of course, now been removed.

D. AGREEMENTS TO MARRY OR FORM A CIVIL PARTNERSHIP

1. AGREEMENTS TO MARRY

A marriage is commonly preceded by an agreement to marry, or 'engagement'. At common law such agreements amounted to contracts provided that there was an intention to enter into legal relations (as there probably would not be in the case of an 'unofficial engagement'). Their highly personal and non-commercial nature gave them certain peculiar characteristics, but as a general rule they were governed by the general principles of the law of contract. Consequently, if either party withdrew from the engagement without lawful justification, the other could sue for breach of contract (commonly referred to as breach of promise to marry). Such actions became rare after the Second World War (and were seldom, if ever, brought by men), partly no doubt because of the difficulty of proving damage, but probably largely as a result of a change in social views.[47]

The fact that actions for breach of promise of marriage were only rarely brought raised the question of their continuing utility. If either party to an engagement was convinced that he (or she) ought not to marry the other, it was highly doubtful whether public policy was served by letting the threat of an action push him into a potentially unstable marriage or by penalising him in damages if he resiled. The Law Commission therefore recommended the abolition of these actions[48] and this recommendation was implemented by s 1 of the Law Reform (Miscellaneous Provisions) Act 1970. This provides that no agreement to marry shall take effect as a legally enforceable contract and that no action shall lie in this country for breach of such an agreement, wherever it was made.

However, the fact that a couple have agreed to marry each other is not without all legal significance. There may still be advantages to being able to show an engagement having taken place, in relation to certain types of property disputes.[49] Problems can therefore arise in establishing what constitutes a legally recognisable agreement to marry, and in proving that it was ever made.

(a) The meaning of an agreement to marry

It could be argued that an engagement should only be recognised if it would have amounted to a legally enforceable contract at common law. In *Shaw v Fitzgerald,*[50] however, Scott Baker J held that an agreement to marry was capable of recognition under s 2 of the Law Reform (Miscellaneous Provisions) Act 1970 even though at common law the contract would have been regarded as contrary to public policy because one of the parties was married to a third person. The test must therefore be whether there was an unconditional agreement to marry.

---

[47] The civil judicial statistics do not disclose how many actions were brought. Nor do we know how far the existence of the action led to settlements out of court.

[48] Law Com No 26 *Breach of Promise of Marriage* (1969).

[49] See Ch 4, Gifts between engaged couples and couples intending to become civil partners, p 109 and Ch 4, Disputes between engaged couples, p 118.

[50] [1992] 1 FLR 357.

(b) Proof of an engagement

The difficulty of proving an engagement actually took place has been recognised in s 44 of the Family Law Act 1996. This provides that where an engagement is relied upon as the basis for seeking orders under Part IV of that Act,[51] there must be produced to the court evidence in writing of the existence of the agreement to marry, or evidence by the gift of an engagement ring by one party to the agreement to the other, in contemplation of their marriage, or evidence of a 'ceremony entered into by the parties in the presence of one or more other persons assembled for the purpose of witnessing the ceremony'.[52] The aim of these requirements is to avoid lengthy enquiries into whether an engagement had, or had not been entered into.[53] But the section seems to leave room for dispute as to its interpretation. For example, does an engagement party constitute a 'ceremony', since the choice of this word might more naturally imply some kind of formal betrothal procedure?

In other contexts, no statutory test is laid down for proving that an engagement existed, but the court is likely to seek evidence of a similar kind as is required under s 44.

2. CIVIL PARTNERSHIP AGREEMENTS

These are the equivalent to an engagement in the case of prospective civil partners. Section 73 of the Civil Partnership Act 2004 mirrors s 1 of the Law Reform (Miscellaneous Provisions) Act 1970 in providing that an agreement to register as civil partners[54] does not have effect as a contract giving rise to legal rights and is not actionable for breach. Oddly, the section borrows the language of s 1(2) to provide that it does not affect any action commenced before it came into force, but unlike engagements to marry, an agreement to register as a civil partner would have had no prior legal validity anyway.[55]

E. ENTRY INTO MARRIAGE

In order that a couple may become spouses, two conditions must be satisfied: first, they must both possess the capacity to contract a marriage, and secondly, they must observe the necessary formalities.[56]

1. CAPACITY TO MARRY

In order that a person domiciled in England and Wales should have capacity to contract a valid marriage, the following conditions must currently be satisfied:

---

[51] Non-molestation or occupation orders, discussed in Ch 6, The Family Law Act 1996 Part IV, pp 179 et seq.   [52] Section 44(2)(b).

[53] Law Com No 207 *Domestic Violence and Occupation of the Family Home* (1992) para 3.24.

[54] Including entering into an overseas relationship in accordance with Part 5, Chapter 2 of the Act.

[55] Section 44 of the Family Law Act 1996 also applies to proof of a civil partnership agreement for the purposes of the domestic violence provisions of that Act. It is hard to imagine what sort of 'ceremony' could be contemplated in this context.

[56] Where a couple come from different countries, or are married abroad, the question may arise as to which law is to be applied to determining these two matters. As regards the formalities for marriage, these are determined by the law of the place where the marriage is celebrated (the *lex loci celebrationis*): see e.g. *Shagroon v Sharbatly* [2012] EWCA Civ 1507 [2013] Fam 67. The position regarding capacity is more difficult, but is broadly based on the law of the parties' domicile (*lex domicilii*), though whether this depends exclusively

(a) neither party must be already married or in a civil partnership;

(b) both parties must be over the age of 16; and

(c) the parties must not be related within the prohibited degrees of consanguinity or affinity.[57]

(a) Sex

Until the Marriage (Same Sex Couples) Act 2013 came into force, it was also a require-ment that one party be male and the other female. Apart from the difficulties this caused to people who wished to marry their homosexual partner, it caused particular problems for transgender, or transsexual people.

> Transsexual people[58] are born with the anatomy of a person of one sex but with an unshakeable belief or feeling that they are persons of the opposite sex. They experience themselves as being of the opposite sex . . . The aetiology of this condition remains uncer-tain. It is now generally recognised as a psychiatric disorder, often known as gender dys-phoria or gender identity disorder. It can result in acute psychological distress.[59]

The treatment for this condition is often to provide the person with the outward physi-cal characteristics of his or her preferred gender, through both hormone treatment and gender-reassignment surgery—operations to effect a 'sex-change'. The condition was first considered by an English court in the nullity case of *Corbett v Corbett*.[60] The appli-cant in this case was born a male; before the marriage the respondent had undergone a surgical operation for the removal of her male genital organs and the provision of artificial female organs. After dealing at length with the medical evidence Ormrod J (who was also a qualified medical practitioner) concluded that a person's biological sex is fixed at birth (at the latest) and cannot subsequently be changed by artificial means. That being so, the respondent, who was male at birth, was not a woman and the mar-riage was therefore void.

In this case the respondent was to be regarded as male by three independent biological criteria: chromosomal, gonadal and genital. There are persons, however, who are male by one test and female by another (known as 'inter-sex'). Ormrod J deliberately left open the question of capacity to marry in such cases, but he was inclined to give greater weight to

---

upon each party's ante-nuptial domicile, or upon the intended matrimonial domicile, is problematic: see *Westminster City Council v C and Others* [2008] EWCA Civ 198 [2009] Fam 11 at [28]–[30] and [61]–[90].

[57] A further prohibition is to be found in the Royal Marriages Act 1772, which was passed to prevent the contracting of highly undesirable marriages by the younger brothers of King George III. It provides that no descendant of King George II (other than the issue of princesses who have married into foreign families) may marry without the previous consent of the Sovereign formally granted under the great seal and declared in Council. The Act is prospectively repealed, and replaced by provisions limited to those who are within six of succession to the throne, by s 3 of the Succession to the Crown Act 2013. For discussion of the Act see S Cretney 'Royal Marriages: Some Legal and Constitutional Issues' (2008) 124 LQR 218; R Probert 'The wedding of the Prince of Wales: royal privileges and human rights' [2005] CFLQ 363; R Probert *The Rights and Wrongs of Royal Marriage: How the Law Has Led to Heartbreak, Farce and Confusion, and Why it Must be Changed* (2011).

[58] See S Edwards *Sex and Gender in the Legal Process* (1996) ch 1. The term preferred nowadays is 'transgender', often abbreviated to 'trans'.

[59] Per Lord Nicholls of Birkenhead in *Bellinger v Bellinger* [2003] UKHL 21, [2003] 2 AC 467 at [7].

[60] [1971] P 83. For discussion of the case and its significance, see S Gilmore '*Corbett v Corbett*: Once a Man, Always a Man?' in S Gilmore, J Herring and R Probert (eds) *Landmark Cases in Family Law* (2011).

the appearance of the genital organs. However, in *W v W (Nullity)*[61] Charles J held that, in the case of an inter-sex, the decision as to whether the person is male or female for the purpose of marriage should be made having regard also to psychological and hormonal factors, and secondary sexual characteristics. There, the respondent had been born of indeterminate sex but her parents had registered her as a male. As she grew up, she regarded herself as female and developed a female body shape, although her chromosomal and gonadal sex was male. She underwent surgery to enable her to have penetrative sex as a woman. It was held that she was a female for the purposes of marriage and thus her marriage to a man was valid.[62]

It has been suggested that from a social and domestic point of view the psychological gender of a transgender person (that is the sex to which the individual feels that he or she belongs) is of greater importance than biological sex.[63] Accordingly, as the parties to such a union regard themselves as belonging to opposite sexes (a view presumably shared by others), a marriage between them should be valid, at least provided that the transgender party has undergone surgery of the type described. This, coupled with other arguments based on human rights and, more recently, further medical evidence concerning differences in brain structure of transsexuals, was argued in a number of cases taken to the European Court of Human Rights following *Corbett v Corbett*. In a number of decisions, the European Court upheld the approach taken in *Corbett v Corbett* but recognised the hardship which transsexuals might suffer from an inflexible law and noted that social attitudes in Europe have been changing. It stressed the need for the United Kingdom to keep the law under review but no legal changes were made.[64] Finally, in *Goodwin v United Kingdom*[65] and *I v United Kingdom*[66] the Court ran out of patience with the United Kingdom and found that the lack of any means of a transgender person altering his or her birth registration as being of a particular sex amounted to a breach of Arts 8 (in respect of the right to respect for *private* life) and 12. In essence, the Court considered that English law did not respect the dignity of the transgender individual, because of the embarrassment and intrusion such people may suffer when called upon to reveal their birth registration, and their inability to live fully under the law as persons of their chosen gender.

This ruling placed the United Kingdom Government under an obligation to bring the law into line with the Convention. This obligation was strengthened when the House of Lords found that s 11(c) of the Matrimonial Causes Act 1973, which provided that the parties to the marriage must be respectively male and female,[67] was incompatible with the Convention and made a declaration of incompatibility. In *Bellinger v Bellinger*[68] a male to

---

[61] [2001] Fam 110. See also P-L Chau and J Herring 'Defining, Assigning and Designing Sex' (2002) 16 Int Jo Law, Policy and the Family 327.

[62] Several jurisdictions provide for a person to be registered as of 'indeterminate sex' thus avoiding the need to opt for male or female, but have not resolved the effect of such registration on the capacity to marry: see BBC, 'Germany allows "indeterminate" gender at birth' [online] 1 November 2013 http://www.bbc.co.uk/news/world-europe-24767225 (accessed 20 April 2014).

[63] See I Kennedy 'Transsexual and Single Sex Marriage' (1973) 2 *Anglo-American Law Review* 112.

[64] *Rees v United Kingdom* (1986) 9 EHRR 56; *Cossey v United Kingdom* [1991] 2 FLR 492; *X, Y and Z v United Kingdom* [1997] 2 FLR 892; *Sheffield and Horsham v United Kingdom* [1998] 2 FLR 928.

[65] [2002] 2 FLR 487. See C Bessant 'Transsexuals and Marriage after *Goodwin v United Kingdom*' [2003] Fam Law 111, R Sandland 'Crossing and Not Crossing: Gender, Sexuality and Melancholy in the European Court of Human Rights' (2003) 11 Fem LS 191.   [66] [2002] 2 FLR 518.

[67] This provision was repealed by the Marriage (Same Sex Couples) Act 2013 Sch 7 para 27.

[68] [2003] UKHL 21, [2003] 2 AC 467. See S Gilmore '*Bellinger v Bellinger*—Not quite between the ears and between the legs—Transsexualism and marriage in the Lords' [2003] CFLQ 295; A Bradney 'Developing Human Rights? The Lords and Transsexual Marriages' [2003] Fam Law 585, S Cowan ' "That Woman Is a Woman!" The Case of *Bellinger v Bellinger* and the Mysterious (Dis)appearance of Sex' (2004) 12 Fem LS 79.

female transgender person sought a declaration that the marriage she had entered into in 1981 was valid. Her application was dismissed and the House of Lords dismissed her final appeal. Although it was potentially open to the House to read the provision as referring to gender, rather than biological sex,[69] it rejected this argument, holding that it would 'necessitate giving the expressions "male" and "female" in that Act a novel, extended meaning: that a person may be born with one sex but later become, or become regarded as, a person of the opposite sex.'[70] Instead, recognising the complexity of amending the law, the House concluded that the matter must be left to Parliament.

With commendable speed, once it was finally galvanised into action, the Government duly brought forward and Parliament enacted the Gender Recognition Act 2004.[71] This did not alter the law on capacity to marry,[72] but provides a means whereby a transgender person may be given legal recognition of his or her acquired gender through the grant of a 'gender recognition certificate'. The person must apply under s 1 of the Act to a Gender Recognition Panel which will determine the application.[73] The basis for grant of a certificate is that the applicant is living in the other gender, or has changed gender under the law of another country or territory outside the United Kingdom. One of the reasons for the reluctance of the House of Lords simply to re-interpret the existing law was concern regarding the point at which a person may be said to have 'acquired' their new gender and be recognised as such—must he or she have had full surgery, for example? Section 2 of the Act requires that the panel must be satisfied that the applicant has, or had, gender dysphoria, that he or she has lived in the acquired gender throughout the period of two years ending with the date on which the application is made, intends to continue to live in the acquired gender until death, and complies with the requirements imposed by and under s 3. These requirements include evidence as to the treatment he or she is having or has undergone.

When marriage was restricted to opposite sex couples, the acquisition of the certificate enabled the transgender person to enter into a valid marriage with a person of the opposite sex to his or her acquired gender.[74] This is now no longer necessary. Moreover, a 'full' certificate will be granted where the applicant is *already* married provided that their spouse consents[75] and the continuity of the marriage is not affected by the change of gender.[76] If they do not consent, an 'interim' certificate will be issued.[77]

However, because civil partnerships currently remain open only to same sex couples, where a party to a civil partnership seeks a full certificate, it may not be issued unless the other party does so as well, in which case both certificates must be issued on the

[69] See S Poulter 'The Definition of Marriage in English Law' (1979) 42 MLR 409 at 421–5. Section 11 of the Matrimonial Causes Act 1973 re-enacted s 1 of the Nullity of Marriage Act 1971, which received Royal Assent 17 months after judgment was delivered in *Corbett v Corbett*.

[70] Per Lord Nicholls of Birkenhead at para 36.

[71] See S Gilmore 'The Gender Recognition Act 2004' [2004] Fam Law 741, R Sandland 'Feminism and the Gender Recognition Act 2004' (2005) 13 Fem LS 43.

[72] Although it does make some changes to marriage law, see Ch 3, Gender reassignment, p 83.

[73] Sch 1(1). Those eligible to sit on such a panel must be legally or medically qualified.

[74] So long as the spouse is aware that he or she has changed gender: see Ch 3, Bars to relief, Petitioner's knowledge, p 85. For equivalent provision for civil partners, see Ch 3, Voidable civil partnerships, p 88.

[75] The marriage must be a 'protected' marriage, which is defined by s 25 of the Gender Recognition Act 2004 (as amended) as a marriage under the law of England and Wales or a marriage under the law of a country or territory outside the United Kingdom. If the marriage is not 'protected', an interim certificate may be granted.

[76] Gender Recognition Act 2004 s 11A, inserted by Marriage (Same Sex Couples) Act 2013, Sch 5, para 10.

[77] Section 4 as amended by Marriage (Same Sex Couples) Act 2013 Sch 5 para 3. For the effect of this, and its conversion to a full certificate, see Ch 3, Gender reassignment, p 83.

same day.[78] It seems rather unlikely that both parties—formerly say, male—would wish to acquire a female gender identity which would enable them to retain their status as civil partners. Fortunately, where the other partner does not wish to change gender as well, the couple may take advantage of s 9 of the 2013 Act which enables them to convert the civil partnership into a marriage.[79]

Where a full certificate is granted, the Secretary of State must send a copy to the Registrar General, who will maintain a gender recognition register, not open to the public. The Registrar enters the person's details in the gender recognition register and annotates the original birth register to enable a confidential trace between the two to be made. The effect is that:[80]

> the person's gender becomes for all purposes[81] the acquired gender (so that, if the acquired gender is the male gender, the person's sex becomes that of a man and, if it is the female gender, the person's sex becomes that of a woman).

(b) Age

Both by canon law and at common law a valid marriage could be contracted only if both parties had reached the legal age of puberty, viz. 14 in the case of a boy and 12 in the case of a girl.[82] If either party was under this age when the marriage was contracted, it could be avoided by either of them when that party reached the age of puberty; but if the marriage was ratified (as it would impliedly be by continued cohabitation), it became irrevocably binding.[83]

It is perhaps surprising that this remained the law until well into the twentieth century. In the words of Pearce J:[84]

> According to modern thought it is considered socially and morally wrong that persons of an age, at which we now believe them to be immature and provide for their education, should have the stresses, responsibilities and sexual freedom of marriage and the physical strain of childbirth. Child marriages by common consent are believed to be bad for the participants and bad for the institution of marriage.

This change of thought led to the passing of the Age of Marriage Act in 1929. Section 1 (now re-enacted in the Marriage Act 1949 s 2) effected two changes in the law. First, it was enacted that a valid marriage could not be contracted unless both parties had reached the age of 16, and secondly any marriage in which either party was under this age was made *void* and not voidable as before.[85] However, the problems identified by Pearce J do not seem

---

[78] Section 5B as inserted by Marriage (Same Sex Couples) Act 2013 Sch 5 para 5.

[79] See later, Conversion of civil partnership into marriage, p 61.   [80] Section 9(1).

[81] But not in respect of things done, or events occurring, before the certificate is issued: s 9(2), and the fact that a person's gender has been altered does not affect his or her status as the father or mother of a child: s 12. Thus, a male to female transgender person who had fathered a child outside marriage and had not acquired parental responsibility would not automatically acquire it on becoming a female. See Ch 11, Acquisition of parental responsibility by unmarried fathers, p 370.

[82] For discussion of the international law aspects, see R Gaffney-Rhys 'A comparison of child marriage and polygamy from a human rights perspective: are the arguments equally cogent?' (2012) 34 JSWFL 49.

[83] Co Litt 79; Blackstone *Commentaries*, i, 436.

[84] *Pugh v Pugh* [1951] P 482 at 492. See further Law Com No 33 *Nullity of Marriage* (1970), paras 16–20; Report of the Latey Committee on the Age of Majority 1967, Cmnd 3342, paras 166–177.

[85] In Australia, a court may authorise the marriage of a person aged up to two years under the minimum age (18) in 'exceptional and unusual' circumstances: Marriage Act 1961 s 12 (as amended). For discussion of this provision meeting the needs of ethnic minorities, see P Parkinson 'Multiculturalism and the Regulation of Marital Status in Australia' in NV Lowe and G Douglas (eds) *Families across Frontiers* (1996) p 309.

to be affected by marriage age—the number of people marrying at a young age has steeply declined, while sexual experience among young people has increased enormously.[86]

(c) Prohibited degrees

Most, if not all, states prohibit certain marriages as incestuous. The prohibited relationship may arise from consanguinity (ie blood relationship) or from affinity (ie relationship by marriage). Before the Reformation, English law adopted the canon law of consanguinity and affinity,[87] but one of the results of the break with the Roman Catholic Church was the adoption of a modified table of prohibited degrees. Since 1949 the prohibitions have been statutory and are contained in the First Schedule to the Marriage Act, as amended:[88]

PART I
Adoptive child
Adoptive parent
Child
Former adoptive child
Former adoptive parent
Grandparent
Grandchild
Parent
Parent's sibling[89]
Sibling
Sibling's child

PART II
Child of former civil partner
Child of former spouse
Former civil partner of grandparent
Former civil partner of parent
Former spouse of grandparent
Former spouse of parent
Grandchild of former civil partner
Grandchild of former spouse

Consanguinity

In the case of consanguinity, prohibition is based on moral and eugenic grounds. Most people view the idea of sexual intercourse (and therefore marriage) between, say, father and daughter or brother and sister with abhorrence; furthermore, the more closely the parties are related, the greater will be the risk of their children inheriting undesirable genetic characteristics. The degrees of relationship based on consanguinity are set out in Part I of the Schedule to the Marriage Act; marriage within these degrees is completely

---

[86] The number of women aged 16 to 19 who married in 2010 was 2,754 (8 of whom had already been divorced), out of a total of 243,808 women getting married. Only 832 men aged under 20 married in 2010: ONS, *Marriages in England and Wales (provisional), 2011* (2013), Age at marriage by sex and previous marital status, Table 1. 'Almost all' women and men in this age group have their first sexual intercourse outside marriage: K Wellings et al *Sexual Behaviour in Britain* (1994) pp 74–5.

[87] See F Pollock and F Maitland *History of English Law*, pp ii and 383–7. The rules that emerged lacked theological or sociological justification and 'are the idle ingenuities of men who are amusing themselves by inventing a game of skill which is to be played with neatly drawn tables of affinity and doggerel hexameters': ibid, 387.   [88] Most recently by the Civil Partnership Act 2004 Sch 27 para 17.

[89] Sibling means a brother, sister, half-brother or half-sister: Sch 1, para 1(2), as amended.

prohibited.[90] It is notable, however, that marriage between first cousins is *not* prohibited.[91] Because of the eugenic basis of the prohibition it includes not only relationships traced through the whole blood but also those traced through the half blood,[92] and it is immaterial that the parents of either of the parties (or of any person through whom the relationship is traced) have not been married to each other.[93]

Affinity

In the case of affinity, prohibition was originally based on the theological concept that husband and wife were one flesh, so that marriage with one's sister-in-law was as incestuous as marriage with one's own sister.[94] Today, the justification must be sought on social and moral grounds. (Some will also have religious objections to certain marriages,[95] but in a pluralist society this must be a matter for the individual's conscience.) Marriage with a near relation of a former spouse is liable to create tensions within the family, particularly if the spouse is still alive, and the possibility of marriage to a stepchild could in some cases lead to sexual exploitation. Even if this were not so, difficulties could well arise if, say, a man were to become the brother-in-law of his other stepchildren and the stepbrother-in-law of his own children. There is a stronger reason for forbidding marriage with a stepchild to whom the other party has been in loco parentis, for this can readily be seen as an abuse of the relationship. In circumstances of this sort prohibition could be justified on the ground that the function of the marriage laws is to support the family and the relationships that uphold it. On the other hand, it must be remembered that degrees of affinity can be created only by marriage (and civil partnership): there is nothing to prevent a man from cohabiting with his stepdaughter outside marriage or marrying the daughter (by another man) of a woman with whom he has himself been living.[96]

Dissatisfaction with the rules relating to affinity resulted in a gradual relaxation of the restrictions, notably in 1986 by the Marriage (Prohibited Degrees of Relationship) Act, passed after the publication of *No Just Cause*, the report of a group set up by the Archbishop of Canterbury to consider the problem following four private Acts to permit marriage within the prohibited degrees. The remaining prohibited degrees of affinity are retained in order to protect stepchildren against possible exploitation. A person may not marry his or her stepchild or stepgrandchild unless both parties have attained the age of 21 and the latter was not at any time before reaching the age of 18 a 'child of the family' in relation to the other.[97] 'Child of the family' is defined as a child who has lived in the same household as the other and been treated by the latter as a child of his or her family.[98] It will thus be seen that there is nothing to

---

[90] Marriage Act 1949 s 1(1). The list relating to relatives between whom sexual intercourse is a criminal offence is congruent with this Schedule: see Sexual Offences Act 2003 s 64.

[91] For discussion of cousin marriage, and the genetic problems that can result, see R Deech 'Cousin Marriage' [2010] *Fam Law* 619.

[92] See the definitions of 'brother' and 'sister' in the Marriage Act 1949 s 78(1).

[93] *Hains v Jeffell* (1696) 1 Ld Raym 68; *R v Brighton Inhabitants* (1861) 1 B & S 447.

[94] For the same reason in the Middle Ages extra-marital sexual intercourse created prohibited degrees.

[95] See Archbishop of Canterbury's Group, *No Just Cause, The Law of Affinity in England and Wales* (1984) pp 30–2.

[96] For an example, see *Smith v Clerical Medical and General Life Assurance Society* [1993] 1 FLR 47.

[97] Marriage (Prohibited Degrees of Relationship) Act 1986 s 1(1); Marriage Act 1949 s 1(2), (3) and Sch 1 Pt II, as amended by Sch 1 to the Act of 1986.

[98] Marriage (Prohibited Degrees of Relationship) Act 1986 s 1(5); Marriage Act 1949 s 78 (as amended). The phrase 'treated as a child of the family' also appears in the definition of 'child of the family' in the Matrimonial Causes Act 1973 and is presumably intended to be interpreted in the same way: see Ch 9, The meaning of 'child of the family', p 296.

prevent a man from marrying his stepdaughter if, say, she was brought up by her grandparents so that he was never in loco parentis to her.

The Act also allowed a person to marry their parent-in-law, provided that both parties were over the age of 21, and the corresponding spouses of the two were both dead (e.g. a man could marry his daughter-in-law provided both his wife—the son's mother—and his son were dead). However, in 2005, the European Court of Human Rights held[99] that this was an unnecessary restriction on the right to marry under Art 12 of the European Convention on Human Rights, on the basis that, since parties could obtain a private Act of Parliament to circumvent its provisions, its ostensible objective of protecting the integrity of the family was not sustainable. The limitation was therefore repealed.[100]

(d) Monogamy

As a result of the English view of marriage as a monogamous union,[101] neither party may contract a valid marriage whilst he or she is already married to someone else, or in a civil partnership. If a person has already contracted one marriage, he cannot contract another until the first spouse dies or the first marriage is annulled or dissolved.[102] It follows that a mistaken belief that the first marriage has been terminated, for example, by the death of the spouse,[103] is immaterial: what is relevant is whether it has in fact been terminated. Consequently, the second marriage may be void even though no prosecution for bigamy will lie in respect of it.[104]

2. FORMALITIES OF MARRIAGE

(a) Historical introduction

The history of the English law relating to the formalities of marriage has been a matter of considerable doubt.[105] Canon law emphasised the consensual aspect of the contract and before the Council of Trent in 1563 no religious ceremony had to be performed: all that was necessary was a declaration by the parties that they took each other as husband and wife, either by a promise expressed in the present tense—'*per verba de praesenti*'—(eg 'I take you as my wife [or husband]'), in which case the marriage was binding immediately, or by a promise for the future—'*per verba de futuro*'—(eg 'I shall take you as my wife [or husband]'), in which case it became binding as soon as it was consummated. But it became customary for the marriage to be solemnised in church after the publishing of

---

[99] *B and L v United Kingdom (Application No 36546/02)* [2006] 1 FLR 35.

[100] By the Marriage Act 1949 (Remedial Order) 2007, SI 2007/438.

[101] For discussion of the English position and its impact on cultural minorities, see P Shah, *Legal Pluralism in Context* (2005) Chap 5. For a discussion of the human rights dimension, see R Gaffney-Rhys, 'A comparison of child marriage and polygamy from a human rights perspective: are the arguments equally cogent?' (2012) 34 JSWFL 49.

[102] But this does not apply if the first marriage was *void*: see Ch 3, The current distinction between void and voidable marriages, Necessity for decree, p 66.

[103] Or by the grant of a divorce decree which is void, eg *Butler v Butler (Queen's Proctor Intervening)* [1990]1 FLR 114; *Manchanda v Manchanda* [1995] 2 FLR 590, CA.

[104] For the position regarding polygamous marriages celebrated abroad, see Ch 3, Grounds on which a marriage will be void, Lack of capacity, p 71.

[105] See the conflicting opinions expressed in *R v Millis* (1844) 10 Cl & Fin 534, HL. See Swinburne *Spousals* (1686); F Pollock and F Maitland *History of English Law* pp ii, 362 *et seq*; the judgment of Sir W Scott in *Dalrymple v Dalrymple* (1811) 2 Hag Con 54; the opinion of the judges in *Beamish v Beamish* (1861) 9 HL Cas 274, HL. The leading text is now R Probert *Marriage Law and Practice in the Long Eighteenth Century: A Reassessment* (2009).

banns (unless this was dispensed with by papal or episcopal licence) and with the consent of the parents of either party who was under the age of 21. The marriage would then be contracted at the church door in the presence of the priest, after which the parties would go into the church itself for the celebration of the nuptial mass.

The common law favoured such open ceremony, for upon the existence of the union might depend many property rights and the identity of the heir at law. But in the course of time the reason for the common law's preference for such a marriage was forgotten, and neither the publishing of banns nor the presence of any other witness was any longer considered necessary; the emphasis shifted to the presence of simply the priest (or, after the Reformation, a clerk in holy orders). The 'clandestine marriage' carried out in secret was thus as binding as if it had been solemnised in church. Indeed, even where the couple exchanged vows without the presence of an ordained priest or deacon, either *per verba de praesenti* or *per verba de futuro* with subsequent sexual intercourse, it became accepted—incorrectly—that a valid marriage was created[106] and, if either party to it subsequently married another, the later marriage could be annulled.[107]

Reform of the common law

Numerous problems resulted from such a state of law. A person who had for years believed him- or herself to be validly married would suddenly find that the marriage was a nullity because of a previous clandestine or irregular union, the existence of which had never been suspected. Children could marry without their parents' consent, and if the minor was a girl with a large fortune, the common law rule that a wife's property vested in her husband on marriage made her a particularly attractive catch. The 'Fleet' parsons thrived—profligate clergy who traded in clandestine marriages. By the middle of the eighteenth century matters had come to such a pass that there was a danger in certain sections of society that such marriages would become the rule rather than the exception.[108]

It was to stop these abuses that Lord Hardwicke's Act was passed in 1753.[109] The principle underlying this Act was to secure publicity by enacting that no marriage[110] should be valid unless it was solemnised according to the rites of the Church of England in the parish church of the parish in which one of the parties resided, in the presence of a clergyman and two other witnesses. Unless a licence had been obtained, banns had to be published in the parish church of the parish in which each party resided for three Sundays. If either party was under the age of 21, parental consent had to be obtained as well, unless this was impossible to obtain or was unreasonably withheld, in which case the consent of the Lord Chancellor had to be obtained. If these stringent provisions were not observed, the marriage would in the vast majority of cases be void.

Lord Hardwicke's Act effectively put a stop to clandestine marriages in England, but many couples deliberately evaded it by getting married in Scotland, particularly when one of the parties was a minor and parental consent was withheld, and the 70 years following the passing of the Act saw an increasing number of 'Gretna Green' marriages. It was in an attempt to prevent this state of affairs that the Marriage Act 1823 was passed to

[106] *Dalrymple v Dalrymple* (1811) 2 Hag Con 54. Probert argues convincingly that the decision was based on a misunderstanding of the medieval law: see R Probert *Marriage Law and Practice in the Long Eighteenth Century: A Reassessment* (2009), Ch 2.

[107] *Bunting v Lepingwell* (1585) 4 Co Rep 29a. See R Probert *Marriage Law and Practice in the Long Eighteenth Century: A Reassessment* (2009).

[108] See L Stone *Uncertain Unions: Marriage in England 1660–1753* (1992).

[109] S Parker 'The Marriage Act 1753: A Case Study of Family Law-Making' (1987) 1 Int J Law and Fam 133.

[110] Marriages according to the usages of the Society of Friends (Quakers) and according to Jewish rites were exempt from the provisions of the Act.

replace Lord Hardwicke's Act. A marriage was now to be void only if both parties *knowingly and wilfully* intermarried in any other place than the church wherein the banns might be published, or without the due publication of banns or the obtaining of a licence, or if they *knowingly and wilfully* consented to the solemnisation of the marriage by a person not in holy orders. In all other cases the marriage was to be valid notwithstanding any breach in the prescribed formalities.

Subsequently, the Marriage Act 1836, reflecting the growth of religious toleration in the early years of the nineteenth century, was enacted to deal with the criticism that the law forced Roman Catholics and Protestant dissenters to go through a religious form of marriage which might well be repugnant to them. This Act, together with the Births and Deaths Registration Act 1836, accordingly created superintendent registrars of births, deaths and marriages, who were empowered to issue certificates to marry as an alternative to the publication of banns or the obtaining of a licence. But its real importance lay in the fact that it permitted marriages to be solemnised in other ways than according to the rites of the Church of England, including by a civil rather than religious ceremony, and it enabled places of worship of members of other denominations to be registered for the solemnisation of marriages.

Marriage Acts 1949–1994

By 1949 the law relating to the formalities of marriage could be found only by reference to more than 40 statutes, quite apart from the case law which had grown up as the result of their judicial interpretation. The purpose of the Marriage Act 1949 was to consolidate these enactments.

The 1949 Act itself was amended by a series of Acts.[111] Notably, restrictions governing the place in which the marriage ceremony may be performed have been liberalised,[112] and the reduction of the age of majority to 18 by the Family Law Reform Act 1969 meant that anyone aged 18 or over may now marry without the consent of any other person.[113] There are also additional requirements imposed on couples where one is subject to immigration control. Such requirements are intended to restrict the use of marriage (or civil partnership) as a device to facilitate entry into, or remaining in, the United Kingdom.[114]

In addition to laying down the legal requirements relating to the preliminaries to marriage and the place and method of solemnisation, the Marriage Acts also regulate the registration of marriages.[115] Proper registration is of extreme importance not only to the

---

[111] The Marriage Act 1949 (Amendment) Act 1954; Marriage Acts Amendment Act 1958; Marriage (Enabling) Act 1960; Marriage (Wales and Monmouthshire) Act 1962; Marriage (Registrar General's Licence) Act 1970; Marriage Act 1983; Marriage (Wales) Act 1986; Marriage (Prohibited Degrees of Relationship) Act 1986; Marriage Act 1994, Marriage Ceremony (Prescribed Words) Act 1996, Immigration and Asylum Act 1999.

[112] The Marriage (Registrar General's Licence) Act 1970 permits a licence to be issued to authorise a marriage anywhere when one of the parties is suffering from a serious illness and cannot be moved; the Marriage Act 1983 permits a certificate to be issued to authorise a marriage of a house-bound or detained person in the place where he or she is confined or detained; and the Marriage Act 1994 permits the solemnisation of civil marriages in premises approved by local authorities.

[113] Section 2(1) implementing the recommendations of the Latey Committee on the Age of Majority 1967, Cmnd 3342.

[114] See eg Asylum and Immigration (Treatment of Claimants, etc) Act 2004, ss 19 et seq held in breach of Arts 12, 14 ECHR in *R (Baiai and others) v Secretary of State for the Home Department* [2008] UKHL 53 [2009] AC 287.

[115] See Pt IV of the Marriage Act 1949 (as amended) and the Marriage (Registrar General's Licence) Act 1970 s 15.

parties themselves but also to others (including Government departments) who may wish to have evidence of the marriage.

Marriage (Same Sex Couples) Act 2013

The strongest objections to the legislation opening up marriage to same sex couples came from religious organisations concerned that they would be compelled to perform marriage ceremonies for such couples despite these being contrary to their beliefs. We noted above that the Government decided to widen their original proposals beyond permitting civil marriage ceremonies to enable those religious groups that *did* wish to perform weddings for same sex couples to do so, but they were also at pains to reassure those which saw this as anathema that they would be protected from legal challenge. In the case of the Church of England, as the established church of England, this entails the creation of a 'quadruple lock' intended to ensure 'that there is a negligible chance of a successful legal challenge in any domestic court, or the ECtHR that would force any religious organisation to conduct marriages for same-sex couples against their will'.[116] The lock consists of the following safeguards. First, the 2013 Act explicitly provides that no religious organisation, or individual minister, can be compelled to marry same-sex couples or to permit this to happen on their premises.[117] Secondly, however, it provides for an 'opt-in' system for religious organisations which do wish to conduct marriages for same-sex couples.[118] Thirdly, it amends the Equality Act 2010 so that no discrimination claims can be brought against religious organisations or individual ministers for refusing to marry a same-sex couple or allow their premises to be used for this purpose.[119] Finally, it ensures that the legislation does not affect the Canon law of the Church of England or the Church in Wales.[120]

(b) Preliminaries

Marriages of persons under the age of 18

If either party to the marriage is over the age of 16 but under the age of 18, certain persons are normally required to give their express consent to the marriage or are given a power to dissent from it. The purpose of this provision is to prevent children contracting unwise marriages. Doubtless in 1753 Parliament was primarily concerned to see that property did not get into the hands of undesirable suitors; today the object is to cut down the number of potentially unstable unions.[121]

The law relating to those whose consent is required was extensively changed by the Children Act 1989. Normally it will be that of each parent with parental responsibility and each guardian (if any). Hence an unmarried father cannot withhold consent unless he has acquired parental responsibility by means of being registered as the child's father or by virtue of a parental responsibility agreement or order.[122] But if a child arrangements or special guardianship order is in force with respect to the child, the consent required is that of the person or persons with whom the child is living or is to live under the order, or each of the special guardians, and not that of parents or guardians.[123] If a care order is in force, the

---

[116] HM Government *Equal marriage: The Government's response* (2012) para 4.24.

[117] Section 2.   [118] Sections 4, 5.

[119] Section 2(5)(6) amending Equality Act 2010 s 110 and inserting para 25A into Sch 3.

[120] Section 1(3)(4). For discussion, see J Oliva and H Hall 'Same-Sex Marriage: An Inevitable Challenge to Religious Liberty and Establishment?' (2014) 3(1) Ox J Law and Religion 25.

[121] Report of the Latey Committee on the Age of Majority 1967, Cmnd 3342 paras 135–177; J Priest 'Buttressing Marriage' [1982] Fam Law 40 pp 43–5.

[122] See Ch 11, Acquisition of parental responsibility by unmarried fathers, pp 370 *et seq*. Registration bestows parental responsibility only in respect of registrations after 1 December 2003.

[123] If a child arrangements order was in force immediately before the child reached the age of 16 but is no longer in force, the consent required is that of the person or persons with whom the child lived or was to live.

local authority designated in the order must consent *in addition to* parents, guardians or special guardians.[124]

If consent cannot be obtained by reason of absence or inaccessibility, the Registrar General may dispense with it. Alternatively, if the consent is withheld, the consent of the court may be obtained instead.[125]

The Law Commission recommended that the consent requirement be repealed, considering it 'illogical, easily circumvented or surmounted, and of doubtful benefit to the very children whom it is trying to help.'[126] It noted that there has never been a consent requirement in Scotland, yet the divorce rate for teenage marriages there was lower than in England and Wales.

Given the declining number of teenage marriages, this issue may well wither away. However, it is worth noting that it has been manifested in a slightly different context—that of arranged and forced marriages,[127] where the issue is one of the *child's* rather than the *parent's* consent. Concern that young people from certain ethnic and religious communities might be subject to pressure to enter into marriages against their will led the Government in 2004 to impose a ban on the entry of foreign spouses into the United Kingdom for settlement purposes if either of the parties to the marriage was aged under 18, unless there were 'clear exceptional compassionate circumstances'. The ban was subsequently extended to those aged under 21 in 2008.[128] This was challenged in *R (Quila); R (Bibi) v Secretary of State for the Home Department*[129] by two applicants who married British citizens but were denied the right to live with them in this country. The Supreme Court held that the ban was an interference with the applicants' Art 8 right to respect for family life which was disproportionate to the legitimate aim of trying to deter or prevent forced marriages, since the Government was unable to show that the measure would have more impact on such marriages rather than on genuinely consensual ones (such as those of the applicants). The restriction concerning those aged under 18 remains.

Giving notice and obtaining authorisation to marry

The rules differentiate between marriages to be performed according to the rites of the Church of England and the rest, be they religious or civil. Civil weddings made up two-thirds (67.9%) of weddings in 2010.[130]

Marriages according to the rites of the Church of England

A heterosexual marriage may be solemnised according to the rites of the Church of England[131] (which includes the Church in Wales)[132] only after the publication of banns or on the authority of a common licence, a special licence issued by the Archbishop of Canterbury or a superintendent registrar's certificate.[133] The Church of England and currently the Church in Wales

---

[124] Marriage Act 1949 s 3(1), (1A), and (1B), as amended. If the child is a ward of court, the court's consent must be obtained: ibid s 3(6). No consent is required at all if the child is a widow or widower: s 3(1), (3).

[125] Marriage Act 1949 s 3(1)(b), (5), as amended. The 'court' for this purpose is the family court. There is no statutory right of appeal from an order of the court giving or withholding consent: *Re Queskey* [1946] Ch 250.

[126] *Review of Child Law: Guardianship and Custody,* Law Com No 172 (1988) para 7.11.

[127] Discussed further in Ch 3, Duress, p 76 and Ch 6, Forced Marriage Protection Orders, p 197.

[128] Immigration Rules 1994 (HC 395) r 277. See G Gangoli and K Chantler 'Protecting Victims of Forced Marriage: Is Age a Protective Factor?' (2009) 17 Fem LS 267.

[129] [2011] UKSC 45 [2012] 1 FLR 788

[130] ONS *Marriages in England and Wales (provisional) 2010* (2013). Marriages by area of occurrence, type of ceremony and denomination, Table 2.

[131] Marriage Act 1949, Part II.   [132] Marriage Act 1949 s 78(2).

[133] Marriage Act 1949 s 5. For details, see pp 56–57 of the 10th edition of this work.

do not permit same sex couples to marry according to their rites, and s 1(3) and (4) of the Marriage (Same Sex Couples) Act 2013 provide that any Canon providing that marriage is a union between a man and woman is not contrary to the law, and that no duty to solemnise marriages imposed upon members of the Anglican clergy (in England or Wales) is extended to same sex marriage by the Act. Section 8 of the Act provides that the Church in Wales may choose to opt in to performing same sex marriages as can other religious organisations, but the Church of England is not given the same dispensation.

Marriages to be solemnised otherwise than according to the rites of the Church of England

All marriages other than those celebrated according to the rites of the Church of England may be solemnised only on the authority of a superintendent registrar's certificate or the Registrar General's licence.[134] The certificate corresponds roughly to banns or a common licence, and the Registrar General's licence to a special licence.

(c) Solemnisation of the marriage

According to the rites of the Church of England

All marriages according to the rites of the Church of England must be solemnised[135] by a clerk in holy orders of that Church in the presence of at least two other witnesses.[136] The marriage must be solemnised within three months of the completion of the publication of the banns or the grant of the licence or twelve months from the entry of notice in the superintendent registrar's marriage notice book, as the case may be.[137]

According to other religious rites

A marriage on the authority of a superintendent registrar's certificate may be solemnised in a registered building; according to the usages of the Society of Friends or of the Jews; or the place where a house-bound or detained person is.[138] In every case the marriage must be solemnised within 12 months of the entry being made in the marriage notice book [139] in the presence of at least two witnesses in addition to the superintendent registrar and registrar or, alternatively, the registrar or authorised person and with open doors.[140]

---

[134] For details, see pp 57–59 of the 10th edition.

[135] Matrimonial Causes Act 1965 s 8(2); Marriage Act 1949 s 5A (added by the Marriage (Prohibited Degrees of Relationship) Act 1986 s 3 and Gender Recognition Act 2004 Sch 4 para 3). No clergyman is obliged to solemnise the marriage of a divorced person whose former spouse is still alive; a marriage which would have been void before the passing of the Marriage (Prohibited Degrees of Relationship) Act 1986 because of the relationship of the parties; a marriage of a person whose gender has become the acquired gender under the Gender Recognition Act 2004, or a marriage between two people of the same sex. Nor can he be forced to permit such a marriage to be solemnised in the church or chapel of which he is the minister.

[136] Marriage Act 1949 s 22, s 25. There are no longer restrictions upon the time of day when the marriage may be solemnised: Act 1949 ss 4, 75(1)(a) repealed by s 114(1) of the Protection of Freedoms Act 2012.

[137] Marriage Act 1949 s 12(2), s 16(3), s 33.

[138] Ibid s 26(1) (as amended by the Marriage Act 1983 Sch 1 and the Marriage Act 1994 s 1(1)).

[139] Unless one of the parties is house-bound or detained, or resident in Scotland or N Ireland: s 33.

[140] Ibid s 44(2), As with Anglican ceremonies, there are no longer restrictions upon the time of day when the marriage may be solemnised: ss 4, 75(1)(a) repealed by the Protection of Freedoms Act 2012 s 114(1). The requirement that the marriage must be solemnised with open doors does not apply to the marriage of a house-bound or detained person: s 45A(2), (3).

Marriage in a registered building

Any building which is certified as a place of religious worship[141] may be registered by the Registrar General for the solemnisation of marriages.[142] Bradney has suggested that relatively few buildings used by non-Christian faiths are registered, owing, in his view, to the stringent requirements for such registration.[143]

A marriage in a registered building may take place only if there is present a registrar of marriages or an 'authorised person'[144] who will normally be a minister of the particular faith or denomination. The functions of the registrar (or authorised person) are to ensure that certificates have been issued, that the provisions of the Marriage Act relating to the solemnisation are complied with, and to register the marriage. The marriage may be in any form, provided that, at some stage in the ceremony, a declaration is made similar to that required when the marriage is in a register office.[145] A same sex marriage may only be solemnised where the relevant governing authority of the religious organisation concerned has 'opted in' by written consent to performing such weddings.[146]

Quaker and Jewish marriages

Quakers, the Society of Friends, continue to be free to solemnise marriages according to their own usages. Provided that the rules of the Society permit it, a marriage may be contracted in this way even though one or both parties are not members of the Society.[147] The Jewish community may also celebrate marriages according to their own rites. In this case, however, both parties must profess the Jewish religion.[148] Both religious groups may opt in to performing same sex marriages by written consent of their governing authorities.[149]

Civil marriages

Marriage in a register office. The parties may marry in a register office[150] in the presence of the superintendent registrar and also of a registrar of marriages. They must declare that they know of no impediment why they should not be joined in matrimony and then contract the marriage.[151] No religious service may be used in a superintendent registrar's office, but, if the parties so wish, the marriage there may be followed by a religious

---

[141] Under the Places of Worship Registration Act 1855. See *R (on the application of Hodkin and another) v Registrar General of Births, Deaths and Marriages* [2013] UKSC 77 [2014] 1 All ER 737 for consideration of the purpose and application of the Act, in the context of an application by the Church of Scientology for registration of premises for the purpose of performing marriages.

[142] See the Marriage Act 1949 s 41 and s 42, as amended by the Marriage Acts Amendment Act, 1958 s 1(1), and the Marriage (Registration of Buildings) Act 1990 s 1(1). The marriage must normally be solemnised in the registration district in which one of the parties resides: s 34, s 36; but see s 35 for exceptions.

[143] A Bradney 'How not to marry people' [1989] Fam Law 408. In 2010, out of 40,325 buildings of worship in England and Wales in which marriages could be solemnised, 16,389 were Anglican, 3,279 Roman Catholic, but only 198 Muslim: ONS, *Marriages in England and Wales (provisional), 2010* Area of occurrence, type of ceremony and denomination (2013) Table 7. [144] Marriage Act 1949 s 44(2).

[145] Marriage Act 1949 s 44(1), (3).

[146] Marriage Act 1949 s 26A, inserted by Marriage (Same Sex Couples) Act 2013 s 4.

[147] Marriage Act 1949 s 47. This privilege was first granted by the Marriage (Society of Friends) Act 1860.

[148] Marriage Act 1949 s 26(1)(d).

[149] Marriage Act 1949 s 26B, inserted by Marriage (Same Sex Couples) Act 2013 s 5.

[150] Which may be in a district other than that where the certificate or licence was issued: Marriage Act 1949 s 35, s 36 (as amended).

[151] Marriage Act 1949 s 45(1), s 44(3). The form of words to be used is: 'I call upon these persons here present to witness that I, *AB*, do take thee, *CD*, to be my lawful wedded wife [or husband].' A Welsh form may be used: s 52. As to marriages of mute persons, see *Harrod v Harrod* (1854) 1 K & J 4.

ceremony in a church or chapel.[152] In this case the marriage which is *legally* binding for all purposes is that in the register office.[153]

Marriage in approved premises.   The Marriage Act 1994[154] permitted local authorities to give approval for certain premises to be used for weddings,[155] so that couples who do not want a religious ceremony may marry in more pleasant surroundings than those at many register offices. Guidance from the Registrar General explains that the Act is intended:

> . . . to allow civil marriages to take place regularly in hotels, stately homes, civil halls and similar premises without compromising the fundamental principle of English marriage law and Parliament's intention to maintain the solemnity of the occasion.[156]

'Premises' is defined in r 2(1) of the Marriages (Approved Premises) Regulations 1995 as 'a permanently immovable structure comprising at least a room, or any boat or other vessel which is permanently moored.' Marriages may not take place in the open air or on a moving vehicle, nor in a building with a recent or continuing religious connection. Thus, while a wedding could take place in the Brighton Pavilion, it could not be celebrated under the posts at the Cardiff Millennium Stadium; 'an old ironclad battleship'[157] would be suitable, but the Mersey ferry would not. Weddings at home are not permitted, and the provision of Las Vegas-style wedding chapels is unlikely to satisfy the requirement that the solemnity of the occasion be maintained. Weddings in approved premises accounted for 75.8% of all civil weddings in 2010.[158]

Only civil weddings may be performed in approved premises; the marriage must be solemnised in the presence of two witnesses and the superintendent registrar and a registrar of the registration district in which the premises are situated. There must be access to the general public, and each of the parties must make the same declaration and use the same form of words as are used in weddings in registered buildings in the presence of a registrar.[159]

Marriages of house-bound and detained persons

The requirement that the marriage must be solemnised in a register office or a registered building (or now on approved premises) meant that a person could not marry on a superintendent registrar's certificate at all if he or she was incapable of leaving home or any other building (for example, a hospital or prison).[160] The position was partly ameliorated by the provisions of the Marriage (Registrar General's Licence) Act 1970, but these apply only to those who are fatally ill. A complaint to the European Commission of Human Rights was made by a prisoner that Art 12 of the European Convention on Human Rights—the right to marry—had been infringed when he was refused permission to leave the prison to get married, and there was no mechanism to enable him to marry inside the prison.[161]

---

[152]   This may be a religious marriage rite, or, as was the case for the Prince of Wales in 2005, a blessing.

[153]   Marriage Act 1949 s 45(2), s 46.

[154]   See C Barton 'Weddings to Go—the Marriage Act 1994' [1995] Fam Law 153.

[155]   Inserting s 46A into the Marriage Act 1949.

[156]   *Guidance in pursuance of s 26(1)(bb) of the Marriage Act 1949*, para 3.

[157]   ONS *First data for marriages at 'approved premises'* ONS (98) 62 (1998).

[158]   ONS, *Marriages in England and Wales (provisional) 2010* Marriages by area of occurrence, type of ceremony and denomination (2013) Table 2.

[159]   Marriage Act 1949 s 46B inserted by the Marriage Act 1994.

[160]   Although it was not uncommon for a prisoner to be released for a short period to enable him to marry.

[161]   *Hamer v United Kingdom* (1982) 24 D & R 5; see also *Draper v United Kingdom* (1980) 24 D & R 72 (European Commission on Human Rights).

As part of a friendly settlement of the case, the Government introduced a wider relaxation in the Marriage Act 1983, which enables a house-bound or detained person to be married in the place where he or she is for the time being.

The marriage may take the form of a civil ceremony or a religious ceremony[162] (including a ceremony according to the rites of the Church of England) but Quaker and Jewish marriages are not covered by the Act.[163] Unless the marriage is solemnised according to the rites of the Church of England (when the service must be taken by a clerk in holy orders), a registrar must be present and, if the ceremony is a purely civil one, the superintendent registrar must be present as well.[164] About 100 such marriages are performed each year.[165]

(d) Reforming formalities

The present law relating to the formalities of marriage is still in principle based upon the provisions of Lord Hardwicke's Act and the Marriage Act 1836. It thus reflects the desire to prevent the clandestine marriages which were a concern for eighteenth-century society, but which are hardly a major social mischief today.

A more significant problem, so far as Government is concerned, is that of 'sham marriages', intended, usually, to enable a person otherwise not entitled to do so under the immigration rules, to remain in this country. Attempts to control these through the imposition of additional preliminary requirements were struck down by the House of Lords in *R (Baiai) and others v Secretary of State for the Home Department*.[166] Under the Asylum and Immigration (Treatment of Claimants, etc) Act 2004 s 19(3), any person subject to immigration control and not settled in the United Kingdom was required to obtain the written permission of the Secretary of State to marry in the UK, unless the marriage was to be celebrated according to the rites of the Church of England or the person had entry clearance granted expressly for the purpose of the marriage. Permission would normally only be granted if the applicant had a valid leave to enter or remain in the UK for more than six months, with more than three months of that period still outstanding. Permission could be granted in addition if there were 'exceptionally compassionate features' making it unreasonable for the applicant to travel abroad to marry or to seek entry clearance from there. Three applicants successfully challenged the Secretary of State in judicial review proceedings. Applying Art 12 of the European Convention on Human Rights, the House of Lords held that while a national authority can impose conditions on the right of a third country national to marry (and that there is no right to marry in order to secure an 'adventitious advantage'), in order to control marriages of convenience, it was disproportionate to impose restrictions which would affect genuine marriages as well, with no reliable means of distinguishing between the two. Insofar as the legislation did not apply to those marrying according to Anglican preliminaries, it was moreover discriminatory. Parliament repealed the offending provision in 2011[167] but came up with no other more effective and compatible means of deterring or detecting such marriages of convenience.

---

[162] A religious wedding between a same sex couple may be performed if the religious organisation has opted in to doing so: s 1 of the 1970 Act as amended by Marriage (Same Sex Couples) Act 2013 s 7.

[163] They require a Registrar General's licence: see earlier, Marriages to be solemnised otherwise than according to the rites of the Church of England p 52.

[164] Marriage Act 1949 s 17 and s 45A (as amended and added); Marriage Act 1983 s 1(6).

[165] General Register Office, *Civil Registration: Delivering Vital Change* (2003) para 3.5.1.

[166] [2008] UKHL 53 [2009] AC 287.

[167] Asylum and Immigration (Treatment of Claimants, etc) Act 2004 (Remedial) Order 2001 (SI 2011/1158).

Leaving aside the immigration dimension, proposals to modernise and simplify marriage formalities have been made on several occasions. In particular, the Labour Government produced proposals in 2002,[168] but these proved controversial and were abandoned. The enactment of the Marriage (Same Sex Couples) Act 2013 was a missed opportunity to have updated the requirements, but no doubt attempting to do so would have made the passage of the Bill even more difficult. Moreover, the question of how far the state should control the formalities of entry into marriage clearly raises wider issues than permitting same sex couples to marry. For example, religious minorities (particularly the Muslim community) seek greater freedom and flexibility in determining how members of their community may simultaneously contract both a legally and religiously recognised marriage, and non-religious 'belief organisations' have also pressed to be permitted to conduct weddings. Indeed, the law is currently being reviewed in this regard, which may offer a further opportunity to grasp the nettle.[169]

F. PRESUMPTION OF MARRIAGE

It has long been established that, if a man and woman cohabit and hold themselves out as husband and wife,[170] this in itself raises a presumption that they are legally married.[171] It is important, however, not to fall into the trap of regarding such a situation as a 'common law marriage'. The presumption of marriage asserts that the parties *are* validly married, albeit that there is a lack of evidence conclusively to show this. By contrast, the phrase 'common law marriage' is frequently used, completely erroneously, to suggest that a couple who plainly never did enter into a marriage (or even intend to marry), have *acquired* the status of marriage through mere cohabitation.[172]

Under the presumption, if the marriage is challenged, the burden lies upon those challenging it to prove that there was in fact no marriage, and not upon those alleging it to prove that it has been solemnised. It might be thought that, in an age where cohabitation is so readily socially accepted, a wish to establish that a marriage had taken place would no longer be of much concern, but on the contrary, it may be important to establish the position where, for example, the parties have been married abroad and have no written or other evidence of the solemnisation, and if the validity of the marriage is called into question where entitlement to immigration, benefits or property depends upon the answer.[173]

---

[168] ONS, *Civil Registration: Vital Change* Cm 5355 (2002), see C Barton 'White Paper Weddings—The Beginnings, Muddles and Ends of Wedlock' [2002] Fam Law 431; R Probert 'Lord Hardwicke's Marriage Act—Vital Change 250 Years On?' [2004] Fam Law 585. The General Synod of the Church of England conducted a parallel review: *Just Cause or Impediment? A Report from the Review of Aspects of Marriage Law Working Party* (2001) and *The Challenge to Change* (2002). The Church in Wales also reviewed the law. The government's final proposals incorporated those of the Anglican churches.

[169] Marriage (Same Sex Couples) Act 2013 s 14.

[170] A Borkowski notes that some of the authorities appear to require both cohabitation and 'repute' whilst others focus on cohabitation, but he concludes that, even in such cases, the element of repute was present: 'The Presumption of Marriage' [2002] CFLQ 251 p 253. Cf the rule of Scottish common law which recognised 'marriage by cohabitation with habit and repute', abolished by s 3 of the Family Law (Scotland) Act 2006.   [171] See A Borkowski 'The Presumption of Marriage' [2002] CFLQ 251.

[172] A Barlow et al 'Just a piece of paper? Marriage and cohabitation' in A Park et al (eds) *British Social Attitudes* (2001) pp 45–6, found 59% of cohabitants believed such status exists. Despite various public information campaigns, when people were interviewed again in 2006, the proportion believing in the existence of common law marriage had declined only to 51%: A Barlow et al, 'Cohabitation and the law: myths, money and the media' in A Park et al (eds) *British Social Attitudes: the 24th report* (2008).

[173] See eg *Mahadervan v Mahadervan* [1964] P 233; *Re Spence* [1990] Ch 652, CA.

There are two forms of the presumption—the first where there is insufficient proof that the parties went through a ceremony of marriage and the second where the parties are proved to have gone through a ceremony but there are doubts as to its validity.[174] A number of modern cases have arisen relating to scenarios of the second type. In *Chief Adjudication Officer v Bath*[175] the respondent had undergone a Sikh marriage ceremony in a temple in London in 1956 and then lived with her 'husband' for 37 years and had two children. On his death, she claimed a widow's pension but the Department for Social Security dismissed her claim on the basis that she had not gone through a ceremony in accordance with the Marriage Act 1949, there being no evidence that the temple had been registered for marriages.[176] The Benefits Agency appealed against the ruling of the Social Security Commissioner that she could rely on the common law presumption of marriage. The Court of Appeal rejected their appeal, confirming the existence of the presumption based on cohabitation for a significant period of time.[177] As Evans LJ put it:[178]

> when the man and woman have cohabited as man and wife for a significant period there is a strong presumption that they have agreed to do so, in proper form . . . When there is, as there is in England, a legal requirement that the marriage ceremony shall take a certain form, then the presumption operates to show that the proper form was observed, and it can only be displaced by what I would call positive, not merely "clear" evidence. . . . How positive, and how clear, must depend among other things upon the strength of the evidence which gives rise to the presumption—primarily, the length of cohabitation and evidence that the parties regarded themselves and were treated by others as man and wife.

Here, although the tribunal had found that the temple was not a registered building, this did not, of itself, render the marriage void.[179] As Evans LJ pointed out, to hold that a failure to comply with all the formal requirements of a ceremony prevents reliance on the presumption, yet to permit such reliance in the absence of evidence of the parties having gone through any ceremony at all would be a remarkable and unjust conclusion to draw.[180]

Subsequent cases have concerned divorce proceedings, where the respondent has cast doubt on the validity of the marriage in order to seek to frustrate the applicant's claims. In *Pazpena de Vire v Pazpena de Vire*[181] the petitioner claimed that the parties were married, by proxy, in Uruguay. The respondent claimed that the marriage certificate he had brought back from there was a forgery. But the couple lived together for 35 years, their child's birth certificate showed the petitioner as the respondent's 'wife' and she was granted an Argentine passport on that basis. It was held that the length of cohabitation and the public and official recognition of the marriage raised the presumption of marriage which the opposing evidence, including flaws in the drafting of the marriage certificate, was inadequate to rebut. In *A-M v A-M (Divorce: Jurisdiction: Validity of Marriage)*[182] the parties, both Muslims, went through an Islamic ceremony in a flat in London and were advised that the wedding would not be recognised in English law. In order to regularise the position, they went to Sharjah where the husband attempted to divorce his wife by talaq so that he could then re-marry her in accordance with local law, which would have been recognised as effective in England and Wales. However, the local judge advised him that it was immoral to divorce the wife simply to protect her position in English law and

---

[174] Eg *Wilkinson v Payne* (1791) 4 Term Rep 468.   [175] [2000] 1 FLR 8, CA.
[176] See earlier, Marriage in a registered building, p 53.   [177] 37 years.
[178] [2000] 1 FLR 8, CA at para 31.
[179] See Ch 3, Defects which *may* invalidate a marriage, p 72.
[180] [2000] 1 FLR 8, at para 32.   [181] [2001] 1 FLR 460.   [182] [2001] 2 FLR 6.

the talaq was revoked. The wife was not told of this. The parties continued to live together for a number of years. It was held that the husband *might* have subsequently organised a second, valid marriage ceremony in the Middle East without telling the wife, and that she could rely on the presumption that a valid marriage existed, raised by the parties' cohabitation and their public reputation of being husband and wife, which could be rebutted only by strong and weighty evidence to the contrary.

By contrast, in *Dukali v Lamrani (Attorney-General Intervening)*[183] the couple, who were dual Moroccan and British citizens, went through a civil marriage ceremony in the Moroccan Consulate in London. After about seven years of cohabitation, the husband divorced the wife in Morocco and she sought leave to seek financial provision under English law.[184] The Moroccan Consulate was deemed part of British territory for the purposes of marriage, and thus subject to the English law of formalities. The failure to comply in any way with the requirements of the Marriage Act could not be saved by the 'short' period of cohabitation. Whilst eschewing the suggestion that he lay down how long the parties should have lived together, Holman J opined that 'a longer period than seven or eight years must be required.' However, it appears that counsel failed[185] to refer the judge to the old decision in *Mahadervan v Mahadervan*,[186] which concerned a marriage allegedly performed in breach of the required preliminaries, in what was then Ceylon, where the parties had only lived together for some six months.

Dukali also shows that if the evidence *establishes* that a ceremony was performed in breach of the statutory requirements, the parties cannot rely upon the presumption by cohabitation. Thus, in *A v A (Attorney General Intervening)*[187] where a Muslim marriage ceremony was performed without having given notice to the registrar and hence without a certificate being issued, the marriage could not be saved by the presumption, although, as discussed in Chapter 3, it was upheld as valid on other grounds.[188]

The purpose of the presumption seems clearly protective: in former times, and still for members of minority ethnic communities, upholding the validity of a marriage avoids the stigma that would otherwise be attached to mere cohabitation. There are still significant legal advantages, as we shall see,[189] to being married, not the least of which is the availability of the courts' powers on divorce, and where a couple have held themselves out as married,[190] it is desirable—but only where it is possible—to give the benefit of the doubt and the legal protection that follows, to the party, usually economically weaker than the other, who asserts the existence of the marriage.

G. ENTRY INTO A CIVIL PARTNERSHIP

As we have seen, the Civil Partnership Act 2004 creates an institution for same sex couples which is effectively the same as marriage. Originally, a major difference was that civil partnership was a purely legal, not a religious, status and no provision was made in the

---

[183] [2012] EWHC 1748 (Fam) [2012] 2 FLR 1099.

[184] Under Part III, Matrimonial and Family Proceedings Act 1984, see Ch 23, Financial relief after foreign divorce, Dissolution, annulment or legal separation, pp 920 *et seq*.   [185] See para 33.

[186] [1964] P 233.   [187] [2012] EWHC 2219 (Fam) [2013] Fam 51.

[188] See too, *Al-Saedy v Musawi (Presumption of Marriage)* [2010] EWHC 3293 (Fam) [2011] 2 FLR 287 and *Asaad v Kurter* [2013] EWHC 3852 (Fam) [2014] Fam Law 459.

[189] See Chs 4 *et seq*.

[190] Note, however, that in *Pazpena de Vire v Pazpena de Vire* [2001] 1 FLR 460 (see earlier) at para 68, the judge considered that a party could not be estopped by his conduct from seeking to rebut the presumption.

Act to enable it to be brought into existence via any religious ceremony, even if the parties might be adherents of a religion which would, for example, bless their union. However, s 202 of the Equality Act 2010 amended the Act so that those religious organisations which wish to do so may carry out civil partnership ceremonies provided that their premises are approved in the same way as for marriages,[191] discussed earlier. The extension of civil partnerships to religiously created unions was as controversial as the debate on whether same sex marriage should be permitted, with the same objection by those opposed to it that the public sector equalities duty would be used to require religious organisations to permit civil partnership ceremonies on their premises, or otherwise lose their registration to perform marriages. As with the protections in place for religious organisations not wishing to perform same sex marriages (discussed earlier), s 6A(3A) provides that 'nothing in this Act places an obligation on religious organisations to host civil partnerships if they do not wish to do so' and there is no meaningful prospect of a successful challenge to churches refusing to perform them.[192]

We explain the rules governing the creation of a civil partnership in the same way as we have discussed those governing marriage. The parties must satisfy the requirements both as to capacity and formalities.

1. CAPACITY

Section 3(1) of the 2004 Act provides that:

> Two people are not eligible to register as civil partners of each other if—
>
> (a) they are not of the same sex,
> (b) either of them is already a civil partner or lawfully married,
> (c) either of them is under 16, or
> (d) they are within prohibited degrees of relationship.

This negative formulation of eligibility provides that, apart from the requirement that the parties to a civil partnership *must* be of the same sex, the rules of capacity are otherwise the same as for a marriage. The question whether those *within* family relationships, who fall, of course, within the prohibited degrees, should be permitted to register was debated in Parliament, the argument being that the advantages of civil partnership (in particular, exemption from say, inheritance tax liability) should be extended to, for example, elderly siblings. The House of Lords did in fact pass such a clause, deliberately intended as a wrecking amendment by those opposed to legal recognition of same sex relationships, but it was overturned in the House of Commons and eventually defeated.[193] The matter was subsequently brought to the European Court of Human Rights in *Burden v United Kingdom*[194] where two elderly unmarried sisters who had lived together all their lives complained that they were discriminated against under the tax system since whoever survived would be liable to pay inheritance tax which does not apply (below a high threshold) as between spouses and civil partners. However, the Court held that a sibling relationship is qualitatively different to that of spouses or civil partners, the former being a connection based on consanguinity while the latter expressly excludes the blood tie. It

---

[191] Marriages and Civil Partnerships (Approved Premises) (Amendment) Regulations 2011, SI 2011/2661.
[192] For full discussion, see C Fairbairn *Same sex marriage and civil partnerships SN/HA/5882* House of Commons Library Standard Note (2012) Section 3.
[193] See the discussion by M Harper et al *Civil Partnership: The New Law* (2005) paras 4.8–4.11.
[194] (Application No 13378/05) [2008] 2 FLR 787.

viewed marriage and civil partnership as a 'public undertaking, carrying with it a body of rights and obligations of a contractual nature' and 'the absence of such a legally binding agreement between the applicants renders their relationship of cohabitation, despite its long duration, fundamentally different to that of a married or civil partnership couple.'[195] The reasoning is unconvincing, since marriage and civil partnership are deliberately defined to exclude close blood relationships, but they could equally be redefined to include them—just as the prohibited degrees of relationship have been altered over many centuries, and there is nothing to stop two siblings from publicly entering into a binding agreement in the nature of a civil partnership—if the law allowed it. Be that as it may, there had been no further challenge to the nature of civil partnership until its recent contestation by heterosexual couples who wish it to be made available to them.[196]

2. FORMALITIES

Since there is no provision for a religious ceremony as a means of creating a civil partnership, the formalities that must be satisfied are all variants of those that apply to civil marriages.

(a) Preliminaries

Civil partner under 18

Section 4 provides that consent must be given by the appropriate persons where a child aged 16 or 17 wishes to enter into a civil partnership. These are the same as for a marriage.[197] However, if a person whose consent is required objects, he or she may forbid the issue of a civil partnership document[198] by giving written notice to that effect.

Registration procedure

The Act provides for four different registration procedures—the standard procedure; the procedure for house-bound persons; that for detained persons; and the special procedure for cases where a person is seriously ill and not expected to recover.[199] It will be seen that these reflect the provisions for marriage by Superintendent Registrar's certificate, marriage of house-bound or detained persons; and the Registrar General's licence.

(b) Registration

Registration must take place in England and Wales.[200] The place must be specified in the notice of proposed civil partnership. If registering under the standard procedure, the place must be one open to the public and will have to have been agreed with the registration authority in whose area it is located. That authority may itself provide a place in its area for registrations to be held, but is not required to do so.[201]

---

[195] *Burden v United Kingdom* (Application No 13378/05) [2008] 2 FLR 787 at [65].

[196] A challenge has been made to this provision to the European Court of Human Rights: *Ferguson and Others v United Kingdom* (Application lodged 2 February 2011). For the arguments, see http://equallove.org.uk/the-legal-case/ (accessed 14 August 2012) and Conversion of civil partnership into marriage, p 61.

[197] See earlier, Marriages of persons under the age of 18, p 55 and Civil Partnership Act 2004 Sch 2.

[198] See later, Registration, p 97.   [199] Civil Partnership Act 2004 s 5(1).

[200] Note that s 210 of the Civil Partnership Act 2004 allows for an Order in Council to be made to permit partners to register at a British consulate in an overseas territory if, inter alia, one of them is a United Kingdom national and there are insufficient facilities for them to enter into the equivalent of a civil partnership under the law of that territory. Section 211 makes similar provision for armed forces personnel.

[201] Civil Partnership Act 2004 s 6.

Unlike a wedding, where the marriage comes into existence on the parties' exchange of the requisite words, a civil partnership is created when each partner has signed, in the presence of the civil partnership registrar and their two witnesses,[202] the civil partnership document—the schedule or licence that has been issued tö them.[203] No religious service may be used while the civil partnership registrar is officiating at the signing of the document,[204] even where performed on religious premises, and the civil partnership registration itself must be kept separate from the religious ceremony.

3. CONVERSION OF CIVIL PARTNERSHIP INTO MARRIAGE

Clearly, many couples who entered into civil partnerships between 2005 and 2014 will have done so because marriage was not open to them, rather than because they considered the status a less patriarchal, less traditional one than marriage. Such couples may wish to get married now that same sex marriage is permitted. The Marriage (Same Sex Couples) Act 2013 accordingly provides for regulations to enable the civil partnership to be converted into a marriage. Where this is done, the civil partnership will end 'on the conversion', and the marriage will be treated as having subsisted since the date the civil partnership was formed.[205] However, although the couple might have a religious ceremony, such as a blessing of their union, this will not be a wedding having legal effect—the status of marriage will flow from the conversion procedure only.[206]

The creation of such a procedure raises the question once again of whether it makes sense to limit civil partnerships to same sex couples. There are heterosexual couples who reject marriage as an outmoded institution but who would value the chance to formalise their relationship through a civil partnership, as the pending litigation in the European Court of Human Rights demonstrates.[207] In the Netherlands, both marriage and civil partnership are open to heterosexual and same sex couples, with the possibility of converting either relationship into the other. At first, it was possible to convert the marriage into a civil partnership and then take advantage of easier termination rules for that relationship, known as 'flitsscheidingen' or 'lightning divorce',[208] but the Dutch Civil Code was amended to prevent this in 2009. Given that civil partnerships are terminable on the same basis as divorce in England and Wales, their extension to heterosexual couples could not give rise to the same circumventing of the marriage rules as happened at first in the Netherlands, so there could be no risk of 'undermining' marriage if the law were changed. A review of the law of civil partnership required by s 15 of the Marriage (Same Sex Couples) Act 2013 concluded that it was premature to determine the issue, while most respondents were against any change.[209]

---

[202] A person so designated by a registration authority for its area: Civil Partnership Act 2004 s 29(1).
[203] Civil Partnership Act 2004 ss 2(1) and 7(1).   [204] Civil Partnership Act 2004 s 2(5).
[205] Civil Partnership Act 2004 s 9(1), (6).   [206] Civil Partnership Act 2004 s 9(5)(c).
[207] *Ferguson and Others v United Kingdom* (Application lodged 2 February 2011).
[208] R Gaffney-Rhys, 'Same-sex marriage but not mixed-sex partnerships: should the Civil Partnership Act 2004 be extended to opposite-sex couples?' [2014] CFLQ 173.
[209] DCMS *Civil Partnership Review (England and Wales)—Report on Conclusions* (2014).

3

DETERMINING THE VALIDITY OF A MARRIAGE OR CIVIL PARTNERSHIP

A. INTRODUCTION

Certain consequences flow from marital (or civil partnership) status and it may be necessary to establish whether a valid marriage or civil partnership exists in order to take advantage of them. There are two mechanisms, in particular, which may be used to obtain a ruling on this point: namely, the grant of a declaration regarding marital status or a decree (or order in the case of a civil partnership) of nullity. In recent years, a number of cases have arisen, seeking either or both of these orders, usually where all of the formal requirements for a valid marriage have not been complied with, often because a religious ceremony has been undergone instead. We begin by considering the position in relation to marriages.

B. DECLARATION AS TO MARITAL STATUS

Section 55 of the Family Law Act 1986 confers a power on the family court and High Court to make a declaratory order regarding marital status.[1]

An application may be made for one or more of the following declarations:

(a) that a marriage was at its inception a valid marriage;

(b) that a marriage subsisted, or did not subsist, on a given date;

(c) that a divorce, annulment or legal separation obtained outside England and Wales is, or is not, entitled to recognition in this country.

It will be observed that there is no power to apply for a declaration that a marriage was void at its inception: in this case the correct procedure is to petition for a decree of nullity, when the court may make orders relating to children and financial relief.[2] However,

---

[1] These provisions implemented the Law Commission's recommendations in Law Com No 132 (*Report on Declarations in Family Matters*). Previously the power had derived partly from statute (going back to the Legitimacy Declaration Act 1858) and partly from the inherent jurisdiction of the High Court (which was abolished in this respect by s 58(4)). There was also a decree of jactitation of marriage which restrained the respondent from wrongfully boasting or asserting that he or she was married to the petitioner. Proceedings for jactitation were obsolete, and were abolished by s 61 of the Family Law Act 1986. See further, S Cretney *Family Law in the Twentieth Century: A History* (2003) at 143, n 6.

[2] Family Law Act 1986 s 58(5)(a); *A Local Authority v X and A Child* [2013] EWHC 3274 (Fam) [2014] 2 FLR 123. See later, Chs 22, 23.

it has been held[3] that a declaration may be made under the inherent jurisdiction of the High Court if and for so long as it is made to declare that there never was a marriage, as distinct from being a declaration (which is not permitted) that a given marriage was void at its inception. For example, in *Galloway v Goldstein*,[4] the parties married lawfully in the USA then underwent a second ceremony at approved premises in England and Wales. The American marriage was subsequently dissolved and the husband sought a declaration so as to avoid any future confusion over his marital status. He was granted both a s 55 declaration that the marriage did not subsist after the date of the American divorce and a declaration under the inherent jurisdiction that the second ceremony had had no legal effect. A further example, is *Westminster City Council v C and others*,[5] where the Court of Appeal held that a ceremony conducted over the telephone between England and Bangladesh, which purported to create a marriage between a man with profound learning difficulties and a Bangladeshi woman, could be the subject of a declaration under the inherent jurisdiction, refusing it recognition on grounds of public policy.

Although a declaration will normally be sought by one of the parties to the marriage, others may be legitimately interested in its validity. For example, the trustees of a pension fund may wish to establish whether a woman is the widow of a former employee. Applications for a declaration may therefore be brought by anyone, but the court must refuse to hear a case if it considers that the applicant does not have a sufficient interest in the outcome of the proceedings.[6] In any event it may refuse to make a declaration if to do so would be manifestly contrary to public policy.[7]

A declaration is a judgment *in rem* and binds everyone including the Crown (which may be important if, for example, the applicant is seeking British citizenship or claiming the right to live in this country).[8] Consequently, the Attorney-General must be given notice of an application and may intervene in any proceedings.[9]

The court has jurisdiction only if one of the parties to the marriage is domiciled in England and Wales at the time of the application or has been habitually resident there for one year before that date or, alternatively, if one of them is dead and he or she satisfied either of these conditions at the time of his or her death.[10]

C. DECREE OF NULLITY

Whilst a declaration is perhaps more likely to be obtained where it is sought to establish that a valid marriage subsists, a decree of nullity may be sought in order clearly to establish that the requirements for a valid marriage have *not* been satisfied.[11] This may

---

[3] In *Hudson v Leigh* [2009] EWHC 1306 (Fam), [2013] Fam 77 discussed further at A void marriage—or no marriage at all? p 68.   [4] [2012] EWHC 60 (Fam) [2012] Fam 129.

[5] [2008] EWCA Civ 198 [2009] Fam 11. In *SH v NB (Marriage: Consent)* [2009] EWHC 3274 (Fam) [2010] 1 FLR 1927 Moylan J granted a declaration that a marriage ceremony conducted in Pakistan was of no effect because it was a forced marriage (see later, Duress at p 78).

[6] Family Law Act 1986 s 55(3).   [7] Family Law Act 1986 s 58(1).

[8] Family Law Act 1986 s 58(2). But no declaration is to affect any judgment or decree already made: s 60(3).

[9] Family Law Act 1986 s 59 and s 60(2)(c). Other interested persons may also be required to be made parties: s 60(2)(b). For a recent example, see *A v A (Attorney General intervening)* [2012] EWHC 2219 (Fam) [2013] Fam 51, discussed later, 'A void marriage—or no marriage at all? p 69.

[10] Family Law Act 1986 s 55(2).

[11] Jurisdiction to grant decrees of nullity (whether the marriage was alleged to be void or voidable) was transferred from the ecclesiastical courts to the new Divorce Court set up by the Matrimonial Causes Act

result in the marriage being held to be either 'void' or 'voidable', or, where there has been a *complete* failure to comply with the requirements, even a 'non-marriage', that is, something not capable of even being classed as a void marriage. It is necessary to examine the development of these distinctions in order to understand their significance.

1. HISTORICAL BACKGROUND

The view of the Roman Catholic church that marriage is a sacrament meant that the law relating to marriage became a part of the canon law, over which the ecclesiastical courts claimed exclusive jurisdiction.[12] This had a profound effect on subsequent legal developments. Not only were these courts the only tribunals competent to declare whether the parties were validly married, but the Roman Catholic doctrine of the indissolubility of marriage became a tenet of English law.

Whilst this doctrine precluded the courts from granting decrees of divorce, it did not stop them from declaring that, although the parties had gone through a ceremony of marriage, some impediment prevented their acquiring the status of husband and wife. The same principles were applied by the English ecclesiastical courts after the breach with Rome in the sixteenth century. Such marriages were said to be *void* for, although the parties by going through a ceremony had apparently contracted a marriage, the result of the impediment was that there was never a marriage either in fact or in law. Consequently, the marriage could be formally annulled by a decree of an ecclesiastical court and, even without such a decree, either party was free to contract another union (unless he or she was already married to somebody else). As the marriage was a complete nullity, its validity could also be put in issue by any other person with an interest in so doing, even after the death of one or both of the parties to it. So, for example, after his death, a man's brother might claim his estate on the ground that his marriage had been void, with the result that his children, being illegitimate, could not inherit and his 'widow', never having been married, could not claim dower.[13]

By the beginning of the seventeenth century, however, the royal courts were becoming concerned at the ease with which marriages could be set aside and the issue declared illegitimate. This was more likely to cause injustice after the parties' death, when relevant evidence might no longer be available. Accordingly, they cut down the ecclesiastical courts' jurisdiction by forbidding them to annul marriages in certain cases after the death of either party.[14] This had the result of dividing impediments into two kinds: civil and canonical. If the impediment was civil—for example, the fact that one of the parties was married to a third person at the time of the ceremony—the marriage was still void from the start and its validity could be put in issue by anyone at any time, whether or not the parties were still alive. If the impediment was canonical—for example, the fact that one of the parties was impotent—the validity of the marriage could not be questioned after either party had died. The rule thus developed that such a marriage must be regarded as valid unless it was annulled during the lifetime of both parties. Until that time it had the capacity to be turned into a void marriage: in other words, it was *voidable*. Once a decree of nullity had been pronounced, however, it acted retrospectively and the marriage was

---

1857, and was vested in the High Court by the Judicature Act 1873. The family court now has jurisdiction to hear all applications.

[12] F Pollock and F Maitland *History of English Law*, pp ii and 364–6.

[13] See Ch 4, Property consequences of marriage and civil partnership, Historical introduction, p 105.

[14] See J Jackson *Formation and Annulment of Marriage* (2nd edn, 1969) pp 54–5.

then regarded as having been void from the beginning. Consequently, the parties reverted to their pre-marital status and their children were automatically bastardised. The distinction between void and voidable marriages was described by Lord Greene MR:[15]

> A void marriage is one that will be regarded by every court in any case in which the existence of the marriage is in issue as never having taken place and can be so treated by both parties to it without the necessity of any decree annulling it: a voidable marriage is one that will be regarded by every court as a valid subsisting marriage until a decree annulling it has been pronounced by a court of competent jurisdiction.

After the introduction of judicial divorce in 1857, the voidable marriage came to occupy a position midway between the void marriage and the valid marriage. The annulment of a voidable marriage, like divorce, changes the parties' status by a judicial act, and whatever the theoretical differences between them are, both are a means of terminating a marriage that has broken down. Divorce,[16] however, does not act retrospectively; the parties are still regarded as having been husband and wife up to the time when the decree was made absolute. Some of the inconveniences of the retrospective operation of the decree of nullity of a voidable marriage were removed by statute or avoided by the courts: for example, children of the marriage remain legitimate[17] and it has never been possible to set aside transactions carried out on the assumption (valid at the time) that the parties to a voidable marriage were husband and wife.[18] Nevertheless, many anomalies remained and the retrospective effect of the decree was artificial and confusing and 'in truth perpetuated a canonical fiction'.[19]

The law of nullity was reviewed by the Law Commission in 1970.[20] In view of the criticisms that had been levelled against the anomalous nature of the voidable marriage, the Law Commission examined the question whether the concept should be abolished altogether and the grounds for annulling a voidable marriage included amongst the facts from which irretrievable breakdown of the marriage might be inferred as the ground for divorce. They rejected the proposal for three reasons. First, certain Christian denominations and their members draw a clear distinction between the annulment and the dissolution of marriage and would be offended if the distinction were blurred. Secondly, some people, associating divorce with stigma, preferred to keep matters involving no moral blame such as impotence and mental disorder as grounds for nullity.[21] Thirdly, the bar which then applied to divorce within the first three years of marriage was clearly inappropriate to the grounds for nullity. The Law Commission, however, made extensive recommendations with the object of resolving uncertainties and removing anomalies. Effect was given to these by the Nullity of Marriage Act 1971, which to a large extent codified the law of nullity. This Act was in turn repealed and its provisions re-enacted in the Matrimonial Causes Act 1973. When same sex marriage was permitted by the Marriage (Same Sex Couples) Act 2013, further amendments were made.

---

[15] *De Reneville v De Reneville* [1948] P 100 at 111, CA.   [16] See Ch 7.

[17] Originally, Law Reform (Miscellaneous Provisions) Act 1949 s 4 (1), but see now the Matrimonial Causes Act 1973 s 16, discussed later, Effect of decree on voidable marriage, p 85.

[18] See *Re Eaves* [1940] Ch 109, CA.

[19] Per Lord Goddard CJ in *R v Algar* [1954] 1 QB 279 at 288, CCA.

[20] Law Com No 33, *Nullity of Marriage* (1970).

[21] But this overlooks the fact that moral blame attaches to some of the grounds for nullity (eg pregnancy by another man).

2. THE CURRENT DISTINCTION BETWEEN VOID AND VOIDABLE MARRIAGES

(a) Grounds for annulment

Essentially, a marriage will be *void* if either party lacks capacity to contract it or if the ceremony is formally defective. It was once doubtful whether lack of consent made a marriage void or voidable, but in the case of marriages contracted after 31 July 1971, the Matrimonial Causes Act 1973 specifically provides that this will make them voidable.

With the doubtful exception of lack of consent, the only ground on which a marriage could be voidable after 1929[22] was that one of the parties was impotent. The Matrimonial Causes Act 1937 added four new grounds: the respondent's wilful refusal to consummate the marriage, either party's mental disorder, the respondent's venereal disease, and the respondent wife's pregnancy by another man. Under the 1973 Act, impotence, the four statutory grounds (with some modifications) and lack of consent are grounds on which a marriage is *voidable* and the Gender Recognition Act 2004[23] added two further grounds relating to cases where one of the parties has undergone gender re-assignment.

(b) Necessity for decree

The vital distinction between a void and a voidable marriage is that the former, being void *ab initio*, needs no decree to annul it, whilst the latter is in all respects a valid marriage until a decree absolute of nullity is pronounced. Hence, if either party dies before a decree is granted, a voidable marriage must be treated as valid for all purposes and for all time.[24] On the other hand, either party to a *void* marriage may lawfully contract a valid marriage with someone else without having the first marriage formally annulled.

Even though, in respect of a void marriage, a decree of nullity can only be declaratory and cannot effect any change in the parties' status, there may be good reason for obtaining such a decree. First, there may be some doubt whether on the facts or the law applicable the marriage is void: whether, for example, one party was already married or there was a due publication of banns. Secondly, a decree of nullity is a judgment *in rem*, so that no one may subsequently allege that the marriage is in fact valid. But the most important reason for bringing proceedings is that the court has power on granting a decree to make certain ancillary orders, and a party may therefore present an application in order, for example, to obtain a property adjustment order or financial provision for herself[25] and any children of the family.[26] As the parties are not married, this is in fact the only way in which a 'spouse' may obtain financial provision purely for him- or herself.

(c) Third parties' rights

From what has been said, it follows that third parties must treat a voidable marriage as valid unless a decree has been pronounced. On the other hand, if it is alleged that a marriage is void, any person with an interest in so doing may prove as a question of fact that there has never been a marriage at all. Suppose that property is settled on trust for A for

---

[22] When the Age of Marriage Act 1929 rendered a marriage void if either party was under the age of 16: see Ch 2, Capacity to marry, Age p 44.   [23] See later, Gender reassignment p 83.

[24] *Re Roberts* [1978] 3 All ER 225, CA (revocation of will executed before marriage).

[25] See eg *J v S-T (Formerly J) (Transsexual: Ancillary Relief)* [1997] 1 FLR 402, CA, explaining *Whiston v Whiston* [1995] Fam 198, CA.

[26] The powers to order financial provision for children are subject to the restrictions under the Child Support Act 1991, discussed in Ch 21, Maintenance under the Child Support Act, The residual role of the courts, pp 820ff. The meaning of 'children of the family' is discussed in Ch 9, The meaning of 'child of the family', p 296.

life with remainder to his widow or, if he leaves no widow, to B absolutely. A goes through a ceremony of marriage with W who survives him. Even though the marriage between W and A was voidable, B cannot dispute its validity to prove that W is not A's widow: but he can show, even after A's death, that the marriage between them was void and that consequently the remainder over to him takes effect, for W, never having been A's wife, cannot now be his widow. But if a decree of nullity had been pronounced before A's death, then, whether the marriage was void or voidable, everyone is bound by it and W may not now assert that she is A's widow. It is easy to imagine other cases in which the validity of a marriage might be impeached: for example, others interested in property might wish to prove that the alleged marriage had not revoked the will of one of the parties to it.[27]

Conversely, it might be in the interest of one of the parties to prove that the marriage was void. Suppose that a testator devises property to W so long as she remains his widow and, if she remarries, to X. W subsequently goes through a ceremony of marriage with K. In the event of a dispute between W and X over the beneficial interest in the property after the ceremony, W clearly succeeds if she can show that the marriage between herself and K is void.[28]

(d) Effect of the decree

If the marriage is void, the decree does not affect the parties' status at all. In the case of a voidable marriage, effect has been given to the Law Commission's recommendation that to remove the difficulties caused by the retrospective effect of the decree, it should operate to annul the marriage only with regard to any time after it had been made absolute and that the marriage should continue to be treated as having existed up to that time.[29]

A decree of nullity is made in two stages: the decree nisi followed by the decree absolute.[30] The rules relating to the application for a decree nisi to be made absolute are the same as in divorce.[31] The marriage is finally annulled when the decree is made absolute and a party to a voidable marriage may not remarry until then.

3. A VOID MARRIAGE—OR NO MARRIAGE AT ALL?

A void marriage is strictly speaking a contradiction in terms: to speak of a void marriage is merely a compendious way of saying that, although the parties have been through a ceremony of marriage, they have never acquired the status of husband and wife owing to the presence of some impediment.[32] And if they have never been through a ceremony at all, their union cannot even be termed a void marriage. However, this in turn raises the difficult problem of what form of ceremony will be sufficient to enable the court to grant a decree of nullity. The matter may be of considerable practical importance, because only if the court pronounces a decree does it have power to make orders relating to financial provision for the spouses and the adjustment of their rights in property.[33]

---

[27] See *Harrod v Harrod* (1854) 1 K & J 4; *Re Peete* [1952] 2 All ER 599; *Re Park's Estate* [1954] P 89; and *Re Spence* [1990] Ch 652, CA.   [28] *Allen v Wood* (1834) 1 Bing NC 8.

[29] Matrimonial Causes Act 1973 s 16, discussed later, Effect of decree on voidable marriage, p 85.

[30] Matrimonial Causes Act 1973 s 15.

[31] See Ch 7, Decrees p 228.

[32] See R Probert 'When are we married? Void, non-existent and presumed marriages' (2002) 22 *Legal Studies* 398; R Probert 'The evolving concept of the "non-marriage"' [2013] CFLQ 314. For the view that the concept of 'non-marriage' is based on a misunderstanding of the early authorities, see V Le Grice 'A critique of non-marriage' [2013] Fam Law 1278.

[33] Though it by no means follows that the court will grant financial relief following the granting of a nullity decree: see *J v S-T (Formerly J) (Transsexual: Ancillary Relief)* [1997] 1 FLR 402, CA and *Whiston v Whiston* [1995] Fam 198, CA.

The first reported case where this precise issue was raised was *Gereis v Yagoub*.[34] The parties went through a purported ceremony of marriage at a Coptic Orthodox Church not registered for marriages,[35] the ceremony being conducted by a priest who was not authorised to conduct marriages and without notice of the marriage having been given to the superintendent registrar. In fact the parties had been advised by the priest to go through a civil ceremony of marriage first, but no civil ceremony was performed. After the church ceremony the parties lived together for nearly a year, but after the breakdown of their relationship the petitioner sought a decree of nullity, which the respondent opposed on the basis that there had not even been a void marriage.

In granting the decree the judge, relying on earlier statements[36] that the ceremony 'must be at least one which will prima facie confer the status of husband and wife', considered that the ceremony in this case 'bore the hallmarks of an ordinary Christian marriage and . . . both parties treated it as such, at least to the extent that they cohabited after it, whereas they had not before, that they had sexual intercourse, which they had not before, and that the respondent had claimed married man's tax allowance, which he had not before'.[37] Moreover, he was satisfied that those who attended the ceremony clearly assumed that they were attending an ordinary Christian marriage. Having found as a fact that both parties were aware of the need to go through some form of ceremony at the civil register office, the judge held that the marriage was void in that both had knowingly and wilfully intermarried in disregard of the formalities required by the Marriage Act 1949.[38]

Gereis v Yagoub has been followed by several similar cases. For example, *A-M v A-M (Divorce: Jurisdiction: Validity of Marriage)*[39] concerned a Muslim religious marriage conducted by a Mufti in a private flat in London. Hughes J relied on the earlier decision in *R v Bham*[40] in which a prosecution had been brought against the accused for performing a ceremony of marriage contrary to s 75(2)(a) of the Marriage Act 1949. In that case a religious ceremony in accordance with Islamic form was performed in a private house in England between a Muslim man and a 16-year-old English girl who had adopted the Muslim faith. Quashing a conviction for knowingly and wilfully solemnising a marriage, the Court of Criminal Appeal said:[41]

> What, in our judgment, was contemplated by [the Marriage Act] . . . in dealing with marriage and its solemnisation, and that to which alone it applies, was the performing in England of a ceremony in a form known to and recognised by our law as capable of producing, when there performed, a void marriage.

Hughes J concluded that the ceremony in *A-M v A-M* 'did not begin to purport to be a marriage according to the Marriage Acts, with or without fatal defects.'[42]

A more unusual situation arose in *Hudson v Leigh*.[43] The wife was a devout Christian, the husband an athiest Jew, and they lived most of the time in South Africa. They agreed

[34] [1997] 1 FLR 854.

[35] See Ch 2, Marriage in a registered building, p 53.

[36] Such as that of Humphreys J in *R v Mohamed (Ali)* (1943) [1964] 2 QB 350n, cited by Thompson J in *R v Bham* [1966] 1 QB 159 at 169B, CCA.   [37] [1997] 1 FLR 854, at 858.

[38] And therefore within the Matrimonial Causes Act 1973 s 11(a)(iii): see later, Defects which *may* invalidate a marriage, p 72.   [39] [2001] 2 FLR 6 at [55]. See Ch 2, Presumption of marriage, p 57.

[40] [1966] 1 QB 159.   [41] At 169.

[42] [2001] 2 FLR 6 at [58]. Followed in relation to a Hindu wedding ceremony performed in a London restaurant by a Brahmin priest in *Gandhi v Patel* [2002] 1 FLR 603.

[43] [2009] EWHC 1306 (Fam) [2013] Fam 77. See R Gaffney-Rhys '*Hudson v Leigh*—the concept of non-marriage' [2010] CFLQ 351.

to ask her church minister to perform a religious 'marriage' ceremony at the husband's South African home, omitting certain words as to the 'lawfulness' of the ceremony, and then to follow this by a civil ceremony at a register office in England. They separated before the civil ceremony was performed and the husband sought a declaration that the South African ceremony had not brought about a valid marriage between them. The wife claimed the marriage was either valid or should be annulled on the basis of non-compliance with South African formalities. Bodey J granted a declaration that the ceremony had not created the status of marriage, inter alia, because the parties had been 'play-acting' in the knowledge that this was not a lawful ceremony: neither of the parties, nor the minister, had intended or believed it to be legally binding. In considering the prior case law, he rejected the invitation by counsel to articulate precisely the test to be applied in such circumstances, considering instead that they should be dealt with on a case by case basis, taking account of, but not limited to the following factors:

(a) whether the ceremony or event set out or purported to be a lawful marriage;
(b) whether it bore all or enough of the hallmarks of marriage;
(c) whether the three key participants (most especially the officiating official), believed, intended and understood the ceremony as giving rise to the status of lawful marriage; and
(d) the reasonable perceptions, understandings and beliefs of those in attendance.[44]

He cautioned that the 'ascertainment of intentions and beliefs will often be difficult and unreliable and their use alone could run into the problem of different participants in or at the ceremony intending or believing different things';[45] nonetheless, one would expect that the parties' and celebrant's intentions must carry the most weight. Indeed, if *none* of these thinks they are formalising a legally binding union, it must be difficult surely to hold that they in fact have done so. However it does not follow that the reverse will make a marriage valid. Thus, he went on to hold, in *El Gamal v Al Maktoum*,[46] another example of a Muslim ceremony conducted in a private home, that the mere fact that the parties *hoped* that the marriage would be valid was not enough to override their failure to attempt to comply with English formalities.

Most of these cases have arisen where one party is attempting to impugn the validity of the marriage and thus avoid financial liability to make provision for the other. However, in *A v A (Attorney General Intervening)*,[47] the parties sought a declaration under s 55 that the marriage, conducted in a mosque in Middlesbrough in 2002, was *valid*. The mosque was registered to solemnise marriages and members of the mosque had at various times been authorised under the Marriage Acts. However, the Imam who performed the ceremony was not authorised at the time and he believed he was merely conducting a religious ceremony

---

[44] At [79]. Followed in *Galloway v Goldstein* [2012] EWHC 60 (Fam) [2012] Fam 129. In *Asaad v Kurter* [2013] EWHC 3852 (Fam) [2014] Fam Law 459 in relation to a marriage performed in a Syriac Orthodox Church in Syria but not registered with the authorities there, Moylan J noted that as Syrian law had no concept of 'non-marriage', it would be wrong to regard the expert witness as having opined that the marriage was a 'non-marriage' in the English sense, and he held it to be void given the parties' knowledge and intention as to the effect of the ceremony.

[45] At [77]. For criticism of the focus on intention, see R Probert 'The evolving concept of "non-marriage"' [2013] CFLQ 314 at pp 328–34.

[46] [2011] EWHC 3763 (Fam) [2012] 2 FLR 387. See too, *Dukali v Lamrani (Attorney-General Intervening)* [2012] EWHC 1748 (Fam) [2012] 2 FLR 1099 (marriage ceremony in Moroccan Consulate in London); *Shagroon v Sharbatly* [2012] EWCA Civ 1507 [2013] Fam 267 (couple married at a London hotel by Islamic ceremony: husband already married: held a non-marriage).

[47] [2012] EWHC 2219 (Fam) [2013] Fam 51. See C Bevan 'The role of intention in non-marriage cases post *Hudson v Leigh*' [2013] CFLQ 80.

in accordance with Islamic law. The parties did not seek a certificate from the registrar and relied totally on the officials at the mosque.

Moylan J thoroughly reviewed all the authorities, and concluded that 'the central issue is whether what took place in this case is sufficiently within the 1949 Act for the marriage to be capable of being a valid marriage under English law.'[48] He applied the range of criteria set out by Bodey J in *Hudson v Leigh* to the question. He noted that: (a) the parties intended to contract a valid marriage; (b) the evidence had not suggested that the Chairman of the mosque, who was an authorised person present at the marriage, did not consider that the parties were indeed marrying validly; (c) the ceremony was sufficient 'as a ceremony' to constitute a valid marriage—the fact it was in Islamic form did not matter since the parties are free, under the Marriage Acts, to adopt such form of ceremony as they see fit; and (d) the ceremony was performed in a registered building in the presence of an authorised person. He considered that the ceremony was therefore 'within the scope' of the 1949 Act. Given that the parties themselves had not 'knowingly and wilfully' married in breach of the requirements as to notice or certification, he concluded that the marriage was therefore valid.[49]

It is worth noting the public policy dimension to Moylan J's judgment. He considered that 'there is a public interest in marriages which have been contracted in England resulting in the obligations and rights consequent on marriage (including a void marriage) being imposed on and afforded to the parties to such marriages.'[50] This particular couple had lived together in reliance on the supposed validity of their marriage, having been reassured by the mosque authorities that there was nothing else they needed to do. They wished to remain married. These factors may well have influenced his Lordship in reaching his conclusion, but there is now considerable uncertainty in the case law as to when a court may decide that a marriage is so far outside the scope of the legislation as to be classed as 'non-existent' on the one hand, or 'merely' void, on the other.

D. GROUNDS ON WHICH A MARRIAGE WILL BE VOID

Section 11 of the Matrimonial Causes Act 1973 expressly provides that a marriage celebrated after 31 July 1971 (when the Nullity of Marriage Act 1971 came into force) shall be void only on the grounds there set out.[51] The present grounds can be divided into two: those relating to capacity and those relating to formal requirements.

---

   [48] [2012] EWHC 2219 (Fam) [2013] Fam 51 at [82].

   [49] See too his judgment to similar effect in *Asaad v Kurter* [2013] EWHC 3852 (Fam) [2014] Fam Law 459 where the marriage was carried out in a Syriac Orthodox Church in Syria but never registered there. He regarded the ceremony as not 'so deficient' as to amount to a non-marriage.

   [50] [2012] EWHC 2219 (Fam) [2013] Fam 51 at [87]. For a similar view that marriages should, at the least, be found void rather than non-existent so as to provide some protection to the vulnerable spouse, see V Le Grice 'A critique of non-marriage' [2013] Fam Law 1278.

   [51] These are all grounds on which a marriage celebrated before that date would be void. In addition, it is probable that lack of consent on the part of one of the parties formerly made a marriage void, in which case a marriage celebrated before 1 August 1971, affected by lack of consent, will remain void. It is also possible that a marriage celebrated before 1 August 1971 was void if one of the parties was divorced and the time for appealing against the decree absolute had not expired: see *Dryden v Dryden* [1973] Fam 217 at 239.

1. LACK OF CAPACITY

Obviously lack of capacity to marry, which was discussed in Chapter 2,[52] will make the marriage void. If the relevant law is English, the marriage will be void on the following grounds:[53]

(i) That the parties are related within the prohibited degrees of consanguinity or, if the conditions set out in the Marriage Act 1949 are not observed, within the prohibited degrees of affinity.[54]

(ii) That either of them is under the age of 16.[55]

(iii) That either of them is already married or a civil partner.[56]

(iv) That either party to a polygamous marriage celebrated abroad was at the time of the ceremony domiciled in England and Wales.[57] This is subject to the overriding principle that a foreign rule of law must be applied instead of the English rule when the conflict of laws so requires.[58] Consequently, if the proper law to apply is that of the proposed matrimonial home, the marriage may still be valid notwithstanding that one of the parties is domiciled in this country.[59]

2. FORMAL DEFECTS

Whether failure to comply with the formal requirements relating to the marriage ceremony will make the marriage void must be determined by reference to the *lex loci celebrationis*—the law of the place where the ceremony was performed.[60]

If the marriage is solemnised in England and Wales, not every defect in the formalities set out in the Marriage Act 1949 will render the ceremony a nullity, as we saw earlier in relation to *A v A (Attorney General Intervening)*.[61] Whilst public policy requires that these formalities should be strictly observed, the consequences of avoiding any marriage where there was some technical defect, however slight, would be socially even more undesirable. English law has reached a compromise between these conflicting demands of public policy in that some formal defects will not render the marriage void at all, whilst in the case of the rest the marriage will be void only if *both* parties contracted it with knowledge of the defect. In other words, it is impossible for a person in England and Wales innocently to contract a marriage which is void because of a formal defect. The real sanction is afforded by the criminal law, for if a party knowingly fails to comply with the Marriage Act, he or she will frequently have to make a false oath or declaration and thus commit perjury.[62]

---

[52] At Capacity to marry pp 40–47.

[53] Matrimonial Causes Act 1973 s 11(c), which applied where the parties were not respectively male and female, was repealed by the Marriage (Same Sex Couples) Act 2013 Sch 7 para 27.

[54] Matrimonial Causes Act 1973 s 11(a)(i),(iii).

[55] Matrimonial Causes Act 1973 s 11(a)(ii). See *A Local Authority v X and A Child* [2013] EWHC 3274 (Fam) [2014] 2 FLR 123.

[56] Matrimonial Causes Act 1973 s 11(b) as amended by Civil Partnership Act 2004 Sch 27 para 40. See, for example, *Whiston v Whiston* [1995] Fam 198, CA.   [57] Matrimonial Causes Act 1973 s 11(d).

[58] Matrimonial Causes Act 1973 s 14(1).   [59] See *Radwan v Radwan (No 2)* [1973] Fam 35.

[60] See Ch 2 Entry into marriage, Capacity to marry, n 56.

[61] [2012] EWHC 2219 (Fam) [2013] Fam 51.

[62] See the Perjury Act 1911 s 3, and the discussion in *J v S-T (Formerly J) (Transsexual: Ancillary Relief)* [1997] 1 FLR 402 at 425–6, per Ward LJ. See also the Marriage Act 1949 s 75, and the Marriage (Registrar General's Licence) Act 1970 s 16 (punishment of offences relating to the solemnisation of marriages).

(a) Defects which will never invalidate a marriage

The Marriage Act 1949 specifically enacts that a marriage shall *not* be rendered void on any of the following grounds:[63]

(a) that any of the statutory residence requirements was not fulfilled;

(b) that the necessary consents had not been given in the case of the marriage of a minor by common licence or a superintendent registrar's certificate;[64]

(c) that the registered building in which the parties were married had not been certified as a place of religious worship or was not the usual place or worship of either of them; or

(d) that an incorrect declaration had been made in order to obtain permission to marry in a registered building.

Although these are the only formal defects specifically stated *not* to invalidate a marriage, it is a general rule that, if the irregularity is not one which the Act expressly states may invalidate it, the defect will never make the ceremony a nullity.[65] Hence, for example, even though the parties are aware that two witnesses are not present at the ceremony, the marriage will still be perfectly valid.[66]

(b) Defects which *may* invalidate a marriage

There is then a group of cases where a failure to comply with the provisions of the Marriage Act will make the marriage void, but only if *both* parties were aware of the irregularity at the time of the ceremony.[67] For marriages according to the rites of the Church of England, these include failures to publish banns correctly or to obtain a common licence or certificate, solemnisation in a place other than one where banns may be published or to which the certificate applied, solemnisation by a person not in Holy Orders, marriage outside the time limit after publication of banns or issue of the licence or entry of notice or marriage, and marriage of a minor after a person entitled to do so has dissented.[68] There are equivalent provisions for other marriages.[69]

It should be noted that in the case of a same sex couple who marry in a religious ceremony (including a Church of England wedding) where the religious authority has *not* given its written consent to opt in to perform such a marriage, the marriage is void, but again, the parties must do so 'knowingly and wilfully'.[70] But given the 'quadruple lock' intended to protect

---

[63] Section 24 and s 48. See also s 47(3) (authorisation of marriage according to the usages of the Society of Friends), s 71 (evidence of marriages in naval, military and air force chapels) and s 72 (usual place of worship), and the Marriage (Registrar General's Licence) Act 1970 s 12 (marriages solemnised on the Registrar General's licence).

[64] The Act refers to consents only where the parties are married on the authority of a superintendent registrar's certificate, but the same is true where they are married by common licence: *R v Birmingham Inhabitants* (1828) 8 B & C 29.   [65] *Campbell v Corley* (1856) 28 LTOS 109.

[66] *Campbell v Corley*; *Wing v Taylor* (1861) 2 Sw & Tr 278.

[67] The Act speaks of 'knowingly and wilfully' intermarrying, and it is not clear whether it is sufficient that both parties should know as a question of fact that the formality is not complied with or whether in addition they must know as a question of law that the defect will invalidate the marriage. The point was left open by Lord Penzance in *Greaves v Greaves* (1872) LR 2 P & D 423 at 424–5. The former construction seems the more natural, even though its adoption would have the effect of invalidating more marriages. The issue was not adverted to in *Gereis v Yagoub* [1997] 1 FLR 854 or in *A v A (Attorney General Intervening)* [2012] EWHC 2219 (Fam) [2013] Fam 51.

[68] Marriage Act 1949 s 25 (as amended by the Marriage Act 1983, Sch 1).

[69] Marriage Act 1949 s 49 (as amended).

[70] Marriage Act 1949 ss 25(2), 49A and Marriage (Registrar General's Licence) Act 1970 s 13A, inserted by Marriage (Same Sex Couples) Act 2013 Sch 7 paras 4, 15 and 25.

religious groups from being required to perform same sex weddings,[71] it must be open to question whether the marriage would be upheld if one of the parties was unaware that consent had not been given, and very doubtful indeed in the case of a marriage in the Church of England which has no power under the legislation to opt in at all.

3. PROPOSALS FOR REFORM

The present rule that a marriage will not be void on the ground of a formal defect unless both parties were aware of it has the advantage that it is impossible for a party mistakenly to contract such a marriage. It also produces uncertainty, however. If there has been some irregularity which could invalidate the marriage, dishonest parties may have the option of deciding whether it is to be regarded as valid or void, for it may be extremely difficult to disprove whatever evidence they give about their knowledge or lack of knowledge of the defect at the time of the ceremony. Similar uncertainty could surround the validity of the marriage of the scrupulous 'for most people have no difficulty in sincerely convincing themselves that what they would like to have occurred is what in fact occurred'.[72] Consequently, the Law Commission concluded that the test of whether a marriage is void on the ground of formal irregularity should be objective and not depend on the parties' knowledge or complicity.[73] This would certainly address the problem noted above of a same sex marriage performed in breach of the 'opt in' requirements.

E. VOIDABLE MARRIAGES

The six grounds on which a marriage celebrated after 31 July 1971 will be voidable are set out in s 12 of the Matrimonial Causes Act 1973.[74]

1. THE UNCONSUMMATED MARRIAGE

Even in canon law a marriage was not always finally and irrevocably indissoluble if it had not been consummated by the sexual act. If at the time of the ceremony either spouse was incapable of consummating it, he or she was regarded as lacking the physical capacity (as distinct from the legal capacity) to contract a valid marriage, and the union could therefore be annulled. If, on the other hand, the marriage remained unconsummated because of one party's refusal to have sexual intercourse, canon law offered no relief, because the ground of complaint was conduct following the ceremony.[75] Despite this, decrees were probably in fact given in some cases in reliance on the presumption that, if the marriage had not been consummated after three years' cohabitation through no fault of the petitioner, the respondent must be impotent.[76] The law was put on a more rational footing by

---

[71] See Ch 2, Formalities of marriage, Marriage (Same Sex Couples) Act 2013, p 50.

[72] Law Com No 53 *Report on Solemnisation of Marriage in England and Wales*, Annex, para 121.

[73] See further, Law Com No 53 *Report on Solemnisation of Marriage in England and Wales* (1973), Annex, paras 121–133.

[74] Re-enacting the Nullity of Marriage Act 1971 s 2, which came into force on 1 August 1971. The section was amended by the Marriage (Same Sex Couples) Act 2013 Sch 4 para 4 and the following discussion takes account of the amendments.   [75] *Napier v Napier* [1915] P 184, CA.

[76] *G v M* (1885) 10 App Cas 171, HL, at 189–90; cf *S v S (otherwise W)* [1963] P 162 at 171, CA. The petitioner did not have to rely on this presumption and could always allege impotence during the first three years of marriage.

the Matrimonial Causes Act 1937, which enacted that a marriage should be voidable if it had not been consummated owing to the respondent's wilful refusal to do so. This was frequently criticised because it offended against the principle that an impediment avoiding a marriage should exist at the time of the ceremony. The Law Commission, however, recommended that it should remain a ground for nullity; the most cogent reason they advanced was that the petitioner might be uncertain whether failure to consummate is due to the respondent's impotence or wilful refusal, and in practice would then plead both grounds in the alternative. Notwithstanding this practical justification, the whole concept seems artificial. The applicant's real complaint is that he (or she) is being deprived of normal sexual relations because of the respondent's impotence or conduct.[77] If intercourse takes place once (perhaps after great delay and difficulty), the applicant's power to apply for nullity disappears and his or her sole remedy lies in divorce if the respondent is unable or unwilling to have further sexual relations.

It must be emphasised that non-consummation as such does not make a marriage voidable. There are two separate grounds on which a party may bring an application: that the marriage has not been consummated owing to the incapacity of either party to consummate it, or that it has not been consummated owing to the respondent's wilful refusal to do so.[78] It must also be noted that neither of these grounds is available to spouses in a same sex marriage[79] since the concept of consummation is defined in terms of heterosexual sexual intercourse only.

(a) Meaning of consummation

A marriage is said to be consummated as soon as the parties have sexual intercourse after the solemnisation.[80] The distinction between the act of intercourse and the possibility of that act resulting in the birth of a child must be kept clear: once the parties have had intercourse the marriage is consummated even though one or both are infertile.[81] If this were not so, the marriage could never be consummated if, for example, the wife were beyond the age of child-bearing. Conversely, if the spouses have not had intercourse, the birth of a child as the result of *fecundation ab extra* or artificial insemination or other methods of assisted reproduction will not amount to consummation.[82]

To amount to consummation, the intercourse must, in the words of Dr Lushington in *D-E v A-G*[83] be 'ordinary and complete, and not partial and imperfect'. Hence, as in *D-E v A-G*, there will be no consummation if the husband does not achieve full penetration in the normal sense. The necessity of complete intercourse has raised difficulties where the spouses use some form of contraception. In *Baxter v Baxter*,[84] however, the House of Lords held that the marriage had been consummated notwithstanding the husband's use of a condom. As Lord Jowitt LC pointed out, the possibility of conception is irrelevant to the question of consummation, and when Parliament passed the Matrimonial Causes Act in 1937 (the statute on which the petition was based) it was common knowledge that many people used contraceptives and that in common parlance this would amount to

---

[77] For discussion of the significance of sexual conduct within family relationships, see C Barton 'Sex and the Family' [2005] Fam Law 628.   [78] Matrimonial Causes Act 1973 s 12(1)(a), (b), as amended.
[79] Matrimonial Causes Act 1973 s 12(2) as inserted by the Marriage (Same Sex Couples) Act 2013 Sch 4 para 4.
[80] Not before the solemnisation. Hence the marriage is not consummated by reason of the fact that the parties have had pre-marital intercourse: see *Dredge v Dredge* [1947] 1 All ER 29.
[81] *D-E v A-G* (1845) 1 Rob Eccl 279; *Baxter v Baxter* [1948] AC 274, HL.
[82] See *Clarke v Clarke* [1943] 2 All ER 540; *L v L* [1949] P 211.   [83] (1845) 1 Rob Eccl 279.
[84] [1948] AC 274, HL, overruling in this respect *Cowen v Cowen* [1946] P 36, CA.

consummation.[85] The House of Lords deliberately left open the question whether coitus interruptus would amount to consummation,[86] but it has since been held at first instance that it does.[87] It has also been held that a marriage is consummated even though the husband is physically incapable of ejaculation after penetration,[88] but not if he is incapable of sustaining an erection for more than a very short period of time after penetration.[89]

(b) Inability to consummate

A marriage is voidable if it has not been consummated owing to the incapacity of either party to consummate it.[90] Inability to consummate may be due to physiological or psychological causes and may be either general or merely as regards the particular spouse.[91] As s 12(1)(a) of the Matrimonial Causes Act 1973 enacts the common law rule that a petitioner may show that the marriage has not been consummated because of *either* spouse's incapacity, petitions can be based on the petitioner's own impotence.[92]

At common law it was said that relief would be granted only if the impotence was incurable, and the term 'incapacity' presumably still imports this element. In this context, however, 'incurable' has received an extended meaning and impotence will be considered incurable not only if it is wholly incapable of any remedy, but also if it can be cured only by an operation attended by danger or, in any event, if it is improbable that the operation will be successful or the party refuses to undergo it.[93]

The petitioner's knowledge of the respondent's impotence before marriage is not necessarily a bar to the petition,[94] although if he or she knew that impotence was a ground for nullity, marrying the respondent in the circumstances might amount to such conduct as would entitle the latter to invoke the statutory bar under s 13 of the 1973 Act.[95]

(c) Wilful refusal to consummate

A marriage will be voidable if it has not been consummated owing to the *respondent's* wilful refusal to do so.[96] Wilful refusal connotes 'a settled and definite decision come to without just excuse', and the whole history of the marriage must be looked at.[97] In *Kaur v Singh*[98] where the parties, who were both Sikhs, married in a register office on the understanding that they should not cohabit until they had gone through a religious ceremony of marriage in a Sikh temple, it was held that in the circumstances the husband's refusal without excuse to make arrangements for such a ceremony amounted to wilful refusal to consummate the marriage.

---

[85] At 286.   [86] At 283.

[87] *White v White* [1948] P 330; *Cackett v Cackett* [1950] P 253. But the contrary was held in *Grimes v Grimes* [1948] P 323.   [88] *R v R* [1952] 1 All ER 1194.

[89] *W (otherwise K) v W* [1967] 3 All ER 178n. Note also that there can be consummation even though the wife's vagina has been artificially extended: *SY v SY (otherwise W)* [1963] P 37, CA (or, presumably, now that change of gender can be legally recognised, where it has been wholly constructed).

[90] Matrimonial Causes Act 1973 s 12(1)(a).

[91] Impotence from psychological causes must amount to invincible repugnance and not merely unwillingness or reluctance: *Singh v Singh* [1971] P 226, CA.

[92] This rule was finally established in *Harthan v Harthan* [1949] P 115, CA.

[93] *S v S (otherwise C)* [1956] P 1 at 11; *M v M* [1957] P 139; cf *L v L* (1882) 7 PD 16; *G v G* (1908) 25 TLR 328.

[94] *Nash v Nash* [1940] P 60 at 64–5; *J v J* [1947] P 158 at 163, CA at 44 (overruled on another point by *Baxter v Baxter*, see earlier).   [95] See later, Bars to relief, Petitioner's knowledge, p 85.

[96] Matrimonial Causes Act 1973 s 12(1)(b).

[97] Per Lord Jowitt LC in *Horton v Horton* [1947] 2 All ER 871, HL at 874. Cf *Potter v Potter* (1975) 5 Fam Law 161, CA (husband's refusal due to loss of sexual ardour for wife in similar circumstances not wilful).

[98] [1972] 1 All ER 292, CA, following *Jodla v Jodla* [1960] 1 All ER 625. See also *A v J* [1989] 1 FLR 110 (wife's decision to postpone indefinitely a religious ceremony was found to be 'adamant and uncompromising').

Refusal to have intercourse in any form will clearly come within the statute, and so may wilful refusal to undergo treatment (attended by no danger) to remove a physical or psychological impediment to consummation.[99] If there has been no opportunity to consummate the marriage (for example, because one party is in prison), an indication by one of them that he will not consummate it at any time in the future has been held to entitle the other to bring an application: the latter is not bound to wait to see whether the respondent changes his mind when the opportunity arises.[100]

Once the marriage has been consummated, it will not be voidable if one spouse subsequently refuses to continue to have intercourse. In these circumstances, the latter's only remedy lies in divorce.

2. LACK OF CONSENT

Section 12(1)(c) of the Matrimonial Causes Act 1973 provides that a marriage shall be voidable if either party did not validly consent to it, whether in consequence of duress, mistake, unsoundness of mind or otherwise. Lack of consent probably made the marriage void at common law.[101] The reason for making such a marriage voidable is that the parties themselves may wish to ratify it when true consent can be given and consequently third parties should not be able to impeach it.[102]

It will be seen that the applicant may rely on the fact that the respondent did not consent to the marriage even though the applicant him- or herself was responsible for this state of affairs, for example by inducing a mistake or uttering threats.

We must now consider what facts will be regarded in law as vitiating consent.

(a) Duress

If, owing to fear or threats, one of the parties is induced to enter into a marriage which, in the absence of compulsion, he or she would never have contracted, the marriage will be voidable.

It is not necessary that the fear should have been inspired by any acts on the other party's part. A striking example is to be seen in *Szechter v Szechter*.[103] The petitioner was a Polish national who had been arrested by the security police in Warsaw. After 14 months' interrogation and detention in appalling conditions she was sentenced to three years' imprisonment for 'anti-state activities'. The respondent was a distinguished Polish historian of Jewish origin whose presence in Poland was something of an embarrassment to the authorities and whom they were prepared to allow to emigrate. In order to effect the petitioner's release he divorced his wife and went through a ceremony of marriage with the petitioner in prison. The scheme was successful, and eventually all the parties reached England, where the petitioner brought proceedings for nullity so that the respondent and his first wife could remarry. A decree was granted. In so doing Simon P applied the following test:[104]

---

[99] *S v S (otherwise C)* [1956] P 1 at 15–16.   [100] *Ford v Ford* [1987] Fam Law 232.

[101] See the discussion in the 4th edition of this book at pp 79–83.

[102] See Law Com No 33, paras 11–15. Cf Marriage (Scotland) Act 1977 s 20A (inserted by s 2 of the Family Law (Scotland) Act 2006) codifies the Scots common law rule that the marriage is void where a party gave consent by duress or error, or was incapable of understanding the nature of marriage.

[103] [1971] P 286. For discussion of the extraordinary background to the case and its significance, see D McClean and M Hayes ' "But I Didn't Really Want to Get Married" ' in S Gilmore, J Herring and R Probert (eds) *Landmark Cases in Family Law* (2011). See also *H v H* [1954] P 258 (marriage contracted in Budapest to enable woman to escape from Hungary where she was likely to be sent to prison or concentration camp); *Parojcic v Parojcic* [1959] 1 All ER 1 (fear imposed by petitioner's father).   [104] At 297–8.

It is, in my view, insufficient to invalidate an otherwise good marriage that a party has entered into it in order to escape from a disagreeable situation, such as penury or social degradation. In order for the impediment of duress to vitiate an otherwise valid marriage, it must, in my judgment, be proved that the will of one of the parties thereto has been overborne by genuine and reasonably held fear caused by threat of immediate danger (for which the party is not himself responsible),[105] to life, limb or liberty, so that the constraint destroys the reality of consent to ordinary wedlock.

There may be rare cases where the party is so terrified that he (or she) does not know what he is doing at all: a marriage contracted in such circumstances must be voidable as there is no consent whatever. In other cases the reference to the party's will being overborne has been criticised on the ground that she does in fact consciously choose to enter into marriage rather than accept the alternative presented to her.[106] The court must then decide whether the circumstances were such that it would be socially more objectionable to tie the party to the union than to permit her to repudiate it: the need to uphold the institution of marriage must be balanced against the need to do justice to the individual. This must depend on what she perceived to be the probable consequences of refusing to enter into the marriage and her capacity to resist the pressure brought to bear on her. Simon P's test has been subjected to criticism as being too restrictive, and it has certainly been liberalised in the modern application of the duress ground which has arisen in cases of forced marriage.

For example, Simon P's third condition, namely that the fear must be caused by 'threat of immediate danger to life, limb or liberty' should no longer be regarded as correct. The Court of Appeal applied it in *Singh v Singh*[107] and *Singh v Kaur*,[108] but only a year after the latter case Ormrod LJ, delivering the leading judgment of the court in *Hirani v Hirani*,[109] denied the need for such threats. The petitioner was a 19-year-old woman of Hindu Indian origin. She formed a relationship with a Muslim man and within a fortnight of discovering this, her parents arranged for her to marry a man from their own community, telling her that if she refused, they would throw her out of the home. Having nowhere to go and no financial means, she went through with the ceremony at a register office, but the marriage was not consummated and she left after six weeks. She petitioned for nullity and on appeal, Ormrod LJ stated that the relevant question is 'whether the pressure . . . is such as to destroy the reality of consent and overbears the will of the individual'.[110]

Hirani was followed in *P v R (Forced Marriage: Annulment: Procedure)*[111] where the petitioner was compelled to enter into a marriage with her cousin while she was staying in Pakistan. Such cases are increasingly recognised as examples of the phenomenon of 'forced marriage'[112] imposed on some young people and vulnerable adults from minority

---

[105] The dictum derives from *Buckland v Buckland* [1968] P 296 where the petitioner had been falsely accused of unlawful intercourse with a young girl and threatened with prison if he did not marry her. Query if innocence is a necessary requirement for reliance on duress, however. See AH Manchester 'Marriage or Prison: The Case of the Reluctant Bridegroom' (1966) 29 MLR 634.

[106] T Ingman and B Grant 'Duress in the Law of Nullity' [1984] Fam Law 92.

[107] [1971] P 226, CA.   [108] (1981) 11 Fam Law 152, CA.

[109] (1983) 4 FLR 232, CA. Ormrod LJ had also given the leading judgment in *Singh v Kaur*.

[110] In Scotland the '*Hirani* test' rather than the '*Szechter* test' was followed in two cases in which the petitioning Pakistani woman was forced to go through with an arranged marriage due to family pressure: see *Mahmood v Mahmood* 1993 SLT 589 and *Mahmud v Mahmud* 1994 SLT 599. For an interesting analysis of these cases see A Bradney 'Duress, Family Law and the Coherent Legal System' (1994) 57 MLR 963.

[111] [2003] 1 FLR 661. See also *NS v MI* [2006] EWHC 1646 (Fam) [2007] 1 FLR 444.

[112] See Home Office *A Choice by Right* (2000).

ethnic communities and there is an awareness of the need for greater understanding of the pressures faced by them in these situations and for sensitivity in laying down an appropriate test of duress.

Indeed, such awareness has resulted in the establishment of a Forced Marriage Unit by the Home Office and Foreign Office to provide guidance,[113] advice and practical aid concerning the issue, and the enactment of the Forced Marriage (Civil Protection) Act 2007 to provide remedies to deter and forestall actions intended to coerce a person into marriage.[114] Section 63A of the Family Law Act 1996, inserted by the 2007 Act, defines a forced marriage as follows:

> (4) ... a person ('A') is forced into a marriage if another person ('B') forces A to enter into a marriage (whether with B or another person) without A's free and full consent.
> (5) For the purposes of subsection (4) it does not matter whether the conduct of B which forces A to enter into a marriage is directed against A, B or another person.
> (6) In this part –
> 'force' includes coerce by threats or other psychological means (and related expressions are to be read accordingly) ...

This rather circular definition is more usefully elaborated by guidance issued by the Forced Marriage Unit:

> There is a clear distinction between a forced marriage and an arranged marriage. In arranged marriages, the families of both spouses take a leading role in arranging the marriage but the choice whether or not to accept the arrangement remains with the prospective spouses. In forced marriage, one or both spouses do not (or, in the case of some adults with disabilities, cannot) consent to the marriage and duress is involved. Duress can include physical, psychological, sexual, financial and emotional pressure.[115]

It is submitted that such initiatives reflect an understanding that non-physical threats can be just as stressful and over-powering as the threat of physical violence,[116] and there should be no question of preventing a victim of such abuse from receiving redress. Moreover, as Coleridge J noted in *P v R (Forced Marriage: Annulment: Procedure)*,[117] it is important that a decree of nullity, rather than of divorce, is made available, to avoid the stigma that would otherwise attach to the petitioner within her community. However, it has been pointed out[118] that the three-year time bar on bringing petitions for nullity on the basis of lack of consent[119] may be too short a time in which to enable a victim of forced marriage to seek a remedy, leaving her, apparently, with the stigmatic use of divorce as

---

[113] See Joint FCO/Home Office Action Plan *Forced Marriage—The Overseas Dimension* (2000); Home Office/FCO/ACPO *Dealing with Cases of Forced Marriage: Guidance for Police Officers* (2nd ed, 2005); see also The Law Society *Family Law News* (April 2004) special issue.

[114] Forced marriages are discussed further in Ch 6, Forced Marriage Protection Orders, pp 197–201.

[115] HM Government *Multi-agency practice guidelines: Handling cases of Forced Marriage* (2009) p 10. For the argument that the supposed distinction between forced and arranged marriage is not as straightforward as this might seem to suggest, see M Enright 'Choice, Culture and the Politics of Belonging: The Emerging Law of Forced and Arranged Marriage' (2009) 72 MLR 331.

[116] See *Scott v Sebright* (1886) 12 PD 21, where the respondent's threats to see that bankruptcy proceedings were taken against the petitioner and to 'accuse her to her mother and in every drawing-room in London of having been seduced by him' were apparently regarded as grounds (along with a threat to shoot her) for annulling the marriage.

[117] [2003] 1 FLR 661. See also, *NS v MI* [2006] EWHC 1646 (Fam) [2007] 1 FLR 444.

[118] R Gaffney-Rhys 'The Legal Status of Forced Marriages: Void, Voidable or Non-Existent?' [2010] Int Fam Law 336.   [119] See later, Bars to relief, Lapse of time, p 85.

the only alternative. The courts have therefore utilised the developing jurisprudence on the 'non-existent' marriage, discussed earlier, to provide another form of redress, at least where the ceremony was performed abroad, through the grant of a declaration denying the marriage recognition on grounds of public policy.[120] However, this is not ideal since it does not enable the victim to seek financial provision from the respondent, and any children born from the union will be treated as illegitimate which, whilst carrying few if any civil law penalties, may still cause problems for them within their communities.

(b) Mistake

A mistake will affect the marriage in two cases only. First, a mistake as to the identity (but not as to the attributes) of the other contracting party will make the marriage voidable if this results in one party's failing to marry the individual whom he or she intends to marry. In the New Zealand case *C v C*,[121] the woman married the man in the erroneous belief that he was a well-known boxer called Miller. It was held that the marriage was not invalidated by the mistake because she married the very individual she meant to marry. Secondly, the marriage will be voidable if one of the parties is mistaken as to the nature of the ceremony and does not appreciate that he is contracting a marriage. In *Valier v Valier*[122] the husband, who was an Italian and whose knowledge of the English language was poor, was taken to a register office by the wife and there went through the usual form of marriage. He did not understand what was happening at the time, the parties never cohabited and the marriage was never consummated. It was held that he was entitled to a decree of nullity. But if each party appreciates that he or she is going through a form of marriage with the other, no other type of mistake apparently can affect the contract.[123] Thus, it has been held that the marriage will not be invalidated by a mistake as to the monogamous or polygamous nature of the union,[124] the other party's fortune,[125] the woman's chastity[126] or the recognition of the union by the religious denomination of the parties.[127]

(c) Unsoundness of mind

This will affect a marriage only if, as a consequence, *at the time of the ceremony* either party was unable to understand the nature of the contract they were entering into. There is a presumption that a party was capable of doing so, and the burden of proof therefore lies upon the party impeaching the validity of the marriage.[128] In *Sheffield City Council*

---

[120] See *SH v NB (Marriage: Consent)* [2009] EWHC 3274 (Fam) [2010] 1 FLR 1927; *B v I* [2010] 1 FLR 1721; *Re P (Forced Marriage)* [2011] EWHC 3467 (Fam) [2011] 1 FLR 2060. But note Holman J's refusal to do so where the victim could bring an application for a nullity decree based on being under 16 at the time of the marriage: *A Local Authority v X and A Child* [2013] EWHC 3274 (Fam) [2014] 2 FLR 123.

[121] [1942] NZLR 356. But if A becomes engaged to B, whom she has never seen before, by correspondence, and C successfully personates B at the wedding, the marriage would be voidable because A intends to marry B and nobody else: ibid, p 359. It would be void if the personation invalidated the publication of banns: see Ch 2, Preliminaries, Marriages according to the rites of the Church of England, p 51.

[122] (1925) 133 LT 830. See also *Ford v Stier* [1896] P 1, and *Kelly v Kelly* (1932) 49 TLR 99 (mistaken belief that ceremony was formal betrothal); *Mehta v Mehta* [1945] 2 All ER 690 (mistaken belief that Hindu marriage ceremony was ceremony of religious conversion); *Alfonso-Brown v Milwood* [2006] EWHC 642 (Fam) [2006] 2 FLR 265 (Ghanaian engagement ceremony).

[123] *Moss v Moss* [1897] P 263 at 271–3; *Kenward v Kenward* [1950] P 71 at 79 (per Hodson J); revsd [1951] P 124 at 133–4 (per Evershed MR). [124] *Kassim v Kassim* [1962] P 224.

[125] *Wakefield v Mackay* (1807) 1 Hag Con 394 at 398.

[126] Even though she is pregnant by another man: *Moss v Moss* [1897] P 263.

[127] *Ussher v Ussher* [1912] 2 IR 445.

[128] *Harrod v Harrod* (1854) 1 K & J 4, 9. But if the person is proved to have been generally insane, there will be a presumption that he was insane at the time of the marriage, and the burden of proof will consequently shift onto the party seeking to uphold its validity: *Turner v Meyers* (1808) 1 Hag Con 414 at 417.

v E and S,[129] E, who was aged 21, had hydrocephalus and spina bifida and was said to function at the level of a 13-year-old. She moved in with a man, S, aged 37, who had a history of sexual violence. The local authority discovered that they were planning to marry and sought an order under the inherent jurisdiction of the High Court to stop them from marrying or associating, asserting that it was in E's best interests neither to marry, nor to associate with, S and that she lacked the capacity to make decisions about where she should live, whether she should have contact with S and whether she should marry him. In determining a preliminary issue concerning what questions E should be asked by experts appointed to advise on her capacity to marry, Munby J followed the test formulated by Singleton LJ in *In the Estate of Park*:[130]

> Was the [person] . . . capable of understanding the nature of the contract into which he was entering, or was his mental condition such that he was incapable of understanding it? To ascertain the nature of the contract of marriage a man must be mentally capable of appreciating that it involves the responsibilities normally attaching to marriage. Without that degree of mentality, it cannot be said that he understands the nature of the contract.

He held that the court had no jurisdiction to consider whether it was in E's best interests to marry, or to marry S. Its task in cases of this type is to determine whether a person has capacity to marry, pure and simple. This involves determining whether he or she can understand the nature of the marriage contract, ie that he or she is mentally capable of understanding the duties and responsibilities that normally attach to marriage. It is not enough that someone appreciates that he or she is taking part in a marriage ceremony or understands its words. 'That said, the contract of marriage is in essence a simple one, which does not require a high degree of intelligence to comprehend. The contract of marriage can readily be understood by anyone of normal intelligence.'[131] He was also at pains to stress that:

> There are many people in our society who may be of limited or borderline capacity but whose lives are immensely enriched by marriage. We must be careful not to set the test of capacity to marry too high, lest it operate as an unfair, unnecessary and indeed discriminatory bar against the mentally disabled . . . Equally, we must be careful not to impose so stringent a test of capacity to marry that it becomes too easy to challenge the validity of what appear on the surface to be regular and seemingly valid marriages.[132]

It is worth noting also that s 1(4) of the Mental Capacity Act 2005 provides that a person 'is not to be treated as unable to make a decision merely because he makes an unwise decision' and s 27(1)(a) of the 2005 Act provides that no decision under the Act can be taken on behalf of a person in relation to consent to marry. However, in *Westminster City Council v C and others*,[133] the Court of Appeal regarded a man with profound

---

[129] [2004] EWHC 2808 (Fam) [2005] Fam 326.

[130] [1954] P 112 at 127, CA; cf Karminski J (in the Div Court) [1954] P 89 at 99; Birkett LJ at 134–5; Hodson LJ at 137; *Hunter v Edney* (1881) 10 PD 93 at 95; *Durham v Durham* (1885) 10 PD 80 at 82.

[131] *Sheffield City Council v E and S* [2004] EWHC 2808 (Fam) [2005] Fam 326 at para 68.

[132] [2004] EWHC 2808 (Fam) [2005] 1 FLR 965 paras 144, 145. Note, however, that an injunction may be granted to restrain those responsible for an adult lacking capacity from taking steps to arrange a marriage for her: *M v B, A, S (By her Litigation Friend, the Official Solicitor)* [2005] EWHC 1681 (Fam) [2006] 1 FLR 117; *Re SA* [2005] EWHC 2942 (Fam) [2006] I FLR 867. Query whether such an injunction could be issued against the intending spouse?

[133] [2008] EWCA Civ 198 [2009] Fam 11.

learning difficulties rendering him unable to function even at the level of a three-year old child, as lacking capacity to enter into a marriage, and therefore refused recognition of the marriage, conducted by proxy in Bangladesh. By contrast, Holman J, sitting as a Judge of the Court of Protection, which deals with cases concerning vulnerable adults who lack mental capacity, refused to authorise the issue of a petition for nullity in the case of a Sikh man with learning difficulties who had been married to a woman on a visit to India who had been unaware of his condition until the wedding day. He took into account her own wish to remain married to the man, and the case highlights how complex the phenomenon of 'forced' marriage may be—for who was the victim in this case, the man or the woman, or both—and what would be the best remedy for them?[134]

In the absence of any binding English authority, it is submitted that the effect of drunkenness and drugs will be the same as that of unsoundness of mind. Consequently, the marriage will be voidable if, as a result of either, one of the parties was incapable of understanding the nature of the contract into which he was entering.[135]

(d) 'Sham marriages'

Cases like *Szechter v Szechter*[136] raise a further question: is a 'sham marriage'—that is, where the parties go through the form of marriage purely for the purpose of representing themselves as married to the outside world with no intention of living together as husband and wife—to be regarded in law as a nullity?

Since the House of Lords' decision in *Vervaeke v Smith*[137] there can be no doubt that such marriages are perfectly valid provided the parties freely consented to contracting them. In that case a Belgian prostitute went through a ceremony of marriage with a British subject so that she could apply for British citizenship and thus escape deportation. The parties had no intention of living together and saw each other again on only one or two occasions. The majority of the House considered it indisputable that the marriage was valid.

This problem is most likely to arise in the context of the United Kingdom's restrictive immigration laws. For these purposes, s 24(5) of the Immigration and Asylum Act 1999 defines a sham marriage as:

a marriage (whether or not void)—

(a) entered into between a person ('A') who is neither a British citizen nor a national of an EEA State other than the United Kingdom and another person (whether or not such a citizen or such a national); and

(b) entered into by A for the purpose of avoiding the effect of one or more provisions of United Kingdom immigration law or the immigration rules.

Under the same section, if a superintendent registrar to whom a notice of marriage has been given, or who has been present at the solemnisation of a marriage, has reasonable grounds for suspecting that the marriage will be or is a sham marriage, he or she must

---

[134] *Sandwell Metropolitan Borough Council v RG and Others* [2013] EWHC 2373 (COP) [2013] COPLR 643.
[135] See *Legey v O'Brien* (1834) Milw 325; *Sullivan v Sullivan* (1818) 2 Hag Con 238 at 246 (per Sir W Scott).
[136] [1971] P 286.
[137] [1983] 1 AC 145, per Lord Hailsham LC at 151–2 and Lord Simon at 162. Lord Brandon agreed with both speeches. For discussion of the case, see D McClean and M Hayes '"But I Didn't Really Want To Get Married"' in S Gilmore, J Herring and R Probert (eds) *Landmark Cases in Family Law* (2011) pp 82–84.

report their suspicion to the Immigration and Nationality Directorate of the Home Office without delay.[138]

Such cases may come to light in contexts some way removed from suspicions raised at the time of the marriage, or through a party seeking a nullity decree. For example, in *Bhaiji v Chauhan, Queen's Proctor Intervening (Divorce: Marriages Used for Immigration Purposes)*[139] they emerged at the divorce stage. Five divorce petitions, all involving couples of Indian ethnicity, one party having British and the other Indian citizenship, were found to be strikingly similar and appeared to involve marriages entered into so as to enable the Indian spouse to obtain indefinite leave to remain. All the petitions were dismissed. In *R (K) v London Borough of Lambeth*[140] the claimant was a Kenyan national whose claim for asylum was rejected. She married an Irish national but the marriage was regarded as a sham and instructions for her removal from the country were issued. Meanwhile, she was refused benefits on the basis that she was a dependant of an EEA national (the Irish husband). She appealed on the basis that she was not his dependant, the marriage being one of convenience only. It was held that the motive for her entering into the marriage was irrelevant, as was the fact that she and her husband might have separated. She was a 'spouse'—a lawfully married person—within the meaning of the relevant regulations and therefore ineligible for support, even though, simultaneously, she was not regarded as a 'spouse' for the purpose of remaining in the jurisdiction.[141]

3. MENTAL DISORDER

A marriage is voidable if, at the time of the ceremony, *either party*, though capable of giving a valid consent, was suffering (whether continuously or intermittently) from mental disorder within the meaning of the Mental Health Act 1983 of such a kind or to such an extent as to be unfitted for marriage.[142] 'Unfitted for marriage' in this context has been defined as 'incapable of carrying out the ordinary duties and obligations of marriage'.[143]

This ground must be distinguished from that already considered, namely, unsoundness of mind producing lack of consent. In the case of mental disorder it is presumed that the party was capable of giving a valid consent to the marriage but that the general state of his or her mental health at the time of the ceremony was such that it is right that the marriage should be annulled. It will be observed that the applicant does not have to rely on the respondent's mental disorder, but may rely on his or her own. This is necessary to enable a party to withdraw from a marriage entered into in ignorance of the existence or extent of his or her illness or the effect which it would have upon his or her married life.

---

[138] Immigration and Asylum Act 1999 s 24. See also *R (Baiai and Others) v Secretary of State for the Home Department* [2008] UKHL 53, [2009] AC 287, discussed in Ch 2, Reforming formalities, p 55.

[139] [2003] 2 FLR 485.   [140] [2003] EWHC 871 (Admin) [2003] 2 FLR 439.

[141] Equally, of course, she was seeking to argue simultaneously that she should be regarded as a spouse for the purpose of remaining in the jurisdiction, but that she should not be so regarded for the purpose of claiming support.

[142] Matrimonial Causes Act 1973 s 12(1)(d). 'Mental disorder' means mental illness, arrested or incomplete development of mind, psychopathic disorder and any other disorder or disability of mind: Mental Health Act 1983 s 1(2).

[143] *Bennett v Bennett* [1969] 1 All ER 539.

4. VENEREAL DISEASE AND PREGNANCY BY ANOTHER

A marriage is voidable if at the time of the ceremony *the respondent* was suffering from venereal disease in a communicable form.[144] 'Venereal disease' is not defined in the Act.[145]

A spouse may bring an application for nullity if at the time of the marriage *the respondent* was pregnant by someone else.[146] Since same-sex spouses cannot conceive together, whenever a respondent is pregnant, she will always have become so by means of a person other than the petitioner. Quite possibly in this context, a sperm donor will be the father. Moreover, whilst the original motivation for including this ground as a basis for annulling a marriage was to prevent a man having spurious children foisted upon him, for a same sex marriage, this ground will only ever be available to female spouses, the reason for whose objection to the partner being pregnant will presumably be rather different from that of a heterosexual man.

Both these grounds, which were introduced by the Matrimonial Causes Act 1937, were thought necessary because there was otherwise no matrimonial relief for fraud or misrepresentation, and it was thought unjust to bind a person to marriage in these circumstances.[147]

5. GENDER REASSIGNMENT

The Gender Recognition Act 2004 introduced two new grounds into s 12 of the Matrimonial Causes Act 1973, to provide for situations where one of the parties has undergone gender reassignment. Section 12(1)(g)[148] provides that a decree may be granted where an interim gender recognition certificate has been issued to either party to the marriage, provided that proceedings are brought within six months of the date of issue of that certificate.[149] The aim of this provision was to prevent the parties to the marriage from effectively, and legally, becoming same-sex spouses[150] although they were (and remain) enabled to register as civil partners through an abridged procedure.[151] Now that same sex marriage is lawful, we have seen that the marriage may be continued where the other spouse consents to the issue of the certificate[152] but if the spouse does not wish to remain married to the trans-gender person, this provision offers him or her an annulment rather than having to obtain a divorce.

Section 12(1)(h)[153] provides that a decree may be granted where the respondent is a person who has changed gender within the terms of the 2004 Act before the marriage. This provision appears intended to provide the same protection for a petitioner against fraud or misrepresentation on the part of the other party, as those earlier concerning venereal disease or pregnancy, but the analogy is questionable. It must be at least arguable that a person's gender is a fundamental aspect of his or her identity—this certainly seems to

---

[144] Matrimonial Causes Act 1973 s 12(1)(e).
[145] The 8th edition of this work (at p 96) discussed whether venereal disease includes AIDS, but we do not think that that point is arguable given the various ways in which the HIV infection can be transmitted.
[146] Matrimonial Causes Act 1973 s 12(1)(f).
[147] Query whether the case for their continued retention as grounds for nullity is now so compelling?
[148] Inserted by Gender Recognition Act 2004 Sch 2 para 2.
[149] Matrimonial Causes Act 1973 s 13(2A) inserted by Gender Recognition Act 2004 Sch 2 para 3.
[150] S Gilmore 'The Gender Recognition Act 2004' [2004] Fam Law 741 at 743 notes that the Parliamentary Joint Committee on Human Rights considered it to be a disproportionate measure and recommended its reconsideration.   [151] Civil Partnership Act 2004 Sch 3 paras 1–4.
[152] See Ch 2, Capacity to marry, Sex, p 41. Requiring a couple to convert a marriage into a civil partnership, or divorce, before allowing one partner a legal change of gender, is not in any event a breach of the ECHR: *Hamalainen v Finland* (Application No 37359/09) ECtHR,16 July 2014.
[153] Inserted by the Gender Recognition Act 2004 Sch 4 para 5.

have been the view taken by the European Court of Human Rights in *Goodwin v United Kingdom*[154]—and not merely an 'attribute'. On this basis, a mistake as to the partner's gender would be covered by s 12(1)(c) and this provision is unnecessary.

6. BARS TO RELIEF

Like any other voidable contract at common law parties to a voidable marriage might effectively put it out of their own power to obtain a decree of nullity by their own conduct.[155]

(a) Petitioner's conduct

Section 13(1) of the Matrimonial Causes Act 1973 provides:

> The court shall not . . . grant a decree of nullity on the ground that the marriage is voidable if the respondent satisfies the court—
>
> (a) that the petitioner, with knowledge that it was open to him to have the marriage avoided, so conducted himself in relation to the respondent as to lead the respondent reasonably to believe that he would not seek to do so; and
> (b) that it would be unjust to the respondent to grant the decree.

The principle underlying the forerunner to this bar was summarised by Lord Watson:[156]

> In a suit for nullity of marriage there may be facts and circumstances proved which so plainly imply, on the part of the complaining spouse, a recognition of the existence and validity of the marriage, as to render it most inequitable and contrary to public policy that he or she should be permitted to go on to challenge it with effect.

The same principle underlies the statutory bar. It should be noted however, that the court will be bound to apply the bar only if the respondent satisfies it that the statutory conditions are fulfilled. Not only does this mean that the burden of proof is on the respondent, but if he or she chooses not to raise the bar at all, the court must grant a decree if a ground has been made out even if it is clear from the facts that these conditions are satisfied.[157] Secondly, no conduct on the petitioner's part can raise the bar unless he (or she) knew at the time that it was open to him to have the marriage avoided. Thirdly, only conduct in relation to the petitioner can act as a bar.

Any positive act by the petitioner may raise the bar if a reasonable person in the respondent's position would have concluded that the petitioner intended to treat the marriage as valid and the respondent in fact drew this conclusion. In *D v D (Nullity: Statutory Bar)*[158] the parties adopted two children at a time when the husband knew that he could have the marriage annulled because of his wife's refusal to consummate it. He later brought nullity proceedings. It was held that by agreeing to the adoption he had so conducted himself in relation to the wife as to lead her to believe that he would not seek to do so.

In addition to proving that the petitioner has led the respondent to believe that he or she will not seek to have the marriage avoided, the latter must also show that it would be unjust to him (or her) to grant the decree. Among the matters which the court should take

---

[154] [2002] 2 FLR 487.   [155] See Law Com No 33, paras 36–45 and 76–86.

[156] *G v M* (1885) 10 App Cas 171, HL at 197–8.

[157] This point was not taken in *D v D* [1979] Fam 70, where the wife, having raised the defence, then elected not to pursue it. Dunn J, however, held that in such circumstances it could not be said to be unjust to grant the decree.   [158] [1979] Fam 70.

into account in deciding whether to grant a decree are the length of time the marriage has lasted, the existence of any children of the family, any religious or other personal objections that the respondent has to the decree, and the financial loss that he (or she) might suffer as a result of nullity (for example, the loss of pension rights). As in the case of divorce, justice will rarely be served by refusing to set aside a marriage that is already dead.

(b) Lapse of time

In all cases, except those based on impotence or wilful refusal to consummate or where an interim gender recognition certificate has been issued, a decree of nullity must normally be refused if the proceedings were not instituted within three years of the date of the marriage.[159]

The reason for this bar is to ensure that the parties' status is not left in doubt for too long: consequently there is no power to extend the period, even though the petitioner was unaware of the facts or that they made the marriage voidable. As we have seen in relation to forced marriages, however, this may well work injustice. The Law Commission concluded that hardship was most likely to arise if the complaining party was mentally disordered. They had in mind two problems in particular: old and lonely people not fully in possession of their faculties may well become the object of attention of fortune hunters, and a petition may have to be presented by the party's litigation friend who may not become aware of all the facts during the first three years of the marriage.[160] Following the Commission's recommendation, the court is thus empowered[161] to grant leave for the presentation of a petition based on any ground, notwithstanding that more than three years have elapsed since the date of the marriage, provided that the petitioner has suffered from mental disorder within the meaning of the Mental Health Act 1983 at any time during the first three years of the marriage and that the court considers that it would be just to do so.

Lapse of time is not a bar in the case of inability or wilful refusal to consummate the marriage, because the petitioner may properly try to overcome the impediment or aversion for a longer period than three years.[162]

A six-month period is allowed for a petition to be brought under s 12(1)(g). If that is not done, it would still be open to a party to petition on another ground (or to seek a divorce).

(c) Petitioner's knowledge

If the petition is based on the respondent's venereal disease, pregnancy by another man, or acquired gender, the decree must be refused unless the court was satisfied that the petitioner was ignorant of the facts alleged at the time of the marriage.[163]

F. EFFECT OF DECREE ON VOIDABLE MARRIAGE

Although a decree has always been necessary to annul a voidable marriage, at common law (as in the case of a void marriage) it pronounced the marriage 'to have been and to be

---

[159] Matrimonial Causes Act 1973 s 13(2). This is independent of the bar last considered, and even if the petition is brought within three years, the respondent may still raise the petitioner's delay or other conduct as a bar if it reasonably led him or her to conclude that the petitioner would not seek to have the marriage annulled.

[160] See Law Com No 116 (*Time Restrictions on Presentation of Divorce and Nullity Petitions*, 1982), Pt III.

[161] Matrimonial Causes Act 1973 s 13(2) and (4) as amended by the Matrimonial and Family Proceedings Act 1984 s 2. Note that the petition does not have to be based on the petitioner's mental disorder.

[162] See Law Com No 33, paras 79–85.

[163] Matrimonial Causes Act 1973 s 13(3) as amended.

absolutely null and void to all intents and purposes in the law whatsoever'. Consequently, before the decree the parties were regarded as husband and wife both in law and in fact but after the decree absolute they were deemed in law never to have been married at all. It is now provided however, that:[164]

> A decree of nullity granted after 31st July 1971 in respect of a voidable marriage shall operate to annul the marriage only as respects any time after the decree has been made absolute, and the marriage shall, notwithstanding the decree, be treated as if it had existed up to that time.

This leaves no doubt that the parties must now be regarded as having been married throughout the whole period between the celebration of a voidable marriage and the decree absolute.

G. IS THERE A CONTINUING NEED FOR NULLITY?

In practical terms the law of nullity has little current relevance. The number of orders is small[165] and for the most part those who want to end the marriage tie can do so by divorcing. Moreover, since annulments only affect voidable marriages *after* the decree, it has now become conceptually hard to distinguish voidable marriages ended by an annulment and marriages ended by divorce. Whether the law of nullity in its current form should be retained, and if not, how it should relate to the law of divorce, are questions that need to be addressed.

Although the inevitable corollary of having criteria governing the validity of marriage is to have a concept of a void marriage, it may be more questionable to retain the concept of a voidable marriage. It seems particularly hard to justify having wilful refusal to consummate as a ground of voidability since that arises purely from a post-marital decision and is surely properly regarded as a reason for divorce.[166] The same could now be said regarding a spouse's change of gender after the marriage. However, the problem of forced marriage does suggest that there is a need for a remedy other than divorce which is available to those from the communities in which this practice occurs. If voidable marriage were to be abolished, lack of consent would have to be reinstated as a ground for declaring the marriage *void* as it probably was at common law, yet this would prevent the parties from ratifying it should they choose.[167] Alternatively, a specific remedy might have to be created to deal with the phenomenon, expanding on the measures already enacted under the Forced Marriage (Civil Protection) Act 2007.[168]

---

[164] Matrimonial Causes Act 1973 s 16, re-enacting the Nullity of Marriage Act 1971 s 5, and implementing the recommendations of the Law Commission: Law Com No 33, paras 21–22 and 25.

[165] The number of petitions for nullity has been in decline since the 1980s when there were around 1,000 petitions per annum. In 2013 there were 365 decrees absolute: *Court Statistics (quarterly) January to March 2014* [online] CSV Divorce_National.csv (accessed 4 August 2014).

[166] Compare the Law Commission's view (Law Com No 33, *Nullity of Marriage*, 1970), discussed earlier, The unconsummated marriage, p 74. The Government's White Paper on Divorce *Looking to the Future* (1995) Cm 2799, para 4.52 stated that 'consultees did not view the law of nullity as relevant to a revision of the divorce law' and that the 'possibility that the ground for nullity of wilful refusal to consummate the marriage should be removed because of the need to prove fault was not supported.'

[167] See discussion earlier, Lack of consent, p 76.

[168] See Ch 6, Forced marriage protection orders, p 197.

H. ESTABLISHING THE VALIDITY OF A CIVIL PARTNERSHIP

1. DECLARATION

As with a marriage, a person may apply to the High Court or county court for a declaration regarding the validity of a civil partnership.[169] The provisions are similar to those applying to marriage and are not discussed further here.[170]

2. ANNULMENT OF A CIVIL PARTNERSHIP

As with a marriage, provision is made for the annulment of a civil partnership and the same distinction is drawn between partnerships that are void and those that are voidable. A nullity *order*, rather than decree, is granted by the court, although it is given in two stages, a conditional and final order, akin to a decree nisi and absolute.[171]

The following are the grounds for annulment.

3. VOID CIVIL PARTNERSHIPS

A civil partnership is void if, at the time when they do so, the couple are not eligible to register under s 3, discussed earlier.[172] It is also void[173] if both parties know, at the time of registering, that due notice of the proposed civil partnership has not been given; that the civil partnership document has not been duly issued; that the applicable period for registration has expired; that the place where they are registering is not that which was specified in the notice they have given; that a civil partnership registrar is not present; or that, in the case of a minor, a person whose consent is required has forbidden the issue of the civil partnership document.[174] It may be noted that this last instance is different from the position in relation to marriage. There, unless a relevant person has objected to the calling of banns, a marriage contracted in the absence of a necessary consent is *not* void.[175] The reason for the distinction may be that the drafters of the Civil Partnership Act wished to make a process equivalent to objecting to banns available to parents etc. Alternatively, though less likely, perhaps, it may have been thought that parents may be more likely to seek to prevent an adolescent child from entering into a same sex union than from getting married. But it is hard to see how making the partnership *void* would support such parents' concerns. Given that the legal position is different with most marriages, the provision is arguably both disproportionate and discriminatory.

---

[169] Civil Partnership Act 2004 s 58.

[170] See earlier, Declaration as to marital status p 62. For the provisions governing recognition of civil partnerships (or the equivalent) entered into overseas, see ss 212–17 and the discussion by M Harper et al *Civil Partnership—The New Law* (2005) paras 4.38–4.42. A Canadian same-sex marriage was recognised only as a civil partnership in *Wilkinson v Kitzinger (No 2)* [2006] EWHC 2022 (Fam) [2007] 1 FLR 295 Potter P rejecting the argument that this was discriminatory. For discussion, see Ch 2, The right to marry, p 36.   [171] Section 37.

[172] Ch 2, Entry into a civil partnership, Capacity, p 59.

[173] Civil Partnership Act 2004 s 49(b).

[174] Under Sch 2 para 6 or 12. See Ch 2, Entry into a civil partnership, Formalities p 60.

[175] See earlier, Formal defects, Defects which *may* invalidate a marriage, p 72.

4. VOIDABLE CIVIL PARTNERSHIPS

Section 50 sets out the grounds on which a civil partnership is voidable. These are the same as for marriage, except for two omissions. First, as with same sex marriages, there is no provision for an inability or wilful refusal to consummate to constitute a ground for annulment. This is because the concept of consummation, which is inherently hetero-normative, does not apply to a same-sex relationship. Secondly, the fact that the respondent was suffering from venereal disease at the time of the registration is not a ground for nullity. It is unclear why this ground has been omitted.

The same bars to relief apply to voidable civil partnerships as to voidable marriages.[176] The same objections to the concept of voidable civil partnerships may also be made and indeed, the grounds are arguably even more anomalous, as noted earlier. It is understandable that the Civil Partnership Act includes them as currently drafted, since the approach of the legislation was to import, as far as possible, the provisions relating to marriage into the legal concept of civil partnership.

---

[176] Section 51, and see earlier, Bars to relief, pp 84–85.

4

THE PERSONAL AND PROPERTY CONSEQUENCES OF MARRIAGE AND CIVIL PARTNERSHIP

A. INTRODUCTION

This chapter explores the key personal legal consequences of marriage (including same sex marriage) and civil partnership, and then considers the property consequences. The number of people entering into marriage has been in long-term decline, from a peak of 426,241 marriages in England and Wales in 1972, to 247,890 in 2011.[1] However, the proportion of British *households* made up of married couples,[2] at 46% of the total in 2011, is still much greater than that of cohabiting couples, who formed only 9% of the total (by contrast, 32% of households consisted of one person).[3] Marriage therefore remains the most popular form of relationship,[4] and it is helpful to view it as the benchmark against which other intimate relationships can be measured. We thus consider the different consequences of marriage and then examine how far civil partnership mirrors these. We consider the position of cohabitants, insofar as the law distinguishes their partnership from other intimate relationships, in Chapter 24.

In examining the legal effects of marriage (or civil partnership),[5] two issues need to be considered. First, how does their marriage affect the parties' legal relationship vis-à-vis each other? Here, the common law doctrine of unity of the spouses, explained later, is important historically, but now has little continuing significance in the wake of the political and social movement towards sexual equality between men and women.[6] Secondly, how far is the parties' relationship legally privileged over other domestic relationships? Here, one can see, in the face of the declining marriage rate, a trend towards providing uniform rules to deal with people's relationships, regardless of their legal form and this is particularly so in relation to the parent–child relationship as we discuss in later chapters.[7] But now that the Marriage (Same Sex Couples) Act 2013 has been passed, one could argue

---

[1] ONS *Marriage summary statistics 2011(provisional)* (2013) Table 2b. There were 6,152 civil partnerships formed in 2011 in England and Wales: ONS *Civil Partnership Formations 2011* (2012) Table 1.

[2] The total includes civil partnerships.   [3] ONS, *General Lifestyle Survey 2011* (2013) Table 3.5.

[4] For the view that non-legal measures have been more powerful in de-centring the significance of marriage than law reform, see R Auchmuty 'Law and the Power of Feminism: How Marriage Lost its Power to Oppress Women' (2012) 20(2) Feminist LS 71.

[5] Civil partnerships are included within our discussion of marriage except where the provision made for them is different.

[6] For a fascinating global historical comparison of marriage laws, see A Gautier 'Legal Regulation of Marital Relations: An Historical and Comparative Approach' (2005) 19 Int Jo of Law, Policy and the Family 47.

[7] See Chapters 8 to 11.

that the importance of marriage as a status which carries legal consequences has been reaffirmed, and, as will be seen, it is premature to argue that marital status is irrelevant to determining a person's legal rights and obligations.

Both same sex marriage and the concept of civil partnership are purely statutory creations. However, s 11(1) of the Marriage (Same Sex Couples) Act 2013 provides that:

> (1) In the law of England and Wales, marriage has the same effect in relation to same sex couples as it has in relation to opposite sex couples.

Schedule 3 para 1 to the Act provides

> (1) In existing England and Wales legislation—
>   (a) a reference to marriage is to be read as including a reference to marriage of a same sex couple;
>   (b) a reference to a married couple is to be read as including a reference to a married same sex couple; and
>   (c) a reference to a person who is married is to be read as including a reference to a person who is married to a person of the same sex.
> (2) Where sub-paragraph (1) requires a reference to be read in a particular way, any related reference (such as a reference to a marriage that has ended, or a reference to a person whose marriage has ended) is to be read accordingly.
> (3) For the purposes of sub-paragraphs (1) and (2) it does not matter how a reference is expressed.

Perhaps reflecting social and cultural norms concerning how same sex couples refer to themselves and are referred to, Schedule 3 para 5(2) provides that new legislation referring to husbands or wives is to be interpreted so that 'husband' includes a man married to another man, and 'wife' includes a woman married to another woman. Thus, Parliament has taken the view that these terms should remain gendered—two women married to each other are both to be regarded as 'wives' rather than having one assume the role of 'husband'.[8]

In light of these provisions, the discussion which follows assumes that spouses in a same sex marriage will be treated in exactly the same way as a heterosexual couple would be, unless the opposite is expressly provided or inevitably follows from the context or the way the law has been interpreted. However, it should be noted that the Civil Partnership Act 2004 does not contain equivalent provisions, although the Act itself seeks (exhaustively) to extend legislation relating to spouses, to civil partners except where expressed to the contrary. Where this may have a bearing on the position of civil partners, this will be made clear.

1. THE DOCTRINE OF UNITY

At common law the principal effect of marriage was that for many purposes it fused the legal personalities of husband and wife into one. According to Blackstone:[9]

> By marriage, the husband and wife are one person in law; that is, the very being or legal existence of the woman is suspended during the marriage, or at least is incorporated and consolidated into that of the husband; under whose wing, protection, and *cover*, she

---

[8] Compare the Human Fertilisation and Embryology Act 2008 s 44 which refers to the female partner of a woman receiving assisted reproduction treatment as having to meet the 'agreed female parenthood' (not 'motherhood') conditions whilst s 37 provides equivalent provisions for the male partner, known as the 'agreed fatherhood' conditions. See Ch 8, Legal parentage, pp 255–257.

[9] *Commentaries* (1753) pp i and 442.

performs everything; and is therefore called in our law-French a *feme-covert* ... Upon this principle of a union of person in husband and wife, depend almost all the legal rights, duties, and disabilities, that either of them acquire by the marriage.

Neither equity nor the ecclesiastical law accepted the doctrine of unity of personality, and both gave married women access to their courts and even permitted actions between spouses. But it was not until the Married Women's Property Act 1870 that a wife was given an extremely limited right to maintain an action in her own name in the courts of common law. Whilst a series of statutes culminating in the Law Reform (Married Women and Tortfeasors) Act 1935 substantially put a married woman in the same legal position as a single woman, they created extensive exceptions to the old rules without abolishing outright the fundamental principle on which the anomalies were based.

The doctrine of unity was doubtless biblical in origin[10] but in time, it became the legal justification for subordinating the wife's will and acts to those of her husband, and the embodiment of patriarchy. The equality of the spouses (and of men and women in general) is a fundamental feature of international law, so that, for example, Art 16 of the United Nations Convention on the Elimination of All Forms of Discrimination against Women 1979 (CEDAW) provides that 'both spouses have the same rights in respect to the ownership, acquisition, management, administration, enjoyment and disposition of property'.[11] This position had also been reached in English law around the same time that the CEDAW was drawn up and the view that marriage as such creates a legal unity of personalities, irrespective of the social implications, did not survive the decision of the Court of Appeal in *Midland Bank Trust Co Ltd v Green (No 3)*.[12] A husband and wife were sued for conspiracy; it was argued that they could not be liable on the ground that they were one person in law and therefore could not conspire with each other. This defence failed. At first instance Oliver J concluded:[13]

Unless I am compelled by authority to do so—and I do not conceive that I am—I decline to apply, as a policy of law, a mediaeval axiom which was never wholly accurate and which appears to me now to be as ill-adapted to the society in which we live as it is repugnant to common sense.

The same sentiments were expressed in the Court of Appeal, where Oliver J's judgment was affirmed. Lord Denning MR expressed himself in these words:[14]

Nowadays, both in law and in fact, husband and wife are two persons, not one ... The severance in all respects is so complete that I would say that the doctrine of unity and its ramifications should be discarded altogether, except in so far as it is retained by judicial decision or by Act of Parliament.

In more picturesque language Sir George Baker P said that to hold that a husband and wife could not be liable in the tort of conspiracy because they were one person:

... would ... be akin to basing a judgment on the proposition that the Earth is flat, because many believed that centuries ago. We now know that the Earth is not flat. We now know that husband and wife in the eyes of the law and in fact are equal.[15]

---

[10] Genesis 2:24; Genesis 3:16.

[11] For discussion of this and other international measures promoting equality, see K Boele-Woelki et al *Principles of European Family Law Regarding Property Relations Between Spouses* (2013) pp 38–41.

[12] [1982] Ch 529, CA.   [13] [1979] Ch 496 at 527.   [14] [1982] Ch 529, CA at 538–9.

[15] [1982] Ch 529, CA at 542.

However, a residual notion of married couples as forming one unit is still to be found in the statutory taxation system, and is applicable to eligible civil partners.[16] For example, both spouses and civil partners are exempt from tax on lifetime gifts and inheritance tax in relation to transfers between each other.[17] Moreover, there is still a tax allowance payable to married people (and now civil partners) where one of the couple was born before 6 April 1935.[18] This was previously available to all married couples. It may be payable to either spouse or civil partner, or apportioned between them. It might once have been justified as reflecting the economic reality that in many instances the husband was the main breadwinner in the family and the head of the household. Its continued limited existence could be justified as reflecting the fact that, in the case of older couples, who have had that traditional division of labour during their marriage, the wife is less likely to have significant pension entitlements and is more likely to be dependent upon the husband's pension and other resources built up over his career. However, it is more difficult to make the same justification in the case of same sex couples. The more likely reason for its retention is that it is politically expedient to provide certain tax benefits to the married. Indeed, the Conservative party committed itself to reintroducing a rather tokenistic tax allowance for all married couples and civil partners regardless of their age,[19] to be implemented in 2015.[20]

2. CONSORTIUM

The slow movement toward equality of the spouses was reflected by changes in the common law concept of consortium, an abstract notion which appears to mean living together as husband and wife with all the incidents (insofar as these can be defined) that flow from that relationship.[21] At one time it would have been said that the husband had the right to his wife's consortium whilst the latter had not so much a reciprocal right to her husband's consortium as a correlative duty to give him her society and her services—a view which was not entirely obsolete in the middle of the nineteenth century. A clear illustration of the wife's legal subjection to her husband can be seen in the old common law rule that a woman who murdered her husband was guilty of petit treason, like the vassal who slew his lord or the servant who slew his master.[22] The wife's basic duty was to submit to the husband, in return for which the husband would protect and support her. As one judge described marriage:

> It is an engagement between a man and woman to live together, and love one another as husband and wife, to the exclusion of all others. This is expanded in the promises of the marriage ceremony by words having reference to the natural relations which spring from that engagement, such as protection on the part of the man, and submission on the part of the woman.[23]

[16] See too the Married Women's Property Act 1882 s 11 and the Life Assurance Act 1774: a spouse (or civil partner—Civil Partnership Act 2004 s 70) may insure own life for benefit of spouse or children and may insure the other's life and recover without showing financial loss—*Reed v Royal Exchange Assurance Co* (1795) Peake Add Cas 70; *Griffiths v Fleming* [1909] 1 KB 805, CA.

[17] Inheritance Taxes Act 1984 s 18, as amended.   [18] Income Tax Act 2007 s 45.

[19] Conservative Party *Invitation to Join the Government of Britain* (2010) p 35.

[20] HM Treasury 'Marriage Transferable Tax Allowance announced by government' 30 September 2013. Basic rate taxpayers may benefit by up to £200 p.a. by one spouse transferring up to £1,000 of their personal tax allowance to the other.   [21] Per Lord Campbell in *Lynch v Knight* (1861) 9 HL Cas 577 at 589.

[22] The distinction between petit treason and murder was abolished in 1828 by 9 Geo 4, c 31 s 2.

[23] *Durham v Durham* (1885) 10 PD 80 at p 82 per Sir James Hannen P.

The husband was also accepted at one time as having the right physically to restrain or confine his wife to the house,[24] and it was only in 1891 that this view was finally rejected. In *R v Jackson*[25] (known as the 'Clitheroe Case')[26] the wife had gone to live with relations whilst her husband was absent in New Zealand. After his return she refused to live with him again. Consequently he arranged with two men that they should seize her as she came out of church one Sunday afternoon. She was then put into a carriage and taken to her husband's residence, where she was allowed complete freedom of the house but was not permitted to leave the building. She then applied for a writ of habeas corpus and it was unanimously held by the Court of Appeal that it was no defence that the husband was merely confining her in order to enforce his right to her consortium. This principle was reinforced subsequently by the Court of Appeal in *R v Reid*,[27] where it was held that a husband who steals, carries away or secretes his wife against her will is guilty of the common law offence of kidnapping her.[28] As Cairns LJ said:[29]

> The notion that a husband can, without incurring punishment, treat his wife, whether she be a separated wife or otherwise, with any kind of hostile force is obsolete.

A further aspect of the husband's right to consortium was the action at common law to obtain damages against anyone who interfered with his right. This could take the form of enticement (a tort also available to a wife),[30] harbouring the wife, or adultery. The last began as the common law action for criminal conversation[31] by which the husband could obtain compensation for the loss of his wife's comfort and society as the result of the adulterer's wrongful act. This action was abolished by the Matrimonial Causes Act 1857 and replaced by a statutory claim for damages in the divorce court which was almost always made on a petition for divorce. In addition, if the husband lost his wife's services as the result of a tort committed against *her*, he could maintain a separate and independent action against the tortfeasor. This served a useful purpose: if, for example, the wife was seriously injured as the result of the defendant's negligence, it provided a means by which the husband could recover the expenses to which he had been put, such as for medical and nursing care, the provision of help to look after himself and the children, and visiting her whilst she was in hospital. But although a wife might be put to similar expense if her husband was injured, the action was not available to her.[32] Actions of this kind came to be regarded as outmoded and patriarchal, and by 1982, had all been abolished.[33] However, more general provisions to compensate family members where a relative is *killed* as a result of wrongdoing were introduced by statute as early as 1846 by the Fatal Accidents Act (commonly called Lord Campbell's Act). This permitted certain dependants of a person killed as the result of the defendant's wrongful act, neglect or default to recover the financial loss suffered as a result of

[24] And thus also physically to punish her. See *R v Lister* (1721) 1 Stra 478, *Re Cochrane* (1840) 8 Dowl 630.
[25] [1891] 1 QB 671, CA.
[26] See *The Northern News* March 26, 1898 [online] http://www.cultrans.com/the-northern-news/march-26-1898/4095-march-26-1898-clitheroe-abduction-case (accessed 8 May 2014).
[27] [1973] QB 299, CA.
[28] See Law Commission, Consultation Paper No 200, *Simplification of Criminal Law: Kidnapping* (2011).
[29] [1973] QB 299, CA at 303.
[30] *Gray v Gee* (1923) 39 TLR 429. This replaced an earlier writ of ravishment or trespass *vi et armis de uxore rapta et abducta* available only to the husband.
[31] See L Stone *Road to Divorce* (1990) Part IX.   [32] *Best v Samuel Fox & Co Ltd* [1952] AC 716, HL.
[33] It is, however, possible to obtain compensation in tort for losses incurred where a relative gives up work or incurs expenses to care for a family member injured by the defendant's negligence (so long as that relative is not himself the defendant): *Hunt v Severs* [1994] 2 AC 350, but in such a situation the nature of the relationship is immaterial, and damages would be payable whether it is a cohabitant, spouse, parent or other who gives up work to look after the injured claimant.

the death. The Act was amended extensively by further legislation in the course of the next 100 years, and eventually consolidated in the Fatal Accidents Act 1976.[34]

This movement for the equality of the rights of the sexes also gradually extended into other fields of private law. In 1923 Parliament equated the rights of the spouses to petition for divorce;[35] in 1925 it established the principle that they have equal rights with respect to their children;[36] in 1967 it gave each of them the power to apply for an order regulating their rights to occupy the matrimonial home;[37] and in 1978 it gave them reciprocal rights to seek maintenance from each other.[38] All these changes reflect the modern view that the wife is no longer the weaker partner subservient to the stronger, but that both spouses are the joint, co-equal heads of the family. It seems to be clear that, insofar as consortium still exists, 'a husband has a right to the consortium of his wife, and the wife to the consortium of her husband',[39] and these rights must now be regarded as exactly reciprocal.[40]

But the question arises whether it makes sense to talk of consortium as continuing to exist at all. In *Macleod v Macleod*[41] the Privy Council held that 'there is no longer an enforceable duty upon husband and wife to live together' and this was confirmed by the Supreme Court in *Granatino v Radmacher (Formerly Granatino).*[42] It could be argued that this is open to argument, since the law does still recognise, through the concept of desertion, that a failure to cohabit without just cause or the consent of the other spouse, or living separately from each other for a certain period of time, is a basis for establishing the irretrievable breakdown of the marriage justifying a divorce. But the *ground* for the divorce is not a breach of marital duty, but the irretrievable breakdown itself, which is merely *proved* by the period of desertion or separation (or by other forms of 'behaviour' which the applicant cannot reasonably be expected to live with, which could range from lack of personal hygiene to alcoholism, avoidance of which has never been regarded as an enforceable marital *obligation*).[43] Harder to explain away is the fact that a judicial separation, as distinct from a divorce, is understood as removing the duty to cohabit from the spouses so that neither can be held in desertion.[44] The matter requires a definitive decision. If the essence of consortium is the 'cohabitation' of the spouses, and if the view of the Privy Council and Supreme Court is correct that this is no longer enforceable by law, the whole concept is an empty one. It thus seems more sensible to consider what the 'consequences of marriage' may be rather than to attempt to pigeonhole some of these into 'aspects of consortium'.

B. PERSONAL CONSEQUENCES

1. USE OF SURNAME

Adults may use any surname they choose provided that there is no intention to perpetrate a fraud.[45] Many wives still take their husband's surname on marriage, although they may

---

[34] As amended.   [35] Matrimonial Causes Act 1923.

[36] Guardianship of Infants Act 1925; see S Cretney 'What Will the Women Want Next?' (1996) 112 LQR 110. In point of fact, their position was not exactly equal until implementation of the Children Act 1989: see, Ch 9, The strenghening of the mother's position, Twentieth century developments, p 312.

[37] Matrimonial Homes Act 1967.   [38] Domestic Proceedings and Magistrates' Courts Act 1978.

[39] Per Scrutton LJ in *Place v Searle* [1932] 2 KB 497 at 512, CA.

[40] See *Sheffield City Council v E and S* [2004] EWHC 2808 (Fam) [2005] 1 FLR 965 [109]–[132].

[41] [2008] UKPC 64 [2010] 1 AC 298 at [38].   [42] [2010] UKSC 42 [2011] 1 AC 534 at [52] and [157].

[43] See Ch 7, The respondent's behaviour, pp 215–218.   [44] See Ch 7.

[45] The execution and enrolment of a deed poll merely provide evidence of the executant's intention to be known by a different name and have no other legal significance.

continue to be known by their former names for professional or business purposes.[46] Likewise a woman may retain her former husband's name after the marriage has been terminated either by death or by divorce, and a man has no such property in his name as to entitle him to sue for an injunction to prevent his divorced wife from using it unless she is doing so for the purpose of defrauding him or some other right of his is being invaded.[47] Similarly, an unmarried woman may use the surname of the man with whom she is living if she wishes (and vice versa), although she may be civilly or criminally liable if she does so for the purpose of defrauding another.

There is no reason why same sex spouses or civil partners should not be able to adopt a common surname in accordance with these rules should they wish. Clearly, there is no norm as to which partner's name is more likely to be used: perhaps a combined surname may prove popular.

2. SEXUAL INTERCOURSE

As we discussed in Chapter 3,[48] neither same sex marriage nor civil partnership imports a *requirement* of consummation to confirm the validity of the union, so that there could be no question of a *duty* to have sexual relations as forming part of the consequences of the status nor of the 'right' of a same sex spouse or civil partner to demand sex from the other. But in the case of *heterosexual* spouses, the incapacity of either spouse or the wilful refusal of the respondent to consummate the marriage still entitles the petitioner to a decree of nullity.[49] As regards sexual intercourse *after* consummation, Hale wrote in the eighteenth century:[50]

> But the husband cannot be guilty of a rape committed by himself upon his lawful wife, for by their mutual matrimonial consent and contract the wife hath given up herself in this kind unto her husband which she cannot retract.

Although Hale cited no authority for this view, it was generally regarded as a correct statement of the common law.[51] But the change in attitude towards the relationship of the spouses during the twentieth century led the courts to seek ways of limiting the scope of the husband's immunity,[52] and the issue was ultimately reviewed by the House of Lords in *R v R*[53] in 1991.

---

[46] Other countries take a much stricter approach and lay down firm rules to determine whose surname may be used, but this may amount to a breach of Arts 8 and 14 of the European Convention on Human Rights: see *Burghardz v Switzerland* [1995] Fam Law 71 (ECHR).

[47] *Cowley v Cowley* [1900] P 305, CA; affd [1901] AC 450, HL; cf *Du Boulay v Du Boulay* (1869) LR 2 PC 430, PC at 441. Thus, if she holds herself out as his wife after he has remarried, she may be guilty of libel or slander if the reasonable inference is that he is not legally married to his second wife.

[48] At Ch 3, The unconsummated marriage, p 74.

[49] Ch 3, The unconsummated marriage, p 75. It will be recalled that the Marriage (Same Sex Couples) Act 2013 Sch 4 para 4 inserts subs (2) into the Matrimonial Causes Act 1973 s 12 to provide that these grounds do not apply to the marriage of a same sex couple.

[50] 1 Hale PC 629. But he could be guilty of aiding and abetting another to rape her: *Lord Audley's Case* (1631) 3 State Tr 401, HL; *R v Leak* [1976] QB 217, CA.

[51] It was not until *R v Clarence* (1888) 22 QBD 23 that judicial doubts were expressed about its correctness.

[52] A number of cases held that consent could be retracted following a court order or by the parties' agreement: *R v Clarke* [1949] 2 All ER 448 (consent withdrawn after decree of judicial separation); *R v O'Brien* [1974] 3 All ER 663 (decree nisi of divorce); *R v Steele* (1976) 65 Cr App Rep 22, CA (non-molestation injunction); *R v Roberts* [1986] Crim LR 188, CA (separation deed). In *R v Miller* [1954] 2 QB 282 it was also held that a husband could not insist on his right to have intercourse by force, and thus would be guilty of assault on his wife. See also *R v Kowalski* [1988] 1 FLR 447, CA (husband guilty of indecent assault by forcing wife to submit to fellatio before sexual intercourse).

[53] [1992] 1 AC 599, HL on which see J Herring 'No More Having and Holding: The Abolition of the Marital Rape Exemption' in S Gilmore et al (eds) *Landmark Cases in Family Law* (2011).

The wife left the husband and told him that she intended to petition for divorce. Some three weeks later he broke into her parents' house, where she was living, and attempted to have sexual intercourse with her against her will. The trial judge ruled that the husband's immunity had been lost, whereupon he pleaded guilty to attempted rape. He then appealed to the Court of Appeal and, when his appeal was dismissed, to the House of Lords. Lord Keith, with whose speech the other members of the House agreed, maintained that the common law is capable of evolving in the light of changing social, economic and cultural developments. Marriage, he pointed out, 'is in modern times regarded as a partnership of equals and no longer one in which the wife must be the subservient chattel of the husband'. Consequently any reasonable person must now regard Hale's proposition as unacceptable.[54] The only obstacle to declaring that a husband had no immunity was s 1 of the Sexual Offences (Amendment) Act 1976 which, for the first time, laid down a statutory definition of rape including the words '*unlawful* sexual intercourse'. This phrase usually connotes extra-marital intercourse[55] and consequently it could be argued that the Act had reintroduced the old common law rule by making it impossible for a husband to rape his wife in any circumstances. Lord Keith rejected this argument on the grounds that it was inconceivable that Parliament had this intention and that 'unlawful' in this context could not reasonably import the existing common law exceptions. The House therefore concluded that the word was mere surplusage and that 'in modern times the supposed marital exception in rape forms no part of the law of England'.[56]

The European Court of Human Rights subsequently rejected a complaint by R that the House of Lords' ruling was in breach of Art 7 of the European Convention because it had retrospectively criminalised his act, the court holding that the line of cases which had already eroded the marital immunity had rendered their Lordships' ultimate ruling reasonably foreseeable, and further that:

> . . . the abandonment of the unacceptable idea of a husband being immune against prosecution for rape of his wife was in conformity not only with a civilised concept of marriage but also, and above all, with the fundamental objectives of the Convention, the very essence of which is respect for human dignity and human freedom.[57]

3.　EVIDENCE IN LEGAL PROCEEDINGS

When one considers the question of testimony in legal proceedings, two principles of public policy may come into conflict. The first is the view that a person should be protected from having to give evidence against his or her spouse or civil partner. The second is that in any proceedings, civil or criminal, no evidence should be excluded if it will help the court or the jury to arrive at the truth.

(a) Competence

At common law neither the parties nor their spouses were competent witnesses in civil proceedings or (with very few exceptions) in criminal proceedings. A spouse's evidence was excluded for a number of reasons: the fact that it might be untrustworthy, the wish to preserve marital harmony, the undesirability of having a witness giving evidence *against*

---

[54] [1992] 1 AC 599, HL at 616D–E.　　　[55] See *R v Chapman* [1959] 1 QB 100, CCA.

[56] At p 489. Section 1 was subsequently amended by the Criminal Justice and Public Order Act 1994 s 142 to delete the reference to 'unlawful' sexual intercourse. See also Law Com Report No 205 *Rape within Marriage* (1992).

[57] *CR v United Kingdom; SW v United Kingdom* [1996] 1 FLR 434 para 42 (at 448–9).

his or her spouse and the consequent unfairness of permitting evidence to be given *for* the spouse. In civil proceedings this rule was abolished by the Evidence Amendment Act 1853 and spouses became competent to give evidence for any party. In criminal proceedings, the Criminal Evidence Act 1898, which also for the first time made the accused generally competent to give evidence on his or her own behalf, enabled a spouse to give evidence for the *defence* subject to some qualifications. Various statutes also made the spouse a competent witness for the *prosecution* in the case of certain crimes, mainly of a sexual nature or against children.

The Police and Criminal Evidence Act 1984 s 80 made the accused's spouse a competent witness for the prosecution, the accused and any co-accused in all cases unless the couple were charged jointly. The Youth Justice and Criminal Evidence Act 1999 amended the general competence rules and s 53 of that Act now provides that all persons are competent at every stage in criminal proceedings to give evidence. Where they are witnesses for the prosecution, they are competent unless charged and liable to conviction in the proceedings. A spouse, civil partner (or cohabitant) is therefore a competent witness for the prosecution where he or she has pleaded guilty or the charges against him or her have been dropped.

(b) Compellability

Once spouses became competent in civil proceedings, the main reason for their not being compelled to give evidence disappeared. The Evidence Amendment Act 1853 accordingly made them compellable as well as competent. The Civil Partnership Act 2004 s 84 extends this (as an enactment or rule of law concerning a spouse giving evidence) to civil partners.

The arguments against forcing a person to give evidence against his or her spouse or partner in *criminal* proceedings are, however, more cogent.[58] The Police and Criminal Evidence Act 1984 struck a compromise.[59] For the first time the spouse was made a compellable witness for the *accused* in all cases unless the spouses are charged jointly. But he or she (and now a civil partner)[60] may be compelled to give evidence for the *prosecution* or a person jointly charged with the accused in only three cases. These are:

(a) if the offence charged involves an assault on, or injury or a threat of injury to, the spouse or civil partner or a person under the age of 16;

(b) if the offence charged is a sexual offence[61] against a person under the age of 16; and

(c) if the offence charged consists of attempting or conspiring to commit any of the above offences or of aiding, abetting, counselling, procuring or inciting their commission.[62]

However repugnant it may seem to force a person to give evidence against his or her spouse or partner facing a criminal charge, in these cases the principle is outweighed by the need to enable the prosecution to produce evidence without which it would often be impossible to prove the offence. This will be effective, however, only if the witness is prepared to give evidence, and there is no doubt that a number of prosecutions, particularly

---

[58] See *Hoskyn v Metropolitan Police Comr* [1979] AC 474, HL, and the critique by S Edwards *Sex and Gender in the Legal Process* (1996) pp 202–5.

[59] Section 80. See P Creighton 'Spouse Competence and Compellability' [1990] Crim LR 34.

[60] Section 80 as amended by Civil Partnership Act 2004 Sch 27 para 97.

[61] As defined in s 80(7).

[62] Prospectively replaced by offences of encouraging or assisting crime under Part 2 of the Serious Crime Act 2007.

of offences involving assault, are not brought because of the victim's unwillingness to testify, whether from fear or some other cause.[63]

The arguments for and against the compellability of spouses apply equally to unmarried couples and to other family relationships. Although the policy decision was taken to align civil partnerships as far as possible with marriages and thus extend this provision to civil partners, in view of the current trend to bring spouses more into line with other witnesses, it is highly unlikely that these rules would be extended to other relationships.

4. CONTRACTS

(a) Between the spouses

The fact that a couple are spouses has played a significant part in the court's determination of whether any agreement they have reached between them should be regarded as a binding contract.[64] An agreement between spouses will clearly be enforceable if it represents a business arrangement, but the courts have traditionally refused to interfere in the running of the home by giving legal effect to the sort of arrangements that spouses living together make every day in order to regularise their domestic affairs. The leading case is still *Balfour v Balfour*[65] where the Court of Appeal held that an agreement, under which the husband, who was about to go abroad, promised to pay the wife £30 a month in consideration of her not looking to him for further maintenance, was unenforceable because there was no intention to enter into legal relations. If the spouses are living together when they enter into the agreement, there is a presumption that they do not intend to be legally bound.[66]

The presumption does not operate if the parties have separated or are at arm's length and about to separate: in these circumstances their intention becomes a question of fact to be inferred from all the evidence. In most cases of this kind, where the agreement relates to financial arrangements, it will be almost impossible to conclude that they did not intend to be legally bound by the terms. However, it should be noted that spouses or civil partners cannot oust the jurisdiction of the courts to determine with finality their financial and property relations, because the courts assert a public interest in ensuring both that a party is financially protected as far as possible and that the state's burden in covering any shortfall in such protection is limited.[67]

(b) Contracts with third parties

At common law a married woman had no contractual capacity and neither she nor her husband could sue or be sued on any contract made by her except as his agent. Equity did not

---

[63] See S Edwards *Sex and Gender in the Legal Process* (1996). Where not compellable, the failure of the spouse or civil partner of a person charged in any proceedings to give evidence in the proceedings shall not be made the subject of any comment by the prosecution: Police and Criminal Evidence Act 1984 s 80A. See further, in the context of domestic abuse, Ch 6, The criminal justice system, Reluctance of the victim, p 171.

[64] For discussion of the role and limitations of contract in regulating agreements between intimate partners, see J Wightman 'Intimate Relationships, Relational Contract Theory, and the Reach of Contract' (2000) 8 Fem LS 93.

[65] [1919] 2 KB 571, CA. See also *Spellman v Spellman* [1961] 2 All ER 498, CA (agreement as to ownership of car unenforceable).

[66] This appears to be the view of the majority of the Court of Appeal in *Gould v Gould* [1970] 1 QB 275.

[67] *Hyman v Hyman* [1929] AC 601, *Sutton v Sutton* [1984] Ch 184. For further discussion of this issue, and for the separate question of pre-nuptial agreements, see Ch 21, Private agreements, Void provisions in maintenance agreements, p 782 and Ch 22, Consent orders, Pre- and post-nuptial agreements, pp 853–862.

take the same strict view, and if a wife had separate property, she could bind this by contract although she could not render herself *personally* liable on any agreement. To enable wives to carry on dealings with tradesmen for household goods, clothes etc, the law recognised them as agents for their husbands, and would enforce, against the husband, the pledging of his credit for the purchase of such articles. The agency device was particularly important for deserted wives with no means of support, who had what was called an 'agency of necessity', finally abolished only in 1970, which permitted them to incur debts against the husband's liability.[68]

Legislation gradually recognised the contractual capacity of married women. The Married Women's Property Act 1882 (which provided that all property acquired by a wife after 1882 should remain her separate property) gave a wife full contractual capacity and enacted that every contract entered into by her otherwise than as an agent should be deemed to be a contract with respect to her separate property and should bind it. Section 1 of the Law Reform (Married Women and Tortfeasors) Act 1935 provided that a married woman is capable of rendering herself and being rendered liable in respect of any contract, debt or obligation, and of suing and being sued in contract, and also that she is subject to the law relating to bankruptcy and the enforcement of judgments and orders as if she were a feme sole (an unmarried woman).

5. TORTS

The fiction of legal unity produced two separate rules in tort. First, if a tort was committed by or against a married woman, her husband had to be joined as a party to the action. Secondly, no liability in tort could arise between spouses and no action in tort could be brought by either of them against the other.

A married woman was given the power to maintain an action in her own name to recover her separate property by the Married Women's Property Act 1870[69] and a full power to sue in respect of any tort committed against her by the Married Women's Property Act 1882.[70] But it was not until the Law Reform (Married Women and Tortfeasors) Act 1935 that husbands *as husbands* finally ceased to be liable for their wives' torts in all circumstances. And it was only by the Law Reform (Husband and Wife) Act 1962 s 1 that each spouse was given the right of action against the other in tort as though they were not married. This applies equally to an action brought after the marriage has been dissolved (or presumably annulled) in respect of a tort committed during matrimony,[71] but in one respect the law here is different, for if the action is brought during the subsistence of the marriage, the court has a discretion to stay the action in two cases. First, it may do so if it appears that no substantial benefit would accrue to either party from the continuation of the proceedings. This is designed to prevent trivial actions brought to air matrimonial grievances;[72] consequently, it is not contemplated that the power would be exercised if the parties were no longer living together as an economic unit and the damage was real, or if the spouse was a purely nominal defendant and the real purpose of the action was to recover damages from a source outside the family. Such would be the case, for example, if the driver of a car wished to claim an indemnity from his insurance company. Secondly,

[68] Matrimonial Proceedings and Property Act 1970 s 41. His agency was distinct from that pertaining while the spouses lived together, and was lost if the wife were herself guilty of a matrimonial offence.

[69] Section 11.

[70] See now the Law Reform (Married Women and Tortfeasors) Act 1935 s 1(c).

[71] Section 3(3).

[72] See Ninth Report of the Law Reform Committee 1961, Cmnd 1268, paras 10–13.

the court may stay the action if it relates to property and the questions in issue could more conveniently be disposed of by an application under s 17 of the Married Women's Property Act 1882, discussed later. Equivalent provision has been made for civil partnerships.[73]

6. CRIMINAL LAW

The doctrine of unity never applied generally in the criminal law so as to make a husband vicariously liable for his wife's crimes or to prevent either of them from being liable in most cases for a crime committed against the other, but it does still have certain consequences which should be considered.

(a) Marital coercion

There was a rule of common law that if a married woman committed certain offences in the presence of her husband, this raised a rebuttable presumption[74] that she had committed the crime under his coercion and consequently he and not she was prima facie liable to be convicted. Both the origin and the extent of this rule are uncertain, and it had become anomalous by the twentieth century. It was abolished by the Criminal Justice Act 1925 s 47, which replaced it with the following statutory defence:

> On a charge against a wife for any offence other than treason or murder it shall be a good defence to prove that the offence was committed in the presence of, and under the coercion of, the husband.

In other words, this section changed the law by placing the burden of proof upon the wife to prove the coercion.[75] Coercion means something other than a threat of serious injury, which is a defence available to anyone charged with a criminal offence except murder and treason. It is apparently sufficient for the wife to show that her will was overborne by the wishes of her husband so that she is forced against her will to commit the offence.[76]

This defence is strictly construed. Hence it is not available to a woman cohabiting with a man outside marriage[77] or to a woman who mistakenly believes that she is married to the man applying coercion.[78] Nor has it been extended to civil partners, reflecting one of the few differences between marriage and civil partnership. It is clearly discriminatory and hence potentially challengeable under the European Convention on Human Rights. Indeed, the Law Commission recommended its abolition as long ago as 1977 as being outmoded.[79] There is no reported modern example of the defence having succeeded, although it was argued in 2013 in the high-profile case of Vicky Pryce, the former wife of a disgraced politician, who was charged with having perverted the course of justice by accepting speeding points on her driving licence to cover up for her husband who faced a ban from driving had he been convicted.[80] The case was striking as Ms Pryce was an eminent economist who presented a very different picture to the public—and the jury—than one might expect of a wife arguing that she felt under such pressure from her husband that she was prepared to commit a crime for him. Similarly, in *R v Darwin*[81]

---

[73] Civil Partnership Act 2004 s 69.

[74] *R v Smith* (1916) 12 Cr App Rep 42, CCA; *R v Torpey* (1871) 12 Cox CC 45.

[75] On the balance of probabilities: *R v Shortland* [1996] 1 Cr App Rep 116.

[76] *R v Shortland* [1996] 1 Cr App Rep 116.   [77] *R v Court* (1912) 7 Cr App Rep 127, CCA.

[78] *R v Ditta, Hussain and Kara* [1988] Crim LR 42, CA. The court also queried, obiter, whether a wife could raise the defence if the marriage were polygamous.

[79] Law Commission, Law Com No 83 *Defences of General Application* (1977).

[80] See *The Guardian* 8 March 2013.   [81] [2009] EWCA Crim 860.

the wife was regarded as someone who, far from being under her husband's thumb, had wholeheartedly co-operated in his insurance fraud, to the extent of pretending to their own children that he had died in a boating accident at sea. It is clearly difficult in a society that proclaims the equality of the spouses to envisage situations where a person could have their will overborne as required, but it has been argued that the defence still has a place for wives who face duress from abusive partners, particularly in some minority ethnic communities.[82] The problem is that many people in diverse intimate relationships do face duress and domestic abuse, as is discussed in Chapter 6—but the category is not confined to wives. It may well be that a new and broader defence of duress is needed, but the retention of the defence of coercion is not the correct response to the problem and it is surely time it was abolished.

(b) Conspiracy

It is provided by statute that a husband and wife may not be convicted of conspiring together,[83] and it is generally believed that this was the position at common law. But this does not prevent them from being convicted of conspiring with the other and a third person.[84]

(c) Theft

Under the doctrine of unity husband and wife were deemed to have unity of possession, so that neither could be guilty of stealing the other's property. But once the concept of separate property had been extended by the Married Women's Property Act 1882, it was obvious that the fiction once more worked an anomaly. Under the current law, for the purposes of the Theft Acts, a husband and wife are to be regarded as separate persons and each can now be convicted of theft of the other's property, obtaining it by deception and so forth.[85] But the consent of the Director of Public Prosecutions is required for prosecution for any offence of stealing or doing unlawful damage to property which at the time belongs to the accused's spouse (or civil partner), or for any attempt, incitement or conspiracy to commit such an offence.[86] The purpose of this provision is to reduce the risk of a prosecution which might prejudice a continuation of the parties' relationship, though one must question how stable that relationship could be in such circumstances.

7. CITIZENSHIP AND RIGHT TO LIVE IN THE UNITED KINGDOM

(a) British citizenship

Only a very brief outline of the position is provided here.[87] The doctrine of unity had no application at common law with respect to nationality. A foreign woman did not acquire British nationality by marrying a British subject, and a woman who was a British subject did not lose her status by marrying a foreigner. This rule was reversed by legislation

---

[82] S Edwards 'In defence of the defence of marital coercion' [2013] Fam Law 996.

[83] Criminal Law Act 1977 s 2(2)(a), extended to civil partners: Civil Partnership Act 2004 Sch 27 para 56. Either may be convicted of inciting the other to commit a crime.

[84] *R v Chrastny* [1992] 1 All ER 189, CA.

[85] Theft Act 1968 s 30(1); Theft Act 1978 s 5(2). Either of them may also be guilty of the theft of property belonging to them both jointly.   [86] Theft Act 1968 s 30(4).

[87] For detailed rules governing the right to enter to live in the United Kingdom see M Phelan and J Gillespie *Immigration Law Handbook* (2013, 8th edn).

during the nineteenth century,[88] but a series of statutes passed since 1914 reflected the change in status of married women by reverting to the common law principles.[89] This meant that a woman who was not a citizen of the United Kingdom and Colonies did not become such a citizen by marrying a man who possessed citizenship; however, she was entitled to acquire it by registration.

The British Nationality Act 1981 removed this entitlement and placed both husbands and wives of citizens on the same footing. The Civil Partnership Act 2004 amended these provisions to cater for civil partners. Now, if a woman (or man), who is not a British citizen, marries or forms a civil partnership with a citizen and wishes to acquire citizenship herself, she must apply for naturalisation unless she qualifies to be registered as a citizen in her own right.[90] However the applicant need have been in the United Kingdom for only three years (and not five years as is usually the case).[91] She must be of good character, have sufficient knowledge of English, Welsh or Scots Gaelic, and sufficient knowledge about life in the United Kingdom,[92] and not be subject to any restriction under the immigration laws on the period for which she may remain here.[93]

(b) Living in the UK

Citizens of the European Economic Area (EEA)[94] may exercise the right to enter and remain in the United Kingdom for work or study purposes,[95] and their spouses (regardless of their nationality) may come with or join them.[96] But otherwise, under the Immigration Rules (HC 395), entry clearance or leave to remain in the United Kingdom for the purpose of marriage or civil partnership, or entry clearance or leave to remain having married abroad, will not be granted if either the applicant or the sponsor will be aged under 18 on the date of arrival in the United Kingdom or (as the case may be) on the date on which the leave to remain would be granted.[97] Formerly, the age limit was 16 but it was raised to deter early marriages as a means of gaining entry to the United Kingdom. In 2008, it was further raised to 21 ostensibly to deter forced marriages, but this was challenged in *R (Aguilar Quila); R (Bibi) v Secretary of State for the Home Department*.[98] The first respondent was a Chilean national who married his British wife when both were under the age of 21. He was refused entry into the UK and the couple moved to Dublin where the wife had obtained a place to study and where, as noted earlier, as an EEA citizen exercising treaty rights to live in an EU state, she had a right to live with her spouse. In the second

---

[88] Aliens Act 1844 s 16; Naturalisation Act 1870 s 10(1).

[89] Status of Aliens Act 1914 s 10; British Nationality and Status of Aliens Act 1918 s 2(5); British Nationality and Status of Aliens Act 1933 s 1(1); British Nationality Act 1948.

[90] The basic requirements are that the person is a British Dependent Territories or Overseas citizen, a British subject (but not citizen) or a British protected person under the Act; has lived here for five years and is not in breach of the immigration laws or subject to immigration restrictions under those laws: British Nationality Act 1981 s 4.

[91] The Borders, Citizenship and Immigration Act 2009 s 40 prospectively amends these provisions to cater for those in a 'relevant family association' rather than spouses and civil partners.

[92] A spouse was not formerly required to have knowledge of the language. This extension and the provision regarding knowledge of life in the United Kingdom were added by the Nationality, Immigration and Asylum Act 2002 s 1.

[93] British Nationality Act 1981 s 6(2) and Sch 1 paras 3 and 4. The applicant must not have been in breach of the immigration laws at any time during the three years.

[94] The EEA includes the member states of the European Union and Iceland, Liechtenstein and Norway; Switzerland is not a member but has a separate agreement which gives the same rights.

[95] A person who is financially self-sufficient also has the right of free movement.

[96] EU, Free Movement of Persons Directive 2004/38 EC; Immigration (European Economic Area) Regulations 2006 (SI 2006/1003).   [97] HC 395 para 277.   [98] [2011] UKSC 45 [2012] 1 AC 621.

case, the spouses were again both under 21 and had an arranged marriage in Pakistan. The second respondent was a Pakistani citizen, her husband British. She was denied entry clearance to join him in the UK. The Supreme Court held that, in the absence of the immigration dimension, there could be no doubt that forcing a married couple either to live separately for some years or suspend their plans to live in one place and go to live where neither wished to live would be a colossal interference with their right to respect for family life. The burden was on the Secretary of State to establish that the interference was justified, but she had failed to demonstrate that when she introduced the higher age limit she had robust evidence of any substantial deterrent effect of the rule change upon forced marriages. By contrast, it was clear that the operation of the rule would interfere with many more entirely voluntary marriages than it would prevent, deter or delay forced marriages. The Court accordingly found that the rule was a disproportionate and unjustified interference with the couples' Art 8 rights and the Government reverted to the age of 18 as the minimum.

Because problems were apparently being caused by men entering the country with two or more wives, a woman, W, will not be given permission to enter or stay here as the wife of a man, H, if (a) her marriage is de facto polygamous (even though the husband had no other wife when she married him) and (b) another wife of H has been in the United Kingdom since her marriage or has been granted entry clearance to enter this country as H's wife, unless W has been lawfully in this country otherwise than as a visitor at a time when there was no such wife satisfying condition (b).[99]

If a person of either sex is present and settled[100] in the United Kingdom or is admitted for settlement, his or her spouse[101] will be granted entry clearance provided that they show that their marriage or civil partnership is genuine, ie that the parties have met and intend to live together permanently as spouses or civil partners. They must also demonstrate that they can maintain and accommodate themselves and any dependants without recourse to public funds.[102] Before 1997, there was an additional requirement to show that the 'primary purpose' of the marriage was *not* to obtain entry into the United Kingdom. The restriction was imposed because of the belief that in the past some men (particularly from the Indian subcontinent) were obtaining entry into this country by contracting arranged marriages, sometimes by proxy, to women (or possibly young girls) whom they had never met.[103] The rule was abolished because, in the words of the Home Secretary, it was 'arbitrary, unfair and ineffective and has penalised genuine marriages, divided families and unnecessarily increased the administrative burden on the immigration system'.[104] He could also have added that the rule was racially discriminatory and placed the applicants in the frequently hopeless position of having to prove a negative.

---

[99] HC 395 paras 278–280.

[100] If he is here lawfully, is ordinarily resident here and is free from any restriction on the period for which he may remain: HC 395 para 5.   [101] The same requirements apply to fiancé(e)s: HC 395 para 290.

[102] HC 395 para 281 as amended.

[103] For the problem of sham marriages, see Ch 2, 'Sham marriages', p 81 and *Bhaiji v Chauhan, Queen's Proctor Intervening (Divorce: Marriages Used for Immigration Purposes)* [2003] 2 FLR 485. In *R (Kimani) v Lambeth London Borough Council* [2003] EWCA Civ 1150 [2004] 1 WLR 272 the appellant, a Kenyan national, married an Irish citizen and sought entry to the UK as a spouse of a EEA national (see later). The Secretary of State considered the marriage one of convenience and she appealed. Meanwhile, the local authority declined to support her on the basis that she was the spouse and thus dependant of an EEA national of a state other than the UK. Her argument that, for this purpose, 'spouse' should mean someone not in a marriage of convenience was, perhaps unsurprisingly, rejected.

[104] HC, Hansard Written Answers, 5 June 1997 col 219. The rule was abolished with effect from that date in respect of both pending and future applications.

(c) Deportation

Where a person who is not a British citizen is liable to deportation (eg because he has overstayed the limit on his permission to remain in the country, or has been convicted of a criminal offence and the court has recommended his deportation), he or she may claim that removing them would breach their Art 8 right to respect for family life. In *Boultif v Switzerland*[105] the European Court of Human Rights held that the following factors would be relevant to the decision:

> [in the case of someone who has been convicted of an offence] the nature and seriousness of the offence; the length of the applicant's stay in the country from which he is going to be expelled; the time elapsed since the offence was committed as well as the applicant's conduct in that period; the nationalities of the various persons concerned; the applicant's family situation, such as the length of the marriage; and other factors expressing the effectiveness of a couple's family life; whether the spouse knew about the offence at the time when he or she entered into a family relationship; and whether there are children in the marriage, and if so, their age. Not least, the Court will also consider the seriousness of the difficulties which the spouse is likely to encounter in the country of origin, though the mere fact that a person might face certain difficulties in accompanying her or his spouse cannot in itself exclude an expulsion.

Deportation may be ordered against the spouse or civil partner of a deportee where he or she has no right of abode. The Home Secretary will not normally order the deportation of a spouse who has qualified for settlement in his or her own right or who has been living apart from the other spouse.[106]

C. PROPERTY CONSEQUENCES OF MARRIAGE AND CIVIL PARTNERSHIP

1. HISTORICAL INTRODUCTION

Reflecting the previous pre-eminent importance that society attached to marriage, the law of 'family' property was, until the 1970s and 1980s, virtually exclusively concerned with the effects of marriage. In this regard, however, the development of the law clearly reflects the development of the status of the wife from being a subservient member of the family to becoming its co-equal head. We consider here the implications of marriage on general property law, and focus on the particular issues regarding the ownership and occupation of the family home in Chapter 5, We begin our discussion with a brief historical résumé of the effects of marriage upon rights in property.

(a) Common law

Interests in land

At common law[107] the husband gained control over all freehold lands which his wife held at the time of marriage or which she subsequently acquired during marriage. The wife

---

[105] [2001] 2 FLR 1228 at para 48.

[106] Immigration Act 1971 s 5, as amended and HC 395 para 365. A deported spouse may seek re-admission if the marriage comes to an end: para 389.

[107] For further details and authorities, reference must be made to the editions of standard works on real and personal property and equity published during the nineteenth and early twentieth centuries. The classic

had no power to dispose of her real property during marriage, although the spouses could dispose of the whole estate together. The wife's leasehold property belonged absolutely to her husband. If the husband died before the wife, she immediately resumed the right to all her freeholds; if she predeceased him, her estates of inheritance descended to her heir, subject to the husband's right, as 'tenant by the courtesy of England', to an estate for his life in all her freeholds in possession.

During the marriage the wife took no interest in her husband's real property but, if she survived him, she became entitled by virtue of her 'dower' to an estate for life in a third of all her husband's freeholds of which he had been seized in possession at any time during marriage, provided that she could have borne a child capable of inheriting (ie such a child would have been a valid heir), whether such a child was ever born or not.

If land were granted to a husband and wife together, they were said to take *by entireties* and received an interest which could not be turned into a tenancy in common by severance. Hence, unless they disposed of the estate during marriage, the survivor was bound to take the whole. If land were granted to a husband, his wife and a third person, then by virtue of the doctrine of unity, the spouses were regarded as one person and consequently they were entitled to only one-half of the rent and profits and the third person was entitled to the other half.

Interests in personal property

All personalty in possession belonging to the wife at the time of the marriage, or acquired by her during the marriage, vested absolutely in the husband, who therefore had the power to dispose of them *inter vivos* or by will. Even if he died intestate during the wife's life, they did not revert to her. The only exception to this rule applied to those articles of apparel and personal ornament (known as the wife's *paraphernalia*) which were suitable to her rank and degree. Whilst the husband could dispose of these during his lifetime, he could not deprive her of them by bequest, and on his death they became her property and did not form a part of his estate.[108]

(b) Equity

The wife's separate estate

The most important contribution of equity to the law relating to a married woman's property was the development of the concept of the separate estate. By the end of the sixteenth century[109] it was established that if property (both realty and personalty) was conveyed to trustees *to the separate use* of a married woman, she retained in equity the same right of holding and disposing of it as if she were a feme sole, in other words, an unmarried woman. She could therefore dispose of it *inter vivos* or by will and, like any other beneficiary of full age who was absolutely entitled, she could call upon her trustees to convey the legal estate. Moreover, even if property were conveyed, devised or bequeathed to a married woman to her separate use with the legal estate vested in the husband, he was deemed in equity to hold it on trust for her and he acquired no greater interest in it than he would have done if it had been conveyed to trustees on similar terms.

---

exposition of the common law position is to be found in Blackstone's *Commentaries* (1753), vol ii. See also A V Dicey *Law and Public Opinion* (1914, 2nd edn) pp 371–95.

[108] Unless the husband's estate was insolvent, in which case his creditors could take the wife's paraphernalia in satisfaction but not her necessary clothing.

[109] See W Holdsworth *History of English Law* (1945) vol v pp 310–15.

The restraint upon anticipation

Whilst the separate estate in equity did much to mitigate the harshness of the common law rule, there remained one situation which it did not meet. There was nothing to prevent a married woman from assigning her beneficial interest to her husband, thereby vesting in him the interest which the separate use had sought to keep out of his hands. To circumvent this, equity developed about 1800 the concept known as the restraint upon anticipation.[110] This prevented the wife from anticipating and dealing with any income until it actually fell due and was designed to protect not only the wife but also the members of her family who would be entitled to the property on her death. Whilst it effectively kept the property out of the hands of her husband and his creditors, it had one obvious drawback in that even where it was in the wife's interest to deal with property subject to a restraint, nothing short of a private Act of Parliament could remove it.

(c) Statutory reform

By the middle of the nineteenth century it was clear that the old rules would have to be reformed.[111] More middle-class women were earning incomes of their own, and there were a number of scandalous cases of husbands impounding their wives' earnings for the benefit of their own creditors, or even mistresses. No relief could be obtained by the woman whose husband deserted her and took all her property with him. The separate use and restraint upon anticipation were clumsy devices which in practice only affected the property of the daughters of the rich, who would have carefully drawn marriage settlements and would be the beneficiaries under complicated wills. Agitation for reform eventually produced a series of Acts of ever wider scope.

Married Women's Property Acts

The most important of these was the Married Women's Property Act 1882.[112] It provided that any woman marrying after 1882 should be entitled to retain all property owned by her at the time of the marriage as her separate property and that, whenever she was married, any property acquired by a married woman after 1882 should be held by her in the same way.[113] Section 1(1) stated:

> A married woman shall . . . be capable of acquiring, holding and disposing, by will or otherwise, of any real or personal property as her separate property, in the same manner as if she were a feme sole, without the intervention of any trustee.

The sweeping nature of these changes should be appreciated. It became impossible for a married man to acquire any further interest in his wife's property by operation of law. No further tenancies by entireties could be created. But more fundamentally, whilst the statute adopted the *equitable* concept of separate property, it went further by vesting in the wife the *legal* interest in her property. Indeed, subject to the restraint on anticipation, which was left unaffected, a married woman's capacity to hold and dispose of property was very nearly the same as that of an unmarried woman.

---

[110] See WG Hart 'The Origin of the Restraint upon Anticipation' (1924) 40 LQR 221.

[111] See D Stetson *A Woman's Issue: the politics of family law reform in England* (1982) and M Shanley *Feminism, Marriage and the Law in Victorian England* (1989).

[112] In fact many of the 1882 Act's wider provisions had been anticipated in an earlier Bill which, in its cut-down form, became the Married Women's Property Act 1870, which was repealed by the 1882 Act.

[113] Sections 2 and 5.

The 1925 property legislation changed the rules of succession on intestacy;[114] in particular dower was abolished. Any remaining tenancies by entireties were abolished, and a grant to a husband, his wife and a third person will now give each of them a third interest in the property.[115]

By 1935 to speak of 'separate property' was becoming something of an anomaly. The Law Reform (Married Women and Tortfeasors) Act 1935 therefore abolished the concept of the separate estate and gave to the wife the same rights and powers as were already possessed by other adults of full capacity. However, it did not affect the validity of any restraints already imposed. The Married Women (Restraint upon Anticipation) Act 1949 finally removed all restraints whenever imposed, and thus rendered the property to which they were attached freely alienable.

By extending the equitable principle of the separate estate, the Married Women's Property Acts replaced the total incapacity of a married woman to hold property at common law with a rigid doctrine of separate property. In Dicey's words,[116] 'the rules of equity, framed for the daughters of the rich, have at last been extended to the daughters of the poor'. But, as Kahn-Freund pointed out,[117] the effects of the Acts were much wider than this. Spouses' property may be broadly divided into that intended for common use and consumption in the matrimonial home and that intended for personal use and enjoyment. The latter may be in the form of savings or investments or derived from the interest on these, and it is obvious that, whilst in a poor family almost the whole of the property will fall into the first category, the richer the spouses the greater the fraction of their property which will fall into the second. Before 1883 the matrimonial home and its contents would almost invariably be vested in the husband to the exclusion of the wife, and the latter's separate property did little more than protect her investments. But, impelled by a movement which was ultimately to secure the almost complete legal equality of the sexes, Parliament extended the doctrine of separation to property forming the matrimonial home as well—a situation which the equitable concept was never intended to cover and with which it was ill adapted to deal.

This was inevitably bound to produce difficulties. During the Second World War many married women were wage earners as well, and what before then had been something of an exception had now become the usual situation in most families. To apply the strict doctrine of separate property to matrimonial assets in such circumstances was manifestly absurd. As a result, judges sought to adapt the principle by regarding both spouses as having an interest in the matrimonial home in many cases, even though the legal estate was vested solely in the husband.[118]

Impact of divorce reform in 1969 and 1970

Although property ownership can be in issue while the spouses are living together, in practice most problems arise following marital breakdown. Until the reforms governing divorce which came into operation in 1971,[119] spouses, like anyone else, had to resolve their disputes under the strict law, and for the most part they would do so by applying under s 17 of the Married Women's Property Act 1882.[120] In the early 1970s, however,

---

[114] See Ch 25, Intestate succession, pp 967ff.

[115] Law of Property Act 1925 s 37. After 1882 the spouses could sever their half-share because *between themselves* they took as ordinary joint tenants.

[116] AV Dicey *Law and Public Opinion* (1914, 2nd edn) p 395.

[117] In W Friedmann (ed) *Matrimonial Property Law* (1955) pp 267 *et seq*. See also his article, 'Recent Legislation on Matrimonial Property' (1970) 33 MLR 601.

[118] See Ch 5, The background to the current law, p 123.   [119] See Chapters 22, 23.

[120] Discussed later at Proceedings under s 17 of the Married Women's Property Act 1882, p 117.

this picture changed dramatically, for the court was given wide powers for the transfer and settlement of property on divorce, nullity and judicial separation.[121] In *Williams v Williams*[122] the Court of Appeal made it clear that whenever possible spouses should rely on these wide powers to adjust property rights. Consequently, the need to make an enquiry into the precise interest that each spouse has in the matrimonial home or other assets was largely removed. However, as we discuss in Chapter 23, whether and how far holding title to property, particularly that brought into the marriage or acquired by gift, inheritance, or one's sole efforts, should affect how that property is allocated on divorce, have become major issues. In the 1880s, it was seen as a major feminist triumph not to introduce any concept of a special 'matrimonial regime' governing the holding of marital property, as is common in civil law systems.[123] But it could now be argued that this did wives no favours by failing to protect those who did not have any separate property of their own anyway, for it meant that they could make no claim to a share of what was held by their husbands. And it continues to disadvantage spouses with inferior earning capacity and thus less ability to acquire such property for themselves.[124]

2. THE MODERN LAW

Regardless of the operation of the divorce jurisdiction, strict property rights are still of the greatest importance on the death or insolvency of one spouse, because they alone will have to be applied to resolve any dispute between the other spouse and the personal representatives or creditors. Furthermore, a spouse may not wish to take matrimonial proceedings, or may not be able to apply for a property adjustment order because she (or he) has remarried or formed a civil partnership.

(a) Property acquired by the spouses or civil partners

Couples, both married and unmarried, have a variety of arrangements regarding how they hold and use property and there is no particular 'norm' applying to spousal as distinct from cohabiting couples. Some make use of joint accounts and pool everything. Others may keep all property and money strictly separate and divide bills either in half or in proportion to their incomes. Yet others may hold some assets jointly and keep others separate.[125] Clearly, this can present considerable evidential difficulties if the parties subsequently dispute who owns what and the law may have to apply a variety of rules and presumptions to determine the answer.

Property owned on entering the relationship

Presumptively, marriage, civil partnership or engagement will not affect the ownership of property vested in either of the couple at the time. This will also be true of property which is used by them jointly in the family home (for example, furniture), in the absence of an express gift of a joint interest in law or in equity.

---

[121] Under what was originally s 4 of the Matrimonial Proceedings and Property Act 1970 and later re-enacted as s 24 of the Matrimonial Causes Act 1973.   [122] [1976] Ch 278, CA.

[123] See E Cooke, A Barlow and T Callus *Community of Property: A regime for England and Wales?* (2006); K Boele-Woelki et al *Principles of European Family Law Regarding Property Relations Between Spouses* (2013) ch 3 section B.

[124] C Smart *The Ties that Bind: Law, marriage and the reproduction of patriarchy* (1984).

[125] C Vogler 'Managing Money in Intimate Relationships: similarities and differences between cohabiting and married couples' in J Miles and R Probert (eds) *Sharing Lives, Dividing Assets: An Inter-disciplinary study* (2009). A Barlow et al, 'Cohabiting relationships, money and property: the legal backdrop' (2008) 37(2) *Journal of Socio-economics* 502.

Gifts between engaged couples and couples intending to become civil partners

At common law a gift made by one party to an engagement to the other in contemplation of marriage could not be recovered by the donor if he was in breach of contract. This meant, for example, that if the man broke off the engagement without legal justification, he could not recover the engagement ring, but he could do so if the woman was in breach of contract.[126]

In conformity with the principle[127] that the parties' rights with respect to property should not depend upon their responsibility for the termination of the agreement, s 3(1) of the Law Reform (Miscellaneous Provisions) Act 1970 provides:

> A party to an agreement to marry who makes a gift of property to the other party on the condition (express or implied) that it shall be returned if the agreement is terminated shall not be prevented from recovering the property by reason only of his having terminated the agreement.[128]

Whether a particular gift was made subject to an implied condition that it should be returned if the marriage did not take place must necessarily be a question of fact to be decided in each case. Normally, birthday and Christmas presents will vest in the donee absolutely, whilst property intended to become a part of the family home (for example, furniture) will be conditional. It is suggested that the general test to be applied should be: was the gift made to the donee as an individual or solely as the donor's future spouse (or civil partner)? If it is in the latter class, it will be regarded as conditional, whereas if it is in the former, it will be regarded as absolute and recoverable only in the same circumstances as any other gift—for example, on the ground that it was induced by fraud or undue influence.

The engagement ring is specifically dealt with by the 1970 Act.[129] The gift is presumed to be absolute, but this presumption may be rebutted by proving that the ring was given on the condition (express or implied) that it should be returned if the marriage did not take place for any reason.[130] One would have thought that by current social convention an engagement ring was still regarded as a pledge and that the presumption ought to have been the other way. As it is, the ring is likely to be recoverable only in the most exceptional circumstances, for example if it can be shown that it was an heirloom in the man's family.

If a gift in contemplation of marriage is made to one or both of the engaged couple by a third person (as in the case of wedding presents), it is, in the absence of any contrary intention, conditional upon the celebration of the marriage and must therefore be returned if the marriage does not take place for any reason at all. A contrary intention will clearly be shown if the gift is for immediate use before the marriage.[131]

---

[126] *Cohen v Sellar* [1926] 1 KB 536; *Jacobs v Davis* [1917] 2 KB 532. There is no direct authority for the position if the agreement was terminated otherwise than by breach, eg by agreement or death. It was generally assumed that the donor (or his personal representatives) could recover conditional gifts: see *Cohen v Sellar*.

[127] See Ch 2, Agreements to marry or form a civil partnership, p 39.

[128] The equivalent provisions for those agreeing to form a civil partnership may be found in s 73(3) and 74(5) of the Civil Partnership Act 2004.

[129] There is no equivalent provision for those agreeing to enter into a civil partnership, presumably because a tradition of giving a ring on such an occasion has not yet been established.

[130] Law Reform (Miscellaneous Provisions) Act 1970 s 3(2). For an illustration of the evidential difficulties in establishing such a condition, see *Cox v Jones* [2004] EWHC 1486 (Ch) [2004] 2 FLR 1010.

[131] See *Jeffreys v Luck* (1922) 153 LT Jo 139. One would expect the same principle to apply to civil partnerships.

Income and investments

The income of either spouse, whether from earnings or from investments, will prima facie remain his or her own property.[132] But where the couple pool their incomes and place them into a common fund, it seems that they both acquire a joint interest in the whole fund. Further, it seems clear that the principle of a joint interest in a common fund rests not upon the relationship between the contributors, but upon the purpose for which the fund was founded and the use to which it is put.[133]

In *Jones v Maynard*[134] the husband, who was about to go abroad with the RAF, authorised his wife to draw on his bank account, which was thereafter treated as a joint account. Into this account were paid dividends on both the husband's and the wife's investments, the husband's pay and allowances, and rent from the matrimonial home which was their joint property and which had been let during the Second World War. The husband's contributions were greater than the wife's; the spouses had never agreed on what their rights in this fund were to be, but they regarded it as their joint savings to be invested from time to time. The husband withdrew money on a number of occasions and invested it in his own name, and finally, after the spouses had separated, he closed the account altogether. The marriage was later dissolved and the wife sued her former husband for a half share in the account as it stood on the day it was closed and in the investments which he had previously purchased out of it. Vaisey J held that the claim must succeed. He said:[135]

> In my judgment, when there is a joint account between husband and wife, a common pool into which they put all their resources, it is not consistent with that conception that the account should thereafter . . . be picked apart, and divided up proportionately to the respective contributions of husband and wife, the husband being credited with the whole of his earnings and the wife with the whole of her dividends . . . In my view a husband's earnings or salary, when the spouses have a common purse and pool their resources, are earnings made on behalf of both; and the idea that years afterwards the contents of the pool can be dissected by taking an elaborate account as to how much was paid in by the husband or the wife is quite inconsistent with the original fundamental idea of a joint purse or common pool.
>
> In my view the money which goes into the pool becomes joint property. The husband, if he wants a suit of clothes, draws a cheque to pay for it. The wife, if she wants any housekeeping money, draws a cheque, and there is no disagreement about it.

What, then, constitutes a 'common purse'? It would seem on principle to be essential that there must be a fund intended for the use of both partners from which either may withdraw money, and this will normally take the form of a joint bank account. Where they both contribute to this fund, as in *Jones v Maynard*, this intention will be imputed to the parties in the absence of any other agreement; where, however, the fund is derived from the income of one partner alone, it is a question of fact whether this is to remain his or her exclusive property, or whether there is an intention to establish a common fund.

In this instance, as between spouses and, possibly, engaged couples,[136] the equitable doctrine of the 'presumption of advancement' could at one time have come into play. This

---

[132] See *Dixon v Dixon* (1878) 9 Ch D 587 (stock settled to the wife's separate use); *Barrack v M'Culloch* (1856) 3 K & J 110 (rents from houses settled to the wife's separate use); *Heseltine v Heseltine* [1971] 1 All ER 952 (income from wife's investments).   [133] *Paul v Constance* [1977] 1 All ER 195, CA.

[134] [1951] Ch 572.   [135] At 575.

[136] The presumption also extended to a transfer from father (query mother?) to child: *Dyer v Dyer* [1775–1802] All ER Rep 205. It appears to have been assumed applicable to mothers (though not on the facts in the particular case) in *Laskar v Laskar* [2008] EWCA Civ 347 [2008] 2 FLR 589 at [20].

held that a transfer of property from husband to wife was prima facie to be regarded as an outright gift rather than, as would otherwise be presumed the case, giving rise to a resulting trust under which the recipient holds the property on trust for the transferor. The reason for the presumption was the recognition that wives were financially dependent upon their husbands, who had a duty to maintain them. The presumption of advancement between husband and wife has been prospectively abolished, as incompatible with the equal position of the spouses[137] and there is no modern authority which has applied it.[138]

If either partner withdraws money from the common purse, property bought with it prima facie belongs solely to that person if it is for his or her personal use (for example, clothes), but to both jointly if it is for their joint use (for example, a car). Investments purchased by means of the common purse will similarly belong to the purchaser unless it is clear that they are intended to represent the original fund. In *Re Bishop*[139] large sums had been withdrawn by both spouses to purchase investments in their separate names. In many cases blocks of shares were bought and half put in one name and half in the other; other money was spent in taking up shares offered to the husband by virtue of rights which he possessed as an existing shareholder in the companies concerned. In these circumstances Stamp J held that the presumption could not be rebutted, so that the spouse in whose name the shares had been purchased was entitled to the whole beneficial interest in them. He distinguished *Jones v Maynard*, where Vaisey J held that the husband was to be regarded as trustee for them both of investments which he had purchased; for in that case the spouses had agreed that when there had been a sufficient accumulation the money should be invested and that that was to be their savings.

Like any other joint interest the balance of the fund will accrue to the survivor on the death of either partner, as it did in *Re Bishop*.

Allowances for housekeeping and maintenance

Originally the same principles were applied to the question of ownership of a housekeeping allowance as to income and investments. Hence, it was held that if a husband supplied his wife with a housekeeping allowance out of his own income, any balance and any property bought with the allowance prima facie remained his property.[140] This could work an injustice, for it took no account of the fact that any savings from the housekeeping money were as much due to the wife's skill and economy as to her husband's earning capacity.[141] It was to remedy this that the Married Women's Property Act 1964,[142] was passed. Section 1 provides:

> If any question arises as to the right of a husband or wife to money derived from any allowance made by either of them for the expenses of the matrimonial home or for similar purposes, or to any property acquired out of such money, the money or property shall, in the absence of any agreement between them to the contrary, be treated as belonging to them in equal shares.

---

[137] Equality Act 2010 s 199. For a critique of the view that the presumption is based on the duty to maintain, and of the rationale for and drafting of s 199, see J Glister 'Section 199 of the Equality Act 2010: How Not to Abolish the Presumption of Advancement' (2010) 73(5) MLR 785.

[138] See comment by Nourse LJ in *McGrath v Wallis* [1995] 2 FLR 114 at 115.   [139] [1965] Ch 450.

[140] *Blackwell v Blackwell* [1943] 2 All ER 579, CA; *Hoddinott v Hoddinott* [1949] 2 KB 406, CA, in which the husband was held entitled to winnings from the football pools, the stake for which had been paid by the wife out of the housekeeping allowance.

[141] See the judgments of Denning LJ in *Hoddinott v Hoddinott* at 416, and *Rimmer v Rimmer* [1953] 1 QB 63, CA at 74.

[142] Prospectively to be called the Matrimonial Property Act by virtue of the Equality Act 2010 s 200(2).

As originally drafted, the Act applied only if the allowance was provided *by the husband* and so did not apply to the case where the wife goes out to work to support a husband who does the housekeeping. It is prospectively amended by the Equality Act 2010 to ensure that either spouse may provide the money, and an equivalent provision was inserted into the Civil Partnership Act 2004.[143]

So far as the application of the 1964 Act is concerned, it is not clear what the phrase 'expenses of the matrimonial home or similar purposes' covers. If, for example, a husband gives his wife money to pay off instalments of the mortgage on the matrimonial home, she may well be regarded as no more than his agent and thus acquire no interest in the house; but if he gives her a housekeeping allowance out of which it is intended that she should pay the instalments, it has been suggested that the effect of the section is to give her a half share in the fraction represented by each payment.[144]

The rule applies not only to the money but also to any property bought with it. Hence, if the wife were to buy furniture with the housekeeping savings, it would presumptively belong to her and her husband equally. This can be rebutted by proof of an agreement between the spouses. Presumably, such agreements may be express or implied. It would be absurd, for example, where the wife uses part of the allowance to buy clothes for herself, that a half share of them should belong to the husband.

The Act has a further weakness. The money or property is to be treated as belonging to the spouses in equal shares. Consequently, on the death of one, the whole beneficial interest will *not* automatically pass to the survivor (as it does in the case of the 'common purse'),[145] but half will go to the personal representatives of the other. It is highly doubtful whether this is what the spouses will want or expect.[146] Neither this rule nor its consequences will be known to the vast majority of spouses and it is not inconceivable that a half-share of furniture will inadvertently pass under a residuary bequest.

Given these difficulties, it is hardly surprising that little use seems to have been made of the Act. Notwithstanding the legislative change to render it gender-neutral, the very concept of a 'housekeeping allowance' appears outmoded. The Law Commission[147] long ago recommended repeal of the Act and that instead there should be a statutory presumption that property bought for the joint use or benefit of spouses should belong to them jointly.

Personal property

Any property purchased by one spouse with his or her own money will presumptively belong exclusively to the purchaser. Property bought out of money coming from the 'common purse' will also presumptively belong to the purchaser if it is for his or her own use.[148] But this presumption is obviously rebuttable. Thus, property bought by one partner as a gift for the other will become the donee's. Hence, if a man buys clothes for his partner or gives her money to buy them for herself, they become her property,[149] and

---

[143] Equality Act 2010 ss 200, 201 (inserting s 70A into the 2004 Act).

[144] See the conflicting views in *Tymoszczuk v Tymoszczuk* (1964) 108 Sol Jo 676, and *Re Johns' Assignment Trusts* [1970] 2 All ER 210n at 213.

[145] See earlier, Income and investments, p 110.

[146] In their desire to remedy the injustice caused by earlier cases where the marriage had broken down, the promoters of the Bill apparently overlooked the obvious fact that most marriages survive and that, whilst a joint interest can always be severed by the unilateral act of one party, it requires the conscious act of both to turn a tenancy in common into a joint tenancy.

[147] Law Com No 175 *Matrimonial Property* (1985).

[148] See earlier, Income and investments, p 110.

[149] *Masson, Templier & Co v De Fries* [1909] 2 KB 831, CA. Contrast *Rondeau, Le Grand & Co v Marks* [1918] 1 KB 75, CA, where it had been agreed that they should remain the husband's property.

the same rule will prima facie apply in any other case where goods are bought for the other's personal use.[150] Property bought by one party but intended for both to enjoy may be subject to an express trust. For example, in *Rowe v Prance*[151] a man bought a boat from the proceeds of sale of his former matrimonial home, telling his mistress that they would live together on it and sail round the world. She accordingly gave up her rented house and put her furniture in storage. The man told her that the title to the boat was in his name because only he had an Ocean Master's certificate, but that the boat was 'ours'. When the relationship ended, it was held that an express trust existed, under which the couple held equal shares.[152]

Difficulties can arise if one partner's money is used to buy property which is conveyed into the other's name or into joint names or, alternatively, if both partners' money is used to buy property which is conveyed into the name of only one of them. At one time, the presumption of advancement could have been used to resolve the question as between husband and wife, although it could come into conflict with the presumption of resulting trust,[153] but as we have seen, the presumption of advancement is to be abolished and is not, in any case, relied upon in the modern law, so the position is the same regardless of the couple's marital status. We will see in Chapter 5 that the *constructive* trust is generally relied on in relation to establishing interests in the family *home*. However, a resulting trust may be used in the absence of any contrary evidence[154] in the case of personal property. In *The 'Up Yaws'*[155] for example, a cohabiting couple bought first a home, held in the woman's sole name, then a boat, in the man's sole name, with money raised from the man's father, and mortgages paid by the woman. They then bought a more expensive boat for which the woman took out another mortgage. When their relationship ended she claimed an interest in the second boat. It was held that they had never discussed whether or how to share the beneficial interest in the boat and there was no evidence to rebut the presumption of resulting trust based on her contribution through the mortgage, and she was awarded a 55% share.

Gifts from third parties

Whether a gift made by third parties belongs to one partner alone or to both of them is a question of the donor's intention. In the case of wedding presents it has been held that it is reasonable to assume in the absence of any evidence to the contrary that the husband's friends and relations intended to make the gift to him and the wife's to her,[156] but one might regard this approach as outmoded and consider that today it would be more

---

[150] *Re Whittaker* (1882) 21 Ch D 657 (piano). But cf *Windeler v Whitehall* [1990] 2 FLR 505 at 517 (dressing table bought for unmarried cohabitant remained purchaser's property).   [151] [1999] 2 FLR 787.

[152] Note that no writing was required, nor was it necessary to establish an implied, resulting or constructive trust, because the boat constituted personal, not real, property. For the position regarding land, see Ch 5, The primary importance of the documents of title, pp 125ff.

[153] See *Mercier v Mercier* [1903] 2 Ch 98, CA (presumption of resulting trust for wife); *Silver v Silver* [1958] 1 All ER 523, CA (presumption of advancement).

[154] The husband may not rebut the presumption by adducing evidence of his own fraudulent or unlawful intention: *Re Emery's Investments' Trusts* [1959] Ch 410 (evasion of tax in the USA); *Tinker v Tinker* [1970] P 136, CA (defrauding creditors). Where the transferor is not obliged to rely on the illegality in order to establish his interest, the claim can succeed: see *Tribe v Tribe* [1995] 2 FLR 966, CA (father and son).

[155] [2007] EWHC 210 (Admlty) [2007] 2 FLR 444.

[156] *Samson v Samson* [1960] 1 All ER 653, CA. Spouses' subsequent conduct may turn a gift to one of them into joint property: *Samson v Samson*. Presumably, a similar approach is applicable to engagement presents, assuming that they are intended as an unconditional gift (ie they are not returnable if the marriage does not take place).

reasonable to assume that a gift, at least where use of the item will be joint, should be regarded as made to both spouses or civil partners.[157]

(b) Transactions between spouses

Undue influence

With the exceptions about to be discussed in the case of chattels, gifts between spouses are subject to the general law. Indeed, it should be noted that the relationship of marriage does not of itself give rise to a presumption that either has exercised undue influence over the other.[158] Undue influence may be described as occurring:

> whenever the consent thus procured ought not fairly to be treated as the expression of a person's free will . . . Equity identified broadly two forms of unacceptable conduct. The first comprises overt acts of improper pressure or coercion such as unlawful threats . . . The second form arises out of a relationship between two persons where one has acquired over another a measure of influence, or ascendancy, of which the ascendant person then takes unfair advantage.[159]

Whilst the relationship between spouses,[160] fiancés,[161] or cohabitants or same sex partners,[162] *can* be regarded as giving rise to circumstances in which undue influence may occur, this must be established on the individual facts. For example, in *Wallbank v Price*[163] after they separated, a wife had signed a document at her husband's dictation, transferring her share in the matrimonial home to her daughters upon its eventual disposal. She claimed that she had done so either through fear or undue influence, but the court did not find evidence either of coercion or that the spouses' relationship had been one of dominance and subordination.[164] However, once the complainant brings forward evidence showing that he or she placed trust and confidence in the other party in relation to the management of his or her financial affairs, and that a transaction has taken place which is not readily explicable simply by virtue of the relationship of the parties,[165] the

---

[157] See *Midland Bank plc v Cooke* [1995] 4 All ER 562, CA (a cash wedding present provided by the groom's parents held to be intended to be a gift to both spouses equally) and *Kelner v Kelner* [1939] P 411, (£1,000 deposited by the wife's father at the time of the marriage in a joint bank account in both spouses' names ordered to be divided equally between them).

[158] *Howes v Bishop* [1909] 2 KB 390, CA; *Mackenzie v Royal Bank of Canada* [1934] AC 468, PC; *Bank of Credit and Commerce International SA v Aboody* [1990] 1 QB 923, CA; *Barclays Bank plc v O'Brien* [1994] 1 AC 180, HL. Contrast *Bank of Montreal v Stuart* [1911] AC 120, PC, where undue influence was in fact exercised.

[159] *Royal Bank of Scotland plc v Etridge (No 2)* [2001] UKHL 44 [2002] 2 AC 773 per Lord Nicholls of Birkenhead at [7]–[8]. See M Haley 'Royal Bank of Scotland plc v Etridge (No 2): The O'Brien defence—a compromise reworked?' [2002] CFLQ 93.

[160] *Barclays Bank plc v Rivett* [1999] 1 FLR 730, CA (wife exercising undue influence over husband).

[161] *Zamet v Hyman* [1961] 3 All ER 933, CA.

[162] *Barclays Bank plc v O'Brien* [1994] 1 AC 180 at 188E per Lord Browne-Wilkinson. The parties to an intimate sexual relationship need not live together: *Midland Bank plc v Massey* [1994] 2 FLR 342, CA. But for the view that undue influence is much less likely to arise in same sex relationships because of the absence of a gendered power dynamic, see R Auchmuty 'When Equality is not Equity: Homosexual Inclusion in Undue Influence Law' (2003) 11 Fem LS 163.   [163] [2007] EWHC 3001 (Ch) [2008] 2 FLR 501.

[164] To similar effect, see *Dailey v Dailey* [2003] UKPC 65 [2003] 3 FCR 369, PC—while husband had entrepreneurial instinct, he was an unlettered man and the wife handled the paperwork in their business. She did not establish that he had exercised undue influence over her when she transferred her interest in a jointly owned parcel of land to him. Cf *Simpson v Simpson* [1992] 1 FLR 601: husband suffering from fatal brain tumour held to be under wife's undue influence when he transferred the bulk of his estate to her.

[165] Explaining the meaning of the requirement to show that the transaction was 'manifestly disadvantageous', as stated by Lord Scarman in *National Westminster Bank plc v Morgan* [1985] AC 686, 703–7.

evidential burden will then shift to the other to produce evidence to counter the inference of undue influence which otherwise should be drawn.[166] In *Humphreys v Humphreys*[167] the defendant failed to discharge this evidential burden. The mother wished to exercise her right to buy the council house she had lived in for many years. She agreed with one of her sons that he would supply part of the purchase price by obtaining a mortgage and in return she would hold the whole of the beneficial interest on trust for him. Some years later, when she wished to sell the property, he placed a caution on the Land Registry title and refused to remove it. The court held that the agreement with the son was not readily explicable by the relationship between the parties and that on the evidence, the son had a dominant position over the mother. The presumption therefore arose and he could only have rebutted it if he had been able to show that she had received full and independent legal advice about the transaction, which she had not.

The possibility of undue influence having occurred is of particular importance in the context of disputes with third parties regarding the fate of the matrimonial home, and is discussed further in Chapter 5.[168]

Chattels

To perfect a gift of a chattel there must be an intention on the part of the donor to pass property to the donee and, in addition, either a deed executed by the former or a delivery of the chattel to the latter. Gifts by deed will be rare between couples in intimate relationships but, when they do occur, will usually present no difficulties since the intention can be inferred from the execution of the deed.[169] But a spouse[170] who alleges that the other has effected a gift by delivery has to surmount two obstacles. First, since spouses frequently use each other's property, an intention to make a gift cannot readily be inferred from permission to use the chattel in question, and consequently the burden of proof upon a spouse alleging a gift will probably be harder to discharge than for a stranger.[171] Secondly, it may be well-nigh impossible in many cases to prove delivery. Where the goods are intended for the exclusive use of the donee (for example, clothes or jewellery), delivery will normally take place at the time the gift is made by a physical handing over and taking; but if the goods in question have already been used by both partners in the family home and will continue to be used in this way (for example, articles of furniture), there is not likely to be any apparent change of possession. There may indeed be an effective symbolic delivery of one chattel as representing the whole, but partners are hardly likely to carry out such an artificial act, the significance of which will not occur to them.[172]

English courts have been slow to infer a delivery of a chattel from one spouse to the other,[173] doubtless because of the danger that they may fraudulently allege a prior gift of the

---

[166] *Royal Bank of Scotland plc v Etridge (No 2)* [2001] UKHL 44, [2002] 2 AC 773 per Lord Nicholls at [17]; Lord Hobhouse of Woodborough at [107], Lord Scott of Foscote at [161]. The 'presumption' 'has the same function in undue influence cases as *res ipsa loquitur* has in negligence cases. It recognises an evidential state of affairs in which the onus has shifted': per Lord Scott ibid.

[167] [2004] EWHC 2201 (Ch) [2005] 1 FCR 712.

[168] See Consent to transaction by spouse or partner, p 150.

[169] But for a dispute between former fiancés as to the true intention behind an apparent bill of sale transferring ownership of a car from one to the other, see *Cox v Jones* [2004] EWHC 1486 (Ch) [2004] 2 FLR 1010 (transfer found to be effective although no money changed hands).

[170] The law would be the same for a fiancé, civil partner or cohabitant.

[171] See *Bashall v Bashall* (1894) 11 TLR 152, CA.

[172] *Lock v Heath* (1892) 8 TLR 295 (husband held to have given all his furniture to wife by symbolic delivery of chair). For an effective constructive delivery by a father to his daughter, see *Kilpin v Ratley* [1892] 1 QB 582.

[173] Nor is there any reason to think that any different attitude would be taken in the case of alleged gifts between other partners.

husband's goods to the wife in order to keep them out of the hands of the former's creditors. A good example of this reluctance is *Re Cole*,[174] in which the husband completely furnished a new house before his wife set foot in it. When she arrived, he put his hands over her eyes, took her into the first room, uncovered her eyes and said, 'Look'. She then went into all the other rooms and handled various articles; at the end the husband said to her, 'It's all yours'. The furniture nevertheless remained insured in his name. He subsequently became bankrupt and the question arose whether the trustee or wife was entitled to the goods in question. It was held that the wife had failed to establish an effective delivery, and consequently the gift to her was never perfected. In the circumstances it would always seem wisest (however unrealistic) for a gift of goods used by both spouses to be made by means of a deed.

Voidable transactions

It is easy to see how transactions between partners might be used as a means of defrauding creditors. To a person who is on the verge of bankruptcy or who is about to engage in a hazardous business operation, there is a great temptation to settle the bulk of his property on trust for his partner and children and thus keep it out of the hands of his creditors and at the same time ensure that his family will be provided for. Parliament has sought to protect the creditors of the rogue who incidentally benefits his family, whilst not prejudicing the members of the family of a person who settles property in good faith and then runs into financial difficulties. If, for example, a husband, fearing insolvency, transfers property to his wife or children, his creditors or trustee in bankruptcy may seek to have the transfer set aside. This may be done under the Insolvency Act 1986 where the transaction was at an undervalue, either under s 423 if done with the intention of defeating the creditor,[175] or under s 339 where, regardless of intent, the debtor has been made bankrupt and the transaction was entered into during the previous five years. In that case, if the transaction was carried out more than two years before the bankruptcy, the bankrupt must have been insolvent or become insolvent because of it. There is a rebuttable presumption that this condition is satisfied if the transaction was entered into with 'an associate', including, among others, the bankrupt's spouse or former spouse, civil partner or former civil partner, reputed spouse, or relative.[176] The phrase 'reputed husband or wife' is unusual and may have been intended to refer to the old Scots law of presumption of marriage by cohabitation with habit and repute, but this form of marriage was abolished in 2006.[177]

The court may make such order as it thinks fit to restore the position to what it would have been had the transaction not been made; however, it cannot be recovered from a bona fide purchaser for value and without notice of the circumstances entitling the court to make an order.[178]

Money lent by one partner to the other

A loan by one partner to the other usually raises no presumption of a gift by way of advancement, so that the lender will be able to recover the sum lent in the absence of evidence that a gift was intended.[179]

---

[174] [1964] Ch 175, CA. Would the court have arrived at the same decision if, say, after the husband's death the question had arisen whether the goods belonged to the wife or to his personal representatives? See also *Bashall v Bashall; Valier v Wright & Bull Ltd* (1917) 33 TLR 366.

[175] Under Insolvency Act 1986 s 436, see e.g. *Agricultural Mortgage plc v Woodward* [1996] 1 FLR 226, CA (farm tenancy to wife by husband set aside when done in order to deprive the mortgagees of the land of the right to take vacant possession).   [176] Insolvency Act 1986 s 339, s 341(1)(a), (2) and s 435.

[177] Family Law (Scotland) Act 2006 s 3.   [178] Insolvency Act 1986 ss 425 (2)–(3) and 342(2), (4).

[179] *Hall v Hall* [1911] 1 Ch 487 (mortgage of the wife's property to secure a loan to the husband). Contrast *Paget v Paget* [1898] 1 Ch 470, CA, where the facts indicated that a gift was intended.

If the borrower becomes bankrupt, his or her spouse or civil partner is not entitled to any payment out of his estate until all other creditors have been paid in full.[180]

(c) Disputes between spouses

So long as spouses (or civil partners) are living amicably together, the questions of who owns what and what rights short of ownership one may have in the property of the other rarely have to be answered, but they become vital if the relationship breaks down. This adds considerably to the difficulty, for the parties rarely contemplate the collapse of the relationship when they acquire property, and their respective rights in it are never discussed, let alone defined. Hence the courts are faced with the problem of having to infer an intention which the partners never formulated at all.[181]

As regards property apart from land (which is discussed in Chapter 5), there are three different ways of solving disputes open to them. Either spouse or partner may protect his or her interests in property by suing the other in tort.[182] As we have seen, there are difficulties in establishing legally binding contractual ties between intimate partners, but actions on the contract may certainly be attempted. Either spouse may also seek an injunction to prevent the other from committing a continuing or threatened wrong against the claimant's property.[183]

Proceedings under s 17 of the Married Women's Property Act 1882

Section 17[184] provides that 'in any question between husband and wife as to the title to or possession of property' either of them may apply for an order to the High Court or a county court and the judge 'may make such order with respect to the property in dispute . . . as he thinks fit'.[185]

For some years there was considerable judicial controversy over the width of the powers which the wording of the section gave to the judges.[186] It was, however, finally settled by the House of Lords in *Pettitt v Pettitt*[187] that the court has no jurisdiction under this section to vary existing titles and no wider power to transfer or create interests in property than it would have in any other type of proceedings. At the most it has, in the words of Lord Diplock, 'a wide discretion as to the enforcement of the proprietary or possessory rights of one spouse in any property against the other'.[188] Furthermore, the fact that the marriage has broken down, the circumstances of the breakdown and the conduct of the parties cannot affect title in the absence of an agreement between the spouses, and are

---

[180] Insolvency Act 1986 s 329 as amended. This applies if the lender was the bankrupt's spouse or civil partner at the commencement of the bankruptcy, whether or not they were married or had formed a civil partnership when the loan was made.

[181] See *Re Rogers' Question* [1948] 1 All ER 328, CA; *Cobb v Cobb* [1955] 2 All ER 696 at 699, CA.

[182] See earlier, Torts, p 99. The court may stay the action if the questions in issue could be disposed of more conveniently by an application under s 17 of the Married Women's Property Act 1882: see next.

[183] This may be done by bringing an action in tort under the Law Reform (Husband and Wife) Act 1962, in proceedings under the Family Law Act 1996, or by way of financial relief in other matrimonial proceedings (such as freezing orders).

[184] Equivalent provision is made for civil partners by s 66 of the Civil Partnership Act 2004.

[185] Section 17 was extended to enable former spouses to make an application for a period of three years after a decree absolute of divorce or nullity by the Matrimonial Proceedings and Property Act 1970 s 39. If the property has been disposed of, the court may either order the defendant to pay to the applicant such sum of money as represents the latter's interest in the property or fund, or to make an order with respect to any other property which now represents the whole or part of the original: Matrimonial Causes (Property and Maintenance) Act 1958 s 7 and Civil Partnership Act 2004 s 67.

[186] See further Ch 5, The background to the current law, p 123.   [187] [1970] AC 777, HL.

[188] [1970] AC 777, HL at 820.

therefore all irrelevant to the outcome of proceedings brought under s 17.[189] But by using its powers to make different types of orders, the court may effectively control the way in which the property is used without departing from the principle that it cannot alter the title. Thus it may order a spouse to give up possession of a house, to deliver up chattels, to transfer shares and other choses in action, or to pay over a specific fund, and it may even forbid him or her to dispossess the other spouse or to deal with the property in any way inconsistent with the other's rights.[190] Similarly, the court may order the property to be sold and direct how the proceeds of sale are to be divided[191] or, if both spouses have an interest, it may order one of them to transfer his or her share to the other on the latter's paying the value of the property transferred.[192]

On the breakdown of a marriage or civil partnership, one of the spouses or partners will normally seek a divorce, annulment or separation and invoke the court's wider powers to make a property adjustment order under s 24 of the Matrimonial Causes Act 1973 or Sch 5 Part 2 to the Civil Partnership Act 2004. Consequently proceedings under s 17 are unlikely to be invoked unless the person seeking relief is unable or unwilling to take other proceedings, or has remarried or repartnered before applying for a property adjustment order.

Disputes between engaged couples

Property adjustment orders are not available to engaged couples.[193] However, s 2(1) of the Law Reform (Miscellaneous Provisions) Act 1970 provides that any rule of law relating to spouses' rights in relation to property in which either or both has or have a beneficial interest, shall apply in like manner to the former fiancés and they can apply for an order under the Married Women's Property Act 1882 s 17.[194] Engaged couples could well start to buy a house in contemplation of their marriage, and this may give them rights in property which are virtually indistinguishable from those acquired by married couples. However, it was the abolition of actions for damages for breach of promise of marriage (which deprived them of the means of recovering the expenses they had lost if the marriage did not take place) that prompted[195] making the summary procedure of s 17 available to the parties to an agreement to marry which has been terminated.[196] Where land is concerned, there seems little advantage in applying under s 17 rather than under s 14 of the Trusts of Land and Appointment of Trustees Act 1996, for while the powers under the latter are at least as extensive,[197] they are not fettered, as are those under s 17, by having to relate to property in which either or both had an interest while the agreement was in force or by the requirement to bring the action within three years of the termination of the agreement.[198]

[189] *Pettitt v Pettitt* [1970] AC 777, HL.

[190] As in *Lee v Lee* [1952] 2 QB 489n, CA and *Halden v Halden* [1966] 1 WLR 1481, CA. In *Re Bettinson's Question* [1956] Ch 67, it was held that an order could be made with respect to property which was subject to the doctrine of community of property under the law of the parties' domicile (California).

[191] Matrimonial Causes (Property and Maintenance) Act 1958 s 7(7); Civil Partnership Act 2004 s 66(2).

[192] *Bothe v Amos* [1976] Fam 46, CA.

[193] See *Mossop v Mossop* [1989] Fam 77.

[194] For couples who had agreed to register their partnership see Civil Partnership Act 2004 ss 68, 74.

[195] See Law Com No 26, *Breach of Promise of Marriage*, paras 35–42. For the abolition of actions for breach of promise, see Ch 2, Agreements to marry or form a civil partnership, p 39.

[196] By the Law Reform (Miscellaneous Provisions) Act 1970 s 2(2). For an example, see *Marsh v Von Sternberg* [1986] 1 FLR 526. For civil partners, see Civil Partnership Act 2004 s 66.

[197] Discussed in Ch 5, Enforcing the trust, pp 144–147.

[198] These requirements for an application under s 17 are set out in s 2(2) of the Law Reform (Miscellaneous Provisions) Act 1970 and, for civil partners, under s 74(4) of the Civil Partnership Act 2004.

Furthermore, an action under s 14 avoids any problems of deciding whether there was an agreement to marry in the first place.[199]

(d) Disputes between one of the spouses and a stranger

The question to be considered here is how far rights in property created or affected by marriage, civil partnership or engagement can be enforced by one of the partners against a third person. The latter may claim in one of a number of capacities, for example, as a purchaser for value from the other partner, as the other's creditor or trustee in bankruptcy, or as a beneficiary entitled to a deceased partner's estate. It is essential to decide first what rights the claiming spouse or partner has against the other and then how far these rights are enforceable against the third person. This will depend upon the application of general principles of the law of property, and in particular the nature of the latter's title. If he is, say, the husband's donee, the woman may enforce against him all those rights (other than purely personal rights) which she would have against her partner; if he is a purchaser of a legal estate or interest for value, he will take the property subject to the woman's legal rights, but will not be bound by her equitable interests if he purchased in good faith and without notice of them.[200]

3. REFORM PROPOSALS

There needs to be a complete overhaul of the whole field of family property law, which, as can be seen, is complex and often outmoded in its approach. Leaving aside the question of how those who have not married or registered their partnership should be dealt with,[201] there is still a need to clarify and update the law as it should apply to those who do acquire the status of spouse or civil partner. Solutions adopted by other legal systems include community of property (under which the property belonging to both spouses or partners is administered by the husband or both and divided between them or their personal representatives when the marriage/partnership comes to an end), community of gains (which limits community to property acquired during the marriage/partnership otherwise than by gift or inheritance), and deferred community (under which each remains free to acquire and dispose of his or her own property, but at the end of the marriage/partnership any net gain or surplus is divided equally between them).[202] English courts already have a wide discretion to adjust rights by ordering the transfer and settlement of property following divorce, dissolution of partnership, nullity and separation. There are also extensive powers to order provision for members of the family and other dependants out of the estate of a deceased person. Bearing these points in mind, the Law Commission, considering the position of spouses in 1978, concluded that it was not necessary to introduce any form of community of property in this country: most remaining hardship would be avoided if the spouses were co-owners of the matrimonial home, which is the most substantial asset in the majority of families. Even at that time well over a half of all married couples who owned their homes did so jointly,[203] and the Commission recommended that the principle of co-ownership should be extended by statute to all spouses.[204]

---

[199] See, for example, *Shaw v Fitzgerald* [1992] 1 FLR 357, discussed in Ch 2, The meaning of an agreement to marry, p 39.

[200] See further Ch 5, Protection of beneficial interests p 147.   [201] See Ch 24.

[202] See E Cooke, A Barlow and T Callus *Community of Property: A regime for England and Wales?* (2006); K Boele-Woelki et al *Principles of European Family Law Regarding Property Relations Between Spouses* (2013) ch 3 section B.   [203] See J Todd and L Jones *Matrimonial Property* (1971) p 10.

[204] Law Com No 86 (Third Report on *Family Property*). See also Law Commission Working Paper No 42 and Law Com No 52 (First Report on *Family Property*); report of the Morton Commission, Cmd 9678, Pt IX.

What they envisaged was that spouses should be statutory co-owners of any property, freehold or leasehold, used as their matrimonial home unless they otherwise agreed or, in the case of a gift, the donor, settlor or testator otherwise stipulated.[205] Once the statutory trust attached to the land, neither would be able to dispose of it unless the other consented or the court dispensed with his or her consent.[206] The Commission rejected the possibility of introducing compulsory co-ownership of goods, partly because the value of used goods is so much less than half that of new goods that compensation in the form of half their actual value would not enable the loser to replace them. Instead they proposed that either spouse should be able to apply for an order concerning the use and enjoyment of 'household goods'.[207] In deciding whether to make such an order, the court should be guided particularly by the extent to which the applicant needed them to meet the normal requirements of his or her daily life and family responsibilities. If the other spouse contravened an order, the court could order him to pay the applicant such sum (which could be the replacement value) as it thought fair and reasonable by way of compensation.

These proposals represented a compromise between the present English system of separate property and a comprehensive adoption of a system of community. They did not, however, command wide support and were not implemented. The Law Commission re-examined the issue of ownership of the family home some years later, and its arguments and conclusions are discussed in Chapter 5 and Chapter 24 as regards cohabitants.

Meanwhile, in 1985, the Law Commission considered the problem again insofar as it concerns pure personalty.[208] They highlighted a number of anomalies and inequalities in the law, including the rules relating to the acquisition of property out of a housekeeping allowance and the operation of the presumption of advancement, which, as we saw earlier, have now been addressed.[209] They also pointed out that the law can work arbitrarily: for example, if the wife pays all the housekeeping bills out of her own earnings and the husband uses his to buy a car for the parties' joint use, the car will belong to him, whilst if they pool their earnings in a joint account, it will belong to them both. The Commission went back on their earlier recommendation and proposed that, if one spouse acquires property intended wholly or mainly for the use or benefit of both, beneficial ownership should vest in both jointly. This would be subject to a contrary intention on the part of the purchaser or transferor, provided that it was made known to the other at the time, and would not apply to property acquired by way of gift or inheritance or purchased or transferred wholly or mainly for the purpose of business.[210] The reason for proposing that the property should be held jointly and not in equal shares was the belief that this is what the parties themselves would wish and intend.[211]

---

[205] The Law Commission contemplated other exceptions. The most important was the ability of a spouse to exclude the house from co-ownership if he owned it at the time of the marriage.

[206] If one spouse's name did not appear on the title, she (or he) would be able to protect her interest by registering it as a land charge.

[207] That is, 'any goods, including a vehicle, which are or were available for use and enjoyment in or in connection with any home which the parties to the marriage have at any time during the marriage occupied as their matrimonial home'. Goods would be excepted if third parties had an interest in them, eg goods subject to hire, hire-purchase and conditional sale agreements.

[208] Law Com No 175 (*Matrimonial Property*, 1985). Land was excluded from the Commission's recommendations because of its peculiar nature.

[209] See Law Com Working Paper No 90 (*Transfer of Money between Spouses*).

[210] The Commission would also exclude policies of life assurance, which could mature many years after the termination of the parties' relationship. It will be seen in Ch 23, Matrimonial and non-matrimonial property, pp 882ff that the question of whether such 'non-matrimonial' assets should be shared between divorcing spouses continues to challenge legal policy.

[211] Cf s 25 of the Family Law (Scotland) Act 1985, under which there is a presumption that each spouse has an equal share in any household goods (excluding money or securities; cars, caravans or other road vehicles; or domestic animals) obtained in prospect of or during the marriage other than by gift or succession from a third party.

The implementation of this proposal would obviously lead to a considerable increase in the number of chattels jointly owned and there is the risk that a purchaser from one party only would not acquire a good title. This risk, however, exists already: the buyer of a family car assumes that the seller is the absolute owner and does not enquire about the source of the funds with which it was originally bought. The Law Commission believed that the proposed change would introduce a fair rule and provide much greater certainty in this area of the law. It is certainly less complex than their earlier recommendations, but as can be seen from the passage of time that has passed since the Law Commission made these proposals, reform of this area of the law is not on the policy agenda. It has been superseded by a focus on resolution of financial and property disputes after the parties' relationship terminates. However, it could be argued that if attention were paid to the 'matrimonial property regime' that should apply to couples *during* their marriage, it would be much simpler to determine what is to happen when they divorce. Such matters are considered further in Chapters 22 and 23.

5

THE FAMILY HOME

A. INTRODUCTION

The right to respect for one's home, enshrined in Art 8(1) of the European Convention on Human Rights, has been described as an aspect of the broader right to privacy contained in that article,[1] and one's home as:

> the place where [a person] and his family are entitled to be left in peace free from interference by the state or agents of the state. It is an important aspect of his dignity as a human being, and it is protected as such and not as an item of property.[2]

The word 'home' in Art 8 is a concept with an autonomous meaning under the Convention and thus does not depend on its meaning under domestic law. Whether or not a particular habitation constitutes a 'home' will depend on the facts—it is the place where a person lives (or intends to live)[3] on a settled basis, but it is not necessary to show that one has the legal right to occupy the property.[4] The right to respect for one's home (not, it should be noted, a right *to a home*)[5] has been prayed in aid primarily in support of claims to occupy public-sector rented property, but arguably it may have significance in litigation between private individuals where the court has to determine whether to order possession or sale, and this is discussed later in this chapter.

The family home may have two functions.[6] Its primary purpose, reflected in this interpretation of the European Convention, is to provide shelter for the parties and their family. At the same time, if it is held in freehold or on a long lease, it will very often constitute the most significant asset that most couples own and is thus an extremely valuable investment.[7] If the relationship breaks down, these two aspects may come into conflict. Both parties may wish to continue in exclusive occupation (with or without children); alternatively, one may wish to do so while the other may wish to realise his or her investment. A party deprived of both the value of the home and the right to occupy it will often find it

---

[1] By Lord Hope of Craighead in *Harrow London Borough Council v Qazi* [2003] UKHL 43 [2004] 1 AC 983 at para 50. For criticism of the linkage of the right to respect for one's home with the right to privacy, rather than as importing a clear right to 'occupancy', see I Loveland 'The Impact of the Human Rights Act on Security of Tenure in Public Housing' [2004] *Public Law* 594 at 601–3.

[2] Per Lord Millett *Harrow London Borough Council v Qazi* [2003] UKHL 43 [2004] 1 AC 983 at para 89.

[3] As in *Gillow v United Kingdom* (1986) Series A, No 109; 11 EHRR 335.

[4] *Wiggins v United Kingdom* (1978) 13 DR 40; *Harrow London Borough Council v Qazi*.

[5] *Chapman v United Kingdom* (2001) 33 EHRR 399.

[6] For a full analysis, see L Fox O'Mahony, *Conceptualising Home: Theories, Law and Policies* (2006).

[7] Its proprietary nature may be protected by Protocol 1, Art 1 to the Convention—the right to peaceful enjoyment of possessions. For consideration of the tension between these two functions, and the ambivalence of legal responses to it, see N Hopkins 'Regulating trusts of the home: private law and social policy' (2009) 125 LQR 310.

impossible to purchase other accommodation, and if the house is sold and the proceeds divided between them, both may face the same predicament. The problem may also arise if one party is insolvent, for a mortgagee may wish to realise his security or a trustee in bankruptcy may wish to sell the home to enlarge the assets available to the creditors. It will therefore be seen that the interests of the creditors may come into direct conflict with those of the rest of the family who still need a roof over their heads.

There are thus two distinct but interrelated problems: ownership and occupation. The first is concerned with the question, in whom are the legal and beneficial interests in the property vested? The second is concerned with the question, what rights of occupation does each party have in the home irrespective of ownership? After discussing the current law governing ownership, we consider the proposals that have been suggested for reform, and compare the English approach with that taken in other jurisdictions. We then consider occupation rights. [8]

B. OWNERSHIP

1. THE BACKGROUND TO THE CURRENT LAW

Unlike continental European systems,[9] English law has never developed a special regime for dealing with matrimonial or family property.[10] Consequently, whenever ownership of family assets is in issue recourse must be had to the ordinary rules governing property law.

Before the Second World War the potential injustice of applying ordinary property rules to the ownership of family assets was barely an issue. At that stage few working class families owned their own homes,[11] and cohabitation outside marriage was rare. In the vast majority of middle class families the husband was the sole earner and, if the home was purchased, it was conveyed into his name, with the result that the whole beneficial interest would vest in the husband to the exclusion of the wife. With low divorce rates and stable house prices, litigation was uncommon.

After the war the social and economic climate changed. It became common for wives to work during marriage. Property ownership increased,[12] with purchases being made with the aid of mortgages. Property prices began to rise and divorce rates spiralled upwards. The combination of these factors resulted in much more litigation being brought in respect of what for most was the key asset, the family home. This in turn brought into

---

[8] This chapter is limited to discussion of the rights family members enjoy as between themselves and in relation to third parties claiming rights through a family member (eg a mortgagee or trustee in bankruptcy). General rights to occupy property under a rented tenancy are not discussed but readers may wish to refer to the previous edition pp 196–202 for an outline.

[9] For a comparative analysis of these, see K Boele-Woelki et al (eds) *European Family Law in Action Volume IV: Property Relations between Spouses* (2009).

[10] For the changing pattern of home ownership and renting over the past 100 years see ONS *A Century of Home Ownership and Renting in England and Wales (full story)* (2013) http://www.ons.gov.uk/ons/rel/census/2011-census-analysis/a-century-of-home-ownership-and-renting-in-england-and-wales/short-story-on-housing.html (accessed 20 April 2014).

[11] In 1918, 77% of households lived in rented accommodation: ONS *A Century of Home Ownership and Renting in England and Wales (full story)* (2013).

[12] The proportion of owner-occupied households reached 50% in 1971 and a peak of 69% in 2001. It has since fallen back to 64% in 2011: ONS *A Century of Home Ownership and Renting in England and Wales (full story)* (2013).

sharp relief the starkness of the application of strict rules of property ownership and the doctrine of separation of ownership as between the spouses. It thus became crucial to determine which spouse paid what bills and expenses, since only payments related to the purchase of the property could give rise to ownership. The iniquities of this approach were only too plain to see for, as Lord Denning MR pointed out, it may be purely a matter of convenience which spouse pays off the mortgage and which pays the other household expenses: they give no thought to the legal consequences of their acts (of which they are probably ignorant) and it is unjust to give the wife an interest in the house if she happens to pay the mortgage but not if she pays the household bills instead.[13]

True to form Lord Denning MR was not content to allow what he considered to be an injustice. Seizing on the wording of s 17 of the Married Women's Property Act 1882:

> In any question between husband and wife as to the title to or possession of property, either party . . . may apply by summons or otherwise in a summary way to any judge of the High Court of Justice . . . and the judge . . . may make such order with respect to the property in dispute . . . as he thinks fit.

He held that the court had a discretionary power over family assets. In his view, therefore, provided the spouse (normally the wife at that time) had made a substantial contribution to the overall household expenses she would be held to have a beneficial share of the property, regardless of whether the money was put towards the deposit or mortgage, even though the property was in the husband's name alone.[14]

Lord Denning MR's approach was controversial, and eventually the issue came before the House of Lords, first in *Pettitt v Pettitt*[15] and then in *Gissing v Gissing*,[16] where it was delivered a death blow. As we saw in Chapter 4, it was held that properly interpreted, s 17 is purely a procedural provision designed to facilitate the speedy disposal of property disputes between the spouses, whereby the court could make a declaration of ownership. As Lord Morris put it in *Pettitt v Pettitt*,[17] under s 17 the question for the court was ' "Whose is this?" and not "To whom shall this be given?" '. Following this unanimous ruling, two fundamental rules emerged. First, it is clear from *Pettitt v Pettitt* that English law knows of no doctrine of community of property or any separate rules of law applicable to family assets.[18] Consequently, if one spouse buys property intended for common use with the other—whether it is a house, furniture or a car—this cannot per se give the latter any proprietary interest. From this follows the second principle, stated in *Gissing v Gissing*,[19] that if either of them seeks to establish a beneficial interest in property, the legal title to which is vested in the other, he or she can do so only by establishing that the legal owner holds the property on trust for the claimant. This latter principle, however, masks considerable difficulties which, as we discuss shortly, continue to arise.

The injustice which Lord Denning sought to avoid was largely removed by the Matrimonial Proceedings and Property Act 1970, which gave the court a power to make property adjustment orders on pronouncing a decree of divorce, nullity or judicial separation and expressly required it to take into account inter alia 'the contributions which

---

[13] See eg *Fribance v Fribance* [1957] 1 All ER 357 at 360, CA, and *Falconer v Falconer* [1970] 3 All ER 449 at 360, CA.

[14] *Hine v Hine* [1962] 1 WLR 1124, CA. Formerly engaged couples may also use s 17 of the Married Women's Property Act 1882: Law Reform (Miscellaneous Provisions) Act 1970 s 2(1).

[15] [1970] AC 777, HL.   [16] [1971] AC 886, HL.   [17] [1970] AC 777 at 798E–F.

[18] [1970] AC 777 at 800–1 (per Lord Morris), 810 (per Lord Hodson) and 817 (per Lord Upjohn).

[19] [1971] AC 886 at 896 (per Lord Reid), 900 (per Lord Dilhorne) and 904–5 (per Lord Diplock).

each of the parties has made . . . to the welfare of the family'.[20] This jurisdiction makes it unnecessary to resort to other means to compensate a spouse, and that proceedings to establish property rights should not be taken when an application could be made for an order in matrimonial proceedings (or the equivalent jurisdiction applicable to civil partners). But it may still be necessary to determine what interest in property a spouse or civil partner has where:

(a) she (or he) is unable or unwilling to take matrimonial or equivalent proceedings;

(b) she has remarried or repartnered without applying for a property adjustment order in proceedings for dissolution or nullity (when her power to do so will be barred);[21]

(c) it has to be decided, on the death of one of the spouses or partners, whether an interest forms part of his or her estate or vests in the survivor;

(d) it has to be decided, on the insolvency of one of the spouses or partners, what property is available for his or her creditors.

Furthermore, as cohabitants are unable to apply for divorce or dissolution, they cannot apply for a property adjustment order. Hence, unless they have children (when a property adjustment order can be made under the Children Act 1989),[22] any claims they may have must be resolved solely by reference to the law of property. With the growing incidence of cohabitation this particular use of property law has become of major concern. It is perhaps ironic that the law evolved to settle the property claims of spouses now derives much of its contemporary significance in relation to unmarried couples.[23] The position has also become more complex because while it would have been the norm for property to be vested in the husband's sole name when these cases first began to arise, as he was probably (regarded as) the sole breadwinner in the family, cohabitants may buy property in joint names, or solely, depending on a variety of circumstances including their views on the stability of their relationship, their respective earning capacities, prior ownership and the approach taken by mortgage lenders.[24] Thus, cases are now as likely to arise where the home is owned in joint, as in sole, names.

2. THE CURRENT LAW

(a) The primary importance of the documents of title

As we have said, *Pettitt v Pettitt* and *Gissing v Gissing* established that no special rules apply to the ownership of family assets and that instead one must apply ordinary property principles. The application of these principles requires first having to establish legal ownership and then to determine equitable or beneficial ownership. To determine these issues one should first have recourse to the document of title. As the Court of Appeal held in *Goodman v Gallant*,[25] if this expressly declares in whom not only the legal title but also the beneficial interests are to vest, it will be conclusive in the absence of fraud or

---

[20] See now the Matrimonial Causes Act 1973 s 24 and s 25(2)(f) and Ch 22, Transfer and settlement of property, p 845 and Ch 23, Contribution, p 896.

[21] See Ch 22, Application for orders, p 831.

[22] See Ch 21, Proceedings under Schedule 1 to the Children Act 1989, p 794.

[23] For a cogent discussion of the way that property law has been 'familialised' by courts having to apply it to the family context, and consideration of how that context has changed, see A Hayward '"Family property" and the process of "familialisation" of property law' [2012] CFLQ 284.

[24] See eg *Singla v Browne* [2007] EWHC 405 (Ch) [2008] 2 FLR 125. For the empirical picture, see G Douglas et al *A Failure of Trust: Resolving Property Disputes on Cohabitation Breakdown* (2007) ch 4.

[25] [1986] Fam 106, CA. Contrast *Re Gorman* [1990] 1 All ER 717, where the parties were not bound by the declaration because they had not signed the transfer. The transfer was nevertheless evidence (in the circumstances conclusive) of their common intention at the time the property was acquired.

mistake.[26] Accordingly, if, as is common in the case of spouses, the family home is conveyed to both partners on express trust for themselves as joint tenants in equity, this must
give them a joint interest in the proceeds of sale, and if either of them severs the joint
interest, they will become equitable tenants in common in equal shares.[27] If the conveyance declares they are to hold as tenants in common in equal shares or in some other proportion, they will be similarly bound by the wording. Solicitors acting for parties buying
their home should enquire what their intentions are and spell them out in the conveyance
to prevent dispute in the future but this is not always done.[28]

If the document is silent as to the beneficial ownership, then it is open to the non-legal
owner and even the joint legal owners to claim entitlement to a (different) share of the
property under a trust. To substantiate such a claim the claimant must establish that the
legal owner holds the property on trust for the claimant. There are two distinct 'hurdles'[29]
to be surmounted. The claimant must first establish whether they have an interest at all.
How this is done will depend upon whether the property is held in joint names or there is
only one legal owner. As Baroness Hale made clear in *Stack v Dowden*:[30]

> Just as the starting point where there is sole legal ownership is sole beneficial ownership,
> the starting point where there is joint legal ownership is joint beneficial ownership. The
> onus is upon the person seeking to show that the beneficial ownership is different from the
> legal ownership. So in sole ownership cases it is upon the non-owner to show that he has
> any interest at all. In joint ownership cases, it is upon the joint owner who claims to have
> other than a joint beneficial interest.

Once an interest is established, the second issue is to quantify it. As the quotation
indicates, the starting-point in a joint names case is that the parties hold a joint—and
equal—beneficial interest, but this may be rebutted through suitable evidence. In a sole
name case, the question will be to determine precisely how large a share the claimant
holds. We discuss each issue in turn.

---

[26] As in *Thames Guaranty Ltd v Campbell* [1985] QB 210, CA. The spouses had agreed that the property
should belong beneficially to the wife but that it should be conveyed into their joint names. The solicitor,
assuming that they wished to take a joint beneficial interest, drafted the transfer to them as joint tenants in
law *and equity*. It was held that the transfer could be rectified by deleting the words italicised, thus leaving
both spouses as trustees for the wife alone. A declaration in the transfer deed that the survivor is entitled to
give a valid receipt for capital does not constitute an express trust of the beneficial interests: *Stack v Dowden*
[2007] UKHL 17 [2007] 2 AC 432.

[27] *Goodman v Gallant* [1986] Fam 106, CA. The presentation of a divorce petition including a prayer for a
property adjustment order does not effect a severance, so that if one spouse dies before the order is made, the
whole interest will vest in the other by survivorship: *Harris v Goddard* [1983] 3 All ER 242, CA. Cf *Kinch v
Bullard* [1999] 1 WLR 423: terminally ill wife initiated divorce proceedings and instructed solicitors to sever
joint tenancy in matrimonial home so that her half share could form part of her estate. Husband then suffered heart attack and was taken to hospital and the wife, wishing to take the whole of the beneficial interest,
destroyed the solicitor's letter severing the tenancy, which had been addressed to the husband and posted
to the house. Husband died before wife—held severance effective to prevent her from taking whole interest.

[28] Per Bagnall J in *Cowcher v Cowcher* [1972] 1 All ER 943 at 959; *Springette v Defoe* [1992] 2 FLR 388 at
390. Although Form TR1 which is used in the land registration process provides for the parties to declare
how they hold the property it is not mandatory to complete the relevant panel: see G Douglas et al *A Failure
of Trust: Resolving Property Disputes on Cohabitation Breakdown* (2007) ch 5. A proposal to make it so (or to
enable the parties to declare their interests in a separate form, JO) was rejected by the Government although
the JO form is now available on a voluntary basis: see E Cooke 'In the Wake of *Stack v Dowden*: The Tale of
TR1' [2011] Fam Law 1142.

[29] As Baroness Hale described them in *Stack v Dowden* [2007] UKHL 17 [2007] 2 AC 432 at [61], [63].
See G Battersby 'Ownership of the family home: *Stack v Dowden* in the House of Lords' [2008] CFLQ 255.

[30] [2007] UKHL 17 [2007] 2 AC 432 at [56].

(b) Establishing a beneficial interest

Under the Law of Property Act 1925 s 53(1)(b) a valid declaration of trust of a beneficial interest in land[31] needs to be in writing. This means that if, for example, one partner purchases the home entirely out of his own money and has it conveyed into his own name, an oral agreement between the partners that the other is to take a beneficial share will not per se give her an interest. It will amount to no more than an imperfect gift, which equity will not perfect, or to a declaration of trust, which is required to be evidenced in writing. Section 53(2) of the 1925 Act, however, does not require 'the creation or operation of resulting, implied or constructive trusts' to be in writing. Accordingly, as Lord Diplock said in *Gissing v Gissing*,[32] in the absence of writing the claimant to a beneficial interest will need to establish an interest under a resulting, implied or constructive trust. Although his Lordship went on to say that from this point of view it does not matter what type of trust it is, such a classification may be important when it comes to assessing the quantum of any interest established. As we shall see, this classification issue is not without its problems.

A further complicating factor is that, while the creation of a beneficial interest depends upon the parties' intentions, all too frequently the parties themselves have given no thought to the question of ownership. According to the majority in *Pettitt v Pettitt* it was not open to the court to impute an agreement to the parties where the evidence adduced showed there was none. As Lord Morris put it:[33] 'The court does not devise or invent a legal result.' In *Gissing v Gissing* Lord Diplock (who had been in the minority in *Pettitt v Pettitt*) accepted that it was not open to the court to impute an agreement to the parties but held that it could nevertheless *infer* an intention from their conduct or words insofar as they would be reasonably understood by the other party. In other words, the court may have to infer an intention the parties never articulated, but it cannot impute to them an agreement they clearly did not make. In *Jones v Kernott*[34] Lord Wilson noted that this issue will 'merit careful thought' in light of the Supreme Court's decision in that case to accept that such imputation may be applied at the quantification stage.

Although *Pettitt* and *Gissing* were important decisions, settling once and for all that there was no power under s 17 of the Married Women's Property Act 1882 to vary property interests and that non-economic contributions to the purchase of the family home could never give rise to a beneficial interest, they nevertheless left a number of uncertainties. In particular, it was unclear precisely what type of conduct could properly be considered to give rise to an inference that the parties intended to share the property. There was also uncertainty as to whether their Lordships, particularly in *Gissing v Gissing*, were really considering the creation of resulting or constructive trusts.

(c) Resulting trust

Property bought by one party and put into the name of the other is presumptively[35] held on a resulting trust by the latter for the purchaser, according to the proportions in

---

[31] Note, however, there is no requirement for writing to create express trusts in respect of chattels. *Paul v Constance* [1977] 1 All ER 195, CA (furniture); *Rowe v Prance* [1999] 2 FLR 787 (boat).

[32] [1971] AC 886, HL at 905.   [33] [1970] AC 777 at 804.

[34] [2011] UKSC 53 [2012] 1 AC 776 at [84].

[35] The presumption does not apply where there is evidence of *actual* intention to create a resulting trust: *M v M and Others* [2013] EWHC 2534 (Fam) [2014] 1 FLR 439 (where the husband had put various properties into the names of offshore companies that he controlled in order to attempt to defeat the wife's claims for financial remedies on divorce). For actual intention, see *Lavelle v Lavelle* [2004] EWCA Civ 223 [2004] 2 FCR 418.

which they provided the purchase money.[36] Until the House of Lords' decision in *Stack v Dowden*[37] this presumption had been regularly utilised as a means of establishing whether a claimant had an interest (or the size of their interest) in property owned by or with a partner.[38] However, the House of Lords (Lord Neuberger dissenting), there held that in the usual domestic case about the beneficial ownership of a family home (at least one which is owned in joint names), the resulting trust should not operate as a legal presumption. Lord Walker and Baroness Hale explained the rationale for moving away from reliance upon the resulting trust presumption in *Jones v Kernott*:[39]

> In the context of the acquisition of a family home, the presumption of a resulting trust made a great deal more sense when social and economic conditions were different and when it was tempered by the presumption of advancement. The breadwinner husband who provided the money to buy a house in his wife's name, or in their joint names, was presumed to be making her a gift of it, or of a joint interest in it. That simple assumption—which was itself an exercise in imputing an intention which the parties may never have had—was thought unrealistic in the modern world by three of their Lordships in *Pettitt v Pettitt*... It was also discriminatory as between men and women and married and unmarried couples. That problem might have been solved had equity been able to extend the presumption of advancement to unmarried couples and remove the sex discrimination. Instead, the tool which equity has chosen to develop law is the 'common intention' constructive trust. Abandoning the presumption of advancement while retaining the presumption of resulting trust would place an even greater emphasis upon who paid for what, an emphasis which most commentators now agree to have been too narrow...

They went on to state:

> The time has come to make it clear, in line with *Stack v Dowden*..., that in the case of the purchase of a house or flat in joint names for joint occupation by a married or unmarried couple, where both are responsible for any mortgage, there is no presumption of a resulting trust arising from their having contributed to the deposit (or indeed the rest of the purchase) in unequal shares. The presumption is that the parties intended a joint tenancy both in law and in equity. But that presumption can of course be rebutted by evidence of a contrary intention, which may more readily be shown where the parties did not share their financial resources.[40]

It will be noted that in this paragraph, Lord Walker and Baroness Hale were clearly referring to cases where the home is in joint names, and it might be thought that, as they stressed

---

[36] *Walker v Hall* [1984] FLR 126. The presumption of advancement could still apply in the case of property bought by the husband and put in the wife's name, but as noted in Ch 4, Income and investments, p 110, that presumption is readily rebutted: *McGrath v Wallis* [1995] 2 FLR 114, CA and will in due course be abolished by the Equality Act 2010 s 199. Moreover, the function of this presumption (protection of the wife) is now performed by the presumption of joint beneficial ownership arising in joint ownership cases: *Gibson v Revenue and Customs Prosecution Office* [2008] EWCA Civ 645 [2009] QB 348. The presumption does not, in any case, apply to cohabitants: *Chapman v Jaume* [2012] EWCA Civ 476 [2012] 2 FLR 830.

[37] [2007] UKHL 17 [2007] 2 AC 432.

[38] See eg *Evans v Hayward* [1995] 2 FLR 511, CA; *Springette v Defoe* [1992] 2 FLR 388, CA; *Huntingford v Hobbs* [1993] 1 FLR 736, CA; *Carlton v Goodman* [2002] EWCA Civ 545, [2002] 2 FLR 259. See also *Tinsley v Milligan* [1994] 1 AC 340, HL (property put into sole name of partner, to enable the couple to claim social security benefits fraudulently. Held, no evidence to rebut the presumption of a resulting trust having arisen by virtue of defendant's contribution to the purchase price, the defendant was therefore entitled to succeed on her counterclaim).

[39] [2011] UKSC 53 [2012] 1 AC 776 at [24], [25]. See the discussion by J Mee '*Jones v Kernott*: Inferring and Imputing in Essex' [2012] Conv 167.   [40] At [25].

both here and in *Stack v Dowden* that sole name cases must be approached differently, they were intending to confine their disapproval of the resulting trust to cases of joint ownership. Nonetheless, they subsequently contended that the 'assumptions as to human motivation, which led the courts to impute particular intentions by way of the resulting trust, are not appropriate to the ascertainment of beneficial interests in a family home'[41] and applied this approach in the Privy Council case of *Abbott v Abbott*[42] where the property was held in the husband's sole name.

However, Lord Walker did consider that the resulting trust approach might apply where the couple had both an emotional and commercial partnership.[43] This may be important given the rise of the 'buy to let' phenomenon, whereby people buy a property to rent out to generate an income in a buoyant housing market, as well as in relation to more straightforward commercial ventures between cohabiting partners. In *Geary v Rankine*[44] the man owned a guest house which the couple did not live in but in which the woman helped out. She failed to establish a beneficial interest on a *constructive* trust basis and analysis using a resulting trust would have benefited him since he had put up the whole of the purchase price. By contrast, in *Laskar v Laskar*[45] a mother bought her council flat with a 'right to buy' discount in order to rent it out, but needed her daughter's help to obtain a mortgage. Lord Neuberger applied the resulting trust approach on the basis that this was a commercial undertaking so that a constructive trust was inapplicable, and on that basis the daughter received a share of one-third, representing her 'contribution' via her liability for the mortgage.

(d) 'Common intention' constructive trust

As we have seen, equity follows the law in that the starting point will be that in the case of a jointly owned property, the parties hold the beneficial interest jointly, and that for a property in one person's name, the other party must establish that he or she has any beneficial interest at all.[46] Given this position, cases of joint ownership based on a constructive trust revolve around the second 'hurdle' of quantification (although sometimes the claim is for 100%);[47] the prior issue of establishment of an interest has been elucidated through the case-law on properties held in one partner's sole name.

It should be appreciated at the outset that the concept of 'intention' in this context is a notional one.[48] It does not necessarily reflect both parties' intentions, for, as Lord Diplock pointed out in *Gissing v Gissing*,[49] a party's intention in this context must mean that which his words and conduct led the other to believe that he holds. It is therefore no objection that the party making the representation actually intended to hold the property

---

[41] At [53].   [42] [2007] UKPC 53 [2008] 1 FLR 1451.

[43] At [32] *per* Lord Walker and reiterated by Lord Walker and Baroness Hale in *Jones v Kernott* [2011] UKSC 53 [2012] 1 AC 776 at [31].   [44] [2012] EWCA Civ 555 [2012] 2 FLR 1409.

[45] [2008] EWCA Civ 347 [2008] 2 FLR 589. See M Pawloswki 'Resulting Trusts, Joint Borrowers and Beneficial Shares' [2008] Fam Law 654. See also *Chaudhury v Chaudhury* [2013] EWCA Civ 758 [2013] 2 FLR 1526 where a father and his second wife put up the deposit for a home purchased in the sole name of a son by the father's first marriage, intending that the father would take over the purchase: held surviving wife entitled to 8% share equivalent to the deposit.

[46] T Etherton 'Constructive Trusts: A new model for equity and unjust enrichment' (2008) 67 CLJ 265; S Gardner 'Family Property Today' (2008) 124 LQR 422.

[47] See eg *Chopra v Bindra* [2009] EWCA Civ 203 [2009] 2 FLR 786 where there was a declaration of trust providing for a right of survivorship if one owner died, and a tenancy in common in unequal shares if both decided to sell.

[48] See the analyses of N Glover and P Todd 'The myth of common intention' (1996) 16 *Legal Studies* 325 and S Gardner 'Rethinking Family Property' (1993) 109 LQR 263 at 264–5. Note too that the evidence may establish an agreement for a *loan* rather than a trust: see, for example, *Chapman v Jaume* [2012] EWCA Civ 476 [2012] 2 FLR 830.   [49] [1971] AC 886 at 906.

for himself.[50] Further, it was held in *Midland Bank plc v Cooke*[51] that even if both parties admit that neither had discussed nor intended any agreement as to the proportion of their interests, this did not preclude the court from inferring one.

Such common intention may be demonstrated in two ways, laid down definitively by the House of Lords in *Lloyds Bank plc v Rosset*[52] which drew a distinction between cases where there has been an agreement between the parties to share the property and those where there has not.

Cases where there is evidence of agreement—'Rosset 1'
According to Lord Bridge:[53]

> The first and fundamental question *which must always be resolved* is whether independently of any inference to be drawn from the conduct of the parties in the course of sharing the house as their home and managing their joint affairs, there has at any time prior to acquisition, or exceptionally at some later date, been any agreement, arrangement or understanding reached between them that the property is to be shared beneficially.

Such a finding must be based upon evidence of express discussions between the parties 'however imperfectly remembered and however imprecise their terms must have been'. As Waite J subsequently observed in *Hammond v Mitchell*,[54] this first requirement means:

> . . . that the tenderest exchanges of a common law courtship may assume an unforeseen significance many years later when they are brought under equity's microscope and subjected to an analysis under which many thousands of pounds of value may be liable to turn on this fine question as to whether the relevant words were spoken in earnest or in dalliance and with or without representational intent.

Yet it is clear that such discussions must be pleaded in the greatest detail both as to the language and to the circumstance.[55] In *Hammond* itself it was held sufficient that the man had said to the woman soon after completion:

> Don't worry about the future because when we are married [the house] will be half yours anyway and I'll always look after you and [their child].

In contrast, in *Springette v Defoe*[56] it was held insufficient that the parties had a mutual but un-communicated belief or intention to share the property for, as Steyn LJ said,[57] 'Our trust law does not allow property rights to be affected by telepathy.'

Other instances where the court has found sufficient evidence of an agreement to share include the owner telling his partner that, although her name would not go onto the deeds, her assumption of joint liability for a mortgage debt charged to his farm would be

---

[50] As in *Eves v Eves* [1975] 3 All ER 768, CA and *Grant v Edwards* [1986] Ch 638, CA.
[51] [1995] 4 All ER 562 at 574–5, CA.   [52] [1991] 1 AC 107, HL.
[53] [1991] 1 AC 107, HL at 132.   [54] [1992] 2 All ER 109 at 121.
[55] But in the absence of any contrary evidence the court may have no choice but to believe the case presented by the claimant: see *Re Lorraine Share* [2002] 2 FLR 88—claimant's case flatly contradicted earlier representations made by her when she was made bankrupt, but the trustee in bankruptcy declined to cross-examine her.
[56] [1992] 2 FLR 388, CA.
[57] [1992] 2 FLR 388, CA at 394. For the view that the court should have found a constructive trust based on 'Rosset 2' (see later), see *Oxley v Hiscock* [2004] EWCA Civ 546 [2005] Fam 211 per Chadwick LJ at para 46.

sufficient proof that she had a 'right' to it,[58] a man assuring his partner that if she would help run his business affairs for him while he was in prison he would share various of his assets with her, even though the precise extent of his promise was unclear,[59] and a man telling his partner that he would put her name on the title when he had time.[60]

Lord Bridge himself instanced two 'outstanding examples' of cases falling into this first category, namely *Eves v Eves*[61] and *Grant v Edwards*.[62] Both cases involved cohabiting couples, and in both the female partner had clearly been led by the male partner to believe that when they set up home together the property would belong to them jointly. In *Eves* the man told his female partner that the only reason the home was to be in his name alone was because she was under 21 and that but for her age he would have had the house put in joint names.[63] Subsequently the woman did a great deal of manual work including breaking up concrete, demolishing and rebuilding a shed, stripping wallpaper and painting the woodwork, to renovate the dirty and dilapidated house that the man had bought. In *Grant v Edwards* the defendant told the plaintiff that her name was not going on the title because that would prejudice her in matrimonial proceedings between her and her husband. The plaintiff made no contributions to the initial purchase price but, despite having four children, went out to work and applied her earnings to the household expenses without which, the Court of Appeal accepted, the mortgage could not have been paid whilst at the same time leaving the family enough money to live on.

Evidence of detrimental reliance on the agreement

Provided an agreement can be proved then, according to Lord Bridge:

> . . . it will only be necessary for the partner asserting a claim to a beneficial interest against the partner entitled to the legal estate to show that he or she has acted to his or her detriment or significantly altered his or her position in reliance on the agreement in order to give rise to a constructive trust.[64]

In *Eves and Eves* and *Grant v Edwards* what seemed to characterise the contributions made by the women was that they comprised conduct on which, in Nourse LJ's words,[65] 'the woman could not reasonably have been expected to embark unless she was to have an interest in the house.' In other words, even where there has been a prior agreement to share, detrimental reliance requires more than living with the man, having a baby by him and looking after the family and home. Thus, in *Midland Bank plc v Dobson*[66] the wife's claim to a beneficial interest in the matrimonial home, which was in her husband's name alone, failed because it was held that the wife's using part of her income for household expenses, including the purchase of domestic equipment, and doing some ordinary decorating, did not amount to detrimental reliance.[67]

---

[58] *Hyett v Stanley* [2003] EWCA Civ 942 [2004] 1 FLR 394.

[59] *Chan Pui Chun v Leung Kam Ho* [2002] EWCA Civ 1075 [2003] 1 FLR 23.

[60] *Drake v Whipp* [1996] 1 FLR 826, CA.   [61] [1975] 3 All ER 768, CA.

[62] [1986] Ch 638, CA.   [63] He admitted in evidence that this was just an excuse.

[64] *Lloyd's Bank plc v Rosset* [1991] 1 AC 107, 132G. Note *Wayling v Jones* [1995] 2 FLR 1029, CA, in which it was held that once conduct had been proved from which detrimental reliance could be inferred, the burden switched to the defendant to show that the claimant had not acted in reliance upon the promise. See *G v G (Matrimonial Property: Rights of Extended Family)* [2005] EWHC 1560 (Admin) [2006] 1 FLR 62 where the husband's claim that members of his extended family had beneficial interests in the large family home was rejected as there was no evidence of any having acted to their detriment in reliance of a share.

[65] [1986] Ch 638 at 648.   [66] [1986] 1 FLR 171 at 177, CA.

[67] Cf *Cox v Jones* [2004] EWHC 1486 (Ch) [2004] 2 FLR 1010. The couple were both barristers whose relationship ended in acrimony and dispute over several items of property. Inter alia, detrimental reliance by the

Whether detrimental reliance can be established otherwise than by contributions of money or money's worth is doubtful. There are some hints, however, in *Hammond v Mitchell*[68] that non-financial contributions can be relevant. In that case the main evidence of detrimental reliance lay in the claimant agreeing to postponing her interest in the property to that of the bank's charge (executed to secure a loan for the defendant's business ventures, which, had they had been unsuccessful, might have involved the whole property having to be sold), but Waite J also took account, at any rate when considering the quantum of the claimant's interest, of the claimant's contribution as 'mother/helper/unpaid assistant and at times financial supporter to the family prosperity.'

Notwithstanding that conduct considered sufficient to establish detrimental reliance may be limited to contributions in money or money's worth, the test of such reliance appears less onerous than having to establish an interest where there is no prior agreement to share. As Lord Bridge observed in *Lloyds Bank plc v Rosset*,[69] the contributions made in both *Eves v Eves* and *Grant v Edwards*, 'fell far short of such conduct as would by itself have supported the claim in the absence of an express representation by the male partner that she was to have such an interest.'

Cases where there is no evidence of agreement—'Rosset 2'
According to Lord Bridge in *Rosset*:[70]

> In sharp contrast with this situation [ie *Rosset 1*] is the very different one where there is no evidence to support a finding of an agreement or arrangement to share, however reasonable it might have been for the parties to reach such an arrangement if they had applied their minds to the question, and where the court must rely entirely on the conduct of the parties both as the basis from which to infer a common intention to share the property beneficially and as the conduct relied on to give rise to a constructive trust. In this situation direct contributions to the purchase price by the partner who is not the legal owner, whether initially or by payment of mortgage instalments, will readily justify the inference necessary to the creation of a constructive trust. But, as I read the authorities, it is at least extremely doubtful whether anything less will do.

In *Rosset* itself, where there was found to be no prior agreement or arrangement to share the property, it was held that neither a common intention that the house was to be renovated as a joint venture nor a common intention that it was to be shared as the family home was sufficient to indicate that both parties were to take an interest; nor could such an inference be drawn from the wife's own renovations to the property and her supervision of the building works over a period of some six weeks before completion and for another six weeks after that. Echoing earlier sentiments as to what type of work a woman could normally be expected to do, Lord Bridge commented:[71]

> . . . it would seem the most natural thing in the world for any wife, in the absence of her husband abroad, to spend all the time she could spare and to employ any skills she might have, such as the ability to decorate a room, in doing all she could to accelerate progress of the work quite irrespective of any expectation she might have of enjoying a beneficial interest in the property.

woman was established in her having given up the chance to purchase a flat in her own name by agreeing to her partner, who could more easily raise the money, doing so on the understanding that he would hold the property as her nominee.

---

[68] [1992] 2 All ER 109 at 119e.   [69] [1991] 1 AC 107 at 133.
[70] [1991] 1 AC 107 at 132–3.   [71] [1991] 1 AC 107 at 131.

Lord Bridge instanced both *Pettitt v Pettitt*[72] and *Gissing v Gissing*[73] as falling into this second category and in neither did the claim for a beneficial interest succeed. In the former, where the house was bought in the wife's name, the husband failed to establish an interest by reason of the 'ephemeral' improvements he effected to the property by his internal decoration, the laying of a lawn and his construction of a well and a garden side wall.[74] Similarly, Mrs Gissing failed since, rather than paying for the deposit or mortgage on the home, she paid for her own and the son's clothes and supplemented the housekeeping allowance.

Perhaps the most infamous example of a second category case where the claim failed is *Burns v Burns*.[75] In that case Mrs Burns (as she was known), who had lived with her partner for 19 years, failed to establish a beneficial interest in the family home, having given up her job to have the couple's two children and then, when she did begin to earn money, having spent it on the household's expenses, fixtures and fittings in the house and the family's clothing.

By contrast, sufficient direct contributions were found to establish an interest in *Aspden v Elvy*.[76] There, a couple separated and the man transferred title in a barn (which he then worked on to convert to a dwelling-house) and some land to his ex-partner. After discharging his debts he was left with some capital but was living in a caravan. It was held that his work on the property and substantial payments made towards its improvement demonstrated that he 'did hope and expect to be able to live in and have an interest in [the barn] when it was complete and that [his ex-partner] was fully aware of it' such that their common intention was that he should have a share.

Where there is a direct financial contribution to the property, even if it is relatively small, the court will readily infer a common intention to share the property. This is implicit in all the speeches in *Gissing v Gissing* and was spelled out by Viscount Dilhorne and Lord Diplock,[77] as well as by Lord Bridge in *Rosset*. This contribution may come directly out of the claimant's own earnings or resources, or out of a common fund to which both parties contributed.[78]

A most extreme example of a finding of a direct contribution of this nature is *Midland Bank plc v Cooke*,[79] in which it was held that a wedding present of just over £1,000 cash provided by the groom's parents was intended to be a gift to both spouses equally, so that the wife could be credited with half of it. Since it was used towards the payment of the initial deposit on the house, it was held there could properly be inferred a common intention to share the property.

Whether anything less than direct contributions will give rise to an inference that the parties intended to share the property is uncertain. Lord Bridge was clearly of the view that indirect contributions by way of payments to the household expenses could never give rise to such an inference, even if it could be shown that without these contributions the legal owner could not have paid the mortgage instalments. However, his comments are obiter and seem at variance with those of Lord Diplock in particular in

---

[72] [1970] AC 777, HL. But note that substantial improvements can be sufficient for a spouse to obtain an interest under s 37 of the Matrimonial Proceedings and Property Act 1970, discussed later, Improvements to the family home, p 143.   [73] [1971] AC 886, HL.

[74] See also *Midland Bank plc v Cooke* [1995] 4 All ER 562, CA, in which it was held that the wife's contribution to the maintenance and improvement of the property was not itself sufficient to raise an inference that the property was to be shared.

[75] [1984] Ch 317, CA. For definitive discussion of the significance of this case, see J Mee '*Burns v Burns*: The Villain of the Piece?' in S Gilmore, J Herring and R Probert (eds) *Landmark Cases in Family Law* (2011).

[76] [2012] EWHC 1387 (Ch) [2012] 2 FLR 807 at [124].   [77] [1971] AC 886 at 900 and 907.

[78] See eg *Gordon v Douce* [1983] 2 All ER 228; *Risch v McFee* [1991] 1 FLR 105, CA.

[79] [1995] 4 All ER 562, CA,

Gissing v Gissing. In that case Lord Diplock pointed out that if the wife had made an initial contribution to the deposit or legal charges which indicated that she was to take some interest in the property, the court should also take account of her contribution to the mortgage instalments, even though these were indirect, because this would be consistent with a common intention that the payment of other household expenses would release the husband's money to pay off the mortgage and would thus be her contribution to the purchase of the home. But, he added, if the wife had made no initial contribution to the purchase, no direct contribution to the repayment of the mortgage, and 'no adjustment to her contribution to other expenses of the household which it can be inferred was refer-able to the acquisition of the house', she cannot claim an interest in it 'merely because she continued to contribute out of her own earnings or private income to other expenses of the household'.[80] Lord Pearson similarly considered that there could be a contribution 'if by arrangement between the spouses one of them by payment of the household expenses enables the other to pay the mortgage instalments'.[81]

Notwithstanding Lord Bridge's comment to the contrary, it was held in *Le Foe v Le Foe and Woolwich plc*[82] that an inference that the property is to be shared can be drawn where the claimant makes only indirect contributions to the mortgage, thus enabling the family economy to function. As the trial judge noted, to hold that only an initial direct contribution could give rise to a share would be to decide such cases 'by reference to mere accidents of fortune, being the arbitrary allocation of financial responsibility as between the parties.'[83] A similar concern seems to underlie the view taken by Baroness Hale in *Stack v Dowden* that the dictum of Lord Bridge may 'have set that hurdle rather too high in certain respects'.[84] Lord Walker in that case went further:

> the court should in my opinion take a broad view of what contributions are to be taken into account. In *Gissing*... Lord Diplock referred to an adjustment of expenditure 'refer-able to the acquisition of the house'. 'Referable' is a word of wide and uncertain meaning. Now that almost all houses and flats are bought with mortgage finance, and the average period of ownership of a residence is a great deal shorter than the contractual term of the mortgage secured on it, the process of buying a house does very often continue, in a real sense, throughout the period of its ownership. The law should recognise that by taking a wide view of what is capable of counting as a contribution towards the acquisition of a residence, while remaining sceptical of the value of alleged improvements that are really insignificant, or elaborate arguments (suggestive of creative accounting) as to how the family finances were arranged.[85]

Nonetheless, in *James v Thomas*[86] a contribution by the woman through working without pay in her partner's *business* was held to give rise to no inference that she should thereby take a share in their home, funded by mortgage payments made from that business. As Sir John Chadwick put it, what she had done was wholly explicable on other grounds—establishing that the contribution is *referable to the purchase* thus remains important.

---

[80] [1971] AC 886 at 907–10, HL.   [81] At 903.

[82] [2001] 2 FLR 970.   [83] At para 49. See also *Bernard v Josephs* [1982] Ch 391 at 403–4, CA.

[84] [2007] UKHL 17 [2007] 2 AC 432 at [63].

[85] [2007] UKHL 17 [2007] 2 AC 432 at [34].

[86] [2007] EWCA Civ 1212 [2008] 1 FLR 1598. See also *Walsh v Singh* [2009] EWHC 3219 (Ch) [2010] 1 FLR 1658: woman's contributions were referable to her recognition of the relationship, not to the acquisition of a share in the property.

(e) Quantification of shares

Up to now we have been discussing the circumstances in which a spouse or partner can establish a beneficial interest in the family home by way of trust. We must now consider the second issue: what is the size of the interest that each acquires? The interest may be created by means of an express trust (if in writing), a resulting trust or a constructive trust. If the conveyance spells out the beneficial interests, the court must give effect to it.[87] If the property is vested in the parties jointly on an express trust for themselves as joint tenants, they will become equitable tenants in common in equal shares if either of them severs the joint interest.[88] Similarly, if they take as tenants in common, the court must give effect to the trust thereby created and divide the proceeds in the proportions stated.

Quantification in cases of resulting trust

If the circumstances in which the property was bought are held to give rise to a resulting trust, the beneficial interests will be proportionate to the parties' contributions.[89] As we have seen, it has been firmly stated that the constructive, rather than resulting trust, should generally be applied in domestic cases (unless there is a commercial dimension to the transaction). Occasionally, however, it may still be proper to rely on a resulting trust where, for example, a constructive trust would be held void under the insolvency rules.[90] Thus in *Re Densham*,[91] although the Court of Appeal was prepared to accept that the parties' pooling of resources was clear evidence of an intention to share the property equally, since such an interest would have been void as against the trustee in bankruptcy on the basis that it was a 'voluntary' gift by the legal owner, reliance had instead to be placed on a resulting trust based upon the claimant's financial contribution to the initial deposit, giving her a one ninth share in the property instead of one half.

Quantification in cases of constructive trust

Property held in joint names

Quantifying the interests held under a constructive trust has been made slightly more straightforward in relation to a property held in joint names as a result of the decision in *Stack v Dowden*.[92] There, the House of Lords held that in such a case the onus is on the party who wishes to show that the beneficial interests are divided other than equally.[93]

Baroness Hale made clear that rebutting the presumption of equal shares will be difficult:

> The burden will therefore be on the person seeking to show that the parties did intend their beneficial interests to be different from their legal interests, and in what way. This is not a task to be lightly embarked upon. In family disputes, strong feelings are aroused

---

[87] Unless the conveyance can be rectified as a result of fraud or mistake: see earlier, The primary importance of the documents of title, p 125.   [88] *Goodman v Gallant* [1986] Fam 106, CA.

[89] This is not to say that it is always easy to quantify the contributions. For some examples of the application of resulting trusts see eg *Huntingford v Hobbs* [1993] 1 FLR 736, CA; *Springette v Defoe* [1992] 2 FLR 388, CA; *Cowcher v Cowcher* [1972] 1 All ER 943; and *Marsh v Von Sternberg* [1986] 1 FLR 526.

[90] Discussed later, Insolvency and the Family Home, pp 158ff.

[91] [1975] 3 All ER 726, CA. Incidentally, perhaps contrary to the view of Baroness Hale in *Stack v Dowden* [2007] UKHL 17 [2007] 2 AC 432 at [66], who suggested there has been no such case, this decision provides an example of a case where a sole legal owner (there being no declaration of trust) *was* held to hold the property on a beneficial joint tenancy (albeit one that was ineffective as against the trustee in bankruptcy). See also *McHardy & Sons (A Firm) v Warren and Hutton* [1994] 2 FLR 338, CA (resulting trust relied upon because of a third party claim).

[92] [2007] UKHL 17 [2007] 2 AC 432.   [93] [2007] UKHL 17 [2007] 2 AC 432 per Lord Hope at [4].

when couples split up. These often lead the parties, honestly but mistakenly, to reinterpret the past in self-exculpatory or vengeful terms. They also lead people to spend far more on the legal battle than is warranted by the sums actually at stake. A full examination of the facts is likely to involve disproportionate costs. In joint names cases it is also unlikely to lead to a different result unless the facts are very unusual.[94]

What are the facts which might render a case 'very unusual'? Of course, if the parties have evidence of a clear agreement to share in some other proportions, that will determine the issue, but usually there is no such evidence. Her Ladyship suggested that the following may be relevant issues to consider:

In law, 'context is everything' and the domestic context is very different from the commercial world. Each case will turn on its own facts. Many more factors than financial contributions may be relevant to divining the parties' true intentions. These include: any advice or discussions at the time of the transfer which cast light upon their intentions then; the reasons why the home was acquired in their joint names; the reasons why (if it be the case) the survivor was authorised to give a receipt for the capital moneys; the purpose for which the home was acquired; the nature of the parties' relationship; whether they had children for whom they both had responsibility to provide a home; how the purchase was financed, both initially and subsequently; how the parties arranged their finances, whether separately or together or a bit of both; how they discharged the outgoings on the property and their other household expenses. When a couple are joint owners of the home and jointly liable for the mortgage, the inferences to be drawn from who pays for what may be very different from the inferences to be drawn when only one is owner of the home. The arithmetical calculation of how much was paid by each is also likely to be less important. It will be easier to draw the inference that they intended that each should contribute as much to the household as they reasonably could and that they would share the eventual benefit or burden equally. The parties' individual characters and personalities may also be a factor in deciding where their true intentions lay. In the cohabitation context, mercenary considerations may be more to the fore than they would be in marriage, but it should not be assumed that they always take pride of place over natural love and affection. At the end of the day, having taken all this into account, cases in which the joint legal owners are to be taken to have intended that their beneficial interests should be different from their legal interests will be very unusual.[95]

Stack v Dowden was found to be an example of such a sufficiently unusual case. There, the couple cohabited for 20 years and had four children. Their first home was purchased by the woman who then used the proceeds of its sale to help buy their second, which was put in joint names. She earned, and contributed, 'far more' than the man. Throughout their relationship, they had kept their bank accounts and various savings and investments 'rigidly' separate and made separate payments for their outgoings and expenses. On this evidence, the House concluded that the woman's share of the beneficial interest should be 65%. They seem to have assumed that keeping one's finances separate is an unusual feature of a long relationship, but in fact, empirical evidence shows a very wide diversity of arrangements reached by both spouses and cohabiting couples these days.[96] Such

---

[94] [2007] UKHL 17 [2007] 2 AC 432 at [68].   [95] [2007] UKHL 17 [2007] 2 AC 432 at [69].
[96] See G Douglas et al *A Failure of Trust: Resolving Property Disputes on Cohabitation Breakdown* (2007) ch 4; C Vogler 'Managing Money in Intimate Relationships: similarities and differences between cohabiting and married couples' in J Miles and R Probert (eds) *Sharing Lives, Dividing Assets: an inter-disciplinary study* (2009).

arrangements, like the decision to purchase in sole or joint names, may have as much to do with inertia, convenience or force of circumstances, as with a conscious decision to live financially separate lives and may therefore have little real significance in casting light on how the parties intended (or can be taken to have intended)[97] to share the beneficial interest in their home.

By holding that there is a strong presumption of equal shares, their Lordships were seeking to discourage the kind of 'detailed examination of the parties' relationship and finances' that adds significantly to the cost of litigation in these cases—particularly since it is often very difficult to recreate at all accurately how the pattern of agreements and arrangements was arrived at. The strength of the presumption is illustrated by the subsequent decision of *Fowler v Barron*.[98] There, as in *Stack,* the couple lived together for over 20 years and had children. The home was purchased in joint names but all payments towards the purchase and outgoings were made by the man. The couple had no joint bank account. The woman worked but her money was spent on herself and their children. Arden LJ stated that 'In determining whether the presumption is rebutted, the court must in particular consider whether the facts as found are inconsistent with the inference of a common intention to share the property in equal shares to an extent sufficient to discharge the civil standard of proof on the person seeking to displace the presumption arising from a transfer into joint names.'[99] The court found no evidence of such inconsistency. Although the man gave evidence that he had not understood the implications of the joint tenancy, and had not intended the woman to share in the property other than on his death, since he had not communicated this to his partner, it could not constitute their 'common intention' and thus serve to rebut the presumption.[100]

Property in sole name

Where the property is in one party's name, but the other has succeeded in establishing that they had a common intention to share the beneficial interest, the approach to determining the size of that share should, in the opinion of Lord Walker and Baroness Hale in *Jones v Kernott,* be the same as just outlined. But since the starting-point is different, the outcome is likely to be different too. We have seen that a presumption of equal shares in a joint names case will be difficult to overcome. An assertion that equal shares were intended in a sole name case may be just as difficult. Thus, in *Thompson v Hurst*[101] where the couple cohabited for 20 years, the man was awarded a 10% share in the former home, which the woman had acquired under the right to buy scheme four years before they separated. In *Gallarotti v Sebastianelli*[102] two men who were long-standing friends bought a flat which was put into S's sole name. On their cash contributions to the initial purchase and mortgage, the shares were 86% and 14% but the judge found they had intended to share equally. However, G had been unable to pay his due share of the mortgage instalments and it was concluded that they had ultimately agreed to share on the basis of their actual contributions.

Inference or imputation: intention or fairness?

In holding that the court may take a broad view of the range of contributions that may be relevant to determining the size of each party's share, the House of Lords in *Stack v*

---

[97] Which we discuss later, Inference or imputation: intention or fairness?

[98] [2008] EWCA Civ 377 [2008] 2 FLR 831.See A Hayward 'Family values in the home: *Fowler v Barron*' [2009] CFLQ 242. [99] [2008] EWCA Civ 377 [2008] 2 FLR 831 at [35].

[100] Compare the situation of an uncommunicated desire not to share the beneficial interest which was held not to prevent a constructive trust arising in a sole name case, in *Eves v Eves* [1975] 3 All ER 768, CA and *Grant v Edwards* [1986] Ch 638, CA.

[101] [2012] EWCA Civ 1752 [2013] 1 FCR 522. [102] [2012] EWCA Civ 865 [2012] 2 FLR 1232.

Dowden drew on an earlier Court of Appeal decision, *Oxley v Hiscock*[103] (which was actually a sole-name case). There, Chadwick LJ had concluded that:

> each [party] is entitled to that share which the court considers fair having regard to the whole course of dealing between them in relation to the property.[104]

Despite agreeing with Chadwick LJ that 'the whole course of dealing' between the parties could be considered, the House appeared to reject his view that the court's task is one of arriving at the *fair* outcome. As Baroness Hale put it:

> ... the search is still for the result which reflects what the parties must, in the light of their conduct, be taken to have intended ... therefore, it does not enable the court to abandon that search in favour of the result which the court itself considers fair. For the court to impose its own view of what is fair upon the situation in which the parties find themselves would be to return to the days before *Pettitt v Pettitt*. . . . [105]

Lord Neuberger agreed, but approached the issue differently. We have seen earlier that he preferred to apply the presumption of a resulting trust in any event. However he also considered that in attempting to rebut that presumption, the court could consider evidence which:

> would often enable the court to deduce an agreement or understanding amounting to an intention as to the basis on which the beneficial interests would be held. Such an intention may be express (although not complying with the requisite formalities) or inferred, and must normally be supported by some detriment, to justify intervention by equity. [However] ... While an intention may be inferred as well as express, it may not, at least in my opinion, be imputed ... The distinction between inference and imputation may appear a fine one ... but it is important.

An inferred intention is one which is objectively deduced to be the subjective actual intention of the parties, in the light of their actions and statements. An imputed intention is one which is attributed to the parties, even though no such actual intention can be deduced from their actions and statements, and even though they had no such intention. Imputation involves concluding what the parties would have intended, whereas inference involves concluding what they did intend.[106]

The other judges in *Stack* did not particularly distinguish between inference and imputation, although their decisions were explicable on the basis of *inferring* what the parties had intended. But they did deal with the distinction subsequently, in *Jones v Kernott*[107] and in so doing, agreed with Chadwick LJ that the task of quantification is indeed ultimately to arrive at a *fair* outcome. The couple bought their home in joint names, but separated eight years later. The woman and their children remained in the property. The couple tried unsuccessfully to sell it, and instead, cashed in a life assurance policy to enable the man to purchase his own property. After that, the woman met all the outgoings. Ten years later (the value of the house having substantially increased), the man sought to claim his share of the value of the property and the woman served a notice severing the joint tenancy. The Supreme Court overruled the decision of the Court of Appeal that there was no evidence to rebut the presumption that the parties had intended their shares to

---

[103] [2004] EWCA Civ 546 [2005] Fam 211.   [104] At para [69].
[105] *Stack v Dowden* [2007] UKHL 17 [2007] 2 AC 432 at [61].
[106] [2007] UKHL 17 [2007] 2 AC 432 at [124]–[126].   [107] [2011] UKSC 53 [2012] 1 AC 776.

be equal and they restored the first instance judge's decision that the woman held 90% of the interest.

In so holding, Lord Walker and Baroness Hale now expressly endorsed Chadwick LJ's formulation. They stated that while they accepted that the search is primarily to ascertain the parties' actual shared intentions, whether expressed or to be inferred from their conduct, there are at least two exceptions to this—the first is where the resulting trust applies (as discussed earlier), and the second:

> is where it is clear that the beneficial interests are to be shared, but it is impossible to divine a common intention as to the proportions in which they are to be shared. In those two situations, the court is driven to *impute* an intention to the parties which they may never have had . . . [and] if it cannot deduce exactly what shares were intended, it may have no alternative but to ask what their intentions as reasonable and just people would have been, had they thought about it at the time.[108]

They considered that while the conceptual difference between inference and imputation is clear, the difference in practice may not be so great.[109] In fact, they were satisfied that they could indeed *infer* that the parties' common intention had changed after they separated and cashed in their life insurance policy. They concluded that the intention was that the man's beneficial interest should 'crystallise' at that point.[110]

Lord Kerr and Lord Wilson considered that imputation squarely concerns determining what would be fair, regardless of what the parties might be supposed to have intended, and they both considered that it could *not* be inferred here that the parties had intended the man to lose his interest in the home when he left. Both were happy to *impute* that intention to them, with the outcome described by Lord Kerr as being 'eminently fair'.[111] It would be inaccurate and premature to suggest that the law has now come close to turning full circle back to Lord Denning's willingness to assume a discretionary jurisdiction to produce a fair outcome in such cases, but recognition that, as Lord Collins reminded us in *Jones v Kernott*,[112] the courts 'are courts of law, but they are also courts of justice' does indicate a willingness to move the law forward in line with social change. We will see later that this is all the more important given the difficulty of achieving statutory reform on this issue.

(f) Proprietary estoppel

According to Lord Bridge in *Lloyds Bank plc v Rosset*,[113] once an agreement to share property has been found the claimant must show:

> . . . that he or she has acted to his or her detriment or significantly altered his or her position in reliance on the agreement in order to give rise to a constructive trust or proprietary estoppel.

In so commenting his Lordship seemed therefore to equate constructive trusts with proprietary estoppel. This in turn has led to much academic speculation[114] as to whether

---

[108] At [31], emphasis added and [47].   [109] At [34]. Lord Collins agreed (at [65]).

[110] At [48]. It has been held that 'in the absence of an express post-acquisition agreement, a court will be slow to infer from conduct alone that parties intended to vary existing beneficial interests established at the time of acquisition': *James v Thomas* [2007] EWCA Civ 1212 [2008] 1 FLR 1598 at [24]. See also *Morris v Morris* [2008] EWCA Civ 257 [2008] Fam Law 521.   [111] At [74], [77], [89].

[112] At [66].   [113] [1991] 1 AC 107 at 132.

[114] See S Gardner 'Rethinking Family Property' (1993) 109 LQR 263; S Nield 'Constructive trusts and estoppel' (2003) 23 *Legal Studies* 311.

the two concepts have been assimilated. The two have very similar features and are often pleaded in the alternative. As Browne-Wilkinson V-C's noted in *Grant v Edwards*:[115]

> . . . In both, the claimant must to the knowledge of the legal owner have acted in the belief that the claimant has or will obtain an interest in the property. In both, the claimant must have acted to his or her detriment in reliance on such belief. In both, equity acts on the conscience of the legal owner to prevent him from acting in an unconscionable manner by defeating the common intention. The two principles have been developed separately without cross-fertilisation between them: but they rest on the same foundation and have on all other matters reached the same conclusions.

Similar views have been expressed in subsequent cases.[116] However, in *Stack v Dowden*[117] Lord Walker indicated that he was 'now rather less enthusiastic' about the notion that proprietary estoppel and 'common interest' constructive trusts can or should be completely assimilated, because while proprietary estoppel consists of asserting an equitable claim against the conscience of the 'true' owner, which is to be satisfied by the minimum award necessary to do justice, a constructive trust identifies the true beneficial owner or owners, and the size of their beneficial interests.[118] One plausible distinction is that recourse to constructive trusts needs to be had in cases where the claim is that the property in issue has been jointly acquired, whereas estoppel becomes relevant where the property has unquestionably already been acquired by one person who, by his or her *subsequent* conduct, has led the claimant to think that he or she will share it.

The essence of proprietary estoppel was outlined by Lord Walker in *Thorner v Majors*:[119]

> a representation or assurance made to the claimant
>
> reliance on it by the claimant; and
>
> detriment to the claimant in consequence of his or her (reasonable) reliance

Representation

In *Thorner,* the House of Lords held that while the representation or assurance must have been in sufficiently clear terms, this will depend on the context. In that case, the claimant had worked unpaid on his cousin's farm for nearly 30 years. They were both 'taciturn and undemonstrative men committed to a life of hard and unrelenting physical work, by day and sometimes by night, largely unrelieved by recreation or female company.'[120] Although the cousin did not say so expressly, he made oblique comments over the years to the effect that he planned to leave the farm to the claimant, and at one point, handed him a bonus statement relating to two life assurance policies stating 'that's for my death duties', after

---

[115] [1986] Ch 638 at 656.

[116] See eg Chadwick LJ in *Oxley v Hiscock* [2004] EWCA Civ 546 [2005] Fam 211 at para 66; Robert Walker LJ in *Yaxley v Gotts* [2000] Ch 162 at 176 and 180.

[117] [2007] UKHL 17 [2007] 2 AC 432 at [37]. See also T Etherton 'Constructive Trusts: A new model for equity and unjust enrichment' (2008) 67 CLJ 265, who argues (at p 286) that they perform 'quite different legal functions'.

[118] However, it has been held that the exception provided for resulting, implied or constructive trusts by s 2(5) of the Law of Property (Miscellaneous Provisions) Act 1989 to the requirement that a contract for the sale or other disposition of an interest in land must be in writing, applies also to proprietary estoppel: *Yaxley v Gotts and Gotts* [2000] Ch 162, CA.

[119] [2009] UKHL 18 [2009] 2 FLR 405 at [29]. The case is cited variously as *Major* and *Majors*. See J Mee 'The Limits of Proprietary Estoppel: *Thorner v Major*' [2009] CFLQ 367.

[120] [2009] UKHL 18 [2009] 2 FLR 405 at [59].

which the claimant had an 'expectation' rather than just a 'hope' that he would inherit. The House upheld the first instance judge's decision that this gave rise to an estoppel. A surely less deserving claim was accepted in *Suggitt v Suggitt*,[121] another farming case. There, a son had been a 'disappointment' to his father, having failed to complete his agricultural course or make a success of his own farming ventures. He had received various inheritances from family members, and was supported by his father, including living rent-free and receiving a regular income from a family trust, whilst working on the father's land. The father left the farm to his daughter, but with the instruction that she should transfer it to the son if she felt him capable of managing it and the court held that this, coupled with various comments and assumptions over the years that indicated the father wished him to inherit, gave rise to an estoppel. The judge set much store by the importance of context as asserted by the House of Lords in *Thorner* and thus considered that 'all due allowance' must be made for the fact that much of the evidence was 'full of ambiguities and conjectures'. By contrast, in *Shirt v Shirt*[122] where father and son had a farming partnership but had fallen out bitterly before the father died, the Court of Appeal held that alleged promises that 'the farm would be coming to' the claimant and that it was his if he wanted to work for it did not give rise to an estoppel as they were inconsistent with subsequent actions by the claimant intended to ensure he secured part, rather than all, of the farm.

An assurance need not be oral; in *Stallion v Albert Stallion Holdings (Great Britain) Ltd*[123] a wife agreed to a divorce so that her husband could marry again, and they drafted a written agreement that, inter alia, she could live rent-free for life in an apartment in a building owned by his business. After he died, his company wished to redevelop the site and sought possession, and the wife was held entitled to rely on the agreement.

The assurance or promise must relate to identified property,[124] rather than a vague commitment that the claimant will be given 'financial security' or some unspecified piece of someone's estate.[125] In *Thorner*, it was held sufficient that, although the exact extent of the deceased's farm varied through sales and acquisitions over the years, the assurance extended to whatever it consisted of, at the time of his death.[126]

Detrimental reliance

As with constructive trusts, the claimant must have acted to his or her detriment, but such detriment need not consist of the expenditure of money or other quantifiable financial detriment, so long as it is something substantial. In *Gillett v Holt*,[127] for example, the appellant left school without obtaining any qualifications at the urging of a wealthy farmer who became his 'patron'. On the strength of assurances that he would be left his estate, the appellant worked as the farm manager for many years, and, as Robert Walker LJ put it, he and his wife 'deprived themselves of the opportunity of trying to better themselves in other ways'.[128]

The claimant's acts must have been induced by his or her mistaken belief.[129] So in *Lissimore v Downing* the claimant failed to establish estoppel after she moved in with a founder member of the rock band, 'Judas Priest', on his lavish country estate, because this

---

[121] [2011] EWHC 903 (Ch) [2011] 2 FLR 875.
[122] [2012] EWCA Civ 1029 [2013] 1 FLR 232.   [123] [2009] EWHC 1950 (Ch) [2010] 2 FLR 78.
[124] *Cobbe v Yeoman's Row Management Ltd* [2008] UKHL 55, [2008] 1 WLR 1752.
[125] *Layton v Martin* [1986] 2 FLR 227 at 239; *Lissimore v Downing* [2003] 2 FLR 308. Cf *Re Basham (decd)* [1986] 1 WLR 1489 at 1503H; *Jennings v Rice* [2002] EWCA Civ 159, [2003] 1 FCR 501.
[126] [2009] UKHL 18 [2009] 2 FLR 405 at [95].   [127] [2001] Ch 210, CA.
[128] See also *Q v Q* [2008] EWHC 1874 (Fam) [2009] 1 FLR 935.
[129] See *Van Laethem v Brooker* [2005] EWHC 1478 (Ch) [2006] 2 FLR 495. Hence there can be no estoppel if the claimant knew that the other reserved his right to change his mind or to revert to the original position: see *A-G of Hong Kong v Humphreys Estate (Queen's Gardens) Ltd* [1987] AC 114, PC.

'represented an exciting opportunity . . . which lifted her out of a humdrum life' and not because she expected a share of his assets.[130] The owner of the property must also know of the claimant's mistake: he cannot encourage a belief of which he was ignorant.[131] On the other hand, as the Court of Appeal held in *Wayling v Jones*,[132] once it is established that the promise has been made and that there has been conduct by the claimant of such a nature that an inducement could be inferred, the burden of proof shifts to the defendant to establish that the plaintiff had not relied on the promise.

A good example of the operation of proprietary estoppel is *Pascoe v Turner*,[133] in which the plaintiff and defendant, who was his housekeeper, began to live together as husband and wife. After the relationship broke down, the plaintiff, who had moved out, told the defendant, 'The house is yours and everything in it'. Relying on his statement, she spent money on redecoration, improvements and repairs. On his claim to possession of the house, the Court of Appeal held that, by encouraging or acquiescing in the defendant's belief that the house was hers, he was estopped from denying this.

Quantification

The remedy granted where a proprietary estoppel is made out is whatever is necessary to satisfy the equity which has arisen in consequence of the misrepresentation. This has resulted in the extremely generous outcome, in *Pascoe v Turner*, of the complete transfer of the property to the claimant.[134] However, an estoppel may be remedied by means of devices other than a share in the beneficial interest such as, in *Greasley v Cooke*,[135] a right of occupation. An important criterion is the reminder in *Gillett v Holt*[136] that:

> The court's aim is, having identified the maximum, to form a view as to what is the minimum required to satisfy it and do justice between the parties. The court must look at all the circumstances, including the need to achieve a 'clean break' so far as possible and avoid or minimise future friction.[137]

This test of proportionality was also applied in *Jennings v Rice*.[138] There, the appellant had been a part-time gardener and odd-job man for an elderly lady since 1970. By the late 1980s, she had stopped paying him for his work but gave him £2,000 to put towards acquiring a property. She reassured him that she would 'see him right' in her will. During the 1990s, he provided her with personal care as she became more infirm, and slept at her house so that she could feel secure. On being left nothing when she died, he claimed her entire estate, valued at over £1.2 million. The Court of Appeal upheld the trial judge's decision to award the appellant a sum of £200,000, considering him to have been correct to consider the likely cost of providing the lady with the kind of personal care that the appellant had provided at around £200,000, as the appropriate sum to award him. As Aldous LJ put it:

> The value of that equity will depend upon all the circumstances including the expectation and the detriment. The task of the court is to do justice. The most essential requirement is that there must be proportionality between the expectation and the detriment.[139]

---

[130] [2003] 2 FLR 308 *per* HH Judge Norris QC at para 55. See to similar effect, *Coombes v Smith* [1986] 1 WLR 808; cf the same principle applied to constructive trusts: earlier, Evidence of detrimental reliance on the agreement, p 131.   [131] *Brinnand v Ewens* (1987) 19 HLR 415, CA.

[132] [1995] 2 FLR 1029.   [133] [1979] 2 All ER 945, CA. See B Sufrin (1979) 42 MLR 574.

[134] See also *Wayling v Jones*, where the plaintiff was awarded the proceeds of sale of the deceased's hotel that he had promised the plaintiff.   [135] [1980] 3 All ER 710, CA.

[136] [2000] 2 FLR 266 at 292B.   [137] See also *Pascoe v Turner* [1979] 1 WLR 431, 438–9.

[138] [2002] EWCA Civ 159, [2003] 1 FCR 501   [139] At para [36].

(g) Improvements to the family home

It may be argued that the parties' interests in the home have been varied if, after purchase, one of them has been solely responsible for enhancing its value by extension or improvement (either by cash payments or by doing the work himself). Unlike a contribution to the purchase price, the mere fact that A does work on B's property does not of itself give A any interest in it. To establish such an interest, A must show that the expenditure was incurred or the work done in pursuance of an agreement or common intention that it should do so or, alternatively, that B has led A to believe that the improvement would confer an interest on him so as to give rise to a proprietary estoppel.[140] In *Pettitt v Pettitt*[141] the husband alleged that as the result of doing work on the matrimonial home (which had been purchased by the wife out of her own money) he had increased its value by over £1,000. Most of the work consisted of redecorating the bungalow in question, but he had also made a garden, built a wall and patio, and done other jobs outside. The House of Lords unanimously held that he could claim nothing on the ground that, in the absence of an express agreement, he could acquire no interest by doing work of an ephemeral nature or 'do-it-yourself' jobs which any husband could be expected to do in his leisure hours.

Leaving aside the gendered nature of this approach, which assumes certain roles for husbands and wives, it can clearly work injustice. Recognition of this led to the passing of s 37 of the Matrimonial Proceedings and Property Act 1970.[142] This provides:

> . . . where a husband or wife[143] contributes in money or money's worth to the improvement of real or personal property in which or in the proceeds of sale of which either or both of them has or have a beneficial interest, the husband or wife so contributing shall, if the contribution is of a substantial nature and subject to any agreement to the contrary express or implied, be treated as having then acquired by virtue of his or her contribution a share or an enlarged share, as the case may be, in that beneficial interest . . .

Section 37 (which refers to the improvement of any property and not merely to that of the home) applies whether the contribution is in money or money's worth: in other words, it does not matter whether the claimant does the job himself or pays a contractor to do it. In the latter case, however, he must show that his contribution is identifiable with the improvement in question: a general contribution to the family's finances (like an indirect contribution to the price) will give him an interest in the home only if it is referable to the improvement.[144]

There are two limitations on the operation of the section. First, it will apply only if the contribution is of a substantial nature. Whether any particular improvement is sufficiently substantial to bring it within the ambit of the section is a question of fact.[145] Secondly, the section applies 'subject to any agreement between the spouses to the contrary express or

---

[140] *Pettitt v Pettitt* (earlier), particularly at 818 (per Lord Upjohn). See also *Thomas v Fuller-Brown* [1988] 1 FLR 237, CA; *Harwood v Harwood* [1991] 2 FLR 274 at 294, CA. Where there is evidence that would give rise to the inference of a constructive trust, the court must examine it and make findings: *Dibble v Pfluger* [2010] EWCA Civ 1005 [2011] 1 FLR 664.

[141] [1970] AC 777, HL. The husband had to rely on the general law because the case was decided before the passing of the Matrimonial Proceedings and Property Act 1970.

[142] Enacted on the recommendation of the Law Commission: see Law Com No 25, paras 56–8 and pp 102–5. It applies to engaged couples by virtue of s 2(1) of the Law Reform (Miscellaneous Provisions) Act 1970. A similar provision applies to civil partners under s 65 of the Civil Partnership Act 2004.

[143] The provision extends to same-sex spouses by virtue of Sch 3 para 1 to the Marriage (Same Sex Couples) Act 2013.

[144] *Harnett v Harnett* [1973] Fam 156 at 167, per Bagnall J. (The question did not arise on appeal: [1974] 1 All ER 764, CA.)

[145] *Re Nicholson* [1974] 2 All ER 386.

implied', so that if they agreed that the improvements should confer no interest on the party making them, this will be conclusive. If the parties agreed on the size of the interest which the improvements were to confer on the spouse making them, the court must give effect to the agreement; in other cases it has power to make such order as appears just in all the circumstances. Normally this should reflect the amount by which the value of the property was increased at the time: if, for example, the wife puts the value of the husband's house up from £80,000 to £100,000, she should obtain one-fifth of the price when it is sold.[146]

In practice, the provision is rarely used, being superseded by the courts' wider powers of financial relief on divorce, although it might conceivably be relied on by a spouse in cases involving third party claims to the family home, such as on insolvency. However, it should not be forgotten, and in particular, the fact that it extends to engaged couples is important. In *Dibble v Pfluger*[147] the cohabitants had been engaged for 10 years when they separated. The male partner claimed a share in the interest of a property held in the woman's name in Poland, on which he had contributed sums for renovation and improvement, and no one, until the case reached the Court of Appeal and Ward LJ pointed it out, noticed that s 37 might be applicable.

3. ENFORCING THE TRUST

(a) The court's powers under s 14 of the Trusts of Land and Appointment of Trustees Act 1996

Before implementation of the Trusts of Land and Appointment of Trustees Act 1996, a trust for sale arose whenever land was conveyed to two or more people either as beneficial joint tenants or as tenants in common. As its name implied, the creation of such trusts imposed an ultimate obligation upon the trustees to sell the property, and, if the trustees refused to sell the trust property, s 30 of the Law of Property Act 1925 enabled any person interested to apply to the court for an order directing them to give effect to the trust, whereupon the court could make such order as it thought fit. Section 30 could be used to force the sale of a matrimonial home, because, if both spouses had a beneficial interest in it either as joint tenants or as tenants in common, a trust for sale was automatically created. Following the Law Commission's recommendations,[148] trusts for sale were replaced by trusts of land. Under the 1996 Act all existing trusts for sale, whether express or implied, became trusts of land. One of the crucial differences between trusts of land and trusts for sale is that *implied* trusts of land no longer carry an obligation to sell, and even in *express* trusts there is an implied power to postpone a sale indefinitely.[149]

While the parties are living together, they are likely to agree on the disposal of their home, but if their relationship breaks down and they separate, one may well wish to remain in the former home and the other to have it sold so as to realise the capital. If the parties are married or civil partners, the courts prefer to use their wide powers to make property adjustment orders under the Matrimonial Causes Act 1973 and Civil Partnership Act 2004, because they can then make a fair order after taking all relevant facts into account.[150] But this can be done only if one of them seeks to end the marriage

---

[146] Query the position if the 'improvement', although substantial in money terms, does not actually increase the value of the property in the market, eg the installation of double glazing?

[147] [2010] EWCA Civ 1005 [2011] 1 FLR 664.

[148] See Law Com No 181, *Transfer of Land, Trusts of Land* (1989).   [149] See s 5 and s 4 respectively.

[150] *Tee v Tee and Hillman* [1999] 2 FLR 613, CA. Civil partners may take advantage of the equivalent jurisdiction: Civil Partnership Act 2004 s 72 and Sch 5.

or partnership. If no such proceedings are taken or they are unmarried, this course is not open to them, and they will be compelled to invoke the court's powers under s 14 of the 1996 Act, which replaced s 30 of the 1925 Act.

This provision enables any person who is a trustee of land or who has an interest in property subject to a trust of land[151] to seek a court order either relating to the exercise by the trustees of any of their functions or to 'declare the nature or extent of a person's interest in property subject to the trust'.[152] In each case the court may make such order as it thinks fit. Although s 14 allows a court to order a sale, its powers are not limited to this. It also includes the power to declare the nature and extent of a person's interest in the land in question, which is the same power as under s 17 of the Married Women's Property Act 1882 and s 66 of the Civil Partnership Act 2004.

Section 15 of the 1996 Act provides a set of guidelines on matters to be taken into account when exercising the powers under s 14. The aim of the guidelines is, in the Law Commission's words,[153] to 'consolidate and rationalise' the former approach adopted by the courts under s 30 of the Law of Property Act 1925, without, however, restricting the exercise of judicial discretion.[154]

Under s 15(1) the matters to which the court is to have regard include:

(a) the intentions of the person or persons (if any) who created the trust,
(b) the purpose for which the property subject to the trust is held,
(c) the welfare of any minor who occupies or might reasonably be expected to occupy any land subject to the trust as his home, and
(d) the interests of any secured creditor or any beneficiary.

Section 15(3) also requires the court to have regard to the circumstances and wishes of any beneficiaries of full age and entitled to an interest in possession in property subject to the trust. The matters in s 15 are not listed in order of priority, and, in the view of Arden LJ,[155] are not exhaustive in structuring the court's discretion under s 14. Thus, a judge was entitled under s 15(3) to have regard to the mother's wishes and circumstances in seeking a sale of the former family home when the father wished to postpone sale to enable him to remain there bringing up the children. It should be noted that these guidelines do not apply where a trustee in bankruptcy is seeking an order;[156] in such a case different guidelines apply.[157]

Although in general terms these guidelines reflect the factors formerly considered by the court under the 1925 Act, the approach of the courts to balancing the competing interests of the parties, especially in a case of bankruptcy, has changed and the old authorities relating to s 30 should be treated with caution.[158] For example, one important change is the guideline relating to children's welfare. By making such welfare an independent

[151] This is narrower than recommended by the Law Commission, in that it does not permit *any* interested person to apply. See also *Re Ng (A Bankrupt), Trustee of the Estate of Ng v Ng* [1998] 2 FLR 386.
[152] In the case of unmarried partners, where there are children, and both parties have an interest in the property, there should usually be an application under s 15 and Sch 1 to the Children Act 1989 made at the same time and dealt with by the court simultaneously: *W v W (Joinder of Trusts of Land Act and Children Act Applications)* [2003] EWCA Civ 924 [2004] 2 FLR 321.
[153] Law Com No 181 (*Transfer of Land, Trusts of Land,* 1989) para 12.9.
[154] Ibid at 12.10. See also *TSB Bank plc v Marshall, Marshall and Rodgers* [1998] 2 FLR 769.
[155] *W v W (Joinder of Trusts of Land and Children Act Applications)* [2003] EWCA Civ 924, [2004] 2 FLR 321 at para [26]. [156] Section 15(4).
[157] Viz. those under the Insolvency Act 1996 s 335A, discussed later, Protection of members of the bankrupt's family, p 159. [158] *The Mortgage Corporation v Shaire* [2001] 4 All ER 364.

consideration, the Act has implemented the Law Commission's recommendations[159] aimed at ensuring that a case such as *Re Evers' Trust*,[160] in which the mother's need for a home with her three children was fully taken into account, is likely to be preferred to those such as *Re Holliday (a bankrupt)*,[161] in which the court dismissed the notion that it was a collateral object of the trust to preserve the house as a home for the children.

On the other hand, there is no reason to suppose that the new powers have altered the court's basic stance, that if two people (whether married or not) buy property as a home for themselves (together with any children they may have), the underlying purpose of the trust is to provide a home and not an investment.[162] Consequently, so long as that purpose subsists, the trust should not be executed and the property should not be sold.[163] Relevant to the question of whether the purpose still subsists is s 12(1) of the 1996 Act, which provides that a person who is beneficially entitled to an interest in possession in land subject to a trust of land is entitled, by reason of his interest, to occupy the land at any time if at that time (a) the purposes of the trust include making the land available for his occupation, or (b) the land is held by the trustees so as to be so available. Subsection (1) does not, however, confer on a beneficiary a right to occupy land if it is either 'unavailable or unsuitable for occupation by him'.[164]

Once the purpose for which the property was acquired has been discharged, the court is likely to order a sale.[165] It has been suggested that the 'intentions of the persons or persons who created the trust' must be an intention which they had in common, such that the original intention as to the purpose of the trust may only be changed by agreement of all those concerned. If, then, the original intention in acquiring the property is found to be to provide a home for the adult partners, there must be evidence that they have *agreed* to change the purpose to make it a home for themselves and their children subsequently if one partner wishes to rely on this as a reason for postponing sale.[166]

(b) Compensation for occupation

Where one party remains in occupation after the other has left (or been excluded), s 13 provides that the occupier may be required to pay, inter alia, for the outgoings and expenses on the property, and also to compensate the other for his or her loss of occupation (previously known as 'equitable accounting'). A court may make orders in relation to these matters under s 14, applying the criteria set out in s 15 (see earlier). Thus, in *Stack v*

---

[159] Law Com No 181 at para 12.9.   [160] [1980] 3 All ER 399, CA.

[161] [1980] 3 All ER 385, CA. See also *Chhokar v Chhokar* [1984] FLR 313 and *Dennis v McDonald* [1982] Fam 63, CA.

[162] But the precise scope of such purpose may be difficult to identify: see *Laird v Laird* [1999] 1 FLR 791, where the district judge and circuit judge on appeal differed in their assessment of what the parties had intended.

[163] *Re Buchanan-Wollaston's Conveyance* [1939] Ch 738 [1939] 2 All ER 302, CA; *Williams v Williams* [1976] Ch 278 [1977] 1 All ER 28, CA; *Re Evers' Trust* [1980] 3 All ER 399, CA; *Bernard v Josephs*, CA, earlier; *Chhokar v Chhokar*, earlier; *Abbey National plc v Moss* [1994] 1 FLR 307, CA.

[164] Section 12(2). See *Chan Pui Chun v Leung Kam Ho* [2003] 1 FLR 23.

[165] *Jones v Challenger* [1961] 1 QB 176CA. Cf *Bedson v Bedson* [1965] 2 QB 666, CA, where the wife had deserted her husband, and the property in question (a draper's shop with a flat over it) had been bought out of the husband's savings and was his sole livelihood, the sale was refused.

[166] According to Arden LJ in *W v W (Joinder of Trusts of Land Act and Children Act Applications)* [2003] EWCA Civ 924, [2004] 2 FLR 321 at paras [22]–[24]. For an example of the purpose of a trust changing to encompass the provision of a home for the wife and children, and hence requiring the postponement of sale for 10 years until the home was no longer needed for the children, see *F v F (S Intervening) (Financial Provision: Bankruptcy: Reviewable Disposition)* [2002] EWHC 2814 (Fam) [2003] 1 FLR 911.

Dowden,[167] the parties agreed (after the woman had initially taken exclusion proceedings against the man) that he would stay out of the property and that she would compensate him for this at the level of the rent he was paying. After this temporary agreement expired, they disputed how much compensation he should receive. The trial judge ordered the woman to pay £900 per month (the same figure that had previously been agreed), primarily because, as the occupier, she was in control of marketing it for sale and could therefore determine how long the man would be kept out of his money. The majority in the House of Lords agreed with the Court of Appeal that the man was not entitled to any payment, the House placing emphasis on the facts that the purpose of the trust had been to provide a home for the parties and their children, three of whom still remained at home; the man was not contributing to the outgoings; and he had agreed to leave.[168]

In *Jones v Kernott*,[169] where, it will be recalled, the parties had separated *ten years* before the litigation, the Supreme Court noted that, had the parties' beneficial interests remained equal, they could have cross-claimed against each other—the woman for payments due under the mortgage, which she had had to make, and the man for his housing costs, during that period. Lord Walker and Baroness Hale considered it quite likely that no occupation rent would be ordered, since the home had still been needed for the couple's children, and would be cancelled out by the man's liability to contribute to the mortgage. They commented that the exercise had wisely not been attempted, since it would have involved 'a quite disproportionate effort, both to discover the requisite figures (even supposing that they could be discovered) and to make the requisite calculations, let alone to determine what the ground rules should be.'

This suggests that courts may be reluctant to engage—or encourage the parties to engage—in the exercise, and that a rough and ready trade-off may be the preferred option,[170] which would be in keeping with the general message both to avoid the litigation in the first place, and to accept (in a joint names case at least) the presumption of equality as determining the issue, which so strongly permeates the current case-law.

4. PROTECTION OF BENEFICIAL INTERESTS

(a) Overriding interests

Although the Trusts of Land and Appointment of Trustees Act 1996 in some ways strengthens the beneficiary's right to be consulted before trustees can exercise any of their powers,[171] it does not obviate the problem that if the house is sold or mortgaged, the beneficiaries' equitable interests are overreached and a purchaser of a legal estate (including a legal mortgagee or chargee) is not bound by them even though he has notice of them, provided that he pays the proceeds of sale or other capital money to two or more trustees (or a trust corporation).[172] Hence, once the property is sold and the beneficial interests

---

[167] [2007] UKHL 17 [2007] 2 AC 432.

[168] Note that in *Dennis v McDonald* [1982] Fam 63, CA, it was held that where a co-owner voluntarily leaves the property, he or she is not entitled to any compensation by way of occupation rent.

[169] [2011] UKSC 53 [2012] 1 AC 776 at [50].

[170] Compare *Leake v Bruzzi* [1974] 2 All ER 1196, CA, where the interest element of the mortgage payment was regarded as equivalent to 'rent', and compensation was limited to payments equivalent to the capital portion. As many mortgages these days pay only the interest on the debt, the argument that one party's rent effectively balances out the mortgage cost is strengthened.   [171] Viz. by s 11 of the 1996 Act.

[172] Law of Property Act 1925 s 27(1) as amended by the Trusts of Land and Appointment of Trustees Act 1996 Sch 3, para 4(8). The TR1 form, discussed earlier, The primary importance of the documents of title (n 29) at p 126 is intended, in part, to alert a purchaser to the need to ensure a valid receipt can be given.

overreached, the beneficiaries cannot enforce any right of occupation or possession even though they were not parties to the conveyance. Similarly, if the property is mortgaged by two or more trustees, the beneficiaries' interest shifts onto the equity of redemption, and whilst they will be able to remain in possession so long as the mortgage remains in existence, they cannot enforce any right to do so if the mortgagee exercises his statutory right of sale. In *City of London Building Society v Flegg*[173] a husband, wife and the wife's parents agreed to buy a house in which all four could live. The property was conveyed to the husband and wife alone but the wife's parents, who had provided part of the purchase money, also had a beneficial interest. The husband and wife later mortgaged the property to the plaintiffs, who sought possession of the premises when the spouses became insolvent. It was held that, although the wife's parents had a right to occupy the premises against their son-in-law and daughter, they had none whatever against the building society which was protected by having paid the sum borrowed to the two trustees.

The same conclusion would be reached if the husband and another were joint legal tenants of the matrimonial home in which the wife had a beneficial interest either under an express trust or by virtue of a resulting or constructive trust. If the owners of the legal estate sold or mortgaged it, the wife's interest would be overreached and so unenforceable against the purchaser or mortgagee. A similar result would obtain in the case of cohabitants. In practice difficulty arises if the legal estate is vested in one partner only (say, the man) and the woman has a beneficial interest under a resulting or constructive trust. The man should appoint another trustee (who would normally be his partner) but in many cases this will not be done, and if the man sells or mortgages the house, the purchaser or mortgagee will deal with him alone. If the man acts without the knowledge or consent of the woman, can she enforce her rights against the new legal owner if he seeks possession of the premises or takes steps to realise his security?

If the legal title is registered under the Land Registration Act 2002, she may enter a restriction against the property.[174] In practice this may be of little use unless the wife or cohabitant seeks legal advice on the breakdown of her relationship before the man deals with the land. The woman is much more likely to be helped by the fact that her undivided share gives her an 'overriding interest'. In *Williams and Glyn's Bank Ltd v Boland*[175] the husband was registered as the sole proprietor of the legal estate of the matrimonial home, but the wife had contributed a substantial sum towards the purchase and was admittedly an equitable tenant in common to the extent of her contribution. The husband later executed a legal mortgage to the appellant bank, which made no enquiries of the wife. When the husband failed to pay the sum secured, the bank started proceedings for possession of the house with a view to selling it under their powers as mortgagees. The wife resisted the action on the ground that her interest took priority over the bank's by virtue of what was then s 20(1) of the Land Registration Act 1925. The House of Lords held that the wife's physical presence in the house coupled with the right to exclude others without a right to occupy clearly gave her actual occupation, and the fact that the husband (the owner of the legal estate) was also in actual occupation could not affect this. Furthermore, although the land was held on (what was then a) trust for sale, pending sale the wife had an interest subsisting in reference to the land itself. Her claim must therefore succeed.

---

[173] [1988] AC 54, HL. Some caution must be exercised when reading Lord Oliver's judgment, since some of his reasoning is based on the doctrine of conversion, which has since been abolished by the Trusts of Land and Appointment of Trustees Act 1996. Nevertheless, it seems clear that the decision survives the 1996 Act.

[174] Land Registration Act 2002 s 42. For the value of seeking a restriction order under s 46 of the Act, see S Carrigan 'Land Registration Act 2002, s 46: A Guided Missile' [2005] Fam Law 722. A spouse or civil partner with no beneficial interest could register her home rights by a notice against the property: Family Law Act 1996 s 31(10).   [175] [1981] AC 487, HL.

Williams and Glyn's Bank Ltd v Boland created a number of difficulties for prospective purchasers (and particularly prospective mortgagees).[176] First, what if a person moved into a property, thus taking up 'actual occupation', between the creation of a charge (such as a mortgage) and its registration? Schedule 3 para 2 to the Land Registration Act 2002 dealt with this issue by referring to an overriding interest belonging to the person in actual occupation 'at the time of the disposition', thus ensuring that the chargee will take priority.

A further problem arose concerning the meaning of 'actual occupation'. It should be given its ordinary meaning of possession or presence on the land: 'actual' indicates physical possession as distinct from legal possession by receipt of rents and profits.[177] The term is apparently not synonymous with 'reside':[178] a person can obviously occupy one property and reside in another, and he can occupy premises by an agent, eg a caretaker. The facts of *Lloyds Bank plc v Rosset*[179] illustrate the difficulties that can arise. The husband purchased a semi-derelict house, partly with the aid of a charge in favour of the appellant bank. The vendor let the husband and his wife into possession some six weeks before completion and the creation of the charge, and during this time the wife spent almost every day on the premises directing building work and doing some decorating herself, and she occasionally slept there. The majority of the Court of Appeal held that the presence of the builders (who were agents of both parties) coupled with that of the wife amounted to actual occupation by her because 'there was . . . physical presence on the property by the wife and her agent of the nature that one would expect of an occupier having regard to the then state of the property'.[180] Mustill LJ, dissenting on this point, thought that the tradesmen's presence would not indicate to an enquirer that a person with a claim adverse to the owner's was in occupation: they were working on the site rather than in occupation of it, and the wife's activities were more in keeping with preparing the house for occupation than with occupation itself.[181] This view certainly accords with that of the House of Lords in *Abbey National Building Society v Cann*,[182] where they held that the activities of the workmen laying carpets and carrying in furniture were no more than preparatory steps leading to the assumption of actual residential occupation later, and that consequently the respondent's mother could not be said to be in actual occupation of the house when the charge was created. Like possession, 'occupation' connotes some form of continuity rather than periodic visits and, it is submitted, should be unambiguous.

Schedule 3 para 2 to the 2002 Act provides that a relevant interest will override unless it is:

(b) an interest of a person of whom inquiry was made before the disposition and who failed to disclose the right when he could reasonably have been expected to do so; or
(c) an interest—
  (i) which belongs to a person whose occupation would not have been obvious on a reasonably careful inspection of the land at the time of the disposition, and
  (ii) of which the person to whom the disposition is made does not have actual knowledge at that time.

[176] See Law Com No 115 (*Implications of Williams and Glyn's Bank Ltd v Boland*) 1982; Law Com 188 (*Overreaching: Beneficiaries in Occupation*) 1989.
[177] Per Lord Wilberforce in *Williams and Glyn's Bank Ltd v Boland* [1981] AC 487 at 505.
[178] See *Lloyds Bank plc v Rosset* [1989] Ch 350, CA.
[179] [1989] Ch 350, CA. Having held that the wife acquired no beneficial interest (see earlier, 'Common intention' constructive trust, p 132), the House of Lords found it unnecessary to consider whether she was in actual occupation when the charge was created: [1991] 1 AC 107, HL.
[180] Per Nicholls LJ at 379.　　[181] At 398–9.　　[182] [1991] 1 AC 56, HL.

Sub-paragraph (b) replaces the old law which referred to enquiry being made of the person in occupation and their rights not being disclosed. Sub-paragraph (c), however, is intended to lessen the burden on those enquiring about title. It is not the person's interest that has to be obvious, but the occupation. The test is not one of constructive notice but the less demanding one of being obvious on a reasonably careful inspection of the land. However, even if the occupation is not apparent, the exception does not apply where the buyer has actual knowledge of the occupation.

(b) Unregistered land

If the land is unregistered, the position is more complex. A partner cannot register her interest under the Land Charges Act 1972.[183] The basic principle was summarised by Lord Oliver in *City of London Building Society v Flegg*:[184]

> The reason why a purchaser of the legal estate (whether by way of outright sale or by way of mortgage) from a single proprietor takes subject to the rights of the occupying spouse is . . . because, having constructive notice of the trust as a result of the beneficiary's occupation, he steps into the shoes of the vendor or mortgagor and takes the estate subject to the same equities as those to which it was subject in the latter's hands, those equities and their accompanying incidents not having been overreached by the sale . . .

This implies that anyone dealing with the land will be protected only by the general equitable doctrine that a bona fide purchaser of a legal estate for value will take it free of any equitable interest of which he does not have actual or constructive notice. Hence, if he takes an equitable interest (for example, if a bank takes an equitable charge from the husband), the partner must have priority. A purchaser of a legal estate will normally have constructive notice of the rights of any person in occupation of the land: this raises the question whether the fact that the spouse or cohabitant is residing in the house will itself be sufficient notice of their interest to give priority over the purchaser. In *Williams and Glyn's Bank Ltd v Boland* the House of Lords was obviously more concerned to protect the wife than the purchaser in such circumstances. In the words of Lord Wilberforce:[185]

> The extension of the risk area follows necessarily from the extension, beyond the paterfamilias, of rights of ownership, itself following from the diffusion of property and earning capacity. What is involved is a departure from an easy-going practice of dispensing with enquiries as to occupation beyond that of the vendor and accepting the risks of doing so. To substitute for this a practice of more careful enquiry as to the fact of occupation and, if necessary, as to the rights of occupiers cannot, in my view of the matter, be considered as unacceptable except at the price of overlooking the widespread development of shared interests in ownership.

(c) Consent to transaction by spouse or partner

If the wife or partner consents to the transaction—and a fortiori if she is a party to the conveyance of mortgage—she cannot argue that any interest she may have in the property takes priority over the purchaser's or mortgagee's. Furthermore, if she knows that the house can be bought only with the help of a loan and supports the husband's proposal that this would be

---

[183] Interests arising under a trust of land are expressly excluded from the definition of a general equitable charge: Land Charges Act 1972 s 2(4) (as amended). A spouse or civil partner with no beneficial interest could register home rights as a Class F land charge under s 2(7).   [184] [1988] AC 54 at 83, HL.
[185] [1981] AC 487, HL at 508–9.

secured by a mortgage, then, as the Court of Appeal held in *Bristol and West Building Society v Henning*,[186] it must have been the parties' common intention that the charge should take priority over both their beneficial interests. To secure his position the mortgagee may insist on the wife's being party to the charge, and this will in any event be necessary if the legal estate is vested in both spouses jointly. He runs an obvious risk, however, if he leaves the husband to procure the wife's signature to the instrument. In practice, this is most likely to occur if the husband seeks a secured loan or overdraft to finance a business venture and the only security he can offer is that of the matrimonial home.[187] If the husband knows that the wife may be unwilling to agree, he may resort to undue influence or misrepresentation to obtain her consent. The House of Lords laid down definitive guidance to lenders to deal with this situation and to avoid being bound by the wife's interest in *Royal Bank of Scotland v Etridge (No 2)*.[188] First, they held that a lender will be put on inquiry whenever one party to a personal relationship of which the lender is aware offers to stand surety for another's debts. The lender should insist on the prospective surety attending a private meeting with its representative, at which she will be told of the extent of her liability and risk, and urged to take independent legal advice. The lender is not obliged, itself, to provide such advice. The independent legal adviser must explain to the surety the purpose of her involvement and obtain her confirmation that she wishes him to act and advise her on the legal and practical implications of the proposed transaction. In advising the surety, the solicitor does not act as agent for the lender, which is entitled to proceed on the basis that the solicitor has given her proper advice. Where such steps are taken, the lender will be protected from any attempt to resist enforcement of the charge by the surety based on misrepresentation or undue influence.

If the purchaser or mortgagee takes a legal estate subject to the wife's beneficial interest, the transaction will still have the effect of granting him whatever beneficial interest the husband has.[189] But even if he finds himself saddled with the wife's interest, it does not follow that she will be able to stay in occupation indefinitely. The purchaser will be entitled to take proceedings for an order for sale: in deciding whether to order the property to be sold, the court must take into account the same facts as it would if the proceedings had been brought by the husband, in whose shoes the purchaser now stands. If the husband is insolvent, the court may enforce a sale in bankruptcy proceedings and leave the wife to claim her share of the proceeds.[190]

C. OCCUPATION

Legal and beneficial ownership of land carries with it a prima facie right of occupation. Furthermore, at common law a wife had a right to occupy the matrimonial home by virtue of

---

[186] [1985] 2 All ER 606, CA (unregistered land). See also *Paddington Building Society v Mendelsohn* (1985) 50 P & CR 244, CA (registered land); *Equity and Law Home Loans Ltd v Prestidge* [1992] 1 All ER 909, CA (replacement mortgage). Had the House of Lords found in *Abbey National Building Society v Cann*, that the respondent's mother had an overriding interest, they would have held that it would not have prevailed over the appellant's interest for the same reason.

[187] For an empirical study of this phenomenon, see B Fehlberg 'Money and Marriage: Sexually Transmitted Debt in England' (1997) 11 Int Jo of Law and Family 320.

[188] [2001] UKHL 44, [2002] 2 AC 773, discussed in Ch 4, Transactions between spouses, Undue influence, p XXX. The same principles apply whether the case is one of undue influence or misrepresentation: *Annulment Funding Company Ltd v Cowey* [2010] EWCA Civ 711.

[189] *Ahmed v Kendrick* [1988] 2 FLR 22, CA. In this case the husband and wife were joint tenants in law and equity. The husband sold the house to the defendant and forged the wife's signature on the transfer. It was held that, whilst this could not convey the legal estate, it severed the husband's joint tenancy in equity so that the spouses now held the property on trust for the wife and the defendant in equal shares.

[190] See later, Insolvency and the family home, p 158ff.

her right to her husband's consortium. This latter right has now become a statutory right for both spouses and civil partners, as provided for by the Family Law Act 1996.[191]

1. 'HOME RIGHTS'

It was at one time accepted as the duty of the spouses to live together as far as their circumstances would permit, and remedies are still available to a spouse who has been deserted.[192] In accordance with the view that the husband was the head of the household, the earlier opinion was that he had the right to determine where the matrimonial home was to be, and a judicial dictum to this effect is to be found as late as 1940.[193] Today, however, this, like other domestic matters of common concern, is something in which both spouses have a right to be heard and which they must settle by agreement,[194] or, failing that, ultimately by separation and divorce.

It is uncertain whether a duty to live together is imposed upon civil partners. Whereas a decree of judicial separation lifts the obligation from spouses[195] a separation order has no such stated effect in relation to civil partners.[196] Yet desertion and separation form bases for applications for divorce or dissolution[197] and for applications for financial support.[198] Given that there is no means of enforcing the obligation in a marriage there would seem to be no difference in practice in either case. The important dimension of the status of marriage or civil partnership is the right to occupy the family home which it brings with it.

(a) Background

If spouses are joint tenants in law or if both of them have a beneficial interest in the matrimonial home, each will prima facie be entitled to occupy it as owner, and have equal rights to stay in the property or seek to dispose of it. If the legal and equitable title is vested in the husband alone, the wife could claim a common law right of occupation by virtue of her right to her husband's consortium and her right to be maintained by him, which right would be primarily discharged by his providing her with a home.[199] However, in *National Provincial Bank Ltd v Ainsworth*[200] the House of Lords rejected a series of cases stemming from a decision by Lord Denning in 1952[201] which had created the so-called 'deserted wives' equity' under which it had been held that a deserted wife could assert her common law right to remain in the matrimonial home not only against her husband, but also against third parties. They ruled that, where the husband had left the wife and children in the matrimonial home, and then conveyed it to a company in which he had a controlling interest, which in turn charged the home to the appellant bank as security for a loan, the wife's interest in remaining in the home could not prevail against the creditors' interest in realising their security in the property.[202]

---

[191] As amended by s 82 and Sch 9 para 1 to the Civil Partnership Act 2004.

[192] See Ch 7, The respondent's desertion, p 218 and Ch 21, Applications under s 1, p 787.

[193] *Mansey v Mansey* [1940] P 139 at 140. See also *King v King* [1942] P 1 at 8.

[194] *Dunn v Dunn* [1949] P 98 at 103 at 823, CA.

[195] Matrimonial Causes Act 1973 s 18(1), discussed in Ch 7, Judicial separation in marriage, p 241.

[196] Civil Partnership Act 2004 ss 56, 57.

[197] Matrimonial Causes Act 1973 s 1(2); Civil Partnership Act 2004 s 44(5).

[198] Domestic Proceedings and Magistrates' Courts Act 1978 s 1 and Civil Partnership Act 2004 Sch 6 para 1.

[199] See *Price v Price* [1951] P 413 at 420–1, CA. Husbands had the same right where the wife was sole legal and equitable owner, arising from the wife's duty to cohabit with the husband: *Shipman v Shipman* [1924] 2 Ch 140, CA.

[200] [1965] AC 1175, HL.   [201] *Bendall v McWhirter* [1952] 2 QB 466.

[202] In many cases, the wife could have the sale set aside as a transaction intended to defeat her claim for financial relief in divorce proceedings (see Ch 23, Attempts to defeat claims for financial relief, p 918) but

The Matrimonial Homes Act 1967 was enacted to improve the position of such 'deserted wives' by clarifying what rights to occupy the home arise on marriage, and by providing a mechanism whereby third parties could be bound by spousal rights. The legislation, which laid down 'rights of occupation' was amended and consolidated,[203] and is now contained in Part IV of the Family Law Act 1996. This has in turn been amended by the Civil Partnership Act 2004 so that civil partners are treated in the same way as spouses. The amended provisions adopt slightly different terminology, now referring simply to 'home rights'.[204]

(b) The definition of 'home rights'

By s 30(1) and (2) of the 1996 Act, if:

(a) one spouse or civil partner ("A") is entitled to occupy a dwelling-house by virtue of—
  (i) a beneficial estate or interest or contract; or
  (ii) any enactment giving A the right to remain in occupation; and
(b) the other spouse[205] or civil partner ("B") is not so entitled,

. . .

B has the following rights ("home rights")—

(a) if in occupation, a right not to be evicted or excluded from the dwelling-house or any part of it by A except with the leave of the court given by an order under s 33;[206]
(b) if not in occupation, a right with the leave of the court so given to enter into and occupy the dwelling-house.

One spouse or civil partner entitled to occupy

Home rights only arise where one of the parties is entitled to occupy the dwelling-house. Such entitlement may be by virtue of a beneficial estate or interest, contractual right or a statutory right, and applies regardless of whether the party shares his interest with another person who is not the spouse.[207] Where entitlement depends upon an estate or interest, any right to possession conferred on a mortgagee under or by virtue of the mortgage, is disregarded.[208] A party who lives in a house because he is a lodger or domestic servant will have a contractual right to occupy, while a statutory tenant under the Rent Acts will have a statutory right.

---

the argument failed in *Ainsworth* as against the bank, because the bank was a bona fide purchaser for value without notice of the husband's intention.

[203] Matrimonial Homes Act 1983.

[204] See Civil Partnership Act 2004 s 82 and Sch 9, amending Family Law Act 1996 s 30 *et seq.*

[205] It may be necessary first to determine whether the parties are validly married (or registered in a civil partnership): *Ramsamy v Babar* [2003] EWCA Civ 1253 [2005] 1 FLR 113 (husband separated from first wife who was holding the home on trust for him claimed the second marriage was void and thus the second wife was not entitled to occupy the home under s 30. County court should have investigated the validity of the marriage to decide whether s 30 was applicable). The provisions apply even though one party is, or has been, married polygamously: s 63(5).

[206] See Ch 6, Occupation orders, Entitled applicants, p 184.

[207] *Abdullah v Westminster City Council* [2011] EWCA Civ 1171: husband and mother of wife held a joint tenancy of the home in which all lived—held it would be contrary to the objective of the statute and downright absurd, if the wife were to be denied the protection of the Act simply because her husband had taken the tenancy of the home jointly with another person who was not his spouse.

[208] Section 54(1)(2).

Other spouse or civil partner not entitled

Where the other party in fact has an equitable interest in the dwelling-house, he or she is to be treated as *not* having such an interest for the purpose of establishing home rights.[209] This enables him or her to take advantage of the protection offered by s 30 and s 31 in the event of a sale of the property by the entitled party.

Dwelling-house

Section 63 provides that 'dwelling-house' includes:

(a) any building, or part of a building which is occupied as a dwelling,[210]
(b) any caravan, house-boat or structure occupied as a dwelling,and any yard, garden, garage or outhouse belonging to it and occupied with it.[211]

The dwelling-house must have been, or been intended by the spouses to be, a matrimonial home of theirs (or, in the case of civil partners, a 'civil partnership home of theirs').[212] This means that where, for example, a property has been bought by one spouse, with the intention that it will be the matrimonial home, but the parties separate before they move into it, the non-entitled spouse may claim home rights in respect of it. Similarly, if one party has rented a property and then leaves, the other has the right to occupy even if the party's continuing entitlement stems from a newly-granted tenancy.[213]

If the couple live in a town house and have a country cottage, each property may be a dwelling-house in respect of which home rights may arise.[214] On the other hand, if the couple live in one home, and rent out another, never intending to live in it, home rights do not exist in respect of the rented-out property,[215] nor do they arise in respect of property acquired by one party for him- or herself to live in subsequent to their separation.

(c) The effect of having home rights

Where a spouse or civil partner has rights under s 30, he or she cannot be excluded from the dwelling-house by the other except by a court order[216] and, where not currently in occupation, may be given the right to enter by order. In either case, the order to be sought is an occupation order under s 33 of the Act, and the spouse or civil partner is an 'entitled applicant' for the purposes of that section.[217]

Where the party who is the owner or tenant etc leaves home and stops paying the mortgage, rent or other outgoings, the party with home rights has the right to keep up the payments in order to preserve his or her occupation and prevent the mortgagee or landlord from seeking possession.[218]

Where the property is held on a joint tenancy, any one of the tenants may serve a notice to quit in order to bring the contractual tenancy to an end before the term expires, but the

---

[209] Section 30(9).

[210] In *Kinzler v Kinzler* [1985] Fam Law 26, CA, it was held that the whole of a hotel owned by the parties, and not just their living quarters, was the matrimonial home, because there was only one front door and one kitchen.

[211] Para (b) does not apply where home rights are being asserted against third parties under s 31: s 63(4).

[212] Section 30(7).   [213] *Moore v Moore* [2004] EWCA Civ 1243 [2005] 1 FLR 666.

[214] But a party may only register rights against one home at a time: see later, Registration of home rights, p 155.   [215] See *Collins v Collins* (1973) 4 Fam Law 133, CA, for an example.

[216] '[T]he right is in essence a personal and non-assignable statutory right not to be evicted from the matrimonial home in question during marriage or until the court otherwise orders' per Megarry J in *Wroth v Tyler* [1974] Ch 30 at 46G.   [217] See Ch 6, Entitled applicants, p 184.

[218] Section 30(3)–(6).

consent of all is required to continue a periodic tenancy. Consequently if the couple are joint tenants and one of them indicates to the landlord that he or she does not intend to renew the tenancy at the end of the current period, the other will lose her or his protection on expiry of the tenancy.[219] The same position applies where the spouse or civil partner is a sole tenant who surrenders the lease.[220] However, pending actual termination, the spouse or partner retains her home rights as against the other partner, which may give her some short-term relief.[221]

(d) Registration of home rights

The main aim in enacting the original Matrimonial Homes Act 1967 was to strike a balance between protecting a non-entitled spouse from eviction and ensuring that those who *bona fide* acquired rights in the dwelling-house from her husband should not be prevented from enjoying those rights. The mechanism chosen to achieve this balance was by enabling, and requiring, the non-entitled spouse to register her rights as a charge on the dwelling-house where that was held by virtue of an estate or interest.

Section 31 of the 1996 Act provides that a spouse's or civil partner's home rights are a charge on the estate or interest.[222] To bind a third party, the charge *must* be registered.[223] In the case of registered land, this is done by means of a notice under the Land Registration Act 2002.[224] Where the title is unregistered, registration is achieved by means of a Class F land charge under the Land Charges Act 1972.[225] The charge will bind any person deriving title under the other spouse or civil partner, except that it will be void against any purchaser of the land or any interest in it for value if it is not registered before completion.[226] As a party out of occupation may need even greater protection than one physically in the house, her charge may be registered even though she has not yet been given leave by the court to enter and occupy.[227]

A spouse or civil partner is entitled to have only one charge registered at a time. Consequently, if the couple have two homes, she must decide against which one she will register her charge. If, after registering one, she registers another, the first registration must be cancelled.[228]

(e) Duration of home rights

Home rights will usually come to an end on the death of the other spouse or civil partner or on the dissolution or annulment of the marriage or civil partnership, unless the court has ordered that they should continue after the termination of the relationship (whether

---

[219] *Hammersmith and Fulham London Borough Council v Monk* [1992] 1 AC 478, HL. See Ch 6, Victim terminating tenancy, p 204. An alternative device may be to convert the tenancy into a sole one via a deed of release: *Burton v Camden London Borough Council* [1998] 1 FLR 681, CA.

[220] *Sanctuary Housing Assocation v Campbell* [1999] 2 FLR 383, CA.

[221] *Moore v Moore* [2004] EWCA Civ 1243 [2005] 1 FLR 666.

[222] Section 31(2), (3).

[223] But for discussion of the development of the doctrine of undue influence as a mechanism to protect a spouse's (or other intimate partner's) continuing occupation of the home against attempts by purchasers and creditors to obtain possession, see Ch 4, Undue influence, p 114.

[224] Section 31(10). Home rights are not capable of amounting to an overriding interest within para 2 of Schs 1 or 3 to the 2002 Act: s 31(10)(b).   [225] Section 2(7).

[226] Land Charges Act 1972 s 4(8); 'purchaser' includes a mortgagee, but in the usual situation where a property is purchased with the aid of a mortgage, the home rights charge is not protected by registration until after the mortgage is created, and hence the mortgagee takes priority.

[227] *Watts v Waller* [1973] QB 153, CA. If the party subsequently makes an unsuccessful application for such leave, the registration will be cancelled.   [228] Family Law Act 1996 Sch 4, para 2.

by death or a court order).[229] Rights will also come to an end if the owning party disposes of his estate or interest in the home, unless they have been registered and hence are binding upon the purchaser.[230] It may be advisable to seek an order extending rights beyond the termination of the marriage, as this may be the only way of protecting the spouse if the home cannot be made the subject of a property adjustment order.[231] However, where the object of registration is purely to freeze assets with a view to a financial remedies claim, the court may set the registration aside.[232] A court has also awarded damages to a purchaser where a wife registered her charge without informing her husband before he could complete a sale, thus preventing him from giving the purchaser vacant possession.[233]

2. OTHER FORMS OF PROTECTED OCCUPATION

What we are now concerned to discuss are other means by which rights of occupation may be acquired. This issue is of principal relevance to cohabiting couples, since if ownership is vested in one of them alone the other's right of occupation must be found by reference to the general law of property. In the following discussion we assume for the purpose of illustration that the couple are heterosexual and that the property is vested in the man but the position would be precisely the same for a same sex couple.

(a) Contractual licence

If the woman has given up some existing right or suffered some other detriment to go and live with the man, it may be possible to regard this as consideration and thus give the woman a contractual licence. In *Tanner v Tanner*,[234] for example, the plaintiff bought a house for the defendant and their twin daughters and the defendant surrendered a rent-controlled tenancy to move into it. When the plaintiff later claimed possession of the house, it was held that, as the defendant had furnished consideration by giving up the security of her flat, the licence was a contractual one.

The facts of *Tanner* were unusual in that the parties never lived in the house together. The problem more likely to arise is that facing a woman who, having set up home with a man in property belonging to him, is required to leave when their relationship breaks down. Even if she suffered a detriment, for example by giving up a secure tenancy like the defendant in *Tanner*, it would usually be impossible to spell out any promise by the man that she could continue to reside in the house if he no longer wished to live with her. Any such undertaking is more likely to be given at the point of breakdown if the man leaves, but unless the woman suffers some fresh detriment (such as a reciprocal undertaking to pay rent or other outgoings), any consideration would be past and therefore ineffective to establish a contract.

Even if it is possible to spell out a contractual licence, it may well be difficult to infer the period for which the parties intended that the woman should be entitled to stay in the premises. In *Tanner v Tanner* the Court of Appeal took the view that the defendant had a licence to remain in the house so long as the parties' children were of school age and it was reasonably required as a home for them and their mother. There was necessarily

---

[229] Section 33(5).
[230] See earlier. But see *Moore v Moore* [2004] EWCA Civ 1243, [2005] 1 FLR 666: entitlement to occupy continued during the notice period, and should the entitled spouse have entered into a new lease on the property, the other spouse would have continued to be able to exercise her rights.
[231] See Ch 22, Transfer and settlement of property, p 845.
[232] *Barnett v Hassett* [1981] 1 WLR 1385.   [233] *Wroth v Tyler* [1974] Ch 30.
[234] [1975] 3 All ER 776, CA. Cf *Horrocks v Forray* [1976] 1 All ER 737, CA.

something arbitrary about terminating the licence when the children reached the age of 16 because they might continue in full-time education after that, but it was reasonable to imply that it should cease, say, if their mother married. The woman is likely to be less favourably treated if the children of the owner of the property are not living with her. In *Chandler v Kerley*[235] the defendant and her husband had sold their former matrimonial home to the plaintiff on the understanding that the defendant (who proposed to marry the plaintiff after her divorce) would continue to live there with him and the two children of her marriage. The relationship between the parties broke down very shortly afterwards and the plaintiff sought possession of the house. The Court of Appeal held that he could not have intended to assume the burden of housing the defendant and another man's children indefinitely, and that the licence was terminable on her being given 12 months' notice, which would enable her to find other accommodation.

(b) Licence by estoppel

By analogy with proprietary estoppel, one party may claim a licence if the other has led her to believe (or has acquiesced in her belief) that she has, or will be given, permission to remain in the house and she acts to her detriment in reliance on this belief. The extent of the resulting equity is to make good the expectations which the owner has encouraged, insofar as fairness between the parties permits this to be done.[236] As in other cases of proprietary estoppel, it must be shown that the woman acted in reliance on the belief that she was to have a licence; the fact that she goes to live with the owner of the property and permits herself to become pregnant will not of itself give her any right to remain there.[237]

(c) Rights against third persons

Even where the owner of the parties' home or former home cannot evict the other party, the latter's position may become precarious if the former dies or disposes of the property.

If the occupant holds under a trust, a purchaser will be bound by her right of occupation in the same circumstances as he would be bound by a beneficial interest in the property itself, and her presence there may give him notice of her rights.[238] In particular, a volunteer (for example, a devisee of the home) will take subject to them. A contractual licence, on the other hand, confers only a personal right on the licensee.[239] Consequently, a cohabitant who has such a licence could enforce it against the other party's personal representatives, who are bound by his contractual obligations,[240] but not against a purchaser (even though he took with notice of it) unless the circumstances of the purchase make him a constructive trustee. A constructive trust will not be imposed in reliance on slender material:[241] the purchaser must have behaved in such a way as to make it unconscionable to permit him to deny the occupant's rights, for example by giving an express assurance

---

[235] [1978] 2 All ER 942, CA. It is not clear what the consideration for the licence was: presumably it was the defendant's taking less than half the proceeds of sale because she was to continue to live in the house.

[236] See *Greasley v Cook* [1980] 3 All ER 710, CA: defendant worked as housemaid for a family, and then cohabited with one of the sons for nearly 30 years. She looked after the family as a whole and in particular cared for the daughter who was mentally ill. She received no payment and asked for none because the members of the family had led her to believe that she would be entitled to remain in the house as long as she wished. In those circumstances, it was held that she should be able to do so and the plaintiffs' action for possession failed.   [237] *Coombes v Smith* [1986] 1 WLR 808.

[238] See earlier, Overriding interests, p 147.   [239] *Ashburn Anstalt v Arnold* [1989] Ch 1, CA.

[240] This was apparently assumed in *Horrocks v Forray* [1976] 1 All ER 737, CA, although the executor's claim for possession succeeded because it was held that the defendant did not have a contractual licence.

[241] *Ashburn Anstalt v Arnold*, above, at 26.

that they would be respected,[242] or paying a lower price because the land was subject to them.[243] The threat of litigation may be sufficient to deter a prospective purchaser, but a vendor anxious to dispose of the property at the highest price is unlikely to impose terms which would create a trust. A licence by estoppel may put the occupant in a stronger position, because an equity by estoppel is capable of binding successors in title.[244]

D. INSOLVENCY AND THE FAMILY HOME

1. MORTGAGES AND CHARGES

If the sole legal owner of the family home mortgages it and later fails to pay the mortgage instalments, the mortgagee may wish to obtain vacant possession in order to realise his security. Even though the mortgagor has no defence to the claim, his or her spouse or partner may be protected if she or he did not concur in the mortgage, in which case of course the mortgagor will be able to remain in occupation as well. For the purpose of illustration it will be assumed that legal ownership is vested in the husband or male cohabitant.

We have already considered the circumstances in which a mortgagee will take subject to any beneficial interest which the wife or partner has in the property.[245] If that interest takes priority over a mortgage, the mortgagee, as a person interested, may bring proceedings to enforce the trust of land under the Trusts of Land and Appointment of Trustees Act 1996 s 14. On principle, the mortgagee should have no greater right than the husband or partner. Hence, it could be argued that if the wife (or partner) and children are occupying the house as the family home, the primary object of the trust will still be in existence and the court should not order a sale. But in *Bank of Ireland Home Mortgages Ltd v Bell and Bell*,[246] it was held that a powerful consideration for the court to take into account is whether the creditor is receiving proper recompense for being kept out of his money, for which repayment is overdue. Thus, where the husband left the wife soon after executing a charge on the matrimonial home, and where no payments of capital or interest were received by the lender for several years and the debt was now some £300,000, the first instance judge had been wrong to refuse to order a sale because he considered that the wife and her son were still fulfilling the purpose of the trust in living there. Moreover, the wife's ill health, according to the Court of Appeal, was a factor relevant to determining *when* the sale should take place, but not *whether* it should do so.[247]

If the mortgagee is aware of the spouse's or partner's rights, he will insist on her agreeing that the charge should take priority over them, and it would be prudent for him to give himself the maximum protection by insisting on her concurring in the mortgage in any event. Even if she does so, a wife or civil partner (as distinct from an unmarried cohabitant) is still given a degree of protection by the Family Law Act 1996. This provides that, if a spouse or civil partner entitled under the Act to occupy the whole or part of the home makes any payment or tender in respect of rent, mortgage payments or other outgoings

---

[242] As in *Lyus v Prowsa Developments Ltd* [1982] 2 All ER 953. The fact that the land is transferred expressly subject to the occupant's rights does not of itself create a constructive trust, because this merely gives the transferee notice of their existence.   [243] As in *Binions v Evans* [1972] Ch 359, CA.

[244] Land Registration Act 2002 s 116.

[245] See earlier, Overriding interests, p 147.   [246] [2001] 2 FLR 809, CA.

[247] See also *First National Bank plc v Achampong* [2003] EWCA Civ 487 [2004] 1 FCR 18; *Putnam & Sons v Taylor* [2009] EWHC 317 (Ch) [2009] BPIR 769.

affecting the home, this shall be as effective as though it were made by the owner.[248] If the mortgagee brings proceedings to enforce his security, the court may stay or suspend the execution of any order made, if the mortgagor is likely to be able to pay all sums due within a reasonable time.[249] The wife or civil partner is given further protection by the requirement that the mortgagee must serve her with notice of proceedings if her right of occupation is registered; in any event she is generally entitled to be made a party if the court is satisfied that she may be expected to make such payments (or do anything else in satisfaction of the mortgagor's obligations) as might affect the outcome of the proceedings.[250] The difficulty is that the mortgagee is not bound to give her notice of the husband's default. As a result, such massive arrears may have accumulated before she gets to hear of them that she will find it impossible to pay them off within a reasonable time, even though she might have been able to pay each instalment as it fell due.

The provisions mentioned in the last paragraph do not apply to an unmarried cohabitant, whose only hope of preserving her right would be to seek an agreement with the mortgagee that she should pay off the arrears.

2. BANKRUPTCY

If the family home forms part of the assets of a bankrupt, his interest in it will vest in the trustee in bankruptcy immediately his appointment takes effect. Hence, if the bankrupt and his (or her) spouse or partner are tenants in common,[251] the latter will retain her equitable share which will not be available for the other's creditors. Consequently, in bankruptcy the parties' interests in property will be of paramount importance.

(a) Voidable transactions

The trustee may wish to have the spouse's or cohabitant's interest set aside under s 339 or s 423 of the Insolvency Act 1986, the details of which have already been discussed.[252] Homes recently purchased may well be caught by s 339. If within the period of two years preceding the presentation of the bankruptcy petition the man had bought the family home with his own money and had it conveyed into the partners' joint names as equitable beneficial owners, the trustee may claim the spouse's or cohabitant's beneficial interest as one obtained in a transaction at an undervalue. The same result would follow if the partner had contributed significantly less than the value of her equitable share or, in similar circumstances, if the house had been purchased more than two years but less than five years before the petition and the purchaser was then insolvent.

(b) Protection of members of the bankrupt's family

Whether the bankrupt (who, for the sake of example, will be assumed to be the husband) is the sole beneficial owner of the matrimonial home or has a limited beneficial interest, the trustee in bankruptcy will normally wish to sell it to increase the assets available for the creditors. This will bring their interests into direct conflict with those of the members of the bankrupt's family who wish to retain the property as a family home.

---

[248] Section 30(3).

[249] Administration of Justice Act 1973 s 8; *Halifax Building Society v Clark* [1973] 2 All ER 33, CA; *Governor & Co of the Bank of Scotland v Grimes* [1985] 2 All ER 254, CA.

[250] Family Law Act 1996 ss 55–6. The right extends to those other than spouses or civil partners, who have an occupation order in their favour: Family Law Act 1996 Sch 8, paras 53, 59.

[251] If they are equitable joint tenants, the joint tenancy will be severed when the property vests in the trustee, and the trustee and the other party will become equitable tenants in common in equal shares.

[252] See Ch 4, Voidable transactions, p 116.

Rights of the bankrupt's spouse

Section 336 of the Insolvency Act 1986 protects the occupation rights of the bankrupt's spouse. No home right under Part IV of the Family Law Act 1996 may be acquired in the period between the presentation of the petition and vesting of the bankrupt's property in the trustee, so that if the bankrupt marries during that period his spouse will have no statutory rights. But existing rights of occupation under the Act will continue in force and bind the trustee, whether or not they are registered. The trustee has the same power to apply to the court to have these rights terminated, suspended or restricted as the husband would have had.[253] It will be observed that these provisions do not apply to an unmarried cohabitant.

The rights of children

Children (whether or not they are related to the bankrupt) are given protection by s 337, which applies when the bankrupt is entitled to occupy a dwelling house[254] by virtue of any estate or interest. If any person under the age of 18, who had his home with the bankrupt both when the bankruptcy petition was presented and when the bankruptcy order was made, had at any time occupied that house with the bankrupt, the bankrupt has the same right of occupation against the trustee as a spouse under the Family Law Act 1996 and cannot be evicted from the house without the leave of the court.[255] This protection is additional to that given by s 336 and is of importance if the children are living with the bankrupt but not with his wife (e.g. because she is dead or the spouses are divorced), or if the mother is living with the bankrupt but is not married to him.

  If the bankrupt and his spouse or former spouse are trustees of land or the beneficial owners of a dwelling house, the trustee in bankruptcy may apply to the court for an order to sell the property under s 14 of the Trusts of Land and Appointment of Trustees Act 1996. Alternatively, he may apply to have the occupation rights of the bankrupt's spouse or former spouse terminated. In either case, the court must make such order as it thinks just and reasonable, having regard to the interests of the creditors, to the conduct of the spouse or former spouse so far as contributing to the bankruptcy, to the needs and financial resources of [that person], to the needs of any children and to all the circumstances of the case other than the needs of the bankrupt.[256]

The bankrupt

If the application is made to terminate the bankrupt's own rights of occupation given by s 337, regard must similarly be had to 'the interests of the creditors, the bankrupt's financial resources, the needs of the children and all the circumstances of the case other than the needs of the bankrupt'.[257] The court may make any order that it could make under Part IV of the Family Law Act 1996 and so could permit the bankrupt to remain in occupation if he paid an occupation rent or other outgoing.[258]

---

[253] Insolvency Act 1986 s 336(1)–(2), as amended.

[254] This is defined as in the Family Law Act 1996: see earlier, Dwelling-house, p 154; Insolvency Act 1986, s 385(1).

[255] Insolvency Act 1986, s 337(1)–(4). Note that the children need not be the bankrupt's own children.

[256] Insolvency Act 1986 s 335A and s 336(4), added by the Trusts of Land and Appointment of Trustees Act 1996 Sch 3, para 23.

[257] Insolvency Act 1986 s 337(5). It has been held at first instance that the same factors must be considered where the proceedings are to enforce a charging order: *Close Invoice Finance Ltd v Pile* [2008] EWHC 1580 (Ch) [2009] 1 FLR 873: *Pickering v Wells* [2002] 2 FLR 797 not followed.

[258] The payment of outgoings will not give him any proprietary interest in the property: Insolvency Act 1986, s 338.

12 months' grace period

If the application is made more than a year after the property vested in the trustee, it is to be assumed that the creditors' interests outweigh all other considerations, unless the circumstances are exceptional.[259] In *Barca v Mears*[260] it was doubted whether the requirement to show that the circumstances are exceptional is compatible with the ECHR, but the matter did not fall for resolution on the facts. However, in *The Official Receiver for Northern Ireland v Rooney and Paulson*[261] the court considered that a *twelve year* delay in taking proceedings for possession, during which the bankrupts' spouses had spent money on improving the properties, was a disproportionate interference with the wives' Art 8 rights. It concluded that 'little more than a nod' had been accorded to the effect of the Human Rights Act on the question of how 'exceptional circumstances' should be understood, and in so holding, was clear that human rights issues *must* be taken into account. However, in *Foyle v Turner*[262] it was held that Art 8 did not require any modification to the traditional approach. Section 283A of the Insolvency Act 1986 now gives the trustee in bankruptcy three years from the commencement of the bankruptcy in which to decide whether to realise any interest of the bankrupt in a dwelling-house which was his sole or principal residence. If the trustee fails to take any steps, the dwelling-house in question re-vests automatically in the bankrupt.

Insolvency practitioners will generally delay making any application under either section for a year so as to be able to take advantage of the presumption in favour of making an order after that time. This will effectively give the bankrupt and his spouse or partner a year in which to find other accommodation. The fact that the family will be rendered homeless is an inevitable consequence of the sale and is not exceptional;[263] although the bankrupt or his wife would not usually be ordered to surrender possession until they had had reasonable time to make other arrangements.[264] Examples of the court finding exceptional circumstances include cases of ill-health, such as *Judd v Brown*,[265] in which the bankrupt's wife had had recent major surgery for cancer and was about to undergo extensive chemotherapy treatment. There, a sale was refused. It is more common to find the court *postponing* sale for an appropriate period of time.[266] Sale may also be postponed to enable the spouse to take negligence proceedings against her legal advisers in respect of their advice to her regarding the property.[267] It has, by contrast, been held not to amount to exceptional circumstances that the value of the bankrupt's share of the property will be exceeded by the debt owed, or the expenses incurred in the bankruptcy proceedings.[268] It is suggested that the circumstances pertaining in a case under the earlier law,

---

[259] Insolvency Act 1986, s 335A(3), s 336(5) and s 337(6).

[260] [2004] EWHC 2170 (Ch) [2005] 2 FLR 1.

[261] [2008] NICh 22 [2009] 2 FLR 1437. Cf *Turner v Avis and Avis* [2009] 1 FLR 74 where a 15 year delay was not regarded as exceptional.   [262] [2007] BPIR 43.

[263] *Re Lowrie* [1981] 3 All ER 353 at 356, CA.

[264] *Barclays Bank plc v Hendricks; Re Turner* [1975] 1 All ER 5; *Re McCarthy* [1975] 2 All ER 857. But immediate possession might be given to the trustee eg if the spouse was being obstructive: *Re McCarthy* at 859.

[265] *Judd v Brown, Bankrupts (Nos 9587 and 9588 of 1994)* [1998] 2 FLR 360. This decision was not affected by a successful appeal in respect of other properties involved: *Judd v Brown* [1999] 1 FLR 1191, CA.

[266] See eg *Re Bremner (A Bankrupt)* [1999] 1 FLR 912—home not to be put up for sale until three months after the death of the bankrupt (aged 79 and in poor health; sale postponed to enable his wife to care for him); *Claughton v Charalambous* [1999] 1 FLR 740—sale suspended so long as the wife, who was aged 60 and had reduced life expectancy due to renal failure, continued to live in the property, which had been fitted with a stair-lift.

[267] *Re Gorman (A Bankrupt) ex parte the Trustee of the Bankrupt v The Bankrupt and Another* [1990] 2 FLR 284; cf *Trustee of the Estate of Eric Bowe (A Bankrupt) v Bowe* [1998] 2 FLR 439.

[268] *Re Ng (A Bankrupt), Trustee of the Estate of Ng v Ng* [1998] 2 FLR 386; *Trustee of the Estate of Eric Bowe (A Bankrupt) v Bowe.*

Re Holliday[269] should still be classed as falling within the 'exceptional' category. The husband and wife were beneficial joint tenants of the matrimonial home. The husband presented a petition in his own bankruptcy to frustrate the wife's application for a property transfer order in divorce proceedings, and there was no evidence that any of his creditors would have petitioned. If an immediate sale had been ordered, the wife was unlikely to have been able to find alternative accommodation for herself and her three children in the neighbourhood, so that their education would have been upset, and in the particular circumstances of the case a postponement would not have worked undue hardship on the creditors. The Court of Appeal held that in these exceptional circumstances 'the voice of the wife seeking to preserve a home for herself and the children ought in equity to prevail' and ordered that the house should not be sold for five years.

However, in the more usual type of case, it will be rare for creditors not to be prejudiced by a delay in the sale of more than a few months; consequently, if the trustee applies for an order after the first year, the court is likely to order an immediate sale unless the welfare of the children makes it imperative that they should stay in the matrimonial home, eg because they have reached a critical stage in their education or have a disability.[270]

E. REFORM

While the law relating to the family home has been the subject of statutory reform in relation to occupation, and the position on insolvency, the problem of devising a workable and fair system governing ownership remains elusive. The issue was referred to the Law Commission for review in 1995 and they published a Discussion Paper on the issue in 2002.[271] They identified the following key problems with the current law:[272]

(i)   the search for the parties' common intention can be an unrealistic exercise yet much depends upon the court's conclusion as to what that common intention was;

(ii) the line between which types of contributions will, and will not, count towards the acquisition of an interest in the property is not clear;

(iii) extensive work in and around the home, which may include looking after the children of a relationship, appears not to 'count' in giving rise to an interest;

(iv) quantifying the share may be extremely difficult and has led to decisions which are inconsistent and difficult to reconcile;

(v)   the uncertainty of the law can lead to lengthy and costly litigation.

The Law Commission sought to produce a scheme which (a) would not depend upon the nature of the relationship between the claimant and the owner—thus, they sought to include not only cohabiting partners, but also relatives such as an adult child living with parents or two siblings sharing a home, or indeed any combination of 'home sharers'; and (b) would be based on contributions to the shared home, and not on the parties' intentions (save in the case of an express declaration of trust). They considered that a contribution-based scheme would have the advantages of certainty and predictability as it would be possible to value contributions objectively and there would be no need to rely

---

[269] [1981] Ch 405, CA.

[270] See *Re Haghighat (A Bankrupt)* [2009] EWHC 90 (Ch) [2009] 1 FLR 1271: child had severe disabilities and alternative suitable accommodation not available, sale postponed for three years.

[271] Law Commission, *Sharing Homes: A Discussion Paper* (2002).

[272] Law Commission, *Sharing Homes: A Discussion Paper* (2002) Executive Summary para 7 and Report paras 2.105–2.112.

on vaguely remembered, or imputed, agreements. Ignoring the nature of the parties' relationship was intended to ensure that the scheme could operate without discrimination between different classes of relationship.

However, they found themselves unable to arrive at a workable set of proposals. In particular, they could not produce a scheme which would result in a fair outcome based on contributions alone, without taking account of the different nature of the relationships between different sorts of parties, but they considered that the policy implications of a scheme which would only apply, say, to cohabitants, would take the project beyond the remit of a law reform body and lay properly with Government instead. They therefore confined themselves to urging legal advisers to encourage parties to make express written arrangements setting out what they intend their rights to be, most often by means of a declaration of trust; of course, this does not assist the situation where one party joins another in a home that has already been acquired and where it is most unlikely that the parties will think that they need to consult a lawyer. The Law Commission accordingly urged the courts to adopt greater flexibility in recognising an indirect contribution to the mortgage (by means of paying the household bills and thereby enabling the other party to pay the mortgage instalments) but they stopped short of recommending that the courts take account of non-financial contributions such as caring for the home and family.

It is this failure to produce reform which could be implemented through legislation which has made the rulings of the highest courts in *Stack v Dowden*[273] and *Jones v Kernott*[274] so important, because there is no other means of keeping the law in step with social change. An earlier attempt[275] to recommend automatic co-ownership of the matrimonial home received no political support, and there is still no scope nor appetite for introducing into English law a 'matrimonial property regime' along the lines of those common in civil law systems whereby specified property (which might apply to everything the parties bring into, or acquire during, the marriage, or be limited to the home) is automatically co-owned. Spouses (and civil partners) will usually be catered for through the courts' adjustive powers when their relationship breaks down, so that the matter is not so pressing for them. However, tackling the law as it applies to cohabitants has become bound up in the political issue of whether improving their rights would 'undermine' marriage. We discuss the proposals that the Law Commission has made to tackle this problem in Ch 24[276] after we have examined financial remedies on divorce and dissolution so that a proper evaluation can be made. For now, it can be noted that the Government has attempted to address the high level of public ignorance as to the lack of rights accorded to cohabitants,[277] through the provision of internet publicity and information in the hope of encouraging such partners to take specific legal advice to protect themselves.[278]

---

[273] [2007] UKHL 17 [2007] 2 AC 432.   [274] [2011] UKSC 53 [2012] 1 AC 776.

[275] Law Commission, *Third Report on Family Property: The Matrimonial Home (Co-Ownership and Occupation Rights) and Household Goods* Law Com No 86 (1978).

[276] At Reform proposals by the Law Commission, p 952.

[277] See in particular, A Barlow et al 'Just a piece of paper? Marriage and cohabitation in Britain' in A Park et al *British Social Attitudes: The 18th report* (2001) and 'Cohabitation and the law: myths, money and the media' in A Park et al *British Social Attitudes: The 24th report* (2008); G Douglas et al *A Failure of Trust: Resolving Property Disputes on Cohabitation Breakdown* (2007).

[278] See http://www.advicenow.org.uk/living-together/ (accessed 20 April 2014) and A Barlow et al *The Living Together Campaign: an investigation of its impact on legally aware cohabitants* (2007). For the view that modern social conditions may not be so adverse to the average cohabiting woman as might be thought from 'hard cases' such as *Burns v Burns* [1984] Ch 317, CA, see R Probert 'Trusts and the Modern Woman—Establishing an Interest in the Family Home' [2001] CFLQ 275 but cf G Douglas et al *A Failure of Trust: Resolving Property Disputes on Cohabitation Breakdown* (2007).

6

DOMESTIC VIOLENCE
AND ABUSE

A. INTRODUCTION

1. THE DEFINITION OF DOMESTIC VIOLENCE AND ABUSE

This chapter deals with the legal responses to a variety of forms of personal behaviour within the domestic sphere which may amount to physical or emotional abuse. 'Domestic violence' is a term that can be criticised, as it appears to signify a concern purely with violent behaviour.[1] It is now therefore common to refer to both domestic violence and *abuse*. The range of behaviour encompassed within the term, and the range of relationships which ought to be classed as 'domestic', have gradually been widened as understanding of the nature and scope of such abuse has grown. Following public consultation, the Government introduced a new definition of domestic violence and abuse in 2013 to be 'used by Government departments to inform policy development and . . . the police, the Crown Prosecution Service (CPS) and the UK Border Agency to inform the identification of domestic violence cases'[2] (but not as a legal definition). It is defined as:

> Any incident or pattern of incidents of controlling, coercive or threatening behaviour, violence or abuse between those aged 16 or over who are or have been intimate partners or family members regardless of gender or sexuality.
>
> This can encompass, but is not limited to, the following types of abuse:
>
> - psychological
> - physical
> - sexual
> - financial
> - emotional
>
> 'Controlling behaviour' is: a range of acts designed to make a person subordinate and/or dependent by isolating them from sources of support, exploiting their resources and capacities for personal gain, depriving them of the means needed for independence, resistance and escape and regulating their everyday behaviour.
>
> 'Coercive behaviour' is: an act or a pattern of acts of assault, threats, humiliation and intimidation or other abuse that is used to harm, punish, or frighten their victim.[3]

---

[1] See L Smith *Domestic Violence: an overview of the literature* Home Office Research Study No 107 (1989) ch 1.

[2] Home Office *Cross-Government Definition of Domestic Violence: A Consultation* (2011) p 6.

[3] Home Office, https://www.gov.uk/government/news/new-definition-of-domestic-violence-and-abuse-to-include-16-and-17-year-olds (accessed 20 April 2014). It does not help that this 'definition' appears in slightly different forms in different Government online publications, but this appears to be the most comprehensive version.

The definition includes so called 'honour' based violence, female genital mutilation (FGM) and forced marriage.[4]

The range of legal mechanisms used to control the perpetrator's behaviour and provide effective protection for the victim may go well beyond the traditional criminal responses normally associated with the terms 'violence' or 'abuse'. In particular, the use of the civil law, to control personal behaviour or the occupation of the family home, or the use of public law through the provision of alternative accommodation for the family or individual family members, have been seen as being potentially more helpful to victims than reliance on penal sanctions. However, this approach has been challenged in recent years, with a renewed emphasis in Government policy on viewing domestic abuse as a criminal matter.

2. THE SCALE OF DOMESTIC ABUSE

It is difficult to estimate the scale of domestic violence or abuse with any confidence. The Home Office state that:

> Each year, over 1 million women suffer domestic abuse, over 300,000 women are sexually assaulted, 60,000 women raped and thousands more stalked. These crimes are often hidden away behind closed doors, with the victim suffering in silence.
>
> Fewer than 1 in 4 people who suffer abuse at the hands of their partner – and only around 1 in 10 women who experience serious sexual assault – report it to the police.[5]

Thirty per cent of domestic violence is estimated to start during a woman's pregnancy, and where there is a history of violence, it often escalates during it.[6] The period after a couple have separated is a particularly vulnerable time for women, with 22% of separated women reporting having been assaulted in the previous year.[7] Around two women per week are killed by their partners or ex-partners in the UK, and around 42% of the total number of murdered women, are killed by a partner or ex-partner.[8] Yet non-reporting of domestic violence is a particular problem: it has been estimated that the average victim will undergo 35 or more assaults, over a seven-year period, before approaching the police or another domestic violence agency, for help.[9]

[4] For the range of behaviour and criminal offences which may be involved, see Crown Prosecution Service *Policy for Prosecuting Cases of Domestic Violence* (2009) Annex A http://www.cps.gov.uk/publica tions/prosecution/domestic/domv.html#a02 (accessed 20 April 2014).

[5] Home Office, https://www.gov.uk/government/policies/ending-violence-against-women-and-girls-in-the-uk (accessed on 20 April 2014). See also the speech by the Director of Public Prosecutions, Keir Starmer QC 'Domestic Violence: the facts, the issues, the future' (2011) http://www.cps.gov.uk/news/articles/domes-tic_violence_-_the_facts_the_issues_the_future/ (accessed 20 April 2014).

[6] Home Office *Safety and Justice: The Government's Proposals on Domestic Violence* (2003) Cm 5487, para 23.

[7] C Mirrlees-Black and C Byron *Domestic Violence: Findings from the BCS Self-Completion Questionnaire: Research Findings No 86* (1999) Home Office Research, Development and Statistics Directorate. See also C Humphreys and R Thiara 'Neither justice nor protection: women's experiences of post-separation violence' (2003) 25 JSWFL 195.

[8] C Flood-Page and J Taylor (eds) *Crime in England and Wales 2001/2002: Supplementary Volume* (2003) (Home Office) p 12.

[9] T Hall and S Wright *Making it count: A practical guide to collecting and managing domestic violence data* (2003) (NACRO).

3. HISTORICAL DEVELOPMENTS

Violence in the home is a phenomenon long recognised by legal commentators. Although Sir Matthew Hale had denied that a husband had a legal power to administer corporal punishment to his wife,[10] it was stated in Bacon's *Abridgment* in 1736 that a husband might beat his wife (but not in a violent or cruel manner) and confine her.[11] Blackstone, writing some 30 years later, maintained that, whilst the practice had become obsolete in polite society, 'the lower rank of people, who were always fond of the old common law, still claim and exert their ancient privilege'.[12] Little was heard of the problem for another century until Parliament intervened in 1878 following a campaign drawing attention to the brutal treatment of many working-class women.[13] The Matrimonial Causes Act 1878 gave a criminal court, before which a man was convicted of aggravated assault on his wife, the power to make a separation and maintenance order in her favour and to vest in her the legal custody of the children of the marriage under the age of 10 years if it felt that her future safety was in peril.[14]

Almost another 100 years passed before the question again became one of public concern. Publicity was generated by the setting up of women's refuges[15] to which women and their children could flee from violence, and the feminist movement lobbied for action. A House of Commons Select Committee heavily criticised the effectiveness of the existing remedies open to women who were the victims of violence at the hands of their husbands or the men with whom they were cohabiting.[16] At that time, remedies were limited to taking criminal proceedings or to pursuing civil actions (eg for damages in tort for a battery, or to assert a property right in the home), and seeking to have an injunction attached, under which the respondent was prohibited from 'molesting, assaulting or otherwise interfering with' the applicant and/or any children. It was also possible during the course of divorce or other matrimonial or family proceedings between the parties, to apply for an injunction to require a party to leave the matrimonial home or let the applicant back in. However, it was considered that it was unduly burdensome to require an applicant to take substantive proceedings when she really only wanted the injunction, and accordingly it was provided in the Domestic Violence and Matrimonial Proceedings Act 1976 that a spouse or cohabitant could seek a non-molestation or ouster injunction from the county court without having to take any other proceedings. Magistrates were subsequently given similar powers by the Domestic Proceedings and Magistrates' Courts Act 1978 to make 'personal protection' and 'exclusion orders', although only in respect of physical violence inflicted by a spouse.[17]

Notwithstanding these express statutory provisions, it continued to be common for a party to seek an injunction, especially to exclude the other party from the home, during divorce or other proceedings relating to the children. In 1983, the House of Lords held in

---

[10] *Lord Leigh's Case* (1674) 3 Keb 433.   [11] Tit Baron and Feme (B).

[12] *Commentaries* i 455.

[13] See Frances Power Cobbe *Wife Torture in England* (1878); and for modern examinations of the Victorian response, see A James Hammerton *Cruelty and Companionship: Conflict in Nineteenth-Century Married Life* (1992), M Doggett *Marriage, Wife-Beating and the Law in Victorian England* (1992). See also S Cretney *Family Law in the Twentieth Century: A History* (2003) pp 752–6.   [14] Section 4.

[15] Particularly by Erin Pizzey in Chiswick. See her *Scream Quietly or the Neighbours will Hear* (1974). See also M Borkowski, M Murch and V Walker *Marital Violence* (1983).

[16] See the *Report of the Select Committee on Violence in Marriage* HC 553 (1974–75) and on *Violence in the Family* HC 329 (1976–77).

[17] Sections 16–18, following the recommendations of the Law Commission in Law Com No 77, *Report on Matrimonial Proceedings in Magistrates' Courts.*

Richards v Richards[18] that a spouse with statutory rights of occupation of the matrimonial home given under the Matrimonial Homes Act 1967 (later consolidated in the 1983 Act of the same name)[19] could not be evicted or excluded from the matrimonial home by the other except with the leave of the court *given by an order under that Act*. It followed that the owner of the property could be evicted only under a like order, and the same argument would apply if both had a legal estate in the land. Consequently, if the parties were married, an ouster injunction could be granted only in proceedings taken under that Act or under the Domestic Violence and Matrimonial Proceedings Act 1976. In *Richards v Richards* Lord Scarman observed:[20]

> The statutory provision is a hotchpotch of enactments of limited scope passed into law to meet specific situations or to strengthen the powers of specified courts. The sooner the range, scope and effect of these powers are rationalised into a coherent and comprehensive body of statute law, the better.

The Law Commission accordingly examined the civil law[21] and their recommendations, with some changes, were eventually enacted in Part IV of the Family Law Act 1996, which is discussed later.[22]

4. GOVERNMENT STRATEGY

Since the enactment of Part IV, Government strategy has shifted away from a focus on civil, to criminal justice, responses to domestic abuse. The Labour Government set out its approach to tackling the issues in a White Paper published in 2003, *Safety and Justice*, based on 'prevention, protection and justice, and support'[23] and the coalition Government issued its own *Action Plan* in 2011, subsequently updated in 2012.[24] Both sought to bring together measures aimed at prevention of abuse in the first place, primarily through public education and seeking to shift social attitudes; the effective provision of support and services for victims;[25] and improvements in the criminal justice system. Both governments had relatively little to say regarding the provision of civil remedies, with the emphasis overwhelmingly on the role of the police and criminal justice system.

Delivery of this strategy requires a multi-agency approach, utilising a range of services in both the statutory and voluntary sectors, including the police and Crown Prosecution Service, health, housing and social services authorities, and organisations such as Victim Support and Women's Aid.[26] Work on creating such an approach had already begun with the establishment of local 'domestic violence fora' designed to co-ordinate the development

---

[18] [1984] AC 174, HL.   [19] See Ch 5, 'Home rights', p 152.   [20] [1984] AC 174, HL at 206–7.
[21] *Report on Domestic Violence and Occupation of the Family Home*, Law Com No 207, 1992 following Law Com Working Paper No 113 *Domestic Violence and Occupation of the Matrimonial Home*.
[22] See The Family Law Act 1996 Part IV, p 179ff.   [23] Cm 5487, para 19.
[24] HM Government, *Call to End Violence against Women and Girls: Action Plan* (2011), https://www.gov.uk/government/publications/call-to-end-violence-against-women-and-girls-action-plan (accessed 20 April 2014), and *Call to End Violence against Women and Girls: Action Plan. Taking Action: the next chapter* (2012) https://www.gov.uk/government/publications/call-to-end-violence-against-women-and-girls-taking-action-the-next-chapter (accessed 20 April 2014). See also, Welsh Government, Gender-based Violence, Domestic Abuse and Sexual Violence (Wales) Bill, Explanatory Memorandum (2014).
[25] See R Moorhead et al *The Advice Needs of Lone Parents* (2004) pp 44–5.
[26] See N Harwin, G Hague and E Malos (eds) *The Multi-Agency Approach to Domestic Violence: New Opportunities, Old Challenges* (1999).

of services, improve practice via training, support new projects to aid victims, raise aware-ness of domestic violence amongst the general public and set up preventative programmes in schools and for perpetrators. It is now standard practice to hold Multi-Agency Risk Assessment Conferences (MARACs) where information about high risk domestic abuse vic-tims (those at risk of murder or serious harm) is shared between local agencies and where the victim is supported by an Independent Domestic Violence Advisor.[27] The aim of the meeting is to draw up a safety plan to protect the victim and they deal with over 57,000 cases a year.

A scheme (known as 'Clare's Law' after a victim who was murdered despite the police knowing of her partner's previous convictions for harassment) for the police to provide information about the previous history of violence or abuse of a person to their partner so that they are made aware of their risk, was piloted in 2012 and implemented nation-ally in 2014. The 'Domestic Violence Disclosure Scheme' relies on common law powers vested in the police to provide such information,[28] but sets out a procedure and criteria to be applied consistently to enable a person who has concerns to ask, and to empower the police proactively to tell her (a 'right to ask' and a 'right to know'), regarding the perpetra-tor's prior record as contained in the Police National Database. The 'right to know' will depend upon a MARAC being held and concluding that there is a 'pressing need' for the information to be given.[29]

As a further measure intended to promote and utilise multi-agency working, s 9 of the Domestic Violence, Crime and Victims Act 2004 provides for 'domestic homicide reviews'. These are held into the circumstances in which the death of a person aged 16 or over has, or appears to have, resulted from violence, abuse or neglect by a person to whom he was related or with whom he was or had been in an intimate personal relationship, or a member of the same household as himself, in order to identify the lessons to be learnt from the death. Those participating include police, local authorities, probation boards and health authorities and trusts. Such reviews mirror those carried out after the deaths of children in suspected child abuse and neglect cases.[30]

5. GENDER-BASED ABUSE AS A BREACH OF HUMAN RIGHTS

While men and boys may be victims of violence and abuse, the preponderance of abuse is inflicted by men on women, and male abuse is likely to be more serious than that of women.[31] The gender-based nature of domestic abuse has been recognised in international law.[32] The view of the Committee on the United Nations Convention on the Elimination of All Forms of Discrimination Against Women 1979 (CEDAW) is that gender-based violence is a form of discrimination that seriously inhibits women's ability to enjoy rights and freedoms on a basis of equality with men and is therefore prohibited under Art 1 of the Convention. The Committee's *General Recommendation No. 19 on Violence Against*

---

[27] For evaluation, see E Howarth et al *Safety in Numbers: A Multi-Site Evaluation of Independent Domestic Violence Advisor Services* (2009).

[28] *R v Chief Constable of North Wales Police ex p Thorpe* [1998] 2 FLR 571; *R v Local Authority and Police Authority in the Midlands ex p LM* [2000] 1 FLR 612.

[29] Home Office *Domestic Violence Disclosure Scheme: A Consultation* (2011), *Summary of Responses* (2012), *Domestic Violence Disclosure Scheme: Impact Assessment* (2013).   [30] See Ch 16.

[31] M Hester *Who Does What to Whom? Gender and Domestic Violence Perpetrators* (2011).

[32] See R McGuigg *International Human Rights Law and Domestic Violence: The effectiveness of human rights law* (2013); M Madden Dempsey 'Toward a Feminist State: What Does "Effective" Prosecution of Domestic Violence Mean?' (2007) 70(6) MLR 908; S Subedi 'Protection of Women Against Domestic Violence: the response of international law' (1997) 6 EHRLR 587.

Women[33] sets out duties owed by member states to 'take all legal and other measures that are necessary to provide effective protection of women against gender-based including penal sanctions, civil remedies and compensatory provisions to protect women against all kinds of violence'. In *Opuz v Turkey*,[34] the European Court of Human Rights referred to CEDAW's views, and held that the general passivity and degree of tolerance of violence against women by the legal authorities in Turkey amounted to a form of gender-based discrimination within Art 14 of the ECHR in conjunction with the applicants' rights under Arts 2 and 3 (which were also broken).[35] The Council of Europe subsequently drafted the Convention on Preventing and Combating Violence against Women and Domestic Violence (which is known as the Istanbul Convention) which opened for signature in 2011 and which is intended to promote awareness of abuse and encourage states to take a co-ordinated and effective approach to combating it.[36] Turkey has, perhaps not surprisingly in light of *Opuz*, ratified the Convention. The UK has signed but not yet ratified, and the Convention is not yet in force.

B. PROTECTION AFFORDED BY THE CRIMINAL LAW

1. THE CRIMINAL JUSTICE SYSTEM

(a) Police policy

A family member is in a similar legal position to any other person who may be prosecuted for assaulting another (whether for common assault or an assault occasioning actual bodily harm) or for committing one of the more serious offences of wounding, causing grievous bodily harm, rape (within or outside marriage)[37] or even attempted murder. In practice, however, the criminal law was little used by victims of domestic violence until the past decade.[38] The reasons are numerous. First, there was a traditional reluctance by the police to become involved in a 'domestic' incident, partly because of a perception that the complainant would decline to press charges and so waste police time, and partly because of the strongly male, and sexist, 'canteen culture' which pervaded the police service.[39] Recognition of the seriousness of violence within the family led to an attempt by Government to change this attitude by issuing a Home Office Circular in 1990 reminding police officers 'of their responsibility to respond as law enforcement officers to requests

---

[33] UN doc. CEDAW/C/1992/L.1/Add.15 (1992).

[34] App no 33401/02 (2009) 50 EHRR 695. See M Burton 'The human rights of victims of domestic violence: *Opuz v Turkey*' [2010] CFLQ 131.

[35] For the view that human rights law should be used as a means of compelling state action to protect those harmed by domestic violence, see S Choudhry and J Herring 'Righting Domestic Violence' (2006) 29 *Int Journal of Law, Policy and the Family* 95 and *European Human Rights and Family Law* (2010) ch 9.

[36] It may also be noted that a proposal for a Regulation to provide reciprocal recognition and enforcement of non-molestation etc. orders across the EU has been agreed by the EU Commission and Parliament: http://europa.eu/citizens-2013/en/news/eu-wide-protection-victims-domestic-violence-become-law.

[37] See Ch 4, Sexual intercourse, p 95.

[38] See S Edwards *Policing 'Domestic' Violence* (1989) ch 2 and *Sex and Gender in the Legal Process* (1996) ch 5; HM Inspectorate of Constabularies and HM Inspectorate of the Crown Prosecution Service *Violence at Home* (2004); M Madden Dempsey *Prosecuting Domestic Violence: A Philosophical Analysis* (2009).

[39] See S Edwards *Sex and Gender in the Legal Process* (1996) pp 196–8. The European Court of Human Rights criticised a similar mind-set amongst the Turkish authorities in *Opuz v Turkey* App no 33401/02 (2009) 50 EHRR 695.

from victims for help, and of their powers to take action in cases of violence'.[40] A number of police services revised their policies in respect of domestic violence as a result of this circular, and several established domestic violence units (now called community safety units) to provide a specialist service offering liaison between police and victims, advice to investigating officers, training in how to handle domestic violence incidents, and co-operation with other agencies in tackling the problem.[41] Continuing evidence that the police were still sometimes failing to arrest an attacker at the scene of the crime, or of failing to record a domestic incident as a crime, resulted in a revised Circular, issued in 2000, which, inter alia, created a presumption of arrest, requiring an officer to justify in writing any decision not to arrest.[42] The Government also identified complexity in the grounds on which police officers may arrest for common assault, and uncertainty on their part as to whether they could arrest for this offence where they have not themselves witnessed it. The Police and Criminal Evidence Act 1984 was accordingly amended to add common assault to the list of offences arrestable without a warrant[43] but subsequently, the distinction between arrestable and non-arrestable offences was abolished anyway.[44]

(b) The Crown Prosecution Service

Where police action is taken, the criminal justice system may still operate to deter or discourage victims from pursuing a complaint. The Crown Prosecution Service (CPS), which must decide on whether to proceed with a charge, and on what offence to prosecute, has been accused of frequently discontinuing, or 'down criming' a charge,[45] thus reinforcing the perception that 'domestic' violence is regarded as less serious than other crime, and deterring victims from making complaints. Its policy was in turn revised in 2001, with an emphasis on seeking to overturn this perception, and violence against women co-ordinators were appointed to handle domestic violence cases, identify and take forward strategic issues such as training, and work closely with domestic violence fora in their areas.

Yet a joint inspection[46] of police and CPS practice in relation to domestic violence cases found that, in a study of 463 domestic violence incidents in six police forces, only 25% resulted in a crime being recorded. The basis for not recording incidents as crimes was mainly because the victim withdrew the allegation or declined to provide a statement. In all, charges were brought in 21% of recorded incidents but a number of cases were dropped by the CPS, either because of insufficient evidence or, more rarely, because it was not in the public interest to proceed. In a similar sample of 418 cases dealt with by the CPS, the prosecution dropped the case in 28% of cases, compared with a national discontinuance average of around 13%. Where cases proceeded to court, over three-quarters of defendants pleaded guilty, but those contesting charges were more likely to be acquitted than for other offences. Summing up the situation, at each stage in the criminal justice process, the Inspectorates found around a 50% drop out rate, with only 11% of domestic violence matters recorded as crimes resulting in a conviction. More recently, a Freedom

---

[40] Home Office Circular 60/1990, quoted in Home Affairs Committee Third Report, *Domestic Violence* HC 245 para 14.

[41] Home Affairs Committee Third Report, *Domestic Violence* HC 245 paras 23–32, and see S Edwards *Sex and Gender in the Legal Process* (1996) pp 193–5.   [42] Home Office Circular 19/2000.

[43] Police and Criminal Evidence Act 1984 Sch 1A para 14A inserted by the Domestic Violence, Crime and Victims Act 2004 s 10.   [44] Serious Organised Crime and Police Act 2005 s 110.

[45] S Edwards *Sex and Gender in the Legal Process* (1996), p 200–1; A Cretney and G Davis 'Prosecuting "Domestic" Assault' [1996] Crim LR 162.

[46] See HM Inspectorate of Constabularies and HM Inspectorate of the Crown Prosecution Service *Violence at Home* (2004) ch 6.

of Information request by the Labour party in 2013 found that the police used 'community resolution' methods—restorative justice entailing admission of guilt and apology to the victim, as an alternative to cautioning or prosecuting the offender—in up to 14% of recorded violent offences in 2012, with 2,225 offences of domestic violence dealt with in this way in those forces that responded to the FOI request.[47]

(c) Reluctance of the victim

It can be seen that a key factor influencing whether a case will proceed through the criminal justice process is the attitude of the victim.[48] In *Opuz v Turkey* the authorities cited the victims' unwillingness to give evidence as a basis for dropping a case against the perpetrator or a resulting acquittal. The European Court of Human Rights referred with approval to the approach of the CPS in expressly balancing the victim's (and any children's) Art 2 and 3 rights against their Art 8 right to respect for private and family life, in deciding whether to pursue a prosecution despite the victim's reluctance to press charges or act as a witness.[49] Reluctance to give evidence against the perpetrator is hardly surprising. There has been a strong tendency to disbelieve allegations, particularly where they involve sexual assaults, with victims even being prosecuted themselves on the basis of perverting the course of justice for making claims which they later retract.[50] Where a prosecution is brought, the complainant may be placed under considerable emotional strain and may have good reason to fear reprisals if the accused is released on bail pending his trial or, in any case, after his ultimate release. Although an accused's spouse is a compellable witness for the prosecution in cases of assault and unmarried partners have always been compellable,[51] there were instances in the past of insensitive handling of victims who are too scared to testify and there are still such examples.[52] Attempts to support victims and witnesses have been enacted alongside attempts to promote greater sensitivity in both the police and CPS to handling witnesses' concerns.[53] Complainants may not always have to give oral testimony, since under s 23 of the Criminal Justice Act 1988 a statement made in a document by a person to a police officer may be admissible as evidence of any fact of which direct oral evidence by that person would be admissible, where the witness does not give oral evidence through fear. The court has a discretion whether to admit the statement, and must take account of the risk of unfairness to the accused in the lack of an opportunity to cross-examine the witness. This could provide a means of protecting a victim from some of the stress of giving evidence, but appears to have been rarely invoked by the prosecution in domestic violence cases.[54] Of greater significance, Part II, Chapter I of the Youth Justice and Criminal Evidence Act 1999 sets out 'special measures' that can be taken where the court is satisfied that the quality of evidence given by a witness is

[47] *The Guardian* 30 April 2013.

[48] See M Burton 'Prosecution decisions in cases of domestic violence involving children' (2000) 22, 2, JSWFL 175; L Ellison 'Prosecuting Domestic Violence without Victim Participation' (2002) 65 MLR 834; D Cook et al *Evaluation of Specialist Domestic Violence Courts/Fast Track Systems* (2006) para E17.3; M Madden Dempsey *Prosecuting Domestic Violence: A Philosophical Analysis* (2009) chs 8, 9.

[49] *Opuz v Turkey* at paras 89, 138.

[50] See for example, *R v A* [2012] EWCA Crim 434 [2012] 2 Cr App Rep 80. The CPS issued a report in 2013 noting that false allegations are much rarer than the popular (and police and CPS) perception: http://www. cps.gov.uk/news/latest_news/under_the_spotlight/ (accessed 9 May 2014).

[51] Police and Criminal Evidence Act 1984 s 80, see Ch 4, Compellability, p 97.

[52] HMCPSI, HMICA, HMIC *Criminal Justice Joint Inspection: Report of a Join Thematic Review of Victim and Witness Experiences in the Criminal Justice System* (2009).

[53] See CPS *Policy on Prosecuting Cases of Domestic Violence* (2005).

[54] See S Edwards *Reducing Domestic Violence . . . What Works? Use of the Criminal Law* (2000) Home Office Policing and Reducing Crime Unit.

'likely to be diminished by reason of fear or distress on the part of the witness in connection with testifying in the proceedings.' The measures that can be taken include enabling the witness to give evidence from behind a screen so that she cannot see the accused,[55] providing a live video link to give evidence from outside the court,[56] excluding persons (other than the accused and his representatives) from the court where it appears to the court that there are reasonable grounds for believing that the person will seek to intimidate the witness,[57] video-recording the witness's evidence in chief,[58] and enabling cross-examination also to take place by video-recording.[59] Despite such measures, the Director of Public Prosecutions reported that over 6,500 domestic violence cases failed in 2009/10 because the victim either failed to attend court or retracted her evidence—a third of all failed cases, compared with a general figure of about 9% for all prosecutions.[60]

(d) Courts and sentencing

One further measure intended to improve the criminal justice response has been the creation of specialist domestic violence courts. First established in 2005, there are now 143 such courts, which are staffed by magistrates who have usually received additional training in dealing with domestic violence cases and who work with agencies including probation and specialist support services for victims. These courts list domestic violence cases for a single dedicated session, and promote multi-disciplinary working amongst the relevant agencies.[61] Evaluation suggests that they can speed up the processing of cases and help victims feel more able to proceed with cases, although they have not altered the types of charge, outcome, or sentence imposed. Such findings parallel those in the United States, which have also found greater use of plea-bargaining.

A major priority is to ensure that information is shared across agencies so that a realistic assessment of the risk to the victim can be conducted, since even where a prosecution is successful, the victim may be concerned about what will happen after the trial. In particular, there remains the question of the appropriate sentence. In the past, it appeared that leniency was frequently shown to 'domestic' violence perpetrators. However, the Court of Appeal has reiterated that any such leniency is misplaced. For example, in *R v McNaughten*,[62] it stated that:

> . . . we must firmly emphasise that the seriousness of an incident of violence is not diminished merely because it takes place in a 'domestic environment'. Whenever and wherever it happens an offence of violence is an offence of violence.

This approach is reflected in the *Overarching Principles* issued by the Sentencing Guidelines Council in 2006,[63] which also identify both aggravating and mitigating factors that may affect sentence. Aggravating factors include abuse of trust or power, the particular vulnerability of the victim (such as age, or current or recent pregnancy), an offender exploiting contact arrangements with a child to carry out an offence, and where

---

[55] Section 23.   [56] Section 24.

[57] Section 25(4)(b).   [58] Section 27.   [59] Section 28 (not yet in force).

[60] Keir Starmer, 'Domestic Violence: the facts, the issues, the future' (2011) http://www.cps.gov.uk/news/articles/domestic_violence_-_the_facts_the_issues_the_future/ (accessed 20 April 2014).

[61] For consideration of the use of social work support and mediation as an adjunct to the courts in such cases, see H Laufer 'Managing Domestic Violence Cases in Family Court Social Services in Israel' (2004) 18 Int Jo of Law, Pol and Fam 38.   [62] [2003] 2 Cr App R (S) 142.

[63] Sentencing Guidelines Council *Overarching Principles: Domestic Violence* (2006) passim.

the victim is required to leave home because of the offence. Mitigation may be found in positive good character or provocation by the victim, but the *Principles* stress that perpetrators may frequently avoid detection and conviction because of an apparently 'good' public face and that provocation would need to have been of itself a form of actual or anticipated violence.[64] The wish of the victim that the perpetrator be 'spared' should also be treated with caution with due account taken of the nature of the relationship and the needs of any children.[65]

The matter is complex. Whilst a non-custodial sentence may leave the victim vulnerable to further abuse, imprisonment may be equally damaging, curtailing the perpetrator's income which may have supported the family, and, unless some form of treatment is available during his sentence, leaving him no better able to manage his behaviour than before.[66]

2. THE PROTECTION FROM HARASSMENT ACT 1997

During 1995 and 1996, a number of cases of 'stalking' appeared in the media. 'Stalking' has been defined as:

> ... a campaign of harassment or molestation of another, usually with an undertone of sexual attraction or infatuation.[67]

The recognition of such behaviour as deserving of criminal sanction led to a number of initiatives to widen the ambit of existing offences.[68] For example, a series of unwanted telephone calls during which the caller simply remained silent, but which put the recipients in immediate fear for their safety and caused them psychological injury, was held capable of amounting to assault occasioning actual bodily harm in *R v Ireland, R v Burstow*.[69] Nonetheless, it seemed at that time that the criminal law could not be used successfully to cope with all forms of such conduct, and calls were made to introduce new legislation to plug the gap. The Protection from Harassment Act 1997 was enacted, containing both criminal and civil powers.[70] The former are dealt with here, and the latter in a later section of this chapter.[71]

The Protection from Harassment Act 1997 was intended to apply primarily to 'stalkers',[72] who may often be strangers to the victim, but it was drafted in broad terms, and may be invoked by a spouse or partner, or by someone who falls outside the range of those covered by the Family Law Act 1996 Part IV, discussed later. However, concern that stalking itself was not being taken sufficiently seriously by the police and prosecuting authorities led to the insertion into the Act, by the Protection of Freedoms Act 2012, of two further, specific offences of 'stalking'.

---

[64] *Overarching Principles: Domestic Violence* (2006) paras 3.20, 3.23.

[65] *Overarching Principles: Domestic Violence* (2006) paras 4.1–4.4.

[66] *Overarching Principles: Domestic Violence* (2006).

[67] C Wells 'Stalking: The Criminal Law Response' [1997] Crim LR 463.

[68] T Lawson-Cruttenden 'Psychological assault and harassment' (1996) 146 NLJ 1326; C Wells 'Stalking: The Criminal Law Response' [1997] Crim LR 463 at pp 465–9.   [69] [1998] AC 147, HL.

[70] See T Lawson-Cruttenden and N Addison *Guide to the Protection from Harassment Act 1997* (1997).

[71] See Civil law remedies, Protection from Harassment Act 1997, p 195.

[72] The term probably derives from the United States, where the first 'anti-stalking' law was enacted by California; see D Morville 'Stalking Laws: Are They Solutions for More Problems?' (1993) 71 Wash ULQ 921.

(a) Harassment

Section 1 of the Act provides that:

(1) A person must not pursue a course of conduct—
 (a) which amounts to harassment of another; and
 (b) which he knows or ought to know amounts to harassment of the other.

(2) For the purposes of this section, the person whose course of conduct is in question ought to know that it amounts to harassment of another if a reasonable person in possession of the same information would think the course of conduct amounted to harassment of the other.

Although the Act does not define harassment, s 7(2) provides that 'references to harassing a person include alarming the person or causing the person distress'. It also provides that a '"course of conduct" must involve conduct on at least two occasions'.[73] Under s 2, a person who pursues a course of conduct in breach of s 1 is guilty of the offence of harassment.[74] It is clear that the objective test of *mens rea* utilised in s 1(1)(a) is designed to overcome the problems of other offences where establishing subjective intent has proved difficult, and it has been held that a person suffering from schizophrenia, who made threats in letters to his local MP, was rightly convicted of the offence.[75] The provision that harassment includes causing alarm or distress also obviates the need to prove psychological injury which is required for a charge of assault.

It is necessary, however, to show that the conduct complained of has occurred on at least two occasions, so that a single incident, for example, bursting in on the estranged spouse while he or she is at work, and shouting and swearing at her in front of colleagues, or sending photographs of the victim in a semi-nude state to a national newspaper[76] would not be an offence under this Act, though the former activity might be under the Public Order Act 1986 s 4A, and the latter might be covered by the 1997 Act if the perpetrator gave the 'exclusive' prints to a number of different tabloid newspapers.[77] The requirement to show a course of conduct appears to differentiate the kind of harassment intended to be covered from, eg sexual harassment in the workplace, where a single incident would suffice.[78] It is not always easy to establish that a course of conduct has occurred. There must be a nexus or link between the incidents complained of, and each incident must be proved. Thus, in *Lau v DPP*[79] the appellant was found to have slapped his girlfriend on one occasion and then, some months after that incident, and after she had ended the relationship, to have threatened her new boyfriend with violence. The Divisional Court held that although a

---

[73] Section 7(3).

[74] Section 2(2). The offence carries a maximum penalty on summary conviction of imprisonment for up to six months or a fine not exceeding level 5 on the standard scale or both.

[75] *R v Colohan* [2001] EWCA Crim 1251 [2001] 2 FLR 757.

[76] *Johnson v Walton* [1990] 1 FLR 350, CA.

[77] But cf *C v C (Non-Molestation Order: Jurisdiction)* [1998] Fam 70, where a former husband was refused a non-molestation order under Part IV of the Family Law Act 1996 to restrain his ex-wife from making revelations to a tabloid newspaper, because, inter alia, the aim was to seek to impose a gagging order which would threaten the freedom of the press. It is arguable that a court would apply similar reasoning to refuse to find the offence under s 2 made out, and in *Trimingham v Associated Newspapers Ltd* [2012] EWHC 1296 (QB) [2012] 4 All ER 717, the right to freedom of expression was used successfully to resist a civil claim of harassment relating to a series of articles mocking the applicant's appearance and sexuality because, according to the court, a reasonable person would have regarded her as a strong character unlikely to have been upset by them.

[78] *Porcelli v Strathclyde Regional Council* [1986] ICR 564, Court of Session; *Scott v Combined Property Services Ltd* (1996) EAT/757/96.

[79] [2000] 1 FLR 799. See also *R v Patel* [2004] EWCA Crim 3284, [2005] 1 FLR 803.

mere two incidents may amount to a course of conduct, one has to examine the context in which they occur.[80] Here, there was insufficient evidence (on the facts as proved) to justify linking the two incidents together. It has been suggested that it may therefore be sensible to base a prosecution on individual counts of assault where there is doubt whether the incidents can be sufficiently linked to each other.[81] It appears that the police may tend to wait before arresting a suspect until at least three complaints have been made by the victim in order to ensure that a course of conduct can be proved.[82]

(b) Stalking

Following a campaign for greater protection for victims of stalking, and the creation of a specific offence in Scotland, a new offence of stalking was inserted into the Act in 2012.[83] Section 2A provides that a person is guilty of an offence[84] if:

(a) the person pursues a course of conduct in breach of section 1(1), and
(b) the course of conduct amounts to stalking.

A person's course of conduct amounts to stalking of another person if:

(a) it amounts to harassment of that person,
(b) the acts or omissions involved are ones associated with stalking, and
(c) the person whose course of conduct it is knows or ought to know that the course of conduct amounts to harassment of the other person.

Thus, the offence is a more specific form of the activity covered by s 1. Stalking, like harassment, is not itself defined, but the section goes on to provide examples of acts or omissions which 'in particular circumstances, are ones associated with stalking'. These are:

(a) following a person,
(b) contacting, or attempting to contact, a person by any means,
(c) publishing any statement or other material—
    (i) relating or purporting to relate to a person, or
    (ii) purporting to originate from a person,
(d) monitoring the use by a person of the internet, email or any other form of electronic communication,
(e) loitering in any place (whether public or private),
(f) interfering with any property in the possession of a person,
(g) watching or spying on a person.

The CPS have explained that the effect of stalking is 'to curtail a victim's freedom, leaving them feeling that they constantly have to be careful. In many cases, the conduct might appear innocent (if it were to be taken in isolation), but when carried out repeatedly so

---

[80] See *Hipgrave and Hipgrave v Jones* [2004] EWHC 2901 (QB), [2005] 2 FLR 174 where the Divisional Court stressed that whether two acts eight months apart amounted to a course of conduct was a factual question for the judge (who held that they did).

[81] See the comment by R Bailey-Harris at [2001] Fam Law 185 on *R v Hills* [2001] 1 FLR 580, CA, a decision relating to the more serious offence under s 4 (see later).

[82] J Harris *The Protection from Harassment Act 1997—An Evaluation of its Use and Effectiveness, Research Findings No 130* (2000) (Home Office Research, Development and Statistics Directorate).

[83] By the Protection of Freedoms Act 2012 s 111. See P Strickland *Stalking* (2013) (Commons Library Standard Note, SN/HA/6261): http://www.parliament.uk/briefing-papers/SN06261 (accessed 20 April 2014).   [84] It carries a penalty of up to 51 weeks' imprisonment.

as to amount to a course of conduct, it may then cause significant alarm, harassment or distress to the victim.'[85] It is unclear whether the insertion of this new offence will make the basic crime of harassment redundant or whether the latter will become the 'default' offence for intra-familial abuse whilst stalking is reserved for where the perpetrator is a (comparative) stranger to the victim.

(c) Putting in fear of violence

The Protection from Harassment Act 1997 also created a still more serious offence under s 4, which provides that:

> (1) A person whose course of conduct causes another to fear, on at least two occasions, that violence will be used against him is guilty of an offence if he knows or ought to know that his course of conduct will cause the other so to fear on each of those occasions.

It was suggested, by Lord Steyn in *R v Ireland*, that it will be difficult to prove that a victim has cause to fear that violence *will*, rather than *may* be used against her, and that therefore this provision is not well-suited to dealing with the problem of menacing phone calls.[86] However, the *mens rea* is to be judged objectively, which should make the burden of proof somewhat easier for the prosecution. Where a person is tried on indictment,[87] the jury may return a verdict under s 2 where they find him not guilty under s 4.[88]

The 2012 Act similarly inserted a new s 4A to create an offence[89] where the form of activity which puts the person in fear is stalking. It provides that:

> (1) A person ("A") whose course of conduct—
>   (a) amounts to stalking, and
>   (b) either—
>   (i) causes another ("B") to fear, on at least two occasions, that violence will be used against B, or
>   (ii) causes B serious alarm or distress which has a substantial adverse effect on B's usual day-to-day activities,
> is guilty of an offence if A knows or ought to know that A's course of conduct will cause B so to fear on each of those occasions or (as the case may be) will cause such alarm or distress.

The scope of the offence is wider than s 4. Here, the *actus reus* will have occurred not only where the victim is caused to fear violence, but also where the victim is caused 'serious alarm or distress' which interferes with her daily activities.

(d) Restraining orders

An important feature of the Protection from Harassment Act 1997 is the power, contained in s 5, to enable a court sentencing a person for any offence[90] to make an order,

---

[85] http://www.cps.gov.uk/legal/s_to_u/stalking_and_harassment/ (accessed 20 April 2014).

[86] [1998] AC 147 at 153C.

[87] The maximum sentence, if the accused is convicted on indictment, is five years' imprisonment, a fine, or both, or, on summary conviction, to imprisonment for six months, the statutory maximum fine, or both: s 4(4).

[88] Section 4(5). Though it is preferable to add a count to the indictment to allow for this: *R v Patel* [2004] EWCA Crim 3284 [2005] 1 FLR 803.

[89] The maximum sentence on indictment is the same as for an offence under s 4 but is a maximum of 12 months on summary conviction.

[90] As originally enacted, this power applied only to convictions under the 1997 Act. Section 12 of the Domestic Violence, Crime and Victims Act 2004 extended the power to conviction for any offence.

similar to a civil injunction, called a 'restraining order', which prohibits the defendant from doing anything which amounts to further harassment or will cause a fear of violence on the part of the victim of the offence or any other person mentioned in the order. Thus, a criminal court, sentencing the defendant for an offence of assault of his wife, could make a restraining order against him in respect of their children as well. Conditions may be attached to the order, such as requiring the defendant not to contact the victim or her family or to keep away from the victim's home or workplace. The order may be of fixed or indefinite duration.[91] The court will decide whether to make a restraining order applying the civil standard of proof, and the civil rules on admissibility of evidence. Yet breach of the terms of an order without reasonable excuse is itself an offence punishable by imprisonment of up to five years and/or a fine.[92] Such an order is intended to deal with the problem, noted earlier, that criminal penalties may be inadequate to protect the victim from further offences. But putting a person at risk of a criminal sanction (albeit applying the criminal standard of proof) for breach of a civil order is controversial as an erosion of civil liberties—although, as we discuss later, it has been utilised in relation to other civil law remedies for domestic abuse.[93]

The potential interference with the freedom of the individual has also been made much more significant by s 5A[94] of the Act. This provides for a restraining order to be made even where the defendant has been acquitted,[95] if the court considers it *necessary* to do so to protect a person from harassment by the defendant. This is an even more controversial innovation since it means that a person who has been found not guilty of the substantive offence may still be made subject to penal consequences. Awareness of the draconian nature of this provision led the Court of Appeal in *R v Smith*[96] to stress that the court must be satisfied that the defendant is likely—and therefore intends—to pursue a course of conduct amounting to harassment in the future, and that the word 'necessary' in the section should not be diluted.

(e) Use of the Protection from Harassment Act 1997

The Government had predicted that there would be no more than around 200 prosecutions per annum,[97] but the 1997 Act proved more popular with prosecutors than expected, with nearly 6,000 prosecutions in the Act's first full year of operation.[98] This is probably because relatively few cases of 'stalking' actually occur. Instead, the Act has been used overwhelmingly where the perpetrator and victim know each other, either as

[91] Section 5(3)(b). The prosecutor, defendant or any person mentioned in the order may apply to the court for it to be varied or discharged: s 5(4).

[92] Where convicted on indictment; on summary conviction, the penalty is imprisonment for up to six months and/or the maximum statutory fine: s 5(5).

[93] See Civil law remedies, Protection from Harassment Act 1997 at p 195.

[94] Inserted by s 12(5) of the Domestic Violence, Crime and Victims Act 2004.

[95] Or where an appeal has been allowed, in which case, the matter may be remitted to the Crown Court: s 5A(3).

[96] [2012] EWCA Crim 2566 [2013] 2 All ER 804. This decision was applied in *R v R(AJ)* [2013] EWCA Crim 591 [2013] 2 Cr App Rep 128 where a man acquitted by reason of insanity of charges of attempted murder and wounding of his daughter was initially made subject to a five-year restraining order. The Court of Appeal ruled this had been wrongly imposed because the offences had occurred on a single occasion and the appellant had since been treated for his mental disorder. There was therefore no evidence to suggest that he was likely to pursue the necessary 'course of conduct' in the future.

[97] Figure cited by T Lawson-Cruttenden and N Addison 'The Protection from Harassment Act' (1997) 147 *NLJ* 983.

[98] J Harris *The Protection from Harassment Act 1997—An Evaluation of its Use and Effectiveness, Research Findings No 130* (2000) (Home Office Research, Development and Statistics Directorate).

neighbours or having had an intimate relationship which has ended badly, and the Act has proved a useful alternative to civil remedies or to other criminal offences. Indeed, it has been said that where breach of a non-molestation order under the Family Law Act 1996[99] requires a sentence near the top of the range, proceedings may be better brought under the Protection from Harassment Act 1997 than the former.[100]

However, the proportion of harassment cases dropped by the CPS—39%—is much higher than the average for all offences of 14%. The majority of cases were dropped because of inadequate evidence, but a third were terminated because the victim did not wish to proceed,[101] suggesting that the Act is not a panacea for the problems discussed earlier with using other substantive criminal offences in domestic violence cases. Around half of all convictions have resulted in a restraining order being made, but the most frequent sentence given for the offence itself has been a conditional discharge, in 46% of one sample of cases.[102] This lenient attitude to the offences under the Act may explain why it has been felt necessary to strengthen the courts' powers to make restraining orders, but a rate of breach of these orders at around 40%[103] suggests that offenders may not take them too seriously. Moreover, only around a third of those in breach receive a custodial sentence,[104] suggesting that the courts are wary of treating these offenders in a harsh way. This may reflect attitudes to sentencing for harassment in courts used to dealing with offences that they consider much more serious and deserving of longer sentences. But the result is that victims may continue to worry that offenders are not being robustly dealt with despite the array of measures apparently available to the courts. Whether the new specific offences of stalking will encourage a more punitive approach by prosecutors and courts remains to be seen—the effect might actually be to downgrade the seriousness of the 'basic' harassment offence in the domestic setting, in comparison with stalking which may be perceived as applying to more dangerous offenders.

C. CIVIL LAW REMEDIES

As noted earlier, the law relating to the grant of orders intended to enjoin the respondent from attacking or pestering the victim, or to exclude him from the family home, had become a confused and complicated jumble of jurisdictions. Part IV of the Family Law Act 1996 was intended to simplify and improve the protection given by the civil courts, largely by bringing jurisdictions together, but there is still a range of different statutory powers, some very new, under which varying forms of protection can be provided.[105] We discuss these in turn.

[99] See later, Breach of a non-molestation order made a criminal offence, p 192.
[100] *Robinson v Murray* [2005] EWCA Civ 935 [2005] 3 FCR 504.
[101] J Harris *The Protection from Harassment Act 1997—An Evaluation of its Use and Effectiveness, Research Findings No 130* (2000) (Home Office Research, Development and Statistics Directorate).
[102] J Harris *The Protection from Harassment Act 1997—An Evaluation of its Use and Effectiveness, Research Findings No 130* (2000) (Home Office Research, Development and Statistics Directorate). Binding over was equally common.
[103] See Sentencing Advisory Panel, *Sentencing Guidelines on Domestic Violence Cases: Consultation Paper* (2004) para 53.
[104] See Sentencing Advisory Panel, *Sentencing Guidelines on Domestic Violence Cases: Consultation Paper* (2004) para 53.
[105] There is also power, available to courts dealing with both spouses and cohabitants whose home is held on a tenancy, to provide a long-term solution to their problem by transferring the home between them and this is discussed in Ch 23, Transfer of tenancy p 907 and Ch 24, Transfer of tenancies at p 950.

1. THE FAMILY LAW ACT 1996 PART IV

(a) The scheme of Part IV

Part IV sets out the rights of spouses to occupy the matrimonial home where they lack a proprietary right to do so.[106] It provides for two categories of orders to be made, occupation orders[107] and non-molestation orders.[108]

(b) Non-molestation orders

Although the Family Law Act 1996 deals with non-molestation orders after occupation orders, we discuss them first, because they are the more likely and common order to be granted: over eight times as many non-molestation orders as occupation orders were granted by county courts in 2013.[109]

Section 42(1) provides that a non-molestation order:

... means an order containing either or both of the following provisions—

(a) prohibiting ... the respondent from molesting another person who is associated with the respondent;
(b) prohibiting the respondent from molesting a relevant child.[110]

What is molestation?

Reflecting the response to the Law Commission's proposals that any attempt at a definition might reduce the level of protection afforded by the former law, 'molestation' is deliberately not defined in the Act.[111] Instead, its meaning is left to case law, including that under the previous legislation, where it had been regarded as meaning 'deliberate conduct which substantially interferes with the applicant or child, whether by violence, intimidation, harassment, pestering or interference sufficiently serious to warrant intervention by a court.'[112] In *C v C (Non-Molestation Order: Jurisdiction)* Sir Stephen Brown P stated that 'it implies some quite deliberate conduct which is aimed at a high degree of harassment of the other party, so as to justify the intervention of the court.'[113] This clearly overlaps with, though is wider in terms than, the concept of harassment under the Protection from Harassment Act 1997, since there is no requirement to prove a 'course of conduct', meaning conduct on at least two occasions. On the other hand, the 1997 provision may be broader in scope, since it provides that harassment includes causing alarm or distress, whereas molestation must pass a 'seriousness' hurdle, and it is open to a court to consider that the conduct complained of is not sufficiently serious to warrant its intervention. Indeed, In *C v C (Non-Molestation*

---

[106] These are called 'home rights' and are discussed in detail in Ch 5, 'Home rights', p 152.
[107] Sections 33–41.   [108] Section 42.
[109] *Court Statistics (quarterly) January to March 2014, Main Tables* (2014), Table 2.7. In 2013, 22,269 non-molestation orders and 2,746 occupation orders were granted in the county courts. Both types of order are declining but occupation orders have declined more rapidly: in 2004, 24,040 non-molestation orders and 9,207 occupation orders were made.
[110] A 'relevant child' is defined by s 62(2) (as amended) as any child who is living with, or might reasonably be expected to live with either party to the proceedings, any child in relation to whom an order under the Adoption Act 1976, the Adoption and Children Act 2002 or the Children Act 1989 is in question in the proceedings, or any other child whose interests the court considers relevant.
[111] Law Com No 207 at para 3.1.
[112] His Honour Judge Fricker 'Molestation and Harassment after *Patel v Patel*' [1988] Fam Law 395 at 399. See too, *Davis v Johnson* [1979] AC 264 at 334, *Vaughan v Vaughan* [1973] 3 All ER 449 at p 452E, *Horner v Horner* [1982] Fam 90 at 93.   [113] [1998] Fam 70.

Order: Jurisdiction) itself, Sir Stephen Brown P refused an order to prevent a former wife passing details about her ex-husband and their marriage to a tabloid newspaper.

Who may apply for an order?

Under the former law, problems arose because only spouses or cohabitants could seek an injunction or order without also having to take civil proceedings, usually in tort. The Law Commission were concerned to extend the range of applicants for non-molestation orders, but were against providing a remedy open to anyone, regardless of their relationship with the respondent.[114] They reasoned that a domestic or family relationship justifies special remedies and procedures because the proximity of the parties gives rise to heightened emotions in situations of stress, and because of the likelihood that the relationship will continue. They considered that extending equal protection to neighbours, tenants and victims of sexual harassment would be going too far.[115] (As we shall see, however, the Protection from Harassment Act 1997 opens up the possibility of obtaining an injunction to restrain harassment to any person who can prove that the respondent has acted in breach of s 1.)

Instead, the Law Commission proposed basing eligibility upon a person's 'association' with another, and suggested a range of such associations. Not all of these were accepted by the Government at first but the list was subsequently widened by the Domestic Violence, Crime and Victims Act 2004.[116] Those eligible are set out in s 62(3) as follows:

a person is 'associated with' another person if—

(a)   they are, or have been married to each other;[117]

(aa)   they are or have been civil partners of each other;[118]

(b)   they are cohabitants[119] or former cohabitants;

(c)   they live or have lived in the same household, otherwise than merely by reason of one of them being the other's employee, tenant, lodger or boarder;

(d)   they are relatives;[120]

(e)   they have agreed to marry one another (whether or not that agreement has been terminated);[121]

(eza) they have entered into a civil partnership agreement (as defined by section 73 of the Civil Partnership Act 2004) (whether or not that agreement has been terminated);[122]

(ea)   they have or have had an intimate personal relationship with each other which is or was of significant duration;[123]

---

[114] As is possible in New South Wales, South Australia, Western Australia and Tasmania: see the discussion by the Law Commission in Report No 207 para 3.9.

[115] Law Commission in Report No 207 paras 3.17, 3.19.   [116] Sections 3 and 4.

[117] The provisions of Part IV apply to polygamous as well as monogamous marriages: s 63(5).

[118] Amended by Sch 9 para 13 to the Civil Partnership Act 2004.

[119] Defined by s 62(1)(a), as amended by Sch 9 para 13 to the Civil Partnership Act 2004, as meaning 'two persons who are neither married to each other nor civil partners of each other but are living together as husband and wife or as if they were civil partners'.

[120] Extensively defined in s 63(1) (as amended).

[121] Section 44 provides that such an agreement must be evidenced in writing, or by the gift of an engagement ring, or by a ceremony entered into by the parties in the presence of witnesses—which looks like the definition for an old-fashioned betrothal ceremony, but *quaere* whether it would be satisfied by an engagement party? See Ch 2, Proof of an engagement, p 40. No application for a non-molestation order may be brought in reliance on a former engagement more than three years after the date on which it was terminated: s 42(4).

[122] Amended by Sch 9 para 13 to the Civil Partnership Act 2004.

[123] Added by s 4 of the Domestic Violence, Crime and Victims Act 2004.

(f) in relation to any child, they are both persons falling within subsection (4); or

(g) they are parties to the same family proceedings.[124]

Section 62(4) provides that:

a person falls within this subsection in relation to a child if—

(a) he is a parent of the child; or

(b) he has or has had parental responsibility for the child.[125]

Under s 43, a child under the age of 16 may seek an order, with leave of the court, which may only be granted if the court is satisfied that the child has sufficient understanding to make the application. The test is the same as applies in relation to a child seeking leave to seek a s 8 order under the Children Act 1989, and the case law relating to that test is equally applicable.[126]

This list covers the main groups who are regarded as needing protection by virtue of an order, although it is not unproblematic. Couples whose marriage or cohabitation relationship has ended were excluded from the ambit of the former law, yet it appears that a significant number of cases of domestic violence may involve such couples,[127] and hence they are now included.[128] But the difficulty of establishing whether a relationship involved cohabitation may still occur. For example, in *G v G (Non-molestation Order: Jurisdiction)*[129] the applicant had maintained to the Department of Social Security that she and the respondent did *not* live together, but then sought an order from the magistrates asserting that they spent about five nights a week together. On appeal against the magistrates' refusal to make an order, the court held that three of the 'signposts' which may establish a cohabiting relationship were present[130] and the court was clear that the 1996 Act should be given a purposive interpretation in order to bring someone within, rather that outside, its protection unless this was clearly impossible. A similar purposive approach was taken in *Chechi v Bashier*.[131] Here, a man engaged in a land dispute with his relatives in Pakistan sought non-molestation orders against his brother and nephews. The trial judge discharged the *ex parte* orders that had been made, considering that the dispute was better dealt with as a civil matter and that the family relationship between the parties was incidental. The Court of Appeal, whilst upholding the judge's exercise of his discretion, nonetheless affirmed that the Family Law Act 1996 is intended to extend protection to a wide class of 'family' relationships and that suitable cases should certainly be within its ambit.[132]

---

[124] These are defined in s 63(1) and (2) as amended.

[125] Additionally, s 62(5), as amended, provides that, if a child has been adopted or subject to placement for adoption, two persons are also associated with each other if one is the natural parent, or parent of such a natural parent, and the other is the child, or any person who is an adoptive parent of the child, or has had the child placed with him for adoption. The aim of this provision is presumably to enable adopters to utilise the Act to obtain orders to prevent birth relatives from 'pestering' the adoptive family.

[126] Children Act 1989 s 10(8), discussed in Ch 14, The application of s 10(8), p 518.

[127] See Law Com No 207 para 3.18.

[128] But note that former spouses, partners or cohabitants of a person's current spouse, partner or cohabitant are not 'associated' with each other.   [129] [2000] 2 FLR 532.

[130] See *Kimber v Kimber* [2000] 1 FLR 383, discussed in Ch 24, 'As Husband and wife', at p 942.

[131] [1999] 2 FLR 489, CA.

[132] For the Court's consideration of the power of arrest which may be attached to an order, see later, Power of arrest for breach of occupation order, at p 193.

Once it is decided that those in a relationship which does not *presently* involve cohabitation ought to be able to seek an order, but not to open up the jurisdiction to all-comers, it then becomes necessary to determine where to draw the boundaries and thereby define what apparently amounts to a domestic or family relationship.[133] This list gives us a picture of modern thinking on this issue, and it is interesting how rapidly such thinking has changed. As originally provided in the 1996 Act, for example, same sex couples were not expressly included, although if they lived together, they would fit within category (c). Nor were intimate relationships which did not involve cohabitation included, although the Law Commission had recommended that they should be.[134] The experience of working with the limitations of the original provisions, the human rights-led inclusion of same-sex relationships within the definition of 'family' and recognition that personal relationships are taking a more diverse range of forms than hitherto, led to their inclusion through the further broadening of the definitions in s 62.

When may an order be made?

The court may make an order on a free-standing application, or where an application is made in other family proceedings.[135] It may also make an order of its own motion in any family proceedings to which the respondent is a party, if it considers that the order should be made for the benefit of any other party, or of any relevant child,[136] and, when the court is considering whether to make an occupation order, it must also consider whether to make a non-molestation order of its own motion.[137] This is to enable breach of the order to be dealt with more effectively by the police, who may arrest for breach of a non-molestation, but not an occupation, order unless the latter has a specific power of arrest attached.[138] These provisions give flexibility both to parties and the court. Clearly, an applicant should be able to obtain an order without having to take other proceedings, but it is equally useful to enable an application to be attached to proceedings already under way, and to give the court a reserve power to make an order even where no application has been made. Indeed, such a power might prove helpful where a party is reluctant to be seen to be seeking an order for fear of antagonising the respondent.

Criteria for the grant of an order

In deciding whether to make the order, and if so, in what manner:

> . . . the court shall have regard to all the circumstances, including the need to secure the health, safety and well-being—
>
> (a) of the applicant; and
> (b) of any relevant child.[139]

---

[133] For a convincing critique of this approach, and the argument that the concept of 'associated person' has neither an empirical nor a principled basis, see H Reece 'The End of Domestic Violence' (2006) 69(5) *Modern Law Review* 770.   [134] Law Com No 207 para 3.26.

[135] Section 42(2)(a). Family proceedings are defined in s 63(1), (2) and, by virtue of s 42(3), include proceedings where the court has made an emergency protection order under s 44 of the Children Act 1989 which includes an exclusion requirement: see Ch 16, The power to add an exclusion requirement, p 587.

[136] Section 42(2)(b). A relevant child is any child who is living with or might reasonably be expected to live with either party to the proceedings; any child in relation to whom an order under the Adoption and Children Act 2002 or the Children Act 1989 is in question in the proceedings; and any other child whose interests the court considers relevant: s 62(2).

[137] Section 42(4A) and (4B), inserted by Sch 10 para 36 to the Domestic Violence, Crime and Victims Act 2004.

[138] Section 47(2). See further later, Enforcing orders, at p 192.   [139] Section 42(5) as amended.

The purpose of this test is to focus the court's attention upon the victim's need for protection, rather than to scrutinise the nature and quality of the perpetrator's conduct,[140] and to give guidance in exercising the powers under the section.

Terms of a non-molestation order

Under s 42(6), a non-molestation order may refer to molestation in general, to particular acts of molestation, or to both, which gives the court flexibility to outline certain kinds of prohibited conduct or to leave the prohibition in general terms.[141] For example, a court could prohibit the respondent from telephoning the victim, or from loitering outside her place of work, or from coming within a certain distance of her home.[142]

The order may be for a fixed period or until further order. The Court of Appeal has held that the purpose of a non-molestation order is not, as was the understanding under the former law, simply to give a breathing space to the parties for the tensions to die down between them. There may be cases where it may be appropriate for the order to last for a much longer period, and the courts are not obliged to consider whether such cases are 'exceptional' or 'unusual' before making an order of indefinite duration.[143]

The order may be varied or discharged on application by the respondent or applicant, and, where it was made on the court's own motion, may be varied or discharged by the court, even though no application has been made.[144]

(c) Occupation orders

The second type of order which can be made under the Family Law Act 1996 is more complicated. An occupation order may declare or regulate the right to occupy the family home, but the detailed terms of the order will vary according to the eligibility of the applicant, as will the criteria determining whether the order should be granted. Declaratory orders may 'declare, confer or extend occupation rights', while regulatory orders 'just control the exercise of existing rights'.[145]

Who may apply?

Applications may be free-standing or made in other family proceedings, but the court has no power to make an order of its own motion.[146] The range of permitted applicants is much narrower than in the case of non-molestation orders, because the Law Commission were concerned that the interference with the enjoyment of property rights when requiring a respondent to leave his own home or let the applicant into it is harder to justify where the applicant has no such property rights herself.[147] They also considered that, for non-entitled applicants, the purpose of seeking an order is to obtain short-term protection until they can find an alternative home, whereas entitled applicants might be seeking medium- or long-term regulation of the property.[148] The Act accordingly does not employ the concept of the 'associated person' used in relation to non-molestation orders, but instead distinguishes between two categories of applicant: those deemed 'entitled',

---

[140] Although it has been held that, where the respondent could not help her conduct, which was due to dementia, a non-molestation order should not be made: *Banks v Banks* [1999] 1 FLR 726 (county court); cf *P v P (Contempt of Court: Mental Capacity)* [1999] 2 FLR 897, CA: as long as the respondent understands that an order has been made forbidding him from doing certain things, and that he will be punished if he does them, he has sufficient understanding for an order and for a finding of contempt to be made.

[141] Law Com No 207 para 3.2.   [142] As in *Burris v Azadani* [1995] 1 WLR 1372, CA.

[143] *Re B-J (Power of Arrest)* [2000] 2 FLR 443, CA.   [144] Section 49(1) and (2).

[145] Law Com No 207 para 4.1.   [146] Section 39(2).   [147] Law Com No 207 para 4.7.

[148] Law Com No 207 para 4.7.

and those who are 'non-entitled' applicants, in property law terms. We deal with the position of entitled applicants first, and then with non-entitled applicants.

Entitled applicants

Under s 33(1)(a), an entitled applicant is a person who:

> (i) is entitled to occupy a dwelling-house by virtue of a beneficial estate or interest or contract or by virtue of any enactment giving him the right to remain in occupation, or
> (ii) has home rights[149] in relation to a dwelling-house.

Such an applicant may seek an order where the dwelling-house[150] is or at any time has been the home of the applicant and a person with whom he is associated,[151] or was intended by them to be their home.[152]

Types of occupation orders in favour of entitled applicants

Under s 33, the applicant may seek an order containing any of a list of provisions specified. Declaratory orders may simply declare that the applicant is entitled to occupy the home by virtue of property law or home rights,[153] or may provide that the applicant's home rights are to continue beyond the death of the other spouse or civil partner, or the termination of the marriage or civil partnership.[154] Such orders seem to have limited utility, except in situations where, perhaps, the applicant is contesting a property claim by a third party with whom he or she is associated, such as, for example, her brother-in-law who is a joint owner of the family home,[155] or where there is a need to safeguard the applicant's position after divorce or death of the other party, perhaps pending resolution of any financial relief or family provision claim which might be made.

Of greater utility are regulatory orders. These may:[156]

> (a) enforce the applicant's entitlement to remain in occupation as against the . . . respondent . . .;
> (b) require the respondent to permit the applicant to enter and remain in the dwelling-house or part of the dwelling-house;
> (c) regulate the occupation of the dwelling-house by either or both parties;
> (d) if the respondent is entitled [as mentioned in s 33(1)(a)(i)], prohibit, suspend or restrict the exercise by him of his right to occupy the dwelling-house;
> (e) if the respondent has home rights in relation to the dwelling-house and the applicant is the other spouse or civil partner, restrict or terminate those rights;
> (f) require the respondent to leave the dwelling-house or part of the dwelling-house; or
> (g) exclude the respondent from a defined area in which the dwelling-house is included.

---

[149] Home rights are granted by s 30(2) and discussed in Ch 5, 'Home rights' at p 152.

[150] Section 63(1) defines a dwelling house, for the purposes of an occupation order, as including (a) any building, or part of a building which is occupied as a dwelling, (b) any caravan, house-boat or structure which is occupied as a dwelling, and any yard, garden, garage or outhouse belonging to it and occupied with it.

[151] As defined by s 62(3). No application may be brought based on a former agreement to marry or form a civil partnership after the period of three years beginning with the date the engagement or agreement was terminated: s 33(2).

[152] Section 33(1)(b). See *Moore v Moore* [2004] EWCA Civ 1243, [2005] 1 FLR 666 noted in Ch 5, Dwelling-house, at p 154, n 213.   [153] Section 33(4).

[154] Section 33(5), but an order may not be made after the death of either of the former parties: s 33(9)(a).

[155] But cf *Kalsi v Kalsi* [1992] 1 FLR 511, CA: a wife was not entitled to declaration of her rights of occupation in the matrimonial home as against her husband's three brothers who were legal owners, with her husband, of the property.   [156] Section 33(3).

These provisions can be used flexibly to meet the circumstances of the particular case. For example, an order could prevent the respondent from changing the locks of the home to keep the applicant out, or require him to let her back in; require either party to quit the home at certain times, for example, at weekends; require the respondent to leave the home, or prohibit him from entering certain parts of it, eg a bedroom; or, as in *Burris v Azadani*,[157] prohibit him from entering within a certain distance of the home.

Criteria for an order in favour of entitled applicants

No test is laid down for the court to apply when deciding whether to make a simple *declaratory* order that the applicant is a person entitled, since the issue will depend purely on whether the court finds that the applicant has the property or home rights contended for. Where the court is considering whether to extend home rights beyond the death of the other spouse or civil partner, or after the termination of the marriage or civil partnership, it may do so whenever it considers that, in all the circumstances, it is just and reasonable.[158]

The balance of harm test

In relation to making a *regulatory* order, the Law Commission were concerned to provide a test which would meet the varied circumstances which might arise in individual cases, such as the degree of danger being faced by the applicant, the ability to find alternative accommodation at short notice, and any need for a longer-term solution to the problem. They were also keen to deal with the perceived shortcomings of the test under the old law which had placed emphasis upon the misconduct of the respondent rather than upon the needs of the applicant and any children, effectively reintroducing the concept of fault into the law when the trend has been to promote settlement of problems without recrimination.[159] Accordingly, they proposed a 'balance of harm' test, which would enable the court to strike a balance between being fair to respondents on the one hand, and ensuring the protection of the victims on the other, and which would elevate the court's *power* to make an order into a *duty* to do so, where the effects upon the victims are sufficiently grave.

The court is therefore required to consider first of all, whether the terms of s 33(7) are satisfied. This provides that if it appears to the court that the applicant or a relevant child is likely to suffer significant harm attributable to the conduct of the respondent if an order is not made, the court *must* make an order unless it appears that the respondent or a relevant child is likely to suffer greater harm in consequence of the order being made. 'Significant harm' is a term taken from the Children Act 1989.[160] 'Harm' is defined in s 63(3) to mean, in relation to a person aged 18 or over, ill-treatment or the impairment of health, and, in relation to a *child*, ill-treatment or the impairment of health or development. Interestingly, the section provides that ill-treatment includes sexual abuse only in relation to a child. The reason for this limitation is unclear.

The working of s 33(7) is usefully illustrated by *B v B (Occupation Order)*.[161] The wife left the husband after suffering serious violence, and took their two-year-old daughter with her. She was housed temporarily by the local authority in bed and breakfast accommodation. Meanwhile, the husband remained in the matrimonial home, with his six-year-old son by a former partner. The husband appealed against the making

---

[157] [1995] 1 WLR 1372, CA; 250 yards from the home.   [158] Section 33(8).

[159] Law Com No 207 paras 4.20, 4.23.

[160] See s 31, discussed in Ch 17, The significant harm condition, p 600.

[161] [1999] 1 FLR 715, CA. See F Kaganas 'B v B (Occupation Order) and Chalmers v Johns: Occupation Orders under the Family Law Act 1996' [1999] CFLQ 193.

of an occupation order requiring him (and his son) to leave. The Court of Appeal held that, weighing the respective likelihood of harm, the husband's son would suffer more harm if an occupation order were made than the wife and daughter would if it were not, because the husband would be regarded by the local authority as having made himself intentionally homeless and therefore entitled only to temporary accommodation. His child might then have to be taken into care. By contrast, the mother would eventually be rehoused by the authority in suitable permanent accommodation. Thus, even though the Court was at pains to condemn the husband's conduct, it did not consider it appropriate to make the order sought.

It should be noted that the Law Commission's formulation of this presumption did not require a causal connection between the harm and the respondent's conduct. This was inserted by Parliament. However, the Court of Appeal has stressed that it is the effect of the conduct, rather than the intention of the doer, on which the court must concentrate. Thus, a judge was wrong to consider that harm suffered by the two sons of the marriage was not attributable to the husband's conduct because he had not intentionally contributed to the strained atmosphere in the home pending resolution of the spouses' divorce.[162]

The discretionary test

Where the balance of harm test is not satisfied, it does not follow that an order will not be made. The court must then go on to consider whether, as a question of discretion, it should make an order, taking into account the factors listed in s 33(6).[163]

Under s 33(6), the court is required to have regard to all the circumstances, including:

(a) the housing needs and resources of each of the parties and of any relevant child;
(b) the financial resources of each of the parties;
(c) the likely effect of any order, or of any decision by the court not to exercise its powers under subsection (3), on the health, safety or well-being of the parties and of any relevant child; and
(d) the conduct of the parties in relation to each other and otherwise.

In exercising its discretion whether to make an order, the court must bear in mind, according to the Court of Appeal, that occupation orders continue to be regarded as draconian measures to be confined to exceptional cases, as they were under the former law.[164] However, it was held in *Dolan v Corby*[165] that it does not follow that only violence will constitute such exceptional circumstances. There, although the respondent had not subjected the victim to any physical violence, the victim's psychiatric state was sufficient to justify the first instance judge excluding the respondent from the property. Similarly, in *Re L (Occupation Order)*,[166] the Court of Appeal stressed that proof of violence is not a requirement for the making of an occupation order, nor need reprehensible conduct on the part of the respondent be established.

---

[162] *G v G (Occupation Order: Conduct)* [2000] 2 FLR 36, CA. Nonetheless, they upheld his refusal of an order because it would have been draconian in the circumstances: see further below. Cf *Banks v Banks* [1999] 1 FLR 726 (county court), where the judge refused to make the order, inter alia, because the wife, who suffered from dementia, could not help her conduct.

[163] Per Thorpe LJ in *Chalmers v Johns* [1999] 1 FLR 392, at p 396D, CA; *G v G (Occupation Order: Conduct)* [2000] 2 FLR 36, CA.

[164] Ibid. For criticism of this view, see M Humphries 'Occupation Orders Revisited' [2001] Fam Law 542.

[165] [2011] EWCA Civ 1664 [2012] 2 FLR 1031.   [166] [2012] EWCA Civ 721 [2012] 2 FLR 1417.

Duration of orders in favour of entitled applicants

By s 33(10), orders may be made for a specified period, until the occurrence of a specified event, or until further order. Under the former law, orders were generally limited to three months' duration with the possibility of renewal,[167] but this was felt to be inadequate in many instances to achieve a resolution of the parties' problems, and 'not obviously appropriate to the regulation of occupation between those who have equal rights to occupy'.[168] As with non-molestation orders, either party may apply for a variation or discharge of the order.[169]

Non-entitled applicants

The Law Commission considered that, where a person has no property right in the home, the possibility of obtaining an occupation order should be limited to cohabitants (who were protected under the Domestic Violence and Matrimonial Proceedings Act 1976 anyway), former cohabitants, and former spouses, as these were the classes of relationship most in need of protection.[170] Accordingly, the Act provides that where the respondent is entitled under property law to occupy the dwelling-house but the applicant is not, he or she may seek an occupation order as a 'non-entitled applicant'.[171] The Civil Partnership Act 2004 extends this protection to former civil partners.[172] The order must be in respect of a dwelling-house which is the home they are living in, or have at any time lived in or intended to live in together (if formerly married, as their matrimonial home; if former civil partners, as their civil partnership home).[173] Additionally, spouses, former spouses, civil partners or former civil partners, cohabitants and former cohabitants may seek an order where *neither* party is entitled to occupy the dwelling-house, in respect of the home they are currently living in.[174] This category is intended to deal with the, perhaps relatively uncommon, situation where the couple are occupying a property either as squatters or, more likely, as bare licensees.

Non-entitled applicants where the respondent has property rights

In respect of applications brought by non-entitled applicants where the respondent has property rights, it is necessary to consider three separate issues. First, what provisions may be included in an order? Secondly, what criteria apply to the grant of an order, and to the provisions included within it? Thirdly, how long may an order last? On these last two issues the Act distinguishes between former spouses and former civil partners on the one hand, and current or former cohabitants on the other.

---

[167] *Practice Note* [1978] 1 WLR 1123. Orders of indefinite duration were occasionally made: see *Spencer v Camacho* (1983) 4 FLR 662, CA and *Galan v Galan* [1985] FLR 905, CA.

[168] Law Com No 207 para 4.35, 4.36.   [169] Section 49.   [170] See Law Com No 207 para 4.8.

[171] Under the former law, it was clearly established by the House of Lords in *Davis v Johnson* [1979] AC 264, HL that non-entitled cohabitants could obtain ouster injunctions under the Domestic Violence and Matrimonial Proceedings Act 1976, but the jurisdiction did not extend to those whose cohabitation had ceased a significant time before proceedings were brought: *Harrison v Lewis* [1988] 2 FLR 339, CA, *McLean v Nugent* (1980) 1 FLR 26, CA. Former spouses were outside the ambit of the 1976 Act.

[172] Civil Partnership Act 2004 Sch 9 para 6.

[173] Section 35(1)(c) as amended—former spouses or former civil partners; s 36 (as amended by the Domestic Violence, Crime and Victims Act 2004 Sch 10 para 34)—cohabitants or former cohabitants.

[174] Section 37(1)—spouses and former spouses; s 37(1A)—civil partners and former civil partners; and s 38(1) (as amended)—cohabitants and former cohabitants.

Provisions in the order

Declaratory provisions.   If the applicant is currently in occupation in the dwelling-house an order must contain the following provisions:

> (a) giving the applicant the right not to be evicted or excluded from the dwelling-house or any part of it by the respondent for the period specified in the order; and
>
> (b) prohibiting the respondent from evicting or excluding the applicant during that period.[175]

Where the applicant is not in occupation, the order must include provision:

> (a) giving the applicant the right to enter into and occupy the dwelling-house for the period specified in the order; and
>
> (b) requiring the respondent to permit the exercise of that right.[176]

These provisions were termed by the Law Commission as 'occupation rights orders', granting a right to occupy the home to applicants who do not already possess such a right.[177]

Regulatory provisions.   Additionally, it is provided that a court may also include provisions in the order to:

> (a) regulate the occupation of the dwelling-house by either or both of the parties;
>
> (b) prohibit, suspend or restrict the exercise by the respondent of his right to occupy the dwelling-house;
>
> (c) require the respondent to leave the dwelling-house or part of the dwelling-house; or
>
> (d) exclude the respondent from a defined area in which the dwelling-house is included.[178]

Taken together, these two types of provisions provide the same protection in practice to a non-entitled applicant as to an entitled applicant.[179]

Criteria for an order

Former spouses and former civil partners.   In respect of the declaratory provisions in an order, s 35(6) provides that the court must have regard to all the circumstances, including:

> (a) the housing needs and housing resources of each of the parties and of any relevant child;
>
> (b) the financial resources of each of the parties;
>
> (c) the likely effect of any order, or of any decision by the court not to [grant an order], on the health, safety or well-being of the parties and of any relevant child;
>
> (d) the conduct of the parties in relation to each other and otherwise;
>
> (e) the length of time that has elapsed since the parties ceased to live together;

---

[175] Section 35(3) as amended—former spouses and former civil partners; and s 36(3)—cohabitants and former cohabitants.

[176] Section 35(4)—former spouses and former civil partners; and s 36(4)—cohabitants and former cohabitants.   [177] Law Com No 207 para 4.3.

[178] Section 35(5)—former spouses and former civil partners; and s 36(5)—cohabitants and former cohabitants.

[179] But the permitted duration of an order is different: see Duration of an order, p 190.

(f) the length of time that has elapsed since the marriage or civil partnership[180] was dissolved or annulled; and

(g) the existence of any pending proceedings between them [relating to financial relief or property].[181]

The first four of these factors are the same as apply to applications by entitled applicants. The last three factors are intended to focus attention upon the 'qualification' of the applicant for an order. By this, the Law Commission appear to have meant that, where an applicant is not on an equal footing in property rights terms with the respondent, she needs to show some justification for obtaining a declaratory order giving rights she would not otherwise have, separate from the basic need for protection which is catered for in the regulatory parts of the order.[182]

As far as determining which regulatory provisions might be included, the court is directed to consider the factors in paragraphs (a) to (e)—which may perhaps be viewed as the 'practical' issues, as distinct from ones concerning legal status and proceedings—and then apply the same 'balance of harm' presumption as applies to entitled applicants.[183]

Cohabitants and former cohabitants.   Clearly, some of the factors relevant to former spouses or civil partners, such as the length of time which has elapsed since their marriage or partnership ended, cannot be applicable to cohabitants. Equally, the length and nature of a cohabiting relationship can vary enormously, and may be highly relevant to the question whether it would be just to make an order against a respondent. Accordingly, the Law Commission recommended that courts consider certain specific factors pertaining to the cohabitants' relationship when determining whether to make a declaratory order.[184] Parliament chose to emphasise the distinction in the 'quality' of the relationship of those who have made a public commitment to each other by being married or having formed a civil partnership as compared with cohabitants, and added to the relevant criteria. Thus, by s 36(6), the court is obliged to consider, in addition to the factors common to entitled applicants and former spouses and former civil partners:

(e) the nature of the parties' relationship and in particular the level of commitment involved in it;[185]

(f) the length of time during which they have cohabited;[186]

(g) whether there are or have been any children who are children of both parties or for whom both parties have or have had parental responsibility;

(h) the length of time that has elapsed since the parties ceased to live together; and

(i) the existence of any pending proceedings between them over property.[187]

It will be seen that in assessing the nature of the parties' relationship, the court must have regard in particular to the level of commitment involved in it. This replaces a more pejorative formulation, originally included as s 41 of the 1996 Act, which required the court 'to

[180] Inserted by Sch 9 para 5 to the Civil Partnership Act 2004.

[181] The proceedings specified are those for a property adjustment order under the Matrimonial Causes Act 1973 or Civil Partnership Act 2004, for a property order against a parent under the Children Act 1989 Sch 1, or relating to the legal or beneficial ownership of the dwelling-house: s 35(6)(g).

[182] See Law Com No 207 para 4.10.

[183] Section 35(7)–(8); see the discussion earlier, The balance of harm test, p 185.

[184] Law Com No 207 paras 4.10–4.13.

[185] Amended by s 2(2) of the Domestic Violence, Crime and Victims Act 2004.

[186] Amended by Sch 10 para 34(3) to the Domestic Violence, Crime and Victims Act 2004.

[187] The proceedings specified are those for a property order under the Children Act 1989 Sch 1 or those relating to the legal or beneficial ownership of the dwelling-house.

have regard to the fact that they have not given each other the commitment involved in marriage.' This provision was inserted by Parliament to stress the symbolic significance of marriage and to penalise cohabitation, but it is doubtful whether it added very much to the other factors which are specified. It is unlikely that a court, hearing an application by a woman who had lived with her partner for twenty years, raised their children and run a business together, was going to reject her application because they 'did not get round to the paperwork'. By the same token, a court is, under the revised wording, just as unlikely as before to show much sympathy to a financially independent applicant with no children who moves into her boyfriend's house for a month and then, having given up her own rented property, attempts to exclude him from his home.

When determining whether to include any regulatory provisions in the order, the court is required to consider the same common factors as before, and the balance of harm test.[188] However, for cohabitants and former cohabitants, this test does not operate as a *presumption* in favour of making an order but only as a further consideration. This differentiation was made by Parliament as a further attempt to distinguish marriage (and presumably, now, civil partnership) from cohabitation, and out of concern that courts should not be constrained to make orders where the applicant could point neither to property entitlement nor to recognised relationship status as a qualification for an order.

Duration of an order

The Law Commission considered that the purpose of occupation orders for non-entitled applicants is to provide relatively short-term protection to enable the applicant to find alternative accommodation, await the outcome of any legal proceedings over the property, or, potentially, to reconcile with the respondent.[189] So while entitled applicants are able to obtain orders of unlimited duration, the Act restricts this for non-entitled applicants, once again distinguishing between those who have been married (or in a civil partnership) and those who have not.[190]

Former spouses and former civil partners.   Section 35(10) limits the length of an order in favour of a non-entitled former spouse or former civil partner to a specified period not exceeding six months, although the order may be extended on one or more occasions.

Cohabitants and former cohabitants.   Section 36(10) similarly limits the duration of an order to a *maximum* period of six months, but, in line with Parliament's concern to restrict protection for this group of applicants, additionally provides that only one extension may be given, for a further maximum period of six months.

The consequence of these provisions, especially for cohabitants, is to provide a clear advantage, not simply to those who are married or in a civil partnership, as opposed to those who cohabit, but to those who can establish property rights compared with those who cannot. If Parliament had really wished to stress the value it attached to the formal legal commitment demonstrated by entry into marriage or civil partnership, it could have discriminated against even those cohabitants who have property rights, for example, by requiring the court to consider the nature of their relationship with the respondent, or by imposing a limit on the duration of any order, but it chose to do so only against those applicants who are the most vulnerable—those who have not acquired a proprietary right or interest in their home.

---

[188] Section 36(7)–(8).   [189] Law Com No 207 paras 4.7 and 4.19.
[190] The order may be varied or discharged on the application of either party: s 49.

Neither party entitled to remain in occupation of the home

Where neither spouse nor civil partner has a property right in respect of the family home, then neither can have home rights, and therefore cannot be classed as an entitled applicant.[191] Similarly, former spouses, civil partners or cohabitants may be living in a property in which neither has the right to remain, for example, as bare licensees or squatters. Since the former law permitted spouses and cohabitants to obtain ouster injunctions in such circumstances, the Law Commission recommended that the protection continue, and be extended to the other classes of non-entitled applicants.[192] Sections 37[193] and 38 duly permit applicants to obtain regulatory orders[194] to control occupation of the property by the applicant and respondent. In respect of spouses and civil partners, and former spouses and former civil partners, the criteria for making such an order are the same as apply to entitled applicants, including the balance of harm presumption.[195] No consideration of the applicant's qualification to seek an order is required, since she has no lesser entitlement to occupy the property than the respondent. However, any order made is subject to a maximum duration of six months, although it may be extended on more than one occasion.[196] A court considering whether to make an order in favour of a cohabitant or former cohabitant must have regard to the factors common to all applications,[197] and then consider the balance of harm test, although again, not as a presumption.[198] The order may have effect for up to six months, and may be renewed once.[199]

(d) Additional provisions

Where the court makes an order under s 33, s 35 or s 36, it may, at the same time, or at any time afterwards, include additional provisions.[200] It may impose on either party an obligation as to the repair and maintenance of the property or the payment of rent, mortgage or other outgoings. This may be important to preserve the long-term security of the property. For example, it would clearly be regrettable to control the parties' occupation but leave it open to the occupant to neglect the property, or for the party in a position to pay, but now excluded, to fall behind with payments, resulting in repossession. It may also require the occupying party to make periodical payments to the other, as compensation for that person's loss of occupation. Further, it may grant either party the possession or use of furniture or other contents of the home; order either party to take reasonable care of these, and order either party to take reasonable steps to keep the dwelling-house and contents secure. Such provisions may be important, as it is not unknown for a party, before letting an applicant back into the property, to strip the home of its contents, or to damage it.[201] Unfortunately, however, they are unenforceable. In *Nwogbe v Nwogbe*[202] the Court of Appeal upheld the trial judge's view that, since the provisions in s 40 are not expressly mentioned in any of the legislation concerning the enforcement of debts and judgments,[203] there was no power to commit the husband, who had failed to pay

---

[191] See s 30(1)(a).   [192] See Law Com No 207 para 4.8.

[193] As amended by Sch 9 para 8 to the Civil Partnership Act 2004.

[194] Declaratory orders cannot be made, since, by definition, the parties have no right to occupy the property. The provisions which may be included in the order are set out in s 37(3)—spouses and former spouses—and s 38(3)—cohabitants and former cohabitants.

[195] Section 37(4).   [196] Section 37(5).

[197] Section 38(4). Viz. housing needs, financial resources, likely effect of any order on the health, safety or well-being of the parties or a relevant child and the parties' conduct.   [198] Section 38(5).

[199] Section 38(6).

[200] Section 40.   [201] See *Davis v Johnson* [1979] AC 264, HL.   [202] [2000] 2 FLR 744, CA.

[203] Debtors Act 1869, ss 4 and 5, Administration of Justice Act 1970, s 28 and Sch 8, Attachment of Earnings Act 1971, Sch 1.

the monthly rent on the matrimonial home, to prison for contempt of court. Despite the court's opinion that this required urgent attention, the lacuna has not yet been closed.

(e) Enforcing orders

Introduction of power of arrest

Breach of the terms of a court order may be a civil contempt of court, but contempt procedures normally take a number of days and in the meantime the victim may be at risk. Consequently, the former legislation empowered the court, on making an order restraining the respondent from using violence (but not just molestation), or excluding a respondent from the home, to attach a power of arrest to the order. However, courts considered that the civil liberties implications of empowering summary arrest and detention for breach of a civil order were such that the power should only be used 'where men or women persistently disobey injunctions and make a nuisance of themselves to the other party and to others concerned'.[204] Thus, the power was attached in only a minority of cases.[205]

The Law Commission were impressed by the weight of opinion supporting a presumption in favour of attaching a power of arrest in any case where there had been violence or threatened violence, viewing the power as 'a simple, immediate and inexpensive means of enforcement which underlines the seriousness of the breach to the offending party',[206] and they recommended accordingly. Section 47 of the Family Law Act 1996 therefore originally provided that if a court made an occupation or non-molestation order and it appeared to the court that the respondent had used or threatened violence against the applicant or a relevant child, it had to 'attach a power of arrest. . . unless satisfied that in all the circumstances of the case the applicant or child will be adequately protected without such a power of arrest.'[207]

Breach of a non-molestation order made a criminal offence

The incorporation of a presumption in favour of attachment tilted the balance towards a focus upon protection of the victim from further harm, resulting in a much higher proportion of orders being made with the power attached.[208] However, the Government considered that police officers were often unclear about whether they could arrest a respondent under the attached power or not, especially where it was attached only to particular provisions in the order. They noted that information on orders and powers of arrest is not recorded centrally, with inconsistent arrangements for exchanging information between police forces. They were also concerned that, where the victim had to apply for an arrest warrant because no power had been attached, she was at risk of further violence pending its issue.[209] The Domestic Violence, Crime and Victims Act 2004 therefore inserted s 42A into the 1996 Act, to provide that:

> (1) A person who without reasonable excuse does anything that he is prohibited from doing by a non-molestation order is guilty of an offence.

Those seeking to enforce the non-molestation order have to choose whether to ask for the offence to be charged or proceed via contempt proceedings, as the defendant cannot be

---

[204] Per Ormrod LJ in *Lewis v Lewis* [1978] Fam 60 at 63, CA. A similar approach was taken under the magistrates' jurisdiction: *Widdowson v Widdowson* (1982) 4 FLR 121.

[205] In 1996, of 22,652 injunctions granted under the 1976 Act, 10,049 (44%) had powers of arrest attached: *Judicial Statistics 1996* Table 5.9.   [206] Law Com No 207 para 5.13.

[207] Section 47(2).

[208] For a useful discussion, see DJ R Hill 'The Domestic Violence, Crime and Victims Act 2004' [2005] Fam Law 281.   [209] Home Office *Safety and Justice* (2003) para 46.

punished twice over.[210] One would expect the criminal route to be preferred, both because it clarifies the powers of the police and because the maximum sentence on conviction on indictment is a term of imprisonment of five years plus a fine,[211] compared with two years imprisonment for contempt.[212] The objective test imposed for liability for the offence appears in line with the mental element required for the offence of harassment under the Protection from Harassment Act 1997.

Unlike the original power of arrest under s 47, which was limited to cases where it appeared to the court that the respondent had used or threatened violence, the criminal offence may apply to a breach in respect of non-violent incidents of 'molestation'.

Power of arrest for breach of occupation order

Breach of an occupation order has *not* been made a criminal offence, but when a court is deciding whether to make an occupation order, it must consider whether to make a non-molestation order of its own motion. Doing so will bring in the criminal sanction for breach of the latter order which, one might assume, will usually encompass acts in breach of the occupation order as well. However, the court might decide that it is inappropriate to make the respondent subject to a non-molestation order, or that breach of the occupation order requires separate enforcement. Section 47 therefore now provides that, while it is no longer possible to attach a power of arrest to a non-molestation order, the court may continue to do so, in the same circumstances as hitherto, when making an occupation order.[213] Where such a power is attached, a police constable may arrest without warrant a person whom he has reasonable cause for suspecting to be in breach of any provision in the occupation order to which the arrest power is attached.[214]

In *Re B-J (Power of Arrest)* the Court of Appeal held that the duration of the power of arrest may be shorter than that of the order to which it is attached.[215] This may seem illogical, since the point of attaching the power is to enable enforcement of the order. However, the court considered that while it may be appropriate to make the substantive order of indefinite or long duration because of the circumstances between the parties, it would put the cart before the horse to limit the order because the court feels that it is unnecessary that the power of arrest last so long.[216] Equally, it is unjust to the respondent to hold him at risk of arrest for a period longer than is necessary to ensure his compliance.[217]

Dealing with the respondent after arrest

If the respondent is arrested for breach of the non-molestation order under s 42A, he will be subject to the usual criminal justice processes regarding detention, charge and remand. Where, however, the arrest is made under s 47, its purpose is to bring the respondent

---

[210] Section 42A(3)(4). See C Bessant 'Enforcing Non-Molestation Orders in the Civil and Criminal Courts' [2005] Fam Law 640.

[211] Section 42A(5)(a). The maximum for summary conviction is imprisonment for 12 months plus a fine not exceeding the statutory maximum. [212] Contempt of Court Act 1981 s 14(1).

[213] As amended by the Domestic Violence, Crime and Victims Act 2004 Sch 10 para 38. See DJ R Hill 'Abolition of the Power of Arrest' [2005] Fam Law 474.

[214] Section 47(6). [215] [2000] 2 FLR 443, CA.

[216] Cf the Court of Appeal's view, in *Chechi v Bashier* [1999] 2 FLR 489, that the trial judge had correctly declined to make a non-molestation order where the power of arrest that would have been attached to it would have given the applicant too much power over his relatives, in the particular family dynamics in that case: see earlier, Non-molestation orders, Who may apply for an order? p 180.

[217] Where the court has made a non-molestation order, or a power of arrest has not been attached to an occupation order (or only to certain provisions of it), the applicant may apply for the issue of a warrant for the respondent's arrest if she considers that he has failed to comply with the order: s 47(8) as amended.

before the relevant judicial authority for punishment for contempt. This must be done within 24 hours from the time of the arrest,[218] and he may then be remanded, on bail or in custody, or dealt with for the breach.[219]

(f) *Ex parte* orders

It was possible under the former legislation to obtain an order *ex parte* (without notice), although this was rare, especially in respect of what were then called ouster orders. The courts considered that orders should only be made where it was necessary to act quickly to avert a real and immediate danger of serious injury or irreparable damage,[220] and that, where possible, substituted service or abridgement of the period of notice should be used instead. The Law Commission recognised the drawbacks of without notice orders: they might be based on misconceived or malicious allegations with no opportunity for the court to test these out. There is, moreover, no opportunity to try to resolve the parties' differences by agreed undertakings,[221] nor is there scope for bringing home to the respondent the seriousness of the situation and the importance of compliance with the order.[222] However, the need to provide a protective remedy as a matter of urgency, or to provide a breathing-space to enable an applicant to pursue her remedy, led them to recommend a test which would balance these competing considerations. The vast majority of applications for both non-molestation and occupation orders (20,224 out of 23,885 in 2013)[223] are in fact made *ex parte*.

Section 45 provides that a court may make either a non-molestation or occupation order *ex parte* where 'it considers it just and convenient to do so', but must have regard to all the circumstances, including:

(a) any risk of significant harm to the applicant or a relevant child, attributable to conduct of the respondent, if the order is not made immediately;

(b) whether it is likely that the applicant will be deterred or prevented from pursuing the application if an order is not made immediately; and

(c) whether there is reason to believe that the respondent is aware of the proceedings but is deliberately evading service and that an applicant or a relevant child will be seriously prejudiced by the delay involved [in effecting service].[224]

The court making an order must afford the respondent the opportunity of a full hearing as soon as is just and convenient, and the duration of any occupation order made at the full hearing must be calculated taking into account the date when the *ex parte* order was made.[225] The court may attach a power of arrest to an *ex parte* occupation order[226] if it appears that the respondent has used or threatened violence against the applicant or a relevant child, and there is a risk of significant harm to them, attributable to the respondent's conduct, if the power of arrest is not attached to the order immediately. In such a case, the court may provide that the power of arrest is to last for a shorter period than the other provisions in the order, which reflects the concern that the respondent's civil liberties are

[218] Excluding Christmas Day, Good Friday or any Sunday: s 47(7). Where the arrest is pursuant to a warrant, the respondent must be brought before the court immediately.
[219] For guidance on sentencing for breach, see *Hale v Tanner* [2000] 1 WLR 2377, CA.
[220] *Ansah v Ansah* [1977] Fam 138, CA; *G v G (Ouster: Ex Parte Application)* [1990] 1 FLR 395, CA; *Practice Note* [1978] 2 All ER 919.   [221] Discussed in the next section, Undertakings, p 195.
[222] Law Com No 207, para 5.6.
[223] *Court Statistics (quarterly) January to March 2014* Table 2.7 [online] CSV_Domestic_Violence_National.csv (accessed 4 August 2014).
[224] Section 45(2).   [225] Section 45(3), (4).
[226] Section 47(3) as amended by Sch 10 para 38(4) to the Domestic Violence, Crime and Victims Act 2004.

doubly jeopardised in a case where, first, he is at risk of arrest for a civil matter, and secondly, he has had no opportunity to contest the making of the order.[227]

(g) Undertakings

An undertaking whereby the respondent gives a promise to the court in the terms of the proposed order, for example, that he will not molest the applicant, and will leave the home within seven days, became a common[228] and popular alternative mechanism to the making of an order under the former law. It was to the respondent's advantage, since no finding of fact would be made on the applicant's allegations against him. It was to the court's advantage, because it obviated the need for a full hearing and thus saved time. And it was to the applicant's advantage, inter alia because she did not need to give evidence against the respondent in court, and because an undertaking has the effect of an order of the court and is therefore enforceable through contempt proceedings. It was also said to reduce confrontation and defuse explosive situations.[229] Section 46 (as amended) accordingly empowers the court to accept an undertaking from any party to the proceedings. However, a police power of arrest may not be attached to an undertaking[230] so an applicant who agrees to an undertaking rather than proceeding with her application runs the risk of facing difficulty if she needs practical enforcement measures to be taken in the future.[231] Section 46(3) therefore provides that a court shall not accept an undertaking 'instead of making an occupation order in any case where, apart from this section a power of arrest would be attached to the order.'[232] Section 46(3A)[233] also directs a court not to accept an undertaking instead of making a non-molestation order where it appears that the respondent has used or threatened violence against the applicant or a relevant child (the same test as for attaching a power of arrest) and, for their protection, it is necessary to make a non-molestation order so that any breach may be punishable under s 42A. Accordingly, a court ought not to accept an undertaking where it would otherwise make an order which could be enforceable by a power of arrest.

2. PROTECTION FROM HARASSMENT ACT 1997

Before the Protection from Harassment Act 1997, attempts were made to extend the existing law of tort to cover harassment. It was held in *Patel v Patel*[234] that harassment does not amount to a distinct tort. However, relying upon old cases,[235] where it had been held

---

[227] See *President's Direction: Family Law Act 1996 Part IV* [1998] 1 FLR 496. Compare 'go orders', discussed later, Domestic Violence Protection Notices and Orders, p 202.

[228] G Jones et al 'Domestic violence applications: an empirical study of one court' (1995) 17 JSWFL 67, Tables 15 and 16 found nearly half of non-molestation applications were resolved by means of an undertaking in the court they studied, and District Judge Bird put the proportion at 80% in his memorandum to the House of Lords Special Public Committee *Written Evidence* p 7. Magistrates did not have the power to accept undertakings.

[229] DJ S Gerlis 'The Family Homes and Domestic Violence Bill—Undermining the Undertaking' [1994] Fam Law 700. The problems of utilising mediation to deal with domestic violence are discussed by F Kaganas and C Piper 'Domestic Violence and Divorce Mediation' (1994) 16 JSWFL 265 and F Raitt 'Domestic Violence and divorce mediation: A rejoinder' (1996) 18 JSWFL 11.   [230] Section 46(2).

[231] See the concerns expressed by A Kewley 'Pragmatism before principle: the limitations of civil law remedies for the victims of domestic violence' [1996] JSWFL 1.

[232] As amended by Sch 10 para 37 to the Domestic Violence, Crime and Victims Act 2004. See earlier, Power of arrest for breach of occupation order, p 193.

[233] As amended by Sch 10 para 37 to the Domestic Violence, Crime and Victims Act 2004.

[234] [1988] 2 FLR 179, CA.

[235] *Wilkinson v Downton* [1897] 2 QB 57; *Janvier v Sweeney* [1919] 2 KB 316, CA.

that conduct calculated to impair the plaintiff's health, and having that effect, was a tort, the Court of Appeal in *Burnett v George*[236] was able to hold that pestering having the like consequence could be restrained by injunction.

The civil law was extended by the 1997 Act, which, as well as creating the new criminal offences of harassment and putting a person in fear of violence, also created a statutory tort of harassment, based on a claim brought 'by the person who is or may be the victim of the course of conduct in question'.[237]

Section 3(2) provides for damages to be awarded for, inter alia, any anxiety caused by the harassment, and any financial loss which results. It has been said that the prospect of damages may be attractive in cases (perhaps few?) where the perpetrator has the means to satisfy the award, and it has been held that there is no bar on concurrent applications under both s 42 of the 1996 Act and this provision. The High Court or county court may also issue an injunction to prohibit further harassment, and the plaintiff may apply for a warrant for arrest to be issued where he or she considers that the defendant has broken the terms of such an injunction.[238] Breach of the injunction may be punishable either as a contempt of court or, where the defendant has no reasonable excuse, as an offence.[239]

3. INJUNCTIONS IN OTHER CIVIL PROCEEDINGS

The 1996 Act is intended to cater for a wide range of family relationships where some form of protective order is required, and the Protection from Harassment Act 1997 provides a jurisdiction dealing with harassment, but the general jurisdiction of the courts to provide injunctions, ancillary to substantive proceedings, may still be relevant in situations which might fall outside these two statutes. Injunctions may be granted either under the Senior Courts Act 1981 s 37 in respect of the High Court or the County Courts Act 1984 s 38 'in all cases in which it appears to the court to be just and convenient to do so.'

The High Court also has an 'inherent jurisdiction' to grant injunctions which has been relied upon to protect litigants in pending proceedings, and to protect children and recently, parents, from abusive behaviour. However, the basis for the exercise of this juris-diction is not particularly clear. It is undoubtedly the case that the High Court exercising its *parens patriae* jurisdiction may make orders to protect children where necessary,[240] and old decisions asserting an 'inherent jurisdiction' may be examples of the exercise of that power.[241] One manifestation of the High Court's power is through wardship.[242] On this basis, it has been held that the inherent jurisdiction may be invoked by a local author-ity to obtain an injunction preventing a suspected sexual abuser from visiting the home and children of his woman friend.[243] More controversially, in *Re S (Minors)(Inherent Jurisdiction: Ouster)*,[244] the same approach was taken by Connell J in response to a local authority's application to have the children's father excluded from the home. The father conceded that the court had power to make the order, but his Lordship's view that the

---

[236] [1992] 1 FLR 525, CA.

[237] Section 3(1). For procedural issues, see DJ R Hill 'Protection from Harassment' [2005] Fam Law 364 at pp 366–367.

[238] But the court cannot attach a power of arrest at the time of issuing the injunction.

[239] Section 3(6)–(8). The offence is punishable on indictment by imprisonment for a term not exceeding five years and/or a fine; or, on summary conviction, to imprisonment for a term not exceeding six months, and/or a fine: s 3(9).

[240] *Re Spence* (1847) 2 Ph 247.

[241] *Stewart v Stewart* [1973] Fam 21. *Wilde v Wilde* [1988] 2 FLR 83, CA.

[242] See Ch 20, Wardship, p 742.   [243] *Devon County Council v S* [1994] Fam 169.

[244] [1994] 1 FLR 623.

inherent jurisdiction was applicable and appropriate took no account of the statutory regime governing exclusion from the matrimonial home, and on that account appears to be in conflict with the House of Lords' approach in *Richards v Richards*.[245]

As Wall J once put it, there remains 'a substantial degree of confusion, both about the nature of the inherent jurisdiction and the extent of the powers exercisable under it.'[246] Such confusion has arguably been compounded by a case, *Re L (Vulnerable Adults with Capacity: Court's Jurisdiction) (No 2)*[247] initially decided on a without notice basis by his Lordship when he was President of the Family Division,[248] and subsequently by Theis J after a full hearing.[249] An elderly couple were, allegedly, being threatened with violence and abusive behaviour by their adult son, who lived with them. They were mentally competent[250] but declined to seek any legal remedies against him. The local authority, which was supplying care services to the disabled mother, applied to the High Court for an order restraining the son from molesting the parents. The Court of Appeal upheld both judges' view that this could be done under the inherent jurisdiction in order to fill a lacuna whereby the parents were in need of protection but there was no other mechanism of providing this for them. In so holding, the Court approved of the approach to the law set out in an earlier decision by Munby J,[251] who had considered that the jurisdiction may be exercised in relation to 'a vulnerable adult who, even if not incapacitated by mental disorder or mental illness, is, or is reasonably believed to be, either: (i) under constraint; or (ii) subject to coercion or undue influence; or (iii) for some other reason deprived of the capacity to make the relevant decision, or disabled from making a free choice, or incapacitated or disabled from giving or expressing a real and genuine consent.' However, the question of whether and when such intervention should be attempted is not straightforward, involving a difficult balancing exercise between potentially upholding the parties' rights under Art 3 of the ECHR whilst simultaneously interfering with their rights under Art 8.

4. FORCED MARRIAGE PROTECTION ORDERS

Alongside a deeper appreciation of the variety of forms in which abuse can be perpetrated on family members, there has grown an awareness that some cultural norms may also be coercive and that vulnerable people, particularly in certain minority ethnic groups, may be subjected to abusive practices.[252] We saw in Chapter 3 that while arranged marriages are seen as perfectly acceptable, *forced* marriages are an abuse of human rights.[253] Recognition that this constitutes a serious problem resulted in the introduction of a private members' bill by Lord Lester of Herne Hill in 2006. There was wide parliamentary support for this and the Government took over the bill, which was enacted as the Forced Marriage (Civil Protection) Act 2007. This inserted Part 4A into the Family Law Act 1996

---

[245] [1984] AC 174, HL. It would probably now be regarded as also conflicting with the power of a court to include an exclusion requirement in the terms of an emergency protection or interim care order, under Sch 6 to the Family Law Act 1996, discussed in Ch 16, The power to add an exclusion requirement, p 587.

[246] In *C v K (Inherent Powers; Exclusion Order)* [1996] 2 FLR 506 at 511.   [247] [2013] Fam 1.

[248] [2010] EWHC 2675 (Fam) [2011] Fam 189. See the discussion by J Miles 'Family abuse, privacy and state intervention' [2011] CLJ 31.

[249] Sub nom *A Local Authority v DL* [2011] EWHC 1022 (Fam) [2012] 1 FLR 1119.

[250] Although by the time of the Court of Appeal hearing, one had lost mental capacity.

[251] *Re SA (Vulnerable Adult with Capacity: Marriage)* [2005] EWHC 2942 (Fam) [2006] 1 FLR 867.

[252] See Home Office *A Choice by Right* (2000) and FCO *Forced Marriage, A Wrong Not a Right* (2005).

[253] See C Dauvergne and J Millbank 'Forced Marriage as a Harm in Domestic and International Law' (2010) 73 MLR 57.

to enable courts to make 'forced marriage protection orders'.[254] Its position immediately following the provisions on non-molestation and occupation orders underscores the association of forced marriage with domestic abuse. The use of civil, rather than criminal, measures as a response was intended to reassure victims that they could seek help without placing their families at risk of criminal sanctions—the same rationale for the introduction of non-molestation and occupation orders.

(a) The order

Under s 63A, a court may make a forced marriage protection order:

> for the purposes of protecting—
>
> (a) a person from being forced into a marriage or from any attempt to be forced into a marriage; or
> (b) a person who has been forced into a marriage.

Section 63A(4) provides that 'a person ("A") is forced into a marriage if another person ("B") forces A to enter into a marriage (whether with B or another person) without A's free and full consent.' The conduct forcing A to enter into the marriage need not be directed against A her- or himself and 'force' includes to 'coerce by threats or other psychological means'[255] so that a threat that a sibling will be prevented from continuing their education, or that a parent will be shamed before the community, if the victim does not go through with the marriage could amount to sufficient coercion. The burden of proof is on the applicant and the standard of proof is the simple balance of probabilities.[256]

As with non-molestation orders under s 42, in deciding whether to make an order, the court must have regard to all the circumstances including the need to secure the health, safety and well-being of the person to be protected and in 'ascertaining that person's well-being, the court must, in particular, have such regard to the person's wishes and feelings (so far as they are reasonably ascertainable) as the court considers appropriate in the light of the person's age and understanding.'[257] An order may be made without notice and the court may accept an undertaking instead of making an order.[258] It may be made for a specified period or until varied or discharged.[259]

An order made under the section may contain such prohibitions, restrictions or requirements (which could include prohibitions on travel abroad or surrender of passports, or an order to reveal the whereabouts of the victim) and such other terms as the court considers appropriate and may in particular, 'relate to conduct outside England and Wales as well as (or instead of) conduct within England and Wales'.[260] Respondents may include those who aid, abet, counsel, procure, encourage, assist or conspire to force, or attempt to force, a person into a marriage. The aim is thus to ensure that the order can

---

[254] An excellent overview of the background and detail of the provisions is contained in P Strickland *Forced Marriage: Standard Note* SN/HA/1003 Updated 16 September 2013 (2013, House of Commons Library). Similar provisions exist in Scotland, in the Forced Marriage etc. (Protection and Jurisdiction) (Scotland) Act 2011.   [255] Section 63A(6).

[256] *A v SM and HB (Forced Marriage Protection Orders)* [2012] EWHC 435 (Fam) [2012] 2 FLR 1077.

[257] Section 63A(2)(3).   [258] Sections 63D, 63E.

[259] Sections 63F, 63G. For an order made without limit of time, see *A v SM and HB (Forced Marriage Protection Orders)* [2012] EWHC 435 (Fam) [2012] 2 FLR 1077.

[260] However, orders are not enforceable abroad and it would be necessary to utilise local legal or intergovernmental procedures to put them into effect.

apply even where the coercion takes place abroad, and even where others (who may or may not be part of the victim's own family) are involved.

Unlike non-molestation and occupation orders, only designated courts of the Family Court, and the High Court, have jurisdiction to make forced marriage protection orders. The courts so designated are situated in main urban centres and are expected to have specialist court staff and procedures in place to ensure safety and confidentiality for victims and those supporting them.[261]

(b) Who can apply?

Importantly, under s 63C, a court may make an order on application or when already hearing family proceedings[262] in which the respondent to the order is a party. An application may be made by the victim, a 'relevant third party' (specified by the Lord Chancellor[263] as a local authority) or any other person who is given leave, such as a concerned family member. In deciding whether to grant leave, the court:

> must have regard to all the circumstances including—
>
> (a) the applicant's connection with the person to be protected;
> (b) the applicant's knowledge of the circumstances of the person to be protected; and
> (c) the wishes and feelings of the person to be protected so far as they are reasonably ascertainable and so far as the court considers it appropriate, in the light of the person's age and understanding, to have regard to them.[264]

(c) Power of arrest

Under the provisions as originally enacted, if the court intended to make a forced marriage protection order and considered that the respondent had used or threatened violence against the person being protected or otherwise in connection with the matters being dealt with, then it *had to* attach a power of arrest to the order unless it considered that, in all the circumstances of the case, there would be adequate protection without such a power.[265] The court also had the discretion to attach a power of arrest order if it considered that there was a risk of significant harm to a person, attributable to conduct of the respondent (or any person to whom the order is directed), if the power of arrest was not attached to the provisions immediately.[266] Breach of an order was punishable as a contempt of court.[267] Under the Anti-Social Behaviour, Crime and Policing Act 2014, Part 10, breach of an order has become a criminal offence so that a power of arrest automatically exists and these provisions have been repealed.[268]

---

[261] See MoJ/HMCTS *Forced Marriage Protection Orders: A Guide to the Court Process* (2012, 2nd edn).

[262] Which for these purposes include proceedings under the inherent jurisdiction of the High Court in relation to adults, proceedings in which an emergency protection order including an exclusion requirement has been made, and proceedings where an order has been made under s 50 of the Children Act 1989 for the recovery of abducted children: s 63C(7).   [263] Section 63C(7).

[264] Section 63C(4).   [265] Section 63H(1) and (2).

[266] Section 63H(4). Under s 63J an interested party may apply for the issue of a warrant for arrest where no power has been attached or it does not apply to certain provisions in the order or has expired.

[267] However, contempt proceedings could not be initiated by the police, but only by a local authority or the Attorney General: *Bedfordshire Police v U and another* [2013] EWHC 2350 (Fam) [2014] Fam 69.

[268] Section 120 inserting s 63CA into Part 4A of the Family Law Act 1996. The provisions operate in the same way as those relating to breach of a non-molestation order, discussed earlier, Breach of a non-molestation order made a criminal offence, p 192.

(d) Effectiveness

In 2013, 103 orders were made under the provisions in Part 4A, 80 of which had powers of arrest attached.[269] However, there are no reliable statistics concerning the actual extent of forced marriage in the UK. In the same year, the government's Forced Marriage Unit (FMU) provided advice or support in almost 1,500 cases, but research published in 2009 estimated there were between 5,000 and 8,000 cases reported to the authorities—and the number of *unreported* cases is of course unknown.[270] In 2012, of the 1,485 cases handled by the FMU, where the victim's age was known, 13% were under 15, 22% aged 16 or 17, 30% aged 18 to 21—but the oldest victim was 71 and the youngest was 2. 82% of victims were female and 18% male. While the largest proportion (47.1%) involved families from Pakistan, victims' family of origin came from a further 59 countries. 114 cases involved victims with disabilities and 22 involved victims who identified as lesbian, gay, bisexual or transgender.[271]

In *Bedfordshire Police v U and another*[272] Holman J, in holding that the police had no standing to commit persons suspected of breach of an order for contempt of court, concluded that in his view, the case revealed 'a grave weakness in the existing forced marriage protection order machinery'. He described forced marriages as 'a scourge, which degrade the victim and can create untold human misery' and urged that orders should have 'real teeth' to ensure that those bound by them appreciate that they will be enforced. He called on the Government to give urgent consideration to improving the effectiveness of forced marriage protection orders and the means of their enforcement but noted that it was not for him to suggest how that should be done.

Similar concern that the provisions of the Act were not providing effective protection led the House of Commons Home Affairs Select Committee to recommend the criminalisation of forced marriage itself.[273] Initially, the Government opposed this, arguing that it would be difficult to define the offence, would be hard to prove to the criminal standard and could result in intimidation or worse of victims and witnesses.[274] However, after a public consultation,[275] the Government announced in 2012 that it would seek to criminalise both breach of an order, and forced marriage.[276]

The Anti-Social Behaviour, Crime and Policing Act 2014 s 121 provides that a person commits an offence if he or she:

> (1) (a) uses violence, threats or any other form of coercion for the purpose of causing another person to enter into a marriage, and
>   (b) believes, or ought reasonably to believe, that the conduct may cause the other person to enter into the marriage without free and full consent.

---

[269] *Court Statistics (quarterly) January to March 2014, Main Tables* Table 2.8.

[270] Department for Children, Skills and Families, Research Brief No DCSF-RB128, *Forced Marriage: Prevalence and Service Response* (2009).

[271] https://www.gov.uk/government/uploads/system/uploads/attachment_data/file/141823/Stats_2012.pdf (accessed on 20 April 2014).

[272] [2013] EWHC 2350 (Fam) [2014] Fam 69 at [38]–[40].

[273] See HC Home Affairs Select Committee *Domestic violence, forced marriage and 'honour-based' violence* 20 May 2008, HC 263 of 2007–08 and *Forced Marriage* 10 May 2011, HC 880 of 2010–2012.

[274] Home Office *Forced Marriage: The Government response to the Eighth report from the Home Affairs Committee, Session 2010–12 HC 880*, Cm 8151, July 2011.

[275] Home Office *Forced Marriage Consultation* (2011).

[276] Number 10 Downing Street Press Release *Forced Marriage to become a criminal offence* 8 June 2012. See earlier regarding criminalisation of breach of an order, Power of arrest, p 199.

(3) ... (a) practises any form of deception with the intention of causing another person to leave the United Kingdom, and

(b) intends the other person to be subjected to conduct outside the United Kingdom that is an offence under subsection (1) or would be an offence under that subsection of the victim were in England and Wales.[277]

It can be seen that the offence would cover actions such as direct threats and intimidation as well as violence, and tricking the victim into going abroad (eg for a 'holiday') intending the marriage to take place outside the United Kingdom. Moreover, in the case of a victim who lacks capacity to consent to marriage, sub-section (2) provides that '... the offence under subsection (1) is capable of being committed by any conduct carried out for the purpose of causing the victim to enter into a marriage (whether or not the conduct amounts to violence, threats or any other form coercion).' Section 121(4) provides that 'marriage' 'means any religious or civil ceremony of marriage (whether or not legally binding)'. Some people (particularly in the Muslim community) may hold a religious wedding which is not recognised under the civil law, leaving them without the protections that accrue to spouses (for example, if the relationship breaks down and financial support is needed).[278] The status of the marriage has not been discussed in any reported decision on the making of a forced marriage protection order, but the same definition applies to the Family Law Act under s 63S.

The criminalisation of forced marriage is a controversial measure, with strong voices arguing that it will increase the risk to victims, whilst those in favour argue that it is an essential step in deterring forced marriage.[279] It will be interesting to see what use is made of the new provisions.

5. DOMESTIC VIOLENCE PROTECTION NOTICES AND ORDERS

The Family Law Act 1996 contains a power, never brought into force, in s 60, to provide for rules of court setting out when 'prescribed persons' may act on behalf of another to bring proceedings under Part IV of the Act. This stemmed from a Law Commission recommendation[280] that the police be given the power, as in certain Australian states, to seek civil remedies on the victim's behalf. This was said, inter alia, to remove the burden of stress upon the victim to take action. This recommendation was not accepted by the Government, on the basis that introducing a power to seek a civil remedy would represent too radical a departure from the core criminal justice functions of the police, but the opposition successfully pressed an amendment to the legislation, which became s 60 of the Act, to enable some form of representative action to be introduced through rules of court.[281]

---

[277] An offence is committed only if either the perpetrator or victim are in England and Wales at the time of the coercion or deception, or if both are abroad, one of them is habitually resident in England and Wales or a UK national: s 109(5). The offence is punishable on summary conviction to imprisonment for up to 12 months or a fine or both, and on indictment, to imprisonment for up to seven years. Section 110 provides for an equivalent offence under Scots law, but the maximum term of imprisonment there is two years.

[278] For the interaction of civil and religious law in relation to marriage, see G Douglas et al 'The role of religious tribunals in regulating marriage and divorce' [2012] CFLQ 139.

[279] For a summary of the arguments, see P Strickland *Forced Marriage: Standard Note* SN/HA/1003 Updated 16 September 2013 (2013, House of Commons Library) pp 9–11.

[280] Law Com No 207 paras 5.18, 5.20.

[281] See M Burton 'Third party applications for protection orders in England and Wales: service providers' views on implementing Section 60 of the Family Law Act 1996' (2003) 25 JSWFL 137.

As we have seen, forced marriage protection orders may be sought on behalf of a victim by a local authority or concerned person with leave of the court. A Government consultation in 2009[282] resulted in two additional measures being included in the Crime and Security Act 2010—domestic violence protection notices (DVPN) and orders (DVPO). Such measures, known also as 'go orders', enable the police to take action beyond charging for an offence, on behalf of a victim. Having been the subject of pilot schemes in various police areas they were implemented nationally in 2014.

(a) Domestic violence protection notice

Section 24 of the Crime and Security Act 2010 provides that an 'authorising officer' (not below the rank of superintendant) may issue a DVPN to a person ('P') aged 18 or over where the officer has reasonable grounds for believing that –

(a) P has been violent towards, or has threatened violence towards, an associated person, and
(b) the issue of the DVPN is necessary to protect that person from violence or a threat of violence by P.

'Associated person' bears the same meaning as under Part IV of the Family Law Act 1996.[283] Although the officer must consider the views of the victim, her consent to the issuing of the notice is not required, thus raising the issue again of how far the state should take to itself the decision whether to impose restraints upon a person who may have committed no crime, against the personal wishes of the victim.[284]

The notice must contain 'provision to prohibit P from molesting the person for whose protection it is issued'[285] and if the person lives in the same premises as the victim, it may also prohibit P from evicting or excluding the victim from the premises and exclude P from those premises and from coming within a certain distance,[286] in the same way as an occupation order under Part IV of the Family Law Act 1996. It must be in writing and served on P personally by a police constable.[287]

Although the officer must consider any representations made by P, he or she has the power in effect to make a non-molestation or occupation order without any of the protections for the defendant contained in Part IV of the 1996 Act. The notice remains in effect for up to 48 hours so it is a limited interference with the rights of the person but a police officer may arrest without warrant if he has reasonable grounds for believing that P is in breach of its terms[288] and P must then be kept in custody for up to 24 hours and brought to court.[289]

(b) Domestic violence protection order

Section 25(1)(c) provides that the notice must include the information that an application (made under s 27) for a domestic violence protection order will be heard (by a magistrates' court) within 48 hours of the time of service of the DVPN and that notice of the hearing will be given to P. The notice continues in effect until that application is determined.

---

[282] HM Government *Together We can End Violence against Women and Girls: A Consultation Document* (2009).
[283] Section 24(9).
[284] The welfare of any relevant child and the opinion of anyone else living in the premises, must also be considered: s 24(3).
[285] Section 24(6).   [286] Section 24(8).   [287] Section 25(2).
[288] Section 25(1)(b).   [289] Section 26.

At the hearing, the court may make a DVPO under s 28 provided that two conditions are met. First, it must be satisfied 'on the balance of probabilities that P has been violent towards, or has threatened violence towards, an associated person.' Secondly, the court must consider that making the DVPO 'is necessary to protect that person from violence or a threat of violence by P.'[290] The court must consider the same range of persons interested as the police officer, including the victim and any relevant child, but again, it may make the order against their wishes.[291] Like a notice, the order may include occupation provisions as well as those focused on non-molestation and it must include a power of arrest.[292] It may last between 14 and 28 days.[293] The order cannot be varied or revoked, and it will lapse automatically at the end of its stated duration. Breach is a contempt of court.

It has been convincingly argued that the human rights implications of these provisions have not been adequately considered.[294] It would be regrettable if measures intended to aid those at risk of violence become vulnerable to challenge by perpetrators and the protections promised cannot be delivered.

D. REMEDIES THROUGH HOUSING LAW

Even if a victim of violence obtains an order under the jurisdictions discussed so far in this chapter or criminal proceedings are successfully taken, this may provide only an interim solution to the problem. Many victims will seek to leave the home and put themselves and their children out of harm's way rather than rely on the uncertain compliance of the perpetrator with any court order. Some victims will have to flee the home at short notice. All will require some form of accommodation, be it temporary or permanent. The provision of temporary refuges is one means by which urgent accommodation needs may be met, but many victims must find alternatives, such as staying with friends and relatives, being placed in hostels, or in temporary accommodation such as bed and breakfast hotels.

1. ACTIONS IN RELATION TO RENTED PROPERTIES

(a) Transfer of tenancy

One long-term solution to the housing dilemma of a victim of violence, which is available to a spouse, civil partner or cohabitant whose home is rented, is to seek a transfer of the tenancy by court order. The courts have the power to effect such a transfer in respect of couples whose marriage or partnership has been terminated, under the Matrimonial Causes Act 1973 s 24,[295] Civil Partnership Act 2004 s 72 and Sch 5,[296] and the Family Law Act 1996 s 53 and Sch 7.[297] There is also power to make such a disposition for the benefit of children, under Sch 1 to the Children Act 1989.[298] Sch 7 of the Family Law Act 1996

---

[290] Section 28(2)(3).   [291] Section 28(4)(5).
[292] Section 28(9).   [293] Section 28(10).
[294] L Crompton 'DVP notices and orders: vulnerable to human rights challenge?' [2013] Fam Law 1588.
[295] See Ch 23, Transfer of tenancy, p 907.
[296] Ch 23, Financial provision after divorce etc or dissolution: Comparable provisions under the Matrimonial Causes Act 1973 and Civil Partnership Act 2004, p 865.
[297] Ch 24, Transfer of tenancies, p 950.
[298] See Ch 21, Proceedings under Schedule 1 to the Children Act 1989, Powers, p 794.

extended the court's power to apply to cohabitants who have ceased to cohabit.[299] The Law Commission recommended this latter extension (which already existed in Scotland), to ensure that a tenancy, probably granted by a local authority or housing association on the assumption that it would provide a home for the cohabiting couple and their children, should continue to provide a secure home for the children even though their parents' relationship has broken down,[300] and also to do justice between the couple.

If the victim could therefore obtain some short- to medium-term protection, possibly under Part IV of the 1996 Act, she might then be able to seek an order under these powers for a permanent solution to her housing problem.

(b) Eviction

Alternatively, where a dwelling-house held on a secure or assured tenancy was occupied by a married couple, civil partners or a cohabiting couple, and one partner has left because of violence or threats of violence against him or her or a member of his or her family, the landlord may seek an order for possession.[301] It might be thought that this could be a useful device to justify the landlord terminating the violent partner's right to occupy, and then granting the victim a new tenancy for herself. However, the court must be satisfied that the partner who has left is unlikely to return.[302]

(c) Victim terminating tenancy

A more effective device is for a victim who is herself a joint tenant of the property to give notice of termination to the landlord,[303] on the understanding that the landlord will then grant her a fresh tenancy in her sole name. It was held by the House of Lords in *Hammersmith and Fulham London Borough Council v Monk*[304] that the appropriate notice, as required under the tenancy, given unilaterally by one joint tenant is effective to bring the tenancy to an end, notwithstanding the other tenant's lack of agreement, or even knowledge.[305] Such a device avoids the usual requirement of notice before eviction, and enables the victim effectively to obtain a transfer of the tenancy which could normally only be done by order under Sch 7 to the Family Law Act 1996. Despite the potentially draconian nature of the remedy, the argument that it is in breach of the other tenant's Art 8 right to respect for his home has been rejected and the principle has been upheld in numerous later cases.[306]

There is an undoubted difficulty in balancing the interest of the victim of violence to be rehoused safely, against that of the remaining partner who might have had security of tenure until the joint tenancy was unilaterally terminated, and whose interest must in turn be weighed against that of the landlord in controlling and allocating limited housing stock. The Law Commission recommended that a joint occupier should be able to withdraw from a

---

[299] Defined, as under Part IV of the Act, in s 62(1). See S Bridge 'Transferring Tenancies of the Family Home' [1998] Fam Law 26.   [300] Law Com No 207 para 6.3.

[301] Housing Act 1985 Sch 2 Part 1, Ground 2A (secure tenancy); Housing Act 1988 Sch 2 Part 2, Ground 14A (assured tenancy).

[302] Housing Act 1985 Sch 2 Part 1, Ground 2A (secure tenancy); Housing Act 1988 Sch 2 Part 2, Ground 14A (assured tenancy).

[303] For a valuable discussion, see M Davis and D Hughes, 'An End of the Affair—Social Housing, Relationship Breakdown, and the Human Rights Act 1998' [2004] Conv 19.

[304] [1992] 1 AC 478, HL.

[305] A joint tenant who gives notice without the other's knowledge does not act in breach of trust: *Crawley Borough Council v Ure* [1996] QB 13, CA.

[306] See eg *Harrow London Borough Council v Johnstone* [1997] 1 WLR 459, HL, *Sims v Dacorum Borough Council* [2013] EWCA Civ 12 [2013] 1 EGLR 52; *Muema v Muema* [2013] EWHC 3864 (Fam).

joint tenancy by giving notice to the landlord, without at the same time destroying the whole tenancy. They also argued that it would be fairer, and more transparent, for the landlord to seek possession and have proposed a newly defined ground for eviction which could be used against a violent tenant—though only in respect of physical violence (since they regarded the broader definition of abuse noted at the start of this chapter as too wide to justify possession proceedings).[307] These proposals are to be enacted in Wales[308] but were rejected for England.

2. SEEKING HELP UNDER THE HOMELESSNESS LEGISLATION

A victim of domestic abuse may seek help from the local authority in finding alternative accommodation, on the basis that she is homeless, as defined by statute.[309] Relationship breakdown was the cause of homelessness in 18% of cases in 2012/13, of which 69% involved violence.[310]

Part VII of the Housing Act 1996[311] imposes a duty on all local housing authorities to secure that advice and information about homelessness and its prevention, are available free of charge to any person in their district;[312] where they have reason to believe that a person may be homeless or threatened with homelessness. They must enquire into the circumstances to determine whether he is eligible for assistance, and if so, whether any duty is owed to him under the Act;[313] and secure that suitable accommodation is made available to a person[314] who is homeless, in priority need of accommodation, and who did not become homeless intentionally (subject to the requirements of Part VI of the 1996 Act concerning allocation of their own accommodation).[315]

(a) Definition of homeless

A person is homeless for the purpose of the Act if he has no accommodation available for his occupation in the United Kingdom or elsewhere, which he (together with any other person who normally resides with him as a member of his family or any other person who might reasonably be expected to reside with him):[316]

(a) is entitled to occupy by virtue of an interest in it or by virtue of an order of a court, or
(b) has an express or implied licence to occupy, or
(c) occupies as a residence by virtue of any enactment or rule of law giving him the right to remain in occupation or restricting the right of another person to recover possession.[317]

---

[307] Law Commission, Law Com No 297, *Renting Homes: The Final Report Volume 1: The Report* (2006) Cm 6781-1 paras 2.44, 2.46; Law Com No 337, *Renting Homes in Wales* (2013) Cm 8578, para 5.21. Compare with the discussion later regarding the meaning of domestic violence within s 177 of the Housing Act 1996.

[308] Welsh Government, *Renting Homes: A Better Way for Wales* White Paper (2013) http://wales.gov.uk/docs/desh/consultation/130520rentinghomesbillen.pdf.

[309] See A Arden et al *Homelessness and Allocations* (2010, 8th edn).

[310] DCLG *Housing Statistical Release: Statutory Homelessness January to March 2013 and 2012/13, England* (2013) p 4.

[311] As amended by the Homelessness Act 2002. For Wales, see Housing (Wales) Bill 2013, Part 2.

[312] Housing Act 1996 s 179.   [313] Section 184.

[314] Excluding persons from abroad and asylum seekers: Housing Act 1996 ss 185, 186, as amended.

[315] Section 193. There is an interim duty to accommodate where the authority have reason to believe that the person would be eligible, pending their decision: s 188.

[316] Section 176; an unborn child is not such a person—*R v London Borough of Newham, ex p Dada* [1996] QB 507, CA.   [317] Section 175(1). Paragraph (c) covers a spouse with home rights.

He is also homeless if he has such accommodation but he cannot secure entry to it.[318]

Section 175(3) provides that a person shall not be treated as having accommodation unless it is accommodation which it would be reasonable for him to continue to occupy, and in so determining, under s 177, domestic violence is expressly to be taken into account:

(1)   It is not reasonable for a person to continue to occupy accommodation if it is probable that this will lead to domestic violence or other violence[319] against him, or against—
      (a)   a person who normally resides with him as a member of his family, or
      (b)   any other person who might reasonably be expected to reside with him.

(1A) For this purpose 'violence' means
      (a)   violence from another person; or
      (b)   threats of violence from another person which are likely to be carried out; and violence is 'domestic violence' if it is from a person associated with the victim.

In *Yemshaw v Hounslow London Borough Council*,[320] a woman with two young children left her husband and applied to the local authority for housing as a homeless person. She told the authority that her husband hated her and that she was scared of him, although he had never actually threatened or used force against her. She also complained that he shouted at her in front of the children, did not give her money for housekeeping and that she feared that he would take the children away from her. The local authority decided that she was not homeless on the basis of threatened domestic violence. The Supreme Court held that 'violence' is not a term of art but is capable of bearing several meanings and applying to many different types of behaviour which can change and develop over time. It considered that whatever may have been the position when the original legislation was enacted in the 1970s, the general understanding of the harm which intimate partners or other family members may do to one another has moved on—as we indeed noted at the beginning of this chapter. The Court held that the purpose of the legislation is first to ensure that a person is not obliged to remain living in a home where she, her children or other members of her household are at risk of harm and secondly 'that the victim of domestic violence has a real choice between remaining in her home and seeking protection from the criminal or civil law and leaving to begin a new life elsewhere.'[321] It concluded that these purposes could be achieved if the term 'domestic violence' were interpreted in the same sense as that provided by the President of the Family Division in his *Practice Direction (Residence and Contact Orders: Domestic Violence) (No 2)*: '"Domestic violence" includes physical violence, threatening or intimidating behaviour and any other form of abuse which, directly or indirectly, may give rise to the risk of harm.'[322] This broader definition of violence is welcome, and of course in keeping with the

---

[318] Section 175(2)(a). Thus, a spouse who cannot gain entry because the locks have been changed may be regarded as homeless.

[319] Other violence added by s 10(1)(a) Homelessness Act 2002. Such violence could include racial harassment, or intimidation.

[320] [2011] UKSC 3 [2011] 1 WLR 433. For criticism of the approach by the Court, see CJS Knight 'Doing (linguistic) violence to prevent (domestic) violence? *Yemshaw v Hounslow LBC* in the Supreme Court' [2012] CFLQ 95; C Bevan 'Interpreting Statutory Purpose—Lessons from *Yemshaw v Hounslow London Borough Council*' (2013) 76(4) MLR 735.   [321] Per Baroness Hale at [27].

[322] [2009] 1 WLR 251, para 2. An authority should not take into account whether the victim could have taken action against the perpetrator to restrain his violence: the relevant question is whether domestic violence will probably follow if the person remains in occupation, and the availability of other remedies does not answer the probability question: *Bond v Leicester City Council* [2001] EWCA Civ 1544, [2002] 1 FCR 566 per Hale LJ at para 27.

modern understanding of the term, but it creates yet another definition, tied to a particular statutory jurisdiction, to consider, making the law yet more complex.

Interestingly, while the Act incorporates the same definition of 'associated person' in relation to the person who is inflicting the violence as is to be found in Part IV of the Family Law Act 1996, it does not define what is meant by 'family'. Although the term 'associated person' is intended to convey some form of domestic relationship, it is wider than what is conveyed by the word 'family'. The Code of Guidance, to which housing authorities are to have regard in discharging their functions under the Act, suggests that it would include cohabiting couples, foster children, housekeepers and companions, and carers of the elderly or disabled.[323]

'Accommodation' means a place which can fairly be described as accommodation and which it would be reasonable, having regard to the general housing conditions in the district, for the person to continue to occupy, and in *R v Brent London Borough Council, ex p Awua*[324] the House of Lords held that there is no requirement that it be settled or permanent. The question arises whether a woman who has fled with her children to a refuge may be regarded as homeless notwithstanding that she has a roof over her head. In *R v Ealing London Borough Council, ex p Sidhu*[325] it was held that she should be so regarded, otherwise she could not call on the housing authority for assistance unless the refuge gave her 28 days' notice to leave, in which case she would be 'threatened with homelessness': a procedure which would merely pile stress on stress unnecessarily. Lord Hoffmann in *Awua* agreed that a person whose only accommodation was a night shelter or hostel which he had to leave during each day and could only return to at night would not be regarded as 'having accommodation'[326] and the Code of Guidance advises that it should not be regarded as reasonable to expect a person to remain in a refuge in the medium or longer term.[327]

(b) Priority need

Persons with a priority need include inter alia:

(a) a pregnant woman or a person with whom she resides or might reasonably be expected to reside;

(b) a person with whom dependent children reside or might reasonably be expected to reside;

(c) a person who is vulnerable as a result of old age, mental illness or handicap or physical disability or other special reason,[328] or with whom such a person resides or might reasonably be expected to reside . . .[329]

In addition, under the relevant regulations, in England, if an applicant has had to cease to occupy accommodation because of violence or threats of violence which are likely to be carried out, she will be in priority need if she is vulnerable as a result.[330] A person is

---

[323] ODPM *Homelessness Code of Guidance for Local Authorities* (2002) para 6.3. The Code is not binding upon housing authorities, although they are obliged to have regard to it under s 182: *De Falco v Crawley Borough Council* [1980] QB 460, CA. For Wales, see Housing (Wales) Bill 2013, cl 43.

[324] [1996] AC 55. It was held that temporary accommodation is not, *ipso facto*, unsuitable, although accommodation likely to be available for under 28 days would not be sufficient, as the applicant would then be threatened with homelessness within the statutory definition. [325] (1982) 3 FLR 438.

[326] At 67A. [327] At para 6.26.

[328] This could include a young person or an adult with no children who has left home to escape abuse or violence: *Kelly v Monklands District Council* 1986 SLT 169, Ct of Sess (young person); *R v Kensington and Chelsea London Borough Council, ex p Kihara* (1996) 29 HLR 147, CA. [329] Section 189(1).

[330] Homelessness (Priority Need for Accommodation) (England) Order 2002 (SI No 2051).

'vulnerable' where he is 'less able to fend for oneself so that injury or detriment will result where a less vulnerable man will be able to cope without harmful effects.'[331] This may well exclude many applicants from eligibility. A more generous approach is taken in Wales, where applicants who have been subject to domestic (but not other) violence or are at risk of such violence, or would be if they returned home, are also included.[332]

The applicant's dependent child need not be wholly and exclusively dependent on or reside solely with her.[333] Nor is it necessary to have a residence order in the applicant's favour to demonstrate that she has a child residing, or reasonably expected to reside, with her.[334] Equally, however, a parent will not be regarded as in priority need because a court has made a shared residence order providing for children to live with him. The Supreme Court held in *Holmes-Moorhouse v Richmond-upon-Thames London Borough Council*[335] that the housing authority must ask whether it is reasonably to be expected, in the context of a scheme for housing the homeless, that children who already have a home with one parent should be able also to reside with the other. This may well run counter to the trend towards shared residence, but the authority are entitled to consider the impact of allocating property which will be under-occupied on the scarcity of their housing stock.[336]

(c) Intentional homelessness

The extent of the authority's duty to a homeless person in priority need depends upon whether or not they are satisfied that she became homeless (or threatened with homelessness) intentionally. If they are not so satisfied, they must secure that accommodation is available for her occupation.[337] If they are so satisfied, they are bound only to secure accommodation for her occupation for such period as they consider will give her a reasonable opportunity of securing accommodation for herself, and provide her with advice and appropriate assistance to help her find accommodation.[338] The question of whether a person is or is not intentionally homeless is therefore a crucial one.

A person is to be regarded as becoming homeless intentionally if she deliberately does or fails to do something as a result of which she ceases to occupy accommodation which is available for her occupation and which it would have been reasonable for her to continue to occupy.[339]

The question is whether the tenant *became* homeless intentionally, not whether he is now homeless intentionally. Consequently if, as in *Din v Wandsworth London Borough Council*[340] the applicant deliberately left available accommodation, he will be considered to have become homeless intentionally even though he would probably have been evicted later and thus have become homeless unintentionally. Conversely, if, as in *Gloucester City Council v Miles*,[341] the applicant became homeless because her husband had vandalised her home to such an extent that it became uninhabitable, she will not be homeless intentionally even though, had she stayed there, she would probably have become so through non-payment of rent.[342]

---

[331] *R v Waveney DC ex p Bowers* [1983] QB 238 at 244H–245A.

[332] Homeless Persons (Priority Need) (Wales) Order 2001 (SI No 607). See also, Housing (Wales) Bill 2013 cl 55.

[333] *R v London Borough of Lambeth, ex p Vagliviello* (1990) 22 HLR 392, CA (applicant could have priority need although child residing with him only 312 days a year).

[334] *R v Ealing London Borough Council, ex p Sidhu* (1982) 3 FLR 438.

[335] [2009] 1 WLR 413.

[336] *Holmes-Moorhouse v Richmond-upon-Thames London Borough Council* [2009] UKHL 7 [2009] 1 FLR 904 [16], [21].

[337] Section 193(2).   [338] Section 190.   [339] Section 191(1).

[340] [1983] 1 AC 657, HL.   [341] [1985] FLR 1043, CA.

[342] The same test is to be applied to determine whether a person is *threatened* with becoming homeless intentionally.

(d) Local connection

Where a victim of violence leaves not simply her home, but also the area where it is situated, the housing authority to whom she applies for help may argue that she has no close connection with their area, and should be housed by the authority for the area from which she came. They may seek to refer her case to that other authority under s 198 of the Act. However, they cannot do this where the applicant or any person who might reasonably be expected to reside with the applicant will run the risk of domestic violence from a person with whom they are associated, or of threats of violence from such a person which are likely to be carried out.[343]

E. A CRIMINAL OR CIVIL MATTER?

In *Lomas v Parle*, the Court of Appeal drew attention to the:

> unsatisfactory nature of the present interface between the criminal and family courts in [domestic violence] cases. It is expensive, wasteful of resources and time-consuming. It is stressful for the victim to move from court to court in order to obtain redress and protection from the perpetrator.[344]

They suggested that the possibility of integrated courts be explored to see if these might avoid the problems they had identified. However, although the Government sought opinions on the creation of specialised courts,[345] no legislative measures have been taken to develop them. Instead, as we have seen, local initiatives have been taken to establish courts, operating only in the criminal jurisdiction, and only at the magistrates' level as yet, to focus on domestic violence cases. The next step, of providing criminal and civil jurisdiction in the same court, has been taken in several states in the USA, in Canada and in Europe. But whilst judges and prosecutors apparently consider that these produce administrative efficiency and reduced recidivism, defendants' lawyers considered the courts to be biased. A chief advantage of the integrated court appears to be, as the Court of Appeal had hoped, that it can prevent the victim being shifted from pillar to post and ensure that there is full awareness of all the circumstances in the case, but concern has also been expressed that women can be pressurised into pursuing the criminal justice route against their will, or that they may even be deterred from using the court at all, for fear of having their children removed.[346]

Whether the legal response to domestic violence should primarily be the use of the criminal law, with the focus on punishment and deterrence, or through the civil law, where the primary object is to secure the safety of the victims, is a continuing question for policy makers. The much greater focus in recent policy making on the criminal justice route as the response to domestic violence may admirably reflect an increased awareness of the criminal nature of such behaviour and a determination to leave behind patriarchal value judgments about its seriousness. On the other hand, there is a danger that the views of the victim can be lost in a willingness to react 'toughly' and to ignore her longer-term needs. Moreover, there is still a need for greater recognition of the emotional

---

[343] Section 198(2), (3).   [344] [2003] EWCA Civ 1804 [2004] 1 All ER 1173 at para [51].

[345] Home Office *Safety and Justice* (2003) paras 19, 20.

[346] See M Burton 'Domestic Violence—From Consultation to Bill: Closer integration of the civil and criminal justice systems' [2004] Fam Law 128.

dimension, especially when set in the context of a failed or terminated relationship. It was noted earlier that women who have separated from their partners are at increased risk of violence.[347] It is also clear that disputes between parents over their children, especially concerning contact, may often take place in a setting in which violence, or fear of violence, is alleged by a resident parent as a reason for refusing contact and where violence is indeed inflicted by the non-resident parent as a means of exerting power over the other.[348] It is also increasingly accepted that violence against an adult partner is associated with violence against a child[349] and indeed, s 31(9) of the Children Act 1989 provides that 'harm' includes 'impairment suffered from seeing or hearing the ill-treatment of another'. The 'family' context of such violence cannot be ignored when determining how best to respond to it in the search to protect those at risk.

Government attempts to 'join up' thinking and strategy through a three-pronged approach which utilises education and prevention, protection and legal processes, and support through housing and other services such as information and advice, would appear to be the correct way forward. However, translating principles into practice is a formidable task, in the face of limited resources, especially for alternative accommodation for victims, and a legal system (in both its criminal and civil forms) which remains complex and fragmented. Of particular concern is the continuing multiplicity of definitions and understandings of 'domestic violence' or 'abuse'. We set out at the beginning of this chapter the expansive definition used by Government; we have also discussed the fact that the term 'violence' is *not* used in Part IV of the Family Law Act 1996 at all to determine whether a non-molestation order should be granted. We have also seen that the Supreme Court has adopted yet another variant in considering the scope of 'violence' for the purposes of the homelessness legislation. Moreover, we saw in Chapter 1[350] that when a person is seeking legal aid for representation in relation to a matter arising out of a family relationship, then under the Legal Aid, Sentencing and Punishment of Offenders Act 2012, they must establish that '(a) there has been, or is a risk of, domestic violence between A and B, and (b) A was, or is at risk of being, the victim of that domestic violence.'[351] For the purposes of that Act, yet another definition of 'domestic violence' is provided— it means 'any incident, or pattern of incidents, of controlling, coercive or threatening behaviour, violence or abuse (whether psychological, physical, sexual, financial or emotional) between individuals who are associated with each other'.[352]

A truly integrated, joined-up and coherent strategy for tackling domestic abuse would, surely, begin by setting out a comprehensive definition to be applied consistently in all areas of the law and social policy where the intention is to protect and support the victim. The current law is a very long way from that position.

---

[347] See The scale of domestic abuse, p 165.

[348] See Lord Chancellor's Advisory Board on Family Law, Children Act Sub-Committee *A Report to the Lord Chancellor on the Question of Parental Contact in Cases where there is Domestic Violence* (2000).

[349] See the literature cited by C Humphreys and C Harrison 'Focusing on safety—domestic violence and the role of child contact centres' [2003] CFLQ 237.

[350] Ch 1, Private ordering and the withdrawal of legal aid, p 10.   [351] Sch 1 para 1.

[352] Sch 1 para 12(9) as amended by SI 2013/748.

7

DIVORCE AND DISSOLUTION

A. INTRODUCTION

Divorce law has always been one of the most contentious subjects in family law.[1] Marriage and its place in modern society are seen as significant political and cultural issues, with the 'health' of society somehow bound up with the extent to which marriages appear to be stable or 'failing'. Since the English law of marriage derives from the Canon law, religious sensibilities have also been engaged and the Church of England has wielded considerable influence in the shape and rate of reform. Making divorce 'too easy' has been seen by some as a means of undermining traditional family life and hence the stability of society whilst others have sought to liberalise divorce precisely in order to assist the emancipation of women from the traditional role of housewife.

Confusion between the rate of marriage breakdown and the rate of divorce has often marked the debates over whether and how the law should be reformed. It is true to say that the number of divorces granted each year increased substantially during the past century and particularly in the post-war period. For example, just before the Second World War, in 1938, the number of divorce decrees granted was 6,092. By 1968, the number had increased to 45,036. The law then underwent a major reform, which made it easier to obtain a divorce against the other spouse's will, and the number of divorces began a steep climb, reaching a high point of 165,018 in 1993 and then falling back gradually, to 117,558 in 2011.[2] The decline is probably due to the falling marriage rate, with less stable relationships now formed by cohabitation rather than marriage.[3] But all that these figures show is the number of divorces granted in any given year, not the number of marriages which broke down. We cannot say for certain what the marriage breakdown rate is, nor whether it is higher than in previous times when divorce was harder to obtain, although it is likely that this is the case because of changing social attitudes to personal relationships. A bar or restriction on divorce does not, of itself, prevent marriage breakdown, although it is a matter of debate as to how far a restrictive divorce law would restrain breakdowns or encourage couples to reconcile.[4]

The enactment of the Civil Partnership Act 2004 introduced a new form of legal status[5] with its own rules for termination. Rather than refer to civil partners as obtaining a 'divorce', the Act instead uses the term 'dissolution'; however, the provisions are very

---

[1] See L Stone *Road to Divorce: England 1530–1987* (1990) and *Broken Lives: Separation and Divorce in England 1660–1857* (1993); S Cretney *Family Law in the Twentieth Century: A History* (2003) Part II.

[2] ONS, *Divorces in England and Wales, 2011* (2012).

[3] See Ch 24, The extent of cohabitation, p 935.

[4] Compare R Deech 'Divorce Law and Empirical Studies' (1990) 106 LQR 229 with J Eekelaar and M Maclean 'Divorce Law and Empirical Studies—A Reply' (1990) 106 LQR 621.

[5] See Chapter 2, The introduction of civil partnerships, pp 31.

similar to those pertaining on divorce, and are therefore discussed after we have examined the development and detail of the current divorce law.[6]

1. DIVORCE BEFORE 1857

The doctrine of the indissolubility of marriage was accepted by the English ecclesiastical courts after the Reformation, so that these courts had no power to pronounce a decree of divorce (as opposed to nullity) which would permit the parties to remarry.[7] The only way in which an aggrieved party could obtain a full divorce ('*divorce a vinculo matrimonii*') was by Act of Parliament, the expense of which was beyond the reach of most.[8]

2. THE MATRIMONIAL CAUSES ACT 1857

The possibility of obtaining a divorce without having to petition Parliament was eventually introduced by this Act. In addition to vesting the existing jurisdiction of the ecclesiastical courts in a new statutory Divorce Court (from which it was transferred to the High Court in 1875)[9] the Act permitted full divorce by judicial process for the first time in English law. But the law retained a distinction between the position of the husband and that of the wife which had applied to parliamentary divorce. A husband could petition for divorce on the ground of adultery alone, whilst a wife had to prove either adultery coupled with incest, bigamy, cruelty or two years' desertion, or, alternatively, rape or an unnatural offence.[10]

The purpose of the Act was primarily to change the process by which divorce was obtained from a legislative one to a judicial one: the principle that divorce was a remedy for a matrimonial wrong remained, and adultery was regarded as the only matrimonial offence which would justify the dissolution of the marriage bond. Here one sees reflected the mid-Victorian attitude to sexual morality: whilst one act of adultery by a wife was considered unforgivable and gave the husband the power to petition for divorce without more, she could not even rely on a series of associations by him unless the adultery was 'aggravated'.[11]

3. EXTENSION OF THE GROUNDS FOR DIVORCE

The law remained in this state until the Matrimonial Causes Act 1923[12] put the husband and wife in the same position by permitting the latter to petition on the ground of adultery alone without having to show an aggravating factor. A P Herbert's Matrimonial Causes Act 1937 further extended the grounds for divorce by permitting either spouse to base a petition on the other's cruelty, desertion for three years, or (subject to certain other conditions)

---

[6] See Dissolution of civil partnership, p 240.

[7] Although they could pronounce decrees of restitution of conjugal rights (which called upon a deserting spouse to resume cohabitation), and of divorce '*a mensa et thoro*', which was a decree of separation relieving the applicant from the duty of cohabiting with the respondent.

[8] There were on average fewer than two divorces by statute a year on the husband's petition, while in total only four were granted on the wife's petition. See L Stone *Road to Divorce: England 1530–1987* (1990); and for discussion of the 'first' 'modern' divorce case, see R Probert 'The *Roos* Case and Modern Family Law' in S Gilmore et al (eds) *Landmark Cases in Family Law* (2011).   [9] By the Judicature Acts 1873–75.

[10] Matrimonial Causes Act 1857 s 27.

[11] For a fascinating account of one of the earliest judicial divorce suits, see K Summerscale *Mrs Robinson's Disgrace: The Private Diary of a Victorian Lady* (2012).   [12] Section 1.

supervening incurable insanity.[13] This last provision introduced, for the first time, the possibility of obtaining a divorce even though the respondent was in no way at fault.

4. THE DIVORCE REFORM ACT 1969

In the decades following the Second World War there was a vast increase in the number of divorces, and although this must in some measure reflect an increase in the number of marriages that had broken down, other factors came into play. Legal aid enabled many to obtain a divorce who could not previously have afforded it; the attitude of society towards divorced spouses (particularly 'guilty' spouses) had changed; and many religious bodies were taking a far less rigid attitude. More than 90% of all petitions were undefended, and some of these undoubtedly amounted to divorce by consent.

Consequently, the idea that the purpose of divorce was to provide a remedy available only to the 'innocent' spouse for a matrimonial wrong committed by the other seemed to many to be an outdated concept. It was argued that divorce should be available to either spouse when the marriage has irretrievably broken down: to insist on the commission of a matrimonial offence lays stress upon the symptoms of breakdown rather than on the breakdown itself. The introduction of this principle would, it was argued, reduce the number of stable illicit unions[14] where there was no foreseeable chance of the parties being able to marry or of their children being legitimated because the spouse of one of them refused to release his or her partner on account of religious or moral scruples, financial advantage or vindictiveness. On the other hand, some regarded the idea as fundamentally unjust in that it would enable a party to take advantage of his own wrong and obtain a divorce against the will of an innocent spouse, who might have a conscientious objection to divorce, and because an 'innocent' wife in particular might suffer serious financial hardship as a consequence of the decree.

A Royal Commission (the Morton Commission)[15] was appointed in the 1950s to consider the law but its members were divided on how far the concept of the matrimonial offence should remain the exclusive basis for divorce, and could not reach a clear consensus on reform. Consequently nothing significant happened until two major publications appeared in 1966. In the first, *Putting Asunder*, a group appointed by the Archbishop of Canterbury to consider the law of divorce in contemporary society came down in favour of the breakdown theory. Logically they argued that this must be the sole ground of divorce and that possible abuse of the concept must be guarded against by a judicial inquest in each case. Their report was referred to the Law Commission, who in turn produced a report, *Reform of the Grounds of Divorce: the Field of Choice*. They concluded that the Archbishop's group's proposals for a full judicial enquiry in every case were impracticable, and put forward a number of possible alternatives based on the fundamental assumption that the aims of a good divorce law are:

> . . . to buttress, rather than undermine, the stability of marriage, and when, regrettably, a marriage has irretrievably broken down, to enable the empty legal shell to be destroyed with the maximum fairness and the minimum bitterness, distress and humiliation.[16]

[13] The Act largely gave effect to the recommendations of the majority of members of a Royal Commission appointed in 1909 (the Gorrell Commission, Cmd 6478). For a lively account of the history of the passage of this bill through Parliament, see Sir Alan Herbert's *The Ayes have it* (1937), and for a more recent discussion, see S Redmayne 'The Matrimonial Causes Act 1937: A Lesson in the Art of Compromise' (1993) 13 OJLS 183.

[14] But the change in the law which followed did not have this effect: see R Probert *The changing legal regulation of cohabitation: from fornicators to family 1600–2010* (2012) ch 6.   [15] Cmd 9678.

[16] Cmnd 3123 para 15.

Their own preference was for introducing as an additional ground for divorce the break-down of the marriage as evidenced by a period of separation, which should be shorter if the respondent consented than if he or she did not.

The consequence was the passing of the Divorce Reform Act 1969. It represented a compromise between the views put forward by the Archbishop's group and the Law Commission. All the old grounds for divorce were abolished and replaced by one ground—that the marriage had irretrievably broken down. This, however, could only be established by proof of one or more of five facts set out in the Act. Various safeguards for the financial protection of the respondent, who was now potentially at risk of being divorced against his or her will, and after having committed no matrimonial wrong, were introduced.

B. THE MATRIMONIAL CAUSES ACT 1973

This Act consolidated the Divorce Reform Act together with reforms relating to the financial and property consequences of divorce.[17]

1. THE SUBSTANTIVE LAW

(a) Irretrievable breakdown the sole ground for divorce

By s 1(1) of the Matrimonial Causes Act 1973 there is only one ground for divorce: that the marriage has broken down irretrievably. Irretrievable breakdown, however, may be established only by proving one or more of the five facts set out in s 1(2). If none of these is established, the court may not pronounce a decree even though it is satisfied that the marriage is at an end.[18] Although it is the duty of the court 'to inquire, so far as it reasonably can, into the facts alleged' by both parties,[19] in practical terms the burden on the applicant[20] is solely to establish one of the facts and it is for the respondent in a defended suit to show, if he or she wishes, that the marriage has not broken down irretrievably. Most applications are undefended, and, as we will see, are processed without an oral hearing. However, it is necessary to consider the substantive law in a little detail to understand the way in which the justification for divorce is understood in English law.

It should be noted that no application may be brought during the first year of the marriage, in order to discourage couples from 'giving up' too easily should their marriage fall into difficulties early on.[21] Whether the bar serves this purpose may be questioned: Scottish law manages quite well without it.

(b) The five facts for proving irretrievable breakdown

The respondent's adultery

The first fact on which the applicant may rely is that the respondent has committed adultery and that the applicant finds it intolerable to live with him or her.[22] It will be seen that there are two limbs. Adultery by itself is not sufficient: Parliament accepted that infidelity

---

[17] Matrimonial Proceedings and Property Act 1970, discussed in Chapters 22 and 23.

[18] As in *Richards v Richards* [1972] 3 All ER 695.   [19] Matrimonial Causes Act 1973 s 1(3).

[20] Note that the statute refers to a 'petition' for divorce, and the 'petitioner'. However, the Family Procedure Rules 2010 (FPR 2010) refer to an 'application' and 'applicant', and these terms are used interchangeably when discussing the current legal position.

[21] Matrimonial Causes Act 1973 s 3 as amended by the Matrimonial and Family Proceedings Act 1984.

[22] Matrimonial Causes Act 1973 s 1(2)(a).

may be a symptom of breakdown rather than a cause of it and that an isolated act of adultery may not even be a symptom.

Adultery may be defined as voluntary sexual intercourse between two persons of the opposite sex, of whom one or both are married but who are not married to each other.[23] Receiving donor insemination does not constitute adultery[24] and nor do anal intercourse or non-penetrative sex. A spouse in a same sex marriage commits adultery only if he or she has intercourse with a person of the opposite sex.[25] The adultery must be voluntary, so a married woman who is raped is of course not regarded as having committed adultery.[26]

Whether or not the applicant finds it intolerable to live with the respondent is clearly a question of fact and the test is subjective: did this applicant find it intolerable to live with this respondent?[27]

The Act does not require any causal connection between the two limbs. After some initial doubts, when it was suggested that the applicant should be able to allege that he found it intolerable to live with the respondent only if this was in consequence of the adultery, the Court of Appeal held in *Cleary v Cleary*[28] that the statute must be interpreted literally and that the applicant may therefore rely not only on the adultery but also on any other matter to show that further cohabitation would be intolerable. In that case, the husband took the wife back after the adultery but she continued to correspond with the man in question, went out at night and finally left the husband to live with her mother. The court held that the husband had established irretrievable breakdown even though he found life with the wife intolerable not on account of her adultery but because of her subsequent conduct.[29] This approach is open to criticism: it is difficult to reconcile it with the provision, intended to encourage the parties to attempt a reconciliation, that cohabitation for a period not exceeding six months after the applicant discovers the respondent's adultery shall be disregarded in determining whether he finds it intolerable to live with the respondent,[30] which implies that it must be the discovery of the adultery that makes cohabitation intolerable.

The respondent's behaviour

The applicant may establish that the marriage has irretrievably broken down by showing that the respondent has behaved in such a way that the applicant cannot reasonably be expected to live with him or her.[31] This provision is frequently, but erroneously, abbreviated to 'unreasonable behaviour',[32] thereby suggesting that all one has to look at is the

---

[23] *Dennis v Dennis* [1955] P 153.

[24] So held in Scotland in *Maclennan v Maclennan* 1958 SLT 12. Nor would a husband commit adultery by acting as a sperm donor so long as insemination was the treatment method used. Acting without the spouse's knowledge or consent could well be sufficient for a petition based on behaviour, however, see later.

[25] Matrimonial Causes Act 1973 s 1(6), inserted by Marriage (Same Sex Couples) Act 2013 Sch 4 para 3. Sexual infidelity with a person of the same sex may be regarded as 'behaviour' under s 1(2)(b).

[26] *Clarkson v Clarkson* (1930) 143 LT 775.

[27] *Goodrich v Goodrich* [1971] 2 All ER 1340 at 1342; *Pheasant v Pheasant* [1972] Fam 202 at 207.

[28] [1974] 1 All ER 498, CA.

[29] See also *Carr v Carr* [1974] 1 WLR 1534, CA, where, although the Court of Appeal doubted whether *Cleary v Cleary* was correct, it regarded itself as bound to apply it—applicant found life intolerable because of respondent's treatment of their children.

[30] Matrimonial Causes Act 1973 s 2(2). Cohabitation for more than six months prevents the applicant from relying on the previous acts of adultery in any subsequent petition: s 2(1).

[31] Matrimonial Causes Act 1973 s 1(2)(b).

[32] Described as a 'linguistic trap' by Ormrod LJ in *Bannister v Bannister* (1980) 10 Fam Law 240, CA.

quality of the respondent's behaviour, whereas in fact what is important is the effect of that conduct upon the applicant.[33]

Whether the respondent's behaviour has been such that the applicant can no longer reasonably be expected to live with him or her is essentially a question of fact. In contrast to the test of intolerability under s 1(2)(a), however, the question is whether the applicant can reasonably be expected to live with the respondent, and it is for the court, and not the applicant, to answer it.[34] The test is thus objective, but this is not the same as asking whether a hypothetical reasonable spouse in the applicant's position would continue to live with the respondent. The court must have regard to the personalities of the individuals before it, however far these may be removed from some hypothetical norm, and it must assess the impact of the respondent's conduct on the particular applicant in the light of the whole history of the marriage and their relationship. The test generally accepted is that formulated by Dunn J in *Livingstone-Stallard v Livingstone-Stallard*[35] and adopted by the majority of the Court of Appeal in *O'Neill v O'Neill*:[36]

> Would any right-thinking person come to the conclusion that this husband has behaved in such a way that this wife cannot reasonably be expected to live with him, taking into account the whole of the circumstances and the characters and personalities of the parties?

The question is one of fact. Thus a wife has obtained a decree against a husband who has treated her with violence;[37] whose domineering manner led him to belittle her and level abuse and unwarranted criticism at her;[38] who made the matrimonial home virtually uninhabitable for months by carrying out building operations (which he was not qualified to do) as well as quite unjustifiably alleging that the two children of the marriage were not his;[39] and whose controlling and undermining behaviour carried on during the divorce proceedings in which he alleged that she had committed adultery and that she had improper financial motives for both marrying and then divorcing him so that 'the husband had pulled away every foundation and cornerstone of the matrimonial relationship.'[40] Similarly, a husband has successfully relied on his wife's association with another man stopping short of adultery,[41] from which it appears to follow that an applicant could complain of the respondent's adultery under this head without having to show that he found life with the other intolerable. Homosexual sexual intercourse, which, as we have seen earlier, does not come within the definition of adultery, could nonetheless amount to behaviour such that it is unreasonable to expect the applicant spouse to live with the other.

However, the application must amount to more than a complaint that the parties are incompatible, that they no longer have anything in common and cannot communicate,[42] or that one of them is bored with the marriage.[43] In *Pheasant v Pheasant*,[44] Ormrod J dismissed the petition of a husband whose sole charge against the wife was that she was unable to give him the demonstrative affection for which he craved whereas, as the judge found, she had

---

[33] *Ash v Ash* [1972] Fam 135; *Pheasant v Pheasant* [1972] Fam 202; *Livingstone-Stallard v Livingstone-Stallard* [1974] Fam 47; *O'Neill v O'Neill* [1975] 1 WLR 1118, CA.

[34] See *Ash v Ash* [1972] Fam 135, 139–140.   [35] [1974] Fam 47, 54.

[36] [1975] 1 WLR 1118, CA.   [37] *Ash v Ash* [1972] Fam 135.

[38] *Livingstone-Stallard v Livingstone-Stallard* [1974] Fam 47.

[39] *O'Neill v O'Neill* [1975] 1 WLR 1118, CA.

[40] *Hadjimilitis (Tsavliris) v Tsavliris (Divorce: Irretrievable Breakdown)* [2003] FLR 81.

[41] *Wachtel v Wachtel (No 1) Times*, 1 August 1972.

[42] As in *Buffery v Buffery* [1988] 2 FLR 365, CA.   [43] As in *Kisala v Kisala* (1973) 117 Sol Jo 664.

[44] [1972] Fam 202.

given him all the affection she could and nothing in her behaviour could be regarded as a breach of any of the obligations of a marriage.

Behaviour implies some form of conduct and not just a state of mind. As Baker P put it in *Katz v Katz*:[45]

> Behaviour is something more than a mere state of affairs or a state of mind, such as for example a repugnance to sexual intercourse, or a feeling that the wife is not reciprocating the husband's love, or not being as demonstrative as he thinks she should be. Behaviour in this context is action or conduct by one which affects the other. Such conduct may either take the form of acts or omissions or may be a course of conduct, and, in my view, it must have some reference to the marriage.

The whole history of the marriage must be looked at: the cumulative effect of a series of acts might well amount to behaviour which the applicant cannot reasonably be expected to put up with, even though each of them taken separately might be too trivial.[46]

How far can one regard as 'behaviour' conduct over which the respondent has no control? In *Thurlow v Thurlow*,[47] as a result of severe epilepsy, the wife became progressively less able to function. She threw things at her mother-in-law (with whom the parties lived), burnt articles on the electric heater and wandered into the street. Eventually, she became bedridden and incontinent and was admitted to hospital when her husband could no longer cope with the situation. There was no reasonable hope that her condition would improve and the husband sought a divorce on the basis of her behaviour. Rees J granted him a decree. He stated explicitly that, if the behaviour in question stems from misfortune, such as mental or physical illness or an accident, the court must take full account of all the obligations of the married state including the normal duty to accept and share the burdens imposed by the respondent's ill-health. But it must also consider the length of time the applicant has had to bear them, the effect upon his health and his capacity to bear the stresses imposed, and in the end must decide whether he can fairly be required to live with the respondent.[48]

As with adultery, if the parties have lived with each other in the same household for a period or periods not exceeding six months after the last act or incident relied on by the applicant, this is to be disregarded in determining whether he or she can reasonably be expected to live with the respondent.[49] But where the parties have continued to live together in excess of six months, the statute gives no guidance on whether the applicant can continue to rely on the acts complained of. In *Biggs v Biggs and Wheatley*,[50] a case where the parties had reconciled after decree nisi, Payne J held that either there is an absolute bar on making the decree absolute if there has been more than six months' cohabitation after knowledge of the adultery, or that there is a discretion, which should not be exercised in the petitioner's favour on the facts. Alternatively he could be taken (according to Parker J in *Kim v Morris*)[51] to be holding that the basis for establishing irretrievable breakdown is no longer made out and that therefore any discretion to make the decree absolute can no longer be exercised. Yet there may be good reasons, such as a lack of anywhere else to go, which prevent the applicant from leaving and which should not therefore prevent him or her from subsequently obtaining decree absolute.[52]

[45] [1972] 3 All ER 219, 223.   [46] *Stevens v Stevens* [1979] 1 WLR 885.
[47] [1976] Fam 32.   [48] *Thurlow v Thurlow* [1976] Fam 32 at 44.
[49] Matrimonial Causes Act 1973 s 2(3).   [50] [1977] Fam 1.
[51] [2012] EWHC 1103 (Fam) [2013] 2 FLR 1197.
[52] See eg *Bradley v Bradley* [1973] 3 All ER 750, CA.

It might still be argued that, for a heterosexual couple, there remains a legitimate expectation of sexual intercourse after the marriage has been consummated, and that a refusal to have intercourse, or perhaps an unreasonable rationing of its frequency, might ground an application for divorce based upon behaviour such that one spouse could not reasonably be expected to live with the other.[53] It is less certain what the position is in relation to a same sex marriage or civil partnership. We have seen[54] that consummation is not a requirement of either union, and the opportunity to redefine adultery to include homosexual sexual intercourse was declined by the Government when steering the Marriage (Same Sex Couples) Act 2013 through Parliament. How far the partnership was nonetheless intended or expected to have a sexual dimension to it in the minds of the legislators is unclear. After all, Parliament rejected an attempt to open up civil partnerships to couples who are clearly not engaged in a sexual relationship, such as two elderly sisters.[55] A reluctance to contemplate the details of sexual behaviour in same sex relationships and to attempt to prescribe what these should entail no doubt influenced this approach. It might therefore be left to the parties themselves, in the context of dissolution of the partnership, to determine how important the sexual aspect was to them and thus whether a 'failure' of it could lead to an application based on 'behaviour' as discussed in this section.

The respondent's desertion

The applicant may show that the marriage has irretrievably broken down by proving that the respondent has deserted the applicant for a continuous period of at least two years immediately preceding the presentation of the petition.[56] Desertion consists of the unjustifiable withdrawal from cohabitation without the consent of the other spouse and with the intention of remaining separated permanently.

There can be no desertion unless there is a factual separation between the spouses. Usually, this will occur when one spouse leaves the matrimonial home. But it may be impossible for the spouse wishing to leave to find accommodation elsewhere and the situation may arise where the spouses continue to live under the same roof but where one shuts him or herself off from the other so that they are living as two units rather than one. The correct test to be applied in such a case is: Are the spouses living as two households or as one?[57] This is strictly construed: it cannot be desertion if any matrimonial services are performed even though these are isolated and intermittent.[58]

---

[53] *P(D) v P(J)* [1965] 2 All ER 456 (wife guilty of cruelty in refusing intercourse, although due to invincible fear of conception and childbirth) but cf *Mason v Mason* (1980) 11 Fam Law 143 (wife's refusal to have intercourse more than once a week was not behaviour such that the husband could not be expected to live with her).

[54] At Ch 3, The unconsummated marriage pp 73–76 and Voidable civil partnerships p 88.

[55] 'This Bill is about same sex couples whose relationships are completely different from those of siblings.' Per Lord Alli, HL Deb 24 June 2004, vol 662, col 1369. In *Burden v United Kingdom* (Application No 13378/05) [2008] 2 FLR 787 the relationship between two elderly sisters was found by the Grand Chamber of the European Court of Human Rights not to be analogous to that of spouses and civil partners.

[56] Matrimonial Causes Act 1973 s 1(2)(c). For the computation of the period of two years, see *Warr v Warr* [1975] Fam 25. Where the spouses attempt a reconciliation, which fails, the court must disregard any period or periods not exceeding six months in which the parties have lived together in the same household. But the periods of cohabitation must be ignored in calculating the length of time the parties have been apart: Matrimonial Causes Act 1973 s 2(5), so that a trial reconciliation of say, three months will require the applicant to wait until two years and three months have elapsed from the initial point of desertion before he or she can present a petition based on this fact.

[57] *Hopes v Hopes* [1949] P 227, at 231, 236.

[58] Cf *Naylor v Naylor* [1962] P 253—desertion established where parties lived separately under same roof; with *Hopes v Hopes*—no desertion where husband joined in certain activities with rest of family and an outsider would not have seen anything abnormal in the situation.

Even though there is a de facto separation, there will be no desertion unless the guilty spouse has the intention of remaining permanently separated from the other. There is no question of desertion if one spouse is temporarily absent on holiday or business, or for reasons of health.[59] Nor will there be desertion if the absence is involuntary, for example owing to service in the armed forces or imprisonment. But in such cases there will be desertion if the intention can be specifically proved, for example, if the respondent makes it clear that he wishes to have nothing more to do with the applicant.[60]

Historically, desertion is a matrimonial offence; consequently there can be no desertion if the separation is by consent.[61] Whether consent has been given is a question of fact. It may be expressly given as a simple licence to go, or be embodied in a separation agreement, or it may be implied by the party's conduct. For example, in *Joseph v Joseph*[62] the wife persuaded the husband to grant her a *get* which by Jewish law effects a divorce.[63] Although this would not dissolve the marriage by English law it was held by the Court of Appeal that the wife had thereby shown her consent to living apart from her husband and could therefore no longer assert that he was in desertion.

If one spouse has a reasonable cause or excuse for leaving the other, then there will be no unjustifiable separation and consequently he will not be in desertion. For example, in *Quoraishi v Quoraishi*[64] where the couple were Muslims and the husband took a second wife in Bangladesh against the will of the first wife, the latter was held not to be in desertion when she left him. Such conduct on his part would also found a petition based on his behaviour.

Finally, it should be noted that it need not be the spouse who takes the physical step of leaving the matrimonial home who will be in desertion. Where one spouse behaves in such a way that the other is virtually compelled to leave, the former may be in law the deserter, and is said to be in constructive desertion.[65]

This fact has come to be relied upon only rarely,[66] because the application will usually be based on two years' separation if the respondent consents. An applicant might wish to use it, however, if the respondent is in desertion and refuses to consent to a decree; and even after five years' separation (when the respondent's consent is not required) it avoids the possibility that the respondent will use s 5 or s 10 of the Matrimonial Causes Act to oppose or delay the granting of the decree absolute.[67]

Two years' separation and the respondent's consent to the decree

The applicant may establish that the marriage has broken down irretrievably by showing that the spouses have lived apart for a continuous period of at least two years immediately preceding the presentation of the petition and that the respondent consents to the decree being granted.[68] This was one of the most controversial provisions of the Divorce Reform Act, because it introduced, albeit to a limited extent, divorce by consent.

---

[59] *G v G* [1964] P 133.
[60] *Beeken v Beeken* [1948] P 302, CA.   [61] *Pardy v Pardy* [1939] P 288.
[62] [1953] 2 All ER 710, CA.
[63] See later, Postponement of decree absolute, In cases of religious divorce, p 225.
[64] [1985] FLR 780, CA.
[65] *Graves v Graves* (1864) 3 Sw & Tr 350; *Hall v Hall* [1962] 3 All ER 518, CA; *Saunders v Saunders* [1965] P 499.
[66] Only around 0.5% of all divorces in 2011. See ONS *Divorces in England and Wales, 2011* (2012) Table 8.
[67] See later, Protection of the respondent and children, p 221.
[68] Section 1(2)(d). As with computing the period for desertion, periods not exceeding six months' cohabitation since separation began do not prevent the period from running, but must be added on to ensure that a full two years' separation has elapsed before a petition can be presented: s 2(5).

The 1973 Act provides that spouses are to be treated as living apart unless they are living with each other in the same household.[69] On this basis, the courts have built up two principles. First, if the spouses are living under the same roof, they can be regarded as living apart only if they are living in two households: in other words there must be the same degree of separation as is necessary to constitute desertion.[70] Hence they will not be living apart if they share their meals and living accommodation, even though they sleep in separate rooms, no longer have sexual intercourse and largely live their own lives.[71] Conversely, they will be treated as still living apart if the wife, having left her husband for another man, subsequently takes him in as a lodger because he is ill and has nowhere else to go.[72]

But even if the spouses are physically separated, it does not follow that they are living apart for the purpose of the Act. The second principle, formulated by the Court of Appeal in *Santos v Santos*[73] is that they will not be so treated unless 'consortium'—or living 'as husband and wife'—has come to an end.[74] So long as both spouses intend to share a home when circumstances permit them to do so, consortium would traditionally be regarded as continuing. Consequently, before a couple could be said to be living apart, one of them at least must regard the marriage as finished. If they agree to separate or one deserts the other, it will be obvious to both that consortium is at an end; if the separation is temporary or enforced (for example, because of a business trip or treatment in hospital), consortium will usually continue, but it will come to an end if either spouse decides not to return to the other. In the latter case it was further held in *Santos* that it is not necessary for that spouse to communicate his or her decision to the other and the statutory period can begin to run immediately. Suppose, for example, that a husband is serving a long term of imprisonment and his wife stands by him and regularly visits him; one of them resolves not to live with the other again but says nothing and the visits continue as before. Two years after making this decision he or she may apply for divorce with the other's consent. At first sight this seems surprising, but it accords with the policy of the Act. The period of separation is designed to provide evidence that the marriage has broken down irretrievably and this of itself justifies a restrictive interpretation of the words 'living apart' by requiring evidence that consortium was at an end during the whole of the period. But equally, the fact that one spouse has regarded the marriage as dead for at least two years must normally be pretty clear evidence that it has broken down irretrievably whether or not the other knew of this. As we will see, the procedural mechanisms for satisfying the court that the marriage has broken down irretrievably make it easy for a spouse to indicate that he or she did indeed regard the marriage as over for the requisite length of time prior to issuing the application.

The respondent must affirmatively consent to the decree; it is not sufficient that he or she does not oppose it.[75] Information must be given so as to enable him or her to understand the effect of the decree being granted.[76] The respondent may withdraw his or her consent at any time before a decree nisi is pronounced. After decree nisi[77] the respondent has only a qualified power to withdraw his or her consent and to attempt to prevent the decree from being made absolute. If the court grants a decree solely on the fact of

---

[69] Matrimonial Causes Act 1973 s 2(6), see *Santos v Santos* [1972] Fam 247, CA.

[70] *Mouncer v Mouncer* [1972] 1 All ER 289.

[71] *Mouncer v Mouncer* [1972] 1 All ER 289. Cf *Hopes v Hopes* [1949] P 227.

[72] *Fuller v Fuller* [1973] 2 All ER 650, CA.   [73] [1972] Fam 247, CA.

[74] See Ch 4, Consortium, p 92.

[75] *McG v R* [1972] 1 All ER 362. The usual way of proving consent is by producing the completed acknowledgement of service stating that the respondent consents to the decree, which must be signed by him or her personally: see FPR 2010 r 7.12.

[76] Matrimonial Causes Act 1973 s 2(7).   [77] See later, Decrees, p 228.

two years' separation coupled with the respondent's consent, the respondent may apply to have the decree nisi rescinded on the ground that the applicant misled him (whether intentionally or unintentionally) about any matter which he took into account in deciding to give his consent.[78] The court is not bound to rescind the decree; presumably it will do so only if the respondent has been seriously misled. A change of mind after the decree has been made absolute[79] will be too late.

Five years' separation

The fifth fact on which an applicant may rely is that the spouses have lived apart for a continuous period of at least five years immediately preceding the presentation of the application.[80] This fact is identical with the last except that the period of separation is five years and the respondent's consent to the divorce is not required: hence it has been dubbed 'divorce without consent'. This provision was even more controversial than that based on two years' separation with consent, because it enables the marriage to be dissolved against the will of a spouse who has committed no matrimonial offence and who has not been responsible for the breakdown of the marriage. On the one hand it was hailed as a measure that would bring relief to hundreds of couples who would otherwise live in stable illicit unions unable to marry because one or both of them could not secure release from another union; on the other hand it was castigated as a 'Casanova's charter', permitting middle-aged men to put away their first wives in preference for new, younger spouses. If five years' separation is established, a decree can still be refused if it would cause the respondent grave financial or other hardship, discussed later.

It is worth noting that despite the shift towards the 'no fault' concept of irretrievable breakdown, three of the five 'facts' are fault-based, and the majority of applicants continue to rely upon these as the basis for their divorce. In 2011, 51% of husband applicants, and 69% of wives, relied upon the first two facts, while a third of husbands, and 22% of wives, relied upon two years' separation with consent and 16% of husbands and only 9% of wives on the basis of five years' separation.[81] We examine the reasons for and implications of these statistics later.

(c) Protection of the respondent and children

The Matrimonial Causes Act as originally drafted set out various provisions designed to give protection to the respondent to the petition, and to the parties' children, but the latter were repealed by the Children and Families Act 2014.[82] Their rationale was to try to ensure that those most directly affected by the applicant's decision to seek a divorce are not *unduly* adversely affected by the ending of the marriage (no one could claim that a divorce could very easily be made painless for all concerned). In the case of the respondent, it is for him or her to raise the relevant provision as part of the case, either to prevent or to delay the divorce going through. In the case of children, there was automatic consideration of the arrangements proposed for their future care and upbringing in every case (see later).

Protection of the respondent

One way of ensuring that the court properly considers the respondent's perspective could be for him or her simply to defend the divorce and argue that the applicant has not proved one of the five facts for establishing that the marriage has irretrievably broken down.

---

[78] Matrimonial Causes Act 1973 s 10(1). The matters on which a respondent is most likely to be misled are those relating to financial provision.   [79] See Decrees, p 228.

[80] Matrimonial Causes Act 1973 s 1(2)(e). Section 2(5) applies to the computation of the five-year period.

[81] ONS *Divorces in England and Wales, 2011* (2012) Table 8.   [82] Section 17.

However, in practice, very few applications are defended. The courts, and hence lawyers advising their clients, have taken the view that, if one party adamantly asserts that the marriage is over, there is usually little to be gained from allowing the other to try to contest the assertion. Where a spouse nonetheless insists on resisting the application, it can be seen from cases like *Hadjimilitis (Tsavliris) v Tsavliris (Divorce: Irretrievable Breakdown)*[83] that the very act of defending may persuade the court that the marriage is indeed over. There, the husband's attacks on the wife's marital 'failings' and motives somewhat undermined his claims that he wanted a reconciliation with her, and the court concluded that the wife had made out her case.

So instead of a general attempt to defend the application, the respondent may, in appropriate cases, be advised to ask the court to utilise either of two mechanisms: the refusal of the divorce entirely, under s 5, or the postponement of the decree absolute, under s 10 of the Act.

Refusal of the decree

If the applicant relies on five years' separation, s 5 of the Act permits the respondent to oppose the grant of a decree nisi on the ground that the dissolution of the marriage would result in grave financial or other hardship to him and that it would be wrong in all the circumstances to dissolve the marriage. This provision was introduced in response to those concerns noted earlier that the five-year separation fact could be used to divorce an 'innocent' spouse against his or her will. In the vast majority of cases, the wife is much more likely to suffer hardship, particularly financial hardship, from the granting of a decree than the husband and so the following discussion is based on the assumption that it is the wife who is resisting the husband's petition, but it must be remembered that precisely the same principles apply if the respondent is the husband.

The hardship must result from the dissolution of the marriage: it is not enough for the respondent to show that hardship would result if the divorce were based on five years' separation, as distinct from some other fact. In *Grenfell v Grenfell*[84] the wife presented a petition based on her husband's behaviour. He cross-petitioned on the basis of five years' separation, and in her reply the wife pleaded that, as she was a practising member of the Greek Orthodox Church, her conscience would be affronted if the marriage were to be dissolved 'otherwise than on grounds of substance'. It was held that, as she was seeking a divorce herself, she could not argue that she would suffer hardship if the marriage were to be dissolved and so her answer was struck out.

Additionally, the hardship must be the result of the dissolution and not of the breakdown of the marriage.[85] Hence, the fact that the husband will be supporting two families and have less money with which to support his wife and first family will be irrelevant if he is already living with the woman he wishes to marry and has children by her. Moreover, the hardship must be 'grave'. Whether or not there would be grave hardship must be considered 'subjectively in relation to the particular marriage and the circumstances in which the parties lived while it subsisted',[86] but what matters is not whether the respondent feels that she would suffer but whether sensible people knowing all the facts would think so.[87] It has been said that one must look at the situation through the eyes of the respondent and then judge objectively the reality of the apprehension.[88]

---

[83] [2003] 1 FLR 81.   [84] [1978] Fam 128, CA.   [85] *Talbot v Talbot* (1971) 115 Sol Jo 870.
[86] Per Dunn LJ in *Talbot v Talbot* (1971) 115 Sol Jo 870 approved in *Mathias v Mathias* [1972] Fam 287, 299.
[87] Per Lawton LJ in *Rukat v Rukat* [1975] Fam 63, 73. To quote his example, 'The rich gourmet who because of financial stringency has to drink *vin ordinaire* with his grouse may well think he is suffering hardship, but sensible people would say he was not.'
[88] *Balraj v Balraj* (1980) 11 Fam Law 110, CA. See also *Rukat v Rukat* [1975] Fam 63 at 72.

Hardship includes the loss of the chance of acquiring any benefit which the respondent might acquire if the marriage were not dissolved.[89] The potential loss of rights on the husband's intestacy will usually be immaterial because he will usually be advised to make a will in favour of other beneficiaries; and whether the marriage is dissolved or not, the wife may have a claim under the Inheritance (Provision for Family and Dependants) Act 1975.[90] In practice, grave financial hardship will be due to one (or both) of two causes. First, the wife may no longer be able to claim certain social security benefits (such as bereavement benefits or retirement pension) by virtue of her husband's contributions. However, the Court of Appeal in *Reiterbund v Reiterbund*[91] laid down the principle that the court must not ignore the claims the wife has to means-tested benefits such as income support. There is no stigma attached to the receipt of such benefits and it can make no difference to the wife which public fund the money comes from. If, therefore, the amount she would receive from such benefits is not substantially less than what she would receive from the contribution-based benefit, she will suffer no hardship as a result of the divorce.

The other likely cause of grave financial hardship will be the potential loss of pension rights, other than those payable under the state retirement pension scheme, accruing to an employee's widow. This is much less significant a problem than hitherto, because provisions were introduced into the law in 1995 and 1999 to enable a court to allocate either pension payments, or pension rights, to the divorced spouse, as part of the overall financial settlement reached in the suit.[92] Even before these provisions came into effect, the courts were wary about refusing a divorce on this ground and applicants were usually able to persuade the court that the offer of some alternative form of financial provision would adequately compensate for the wife's loss or that her overall financial situation would cushion her sufficiently.[93] But where the court is not satisfied that the wife's loss has been offset, it is likely to adjourn the proceedings, to enable (or persuade) the husband to find some better means of meeting the wife's needs.

The position of the children may also be relevant in determining whether the respondent would suffer financial hardship. In *Lee v Lee*[94] the wife needed accommodation to look after her son, who needed constant nursing and care. The husband's proposal to sell the matrimonial home and give the wife half the proceeds of sale would not have enabled her to buy a flat for this purpose, and his petition was dismissed.[95]

There is no clear judicial definition of what hardship other than financial hardship might mean, but the reported cases involve respondents alleging that divorce is anathema to them on religious grounds or that it would result in social ostracism. For example, in *Banik v Banik*[96] the wife was a Hindu still living in India. It was held by the Court of Appeal that it was not sufficient that the divorce would cause her distress and unhappiness or that she personally would regard it as immoral or contrary to the rules of her community; she must establish that shame, disgrace or degradation would fall on her.

[89] Matrimonial Causes Act 1973 s 5(3).
[90] See Ch 25, Who may apply for an order, p 977.   [91] [1975] Fam 99, CA.
[92] The Pensions Act 1995 s 166, which came into force in 1996, amended the Matrimonial Causes Act 1973 by inserting ss 25B–D to enable the 'earmarking' of pension payments to the divorced spouse. The Welfare Reform and Pensions Act 1999 Sch 3, which came into force in 2000, inserted s 21A and ss 24B–D into the 1973 Act to enable the making of a pension sharing order in respect of pension rights. See Ch 22, Orders in relation to pensions, p 842.
[93] See *Le Marchant v Le Marchant* [1977] 3 All ER 610, CA; *Archer v Archer* [1999] 1 FLR 327, CA.
[94] (1973) 117 Sol Jo 616.
[95] On appeal, the divorce was granted because the son had died in the meantime: (1975) 5 Fam Law 48.
[96] [1973] 3 All ER 45, CA. The court remitted the case for rehearing and a decree was later pronounced because the wife's statement that she would become a social outcast could be discounted and it would not be wrong to dissolve the marriage: see 117 Sol Jo 874.

Whether this would amount to grave hardship if it were established is a question of fact and degree: the defence has not been successful in any reported case.[97]

Even if the respondent does prove that the decree would cause her grave hardship, the court must still pronounce a decree unless it also considers that it would be wrong to do so. The use of 'wrong' in this context is unusual and its meaning is ambiguous and obscure; in *Brickell v Brickell*[98] Davies LJ thought that it meant 'unjust or not right in all the circumstances of the case'. The court has to take into account specifically the conduct and interests of the parties and the interests of any children[99] and other persons concerned (for example, the person whom the applicant wishes to marry), and in the end will have to balance those interests against the hardship that the divorce would cause the respondent.[100]

Even though reliance on s 5 is rarely, if ever, successful, it has been regarded as 'an important protection for a small group of people who may still face serious hardship which the law is unable at present to redress in other ways' and its retention in the law has been recommended.[101] How often it in fact plays a part in the negotiations over the relatively small proportion of divorces brought under the five years' separation fact is unknown.

Postponement of decree absolute

In cases based on two and five years' separation

If a decree nisi is granted on the basis of two or five years' separation, the respondent may apply for it not to be made absolute[102] unless the court is satisfied:

(a) that the applicant should not be required to make financial provision for the respondent; or

(b) that the financial provision made by the applicant for the respondent is reasonable and fair or the best that can be made in the circumstances.[103]

This is another weapon given to the respondent to use against the applicant. The threat to delay the applicant's remarriage, for example, by holding up the decree absolute, may be regarded as a legitimate tactic if the applicant is deliberately evading his or her financial responsibilities. But in order to prevent a respondent from abusing the provision, the court may, even if it finds that the applicant has not made such reasonable financial provision as should have been made, nonetheless make the decree absolute if it appears that there are circumstances making it desirable that this should not be delayed *and* the court has obtained a satisfactory undertaking from the applicant that he or she will make such financial provision as the court may approve.[104] In practice, it should rarely be necessary for a respondent to a petition based on two years' separation to rely on s 10 since he or she could simply decline to give consent to the decree. In the case of a petition based on five years' separation, the potential of s 10 as another bargaining chip for the respondent should not be underestimated, and a failure to explore the possibility of using it may result in a finding of professional negligence against the wife's legal adviser.[105]

---

[97] See also, *Parghi v Parghi* (1973) 117 Sol Jo 582 (Hindu wife resident in Bombay); *Rukat v Rukat* [1975] Fam 63 (Roman Catholic wife with family in Sicily); *Balraj v Balraj* (1980) 11 Fam Law 110, CA (wife resident in Kshatriya community in India; divorce would also reduce daughter's marriage prospects).

[98] [1974] Fam 31, CA.

[99] Who include children over the age of 18: *Allan v Allan* (1973) 4 Fam Law 83.

[100] See *Rukat v Rukat* [1975] Fam 63 at 75, *Mathias v Mathias* [1972] Fam 287, 299 CA.

[101] Law Commission, Report No 192 para 5.75.

[102] The court's general power to withhold a decree absolute is discussed later, Decrees, p 228.

[103] Matrimonial Causes Act 1973 s 10(2), (3).

[104] Section 10(4).   [105] *Griffiths v Dawson & Co* [1993] 2 FLR 315.

In cases of religious marriage

Since the Act was originally passed, Orthodox Jewish women seeking a divorce have publicised the problem of the *'agunah'*, or 'anchored woman'.[106] Under Jewish law, only the husband can divorce his wife. Where he refuses to do so, then, although she may have obtained a divorce under English law, she remains married in the eyes of her religion and is unable to remarry according to Jewish rites. A husband could exploit this rule by only agreeing to divorce the wife under Jewish law (referred to as giving her a *get*) upon her acceptance of a smaller financial settlement. Section 10A of the Matrimonial Causes Act 1973[107] seeks to redress this unfairness. It provides that if the parties were married to each other in accordance with usages of the Jews, or any other prescribed religious usages, and are required to co-operate if the marriage is to be dissolved in accordance with those usages, the court may, on the application of either party, order that a decree of divorce is not to be made absolute until a declaration made by both parties that they have taken such steps as are required to dissolve the marriage in accordance with those usages is produced to the court. The order may only be made if the court is satisfied that in all the circumstances of the case it is just and reasonable to do so, and it may be revoked (presumably on the application of either party) by the court at any time.[108] Thus, if a Jewish husband sought a civil divorce from his wife, she could apply to the court for an order, in effect, that he give her a *get*. However, where the wife seeks the divorce and the husband either opposes or does not care if the marriage is terminated, it would seem that he could still frustrate her, since he could simply ignore the order or delay his compliance, again potentially exploiting the wife's financial vulnerability by forcing her to agree to an inferior settlement.

Protection of children

Until the Children and Families Act 2014, in every case where there were children of the family under the age of 16 (or whom the court expressly directed should be included)[109] the court had to consider the arrangements proposed for the children's future after their parents' divorce. At one time, the court had to be positively satisfied with these arrangements, or consider that they were the best that could be devised in the circumstances, before it could grant the decree absolute. However, research showed that this was an ineffective means of checking that arrangements were suitable.[110] The provision was therefore amended by the Children Act 1989, so that all the court had to do was to consider the arrangements, as set out on a detailed 'statement of arrangements form', and decide whether it should exercise any of its powers under the Children Act 1989 with respect to them. In exceptional circumstances the court might still direct that the decree was not to be made absolute until further order, if it was of the opinion that it was likely to have to exercise its powers under the Children Act with respect to the children of the family and it needed to give further consideration to the case.[111] This was rarely done.[112] In practice, as the Law Commission intended, the court trusted the parents, and the lawyers trusted their clients, to make suitable arrangements for their children, and expected a respondent

---

[106] See M Freeman 'The Jewish Law of Divorce' [2000] *International Family Law* 58. For consideration of religious divorces, see G Douglas et al 'The role of religious tribunals in regulating marriage and divorce' [2012] CFLQ 139.   [107] Added by the Divorce (Religious Marriages) Act 2002.
[108] Section 10A(3).   [109] For example, because a child is disabled.
[110] See G Davis, A Macleod and M Murch 'Undefended divorce: Should s 41 of the Matrimonial Causes Act 1973 be Repealed?' (1983) 46 MLR 121.   [111] Matrimonial Causes Act 1973 s 41 (as amended).
[112] For an assessment of the working of this provision, see G Douglas et al 'Safeguarding children's welfare in non-contentious divorce: towards a new conception of the divorce process' (2000) 63 MLR 177.

to raise any concerns he or she might have when acknowledging service of the petition or by issuing an application for an order under the Children Act 1989.

When the Government formulated their response to the recommendations of the Family Justice Review[113] in 2012, they took the logical step of proposing that this process should be abolished, leaving parents to make use of dispute resolution processes if they cannot agree on arrangements for the children.[114] This change ends over half a century of practice which viewed the fact of divorce proceedings as in itself sufficient justification for the state taking a supervisory role over the arrangements parents choose to make for their children after they separate. That stance arose at a time when divorce was relatively uncommon, stigmatic both to the parents and their children, and where it was assumed that the children might be in need of particular protection.[115] Given the increase in the number of children raised in cohabiting relationships, for whom no such oversight is (or can be) provided, and given the shift in approach to regarding divorce as a common experience for very many parents and their children rather than a dramatic deviation from 'normal' family behaviour, the s 41 requirement had become an outmoded and unnecessary addition to the paperwork entailed in ending a marriage.

2. THE PROCEDURE FOR OBTAINING THE DIVORCE

(a) The special procedure

Consideration of the substantive law governing the grant of a divorce provides only a partial and inaccurate picture of what the experience of obtaining a divorce is like for those involved. This is because, as noted, virtually all divorce petitions are undefended: in other words, the respondent does not attempt (either from the start, or once he or she has taken advice or realised that the marriage is indeed over) to resist the grant of the divorce. This is not to say that most couples experience an amicable divorce; there may be much to argue over when it comes to determining how the financial and property consequences are to be dealt with, and what pattern of arrangements is to be made for the future care of the couple's children. But as far as the decree itself is concerned, there is no effective contest between the parties, and this state of affairs long pre-dated the advent of the Matrimonial Causes Act.

Yet notwithstanding the fact that the suit was uncontested, before 1973, the petitioner's evidence was heard in open court together with that of any other witness necessary to support his or her case. Appearance in court often led to considerable anxiety for the petitioner and to costs which, whether borne by the parties or the legal aid fund, were significant and growing rapidly. It also involved a great deal of judicial time.[116] Consequently, in 1973 a 'special procedure'[117] was introduced to dispense with the need to give evidence in court if the case was not defended.[118] Originally it applied only to petitions based on

---

[113] See Ch 1, Pressure for a family court and the *Family Justice Review* p 17.

[114] Ministry of Justice *The Government's Response to the Family Justice Review: A system with children and families at its heart* (2012) Recommendation 130; Children and Families Act 2013 s 17.

[115] The 'welfare check' was enacted by the Matrimonial Proceedings (Children) Act 1958, s 2(1), following the recommendation of the Morton Commission (see *Royal Commission on Marriage and Divorce* Cmd 9678 (1956) at para 372), which in turn built on proposals of the *Committee on Procedure in Matrimonial Causes* Cmd 7024 (1947) (the Denning Committee).

[116] E Elston, J Fuller and M Murch 'Judicial Hearings of Undefended Divorce Petitions' (1975) 38 MLR 609.   [117] Now see Family Procedure Rules 2010 Part 7.

[118] Where the petition is defended, the respondent must file an answer to the petition within 21 days after the expiration of the time limit for giving notice of intention to defend: FPR 2010 r 7.12(8). The case is

two years' separation, but since 1977 all undefended petitions for divorce have been dealt with under this procedure. At the same time, legal aid for the divorce petition itself was withdrawn.[119] This change in procedure may in some ways be seen as the most fundamental, yet relatively unremarked-upon change in divorce since the introduction of judicial divorce in 1857, since it seems to have marked the end of attempts to provide any effective scrutiny of a party's case for obtaining a divorce and has rendered the substantive law outlined earlier no more than a template to which the spouse or the lawyer must fit the facts on which the applicant chooses to rely in establishing irretrievable breakdown.

Under the special procedure, the applicant commences proceedings by issuing an application giving details of the marriage, of any children of the family, and of the facts on which the applicant relies to establish irretrievable breakdown. The district judge then enters the cause in the special procedure list. If the judge is satisfied that the applicant has proved his or her case and is entitled to a decree, the judge makes and files a certificate to this effect and a day is fixed on which the decree nisi is pronounced in open court. Neither party needs to be present when this is done. While scrutiny of the documentation might reveal technical errors, it is unlikely to reveal defects of substance.[120]

The effect of the introduction of this procedure was inevitably to ensure that there can be no real investigation of the truth of the allegations made in the divorce petition if the respondent chooses not to challenge them,[121] or is not in a position to do so.[122] However, there is still an outside chance that an abuse may come to light. In *Bhaiji v Chauhan, Queen's Proctor Intervening (Divorce: Marriages Used for Immigration Purposes)*[123] for example, court staff became suspicious when they found strong similarities between five petitions presented by litigants acting in person. All the parties were of Indian ethnicity and in each case one spouse was a UK citizen and resident and the other a recent entrant to the UK who had relied on the marriage to obtain indefinite leave to remain. In four of the cases, the period of time between obtaining such leave and the alleged breakdown of the marriage was very short. The cases were transferred for full hearing in the High Court which dismissed all but one (which was withdrawn), on the basis that the allegations made in the petitions were false.

Parties seeking a quick divorce have little to lose by bringing the petition on the basis of one of the fault facts—adultery or behaviour—rather than waiting the two years for a no fault decree. As we have seen, the large majority of applications are based on the 'fault' facts, and around two-thirds are sought by wives rather than husbands.[124]

---

then heard in open court in the usual way. In *N v N* [1992] 1 FLR 266, the wife presented a petition based on the husband's behaviour. They agreed to try a reconciliation during which the wife would not proceed with her suit and that, if the reconciliation attempt failed, the husband would not defend the petition. Five months later, the wife decided the reconciliation attempt had failed and she renewed her petition. The husband applied to file an answer out of time, but it was held that the agreement not to defend was perfectly proper.

[119] Funding for legal 'help' (basic advice but not representation) remained available. The more recent withdrawal of legal aid from most other forms of family proceedings, and the implications for the conduct of family cases, are discussed at Ch 1, Private ordering and the withdrawal of legal aid, p 10.

[120] Law Com No 192 *The Ground for Divorce* (1990) para 2.2.

[121] See *Callaghan v Hanson-Fox* [1992] Fam 1; *Moynihan v Moynihan (Nos 1 and 2)* [1997] 1 FLR 59.

[122] *Akhtar v Rafiq* [2006] 1 FLR 27: wife had returned to Pakistan, husband forged wife's thumbprint on acknowledgement of service form and decree was granted in 1992. Husband 'remarried' and had five children. Wife sued for divorce in 2003 and the forgery came to light. Held decree must be set aside where there had been no proper service and the irregularity was only discovered after the event.

[123] [2003] 2 FLR 485.   [124] ONS *Divorces in England and Wales, 2010* (2011) Table 8.

The artificiality of the 'special procedure' was noted by the Family Justice Review in 2011. They pointed out that it requires (highly paid) judges 'to spend time in effect to do no more than check that forms have been filled in correctly, with accurate names and dates. This is a waste'.[125] They proposed instead that more of this work could be done by administrators, leaving judges to deal with the small number of contested divorces or to handle any queries or doubts in the paperwork that the administrators might identify, a proposal with which the Government agreed but on which action is awaited.[126]

(b) Decrees

The divorce decree is made in two stages: the decree nisi, followed by the decree absolute.[127] The applicant may apply for the decree to be made absolute at any time after the expiration of six weeks from the granting of the decree nisi unless the court fixes a shorter time in the particular case;[128] if the applicant fails to apply for a decree absolute, the respondent may apply at any time after the expiration of three months from the earliest date on which the applicant could have applied.[129] Should the respondent apply before this period has expired, and the court wrongly grants the decree absolute, it is void.[130] There is a discretion whether to permit the respondent's application, and it may be refused where financial matters are outstanding and the applicant will be prejudiced if the respondent is permitted to obtain the freedom to remarry before these are resolved.[131]

The delay is intended to provide an opportunity for an unsuccessful respondent to appeal against the granting of the decree nisi, or for the Queen's Proctor[132] or any other person to intervene to show cause why the decree should not be made absolute. One or both of the parties themselves may have reasons for wishing to have the decree rescinded. For example, in S v S (Rescission of Decree Nisi: Pension Sharing Provision)[133] the court rescinded a decree nisi granted in 1999, on the wife's application with the husband's consent, so that they could take advantage of the power, only granted to courts in respect of petitions presented after 1 December 2000, to make a pension sharing order.[134] Upholding public policy may also be in issue. In the old days of the matrimonial offence, the Queen's Proctor investigated allegations of collusion or other abuse of the divorce process by the spouses (primarily in order to prevent them obtaining a divorce 'by consent'). The office still exists to enable the court to call on the Queen's

---

[125] Ministry of Justice *Family Justice Review Final Report* (2011) para 4.166.

[126] Ministry of Justice *The Government's Response to the Family Justice Review: A system with children and families at its heart* (2012) Recommendation 130.

[127] Subject to the provisions of s 10 and s 41 of the 1973 Act discussed earlier. For the reasons for the two-stage process, see S Cretney *Family Law in the Twentieth Century: A History* (2003) p 178.

[128] Matrimonial Causes Act 1973 s 1(5) and *Practice Direction* [1977] 2 All ER 714.

[129] Matrimonial Causes Act 1973 s 9(2). Where notice for the grant of decree absolute is lodged more than 12 months after the making of the decree nisi, the applicant must explain in writing why it was not made sooner and indicate whether a child has been born to them: FPR 2010 r 7.32(3). If a longer period elapses, the decree nisi may be rescinded and a fresh petition required *Kim v Morris* [2012] EWHC 1103 (Fam) [2013] 2 FLR 1197.

[130] *Manchanda v Manchanda* [1995] 2 FLR 590, CA; *Dennis v Dennis* [2000] 2 FLR 231.

[131] *Smith v Smith* [1990] 1 FLR 438; *Wickler v Wickler* [1998] 2 FLR 326. Cf *Re G (Decree Absolute: Prejudice)* [2002] EWHC 2834 (Fam) [2003] 1 FLR 870—no prejudice to wife to grant husband's application for decree absolute where husband not proved likely to obstruct financial proceedings.

[132] Discussed by S Cretney *Family Law in the Twentieth Century: A History* (2003) pp 178–181.

[133] [2002] 1 FLR 457.

[134] Cf *H v H (Pension Sharing: Rescission of Decree Nisi)* [2002] EWHC 767 (Fam) [2002] 2 FLR 116: application refused because of husband's lack of consent and unfairness to him in such circumstances to permit wife to circumvent the commencement date set by Parliament. To similar effect, see *Rye v Rye* [2002] EWHC 956 (Fam) [2002] 2 FLR 981.

Proctor's services either to investigate modern day abuses,[135] or to act as amicus curiae (as was done in *S v S*).

The marriage ceases as soon as the decree is made absolute, and either spouse is then free to remarry. The decree nisi does not have this effect, and if either party remarries before it has been made absolute, the second marriage is void.[136] The Family Justice Review noted that they had received evidence that some couples do not understand that they remain married until decree absolute. They recommended that the terms 'decree nisi' and 'absolute' be abolished, and were shocked to discover that such a change (to 'conditional and final' order) which the Family Procedure Rules Committee had also advocated, had not been made due to the cost of changing the courts' IT systems![137]

3. RECONCILIATION

The emphasis of the law is on *irretrievable* breakdown and certain provisions in the Matrimonial Causes Act are designed to promote reconciliation between the parties. For example, if the applicant instructs a legal representative to act for him or her in the proceedings, the latter is required to certify whether or not he or she has discussed with the applicant the possibility of reconciliation and has given the applicant the names and addresses of persons qualified to help effect a reconciliation between estranged spouses.[138] However, many and increasing numbers of applicants are self-represented, a trend which is of course likely to continue following the withdrawal of legal aid in most family proceedings, and the provision has long been regarded as serving little purpose.[139] The disregard of periods of cohabitation following instances of 'fault' or during separation is also intended to encourage the parties to try to repair the marriage without feeling that they would thereby 'lose' the basis of their petition.

There is little empirical evidence on the extent to which those contemplating divorce may attempt reconciliation nor how successful such attempts may be. Davis and Murch have suggested that there is potential for reconciliation in a significant number of cases, based on their findings that some couples may feel swept along the divorce track without adequate time to stop and reflect on whether this is what they really want. But they also note that it does not follow that such couples' marriages could have been 'saved' by the legal process seeking to facilitate their reconciliation.[140] One study, following up 1,491 people who had taken part in a pilot scheme intended to test out certain provisions aimed at reforming the Matrimonial Causes Act (and which are discussed later), found that 19% of those contacted, who had been contemplating divorce at the time of the pilot, were still living with their spouse two years later. The researchers commented, however, that while some respondents felt their marriages had been strengthened, the interview data left an impression of marriages 'continuing largely because spouses have learnt to make the best of imperfect circumstances . . . There is no doubt that the continuation of co-residence is not necessarily an indicator that the marriage has been "saved".'[141]

As discussed in Chapter 1, over the past 30 years, there has been a growing realisation that the *consequences* of family breakdown may not be best resolved through the legal

---

[135] As in *Bhaiji v Chauhan, Queen's Proctor Intervening (Divorce: Marriages Used for Immigration Purposes)* [2003] 2 FLR 485, noted earlier.
[136] As happened in both *Manchanda v Manchanda* [1995] 2 FLR 590, CA and *Dennis v Dennis* [2000] 2 FLR 231.   [137] Ministry of Justice, *Family Justice Review* para 4.168.
[138] Ibid, s 6(1); Family Procedure Rules 2010.
[139] *Report of the Matrimonial Causes Procedure Committee* (the Booth Committee) (1985) paras 4.42–4.43.
[140] G Davis and M Murch *Grounds for Divorce* (1988) ch 4.
[141] J Walker and P McCarthy 'Picking Up the Pieces' [2004] Fam Law 580.

system, and that the emotional and practical problems arising when a relationship ends can be exacerbated by an adversarial system of law designed to produce a 'winner' and 'loser'.[142] Indeed, the argument that the irretrievable breakdown of the marriage, rather than the fault of one or both of the spouses, should be the justification for terminating the relationship, is itself a demonstration of this realisation. We saw in Chapter 1 that a variety of mechanisms, initially introduced as local initiatives, both within and outside the courts, and then expanded to become an embedded feature of the family justice 'system' as a whole, have been used to attempt to bring a more 'conciliatory' and less confrontational dimension to family disputes. The growth of these mechanisms became allied with a wish to control and then reduce spending on legal aid for family matters. Consideration of mediation or other forms of dispute resolution became a mandatory step before a party could bring applications relating to children or financial matters connected with divorce to the court and legal aid for such proceedings is now only available if the applicant or a child is at risk of violence.

These procedural reforms have been interwoven with calls for reform of the substantive divorce law, as we explain in 'C. Proposals for Reform'.

C. PROPOSALS FOR REFORM

During the 1980s and 1990s, criticisms of the substantive and procedural law governing divorce resulted in several reform proposals being advocated. Legislation eventually followed in the shape of the Family Law Act 1996, but uncertainty about the viability and desirability of the new legislative process eventually led to a decision not to bring the relevant provisions of the Act into force and to their subsequent repeal. We trace below the sequence of events, to outline what the criticisms of the law were, how it was suggested they be dealt with, and why, in the end, the legislative changes were not implemented. A notable feature in this chronology is the recurrent identification of the same problems and issues, the proposal of similar recommendations to address them and the ultimate shying-away from their implications, either in cost or political fall-out.

1. THE BOOTH COMMITTEE ON MATRIMONIAL CAUSES PROCEDURE

In 1982 a committee chaired by Booth J was established to examine divorce procedure. The main thrust of their Report, published in 1985, was that bitterness between the parties might be reduced if unnecessary acrimonious allegations were eliminated and defended suits kept to a minimum; furthermore, parties should be encouraged and helped to settle financial matters and questions relating to children themselves with the benefit of legal advice and, if necessary, the assistance of mediators.

They also proposed that there should be an initial hearing within about 10 weeks of filing the application in every case involving children to whom s 41 of the 1973 Act applied[143] and also in cases where the respondent had stated an intention to oppose the grant of the decree. The purpose of the hearing would be to make orders in respect of agreed matters, to refer the parties to mediation where appropriate, to define the issues remaining between them, and to give directions.[144]

---

[142] For an interesting comparative perspective on this issue, which finds little clear link between the nature of the process and post-divorce adjustment, see O Cohen, R Savaya and S Tali 'Predictors of Adjustment to Divorce of Palestinian Israelis: Shari'a Court Procedure and Outcomes' (2007) 29 JSWFL 33–48.

[143] See earlier, Protection of children, p 225.   [144] Report para 3.5.

The Committee recommended that the terms 'decree nisi' and 'decree absolute' be replaced by 'provisional decree' and 'final decree', and that the latter should normally issue automatically four weeks after the grant of the former. To protect a party where this would work hardship (for example, because no order had been made for financial relief) the court would be given a power to delay the final decree in appropriate cases.

No action was taken on most of their recommendations, although a number were later developed by the Law Commission in their own proposals for more thorough-going reform of the law.

2. THE LAW COMMISSION'S PROPOSALS

Research showed that the objectives of the law, as laid down by the Law Commission in their 1966 Report, were not being met,[145] and the Law Commission looked again at the problem, issuing a Discussion Paper in 1988[146] and a report in 1990.[147]

(a) The Law Commission's criticisms of the 1973 Act

'It is confusing and misleading'

The sole ground for divorce is stated to be the irretrievable breakdown of the marriage, suggesting that fault is not the basis for granting a divorce, but such breakdown, no matter how profound, will not lead to a divorce decree unless a spouse can point to one of the five facts, three of which do involve fault. Further, the real reason for the breakdown might have nothing to do with the fact presented in the application, the allegations becoming a peg on which to hang the application, regardless of their significance (or insignificance) for the parties. No real scrutiny can be conducted into the truth of the allegations, and an applicant might be encouraged to bolster the petition with trivial or exaggerated allegations.[148]

'It is discriminatory and unjust'

The two years' separation with consent fact is relied upon more often by those in the higher socio-economic groups, while the poorer have to rely on the less satisfactory fault facts in order to obtain a speedier divorce and hence resolution of their financial and property problems.[149] It is discriminatory and unjust to provide a civilised no fault basis for divorce which is, in practice, unavailable to a large part of the population because many couples cannot afford to part and live in separate households for two years before the divorce. The fault facts themselves do not result in a clear allocation of 'blame' for the breakdown of the marriage, since the applicant might have been equally to blame although his conduct is not raised because the respondent does not defend the case. Even where respondents wish to dispute the allegations made in the petition by defending the suit, they are usually told that it would be a waste of time and money because the divorce will be granted anyway.

'It distorts parties' bargaining positions'

Given the difficulty facing a spouse in challenging allegations in the divorce suit itself, the scope for dispute is usually displaced from the divorce petition itself to the ancillary

---

[145] See, in particular, G Davis and M Murch *Grounds for Divorce* (1988).
[146] *Facing the Future—A Discussion Paper on the Ground for Divorce* Law Com No 170.
[147] *The Ground for Divorce* Law Com No 192.   [148] Law Com No 192 paras 2.8–2.12.
[149] Examination of 477 cases begun in the years 1980 to 1984 revealed that 36% of those in the highest socio-economic group relied upon the two years' separation fact, compared with 17% in the lowest: Law Com No 192 Appendix C, Table 2.

matters. One party who is more anxious or reluctant for the divorce to occur might be placed in a correspondingly weaker or stronger position in bargaining over matters relating to money and the children.

'It provokes unnecessary hostility and bitterness'

A fundamental objective of the Divorce Reform Act 1969 was to minimise the bitterness, distress and humiliation experienced by the parties in obtaining their divorce. But the system encourages each to make allegations against the other and to portray the other in as bad a light as possible to support the application. This provokes resentment, hostility and distress in the other spouse at a time when the couple are experiencing severe stress and unhappiness in coming to terms with the ending of their marriage. Their emotional misery is simply compounded by the legal process.

'It does nothing to save the marriage'

Despite the provisions intended to promote reconciliation which, as we saw,[150] have had little effect, the law in fact drives the parties further apart by encouraging the making of allegations of misconduct against each other or by requiring them to separate. Attention is placed upon how to prove irretrievable breakdown rather than on how to try to mend the marriage.

'It can make things worse for the children'

Children whose parents divorce may suffer more subsequently if the parents remain in conflict.[151] The law does nothing to reduce such conflict: indeed, it frequently exacerbates it.

(b) The options for reform

These criticisms convinced the Law Commission that the law required further reform. In deciding how to achieve this, the Law Commission drew up a new set of objectives for the law, which show interesting differences from their 1966 formulation noted earlier. It was 'generally agreed' that the law should:

> . . . try to support those marriages which are capable of being saved. . . enable those which cannot be saved to be dissolved with the minimum of avoidable distress, bitterness and hostility . . . encourage, so far as possible, the amicable resolution of practical issues relating to the couple's home, finances and children and the proper discharge of their responsibilities to one another and to their children . . .

and

> . . . seek to minimise the harm that the children of the family may suffer, both at the time and in the future, and to promote so far as possible the continued sharing of parental responsibility for them.[152]

These objectives reflect both an emphasis on mediation, in response to the developments in the provision of mediation pioneered during the 1970s and 1980s, and the shift of attention towards the children of the marriage and the fundamental ideology of parental

---

[150] See Reconciliation, p 229.
[151] J Pryor and B Rodgers *Children in Changing Families: Life after Parental Separation* (2001).
[152] Law Com No 192 para 3.1.

responsibility which underpins the Children Act 1989 (enacted shortly before this report was published).

The Commission rejected a return to a fault-based system on the basis that, first, the law is capable of assessing fault only in the crudest way, and secondly, that denying divorce except on grounds of fault is an illogical and ineffective way of promoting good marital conduct. Equally, divorce by immediate unilateral demand was rejected as providing no means of protecting the respondent, and divorce by mutual consent would not cater for cases where one spouse steadfastly refuses to consent. In many other jurisdictions which reformed their law after the Divorce Reform Act, the preferred model was a simple period of separation, but the Law Commission criticised this for its discriminatory effects against those who are poor. Instead, they recommended that divorce should no longer be seen as a single event but should be granted only after a process continuing over a period of time, during which the parties could reflect on whether they truly wished to end the marriage and if so, decide on the practical arrangements for doing so.

(c) The Law Commission's proposed scheme

The process they contemplated would begin by either (or preferably both) of the parties lodging at a court a sworn statement that he or she (or both) believes that the marriage has broken down. Each party would then be given a comprehensive information pack explaining inter alia the purpose of the period of consideration and reflection, the effects of divorce and separation, the powers of the court, and the nature and purpose of counselling, reconciliation and mediation. No later than 12 weeks after the making of the statement, the court would hold a preliminary assessment to review progress, make directions and consider whether mediation might be appropriate in helping the parties reach agreements.[153] After 11 months either or both of them would be able to apply for an order for divorce on making a declaration that the maker (or makers) believed that the breakdown of their marriage is irretrievable. In the intervening period the parties could be offered counselling or mediation, and the court could make orders relating to children, financial provision and property adjustment. This would reflect the principle that the practical consequences of divorce should ideally be settled before the marriage is dissolved. The court would normally make an order for divorce a month after the application (giving a minimum period of 12 months from the lodging of the initial statement). As under the 1973 Act, however, it should be able to postpone the order in exceptional circumstances and to refuse an order for divorce if this would result in grave financial or other hardship to one of the parties and it would be wrong in the circumstances to dissolve the marriage.

(d) The government's response

In response to the Law Commission's report, and notwithstanding the fact that hitherto divorce legislation had been regarded as too controversial to be handled as a Government measure, the Lord Chancellor decided to introduce plans to reform the divorce law.[154] The Government accepted the Law Commission's recommended scheme for a period of

---

[153] The assessment would have been roughly equivalent to the initial hearing recommended earlier by the Booth Committee: see earlier, The Booth Committee on Matrimonial Causes Procedure, p 230.

[154] *Looking to the Future: Mediation and the Ground for Divorce* Cm 2424 (hereafter, 'Green Paper'), Cm 2799 (hereafter, 'White Paper'). The White Paper had the same title as the earlier Consultation Paper. For assessments of the government's proposals, see A Bainham 'Divorce and the Lord Chancellor: Looking to the Future or Getting Back to Basics?' (1994) 35 *Cambridge Law Journal* 253; S Cretney 'Divorce Reform in England: Humbug and Hypocrisy or a Smooth Transition?' in M Freeman (ed) *Divorce, Where Next?* (1996).

consideration and reflection having to elapse as evidence of the irretrievable breakdown of the marriage. It also seized upon mediation as a mechanism which would, it said, be better able than the legal process to identify marriages capable of being saved, and would thus enhance the opportunities for reconciliation. Where reconciliation was not achievable, the couple would be encouraged to resolve their differences and co-operate in sorting out the arrangements necessary for their, and their children's, future lives more amicably. The Government regarded mediation as cheaper than litigation and estimated that the average cost of comprehensive mediation (in which both financial and child issues are dealt with) was about £550 per case, while the average cost of a matrimonial bill paid by the Legal Aid Fund in 1992/93 was £1,565.[155]

The Government's proposals differed from those of the Law Commission in significant respects. First, they placed much greater emphasis upon the role of mediation and sought to minimise the input of lawyers, whom they regarded as adding to the costs and adversarial nature of the proceedings. Secondly, instead of having a preliminary assessment during the period for consideration and reflection, they proposed that the initial appointment become a purely information-giving service which would be compulsory for anyone initiating the divorce process.[156]

A third important change related to the settling of the financial and other arrangements before the divorce would be granted. The Law Commission argued that, while one of the strengths of the period for consideration and reflection would be that it would enable the parties to decide upon the arrangements consequent upon the divorce, and while there should be power for the courts to make final orders relating to these before the dissolution of the marriage, it would be wrong to require the parties to have resolved all issues concerning children, property and finance before a divorce order could be made. They reasoned that this would 'create a formidable bargaining chip for the more powerful or determined party', who could thereby delay the grant of the divorce.[157] Instead, they proposed that the court should have the power to postpone the divorce where granting it without any delay would cause hardship to the spouse or children.[158] The Government, however, reversed this position. They were influenced by the argument that 'people who marry should discharge their obligations undertaken when they contracted their earlier marriage, and also their responsibilities which they undertook when they became parents, before they became free to remarry.'[159] Accordingly, there should be no divorce until arrangements have been finalised, unless delay would cause hardship to a spouse or child.

3. DIVORCE UNDER THE FAMILY LAW ACT 1996

The government's Family Law Bill had a difficult passage through Parliament, and several further changes were made to the legislation before it received the Royal Assent in 1996.[160] Part I, which contains 'general principles' in s 1, and Part III, which concerned legal aid,[161] were implemented. Part II, which set out the new divorce law, was not, for reasons explained once an outline of the proposed law has been given in the following sections.

---

[155] Green Paper paras 9.28, 9.30.   [156] Green Paper para 8.12; White Paper para 6.15.
[157] Law Com No 192 para 5.56.   [158] Law Com No 192 para 5.58.
[159] White Paper para 4.26 and Hansard HL Debs, 30 November 1995, col 703.
[160] For a critical analysis of the ideology and philosophy of the Act, see H Reece *Divorcing Responsibly* (2003) and 'Divorcing Responsibly' (2000) 8 Fem LS 65.
[161] Subsequently replaced by the Access to Justice Act 1999 and the LSC Funding Code.

(a) The 'general principles'

Section 1 of the Act requires the court, and any person exercising functions under Part III of the Act, to have regard to the following general principles:

> (a) that the institution of marriage is to be supported;
> (b) that the parties to a marriage which may have broken down are to be encouraged to take all practicable steps, whether by marriage counselling or otherwise, to save the marriage...[162]

These principles were intended to guide courts and others in their application of the relevant provisions. They now appear to be redundant, other than to serve as a legislative statement of Parliament's view of what constitutes a good divorce law.

(b) Divorce procedure under Part II

In line with the Law Commission's proposed scheme, Part II would have required the person seeking a divorce to go through a series of steps, over a period of time, designed to ensure that the marriage could not be saved, that the applicant understood the implications of the divorce, and that sufficient attention had been paid to the consequences both for the spouses and their children, before the marriage was finally legally terminated. The complexity and controversy of the proposed system, and experience of introducing the child support scheme in 1993 without first having tested it out, to disastrous political effect,[163] led the incoming Labour Government in 1997 to tread carefully when it was attempting to decide how to implement Part II. The key innovations proposed were therefore made the subjects of pilot schemes, designed and monitored by independent researchers, to measure their feasibility and effectiveness.

The information meeting

The Act provided that a spouse (or both spouses) initiating the divorce, or contesting it, or seeking an order to be made in connection with the divorce, must have attended an information meeting first.[164] The purpose of the meeting was to communicate a range of information relating to divorce, the process and its consequences, and also to 'mark the seriousness of the step being taken'.[165] The Government had wanted meetings to be organised for groups of intending divorcees, as is done in Australia and parts of the USA, but this was rejected by Parliament as demeaning and embarrassing.[166]

The information to be given reflected the greater attention which is now paid to the needs of the children of divorced couples and the desire to ensure that couples understood the implications of starting the divorce process.[167] It was also hoped that it would give

---

[162] Subsections (c) and (d), which referred to the desirability of minimising distress to the parties and children, and the importance of minimising the risk of violence, were repealed by the Children and Families Act 2014 s 18.   [163] See Ch 21, pp 800ff.

[164] Family Law Act 1996 s 8(2).

[165] Hansard HL Debs, 30 November 1995, col 702 (Lord Mackay LC).

[166] See the White Paper: Cm 2799, paras 7.14–7.16 and for withering criticism of such an innovation, see S Cretney 'Divorce Reform in England: Humbug and Hypocrisy or a Smooth Transition?' in M Freeman (ed) *Divorce, Where Next?* p 48, G Davis 'Divorce Reform—Peering Anxiously into the Future' [1995] Fam Law 564.

[167] Compare the findings of G Davis and M Murch *Grounds for Divorce* (1988) pp 57–67 and the government's findings that there is widespread ignorance of the possibilities open to couples whose marriage is in difficulty but who have not yet decided on a divorce: See White Paper para 7.1.

them an opportunity to consider the value of attending marriage counselling and of an attempt at reconciliation.

The researchers monitoring the information meetings developed a variety of formats for delivery of the requisite information in order to see which might be most effective. These included group meetings, because even though the legislation required individual meetings, it was felt, given the successful experience in other jurisdictions, that group meetings could be offered as an additional facility to users, postal packs, videos and CD roms as well as more traditional talks. Since the legislation was not in force, the researchers had to rely on volunteers who were invited to participate in the study and this, inevitably, meant that the pilot could not completely mimic the effect that a compulsory scheme might have had. Even so, the researchers recruited nearly 8,000 people to attend meetings and nearly 1,500 who received postal packs of information. These were sufficiently large numbers to enable some reliable findings to be reached. Whilst 90% of those attending meetings were glad they had gone and valued the information they received, the findings revealed more problems than successes with the shape of the legislative scheme. First, the scheme required the delivery of standard form 'information' to all those participating, but this took no account of the individual circumstances and stages in the marriage breakdown that different participants might have experienced. Whilst some, whose marital problems were relatively new, simply wanted advice on what they should do next, others were much clearer about what they were going to do and wanted information on specific issues such as the financial implications. A 'one size fits all' package of information meant that many participants would find parts of the meeting of no use to them and for those who had determined on a divorce, receiving information about attempting marriage counselling and reconciliation was a waste of time. Moreover, participants wanted *advice* tailored to their individual needs, but those providing the meetings were not empowered to give this.

The headline statistics that most disappointed the Government, however, were that only 7% of those attending marriage-support focused meetings indicated that their attendance meant that a divorce was now less likely; indeed the information meeting 'tended to tip those who were uncertain about their marriage into divorce mode'. Only 23% of participants went to marriage counselling in the two years following their attendance at a meeting and only 10% of participants went to mediation over the two year period, of whom 37% reached agreement on the matters in dispute with their spouse. By contrast, 73% of participants went to a solicitor in the two year period, demonstrating that, contrary to the government's hope, people still saw solicitors as a legitimate and authoritative source of information and advice and viewed counselling and mediation as less relevant to them.[168]

Statement of marital breakdown

Once three months had elapsed since the applicant had attended an information meeting, he or she (or both spouses together) would have been permitted to file with the court a statement of marital breakdown.[169] The object of this delay was to provide a 'cooling-off period' during which the parties could explore the scope for reconciliation. The statement would declare that the maker or makers believed that the marriage had broken down, although *not* that they believed it had broken down irretrievably, since it was the purpose

---

[168] All data are taken from J Walker et al *Information Meetings and Associated Provisions within the Family Law Act 1996: Final Evaluation Report* (2001). For Walker's reflections on the research, see J Walker 'Information Meetings Revisited' [2000] Fam Law 330 and 'The Information Meeting Pilots—Using and Abusing Evidence?' [2001] Fam Law 817.   [169] Family Law Act 1996 s 6.

of the period for reflection and consideration (see next) to establish this. As with the current law one year time bar on presenting an application, a spouse would not have been permitted to file a statement before the first anniversary of the marriage.[170]

Period for reflection and consideration

The irretrievable breakdown of the marriage would have been established by the passing of a period for reflection and consideration, lasting for a basic period of nine months.[171] The aim of the period was for the parties to use it to explore further the scope for reconciliation, with the help of marriage counselling if desired, or to seek to come to terms with the ending of the marriage and settle their post-divorce arrangements, preferably via mediation.[172] A second pilot scheme was undertaken in order to test out how publicly-funded mediation on a mass scale might work during this proposed period.

Unlike the information meeting pilot, the researchers monitoring mediation had a semi-captive sample to investigate, because the provision of legal aid for family matters had, under Part III of the Family Law Act, which *was* brought into force, been made dependent on a prior exploration of whether the case was suitable for mediation. The researchers thus were able to monitor the use of mediation in conditions more or less akin to those that would pertain if the legislation were fully implemented. They were able to scrutinise over 4,500 monitoring forms compiled by mediation providers on individual clients and to interview over 1,000 of these clients. But they found that the number of mediations undertaken as a result of the new legal provisions was lower than expected, so that although many clients underwent an assessment to determine if mediation was suitable for them, this did not translate into a major increase in the resort to mediation proper; in other words, for various reasons (most often the unwillingness of the other spouse to attempt it) mediation was not regarded as 'suitable' for this particular legal aid client. Of those who did go to mediation, the response was generally favourable, with around 70% of those using mediation to resolve disputes finding it fairly helpful or very helpful. The researchers urged caution in assessing 'success rates' for mediation, since the lack of a complete agreement does not mean that the parties did not make progress in improving their communication with each other or in getting closer to some sort of settlement. Nonetheless, they found that 45% of those experiencing mediation about children issues, and 34% using mediation for financial disputes, had reached agreement.

Overall, these figures suggested that mediation can provide a useful service for a number of divorcing spouses. But when the researchers also asked clients about their attitudes to solicitors, they found that these scored even higher in terms of client satisfaction. Moreover, they could not find that use of mediation had a significant impact on legal costs incurred, although they did find that, as might be expected, those mediation services operating in the not-for-profit sector, as compared with solicitor-mediators, were cheaper.[173] The conclusion drawn by the Government was thus once again a negative one—mediation was unlikely to be taken up in the numbers required to have a major impact on legal aid expenditure, and it could not be regarded as the corner-stone, or panacea, that some policy-makers had originally hoped at the time the Act was drafted.

---

[170] Family Law Act 1996 s 7(6).

[171] The time would begin to run 14 days after the day the statement was received by the court: s 7(3).

[172] White Paper paras 6.17–6.21.

[173] All data are taken from G Davis et al *Monitoring Publicly Funded Mediation* (2001). See also G Davis et al 'Medation and Legal Services—The Client Speaks' [2001] Fam Law 110; G Bevan et al 'Can Mediation Reduce Expenditure on Lawyers?' [2001] Fam Law 187, G Davis et al 'Family Mediation—Where Do We Go from Here?' [2001] Fam Law 265; and R Dingwall and D Greatbatch 'Family Mediators—What Are They Doing?' [2001] Fam Law 378.

That cautious view has now been superseded, as we saw in Chapter 1, by the Coalition Government's determination to press the use of mediation, or other dispute resolution procedures, before or instead of resort to court in family proceedings.

The 1996 Act provided that the reflection and consideration period could be extended in certain circumstances, such as where the parties wished to attempt a reconciliation, or one party did not accept that the marriage was over and applied to the court for an extension of time. The period would also be automatically extended for six months where there was a child of the family under the age of 16. This was a significant change from previous thinking. The argument that divorce should be harder—or, at least, take longer—where children are involved had been resisted by the Law Commission on the basis that it could cause the parties to feel bitter and resentful towards their children,[174] but parliamentarians considered that parents should be required to take more time to ensure that the marriage was truly over for the sake of their children and voted through the amendment to require the extension (except where there was a non-molestation or occupation order in force or the court was satisfied that delaying the divorce would be significantly detrimental to the welfare of any child of the family).[175] It is striking to note how attitudes have changed again, as evidenced by the repeal by the Children and Families Act 2014 of the s 41 statement of arrangements for children, discussed earlier.

The divorce order

At the end of the requisite period, either or both of the parties would have been able to apply for the divorce order (not 'decree'). Under a provision akin to s 5 of the Matrimonial Causes Act 1973, a court could have refused to grant the divorce order on the application of a spouse claiming that dissolution of the marriage would result in substantial financial or other hardship to him or her or to a child of the family; and that it would be wrong, in all the circumstances (including the conduct of the parties and the interests of any child of the family), for the marriage to be dissolved.

The divorce order would have dissolved the marriage, coming into force on its being made and thus doing away with the two-stage process of decree nisi and absolute.

D. THE FUTURE OF DIVORCE REFORM

One of the 'presentational' problems which had faced the Law Commission and the Government when issuing their original proposals was how to avoid the trap of being accused of making divorce 'harder' or 'easier'. On the one hand, by requiring parties to wait at least a year from start to finish of the divorce process, it could be said that the proposed new law would make divorce harder than under the Matrimonial Causes Act where, when the 'fault' facts are relied on, it is possible to go from angry break-up to final decree within the space of a few weeks, as in the case of 'domestic goddess', TV chef Nigella Lawson, who obtained a decree nisi less than eight weeks after her husband was photographed apparently grabbing her round the throat in a London restaurant.[176] The waiting stage under the 1996 Act was a deliberate attempt to answer those critics of the current law that it does not sufficiently help couples to explore the scope for reconciliation

---

[174] Law Com No 192 para 5.28; White Paper para 4.18.

[175] Section 7(12)(b). Lord Irvine of Lairg considered that there would be 'very many cases' where concern that delaying the divorce would be detrimental to a child's interests would be justified: Hansard HL Debs, 27 June 1996, col 1071.

[176] Reported in *The Daily Telegraph* 31 July 2013.

or to give them time to come to terms with the implications of ending their marriage. A period of careful 'reflection and consideration' could be a challenging and sobering experience requiring spouses to face up to the consequences of their actions, both for themselves and for their children. The new divorce law, on this view, would be 'harder', but better. Equally, it was argued by some that removing any reference to 'fault' as a basis for divorce would make divorce much easier, and potentially quicker, than now. No longer would a spouse have to justify their petition to end their marriage by asserting one of the five facts proving irretrievable breakdown, but simply wait things out for the appropriate length of time. Marriage obligations would be rendered nugatory since nothing would turn on a spouse's fulfilment or abandonment of the marriage oath—an entirely 'blameless' spouse could now be divorced in not much more than a year, instead of being able to hold the other to their marital commitments for five years.

Those commentators who rejected both of these arguments, and who, by and large, welcomed the abolition of the doctrine of fault as completing the job which should have been achieved in the 1960s, still found flaws in the proposed divorce regime. The requirement to go through a series of procedural steps in the right order appears based on an assumption that nearly all couples have similar needs and have similar powers of rational behaviour and can thus divorce in a 'civilised' fashion, but the information meeting pilot demonstrated that people have different agendas and different capacities to make use of counselling and mediation. The mediation pilot also showed that mediation cannot easily replace the more familiar mechanisms of lawyer support and negotiation and that most people still regard divorce as a primarily 'legal' issue on which they want an expert's advice and assistance. Of course, the subsequent withdrawal of legal aid from most family proceedings by the Coalition Government will test whether such attitudes can be changed, and how smoothly or otherwise.

Nor would the new regime have done away with all the criticisms levelled at the current law by the Law Commission. Although it would not have been necessary for the spouses to separate in order to establish irretrievable breakdown, the prospect of remaining under the same roof whilst the period of reflection and consideration elapsed (for 15 months where there were children, plus the three months initial 'cooling off' time) would not be an easy one to contemplate. Those financially better off would be able to separate and negotiate at a distance; those not able to do so would be forced to live in what might be an extremely difficult atmosphere for many months, which could hardly be conducive to the well being of any children of the family. There would still be opportunities to exploit one spouse's stronger bargaining position, by seeking to spin things out through extensions, or attempts to block the divorce order, at the cost of the other party's compromising on the financial or other consequences to their detriment.[177]

But there were valuable features of the new law, which remain pertinent. Opportunities to receive well-devised information about the process and the implications of divorce, and to meet a marriage counsellor, were important innovations which could be very helpful, if delivered at a time and manner suited to those involved. The Family Justice Review's proposals for an 'information hub'[178] to fulfil a similar role (albeit primarily online and by telephone) were accepted by the Government[179] and may go some way to meeting the clear

---

[177] It has also been argued that the law was hijacked by a lobby more concerned to uphold traditional notions of marriage and morality than to grapple with the realities of family life: see E Hasson 'Setting a Standard or Reflecting Reality? The "Role" of Divorce Law, and the Case of the Family Law Act 1996' (2003) 17 Int Jo of Law, Policy and the Family 338; and E Hasson 'The Street-Level Response to Relationship Breakdown: A Lesson for National Policy?' [2004] JSWFL 35.   [178] *Final Report* para 4.74 ff.

[179] *Response* Recommendation 111.

need for reliable information and advice when going through the divorce process, although it is highly doubtful that they can meet the gap left by the loss of legal aid and representation provided by lawyers for the many who cannot afford to fund this themselves.

The greater emphasis on children's welfare chimed very closely with modern thinking on its central importance and could have encouraged parents to pay greater attention to these than they are currently required to do. The Government's response to the Family Justice Review *attempts* to reflect this importance, although it has been criticised, as we will see,[180] for focusing on parents' (especially fathers') rights and interests and failing to put children's welfare truly at centre-stage. And its proposed abolition of the statement of arrangements delivers the opposite message that the state is not actually very interested in children's welfare at all except where parental disagreement forces this to the attention of the family justice system.

Finally, the abolition of fault would have brought English law up to date at last with majority views about the limits of the law in seeking to impose moral judgments on intimate conduct. It is regrettable indeed that the Coalition Government did not feel able to adopt this most fundamental and overdue reform of divorce law, and one which, increasingly, some members of the judiciary themselves have openly called for.[181]

At the same time as greater access to information and non-legal services is being promoted as a means of helping couples deal with the practical and non-legal aspects of divorce, further restrictions on access to legal aid have been introduced to attempt to pin back the costs of legal assistance. The logic of such a development is to move to an overtly administrative system of divorce, at least for 'straightforward' cases, as is done in some other jurisdictions, and this is precisely what the Coalition Government are now proposing on the strength of the Family Justice Review's recommendations noted earlier. Just as one does not need to visit a lawyer (although the growth in acceptability of pre-nuptial agreements[182] may render such a visit increasingly useful), still less a court, to get married so we might one day conclude that there is no need to send papers to a court to sanction the ending of that marriage. Increasing attempts to harmonise law across Europe may provide a way forward in order both to simplify and unify divorce laws for an ever more mobile population.[183]

E. DISSOLUTION OF CIVIL PARTNERSHIP

The basic approach of the Civil Partnership Act 2004 was to assimilate as closely as possible the rules governing such partnerships with those already applicable to marriage, without actually referring to the former as a type of 'marriage'. The rules on terminating a valid civil partnership are therefore similar to those applying to divorce.[184]

No application to dissolve a civil partnership may be brought within one year of its formation, although the application may be based on matters which occurred during

---

[180] See Ch 14, Changes made by the Children and Families Act 2014, p 481.

[181] See, for example, the speech of Sir Nicholas Wall, former President of the Family Division to the Resolution Annual Conference, 24 March 2012:

http://www.judiciary.gov.uk/Resources/JCO/Documents/Speeches/pfd-speech-resolution-annual-conference-240312.pdf (accessed 3 August 2012).

[182] See Ch 22, Pre- and post-nuptial agreements, pp 853ff.

[183] For a distillation of common European principles and a resulting suggested common divorce law based on consent, or separation in the absence of consent, see K Boele-Woelki, F Ferrand, C Gonzales Beilfuss, M Jantera-Jareborg, N Lowe, D Martiny and W Pintens *Principles of European Family Law Regarding Divorce and Maintenance Between Former Spouses* (2004).

[184] See Civil Partnership Act 2004 Part 2, Ch 2; M Harper et al, *Civil Partnership: The New Law* (2005) paras 4.43–4.50.

this period.[185] Secondly, the ground for dissolution is the irretrievable breakdown of the civil partnership, to be established by proof of one or more of *four* facts.[186] These are the same as for divorce, with the omission of adultery and intolerability, it being accepted that adultery is defined as sexual intercourse between parties of the opposite sex, one of whom is married.[187] It will have been noted earlier that in a same sex marriage, adultery *may* be relied upon—but the definition requires that the spouse have had intercourse with a person of the opposite sex. It might have been sensible to amend the Civil Partnership Act 2004 in order to be consistent with this (even if heterosexual intercourse may be unlikely where same sex couples are involved). As Harper et al comment, one party's infidelity is as likely to be the cause of (or perhaps one should say, contribute to) the irretrievable breakdown of a civil partnership as it is in a marriage. Meanwhile, such unfaithfulness may be embraced within the concept of 'behaviour'.[188]

The Act includes the same provisions designed to facilitate reconciliation as appear in the Matrimonial Causes Act, that is, providing for rules of court to require the solicitor to certify whether he or she has discussed the possibility with the applicant,[189] and disregarding periods of living together for up to six months.[190] The Act also applies the same protection[191] concerning financial provision for respondents in cases based on separation by enabling the court to refuse an order based on five years' separation,[192] rescind a conditional order if satisfied that the respondent was misled by the applicant into giving his or her consent to the dissolution, or postpone the finalising of the dissolution until satisfied as to the financial settlement proposed.[193] However, since, when first enacted, it was provided that a civil partnership was an exclusively non-religious union, there is no equivalent to s 10A (postponement of decree absolute to encourage dissolution according to religious rites) of the Matrimonial Causes Act 1973.

The special procedure, being a product of secondary legislation, is not mentioned in the Act, but dissolution proceedings are governed by the same procedural rules as for a divorce.[194] A dissolution 'order'[195] (not 'decree') is pronounced in two stages, referred to as a 'conditional' and 'final' order[196] with the same usual minimum interval of six weeks between the two, with the possibility of the court shortening the period, as for divorce.[197] The Queen's Proctor may investigate issues arising during the proceedings.[198]

F. JUDICIAL SEPARATION AND SEPARATION ORDERS

1. JUDICIAL SEPARATION IN MARRIAGE

Before the introduction of judicial divorce in 1857, a spouse could obtain an order from the ecclesiastical courts, called a divorce *a mensa et thoro*,[199] relieving the applicant of the duty to cohabit with the respondent, so that neither spouse could be held in desertion

---

[185] Civil Partnership Act 2004 s 41.   [186] Section 44.
[187] *Dennis v Dennis* [1955] P 153. Confirmed by s 1(6) of the Matrimonial Causes Act 1973 inserted by Sch 4 para 3 to the Marriage (Same Sex Couples) Act 2013.
[188] See M Harper et al, *Civil Partnership: The New Law* (2005) para 4.48.   [189] Section 42.
[190] Section 45.
[191] Until repealed by the Children and Families Act 2014 s 17, the court was also required, as in divorce, to scrutinise the arrangements proposed for any children of the family.
[192] Section 47.   [193] Section 48.   [194] Family Procedure Rules 2010 Part 7.
[195] Section 37(1)(a).   [196] Section 37(2).   [197] Section 38.   [198] Section 39.
[199] Meaning 'from bed and board'.

while it was in force. But the parties remained husband and wife, so that neither of them was free to remarry. An equivalent power was given to the civil courts in 1857, through the grant of a decree of 'judicial separation', under which the applicant had to prove exactly the same grounds as for a divorce.

The advantage of the decree lay mainly in the fact that it gave the court jurisdiction to order financial provision for the wife; consequently, as long as the grounds for divorce were limited, she could obtain a measure of both financial and physical protection. But alternative ways of obtaining maintenance, the ease with which divorce can now be obtained, and the possibility of obtaining remedies for domestic violence, have long tended to provide more appropriate mechanisms for spouses than judicial separation per se, and a mere 136 decrees were granted in 2013.[200] Nonetheless, an order denoting a legal separation rather than a divorce may still be useful. First, a spouse may have a conscientious or religious objection to divorce (although the religion itself may not recognise the civil divorce anyway);[201] secondly, an elderly spouse whose marriage has broken down will remain entitled to a widow's or widower's pension on the death of the other, which may be of substantial financial importance.

When divorce law was reformed by the Divorce Reform Act 1969, the basis for obtaining a judicial separation was also amended to keep the law in line.[202] However, since the marriage is not terminated by the decree, it is not necessary to establish its 'irretrievable breakdown' but simply one or more of the five 'facts' which, for this purpose, constitute the 'grounds' for the decree.[203] Moreover, a petition may be presented during the first year of the marriage.

Sections 5 and 10 of the Matrimonial Causes Act do not apply because the decree does not alter the parties' marital status. For the same reason, the decree is not pronounced in two stages, but takes effect immediately it is pronounced.[204]

The principal effect of the decree is that it relieves the applicant from any duty to cohabit with the respondent.[205] The court has power to make a number of orders relating to the children of the family and to financial relief.[206] The decree will also affect the devolution of a spouse's property if he or she dies intestate.[207] But for all other purposes the spouses remain married; neither of them is at liberty to remarry, for example, and such of the common law disabilities arising from marriage as remain will continue in force.[208]

---

[200] Ministry of Justice *Court Statistics (quarterly) January to March 2014* [online] CSV divorce_National.csv (accessed 4 August 2014).

[201] See G Douglas et al 'The role of religious tribunals in regulating marriage and divorce' [2012] CFLQ 139.

[202] See Matrimonial Causes Act 1973 s 17. When considering divorce reform in 1990, the Law Commission accepted that the possibility of obtaining a 'separation' as distinct from a divorce should be retained: Law Com No 192 para 4.8 so that when the Family Law Act 1996 was enacted, new provisions for 'separation orders' were included. Unless the arguments change, one would expect any further reform of divorce to require similar provision to be made for those objecting to divorce on conscientious or other grounds.

[203] A spouse who later seeks a divorce may (subject to the provisions of s 2 regarding resumed cohabitation) rely on the facts presented for the judicial separation decree, and the decree is to be treated as sufficient proof of any fact by reference to which it was granted: Matrimonial Causes Act 1973 s 4(1)(2).

[204] A statement of arrangements for children was required until the repeal of s 41 by the Children and Families Act 2014.

[205] Matrimonial Causes Act 1973 s 18(1). But see Ch 4, Consortium, p 94, for discussion of the view expressed in *Macleod v Macleod* [2008] UKPC 64 [2010] 1 AC 298 that the duty to cohabit was removed when the action for restitution of conjugal rights was abolished.

[206] See Ch 22.

[207] See Ch 25 Intestate succession, Judicial separation or separation order in relation to a civil partnership, p 971.   [208] Eg as to compellability as a witness: see Ch 4, Compellability, p 97.

2. SEPARATION IN CIVIL PARTNERSHIP

Equivalent provisions apply to separation orders, as they are known,[209] in cases of civil partnership. The basis of the order is proof of one of the four facts which may be relied on in dissolution, without the need to establish irretrievable breakdown.[210] However, the effect of a separation order does not include the lifting of an obligation to cohabit with each other, as has been understood to be the case in judicial separation. It is uncertain whether such an obligation exists in a civil partnership but of course, the same restriction on entering into a new civil partnership (or marriage) applies as on judicial separation.

[209] Civil Partnership Act 2004 s 37(1)(d).   [210] Section 56.

8

PARENTS AND GUARDIANS

A. INTRODUCTION

A fundamental legal status and one that is critical to family law is that of parenthood, which is the focus of this chapter. In addition we discuss guardianship which, as it has now been developed, is a status akin to parenthood acquired through formal testamentary or judicial appointment by which appointed persons replace deceased parents for certain purposes during the child's minority.

B. LEGAL PARENTAGE

Although a number of persons could be considered 'parents',[1] English law, in common with many legal systems, has chosen to accord the *legal* status of parentage in the first instance to those who have been responsible for creating the child (principally those whose genetic material created the child) rather than to those (sometimes referred to as 'social parents') who care for the child after the birth (though, of course most persons responsible for creating the child also bring up the child).[2]

At common law, the position was simple—legal parentage was based upon the genetic or presumed genetic connection with the child, but with the advancement of medical reproductive techniques and societal changes, the position is now much more complicated. Furthermore, while at common law legal parentage was inalienable, now, following the introduction of adoption and subsequently parental orders it is possible to transfer parentage after the child's birth. In short, legal parentage is either conferred at the time of the child's birth, or it can be acquired through its subsequent transfer by adoption or by the making of a parental order under the Human Fertilisation and Embryology Act (HFEA) 2008. It has been observed[3] that this multiplicity of mechanisms operates on a continuum of state regulation, from minimal, if any, control in the case of the mother who happens to be unmarried, to lengthy state investigation into the applicant's suitability to be a parent in the case of adoption.

In this chapter we discuss legal parentage at the time of the child's birth and parental orders, deferring to Chapter 19 the discussion of adoption.

---

[1] See the analysis by Baroness Hale in *Re G (Children) (Residence: Same Sex Partner)* [2006] UKHL 43 [2006] 1 WLR 2305 at [32]–[36], in which she refers to natural parents, gestational parents and social and psychological parents. See also M Richards 'A Biomedical Perspective on Parenthood' in A Bainham, S Day Sclater and M Richards (eds) *What is a Parent?* (1999) pp 47–48.

[2] As we discuss in Chapter 10, the means by which English law confers power to act as a parent during the child's minority is by the vesting of parental responsibility in that person.

[3] G Douglas and N Lowe 'Becoming a Parent in English Law' (1992) 108 LQR 414.

1. WHO ARE THE LEGAL PARENTS OF A CHILD?

(a) Introduction

At one time it went without saying that the person who gave birth to the child was the mother and the person by whom she conceived was the father. Indeed, traditionally the law has taken the blood tie or genetic link as the test of parenthood.[4] However, the advent of human assisted procreation led to a reappraisal of this position particularly in the light of a detailed inquiry into the whole subject by the Warnock Committee on Human Fertilisation and Embryology.[5] There is now comprehensive legislation in the form of the HFEAs of 1990 and 2008 governing issues arising from assisted procreation, including, inter alia, the question of who is to be regarded as a parent.[6]

Before discussing who in law are regarded as parents of a child it is helpful to say a little about the different techniques of assisted reproduction.[7]

(b) Techniques of human assisted procreation

Artificial insemination

Artificial insemination refers to the placing of semen into a woman's vagina, cervix or uterus (ie womb) by means other than sexual intercourse. If the woman's husband's sperm is used, the process is referred to as artificial insemination by husband or AIH. If someone else's sperm is used, it is known as artificial insemination by donor, or DI—donor insemination. It is estimated that there are between 800 and 1,000 births by DI each year.[8]

In vitro fertilisation (IVF)

The technique of in vitro fertilisation is to take a ripe egg from the woman's ovary just before ovulation (ie when the egg would have been released naturally). It is then mixed with sperm in a dish (in vitro) so that fertilisation can occur. If the egg is fertilised, it is returned to the uterus, where it may implant, and then develop as normal. In 2010 about 2% of all live births in the United Kingdom were from IVF conceptions.[9]

---

[4] Hence the use of blood tests (now known as 'scientific tests') to determine parentage: see, The use of blood and DNA tests to establish parentage p 263. For the legal significance of parentage see p 274.

[5] Report on the Committee of Inquiry into Human Fertilisation and Embryology (1984) Cmnd 9314 whose recommendations were essentially accepted in the government's White Paper *Human Fertilisation and Embryology: A Framework for Legislation* (1987) Cm 259.

[6] For interesting discussion of this issue see A Bainham 'Parentage, Parenthood and Parental Responsibility: Subtle, Elusive, Yet Important Distinctions' in A Bainham, S Day Sclater and M Richards (eds) *What is a Parent?* (1999) ch 2, J Herring 'Parents and Child' in J Herring (ed) *Family Law, Issues, Debates, Policy* (2001) ch 4 and R Probert 'Families, Assisted Reproduction and the Law' [2004] CFLQ 273.

[7] See generally G Douglas *Law, Fertility and Reproduction* (1991) ch 6; E Jackson, *Regulating Reproduction: law, technology and autonomy* (2001) and the Warnock Report, Cmnd 9314 chs 3–7. New techniques are being continually developed and refined, and the text refers only to the main types used, which have particular significance for family law. For a historical perspective on artificial insemination and other techniques of human assisted reproduction, see S Cretney *Family Law in the Twentieth Century* (2003) pp 540–4. For valuable overviews see R Deech 'The Legal Regulation of Infertility Treatment in Britain' in S Katz, J Eekelaar and M Maclean (eds) *Cross-Currents—Family Law Policy in the US and England* (2001) ch 8 and S Sheldon 'Fragmenting Fatherhood: The Regulation of Reproductive Technologies' (2005) 68 MLR 523.

[8] See S Cretney *Family Law in the Twentieth Century* (2003) and R Probert 'Families, Assisted Reproduction and the Law' [2004] CFLQ 273 at 279.

[9] Human Fertilisation and Embryology Authority *Fertility Treatment in 2011—Trends and Figures* (2012). Note in *H v Austria* (App No 57813/00), [2012] 2 FCR 291 the restriction of access to IVF treatment was held by the ECtHR (Grand Chamber) not to violate human rights.

Egg and embryo donation

Egg collection technology coupled with IVF makes it possible to obtain an egg from a donor for transfer to another woman having been fertilised with either the husband's or a donor's sperm in vitro.[10] It will be appreciated that IVF treatment has therefore created the possibility that the woman who gives birth to a child may not be the genetic mother. In the case of embryo transfer neither the woman nor her partner (unless his sperm is used) will be genetically related to the child.

Surrogacy

Surrogacy[11] involves one woman carrying a child for another with the intention that the child be handed over. It is not to be confused with the techniques for human assisted reproduction just described, though the surrogate may well have conceived by one of those methods. We discuss the effect and regulation of surrogacy agreements later in this chapter.

2. WHO IS THE LEGAL MOTHER?

Until the advent of in vitro fertilisation, provided the fact of the birth could be proved, there could be no doubt that the woman giving birth must in law be the child's mother. As Lord Simon said in *The Ampthill Peerage* case,[12] 'Motherhood, although also a legal relationship, is based on a fact, being proved demonstrably by parturition.'

There is no doubt that, where the woman has conceived by artificial insemination or by in vitro fertilisation of her ovum, she is the legal mother. The difficulty arises where the woman giving birth is not the child's genetic mother but is the carrying or gestational mother as a result of egg or embryo donation. As Scott Baker J said in *Re W (Minors) (Surrogacy)*,[13] 'The advent of IVF presented the law with a dilemma: whom should the law regard as the mother?' Arguments can be led either way. On the one hand, given the biological connection, it could be argued that the genetic mother should be regarded as the child's legal mother. On the other hand, because of the consequences that would follow if the genetic mother is unknown (for example, the child's birth would have to be registered with the name of the mother unknown and in most cases would result in the child having no legal parents at birth),[14] there would seem a strong case for considering the carrying mother the legal mother.[15] An alternative approach altogether is to hold the *intending* parent the legal parent.

This latter approach was adopted in the Californian decision of *Johnson v Calvert*.[16] In that case, in pursuance of a surrogacy agreement, one of the commissioning mother's

---

[10] Including *gamete intrafallopian transfers* (GIFT) by which a donated egg is placed with the sperm in the womb and *intra-cytoplasmic sperm injection* (ICSI) which involves injecting sperm in to an egg and placing the resulting embryo in the womb.

[11] See the definition in the Surrogacy Arrangements Act 1985 s 1(2).

[12] [1977] AC 547 at 577, HL.   [13] [1991] 1 FLR 385 at 386.

[14] But note the practice in France and Italy to permit mothers to give birth anonymously—a practice which was controversially held not to be in breach of Art 8 of the European Convention on Human Rights see *Odièvre v France* [2003] 1 FCR 621 on which see E Steiner 'Odièvre v France—Desperately seeking mother—anonymous births in the European Court of Human Rights' [2003] CFLQ 425.

[15] See P Bromley 'Aided Conception—the Alternative to Adoption' in P Bean (ed) *Adoption, Essays in Social Policy, Law and Sociology* (1984) ch 11 at pp 189–90.

[16] 5 Cal 4th 84 (1993), noted by G Douglas (1994) 57 MLR 636. But cf *Moschetta v Moschetta* (1994) 25 Cal App 4th 1218, in which the Californian Court of Appeal held that the surrogate was the only mother of the child and refused to enforce the surrogacy agreement and on which see S Bridge 'Assisted Reproduction and Parentage in Law' in A Bainham, S Day Sclater and M Richards (eds) *What is a Parent?* (1999) 73

eggs was fertilised in vitro with her husband's sperm and transferred to the surrogate, who successfully carried it to term. During the pregnancy the surrogate and the commissioning couple fell out, and each sought a declaration of parentage of the child. It was accepted that blood tests showed the commissioning parents to be the genetic parents of the child. In holding that it was the commissioning parents who were the child's legal parents, Panelli J commented that it was they who 'affirmatively intended the birth of the child, and took the steps necessary to effect in vitro fertilisation. But for their acted-on intention the child would not exist' and the commissioning mother, 'who intended to procreate the child–that is she who intended to bring about the birth of a child that she intended to raise as her own–is the natural mother under California law'.

   Although the application of this notion of intending to be a parent is a rational way of solving the so-called 'womb leasing' problems as in *Johnson v Calvert*, one important problem in using it as a *general* test of determining parenthood is that it would involve accepting the corollary that lack of intention is a means of avoiding parenthood. As one commentator[17] has pointed out:

> Hitherto, the law in the United Kingdom has generally refused to permit someone to avoid liability (if not responsibility) for a child on the ground that he or she had not *intended* the child's conception or birth. It is no answer to the Child Support Agency for the absent parent to say that he thought the child's mother was on the pill, or even that his condom split during intercourse.

But she adds:

> . . . it is possible for a sperm or egg donor to waive their parental status and responsibility in respect of any resulting child under the terms of the Human Fertilisation and Embryology Act 1990. Parents may also give their child up for adoption. So our law does recognise the intention *not* to be a social parent in certain circumstances.

So far as English law is concerned, the position at common law has still to be determined. The matter was raised in *Re W (Minors) (Surrogacy)* (which, like *Johnson v Calvert*, was a womb leasing case), but left open upon an undertaking by the commissioning genetic parents[18] that they would apply for a 'parental order' under what was then s 30 of the Human Fertilisation and Embryology Act 1990[19] as soon as the provision was implemented. However, adopting the Warnock Committee's recommendation,[20] what is now s 33 (1) of the Human Fertilisation and Embryology Act 2008 provides:

> The woman who is carrying or has carried a child as a result of the placing in her of an embryo or of sperm and eggs, and no other woman, is to be treated as the mother of the child.

---

at pp 86–7. For the view that a person's intention or desire to be regarded as a parent and to fulfil the functions of parent is in fact the primary test of legal parentage in English law, see C Barton and G Douglas *Law and Parenthood* (1995) pp 50ff.

[17] G Douglas (1994) 57 MLR 636, at 640.

[18] The genetic mother had no womb but was able to produce the eggs, which were taken from her medically and fertilised in vitro by her husband's sperm. Two resultant embryos were implanted in the surrogate host mother, who gave birth to the twins who, having been handed over by the surrogate, had lived with the 'commissioning couple' ever since. The local authority argued that the couple should register themselves as private foster parents, which prompted them to seek a declaration of parentage.

[19] Now s 54 of the 2008 Act, discussed at Parental orders, pp 277ff.   [20] At para 6.8.

Where this provision applies, the woman giving birth and no other woman will, unless the child is subsequently adopted or a parental order is subsequently made, be treated as the legal mother regardless of genetic connection.[21] Section 33 applies regardless of whether the woman was in the United Kingdom or elsewhere at the time of the placing in her of the embryo or the sperm and eggs.[22] It does not, however, have retrospective effect[23] and only applies in relation to children carried by women as a result of the placing in them of embryos or of sperm and eggs, or of their artificial insemination on or after 5 April 2009. In the case of children being so carried before 5 April 2009 but after 1 August 1991 the position is governed by the identically worded s 27 of the 1990 Act. But s 27, too, does not have retrospective effect[24]and for this reason it may still be necessary to resolve the position at common law with regard to children being carried etc before 1 August 1991.

Following the Gender Recognition Act 2004 the woman giving birth remains the mother notwithstanding a subsequent change of gender.[25]

3. WHO IS THE LEGAL FATHER?

At common law, the genetic father is regarded as the legal father. Accordingly, unless a statutory exception (discussed shortly) applies, or there has been a formal change of status as afforded by adoption, or the making of a parental order, the man whose sperm fertilised eggs is the child's legal father.[26]

(a) When genetic fathers are not legal fathers

Two exceptions to the general rule that the genetic father is the legal father are provided in the case of children carried by women as a result of the placing in them of embryos or of sperm and eggs or their artificial insemination after 5 April 2009,[27] by s 41 of the Human Fertilisation and Embryology Act 2008. These are:

(a) where he is a donor whose sperm is used for assisted procreation treatment at a clinic licensed[28] to offer such treatment and whose consent to the use of his sperm has been obtained in accordance with the requirements of para 5 of Sch 3 to the 1990 Act; and
(b) where his sperm is used without his written consent after his death.[29]

---

[21] Note also by s 47 a woman will not be treated as parent merely by reason that she donated the egg. See further Female parenthood p 256.

[22] HFEA 2008 s 33(3). But there is no domicile requirement, nor is there a requirement that the child be born in England and Wales, but the provisions can only apply where, by the conflict of law rules, English law is held to be the applicable law.   [23] HFEA 2008 s 57 (1).

[24] HFEA 1990 s 49(3). See also Re M (Child Support Act: Parentage) [1997] 2 FLR 90.

[25] Section 12. Query the position where, in the admittedly unlikely event, a person becomes pregnant after acquiring a change of gender to a male?

[26] As Bracewell J pointed out in Re B (Parentage) [1996] 2 FLR 15 at 21, it is irrelevant how the sperm fertilises the egg; sexual intercourse is not a prerequisite to fatherhood.

[27] For children so carried between 1 August 1991 (but not before) and 5 April 2009, the controlling provision is s 28(6) of the HFEA 1990, which is of similar effect to s 41 of the 2008 Act.

[28] Under HFEA 1990 Sch 2.

[29] Cf R v Human Fertilisation and Embryology Authority, ex p Blood [1999] Fam 151, CA, in which, following the Court of Appeal ruling that the Human Fertilisation and Embryology Authority had failed to pay sufficient regard to the effect of the EC Treaty whereby a citizen was entitled to receive services in another Member State, the applicant was allowed to take her dead husband's sperm to Belgium for treatment. This was notwithstanding that written consent to the obtaining of his sperm had not been given by the husband before his death. Mrs Blood subsequently had two children by such treatment.

It should be noted that before sperm can be used or stored the donor must have consented in writing.[30] Furthermore either the man or the woman have an unconditional right to withdraw consent to the continued storage and subsequent use of embryos and following that withdrawal the embryo(s) must be destroyed.[31]

One incidental but important effect of these exceptions is that there will be occasions when a child has no legal father.[32]

Donors giving sperm at licensed clinics

This exception only applies to donors who give their sperm to licensed clinics. All other 'donors' are regarded as fathers.[33] But even where the donation is to a licensed clinic the donor can, on rare occasions, still be regarded as the legal father of a resulting child. In *Leeds Teaching Hospitals NHS Trust v A*[34] a man consented to his sperm being used for his wife but the clinic mistakenly injected the sperm into another woman's eggs. It was held[35] that he was the legal father of the resulting twins, because the use of his sperm was not in conformity with the terms of his consent as the statute requires.[36] This seems a harsh decision and surely not what Parliament intended.

Formerly, the legal absence of parental status was coupled with anonymity for the donor but in an important policy change this right was ended with respect to children conceived as a result of sperm donated on or after 1 April 2005. Such children will, upon attaining the age of 18 (ie from April 2023 at the earliest), have the right to be given identifying information provided by donors to the relevant clinic.[37] While this change is designed to promote children's right to identity[38] there was a danger that it might operate

---

[30] HFEA 1990 Sch 3, para 1.

[31] *Evans v Amicus Healthcare Ltd* [2004] EWCA Civ 727, [2005] Fam 1 upheld as human rights compliant in *Evans v United Kingdom* [2007] 1 FLR 1990 (ECtHR (Grand Chamber)). Note also *L v Human Fertilisation and Embryology Authority and the Secretary of State for Health* [2008] EWHC 2149 (Fam) [2008] 2 FLR 1999, in which it was held that while the HFEA 1990 clearly precluded the storage of sperm in the UK and use in the UK without effective consent (in this respect Charles J rejected the contention that notwithstanding *Evans* a regime which precluded argument in any given case that the prohibition on the storage and subsequent use of sperm in the UK was in breach of Art 8 of the ECHR), it did not set such an absolute rule for the storage and subsequent use of sperm outside the UK given the discretion provided by HFEA 1990, s 24(4).But cf *Warren v CARE and HFEA* [2014] EWHC 602 (Fam), [2014] Fam Law 803.

[32] Such as in those cases where such children are born to a woman who has no husband or partner deemed to be the legal father under s 28(2) and (3), discussed at The position under the Human Fertilisation and Embryology Act 1990, p 252.

[33] See eg *Re M (Sperm Donor Father)* [2003] Fam Law 94 where the man concerned responded to an advertisement by a lesbian couple. Note also *M v F and H (Legal Paternity)* [2014] 1 FLR 352—where a married mother made contact with a man advertising his services on a website who not only provided sperm but had intercourse with her. In that case it was found that the child resulted from the intercourse and that therefore the HFEA 2008 was irrelevant.

[34] [2003] EWHC 259 (QB) [2003] 1 FLR 1091.

[35] This was an incidental decision, the main suit being the (unsuccessful) seeking of a declaration of parentage by the husband of the woman giving birth. See further at The position under the Human Fertilisation and Embryology Act 1990 p 252.   [36] See Sch 3 para 5.

[37] Human Fertilisation and Embryology Authority (Disclosure of Donor Information) Regulations 2004 (SI 2004/1511) reg 2(3). For some background discussion of events leading to this change see S Sheldon 'Fragmenting Fatherhood: The Regulation of Reproductive Techniques' (2005) 68 MLR 523 at 547. See also A Bainham 'Arguments about Parentage' [2008] CLJ 322.

[38] See Department of Health *Donor Information Consultation* (2002) and Human Fertilisation and Embryology Authority *Response to the Department of Health's consultation on donor information* (2002). But note the criticism eg by J Wallbank 'Reconstructing the HFEA 1990: is blood really thicker than water?' [2004] CFLQ 387 at 393, who points out that even with these changes there is no obligation upon parents to tell their children of their mode of conception.

as a powerful disincentive to would-be sperm donors but this is not entirely borne out by statistics.[39]

Posthumous use of sperm

Formerly, the rule was both simple and strict: in no circumstances could a man be regarded as the father where his sperm was used after his death. This was so regardless of whether he consented to such use before his death. However, this strict rule was amended initially by the Human Fertilisation and Embryology (Deceased Fathers) Act 2003 which was passed in part as a response to a ruling in a case brought by the children born to Diane Blood in which the judge declared that to deny the children the right to name Mr Blood as their father was incompatible with their Art 8 rights under the ECHR.[40] In the case of children carried by a woman as a result of the placing in her of embryos or of sperm and eggs or her artificial insemination after 5 April 2009, the position is governed by s 39 of the 2008 Act.

Under s 39 if a man has given written consent (which has not been withdrawn) to the use of his sperm after his death which brought about the creation of the embryo carried by the mother[41] or, as the case may be, to the placing in the mother after his death of the embryo, which was brought about using his sperm before his death; and to being treated as the father for the purpose of being registered as the child's father, he will so be treated for this limited purpose once the mother elects in writing not later than the end of the period of 42 days after the child's birth, for the man to be so treated. Unlike the 1990 Act, s 39 of the 2008 Act applies regardless of the man's relationship with the mother.[42] This last point apart, a similar position obtains with respect to such use of sperm in cases controlled by HFEA 1990.[43]

The effect of being acknowledged as the father in these circumstances is largely symbolic. It has no effect on succession rights nor does it confer citizenship.[44] But it does impact upon the child's status with regard to legitimacy which is discussed in Chapter 9.

(b) Where non-genetic 'fathers' are treated as legal fathers

The position at common law

The strictness of the common law position that only genetic fathers could be regarded as legal fathers made no allowance for the use of the various techniques of assisted procreation, the object of which is for childless couples to have children that they can regard as their own. A good example is the DI child conceived by a wife because her husband was infertile or because he was the possible carrier of an inheritable disease, but whom (as usually will be the case) the couple wished to treat as though he or she were the husband's child.[45] The absence of legal fatherhood made little difference to the legal relationship

---

[39] According to Human Fertilisation and Embryology Authority *Fertility Treatment in 2011—Trends and Figures* (2012) the number of registered sperm donors from the UK has increased but at the same time there is a greater proportion of registered donors from overseas.

[40] *Blood and Tarbuck v Secretary of State for Health* (unreported 28 February 2003) cited in the Appendix to Lord Steyn's judgment in *Ghaidan v Godin-Mendoza* [2004] UKHL 30 [2004] 2 AC 557. Note: the amendments to the HFEA 1990 made by the Human Fertilisation and Embryology (Deceased Fathers) Act 2003 apply retrospectively to 1 August 1991.

[41] Regardless of whether the mother was in the UK or elsewhere at the time of the placing of the embryo: HFEA 2008, s 39(2).

[42] Ie no distinction is drawn between spouses and other relationships.

[43] HFEA 1990 s 28(5A)–(5I), added by the Human Fertilisation and Embryology (Deceased Fathers) Act 2003.   [44] See s 39(3) and 48(3) of the 2008 Act and s 29(3A), (3B) of the 1990 Act, as amended.

[45] They might even register the husband as the father. If the husband is known not to be the father, the person registering the birth will commit an offence under the Perjury Act 1911 s 4.

between him and the child, because his treating the child as his own made the latter a 'child of the family'[46] and, since the sperm donor's identity would not normally be divulged, there was virtually no risk of legal claims arising between the donor and the child.[47] Nevertheless, there were potentially a number of longer-term problems. For example, the child had no entitlement to the husband's estate, if the latter died intestate,[48] nor if property was held on trust for the husband's children or the wife's legitimate children. If the child made such a claim and the spouses knew that the husband was not the father, they had either to connive at the deception or be forced to disclose facts which they had wished to keep secret.

These shortcomings of the common law led to calls for reform.[49] Now, following changes introduced by the Family Law Reform Act (FLRA) 1987, the Human Fertilisation and Embryology Acts of 1990 and 2008 it is possible for a man to be regarded as the legal father notwithstanding that he has no genetic connection with the child. Since none of the three statutes has retrospective effect, each must be considered because their application depends on the date of the child's birth.

The position under the Family Law Reform Act 1987

By s 27(1) of the 1987 Act, a child born in England and Wales between 4 April 1988[50] and 1 August 1990[51] and conceived as a result of artificial insemination (whether or not as a result of 'licensed treatment')[52] of a married woman will be treated in law as the child of both spouses, unless the husband can prove to the court's satisfaction that he did not consent to the insemination. For these purposes marriage includes a void marriage if, as will be presumed to be the case unless the contrary is shown, at the time of the insemination resulting in the birth both or either of the parties reasonably believed that the marriage was valid.[53] In *J v C (Void Marriage: Status of Children),*[54] however, it was held, that this provision did not apply where the parties to the 'void marriage' were both female. Hence, the applicant (whom the mother had 'married' in the mistaken belief that she was a man) could not be treated as the father of a child conceived as a result of artificial insemination by donor.

In summary, under s 27, a DI child born to a married couple is presumptively the child of both parties, and the presumption can be rebutted only by showing that the husband did not consent to the artificial insemination of his wife.

The position under the Human Fertilisation and Embryology Act 1990

Section 27 only applies to DI children. Section 28 of the Human Fertilisation and Embryology Act 1990 (which applies to children born between 1 August 1990 and

---

[46] Unless the spouses separated before the child's birth. See Ch 9, The meaning of 'child of the family', p 296.

[47] Before the 1990 Act good clinical practice required the doctor carrying out the insemination not to divulge the donor's identity.

[48] Although he would have a claim to provision under the Inheritance (Provision for Family and Dependants) Act 1975 as a 'child of the family': see Ch 25.

[49] Both the Law Commission (Law Com No 118 paras 12.9 and 12.11) and the Warnock Committee (at para 4.17) had recommended change.

[50] But not *before* 4 April 1988: see *Re M (Child Support Act: Parentage)* [1997] 2 FLR 90.

[51] Ie the commencement date of HFEA 1990 ss 27–29. For an example of where the FLRA 1987 rather than HFEA 1990 applied see *J v C (Void Marriage: Status of Children)* [2006] EWCA Civ 551, [2007] Fam 1.

[52] Ie treatment covered by the HFEA 1990, Sch 2.   [53] FLRA 1987 s 27(2).

[54] [2006] EWCA Civ 551 [2007] Fam 1. Note that this ruling can only apply to 'marriages' before March 2014, that is, when the Marriage (Same Sex Couples) Act 2013 came into force, since marriages between two females after that date are valid and the circumstances arising in *J v C* would only make the marriage voidable.

6 April 2009), however, makes provision for other forms of assisted procreation, as well as artificial insemination. Section 28(2) provides that where a married woman[55] is carrying or has carried a child as the result of the placing in her of an embryo, or sperm and eggs, or of her insemination, then notwithstanding that the sperm was not that of her husband, he and no other person[56] is treated as the father of the child,[57] unless it is shown that he did not consent to his wife's treatment. This provision is subject to s 28(5)(a), by which the common law presumption of legitimacy based on marriage[58] takes priority over the requirement of the husband's consent. What this seems to mean[59] is that the husband will be regarded as the father unless the issue is raised, when, if he did not consent, the presumption will have to be rebutted, usually by means of scientific tests.

As between spouses the issue of consent rarely arises not least because a clinic is unlikely to provide services to a married woman without her husband's consent,[60] but one case where it did—albeit by accident—was *Leeds Teaching Hospital NHS Trust v A*.[61] In that case two couples, Mr and Mrs A, a white couple, and Mr and Mrs B, a black couple, were undergoing sperm injection treatment (the mixing of the husband's sperm with his wife's eggs) at the same clinic. Due to a mix-up by the clinic Mr B's sperm was used to impregnate Mrs A, who later gave birth to twins. It was held that Mr A was not the father under the terms of s 28(2) since, because of the fundamental mistake by the clinic,[62] he could not be taken to have consented to the actual treatment of his wife, viz., being impregnated by someone else's sperm.[63]

Section 28(3) of the 1990 Act goes further providing that, where donated sperm is used for a woman in the course of licensed 'treatment services'[64] provided for her and a man together, then that man, and no other person, shall be treated as the father of the child if s 28(2) does not apply (for example, where the woman is not married or where there is a judicial separation order in force). As Hale LJ observed,[65] s 28(3):

> is an unusual provision, conferring the relationship of parent and child on people who are related neither by blood nor by marriage. Conferring such relationships is a serious matter, involving as it does not only the relationship between father and child but also between the whole of the father's family and the child. The rule should only apply to those cases which clearly fall within the footprint of the statutory language.

---

[55] For these purposes, marriage includes (subject to what is said below) a void marriage if, as is presumed until the contrary is shown, at the time of the treatment resulting in the child's birth, one of the parties reasonably believed that the marriage was valid: s 28(7)(b); but it does not include the case where a judicial separation was in force: s 28(7)(a).   [56] Section 28(4).

[57] See, for example, *Re CH (Contact: Parentage)* [1996] 1 FLR 569. It will be noted that unlike s 27 of the 1987 Act which merely provided for the child to be 'treated in law as the child of the parties to [the] marriage', s 28(2) of the 1990 Act specifically confers legal *fatherhood* upon the husband.

[58] See Ch 9, The concept of legitimacy, pp 299ff.

[59] See Douglas *Law, Fertility and Reproduction* (1991) at p 129.

[60] See generally the Human Fertilisation and Embryology Authority *8th Code of Practice*.

[61] [2003] EWHC 259 (QB) [2003] 1 FLR 1091.

[62] At para [29] Butler-Sloss P accepted that non-fundamental mistakes may not vitiate consent.

[63] Neither could he rely on the common law presumption of paternity (discussed later at Presumption that the mother's husband is the father, p 260) since that was overridden by DNA tests showing Mr B to be the father. It was precisely because the treatment fell outside that to which Mr B had consented that he was to be regarded as the father ie s 28(6) did not apply, see n 27, earlier.   [64] See s 2(1).

[65] *Re R (A Child) (IVF: Paternity of Child)* [2003] EWCA Civ 182 [2003] Fam 129 at [20] cited, with apparent approval, by Lords Hope and Walker on appeal to the HL, see [2005] UKHL 33 [2005] 2 FLR 843 at [6] and [39] respectively.

Although Parliament had unmarried couples in mind when passing this provision[66] (it is established that the provision has no application to married couples),[67] proof of cohabitation is not required, nor, conversely, does it follow that 'simply because a man is living with a treated woman he is being provided with treatment services'.[68] The key test is whether the man and woman had 'treatment together'. This concept, however, proved troublesome with various different approaches being suggested.[69] But one approach that gained general favour was that of Bracewell J in *Re B (Parentage)*,[70] namely to consider on all the facts whether the man and woman could be said to have embarked on a 'joint enterprise' the object of which is for the woman to conceive and give birth, rather than to concentrate on what happens to the individual partner. Bracewell J's approach was approved by the Court of Appeal in *R v Human Fertilisation and Embryology Authority, ex p Blood*,[71] though in that case itself it was held that the posthumous use of sperm taken from the husband while in a coma was not capable of constituting 'treatment . . . together'. In *Re R (IVF: Paternity of Child)*[72] Lord Walker said:

> where there is IVF treatment using embryos created with donor sperm, the infertile male partner cannot easily be described as participating in the treatment. If he is to be regarded as participating he must do more than simply consent to his partner's treatment. His conduct must be such as to make his partner's treatment something of a joint enterprise (an expression used by Bracewell J in *Re B (Parentage)* . . .

Whether there was a joint enterprise is a question of fact to be determined in each case taking into account the parties' conduct and, where relevant, the clinic's perspective as demonstrated by the records that are required to be kept.[73] Examples of 'treatment together' are *Re B (Parentage)* where the couple attended the hospital together and, knowing that the sperm which the man donated[74] was not to be used for impregnation that day, had waited a short time to ensure that the donation was satisfactory[75] and *U v W (A-G Intervening)*,[76] in which an unmarried couple voluntarily attended a fertility clinic after they knew that donor sperm as well as the man's own sperm was to be used.

In *Re B* Bracewell J held in effect that once it had been established that a joint enterprise existed the parties' consent to the treatment continued until it was withdrawn. Hence in that case it did not matter that the man and woman had separated by the time of insemination. But this approach is now established to be wrong. According to *Re R (IVF: Paternity*

---

[66] See Lord Mackay, Hansard, HL Debs 20 March 1990, cols 209–10.

[67] See *Leeds Teaching Hospital NHS Trust v A*, earlier.

[68] Per Johnson J in *Re Q (Parental Order)* [1996] 1 FLR 369 at 372.

[69] According to Johnson J in *Re Q (Parental Order)* [1996] 1 FLR 369, the provision envisages a situation in which the man involved receives medical treatment. But this was clearly too restrictive and as Johnson J himself observed, at 371, begs the question as to what 'treatment' is envisaged. Another approach was to equate 'treatment together' with treatment 'as a couple', see *U v W (A-G Intervening)* [1998] Fam 29, per Wilson J, but that was regarded by Hale LJ in *Re R (A Child) (IVF: Paternity of Child)* [2003] EWCA Civ 182 [2003] Fam 129 at [23] as an 'unnecessary gloss' on the wording of the statute.

[70] [1996] 2 FLR 15.

[71] [1999] Fam 151 at 179, per Lord Woolf MR. See also *Evans v Amicus Healthcare Ltd* [2004] EWCA Civ 727, [2005] Fam 1 at [93], per Arden LJ.   [72] [2005] UK HL 33 [2005] 2 FLR 843 at [26].

[73] See Lord Hope in *Re R (IVF: Paternity of Child)* [2005] UKHL 33 [2005] 2 FLR 843 at [19].

[74] Bracewell J rejected the man's argument that his donation of sperm had been a casual favour and there had been no joint enterprise to conceive a child.

[75] It did not matter for these purposes that the father had not been counselled, for as Bracewell J (*Re B (Parentage)* [1996] 2 FLR 15 at 21) pointed out, s 2(1) which defines treatment services as 'medical, surgical or obstetric services', makes no mention of counselling.   [76] [1998] Fam 29, per Wilson J.

of Child)[77] the correct test is to judge the issue at the time of the treatment leading to the birth. In *Re R* itself both the woman and man signed a consent form for in vitro fertilisation and the man acknowledged that they were being treated together even though his sperm would not be used. The initial embryo placement was unsuccessful and before the second placement, which was successful, the couple had separated. The woman, however, did not reveal this separation to the clinic and on the contrary led them to believe that they were still a couple. It was held that the second embryo placement leading to the birth of child could not be considered to be the result of 'treatment together' and that therefore the man could not be regarded as the father, within the terms of s 28(3).

It is established[78] that where the wrong sperm is used due to a mix-up by the clinic the child's birth cannot be regarded as the result of 'treatment together'. A fortiori an express withdrawal of consent will negate the idea of treatment altogether.[79]

Unlike the Family Law Reform Act 1987 there is no requirement that the resulting child be born in England and Wales, but s 28 can only apply where, by the conflict of laws rules, English law is the applicable law, which means that at least one of the parties must either be domiciled or habitually resident here at the time of the treatment or insemination.[80] On the other hand, s 28(8) expressly states that the provisions apply 'whether the woman was in the United Kingdom or elsewhere at the time of placing in her of the embryo or the sperm and eggs or her artificial insemination.' However, this provision is effectively limited to children born to married women since, as Wilson J pointed out in *U v W*,[81] in the case of an unmarried mother, for the man to be regarded as the father under s 28(3), the 'treatment services' must be provided by a 'licensed person'. Accordingly, treatment abroad will fall outside the provision, even though that could be said to be restrictive of the freedom to provide services for all nationals of member states within the European Union.[82]

The position under the Human Fertilisation and Embryology Act 2008

In the case of children born on or after 6 April 2009 the position is governed by the 2008 Act. As under the 1990 Act, s 35 of the 2008 Act provides that a man will be treated as the legal father of the child carried by his wife as a result of the placing in her[83] of the embryo or of the sperm and eggs or of her artificial insemination, notwithstanding that the creation of the embryo carried by her was not brought about with his sperm, unless it is shown that he did not consent to the placing in her of the embryo etc. 'Marriage' for these purposes includes a void marriage but does not include the case where a judicial separation was in force.[84] As under s 28(2) of the 1990 Act, this provision applies whether or not the artificial insemination was 'licensed'.[85] It has been held[86] that absence of consent is not destroyed by acquiescence per se but only if this amounts to an outward sign of an

---

[77] [2005] UK HL 33 [2005] 2 FLR 843.   [78] *Leeds Teaching Hospital NHS Trust v A*, earlier.

[79] See *Evans v Amicus Healthcare Ltd*. Note: the applicant subsequently failed in her claim that the destruction of 'her' embryos, following her former partner's consent to use them, violated her Art 8 rights, see *Evans v United Kingdom* [2007] 1 FLR 1990, ECtHR (Grand Chamber).

[80] In *Re X (Children) (Parental Order: Surrogacy)* [2008] EWHC 3030 (Fam) [2009] 2 WLR 1274 it was held that ss 27 and 28(2) have extraterritorial effect such that in the case of a surrogacy agreement made between an English couple and a married women living abroad (in this case, Ukraine) the surrogate mother and her husband were, respectively the legal mother and father.   [81] [1998] Fam 29 at 37.

[82] Viz. under what was then Art 59 of the Treaty of Rome (now Art 56 TFEU): see *U v W* [1998] Fam 29 at 40ff.   [83] Regardless of whether the mother was in the UK or elsewhere: s 35(2).

[84] HFEA 2008 s 58 (2).

[85] See *M v F and H (Legal Paternity)* [2014] 1 FLR 352.

[86] *M v F and H (Legal Paternity)* [2014] 1 FLR 352 at [27] and [26] respectively.

inward consent, nor is it a requirement that the absence of consent has to be communicated to all those affected.

As under the 1990 Act, s 40(1) of the 2008 Act provides that the husband will be treated as the father if, in the case of an embryo created before his death, but with the sperm of someone else, he gave written consent (which had not been withdrawn) to the placing of the embryo in his widow and to being treated as the father of any resulting child for the purpose of being so entered on the birth register provided (a) the mother elected in writing not later than the end of 42 days following the child's birth for the man's particulars to be entered on the birth register and (b) no-one else is to be treated as the father or as a parent. The effect of being treated as the legal father in these circumstances is confined to being registered as the father. It does not in particular have any effect upon succession or citizenship rights.[87]

As under the 1990 Act, s 36 of the 2008 Act makes provision for an unmarried man to be considered the legal father of a donor-conceived child even though his sperm has not been used to create the embryo carried by the woman. For this to be the case three conditions need to be satisfied, namely (a) the placement of the embryo or the sperm and eggs in the woman or her artificial insemination must be 'in the course of treatment services provided in the United Kingdom by a person to whom a licence applies', (b) at the time of the placement of the embryo or the sperm and eggs in the women or her artificial insemination, the 'agreed fatherhood conditions' 'were satisfied in relation to a man, in relation to treatment provided to [the woman] under licence' and (c) the man remained alive at the time of the treatment.

The 'agreed fatherhood conditions' are defined by s 37 and may be summarised as requiring the couple each to give to 'the person responsible' (ie the person under whose supervision licensed activities are carried out) notice agreeing to the man being treated as the father.[88] Such notices must remain effective inasmuch as neither must be withdrawn[89] nor must the woman have given a further notice stating that she consents to another man or woman being treated as the resulting child's 'parent'.[90]

Notices must be written and signed by the person giving it,[91] but whilst they must be given to the person responsible at the clinic they do not necessarily have to be drawn up there.[92] The notice requirement is waived if any of the parties involved is unable to sign because of illness, injury or physical disability.[93] Notices cannot be given by those within prohibited degrees of relationship.[94] The 'agreed fatherhood conditions' replace the troublesome requirement under the 1990 Act of a licensed treatment 'for the man and woman together' and are intended to avoid the type of problem that arose in *Evans v Amicus Healthcare Ltd*.[95]

As under the 1990 Act,[96] s 40(2) of the 2008 Act provides that an unmarried man can also be treated as the father if in the course of licensed treatment in the United Kingdom[97] an embryo was created with the sperm of another man but the man died before the placing of the embryo in the woman provided he consented in writing (and did not withdraw that consent) to the placing of the embryo after his death and to being treated as the father; the

---

[87] HFEA 2008 ss 40(4) and 48(3).

[88] Cf *AB v CD and Z (Fertility Clinic)* [2013] EWHC 1418 (Fam) [2013] 2 FLR 1357, in which the equivalent 'agreed female parenthood conditions' under s 44 were not complied with because of lack of adequate notice.

[89] Withdrawal is effected by written notice being given to the person responsible: s 37(1)(c).

[90] HFEA 2008 s 37(1)(d).   [91] HFEA 2008 s 37(2).

[92] See the Explanatory Notes to HFEA 2008 at para 172.   [93] HFEA 2008 s 37(3).

[94] HFEA 2008 ss 37(2), 58(2).   [95] Earlier at fn 31.

[96] HFEA 1990 s 28(5D), added by the added by the Human Fertilisation and Embryology (Deceased Fathers) Act 2003.

[97] But note it does not matter whether the resulting embryo was placed in the woman in the UK or elsewhere: s 40(3).

agreed fatherhood conditions were satisfied, and the woman elected within 42 days of the child's birth to enable the man's particulars to be entered on the birth register. The effect of being treated as a father in these circumstances is confined to being registered as the father, ie it does not in particular have any effect upon succession or citizenship rights.[98]

4. FEMALE PARENTHOOD

A fundamental change introduced by the 2008 Act was to provide that in the case of children born on or after 6 April 2009 the female civil partner or cohabitant of the mother be treated as the legal parent to the exclusion of any man being treated as the father.[99] Following the enactment of the Marriage (Same Sex Couples) Act 2013 these provisions now equally apply to a mother's female spouse.[100] It will be noted that under these provisions, the woman concerned is treated as 'a parent' and not a second or co-'mother'.

Bringing provision for female spouses and civil partners into line with that applying to married couples, s 42 provides that where a woman gives birth to a child conceived as a result of donor insemination (anywhere in the world), she is the mother of the child and her female spouse or civil partner will automatically be the other parent, unless she did not consent to the mother's treatment ('s 42 parent'). In short, s 42 replicates, with appropriate modification of wording, s 35.

In the case of same-sex female couples who are neither married nor civil partners, ss 43 and 44 mirror ss 36 and 37 in the case of different-sex unmarried couples. Accordingly the mother's female partner will be treated as the other parent (a 's 43 parent') provided:

(i) the placement of the embryo or the sperm and eggs in the woman or her artificial insemination took place as a result of licensed treatment within the UK;

(ii) the 'agreed female parenthood conditions' have been satisfied; and

(iii) the other woman remained alive at the time of the treatment.

The 'agreed female parenthood conditions' provided for in s 44 mirror, with appropriate changes of wording, the 'agreed fatherhood conditions' as defined in s 37. Consequently exactly the same rules apply with regard to the requisite notices.

Where a woman is treated as a parent either under s 42 or s 43, then, by s 45 'no man is to be treated as the father of the child'.

Akin to the provision made for different sex couples, s 46 (as amended by the Marriage (Same Sex Couples) 2013) makes provision for certain cases where the child is born after the death of the mother's female spouse or partner. In the case of a child carried by the mother as a result of placing in her of an embryo created during her marriage to or civil partnership with another woman but placed in the mother (whether in the UK or elsewhere) after the woman's death, that woman will, solely for the purposes of registration, be treated as a parent provided she gave written consent both to the placement of the embryo after her death and to being treated as a parent.[101] A similar position obtains where the embryo was not created during such a marriage or civil partnership but in the course of licensed treatment, and another woman gave the requisite consents.[102]

---

[98] HFEA 2008 ss 40(4) and 48(3).

[99] See s 45, on which see *Re G, Re Z (Children: Sperm Donors: Leave To Apply For Children Act Orders)* [2013] EWHC 134 (Fam) [2013] 1 FLR 1334. For the background to this reform, see the *Review of the Human Fertilisation and Embryology Act: Proposals for revised legislation (including establishment of the Regulatory Authority for Tissues and Embryos)* Cm 6989 (2006).

[100] Marriage (Same Sex Couples) Act 2013 Sch 7 paras 37–41.

[101] HFEA 2008 s 46 (1), (3), (4).   [102] HFEA 2008 s 46 (2), (3), (4).

Save where the conditions set out in ss 42, 43 and 46 are satisfied, as s 47 makes clear,[103] a woman is not to be treated as a parent merely because she has donated the egg.

5. OVERALL SUMMARY AND COMMENTARY

As the previous discussion amply demonstrates, to the question who are the legal parents English law gives an exceedingly complicated reply. Whether the law needs to be so complex can be debated. It is certainly not helped by the fact that the three successive Acts dealing with the issue do not have retrospective effect. On the other hand, some complexity seems inevitable as the law has sought to keep up with the scientific and societal developments.

(a) Breaking the exclusivity of the genetic link to establish legal parentage

Although, as others have pointed out,[104] it is by no means the only solution, for quite understandable reasons the common law, in line with many other systems, chose to base legal parentage on the biological link with the child and that indeed remains the fundamental basis of the current law. In fact, as we have seen, excluding adoption which concerns the *transfer* of parenthood, the exclusivity of the blood tie as the determinant of legal parentage was not broken until the Family Law Reform Act 1987, when provision was made to treat the husband as the legal father of a child born to his wife a result of her artificial insemination by the sperm of someone else. Given that the practice of artificial insemination by donor was a developing service even in the 1930s and 1940s,[105] it is perhaps surprising that it took so long to regulate its legal effect. But that in part was because of the ambivalence towards the practice—in 1948 the Archbishop of Canterbury recommended it to be a criminal offence[106] and even in 1960 the Faversham Committee[107] concluded that DI was an undesirable practice and strongly to be discouraged.[108] In contrast, in 1973 the Peel Report recommended that for a small proportion of couples for whom DI would be appropriate the practice should be available within the NHS at accredited centres.[109] But it was the recommendations both of the Law Commission[110] and the Warnock Report[111] that eventually led to the 1987 Act changes.

---

[103] Though it may noted that the wording of the headnote to the section, which is clear, is not replicated in the section itself.

[104] See eg the summary by S Harris-Short and J Miles *Family Law: Text, Cases, and Materials* (2nd edn, 2011) pp 586ff. See also I Schwenzer *Model family Code—From a global perspective* (2006) who considers that legal parenthood could simply be based on the woman giving birth ('parentage by birth') coupled with 'the person who, with the consent of the birth mother, intentionally assumes parentage for the child' ('parentage by intention').

[105] Artificial insemination by donor (AID) was first developed in the late nineteenth century, see G W Bartholomew 'The Development and Use of Artificial Insemination' (1958) 49 *The Eugenics Review* 187, relied upon by M Richards in 'Assisted Reproduction and Parental Relationships' in A Bainham, B Lindley, M Richards and L Trinder (eds) *Children and Their Families: Contact, Rights and Welfare* (2003) p 301.

[106] See *Artificial Human Insemination: the report of a Commission appointed by His Grace the Archbishop of Canterbury Society for the Propagation of Christian Knowledge* (1948).

[107] HMSO Departmental Committee on Human Artificial Insemination (1960) (Cmnd 1105).

[108] Another reason was that although in theory the legal position was that the child was illegitimate, the donor was the legal father and therefore liable to maintain the child and the mother guilty of perjury if she registered her husband as the father.

[109] British Medical Association *Annual Report of the Council, Appendix V: Report of the Panel on Human Artificial Insemination* (British Medical Journal Supplement, 7 April 1973) vol II 3–5 cited by the *Report of the Committee of Inquiry into Human Fertilisation and Embryology* (the 'Warnock Report') (1974) Cmnd 9314 at 4.7.   [110] Law Com No 118, *Illegitimacy* paras 12.9, 12.11 and 12.26.

[111] *Report of the Committee of Inquiry into Human Fertilisation and Embryology* at 4.16 ff.

Although the 1987 Act reform was significant, it provided a narrow exception to the rule that legal parentage was based upon the genetic link, as it only applied to the artificial insemination of a married woman. This narrowness was, however, rapidly addressed by the Human Fertilisation and Embryology Act 1990 such that it applied deemed father-hood to other forms of assisted procreation and extended the law to allow men who were not married to the woman giving birth to be regarded as the legal father. Given that in these situations the man in question is regarded as the sole father the inevitable corollary is that the genetic father is not regarded as the legal father.

Not only did the 1990 Act expand the concept of deemed fatherhood it also provided that legal motherhood was confined to the woman giving birth regardless of her genetic connec-tion to the child. Although, as previously discussed, it is not beyond the realms of possibility that the common law could still reach the same conclusion, what it undoubtedly could not contemplate, is the recognition of the second female parent as provided for by the Human Fertilisation and Embryology Act 2008. Although it could be said that once the imperative of genetic connection as the arbiter of legal parentage has been disconnected, it is not such a large step to designate the female spouse or partner of the mother as a 'parent' any more than it was to designate a man as the father in cases where his wife or 'partner' conceives by another man's sperm, there can be little doubt of the enormity of providing that a child can have two female parents and no father, a position scarcely imaginable even a few years ago. Not surprisingly, these provisions were not passed without heated controversy though in fact most of the debate centred on what became s 14(1) and (2) of the 2008 Act. Those provi-sions amend s 13(5) of the 1990 Act so that instead of directing the Human Fertilisation and Embryology Authority not to provide a woman with treatment services unless account has been taken of the welfare of any child who may be born as a result of the treatment (includ-ing the need of that *child for a father*), or of any other child that may be affected by the birth, it must have regard to the potential child's welfare 'including the need for *supportive parenting*'. In other words the reference to the need for a father has been replaced by a need for supportive parenting. This change was condemned by some as undermining fatherhood and as sending out signals that fatherhood does not matter.[112]

There are few other European jurisdictions, outside the United Kingdom, that make provision for legal parenthood in the case of same sex partnerships.[113] The issue is sensitive and attempts to provide for such developments in a Council of Europe Recommendation failed.[114] Notwithstanding that it is in the vanguard, the 2008 Act can be criticised for stopping short of designating the second female parent as a 'co mother' as is done in the Norwegian legislation. As one commentary put it: 'While English law has become increasingly open to the idea that a child can have two parents of the same gender, the sexual family model continues to resonate in a steadfast resistance to the possibility that a child can have two mothers (or indeed two fathers).'[115] The law's reticence in this regard may be contrasted with its readiness to refer to a woman who is married to another woman as a 'wife'[116] with the paradoxical result that a family can comprise two wives but only one mother yet both being the legal parents of their common child.

[112] For a comprehensive discussion of the issues, see L Smith 'Clashing Symbols? Reconciling support for fathers and fatherless families after the Human Fertilisation and Embryology Act 2008' [2010] CFLQ 46.
[113] Only Norway, Spain and Sweden do so, see N Lowe 'A Study into the Rights and Legal Status of Children Being Brought up in Various Forms of Marital or Non-Marital Partnerships and Cohabitation' CJ-FA (2008) 5.
[114] See N Lowe 'The Impact of the Council of Europe on European Family Law' in J Scherpe (ed) *Research Handbook on European Family Law* (2015).
[115] J McCandless and S Sheldon 'The HFEA (2008) and the Tenacity of the Sexual Family Norm' (2010) 73 MLR 175.
[116] See the Marriage (Same Sex Couples) Act 2013 Sch 3 para 5(2)(b).

(b) Why can there only be two legal parents?

As is evident from the foregoing discussion, despite all the legal changes, English law, in common with other jurisdictions, has stuck rigidly to the idea that a child can only two legal parents, yet with the abandonment of the gestational link as the sole determinant of legal parentage the question arises as to why this should be so. There has been interesting discussion of a 'three parent solution' particularly in the context of lesbian couples making a private arrangement for one of them to conceive with the help of a known sperm donor[117] and indeed there have been court decisions both in Canada and the USA that for the purposes of child support a child may have three parents.[118] But while a three parent solution might work for child support it may not be so appropriate for such issues as succession and citizenship. It remains to be seen what, if any, further reform there may be, but in the meantime those such as known donors will have to seek parental responsibility orders to have any legal responsibility vis à vis the child.[119]

(c) Should the concept of legal parentage be revised?

Since the first breaking of the exclusivity of blood tie as the basis of parentage by the Family Law Reform Act 1987 English law has developed significantly such that it is now among the most liberal of jurisdictions in its recognition of who is to be regarded as a legal parent. The motivation for these changes has not been a radical re-think of parentage as such but rather a pragmatic response to medical advances and societal changes. It is possible that there may be further changes in the wake of further medical advances, for example, the law may have to come to terms with the possibility of having three genetically related parents. Consideration might also be given to improving the position of known sperm donors.[120] It might also be pointed out that while the biological link lies at the heart of notions of legal parenthood in other European legal systems, the continental systems tend to be more formal particularly in the context of unmarried parents, requiring the man to recognise his paternity, and it may be that if there is to be closer uniformity within Europe, English law may have to adapt its thinking.[121]

The pragmatic rather than the principled development of notions of parenthood raises the question whether the time has now come for the whole concept to be reassessed. There can, for example, be sensible debate as to what should now be the overall test. However, there is unlikely to be such a reassessment of the English position, at any rate, in the near future and, arguably, since most current issues are catered for, there is no need to do so. Moreover, the biological basis of parenthood, which after all continues to apply in the vast majority of cases, provides reasonable certainty and clarity.[122]

---

[117] L Smith 'Tangling the web of legal parenthood: legal responses to use of known donors in lesbian parenting arrangements' (2013) 33 LS 355, L Smith 'Is three a crowd? Lesbian mothers' prospects' [2006] CFLQ 231, M Vonk 'One, Two or Three Parents? Lesbian Co-Mothers and a Known Donor with "family life" under Dutch Law' (2004) 18 Int Jo of Law, Policy and the Family 103.

[118] See respectively *AA v BB* (2007) 83 OR (3d) 561 and *Jennifer L Schultz v Jodilynn and Carol Frampton* 2007 PA Super 118.

[119] See eg *Re D (contact and parental responsibility: lesbian mothers and known father)* [2006] EWHC 2 (Fam) [2006] 1 FCR 556, on which see L Smith 'Tangling the web of legal parenthood: legal responses to use of known donors in lesbian parenting arrangements' (2013) 33 LS 355.

[120] See L Smith, 'Tangling the web of legal parenthood: legal responses to use of known donors in lesbian parenting arrangements' (2013) 33 LS 355 at 378–379 and J Wallbank and C Dietz 'Lesbian mothers, fathers and other animals: is the political personal in multiple parent families?' [2013] CFLQ 451.

[121] See N Lowe 'Working Towards A European Concept Of Legal Parenthood' in A Büchler and M Müller-Chen (eds) *Private Law, national–global comparative. Festschrift für Ingeborg Schwenzer* (2011) p 1105.

[122] See in particular A Bainham 'Parentage, Parenthood and Parental Responsibility' in A Bainham, S Day Sclater and M Richards (eds) *What is a Parent? A Socio-Legal Analysis* (1999) ch 2.

6. ESTABLISHING OR CONTESTING PARENTAGE

One consequence of essentially basing parenthood on the biological link with the child is that parentage can either be established or contested on the factual basis of that link.[123] English law has long taken the view that such actions can be brought at any time. Indeed it has been said in the context of court proceedings that where parentage is in doubt it is normally wrong to leave the matter unresolved.[124] In making a finding, the court is not bound by any decision by an Immigration Judge and indeed the court should be cautious about basing any judgment on the child's immigration status.[125]

(a) Mothers

Normally, proving who the mother is presents no difficulties, because the fact of birth and identity can be established by the evidence of the doctor or other persons present at the birth and, as Lord Simon said in the *Ampthill Peerage* case,[126] motherhood is proved demonstrably by parturition: *mater est quam gestatio demonstrat*. However, it is not unknown for mothers to be given the wrong children in maternity hospitals and there have been cases where parents have attempted to pass off a suppositious child as their own, usually in order to defraud others who would be entitled to property in default of children of the marriage.[127] Difficult problems of proof may also arise in the context of immigration where first-hand evidence of the birth may be absent.[128]

(b) Fathers

Use of presumptions

Presumption that the mother's husband is the father

Before the advent of blood tests, paternity could normally be inferred only from the fact that the alleged father had sexual intercourse with the mother about the time when the child must have been conceived.[129] Consequently, if two men had intercourse with her during the relevant period, it would be impossible to prove affirmatively which was the father. Moreover, the fact that intercourse took place can, in most cases, be proved only by the evidence of the parties themselves or circumstantially from their conduct and the opportunities which were presented to them.

The impossibility of proving affirmatively the paternity of the child led at least as early as the twelfth century to the adoption of the civil law maxim: *pater est quem nuptiae demonstrant*—that is, if a child is born to a married woman, her husband is presumed

---

[123] For a fascinating historical discussion of the law in this respect see S Cretney *Family Law in the Twentieth Century* (2003) pp 529–36. See also N Lowe 'The Establishment of Paternity under English Law' ICCS Colloquy (Strasbourg, 1999) 80–96. For a discussion of the position in certain European decisions see R Blauwhoff ' "Motherless" Paternity Tests and Minors in Europe' [2005] IFL 146.

[124] Per Wall P in *Re P (Identity of Mother)* [2011] EWCA Civ 79 [2012] 1 FLR 351.

[125] Per Wall P in *Re P (Identity of Mother)* [2011] EWCA Civ 79 [2012] 1 FLR 351, applying *Re A (Care Proceedings: Asylum Seekers)* [2003] EWHC 1086 (Fam) [2003] 2 FLR 921.   [126] [1977] AC 547.

[127] See eg *Slingsby v A-G* (1916) 33 TLR 120, HL, where the wife deceived her own husband; cf the popular belief, current at the time, that the son born to James II's consort was smuggled into the queen's room in a warming pan in order to prevent the descent of the Crown to James's Protestant daughters. For modern examples of so-called 'miracle babies', see *Re D (Nigerian Fertility Clinic: Fact Finding)* [2012] EWHC 4231 (Fam), [2013] 2 FLR 1417 and *A Local Authority v S and Others* [2012] EWHC 3764 (Fam) [2014] 1 FLR 1313.

[128] See eg *Re P (Identity of Mother)* [2011] EWCA Civ 79 [2012] 1 FLR 351.

[129] See C Barton and G Douglas *Law and Parenthood* (1995) p 54ff.

to be his father until the contrary is proved.[130] This means that, if it is alleged that the husband is not the father, the burden of rebutting the presumption is cast on the asserter. This presumption applies even though the child is born so soon after the marriage that he must have been conceived beforehand[131] and, in the case of a posthumous child, if he was born within the normal period of gestation after the husband's death.[132] Difficulty arises, however, if the birth takes place an abnormally long time afterwards. In *Preston-Jones v Preston-Jones*[133] the House of Lords agreed that judicial notice could be taken of the fact that there is a normal period of gestation (although the period is variously given as 270 to 280 days or as nine months),[134] but Lord MacDermott added that judicial notice must also be taken of the fact that the normal period is not always followed. Although the longer the period deviates from the normal, the more easily will the presumption be rebutted until there comes a time when it is not raised at all, it is difficult to say where the line is to be drawn.

The presumption applies equally to a child born after a decree of divorce. In *Knowles v Knowles*[135] the child could have been conceived before or after the decree absolute. Wrangham J held that the presumption of legitimacy operated in favour of presuming that conception took place whilst the marriage was still subsisting and that the husband was the father, although, as he pointed out, in such circumstances the presumption may be rebutted much more easily.

Conflicting presumptions arise if the child must have been conceived during the subsistence of a marriage since terminated by the husband's death or divorce and the mother has remarried before the birth. However, in the absence of evidence to the contrary the first husband should be presumed to be the father, since it ought to be presumed that the mother had not committed adultery.[136]

A Lord Chancellor's Consultation Paper[137] raised the question whether the presumption of paternity should be put on a statutory footing in line with Scotland,[138] but in the event no action was taken.

The position where the child is born to an unmarried mother

At common law, since the presumption of paternity was based on the presumption of legitimacy, there could be no presumption of fatherhood outside marriage. This meant and still means that the birth of a child to a cohabiting couple does not in itself raise any presumption and that consequently the man must prove his paternity if he wishes to assert fatherhood. However, it has long been accepted that entry of a man's name as

---

[130] Glanvil, book 7, ch 12. See also Bracton, col 6, Co Litt 373; Blackstone's *Commentaries*, 457; Nicolas *Adulterine Bastardy*; and Lord Simon who said in the *Ampthill Peerage* case [1977] AC 547 at 577: ' "Fatherhood". . . is a presumption'.

[131] See *Gardner v Gardner* (1877) 2 App Cas 723, HL; *R v Luffe* (1807) 8 East 193; *Anon v Anon* (1856) 23 Beav 273; *Turnock v Turnock* (1867) 36 LJP & M 85. A similar position obtained throughout Europe.

[132] *Re Heath* [1945] Ch 417 at 421–2 per Cohen J.   [133] [1951] AC 391.

[134] Per Lord Simonds at 401, Lord Morton at 413, Lord MacDermott at 419.

[135] [1962] P 161; cf *Re Leman's Will Trusts* (1945) 115 LJ Ch 89. It is submitted that the dictum to the contrary in *Re Bromage* [1935] Ch 605 at 609 cannot be supported.

[136] See *Re Overbury* [1955] Ch 122, where Harman J found in favour of the first husband's paternity on the facts. Aliter, according to *Hetherington v Hetherington* (1887) 12 PD 112; *Ettenfield v Ettenfield* [1940] P 96 at 110, if the child must have been conceived when the husband and wife were living apart under a decree of judicial separation since it is presumed that the spouses observed the decree and did not have intercourse. But it is doubtful that these decision would still be applied since they rested on the outdated premise that there is a spousal duty to cohabit from which the petitioner was relieved by reason of the decree.

[137] *Court Procedures for the Determination of Paternity* (1998) paras 31ff.

[138] Viz. Law Reform (Parent and Child) (Scotland) Act 1986 s 5.

that of the father on the registration of the child's birth is prima facie evidence of his paternity,[139] a point that can only be strengthened by the fact that such registration now confers parental responsibility on the man.[140] In such cases, given the relative weakness of the presumption of a married man's paternity (discussed shortly), it is hard to distinguish the legal position of the married man and the unmarried man named as the father. In both cases the onus in any court proceedings lies on those wishing to prove that the man is not the father. Although it has still not been authoritatively resolved, the better view is that the making of a parental responsibility agreement also provides prima facie evidence of paternity.[141]

Whether there should be a presumption of paternity in the case of cohabiting couples, as there is in some Commonwealth jurisdictions,[142] was considered but rejected by the Law Commission[143] on the basis that, unlike marriage, which requires no further evidence, cohabitation is not so easy to prove. It is submitted, however, that there is no reason why there should not be a *presumption* of paternity in cases where a couple have made a parental responsibility agreement.

The position where the child is born to a mother married to another woman

As Sch 4 Part 2 to the Marriage (Same Sex Couples) Act 2013 makes clear, where a child is born to a woman during her marriage to another woman the common law presumption 'is of no relevance to the question of who the child's parents are.' In other words, there is no presumption that the mother's spouse is a parent.

Rebutting the presumption

Standard of proof

At common law the generally accepted view was that the presumption could only be rebutted by evidence establishing beyond reasonable doubt that the husband could not be the father.[144] However, the Family Law Reform Act 1969 s 26 fundamentally altered that position by providing that the presumption may be rebutted upon the balance of probabilities.[145]

Although certain post 1969 Act decisions[146] held that, given the seriousness of the issue, something more than a mere balance of probabilities was required to rebut the presumption of legitimacy, the House of Lords decisively rejected the notion that there are different civil standards of proof. As Baroness Hale said 'loud and clear' in *Re B (Children) (Care Proceedings: Standard of Proof) (CAFCASS intervening)*[147] there is but one civil standard

---

[139] *Brierley v Brierley* [1918] P 257; Births and Deaths Registration Act 1953 s 34(2). See also the Lord Chancellor's Consultation Paper *Court Procedures for the Determination of Paternity* (1998), at para 26, which observes that a certified copy of registration is accepted as prima facie evidence of paternity in most matters of inheritance nationality and citizenship.

[140] See Ch 11, Registration as the father, p 371.

[141] See the Lord Chancellor's Consultation Paper *Court Procedures for the Determination of Paternity* (1998) at para 28. Parental responsibility agreements are discussed in Ch 11, Parental responsibility agreements, pp 372ff.

[142] Such as Tasmania, New South Wales and Ontario; see Law Com No 118 at para 10.53, n 120.

[143] Law Com No 118 para 10.54.

[144] See *Watson v Watson* [1954] P 48 and see Law Com No 16 *Blood Tests and the Proof of Paternity in Civil Proceedings* (1968) at paras 12ff.

[145] This implemented the recommendations of the Law Commission: see Law Com No 16 para 15.

[146] In particular *Serio v Serio* (1983) 4 FLR 756 and *Re Moynihan* [2000] 1 FLR 113.

[147] [2008] UKHL 35 [2009] 1 AC 11, at [70]. *Re B* reinforced the decision to the same effect in *Re H (Minors) (Sexual Abuse: Standard of Proof)* [1996] AC 563 in which Lord Lloyd (at 577) specifically criticised *Serio* for

of proof, namely the balance of probabilities, and neither 'the seriousness of the allegations nor the seriousness of the consequences' makes any difference to that standard.
Consequently, as Lord Reid observed in *S v S, W v Official Solicitor (or W)*,[148] s 26 means
that even weak evidence must prevail if there is no other evidence to counterbalance it. It
has been held that the inference of paternity drawn from an unjustified refusal to undertake a DNA test (discussed later) is sufficient to rebut the presumption of legitimacy.[149]

In fact, given the existence of DNA testing, it will be rare for the presumption to be
relied upon and that in turn has led one judge to question the continued relevance of
s 26, commenting that 'as science has hastened on and as more and more children are
born out of marriage it seems to me that the paternity of any child is to be established
by science and not by legal presumption or inference.'[150] While in general terms there
is clearly force in this observation there can still be cases, for example where succession
is in issue and one or more of the relevant persons are dead, where such tests are not
practical.

What has to be rebutted

Although disputed issues of paternity are normally settled by DNA tests, the presumption of paternity can be rebutted by showing the husband and wife did not have intercourse at the relevant time.[151] Where such marital intercourse cannot be excluded the
husband must show that the child is not the issue of that intercourse to rebut the presumption of paternity. This normally implies that the wife has committed adultery. It is
established, however, that the fact that the wife has committed adultery does not in itself
(save where it can shown that the husband is sterile) rebut the presumption, because this
evidence merely shows that the husband or the adulterer could be the father.[152] In these
circumstances, although it is possible to seek to rebut the presumption by the admission of
evidence of facial resemblance,[153] racial[154] or genetic characteristics (sometimes referred to
as 'anthropological tests'),[155] the practice in England and Wales is to determine disputes with
the aid of DNA tests.

The use of blood and DNA tests to establish parentage

The nature of the tests

In cases where parentage (usually paternity) is in issue the most cogent evidence is likely to be
obtained by DNA tests. Such tests may be used either to rebut the presumption or allegation
of paternity or to establish parentage.

---

reading words into the statute which are not there. See C Cobley and N Lowe 'Interpreting the Threshold
Criteria under section 31 (2) of the Children Act 1989—the House of Lords decision in *Re B*' (2009) 72
MLR 463.
                                                          [148] [1972] AC 24, HL at 41.

[149] *Secretary of State for Work and Pensions v Jones* [2003] EWHC 2163 (Fam) [2004] 1 FLR 282.

[150] Thorpe LJ in *Re H and A (Paternity: Blood Tests)* [2002] EWCA Civ 383 [2002] 1 FLR 1145 at [30].

[151] Indeed before the advent of blood tests this was the ground on which a husband was most likely to
succeed. See eg *Preston-Jones v Preston-Jones* [1951] AC 391, HL, husband's absence from wife; the *Banbury
Peerage Case* (1811) 1 Sim & St 153, HL, husband's impotence and the *Aylesford Peerage Case* (1885) 11 App
Cas 1, HL, and *Morris v Davies* (1837) 5 CL & Fin 163, HL, intrinsic unlikelihood of sexual intercourse
between the spouses.

[152] *Francis v Francis* [1960] P 17 and *Gardner v Gardner* (1877) 2 App Cas 723, HL.

[153] See *C v C and C (legitimacy: photographic evidence)* [1972] 3 All ER 577.

[154] See *Slingsby v A-G* (1916) 33 TLR 120 at 122, HL.

[155] The Law Commission (Law Com No 16 *Blood Tests and the Proof of Paternity in Civil Proceedings*,
para 16) did not recommend the introduction of such tests in England because of doubts about their medical
validity.

Until DNA tests became publicly available[156] reliance was placed on blood tests.[157] Based on the fact that certain characteristics of a person's blood are inherited and that if the mother's blood does not possess a characteristic possessed by the child, he must have inherited it from the father, blood tests could go some way in resolving issues of paternity. The great drawback of such tests, however, is that, although they can definitely show that a man *cannot* be the father, they can only show with varying degrees of probability that he *is* the father.[158] In contrast, DNA tests can, by matching the alleged father's DNA bands with those of the child's (having excluded those bands that match the mother's) make positive findings of paternity with virtual certainty.[159] Furthermore, such tests can be carried out on a variety of bodily tissue (including hair, for example) or bodily fluids (for example, saliva which can be tested by taking mouth swabs)[160] and not simply on blood.

Reflecting these advancements, whereas formerly directions could only be made for the use of blood tests, courts currently make directions for the use of 'scientific tests' which permits, subject to necessary consents, tests to be carried on bodily samples taken from the relevant persons.

Although much of the jurisprudence about to be discussed concerned the use of 'blood' rather than 'scientific' tests no legal significance is attached to this. In other words case law developed on blood tests applies without qualification to scientific tests.

The power to give directions for the use of scientific tests

The power to give directions for the use of scientific tests is governed by s 20 of the Family Law Reform Act 1969. This provides that any court may, of its own motion or upon application by any party to the proceedings, direct scientific tests to be used in any *civil* proceedings[161] in which the parentage of any person is to be determined. The power under s 20 is sometimes loosely referred to as a power to *order* scientific tests, but as Ward LJ pointed out in *Re H (A Minor) (Blood Tests: Parental Rights)*:[162]

> . . . section 20 does not empower the court to order blood tests, still less to take blood from an unwilling party: all it does is permit a direction for the use of blood tests to ascertain paternity.

Accordingly, the appropriate wording of the direction is not to direct the parties to provide bodily samples but to direct that scientific tests be used to show that a party to the proceedings is or is not the father or mother of the child in question.

Notwithstanding Ward LJ's clear statement, a distinction should be drawn between adults and children. As Hale J pointed out in *Re R (A Minor) (Blood Tests: Constraint)*,[163] while there is an absolute embargo against forcing an adult to supply a sample against his will, there is no such bar against ordering a sample from a child even to the extent of ordering physical restraint against him or her.

---

[156] 1 June 1987—see *Re J (A Minor) (Wardship)* [1988] 1 FLR 65.

[157] See generally S Cretney *Family Law in the Twentieth Century* (2003) pp 536–540.

[158] Though, as these tests were being perfected, the degree of probability could be very high, in some cases over 99.8%: see the scales referred to in *Armitage v Nanchen* (1983) 4 FLR 293.

[159] See C Barton and G Douglas *Law and Parenthood* (1995) at pp 59–60, R Yaxley 'Genetic Fingerprinting' [1988] Fam Law 403; and A Bradney 'Blood Tests, Paternity and the Double Helix' [1986] Fam Law 378.

[160] This is the most common way in which DNA tests are conducted.

[161] 'Civil proceedings' includes proceedings under the Child Support Act 1991 s 27: *Re E (A Minor) (Child Support Act: Blood Test)* [1994] 2 FLR 548.

[162] [1996] 4 All ER 28 at 36, CA. For the human rights implications of the inability to enforce a direction, see The inferences from a refusal to consent, p 268.   [163] [1998] Fam 66.

Where no issue of parentage falls to be directed then there is no power to make a direction under s 20. Hence, in *Hodgkiss v Hodgkiss*,[164] for example, the judge was held wrong to have made a direction in divorce proceedings to settle the paternity of two children since no issue of paternity had been raised in the proceedings, the husband having conceded that the children were 'children of the family'. Similarly, if there are no 'civil proceedings' in existence there is no freestanding power to direct tests to be taken.[165]

It is important to appreciate that s 20 does not inhibit the giving of evidence. If all the parties agree, they do not have to obtain the court's consent before having a test carried out.[166] What the Act does is to give the court a discretion to direct a test if they do not agree. Section 20 is silent as to when such a direction should be made, but in *S v S, W v Official Solicitor (or W)*[167] Lord Reid expressed the view that the provision could not have possibly been intended to confer an unfettered discretion on what were then lower court judges and magistrates and that instead it must be left to the superior courts to settle the principles.

S v S establishes the important point that, when considering whether to make a direction, the court was not exercising its so-called custodial jurisdiction, but was instead exercising its protective jurisdiction.[168] This meant that the correct test was not to make a direction where it is in the child's best interests to do so, but only to refuse to make a direction where it would be against the child's interests to do otherwise,[169] for example, where, 'having regard to the facts and circumstances of a particular case, his interests are such that their protection necessitates the withholding from a court of evidence which may be very material',[170] or if 'it would be unjust to order a test for a collateral reason to assist a litigant in his or her claim'.[171] The House of Lords refused to accept that the mere fact that a test could establish conclusively that the child was illegitimate was sufficiently against his interest to withhold consent, even though, as in *W v Official Solicitor*, this would leave him with no known father at all. This danger is far outweighed by the demands of public policy that all relevant evidence should be made available. Furthermore, the suppression of evidence would not encourage the mother's husband, whose suspicions would be unallayed, to accept the child as his, whereas he might be prepared to do so if a test did not exclude his paternity; and the child himself in later life might resent the fact that a full investigation was not conducted at the time. It will usually be in the child's interest—as well as in the public interest—that the truth should out.[172]

As Balcombe LJ later put it in *Re F (A Minor) (Blood Tests: Parental Rights)*,[173] *S v S* established inter alia that:

> Public policy no longer requires that special protection should be given by the law to the status of legitimacy . . . The interests of justice will normally require that available evidence

---

[164] [1984] FLR 563, CA. But see the comment at [1985] Fam Law 87.

[165] Per Balcombe LJ in *Re E (Parental Responsibility: Blood Tests)* [1995] 1 FLR 392 at 400–1, CA.

[166] See for example the practice under the Child Support Act, discussed in Ch 22.

[167] [1972] AC 24 [1970] 3 All ER 107, HL. See M Hayes 'The Use of Blood Tests in the Pursuit of Truth' (1971) 87 LQR 86. For an extensive analysis of this decision, see A Bainham 'Welfare, Truth and Justice' in S Gilmore, J Herring and R Probert (eds) *Landmark Cases in Family Law* (2012) ch 7.

[168] The distinction between the two jurisdictions is explored further in Ch 12, The paramountcy principle does not apply to issues only indirectly concerning the child, p 422.   [169] Per Lord Reid at 45.

[170] Per Lord Morris at 53.   [171] Per Lord Hodson at 58.

[172] *S v S* [1972] AC 24 [1970] 3 All ER 107, HL at 45 (per Lord Reid) 55–6 (per Lord Morris), 59 (per Lord Hodson).

[173] [1993] Fam 314 at 318, CA, on which see J Fortin 'Re F: The Gooseberry Bush Approach' (1996) 57 MLR 296, J Fortin 'Children's right to know their origins – too far, too fast?' [2009] CFLQ 336, and C Barton and G Douglas *Law and Parenthood* (1995) at p 61.

be not suppressed and that the truth be ascertained whenever possible. . . In many cases the interests of the child are also best served if the truth is ascertained. . . However, the interests of justice may conflict with the interests of the child. In general the court ought to permit a blood test of a young child to be taken unless satisfied that that would be against the child's interests; it does not first need to be satisfied that the outcome of the test will be for the benefit of the child . . . It is not really protecting the child to ban a blood test on some vague or shadowy conjecture that it may turn out to be for its advantage or at least to do it no harm.

Notwithstanding general agreement as to what the test is, there has been some difficulty and inconsistency in applying it.[174] In *Re F* itself, the Court of Appeal upheld a refusal to make a direction upon the application of a man claiming to be the father (and who had never seen the child) and opposed by the mother, in a case where the child had been conceived and brought up in an existing marriage, albeit that at the time of conception the mother had been having sexual relations with her husband and the applicant. The court held that the child's welfare depended upon her relationship with the mother and on the stability of the family unit, which included the mother's husband. Anything which might disturb that stability was likely to be detrimental to the child's welfare and therefore, unless this could be counter-balanced by other advantages to her of ordering a test, it would be wrong to do it.

In *Re F* the Court of Appeal seemed to be saying that, if the child is being brought up in an intact family and the test is opposed by the parent, then it is likely to be thought contrary to the child's interests for a direction to be made. But if that was what was meant it cannot stand with subsequent case law. For example, in *Re H (A Minor) (Blood Tests: Parental Rights)*,[175] soon after a married woman began a sexual relationship with another man she became pregnant. However, notwithstanding this affair she continued to have sexual relations with her husband, who five years previously had had a vasectomy (though he had never checked on the success of that operation). At first the mother intended to leave her husband and set up home with her lover, but she ended the affair before the child was born. When the child was born, his birth was registered in her husband's name. As in *Re F*, the mother opposed the making of a blood test direction upon an application by the lover, who was seeking contact. She argued that pursuing contact would destabilise her own marriage which had only recently been put together again, and that that would be to the child's disadvantage.

In making the direction the Court of Appeal emphasised that the mother's refusal to undergo a test herself was *not* determinative of whether the court should direct such a test,[176] though it remained a factor to be taken into account.[177] But a more important factor was, according to Ward LJ, the right of every child to know the truth about their parentage unless their welfare clearly justifies the 'cover up'. As he pointed out, this right to know is underlined by Article 7 of the UN Convention on the Rights of the Child. Among other factors to be considered, his Lordship considered that[178] any gain to the child from preventing any disturbance to his security had to be balanced against the loss to him of the certainty of knowing who he was. Accordingly, while the risk of disruption to the

---

[174] See generally J Fortin *Children's Rights and the Developing Law* (3rd edn, 2009) pp 475–481.

[175] [1997] Fam 89, CA.

[176] Wall J's conclusion to the contrary in *Re CB (A Minor) (Blood Tests)* [1994] 2 FLR 762 at 773H was therefore disapproved.

[177] In the case of a haemophiliac father, for example, it may be a very powerful argument: per Ward LJ, in *Re H (A Minor) (Blood tests: Parental Rights)* [1997] Fam 89 at 101.   [178] Ibid at 105.

child's life both by the continuance of the paternity issue as well as the pursuit of the s 8 order were obviously factors which impinged on the child's welfare, they were not, in his judgment, determinative of whether to make a direction. Although Ward LJ himself did not accept that the two cases were indistinguishable,[179] it is hard to reconcile Re F and Re H, though the latter seems more in tune with the House of Lords' approach in S v S. The normality of making directions was again emphasised in Re H and A (Paternity: Blood Tests)[180] and in which Thorpe LJ stressed the application of two key principles, namely (1) that the interests of justice are best served by the ascertainment of truth; and (2) the court should be furnished with the best available science and not to have to rely upon presumptions and inferences. However, in that case, notwithstanding the 'profoundest misgivings' about the first instance refusal to make a direction on the basis that it would damage the twins' family (the husband intimated that he would very likely leave home if tests established that he was not the father)[181] the case was remitted for a re-trial.

Notwithstanding their normality, directions are not always made. One profitable line of argument has been to persuade the court that there is no need to determine paternity to settle an issue at all. In K v M (Paternity: Contact),[182] for example, it was held unnecessary to consider the paternity of the child to determine the only live issue, namely contact. Similarly, in O v L (Blood Tests),[183] in which the mother asserted that the husband was not the father of the child after they separated nearly three years after the child's birth and, in response to her husband's application for contact, only sought a blood test in an effort to forestall this, it was held unnecessary to define the precise nature of the relationship between the husband and the child in order for contact between them to be fostered. What these cases seem to demonstrate at any rate in this context is that the child's welfare in having contact is more important than establishing so-called father's rights.

Another circumstance that may justify a refusal to make a direction is where the child him- or herself objects. In L v P (Paternity Test: Child's Objection),[184] for example, a direction for a DNA test was refused because of the reasonable objections of a mature 15 year old.

The need for consent

In the case of adults (and those aged 16 or 17) there is no compulsion attached to the direction. This is made clear by s 21 which provides that, except in the case of a person suffering from mental disorder, bodily samples may not be taken from a person aged 16 or over unless he or she consents. In the case of those under the age of 16, s 21(3), as originally enacted, simply provided that a sample could be taken for such a person 'if the person who has care and control agrees'. This led to a conflict of view as to whether this provision meant that those with care and control had a right of veto.[185] To resolve that conflict

---

[179] Ibid at 106.

[180] [2002] EWCA Civ 383, [2002] 1 FLR 1145. Note also Re T (Paternity: Ordering Blood Tests) [2001] 2 FLR 1190 in which a direction was made notwithstanding the mother's opposition on the basis it would create a serious risk of destabilising the present arrangements viz. a husband and wife bringing up a seven-year-old boy. Note also that six years previously a magistrates' court had refused to make a direction.

[181] Thorpe LJ was not convinced that the marriage was as stable as alleged.

[182] [1996] 1 FLR 312.

[183] [1995] 2 FLR 930, CA. See also M (D) v M (S) and G (M (DA) Intervening) [1969] 1 WLR 843—direction refused where sole reason for application was to prove the wife's adultery.

[184] [2011] EWHC 3399 (Fam) [2013] 1 FLR 578. See also Re D (Paternity) [2006] EWHC 3565 (Fam) [2007] 2 FLR 26—in the face of strong opposition of an 11 year old, a paternity test was stayed on the basis that it was not in his immediate interests that the issue be resolved.

[185] See Re R (A Minor) (Blood Tests: Constraint) [1998] Fam 66 in which Hale J held that to get round the lack of parental consent the child could be ordered to be delivered into the care and control of the Official

s 21(3) was amended to provide that in the absence of the requisite consent a sample may be taken 'if the court considers that it would be in [the child's] best interests for the sample to be taken'.[186] This enjoinder to consider the child's best interests seems, however, to lie at odds with the general test established by *S v S, W v Official Solicitor*[187] as to when to make a direction in which the House of Lords expressly rejected the 'best interests of the child' approach. In *Re T (Paternity: Ordering Blood Tests)*[188] Bodey J solved this potential dilemma by ruling that while the child's welfare is not paramount when considering whether to make a direction instead 'one has to apply the test of his best interests, weighing those best interests against the competing interests of the adults who would be affected one way or another, according to whether the applications were granted or refused'. He further pointed out that under Art 8 of the European Convention on Human Rights while all the parties had the right to respect for their private and family life if those rights pulled in different directions, then the child's right to know his true identity was the weightiest consideration.[189] On the facts, Bodey J had little difficulty in making a direction on the basis that the 7 year old child's interest in knowing his true identity (which issue was in the public domain following the mother's husband's proclamation of his paternity on citizen's band radio) outweighed the interests of both the mother and her husband.

Although there can be few quibbles with the overall outcome, one might nevertheless question whether Bodey J's approach was strictly correct. His interpretation of the test to be applied in making a direction is dubious (the House of Lords in *S v S* held that a direction should only be refused where it could be shown to be against the child's interests) and in any event seems to conflate the question of whether to make a direction with whether to override a person with care and control's refusal to allow a sample to be taken from a child. The correct approach, it is submitted, is first to decide according to the principles set out in *S v S* whether to make a direction and then to apply s 21(3) to determine whether or not a sample should be taken from the child. Although the tests are not the same it has, however, to be admitted that once it has been shown not to be harmful to the child for a direction to be made, it will almost inevitably follow that it will be in the child's best interests to have a sample taken from him or her to establish parentage.

In the case of a person (including those under the age of 16) suffering from a mental disorder and who does not understand the nature of the test, consent must be obtained from the person who has care and control and in addition the medical practitioner responsible for the person's care must certify that the taking of a sample will not be prejudicial to his welfare.[190]

The inferences from a refusal to consent

Although there is a power of refusal under s 21, s 23(1) permits the court to draw such inferences as appear proper from a person's failure to give consent or to take steps to give effect to the direction.

Solicitor, who could then consent on the child's behalf. Cf *Re O (A Minor) (Blood Tests: Constraint)* [2000] Fam 139 in which Wall J considered that Hale J's stratagem was wrong because it was a device to circumvent the plain provision of the Act. He nevertheless thought that the resulting right of veto was not human rights compliant.

[186] Section 21(3)(b) added by the Child Support, Pensions and Social Security Act 2000 s 82.
[187] [1972] AC 24, HL, discussed at The power to give directions for the use of scientific tests, p 265.
[188] [2001] 2 FLR 1190.
[189] See eg *Mikulić v Croatia* [2002] 1 FCR 720, ECtHR and 'The Gaskin case' [1990] 1 FLR 167, ECtHR.
[190] Section 21(4).

In *Re A (A Minor) (Paternity: Refusal of Blood Test)*[191] Waite LJ commented that given the background of scientific advance:

> ... if a mother makes a claim against one of the possible fathers,[192] and he chooses his right not to submit to be tested, the inference that he is the father of the child should be virtually inescapable. He would certainly have to advance very clear and cogent reasons for his refusal to be tested—reasons which it would be just and fair and reasonable for him to be allowed to maintain.

The inference from a refusal to provide a sample for a scientific test is stronger than the presumption of legitimacy. In *Secretary of State For Work and Pensions v Jones*,[193] for example, it was held that the justices had erred in giving greater weight to the presumption of legitimacy than to the inference of paternity drawn from the respondent's failure to provide a sample for a DNA test. In this case the mother, although married to someone else, had been exclusively living with the respondent for nine months around the time of conception. She named him as the father in her application for child support, but the respondent whilst indicating his possible paternity, nevertheless failed to provide a sample to enable a test to be carried out. Butler-Sloss P, setting aside the magistrates' decision, declared the respondent to be the father. In *Re G (Parentage: Blood Sample)*[194] Ward LJ said:

> ... the forensic process is advanced by presenting the truth to the court. He who obstructs the truth will have the inference drawn against him.

In that case the trial judge was held to have misdirected himself when failing to draw the inference from a man's his refusal to submit to a test.[195]

Under s 23(2), if a party makes a claim relying on the presumption of legitimacy, the court may dismiss the claim even though there is no evidence to rebut the presumption.

In *Re O (A Minor) (Blood Tests: Constraint)*[196] Wall J suggested that notwithstanding the power to draw inferences from a refusal to comply with a direction, the inability simply to enforce a direction may mean that Part III of the 1969 Act will need to be reformed to become human rights compliant. But whether this is right remains to be seen for although the establishment of parentage engages both Article 6 and 8,[197] given that inferences can be drawn from a refusal to comply with a direction thereby leading to a finding, it is not at all clear that a breach of Article 8 would be established.[198]

(c) Commentary

The readiness of English law to allow challenges to parentage in subsequent court proceedings without condition is by no means the norm among other European jurisdictions.

---

[191] [1994] 2 FLR 463 at 473, CA. For an earlier example of a husband reasonably refusing to submit to a blood test, see *B v B and E (B intervening)* [1969] 3 All ER 1106, CA.

[192] At the time of conception the mother was having sexual relationships with three different men.

[193] [2003] EWHC 2163 (Fam) [2004] 1 FLR 282. See also *F v Child Support Agency* [1999] 2 FLR 244.

[194] [1997] 1 FLR 360 at 366, CA.

[195] Though in fact in the appeal he was given a further opportunity to change his mind.

[196] [2000] Fam 139 at 155.

[197] See eg *Ramussen v Denmark* (1985) 7 EHRR 371, ECtHR.

[198] Cf *Mikulić v Croatia* [2002] 1 FCR 720, ECtHR where a breach was found only because under Croatian law there was no alternative means of establishing paternity other than a DNA test. See also *Odièvre v France* [2003] 1 FCR 621, ECtHR, in which the French law permitting a mother to give birth anonymously was held not to violate the child's Art 8 rights.

Many take the view that an unrestricted right to contest parentage threatens family stability particularly where that family unit has been happily in existence for some time. Consequently it is not unusual for restrictions to be placed on the ability to bring court proceedings.[199] So far as human rights is concerned, it is established that while there should be a legal mechanism to contest parentage[200] provided they are reasoned and proportionate and not arbitrary, restrictions are human rights compliant.[201] English law is necessarily human rights compliant in this regard since it imposes no formal restrictions on the right of challenge.

7. DECLARATIONS OF PARENTAGE

There are two ways[202] in which the issue of parentage may be determined by the court, namely, by a finding in the course of existing proceedings, or by a formal declaration of parentage. The drawback of the former is that any judicial decision is a judgment in personam and consequently only binds the parties to it and their privies, ie persons claiming through them. Formal declarations, on the other hand, are binding for all purposes.

Under s 55A of the Family Law Act 1986 any person may apply for a declaration as to whether or not a person named in the application is or was the parent of another person so named. The limits of this procedure need to be appreciated—a declaration cannot transform the child's legal status. A good example is *M v W (Declaration of Parentage)*,[203] in which the court made a declaration of biological parentage in respect of a child who had subsequently been adopted but, as Hogg J observed, the declaration did not affect the validity of the adoption. It is for this reason that declarations are no substitute for obtaining parental orders or adoption in cases of foreign surrogacy agreements.[204] The court's power in s 55A proceedings is limited to determining whether or not to make the declaration; it cannot, for example, make an order relating to separate enforcement proceedings, for example, for child support arrears.[205]

Jurisdiction to entertain an application is based on either person's[206] domicile or habitual residence for one year in England and Wales either the date of application, or if dead, at the time of death.[207] To guard against vexatious applications (typically from third parties) courts have (except where the declaration sought is as to whether or not the applicant is the parent of the named person; the named person is the parent of the applicant, or the named person is

---

[199] See N Lowe 'A Study into the Rights and Legal Status of Children Being Brought up in Various Forms of Marital or Non-Marital Partnerships and Cohabitation' (Council of Europe, 2008, CJ-FA (2008) 5). See also A Spickhoff, D Schwab, D Heinrich and P Gottwaid (eds) *Strei um die Abstammung—ein Europäischer Vergliech* (2007).

[200] See *Kautzor v Germany* [2012] 2 FLR 396, *Ahrens v Germany* [2012] 2 FLR 483, *Kroon v The Netherlands* (1995) 19 EHRR 263 and *Mikulić v Croatia* [2002] 1 FCR 720.

[201] See eg *Znameskaya v Russia* (2007) 44 EHRR 15, *Różański v Poland* (2007) 45 EHRR 26, *Shoffmann v Russia* (2007) 44 EHRR 35, *Missi v Malta* (2008) 46 EHRR 27 and *Paulík v Slovakia* (2009) 46 EHRR 1. For two more recent examples of where the restrictions were held not to violate human rights see *Ahrens v Germany* (App No 45071/09) [2012] 2 FLR 483 and *Kautzor v Germany* (App No 23338/09) [2012] 2 FLR 396.

[202] Formerly, a declaration could be obtained under the Child Support Act 1991 s 27 but that was only effective for child support and maintenance purposes. This method was abolished by the reforms introduced by the Child Support, Pensions and Social Security Act 2000.

[203] [2006] EWHC 2341 (Fam) [2007] 2 FLR 270.

[204] See *A v P* [2011] EWHC 1738 [2012] Fam 188.

[205] *Law v Inostroza Ahumada* [2010] EWCA Civ 1145 [2011] 1 FLR 708.

[206] Ie the applicant or the person named in the application. Formerly, jurisdiction was founded only upon the applicant's domicile or habitual residence.   [207] Section 55A(2).

the other parent of a named child of the applicant),[208] a discretion not to hear an application if it considers that the applicant does not have a sufficient personal interest.[209] Furthermore, where one of the named persons in the application is a child the court may refuse to hear it 'if it considers that the determination of the application would not be in the child's best interests'.[210] Where a court refuses to hear an application it may order that the applicant should not apply for the same declaration without leave of the court.[211] It has been held that under this provision the focus is firmly on the child's interests.[212]

Where the truth of the proposition sought to be declared is proved to the court's satisfaction the court must make a declaration of parentage unless to do so would be manifestly contrary to public policy.[213] If a declaration is made, it is binding upon the Crown and all other persons,[214] and the Registrar-General will be informed.[215] If the declaration is refused, the court cannot grant a declaration for which an application was not made.[216]

8. REGISTRATION OF BIRTHS

As we have seen,[217] inclusion of the father's name in the register of births is prima facie evidence of his paternity.[218] Under the Births and Deaths Registration Act 1953 s 2, as amended, the child's mother, married father and s 42 parent[219] are obliged to register the birth within 42 days.[220] In contrast, neither the unmarried father nor a woman (a s 43 parent)[221] who is not married to nor the civil partner of the mother has an obligation to register himself as the father or herself as the second female parent and indeed has no general right to do so, in striking contrast to continental European legal systems which permit a man to make a binding voluntary recognition of his paternity.[222] The unmarried father's or second female parent's name may, however, be entered on the register in the following circumstances:[223]

    (i) at the joint request of the mother and the father or the woman concerned, in which case both must sign the register;

---

[208] Section 55A(4), on which see *Re R (Parental Responsibility)* [2011] EWHC 1535 (Fam) [2011] 2 FLR 1132.

[209] Section 55A(3). For these purposes where an application for a declaration of parentage is made by the Secretary of State in connection with a maintenance calculation under the Child Support Act 1991 the person with care is deemed to have a sufficient interest if she is seeking a declaration: s 27 of the Child Support Act 1991, to which s 55A(3) is expressly made subject.

[210] Section 55A(5). This provision might be thought to raise similar issues to those under s 21(3) of the Family Law Reform Act 1969, discussed earlier, The need for consent, p 267.   [211] Section 55A(6).

[212] *Re S (a child) (declaration of parentage)* [2012] EWCA Civ 1160 [2012] All ER (D) 140 (Aug). Cf the position under s 58(1), discussed in Ch 9, Declarations of status, p 303, which is concerned with the more general issues of public policy.

[213] Section 58(1).   [214] Section 58(2).

[215] Section 55A(7), FPR 2010 r 8.22 (2). There is a limited discretion to extend the 21 days period of notice, see *Re F (Paternity: Registration)* [2011] EWCA Civ 1765 [2013] 2 FLR 1036.   [216] Section 58(3).

[217] See earlier, The position where the child is born to an unmarried mother, p 262. Registration also vests parental responsibility if the man is not married to the mother, see Ch 11, Registration as the father, p 371.

[218] See generally A Bainham 'What is the point of birth registration?' [2008] CFLQ 449.

[219] Ie a woman married to or civil partner of the mother and who satisfies the requirements of HFEA 2008, s 42, discussed earlier, see Female parenthood, p 256.

[220] For registering posthumous fathers of children conceived after their death, see s 10ZA of the 1953 Act, as substituted by HFEA 2008, Sch 6, para 6.

[221] Ie a woman who satisfies the requirements of HFEA 2008, s 43, discussed earlier at Female parenthood, p 256.

[222] See N Lowe 'A Study into the Rights and Legal Status of Children Being Brought up in Various Forms of Marital or Non-Marital Partnerships and Cohabitation' CJ-FA (2008) 5.

[223] Births and Deaths Registration Act 1953 s 10 as substituted by the Family Law Reform Act 1987 s 24 and amended by the Children Act 1989 Sch 12 para 6.

(ii) at the mother's request upon production of a declaration[224] by her and the man to the effect that he is the father, or by her and the woman concerned that she is a parent;

(iii) at the father's or the woman concerned's request upon production of a declaration by him or her and the mother to the effect that he is the father or that she is a parent;

(iv) at the written request of either the mother or the father or the woman concerned, upon the production of a copy of a parental responsibility agreement, a parental responsibility order or a court order requiring him or her to make financial provision for the child.

If the child's birth has been registered with no father or second female parent named, it may be re-registered showing the father's or the woman concerned's name if one of the listed conditions is satisfied.[225] Re-registrations can also be made by the Registrar-General upon receiving satisfactory evidence that the child has become a legitimated person[226] or upon being notified of a declaration of parentage or of non-parentage[227] being made either under s 55A or s 56 of the Family Law Act 1986.[228] Notwithstanding that declarations of parentage offer the only means by which unmarried fathers or s 43 parents can respectively have their paternity or parentage registered without the mother's consent, such re-registrations have no effect on the allocation of parental responsibility.[229]

Much criticised provisions for compulsory joint birth registration by unmarried parents are contained in the Welfare Reform Act 2009 Sch 6, but they have not been implemented and are unlikely to be so.[230]

9. DISCOVERING GENETIC PARENTAGE

Children may consult the birth register to discover who their registered parents are. Moreover, as we discuss in Chapter 19, when they reach 18, adopted children are generally entitled to see their original birth certificate, thus enabling them to trace their birth parents. In addition, following the recommendations of the Warnock Committee[231] that a child should have a right, to basic information about his ethnic and genetic origins,[232]

---

[224] Namely, a duly signed and witnessed declaration on a prescribed from—viz. Form 2 under Sch 1 to the Registration of Births and Deaths Regulations 1987.

[225] Births and Deaths Registration Act 1953 s 10A, as amended. Special arrangements are made for the registration of parental orders under s 54 of HFEA 2008 by Sch 1 to the Parental Orders (Human Fertilisation and Embryology) Regulations 2010 and for adoptions under the Adoption and Children Act 2002 Sch 1.

[226] Births and Deaths Registration Act 1953 s 14.

[227] See *AB v CD and Z (Fertility) Clinic* [2013] EWHC 1418 (Fam) [2013] 2 FLR 1357 and *M v F and H* [2014] 1 FLR 352.

[228] Section 14A, added by the Family Law Reform Act 1987 s 27 and amended by the Child Support, Pensions and Social Security Act 2000 s 83(5). Declarations are discussed at Declarations of parentage, p 270 and in Ch 9, Declarations of status, p 303.

[229] Responsibility is only conferred when the man or second female parent is registered as the unmarried father under s 10(1) and 10A(1) of the 1953 Act and not, therefore, under s 14A, see Children Act 1989 s 4(1A), discussed in Ch 11, Registration as the father, p 371 and Acquisition of parental responsibility by female parents who are neither married to nor in civil partnership with the mother, p 385.

[230] For critical discussion see A Bainham 'What is the point of birth registration?' [2008] CFLQ 449, and J Wallbank '"Bodies in the Shadows": joint birth registration, parental responsibility and social class' [2009] CFLQ 267.

[231] Report of the Committee of Inquiry into Human Fertilisation and Embryology (1984) Cmnd 9314, para 4.21.

[232] See generally J Fortin 'Children's right to know their origins – too far, too fast?' [2009] CFLQ 336, J Masson and C Harrison 'Identity: Mapping the Frontiers' in N Lowe and G Douglas (eds) *Families Across Frontiers* (1996) pp 277–94, and C Barton and G Douglas *Law and Parenthood* (1995) pp 83–9.

s 31ZA of the Human Fertilisation and Embryology Act 1990[233] provides that a person who has attained the age of 16[234] having been given a suitable opportunity to receive proper counselling,[235] may apply to the Human Fertilisation and Embryology Authority to give him notice stating whether or not the information contained in the Authority's register shows that, but for ss 27–29 of the 1990 Act or ss 33 to 47 of the 2008 Act, some other person would or might be his parent. If it does, the Authority must generally give the applicant such information as relates to the donor as is permitted by the Regulations but no other information.[236] Only non-identifying information can be given while the child is under 18.[237] A donor conceived person can also request information about genetic half siblings. As discussed earlier in this chapter, the right to anonymity for donors giving sperm at a licensed clinic has been ended with respect to children conceived as a result of sperm donated on or after 1 April 2005. Consequently such donor conceived children will, upon attaining the age of 18 (ie as from April 2023 at the earliest), be able to obtain identifying information from the Human Fertilisation and Embryology Authority.[238]

At the time of the legislation there was a sharp division of opinion as to whether it is in the child's interests to learn of the fact of donation[239] and concerns continue to be expressed.[240]

By 34 of the 1990 Act[241] where in any proceedings before a court the question whether a person is or is not the parent of a child by virtue of ss 27–29 of the 1990 Act or ss 33 to 47 of the 2008 Act, falls to be determined, the court may, on the application of any party to the proceedings make an order requiring the Human Fertilisation and Embryology Authority to disclose such information as is specified in the order.

It is accepted that there is power to make a specific issue order to inform children about their father's identity[242] and even very existence.[243]

It is equally accepted that claims by donor conceived person for information about the donors engage Art 8 rights but that does not necessarily mean that restrictions, for example, those currently preventing the disclosure of identifying information, violate those rights.[244]

---

[233] Substituting s 31 by HFEA 2008 s 24.   [234] Note the 2008 Act lowered this age from 18.

[235] Section 31(3) of the HFEA 1990.

[236] Section 31ZA(2)(a). But the Authority has a discretion not to comply with applicant's request if it considers that special circumstances exist which increase the likelihood inter alia of the applicant identifying the donor, s 31ZA(6).   [237] Section 31ZA(4).

[238] For the background to this change, see Department of Health *Donor information consultation* (2002) and Human Fertilisation and Embryology Authority *Response to the Department of Health's consultation on donor information* (2002).

[239] See G Douglas *Law, Fertility and Reproduction* (1991) pp 132–6. But see the criticisms of S Maclean and M Maclean 'Keeping secrets in assisted reproduction: the tension between donor anonymity and the need of the child for information' (1996) 8 CFLQ 243; and K O'Donovan 'What shall we tell the children?' in R Lee and D Morgan (eds) *Birthrights* (1994) pp 105–8.

[240] See J Fortin 'Children's right to know their origins – too far, too fast?' [2009] CFLQ 336. For an interesting discussion of the Swedish experience, see J Stoll *Swedish donor offspring and their legal right to information* (2008).   [241] As amended by HFEA 2008.

[242] See *Re F (Paternity: Jurisdiction)* [2007] EWCA Civ 873 [2008] 1 FLR 225. The court can even do so on its own motion: *Re J (Paternity: Welfare of Child)* [2006] EWHC 2837 (Fam) [2007] 1 FLR 1064—but declined on the facts to do so. See also *Re L (Identity of Birth Father)* [2008] EWCA Civ 1338 [2009] 1 FLR 1152—case remitted because welfare decision had been taken on incomplete evidence (not hearing the child's psychiatrist by agreement between the parents). Specific issue orders are discussed in Ch 14.

[243] *Re K (Specific Issue Order)* [1999] 2 FLR 280—application rejected.

[244] See *Rose v Secretary of State for Health and Human Fertilisation and Embryology Authority* [2002] EWHA 1593 (Admin) [2002] 2 FLR 962 and 'The Gaskin case' [1990] 1 FLR 167, ECtHR.

10. THE LEGAL SIGNIFICANCE OF PARENTAGE

Like a number of other legal systems, English common law refused to accept that the mere fact of parentage gave rise to a legally recognised relationship between parent and child. Instead it chose to recognise only the legal relationship between parent and *legitimate* child. We discuss the concept and significance of legitimacy when considering the child's position in Chapter 9. Suffice to say here that, although the significance of status has declined, English law continues to distinguish parents, and in particular fathers, whose children have been born in lawful wedlock from those whose children have not. Hence, while all mothers automatically have parental responsibility, only fathers whose children are legitimate automatically have such responsibility.[245]

That is not to say, however, that parentage per se has no legal significance.[246] For example, each parent is liable to maintain his child, and an application for child support may be brought under the Child Support Act 1991 against non-resident parents. Rights of succession automatically flow from the parent–child relationship,[247] as do the rules on prohibited degrees of marriage[248] and incest. All parents have a right to apply without leave for a s 8 order under the Children Act 1989[249] and there is a presumption that a child in local authority care should have reasonable contact with each parent.[250] Another consequence of legal parentage is the conferment upon the child of citizenship and the right to remain and settle in the United Kingdom. Overall, as Baroness Hale observed in *Re G (Children) (Residence: Same Sex Partner)*,[251] legal parenthood makes the child a member of that person's family. But over and above these legal consequences and not to be overlooked is the symbolic consequence of legal parentage not least for the child.[252]

11. SURROGACY AGREEMENTS

Although the precise arrangements may differ, a surrogacy agreement[253] is basically one by which a woman ('the carrying mother') agrees to bear a child for someone else ('the commissioning parents'). For the purposes of the Surrogacy Arrangements Act 1985, a 'surrogacy arrangement' is one made before the woman began to carry the child 'with a view to any child carried in pursuance of it being handed over to, and parental responsibility being met (so far as practicable) by another person or persons'.[254] It is the essence of such agreements that the carrying mother agrees to hand over the baby at birth to

---

[245] Children Act 1989 s 2(1) and (2), discussed in Ch 11, Married mothers and fathers, p 368.

[246] For a summary, see *AB v CD and Z (Fertility) Clinic* [2013] EWHC 1418 (Fam) [2013] 2 FLR 1357 at [2], per Cobb J.[247] See Ch 25.

[248] See Ch 3.   [249] See Ch 14, Persons entitled to apply for any s 8 order, p 513.

[250] Children Act 1989 s 34, discussed in Ch 18, Contact with children in care, pp 654ff.

[251] [2006] UKHL 43 [2006] 1 WLR 2305 at [32]. This is a point strongly made by A Bainham 'Parentage, Parenthood and Parental Responsibility' in A Bainham, S Day Sclater and M Richards (eds) *What is a Parent? A Socio-Legal Analysis* (1999) ch 2.

[252] See K Everett and L Yeatman 'Are some parents more natural than others?' [2010] CFLQ 290 at 306–7.

[253] See generally *Surrogacy: Review for Health Ministers* (Chair: Professor Margaret Brazier, 1998) Cm 4068; G Douglas *Law, Fertility and Reproduction* (1991) ch 7; P Bromley 'The Legal Aspects of Surrogacy Agreements' in D Freestone (ed) *Children and the Law* (1990) p 1; and the Report of the Committee of Inquiry into Human Fertilisation and Embryology (the Warnock Report) Cmnd 9314, ch 8. See also M Hibbs 'Surrogacy Legislation—Time for Change' [1997] Fam Law 564 and L Harding 'The Debate on Surrogate Motherhood' [1987] JSWL 37.

[254] Section 1(2) as amended by the Children Act 1989 Sch 13 para 56.

the commissioning parents and not to exercise any parental responsibility that she may have in respect of the child. As one commentator has put it,[255] '[s]urrogacy arrangements have become an increasingly popular alternative for childless couple, and singles, seeking to fulfil their dream of becoming parents.' Indeed in some countries, notably the USA and India, surrogacy has become a multi-million pound industry. Yet despite its growth, many countries have no legislation governing surrogacy, while some others have banned the practice. In between are countries that have chosen to regulate surrogacy. The United Kingdom was one of the first to legislate on the issue.

Surrogacy agreements came into prominence in the United Kingdom as a result of the much publicised 'Baby Cotton' case,[256] which was believed to be the first UK case of a commercially arranged surrogacy agreement.[257] That case aroused public debate about the desirability of such agreements in general and of commercial surrogacy in particular. Notwithstanding that the weight of public opinion seemed to be against the practice of surrogacy,[258] the Warnock Committee did not recommend imposing a complete ban. Instead they recommended that it be a criminal offence for a person to be involved in negotiating or making a surrogacy arrangement on a commercial basis.[259]

Adopting the Warnock recommendation, s 2(1) of the Surrogacy Arrangements Act 1985 provides:

> No person shall on a commercial basis do any of the following acts in the United Kingdom, that is—
>
> (a) initiate or take part in any negotiations with a view to the making of a surrogacy arrangement,
> (b) offer or agree to negotiate the making of a surrogacy arrangement, or
> (c) compile any information with a view to its use in making, or negotiating the making, of surrogacy arrangements,
>
> and no person shall in the United Kingdom knowingly cause another to do any of those acts on a commercial basis.

These offences have since been relaxed inasmuch as a non-profit making body does not commit an offence because it or another receives any 'reasonable payment.[260]

Section 3 also makes it an offence for *anyone* to advertise that a woman is willing to enter into or to facilitate the making of a surrogacy arrangement or that any person is looking for a woman to become a surrogate mother.[261] Again this offence has been relaxed in relation to non-profit making bodies.[262]

To constitute an offence, the arrangement must be made before the surrogate mother begins to carry the child, and it must be made with a view to the child being handed over to, and the parental responsibility being exercised (so far as practicable) by, another person or persons. The surrogate mother and the commissioning parents are excluded from

---

[255] J Stoll *Surrogacy Arrangements and Legal Parenthood* (2013) at p 31.

[256] Reported as *Re C (A Minor) (Wardship: Surrogacy)* [1985] FLR 846.

[257] But it was not the first surrogacy agreement to come before the court: see *A v C* [1985] FLR 445, CA (decided in 1978).

[258] Cmnd 9314 at para 8.10.   [259] At para 8.18.

[260] Surrogacy Arrangements Act 1985 s 2(2A)–(2C), added by the HFEA 2008 s 59. For a case in which solicitors acted in breach of s 2(1), see *JP v LP and Others (Surrogacy Arrangement: Wardship)* [2014] EWHC 595 (Fam), [2014] Fam Law 813.

[261] The maximum penalty for involvement in a surrogacy arrangement is imprisonment for up to three months and a fine not exceeding level five, and for unlawful advertising, a fine not exceeding that level. The consent of the Director of Public Prosecutions is necessary for prosecution to be brought.

[262] Surrogacy Arrangements Act 1985 s 3(1A), added by the HFEA 2008 s 59(7).

liability for their participation in the arrangements (though they can be liable for the advertising offence). Furthermore, it is only an offence knowingly to assist in the negotiations for a commercial surrogacy arrangement.[263]

Although the participating individuals might not commit an offence under the 1985 Act, in cases where the arrangement was expressly made *with a view to the child's adoption* by the commissioning parents, if money is paid or agreed to be paid, the contracting parties prima facie commit an offence under the adoption legislation.[264] Now, however, as discussed in the next section, courts can make a 'parental order', so that a child born as a result of a surrogacy arrangement will be treated as that of the commissioning parents, if a number of conditions are met. Hence, provided arrangements do not infringe the Surrogacy Arrangements Act 1985, those made in contemplation of a parental order cannot be held illegal.

The availability of a parental order does not solve all problems about enforceability. What, for example, is the position if the surrogate mother refuses to hand over the child, or if the commissioning parents refuse to accept the child? In its original form, notwithstanding the recommendation of the Warnock Committee,[265] the 1985 Act was silent on whether surrogacy arrangements were enforceable, although the generally accepted view was that they were not. The matter was settled by s 1A of the Surrogacy Arrangements Act 1985,[266] which unequivocally states that 'No surrogacy arrangement is enforceable by or against any of the persons making it'.

Given that such arrangements are unenforceable, what then happens to the child? If there is no dispute between the parties, there is no compulsion to go to court. However, given that the surrogate mother will be treated as the child's legal mother even if she is not the genetic mother,[267] it is advisable for the commissioning parents to seek a parental order. As Theis J commented in *J v G (Parental Orders)*, 'The legal relationship between a child born as a result of surrogacy arrangements and their intended parents is not on a secure footing without a s 54 order being made. The message needs to go out loud and clear to encourage parental order applications to be made in respect of children being born as a result of international surrogacy agreements, and for them to be made promptly.'[268]

If they are unable to apply for a parental order because, for example, the surrogate mother has withdrawn her consent or has refused to hand over the child, the commissioning parents can still seek a s 8 order[269] under the Children Act 1989.

It is clear that in resolving any disputes the court is bound to treat the child's welfare as its paramount consideration and is not bound by the terms of the agreement.[270] In

---

[263] It is not an offence to help in carrying out the arrangement after it has been made. An unsuccessful attempt was made to change this in the Surrogacy Arrangements (Amendment) Bill 1986.

[264] Viz. Adoption and Children Act 2002 s 95, though the court can subsequently authorise payment, see the discussion in Ch 19, Illegal payments, pp 729ff. For the position with regard to parental orders, see Conditions for making orders, p 278.   [265] Cmnd 9314 at para 8.19.

[266] Introduced by s 36(1) of the HFEA 1990.

[267] Under s 33 of the HFEA 2008, discussed at Who is the legal mother? p 246. Furthermore, if she is married and conception has resulted from assisted reproduction methods (commonly surrogacy agreements take the form of the woman agreeing to be artificially inseminated with the commissioning man's semen), her husband may be treated as the legal father pursuant to s 35 of the 2008 Act (discussed at The position under the Human Fertilisation and Embryology Act 2008, p 254).

[268] [2013] EWHC 1432 (Fam) [2014] 1 FLR 297, at [30].   [269] Discussed in Ch 14.

[270] Section 1(1) of the Children Act 1989. Nevertheless, it seems likely that if the carrying mother wishes to keep the child and is in a position to give the child a loving and caring home, she will be allowed to do so—cf *Re P (Residence: Appeal)* [2007] EWCA Civ 1053 [2008] 1 FLR 198; *A v C* [1985] FLR 445, CA and *Re P (Minors) (Wardship: Surrogacy)* [1987] 2 FLR 421; cf in the USA the notorious decision *Re Baby M* 537 A 2d 1227 (1988) in which the terms of the agreement were applied.

applying the welfare test in this context it has been said[271] that the court should ask itself in which home the child was most likely to mature into a happy and balanced adult and to achieve his or her fullest potential. Another possibility, provided the child is handed over, is for the commissioning parents to apply to adopt the child.[272]

Whether the current law adequately balances all the relevant interests can be debated. Some additional protection is afforded to the child, or potential child, inasmuch as local authorities have responsibilities to ensure that the child is not at risk of harm as a result of a surrogacy agreement, whether or not it is for money.[273] However, the difficulty of the English position in not banning such arrangements even where money changes hands,[274] yet not allowing such arrangements to be enforceable, was highlighted in the Karen Roche case. It seems[275] that this woman, having made an arrangement with a Dutch couple, falsely claimed that she had terminated the pregnancy, and then entered into a second arrangement. Following the disquiet raised by this case, the Government commissioned a review which was conducted under the Chairmanship of Professor Margaret Brazier.[276] That review recommended inter alia that payments to surrogate mothers should only cover genuine expenses associated with the pregnancy and that additional expenses should be prohibited to prevent surrogacy arrangements being entered into for financial benefit and that legislation should define expenses in broad terms of principle and empower Ministers to issue directions on what constitutes reasonable expenses and the methods by which expenses shall be proven. It also recommended that agencies should be required to be registered by UK Health Departments and operate in accordance with a Code of Practice to be drawn by the Department of Health in consultation with the other UK Health Departments. In the event, however, no action has been taken.

12. PARENTAL ORDERS

Notwithstanding that surrogacy arrangements are unenforceable, in cases where the child is handed over to the commissioning parents, legal certainty as to the child's legal parentage can be achieved by the subsequent making of a 'parental order' by which the commissioning parents become the child's legal parents. This order was first introduced (in 1994) by s 30 of the Human Fertilisation and Embryology Act 1990 but has since (from April 2010) been replaced by s 54 of the Human Fertilisation and Embryology Act 2008.[277]

Under s 54 courts are empowered to make an order providing for a child to be treated in law as the child of the applicants in circumstances where the child has been carried by a woman other than one of the applicants as a result of the placing in her of an embryo or sperm and eggs or her artificial fertilisation (whether in the United Kingdom or elsewhere)[278] following the use of gametes of at least one of the applicants. This power is subject to a number of conditions not least of which is that s 54 does not apply if the child

---

[271] Per Baker J in *Re T T (Surrogacy)* [2011] EWHC 33 (Fam) [2011] 2 FLR 392.

[272] As happened in *C and C (Petitioners and Respondents to Adopt X)* [1997] Fam Law 226.

[273] See DHSS Circular LAC 85 (12).

[274] Under British Medical Association guidelines, surrogate mothers can be paid 'reasonable expenses' of up to £10,000. See M Hibbs 'Surrogacy Legislation—Time for Change' [1997] Fam Law 564 at 565.

[275] See M Hibbs 'Surrogacy Legislation—Time for Change' [1997] Fam Law 564.

[276] *Surrogacy: Review for Health Ministers of Current Arrangements for Payments and Regulation* (1998) Cm 4068.

[277] Orders made under s 30 of the HFEA 1990 remain in force: HFEA 2008 s 57(4).

[278] Section 54(10).

was conceived as the result of normal intercourse between the husband and the surrogate mother.[279]

(a) Who can apply

The key change introduced by the 2008 Act was to broaden those entitled to apply for such an order beyond a married couple. By s 54(2) applications for parental orders can be made not just by a husband and wife but also civil partners or two persons who are living as partners in an enduring family relationship and who are not within the prohibited degrees of relationship to each other.[280] 'Partners living in an enduring relationship' is not defined but is intended to cover different and same sex couples living together but precisely what ranks as an 'enduring relationship' remains to be seen.

Applications can only be made by couples and not a single individual but it has been held,[281] provided an application was duly made by a couple, it is no objection that one dies before the application is heard. Why individuals are barred from applying may in any event be questioned particularly as there is no equivalent bar for adoptive applicants, nor are single women denied access to assisted procreation treatment.[282]

(b) Conditions for making orders

Both applicants must be at least 18 and at least one must be domiciled in part of the United Kingdom or the Channel Islands or Isle of Man.[283] The Act is silent as to whether the *child* should be habitually resident in the UK but according to Hedley J in *Re K (Foreign Surrogacy)*,[284] there is such a requirement and in consequence there is no power to 'progress a case' until the child is in the jurisdiction. Accordingly, it is not possible for the court to give an indication to the immigration authorities as to the likelihood of success of the parental order application. This is likely to cause difficulties in inter-country surrogacy arrangements in which the commissioning parents are seeking entry clearance for the child in order to make a s 54 application.[285]

The application must be made within six months of the child's birth.[286] At the time of the application the child's home must be with the applicants[287] (or applicant, if one of them has died).[288]

Before any order can be made, the court must be satisfied that the carrying woman *and* any other person who is a parent of the child but is not one of the applicants (including a man who is the father by virtue of HFEA 2008 ss 35 or 36[289] or any woman who is a parent by virtue of HFEA ss 42 or 43 (which have extra-territorial effect)[290] have freely and with full understanding of what is involved, agreed unconditionally to the making of an

---

[279] See eg *Re Adoption Application (Payment for Adoption)* [1987] Fam 81. See also *M v F and H (Legal Paternity)* [2014] 1 FLR 352.
[280] Section 54(2)(c). See s 58(2) for those persons who fall within the prohibited degrees. See further Ch 24.   [281] *A v P* [2011] EWHC 1738 (Fam) [2012] Fam 188.
[282] See the comment by R Fenton, S Heenan, and J Rees 'Finally fit for purpose? The Human Fertilisation and Embryology Act 2008' (2008) 32 JSWFL 275 at 281.
[283] HFEA 2008 s 54(4)(b) and (5), on which see *Z and B v C (Parental Order: Domicile)* [2011] EWHC 3181 (Fam) [2012] 2 FLR 797 and *Re A and B (Parental Order: Domicile)* [2013] EWHC 426 (Fam) [2014] 1 FLR 169. In both these cases the applicants discharged the burden that on the balance of probabilities they had abandoned their domicile of origin and acquired a domicile of choice in the UK.
[284] [2010] EWHC 1180 (Fam) [2011] 1 FLR 533, at [6].
[285] On which, see the UK Border Agency's guidance 'Inter-Country Surrogacy and Immigration Rules'.
[286] Section 54(3).   [287] Section 54(4)(a).
[288] *A v P* [2011] EWHC 1738 (Fam) [2012] Fam 188.
[289] Or by virtue of HFEA 1990 s 28(2) or (3), see *Re Q (Parental Order)* [1996] 1 FLR 369.
[290] *Re X (Children) (Parental Order: Surrogacy)* [2008] EWHC 3030 (Fam) [2009] 2 WLR 1274.

order[291] (ie not to the application). Unlike adoption there is no general power to dispense with the required agreements, although agreement is not required of a person who cannot be found or is incapable of giving agreement.[292] Furthermore, the agreement of the woman who carried the child is ineffective if given by her less than six weeks after the child's birth.[293] As Hedley J pointed out in *Re IJ (Foreign Surrogacy Agreement: Parental Order)*[294] this latter requirement will often mean that a second consent be obtained since overseas law may require consent at or before birth or on handing over the child.

The court must be satisfied that no money or other benefit (save for expenses reasonably incurred, such as the surrogate's expenses for maternity clothes, travel for the assisted reproduction treatment and for antenatal check-ups, and possibly for her loss of earnings consequent on giving up work to have the baby) has been given, paid or received by the spouses in connection with the making of the order, the giving of agreement, the handing over of the child or the making of any arrangements with a view to the making of the order.[295] 'Payments' for these purposes include not just those paid to the surrogate but also those paid, for example, to the organisation or agency making the arrangements.[296]

It is for the applicants to establish that any payments do not offend this restriction.[297] Payments can, however, be authorised by the court and it is well established that such authorisation can be given retrospectively. Indeed there is a growing jurisprudence on the approach that a court should adopt when considering authorising payments. In *Re X (Children) (Parental Order: Surrogacy)*,[298] Hedley J considered there were two basic questions namely (a) whether the payment is indeed for 'expenses reasonably incurred' (a pure question of fact); and (b) if not, whether the court should authorise such payments. However, there is no statutory guidance as to the basis upon which approval should be given though it is clearly a policy decision that on the one hand commercial surrogacy agreements should not be regarded as lawful and on the other that there may be reasons for making payments over and above reasonable expenses based upon the child's welfare. With this in mind Hedley J considered that the court should pose itself these questions:

(1) Was the sum paid disproportionate to reasonable expenses?

(2) Were the applicants acting in good faith and without 'moral taint' in their dealings with the surrogate mother?

(3) Were the applicants party to any attempt to defraud the authorities?

In practice payments are normally authorised.[299] In *Re S (Parental Order)*,[300] a couple having made a 'Gestational Surrogacy Agreement' in California sought a parental order in England.

---

[291] HFEA 2008 s 54(6). Agreements may be in the form referred to in *Practice Direction 5A* or in a form to like effect: FPR 2010 r 13.11, on which see *Re A and B (Parental Order: Domicile)* [2013] EWHC 426 (Fam) [2014] 1 FLR 169.

[292] HFEA 2008 s 54(7). To satisfy the court that the person cannot be found, all reasonable steps to locate that person must have been taken: *Re D (Children) (Parental Order: Foreign Surrogacy) (Practice Note)* [2012] EWHC 2631 (Fam) [2013] 1 WLR 3135.   [293] HFEA 2008 s 54(7).

[294] [2011] EWHC 921(Fam) [2011] 2 FLR 646.

[295] HFEA 2008 s 54(8). As a matter of practice whenever a s 54(8) issue arises for serious consideration, the children should ordinarily be separately represented by a guardian: *Re S (Parental Order)* [2009] EWHC 2977 (Jud) [2010] 1 FLR 1156 at [9], per Hedley J.

[296] *Re PM (Parental Orders: Payments To Surrogacy Agency)* [2013] EWHC 2328 (Fam) [2014] 1 FLR 725.

[297] *Re S (Parental Order)* [2009] EWHC 2977 (Jud), [2010] 1 FLR 1156.

[298] [2008] EWHC 3030 (Fam) [2009] 2 WLR 1274. This approach was endorsed by Wall P in *Re X and Y (Parental Order: Retrospective Authorisation of Payments)* [2011] EWHC 3147 (Fam) [2012] 1 FLR 1347.

[299] Indeed, at the time of writing there has been no reported instance of payments not being authorised.

[300] [2009] EWHC 2977 (Jud) [2010] 1 FLR 1156.

It was found that payments had been made to the surrogate mother which, though lawful in California, nevertheless contravened what is now HFEA 2008 s 54(8) (then HFEA 1990 s 30(7)). In Hedley J's view that arrangement clearly raised matters of public policy such that it was incumbent upon the court to (a) ensure that commercial surrogacy arrangements are not used to circumvent childcare laws resulting in the approval of arrangements in favour of people who would not have been approved as parents under any set of circumstances; (b) be astute not to be involved in anything that looks like the simple payment for effectively buying children overseas; and (c) be astute to ensure that sums of money which might look modest in themselves are not in fact of such a substance that they overbear the will of a surrogate. In *Re S*, however, the payments were found not to offend any broad issue of principle and they were accordingly approved and the order made. Similarly, in *Re L (A Child) (Parental Order: Foreign Surrogacy)*, in the context of a commercial surrogacy arrangement made lawfully in Illinois, USA, Hedley J again authorised the payments and made a parental order. In doing so, he observed that the approach set out in *Re S* above, in relation to the 1990 Act, continues to hold good under the 2008 Act but, given that the weight that is now to be put on the child's welfare in these cases has shifted from being 'first' to being 'paramount', the balance between public policy considerations and welfare had shifted decisively in favour of the latter. Consequently 'it will only be in the clearest case of abuse of public policy that the court will be able to withhold an order if otherwise welfare considerations support its making'.[301] Whilst acknowledging that 'reasonable expenses' remains a somewhat opaque concept, he nevertheless treated any payment described as 'compensation' as prima facie being payments going beyond reasonable expenses. At the same time he emphasised that each case has to be scrutinised on its own facts.

Failure to meet any of the above requirements is fatal to a s 54 application.[302]

(c) The governing principles in determining applications

Somewhat questionably, the governing principles in determining whether or not to make a parental order are not provided by the 2008 Act but by secondary legislation, namely, the Human Fertilisation and Embryology Regulations 2010,[303] which in turn apply s 1 of the Adoption and Children Act 2002.

The 2010 Regulations brought about the long overdue but important change that, by applying s 1(2) of the 2002 Act, the court must give *paramount* consideration to the child's welfare throughout his life when deciding whether or not to make a parental order. Previously, the court was bound by s 6 of the Adoption Act 1976, to give *first* (but not paramount) consideration 'to the need to safeguard and promote the welfare of the child throughout his childhood'. Anomalously, this enjoinder remained in place notwithstanding the changed position for adoption under the 2002 Act. Now, however, the governing principles for making parental orders have been brought into line with those governing adoption. As has just been discussed, the switch to the paramountcy test means that it is even less likely that an order which is otherwise in the child's interests will be refused because of payments made by the applicants.

---

[301] [2010] EWHC 3146 (Fam) [2011] Fam 106, at [10]. See also *D v L (Surrogacy)* [2012] EWHC 2631 (Fam) [2013] 2 FLR 275; *J v G (Parental Orders* [2013] EWHC 1432 (Fam) [2014] 1 FLR 297; and *Re PM (Parental Orders: Payments To Surrogacy Agency)* [2013] EWHC 2328 (Fam) [2014] 1 FLR 725.

[302] See *JP v LP and Others (Surrogacy Arrangement: Wardship)* [2014] EWHC 595 (Fam), [2014] Fam Law 813—time limit not complied with but a solution was found in wardship (discussed at Use in private law cases, p 761) and *Re G (Surrogacy: Foreign Domicile)* [2007] EWHC 2814 (Fam) [2008] 1 FLR 1047—applicants were domiciled in Turkey. In the event an order was made under the Adoption and Children Act 2002 s 84 giving them exclusive parental responsibility. This power is discussed in Ch 26.

[303] SI 2010/985. See reg 2 and Sch 1. The 2010 Regulations replaced the Parental Orders (Human Fertilisation and Embryology) Regulations 1994.

In applying the paramountcy principle the court is bound to apply the welfare checklist under s 1(4) of the 2002 Act, as amended. It is also bound by s 1(6) to consider the whole range of its powers and only to make an order if it is better for the child to do so than making no order.[304]

The procedure for applying for parental orders is governed by the Family Procedure Rules 2010 Part 13. As soon as practicable after the issue of proceedings the court must set a date for the first directions hearing (or, if it is appropriate, give such directions) and for the hearing of the application.[305] It must also appoint a parental order reporter. Such a reporter is appointed to act on behalf of the child who is the subject of the proceedings and has a duty to safeguard the interests of that child. The reporter's duties are to (a) investigate the matters set out in s 54(1)–(8) of HFEA 2008; (b) investigate, so far as the reporter considers necessary, any matter (contained in the application form or otherwise) which appears relevant to the making of a parental order; and (c) advise the court on whether there is a reason under s 1 of the 2002 Act to refuse the making of a parental order. The reporter's confidential report is filed with the court which then has to consider whether or not it should be disclosed to a party.[306] It has been observed[307] that 'an application for a parental order should be treated with the same care and caution that attends every application for an adoption order.'

(d) The effect of making an application and of making an order

The effects of making an application and order are governed by the Adoption and Children Act 2002, as applied by the 2010 Regulations.

While an application is pending, no parent or guardian can remove the child from the applicant's home against the applicant's will without leave of the court.[308]

The effect of parental orders is the same as adoption. Consequently, such orders vest parental responsibility for the child exclusively in the applicants, and extinguish the parental responsibility any person had before the order.[309] They also extinguish any prior order under the Children Act 1989 and any previous duty to make maintenance payments.[310] They confer British citizenship upon the child if one of the applicants is such a citizen.[311]

The child who is the subject of a parental order is treated in law 'as if he had been born as the child of the' persons who obtained the order and as the legitimate child of such persons.[312] However, notwithstanding the making of a parental order the child stays within the prohibited degrees with his birth family for the purpose of marriage and incest.[313] For the purpose of disposition of property, while the 'section 54 child' is not to be treated as the child of any other person other than the new parents this does not prejudice any interest or expectant interest vested in possession before the making of the parental order.[314]

---

[304] See *Re L (A Child) (Parental Order: Foreign Surrogacy)* [2010] EWHC 3146 (Fam) [2011] Fam 106. Note also *A v P* [2011] EWHC 1738 (Fam) [2012] Fam 188.

[305] FPR 2010 r 13.5.   [306] FPR 2010 r 13.12.

[307] Per Hedley J in *G v G (Parental Order: Revocation)* [2012] EWHC 1979 (Fam) [2013] 1 FLR 286 at [45].

[308] Adoption and Children Act 2002 s 36(1) as applied to parental orders by the 2010 Regulations.

[309] Section 46, as applied by the 2010 Regulations.

[310] Section 46 (2)(d) as applied by the 2010 Regulations.

[311] British Nationality Act 1981 s 1 (5). Nevertheless, it is not necessary, as a matter of course in cases involving overseas surrogacy agreements, to give notice to the Home Office, per Hedley J in *Re IJ (Foreign Surrogacy Agreement: Parental Order)* [2011] EWHC 921 (Fam) [2011] 2 FLR 646.

[312] Section 67(1) and (2) of the 2002 Act, as applied by the 2010 Regulations.

[313] Section 74(1) and (2) of the 2002 Act, as applied by the 2010 Regulations.

[314] Sections 67 and 69–73 of the 2002 Act, as applied by the 2010 Regulations.

Parental orders take effect from the date when they are made or such later date as the court may specify.[315] Once made, since the effect of a parental order is akin to that of adoption and in the absence of a statutory power to set aside such orders, the court should only exercise its inherent power to do so in the same type of extreme circumstances as established for adoption. This was Hedley J's reasoning in *G v G (Parental Order: Revocation)*[316] in refusing to set aside a parental order notwithstanding the commissioning couple's subsequent separation (which the mother had anticipated at the time of the order being made) and the undoubted serious procedural flaws in the proceedings leading to the order.

Within seven days of the making of the final order, or such shorter time as the court may direct, copies of the order should be sent by the court officer inter alia to the applicant and to the Registrar General.[317] All parental orders are registered in a Parental Order Register maintained by the Registrar General in the General Register Office.[318] Upon request, the Registrar General is obliged to cause a search to be made of the register on behalf of an applicant or to permit that person to search himself and to issue to any person a certified copy of any entry on the register.[319] Provision is also made for the person who is the subject of a parental order and who has attained the age of 18 years, to be supplied with information enabling him to obtain a certified copy of the record of his birth, having first been advised of the counselling services available to him.[320]

(e) Use made of parental orders

Official statistics on parental orders are not published but figures have been obtained by Crawshaw et al.[321] These show that between 1995 and 2011 833 parental orders were registered in the United Kingdom, the vast majority being in England and Wales. In 2011, 149 parental orders were registered in the United Kingdom, 133 of which were registered in England and Wales. The number of such orders seems to be rising. One surprising finding was that of the orders registered in 2011, only 26% involved children born abroad, though this finding should be treated with some caution as there is no obligation to record the child's place of birth and the finding is based on a low number of cases where the information was recorded.

(f) Commentary

Parental orders are sometimes referred to as 'fast-track' adoptions but while there is an obvious analogy between the two orders not least in their effect, the crucial difference lies at the initial stages of the arrangements. Whereas adoption is subject to close control throughout and indeed it is an offence for an individual to place a child for adoption

---

[315] FPR 2010 r 13.20(1). In proceedings in Wales a party may request that an order be drawn up in Welsh, r 13.20(2).

[316] [2012] EWHC 1979 (Fam) [2013] 1 FLR 286. The power to set side adoption orders is discussed in Ch 19, Setting adoptions aside, p 723.

[317] FPR 2010 r 13.21(1). Notice of the making of a final order or an order quashing or revoking a parental order or allowing an appeal against an order in proceedings should also be sent by the court officer to every respondent and, with court permission, any other person: FPR 2010 r 13.21(c). Notice of an order should also be sent to the principal registry if it appears to the court officer that a parental responsibility agreement has been recorded there: FPR 2010, r 13.21(2)(b).   [318] Section 77 as applied by the 2010 Regulations.

[319] Section 78 as applied by the 2010 Regulations.

[320] Section 79(7) as applied by the 2010 Regulations.

[321] M Crawshaw, E Blyth and O van den Akker 'The changing profile of surrogacy in the UK—Implications for national and international policy' (2012) 34 JSWFL 267, Table 1. Slightly updated figures can be found in J Stoll *Surrogacy Arrangements and Legal Parenthood* (2013) at 188, who found that in England, 586 orders were registered between 2002 and 2012, 409 being made under s 30 of the HFEA 1990 and 177 under s 54 of HFEA 2008.

privately with a non-relative,[322] in the case of parental orders there is a complete absence of regulation on the placement of the child with the applicants[323] and indeed of making a surrogacy agreement in the first place. Another difference is that there is no equivalent to the post adoption support service in the context of parental orders though some UK surrogacy agencies do offer ongoing support.[324] A third difference, which might merit further review, is that unlike adoption there is no general power to dispense with parental consent to the making of parental orders, indeed save where a parent cannot be found, parental consent is required to the making of the application.

Parental orders should be seen as part of the overall legal response to surrogacy. They were originally introduced as a hurried response to the high profile Cumbria case,[325] which at the time of the passage of the 1990 Human Fertilisation and Embryology Bill, drew attention to the difficulties (viz. the illegality of private placements, if neither were genetically connected to the child) and the questionable appropriateness of commissioning couples having to adopt the child if one of them was the genetic parent, which was then the only legal means of securing their position as parents. Although it would have been possible to have adapted adoption to meet the needs of commissioning parents and although s 30 bore all the hallmarks of being drafted to meet a specific case, nevertheless having such a dedicated order has its merits since the regularisation of a successful surrogacy arrangement is not on all fours with adoption.

In fact the United Kingdom is not alone in having such dedicated orders. A similar scheme operates in Australia for example.[326] Such orders also exist in Israel, though in that jurisdiction, there is strict State control on who can enter into surrogacy agreements in first place.[327] An altogether different approach has been adopted in Greece.[328] There, it is necessary to obtain prior court approval for what are known as gestational surrogacies (the only circumstance in which surrogacy is permitted in Greece), but where that has been obtained the commissioning mother is the legal mother regardless of her genetic connection with the child and not the woman giving birth. In many other countries, however, there is a striking absence of legislation.[329]

Notwithstanding the figures just mentioned it is evident that a significant number of surrogacy arrangements even in the United Kingdom are made abroad and as the

---

[322] Adoption and Children Act 2002 s 92.

[323] One possible control, namely the requirement to register as a private foster parent, does not apply during the pendency of an application for a parental order: Children Act 1989 Sch 8 para 5 as applied by the 2010 Regulations Sch 4 para 12.

[324] See M Crawshaw, E Blyth and O van den Akker 'The changing profile of surrogacy in the UK – Implications for national and international policy' (2012) 34 JSWFL 267.

[325] Subsequently reported as *Re W (Minors) (Surrogacy)* [1991] 1 FLR 385 and discussed earlier at Who is the legal mother? p 246.

[326] Such orders are known as 'parentage orders', see M Keyes in K Trimmings and P Beaumont (eds) *International Surrogacy Arrangements Legal Regulation at the International Level* (2013) ch 2, p 27. See also M Henaghan 'International commercial surrogacy and the judiciary' [2013] IFL 198.

[327] Such orders are also known as 'parentage orders', see J Stoll *Surrogacy Arrangements and Legal Parenthood* (2013) ch 5 and S Shakargy in K Trimmings and P Beaumont (eds) *International Surrogacy Arrangements: Legal Regulation at the International Level* (2012) ch 14.

[328] See J Stoll *Surrogacy Arrangements and Legal Parenthood* (2013) at 2.9 and 7.4.2; K Rokas in K Trimmings and P Beaumont (eds) *International Surrogacy Arrangements Legal Regulation at the International Level* (2012) ch 9; and E Kounougeri-Manoledaki 'Surrogate motherhood in Greece (according to the new law on assisted reproduction)' in A Bainham (ed) *The International Survey of Family Law* (2005) p 267.

[329] See the various country reports in K Trimmings and P Beaumont (eds) *International Surrogacy Arrangements: Legal Regulation at the International Level* (2012).

judiciary have commented on several occasions they are fraught with difficulty. It would seem desirable therefore that there should be some form of international control along the lines, perhaps of the 1993 Hague Intercountry Convention and indeed this is a project high on the agenda of the Hague Conference.[330]

C. GUARDIANSHIP

As we discuss at the end of this chapter, the term 'guardian' has a variety of meanings, but the specific concern here is the institution of legal guardianship over children during their minority. Formerly, the concept of guardianship was complex but following its reform by the Children Act 1989 it can now be said to be the legal status under which a person has parental responsibility for a child following the death of one or both of the child's parents. In short, a 'guardian' is someone who has been formally appointed to take the place of the child's deceased parent during the child's minority.

1. THE POSITION BEFORE THE CHILDREN ACT 1989

Before its reform, guardianship had become a complicated product of common law, equity and statute.[331] Its early history was succinctly described by the Law Commission as follows:[332]

> The institution of guardianship was originally of concern only to those who had property. It began as a lucrative incident of feudal tenure and developed as a means of safeguarding a family's property and securing its transmission from one generation to another. Subsequently it became the instrument for maintaining the authority of the father over the upbringing of his children.

The pre-1989 Act law recognised both parental and non-parental guardianship. With regard to the former, notwithstanding the general equalisation of spouses' rights,[333] it remained the case that during his lifetime the father was the sole guardian of his legitimate children. It was only upon his death that the mother became a guardian either alone or jointly with any other guardians appointed by the father. The common law made no provision for guardianship of illegitimate children and, even though the mother was eventually recognised[334] as having exclusive parental rights and duties, she was not formally regarded as a guardian.[335] In relation to non-parental guardianship, statute

---

[330] See the thoughtful contribution by H Baker 'A Possible Future Instrument on International Surrogacy Arrangements: Are There Lessons to be Learnt from the 1993 Hague Intercountry Adoption Convention?' in K Trimmings and P Beaumont (eds) *International Surrogacy Arrangements: Legal Regulation at the International Level* (2012) ch 26. The 1993 Convention is discussed in Ch 26.

[331] For an excellent summary of the history see the Law Commission Working Paper No 91 on *Guardianship* (1985), Part 11. For a detailed history see eg Holdsworth *History of English Law* (7th edn, 1966) Vol 111. See also H Bevan *Child Law* (1989) ch 4, and ch 10 of the 7th edition of this work.

[332] In their Working Paper No 91 at para 3.1.

[333] See Ch 9, The changing nature of the parent–child relationship, pp 307ff.

[334] Children Act 1975 s 85(1).

[335] Though in *Re A* (1940) 164 LT 230 it was held that the Guardianship of Infants Act 1925 had given the mother the right to appoint a testamentary guardian for her illegitimate child.

eventually conferred[336] equal rights on mothers and fathers to appoint a testamentary guardian in respect of legitimate children, with the mother having the exclusive right to do so in the case of her illegitimate children. Testamentary appointments took effect upon the death of the appointing parent even if the other parent was still alive. However, if the latter objected, he or she could apply to the court to prevent the appointee from acting. A guardian could also apply to court if he considered the parent unfit to have custody, and the court had various powers to resolve such disputes.[337]

Historically, the law recognised two separate functions of guardians: the protection of the person and the protection of the property of the ward. These functions could be split between guardians of the person, with no right to control the ward's property, and guardians of the estate, with no right to control the ward's person.

Guardians (unless of the estate only) had broadly similar rights and duties with respect to the child as a parent,[338] but they were not in exactly the same position.[339] For example, unlike parents, guardians could not be made liable to maintain their wards, nor could they appoint a guardian themselves. On the other hand, they probably had wider powers than parents in respect of the child's property.[340] There was uncertainty as to whether a guardian had a right of access to the child and, indeed, as to who had the right to care and control of the child where the parent was still alive.

As the Law Commission concluded,[341] the interrelationship between the legal status of parent and guardian was obscure, particularly where the parent was also described as a guardian. Furthermore, the notion of parental guardianship confused the separate legal concepts of parenthood and guardianship. The Commission considered that it was both sensible and practical to regard parenthood as the primary concept and to distinguish it from the role of a guardian who acts in loco parentis.[342] Accordingly they recommended abolishing the rule under which parents, who for all practical purposes had the same rights and authority, were sometimes guardians and sometimes not.[343] On the other hand, although little was known about the frequency of guardianship appointments,[344] the Commission considered[345] that the law should provide some means of appointing a person or persons who could step into the shoes of a parent or parents who have died. Following consultation the Commission found unanimous support for the power both of the parents and courts to appoint guardians.[346] Save for the abolition of guardians of the estate,[347] the Law Commission's recommendations for reforming guardianship were enacted by the Children Act 1989.

---

[336] Restricted rights were first conferred by the Guardianship of Infants Act 1886 and equal rights by the Guardianship of Infants Act 1925, which was then consolidated by the Guardianship of Minors Act 1971.

[337] See pp 352–3 of the 7th edition of this work.

[338] For example, both had a statutory right to consent to the marriage of a child under the age of 18 and to agree to the child's adoption.

[339] For a detailed analysis of the former position see Law Commission Working Paper No 91, paras 2.24–2.35, and pp 355–60 of the 7th edition of this work.

[340] For example, a guardian but not a parent could give a valid receipt on the child's behalf for a legacy: see Law Com Working Paper No 91, para 2.33.   [341] Working Paper No 91 para 2.35.

[342] Working Paper No 91 para 3.2.

[343] Law Com Report No 172 on *Guardianship and Custody* (1988) para 2.2.

[344] Though they did commission a small study undertaken by Priest in the North East of England—see Appendix B of Working Paper No 91.

[345] Working Paper No 91 para 3.17.

[346] Law Com No 172 para 2.2.   [347] Law Com No 172 para 2.24.

2. THE CURRENT LAW

The law of guardianship is now governed by s 5 and s 6 of the Children Act 1989.[348] The concept of *parental* guardianship has been abolished[349] and, save for the exceptional case where the unmarried father without parental responsibility becomes a guardian,[350] the status is now confined to those non-parents formally appointed to take the place of a deceased parent or parents.

With one exception different types of guardians cannot be appointed. This exception, preserved by s 5(11) and (12), is the High Court's inherent power to appoint a guardian of a child's estate. This power is limited in that only the Official Solicitor can be so appointed, and even then only when persons with parental responsibility have signified their consent to the court or when, in the court's opinion, such consent cannot be obtained or may be dispensed with.[351] Appointments may be made only in certain defined circumstances, for example, when the Criminal Injuries Compensation Authority has made or intends to make an award to the child, when payment to the child has been ordered by a foreign court or tribunal, or when the child is entitled to the proceeds of a pension fund, and in any other case where, in the court's view, such an appointment seems desirable.[352] In practice such appointments are likely to be confined to cases where the parents are dead or where it is unsuitable for them to be involved (for example, where they had caused injuries to the child in respect of which compensation has been paid).

Guardians of the estate apart, all guardians have parental responsibility for the child,[353] which effectively places them in the same legal position as parents, at least so far as the care and upbringing of the child is concerned. The conferment of full parental responsibility was central to the role of guardians as envisaged by the Law Commission. As they put it:[354]

> The power to control a child's upbringing should go hand in hand with the responsibility to look after him or at least to see that he is properly looked after. Consultation confirmed our impression that it is now generally expected that guardians will take over any responsibility for the care and upbringing of a child if the parents die. If so, it is right that full legal responsibility should also be placed upon them.

One consequence of having parental responsibility is that guardians can themselves appoint guardians. Appointments can also be made by a parent with parental responsibility or by a court.

[348] This is not to say that an English court will not recognise a guardianship appointment made abroad. Indeed it is bound to recognise a guardianship order competently made in another EU State (other than Denmark) under the terms of Council Regulation (EC) No 2201/2003 of 27 November 2003 ('Brussels II Revised') see Art 21, guardianship being expressly included in the meaning of 'parental responsibility' by Art 2(b). Nevertheless it remains a moot point whether a foreign appointed guardian qualifies as a 'guardian' for the purposes of adoption, see generally, N Lowe 'Do Foreign Appointed Guardians Qualify as "Guardians" for the purposes of the Adoption and Children Act 2002?' [2008] Fam Law 163, and see Whose consent is required? p 709.

[349] Following the express abolition of the rule of law that a father is the natural guardian of his legitimate children by the Children Act 1989 s 2(4), and the repeal (by Sch 15) of s 3 of the Guardianship of Minors Act 1971 which provided that upon the death of one parent the other became the guardian of any legitimate child.

[350] Such as upon the mother's death following an appointment by her or by the court.

[351] CPR 1998 r 22.12(2).   [352] CPR 1998 r 22.12(1).   [353] Children Act 1989 s 5(6).

[354] Law Com No 172 para 2.23.

(a) Appointment of guardians

Private appointment of guardians

Any parent with parental responsibility (ie not an unmarried father without such responsibility), any guardian and any special guardian may appoint an individual to be the child's guardian.[355] More than one person may be appointed.[356] Furthermore, an additional guardian or guardians can be appointed at a later date.[357] There is nothing to prevent an appointment being made by two or more persons jointly.[358]

There is no restriction or control upon who may be appointed (even another child, it seems, could be appointed),[359] nor are there any means of scrutinising an appointment unless a dispute or issue is subsequently brought before the court.[360] Appointments can be made only in respect of children under the age of 18.[361]

By s 5(5) an appointment must be made in writing, dated and signed by the person making it. This simpler method of appointment (formerly an appointment had to be by deed or will) was intended to encourage parents (particularly young parents who are notoriously reluctant to make wills) to appoint guardians.[362] Section 5(5) does not preclude appointments being made in a will since such means will satisfy the minimum requirements.[363] An appointment made by will but not signed by the testator will be valid if it is signed at the direction of the testator in accordance with the Wills Act 1837 s 9.[364] An appointment will also be valid in any other case provided it is signed at the direction of the person making the appointment, in his presence and in the presence of two witnesses who each attest the signature.[365] These latter provisions cater for the blind or physically disabled persons who cannot write.[366]

Revoking an appointment

By s 6(1) a later appointment revokes an earlier appointment (including one made in an unrevoked will or codicil) made by the same person in respect of the same child, unless it is clear that the purpose of the later appointment is to appoint an additional guardian. Under s 6(2) the person who made the appointment (including one made in an unrevoked will or codicil) can expressly revoke it in a signed written and dated instrument. Under

---

[355] Section 5(3)–(4) as amended by the Adoption and Children Act 2002.

[356] This is implicit in s 6(1) which refers to 'an additional guardian'. In any event, under the Interpretation Act 1978 s 6(c), unless there is a contrary intention, words in the singular in a statute presumptively include the plural. But 'individual' does not include a 'body': see further, The court's power to appoint guardians, p 290.   [357] Section 6(1).

[358] Section 5(10). Such an appointment only takes effect on the death of all the appointers: see further, When the appointment takes effect, p 288.

[359] Although it seems questionable that one child should have parental responsibility over another, the power can nevertheless occasionally be useful: see *Re A, J and J (minors) (Residence and Guardianship Orders)* [1993] Fam Law 568; see further, When the power may be exercised, p 290 n 391.

[360] See also, Removal by the court, p 291 for discussion of the courts' powers to remove a guardian. The complete absence of regulation is commented upon by G Douglas and N Lowe 'Becoming a Parent in English Law' (1992) 108 LQR 414 at 428.

[361] Section 105(1). Query whether (a) an appointment can take effect once the child is married, or (b) an appointment is valid if made before the child is born but where the child is alive at the appointer's death? See further, Evaluating the law, p 292.   [362] See Law Com No 172 para 2.29.

[363] See Lord Mackay LC's comments at 502 HL Official Report (5th Series), col 1199.

[364] Section 5(5)(a).   [365] Section 5(5)(b).

[366] But not those who are mentally incapacitated: the original Department of Health's *Children Act 1989: Guidance and Regulations*, Vol 1 *Court Orders*, para 2.18. The revised *Children Act 1989: Guidance and Regulations*, Vol 1 *Court Orders* (2008) Department for Children, Schools and Families, para 2.22, however, omits this comment.

s 6(3A) a dissolution or annulment of marriage on or after 1 January 1996 revokes an appointment of the former spouse as a guardian unless a contrary intention appears from the appointment.[367] Similarly, under s 6(3B), in the case of a registered civil partnership the dissolution or annulment of the partnership by a court order revokes an appointment by the former partner unless a contrary intention appears by the appointment.[368] Section 6(4) further provides that an appointment made in a will or codicil is revoked if the will or codicil is revoked. An appointment, *other than* one made by will or codicil, will also be revoked if the person making it destroys the document with the intention of revoking the appointment.[369]

When the appointment takes effect

The appointment normally takes effect upon the death of the sole surviving parent with parental responsibility.[370] If the appointing person is already the sole parent with parental responsibility, then the appointment will take effect immediately upon his death.[371] Under s 5(7)(b),[372] however, an appointment takes effect immediately upon the death of the appointing person if a child arrangements order was in force naming that person as a person with whom the child was to live or upon the death of the only or last surviving special guardian. In these instances, the surviving parent has no right to object, but he can apply to the court for an order ending the appointment.[373] The rationale for delaying the operation of a guardianship appointment is to avoid unnecessary conflict between a surviving parent and a guardian appointed by the deceased parent. As the Law Commission said,[374] there seems little reason why the surviving parent should have to share parental responsibility with a guardian who almost invariably will not be living in the same household. In effect the law protects the surviving parent from interference by an outsider; though, of course, if that parent wishes informally to seek the help of the appointee, he can do so without jeopardising his parental status. In such circumstances, however, the surviving parent cannot object to the appointment, although under s 6(7) he can seek a court order to end it. On the other hand, if the *appointee* wishes to challenge this position, he will need to seek the court's leave to obtain a s 8 order.

While it seems right that appointments should only take effect upon the death of the sole surviving parent with parental responsibility (and furthermore, brought English law into line with the Council of Europe recommendation on guardianship)[375] where the child was living with both parents in a united family before the death of one of them, different considerations apply where the parents are divorced or separated. Endorsing the Law Commission's view,[376] the law takes the position that, if there was a court order that

---

[367] This provision was added by the Law Reform (Succession) Act 1995 (on which see C Barton and R Wells 'A Matter of Life and Death—The Law Reform (Succession) Act 1995' [1996] Fam Law 172 at 174, who make the point that an appointment of a cohabitant would *not* be revoked by the couple's subsequent estrangement). For the purposes of this provision the dissolution or annulment includes both those made by a court of civil jurisdiction in England and Wales and those recognised in England and Wales by Part II of the Family Law Act 1986.

[368] This provision was added by the Civil Partnership Act 2004, s 76. Dissolution or annulment, for these purposes, includes both those made by a court in England and Wales and those recognised in England and Wales: Civil Partnership Act 2004, Part 5, Ch 3: s 6(3B)(b) of the 1989 Act.   [369] Section 6(3).

[370] Section 5(8).   [371] Section 5(7)(a).

[372] As amended by the Children and Families Act 2014 Sch 2 para 2(3).   [373] Section 6(7).

[374] Law Com No 172 para 2.28.

[375] Recommendation R84(4) *Parental Responsibilities*, Principle 9. Indeed, as the Law Commission pointed out (ibid at para 2.27), before the Children Act amendments the UK was the only member country of the Council of Europe that permitted guardianship to operate during the lifetime of a surviving parent.

[376] Law Com No 172 at para 2.28.

the child should live with the parent who had died, that parent should be able to provide for the child's upbringing in the event of his death. Against this, however, it has been commented:[377]

> The survivor will, of course, have joint parental responsibility with the guardian but will have the onus of bringing the child's position before the court in the event of a disagreement between them.[378] This is not very easy to reconcile with the ethos of continuing parental responsibility following divorce. It casts the non-residential parent in the role of an outsider who is liable to interfere with the child rather than that of a concerned parent who is anxious to step into the breach left by the deceased.

In any event, this position creates uncertainty about who is entitled to take over the physical care of the child, since prima facie both the guardian and the surviving parent have equal claims.[379] This standpoint has also been criticised for *not* making provision for cases where the spouses are separated, or even divorced, but where there is no order governing the child's living arrangements.[380] The father, for example, may simply have abandoned his family. As the Scottish Law Commission said:[381]

> In many of these cases it might well be desirable for an appointment of a guardian to be capable of coming into operation, even though there is a surviving parent somewhere.

Disclaiming the appointment

Under s 6(5) there is a formal right for a guardian to disclaim an appointment. This right, which only applies to appointments made by a parent or a guardian (ie not to court appointments), must be exercised 'within a reasonable time of his first knowing that the appointment has taken effect'.[382] Furthermore, it must be disclaimed by a written instrument, signed by the appointee.[383] This power to disclaim an appointment was new to the 1989 Act and, in the words of one commentary,[384] makes 'it all the more important for parents to discuss their proposed appointment with the person concerned. It seems desirable for some official guidance to be published reminding parents of the desirability of prior consultation.'

---

[377] A Bainham *Children: The New Law* (1990), para 2.40.

[378] Under s 6(7), for example, he can seek a court order to end the appointment.

[379] A Bainham and S Gilmore *Children: The Modern Law* (4th edn, 2013) conclude, at p 185 'The rather unsatisfactory outcome . . . is that the onus to commence proceedings will be on the person wishing to change the existing arrangements.'

[380] Such a scenario is now more likely to arise, since it will be by no means uncommon, because of the so-called non-intervention principle under s 1(5), for no orders to have been made.

[381] Scot Law Com No 135 *Report on Family Law* (1992), paras 3–11, repeating what was said in Discussion Paper No 88 *Parental Responsibilities and Rights, Guardianship and the Administration of Children's Property* (1990) para 3.11. Accordingly, no change was recommended, so that in Scotland (see the Children (Scotland) Act 1995 s 7) it remains the case that a guardianship appointment made by the deceased parent comes into effect notwithstanding the survival of the other parent. For an example of where the Scottish position could be advantageous see *Re A, J and J (Minors) (Residence and Guardianship Orders)* [1993] Fam Law 568: see When the power may be exercised, p 290 n 391.

[382] See, by way of example, *Re SH (Care Order: Orphan)* [1995] 1 FLR 746 in which it was said that local authority foster parents intended to revoke a guardianship appointment by the mother.

[383] Under s 6(6). There is provision to make regulations for the recording of such disclaimers (which would then be ineffective unless recorded) but at the time of writing no regulations have been made.

[384] R White, P Carr and N Lowe *The Children Act in Practice* (4th edn, 2008) para 3.124.

(b) The court's power to appoint guardians

When the power may be exercised

By s 5(1) of the 1989 Act a court may appoint an 'individual' to be a child's guardian. By confining the power to the appointment of an 'individual',[385] a court cannot appoint a *body* such as a local authority to be a guardian.[386] This latter restriction is contrary to the recommendations made in the Government White Paper, *The Law on Child Care and Family Services*,[387] and has proved inconvenient.[388] It is suggested that this restriction could usefully be removed.

In line with the general restriction against appointing guardians during the lifetime of a parent with parental responsibility, the court's power arises only if:

(a) the child has no parent with parental responsibility for him; or

(b) a child arrangements order was in force naming the child's parent, guardian or special guardian as a person with whom the child was to live has died [389] or;

(c) paragraph (b) does not apply, and the child's only or last surviving special guardian dies. [390]

Although the first embargo is strict,[391] it nevertheless only applies where the child has no *parent* with parental responsibility. The court can therefore make an appointment even though the child already has a guardian (other than the child's unmarried father)[392] and it can also make an appointment notwithstanding that the child's unmarried father is still alive, provided he does not have parental responsibility.

Who may apply?

The Act is silent as to who can apply to become a guardian, but it is generally thought that *any* individual[393] (including, in theory, a child) may apply to be appointed. There is no requirement that leave of the court must first be obtained.

In respect of whom may applications be made?

An application may be made only in respect of a 'child', that is, a person under the age of 18.[394] There is no express embargo against making an appointment in respect of a married

---

[385] Notwithstanding the use of the singular, by reason of the Interpretation Act 1978 s 6 (c) the court may appoint more than one guardian.

[386] Nor can this embargo be overcome by seeking the appointment of what was described as an 'artificial individual', namely the director of children services: per Hollis J in *Re SH (Care Order: Orphan)* [1995] 1 FLR 746 at 749.   [387] Cm 62, 1987.

[388] See *Birmingham City Council v D, Birmingham City Council v M* [1994] 2 FLR 502, in which the local authority unsuccessfully sought care orders in respect of orphans accommodated by them, essentially in order to obtain parental responsibility; cf *Re SH (Care Order: Orphans)* [1995] 1 FLR 746 and *Re M (Care Order: Parental Responsibility)* [1996] 2 FLR 84, in which, in rather different circumstances, care orders *were* made in respect of orphans.

[389] Section 5(1) as amended by the Children and Families Act 2014, Sch 2, para 2 (2). An exception is where the surviving parent is also named in such a child arrangements order [a residence order was also made in favour of the surviving parent: s 5(9), as amended by Sch 2 Part I para 2 (4) of the 2014 Act.

[390] The references to special guardianship were added by the Adoption and Children Act 2002 s 115(4).

[391] See eg *Re A, J and J (Minors) (Residence and Guardianship Orders)* [1993] Fam Law 568—no power to appoint an elder sibling to be a guardian because father was still alive, notwithstanding that he was living out of the jurisdiction and was believed to be suffering from mental illness.

[392] Since a guardian has parental responsibility (s 5(6)), presumably an unmarried father who is a guardian will be regarded as a 'parent' with parental responsibility for these purposes.

[393] But not a 'body' such as a local authority.   [394] Section 105(1).

child, although it remains to be seen whether in practice the courts would be prepared to make an appointment in such a case.[395] On normal principles of construction there would appear to be no power to appoint a guardian of a child until it is born.[396]

Exercising the power

In accordance with the general principles under s 1, when deciding whether to make an appointment, the court is enjoined to regard the child's welfare as the paramount consideration and to be satisfied that making an order is better than making no order at all. It is not, however, obliged to have specific regard to the welfare checklist set out in s 1(3), though the court is free to do so if it so wishes. There is no restriction comparable to that under s 9(6) with regard to s 8 orders that appointments with respect to 16- or 17-year-olds should only be made in 'exceptional circumstances'.

Since s 5 proceedings rank as 'family proceedings' the court can make, either upon application or upon its own motion, any s 8 order in addition to or instead of appointing a guardian.[397]

Although, the court is empowered to appoint more than one guardian at one time or indeed on different occasions, as has been pointed out,[398] it seems unlikely that a court would appoint a subsequent guardian knowing that the two or more guardians would be in conflict. It has also been said[399] that it would be unusual, though not an absolute bar, to appoint persons as guardians who have never actually seen the children.

In those cases where more than one guardian has been appointed and they are in dispute with each other over the child's upbringing they are free to apply to the court for a s 8 order or alternatively under s 6(7) to terminate theirs or the other's appointment.

(c) Termination of guardianship

Automatic termination

The guardian's duties cease if the child dies,[400] and automatically end when he attains the age of 18.[401] Whether the guardian's powers cease upon the child's marriage is perhaps debatable for, while s 5 imposes no such express limitation, it may well be that there is no scope for the operation of guardianship, save perhaps in respect of the child's property. In any event, it seems unlikely that a guardian would be permitted to interfere with the activities of a married child even if the guardianship continues. Guardianship also ends upon the death of a sole guardian. If a guardian dies leaving others in office, the survivors continue to be guardians.

Removal by the court

Under s 6(7) of the 1989 Act a court can make an order bringing any appointment made under s 5 to an end. Such an order can be made at any time upon the application of:

(1) any person who has parental responsibility including the guardian; or

(2) the child himself, with leave of the court; or

---

[395] A similar problem obtained in respect of the former law, but the Law Commission (see Working Paper No 91 para 3.64) was inclined to leave the question open.

[396] See *Elliot v Joicey* [1935] AC 209, HL.   [397] Section 10(1).

[398] Hershman and McFarlane, *Children—Law and Practice*, at A [288] relying on *Re H (An Infant)* [1959] 1 WLR 1163.   [399] Per Purchas LJ in *Re C (minors) (adoption by relatives)* [1989] 1 All ER 395, CA.

[400] Though query whether a guardian has a duty to bury or cremate the child?—cf *R v Gwynedd County Council, ex p B* [1992] 3 All ER 317, CA, discussed in Ch 10, Disposing of the child's corpse, p 359.

[401] Section 91(7)–(8). Butterworths *Family Law Service* at 3A [1536] points out that there is nothing in the 1989 Act to prevent a guardian being appointed conditionally or until the child reaches a specified age below 18, in which cases the appointment will end in accordance with its terms.

(3) upon the court's own motion in any family proceedings, if the court considers that the appointment should be brought to an end.

In deciding whether to end the guardianship, the court must be guided by the welfare principle, pursuant to s 1(1) of the 1989 Act.[402] If, for example, the guardian expresses an unwillingness to continue, the court is unlikely to consider it to be for the child's welfare that the appointment should continue. But the power to end the appointment is not confined to cases where the guardian wishes to be released. In the past appointments have been brought to an end because of actual or threatened misconduct of the guardian (for the court will attempt to avert a possible danger to the child rather than wait for it to happen),[403] the abandonment of his rights for such a length of time that it would not be in the child's interests to permit him to reassert them,[404] or merely because of a change of circumstances which rendered it for some reason better for the child to have a new guardian.[405] If it decides to end the guardianship, the court may appoint another individual to take the former guardian's place. It is also open to the court to make a s 8 order. Indeed, it has been pointed out[406] that where the court orders a guardian's removal it may have to consider the appointment of a new guardian to prevent a hiatus in parental responsibility for the child.

(d) Evaluating the law

Following the 1989 Act reforms, guardianship has the clearly defined role of facilitating the replacement of a deceased parent by another person in who is vested parental responsibility. Furthermore, by simplifying the procedure for making private appointments, the law has arguably done all that it can to encourage the making of such appointments. However, the complete absence of control on private appointments is striking and is in marked contrast, for example, to the plethora of controls on adoption and even private fostering.[407] The closest analogy is with making parental responsibility agreements, but such agreements can only be made between unmarried parents and between parents and step-parents, and even these have to be witnessed in court and centrally recorded.[408] This absence of control could be justified on the basis that parents are in a better position than either the courts or local authorities to decide who is best able to care for their children after their death. In any event, there remains the safeguard of the local authority's investigative powers to protect children in need or at risk.

In practice, little is known about the use made of testamentary guardianship and in the previous edition we said that research was needed, for example, to discover how common such appointments are; how many are made without even the appointee's knowledge or consent; how many such appointments are disclaimed; and most important, whether there is any evidence to suggest that children may be at risk of abuse by guardians. Since then a small study focussing upon testamentary appointments has been undertaken.[409]

---

[402] It is not, however, *bound* to apply the checklist in s 1(3)—see s 1(4)—but it should only, pursuant to s 1(5), make an order upon being satisfied that to do so is better than making no order at all.

[403] *Beaufort v Berty* (1721) 1 P Wms 703 at 704–5; *Re X* [1899] 1 Ch 526, at 531, CA.

[404] *Andrews v Salt* (1873) 8 Ch App 622.

[405] *Re X* (above) at 535–6; *F v F* [1902] 1 Ch 688, in which a guardian who had become a Roman Catholic was removed although she had made no attempt to influence her ward, a Protestant.

[406] A Bainham and S Gilmore *Children—The Modern Law* (2013, 4th edn) 183.

[407] See G Douglas and N Lowe 'Becoming a Parent in English Law' (1992) 108 LQR 414, at 428 and 432.

[408] See Ch 11, Parental responsibility agreements, pp 372ff.

[409] See E Hasson 'Navigating family and personal relationships: the appointment of testamentary guardians' (2012) JSWFL 279. The study comprised open ended qualitative interviews with 26 practitioners in the East Midlands who specialised in drafting wills. Its methodology was not dissimilar to the study

Inter alia what this interesting study found was that clients seeking advice about making wills were typically aged over 50 so that it was in a minority of cases that guardianship was relevant. On the other hand, having children was not an insignificant trigger for seeking advice about making a will though not surprisingly clients' awareness of guardianship varied from total ignorance to being 'very clued up'. An interesting finding concerned the choice of guardian which for some was a real cause for concern. The professional advice was to focus upon the child-guardian relationship and to think about securing stability in bereavement. As a result of this advice most clients appointed fellow family members but a significant proportion chose friends.

It remains the case that little is known about the use made of the court's powers to make guardianship appointments. There are no national statistics of the numbers of applications and orders made under s 5. However, judging from the paucity of case law, little use seems to be made of the courts' powers. Again, further research is needed.

3. DISTINGUISHING GUARDIANSHIP FROM OTHER RELATIONSHIPS

(a) Distinguishing guardians from parents

Following the 1989 Act reforms, the *concepts* of parenthood and guardianship are legally distinct: parents are no longer regarded as guardians and, apart from the exceptional case where an unmarried father without parental responsibility is appointed a guardian, no guardians will be parents. Guardians are nevertheless in a similar legal position to parents with parental responsibility. The key difference is that, unlike a parent, a guardian is not a 'liable relative' under the Social Security Administration Act 1992,[410] nor a 'non-resident parent' under the Child Support Act 1991,[411] and no court may order a guardian to make financial provision for, or a transfer of property to a child, under the Children Act 1989.[412] This means that although guardians have a duty to see that the child is provided with adequate food, clothing, medical aid and lodging[413] and to educate the child properly,[414] no financial orders can be made against them nor are they liable to contribute to the maintenance of a child who is being looked after by a local authority.[415] The absence of any general legal liability on guardians to maintain children might seem at odds with the general policy of awarding them full parental responsibility. The Law Commission, however, considered[416] that, apart from representing a major change of policy, the imposition of financial liability upon guardians might 'act as a serious deterrent to appointments being made or accepted'. Guardians have no rights of succession upon the child's death, nor can a child take British citizenship from his guardian.

(commissioned by the Law Commission) conducted by J Priest and appended to Law Com Working Paper No 91. See also Scot Law Com, Discussion Paper No 88 para 3.2.   [410] Section 78(6) and s 105(3).

[411] Section 3, discussed in Ch 21, The relevant parties, p 806.

[412] Viz s 15 and Sch 1, discussed in Ch 21, Proceedings under Schedule 1 to the Children Act 1989, pp 793ff. However, in divorce, nullity and separation proceedings between a guardian and his or her spouse or the equivalent proceedings between a guardian and his or her civil partner, there is power under the Matrimonial Causes Act 1973 and the Civil Partnership Act 2004 to make financial provision for the child, provided he or she is a 'child of the family'.

[413] Pursuant to the Children and Young Persons Act 1933 s 1(2)(a): see Ch 10, Protection, p 340.

[414] Pursuant to the Education Act 1996 s 7, s 8 and s 576(1): see Ch 10, Education, p 347.

[415] Only parents are so liable, see Children Act 1989 Sch 2 para 21(3). Similarly guardians cannot be liable to contribute to the costs of services provided by a local authority for a child and his family, see 29(4) of the 1989 Act.   [416] Law Com No 172 at para 2.25.

(b) Distinguishing guardians from 'non-parents' named in child arrangements orders as a person with whom the child is to live

Guardianship, like a child arrangements order naming a non-parent as a person with whom the child is to live, vests parental responsibility for the duration of the order but, unlike the latter,[417] it also gives a guardian the right to consent to or withhold consent to the child's placement for adoption and to the making of an adoption order and to appoint a guardian. Furthermore, although the process of making child arrangements orders in favour of non-parents bears some resemblance to the court process of appointing guardians, the resulting orders are conceptually different in that the guardian replaces the deceased parent or parents, whereas a person will normally be named in a child arrangements order as a person with whom the child is to live whilst the child's parents are alive and will therefore share parental responsibility with them.

(c) Distinguishing guardians from special guardians

Special guardians are persons who have been appointed as such by a court.[418] Only non-parents can be appointed as special guardians. An appointment places the individual in stronger legal position than non-parents named in a child arrangements order as a person with whom the child is to live. They are empowered, for example, to appoint a guardian as well as having parental responsibility for the child. Special guardians are distinguishable from guardians in that they do not replace the deceased parent but are normally appointed whilst the child's parents are alive and share parental responsibility with them. Furthermore special guardians can only be appointed by a court; they cannot be appointed privately.

(d) Distinguishing guardians from de facto carers

The key difference between guardians and de facto carers is that the latter, even though they have de facto control, have no parental responsibility for the child. If a parent is dead or is unfit to exercise his responsibilities, it is clearly essential for someone to stand in loco parentis to a child; but by English law parental responsibility will not vest in a person unless he has been formally appointed as a guardian either by a deceased parent or by a court order. In a large number of cases this never happens; and if both parents die, a child's grandparents or other near relations will assume de facto control of the child without taking steps to have themselves appointed legal guardians. Although such persons do not have parental responsibility, nevertheless under s 3(5) of the 1989 Act they 'may (subject to the provisions of this Act) do what is reasonable in all the circumstances for the purpose of safeguarding or promoting the children's welfare'. There is also a duty to afford protection, both at common law and under the Children and Young Persons Act 1933.[419] Furthermore, anyone who cares for a child will be criminally liable under the 1933 Act[420] if they wilfully fail to provide the child with adequate food, clothing, medical aid or lodging. Similarly, the Education Act 1996 places such persons under a duty to see that the child receives full-time education.[421]

(e) Distinguishing guardians from private foster parents

An important difference between a privately appointed guardian and a private foster parent is that, unlike the former, the latter, despite the absence of any formal legal status, is

---

[417] See Children Act 1989 s 12(3), discussed in Ch 11, Acquisition of parental responsibility by other individuals, p 389.   [418] See the Children Act 1989 ss 14A–G, discussed in Ch 19.
[419] See Ch 10, Protection, pp 340ff.   [420] Section 1 and s 17.
[421] Sections 7–8 and s 576(1).

nevertheless still subject to public scrutiny and regulation. If a child is deemed to be privately fostered, then the carers will be subject to the provisions of Part IX of the Children Act 1989, the purpose of which is to ensure that the child is visited periodically by local authority officers, who must satisfy themselves that the child's welfare is being satisfactorily safeguarded and who must give any necessary advice to the foster parents.[422]

A privately fostered child is a child, under the age of 16, who is cared for and accommodated (whether for reward or not) by someone *other than* his parent (including the unmarried father), a person having parental responsibility for the child or a relative[423] for a period or intended period of 28 days or more.[424] However, to ensure that normal domestic arrangements are not within the scope of these provisions, they do not apply if the child lives in the same premises as a parent or a person having parental responsibility for the child, or a relative who has assumed responsibility for him. The provisions are also excluded where the child is being looked after by a local authority,[425] or lives in accommodation provided by a voluntary organisation, or in a school in which he is receiving full-time education,[426] a hospital, a nursing or mental nursing home, or is subject to a supervision order.[427]

---

[422] Children Act 1989 s 67(1) and the Children (Private Arrangements for Fostering) Regulations 2005. For a discussion of private fostering under the Children Act see Vol 8 of the Department of Health's *Guidance and Regulations* (1991). There is no comparable revised guidance.

[423] Defined by s 105(1) of the 1989 Act as 'grandparent, brother, sister, uncle or aunt (whether of the full blood or half blood or by affinity) or a step-parent'.

[424] Children Act 1989 s 66. An intention to look after a child for more than 28 days may be inferred from the facts: cf *Surrey County Council v Battersby* [1965] 2 QB 194.

[425] The selection and supervision of *local authority* foster parents is highly regulated under the Fostering Services (England) Regulations 2011 and the Fostering Services (Wales) Regulations 2003.

[426] Children under 16 who are pupils at a school which is not maintained by a local education authority are treated as privately fostered if they live at the school during school holidays for more than two weeks: Sch 8 para 9.

[427] As these provisions are complementary to those relating to protected children under the Adoption and Children Act 2002, they do not apply to such children either: Sch 8 para 5. A similar exemption applies to children living with applicants for a parental order: Human Fertilisation and Embryology Regulations 2010 Sch 4 para 12.

9

THE LEGAL POSITION OF CHILDREN

A. INTRODUCTION

Having discussed in Chapter 8 who is the legal parent, we turn our attention in this chapter to the legal position of children. We consider first the relatively simple issues of who the law regards as a child and the meaning of 'child of the family'. We then discuss the child's legal status. We continue with a discussion of the changing nature of the parent–child relationship and conclude with consideration of the still developing notion of the child's independent or autonomy rights.

B. THE MEANING OF 'CHILD'

At common law a child attained his majority at the age of 21 but, following the Latey Committee's recommendation,[1] the age of majority, as enacted by s 1(1) of the Family Law Reform Act 1969, is now 18. A 'child' may therefore be said to be a person under the age of 18.[2] This definition is in line with Article 1 of the UN Convention on the Rights of the Child 1989 which states:

> For the purposes of the present Convention a child means every human being below the age of 18 years unless, under the law applicable to the child, majority is attained earlier.

Although for some purposes an unborn child may be regarded as a 'child', whenever the term is used in a statute it is presumed, unless the contrary intention can be shown, only to refer to a live child, that is to a child after he or she has been born.[3]

C. THE MEANING OF 'CHILD OF THE FAMILY'

A recurring concept employed in family legislation is that of 'child of the family'. Broadly speaking, this concept is intended to embrace those children who have been brought up

---

[1] Committee on the Age of Majority 1967, Cmnd 3342, para 134.

[2] This is the definition of 'child' under s 105(1) of the Children Act 1989. It is to be noted that not all laws relating to children are linked to the age of majority. In fact there is little consistency in the age below which legislation concerning children applies.

[3] See *Elliot v Joicey* [1935] AC 209, HL; *D (A Minor) v Berkshire County Council* [1987] AC 317; and *R v Newham London Borough Council, ex p Dada* [1996] QB 507, CA.

as if they were members of the spouses' or civil partners' family, it being felt reasonable to fix on those spouses' or partners' duties of maintenance and protection whether or not they are the biological parents. At one stage, the definition differed according to which legislation was involved but, although the concept is employed in a number of different statutes,[4] the core definition is now the same. It is to be noted that a child may only be a 'child of the family' where he has been brought up by parties to a marriage or civil partnership, and not therefore by cohabitants.

The common definition is that a child of the family is:

(a) a child of both spouses or civil partners; and

(b) any other child, not being a child who is placed with those parties as foster parents by a local authority or voluntary organisation,[5] who has been treated by both of those parties as a child of the family.

In the case of different sex marriages, category (a) refers to any child, including an adopted child or a child in respect of whom there is a parental order, who is treated in law as being a child of both the spouses. In the case of same sex marriages and civil partnerships, category (a) applies to the parties' adopted children and those subject to a parental order and, presumably, also to cases where the female spouse or partner is regarded as a parent ('the second female parent') under s 42 or s 43 of the Human Fertilisation and Embryology Act 2008.[6]

Children falling outside category (a) will still be regarded as children of the family if they fall within category (b). This latter category embraces any child who has been treated as a member of the family by both parties to a marriage or civil partnership. There is no requirement that either spouse or partner be the natural parent of the child. Hence, relatives (or even foster parents, provided the child is not in the care of a local authority or voluntary organisation) caring for the child on a long-term basis may be held to be treating the child as one of the family. In the case of grandparents it has been said[7] that the court should always give due weight to the pre-existing relationship between the grandparent and the child and in particular investigate whether the grandparents were simply providing everyday or secondary cover, or whether the parents had left them to assume primary responsibility for their child in the foreseeable future. Whether a child has been so treated is a question of fact.

Common sense excludes some children, for example, young lodgers, and relatives who are being looked after during their parents' temporary absence. In all cases, however, the test is an objective one, namely to consider as an independent outside observer whether the evidence shows that the child was treated as a member of the family.[8] It has been held, for instance, that a child can be a 'child of the family' even though a maintenance order against the natural father in respect of the child remains in force,[9] and the fact that the

---

[4] See Matrimonial Causes Act 1973 s 52, as amended by the Children Act 1989 Sch 12 para 33; Domestic Proceedings and Magistrates Court Act 1978 s 38, as amended by the Children Act 1989 Sch 12 para 43; and the Children Act 1989 s 105(1), as amended by the Civil Partnership Act 2004 s 75(3). Note also the Marriage Act 1949 s 1(3) and the truncated definition in s 78(1), discussed in Ch 2, Affinity, p 46.

[5] This is in line with the general policy of limiting the right of foster parents to apply for orders vesting some control over the child so as not to discourage parents from allowing their child to be fostered. See Ch 14, Persons entitled to apply with leave, p 515.

[6] Adoption is discussed in Ch 19; parental orders and s 42 and 43 parenthood are discussed in Ch 8.

[7] Per Thorpe LJ in Re A (Child of the Family) [1998] 1 FLR 347 at 350.

[8] See Teeling v Teeling [1984] FLR 808 at 809, CA, per Ormrod LJ and D v D (Child of the Family) (1981) 2 FLR 93, CA.

[9] See Carron v Carron [1984] FLR 805, CA, where, following their marriage, the mother and stepfather took the mother's two children into their household and lived together for four years. That, according to

husband mistakenly believed the child to be his will not prevent the child from being a child of the family if the husband treated him as such.[10] A similar position applies to partners to a civil partnership.

There are two sets of circumstances in which it may be legally impossible for a child to be treated as a child of the family. First, there must be a family of which the child may be treated as a member: consequently a child may not become a child of the family if the unit never existed in the first place,[11] or if it has ceased to exist. In the latter regard, if, for instance, the wife has a child by another man after her husband has left her, but the husband agrees to treat the child as his own even though they continue to live apart, such a child cannot be a child of the family.[12] Once a family has been shown to exist, however, a child can be a child of the family even if the spouses have lived together for an extremely short period.[13] A similar position applies to partners to a civil partnership. Secondly, a child cannot be treated as a child of the family before he is born. In *A v A (Family: Unborn Child)*[14] the husband had married the wife knowing her to be pregnant and believing himself to be the father. Six days after the marriage the wife left him. When the child was born five months later, she was obviously not the husband's child but the daughter of a Pakistani man with whom the mother had also had intercourse before the marriage. The only evidence that the husband had treated the child as his own was the fact that he had married the mother, but Bagnall J held that 'treatment' involved behaviour towards a child who must be in existence. Although the decision was correct on the facts, its reasoning seems narrow and technical and capable of working injustice[15] and it is urged that it ought not to be followed.[16]

A child of the parties who has subsequently been adopted by someone else cannot normally be a 'child of the family'. An adopted child ceases in law to be a child of the birth parents and therefore falls outside the first part of the definition, and the provisions about treating a child cannot refer to conduct before the adoption. A husband's failure to deny that a child is a child of the family in undefended divorce proceedings does not stop him from asserting otherwise in subsequent proceedings.[17] A similar position applies to a partner involved in dissolution proceedings to end a civil partnership.

D. THE CHILD'S STATUS

1. INTRODUCTION

Historically, most systems of jurisprudence have, at any rate in the past, drawn a distinction between the legal position of a child born of a legally recognised union and that of a

---

Ormrod LJ, made it inevitable that there should be a finding that the two children were children of the family. In the case of private foster parents, the fact that a child is still being maintained by the natural parents could well indicate that the child was not a child of the foster parents' family, but it will not be decisive: see Law Com No 25, *Report on Financial Provision in Matrimonial Proceedings*, paras 23–32.

[10] See *W (RJ) v W(SJ)* [1972] Fam 152.   [11] See *W v W (Child of the Family)* [1984] FLR 796, CA.

[12] *M v M (Child of the Family)* (1980) 2 FLR 39, CA. Aliter if the parties resume living together: see *Teeling v Teeling* [1984] FLR 808.

[13] See *W v W (Child of the Family)* [1984] FLR 796, CA where the man spent barely a fortnight with his wife and the child.   [14] [1974] Fam 6.

[15] This may be particularly harsh with regard to family provision after death, where the same definition is used under the Inheritance (Provision for Family and Dependants) Act 1975 s 1(1)(d), discussed in Ch 25.

[16] However, the decision was subsequently approved by Sheldon J, sitting in the Court of Appeal, in *W v W (Child of the Family)* [1984] FLR 796, CA. See also *Re Leach* [1986] Ch 226 at 223, CA, per Slade LJ.

[17] *Rowe v Rowe* [1980] Fam 47, CA. See also *Healey v Healey* [1984] Fam 111.

child born of an illicit union or as a result of a casual act of intercourse. Children born in the latter circumstances were commonly accorded an inferior legal status and had markedly fewer rights, if any, than those born to formal unions. This was certainly true of the common law, which, like Roman law and the modern systems based on it,[18] adhered rigidly to the rule that no child could be legitimate unless he was born or conceived in wedlock.[19] At common law an illegitimate child had no legal relationship with his father or, initially, with his mother. However, as a result of successive Acts of Parliament, the harshness of this position was significantly mitigated and the concept of legitimacy widened; children born illegitimate may be legitimated if their parents subsequently intermarry and, most importantly, the legal disadvantages attached to illegitimacy have all but been removed.[20] As a result of these changes the question whether a child is legitimate or illegitimate has become markedly less important. Nevertheless, unlike some jurisdictions such as Scotland[21] and New Zealand,[22] and despite a suggestion by the Law Commission that the concept should be abolished here,[23] the basic status of legitimacy and illegitimacy remains and is to some extent still relevant in determining the legal relationship between a child and his parents.

2. THE CONCEPT OF LEGITIMACY

(a) The position at common law

At common law a child is legitimate[24] if his parents were married at the time of his conception or at the time of his birth.[25] Commonly, legitimate children are both conceived and born in wedlock, but a similar status is accorded to other classes of children:

(a) those whose parents were married when they were born even though they must have been conceived before the marriage;[26] and

(b) those whose parents were married at the time of their conception, even though the marriage was terminated before their birth.

---

[18] But this was not the only criterion accepted in Western Europe. See, further, M Woolf *Private International Law* (1975, 2nd edn) p 385, and the *American Restatement of the Conflict of Laws* s 137 and *Comment*, where it is pointed out that in some legal systems a person may be the legitimate child of one parent but not of the other.

[19] Though it has always been possible to sponsor private legislation to legitimate a person who is illegitimate at common law.

[20] For the drawing of an interesting parallel between the decline in importance of legitimacy and the decline of the great landed families for whom the protection of patrilineal descent was crucial, see J Eekelaar *Family Security and Family Breakdown* (1971) p 13.

[21] See s 21 of the Family Law (Scotland) Act 2006, which 'abolished' illegitimacy.

[22] Where as a result of the Status of Children Act 1969 s 3(1) (since amended by the Care of Children Act 2004 Part 4) no distinction is drawn between the status of children born to married parents and those born to unmarried parents: see *Butterworth's (NZ) Family Law in New Zealand* (2013, 13th edn) 6.502, and P Bromley and PHR Webb *Family Law* pp 429–39. The New Zealand enactment has served as a model for other legislation in parts of Australia and Canada: see J Eekelaar *Family Law and Social Policy* (1984, 2nd edn) p 139.

[23] Law Com Working Paper No 74, *Illegitimacy*. But note the Lord Chancellor's Consultation Paper (1998) on *The Law on Parental Responsibility for Unmarried Fathers* canvassed views on whether all fathers should have parental responsibility.

[24] For the historical development of the law see generally, S Cretney *Family Law in the Twentieth Century* (2003) ch 15.

[25] Blackstone's *Commentaries* 446 and 454–7. For a full account of the common law relating to legitimacy and a detailed examination of the cases before 1836, see Nicolas *Adulterine Bastardy*.

[26] Co Litt 244 a; Blackstone's *Commentaries* i 454. See also N Nicolas, *Adulterine Bastardy* (1836), and the cases cited in Ch 8, Presumption that the mother's husband is the father, p 260.

Consequently, a posthumous child may be legitimate, as will be the child whose parents' marriage was terminated by divorce between the time of his conception and his birth.[27]

In the absence of authority, it is thought that a child conceived as a result of pre-marital intercourse, whose parents then marry but whose father dies before his birth, is legitimate. Had the father survived, the child would certainly have been legitimate[28] and, as we have seen, the common law does not bastardise a child merely because he is born posthumously.

It seems beyond argument that a child conceived during the marriage as a result of artificial insemination with the husband's own semen (AIH) is legitimate and, conversely, at common law, the child conceived as a result of artificial insemination by the semen of a donor other than the husband (DI) is illegitimate. What, however, is the child's status if the wife conceives by AIH after her husband's death? At common law, such a child must surely be illegitimate since conception has taken place outside marriage and, were the position otherwise children *conceived* by the parties *after* their divorce would also have to be regarded as legitimate,[29] unless the view is taken that there is a material difference between marriages ending because of death and those ending by reason of divorce The common law has still to determine the status of a child born to a host or carrying mother but genetically of commissioning parents.[30]

(b) Statutory changes

Legitimacy of children of void marriages

Since a void marriage is a marriage neither in fact nor in law, children of such a marriage were necessarily illegitimate at common law. However, following the recommendation of the Morton Commission on Marriage and Divorce,[31] the law was changed by the Legitimacy Act 1959, since replaced by the Legitimacy Act 1976. Section 1(1) provides:[32]

> The child of a void marriage, whenever born, shall . . . be treated as the legitimate child of his parents if at the time of the insemination resulting in the birth or, where there is no such insemination, the child's conception (or the time of the celebration of marriage if later) both or either of the parties reasonably believed that the marriage was valid.

In common with other provisions relating to status, s 1(1) only applies if the child's father was domiciled in England and Wales at the time of the child's birth or, if he died before the birth, immediately before his death.[33]

In *Re Spence*[34] it was held that s 1(1) does not apply to a child *born*[35] before his parents entered into a void marriage. It must also be the case that s 1(1) has no application where

---

[27] *Knowles v Knowles* [1962] P 161.

[28] Similarly, if the child was born to a mother who is 'brain dead' but kept alive on a life support machine until the child's birth.

[29] See P Bromley 'Aided Conception: The Alternative to Adoption' in P Bean (ed) *Adoption: Essays in Social Policy, Law and Sociology* (1984) 174 at 175.

[30] Which remains relevant in the case of children conceived by means of in vitro fertilisation taking place before 1 August 1991, ie before the Human Fertilisation and Embryology Act 1990 came into force. See also the discussion in Ch 8.

[31] Cmnd 9768, paras 1184–6. This recommendation was intended to reflect the position in Scottish common law and many other jurisdictions which recognised the harshness of declaring as illegitimate children of parents whose marriage turned out to be void, as least where one, if not both, of the parents was ignorant of the invalidity.   [32] As amended by the Family Law Reform Act 1987 s 28(1).

[33] Section 1(2). Compare the provisions relating to *legitimatio per subsequens matrimonium*, at Legitimation, p 302.   [34] [1990] Ch 652, CA.

[35] Aliter if conceived before, but born after the putative ceremony.

the child is born of parents whose purported marriage was so defective as to rank as no marriage at all rather than a void marriage.[36]

As originally worded, the Act seemed to lay the burden of proof upon the person asserting the legitimacy, a burden which might be difficult to discharge, particularly if the issue is raised many years after 'the marriage'. However, s 1(4) now provides[37] that, in relation to any child born on or after 4 April 1988,[38] it is to be presumed, unless the contrary is shown, that one of the parties reasonably believed, at the relevant time, that the marriage was valid. Another problem with s 1 is the meaning of 'reasonably believed'. As it had been held[39] that this imports an objective test, ie the belief must be one that a reasonable person would have held in the circumstances, there was some doubt as to whether a mistake of law would support a reasonable belief. However, following the Law Commission's recommendations,[40] s 1(3)[41] provides that such a mistake can support a reasonable belief.

Legitimacy of children of voidable marriages

At common law a decree of nullity, where the marriage was voidable, had retrospective effect and automatically bastardised the issue of the marriage.[42] When the grounds for nullity were extended by the Matrimonial Causes Act 1937, it was appreciated that this rule might work hardship in those cases where the marriage was annulled because the respondent was of unsound mind, or epileptic, or was suffering from a venereal disease in a communicable form, since the wife might conceive before the petitioner discovered the existence of the impediment. Consequently the 1937 Act provided that in these cases any child born of the marriage should be legitimate notwithstanding the annulment of the marriage.[43] Where the respondent was pregnant by a man other than the petitioner, the question of the legitimacy of the child did not arise, and apparently the legislature did not foresee that any child would be born if the marriage had not been consummated. Since then, however, cases concerning children born as a result of pre-marital intercourse,[44] or *fecundatio ab extra*,[45] and of artificial insemination (using the husband's sperm) have come before the courts.[46]

This anomaly was first removed by the Law Reform (Miscellaneous Provisions) Act 1949 s 4(1) which provided that any child who would have been the legitimate child of the parties to a voidable marriage had it not been annulled should be deemed to be their legitimate child.[47] The same result is now reached by s 16 of the Matrimonial Causes Act 1973 which, by enacting that a voidable marriage shall be treated as if it had existed up to the date of the decree absolute, must necessarily preserve the legitimacy of any child born or conceived between the date of the marriage and the date of the decree, as well as that of any child legitimated by the marriage.[48]

---

[36] See eg *Hudson v Leigh* [2009] EWHC 1306 (Fam) [2009] 2 FLR 1129, discussed in Ch 3.

[37] Added by s 28(2) of the Family Law Reform Act 1987 following the Law Commission's recommendation in Law Com No 118 *Illegitimacy* at para 10.51.

[38] The date on which the amendment came into force.

[39] *Hawkins v A-G* [1966] 1 All ER 392 at 397, criticised by H Bevan *Child Law* (1989) 247.

[40] Law Com No 118, para 10.52.   [41] Added by the Family Law Reform Act 1987 s 28(2).

[42] See Ch 3, Effect of decree on voidable marriage, p 85.   [43] Section 7(2).

[44] As in *Dredge v Dredge* [1947] 1 All ER 29.   [45] As in *Clarke v Clarke* [1943] 2 All ER 540.

[46] As in *REL v EL* [1949] P 211.

[47] This provision, however, did not have retrospective effect. Consequently, except in those cases provided for in s 7(2) of the Matrimonial Causes Act 1937, the children of voidable marriages annulled before 16 December 1949 remain illegitimate: *Re Adams* [1951] Ch 716.

[48] For discussion of s 16, see Ch 3, Effect of decree on voidable marriage, p 85. The section cannot legitimate a child who never was legitimate (eg because the husband was not the father): *Re Adams* [1951] Ch 716.

Legitimacy of children with a second female parent

The concept of legitimacy has been further extended to include children conceived by assisted reproduction after the coming into force of Part 2 of the Human Fertilisation and Embryology Act 2008[49] and born to a same sex female couple who are either married or who have entered a civil partnership. Section 48 (6) of the 2008 Act provides that a child who has a parent, by virtue of s 42 of that Act or by s 43,[50] who is (at any time beginning with the placing of the embryo or the sperm or eggs in the mother and ending with the resulting child's birth) a civil partner of the mother is the legitimate child of the parents. However, such a child cannot succeed to any dignity or title of honour.[51]

Legitimation

Canon law adopted the Roman law rule that a bastard would become legitimate[52] if his parents subsequently intermarried, provided that they had been free to marry each other at the time of the child's birth. But the importance of establishing the identity of the heir at law, to whom descended the valuable private rights and important public duties of the ownership of an inheritable estate of freehold land in the Middle Ages, led the common law to reject this doctrine of *legitimatio per subsequens matrimonium*, and an attempt to introduce it by the Statute of Merton in 1235 was successfully resisted by the temporal peers. Consequently, no form of legitimation was recognised by English law until the passing of the Legitimacy Act 1926, by which time the property legislation of 1925 had rendered it almost wholly unnecessary to establish the identity of the heir save in the case of the descent of an unbarred entailed interest.

The Legitimacy Act 1926 provided that a child should be legitimated by the subsequent marriage of his parents. But it also adopted the canon law rule that legitimation was impossible if either parent was married to any other person at the time of the child's birth.[53] However, a child conceived whilst one of his parents was married could still be legitimated if this marriage was terminated before his birth, and in many cases decrees of divorce were expedited for this reason. The Legitimacy Act 1959 s 1 extended those provisions to children born when either or both of their parents were married. These Acts were repealed and their provisions re-enacted in the Legitimacy Act 1976. Section 2 provides:

> . . . where the parents of an illegitimate person marry one another, the marriage shall, if the father of the illegitimate person is at the date of the marriage domiciled in England and Wales, render that person, if living, legitimate from the date of the marriage.

A person will be legitimated by this section provided the marriage is not void[54] and only if his father was domiciled in England and Wales at the time of the marriage. Legitimation does not have retrospective effect, so that no one can be legitimated unless he is still alive when his parents marry.[55] The fact that an adopted child is to be regarded as the child of

---

[49] Ie 6 April 2009.   [50] Sections 42 and 43 are discussed in Ch 8.   [51] HFEA 2008 s 48 (7).

[52] For a fascinating account of the historical development of the law on legitimation, see S Cretney *Family Law in the Twentieth Century* (2003) pp 547–54.

[53] Section 1(2). Cf the similar former French position condemned by the ECtHR in *Mazurek v France* (2006) 42 EHRR 9.

[54] Cf *Re Spence* [1990] Ch 652, CA. Note a child *will* be legitimated by the parents' subsequent *voidable* marriage by reason of s 16 of the Matrimonial Causes Act 1973.

[55] Or, if they were married before the date on which the Act by virtue of which he was legitimated came into force, on that date. Legitimacy Act 1926 s 1(1); Legitimacy Act 1959 s 1(2); Legitimacy Act 1976 Sch 1 para 1. But if the parents had married before the relevant Act came into force, the children could be legitimated on that date, even though one or both parents had already died: *Re Lowe* [1929] 2 Ch 210.

the adoptive parent and of no other person does not prevent an illegitimate child from being legitimated if he has been adopted solely by one of his parents who then marries the other parent.[56]

The provisions just mentioned have been extended to include children whose 's 43 parent'[57] enters into a civil partnership with the mother subsequent to the child's birth.[58]

3. DECLARATIONS OF STATUS

Although the question of a child's status may be put in issue in a number of ways, any judicial decision about status[59] will normally be a judgment *in personam* which only binds the parties to it and their privies, ie persons claiming through them. The desirability of a procedure to enable a disputed question of legitimacy to be settled once and for all led to the passing of the Legitimacy Declaration Act 1858, which was repealed and substantially re-enacted in the Matrimonial Causes Act 1973 s 45. Under s 45 any person could petition for a decree that he was legitimate or that he or his parents or grandparents were validly married. But a petitioner could not obtain a declaration of legitimacy of anyone other than himself,[60] nor was there any power to declare anyone illegitimate,[61] or to make a declaration of paternity of any illegitimate child.[62]

Following a review by the Law Commission,[63] s 45 was repealed and replaced by s 56 of the Family Law Act 1986 and rewritten by the Family Law Reform Act 1987 s 22.[64] Under s 56 the 'child' but no one else can seek a declaration that he or she is the legitimate child of his or her parents; and that the applicant has become or has not become a legitimated person. Such applications may be made either in the High Court or Family Court.[65]

These provisions are subject to a number of safeguards, reflecting the Law Commission's concern that bare declarations could be abused. Hence, no application can be made unless the applicant is domiciled or has been habitually resident for one year in England and Wales at the date of the application.[66] There is power, at any stage of the proceedings, to send the papers to the Attorney General and, whether or not such papers are sent, the Attorney General can intervene in the proceedings.[67]

Where the truth of the proposition to be declared has been proved to the court's satisfaction, the court shall make that declaration 'unless to do so would be manifestly contrary to public policy'.[68] It has been held[69] that in contrast to refusing declarations of parentage where the focus is firmly on the child's interests, refusals of declarations of

---

[56] Legitimacy Act 1976 s 4. Indeed in such circumstances the adoption can be revoked upon application of any of the interested parties: Adoption and Children Act 2002 ss 55(1), discussed in Ch 19, Revocation of adoption orders, p 723.   [57] Discussed in Ch 8, Female parenthood, p 256.

[58] Legitimacy Act 1976, ss 2A and 3(2) added respectively by HFEA 2008 Sch 6 paras 16 and 17.

[59] For declarations in other family matters, see Ch 3, Declaration as to marital status, p 63, and Ch 8, Declarations of parentage, pp 270ff.   [60] *Aldrich v A-G* [1968] P 281.

[61] *B v A-G* [1966] 2 All ER 145n.

[62] *Re JS (A Minor) (Declaration of Paternity)* [1981] Fam 22, CA.

[63] See Law Com No 118, paras 10.1–10.27 and Law Com No 132, *Declarations in Family Matters*, paras 3.9–3.14.

[64] Note also the amendments made by the Child Support, Pensions and Social Security Act 2000, which removed the power to make a declaration of *parentage* under s 56 of the 1986 Act.

[65] Family Law Act 1986 s 63 and the Matrimonial and Family Proceedings Act 1984 s 31E, as added by the Court and Crimes Act 2013 Sch 10. The procedure is governed by the Family Proceedings Rules 2010, rr 8.18–8.20.

[66] Family Law Act 1986 s 59(1).   [67] Section 59(2).

[68] Section 58(1). This proviso puts into statutory form the power exercised in *Puttick v A-G* [1980] Fam 1.

[69] *Re S (a child) (declaration of parentage)* [2012] EWCA Civ 1160 [2012] All ER (D) 140 (Aug).

legitimacy under s 58 are concerned with the more general issues of public policy. If a dec-laration is made, it is binding upon the Crown and all other persons,[70] and the Registrar General will be informed.[71] If the declaration is refused, the court cannot grant another declaration for which an application has not been made.[72]

4. THE SIGNIFICANCE OF THE CHILD'S STATUS

At common law the illegitimate child, being *filius nullius*, had no legal relationship with either parent and consequently had no rights, for example, to receive maintenance,[73] to succeed to their property, or to other benefits normally accruing from the relationship of parent and child. Many of these disabilities subsisted until well after the Second World War, but have since been whittled away. For example, following the reforms of the Family Law Reform Acts of 1969 and 1987, children whose parents are not married now have full rights of intestate succession.[74] They can also succeed as an heir to an entailed estate.[75] Such children can now make claims as dependants both under the Inheritance (Provision for Family and Dependants) Act 1975 and the Fatal Accidents legislation.[76] Substantial improvements have been made to the right of support both under the private law (under the Children Act 1989 Sch 1 either parent can be ordered to pay to the other or to the child secured or unsecured periodic payments, lump sum payments, or make property trans-fers)[77] and the public law (all parents are liable to support their children now enforceable through the Child Support Act 1991).[78]

One further difference more recently addressed was that, whereas parties seeking a divorce must necessarily have their plans for their child's future scrutinised by the court,[79] there was no similar scrutiny in cases where unmarried parents separate. However, this statutory duty has been repealed by s 17 of the Children and Families Act 2014, though it remains the case that since divorce requires a court procedure the issue of the future well-being of any children of the family is still more likely to come to judicial notice than in the case of separating families.

(a) Titles of honour

Despite all these important changes it cannot yet be said that children whose parents are unmarried are in exactly the same legal position as those whose parents are married (though as one commentator has put it,[80] the fact that the child's parents are unmarried no longer stamps the child as legally fundamentally different from the child whose par-ents are married) since there remains one further area of discrimination, namely with regard to succession to a title of honour. Section 19(4) of the 1987 Act makes it clear that, despite the new construction of the term 'heir', children of unmarried parents will not be able to succeed to property which is limited to devolve along with a dignity or title of hon-our. However, this should not be read as meaning that such children will never be able to succeed, since that will depend upon the terms of the letters patent issued under the Great

---

[70] Section 58(2).   [71] Section 56(4).   [72] Section 58(3).
[73] But see S Cretney *Principles of Family Law* (1984, 4th edn) p 594.   [74] See Ch 25.
[75] Family Law Reform Act 1987 s 19(2).
[76] Fatal Accidents Act 1976 as substituted by the Administration of Justice Act 1982.
[77] Discussed in Ch 21, Proceedings under Schedule 1 to the Children Act 1989, pp 793ff.
[78] Discussed in Ch 22.
[79] Under s 41 of the Matrimonial Causes Act 1973. There was a similar scrutinising process when dissolv-ing a civil partnership, see s 63 of the Civil Partnership Act 2004.
[80] S Cretney *Family Law in the Twentieth Century* (2003) p 565.

Seal. Currently, they are in a form[81] which limits succession to the 'heirs . . . of his body lawfully begotten', which is enough to show a contrary intention against devolvement to children whose parents are unmarried. However, if in the future the form 'to X and the heirs of his body' were used, then any child could succeed under the terms of s 19(2).

(b) The position of legitimated children

By s 8 of the Legitimacy Act 1976 a legitimated person has the same rights and obligations in respect of the maintenance and support of himself and other persons as if he had been born legitimate, and any legal claim for damages, compensation, allowances, etc, by or in respect of a legitimate child shall apply in the case of one legitimated. Similarly, for the purpose of determining whether he is a British citizen he is to be treated as being born legitimate as from the date of his parents' marriage.[82] Subject to what is said later with respect to rights in property,[83] a legitimated person is in the same position as if he had been born legitimate. On the other hand, a legitimated person is not entitled to succeed to a title of honour.[84]

5. SHOULD REFERENCE BE MADE TO LEGITIMACY AND ILLEGITIMACY?

(a) Background to the Family Law Reform Act 1987

At one time the Law Commission favoured what at the time was thought to be a radical plan that the status of illegitimacy should be abolished altogether.[85] They argued that since the label was itself discriminatory, true equality demanded not simply the removal of the remaining areas of legal discrimination but the abolition of the very status.[86] Indeed, so strongly were they committed to this view that they were prepared to countenance the necessary corollary of their recommendations: that all fathers should be treated equally. The overwhelming response, however, was against giving all fathers automatic rights,[87] and accordingly, in their full report on *Illegitimacy*,[88] the Law Commission did not advocate abolition of that status, but recommended instead a change in terminology, with the terms 'marital' and 'non-marital' replacing so far as possible 'legitimate' and 'illegitimate'.

Before these recommendations were acted upon, the issue was examined by the Scottish Law Commission. They observed that:

> . . . so long as marriage exists and children are born there will be children born out of marriage. In some cases of children born out of marriage, the parents will marry each other after the birth: in others they will not. These are facts and, short of abolishing marriage, there is nothing the law can do about them.[89]

---

[81] See the discussion in Law Com No 118 at para 8.26.   [82] British Nationality Act 1981 s 47(1).

[83] See the Legitimacy Act 1976 s 5 discussed in Ch 25.

[84] Legitimacy Act 1976 Sch 1, para 4(2).

[85] For an influential argument against giving all fathers automatic rights, see M Hayes 'Law Commission Working Paper No 84: Illegitimacy'(1980) 43 MLR 299, though J Eekelaar 'Second Thoughts on Illegitimacy Reform' [1985] Fam Law 261 argued that the status could have been abolished without giving all fathers equal rights.

[86] See generally A Bainham 'The Illegitimacy Saga' in R Probert and C Barton (eds) *50 Years in Family Law* (2012) p 83.   [87] See their Working Party No 74 on *Illegitimacy* (1979).

[88] Law Com No 118 (1982), particularly at Part IV.

[89] Scot Law Com No 82 (1984), para 9.1. The issue was also examined by the Irish Law Reform Commission: see W Duncan 'Abolishing Illegitimacy—A Discussion of the Law Reform Commission's Proposals' (1983) 5 *Dublin University Law Journal* 29–41.

Like the English Law Commission they did not recommend abolishing the status of ille-gitimacy, but unlike that body the Scots could see no merit in introducing the new terms 'marital' and 'non-marital'. As they said,[90] that 'was just another way of labelling children, and experience in other areas, such as mental illness, suggests that new labels can rapidly take on old connotations'. They concluded that they did not wish to see 'a discrimina-tory concept of "non-maritality" gradually replace a discriminatory concept of "illegiti-macy" '. Accordingly, they recommended that the terms 'legitimate' and 'illegitimate' as applied to people, should wherever possible cease to be used in legislation. To achieve this they recommended that, where distinctions based on marriage were necessary, future legislation should distinguish between fathers rather than children. Where it was thought necessary to distinguish people on the basis of whether or not their parents were married to each other at any relevant time (which they hoped would be a 'very rare exception') it should be done expressly in those terms. The Scottish Law Commission's proposals were enacted in the Law Reform (Parent and Child) (Scotland) Act 1986.

Following these developments, the English Law Commission reconsidered its pro-posals and in a second report, published in October 1986,[91] advocated reform along the Scottish lines. Their recommendations were enacted by the Family Law Reform Act 1987.

(b) The Family Law Reform Act 1987

Apart from making important changes to the status of some children born as a result of donor insemination and amending the provision dealing with children of void marriages, the 1987 Act left untouched the basic concept of legitimacy. However, in order to imple-ment the strategy of reducing the need to refer to the concept, in cases where it is still nec-essary to distinguish between children born within marriage and those born without, the Act introduced the important change that reference be made to the parents and whether or not they are married to each other, rather than to the children. This general approach is set out by s 1 of the 1987 Act.

Section 1(1) provides that references in the 1987 Act and any succeeding Act or statu-tory instrument to 'mothers' or 'fathers' or 'parents' refers, unless the contrary intention appears, to all such persons regardless of whether they have or had been married to each other at any time. The clarity of this opening provision is immediately obscured by defi-nitional provisions designed to distinguish (in simple terms) parents (primarily fathers) of legitimate from those of illegitimate children. To avoid using the words 'legitimate' or 'illegitimate', s 1(2) refers instead to a person whose parents were not married to each other at the time of the child's birth. However, it was recognised that this shorthand defi-nition was insufficient by itself, because a child can be legitimate even though his parents were not married at the time of his birth. Accordingly s 1(2) is made subject to s 1(3), so that references to 'a person whose father and mother were not married to each other at the time of the child's birth'[92] do not include (and correspondingly, references to a person whose parents were married to each other at the time of his birth *do* include) cases where the child is:

(a) rendered legitimate by s 1 of the Legitimacy Act 1976 even though his parents' marriage is void;

(b) legitimated by reason of his parents' subsequent marriage;

---

[90] Scot Law Com No 82 (1984) at para 9.2.   [91] Law Com No 157.

[92] By s 1(4) a child's birth is to be taken to include the period beginning with insemination resulting in his birth or, where there was no such insemination, his conception, and ends with his birth.

(c) adopted; and

(d) 'otherwise treated in law as legitimate'.[93]

The resulting law can be confusing. For example, as we discuss in Chapter 11, s 2(1) of the Children Act 1989 states that: 'where a child's father and mother were married to each other at the time of his birth, they shall each have parental responsibility for the child', whereas according to s 2(2) if they were not so married then only the mother has such responsibility. The unsuspecting reader might think that these provisions mean what they say and conclude that parental responsibility is only automatically vested in a father if he is married to the mother at the time of the child's birth. In fact, however, he will also have responsibility if he had divorced his wife at the time of the child's birth, and he will acquire it automatically if he subsequently marries the mother.

Whether the law needed to have been so complex is debatable.[94] Despite its resulting complexity, in deference to the clear spirit of the 1987 Act, we shall avoid where possible labelling children and, as a matter of shorthand convenience, will refer to mothers or fathers as 'unmarried' when referring to parents of a child whose mother and father are not and have not been married to each other.

E. THE CHANGING NATURE OF THE PARENT–CHILD RELATIONSHIP

1. INTRODUCTION

Like society's views about the role of the family and of the individual members within the unit, the legal attitude towards the parent–child relationship has not remained static.[95] The principal catalyst for legal change in the past was the rise of individualism, first with respect to women and then with respect to children.[96] With regard to the former, the growing calls for women's equality during the nineteenth century led eventually to the fundamental change that, whereas parental rights were formerly vested in the father (at any rate in respect of legitimate children), they are now shared between the father and the mother. The growing acceptance that a child is a person in his own right[97] led first to concern about his welfare and protection and then to the recognition that in certain circumstances at least he might have rights of his own. This in turn led to a fundamental change in the nature of parental authority. In the past it was accurate to think of the parental position in terms of rights and duties, for at common law fathers had almost complete autonomy over their legitimate children, and their interest was akin to a proprietorial

---

[93] This covers the case, for example, where the child is conceived through the placing in a married woman of an embryo or of the sperm and eggs or of her artificial insemination and who therefore, by virtue of ss 33–35 of the Human Fertilisation and Embryology Act 2008, is treated as being the child of the woman and her husband.

[94] See eg N Lowe 'The Family Reform Act 1987—Useful Reform but an Unhappy Compromise?' (1988) Denning LJ 77.

[95] See generally S Cretney, *Family Law in the Twentieth Century* (2003) ch 16 and N Lowe 'The Legal Position of Parents and Children in English Law' [1994] *Singapore Journal of Legal Studies* 332.

[96] The legal and social background to these developments is well summarised by S Maidment *Child Custody and Divorce* (1985) chs 4 and 5.

[97] There are those who maintain that until the seventeenth century the concept of childhood did not exist: see eg P Ariès *Centuries of Childhood* (1960), though this view has not escaped criticism. See the references in S Maidment *Child Custody and Divorce* (1985) at pp 91–2.

one;[98] by the 1980s the emphasis had clearly shifted towards parental responsibility,[99] which position was firmly entrenched in the Children Act 1989.

Although the overall effect of these developments has been to weaken the parents' position, it would be a mistake to infer that the issue of parental responsibility is no longer important. On the contrary, the position of parents remains of key importance in English law. Indeed, it is through the medium of parental responsibility that the law in effect recognises the general *right* of parents both to bring up their own children and to a large extent to do so in their own way.[100]

2. THE INITIAL STRENGTH OF THE FATHER'S POSITION

(a) Legitimate children

The position at common law

Common law recognised the natural duties of protecting and maintaining one's legitimate minor children, and although the machinery for enforcing these duties was almost wholly ineffective, nevertheless they could properly be regarded as unenforceable legal obligations.[101] Moreover, it was obvious that, at any rate in early law, these duties could be performed only if the parent actually had the custody of the child, and in many cases the father would be the only member of the family who would be physically capable of carrying them out. Consequently, it is not surprising to discover that his duty to protect carried with it the correlative right to the custody of all minor children and that this right was absolute even against the mother, except in the rare cases where the father's conduct was such as gravely to imperil the children's life, health or morals.[102]

Custody carried with it many rights and powers in addition to care and control. A father was entitled to the services of his children in his custody and to correct them by administering reasonable corporal punishment. He alone might determine the form of their religious and secular education. Whilst his powers were never as wide as those of the paterfamilias in Roman law, the same fundamental approach is apparent. Physical control represented the kernel of this right; without it the others could not be enforced, and the procedural machinery of the common law was such that only his right could be specifically enforced by the writ of habeas corpus.

At common law the father was entitled to the legal custody of his legitimate children until they reached the age of 21,[103] but his rights could be lost if to enforce them would probably lead to the physical or moral harm of the child,[104] or if his claim was not made bona fide.[105] After his death, the mother was entitled to the legal custody of her

---

[98] Ironically, the common law has not been entirely immutable: see, for instance, *R v D* [1984] AC 778, HL, where in holding that even a father could be guilty of the common law offence of kidnapping his own child, Lord Brandon said (at 805), 'The common law, however, while generally immutable in its principles . . . is not immutable in the way it adapts those principles in a radically changing world and against the background of radically changed social conventions and conditions.'

[99] See eg Woolf J in *Gillick v West Norfolk and Wisbech Area Health Authority* [1984] QB 581 at 596, who said that the interests of parents are more accurately described as responsibilities and duties.

[100] See further the discussion in Ch 10.

[101] For a more detailed account see P Pettit 'Parental Control and Guardianship' in R Graveson and F Crane (eds) *A Century of Family Law* (1957) ch 4.

[102] See *Re Agar-Ellis* (1883) 24 ChD 317 at 334, per Cotton LJ.

[103] *Thomasset v Thomasset* [1894] P 295, CA; *Re Agar-Ellis* (1883) 24 Ch D 317, CA.

[104] Such as apprehension of cruelty or grossly immoral or profligate conduct: *Re Andrews* (1873) LR 8, QB 153 at 158.

[105] If his purpose was to hand the child over to another, for example: *Re Turner* (1872) 41 LJQB 142.

minor children for nurture,[106] but even this right was superseded after 1660 if the father appointed a testamentary guardian under the provisions of the Tenures Abolition Act.[107] Common law accorded no other right to the mother as such, and so absolute against her were the father's rights that he could lawfully claim from her possession even a child at the breast.[108]

The intervention of equity

The common law position was tempered by the intervention of equity. The jurisdiction of equity to intervene between parent and child is derived from the prerogative power of the Crown as *parens patriae* to interfere to protect any person within the jurisdiction not fully *sui juris*. This power was exercised by the Lord Chancellor, and although it fell into abeyance when the Court of Wards was set up in 1540, successive Chancellors began to use their powers more and more extensively when this court was abolished in 1660.[109] From the Court of Chancery the jurisdiction passed to the High Court under the Judicature Acts of 1873 and 1875.

One advantage that equity had over the common law was that its procedure was much better adapted to deal with disputes concerning children. Common law, limited as it was to the issue of a writ of habeas corpus, could only enforce the right to physical control; equity, on the other hand, acts *in personam*, so that it could not only make orders concerning, for example, the child's education, but also effectively ensure that they were carried out. A further step that could be taken was to have the child made a ward of court.[110] This procedure had a number of advantages. Not only could the person to whom care and control was given always turn to the court for advice, but the ward remained under the permanent control of the court during minority, so that any dereliction of duty on the part of the carer and any interference with the ward were punishable as a contempt of court. Furthermore, the court could give care and control of the child to his own parent, which meant that the child would remain in the latter's possession whilst the court could ensure that the parental powers were exercised in the child's best interests.

The increasing influence of equity

At first the intervention of equity scarcely had any impact upon the father's position. It left untouched the common law duties of a parent and indeed gave prima facie effect to the father's right to custody of his legitimate children, unless he had forfeited it by his immoral or cruel conduct, or was seeking to enforce it capriciously or arbitrarily. As Cotton LJ said in *Re Agar-Ellis*:[111]

---

[106] *R v Clarke* (1857) 7 E & B 186 at 200.   [107] See the 7th edition of this work at p 350.

[108] *R v De Manneville* (1804) 5 East 221—a father who had separated from his wife forcibly removed an eight-month child while it was actually at the breast and carried it away almost naked in an open carriage in inclement weather. The court, in upholding his right to custody, said it could draw no inferences to the disadvantage of the father. See also *R v Greenhill* (1836) 4 Ad & El 624—a father's right to custody of his three daughters aged five and under was upheld notwithstanding he was living with an adulteress and nothing could be said against the mother. The children went to live with their paternal grandmother.

[109] W Holdsworth *History of English Law*, vi 648. The Court of Wards was set up by the 32 Hen 8, c 45, and abolished by the Tenures Abolition Act 1660.

[110] For the history and development of wardship see N Lowe and R White *Wards of Court* (1986, 2nd edn), ch 1 and J Seymour '*Parens Patriae* and Wardship Powers: Their Nature and Origins' (1994) 14 Ox J of Legal Studies 159. Wardship is discussed further in Ch 20.

[111] (1883) 24 ChD 317, at 334, CA in which the father's right to custody was upheld and communication with her mother prevented on the grounds that his daughter's affection for him might thereby be alienated. This decision was referred to as a 'dreadful case' by Lord Upjohn in *J v C* [1970] AC 668 at 721, an observation repeated by Munby LJ in *Re G (Education: Religious Upbringing)* [2012] EWCA Civ 1233, [2013] 1 FLR 677 at [20].

> This court holds this principle—that when, by birth, a child is subject to a father, it is for the general interest of families, and for the general interest of children, and really for the interest of the particular infant, that the Court should not, except in very extreme cases, interfere with the discretion of the father, but leave to him the responsibility of exercising that power which nature has given him by the birth of the child.

On the other hand there was a growing view,[112] which ultimately prevailed, that the welfare of the child was the first consideration[113] and equity would not hesitate to deprive a father of his rights if it would clearly be contrary to the child's interests to give effect to them. In the words of Lord Esher MR in *R v Gyngall*:[114]

> The court is placed in a position by reason of the prerogative of the Crown to act as supreme parent of the child, and must exercise that jurisdiction in the manner in which a wise, affectionate, and careful parent would act for the welfare of the child. The natural parent in the particular case may be affectionate, and may be intending to act for the child's good, but may be unwise, and may not be doing what a wise, affectionate, and careful parent would do. The Court may say in such a case that, although they can find no misconduct on the part of the parent, they will not permit that to be done with the child which a wise, affectionate, and careful parent would not do. The court must, of course, be very cautious in regard to the circumstances under which they will interfere with the parental right . . . The court must exercise this jurisdiction with great care, and can only act when it is shown that either the conduct of the parent, or the description of the person he is, or the position in which he is placed, is such as to render it not merely better, but—I will not say "essential", but—clearly right for the welfare of the child in some very serious and important respect that the parent's rights should be suspended or superseded; but . . . where it is so shown, the Court will exercise its jurisdiction accordingly.

Hence, although originally equity interfered with the father's rights hardly less readily than the common law, by the end of the nineteenth century it would do so if there was any threat of physical or moral harm to the child; and if a father once abandoned or abdicated his right, he would not be allowed to reassert it arbitrarily if this would be contrary to the child's interests.[115]

As in other fields, equity ensured that, where its own rules were in conflict with those of common law, the former should prevail. It would not only grant an injunction to restrain a person from applying for a writ of habeas corpus to obtain the custody of a child,[116] but would also prevent a person who had already obtained the writ from interfering with the child if this was not in his interests.[117] The Judicature Act 1873 expressly provided that the rules of equity relating to the custody and education of minors should prevail over those of common law.[118] Notwithstanding this enjoinder, it seems evident that on occasion at least the courts

---

[112] Arguably the 'germ' of the welfare principle was sown in two early House of Lords' decisions, *Johnstone v Beattie* (1843) 10 Cl & Fin 42 and *Stuart v Marquis of Bute* (1861) 9 HL Cas 440, both of which concerned guardians rather than parents.

[113] See N Lowe 'The House of Lords and the Welfare Principle' in C Bridge (ed) *Family Law Towards the Millennium—Essays for P M Bromley* (1997) pp 125 and 127–34.

[114] [1893] 2 QB 232 at 241–2, CA. See also *Re O'Hara* [1900] 2 IR 232, CA; *Official Solicitor v K* [1965] AC 201, HL.   [115] See *Re O'Hara* [1900] 2 IR 232 at 240–1; *Re Fynn* (1848) 2 De G & Sm 457 at 474–5.

[116] Per Lindley LJ in *R v Barnardo, Jones's Case* [1891] 1 QB 194 at 210, CA.

[117] *Andrews v Salt* (1873) 8 Ch App 622.

[118] Section 25(10) (now the Senior Courts Act 1981 s 49). But even before this the common law courts recognised the superiority of the jurisdiction of the Court of Chancery to the extent that, if proceedings were

continued to apply common law principles at the expense of equity even into the twentieth century.[119] Moreover, it seems fair to say that at the end of the nineteenth century, notwithstanding the growing influence of equity, the courts remained 'parent focused', though the seeds had been sown for the development of the welfare principle which would eventually take precedence over parents' rights.

(b) The position with regard to illegitimate children

At common law a child born outside marriage was *filius nullius* and consequently none of the legal powers or duties which flowed from the relationship of parent and legitimate child was accorded him or his parents.[120] This meant, inter alia, that the father could not claim custody.[121] Eventually it became accepted that the right of control vested in the mother,[122] who indeed as against third parties was in as strong a position as the father in respect of his legitimate children.[123]

Although virtually all of the legal disabilities attaching to illegitimacy have now been removed by statute, it remains the case that unless he subsequently acquires it by being formally registered as the father, by court order or by agreement, parental responsibility is vested in the mother to the exclusion of the father, even where the latter's paternity is not in doubt.[124]

3. THE STRENGTHENING OF THE MOTHER'S POSITION

The inevitable corollary of the strength of the father's position was the weakness of the mother's in respect of legitimate children. However, during the nineteenth century a series of statutes began to whittle down the father's rights and also gave the mother positive rights to custody which even equity did not accord to her. The history of this change in attitude can best be seen by a brief examination of the principal provisions of each statute.

(a) Talfourd's Act 1839

This Act marks a decisive point in the history of family law, for it empowered the Court of Chancery to give the mother custody of her children until they reached the age of seven and access to them until they came of age. But the Act specifically provided that no order was to be made if the mother had been guilty of adultery.

(b) Custody of Infants Act 1873

This extended the principle of Talfourd's Act by empowering the court to give the mother custody until the child reached the age of 16. It did not, however, repeat the proviso

---

pending in the latter court, an application for habeas corpus would be stayed until the decision of Chancery was known: *Wellesley v Duke of Beaufort* (1827) 2 Russ 1 at 25–6, *R v Isley* (1836) 5 Ad & El 441.

[119] See eg *Re Agar-Ellis* (1883) 24 ChD 317 and *R v New* (1904) 20 TLR 583; see further, n 123.

[120] Blackstone *Commentaries* i, 458–9.   [121] See eg *R v Soper* (1793) 5 Term Rep 278.

[122] See eg *Barnardo v McHugh* [1891] AC 388, HL, in which an unmarried mother successfully invoked habeas corpus proceedings following Dr Barnardo's failure to deliver her illegitimate son to a person named by her.

[123] See eg *R v New* (1904) 20 TLR 583, in which the Court of Appeal upheld a mother's right of custody to her illegitimate daughter, as against foster parents with whom the child had been living for 10 years, to the extent of removing the child and placing her in a Church of England Home where no one would be allowed to visit her until she had been there for two years.

[124] See the Children Act 1989 s 2 (1)–(2), discussed in Ch 11.

relating to her adultery. The Act provided that arrangements as to custody or control in separation deeds (which had formerly been held void as contrary to public policy) were to be enforceable so long as they were in the child's interests.

(c) Guardianship of Infants Act 1886

Neither of the two earlier Acts gave mothers rights as such, but were concerned to extend the court's discretion to grant orders in the mother's favour. However, the Guardianship of Infants Act 1886 not only extended judicial discretion by empowering the court to give the mother custody of her children until they reached the age of 21, but also prevented the father from defeating the mother's right after his death by appointing a testamentary guardian and enacted, that the mother was to act jointly with any guardian so appointed. Furthermore, for the first time it gave limited powers to a mother to appoint testamentary guardians.

(d) Twentieth century developments

Although the move to establish maternal rights proved to be of passing significance with attention becoming more focused on the child's welfare, the process of equalising parental rights continued in the twentieth century. The Guardianship of Infants Act 1925 provided that in any proceedings before any court[125] neither the father nor the mother should be regarded as having a claim superior to the other in respect of the custody or upbringing of the child.[126] It also gave the mother the same right to appoint testamentary guardians as the father. The Guardianship Act 1973 gave each parent (of a legitimate child) equal and separately exercisable rights. Finally, with the abolition by s 2(4) of the Children Act 1989 of the archaic rule that during his lifetime the father was the sole guardian of his legitimate child, it can now be said that the legal position of married parents with respect to their children is equal.[127]

4. THE INCREASING RECOGNITION OF THE CHILD'S POSITION

(a) The evolution and development of the welfare principle

The position before 1925

A striking feature of the early law was its apparent lack of concern for the child. By the end of the nineteenth century, however, there was a growing awareness[128] of the child's welfare, possibly triggered by the development starting in the mid-nineteenth century

---

[125] Jurisdiction to make orders relating to custody etc, which had formerly been exercisable only by the High Court and (since 1886) by county courts, was extended (subject to certain exceptions) to magistrates' courts. For further discussion of this Act see S Cretney '"What will the Women Want Next?" The Struggle for Power within the Family 1925–1975' (1996) 112 LQR 110.

[126] This direction was repeated in s 1 of the Guardianship of Minors Act 1971, but as Baroness Hale observed in *Re J (A Child) (Custody Rights: Jurisdiction)* [2005] UKHL 40 [2005] 3 WLR 14 at [18], the proposition that the court should disregard whether the claim of the father was superior to that of the mother and vice versa was regarded as 'too obvious' to require repetition in s 1(1) of the Children Act 1989.

[127] Note, however, that in relation to unborn children fathers have no rights: see *Paton v British Pregnancy Advisory Service Trustees* [1979] QB 276, and *C v S* [1988] QB 135, CA, discussed in Ch 11, In respect of whom is there parental responsibility? pp 390–91.

[128] See generally N Lowe 'The House of Lords and the Welfare Principle' in C Bridge (ed) *Family Law Towards the Millennium—Essays for P M Bromley* (1997) pp 127ff; S Maidment *Child Custody and Divorce* (1985) ch 4. See also J Hall 'The Waning of Parental Rights' [1972] CLJ 248 and S Cretney *Family Law in the Twentieth Century* (2003) ch 15. For a modern judicial view of this development see *Re G (Education: Religious Upbringing)* [2012] EWCA Civ 1233 [2013] 1 FLR 677 at [20]–[24], per Munby LJ.

that children should have a right to basic education and the general rise of individualism.[129] For example, under the Custody of Infants Act 1873 a parental agreement about custody could not be enforced if the court did not think that it was for the child's benefit. Further, the Guardianship of Infants Act 1886 directed the court to have regard to the child's welfare as well as to the conduct and wishes of the parents when deciding custody applications. The most obviously child-centred statute was the Custody of Children Act 1891, which was passed as the direct result of a number of cases in which parents had succeeded in recovering children whom they had placed in Dr Barnardo's 'homes', or whom they had abandoned and had been taken in by him. It provided that if a parent had abandoned or deserted his child or allowed him to be brought up by, and at the expense of, another person, school, institution or local authority, in such circumstances as to show that he was unmindful of his parental duties, he had to prove that he was fit to have custody of the child claimed.

The more enduring development, however, was judicially inspired. Equity's changing attitude during the nineteenth century, beginning with a marked reluctance to interfere with a father's right to custody and ending with its increasing readiness to interfere if it was in the child's interests to do so, has previously been noted. It is evident that during the early part of the twentieth century still more weight was being placed upon the child's welfare.[130]

A key case is *Ward v Laverty*,[131] in which a paternal great-aunt of three orphaned children applied for a writ of habeas corpus with a view to the children being placed in the custody of their paternal relatives and being brought up, according to their deceased father's wishes as set out in his will, as Roman Catholics. At the time of the application the children were living with their maternal grandparents and being brought up as Presbyterians having been placed with them nearly four years previously by their mother when she left their father before his death. Immediately after leaving her husband she removed her eldest daughter from the Catholic school she had been attending and sent her instead to a Protestant school. After his death the mother herself reverted to being a Presbyterian and died a member of that church nearly three years later. Viscount Cave LC, with whom the other Law Lords agreed, considered the law to be well settled:[132]

> On the question of religion in which a young child is to be brought up, the wishes of the father of the child are to be considered; and if there is no other matter to be taken into account, then according to the practice of our Courts, the wishes of the father prevail. But that rule is subject to the condition, that the wishes of the father only prevail if they are not displaced by considerations relating to the welfare of the children themselves. *It is the welfare of the children, which according to rules which are now well accepted, forms the paramount consideration in these cases.* Some of the earlier judgments contain sentences in which perhaps greater stress is laid upon the father's wishes than would be placed upon them now, but in the more recent decisions and especially since the passing of the Guardianship of Infants Act, 1886, s 5 of which Act shows the modern feeling in these matters, the greater stress is laid upon the welfare and happiness of the children. (Emphasis added)

---

[129] See further I Pinchbeck and M Hewitt *Children in English Society* Vol 1 (1969) and Vol 2 (1973).

[130] In fact the first recorded judicial use of the word 'paramount' in this context seems to be in *Re A and B (Infants)* [1897] 1 Ch 786 at 792, per Lopes LJ; see Lord Upjohn in *J v C* [1970] AC 668 at 722C. Note also the reference to the paramountcy of the child's welfare in *Scott v Scott* [1913] AC 417, HL at 437, per Viscount Haldane.

[131] [1925] AC 101.   [132] At 108.

Viscount Cave observed that before the mother's death the father's family had shown little interest in the children. In contrast, the children were happy where they were and the grandparents were fond of them and ready and willing to care for them. The eldest child was found to be bright and intelligent and had strong convictions in favour of the Presbyterian faith. Moreover, she was happy where she was. The court had no doubt that her welfare was best served by leaving her with her maternal grandparents. With regard to the two younger children the court considered that they were too young to have religious convictions, but it was accepted that it was not for their welfare to be separated from their elder sister nor from their loving grandparents. Accordingly, these considerations were held to 'prevail over the wishes of the father'.

Ward v Laverty has generally been overlooked by academic writers,[133] yet by applying a child-centred approach to a habeas corpus application, it seemed to establish that no matter which jurisdiction was being invoked, the court was bound to apply the paramountcy of the child's welfare test to resolving the dispute. Whether Viscount Cave was right to say that it was 'settled law' that the child's welfare was 'paramount' is debatable[134] but, given that this was a House of Lords decision, it was surely authoritative in its own right.

Perhaps the reason why *Ward v Laverty* has never really been regarded as a leading decision was that it was overtaken by s 1 of the Guardianship of Infants Act 1925,[135] which provided that in:

> ... *any proceedings* before *any* court [in which] ... the custody or upbringing of an infant or the administration of any property belonging to or held on trust for an infant, or the application of the income thereof, is in question, the court, in deciding that question, shall regard the welfare of the infant as the first and paramount consideration. (Emphasis added)

Whatever the true position was before 1925, the striking difference between this Act and that of 1886 with regard to the weight to be placed on the child's welfare is evidence of quite a remarkable change of thought. Whether the 1925 Act was intended to do anything more than further the process of equalising parental rights, whilst at the same time extending the courts' discretionary power to override the absolute rights of the father in custody cases, seems open to question. Furthermore, it now seems clear that at that time Parliament was certainly not intending the child's welfare to be the court's *sole* consideration.[136]

J v C

Notwithstanding *Ward v Laverty*, the courts began to interpret s 1 of the 1925 Act narrowly and indeed, prior to the House of Lords' decision in *J v C*,[137] there remained Court

---

[133] See the analysis by N Lowe 'The House of Lords and the Welfare Principle' in C Bridge (ed) *Family Law Towards the Millennium—Essays for P M Bromley* (1997) at p132.

[134] See P Pettit 'Parental Control and Guardianship' in R Graveson and F Crane (eds) *A Century of Family Law* (1957) ch 4 at 76.

[135] Which ironically (given that the case was on appeal from Northern Ireland), as Lord Upjohn observed in *J v C* [1970] AC 668 at 723, was destined never to apply to Northern Ireland.

[136] See the scholarly analysis of the history of the 1925 legislation by S Cretney ' "What will the Women Want Next?" The Struggle for Power within the Family 1925–1975' (1996) 112 LQR 110 at 129–31, who convincingly shows that it was definitely intended not to be the sole consideration, since, ironically, it was Viscount Cave who had the word 'sole' removed from the Bill and replaced by the words 'first and paramount'.

[137] [1970] AC 668, on which see N Lowe 'J v C—Placing The Child's Welfare Centre Stage' in S Gilmore, J Herring and R Probert (eds) *Landmark Cases in Family Law* (2011) ch 3.

of Appeal authority[138] for saying that the Act only applied to disputes between fathers and mothers over their legitimate children, and apparent authority[139] for saying that the wishes of an unimpeachable parent were to be preferred to the welfare of the child. Both propositions, however, were firmly laid to rest by *J v C*. In that case a Spanish couple came to England looking for work. Whilst here the mother gave birth to a boy, but because she was ill the baby went to live with English foster parents. When the couple later returned to Spain they took the boy with them, but whilst in Spain his health deteriorated and at the parents' request he was returned to the foster parents in England. The parents meanwhile went to West Germany to look for work and, having successfully improved their economic position, returned to Spain some two years later. Whilst in West Germany the parents made no attempt to contact their son and were only prompted to seek his return after receiving a somewhat tactless letter from the foster parents describing how 'English' the boy had become. The ensuing proceedings proved protracted and in any event the parents were poorly advised and only belatedly formally applied for the return of the child. Consequently, it took a further five years before the case was heard by the House of Lords. By that time the boy, who had spent all but 18 months of his 10 and a half years with the foster parents in England, had become well integrated into the family. Moreover, he had been brought up as an English boy, spoke little Spanish and scarcely knew his parents. On the other hand, the Spanish parents now lived in 'an entirely suitable' modern three-bedroomed flat in Madrid. The father had a good job and the mother's health was completely restored.[140]

At first instance Ungoed-Thomas J awarded care and control to the English foster parents, and this decision was upheld by the Court of Appeal. On appeal to the Lords it was accepted that the decision was only challengeable if it could be shown that the trial judge had exercised his discretion upon some wrong principle. Accordingly, it was submitted that united parents were prima facie entitled to the custody of their infant children and the court should only deprive them of care and control if they were unfitted by character, conduct or position in life to have this control. Thus in the case of unimpeachable parents (which for the purposes of argument the appellants were assumed to be) the court should, save in very exceptional cases, give care and control to those parents. It was consequentially argued that, notwithstanding s 1 of the Guardianship of Infants Act 1925 which, it was contended, only applied to disputes between parents and not between parents and non-parents, the child's welfare was not the first and paramount consideration. This argument was said to be supported by the preamble to the Act which stated 'Whereas Parliament by the Sex Disqualification (Removal) Act 1919, and various other enactments has sought to establish equality in law between the sexes, and it is expedient that this principle should obtain with respect to the guardianship of infants and the rights and responsibilities conferred thereby'.

The House of Lords rejected these submissions.

It was unanimously agreed that s 1 of the 1925 Act was not confined, as the preamble seemed to imply,[141] to disputes between parents, but was of 'universal application',

---

[138] *Re Carroll* [1931] 1 KB 317 in which the Court of Appeal upheld the mother's wish to remove her illegitimate daughter from a Protestant Adoption Society so as to place her with another Society where she would be brought up as a Catholic, notwithstanding the lower court's finding that the child's welfare would be best served by leaving her where she was.

[139] *Re Thain* [1926] Ch 676, although in *J v C* [1970] AC 668 at 711, Lord MacDermott considered the headnote misleading.

[140] All this was in stark contrast to the position when the parents first returned to Spain after leaving England, when the father was a lowly paid worker and the family lived in what were virtually slum conditions.

[141] As their Lordships pointed out, relying on *A-G v Prince Ernest Augustus of Hanover* [1957] AC 436, preambles cannot control the ambit of sections of an Act.

and insofar as *Re Carroll*[142] held otherwise, it was overruled. As Lord MacDermott (with whom Lord Pearson expressly agreed) pointed out, the wording of s 1 seemed to be deliberately wide and general, relating to *any* proceedings before any court and, so worded,[143] 'would apply to cases, such as the present, between parents and strangers'.

Whether the House of Lords were right in their interpretation of the 1925 Act has been questioned. After a detailed examination of the Parliamentary history, Cretney concluded[144] 'It seems inconceivable that legislation which would have resulted in a child being kept from his family by an outsider able to offer a better upbringing would have been well received in 1925; and this outcome was certainly unforeseen by anyone involved in drafting the 1925 Act.' The more likely Parliamentary intention was to further the process of placing mothers and fathers in the same legal position vis-à-vis their children. Indeed in a later House of Lords decision, *A v Liverpool City Council,* Lord Wilberforce described the provision as a 'sex equality' enactment.[145]

Notwithstanding these doubts, the significance of *J v C* cannot be over-emphasised. First, it established that s 1 of the 1925 Act applied as much to disputes over a child's upbringing between parents and third parties as it did to disputes between parents. Indeed, it is clear that the decision was meant to have a general application to proceedings concerning the upbringing of children. As Lord Guest put it, s 1 had 'universal application'. Secondly, it unequivocally established that the child's welfare is so overwhelmingly important that it can outweigh the interests of even so-called unimpeachable parents in seeking to look after their own child against a third party. A fortiori it is the dominant consideration in disputes between parents.

Subsequent applications of *J v C*

Shortly after *J v C* was decided, s 1 of the 1925 Act was repealed and re-enacted in s 1 of the Guardianship of Minors Act 1971. The influence of *J v C* became more apparent. For example, the Court of Appeal in *S (BD) v S(DJ) (Children: Care and Control)*[146] finally quashed the notion that the so-called 'unimpeachable parent' stood in a more favourable position as against the other who was guilty of matrimonial misconduct, and established in effect that the interests of justice as between the parents do not outweigh the welfare principle. In other words, if the welfare of the child so demands, he or she should be looked after by the so-called 'guilty' parent, however unjust the other will believe the decision to be. Hence, matrimonial misconduct is relevant only insofar as it reflects on that person as a parent. This approach reflected the shift in attitude to divorce espoused by the Divorce Reform Act 1969 to the concept of irretrievable breakdown away from matrimonial fault. In *S (BD) v S (DJ)* Ormrod LJ (who was a great champion of children's welfare) deprecated the use of the term 'unimpeachable' parent in this context. As he said:[147]

> I have never known and still do not know what it means. It cannot mean a parent who is above criticism because there is no such thing. It might mean a parent against whom no matrimonial offence has been proved. If so it adds nothing to the record which

[142] [1931] 1 KB 317.   [143] [1970] AC 668 at 710.

[144] ' "What will the Women Want Next?" The Struggle for Power within the Family 1925–1975' (1996) 110 LQR 110 at 128–33.

[145] [1982] AC 363 at 371. See also in similar vein *Richards v Richards* [1984] AC 174 at 203, per Lord Hailsham LC.

[146] [1977] Fam 109. See also *Re K (Minors) (Children: Care and Control)* [1977] Fam 179, CA. See J Hall 'Custody of children—welfare or justice?' [1977] CLJ 252.

[147] At 115–16. In *Re R (Minors) (Wardship: Jurisdiction)* (1981) 2 FLR 416 at 425, Ormrod LJ referred to the 'unimpeachable parent' as being in 'forensic limbo'.

is before the court and in any event is now outmoded. I think in truth it is really an advocate's phrase.

In *Re B (A Minor) (Wardship: Sterilisation)*[148] the application of the welfare principle can be seen in another context. An application was made to sanction the sterilisation of a 17-year-old girl who had a severely limited intellectual capability. Evidence was adduced that, while she had already been shown to be vulnerable to sexual approaches, she could not be placed on any contraceptive regime and was incapable of knowing the causal connection between intercourse and childbirth. It was further shown that she could not understand the nature of pregnancy nor what was involved in delivery. In sanctioning the operation notwithstanding its irreversible nature, the Lords rejected the argument based on the Canadian Supreme Court decision, *Re Eve*[149] and an earlier English High Court decision, *Re D (A Minor) (Wardship: Sterilisation)*[150] that, because what was in issue was 'non-therapeutic' treatment, the court had no power to act. As Lord Bridge put it:[151]

> To say that the court can never authorise sterilisation of a ward as being in her best interests would be patently wrong. To say that it can only do so if the operation is "therapeutic" as opposed to "non therapeutic" is to divert attention from the true issue, which is whether the operation is in the ward's best interest, and remove it to an area of arid semantic debate as to where the line is to be drawn between "therapeutic" and "non therapeutic" treatment.

Similarly, Lord Oliver observed[152] that if:

> ... the expression "non-therapeutic" was intended to exclude measures taken for the necessary protection from future harm of the person over whom the jurisdiction is exercisable, then I respectfully dissent from it for it seems to me to contradict what is the sole and paramount criterion for the exercise of the jurisdiction, viz the welfare and benefit of the ward.

Further important reaffirmation of *J v C* was made by the House of Lords in *Re KD (A Minor) (Ward: Termination of Access)*,[153] in which a local authority sought the termination of a mother's already limited contact with her son, who for the previous four of his four-and-three-quarter years of life had been living with foster parents. The mother argued that the right to see her son was a parental right which could only be displaced where the court was satisfied that the exercise of the right would be positively inimical to the interest of the child. It was further contended that this right had been affirmed as a fundamental human right under the European Convention on Human Rights. Both contentions were rejected. As Lord Oliver put it:[154]

> ... the contention that a parent has a right of access was out of line with an approach which has been universally acted upon ever since the decision of your Lordships' House in *J v C*.

In Lord Oliver's view, the law recognised the parent's position by taking it to be a normal assumption that a child benefits from having continued contact with both parents.

---

[148] [1988] AC 199, HL.   [149] (1986) 31 DLR (4th) 1.
[150] [1976] Fam 185. See also N Lowe and R White *Wards of Court* (1986, 2nd edn) paras 7–6, note 6, and 7–11.
[151] [1988] AC at 205.   [152] At 212.   [153] [1988] AC 806.   [154] at 827.

Nevertheless that position must always be qualified by considerations of what is best for the welfare of the particular child in question. So understood, his Lordship could find nothing in the European Court of Human Rights' decision in *R v UK*[155] which 'contradicts or casts any doubt upon that decision [ie in *J v C*] or which calls now for any reappraisal of it by your Lordships'.

Notwithstanding these decisions it should not be thought that parents have no standing. In *Re G (Children) (Residence: Same-sex Partner)* the House of Lords overturned a decision of the lower courts to award primary residence to the former same-sex partner of the biological mother's two children after the mother had flouted the terms of a shared residence order. The House emphasised that, in Baroness Hale's words,[156] the fact that a person who is the natural parent (ie in this case, both the biological and psychological parent) of the children 'while raising no presumption in her favour, is undoubtedly an important and significant factor in determining what will be best for them now and in the future.' Lord Nicholls went further, saying 'in the ordinary way the rearing of a child by his or her biological parent can be expected to be in the child's best interests, both in the short term and also, importantly, in the longer term. I decry any tendency to diminish the significance of this factor. A child should not be removed from the primary care of his or her biological parents without compelling reason.'[157]

By the end of the 1980s it was clear that when called upon to determine a child's upbringing the courts were effectively treating the child's welfare as the sole consideration in the sense that all the circumstances of the case were weighed in the balance to determine what was in the best interests of the child concerned. Nevertheless the fact remained that under the 1971 Act the child's welfare was still expressed to be '*the first* and paramount interest'.

However, reflecting the fact that the words 'first and' had become redundant, the Children Act 1989 s 1(1) simply states that:

> When a court determines any question with respect to—
>
> (a) the upbringing of a child; or
> (b) the administration of a child's property or the application of any income arising from it, the child's welfare shall be the court's paramount consideration.

We consider in more detail the history and application of s 1 in Chapter 12. Suffice to say here that the new formulation was neither intended nor has it in fact altered the pre-1989 Act position, though that is not to say that there have been no problems concerning its application, not least of which has been its compatibility with human rights following the implementation of the Human Rights Act 1998.

(b) Children's ability to make decisions for themselves

Although the application of the welfare principle obviously dilutes parental authority it does not in itself give a child rights as such.[158] Indeed, until the issue comes before the

---

[155] (1988) 10 EHRR 74, [1988] 2 FLR 445 in which the United Kingdom was found to be in breach of Article 8 of the Convention (right of respect for family life) because under the law at the time parents had no means of challenging access decisions in relation to a child in local authority care. In fact, this and other European Court of Human Rights' decisions did cause the Government to provide under s 34 of the Children Act 1989 a presumption of reasonable contact between a child in care and his family. See R White, P Carr and N Lowe *The Children Act in Practice* (2008, 4th edn) para 1.7.

[156] [2006] UKHL 43 [2006] 1 WLR 2305 at [44].   [157] [2006] UKHL 43 [2006] 1 WLR 2305 at [2].

[158] See generally M Freeman *The Rights and Wrongs of Children* (1983) particularly ch 2; J Fortin *Children's Rights and the Developing Law* (2009, 3rd edn) particularly ch 1 and J Eekelaar 'The Eclipse of Parental Rights' (1986) 102 LQR 4.

court, parents still generally have considerable authority over their children. There has, however, been a discernible trend towards the greater empowerment of children, though, as will be seen, English law has (so far) generally stopped short of giving children what are sometimes referred to as autonomy rights.

R v D 1984

In *R v D*[159] the question was raised as to whether at common law a father could be guilty of kidnapping his own child. In his defence the father sought to rely on the alleged paramountcy of his position at common law. In rejecting this defence the House of Lords, whilst acknowledging that it might well have succeeded in the nineteenth century, were not prepared to apply it in the case before them. As Lord Brandon put it:[160]

> The common law . . . while generally immutable in its principles, unless different principles are laid down by Statute, is not immutable in the way in which it adapts, develops and applies those principles in a radically changing world and against the background of radically changed social conventions.

He continued:

> . . . the paramountcy of a father's position in the family home [has] been progressively whittled away, until now, in the second half of the 20th century, [it] can be regarded as having disappeared altogether.

Having rejected this defence, the House of Lords further considered whether the child's consent to removal would be a defence. In ruling that it could, Lord Brandon said:[161]

> I see no good reason why, in relation to the kidnapping of a child, it should not in all cases be the absence of the child's consent which is material, whatever its age may be. In the case of a very young child, it would not have the understanding or intelligence to give its consent, so that absence of consent would be a necessary inference from its age. In the case of an older child, however, it must, I think be a question of fact for a jury whether the child concerned has sufficient understanding and intelligence to give its consent . . . While the matter will always be for the jury alone to decide, I should not expect a jury to find at all frequently that a child under 14 had sufficient understanding and intelligence to give its consent.

The significance of *R v D* is twofold. First, it put the final nail in the coffin of the father's supremacy within the family even under the common law. Secondly, it accepted the proposition that children even as young as 14 might be competent to make some decisions for themselves. It is this latter point that became developed further in the next House of Lords decision, *Gillick v West Norfolk and Wisbech Area Health Authority*.

Gillick v West Norfolk and Wisbech Area Health Authority

Gillick[162] concerned a Government circular in which doctors were advised that in 'most unusual circumstances' it would be proper for them to give contraceptive advice and

---

[159] [1984] AC 778, HL, on which see Law Commission Consultation Paper No 200 *Simplification of Criminal Law: Kidnapping* (2013) ch 2 and N Lowe 'Child Abduction and Child Kidnapping—II: The Common Law Position and its Relationship with the Child Abduction Act 1984' (1984) 134 NLJ 995.

[160] [1984] AC 778, HL at 805.   [161] [1984] AC 778, HL at 806.

[162] [1986] AC 112, HL, for an extended analysis of which see J Fortin 'The *Gillick* Decision—Not Just a High-water Mark' in S Gilmore, J Herring and R Probert (eds) *Landmark Cases in Family Law* (2011) ch 11;

treatment to a girl under the age of 16 without her parents' knowledge or consent. The applicant, a mother of four daughters under the age of 16, sought a declaration that this was unlawful, because it infringed her parental right to be informed and to veto any medical treatment of her children, at any rate until they were 16.[163] The action failed. The contention about parental rights was rejected on the basis that the law does not recognise any rule of absolute parental authority until a fixed age and that even with regard to contraceptive treatment a girl of sufficient maturity and understanding could give a valid consent. The circular could not therefore be said to be unlawful since girls of sufficient maturity, even if under the age of 16, could themselves consent to the contraceptive treatment. Indeed, the majority view seemed to be that as parental authority exists for the benefit of the child and not for the parent, it lasts only as long as a child needs protection, and will consequently end when the child is sufficiently mature to make the decision for himself. As Lord Scarman put it:[164]

> The underlying principle of the law . . . is that parental right yields to the child's right to make his own decisions when he reaches a sufficient understanding and intelligence to be capable of making up his own mind on the matter requiring decisions.

Of course, even under this analysis a crucial question is, when will a child be considered to have sufficient understanding to be considered what has since become known as 'Gillick competent'? This will depend upon the nature of the issue involved for, as has since been observed in the context of a vulnerable adult's capacity to consent to sexual relations, the Gillick test of competence 'is act not person specific'.[165] In the context of consenting to medical treatment, for example, it would not require much intelligence to appreciate that a broken leg needs mending whereas, as Gillick itself shows, considerable understanding is required in the case of consenting to the prescription of contraceptive treatment. In that context Lord Scarman said:[166]

> It is not enough that she should understand the advice which is being given: she must also have sufficient maturity to understand what is involved. There are moral and family questions, especially her relationship with her parents, long-term problems associated with the emotional impact of pregnancy and its termination; and there are risks to health of sexual intercourse at her age, risks which contraception may diminish but cannot eliminate.

With respect to Lord Scarman this looks suspiciously like importing into this area of law the doctrine of informed consent, which in the context of the tort of negligence at least the House of Lords had previously rejected.[167] It may indeed be doubted whether many adults—let alone

S Gilmore 'The Limits of Parental Responsibility' in R Probert, S Gilmore and J Herring (eds) *Responsible Parents and Parental Responsibility* (2011) ch 4; C Barton and G Douglas, *Law and Parenthood* (1995), 118ff; J Fortin *Children's Rights and the Developing Law* (2009, 3rd edn) chs 3 and 5; J Eekelaar (1986) 102 LQR 4; A Bainham 'The Balance of Power in Family Decisions' [1986] CLJ 262; and J Eekelaar 'The Emergence of Children's Rights' [1986] 6 OJLS 161. For an interesting discussion of the contrasting position of mentally incapacitated persons (including children) under the Mental Capacity Act 2005, see E Cove 'Maximisation of minors' capacity' [2011] CFLQ 431.

[163] When by reason of s 8 of the Family Law Reform Act 1969 children can give a valid consent.

[164] [1986] AC 112 at 184A.

[165] See *D Borough Council v AB* [2011] EWHC 101 (COP) [2011] 2 FLR 72 at [18] per Mostyn J, who also observed that in *Gillick* the doctor did not need to know the identity of the person with whom the girl proposes to have sex.   [166] [1986] AC 112 at 189.

[167] In *Sidaway v Board of Governors of the Bethlem Royal Hospital and the Maudsley Hospital* [1985] AC 871, HL. See also S Cretney *All ER Annual Review 1985* at 175, though that decision has since been heavily criticised in *Chester v Afshar* [2004] UKHL 1 AC 134 [2005] 1 AC 134.

a child under the age of 16—could validly consent to contraceptive treatment under Lord Scarman's test. In practice it seems likely that consideration is mainly given to whether the child has sufficient maturity to understand the advice.[168] Even this, however, will not be easy for a practitioner to judge.

It might have been supposed that once it is established that a *Gillick* competent child has consented to the proposed treatment, no further inquiry need be made and the continued involvement of the parent may be ignored. In fact, however, the *Gillick* decision does not go that far. It does not give doctors a carte blanche to prescribe contraceptives to girls under the age of 16. According to Lord Fraser,[169] in addition to being satisfied that the girl understands his advice, the doctor must also be satisfied that he cannot persuade her to allow him to inform her parents, that she is very likely to begin or continue to have sexual intercourse with or without contraceptive treatment, that without the advice or treatment her health is likely to suffer and that her best interests require him to give the advice, treatment or both without parental consent. Even with respect to simpler treatment Lord Fraser seemed to contemplate some parental involvement. Hence, while he did not doubt the capacity of a 15-year-old to consent to having a broken arm set, he added that 'of course the consent of the parents should normally be asked.'[170]

R (Axon) v Secretary of State for Health and the Family Planning Association

Gillick was subsequently applied in *R (Axon)*,[171] in which a parent sought a declaration that Guidance issued by the Department of Health document[172] in 2004 was unlawful. The Guidance stated that a medical professional could provide advice and treatment on sexual matters for young people under the age of 16 without the knowledge and consent of their parents. In so providing, the Guidance clearly stated that children under the age of 16 are owed the same duty of confidentiality as any other person. It was sought to impugn the Guidance on the basis that it (a) misrepresented *Gillick* while purporting to clarify it, (b) made doctors the sole arbiters of what is in a child's best interests, (c) made informing the parents the exception rather than the rule, (d) excluded parents from decision making about the child's life and welfare, and (e) failed to discharge the State's positive obligation to give practical and effective protection of the claimant's Art 8 Rights under the European Human Rights Convention.

In an extensive and carefully considered judgment Silber J rejected all the contentions and refused to make the declaration sought, holding that the *Gillick* decision was determinative of the issues raised. In particular he held, following Lord Scarman's judgment in *Gillick*, that where the young person understood the advice provided by the medical

---

[168] Which is all Lord Fraser seemed to require: see *Gillick v West Norfolk and Wisbech Area Health Authority* [1986] AC 112, HL at 174. Cf *A Local Authority v Mrs A (Test For Capacity As To Contraception)* [2010] EWHC 1549 (COP) [2011] 1 FLR 26 where, in the context of determining a vulnerable adult's capacity to consent to contraceptive treatment, Bodey J considered (at [60]–[61]) that requiring a wide understanding such as envisaging the wider practicalities of bringing up a child would 'create a real risk of blurring the line between capacity and best interests'.

[169] [1986] AC 112, HL at 174. It must be a matter of doubt whether in practice a medical practitioner will always be so thorough as Lord Fraser's test demands.

[170] [1986] AC 112, HL at 169 and 409 respectively.

[171] [2006] EWHC 37 (Admin) [2006] 2 FLR 206, on which see R Taylor 'Reversing the retreat from *Gillick*? *R (Axon) v Secretary of State for Health*' [2007] CFLQ 81.

[172] 'Best Practice Guidance for Doctors and other Health Professionals on the Provision of Advice and Treatment to Young People under Sixteen on Contraception, Sexual and Reproductive Health', which replaced the Guidance that had been upheld in *Gillick*.

professional and its implication (ie had satisfied the '*Gillick* competence' test) the parent ceased to retain an Art 8 right in relation to that decision.[173]

The interest of *Axon* is twofold. It is one the few decisions, albeit a first instance one, to expressly apply Lord Scarman's reasoning in *Gillick*. Secondly, it was the first case to consider the *Gillick* ruling in the light of human rights following the Human Rights Act 1998. That *Gillick* was applied should occasion no real surprise since the facts of *Axon* were remarkably similar to the earlier decision. However, it is the analysis of the application of Art 8 of the European Convention on Human Rights that merits close attention. In this respect Silber J said:[174]

> There is nothing in the Strasbourg jurisprudence that persuades me that any parental right or power of control under Art 8 is wider than in domestic law, which is that the right of parents, in the words of Lord Scarman 'exists primarily to enable the parent to discharge his duty of maintenance, protection and education until he reaches such an age as to be able to make his own decisions' . . . The parental right to family life does not continue after that time and so parents do not have Art 8 rights to be notified of any advice of a medical professional after the young person is able look after himself or herself and make his or her own decisions.

This approach has been criticised on a number of fronts. In particular it has been well pointed out that the Strasbourg jurisprudence does not support the idea that parents lose their Art 8 rights when their children gain sufficient understanding to make decisions for themselves. The better analysis, it has been said, is that family life continues to exist between parents and children but that the rights do not require 'respect' or legal promotion once the child matures.[175] Silber J's analysis has also been criticised for paying scant regard to the position of the child involved in *Axon* and its inadequate dismissal (on the basis that it was only concerned with Art 5) of the Strasbourg decision, *Nielsen v Denmark*[176] in which the European Court of Human rights considered that Art 8 covered a wide range of parental decisions. It was mooted that *Nielsen* could be reconciled with adolescent autonomy by balancing the child's own Art 8 rights with those of parents giving greater weight to an older child's psychological integrity including the right to self-determination.[177]

Despite these criticisms *Axon* has been said to be 'important for its place in the emerging emphasis on the autonomy of competent children'[178] and for usefully emphasising 'the relevance of *Gillick* within the rights framework superimposed on family law by the Human Rights Act.'[179]

Gillick—a false dawn?

Although *Gillick* should certainly be seen as a further important example of the diminution of parental authority in the eyes of English law, potentially it was (and still is) of much

---

[173] [2006] EWHC 37 (Admin) [2006] 2 FLR 206 at [130].

[174] [2006] EWHC 37 (Admin) [2006] 2 FLR 206 at [132].

[175] By R Taylor 'Reversing the retreat from *Gillick? R (Axon) v Secretary of State for Health* [2007] CFLQ 81.

[176] (1989) 11 EHRR 175.

[177] J Fortin 'The *Gillick* Decision—Not Just a High-water Mark' in S Gilmore, J Herring and R Probert (eds) *Landmark Cases in Family Law* (2011) pp 220–221. This analysis, it was contended, would mean that the two Court of Appeal decisions, *Re R* and *Re W*, about to be discussed, would not survive a human rights challenge.

[178] R Taylor 'Reversing the retreat from *Gillick? R (Axon) v Secretary of State for Health* [2007] CFLQ 81 at 97.

[179] J Fortin 'The *Gillick* Decision—Not Just a High-water Mark' in S Gilmore, J Herring and R Probert (eds) *Landmark Cases in Family Law* (2011) at p 222.

greater significance, for it seemed to acknowledge that children themselves have the power to make their own decisions.[180] Had this been how the decision was interpreted, then it might fairly have been described as a landmark of children's rights.[181] However, as we now discuss, it has been restrictively interpreted, and for those who saw *Gillick* as establishing autonomy rights for mature children it has so far proved a false dawn. The two leading cases are *Re R (A Minor) (Wardship: Consent to Medical Treatment)*[182] and *Re W (A Minor) (Medical Treatment: Court's Jurisdiction)*,[183] both decided by the Court of Appeal.

Re R concerned a 15-year-old girl who had suffered emotional abuse and had become suicidal. Fears for her mental state led the local authority to intervene and a place was found for her at an adolescent psychiatric unit. Her condition was felt to warrant the use of sedatives and drugs. However, during a lucid period the girl indicated that she would refuse any such treatment. Despite the unit's insistence on the necessity of the treatment the local authority declined to consent and instead took the issue to court. Perhaps controversially, the court unanimously held that R lacked the necessary maturity to decide whether to take the medication on the basis that '*Gillick* competence' could not fluctuate on a day-to-day basis, so that the child is one day regarded as competent, while on another day she is not. Accordingly, the unanimous decision was to sanction the treatment. Lord Donaldson MR, however, went further. He held (obiter) that all *Gillick* had decided was that a competent child could consent to medical treatment but that it did not decide that such a child could veto medical treatment. In his view, both parents (and presumably anyone with parental responsibility) and the court retain the power to consent to treatment even of a '*Gillick* competent child', notwithstanding that the child has refused treatment. He considered that there are concurrent powers to consent (which he described as being 'keys which unlock the door') and only if *all* the 'key holders' fail or refuse to consent will a veto be treated as binding.

This important limitation on the effect of *Gillick* was confirmed in *Re W*, which concerned a 16-year-old girl who suffered anorexia and who refused treatment. Her condition was such that without treatment she would shortly die. Because the child was 16 she had a statutory right (under Family Law Reform Act 1969 s 8) to give a valid consent to treatment. The question was, however, did s 8 or *Gillick* give her an absolute power of veto? The Court of Appeal again held that neither s 8 nor *Gillick* could be considered to vest in the child a power of veto. Instead they held that the High Court could (and in this case, should) overrule the child's wishes. They rejected the argument that implicit in a right to consent must also be a power of veto. In so concluding, Lord Donaldson MR and Balcombe LJ acknowledged that

---

[180] But note the scepticism about whether *Gillick* really did provide for competent children's autonomy expressed by S Gilmore 'The Limits of Parental Responsibility' in R Probert, S Gilmore and J Herring (eds) *Responsible Parents and Parental Responsibility* (2011) ch 4.

[181] As it was heralded by the Children's Legal Centre at (1985) 22 *Childright* 11.

[182] [1992] Fam 11, CA; G Douglas 'The Retreat from *Gillick*' (1992) 55 MLR 569.

[183] [1993] Fam 64 [1992] 4 All ER 627, CA; N Lowe and S Juss 'Medical Treatment—Pragmatism and the Search for Principle' (1993) 56 MLR 865; A Bainham 'The judge and the competent child' (1992) 108 LQR 194; J Eekelaar 'White Coats and Flak Jackets—Doctors, Children and the Courts Again' (1993) 109 LQR 182; and J Masson '*Re W*: Appealing from a golden cage' (1993) 5 Jo of Child Law 37. See also *Re P (Medical Treatment: Best Interests)* [2003] EWHC 2327 (Fam) [2004] 2 FLR 1117 (in which Johnson J, though accepting that a refusal of medical treatment by a child can be determinative, nevertheless overrode a 16 year old Jehovah's Witness's objections by permitting the hospital to administer blood or blood treatments provided there was no other form of treatment available); *Re M (Medical Treatment: Consent)* [1999] 2 FLR 1097 (in which Johnson J overrode an intelligent 15 year old girl's refusal to have a heart transplant because she did not want someone else's heart). Note also *Re L (Medical Treatment: Gillick Competence)* [1998] 2 FLR 810 at 813E per Sir Stephen Brown B (14-year-old Jehovah's Witness found not to be competent but even if she had been the court would have overridden her wishes) and *Re C (Detention: Medical Treatment)* [1997] 2 FLR 180.

Lord Scarman's reference to the termination of parental authority upon the child's reaching competence could be taken to suggest that the refusal of a child below the age of 16 to accept medical treatment was determinative. Both, however, doubted whether Lord Scarman meant anything more than that the child's parents lose their exclusive rights to consent upon the child becoming '*Gillick* competent'. Even if he had meant that such children have a right of veto, then both their Lordships thought he was wrong.

Rejecting the notion that the child's views were determinative did not mean that the court would pay no regard to the child's wishes. On the contrary, as Lord Donaldson MR said, 'good parenting involves giving minors as much rope as they can handle without an unacceptable risk that they will hang themselves'. Yet, as Balcombe LJ said, 'if the court's powers are to be meaningful there must come a point at which the courts, whilst not disregarding the child's wishes, can override them in the child's own best interest, objectively considered'. In his view, such a point comes when the child, in refusing treatment, is threatened with death or severe permanent injury. He cited in support Ward J's trenchant comment in *Re E (A Minor)*[184] that the court, 'in exercising its prerogative of protection, should be very slow to allow an infant to martyr himself'. Put less dramatically, as Hedley J said,[185]in the context of a 15 year old's objections to being DNA tested for paternity purposes, a *Gillick* competent child 'does not have a right to refuse consent; a refusal of consent, unless statute otherwise indicates, always triggers the issue of welfare'.

Not surprisingly, these decisions have generated considerable comment, for they bring into sharp relief the issue of allowing competent children to make decisions for themselves (ie whether they have autonomy rights) as against the paternalistic approach of protecting them from doing (at any rate, irreparable) harm to themselves. As can be seen, the Court of Appeal favour the latter approach, though one of the intrinsic difficulties of doing so is being able to accept that a child can be competent to give a valid consent yet not be competent to exercise a power of veto.[186] One suggestion, however,[187] is that based on the premise that, since a doctor will act in the best interests of his patient, it is perfectly rational for the law to facilitate this and hence allow a '*Gillick* competent' child to give a valid consent, and also to protect the child against parents opposed to what is professionally considered to be in his or her best medical interests. In contrast, it is surely right for the law to be reluctant to allow a *child* to be able to veto treatment designed for his or her benefit, particularly if a refusal would lead to the child's death or permanent damage. In other words, the clear and consistent policy of the law is to protect children against wrong-headed parents and against themselves with the final safeguard, as *Re W* establishes, of giving the court the last word in cases of dispute. In the mean time the debate continues.[188]

Such an argument, however, by no means commands widespread support and many commentators remain keen for the law to recognise competent children's autonomy. They

[184] (1990) 9 BMLR 1.
[185] In *L v P (Paternity Test: Child's Objection)* [2011] EWHC 3399 (Fam) [2013] 1 FLR 578 at [17]. In fact faced with child's objections the application for a DNA test on the child was refused but on the basis of welfare considerations.
[186] With respect to Lord Donaldson MR, it is difficult to follow his distinction between consenting to and determining treatment.
[187] See N Lowe and S Juss 'Medical Treatment—Pragmatism and the Search for Principle' (1993) 56 MLR 865, pp 871–2. See also S Gilmore and J Herring ' "No" is the hardest word: consent and children's autonomy' [2011] CFLQ 3 for a partial defence of the Court of Appeal decisions, though drawing a distinction between refusing consent and refusing treatment.
[188] See the reply to Gilmore and Herring's article in [2011] CFLQ 3, by E Cave and J Wallbank 'Minors' Capacity to Refuse Treatment: A Reply to Gilmore and Herring' [2012] *Medical Law Review* 423 and the subsequent riposte by S Gilmore and J Herring 'Children's refusal of treatment: the debate continues' [2012] Fam Law 973.

will no doubt derive encouragement from a number of comments to the effect that a *Gillick* competent child has a right to make informed decisions on his or her own behalf made by the now President of the Family Division, Sir James Munby.[189] It remains to be seen how the law will develop.

(c) The international dimension

The UN Convention on the Rights of the Child

Discussion of the legal relationship between parent and child can no longer focus solely on the domestic position.[190] Regard must also be had to international instruments and in particular to the UN Convention on the Rights of the Child 1989, to which the UK is a party; to the initiatives of the Council of Europe, which have increasing influence; and to the European Union's Charter of Fundamental Rights of the European Union.

So far as the UN Convention is concerned, note may be taken in particular of Art 3(1), which provides:

> In all actions concerning children, whether undertaken by public or private social welfare institutions, courts of law, administrative authorities or legislative bodies, the best interests of the child shall be a primary consideration.

As can be seen, this Article provides an international obligation to apply the best interests of the child test and as such is clearly similar to the paramountcy test under s 1(1) of the Children Act 1989. It may be observed, however, that in one sense Art 3 is narrower than the domestic provision, in that the enjoinder to regard the best interests as *a primary* consideration is not as strong as to regard the child's welfare as the *paramount* consideration. On the other hand, Art 3, by applying to administrative authorities and legislative bodies, is wider than s 1(1) which only applies to court proceedings.[191] We discuss this provision further in Chapter 12.

A second important Article is Art 12 which provides:

> 1. States parties should assure to the child who is capable of forming his or her own views the right to express those view freely in all matters affecting the child, *the view of the child being given due weight in accordance with the age and maturity of the child.*
> 2. For this purpose the child shall in particular be provided the opportunity to be heard in any judicial and administrative proceedings affecting the child, either directly, or through a representative or an appropriate body, in a manner consistent with the procedural rules of national law. (Emphasis added)

Article 12(1) stops short of giving even mature children autonomy rights. Although the precise meaning of the phrase 'the views of the child being given due weight in accordance

---

[189] See *Re Roddy (A Child) (Identification: Restriction on Publication)* [2003] EWHC 2927 (Fam) [2004] 2 FLR 949 at [57] and in *E (By Her Litigation Friend The Official Solicitor) v Channel Four and St Helens Borough Council* [2005] EWHC 1144 (Fam) [2005] 2 FLR 913 at [56]. In *Re G (Education: Religious Upbringing)* [2012] EWCA Civ 1233 [2013] 1 FLR 677 at [21], Munby P commented that Lord Scarman's speech in *Gillick* 'demands particular attention'.

[190] See inter alia J Fortin *Children's Rights and the Developing Law* (2009, 3rd edn) ch 2; C Barton and G Douglas, *Law and Parenthood* (1995), 34–43; G Van Bueren *The International Law on the Rights of the Child* (1993); S Detrich 'Family Rights Under the United Nations Convention on the Rights of the Child' and K O'Donnell 'Parent-Child Relationships Within the European Convention', both in N Lowe and G Douglas (eds) *Families Across Frontiers* (1996) at pp 95–114, and 135–50 respectively.

[191] Though local authorities have a general duty to safeguard and promote the welfare of children in need in their area and of those they are 'looking after' under s 17 and s 22 of the Children Act 1989 (discussed in Chs 15 and 18, respectively).

with the age and maturity of the child' is unclear, it is submitted that the English position of reserving the power of the court to override the wishes of a *Gillick* competent child does not breach Art 12(1). Neither *Re R* nor *Re W* establishes that the views of such competent children are ignored; far from it: considerable stress was placed on the need to have the greatest regard to such views. Further, as we discuss in Chapters 12 and 13, s 1(3)(a) of the Children Act 1989 specifically directs the court, at any rate in contested private law proceedings for s 8 orders, to have regard to the ascertainable wishes and feelings of the child. The Act also provides a mechanism for children of sufficient understanding to initiate proceedings in their own right.[192] Furthermore r 16.6 of the Family Procedure Rules 2010 permits competent children to initiate proceedings without the need of a litigation friend.[193] The judiciary have been acutely aware of the need to safeguard Art 12 rights with Thorpe LJ going as far to say[194] that 'we must, in the case of articulate teenagers, accept that the right to freedom of expression and participation outweighs the paternalistic judgment of welfare.'

Although the provisions just mentioned go a long way to satisfying the requirements of Art 12, it can be argued[195] that a possible breach could be occasioned in cases where the parents are agreed and the views of children are consequently overlooked.[196]

A third Article sometimes referred to in domestic jurisprudence is Art 9 by which a child has the right to live with or maintain contact with both parents inasmuch as Art 9(1) requires States Parties to:

> ensure that a child shall not be separated from his or her parents against their will, except when competent authorities subject to judicial review determine, in accordance with applicable law and procedures, that such separation is necessary for the best interests of the child.

Where the child is separated from one or both parents, Art 9(3) requires States to:

> respect the right of the child . . . to maintain personal relations and direct contact with both parents on a regular basis, except if it is contrary to the child's best interests.

Other Articles that might be mentioned are Article 6 which requires States Parties that 'every child has inherent right to life' and to 'ensure to the maximum extent possible the survival and development of the child'; and Arts 7 and 8 which effectively provide the child with a right to an identity inasmuch as Article 7 provides:

1. The child shall be registered immediately after birth and shall have the right from birth to a name, the right to acquire a nationality and, as far as possible, the right to know and be cared for by his or her parents.
2. State Parties shall ensure the implementation of these rights in accordance with their national law and their obligation under the relevant international instruments in this field, in particular where the child would otherwise be stateless.

---

[192] Children Act 1989 s 10(2)(b), discussed in Ch 14, The leave criteria, pp 515ff.

[193] Discussed further in Ch 13.

[194] In *Mabon v Mabon* [2005] EWCA Civ 634 [2005] Fam 366, at [28]. But note also *Re P-S (Children: Family Proceedings: Evidence)* [2013] EWCA Civ 223 [2013] 1 WLR 3831, discussed further in Ch 13.

[195] See N Lowe 'The Legal Position of Parents and Children in English Law' [1994] *Singapore Journal of Legal Studies* 332 at 346.

[196] See further Ch 12, The interrelationship of human rights and section 1(5), p 444.

Article 8 further requires States Parties:

> to respect the right of the child to preserve his or her identity, including nationality, name and family relations as recognised by law without unlawful interference.

In addition, the Convention confers upon the child the right to recover maintenance from the parents or other persons having financial responsibility for the child (Art 27(4)); right of freedom of expression (Art 13); freedom of thought, conscience and religion (Art 14); freedom of association (Art 15); right to education (Art 28) and in general not to be subjected to arbitrary or unlawful interference with privacy, family, home or correspondence (Art 16).

The European Convention on Human Rights and other Council of Europe instruments

Most of the UN rights mentioned are also effectively provided for by the European Convention on Human Rights[197] although neither expressed in a child specific way nor expressly as a positive obligation.[198] Thus the right to life (though not development); freedom of expression; freedom of thought; conscience and religion; freedom of association; the right to education; and the right to respect for private and family life are protected by respectively Articles 2, 10, 9, 11, Article 2 of Protocol 1 and Article 8. Although there is no direct counterpart to UN's Article 7, some argue[199] that the child's right to identity is embodied in Article 8, while the right of the child to maintain regular contact with his or her parents is provided for by Article 4 of the 2003 European Convention on Contact Concerning Children (to which, however, the UK is not a party).

The point has been well made that because the Convention is not child centred it is not the easiest of vehicle by which to develop children's rights as such.[200] Indeed the Strasbourg Court only seems prepared to do so when applications are brought on behalf of children, which is the case in only a tiny minority of applications. That said, the Court has imaginatively interpreted Art 3 to equate severe forms of physical abuse with torture and degrading treatment.[201] It has also, via Art 8 (which clearly offers the most scope to develop children's right), secured for the child a right to information about themselves held by public authorities,[202] a right to resolve uncertainty about their parent's identity without unnecessary delay, [203] and also held that the notion of personal integrity is an important principle incorporated by the Article, which has obvious significance for adolescents' rights.[204]

---

[197] See generally G Van Bueren *Child Rights in Europe* (2007) and U Kilkelly *The Child and the European Convention* (1999).

[198] Though it is well established that certain Articles of the Convention (Articles 2, 3 and 8 in particular) not only compel States to abstain from interfering with the rights they protect but also require them to take positive steps to secure those rights. See *Marckx v Belgium* (1979) 2 EHRR 330, on which see J Scherpe and W Pintens 'The Marckx Case: A "Whole Code of Family Law"?' in S Gilmore, J Herring and R Probert (eds) *Landmark Cases in Family Law* (2011) ch 9. See also S Choudry and J Herring *European Human Rights and Family Law* (2010).

[199] See Van Bueren *Child Rights in Europe* (2007) 16 at pp 64ff and the authorities there cited. See also J Fortin *Children's Rights and the Developing Law* (2009, 3rd edn) p 61.

[200] See the interesting discussion by J Fortin *Children's Rights and the Developing Law* (2009, 3rd edn) pp 60ff.

[201] See eg *A v United Kingdom (Human Rights: Punishment of Child)* [1998] 2 FLR 959 and *Z v United Kingdom* [2001] 2 FLR 612. [202] See eg 'The Gaskin case' [1990] 1 FLR 167, ECtHR.

[203] See eg *Mikulić v Croatia* [2002] 1 FCR 720.

[204] See *Pretty v United Kingdom* [2002] 2 FLR 45, on which see J Fortin *Children's Rights and the Developing Law* (2009, 3rd edn) at p 62.

Quite apart from the Human Rights Convention the Council of Europe has been very active in promoting children's rights.[205] Examples of its work include its 1975 Convention on the Legal Status of Children Born Out of Wedlock, which aimed to improve the legal status of children born outside marriage, including through Art 9, that they should have the same rights of succession as those born to married parents; the 1996 European Convention on the Exercise of Children's Rights, which is aimed at supplementing the UN Convention by assisting children to exercise their substantive rights set out in the latter Convention; the 2003 European Convention on Contact Concerning Children, which aims to provide common European rules concerning contact; and the 2007 European Convention on the Protection of Children Against Sexual Exploitation and Sexual Abuse which aims to secure for every child the right to measures of protection against sexual exploitation and sexual abuse. Among its many Recommendations, mention may be made of the 1985 Recommendation on Violence in the Family,[206] in which States are recommended to review their legislation on the power to punish children 'in order to limit or indeed prohibit corporal punishment'; a 1990 Recommendation[207] inter alia to appoint a special ombudsman for children; and another 1990 Recommendation[208] to encourage governments to adopt co-ordinated and child-focused policies at national and local levels.

At one time the Council of Europe was the major institutional driver for family law reform but it has become markedly less so particularly with the growing influence of the European Union. One indicator of this decline is the lack of take-up of some of the Conventions mentioned. Indeed, at the time of writing, the UK has not ratified the 1996, 1997, 2003 and the 2007 Conventions, nor has it complied with all the Recommendations.

The Charter of Fundamental Rights of the European Union

Art 24 of the Charter of Fundamental Rights of the European Union embodies three of the major principles of the UN Convention, namely that:

(1) children have the right to such protection and care as is necessary for their well-being and to express their views freely (such views to be taken into account on matters which concern them in accordance with their age and maturity);
(2) that in all actions the child's best interests must be a primary consideration; and
(3) the right to maintain on a regular basis a personal relationship and direct contact with both parents unless it is contrary to their interests.

The European Charter was first drawn up in 1999–2000 and was 'solemnly proclaimed' by the Commission, Parliament and Council and politically approved by Member States at Nice in 2000. Its precise legal status, however, remained unclear. The Charter was subsequently formally approved by the Treaty of Lisbon in December 2009. Although it is not incorporated into the EU Treaties, by Art 6 TEU, it has the same legal status as the Treaties themselves. However, a further complication is that under Protocol 30 to the Lisbon Treaty the Charter on its face seems to have limited effect in the United Kingdom since it is said the:

The Charter does not extend the ability of the Court of Justice of the European Union, or any court or tribunal of . . . the United Kingdom to find that the laws, regulations or

---

[205] See generally *Council of Europe Achievements in the field of law—Family law and the protection of children* (2008) and N Lowe 'The Impact of the Council of Europe on European Family Law' in J Scherpe (ed) *Research Handbook on European Family Law* (2015).   [206] No R (85)4.

[207] Recommendation No 1121 on the *Rights of Children*.

[208] Recommendation No 1286 on a *European Strategy for Children*.

administrative provisions or action of . . . the United Kingdom are inconsistent with the fundamental rights freedoms and principles that it reaffirms.

The general view[209] seems to be that this Protocol has little more than a declaratory effect and so may not have the limiting effect intended.

It remains to be seen what impact the Charter will have on the developments of children's rights.

---

[209] See eg P Craig and G De Búrca, *European Law: Text, Cases and Materials* (2011, 5th edn) pp 394–395. Though in *R (AB) v SSHD* [2013] EWHC 3453 (Fam) Mostyn J suggested that the Charter was binding on the UK.

10

WHAT IS PARENTAL RESPONSIBILITY?

A. INTRODUCTION

Before the Children Act 1989, statutes referred to 'parental rights and duties' or 'parental powers and duties' or the 'rights and authority' of a parent. Not only were these terms inconsistent with one another but, as the Law Commission commented:[1] 'It can be cogently argued that to talk of "parental rights" is not only inaccurate as a matter of juristic analysis but also a misleading use of ordinary language.' In their *Report on Guardianship and Custody* the Commission recommended the introduction of the concept of 'parental responsibility' to replace all the ambiguous and misleading terms previously employed in statutes, a concept which in the Commission's view, 'would reflect the everyday reality of being a parent and emphasise the responsibility of all who are in that position'.[2]

The Government accepted the Commission's recommendation, and 'parental responsibility' is a pivotal concept of the 1989 Act.

In this chapter we discuss the meaning of parental responsibility, leaving discussion of who has that responsibility to Chapter 11.

1. INTERNATIONAL ACCEPTANCE OF THE CONCEPT OF PARENTAL RESPONSIBILITY

The shift away from parental power as reflected by such expressions as 'parental rights and duties' or 'parental power and duties' to that of parental care as encapsulated by the concept of 'parental responsibility' was by no means peculiar to English law. Such a change was effected, for instance, in what was then West Germany, when the term 'parental power' (*elter Gewalt*) was replaced by 'parental care' (*elterliche Sorge*) in 1970.[3] In Norway,

---

[1] Law Com No 118 *Illegitimacy* (1982) para 4.18.

[2] Law Com No 172 (1988) para 2.4. The Commission also noted that such a change would bring English law into line with the Recommendation No R(84)4 on Parental Responsibilities adopted in 1984 by the Committee of Ministers of the Council of Europe.

[3] See R Frank 'Family Law and the Federal Republic of Germany's Basic Law' (1990) 4 Int Jo of Law, Policy and the Family 214. See also N Dethloff and D Martiny 'German Report' particularly the response to Q5 in K Boele-Woelki, B Bratt and I Curry-Sumner (eds) *European Family Law in Action, Vol III Parental Responsibilities* (2005). This useful volume contains the responses to a detailed questionnaire on parental responsibilities written by experts from 22 different European jurisdictions. For the follow up to this, see K Boele-Woelki, F Ferrand, C González Beilfuss, M Jänterä-Jareborg, N Lowe, D Martiny and W Pintens *Principles of European Family Law Regarding Parental Responsibilities* (2007). For the position in several jurisdictions worldwide see 'The Symposium on Comparative Custody Law' in (2005) 39 FLQ 247.

the term 'parental responsibility' was introduced in their Children Act 1981, replacing such terms as 'parental authority' and 'parental power'.[4] A similar reform was introduced in Austria in 1989.[5] Since then the term has been adopted in the domestic legislation of, for example, Australia, the Isle of Man, Northern Ireland and Scotland. [6]

International impetus for change was first given by the already mentioned Council of Europe 1984 Recommendation on Parental Responsibilities, the Council agreeing that:[7]

> The term 'parental responsibilities' describes better the modern concept according to which parents are, on a . . . basis of equality between parents and in consultation with their children, given the task to educate, legally represent, maintain, etc their children. In order to do so they exercise powers to carry out duties in the interests of the child and not because of an authority which is conferred on them in their own interests.

Global recognition of the concept of parental responsibility has been given by its use in the UN Convention on the Rights of the Child[8] and the term is now regularly used in international instruments concerning children.[9]

2. CONTEXTS IN WHICH PARENTAL RESPONSIBILITY IS RELEVANT

To have a better understanding of the concept of parental responsibility it is important to appreciate that it is concerned with a number of different relationships. In his leading analysis, Eekelaar[10] argues that the concept can represent two ideas: one, that parents must behave dutifully towards their children; the other, that responsibility for bringing up a child belongs to parents, not the State. Both these ideas are important and both are

---

[4] See L Smith and P Lødrup *Children and Parents—The relationship between children and parents according to Norwegian Law*, ch 5 (2004). See also T Sverdrup and P Lødrup 'Norwegian Report', particularly the response to Q5 in K Boele-Woelki, B Bratt and I Curry-Sumner (eds) *European Family Law in Action, Vol III Parental Responsibilities* (2005).

[5] See M Roth, 'Austrian Report', particularly the response to Q5 in K Boele-Woelki, B Bratt and I Curry-Sumner (eds) *European Family Law in Action, Vol III Parental Responsibilities* (2005).

[6] See respectively, the Family Law Reform Act 1995 (Cth), the Manx Family Law Act 1991, the Children (Northern Ireland) Order 1995 and the Children (Scotland) Act 1995. Note also the amendment to the definition of guardianship in New Zealand in the Care of Children Act 2004 Part 2, to include reference to 'responsibilities'.

[7] See para 6 of the Explanatory Memorandum to the Recommendation. Note also the Council of Europe's 'White Paper' of 15 January 2002 on principles concerning the establishment and legal consequences of parentage, initially published as a consultation paper (CJ-FA (2001) 16 rev but later published as a stand-alone document, see CJ-FA (2006) 4).

[8] See in particular Art 18(1) which states: 'States Parties shall use their best efforts to ensure recognition of the principle that both parents have common responsibilities for the upbringing and development of the child. Parents or, as the case may be, legal guardians, have the primary responsibility for the upbringing and development of the child. The best interests of the child will be their basic concern.' See also Arts 5 and 9.

[9] See, for example, the 1993 Hague Convention on the Protection of Children and Co-operation in Respect of Intercountry Adoption, Art 21(1)(b); the 1996 Hague Convention on Jurisdiction, Applicable Law, Recognition, Enforcement and Co-operation in respect of Parental Responsibility and Measures for the Protection of Children, Art 16(1); and Council Regulation (EC) No. 2201/2003 of 27 November 2003 concerning jurisdiction and the recognition and enforcement of judgments in matrimonial matters and the matters of parental responsibility, repealing Regulation (EC) No. 1347/2000 (the revised Brussels II Regulation).

[10] J Eekelaar 'Parental responsibility: State of Nature or Nature of the State?' [1991] JSWFL 37.

embodied in the Act. The former idea is well summed up by Lord Mackay LC, who said[11] when introducing the Bill, that the concept of 'parental responsibility':

> . . . emphasises that the days when a child should be regarded as a possession of his parents, indeed when in the past they had a right to his services and to sue on their loss, are now buried forever. The overwhelming purpose of parenthood is the responsibility for caring and raising the child to be a properly developed adult both physically and morally.

This comment is echoed by the Department of Health's introductory guide to the Children Act[12] which states that parental responsibility:

> . . . emphasises that the duty to care for the child and to raise him to moral, physical and emotional health is the fundamental task of parenthood and the only justification for the authority that it confers.

Both these comments reflect in turn the earlier landmark decision of *Gillick v West Norfolk and Wisbech Area Health Authority*,[13] in which Lords Fraser and Scarman emphasised that parental power to control a child exists not for the benefit of the parent but for the benefit of the child.

Although the Law Commission themselves considered[14] that the change of terminology from rights and duties to responsibility would make little change in substance to the law, symbolically saying a parent has responsibilities rather than rights in itself conveys a quite different message. Ironically, however, following the implementation of the Human Rights Act 1998, this symbolic change has had to operate in a much more 'rights' orientated context. Indeed it can be at least as important to determine whether a parent has a Convention right as it is to determine whether he or she has parental responsibility, since public authorities must respect that right.[15]

It is the enduring nature of responsibility, particularly when allied with the so-called principle of non-intervention under s 1(5),[16] that embodies the second idea referred to by Eekelaar, namely that responsibility for child care belongs to parents rather than the State. As another commentator has put it,[17] by providing that responsibility should continue despite, for example, a court order that the child should live with one of them, parents 'are to understand that the state will not relieve them of their responsibilities'. This is further underscored by the fact that responsibility cannot be voluntarily surrendered to a public body[18] and that, even where a care order is made compulsorily placing the child in local authority care, the parents still retain their responsibility.[19] In short, through the concept of parental responsibility, the 1989 Act emphasises the idea that 'once a parent always a

---

[11] 502 HL Official Report (5th series) col 490.

[12] *Introduction to the Children Act 1989* (HMSO, 1989) para 1.4.

[13] [1986] AC 112, HL, discussed in Ch 9, *Gillick v West Norfolk and Wisbech Area Health Authority* at pp 319ff.   [14] Law Com No 172 at para 2.4.

[15] Note also that having parental responsibility also means that, for the purposes of the Hague Convention on Civil Aspects of International Child Abduction 1980, the individual has 'rights of custody'. See further Ch 26.

[16] Discussed in Ch 12, Orders to be made only where better than no order, pp 438ff.

[17] S Cretney 'Defining the Limits of State Intervention: The Child and the Courts' in D Freestone (ed) *Children and the Law* (1990) 58 at p 67.

[18] When the child is 'accommodated' by a local authority under s 20, discussed in Ch 17, parental responsibility is not acquired by the authority: see the discussion by J Eekelaar 'Parental responsibility: State of Nature or Nature of the State?' [1991] JSWFL 37 at pp 40–2.

[19] The effect of care orders is discussed in Ch 17, The effects of a care order, pp 438ff.

parent', and that prima facie the primary responsibility for deciding what should happen to their children even upon their separation should rest with the parents themselves.

Apart from the parent–child and the parent–state relationships, there is another relationship in which the concept of parental responsibility is relevant, namely, as between parents and other individuals. It can be as important to parents that they can look after their children without interference by other individuals as by the State. On the other hand, de facto carers (whether short-term or long-term) need some authority to take normal 'day-to-day' decisions whilst looking after the child. These potentially conflicting standpoints are accommodated by the 1989 Act since, although in the first instance only those with parental responsibility are entitled to make decisions in relation to the child, such persons are nevertheless permitted to 'arrange for some or all [of their responsibility] to be met by one or more persons acting on his behalf.'[20] Furthermore, those without parental responsibility but who have care of the child can 'do what is reasonable in all the circumstances of the case for the purpose of safeguarding or promoting the child's welfare.'[21] In other words, while those with parental responsibility are, as against other individuals, primarily in control of the child's upbringing, other persons can take decisions about the child either on the basis of parental delegation or, in the case of de facto carers, on the basis of (short-term) necessity.

As s 2 makes clear, not only can more than one person have parental responsibility at the same time but, perhaps more importantly, a person does not cease to have responsibility just because someone else acquires it.[22] Furthermore, each holder of responsibility can in theory[23] continue to exercise it without the need to consult any other holder, subject only to the overriding condition that the holder must not act incompatibly with any existing court order.[24]

B. THE MEANING AND FUNCTION OF 'PARENTAL RESPONSIBILITY'

1. THE NEED TO DEFINE PARENTAL RESPONSIBILITY

Parental responsibility needs to be definable by some means,[25] so that parents can know what they can or cannot do in relation to their child and, as importantly, so that others can know what the parents' position is. For example, is parental permission required to take a child on an educational outing? Do doctors need parental consent before medically treating the child and is that consent binding on the child?

Quite apart from the individual's point of view, the courts' powers can sometimes be dependent upon the scope of parental responsibility. They can only make a 'prohibited

---

[20] Section 2(9).   [21] Section 3(5)(b).   [22] Section 2(5) and (6).

[23] But note *Re C (Welfare of Child: Immunisation)* [2003] EWCA Civ 1148 [2003] 2 FLR 1095, *Re PC (Change of Surname)* [1997] 2 FLR 730, and *Re G (Parental Responsibility: Education)* [1994] 2 FLR 964, CA, discussed in Ch 11, Sharing parental responsibility for a child, p 392.   [24] Section 2(7) and (8).

[25] See generally R Probert, S Gilmore and J Herring (eds) *Responsible Parents & Parental Responsibility* (2009), J Bridgemen, H Keeting and C Lind (eds) *Responsibility, Law and the Family* (2008) and N Lowe 'The Meaning and Allocation of Parental Responsibility—A Common Lawyer's Perspective' (1997) 11 Int Jo of Law, Policy and the Family 192 at 193–197. For a survey of the position in 22 different European jurisdictions see K Boele-Woelki, B Bratt and I Curry-Sumner (eds) *European Family Law in Action, Vol III Parental Responsibilities* (2005). See also, for a wider global view, the 'Symposium on Comparative Custody Law' in (2005) 39 FLQ 247.

steps order' to prevent any 'step which could be taken by a parent in meeting his parental responsibility for a child' and a 'specific issue order' to determine 'a specific question which has arisen, or which may arise in connection with any aspect of parental responsibility for a child.'[26]

Notwithstanding the demonstrable need to be able to define what parental responsibility comprises, the question remains as to whether this should be done by means of a general statutory provision or simply left to case law and statutory provisions dealing with specific points. The Scottish Law Commission considered that there are advantages in having a general statutory statement of parental responsibilities, namely:[27]

(a) that it would make explicit what is already implicit in the law;

(b) that it would counteract any impression that a parent has rights but no responsibilities; and

(c) that it would enable the law to make it clear that parental rights are not absolute or unqualified, but are conferred in order to enable parents to meet their responsibilities.

These arguments seem convincing. It is surely right that some attempt be made to give general statutory guidance on the meaning of what is after all a pivotal concept of child law.

2. CAN THERE BE A MEANINGFUL GENERAL DEFINITION?

In contrast to the Scottish Law Commission, the earlier inquiry of the English Law Commission concentrated on whether there could be a comprehensive definition of parental responsibility. They concluded[28] that although there was a superficial attraction in providing a comprehensive list of the incidents of responsibility, it was impracticable to do so. They pointed out that such a list would have to change from time to time to meet differing needs and circumstances, and would have to vary with the age and maturity of the child and circumstances of the case.

While there is some validity in this view, particularly if it is sought to provide a comprehensive definition, it by no means follows that *some* useful guidance cannot be given. In the event, implementing the strategy recommended by the Law Commission, s 3(1) simply provides that:

... 'parental responsibility' means all the rights, duties, powers, responsibility and authority which by law a parent of a child has in relation to the child and his property.

This provision seems a poor one, for not only might it rightly be said to be 'a non-definition',[29] but it also refers back to the rights and duties model which 'responsibility' was supposed to replace.[30]

---

[26] Under s 8(1) of the Children Act, discussed in Ch 14, Limits on the courts' powers to make specific issue and prohibited steps orders, pp 501ff. Jurisdiction may also depend upon its scope since within Member States of the EU (other than Denmark) matters relating to parental responsibility are governed by the revised Brussels II Regulation, discussed in Ch 26. In this respect, however, regard must be had to its international meaning under the Regulation, the final arbiter upon which is the Court of Justice of the European Union at Luxembourg.

[27] See Scot Law Com, Discussion Paper No 88 *Parental Responsibilities and Rights, Guardianship and the Administration of Children's Property* (1990) para 2.3.   [28] Law Com No 172 para 2.6.

[29] So described by Lord Meston in the debate on the Bill: HL Debs Vol 502, col 1172.

[30] Note Ward LJ's criticisms in *Re S (Parental Responsibility)* [1995] 2 FLR 648 at 657. A not dissimilar 'definition' is provided in the Australian legislation: see Family Law Act 1975 (Cth) s 61B, save that there is no mention of 'rights'. Note also Council Regulation (EC) No. 2201/2003 of 27 November 2003 (the revised

In contrast to the English position, the Children (Scotland) Act 1995, implementing the recommendation of the Scottish Law Commission,[31] provides first by s 1(1) that:

A parent has in relation to his child the responsibility—

(a) to safeguard and promote the child's health, development and welfare;
(b) to provide, in a manner appropriate to the stage of development of the child—
  (i) direction;
  (ii) guidance,

  to the child;
(c) if the child is not living with the parent, to maintain personal relations and direct contact with the child on a regular basis; and
(d) to act as the child's legal representative,

  but only in so far as compliance with this section is practicable and in the interests of the child.

To enable a parent to fulfil those parental responsibilities, s 2(1) provides that a parent:

has the right—

(a) to have the child living with him or otherwise to regulate the child's residence;
(b) to control, direct or guide, in a manner appropriate to the stage of development of the child, the child's upbringing;
(c) if the child is not living with him, to maintain personal relations and contact with the child on a regular basis; and
(d) to act as the child's legal representative.

The Scottish legislation shows that it is possible to provide helpful general guidance as to the meaning of parental responsibility. It neatly handles the problem of dealing with children of different ages and maturity by the simple expedient of stating that the responsibility to give direction and guidance should be 'in a manner appropriate to the stage of development of the child.' By making separate provisions for responsibilities and rights, it grapples with the problem of having to deal not only with the parent–child relationship (in which context the expression 'responsibility' seems absolutely right, because parents ought to act on their children's behalf rather than on their own)[32] but also with the relationship both between the parents themselves and between parents and the State and other individuals (in which context the expression 'rights' still seems appropriate, since, as against others, parents can still be regarded as having the power and authority to bring up their children as they see fit).[33] It also avoids the problem of being too specific and instead leaves the courts free to determine particular issues on a case by case basis.

Brussels II Regulation) under which parental responsibility is defined (see Art 2(7)) as meaning 'all rights and duties relating to the person or the property of a child which are given to a natural or legal person by judgment, by operation of law or by agreement having legal effect. The term shall include rights of custody and rights of access'. Article 1(2) and (3) respectively set out what is and what is not included in the concept. The Council of Europe's 'White Paper' on *Principles Concerning the Establishment and Legal Consequences of Parentage* defines in Principle 18 parental responsibilities as 'a collection of duties and powers, which aims at ensuring the moral and material welfare of children, in particular: Care and protection; Maintenance of personal relationship; Provision of education; Legal representation; Determination of residence and Administration of property'.

[31] Scot Law Com No 125 *Report on Family Law* (1992) paras 2.1 ff.
[32] See C Barton and G Douglas *Law and Parenthood* (1995), pp 18–28.
[33] Using Hohfeld's analysis (Hohfeld *Fundamental Legal Conceptions as Applied in Judicial Reasoning* (1919)), it might be more accurate to say that, at any rate as against third parties, parents have a 'privilege'

However, although the Scottish approach seems preferable,[34] English law seems to have worked reasonably well and it is probably not now worth amending the 1989 Act.

This discussion presupposes that the function of parental responsibility is to confer the ability to make decisions about a child's upbringing and indeed this does seem the underlying purpose of the concept as is discussed in the Department of Health's *Introduction to the Children Act 1989* which observes:[35]

> . . . the effect of having parental responsibility is to empower a person to take most decisions in the child's life.

It is evident, however, that the judiciary do not always share this view for in some cases[36] they have stressed that the attribution of parental responsibility confers a type of status[37] rather than real rights. However, as has been observed,[38] they are not always consistent about this and there is therefore a 'tension about whether parental responsibility is about real decision-making power, or whether it is of more symbolic value, recognising the [parents'] commitment to the child'.

3. FURTHER PRELIMINARY OBSERVATIONS

Before examining parental responsibility further, some preliminary observations may be made. First, although the broad definition under s 3(1) necessarily refers to the pre-1989 Act position,[39] it must do so subject to the change of emphasis from rights to responsibilities. One problem in particular is deciding whether a former 'right' attaches only to a parent or guardian or to anyone with parental responsibility.[40] As the Law Commission commented,[41] the incidents of parenthood with which they were concerned were those that related to the care and upbringing of a child and not specifically incidents that attached to parents qua parents.

Secondly, the exercise of parental responsibility may be qualified by agreement of the parties (for example, the father agreeing that the child is to live with the mother) or by order of the court. In the latter instance the extent to which responsibility can be asserted

---

to bring up children as they see fit in the sense that others have 'no right' to interfere. As against the State, however, this privilege is more limited, since the State can interfere with parental upbringing once it falls below the accepted threshold as set out in s 31 of the Children Act 1989, discussed in Ch 17, The threshold criteria, pp 597ff.

[34] Reform along the Scottish lines had been recommended in *People Like Us* (Report of the Review of the Standards for Children Living Away from Home—the Utting Report) (Department of Health and Welsh Office, 1997) para 6.2 and recommendation 9. [35] Para 2.4.

[36] See in particular *Re S (Parental Responsibility)* [1995] 2 FLR 648, *Re S (A Minor) (Parental Responsibility)* [1995] 3 FCR 564, and *Re C and V (Contact and Parental Responsibility)* [1998] 1 FLR 392, discussed in Ch 11, The disposition to make orders, p 376.

[37] According to J Eekelaar 'Parental Responsibility—A New Legal Status?' (1996) 112 LQR 233, this status is best understood as the legal recognition of the exercise of social parenthood. For a particularly scathing analysis of how the attribution of parental responsibility has been developed, see H Reece 'The Degradation of Parental Responsibility' in R Probert, S Gilmore and J Herring (eds) *Responsible Parents & Parental Responsibility* (2009) ch 5. See also PG Harris and R George 'Parental responsibility and shared residence orders: parliamentary intentions and judicial interpretations' [2010] CFLQ 151.

[38] J Herring *Family Law* (2nd edn, 2004) at pp 358–359.

[39] For which see J Eekelaar 'What are Parental Rights?' (1973) 89 LQR 210; J Hall 'The Waning of Parental Rights' [1972B] CLJ 248; S Maidment 'The Fragmentation of Parental Rights' [1981] CLJ 135 and Law Com Working Paper No 91 *Guardianship* paras 2.25 et seq.

[40] For example, with regard to the right to confer a child's name or to dispose of a child's corpse discussed later in this chapter. [41] Law Com No 172 para 2.7.

is effectively limited by the paramountcy of the child's welfare, which principle the court is bound to apply in any proceedings concerning his upbringing or the administration of his property.[42]

Thirdly, the older the child the less extensive and important parental responsibility may become. As Lord Denning MR eloquently put it in respect of custody:[43]

> ... it is a dwindling right which the court will hesitate to enforce against the wishes of the child, the older he is. It starts with the right of control and ends with little more than advice.

Fourthly, the ambit of responsibility varies. It is widest when enjoyed by parents or guardians, but less extensive when vested in others by means of a child arrangements order, or in local authorities by reason of a care order.[44] It is narrowest when vested in those who have obtained an emergency protection order.[45]

Fifthly, the absence of responsibility does not necessarily mean that a person has no obligation towards the child. For example, unmarried fathers have a statutory duty to maintain their children regardless of whether they also have parental responsibility.[46] On the other hand, the absence of responsibility does not automatically mean that an individual has no 'rights', for if a person has a relationship with the child which amounts to 'family life' within the meaning of Art 8 of the European Convention on Human Rights then that right must be respected by public authorities.[47]

Lastly, as the Department of Health's *Introduction* observes:[48]

> the effect of having parental responsibility is to empower a person to take most decisions in the child's life. It does not make him a parent or relative of the child in law, for example, to give him rights of inheritance, or to place him under a statutory duty to maintain a child.

4. WHAT PARENTAL RESPONSIBILITY COMPRISES

In the absence of an agreed list it is suggested that parental responsibility comprises[49] at least the following:[50]

– Bringing up the child.

– Having contact with the child.

[42] Children Act 1989 s 1(1), discussed in Ch 12.

[43] *Hewer v Bryant* [1970] 1 QB 357 at 369, CA and cited by Ward LJ in *Re D (Local Authority Responsibility)* [2012] EWCA Civ 627 [2013] 2 FLR 673 at [29] in holding that the parental responsibility acquired by a local authority similarly dwindles as the child matures. Even so, parents do not lose all their responsibility even where their child is '*Gillick* competent': see Ch 9, *Gillick v West Norfolk and Wisbech Area Health Authority*, pp 319ff.

[44] See Ch 14, Effect of child arrangements orders, p 520 and Ch 17, Effects of a care order, p 636 respectively.   [45] See Ch 16, Effects of an order, p 586.

[46] See Ch 21, Parents' duty to maintain children, p 775.

[47] See eg *Sahin v Germany, Sommerfeld v Germany* [2003] 2 FLR 671, ECtHR in which treating an unmarried father's position differently from that of married fathers with regard to contact was held to violate Art 14 taken in conjunction with Art 8.Under English law most unmarried fathers, but not all, will have parental responsibility because they have registered as the child's father, see Ch 11.   [48] At para 2.4.

[49] See also the *Family Law Review* (the 'Norgorve Report') Final Report (November, 2011) at paras 4.6 and 4.7; C Barton and G Douglas *Law and Parenthood* (1995) pp 114 ff; and K Boele-Woelki et al *Principles of European Family Law Regarding Parental Responsibilities* (2007) Principles 3:19–3:29.

[50] Some commentaries include children's services, but as will be seen (see Child's services, p 337) parental responsibility cannot now be said to include a right to domestic services.

-   Protecting and maintaining the child.
-   Disciplining the child.
-   Determining and providing for the child's education.
-   Determining the child's religion.
-   Consenting to the child's medical treatment.
-   Consenting to the child's marriage.
-   Consenting to the child's adoption.
-   Vetoing the issue of a child's passport.
-   Taking the child outside the United Kingdom and consenting to the child's emigration.
-   Administering the child's property.
-   Naming the child.
-   Representing the child in legal proceedings.
-   Disposing of the child's corpse.
-   Appointing a guardian for the child.

Whether parental responsibility can also be said to comprise the right to receive information about the child and the power to control publicity about the child can be debated and will be discussed later in this chapter. It can also be debated whether sharing liability for criminal offences should now also be added to the list.[51]

Not all of these listed attributes are the responsibility or duties solely of holders of parental responsibility. Some, for example, the duty to protect the child, are owed by any adult de facto carer.

Consenting to a child's marriage was considered in Chapter 2. Appointment of a testamentary guardian, consenting to a child being adopted and maintenance are discussed respectively in Chapters 8, 19 and 21.

(a) Bringing up the child

A key aspect of parental responsibility is that of looking after and bringing up the child. How best this responsibility should be expressed is a matter of debate. At common law parents (originally fathers of legitimate children) were said to have a right to possession of the child.[52] But in the modern context, it seems better to say that those with responsibility have a prima facie right to bring up their own children and the power to determine where they should live. To speak of possessory rights, particularly in the context of the parent–child relationship, harps back to a concept from which that of parental responsibility was seeking to escape[53] and in any event to speak of possession only makes real sense in the case of babies. However, both in the context of the parent-state relationship and that between parents and other individuals, it makes more sense to dwell on rights and indeed it has been forcefully argued[54] that the 'possessory right is now justified, not as an archaic relic of patriarchal domination over other family members, but as reflecting the liberal view that the family and the members who comprise it should be free from arbitrary state inference'. Nevertheless 'possession' seems too strong a concept even in this context. In the final analysis, however, this may be a sterile debate for it is

[51] Ie in cases of breach of parenting orders—see Liability for children's acts, p 363.
[52] See eg *Re Agar-Ellis* (1883) 24 Ch D 317.
[53] See the speech of Lord Mackay LC when introducing the Children Bill to Parliament, see Contexts in which parental responsibility is relevant, p 332, n 11.
[54] See G Douglas *An Introduction to Family Law* (2004, 2nd edn) p 85.

common ground that parental responsibility embodies the right to bring up a child free both from arbitrary interference by the State (which right is protected by Art 8 of the European Convention on Human Rights)[55] and from interference by other individuals. In this latter context the right to bring up the child is protected by the criminal law to the extent that persons without responsibility commit the crime of child abduction if they remove the child without lawful authority.[56] As between individuals with parental responsibility the right is qualified to the extent that removal of a child outside the United Kingdom without the consent of other individuals with parental responsibility can amount to a crime.[57]

Associated with bringing up the child is the power physically to control a child's movements, at any rate until the years of discretion.[58] It is established that responsibility includes the power to control the child's movements whilst in someone else's care.[59] On the other hand, it is also the case that a parent, and therefore presumably any other person with parental responsibility, can commit the common law crime of kidnapping[60] or unlawful imprisonment[61] if a child (old enough to make up his own mind) is forcibly taken or detained against his will.

(b) Contact with the child

Prima facie, parental responsibility encompasses seeing or otherwise having contact with the child (though it is commonly said that contact is a right of the child rather a right of the parent).[62] While not an absolute right, since in any litigation it will be contingent upon the child's welfare, nevertheless as Lord Oliver said in *Re KD (A Minor) (Ward: Termination of Access)*:[63]

> As a general proposition a natural parent has a claim to [contact with] his or her child to which the court will pay regard and it would not I think, be inappropriate to describe such a claim as a 'right'.

By an amendment to the Children Act 1989 introduced by the Children and Families Act 2014, the 'right' of a parent to be continually 'involved'[64] with the child is protected to the extent that provided there is no evidence that the involvement of a parent in the child's life would put that child at risk of harm, the court is to presume unless the contrary is shown that such continued involvement will further the child's welfare.[65] However, when applying this presumption the court is not bound to provide for any particular division of the child's time and therefore is not bound to provide for equal division; rather the court must

---

[55] See eg *TP and KM v United Kingdom* [2001] 2 FLR 549 in which the failure of a local authority properly to investigate an allegation of child abuse resulting in a mother and child being wrongly separated for a year was held to violate Art 8. For further discussion of this case see Ch 18, Taking the case to the European Court of Human Rights, p 677.　　　　　　　　　　　　　　　　　　[56] Child Abduction Act 1984 s 2.

[57] Under the Child Abduction Act 1984 s 1 (as amended by the Children Act 1989). Note the defences, however, under s 1(5).

[58] *R v Rahman* (1985) 81 Cr App Rep 349, CA at 353, per Lord Lane CJ. See also *Hewer v Bryant* [1970] 1 QB 357 at 373, CA, per Sachs LJ.　　　　　　　　　　　　　　[59] *Fleming v Pratt* (1823) 1 LJOS 194.

[60] *R v D* [1984] AC 778, HL: see N Lowe 'Child Abduction and Child Kidnapping—II: The Common Law Position and its Relationship with the Child Abduction Act 1984' (1984) 134 NLJ 995.

[61] *R v Rahman* (1985) 81 Cr App Rep 349. See Khan 'False Imprisonment of a Child by a Parent' [1986] Fam Law 69.　　　　　　　　　　　　[62] See eg *M v M (Child: Access)* [1973] 2 All ER 81, per Wrangham J.

[63] [1988] AC 806 at 827, HL.

[64] By s 1(2B) 'involvement' means 'involvement of some kind, either direct or indirect, but not any particular division of a child's time.'

[65] Children Act 1989 s 1(2A), inserted by s 11(2) of the 2014 Act, discussed further in Ch 12.

make its final decision according to the paramountcy principle under s 1(1).[66] In short, there is no presumption that a parent should have direct contact with his or her child.

There is a statutory presumption of reasonable contact between a child in local authority care or under emergency protection and, amongst others, those with parental responsibility.[67] These provisions were enacted following the European Court of Human Rights ruling[68] that the absence of any right to challenge a termination of contact by a local authority amounted to a breach of Arts 8 and 13 of the Convention. It should also be noted that Art 9(3) of the UN Convention on the Rights of the Child 1989 provides:

> States Parties shall respect the right of the child who is separated from one or both parents to maintain personal relations and direct contact with both parents on a regular basis, except if it is contrary to the child's best interests.

Given that it is a normal assumption that a child will benefit from continued contact with both parents,[69] it may be that parental responsibility also properly encompasses the prima facie *duty* to allow the child to have contact with either or both parents. Whether such responsibility extends to a parent having an obligation him- or herself to maintain contact with the child can, in the absence of any ruling by a domestic court or the European Court of Human Rights, be debated.[70]

If parental responsibility encompasses the power to control the child's movements, it would seem to follow that it includes the power to restrict those with whom the child may have contact. In *Nottingham County Council v P*,[71] in which it was sought to exclude the father from the matrimonial home and to restrict his contact with his children (on the basis of his sexual abuse), Ward J saw 'the force of the submission' that steps taken by a parent in meeting his parental responsibility are necessarily wide steps and could extend to controlling contact with the other parent. In *Re M (Care: Leave to Interview Child)*[72] Hale J was more forthright, commenting: 'Until the child is old enough to decide for himself, a parent undoubtedly has some control over whom he may see and who may see him'.

(c) Protection

Physical and moral protection

As previously mentioned, affording physical protection to the child is not just an aspect of parental responsibility but is also a common law duty owed by anyone who willingly undertakes to look after another who is incapable of looking after himself. Hence this duty can be owed to a step-child or foster child[73] and can continue after the child reaches

---

[66] Children Act 1989 s 1(2B), discussed further in Ch 12.

[67] Children Act 1989 s 34(1) and s 44(13) discussed in Ch 18, The presumption of reasonable contact, p 655 and Ch 16, The effects of an order, p 586, respectively.

[68] See *R v UK, O v UK, W v United Kingdom* [1988] 2 FLR 445. See also, among many decisions, *Kosmopoulou v Greece* [2004] 1 FLR 800, ECtHR and *Hokkanen v Finland* [1996] 1 FLR 289, ECtHR, in which the failure by the State to enforce a parent's right of access was held to be a breach of Art 8, and *Ciliz v The Netherlands* [2000] 2 FLR 469, ECtHR, deportation of a divorced father before the conclusion of a contact hearing held to violate Art 8.

[69] See eg Lord Oliver in *Re KD (A Minor) (Ward: Termination of Access)* [1988] AC 806 at 827, HL at 827 and *M v M (Child: Access)* [1973] 2 All ER 81, per Wrangham J at 85 and per Latey J at p 88.

[70] In Scotland the Children (Scotland) Act 1995 s 1(1)(d) clearly states that a parent has a responsibility to maintain personal relations and direct contact with the child. But even supposing that there is a theoretical duty to see the child, it would be difficult to impose this order on an unwilling parent.

[71] [1994] Fam 18, 23.

[72] [1995] 1 FLR 825. See also *Re F (Specific Issue: Child Interview)* [1995] 1 FLR 819, CA.

[73] *R v Bubb* (1850) 4 Cox CC 455; *R v Gibbins and Proctor* (1918) 13 Cr App Rep 134, CCA.

his majority, if he is unable to look after himself owing to some physical or mental disability.[74] Whether the duty exists in any given case depends inter alia upon the necessity of protection. A disabled mother, for example, would not be under any duty to protect a healthy son aged 17. In *R v Shepherd*,[75] where a girl aged 18, who normally lived away in service but returned home from time to time, died there in childbirth, it was held that her mother was under no duty to send for a midwife because the girl was beyond the age of childhood and was entirely emancipated.

As we now discuss, breach of the duty can lead both to criminal and civil liability.

Criminal liability

Any person, whether or not a holder of parental responsibility, will be criminally liable for assault if he inflicts physical injury on a child or puts him in fear that he will do so. However, where breach of the duty to protect the child takes the form of neglect, abandonment or some other omission, the common law criminal sanctions are wholly inadequate to ensure the child's protection, not least because no offence is committed unless the child's health actually suffers as a result. In practice, so far as the criminal law is concerned, the common law duty has been superseded by the statutory duty contained in the Children and Young Persons Acts 1933 to 1969.[76]

Section 1(1) of the 1933 Act provides:

> If any person[77] who has attained the age of sixteen years and has responsibility for any child or young person under that age, wilfully assaults, ill-treats, neglects, abandons, or exposes him, or causes or procures him to be assaulted, ill-treated, neglected, abandoned, or exposed, in a manner likely[78] to cause him unnecessary suffering or injury to health (including injury to or loss of sight, or hearing, or limb, or organ of the body, and any mental derangement), that person shall be guilty of [an offence] . . .[79]

By s 17 of the Act the following are liable under s 1:[80]

> (a) any person who—
>   (i) has parental responsibility for him (within the meaning of the Children Act 1989); or
>   (ii) is otherwise legally liable to maintain him; and
> (b) any person who has care of him.

---

[74] *R v Chattaway* (1922) 17 Cr App Rep 7, CCA (starvation of a helpless daughter aged 25).

[75] (1862) Le & Ca 147 (the age of majority was then 21).

[76] Viz. the Children and Young Persons Act 1933; Children and Young Persons (Amendment) Act 1952; Children and Young Persons Act 1963; Children and Young Persons Act 1969 as amended by the Children Act 1989 Schs 12 and 13.

[77] There can be joint liability: see *R v Gibson and Gibson* [1984] Crim LR 615, CA.

[78] It has been held that 'likely' should be understood as excluding only what would fairly be described as highly unlikely: *R v Willis* [1990] Crim LR 714, applying remarks of Lord Diplock in *R v Sheppard* [1981] AC 394 at 405.

[79] The phrase 'in a manner likely to cause . . . injury to health' governs the whole of the preceding phrase 'wilfully assaults . . . abandoned, or exposed': *R v Hatton* [1925] 2 KB 322, CCA. The section has virtually superseded the Offences against the Person Act 1861 s 27, which relates to the abandonment and exposure of children under two years of age. The former defence under s 1(7) permitting parents, teachers and those having lawful charge of the child to administer punishment was repealed by the Children Act 2004 s 58, discussed at p 347.

[80] The Act says 'presumed to be liable', but the presumption is apparently irrefutable: *Brooks v Blount* [1923] 1 KB 257.

This wording is extremely wide and would cover, for example, a schoolteacher and anyone over the age of 16 acting as a babysitter.

The object of the Act is to make criminal any wilful course of conduct likely to cause physical or mental injury to the child. The Act specifies that neglect shall include failure to provide adequate food, clothing, medical aid[81] or lodging or, if the parent or guardian is unable to provide any of these, failing to take steps to procure them through the State.[82] But clearly many other types of cruelty and neglect are covered, such as beating a child, locking him up alone, leaving him in an otherwise deserted house or shutting him out in inclement weather, if such acts are likely to cause the child concerned suffering or ill-health. A person will be liable, however, only if his act is wilful: hence he must either know that his conduct might cause suffering or injury to health, or not care whether this results or not.[83] A parent who does not know that the child's health is at risk will not be guilty of an offence if he fails to summon medical aid even though a reasonable person would be aware of this fact: if he does know this, however, he will presumably be guilty even though he has some religious or other reason for refusing to provide assistance.[84]

Under s 5 of the Domestic Violence, Crime and Victims Act 2004, as amended,[85] a person is guilty of an offence if a child dies, or suffers serious physical harm, as a result of an unlawful act (which includes a course of conduct or omission) of a person who was a member of the same household or had frequent contact with the child. Parents (and others having responsibility for children) may also be criminally liable for causing the death of a child under the age of three by overlying it in bed whilst drunk,[86] for allowing a child under the age of 12 to be in a room containing an unguarded fire or other heating appliance with the result that the child is killed or seriously injured,[87] or for permitting children under the age of 16 (subject to certain exceptions) to take part in or train for dangerous performances.[88] Similarly it is an offence to allow a child under the age of 16 to beg,[89] and penalties are imposed upon parents who permit children to take part in entertainments or to go abroad for the purpose of performing for profit except under stringent conditions.[90]

Civil liability

There are two possible civil actions arising from a breach of the duty to protect: an action for assault and a common law action for damages in negligence. So far as the former is concerned, parents or others having responsibility or care of the child stand in no special position. Like anyone else they can be liable in damages for such assaults and, though such actions are rare, an example is *Pereira v Keleman*[91] in which a father was held liable in damages to each of his three daughters in respect of his physical and indecent assaults.

With regard to negligence claims, the child must prove that he has been injured as a result of the other's breach of duty to take care to avoid such acts or omissions as are foreseeably likely to injure him. Where a duty of care exists independently so that, had

---

[81] Unreasonable refusal to permit a surgical operation may amount to wilful neglect: *Oakey v Jackson* [1914] 1 KB 216.   [82] Children and Young Persons Act 1933 s 1(2)(a).

[83] *R v Sheppard* [1981] AC 394, HL.

[84] As in *R v Senior* [1899] 1 QB 283 (religious objection to calling in medical aid), which appears to have been approved on its facts in *R v Sheppard* [1981] AC 394, HL.

[85] By the Domestic Violence, Crime and Victims (Amendment) Act 2012 s 1.

[86] Children and Young Persons Act 1933 s 1(2)(b).

[87] Section 11 as amended by the Children and Young Persons (Amendment) Act 1952 s 8.

[88] Sections 23–24; Children and Young Persons Act 1963 s 41 and Schs 3 and 5.

[89] Children and Young Persons Act 1933 s 4.

[90] Section 25; Children and Young Persons Act 1963 ss 37–40 and 42.   [91] [1995] 1 FLR 428.

the injured person been a stranger, he could have recovered from the tortfeasor, the relationship of parent and child should not *ipso facto* bar the action. An obvious example is where a child, who is a passenger in his father's car, is injured as a result of the latter's negligent driving. The father's duty of care similarly extends to an unborn child, whereas the mother's duty to an unborn child arises only when she is driving a motor vehicle.[92]

Where there is no independent duty, so that the child has to rely solely on the common law duty to protect owed to him by his parent or other person having parental responsibility or of those simply looking after him, the position is less clear. In *Surtees v Kingston-upon-Thames Borough Council*[93] the claimant, then aged two, had, whilst in foster care, an accident in which she sustained serious injuries to her foot. The injuries were caused by immersion in water hot enough to cause third degree burns. Although the precise circumstances were disputed, the court accepted the foster parents' explanation that whilst the foster mother was out of the bathroom the plaintiff somehow placed her foot in the wash basin and switched on the hot water tap. The foster mother took the child immediately to a doctor, who treated her daily. It was held that on these facts the action for negligence should fail.[94] With respect to the foster parents it was held that, in the domestic circumstances in which the foster mother was performing her normal household duties, the kind of injury sustained by the plaintiff was not foreseeable. In reaching this decision both Stocker LJ and Browne-Wilkinson V-C were mindful of the danger of imposing an impossibly high standard of care in domestic situations. It was accepted that for this purpose the duty owed by foster parents was exactly the same as that owed by a parent. Browne-Wilkinson V-C further observed:[95]

> There are very real public policy considerations to be taken into account if the conflicts inherent in legal proceedings are to be brought into family relationships . . . The studied realm of the Royal Courts of Justice . . . is light years away from the circumstances prevailing in the average home. The mother is looking after a fast-moving toddler at the same time as cooking the meal, doing the housework, answering the telephone, looking after the other children and doing all the other things that the average mother has to cope with simultaneously, or in quick succession, in the normal household. We should be slow to characterise as negligent the care which ordinary loving and careful mothers are able to give to individual children, given the rough-and-tumble of home life.

The reluctance to impose too high a standard of care upon those looking after children should not be taken to imply that such carers will never be held to be negligent. An instructive decision is that of the New Zealand Court of Appeal in *McCallion v Dodd*.[96]

---

[92] The Congenital Disabilities (Civil Liability) Act 1976 s 2. Liability can only accrue provided the child is born alive: s 4(2)(a).

[93] [1991] 2 FLR 559, CA. But note also *X (Minors) v Bedfordshire County Council* [1995] 2 AC 633, HL; *Barrett v Enfield London Borough Council* [2001] 2 AC 550, HL; *W v Essex County Council* [2001] 2 AC 592, HL and *D v East Berkshire Community Health NHS Trust* [2005] UKHL 23 [2005] 2 AC 373 on the possible liability of local authorities, discussed in Ch 18, Suing the local authority for negligence, p 673. For the position in Australia see N Mullany 'Civil Actions for Childhood Abuse in Australia' (1999) 115 LQR 565 and the authorities there cited.

[94] It was conceded that the authority could not be liable if the foster parents were exonerated from blame, though in any event Stocker LJ considered obiter that as a matter of causation the claim against the authority was bound to fail unless the injuries were deliberately inflicted. For a criticism of this observation see G Douglas [1991] Fam Law 426–7. It is established that foster parents are not agents of the local authority: *S v Walsall Metropolitan Borough Council* [1986] 1 FLR 397, CA.

[95] [1991] 2 FLR at 583–4; but cf Beldam LJ, who dissented.

[96] [1966] NZLR 710. See D Mathieson 'Can a Child Sue his Parents in Tort?' (1967) 30 MLR 96. See also *S v Walsall Metropolitan Borough Council* [1986] 1 FLR 397, CA, where damages were awarded against foster parents in respect of injuries suffered by a child whilst in their care.

In that case parents alighted from a bus at night with their two children and started to walk along the road in the dark. The mother, who was deaf and, as the father knew, was not wearing her hearing aid, took the plaintiff, aged four, by the hand and the father carried the baby in his arms. A car driven by the defendant hit the mother and the plaintiff, killing the mother and severely injuring the boy. The plaintiff sued the defendant in negligence, and the defendant claimed contribution from the father on the ground that he had also broken a duty of care owed to the plaintiff. The jury found that the defendant had been negligent and that the father had been negligent in permitting the boy to walk in the road on the wrong side and in the path of oncoming traffic. On appeal it was held that, even though the boy was under the immediate control of his mother, the father continued to be under a special duty because of her deafness. Turner and McCarthy JJ thought that no duty of care was created purely by the relationship of parent and child, but that it arose from the fact that the father had taken the boy onto the road,[97] although admittedly the relationship is evidence of the fact that the parent has undertaken the duty to supervise and control the child's conduct.[98] North P, however, thought that, although a stranger would be liable in negligence only if he had assumed or accepted the care of the child, parents 'at all times while present are under a legal duty to exercise reasonable care to protect their children from foreseeable dangers' and that duty cannot be shed by a parent who is present.[99] In most cases it will make little difference which view is correct, but the wider rule formulated by North P is to be preferred. Indeed, it is submitted that it should be even more broadly based. If a parent leaves a child in the care of one known to be unreliable and the child comes to harm as the result of the latter's irresponsibility, the parent should be civilly liable.

It was unanimously held that there was no question of the plaintiff's damages being reduced as the result of the father's negligence. The court followed *Oliver v Birmingham and Midland Omnibus Co Ltd*[100] in which the plaintiff, aged four, was crossing a road with his grandfather, who was holding his hand, when an omnibus bore down on them. The grandfather let go of the plaintiff's hand and jumped to safety; the plaintiff was struck by the omnibus owing to the driver's negligence and was injured. It was held that his action for damages against the omnibus company was not affected by his grandfather's contributory negligence.

(d) Discipline

The common law position

A necessary part of bringing up a child is the power to exercise discipline[101] over the child. Discipline can take different forms, for example, it has been held[102] that restraint of a child's movement is usually well within the realms of reasonable discipline. But analyses have tended to concentrate on the more controversial aspect of discipline, namely, the power to inflict corporal punishment. At common law a person with parental responsibility could lawfully chastise and inflict moderate and reasonable corporal punishment for the purpose of correcting a child or punishing an offence.[103] Moreover, it was established

---

[97] At 725 and 728.

[98] Per McCarthy J at 729.   [99] At 721.   [100] [1933] 1 KB 35.

[101] See generally J Fortin *Children's Rights and the Developing Law* (2009, 3rd edn) pp 325–334, S Choudry 'Parental Responsibility and Corporal Punishment' in R Probert, S Gilmore and J Herring (eds) *Responsible Parents & Parental Responsibility* (2008) ch 9 and R Smith ' "Hands-off parenting?" towards a reform of the defence of reasonable chastisement in the UK' [2004] CFLQ 261.

[102] Per Lord Lane CJ in *R v Rahman* (1985) 81 Cr App Rep 349 at 353, CA.

[103] *R v Hopley* (1860) 2 F & F 202; *R v Woods* (1921) 85 JP 272.

that these powers could be delegated either expressly[104] or impliedly but they could only be exercised by those in loco parentis to the child.[105] It was in this way that teachers were empowered to administer corporal punishment.[106] This power was given statutory form by s 1(7) of the Children and Young Persons Act 1933.

Even at common law the power to administer punishment only extended to inflicting *reasonable* corporal punishment.[107] If it went beyond that it was unlawful and would render the individual criminally liable for assault or, depending on the gravity, for more serious offences.[108] It was also established that disciplinary acts amounting to degrading punishment[109] or inflicted without parental consent, are in breach of the European Convention on Human Rights.[110]

Calls for reform

There had been mounting pressure to reform this position on the basis that it is morally wrong to permit physical punishment of children and symbolically important that the State should respect the physical integrity of all its citizens, and because of the danger that punishment can quickly degenerate into abuse. The principal argument for maintaining the status quo was that many parents think that some punishment is justified and that a complete ban would be unenforceable.

An important catalyst for change was the European Court of Human Rights with a series of decisions, notably *Tyrer v United Kingdom*,[111] *Campbell and Cosans v United Kingdom*[112] and *Costello-Roberts v United Kingdom*, leading to the ending of the power to inflict corporal

---

[104] See *Sutton London Borough Council v Davis* [1994] 1 FLR 737 in which a local authority's refusal to register a child minder who would not comply with their 'no smacking policy' (the child minder had had the parents' permission to smack their daughter) was overturned by the court. But see now the Day Care and Child Minding (National Standards) (England) Regulations 2003 (SI 2003/1996) reg 3.

[105] See eg *R v Woods* (1921) 85 JP 272 in which it was held to be unlawful for an elder brother to administer corporal punishment on his younger sibling where both were living with their father.

[106] See the review of Elias J in *R (On the Application of Williamson) v Secretary of State for Education and Employment* [2001] EWHC Admin 960 [2002] 1 FLR 493 at [19] et seq (judgment upheld on appeal at [2005] UKHL 15, [2005] 2 AC 246) citing *Cleary v Booth* [1893] 1 QB 465 and *Ryan v Fildes and Others* [1938] 3 All ER 517.

[107] Note *R v H (Assault of Child: Reasonable Chastisement)* [2001] EWCA Crim 1024 [2001] 2 FLR 431 in which it was held that where reasonable chastisement was raised as a defence to criminal charges, a judge should direct the jury to consider the following: '(i) the nature and context of the defendant's behaviour; (ii) the duration of that behaviour; (iii) the physical and mental consequences in respect of the child; (iv) the age and personal characteristics of the child; [and] (v) the reasons given by the defendant for administering the punishment'.

[108] Children and Young Person Act 1933 s 1; *R v Derriviere* (1969) 53 Cr App Rep 637, CA—West Indian father convicted of occasioning actual bodily harm to his 13-year-old son. If the child dies, the parent could be guilty of manslaughter or even murder. An unreasonable restraint of a child's movement can render a parent guilty of unlawful imprisonment: *R v Rahman* (1985) 81 Cr App Rep 349.

[109] See *Costello-Roberts v United Kingdom* (1996) 19 EHRR 293, in which slippering a seven-year-old was held not to be degrading.

[110] Corporal punishment without parental consent was held to be in breach of the European Convention on Human Rights: see *Campbell and Cosans v United Kingdom* (1982) 4 EHRR 293, (albeit in the context of a parent's right to determine the child's education), discussed by G Douglas (1988) 2 Int J Law and Fam 76. Note also Art 37 of the UN Convention on the Rights of the Child, which inter alia states that no child shall be subject to degrading treatment.

[111] (1979–80) 2 EHRR 1—which concerned judicial corporal punishment (birching) in the Isle of Man—held to have violated Art 3.

[112] (1979–80) 2 EHRR —which involved a Scottish school's use of the 'tawse' (a split leather belt).

punishment on children in all schools,[113] children's homes,[114] foster placements[115] and nurseries.[116] These embargos do not outlaw forms of discipline falling short of corporal punishment.[117]

Notwithstanding the changes just mentioned, there was continued resistance to curbing parents' power to administer corporal punishment. This remained so in spite of a Council of Europe Recommendation that legislation on corporal punishment of children be reviewed;[118] that it had been banned in a growing number of European countries;[119] that Art 19 of the United Nations Convention on the Rights of the Child enjoins States to take appropriate measures to protect children from violence inter alia whilst in care of their parents;[120] and despite a recommendation by the Scottish Law Commission[121] that striking a child with an implement should be banned. However, once again the catalyst for reform was a European Court of Human Rights' ruling, namely, *A v United Kingdom (Human Rights: Punishment of Child)*.[122] In that case a step-father of a nine-year-old boy repeatedly hit him with a garden cane, causing bruises which lasted up to a week. The

[113] Education Act 1996 s 548 (as substituted by s 131 of the School Standards and Framework Act 1998) which, as Elias J pointed out in *R (On the Application of Williamson) v Secretary of State for Education and Employment* [2001] EWHC Admin 960 [2002] 1 FLR 493 at [16], removes the defence of justification, which is necessary if the intentional infliction of physical harm is not to be considered unlawful, rather than prohibiting corporal punishment as such. In *Williamson* the House of Lords (at [2005] UKHL 15 [2005] 2 AC 246) rejected a claim by head teachers, teachers and parents of four independent schools that this statutory prohibition breached their right to freedom of religion under Art 9 or Art 2 of Protocol 1.

[114] Children's Homes Regulations 2001 (SI 2001/ 3967) reg 17(5)(a) (England) and Children's Homes (Wales) Regulations 2002 (SI 2002/327) reg 17(5)(a), which simply prohibit the use of any form of corporal punishment.

[115] Fostering Services Regulations 2011 (SI 2011/581) Sch 5 para 2 (c) (England) and Fostering Services (Wales) Regulations 2003 (SI 2003/237) Sch 5 point 8 paras which require foster parents in England to make a written agreement not to administer corporal punishment.

[116] The Day Care and Child Minding (National Standards) (England) Regulations 2003 (SI 2003/1996) reg 5. This follows the earlier ban imposed in Wales, see R Smith ' "Hands-off parenting?" towards a reform of the defence of reasonable chastisement in the UK' [2004] CFLQ 261, at 263.

[117] Under the Education Act 1996 s 550A, school staff are empowered to use 'such force as is reasonable in the circumstances' to prevent a pupil committing an offence. The distinction between this so-called restraining power and corporal punishment can be a fine one. See the discussion by C Hamilton 'Rights of the child—a right to and a right in education' in C Bridge (ed) *Family Law Towards the Millennium, Essays for P M Bromley* ch 6.

[118] Recommendation No R85(4) on Violence in the Family (1985), para 12. As the explanatory memorandum notes: 'It is the very assumption that corporal punishment of children is legitimate that opens the way to all kinds of excesses and makes the traces or symptoms of such punishment acceptable to third parties'.

[119] Eg in Sweden (1979), Finland (1984), Denmark (1986), Norway (1987), Austria (1989) and Italy (1996). For the position in 22 European jurisdictions see K Boele-Woelki, B Bratt and I Curry-Sumner (eds) *European Family Law in Action, Vol III Parental Responsibilities* (2005), answer to Q8(d) and see J Fortin *Children's Rights and the Developing Law* (2009, 3rd edn).

[120] Indeed in 2002 the UN Committee on the Rights of the Child recommended that the UK should as a matter of urgency prohibit all corporal punishment in the family: *Concluding Observations of the Committee on the Rights of the Child: United Kingdom of Great Britain and Northern Ireland* UN Doc E/C. 12/1/Add 79, para 36.

[121] See Scot Law Com Discussion Paper No 88 *Parental Responsibilities and Rights, Guardianship and Administration of Children's Property* (1980) paras 2.44ff and Scot Law Com No 135 *Report on Family Law* (1992) paras 2.67ff. Notwithstanding public support for their recommendation that striking a child with an implement should be banned, no such provision was included in what became the Children (Scotland) Act 1995. However, under s 51 of the Criminal Justice (Scotland) Act 2003, blows to the head, shaking, or the use of an implement are banned.

[122] [1998] 2 FLR 959 on which see A Bainham 'Corporal Punishment of Children: A Caning for the United Kingdom' [1999] CLJ 29 and C Barton 'The Thirty Thousand Pound Caning—an "English Vice" in Europe' [1999] CFLQ 63.

step-father was tried but acquitted for assault causing actual bodily harm. The European Court ruled that the UK had failed to provide the child with sufficient protection against a punishment that amounted to degrading treatment and had accordingly violated Art 3. In response to this decision the Government issued a Consultation Paper[123] and seemed prepared to accept that domestic law needed amending in the light of *A v United Kingdom*. However, after analysing the responses to the Consultation Paper,[124] the Government concluded that there was no need for change as s 3 of the Human Rights Act 1998 obliged the courts to take account of the European Court of Human Rights' ruling. This conclusion did not dampen calls for reform. The House of Commons Health Committee,[125] for instance, when considering the report of the Victoria Climbié inquiry,[126] urged the Government to 'remove the increasingly anomalous reasonable chastisement defence'. Eventually, some reform was achieved when Lord Lester's amendment to what is now the Children Act 2004 was accepted in the House of Lords.[127]

The Children Act 2004 s 58

Section 58(1) of the Children Act 2004 provides that in relation to charges[128] of wounding and causing grievous bodily harm, assault occasioning actual bodily harm and cruelty to persons under the age of 16, 'battery of a child cannot be justified on the ground that it constituted reasonable punishment'. Section 58(3) additionally provides that 'Battery of a child causing actual bodily harm to the child cannot be justified in any civil proceedings on the ground that it constituted reasonable punishment'.

Although the general defence under s 1(7) of the Children and Young Persons Act 1933 was also repealed,[129] these reforms did not *ipso facto* remove the right to smack children. The defence of reasonable chastisement can still be pleaded in proceedings for common assault before magistrates[130] while batteries *not* occasioning actual bodily harm (popularly translated as hitting without leaving a mark) are still permitted. In other words, s 58 stops short of imposing an outright ban on corporal punishment, which even whilst the provision was being debated in Parliament was criticised for not going far enough.[131]

(e) Education

As Ward LJ observed in *Re Z (A Minor) (Identification: Restrictions on Publication)*[132] 'arranging for education[133] commensurate with the child's intellectual needs and abilities is [an] . . . incident of the parental responsibility which arises from the duty of the parent to secure the child's education'. This responsibility is long established and derives from

---

[123] *Protecting Children, Supporting Parents: A Consultation Document on the physical punishment of children* (2000).

[124] *Analysis of Responses to the Protecting Children, Supporting Parents Consultation Document* (2001).

[125] *Sixth Report of the House of Commons Health Committee—The Victoria Climbié Inquiry Report* HC 270 (TSO, 2003).   [126] Lord Laming, *The Victoria Climbié Inquiry*, Cm 5730 (2003).

[127] On which see R Smith ' "Hands-off parenting?" towards a reform of the defence of reasonable chastisement in the UK' [2004] CFLQ 261 at pp 271–2.

[128] Respectively under ss 18 or 20 of the Offences Against the Person Act 1861, s 47 of the 1861 Act and s 1 of the Children and Young Persons Act 1933.   [129] By s 58(5) of the 2004 Act.

[130] See the Explanatory Notes to the 2004 Act at para 236.

[131] See the Joint Committee on Human Rights HL 161/HC 537 discussed by R Smith ' "Hands-off parenting?" towards a reform of the defence of reasonable chastisement in the UK' [2004] CFLQ 261, at 272.

[132] [1997] Fam 1 at 26.

[133] See D Monk 'Parental Responsibility and Education: Taking a Long View' in R Probert, S Gilmore and J Herring (eds) *Responsible Parents & Parental Responsibility* (2009) ch 8 and N Harris *Education, Law and Diversity* (2007).

the common law right of a parent to determine what education the child should receive.[134] Parents' rights to determine their children's education are also protected by the European Convention on Human Rights to the extent of respecting their religious and philosophical convictions.[135]

Duty to ensure children receive appropriate education

At common law, because the duty was unenforceable,[136] parents could choose not to have their children educated. This right, however, has long since been removed. Now, parents of every child between the ages of five and 16 have to ensure that the child receives 'efficient full-time education suitable (a) to his age, ability and aptitude and (b) to any special educational needs he may have, either by regular attendance at school or otherwise'.[137]

'Parent' for these purposes includes any person who is not a parent but who has parental responsibility for the child or who has care of the child.[138]

Those with parental responsibility or who have care of children can discharge their duty by ensuring that they attend independent[139] rather than state schools or even by educating them at home, provided in this latter instance the local education authority is satisfied that the child is receiving efficient and full-time education suitable to his age etc. Where state education is relied upon, except where the child has been permanently excluded from two or more schools, education authorities and governing bodies of maintained schools are required to comply with 'parental' wishes as to choice of school, save, importantly, where compliance would 'prejudice the provision of efficient education or the efficient use of resources' or, if the admission arrangements to the preferred school are based on pupils with high ability or with aptitude and compliance would be incompatible with those criteria.[140] To enable a reasoned choice to be made 'parents' must be given information about the primary and secondary education available[141] and inter alia the curriculum and subject choice.[142]

Enforcing the duty

The obligation to ensure that a child is receiving education suitable to his or her needs is enforceable in different ways. For example, it remains possible for a local authority social services department to institute care proceedings in cases of persistent non-school

---

[134] For a striking example see *Tremain's Case* (1719) 1 Stra 167, discussed by S Cretney, J Masson and R Bailey-Harris, *Principles of Family Law* (2003, 7th edn) at 18–013. See also *Andrews v Salt* (1873) 8 Ch App 622—father's wishes to be respected after his death.   [135] Protocol No 1, Art 2.

[136] See *Hodges v Hodges* (1796) Peake Add Cas 79.

[137] Education Act 1996 ss 7–8. If the child is living with both parents, the statutory duty is cast on both of them: *Plunkett v Alker* [1954] 1 QB 420. For a useful discussion of the 1996 Act see Clarke Hall & Morrison *On Children* Division 12. Following reforms made by the Education and Skills Act 2008, Part 1, young persons aged between 16 and 18 have a duty to participate in education or training. Under Part 4 where the young person is failing to fulfil that obligation, the Local Education Authority can enter into a parenting agreement with the parent or, more drastically, seek a parenting order to enforce their child's obligation.

[138] Education Act 1996 s 576(1). This definition can cover a local authority foster parent: *Fairpo v Humberside County Council* [1997] 1 FLR 339.

[139] Disputes between the parents about appropriate schooling may be resolved by means of a specific issue or prohibited steps order under s 8 of the Children Act 1989, see Ch 14, Prohibited steps orders, pp 498ff.

[140] Education Act 1996 s 9 and the School Standards and Framework Act 1998 s 86; it will be noted therefore that education authorities are not under an absolute duty to comply with parental wishes. See further Clarke Hall and Morrison at 12 [12]. For the position of children with special educational needs, see Clarke Hall and Morrison at 2 [1101]ff.   [141] School Standards and Framework Act 1998 s 92.

[142] Education Act 1996 s 408.

attendance.[143] However, action is more likely to be taken by the local education authority. If it appears to an education authority that a child is not receiving suitable education, they may serve a notice requiring a parent to satisfy the authority that the child is receiving such education.[144] If a parent on whom a notice has been served fails to satisfy the authority that the child is receiving suitable education or in the authority's opinion it is expedient for the child to attend school, the authority must then serve on the parent a school attendance order.[145] Failure to comply with the order is an offence.[146] However, before instituting proceedings for the offence, the education authority must consider whether it would be appropriate to apply instead, or in addition, for an education supervision order under s 36 of the Children Act 1989.[147]

Before instituting proceedings for an education supervision order, the education authority must consult the appropriate social services authority.[148] The latter may decide to provide support for the child and family under Part III of the 1989 Act[149] or to institute care proceedings.

An education authority may apply for an education supervision order on the ground that the child concerned is of compulsory school age and is not receiving full-time education suitable to his age, ability and aptitude and any special education needs he may have.[150] Unless proved to the contrary, the ground is deemed to be satisfied if a school attendance order is not complied with or the child is not regularly attending the school at which he is a registered pupil.[151]

Under an education supervision order, the supervisor has the duty to advise, assist and befriend and give directions to the child and the parents so as to secure that the child is properly educated.[152]

The supervisor must also consider what further steps to take if his directions are not complied with.[153] He may seek new directions or apply for a discharge of the order. A parent who persistently fails to comply with a direction is guilty of an offence.[154] Where a child persistently fails to comply with a direction, the education authority must notify the social services authority, which is obliged to investigate the child's circumstances.[155]

An education supervision order may last up to one year but may be extended for up to a further three years at a time.[156] It ceases to have effect when the child reaches the

---

[143] Formerly, truancy was a specific ground for making a care order, but now under the Children Act application has to be made under s 31. But for a case where such an application succeeded see *Re O (A Minor) (Care Proceedings: Education)* [1992] 1 WLR 912, discussed in Ch 17, The significant harm condition, p 603.

[144] Education Act 1996 s 437(1).   [145] Section 437(3).

[146] Section 443. There is also a separate offence under s 444 if a child of compulsory school age and who is a registered pupil fails to attend school regularly. Formerly, parents could be fined but not imprisoned for such offences. However, under s 444(8A) (added by the Criminal Justice Act 2003) parents can be imprisoned for up to three months. An alternative sanction is for the court to make a parenting order (ie an order requiring a parent to comply for a period not exceeding 12 months with such requirements as are specified in the order and to attend for a concurrent period not exceeding three months such counselling or guidance programme as may be specified by the responsible officer) if the court is satisfied that such an order would prevent further offences: Crime and Disorder Act 1998 ss 8 and 9. See further Clarke Hall and Morrison at 12 [780]. Note the further powers under Part 4 of the Education and Skills Act 2008, on which see n 137.

[147] Section 447. Where prosecutions are brought, the court trying the case may direct the education authority to apply for an education supervision order, but the latter has a discretion not to apply if, after consulting the local authority, it is thought that the child's welfare will be satisfactorily safeguarded without an order: s 447(2).   [148] Children Act 1989 s 36(8)–(9).

[149] Discussed in Ch 15, Local authority support for children and families, p 559.

[150] Section 36(3)–(4).

[151] Section 36(5).   [152] Sch 3 para 12(1)(a).   [153] Sch 3 para 12(1)(b).

[154] Sch 3 para 18.   [155] Sch 3 para 19.   [156] Sch 3 para 15(1)–(5).

compulsory school leaving age or when he becomes subject to a care order.[157] The order may be discharged upon the application of the child, parent or education authority.[158]

(f) Religious upbringing

A person with parental responsibility has a right to determine the child's religious education, though there is no duty to give a child a religious upbringing.[159] As Wall J said in *Re J (Specific Issue Orders: Muslim Upbringing and Circumcision)*[160] '[p]arental responsibility . . . clearly includes the right to bring up children in a particular religious faith, or in none'. Based on the common law,[161] this right to determine the child's religious education is protected to the extent that a local authority cannot cause a child in their care 'to be brought up in any religious persuasion other than that in which he would have been brought up if the order had not been made'.[162] Parents with parental responsibility and those caring for the child can require a child's exclusion from religious studies lessons and school assembly.[163] Although the courts will seek to pay 'serious heed to the religious wishes of a parent'[164] (and indeed to prevent a parent bringing up his child *simply* on the basis of his religious belief is contrary to Art 9 of the European Convention on Human Rights),[165] in the event of a dispute the court must treat the child's welfare as the paramount consideration.[166] It is not for a judge to weigh one religion against another.[167]

(g) Medical treatment

Any person over the age of 16 who has responsibility (in the sense of having de facto control) for a child under the age of 16 has a duty to obtain essential medical assistance[168] for

---

[157] Sch 3 para 15(6).   [158] Sch 3 para 17.

[159] See generally R Taylor 'Parental Responsibility and Religion' in R Probert, S Gilmore and J Herring (eds) *Responsible Parents & Parental Responsibility* (2009) ch 7, C Hamilton *Family Law and Religion* (1995) and A Mumford 'The Judicial Resolution of Disputes Involving Children and Religion' (1998) 47 ICLQ 117.

[160] [1999] 2 FLR 678 at 685—decision upheld by the Court of Appeal at [2001] 1 FLR 571.

[161] See *Andrews v Salt* (1873) 8 Ch App 622. The rule, see eg *Hawksworth v Hawksworth* (1871) LR Ch App 539, that unless there were exceptional circumstances children had to be brought up in the religion of their father was abolished by the Guardianship of Infants Act 1925 s 1. See generally H Bevan *Child Law* (1989) paras 11.02–11.16.

[162] Children Act 1989 s 33(6)(a). Note that under the Adoption and Children Act 2002 s 1(5) (which now only applies in Wales, see Religious, racial, cultural and linguistic considerations, p 696) there is a general requirement that adoption agencies 'must give due consideration' to the child's religious persuasion when placing for adoption, rather than specifically having to have regard to parental wishes.

[163] School Standards and Framework Act 1998 s 71, discussed in Clarke Hall and Morrison at 12 [407]. More generally, see N Harris *Education, Law and Diversity* (2007) 429–441.

[164] *J v C* [1969] 1 All ER 788 at 801, per Ungoed-Thomas J.

[165] See *Palau-Martinez v France* [2004] 2 FLR 810, ECtHR and *Hoffmann v Austria* (1993) 17 EHRR 293, ECtHR (note the comment at [1994] Fam Law 673). But a parent's right to manifest his religion has to be balanced against the welfare of the child and the rights of the other parent—see Thorpe LJ in *Re J (Specific Issue Orders: Muslim Upbringing and Circumcision)* [2000] 1 FLR 571 at 575, CA. Note also *R (On the Application of Williamson) v Secretary of State for Education and Employment* [2005] UKHL 15, [2005] 2 AC 246. For further commentary, see N Harris *Education, Law and Diversity* (2007) 66–85.

[166] See eg *Re G (Education: Religious Upbringing)* [2012] EWCA Civ 1233, [2013] 1 FLR 677, *Re S (Minors) (Access: Religious Upbringing)* [1992] 2 FLR 313, CA, *Re P (A Minor) (Residence Order: Child's Welfare)* [2000] Fam 15 and *Re J (Specific Issue Orders: Muslim Upbringing and Circumcision)* [2000] 1 FLR 571, CA.

[167] *Re G (Education: Religious Upbringing)* [2012] EWCA Civ 1233 [2013] 1 FLR 677 at [36] per Munby LJ, on which, see R Taylor 'Secular values and sacred rights' [2013] CFLQ 336.

[168] See L Hagger 'Parental Responsibility and Children's Health Care Treatment' in R Probert, S Gilmore and J Herring (eds) *Responsible Parents & Parental Responsibility* (2009) ch 10. For consent to medical treatment see generally E Jackson *Medical Law: Text, Cases and Materials*, Ch 4; and J Mason and A McCall Smith *Law and Medical Ethics* (9th edn by J Mason and G Laurie, 2011) Ch 4. See also J Munby 'Consent and Treatment: Children and the Incompetent Patient' in A Grubb, J Laing and J McHale (eds) *Principles of Medical Law* (2010, 3rd edn) 491.

that child.[169] However, in most cases, before any treatment can be given, medical practitioners need a valid consent, for without it they may be open to a prosecution for battery upon the child or for one of the graver forms of assault, or be subject to a claim in tort for trespass for which the practitioner may be liable regardless of fault.[170] Absent an emergency, a medical examination of a child conducted against the parents' wishes will also constitute a violation of the child's Art 8 rights under the European Convention on Human Rights.[171]

Such consent is not always required: practitioners have long been advised that in an emergency treatment may be given if the well-being of the child could suffer by delay caused in obtaining consent.[172] There is also some authority[173] for saying that consent is not required if those with parental responsibility have abandoned or, possibly, neglected the child. In cases of doubt, however, a ruling can be sought from the court because it is well established (see later) that the High Court (and now the Family Court) can override either the giving or the refusal to give consent. Conversely, consent might not always exonerate a medical practitioner, as for example where the treatment is clearly against the child's interests, though even then there might be some situations where leave can properly be given. For example, the transplant of a child's kidney to a twin may not be in the donor's medical interests, but if, having been properly guided by medical advice, a reasonable person with parental responsibility, weighing the risks to the donor against the advantage to the other, would give his consent, all concerned should be given legal protection.[174] Although this absence of any consent may lay the practitioner open to an action *by or on behalf of the child*, apart from seeking an injunction to prevent the proposed treatment, it is difficult to see what other legal action a person with parental responsibility could bring in his own right.[175]

No practitioner can be forced to give treatment contrary to his clinical judgment.[176] Hence, as Lord Donaldson MR observed in *Re W (A Minor) (Medical Treatment: Court's Jurisdiction)*,[177] no question of consenting or refusing consent arises unless and until a medical or dental practitioner advises such treatment and is willing to undertake it.

The position of those with parental responsibility

As a general rule anyone with parental responsibility (including a local authority)[178] can give a valid consent to the child's medical treatment. This power, however, is subject to a number of qualifications. First, not all those with parental responsibility are in the same

---

[169] Children and Young Persons Act 1933 s 1. Note especially s 1(2)(a) under which parents, guardians and other persons legally liable to maintain the child are deemed to have neglected the child in a manner likely to cause injury to the child's health by failing to provide, or to take steps to procure the provision of, inter alia, medical aid.

[170] See eg *Re R (A Minor) (Wardship: Consent to Medical Treatment)* [1992] Fam 11 at 22, per Lord Donaldson MR.

[171] See *MAK and RK v United Kingdom* (App Nos 45901/05 and 40146/06) [2010] 2 FLR 451, ECtHR—in which a hospital, contrary to the parent' instructions took a blood test and intimate photographs of the child.

[172] Upon the basis of the common law defence of necessity: cf Ministry of Health Circular F/19/113 1967 and Home Office Circular 63/1968. See also *Re F (Mental Patient: Sterilisation)* [1990] 2 AC 1 at 52, per Lord Bridge and *Re A (Children) (Conjoined Twins: Surgical Separation)* [2001] Fam 147, CA, per Brooke LJ.

[173] *Gillick v West Norfolk and Wisbech Area Health Authority* [1986] AC 112, HL per Lord Scarman at 189 and Lord Templeman at 204.

[174] Though perhaps it is an interesting point as to whether a parent has any power to consent to such irreversible treatment, see The position of those with parental responsibility, p 352.

[175] Parents no longer have the right to sue for the loss of their child's services: see Damages for loss of services, p 366. However, practitioners could be subject to disciplinary action by their professional body.

[176] *Re J (A Minor) (Child In Care: Medical Treatment)* [1993] Fam 15, CA. See also *Portsmouth NHS Trust v Wyatt* [2005] EWHC 2293 (Fam), [2006] 1 FLR 652.   [177] [1993] Fam 64 at 83.

[178] See *R v Kirklees Metropolitan Borough Council, ex p C (A Minor)* [1992] 2 FLR 117 and *A Metropolitan Borough Council v DB* [1997] 1 FLR 767.

position. In particular, those having responsibility by virtue of an emergency protection order only have authority to take such action 'as is reasonably required to safeguard
or promote the welfare of the child'.[179] Hence, while such persons may be able to give a
valid consent to day-to-day treatment, they cannot agree to major elective surgery. In
Re B (Medical Treatment)[180] it was thought to be 'probably right' that a local authority
should take the view that their parental authority did not extend to consenting to a declaration that a child in their care be withheld intensive resuscitation in certain defined
circumstances.

Secondly, even parents with parental responsibility are not empowered to consent
to all forms of treatment. According to Lord Templeman in Re B (A Minor) (Wardship:
Sterilisation)[181] sterilisation of a girl under the age of 18 can only be lawfully carried out with
leave of a High Court judge. Notwithstanding that Lord Templeman was the only Law Lord
to say this and that the precise legal basis for his assertion remains uncertain, it has since
been accepted as the basic position,[182] though whether a similar requirement extends to
other forms of treatment has yet to be decided.[183] However, High Court leave is not required
to perform an operation for therapeutic reasons even though a side effect (but not its main
purpose) will be to sterilise the child. Furthermore, notwithstanding that a decision as to
sterilisation is a matter for the judge, not all responsibility is thus removed from parents (or
others with parental responsibility) since they retain the responsibility to bring the issue
before the High Court.[184]

Apart from these qualifications, the power of consent vested in those with parental
responsibility extends to most forms of surgical, medical or dental treatment including treatment by drugs or for drug abuse and, by analogy with s 8(2) of the Family Law
Reform Act 1969, diagnostic procedures such as HIV testing and, by reason of s 21(3) of that
Act (as amended), the taking of bodily samples from the child to be used in tests to determine
parentage and ritual circumcision.[185] The extent to which a parent or other holder of parental
responsibility can consent to the withdrawal of treatment has yet to be fully explored but it is
at least implicit in Re RB,[186] in which the father withdrew his opposition to the hospital taking his son off ventilation, that it is within the power of parents to consent to the withdrawal
of treatment by a hospital even if that inevitably means that the child will die.

The third qualification on the power of consent vested in those with parental responsibility is the age of the child. Although the matter is not entirely free from doubt, following Re W (A Minor) (Medical Treatment: Court's Jurisdiction),[187] it seems that those with
parental responsibility retain their power to give a valid consent throughout the child's
minority.[188] This, however, is subject to three important qualifications namely:

---

[179] Children Act 1989 s 44(5)(b).
[180] [2008] EWHC 1996 (Fam) [2009] 1 FLR 1264 at [7], per Coleridge J.
[181] [1988] AC 199 at 205, HL, discussed by A Grubb and D Pearl 'Sterilisation and the Courts' [1987] CLJ
439. A similar conclusion was reached by the Australian High Court in Department of Health v JWB and
SMB (1992) 66 ALJR 300.
[182] At any rate, as Lord Donaldson MR put it in Re W (A Minor) (Medical Treatment) [1993] Fam 64 at
79: 'parties might well be advised to apply to the court for assistance'.
[183] It might conceivably cover all irreversible treatment for non-therapeutic reasons.
[184] Re HG (Specific Issue Order: Sterilisation) [1993] 1 FLR 587. See also Practice Note [1993] 3 All ER 222.
[185] Re J (Specific Issue Orders: Child's Religious Upbringing and Circumcision) [2000] 1 FLR 571, CA.
[186] [2009] EWHC 3269 (Fam) [2010] 1 FLR 946.   [187] [1993] Fam 64, CA.
[188] This view was most clearly expressed by Lord Donaldson MR, but it seemed also to be accepted by
Balcombe LJ, both of whom expressly rejected the contention that Lord Scarman should have been taken to
have been saying in Gillick v West Norfolk and Wisbech Area Health Authority [1986] AC 112, HL that parents
of a 'Gillick competent' child had no right at all to consent to the medical treatment of the child. But note to the

(1) that a child aged 16 or 17 or who is 'Gillick competent' if under the age of 16 can give a valid consent—which cannot be countermanded by an adult;[189]

(2) although in theory a valid consent may be given by an adult with parental responsibility notwithstanding the opposition of the 'Gillick competent' or 16- or 17-year-old child, in practice no treatment should be given without prior court sanction;[190] and

(3) any decision by a parent can be overridden by the High Court.

The court's powers

It is well established that the High Court can override a decision by a parent to consent or refuse consent to the child's medical treatment. For example, in *Re D (A Minor) (Wardship: Sterilisation)*[191] a gynaecologist intended to sterilise a mentally impaired girl aged 11 (with her parent's consent) to prevent the possibility of her having children in the future. It was held that as there was no foreseeable risk of an unwanted pregnancy and that, as the girl would have sufficient understanding to be able to make up her own mind on the matter when she was older, the operation should not take place. Conversely, in *Re A (Children: Conjoined Twins: Surgical Separation)*[192] the court sanctioned, contrary to the parents' wishes, the separation of conjoined twins notwithstanding that the inevitable result would be to kill the weaker twin but preserve the life of the stronger twin. In *Re C (HIV Test)*[193] the court ordered, contrary to the parents' wishes, an HIV test to be carried out on a baby, and in *Re C (Welfare of Child: Immunisation)*[194] the court ordered, contrary to the wishes of the one-parent carer, that the children concerned should have the MMR vaccination. Other examples include *An NHS Trust v SR (Radiotherapy and Chemotherapy)*[195] in which the court overruled a mother's refusal to consent to follow-up radiotherapy and chemotherapy treatment for her 7 year old son following surgery for removal of a brain tumour; *Re B (A Minor) (Wardship: Medical Treatment)*[196] in which the court sanctioned, contrary to the parents' wishes, a life-saving operation for a newly born Down's Syndrome child; *Re B (Wardship: Abortion)*[197] in which the court, overruling the mother's objections, gave permission for a 12-year-old to have an abortion; and *Re R (A Minor) (Blood Transfusion)*[198] in which the court overrode opposition to a blood transfusion by parents who were Jehovah's Witnesses.

---

contrary *R (Axon) v The Secretary of State For Health and the Family Planning Association* [2006] EWHC 37 (Admin) [2006] 2 FLR 206, per Silber J.

[189] See Lord Donaldson MR in *Re W* [1993] Fam at 83–4. Note: s 8 of the Family Law Reform Act 1969, confers a statutory right of consent to medical treatment on 16 and 17 year olds.

[190] This, at any rate, was Nolan LJ's view in *Re W* [1993] Fam at 94. Even Lord Donaldson MR, at 84, thought that a child's refusal was a very important consideration for parents deciding whether themselves to give consent.

[191] [1976] Fam 185. The case had been brought by an educational psychologist concerned with the case.

[192] [2001] Fam 147.

[193] [1999] 2 FLR 1004. But note at first instance Wilson J declined to order the mother to stop breast feeding her baby. After detailed consideration the Court of Appeal refused permission to appeal against this judgment, see [1999] 2 FLR at 1017. For a comment on this decision, see A Downie 'Re C (HIV Test): The Limits of parental autonomy' [2000] CFLQ 197.

[194] [2003] EWCA Civ 1148 [2003] 2 FLR 1095, on which see K O'Donnell 'Re C (Welfare of Child: Immunisation)—Room to Refuse? Immunisation, welfare and the role of parental decision making' [2004] CFLQ 213. A similar decision was reached in *F v F (MMR Vaccine)* [2013] EWHC 2683 (Fam) [2014] 1 FLR 1328 in which both parents refused to give their consent.

[195] [2012] EWHC 3842 (Fam) [2013] 1 FLR 1297.   [196] [1981] 1 WLR 1421, CA.

[197] [1991] 2 FLR 426.   [198] [1993] 2 FLR 757.

The High Court's powers of consent are wider than those of a parent and can extend, for example, to sanctioning a child's sterilisation.[199] It has been held in relation to a terminally ill child that a court can authorise treatment to relieve the child's suffering even if this means shortening the child's life.[200] In deciding what order to make it is established that the court's paramount duty is to decide what is in the best interests of the child,[201] not the reasonableness of the parents' refusal of consent.[202] There is therefore no proposition of law that the court cannot order non-essential invasive medical treatment in the face of rooted opposition by the child's primary carer.[203] This approach does not, however, mean that the parents' standpoint can be ignored. A good, if controversial, example is Re T (a minor) (wardship: medical treatment),[204] which concerned a child aged 18 months suffering from a life-threatening liver defect. The medical advice was that the child should have a liver transplant as the prospects of success were good, whereas without the transplant the child's life expectancy was just over two years. The parents refused to consent. The child had already undergone surgery which had caused much pain and distress, and the mother, who had a deep-seated concern as to the benefits of major invasive surgery and post-operative treatment and about the dangers of failure long-term as well as short-term, took the view that it was better for her child to spend the rest of his short life without the pain, stress and upset of intrusive surgery. No one doubted the sincerity of the mother's views and both parents were described as caring and devoted to the child. An added complication of the case was that at the time of the action the family were living abroad, so that it was not certain that an order authorising the treatment would be implemented.

The court was acutely aware of the difficulties that the case presented—was it in the best interests of the child to have a peaceful if short life with devoted parents, or should the court give its consent to the liver transplant and order the child's return to this country with all the distress and uncertainties that that would entail? In the exceptional circumstances of the case it was held that the child's best interests required that decisions as to his future treatment should be left in the hands of his devoted parents.

(h) Vetoing the issue of a passport

Since 5 October 1998 it has not been possible to apply to put children's names on adults' passports. Instead applications have to be made for children to be issued with their own

---

[199] See Re B (A Minor) (Wardship: Sterilisation) [1988] AC 199 at 205, per Lord Templeman. See also Re R (A Minor) (Wardship: Consent To Medical Treatment) [1992] Fam 11 at 25B and 28C–F.

[200] Re C (A Minor) (Wardship: Medical Treatment) [1990] Fam 26, CA. Note also Re C (A Baby) [1996] 2 FLR 43 in which the court authorised the discontinuation of artificial ventilation of a brain-damaged child. See also Re C (Medical Treatment) [1998] 1 FLR 384 in which the court approved a hospital's proposal—opposed by the child's parents who, being Orthodox Jews, could not contemplate a course of action which would indirectly shorten life—to withdraw ventilation and thereafter not to reinstate it in the case of a 16-month-child suffering from a fatal disease, since life-sustaining treatment would simply delay death without significantly alleviating suffering. For a similar type of decision see A National Health Service Trust v D [2000] 2 FLR 677 in which Cazalet J observed that allowing a child to die with dignity fell within Art 3 of the European Convention on Human Rights (as established by D v United Kingdom (1997) 24 EHRR 423) and could not therefore be considered to be in breach of the right to life under Art 2.

[201] For a discussion of whether the test is different when considering whether to overrule a competent child's decision, see N Lowe 'The House of Lords and the welfare principle' in Bridge (ed) Family Law Towards the Millennium, Essays for P M Bromley (1997) 125 at 170.

[202] Per Butler-Sloss LJ in Re T (a minor) (wardship: medical treatment) [1997] 1 All ER 906 at 913, applying inter alia Re B (A Minor) (Wardship: Sterilisation) [1988] AC 199, HL.

[203] Per Thorpe LJ in Re C (Welfare of Child: Immunisation) [2003] EWCA Civ 1148 [2003] 2 FLR 1095 at [22].

[204] [1997] 1 All ER 906. For a criticism of this decision see C Bridge 'Parental power and the medical treatment of children' in Bridge (ed) Family Law Towards the Millennium, Essays for P M Bromley (1997) 295 at 325–8, who considers the decision to be too parent-centred. It is instructive to compare this decision with that in Re D (A Minor) (Wardship: Sterilisation).

passports though passports already issued to parents with their children's names upon them remain valid.[205] As the guidance issued by what was then the UK Passport Agency (now HM Passport Office) explains,[206] in the absence of any objection being lodged at the Agency's passport office, standard passport facilities are normally granted to children with the consent of either parent or a person acting in loco parentis. Where the child's parents are not married to each other, the mother's consent is required if the father does not have parental responsibility.[207] Where it is known that the child is a ward of court,[208] the court's consent is required.

(i) Taking the child abroad and arranging for the child's emigration

Subject to obtaining the necessary passports, parents with parental responsibility acting in unison have the power to take their child outside the United Kingdom and can therefore arrange for his emigration. Neither parent has the *unilateral* right, if the other parent has parental responsibility, to take or remove the child, under the age of 16, from the United Kingdom without the other's consent,[209] since to do so is an offence under the Child Abduction Act 1984 s 1(1). Guardians and special guardians are empowered to remove the child from the United Kingdom unless there are other persons with parental responsibility, in which case their consent is also required.[210]

The powers of removal are further fettered in the event of the making of a child arrangements order or care order. A person named in a child arrangements order as a person with whom the child is to live is made is thereby entitled to remove the child from the United Kingdom for a period of less than one month without anyone's permission,[211] but can only remove the child for a period in excess of one month with the *written* consent of every person having parental responsibility or with leave of the court.[212] The making of a care order prevents any person from removing the child from the United Kingdom without the written consent of every person with parental responsibility[213] or leave of the court, although the local authority themselves can arrange for the child's removal for a

[205] Home Office News Release 142/98. It is to be noted that arrangements for obtaining a one-year British Visitor's Passport having ended, these controls govern *all* applications for British passports for children.
[206] Reproduced at [1994] Fam Law 651. See also *Practice Direction* [1986] 1 All ER 983. According to *Practice Direction 12F—International Child Abduction* para 4.10, what is now the HM Passport Office will only take action to prevent a United Kingdom passport or replacement passport being issued where it has been served with a court order expressly requiring a United Kingdom passport to be surrendered or expressly prohibiting the issue of any further United Kingdom passport facilities to the child without consent of the court or the holder of such an order.
[207] For the position of unmarried fathers with respect to parental responsibility see Ch 11.
[208] Wardship is discussed in Chapter 20.
[209] 'United Kingdom' means England and Wales, Scotland and Northern Ireland: Interpretation Act 1978 Sch 1. For the purposes of this Act the 'consent' required does not have to be in writing. It is a defence under s 1(5) of the Child Abduction Act 1984 if the child is removed: (a) in the belief that the other person has consented or would have done had he been aware of all the relevant circumstances; (b) after taking all reasonable steps to communicate with the other person, the accused had been unable to do so; or (c) the other person has unreasonably refused to consent. Section 1(5)(c) does not apply if the person refusing consent is named in a child arrangements order as a person with whom the child is to live: s 1(5A), as amended. Where there is sufficient evidence to raise the application of s 1(5) the burden is on the prosecution to show that s 1(5) does not apply: s 1(6).
[210] Special guardians only require consent to take the child out of the United Kingdom for more than three months: Child Abduction Act 1984 s 1(4)(b), as amended by the Adoption and Children Act 2002. Special guardianship is discussed in Ch 19.
[211] Children Act 1989 s 13(2), as amended by Sch 2 Part 1 para 22 (3) of the Child and Families Act 2014.
[212] Children Act 1989 s 13(1). Cf the position of special guardians, see n [210].
[213] Children Act 1989 s 33(7)(b).

period of less than one month without anyone's permission[214] and, with approval of the court, may make arrangements for the child in their care to live outside England and Wales.[215] The net result of these provisions is that where the child is to be removed from the United Kingdom for more than one month the consent of all those who have parental responsibility or leave of the court must be obtained.

(j) Naming the child

Although it can simply be said that naming a child[216] is an aspect of parental responsibility the law on this issue is surprisingly complicated. There are two aspects: the initial conferring of the name and the subsequent changing of it. A distinction can also be made between first or given names and surnames.

Conferring names

The power to confer the name is vested in those who can register the child's birth, which in turn is governed by the Births and Deaths Registration Act 1953, as amended. As Butler-Sloss LJ explained in *Re W (A Child) (Illegitimate Child: Change of Surname)*,[217] the 1953 Act:[218]

> requires registration of the birth of a child within 42 days of birth. The Registration of Births and Deaths Regulations 1987, as amended by the Registration of Births and Deaths (Amendment) Regulations 1994, set out the requirements for registration. These include the name and surname of the child. Regulation 9(3)(b) provides
>
> "... the surname to be entered shall be the surname by which at the date of the registration of the birth it is intended that the child shall be known".
>
> When the parents are married the duty to provide the relevant information lies on both parents. When the parents are not married at the time of his birth the mother alone has the duty to register the birth.

To this may be added that in the case of abandoned children the person having charge of the child can apply to the Registrar General to have the birth registered.[219]

The 1953 Act, therefore, effectively confines the power to confer a name on the child (other than an abandoned child) to each of the married parents or the unmarried mother, i.e. parents who have parental responsibility for the child immediately he or she is born.

Although the 1953 Act places an obligation on married parents and unmarried mothers to register the child's birth and name it does not dictate what surname to register. Hence, although by convention a child born to married parents takes his father's surname, the father cannot insist upon this.[220] Conversely, while a child whose parents are

---

[214] Children Act 1989 s 33(8)(a).   [215] Children Act 1989 s 33(8)(b) and Sch 2 para 19.

[216] See generally J Herring 'The Shaming of Naming: Parental Rights and Responsibilities in the Naming of Children' in R Probert, S Gilmore and J Herring (eds) *Responsible Parents & Parental Responsibility* (2009) ch 6 and A Bond 'Reconstructing families—changing children's surnames' [1998] CFLQ 17.

[217] [2001] Fam 1 at [2].

[218] Sections 2 and 10. This compulsory method of registration conforms with the requirement under Art 7 of the United Nations Convention on the Rights of the Child that children be registered immediately after birth and from birth, have the right to a name and nationality. For the background to Art 7 see J Fortin *Children's Rights and the Developing Law* (2009, 3rd edn) 470 ff.   [219] Section 3A.

[220] There is nothing in the Registration of Births and Deaths Regulations 1987 requiring the father's name to be given priority and it seems that the mother is entitled to register the child in her name: *D v B (Surname: Birth Registration)* [1979] Fam 38, CA.

not married may take the mother's surname, he may be known by his father's,[221] although the father has no right to insist upon this.[222]

While it is mandatory to register a surname there is no similar obligation to register first names,[223] and even where they are registered, as Thorpe LJ pointed out in *Re H (Child's Name: First Name)*[224] it is 'commonplace for a child to receive statutory registration with one or more given names and, subsequently, to receive different given names, maybe at baptism or, maybe, by custom or adoption'. In short, as Thorpe LJ said, given names 'have a much less concrete character'.

Notwithstanding their significance with regard to names, registration is essentially a matter of record. Hence, as Thorpe LJ has pointed out,[225] '[O]nce a child has received official registration, then that registration stands indefinitely, save perhaps in quite exceptional circumstances.' The finality of registrations is well illustrated by *Re H (Child's Name: First Name)*,[226] in which a father, without informing his wife, registered the child with his own choice of given names. The wife subsequently registered the child with a different given name. It was accepted that the father's registration, being the first in time, prevailed and the mother's registration was cancelled. The Court of Appeal, however, ruled that the mother was free to use her chosen given name.

Changing names

Notwithstanding the finality of registration, the child's name can be changed[227] either formally by court order,[228] or by deed poll or informally. Although there is no requirement to execute a formal deed to change a surname, since a person may call himself what he likes, the execution and enrolment of a deed may be useful for evidential purposes.[229] There is no formal provision for changing a child's first or given name.

Where only one person has parental responsibility (as, for example, where a married parent survives the other or in the case of unmarried parents where only the mother has parental responsibility) then, as Holman J said in *Re PC (Change of Surname)*,[230] 'that person has the right and power lawfully to cause a change of surname without any other permission or consent'. However, once the child's name has been registered then, in Holman J's words,[231] '[w]here two or more people have parental responsibility for a child then one of those people can only cause a change of surname if all other people having parental responsibility consent

---

[221] See eg *Re P (Parental Responsibility)* [1997] 2 FLR 722, CA.

[222] See eg *Dawson v Wearmouth* [1999] 2 AC 308, HL, on which see M Hayes '*Dawson v Wearmouth*—What's in a name? A child by any other name is surely just as sweet?' [1999] CFLQ 423.

[223] See reg 9(3)(a) of the 1987 Regulations which directs the registrar, if a first name is not given to 'enter only the surname, preceded by a horizontal line'.

[224] [2002] EWCA Civ 190, [2002] 1 FLR 973 at [14]. But note *Re D, L and LA (Care: Change of Forename)* [2003] 1 FLR 339, discussed later in this section, at p 358.

[225] In *Re H (Child's Name: First Name)* [2002] EWCA Civ 190, [2002] 1 FLR 973 at [12].

[226] [2002] EWCA Civ 190, [2002] 1 FLR 973. The couple had separated when the wife was six weeks' pregnant. The father had no further contact until the day of the birth when he visited the hospital to discuss the names which the child should be given.

[227] See Chapter 14 for discussion of the resolution of disputes over names.

[228] An adoption order entitles the adopters to change the child's name which is entered on the Adopted Children Register (see Ch 19, The adopted children register, p 721). The court can also sanction a change of surname when making a special guardianship order: Children Act 1989 s 14B(2)(a) (see Ch 19, Powers when making a special guardianship order, p 733) or by making a specific issue order under s 8 or when granting leave under s 13(1)(a) of the 1989 Act (see Ch 14, Change of child's surname, p 520).

[229] See the Enrolment of Deeds (Change of Name) Regulations 1994, SI 1994/604.

[230] [1997] 2 FLR 730 at 739.

[231] In *Re PC (Change of Surname)* [1997] 2 FLR 730 at 739, Holman J left open whether in the case of older children, particularly those over the age of 16, the child's own consent was also required.

or agree' or he or she obtains an appropriate court order. This is clearly the position where a child arrangements order determining with whom the child is to live is in force, since s 13(1)(a) of the 1989 Act expressly states that no person may cause the child to be known by a new surname without either the written consent of every person who has parental responsibility for the child or leave of the court. A similar position obtains upon the making of a special guardianship order,[232] a care order[233] and a placement order for adoption.[234] The position where there are no court orders is less clear. In *Re PC* it was argued that in such cases there was no restriction on any person unilaterally changing a child's name. Holman J, however, ruled otherwise pointing out the bizarre consequences of the argument, namely that where:

> parents have not agreed about their child or not been able to trust each other so that a residence order had to be made; or where (putting it loosely) they have caused or risked significant harm to their child so that a care order has had to be made, the "rights" of both parents in relation to a change of name are carefully preserved; whereas where parents have been able to agree and have not caused or risked harm to their child the "rights" of either parent can be literally overborne by the other.[235]

He also rejected the argument, based on s 2(7) of the 1989 Act (which allows any one holder of parental responsibility to act alone without the other), that one spouse can unilaterally change a child's surname. In his Lordship's view, in the absence of an order determining with whom the child is to live, the 1989 Act cannot be taken to have altered the former law[236] under which it was clear that one married parent could not change his child's name without his spouse's consent.[237]

One interesting result of the current position is that whereas conferring names is exercisable only by parents with parental responsibility, the power to agree or refuse to agree to its change is exercisable by *any* person with parental responsibility.

The statutory provisions already referred to and the decision in *Re PC* are concerned with changing surnames but it cannot be assumed that there is unlimited freedom to change given names. In *Re D, L and LA (Care: Change of Forename)*,[238] for example, it was held that foster carers (who do not have parental responsibility) had no power to change the child's given names. There is perhaps less concern about parental carers changing forenames than surnames but even this issue has been litigated.[239]

(k) Representation

In general a child can only bring or defend legal proceedings,[240] in the Family Court and in the High Court, by his 'litigation friend'.[241] Similarly, if civil proceedings are brought

---

[232] Children Act 1989 s 14C(3), discussed in Ch 19, The effects of special guardianship orders, p 735.

[233] Section 33(7), discussed in Ch 17, The effects of a care order, p 636.

[234] Adoption and Children Act 2002 s 28(2), (3)(a), discussed in Ch 19, The legal effects of placement, p 703.   [235] [1997] 2 FLR 730 at 736.

[236] His Lordship relied upon *Y v Y (Child: Surname)* [1973] Fam 147 [1973] 2 All ER 574, but for an earlier authority to the same effect see *Re T (otherwise H) (An Infant)* [1963] Ch 238 [1962] 3 All ER 970.

[237] *Practice Direction* [1995] 1 All ER 832.

[238] [2003] 1 FLR 339. Butler-Sloss P held the correct course where foster carers think a change of name is desirable is to inform the social worker in charge of the case. In foster placements the parents should always be consulted and if a change cannot be achieved by consent, it might be necessary to involve the High Court's inherent jurisdiction (query why a specific issue order could not be sought instead?).

[239] See *Re H (Child's Name: First Name)* [2002] EWCA Civ 190 [2002] 1 FLR 973.

[240] See C Sawyer 'Children's Representation by Their Parents in Legal Proceedings' in R Probert, S Gilmore and J Herring (eds) *Responsible Parents & Parental Responsibility* (2009) ch 12.

[241] CPR 1998 r 21.2(2).

against him he must be represented by a guardian. Parents have long been regarded as having the prima facie[242] entitlement to act in each of those capacities, and presumably anyone with parental responsibility is in the same position.[243] However, with respect to proceedings under the Children Act 1989 and under the High Court's inherent jurisdiction special rules apply, so that children of sufficient age and understanding do not need to act through a litigation friend or guardian.[244]

(l) Disposing of the child's corpse

A parent who has the means to do so is bound to provide for the burial (or presumably, cremation) of his deceased child.[245] Such an obligation, which can be seen both as a duty vis-à-vis the State and right as against other individuals, may therefore properly be considered to be an aspect of parental responsibility.[246] In *R v Gwynedd County Council*[247] it was held that, as the local authority's responsibility towards a child in care ceases upon the child's death, the obligation/right to bury the child vests in the parent. Hence in that case the foster parent had no such rights. Put into the language of the 1989 Act it can be said that, as the local authority's responsibility ended upon the child's death, the right to bury the child vested exclusively in the parents with parental responsibility.[248] Similarly, those who have parental responsibility by means of a child arrangements order will lose it upon the child's death. Accordingly, the right to dispose of a child's corpse seems exclusively to be vested in parents with parental responsibility and guardians.

This aspect of parental responsibility falls outside the scope of the Children Act 1989, since that Act is properly considered to be confined to dealing with live children.[249] In *Fessi v Whitmore*,[250] which concerned a dispute as to the right to determine how the child's remains should be disposed, it was accepted that the 1989 Act was not the appropriate statutory vehicle to decide the matter, but neither was it considered to be a matter of administering the child's estate. In the judge's view the issue was more in the nature of a dispute between two equally entitled trustees (ie the mother and father) and decided the case on the basis of an evaluation of the arguments advanced by each parent. In *Buchanan v Milton*,[251] which involved a dispute between the birth mother and adoptive mother over

[242] *Woolf v Pemberton* (1877) 6 Ch D 19. Note there is a power of removal if a proper case is made out: *Re Taylor's Application* [1972] 2 QB 369 (successful application to remove a parent who refused to accept compromise of thalidomide application, though decision to remove the particular parent was reversed on appeal).

[243] In Scotland the matter is put beyond doubt by s 2(1)(d) of the Children (Scotland) Act 1995: see Can there be a meaningful general definition? p 334.

[244] Family Procedure Rules 2010 r 16.6, on which see *Re T (A Minor) (Child: Representation)* [1994] Fam 49, CA, discussed at Ch 13, Children as litigants, p 470. For an overview see C Sawyer 'The competence of children to participate in family proceedings' [1995] CFLQ 180.

[245] *R v Vann* (1851) 2 Den 325, 15 JP 802, approved by Lord Alverstone LJ in *Clark v London General Omnibus Co Ltd* [1906] 2 KB 648, CA at 659 and followed in *R v Gwynedd County Council, ex p B* [1992] 3 All ER 317, CA.

[246] See J Bridgeman 'Parental Responsibility, Relationship Responsibility: Caring for and Protecting Children after their Death' in R Probert, S Gilmore and J Herring (eds) *Responsible Parents & Parental Responsibility* (2009) ch 14.   [247] [1992] 3 All ER 317, CA.

[248] It should be noted, however, that local authorities have permissive powers to arrange for the child's burial or cremation should the parents not wish or be able to exercise their rights: Children Act 1989 Sch 2 para 20.

[249] Section 105(1) defines child as 'a person under the age of eighteen' and following the normal rules of construction 'person' presumptively refers to a live person: see eg *Elliot v Joicey* [1935] AC 209, HL, and *R v Newham London Borough Council, ex p Dada* [1996] QB 507, CA. For a similar interpretation of 'child' under the Children and Young Persons Act 1969 s 70(1) see *Re D (A Minor)* [1987] AC 317, HL.

[250] [1999] 1 FLR 167.

[251] [1999] 2 FLR 844. Cf *Burrows v HM Coroner For Preston* [2008] EWHC 1387 (QB) [2008] 2 FLR 1225, in which the dispute was resolved by reference to the Non-Contentious Probate Rules.

the disposal of an adult child's remains, the case was determined with reference to s 116(1) of (what is now) the Senior Courts Act 1981 under which applications can be made to be appointed as administrator of the deceased's estate. An alternative procedure for resolving disputes of this kind is to invoke the High Court's inherent jurisdiction.[252]

(m) Child's services

At common law, persons with parental rights were entitled to the domestic services of their unmarried children under the age of 18 actually living with them as part of the family. The significance of this lay in the fact that it provided the parent with his only common law remedy against a stranger for interference with parental rights.[253] However, insofar as the loss of service is due to a tort committed against the child, the parents' cause of action was abolished by the Administration of Justice Act 1982 s 2(b). Furthermore, it has been held[254] that there is no cause of action against a stranger for interference with parental rights in respect of the relationship with their children. For practical purposes, therefore, parental responsibility cannot be said to include a right to domestic services.

(n) Administration of property

Parental responsibility includes the rights, powers and duties which a guardian of the estate (appointed before the Children Act 1989 came into force) would have had in relation to the child and his property.[255] Such rights include the right 'to receive or recover in his own name, for the benefit of the child, property of whatever description and wherever situated which the child is entitled to receive or recover.'[256]

Parental responsibility does *not* include rights of succession to the child's property.[257] Indeed, it seems that parents have no rights as such in the property of a child of any age and therefore, in the absence of any agreement, have no claim, for instance, on the child's wages.[258] The ownership of gifts to a child is more problematic. In the case of gifts to young children, the legal interest probably vests in the parents (or other persons having parental responsibility for the child), but as a result of s 3(3) of the 1989 Act such goods would then be held on trust for the child. In the case of gifts to older children,[259] it is thought that the property belongs to the child. In practice, if a minor is entitled to property of any value, he will normally derive it under a settlement or will or on an intestacy, and the legal ownership will therefore usually vest in trustees.[260]

Notwithstanding that parental responsibility does not include a right of succession, since children cannot generally[261] make a valid will, in practice parents (but not others with parental responsibility) have a right to inherit their children's property.[262]

---

[252] See *Hartshorne v Gardner* [2008] EWHC B3 (Ch), [2008] 2 FLR 1681.The inherent jurisdiction is discussed in Ch 20.   [253] Discussed *in extenso* in the 6th edition of this work at pp 329 et seq.
[254] *F v Wirral Metropolitan Borough Council* [1991] Fam 69, CA and *Re S (A Minor) (Parental Rights)* [1993] Fam Law 572, discussed further at Damages for interference with parental responsibility, p 366.
[255] See Children Act 1989 s 3(2). See generally E Cooke 'Don't Spend It All at Once! Parental Responsibility and Parents Responsibilities in Respect of Children's Contracts and Property' in R Probert, S Gilmore and J Herring (eds) *Responsible Parents & Parental Responsibility* (2009) ch 11.
[256] Section 3(3).   [257] Section 3(4)(b).   [258] See *Williams v Doulton* [1948] 1 All ER 603.
[259] At what stage a child makes the transition from younger to older for these purposes is uncertain and will be a question of fact to be determined in each case.
[260] If a child is absolutely entitled to property under a will or on an intestacy, the personal representatives may appoint trustees of the gift for the beneficiary and vest the property in them: Administration of Estates Act 1925 s 42(1). Depending upon the terms of the instrument creating the interest, parents (or others with parental responsibility) may be able to make a claim on the fund for the child's maintenance and education.
[261] Aliter if they are on actual military service: Wills (Soldiers and Sailors) Act 1918 s 1 (as amended by the Family Law Reform Act 1969 s 3(1)(b)).
[262] Administration of Estates Act 1925 Pt IV and the Family Law Reform Act 1987 s 18(2), discussed further in Ch 25.

(o) Information about the child

There is a growing jurisprudence both as to the right to obtain information about a child and as to whether parental responsibility carries with it the power to control publicity about a child. Nevertheless, as will be seen, it remains unclear both as to whether parental responsibility confers a right per se to the obtaining of information about the child and, insofar as it confers the power to control publicity, whether this can be said be a separate incident of responsibility or simply another aspect of the power to protect the child. It is for these reasons that rights in respect of information about a child were not included in the 'list' of what parental responsibility comprises. Nevertheless it is convenient to discuss the foregoing issues under the one umbrella heading. We begin by considering the power to obtain information about the child.

Obtaining information about the child

The common law is largely silent on a parent's position with regard to having access to information about the child. Case law has been concerned with the issue of disclosure of evidence in court proceedings, but in those cases the parents claimed a right to see the evidence on the basis of their alleged rights as parties to the litigation rather than as parents per se.[263] In *Re C (Disclosure)*, however, a guardian successfully sought leave to withhold information gained in care proceedings and which the 16-year-old child concerned did not want to be revealed, from the mother who was party to the proceedings, Johnson J commented that quite apart from her entitlement as a party to the proceedings to know all the evidence 'her very status as . . . mother must give her some strong entitlement to information about her daughter.'[264] On the facts, however, he held that, because he was satisfied that there was a high degree of probability that disclosure would be harmful to the child, the information should be withheld.

Access to information about a child is governed by the Data Protection Act 1998. In general terms, parents, or those with parental responsibility, can request disclosure of information held about the child.[265] However, one commentary advises[266] that if the data controller has any doubts as to the entitlement of the person making the request to do so, 'it will be prudent to refuse access and leave the issue to be decided by a competent court which can weigh what is in the best interests of the child'.

In relation to information relating to the child's health, a person with parental responsibility can make a request for information but over and above other restrictions[267] health data are exempt from disclosure if the information was:

(a) provided by the data subject in the expectation that it would not be disclosed to the person making the request;
(b) obtained as a result of any examination or investigation to which the data subject consented in the expectation that the information would not be disclosed; or
(c) which the data subject has expressly indicated should not be so disclosed.

---

[263] See, for example, *Official Solicitor v K* [1965] AC 201, HL.

[264] [1996] 1 FLR 797 at 803. For an exceptional case of a local authority justifiably denying a parent a right to information about any matter concerning that child's welfare, see *Re C (Care: Consultation with Father not in Child's Best Interests)* [2005] EWHC 3390 (Fam) [2006] 2 FLR 787.

[265] Formerly there were disparate provisions as, for example, under the Access to Health Records Act 1990, the Access to Personal Files Act 1987 and the Access to Personal Files (Social Services) Regulations 1989.   [266] R Jay and A Hamilton *Data Protection, Law and Practice* (2007, 3rd edn) at 10.07.

[267] There is a general exemption on having to reveal information that is likely to cause serious harm to the physical or mental health or condition of the data subject or any other person: Data Protection (Subject to Access Modification) (Health) Order 2000 (SI 2000/413) reg 5(1).

But it is expressly provided that the child (data subject) can change his mind and allow access which had been previously vetoed.[268]

So far as education is concerned, the data controller is exempt from the need to comply with a request in circumstances where the data consists of information as to actual or potential child abuse, and compliance would not be in the interests of the data subject.[269]

So far as social work information is concerned, there is no entitlement in respect of information:

> (a) provided by the data subject in the expectation that it would not be disclosed to the person making the request;
> (b) obtained as a result of any examination or investigation to which the data subject consented in the expectation that the information would not be disclosed; or
> (c) which the data subject has expressly indicated should not be so disclosed.

Controlling publicity about the child

At one time it was thought that questions concerning publicity about a child fell outside the ambit of parental responsibility.[270] It has become evident, however, that the position is not so straightforward. As Ward LJ pointed out in *Re Z (A Minor) (Identification: Restrictions on Publication)*,[271] there are a number of different situations in which the issue of publicity can be involved. At one end of the spectrum is the situation where some third party, such as the media, simply publishes, without making any approaches to the parents, information about the child and/or his family. It seems clear that in this type of instance the issue of publicity cannot be regarded as an aspect of parental responsibility.[272] At the other end of the spectrum is the publication of information that is properly regarded as being confidential to the child. That, according to Ward LJ, clearly involves an aspect of parental responsibility. In *Re Z* a mother sought the discharge of an injunction restraining publicity about her child so that a film could be broadcast publicising treatment of the child (who would have been clearly identified in the film) at a unit specialising in the treatment of children with special educational needs. In holding that the restraint of publicity in these circumstances was an aspect of parental responsibility, Ward LJ held that:[273]

> Placing this particular child at this institute is a proper discharge by this mother of her responsibility to secure her [ie the child's] medical and educational advancement. It then becomes her duty to respect the confidence of her treatment and/or education at the institute. *It is an incident of her parental responsibility to decide whether to preserve or to publish matters relating thereto which are confidential to the child.* (Emphasis added)

---

[268] Reg 5(3).

[269] Data Protection (Subject to Access Modification) (Education) Order 2000 (SI 2000/414) reg 5.

[270] See, for example, the Department of Health's *Guidance and Regulations*, vol 1 *Court Orders* (1991) at para 2.31 which is repeated in the Guidance to the Northern Ireland Order, vol 1, *Court Orders and Other Legal Issues* (1995), para 5.17, but not repeated in the revised *Guidance* issued in 2008 by the Department for Children, Schools and Families.

[271] [1997] Fam 1, CA, discussed also in Ch 12, The paramountcy principle does not apply to issues only indirectly concerning the child, p 422. See the comments on this case by H Fenwick 'Clashing Rights, the Welfare of the Child and the Human Rights Act' (2004) 67 MLR 889.

[272] See eg *Re M and N (Minors) (Wardship: Publication of Information)* [1990] Fam 211, CA and *R v Central Independent Television plc* [1994] Fam 192, CA, discussed in Ch 12, The paramountcy principle does not apply to issues only indirectly concerning the child, p 422.   [273] [1997] Fam 1, CA at 26.

In between these two extremes is the type of situation that arose in *Re W (Wardship: Discharge: Publicity)*[274] in which a father stood by and acquiesced in his teenage sons taking their story to the press.[275] The majority view[276] in that case was that it was at least 'arguable' that publishing information about a child was a 'non-parental activity' and, as such, was not an aspect of parental responsibility. However, Hobhouse LJ disagreed, commenting:[277]

> Whether or not an immature child should become involved with the media is something which clearly can affect the welfare of the child and falls within the scope of the proper discharge of parental duties . . . An immature child will often be unable to judge when it is truly to his advantage to invite the media into his life; he may not appreciate the distress and harm it may cause him and not be able to cope with it when it occurs. There is a risk of harm to the child which requires the exercise of parental responsibility in the interests of the child's welfare. A parent has the responsibility and the authority and power as part of his upbringing of the child to control, if needs be, his child's contact with the media.

Notwithstanding that his was a dissenting judgment, Hobhouse LJ's view seems a powerful one, and moreover is in line with the cases that establish[278] that giving leave to interview a child by solicitors acting for the father in criminal proceedings is an aspect of parental responsibility. It remains to be seen whether the law will be developed along these lines.

Recent concern about the so-called secrecy of family court proceedings, particularly care proceedings, has led to a much more open approach. A case in point is *Re P (Enforced Caesarean: Reporting Restrictions)*[279] in which an Italian mother had been made the subject of a declaration authorising the performance of a caesarean section due to her lack of capacity and her child had been taken into care at birth and subsequently placed for adoption. As Munby P said, the 'public has an interest in knowing and discussing what has been done in this case, both in the Court of Protection and the county court. It is hard to imagine a case which more obviously and compellingly requires that public debate be free and unrestricted.' Nevertheless the judge still had to conduct a balancing exercise, focusing on the comparative importance of the specific rights in play in the individual case and treating the interests of the child, although not paramount, as a primary consideration.[280]

5. LIABILITY FOR CHILDREN'S ACTS

Hitherto we have been concerned with what responsibility comprises, but a related issue is the potential liability of those having parental responsibility.

(a) Contracts

It is established that a parent (and therefore any person with parental responsibility) will never be liable qua parent for any contract made by the child.[281] Such persons

---

[274] [1995] 2 FLR 466, CA.

[275] An article was published in the *Independent* newspaper entitled 'Our fight to stay with Dad', together with a picture of the boys in silhouette from which they could nevertheless be identified.

[276] Per Balcombe LJ, [1995] 2 FLR 466, CA at 472, with whom Waite LJ agreed.

[277] [1995] 2 FLR 466, CA at 476–7.

[278] See *Re M (Care: Leave to Interview Child)* [1995] 1 FLR 825 and *Re F (Specific Issue: Child Interview)* [1995] 1 FLR 819, CA, discussed in Ch 12, The paramountcy principle does not apply to issues only indirectly concerning the child, p 427 n 230. It also seems to be favoured by Ward LJ in *Re Z* [1997] Fam 1, CA at 27, who also pointed out that in any case the majority's views were obiter.

[279] [2013] EWHC 4048 (Fam) [2014] Fam Law 949.

[280] Applying *Re J (a Child)* [2013] EWHC 2694 (Fam). [281] *Mortimore v Wright* (1840) 6 M & W 482.

may, however, be liable on the ordinary principles of agency if they have authorised the child to make the contract or, in the case of unauthorised contracts, by estoppel or ratification.[282]

(b) Torts

As in the case of contracts, neither parents nor others with parental responsibility will be liable for a child's tort[283] qua parent unless they have authorised its commission. Such persons may, however, may be personally liable if they themselves have been negligent by affording the child an opportunity of injuring another. This is a particular application of the tort of negligence, and the test is therefore: did the parent by his act or omission cause or permit his child to do an act which was foreseeably likely to harm the person injured and against which a reasonably prudent parent would have guarded? If so, he will be liable. In *Newton v Edgerley*[284] a father permitted his son aged 12 to have possession of a shotgun but did not instruct him how to handle it when others were present. Although the father had forbidden his son to use the gun when other children were near, he was nonetheless held personally liable in negligence for the injury to a child who was accidentally shot by his son, because he ought to have foreseen that his son would succumb to temptation and consequently should either have forbidden him to use the gun at all or have instructed him how to handle it in the presence of others. On the other hand, in *Donaldson v McNiven*[285] a father had let his son aged 13 buy an airgun. He forbade him to fire it outside the house (he was only permitted to fire it in the cellar) and the boy gave his word that he would not do so. One day, however, he took it outside, fired it and put out the claimant's eye. The father was held not to be liable, for he had taken all reasonable precautions to ensure that the gun was fired in a safe place and no damage would have resulted but for the son's disobedience and folly, which the defendant could not reasonably have foreseen.

Although these cases both deal with liability for permitting a child to have a dangerous toy or weapon, there is no reason why it should be restricted to this field. Thus, if an adult in charge of a young child on a busy road negligently lets him run into the traffic with the result that the driver of a car, in swerving to avoid the child, injures himself or another, that adult must on principle be liable for the damage.[286]

(c) Crimes

At common law a parent was not liable for his child's crimes[287] unless he himself was guilty of aiding and abetting. But the fact that a child's criminal propensities may be due to bad home influence or a lack of parental supervision has long been recognised by

---

[282] See generally works on the law of contract and agency.

[283] See generally P Giliker 'Parental Liability for Harm Caused by Children: A Comparative Analysis' in R Probert, S Gilmore and J Herring (eds) *Responsible Parents & Parental Responsibility* (2009) ch 18.

[284] [1959] 3 All ER 337. See also *Bebee v Sales* (1916) 32 TLR 413.

[285] [1952] 2 All ER 691, CA. See also *Jauffir v Akhbar, The Times*, 10 February 1984; *Gorely v Codd* [1966] 3 All ER 891.

[286] See *Carmarthenshire County Council v Lewis* [1955] AC 549, HL, where a school authority was liable in similar circumstances for negligently letting a child run out of the school premises onto a road with the result that a lorry driver was killed. See further P Waller 'Visiting the Sins of the Children' (1963—65) 4 Melbourne ULR 17 and for discussion of parents' civil liability for failing to protect their child, see Civil liability, pp 366ff.

[287] See generally R Leng 'Parental Responsibility for Juvenile Offending in English Law' in R Probert, S Gilmore and J Herring (eds) *Responsible Parents & Parental Responsibility* (2009) ch 17.

statute.[288] The court before which a child has been found guilty of an offence can, with the consent of the offender's parent or guardian, order the parent or guardian to enter into a recognizance to take proper care of him and exercise proper control over him (failure unreasonably to consent is punishable by a fine not exceeding £1,000).[289] Where the offending child is aged between 10 and 15 the court has a duty to exercise the powers just mentioned if it is satisfied in all the circumstances that their exercise would be desirable in the interests of preventing the child committing further offences.[290] Alternatively, if a court imposes a fine or costs or makes a compensation order for the commission of an offence by a child under the age of 17, it may order that these be paid by the child's parent or guardian (but not other persons even if they have parental responsibility) unless the latter cannot be found or the court is satisfied that he has not conduced to the commission of the offence by neglecting to exercise due care or control of the child.[291] Under the Crime and Disorder Act 1998, as amended, where a court makes a child safety order or an anti-social behaviour order in respect of a child or the child has committed an offence or the parent has failed to comply with a school attendance order or to secure the regular attendance of a registered pupil, the court may make a parenting order.[292] In the case of a child under the age of 16 who has been convicted of an offence where the court is satisfied that a 'parenting order' would help prevent a re-occurrence of the offending behaviour, it is obliged to make such an order.[293] The parenting order requires a parent to comply for up to 12 months with such requirements as are specified in the order and in particular may require the parent to attend a counselling or guidance programme for up to three months. A parent can subsequently be fined up to a maximum of £1,000 for failing to comply with the parenting order. As an alternative to being made subject to parenting orders, under the scheme introduced by the Anti-Social Behaviour Act 2003 parents may voluntarily enter into parenting contracts, inter alia with schools, local education authorities or youth offending teams as appropriate. Under these contracts parents, on the one hand agree to comply with the requirements set out in the contract for a specified period while on the other hand the school, local education authority or youth offending team provides or arranges support to the parent to help with compliance.[294]

[288] The earliest imposition of criminal liability on parents was the Children and Young Person Act 1993 s 55, see generally R Leng 'Parental Responsibility for Juvenile Offending in English Law' in R Probert, S Gilmore and J Herring (eds) *Responsible Parents & Parental Responsibility* (2009) at p 316.

[289] Powers of Criminal Courts (Sentencing) Act 2000 s 150(1), (2).

[290] Section 150(1)(a). If the court decides not to exercise these powers it must state in open court why it is not so satisfied: s 150(1)(b).

[291] Children and Young Persons Act 1933 s 55; Children and Young Persons Act 1969 s 3(6) and Schs 5 and 6; Administration of Justice Act 1970 Sch 11; Criminal Justice 1972 Sch 5. The court must exercise this power if the child is under 14. A local authority having parental responsibility for a child or young person who is in their care or who is being provided with accommodation by them is regarded as a parent or guardian for these purposes: Children and Young Persons Act 1933 s 55(5) (added by the Criminal Justice Act 1991 s 57(2)), reversing *Leeds City Council v West Yorkshire Metropolitan Police* [1983] 1 AC 29, HL. See also *D (a minor) v DPP* [1995] 2 FLR 502 in which it was held to be a defence for the local authority (as for a parent) that they have done everything that could reasonably and properly be done to protect the public from the offender. Where a local authority allows a child to be under the charge or control of a parent or guardian, that person can be liable, though it is a question of fact whether the arrangements made between the parties constitute a transfer of control: *Leeds City Council v West Yorkshire Metropolitan Police*, above. See G Samuel 'Legal Reasoning and Liability for People' (1982) 98 LQR 358. See also the Criminal Law Act 1977 s 36 (liability of parent or guardian for unpaid fine).

[292] Crime and Disorder Act 1998 s 8. For a full discussion of parenting orders see eg Clarke Hall & Morrison on *Children* 14 [70]ff.

[293] Section 9. If it is not so satisfied the court should state in open court the reasons why: s 9(1)(b).

[294] Anti-Social Behaviour Act 2003 s 25.

6. LIABILITY FOR INTERFERENCE WITH PARENTS' AND CHILDREN'S RIGHTS

(a) Criminal liability

Although the contrary view was once held,[295] there is no common law offence of taking a child against his parents' will.[296] However, under the Child Abduction Act 1984 s 2, it is an offence for a person 'unconnected'[297] with the child to take or detain, without lawful authority or reasonable excuse, a child under the age of 16 so as to remove him from or to keep him out of the lawful control[298] of any person having or entitled to lawful control of him.[299] The offence may be committed in respect of a child of either sex, and regardless of whether the interference is permanent or temporary. There is no need to prove force or fraud, so it can be an offence to persuade a child to leave his parents. Under this Act a person is regarded as 'taking' a child if he causes or induces the child to accompany him or any other person or causes the child to be taken.[300] It is a defence if the accused can show that he reasonably believed that the child was 16[301] or, in the case of an unmarried father, that he was or reasonably believed himself to be the child's father.[302]

(b) Civil liability

Damages for loss of services

The former tort of wrongfully depriving a parent of his child's services was abolished by the Administration of Justice Act 1982.[303]

Damages for interference with parental responsibility

There is no known tort of interference with parental rights nor therefore with parental responsibility.[304] The leading case is *F v Wirral Metropolitan Borough*

---

[295] East *Pleas of the Crown*, 429–30.

[296] The removal must be against the *child's* will: *R v Hale* [1974] QB 819. It is, however, established that a parent can be guilty of the common law offence of kidnapping his own child: *R v D* [1984] AC 778, HL, and see N Lowe 'Child Abduction and Child Kidnapping—II: The Common Law Position and its Relationship with the Child Abduction Act 1984' (1984) 134 NLJ 995; and of unlawfully imprisoning his own child: *R v Rahman* (1985) 81 Cr App Rep 349; CA; see A Khan 'False Imprisonment of a Child by a Parent' [1986] Fam Law 69. For a discussion of the statutory offence under s 1 of the Child Abduction Act 1984, see Ch 26.

[297] One who is not a parent, guardian or special guardian or named in a child arrangements order as a person with whom the child is to live: Child Abduction Act 1984 s 1(2), as amended by the Children and Families Act 2014 Sch 2 para 47 (2).

[298] Lawful control is a question of fact and the concept of control may vary according to the person having the control, whether it be a parent, a schoolmaster or a nanny: *R v Mousir* [1987] Crim LR 561, CA. 'Control' does not have a spatial element and 'taking' does not involve detaining: *R v Leather* [1993] 2 FLR 770, CA—the accused was held rightly convicted for asking two children to help him look for a stolen bicycle since the children were deflected from what they would have otherwise been doing.

[299] This provision implements with some modification the recommendations of the Criminal Law Revision Committee in their 14th Report, *Offences Against the Person*, 1980 Cmnd 7844, paras 239–49. The offence carries a maximum penalty of seven years' imprisonment: Child Abduction Act 1984 s 4.

[300] Child Abduction Act 1984 s 3(a). There is a similar definition of 'detain' under s 3(c).

[301] Section 2(3)(b).

[302] Section 2(3)(a). But note there can be no such defence where a man abducts the wrong child by mistake: *R v Berry* [1996] 2 Cr App R 226, CA.

[303] Section 2(b). But cf *Donnelly v Joyce* [1974] QB 454, CA on the question of damages in an action brought by the child. See also *Hunt v Severs* [1994] 2 AC 350, HL.

[304] Note, however, *C v K (Inherent Powers: Exclusion Order)* [1996] 2 FLR 506, in which Wall J pointed out that persons can be restrained from interfering with the exercise of parental responsibility and that the courts could use their powers to exclude a third party from the family home to protect the exercise of parental responsibility. For the court's power generally to exclude persons from the family home, see Ch 5.

Council,[305] which involved a complaint by the parents that what was originally under-stood by them to be a short-term placement with foster parents, to which arrangement they had agreed, became a long-term arrangement, to which they had not agreed, and that this therefore constituted a wrongful interference with their rights. In support of this argument they prayed in aid Art 8 of the European Convention on Human Rights and the European Court's decision in *R v United Kingdom*[306] as recognising a right of consortium between parent and child as one of the 'fundamental elements of family life'. After an exhaustive review of the law the Court of Appeal unanimously concluded, in Purchas LJ's words that 'neither under the old common law, apart from the action *per quod servitium amisit,* nor under modern authority is there a parental right necessary to found a cause of action against a stranger upon which the common law would grant a remedy in damages.'

The Fatal Accidents Act 1976

Parents and children come within the category of dependants for the purposes of the Fatal Accidents Act 1976,[307] so that either may sue any person who has unlawfully caused the death of the other for compensation for pecuniary loss resulting from the death.

---

[305] [1991] Fam 69, CA, on which see A Bainham 'Interfering with Parental Responsibility: A New Challenge for the Law of Torts?' (1990) 3 Jo of Child Law 3. See also *Re S (A Minor) (Parental Rights)* [1993] Fam Law 572. [306] [1988] 2 FLR 445, ECtHR.

[307] Section 1, as substituted by the Administration of Justice Act 1982 s 3(1).

11

WHO HAS PARENTAL RESPONSIBILITY?

A. INTRODUCTION[1]

Having discussed the concept of parental responsibility in Chapter 10, in this chapter we concentrate first of all on the important question of who has parental responsibility, or put another way, who the holders of parental responsibility are. We begin that discussion by examining the position at the child's birth and then subsequently. The chapter continues by examining over whom such responsibility exists. It ends by discussing the duration of parental responsibility, the position where responsibility is shared between different holders, delegation of responsibility and finally the legal position of those caring for a child without having parental responsibility.

B. THE ALLOCATION OF PARENTAL RESPONSIBILITY AT THE CHILD'S BIRTH

1. THE POSITION AT THE CHILD'S BIRTH

(a) Married mothers and fathers

Section 2(1) of the Children Act 1989 provides that where the father and mother of the child were married to each other at the time of the child's birth, they each have parental responsibility. By s 2(3), the phrase 'married to each other at the time of the child's birth' has to be interpreted in accordance with s 1 of the Family Law Reform Act 1987. Read with s 1(2)–(4) of the 1987 Act,[2] s 2(1) refers to a child whose parents were married to each other at any time during the period beginning with insemination or (where there was no insemination) conception and ending with birth, but also includes a child who:

(a) is treated as legitimate by virtue of the Legitimacy Act 1976, s 1;

(b) is a legitimated person within the meaning of s 10 of the 1976 Act;

(c) is an adopted child; or

(d) is otherwise treated in law as legitimate.

---

[1] See generally N Lowe 'The Meaning and Allocation of Parental Responsibility—A Common Lawyer's Perspective' (1996) 11 Int Jo of Law, Policy and the Family 192 at 197ff.

[2] Discussed in Ch 9, The Family Law Reform Act 1987, p 306. For a discussion of the legal position of the husband whose wife makes a parental responsibility agreement with another man, see Parental responsibility agreements, p 372.

Stated simply, this means that both the married father and the mother automatically each have parental responsibility in respect of their legitimate children.[3]

(b) Female spouses and civil partners

A mother's spouse or civil partner who is a parent by virtue of either (a) s 42 of the Human Fertilisation and Embryology Act 2008 (which relates to assisted reproduction treatment of a woman who is at the time of treatment a party to a marriage or civil partnership); or (b) s 43 of the 2008 Act (which relates to assisted reproduction treatment provided to a woman who agrees that that second woman is to be the parent of any resulting child)[4] and to whom s 1(3) of the Family Law Reform Act 1987[5] applies (ie where the mother marries the woman or enters into a civil partnership with her after the commencement of the treatment and before the child's birth)[6] will, together with the mother, each have automatic parental responsibility.[7]

These provisions are not retrospective which means that they only apply in relation to children carried by women as a result of the placing in them of embryos or of sperm and eggs, or their artificial insemination on or after 6 April 2009.[8]

(c) Unmarried mothers and fathers

Where the father and mother of the child were not married to each other at the time of the child's birth (effectively meaning where the child is illegitimate) then s 2(2) of the Children Act 1989 provides that the mother but not the father has parental responsibility for the child.[9]

(d) Unmarried mothers and female partners

Where the mother and female partner are neither married nor in a civil partnership then notwithstanding that the partner may be a 's 43 parent', then, as in the case of mothers and fathers who are not married to each other, the mother but not her female partner has parental responsibility for the child.[10]

Since only parents have automatic parental responsibility for a child, then no other person has such responsibility at the time of the child's birth.

(e) Gender change

Section 12 of the Gender Recognition Act 2004 states: 'The fact that a person's gender has become the acquired gender under this Act does not affect the status of the person as the father or mother of the child.' Consequently a subsequent change of gender will not affect the attribution or non-attribution of parental responsibility. Consequently a mother who subsequently becomes a man will continue to have parental responsibility regardless of her marital or partnership status. Conversely, an unmarried father who does not have parental responsibility will not acquire it by reason of a change of gender.

---

[3] Which expression should also be taken to include children in respect of whom a parental order has been obtained under the Human Fertilisation and Embryology Act 2008 s 54, discussed in Ch 8 Parental orders, p 277.

[4] Discussed in Ch 8 Female parenthood, p 256.   [5] As amended by HFEA 2008.

[6] But for the position where the marriage or civil partnership takes place after the child's birth, see Ch 9, Legitimation, p 302.

[7] Children Act 1989 s 2(1A) as inserted by HFEA 2008 Sch 6 para 26 (1), (2). For the position where the woman marries or enters into a civil partnership after the birth, see Ch 9, Legitimation, p 302.

[8] Ie the date when Part 2 of the HFEA 2008 came into force (see SI 2009/479): HFEA 2008 s 57(1).

[9] This position has been ruled Human Rights compatible, see *B v UK* [2000] 1 FLR 1, ECtHR.

[10] Children Act 1989 s 2(2A) as inserted by HFEA 2008 Sch 6 para 26(3).

C. ACQUISITION OF PARENTAL RESPONSIBILITY SUBSEQUENT TO THE CHILD'S BIRTH

Although parental responsibility is automatically assigned to mothers, married fathers and female spouses or civil partners at the time of the child's birth, as just discussed, the Act makes clear provision for others to acquire responsibility after the child's birth.

1. ACQUISITION OF PARENTAL RESPONSIBILITY BY UNMARRIED FATHERS

The unmarried father does not automatically have parental responsibility but, as s 2(2)(b) states, he can subsequently acquire it in accordance with the provisions of the 1989 Act. He can acquire responsibility in the following ways:

(a) by subsequently marrying the child's mother;

(b) by being registered as the father on the child's birth certificate;

(c) upon taking office as a formally appointed guardian of the child;

(d) by making a parental responsibility agreement with the mother;

(e) by obtaining a parental responsibility order;

(f) by being named in a child arrangements order as a person with whom the child is to live, in which case a separate parental responsibility order *must* be made;

(g) by being named in a child arrangements order as a person with whom the child is to spend time or otherwise have contact, in which case a separate parental responsibility order must be *considered* and, depending upon the child's welfare, *may* be made.

(a) Subsequent marriage

By subsequently marrying the mother, the father brings himself within s 2(1) of the 1989 Act[11] and, provided the child is under the age of 18 at the time,[12] will therefore automatically have parental responsibility. Although the Act does not expressly say so, because conferment of responsibility is an *automatic* consequence, the parents' subsequent marriage must be regarded as superseding the effect of registration and overriding any prior parental responsibility order or agreement which means that responsibility cannot then be ended by a court order other than adoption or a parental order.[13]

---

[11] Which, pursuant to s 2(3), must be interpreted in line with the FLRA 1987 s 1(3)(b) of which, includes the parents' subsequent marriage. For an example, see *DN v MD and AR (Contact)* [2011] EWHC 2290 (Fam) [2012] Fam Law 127 where the biological mother subsequently married (though for 'convenience' only) the sperm donor. The mother and her female partner continued to bring up the child and the application to limit the father's parental responsibility was refused.

[12] It is therefore possible for a person to be legitimated by his parents' subsequent marriage, yet for the father not to have or to have had parental responsibility.

[13] Viz. under s 54 of the Human Fertilisation and Embryology Act 2008. For the court's power to end agreements see Ending parental responsibility acquired by registration, court orders or agreements, p 382.

(b) Registration as the father

Based on a suggestion canvassed in a Lord Chancellor's Consultation Paper,[14] the 1989 Act was amended[15] to provide for the unmarried father's acquisition of parental responsibility following his registration as the child's father. For these purposes the registration must be under either s 10(1)(a)–(c) or s 10A(1)(a)–(c) of the Births and Deaths Registration Act 1953[16] (or their Scottish or Northern Irish equivalents).[17]

Although *re-registrations* can confer parental responsibility they will do so only providing they fall within the terms of s 10A(1) of the 1953 Act, namely, where no father has previously been named and the re-registration is with the mother's consent. Re-registrations following a declaration of parentage[18] (which is the only means that an unmarried man has of registering his fatherhood without the mother's consent) do not confer parental responsibility since they fall under s 14A of the 1953 Act.[19] Although, at first sight, this might seem anomalous, this prevents men who have not been registered as fathers circumventing the requirement when seeking parental responsibility orders, effectively against the mother's wishes, of having to show that the making of such an order is in the child's best interests.[20] Because the legislation is *not* retrospective[21] only relevant registrations made on or after 1 December 2003[22] confer parental responsibility.

Although the acquisition of parental responsibility is an automatic consequence of a relevant registration it does not put unmarried fathers in exactly the same position as married fathers since, unlike the latter, the court can, upon application by any person with parental responsibility or, with court leave, the child, order that the father shall cease to have that responsibility.[23] Moreover, parental responsibility dates from the registration, not the child's birth.[24]

(c) Guardianship

To become a guardian, the father must formally have been appointed as such by the child's mother, or by the court in accordance with the terms set out in s 5 of the 1989 Act (discussed in Chapter 8). Such an appointment can only take effect after the mother's death. As a guardian the father will have parental responsibility.

---

[14] *(1) Court Proceedings for the Determination of Paternity; (2) The Law on Parental Responsibility for Unmarried Fathers* (1998) paras 39 et seq. See also R Pickford *Fathers, marriage and the law* (1999) who concluded that her research showed that the then law for conferring parental responsibility on unmarried fathers was 'seriously defective'.

[15] By the Adoption and Children Act 2002 s 111. A similar change was made in Scotland; see the Family Law (Scotland) Act 2006 s 23.   [16] Discussed in Ch 8, Registration of births, p 271.

[17] Viz. the Registration of Births, Deaths and Marriages (Scotland) Act 1965 ss 18(1)(a)–(c), 2(6) and 20(1)(a) and the Births and Deaths Registration (Northern Ireland) Order 1976 Art 14(3)(a)–(c). Note, therefore that registrations in the Isle of Man or Channel Islands or foreign registrations do *not* confer parental responsibility, see, for example, *Re S (Relocation: Parental Responsibility)* [2013] EWHC 1295 (Fam) [2013] 2 FLR 1453 (an estranged husband registered as the father in Colombia). But note, under s 4(1B) of the 1989 Act the Secretary of State has the power to add to the list of enactments under which registration confers parental responsibility. At the time of writing no additions have been made.

[18] Ie under the Family Law Act 1986 s 55A(7) or s 56(4), see Ch 8, Declarations of parentage, p 270 and Ch 9, Declarations of status, p 303.

[19] See *M v F and H (Legal Paternity)* [2014] 1 FLR 352, at [31], per Peter Jackson J.

[20] Discussed at Deciding whether to make a s 4 order, p 374.

[21] See s 111(7) of the Adoption and Children Act 2002.

[22] Ie when s 111 was brought into force, see Adoption and Children Act 2002 (Commencement No. 4) Order 2003.   [23] Children Act 1989 s 4(2A), (3).

[24] If the mother dies before registration, since he cannot register himself as the father, the unmarried father can only acquire parental responsibility by court order or on being appointed a guardian.

(d) Parental responsibility agreements

Although now of much less significance, given the effect of registration, an innovation of the 1989 Act, was to provide a means for unmarried fathers to acquire parental responsibility by agreement with the mother. This power implemented the recommendation of the Law Commission, which pointed out,[25] that although the father could apply for what was then a parental rights and duties order under s 4 of the Family Law Reform Act 1987, the need to resort to judicial proceedings to obtain parental responsibility seemed 'unduly elaborate, expensive and unnecessary unless the child's mother object[ed]'.

By s 4(1)(b) an unmarried father and mother may, by a 'parental responsibility agreement', provide for the father to have parental responsibility for the child. Such agreements, however, only have effect if they are made in prescribed form and recorded in the prescribed manner.[26]

There are no prescribed age limits on those making agreements and there is no reason to suppose that valid agreements cannot be made by parents under the age of 18.[27] On the other hand, it seems unlikely that valid agreements can be made with respect to an unborn child.[28] A local authority, in whose care the child is, cannot prevent the mother from making a parental responsibility agreement with the father.[29]

Although it is clear from the prescribed formalities (discussed shortly) that binding agreements can only be made in England and Wales there is some uncertainty as to the required connection of the parties to this jurisdiction, though the better view is that jurisdiction must normally be based on the child's habitual residence.[30]

When first introduced, all that was formally required was that the agreement in prescribed form should be signed by both parents and witnesses and subsequently filed in the Principal Registry of the Family Division. However, as the Children Act Advisory Committee observed,[31] this relatively informal scheme was not without its difficulties. In some cases agreements were apparently filed with the mother's signature forged. Accordingly, a new procedure was introduced in 1995[32] under which applicants must take their completed form to a local office of the Family Court or to the Central Family Court (formerly the Principal Registry), where a justice of the peace, a justices' clerk or court officer authorised by a judge to administer oaths will witness the parents' signature and sign the certificate of the witness. As before, the duly completed form, together with two copies, should then be taken or posted to the Central Family Court.[33] Sealed copies will be returned to the mother

---

[25] Law Com No 172 para 2.18.

[26] Section 4(2). The prescribed form and manner of recording are provided for by the Parental Responsibility Agreement Regulations 1991 (SI 1991/1478), as amended by (SI 1994/3157). These Regulations were further amended in 2005 (see SI 2005/2808) to apply to agreements with step-parents, discussed at Acquisition of parental responsibility by step-parents, p 386, and in 2009 (see SI 2009/2026) so as to ask for the child's gender.

[27] An analogy should *not* be drawn with capacity to make contracts: parental responsibility agreements are probably best regarded as being agreements *sui generis* and not strict contracts, since it is difficult to see what consideration is given by the father when making the agreement.

[28] Agreements may only be made in respect of a 'child' as defined by s 105(1). There is a presumption against interpreting such definitions as including children *en ventre sa mere*: see *Elliot v Joicey* [1935] AC 209, HL, and *R v Newham London Borough Council, ex p Dada* [1996] QB 507, CA.

[29] *Re X (Minors) (Care Proceedings: Parental Responsibility)* [2000] Fam 156 in which Wilson J held that the 'facility' under s 4(1)(b) is self-contained and does not depend upon the exercise of parental responsibility. Compare *Re W (minors) (removal from jurisdiction)* [1994] 1 FCR 842 in which the High Court accepted an undertaking not to make a parental responsibility agreement.

[30] See further When orders may be made, p 373.   [31] In their Report 1992/93, p 13.

[32] See the Parental Responsibility Agreement (Amendment) Regulations 1994 (SI 1994/3157). Note: a new form (C (PRA 1)) has been issued to take account of the creation of the Family Court.

[33] Art 3(1).

and father,[34] while the record is open to public inspection. No fee is charged to the parents for the formal recording of their agreement, though a charge is payable by those wishing to inspect the record.[35]

Notwithstanding the 1994 changes, the formalities for making binding parental responsibility agreements remain perfunctory. In particular, there is no investigation as to whether the agreement is in the child's best interests or why the parents are entering into it. Indeed there is no effective check on whether, for example, the man is the father of the child concerned. Notes attached to the Agreement Form[36] explain that the agreement will not take effect until the form has been received and recorded at the Central Family Court but that, once it has, it can only be brought to an end by a court order or upon the child reaching 18. It also warns: 'The making of this agreement will affect the legal position of mother and father. You should both seek legal advice before you make the Agreement.'

Whether such warnings, together with the need to take the agreement to court, provide a sufficient safeguard to allay the fears, expressed both by the Law Commission and during the passage of the Bill,[37] that mothers may be bullied into conferring rights upon the fathers at a time when they are particularly vulnerable to pressure, is hard to say.[38] In the wake of the 1994 reform, after a steady rise between 1992 and 1994, the number of agreements fell sharply in 1995 but rose again in 1996.[39] Since 1996 no national statistics have been published. However, it must be assumed that now that unmarried fathers acquire parental responsibility by reason of their registration on the child's birth certificate few agreements are now made.

(e) Parental responsibility orders

When orders may be made

Under s 4(1)(c) of the 1989 Act the court may, upon the application of an unmarried father (ie not upon its own motion), order that he shall have parental responsibility for the child. Applications may be made to the Family Court or to the High Court.[40] If the applicant's paternity is in doubt and especially if it is disputed, it will have to be proved before the action may proceed.[41] Indeed it has been held[42] that it is implicit in every order made under s 4 that the man in question has been found or adjudged to be the father of the child in question.

---

[34] Art 3(2). [35] Art 3(3).

[36] Amended on several occasions, the latest being in 2009.

[37] See particularly Lord Banks, 502 HL Official Report (5th series) cols 1180–82 and 503 HL Official Report col 1319.

[38] In *Re W (A Minor) (Residence Order)* [1992] 2 FLR 332, CA, a mother did assert that she had signed an agreement under pressure, though this was under the old procedure.

[39] According to the CAAC Report 1993–94 (Appendix 1) 2,941 agreements were registered in 1992, 4,411 in 1993 and 'around' 5,280 in 1994. In 1995, the numbers fell 36% to an 'estimated' 3,455 (CAAC Report 1994/1995 Appendix 1). In 1996 the number of agreements rose 4% to an estimated 3,590 (CAAC Final Report, 1997, Appendix 2). Many have commented on the low number of agreements (a phenomenon also noted in Scotland where in 2003 there were 20,542 joint registrations by unmarried parents but only 502 formal agreements: Registers of Scotland, Scottish Executive). However, as G Douglas *Introduction to Family Law* (2004, 2nd edn) 59, has said (relying on research by R Pickford *Fathers, Marriage and the Law* (1999)) while the main reason for the low take-up is ignorance of the procedure, in addition 'inertia and a diffidence about raising the issue with the child's mother may also play a part'.

[40] Section 92(7), which has to be interpreted in the light of the creation of the Family Court.

[41] See *Re F (A Minor) (Blood Tests: Parental Rights)* [1993] Fam 314, CA.

[42] See *R v Secretary of State for Social Security, ex p W* [1999] 2 FLR 604, per Johnson J.

An application may be made only in respect of a 'child', that is a person under the age of 18.[43]

As confirmed by *A v B (Jurisdiction)*,[44] the making of parental orders clearly falls within the scope of the revised Brussels Regulation.[45] That Regulation requires for recognition and enforcement purposes within Member States of the European Union (other than Denmark) that jurisdiction be founded on the child's habitual residence or, failing that, presence in the Member State.[46] In exceptional cases, however, that is, where *no* court within the EU (except Denmark) has jurisdiction, Art 14 of the Regulation permits courts to apply their own rules.[47] In the case of parental orders there is authority, namely *Re S (A Minor) (Parental Responsibility: Jurisdiction)*,[48] that it is not necessary for the child to be habitually resident, present or even born in England and Wales to found jurisdiction to make a s 4 order. That case concerned a child who had reputedly been born in India and who had never set foot outside that country. Whether the passing of the Regulation will provide a reason for revisiting *Re S* remains to be seen but even were it to be applied in cases falling within Art 14 (ie where the child concerned is neither habitually resident nor present elsewhere within the EU as was the case in *Re S*) then, presumably, though this is by no means clear from *Re S*, the applicant (or mother) must have some real connection with England and Wales.

Applications under s 4 are sometimes referred to as free-standing applications to distinguish them from child arrangements order applications by unmarried fathers, in which s 4 orders are made as an ancillary but automatic consequence of naming him in the order as a person with whom the child is to live.[49] As Waite J commented in *Re CB (A Minor) (Parental Responsibility Order)*:[50]

> . . . there is an unusual duality in the character of a parental responsibility order: it is on the one hand sufficiently ancillary by nature to pass automatically to a natural father without inquiry of any kind when [what was then] a residence order is made in his favour; and, on the other hand, sufficiently independent, when severed from the context of a residence order, to require detailed consideration upon its merits as a free-standing remedy in its own right.

Deciding whether to make a s 4 order

It is accepted that in deciding whether or not to make a parental responsibility order the court must, in line with the general principles laid down by s 1 of the 1989 Act, treat the child's welfare as its paramount consideration[51] and be satisfied that making the order

---

[43] Section 105(1). For the reasons discussed in Ch 14, Any child, at p 537 n 442 it is not thought orders can be made in respect of unborn children.

[44] [2011] EWHC 2752 (Fam) [2012] 1 FLR 768, per Wall P.

[45] Viz. Council Regulation (EC) No. 2201/2003 of 27 November 2003, which applies to *all* civil matters relating to the *attribution* of parental responsibility, see Art 1(b) and Recital 5. This Regulation is discussed in Ch 26.   [46] See Arts 8 and 13 respectively.

[47] Note the strictness of this requirement, see *Lopez v Lizazo* Case C-68/07 [2008] 3 WLR 338, CJEU. But for an application of Art 14 in wardship, see *A v A (Children: Habitual Residence) (Reunite International Child Abduction Centre Intervening)* [2013] UKSC 60 [2014] AC 1, discussed in Ch 20, The Supreme Court decision in *A v A*, p 747.

[48] [1998] 2 FLR 921, CA, per Butler-Sloss LJ who pointed out that the jurisdictional rules contained in the Family Law Act 1986 do not expressly apply to s 4 orders and should not therefore be used to curb jurisdiction to make such orders.

[49] Section 12(1), discussed at The effect of parental responsibility orders and agreements, p 380.

[50] [1993] 1 FLR 920 at 929.

[51] *Re M (Parental Responsibility Order)* [2013] EWCA Civ 969 [2014] 1 FLR 339, at [15]. *R v E and F (Female Parents: Known Father)* [2010] EWHC 417 (Fam) [2010] 2 FLR 383 and *Re H (Parental Responsibility)* [1998]

would be better for the child than making no order at all.[52] There is no enjoinder to have regard to the checklist set out by s 1(3),[53] though there is nothing to prevent the court from considering it if it so wishes. This means that the court is not obliged to have regard to older children's wishes: yet, as has been pointed out,[54] given that, if the father applies instead for a child arrangements order which is opposed by the mother, the court must have regard to the child's wishes, it is difficult to see why the checklist should not apply at the very least to contested s 4 applications. Furthermore, since a child with sufficient understanding may, with leave, apply to have the order ended[55] it is logical to assume that such a child's view may be relevant to deciding whether to make the order in the first place.[56]

The restriction under s 9(6) which prevents the court from making a s 8 order in respect of a child aged 16 or over save in 'exceptional circumstances'[57] does not apply to the making of s 4 orders.

The Re H/Re S *discipline*

According to *Re H (Minors) (Local Authority: Parental Rights) (No 3)*[58] in deciding whether or not to make an order the following factors are material:

> (1) the degree of commitment which the father has shown towards the child; (2) the degree of attachment which exists between the father and the child; (3) the reasons of the father for applying for the order.[59]

Re H and subsequent case law was examined in detail by Ward LJ in *Re S (Parental Responsibility)*[60] from whose judgment the following non-exhaustive factors (referred to as the '*Re S* factors') were extracted by Ryder LJ in *Re M (Parental Responsibility Order)*:[61]

i)   The court should take into account the degree of commitment which the father has shown towards the child, the degree of attachment which exists between the father and the child and the reasons of the father for applying for the order.

ii) It is a relevant but not overriding consideration that the court considers the prospective enforceability of parental rights.

iii) It is important to observe the interrelation between the rights and status and the exercise of those rights and restrictions upon the exercise of those rights that exists or that can be imposed. One of the examples given of this was the 'cruel and callous' behaviour of a father who abducted a child from her mother for a few days who was not granted parental responsibility and other circumstances where a

---

1 FLR 855, CA at 859 per Butler-Sloss LJ. But note *Re G (A Minor) (Parental Responsibility Order)* [1994] 1 FLR 504 at 508 in which Balcombe LJ seemed not to have regarded as beyond argument that an application for a parental responsibility order is not a question relating to the child's upbringing and is therefore not governed by s 1(1).

[52]   Pursuant to s 1(5), discussed at Orders to be made only where better than no order p 349, and on which see *Re B (Role of Biological Father)* [2007] EWHC 1952 (Fam) [2008] 1 FLR 1015.

[53]   Discussed in Ch 12, The welfare checklist, pp 399ff.

[54]   By M Doggett, 'Unmarried fathers and section 4 before and after the Children Act 1989' (1992) JCL 39 at 41.

[55]   Section 4(3)(b) and (4), discussed at Ending parental responsibility acquired by registration, court orders or agreements, p 382.

[56]   In practice it is not unusual to ask for a welfare report, when no doubt the child's view can be brought to the court's notice.   [57]   Discussed in Ch 14, General restrictions on making s 8 orders, p 510.

[58]   [1991] Fam 151 at 158, CA.

[59]   The basic application form for a parental responsibility order specifically asks the applicant to state his reasons for making the application: Form C (PRA) 1.

[60]   [1995] 2 FLR 648 at 652H–657B.   [61]   [2013] EWCA Civ 969 [2014] 1 FLR 339 at [15].

misuse of 'rights' could be controlled by a specific issue or prohibited steps order or in the last resort the discharge of the parental responsibility order.

iv) While not wholly irrelevant to each other, a section 8 welfare decision and a decision whether to grant the father parental responsibility are separate and distinct questions to be examined from different perspectives.

v) Where a concerned though absent father has established a degree of commitment to his child, there is a degree of attachment between them and his reasons for applying for parental responsibility are neither demonstrably improper nor wrong, then *prima facie*, it would be in the interests of the child for a parental responsibility order to be made and the court will need cogent evidence that the child's welfare would be adversely affected before considering otherwise.

Possible impact of the s 1(2A) presumption that continued involvement with each parent after their separation will further the child's welfare

The extent to which the *Re H/Re S* discipline is affected by the s 1(2A) presumption that unless the contrary is shown and provided the child will not thereby be put at the risk of harm, the continued involvement of each parent in the life of the child will further that child's welfare,[62] has yet to be determined. It is a mandatory requirement that the courts apply the presumption to parental responsibility order applications[63] and, at the very least this will complicate matters. But it does not necessarily render the *Re H/Re S* discipline irrelevant. Rather that discipline will have to be considered in the context of the application of s 1(2A).

However, while s 1(2A) will no doubt provide a further peg on which applicants can hang their arguments, it is submitted that it ought not to make much difference to the overall outcome of applications. Point v) of the *Re H/Re S* discipline came close to establishing a presumption that a devoted father should be granted an order although it should be said that in *Re H (Parental Responsibility)*[64] Butler-Sloss LJ had disapproved of the notion that case law had created a presumption that a devoted father will ordinarily be granted an order. However, her comment that the '*Re H* requirements' are an important starting point when considering the making of a section 4 order but they are not the only factors and even if they are satisfied the court still has an overriding duty to apply the paramountcy test and to determine whether the making of an order is for the child's welfare, is equally true when applying 1(2A). As the Explanatory Notes to the 2014 Act say,[65] the s 1(2A) presumption is subject to the application of the overriding principle of the paramountcy of the child's welfare. It is therefore submitted that the point well put by Black J in *Re M (handicapped child: parental responsibility)*[66] that:

> parental responsibility is not a reward for the father for his commitment to and involvement with [the child] but an order which would only be made in [the child's] best interests

is equally apposite to the application of s 1(2A).

The disposition to make orders

A further reason for thinking that s 1(2A) will make little difference in practice is that it was evident that the courts were readily disposed to grant orders to committed fathers.[67]

---

[62] Section 1(2A) was inserted into the 1989 Act by s 11 of the Children and Families Act 2014, see The section 1 (2A) presumption, p 433.

[63] See s 1(2A) and 1(7).   [64] [1998] 1 FLR 855, CA.   [65] At para 109.

[66] [2001] 3 FCR 454 at 479b.

[67] According to the *Judicial and Court Statistics* for 2011, there were only 45 refusals (0.8%) out of 5,586 disposals of private law applications.

As Ward LJ put it in *Re C and V (Contact and Parental Responsibility)*,[68] because it is desirable for the sake of a child's self-esteem to grow up, wherever possible, having a favourable and positive image of an absent parent, then applying the paramountcy test: 'wherever possible, the law should confer on a concerned father that stamp of approval because he has shown himself willing and anxious to pick up the responsibility of fatherhood and not to deny or avoid it'. This standpoint echoes that taken in *Re S (Parental Responsibility)*.[69] In that case, after the breakdown of his relationship with the mother, an unmarried father was convicted of possession of obscene literature (comprising indecent photographs of children). Because of this the mother severed contact between the father and his daughter but resumed it when the child's resulting distress and deterioration of her behaviour became apparent. That contact later developed into unsupervised staying contact. The father then applied for a parental responsibility order, which the mother vigorously opposed upon the basis of the father's conviction and his unreliability about money. At first instance the application was rejected primarily because it would 'give him scope to interfere in many different ways with the present arrangements for the child'. On appeal this decision was reversed, Ward LJ stressing[70] that objecting to the order because of the rights and power that it would confer demonstrated 'a most unfortunate failure to appreciate the significant change that the Act has brought about where the emphasis is to move away from rights and to concentrate on responsibilities.' His Lordship continued:

> It is wrong to place undue and therefore false emphasis on the rights and duties and the powers comprised in 'parental responsibility' and not to concentrate on the fact that what is at issue is conferring upon a committed father the status of parenthood for which nature has already ordained that he must bear responsibility.

He added that it seemed to him to be important to ensure that wherever possible:

> . . . the law confers upon a committed father that stamp of approval, lest the child grow up with some belief that he is in some way disqualified from fulfilling his role and that the reason for the disqualification is something inherent which will be inherited by the child, making her struggle to find her own identity all the more fraught.

A similar point was made in *Re S (Parental Responsibility)*[71] in which Sir Stephen Brown P emphasised that a s 4 order does not affect the day-to-day care of children,[72] but does provide status for the father; and *Re W (Direct Contact)*,[73] in which McFarlane LJ commented 'Whether or not a parent has parental responsibility is not a matter that achieves the ticking of a box on a form. It is a significant matter of status as between parent and child and, just as important, as between each of the parents.'

Consistent with the emphasis upon the consequent status conferred by a s 4 order it has been held that orders can be made notwithstanding that the child is in local authority care,[74] nor is the question of enforcement necessarily decisive.[75] In *Re H (A Minor) (Contact and*

---

[68] [1998] 1 FLR 392 at 397, CA.

[69] [1995] 2 FLR 648, CA, on which see J Eekelaar 'Parental Responsibility—A New Legal Status?' (1996) 112 LQR 233.

[70] [1995] 2 FLR 648, CA at 657. [71] [1995] 2 FLR 648, CA.

[72] For the effects of a s 4 order see The effect of parental responsibility orders and agreements, p 380.

[73] [2012] EWCA Civ 999 [2013] 1 FLR 494 at [80].

[74] *D v Hereford and Worcester County Council* [1991] Fam 14. But cf *W v Ealing London Borough Council* [1993] 2 FLR 788, CA, in which the application was dismissed because the children were being prepared for a termination of contact with their parents pending their introduction to prospective adopters, and to change that would have left them in limbo and confused. [75] *Re C (Minors)* [1992] 2 All ER 86.

Parental Responsibility),[76] an order was made even though the father had been denied what was then a contact order. Indeed in *Re C and V (Contact and Parental Responsibility)*[77] the Court of Appeal stressed that applications for contact and parental responsibility were to be treated as wholly separate applications, so that the dismissal of the former did not necessarily mean that the latter should also be dismissed. It has also been held[78] that the court should not use its power to make a parental responsibility order as a weapon to force a father to make maintenance payments for the upkeep of his child.

In all cases the test remains whether it is for the child's welfare that an order be made. Lack of insight into a daughter's needs and an inability to get on with social workers is not reason in itself to refuse an order,[79] nor similarly is it justifiable to base a refusal solely on the acrimony between the parents,[80] nor because of transsexuality.[81]

Once it is found to be in the child's interests that both parents should have parental responsibility, this should be reflected by the making of a s 4 order and not by making 'no order' pursuant to s 1(5).[82] It is within the court's power to accept, when making a s 4 order, an undertaking from the unmarried father not to exercise certain aspects of that responsibility,[83] Although there is no power to suspend a parental responsibility order,[84] applications can be adjourned to see whether the commitment and attachment criteria can be established in the future.[85]

Examples of refusals

While parental responsibility orders were commonly granted, not all applications succeeded. One telling factor was violence. In *Re H (Parental Responsibility)*,[86] for instance, the order was refused because the father had been found to have injured his son in circumstances indicating deliberate cruelty and possibly sadism. In *Re T (A Minor) (Parental Responsibility: Contact)*[87] an order was refused where the father had treated the mother with hatred and violence, showing no regard for the child's welfare. Improper motive is another relevant factor: in *Re P (Parental Responsibility)*[88] an order was refused because it was found that the father intended to use

---

[76] [1993] 1 FLR 484, CA.

[77] [1993] 1 FLR 484, CA, followed in *Re W (Parental Responsibility Order: Inter-Relationship With Direct Contact)* [2013] EWCA Civ 335 [2013] 2 FLR 1337.

[78] *Re H (Parental Responsibility: Maintenance)* [1996] 1 FLR 867, CA.

[79] *Re G (A Minor) (Parental Responsibility Order)* [1994] 1 FLR 504.

[80] *Re P (A Minor) (Parental Responsibility Order)* [1994] 1 FLR 578.

[81] *Re L (Contact: Transsexual Applicant)* [1995] 2 FLR 438, in which a 'father' who to outward appearances was a woman was granted a s 4 order.

[82] Per Wilson J in *Re P (A Minor) (Parental Responsibility Order)* [1994] 1 FLR 578. For discussion of the application of s 1(5), see Ch 12, The application of s 1(5) in practice, p 442. In 2011, just 40 (0.7%) out of 5,586 court disposals were 'no order' disposals: Table 2.4 *Civil Judicial Statistics 2011*.

[83] *Re D (contact and parental responsibility: lesbian mothers and known father)* [2006] EWHC 2 (Fam) [2006] 1 FCR 556, undertaking not to visit the child's school nor to contact any health professional connected with the child's care. For commentaries on this decision see fns [137–8]. Cf *Re B (Role of Biological Father)* [2007] EWHC 1952 (Fam) [2008] 1 FLR 1015 in which in not dissimilar circumstances Hedley J made a 'no order'.

[84] *Re G (A Child) (Parental Responsibility Order)* [2006] EWCA Civ 745 [2006] 2 FLR 1093.

[85] See *Re D (Parental Responsibility)* [2001] EWCA Civ 230 [2001] 1 FLR 971.

[86] [1998] 1 FLR 855, CA. See also *Re G (a child) (domestic violence: direct contact)* [2001] 2 FCR 134, CA— order refused because of the child's fear and anxiety about the father and *Re L (A Child) (Contact: Domestic Violence)* [2001] Fam 260, CA—order refused because of the father's violence and desire to control the child.

[87] [1993] 2 FLR 450, CA.

[88] [1998] 2 FLR 96, CA. The father was deeply confused over sexual boundaries (he was in possession of a number of photographs of pre-pubescent children) and had little appreciation of the difference between abusive and appropriate behaviour. See also *Re M (handicapped child: parental responsibility)* [2001] 3 FCR 454—order refused because the father was likely to misuse it to interfere with the mother's care thus causing her stress and potentially undermining her ability to care properly for the child.

the order for improper or inappropriate ends to try to interfere with and possibly undermine the mother's care. Similarly in *Re M (Parental Responsibility Order)*[89] an order was refused because of the fear that the father would use the order to control the child and, through him, the mother.

Another scenario in which orders were sometimes refused involved known sperm donors. For example, in *R v E and F (Female Parents: Known Father)*[90] in the context of a child being brought up by his mother and civil partner, the father, the 'known sperm donor' and who himself was living in a same sex relationship and with whom the child had some contact, was refused a parental responsibility order.

Other examples of refusal include *Re J (Parental Responsibility)*[91] in which the child (then aged 12) and who was born after the parents' separation, had infrequent contact with her father and did not want contact. Moreover the raison d'étre for the father's application, namely his concern about the mother's involvement with drugs, no longer existed. In *M v M (Parental Responsibility)*[92] an order was refused because the father was found to be mentally incapable of discharging the functions embraced within the concept of parental responsibility. In *Re P (Parental Responsibility)*[93] the Court of Appeal declined to interfere with a refusal to make an order based in part on the father's criminal conduct, holding that a court was entitled to take into account, as relevant but not conclusive, factors such as that the father was in prison and the circumstances of the criminal conduct for which the sentence was imposed.

Although there is no reason to think that these cases would be decided differently in the light of the 2014 reforms, they would nevertheless have to be expressed differently. Some could simply be decided upon the basis that the presumption of continued involvement did not apply because of the risk of harm to the child. Obvious examples are the refusals based on the man's violence, but could also include cases of the father's incapacity. The refusals based on the fear that the father would misuse the order to exert undesirable control of or interference with the child's upbringing would be justified upon the overarching welfare principle. A similar reasoning would apply to refusal based upon the child's objections.

(f) Being named in a child arrangements order as a person with whom the child is to live

If an unmarried father who does not otherwise have parental responsibility is named in a child arrangements order as a person with whom the child is to live then, by s 12(1), the court is required to make a *separate* s 4 order. The importance of the s 4 order being made separately is that it will not automatically come to an end if the child arrangements order is ended, but will require an express order ending it, if the child is still a minor.

(g) Being named in a child arrangements order as a person with whom the child is to spend time or otherwise have contact

If an unmarried father who does not otherwise have parental responsibility is named in a child arrangements order as a person with whom the child is to spend or otherwise have

---

[89] [2013] EWCA Civ 969 [2014] 1 FLR 339.

[90] [2010] EWHC 417 (Fam) [2010] 2 FLR 383. See also *Re B (Role of Biological Father)* [2007] EWHC 1952 [2008] 1 FLR 1015—no order made pursuant to s 1(5) in respect of a brother of one of the partners to a lesbian relationship who provided sperm for artificial insemination on the understanding he would have nothing to do with the child.

[91] [1999] 1 FLR 784.   [92] [1999] 2 FLR 737.

[93] [1997] 2 FLR 722, CA. But cf *Re S (Parental Responsibility)* [1995] 2 FLR 648, discussed at The disposition to make orders, p 376.

contact but is not named as a person with whom the child is to live, the court must decide whether it is appropriate for him to have parental responsibility and, if the court decides that it is appropriate, it must make a s 4 order in the father's favour.[94]

(h) The effect of parental responsibility orders and agreements

The effect of a court order or a properly recorded agreement is the same, namely it confers parental responsibility upon the unmarried father. In most cases he will share responsibility jointly with the mother or, if the mother is dead, with any formally appointed guardian. He could also share responsibility with a special guardian or some other person who is named in a child arrangements order as a person with whom the child is to live. The legal position of a husband whose wife makes a parental responsibility agreement with another man is not clear. Prima facie that agreement confers responsibility on that other man, yet because of the presumption of paternity[95] the woman's husband would also be regarded as having responsibility. Of course, once the issue is before the court the conundrum can be solved by a finding of paternity, but what is the position before that? There is no objection in principle to two men having parental responsibility in relation to a child, but because in this situation only one man can actually be the child's father, only one of them can be regarded as having responsibility. Although the making of an agreement is some evidence that the husband might not be the father, it seems unlikely that an agreement alone would be regarded as sufficient to rebut the presumption of the husband's paternity unless a court so holds. One cannot shut one's eyes to the possibility that both the mother and the other man might know that the husband is or could be the father, but want to exclude him if the other man is prepared to accept the child as his. In many cases, however, there is likely to be other evidence, for example that before the birth the woman had left her husband to live with the other man.[96]

Although in general terms it is correct to say that an unmarried father with parental responsibility is in the same legal position with regard to the child as if he had married the mother, the effect should be neither overestimated nor under-estimated. Even without responsibility the father is regarded as a 'parent' for most purposes of the Children Act 1989. He has, for example, the right to apply to the court for a s 8 order[97] and is entitled to reasonable contact with a child in local authority care.[98] Furthermore, the lack of parental responsibility does not mean that such fathers have no statutory duty to maintain their children.[99] On the other hand, conferring parental responsibility upon unmarried fathers does not alter the status of the child. Hence the child will still not be able to succeed to a title of honour through his parents. Furthermore, as the courts have stressed,[100] the granting of a s 4 order does not per se entitle the father to interfere with the day-to-day running of affairs affecting the child, at any rate whilst the child is living with another carer.[101]

---

[94]   Children Act 1989 s 12(1A), added by the Children and Families Act 2014 Sch 2 para 21(2).

[95]   Discussed in Ch 8, Presumption that the mother's husband is the father, pp 260ff.

[96]   It is also relevant to know who is registered as the father.

[97]   Under s 10(4), discussed in Ch 14, Persons entitled to apply without leave, p 513.

[98]   Under s 34, discussed in Ch 18, The presumption of reasonable contact, p 655.

[99]   On the contrary, unmarried fathers can be 'non-resident parents' for the purposes of the Child Support Act 1991: see Ch 21. For this reason Waite J must be regarded as being mistaken when he commented in *Re C (Minors) (Parental Rights)* [1992] 1 FLR 1 at 9 that *upon* being vested with parental responsibility the father assumes 'an immediately enforceable burden' to maintain the child.

[100]   *Re S (A Minor) (Parental Responsibility)* [1995] 3 FCR 564; *Re A (A Minor) (Parental Responsibility)* [1996] 1 FCR 562; *Re P (A Minor) (Parental Responsibility Order)* [1994] 1 FLR 578.

[101]   And note eg *Re P (Parental Responsibility)* [1998] 2 FLR 96, CA, where the motivation to undermine the mother's care was held to justify refusing to make an order in favour of a devoted father.

Notwithstanding the courts' entreaties not to concentrate on the rights conferred by a s 4 order, it is nevertheless instructive to enquire how the legal position of an unmarried father changes upon being vested with parental responsibility. The principal effects are:

(1) he becomes a 'parent' for the purposes of the adoption legislation and can therefore withhold his consent to a proposed adoption or placement order;[102]

(2) he becomes entitled to remove his child (under the age of 16) from local authority accommodation, and, if he is willing and able to provide accommodation or to arrange for accommodation to be provided for his child, may object to his child being accommodated in the first place;[103]

(3) he will automatically be a party to care proceedings;[104]

(4) he can appoint a guardian;[105]

(5) he can give a valid consent to his child's medical treatment[106] and require full medical details from the child's medical practitioner;[107]

(6) he has the power to consent to his child's marriage;[108]

(7) he is empowered to express a preference as to the school at which he wishes his child's education to be provided; to initiate and be involved in the procedure for statementing of a child with special needs; to withdraw his child from sex education in local education authority schools and to receive full comprehensive reports from his child's school;[109]

(8) the mother will need to obtain his consent to take the child (under the age of 16) outside the United Kingdom;[110]

(9) he will be entitled to sign passport applications and to oppose the granting of a passport for his child;[111]

(10) he will be considered to have 'rights of custody' for the purposes of the Hague Convention on International Child Abduction.[112]

Notwithstanding that a s 4 order undoubtedly strengthens the unmarried father's legal position in relation to his child, it is worth stressing that the mother loses relatively little by the making of the order. She is under no general obligation (but see later) to consult the father about the child's upbringing[113] and, so long as the child is living with her, the father has no right to interfere with the day-to-day management of the child's life, and indeed any attempt or threat to do so can be controlled by a s 8 order.[114] What the

---

[102] Adoption and Children Act 2002 ss 21, 47(2) and 52(6), see Ch 19.

[103] Children Act 1989 s 20(8) and s 20(7) respectively, discussed in Ch 15, Limits on providing accommodation, p 568.

[104] FPR 2010 r 12.3.   [105] Section 5(3).

[106] See Ch 10, Medical treatment, p 350.

[107] For instance, under the Access to Health Records Act 1990: see Ch 10, Obtaining information about the child, p XXX. See also *Re H (A Minor) (Shared Residence)* [1994] 1 FLR 717, CA.

[108] Marriage Act 1949 s 3(1A)(a)(i): see Ch 2, Marriages of persons under the age of 18, p 50.

[109] Under the School Standards and Framework Act 1998 ss 71 and 86 and Education Act 1996 Part IV: see Ch 10, Education, p 347.

[110] Child Abduction Act 1984 s 1(3)(a)(ii): see Ch 10, Taking the child abroad and arranging for the child's emigration, p 355.

[111] See the Guidance issued by the then UK Passport Agency reproduced at [1994] Fam Law 651, discussedin Ch 10, Vetoing the issue of a passport, p 354.

[112] He will have *locus standi* to seek the child's return under the Hague Convention: see the discussion in Ch 26.

[113] By reason of s 2(7), discussed further at Sharing parental responsibility for a child, p 392.

[114] See eg Ward LJ's comments in *Re S (Parental Responsibility)* [1995] 2 FLR 648 at 657.

mother undoubtedly loses is the *unilateral* right to remove the child from the UK[115] and, more controversially, it may be that she needs to consult the father about a change of school,[116] or surname,[117] and about the immunisation[118] and circumcision of their child.[119] She also loses the ability to appoint a guardian to take effect upon her death, unless she has named in a child arrangements order as a person with whom the child is to live.[120]

The fact that a s 4 order does not entitle an unmarried father to intermeddle in the day-to-day management of the child prompts the question as to why applications are made. Indeed the judiciary themselves have sometimes commented that applications are sometimes based on a fundamental misunderstanding of the nature of the order.[121] For some, however, the judicial recognition of what has been described[122] as the exercise of their 'social parenthood' will undoubtedly be important. Whatever the reasons, the numbers of such orders have steadily increased, from 2,762 in 1992, 5,587 in 1996, 7,786 in 2000 to 10,522 in 2004.[123] It was anticipated, however, that in time the number would drop, given that unmarried fathers registered as such on or after 1 December 2003 thereby obtain parental responsibility and to an extent this is borne out by the statistics with 7,570 orders being made in 2007 declining to 5,224 in 2011.[124]

(i) Ending parental responsibility acquired by registration, court orders or agreements

Parental responsibility orders and agreements remain effective notwithstanding that the couple live together or subsequently separate. They will, however, automatically end once the child attains his majority.[125] Parental responsibility acquired by registration similarly ends upon the child attaining his majority. It is submitted that parental responsibility acquired upon registration is superseded and that both an order and an agreement are automatically overridden if the father subsequently marries the mother during the child's minority. This is because, by virtue of s 2(1), marriage confers parental responsibility upon the father which, unlike a court order or agreement, cannot subsequently be ended by a court order, save upon adoption or the making of a parental order.

---

[115] Under s 1 of the Child Abduction Act 1984 she will require the father's consent to leave the United Kingdom.

[116] See *Re G (Parental Responsibility: Education)* [1994] 2 FLR 964, CA, discussed at Sharing parental responsibility for a child, pp 393–394.

[117] See *Re PC (Change of Surname)* [1997] 2 FLR 730, discussed at Sharing parental responsibility for a child, p 394.

[118] See *Re C (Welfare of Child: Immunisation)* [2003] EWCA Civ 1148, [2003] 2 FLR 1095. See also *F v F (MMR Vaccine)* [2013] EWHC 2683 (Fam) [2014] 1 FLR 1328 in which a mother's objection to her child having the MMR vaccine was overruled by the court. See further Ch 10, Medical treatment, p 350.

[119] See *Re J (Specific Issue Orders) (Muslim Upbringing and Circumcision)* [2000] 1 FLR 571, discussed at Sharing parental responsibility for a child, p 394.

[120] Children Act 1989 s 5(7), as amended by the Children and Families Act 2014 Sch 2 para 2, discussed in Ch 8 When the appointment takes effect, p 288.

[121] See eg *Re S (Parental Responsibility)*, above, per Ward LJ who said that s 4 applications 'have become one of those little growth areas born of misunderstanding', see also *Re S (A Minor) (Parental Responsibility)* [1995] 3 FCR 564.

[122] J Eekelaar 'Parental Responsibility—A New Legal Status' (1996) 112 LQR 233 at 235.

[123] See Table 5.3 of *Judicial Statistics* of the relevant year. But as I Butler, G Douglas, N Lowe, L Noakes and A Pithouse 'The Children Act 1989 and the unmarried father' (1993) 5 *Journal of Child Law* 157, pointed out such figures only represented a tiny proportion of the overall number of unmarried fathers.

[124] See the *Judicial and Court Statistics* respectively for 2007 (Table 5.4) and 2011 (Table 2.4).

[125] Children Act 1989 s 91(7) and (8).

Apart from these instances parental responsibility may be brought to an end only upon a court order to that effect.[126] Such an order may be made upon the application (ie *not* of the court's own motion) of:

(1) any person who has parental responsibility for the child (this will include the father himself), or

(2) with leave of the court, the child himself.[127]

In the latter case, the court may grant leave only if it is satisfied that the child has sufficient understanding to make the proposed application.[128] The court may not end a s 4 order while a child arrangements order naming an unmarried father as a person with whom the child is to live remains in force.[129]

In deciding whether to order the cessation of parental responsibility, the court must regard the child's welfare as its paramount consideration and be satisfied that making such an order is better than making no order at all.[130] However, notwithstanding the application of the paramountcy principle there is, as Ryder LJ accepted in *Re D (Withdrawal of Parental Responsibility)*, there is ample case-law 'describing the imperative in favour of a continuing relationship between both parents and a child so that ordinarily a child's upbringing should be provided by both of his parents and where that is not in the child's interests by one of them with the child having the benefit of a meaningful relationship with both. A judge would not be criticised for identifying that, as a very weighty, relevant factor, the significance of the parenthood of an unmarried father should not be under estimated.'[131] Whether similar considerations apply to applications to terminate parental responsibility vested by reason of an agreement can be debated. One can imagine the situation, where for example, the mother had been subjected to undue pressure to sign the agreement.

Given that parental responsibility vested in the married father may be ended only upon the child's adoption, the ending of a child arrangements order naming the unmarried father as a person with whom the child is to live should not automatically mean that parental responsibility should also come to an end. In any event, a separate order expressly ending the s 4 order will be required to end the father's parental responsibility.

In *Re P (Terminating Parental Responsibility)*,[132] Singer J considered that when faced with an application to terminate parental responsibility the considerations relevant to the making of a parental responsibility order are equally relevant to determining whether to terminate it. This approach was subsequently endorsed in *Re D (Withdrawal of Parental Responsibility)*[133] in which the Court of Appeal rejected the argument that the changes introduced by the Adoption and Children Act 2002 had narrowed the scope of the court's powers to terminate parental responsibility and that such powers were incompatible with Arts 8 and 14 of the European Convention on Human Rights.[134] In *Re P* (in which Singer J emphasised that the ability to apply to terminate parental responsibility should not be used as a weapon by the dissatisfied mother of a non-marital child) responsibility was terminated, the father having been found to be responsible for inflicting appalling injuries on the

---

[126] Section 4(2A).   [127] Section 4(3).

[128] Section 4(4). For a similar requirement when seeking leave to apply for a s 8 order, see s 10(8), discussed in Ch 14, The application of s 10(8), p 518.   [129] Section 11(4).

[130] Pursuant to s 1(1) and (5); and see *Re P (Terminating Parental Responsibility)* [1995] 1 FLR 1048 and *CW v SG (Parental Responsibility: Consequential Orders)* [2013] EWHC 854 (Fam) [2013] 2 FLR 655.

[131] [2014] EWCA Civ 315 [2014] Fam Law 971, at [14].   [132] [1995] 1 FLR 1048 at 1052.

[133] [2014] EWCA Civ 315, [2014] Fam Law 971, at [18].

[134] In this respect *Smallwood v United Kingdom* (App No 29779/96),(1999) 27 EHRR 155 remains good law.

child. Similarly, in *Re D* parental responsibility was terminated where the father had been convicted of several offences of child abuse.[135]

(j) Commentary

The legal position of unmarried fathers has progressed a long way from the common law position of having no legal relationship at all with his child (nor little possibility of establishing one)[136] to the current position of being able to acquire parental responsibility upon being registered as the father, or by court order or by agreement. This raises two opposing questions, namely, has the reform gone too far or has it not gone far enough?

With regard to the former it has been observed by some commentators[137] that, at any rate in the context of making parental responsibility orders in favour of unmarried fathers, the courts have tended to treat such orders as vesting status rather than parental authority. This trend, it is said,[138] blurs the distinction between parenthood and parental responsibility and by so doing effectively so degrades the concept of parental responsibility as to strip it of any meaning.[139]

While undoubtedly the courts have stressed the status element of parental responsibility that does not mean that such orders have no legal effect (see the discussion earlier in this chapter) even for unmarried fathers. It may also be pointed that for non-parents the conferring of parental responsibility has very real effect. Nevertheless what the commentaries point up is whether parental responsibility orders are the right vehicle by which to confer the 'status' of being a holder of parental responsibility. This raises the question of whether reform has gone far enough.

The current law stops short of giving *all* fathers parental responsibility simply on the basis of their biological fatherhood and thus equating the position of unmarried fathers with that of married fathers and all mothers. Should all fathers be treated equally?

Following a comprehensive review of and public consultation on this issue[140] the Scottish Law Commission recommended:[141] 'In the absence of any court order regulating the position, both parents of the child should have parental responsibilities and rights

---

[135] See also *Re A (Termination of Parental Responsibility)* [2013] EWHC 2963 (Fam), [2014] 1 FLR 1305, in which a violent father posed a real threat to the life and limb of the mother and *Re F (Indirect Contact)* [2006] EWCA Civ 1426 [2007] 1 FLR 1015, in which the father's anger towards the mother and propensity to violence justified the 'revocation' of the parental responsibility order. Cf *Re G (Child Case: Parental Involvement)* [1996] 1 FLR 857, CA, in which an appeal against a revocation of a parental responsibility agreement was successful, inter alia because he had not been given sufficient opportunity to be heard.

[136] Unmarried fathers only acquired the right to apply for custody under the Legitimacy Act 1959 s 3 (subsequently re-enacted by the Guardianship of Minors Act 1971 s 14). Before that, the only legal means for an unmarried father to acquire care and control was by instituting wardship proceedings.

[137] See eg J McCandless 'Status and Anomaly: *Re D (contact and parental responsibility: lesbian mothers and known father)*' (2008) 30 JSWL 63. The point about status was first made by J Eekelaar 'Parental Responsibility—A New Legal Status?' (1996) 112 LQR 233.

[138] See C Lind 'Responsible Fathers: Paternity, the Blood Tie and Family Responsibility' in J Bridgeman, H Keeting and C Lind (eds) *Responsibility, Law and the Family* (2008) 191 at 192.

[139] See the thoughtful article by H Reece 'The Degradation of Parental Responsibility' in R Probert, S Gilmore and J Herring (eds) *Responsible Parents & Parental Responsibility* (2009) ch 5.

[140] See Scot Law Com Discussion Paper No 88 *Parental Responsibilities and Rights, Guardianship and Administration of Children's Property* (1990) and Scot Law Com No 135 *Report on Family Law* (1992). Earlier discussion in England and Wales had first been prompted by the English Law Commission's proposal in their Working Paper No 74 *Illegitimacy* (1979) to abolish the status of illegitimacy with the consequence that all fathers would be in the same legal position. That suggestion met with little favour (for a summary of the criticisms, see Law Com No 118 (1st Report on *Illegitimacy*, 1982) on which see M Hayes (1980) 43 MLR 299) and in their later review, the Commission (Law Com No 172, *Guardianship and Custody*, 1988) the Commission considered that the issue of giving unmarried fathers automatic status had been fully canvassed and rejected.

[141] Scot Law Com No 135 *Report on Family Law* (1992) para 2.50.

whether or not they are or have been married to each other.' As the Commission power-fully observed:[142]

> The question is whether the starting position should be that the father has, or has not, the normal parental responsibilities and rights. Given that about 25% of all children born in Scotland in recent years have been born out of wedlock,[143] and that the number of couples cohabiting outside marriage is now substantial, it seems to us that the balance has now swung in favour of the view that parents are parents, whether married to each other or not. If in any particular case it is in the best interest of a child that a parent should be deprived of some or all of his or her parental responsibilities and rights, that can be achieved by means of a court order.

In the event, the Commission's recommendation was rejected, so that under the Children (Scotland) Act 1995, as under the English Children Act 1989, the unmarried father does not automatically have parental responsibility simply by reason of being the biological father, though, as in England and Wales, they do acquire it upon being registered as the father.[144]

The practical difficulty of going beyond giving parental responsibility to unmarried fathers upon being registered as the child's father is the uncertainty that it would create. Short of going to court, on what evidence could parental responsibility be based? The marital presumption of paternity is not so easily translated to relationships outside marriage.

One possible way forward that at one time was favoured by Government is to make provision for compulsory joint registration of birth but though legislation was passed to that effect,[145] it has not been implemented and seems unlikely to be so.[146]

2. ACQUISITION OF PARENTAL RESPONSIBILITY BY FEMALE PARENTS WHO ARE NEITHER MARRIED TO NOR IN CIVIL PARTNERSHIP WITH THE MOTHER

A woman who is a 's 43 parent'[147] but to whom s 1(3) of the Family Law Reform Act 1987 does not apply, that is, a woman who was neither the spouse nor the civil partner of the mother at any time beginning with the placement of the embryo or the sperm and eggs in the mother or her insemination and ending with the child's birth, does not automatically have parental responsibility but 'shall have it if she has acquired it (and has not ceased to have it) in accordance with the provisions of this Act.'[148] Section 4ZA(1) of the 1989 Act[149] specifically provides that a s 43 parent will acquire parental responsibility for the child

(1) by becoming registered as the child's parent,[150]

(2) by making a parental responsibility agreement with the mother;[151] or

(3) by obtaining a parental responsibility order.

---

[142] Scot Law Com No 135 *Report on Family Law* (1992) at para 2.48.

[143] In England and Wales, according to the figures from the Office for National Statistics, in 2012 47.5% of children were born out of wedlock.

[144] See Family Law (Scotland) Act 2006 s 23. Like English law, this provision is *not* retrospective.

[145] See the Welfare Reform Act 2009 Sch 6. [146] See the discussion in Ch 8.

[147] Discussed in Ch 8, Female parenthood, p 256.

[148] Children Act 1989 s 2(2A), added by HFEA 2008 Sch 2 para 26(3).

[149] Added by HFEA 2008 Sch 6 para 27.

[150] The birth registration forms have also been consequently amended specifically to permit the registration of the female parent rather than a father, see the Registration of Births and Deaths (Amendment) (England and Wales) Regulations 2009 (SI 2009/2165) which came into force on 1 September 2009.

[151] The relevant form, Form C(PRA) 1 was amended in April 2014 in the light of the creation of the Family Court. The procedure is the same as that for agreements between the unmarried mother and father and is discussed at Parental responsibility agreements, p 372.

In addition to this, as with unmarried fathers, parental responsibility will also be acquired by a s 43 parent upon taking office as a formally appointed guardian;[152] by being named in a child arrangements order as a person with whom the child is to live, in which case a separate parental responsibility order *must* be made[153] or being named in a child arrangements order as a person with whom the child is to spend or otherwise have contact but is not named as a person with whom the child is to live, the court must decide whether it is appropriate for him to have parental responsibility and, if the court decides that it is appropriate, it must make a s 4ZA order in the second female parent's favour.[154]

As with unmarried fathers a s 43 parent will acquire parental responsibility upon subsequently marrying the mother but whether she will do so upon entering into a civil partnership with the mother subsequent to the child's birth can perhaps be debated. As already discussed, responsibility is acquired by the unmarried father subsequently marrying the mother but this is because s 2(3) of the 1989 Act directs that regard be had to the extended meaning of the phrase 'married at the time of birth' given by the Family Law Reform Act 1987 s 1 and which consequently includes the child's legitimation by the parents' subsequent marriage.[155] However, s 2(3) has not been amended to include s 43 parents. On the other hand, the Legitimacy Act 1976 has been specifically amended[156] to provide for the child's legitimation by a s 43 parent entering into a civil partnership with the mother subsequent to the child's birth. Given that the general overall strategy of the 2008 legislation is to place the s 43 parent in the same legal position as the unmarried father, it is submitted that entering into a civil partnership with the mother following the child's birth does automatically confer parental responsibility on that parent.[157]

As in the case of unmarried fathers, parental responsibility acquired by the s 43 parent by registration, court order or agreement ends upon the child obtaining his or her majority or by a court order to that effect.[158]

3. ACQUISITION OF PARENTAL RESPONSIBILITY BY STEP-PARENTS

As originally enacted the Children Act 1989 made no special provision for step-parents to acquire parental responsibility. Instead they were treated like any other individual non-parent (see the discussion in the next section). However, following reform introduced by the Adoption and Children Act 2002[159] provision is made for a step-parent who

---

[152] Viz. by the mother or the court under the terms of s 5 of the 1989 Act (discussed in Ch 8).

[153] Children Act 1989 s 12(1A) as substituted by the Children and Families Act 2014 Sch 4 Part 2 para 21(2).

[154] Children Act 1989 s 12 (1A), added by the Children and Families Act 2014, Sch 2 para 21(2).

[155] See s 1(3) of the 1987 Act.

[156] Legitimacy Act 1976, ss 2A and 10 respectively added and amended by HFEA 2008, Sch 6 paras 16 and 19.

[157] This conclusion is not without significance since unlike the other methods of acquiring parental responsibility, acquisition of responsibility by reason of civil partnership cannot be ended by a court order, see the arguments in respect of unmarried fathers discussed at Subsequent marriage, p 370.

[158] See respectively s 91(7) and (8), as amended by HFEA 2008 Sch 6 para 29 and s 4ZA(5), as amended by HFEA 2008 Sch 6 para 27.

[159] Section 112 inserting s 4A into the Children Act 1989 with effect from 30 December 2005 (see Adoption and Children Act 2002 (Commencement No 9) Order 2005 (SI 2005/2213)). This in turn was amended by the Civil Partnership Act 2004 s 75(2).

is married[160] to or is a civil partner[161] of the parent who has parental responsibility for the child,[162] to obtain parental responsibility either by agreement or court order. Section 4A(1) of the 1989 Act provides:

> Where a child's parent ('parent A') who has parental responsibility for the child is married to or is a civil partner of a person who is not the child's parent ('the step-parent')—
>
> (a) parent A or, if the other parent also has parental responsibility for the child, both parents may by agreement with the step-parent provide for the step-parent to have parental responsibility for the child; or
> (b) the court may, on the application of the step-parent, order that the step-parent shall have parental responsibility for the child.

Although there had been calls to improve the status of step-parents,[163] the motivation for the reform was to provide an alternative to adoption. As the Explanatory Notes to the 2002 Act[164] say, the intention of the provision is 'to provide an alternative to adoption where a step-parent wishes to acquire parental responsibility for his or her step-child. It has the advantage of not removing parental responsibility from the other birth parent and does not legally separate the child from membership of the family of the other birth parent'. Given this background and given that the 2002 Act permits joint adoption by couples whether or not they are married to each other[165] it is perhaps ironic that it is not open to a *cohabiting* partner of the parent to seek parental responsibility by agreement or order.[166]

Although the clear intention of s 4A is to provide a means by which an 'incoming parent' (ie a person who lives with a parent with parental responsibility following, typically, the breakdown of the latter's relationship with the other parent and who will be centrally participating in the future upbringing of the child) can acquire parental responsibility, as a matter of strict law it can also apply to a partner of the parent who helped bringing up the child upon the mistaken assumption that he was the biological father. Whether

---

[160] Including same sex marriages.

[161] Ie a party to a formally registered civil partnership under the Civil Partnership Act 2004.

[162] Accordingly the provisions only apply to a step-mother if she is married to a father with parental responsibility. Presumably, however, s 4A(1) will be triggered if the father acquires parental responsibility *after* his marriage to the step-mother, as for example, by becoming the child's guardian. Note *Re A and B (Parental Order: Domicile)* [2013] EWHC 426 (Fam) [2014] 1 FLR 169, in which a parental responsibility order was erroneously made in favour of the civil partner of a biological father whose child was born as a result of a surrogacy agreement made in India which did not thereby give him parental responsibility.

[163] See eg J Masson 'Old families into new: a status for step-parents' in M Freeman (ed) *State, Law and the Family* (1984) ch 14 pp 237 et seq and see p 391 of the previous edition of this work.

[164] Para 268. This reform implements a long standing proposal first made in *Adoption: The Future* Cm 2288 (1993) paras 5.20–5.22 and cl 85 of the Draft Bill attached to *Adoption—A Service for Children* (Department of Health and Welsh Office, 1996). Interestingly, the Law Commission had much earlier (see Working Paper No. 91 *Guardianship* (1985) paras 4.15–4.19) canvassed views about the possibility of step-parents acquiring responsibility by administrative rather than judicial means, but did not pursue the point because it attracted little support at the time: Law Com No. 172 *Guardianship and Custody* (1988) para 2.22. It might also be noted that no such reform has been introduced in Scotland despite the reform of the unmarried father's position made in the Family Law (Scotland) Act 2006.

[165] See Adoption and Children Act 2002 ss 50 and 144(a)(b), discussed in Ch 19, Adoptions by one person or a couple, p 705.

[166] But such a couple can apply for each to be named in a child arrangements order as a person with whom the child is to live, the effect of which is to vest parental responsibility in the parent's partner, see Acquisition of parental responsibility by other individuals, p 389.

in these circumstances it will be in the child's best interests for an order to be made is another issue.[167]

So far as parental responsibility agreements are concerned, if the mother and father or female parent have parental responsibility then the agreement must be made between the step-parent and *both* the child's mother and father or female parent as the case may be.[168] The non-resident parent's involvement in this regard can be questioned for, as has been pointed out,[169] while on the one hand it could be seen as giving the non-resident parent a bargaining chip, on the other the non-resident parent essentially loses nothing by the step-parent gaining parental responsibility.[170] The non-resident parent's involvement, however, is in line with the judicially imposed requirement that important decisions in a child's life should not be unilaterally taken by one parent.[171] But whatever the merits of doing so, the mandatory involvement of the non-resident parent in making agreements is likely to lead to conflict and one must doubt whether many such tri-partite agreements are made.

As the same formalities are required for making the agreement with step-parents as for making one between parents,[172] there is no scrutiny of whether the agreement is in the child's interests nor is there any requirement to involve the child him or herself. Although this means that the child cannot veto the making of the agreement, he or she can apply to a court to end the agreement. Whether this is human rights compliant remains to be seen. As with unmarried fathers no specific provision is made regarding age requirements for those making an agreement; nor whether the agreement can be made in respect of an unborn child or a child has married. However, the position must be the same as for unmarried mothers and fathers.[173]

The court's power to make a parental responsibility order is exercisable only upon the application of the step-parent[174] which is the same position as for orders for unmarried fathers. This means, for instance, that upon an adoption application there is no power to make a parental responsibility order instead. Unlike for unmarried fathers, no provision is made for the automatic making of a parental responsibility order following the making of a child arrangements order naming a step-parent as a person with whom the child is to live.[175] Consequently in such cases unless the step-parent has responsibility by way of a separate order or agreement, responsibility will cease upon the ending of the residence order.[176]

---

[167] See *Re R (Parental Responsibility)* [2011] EWHC 1535 (Fam) [2011] 2 FLR 1132, where the order was not made, although the mother was ordered to provide the husband with regular information about the child.

[168] Of course, where only the mother has parental responsibility an agreement only needs to be with her, ie the father need not be involved but A Bainham and S Gilmore *Children—The Modern Law* (2013, 4th edn) at p 177 question whether this is human rights compliant.

[169] See S Cretney, J Masson and R Bailey-Harris *Principles of Family Law* (2003, 7th edn) at 18–042.

[170] A Bainham and S Gilmore *Children—The Modern Law* (2013, 4th edn) at pp 178–79, takes issue with the diminution argument arguing that the enhanced status for step-parents 'could be seen as shutting out, or at least diluting, the parental contribution of the non-resident parent'. The counter to this is surely that the de facto position will already be seen as diluting the non-resident parent's position and, in any event, as Cretney et al point out, there is nothing to prevent the resident parent delegating responsibility to the step-parent.

[171] See eg *Re G (Parental Responsibility: Education)* [1994] 2 FLR 964, CA and *Re C (Welfare of Child: Immunisation)* [2003] EWCA Civ 1148 [2003] 2 FLR 1095, discussed at Sharing parental responsibility for child, p 394.

[172] Children Act 1989 s 4A(2) and the Parental Responsibility Agreement Regulations 1991 as amended by the Parental Responsibility Agreement (Amendment) Regulations 2009 (SI 2009/2026).

[173] See the discussion at Parental responsibility agreements, p 372.

[174] See s 4A(1)(b).   [175] Ie s 12(1) of the Children Act 1989 only applies to unmarried fathers.

[176] For this reason step-parents might well be advised when applying for a residence order also to seek a parental responsibility order.

No specific provision is made regarding jurisdiction to make orders but the position must be the same as for making orders in favour of unmarried fathers.[177] Similarly, by analogy with unmarried fathers, and in line with the general principles of the 1989 Act, in deciding whether or not to make an order, the court must treat the child's welfare as its paramount consideration and be satisfied that making the order is better than making no order at all. On the other hand, there is no obligation to apply the welfare checklist under s 1(3) and thus no necessity to have regard even to an older children's wishes, though whether it would be human rights compliant to ignore those wishes can be debated. No doubt the jurisprudence on whether to make a parental responsibility order in favour of the unmarried father is relevant to step-parent applications but the analogy is not exact since in most cases the application will be made with the mother's consent and the opposition will come from the non-resident father.

Parental responsibility agreements and orders remain effective notwithstanding the couple's subsequent separation or even divorce. They will, however, automatically end once the child attains his majority.[178] As with unmarried fathers, agreements and orders in favour of step-parents can be brought to an end by a subsequent court order. Such orders can be sought by *any* person with parental responsibility (including, therefore, the non-resident parent) or with leave of the court, by the child himself.[179] In this latter case, leave can only be granted if the court is satisfied that the child has sufficient understanding to make the application.[180] As we have seen, seeking the ending of an agreement is the only way a child can be directly involved and the only guaranteed way of being involved in respect of court orders. By analogy with unmarried fathers, in deciding whether to end an order the court must apply the welfare principle.[181]

4. ACQUISITION OF PARENTAL RESPONSIBILITY BY OTHER INDIVIDUALS

Those who are not parents do not have parental responsibility automatically, but they can acquire it. Any person taking office as a guardian has parental responsibility for the child concerned.[182] Similarly any person (who is not a parent or guardian) named in a child arrangements order as a person with the child is to live, has parental responsibility for the duration of the order[183] though this will not entitle him to agree or refuse to consent to the making of an adoption order, nor may he appoint a guardian.[184]

In a change brought about by the Children and Families Act 2014 the court may provide that a person (who is not a parent or guardian) named in a child arrangements order as a person with whom the child is to spend time or otherwise to have contact but who is not named as a person with whom the child is to live, have parental responsibility for the duration of the order.[185] This new power would meet the type of situation encountered in *Re WB (Residence Orders)*[186] in which a man, who thought he was the child's father and only discovered he was not as a result of a paternity test, could not be given parental

---

[177] For a discussion of which see When orders may be made, p 373.
[178] Children Act 1989 s 91(7), (8) as amended by the Adoption and Children Act 2002 Sch 3 para 68(b) and (c).
[179] Children Act 1989 s 4A(3).   [180] Section 4A(4).
[181] Discussed at Ending parental responsibility acquired by registration, court orders or agreement, p 382.   [182] Section 5(6).
[183] Section 12(2), as amended by Sch 2 Part 1 para 21(3) of the Children and Families Act 2014.
[184] Section 12(3)(b) and (c).
[185] Section 12(2A) added by Sch 2 Part1 para 21(4) to the 2014 Act.
[186] [1995] 2 FLR 1023. For a different type of example see *Re W (Arrangements to Place for Adoption)* [1995] 1 FLR 163.

responsibility under the law as it then stood following the decision that the child should live with the mother. Now, provided he is named in a child arrangements order as a person with whom the child is to spend time etc, he can be given parental responsibility. However, it may give scope for others, such as grandparents, to seek to play a more significant role in the upbringing of a child contrary to the wishes of the parents, which will need to be controlled by the court.

Individuals who are appointed as special guardians[187] have parental responsibility for the child which they can exercise to the exclusion of anyone else apart from another special guardian.[188] Unlike those named in a child arrangements order as a person with whom the child is to live special guardians can appoint a guardian[189] and can consent or withhold consent to the child's adoption (though not to the exclusion of the parent's right to do so).[190]

An individual also acquires parental responsibility upon being granted an emergency protection order, though this will only entitle him to take 'such action in meeting his responsibility for the child as is reasonably required to safeguard or promote the welfare of the child (having regard in particular to the duration of the order)'.[191]

5. ACQUISITION OF PARENTAL RESPONSIBILITY BY LOCAL AUTHORITIES

Local authorities acquire parental responsibility upon the making of a care order,[192] when they will share responsibility with any parent, special guardian or step-parent who has parental responsibility. If they are satisfied that it is necessary to do so to safeguard or promote the child's welfare, however, they may determine the extent to which a parent, guardian, or special guardian of the child may meet his parental responsibility for him.[193] In no event, however, will a local authority be empowered to change the child's religion, to agree to his adoption, or to appoint a guardian[194] and it may be that they cannot consent to a declaration that a child in their care should not receive intensive resuscitation in certain defined circumstances.[195]

Local authorities also acquire parental responsibility to the same limited extent as individuals upon being granted an emergency protection order.

There are no other means by which local authorities can acquire parental responsibility.

D. IN RESPECT OF WHOM IS THERE RESPONSIBILITY?

Parental responsibility exists in respect of a 'child', that is, a person under the age of 18.[196] It is a moot point as to whether responsibility exists for a married child.[197]

---

[187] Special guardianship is discussed in Ch 19.   [188] Children Act 1989 s 14C(1).

[189] Section 5(4), as amended by s 115(4)(b) of the Adoption and Children Act 2002.

[190] The power of consent is vested in parents and guardians, see s 47(2) of the 2002 Act and for these purpose 'guardians' include 'special guardians': see s 144(1). However, s 14C(2)(b) of the Children Act 1989 preserves the parents' right to consent.

[191] Children Act 1989 s 44(4)(c) and s 44(5)(b). Emergency protection orders are discussed in Ch 16.

[192] Section 33(3)(a). The effect of care orders is discussed in Ch 17, The effects of a care order, pp 636ff.

[193] Section 33(3)(b) and (4), as amended by the Adoption and Children Act 2002 Sch 3 para 63.

[194] Section 33(6), as amended by the Adoption and Children Act 2002 Sch 3 para 63.

[195] See *Re B (Medical Treatment)* [2008] EWHC 1996 (Fam) [2009] 1 FLR 1264, in which Coleridge J commented at [7] that the local authority had been 'probably right' to think that they had no power to consent to the withdrawal of life saving treatment.

[196] Children Act 1989 s 105(1).   [197] See Duration of parental responsibility, p 391.

The 1989 Act is silent on when parental responsibility begins but, in the absence of any indication to the contrary, references to 'child' in the Act must be taken to mean a live child.[198] Accordingly, no one has parental responsibility until the child is born.

Fathers have no rights over foetuses. This was the reasoning of Sir George Baker P in *Paton v British Pregnancy Advisory Service Trustees*[199] when he refused a husband's application for an injunction to prevent his wife from having an abortion. An unmarried father was similarly refused an injunction in *C v S*.[200] In *Paton's* case strong obiter doubts were also expressed as to whether the court should interfere even if the medical practitioners involved had not acted in good faith in issuing the certificate required by the Abortion Act 1967 and there was an obvious attempt to commit a crime: it is not for the civil courts to interfere with the exercise of doctors' discretion under the Act. This view may appear to have been weakened by the fact that both Heilbron J and the Court of Appeal in *C v S* were prepared to hear argument that the proposed abortion was contrary to the provisions of the Infant Life (Preservation) Act 1929 s 1. However, Sir John Donaldson MR commented that even if a breach of the 1929 Act could have been proved, 'strong consideration' would still have been paid to Sir George Baker P's comment that the matter would be better left to the Director of Public Prosecutions, who could then consider whether prosecutions should be brought. It is submitted that even if the abortion were ex facie illegal the father still could not obtain an injunction to prevent the commission of the proposed criminal act once it is accepted that he has no right which would be affected.[201]

E. DURATION OF PARENTAL RESPONSIBILITY

An important aspect of parental responsibility is its enduring nature, and in particular that it is not lost merely because someone else acquires it. Nevertheless, responsibility does not have an unlimited duration. As it can only exist in respect of a 'child', parental responsibility ends upon the child attaining his majority. It will clearly end upon the child's death.[202] Upon the making of a parental order[203] or an adoption order,[204] parental responsibility is transferred to the person or persons in whose favour the order is made.[205] Non-parents who have responsibility by reason of a child arrangements order,

---

[198] See *Elliot v Joicey* [1935] AC 209, HL. For a similar interpretation of the meaning of 'child' under the Children and Young Persons Act 1969 s 70(1) see *Re D (A Minor)* [1987] AC 317, HL. Note also *R v Newham London Borough Council, ex p Dada* [1996] QB 507, CA interpreting the Housing Act 1985 s 75.

[199] [1979] QB 276. See further I Kennedy (1979) 42 MLR 324; Phillips (1979) 95 LQR 332; N Lowe (1980) 96 LQR 29 and N Lowe and R White *Wards of Court* (1986, 2nd edn) paras 2–3. The husband also failed before the European Commission of Human Rights, which ruled that although he had *locus standi* to bring the complaint, there had been no breach of the Convention since the abortion was certified as being necessary for the wife's health: *Paton v United Kingdom* (1980) 3 EHRR 408.   [200] [1988] QB 135, CA.

[201] See *Gouriet v Union of Post Office Workers* [1978] AC 435, HL. But see Kennedy, above.

[202] It is established, however, that even if the child had been in care the parent retains the right to bury (or, presumably, cremate) the child: *R v Gwynedd County Council, ex p B* [1992] 3 All ER 317, CA, discussed in Ch 10, Disposing of the child's corpse, p 359.

[203] Viz. an order made under the Human Fertilisation and Embryology Act 2008 s 54, discussed in Ch 8.

[204] Adoption and Children Act 2002 s 46 discussed in Ch 19, The effects of an adoption order, p 722.

[205] Apart from these orders there is no other means of depriving parents of their *automatic* parental responsibility during the child's minority. However, if such power exists in a foreign jurisdiction then the English courts may be forced to recognise it, see *Re AMR (Adoption: Procedure)* [1999] 2 FLR 807—Polish order depriving parents of their parental authority held to deprive them of parental responsibility under English law.

local authorities which have responsibility by reason of a care order, and anyone who has responsibility by reason of an emergency protection order, only do so for the duration of the order.[206]

Apart from in the circumstances just mentioned there is uncertainty as to whether other events can end parental responsibility. Before the Children Act 1989 there was authority for saying that the right of custody ended upon the child's marriage[207] and that it was suspended whilst the child was serving in the armed forces,[208] but it remains to be decided whether a similar position applies with regard to parental responsibility. There is also conflicting opinion as to whether responsibility ceases in respect of any aspect of a child's upbringing about which the child himself is sufficiently mature to make his own decisions.[209] Perhaps the better view in each of these situations is that parental responsibility does not end, but that the scope for its exercise is limited.

Unlike Scottish law[210] there is no general power under English law to divest a mother or married father[211] of parental responsibility. Whether there should be a general divesting power can be debated. On the one hand, where a parent has behaved so appallingly, either towards the child or other members of the family, it could certainly be argued that that person should no longer have responsibility. On the other hand, a general divesting power cuts across the principle that responsibility should be enduring.[212] On balance, however, provided any divesting power is subject to the overarching principle of the paramountcy of the child's welfare, there seems a good case for amending English law.[213]

F. SHARING PARENTAL RESPONSIBILITY FOR A CHILD

As s 2(5) provides, more than one person may have parental responsibility for the same child at the same time while s 2(6) makes it clear that a person with parental responsibility does not cease to have it solely because some other person subsequently acquires it. This latter provision which, in the words of one commentator,[214] 'encapsulates the ethos of continuing parental responsibility' means, for example, that a parent will not lose

---

[206] See respectively s 12(2), s 33(3) and s 44(4)(c).

[207] See eg *Hewer v Bryant* [1970] 1 QB 357 at 373, CA, per Sachs LJ; *R v Wilmington Inhabitants* (1822) 5 B & Ald 525 at 526 and *Lough v Ward* [1945] 2 All ER 338 at 348.

[208] *R v Rotherfield Greys Inhabitants* (1823) 1 B & C 345 at 349–50.

[209] See the comment of Lord Scarman in *Gillick v West Norfolk and Wisbech Area Health Authority* [1986] AC 112 at 186, which suggests it does, but which was specifically rejected by Lord Donaldson MR in *Re R (A Minor) (Wardship: Consent to Medical Treatment)* [1992] Fam 11 at 23, and both by Lord Donaldson MR and Balcombe LJ in *Re W (A Minor) (Medical Treatment) (Court's Jurisdiction)* [1993] Fam 64 at 75–6 and 87, discussed in Ch 9, *Gillick*— a false dawn? pp 322–325.   [210] See s 11(2)(a) of the Children (Scotland) Act 1995.

[211] Parental responsibility orders and agreements can be ended by the court under s 4(3):. Those who acquire responsibility via a child arrangements order only have it for the duration of the order.

[212] The enduring nature of responsibility is emphasised, in the case of an unmarried father acquiring responsibility by virtue of being named in a child arrangements order as a person with whom the child is to live, by the requirement under s 12(1) to make a separate parental responsibility order, so that the subsequent ending of the residence order will not *ipso facto* end the responsibility.

[213] Compare Principle 3:33 of the Commission on European Family Law (CEFL)'s Principles of European Family Law on Parental Responsibilities which does provide for a general divesting power, though this counterbalanced by Principle 3:34 which would allow the competent authority to restore such responsibilities, see K Boele-Woelki, F Ferrand, C González Beilfuss, M Jänterä-Jareborg, N Lowe, D Martiny, W Pintens *Principles of European Family Law Regarding Parental Responsibilities* (2007).

[214] A Bainham *Children, The New Law, The Children Act 1989* (1990) para 2.18.

responsibility because someone else such as a step-parent, grandparent, foster parent or, even, a local authority acquires it. Section 2(6) should not, however, be read as meaning that a court order can never end a parent's responsibility. An adoption order clearly does, because the statute expressly says so.[215]

Where parental responsibility is shared, then, by s 2(7), each person in whom it is vested 'may act alone and without the other (or others) in meeting that responsibility' except where a statute expressly requires the consent of more than one person in a matter affecting the child.[216] This power to act independently, however, is subject to the important limitation under s 2(8), namely, that a person with parental responsibility is not entitled to act in any way that could be incompatible with a court order.[217]

The ability to act independently was intended to mean, not simply that neither parent has a right of veto, but also that there is no legal duty upon parents to consult each other[218] since, in the Law Commission's view,[219] such a duty was both unworkable and undesirable. It was expressly contemplated that even where a parent has been named in a child arrangements order as a person with whom the child is to live, subject to not acting incompatibly with a court order, each parent could still exercise that responsibility without having to consult the other and with neither having a right of veto over the other's action. Referring to the example of a child living with one parent and going to a school nearby, the Commission considered that while it would be incompatible for the other parent to arrange for the child to have his hair done in a way which would exclude him from the school, it would be permissible for that parent to take the child to a sporting occasion over the weekend, no matter how much the parent with whom the child lived might disapprove. According to the Commission the intended independence of each parent was to be seen as part of the general aim of encouraging both parents to feel concerned and responsible for the welfare of the children.[220]

This intended scheme had been criticised on the basis that it was difficult to see how failing to provide for consultation, at any rate with respect to serious or long-term decisions affecting the child, could promote joint parenting following breakdown.[221] Evidently the courts sympathised with that point of view for, despite the apparently clear wording of s 2(7), the Court of Appeal in *Re G (Parental Responsibility: Education)*[222]

---

[215] Adoption and Children Act 2002 s 46(2)(a). As Lord Mackay LC said, during the Debates on the Children Bill (588 HL Official Report (5th series) col 1175), the word 'solely' is used advisedly in s 2(6), ie an adoption order deprives a parent of responsibility not solely because adoptive parents acquire it but because the 2002 Act expressly extinguishes it. Parental orders similarly extinguish previously held parental responsibility: see Ch 8, The effect of making an application and of making an order, p 281.

[216] This latter qualification preserves, for example, the embargo imposed by the Child Abduction Act 1984 s 1 against one parent taking the child (under the age of 16) outside the United Kingdom without the other's consent (in this regard it will be noted that neither parent can unilaterally change the child's habitual residence: *Re S (Minors) (Child Abduction: Wrongful Retention)* [1994] 1 FLR 82 per Wall J and *Re A (Wardship: Jurisdiction)* [1995] 1 FLR 767 per Hale J) and maintains the need to obtain *each* parent's consent to an adoption order as laid down by s 47(2) of the Adoption and Children Act 2002.

[217] The absence of a court order does not necessarily mean that parental responsibility may be exercised without qualification. For example, since ultimate responsibility for a ward of court rests with the court (see Chapter 20), the warding of a child must immediately operate at least to limit freedom of action.

[218] This resolved the uncertainty of the former law, which seemed to impose no duty to consult but did confer a power of veto: see Law Com Working Paper No 96 *Custody* para 2.34 *et seq.*

[219] Law Com No 172 para 2.07.   [220] At para 2.10.

[221] See A Bainham [1990] Fam Law 192 at 193. But for a strong counter view see J Eekelaar 'Rethinking Parental Responsibility' [2001] Fam Law 426 at 429 and by the same author 'Do parents have a duty to consult?' (1998) 114 LQR 337. See also the thoughtful analysis, including the notion that a right of veto is not synonymous with the 'right to be consulted', by S Maidment, 'Parental Responsibility—Is There A Duty To Consult? [2001] Fam Law 518. For an interesting empirical survey of the general public's view as to who should be in control over decision making see G Potter and C Williams 'Parental responsibility and the duty to consult—the public's view' [2005] CFLQ 207.   [222] [1994] 2 FLR 964, CA.

assumed that there remains[223] a duty to consult, at any rate over long-term decisions. In that case a father who had custody, care and control under a court order arranged for his son to attend a local education authority boarding school without informing the mother. In Glidewell LJ's view the '. . . mother, having parental responsibility, was entitled to and indeed ought to have been consulted about the important step of taking her child away from the day school that he had been attending and sending him to boarding school. It is an important step in any child's life and she ought to have been consulted.'

Since *Re G* it has been held that s 2(7) does not entitle one spouse to change the child's surname without consent of the other;[224] nor to permit the circumcision of a child against the wishes of the other.[225] It has also been held[226] that hotly contested issues of immunisation belong to that small group of important decisions that ought not to be carried out or arranged by the one-parent carer in the absence of agreement of those with parental responsibility.

What other examples will fall into this group of important decisions is a matter of speculation but in one sense, it makes no difference whether or not there is a duty to consult, for in either case in the event of a disagreement the burden will be on the complaining parent to take the issue to court. Even so, the courts' approach to s 2(7) is questionable.

G. EFFECT OF THIRD PARTIES ACQUIRING PARENTAL RESPONSIBILITY

As previously noted, by s 2(6) neither parent loses parental responsibility solely because someone else has acquired it through a court order. This means, for example, that upon divorce a father does not lose responsibility even if a step-father also acquires it under a court order or agreement.[227] In this situation the mother, step-father and father all share responsibility for the child and, subject to not acting incompatibly with a court order and, subject to the case-law just discussed, each can exercise their responsibility independently of the others. A similar situation arises if grandparents or other relations or foster parents have residence orders or special guardianship orders[228] made in their favour. Another effect of s 2(6) is that parents do not lose parental responsibility when a local authority obtains a care order, nor where an emergency protection order is made.[229]

---

[223] This seems a throw-back to the pre-1989 Act law and in particular to *Dipper v Dipper* [1981] Fam 31, CA, discussed in the 7th edition of this work at pp 295 and 302.

[224] *Re PC (Change of Surname)* [1997] 2 FLR 730 per Holman J.

[225] *Re J (Specific Issue Orders) (Muslim Upbringing and Circumcision)* [2000] 1 FLR 571, CA. In that case Butler-Sloss P also included sterilisation among the group of important decisions needing more than just the one-parent carer's consent.

[226] *Re C (Welfare of Child: Immunisation)* [2003] EWCA Civ 1148 [2003] 2 FLR 1095 at [16]–[17], per Thorpe LJ.

[227] It will be noted that step-parents may acquire parental responsibility only through an order or agreement or upon being appointed a guardian. They do not acquire responsibility simply by marrying the child's parent. This 'disconnection' between responsibility and divorce is a trend noted in other jurisdictions, see the observations by D Blair and M Weiner 'Resolving Parental Custody Disputes—A Comparative Explanation' (2005) 39 Fam LQ 247 at 255.

[228] This is stated more forcibly by s 14C(1)(b), discussed in Ch 19, The effects of special guardianship orders, p 735.

[229] Discussed in Ch 17, The effects of a care order, p 636 and Ch 16, The effects of an order, p 586 respectively.

H. DELEGATION OF PARENTAL RESPONSIBILITY

Whilst preserving the previous position that a person with parental responsibility may not surrender or transfer any part of that responsibility to another, s 2(9) permits those with responsibility to 'arrange for some or all of it to be met by one or more persons acting on his behalf'. Such delegation can be made to another person who already has parental responsibility[230] or to those who have not, such as schools or holiday camps. The aim of s 2(9) is to encourage parents (regardless of whether or not they are separated) to agree among themselves on what they believe to be the best arrangements for their children. Section 2(9) does not, however, make such arrangements legally binding. Consequently, they can be revoked or changed at will. Furthermore, as s 2(11) provides, delegations will not absolve a person with parental responsibility from any liability for failure on his part to discharge his responsibilities to the child.[231]

I. CARING FOR A CHILD WITHOUT HAVING PARENTAL RESPONSIBILITY

The 1989 Act clarifies the legal position of those who are caring for a child but who do not have parental responsibility, by providing that they 'may (subject to the provisions of this Act) do what is reasonable in all the circumstances for the purpose of safeguarding or promoting the child's welfare'. As the revised Health's *Guidance and Regulations* observe,[232] what is reasonable 'will depend upon the urgency and gravity of what is required and the extent to which it is practicable to consult a person with parental responsibility'. In other words all that s 3(5) does is to clothe the de facto carers with the *minimum* power necessary to provide for the day-to-day care of the child. So, for example, while a carer may be able to consent to the child's medical treatment in the event of an accident, he or she will not be able to consent to major elective surgery. Indeed, it may be difficult for the carer to convince a doctor that he has sufficient authority to consent to medical treatment which may be desirable but not essential.[233] Whether a significantly greater latitude for action should be given to those caring for orphans remains an interesting point.

It is on the basis of s 3(5) that it is thought that a foster parent of a child being accommodated by a local authority could properly refuse immediately to hand over the child to a parent who is drunk or who turns up in the middle of the night. On the other hand, it is clear that s 3(5) does not empower a de facto carer to change a child's habitual residence merely by taking the child out of the jurisdiction[234] nor to obtain a passport for the child,[235]

---

[230] Section 2(10).

[231] For example, not to neglect, abandon, expose or cause or procure a child under the age of 16 to be assaulted or ill-treated etc under s 1 and s 17 of the Children and Young Persons Act 1933: see Ch 8, Protection, p 340.

[232] Children Act 1989 *Guidance and Regulations* Vol 1, *Court Orders* (2008), Department for Children Schools and Families para 2.16.

[233] See, for example, Johnson J's comments in *B v B (A Minor) (Residence Order)* [1992] 2 FLR 327 at 330. His Lordship also observed that notwithstanding s 3(5) a maternal grandmother, who was the de facto carer, found in practice that the education authorities were reluctant to accept her authority to give consent, for example, to the child going on a school trip, and insisted upon having the mother's written authority.

[234] See *Re S (A Minor) (Custody: Habitual Residence)* [1998] AC 750, HL, per Lord Slynn.

[235] Per Butler-Sloss LJ in *Re S (Abduction: Hague and European Convention)* [1997] 1 FLR 958 at 962.

or to change the child's surname.[236] It has also been held[237] that because they do not have parental responsibility local authorities have no power to transfer an 'accommodated' child from residential care to foster care without the parents' permission.[238] Anyone who cares for a child is obliged not to assault, ill-treat, neglect, abandon or expose the child in a manner likely to cause unnecessary suffering or injury to health.[239]

[236] *Re D, L and LA (Care: Change of Forename)* [2003] 1 FLR 339.
[237] *R v Tameside Metropolitan Borough Council, ex p J* [2000] 1 FLR 942.
[238] Accommodation is discussed in Ch 15.   [239] Children and Young Persons Act 1933 s 1.

12

THE WELFARE PRINCIPLE

A. INTRODUCTION

This chapter is concerned with the fundamental principle, commonly known as the welfare principle, which the courts are called upon to apply when determining any question concerning a child's upbringing or the administration of his property. This is governed by s 1 of the Children Act 1989. Section 1(1) provides for the paramountcy of the child's welfare and is essentially based on s 1 of the Guardianship of Minors Act 1971 (which was itself a re-enactment of s 1 of the Guardianship of Infants Act 1925). The 1989 Act, however, broke new ground by providing a checklist of factors to help the courts determine what is for the child's welfare in any particular case, directing the court to have regard to the likely prejudicial effect on the child's welfare of delay in making decisions and directing courts only to make orders where it is better to do so than making no order.

Apart from an indirect refinement to the checklist,[1] s 1 remained unaltered until the amendment, made by the Children and Families Act 2014 s 11,[2] directing the courts to presume, unless the contrary is shown, that involvement of each parent in the child's life will further the child's welfare.

B. THE PARAMOUNTCY OF THE CHILD'S WELFARE

Section 1(1) of the Children Act 1989 lays down the cardinal principle that:

> When any court determines any question with respect to:
>
> (a) the upbringing of a child; or
> (b) the administration of a child's property or the application of any income arising from it,
>
> the child's welfare shall be the court's paramount consideration.

Section 1(1), which is mandatory in effect,[3] immediately poses two questions, namely, the meaning of 'welfare' and the meaning of 'paramount'. The meaning of the latter assumed some importance immediately after the implementation of the Human Rights Act 1998 insofar as whatever it meant it had to be compatible with the European Convention of Human Rights. Another not unrelated issue is the relationship between s 1(1) and Art

---

[1] Namely in relation to the definition of 'harm' in s 1(1)(e), discussed at Any harm which the child has suffered or is at risk of suffering, p 412.   [2] Adding s 1(2A) to the 1989 Act.
[3] As emphasised by Ward LJ in *Re A (Children) (Conjoined Twins: Surgical Separation)* [2001] Fam 147.

3(1) of the UN Convention on the Rights of the Child. The other fundamental question is when the 'paramountcy principle' does or does not apply. Each of these questions will be addressed in turn.

1. THE MEANING OF 'WELFARE'

The term 'welfare' is not defined in the 1989 Act and, although the welfare principle had been the cornerstone of child law for some considerable time before that Act, it was surprisingly difficult to find judicial articulation of its meaning. Indeed it is its very vagueness that has led to the criticism that it fails to provide a predictive basis upon which decisions may be made.[4]

An early attempt at a definition was made by Lindley LJ who said:[5]

> . . . the welfare of the child is not to be measured by money alone nor by physical comfort only. The word welfare must be taken in its widest sense. The moral and religious welfare must be considered as well as its physical well-being. Nor can the ties of affection be disregarded.

In a New Zealand case, *Walker v Walker and Harrison*[6] Hardy Boys J said:

> 'Welfare' is an all-encompassing word. It includes material welfare, both in the sense of an adequacy of resources to provide a pleasant home and a comfortable standard of living and in the sense of an adequacy of care to ensure that good health and due personal pride are maintained. However, while material considerations have their place, they are secondary matters. More important are the stability and the security, the loving and understanding care and guidance, the warm and compassionate relationships, that are essential for the full development of the child's own character, personality and talents.

At one time there was a similar dearth of post-Children Act judicial discussion of the meaning of 'welfare' but this gap has now been filled by the comprehensive discussion of the meaning of the term by Munby LJ in *Re G (Education: Religious Upbringing).*[7] But before referring to this, it also worth mentioning another point made by Munby J (as he then was) in an earlier case,[8] namely, that conceptions of the concept of welfare have changed and will continue to change as society's understandings and values are also developing.

(a) *Re G (Education: Religious Upbringing)*

As Munby LJ put it in *Re G,*[9] 'welfare' is synonymous with 'well being' and 'interests' and extends to and embraces 'everything that relates to the child's development as a human

---

[4] See in particular R Mnookin 'Child Custody Adjudication: Judicial Functions in the Face of Indeterminancy' (1975) 39 *Law and Contemporary Problems* 226. For further criticism of the welfare principle see Criticisms of the welfare principle, p 430.

[5] *Re McGrath (Infants)* [1893] 1 Ch 143 at 148.

[6] Noted in [1981] NZ Recent Law 257 and cited by the Law Commission Working Paper No 96, *Custody* (1985), para 6. 10.

[7] [2012] EWCA Civ 1233 [2013] 1 FLR 677, on which see R Taylor 'Secular values and sacred rights: *Re G (Education: Religious Upbringing)*' [2013] CFLQ 336. See also Butler Sloss P's comment in *Re A (Male Sterilisation)* [2000] 1 FLR 549 at 555 that a child's best interests 'encompasses medical, emotional and all other welfare issues'.

[8] *CF v Secretary of State For The Home Department* [2004] EWHC 111 (Fam) [2004] 2 FLR 517 at [103].

[9] At [26], referring, en passant, to Lord Hailsham LC's observations in *Re B (A Minor) (Wardship: Sterilisation)* [1988] AC 199 at 202. Regard was also had to J Herring and C Foster 'Welfare means rationality, virtue and altruism' (2012) 32 *Legal Studies* 480.

being and to the child's present and future life as a human being. The judge must consider the child's welfare now, throughout the remainder of the child's minority and into and through adulthood.' The court should take a medium to long-tem view and not, as Sir Thomas Bingham MR pointed out,[10] 'accord excessive weight to what appear likely to be short-term or transient problems.' How far into the future the judge must peer, and, as Munby LJ pointed out, with modern life expectancy a judge dealing with a young child today may be looking to the 22nd century, must depend upon the context and nature of the issue. A dispute over a school trip is clearly very much an issue of the present. In contrast, if the question is whether a teenager should be sterilised, 'the judge will have to think a very long way ahead indeed.'

Munby LJ observed[11] that evaluating a child's best interests involves a welfare appraisal in the widest sense 'taking into account, where appropriate, a wide range of ethical, social, moral, religious, cultural, emotional and welfare considerations. Everything that conduces to a child's welfare and happiness or relates to the child's development and present and future life as a human being, including the child's social, cultural, ethnic and religious community, is potentially relevant and has, where appropriate, to be taken into account.' 'Happiness' in this context, is not pure hedonism and can include 'such things as the cultivation of virtues and the achievement of worthwhile goals, and all the other aims which parents routinely seek to inculcate in their children.'

In conducting this evaluation the judge must adopt a holistic approach. As Thorpe LJ once said[12] 'it would be undesirable and probably impossible to set bounds to what is relevant to a welfare determination.' Munby LJ also made the point[13] that the well-being of a child cannot be assessed in isolation and that it is 'only by considering the child's network of relationships that their well-being can be properly considered. So a child's relationships, both within and without the family, are always relevant to the child's interests: often they will be determinative.'

It might be noted that in his analysis Munby LJ referred at one point to the 'child's best interests'. It is not uncommonly said that in applying the welfare principle the court must act in the child's best interests and indeed, that is the phrase used by Art 3(1) of the UN Convention on the Rights of the Child 1989 (discussed later in this chapter). However, this may put an unduly sanguine gloss on the court's function: it should be appreciated that a judge may not be dealing with what would be ideal for the child but simply with what is the best that can be done in the circumstances. Perhaps not untypical of the dilemmas faced by the court is that described by Cumming-Bruce LJ as being before the trial judge in *Clarke-Hunt v Newcombe*:[14]

> There was not really a right solution; there were two alternative wrong solutions. The problem for the judge was to appreciate the factors in each direction and to decide which of the two bad solutions was the least dangerous, having regard to the long-term interests of the children . . .

(b) The welfare checklist

Although the 1989 Act does not define 'welfare', it provides a checklist of factors to which in certain circumstances the court must have regard when deciding what, if any, order to

[10] In *Re O (A Minor) (Contact: Indirect Contact)* [1995] 2 FLR 124 at 129 and reiterated by Munby P in *Re B-S (Children) (Adoption Order: Leave to Oppose)* [2014] 1 WLR 563, at [74 (viii)]. There will, however, be some cases where the short-term disadvantages are so overwhelming as to rule out the long-term option: see eg *Thompson v Thompson* [1987] Fam 89, CA.

[11] [2012] EWCA Civ 1233 [2013] 1 FLR 677, at [27].

[12] In *Re SL (Adult Patient) (Medical Treatment)* [2001] Fam 15, at 30.

[13] In *Re G* [2012] EWCA Civ 1233 [2013] 1 FLR 677 at [30]. [14] (1983) 4 FLR 482 at 486, CA.

make. The introduction of a checklist had been recommended by the Law Commission,[15] both as 'a means of providing greater consistency and clarity in the law' and 'as a major step towards a more systematic approach to decisions concerning children'.

In other words, the object was not to redefine what is meant by 'welfare' but to provide a means by which greater homogeneity can be achieved in exercising the court's undoubtedly wide discretion in determining what is best for the child. The advantage of a list is that it enables everyone from the judge to the litigant, the advocate to the Cafcass officer, to focus on the same issues at the same time.

The contents of the list

The checklist, which is contained in s 1(3) is as follows:

(a) the ascertainable wishes and feelings of the child concerned (considered in the light of his age and understanding);

(b) his physical, emotional and educational needs;

(c) the likely effect on him of any change in his circumstances;

(d) his age, sex, background and any characteristics of his which the court considers relevant;

(e) any harm which he has suffered or is at risk of suffering;

(f) how capable each of his parents, and any other person in relation to whom the court considers the question to be relevant, is of meeting his needs;

(g) the range of powers available to the court under this Act in the proceedings in question.

Before considering how the checklist applies in particular cases, it is relevant to make the following general observations.

First, the checklist is not exhaustive and indeed might properly be regarded as the minimum that will be considered by the court. It has been held, for instance, that it is quite proper to take into account financial considerations as well.[16] In any event, it is always open to the court to specify other matters which it would like to see included in a welfare report.[17]

Secondly, the content of the checklist follows that recommended by the Law Commission save for the addition of s 1(3)(g), the purpose of which is to emphasise the court's duty to consider not only whether the order being sought is the best for the child but also the alternatives that the Act makes available. This, as we discuss in Chapter 18, has particular application in care proceedings, in which it is incumbent upon the court to consider not just whether or not to make the care order but whether, for example, a child arrangements order dealing with the child's living arrangements under s 8 would better serve the child's interests. This duty also reflects the general policy of the 1989 Act and consistent with human rights considerations, to take the 'least interventionist approach'.[18]

Thirdly, although the statutory checklist was new to the Children Act, with the exception of s 1(3)(g), the factors themselves were drawn from previous practice. Nevertheless, it is to be noted that s 1(3)(a) provided the first mandatory direction to the courts to have regard[19] to the child's own wishes both in the context of private disputes over children

---

[15] Law Com No 172, paras 3.17 ff.   [16] *Re R (Residence Order: Finance)* [1995] 2 FLR 612, CA.

[17] Ie a report ordered by the court under s 7 of the 1989 Act in which an investigation is made into the child's circumstances. Welfare reports are discussed in Ch 13.

[18] See *Re B-S (Children) (Adoption Order: Leave to Oppose)* [2014] 1 WLR 563, at [23], per Munby P.

[19] Though note: the child's wishes are *not* expressed to be determinative. See further Ch 13.

following their parents' separation or divorce and in care proceedings.[20] Whether the child's wishes should have been part of the checklist can be debated. It could be argued that such wishes are independent of their welfare.[21] Moreover, making it a separate requirement to listen to children would have given greater recognition to children being treated as individuals in their own right.

Whether and to what extent the list should be amended can be debated. It has been suggested, [22] for instance, that to be consistent with human rights the rights of parents should be included in the list. Another issue, to which we will return shortly, is whether the checklist should be amended to ensure that the courts have regard to the importance of sustaining a relationship between the child and both parents.

When the list applies

Section 1(4) directs the courts to have regard to the checklist in *contested* s 8 applications, all applications for special guardianship orders[23] and in *all* proceedings for care and supervision orders, including applications to vary or discharge such orders.[24] There is, however, nothing to prevent the courts from considering the factors in other proceedings if they so choose,[25] and indeed, particularly in contested applications for parental responsibility orders and guardianship appointments under s 4 and s 5, it would seem prudent to do so. In *Re B (Change of Surname)*,[26] Wilson J commented that, notwithstanding that he did not have to apply the checklist to determine an application for leave to change a child's surname, the list remained 'a most useful aide memoire of the factors that may impinge on the child's welfare'. In *Payne v Payne*,[27] in which an application for leave to remove a child from the jurisdiction was made under s 13, Thorpe LJ went further, commenting:

> Although technically an application brought under s 13(1) is not subject to the welfare checklist the trial judge should nevertheless take the precaution of regarding the checklist factors when carrying out his welfare appraisal.

The reason for restricting the application of s 1(3) to contested s 8 cases is that in many family proceedings such as divorce there is often no choice as to where and with whom the child should live. If s 1(3) applied to all s 8 cases, courts might feel compelled to investigate even these cases in depth.[28] Such an investigation would not only be a waste of resources but also, arguably, an unwarranted intrusion into family autonomy.

Although s 1(3) specifically directs *the court* to have regard to the checklist, it is clearly useful to legal advisers and their clients both in preparing and in arguing their case. Furthermore, as Holman J pointed out in *Re B (Care Proceedings: Notification of Father*

---

[20] Compare adoption, where it has always been incumbent upon the court to give due consideration to the child's wishes having regard to his age and understanding, see the Adoption Act 1926 s 3(b) re-enacted in the Adoption Acts of 1950 s 5(1)(b), 1958, s 7(2), 1976, s 6. See now s 1(4)(a) of the Adoption and Children 2002, discussed in Ch 20.

[21] For the importance of listening to children and the impact of the Children Act 1989 in this respect see *The Children Act Now—Messages from Research* (Dept of Health, 2001), ch 5.

[22] A Bainham 'Family Rights in the Next Millennium' (2000) 53 *Current Legal Problems* 473 at 490.

[23] Children Act 1989 s 4 (1)(b), as amended by the Adoption of Children Act 2002 s 115 (3).

[24] But note: leave to withdraw applications falls outside the terms of s 1(4)(b) on the basis that a withdrawal is neither a variation nor a discharge and therefore falls outside the terms of s 1(4)(b), see *Southwark London Borough v B* [1993] 2 FLR 559 applied in *WSCC v M, F, W, X Y and Z* [2010] EWHC 1914 (Fam) [2011] 1 FLR 188.

[25] *Southwark London Borough v B* [1993] 2 FLR 559, CA; *Re W (A Minor) (Medical Treatment: Court's Jurisdiction)* [1993] Fam 64, CA, per Thorpe J.   [26] [1996] 1 FLR 791 at 793, CA.

[27] [2001] EWCA Civ 166 [2001] 1 FLR 1052 at (30).   [28] See Law Com No 172 at para 3.19.

Without Parental Responsibility),[29] the rules[30] require Cafcass officers to have regard to the checklist. The Law Commission envisaged[31] that the list would enable parties to prepare relevant evidence and that focusing clients' minds on the real issues might help to promote settlements.

Where it is mandatory to apply the checklist it is clearly preferable that express reference is made to it. However, it seems to be accepted that higher court judges (ie not magistrates) are entitled to have it assumed in their favour that the checklist was in their mind without subjecting them to the laborious necessity of relating their findings to the specific item in the list 'one by one'.[32] Nonetheless, as Baroness Hale said in *Re G (Children) (Residence: Same Sex Partner)*[33] in any difficult or finely balanced case 'it is a great help' for all trial judges (even High Court judges) 'to address each of the factors in the list, along with any others which may be relevant, so as to ensure that no particular feature of the case is given more weight than it should properly bear. This is perhaps particularly important in any case where the real concern is that the children's primary carer is reluctant or unwilling to acknowledge the importance of another parent in the children's lives'.

As the Court of Appeal has observed,[34] the checklist represents an extremely useful and important discipline and ensures that all relevant matters are considered and balanced.[35]

Applying the checklist

The ascertainable wishes and feelings of the child concerned (considered in the light of his age and understanding)

The enjoinder to consider the child's wishes and feelings[36] is reflective of the international obligation under the UN Convention on the Rights of the Child 1989, Art 12(1).[37] However, by referring to the child's 'wishes and feelings', s 1(3)(a) is wider than Art 12, which is confined to 'views'. Very young children have discernible 'feelings', even if they cannot yet express their views. At the other end of the spectrum, it was accepted in *R (CD) v Isle of Anglesey County Council*[38] that the wishes and feelings of a 15 year old with grave disabilities should carry no less weight than for any other 15 year old.

Despite being placed first in the welfare checklist, the child's view is not expressed to be determinative.[39] As Butler-Sloss LJ put it in *Re P (Minors) (Wardship: Care and Control)*:[40]

---

[29] [1999] 2 FLR 408 at 415.

[30] Viz. what is now FPR 2010 r 16.33(4).   [31] Law Com 172 at para 3.18.

[32] See eg *Oldham Metropolitan Borough Council v E* [1994] 1 FLR 568 at 576, per Waite LJ and *Re V (Residence: Review)* [1995] 2 FLR 1010 at 1018, per Russell LJ.

[33] [2006] UKHL 43 [2006] 1 WLR 2305, at [40].

[34] *B v B (Residence Order: Reasons for Decision)* [1997] 2 FLR 602, CA—what was then a residence order made by a recorder without reference to the checklist because neither party had made complaints against the other, remitted for a re-hearing.

[35] For a reminder of the importance of correctly applying the checklist, see *Re H (Contact Order)* [2010] EWCA Civ 448 [2010] 2 FLR 866—trial judge held to have ignored the most relevant features of the checklist when ordering a mother who was still partially breast feeding the baby, to give staying contact to a father who was assumed to have good parenting skills because he was a general practitioner who had paediatric experience. See also *Re H (Contact With Biological Father)* [2012] EWCA Civ 281 [2012] 2 FLR 627—failure to run up the issue of contact with the biological father against the yardstick of the welfare checklist.

[36] For the background to this provision see Law Com No 172, paras 3.22 et seq. See also J Eekelaar 'The Interests of the Child and the Child's Wishes—The Role of Dynamic Self-Determinism' (1994) 8 Int Jo of Law and the Family 42.   [37] See Ch 13, International obligations, p 448.

[38] [2004] EWHC 1635 (Admin) [2005] 1 FLR 59.

[39] *Re W (Minors) (Residence Order)* [1992] 2 FCR 461, CA; *Re W (A Minor) (Residence Order)* [1993] 2 FLR 625, CA.

[40] [1992] 2 FCR 681 at 687. See also *M v M (Minor: Custody Appeal)* [1987] 1 WLR 404, at 411, CA, per May LJ.

How far the wishes of children should be the determinative factor in their future placement must of course vary on the particular facts of each case. Those views must be considered and may, but not necessarily must, carry more weight as the children grow older.

This point was re-emphasised by Sir Alan Ward in *Re P-S (Children) (Family
Proceedings: Evidence)*[41] when commenting that s 1(3)(a) cannot be construed as creating a rebuttable presumption that the mature child's wishes should prevail. Each case
is fact specific.

On the other hand, it has also been said that where all other factors are evenly balanced it is appropriate to recognise the extra significance of an older child's views.[42]
Nevertheless, the court's obligation is to *consider* the child's wishes and feelings but not
necessarily to give effect to them. It must be remembered that the child may have been
coached or brainwashed[43] by one parent or have become enmeshed in the parents' problems and have learned to say what they think is expected of them,[44] and that sometimes
even an older child's own wishes are so contrary to his or her long-term welfare that the
court may feel justified in overriding them. In *Re M (Family Proceedings: Affidavits)*,[45] for
example, a father applied for what was then a residence order based largely on his 12-year-
old daughter's wishes. Although the welfare report indicated that either parent was suitable as a carer, given that the child had hitherto lived with her mother and had not had the
opportunity to have any clear idea of what living with her father would really be like (the
contact visits to her father had always taken place at the paternal grandparents' home),
the judge upheld the welfare officer's 'instinct' that the child's long-term welfare would be
better governed by her remaining with her mother. In upholding the first instance decision, the Court of Appeal rejected the argument that, given either parent was suitable,
the child's views should have tipped the balance. The court accepted that the judge had
properly taken the child's wishes into account but was not obliged to follow them, if, as
here, it was not felt to be in the child's interests to do so.

The child's physical, emotional and educational needs

Although some have argued that to speak of needs may be simply a way of expressing adult
preferences in an apparently child-centred way,[46] it is nevertheless clear that in practice the
child's needs together with the parents' capabilities are the major concern in most cases.

---

[41] [2013] EWCA Civ 223 [2013] 1 WLR 3831 at [43].

[42] *Re F (Minors) (Denial of Contact)* [1993] 2 FLR 677, CA. Note Wilson J's comment in *Re B (Change of
Surname)* [1996] 1 FLR 791, CA, that it was virtually unknown to make what were then residence or contact
orders that run contrary to the wishes of normal adolescent children. However, this comment should perhaps be treated with some caution. It certainly should not be regarded as a statement of principle.

[43] See eg *Re R (A Minor) (Residence: Religion)* [1993] 2 FLR 163, CA, in which the wishes of a nine-year-old
boy to remain with a member of the Exclusive Brethren were overridden.

[44] See *V v V (Contact: Implacable Hostility)* [2004] EWHC 1215 (Fam) [2004] 2 FLR 851 at [44] where
Bracewell J also commented that the children in that case had become skilled in reiterating the view of their
principal carer.

[45] [1995] 2 FLR 100, CA; cf *Re M (Child's Upbringing)* ('the Zulu boy case') [1996] 2 FLR 441, where the
10-year-old's wishes seemed to be ignored—see the editorial at (1996) 146 NLJ 669. See also cases such as *Re
P (Medical Treatment: Best Interests)* [2003] EWHC 2327 (Fam) [2004] 2 FLR 1117; *Re W (A Minor) (Medical
Treatment: Court's Jurisdiction)* [1993] Fam 64, CA; *Re E (an infant)* (1990) 9 BMLR 1 and *Re M (Child:
Refusal of Medical Treatment)* [1999] 2 FLR 1097 (discussed in Ch 9, *Gillick*—a false dawn?, p 322), where
respectively a 17, a 16 and two 15-year-olds' refusal to have medical treatment was overridden.

[46] See eg S Maidment *Child Custody and Divorce* (1985) p 149, who comments, 'when a court makes a . . .
decision it may attempt to heed the child's needs but it is essentially making a decision as to which available
adult . . . is to care for the child . . .'

Physical needs. Physical needs can include the need for adequate accommodation but, as Wood J said in *Stephenson v Stephenson*,[47] in most cases 'disadvantages of a material sort must be of little weight'. The court's major concern is for the child's security and happiness, not his material prospects. Any other approach would automatically put a poor parent (and mothers in particular) at a disadvantage. Nevertheless, a party's financial position cannot be entirely ignored: for example, if he is so poor that he cannot even provide a home, this in itself might be sufficient to refuse him an order that child should live with him.[48] Even in a less extreme case a parent who can offer a child good accommodation must, other things being equal, have the edge over the one who cannot.[49] But again the quality of the home life that the child will have must not be measured in purely material terms: the amount of time and energy that a parent can devote to his care and upbringing is of considerable importance. This may mean that a mother who can spend the whole of her time with her children will have an advantage over a father who is out at work all day, whatever alternative arrangements he can make to have them looked after.[50] However, in *B v B (Custody of Children)*,[51] where an unemployed father was successfully looking after his child, it was held that the judge had erred in law in putting into the balance as a determining factor the man's moral duty to find work and not to rely upon the benefits provided by the welfare state.[52]

Emotional needs. The child's emotional needs will often be a crucial element in the case. Chief among these needs is that of attachment perhaps to a particular parent or to a sibling or even to a family. As Munby LJ commented in *Re G (Education: Religious Upbringing)*[53] 'a child's relationships both within and without the family are always relevant to the child's interests; often they will be decisive.'

With regard to attachment to a particular parent one influential notion in the past had been that young children need their mothers.[54] Indeed, in *Re W (A Minor) (Residence Order)*[55] Lord Donaldson MR went so far as to say that 'there is a rebuttable presumption of fact that the best interests of a baby are served by being with its mother', but this is difficult to square with *Re G (Children) (Residence: Same Sex Partner)*[56] in which the House of Lords eschewed the application of any presumptions in this context stressing the general application of the paramountcy principle. Nevertheless within this approach the court is prepared to acknowledge that certain arrangements are more often consistent with good child raising than others. As Lord Jauncey put it in *Brixey v Lynas*:[57]

---

[47] [1985] FLR 1140 at 1148, CA.

[48] Though note that for the purposes of the Housing Act 1996 a person caring for a child and who is unintentionally homeless has a priority need: see Ch 6.   [49] *Re F (An Infant)* [1969] 2 Ch 238.

[50] See *Re K (Minors) (Children: Care and Control)* [1977] Fam 179, CA; *S (BD) v S (DJ) (Children: Care and Control)* [1977] Fam 109, CA.

[51] [1985] FLR 166, CA.

[52] Compare *Re S (Children)* [2002] EWCA Civ 583 in which a residence order was granted to the mother notwithstanding that she was the 'bread winner' and the father had taken on a 'house husband' role in which Thorpe LJ, perhaps tellingly, referred to the 'very different role and functions of men and women'.

[53] [2012] EWCA Civ 1233 [2013] 1 FLR 677 at [30].

[54] This maternal preference was undoubtedly influenced by Bowlby's and others' theories of maternal deprivation: see the discussion in S Maidment *Child Custody and Divorce* (1984) at pp 182–4.

[55] [1992] 2 FLR 332 at 336, CA. In this case the baby was less than four weeks old.

[56] [2006] UKHL 43 [2006] 1 WLR 2305. See particularly [30]–[31], per Baroness Hale.

[57] 1996 SLT 908 at 9111 [1996] 2 FLR 499 at 505, on which see E Sutherland 'The unequal struggle— Fathers and children in Scots Law' [1997] CFLQ 191. For previous expressions of the common advantages of motherhood, see for example, *Re W (A Minor) (Custody)* (1983) 4 FLR 492 at 504, per Cumming-Bruce LJ and *Re S (A Minor) (Custody)* [1991] 2 FLR 388, CA at 390 and *Re A (A Minor) (Custody)* [1991] 2 FLR 394, CA at 400, per Butler-Sloss LJ.

... the advantage to a very young child of being with its mother is a consideration which must be taken into account in deciding where lie its best interests in custody proceedings in which the mother is involved. It is neither a presumption nor a principle but rather recognition of a widely held belief based on practical experience and the workings of nature. Its importance will vary according to the age of the child and to the other circumstances of each individual case such as whether the child has been living with or apart from the mother and whether she is or is not capable of providing proper care. Circumstances may be such that it has no importance at all. Furthermore it will always yield to other competing advantages which more effectively promote the welfare of the child. However, where a very young child has been with its mother since birth and there is no criticism of her ability to care for the child only the strongest competing advantages are likely to prevail.

In that case (an appeal from Scotland) the House of Lords were asked to consider what weight, if any, should be attached to the natural ability of mothers to care for very young children. At first instance, despite the fact that the 15-month-old girl was happy and well cared for by her mother, custody was granted to the father on the basis of the latter's more advantageous social background. This decision was overruled on appeal because it had overlooked the advantages both of maternal care of very young children and of maintaining the status quo. In dismissing the father's further appeal the Lords rejected the argument that the court had erred in allegedly accepting the principle of maternal preference.

Another 'emotional need' is that of sibling support. In general the courts dislike separating children. As Purchas LJ said in *C v C (Minors: Custody)*:[58]

It is really beyond argument that unless there are strong features indicating a contrary arrangement . . . brothers and sisters should wherever possible, be brought up together, so that they are an emotional support to each other in the stormy waters of the destruction of their family.

Occasionally this consideration can be decisive. In *Adams v Adams*,[59] for example, the mother sought an order to look after her daughter but not her son, but her application failed because it was held preferable to keep the two children together. In *Clarke-Hunt v Newcombe*[60] it was held that, as it was in the younger boy's interests to be with his mother and it was inappropriate to separate the brothers, both boys should live with her, even though it was against the elder boy's wishes and possibly slightly detrimental to his interests. However influential this consideration may be, it is of course not a rule and there will be cases when separation of siblings is appropriate or unavoidable. In *B v B (Residence Order: Restricting Applications)*,[61] for example the trial judge had ordered two brothers to live with their mother, but the older boy then 'voted with his feet' by going to live with his

---

[58] [1988] 2 FLR 291, CA at 302. See also *Adams v Adams* [1984] FLR 768, CA at 772, CA, where Dunn LJ said: 'All these cases depend upon their own facts, but it is undesirable, other things being equal, that children should be split when they are close together in age and obviously fond of one another . . . Children do . . . support one another and give themselves mutual comfort, perhaps more than they can derive from either of their parents.' But the disapproval of splitting siblings is not new: see *Re Besant* (1879) 11 Ch D 508 at 512, CA, per Jessel MR.

[59] [1984] FLR 768, CA.   [60] (1982) 4 FLR 482, CA.

[61] [1997] 1 FLR 139, CA. See also *Re D (Care: Natural Parent Presumption)* [1999] 1 FLR 134, CA in which it was held that too much importance had been attached in that case to the need to keep the siblings together; *Re B (T) (A Minor) (Residence Order)* [1995] 2 FCR 240, CA, in which on the facts, maintaining the status quo was held to be more important to the child than being with his siblings; and *Re O (Infants)* [1962] 2 All ER 10, CA (boy's long-term future thought to be better served by being with his father in the Sudan, whereas the girl's was with her mother in England).

father. The judge subsequently and reluctantly concluded that the younger child should remain with the mother because she met his needs and that the older child should continue to live with the father. His decision was upheld by the Court of Appeal.

Another aspect of emotional need is that of attachment to the family. Clearly this will come into play where the dispute is between parents and third parties. Although, as *J v C*[62] made clear, the paramountcy of the child's welfare principle applies equally to disputes between parents and other individuals as well as to disputes between parents, nevertheless the courts have also recognised the prima facie strength of the parents' position based on their view that children have a basic interest in being brought up by their own family. But it is important not to go too far in this respect[63] for as has been pointed out,[64] there is no presumption in favour of the natural parent to be found anywhere in the 1989 Act and consequently any judicial overlay of the words of the statute had to be treated with caution. In any event, the biological parents might not always be their 'parents' in the eyes of the child and in cases where the child had been in the long-term care of a non-parent it will be the latter person who is the child's psychological parent.

How best to express the notion of the significance of parenthood without undermining the paramountcy principle has continued to trouble the courts. In *Re G (Children) (Residence: Same-Sex Partner)* Baroness Hale said:[65]

> The statutory provision is plain: the welfare of the child is the paramount consideration. As Lord MacDermott explained [in *J v C*], this means that it 'rules upon or determines the course to be followed'. There is no question of a parental right. As the Law Commission explained,[66] 'the welfare test itself is well able to encompass any special contribution which natural parents can make to the emotional needs of their child' or, as Lord MacDermott put it, the claims and wishes of parents 'can be capable of ministering to the total welfare of the child in a special way.

However, Baroness Hale added that none of this means that the fact of parentage[67] is irrelevant and she expressly approved the following comment by an Australian judge:[68]

> I am of the opinion that the fact of parenthood is to be regarded as an important and significant factor in considering which proposals better advance the welfare of the child. Such fact does not, however, establish a presumption in favour of the natural parent, nor generate a preferential position in favour of the natural parent from which the Court commences its decision-making process . . . Each case should be determined upon an examination of its own merits and of the individuals there involved. (Emphasis added)

While this positional statement is clear, it was arguably tempered by a different line taken by Lord Nicholls who, having referred to the paramountcy of the child's welfare, said:[69]

---

[62] [1970] AC 668, HL, discussed in Ch 9, *J v C*, pp 314ff.

[63] Decisions such as *Re D (Care: Natural Parent Presumption)* [1999] 1 FLR 134 went as far as to say that positive reasons were required before residence orders would be made in favour of non-parents.

[64] *Re H (A Child: Residence)* [2002] 3 FCR 277, CA in which the child had lived most of her life with the maternal grandparent.

[65] [2006] UKHL 43 [2006] 1 WLR 2305 at [30]. See L Smith 'Re G (Children: Same Sex Partner)' (2006) 29 JSWFL 307.   [66] Law Com Working Paper No 96, *Custody* (HMSO 1986) para 6.22.

[67] Note: Baroness Hale was at pains to stress (see *Re G* at [32]–[38]) that one should be wary of placing too much stress on the *biological* parenthood given that parenthood can comprise genetic, gestational, social and psychological parenthood.

[68] Namely Lindenmayer J in *Hadak, Newman and Hadak* (1993) FLC 92-421 approved by the Full Court of the Family Law Court of Australia in *Rice v Miller* (1993) FLC 92-415 and *Re Evelyn* [1998] Fam CA 55.

[69] At [2].

> In reaching its decision the court should always have in mind that in the ordinary way the rearing of a child by his or her biological parents can be expected to be in the child's best interests, both in the short term also, and importantly, in the longer term. *I decry any tendency to diminish the significance of this factor. A child should not be removed from the primary care of his or her biological parents without compelling reason. Where such a reason exists the judge should spell this out explicitly.* (Emphasis added)

But any notion that Lord Nicholls was to be taken as espousing a different approach to Baroness Hale was firmly quashed by the Supreme Court *Re B (A Child) (Residence: Biological Parent)*. Giving the judgment of the court, Lord Kerr pointed to Lord Nicholls' qualification of his statement by his reference to 'the ordinary way' of rearing a child and commented[70]'But many disputes about residence and contact do not follow the ordinary way. Therefore although one should keep in mind the common experience to which Lord Nicholls was referring, one must not be slow to recognise those cases where that common experience does not provide a reliable guide'.

Referring to Baroness Hale's judgment just quoted, Lord Kerr said:

> It is a message which should not require reaffirmation but, if and in so far as it does, we would wish to provide it in this judgment. All consideration of the importance of parenthood in private law disputes about residence must be firmly rooted in an examination of what is in the child's best interests. This is the paramount consideration. It is only as a contributor to the child's welfare that parenthood assumes any significance. In common with all other factors bearing on what is in the best interests of the child, it must be examined for its potential to fulfil that aim.[71]

It is one thing to agree upon the principle but quite another to agree upon its application. In *Re B*, however, the application of the paramountcy test, as properly understood,[72] seemed straightforward. In that case the Supreme Court restored the magistrates' decision that a four year old who had lived virtually all his life with his grandmother should remain with her and not be moved to live with his father. *Re G*, in contrast, was not so straightforward. It involved a dispute between a lesbian couple over the future upbringing of two children who the couple had together by means of donor insemination of one of them. In reinstating an order giving primary residence to the birth mother, the House of Lords considered that insufficient weight had been given to the fact that she was their natural parent. As Baroness Hale said the fact that the respondent was 'the natural mother of those children in every sense of the term,[73] while raising no presumption in her favour, is an important and significant factor in determining what will be best for them now and in the future'.

---

[70] [2009] UKSC 5 [2009] 1 WLR 2496, at [35].   [71] At [37].

[72] The original decision was overturned in the father's favour on the basis of Lord Nicholls' judgment in *Re G* that the justices had failed to give weight to the notion that children should be raised by their biological parent or parents. The Court of Appeal (see *Re B (Residence: Second Appeal)* [2009] EWCA Civ 548 [2009] 2 FLR 632) refused to interfere with the appeal judge's ruling upon the basis that his fundamental approach was not plainly wrong. The Supreme Court disagreed, holding that as the exercise of the justices' discretion, though flawed, could not be said to be plainly wrong, the appeal judge had in turn been wrong to interfere with their decision. It is an interesting point as to how the appeal would now have been decided in view of the Supreme Court's subsequent decision in *Re B (A Child) (Care Proceedings: Threshold Criteria)* [2013] UKSC 33, [2013] 1 WLR 1911, discussed at The power of the appellate courts, p 426 and in Ch 14, Appeals, p 545 and Ch 17, Appeals, p 650.

[73] Ie she was the genetic, gestational, social and psychological parent.

A controversial application of the view that a child is better off being brought up in his own family is *Re M (Child's Upbringing)*.[74] There the Court of Appeal ordered the immediate return of a 10-year-old boy of Zulu origin to his natural parents (who had previously been retained by the applicant whilst in South Africa as household employees) in South Africa, notwithstanding that he had been brought up for the last four years exclusively by the white applicant in England, and apparently ignoring both the child's own wishes and strong medical advice that an immediate return would be harmful. As Neill LJ put it:[75]

> Of course there will be cases where the welfare of the child requires that the child's right to be with his natural parents has to give way in his own interest to other considerations. But I am satisfied that in this case, as in other cases, one starts with the strong supposition that it is in the [child's] interests . . . that he should be brought up with his natural parents.

Educational needs.   Education is an important aspect of a child's upbringing. In *Re G (Education: Religious Upbringing)*[76] Munby LJ observed, that, given the court's objective to maximise the child's opportunities in every sphere of life as they enter into adulthood, judges should be cautious about choosing a regime which may have the effect of foreclosing or unduly limiting the child's ability to make such decisions in the future. Occasionally, parental attitude to education can be significant. In *May v May*[77] care and control was granted to the father inter alia because he laid greater emphasis on academic achievements in contrast to the freer and easier attitude of the mother and her cohabitant to the time the children (aged eight and six!) should be doing homework. It has been said[78] that the question of religion can also be embraced under the heading of 'educational needs' and, indeed, on occasion, are closely inter-related issues.

Other needs.   Needs have also been held to include medical needs and hence, provided it is for the child's benefit, it is within the court's power to make an order for the taking of a blood sample to ascertain whether the child is HIV positive.[79] In extreme cases in which the court has to decide whether or to sanction the withdrawal of life prolonging treatment, it has been said:

> The court must, taking account of all relevant matters and treating the child's welfare in the widest sense as its paramount consideration, decide what is in the child's best interests, looking at it from the child's point of view and applying a strong, though rebuttable, presumption in favour of a course of action that would prolong life.[80]

---

[74] [1996] 2 FLR 441, CA. For a critique of this case see N Lowe 'The House of Lords and the Welfare Principle' in Bridge (ed) *Family Law Towards the Millennium—Essays for P M Bromley* 125 at 164–5, and as Thorpe LJ subsequently said in *Note: Re O (Family Appeals: Management)* [1998] 1 FLR 431 that 'with the advantage of hindsight' it might be said that the court fell into error in placing the weight that it did on the biological attachment.

[75] At 453. In fact, the boy later returned to England with the mother's consent to resume living with the applicant.

[76] [2012] EWCA Civ 1233 [2013] 1 FLR 677.   [77] [1986] 1 FLR 325, CA.

[78] Per Wall J in *Re J (Specific Issue Orders: Muslim Upbringing and Circumcision)* [1999] 2 FLR 298 – decision upheld by Court of Appeal, see [2000] 1 FLR 571.

[79] See *Re C (HIV Test)* [1997] 2 FLR 1004, FD and CA and *Re W (A Minor) (HIV Test)* [1995] 2 FCR 184, per Kirkwood J.

[80] Per Peter Jackson J in *An NHS Trust v R* [2013] EWHC 2340 [2014] Fam Law 294 at [40] (and on which see the comment by G Douglas at [2014] Fam Law 294) applying *Wyatt v Portsmouth Hospital NHS Trust* [2005] EWCA Civ 1181, [2005] 1 WLR 3995 and *Re J (Wardship: Medical Treatment)* [1991] Fam 33. A similar test has since been applied to vulnerable adults by the Supreme Court in *Aintree University Hospitals NHS Foundation Trust v James* [2013] UKSC 67, [2014] AC 591, in which Baroness Hale said, at [39], 'in considering the best interests of this particular patient at this particular time, decision-makers must look at the

The likely effect on the child of any change in his circumstances

Section 1(3)(c) is the statutory enactment of the 'status quo' or continuity factor, which in practice is particularly important in resolving private law disputes, the courts being well aware of the dangers of removing a child from a well-established home.[81] As Ormrod LJ said in *D v M (A Minor: Custody Appeal)*:[82]

> ... it is generally accepted by those who are professionally concerned with children that, particularly in the early years, continuity of care is a most important part of a child's sense of security and that disruption of established bonds is to be avoided whenever it is possible to do so.

Although good reasons will have to be adduced to justify moving a child from a well established home,[83] even on an interim basis,[84] there is no presumption in favour of the status quo. As Ward LJ put it in *Re F (Shared Residence Orders)*[85] the status quo argument means no more than that if the children are settled in one place then the court is to have regard to s 1(3)(c) and consider the likely effect on them of any change in their circumstances. In other words, the status quo is only a factor and the court may well think that the child's welfare in any particular case might be better served by being moved. As Ormrod LJ elegantly put it:[86]

> ... the status quo argument depends for its strength wholly and entirely on whether the status quo is satisfactory or not. The more satisfactory the status quo, the stronger the argument for not interfering. The less satisfactory the status quo, the less one requires before deciding to change.

The maintenance of the status quo becomes a stronger argument the longer the child has been with one party,[87] and is especially powerful if the other has lost contact with the child. On the other hand, if, as in *Allington v Allington*,[88] the parties have only been separated for a few weeks and the absent parent has maintained regular contact with the child, there can effectively be no status quo argument at all. In assessing what the status quo is the court should examine the whole history of the case and not simply the position immediately before the hearing. Hence, where a parent has 'snatched' a child from the other, the

---

welfare in the widest sense, not just medical but social and psychological; they must consider the nature of the treatment in question, what it involves and its prospects of success; they must consider what the outcome of that treatment for the patient is likely to be; they must try and put themselves in the place of the individual patient and ask what his attitude to the treatment is or would be likely to be; and they must consult others who are looking after him or interested in his welfare ...'

[81] Compare *Re Thain* [1926] Ch 676 in which the traumas of being moved were dismissed as being transitory.　　　　　　　　　　　　　　　　　　　　　　　　　　　　[82] [1983] Fam 33 at 41.

[83] See eg *Re B (Residence Order: Status Quo)* [1998] 1 FLR 368, CA, in which a first instance judge was held wrongly to have placed speculative improvements in contact over and above the consideration of continuity of care. See also *Re B (T) (A Minor) (Residence Order)* [1995] 2 FCR 240, CA in which, on the facts, maintaining the status quo was thought to be more important to the child than being with her siblings, and *Re L (Residence: Justices' Reasons)* [1995] 2 FLR 445 (inadequate reasons given by magistrates for upsetting the status quo).

[84] See eg *Re J (Children: Ex Parte Order)* [1997] 1 FLR 606, in which Hale J observed (at 609) that without notice (*ex parte*) orders handing over a young child to a parent with whom she has not lived for 20 months should surely be exceptional.　　　　　　　　　　　　　　　　　　[85] [2009] EWCA Civ 313 [2010] 1 FLR 354.

[86] In *S v W* (1980) 11 Fam Law 81 at 82, CA.

[87] It also needs to be borne in mind that the younger the child the greater the effect of the passage of time on the child's attachment and adjustment: see J Goldstein, A Freud and A Solnit *Beyond the Best Interests of the Child* (1973).　　　　　　　　　　　　　　　　　　　　　　　　　[88] [1985] FLR 586, CA.

court may properly regard the status quo as being the position before the snatch.[89] There is however, no rule that the child should be returned in snatching cases. The only principle is that the child's welfare is the paramount consideration.[90]

The child's age, sex, background and any characteristics of which the court considers relevant

Consideration of the child's age is obviously linked to other matters such as the child's wishes and when combined with sex can be relevant to the choice of parents, which we have already discussed.

Religious considerations. The child's background can include his religious upbringing. In the past this was of crucial significance, but today this consideration is of much less importance.[91] It is inconceivable, for instance, that a court would refuse to make an order for the child to live with a parent on the sole basis of the latter's atheism.[92] In the case of a very young child (and probably any child where religion has played little or no part in their upbringing) the question of religious upbringing will have little bearing on the outcome of the case.[93] In *Re J (Specific Issue Orders: Muslim Upbringing and Circumcision)*[94] the child concerned (aged 5) was being brought up as a non-practising Christian in accordance with the beliefs of his mother with whom he lived and as a non-practising Muslim when staying with his father. He could therefore be said to have no settled religious faith. Wall J declined to make a specific issue order that the child be brought up in the Muslim religion. A similar decision was made in *Re S (Specific Issue Order: Religion: Circumcision)*[95] where the two children born to a Muslim mother and Hindu father had been brought up as Hindus, with Islamic influences but with neither being strict adherents to their respective faiths.

On the other hand, where religious upbringing is clearly part of the child's upbringing, the court may well consider its continuation vital particularly if the evidence suggests that otherwise the child could suffer emotional disturbance.[96] Nevertheless, even in these circumstances there is no rule that it can never be right to force a child to abandon his religious beliefs, since ultimately such beliefs are subservient to what is perceived as being overall in a child's best interests.[97] This is well illustrated by *Re G (Education: Religious Upbringing)*[98] in which in determining how the children should be educated, the court had to choose between preserving their upbringing in the Chassidic (Hasidic) or Chareidi community of ultra Orthodox Jews and a less strict form of Orthodox Jews. It chose the

---

[89] As in *Edwards v Edwards* [1986] 1 FLR 187; affd [1986] 1 FLR 205, CA.

[90] *Re J (A Minor) (Interim Custody: Appeal)* [1989] 2 FLR 304, CA. But see Ch 26 for the position of international child abduction under the Hague and European Conventions and Brussels II Regulation.

[91] For a full discussion of religious issues see C Hamilton *Family, Law and Religion* (1995) chs 4 and 5 and A Mumford 'The Judicial Resolution of Disputes Involving Children and Religion' (1998) 47 ICLQ 117.

[92] Compare *Shelley v Westbrooke* (1817) Jac 266n in which the poet Shelley was denied custody on this ground.   [93] See *Re C (MA) (An Infant)* [1966] 1 All ER 838 at 856 and 864–5, CA.

[94] [1999] 2 FLR 678—decision upheld by the Court of Appeal at [2000] 1 FLR 571.

[95] [2004] EWHC 1282 (Fam) [2005] 1 FLR 236.

[96] This certainly influenced Willmer LJ in *Re M (Infants)* [1967] 3 All ER 1071 at 1074, CA.

[97] See Balcombe LJ in *Re R (A Minor) (Residence: Religion)* [1993] 2 FLR 163 at 180, CA. Note also *Re R (A Minor) (Residence: Religion)* (1975) 2 FLR 239, CA, in which, faced with the stark choice of either making an order that a nine year old boy should live with his father, thereby effectively excluding the boy from the Exclusive Brethren within which society he had hitherto grown up, or ordering the boy to live with members of the sect, which would mean, because of the strict rules of the fellowship, his son would no longer even see his father, the court ordered that the child should live with his father. The Court of Appeal made it clear that their decision was not based on a value judgment as to the tenets of the particular religion, but rather that it was thought to be in the boy's long-term interests to continue to be brought up by his father.

[98] [2012] EWCA Civ 1233 [2013] 1 FLR 677 at [36].

latter because that afforded wider education prospects. In reaching this decision Munby LJ said 'It is not for a judge to weigh one religion against another. The court recognises no religious distinctions and generally speaking passes no judgment on religious beliefs of parents or on the tenets, doctrines or rules of any particular section of society.' All are entitled to equal respect, so long as they 'legally and socially acceptable' and are not 'immoral or socially obnoxious' or 'pernicious'.[99]

Not being judgmental about religious beliefs means, for example, that being a Jehovah's Witness does not *ipso facto* mean that a child should not be ordered to live with that parent.[100] Indeed to deny an order solely on this ground would violate human rights.[101] In *Re H (A Minor) (Custody: Religious Upbringing)*,[102] the court took the view that:

> mere indoctrination with the beliefs and tenets of this narrow faith is not of itself indicative of harm or that harm will occur to the child so indoctrinated, provided there is an understanding and level-headed parent in charge of the child.

On the other hand a similar latitude might not be given in respect of membership of what the court considers to be an extreme sect. In *Re B and G (Minors) (Custody)*[103] the decisive factor in denying a father and stepmother an order to look after the children which they had been doing for five years was that they were scientologists and held views which were then found to be 'immoral and obnoxious'.

In appropriate cases, for example, where the care-giver has a different religion from that of the child, it is open to the court to make a child arrangements order on condition that the child's religious upbringing will be continued.[104] On the other hand, it could be a condition of an order that the adult does not involve a child in his religion.[105]

Racial, cultural and linguistic background. Racial origin, cultural background and linguistic background[106] are issues that should be considered under this head and are likely on occasion to prove difficult.

[99] Above at [36]. This comment echoes that of Scarman LJ's comment in *Re T (Minors) (Custody: Religious Upbringing)* that: '. . . it was not for the court to pass any judgment on the beliefs of parents where they are socially acceptable and consistent with a decent and respectable life . . .'

[100] Although parties are sometimes asked to undertake not to involve their children, for example, in the house-to-house visiting conducted by Jehovah's Witnesses: see eg *Re C (Minors) (Wardship: Jurisdiction)* [1978] Fam 105, CA. Note also *Re N (A Child: Religion: Jehovah's Witness)* [2011] EWHC 3737 (Fam) [2012] 2 FLR 917, in which neither parent (the father was an Anglican and the mother a Jehovah's Witness) was permitted to prevent the child from participating in school activities and school assemblies.

[101] Viz. Arts 9 and 8 taken in conjunction with Art 14 of the European Convention, see eg *Hoffmann v Austria* [1994] 1 FCR 193, ECtHR, *Palau-Martinez v France* [2004] 2 FLR 810, ECtHR but cf *Ismailova v Russia (App No 37614/02)* [2008] 1 FLR 533.

[102] (1980) 2 FLR 253. See also *Vojnity v Hungary* (App No 29617/07) [2013] 2 FCR 495, EctHR—applicant's insistence on proselytising did not justify denying the father access to his son.

[103] [1985] FLR 493, CA. The court felt that it could not rely on the father's undertaking to remove the children from 'the evil forces of scientology'. Query whether the Supreme Court decision in *R v Registrar General of Births, Deaths and Marriages* [2013] UKSC 77 [2014] 2 WLR 23, that Scientology is a 'religion' for the purpose of celebrating marriages indicates a general change of attitude?

[104] In the past, however, the court has been content to accept undertakings to this effect: see eg *Re E (an infant)* [1963] 3 All ER 874, where a Jewish couple were required to bring up a ward of court as a Roman Catholic; and *J v C* [1970] AC 668, HL, where Protestants gave a similar undertaking to bring up the child as a Roman Catholic.

[105] See eg *Re R (A Minor) (Residence: Religion)* [1993] 2 FLR 163, CA, where an aunt was granted contact upon her undertaking not to speak or communicate with the child in any way in relation to religious or spiritual matters or make any reference to the Exclusive Brethren as a religious group; cf *Re C (Minors) (Wardship: Jurisdiction)*, above.

[106] Considerations to which local authorities must have specific regard under s 22(5)(c): see Ch 18, Local authority duties towards 'looked after children', pp 660 ff.

The preservation of links with the child's culture and heritage are important issues that should not be overlooked.[107] Such considerations were clearly a key motivating force in *Re M (Child's Upbringing)*,[108] in which the Court of Appeal ordered the return of a boy of Zulu origin to his mother in South Africa, while in *Re M (Section 94 Appeals)*[109] the failure to address the question of race when denying contact of a mixed race girl (who was confused about her racial origin) to her black father, was held to justify the Court of Appeal reversing the decision. Nevertheless important though culture and heritage may be, the rule remains that it is the child's welfare that is the paramount consideration. In *Re P (A Minor) (Residence Order: Child's Welfare)*[110] in which Jewish Orthodox parents sought to have their child (born with Down's Syndrome) returned to them, notwithstanding that for the previous four years she had been living with a non-practising Catholic couple under a residence order, the Court of Appeal upheld the first instance decision that on the evidence of the child's limited ability to understand and appreciate the Jewish religion, her religious and cultural heritage was *not* an overwhelming factor.

Any harm which the child has suffered or is at risk of suffering

The 'harm' referred to in s 1(3)(e) has the same meaning as it does for the purposes of care proceedings,[111] and accordingly means both ill-treatment and the impairment of health or development. It clearly covers both physical and psychological trauma. It also covers sexual abuse which, if proved, is obviously likely to be a significant consideration but even so may not inevitably mean that the abuser should not, for example, be allowed contact.[112] Following amendment by the Adoption and Children Act 2002[113] the definition of 'harm' has been extended to include 'impairment suffered from seeing or hearing the ill-treatment of another'. This amendment is intended to emphasise the potential harm caused to a child, for example, by witnessing violence perpetrated by one parent on another.

Note may also be taken of the power, conferred by s 16A,[114] for Cafcass and Welsh family proceedings officers to carry out a risk assessment and provide it to the court, if in the course of carrying out any function in family proceedings under Part II of the 1989 Act, the officer is given cause to suspect that the child concerned is at risk of harm.

Apart from actual harm, s 1(3)(e) also encompasses 'risk' of harm. Such a risk could, for example, emanate from the parents' past alcoholism,[115] or sexual abuse. It is, however, established that s 1(3)(e) deals with actual harm or risk of harm and not with possibilities. As Butler-Sloss LJ said in *Re M and R (Child Abuse: Evidence)*:[116]

---

[107] These issues are particularly relevant in so-called non-Convention abduction cases (discussed in Ch 27), see *Re J (A Child) (Custody Rights—Jurisdiction)* [2005] UKHL 40 [2005] 3 WLR 14.

[108] [1996] 2 FLR 441, CA, discussed earlier.   [109] [1995] 1 FLR 546, CA.

[110] [2000] Fam 15, CA.

[111] Section 105(1) provides that 'harm' has the same meaning as in s 31(9), discussed further in Ch 17, The significant harm condition, p 600.

[112] See *H v H (Child Abuse: Access)* [1989] 1 FLR 212, CA; *L v L (Child Abuse: Access)* [1989] 2 FLR 16, CA; and *C v C (A Minor) (Child Abuse: Evidence)* [1988] 1 FLR 462; cf *Re R (A Minor) (Access)* [1988] 1 FLR 206, CA.

[113] Section 120, which was brought into force on 31 January 2005 by the Adoption and Children Act 2002 (Commencement No 7) Order 2004 (SI 2004/3203).

[114] Added to the 1989 Act by the Adoption and Children Act 2002 s 120.

[115] See eg *Re L (Residence: Justices' Reasons)* [1995] 2 FLR 445.

[116] [1996] 2 FLR 195 at 203, applying the same test as applies to s 31 following the House of Lords' ruling in *Re H (Minors) (Sexual Abuse: Standard of Proof)* [1996] AC 563, discussed in Ch 17. Note: *Re P (Sexual Abuse: Standard of Proof)* [1996] 2 FLR 333, CA. See also *Re W (Residence Order)* [1999] 1 FLR 869, CA (judge not entitled to assume that an uninhibited attitude to nudity posed a risk of harm to the children).

> The court must reach a conclusion based on facts, not on suspicion or mere doubts. If, as in the present case, the court concludes that the evidence is insufficient to prove sexual abuse in the past, and if the fact of sexual abuse in the past is the only basis for asserting a risk of sexual abuse in the future, then it follows that there is nothing (except suspicion or mere doubts) to show a risk of future sexual abuse.

Although *Re M and R* has not escaped criticism,[117] Lord Nicholls subsequently commented in *Re O (Minors) (Care: Preliminary Hearing)*[118] that, without hearing full arguments on the matter, he found the conclusions of the Court of Appeal in *Re M and R* 'attractive' adding:

> It would be odd if, on this point, the approach in proceedings for section 8 orders were different from the approach in care proceedings.

Re M and R was expressly approved by the House of Lords in *Re B (Children) (Care Proceedings: Standard of Proof)*.[119]

Re M and R also establishes that the appropriate standard of proof is the balance of probabilities.[120] However, the undoubted difficulties of proving primary allegations in some cases do not justify not investigating them at all.[121] The proper approach is to consider first whether the primary allegation on which the risk of harm is said to be based can be proved and then, assuming it can, to decide whether or not that is a risk of harm to satisfy s 1(3)(e). The leading case on the application of balance or preponderance of probabilities test is *Re B (Children) (Care Proceedings: Standard of Proof)*, in which Baroness Hale announced 'loud and clear' that:

> the standard of proof in finding the facts necessary to establish the threshold under section 31(2) or the welfare considerations in section 1 of the 1989 Act is the simple balance of probabilities, neither more nor less. Neither the seriousness of the allegation nor the seriousness of the consequences should make any difference to the standard of proof to be applied in determining the facts. The inherent probabilities are simply something to be taken into account, where relevant, in deciding where the truth lies.[122]

How capable each of the child's parents, and any other person in relation to whom the court considers the question to be relevant, is of meeting his needs

A wide variety of circumstances can be brought under this heading, ranging from the capability to provide housing,[123] the parents' medical condition[124] or their lifestyle.[125] As

---

[117] See eg I Hemingway and C Williams '*Re M and R: Re H and R*' [1997] Fam Law 740.

[118] [2003] UKHL 18 [2004] 1 AC at [45].

[119] [2008] UKHL 35 [2009] 1 AC 11, on which see C Cobley and N Lowe 'Interpreting the Threshold Criteria under s 31 (2) of the Children Act 1989—the House of Lords decision in *Re B*' (2009) 72 MLR 463. See further Ch 17.

[120] [2008] UKHL 35 [2009] 1 AC 11 at 203, expressly rejecting the contention that, because the child's welfare was paramount, the standard of proof for establishing harm should be less than the preponderance of probabilities.

[121] See eg *Re L (Residence: Justices' Reasons)* [1995] 2 FLR 445, in which magistrates were held wrong not to deal expressly with the father's contention that the mother's former alcohol problems had resumed.

[122] [2008] UKHL 35 [2009] 1 AC 11 at [70].

[123] See *Holmes-Moorhouse v Richmond-upon-Thames London Borough Council* [2009] UKHL 7 [2009] 1 WLR 413.

[124] See eg *Re C (Appeal From Care and Placement Order)* [2013] EWCA Civ 1257, in which a maternal grandparent's application for a special guardianship order (discussed in Ch 19) failed in part because of her blindness.   [125] See eg *May v May* [1986] 1 FLR 325, CA.

well as that of parents the capability of any other person in relation to whom the court considers the question to be relevant must also be examined. This will clearly include any new partner (formal or informal) of the parent.[126] It can also include, in the public law context, the local authority's capacity to meet the child's needs through, for example, long-term fostering rather than adoption.[127]

2. THE MEANING OF 'PARAMOUNT'

As discussed in Chapter 9, although before the Children Act 1989 courts were directed[128] to treat the child's welfare as their '*first and* paramount consideration', judicial decisions, in particular that of the House of Lords in *J v C*,[129] had effectively rendered the words 'first and' redundant. The 1989 Act's paramountcy formulation therefore simply reflected that previously well established position and, as such, was not intended to alter the law or practice. Indeed, in *Re O and another (Minors) (Care: Preliminary Hearing); Re B*[130] Lord Nicholls said that the approach adopted by Lord MacDermott in *J v C* when applying the welfare principle under what was then the Guardianship of Infants Act 1925 was 'equally applicable' to that under the 1989 Act. In this regard Lord MacDermott had classically stated that the principle connotes:[131]

> a process whereby when all the relevant facts, relationships, claims and wishes of parents, risks, choices and other circumstances are taken into account and weighed, the course to be followed will be that which is most in the interests of the child's welfare as that term has now to be understood.

What *J v C* was commonly taken to have established and therefore confirmed by s 1(1) of the 1989 Act, was that the child's welfare was in effect the court's sole concern and that other factors were relevant only to the extent that they would assist the court in ascertaining the best solution for children. However, the problem with that interpretation is the difficulty of squaring it with the requirement under the European Convention on Human Rights[132] to respect the rights of the parents as well as the child. As we discuss shortly, however, the domestic courts modified their stance on the application of the paramountcy principle, while at the same time the European Court of Human Rights has increasingly recognised the predominant position of the child.

In choosing the paramountcy formulation, the Government rejected the Law Commission's recommendation,[133] that 'when determining any question under the Act the welfare of *any child likely to be affected* shall be the court's *only* concern.' This proposal to consider the welfare of *any* child was open to the objection that it could lead to wide and speculative enquiries, which ultimately could blur the court's view and duty towards the

---

[126] See eg *Scott v Scott* [1986] 2 FLR 320, CA (mother's cohabitant found to have committed acts of indecency against the child), and *M v Birmingham City Council* [1994] 2 FLR 141 at 147, per Stuart-White J.

[127] See *Re G (Care Proceedings: Welfare Evaluation)* [2013] EWCA Civ 965 [2014] 1 FLR 670 at [47], per McFarlane LJ.

[128] Viz. by s 1 of the Guardianship of Minors Act 1971 which in turn re-enacted s 1 of the Guardianship of Infants Act 1925.

[129] [1970] AC 668, for an extensive analysis of which see N Lowe '*J v C*: Placing the Child's Welfare Centre Stage' in S Gilmore, J Herring and R Probert (eds) *Landmark Cases in Family Law* (2011) ch 3.

[130] [2003] UKHL 18 [2004] 1 AC 523 at [24].   [131] [1970] AC 668 at 710–11.

[132] Ie in particular the right to respect for private and family life under Art 8.

[133] Clause 1(2) of the Draft Bill published in Law Com No 172, *Review of Child Law, Guardianship and Custody*, 1988.

welfare of the child before it,[134] and force it to compromise between the interests of two or more children.[135] In any event, once the enjoinder to consider the welfare of the particular child before the court is departed from, there seems no reason to stop at the welfare of other children. A plausible case could be made out to include the welfare of others, for example, an adult but disabled sibling who is still living with the family or an infirm parent or grandparent, each of whom could be argued to have a claim for equal consideration. However, any such broadening might have had the effect of weakening the protection of children, which the Law Commission itself was not prepared to contemplate.[136]

(a) Is the paramountcy principle human rights compliant?

As discussed in Chapter 9, a decade before the Human Rights Act 1998, it had been unsuccessfully argued before the House of Lords in *Re KD (A Minor) (Ward: Termination of Access)*[137] that the paramountcy principle was incompatible with the European Convention on Human Rights. In Lord Templeman's view[138] there was 'no inconsistency of principle or application between the English rule and the Convention rule'. While Lord Oliver concluded:[139]

> such conflict as exists is, I think, semantic only and lies only in differing ways of giving expression to the single common concept that the natural bond and relationship between parent and child gives rise to universally recognised norms which ought not to be gratuitously interfered with and which, if interfered with at all, ought to be so only if the welfare of the child dictates it.

Although this analysis did not go unchallenged in academic circles[140] the House of Lords' ruling might have been taken as definitive but for the fact that the 1998 Act provided an opportunity for a general reappraisal.[141] However, the judiciary were quick to confirm the paramountcy principle's compatibility with human rights. In *Re L (A Child) (Contact: Domestic Violence)*,[142] Butler-Sloss P considered that the prevailing preference for children's interests was entirely compatible with Art 8(2) of the European Convention

---

[134] It will be noted, however, that s 2 of the Child Support Act 1991 does require the Secretary of State or any child support officer to 'have regard to the welfare of any child likely to be affected by his decision'. See Ch 21.

[135] For the application of s 1(1) to more than one child, see Applying the paramountcy principle to more than one child, p 428.   [136] Law Com No 172 at para 3.12.   [137] [1988] AC 806.

[138] [1998] AC 806 at 812.   [139] [1998] AC 806 at 825.

[140] See in particular J Herring 'The Human Rights Act and the welfare principle in family law—conflicting or complementary?' [1999] CFLQ 223, discussed at Criticisms of the welfare principle, p 430. See also the trenchant criticism by J Fortin in *Children's Rights and the Developing Law* (2009, 3rd edn) 523.

[141] Academic speculation about the impact of the 1998 Act on the paramountcy principle was extensive. J Fortin 'The HRA's impact on litigation involving children and their families' [1999] CFLQ 237, for example, was concerned that the Convention would dilute the paramountcy principle. See also the analyses of J Herring 'The Welfare Principle and the Rights of Parents' in A Bainham, S Day Sclater and M Richards (eds) *What is a Parent?* (1999) 89 and 'The Human Rights Act and the welfare principle in family law—conflicting or complementary?' [1999] CFLQ 223; H Swindells 'Crossing The Rubicon—Family Law Post The Human Rights Act 1998' in E Butler-Sloss and S Cretney (eds) *Family Law Essays for the new Millennium* (2000) 55 at 62–6; A Bainham 'Children Law At The Millennium' in *Family Law Essays for the new Millennium*, 113 at 125–6, F Kaganas and C Piper 'Grandparents and contact: "rights or welfare" revisited' (2001) 15 Int Jo of Law Policy and the Family 250; S Choudry and H Fenwick 'Taking the rights of Parents and Children Seriously: Confronting the Welfare Principle under the Human Rights Act' (2005) 25 OJLS 453 and D Bonner, H Fenwick and S Harris-Short 'Judicial Approaches to the Human Rights Act' (2003) 52 ICLQ 549.

[142] *Re L (A Child) (Contact: Domestic Violence) ; Re V (A Child) (Contact: Domestic Violence); Re M (A Child) (Contact: Domestic Violence) ; Re H (Children) (Contact: Domestic Violence)* [2001] Fam 260 at 277.

on Human Rights. As she pointed out, in *Hendricks v Netherlands*[143] it was held that where there was a serious conflict between the interests of a child and one of his or her parents which could only be resolved to the disadvantage of one of them it was the child's interests that had to prevail under Art 8(2). As Butler Sloss P put it:

> The principle of the crucial importance of the best interests of the child has been upheld in all subsequent decisions of the European Court of Human Rights.

She pointed in particular to *Johansen v Norway*[144] in which the Court commented that 'the parent cannot be entitled under Article 8 of the Convention to have such measures taken as would harm the child's health and development'.

In *Payne v Payne*[145] Thorpe LJ similarly had no doubts as to the compatibility of the paramountcy principle with Convention. He observed:

> The acknowledgement of child welfare as paramount must be common to most if not all judicial systems within the Council of Europe. It is of course enshrined in Art 3(1) of the United Nations Convention on the Rights of the Child 1989. Accordingly the jurisprudence of the European Court of Human Rights inevitably recognises the paramountcy principle, albeit not expressed in the language of our domestic statute.

Accordingly, Thorpe LJ concluded:

> whilst the advent of the 1998 Act requires some revision of the judicial approach to conclusion, as a safeguard to an inadequate perception and application for a father's rights under arts 6 and 8, it requires no re-evaluation of the judge's primary task to evaluate and uphold the welfare of the child as the paramount consideration, despite its inevitable conflict with adult rights.

It is noticeable that by analysing the paramountcy principle in terms of prioritising children's welfare where it conflicts with parents' interests, both Butler-Sloss P and Thorpe LJ moved away from the traditional view that children's welfare should be the court's only concern which, as we have said, seems incompatible with human rights law. However, as Thorpe LJ said, this shift is only a semantic one and there seems little doubt that neither he nor Butler-Sloss P thought that the 1998 Act would cause an English court to reach a different decision than it would otherwise have done.[146]

As a matter of fact since these two decisions the European Court of Human Rights has seemingly moved closer to the English position, by commenting in *Yousef v Netherlands*:[147]

> that in judicial decisions where the rights under art 8 of parents and those of the child are at stake, the child's rights must be the paramount consideration. If any balancing of interests is necessary, the interests of the child must prevail . . .

---

[143] (1982) 5 EHRR 223. In fact this case was decided by the Commission and not, as suggested by Butler-Sloss P, the European Court of Human Rights.   [144] (1996) 23 EHRR 33, ECtHR.
[145] [2001] EWCA Civ 166 [2001] 1 FLR 1051 at [38] and [57].
[146] For a similar conclusion see A Bainham 'Protecting Children and their Rights' [2002] Fam Law 279 at 288.
[147] (2003) 36 EHRR 20 [2003] 1 FLR 210 at [73]. In *CF v Secretary of State for the Home Department* [2004] EWHC 111 (Fam) [2004] 2 FLR 517 at [103] Munby J referred to *Yousef* as establishing that the welfare principle was a 'core principle' of human rights law. It might be noted, however, that the Strasbourg Court conflated 'rights' and 'interests'.

This was the first time that the European Court of Human Rights expressly referred to the *paramountcy* of the child's rights and its decision confirms a trend towards greater emphasis on the predominance of children's rights under the Convention.[148] It is now common place for the Strasbourg Court to refer to the paramountcy of the child's welfare.[149]

Notwithstanding the apparent convergence of European human rights jurisprudence with English domestic case law, it can still be argued that there is a real difference between them. Put succinctly and to adopt the words of one commentator,[150] while the scales might apparently start even in the sense that both parents and children have rights under the European Convention, under English domestic law the scales are heavily weighted in favour of children. This difference of approach has been highlighted particularly by Herring.[151] Taking the example of seeking to deny a parent contact with his or her child, he argues that whereas under the Convention the starting point is the parent's right to contact and to justify its breach there must be clear and convincing evidence that the contact would infringe the rights of the child to such an extent as to make the infringement of the parent's right necessary and proportionate; under English domestic law the starting point is that contact is in the child's interests which can be rebutted by evidence that his or her welfare is not enhanced in the particular case. He argues that as a result less evidence is required to deny contact under domestic law than under Convention law and furthermore while it is a factual issue under the domestic law it is a legal issue under the Convention. Arguably, however, the sting has been taken out of this point following the introduction, by the Children and Families Act 2014, of the direction to courts 'to presume, unless the contrary is shown, that a parent's continued involvement in the life of the child will further that child's welfare.'[152]

Notwithstanding this interesting argument one suspects nevertheless that a properly arrived at domestic law outcome based on the paramountcy principle, as it is now understood, is unlikely to be held in breach of the Convention.[153]

---

[148] Compare the statement in *Yousef* with the earlier ones, eg in *W v Federal Republic of Germany* (1985) 50 D & R 219 where the European Commission held that national courts should take into consideration the interests of children; *Hendricks v Netherlands*, earlier, where the Commission referred to the interests of children predominating and *Hoppe v Germany* [2003] 1 FLR 384 at para [49] where the court referred to the interests of children being of 'particular importance'. For an analysis of other European Court decisions at the time, see A Vine 'Is the Paramountcy Principle Compatible with Article 8?' [2000] Fam Law 826 at 828–30.

[149] See, for example the Grand Chamber decision, *Neulinger and Shuruk v Switzerland* (2010) (App No 41615/07) [2011] 1 FLR 122, in which the Court said (at [135]) that 'there is a broad consensus—including in international law—in support of the idea that in all decisions concerning children their best interests must be paramount.' Ironically, this emphasis on children's welfare was misplaced in relation to the 1980 Hague Abduction Convention, see the discussion in Ch 26.

[150] A Bainham 'Family Rights in the Next Millennium' in (2000) 53 *Current Legal Problems* 473 at 489. In fact this comment was made in the context of a possible conflict between the Convention and the United Nations Convention on the Rights of the Child 1989, discussed at Comparison with the UN Convention, p 418.

[151] See 'The Human Rights Act and the welfare principle in family law—conflicting or complementary?' [1999] CFLQ 223 at 230ff and further developed in *Family Law* (2009, 4th edn) at 430–431.

[152] Section 1(2A) of the Children Act 1989, inserted by s 11(2) of the 2014 Act, discussed further at The section 1(2A) presumption, p 433.

[153] A Vine 'Is the Paramountcy Principle Compatible with Article 8?' [2000] Fam Law 826 at 830, considers it significant that in *Scott v United Kingdom* [2000] 1 FLR 958 (in which inter alia a complaint was made under Art 8 about the dismissal of a mother's application for increased contact under the Children Act 1989, s 34 (discussed in Ch 18)), the European Court not only made no criticism of the paramountcy principle but concluded on the facts of the case that a decision based on the welfare of the child fell well within the domestic court's margin of appreciation.

Before leaving the question of the interrelationship between the paramountcy principle and human rights a further issue needs to be considered. The foregoing discussion assumes the application of the paramountcy principle but, as we discuss later, s 1(1) only applies where the child's upbringing is directly in issue. There will, however, be cases falling outside s 1(1) yet still engage a child's Art 8 rights and the question is how the child's interests should then be weighed. A case in point is *ZH (Tanzania) v Secretary of State for the Home Department*,[154] which concerned a mother's deportation. Upon the mother's application that her removal from the country would amount to a disproportionate interference with the family's Art 8 right to respect for private and family life, the issue before the Supreme Court[155] was what weight should be given to the best interest of the children who were affected by the decision. In answering this question Baroness Hale observed that there is a distinction between questions with respect to the upbringing of a child and a decision which may affect them. In this latter instance, of which this case was an example, the child's welfare, though important is nevertheless not paramount. This means that in Convention terms in making the proportionality assessment under Art 8 while the child's best interests must be a primary consideration and must therefore be considered first, they can be outweighed by the cumulative effect of other considerations.

(b) Comparison with the UN Convention

Section 1(1) of the 1989 Act might be compared with Art 3(1) of the UN Convention on the Rights of the Child 1989 (to which the UK is a party) which states:

> In all actions concerning children, whether undertaken by public or private social welfare institutions, courts of law, administrative authorities or legislative bodies, the best interests of the child shall be a primary consideration.

This Article provides an international obligation[156] to apply the 'best interests of the child' test and as such is clearly similar to the paramountcy test under s 1(1) of the 1989 Act.[157] However, the enjoinder to regard the child's best interests as a *primary* consideration is

---

[154] [2011] UKSC 4 [2011] 2 AC 166, on which see J Fortin 'Are Children's Best Interests Really Best?' (2011) 74 MLR 947. See also *Zoumbas v Secrtetary of State for the Home Department* [2014] UKSC 74 [2014] 1 FCR 141.

[155] By the time of the hearing before the Supreme Court, the Secretary of State accepted that on the facts it would be disproportionate to order the mother's removal.

[156] As a matter of strict law since the UN Convention has not been incorporated by statute into English domestic law (though note the different position in Wales with regard to the Rights of Children and Young Persons (Wales) Measure 2011), courts are not bound to apply it: see *British Airways v Laker Airways* [1985] AC 58, HL. Nevertheless in *Smith v Secretary of State for Work and Pensions* [2006] 1 WLR 2024, at [78], Baroness Hale commented 'Even if an international treaty has not been incorporated into domestic law, our domestic legislation has to be construed as far as possible so as to comply with the international obligations which we have undertaken. When two interpretations . . . are possible, the interpretation chosen should be that which better complies with the commitment to the welfare of children which this country has made in ratifying the United Nations Convention on the Rights of the Child'. In *ZH (Tanzania) v Secretary of State for the Home Department* [2011] UKSC 3 [2011] 2 AC 166 at [23], her Ladyship referred to Art 3 of the UN Convention (that the best interests of the child is a primary consideration) was a binding obligation in international law and that 'the spirit, if not the precise language, has also been translated into our national law' by the Children Act 2004 s 11. Note also Lord Neuberger SCJ's comment in *Re B (A Child) (Care Proceedings: Threshold Criteria)* [2013] UKSC 33 [2013] 1 WLR 1911 at [73] that the Adoption and Children Act 2002 (and, implicitly, the Children Act 1989) should be construed and applied bearing in mind the provisions of UNCRC.

[157] Indeed in *Payne v Payne* [2001] EWCA Civ 168 [2001] 1 FLR 1052 at (38) Thorpe LJ went as far as to say that the paramountcy principle was 'enshrined' by Art 3(1).

not as strong as to treat the child's welfare as the *paramount* consideration. As Baroness Hale put it in *ZH (Tanzania) v Secretary of State for the Home Department*[158] 'a primary consideration is not the same as the primary consideration, still less as the paramount consideration'. On the other hand, by applying both to administrative authorities and legislative bodies, Art 3(1) is wider than s 1(1) which, as we discuss shortly, only applies in court proceedings.

Notwithstanding these differences both in the wording and apparent application it is evident from *ZH (Tanzania) v Secretary of State for the Home Department*, in particular, that in application at least, s 1(1), and Art 3 are perfectly compatible. In relation to the latter, Baroness Hale cited with approval[159] the summary contained in the *Guidelines on Determining the Best Interests of the Child* (May 2008), para 1.1, that:

> the best interests must be the determining factor for specific action, notably adoption (Article 21) and separation of a child from parents against their will (Article 9);
> The best interests must a primary consideration for all other actions affecting children whether undertaken by public or private social welfare, institution, courts of law, administrative authorities or legislative bodies (Article 3).

In other words, in disputes directly concerning his or her upbringing, the child's welfare is the determinative factor but in matters affecting the child Art 3 operates so as to make the child's welfare a primary consideration but not the sole one. In this latter respect the Court quoted with approval[160] the High Court of Australia's view[161] that:

> A decision-maker with an eye to the principle enshrined in the Convention would be looking to the best interests of the children as a primary consideration, asking whether the force of any other consideration outweighed it.

(c) When the paramountcy principle applies

As s 1(1) states, the paramountcy principle applies whenever a court is called upon to determine any question about the child's upbringing or the administration of his property. Section 1(1) is therefore of general application and is not restricted to Children Act proceedings. It is established, for example that the provision is applicable to wardship proceedings,[162] including non-Convention[163] child abduction cases,[164] cases brought under the 1980 Hague Abduction Convention, and to the exercise of the High Court's inherent jurisdiction.[165]

As discussed in Chapter 9, *J v C* establishes that the paramountcy principle applies equally to disputes between parents and other individuals, as well as to disputes between parents.[166] So far as Children Act proceedings are concerned, as the Department of

---

[158] [2011] UKSC 3 [2011] 2 AC 166, at [25].   [159] [2011] UKSC 4 [2011] 2 AC 166, at [25].

[160] [2011] UKSC 3 [2011] 2 AC 166, at [26].

[161] *Minister for Immigration and Ethnic Affairs v Teoh* (1995) 183 CLR 273, at [39].

[162] *J v C* [1970] AC 668, HL, discussed in Ch 9. Wardship is discussed in Ch 20.

[163] That is, cases not governed by either the 1980 European Custody Convention or the 1980 Hague Abduction Convention: see Ch 26.

[164] See *Re J (A Child) (Custody Rights: Jurisdiction)* [2005] UKHL 40 [2005] 3 WLR 14, discussed in Ch 26.

[165] See *Re A (Children) (Conjoined Twins: Surgical Separation)* [2001] Fam 147; *Re T (a minor) (wardship: medical treatment)* [1997] 1 All ER 906, CA; and *Re W (A Minor) (Medical Treatment: Court's Jurisdiction)* [1993] Fam 64, CA.

[166] Though this is not to say that parentage is irrelevant, see *Re G (Children) (Residence: Same Sex Partner)* [2006] UKHL 43 [2006] 1 WLR 2305 at [30], per Baroness Hale, discussed further at Emotional needs, pp 404ff.

Health's Guidance on the 1989 Act states,[167] it applies *whenever* a court is considering whether to make a s 8 order (ie regardless of who the parties[168] are, what the issue is[169] or in which proceedings the issue is raised).[170] It also applies when considering whether to make a parental responsibility order under s 4[171] and whether to give leave under s 13 either to change a child's surname[172] or to remove a child from the United Kingdom.[173]

With regard to public law proceedings under the Children Act, it is clear that the paramountcy principle applies at the welfare stage of care proceedings,[174] ie *after* deciding whether or not the statutory threshold under s 31 has been crossed. It also applies to deciding whether to make contact orders under s 34[175] and to applications to discharge care orders under s 39.[176] It has also been held that the paramountcy principle applies to deciding whether leave should be given to a local authority to withdraw their application for a care order.[177]

(d) When the paramountcy principle does not apply

The paramountcy principle is not of unlimited application.[178] It does not apply outside the context of court litigation, and even where an issue is before a court it will only apply provided the child's upbringing or the administration of his property is *directly* in question. In other words, as Baroness Hale put it,[179] questions with respect to the upbringing of a child must be distinguished from other decisions that affect them. Even if such issues are directly in question, the paramountcy principle only applies if it has not been expressly or impliedly excluded either by the 1989 Act itself or by some other statute.

---

[167] *Guidance and Regulations*, Vol 1, *Court Orders* (1991), para 2.57. This comment is not repeated in the revised Guidance (2008) produced by the Department for Children, Families and Schools.

[168] See eg *Re S (Contact: Grandparents)* [1996] 1 FLR 158 at 164 per Wall J, which involved an application for contact by a grandparent.

[169] Including, for example, the child's religious upbringing, see *Re G (Education: Religious Upbringing)* [2012] EWCA Civ 1233 [2013] 1 FLR 677, and determining whether a boy should be ritually circumcised: *Re J (Specific Issue Orders: Muslim Upbringing and Circumcision)* [1999] 2 FLR 678, decision upheld on appeal: [2000] 1 FLR 571.

[170] See *Re RJ (Fostering: Person Disqualified)* [1999] 1 FLR 605, CA, order made in wardship proceedings, see further Ch 20, Use in public law cases, p 755.

[171] Per Butler Sloss LJ in *Re H (Parental Responsibility)* [1998] 1 FLR 855 at 659. This issue, however, may not be beyond argument: see Balcombe LJ in *Re G (A Minor) (Parental Responsibility Order)* [1994] 1 FLR 504 at 507–8 and *Re E (Parental Responsibility)* [1994] 2 FLR 709 at 715 who pointed out that it was arguable that such applications do not concern the upbringing of the child.

[172] Per Wilson J in *Re B (Change of Surname)* [1996] 1 FLR 791 at 793, CA. The paramountcy principle equally applies to applications to change names under s 33(7), see *Re S (Change of Surname)* [1999] 1 FLR 672 at 674, per Thorpe LJ.

[173] *Payne v Payne* [2001] EWCA Civ 166 [2001] 1 FLR 1052, per Thorpe LJ.

[174] See eg *Re O and another (Minors) (Care: Preliminary Hearing); Re B (A Minor)* [2003] UKHL 18 [2004] 1 AC 523 at [23] per Lord Nicholls.

[175] *Re T (Minors) (Termination of Contact: discharge of order)* [1997] 1 All ER 65, CA and *Re B (Minors) (Termination of Contact: Paramount Consideration)* [1993] Fam 301, CA.

[176] See eg *Re T and E (Proceedings: Conflicting Interests)* [1995] 1 FLR 581.

[177] *Southwark London Borough v B* [1993] 2 FLR 559, CA and applied in *WSCC v M, F, X, Y and Z* [2010] EWHC 1914 (Fam) [2011] 1 FLR 188 and *London Borough of Redbridge v B, C and A (A Child)* [2011] EWHC 517 (Fam) [2011] 2 FLR 117. Aliter on applications concerning whether someone should cease to be a party or be served with notice of proceedings see eg *Re W (Discharge of Party to Proceedings)* [1997] 1 FLR 128. The paramountcy principle equally applies to determining whether to stay an order: *Re M (application for stay of order)* [1996] 3 FCR 185, CA.

[178] See N Lowe 'The House of Lords and the welfare principle' in C Bridge (ed) *Family Law towards the Millennium—Essays for P M Bromley* (1997) 125 at 150ff.

[179] *ZH (Tanzania) v Secretary of State for the Home Department* [2011] UKSC 4 [2011] 2 AC 166, at [25].

The paramountcy principle does not apply outside the context of litigation

The paramountcy principle only applies, if at all, in the course of litigation. Unlike Art 3(1) of the UN Convention on the Rights of the Child it has no *direct* application to institutions (such as prison authorities),[180] administrative authorities (such as local authorities)[181] or legislative bodies. Furthermore it does not apply to parents or other individuals with respect to their day-to-day or even long-term decisions affecting the child. As one commentary has put it:[182]

> It can hardly be argued that parents, in taking family decisions affecting a child, are bound to ignore completely their own interests, the interests of other members of the family and, possibly, outsiders. This would be a wholly undesirable, as well as an unrealistic objective.

Accordingly, parents are not bound to consider their children's welfare in deciding, for example, whether to make a career move, to move house or whether to separate or divorce.[183]

It is also established that the paramountcy principle does not govern the application of Part III of the 1989 Act (which deals with support services for children provided by local authorities).[184] As Butler-Sloss LJ said in *Re M (A Minor) (Secure Accommodation Order):*[185]

> The framework of Part III of the Act is structured to cast upon the local authority duties and responsibilities for children in its area and being looked after. The general duty[186] of a local authority to safeguard and promote the child's welfare is not the same as that imposed upon the court in s 1(1) placing welfare as the paramount consideration.

In Butler-Sloss LJ's view[187] s 1 was not designed to be applied to Part III of the Act. Accordingly, in deciding pursuant to s 17(1) what level of services to provide for children in need in their area, local authorities are not obliged to treat the welfare of individual children as their paramount consideration,[188] nor, similarly, when deciding pursuant to s 22 how best to discharge their duties in relation to children looked after by them,[189] though in this latter instance the welfare of the child remains an important consideration.[190]

---

[180] See eg *R (P) v Secretary of State for the Home Department, R (Q) v Secretary of State for Home Department* [2001] EWCA Civ 1151 [2001] 1 WLR 2002 at [89] per Lord Phillips MR.

[181] See eg *R (Howard League for Penal Reform) v Secretary of State For The Home Department)* [2002] EWHC 2497 (Admin) [2003] 1 FLR 484 at [35], per Munby J.

[182] A Bainham and S Gilmore *Children: The Modern Law* (2013, 4th edn) 70.

[183] See B Dickens 'The Modern Function and Limits of Parental Rights' (1981) 97 LQR 462 at 471, who asserts (correctly, it is submitted) that parental responsibility is not to do positive good but to avoid harm.

[184] Part III is discussed in Ch 15.

[185] [1995] Fam 108 at 115. An analysis applied by Black LJ in *R (on the application of O) v Hammersmith and Fulham London Borough Council* [2011] EWCA Civ 925 [2012] 1 WLR 1057 at [49]–[50].

[186] Pursuant to the Children Act 1989 s 17(1) and s 22(3).

[187] [1995] Fam 108 at 115, expressly disagreeing with comments to the contrary in Vols 1 and 4 of the Department of Health, *Guidance and Regulations* (1991) on the 1989 Act.

[188] It is generally thought that s 17 is so phrased as to avoid the duty being applied to individual children: see Ch 15, General duty to children in need, p 560 n [51].

[189] Section 22(6) expressly states that the need to protect members of the public from serious injury overrides any duty even to promote and safeguard the interests of any individual child, let alone treating that child's welfare as the paramount consideration. See also *R (Johns and another) v Derby City Council (Equality and Human Rights Commission Intervening)* [2011] EWHC 375 (Admin) [2011] 1 FLR 2094 at [71], per Munby LJ.

[190] Per Charles J in *Re P (Children Act 1989, ss 22 and 26: Local Authority Compliance)* [2000] 2 FLR 910 at 923.

The paramountcy principle does not apply to issues only indirectly concerning the child

Pre-Children Act authority

An important limitation on the application of the paramountcy principle established by the House of Lords in *S v S, W v Official Solicitor*[191] is that it only applies where the child's upbringing or the administration of his property etc is *directly* in issue. In *S v S* the court was asked to make what was then a blood test direction for the purpose of determining paternity. It had been submitted that no direction should be made unless it could be shown to be in the child's interest that there should be such a test. In other words, the court was bound to apply the paramountcy principle. Rejecting that submission, the House of Lords unanimously held that the correct approach was for the court to make a blood test direction unless it could be shown to be against the child's interests to do so. In Lord MacDermott's view what the court was being asked to do was to exercise its protective rather than its custodial jurisdiction, because the question raised:[192]

> . . . is quite distinct from the question of custody and other questions mentioned in s 1 of the Guardianship of Infants Act. It is true that in deciding as to the custody of a child its welfare may depend on the weighing and assessment of various factors including the rights and wishes of the parents and that the question of paternity may therefore not only arise but be very relevant. But that is not to make the question of paternity a question of custody. It is only part of the process in deciding the ultimate and paramount question, namely, what is best for the welfare of the child.

This distinction between issues directly and indirectly concerning the child's upbringing was adopted by the majority in *Richards v Richards*,[193] in which an application made in divorce proceedings by a mother to exclude her husband from the matrimonial home was held not to be governed by the paramountcy principle. Lord Hailsham LC said:[194]

> In my view the Guardianship of Minors Act criterion is to be applied only in proceedings of the type specified in the section, ie proceedings in which custody, upbringing, or the proprietary jurisdiction implied by s 1(b) fall to be decided as a matter *directly* in issue . . . (Emphasis added.)

Richards vindicates Sir John Pennycuick's view in *Re X (A Minor) (Wardship): Jurisdiction)*[195] that an application to restrain the publication of a book containing salacious details of a child's dead father, on the grounds that it would be harmful to the child, was not governed by the paramountcy principle because the subject-matter only indirectly concerned the child's upbringing.

In summary, what *S v S* established and *Richards v Richards* confirmed was that:

(i) the paramountcy principle only applies when the child's upbringing etc is directly in issue;

(ii) even where the paramountcy principle does not apply, the court retains a protective jurisdiction to prevent a child from suffering harm; but

---

[191] [1972] AC 24, on which see the extensive analysis by A Bainham 'Welfare, Truth and Justice: the Children of Extra-marital Liaisons' in S Gilmore, J Herring and R Probert (eds) *Landmark Cases in Family Law* (2011) ch 7.   [192] [1972] AC 24 at 50G. See also Lord Hodson at 58C–D and G–H.
[193] [1984] AC 174, HL.   [194] At 203H. See also Lord Brandon at 223F.
[195] [1975] Fam 47, CA.

(iii) in exercising the latter jurisdiction, the child's welfare is not the only or necessarily the most important consideration to be taken into account.

Post-Children Act authority

It is clear that s 1(1) of the 1989 Act only applies where the child's upbringing is directly in issue. It was on this basis that it was held by the Supreme Court in *ZH (Tanzania) v Secretary of State for the Home Department*[196] that the child's welfare was not paramount in determining the lawfulness of immigration, asylum, deportation or removal decisions concerning the parents. Similarly, in *R (P) v Secretary of State for the Home Department; R (Q) v Secretary of State for the Home Department*[197] the paramountcy principle was held to have no application to the lawfulness of prison policy to separate children from their imprisoned mothers once they reached 18 months. It was partly on this basis that it was held in *Re A (Minors) (Residence Orders: Leave to Apply)*[198] that s 1(1) does not apply when determining whether to grant adults[199] leave to apply for a s 8 order, since, in Balcombe LJ's words, 'in granting or refusing an application for leave to apply for a section 8 order the court is not determining a question with respect to the upbringing of the child concerned. That question only arises when the court hears the substantive application'.

Other cases in which it has been held that the paramountcy principle does not apply include: determining whether to give directions for blood (now scientific) testing to determine parentage;[200] determining whether an unmarried father should be served with notice of care proceedings;[201] resolving a mother's application that the father cease to be party to the discharge of care proceedings;[202] considering whether a parent be committed to prison for a flagrant breach of a court order concerning a child;[203] determining whether to issue a witness summons against a child;[204] making directions for interim assessments under s 38(6) of the Children Act 1989;[205] resolving a dispute between a birth mother and an adoptive mother over the disposal of their deceased adult child's remains;[206] determining whether costs should be given in family proceedings;[207] questioning, in judicial review proceedings, the activities of a local authority in relation to a

---

[196] [2011] UKSC 4 [2011] 2 AC 166   [197] [2001] EWCA Civ 1151 [2001] 1 WLR 2002.

[198] [1992] Fam 182 at 191G–H. It has been similarly held that the paramountcy principle does not apply to applications for leave under s 91(17): *Re T (Minor) (Termination of Contact: discharge of order)* [1997] 1 All ER 65, CA.

[199] According to Charles J in *Re S (Contact: Application By Sibling)* [1998] 2 FLR 897, Stuart-White J in *Re C (Residence: Child's Application for Leave)* [1995] 1 FLR 927 and Booth J in *Re SC (A Minor) (Leave to Seek Residence Order)* [1994] 1 FLR 96 a similar position obtains in respect of children seeking leave; cf *Re C (A Minor) (Leave to Seek Section 8 Orders)* [1994] 1 FLR 26, per Johnson J, who thought the paramountcy principle did apply.

[200] *Re H (A Minor) (Blood Tests: Parental Rights)* [1997] Fam 89, CA.

[201] *Re X (Care: Notice of Proceedings)* [1996] 1 FLR 186.

[202] *Re W (Discharge of Party to Proceedings)* [1997] 1 FLR 128.

[203] *A v N (Committal: Refusal of Contact)* [1997] 1 FLR 533, CA. It is similarly inapplicable when considering whether to make enforcement orders and order for financial compensation for breaches of contact orders: see respectively ss 11L(7) and 11O(14) of the Children Act 1989, inserted by the Children and Adoption Act 2006, see *Re LW (Enforcement and Committal) ; CPL v CH-W and Others* [2010] EWCA Civ 1253, [2011] 1 FLR 1095.

[204] *Re P (Witness Summons)* [1997] 2 FLR 447, CA. See also *R v Highbury Corner Magistrates Court, ex p Deering* [1997] 1 FLR 683.

[205] Per Holman J in *Re M (Residential Assessment Directions)* [1998] 2 FLR 371 at 381–2 and per Charles J in *Re P (Children Act 1989, ss 22 and 26: Local Authority Compliance)* [2000] 2 FLR 910 at 923.

[206] Per Hale J in *Buchanan v Milton* [1999] 2 FLR 844 at 857.

[207] Per Wilson J in *Q v Q (Costs: Summary Assessment)* [2002] 2 FLR 668 at [14].

child;[208] and determining whether or not to make return orders under the 1980 Hague Abduction Convention.[209]

Notwithstanding that this basic distinction is firmly established, it can still be a matter of fine judgment as to what amounts to 'direct' and 'indirect' for these purposes. There are three areas in particular in which the application of the paramountcy principle has proved problematic, namely with regard to publicity, procedural issues and to appeals.

Publicity

In *Re S (A Child) (Identification: Restrictions on Publication)*,[210] the House of Lords held that since the implementation of the Human Rights Act 1998 the foundation of the jurisdiction to protect children from publicity derives from the European Convention on Human Rights and involves the balancing of the right to respect for private and family life under Art 8 and the right to freedom of expression under Art 10. Consequently it was no longer necessary to consider the preceding case law about the existence and scope of the inherent jurisdiction of the High Court[211] to restrict publicity to protect children. However, such case-law was thought not to be wholly irrelevant to the ultimate balancing exercise to be carried out under the Human Rights Convention. The requirement to balance Art 8 rights with Art 10 rights means that the child's welfare cannot be the paramount consideration and indeed in *Re S* itself the Lords upheld the decision not to grant an injunction prohibiting the identification of the defendant in a criminal trial charged with the murder of her elder son to protect her younger son from harm. In other words the younger child's welfare was *not* paramount (ie s 1(1) of the 1989 Act did not apply). Having to balance the child's Art 8 rights with those of freedom of expression under Art 10 does not inevitably mean that publicity will never be restrained.[212] Indeed in the first post-*Re S* decision, *A Local Authority v W, L, W, T and R (By the Children's Guardian)*[213] an injunction was granted. A mother of two children was awaiting sentence having pleaded guilty to a charge that she had knowingly infected the father of one of the children with HIV. Both children were in foster care and the elder (who was not HIV positive) attended a nursery away in an area where her mother's identity was not known. The applicant local authority, fearing that if publicity was given to the identity and HIV status of the mother that could give rise to a general outcry at the nursery and also make it more difficult to find alternative carers for the children, successfully sought an injunction restraining the publication of the parents' identity in connection with the criminal proceedings and of the details of the nursery placements.

But having to balance Art 8 and Art 10 rights in fact reflected the line generally taken previously, namely, that since the curbing of publicity (even that directly concerning the child) only indirectly concerns the child's upbringing, the child's welfare was not paramount but had instead to be weighed in the balance with the freedom of the press. The *Re S* analysis, however, does call into question the line taken in at least two earlier decisions, namely, *R v Central Independent Television plc*[214] and *Re Z (A Minor) (Identification: Restrictions on Publication)*.[215] In the former it was held that, if the allegedly harmful publication does not relate to the care and upbringing of children over whose welfare the court is exercising a supervisory role, then not only is the child's welfare not paramount

---

[208] Per Black LJ in *R (on the application of O) v Hammersmith and Fulham London Borough Council* [2011] EWCA Civ 925 [2012] 1 WLR 1057 at [51].

[209] *Re E (Children) (Abduction: Custody Appeal)* [2011] UKSC 27 [2012] 1 AC 144.

[210] [2004] UKHL 47 [2005] 1 AC 593.

[211] The High Court's inherent jurisdiction is discussed in Ch 20.

[212] In this regard note might be taken of cl 6 of the Press Complaints Commission's Code of Practice for Journalists which is designed to protect the welfare of children.

[213] [2005] EWHC 1564 (Fam) [2006] 1 FLR 1, per Potter P.   [214] [1994] Fam 192, CA.

[215] [1997] Fam 1, CA.

but it is not relevant at all. This approach could presumably be justified in post *Re S* terms by saying that in such cases the child's Art 8 rights are not engaged at all and therefore only Art 10 has to be considered. More problematic, however, is *Re Z* which was a case in which the mother wanted her child, in Ward LJ's words, 'to perform for the making of the film' about her treatment at the unit dealing with special educational needs. It was held that because, unlike the other cases, the issue was concerned with a parent's exercise of parental responsibility in waiving the child's right to confidentiality with respect to her education the child's welfare was paramount and that therefore the film should not be broadcast. Whether this analysis can survive *Re S*, remains to be seen.[216]

Procedural issues

On one view it may be said that the paramountcy principle can also apply to procedural issues. It is arguable that in deciding that a parent did not have a right to see the Official Solicitor's report compiled in connection with an application to look after the child, and that the court had the power to withhold it from the parties, the House of Lords in *Official Solicitor v K*[217] was applying such a principle.[218] But an alternative analysis[219] is that in certain instances the courts will not rigidly apply certain procedural rules designed to provide overall justice to litigants if in a particular case they are satisfied that to do so would be harmful to the individual child concerned. Such an analysis can be justified by saying that disclosure only indirectly concerned the child's upbringing and is arguably supported by another House of Lords decision, *Re L (A Minor) (Police Investigation: Privilege)*.[220] In that case, to assist an investigation as to whether a criminal offence had been committed, the police sought leave to have sight of a medical report written by an expert engaged by the mother in the course of care proceedings and filed with the court.

Ordering the disclosure Lord Jauncey (giving the majority judgment) drew a distinction between privilege attaching to communications between solicitor and client and that attaching to reports by third parties prepared on the instructions of a client for the purposes of litigation. Whilst the former, perhaps properly referred to as 'legal professional privilege', was absolute,[221] the latter, better described as 'litigation privilege', was a creature of adversarial procedure and as such had no place in proceedings under the Children Act 1989. In drawing this conclusion Lord Jauncey had in mind the approach of *Official Solicitor v K*, namely that the court should not disable itself from being able to safeguard and promote the interests of children involved in Children Act proceedings by rigidly applying procedural rules. As he put it:[222]

> ... if litigation privilege were to apply ... it would have the effect of subordinating the welfare of the child to the interests of the mother in preserving its confidentiality. This would appear to frustrate the primary object of the Act.

---

[216] In *A Local Authority v W, L, W, T and R (By the Children's Guardian)* [2005] EWHC 1564 (Fam) [2006] 1 FLR 1 at [24] Potter P referred specifically to *Re Z* as having limited value but this was in respect of its analysis of the protective powers of the court under its inherent jurisdiction.   [217] [1965] AC 201, HL.

[218] See the headnote statement at [1965] AC 202, 'that the paramount consideration of the Chancery Division in exercising its jurisdiction over wards of court was the welfare of the infants'. The headnote to the All England report is in similar terms: see [1963] 3 All ER 191.

[219] See N Lowe 'The House of Lords and the welfare principle' in C Bridge (ed) *Family Law towards the Millennium—Essays for P M Bromley* (1997) at 153–8.

[220] [1997] AC 16. See also *Re D (Minors) (Adoption Reports: Confidentiality)* [1996] AC 593, HL, which establishes that non-disclosure of reports should be the exception not the norm and should be ordered only when the case for doing so is compelling.

[221] Following the House of Lords' ruling in *R v Derby Magistrates' Court, ex p B* [1996] AC 487.

[222] [1997] AC at 27F.

Having ruled that the court had a discretion to order disclosure even to non-parties, the majority could not fault the trial judge's exercise of discretion. In this respect it should be noted that Bracewell J expressly said:[223]

> The application before me does not relate to the upbringing of the child and, therefore, is not governed by s 1 of the Children Act 1989. Welfare must be weighed, but it can be displaced in some circumstances. The interests of the child or children must always be very important factors, since it is the essence of the proceedings to protect those interests and the reason why the courts have imposed the curtains of privacy. There is the competing claim of public interest in the due administration of justice which requires police forces to make informed decisions before deciding whether to prosecute.

Balancing these interests, Bracewell J came down in favour of disclosure and her approach, endorsed by the House of Lords, is a classic exposition of the exercise of the protective jurisdiction which, as the learned judge pointed out, was relevant here because disclosure did not directly concern the child's upbringing.

The minority (Lords Nicholls and Mustill) did not accept the separate distinction of litigation privilege nor that there was no element of an adversarial character in Children Act proceedings. Lord Nicholls considered that parents and other parties should be entitled to a fair hearing notwithstanding any special role of judges in family proceedings. As he strikingly put it,[224] 'The paramountcy principle must not be permitted to become a loose cannon destroying all else around it.' With respect, this seems to be going too far: the reason for relaxing the procedural rule was not the paramountcy principle but rather not to prevent courts in general from being able to safeguard and promote children's interests as set out in the Children Act. In making this decision the child's interests have to be weighed against other interests. Such a process can hardly be described a loose cannon.

Appeals

It is implicit in *Re L* that not all procedural rules can be changed even to protect children— so for example, legal professional privilege attaching to solicitor-client communications is absolute. The same is arguably true for the rules of appeal though the issue has become complicated following the Supreme Court ruling in *Re B (A Child) (Care Proceedings: Threshold Criteria)*.[225] We return to this ruling in later chapters. Suffice to say here that while the appellate court's enquiries may differ according to the context and in particular to whether the appealed decision was an evaluative one (as in determining whether the statutory threshold under s 31 has been crossed or whether care order was 'proportionate' as in *Re B*) or discretionary (as in determining with which of two parents a child is to live)[226] the basic function is one of review with intervention being justified only if the original decision can be shown to be 'wrong'.[227] In other words, the appellate court is not called upon to make its own independent evaluation of the child's welfare but to consider the propriety of the lower court's decision. Consequently in determining an appeal the paramountcy principle does not apply.[228]

---

[223] [1995] 1 FLR 999 at 1007.   [224] [1997] AC at 13B.   [225] [2013] UKSC 33 [2013] 1 WLR 1911.

[226] As in *G v G (Minors: Custody Appeal)* [1985] 1 WLR 647, HL. But note the comments on this by the NZ Supreme Court in *Kacem v Bashir* [2011] 2 NZLR 1.

[227] In *Re B* there seemed to be a general disapproval of the former test espoused *by G v G*, of having to show that the trial judge was 'plainly wrong', though it is a matter of some doubt whether that remains the test when appealing a discretionary judgment.

[228] Indeed in *G v G* the House of Lords expressly rejected the argument that the paramountcy principle was applicable to appeals.

Perhaps the most convincing reason for reaching this conclusion, which after all in practice still leaves a wide area of discretion to the appellate court, is the point made by Lord Fraser in *G v G* that:[229]

> ... the desirability of putting an end to litigation, which applies to all classes of cases, is particularly strong because the longer legal proceedings last, the more are the children, whose welfare is at stake, likely to be disturbed by the uncertainty.

Put in theoretical terms, the issue of when an appellate court should intervene does not directly concern a child's upbringing and hence the paramountcy principle does not apply. Furthermore, as the normal rules of appeal do not inhibit the courts from performing their proper role of safeguarding the child's interests, there is no need to provide special rules.

Areas of uncertainty

There is uncertainty as to whether the paramountcy principle applies to determining whether to give leave to interview children involved in court proceedings with a view to preparing an adult's defence in criminal proceedings.[230] There is also uncertainty concerning the applicability of the paramountcy principle to the determination of *forum conveniens*, though the predominant view now is that it does not apply.[231]

The paramountcy principle does not apply if excluded by other statutory provisions

Even where a child's upbringing is directly in issue the court is not always bound by the paramountcy principle. It clearly will not be if statute expressly provides an alternative test or expressly excludes its operation. For example, the child's welfare is expressed to be the first consideration in proceedings relating to the adjustment of property and financial matters on divorce,[232] while s 105(1) of the Children Act 1989 expressly excludes maintenance from the definition of child's upbringing and so disapplies the paramountcy principle.[233]

The paramountcy principle can be *impliedly* excluded by statute. For example, it has been held that the paramountcy principle is inconsistent with the duties of local authorities under s 25(1)(b) of the Children Act 1989 and therefore has no application to the question of making secure accommodation orders.[234] Similarly, the criteria set out in

---

[229] [1985] 1 WLR 647 at 652A. But for an excellent critique of this case see J Eekelaar 'Custody Appeals' (1985) 48 MLR 704.

[230] In *Re F (Specific Issue: Child Interview)* [1995] 1 FLR 819, CA, Waite LJ was prepared to assume that s 1(1) of the 1989 Act applied whereas in *Re M (Care: Leave to Interview Child)* [1995] 1 FLR 825 Hale J held that the child's welfare was not the overriding consideration. Relying on the cases concerning the issue of witness summons R White, C Parr and N Lowe, *The Children Act in Practice* (2nd edn, 1995) at 2.23 consider that Hale J's view is to be preferred.

[231] See the review by Munby J in *Re V (Forum Conveniens)* [2004] EWHC 2663 (Fam) [2005] 1 FLR 718 at [18]–[19], preferring the views of Thorpe J in *Re S (Residence Order: Forum Conveniens)* [1995] 1 FLR 314 at 325 and Bracewell J in *Re D (Stay of Children Act Proceedings)* [2003] EWHC 565 (Fam) [2003] 2 FLR 1159 at [21] to those of Waite J in *H v H (Minors) (Forum Conveniens)* [1995] 1 FLR 314 at 324–5. In Scotland, Lord Maclean also preferred Thorpe J's analysis, see *B v B* 1998 SLT 1245 at 1246. *Re S* was also followed by Wilson J in *M v M (Stay of Proceedings: Return of Children)* [2005] EWHC 1159 (Fam) [2006] 1 FLR 138.

[232] By the Matrimonial Causes Act 1973 s 25(1), for the application of which see *N v N (Consent Order: Variation)* [1993] 2 FLR 868, CA and *Suter v Suter and Jones* [1987] Fam 111, CA, discussed in Ch 22. Before the Adoption and Children Act 2002 the child's welfare was only treated as the first consideration in adoption proceedings: Adoption Act 1976 s 6.

[233] This means that s 1(1) has no application to court applications for maintenance (insofar as they are still permitted under the Child Support Act 1991: see Ch 21) and probably has no application to proceedings for lump sums or property orders for the child under Sch 1 to the 1989 Act; cf *K v H (Child Maintenance)* [1993] 2 FLR 61.

[234] *Re M (A Minor) (Secure Accommodation Order)* [1995] Fam 108, CA. Secure accommodation is discussed in Ch 15.

s 10(9) for determining whether to grant adults leave to apply for s 8 orders have been held to exclude the application of the paramountcy principle.[235] It is also clear that while the paramountcy principle applies in proceedings under Parts IV and V of the 1989 Act, it will only come into play provided the applicant can satisfy the court that the preconditions for a care order or for an emergency protection order have been made out.[236] As Bainham pointed out:[237]

> ... the more limited application of the welfare principle in care proceedings reflects the need to set limits to the power of the state to intervene in the family by defining more specifically the circumstances in which this is permissible while in other areas the differing weighting of the child's welfare is the mechanism whereby Parliament stipulates the relative importance to be attached to the often conflicting interests of children and adults.

It has been said that the jurisdictional question of whether the future of children should be decided in one part of the United Kingdom rather than another is determined by statute[238] and that their welfare is not the paramount consideration in reaching that decision.[239]

In other cases, it is the whole scheme of legislation rather than a specific provision that impliedly excludes the paramountcy principle. The courts have refused, for example, to apply the paramountcy principle so as to interfere with discretionary powers clearly vested by Parliament in another body or court. Hence it is clearly established that the principle cannot be invoked to interfere with the discretionary powers vouchsafed to local authorities to look after and manage children in their care,[240] nor to interfere with the discretionary power vested in the immigration service.[241]

(e) Applying the paramountcy principle to more than one child

An inherent difficulty in applying the paramountcy principle is in cases involving two or more children with conflicting interests. This issue can arise either where the applicant is a child or where the application concerns siblings.

Child-parents and babies

The leading case is *Birmingham City Council v H (A Minor)*[242] where a 15-year-old child and her baby had both been made the subjects of interim care orders. The mother was disturbed and aggressive and made attempts to harm herself, as a result of which the baby was removed to foster parents. At the subsequent full care hearing the mother sought contact with her child. The evidence suggested that it was not in the baby's interests for contact to continue but it was in the mother's interests that it should. The question was, therefore, squarely raised as to whose welfare was paramount, the baby's or the mother's?

The House of Lords ruled that the baby's welfare was paramount. According to Lord Slynn (who gave the main judgment), s 34 (which governs contact with a child in care)

---

[235] *Re A (Minors) (Residence Orders: Leave to Apply)* [1992] Fam 182, CA.

[236] See *Re B (A Child) (Care Proceedings: Care Threshold Criteria)* [2013] UKSC 33 [2013] 1 WLR 1911.

[237] *Children—The New Law* (1990) at p 11.

[238] Ie the Domicile and Matrimonial Proceedings Act 1973 Sch 1 para 8(1).

[239] See *M v M (Abduction: England and Wales)* [1997] 2 FLR 263 at 275F, per Millett LJ. The child's welfare is not paramount when deciding whether to make a return order under the 1980 Hague Abduction Convention, see Ch 26. The paramountcy principle is ousted by a successful claim to diplomatic immunity under the terms of the Diplomatic Privileges Act 1964, see *Re P (Children Act: Diplomatic Immunity)* [1998] 1 FLR 624.

[240] *A v Liverpool City Council* [1982] AC 363, HL, discussed further in Ch 18.

[241] *Re Mohamed Arif (An Infant), Re Nirbhai Singh (An Infant)* [1968] Ch 643, CA. Note also *ZH (Tanzania) v Secretary of State for the Home Department* [2011] UKSC 4 [2011] 2 AC 166, discussed earlier in this chapter.

[242] [1994] 2 AC 212, HL (discussed further in Ch 18, The court's powers, p 657) and see G Douglas 'In Whose Best Interests?' (1994) 110 LQR 379.

makes it clear that the subject-matter of the application is the child in care in respect of whom an order is sought (ie in this case, the baby) and that, accordingly:[243]

> [the] question to be determined relates to that child's upbringing and it is that child's welfare which must be the court's paramount consideration. The fact that the parent is also a child does not mean that both parent's and child's welfare is paramount and that each has to be balanced against the other.

Lord Slynn said that the same analysis would be applicable if the child was the applicant, because it would still be:

> . . . that child's welfare which is directly involved and which is paramount even if the other named person is also a child. The welfare of any other named person, even if a child, is not also paramount so as to require a balancing exercise to be carried out.

This decision has been criticised[244] both for being confined to s 34 and for its application of the 'subject-matter-of-the-application' approach even when interpreting s 34. However, with regard to the latter it has become evident that the subject-matter-of-the-application approach has a broad application. In *F v Leeds City Council*[245] the Court of Appeal rejected a 17-year-old mother's argument that in deciding whether to make a care order in respect of her baby (who had been removed from her within hours of the birth) the baby's welfare alone should not be treated as the paramount consideration since she herself was a child whose upbringing was in question. It was held, following *Birmingham*, that, since the baby and not the mother was the subject matter of the application and the only child to be named in the order, no question relating to the mother's upbringing arose and hence there was no requirement to treat her welfare as paramount.

With regard to the House of Lords' interpretation of s 34, it has been pointed out that, while it 'breaks the tie' as between a parent who is a child and her baby, it will not do so where one sibling in care applies for contact with another sibling in care, for it will not be possible to say which child is the subject-matter of the application unless this is to be determined simply by the accident of who brought the application.[246] As against this, however, it seems right to treat a baby's welfare as superior to the mother's for, as was argued in *Birmingham*,[247] 'vulnerable infants ought not to be deprived of the protection of the welfare principle because they have a teenage mother'. Accordingly it is submitted that, instead of leaving it open,[248] the Lords should have adopted the wider argument that an application by a parent (who is still a child) for contact with his or her own child falls outside the scope of s 1(1), since it only relates to the child's position as a parent and not to the child parent's own upbringing. Such an approach would have been well in line with the well developed jurisprudence of confining the paramountcy principle to issues *directly* concerning the child's upbringing and would have provided a simpler test.

Balancing the interests of siblings

As has been suggested, the *Birmingham* decision is not easy to apply, if at all, in cases involving siblings. In *Re F (Contact: Child in Care)*,[249] in which a child in care sought contact with his four siblings who were not in care, Wilson J observed that where an application was properly made under s 34 (viz. where the parents or siblings were content to have contact but

---

[243] At 222.
[244] By G Douglas 'In Whose Best Interests?' (1994) 110 LQR 379.   [245] [1994] 2 FLR 60, CA.
[246] See the detailed analysis by G Douglas 'In Whose Best Interests?' (1994) 110 LQR 379 at 382, and see *Re F (Contact: Child in Care)* [1995] 1 FLR 510.   [247] [1994] 2 AC at 215G.
[248] [1994] 2 AC at 223H.   [249] [1995] 1 FLR 510.

the resistance emanated from the local authority) the child in care's welfare would be the paramount consideration, since that child would be the 'named person'. On the other hand, if that child were to apply for a s 8 order to have contact with his siblings, it would be the latter's welfare that would be paramount. Whether it is sensible for the issue of paramountcy to depend on which application is brought can surely be questioned, but even accepting this analysis it will still not solve the problem of competing interests between sibling children each of whom is in care, in the case of applications by each of them for contact with the other.

In such a situation the Court of Appeal's approach in the *Birmingham* case seems more apposite, that is, to balance the children's interests and find a preponderance in favour of one or the other.[250] A similar approach also seems inevitable in resolving private law applications concerning sibling children where their interests conflict. This was Wall J's view in *Re T and E (Proceedings: Conflicting Interests)*,[251] in which he commented, obiter:

> . . . where a number of children are all the subject of an application or cross-application to the court in the same set of proceedings, and where it was impossible to achieve what was in the paramount interests of each child, the balancing exercise described in the Court of Appeal (in the *Birmingham* case) had to be undertaken and the situation of least detriment to all the children achieved.

This approach has been authoritatively endorsed by the Court of Appeal in *Re A (Children) (Conjoined Twins: Surgical Separation)*[252] which concerned the issue of whether the conjoined twins should be surgically separated when to do so would preserve the life of one (Jodie) but inevitably kill the other (Mary). In sanctioning the operation Ward LJ said,[253] applying the Court of Appeal approach taken in the *Birmingham* case:

> If the duty of the court is to make a decision which puts Jodie's interests paramount and that decision would be contrary to the paramount interests of Mary, then, for my part, I do not see the court can reconcile the impossibility of fulfilling each duty by simply declining to decide the very matter before it. That would be a total abdication of the duty which is imposed on us. Given the conflict of duty, I can see no other way of dealing with it than by choosing the lesser of the two evils and so finding the least detrimental alternative. A balance has to be struck somehow and I cannot flinch from undertaking that evaluation, horrendously difficult though it is.

A less dramatic example of the balancing approach is the pre-Children Act decision in *Clarke-Hunt v Newcombe*,[254] in which the Court of Appeal upheld a decision not to separate two brothers but to place them together with their mother even though it was against the elder boy's wishes and possibly slightly detrimental to his interests.

C. CRITICISMS OF THE WELFARE PRINCIPLE

Although, as already discussed, the paramountcy principle is best regarded as being human rights compliant and is consistent with Art 3(1) of the United Nations Convention on the Rights of the Child, both its paramountcy and indeed the very notion of welfare have been criticised.

The paramountcy principle has been criticised on the grounds that it pays too little attention to the interests of parents and other members of the family and generally ignores the

---

[250] See G Douglas 'In Whose Best Interests?' (1994) 110 LQR 379 at 382.
[251] [1995] 1 FLR 581 at 587.
[252] [2001] Fam 147.   [253] [2001] Fam 147 at 192.   [254] (1983) 4 FLR 482, CA.

reality of family life, namely, that children are not brought up in a vacuum but live in a relationship or series of relationships with other family members. In short, the court's understanding of the welfare principle has been said to be unduly individualistic with the child
wrongly being seen simply in isolation. This has led at least one critic[255] to suggest that the
paramountcy rule be abandoned and replaced within a framework which recognises that
the child is merely one participant in a process in which the interest of all the participants
count. Another[256] has sought to categorise parents' and children's interests as either primary
or secondary and to suggest that a child's secondary interests give way to a parent's primary
interests. A third suggestion[257] is that the concept of welfare be broadened to comprise what
is described as a 'relationship-based welfare approach', whereby instead of conceiving the
problem as a clash between (usually) children and parents in terms of weighing two conflicting interests, the issue should be regarded as deciding what is a proper parent–child relationship which in turn is grounded upon the premise that it is beneficial for a child to be brought
up in a family that is based on relationships which are fair and just (but which may involve
the child having to make some sacrifices).

   While each of these approaches, and particularly the latter two, arguably bring to the
fore a better articulation of a fair balance of family interests, none of the proposals are
problem-free. Abandoning the paramountcy principle is open to the objection that it
would leave the child too unprotected and would, in any event, run counter to the UN
Convention on the Rights of the Child. Thinking of welfare as protecting primary interests and balancing secondary ones will not solve the problem of resolving clashes between
primary interests and in any event is too complicated. Complexity of approach is also a
criticism that may be levelled at the relationship-based welfare suggestion. Moreover, as
Herring himself admitted,[258] the courts may already be thought to have accommodated
the approach 'even if in an unarticulated way'. However, the very chameleon qualities of
the welfare principle as applied by the courts have led to charges that the concept is too
uncertain and value laden, and ironically, 'might fail to provide sufficient protection to
children's interest because its use conceals the fact that the interests of others, or, perhaps,
untested assumptions about what is good for children, actually drive the decision'. This
latter charge has led Eekelaar to speculate[259] about abandoning the welfare principle as it
is currently understood in favour of a concept of 'well-being' (which he defines as being
indicated by the degree of success achieved in realising the person's significant goals in
life) which he argues would offer a more nuanced approach.[260] He concludes:[261]

> Of course, children must be seen to have rights . . . They must be seen to have the right to
> begin writing the script of the way their life is to unfold. But the claims of other parties
> to procedural justice and to the protection of their well-being must not be overlooked.
> Children's rights should be seen as a species of people's rights: in this case, people on their

---

[255] H Reece 'The Paramountcy Principle: Consensus or Construct?' (1996) 49 *Current Legal Problems* 267.
[256] A Bainham 'Non-Intervention and Judicial Paternalism' in P Birks (eds) *Frontiers of Liability* 161 and
developed in ' "Honour Thy Father and Mother": Children's Rights and Children's Duties' in G Douglas and
L Sebba (eds) *Children's Rights and Traditional Values* (1998) 93.
[257] See J Herring 'The Welfare Principle and the Rights of Parents' in A Bainham, S Day Sclater and
M Richards (eds) *What is a Parent?* (1999) 89 and developed in 'The Human Rights Act and the welfare
principle in family law—conflicting or complementary?' [1999] CFLQ 223. But see also by the same author—
'Farewell Welfare?' (2005) 27 Jo of Social Welfare and Family Law 159 for a 'defence' of the welfare principle.
Note also the thoughtful comments of D Bonner, H Fenwick and S Harris-Short 'Judicial Approaches to the
HRA' (2003) 52 ICLQ 549 at 580.   [258] See [1999] CFLQ at 233.
[259] J Eekelaar 'Beyond the welfare principle' [2002] CFLQ 237.
[260] J Eekelaar 'Beyond the welfare principle' at 243.
[261] J Eekelaar 'Beyond the welfare principle' at 249.

> way to becoming adults. In themselves, these rights are no different from adults' rights. Due allowance being made for issues of competence and children's special vulnerability, they should be respected just as adults' rights should be; certainly no less, but also no more.

To an extent, the notion of well-being has since been accommodated by Munby LJ's analysis (discussed earlier in this chapter) of welfare in *Re G (Education: Religious Upbringing)*[262] while reform that we are about to discuss, seeks to underscore the importance of a child's ongoing relationship with both parents despite family breakdown.

D. THE IMPORTANCE OF AN ONGOING RELATIONSHIP WITH BOTH PARENTS AFTER FAMILY SEPARATION

1. BACKGROUND TO REFORM

Against the background of concern expressed by high profile pressure groups such as Families need Fathers and 'Fathers 4 Justice' that the courts were biased against fathers, there was considerable discussion, during the debate leading to the Children and Adoption Act 2006, as to whether the checklist should be amended to ensure that the courts have regard to the importance of sustaining a relationship between the child and both parents in the event of family separation. The Government view at the time was that the checklist was not the place to include it.[263] The issue resurfaced in the course of the *Family Justice Review* ('The Norgrove Review'), though the Final Report retreated from its earlier proposals to introduce a legal presumption of shared parenting.[264] Although the Coalition Government accepted most of the Norgrove proposals, it nevertheless considered[265] that because of the alleged bias against fathers, there was a need to clarify and restore public confidence that the courts recognised the joint nature of parenting and published various options for doing so in a Consultation Paper.[266] That drew a response from a wide range of interested parties from which the Government concluded that a clear presumption that both parents should be involved in a child's life was the most appropriate way to achieve its aims. Although the House of Commons Justice Committee supported the principle that, where there is no potential harm the welfare of the child, both parents should be involved in that child's life they nevertheless had reservations inter alia about the use of

---

[262] [2012] EWCA Civ 1233, [2013] 1 FLR 677

[263] See the *Government Reply to the Report from the Joint Committee on the Draft Children (Contact) and Adoption Bill* Cm 6583 (June 2005) para 121. Ironically, the now repealed s 11(4) of the Family Law Act 1996 which was to have directed the courts admittedly only in divorce and separation cases to have particular regard to, 'the general principle that, in the absence of evidence to the contrary, the welfare of the child will be best served by: (i) his having regular contact with those who have parental responsibility for him and with other members of his family . . .', might have served as a statutory model. Note also Art 4 of the Council of Europe Convention on Contact Concerning Children 2003.

[264] The interim report was published in March 2011 and the final report on 3 November 2011, for a summary of which see [2011] Fam Law 1392.

[265] *The Government Response to the Family Justice Review: A system with children and families at heart* (2012 Cm 8273).

[266] *Co-operative Parenting Following Family Separation: Proposed Legislation on the Involvement of Both Parents in a Child's Life* (TSO, 2012).

the word 'presumption'.[267] Despite the Committee's reservations and those of the wider legal community,[268] the Government proposal eventually became enacted by s 11 of the Children and Families Act 2014.

2. THE SECTION 1(2A) PRESUMPTION

Section 11 inserts a new sub section, s 1(2A), into the Children Act 1989 requiring the court, whenever it is considering making a parental responsibility or a contested s 8 order:[269]

> to presume, unless the contrary is shown, that involvement of [each relevant] parent in the life of the child concerned will further the child's welfare.

This presumption only applies where a 'parent can be involved in the child's life in a way that does not put the child at risk of suffering harm' but a parent is to be so treated 'unless there is some evidence before the court in the particular proceedings to suggest that involvement of that parent in the child's life would put the child at risk of suffering harm whatever the form of the involvement.'[270] By s 1(2B) 'involvement' for these purposes means:

> involvement of some kind, either direct or indirect, but not any particular division of a child's time.

Whatever order is made it is subject to the overarching principle of the paramountcy of the child's welfare as set out by s 1(1).

(a) Determining whether the presumption applies

Although the object of this reform is easy enough to state, namely, in the words of the Explanatory Notes to the Act, 'to reinforce the importance of children having an ongoing relationship with both parents after family separation, where that is safe, and in the child's best interests',[271] the process introduced by the amendments is less straightforward. Indeed, apparently mindful of this complexity the Explanatory Notes to the Act provide both a flow chart and five examples of how the law is expected to work.[272]

In all cases the first question that must be asked is whether the presumption can apply at all, to which the answer is: it will if, but only if, the court has before it an application *by a parent* (ie not a step-parent) for a parental responsibility order or a *contested* application to make, vary or discharge a 8 order (*Step 1*).

---

[267] House of Commons Justice Committee—Pre-legislation scrutiny of the Children and Families Bill, 4th Report of Session 2012–2013, outlined at [2013] Fam Law 229. The Committee also had reservations about whether there was an implication in the proposal that it promoted the equal division of a child's time between separated parents. But in a late amendment, adding s 1(2B), it was made clear that it does not.

[268] See eg the response of the Law Society in 'Law Society, *Cooperative Parenting Following Separation. Response of the Law Society of England and Wales*' (2012), the responses referred to in 'FJR response' [2012] Fam Law 252 at 253 and for critical articles both by academics and practitioners, see eg, F Kanagas 'A presumption that 'involvement' of both parents is best: deciphering law's messages' [2013] CFLQ 270, M O'Grady 'Shared parenting: keeping welfare paramount by learning from mistakes' [2013] Fam Law 448 and D Nickols 'A presumption of shared parenting: long awaited or misguided?' [2012] Fam Law 573.

[269] Children Act 1989 s 1(2A) and (7), inserted by s 11 (3) of the 2014 Act.

[270] Children Act 1989 s 1(6), inserted by s 11(3) of the 2014 Act.   [271] At para 105.

[272] See Annex A.

Assuming this first step is satisfied the second stage is to consider in relation to *each* parent whether there is evidence that the involvement of either of them would put the child at risk of suffering harm (*Step 2*).

If there is no such evidence the court must nevertheless consider whether there is anything other than a risk of harm, to rebut the presumption (*Step 3*).[273]

If there is not, then the court must apply the presumption but in doing so, as 1(2B) makes clear, it is not bound to provide for any particular division of the child's time and therefore it is not bound to provide for equal division, rather the court must make its final decision according to the paramountcy principle under s 1(1) (*Step 4*).

If at Step 2 there is evidence of a risk of harm then the court must consider whether the parent concerned can be involved in the child's life in a way that does not put the child at risk of harm. If there is not, the presumption will not apply and the court must make whatever order it considers to be for the child's welfare. If limited involvement will not put the child at risk then the court must apply Steps 3 and 4 described earlier.

If at Step 3 there is evidence to rebut the presumption then the court must make its final order according to general welfare principles without reference to the presumption.

(b) Examples of the application of the presumption

To illustrate how this process is intended to work reference can usefully be had to the examples provided in the Explanatory Notes. The first example is the straightforward case of a married couple separating but with the left-behind parent, 'Parent B', refusing to let the other parent, 'Parent A', see the child by having, in the eyes of Parent B, forfeited the right to do so by leaving the marital home. There is no evidence that either parent poses a risk of harm to the child nor is it alleged by Parent B that Parent A's involvement would not further the child's welfare. There is evidence that the child had had a good relationship with Parent A and wants to see that parent. In this case the presumption clearly applies and in making its decision the court must weigh that alongside the other considerations in s 1 of the Children Act with the child's welfare remaining at all times the court's paramount consideration.

At the other end of the spectrum is Example 3 in which following the parents' separation contested proceedings are brought over seeing the child. Parent B alleges that Parent A has a history of emotionally and physically abusing both Parent B and the child. A welfare report confirms these allegations. There is also a disputed allegation that Parent A sent threatening letters to the child. After considering all the evidence the court concludes that the prospect of any contact at all (including writing letters to the child) with Parent A would pose a risk of harm to the child and, having ruled that the presumption does not apply, dismissed the argument that a denial of contact would violate Art 8 of the Convention on Human Rights. In making its decision the court must weigh the fact that the presumption does not apply alongside the other considerations in s 1 of the Children Act with the child's welfare remaining at all times the court's paramount consideration.

Examples 2 and 5 are where the risk of harm can be overcome with limited contact such that the presumption will apply. Example 4 is an illustration of where, notwithstanding the absence of a risk of harm, the application of the presumption is rebutted at Step 3. Here the child concerned is 15 and does not want any contact with Parent A because that parent finds it difficult to come to terms with the fact that the child has declared himself to be gay.

---

[273] Cf the flow chart which describes Step 3 as posing the question 'Would the involvement of that parent further the welfare of the child?' But with respect this is not what the section requires and in any event seems to conflate this step with Step 4.

Although these are good examples, it is noticeable that they only concern what may broadly be described as contact issues. They do not deal with the making of parental responsibility orders[274] or with how the presumption might work in the context of relocation applications.[275] The examples also gloss over some potential legal difficulties, for example as to the meaning of 'risk' and of 'harm'.[276]

(c) Commentary

Whether this reform was either necessary or worthwhile can be debated. As we discuss in Chapter 14, the courts have long stressed the general importance of maintaining contact between the child and both parents and it seems doubtful that the reform will make, as the Government maintained, judges 'more mindful' of this, while it is a matter of speculation as to whether the reform will address the problem, as the Government saw it, of the lack of public confidence in the family justice system. The reform is not just aimed at the courts but also 'to send a clear signal to separated parents that the courts will take account of the principle that both should continue to be involved with their children's lives where that is safe and consistent with the child's welfare'.[277] But, as has forcefully been said, there is no evidence that changing the law will improve children's relationships with parents and indeed there is a danger that the symbolic affirmation essentially of the importance of fathers could come at the expense of vulnerable mothers and their children. [278] As one commentator said,[279] 'The concern is that the [presumption] may resolve little and lead to increased acrimony rather than building agreements based on the child's needs.' Much of the debate centred on the Australian experience of their shared parenting legislation introduced in 2006.[280] That legislation seems to have led parents to believe that the reform conferred rights with the consequence that litigation and negotiation has focused more on parental rights than on children's welfare.[281] The fear is that the Australian experience will be repeated here.[282] Time will tell whether these fears prove justified. But even without these concerns the reform is open to the criticism that it is convoluted and to the charge that 'presumptions 'do not sit comfortably in cases concerning children's welfare.'[283] This criticism is all the more serious given that the general withdrawal of legal aid will mean that more proceedings will be brought by litigants in person who will find it hard to understand what, after all, is an extremely difficult provision.

---

[274] See further the discussion in Ch 11.   [275] See further the discussion in Ch 14.

[276] Presumably with regard to 'risk' reference will be have to be had to *Re M and R (Child Abuse: Evidence)* [1996] 2 FLR 195, discussed at Any harm which the child has suffered or is at risk of suffering, p 412; while 'harm' must, by reason of s 105(1), be interpreted in line with s 31(9), as discussed in Ch 17, The significant harm condition, p 600. See also the comments by M O'Grady 'Shared parenting: keeping welfare paramount by learning from mistakes' [2013] Fam Law 448 at 450.

[277] See the Government response to the Norgrove Review.

[278] See F Kanagas 'A presumption that "involvement" of both parents is best: deciphering the messages' [2013] CFLQ 270, at 293.

[279] D Nickols 'A presumption of shared parenting: long awaited or misguided?' [2012] Fam Law 573.

[280] Family Law Act 1975 (Cth) s 60 (CC)(2)(a) and (b).

[281] See R Kaspiew, M Gray, R Weston, L Malony, K Hand and L Qu *Evaluation of the 2006 family law reforms* (2012). See also B Fehlberg 'Legislating for shared parenting: how the Family Justice Review got it right' [2012] Fam Law 709. Cf the reported comments of P Parkinson in 'Shared parenting: UK' [2012] Fam Law 758.

[282] In this respect note may be taken of research by J Fortin, J Hunt and L Scanlan *Taking a Longer View of Contact* (2012), which casts doubt on the claim that a presumption would promote children's best interests. For a general review of the research about shared parenting, see L Trinder 'Shared Residence: A Review of Recent Research Evidence' [2010] Fam Law 1192.

[283] See M O'Grady 'Shared parenting: keeping welfare paramount by learning from mistakes' [2013] Fam Law 448.

E. DELAY PRIMA FACIE PREJUDICIAL TO THE CHILD'S WELFARE

Section 1(2) enjoins the court, in any proceedings in which any question with respect to a child's upbringing arises, 'to have regard to the general principle that any delay in determining the question is likely to prejudice the welfare of the child'.[284] Since this principle applies to all proceedings concerning a child's upbringing[285] it is not confined to proceedings under the 1989 Act, but applies equally, for example, to proceedings under the High Court's inherent jurisdiction (separate provision is made for adoption proceedings).[286]

The case for making some provision about the harmful effect of delay was cogently argued by the Law Commission.[287] They pointed out that 'prolonged litigation about their future is deeply damaging to children, not only because of the uncertainty it brings for them, but also because of the harm it does to the relationship between the parents and their capacity to co-operate with one another in the future'. Despite its importance, however, it was only at the final House of Lords stages that this provision was promoted to the opening section, Lord Mackay commenting:[288]

> After the welfare principle, the need to avoid delay is one of the most important policies underlying the Bill. It is therefore proper that it should appear in clause 1.

The need for speed is also underscored by Art 6 of the European Convention on Human Rights under which everyone is entitled to a fair and public hearing in the determination of his civil rights and obligations *within a reasonable time*.[289]

Notwithstanding s 1(2) it should not be thought that delay[290] is always detrimental to the child's welfare. As Ward J observed in *C v Solihull Metropolitan Borough Council*,[291] while delay is ordinarily inimical to the welfare of the child, planned and purposeful delay may well be beneficial. Hence, the delay of a final decision for the purpose of ascertaining the result of an assessment is obviously for, rather than against, the child's interests. In *Re B (A Minor) (Contact: Interim Order)*,[292] for example, magistrates were held to be wrong to refuse to make an interim contact order during which arrangements for the reintroduction of contact were to be assessed, because such arrangements infringed the principle of the avoidance of delay

---

[284] See generally *Scoping Study on Delay in Children Act Cases* (Lord Chancellor's Department, 2002), on which draft Report see A Finlay 'Delay and the Challenges of the Children Act' in M Thorpe and C Cowton (eds) *Delight and Dole* (2003) 5 at 10ff. A McFarlane 'Delay: A Cause of Significant Harm' [2003] Fam Law 453 and M Booth *Avoiding Delay in Children Act Cases* (1996), summarised at [1996] Fam Law 598–601, 643–5.

[285] But not property and note also the exclusion of maintenance from the definition of 'upbringing' under s 105(1).   [286] Viz. by s 1(3) of the Adoption and Children Act 2002, discussed in Ch 19.

[287] Law Com No 172, para 4.55.   [288] See 512 HL Official Report (5th Series) Vol 720.

[289] For examples where undue delay has been held to be in breach of Art 6 see eg *Süss v* Germany [2006] 1 FLR 522, ECtHR, protracted access dispute for over a decade only ending when the child became 18; *Adam v Germany* [2009] 1 FLR, ECtHR—lengthy delays in enforcing contact; *Jevremovic v Serbia* [2008] 1 FLR 550, ECtHR and *Karcheva v Bulgaria* [2006] 3 FCR 434, ECtHR, both involving protracted proceedings to establish paternity and *EO and VP v Slovakia* [2004] 2 FCR 242, ECtHR—protracted dispute over the education of a 14-year-old which had to be discontinued when child became 18.

[290] See I Butler et al 'The Children Act and the Issue of Delay' [1993] Fam Law 412, who pointed out that 'delay is a relative phenomenon and needs to be distinguished from "duration". A complex case may, quite appropriately and expeditiously, remain in the courts for several weeks while a relatively simple matter that ought to be dealt with within days might take three weeks and hence be subject to significant delay, yet still be of moderate duration.'

[291] [1993] 1 FLR 290 at 304.   [292] [1994] 2 FLR 269.

as set out in s 1(2). It may be similarly beneficial to a child to make a temporary order to allow 'a volatile family situation' involving children to settle down.[293] On the other hand, what s 1(2) aims to prevent is unnecessary and unplanned delay for reasons that have nothing to do with the child's welfare.[294] It has been said, for example, that to delay a harsh decision is to delay for 'no purpose'.[295] As the criterion to be applied is the welfare of the *child*, detriment to the *family* is not of itself a relevant factor. It was on this basis that in *Re T-B (Care Proceedings: Criminal Trial)*[296] it was held that the fact there was a pending criminal trial was not enough to justify delaying the hearing of the care proceedings.

The principal effect of s 1(2) is to place the onus upon the courts[297] to ensure that all proceedings concerning children are conducted as expeditiously as possible. As Wall J put it:[298]

> The non-adversarial approach in children's litigation means . . . that whatever the forensic stance of the litigant, delay in the prosecution of applications relating to children should not be permitted even where it is perceived to be in the interests of one of the adult parties. Furthermore . . . the courts have a duty to be proactive in ensuring that applications once launched are not allowed to moulder.

To this end the courts are directed[299] both in applications for s 8 orders and for orders under Part IV to draw up a timetable and to give appropriate directions for adhering to that timetable. The procedure for the timetabling both private and public law proceedings is governed by the Family Procedure Rules 2010 the general strategy of which is that, until the application is finally disposed of, a definite return date must be fixed before the end of any directions appointment or other hearing of the case. Although these provisions only apply to proceedings under the 1989 Act (though, in practice they are applied to proceedings under the inherent jurisdiction), there is a more generally applicable enjoinder[300] upon the courts actively to manage family proceedings, including fixing timetables and otherwise controlling the progress of the case.

The court may be robust in insisting that any timetable is met. In *Re B and T (Care Proceedings: Legal Representation)*,[301] for example, parents who had failed to comply

---

[293] As in the pre-Children Act decision *Re S (Minors) (Custody)* [1992] 1 FCR 158, CA. See also *Re K (Non-Accidental Injuries: Perpetrator: New Evidence)* [2005] 1 FLR 285 in which while the delay principle was acknowledged, there were thought to be 'powerful' considerations on the other side, namely, the public interest in the identification of the perpetrator of the non-accidental injuries on the children and the possibility, dependent on that finding, of the children being reconciled with their mother.

[294] For examples of cases in which delay was thought to have prejudiced the children's welfare, see *B v B (Minors) (Interviews and Listing Arrangements)* [1994] 2 FLR 489, CA and, most strikingly, *Re A and B (Minors) (No 2)* [1995] 1 FLR 351.

[295] Per Ward LJ in *Re M (Child's Upbringing)* [1996] 2 FLR 441 at 460, CA.

[296] [1995] 2 FLR 801, CA. Note also *Re B and T (Care Proceedings: Legal Representation)* [2001] 1 FLR 485, CA, discussed later in this section.

[297] But note that, according to Wall J in *B v B (Child Abuse: Contact)* [1994] 2 FLR 713 at 736, practitioners too have a duty to ensure that cases do not drift. But s 1(2) does not of itself mean that Cafcass must make an officer available for appointment as a guardian in care proceedings on receiving a request from the court: *R v Children and Family Court Advisory and Support Service* [2003] EWHC 235 Admin [2003] 1 FLR 953.   [298] In *B v B (Minors) (Interviews and Listing Arrangements)* [1994] 2 FLR 489 at 492, CA.

[299] By ss 11(1) and 32(1). Similar but separate timetabling powers are conferred by s 109 of the Adoption and Children Act 2002, in relation to adoption proceedings.   [300] FPR 2010 r 1.4.

[301] [2001] 1 FLR 485. See also *Blunkett v Quinn* [2004] EWHC 2816 (Fam), [2005] 1 FLR 648—application to adjourn proceedings for parental responsibility and contact because of the mother's ill-health was refused, inter alia, because delay would be damaging to the father–child relationship; and *Re C (Section 8 Order: Court Welfare Officer)* [1995] 1 FLR 617, CA in which it was held that in view of s 1(2) a court can, in

with directions were effectively precluded from legal representation by the refusal of an adjournment application made by solicitors who had just been instructed on the first day of a five day hearing. In so ruling the Court of Appeal considered that having regard to the overall fairness of the proceedings and the need to balance the parents' rights against those of the children to an early determination of their future, the parents' Art 6 rights to a fair trial were not violated by the refusal to adjourn. Among the possible sanctions against practitioners for failing to comply with the timetable are being personally penalised in costs, being held guilty of professional misconduct,[302] or ultimately being held guilty of contempt of court.

At the time of implementation of the Children Act 1989 there were expectations that private law cases would generally be disposed of within 16 weeks and public law cases within 12 weeks.[303] Both expectations proved wildly optimistic. The Norgrove Report published in 2011, found that care and supervision order cases took on average 56 weeks with private law cases taking an average of 32 weeks. Norgrove is the latest of a number of investigations into the issue of delay[304] and there have been several initiatives to speed up public law proceedings. One such initiative was to introduce a *Protocol for Judicial Case Management in Public Law Children Act Cases*[305] the object of which was to prescribe a 40-week target for the general completion of such proceedings. This Protocol was replaced by the *Public Law Outline* which was incorporated in *Practice Direction 12A* with a further pilot scheme running from July 2013 to April 2014 as set out by *Practice Direction 36C*, with a view to revising the *Public Law Outline*, with the overall aim of completing proceedings within 26 weeks, in line with the Norgrove recommendation. This has now been made a statutory obligation by the Children and Families Act 2014.[306] We discuss these developments in more detail in Chapter 17.

F. ORDERS TO BE MADE ONLY WHERE
BETTER THAN NO ORDER

1. INTRODUCTION AND BACKGROUND

An important and innovative principle introduced by s 1(5), is that whenever a court is considering whether to make one or more orders under the 1989 Act with respect to a child, it 'shall not make the order or any of the orders unless it considers that doing so would be better for the child than making no order at all'. Section 1(5) is intended to focus attention as to whether any court order is necessary.[307] It can also be seen as part

---

appropriate cases, depart from the recommendation in a welfare report even though the reporter did not attend court to give oral evidence.

[302] See *Re M* (1989) *The Times*, 29 December, CA.

[303] See respectively Law Com No. 172 at para 4.54 the *Scoping Study*, op cit, at para 24, referred to by Baroness Hale in *Re G (A Minor) (Interim Care Order: Residential Assessment)* [2005] UKHL 68, [2005] 3 WLR 1166 at [58].

[304] Eg the *Scoping Study*, see earlier, and the Booth Report, see earlier. See also R Bailey-Harris, G Davies, J Barron and J Pearce *Monitoring Private Law Applications under the Children Act: A Research Report to the Nuffield Foundation* (1998).   [305] [2003] 2 FLR 719.

[306] See s 14 which makes substantial amendments to s 32 of the 1989 Act.

[307] This implements that Law Commission's recommendations with regard to private law proceedings, see Law Com No 172, paras 3.2–3.4, and those of the Child Care Review (DHSS 1985) paras 15.24–15.25 and the government's White Paper *The Law on Child Care and Family Services* Cm 62, 1987, para 59, with respect to public law proceedings.

of the underlying philosophy of the 1989 Act to respect the integrity and independence of the family save where court orders have some positive contribution to make towards the child's welfare. As Sir James Munby P put it in *Re B-S (Children) (Adoption: Leave to Oppose)*[308] there is a well established principle derived from s 1(5) read in conjunction with s 1(3)(g) that when considering what orders, if any, to make, the court should adopt the 'least interventionist approach'.

According to the revised *Children Act 1989 Guidance and Regulations*,[309] s 1(5) has three main aims:

> The first is to discourage unnecessary court orders being made, for example as part of a standard package of orders. If orders are restricted to those cases where they are necessary to resolve a specific problem this should reduce conflict and promote parental agreement and co-operation. The second aim is to ensure that the order is granted only where it will positively improve the child's welfare and not simply because the grounds for making the order are made out. For example, in care proceedings where the court may decide that it would be better for a particular child not to be in local authority care. The application by the court of this 'no order' principle should not deter local authorities from bringing proceedings where they believe that a care or supervision order is necessary in order to safeguard and promote a child's welfare. The third aim is to discourage the making of unnecessary applications.

2. WHEN SECTION 1(5) APPLIES

Section 1(5) applies where a court is considering whether or not to make one or more orders *under the 1989 Act*. Accordingly, it has no direct application in proceedings in which courts are considering whether or not to make orders relating to children outside the Act.[310] In this respect, s 1(5) has a narrower ambit than either s 1(1) or s 1(2).

In *K v H (Child Maintenance)*[311] it was held that s 1(5) does not apply to applications for financial provision[312] for a child under Sch 1 to the Act. The principal reason for so holding was that like s 1(1), which was taken to be the general controlling provision for the overall application of s 1, s 1(5) 'is principally directed to orders relating to the upbringing of a child, the administration of a child's property or the application of any income arising from it'. Accordingly, since an application for financial provision neither concerns the child's upbringing nor the administration of his property, s 1(5) does not apply.

Whether it was right to say that s 1(1) was intended to provide the overall criterion for the operation of s 1 may be debated, but in practice it is likely to be the case that s 1(5) will not apply if s 1(1) does not. For example, in *Re M (Secure Accommodation Order)*,[313] which established that s 1(1) does not apply to the question of whether to make a secure accommodation order under s 25,[314] it was held that, because of the need to protect the public as well as the child, s 1(5) does not apply either. Again, in deciding whether to grant

---

[308] [2014] 1 WLR 563 at [23].

[309] Vol 1, *Court Orders* (2008), Department for Children, Schools and Families, para 1.15.

[310] Such as orders under the wardship or inherent jurisdiction (though presumably, however, there is nothing to prevent the court from taking a similar approach, if they so choose). However, a similar enjoinder now applies in adoption proceedings, see s 1(6) of the Adoption and Children Act 2002, discussed in Ch 19.

[311] [1993] 2 FLR 61 per Sir Stephen Brown P.

[312] That is, periodical payments, which was what *K v H* concerned, or lump sums or property orders.

[313] [1995] 1 FLR 418, CA, per Butler-Sloss LJ.

[314] Secure accommodation is discussed in Ch 15.

leave to apply for a s 8 order where it is established that the paramountcy principle does not apply,[315] it seems right to say that s 1(5) is also subsumed by the criteria set out in s 10(9).[316]

3. APPLYING SECTION 1(5)

The application of s 1(5) has proved problematic. It quickly became referred to as establishing a 'non-intervention principle' or 'no order principle' and was said to reflect a basic philosophy of the 1989 Act, memorably described as 'privatising the family',[317] though perhaps more accurately by others as a policy of deregulation[318] or non-intervention, which in turn rests 'on the belief that children are generally best looked after within the family with both parents playing a full part and without resort to legal proceedings'.[319] However, insofar as these epithets suggest that orders are presumed to be unnecessary, their use has been deprecated in some quarters. As one commentator has pointed out[320] neither the Law Commission nor the statute says that court orders are presumed to be unnecessary and 'most certainly' neither suggested that in public care proceedings there was a legal presumption against the making of care or supervision orders. In his view if epithets are required he suggests a more accurate one could be the 'no *unnecessary* order principle'.

This debate is allied to an important issue as to whether s 1(5) is properly considered as creating a formal burden of proof on those seeking an order to show that its making is for the child's benefit. In *Re X and Y (Leave To Remove From Jurisdiction: No Order Principle)*[321] Munby J held that it did, for as he put it, relying on principles said to be distilled from the House of Lords' decision in *Dawson v Wearmouth*:[322]

> The burden is on the party applying for an order to make out a positive case that on a balance of probabilities it is in the interests of the child that that order should be made. If he fails to make out that positive case the application will fail.

However, this analysis was disapproved by the Court of Appeal first in *Re H (Children) (Residence Order: Condition)*, Thorpe LJ commenting that he did not think that the dicta drawn from the House of Lords' cases bear 'the weight of the edifice that Munby J sought to build on them'[323] and then in *Re G (Children)* in which Ward LJ said:

> [s 1(5)] is perfectly clear. It does not . . . create a presumption one way or another. All it demands is that before the court makes any order it must ask the question: Will it be better for the child to make the order than making no order at all?[324]

---

[315] See *Re A (Minors) (Residence Orders: Leave to Apply)* [1992] Fam 182, CA, discussed in Ch 14, The application of s 10(9), p 516.

[316] In particular s 10(9)(c), which directs the court to consider the risk of harm to the child that the proposed application might cause.

[317] Inter alia by S Cretney 'Privatising the Family: The Reform of Child Law' (1989) Denning LJ 15 and A Bainham 'The Privatisation of the Public Interest in Children' (1990) 53 MLR 206.

[318] See eg G Douglas 'Family Law under the Thatcher Government' (1990) 17 JLS 411 at 425, n 17.

[319] *Introduction to the Children Act 1989* (HMSO 1989) para 1.3.

[320] A Bainham 'Changing families and changing concepts—reforming the language of family law' [1998] CFLQ at 2–4.   [321] [2001] 2 FLR 118, at 147–8 (Point 3).

[322] [1999] 2 AC 308 relying in particular upon comments made by Lord Mackay at 321A and Lord Hobhouse at 325H–326E. According to Munby J there was no difference in substance between what was said by the House of Lords in *Dawson* and what they said in *S v M (Access Order)* [1997] 1 FLR 980 (on appeal from Scotland).   [323] [2001] EWCA Civ 1338 [2001] 2 FLR 1277 at [19].

[324] [2005] EWCA Civ 1283 [2006] 1 FLR 771 at [10].

While there may be no formal burden of proof, it remains the case that the court must be satisfied that an order is for the benefit of the particular child. This requirement is clearly easier to satisfy in contested applications. Indeed it has been said that making 'no order' is inappropriate if the court is clearly charged with the responsibility for settling a dispute. In *Re W (A Minor) (Contact)*,[325] upon a father's application for defined contact following the mother's refusal to comply with a previous order for reasonable contact and her declared intention not to obey any further order, the first instance decision to make a 'no order' was held to be an abdication of responsibility. The point has also been made that there is a clear distinction between dismissing an application and making a 'no order' disposition. If the making of the latter is tantamount to dismissing a parent's application for contact, as opposed to holding that an order was not necessary, then, according to Wall J in *D v D (Application for Contact)*,[326] the court should at least take a proactive role and consider whether any further application should be made and, if so, when and in what circumstances.

Although it might be easier to persuade the court to make an order in contested cases it by no means follows that no order can be granted if the parties are agreed. In this respect reference can be usefully made to the revised *Guidance* on the 1989 Act:[327]

> There are several situations where the court is likely to consider it better for the child to make an order than not. If the court has had to resolve a dispute between the parents, it is likely to be better for the child to make an order about it. Even if there is no dispute, the child's need for stability and security may be better served by making an order. There may also be specific legal advantages in doing so.

In the Guidance as originally issued,[328] two examples were given of where an order might be justified notwithstanding the absence of a dispute. The first is where abduction of the child is thought to be a possibility, since a court order is necessary for enforcement proceedings in other parts of the United Kingdom under the Family Law Act 1986 and, one might add, is useful for enforcement proceedings in other EU Member States.[329] Moreover, under the 1980 Hague Abduction Convention an order will be necessary if the aggrieved party is, for example, an unmarried father or a relative who would not otherwise have 'rights of custody'. The original Guidance also said:

> An advantage of having a residence order [ie of what would now be of being named in a child arrangements order as a person with whom the child is to live] is that the child may be taken out of the country for periods of less than one month without the permission of other persons with parental responsibility or the court, whereas without an order this could amount to an offence under the Child Abduction Act 1984. Also if a person has a sole residence order in his favour and appoints a [testamentary] guardian for the child, the appointment will take effect immediately on that person's death, even where there is a surviving parent. Depending on the circumstances of the case, the court might therefore be persuaded that an order would be in the child's interest.

The *Guidance*'s reference to the need for stability and security needs to be read with caution. It is all too easy to advance this argument, but if s 1(5) is to have any meaning the

---

[325] [1994] 2 FLR 441, CA. Note Thorpe LJ's similar comments in *Re H (Children) (Residence Order: Condition)* [2001] EWCA Civ 1338, [2001] 2 FCR 1277 at [19]. See also *Re P (A Minor) (Parental Responsibility Order)* [1994] 1 FLR 578.

[326] [1994] 1 FCR 694.   [327] (Volume 1) 'Court Orders', (2008) para 2.73.

[328] *Children Act 1989 Guidance and Regulations*, Vol 1 Court Orders (Dept of Health, 1991), para 2.56.

[329] Ie to meet the criteria under Council Regulation (EC) No 2201/2003 of 27 November 2003 (the revised Brussels II regulation). See further Ch 26.

court cannot, as a matter of routine, make orders for this reason. Indeed, in the past, the Children Act Advisory Committee expressed concern[330] that applications were still being made (and presumably granted) so as to provide the parent with care with the security of an order even though there was no dispute about the child's residence or contact.

One circumstance not mentioned in the *Guidance* but which could justify the making of a child arrangements order is where the applicant, for example, a relative, has no parental responsibility, since it can always be argued that unless an order is made he or she will not otherwise have *locus standi* in relation to the child.[331] In *Re G (Children) (Residence: Same Sex-Partner)*,[332] what was then a shared residence order was made specifically to give the non-parent partner parental responsibility. Similarly, in *B v B (A Minor) (Residence Order)*[333] Johnson J accepted this argument when he granted, in what he described as 'the unusual circumstances of the case', an unopposed application for a residence order by a grandparent with whom the child had been living for over 10 years.

The Court of Appeal has warned of the dangers that might result from deciding to make no order simply because the parties appear to be in agreement. In *Re S (Contact: Grandparents)*[334] a grandparent sought a contact order. By the time the matter came to court the judge was persuaded that the mother would permit contact and he therefore made no order relying on s 1(5). On appeal it was held that, having decided it was in the child's welfare to have contact with the grandparent, and given the history of antagonism between the parties, a contact order should have been made even though the parties were in agreement at the time of the court hearing. The making of the order would ensure that contact did take place and avoid the need to return to court in the event of a disagreement.

(a) The application of s 1(5) in practice

Before implementation of the 1989 Act there was much speculation as to how s 1(5) would apply in practice. It was intended to have most impact in private law proceedings and in particular in divorce and separation proceedings, the concern being that orders relating to children should cease to be seen as merely 'part of the divorce package'. The indicators, however, are that the impact of s 1(5) has not been as great as had been expected. A study conducted in the late 1990s by Bristol University found that 'no orders' were made in about 5% of cases.[335] National statistics point to a declining proportion of 'no orders'. Early indicators were that about 9% of all private law orders were 'no orders'.[336] However, in 2000 this proportion dropped to about 4% of orders, to 1.5% in 2006 and to only 0.7% in 2011.[337] What of course cannot be known is how many applications were deterred in the first place by s 1(5).

---

[330] CAAC Report 1992/93, p 25.

[331] See s 10(4) and (6).   [332] [2006] UKHL 43 [2006] 1 WLR 2305.

[333] [1992] 2 FLR 327. Another circumstance that might justify the making of a consent order is where it can be shown that without an order the person looking after the child will not be accorded priority on a local authority housing list, though this practice was deprecated by the Children Act Advisory Committee (see CAAC Report 1992-1993, p 25).   [334] [1996] 1 FLR 158, CA.

[335] See R Bailey-Harris, J Barron and J Pearce 'Settlement culture and the use of the "no order" principle under the Children Act 1989' [1999] CFLQ 53. They also found that at county court level practitioners and district judges took a variety of approaches to s 1(5).

[336] See the analysis in R White, C Parr and N Lowe, *The Children Act in Practice* (2nd edn, 1995) at 2.49 based upon the analysis of the CAAC Reports 1991/92 and 1992/3.

[337] Based respectively on an analysis of Table 5.3 of the Judicial Statistics Annual Report 2000 and Table 5.3 of the Judicial Statistics Annual Report 2006 and Table 2.4 of the Civil Judicial Statistics 2011 (560 out of 183,718 overall disposals).

Although at one time, s 1(5) seemed to have led local authorities not to bring court proceedings, in fact relatively few no order disposals were in the public law context. In the first nine months after implementation of the 1989 Act such dispositions accounted for 3% of the total number of disposals made in public law proceedings[338] but only about 1% based on the 2011 statistics.[339] One would have expected relatively few no order disposals being made in the public law context, particularly in care proceedings under s 31 since if the statutory threshold is satisfied there is likely to be good reason to make an order regardless of whether or not the proceedings are contested.[340] Conversely, if s 31 is not satisfied a dismissal seems more likely than a 'no order'. In fact, however, in 2011 just over 2% of all disposals in care proceedings ended in a no order disposition.[341]

4. FORM OF ORDER

If the court decides that it is in the best interests of the child that no order be made, then a formal order to that effect must be made. A decision not to make an order still ranks as a 'decision', and reasons for making it should therefore be given.[342]

5. THE INTERRELATIONSHIP OF THE PARAMOUNTCY PRINCIPLE AND SECTION 1(5)

Although s 1(5) can be seen as complementing the welfare principle, since it cannot be in the best interest of a child to be the subject of unnecessary court orders, it has been argued[343] that in reality the welfare principle has been 'hijacked by non-interventionism' on the basis that the non-interventionist stance taken in the 1989 Act means that parental wishes, especially where both are in agreement, will determine an increasing number of issues affecting children.

Although there is some tension between s 1(1) and 1(5) it is surely going too far to suggest that the paramountcy principle has been 'hijacked'. As has just been seen even in the private law context, the proportion of 'no orders' made under s 1(5) is relatively small (though of course it is unknown how many applications are simply not being pursued).[344] Furthermore, most agreements are likely to provide the best arrangements that can be made for the children in the circumstances. Nevertheless there is a danger that by making no order in cases where there is parental agreement the court could overlook the child's wishes.[345] If they do so in the case of older children, there could be a breach of Art 12 of

---

[338] See CAAC Report 1991/92 Table 2.

[339] Table 2.4 of Civil Judicial Statistics 2011 (350 out of a total 32,739 disposals).

[340] In many cases, not making an order would amount to a dereliction of the court's duty: see eg *Re B (A Minor) (Care Order: Criteria)* [1993] 1 FLR 815 at 821. Note: the fact that the parties are agreed does not absolve the court from investigating the facts for itself: *Re G (A Minor) (Care Order: Threshold Condition)* [1995] Fam 16.   [341] 260 out of 11,411 overall disposals.

[342] *S v R (Parental Responsibility)* [1993] 1 FCR 331.

[343] A Bainham 'The Privatisation of the Public Interest in Children' (1990) 53 MLR 206 at 221. See also A Bainham 'The Children Act 1989, Welfare and Non-Interventionism' [1990] Fam Law 143 at 145.

[344] Nor should the number of withdrawn applications be overlooked, since a proportion of these withdrawals may have been motivated by a desire to avoid a 'no order'. The number of withdrawals generally exceeds that of 'no orders'. In 2011, for example, 792 public law applications were withdrawn compared with 350 'no orders' and 3,360 private law applications were withdrawn compared with 560 'no orders', see Table 2.4 of the Civil Judicial Statistics 2011.

[345] This is evidence that this is indeed the case in the context of divorce see, G Douglas et al 'Safeguarding Children's Welfare in Non-Contentious Divorce: Towards a Non Conception of the Legal Process?' (2000) 63 MLR 177 at 190–1.

the UN Convention on the Rights of the Child.[346] Accordingly, courts should be alive to this possibility and wherever possible[347] seek some assurance that the child in question does not object to the arrangements agreed between the parents.

6. THE INTERRELATIONSHIP OF HUMAN RIGHTS AND SECTION 1(5)

In the public law context in particular, but not exclusively, another consideration that comes into play is the need from a human rights perspective for the response to any harm to be proportionate.[348] It may be, notwithstanding that harm has been found, that the child will be adequately protected without any order being made. In such a case a 'no order' disposition would be justified both on human rights grounds and on the basis of s 1(5).[349] It is important, however, not to muddle these considerations. Section 1(5) operates to determine whether *any* order should be made, whereas human rights considerations dictate that whatever order is made must be proportionate to the harm found. In other words, even where an order is considered necessary, human rights, but not s 1(5), still operates to determine what type of order is appropriate. But neither consideration should derogate from the overarching principles of the paramountcy of the child's welfare.[350]

---

[346] Under which there is an international obligation for courts to give due weight to a child's views: see Ch 13.

[347] Though with formal repeal of s 41 of the Matrimonial Causes Act 1973 by s 17(1)(a) of the Children and Families Act 2014, the court has no *locus standi* to intervene in divorce proceedings unless separate proceedings over the children are brought.

[348] See *Re B (A Child) (Care Proceedings: Threshold Criteria)* [2013] UKSC 33 [2013] 1 WLR 1911, discussed in Ch 17, Welfare stage, p 625.

[349] See eg *Re K; A Local Authority v N* [2005] EWHC 2956 (Fam) [2007] 1 FLR 399, particularly at [55]–[58], per Munby J.

[350] See *Re M-J (Adoption Order or Special Guardianship Order)* [2007] EWCA Civ 56 [2007] 1 FLR 691, particularly at [19], per Wall LJ.

13

THE VOICE OF THE CHILD

A. INTRODUCTION

As we discussed in Chapter 9, historically the great shift in English law governing parent and child was the move from the position where children were of no concern at all to one where their welfare is the court's paramount consideration. But this has not been the only change, for a no less significant development has been the shift away from treating children as passive victims of family breakdown towards regarding them as participants and actors in the family justice system.[1] In *Re LC (Children) (Reunite International Child Abduction Centre intervening)*[2] Baroness Hale referred to the family justice system's 'increasing recognition of children as people with a part to play in their own lives, rather than as passive recipients of their parents' decisions.' One consequence of this shift is that in various family proceedings it has become incumbent upon the court to ascertain and duly to take into account children's own wishes and views. Judges too have been encouraged to see, at any rate older, children involved in private law proceedings before them. Policy makers and the judiciary have also been informed by a growing body of research into children's experiences of and views on the family justice system.[3]

It is now generally accepted that children should have a voice or, at any rate, the opportunity of expressing a view in legal proceedings which concern them. As the *Family Justice Review* (the 'Norgrove Review') put it:[4]

> Children's interests are central to the operation of the family justice system. Decisions should take the wishes of children into account and children should know what is happening and why.

We begin by discussing what obligation there is to take the child's views into account then we discuss how those views are investigated. Thirdly, we consider the law and practice

---

[1] See N Lowe and M Murch 'Children's participation in the family justice system—translating principles into practice' [2001] CFLQ 137.   [2] [2014] UKSC 1 [2014] 2 WLR 124 at [87].

[3] See, for example, U Kilkelly *Listening to children about justice: report of the Council of Europe consultation on child-friendly justice* (2010); Private Law Consultation *How it looks to me* (Cafcass, 2010); J Timms, S Bailey and J Thorburn *Your shout too! A survey of the views of children and young people involved in court proceedings when their parents divorce or separate* (NSPCC, 2007), the studies in the ESRC programme: *Children 5–16: growing into the twenty-first century*, referred by Lowe and Murch, op cit, 145, n 61; B Neale and C Smart 'Agents or Dependants? Struggling to listen to Children in Family Law and Family Research' Working Paper No 3 (1999); C Thomas, V Beckford, N Lowe, M Murch, *Adopted Children Speaking* (1999), I Butler, L Scanlan, M Robinson, G Douglas, M Murch *Divorcing Children—children's experience of their parents' divorce* (2003) and G Douglas, M Murch, C Miles and L Scanlan *Research into the Operation of Rule 9.5 of the Family Proceedings Rules 1991* (DCA, 2006). For an interesting discussion and research on researching into children's views see J Driscoll 'Children's rights and participation in social research: balancing young people's autonomy rights and their protection' [2012] CFLQ 452.

[4] Final Report, November 2011 at para 8 of the Executive Summary.

governing the child's direct participation in legal proceedings concerning them. We then discuss the needs for and requirements of a child friendly family justice system and finally, we consider the role of the Commissioners for Children to look after children's interests more generally.

B. THE OBLIGATION TO HAVE REGARD TO THE CHILD'S VIEWS

1. DOMESTIC LAW

(a) Adoption

Ever since adoption was introduced into English law in 1927 it has been incumbent upon the courts to give due consideration to the wishes of the children concerned having regard to their age and understanding.[5] Currently, the obligation, which lies on both courts *and* adoption agencies, is to have regard, whenever they are 'coming to decisions relating to the adoption of a child', to the child's ascertainable wishes and feelings considered in the light of the child's age and understanding.[6]

(b) Private law proceedings under the Children Act 1989

For a long time adoption was unique in requiring courts to have regard to children's wishes. No such formal obligation[7] was imposed in private law proceedings concerning children until the Children Act 1989. Now as part of the welfare checklist the court must, as in adoption, have regard to the 'ascertainable wishes and feelings of the child concerned (considered in the light of his age and understanding)'.[8] However, as discussed in Chapter 12 the *obligation* to apply the checklist in private law proceedings only arises in *contested* applications for s 8 orders.[9] This means that even where private law orders are sought under the Act, if the *adults* are agreed such that there is no contest, there is no statutory compulsion to consult the children. Indeed one of the reasons for limiting the application of the checklist to contested cases was to protect family autonomy.

Of course in the absence of any child related proceedings the court has no *locus standi* to consider the child's position. This has a particular impact in the context of divorce especially since the repeal of s 41 of the Matrimonial Causes Act 1973 by s 17 of the Children and Families Act 2014, thereby removing the obligation of the divorce courts to consider whether they should exercise any of their powers under the Children Act 1989 in relation to any children of the family.[10] Not only did the 2014 Act repeal s 41 but it also formally

---

[5] See the Adoption of Children Act 1926 s 3(b).

[6] Adoption and Children Act 2002 s 1(1) and (4)(a).

[7] Though as Butler-Sloss LJ said in the pre-Children Act decision, *Re P (A Minor) (Education)* [1992] 1 FLR 316 at 321: 'The courts over the last few years have become increasingly aware of the importance of listening to the views of older children and taking into account what children say, not necessarily agreeing with what they want nor, indeed, doing what they want, but paying proper respect to older children who are of an age and maturity to make up their minds as to what they think is best for them.'

[8] Children Act 1989 s 1(3)(a).

[9] Section 1(4)(a). The s 8 orders, namely, child arrangement orders, specific issue orders and prohibited steps orders are discussed in Ch 14.

[10] In fact the 1989 Act itself diluted the s 41 obligation. Before that the courts had to be satisfied with the arrangements for the children or consider that they were the best that could be devised in the circumstances. See the discussion in Ch 9, The meaning of 'child of the family', p 296.

repealed[11] s 11 of the Family Law Act 1996, which would have amended s 41 so as to have obliged a divorce court, when deciding whether it should exercise its powers under the Children Act, (a) to treat the child's welfare as the paramount consideration and (b) to have particular regard to a checklist of factors including 'the wishes and feelings of the child considered in the light of his age and understanding and the circumstances in which those wishes were expressed'. It also repealed the insertion of s 8(5) into the Children Act which would have empowered courts in the course of divorce proceedings to make s 8 orders whether or not they had been sought. These repeals reverse the policy underlying the 1996 reforms, which were never brought into force,[12] described by the then Lord Chancellor, Lord Irvine, as being:[13]

> fully in tune with the new and increasing contemporary awareness that a child is a person in his or her own right . . . the divorce process must now have regard to the interests and views of the children. They will now have a right to be consulted about the proposals which parents are making for the future in which they have a vital interest.

The 2014 reforms effectively deny children a voice in divorce proceedings themselves. It can be seen as the ultimate adoption of the non-interventionist policy espoused by the Children Act which in turn has been said[14] to rely upon the assumption that parents may be trusted in most cases, to plan what is best for their children's futures, and that, where they are in agreement on this, it is unnecessary and potentially damaging for the State, in the guise of the court, to intervene. But while in most cases it will no doubt be true that in the absence of dispute between the parents, children's interests will not be furthered by court intervention and that in any event the s 41 scrutiny was effectively a dead letter, the signals sent out by the 2014 reform nevertheless run counter to the general trend of involving children more rather than less in proceedings that concern them. The reform, however, is in line with the general policy of discouraging recourse to the courts in family matters, though whether it is in line with the UN Convention on the Rights of the Child can be debated, as we discuss shortly. It might also be added, however, that the reform places children of divorcing parents in no different a position to that of separating parents or of parents who are unmarried.

Divorce proceedings are not the only proceedings affecting children in which there is no obligation upon the court to ascertain the child's views, a similar gap exists in financial proceedings. Moreover, under s 10 of the Children and Families Act 2014, save in cases of domestic violence any person wishing to make a relevant family application[15] must first attend a family mediation and assessment meeting ('MIAM'). However, there is no statutory compulsion for children's views to be ascertained at these meetings. There is concern, too, that mediators do not always adopt a child inclusive approach.[16]

---

[11] See s 18.   [12] See Ch 7.   [13] Hansard, HL Debs Vol 573, Col 1076 (June 1996).

[14] G Douglas, M Murch, L Scanlan and A Perry 'Safeguarding Children's Welfare in Non-Contentious Divorce: Towards a New Conception of Legal Process?' (2000) 63 MLR 177 at 183–4.

[15] Ie an application made to a court in or to initiate family proceedings and is of a description specified in the Family Procedure Rules 2010: s 10(3).

[16] See J Walker 'How can we ensure that children's voices are heard in mediation?' [2013] Fam Law 191. See also J Norton 'The voice of the child in mediation in NFM services' [2012] Fam Law 84. For an interesting discussion of engaging children in contact centres see L Trinder, C Jenks and A Firth 'Talking children into being *in absentia*? Children as a strategic and contingent resource in family court dispute resolution [2010] CFLQ 234; L Caffrey 'Hearing the "voice of the child"? The role of child contact centres in the family justice system' [2013] CFLQ 357.

(c) Public law proceedings

In contrast to private law proceedings it is incumbent upon the court to have regard to the child's ascertainable wishes and feelings in *all* proceedings (whether or not contested) under Part IV of the Children Act.[17] Furthermore, in such proceedings the child will be represented by a children's guardian.

(d) Is the domestic law human rights compliant?

It is perhaps debatable whether the absence of an obligation to ascertain and consider children's views in proceedings either directly or indirectly concerning them violates the European Convention on Human Rights. Attention has tended to focus[18] upon the human rights implications of the absence of a right to separate representation in private law proceedings[19] (discussed later in this chapter) but there is clearly a case for arguing that the absence of a duty to consider the child's views violates Art 6 which guarantees *everyone* a right to a fair trial and, because the outcome of the case affects the child's family life, it could be said also to infringe procedural rights under Art 8. But this is by no means established by human rights jurisprudence[20] and in relation to Art 6 it could be argued that the absence of an obligation to consider the child's views is a matter of substantive rather than procedural law to which the Article therefore has no relevance.[21] What is accepted is that where the child is party to proceedings, Art 6 operates to guarantee a fair and public hearing within a reasonable time and that to be 'fair' the child's views have to be heard at any rate to the extent of having their wishes and feelings made known to the judge.[22]

2. INTERNATIONAL OBLIGATIONS

(a) UN Convention on the Rights of the Child

International impetus for promoting children's participation in the legal process was given by the United Nations Convention on the Rights of the Child 1989. Article 12 in particular states:

> (1) States Parties shall assure to the child who is capable of forming his or her own views the right to express those views freely in all matters affecting the child, the views of the child being given due weight in accordance with the age and maturity of the child.

---

[17] Children Act 1989 s 1(3)(a) and (4)(b). Part IV proceedings basically refer to care proceedings, see Ch 17. Although this obligation is confined to Part IV hearings and not therefore emergency proceedings under Part V, the court can appoint a guardian for the child for these proceedings, as well, see later in this chapter.

[18] See e.g. Mr Justice Munby 'Making Sure the Child is Heard? Part 2 Representation' [2004] Fam Law 427, J Fortin 'The HRA's impact on litigation and their families' [1999] CFLQ 237 and C Lyon 'Children's Participation in Private Law Proceedings' in M Thorpe and E Clarke (eds) *No Fault or Flaw: The Future of the Family Law Act 1996* (2000) 70.

[19] Discussed at Children as parties, p 467. The implication of Art 6 has also been considered in the context of children giving evidence, see The role of the children's guardian, p 459.

[20] Indeed the decision of the Grand Chamber of the European Court of Human Rights in *Sahin v Germany, Sommerfeld v Germany* [2003] 2 FLR 671 (discussed at Is the lack of automatic party status human rights compliant?, p 469) might be thought to point to the contrary. See also the analysis by J Fortin *Children's Rights and the Developing Law* (2009, 3rd edn) at 239 and 300.

[21] Cf *TP and KM v United Kingdom* [2001] 2 FLR 549.

[22] Per Sir Alan Ward in *Re P-S (Children) (Family Proceedings: Evidence)* [2013] EWCA Civ 223 [2013] 1 WLR 3831 at [37]–[38].

(2) The child shall in particular be provided the opportunity to be heard in any judicial and administrative proceedings affecting the child, either directly, or through a representative or appropriate body, in a manner consistent with procedural rules of national law.

Also not to be overlooked, is Art 9(2) which provides that in any proceedings concerning the separation of a child from his or her parents '*all* interested parties shall be given the opportunity to participate in the proceedings and make their views known' (emphasis added). The reference to all interested parties must include the child.[23]

Although, as mentioned in Chapter 12, the UN Convention is not strictly binding upon the English courts[24] as Sir Alan Ward put it in *Re P-S (Children) (Family Proceedings)*[25] 'the duty of the court is none the less to have regard to it when considering matters relating to it.' Indeed, as we are about to discuss, the English judiciary, inspired by Art 12, have moved considerably in being prepared not just to obtain children's views but also to hearing children directly both in domestic and international cases. Article 12 also very much lay at the heart of the reforms about listening to children recommended by the Norgrove Review[26] and accepted by the Government. In its response to Norgrove the Government said[27] that they 'were committed to giving due consideration to the UNCRC when making new policy and legislation' and that '[t]he key principles of our reforms will truly meet the needs of children and are intrinsically in line with the "general principles" of the UNCRC, which include... respect for the views of the child.'

What then are the obligations under Art 12? As Fortin has said[28] Art 12 'assures the rights set out to *any* child "capable of forming his or her own views", however young. Its phrasing makes it clear that specific age barriers are not acceptable.' It will also be noted that Art 12 applies not just to judicial proceedings but also to administrative proceedings. In this latter regard it was held in *ZH (Tanzania) v Secretary of State for the Home Department*,[29] relying on Art 12, that immigration authorities must be prepared at least to consider hearing directly from a child who wishes to express a view and is old enough to have one.

As Fortin points out,[30] the UN Committee on the Rights of the Child was in no doubt that Art 12 should be interpreted purposefully and indeed criticised the UK for not ensuring that its obligations were more consistently incorporated into legislation in private law proceedings involving divorce.[31] Although States Parties reaffirmed their commitment to Art 12 at the 27th session of the General Assembly in 2002, as Sir Alan Ward has observed,[32] children were still being marginalised. However, following a discussion organised by the Committee on the Rights of the Child in 2006, General Comment Number 12 was published in 2009. That Comment states inter alia:

---

[23] See A Moylan 'Children's Participation in Proceedings—The View from Europe' in M Thorpe and J Cadbury (eds) *Hearing the Child* (2003) 175.

[24] Though note the possibly different position in Wales by reason of the Rights of Children and Young Persons (Wales) Measure 2011, adverted to by Sir Alan Ward in *Re P-S (Children) (Family Proceedings: Evidence)* [2013] EWCA Civ 223 [2013] 1 WLR 3831 at [35].

[25] [2013] EWCA Civ 223 [2013] 1 WLR 3831 at [35].

[26] See para 4 of the Executive Summary to the Interim report (March 2011).

[27] *The Government Response to the Family Justice Review: A system with children and families at its heart* (Cm 8273, 2012) at p 10.   [28] *Children's Rights and the Developing Law* (2009, 3rd edn) p 236.

[29] [2011] UKSC 4 [2011] 2 AC 166 at [37].

[30] *Children's Rights and the Developing Law* (2009, 3rd edn) p 236.

[31] Committee on the Rights of the Child (2002) para 29.

[32] In *Re P-S (Children) (Family Proceedings: Evidence)* at [26].

34. A child cannot be heard effectively where the environment is intimidating, hostile, insensitive or inappropriate for her or his age...
35. After a child has decided to be heard, he or she will have to decide how to be heard: "either directly, or through a representative or appropriate body." The Committee recommends that, wherever possible, the child must be given the opportunity to be directly heard in any proceedings...
38. The opportunity for representation must be "in a manner consistent with procedural rules of national law"...
42. The context in which a child exercises his or her right to be heard has to be enabling and encouraging so that the child can be sure that the adult who is responsible for the hearing is willing to listen and seriously consider what the child has decided to communicate. The person who will hear the views of the child can be ... a decision-maker in an institution (eg a director, administrator or judge) ...
43. Experience indicates that the situation should have the format of a talk rather than a one-sided examination. Preferably, a child should not be heard in open court, but under conditions of confidentiality...
45. Since the child enjoys the right that her or his views are given due weight, the decision maker has to inform the child of the outcome of the process and explain how her or his views were considered. The feedback is a guarantee that the views of the child are not only heard as a formality, but are taken seriously.

There have been some quite wide judicial statements based on Art 12, not least that of Thorpe LJ in *Mabon v Mabon*,[33] who commented that to safeguard Art 12 rights 'we must, in the case of articulate teenagers, accept that the right to freedom of expression and participation outweighs the paternalistic judgment of welfare'. But it is important to keep the provision in perspective. It does not confer autonomy rights even on competent children nor does it prescribe how the child's voice is to be heard, that is, whether directly or through a representative but instead leaves that to be determined by national law.

In *Re P-S* Sir Alan Ward commented[34] that in the light of Art 12, it should now be declared that children have the important but limited right to be heard in legal proceedings. However, given that the Convention does not specify how the child should be heard and indeed expressly recognises that the voice of the child may be conveyed either directly or through a representative or appropriate body, the Convention cannot be said to confer a right to the child to give evidence.

All this said, the impact of Art 12 is not to be underestimated. In a child abduction case, for example, Thorpe LJ has commented[35] that it was implicit in the UN Convention that there is 'a growing perception that the trial judge should hear the voice of the child' and on this basis in another case[36] a trial judge was held to have erred by not raising with parties upon his own motion the need for him to meet the children (aged 15, 13 and 10) face to face. This need to consider the child's own perspective was further underscored by *Re LC (Children) (Reunite International Child Abduction Centre intervening)*[37] in which the Supreme Court held that in determining a child's habitual residence, it was important to address the child's state of mind.

---

[33] [2005] EWCA Civ 63 [2005] Fam 366 at [28].
[34] [2013] EWCA Civ 223 [2013] 1 WLR 3831 at [36].
[35] *Re G (Abduction: Children's Objections)* [2010] EWCA Civ 1232 [2011] 1 FLR 1645 at [15].
[36] *Re J (Abduction: Children's Objections)* [2011] EWCA Civ 1448 [2012] 1 FLR 457.
[37] [2014] UKSC 1 [2014] 2 WLR 124. For further discussion of this decision, see Ch 26.

(b) The European Convention on the Exercise of Children's Rights

Important as Arts 9 and 12 of the UN Convention are, they lack detail, for example, as to how children should be heard, and it was to address this deficiency that the Council of Europe devised its 1996 Convention on the Exercise of Children's Rights.[38]

The 1996 Convention aims to supplement the UN Convention, inter alia, by providing procedural mechanisms by which the voice of the child can be heard in legal proceedings concerning them. In particular Art 3 provides that a child 'considered by internal law as having sufficient understanding' shall, in the case of judicial proceedings affecting him or her, be granted and entitled to request the following rights:

a. to receive all relevant information;
b. to be consulted and express his or her views;
c. to be informed of the possible consequences of compliance with these views and the possible consequences of any decision.

Article 4 further provides for children to have the right:[39]

to apply, in person or through other persons or bodies, for a special representative in proceedings before a judicial authority affecting the child where internal law precludes the holders of parental responsibilities from representing the child as a result of a conflict of interest with the latter.

Despite its good intentions, the Convention has not had an enthusiastic reception particularly in the United Kingdom, with one critic[40] going as far as to say that it is 'weak' and 'toothless' especially when compared with the European Convention on Human Rights.

The United Kingdom has not signed this Convention and has given no indication of an intention to do so.

C. HOW CHILDREN'S VIEWS ARE INVESTIGATED

Even where their views and wishes and feelings have to be taken into account, children are not normally made parties to private law proceedings (and will not therefore be separately represented)[41] though there is a general power to do so.[42] In these proceedings the normal process through which the court will learn of the child's views, wishes and feelings, is by a court welfare report which can be ordered under s 7 of the Children Act 1989. These reports are provided by officers known as Children and Family Reporters. These officers

---

[38] The Convention came into force in 2000 following ratification by Greece, Poland and Slovenia. As of July 2014 there were 18 Contracting States to this Convention.

[39] This is subject to Art 9 which empowers the judicial authority to appoint a special representative for children (irrespective of their capacity or understanding) in cases of a conflict of interest between a child and the holders of parental responsibility. See further the Explanatory Report on the Convention published in 1997 by the Council of Europe.

[40] M Freeman *The Moral Status of Children* (1997) at 39. See also C Sawyer 'One step forward, two steps back—the European Convention on the Exercise of Children's Rights' [1999] CFLQ 151. But for some, albeit ambivalent support, see N Lowe 'Where in the World is International Family Law Going Next?' in G Douglas and N Lowe (eds) *The Continuing Evolution of Family Law* (2009) 260 at 281.

[41] But note the potential power to appoint a child's guardian provided for by s 41(6A) of the 1989 Act, inserted by the Adoption and Children Act 2002 s 122(1)(b), discussed at When guardians should be appointed, p 460.   [42] FPR 2010 r 16.2, discussed at Making a child a party, p 467.

are independent of the parties and are appointed by the court to investigate and report on the child's circumstances.

In public law proceedings the position is different. There, the child *is* a party to the proceedings and is normally represented by the children's guardian who in turn will (usually) instruct a solicitor (the so-called tandem model of representation). The creation of a system for separate representation of children by guardians pre-dates both the Children Act 1989 and the UN Convention on the Rights of the Child, being first introduced in 1984 (before that the child's interests were assumed to be represented by the parents).[43]

Before examining the differing roles of reporters and children's guardians, it is necessary to say something about the service that administers them.

1. CAFCASS

(a) The previous position

Before the reforms introduced in 2001 by the Criminal Justice and Court Services Act 2000 there were three separate services concerned with making reports about and/or representing children in family proceedings: the Guardian ad Litem and Reporting Officer (GALRO) Service, the Family Court Welfare Service and the Children's Branch of the Official Solicitor's Department.

The GALRO service was administered and financed by local authorities each of which had to set up a panel. The guardians ad litem themselves had to be qualified in social work and be a member of a panel. To ensure that the guardian was independent of all the parties, especially the local authority involved in the particular case, the individual appointed could not (a) be a member or officer or servant of the local authority or authorised person bringing the proceedings, or (b) have been at any time in the past an officer of the authority or voluntary organisation who has been directly concerned in that capacity in arrangements relating to the care or accommodation and welfare of the child, or (c) be a serving probation officer. Although the courts jealously protected guardians' independence, for example, in one case[44] quashing an attempt by one authority to lay down in advance the normal maximum time that should be spent on any particular case, the system was open to obvious doubts about the true independence of guardians. A clear conflict arose if, for example, the local authority made a complaint about the conduct of a case by a guardian since it was still involved in considering whether that guardian should continue to serve on the panel.

The Family Court Welfare Service was formerly a branch of the Probation Service (which had had long-standing and substantial involvement in the domestic jurisdiction of magistrates' courts) and what were then called court welfare officers were qualified probation officers.[45]

At one time the Official Solicitor played a significant role in representing children especially in wardship proceedings[46] but even before the creation of Cafcass had gradually

---

[43] The need to give the child a separate voice in care proceedings was first highlighted in 1974 by the Field-Fisher Committee of Inquiry into the death of Maria Colwell (HMSO, 1974).

[44] *R v Cornwall County Council, ex p Cornwall and Isles of Scilly Guardians ad Litem and Reporting Officers Panel* [1992] 2 All ER 471.

[45] For a brief discussion of the history of the service see e.g. S Cretney *Family Law in the Twentieth Century—A History* (2003) at 770, N Lowe and R White *Wards of Court* (1979, 1st edn) ch 9 and the references there cited.

[46] See eg N Lowe and R White *Wards of Court* (1986, 2nd edn) ch 9. Wardship is discussed in Ch 20.

retreated from the role, save in the most difficult cases and particularly those involving medical treatment.[47]

(b) The decision to change the system

There seemed an obvious case for rationalisation of these separate schemes and in 1997 a review concluded that each of the services just mentioned could provide an improved service to the courts, better safeguard the interests of children and reduce wasteful overlaps and increase efficiency.[48] Following this review, the Lord Chancellor decided to set up the Children and Family Court Advisory and Support Service (Cafcass).[49] This was achieved by the Criminal Justice and Court Services Act 2000 which came into force in April 2001. Since April 2005 Cafcass in Wales is the responsibility of the Welsh Government and its role is carried out by Cafcass (Cymru).[50]

(c) The current position

Cafcass is a non-departmental public body. It was initially sponsored by what was then known as the Department for Education and Skills, with ministerial responsibility resting with the Minister for Children, Young People and Families. Following the Family Justice Review, however, from April 2014 the sponsoring department is the Ministry of Justice. The thinking behind this change was to bring court social work functions closer to the court process, to mediation services and to out of court resolution and to give Cafcass 'a strong voice within the wider family justice system to champion the voice of the child in the courts.'[51]

The principal functions of Cafcass are set out by s 12(1) of the 2000 Act, namely, to:

> (a) safeguard and promote the welfare of children,
> (b) give advice to any court about any application made to it in any such [family] proceedings,
> (c) make provision for the children to be represented in such proceedings, and
> (d) provide information, advice and other support for the children and their families.

Following the creation of Cafcass changes were made to the names of its various officers. In particular, court welfare officers became known as 'children and family court reporters'[52] and guardians ad litem became known as 'children's guardians'. The former responsibilities of the Official Solicitor to represent children who are the subject of family proceedings have been taken over by the 'Cafcass High Court team'[53] (formerly known as 'Cafcass Legal', which term is now used to describe the Cafcass in-house lawyers). All Cafcass employees and contractors are expected to work in accordance with the *Cafcass*

---

[47] See eg R White, P Carr and N Lowe *Children Act in Practice* (1995, 2nd edn) 10.22–10.25. For discussion of the Official Solicitor's current role, see Butterworths *Family Law Service* 3A [5065] ff and Clarke Hall & Morrison on *Children* 11[170] ff.

[48] *Support Services in Family Proceedings—Future Organisation of Court Welfare Services* (1998).

[49] *Setting up a unified Children and Family Court Advisory and Support Service (CAFCASS)* 'Children First' (2000).   [50] Children Act 2004 Part IV.

[51] *The Government Response to the Family Justice Review: A system with children and families at its heart* (Cm 8273, 2012) at p 27. No changes were made to the responsibility for Cafcass (Cymru).

[52] Rather confusingly, however, a local authority officer appointed under s 7 of the Children Act 1989 (discussed below) is known as a 'welfare officer'.

[53] For the types of cases that should be handled by the team, see *Cafcass and National Assembly of Wales Practice Note* [2006] 2 FLR 143.

National Standards.[54] Any individual wishing to complain about any aspect of the work of Cafcass may do so according to the terms of its complaints process.[55]

(d) Criticisms of Cafcass

Despite the obvious sense in amalgamating the disparate schemes for safeguarding children's interests, Cafcass was the subject of considerable criticism particularly in its early years. It had a troubled introduction including the quashing of its decision to use only employed staff and not to proceed with the option of self-employment for former guardians ad litem.[56] One consequence of this early dispute was the haemorrhaging away from the service of experienced guardians who decided to retire rather than work for Cafcass.[57] As highlighted in a report by the House of Commons Select Committee on Cafcass[58] a major cause of the initial problems was the unrealistically short timetable for the establishment of the service which, in the Committee's view was a serious misjudgment. Other problems identified by the Committee included unacceptable delays, shortage of qualified staff and confused lines of accountability.

In response to the criticisms, Cafcass introduced national standards which, as already mentioned, are measured by HM Magistrates' Courts Services Inspectorate. It also introduced a complaints procedure. But while the service may well have improved its performance after a poor beginning,[59] it is evident that there remain problems about pressure on resources and consequential backlogs and there have been several so-called 'interim' guidance notes concerning the use of Cafcass resources.[60] However, in its response to the Norgrove Review, the Government commented:[61]

> Cafcass has made substantial progress in its performance, particularly in the light of a significant and sustained increase in demand for care applications over the last three years.

Cafcass has reformed many of its working practices to absorb a much higher volume of cases, and has made a 15% increase in productivity since April 2010, improvements which are now being built on further.

The idea of the already mentioned change of sponsorship to the Ministry of Justice is to 'embed these changes and bring Cafcass into the wider system of family justice'.[62] It remains to be seen how successful the service will be in the future.

---

[54] Published in June 2007 and superseding those published in March 2003.

[55] For details of which see the Cafcass website.

[56] *R (on the application of the National Association of Guardians ad Litem and Reporting Officers) v Children and Family Court Advisory and Support Service* [2001] EWHC 693 (Admin) [2002] 1 FLR 255.

[57] But note the rejection of this allegation by J Tross (the then Cafcass Chief Executive) in 'CAFCASS—Moving Forward' [2002] Fam Law 829, at 830.

[58] Published in July 2003 and summarised in [2003] Fam Law 626. Note also the Government reply: *The Response of the Government and the Children and Family Court Advisory and Support Service to the Constitutional Affairs Committee's Report on Children and Family Court Advisory and Support Service (CAFCASS)* (2003) Cm 6004.

[59] See J Tross 'CAFCASS Present and Future' [2004] Fam Law 731.

[60] See *Practice Direction Interim Guidance to Assist Cafcass* [2009] 2 FLR 1407.

[61] *The Government Response to the Family Justice Review: A system with children and families at its heart* at p 27.

[62] Not everyone is enthusiastic about this change, see the concerns expressed by J Doughty and M Murch 'Judicial independence and the restructuring of family courts and their support service' [2012] CFLQ 333 at 351–354.

2. WELFARE REPORTS

(a) The power under section 7

The principal means of ascertaining the child's view in private law proceedings is through a welfare report.[63] Section 7(1) of the 1989 Act empowers any court, when considering *any* question with respect to a child under the 1989 Act, to ask an officer of the service (ie a Cafcass or a Welsh family proceedings officer) or a local authority to report to the court 'on such matters relating to the welfare of that child as are required to be dealt with in the report'. Insofar as this role is taken on by a Cafcass officer it will be discharged by a children and family reporter. The power to ask for a report in relation to *any* issue under the 1989 Act means that welfare reports may be ordered in care proceedings.[64] However, as we discuss shortly, this role is usually undertaken by children's guardians who, unlike children and family reporters, represent the child in the proceedings. Nevertheless, on occasion it might be necessary for a reporter to act in care cases to save time and resources. Indeed, in some cases such a reporter may have already done so, for example, in family proceedings where the court decides, after hearing the evidence, that it should exercise its powers under s 37 and invite the local authority to investigate the case with a view to the authority applying for a care or supervision order.[65]

Section 7 empowers the courts in private law proceedings to ask a local authority to report rather than a children and family reporter. However, this is not intended to result in local authorities being asked as a matter of routine, but only in those cases where they have an obvious connection with the case.[66] If a local authority is already involved, applications may properly be made to the court hearing the private law proceedings for them to provide a report under s 7.[67] According to the *Child Arrangements Programme*[68] in determining whether a request for a report should be directed to a relevant local authority the court should consider such information as Cafcass has provided about the nature and extent of the local authority's current or recent involvement with the child(ren) and the parties. Where both private law proceedings and investigations are being carried out by the police and social services, then s 7 can and should be used to require the local authority to report to the court on the nature, progress and outcome of the investigation. In this way the court can ensure the co-ordination of the private law proceedings with the statutory local authority child abuse investigations.[69]

Under s 7(5) it is the duty of the local authority or reporter to comply with any court request for a welfare report.[70] However, where the court decides to ask the local authority to report, it can ask them to arrange for this to be done either by one of their officers or 'such other person (other than an officer of the Service or a Welsh family proceedings

---

[63] For a consumer view of the Service see A Buchanan, J Hunt, H Bretherton and V Bream *Families in Conflict: Perspectives of Children and Parents in the Family and Court Welfare Service* (2003).

[64] For an example, see *Re L (Interim Care Order: Extended Family)* [2012] EWCA Civ 179 [2013] 2 FLR 302.   [65] Care and supervision orders are discussed in Ch 17.

[66] See Law Com No 172 para 6.17. For examples of a welfare report being prepared by a local authority in private law proceedings, see *Re M (Intractable Contact Dispute: Interim Care Order)* [2003] EWHC 1024 (Fam) [2003] 2 FLR 636: report ordered in a father's application to enforce a contact order against the mother who had made allegations of sexual abuse by the father and *Re J (Residence and Contact Dispute)* [2012] EWCA Civ 1231 [2013] 1 FLR 716: a seemingly simple dispute over residence and contact. In the context of international child abduction, see *Re C (Jurisdiction and Enforcement Of Orders Relating To Child)* [2012] EWHC 907 [2012] 2 FLR 1191 and *Re H (Abduction: Grave Risk)* [2003] EWCA Civ 355 [2003] 2 FLR 141.

[67] Per Wall J in *W v Wakefield City Council* [1995] 1 FLR 170.   [68] (2014) para 11.12.6(c).

[69] Per Wall J in *Re A and B (Minors) (No 2)* [1995] 1 FLR 351 at 368–9.

[70] See also FPR 2010 r 16.33 (2).

officer) as the authority consider appropriate'.[71] There is no power under s 7 to order a local authority to instruct a child psychiatrist to prepare a report for the court,[72] nor more generally to order any form of residential assessment.[73] It should be appreciated that both a children and family reporter and a local authority welfare officer have an independent role, being neither the child's representative nor a witness for either party. In relation to the reporter (CFR) it has been said[74] that manifestly he (or she):

> acts independently and exercises an independent discretion as to the nature and extent of his investigations and inquiries and no less in the manner in which he approaches them . . . It is through the CFR that the judge most evidently executes that part of his function which is inquisitorial. The CFR in turn depends upon the judge to give due weight in the scales of justice to the outcome of his investigations. Both judge and CFR are united sharing the same ultimate objective, namely, the protection of children and the advancement of their welfare. In pursuit of that overriding objective each must be free to operate independently as well as collaboratively and independent operation includes the exercise of an independent discretion.

It is important to emphasise that the reporter's duty is to report on the child's welfare rather than on the child's wishes and feelings as such, though in discharging this duty, the reporter will investigate those wishes and feelings. In other words, a welfare report provides an indirect voice for the child.

(b) When reports should be ordered

As explained by the 'Best practice note' drafted by the Children Act Advisory Committee (hereinafter referred to as *Best Practice*),[75] the ordering of a welfare officer's report is a judicial act requiring inquiry into the circumstances of the child. A report should not be ordered unless there is a live issue under the Children Act, and before a report is ordered consideration should be given to the power to refer the parties (with their consent) to mediation. This approach is reinforced by the *Child Arrangements Programme*[76] according to which the court should specifically consider whether there are welfare issues that need addressing and that in any event the court should consider whether there are alternative ways of working with the parties such as through mediation. At every First Hearing Dispute Resolution Appointment ('FHDRA') a Cafcass officer is expected to be available to facilitate early dispute resolution rather than the provision of a formal report. Commonly, the decision to order a report will be taken at the FHDRA, though there is power to order a report at any stage. The court has been said to have an unappealable discretion to decide whether or not to ask for a report.[77]

---

[71] Section 7(1)(b). This is intended to cover the situation where, as a result of close co-operation, the NSPCC, for example, acting on behalf of the local authority, is seen to be the key worker for the particular child: see R White, P Carr and N Lowe *A Guide to the Children Act 1989* (1990) para 8.6.

[72] *Re K (Contact: Psychiatric Report)* [1995] 2 FLR 432, CA.

[73] *R v R (Private Law Proceedings: Residential Assessment)* [2002] 2 FLR 953.

[74] Per Thorpe LJ in *Re M (Disclosure: Children and Family Reporter)* [2002] EWCA Civ 1199 [2002] 2 FLR 893 at [26].

[75] See *Handbook of Best Practice in Children Act Cases* (CAAC 1997) Appendix A. Although this was drafted before the creation of CAFCASS, as Clarke Hall and Morrison says at 11 [142], it still appears to remain best practice with appropriate amendments to terminology.   [76] (2014) para 11.12.6(a).

[77] *Re W (Welfare Reports)* [1995] 2 FLR 142, CA. But note the queries on this raised in R White, P Carr and N Lowe *Children Act in Practice* (2008, 4th edn) at 10.20.

If a report is ordered, then, according to the *Child Arrangements Programme*[78] the order should state the specific and other factual issues that are to be addressed in a focused report. General requests are to be avoided, as *Best Practice* explains:

> ... the judge, district judge or justices' clerk should explain briefly to the parties what will be involved and should emphasise the need to co-operate with the welfare officer and specifically to keep any appointments. In particular when the principle of contact is in dispute the parties should be told that the welfare officer will probably wish to see the applicant parent alone with the child. It should also be emphasised that the report, when received, is a confidential document and must not be shown to anyone who is not a named party to the application.

It has long been established[79] that the officer's reporting and mediation roles are quite distinct and to some extent incompatible and that accordingly, as *Cafcass Service Principles and Standards* now states:[80]

> If CAFCASS is subsequently ordered to prepare a report by the Court, another Practitioner should be assigned to the case and should not be given access to any information or statements made during the course of the mediation process.

It also expected that such appointees should carry out their investigative task and not subsequently assume a mediation role.[81]

It has been held that, once the report is ordered, the desirable practice is to ascertain when it can be expected and to fix a specific date in the light of that information.[82]

(c) The form, content and disclosure of reports

Once appointed, 'officers' (as the persons preparing the report are known)[83] must make such investigations as may be necessary and in particular contact or seek to interview such persons as appear appropriate or as the court directs and obtain such professional assistance as is available which the officer thinks appropriate or which the court directs to be obtained.[84] Whenever possible officers should see the child with each of the parties, for as Johnson J commented in *Re P (A Minor) (Inadequate Welfare Report)*:[85]

> The whole point of the ... system is that, because in the nature of things the court cannot itself observe the relationship between the children and the parents, the [reporter or welfare officer] acts as the eyes and ears of the court and provides the court with an independent and objective assessment of the relationships involved. Here the report was inadequate. The inquiry was conducted in such a way as to make it impossible for her to form any views about the relationships involved.

A fortiori all children should be seen by the officer unless there are strong reasons for not doing so. If a child is not seen the reasons for this should be given in the report.[86]

---

[78] (2014) para 11.12.6 (b).

[79] See *Scott v Scott* [1986] 2 FLR 320, CA and *Re H (Conciliation: Welfare Reports)* [1986] 1 FLR 476. The Booth Committee (Report of the Matrimonial Causes Procedure Committee, 1985) at para 4.63 had already recommended that the same officer should not both conciliate and later report in the same case.

[80] Ibid at 3.29.   [81] *Scott v Scott*. See also *National Standards*.

[82] *B v B (Minors) (Interviews and Listing Arrangements)* [1994] 2 FLR 489.

[83] FPR 2010 r 16.33 (1).   [84] *Practice Direction 16A* para 6.2.

[85] [1996] 2 FCR 285 at 291. See also *Re W (A Minor) (Custody)* (1983) 4 FLR 492 at 501, CA, per Cumming-Bruce LJ.   [86] But cf the findings of Buchanan et al, op cit.

The report may be made in writing or orally as the court requires.[87] In practice it is usually made in writing. Beyond directing that in carrying his duties an officer must address the effects of delay and have regard to the welfare checklist,[88] neither statute nor the Rules prescribe the contents of the report. Nevertheless officers are required to structure their report in accordance with the Cafcass format and guidelines.[89] According to those guidelines, reports will:

> 3.11.1 set out all relevant information which the Practitioner has acquired through his/her enquiries, making clear from what service the information has been obtained and distinguishing between matters of fact and matters of opinion;
>
> 3.11.2 make clear recommendations (or explain why recommendations cannot be made) which draw on relevant aspects of the Welfare Checklist;
>
> 3.11.3 explain the basis upon which those recommendations have been made, including reasons both for and against those recommendations.

In response to the recommendation of the Private Law Working Group (chaired by Cobb J)[90] aimed at reducing the duration of a private law case, the *Child Arrangements Programme*[91] states that when preparing a report, officers 'are encouraged to make recommendations for stepped phasing-in of child arrangements (ie recommendations for the medium and longer term future for children) insofar as they are able to do so safely in the interests of the child(ren) concerned'.

It is inevitable that to some extent an officer will rely on hearsay evidence. Indeed, it has been said that in the nature of things such officers could not do what is required of them and comply with the hearsay rule.[92] However, although s 7(4) provides that, regardless of any rule of law which would otherwise prevent it from doing so, the court may take into account any statement contained in (or evidence given in respect of matters referred to in) the report, regard should still be had to *Thompson v Thompson*.[93] In that case it was said that on controversial issues, for example, making adverse findings against a party, if an officer is constrained to pass on second-hand evidence, he should endeavour to make this explicit and indicate his source of information and his reasons, if he has any, for agreeing with such an opinion.

The officer must notify and explain to the child such contents (if any) as the officer considers appropriate to the child's age and understanding including any reference to the child's own views and the recommendation.[94] Written reports should be filed with the court and a copy served on the other parties and any guardian in accordance with the timetable set by the court.[95] The report is a confidential document and should not be disclosed to anyone other than a party, his or her legal representative, the Cafcass officer and the Legal Services Commission without the leave of the court.[96] In exceptional cases the court can order that the report should not be disclosed to the parties.[97] Accordingly, officers should give no undertaking that what they are told will be kept confidential and not disclosed in the report.[98]

---

[87] Section 7(3). The normal expectation is that the report will be written.

[88] See FPR 2010 r 16.33 (4).   [89] See para 3.10 of *Cafcass Services, Principles and Standards*.

[90] Whose Report is published in [2013] Fam Law 1594, see para 13(b).   [91] (2014) para 14.3.

[92] Per O'Connor LJ in *Webb v Webb* [1986] 1 FLR 462 at 463, CA.

[93] [1986] 1 FLR 212n at 216–17, CA. See also *Edwards v Edwards* [1986] 1 FLR 187 and *H v H (A Minor), K v K (minors)* [1990] Fam 86, CA.   [94] *Practice Direction 16A* para 9.3.

[95] *Practice Direction 16A* para 9.4.   [96] FPR 2010 r 16.33.

[97] *Re M (Minors) (Disclosure of Evidence)* [1994] 1 FLR 760, CA and *Re B (Minor) (Disclosure of Evidence)* [1993] Fam 142, CA, but note that the appropriate test is that laid down in *Re D (Minors) (Adoption Reports: Confidentiality)* [1996] AC 593, HL.

[98] *Re G (Minors) (Welfare Report: Disclosure)* [1993] 2 FLR 293, CA.

Notwithstanding the confidentiality of the report it has been held[99] that an officer does *not* require court leave to report concerns about possible child abuse to the relevant statutory authorities.

There is no automatic requirement that the officer attend court, instead that is dependent upon the court direction.[100] If no direction is made the officer is not expected to attend. Such directions will need to be made whenever a party wishes to exercise his right to question the officer about his report.[101] However, officers are not witnesses but are officers of the court[102] and it is important not to draw them into the adversarial battle between the parties. As Thorpe LJ said in *Re B (Residence Order: Status Quo)*,[103] the function of the officer:

> is essentially to submit for the guidance of the judge very carefully considered reports. I cannot imagine a case in which it would be necessary for the [children and family reporter] to be exposed to a whole day of what was effectively cross-examination by one side or the other. It is wasteful of the [reporter's] precious time and, in the end, it does not help the judge who wants to see the wood and is invariably helped by being spared the trees.

The court is not bound by any recommendations contained in a s 7 report but if it departs from it the judge should state the reasons for so doing.[104] Although there are several reported examples of the court not following a recommendation,[105] in practice the children and family reporter's view commands great respect and it should be appreciated that in most cases he is the most influential figure in the decision-making process.[106]

Normally, clear-cut recommendations should only be rejected after hearing the welfare officer's oral evidence.[107] However, bearing in mind the principle of delay set out in s 1(2), it is within the court's power to depart from a recommendation even where the officer does not attend the hearing.[108]

3. THE ROLE OF THE CHILDREN'S GUARDIAN

(a) Distinguishing children's guardians and children and family court reporters

The crucial role of giving children a voice in public law proceedings in particular is provided by the 'children's guardian'.

Unlike children and family court reporters, guardians represent children in public law proceedings, in which the child is a party.[109] They also have the duty to instruct legal

---

[99] *Re M (Disclosure: Children and Family Reporter)* [2002] EWCA Civ 1199 [2002] 2 FLR 893: during preparation of the report the mother and sister alleged that the father had behaved inappropriately in front of the children.

[100] *Practice Direction 16A* para 9.4 (a).   [101] FPR 2010 r 16.33(5).

[102] See the wording of r 16.33 (5).   [103] [1998] 1 FLR 368 at 371.

[104] See eg *Re M (Residence)* [2004] EWCA Civ 1574 [2005] 1 FLR 656 and *Re V (Residence: Review)* [1995] 2 FLR 1010, CA.

[105] See eg *Re P (A Minor) (Inadequate Welfare Report)* [1996] 2 FCR 285; *Re W (A Minor) (Custody)* (1983) 4 FLR 492, CA; *Leete v Leete and Stevens* [1984] Fam Law 21; and *H v H* [1984] Fam Law 112, CA.

[106] See eg M Murch *Justice and Welfare in Divorce* (1980) ch 8.

[107] *Re W (Residence)* [1999] 2 FLR 390, CA; *Re CB (Access: Court Welfare Reports)* [1995] 1 FLR 622, CA. See also *Re F (Minors) (Contact: Appeal)* [1997] 1 FCR 523, CA.

[108] *Re C (Section 8 Order: Court Welfare Officer)* [1995] 1 FLR 617, CA.

[109] For interesting research on this issue see A James, A James and S McNamee 'Constructing Children's Welfare in Family Proceedings' [2003] Fam Law 889.

representation for the child.[110] This method of representation is commonly referred to as the 'tandem model' of representation of children whereby, as Thorpe LJ put it in *Mabon v Mabon*:[111]

> the court appoints a guardian . . . , who will almost invariably have a social work quali-fication and a very wide experience of family proceedings. He then instructs a specialist solicitor who, in turn, usually instructs a specialist family barrister') works well particu-larly in public law proceedings.

Notwithstanding their differences guardians and children and family court reporters have many functions in common. Both have a duty to report to the court and be exam-ined on their report and both are under a duty to safeguard the interests of the child and thus to advise the court independently of the other parties as to what is best for the child. These similarities prompted Butler-Sloss LJ to say that one would not normally expect to have both a guardian and welfare officer appointed in the same case.[112] A further blurring of the distinction between the two roles is with respect to training. Cafcass officers are recruited as 'convergence trained' officers which means that they are trained in the func-tions of both children's guardians and children and family reporters.

Only Cafcass and Welsh family proceedings officers may be appointed as a children's guardian. Independent social workers, for example, cannot be so appointed. Although it is generally good practice for the court to leave it to the service to choose which individual officer to act it seems implicit in the power[113] 'to consider the appointment of anyone who has previously acted as a children's guardian' that the court can appoint a specified person.[114] In any event the point has been made that the court appoints an officer of the service to act and not the organisation.[115]

(b) When guardians should be appointed

Under s 41 of the Children Act 1989 courts are required in 'specified proceedings' to appoint a children's guardian for the child 'unless satisfied that it is not necessary to do so in order to safeguard his interests'. By 'specified proceedings' is essentially meant public law proceedings[116] and, following amendments by the Adoption and Children Act 2002, applications for the making or revoking of adoption placement orders.[117]

At the time of the 1989 Act the intention was that appointment of children's guard-ians would be the norm in care proceedings[118] and indeed it is rare for an appointment

---

[110] These differences were highlighted by Butler-Sloss LJ in *Re S (A Minor) (Guardian Ad Litem/Welfare Officer)* [1993] 1 FLR 110 at 114–15, CA. [111] [2005] EWCA Civ 634 [2005] Fam 366 at [25].

[112] In *Re S (A Minor) (Guardian Ad Litem/Welfare Officer)* at 116. But for a case where this was done see *L v L (Minors) (Separate Representation)* [1994] 1 FLR 156, CA. Note also *Re T and E (Proceedings: Conflicting Interests)* [1995] 1 FLR 581 in which Wall J observed that it was not necessary to appoint more than one guardian to represent children involved in the same proceedings even if their interests conflict.

[113] Conferred by FPR 2010 r 16.3(4).

[114] A point made by *Butterworths Family Law Service* at 3A [5213].

[115] Per Sir Nicholas Wall P in *A County Council v K, CJ and T* [2011] EWHC 1672 (Fam) [2011] 2 FLR 817, at [42].

[116] 'Specified proceedings' are defined by s 41(6) and include care and supervision proceedings, cases where a s 37 direction has been made, discharge applications, applications under Part V of the Children Act and contact in care proceedings under s 34. See also FPR 2010 r 12.27. As *Butterworths Family Law Service* points at 3A [5204] education supervision order applications are not included within the definition.

[117] Children Act s 41(6)(hh). In fact under the FPR 2010, all adoption, placement and related proceedings (referred to as proceedings to which Part 14 applies) are treated as if they were 'specified' proceedings'.

[118] During the debates on the Bill, David Mellor MP said on behalf of the Government that guardians should be appointed in over 90% of cases: HC Official Report, SC B, 23 May 1989, col 255.

not to be made. Nevertheless it was held first in *R v Children and Family Court Advisory and Support Service*[119] and subsequently in *R and Others v Cafcass*[120] that the service is not under a duty to make provision to enable it, immediately on request by the court to make available an officer of the service for appointment as guardian but rather to do so 'as soon as reasonably practicable' having regard to its general functions and duties, its human and financial resources and the various competing demands upon it. In reaching this conclusion the Court of Appeal in the latter case rejected the 'brave submission' that a failure to appoint a children's guardian immediately upon being directed to do so by the court amounted to breach of Arts 6 and 8 of the European Convention on Human Rights. As McFarlane LJ put it, '[o]ther than a blanket policy which, for example, refused to permit a party to proceedings any form of representation, it is difficult to conceive of circumstances where a breach of Art 6, or the procedural requirements of Art 8, could be established "immediately" at the very start of proceedings.'[121] All this said, it is accepted that the sooner an appointment is made the better for the child and that some cases are more urgent than others. Note might still be taken, for example of *X Council v B (Emergency Protection Orders)*[122] in which Munby J held that in the context of emergency protection proceedings, a delay of 10 days was 'wholly unacceptable'. By *Practice Direction 12A* the allocation of an officer is expected within three days.

The appointment normally lasts until the conclusion of the proceedings for which the appointment was made[123] but there is power, solely exercisable by the court,[124] to revoke or change an appointment before the conclusion of proceedings.[125]

The difference between representation in public and private law proceedings is striking and is a vivid illustration that the dichotomy between private and public law proceedings has not been harmonised by the 1989 Act.[126] It may be noted that although s 122(1)(b) of the Adoption and Children Act 2002 extended the definition of 'specified proceedings' by adding s 41(6A) which provides that Rules of Court may bring within the definition proceedings for the making, varying or discharging of a s 8 order,[127] no such action has been taken.

(c) The children's guardian's duties

Pursuant to s 41(2)(b) of the 1989 Act, the children's guardian's general duty is to safeguard the interests of the child as prescribed by the Rules. Rule 16.20 requires children's guardians to act on behalf of the child and to provide the court with such other assistance as it may require. In carrying out these duties regard must be had to the delay principle and to the checklist of factors under the 1989 Act or the Adoption and Children Act 2002 as is appropriate. By *Practice Direction 16A* children's guardians are expected to advise the court on the following:

(a) whether the child is of sufficient understanding for any purpose including the child's refusal to submit to a medical or psychiatric examination or other assessment that the court has power to require direct or order;

---

[119] [2003] EWHC 235 (Admin) [2003] 1 FLR 953.

[120] [2012] EWCA Civ 853 [2012] 2 FLR 1432.

[121] Ibid at [87]. But note that undue delay might violate Art 6 etc in an individual case but that could only be established by looking at the trial process as a whole. [122] [2005] 1 FLR 341.

[123] Which means in the case of supervision orders on the *making* of the order. The decision to the contrary in *Re SB and MB (Children)* [2001] 2 FLR 1334 has been reversed by the repeal of the Criminal Justice and Court Services Act 2000, s 12 (5)(b), see SI 2003/3079.

[124] See Sir Nicholas Wall P's comments to this effect in *A County Council v K, CJ and T* [2011] EWHC 1672 (Fam) [2011] 2 FLR 817 at [43]. [125] FPR 2010 rr 16.19 and 16.25.

[126] See *W v Wakefield City Council* [1995] 1 FLR 170.

[127] On which see M Millin 'Speaking for Children' [2003] Fam Law 217.

(b) the wishes of the child in respect of any matter relevant to the proceedings, including that child's attendance at court;
(c) the appropriate forum for the proceedings;
(d) the appropriate timing of the proceedings or any part of them;
(e) the options available to the court in respect of the child and the suitability of each such option including what order should be made in determining the application;
(f) any other matter on which the court seeks his advice or on which the children's guardian considers that the court should be informed.[128]

By para 6.2 of *Practice Direction 16A* the children's guardian must (save where he is an officer of the service authorised to conduct litigation and intends to conduct the proceedings on the child's behalf)[129] appoint a solicitor to act for the child unless a solicitor has already been appointed.[130] He must also give such advice to the child as is appropriate having regard to that child's understanding and, where appropriate, instruct the solicitor representing the child on all matters relevant to the child's interests arising in the course of proceedings, including possibilities for appeal.

Once both a guardian and a solicitor have been appointed, it is for the former to consider how the case should be presented in court on the child's behalf and to give instructions to the solicitor.[131] However, where the child wishes and is able to give instructions on his or her own behalf[132] which conflict with those of the guardian, the solicitor must take instructions from the child.[133] In that event the guardian continues with his or her duties save for instructing the solicitor.

(d) Discharging the duties

To carry out his duties, a children's guardian must investigate all the circumstances, including interviewing such persons as he thinks appropriate or as the court directs, inspect local authority records (see later), and bring to the court's attention such records and documents which in his opinion may be of assistance to the case. He may also obtain such professional assistance as he thinks appropriate or which the court directs him to obtain.[134] According to the *Cafcass Service Principles and Standards*[135] children's guardians should work in a manner and at a pace which are appropriate to the child's age and understanding and the seriousness of the child's situation. They should develop a comprehensive understanding of the child's needs in the light of the child's age and understanding.

The guardian's investigations are confidential,[136] but it is for the court and not the guardian to waive that confidentiality.[137] Consequently, all information relevant to the

---

[128] Para 6.6.   [129] See *Practice Direction 16A* para 6.3.

[130] But note (1) that under s 41(3), (4) the court may appoint a solicitor for the child if there is no guardian or if the child, having sufficient understanding to instruct a solicitor, wishes to do so, or if the court thinks that it is in the child's interests to be represented, and (2) notwithstanding this duty to instruct a solicitor the Legal Services Commission may decide that the merits of a case do not warrant legal representation and refuse legal aid: *W and Others v Legal Services Commission* [2000] 2 FLR 821.

[131] See The Law Society *Protocol for Working Relationship between Children Panel solicitors and Guardians ad Litem* (2000).

[132] In cases of doubt, expert opinion might be required: *Re H (A Minor) (Care Proceedings: Child's Wishes)* [1993] 1 FLR 440.

[133] See FPR 2010 r 16.29. See C Sawyer 'The competence of children to participate in family proceedings' [1995] CFLQ 180.

[134] See *Practice Direction 16A* para 6.1   [135] See para 2.5.

[136] Per Ward J in *Oxfordshire County Council v P* [1995] Fam 161 and, per Hale J, in *Cleveland County Council v F* [1995] 2 All ER 236.   [137] See *Re G (Minors) (Welfare Report)* [1993] 2 FLR 293, CA.

enquiry should be disclosed in the report. It is not within the guardian's power to promise a child to withhold information from the court.[138] On the other hand, information revealed to the guardian in the course of the investigations should not be disclosed to third parties without prior court leave.[139]

Section 42 of the 1989 Act gives the children's guardian extensive rights to examine and take copies of any records of or held by a local authority or the NSPCC in relation to a child and compiled in connection with any function of the social services committee.[140] These include child protection conference minutes[141] and files prepared in the exercise of the authority's function as an adoption agency.[142] The guardian does not, however, have a right to see Crown Prosecution Service files, although the court may order such disclosure.[143]

At the end of these investigations the guardian produces a written report advising on the interests of the child. The report should make clear recommendations or explain what recommendations cannot be made.[144] As with other court documents, the report is confidential. Furthermore, this confidentiality continues after the conclusion of the hearing.[145]

Children's guardians or the appointed solicitor are, unless specifically excused, required to attend all direction hearings.[146] On a strict reading it would appear that a children's guardian is not bound even to attend a final hearing but it is clear that in practice their attendance at the final hearing is required[147] with the expectation that they can be questioned about their reports. As with court welfare reports, the evidence and recommendations of children's guardians are not binding on the court,[148] but they are very influential and in any event the court should give its reasons for departing from them.[149]

Normally the guardian's appointment ceases at the conclusion of the proceedings and it has been held,[150] for example, that a court cannot order that a guardian should have contact with a child after a care order has been made. It is now clear that the appointment will end upon the making of a supervision order.[151] Nevertheless it seems that the conclusion of proceedings may not *ipso facto* mean that the guardian becomes *functus officio*. At any rate this was the view taken in *Oxfordshire County Council v L and F*[152] in which it was

---

[138] Compare *Re D (Minors) (Adoption Reports: Confidentiality)* [1996] AC 593, HL.

[139] But see *Oxfordshire County Council v P* and *Re G (a minor) (social worker: disclosure* [1996] 2 All ER 65, CA, which establish that guardians can properly disclose parental admissions about the responsibility for non-accidental injuries to their children to the social worker involved in the case without court leave. See further N Lowe 'Guardians Ad Litem and Disclosure' [1996] Fam Law 618.

[140] But not therefore of the housing or education committees.

[141] Children Act 1989 s 42(1) as amended by the Courts and Legal Services Act 1990 Sch 16 para 18.

[142] *Re T (A Minor) (Guardian ad Litem: Case Record)* [1994] 1 FLR 632, CA.

[143] *Nottingham County Council v H* [1995] 1 FLR 115.

[144] See *Cafcass Service Principles and Standards* para 3.

[145] See *Re C (Guardian ad Litem: Disclosure of Report)* [1996] 1 FLR 61, in which it was held that court leave was required to disclose the report to a family centre which was connected with the social services department and which offered therapeutic treatment to the children concerned.

[146] *Practice Direction 16A* para 5.

[147] Cf *Re W (Cross-Examination)* [2010] EWCA Civ 1449 [2011] 1 FLR 1979.

[148] See eg *Buckinghamshire County Council v M* [1994] 2 FLR 506, CA.

[149] See eg *Re W (A Minor) (Secure Accommodation Order)* [1993] 1 FLR 692.

[150] *Kent County Council v C* [1993] Fam 57. For the position in cases where a s 37 direction has been made see *Re CE (Section 37 Direction)* [1995] 1 FLR 26 and *Re S (Contact: Grandparents)* [1996] 1 FLR 158, CA; guardian's appointment should be ended by a judicial rather than an administrative act.

[151] Following the repeal by Sch 4 to the Adoption and Children Act 2002 of s 12(5)(b) of the Criminal Justice and Court Service Act 2000, thus reversing *Re MH (A Child) and Re SB and MB (Children)* [2004] 2 FLR 1334.

[152] [1997] 1 FLR 235. But cf Butler-Sloss LJ in *Re G (Minor) (Social Worker: Disclosure)* [1996] 2 All ER 65 at 71 who commented: 'The guardian has no function outside the proceedings to which he has been appointed. *When these proceedings are completed his function is ended*' (emphasis added).

held that the guardian should continue to be involved in proceedings brought after a care order had been made for the disclosure of documents of those proceedings to the police and for a variation of injunctions controlling publicity.

At all events, the children's guardian must (a) ensure that if it is appropriate to do so the child is notified (in a manner appropriate to the child's age and understanding) of the court's decision and in such cases have the decision explained (again in a manner appropriate to the child's age and understanding)[153] and (b) consider with child's solicitor possibilities for an appeal.[154]

(e) Commentary

One effect of the introduction of children's guardians in public law proceedings was to give them greater authority in the eyes of the court though it may be questioned why greater weight should be given to the guardian's opinion than to that of any other witness of similar expertise. As has been observed,[155] the guardian is likely to have more experience than the average social worker, but is working alone, with limited supervision. There is no evidence that guardians are appointed for their expertise in a particular type of case. If the local authority put forward a cogent case supported by expert evidence based on the considered opinion of experienced staff, surely the court should express with equal clarity its reasons for departing from their recommendations? But this quibble apart, the 'tandem model of representation', which Thorpe LJ referred to as a 'Rolls-Royce' model which is the envy of many other jurisdictions,[156] has in Wall LJ's words, served:[157]

> the interests of . . . children very well. The child has the input of expertise from the different disciplines of lawyer and guardian, who are able, with the court's permission, to call on additional expertise and advice where necessary. In public law proceedings s 42 of the Children Act 1989 gives the court sweeping powers of investigation on the child's behalf. At the same time, the child concerned is protected from the corroding consequences of adversarial litigation. Children are not required to give evidence and be cross-examined: they do not have access to the sensitive documentation generated by the case. The system is, of course, paternalistic in approach, but it usually works well, in my experience, even in cases where the child has sufficient understanding to participate in the proceedings concerned without a guardian.

As McFarlane LJ has observed,[158] 'the availability of the tandem model in childcare proceedings has been under focus in the recent review of the family justice system' but it was very much endorsed by that Review. In its interim report the Norgrove Review stated:[159]

> The tandem model is fundamental to our system and receives strong support . . . the court needs an impartial social work opinion and even though this results in a degree of duplication with the role of the Local Authority social worker.

Importantly, in McFarlane LJ's words, 'the government accepted the recommendation that the tandem model should be retained with resources carefully prioritised and allocated.'[160]

---

[153] *Practice Direction 16A* para 6.11.   [154] *Practice Direction 16A* para 6.2(c).

[155] R White, P Carr and N Lowe *Children Act in Practice* (1995, 2nd edn) at 10.45.

[156] In *Mabon v Mabon* [2005] EWCA Civ 634, [2005] Fam 366 at [25].   [157] In *Mabon v Mabon*, at [40].

[158] In *R and Others v Cafcass* [2012] EWCA Civ 853 [2012] 2 FLR 1432 at [7].

[159] See para 4.243–4.244 of the Interim Report (March 2011). The final report (November 2011) was very much in the same vein.

[160] See the Government Response to the Family Justice Review: A System with children and families at its heart (Cm 8273, 2012) at p 63.

D. THE CHILD'S DIRECT PARTICIPATION IN PROCEEDINGS

1. PRIVATE LAW PROCEEDINGS

As has been said, children's involvement, if at all, in private law proceedings is limited. They are not normally parties to the proceedings and their view will either be conveyed to the court through a welfare report or via the parents. However, it is not always the case that children do not have a direct involvement in a private law case. First, even where they are not parties, it is open to a judge to interview children in private. Secondly, there are occasions when children can be made parties to proceedings brought by the parents. Finally, it is open to children, at least those of sufficient age and understanding, to initiate proceedings themselves.

(a) Judicial interviews with children in private

The question of whether judges should see children in private has generated considerable discussion not least among the judges themselves.[161] It is evident that views on the appropriateness of such a practice, which is the norm in Continental European jurisdictions, have changed. As Sir Alan Ward commented in *Re P-S (Children) (Family Proceedings: Evidence)*:[162]

> It is an odd feature of the law relating to children that under that most paternalistic of all jurisdictions, wardship, the judge in wardship frequently saw his ward, or at least I did as often as I could. Then when wardship effectively disappeared following the Children Act 1989, the practice of seeing children seems to have been actively discouraged. Now the pendulum is swinging back.

In a thoughtful and comprehensive extra-judicial address,[163] Baroness Hale identified three reasons for the then declining frequency of judges seeing children in private, namely (1) there were more professionals involved in ascertaining the child's view and the courts were content to accept their accounts and interpretations; (2) there was a reluctance on the part of the higher courts to allow lay magistrates (who under the Children Act had been given comparable powers and procedures to the higher courts) to interview children in private;[164] and (3) there was (and still is) the difficulty of reconciling a private interview with adversarial procedures and rules of evidence. As Wall LJ commented in *Mabon v Mabon*,[165] the reluctance of the English judge to talk to children in private:

> has several origins, but one of them is undoubtedly rooted in the rules of evidence and the adversarial mode of trial. What is said in private by the child to the judge cannot be tested in evidence or in cross examination. As a consequence a judge in England and

---

[161] For extra-judicial discussion see Sir Mark Potter 'The Voice of the Child: Children's "Rights" in Family Proceedings' [2008] IFL 140; Baroness Hale 'The Voice of the Child' [2007] IFL 171 and Sir Nicholas Wilson 'The Ears of the Child in Family Proceedings' [2007] Fam Law 808.

[162] [2013] EWCA Civ 223 [2013] 1 WLR 3831 at [23].   [163] 'The Voice of the Child' [2007] IFL 171.

[164] In fact there was pre-Children Act authority, namely, *Re T (An Infant)* (1974) 4 Fam Law 48; *Re T (A Minor) (Welfare Report Recommendation)* (1977) 1 FLR 59; and *Re W (Minors)* (1980) 10 Fam Law 120, that only the High Court and county court could see children in private, but after the Act it was held in *Re M (A Minor) (Justices' Discretion)* [1993] 2 FLR 706, per Booth J that in exceptional circumstances magistrates could also see a child in private.   [165] [2005] EWCA Civ 634 [2005] Fam 366 at [38].

Wales cannot promise a child that any conversation with the child will be entirely confidential. That fact may inhibit children from expressing their true wishes and feeling to
the judge . . .

Baroness Hale made it clear that she did not find these reasons convincing, commenting
in relation to the third point in particular that the confidentiality problem is raised just
as much by professionals seeing children as it is by the court doing so. She also pointed to
what she described as 'wake-up calls' both from research[166] which pointed to children's
need to feel involved and from European Court of Human Rights' decisions[167] which
she considered indicated the Court's expectation that the child's Art 8 rights required as
much procedural protection as those of adults. In her view, with safeguards (such as having someone else present and taking notes) the logistical problem of seeing a child in private can be overcome and in appropriate cases and with careful handling there are clear
advantages to the child of doing so, not least of which is engendering in the child a feeling
of being respected, valued and involved. It was equally clear that the then President of
the Family Division, Sir Mark Potter, shared Baroness Hale's views and was in favour of
encouraging judges to see children, particularly those who were keen to see the judge.[168]

While these views were undoubtedly influential and indeed shared by some other senior judges, not least Thorpe LJ,[169] they were at that time by no means the majority view.[170]
In 2008 the matter was referred to a sub-committee of the Family Justice Council, 'The
Voice of the Child', to consider the way forward. That committee came out strongly in
favour of judges seeing children. The resulting guidance from the Council, *Guidelines for
Judges Meeting Children Who Are Subject to Family Proceedings* published in 2010 states its
purpose as being:

to encourage judges to enable children to feel more involved and connected with proceedings in which important decisions are made in their lives and to give them an opportunity to
satisfy themselves that the judge has understood their wishes and feelings and to understand
the nature of the judge's task.[171]

The Guidelines stress that 'the child's meeting with judge is not for the purpose of gathering
evidence. That is the responsibility of the Cafcass officer. The purpose is to enable the child to
gain some understanding of what is going on, and to be reassured that the judge has understood him/her.'[172]

The Guidelines provide that the judge is entitled to expect the child's lawyer and/or the
Cafcass officer to advise on whether the child wishes to meet the judge and whether that
accords with the child's welfare. If a judge decides nevertheless not to meet the child, he
should consider providing the child with a brief written explanation. The other parties are
entitled to make representations about any proposed meeting. If the meeting takes place
before the conclusion of proceedings the judge should explain to the child he cannot hold any
secrets and discuss with the child how his decision (which he should explain is his responsibility) should be communicated.

---

[166] Discussed at Messages from research, p 472.
[167] In particular *Sahin v Germany; Sommerfeld v Germany* [2003] 2 FLR 671, ECtHR (Grand Chamber).
[168] See his extra-judicial address 'The Voice of the Child: Children's "Rights" in Family Proceedings'
[2008] IFL 140.
[169] See eg *Re W (Leave To Remove)* [2008] EWCA Civ 538 [2008] 2 FLR 1170 and *Re G (Abduction: Custody)*
[2010] EWCA Civ 1232 [2011] 1FLR 1645.
[170] See eg the cautious views expressed in *Re W (Leave To Remove)* above in disagreement with Thorpe LJ.
[171] [2010] 2 FLR 1872, in the Preamble.   [172] See para [5].

While the Guidelines preserve the judge's discretion whether to see a child in private in any particular case, note might be taken of *Re J (Abduction: Children's Objections)*[173] in which it was held that the trial judge had erred by not raising upon his own motion the need for him to meet the children. In other words, it is incumbent upon judges to consider the appropriateness of seeing children and to apply the Guidelines. In short the discretion whether or not to see the child can no longer be considered to be entirely unfettered.[174] It is also important not to confuse gathering evidence from children, which is subject to another set of guidelines,[175] and listening to the child's views.[176]

(b) Children as parties

Making a child a party

Children are not automatically parties to private law proceedings. Indeed as we discussed in Chapter 10, the power to conduct litigation on their child's behalf is generally thought to be an aspect of parental responsibility. Nevertheless it is within a court's power[177] to order that a child be made a party to proceedings. This is now provided for by r 16.2 of the Family Procedure Rules 2010.[178] This Rule, which only applies to private law proceedings,[179] simply provides:

> (1) The court that may make a child a party to proceedings if it considers it is in the best interests of the child to do so.

Guidance on the matters that the court should take into consideration in determining whether a child should be made party are provided by *Practice Direction 16A* to which Rule 16.2 draws attention.

As the *Practice Direction* says, making a child a party is 'a step that will be taken only in cases which involve an issue of significant difficulty and consequently will occur in only a minority of cases.' Before taking such a step the court should consider whether an alternative route might be preferable such as asking a Cafcass officer to make further enquiries or possibly by obtaining expert evidence. It should also take into account the risk of delay that such an appointment will inevitably cause. The *Practice Direction* contains the following circumstances that may justify making a child a party:

> (a) where an officer of the service or Welsh family proceedings officer has notified the court that in the opinion of that officer the child should be made a party;
> (b) where the child has a standpoint or interest which is inconsistent with or incapable of being represented by any of the adult parties;
> (c) where there is an intractable dispute over residence or contact, including where all contact has ceased, or where there is irrational but implacable hostility to contact or where the child may be suffering harm associated with the contact dispute;

---

[173] [2011] EWCA Civ 1448 [2013] 1 FLR 457.

[174] Cf earlier decisions such as *D v D (Custody of Child)* (1981) 2 FLR 74 and *Re R (A Minor) (Residence: religion)* [1993] 2 FLR 163, CA, which suggested that it was.

[175] *Guidelines in Relation to Children Giving Evidence in Family Proceedings* (2011).

[176] See *Re A (Fact-finding Hearing: Judge Meeting With Child)* [2012] EWCA Civ 185 [2012] 2 FLR 369.

[177] Note: any level of judge make the appointment. Prior to the 2010 Rules, magistrates had no power.

[178] This rule replaced r 9.5 of the FPR 1991, on which see G Douglas, M Murch, C Miles and L Scanlan *Research into the operation of Rule 9.5 of the Family Proceedings Rules 1991* (2006), J Fortin *Children's Rights and the Developing Law* (2009, 3rd edn) ch 7 and M Murch 'The Voice of the Child in Private Law Proceedings in England and Wales' [2005] IFL 8.

[179] See r 16.2, which excludes the application of r 16.1 to 'specified proceedings' (ie public law proceedings as defined by s 41 (6) of the 1989 Act and FPR 2010, 12.27) and Part 14 proceedings (ie adoption and related proceedings).

(d) where the views and wishes of the child cannot be adequately met by a report to the court;

(e) where an older child is opposing a proposed course of action;

(f) where there are complex medical or mental health issues to be determined or there are other unusually complex issues that necessitate separate representation of the child;

(g) where there are international complications outside child abduction, in particular where it may be necessary for there to be discussions with overseas authorities or a foreign court;

(h) where there are serious allegations of physical, sexual or other abuse in relation to the child or there are allegations of domestic violence not capable of being resolved with the help of an officer of the service or Welsh family proceedings officer;

(i) where the proceedings concern more than one child and the welfare of the children is in conflict or one child is in a particularly disadvantaged position;

(j) Where there is a contested issue about scientific testing.

As Douglas et al observed[180] of the similar guidelines previously contained in a *President's Direction*, paras (b), (c) and (d) all make reference to the child having a position or views contrary to those proposed by adults which is, as they say, reflective of a 'voice'-based approach and is evidence of a greater sensitivity to the need to hear the child's wishes and feelings. The other examples concern either the complexity of the case or the welfare of the child and reflect the more traditional approach of the courts.

Case-law, at any rate in the past, generally reflects the view[181] that welfare is the primary rationale for making separate representation appointments and in particular 'a desire to ensure that a conflict of interests of the parents does not obscure the real needs of the child'. In Douglas et al's view the courts' overall concern when ordering separate representation 'is to obtain a complete picture of the situation, where necessary presented by someone who is independent of the parents' positions. And this will often be motivated less by a concern to hear the child than to explore conflicts of evidence or to hear arguments that neither adult party wishes to put forward'.[182]

The consequences of making a child a party

Where a child is made a party in accordance with r 16.2 then, by r 16.4(c) the court must appoint a children's guardian to act for the child, unless the child has obtained the court's permission to act without such a guardian or a solicitor considers that the child is able, having regard to his understanding to give instructions (which the solicitor has accepted) in relation to the proceedings.[183]

Where an appointment of a children's guardian is required then by r 16.24 the court may appoint an officer of the service or a Welsh family proceedings officer or, if the

---

[180] *Research into the Operation of Rule 9.5 of the Family Proceedings Rules 1991* (2006) at 2.33.

[181] See Douglas et al, op cit at 2.38, relying inter alia upon *Re H (Contact Order) (No 2)* [2002] 1 FLR 22—contact dispute after father threatened to kill himself and the children; *Re A (Contact: Separate Representation)* [2000] 1 FLR 663—contact dispute in which the parents were so antagonistic to each other neither could be regarded as able to put their child's interests first; *Re F (Contact Restraint Order)* [1995] 1 FLR 956, CA—fears about accepting children's, especially young children's, views at face value—in this case children aged seven and six stated that they did not want contact with their father. See also *Re W (Contact: Joining Child as Party)* [2001] EWCA Civ 1830 [2003] 1 FLR 681—a seven-year-old child reluctant to have contact with his father. Note also *Re L (Minors) (Separate Representation)* [1994] 1 FLR 156 in which (what was then) the court welfare officer felt she could not adequately present the children's (aged 14, 12 and nine) views to the court and *Re C (Prohibition on Further Applications)* [2002] EWCA Civ 292 [2002] 1 FLR 1136—a case of alleged 'parental alienation syndrome'.

[182] Douglas et al, op cit at para 2.45.   [183] FPR 2010 r 16.6 (3).

appointee consents, the Official Solicitor or some other person. In no event should a children's guardian be appointed unless the court is satisfied that the appointee '(a) can fairly and competently conduct proceedings on behalf of the child; and (b) has no interest adverse to that of the child.'[184] There is power subsequently to terminate the appointment and to appoint a substitute children's guardian[185] and, in any event, an appointment terminates upon the child reaching 18.[186]

The powers and duties of a 'r 16.4 children's guardian' are set out by *Practice Direction 16A*,[187] namely 'fairly and competently to conduct proceedings on behalf of the child' such that all steps and decisions taken by the children's guardian 'are taken for the benefit of the child.'

According to Thorpe LJ in *Mabon v Mabon*[188] what is now the Rule 16.4 system of representation is:

> essentially paternalistic. The guardian's first priority is to advocate the welfare of the child he represents. His second priority is to put before the court the child's wishes and feelings.

(c) Is the lack of automatic party status human rights compliant?

There has been much speculation as to whether the child's lack of automatic party status in private law proceedings is human rights compliant. The most obvious provision in point is Art 6 which guarantees that in the determination of his civil rights and obligations 'everyone is entitled to a fair and public hearing within a reasonable time by an independent and impartial tribunal established by law'. And there are those who have argued[189] that Art 6 could be thought to vest a right in children to have separate representation in proceedings concerning them. Some[190] have gone further and suggested that 'the way in which children are currently treated by the private family proceedings process might arguably been in breach of Art 14 which prohibits discrimination on any ground and that a child's or young person's age could certainly be included within this'.

To date, however, there is no European Court of Human Rights decision that supports this speculation. Indeed to the contrary the Grand Chamber of the European Court of Human Rights' ruled in *Sahin v Germany; Sommerfeld v Germany*[191] that Germany had not violated the Convention in *Sahin*'s case, by the German court's reliance on the findings of experts concerning a five-year-old's view. As the court pointed out, contrary to its earlier Chamber decision[192] it is going too far to say that domestic courts should always hear evidence from a child in court. Of course that ruling might not apply to older more mature children but in that respect it is important to take into account that a specific duty of a children and family reporter is to consider whether the child should be given party status and to advise the court accordingly.[193] Moreover, it is open to a child of sufficient

---

[184] FPR 2010 r 16.24 (2). An application for such an appointment requires evidence: r 16.24 (4).

[185] FPR 2010 r 16.25.   [186] FPR 2010 r 16.28.   [187] FPR 2010 r 16.27.

[188] [2005] EWCA Civ 634 [2005] Fam 366 at [26].

[189] See J Fortin 'The HRA's impact on litigation involving children and their families' [1999] CFLQ 237 at 244. See also her arguments in *Children's Rights and the Developing Law* (2009, 3rd edn) at 238–39, where she also speculated whether lack of party status could be in breach of procedural rights under Art 8.

[190] C Lyon 'Children's Participation in Private Law Proceedings' in M Thorpe and E Clarke (eds) *No Fault or Flaw: The Future of the Family Law Act 1996* (2000) 70. Query whether this argument would be accepted since the courts might well say that there are good reasons for differentiating between children and adults in the matter of participating in legal proceedings, with the former needing more protection from, for example, the rigours of cross-examination, than the latter.   [191] [2003] 2 FLR 671.

[192] *Sahin v Germany; Sommerfeld v Germany; Hoffman v Germany* [2002] 1 FLR 119.

[193] *Practice Direction 16A* para 9.4 (c).

understanding, to acquire party status according to the procedure set out in the Family Procedure Rules 2010 r 16.6 (discussed shortly). In short, even for older children the lack of automatic party status might not, particularly when these other safeguards and mechanisms for requiring party status are taken into account, be in breach of Art 6.

2. PUBLIC LAW PROCEEDINGS

As previously discussed, the child is a party to public law proceedings and will be represented by the children's guardian. Nevertheless notwithstanding that party status, the Rules[194] give the court a discretion to hear the case in the child's absence if it considers it in the interests of the child, having regard to the matters to be discussed or the evidence likely to be given, and the child is represented by a guardian or solicitor. In other words, the child does not have an absolute right to attend the hearing and indeed there is a general view that it is commonly not in his or her interests to do so.[195]

Notwithstanding the foregoing, the child's evidence may be heard by the court if it is of the opinion that the child understands the duty to speak the truth and has sufficient understanding to justify his evidence being heard.[196] More commonly, however, the child will have been interviewed beforehand and the evidence will be presented in court on the child's behalf by the interviewer.[197]

E. CHILDREN AS LITIGANTS

1. THE SUBSTANTIVE LAW

Before the Children Act 1989, one of the few ways that a child could initiate his or her own proceedings was by making him or herself a ward of court.[198] Even after implementation of the 1989 Act this remains a possible option. However, in most cases the preferable course is to seek leave to apply for a s 8 order under the Children Act. The ability for children to seek s 8 orders was one of the innovations of the 1989 legislation. We discuss this course of action in Chapter 14. Suffice to say here, that court leave (which can only be granted where the court is satisfied that the child has sufficient understanding to make the application)[199] is a necessary prerequisite to seeking a s 8 order.[200]

Apart from the right, subject to leave, to apply for s 8 orders, the 1989 Act confers on a child of sufficient understanding a number of other rights. He can, for example, again subject to court leave, apply to (a) have a parental responsibility order made under s 4, s 4ZA or s 4A brought to an end;[201] (b) to have a guardianship appointment made under s 5 brought to an end;[202] and (c) have a special guardianship order varied or discharged.[203] So far as public law orders are concerned, a child can apply for the discharge or variation

[194] FPR 2010 r 12.14, on which see *A City Council v T, J and K* [2011] EWHC 1082 (Fam) [2011] 2 FLR 803.
[195] See eg *Re C (A Minor) (Care: Child's Wishes)* [1993] 1 FLR 832 in which it was held that guardians ad litem should think carefully about the arrangements for children who are to be present in court.
[196] Children Act 1989 s 96(2).
[197] This hearsay evidence is admissible under the Children (Admissibility of Hearsay Evidence) Order 1993.
[198] See N Lowe and R White *Wards of Court* (1986, 2nd edn) at 3–4. Wardship is discussed in Ch 20.
[199] See s 10(8).   [200] Section 10(1)(a)(ii).
[201] Section 4(3)(b), s 4ZA (6)(b) and s 4A(3)(b), discussed in Ch 11.
[202] Section 6(7)(b), discussed in Ch 8.   [203] Section 14D(1)(e), (3) and (4), discussed in Ch 19.

of a care or supervision order[204] and for the discharge of an emergency protection or child assessment order.[205] However, the child has no right to apply for the review or discharge of a secure accommodation order.[206]

2. THE PROCEDURE

In line with the general inability of children to conduct their own legal proceedings,[207]r 16.5 of the Family Procedure Rules 2010 requires a child who is a party to but not the subject of proceedings to have a litigation friend[208] to conduct proceedings on his behalf. However, as an exception to this general principle, r 16.6[209] enables a child to conduct proceedings under the Children Act 1989 and under the High Court's inherent jurisdiction without a litigation friend or children's guardian. According to r 16.6(3) a child may do so either where the court has given leave or where a solicitor considers that the child is able, having regard to his age and understanding, to give instructions and has accepted instructions from the child to act for him in the proceedings.

The leading decision, *Re T (A Minor) (Child: Representation)*,[210] establishes that where the court considers that the child does not have sufficient understanding, though the solicitor's assessment of the child's capacity to instruct him is otherwise, the court is the final arbiter and can appoint a litigation friend or guardian ad litem. It also established, however, that once it is found that the child has sufficient understanding to instruct a solicitor the court has no power to interfere.

Precisely what level of understanding a child must have to pass the r 16.6(3) test has been the subject of much thought[211] and litigation. According to Thorpe J *Re H (A Minor) (Care Proceedings: Child's Wishes)*[212] the level of understanding required to enable a child to instruct a solicitor is not as high as that required to make an informed decision to refuse psychiatric or medical treatment. The leading case is *Mabon v Mabon*[213] in which the Court of Appeal overturned a refusal to grant three brothers, aged 17, 15 and 13, separate representation. In reaching this conclusion, Thorpe LJ recognised that there is now 'a keener appreciation of the autonomy of the child and the child's consequential right to participate in decision-making processes that fundamentally affect his family life'. Consequently courts must accept that in the case of articulate teenagers 'the right to freedom of expression and participation outweighs the paternalistic judgment of welfare'. However, his Lordship added:

> In testing the sufficiency of a child's understanding, I would not say that welfare has no place. If direct participation would pose an obvious risk of harm to the child, arising out of the nature of the continuing proceedings and, if the child is incapable of comprehending that risk, then the judge is entitled to find that sufficient understanding has not been

---

[204] Section 39, discussed in Ch 17.   [205] Section 45(8) and 43(12), discussed in Ch 17.
[206] Secure accommodation orders are discussed in Ch 15.
[207] Civil Procedure Rules 1998 Part 21.
[208] A litigation friend, formerly known as a 'next friend', is basically a disinterested person who can fairly and competently conduct proceedings on the child's behalf. The procedure for becoming a litigation friend is provided for by FPR 2010 Part 16 Chapter 5.   [209] Formerly r 9. 2A of the FPR 1991.
[210] [1994] Fam 49.
[211] For early discussion see eg Mr Justice Thorpe 'Applications by children under the Children Act' [1994] Fam Law 20; D Burrows 'A child's understanding' [1994] Fam Law 579; E Walsh 'Applications by Children: Paternalism v Autonomy' [1994] Fam Law 663. See also the valuable study by C Sawyer *The Rise and Fall of the Third Party: Solicitors' Assessment of the Competence of Children to Participate in Family Proceedings* (1995).
[212] [1993] 1 FLR 440.   [213] [2005] EWCA Civ 634 [2005] Fam 366.

demonstrated. But judges have to be equally alive to the risk of emotional harm that might arise from denying the child knowledge and participation in the continuing proceedings.

On the facts of *Mabon* Thorpe LJ agreed with the submission that it would be unthinkable to exclude the young men from knowledge of and participation in legal proceedings that affected them so fundamentally.

It is nevertheless the solicitor's duty to assess the child's understanding throughout the case. In this regard the solicitor will be guided by the SFLA's *Guide to Good Practice for Solicitors for Children*.[214] Any leave which has been granted by the court under r 16.6 can subsequently be revoked by the court if it considers that the child does not have sufficient understanding.[215]

Although the gradual move towards child autonomy and away from a welfare based approach will be welcomed by many, the child litigant nevertheless does pose some difficult problems for the family justice system. It may be questioned, for example, whether it is necessary for the child to participate fully in the proceedings as if he were an adult. Should he, for example, be subject to the full rigours of cross-examination or be entitled to examine all the papers?[216] In this regard note should be taken of Lord Wilson's observation in *Re LC (Children) (Reunite International Child Abduction Centre intervening)*[217] 'A grant of party status to a child leaves the court with a wide discretion to determine the extent of the role which she should play in the proceedings.'

F. THE NEEDS FOR AND REQUIREMENTS OF A CHILD-FRIENDLY FAMILY JUSTICE SYSTEM

1. MESSAGES FROM RESEARCH

Research suggests that many practitioners in the family justice system lack the necessary skills and understanding for effective face to face work with children. Hunt and Lawson,[218] for example, comment that many professionals are aware of their lack of training and experience in talking to and listening to children.

Other areas of concern highlighted by various studies include:[219]

(1) Children are not used to being listened to. As Schofield and Thoburn comment[220] 'Children in our society are not accustomed to having their views taken into account in their everyday lives at home or at school. We do not live in a culture which supports participation by children'.

---

[214] 2002, 6th edn.   [215] FPR 2010 r 16.6(8).

[216] See the discussion in R White, P Carr and N Lowe *Children Act in Practice* (1995, 2nd edn) 10.16ff.

[217] [2014] UKSC 1 [2014] 2 WLR 124 at [55].

[218] J Hunt and J Lawson *Crossing the boundaries—the views of practitioners of Family Court Welfare and Guardian ad Litem work on the proposal to create a unified court welfare service* (1999) at p 38.

[219] Much of which is summarised by A O'Quigley *Listening to children's views and representing their best interests—a summary of current research* (1999). See also N Lowe and M Murch 'Children's participation in the family justice system—translating principles into practice' [2001] CFLQ 137 at 143 *et seq.*

[220] G Schofield and J Thoburn *Child Protection: the voice of the child in decision making* (1996) at p 62. Note also the comment by A L James and A James 'Pump up the Volume' (1999) 6(2) *Listening to Children in Separation and Divorce in Childhood* 206: 'Ours is a culture that does not particularly like children. The adage that "children should be seen and not heard" has an authentically English ring about it.'

(2) Many adults seem to have difficulties in listening to children. A number of reasons have been advanced for this. Neale, for example, comments[221] 'Adults view children as essentially other. They are seen as less important and they are dependent and less powerful. Language is a tool used communally or on the basis of shared understandings. Adults interpret what children say. Welfare professionals do so on the basis of their understanding of what is in the child's best interest.' Smith[222] postulates that adults fear they will upset children by talking about difficult experiences such as separation and divorce. Even more challengingly, Day Sclater and Piper assert[223] that adults protect themselves from their own vulnerabilities by projecting them (*unconsciously*) on to the children. They suggest that to keep that anxiety contained, adults rationalise that it is vital *not* to listen to children's own constructions of their needs but instead to act as if they know children's best interests better than they do. Finally, Murch et al believe[224] that many adults (including welfare professionals, solicitors and judges) confuse 'participation' with decision making. They are reluctant even to speak or to listen to children because they see this as inappropriately asking the child to decide. But whatever the reason, as Baroness Hale has said extra-judicially,[225] it is a common criticism that reporters do not accurately report what the child has said or has put his own interpretation or spin upon it.

(3) Children can have disturbing experiences when talking to professionals. In this respect O'Quigley[226] makes five important and troubling points:

(a) Children are generally reluctant to talk to outsiders about family issues as this was seen as disloyal and liable to lead to an escalation of problems.

(b) Professionals are seen as having been interventionist rather than supportive.

(c) The discussions that children have with professionals often feel like interrogations.

(d) Adults are frequently experienced as judgmental and intrusive in their approach.

(e) Discussions are often not treated as confidential.

Neale and Smart concluded:[227] 'Professionals may be perceived as inflexible, intrusive, condescending, deceitful, untrustworthy, disrespectful and reinforcing in a myriad of ways their superiority to the child.'

But not all studies found such dissatisfaction with child representatives. Buchanan, Hunt, Bretherton and Bream,[228] for example, found that most children liked their welfare officer, while in the *Your shout too!* survey[229] about half of those surveyed thought their

---

[221] B Neale 'Dialogues with children in participation and choice in family decision making' (unpublished paper) (1999).   [222] *All Change* UK Youth (Spring 1999) at 12.

[223] S Day Sclater and C Piper *Undercurrents of Divorce* (1999) p 8.

[224] M Murch, G Douglas, L Scanlan, A Perry, C Lisles, K Bader and M Borkowski *Safeguarding children's welfare in uncontentious divorce: a study of section 41 of the Matrimonial Causes Act 1973*, pp 178–85, Lord Chancellor's Department, Research Series No 7/99 (1999).

[225] 'The Voice of the Child' [2007] IFL 171 at 172.

[226] *Listening to children's views and representing their best interests—a summary of current research* (1999).

[227] B Neale and C Smart 'Agents or Dependants? Struggling to listen to Children in Family Law and Family Research' Working Paper No 3 (1999) at 33.

[228] A Buchanan, J Hunt, H Bretherton and V Bream 'Families in Conflict: the Family Court Welfare Service: the perspectives of children and parents' [2001] Fam Law 900.

[229] J Timms, S Bailey and J Thorburn *Your shout too! A survey of the views of children and young people involved in court proceedings when their parents divorce or separate* (NSPCC, 2007).

Cafcass officer helpful or very helpful and more than half thought that the worker's input had made their situation better.

Drawing on the findings of two child focused research projects conducted by Cardiff University,[230] Lowe and Murch[231] identified some common experiences. First, children had misconceptions about the court and the legal process—many associated courts with criminal wrongdoing and many were afraid having to go to court; others were just ignorant of legal process and were often left to 'suss it out' for themselves. Secondly, children felt isolated and ignorant of what was happening and felt the need for reliable information. Thirdly, children needed support particularly through the shock and worry experienced by them on hearing of their parents' separation and, in the adoption context, particularly during the move to the adoptive home. Lowe and Murch concluded from these findings that the ability of both professionals and parents to communicate with children and be sensitive to their needs were 'the absolute minimum requirements of putting into practice legal obligations to ascertain and have regard to children's wishes and feelings'. They also considered that 'there is a crying need to develop ways and means to explain the court process and to familiarise children with the court room and judge before any hearing'.[232]

The findings of a subsequent study of children's experience of separate representation in private law proceedings[233] reinforces these messages. This study found that while most of the children liked the idea of someone appointed by the court to help them have their say in the proceedings, a number were ignorant and confused about the legal process and imagined courts to be ' "scary places" with judges who have the capacity to "punish" their parents'. They felt that the court and the judge should be 'child friendly' and that they needed someone accessible to them, apart from their parents, to support them through the litigation process. A number wanted to be kept informed about the progress of the case. In their eyes a 'good' guardian was someone who gave them enough time to get to know them (hasty interrogations were disliked), who could be trusted and who would communicate at their level and who would give clear explanations as to the role of both the guardian and of the legal process.[234]

2. MOVES TO IMPROVE THE FAMILY JUSTICE SYSTEM

The Norgrove Review made three recommendations that address some of these concerns.[235] It recommended first that children and young persons be given age-appropriate information to explain what is happening when they are involved in public and private law cases. Secondly, and in recognition that by no means all children want to be directly involved in court proceedings,[236] it recommended that children and young persons should, as early as possible, be supported to be able to make their views known and that older children should be offered a menu of options, to lay out the ways in which they could—if they wish—do this. Norgrove also recognised the need for skilled Cafcass officers to be able to present children's wishes and feelings to a court and that the lead for developing

---

[230] Ie I Butler et al *Divorcing Children—children's experience of their parents' divorce* (2003), and C Thomas et al *Adopted Children Speaking* (1999).

[231] N Lowe and M Murch 'Children's participation in the family justice system—translating principles into practice' [2001] CFLQ 137.   [232] Ibid at 154–155.

[233] G Douglas et al *Research into the operation of Rule 9.5 of the Family Proceedings Rules 1991* (2006).

[234] See 'The Summary of children's interviews', in Douglas et al, see n 180, at 3.80–3.85.

[235] *Family Justice Review* Final Report (November 2011), Recommendations 1–3.

[236] Reference being made to the findings of J Timms, S Bailey and J Thorburn in *Your shout too!*

national standards and guidelines on working with children and young people should be taken a newly created Family Justice Service. The service should also ensure consistency of support services, of information for young people and of child-centred practice and oversee the dissemination of up to date research. In its response, the Government agreed with these recommendations stating that it wanted 'to ensure the system listens to children, takes into account their wishes and feelings, and helps professionals to have the necessary skills to support children and young persons to express their views.'[237] To that end it determined to establish a Family Justice Board which would be charged to consider how best to put these recommendations into practice. That Board was created in 2012 and David Norgrove was appointed as its first Chair.

The voice of the child was also a central concern of the 'Cobb Report' of the Private Law Working Group[238] and, based on that report, the *Child Arrangements Programme* directs[239] the court specifically to ask '(a) Is the child aware of the proceedings? (b) Are the wishes and feelings of the child available, and/or to be ascertained (if at all)? (c) How is the child to be involved in the proceedings, if at all? Should this be at or after the FHDRA? (d) Who will inform the child of the outcome of the case, where appropriate?'

The family justice system has come a long way in recognising the needs of children and the reform bodes well, but as ever, the key question is whether sufficient resources will be put in place to achieve its good intentions.

G. LOOKING AFTER CHILDREN'S WIDER INTERESTS—THE COMMISSIONERS FOR CHILDREN

1. BACKGROUND

As one commentary put it,[240] the use of a 'children's Commissioner' or ombudsman has come to be regarded as one of the most effective means of ensuring that the separate and special interests of children[241] promoted by the United Nations Convention on the Rights of the Children 1989 are protected. Many States have accordingly established such an office as part of their response to meeting their obligations under the Convention with Norway being the first to do so in 1981.[242] Calls for an office in the United Kingdom began at least in 1991 with a report promoted by the Gulbenkian Foundation,[243] but it was the criticism by the United Nations Committee on the Rights of the Child (to whom

---

[237] *The Government Response to the Family Justice Review: A System with children and families at its heart* (Cm 8273, 2012) at p 37.

[238] 'Report to the President of the Family Division of the Private Law Working Group (2013) [2013] Fam Law 1594 at para 14.   [239] See para 11.12.7.

[240] K Hollingsworth and G Douglas 'Creating a children's champion for Wales? The Care Standards Act 2000 (Part V) and the Children's Commissioner for Wales Act 2001' (2002) 65 MLR 58.

[241] See J Williams, 'Effective government structures for children?: The UK's four Children's Commissioners' [2005] CFLQ 37.

[242] There are also well-established comparable offices in Australia, Canada, Germany, New Zealand and Switzerland. According to an article (published in 2000) in the *Guardian* newspaper cited by Hollingsworth and Douglas ((2002) 65 MLR 58), there are at least 18 such offices. Ireland created a Children's Ombudsman in 2002. See also M Seneviratne 'Ombudsman for Children' (2001) 23 JSWFL 217.

[243] M Rosenbaum and P Newell *Taking Children Seriously: a Proposal for a Children's Rights Commissioner* (1991).

the United Kingdom had submitted its first compliance report) and the recommendation that a children's ombudsman should[244] be appointed that ultimately led to the creation of the Commissioners in the United Kingdom. That proposal was taken up by the House of Commons Select Committee on Health in 1998 which formally recommended the creation of a UK Commissioner. However, at first the Government resisted these calls and instead the initiative was taken up first in Wales[245] where the Children's Commissioner for Wales took up his appointment in 2001, then in Northern Ireland,[246] with the post being taken up in 2004 and then in Scotland[247] where the first Commissioner was appointed in 2004. Finally, the Government agreed to create a comparable post for England which it did by Part 1 of the Children Act 2004 which came into force in November 2004. The first Commissioner for Children in England was appointed in 2005.

There was general agreement, however, that the functions of the English Commissioner for Children were disappointingly weak with one commentary tellingly concluding[248] what ought to have been:

> a cause for celebratory fireworks . . . more nearly resembles a damp squib. The existing legislation represents an opportunity lost rather than seized, and the post will require a very strong candidate indeed, in addition to changes in the law, to become a true children's champion.

An independent review (conducted by John Dunford) was commissioned by the Secretary of State for Education in 2010. Its central recommendations[249] were accepted by the Government and the consequential reforms incorporated in Part 5 of the Children and Families Act 2014.

2. OVERVIEW OF THE ENGLISH COMMISSIONER'S ROLE

The Children's Commissioner for England has the dual role of being both the Commissioner for England and also for Wales in non-devolved matters, Scotland in reserved matters, and Northern Ireland in excepted matters. This has not been changed by the Children and Families Act 2014.[250]

(a) The original remit

As originally enacted, the Children's Commissioner's mandate was, by s 2(1) of the 2004 Act, to promote awareness of the views and interests of children in England Wales, and, by s 2(2) he or she could:

> (a) encourage persons exercising functions or engaged in activities affecting children, to take account of their views and interests;

---

[244] Children's Rights Office, *Proposal for an Office of Children's Rights Commissioner* (1997). As Clarke Hall and Morrison comment, at 9[3], the appointment of an independent office had been strongly promoted by the Council of Europe through its 'European Strategy for Children' Recommendation 1286 (1996).

[245] The impetus was the Waterhouse report *Lost in care: Report on the Tribunal of Inquiry into the abuse of children in care in the former county council areas of Gwynedd and Clwyd since 1974*, HC, 201 (2000). See generally Hollingsworth and Douglas (2002) 65 MLR 58.

[246] The Commissioner for Children and Young People (Northern Ireland) Order 2003 (SI 2003/439) (NI 11).   [247] The Commissioner for Children and Young People (Scotland) Act 2003.

[248] B Clucas 'The Children's Commissioner For England: The Way Forward?' [2005] Fam Law 290 at 293.

[249] *Review of the Office of the Children's Commissioner (England)* ('the Dunford Review'), December 2010.

[250] Though minor changes have been made to ss 5, 6 and 7 in order to apply the changes to the Commissioner's functions to those in respect of non-devolved, etc, matters.

> (b) advise the Secretary of State on the views and interests of children;
> (c) consider or research the operation of complaints procedures so far as relating to children;
> (d) consider or research any other matter relating to the interests of children: publish a report on any matter research by him under this section.

A major criticism of that remit was that in contrast to the other Commissioners in the United Kingdom who are required by law to promote and safeguard the 'rights' of children, the Commissioner's general function in England was only to promote 'awareness of the views and *interests* of children in England' which was perceived to be more restrictive.

The English Commissioner had two means to launch an investigation: either on his own initiative as provided for by s 3 but subject to prior consultation with the Secretary of State;[251] or pursuant to s 4, on direction by the Secretary of State. Although in each case the trigger for the inquiry was the case of an individual child, its purpose was confined to investigating and making recommendations of issues of public policy of relevance to other children. The Commissioner was specifically barred from conducting an investigation of the issue of an individual child.[252]

The problem with ss 3 and 4 was that they called into question the Commissioner's independence, for implicit in the requirement to consult was that the Commissioner needed the Secretary of State's consent to go ahead or that he or she was at least subject to a ministerial veto. Furthermore, the power to 'direct' an inquiry under s 4 rather than to 'request' one had, as one commentary put it,[253] 'an odd flavour in comparison with the UK Commissioners', who are clearly independent of the relevant devolved governing powers'. The bar on investigating individual cases was clearly a significant limitation on the Commissioner's powers though, arguably, a realistic limitation in terms of resources.

(b) The revised remit

The reforms made by the 2014 Act address, in line with the Dunford Review, some of these criticisms. Section 2 of the 2004 Act is entirely rewritten[254] and provides by s 2(1) that the Commissioner's 'primary function is promoting and protecting the rights of children in England.' This provision brings the Commissioner's mandate in line with the other UK Commissioners and, in the words of the Explanatory Report, 'should, in practice, mean that the Commissioner will be able to challenge any policy or practice which he or she considers may lead, or has led, to an infringement or abuse of children's rights.' However, the Report adds that the Commissioner does not thereby have the power to require a change to that policy or practice.

By s 2(2) the primary function continues to include 'promoting awareness of the view and interests of children in England', while s 2(3) contains a revamped, non-exhaustive, list of activities that the Commissioner may undertake in the exercise of the primary function, namely:

> (a) advise persons exercising functions or engaged in activities affecting children on how to act compatibly with rights of children;
> (b) encourage such persons to take account of the views and interests of children;
> (c) advise the Secretary of State on the rights, views and interests of children;

---

[251] See s 3(3).

[252] Section 2(7). As is the Scottish Commissioner. Compare the Welsh and Northern Ireland Commissioner's powers: see Williams [2005] CFLQ 37, at pp 41, 43, 48–50.

[253] Clucas [2005] Fam Law 290, at 292.   [254] See s 107 of the 2014 Act.

(d) consider the potential effect on the rights of children of government policy proposals and government proposals for legislation;

(e) bring any other matter to the attention of either Houses of Parliament;

(f) investigate the availability and effectiveness of complaints procedures so far as relating to children;

(g) investigate the availability and effectiveness of advocacy services for children;

(h) investigate any other matter relating to the rights or interests of children;

(i) monitor the implementation in England of the United Nations Convention on the Rights of the Child;

(j) publish a report on any matter considered or investigated under this section.

In discharging the primary function the Commissioner 'must take reasonable steps to involve children'[255] while a new s 2A directs the Commissioner to have regard to the UN Convention on the Rights of the Child in considering what constitutes the rights and interests of children. The references to the UN Convention in ss 2(3)(i) and 2A are the first such references in legislation applying to England.[256]

The embargo against investigating individual cases is maintained by s 2(5), the intention being that the Commissioner should concentrate on strategic issues rather than providing 'an ombudsman service for individual children'.[257] However, the Commissioner is able to provide advice and assistance to children living away from home or receiving social care.[258]

No amendments have been made to sections 3 and 4 but among other changes are the creation of an Advisory Board, the removal of the requirement to appoint a Deputy Children's Commissioner, the combining of the functions of the Commissioner with activities formerly carried out by the Children's Rights Director and the removal of the option to renew the Commissioner's appointment such that the appointment will be for a single six year term. The purpose of this last change is to allay the concerns of the Dunford Review that the possibility of a second term might compromise the Commissioner's independence.

The intention behind the reforms just outlined is to remove the barriers that the Dunford Review identified as preventing the English Commissioner for Children from having sufficient impact on children's lives. It remains to be seen whether the changes are successful in this regard. The scope of the English Commissioner's remit remains limited in comparison to that of the Welsh Commissioner.[259]

[255] Section 2B of the 2004 Act, as inserted by s 107 of the 2014 Act.

[256] But the first such reference in UK legislation was in Children's Commissioner for Wales Regulations 2001, reg 22 of which, directs the Commissioner to have regard to the Convention while exercising his functions.

[257] See para 439 of the Explanatory Notes.

[258] See ss 2D and 8A of the 2004 Act, as inserted by ss 108 and 114 respectively of the 2014 Act.

[259] See O Rees 'Devolution and Family Law in Wales: A Potential for Doing Things Differently?' (2012) 33 *Statute Law Review* 192.

14

THE COURT'S POWERS TO MAKE ORDERS UNDER PART II OF THE CHILDREN ACT 1989

A. INTRODUCTION

This chapter considers the courts' powers under Part II of the Children Act 1989 to make orders, other than financial orders,[1] in what are termed 'family proceedings'.

1. THE ORIGINAL SCHEME OF PART II

Part II was originally based on the Law Commission's recommendations contained in its *Report on Guardianship and Custody*.[2] Pointing to research evidence[3] which showed that children who fare best after their parents' separation are those who are able to maintain a good relationship with both parents, but recognising the obvious limitation that the law cannot make people co-operate, the Commission argued that at least it should not stand in their way. Hence, if the parties can co-operate with each other, the law should intervene as little as possible, but if they cannot, the law should at least try to 'lower the stakes' and avoid the impression that the 'loser loses all'.[4]

With these considerations in mind and with the general aim of making the law simpler, clearer and fairer for children and their families the Law Commission recommended[5] that the differing powers of the various courts should be replaced by a new set of powers common to all courts and which were designed to be less emotive and more flexible.

These recommendations were enacted by Part II by which courts are empowered to make a range of orders, collectively known as 's 8 orders'. As originally enacted, s 8 orders comprised residence orders and contact orders, which respectively replaced the former power to make custody and access orders, and prohibited steps orders and specific issue orders, which were new powers. Although s 8 orders are closely associated with private

---

[1] The powers to make financial orders are governed by s 15 and Sch 1, for discussion of which, see Ch 21.
[2] Law Com No 172 (1988).
[3] Notably that of J Wallerstein and J Kelly *Surviving the Breakup* (1980). But see also J Wallerstein and S Blakeslee *Second Chances: Men, Women and Children a Decade After Divorce* (1990); M Richards and M Dyson *Separation, Divorce and the Development of Children: A Review* (1982); and J Pryor and B Rodgers *Children in Changing Families: Life After Parental Separation* (2001).
[4] Law Com No 172 para 4.5.   [5] Para 8.2.

law disputes they can be made in *any* family proceedings[6] including, therefore, in public law proceedings.[7]

As well as providing this range of powers, Part II also makes clear provision for determining who can apply for an order. The basic scheme (under s 10) is that some people, for example parents, guardians or special guardians, are entitled to apply for any s 8 order, while others, eg relatives, are required to seek the court's leave either to intervene in existing family proceedings or to initiate their own proceedings to seek a s 8 order.

An important change introduced by the 1989 Act was the removal of the court's previous power in matrimonial and other private law proceedings concerning children to make committal to care or supervision orders. Instead, under s 37 courts can direct the local authority to investigate the circumstances but it is for the authority and not the court to decide whether an application for a care or supervision order should be made. However, in place of these former powers is the power under s 16 to make 'family assistance' orders, the object of which is to provide short-term help for the family. We discuss these powers at the end of this chapter.

2. CHANGES MADE BY THE CHILDREN AND ADOPTION ACT 2006

After operating for many years virtually unamended there have been a number of changes to Part II. A raft of new powers both to promote contact (for example, to make contact activity directions or conditions) and to enforce contact orders (including the power to impose an unpaid work requirement and to order compensation to another for a financial loss caused by a breach) was introduced by the Children and Adoption Act 2006.[8]

That it was felt necessary to introduce new powers over contact was indicative of the fact that these had proved to be the least successful of the s 8 powers.[9] They were also a response in part to an influential report *Making Contact Work*[10] and in part to a high profile campaign by pressure groups such as Families need Fathers and Fathers 4 Justice which brought alleged gender bias in the judicial resolution of residence and, particularly, contact disputes very much to the fore.[11]

Another important reform made by the 2006 Act was to insert section 16A into the Children Act 1989 which requires Cafcass officers to carry out a risk assessment and provide it to the court, if in the course of carrying out any function in private family law

[6] For the full meaning of which, see Section 8 orders, p 485.

[7] To put these powers to make s 8 orders in both private and public law into context it might be noted that whereas in 2011, 39,123 residence orders were made in private law proceedings, 4,212 orders were made in public law proceedings. The respective figures for contact were 108,552 as against 2,831, for prohibited steps orders 18,076 as against 558 and for specific issue orders there were 5,650 as against 271: Table 2.4 of the 2011 *Civil Judicial Statistics*.

[8] Note also the introduction of special guardianship orders by the Adoption and Children Act 2002, discussed at the end of Ch 19.

[9] Statistically, they were also the order most frequently sought. In 2011, for example, of the 183,718 private law disposals, 111,302 (61%) were for contact and of these, 108,552 (98%) were granted. By way of comparison there were 40,361 disposals for residence (22% of the total number of private law applications) of which 39,123 (97%) were granted.

[10] A Report to the Lord Chancellor by the Advisory Board on Family Law; Children Act Sub-Committee, 2002.

[11] On which see V Peacey and J Hunt *I'm not saying it was easy... Contact problems in separated families* (2009), J Hunt and A Macleod *Outcomes of applications to court for contact orders after parental separation or divorce* (2008) and R Collier 'Fathers 4 Justice, the law and the new politics of Fatherhood' [2005] CFLQ 511.

proceedings under the 1989 Act (including monitoring of contact orders or even working on alternative dispute resolution) the officer is given cause to suspect that the child concerned is at risk of harm.

3. CHANGES MADE BY THE CHILDREN AND FAMILIES ACT 2014

(a) A brief overview of the post 1989 Act experience

Despite the 2006 Act's reforms the s 8 powers themselves remained unchanged. But while in some ways they had stood the test of time, residence and contact orders, in particular, did not develop entirely as intended or anticipated.[12] A major objective of the 1989 Act reforms was to encourage divorcing or separating parents to make their own arrangements for the upbringing of their children and only to use the courts as a last resort.[13] Further, it was hoped that residence and contact orders would be less emotionally charged than their predecessors, custody and access orders, thereby avoiding the impression that there were 'winners and losers' in court proceedings.[14] Further, it was intended that with the automatic continuation of parental responsibility despite the parents' divorce or separation, the courts would only be called upon to settle real as opposed to symbolic disputes.[15]

Although studies had found that 90% of separating parents did not go to court to settle the future arrangements for their children[16] and that only around 10% of children with a contact arrangement had this ordered by the court,[17] the number of children involved in residence and contact order applications rose exponentially over the years. According to the *Family Justice Review*[18] the number of children involved in private law proceedings had increased every year since 2005 and in 2009, 45,000 children were involved in residence order applications and 53,000 in contact order applications—an increase of 11% and 23% respectively on 2008.

Perhaps, predictably, the attempt to make residence and contact order less emotionally charged basically failed. In this regard public perception of these orders had not been helped by the media's refusal to embrace the Children Act terminology and their continued reference to 'custody and access battles'. Similarly, the strategy of providing for the automatic continuation of parental responsibility following divorce such that orders would only deal with real as opposed to symbolic disputes had not been that successful. Although it was true that the former hollow disputes as to whether the court should make sole or joint custody orders regardless with whom the child was to live had been consigned to legal history, a new type of dispute arose, namely, where the child was to spend time with each parent, as to whether this should be reflected by a residence order plus contact or a shared residence order. Residence orders had also been used, at any rate on occasion, as a means of allocating parental responsibility to those who did not already

---

[12] See N Lowe 'A Review of the Developing Law on Residence, Contact, Prohibited Steps and Specific Issue Orders under Section 8 of the Children Act 1989' (2010) 5 *Journal of Children's Services* 39.

[13] See Law Com No 172 *Report on Guardianship and Custody* (1988) and B Hoggett (now Baroness Hale) 'The Children Bill: The Aim' [1989] Fam Law 217.   [14] Law Com No 172 para 4.5.

[15] Ibid para 2.11.   [16] A Blackwell and F Dawe *Non-resident parent contact* (2003).

[17] A Buchanan, J Hunt, H Bretherton and V Bream *Families in Conflict: Perspective of children and parents on the Family Court Welfare Service* (2001) and L Trinder et al *Making contact happen or making contact work* (2006).

[18] See para 5.9 of the Interim Report (March 2011). The *Review* was chaired by David Norgrove and the *Review* is sometimes referred to as the 'Norgrove Review'.

have it. In any event, it is doubtful that the parental responsibility changes really filtered down into public consciousness.

Although the notion of a shared residence order had been contemplated at the time of the 1989 Act, it was not anticipated that such orders would be at all common.[19] That such orders became more common reflected an important culture shift in that fathers were becoming more active parents and were less content just to be given contact. There was a perception, at least, that the courts were not always even handed between parents. That perception also permeated contact disputes, which were certainly no less bitter, and sometimes so protracted that the parent (commonly, though not exclusively, fathers) seeking it would give up.[20]

(B) The Family Justice Review

The Interim Report

In their Interim Report the *Family Justice Review* identified[21] a number of concerns about the then private law concerning children. Underlying these concerns the *Review* noted that research has shown that intense parental conflict can reduce the quality of parenting and can damage children. In particular, prolonged exposure to frequent, intense and poorly resolved conflict is associated with a range of psychological risks for children.[22]

The *Review* also referred to *A v A (Shared Residence)* in which Wall J alluded[23] to 'the distress and damage caused to children by long-standing and continuous hostility between their parents' which, in that case had lasted six years, and was such that one of the children said that 'he could not bear it any longer'.

The *Review* pointed to the criticism that the private law system was overly adversarial. Whilst acknowledging that processes had been designed to overcome this[24] and that the focus at all times is to ensure that parties come to an agreement,[25] it pointed to the fact that by the time a case reached a first hearing accusations and cross-accusations may already have been made. As the *Review* commented:[26]

---

[19] See the Department of Health's *Guidance and Regulations* Vol 1 *Court Orders* (1991) para 2.28. For a summary of the research on shared residence, see L Trinder 'Shared residence: A review of recent research evidence' [2010] CFLQ 475 and for the Australian experience of shared parenting, see H Roades 'Legislating to promote children's welfare and the quest for certainty' [2012] CFLQ 158 and H Roades' evidence to the *Family Justice Review* published as Annex G to the Final Report.

[20] See, for example, *Re D (Intractable Contact Dispute: Publicity)* [2004] EWHC 727 (Fam) [2004] 1 FLR 1226 in which a five year dispute comprised 43 hearings before 16 different judges before the father gave up. See also *Re O (Contact: Withdrawal of Application)* [2003] EWHC 3031 (Fam) [2004] 1 FLR 1258. But even in these type of cases a court should be slow to deny contact, see *Re A (Intractable Contact Dispute: Human Rights Violations)* [2013] EWCA Civ 1104 [2014] 1 FLR 1185. Note also *Re S (Contact: Intractable Dispute)* [2010] EWCA Civ 447 [2010] 2 FLR 1517—wrong to burden the child with the responsibility of deciding whether there should be contact.   [21] See paras 5.27ff of the Interim Report (March, 2011).

[22] See J Hunt and L Trinder *Chronic Litigation Cases: Characteristics, Numbers, Interventions, A Report for the Family Justice Council* (2011) and J McIntosh 'Enduring conflict in parental separation: pathways of impact on child development' (2003) 9 *Journal of Family Studies* 63.

[23] [2004] EWHC 142 (Fam) [2004] 1 FLR 1195 at 1201.

[24] Notably through Separated Parents Information Programmes ('PIPS'), on which see L Smith and L Trinder 'Mind the gap: parent education programmes and the family justice system' [2012] CFLQ 428, and L Trinder, C Bryson, L Coleman, C Houlston, S Purdon, J Reibstein and L Smith *Building bridges? An evaluation of the costs and effectiveness of the Separated Parents Information Programme (PIP)* (2011).

[25] Particularly following the introduction of First Hearings Dispute Resolution Appointments ('FHDERA'), which is further refined by the Child Arrangements Programme, *Practice Direction 12B—Child Arrangements Programme*.   [26] At para 5.31.

Many people have the perception that they will 'have their day in court' and that there will be a winner and a loser. This tends to inflame conflict even though the courts may not allow the issues to play out this way.

Another perception of the system highlighted by the *Review* was that it was more favourable to one parent over the other.[27] Fathers, in particular felt that system was biased. The *Review* pointed to research which showed[28] children still typically lived with their mothers and that because of the slowness of the system the children's living arrangements leading up to the hearing tended to be upheld by the courts. This perception of bias was reinforced by solicitors' apparently common advice to non-resident parents that their case for residence was hopeless.[29] On top of this was the general failure of enforcement measures such that non-resident parents strongly believed that once an order was made the resident parent was free to flout it which again led to the perception of the system's bias.

Other criticisms of the system referred to by the *Review*,[30] were that it was confusing and difficult to navigate, that children did not understand the process or feel listened to and that it was slow and expensive. In this last respect concerns were expressed about what, was then, the possible withdrawal of legal aid.

In the light of these criticisms the Interim Report made a number of recommendations to improve the system. These included promoting awareness of parental responsibility, providing all parents with information about the importance of raising children in a co-operative manner, and developing Parenting Agreements in which parties set out how they will jointly exercise their responsibilities following separation.[31]

So far as substantive law was concerned, the *Review* received evidence for the need to change terminology particularly 'contact' and 'residence' in order to 'promote the fact that both parents retain a role and responsibilities in their child's life following separation.'[32] Taking note of Chief Justice Diana Bryant's view that in Australia the move away from using residence and contact had been very beneficial, the *Review* recommended[33] the removal of the terms 'contact' and 'residence' from all issues between parents with parental responsibility and that disputes over the division of time between parents should be resolved by a specific issue order instead. Consequent upon this removal, the power of the residence order holder to take the child outside the United Kingdom for up to one month, under s 13 (2) of the 1989 Act would be repealed, with the *Review* considering that that issue should be covered in the Parenting Agreement. On other hand, the *Review* recommended that there should be no changes to the continued availability of the full range of s 8 orders with regard to applications made by those who did not have parental responsibility.

The Final Report

A key change in the Final Report (published in November 2011) concerned the abolition of contact and residence orders. The *Review* acknowledged that there was widespread but

---

[27] At paras 5.33–5.38.

[28] A study by V Peacey and J Hunt *I'm not saying it was easy . . . Contact problems in separated families* (2009) found that around 90% of children resided with one parent and of these only 12% lived with their father after divorce.

[29] See the findings of J Hunt and A Macleod *Outcomes of applications to court for contact orders after parental separation or divorce* (2008). [30] See paras 5.39–5.57.

[31] The intention here was to build on Parenting Plans as facilitated via Cafcass.

[32] At para 5.93. [33] At para 5.95.

not universal support for the proposal. Arguments against the change were that it would make no difference, it being pointed out that the terms 'access' and 'custody' remained in common use despite their abolition by the 1989 Act; it would create confusion and would require a large legislative and administrative effort for little appreciable benefit. Others, notably, the Association of Her Majesty's District Judges, argued for a new order, namely, 'parenting time orders'.

The *Review* opted to continue to recommend the removal of the terms 'contact' and 'residence' but, in an important departure from the Interim Report, the Final Report recommended the creation of a new order that would encompass all arrangements for children's care in private law. This new order could, as the Final Report put it,[34] be termed 'a child arrangements order' which would set out the arrangements for the upbringing of children and which 'would focus all discussions on resolving issues related to [children's] care, rather than on labels such as residence and contact.' This new order would be available for all litigants but the powers to make specific issue and prohibited steps orders or to have recourse to the High Court's inherent jurisdiction (discussed in Chapter 20) would be left untouched. Another consequence of this changed stance was the dropping of their earlier recommendation that s 13(2) (permitting a child's temporary removal from the United Kingdom) be repealed.

The *Review* expressed its confidence that the new proposed order would enable more flexible, child-focused arrangements to be made and quoted[35] Lady Hale's view, given to *Review* in response to the consultation:

> The thinking behind the Children Act 1989 was that parents should be encouraged to make their own arrangements and the court would only decide what they could not decide. But their task, and the court's task, was not to allocate status or rights, so much as to settle the practical living arrangements for the child. Over the years, 'residence' and 'contact' have taken on too much of the flavour of the old 'custody' and 'access' orders. These proposals would restore the original vision underlying the 1989 Act.

The Government's response

The Government essentially accepted the *Review*'s recommendations.[36] It announced a two-fold strategy of putting measures in place (a) to support families so that they do not need to bring their issues to court in the first place, and (b) where courts are involved, to ensure that the process is speedy and straightforward, whilst recognising the paramountcy of children's welfare.

With regard to finding solutions outside the court the Government promised to establish an improved dispute resolution process, to support the development of a Parenting Agreement, and making attendance at a Mediation Information and Assessment Meeting (MIAM) compulsory with built in safeguards concerning domestic violence.[37]

Where cases do reach the courts, the Government announced that a single Family Court would be established with a single point of entry but with proceedings being allocated to the appropriate level of judiciary.[38] To speed up cases the Government said it would consider the possibility of providing for cases to follow one of a number of 'tracks' depending on, for example, complexity or urgency.[39]

---

[34] See para 4.60.   [35] At para 4.65.
[36] See *The Government Response to the Family Justice Review: A system with children and families at its heart* (Cm 8273, 2012).   [37] See paras 65–73 and 79–80.
[38] See para 75.   [39] See para 75.

So far as substantive law was concerned the Government accepted the *Family Justice Review*'s recommendation to replace residence and contact orders with what it referred to as a new 'child's arrangement order'.[40] It also accepted the need to improve the enforcement process.[41]

As we discussed in Chapter 1, a new Family Court was created by the Crime and Courts Act 2013, Sch 10 and attendance at MIAMs was made compulsory by s 10 of the Children and Families Act 2014. As we now discuss, child arrangements orders have been introduced by s 12 of the 2014 Act. It should be added that all pre-existing contact and residence orders are deemed to be child arrangements orders.[42]

B. SECTION 8 ORDERS

1. THE POWERS

The expression 'a section 8 order' means any of the orders mentioned in s 8(1), that is: a child arrangements order, a prohibited steps order or a specific issue order. It also includes any order varying or discharging a s 8 order.[43] In making any s 8 order the court has further supplemental powers (designed to ensure maximum flexibility) under s 11(7) inter alia to make directions or impose conditions.[44]

(a) Child arrangements orders

By s 8(1), as amended,[45] a child arrangements order:

> . . . means an order regulating arrangements relating to any of the following–
>
> (a) with whom the child is to live, spend time or otherwise have contact, and
> (b) when a child is to live, spend time or otherwise have contact with any person.

Child arrangements orders deal with the child's living arrangements and, what might still be broadly called, contact under a single umbrella order. This is a significant departure from having separate orders dealing with what can clearly be interwoven issues. The *Family Justice Review* considered that this form of order would 'focus all discussions on resolving issues related to [the care of children] rather than upon labels such as residence and contact'.[46] One practitioner gave a cautious welcome to the new order at least in the sense that it might 'herald a greater concentration on the content and practical workings of s 8 orders'.[47] However, the House of Commons Justice Committee considered that the 'mixing of the different elements of the order' made it 'much more complex and confusing, particularly for litigants in person'.[48] There is also the obvious danger of a court descending into minutiae, thereby exacerbating conflict rather than reducing it. Another consideration, however, is that if orders are too broadly drawn they might not enforceable.[49]

---

[40] See para 77.   [41] See paras 79–80.

[42] The Children and Families Act 2014 (Transitional Provisions) Order 2014 (SI 2014/1042) art 6.

[43] Section 8(2).   [44] Discussed at Additional directions and conditions, pp 504 ff.

[45] By s 12 of the Children and Families Act 2014.   [46] Final Report, para 4.60.

[47] C Bevan 'The devil in the detail: implication of the Children and Families Bill for practitioners' [2013] Fam Law 602 at 604.

[48] *Pre-legislative scrutiny of the Children and Families Bill Fourth Report of Session 2012–2013* para (35), reproduced at [2013] Fam Law 229 at 233.

[49] See the comments of Bevan [2013] Fam Law 602 at 604. For general discussion of enforcement of s 8 orders, see Enforcing section 8 orders, pp 537 ff.

Although it is important to the overall strategy of reducing the emotional significance attached to the order that it should be treated as a single entity, analysis of the order requires distinguishing the living element from the other elements since there are legal effects that attach to the former but not to the latter. In this respect it may be noted that notions of 'living with', 'spending time with', and 'otherwise having contact with' are not defined in the Act. The general intention, however, is to make two basic distinctions, namely, between those orders that provide for the child to spend significant periods with a named parents as opposed to those that just provide for the child to see a named person and between those orders providing for face-to-face time as opposed to non-physical contact.

The following discussion considers first the living element and then the element concerning the child seeing or otherwise having contact with a named person. It is to be emphasised, however, that orders do not have to embrace both these elements and indeed should only do so if both are in issue.

Naming a person with whom the child is to live

Insofar as child arrangements orders deal with the living element, they determine with whom the child is to live. Although by determining with whom the child will live the order effectively determines *where* the child will live, in the absence of a prohibited steps order[50] or, unless the court adds a direction or condition,[51] the person named in a child arrangements order as a person with whom the child is to live is free to live in or subsequently move to any location within the UK.[52]

Since a child arrangements order only settles the arrangements as to the person with whom the child is to live, any other conditions that are needed must be specified separately by the court either acting under the powers vested by s 11(7) or possibly under its inherent powers.[53] Indeed, given that in cases where the child is to live with more than one person under a child arrangements order, neither is obliged to consult the other unless this is specified in the order, it is important that the order is clear on points which are fundamental to the success of the arrangement.[54] One area in particular that will commonly require clarification is the issue of holidays, particularly foreign holidays.

A child arrangements order is broadly defined by s 8 as an order regulating arrangements relating inter alia to with whom the child is to live. However, elsewhere in the Act, for example, in s 12(2) and s 13(1)(b) (which deal with the consequences of such orders concerning the allocation of parental responsibility and the ability to take a child outside the United Kingdom), reference is made to 'a person who has been named in a child arrangements order as a person with whom the child is to live.' Although reference is made here to 'a' person that should not be read as meaning only one person can be so named. Indeed, to the contrary, implicit in the reference to 'a' person is that others can also be named as a person with whom the child is to live. Furthermore the persons named

---

[50] See eg *Re H (Children) (Residence Order: Condition)* [2001] EWCA Civ 1338 [2001] 2 FLR 1277, discussed at Application to living arrangements, p 507.

[51] Viz. under s 11(7) (discussed at Additional directions and conditions, pp 504ff). In practice the courts are reluctant to restrain the residence holder's freedom of movement: see Application to living arrangements, pp 506–507.

[52] But not *outside* the UK without either court leave or the consent of everyone with parental responsibility: s 13(1)(b), discussed at Removal of child from the United Kingdom—'External relocation', p 525.

[53] See *A v A (Shared Residence)* [2004] EWHC 142 (Fam) [2004] 1 FLR 1195 in which a Schedule was attached.

[54] For an attempt to do this see the Schedule attached to the shared care order made in *A v A (Shared Residence)*.

do not have to live together, which means principally, but not necessarily exclusively, that notwithstanding their divorce or separation, each of the parents can be named as a person with whom the child is to live.

It is similarly clear that there is no limitation on who can be so named (apart for the need that the person be an 'individual' as opposed to a 'body' or institution).[55] Consequently although child arrangements orders commonly settle the child's living arrangements as between the parents, orders can also be made in favour of a parent and step-parent,[56] a cohabiting couple,[57] grandparents,[58] or foster parents,[59] as in the past.[60]

As well as determining with whom the child is to live, the court is also empowered to specify the length of time that the child is to live with a particular person. Such stipulations can range from providing that the child is to live full-time with one parent, or some other person or the length of time that the child shall live with different persons, normally, but not necessarily, each parent. The advantage of the order is that whatever living arrangements are ordered, it will be simply referred to as a child arrangements order and, not as previously nor as emotively, as a residence order, a joint residence order (that is, an order made in favour of two people living together) or a shared residence order (that is, an order made in favour of two people living in different households), as the case may be. Moreover arrangements whereby a child spends weekdays with one parent and weekends with the other, which would formerly have been expressed as a residence order to the former parent with staying contact with the latter, will simply be expressed as a child arrangements order for each parent. In cases where the child's living arrangements are split between two persons the court's task has been simplified by the 2014 reforms since it need only determine the appropriate division of care between them and not then to have to decide whether the division of time qualifies as a shared residence order.[61]

While there are no express limits on the court's powers to name a person with whom the child 'is to live', to make a sensible distinction between 'living with' and 'spending time with' it is suggested that, given 'living with' is associated with the notion of where a person has his or her home, at a minimum a person can only be named as someone with whom the child is to live if the child spends some nights in the person's home.[62]

What the court's practice will be on this issue remains to be seen but it needs to be borne in mind that those named as a person with whom the child is to live have the right to take the child outside the United Kingdom for up to one month without the need to seek anyone else's consent.[63] On the other hand, since the whole point of the 2014 reforms is to avoid symbolic labelling disputes, the courts will need to tread warily on this issue so as to avoid disputes about how the order should be framed rather than about its substance.

---

[55] Under s 9 (2), as amended by Sch 2 para 4 (3) to the 2014 Act, there is an express embargo on naming a local authority in a child arrangements order, see further Restrictions in the case of local authorities, p 511. [56] See *Re H (Shared Residence: Parental Responsibility)* [1995] 2 FLR 883, CA.

[57] See eg *Re AB (Adoption: Joint Residence)* [1996] 1 FLR 27 and *Re C (A Minor) (Residence Order: Lesbian Co-parents)* [1994] Fam Law 468 (joint residence order made to the mother and her female cohabitant).

[58] See eg *Re W (A Minor) (Residence Order)* [1993] 2 FLR 625, CA.

[59] See eg *Re M (Adoption or Residence Order)* [1998] 1 FLR 570, CA.

[60] Where a child arrangements order 'has the result that there are times when the child lives is to live with one of the parents', that order will cease to have effect if the parents live together for a continuous period of more than six months: s 11(5), as amended by Sch 2 para 6 to the 2014 Act. For an example of where what was then a residence order came to such an end see *Re P (Abduction: Declaration)* [1995] 1 FLR 831, at 834, CA.

[61] Which was the suggested approach before the 2014 reforms, see *Re K (Shared Residence Order)* [2008] EWCA Civ 526, [2008] 2 FLR 380 at [6], per Wilson LJ.

[62] An analogy might be drawn with the definition of a 'person with care' in the child support legislation, see Child Support Act 1991 s 3(3), discussed in Ch 21.

[63] Section 13(2), discussed at Removal of child from the United Kingdom—'External relocation', pp 525ff.

Although, as we discuss later in this chapter, an order naming a person as someone with whom the child is to live confers parental responsibility on those who do not already have it,[64] a child arrangements order should not be made *solely* for that purpose. Although there was conflicting authority on the pre-2014 position,[65] there is little justification now for naming someone as a person with whom the child is to live just to confer parental responsibility on them since the court has a discretion to make a parental responsibility order where it names a person as someone with whom the child is to spend time or otherwise have contact,[66] and in the absence of any contact it is difficult to see why a *non-parent* should have such responsibility. In any event, it is the clear spirit of the reformed order that it should simply be used for determining with whom the child is to live and nothing more.

In deciding what the child's living arrangements should be, as with all s 8 orders, the court is bound by the overarching principle of the paramountcy of the child's welfare as applied by s 1(1). But, as we discussed in Chapter 12, in contested applications between parents the courts must, provided it is satisfied a parent's involvement will not put the child at risk of suffering harm, also apply s 1(2A) by which they are 'to presume, unless the contrary is shown, that involvement of [each] parent in the life of the child concerned will further the child's welfare.' However as s 1(2B) makes clear, that does not create a presumption of 'any particular division of a child's time.' In other words, there is no presumption that the child's living arrangements should be split between the parents, still less that they should be split equally. All must depend upon the court's assessment of the child's welfare. That said, pre-2014 case law established that it is no necessary objection to splitting the child's living arrangements that the parents do not have a harmonious relationship[67] (though clearly that must be a relevant factor in deciding what order to make)[68] or that they live some distance apart.[69] On the other hand, the court must be satisfied that the proposed arrangements are practical and do not place an undue burden (for example, lengthy travel) upon the child. In determining this, the court must in all contested cases apply the welfare checklist.

'Interim' orders

The combination of s 11(3), which permits the court to make a child arrangements order 'even though it is not in a position to dispose finally of those proceedings' and s 11(7)(c), under which orders can be made for a specified period, enables courts to make interim provision such that it can name a person with whom the child is to live for a limited period. The Act, however, makes no distinction between a final order and one made as an interim measure. Hence *all* such orders naming a person with whom the child is to live,

---

[64] Under s 12(2)–(3), discussed at Effect of child arrangements orders, p 520.

[65] See eg *Re WB (Residence Orders)* [1995] 2 FLR 1023, in which Thorpe J refused to make an order, but compare *Re H (Shared Residence: Parental Responsibility)* [2005] EWCA Civ 642 [2005] 2 FLR 957, and *Re G (Residence: Same-Sex Partners)* [2005] EWCA Civ 462 [2005] 2 FLR 957], upheld at [2006] UKHL 43 [2006] 1 WLR 2305, in which orders were made in part to confer parental responsibility.

[66] Section 12(2A) as added by Sch 2 para 21 (4) and discussed in Ch 12.

[67] See eg *A v A (Shared Residence)* [2004] EWHC 142 (Fam) [2004] 1 FLR 1195 and *D v D (Shared Residence Order)* [2001] 1 FLR 495, CA, children coping well with split living arrangements, even though the parents were at loggerheads.

[68] See *Re W (Shared Residence Order)* [2009] EWCA Civ 592 [2009] 2 FLR 436, at [15], per Wilson LJ.

[69] See eg *Re F (Shared Residence Order)* [2003] EWCA Civ 592 [2003] 2 FLR 397, two young children lived with their mother in southern England during school term times and holidays with their father in Edinburgh, and *Re A (Temporary Removal From Jurisdiction)* [2004] EWCA Civ 1587 [2005] 1 FLR 639, a shared residence order was continued notwithstanding that the mother was permitted to live with the child in South Africa for two years to enable her to complete her PhD.

even those expressed to last for a matter of days, have the same effect and will, for example, discharge any existing care order,[70] confer, for the duration of the order, parental responsibility on those who do not already have it,[71] and empower the person named in the order as someone with whom the child is to live to remove the child from the UK for a period of less than one month.[72]

Naming a person with whom the child is to spend time or otherwise have contact

The nature of the order

As we said earlier, there is no definition of 'spending time' or of 'otherwise having contact' but the broad intention[73] is that the former embraces face-to-face or physical contact and the latter non-physical contact such as by letter, telephone,[74] email, texting or by other means.[75] For the purposes of protection, indirect contact can be facilitated by third parties.[76]

It is within the power to name a person with whom the child is to spend time to provide for short visits or longer ones including overnight stays or weekends. As we discussed earlier, there will come a point at which longer stays raise the question of whether that should be reflected by naming the person as someone with whom the child is to *live* rather than with whom they *spend time*. Orders can provide for contact to take place at Contact Centres, which are a useful means of providing a temporary venue for supported contact in cases where the child's parents are unable to provide an alternative.[77] They are not, however, intended to be places for contact over the long-term, nor are they the equivalent of professionally supervised contact. Orders can also provide for children spending time with a parent abroad.[78]

Orders may name any person (including, where appropriate, a sibling) with whom the child is to spend time or otherwise have contact and more than one person may be so named. In theory, it is within the court's powers to provide for the child to spend time or

---

[70] Under s 91(1), as amended, and s 91(1A) added by the 2014 Act, Sch 2 para 37. Where an 'interim' order is thought justified, careful thought needs to be given to its length and, mindful of the general enjoiner under s 1(2) to treat 'delay' as prima facie detrimental to the child's interest, courts should ensure that it is no longer than absolutely necessary: see, in relation to residence orders, eg *Re O (Minors) (Leave To Seek Residence Order)* [1994] 1 FLR 172, where, on the facts, five weeks' duration was thought too long. See also *Re Y (A Minor) (Ex Parte Interim Orders)* [1993] 2 FCR 422.

[71] Under s 12(2) as amended by Sch 2 para 21(3) to the 2014 Act,: see Effect of child arrangements orders, p 520.

[72] Under s 13(2) (as amended by Sch 2 para 22(3) to the 2014 Act and discussed at Temporary removals for less than one month, p 526. Presumably this power of removal is subject to the length of the order—an order expressed to last only a few days cannot be taken to vest a power of removal in excess of that. 'Interim' orders are recognised and enforceable under various international child law conventions, discussed in Ch 26. They also take effect as a 'superseding' order for the purpose of the Family Law Act 1986, also discussed in Ch 26. [73] See the Explanatory Notes to the Act, at para 112.

[74] For examples of contact by post see eg *A v L (Contact)* [1998] 1 FLR 361 and *Re M (A Minor) (Contact: Conditions)* [1994] 1 FLR 272—both involving letter contact with a father in prison, and *Re L (Contact: Transsexual Applicant)* [1995] 2 FLR 438 (indirect contact with transsexual father). *Re D (Parental Responsibility: IVF Baby)* [2001] 1 FLR 972, CA—indirect contact with a man deemed to be the father under the Human Fertilisation and Embryology Act 1990. For examples of indirect contact with violent or abusive parents being ordered, see eg *Re S (Violent Parent: Indirect Contact)* [2000] 1 FLR 481, *Re H (Contact: Domestic Violence)* [1998] 2 FLR 42, CA and *Re M (Sexual Abuse Allegations: Interviewing Techniques)* [1999] 2 FLR 92.

[75] Including video recordings, see e.g. *Re A (Contact: Witness Protection Scheme)* [2005] EWHC 2189 (Fam) [2006] 2 FLR 551 and skype etc.

[76] Eg via Cafcass, see eg *Re F (Indirect Contact)* [2006] EWCA Civ 1426 [2007] 1 FLR 1015.

[77] See L Caffrey ' "Hearing the voice of the child": The role of contact centres in the family justice system' [2013] CFLQ 357.

[78] See eg *Re A (Temporary Removal From Jurisdiction)* [2004] EWCA Civ 1587 [2005] 1 FLR 639.

otherwise have contact with an unwilling parent[79] but it seems an impracticable option and therefore questionable in terms of the child's welfare. In fact the Joint Committee on the Draft Children (Contact) and Adoption Bill were in favour of such a power[80] but the Government dismissed the suggestion saying:[81]

> We would be concerned about the implications that would arise if contact orders were to be used to force someone, against their wishes, to have contact with a child. The child's welfare must be the paramount consideration in making decisions about their upbringing and there are serious issues raised about the potential distress, or even harm, such contact could cause to the child or children involved.

On the other side of the coin, in *Re W (Contact: Joining Child As Party)* Butler-Sloss P went so far as to say 'the child has a right to relationship with his father even if he does not want it.'[82] However, it should be added that although the appeal against a refusal against an order for no contact was allowed rather than making an order for the father to see his 7 year old son against the child's wishes, the case was referred to Cafcass to work with the family.

This issue was not re-visited by the *Family Law Review*.

Making provision for a child to spend time or otherwise have contact with a named person can be the sole order made, even between parents, and may be appropriate where there is no dispute as to the person with whom the child is to live. Although the courts should avoid making over-detailed orders if satisfied that the parties can work out the arrangements for themselves, making orders that are entirely open-ended raises the question whether, having regard to s 1(5),[83] there is a need to make an order at all. Such an order might, however, be justified where the applicant is not a parent, for example, a grandparent, since without an order such a person has no *locus standi* in relation to the child[84] and it might be valuable if the person with whom the child lives is hostile to the child spending time with the other parent and might therefore seek to prevent it. Where restricted or supervised contact is thought appropriate the court may attach any directions or conditions under s 11(7).

Like those dealing with the child's living arrangements, a child arrangements order providing for the child to spend time or otherwise have contact with one of the child's parents when the child is living with the other parent automatically ceases if the parents subsequently live together for a continuous period of more than six months.[85]

Under the general provisions of s 11(3), a court can make an *interim* order determining with whom the child is to spend time etc in cases where it is not in a position finally to dispose of proceedings. However, it has been held[86] that courts should be cautious about making

---

[79] But note Wall LJ's comment in *Re S (Permission to Seek Relief)* [2006] EWCA Civ 1190 [2007] 1 FLR 482 at [88]: 'There is currently no power to compel an absent parent to have contact with their children.'

[80] See their First Report HL Paper 100–1/HC 400–1.

[81] See the *Government Reply to the Report from the Joint Committee* Cm 6583 (June 2005).

[82] [2001] EWCA Civ 1830 [2003] 1 FLR 681 at [16], on which see the critique by A L James et al 'Turn down the volume— not hearing children in family proceedings' [2004] CFLQ 189 at 201.

[83] Discussed in Ch 12, Orders to be made only where better than no order, pp 438 ff.

[84] See Ch 12, Applying s 1(5), p 440.

[85] Section 11(6), as amended by Sch 2 para 6(4) to the 2014 Act. But note: orders providing for child to spend time with a third party do not end upon the parents' resumed cohabitation.

[86] Per Wall J in *Re D (Contact: Interim Orders)* [1995] 1 FLR 495. An example of where such an order might be justified is where previously satisfactory contact has been arbitrarily terminated by the 'residential parent'.

such interim orders where the principle of contact is in dispute and substantial factual issues, particularly sexual abuse or violence allegations are unresolved.[87]

While the child is spending time with a parent, that parent may exercise parental responsibility, at any rate with respect to short-term matters,[88] without consulting the other, provided he or she does nothing which is incompatible with any existing court order.[89]

Prohibiting a child from spending time or otherwise having contact with a named person

An issue that caused difficulty in the law before the 2014 reforms was how to make an order *preventing* a person from having contact with a child. Although the natural way of doing so was to make a prohibited steps order, the Court of Appeal held in *Nottingham County Council v P*[90] that what were then contact orders embraced not just 'positive' contact orders but also 'negative orders', that is, orders for 'no contact'. Subsequently, however, in *Re H (Minors) (Prohibited Steps Order)*,[91] the Court of Appeal made a prohibited steps order against a mother's former cohabitant preventing him from having or seeking contact with her children, to whom it was considered he posed a risk. It was held that it was only by this means that the order could be directed (and thus enforced) against the man. Butler-Sloss LJ commented that had a 'no contact' order been made it would have been directed against the mother, who would thus have been obliged to prevent contact. That would have been inappropriate in this case, since she neither wanted the children to have such contact nor had she the power to control it. The children were of school age and, as Butler-Sloss LJ said, 'With the best will in the world the mother could not protect her children going to and from school or at play . . .'

Although no doubt similar arguments could be deployed as to whether child arrangements orders only embrace positive orders, it is suggested that the *Nottingham* approach be abandoned so that in all cases where it sought to prohibit a person spending time or otherwise having contact with a child, the order that is sought should be a prohibited steps order.

Deciding what order to make

Disputes over who is to see the child and on what terms are among the greatest problems faced by the courts[92] in the private law context.[93] As Wall J once commented:[94]

> Disputes between separated parents over contact to their children are amongst the most difficult and sensitive cases which judges and magistrates have to hear. Nobody should pretend that they are easy, or that there is any one-size-fits-all solution.

Despite the 2014 reforms there is no reason to think that these disputes will become any easier to resolve.

In all cases, the overarching principle is the paramountcy of the child's welfare but in contested cases between parents the court must, provided it is satisfied that a parent's involvement

---

[87] *Re W (Staying Contact)* [1998] 2 FLR 450, CA. It may not, however, be possible, particularly in domestic violence cases, to make an interim order without hearing oral evidence or the advice of a children and family reporter: see *Re M (Interim Contact: Domestic Violence)* [2000] 2 FLR 377, CA.

[88] But, possibly, not to take important steps that have long term consequences for the child: see eg *Re G (Parental Responsibility: Education)* [1994] 2 FLR 964, CA discussed in Ch 11, Sharing parental responsibility for a child, pp 393–394.   [89] See Ch 11, Sharing parental responsibility for a child, p 393.

[90] [1994] Fam 18 at 38–9, CA, discussed further at No power to order a parent's removal from the family home, p 502.   [91] [1995] 1 WLR 667, CA.

[92] See F Kanagas 'Regulating emotion: judging contact disputes' [2011] CFLQ 63.

[93] See generally Lord Justice Wall 'Enforcement of Contact Orders' [2005] Fam Law 26. For an overview of the position in other jurisdictions see J Hunt and C Roberts *Intervening in litigated contact: ideas from other jurisdictions* (Family Policy Briefing No 4, 2005).

[94] *Re O (Contact: Withdrawal of Application)* [2003] EWHC 3031 (Fam) [2004] 1 FLR 1258 at [6](1).

will not put the child at risk of suffering harm, also apply s 1(2A) by which they are 'to presume, unless the contrary is shown, that involvement of [each] parent in the life of the child concerned will further the child's welfare.' We discuss in detail in Chapter 12 how this presumption is expected to operate. Suffice to say here that once it is determined that the presumption applies in any particular case, then some provision will have to be made to preserve the 'involvement' of the parent with whom the child is not living. Of course that still leaves open the form of that involvement (be it direct or indirect contact or some other form of 'involvement' such as being informed of the child's progress). However, it is well established that contact between a parent and child falls within Art 8(1) of the European Convention on Human Rights as a right to respect for private and family life both within marriage based relationships[95] and to children and parent relationships outside marriage.[96] Consequently to be consistent with human rights considerations and the spirit of the 2014 reforms the court should seek to provide for the maximum involvement that is consistent with the child's welfare. Denial of all involvement will have to be especially justified. It would be wrong, for example, to deny involvement because an application for a parental responsibility order had been refused,[97] nor will implacable hostility over a long time by the carer necessarily justify ending all contact.[98]

All this said, however, and notwithstanding the extensive discussion about the reform, it is not expected that new presumption will make much, if any, change in practice since s 1(2A) essentially puts in statutory form what was clearly established by case-law, namely the court's predisposition to preserving the continued involvement of both parents following their divorce or separation. As Butler-Sloss P put it in *Re S (Contact: Promoting Relationship With Absent Parent)*:[99]

No parent is perfect but 'good-enough parents' should have a relationship with their children for their own benefit and even more in the best interests of the children. It is, therefore, most important that the attempt to promote contact between a child and the non-residential parent should not be abandoned until it is clear that the child will not benefit from continuing the attempt.

As Butler-Sloss LJ pointed out in *Re R (A Minor) (Contact)*,[100] the principle of continuing contact is underlined by the UN Convention on the Rights of the Child 1989, Art 9(3). Furthermore as the European Court of Human Rights held in *Glaser v United Kingdom*, Art 8 of the European Convention on Human Rights 'includes a right for a parent to have measures taken with a view to his or her being reunited with the child and an obligation of national authorities to take measures' both in public and private law proceedings. However, the court also acknowledged that the obligation of national authorities to take measures to facilitate contact by a non-custodial parent after divorce is not absolute and that where it might appear to threaten the child's interests or interfere with his or her Art 8 rights, it is for those authorities 'to strike a fair balance between them'.[101]

---

[95] See e.g. *R v United Kingdom* [1988] 2 FLR 445, ECtHR; *Hokkanen v Finland* [1995] 2 FCR 320, [1996] 1 FLR 289, ECtHR and *Sahin v Germany, Sommerfeld v Germany* [2003] 2 FCR 619 and 647 [2003] 2 FLR 671, ECtHR (Grand Chamber).

[96] See *Lebbink v Netherlands* [2004] 2 FLR 463, ECtHR and *Sahin v Germany, Sommerfeld v Germany*. Art 8 can also be engaged in respect of foster parents, see *Kopf and Liberda v Austria* [2012] 1 FLR 1199.

[97] See *Re W (Parental Responsibility Order: Inter-Relationship with Direct Contact)* [2013] EWCA Civ 335 [2013] 2 FLR 1337.

[98] See eg *Re A (Intractable Contact Dispute: Human Rights Violations)* [2013] EWCA Civ 1104 [2014] 1 FLR 1185.   [99] [2004] EWCA Civ 18 [2004] 1 FLR 1279 at [32].

[100] [1993] 2 FLR 762 at 767, CA.

[101] [2001] 1 FLR 148 at (65)–(66). See also *Haase v Germany* [2004] 2 FLR 39, ECtHR and *Kosmopoulou v Greece* [2004] 1 FLR 800, ECtHR and, with respect to unmarried father's rights, see *Sahin v Germany, Sommerfeld v Germany* [2003] 2 FLR 671, ECtHR.

In *Re M (Contact: Welfare Test)*,[102] Wilson J suggested that the court should consider whether the fundamental need of every child to have an enduring relationship with both parents is outweighed by the depth of harm to the particular child that might thereby be caused by the contact order. The governing principles were referred to by Munby LJ in *Re C (Direct Contact: Suspension)*[103] as follows:

> Contact between parent and child is a fundamental element of family life and is almost always in the interests of the child.
>
> Contact between parent and child is to be determined only in exceptional circumstances, where there are cogent reasons for doing so and where there is no alternative. Contact is to be terminated only if it will be detrimental to the child's welfare.
>
> There is a positive obligation on the State, and therefore on the judge, to take measures to maintain and to reconstitute the relationship between parent and child, in short, to maintain or restore contact. The judge has a positive duty to attempt to promote contact. The judge must grapple with all the available alternatives before abandoning hope of achieving some contact. He must be careful not to come to a premature decision, for contact is to be stopped only as a last resort and only once it has become clear that the child will not benefit from continuing the attempt.
>
> The court should take both a medium-term and long-term view and not accord excessive weight to what appear likely to be short-term or transient problems.
>
> The key question, which requires 'stricter scrutiny', is whether the judge has taken all necessary steps to facilitate contact as can reasonably be demanded in the circumstances of the particular case.
>
> All that said, at the end of the day the welfare of the child is paramount; 'the child's interests must have precedence over any other consideration'.

Even where direct contact might be inappropriate, the court should still consider indirect contact as a means of preserving some kind of relationship with the absent parent. In *A v L (Contact)*,[104] for example, the father was serving a long-term prison sentence and, notwithstanding the unwillingness of any relative to facilitate any form of contact, the court thought it right to make an order for indirect contact (using the good offices of the mother's solicitors), Holman J stressing the child's fundamental right to have some knowledge of and some contact with his natural father. In many other cases the court has been concerned that every effort is made to preserve contact or the possibility of contact to the extent of referring the parents to therapy or other professional help.[105]

Notwithstanding the predisposition to preserve involvement with both parents wherever possible, there are obviously occasions when it would not be in the child's interests to do so. Obvious examples include cases where the parent has sexually abused his child[106]

---

[102] [1995] 1 FLR 274 at 278–9, CA.

[103] [2011] EWCA Civ 521 [2011] 2 FLR 912 at [47]. See also Wall J's summary in *Re P (Contact: Supervision)* [1996] 2 FLR 314 at 328, CA, relying on *Re O (Contact: Imposition of Conditions)* [1995] 2 FLR 124 at 128–30 per Sir Thomas Bingham MR. See also *Re W (Direct Contact)* [2012] EWCA Civ 999 [2013] 1 FLR 494.

[104] [1998] 1 FLR 361. Holman J was anxious that the boy (a three-year-old) should know who his father was, and he therefore held that it was wrong for the justices to have accepted the mother's view (even though this was also accepted by the father) that the child should not be told about his parentage until he grew older. See also the similar concern and approach in *Re R (A Minor) (Contact)* [1993] 2 FLR 762, CA.

[105] See eg *Re M (Contact: Long-Term Interests)* [2005] EWCA Civ 1090, [2006] 1 FLR 627, *Re S (Unco-operative Mother)* [2004] EWCA Civ 597 [2004] 2 FLR 710 and *Re S (Contact: Promoting Relationship With Absent Parent)* [2004] Civ 18 [2004] 1 FLR 1279.

[106] Cf *Re K (Appeal: Contact)* [2010] EWCA Civ 1365 [2011] 1 FLR 1592 and *Re C (Direct Contact: Suspension)* [2011] EWCA Civ 521 [2011] 2 FLR 912. For earlier examples, see eg *S v S* [1988] Fam Law 128,

and where continued contact was shown to be directly harmful to the child either physically[107] or emotionally in the sense of undermining the child's security.[108] In *Re T (A Child: One Parent Killed By Other Parent)*[109] all contact with his eight year old daughter denied to a father guilty of manslaughter of the mother, not on the basis of the killing per se but because there was concern that he was incapable of meeting the child's needs. Other examples include *Re F (Minors) (Denial of Contact)*,[110] in which contact with a transsexual father was refused primarily because of the children's (boys aged 12 and nine) own wishes; *Re T (A Minor) (Parental Responsibility: Contact)*,[111] where an unmarried father was denied contact because of his violence towards the mother and his blatant disregard for the child's welfare; and *Re C and V (Contact and Parental Responsibility)*,[112] in which the child had severe medical problems requiring constant and informed medical attention which the mother, but not the father, was able to give.

As Balcombe LJ commented in *Re J (A Minor) (Contact)*,[113] judges should be very reluctant to allow one parent's so-called 'implacable hostility'[114] to deter them from making a contact order where they believe the child's welfare requires it. In other words implacable hostility, per se, is not a reason for denying continued involvement. In this connection mention may be made that protracted proceedings, which are sometimes associated with implacable hostility, raise Art 8 issues insofar as delay in enforcing orders effectively cause the end of contact.[115]

Mention has been made of domestic violence, which is a frequently encountered allegation particularly in disputes concerning seeing a child. It is established that violence does not per se justify a refusal of contact;[116] it is a matter of discretion, not principle. But in *Re M (Contact: Violent Parent)*[117] Wall J commented that too little weight was sometimes given to the need of a violent parent to change behaviour so as to demonstrate fitness to have contact.

CA and *Re R (A Minor) (Child Abuse)* [1988] Fam Law 129. Though note proof of sexual abuse does not *ipso facto* mean that contact should be denied: see *H v H (Child Abuse: Access)* [1989] 1 FLR 212, CA and *C v C (Child Abuse: Evidence)* [1988] 1 FLR 462.

[107] See eg *Re C (Contact: No Order for Contact)* [2000] 2 FLR 723, in which indirect contact was refused with a father who had been absent for three years and against whom the child had an extreme adverse reaction; and *Geapin v Geapin* (1974) 4 Fam Law 188, CA where a boy suffered serious asthmatic attacks when in contact with his father.

[108] See eg *Re W (Family Proceedings: Applications)* [2011] EWHC 76 (Fam) [2011] 1 FLR 2163, *Re C (Minors) (Access)* [1985] FLR 804, CA; *Williams v Williams* [1985] FLR 509, CA (though the children were being indoctrinated against their father); and *Wright v Wright* (1980) 2 FLR 276, CA.

[109] [2011] EWHC 1195 (Fam) [2012] 1 FLR 472.

[110] [1993] 2 FLR 677, CA. See also *Re L (Contact: Transsexual Applicant)* [1995] 2 FLR 438. For pre-1989 Act cases following the children's wishes, see eg *Re N (A Minor) (Access: Penal Notices)* [1992] 1 FLR 134, CA.

[111] [1993] 2 FLR 450, CA. See also *Carp v Bryon* [2005] EWCA Civ 1035 [2006] 1 FCR 1, *Re A (Contact)* [1998] 2 FLR 171, and *Re D (Contact: Reasons for Refusal)* [1997] 2 FLR 48, CA (mother found to be genuinely fearful for herself and her child). Other examples might include sexual abuse, or physical abuse.

[112] [1998] 1 FLR 392, CA.

[113] [1994] 1 FLR 729 at 736. See also *Re S (Contact: Grandparents)* [1996] 1 FLR 158 and *Re P (Contact: Supervision)* [1996] 2 FLR 314, CA.

[114] See also *Re A (Intractable Contact Dispute: Human Rights Violations)* [2013] EWCA Civ 1104 [2014] 1 FLR 1185., and *Re S (Contact: Intractable Dispute)* [2010] EWCA Civ 447 [2010] 2 FLR 1517. But note *Re D (Contact: Reasons for Refusal)* [1997] 2 FLR 48, CA, in which Hale J observed that the term 'implacable hostility' usually refers to the type of case where no good reason could be discerned for a parent's opposition to contact.

[115] See *Kopf and Liberda v Austria* [2012] 1 FLR 1199, ECtHR and *Re A (Intractable Contact Dispute: Human Rights Violations)* [2013] EWCA Civ 1104 [2014] 1 FLR 1185.

[116] *Re F (A Child) (Contact Order)* [2001] 1 FCR 422 and *Re H (Contact: Domestic Violence)* [1998] 2 FLR 42, CA.   [117] [1999] 2 FLR 321.

In the leading case, *Re L (A Child), Re V (A Child), Re H (A Child) (Contact: Domestic Violence)*,[118] the Court of Appeal dismissed four appeals by fathers against orders allowing them indirect contact, but refusing them direct contact in cases of a background of domestic violence between the spouses and partners. It was held that there were no presumptions for or against contact with a violent parent, and the only principle applicable was the paramountcy of the child's welfare. Drawing both on *A Report to the Lord Chancellor on the Question of Parental Contact in Cases* by the Children Act Sub-Committee of the Lord Chancellor's Advisory Board[119] and on an expert report (later published)[120] prepared by Drs Claire Sturge and Danya Glaser on contact from a child and adolescent psychiatry perspective, Butler-Sloss LJ commented:[121]

> The general principle that contact with the non-residence parent is in the interests of the child may sometimes have discouraged sufficient attention being paid to the adverse effects on children living in the household where violence has occurred . . . In a contact or other s 8 application, where allegations of domestic violence are made which might have an effect on the outcome, those allegations must be adjudicated upon and found proved or not proved. It will be necessary to scrutinise such allegations which may not always be true or may be grossly exaggerated. If however there is a firm basis for finding that violence has occurred, the psychiatric advice becomes very important. There is not, however, nor should there be, any presumption that, on proof of domestic violence, the offending parent has to surmount a prima facie barrier of no contact. As a matter of principle, domestic violence of itself cannot constitute a bar to contact. It is one factor in the difficult and delicate balancing exercise of discretion . . . In this context, the ability of the offending parent to recognise his past conduct, be aware of the need to change and make genuine efforts to do so, will be likely to be an important consideration.

Subsequent to *Re L*, Butler-Sloss P refused direct contact to a violent father who had killed his wife.[122] All contact was also refused in a case[123] where there had been 'unusually high levels of domestic violence', because of the harm to the child living with the mother who was suffering from psychological and emotional conditions induced by that contact. It has been said that a refusal of contact in cases of domestic violence where there is a risk of emotional destabilisation to the child promotes the child's right to family life with its primary carer pursuant to Art 8 of the European Convention on Human Rights.[124]

Another issue that is sometimes raised before the courts is that of parental alienation, that is, an allegation that the children's hostility towards one parent (normally the non-resident parent) has been deliberately fostered by the other (normally the resident parent). There is little doubt about the existence of this as a phenomenon but one debate (particularly prevalent in the United States of America) is whether there is such a thing as 'Parental Alienation Syndrome'.[125] The English court's attitude is that it is inappropriate to call it a 'syndrome'[126] and it should not be assumed that a child's hostility to contact has

---

[118] [2001] Fam 260, CA.

[119] See now the fully published Report *Making Contact Work*.   [120] [2000] Fam Law 615.

[121] [2001] Fam at 272–3.   [122] *Re G (Direct Contact: Domestic Violence)* [2000] 2 FLR 865.

[123] *Re M and B (Children) (Contact: Domestic Violence)* [2001] 1 FCR 116, CA.

[124] *Re Q (Contact: Natural Father)* (2001, unreported).

[125] See the discussion by C Bruch 'Parental Alienation Syndrome and Alienated Children—getting it wrong in child custody cases' [2002] CFLQ 381.

[126] See in particular the paper prepared by Drs Sturge and Glaser for the Court of Appeal in *Re L; V, M and H (Contact: Domestic Violence)* [2001] Fam 260 published under the title 'Contact and Domestic Violence—The Experts' Court Report' [2000] Fam Law 615 at 622–3 and Lord Justice Wall 'Enforcement of Contact Orders' [2005] Fam Law at 29.

been deliberately fostered by the residential parent.[127] As with all issues, the allegation of hostility requires careful investigation and evaluation.[128]

One final point that might be made in this brief overview, and a return to the theme mentioned at the beginning of the chapter, is that contact works best when it is voluntarily agreed between the parents. In other words, recourse to the court should be the last resort. As Wall J observed in *Re O (Contact: Withdrawal of Application):*[129]

> Fortunately, most separating parents are able to negotiate contact without the need to go to court. Contact disputes are best resolved outside the court system . . . Contact in my experience works best when parents respect each other and are able to co-operate; where the children's loyalties are not torn, and where they can move between their parents without tension, unhappiness or fear of offending one parent or the other. Such cases rarely come to court. The courts, therefore, have to deal with the cases in which there is no agreement.

(c) Activity directions and conditions

As part of the original strategy to facilitate contact, powers to make what were then called *contact* activity directions and conditions were introduced by the Children and Adoption Act 2006, adding ss 11A to 11G to the Children Act 1989.[130] These provisions have been amended by the Children and Families Act 2014[131] so as to make them applicable to any type of child arrangements orders and are now simply referred to as activity directions and conditions. In substance, however, the powers remain the same.

Directions can only be made where a court is *considering* whether to make, vary or discharge a child arrangements order. They cannot be given on a final child arrangements order.[132] Conversely, *conditions* can only be made upon the making or varying of a child arrangements order. The latter are part of a formal order and are therefore enforceable on pain of contempt, by an enforcement order or by a financial compensation order.[133] Although there are no formal sanctions for non-compliance with directions, due account can be taken of any breaches[134] in the final disposal of the contact issue.

Activity directions

An activity direction is defined in s 11A(3)[135] as one 'requiring an individual who is a party to the proceedings concerned to take part in an activity that would, in the court's opinion, help to establish, maintain or improve the involvement in the life of the child concerned of—(a) that individual, or (b) another individual who is a party to the proceedings'.

[127] See eg *Re O (Contact: Withdrawal of Application)* [2003] EWHC 3031 [2004] 1 FLR 1279, in which the father's assertion of alienation by the mother was rejected, the children's hostility being found to be due to the father's own behaviour.
[128] See *T (Contact: Parental Alienation: Permission to Appeal)* [2002] EWCA Civ 1736 [2003] 1 FLR 531, where the alienation was held not to have been adequately investigated.
[129] [2003] EWHC 3031 [2004] 1 FLR 1279 at [6](8)–(9).
[130] For the background to these measures see the Government Green Paper's *Parental Separation: Children's Needs and Parents' Responsibilities* Cm 6273 (July 2004), *Parental Separation: Children's Needs and Parent's Responsibilities: Next Steps* Cm 6452 (January 2005); the Draft Children (Contact) and Adoption Bill Cm 6462 (February 2005); the Joint Committee on the Draft Children (Contact) and Adoption Bill: First Report HL Paper 100–1/HL (the so-called 'Scrutiny Committee') and *The Government Reply to the Report from the Joint Committee* Cm 6583 (June 2005). For comments on the proposals see J Masson and C Humphreys 'Facilitating and Enforcing Contact: The Bill and the Ten Per Cent' [2005] Fam Law 548.
[131] The amendments are made in Sch 2 paras 7–13 to the 2014 Act.
[132] Section 11A(7).   [133] Discussed at Enforcing section 8 orders, pp 537ff.
[134] A Cafcass officer can be asked to monitor compliance with a direction and to report to the court any failure to comply, s 11G.   [135] As rewritten by Sch 2 para 7(2) to the 2014 Act.

Directions can only be made in disputed cases and children cannot be made to take part in an activity unless they are the parent of the child in relation to whom the court is considering provision for a child arrangements order.[136] Directions cannot be made in contact applications in adoption proceedings.[137]

A direction must specify both the activity to be undertaken and the person providing the activity.[138] The activities that may be so required include (a) programmes, classes and counselling or guidance sessions of a kind that may assist a person as regards establishing, maintaining or improving contact with a child and, may, by addressing a person's violent behaviour, enable or facilitate contact; and (b) sessions in which information or advice is given as regards making or operating arrangements for contact with a child including making arrangements by means of mediation.[139] On the other hand, a direction cannot be used to require medical or psychiatric examinations or mediation.[140]

In deciding whether to make a direction, 'the welfare of the child concerned is the court's paramount consideration'.[141] The court must also be satisfied that the activity is appropriate in the circumstances of the case; that the provider of the activity concerned is suitable to provide it; and the activity is available in a place to which it is reasonable to expect the person in question to travel.[142] Before making a direction the court must obtain and consider information about the individual who would be subject to the direction and its likely effect upon him in particular with regard to any conflict with his religious beliefs or any interference with the times that he is at work or attending an educational establishment.[143] Courts can seek information on any of these points from a Cafcass or Welsh family proceedings officer.[144]

Activity conditions

Like a direction, under s 11C, as amended by 2014 Act, an activity condition requires an individual to take part in an activity that 'would, in the court's opinion, help to establish, maintain or improve the involvement in the life of the child concerned of—(a) that individual, or (b) another individual who is a party to the proceedings'. Although conditions are made at a later stage than directions, there is no requirement that conditions can only be made following the making of directions.

As with a direction, a condition must specify both the activity to be undertaken and the person providing the activity and the activity conditions are the same as those that can be specified in a direction and are subject to the same prohibitions.[145] Like directions, in deciding whether to make a condition the court must be satisfied that the activity is appropriate in the circumstances of the case; that the provider of the activity concerned is suitable to provide it; and the activity is available in a place to which it is reasonable to expect the person in question to travel.[146]

---

[136] Section 11B(2), as amended by Sch 2 para 8(3) to the 2014 Act.

[137] Section 11B(3). Section 11B(7) also provides that the individual must be habitually resident in England and Wales. [138] Section 11A(4).

[139] Financial assistance to help individuals pay providers for their services might be available from the State: s 11F.

[140] Section 11A(6). [141] Section 11B(9). [142] Section 11E. [143] Section 11E(5), (6).

[144] Section 11E(7). The appropriate officer is bound to comply with such a request.

[145] Section 11C(5). Note in particular that conditions cannot require medical or psychiatric examinations or mediation. Conditions can only be imposed upon a child if he or she is a parent of the child concerned. Conditions cannot be added to contact orders made in adoption proceedings and conditions can only be imposed on individuals who are habitually resident in England and Wales: s 11D.

[146] Section 11E.

Before imposing a condition the court must obtain and consider information about the individual who would be liable to the condition and its likely effect upon him in particular with regard to any conflict with his religious beliefs or any interference with the times that he is at work or attending an educational establishment.[147] Unlike when making directions, there is no *express* requirement to treat the child's welfare as the paramount consideration when making conditions. Although this seems a curious omission, on general principles, applying s 1(1), courts will have to treat the child's welfare as the *paramount* consideration in determining whether to add conditions.

Other differences between conditions and directions are (a) there is no stated requirement that there needs to have been a dispute; (b) unlike directions, which can be imposed upon parties, the individuals upon whom conditions can be imposed are limited to those named in a child arrangements order as a person with whom the child is to live or spend time and a person upon whom the order imposes a condition under s 11(7)(b) of the 1989 Act, and (c) unlike directions, conditions are enforceable on pain of contempt.[148]

(d) Monitoring

In addition to asking Cafcass or Welsh family proceedings officers to monitor compliance with activity directions and conditions, under s 11H a court can also ask such officers to monitor compliance with provisions contained in a child arrangements order and to report to the court on such matters relating to compliance as the court may specify. Such monitoring roles can last up to one year.[149] Those who can be subject to monitoring are those in which a child arrangements order (a) provides for the child concerned to live with different persons at different times and names the individual as one of those persons, (b) imposes requirements on that individual with regard to the child concerned spending time or otherwise having contact with some other person, and (c) which names that individual as a person with whom the child concerned is to spend time or otherwise have contact.[150] A person who is subject to a condition under s 11(7)(b) of the 1989 Act can also be monitored.[151]

(e) Prohibited steps orders

A prohibited steps order:

> ... means an order that no step which could be taken by a parent in meeting his parental responsibility for a child, and which is of a kind specified in the order, shall be taken by any person without the consent of the court.

This is one of two orders under the 1989 Act (the other being a specific issue order), which were modelled on the wardship jurisdiction, and intended to broaden all the courts' powers when dealing with children. It empowers a court to place a *specific* embargo upon the exercise of any aspect of parental responsibility. This is in contrast to the vague requirement in wardship that 'no important step' in the child's life be taken without the court's prior consent.[152]

---

[147] Section 11E(5), (6). Courts can seek information on any of these powers from a Cafcass or Welsh family proceedings officer: s 11E(7). The appropriate officer is bound to comply with such a request.

[148] Though for both directions and conditions Cafcass officers can be asked to monitor the compliance and report to the court any failure to comply: s 11G.   [149] Section 11H(6).

[150] Section 11H(3)(za) added by the Children and Families Act 2014, Sch 2 para 14(4)(b).

[151] Section 11H(3)(c).

[152] Wardship is discussed in Ch 20. It is assumed that an order as vague as prohibiting any important step could not be made as a prohibited steps order.

Prohibited steps orders can be put to a variety of uses. They can, for example, be used to prohibit contact with a parent or someone else,[153] to restrain a particular medical operation, including the ritual circumcision of a boy without the consent of the other parent or the court,[154] to prevent the removal of the child from one parent's care for duration of the child's medical treatment to which the other parent is opposed,[155] to restrain changing the child's surname,[156] to restrain changing the child's schooling or religion,[157] and to prevent the child's removal from his home before the court has had time to decide what order, if any, should be made.[158] Another use is to impose an embargo against removing a child from the United Kingdom in cases of possible child abduction.[159] This power might be useful to prevent a threatened removal in cases where the automatic restriction against removal under s 13 does not apply.[160] Even where s 13 operates to permit temporary removals it might still be possible to obtain a prohibited steps order to prevent repeated removals of children outside the United Kingdom for periods of less than one month by the parent with whom the child lives. Furthermore since s 13 only prevents a child's removal outside the United Kingdom, a prohibited steps order is the preferable option[161] to prevent relocation *within* the United Kingdom.[162]

Although the order itself must relate to an aspect of parental responsibility,[163] it can be made against anyone regardless of whether they hold parental responsibility.[164] Hence orders can be made against an unmarried father whether or not he has responsibility and similarly against a third party, for example to restrain a former cohabitant (notwithstanding that he was not even a party) from contacting or seeking to have contact with the child,[165] or to restrain an individual or group from associating with the child. Applicants

---

[153] *Re H (Minors) (Prohibited Steps Order)* [1995] 1 WLR 667, CA, discussed at Prohibiting a child from spending time or otherwise having contact with a named person, p 494.

[154] *Re J (Specific Issue Orders: Muslim Upbringing and Circumcision)* [1999] 2 FLR 678, per Wall J upheld on appeal: [2000] 1 FLR 571, CA. See also *Re S (Specific Issue Order: Religion: Circumcision)* [2004] EWHC 1282 (Fam) [2005] 1 FLR 236.

[155] See *An NHS Trust v SR (Radiotherapy and Chemotherapy)* [2012] EWHC 3842 (Fam) [2013] 1 FLR 1297.

[156] At any rate in the absence of a child arrangements order relating to the child's living arrangements: see *Dawson v Wearmouth* [1999] 2 AC 308, HL. Where there is such an order, applications concerning a change of name should be made under s 13: see *Re B (Change of Surname)* [1996] 1 FLR 791, CA, discussed at Change of child's surname, p 521.

[157] See the case referred to by C Bevan ('Is welfare faring well? In praise of the welfare principle: a case study from Romford' [2012] Fam Law 1141) concerning a dispute over a child's baptism.

[158] See the revised *Guidance and Regulations*, Vol 1, *Court Orders* (Department for Children, Schools and Families, 2008) at para 2.37.

[159] See eg *Re R (a child)(prohibited steps order)* [2013] EWCA Civ 1115 [2014] 1 FCR 113.

[160] As pointed out by the revised Guidance, at 2.37, in turn repeating the example given by the Law Commission, see Law Com No 172, para 4.20. The embargo under s 13(1)(b) and (2) is discussed at Removal of child from the United Kingdom—'External Relocation', p 525. In the absence of a child arrangements order, the Child Abduction Act 1984 (see Ch 26, Criminal sanctions, p 1018) operates to prevent unilateral removal.

[161] See *Re F (Internal Relocation)* [2010] EWCA Civ 1428 [2011] 1 FLR 1382 at [23], per Wilson LJ who agreeing with Thorpe LJ in *Re B (Prohibited Steps Order)* [2007] EWCA Civ 1055 [2008] 1 FLR 613 at [4], 'provisionally' considered that a prohibited steps order was to be preferred to seeking the imposition of a condition on a child arrangements order dealing with the child's living arrangements, see further Additional directions and conditions, p 504.

[162] See *Re L (Shared Residence Order)* [2009] EWCA Civ 20 [2009] 1 FLR 1157, *Re F* and *Re B* above and *Re H (Children) (Residence Order: Condition)* [2001] EWCA Civ 1338 [2001] 2 FLR 1277, discussed at Application to living arrangements, p 507.

[163] See the discussion at Orders must concern 'an aspect of parental responsibility', p 501.

[164] See the 2008 Guidance at 2.37.

[165] *Re H (Children) (Residence Order: Condition)*. In the case of non-parties, orders cannot be enforced until they have been served on the respondent: see Clarke Hall and Morrison on *Children* 11[531].

do not have to have parental responsibility but in its absence will need court leave to make an application.[166]

A prohibited steps order may be made either in conjunction with another s 8 order or on its own.

(f) Specific issue order

A specific issue order:[167]

> ... means an order giving directions for the purpose of determining a specific question which has arisen, or which may arise, in connection with any aspect of parental responsibility for a child.

These orders enable a specific question relating to the child to be brought before the court, the aim of which is not to give one parent or the other a general 'right' to make decisions in a particular respect, but to enable a particular dispute to be resolved.[168] In doing so, detailed directions may be necessary.

It was held in *Re HG (Specific Issue Order: Sterilisation)*[169] that there is no necessity for there to be a dispute between the parties before the power arises to make a specific issue order; it is sufficient that there is a question to be answered. In that case an unopposed application[170] for a specific issue order was granted giving High Court sanction for the sterilisation of a 17-year-old mentally impaired child. Like prohibited steps orders, specific issue orders may be made either in conjunction with another s 8 order or on their own.[171]

Examples of specific issue orders include *F v F (MMR: Vaccine)*,[172] in which the court ordered, contrary to the mother's wishes, the child's immunisation; *Re R (A Minor) (Blood Transfusion)*,[173] in which the court ordered inter alia that, in an imminently life-threatening situation, the child in question be given a blood transfusion without the consent of her parents, who were Jehovah's Witnesses; *Re D (a minor)*,[174] in which a mother was ordered to return the child to the jurisdiction; and *Re A (Children) (Specific Issue Order:*

---

[166] See *SH v MM and RM (Prohibited Steps Order: Abduction)* [2011] EWHC 3314 (Fam) [2012] 1 FLR 837. Provided the order is of some value to the applicant it can be made even though the child is abroad: See *Re D (a minor)* [1992] 1 All ER 892, CA—a mother, in breach of an undertaking given to the English court, failed to return the child from Turkey: an order for the child's return was thought helpful to the father in bringing proceedings in Turkey. Orders may made without notice: FPR 2010 r 12.16(1)(a). A without notice application is one which made by one party without informing the other. Such orders are sometimes made in the context of international child abduction, often at the request of the abducting parent, to prevent removal by the other, see *SH v MM and RM (Prohibited Steps Order: Abduction)*. But caution should be exercised in making without notice applications and orders, see *B v A (Wasted Costs Order)* [2012] EWHC 3217(Fam) [2013] 2 FLR 958 and *KY v DD (Injunctions)* [2011] EWHC 1277 (Fam) [2012] 2 FLR 200.

[167] See generally S Gilmore 'The nature, scope and use of the specific issue order' [2004] CFLQ 367.

[168] See The Department of Health's *Guidance and Regulations*, Vol 1, *Court Orders* 1991, para 2.32, not precisely replicated in the revised 2008 *Guidance*, see para 2.38.   [169] [1993] 1 FLR 587.

[170] The application was thought necessary in view of Lord Templeman's lone dictum in *Re B (A Minor) (Wardship: Sterilisation)* [1988] AC 199 at 205, (discussed in Chapter 10) that High Court sanction is always required for a child's sterilisation. See also *Practice Note* [1993] 3 All ER 222.

[171] They can also be made without notice: FPR 2010 r 12.16(1)(a). For an example, see *Re D (A Minor) (Child: Removal From Jurisdiction)* [1992] 1 WLR 667, CA. But note *B v A (Wasted Costs Order)* and *KY v DD (Injunctions)* above.

[172] [2013] EWHC 2769 (Fam) [2014] 1 1 FLR 1328. For a similar decision. See *Re C (Welfare of Child: Immunisation)* [2003] EWHC 1376 (Fam) [2003] 2 FLR 1054, upheld on appeal: [2003] EWCA Civ 1148 [2003] 2 FLR 1095. See also *Re C (HIV Test)* [1999] 2 FLR 1004, CA—in which a specific issue order was granted that a baby be tested for HIV.

[173] [1993] 2 FLR 757.   [174] [1992] 1 All ER 892, CA.

Parental Dispute)[175] in which the court ordered, at the French father's request, that the two children should attend the Lycée Français in London even though, since their parents' separation, they were living with their English mother in England.

Specific issue orders can also be sought to resolve disputes over children's religious upbringing;[176] to inform children about their father's identity[177] and even his very existence;[178] to obtain reports from the other parent on their child's progress;[179] to return the children to their home jurisdiction;[180] to obtain court sanction for a defence solicitor to interview children for the purpose of providing evidence in criminal proceedings against their father;[181] and, provided no child arrangements order is in force, to obtain court leave to change a child's name,[182] or to take the child out of the UK,[183] or, though no prior leave is required, to obtain court sanction to take a child to live in another part of the UK.[184]

(g) Limits on the courts' powers to make specific issue and prohibited steps orders

Orders must concern 'an aspect of parental responsibility'

An important limitation both on prohibited and specific issue orders[185] is that they must concern an aspect of parental responsibility. A court cannot, therefore, make a prohibited steps order forbidding contact between the parents,[186] or protecting one parent from being assaulted by the other,[187] nor may it make a specific issue order compelling a local

---

[175] [2001] 1 FLR 121, CA. See also *M v M (Specific Issue: Choice of School)* [2005] EWHC 2769 (Fam), [2007] 1 FLR 251, in which a father was given permission to take his son for a voice test with a view to test the possibility of him obtaining a scholarship to a cathedral school, a move opposed by the mother.

[176] See *Re G (Education: Religious Upbringing)* [2012] EWCA Civ 1233 [2013] 1 FLR 677, which involved a dispute over whether the children should have a Jewish Orthodox or ultra-Orthodox education; *Re S (Specific Issue Order: Religion: Circumcision)* [2004] EWHC 1282 (Fam) [2005] 1 FLR 236 in which a Muslim mother separated from the Hindu father unsuccessfully sought a specific issue order for both children to become practising members of the Islamic faith and for the boy to be circumcised. A similar application was refused in *Re J (Specific Issue Orders: Muslim Upbringing and Circumcision)* [1999] 2 FLR 678, upheld on appeal at [2000] 1 FLR 571.

[177] See *Re F (Paternity: Jurisdiction)* [2007] EWCA Civ 873 [2008] 1 FLR 225. The court can even do so on its own motion: *Re J (Paternity: Welfare of Child)* [2006] EWHC 2837 (Fam) [2007] 1 FLR 1064—but declined on the facts to do so. See also *Re L (Identity of Birth Father)* [2008] EWCA Civ 1338 [2009] 1 FLR 1152—case remitted because welfare decision had been taken on incomplete evidence (not hearing the child's psychiatrist by agreement between the parents).

[178] *Re K (Specific Issue Order)* [1999] 2 FLR 280—application rejected.

[179] See *Re D (Withdrawal of Parental Responsibility)* [2014] EWCA Civ 315, [2014] Fam Law 971—application refused on the facts.

[180] See eg *Re J (A Child) (Custody Rights: Jurisdiction)* [2005] UKHL 40 [2005] 3 WLR 14, discussed in Ch 26.

[181] *Re F (Specific Issue: Child Interview)* [1995] 1 FLR 819, CA. See also *Re M (Care: Leave To Interview Child)* [1995] 1 FLR 825, and *Chief Constable of Greater Manchester v KI and KW (By Their Children's Guardian, CAFCASS Legal) and NP* [2007] EWHC 2090 (Fam) [2008] 1 FLR 504 in which the police were given leave to interview the children for the purpose of investigating their sister's death.

[182] See *Dawson v Wearmouth* [1999] 2 AC 308, HL and *Re W (A Child) (Illegitimate Child: Change of Surname)* [2001] Fam 1, CA discussed at Change of child's surname, p 521.

[183] *Re D (A Minor) (Child: Removal From Jurisdiction)* [1992] 1 WLR 667, CA.

[184] See *Re F (Internal Relocation)* [2010] EWCA Civ 1428 [2011] 1 FLR 1382.

[185] For discussion of the general restrictions on making s 8 orders, see p 510.

[186] *Croydon London Borough Council v A* [1992] Fam 169; cf *F v R (Contact)* [1995] 1 FLR 227 in which Wall J accepted that such an embargo could be incorporated as a condition to what would now be a child arrangements order under s 11(7), though this decision is difficult to square with *D v N (Contact Order: Conditions)* [1997] 2 FLR 797, CA discussed at Conditions concerning arrangements about the child spending time etc with a named person, p 507.

[187] *M v M (Residence Order: Ancillary Injunction)* [1994] Fam Law 440 in which Johnson J also held that an injunction could nevertheless be sought under the appropriate domestic violence legislation, as an ancillary action to the Children Act application.

authority to provide support services,[188] since neither contact between adults nor the provision of support services has anything to do with parental responsibility.

There is uncertainty with regard to making orders concerning publicity about a child. The initial assumption[189] that publicity about a child was not an aspect of parental responsibility which therefore meant that it could neither be restrained or sanctioned by a s 8 order, was reflected in the majority view in *Re W (Wardship: Discharge: Publicity).*[190] However, note may be taken of Hobhouse LJ's well-reasoned dissenting judgment in *Re W*[191] that determining whether an immature child should become involved with the media 'falls within the scope of the proper discharge of parental duties', and of *Re Z (A Minor) (Identification: Restrictions on Publication)*[192] in which the Court of Appeal made a prohibited steps order restraining publicity upon the basis that the mother's waiver of the child's right of confidentiality to the particular information (viz. the attendance at a specialist unit dealing with children's educational needs) was an aspect of parental responsibility.

No power to order a parent's removal from the family home

In *Nottingham County Council v P*[193] Sir Stephen Brown P commented that 'it is very doubtful indeed whether a prohibited steps order could in any circumstances be used to "oust" a father from a matrimonial home.' Similarly, in *Pearson v Franklin*[194] Nourse LJ commented that Parliament could not have intended that ouster orders are capable of being made under the guise of specific issue orders. It was therefore held that a specific issue order (and by implication a prohibited steps order) could not be used to interfere with rights of occupation. In *Re M (Minors) (Disclosure of Evidence)*[195] the Court of Appeal took *Nottingham* to have established that there is no jurisdiction under the Children Act to exclude a parent from the home for the protection of the child, and in *Re D (Prohibited Steps Order)*[196] Ward LJ clearly stated that there is no jurisdiction to make an ouster order under the Children Act.[197]

Aside from justifying this position as a matter of policy (ie that because of their draconian effect Parliament should be taken to confer the power to make ouster orders only where a statute clearly so provides) a possible theoretical justification for this lack of power is that ouster orders relate to matters of occupation rather than parental responsibility.[198]

---

[188] *Re J (Specific Issue Order: Leave To Apply)* [1995] 1 FLR 669, per Wall J.

[189] See original *Guidance and Regulations*, Vol 1, *Court Orders* (1991) at para 2.31. This comment has not been repeated in the revised Guidance (2008), see para 2.37.   [190] [1995] 2 FLR 466.

[191] At 476.

[192] [1997] Fam 1. For analysis of this decision, see inter alia, *Kelly v BBC* [2001] Fam 59, per Munby J and *Medway Council v BBC* [2001] 1 FLR 104, per Wilson J. Query whether Ward LJ's analysis has survived the House of Lord's subsequent ruling in *Re S (A Child) (Identification: Restrictions on Publication)* [2004] UKHL 47 [2005] 1 AC 593 (discussed in Ch 10) that the foundation of the jurisdiction to control publicity about a child derives from the European Convention on Human Rights rather than the inherent jurisdiction?

[193] [1994] Fam 18 at 39E–F, CA.   [194] [1994] 1 WLR 370.   [195] [1994] 1 FLR 760.

[196] [1996] 2 FLR 273. See also *Re D (Residence: Imposition of Conditions)* [1996] 2 FLR 281, CA, applied in *Re K (Contact Order: Condition Ousting Parent From Family Home)* [2011] EWCA Civ 1075 [2012] 2 FLR 635. These cases also establish that the inability to make an ouster order by way of a prohibited steps or specific issue order cannot be overcome by using s 11(7).

[197] Though probably an application for an occupation order under Part IV of the Family Law Act 1996 (discussed in Ch 5) can be brought as an ancillary action to the Children Act application; cf *M v M (Residence Order: Ancillary Injunction)* [1994] Fam Law 440. For the court's power to make ouster orders under the High Court's inherent jurisdiction and upon making an emergency protection or interim care order, see Chs 20, 16 and 17 respectively.

[198] This line of argument was hinted at by Nourse LJ in *Pearson v Franklin*, but it is not beyond question, since ouster orders are viewed as being primarily about protection and only incidentally about occupation. See Ch 6.

No power to make disguised child arrangements orders

Section 9(5)(a)[199] prevents the court from making a prohibited steps or a specific issue order 'with a view to achieving a result which could be achieved by a child arrangements order'. This provision was made to guard against the slight risk, particularly in uncontested cases, that the orders might be used to achieve the same practical results as what are now known as child arrangements orders but without the same legal effects.[200] Clear examples of the types of order forbidden by s 9(5)(a) are *Re S (Contact Order)*[201] in which a judge made an order for the father 'to have the care' of the child at certain times, which on appeal was unsuccessfully argued to have been a perfectly valid specific issue order, and *M v C (Children-Orders: Reasons)*[202] in which justices purported to make a specific issue order returning the children to their mother when this could and should have been achieved by what would now be a child arrangements order. But other examples are less obvious. For instance, in *Re B (Minors) (Residence Order)*[203] it was held that s 9(5)(a) operates to prevent the making of a specific issue order to return a child to a parent in the case of a snatch, since such an order could be made by means of what would now be a child arrangements order with appropriate conditions attached under s 11(7).[204] In *Nottingham County Council v P*[205] it was held to be contrary to s 9(5)(a) to order, upon a local authority application under s 8, that a father vacate the household and that the child should have no further contact with him save under local authority supervision since the application patently sought to determine the children's living arrangements (that is, by regulating who could live in the household) and the degree of contact which the children might have with the father. In this latter regard the Court of Appeal, rejected the argument that an order for 'no contact' could not be made as what was then known as a contact order under s 8.[206] However, in *Re H (Minors) (Prohibited Steps Order)*,[207] the Court of Appeal subsequently held that a prohibited steps order restricting a former cohabitant from contacting or seeking contact with the children did not contravene s 9(5), since unlike an order for no contact under s 8 it could properly be directed and enforced against the man rather than the mother.

No power to make orders that are denied to the High Court acting under its inherent jurisdiction

Section 9(5)(b) prevents the court from exercising its power to make a specific issue or prohibited steps order 'in any way which is denied to the High Court (by s 100(2)) in the exercise of its inherent jurisdiction.'[208] According to the Department of Health's original *Guidance and Regulations*,[209] s 9(5)(b) prevents local authorities applying for a prohibited

---

[199] As amended by the Children and Families Act 2014 Sch 2 para 4. Note also a similar embargo against making such orders with a view to achieving a result which could be achieved by a s 51A order (post adoption contact), see Children Act 1989 s 9 (5)(a), as amended by the Adoption and Children Act 2002, s 51B (7), inserted by 9 of the 2014 Act. Section 51 A orders are discussed in Ch 19.

[200] Law Com No 172 para 4.19 and the revised *Guidance and Regulations, Court Orders* (2008), para 2.40.

[201] [2010] EWCA Civ 705 [2011] 1 FLR 183. [202] [1993] 2 FLR 584.

[203] [1992] Fam 162, CA; cf *Re D (A Minor) (Child: Removal From Jurisdiction)* [1992] 1 WLR 667, CA, in which a specific issue order *was* made ordering a parent abroad to return the child to the jurisdiction.

[204] The power to add conditions etc under s 11(7) is discussed at Additional directions and conditions, pp 504 ff.

[205] [1994] Fam 18, CA.

[206] Discussed at Prohibiting a child from spending time or otherwise having contact with a named person, p 491. There is no reason to think that this position has changed since the introduction of child arrangements orders. [207] [1995] 1 WLR 667, CA.

[208] The High Court's inherent jurisdiction is discussed in Ch 20.

[209] Vol 1, *Court Orders*, at para 2.33. The revised Guidance issued by the Department for Children, Schools and Families, 2008, omits to mention the bar on local authorities obtaining parental responsibility, see para 2.41.

steps or specific issue order as a way of obtaining (a) the care or supervision of a child; (b) an order that the child be accommodated by them; and (c) any aspect of parental responsibility.[210] In *Re S and D (Children: Powers of Court)*[211] it was held by reason of s 9(5)(b) and s 100(2)(b) that there was no power to restrain a parent from removing the child from local authority accommodation[212] pursuant to the rights conferred by s 20(7). It must also follow that there is similarly no power to restrain a parent from objecting to his child being accommodated in the first place pursuant to the right conferred by s 20(7).[213]

(h) Additional directions and conditions

Section 11(7)[214] provides that any s 8 order[215] may:

> (a) contain directions as to how the order is to be carried out;
> (b) impose conditions to be complied with by any person in whose favour the order has been made or any parent or any non-parent who has parental responsibility, or any parent with whom the child is living;
> (c) specify the period for which the order or any provision in it is to have effect; and
> (d) make such incidental, supplemental or consequential provision as the court thinks fit.

Directions and limited duration orders

The power under s 11(7)(a) to give directions as to how an order is to be put into effect was designed[216] to enable the court to smooth the transition in cases where the child's living arrangements are changed or to define more precisely what contact is to take place. However, in these particular instances it may be that such directions can simply be regarded as 'arrangements' in a child arrangements order such that recourse to s 11(7) is unnecessary.[217] On the other hand, s 11(7) continues to provide the means by which a court can stay a s 8 order, which can be important for example, in cases of an appeal.[218]

The power under s 11(7)(c) to specify the period for which a s 8 order, or any provision in it, is to have effect is intended[219] to empower the court to make what are effectively interim orders. Accordingly, the court can make an order for a limited duration coupled with a direction that the matter be brought back to court at a later specific date.[220] Limited duration orders can be useful in cases where more information is required,[221] or to allow time to monitor the effectiveness of contact arrangements.[222]

---

[210] For further discussion of local authority use of prohibited steps and specific issue orders see Restrictions in the case of local authorities, p 511.   [211] [1995] 2 FLR 456, CA.

[212] Local authority accommodation is discussed in Ch 15.

[213] Query whether it is possible for a prohibited steps order to be made upon the parent's application to prevent the other parent from objecting to the child's accommodation?

[214] Occasionally, however, courts accept undertakings rather than imposing conditions. See eg *Re R (A Minor) (Residence:Religion)* [1993] 2 FLR 163, CA (aunt granted contact on the undertaking that she would not speak or communicate with the child in any way in relation to religious or spiritual matters).

[215] But not any other order, for example, a s 91(14) order, see *Re S (Permission To Seek Relief)* [2006] EWCA Civ 1190 [2007] 1 FLR 482 at [73].

[216] See Law Com No 172 para 4.22.

[217] Recourse to s 11(7) will remain necessary to make directions etc in any prohibited steps or specific issue orders.   [218] See *Re J (A Minor) (Residence)* [1994] 1 FLR 369 at 375, per Singer J.

[219] Law Com No 172 para 4.24.

[220] Query whether such orders should be considered 'arrangements' in a child arrangements order?

[221] Under s 11(3) courts can make a s 8 order even though they are not in a position finally to dispose of proceedings.   [222] As in *Re B (A Minor) (Contact: Interim Order)* [1994] 2 FLR 269.

Conditions and other supplemental orders

At first sight the power under s 11(7)(b) and (d) to add conditions and to make 'such incidental, supplemental or consequential provision as the court thinks fit' seems to give the court considerable scope for making a wide range of supporting provisions to s 8 orders. The Law Commission, however, did not contemplate the frequent use of what they considered to be 'supplemental provisions', but they did give[223] three examples of when they could be useful:

(1) in the case of a dispute about which school the child should attend, making it a condition of an order naming the person with whom the child is to live that the child attend a particular school;

(2) where there is a real fear that on a contact visit the parent will remove the child from the country and not return him, making it a condition of the contact order that any such removal is prohibited;[224] and

(3) where there is real concern that the person with whom the child will live will not agree to a blood transfusion, making it a condition of naming the person with whom the child is to live to require the parent to inform the other parent so that the latter can agree to it.[225]

Subsequent case-law established that s 11(7) only vests ancillary or supportive powers to those under s 8. It does not give the courts completely novel and independent powers to make, for example, conditions about the parties' finances or property ownership. It is on this basis that it is established that s 11(7) cannot be used to interfere with rights of occupation. As Ward LJ said in *Re D (Prohibited Steps Order)*:[226]

> Section 11(7), in my judgment, is ancillary to the making of a s 8 order. It is governed by the provisions for the making of a s 8 order and does not allow the importation by the back door of the matters laid down in the Matrimonial Homes Act[227] or proper adjustment of rights of occupation.

As s 11(7)(b) itself states, conditions may only be imposed on the persons there listed and, according to Booth J in *Leeds City Council v C*,[228] the power to make orders under s 11(7)(d) is similarly confined.[229] The list is wide and enables a court to impose obligations not

---

[223] Law Com No 172 para 4.23. All that the original *Guidance and Regulations*, Vol 1, *Court Orders* (1991) at para 2.22 stated is that the supplemental etc powers 'enable the new orders [ie s 8 orders] to be as flexible as possible and so reduce or remove the need to resort to wardship'. Even this minimal guidance is omitted from the revised Guidance (2008), see para 2.27.

[224] Lord Mackay LC at 505 HL Official Report (5th Series) col 345 envisaged conditions being imposed forbidding a parent from moving the child to another town. For examples of where this was done, see *B v B (Residence: Condition Limiting Geographic Area)* [2004] 2 FLR 979 and *Re S (a child) (residence order: condition) (No 2)* [2002] EWCA Civ 1795, [2003] 1 FCR 138. But cf *Re S (a child) (residence order: condition)* [2001] EWCA Civ 847, [2001] 3 FCR 154 and *Re E (Residence: Imposition of Conditions)* [1997] 2 FLR 638, CA, discussed at Application to living arrangements, p 506. But query whether such a 'condition' could be regarded as an 'arrangement' in a child arrangements order?

[225] See the pre-Children Act decision, *Jane v Jane* (1983) 4 FLR 712, CA, in which effectively the father was given the power to consent to medical treatment but the mother (a Jehovah's Witness) looked after the child.

[226] [1996] 2 FLR at 279. Applied in *Re K (Contact Order: Condition Ousting Parent From Family Home)* [2011] EWCA Civ 1075, [2012] 2 FLR 635.

[227] Since repealed and replaced by Part IV of the Family Law Act 1996: see Ch 6.

[228] [1993] 1 FLR 269.

[229] As Booth J pointed out, at 273, if it were not, then s 11(7)(b) would be unnecessary. See also *Re DH (A Minor) (Child Abuse)* [1994] 1 FLR 679 at 700–1, per Wall J.

only upon the person in whose favour the s 8 order is made, but also upon any parent,[230] any other person who has parental responsibility, or any other person with whom the child is living. Furthermore, provided the person is included in the list it is no objection that he is not a party.[231] However, as local authorities are not listed, there is no power under s 11(7) to order contact to be supervised by a local authority.[232]

Application to living arrangements

In *Re E (Minors) (Residence: Condition)*,[233] it was held that s 11(7) does not empower a court to impose upon the carer of a child the condition that he or she should reside at a particular address, since such a restriction 'sits uneasily with the general understanding of what is meant by [what was then] a residence order.' As Butler-Sloss LJ explained:[234]

> A general imposition of conditions on residence orders was clearly not contemplated by Parliament and where the parent is entirely suitable and the court intends to make a residence order in favour of that parent, a condition of residence is in my view an unwarranted imposition upon the right of the parent to choose where he/she will live within the UK or with whom. There may be exceptional cases, for instance, where the court, in the private law context, has concerns about the ability of the parent to be granted a residence order to be a satisfactory carer but there is no better solution than to place the child with that parent. The court might consider it necessary to keep some control over the parent by way of conditions which include a condition of residence. Again, in public law cases involving local authorities, where a residence order may be made by the court in preference to a care order, s 11(7) conditions might be applied in somewhat different circumstances.

In *Re S (a child) (residence order: condition)*[235] Thorpe LJ considered that:

> in defining the possibility of exception [in *Re E*] Butler-Sloss LJ was guarding against the danger of never saying never in family litigation. The whole tenor of her judgment is plain to me, in that she was giving the clearest guide to courts of trial that, whereas it was not safe to say never in cases in which the imposition of such a condition would be justified, it would be highly exceptional and probably restricted to a case, as yet unforeseen and may be difficult to foresee, in which the ability of the primary carer to perform to a satisfactory level required the buttress of a s 11(7) order.

In Thorpe LJ's view Butler-Sloss LJ's judgment in *Re E* was not to be interpreted as giving the trial judges 'general latitude to strive for some sort of ideal over and above the rival proposals of the available primary carers'. It was accordingly held that the judge had been wrong to grant the mother a residence order in respect of a Down's Syndrome child with a serious heart condition coupled with a condition that she should reside in Croydon (she wanted to live in Cornwall) although the matter was remitted to the first instance court for further investigation.

---

[230] Including, therefore, the unmarried father who does not have parental responsibility for the child.

[231] See *Re H and Others (Minors) (Prohibited Steps Order)* [1995] 1 WLR 667, discussed at Orders must concern 'an aspect of parental responsibility', p 501, in which it was held that when making a prohibited steps order against a non-party there was power under s 11(7)(d) to give that person liberty to apply on notice to vary or discharge the order.

[232] In Booth J's view the appropriate remedy is a family assistance order, discussed at Family assistance orders, pp 546ff.

[233] [1997] 2 FLR 638.   [234] [1997] 2 FLR 638 at 642.

[235] [2001] EWCA Civ 847 [2001] 3 FCR 154.

What these decisions make clear is that in the private law context in particular, it will be difficult to justify imposing conditions restricting the primary carer's movements and choice of where and with whom to live because to do so, save in exceptional circumstances, is an unacceptable restriction on adult liberties and would be likely to have an adverse effect on the welfare of the child. So viewed, the same approach should be taken with regard to child arrangements orders.

That said, case-law shows that it can sometimes be thought right to restrict the primary carer's movements even within the United Kingdom. This was done, for example, at the remitted hearing in *Re S* just referred to.[236] Similarly, in *B v B (Residence: Condition Limiting Geographic Area)*[237] a condition that the mother should reside within an area 'bounded by the A4 to the north, the M25 to the west and the A3 to the south and east', was temporarily imposed in the context of the mother making two applications to go to Australia with the prime motive of getting away from the father. However, where such restrictions are thought justified (and note may be taken of Wilson LJ's subsequent criticism[238] of the exceptionality test as being an impermissible gloss of the paramountcy test) the question arises as to how this should be done. One alternative is to couple the main order with a prohibited steps order as was done in *Re H (Children) (Residence Order: Condition)*[239] to prevent the father taking the children to Northern Ireland, inter alia, because their sense of loss of their mother as a close and regular contact would be akin to a bereavement. There seems no obvious reason why a prohibited steps order should be chosen in preference to imposing a s 11(7) condition but it does seem clear that such restrictions cannot be considered as part of the 'arrangements' in a child arrangements order since that order does not encompass ordering *where* the child is to live.

Conditions concerning arrangements about the child spending time etc with a named person

With regard to attaching conditions to child arrangement orders concerning contact, note should be taken of *Re O (Imposition of Conditions)*.[240] In that case Sir Thomas Bingham MR considered that ss 8 and 11(7) give the court a wide and comprehensive power to make orders and set conditions which effectively ensure and facilitate contact between the child and the non care giving parent. Accepting that judges should not impose duties which parents could not realistically be expected to perform, his Lordship considered they could compel the person with whom the child is living and who is hostile to contact to read the other parent's communications with the child without censorship. It was also held to be wrong to place unnecessary limits on the number of letters the absent parent could send.[241] Similarly, in *F v R (Contact: Justices' Reasons)*[242] Wall J approved an agreed condition to an indirect contact order that the father was not to contact or enter a day centre or school at which the child was a pupil without either the mother's or the court's prior permission.

Whether such restrictions could now be included in the 'arrangements' governing contact in a child arrangements order thereby rendering it unnecessary to resort to s 11(7) has yet to be determined. However, no matter how it is done, there are limits to what can be imposed. In *D v N (Contact Order: Conditions)*[243] it was held that when making an order for defined contact it was wholly inappropriate to use s 11(7) to make orders forbidding

---

[236] Which decision was upheld on a further appeal, see *Re S (a child) (residence order: condition) (No 2)* [2002] EWCA Civ 1795 [2003] 1 FCR 138.   [237] [2004] 2 FLR 979.

[238] In *Re F (Internal Relocation)* [2010] EWCA Civ 1428 [2011] 1 FLR 1382 at [25]–[26].

[239] [2001] EWCA Civ 1338 [2001] 2 FLR 1277.   [240] [1995] 2 FLR 124, CA.

[241] Ie disagreeing with Wall J's ruling in *Re M*, that orders permitting absent parents to write to or telephone a child should be carefully defined and usually expressed by reference to a maximum 'not more than' formula.

[242] [1995] 1 FLR 227.   [243] [1997] 2 FLR 797, CA.

the father from molesting the mother or her relatives, from entering or damaging certain premises belonging to those relatives, or from corresponding with the mother's employers, which related more to the protection of the mother from perceived harassment than to the management of contact.

Restricting further applications under s 91(14)

Section 91(4) allows the court on 'disposing of any application for an order' under the Children Act 1989 to restrain future applications without the leave of the court. Although perhaps more associated with private law orders, this power can be exercised both in respect of private *and* public law proceedings.[244] These orders represent a substantial interference with a citizen's right of unrestricted access to the courts and how this should be balanced against the child's welfare was carefully considered in *Re P (A Minor) (Residence Order: Child's Welfare)*.[245] Butler-Sloss LJ commented:

> A number of guidelines might be drawn from the cases . . . It is, however, important to remember that these are only guidelines intended to assist and not to replace the wording of the section . . .
>
> (1) Section 91(14) should be read in conjunction with section 1(1) of the Children Act 1989 which makes the welfare of the child the paramount consideration.
> (2) The power to restrict applications to the court is discretionary and in the exercise of its discretion the court must weigh in the balance all the relevant circumstances.
> (3) An important consideration is that to impose a restriction is a statutory intrusion into the right of a party to bring proceedings before the court and to be heard in matters affecting his/her child.
> (4) The power is therefore to be used with great care and sparingly: the exception and not the rule.
> (5) It is generally to be seen as a useful weapon of last resort in cases of repeated unreasonable applications.
> (6) In suitable circumstances (and on clear evidence) a court might impose the leave restriction in cases where the welfare of the child requires it, although there was no past history of making unreasonable applications.
> (7) In cases under paragraph 6 above, the court will need to be satisfied: first, that the facts go beyond the commonly encountered need for a time to settle to a regime ordered by the court and the all too common situation where there is animosity between the adults in dispute or between the local authority and the family and; second, that there is a serious risk that, without the imposition of the restriction, the child or the primary carers will be subject to unacceptable strain.
> (8) A court may impose the restriction on making applications in the absence of a request from any of the parties, subject, of course, to the rules of natural justice such as an opportunity for the parties to be heard.
> (9) A restriction may be imposed with or without limitation of time.
> (10) The degree of restriction should be proportionate to the harm it is intended to avoid. Therefore the court imposing the restriction should carefully consider the extent of the restriction to be imposed and specify, where appropriate, the type of application to be restrained and the duration of the order.

---

[244] See *Re P (Children Act 1989, ss 22 and 26: Local Authority Compliance)* [2000] 2 FLR 910. But note s 91(15) imposes an automatic bar on making further applications without court leave within six months of a previous application to discharge a care, supervision or education supervision order or for the substitution of a supervision order for a care order or a child assessment order and similarly s 91(17) does so following the refusal of a contact application under s 34.   [245] [2000] Fam 15 at 37–8.

(11) It would be undesirable in other than the most exceptional cases to make the order ex parte.

Her Ladyship continued:

It was suggested to us that s 91(14) may infringe the Human Rights Act 1998 and European Convention for the Protection of Human Rights and Fundamental Freedoms 1950, Art 6(1), by depriving a litigant of the right to a fair trial. I do not consider that submission to be correct. The applicant is not denied access to the court. It is a partial restriction[246] in that it does not allow him the right to an immediate *inter partes* hearing. It thereby protects the other parties and the child from being drawn into the proposed proceedings unless or until a court had ruled that the application should be allowed to proceed.

While *Re P* is the leading authority, reference can also usefully be made to *Re S (Permission to Seek Relief)* which establishes:

(a) that it is not permissible to attach conditions to a s 91(14) order beyond stating how long it is to last and identifying the type of relief to which it applies. As Wall LJ put it, had 'Parliament intended s 91(14) to create a power to impose conditions under it, Parliament we think [especially in view of the express power under s 11(7)] would have said so.' [247]

(b) Although s 91(14) orders can be made without time limit or expressed to last until the child attains the age of 16 such orders should be the exception rather than the rule.[248] Where they are made the reasons for doing so should be fully and carefully expressed. As Wall LJ said:

It behoves the court to consider carefully what mischief the [order] is designed to address, and in particular whether or not it is going to be possible, at the end of the defined period, to re-investigate the question, and to attempt the restoration of the relationship between the absent parent and the child . . . An order which is indeterminate, or which is expressed to last until the sixteenth birthday . . . is, in effect, an acknowledgement by the court that nothing more can be done . . . If the court has indeed reached that stage, it needs to spell out its reasons, clearly, so that the parents – and in particular the parent who is the subject of the s 91(14) order knows precisely where he or she stands, and precisely what issues he or she had to address if an application for permission to apply is going to be possible.[249]

(c) Before a s 91(14) order is made the person affected by it should have a proper opportunity if necessary, by means of a short adjournment, to consider it and be heard on it.[250]

[246] It is, however, possible to impose an absolute prohibition under the inherent jurisdiction, see *Re R (Residence: Contact: Restricting Applications)* [1998] 1 FLR 749. But note *T v S (Wardship)* [2011] EWHC 1608 (Fam) [2012] 1 FLR 230, in which Hedley J considered that the same principles as established with regard to s 91(14) orders applied to the exercise of the inherent jurisdiction in this respect.

[247] [2006] EWCA Civ 1190 [2007] 1 FLR 482, at [74].

[248] A point also made by Thorpe LJ in *A v B and C (Lesbian Co-Parents: Role of Father)* [2012] EWCA Civ 785, [2012] 2 FLR 607 at [22].

[249] At [89]–[90]. See also *Re A and D (Local Authority: Religious Upbringing)* [2010] EWHC 2503 (Fam) [2011] 1 FLR 615 in which Baker J observed that 'along the spectrum of acceptable cases justifying an order under s 91(14), orders without limits of time should only be made in respect of cases at the most egregious end, meriting the strongest degree of forensic protection for the child'.

[250] At [91]. See also *Re M (Section 91 (14) Order)* [2012] EWCA Civ 446 [2012] 2 FLR 758—wrong to make an order after father had 'stormed out' of the court. On occasion informal notice might be sufficient, see *Re F*

2. GENERAL RESTRICTIONS ON MAKING SECTION 8 ORDERS

(a) Children aged 16 or over

Reflecting the reality that 'as young people mature through their teenage years it becomes inappropriate to make orders concerning them against their wishes',[251] s 9(7) provides that a s 8 order (other than a variation or discharge) should not be made in respect of a child who has attained the age of 16 unless the court is satisfied that the 'circumstances of the case are exceptional'. By s 9(6)[252] there is a similar embargo against making s 8 orders, *other than those dealing with whom and when the child is to live*, to have effect beyond a child's 16th birthday, unless the court is satisfied that the 'circumstances of the case are exceptional'.[253] Orders not expressed to extend beyond the child's 16th birthday automatically end when he or she reaches 16.[254] Where a direction is made, the order will cease to have effect when the child reaches the age of 18.[255]

There is no definition of and little judicial guidance on what is meant by 'exceptional circumstances' for the purposes of s 9(6) but the revised Guidance instances[256] the case where the child concerned has impaired cognitive development. The requirement was held to be satisfied in *A v A (Shared Residence)*[257] in which a shared residence order was made until each child reached their majority, coupled with a s 91(14) order as a package designed to put an end to the parents' litigation over the children and to encourage them to exercise their parental responsibility.

(b) Children in local authority care

Where a child is already the subject of a care order courts cannot make a s 8 order, other than a child arrangements order dealing with whom and/or when the child concerned is to live with any person, with respect to a child.[258] This embargo is based on the well established principle,[259] endorsed both by the *Review of Child Care Law*[260] and the Law Commission[261] that in general the court's 'private law' powers should not be used to interfere with local authorities' exercise of their statutory parental responsibility.

However, orders governing the child's living arrangements are different from the other s 8 orders, since their whole purpose is to determine with whom the child is to live. Hence, such orders may be made even though the child is in care. Obviously, if the court thinks

---

(children) (restriction on applications) [2005] EWCA Civ 499 [2005] 2 FLR 950. Although a court may make a s 91(14) order of its own motion, the parties should be warned so as to allow a proper opportunity for representations: *Re S (Contact: Prohibition of Applications)* [1994] 2 FLR 1057. Note also *Re K (Appeal: Contact)* [2010] EWCA Civ 1365 [2011] 1 FLR 1592 in which Wall P observed that the hearing must be Art 6 compliant and the process fair.

[251] See the revised Guidance (2008) at para 2.58.

[252] As amended by the Children and Families Act 2014 Sch 2 para 4(5) and (6).

[253] According to Butler-Sloss LJ in *Re B (Minors) (Application for Contact)* [1994] 2 FLR 1 at 6, though not directly applicable, a similar regime applies to s 34 contact orders.

[254] Children Act 1989 s 91(10).   [255] Section 91(11).

[256] Revised Guidance (2008) para 2.58. The Law Commission, (Law Com No 172 at para 3.25), instanced the case in which it is necessary to protect an older child from the consequences of immaturity, citing *Re SW (A Minor) (Wardship: Jurisdiction)* [1986] 1 FLR 24 where a 17-year-old girl was made a ward for the few remaining months of her minority in an attempt to control her behaviour.

[257] [2004] EWHC 142 (Fam), [2004] 1 FLR 1195, a decision which remains relevant for orders dealing with contact.

[258] But there is no embargo against a s 8 order being made at the behest of a child in care for contact with siblings who are not in care: see *Re F (Contact: Child in Care)* [1995] 1 FLR 510, discussed in Ch 18, and *Re W (Application for Leave: Whether Necessary)* [1996] 3 FCR 337n.

[259] See *A v Liverpool City Council* [1982] AC 363, HL, discussed in Ch 18.

[260] DHSS, 1985, paras 8.2–8.10.   [261] Law Com No 172 para 4.52.

the child ought to be living with someone else (who will also have parental responsibility), this is inconsistent with the continuation of the care order. The Law Commission[262] thought that, in principle, just as care orders may supersede whatever previous arrangements for the child's upbringing have been made, so should orders concerning the child's living arrangements. Accordingly, s 91(1) provides[263] that the making of a child arrangements order with respect to the child's living arrangements discharges any existing care order.

Applications for child arrangements orders with respect to the child's living arrangements operate, therefore, as applications to discharge care orders. For those with parental responsibility this remedy provides an alternative to seeking a discharge under s 39.[264] For others, eg fathers who do not have parental responsibility or relatives, an application for a child arrangements order is the only means open to them to seek a discharge of a care order.

One effect of the embargo under s 9(1) is that the court cannot make a care order *and* a s 8 order.[265] However, because the embargo only applies where a child is subject to a *care* order there is nothing to prevent a court making a supervision order and a s 8 order,[266] nor will s 9(1) apply where the child is being 'accommodated' by a local authority under s 20.[267] Furthermore, even if the child is initially the subject of a care order, once a child arrangements order has been made, since that discharges the care order, any other s 8 order can *then* be made.

(c) Restrictions in the case of local authorities

Section 9(2)[268] prevents local authorities from applying for and the courts from granting them a child arrangements order.[269] The embargo is intended to prevent local authorities from obtaining parental responsibility other than by a care order under s 31.[270] If local authorities wish to restrict contact to a child accommodated[271] by them, they must seek a care order and have the matter dealt with in those proceedings. The combined effect of s 9(1) and (2) is that where a child is in care, a local authority cannot apply for *any* s 8 order. On the other hand, local authorities may seek leave of the court to obtain a prohibited steps or specific issue order in respect of a child *accommodated* by them, but subject to a care order, though this provision may not be used as a disguised route to seeking a child arrangements order.[272] As *Nottingham County Council v P*[273] establishes,

---

[262] Ibid para 4.53.

[263] As amended by the Children and Families Act 2014 Sch 2 para 37.   [264] Discussed in Ch 18.

[265] But where there are competing care and residence order applications the judge is not bound to make a positive finding on the residence order application before considering whether there is jurisdiction to grant a care order: *Oldham Metropolitan Borough Council v E* [1994] 1 FLR 568, CA. On the other hand, a court should not make a final care order if a parent's residence order application is pending and a final assessment is needed: *Hounslow London Borough Council v A* [1993] 1 WLR 291.

[266] See eg *Re M and J (Wardship: Supervision and Residence Orders)* [2003] EWHC 1585 (Fam) [2003] 2 FLR 541 and *Re T (A Minor) (Care Order: Conditions)* [1994] 2 FLR 423, CA.

[267] Note: accommodation (discussed in Ch 15) is not the same as a care order, it is neither compulsory nor court driven.   [268] As amended by the Children and Families Act 2014 Sch 2 para 4 (3).

[269] The embargo also extends to variations of child arrangements orders: see *Re C (Contact: Jurisdiction)* [1995] 1 FLR 777, CA. Query whether an authority could apply for a child arrangements order in favour of someone else? See Applying for orders in favour of someone else, p 519.

[270] Discussed in Ch 17.

[271] Note: accommodation (discussed in Ch 15) is not the same as a care order, it is neither compulsory nor court driven.

[272] Section 9(5), as amended, discussed at No power to make disguised child arrangements orders, p 503.   [273] [1994] Fam 18, CA.

where intervention is thought necessary to protect children from significant harm, local authorities must take direct action under Part IV of the 1989 Act (ie by initiating care proceedings) rather than seeking to invoke the court's powers under Part II. In *Nottingham*, following allegations of sexual abuse made against her father by the eldest daughter, the local authority obtained emergency protection orders in respect of two younger children. The father voluntarily left the family home leaving the two girls residing with their mother. The local authority, resisting judicial encouragement to bring care proceedings,[274] persisted in their application for a prohibited steps order[275] requiring the father neither to reside in the same household as the girls nor to have any contact with them unless they wished it. In rejecting their application, Sir Stephen Brown P commented:[276]

> We consider that this court should make it clear that the route chosen by the local authority in this case was wholly inappropriate. In cases where children are found to be at risk of suffering significant harm within the meaning of section 31 of the Children Act 1989 a clear duty arises on the part of local authorities to take steps to protect them. In such circumstances a local authority is required to assume responsibility and to intervene in the family arrangements in order to protect the child. A prohibited steps order would not afford the local authority any authority as to how it might deal with the children. There may be situations, for example, where a child is accommodated by a local authority, where it would be appropriate to seek a prohibited steps order for some particular purpose. However, it could not in any circumstances be regarded as providing a substitute for an order under Part IV of the 1989 Act.

This comment was endorsed in *Langley v Liverpool City Council*.[277] Indeed, having observed[278] that a prohibited steps order was 'a private law remedy required to prevent threatened or repeated misconduct, generally in a warring family', Thorpe LJ went as far as to say that he had 'yet to encounter a case in which a local authority has decided that it can achieve the end that its child protection duties require by applying for a prohibited steps order'. *Nottingham* was subsequently applied in *F v Cambridge County Council*.[279] In that case the father, a Schedule 1 offender, sought limited contact with his children who were living with their mother. The local authority were opposed to the father having contact, but did not themselves seek a care order since they accepted that the mother was able to look after the children properly. It was held, following *Nottingham*, that unless and until the s 31 threshold had been met, the local authority could not intervene in family life, and hence leave to join them as a party to private law proceedings should be refused.

Although these decisions severely limit local authority use of prohibited steps and specific issue orders, they cannot be regarded as establishing that the powers can never be used. They might be appropriate, for example, where there is concern about a specific aspect of a parent's care of a child and the authority while not wanting to seek a care order nevertheless wishes to protect the child.[280] The classic example is where the authority is

---

[274] Both Judge Heald, at first instance, and Ward J had made s 37 directions. These directions are discussed at Section 37 directions, p 550.   [275] For which they had been granted leave to apply.

[276] [1994] Fam at 39. In any event, it was doubted whether there was any power to make an ouster order under s 8. For a critique of this decision see C Cobley and N Lowe 'Ousting Abusers—Public or Private Law Solution?' (1994) 110 LQR 38.   [277] [2005] EWCA Civ 1173 [2006] 1 FLR 342 at [78].

[278] Ibid at [77]. But note the examples to the contrary outlined later.

[279] [1995] 1 FLR 516. It might, however, be possible to overcome this embargo by invoking wardship proceedings, see eg *Re RJ (Wardship)* [1999] 1 FLR 618 and *Re W and X (Wardship: Relatives Rejected As Foster Carers)* [2003] EWHC 2206 (Fam), [2004] 1 FLR 415, discussed in Ch 20. See also *Re K (Contact: Psychiatric Report)* [1995] 2 FLR 432, CA. See also the comments of Wall J 'The courts and child protection—the challenge of hybrid cases' [1997] CFLQ 354 at 355–6.   [280] See the revised Guidance (2008) at para 2.41.

concerned about the child's medical treatment. In *Re C (HIV Test)*,[281] the local authority successfully applied for a specific issue order that a baby born to an HIV positive mother be tested for HIV. Similarly, in *Re R (A Minor) (Blood Transfusion)*[282] a local authority successfully applied for a specific issue order to sanction a blood transfusion for a child contrary to his parent's (who were Jehovah's Witnesses) wishes. They might also be appropriate, for example, to protect a child accommodated by a local authority from a threat posed by a non-family member[283] or to resolve specific problems concerning an orphan.[284]

(d) Other restrictions

It has been said that what were then residence orders cannot be made in favour of a child applicant, at any rate, where the child is seeking to live with someone else.[285] However, it is submitted that it cannot be said that a child arrangements order can *never* name a minor as the person with whom a child is to live. It must surely be open to the court to make such an order in favour of a mother who herself is a child in respect of her own child, and there seems no objection in principle[286] to granting such an order in appropriate cases in favour of a child applicant in respect of a sibling.

3. WHO MAY APPLY FOR SECTION 8 ORDERS?

The Act adopts an 'open door' policy whereby some persons are entitled to apply, while others can, with leave of the court, apply for s 8 orders either by intervening in existing 'family proceedings' or by initiating their own proceedings.

The detailed scheme, set out by s 10 (which governs both initiating and intervening in family proceedings) is as follows.

(a) Persons entitled to apply without leave

Persons entitled to apply for any s 8 order

Parents, guardians, special guardians, step-parents who have parental responsibility by virtue of a s 4A agreement or order, and those named in a child arrangements order as a person with whom the child is to live are entitled, with one exception, to apply for *any* s 8 order.[287] The one exception is that court leave is required to seek a child arrangements order relating to with whom and/or how long a child is to live with any person whilst a special guardianship order is in force.[288]

For these purposes the expression 'parent' refers to legal parents and includes the unmarried father whether or not he has parental responsibility[289] and those who are parents by virtue of the human fertilisation and embryology legislation, but not 'former parents' whose child has been adopted.[290]

[281] [1999] 2 FLR 1004, CA. [282] [1993] 2 FLR 757.
[283] To prevent abduction by a friend, for example, or possibly, by a relative.
[284] See *Birmingham City Council v D, Birmingham City Council v M* [1994] 2 FLR 502, discussed further in Ch 17, The application of the threshold criteria to orphans and abandoned children, p 607.
[285] Per Booth J in *Re SC (A Minor) (Leave To Seek Residence Order)* [1994] 1 FLR 96 at 100.
[286] It cannot be objected that because the making of the child arrangements order confers parental responsibility on those who do not already have it an order cannot be made in favour of a child, since of course mothers (and fathers named on the birth certificate or who are married to the mother) have parental responsibility even if they are minors. [287] Section 10(4), as amended.
[288] Section 7A as amended by the Children and Families Act 2014 Sch 2 para 5(7), on which see *Re S (Adoption Order or Special Guardianship Order)* [2007] EWCA Civ 54 [2007] 1 FLR 819 at [64], per Wall LJ.
[289] Cf *Re C (Minors) (Adoption: Residence Order)* [1994] Fam 1.
[290] *Re C (Minors) (Adoption: Residence Order)*.

The strategy of giving this group of people such automatic entitlement is that their close connection with the child makes it inappropriate to require them to apply for leave to obtain a court hearing. But one group missing from this list is grandparents. Their position was specifically looked at in the *Family Justice Review*.[291] Whilst acknowledging that grandparents are often extremely important for children and continue to be so if parents separate, the *Review* recommended that the leave requirement remain. In so concluding the *Review* noted that grandparents have no 'right' to contact and, pointed to research conducted at Cardiff University[292] which found that grandparents were unlikely to lose contact with a grandchild if they had meaningful contact whilst the parental relationship was still in being and if they resisted taking sides after the separation. The Government agreed and repeated the *Review*'s comment:

> We do not believe that courts refuse leave unreasonably or that seeking leave is slow and expensive for grandparents. Rather, the requirement to seek leave prevents hopeless or vexatious applications that are not in the interests of the child.[293]

Accordingly, no changes were made to the legal position of grandparents by the Children and Families Act 2014.

Persons entitled to apply for a child arrangements order

In addition to the persons just mentioned, the following are entitled to apply for a *child arrangements order* without leave:[294]

(a) Any party to a marriage (whether or not subsisting) or any civil partner in a civil partnership (whether or not subsisting) in relation to whom the child is a 'child of the family';[295]

(b) Any person with whom the child has lived for a period of at least three years (this period need not be continuous but must not have begun more than five years before, or ended more than three months before the making of the application);[296]

(c) Any person having the consent of:
   (i)   each of the persons named in a child arrangements order which is in force as a person with whom the child is to live;
   (ii) the local authority, if the child is subject to a care order; or
   (iii) in any other case, each of the persons who have parental responsibility for the child.

(d) Any person who has parental responsibility by virtue of provision made under s 12(2A).[297]

---

[291] See the discussion in the Interim Report (February 2011) 5.79–5.84 and in the Final Report (November 2011) 4.42–4.48.

[292] N Ferguson with G Douglas, N Lowe, M Murch and M Robinson *Grandparenting in Divorced Families* (2004).

[293] *The Government Response to the Family Justice Review: A System with children and families at its heart* Cm 8273 (2012) 26.

[294] See s 10(5) and s 10(5)(aa) added by the Civil Partnership Act 2004 s 77, as amended by the Children and Families Act 2014 Sch 2 para 5(3).

[295] This provision primarily refers to step-parents but can include any married person or registered partner, including grandparents, who has treated the child as a child of the family (the meaning of which is discussed in Ch 9, The meaning of 'child of the family', p 296), see *Re A (Child of the Family)* [1998] 1 FLR 347, CA. 'Marriage' for these purposes includes same sex marriages.   [296] Section 10(10).

[297] Section 10(5)(d) added by the Children and Families Act 2014 Sch 2 para 5(3). This refers to an individual named in a child arrangements order as a person with whom the child is to spend time or otherwise

Persons entitled to apply for a child arrangements order naming them as persons with whom the child is to live

Local authority foster parents and relatives can each apply without leave for a child arrangements order naming them as persons with whom the child is to live, if the child has lived with them for at least a year.[298]

Persons entitled to apply to vary a s 8 order

A person not otherwise included in the categories mentioned so far can nevertheless, pursuant to s 10(6),[299] apply without leave for a variation or discharge of a s 8 order if either the order in question was made on his application or, in the case of a child arrangements order, he is named in the provisions of the order regulating arrangements relating to with whom or when the child concerned is to spend time or otherwise have contact. This means, for instance, that a child named in such an order will not require leave to vary it.[300]

(b) Persons entitled to apply with leave

In the general scheme anyone, including the child himself and any 'body', local authority or organisation professionally concerned with children, who is not entitled to apply, can seek leave of the court to apply for any s 8 order.[301] However, as already discussed, local authorities cannot in any event apply for a child arrangements order, while any person 'who is, or was at any time during the last six months, a local authority foster parent'[302] must have the consent of the local authority to apply for the court's leave, unless he is a relative of the child or the child has been living with him for at one year preceding the application.[303]

The purpose of this additional restriction on local authority foster parent applicants is to prevent applications unduly interfering with the local authority's plans for the child and so undermining their efforts to bring stability to the child's life.[304] It is also intended to guard against the risk of deterring parents from voluntarily using the fostering services provided by local authorities which, it is argued, could easily happen if the restrictions were relaxed.

(c) The leave criteria

The leave criteria are set out in s 10(8) and (9). Section 10(8) states:

> Where the person applying for leave to make an application for a section 8 order is the child concerned, the court may only grant leave if it is satisfied that he has sufficient understanding to make the proposed application for a section 8 order.

---

have contact (but not with whom the child is to live) but in whose favour a parental responsibility order has been made under s 12(2A). This latter provision is discussed in Ch 11.

[298] Section 10(5A) and (5B) as amended, and s 10(5C) added by the Children and Families Act 2014 Sch 2 para 5 (4) and (5).   [299] As amended by the Children and Families Act 2014 Sch 2 para 5(6).

[300] See *Re W (Application For Leave: Whether Necessary)* [1996] 3 FCR 337n, per Wilson J.

[301] Section 10(1)(a)(ii). Local authorities are subject to the restrictions in s 9, discussed at Restrictions in the case of local authorities, p 511. Note that it is within the court's power to give a person leave to intervene but not to become a party: see *Re S (Care: Residence: Intervener)* [1997] 1 FLR 497, CA.

[302] Ie any person with whom any child is 'looked after' by a local authority within the meaning of s 22(3), discussed in Chapter 15, and therefore includes those with whom the child is placed as prospective adopters: Per Judge Foster QC, in *re C (Adoption: Notice)* [1999] 1 FLR 384.

[303] Section 9(3), as amended by s 113 of the Adoption and Children Act 2002, which reduced the period from an anomalous three years.

[304] See Lord Mackay LC in 502 HL Official Report (5th series), cols 1221–2. This provision had not been recommended by the Law Commission.

Section 10(9) states:

> Where the person applying for leave to make an application for a section 8 order is not the
> child concerned, the court shall, in deciding whether or not to grant leave, have particular
> regard [to certain criteria set out shortly].

At one time it was thought that the former provision applied to children seeking leave and
the latter to adults seeking leave. However, in *Re S (A Minor) (Adopted Child: Contact)*[305]
Charles J considered that approach too simplistic. He pointed out that the application of
these provisions is not dependent upon whether or not the applicant is a child but upon
whether or not the applicant is 'the child concerned'. He considered that for these purposes the phrase 'the child concerned' means the child who is the subject of the application.[306] If he is not, then s 10(9) applies rather than s 10(8). In *Re S* itself the child (who
was adopted) was seeking contact with another sibling and could not therefore be the
subject-matter of the action and hence was not 'the child concerned'. Accordingly, s 10(9)
was held to apply.

On Charles J's analysis s 10(9) can apply to both adults *and* children seeking leave,
while s 10(8), though confined to child applicants, will apply where the child is regarded
as the subject of the action, as for example, where a child arrangements order with another
adult is being sought. This analysis has not escaped criticism.[307] One problem of applying
s 10(9) to child applicants is that it might appear that the child's age and understanding
(referred to in s 10(8)) are not relevant. However, according to Charles J that factor *can* be
taken into account since the criteria in s 10(9) are not meant to be exhaustive. But even
if this solution is accepted there remains the difficulty that s 10(9)(b) directs the court
to consider 'the applicant's connection with the child' which does not sit easily with the
interpretation that s 10(9) can apply to child applicants.

The application of s 10(9)

Section 10(9) states:

> Where the person applying for leave to make an application for a section 8 order is not the
> child concerned, the court shall, in deciding whether or not to grant leave, have particular
> regard to:
>
> (a) the nature of the proposed application for the section 8 order;
> (b) the applicant's connection with the child;
> (c) any risk there might be of that proposed application disrupting the child's life to such
>   an extent that he would be harmed by it; and
> (d) where the child is being looked after by a local authority—
>   (i)   the authority's plans for the child's future, and
>   (ii) the wishes and feelings of the child's parents.

It was held in *Re A (Minors) (Residence Orders: Leave to Apply)*[308] that in deciding whether
to grant leave the paramountcy principle under s 1(1) has no application for three reasons.
First, in granting or refusing a leave application the court is not determining a question with

---

[305] [1999] Fam 283.

[306] Which interpretation reflects the House of Lords' decision in *Birmingham City Council v H (A Minor)*
[1994] 2 AC 212 on the application of the paramountcy principle under s 34, discussed in Ch 18, The court's
powers, p 658.

[307] See R White, P Carr and N Lowe *The Children Act in Practice* (2008, 4th edn) at 5.149.

[308] [1992] Fam 182, CA.

respect to the child's upbringing. That question only arises when the court hears the substantive application. Secondly, some of the guidelines, for example s 10(9)(a), (c) and (d)(i), would be otiose if the child's welfare was paramount. Thirdly, in any event there 'would have been little point in Parliament providing that the court was to have particular regard to the wishes and feelings of the child's parents, if the whole decision were to be subject to the overriding (paramount) consideration of the child's welfare'. Notwithstanding this ruling, s 10(9) is not to be regarded as providing *exclusive* guidelines, nor as preventing the court from considering the checklist under s 1(3). It is therefore quite proper to consider the child's own views[309] and, when applying s 10(9) to child applicants, to consider the child's age and understanding.[310] In a case involving a sperm donor it was held that the reforms implemented in the Human Fertilisation and Embryology Act 2008 and the policy underlying those reforms, namely, 'to put lesbian couples and their children in exactly the same legal position as other types of parent and children' are relevant factors to be considered alongside those in s 10(9) when determining whether to give leave.[311]

The leading case on the application of s 10(9) is *Re B (Grandmother: Joinder as Party)*[312] in which all the authorities were carefully reviewed. As Black LJ observed, s 10(9) does not contain anything in the nature of a test by which an application should be judged, rather 'it leaves the court to take into account all the material features of the case and merely highlights certain matters which are of particular relevance.' One factor, which is not specifically picked out by s 10(9), but which was the subject of some judicial debate, is the prospect of success of the proposed application. Plainly, as Black LJ said, leave will not be given where an application is unarguable but that leaves open what may be regarded as 'arguable'.[313] But leaving that question aside, as Black LJ pointed out, having an arguable case does not of itself mean that leave should be given as other factors could weigh against it. Where leave has been given there is no consequent presumption that an order will be made.[314]

The requirement of leave is intended to act as a filter to protect the child and his family against unwarranted interference with their comfort and security, whilst ensuring that the child's interests are properly respected.[315] In general terms the more tenuous the applicant's connection with the child the harder it will be to obtain leave. Conversely, the closer the connection the more readily leave should be given. As the Law Commission put it,[316] the requirement of leave will 'scarcely be a hurdle at all to close relatives such

---

[309] *Re A (A Minor) (Residence Order: Leave To Apply)* [1993] 1 FLR 425, per Hollings J.

[310] Per Charles J in *Re S (A Minor) (Adopted Child: Contact)*.

[311] Per Baker J in *Re G; Re Z (Children: Sperm Donors: Leave To Apply For Children Act Orders)* [2013] EWHC 134 (Fam) [2013] 1 FLR 1334 at [132].

[312] [2012] EWCA Civ 737, [2012] 2 FLR 1358. In fact this case concerned an application to be joined as a party to care proceedings rather for leave to apply for a s 8 order. Nevertheless it was accepted, agreeing with Wall J in *W v Wakefield City Council* [1995] 1 FLR 170, that reference was properly had to s 10 (9).

[313] Black LJ did, however, side with Thorpe LJ's concern expressed in *Re J (Leave to Issue Application for Residence Order)* [2002] EWCA Civ 1364 [2003] 1 FLR 114 that the previously accepted test (as established in *Re M (Care: Contact: Grandmother's Application for Leave)* [1995] 2 FLR 86 at 98, per Ward LJ) that there had to be a 'good' arguable case effectively substituted the test that Parliament applied in s 10(9).

[314] See eg *Re A (Section 8 Order: Grandparents' Application)* [1995] 2 FLR 153, CA and *Re W (Contact: Application by Grandparent)* [1997] 1 FLR 793. The refusal to give leave is a serious issue and failure to give reasons for the decision constitutes a fundamental defect: per Connell J in *T v W (Contact: Reasons for Refusing Leave)* [1996] 2 FLR 473. See also *Re W (Contact Application: Procedure)* [2000] 1 FLR 263.

[315] As Lord Mackay LC eloquently put it (502 HL Official Report (5th Series), col 1227): 'There is clearly a danger both in limiting and expanding the categories of person who may apply for orders in respect of children. On the one hand, a too wide and uncontrolled gateway can expose children and families to the stress and harm of unwarranted interference and the harassment of actual or threatened proceedings. If too narrow or overcontrolled the gateway may prevent applications which would benefit or safeguard a child from harm.'

[316] Law Com No 172 para 4.41.

as grandparents . . . who wish to care for or visit the child'. On the other hand, as Lord Mackay LC commented[317] in his response to the many attempts during the passage of the Bill to give grandparents an entitlement to apply for a residence or contact order:

> . . . [t]here is often a close bond . . . between a grandparent and a grandchild . . . and in such cases leave, if needed, will no doubt be granted. Indeed, in many cases it will be a formality; but we would be naive if we did not accept that not all interest shown by a grandparent in a child's life is necessarily benign, even if well intentioned. Arguably, at least until we have some experience of wider rights of application, the law should provide some protection to children and their parents against unwarranted applications by grandparents when they occur.

One concern voiced by judges is the consequential delay in having too many parties to the proceedings, and Butler-Sloss LJ has specifically said that it is undesirable that grandparents whose interests are identical with those of the mother should be separately represented.[318] In contrast in *Re J (Leave to Issue Application for Residence Order)*[319] Thorpe LJ commented:

> it is important that trial judges should recognise the greater appreciation that has developed of the value of what grandparents have to offer, particularly to children of disabled parents. Judges should be careful not to dismiss such opportunities without full enquiry.

But, as Black LJ said in *Re B*, context is everything and the courts have at their disposal various levels of investigation which can be adapted according to the facts of the particular case. With regard to delay Black LJ referred to Ward LJ's comment in *Re M (Care: Contact: Grandmother's Application for Leave)*[320] that s 10(9)(c) (which directs courts to have particular regard to 'any risk there might be of that proposed application disrupting the child's life to such an extent that he would be harmed by it') was directed to the risk to the child arising from the proposed application rather than arising from making any order that might result from it. Nevertheless, as she said, delay occasioned by or associated with the application is an obvious source of harm, and must properly be considered under this heading.

The application of s 10(8)

Where the applicant for leave is the 'child concerned', s 10(8) provides that leave can only be granted provided the court is satisfied that the child has sufficient understanding to

---

[317] 503 HL Official Report (5th series), col 1342. For a discussion of the legal position of grandparents under the 1989 Act see generally *The Children Act—What's in it for Grandparents?* (3rd edn, Grandparents' Federation, 1996) and N Ferguson with G Douglas, N Lowe, M Murch and M Robinson *Grandparenting in Divorced Families* (2004) pp 72–4. For a defence of the leave requirement for grandparents see G Douglas and N Ferguson 'The Role of Grandparents in Divorced Families' (2003) 17 Int Jo of Law, Policy and the Family' 41, G Douglas 'Re J (Leave to Issue Application for Residence Order) Recognising grandparents' concern or controlling their interference?' [2003] CFLQ 103, and G Douglas and N Ferguson 'Grandparents After Divorce' [2003] Fam Law 653.

[318] *Re M (Minors) (Sexual Abuse: Evidence)* [1993] 1 FLR 822 at 825. The difficulty in practice is that the parties themselves will not always consider their interests identical.

[319] [2002] EWCA Civ 1364 [2003] 1 FLR 114 at [19], on which see G Douglas 'Re J (Leave to Issue Application for Residence Order) Recognising Grandparents' concern or controlling their interference?' [2003] CFLQ 103. Cf *L v Finland* [2000] 2 FLR 118 in which the European Court of Human Rights assumed that the grandparent-grandchild relationship was not as significant as the parent–child relationship. Even so in *Re W (Contact Application: Procedure)* [2000] 1 FLR 263 Wilson J suggested that the absence of a presumption that it is in the interests of a grandchild to have contact with a grandparent, may not be human rights compliant.

[320] [1995] 2 FLR 86 at [17].

make the proposed application.[321] There is no hard and fast rule for determining this. As Sir Thomas Bingham MR said in *Re S (A Minor) (Independent Representation)*:[322]

> . . . the rules eschew any arbitrary line of demarcation based on age and wisely so. Different children have differing levels of understanding at the same age. And understanding is not absolute. It has to be assessed relatively to the issues in the proceedings. Where any sound judgment on these issues calls for insight and imagination which only maturity and experience can bring, both the court and the solicitor will be slow to conclude that the child's understanding is sufficient.

Even if the child is found to be competent, leave might not necessarily be granted. In *Re H (Residence Order: Child's Application For Leave)*,[323] for example, a competent child was refused leave because his father could adequately represent his views to the court.

Apart from requiring the court to be satisfied about the child's understanding, the Act itself gives no further guidance, particularly as it is accepted that the guidelines under s 10(9) do not apply where a child is seeking leave.[324] According to Charles J in *Re S (A Minor) (Adopted Child: Contact)*[325] this lack of guidance is indicative that the court is to have regard to the interests of the child. It is, however, generally accepted that in determining whether to grant leave the child's welfare is *not* the paramount consideration. As Booth J held in *Re SC (a Minor) (Leave to Seek Residence Order)*,[326] applying in turn *Re A (Minors) (Residence Orders: Leave to Apply)*,[327] when determining an application for leave under s 10 (whether it be under s 10(8) or (9)) the court is *not* determining a question in respect of the upbringing of the child concerned (that question only arises if leave is granted and the court determines the substantive application) and therefore s 1(1) does *not* apply.[328]

(d) Applying for orders in favour of someone else

The Act is silent on whether applications may be made for a s 8 order in favour of someone else. However, implicit in the ability of a child to obtain leave to apply for such orders is that they, at least, can seek a s 8 order that they should live with a particular person even if that person has not applied for an order. As Booth J said in *Re SC (A Minor) (Leave to Seek Residence Order)*:[329]

> In my judgment the court should not fetter the statutory ability of the child to seek any s 8 order, including a residence order, if it is appropriate for such an application to be made.

---

[321] Though note *Re HG (Specific Issue Order: Sterilisation)* [1993] 1 FLR 587, in which Peter Singer QC (as he then was) held that parents, at any rate when applying for leave that their child be sterilised, can apply for leave on that child's behalf in cases where the child lacks the necessary understanding to apply on his own behalf.

[322] [1993] Fam 263 at 276.   [323] [2000] 1 FLR 780.

[324] The wording of s 10(9) itself makes this quite clear, as was accepted both in *Re C (A Minor) (Leave To Seek Section 8 Orders)* [1994] 1 FLR 26 and *Re SC (A Minor) (Leave To Seek Residence Order)* [1994] 1 FLR 96 both of which were predicated upon the view that s 10(8) applied to children seeking leave, while s 10(9) applied to adults seeking leave. But it was also implicitly accepted by Charles J in *Re S (A Minor) (Adopted Child: Contact)* [1999] Fam 283, who, as already discussed, considered the application of s 10(8) and (9) to be dependent upon whether or not the applicant was the child concerned.   [325] [1999] Fam 283.

[326] [1994] 1 FLR 96 at 99. See also in *Re C (Residence: Child's Application for Leave)* [1995] 1 FLR 927, per Stuart White J; *North Yorkshire County Council v G* [1993] 2 FLR 732, per Douglas Brown J; and *Re S (a Minor) (Adopted Child: Contact)*, per Charles J.   [327] [1992] Fam 182.

[328] See the discussion in Ch 10.

[329] [1994] 1 FLR 96 at 100 E–F. The reference to 'residence orders' must now be read as a child arrangements order relating to with whom the child is to live.

> Although the court will undoubtedly consider why it is that the person in whose favour a proposed residence order would be made is not applying, it would in my opinion be wrong to import into the Act any requirement that only he or she should make the application.

Whether the courts would be disposed to permit applications other than by children for a child arrangements order in favour of someone else remains to be seen. However, it seems unlikely that local authorities would be permitted to do so,[330] for, even supposing that s 9(2) (which provides: 'No application may be made by a local authority for a child arrangements order and no court shall make such an order in favour of a local authority') is interpreted as not barring applications in favour of someone else,[331] there is still the objection that, contrary to the ruling in *Nottingham County Council v P*,[332] local authorities would thereby be permitted to intervene in family life via Part II rather than Part IV of the 1989 Act.

4. EFFECT OF CHILD ARRANGEMENTS ORDERS

(a) Parental responsibility

Whilst in force, child arrangements orders confer parental responsibility on those such as grandparents or other relatives, or foster parents, who would not otherwise have that responsibility provided they are named as a person with whom the child is to live.[333] In the case of 'unmarried fathers' and second female parents[334] who do not otherwise have parental responsibility, however, upon so naming them in a child arrangements order, the court is *bound* to make a *separate* parental responsibility order under s 4 or s 4ZA.[335] In the case of those named in a child arrangements orders as persons with whom the child is to spend time or otherwise have contact but not as someone with whom the child is to live, then in the case of unmarried fathers or second female parents who do not otherwise have parental responsibility, the court *must* consider whether to make a separate parental responsibility order under s 4 or s 4ZA[336] and, in the case of others, *may* consider providing in the child arrangements order that that person has parental responsibility.[337]

(b) Change of child's surname

Under s 13(1)(a),[338] it is an automatic condition of a child arrangements order relating to either with whom the child concerned is to live and/or when the child is to live with any

---

[330] They might plausibly wish to apply, for example, for a child arrangements order in favour of grandparents who, though capable, are reluctant to apply for themselves.

[331] If the word 'and' is read conjunctively rather than disjunctively it could be argued that all that s 9(2) prevents is local authorities applying for child arrangements orders on their own behalf.

[332] [1994] Fam 18, CA, discussed at Restrictions in the case of local authorities, p 511.

[333] Section 12(2), as amended by the Children and Families Act 2014 Sch 2 para 21(3). Note the restrictions on that responsibility under s 12(3).

[334] Ie a woman who is a parent by virtue of s 43 of the Human Fertilisation and Embryology Act 2008, discussed in Ch 8, Female parenthood, p 256.

[335] Section 12(1), as substituted by the Children and Families Act 2014 Sch 2 para 21(2), discussed at p XXX. Note that this power does not extend to step-parents notwithstanding that they are now able to apply for parental responsibility orders, see Ch 11, Acquisition of parental responsibility by step-parents, p 386.

[336] Section 12(1A), added by the Children and Families Act 2014 Sch 2 para 21(2).

[337] Section 12(2A), added by the Children and Families Act 2014 Sch 2 para 21(4).

[338] As amended by the Children and Families Act 2014 Sch 2 para 22.

person[339] that no person may cause the child to be known by a new surname without either the written consent of every person who has parental responsibility or leave of the court.[340]

Although it is not a *statutory* requirement to have the *child's* consent,[341] in *Re PC (Change of Surname)*[342] Holman J expressly left open whether the consent of an older child, particularly if over the age of 16, was both necessary and sufficient. In any event, if the child objects he may seek leave to apply for a prohibited steps order to prevent the change.[343] Furthermore, as Wilson J observed in *Re B (Change of Surname)*,[344] s 13(1)(a) can only operate as an inhibition on the adult carer not to cause the children to be known by a different surname. As he put it:

> It does not, because in effect it cannot, proscribe the surname which the children ask teachers, friends and relatives to attribute to them.

The prevailing view[345] is that, wherever there is a pre-existing order determining with whom the child is to live, applications to change names are properly made under s 13(1)(a) rather than as a specific issue order under s 8. Conversely, where there is no pre-existing order application must be made for a s 8 order.[346] Although technically this means that there is no *obligation* to apply the welfare checklist, it is accepted that it remains a useful aide mémoire.[347] A more serious consequence of requiring applications to be made under s 13 is that the consequential directions are probably not enforceable as they are not injunctive in form.[348]

Section 13(1)(a) implements the recommendation of the Law Commission[349] which, like the Court of Appeal in the pre-Children Act decision, *W v A (Minor: Surname)*,[350] considered a child's surname to be an important symbol of his identity and relationship with his parents and that, while it may be in his interests for it to be changed, it is not

---

[339] For similar rules where the child is subject to a care order, see s 33(7), discussed in Ch 17, Limitations on the exercise of local authority responsibility, p 638.

[340] See J Herring 'The Shaming of Naming: Parental Rights and Responsibilities in the Naming of Children' in R Probert, S Gilmore and J Herring (eds) *Responsible Parents & Parental Responsibility* (2009) ch 6. For the position of *conferring* a name see Ch 10, Conferring names, p 356.

[341] Attempts were in fact made to amend s 13 so as to require the child's consent: see 502 HL Official Reports (5th series) col 1262, by Lord Meston, and 503 HL Official Reports, col 1347 by Lord Elwyn Jones.

[342] [1997] 2 FLR 730 at 739. Nonetheless the support inter alia of a 16-year-old for a name change did not inhibit the court from refusing the change in *Re B (Change of Surname)* [1996] 1 FLR 791, CA, discussed shortly.   [343] See Lord Mackay LC, 502 HL Official Report (5th series), col 1264.

[344] [1996] 1 FLR 791 at 795, CA.

[345] By *Re B (Change of Surname)* [1996] 1 FLR 791, CA and seems implicit in their separate treatment in FPR 2010 rr 12.2(a) and (c) and 12.3. But note the query raised by Hale J in *Re M (Leave To Remove Child From Jurisdiction)* [1999] 2 FLR 334 and the position taken by R George 'Changing Names, Changing Places: Reconsidering s 13 of the Children Act 1989' [2008] Fam Law 1121, discussed further at Removals for more than one month, p 527.

[346] *Dawson v Wearmouth* [1999] 2 AC 308 at 325 per Lord Hobhouse; *Re W (A Child) (Illegitimate Child: Change of Surname)* [2001] Fam 1 at [9], per Butler-Sloss LJ.

[347] Per Wilson J in *Re B*, earlier at 793. In *Re C*, earlier, Butler-Sloss LJ assumed that the checklist applies regardless of whether the application was under s 8 or s 13.

[348] See *Re P (Minors) (Custody order: Penal Notice)* [1990] 1 WLR 613, CA.

[349] Law Com No 172 para 4.14.

[350] [1981] Fam 14, CA, which in turn decisively rejected such cases as *R (BM) v R (DN)* [1978] 2 All ER 33, CA and *D v B* [1979] Fam 38, CA, which had held that the issue was relatively unimportant and that fathers were tending to lay too much emphasis on it when the purpose was to avoid embarrassment and there was no intention of destroying their links with their children.

a matter on which a parent with whom the child lives should be able to take unilateral action.

Case-law since the Act reflects this attitude. In *Dawson v Wearmouth*[351] Lord Jauncey commented:

> The surname is . . . a biological label which tells the world at large that the blood of the name flows in its veins. To suggest that a surname is unimportant because it may be changed at any time by deed poll when the child has obtained more mature years ignores the importance of initially applying an appropriate label to that child.

But this comment, which went further than that of the other Law Lords, has been criticised as being too emotive and overblowing the importance of names and thus encouraging litigation.[352] Moreover, it is clear that not all judges hold to this view. In *Re R (Surname: Using Both Parents)*[353] Hale LJ suggested that Lord Jauncey was effectively dissenting and that his views were not consistent with the modern law. She added[354] that it was a 'matter of great sadness' that:

> it is so often assumed, and even sometimes argued, that fathers need that outward and visible link in order to retain their relationship with, and commitment to, their child. That should not be the case. It is a poor sort of parent whose interest in and commitment to his child depends upon the child bearing his name. After all, that is a privilege which is not enjoyed by many mothers, even if they are not living with the child. They have to depend upon other more substantial things.

Whatever the status of Lord Jauncey's comments, what *Dawson v Wearmouth* undoubtedly establishes is that as with all applications directly concerning children's upbringing, in resolving disputes over children's names, the child's welfare is the court's paramount consideration. Indeed it was precisely because the issue is governed by the paramountcy principle that the Lords in *Dawson* were able to dismiss the father's arguments based on Art 8 of the European Convention on Human Rights since, as Lord Hobhouse put it,[355] 'the issue of name changes is concerned with children's welfare, not fathers' rights.'[356] However, *Dawson* seemed to go further by indicating that a court should not sanction a change of the child's surname unless there is some evidence that it will lead to an improvement in the child's welfare. This view, however, has since been said to be 'not strictly accurate' and that the test is welfare 'pure and simple'.[357]

Comprehensive guidance on the relevant considerations in determining name disputes is to be found in *Re W (A Child) (Illegitimate Child: Change of Surname)*,[358] in which Butler-Sloss LJ said:

---

[351] [1999] 2 AC 308 at 323.

[352] See in particular the analysis by M Hayes '*Dawson v Wearmouth*: "What's in a name? A Child by any other name is surely just as sweet?" ' [1999] CFLQ 423. For other comments on *Dawson* see J Herring 'Name This Child' [1998] CLJ 266 and A Bainham 'In the Name of the Father?' [1999] CLJ 492.

[353] [2001] EWCA Civ 1344 [2001] 2 FLR 1358 at [13].   [354] Ibid at [18].

[355] [1999] 2 AC 308 at 329.

[356] It might be thought that the strictness of English law on name changes is consistent with Arts 7 and 8 of the UN Convention on the Rights of the Child, which respectively provide for a right to name and a right to preserve that name. But as G Douglas *An Introduction to Family Law* (2004, 2nd edn) 88 and J Fortin *Children's Rights and the Developing Law* (2009, 3rd edn) 470 point out, neither Article was designed with parental disputes in mind; rather they were concerned with the problem of stateless children and those abducted from their families by dictatorial military regimes.

[357] Per Ryder LJ in *Re W (Change of Name)* [2013] EWCA Civ 1488 [2014] 2 FLR 221.

[358] [2001] Fam 1 at 7–8.

(e) On any application the welfare of the child is paramount, and the judge must have regard to the section 1(3) criteria.

(f) Among the factors to which the court should have regard is the registered surname of the child and the reasons for the registration, for instance recognition of the biological link with the child's father. Registration is always a relevant and important consideration but it is not in itself decisive. The weight to be given to it by the court will depend upon the other relevant factors or valid countervailing reasons which may tip the balance the other way.

(g) The relevant considerations should include factors which may arise in the future as well as the present situation.

(h) Reasons given for changing or seeking to change a child's name based on the fact that the child's name is or is not the same as the parent making the application do not generally carry much weight.

(i) The reasons for an earlier unilateral decision to change a child's name may be relevant.

(j) Any changes of circumstances of the child since the original registration may be relevant.

(k) In the case of a child whose parents were married to each other, the fact of the marriage is important and I would suggest that there would have to be strong reasons to change the name from the father's surname if the child was so registered.

(l) Where the child's parents were not married to each other, the mother has control over registration. Consequently on an application to change the surname of the child, the degree of commitment of the father to the child, the quality of contact, if it occurs, between father and child, the existence or absence of parental responsibility are all relevant factors to take into account.

These observations are only guidance and each case has to be decided upon its own facts on the basis of the paramountcy principle. Nevertheless court leave for a change of name has generally proved hard to obtain. As Ward LJ put it in *Re C (Change of Surname):*[359]

> . . . there is a heavy responsibility on those who seek to effect a change . . . good reasons have to be shown.

Examples of refusals to sanction name changes

Examples of judicial refusal to sanction name changes include *Re F (Child: Surname),*[360] in which it was held that there was no reason to suppose that a young girl at school was going to be embarrassed or particularly unusual in being registered at a school under a different name from the current surname of her mother. In other words, there was no case for saying that it was in the child's interests to change her name.

Leave was also refused in *Re B (Change of Surname),*[361] in which the Court of Appeal rejected the argument that a first instance judge had erred when refusing to give leave for a change of name because he had not taken notice of the children's views. Whilst agreeing that 'orders which ran flatly contrary to the wishes of normal adolescent children were

---

[359] [1998] 2 FLR 656 at 667, CA.

[360] [1993] 2 FLR 837n. See also *Re T (Change of Name)* [1998] 2 FLR 620, CA and *G v A (Children: Surname)* [1995] 2 FCR 223n, in which an unmarried father obtained a prohibited steps order restraining the mother from changing the children's surnames. For a striking pre-Children Act example, see *W v A (Minor: Surname)* [1981] Fam 14, in which the Court of Appeal refused to reverse a decision declining to permit a change of name even though the child was emigrating to Australia with his mother and stepfather. Query whether it would be sufficient if the father had disappeared from the scene entirely or if his name had notorious associations because of his conduct?   [361] [1996] 1 FLR 791, CA.

virtually unknown to family law', that principle did not extend to the formal change of surname from that of the father to the stepfather.[362] In Wilson J's view that would only serve to injure the link between the father and the children, which was not in the latter's best interests. In so ruling Wilson J rejected the argument that it was embarrassing for the children to be known by a surname other than that of the adult care givers, commenting that 'there is . . . no opprobrium nowadays for a child to have a different surname from that of adults in the household'.

In *A v Y (Child's Surname)*,[363] a name change was refused because the child would be confused by the change, while in both *Dawson v Wearmouth*,[364] in which an unmarried father wanted his one month old child's name to be changed to his (the child had been registered by the mother in her ex-husband's name), and *Re R (Surname: Using Both Parents)*,[365] in which a mother wanted to change the child's surname upon taking up residence in Spain, leave was refused because no benefit to the child could be demonstrated.

Examples of permitted name changes

In contrast to the cases just discussed, leave was granted in *Re S (Change of Names: Cultural Factors)*[366] in which a Muslim mother, divorced from the Sikh father and now living in a Muslim community, was permitted to use Muslim names, including her current Muslim nickname for the child in daily life and at school. She was not, however, given leave to change the name formally as that would contribute to an undesirable elimination of the child's Sikh identity. In *Re W (A Child) (Illegitimate Child: Change of Surname)*,[367] which comprised three separate appeals, one mother was permitted to change her son's name to avoid having the same as his father who was a notorious criminal so as to protect him from what she genuinely feared was a real risk of harm if his identity was revealed in the new locality where they were living. Another mother was similarly allowed to do so following the father's convictions for indecent assaults upon a 17-year-old girl and his 11-year-old niece. In *Re F (Contact)*[368] a change was permitted because of a threat of child abduction by the father.

Reference might also be had to *Re H (Child's Name: First Name)*[369] in which a mother whose registration of name was cancelled because it was made after the father's registration, was permitted to use her chosen first name for the child, though no order to that effect was necessary. In so ruling Thorpe LJ commented that given names 'have a much less concrete character.'

The position where the name has already been changed

Where the name has already been changed (whether lawfully or not), the issue as to what the child should continue to be called is still governed by the welfare principle. However, it may be too stark to concentrate simply on whether it is in the child's interests for the name to be changed back, since attention also needs to be paid to whether it was in the child's interests to change the name in the first place.[370] Nevertheless,

---

[362] This was because the inhibition against a change of name lay against the mother rather than against the child. As Wilson J pointed out, at 795, the child himself is free to ask others to address him in whatever name he chooses regardless of any s 13 directions.

[363] [1999] 2 FLR 5.   [364] [1999] 2 AC 308.

[365] [2001] EWCA Civ 1344 [2001] 2 FLR 1358.   [366] [2001] 2 FLR 1005.

[367] [2001] Fam 1, CA. This case comprised three separate appeals.

[368] [2007] EWHC 2543 (Fam) [2008] 1 FLR 1163.

[369] [2002] EWCA Civ 190 [2002] 1 FLR 973, CA.

[370] See eg *Re T (Change of Name)* [1998] 2 FLR 620, CA.

case-law suggests that it is easier to persuade the court to sanction a change of name that has already occurred than to permit a prospective change. In *Re P (Parental Responsibility)*[371] the court rejected an application by an unmarried father that his name be restored to his two children. The court noted that the names had been changed some time ago, following the father's long-term imprisonment, when the mother decided to make a fresh start both for herself and her children. It was not thought to be in their interest for the name to be changed back. Even in *Re C (Change of Surname)*,[372] where it was held that the unmarried mother's original decision to change her child's surname following the breakdown of her relationship with the father was not justified, the Court of Appeal resolved nevertheless that a further change now was not in the child's interests.

(c) Removal of child from the United Kingdom—'External Relocation'

Under s 13(1)(b),[373] where a child arrangements order is in force and:

> if the arrangements regulated by the order consist of, or include arrangements which relate to either or both of the following
>
> (a) with whom the child concerned is to live, and
> (b) when the child is to live with any person.[374]

no person may remove the child from the United Kingdom[375] without either the *written* consent of every person who has parental responsibility or leave of the court.[376] In *Re H (Children) (Residence Order: Condition)*[377] the Court of Appeal rejected the argument[378] that s 13(1)(b) requires court leave to remove the child from the jurisdiction (and therefore in this case to remove the child to Northern Ireland) rather than from the United Kingdom (ie England and Wales, Scotland and Northern Ireland).[379] Accordingly, any person named in a child arrangements order as someone with whom the child is to live, does not require permission to relocate anywhere *within* the United Kingdom, though, as previously discussed, such internal relocations can be prevented by means of a prohibited steps order or by the imposition of a s 11(7) condition.

---

[371] [1997] 2 FLR 722, CA.

[372] [1998] 2 FLR 656, CA. See also another *Re C (Change of Surname)* [1998] 1 FLR 549, CA where the children concerned were living with their unmarried father and had already assumed his name. The court rejected the mother's application that they should be known by her maiden name since she herself no longer used it as she had married someone else.

[373] As amended by the Children and Families Act 2014 Sch 2 para 22.

[374] This definition is provided by s 13(4) added by Sch 2 para 22(5) to the 2014 Act.

[375] See R George *Relocation Disputes—Law and Practice in England and New Zealand* (2014) and R George 'Relocation Disputes in England and Wales', University of Oxford Legal Research Paper Series Paper No 91/2013, September 2013.

[376] For similar rules where the child is subject to a care order, see s 33(7)–(8) discussed in Ch 17, Limitations on the exercise of local authority responsibility, p 638.

[377] [2001] EWCA Civ 1338 [2001] 2 FLR 1277.

[378] Relying on inter alia the side-note to s 13 which refers to 'removal from jurisdiction' rather than jurisdictions; s 108(12) which applies particular provisions of the 1989 Act, but not s 13, to Northern Ireland (s108(11) does a similar thing in relation to Scotland) and to the exercise of power under s 101 to make delegated legislation in making the Children (Prescribed Orders—Northern Ireland, Guernsey and Isle of Man) Regulations 1991.

[379] Interpretation Act 1978 s 5 and Sch 1. Note: the Isle of Man and the Channel Islands are *not* part of the United Kingdom.

Temporary removals for less than one month

Under s 13(2)[380] *any* person named in a child arrangements order as a person with whom the child is to live (including those with whom the child lives for a period of time rather than the whole time) can, while the order is in force, remove the child for a period of less than one month without anyone's permission (though, note, even temporary removals can be restrained by a prohibited steps order).[381] This latter provision places those so named in a child arrangements order in a special position. It is normally an offence under the Child Abduction Act 1984[382] to remove a child under the age of 16 without the consent[383] either of those having parental responsibility or leave of the court.

Permitting unrestricted temporary removals is intended[384] to allow those named as a person with whom the child is to live to make arrangements for holidays without having to seek the permission of the non-resident parent or parents, and without even having to give notice. Although there is no limit on the number of temporary removals permitted, in cases of dispute parents are entitled to seek a prohibited steps order to curtail the right or to apply for a restriction of the right to be added to the residence order, pursuant to the court's powers to add conditions under s 11(7).[385]

The *Family Justice Review* discussed the possibility of repealing s 13(2) but in the end decided not to pursue this because, upon reflection, the *Review* acknowledged the benefit that the provision 'can bring to those cases where the parents have not expressly agreed matters, helping to avoid the need for uncontroversial applications to court.'[386] Nevertheless the new form of order to which s 13(2) applies, means that a person named as someone with whom the child is to live can take the child abroad for a month regardless of the specified time for which the child is to live with him or her. Consequently the court should either avoid making a child arrangements order naming a person with whom the child is to live for periods of less than one month or, when making such an order, make specific provision dealing with the issue of temporary removals abroad, which it can do under s 11(7).

Removals for more than one month

Seeking leave

Where permission is sought to take the child out of the United Kingdom for more than one month specific application for leave must be made to the court.[387] Where leave is sought under s 13 then, under s 13(3), the court may grant leave either generally or for specified purposes. However, it is not entirely settled whether leave should be sought under s 13

---

[380] As amended by the Children and Families Act 2014 Sch 2 para 22 (3). A child arrangements order for this purpose is defined by s 13(4), the terms of which have just been set out.

[381] See eg *Re R (a child) (prohibited steps order)* [2013] EWCA Civ 1115 [2014] 1 FCR 113.

[382] Discussed in Ch 26, Criminal sanctions, p 1018.

[383] Though, unlike the requirement under the 1989 Act, the consent does not have to be in writing.

[384] Law Com No 172 para 4.15.

[385] See eg the revised *Guidance and Regulations* (Department of Children, Schools and Families, 2008) Vol 1, Court Orders, para 2.33 and Lord Mackay LC, 503 HL Official Report (5th series), col 1354.

[386] See p 149 of the Final Report (2011) and see also the discussion at The interim report, p 482.

[387] According to Thorpe J in *MH v GP (Child: Emigration)* [1995] 2 FLR 106 such cases should be heard either in the High Court or county court depending on the complexity of the decision. In *Re K (Removal From Jurisdiction: Practice)* [1999] 2 FLR 1084 at 1086–7 Thorpe LJ also said that where applications involve considerations of foreign legal systems and which may require the putting in place of mirror orders, they should normally be dealt with by a Family Division judge.

rather than by way of a specific issue order.[388] Applying the approach to names[389] it seems that it should, but this has been queried by Hale J in *Re M (Leave To Remove Child From Jurisdiction)*[390] who pointed to the oddity of having to apply for a s 8 order if no child arrangements order is in force but having to use a different route if such an order is in force. One commentator has gone further and suggested that s 13 does not confer a power to grant leave and that in all cases the appropriate relief is to obtain a s 8 order,[391] but current accepted law is otherwise.

No matter by what route or by whom (it is equally open to the parent with whom the child is not living, for example, to seek leave to remove the child) the matter is raised, the court's general approach is the same,[392] namely, in deciding whether to grant leave the court must apply the principle of the paramountcy of the child's welfare under s 1(1). But the application of this principle in this context is by no means straightforward.

Deciding whether to give leave—the dilemmas

As one commentator has put it:[393]

> Relocation cases are the San Andreas Fault of family law, because they involve a fundamental clash between two competing ideas about post-separation family life, one in which the family is seen to be at an end, ushering in a freedom for people to begin a new life for themselves, and the other in which the family is seen to endure beyond separation.

They are also among the most difficult cases that family courts have to deal with. What is more, with increasing international migration, such disputes are becoming more common which has led another commentator to say that 'it seems inevitable that relocation disputes will become one of the central issues of modern child law.'[394]

Relocation disputes, particularly where leave is sought to take the child to the other side of the world, raise in very acute form the dilemma of having to balance the child's interests with those of each of the parents. As has been well said:

> The desire of one parent to remove the child to another jurisdiction, leaving the other parent behind, frequently produces deep conflicts between the irreconcilable interests of the parents and child. On the one hand the relocating parent's freedom to live where she wishes is threatened, potentially leaving her isolated from the support of her family network or unable to support herself by working within her area of expertise. On the other hand, the parent left behind risks losing any meaningful contact with his child, seeing

[388] Note: that in the absence of a child arrangements order, a specific issue order must be sought to seek permission to take the child out of the UK if such a proposed move is opposed by another holder of parental responsibility. Without such leave a removal constitutes an offence under the Child Abduction Act 1984.

[389] See eg *Re B (Change of Surname)* [1996] 1 FLR 791, discussed at Change of child's surname, p 520.

[390] [1999] 2 FLR 334 at 340.

[391] R George 'Changing Names, Changing Places: Reconsidering s 13 of the Children Act 1989' [2008] Fam Law 1121.But this argument is not supported by authority. Hale J in *Re M* was not suggesting that there was no s 13 route but merely that by whatever route action is brought the applicable principles are the same.

[392] See *Re S (a child) (residence order: condition)* [2001] EWCA Civ 847 [2001] 3 FCR 154. Technically whereas it is mandatory to apply the welfare checklist in contested s 8 applications, it is only discretionary to do so under s 13, though even then Thorpe LJ has said in *Payne v Payne* [2001] EWCA Civ 166 [2001] Fam 473 at [33] that courts should nevertheless take the precaution of doing so. For research findings on the practice, see R George 'Relocation Disputes in England and Wales', University of Oxford Legal Research Paper Series Paper No 91/2013, September 2013.

[393] P Parkinson *Family Law and the Indissolubility of Parenthood* (2011) 150.

[394] R George 'Reviewing relocation? *Re W (Relocation: Removal Outside Jurisdiction)* [2011] EWCA Civ 345 and *K v K (Relocation: Shared Care Arrangement)* [2011] EWCA Civ 793 [2012] CFLQ 110.

contact reduced to a few calls and the occasional holiday visit. The problem is made more difficult by the fact that the interests of the child are rarely clear.[395]

The research evidence

Research,[396] based on international relocation cases decided at first instance in England and Wales in 2012, found that 95% of applicants were mothers; and 70% of applicants were foreign nationals, most of whom, but not all were seeking to return to their home country. Forty per cent were seeking leave to take their child to another EU State and about 25% were seeking leave to go to North America and another 25% to go to Australasia. The average age of a child involved in a relocation dispute was just under seven. In only a small minority of cases (5%) were there equal shared care arrangements but in well over half there were overnight contact arrangements.

Various studies across the world have attempted to look at the impact of relocation disputes on the child and on the parents.[397] Their findings, however, are equivocal and at times contradictory inasmuch as some emphasise detrimental or harmful outcomes for children while others reveal beneficial effects. Perhaps the safest conclusion is that there is a 'heightened risk' to the child who relocates but much will depend upon the child's age and whether or not they are moving to a known or unknown environment and, of course, upon how settled they are in their current environment. What cannot be denied, however, are the harmful effects upon the child of the inter-parental conflict itself (and relocation disputes tend to be high conflict cases), the high financial costs of relocation litigation and, even if satisfactory post-relocation contact arrangements can be agreed, the potential burden upon the child if further travel is involved. The equivocality of the research poses a problem for the law since it makes it harder (a) to predict which children are most at risk and (b) what solution is best for the child concerned.

We discuss first how the English courts have wrestled with this problem. We then briefly advert to international approaches and to international initiatives to harmonise the various approaches.

Payne v Payne

Central to any discussion of the English position on relocation is *Payne v Payne*,[398] in which a mother successfully sought leave to remove her four year old daughter to New Zealand. As Thorpe LJ recognised in that case, before *Payne*, two propositions had been consistently applied: the paramountcy of the child's welfare and the view that refusing the primary carer's reasonable proposals for relocation is likely to impact detrimentally on the welfare of the dependent children. Consequently, a reasonable application to relocate will be granted unless the court concludes that it is incompatible with the children's welfare.[399] *Payne* affirmed both that the Children Act 1989 had not altered this approach

---

[395] R Taylor 'Poels Apart: Fixed Principles and Shifting Values in Relocation Law' in S Gilmore, J Herring and R Probert (eds) *Landmark Cases in Family Law* (2011) 91.

[396] R George 'Relocation Disputes in England and Wales', University of Oxford Legal Research Paper Series Paper No 91/2013, September 2013.

[397] For an excellent summary of the relevant research, see N Taylor and M Freeman 'International Research Evidence on Relocation: Past, Present, and Future' (2010) 44 Fam LQ 317 and M Freeman 'Relocation Research: Where Are We Now?' [2011] IFL 131.

[398] [2001] EWCA Civ 166 [2001] Fam 473 at [27]. For a contemporary comment on this case see A Perry 'Payne v Payne: leave to remove children from the jurisdiction' [2001] CFLQ 455.

[399] In this respect the principles were set out in *Poel v Poel* [1970] 1 WLR 1469, to which, as Thorpe LJ said in *Re H (Application To Remove From Jurisdiction)* [1998] 1 FLR 848, later cases have added little.

and that the application of the European Convention on Human Rights following the implementation of the Human Rights Act 1998 did not 'necessitate a revision of the fundamental approach to relocation applications formulated by this court and consistently applied over so many years'. Nevertheless to guard against a risk of 'too perfunctory an investigation resulting from too ready an assumption that the [primary carer]'s proposals are necessarily compatible with the child's welfare', Thorpe LJ suggested that the courts should adopt the following discipline:[400]

[40] (a) Pose the question: is the mother's application genuine in the sense that it is not motivated by some selfish desire to exclude the father from the child's life? Then ask is the mother's application realistic, by which I mean founded on practical proposals both well researched and investigated? If the application fails either of these tests refusal will inevitably follow. [401]

(b) If however the application passes these tests then there must be a careful appraisal of the father's opposition: is it motivated by genuine concern for the future of the child's welfare or is it driven by some ulterior motive? What would be the extent of the detriment to him and his future relationship with the child were the application granted? To what extent would that be offset by extension of the child's relationship with the maternal family and homeland?

(c) What would be the impact on the mother, either as the single parent or as a new wife, of a refusal of her realistic proposal?

(d) The outcome of the second and third appraisals must then be brought into an overriding review of the child's welfare as the paramount consideration directed by the statutory checklist insofar as appropriate.

[41] In suggesting such a discipline I would not wish to be thought to have diminished the importance that this court has consistently attached to the emotional and psychological well-being of the primary carer. In any evaluation of the welfare of the child as the paramount consideration great weight must be given to this factor.

Although much emphasis has subsequently been placed on Thorpe LJ's guidance, regard should also be had to Butler-Sloss P's summary in *Payne*[402] (to which reference is now increasingly made), namely:

(a) The welfare of the child is always paramount.

(b) There is no presumption created by s 13(1)(b) in favour of the applicant parent.

(c) The reasonable proposals of the parent with a residence order wishing to live abroad carry great weight.

(d) Consequently the proposals have to be scrutinised with care and the court needs to be satisfied that there is a genuine motivation for the move and not the intention to bring contact between the child and the other parent to an end.

(e) The effect upon the applicant parent and the new family of the child of a refusal of leave is very important.

For a detailed discussion of *Poel*, see R Taylor 'Poels Apart: Fixed Principles and Shifting Values in Relocation Law'.

[400] [2001] EWCA Civ 166 [2001] Fam 473 at [40] and [41].

[401] For examples, see *Tyler v Tyler* [1989] 2 FLR 158, in which the mother's dominant motive in seeking to relocate to Australia was bitterness towards her husband, and *M v A (Wardship: Removal From Jurisdiction)* [1993] 2 FLR 715 and *H v F (Refusal of leave to remove a child from the jurisdiction)* [2005] EWHC 2705 (Fam) [2006] 1 FLR 776, in which leave was refused because of the applicant's poorly considered plans.

[402] At [85]–[86].

> (f) The effect upon the child of the denial of contact with the other parent and in some cases his family is very important.
>
> (g) The opportunity for continuing contact between the child and the parent left behind may be very significant.

Butler-Sloss P also explained that her observations were made upon the premise that the question of with whom the child should live (that is, what was then 'residence') is not a live issue. If there is a real dispute as to with which parent the child should live and the decision is finely balanced, then the future plans of each parent are clearly relevant, but if that decision is clear then the plans for removal from the jurisdiction are not likely to be significant in the decision about residence. The corollary of this is that it by no means automatically follows that because an application for leave to remove has been refused, the child should no longer live with the applicant.[403]

Payne, and in particular the discipline espoused by Thorpe LJ, has proved controversial. Indeed it has been described[404] as 'quite possibly the most criticised decision in private family law.' The principal focus of the criticism is that while the discipline is grounded upon the paramountcy of the child's welfare it is said to be too focused upon and too biased towards the primary carer's well-being. Indeed a number of post-*Payne* first instance refusals of leave have either been overturned on appeal or remitted for retrial precisely because too little regard had been paid to the primary carer's well-being.[405] Moreover, as Hayes has pointed out, whereas the discipline instructs a judge to consider the impact of a refusal of leave upon the relocating family there is no similar enjoinder to consider the impact of granting leave upon the left-behind parent. In her view the discipline amounts to an unacceptable gloss upon the welfare principle.[406] The judiciary, too, have acknowledged that there is a respectable argument that the discipline inappropriately relegates the harm done to children by a permanent breach of the relationship which the children have with the left-behind parent to a level below that of the harm likely to be sustained by a child through the negative impact upon the applicant of refusal of the application.[407]

Another charge laid at the door of *Payne* is that it is rooted in a bygone era when (a) the value to the child of a relationship with the non-residential parent was far less well recognised and (b) shared parenting arrangements were virtually unknown. In short there were many who thought that *Payne* had passed its sell-by date. However, talk of *Payne's*

[403] *Re T (Removal From Jurisdiction)* [1996] 2 FLR 352, CA.

[404] By D Eaton and M Reardon 'K v K: The End of the Road for *Payne*?' [2011] IFL 308.

[405] See eg *Re B (Leave To Remove: Impact Of Refusal)* [2004] EWCA Civ 956 [2005] 2 FLR 239; *Re G (Removal From Jurisdiction)* [2005] EWCA Civ 170 [2005] 2 FLR 166 and *Re B (Removal From Jurisdiction)*; *Re S (Removal From Jurisdiction)* [2003] EWCA Civ 1149 [2003] 1 FLR 1043. In fact in *Re H (Children) (Residence Order: Condition)* [2001] EWCA Civ 1338 [2001] 2 FLR 1277 at [17] Thorpe LJ acknowledged that his guidance was unhelpful in its layout inasmuch as it was easy to assume that para [40] contains the totality of the discipline whereas it is important to understand that para [41] (stressing the importance of the primary carer's well-being) is as much a part of the discipline as if it had been expressed in para [40] (c).

[406] M Hayes 'Relocation cases: is the Court of Appeal applying the correct principles?' [2006] CFLQ 351. See also *Re AR (A Child: Relocation)* [2010] EWHC 1346 (Fam) [2010] 2 FLR 1577 at [8] in which Mostyn J referred to the 'strong view that the heavy emphasis on the emotional reaction of the thwarted primary carer represents an illegitimate gloss on the purity of the paramountcy principle', a point echoed by Wilson LJ in *Re H (Leave To Remove)* [2010] EWCA Civ 915 [2010] 2 FLR 1875 at [22]. See also the critique by C Geekie 'Relocation and Shared Residence: One Route or Two?' [2008] Fam Law 446. But cf J Herring and R Taylor 'Relocating relocation' [2006] CFLQ 717.

[407] Per Wilson LJ in *Re H (Leave To Remove)* at [23], adapting an earlier comment made by Wall LJ in *Re D (Leave to Remove: Appeal)* [2010] EWCA Civ 50 [2010] 2 FLR 1605 at [33].

demise has proved premature and pleas to have the whole issue reviewed by the Supreme Court have (so far), perhaps surprisingly, fallen on deaf ears.[408]

K v K (Children: Permanent Removal from Jurisdiction)

In *K v K*,[409] the leading post-*Payne* authority, the court was faced with the classic dilemma of a mother seeking relocation after the failure of the marriage because she felt isolated here and wanted to return home where she would have the support of her family. The father, on the other hand, pointed to his great commitment to the children and to his shared care. In this case, the mother sought leave to remove her two children, aged two and four, to her home country of Canada. At the time of the application there was a shared residence order under which the children spent 59% of their time with their mother and 41% with their father. Notwithstanding this split and the father's clear commitment to the children and contrary to the Cafcass officer's recommendation, at first instance leave was granted. On appeal the judge's decision was found to be flawed by her failure to consider properly both the Cafcass officer's recommendation and the father's contribution to the care of the children. The case was remitted for a rehearing before a different judge.

Although the Court of Appeal was unanimous in its decision, their reasoning differed. In Thorpe LJ's view because 'his' *Payne* discipline was predicated upon the primacy of the applicant's care, it had no application to cases where, as in *K v K*, each parent was providing more or less equal care. Instead regard should be had to the statutory checklist under s 1(3) of the Children Act. In so holding, he specifically commended Hedley J's decision in *Re Y (Leave To Remove From Jurisdiction)*.[410]

Moore-Bick LJ accepted that *Payne* was binding but only for its *ratio decidendi*. He commented:

> having considered *Payne v Payne* itself and the authorities in which it has been discussed, I cannot help thinking that the controversy which now surrounds it is the result of a failure to distinguish clearly between legal principle and guidance.

He continued:

> As I read it, the only principle of law enunciated by *Payne v Payne* is that the welfare of the child is paramount; all the rest is guidance.[411] Such difficulty as has arisen is the result of treating that guidance as if it contained principles of law from which no departure is permitted. Guidance of the kind provided in *Payne v Payne* is, of course, very valuable both in ensuring that judges identify what are likely to be the most important factors to be taken into account and the weight that should generally be attached to them. It also plays a valuable role in promoting consistency in decision-making. However, the circumstances

---

[408] One such plea was made by Mostyn J in *Re AR (A Child: Relocation)*. But the refusal to give leave to appeal against the decision in *Re F (Relocation)* [2012] EWCA Civ 1364 [2013] 1 FLR 645, on 4 February 2013, perhaps indicates the Supreme Court's lack of interest to take up this challenge, at least for the present.

[409] [2011] EWCA Civ 793 [2012] 2 WLR 941, on which see R George 'Reviewing relocation?' [2012] CFLQ 110, S Gilmore 'The *Payne* Saga: Precedent and Family Law Cases' [2011] Fam Law 970 and D Eaton and M Reardon 'K v K: The End of the Road for Payne?' [2011] IFL 308. The last mentioned authors represented the father in *K v K*.

[410] [2004] 2 FLR 330—leave to remove a five-year-old child who was sharing his home equally with each parent and was well settled, bilingual and bicultural, from Wales to Texas, was refused. Note may also be taken of *Re A (Temporary Removal From Jurisdiction)* [2004] EWCA Civ 1587 [2005] 1 FLR 639 in which Thorpe LJ said 'The more temporary the removal, the less regard should be paid to the principles stated in *Payne v Payne*'.

[411] It should be noted that Thorpe LJ agreed with this assessment: see [39].

in which these difficult decisions have to be made vary infinitely and the judge in each case must be free to weigh up the individual factors and make whatever decision he or she considers to be in the best interests of the child. As Hedley J said in *Re Y* ... the welfare of the child overbears all other considerations, however powerful and reasonable they may be. I do not think that the court in *Payne v Payne* intended to suggest otherwise.

Like Moore-Bick LJ, Black LJ reviewed all the relevant case law and similarly concluded that:

the principle – the *only* authentic principle – that runs through the entire line of relocation authorities is that the welfare of the child is the court's paramount consideration. Everything that is considered by the court in reaching its determination is put in the balance with a view to measuring its impact on the child.

However, in Black LJ's view this conclusion did not mean that what she described as 'valuable guidance' could be ignored. In her view it should be heeded but as guidance—nothing more or less. Importantly, she did not accept that *Re Y* was representative of a different line of authority from *Payne* applicable where the child's care is shared between the parents as opposed to being undertaken by one primary carer. Instead she saw it 'as a decision within the framework of which *Payne v Payne* is part. It exemplifies how the weight attached to the relevant factors alters depending upon the facts of the case.' Consequently Black LJ did not 'expect to find cases bogged down with arguments as to whether the time spent with each parent or other aspects of the care arrangements are such as to make the case "a *Payne* case" or an "*In Re Y* case".'

This last point was endorsed by Munby LJ in *Re F (Relocation)* who commented 'The last thing that this very difficult area of family law requires is a satellite jurisprudence generating ever-more detailed classification of supposedly different types of relocation cases.'[412]

Re F (Relocation)

In *Re F* Munby LJ considered that *K v K* should be taken to establish that the governing principle in relocation cases is the paramountcy of the child's welfare and, as such, there is no room for presumptions one way or another. Although there was disagreement about the value of the *Payne* 'discipline' (ironically with its author being the minority) the majority view was that, provided it was treated as non-binding guidance, it was both valuable and applicable even in cases of shared care arrangements in determining where the child's best interests lie, though it does not eclipse the application of the statutory welfare checklist. Perhaps the best overall summary of the case law position is by Munby LJ in *Re F*:

The focus from beginning to end must be on the child's best interests. The child's welfare is paramount. Every case must be determined having regard to the 'welfare checklist', though of course also having regard, where relevant and helpful, to such guidance as may have been given by this court.[413]

Possible impact of the s 1(2A) presumption of the child's continued involvement with each parent after their separation

A theme running through the case-law just discussed is that there are no presumptions for or against relocation. As Munby LJ put it in *Re F*, 'There can be no presumptions in

---

[412] [2012] EWCA Civ 1364 [2013] 1 FLR 645, at [60].
[413] [2012] EWCA Civ 1364 [2013] 1 FLR 645 at [37]. See also *Re TC and JC (Children: Relocation)* [2013] EWHC 292 (Fam) [2013] 2 FLR 484

a case governed by s 1 of the Children Act 1989.' But, as we discussed in Chapter 12, s 1(2A) of the 1989 Act, inserted by the Children and Families Act 2014 has introduced the presumption that unless the contrary is shown and provided the child will not thereby be put at the risk of harm, the continued involvement of each parent in the life of the child will further that child's welfare. What impact this may have on relocation cases has yet to be determined but while this provision will have to be expressly considered, and in that sense will complicate matters, and while no doubt it will provide a further peg on which opponents to relocation can hang their arguments, it is submitted that it ought not to make much difference to the overall outcome of applications. As the Explanatory Notes to the Act stress,[414] s 1(2A) is without prejudice to the overarching principle of the paramountcy of the child's welfare and it certainly should not be regarded as introducing a presumption against relocation. In any event, granting leave does not inevitably mean that the left behind parent has no continuing 'involvement' with the child so that even where the presumption applies it may be perfectly consistent with it to grant leave to relocate with appropriate arrangements being put in place to preserve the child's contact with the left behind parent. However, what the introduction of s 1(2A) will inevitably mean is that there will have to be further test cases to determine the matter.

Powers when granting leave

When granting leave, the court should assess all risks and build in practical safeguards. It may impose conditions, for example, requiring the swearing of a solemn oath on the Quran,[415] or requiring a deposit of a bond which was to be released upon the child's return.[416]

An international perspective

English law is not alone in wrestling with how best to resolve relocation disputes[417] and the issue has been before the highest courts in a number of jurisdictions. In Canada, for example, as early as 1996, the Supreme Court of Canada ruled in *Gordon v Goertz*[418] that the courts must apply the best interests of the child test which requires an individualised assessment in each case without any presumption or onus. More recently in *Kacem v Bashir*[419] the New Zealand Supreme Court said that the ultimate objective is to determine what outcome will best serve the best interests of the particular child in the particular circumstances. A different approach was taken by the Supreme Court of California in *Re Marriage of Burgess*[420] effectively permitting relocation unless it was harmful to the child,

[414] At para 109.
[415] *Re A (Security For Return To Jurisdiction) (Note)* [1999] 2 FLR 1. In this respect regard may be had to the 1996 Hague Convention on the Protection of Children (discussed in Ch 26) under which protective measures can be recognised and enforced in other Contracting States.
[416] *Re L (Removal From Jurisdiction: Holiday)* [2001] 1 FLR 241. In *Re S (Removal From Jurisdiction)* [1999] 1 FLR 850, CA, in which a deposit of a sum of money was required until the parent with leave obtained 'authentication' of the contact order in the foreign court and complied with an order relating to the child's education. The deposit was to be released upon evidence of compliance.
[417] Though English law is unusual in making a distinction between external and internal relocation.
[418] [1996] 2 SCR 27, on which see N Bala and A Wheeler 'Canadian Cases: Heading Towards Guideline' (2012) 30 *Canadian Family Quarterly* 271, who provide an excellent comparative analysis of Canadian relocation cases, and The Hon J Chamberland 'The Canadian Law of Parental Relocation' [2010] IFL 17. For a view of the position in Australia, see Chief Justice D Bryant 'Freedom of Movement in an Era of Shared Parenting: the Differences in Judicial Approaches: a Critique' [2010] IFL 11.
[419] [2010] NZSC 112 [2011] 2 NZLR 1, on which see Judge P von Dadelszen 'Relocation: the First and Paramount Consideration' [2011] IFL 63.
[420] 13 Cal 4th 25 (1996), on which see C Bruch and J Bowermaster 'The Relocation of Children and Custodial Parents: Public Policy, Past and Present' (1996) 30 Fam LQ 245.

though this was later reined back a little in another Supreme Court decision, *LaMusga v LaMusga*.[421]

Of course, below this level of court relocation case-law is legion but even having regard to these decisions it is evident that different approaches are taken across even the common law world.[422] Another concern and a charge levied at *Gordon v Goertz*, for example, is that the so-called pure best interests test provides no guidance and hence no predictability of and for decision making.[423] This has led to calls for a prioritised discipline.[424]

It was in an attempt to address these concerns and to promote a more uniform international approach that an International Judicial Conference was held in Washington in 2010. Drawing on research findings, the conference produced what is now referred to as the 'Washington Declaration',[425] which, though influential, has no legal status.[426] After stating that in all international relocation applications the best interests of the child should be the paramount (primary) test and that 'determinations should be made without any presumptions for or against relocation', the Declaration set out 13 non-hierarchal factors, which, it was hoped would promote a more uniform approach. It was emphasised that the weight to be given to any one factor 'will vary from case to case.' The factors listed are:

i)   the right of the child separated from one parent to maintain personal relations and direct contact with both parents on a regular basis in a manner consistent with the child's development, except if the contact is contrary to the child's best interest;

ii)   the views of the child having regard to the child's age and maturity;

iii) the parties' proposals for the practical arrangements for relocation, including accommodation, schooling and employment;

iv)   where relevant to the determination of the outcome, the reasons for seeking or opposing relocation;

v)   any history of family violence or abuse, whether physical or psychological;

vi)   the history of the family and particularly the continuity and quality of past and current care and contact arrangements;

vii) pre-existing custody and access determinations:

viii) the impact of grant or refusal on the child, in the context of his or her extended family, education and social life, and on the parties;

ix)   the nature of the inter-parental relationship and the commitment of the applicant to support and facilitate the relationship between the child and the respondent after relocation;

x)   whether the parties' proposals for contact after relocation are realistic, having particular regard to the cost to the family and the burden to the child;

---

[421] 32 Cal 4th 25 (2004), discussed by P Parkinson *Family Law and the Indissolubility of Parenthood* (2011) 155.

[422] See R George *Relocation Disputes—Law and Practice in England and New Zealand* (2014). For brief accounts of relocation law across various jurisdictions, see the *The Judges' Newsletter, Special edition on the Washington conference* (2010).

[423] See D Rollie Thompson 'Ten Years After Gordon, No Law, Nowhere' (2007) 35 Reports of Family Law (6th) 307, and 'Movin' On: Parental Relocation in Canada' (2004) 42 *Family Court Review* 398, Bala and Wheeler, op cit and Madam Justice R Diamond 'Moving towards relocation reform in Canada' [2013] IFL 155.

[424] See in particular M Henaghan 'Relocation cases – the rhetoric and the reality of a child's best interests – a view from the bottom of the world' [2011] CFLQ 226.

[425] The Declaration is set out in full at [2010] IFL 211 and for some background, see the Rt Hon Lord Justice Thorpe 'Relocation: The Search for Common Principle' [2010] IFL 241.

[426] See *Re H (Leave To Remove)* [2010] EWCA Civ 915 [2010] 2 FLR 1875 at [26], per Wilson LJ. See also *Re AR (A Child: Relocation)* [2010] EWHC 1346 (Fam) [2010] 2 FLR 1577 at [10]–[13], per Mostyn J.

xi) the enforceability of contact provisions ordered as a condition of relocation in the State of destination;

xii) issues of mobility for family members; and

xiii) any other circumstances deemed to be relevant by the judge.

There can, of course, be debate about both the content and the value of this list but it does represent a genuine international attempt to provide a common approach to this difficult issue. In fact the intention and expectation was that the Declaration would be taken up by the Hague Conference and provide the basis for work on a formal international instrument. In the event, the 6th Special Commission decided not to undertake the task in part because it was seen as a domestic rather than an international law issue. In the meantime a much more modest proposal on relocation is being considered by the Council of Europe, which makes no attempt to list any factors.[427]

Comparison with internal relocations

As previously discussed,[428] there are no formal restrictions on relocating within the United Kingdom though a court prohibition can be sought. Furthermore whereas a principal carer will ordinarily be granted leave to remove a child outside the United Kingdom unless the court concludes that it is incompatible with the child's welfare, no condition restricting the area of residence within the United Kingdom will be imposed on the principal carer save in exceptional circumstances. The rationale for this less stringent approach is that, in Thorpe LJ's words in *Re H (Children) (Residence Order, Condition)*,[429] within 'the same sovereignty there will be the same system of laws, with the same rights of the citizen, rights for instance to education, health care and statutory benefits'. He added 'Equally, it can be said that within Europe, while perhaps the burden on the applicant may be greater, it is equally mitigated by the fact that within the Community there is the same fundamental approach to social issues and a real endeavour to achieve harmonisation, obviously in social policy but also in family justice.'

5. WHEN SECTION 8 ORDERS CAN BE MADE

(a) Family proceedings

Under s 10(1) s 8 orders may be made 'in any family proceedings in which a question arises with respect to the welfare of any child'. The term 'family proceedings' is defined by s 8(3)[430] as meaning any proceedings 'under the inherent jurisdiction of the High Court in relation to children' or under the enactments listed in s 8(4). With regard to the former, which refers both to wardship and to proceedings under the general inherent jurisdiction of the High Court,[431] s 8(3) states that local authority applications to invoke the High Court's inherent jurisdiction fall outside the definition.

The enactments listed in s 8(4), as amended, are as follows:

– Parts I, II and IV of the 1989 Act;

– Matrimonial Causes Act 1973;

---

[427] Draft Recommendation on Resolution of Parental Disputes (Relocation of Children) 2014.

[428] At Removal of child from the United Kingdom—'External relocation', p 525.

[429] [2001] EWCA Civ 1338 [2001] 2 FLR 1277 at [20].

[430] Note s 8(3) only defines 'family proceedings' for the purpose of making s 8 orders. For other purposes, eg the admission of hearsay evidence, recourse must also be had to the definition in s 92(2): *R v Oxfordshire County Council (Secure Accommodation Order)* [1992] Fam 150.   [431] Discussed in Ch 20.

- Domestic Proceedings and Magistrates' Courts Act 1978;
- Matrimonial and Family Proceedings Act 1984, Part III;
- Family Law Act 1996;
- Adoption and Children Act 2002;
- Crime and Disorder Act 1998, ss 11 and 12;[432] and
- Civil Partnership Act 2004, Schs 5 and 6.

Based on the Law Commission's recommendation[433] and intended to rationalise, harmonise[434] and, in some cases, expand the courts' powers, the wide ambit of the definition of 'family proceedings' should be noted. For example, the inclusion of Part IV of the 1989 Act means that the court can make s 8 orders in care proceedings. Similarly, the court can make s 8 orders in adoption, in proceedings under Part IV of the Family Law Act 1996 and in financial relief proceedings. The reason for including these proceedings is that by extending the range of options the court will be better able to meet the child's needs.[435]

The inclusion of wardship proceedings under 'family proceedings' furthers the policy of reducing the need to resort to the jurisdiction[436] because there will be less incentive to use it if the outcome is likely to be the same as in other proceedings. Furthermore, where an application is made the expectation is that, where appropriate, the court will make a s 8 order and discharge the wardship.[437]

Wide though the definition is, however, it does not include all proceedings concerning children. In particular it does not include those under Part V of the 1989 Act. This means that in applications for emergency protection orders and child assessment orders the court cannot make a s 8 order. There is similarly no power to make s 8 orders in international child abduction proceedings,[438] nor in proceedings brought under the Family Law Act 1986.[439]

(b) Any child

Section 10(1) allows an order to be made in respect of 'any child'. In other words, the court's powers are not limited to 'children of the family',[440] or to the biological children of the parties, though, as we have discussed, the powers are restricted when the child reaches

---

[432] Under which a child safety order, placing a child under the age of 10 who has committed an act which would have been an offence had the child been aged 10 or over, under the supervision of a social worker or a member of a youth offending team, can be made. See further Clarke Hall and Morrison on *Children* at 14 [10.2].   [433] Law Com No 172 para 4.37.

[434] Note, however, that, whereas the court is obliged to consider the children in applications for financial relief under the Domestic Proceedings and Magistrates' Courts Act 1978, there is no such duty in an application under s 27 of the Matrimonial Causes Act 1973.

[435] In the case of domestic abuse proceedings, as the Law Commission observed (Law Com No 172 at para 4.25), the needs of the children are frequently an important factor in determining the relief sought and it was 'highly artificial' for the court to be able to exclude one person from the matrimonial home, at least in part for the children's sake, yet not to be able to order that the child should live with the parent remaining in the home. It might be noted, however, that in these proceedings the court is not *obliged* to consider children and that in many cases the matter will be too urgent for it to do so.

[436] Law Com No 172 para 4.25. Wardship is discussed in Ch 20.

[437] As was done in *Re T (A Minor) (Child: Representation)* [1994] Fam 49, CA and *C v Salford City Council* [1994] 2 FLR 926, discussed in Ch 20, Use in private law cases, p 759.   [438] Discussed in Ch 26.

[439] The 1986 Act deals inter alia with abduction within the UK (see Ch 26), and declarations of status, discussed in Ch 8, Declarations of parentage, p 270, and in Ch 9, Declarations of status, p 303.

[440] The meaning of which is discussed in Ch 9, The meaning of 'child of the family', pp 296–298.

the age of 16.[441] By the normal rules of interpretation[442] 'child' only refers to live persons. There is therefore no power to make s 8 orders in respect of unborn or deceased children.

(c) Upon application or upon the court's own motion

By s 10(1) s 8 orders can be made either upon application or, once proceedings have begun, by the court itself whenever it 'considers that the order should be made *even though no such application has been made*' (emphasis added). Although the Law Commission expected[443] that orders would normally be made upon application, the significance of the courts' ability to make s 8 orders of their own motion means that in theory once family proceedings are on foot there is at least a risk that the court might choose to make a s 8 order in respect of the child regardless of the parties' wishes. If, however, a court is minded to make an order that has not been argued for, it should inform the parties of that intention and give them the opportunity to make submissions on the desirability of the proposed option.[444] It has also been said[445] that it could only be in wholly exceptional circumstances that what is now a child arrangements order should be imposed on unwilling recipients.

In *Gloucestershire County Council v P*[446] it was held that the flexibility given to a judge by s 10(1)(b) to make what would now be a child arrangements order upon his own initiative is not limited by the restrictions imposed by ss 9 and 10(3).[447] It was consequently no bar on the court making an order that the child was to live with foster parents that the parties themselves were prohibited from seeking court leave to apply for such an order. However, as Butler-Sloss LJ observed, it would only be in 'a most exceptional' case that it would be right to make an order in favour of foster-parents who could not themselves apply.

6. ENFORCING SECTION 8 ORDERS

Enforcing s 8 orders[448] can be a difficult and protracted matter which in any event needs to be handled sensitively. The imposition of penal sanctions for breaking court orders (discussed later) should not be thought of as being the norm in children cases. On the contrary, they should be sought only where all other alternatives are seen to be ineffective. Even then, careful thought needs to be given to the provocative and emotional effect that applications for enforcement can have in themselves. Above all it is important not

---

[441] Pursuant to s 9(6): see Children aged 16 or over, p 510.

[442] See *Elliot v Joicey* [1935] AC 209, HL; *D (A Minor) v Berkshire County Council* [1987] AC 317; and *R v Newham London Borough Council, ex p Dada* [1996] QB 507, CA.

[443] Law Com No 172 para 4.38.

[444] See eg *Croydon London Borough Council v A* [1992] Fam 169, and *Devon County Council v S* [1992] Fam 176, in which the observations were made in respect of magistrates' court decisions, but the principle ought to be of general application. Query the position on appeal: see eg *Re F (Minors) (Denial of Contact)* [1993] 2 FLR 677 in which the Court of Appeal refused to make a family assistance order inter alia because the point had not been argued at first instance.

[445] Per Stuart-White J in *Re K (Care Order or Residence Order)* [1995] 1 FLR 675 at 683, in which devoted grandparents did not wish to have legal responsibility in respect of two grandsons (who were suffering from a muscle-wasting disease) they were looking after.

[446] [2000] Fam 1, CA, Thorpe LJ dissenting.

[447] Discussed at General restrictions on making section 8 orders, pp 510ff.

[448] See generally N Lowe 'Enforcing orders relating to children' (1992) 4 *Journal of Child Law* 26 and, especially in relation to enforcing contact orders, see *Making Contact Work* (2002) ch 14 and, inter alia, the Government Green Papers *Parental Separation: Children's Needs and Parents' Responsibilities* Cm 6273 (2004) and *Parental Separation: Children's Needs and Parents' Responsibilities: Next Steps* Cm 6452 (2005).

to lose sight of the *child*'s welfare in these disputes though, as we shall see, in deciding whether to impose a penal sanction the child's welfare is a material but *not* the paramount consideration.[449]

(a) Family Law Act 1986 s 34

Under s 34 of the Family Law Act 1986,[450] where a person is required by a s 8 order to give up a child to another person and the court that made the order is satisfied that the child has not been given up, it may make an order authorising an officer of the court or a constable to take charge of the child and deliver him to that other person.[451] Since this power, which is available to *any* court, enables such orders to be enforced without recourse to penal procedures, it should normally be preferred to those latter powers. However, because an order under s 34 cannot be granted unless or until the order to give up the child has been disobeyed,[452] it might be preferable in emergencies to obtain a without notice order under the High Court's inherent jurisdiction[453] authorising the tipstaff to find and recover the child.[454] The court may also pre-empt an unlawful removal of a child from the care of the person or from the jurisdiction by making an order preventing such removal and attaching a penal notice (that is, a notice formally warning the person against whom the order is made that failure to obey it constitutes a contempt of court for which the offender may be sent to prison) thereto.

(b) The Family Court's general enforcement powers for contempt of court

More general powers of enforcement are provided by the law of contempt of court.[455]

Breaking a court order or an undertaking incorporated in an order constitutes a contempt of court for which the contemnor may be fined, imprisoned or have his property sequestered.[456] The first remedy is unusual.[457] The latter remedy (under which the contemnor's assets are frozen)[458] is useful in cases where the offender is abroad but has assets in this country.[459] The major sanction for breaking a s 8 order is by committal, by which means the offender can be imprisoned for a maximum period of two years.[460]

---

[449] As established by *A v N (Committal: Refusal of Contact)* [1997] 1 FLR 533, CA, discussed at Determining whether to impose a penalty, p 539.

[450] See generally N Fricker et al *Emergency Remedies and Procedures* (1993, 2nd edn) 158 *et seq* and N Lowe, M Everall and M Nicholls *International Movement of Children—Law Practice and Procedure* (2004), ch 10.

[451] The police generally have a duty to assist in the handing over of a child where there is a threat of danger or a breach of the peace: *R v Chief Constable of Cheshire ex p K* [1990] 1 FLR 70. Additionally, under s 33 of the 1986 Act a court can order any person whom it has reason to believe may have relevant information as to the child's whereabouts to disclose it to the court.

[452] Though it can be applied to a suitably worded contact order, viz. one that formally requires the handing over of the child for contact purposes.   [453] Discussed in Ch 20.

[454] See Fricker, op cit, at p 248 and N Fricker 'Injunctive Orders Relating to Children' [1993] Fam Law 226 at 229–30.

[455] See the Family Court (Contempt of Court) (Powers) Regulations 2014, SI 2014/883.

[456] These powers are briefly referred to in the Children Act Advisory Committee (CAAC) Report 1992/93 ch 5. For more detail, see the standard works on contempt of court.

[457] See Butler-Sloss P in *Re S (Contact: Promoting Relationship With Absent Parent)* [2004] EWCA Civ 18 [2004] 1 FLR 1279 at [28] in the context of enforcing what were then contact orders.

[458] There is also power both to order the sale of sequestered assets and to direct that money raised by the sequestrators be used to pay for the costs of tracing the child and instituting proceedings abroad: see respectively *Mir v Mir* [1992] Fam 79, and *Richardson v Richardson* [1989] Fam 95.

[459] It is therefore particularly useful in cases of child abduction—see Ch 26.

[460] Contempt of Court 1981, s 14(1).

Before any committal order may be made the court has to be satisfied beyond reasonable doubt[461] that the defendant knowingly broke the order. Furthermore, it is a requirement[462] that a penal notice must have been attached to the order in question.

Orders are normally only enforceable against parties to the proceedings, but it can also be a contempt for someone else knowingly to frustrate a court order.[463]

Determining whether to impose a penalty

Even if the court is satisfied that an order has been knowingly broken by the defendant, it should regard the enforcement powers for contempt to imprison or fine as remedies of the last resort. As Ormrod LJ commented in *Ansah v Ansah*,[464] 'Committal orders are remedies of the last resort; in family cases they should be the very last.' Further, as Hale LJ observed in *Hale v Tanner*:[465]

> Family cases, it has long been recognised, raise quite different considerations from those elsewhere in the civil law. The two most obvious are the heightened emotional tensions that arise between family members and often the need for those family members to continue to be in contact with one another because they have children together or the like . . .

Nevertheless, it would be wrong to extract any general principle from Ormrod LJ's dictum in *Ansah v Ansah*, and in appropriate cases it may well be right to imprison an offender.[466] Indeed, following the Court of Appeal decision in *A v N (Committal: Refusal of Contact)*,[467] in which it was held that, in considering whether to commit a mother for her persistent and flagrant breach of a contact order with the father, the child's welfare was a material but not the paramount consideration, made imprisonment more likely than previously.[468] In *B v S (Contempt: Imprisonment Of Mother)* Wilson LJ commented[469] that the days 'were long gone when mothers could assume that their role as carers of children protected them from being sentenced to immediate terms of imprisonment for clear, repeated and deliberate breaches of court orders.' However, as far as breach of child arrangements orders

---

[461] See eg *Re L-W (Enforcement and Committal: Contact: CPL v CH-W and Others)* [2010] EWCA Civ 1253 [2011] 1 FLR 1095; *Dean v Dean* [1987] 1 FLR 517, CA; and *Re Bramblevale Ltd* [1970] Ch 128, CA.

[462] CPR 1998 r 81.25.

[463] See *Re K (Minors) (Incitement to Breach Contact Order)* [1992] 2 FLR 108 (solicitor held guilty of contempt for advising a client mother to break what was then an access order); *Re S (Abduction: Sequestration)* [1995] 1 FLR 858 (contempt for a friend to assist mother in abducting child).

[464] [1977] Fam 138 at 143, CA. Note also Bennett J's comment in *Re H*, earlier, that magistrates should 'take the greatest possible caution before proceeding with a hearing under s 63—they should only proceed with the greatest possible caution to use a weapon of last resort'.

[465] [2000] 1 WLR 2377, CA at [25]. See the comments thereon by R Kay 'Guidelines on Sanctions for Breach: *Hale v Tanner*' (2001) 64 MLR 595, particularly 598–601.

[466] See eg *Jones v Jones* [1993] 2 FLR 377, CA.

[467] [1997] 1 FLR 533, CA, in which a mother was committed to prison for 42 days for her persistent and repeated breaches of a contact order. *A v N* was approved in this respect by Munby LJ in *L-W (Enforcement and Committal: Contact); CPL v CH-W and Others* [2010] EWCA Civ 1253 [2011] 1 FLR 1095.

[468] Though this is not to say that the penal remedy should be frequently resorted to, cf *Re F (Contact: Enforcement: Representation of Child)* [1998] 1 FLR 691, CA.

[469] [2009] EWCA Civ 548 [2009] 2 FLR 1005 at [16], in which the Court of Appeal declined to suspend a 28 day sentence. See also *Re S (Contact Dispute: Committal)* [2004] EWCA Civ 1790 [2005] 1 FLR 812—mother's committal for seven days (with an interim residence order to father) for repeated breaches, upheld on appeal. Cf *Re K (Contact: Committal Order)* [2002] EWCA Civ 1559 [2003] 1 FLR 377—wrong to impose a committal on a mother without legal representation, notwithstanding her numerous breaches. Note the strict rules governing contempt cases must be followed, see eg *Hammerton v Hammerton* [2007] EWCA Civ 248 [2007] 2 FLR 1133 and *G v G* [2007] EWCA Civ 680 [2007] 2 FLR 1127.

are concerned, regard must also be had to the power to make enforcement orders under the provisions introduced by the Children and Adoption Act 2006 and broadened by the Children and Families Act 2014, which are discussed in the next section.

Although in principle similar caution should be exercised when considering the imposition of penal sanctions upon the non-residential parent there may nevertheless be less concern for the child's welfare in so doing.[470]

Limitations of the contempt powers

Though they have their place in the coercive armoury both to ensure compliance with court orders and to deter breaches, the contempt remedies are limited and increasing criticism has been voiced at the apparent ease with which contact orders in particular could be frustrated or simply ignored. As Bracewell J observed in *V v V (Contact: Implacable Hostility)*[471] the option of committing the contemnor to prison or to suspend the prison term are always at best a blunt remedy and:

> may well not achieve the object of reinstating contact; the child may blame the parent who applied to commit the carer to prison; the child's life may be disrupted if there is no-one capable of or willing to care for the child when the parent is in prison; it cannot be anything other than emotionally damaging for a child to be suddenly removed into foster care by social services from a parent, usually a mother, who in all respects except contact is a good parent.

Nor is a fine any better, for as Bracewell J said: 'This option is rarely possible because it is not consistent with the welfare of the child to deprive a parent on a limited budget'.

It was in response to criticisms such as these that new measures were introduced by the Children and Adoption Act 2006 to increase the options of the court when dealing with breaches of what were then contact orders.[472] The application of these enforcement powers have since been extended by the Children and Families Act 2014 to apply to all child arrangements orders. It is to these remedies that we now turn.

(c) The enforcement powers under the 2006 and 2014 reforms

Warning notices

As part of the package of measures introduced by the Children and Adoption Act 2006 to improve the enforcement of what were then contact orders and now amended by the Children and Families Act 2014 to apply more generally to child arrangements orders, s 11L of the Children Act 1989 (as amended) provides that *whenever* a court makes or

---

[470] See eg *G v C (Residence Order: Committal)* [1998] 1 FLR 43, CA—father imprisoned for eight months for repeated breaches of order not to threaten or abuse the mother.

[471] [2004] EWHC 1215 (Fam) [2004] 2 FLR 851 at [10]. See also *Re S (Contact: Promoting Relationship With Absent Parent)* [2004] EWCA Civ 18 [2004] 1 FLR 1279 at [28] per Butler-Sloss P and Lord Justice Wall 'Enforcement of Contact Orders' [2005] Fam Law 26 at 30–1.

[472] For the background to these measures see the Government Green Papers *Parental Separation: Children's Needs and Parents' Responsibilities* Cm 6273 (July 2004), *Parental Separation: Children's Needs and Parents' Responsibilities: Next Steps* Cm 6452 (January 2005); the Draft Children (Contact) and Adoption Bill Cm 6462 (February 2005); the Joint Committee on the Draft Children (Contact) and Adoption Bill: First Report HL Paper 100–1/HC 400–1 (the so-called 'Scrutiny Committee') and *The Government Reply to the Report from the Joint Committee* Cm 6583 (June 2005). For comments on the proposals see J Masson and C Humphreys 'Facilitating and Enforcing Contact: The Bill and the Ten Per Cent' [2005] Fam Law 548. Note that the more draconian of the suggested sanctions, namely, curfews and tagging, were not included in the 2006 Act.

varies a provision in a child arrangements order, it must attach a notice warning of the consequences for failing to comply.

Enforcement orders

The Children and Adoption Act 2006 introduced a new sanction, the enforcement order, for failing to comply with contact orders by inserting ss 11J–N into the Children Act 1989. These powers have now been amended by the Children and Families Act 2014[473] so as to apply more generally to child arrangements orders.

Under s 11J where the court is satisfied beyond all reasonable doubt that a person has failed to comply with a provision of the child arrangements order it may make an enforcement order which is an order imposing an unpaid work requirement up a maximum of 200 hours[474] on the person who has broken the order. According to the Explanatory Notes to the 2006 Act,[475] a 'breach' for these purposes includes a breach of an activity condition[476] or of a condition attached to child arrangements order under s 11(7) though the Act does not expressly say so. Any enforcement order that is imposed can be suspended for such a period as the court thinks fit.[477] It has been held[478] that because such proceedings are in effect contempt proceedings and the penalties quasi-criminal, anyone faced with such proceedings is entitled to be represented and if successful in their defence is entitled to apply for costs. It is not a 'breach' of an order if it is outside the defendant's power to comply as, for example, where taking a child for contact is prevented or delayed due to unforeseen and insuperable transport problems.[479]

No enforcement order may be made if the court is satisfied that the person in breach had a reasonable excuse for failing to comply though the burden is on the person in breach to prove, on the balance of probabilities,[480] that he had a reasonable excuse; nor can an order be made against someone who was under 18 at the time of the breach. It has been held that this defence only comes into play if a prima facie breach has first been established. A typical 'reasonable' excuse might be where a child falls ill and the defendant, quite reasonably in the circumstances, takes the child to the doctor rather than going to contact.[481]

By s 11J(5), orders may be made on the application of:

(a) a person who is, for the purposes of the child arrangements order; a person with whom the child concerned lives or is to live;

(b) a person whose contact with the child concerned is provided for in the child arrangements order;

(c) any individual subject to a condition under section 11(7)(b) or an activity condition imposed by the child arrangements order; or

(d) the child concerned.

---

[473] See Sch 2 paras 16 to 20.

[474] Sch A1 para 4 to the 1989 Act as added by Sch 1 to the 2006 Act. Note that the more draconian of the suggested sanctions, namely, curfews and tagging were not included in the 2006 Act.

[475] See para 30.

[476] But note, not an activity *direction*. Activity conditions and directions are discussed at Activity directions and conditions, pp 496ff.   [477] Section 11J(9).

[478] *Re R (Costs: Contact Enforcement)* [2011] EWHC 2777 (Fam) [2012] 1 FLR 445.

[479] See *Re L-W (Enforcement and Committal: Contact); CPL v CH-W and Others* [2010] EWCA Civ 1253 [2011] 1 FLR 1095 at [40] in which Munby LJ instanced the grounding of the nation's airlines by volcanic ash but another example might the washing away of parts of the rail network by storms. In *Re L-W* itself the father was held not to have broken the order that he allow the mother to have contact on the basis that it was the child who had refused.

[480] See s 11J(4).   [481] Per Munby LJ in *Re L-W* [40].

In the latter case the child must obtain the leave of the court and leave may only be given if the court is satisfied that the child has sufficient understanding to make the proposed application.

The inclusion of (a) in the sub-section means that in theory a person with whom the child is to live can seek an enforcement order against a person named as someone with whom the child spends time or has contact. In other words, on its face, s 11J(5) contemplates an enforcement action being brought against parent to force him or her to see the child. However, it is by no means clear that such a child arrangements order can be made against an unwilling person.[482]

By s 11L in deciding whether to make an enforcement order the court must be satisfied that its making is necessary to secure compliance and that 'the likely effect on the person of the enforcement order proposed to be made is proportionate to the seriousness of the breach . . .'. The court is also required, before making the order, to obtain and consider information about the person upon whom the order would be imposed. The unpaid work must be local and information must be obtained about the effect of the order on the individual. Importantly, in making an enforcement order the child's welfare is *not* the paramount consideration though the court must take it into account.[483]

On making an enforcement order 'the court is to ask' a Cafcass officer or a Welsh family proceedings officer to monitor compliance and to report to the court.[484]

More than one enforcement order may be made in relation to the same person on the same occasion[485] An enforcement order can subsequently be revoked or amended, and, if it is itself broken, the court may amend it or make it more onerous, or impose another enforcement order.[486] When making the enforcement order the court *must* attach to that order a notice warning of the consequences of non-compliance.[487]

Compensation for financial loss

The second type of order which may be imposed upon breach of a child arrangements order is to order financial compensation for financial loss occasioned by the breach. The example always cited is the cost of a holiday that has been lost because of the breach but it would also include wasted travel costs though presumably these will have to be substantial enough to justify court time being spent on the issue.

Under s 11O where a court is satisfied on the balance of probabilities[488] that an individual has failed to comply with a child arrangements order[489] and a relevant party[490] has suffered financial loss because of the breach, it can order the person in breach to pay

---

[482]   See the discussion at The nature of the order, p 489 and note the similar criticism made by Masson and Humphreys, op cit, at 552. Ironically, the Government itself rejected the proposal, made during the debates on the 2006 Act, that the court should have the power to compel an unwilling parent to have contact with the child, see The nature of the order, p 490.

[483]   This is the implication of s 11L(7) which provides that when making an enforcement order, the court 'must take into account the welfare of the child who is the subject of the child arrangements order'.

[484]   Section 11M(1).

[485]   Section 11J(10).   [486]   Sch A1 Part 2.

[487]   Section 11N. This is the equivalent of a penal notice having to be attached to an order before contempt sanctions may be imposed.

[488]   See Re L-W (Enforcement and Committal: Contact); CPL v CH-W and Others [2010] EWCA Civ 1253 [2011] 1 FLR 1095 at [38], per Munby LJ. The Act itself is silent on the standard of proof.

[489]   According to the Explanatory Notes to the Act, breaching a contact order includes breaching a condition attached to a contact order. 'Breach' has the same meaning as in the case of enforcement orders; Re L-W.

[490]   Ie a person who is entitled to apply for an order under s 11O(6).

compensation up to the amount of the loss. There is a defence of 'reasonable excuse' for which the burden of proof is on the person claiming to have a reasonable excuse.[491]

Only the person suffering loss can apply[492] and, in any event, claimants are limited to those named in a child arrangements order as a person with whom the child is to live or to spend time or otherwise have contact, an individual subject to a condition under s 11(7)(b) or an activity condition, or, with court leave, the child.[493]

In deciding what compensation to order, the court must take into account the financial circumstances of the individual in breach and the child's welfare (which, as for enforcement orders, is not the paramount consideration). An amount ordered to be paid as compensation may be recovered as a 'civil debt'.

Commentary

Although enforcement and compensation orders have their uses, it has to be said that many of the limitations and difficulties attendant on the contempt sanctions[494] apply equally to enforcement orders, while compensation orders are only likely to be appropriate in a minority of cases where the carer has sufficient resources to pay without adversely impacting upon the child(ren) they are looking after.

7. VARYING AND DISCHARGING ORDERS

All s 8 orders may subsequently be varied or discharged. Indeed, this is one of the important distinguishing features between these orders and adoption.[495]

All the substantive and procedural requirements for the making of a s 8 order apply to their subsequent variation or discharge.[496]

8. APPEALS

(a) Routes of appeal and procedure

There is a right of appeal against the making or the refusal to make any s 8 order under the Children Act, including no-orders. Appeals from the Family Court Lay Justice level (ie magistrates) and from the Family Court District Judge level lie to the Family Court Circuit Judge level (or High Court level if that is the most efficient use of resources); those from the District Judge of the Central Family Court (formerly the principal registry of the Family Division) lie to the Family Court High Court Judge level. Appeals from the Family Court Circuit Judge level or High Court judge level lie to the Court of Appeal.[497] Appeals from the Court of Appeal lie to the Supreme Court.

Permission to appeal from a magistrates' decision is not required, nor to appeal against the making of a committal order or a secure accommodation order.[498] Permission is

---

[491] Presumably upon the balance of probabilities, but unlike for enforcement orders, the Act is silent on this. As in the case of enforcement orders, a reasonable excuse only comes into play if a breach is first established, see Re L-W.　　　　　　　　　　　　　　　　　　　　　[492] Section 11O(5).

[493] Section 11O(6), as amended by Sch 2 para 19(5) to the 2014 Act. Leave can only be given if the court is satisfied that the child has sufficient understanding to make the proposed application. It will surely be unusual for a child to have suffered financial loss.

[494] Discussed at Limitations of the contempt powers pp 540ff. See also the findings by C Dyer et al 'Making Contact Work: Is the Children and Adoption Act 2006 Enough for Resident Parents and Children?' [2008] Fam Law 1237.

[495] Adoption is discussed in Ch 19.

[496] Section 8(2), which provides that a section 8 order includes any order varying or discharging such an order.

[497] *Practice Direction 30A Appeals* para 2(1).　　　　　[498] FPR 2010 r 30.3(1) and 30.3(2) respectively.

however, required in all other cases. The idea of requiring permission is to filter out hopeless or vexatious appeals.

The procedure for appealing is governed by Part 30 of the Family Procedure Rules 2010 as augmented by *Practice Direction 30A* and Part 2 of the Family Court (Composition and Distribution of Business) Rules 2014. In these cases an application for permission to appeal should be made orally at the hearing at which the decision to be appealed against is made,[499] but if no such application is made or the lower court refuses permission, then an application for permission may be made to the higher level. Permission to appeal can only be granted if the court considers that the appeal would have a real prospect of success or there is some other compelling reason why the appeal should be heard.[500]

The procedure for appealing to the Court of Appeal is governed by Part 52 of the Civil Procedure Rules 1998. At this level a distinction is made between first appeals and second appeals (that is, appeals from decisions that themselves were the determination of an appeal). In the case of first appeals permission should normally be sought from the trial court first[501] but if that application is refused or if no application was made at the first instance hearing, permission can then be sought from the Court of Appeal.[502] In the case of second appeals permission *must* be sought from the Court of Appeal.[503] The test for determining whether to grant permission is predictably less stringent for first appeals than for second appeals. In the former the court must consider that the appeal would have a real prospect of success or there is some other compelling reason why the appeal should be heard.[504] In the latter leave cannot be given unless the case raises an important principle or practice or there is some other compelling reason for the Court of Appeal to hear it.[505]

The procedure for appealing to the Supreme Court is governed by the Supreme Court Rules 2009. Leave to appeal must be granted either by the Court of Appeal or, more commonly, by the Appeals Committee of the Supreme Court.[506] Leave may be given on the basis that a point of general importance is involved or that point is one that ought to be considered by the Supreme Court.

(b) The position pending appeal

Under the general powers to impose directions and conditions under s 11(7) of the Children Act 1989[507] the operation of any s 8 order can be postponed pending an appeal, or other interim arrangements can be made.[508]

(c) The powers of appellate courts

An appellate court has all the powers of the lower court. It may grant or dismiss the appeal. Alternatively, it can vary the order or remit any issue or even the whole case for a rehearing.[509] Exceptionally, the appellate court can hear fresh evidence to resolve its doubts about the original decision.[510]

---

[499] FPR 2010 r 30.4 and *Practice Direction 30A* para 4.2.   [500] FPR 2010 r 30.3 (7).

[501] *Practice Direction* 52A para 4.6 the rationale being that the first instance court is usually in the best position to determine whether leave to appeal should be given.

[502] CPR 1998 r 52.3(2), (3) and *Practice Direction 52A* para 4.7.

[503] CPR 1998 r 52.13 and *Practice Direction* 52A para 4.9.   [504] CPR 1998 r 52.3(6).

[505] CPR 1998 r 5 52.13(2).   [506] Supreme Court Rules 2009 r 10.   [507] Discussed at pp 504ff.

[508] Magistrates have no powers to order a stay pending an appeal and an application needs to made to a High Court judge: Children Act Advisory Committee: *Handbook of Best Practice in Children Act Cases* (1997) para 92. Stays should not normally be granted for more than 14 days: cf *Hereford and Worcester County Council v EH* [1985] FLR 975 at 977, per Wood J.

[509] See FPR 2010 r 30.11 and CPR 1998 r 52.10(2).

[510] Per Lord Scarman in *B v W (Wardship: Appeal)* [1979] 3 All ER 83 at 95–6, HL. The admission of fresh evidence is at the court's discretion: see *A v A (Custody Appeal: Role of Appellate Court)* [1988] 1 FLR 193, CA;

In deciding whether to allow an appeal there are no special rules governing appeals in cases involving children. Indeed, in *G v G (Custody: Appeal)*,[511] the House of Lords expressly rejected the argument that in children's cases appeals were subject to the paramountcy principle. As the Rules make clear, appeals to the High Court level and beyond are limited to a review of the lower court decision.[512] In other words they do not take the form of a rehearing.

G v G authoritatively established that an appellate court cannot overturn a first instance decision merely because it disagrees with it nor can it simply substitute its own view. Instead, according to *G v G*, it has to be satisfied that either the judge has erred as a matter of law (ie he applied the wrong principle) or that he relied upon evidence that he should have ignored or ignored evidence that he should have taken into account or that the decision was so 'plainly wrong' that the only legitimate conclusion was that the judge had erred in the exercise of his discretion. However, having to be satisfied that the lower court decision was 'plainly wrong' is not reflected in the Rules. According to the Rules an appeal will be allowed where the lower court decision was either 'wrong' or 'unjust because of a serious procedural or other irregularity in the proceedings of the lower court.'[513] What the correct test should be was re-visited by Supreme Court in *Re B (A Child) (Care Proceedings: Threshold Criteria)*.[514]

Re B was a public law case and, as we discuss in Chapter 17, it is authority for saying that *G v G* has no application to appeals against a determination that the statutory threshold has or has not been crossed or to whether a care order is a proportionate response to the harm or risk of harm found. In such cases an appeal will be allowed if the lower court decision is found to be 'wrong', nothing more, nothing less.[515] In reaching this conclusion the Supreme Court drew a distinction between appeals against evaluative decisions such as determining whether or the statutory threshold has been crossed for care proceedings or whether, for human rights purposes, a care order is proportionate and appeals against a judicial exercise of discretion as, for example, determining with whom a child is to live which was the concern of *G v G*.[516] By making this distinction the Supreme Court in *Re B* was able to distinguish *G v G*. On this analysis, and it should be cautioned that the judgments are not clear cut on this,[517] it follows that the ruling in *G v G* continues to apply to appeals against private law discretionary decisions concerning children such that, notwithstanding the Rules, outside legal or factual errors, an appeal can only succeed if the appellate court is satisfied that the lower court decision was 'plainly wrong'. However, the Justices of the Supreme Court, did not decide this point. Indeed, Lord Neuberger expressly left open the continued application of *G v G*.[518] It is also to be noted that in the subsequent decision, *Re A (Intractable Contact Dispute: Human Rights Violations)*[519] McFarlane LJ

M v M (Minor: Custody Appeal) [1987] 1 WLR 404, CA; *Re C (A Minor) (Wardship Proceedings)* [1984] FLR 419, CA; and *Ladd v Marshall* [1954] 3 All ER 745. The admission of fresh evidence may justify upholding the original decision even though it has been held plainly wrong: *M v M (Minor: Custody Appeal)*. Appeals concerning children do not, however, automatically call for an up-to-date welfare report: *M v M (Welfare Report)* [1989] 2 FLR 354, CA.

[511] [1985] 1 WLR 647, HL. See J Eekelaar 'Custody Appeals' (1985) 48 MLR 704 and J Robinson 'Appeals in Custody Cases' [1985] Fam Law 330.   [512] FPR 2010 r 30.12(1) and CPR 1998 r 52.11(1).

[513] FPR 2010 r 30.12(3) and CPR 1998 r 52.11(3).   [514] [2013] UKSC 33 [2013] 1 WLR 1911.

[515] See Lord Wilson at [47].

[516] See Lord Wilson at [44], Lord Neuberger at [96] and Baroness Hale at [202].

[517] As McFarlane LJ subsequently commented in *Re G (Care Proceedings: Welfare Evaluation)* [2014] 1 FLR 670 [2013] EWCA Civ 965 at [26], the decision in Re B is rich in detail in relation to the role of the appellate court and its full impact may fall to be considered in future cases.

[518] At [96].   [519] [2013] EWCA Civ 1104 [2014] 1 FLR 1185 at [46].

considered that even in the private law context, the *Re B* test applied, at any rate, to total denials of contact not least because of the application of human rights. Note might also be taken of Lord Wilson's comment that even where the *G v G* principles are jettisoned, the factors mentioned in the decision, namely that the judge considered an irrelevant matter, failed to consider a relevant matter, erred in law or applied a wrong principle continue to be relevant in determining whether the trial judge was wrong.

What is clear is that the *Re B* test does not apply to appeals from fact-finding determinations, in which an enormous margin of discretion and respect is given to the trial judge.[520]

Although it is a nice point as to the precise difference between 'wrong' and 'plainly wrong', the latter is a harder test than the former. As Lord Clarke said[521] 'if a plainly wrong test is adopted, it will be possible for an appellate court to hold that the judge was wrong to make [the] order but was not plainly wrong to do so.' But it is to be stressed that either test is difficult to satisfy, the underlying rationale being, as Lord Nicholls forcefully observed:[522]

> The Court of Appeal is not intended to be a forum in which unsuccessful litigants, where no error occurred at first instance, may have a second trial of the same issue by different judges under the guise of an appeal. The mere fact that appellate judges might have reached a different conclusion had they been carrying out the evaluation and balancing exercise does not mean that the first instance judge fell into error.

Whether the law should be so restrictive on appeal is debatable.[523] In *G v G* the House of Lords took the view that there is desirability in putting an end to litigation, particularly as in many cases there is no obviously right answer.[524] They also endorsed the view that an appellate court should be chary of overruling a decision, particularly in cases concerning the upbringing of children where it is so important to have seen the parties and witnesses.[525] There is nothing in *Re B* to gainsay these points.

C. OTHER POWERS

1. FAMILY ASSISTANCE ORDERS

Section 16 of the 1989 Act empowers the court to make a 'family assistance order'. Such an order requires either a Cafcass officer to be made available or the local authority[526] to make an officer of the authority available 'to advise, assist and (where appropriate) befriend any person named in the order'.[527] Those who may be named are: any parent

---

[520] See *Re B-S (Children) (Adoption Order: Leave to Oppose)* [2014] 1 WLR 563, per Munby P at [77] and *Re A (children) (Fact-finding appeal)* [2013] EWCA Civ 1026 [2014] 1 FCR 24. But for a rare example of an allowed appeal, see *Re M (Contact Refusal: Appeal)* [2014] Fam Law 148.   [521] At [139].

[522] *Re B (A Minor) (Adoption: Natural Parent)* [2001] UKHL 70 [2002] 1 WLR 258 at [17].

[523] See the excellent critique by Eekelaar, op cit. However, in terms of the non-application of the paramountcy principle, the decision can be justified on the basis that the appeal rules do not *directly* concern the child's upbringing and since those rules do not inhibit the appellate courts from being able to safeguard the child's interests, there is no need for special rules: see N Lowe 'The House of Lords and the welfare principle' in C Bridge (ed) *Family Law Towards the Millennium—Essays for P M Bromley* (1997) 125 at 158.

[524] See Lord Fraser [1985] 1 WLR at 651 referring to *Clarke-Hunt v Newcombe* (1983) 4 FLR 482 at 488, CA, per Cumming-Bruce LJ.   [525] See eg *Re F (A Minor) (Wardship: Appeal)* [1976] Fam 238, CA.

[526] Subject to s 16(7); see later.   [527] Section 16(1).

(which includes the unmarried father), guardian or special guardian of the child, any person named in an existing child arrangements order as a person with whom the child is to live or to spend time or otherwise have contact, and the child himself.[528]

This power replaced the former power to make supervision orders in private law proceedings and must in turn be distinguished from supervision orders made under s 31.[529] As the Department of Health's *Guidance and Regulations* put it:[530]

A supervision order is designed for the more serious cases, in which there is an element of child protection involved. By contrast, a family assistance order aims simply to provide short-term help to a family, to overcome the problems and conflicts associated with their separation or divorce. Help may well be focused more on the adult than the child.

These powers were amended by the Children and Adoption Act 2006.

(a) When orders may be made

Family assistance orders may be made in any 'family proceedings', whether or not any other order has been made.[531] The power may be exercised only by the court acting upon its own motion, though there is nothing to stop parties requesting the court to make such an order during the course of family proceedings.[532] However, the lack of the right to apply for such an order would seem to prevent parties from applying to the court *solely* for a family assistance order.

The former requirement that the circumstances of the case had to be 'exceptional' was removed by the Children and Adoption Act 2006, as part of a policy to enable such orders to be used more often particularly to facilitate contact. Nevertheless, as the revised *Guidance* comments[533] 'it will be particularly important in all orders for the court to make plain at the outset why family assistance is needed and what it is hoped to achieve by it.' In any event before a family assistance order may be made the court must have obtained the opinion of an appropriate officer about whether it would be in the best interests of the child for the order to be made and, if so, how the order could operate and for how long.[534]

Before any order can be made the court must be satisfied that the consent of every person named in the order, *other than the child*, has been obtained.[535] It may be noted that not only is there no formal requirement that the child himself should consent, there is no statutory requirement to ascertain the child's own wishes and feelings about such an order, since the enjoinder to do so under s 1(3) does not apply to making s 16 orders.[536] Nevertheless, there is nothing to prevent the court from discovering the child's view (nor

---

[528] Section 16(2), as amended.   [529] Discussed in Ch 17.

[530] Vol 1, *Court Orders* (1991), para 2.50 and cited by Wall J in *Re DH (A Minor) (Child Abuse)* [1994] 1 FLR 679 at 704. See also Law Com No 172 para 5.19. The revised 2008 Guidance (issue by the Department for Children, Schools and Families) at para 2.67 omits the reference to supervision orders and to adult focused help, commenting 'The nature of the help to be provided will normally be in assessment or case analysis provided by Cafcass to the court'.   [531] Section 16(1).

[532] Though note *Re F (Minors) (Denial of Contact)* [1993] 2 FLR 677 in which the Court of Appeal refused to consider making a family assistance order, since the point had not been argued at first instance and, in the absence of being able to show that the original order was wrong, the court had no power to make such an order or remit the case back.   [533] Vol 1, *Court Orders*, at para 2.69.

[534] *Practice Direction 12M Family Assistance Orders: Consultation.*   [535] Section 16(3)(b).

[536] See Ch 12, When the list applies, p 401. The Government rejected the recommendation of the Joint Committee on the Draft Children (Contact) and Adoption Bill HL Paper 100–1/HL 400–1, that this requirement of consent be removed on the basis that it would not be constructive to 'advise, assist and befriend' an unwilling or even hostile party. This rejection has not convinced everyone. Indeed the President's Interdisciplinary Conference urged the Government to reconsider their opposition to the recommendation.

from applying the whole s 1(3) checklist) and where the child is mature enough to make his own decisions, it would seem prudent to do so.

A family assistance order may not be made requiring a local authority to make one of its officers available unless the authority agrees or the child concerned lives or will live in its area.[537] It is not a proper use of a family assistance order to require a local authority to provide someone for escort duty where no family member is prepared to take the children to visit their father in prison.[538]

(b) Effect and duration of order

Section 16 gives no guidance as to which officer should be appointed nor is it clear whether the court is empowered to appoint a particular Cafcass officer or Welsh family proceedings officer or a particular type of local authority officer (for example, a housing officer rather than one from social services).[539] In the private law context the most appropriate appointee is likely to be the children and family reporter who has compiled the welfare report for the court, while in care proceedings, the obvious candidate is the social worker attached to the particular case.

Under s 16(4) a family assistance order may direct specified persons named in the order to keep the address of any person named in the order so that he can visit them. As originally enacted, if a s 8 order was also in force, the officer was empowered to refer to the court the question of whether a s 8 order should be varied or discharged.[540] However, the Children and Adoption Act 2006 strengthened this provision, which now provides that where a s 8 order is also in force the family assistance order 'may direct the officer concerned to report to the court on such matters relating to the section 8 order as the court may require (including the question whether the section 8 order ought to be varied or discharged)'.[541] In addition, where a child arrangements order containing contact provision is in force the family assistance order 'may direct the officer concerned to give advice and assistance as regards establishing, improving and maintaining contact to such of the persons named in the order as may be specified in the order'.[542]

A family assistance order is intended to be only a short-term remedy. Section 16(5) originally provided that unless a shorter period is specified the order will have effect only for six months from the day on which it is made, but this period was extended to 12 months by the Children and Adoption Act 2006. There is no restriction on making any further order.[543]

(c) Family assistance orders in practice

According to the *Children Act Report 1995–1999*[544] there were about 600 to around 1,000 family assistance order made annually in the 1990s but in recent years the numbers have

---

[537] Section 16(7) and see *Statutory Guidance on court orders and pre-proceedings* (DfE, 2014) para 12. But see *Re C (Family Assistance Order)* [1996] 1 FLR 424 where, having made an assistance order directing the local authority to make an officer available, the local authority subsequently returned to the court to say that it did not have the resources to carry the order out. Johnson J declined to take further action.

[538] *S v P (Contact Application: Family Assistance Order)* [1997] 2 FLR 277. Cf *Re E (Family Assistance Order)* [1999] 2 FLR 512, discussed at Family assistance orders in practice, p 549.

[539] See L Coubrough 'Family Assistance Orders' [1993] Fam Law 598.

[540] Section 16(6).   [541] Section 16(6) as inserted by s 6(5) of the 2006 Act.

[542] Section 16(4A) added by s 6(3) of the 2006 Act and further amended by the Children and Families Act 2014 Sch 2 para 27.

[543] See Department of Health's *Guidance and Regulations*, op cit, at para 2.52, and the implicit acceptance of that proposition by Booth J in *Leeds County Council v C* [1993] 1 FLR 269 at 272.

[544] Cm 4579, January 2000.

fluctuated.[545] According to the Cafcass Annual Report 2012–2013, only 355 orders were made in 2012–2013, a drop from 590 the previous year.[546] Clearly a key factor is the availability of resources.[547]

The few reported cases show that a major role of family assistance orders is in facilitating contact. In *Re G (Children) (Residence: Same Sex Partner)*,[548] for example, a family assistance order was initially made together with a shared residence order in the context of a residence and a contact dispute between same sex partners and was renewed by the House of Lords essentially to help the parties make the contact arrangements work in the light of the decision that the primary residence of the children should be with their biological mother. In *Re M (Contact Family Assistance Order)*[549] the Court of Appeal proposed (subject to obtaining the mother's consent)[550] making a family assistance order to facilitate indirect contact between the children and their father in respect of whom the mother had a genuine fear. In *Leeds City Council v C*,[551] Booth J held that the only appropriate way in which a court could make provision for supervision of contact by a local authority was by an order under s 16 and not by attaching a condition under s 11(7). However, in *Re DH (A Minor) (Child Abuse)*[552] Wall J observed that while:

> . . . in the conventional case a supervision order under s 31 will not be appropriate where the object is simply to achieve contact supervised by a local authority . . . where the threshold criteria under s 31 are met in relation to the necessity for contact to be supervised, it may be appropriate to make a supervision order rather than an order under s 16.

Despite this comment it is evident that family assistance orders have a useful role to play in providing local authority assistance to supervise contact.[553] In *Re E (Family Assistance Order)*[554] a family assistance order was made against the wishes of a local authority (into whose area the family had moved) in order to supervise contact between a child and her mother who was in a psychiatric unit. A family assistance order was also made in *Re U (Application to Free for Adoption)*,[555] where, in the context of adoption proceedings, what

---

[545] See *Assisting Families by Court Order* (HMICA Report, 2007), *Making Contact Work* (A Report to the Lord Chancellor by the Advisory Board on Family Law: Children Act Sub Committee, 2002) Ch 11, L Trinder and N Stone 'Family assistance order—professional aspiration and party frustration' [1998] CFLQ 291 and J Seden 'Family Assistance Orders and the Children Act: Ambivalence About Intervention or a Means of Safeguarding and Promoting Children's Welfare?' (2001) 15 Int Jo of Law, Policy and the Family 226. For an examination of the pre-2006 Act practice see A James and L Sturgeon-Adams *Helping families after divorce: Assistance by order?* (1999).

[546] HC 316 (July 2013), p 17. In 2009, 394 orders were made and in 2010, 528, *Cafcass Annual Report 2010-11* (HC 1198, 2011).

[547] Lack of funding was one of the problems of having effective family assistance orders identified by Bracewell J in *V v V (Contact: Implacable Hostility)* [2004] EWHC 1215 (Fam), [2004] 2 FLR 851 at [11]. But another factor that might weigh against expanded use is the continuing nature of such orders and the consequential problems that that poses for the courts and support services alike in meeting performance indicators.   [548] [2006] UKHL 43 [2006] 1 WLR 2305.

[549] [1999] 1 FLR 75, CA. A s 91(14) order was also added to prevent the father making an application to the court without leave before the expiration of the family assistance order.

[550] This part of the order was directed to lie on the file for 14 days to give the mother (who was not at the appellate hearing), through her solicitors, the opportunity to consent to the order being made.

[551] [1993] 1 FLR 269.   [552] [1994] 1 FLR 679 at 702.

[553] *B v B (Child Abuse: Contact)* [1994] 2 FLR 713 at 738, ironically also per Wall J. See also *Re R (A Minor) (Residence: Religion)* [1993] 2 FLR 163, CA.   [554] [1999] 2 FLR 512.

[555] [1993] 2 FLR 992, CA. See also *T v S (Wardship)* [2011] EWHC 1608 (Fam) [2012] 1 FLR 230, in which a family assistance order was made for six months in the context of continued disputation between the parents and in which a detailed order within wardship was made whereby the child was to live with mother but spend increasing time with the father.

was then a residence order was granted to grandparents, the Court of Appeal felt that a s 16 order was a useful way of monitoring the child's placement with them.

2. SECTION 37 DIRECTIONS

Before the Children Act 1989 courts could, in exceptional circumstances, commit children upon their own motion into local authority care or make supervision orders in private law proceedings. This power ran counter to the policy under the 1989 Act to have just one route into care. Accordingly, it was abolished. Under s 37, however, if in *any* family proceedings, 'it appears to the court that it may be appropriate for a care or supervision order to be made . . . the court may direct the appropriate authority to undertake an investigation of the child's circumstances'.

Section 37 empowers a court to direct that an investigation is undertaken but it has no power to direct a local authority to bring care proceedings.[556] All that an authority is bound to do under the direction is to undertake the investigation but if after doing so they decide not to apply for a care or supervision order they must inform the court of their reasons for so deciding.[557] Nevertheless if the court is satisfied that the local authority has not complied with the direction or has failed to conduct an investigation that meets the court's concerns, it may extend or renew its direction.[558]

Although courts are not empowered to commit a child into care they can, when making a direction, make an interim care order (provided the relevant criteria are satisfied).[559] As the section itself says and the courts have subsequently emphasised, s 37 directions should only be made where it appears that it might be appropriate to make a public law order. It is therefore generally inappropriate in a purely private law dispute but, while not a panacea, it can on occasion be useful in intractable contact disputes provided there is a coherent care plan of which temporary or permanent removal of the children from the parents is an integral part.[560] Even so it is a drastic order and should not be resorted to even in intractable contact disputes unless there is no alternative.[561]

---

[556] The absence of any such power to direct local authorities to take steps to protect children was criticised in *Nottingham County Council v P* [1994] Fam 18, by Sir Stephen Brown P. See also Mr Justice Wall 'The courts and child protection—the challenge of hybrid cases' [1997] 9 CFLQ 345 at 348–50.

[557] Section 37(3). Unless the court directs otherwise, the local authority must inform the court within eight weeks of the direction: s 37(4).

[558] *Re K (children) (care orders: jurisdiction to renew interim care orders* [2012] EWCA Civ 1549 [2013] 1 FCR 87.

[559] Section 38(1)(b). Interim care orders are discussed in Ch 17.

[560] See eg *Re M (Intractable Contact Dispute: Interim Care Order)* [2003] EWHC 1024 (Fam) [2003] 2 FLR 636. But cf *A v A (Shared Residence)* [2004] EWHC 142 (Fam) [2004] 1 FLR 1195 where a direction was held inappropriate because of the substantial delay that it would engender when the children were in urgent need of respite care and crucially because foster care was inappropriate; and *Re L (Section 37 Direction)* [1999] 1 FLR 984 CA where the case was nowhere near the public law threshold. For other cases on the application of s 37 see eg *Re CE (Section 37 Direction)* [1995] 1 FLR 26, on the consequential role of the guardian; *Re M (Official Solicitor's Role)* [1998] 2 FLR 815, CA—inappropriate to use s 37 if the Official Solicitor is invited to investigate, and *Re H (A Minor) (Section 37 Direction)* [1993] 2 FLR 541—where direction is given 'child's circumstances' should be widely construed.

[561] See *Re F (Family Proceedings: Section 37 Investigation)* [2005] EWHC 2935 (Fam) [2006] 1 FLR 1122, a s 37 report not ordered on condition that the father agreed to a child psychiatrist seeing children (whose negative views of the mother had been encouraged by the father) and assessing their views.

D. SOME FINAL REMARKS

Resolving private disputes over the upbringing of children is a major part of the court's family law workload. Despite considerable efforts to encourage parties to settle their disputes through mediation or other alternative dispute mechanisms, the number of applications has continued to rise. Whether they will continue to do so, following the withdrawal of legal aid for most private law disputes and the reforms introduced by the Children and Families Act 2014, for example by making attendance at a Mediation Information and Assessment Meeting (MIAM) compulsory and by replacing residence and contact orders with child arrangements orders, remains to be seen.

As we have discussed, the Children Act 1989, in its radical reform of child law, attempted to overcome the 'win/lose' nature of parental disputes in court by preserving the parents' parental responsibility following their divorce or separation regardless of the subsequent living arrangements for the child, and by replacing custody and access orders with what was intended to be the less emotive residence and contact orders. These reforms were not as effective as had been hoped. The 2014 Act has replaced residence and contact orders with child arrangement orders again with the hope that they do not attract the same emotional baggage that became attached to residence and contact orders. Whether this reform will be any more successful than the 1989 Act reform again remains to be seen, but one fears that it may not. As one High Court Judge has written extra-judicially:[562]

> It might be slightly cynical to ask whether those that loaded the terms residence and contact will find a way to load the new terms as well.

---

[562] The Hon Mr Justice Moylan J 'Custody, care and control: to shared parental responsibility' [2013] Fam Law 1538 at 1546.

15

CHILDREN AND LOCAL AUTHORITIES

A. INTRODUCTION

In this and Chapters 16–18 we are concerned with child protection issues or with what might broadly be called the public law concerning children.

1. SOME BASIC DILEMMAS

As a long list of often headline grabbing tragedies in which children have died at the hands of their parents or family members (notable examples include Baby Peter, Victoria Climbié, Kimberley Carlile, Jasmine Beckford, Maria Colwell and Dennis O'Neill)[1] bear testimony, it is not always safe for children to be brought by their own family. Such children can fairly be said to have been let down by the State. But not all cases are so clear cut for there is a variety of reasons why parents cannot or should not be allowed to look after their own children. They may be prevented from doing so by illness or the child may be beyond their control. Alternatively, they may be unwilling or unfit to bring up their own child: they may have abandoned the child; physically or sexually abused the child; or they may have neglected the child. The dilemma for the State is how, if at all, it should best intervene. If the law is too strict or intervention is too late, the child may be seriously harmed or worse; if the law is too liberal or intervention is too early then family life will have been violated to the detriment of the child and the family. Examples raising the latter issue include the Cleveland crisis[2] in which over 200 children were removed from their families (often at the crack of dawn) on the grounds of suspected child abuse, essentially because two paediatricians had developed a diagnosis (now discredited) based on anal dilation. Although some of the removals were found to be justified, many, too many, were found not to be. Another example of unjustified removal of children occurred in the so-called 'Satanic ring' cases in Rochdale in 1990[3] and Orkneys in 1991[4] based on what turned out to be unfounded allegations of ritual child abuse.

While the issues raised by the cases already mentioned are difficult enough, there are others. For example, should not children be protected from a *risk* of harm? If parents have harmed their first child ought not a second child be removed before any harm can be perpetrated on him or her? But if 'harm' is hard to prove, how much harder is it to show a

---

[1] In the case of Baby Peter, see the serious case review by London Borough of Haringey (2009). For short accounts of the circumstances surrounding the other cases, see S Cretney *Family Law in the Twentieth Century* (2003) ch 20. For a reflective review, see Sir M Hedley 'Family life and child protection: Cleveland, Baby P et al' [2014] CFLQ 7.

[2] See the *Report of the Inquiry into Child Abuse in Cleveland 1987*, Cm 412 1988 (the 'Butler-Sloss Report').

[3] *Rochdale Borough Council v A* [1991] 2 FLR 192.

[4] See W Ackroyd 'The Orkney and Rochdale Cases' [1991] Fam Law 207.

'risk' of harm? Further, what should the position be if it can only be shown that the child was harmed by one of the parents but not which one?

How far is State intervention justified in cases of emotional neglect and how should parental illness, inability or poverty be handled? In some of these cases, at least, the better course of action is for the State to provide support rather than seek to remove the child from his or her family. But for how long should that support be provided?

Last, but not least, by whose standard should 'care' be judged? Is a family's cultural background relevant? In other words, should behaviour that is tolerated in another culture be tolerated here?

The dilemmas mentioned show just how difficult this area is, even in theory, let alone in practice, and it should come as no surprise that the issues have occupied senior court time on numerous occasions.

2. THE GENERAL ROLE OF THE COURTS AND LOCAL AUTHORITIES

Although the law has been shaped by reports on and the lessons to be learned from the tragedies already mentioned,[5] and in the past has oscillated between focussing on child protection and on parental rights, the current position very much concentrates on the child's well-being. In broad terms the current position is that no child may be compulsorily removed from his or her family without a court order (known as a 'care order') to that effect. No care order can be made unless a minimum threshold, provided by s 31(1) of the Children Act 1989 (discussed in Chapter 17), can be established and even where it can, the court must (a) be sure that no other solution is appropriate, and (b) be satisfied, applying the paramountcy principle, that it is in the child's best interests to make the order.

The front line task of supporting families, investigating the child's circumstances and seeking court orders[6] is entrusted to local authorities (more specifically, after the Children Act 2004, children's services authorities). It is a daunting task and one which itself has been the subject of constant review.

In this chapter we explain the basic legal framework and provisions for local authorities to provide services for families. In Chapter 16 we concentrate on the local authorities' investigative powers and duties, while in Chapter 17 we discuss care and supervision orders and, finally, in Chapter 18 we consider the position of children being looked after by local authorities.

3. AN OVERVIEW OF THE DEVELOPMENT OF LOCAL AUTHORITY POWERS

(a) Pre-1989 developments

Before the 1989 Act reforms,[7] the law was based on two Acts, namely the Child Care Act 1980 and the Children and Young Persons Act 1969. The former Act consolidated earlier

[5] It is now a requirement for the local authority to hold a 'serious case review' to investigate the circumstances surrounding the death of a child being looked after by a local authority: Children Act 2004 s 14 (2) and see HM Government *Working Together to Safeguard Children—A guide to inter-agency working to safeguard and promote the welfare of children* (2013) ch 5.

[6] Though, note the NSPCC may also seek court orders, see Ch 17.

[7] For a masterly historical survey see S Cretney *Family Law in the Twentieth Century* (2003) chs 18 and 19 and L Fox Harding *Perspectives in Child Care Policy* (1997) and N Parton *Governing the Family: Child Care, Child Protection and the State* (1991).

Acts, principally the Children Act 1948, parts of the Children and Young Persons Act 1963, and the Children Act 1975. The Children Act 1948 resulted from a report of the Curtis Committee,[8] which was set up to inquire into existing methods of providing for children deprived of a normal home life, particularly as a result of the evacuation of children during the Second World War, and to consider what steps should be taken to ensure that they were brought up under conditions best calculated to compensate for their lack of parental care. Reflecting the concerns of the Committee the 1948 Act imposed on a local authority a duty to receive a deprived child into care in certain circumstances and then to bring him up according to his best interests. Wherever possible the authority had to secure his discharge from care to parents, relatives or friends as soon as may be.

During the 1950s there was an increasing awareness of the need to prevent families breaking up and children being received into care. Social and economic factors were seen to be important in family difficulties. Juvenile delinquency began to be attributed in many instances to 'deprivation' rather than 'depravity'. It was thought that intensive preventative work with families could help to solve the problems of offenders and non-offenders.

The Ingleby Committee,[9] set up in 1956, investigated these matters and subsequently the Children and Young Persons Act 1963 was enacted, under which all local authorities had, as their first duty, to give advice, guidance and assistance to diminish the need to receive children into care.

Prevention and rehabilitation became the keynote of much of the subsequent work of local authorities, and it was expected that this would lead to an improvement in the prevention of delinquency.

These principles were further emphasised in the Children and Young Persons Act 1969. Both offenders and non-offenders were to be dealt with in the same system, and the provisions were designed to discourage either coming before the courts. For both, the powers of the court were directed towards treatment. In fact, the objective of reducing the relevance of criminal law by raising the age of criminal responsibility was never implemented.

In the 1970s questions were again raised about the nature and efficiency of child care services. Difficulties were experienced as a result of changes in the structure of local authorities.[10] Children's departments, previously responsible for services to children and their families, were replaced by larger social services departments with responsibilities not just for children but for the elderly and the vulnerable as well. The creation of a profession to manage all these different needs inevitably lowered the level of child care expertise and raised workloads. All this in a bureaucratic structure made it impossible in many instances for local authorities to provide the personalised services for children envisaged in the 1948 Act.

Lack of constructive long-term planning for children caused increasing concern. In spite of the apparent emphasis on returning children to their parents, it was considered that substantial numbers of children in care were unlikely ever to go back to their families and could not benefit from waiting in vain hope that they would do so.[11]

There was a rising body of opinion that it was not necessarily in a child's interest to return to his or her natural parents. This was given philosophical expression in the book *Beyond the Best Interests of the Child*,[12] where the importance of the 'psychological' parent

---

[8] Cmd 6922. For a full and fascinating discussion both of the circumstances before the setting up of the Committee and of the Report itself see S Cretney *Family Law in the Twentieth Century* (2003) pp 671–85 and 'The State as a Parent: The Children Act 1948 in Retrospect' (1998) 114 LQR 419 and for a shorter version see 'The Children Act 1948—Lessons for today?' [1997] CFLQ 359.   [9] Cmnd 1191.

[10] Under the Local Authority Social Services Act 1970.

[11] See J Rowe and L Lambert *Children Who Wait* (1973).

[12] J Goldstein, A Freud and A Solnit (1973).

(that is, the child's primary carer) was emphasised. The issue came into the public eye, however, in 1973 when a child, Maria Colwell, was killed by her stepfather after she had been removed from foster parents.[13] Inevitably, there was a demand for a curtailment of parental rights, so that children could be better protected from parental rejection, and plans could be made for their long-term welfare. In any event, the trend towards greater recognition of children as individuals could not be ignored. The resulting legislation, the Children Act 1975, accordingly required a local authority to give first consideration to the need to safeguard and promote the welfare of the child throughout his childhood.

Still different concerns were being voiced in the 1980s. Studies had raised awareness of the damage that local authority care (however well-meaning) could do to family links,[14] but this in turn 'encouraged local authorities to operate strong gate-keeping techniques to prevent children entering the system' with the result that care was denied to those who needed it. Yet another concern highlighted by the 'Cleveland crisis'[15] was whether local authorities had become too powerful at the expense of family autonomy.

The Children Act 1989 attempted to take on board the lessons and experience of the past and to draw anew the balance between family autonomy and local authority powers to protect children. Furthermore, in striking contrast to the previous law, the 1989 Act provides a comprehensive and unified scheme for dealing with children in need. However, before examining the position under that Act it is useful to advert to some post-1989 Act developments.

(b) Post-1989 Act developments

Notwithstanding the reforms made by the 1989 Act, a series of inquiries and reports during the 1990s and 2000s showed that there continued to be problems in protecting children and these in turn prompted further legislation. One period of activity began in the late 1990s with the 'Quality Protects' programme in England[16] and 'Children First' in Wales,[17] and continued with the publication in 2002 of the Joint Chief Inspector's report *Safeguarding Children*[18] and in 2003 of the *Report of the Inquiry into the Death of Victoria Climbié*[19] (Victoria had been starved to death by her carers who had repeatedly frustrated attempts by social workers to check on Victoria's well-being) and the Government's response to the latter two reports in its paper *Keeping Children Safe*.[20] One result of these enquiries and reports was to shift the emphasis from child protection to the safeguarding of children. As *Keeping Children Safe* put it,[21] the reports 'show us how to move towards a better children's safeguards system, where child protection services are not separate from support for families, but are part of the spectrum of services provided to help and support children and families'.

The legislative response to the reports mentioned together with the Government's Green Paper *Every Child Matters*,[22] was the Children Act 2004. That Act did a number of things, including strengthening the support services for children and their families,

---

[13] See the *Report of the Committee of Inquiry into the Care and Supervision provided in relation to Maria Colwell* (1974) HMSO.

[14] See eg S Millham, R Bullock, K Hosie and J Haak *Lost in Care* (1986) and *Social Work Decisions in Child Care* (1985).

[15] Which was concerned with the scope of removal of scores of children because of alleged sexual abuse; and on which see the highly influential *Report of the Inquiry into Child Abuse in Cleveland 1987* Cm 412 1988 (the 'Butler-Sloss Report').

[16] See *Quality Protects Circular: Transforming Children's Services* LAC (98) 28.

[17] *The Children First Programme in Wales: Transforming Children's Services*, Welsh Office Circular 20/97.

[18] Department of Health, 2002.   [19] Cm 5730 (2003).   [20] Cm 5861 (2003).

[21] Ibid para 4.   [22] Cm 5860 (2003).

ensuring clear accountability for children's services which has involved, as referred to at the beginning of this chapter, making fundamental changes to local authority organisational structure, and ensuring a voice for children and young people at a national level through the establishment in England of a Children's Commissioner[23] (Wales had already made provision for a Children's Commissioner).[24] The 2004 Act also imposed a new duty on local authorities to promote the educational achievement of children being looked after by them.[25]

The 2004 Act was amended by the Childcare Act 2006,[26] which introduced a new legal framework for the integrated regulation and inspection of early education and childcare services, placed duties on local authorities to improve the outcomes for young children, securing sufficient childcare and providing information to children. That Act also imposed new duties on local authorities to improve the well-being of young children in their area.[27]

Another development was the publication in 2006 of the Review *of the Child Care Proceedings System in England and Wales*, the major concern of which was the spiralling costs of care proceedings (which rose 42% in the five years running up to the review).[28] Overall, the Review's recommendations aimed to avoid court proceedings where possible or desirable and recommended in particular more consistent use of pre-proceedings initiatives such as family group conferences (ie voluntary conferences led by family members to plan and make decisions for a child at risk)[29], the positive engagement with families and children and to improve professional relationships and inter-agency working.

In June 2007 the Government published another White Paper *Care Matters: Time for Change*[30] which set out plans to improve outcomes for children being looked after by local authorities. This led to the passing of the Children and Young Persons Act 2008 which introduced further reform of the statutory framework for the care system in England and Wales. This Act placed a general duty on the Secretary of State to promote the well-being of children in England.[31] It made provision for the accommodation and maintenance of looked after children including a new power to create a mechanism for the independent review of decisions by fostering service providers.

Since the 2008 legislation there have been two further reviews of local authority practice. The more specific review was that conducted by Professor Munro, whose final report (the 'Munro Review') was published in 2011.[32] Many of the Munro recommendations were aimed at improving day-to-day practice but among its more institutional recommendations were that local authorities should have a duty to secure sufficient provision of local early help services for children, young people and families, that they should designate a Principal Child and Family Social Worker who is a senior manager with lead

---

[23] Discussed in Ch 13.

[24] See the Children's Commissioner for Wales Act 2001, discussed in Ch 13.

[25] See s 52 of the 2004 Act adding s 22(3A) to the 1989 Act. This provision has been strengthened by s 9 of the Children and Families Act 2014 (adding s 22(3B) and (3C) to the 1989 Act), which requires local authorities in England to appoint a local authority officer for the purpose of discharging this duty.

[26] By s 16.   [27] Childcare Act 2006 Part 1 (England) and Part 2 (Wales).

[28] Other concerns were the complexity of cases and the unnecessarily adversarial nature of proceedings.

[29] See DfE *Statutory guidance on court orders and pre-proceedings* (2014) p 15.

[30] Cm 7137 (2007).

[31] See s 7. This provision does not apply to Wales where the care of children is a devolved issue. An important measure, though it does not exactly equate to the 2008 Act, is the Children and Families (Wales) Measure 2010, on which see O Rees 'Devolution and Family law in Wales: A Potential for Doing Things Differently?' (2012) 33 *Statute Law Review* 192 at 200.

[32] *The Munro Review of Child Protection: a child-centred system*, for a summary of which see [2011] Fam Law 655. See also [2011] Fam Law 1321–2 and [2012] Fam Law 894–5.

responsibility for practice in the local authority and who is still actively involved in front-line practice, and that a Chief Social Worker should be created in Government inter alia to advise Government on social work practice. The Review also recommended improvement to the recruiting and training of social workers.

In the more general review, the *Family Justice Review* (the 'Norgrove Review'),[33] concern focused on the problem of delay in court proceedings, which is an issue that will be discussed in Chapter 17. However, outside this important issue, concern was expressed about the poor relationship between the courts and local authorities and mechanisms to promote dialogue between the two were recommended. Another concern centred on the working of the independent reviewing officers and the Review recommended that the local authorities review their operation.[34]

4. THE CURRENT LAW: SOME KEY UNDERLYING PRINCIPLES

The powers and duties of local authorities to protect and care for children derive from the Children Act 1989, as amended.

(a) Non-intervention

One of the great achievements of the Children Act 1989 was to provide a single comprehensive code governing both private and public law. As we have seen in previous chapters, one of the underlying philosophies of the Act is that of non-intervention by the State in family life. As Lord Mackay said in his Joseph Jackson Memorial Lecture:[35]

> . . . the integrity and independence of the family is the basic building block of a free and democratic society and the need to defend it should be clearly perceivable in the law. Accordingly, unless there is evidence that a child is being or is likely to be positively harmed because of a failure in the family, the state, whether in the guise of a local authority or a court, should not interfere.

This basic non-interventionist standpoint is emphasised by the fact that compulsory measures affecting children can only be taken following a court order and that no order may be made unless the basic threshold of 'significant harm' can be proved. Moreover, the presumption under s 1(5)[36] that no order should be made at all unless it is for the child's welfare applies equally to proceedings involving local authorities. Consequently, even where some form of court order is thought justified, the court may still not make an order placing the child in local authority care if it thinks that an alternative s 8 order in favour of an individual rather than the State would be better. In any event, to be human rights compliant, any intervention must be proportionate to the harm or risk of harm.

(b) Working in partnership with parents

A second key principle, allied both to the non-intervention principle and to the enduring nature of parental responsibility, is that local authorities must work in partnership with the parents. There is a strong emphasis on authorities making voluntary agreements with

---

[33] The final report of which was published in November 2011.

[34] The Government accepted this recommendation and promised to support the review, see *The Government Response to the Family Justice Review—A system with children and families at its heart* (Cm 8273, 2012), p 59.

[35] (1989) 139 NLJ 505 at 507.   [36] Discussed in detail in Ch 12.

parents for the benefit of their children. As the Department of Health's *Guidance* put it at the time the 1989 Act was implemented:[37]

> One of the key principles of the Children Act is that responsible authorities should work in partnership with the parents of a child who is being looked after and also with the child himself, where he is of sufficient understanding, provided that this approach will not jeopardise his welfare. A second, closely related principle is that parents and children should participate actively in the decision-making process. Partnership will only be achieved if parents are advised about and given explanations of the local authority's powers and duties and of the actions the local authority may need to take, for example, exchanges of information between relevant agencies . . . This new approach reflects the fact that parents always retain their parental responsibility. A local authority may limit parents' exercise of that responsibility when a child is looked after by a local authority as a result of a court order, but only if it is necessary to do so to safeguard and promote the child's welfare . . .
>
> The development of a successful working partnership between the responsible authorities and the parents and the child, where he is of sufficient understanding, should enable the placement to proceed positively so that the child's welfare is safeguarded and promoted.

The encouragement to work in partnership should not, however, be misconstrued: it does not mean that compulsory measures to remove children from their families cannot be taken until voluntary efforts have failed. If the child's welfare demands it, compulsory measures should immediately be taken.[38]

Not unrelated to the partnership ideal is the vision that the services which, under Part III of the Act, local authorities are obliged to provide, should be seen as a positive response to the needs of children and not as a mark of failure by the family or the professionals.

(c) Maintenance of links between the child and his family

In cases where it is necessary for children to live away from home either as a result of voluntary agreement or compulsory intervention, stress is repeatedly placed on the importance of children maintaining links with their family. As *The Care of Children: Principles and Practice in Regulations and Guidance* puts it:[39]

> There are unique advantages for children in experiencing normal family life in their own birth family and every effort should be made to preserve the child's home and family links.

Local authorities are under a general duty when safeguarding the welfare of children in need to promote the upbringing of children by their families[40] and, if they are looking after[41] the child, to endeavour to promote contact between the child and his parents.[42] Even when in local authority care or subject to an emergency protection order there is a presumption that the child will have reasonable contact with his family. Local authorities wishing to restrict this must obtain the prior sanction of the court.[43]

---

[37] Vol 3, *Family Placements* (1991) paras 2.10 and 2.11.
[38] See *Children Act Report 1992* para 2.21.
[39] (HMSO, 1989) p 8.   [40] Children Act 1989 s 17(1)(b).
[41] For the meaning of this see Ch 18, Local authority duties towards 'looked after children', pp 660ff.
[42] Children Act 1989 Sch 2 para 15.
[43] Ibid s 34, discussed in Ch 18, Contact with children in care, pp 654ff.

(d) Summary of good social work practice

Building on the basic principles of the 1989 Act as just described, the Government's revised *Guidance and Regulations*[44] explains that good social care practice recognises the following principles when working with children and their families:

> Time is a crucial element in work with children and should be reckoned in days and months rather than years.
>
> Parents should be expected and enabled to retain their responsibilities and to remain as closely involved as is consistent with their children's welfare, even if that child cannot live at home whether temporarily or permanently.
>
> If children have to live apart from their family, both they and their parents should be given adequate information and helped to consider alternatives and contribute to the making of an informed choice about the most appropriate form of care.
>
> Continuity of relationships is important and attachments should be respected, sustained and developed.
>
> A change of home, carer, social worker or school almost always carries some risk to a child's development and welfare.
>
> All children need to develop their own identity, including self-confidence and a sense of self-worth.

B. LOCAL AUTHORITY SUPPORT FOR CHILDREN AND FAMILIES

Part III of the 1989 Act contains provisions relating to the services that a local authority must or may provide for children and their families.[45] For the first time services for children in need and disabled children were brought together under one statute. The provisions are intended to enable authorities to support family life, although they may in certain circumstances charge for the service. The Children Act 2004 requires local authorities (that is, the children's services authorities) to make arrangements to promote co-operation between themselves and key partner agencies and other relevant bodies, including the voluntary and community sector, to improve the well-being of children in the area.[46] For these purposes 'well-being' refers to physical and mental health and emotional well-being; protection from harm and neglect; education, training and recreation; the contribution made by them to society; and social and economic well-being.[47] Furthermore, in making such arrangements authorities must have regard to the importance of parents and other persons caring for children in improving the well-being of children.[48]

It is tempting for lawyers to overlook this part of the Act, especially as it does not deal with 'court-based' law. Nevertheless, it is not without relevance to the practising lawyer since such services, both in the sense of past support to a particular family and what

---

[44] Vol 2 *Care Planning, Placement and Case Review* (2010) para 1.5.

[45] Note: in Wales there are plans to repeal Part III and replace it with provisions governing both children and adults, see the Social Services and Well-being (Wales) Bill 2014.

[46] Sections 10 (England), 25 (Wales). For a short explanation of the aims and background to the 2004 Act, see the Explanatory Notes to the Act. The key partner agencies are defined in ss 10(4) and 25(4) respectively.

[47] Sections 10(2) and 25(2).

[48] These duties are further widened by the Childcare Act 2006 in three discrete areas: improving outcomes for young children, securing sufficient childcare and providing information to parents. Part 1 applies to England, Part 2 to Wales.

future support might be given, are important factors in deciding whether or not to make a care order. Furthermore as one commentary[49] points out, there is 'an inextricable link between the provision of support and minimal intervention, which shapes the functions of both local authorities and the courts.' Research[50] has shown that, at any rate in the past, this link is 'frequently under-emphasised by professionals'.

1. GENERAL DUTY TO CHILDREN IN NEED

Under s 17(1) every local authority has a general[51] duty:

> (a) to safeguard and promote the welfare of children in their area who are in need; and
> (b) so far as is consistent with that duty to promote the upbringing of such children by their families,
> by providing a range and level of services appropriate to those needs.

A child[52] is defined as being 'in need' if:[53]

> (a) he is unlikely to achieve or maintain, or to have the opportunity of achieving or maintaining a reasonable standard of health or development without the provision for him of services by a local authority under this Part;
> (b) his health or development is likely to be significantly impaired or further impaired, without the provision for him of such services; or
> (c) he is disabled.

For these purposes 'health' means physical or mental health and 'development' means physical, intellectual, emotional, social or behavioural development.[54]

It will be appreciated that this definition is wide. Furthermore, as the Department of Health's 1991 *Guidance* observes:[55]

> Sometimes the needs will be found to be intrinsic to the child, at other times however it may be that parenting skills and resources are depleted or under-developed and thus threaten the child's well-being.

The duties owed to a child in need do not cease merely because the child is in a Young Offenders Institution or other prison establishment.[56]

---

[49] *Butterworths Family Law Service* at 3A [2201.6].

[50] Dept of Health *Child Protection Messages from Research* (2003) 23.

[51] *R (G) v Barnet London Borough Council; R (W) v Lambeth London Borough Council; R (A) v Lambeth London Borough Council* [2003] UKHL 57 [2004] 2 AC 208, on which see D Cowan 'On need and gate keeping' [2004] CFLQ 331. The inclusion of the word 'general' was intended to reverse *A-G (ex rel Tilley) v London Borough of Wandsworth* [1981] 1 All ER 1162, which had held under the former law that the welfare duty applied to individual children.

[52] Ie. a person under the age of 18: Children Act 1989 s 105(1). Under normal canons of interpretation 'child' means a 'live' child and therefore has no application to unborn children: see *Elliot v Joicey* [1935] AC 209, HL and *R v Newham London Borough Council, ex p Dada* [1996] QB 507, CA. The local authority must assess the age of a person claiming to be under the age of 18 and give adequate reasons for deciding that he is not: *R (B) v Merton London Borough Council* [2003] EWHC 1689 (Admin) [2003] 2 FLR 888. Note also *R (A) v Croydon London Borough Council; R (M) v Lambeth London Borough Council* [2009] UKSC 8 [2009] 1 WLR 2557, discussed at The 'duty' to accommodate, p 564.   [53] Section 17(10).

[54] Section 17(11). This is the same definition as in s 31(9) in care proceedings: see Ch 17.

[55] Vol 2 para 2.5.

[56] *R (Howard League for Penal Reform) v Secretary of State for the Home Department* [2002] EWHC 2497 (Admin) [2003] 1 FLR 484 and *R (D) v Secretary of State for the Home Department* [2003] EWHC 155 (Admin) [2003] 1 FLR 979.

In discharging this general duty towards children in need, as s 17(3) states, the services may be provided for the family of a particular child in need or for any member of his family, if they are provided with a view to safeguarding or promoting the child's welfare. For these purposes, 'family' includes any person who has parental responsibility for the child and any other person with whom he had been living.[57] It is thus not limited to relatives. The object of s 17(3) is to promote the upbringing of children by their families. Hence, parents' own circumstances may be such as to require the service provision so as to safeguard or promote their child's welfare within the family. Local authorities have no *duty* to provide accommodation for a child's *parent* to enable the child to live with that parent.[58] Nevertheless the House of Lords in the *Lambeth* case[59] held that an authority has the power to provide accommodation for a child in need and his family. Section 17(6) was specifically amended[60] to include the provision of accommodation. A child so accommodated, however, is not being 'looked after' by a local authority for the purposes of s 22.[61]

A child 'in need' also includes a disabled child, who, for the purposes of the Act, is a child who is:

> blind, deaf or dumb or suffers from mental disorder of any kind or is substantially and permanently handicapped by illness, injury or congenital deformity or such other disability as may be prescribed.[62]

As a child in need, a disabled child is able to benefit from the same services as other children. Accordingly local authorities are obliged to provide such children with services so as to minimise the effect of their disabilities and to give them the opportunity to lead lives that are as normal as possible.[63]

Following an amendment introduced by s 53 of the Children Act 2004, before determining what, if any, services to provide for a child, the local authority is required, so far as is reasonably practical and consistent with the child's welfare, to ascertain the child's wishes and feelings regarding the provision of those services and having regard to his age and understanding give due consideration to such wishes and feelings as they have been able to ascertain.[64]

The services provided under Part III may include giving assistance in kind or in cash,[65] unconditionally or conditionally as to repayment.[66] Direct payments may be made to a person with parental responsibility for a disabled child of 16 or 17, the purpose of which is to enable the recipient(s) to purchase a service which would otherwise have been provided by the authority itself.[67] Authorities are required to have regard to the means of the child and each of his parents, although no person is liable for repayment at any time when he is in receipt of income support, any element of child tax credit other than the family element,

[57] Section 17(10).
[58] *R (G) v Barnet London Borough Council; R (W) v Lambeth London Borough Council; R (A) v Lambeth London Borough Council* [2003] UKHL 57 [2004] 2 AC 208.
[59] Ibid.   [60] By s 116 of the Adoption and Children Act 2002.
[61] Discussed further at Ch 18, Local authority duties towards 'looked after children', pp 660ff.
[62] Section 17(11).
[63] Sch 2 para 6, on which see inter alia *R (BG) v Medway Council* [2005] EWHC 1932 (Admin) [2006] 1 FLR 663. See also the Department of Health's *Guidance* (1991) Vol 2 at para 2.18. Local authorities must keep a register of children with disabilities in their area: Sch 2 para 2.
[64] Children Act 1989 s 17(4A) which gives statutory backing to guidance issued under s 7 of the Local Authority Social Services Act 1970 in relation to s 17, see the Explanatory Notes to the 2004 Act.
[65] The former provision that payments in cash could only be made in exceptional circumstances was repealed by the Children and Young Persons Act 2008 s 24.
[66] Section 17(6), (7). For an example of a potentially re-payable loan see *R (BG) v Medway Council*, earlier.
[67] Section 17A inserted by the Carers and Disabled Children Act 2000 s 17(1).

working tax credit or income-based jobseeker's allowance.[68] An authority may also contribute to the cost of looking after a child who is living with a person under a child arrangements order, such as a relative or foster parent, except where that person is a parent or step-parent.[69]

Authorities are required to facilitate the provision of Part III services by others, in particular, voluntary organisations, and may make such arrangements as they see fit for others to provide such services (eg day care or fostering services).[70]

2. SPECIFIC DUTIES AND POWERS

In pursuance of the general duty, authorities have specific duties and powers which are set out in Sch 2, Pt I, among which are the following.

(a) Identification of children in need

Every local authority must take reasonable steps to identify the extent to which there are children in need in their area.[71] They must also publish information about the services they provide and, where appropriate, that other organisations or bodies provide.[72] They must also take such steps as are reasonably practicable to ensure that those who might benefit from the services receive the information relevant to them.[73]

(b) Promoting the upbringing of children by their families

Local authorities should make provision for advice, guidance, counselling and home help. This could include family aids or perhaps therapists who might advise on improving family dynamics. Occupational, social, cultural or recreational activities or assistance with holidays may be provided.[74] Where a child is being looked after by a local authority, the authority shall, unless it is not reasonably practicable or consistent with his welfare, endeavour to promote contact between the child and his family and shall ensure that they are kept informed of where he is being accommodated. However, the authority is not required to disclose the whereabouts of the child if he is in care and the authority has reasonable cause to believe that disclosure would prejudice the child's welfare.[75] Expenses may be paid for visits to or by children.[76]

Every local authority must provide such family centres (ie a centre at which a child, his parents, a person with parental responsibility or any person looking after the child may attend) for (a) occupational, cultural, social or recreational activities, or (b) advice, guidance or counselling, or (c) be provided with accommodation whilst receiving these) as they consider appropriate in relation to children within their area.[77]

(c) Prevention of abuse and neglect

Every authority shall take reasonable steps through the provision of Part III services to prevent children in their area suffering ill-treatment or neglect. There is a duty to inform

---

[68] Section 17(8), (9) as amended by the Jobseekers Act 1995 Sch 2 para 19(2).

[69] Schedule 1 para 15. In their study *Residence Order Allowance Survey* (1996) the Grandparents' Federation found that the practice among local authorities with regard to what were then residence order allowances varied enormously both as to whether the allowance was paid at all and, where it was, as to its duration. Whilst acknowledging that the provision of allowances is one of the most difficult parts of a residence order policy, the Department of Health has nevertheless recommended that all authorities should have a policy addressing inter alia when they should be considered, whether they should be capped, and how the rates and periods should be set: Social Services Inspectorate *Children Act 1989, Residence Orders Study* (1995) 6.2.

[70] Section 17(5) and see further Department of Health's *Guidance and Regulations* (1991) Vol 2 para 2.11.

[71] Sch 2 para 1.   [72] Sch 2 para 1(2)(a).   [73] Sch 2 para 1(2)(b).   [74] Sch 2 para 8.

[75] Sch 2 para 15.   [76] Sch 2 para 16.   [77] Sch 2 para 9.

another authority, if a child who the authority believe is likely to suffer harm lives or proposes to live in the area of that authority.[78] There is a connected duty to take reasonable steps, through the provision of Part III services, to reduce the need to bring proceedings for care or supervision orders, or to bring criminal proceedings in respect of children.[79]

(d) Provision of accommodation by third party to protect children

Where it appears to an authority that a child is suffering or is likely to suffer ill-treatment at the hands of another person living at the same premises and that other person proposes to move from those premises, the authority may assist that other person to obtain accommodation, including giving assistance in kind.[80] This provision is a response to concern expressed in the Cleveland Report[81] that children, who were allegedly sexually abused, were removed from the family home, when it might have been in their interests for the alleged abuser to have left, if he could have been provided with alternative accommodation. Under this provision local authorities can assist those who are willing to leave voluntarily, but they have no power to order removal of a person from a child's household. However, the Children Act 1989 was amended by the Family Law Act 1996 so that a court may also make an order requiring the alleged abuser to leave the family home, when making emergency protection orders and interim care orders.[82]

(e) Day care

Every local authority is required to provide such day care as is appropriate for children in need within their area who are five or under and not yet attending school.[83] Day care is defined as any form of care or supervised activity provided for children during the day, whether or not on a regular basis.[84] The authority may provide day care for such children even though they are not in need.[85] They may also provide facilities including training, advice, guidance and counselling for those who are caring for children in day care or who accompany children in day care. The provision of day care by others, in particular voluntary organisations should be facilitated by local authorities.[86]

Under s 19 authorities are required to review their day care provision and, according to the Department of Health's *Guidance*,[87] authorities should have an agreed policy for discharging their general duty to provide day care for children in need. However, past research suggests[88] that there has been little progress on co-ordinated action, identification of levels of need or increase in provision. Rather, lack of resources has made it generally difficult to develop or expand day care facilities. This rather patchy provision became the subject of greater Government concern as part of its broader initiatives concerning employment policy.[89]

(f) Duty to consider racial groups

In making any arrangements either for the provision of day care under s 18 or to encourage persons to act as local authority foster parents, the authority shall have regard to the different racial groups to which children in need in their area belong.[90]

---

[78] Sch 2 para 4.
[79] Sch 2 para 6.   [80] Sch 2 para 5.   [81] Cm 412 (1988).
[82] Viz. s 38A and s 44A, discussed in Ch 16.
[83] Section 18(1). See generally Department of Health's *Guidance and Regulations* Vol 2 paras 3.3 *et seq.*
[84] Section 18(4).   [85] Section 18(2).   [86] Section 17(5).   [87] Viz. Vol 2 at ch 9.
[88] Thomas Coram Research Unit *Implementing the Children Act for Children under 8* (1994).
[89] See DSS *New ambitions for our country: A new contract for welfare* Cm 3805 (1998).
[90] Sch 2 para 11.

3. ACCOMMODATING CHILDREN IN NEED

A key service under Part III of the 1989 Act is accommodation, under which local authorities may arrange, *without court intervention,* for the child live away from home either with relatives, foster parents (who may be a relative, friend, or connected person, or unconnected with the child)[91] or in a children's home.[92]

Accommodation replaced what was formerly known as 'voluntary care'[93] but, reflecting the change of philosophy under the Act, whereas voluntary care was perceived to be a mark of failure either on the part of the family or those professionals and others working to support them, accommodation was intended to be seen, in the words of the Government's White Paper.[94]

> . . . as part of the range of services a local authority can offer to parents and families in need of help with the care of their children. Such a service should, in appropriate circumstances, be seen as a positive response to the needs of families.

A typical example of where help might be needed is where a parent falls ill and the rest of the family cannot cope.

An essential characteristic of this service is that it should be voluntary, that is, it should (save where the parents are dead or have abandoned the child) be based on continuing parental agreement, and operate as far as possible on a basis of partnership and co-operation between the local authority and parents. As Hedley J has said,[95] 'The emphasis in Part III is on partnership and it involves no compulsory curtailment of parental responsibility.'

Consistent with this philosophy, the authority do not acquire parental responsibility while they are 'accommodating children',[96] nor are there any formal restrictions on parents with parental responsibility removing their children under the age of 16 out of accommodation.[97]

The adult basis of the scheme is to be noted.[98] It means that children under the age of 16 cannot insist on being accommodated against their parents' wishes even if they are *'Gillick*-competent'.[99]

(a) The *duty* to accommodate

Under s 20(1) local authorities have an obligation to provide accommodation where a 'child' in need appears to require it as a result of:

---

[91] A private fostering arrangement can qualify as 'accommodation', see *R (A) v Coventry City Council* [2009] EWHC 34 (Admin) [2009] 1 FLR 1202.

[92] Section 22C, added by the Children and Young Persons Act 2008 and amended by the Children and Families Act 2014 Sch 2 para 29 'Other arrangements' can include placing a child in residential schooling, see *R (O) v East Riding of Yorkshire Council (Secretary of State for Education Intervening)* [2011] EWCA Civ 196 [2011] 2 FLR 207.

[93] For a brief review of the statutory background to s 20, see *R (A) v Croydon London Borough Council; R (M) v Lambeth London Borough Council* [2009] UKSC 8 [2009] 1 WLR 2557, at [15]–[16], per Baroness Hale.

[94] *The Law on Child Care and Family Services* Cm 62 (1987) para 21. The Government rejected the recommendation of the *Review of Child Care Law* that there should be a dual system of 'shared care' and 'respite care'.

[95] In *Coventry City Council v C, B, CA and CH* [2012] EWHC 2190 (Fam) [2013] 2 FLR 987 at [25].

[96] But see The effect of being accommodated, p 571, for liability for the criminal acts of a child whilst being accommodated by a local authority.

[97] See s 20(8), discussed at Limits on providing accommodation p 568 (aliter where the child is 16 or 17: see s 20(11)).

[98] But note the duty under s 20(6) to ascertain and take account of the child's wishes—see further The wishes of the child, p 567.

[99] Section 20(7) (discussed at Limits on providing accommodation, p 568) seems conclusive on this point.

(a) there being no person who has parental responsibility for him;

(b) his being lost or having been abandoned; or

(c) the person who has been caring for him being prevented (whether or not permanently, and for whatever reason) from providing him with suitable accommodation or care.

As Black J observed in *R (JL) v Islington Borough Council*[100] there is no acknowledgement of future risks in s 20 (1) and it was her view, bearing in mind the stringent duty that it imposes, that the section 'is designed to cope with actual crises and not with possible or prospective ones.'

According to Ward LJ in *R (A) v Croydon London Borough Council; R (M) v Lambeth Borough Council)*,[101] s 20(1) entails a series of judgments, namely (1) Is the person to whom a s 20 duty may be owed, a 'child'? (2) Is he or she a child 'in need', (3) Is the child within the local authority's area? (4) Does the child appear to the local authority to require accommodation? (5) Is that need the result of one of the grounds specified by s 20(1)? (6) What are the child's wishes regarding provision of accommodation for him or her? (7) What consideration (having regard to the child's age and understanding) is duly to be given to those wishes? (8) Does any person with parental responsibility who is willing to provide accommodation for the child object to the local authority's intervention? (9) If there is an objection, does the person named in what would now be a child arrangements order[102] as a person with whom the child is to live, agree to the child being looked after by the local authority?

This analysis was applied by Baroness Hale in *R (G) v Southwark London Borough Council*.[103]

If there are affirmative answers to questions 1-5 and no objections, having regard to questions 6 to 9, then the local authority is under a duty to accommodate the child under s 20 which it cannot divest itself of, for example, by determining to provide services under s 17, which are only 'target duties owed to the whole community rather than to the individual child'.[104] Furthermore another consequence of the s 20 duty is that the child becomes a 'looked after child' which, as we discuss in Chapter 18, triggers wide ranging obligations on the local authority towards that child, including towards those who were formerly accommodated,[105] and obliges local authorities to pay carers an appropriate allowance.[106] As against this, it is established that local authorities' duties under s 20 are owed to the individual child but not to the family. Hence, as the House of Lords held in *R (G) v Barnet London Borough Council; R (W) v Lambeth London Borough Council; R (A) v Lambeth London Borough Council*, a local authority providing a child with accommodation is not under a duty to accommodate the child's family as well. As Lord Hope commented[107] 'the provision

---

[100] [2009] EWHC 458 (Admin) [2009] 2 FLR 515 at [96].

[101] [2008] EWCA Civ 1445 [2009] 1 FLR 1324 at [75]. Not commented upon on appeal to the Supreme Court, see [2009] UKSC 8 [2009] 1 WLR 2557.

[102] Formerly a residence order as referred to by Ward LJ the *Croydon* decision.

[103] [2009] UKHL 26 [2009] 2 FLR 380 at [28].

[104] Per Baroness Hale in *R (M) v Hammersmith and Fulham London Borough Council* [2008] UKHL 14 [2008] 1 WLR 1384 at [18]. See also *R (G) v Southwark London Borough Council*, earlier, and *R (W) v North Lincolnshire Council* [2008] EWHC 2299 (Admin) [2008] 2 FLR 2150.

[105] See *R (M) v Hammersmith and Fulham London Borough Council* at [20]–[24] and *R (TG) v Lambeth London Borough Council (Shelter Intervening)* [2011] EWCA Civ 526 [2011] 2 FLR 1007.

[106] See eg *R(A) v Coventry City Council* [2009] EWHC 34 (Admin) [2009] 1 FLR 1202.

[107] [2004] UKHL 57 [2004] 2 AC 208 at [92] and on which see D Cowan 'On need and gatekeeping' [2004] CFLQ 331. See also *R v Northavon District Council, ex p Smith* [1994] 2 AC 402 in which the House of Lords held that the nature and scope of the functions of the housing and social services departments were not intended to change as a result of the duty to co-operate imposed under the 1989 Act. In other words, the

of residential accommodation to rehouse a child in need so that he can live with his family is not the principal or primary purpose of [the Children Act 1989]'. Further, although technically the s 20 duty is owed to children under the age of 18,[108] in relation to those aged 16 or 17, the duty to accommodate only arises where the local authority consider that their welfare 'is likely to be seriously prejudiced' if they do not provide them with accommodation.[109]

Although some of the questions posed by Ward LJ are essentially for the local authority rather than a court to determine, by no means all are. A good illustration is the age of the child which was the point in issue before the Supreme Court in *R (A) v Croydon London Borough Council; R (M) v Lambeth London Borough Council*.[110] In each of these cases it was sought to challenge the local authorities' assessment that the children concerned were over 18 and therefore fell outside the scope of s 20. It was held that unlike the question of whether the child 'is in need', which requires a number of different value judgments, the question of whether the person is a 'child' (that is, a person under 18, as defined by s 105(1)) was an objective fact. Accordingly, if it is a live issue, it is ultimately for the court to determine. It might be added, however, that although questions as to whether the child is 'in need' and 'requiring accommodation' are questions for the local authority, this does not necessarily mean that they are beyond challenge. For example, it might be difficult to argue that a homeless adolescent is not 'in need' and requires accommodation.[111] As Baroness Hale put it 'Section 20 involves an evaluative judgment on some matters but not a discretion.'[112]

So far as the grounds are concerned, s 20 basically caters for two categories of children, namely, those who have or effectively have no parents and those whose carers are prevented from looking after them. Section 20(1)(a) is straightforward and essentially covers orphaned children. Section 20(1)(b) has still to be interpreted by the courts but the general view is that 'abandoned' is likely to be interpreted as under the adoption legislation as meaning 'leaving the child to its fate'.[113] Presumably, 'being lost', means that the child's parents cannot be found.

The widest ground is that under s 20(1)(c), particularly as it was accepted in *R(G) v Barnet London Borough Council*[114] that the words 'for whatever reason', should be given the widest possible scope and that 'it makes no difference whether the reason is one which the carer has brought about by her own act or is one which she was resisting to the best of her ability'.[115] As Lord Nicholls succinctly put it[116] 'A child is not to be visited with the shortcomings of his parents'. It is clear that accommodation may be provided because of the disability of the child as well as the disability of the parent.[117] Being 'prevented' from providing accommodation imports an objective test which is not satisfied merely by reason of the fact that the child does not wish to live with someone who is willing to provide suitable accommodation.[118]

---

burden of accommodating intentionally homeless children falls on social services whereas the burden of rehousing homeless families falls on the housing authorities.

[108] Formerly the duty applied to children under the age of 17.   [109] Children Act 1989 s 20(3).
[110] [2009] UKSC 8 [2009] 1 WLR 2557.
[111] See the discussion by Baroness Hale in *R (G) v Southwark London Borough Council* [2009] UKHL 26 [2009] 2 FLR 380 at [28].   [112] *R (G) v Southwark London Borough Council*, earlier, at [31].
[113] *Watson v Nikolaisen* [1955] 2 QB 286.
[114] *R (G) v Barnet London Borough Council; R (W) v Lambeth London Borough Council; R (A) v Lambeth London Borough Council* [2003] UKHL 57 [2004] 2 AC 208.
[115] Per Lord Hope, ibid at para [100].
[116] Ibid at para [24], but note Lord Nicholls dissented in this case.
[117] See R White, P Carr and N Lowe *Children Act in Practice* (2008, 4th edn) 6.36.
[118] Per Stanley Burnton J in *R (S) v Sutton London Borough Council* [2007] EWHC 1196 (Admin) [2007] 2 FLR 849 at [40] and 'favoured' by Baroness Hale in *R (M) v Hammersmith and Fulham London Borough Council* [2008] UKHL 14 [2008] 1 WLR 1384 at [42]–[43].

Whether accommodation is best regarded as a short-term remedy or as an appropriate means of solving long term problems has been debated in relation to orphans and those children whose parents cannot be found.[119] In this context it now seems to be accepted that, although in theory local authorities can adequately look after such children without having parental responsibility,[120] it is nevertheless preferable, where possible,[121] for local authorities to obtain a care order, since the consequential acquisition of parental responsibility will avoid any possible difficulties or delays that might ensue in authorising decisions, for example, as to the child's medical treatment.[122]

Although in *R (A) v Croydon London Borough Council; R (M) v Lambeth London Borough Council,* Baroness Hale accepted[123] that it made sense to consider that where the local authority is under a duty to provide accommodation under s 20 there is a correlative 'right' to accommodation, the Supreme Court were nevertheless not prepared to consider those rights to be civil rights for the purpose of Art 6 of the European Convention on Human Rights.[124] Baroness Hale said she 'would be most reluctant to accept, unless driven by Strasbourg jurisprudence to do so, that Art 6 requires the judicialisation of claims to welfare service of this kind.'[125]

(b) The *discretion* to accommodate

In addition to the obligation to provide accommodation, s 20 vests in local authorities a *discretion* to provide accommodation in two instances. First, under s 20(4) in the case of *any* child (ie not simply a child in need) within their area, even though a person who has parental responsibility for him is able to provide him with accommodation, a local authority may provide accommodation 'if they consider that to do so would safeguard or promote the child's welfare'. It is under this provision that so-called respite care may be given.[126] Secondly, under s 20(5) a local authority may provide accommodation in a community home for any person aged 16–21 if they consider that to do so would safeguard or promote the child's welfare. This power may be used to house homeless adolescents.

(c) The wishes of the child

In all cases, before providing accommodation the authority must, as far as is reasonably practicable and consistent with the child's welfare, ascertain the child's wishes and feelings regarding the provision of accommodation and give due consideration to them, having regard to his age and understanding.[127]

---

[119] Such situations are not so uncommon: in the year ending 31 March 1996, for example, 430 children started to be 'looked after' in England and Wales because they had no parents and another 950 because they were abandoned or lost: *Children Looked After by Local Authorities* Dept of Health, Personal Social Services, Local Authority Statistics A/F 96/12, Table J. Current statistics are not so specific.

[120] Since under s 3(5) a local authority may do all that is reasonable to safeguard or promote the child's welfare, while a prohibited steps or specific issue order could solve any particular dispute.

[121] See *Birmingham City Council v D, Birmingham City Council v M* [1994] 2 FLR 502, discussed further, in Ch 17, The application of the threshold criteria to orphans and abandoned children, p 607.

[122] See *Re SH (Care: Order Orphan)* [1995] 1 FLR 746 at 749 per Hollis J, and *Re M (Care Order: Parental Responsibility)* [1996] 2 FLR 84, discussed further in Ch 17, The application of the threshold criteria to orphans and abandoned children, p 607.   [123] [2009] UKSC 8 [2009] 1 WLR 2557 at [35].

[124] Note: Lord Hope was the most forthright in saying that s 20 duty does not give rise to a 'civil right' (see para [65]) the majority were more circumspect, while Lord Walker left the question open.

[125] At [44].

[126] But note *R (O) v East Riding of Yorkshire Council (Secretary of State for Education Intervening)* [2011] EWCA Civ 196 [2011] 2 FLR 207—whether or not provision made by the local authority is classified as respite care under s 20(4) or accommodation under s 20 is a matter of law and is not dependent upon the local authority's own view.   [127] Children Act 1989 s 20(6), as amended by s 53(2) of the Children Act 2004.

Different views have been taken on the application of this provision. On one interpretation s 20(6) only concerns the child's view about the type of accommodation he or she should have rather than whether he or she be accommodated at all.[128] On the other hand, it has been pointed out[129] that it was unlikely that Parliament intended that local authorities should be able to oblige a competent 16 or 17 year old to accept a service that he does not want. As Baroness Hale has said, 'It is a service not a coercive service.'[130] The better view seems to be that s 20(6) does mean that a child's view on whether he or she should be accommodated has to be taken into account, but that these views are not necessarily determinative.[131]

(d) Limits on providing accommodation

It is of the essence of the service that it is voluntary.[132] As Hedley J put it in *Coventry City Council v C, B, CA and CH*,[133] 'the use of s 20 is not unrestricted and must not be compulsion in disguise.' In that case Hedley J gave, with the approval of the President, extensive guidance on what he considered was required in the obtaining of 's 20 consent', namely, that every social worker is under a personal obligation to be satisfied that the person giving the consent has the capacity to do so; to discharge that obligation the social worker must actively address the issue of capacity but if there are any doubts about it no further attempt should be made to obtain consent on that occasion and advice should be sought from the social work team leader or management. If the social worker is satisfied about capacity, then in order to be human rights compliant, he or she must also be satisfied both that the parent is fully informed to give consent and that the giving consent and the child's subsequent removal is fair and proportionate. In the light of this advice Hedley J concluded that 'local authorities may want to approach with great care the obtaining of s 20 agreement from mothers in the aftermath of birth, especially where there is no immediate danger to the child and where probably no order would be made.'[134]

Hedley J's analysis is significant in that it is predicated on s 20 requiring *positive consent* whereas, on its wording, s 20 seems to permit accommodation unless there is *parental objection*. Indeed it is clear that consent is not always required since accommodation may be provided where the parents are dead or where they have abandoned the child. On the other hand, save in those two instances, accommodation agreements (discussed shortly) are required and it is of the essence of 'an agreement' that there be mutual consent.

Express provision is made in the case of objections. By s 20(7) a local authority cannot provide accommodation if any person with parental responsibility for the child, who is willing and able to provide or arrange for accommodation,[135] objects to the authority so doing.[136] Furthermore, any person with parental responsibility may remove the child from accommodation at any time.[137] These powers of objection and removal do not apply:

---

[128] *R (S) v Sutton London Borough Council* [2007 EWHC 1196 (Admin) [2007] 2 FLR 849 at [51] per Stanley Burnton J.

[129] *R (M) v Hammersmith and Fulham London Borough Council* [2008] UKHL 14 [2008] 1 WLR 1384 at [43] per Baroness Hale.

[130] In *R (G) v Southwark London Borough Council* [2009] UKHL 26 [2009] 2 FLR 380 at [28] point (7).

[131] See *R (Liverpool City Council) v Hillingdon Borough Council* [2009] EWCA Civ 43 [2009] 1 FLR 1536 and *R (W) v North Lincolnshire Council* [2008] EWHC 2299 (Admin) [2008] 2 FLR 2150.

[132] Parental consent is not, however, necessarily required.

[133] [2012] EWHC 2190 (Fam) [2013] 2 FLR 987, at [27]. See also *Surrey County Council v M and others* [2013] EWHC 2400 (Fam) [2014] 1 FCR 429.   [134] Ibid, at [46].

[135] These words were added at a later stage of the Bill to prevent a person simply objecting while having no intention of looking after the child.

[136] For an example of an objection, see *Re B (A Minor) (Care Order: Criteria)* [1993] 1 FLR 815.

[137] Section 20(8).

(a) where a child of 16 or over agrees to being provided with accommodation;[138] or

(b) where the person agreeing is named in a child arrangements order as a person with whom the child is to live, is a special guardian, or has the care of the child by virtue of an order made under the High Court's inherent jurisdiction.[139]

The statutory right to remove a child from accommodation without notice was one of the more controversial provisions of the 1989 Act.[140] Formerly, there had been a requirement to give 28 days' written notice of an intended removal once the child had been looked after for six months or more. Such a period of notice was, it was argued, necessary to allow the child to prepare himself for his return home and to protect the child from any rash decision on the part of the parents.[141] The Government's view, however, was that any period of notice 'would blur the distinction between compulsory and voluntary' care.[142] In their view nothing should undermine the voluntary nature of the service. In line with this philosophy it has been held[143] that in the absence of a court order the local authority is powerless to prevent a mother from removing her children from accommodation. In particular the authority could not rely either on its general duty under s 22(3) to safeguard and promote the child's welfare, nor on the power under s 3(5) to do what is reasonable to promote the child's welfare. Precisely what court order Ward J had in mind may be speculated upon, since it is clear that the court cannot make a specific issue or prohibited steps order requiring a local authority to provide accommodation against the wishes of a parent.[144] It may, however, be possible for one parent to obtain a prohibited steps order preventing the other from objecting. Similarly, it remains a moot point as to whether s 3(5) would justify foster parents refusing to hand over a child to an inebriated parent.[145]

Notwithstanding the clear recognition of the right of removal, there has been no reported evidence of any great difficulties in this regard. In practice the period of removal is one of the matters that should be covered in any accommodation agreement, though it is to be emphasised that an agreement can be of no more than persuasive effect. In particular it cannot in itself prevent the parent exercising the right of removal though this is not to say that the local authority cannot then institute care proceedings in appropriate cases.[146]

(e) Accommodation agreements

It is central to the philosophy of the Act that an authority should seek to reach agreement with the parent or other person with parental responsibility on such matters as the

---

[138] Section 20(11).

[139] Section 20(9), as amended by the Adoption and Children Act 2002 s 139(1) and by the Children and Families Act 2014 Sch 2 para 28. The inherent jurisdiction is discussed in Ch 20.

[140] See eg HC Deb, 18 May 1989, Standing Committee B, cols 137–54.

[141] Ibid at col 142 per R Sims.

[142] Ibid at col 149 per D Mellor. Formerly, local authorities not infrequently used the period of notice to decide to take compulsory measures to keep the child, the House of Lords having ruled in *Lewisham London Borough v Lewisham Juvenile Court Justice* [1980] AC 273, that there was no compulsion to return a child immediately upon receiving the request.

[143] *Nottinghamshire County Council v J* (26 November 1993, unreported), per Ward J, cited by D Hershman and A McFarlane *Children Law and Practice* at G [195].

[144] This would seem to be the result of s 9(5)(b); and see *Re S and D (Children: Powers of Court)* [1995] 2 FLR 456 at 462, per Balcombe LJ. But note *Re G (Minors) (Interim Care Order)* [1993] 2 FLR 839 at 843, CA, in which a mother's undertaking not to withdraw her agreement to the continuing accommodation of her children was accepted by the court.

[145] As argued by R White, P Carr and N Lowe *Children Act in Practice* (2008, 4th edn) at 6.54, but cf *Nottinghamshire County Council v J*, earlier.

[146] See *R v Tameside Metropolitan Borough Council, ex p J* [2000] 1 FLR 942 at 949 per Scott Baker J.

purpose of accommodating the child, the period for which accommodation might be provided, schooling and contact with the child.

Provision for making agreements is governed by the Arrangements for Placement of Children Regulations 1991 which, as the Department of Health's *Guidance* explains:[147]

> . . . place a statutory duty on responsible authorities to draw up a plan in writing for a child whom they are proposing to look after or accommodate in consultation with the child, his parents and other important individuals and agencies in the child's life (regulation 3). Planning for the child should begin prior to placement. After placement, the plan should be scrutinised and adjusted (if necessary) at the first review four weeks after the date the child was first looked after and at subsequent reviews.

(f) Challenging a refusal to accommodate

A refusal to accommodate cannot be challenged by means of a specific issue order under s 8. In *Re J (Specific Issue Order: Leave to Apply)*[148] it was held that a specific issue order could not be used to challenge a local authority decision that a particular child was not 'in need', nor therefore to require the authority to provide appropriate support under Part III (which could of course include accommodation). In Wall J's view:[149]

> the question as to whether or not a child is in need does not raise a specific question which arises in connection with any aspect of parental responsibility for the child. A s 8 order is inapplicable to the exercise of a local authority's powers and duties under Part III of the Act.

Wall J did consider that such a decision was amenable to judicial review.[150] Such actions, however, are in practice difficult to win, especially since much of s 20(1) is itself a matter of discretion. The better first recourse is to use the local authority's complaints procedure under s 26.[151]

In *R v Royal Borough of Kingston-upon-Thames, ex p T*[152] an action for judicial review failed, inter alia, because the local authority's offer of accommodation which was different from that sought by the mother and the child in question (ie a project home offering support and accommodation for Vietnamese families), was held not to be perverse or unreasonable (notwithstanding that the child's elder sister was already accommodated at the project) so as to be amenable to judicial review, but to be well within the parameters of reasonableness, particularly taking into account the cost of the sought-after placement. It might be similarly difficult to challenge a local authority decision that a particular child is not a child in need.[153] This is not to say that an action can never succeed. In *Re T (Accommodation by Local Authority)*[154] the court quashed the Director of Social Services' decision not to ratify the decision of a complaints panel that a 17-year-old child should be accommodated under s 20(3). In that case the Director was held to have erred when he decided that past provision of support given to the child under s 17 made it unlikely that her future welfare would be seriously prejudiced if she were not provided

---

[147] See generally Department of Health's *Guidance and Regulations*, (1991) Vol 3 paras 2.17–2.74 and Vol 4 paras 2.17–2.74.

[148] [1995] 1 FLR 669.   [149] Ibid at 673.

[150] Ibid at 673–4. Judicial review is discussed more generally in Ch 18.

[151] See *R v Royal Borough of Kingston-upon-Thames, ex p T* [1994] 1 FLR 798 and *R v Birmingham City Council, ex p A* [1997] 2 FLR 841. The complaints procedure is discussed in Ch 18.

[152] [1994] 1 FLR 798.   [153] See *Re J (Specific Issue Order: Leave to Apply)*, earlier.

[154] [1995] 1 FLR 159.

with accommodation. In Johnson J's view the Director should have concentrated on the future and taken into account the fact that services provided under s 17 were discretionary and could not therefore be guaranteed to continue.

(g) The effect of being accommodated

Accommodated children are not in local authority care nor does the authority thereby acquire parental responsibility.[155] Consequently a local authority cannot transfer an accommodated child from residential care to foster care without the parents' permission[156] nor can foster parents unilaterally change the child's name.[157] However, this is not to say that accommodation has no legal effect. Accommodated children are among those who are 'looked after' by the local authority, upon which certain consequential duties are imposed.[158] Furthermore, it has been held in *McL v Security of State for Social Security*[159] that because an accommodated child was in the de facto care of the local authority the mother could not claim child benefit. Equally, however, the fact of accommodation cannot be ignored when determining liability under s 55 of the Children and Young Persons Act 1933 for a child's criminal act. Accordingly, where a child is in the de facto care of the local authority and the parent has no control over the child at the time, that parent cannot be said to be responsible for the child's actions.[160]

(h) Accommodation in practice

According to the National Statistics, *Children Looked After by Local Authorities in England*, for year ending March 2013 the number of children accommodated under s 20 declined to 18,190 from 19,260 in 2009 and, in terms of the overall 'looked after' population, declined proportionally to 27% from 32% in 2009.[161] Nevertheless because for the most part the period of accommodation is short, generally less than eight weeks,[162] it remains the case that the majority of children, 59% (16,980 out of 28,830) who *began* to be 'looked after' in the year ending 31 March 2013, were those accommodated under s 20.[163] This proportion, too, has declined. In the year ending 31 March 2004, for example, the proportion was 67%. This declining trend is against the upward trend of the looked after population generally and is an indicator that compulsory measures to take children into care are more readily being resorted to.[164]

---

[155] A point emphasised by the Department of Education's *Delegation of Authority: Amendments to the Children Act 1989 Guidance and Regulations* (2013) p 6.

[156] See *R v Tameside Metropolitan Borough Council ex p J* [2000] 1 FLR 942.

[157] *Re D, L and LA (Care: Change of Forename)* [2003] 1 FLR 339.

[158] See Ch 18. Note also *R (Berhe) v Hillingdon London Borough Council* [2003] EWHC 2075 (Admin) [2004] 1 FLR 439.

[159] [1996] 2 FLR 748, giving a wide definition of the words 'in the care of the local authority' contained in Sch 9 to the Social Security Contributions and Benefits Act 1992.

[160] *TA v DPP* [1997] 2 FLR 887, CA, per Sir Ian Glidewell. Local authorities may be liable under s 55(5) of the 1933 Act, added by the Criminal Justice Act 1991 s 57(2).

[161] SFR 36/2013, Table A2. Separate statistics are kept for Wales, see the *Children Looked After Statistics for Wales*. In the year ending 31 March 2013, 1,230 (21%) of the 5,770 looked after children in Wales were accommodated under s 20.

[162] See eg Table 16 of the Department of Health's Statistics *Children Looked After by Local Authorities* for the year ending 31 March 2004. No comparable statistics are currently published.

[163] See Table LAC3.

[164] Interestingly, soon after the implementation of the Children Act some local authorities seemed to think that unless or until accommodation agreements had broken down there was no scope for taking compulsory care proceedings. To counteract this apparent belief the Department of Health published guidance (*Children Act Report 1992*) stressing (at para 2.21) that local authorities should not feel inhibited from

4. SECURE ACCOMMODATION

(a) Introduction

Secure accommodation[165] is not to be confused with s 20 accommodation. Children who are subject to secure accommodation lose their right to leave the secure unit (be it a room or building) of their own free will, though they should at the same time have the benefit of specialist services to promote and safeguard their welfare. Though clearly draconian, secure accommodation may be the only means of dealing with adolescent children who have a history of aggressive behaviour. As the *Statutory Guidance on court orders and pre-proceedings* comments:[166]

> For some children a period of accommodation in a secure children's home will represent the only way of meeting their complex needs, as it will provide them with a safe and secure environment, enhanced levels of staffing, and specialist programmes of support. A secure placement may be the most suitable, and only, way of responding to the likelihood of a child suffering significant harm or injuring themselves or others.

Yet, as the *Guidance* stresses,[167] because the restriction of a child's liberty is a serious step it should only be taken if it is the most appropriate way of meeting the child's assessed needs and 'never because no other placement is available, because of inadequacies of staffing in a child's current placement, or because the child is simply being a nuisance. Secure accommodation should never be used as a form of punishment'.

Secure accommodation was first developed[168] in response to disturbances in open approved schools following which three special units were built, the first one opening in 1964. These buildings were later transferred to the control of local authorities following the implementation of the Children and Young Persons Act 1969. Under that Act, where a care order had been made,[169] the local authority had the power, without court control, to restrict a child's liberty to the extent they considered appropriate. But concern over (a) the extensive use of secure accommodation in community homes[170] and (b) the need to comply with the European Convention on Human Rights[171] led to the introduction of new safeguards by the Child Care Act 1980. Under the 1980 Act, local authorities were precluded from placing children in their care in secure accommodation unless statutory criteria applied and needed to obtain a court order if they wished to keep a child in secure accommodation for more than 72 hours in any period of 28 days.[172] Though not identical

seeking compulsory measures and where an authority 'determines that control of the child's circumstances is necessary to promote his welfare then compulsory intervention . . . will always be the appropriate remedy'.

[165] For wider discussion see D Harris and J Timms *Between Hospital and Prison or thereabouts* (1993) and R Bullock *Secure treatment outcomes—the care careers of very difficult adolescents* (1998). Note that the ensuing discussion is confined to *civil* proceedings for secure accommodation. There are separate provisions dealing with *criminal* proceedings for which, see R White, P Carr and N Lowe *Children Act in Practice* (2008, 4th edn) 9.30ff.   [166] Produced by the Department of Education (2014) at para 42.

[167] Ibid at para 40.

[168] See the summary by M Parry 'Secure accommodation—the Cinderella of family law' [2000] CFLQ 101.

[169] But not otherwise, ie there was no comparable statutory power to restrict the liberty of a child in 'voluntary' care.

[170] See eg a Report of a DHSS Working Party *Legal and Professional Aspects of the Use of Secure Accommodation for Children in Care* (HMSO, 1981), a Report of the Parliamentary Penal Affairs Group (1981) referred to by M Parry, op cit, at 102 and H Bevan *Child Law* (1989) 728.

[171] Viz. Art 5(4) under which 'Everyone who is deprived of his liberty by arrest or detention shall be entitled to take proceedings by which the lawfulness of his detention shall be decided speedily by a court and his release ordered if the detention is not lawful'. In *X v United Kingdom* (1981) 4 EHRR 181 the European Court of Human Rights held that it was unlawful to deprive mentally ill patients of their liberty by executive decision.

[172] Section 21A. Unlike the 1969 Act, the 1980 Act applied inter alia both to children in voluntary care and those subject to a care order.

either in its application or its wording, the scheme introduced by the 1980 Act, was essentially adopted by the Children Act 1989.

(b) Secure accommodation under the Children Act 1989

The basic scheme

It is fundamental to the scheme under the 1989 Act that local authorities[173] should not use secure accommodation unless the criteria set out in s 25(1) are met. Even then, all other options should have been considered and rejected. Indeed, local authorities have an express duty under Sch 2 para 7(c) to the 1989 Act 'to avoid the need for children within their area to be placed in secure accommodation'.

Provided they are satisfied that the s 25(1) criteria are met, local authorities can keep a child looked after[174] by them in secure accommodation for up to 72 hours in aggregate in any period of 28 days without a court order,[175] but beyond this court sanction is required. Before that sanction can be given, the court must be satisfied that 'any relevant criteria' for keeping a child in secure accommodation are met.[176]

The meaning of secure accommodation

Section 25(1) defines accommodation as that 'provided for the purposes of restricting liberty'. This is potentially a wide definition for, as the Department of Health's *Guidance* points out,[177] 'any practice or measure which prevents a child from leaving a room or building of his own free will may be deemed by the court to constitute "restriction of liberty" '. It is established that secure accommodation is *not* limited to accommodation provided with the approval of the Secretary of State;[178] rather the key element is the restriction of liberty. On this basis, a unit for the treatment of mentally disturbed children was held[179] to be secure accommodation since its purpose was to restrict the liberty of children with a view to modifying their behaviour. Similarly, in *A Metropolitan Borough Council v DB*,[180] it was held that a maternity ward at a hospital was secure accommodation since staff had been instructed to confine the child in question to the ward and could utilise a key/pass system to that end. In contrast, in *Re C (Detention: Medical Treatment)*[181] Wall J, whilst agreeing 'that premises which are not designed as secure accommodation may become secure accommodation because of the use to which they are put in the particular circumstances of individual cases', nevertheless considered that the more natural meaning of the phrase 'provided for the purpose of restricting liberty' is ' "designed for, or having as its primary purpose" the restriction of liberty'. He accordingly held that a private hospital clinic designed primarily to provide treatment for eating disorders and which was not equipped with devices to restrict entry or exit (there were no locks on the individual bedroom doors and the main doors were only locked at night), was not secure accommodation.[182]

---

[173] A similar regime applies to certain other bodies providing residential accommodation, namely, health authorities, Primary Care Trusts, National Health Service Trusts, local education authorities, care homes and independent hospitals, see Children (Secure Accommodation) Regulations 1991 (SI 1991/1505). A separate scheme applies to children detained under the Mental Health legislation and the Powers of Criminal Courts (Sentencing) Act 2000 ss 90–91.

[174] Ie children both accommodated by the local authority or subject to a care order, see Ch 18.

[175] Children (Secure Accommodation) Regulations 1991 reg 10(1).

[176] Children Act 1989 s 25(3).   [177] Vol 4, at 8.10.

[178] Secure accommodation in a children's home must have the prior approval of the Secretary of State: Children (Secure Accommodation) Regulations 1991 reg 3.

[179] *R v Northampton Juvenile Court, ex p London Borough of Hammersmith and Fulham* [1985] 1 FLR 193—applying s 21A of the Child Care Act 1980.   [180] [1997] 1 FLR 767.

[181] [1997] 2 FLR 180.

[182] Accordingly, in Wall J's view, this left him free to exercise his inherent jurisdiction to direct the clinic to detain the 12 year old anorexic child as an inpatient using reasonable force if necessary. Had the clinic

Who can be subjected to secure accommodation?

So far as the powers under s 25 are concerned only children being 'looked after' by a local authority may be placed in secure accommodation. As we discuss in Chapter 18, 'looked after' children refers both to those who are subject to a care order and those accommodated by the local authority for a continuous period of more than 24 hours.[183] This means that children who have been accommodated for 24 hours or less cannot be placed in secure accommodation by a local authority. Further restrictions, imposed by Regulations,[184] prohibit the use of secure accommodation for children over 16 who are accommodated under s 20(5)[185] and those kept away from home under a child assessment order.[186] The Regulations also provide[187] that a child under the age of 13 cannot be placed in secure accommodation in a children's home without the Secretary of State's specific approval.

The criteria for restricting liberty by secure accommodation

By s 25(1) a child being looked after by a local authority cannot be placed, and, if placed, may not be kept in secure accommodation,[188] unless it appears:

(a) that—
   (i) he has a history of absconding and is likely to abscond from any other description of accommodation; *and*
   (ii) if he absconds, he is likely to suffer significant harm; *or*
(b) that if he is kept in any other description of accommodation he is likely to injury himself or other persons. (Emphasis added.)

To fall within s 25(1)(a) the criteria set out in *both* sub-paras (i) and (ii) must be satisfied. It is not therefore sufficient just to prove absconding[189] but it must also be shown that if the child absconds he is likely to suffer significant harm.[190] On the other hand, the criteria in s 25(1)(a) and (b) are disjunctive and it is accordingly unnecessary to satisfy both limbs.[191]

---

been secure accommodation s 25 would have operated to oust the inherent jurisdiction. For a critique of Wall J's approach, see A Downie 'Extra-Statutory Confinement—Detention and Treatment under the Inherent Jurisdiction' [1998] CFLQ 101 at 102.   [183] Children Act 1989 s 22(2).

[184] Viz. Children (Secure Accommodation) Regulations 1991 regs 5(2)(a) and (b).

[185] Discussed at The discretion to accommodate, p 567. Note: this restriction does not prevent a court, when making a secure accommodation order in respect of a child under 16, from specifying a length that goes beyond the child's sixteenth birthday, see *Re G (Secure Accommodation)* [2000] 2 FLR 259, CA.

[186] For a discussion of which, see Ch 16.

[187] Reg 4 of the 1991 Regulation, as amended. Before this Regulation the minimum age was 10.

[188] Note the form or wording which, according to Hoffmann LJ in *Re M (A Minor) (Secure Accommodation Order)* [1995] Fam 108 at 117, means that rather than being expressed as a grant of power, sub s (1) amounts to restriction on a power which is presumed to exist. In his Lordship's view that power to restrict liberty 'is an ordinary incident of parental responsibility conferred by the Act on the local authority in respect of children in its care'. Whether this is a fair interpretation of s 25(1) may be questioned. It is certainly questionable whether parental responsibility to restrict liberty goes nearly as far as that permitted under the Act, see *Re K (A Child) (Secure Accommodation Order: Right To Liberty)* [2001] Fam 377, discussed at Is s 25 human rights compliant?, p 577, and the analysis of Parry, op cit, at 104–5.

[189] But note that *one* previous absconding will amount to a 'history' of absconding for the purposes of s 25(1)(a)(i): *R v Calder Justices, ex p C* (4 May 1993, unreported) cited by Clarke Hall and Morrison on *Children* at 7 [176]. 'Absconding' has been interpreted to mean 'to hide oneself; to go away hurriedly and secretly': see *Re C (Secure Accommodation Order: Representation)* [2001] EWCA Civ 458 [2001] 2 FLR 169, CA.

[190] The phrase 'likely to suffer significant harm' has the same meaning as for care proceedings (discussed in Ch 17), see *Re G (Secure Accommodation Order)* [2001] 1 FLR 884, 896, per Munby J.

[191] *Re D (Secure Accommodation Order) (No 1)* [1997] 1 FLR 197—justices held wrong to have refused to make an order in the case of a 14-year-old child who was clearly at risk of self-harm but who could not be found to have absconded.

So far as s 25(1)(a) is concerned it has been held[192] that the word 'likely' has the same meaning in both sub paras (i) and (ii) and as under s 31 should be construed as meaning 'a real possibility or a possibility that cannot sensibly be ignored'.

The strict application of the s 25 criteria is crucial. As the Department of Health's *Guidance* says[193] 'it is unlawful for the liberty of a child to be restricted [either by a local authority or the court] unless one of these criteria is met, no matter how short the period in security'.

Seeking court authorisation

If a local authority wishes to keep a child in secure accommodation for more than 72 hours they need a court order. Applications should be made by the authority looking after the child to the Family Court.[194]

As proceedings under s 25 are 'specified proceedings' for the purpose of s 41,[195] the court must, unless it is considered unnecessary to do so to safeguard the interests of the child, appoint a children's guardian for the child.[196] Notwithstanding this discretion not to appoint a guardian, the court cannot make a secure accommodation order in respect of a child who is not legally represented unless he has been informed of his right to apply for publicly funded representation and, having had the opportunity to do so, has refused, or failed to apply.[197]

The court's function under s 25

According to s 25(3) of the 1989 Act it is the court's duty, on hearing an application, 'to determine whether any relevant criteria for keeping the child in secure accommodation are satisfied'. If they are, then by s 25(4), the court 'shall make an order authorising the child to be kept in secure accommodation and specifying the maximum period for which he may be kept'. If the court is not in a position to decide whether any of the relevant criteria are met and adjourns the hearing it can make an interim secure accommodation order,[198] but there is no power to make a freestanding application for an interim order.[199]

According to Hoffmann LJ in *Re M (A Minor) (Secure Accommodation Order)*[200] the court's function under s 25 is 'to control the exercise of power by the local authority rather than to exercise an independent jurisdiction in the best interests of the child'. In the same case, however, Butler-Sloss LJ commented that whether it was a reviewing power or a general duty to consider the welfare of the child was 'a matter of words'. They both agreed, however, that though important, the child's welfare is *not* the paramount consideration (that is, s 1(1) has no application to s 25 proceedings).[201] Instead the court's duty is similar to that of the local authority. Consequently, as Hoffmann LJ put it, 'the duty of the court is to put itself in the position of a reasonable local authority and to ask, first, whether the

---

[192] See *S v Knowsley Borough Council* [2004] EWHC 491 (Fam) [2004] 2 FLR 716 at [36] ff per Charles J.

[193] Vol 4 at 8.27.

[194] See the Family Court (Compostion and Distribution of Business) Rules 2014 (SI 2014/840).

[195] FPR 2010 r 2.27(1)(a).

[196] FPR 2010 r 16.3(1). According to Bracewell J in *Re AS (Secure Accommodation Order)* [1999] 1 FLR 103 it is only in the most exceptional case that it will not be appropriate to appoint a guardian. Note: children capable of doing so may instruct their own solicitor, see eg *Re C (Secure Accommodation Order: Representation)* [2001] EWCA Civ 458 [2001] 2 FLR 169, discussed Is s 25 human rights compliant? at p 577. As to the right of the child to attend proceedings, see *A City Council v T, J and K* [2011] EWHC 1082 (Fam) [2011] 2 FLR 803, in which Peter Jackson J held, at [33] that it could no longer be presumed that a child's attendance in court was likely to be harmful nor should children have to prove that their attendance at proceedings about then is in their interests.

[197] Children Act 1989 s 25(6).   [198] Section 25(5).

[199] See *Birmingham City Council v M* [2008] EWHC 1085 (Fam) [2008] 2 FLR 542.

[200] [1995] Fam 108. This reflects the view of Ward J at first instance. For a not dissimilar view see *Re K (A Child) (Secure Accommodation Order: Right To Liberty)* [2001] Fam 377 at [60].

[201] For a general discussion as to the application of s 1(1), see Ch 12.

conditions in sub s (1) are satisfied and secondly, whether it would be in accordance with the authority's duty[202] to safeguard and promote the welfare of the child (but subject to the qualification in s 22(6))[203] for the child to be kept in secure accommodation and, if so, for how long'.

Re M is also authority to say that s 1(5)[204] has no application to s 25 proceedings. As Butler-Sloss LJ said, the mandatory requirement of s 25(4) means that it must prevail over s 1(5).

The decision that s 1 has no application to s 25 proceedings resolved previous conflicting case-law and overrode the Department of Health's *Guidance*.[205] Although *Re M* has not escaped academic criticism,[206] Butler-Sloss LJ was surely right to say that the application of the paramountcy principle does not lie easily with the enjoinder to protect others. In any event, the 'compromise' of requiring the court to consider the child's welfare as part of the 'relevant criteria' to the extent of having to safeguard and promote that welfare effectively means that, at any rate with respect to absconding and self-harm, there should be little difference in outcome than if those interests were of paramount importance.

Once the relevant criteria have been found to be satisfied the court must, pursuant to s 25(4), specify the maximum length of the order. Initially, the maximum length that can be specified is three months[207] but orders may subsequently be renewed upon application for periods of up to six months at a time.[208] In determining the length the court must consider carefully the purpose to be achieved and, consistent with the need to be human rights compliant, the order should be proportionate to the harm found,[209] and only be for so long as is necessary and unavoidable.[210]

The effect of an order

A secure accommodation order is permissive inasmuch as it authorises but does not require the local authority to use it.[211] If, during the order, the local authority is satisfied that the criteria cease to apply, then the child must be discharged from the secure accommodation.[212] It is incumbent upon local authorities to keep secure placements under review.[213] Notwithstanding a court order, children who are accommodated by the authority may be

---

[202] See s 22(3).

[203] This provision permits the local authority to exercise their powers where necessary to do so to protect members of the public from serious injury.

[204] By which courts should not make orders unless in doing so it is better than making no order, see Ch 12.

[205] See Vol 1 at 5.9 and Vol 4 at 8.47 which assumed the application of s 1(1) and 1(5). No such assumptions are made in the revised 2008 Guidance.

[206] See P Bates 'Secure accommodation orders—in whose interests?' [1995] CFLQ 70 and Parry, op cit, at 110–11.

[207] Children (Secure Accommodation) Regulations 1991 reg 11. This will *include* the period of a prior interim order, see *C v Humberside County Council* [1994] 2 FLR 759. Time runs from the date of the order and not from when a child is subsequently placed in secure accommodation: *Re B (A Minor) (Secure Accommodation)* [1995] 1 WLR 232.   [208] Reg 12 of the 1991 Regulations.

[209] Cf *Re B (A Child) (Care Porceedings: Threshold Criteria)* [2013] UKSC, [2013] 1 WLR 1911 and *Re O (Supervision Order)* [2001] EWCA Civ 16 [2001] 1 FLR 923, discussed in Ch 17, The use of supervision orders, p 635.   [210] See *R v Oxfordshire County Council (Secure Accommodation Order)* [1992] Fam 150.

[211] See *Re W (A Minor) (Secure Accommodation Order)* [1993] 1 FLR 692 at 695. Note also Charles J's observation in *S v Knowsley Borough Council* [2004] EWHC 491 (Fam) [2004] 2 FLR 716 at [46] that a court is not entitled to dictate how a local authority should exercise their duties.

[212] See *LM v Essex County Council* [1999] 1 FLR 988 in which Holman J left open the question of whether the discharge should be immediate. See also *Re K (A Child) (Secure Accommodation Order: Right to Liberty)* [2001] Fam 377 at [30] per Butler-Sloss P and [97] per Judge LJ.

[213] See regs 16 and 17 of the 1991 Regulations, for the application of which, see Parry, op cit, at 113.

removed from secure accommodation at any time by those with parental responsibility.[214] To prevent this, the local authority must, where they can, obtain a care order.[215]

Appeals etc

An appeal both against the making of or refusal to make an order by magistrates lies to the High Court.[216] Where the appeal is against the making of an order, the child may be kept in secure accommodation but not if it is against a refusal.[217] Appeals in respect of secure accommodation orders remain one of the few cases where permission is *not* required to appeal either to the High Court or to the Court of Appeal.[218]

No provision is made for the discharge of a secure accommodation order. Consequently, if an order has been validly made but it is subsequently alleged that the criteria no longer apply, the local authority's continuing retention of the child in a secure unit must be challenged either by judicial review or habeas corpus proceedings or, possibly under ss 6 and 7 of the Human Rights Act 1998.[219] According to Charles J in *S v Knowsley Borough Council*,[220] judicial review is likely in most cases to be the most appropriate remedy and can be combined with arguments relying on the Human Rights Act 1998.

Is s 25 human rights compliant?

As we discussed at the beginning of this section, the scheme on which s 25 is based, was drafted with the European Convention on Human Rights in mind but the worries then concerned the absence of any court involvement at all. Despite addressing that issue there was, at the time of the implementation of the Human Rights Act 1998, intense speculation as to whether s 25 was compatible with the Convention.[221] That was soon tested in *Re K (A Child) (Secure Accommodation Order: Right To Liberty)*[222] in which a declaration of incompatibility was sought[223] in respect of s 25. It was argued that secure accommodation amounted to a deprivation of liberty within the meaning of Art 5(1) of the Human Rights Convention[224] and could not be justified by any of the exceptions provided for in that Article.

The Court of Appeal rejected the application. While in the majority's view[225] secure accommodation did amount to a deprivation of liberty so as to engage Art 5(1) rights, it was held to be justified by reason of Art 5(1)(d) which allows the detention of a minor by lawful order for the purpose of educational supervision. In reaching this latter conclusion reliance was placed upon *Koniarska v UK*[226] in which the European Commission on Human Rights declared inadmissible a challenge to the use of secure accommodation and highlighted that 'educational supervision' should not be rigidly equated with classroom education and can include the giving of instruction to a minor to correct dysfunctional behaviour. Although it was accepted that it could be a breach to use such an order without providing any educational supervision, it was observed that the complaint would

---

[214] See s 25(9).   [215] See eg *M v Birmingham City Council* [1994] 2 FLR 141.

[216] Children Act 1989 s 94(1).

[217] See the Department of Health's *Guidance* (1991) Vol 4, para 8.49.

[218] See respectively, FPR 2010 r 30.2(b) and the Civil Procedure Rules 1998 r 52.3(1).

[219] See *LM v Essex County Council* [1999] 1 FLR 988 in which Holman J 'provisionally' considered that after making the secure accommodation order the court becomes *functus officio* and hence, some fresh action is required.   [220] [2004] EWHC 491 (Fam) [2004] 2 FLR 716 at [63]ff.

[221] See eg Parry, op cit, at 105.   [222] [2001] Fam 377, CA.

[223] Such actions are brought under s 4 of the Human Rights Act 1998.

[224] By which 'Everyone has the right to liberty and security of person'.

[225] Butler-Sloss P and Judge LJ. Thorpe LJ dissented on this, holding that 'the deprivation of liberty was a necessary consequence of an exercise of parental responsibility for the protection and promotion of his welfare'. For this he relied upon the European Court of Human Rights' decision in *Nielsen v Denmark* (1989) 11 EHRR 175.   [226] Application No. 33670/96 (12 October 2000).

be about the action of the local authority and not about the statutory provision. In any event s 25 was not to be considered incompatible with the Convention merely because it did not itself mention educational supervision.

Although *Re K* authoritatively settled the compatibility of s 25 with human rights its justification on the basis of educational supervision is not without controversy[227] while Thorpe LJ's approach that secure accommodation is within the normal parental powers seems unsustainable.[228]

A different human rights point was raised in *Re C (Secure Accommodation Order: Representation)*.[229] In that case, the child being dissatisfied with the guardian's approach, instructed another solicitor to represent her. Through an oversight that solicitor was not served with notice of the proceedings. Consequently the child in question only had two hours to instruct her on how to respond to a 15 page statement prepared by the local authority. Although the Court of Appeal accepted not only that the child's rights to a fair trial under Art 6 of the Human Rights Convention were particularly important in secure accommodation proceedings where the child's very liberty is at stake, but also that those rights should be the same as those charged with a criminal offence, it nevertheless upheld the propriety of the secure accommodation order.

Re C has been rightly criticised[230] both for making no reference to the requirement under Art 6(3)(c) that the accused should have adequate time and facilities to prepare their defence and for ignoring whether there was a breach of the Art 6(1) right to 'equality of arms'.

(c) Commentary

While secure accommodation may be the only viable means for dealing with highly disturbed adolescents (nor can it be denied that some children undoubtedly benefit from the regime),[231] as one commentator has said,[232] 'the power to restrict a child's liberty strikes at the core of a law relating to the upbringing of children, which purports to place a premium on the welfare of the child and which is of central and increasing importance within family law'. Consequently, if for no other reason, there is an understandable anxiety as to whether secure accommodation is being used, as the revised *Guidance* clearly states[233] that it should be, as a last resort. Some say[234] that in fact far too many orders are obtained unnecessarily, for example, simply to cure the 'absconding habit' of children or as a means of obtaining medical treatment rather than by using the mental health legislation. Nor is it thought that court scrutiny, at any rate at the magistrates' level, is always sufficiently rigorous.[235]

As with all draconian powers, secure accommodation orders should be used with circumspection and, particularly bearing human rights considerations in mind, only where there is no other appropriate remedy.

---

[227] For a critical analysis see J Masson 'Re K (A Child) (Secure Accommodation Order: Right to Liberty) and 'Re C (Secure Accommodation Order: Representation) securing human rights for children and young people in secure accommodation' [2002] CFLQ 77. As Masson points out, the court seems not to have appreciated that the Education Act 1996 s 562 disapplies the educational duties to those detained under a court order.

[228] This seems to be Butler-Sloss P's view see *Re K*, at [29]. Note also the point made by Judge LJ at [101] that under an order far more supervision and attention is provided than any normal parent could reasonably be expected to provide.   [229] [2001] EWCA Civ 458 [2001] 2 FLR 169.

[230] See J Masson [2002] CFLQ 77, 90 and J Fortin *Children's Rights and the Developing Law* (2009, 3rd edn) 279.

[231] See Bullock et al, op cit at n 15.   [232] Parry, op cit, 115.

[233] Vol 1, *Court Orders* (2008) at para 5.2.   [234] See Fortin, op cit, at 620.

[235] Fortin, op cit, for example cites (at 620) *Re W (A Minor) (Secure Accommodation Order)* [1993] 1 FLR 692 in which magistrates were criticised for making an order to last for three months rather than five weeks as recommended by the guardian.

16

CHILDREN AND LOCAL AUTHORITIES: INVESTIGATION OF CHILD ABUSE

A. GENERAL DUTY OF INVESTIGATION UNDER S 47

Local authorities have a statutory duty both to investigate (either themselves or via another agency, such as the NSPCC) the child's circumstances and to determine what action, if any, should be taken. This duty is imposed by s 47(1),[1] under which local authorities are obliged, where they have reasonable cause to suspect that a child who lives or is found in their area is suffering or is likely to suffer significant harm, or upon being informed that a child in their area is the subject of an emergency protection order, is in police protection, or has contravened a curfew order made under the Crime and Disorder Act 1998, to 'make or cause to be made, such enquiries as they consider necessary to enable them to decide whether they should take any action to safeguard or promote the child's welfare'.[2] If the child concerned is subject to an Emergency Protection Order (discussed later in this chapter) and is not in accommodation provided by the local authority, the authority's enquiries should also consider whether it is in the child's best interests (while the order is in force) to be so accommodated.[3] Breaking its s 47 duty can render the local authority liable in damages.[4]

Having reasonable cause to *suspect* that the child is suffering or is likely to suffer significant harm is, as Scott Baker J pointed out in *Re S (Sexual Abuse Allegations: Local Authority Response)*,[5] a low threshold for the understandable reason that the obligation is to make enquiries 'with a view to deciding whether to take any action to safeguard or

---

[1] See generally HM Government *Working Together to Safeguard Children—A guide to inter-agency working to safeguard and promote the welfare of children* (2013) (hereafter *Working Together*) pp 36–37; Department for Children, Schools and Families *Guidance and Regulations Vol 1, Court Orders* (2008) 4.73–4.82; E Isaacs and C Sheppard *Social Work Decision-Making. A guide for Childcare Lawyers* (2012, 2nd edn); Butterworths *Family Law Service* 3A [3707]ff; R White, P Carr and N Lowe *Children Act in Practice* (2008, 4th edn) ch 7 and M Hayes 'Child Protection from Principles and Polices to Practice' [1998] CFLQ 119.

[2] Local authorities are also obliged to investigate the child's circumstances following a court decision made under s 37 in other family proceedings (discussed Ch 14, Section 37 directions, p 550) or upon being notified by a local education authority that a child has persistently failed to comply with a direction given in an education supervision order (Children Act 1989 Sch 3 para 17). [3] Section 47(3)(b).

[4] *ABB, BBB, CBB and DBB v Milton Keynes Council* [2011] EWHC 2745 (QB) [2012] 1 FLR 1157.

[5] [2001] EWHC Admin 334 [2001] 2 FLR 776 at [36].

promote the child's welfare'. As Lord Nicholls later put it,[6] 'local authorities would be prevented from carrying out effective and timely risk assessments if they could only act on the basis of proven facts'. In *Re S* itself an action for judicial review against a local authority for acting upon the result of a s 47 investigation[7] was dismissed despite the claimant's previous acquittal on indecent assault charges. Notwithstanding *Re S* there must still be objectively reasonable grounds for embarking upon a s 47 investigation.[8]

Section 47 is principally directed towards the investigation of the circumstances of children living at home or who have been removed from home in an emergency.[9] Where enquiries substantiate concerns about the child's safety (and care should be taken that this investigation is adequate)[10] the local authority must arrange a 'strategy discussion' which may comprise a telephone discussion or a meeting involving different professionals. The prime tasks of such a discussion are to share information; decide whether a core assessment under s 47 should be initiated or continued; agree on what action is immediately needed to protect the child; and/or, to provide interim services and support and to decide what information should be shared with the family save where that might place a child at risk or jeopardise a police investigation of an offence.[11]

B. CO-OPERATING WITH OTHER AGENCIES TO DISCHARGE INVESTIGATIVE DUTIES

In discharging their child protection duties local authorities do not work alone. As the Department of Health's 1991 *Guidance* put it:[12]

The authority cannot expect to be the sole repository of knowledge and wisdom about particular cases. Full inter-agency co-operation including sharing information and participating in decision-making is essential whenever a possible care or supervision case is identified.

A similar point is made by *Working Together*:[13]

No single professional can have a full picture of the child's needs and circumstance and, if children and families are to receive the right help at the right time, everyone who comes into contact with them has a role to play in identifying concerns, sharing information and taking prompt action.

[6] *Re O and Another (Minors) (Care: Preliminary Hearing); Re B (A Minor)* [2003] UKHL 18 [2004] 1 AC 523 at [18].

[7] The local authority believing that the claimant presented a risk, resolved to share this information with the claimant's new partner who had children of her own.

[8] See *Gogay v Hertfordshire County Council* [2001] 1 FLR 280.

[9] Though as Hale LJ pointed out in *Gogay v Hertfordshire County Council*, at (27), the section can be adapted to cases where children are already subject to a care order. In *Gogay* itself there was some confusion as to whether the case involved a s 47 investigation or a disciplinary action against one of the local authority staff.

[10] See *Birmingham City Council v AG and A* [2009] EWHC 3720 (Fam) [2010] 2 FLR 580, in which the welfare issues which should have been at the forefront of any social work enquiries about the family had not been considered at all.   [11] See *Working Together* at p 36.

[12] *Vol 1 Court Orders*, para 3.10.   [13] Para 10.

Facilitating inter-agency co-operation are, at the planning and policy level, Local Safeguarding Children Boards[14] and, at the local level, Child Protection Conferences.[15] The principal tasks of the former[16] include advice on, and the review of, local practice and procedure for inter-agency co-operation including training. The task of the latter is to decide what action, if any, should be taken in individual cases.

Membership of both the Local Safeguarding Children Boards and the Child Protection Conferences comprises representatives from the various professions and agencies concerned with children, in particular from the social services, Cafcass, the NSPCC, the police, education authorities, the NHS Trusts and Foundation Trusts, general medical practice, the health visiting service, the Local Probation Trust and appropriate voluntary organisations. In the case of the Local Safeguarding Children Boards membership is drawn from senior representatives of each of these agencies.

There are three kinds of Child Protection Conference, the initial child protection conference, the child protection review, and the pre-birth conference.

As *Working Together* states,[17] the purpose of the initial child protection conference is to bring together and analyse in an inter-agency setting, how best to safeguard the welfare of the child. If concerns relate to an unborn child consideration has to be given as to whether to hold a child protection conference before the child's birth (a pre-birth conference).

It is the conference's responsibility to make recommendations as to how agencies work together to safeguard the child in the future. Its key task, as one commentary puts it[18] is 'to formulate a multi-agency outline child protection plan in as much detail as possible.' To that end it must appoint a key worker, identify those who will develop and implement the plan and establish how the parents, children and family should be involved in the process and, crucially, to determine the time scales.

In deciding whether the child should be the subject of a child protection plan, the key question is whether the child is at risk of significant harm.[19] If the child is thought to be so at risk it automatically follows that the child requires emergency help which in turn will require a formal child protection plan. The aim of a child protection plan, which superseded the scheme of placing children on the Child Protection Register (which was phased out in 2008), is to ensure that the child is safe from harm and to prevent him or her suffering further harm, to promote the child's health and development and to support the family and wider family members to safeguard and promote the welfare of the child, provided it is in the best interests of the child.[20]

The purpose of the child protection *review*, which should be held within three months of the initial child protection conference and thereafter at intervals of no more than six months while the child remains the subject of the plan, is to review whether the child is continuing to suffer, or is likely to suffer, significant harm, and to review developmental progress against the child protection plan outcomes. It must also consider whether the child protection plan should continue or be changed.[21]

If it is judged that the child is no longer continuing, or is likely, to suffer significant harm, or that the child and his/her family has moved permanently to another area or that

---

[14] Which all local authorities in England must establish: Children Act 2004 s 13.

[15] See generally *Working Together* pp 40–45.

[16] See Children Act 2004 s 14, the Local Safeguarding Children Boards Regulations 2006 and *Working Together* ch 4.   [17] At p 40.

[18] Isaacs and Shepherd, op cit at 6.27.   [19] This concept is the linchpin of s 31: see Ch 17.

[20] *Working Together* p 42.   [21] *Working Together* p 44.

the child has reached 18,[22] has died, or has permanently left the United Kingdom, then the child should no longer be the subject of a child protection plan.[23]

The Child Protection Conference's dual function of promoting the dissemination of information about a child among various agencies and of co-ordinating the work of these services is crucial to the management of child protection. All too often, tragedies have resulted in cases where vital information about a child's circumstances has not been communicated to the local authority. With properly co-ordinated services there is a better chance of spotting warning signs of abuse or neglect and of constructive action being taken before crisis points have been reached. As against this, however, there is the danger of excessive investigation which in itself may be damaging to the child and family, and of having too many children under investigation. These at any rate were two of the concerns voiced in *Messages from Research*.[24] Other concerns were that too much focus was placed on specific incidents rather than on examination of the child's needs and that in cases where the test of 'significant harm' is not thought to be satisfied there tends to be a failure to provide any Part III services, regardless of the child's needs.

The key message is that the proper discharge of the investigative duties under s 47 requires them to be in proportion to the circumstances. Clearly, the nature of that investigation must depend on the seriousness and possible cause of any harm, whether the child (and other children) is in a safe place, and on what is already known about the family. If the child has already suffered significant harm then there will need to be an investigation of some kind so as to establish cause. If the harm is serious enough to give rise to the possibility that a criminal offence has been committed, or its cause is not adequately explained, the case ought then to be referred to a Police Child Protection Team.

C. SHORT-TERM PROTECTION

1. INTRODUCTION

As the Department of Health's original 1991 *Guidance* pointed out,[25] action under s 47 'should be seen as the usual first step when a question of child protection arises. . .'[26] It may be that, the matters having been investigated, the problems can be solved with the co-operation of the family and no further formal action is necessary. On the other hand, further action may be thought imperative to protect the child. Short-term protection is governed by Part V of the Act, which, as the revised 2008 *Guidance* puts it, is designed:[27]

> . . . to ensure that effective protective action can be taken within a framework of proper safeguards and reasonable opportunities for parents (or others with parental responsibility for the child) to challenge relevant action before a court. The measures are short-term and time-limited, and may or may not lead to further action . . .

---

[22] To end the plan the local authority should have a review around the child's birthday, which should be planned in advance.   [23] *Working Together* p 46.

[24] Department of Health *Child Protection Messages from Research* (1995) which made the point that of the 160,000 annual referrals to the child protection system, 40,000 (25%) were closed after only limited investigation.   [25] Vol 1, *Court Orders* para 4.78.

[26] Without such intervention the local authority is unlikely to succeed on any application for an emergency protection order or child assessment order.   [27] Vol 1, *Court Orders* para 4.6.

No local authority and no social worker has any power to remove a child from his or her parent without the parent's consent unless they have obtained a court order empowering them to do so.[28] The two principal court orders under Part V are emergency protection orders and child assessment orders. In addition, powers are given to the police to take a child into police protection. We discuss each of these powers in turn.

2. EMERGENCY PROTECTION ORDERS

(a) Introduction

The purpose of an emergency protection order ('EPO')[29] is to provide for the immediate removal or retention of a child in a genuine emergency. As the revised 2008 *Guidance* stresses:[30]

> It should be remembered that an EPO, which has the effect of separating a child from his parents, is a 'draconian' and 'extremely harsh' measure and one requiring 'exceptional justification' and 'extraordinarily compelling reasons'...It should not be regarded as being an automatic response in a case of suspected child abuse or as a routine first step to initiating care proceedings.

Orders necessarily engage Art 8 human rights (ie to respect for private and family life) and intervention has to be proportionate to the risk involved.[31]

As Munby J said in *X Council v B (Emergency Protection Orders)*:[32]

> (i) An EPO, summarily removing a child from his parents, is a 'draconian' and 'extremely harsh' measure, requiring 'exceptional justification' and 'extraordinarily compelling reasons'. Such an order should not be made unless the [court] is satisfied that it is both necessary and proportionate and that no other less radical form of order will achieve the essential end of promoting the welfare of the child. Separation is only to be contemplated if immediate separation is essential to secure the child's safety: 'imminent' danger must be 'actually established'.
>
> (ii) Both the local authority which seeks and the [court] which makes an EPO assume a heavy burden of responsibility. It is important that both the local authority and the [the court] approach every application for an EPO with an anxious awareness

---

[28] See *R (G) v Nottingham City Council* [2008] EWHC 152 (Admin) [2008] 1 FLR 1660, at [15], per Munby J.

[29] See generally DfE *Statutory Guidance on court orders and pre-proceedings* (2014) ch 4 paras 13–29; the Department for Children, Schools and Families' *Guidance and Regulations, Vol 1, Court Orders* (2008), paras 4.25ff; and J Masson 'Emergency Intervention to Protect Children: Using and Avoiding Legal Controls' [2005] CFLQ 75. The provisions are based on the recommendations of DHSS *Review of Child Care Law* (1985) ch 13, following widespread criticism (see eg *Report of the Inquiry into Child Abuse in Cleveland in 1987* Cm 412 (1988); T Norris and N Parton 'Administration of Place of Safety Orders' [1987] JSWL 1) of place of safety orders which emergency protection orders replaced. The criticisms included that such orders were routinely used as method of starting proceedings rather than in genuine emergencies and that they were granted too readily, often by a single justice in his own home.

[30] Vol 1, *Court Orders* paras 4.25 and 4.27.

[31] Removal of babies will be particularly hard to justify in the light of the decision of the European Court of Human Rights in *P, C and S v United Kingdom* (2002) 35 EHRR 546 [2002] 2 FLR 631. See also *K and T v Finland* [2001] 2 FLR 707. Compare, however, *Re M (Care Proceedings: Judicial Review)* [2003] EWHC 850 (Admin) [2003] 2 FLR 171.

[32] [2004] EWHC 2005 (Fam) [2005] 1 FLR 341 at para [57]. See also *Re X (Emergency Protection Orders)* [2006] EWHC 510 (Fam) [2006] 2 FLR 701 per McFarlane J. Both approved by the Court of Appeal in *A v East Sussex County Council and Chief Constable of Sussex Police* [2010] EWCA Civ 743 [2010] 2 FLR 1596.

of the extreme gravity of the relief being sought and a scrupulous regard for the European Convention rights of both the child and the parents.

Even if intervention is thought necessary, it should always be done sensitively with a view to promoting the child's interests and, so far as it is consistent to do so, without overlooking the interests of the other members of the family. So-called 'dawn raids' (ie where children are removed from their families during the night), for example, should rarely be necessary.[33] In any event, thought should always be given to whether the alleged abuser, rather than the child, should be removed from the family.[34]

(b) The grounds for an emergency protection order

Likely to suffer harm

Section 44(1) provides the first of three grounds upon which an emergency protection order may be made, namely that on the application of any person[35] the court is satisfied that there is reasonable cause to believe that the child is likely to suffer significant harm if he:

(i)   is not removed to accommodation provided by or on behalf of the applicant; or

(ii) does not remain in the place in which he is then being accommodated.

Although commonly the applicant will be the local authority or NSPCC, *any* person may apply under this provision, including even a parent or relative.[36] Where the applicant is not the relevant local authority, provision has been made for the authority, if they think it is in the child's best interests, to take over the order and therefore the powers and responsibilities for the child that go with it.[37] The court (and not the applicant) must be satisfied about likelihood of significant harm.[38] The ground itself is prospective, so that evidence of past or even current harm is not sufficient unless it indicates that harm is likely to recur in the future. Moreover, the risk of harm contemplated should be that which is anticipated during the period of the order.[39] On the other hand, this prospective test can be satisfied even though the harm to the particular child has not yet occurred, for example, where a convicted sexual offender moves in with the mother.

Denial of access to the child

Under s 44(1)(b) an order can be made upon application of a local authority where they are making enquiries under s 47(1)(b) because they (ie the local authority) have

---

[33] Such removals, for example in Orkney's and Rochdale's satanic child abuse cases (see respectively R Brett 'Orkney: aberration or system?' (1991) 3 Journal of Child Law 143 and *Rochdale Borough Council v A* [1991] 2 FLR 192), caused considerable public disquiet. In *Re A (Minors)(Child Abuse: Guidelines)* [1992] 1 All ER 153 it was held that they should only be effected when there are clear grounds for believing significant harm would otherwise be caused to the children or vital evidence is only obtainable by such means.

[34] Viz. by an exclusion order, discussed at The power to add an exclusion requirement, p 587, or by other means, on which see C Cobley 'Child abuse, child protection and the criminal law' (1992) 4 *Journal of Child Law* 78.   [35] It is clearly envisaged that a local authority can apply.

[36] In such cases the local authority will also have to become involved, because under s 47(1) they have a duty to investigate upon being informed of the existence of such an order. For the difficulties of individuals obtaining an extension, see Duration of order, p 588.

[37] See the Emergency Protection Order (Transfer of Responsibilities) Regulations 1991 (SI 1991/1414), referred to *Guidance and Regulations*, Vol 1 *Court Orders* (2008) at para 4.31.

[38] For discussion of the meaning of 'significant harm' and 'likelihood' see Ch 17.

[39] See *Re C and B (Care Order: Future Harm)* [2001] 1 FLR 611 at [19] per Hale LJ.

reasonable cause to suspect that a child is suffering, or is likely to suffer, significant harm,[40] and 'those enquiries are being frustrated by access to the child being unreasonably refused to a person authorised to seek access and that the applicant has reasonable cause to believe that access to the child is required as a matter of urgency'. Similar provision is made[41] for an application in the same circumstances by an authorised person (ie the NSPCC).[42]

Section 44(1)(b) and (c) were intended[43] to be used in emergencies where enquiries cannot be completed because the child cannot be seen but there is enough cause to suspect the child is suffering or is likely to suffer significant harm. In cases where there is a need for further investigation of a child's health and development but he is thought to be safe from immediate danger, the proper order, if any, is a child assessment order.[44] The Department of Health's 1991 *Guidance and Regulations* put the point well, commenting:[45]

> The hypothesis of the grounds at section 44(1)(b) and (c) is that this combination of factors is evidence of an emergency or the likelihood of an emergency.

It also made the further point:

> The court will have to decide whether the refusal of access to the child was unreasonable in the circumstances. It might consider a refusal unreasonable if the person refusing had had explained to him the reason for the enquiries and the request for access, the request itself was reasonable, and he had failed to respond positively in some other suitable way—by arranging for the child to be seen immediately by his GP, for example. Refusal of a request to see a sleeping child in the middle of the night may not be unreasonable,[46] but refusal to allow access at a reasonable time without good reason could well be.

The revised 2008 *Guidance* points out:[47]

> The circumstances in which the 'frustrated access' grounds justify an EPO must be distinguished from the child assessment order. The local authority should apply for an EPO where access is required as a matter of urgency. If the real purpose of the authority's application is to enable the authority to assess the child i.e. there is a need for further investigation of the child's health and development but he is not considered to be in immediate danger then the child assessment order is the more appropriate route for the local authority to follow.

Section 44(1) provides the minimum conditions that must be satisfied before an order can be made. However, it is not intended that upon being satisfied of the condition under

---

[40] The duties under s 47 are discussed at the beginning of this chapter.   [41] Section 44(1)(c).

[42] Children Act 1989 s 31(9).

[43] The provision was introduced following a recommendation in the Kimberley Carlile Inquiry (*A Child in Mind*, para 7.24). It was a late amendment to the legislation and was little debated.

[44] See points (iii) and (iv) forcibly made by Munby J in *X Council v B (Emergency Protection Orders)* [2004] EWHC 2015 (Fam) [2005] 1 FLR 341 at [57], and re-emphasised by McFarlane J in *Re X (Emergency Protection Orders)* [2006] EWHC 510 (Fam) [2006] 2 FLR 701 who made the point that (a) mere lack of information or a need for assessment can never of themselves establish the existence of a genuine emergency and (b) cases of emotional abuse will rarely, if ever, warrant an emergency protection order. Child assessment orders are discussed at Child assessment orders, pp 589ff.   [45] Vol 1, para 4.39.

[46] Indeed, removals in the middle of the night will require special justification: cf *Re A (Minors) (Child Abuse: Guidelines)* [1992] 1 All ER 153, per Hollings J.   [47] At para 4.35.

s 44(1) the court should automatically make an order. The court must still consider both the welfare principle, pursuant to s 1(1) and whether or not to make an order, pursuant to s 1(5). Since these proceedings are not 'family proceedings'[48] the court cannot make a s 8 order. On the other hand, it can give directions about contact and medical or psychiatric examination or other assessment of the child.[49] It has been said[50] that where the removal of a baby is thought justified 'one would normally expect arrangements to be made by the local authority to facilitate contact on a regular and generous basis'.

(c) Procedure

According to Munby J in *X Council v B (Emergency Protection Orders)*[51] a without notice (then referred to as an ex parte) application is normally only appropriate where the case is of genuine emergency or other great urgency (and even then in most cases some informal notice ought to be able to be given to the parents) and where an application is so made the evidential burden is even heavier with applicants (normally the local authority) being duty bound to make 'the fullest and most candid and fresh disclosure of all the circumstances known to them'. The revised *Guidance*[52] underscores the point emphasised by Munby J[53] that save in wholly exceptional circumstances application for Emergency Protection Orders should be made on notice, with parents being notified that an application is being made.

A court hearing the application may take account of any statement contained in any report made to the court in the course of or in connection with the hearing or any evidence given during the hearing, which is in the opinion of the court relevant to the application.[54] This enables the court to give proper weight to hearsay, opinions, health visiting or social work records and to medical reports.

(d) The effects of an order

An emergency protection order authorises, but does not direct,[55] either the removal to or prevention of removal from accommodation provided by or on behalf of the applicant.[56] In the former instance the order operates as a direction to any person who is in a position to do so to comply with any request to produce the child to the applicant.[57] The court may also authorise an applicant to enter specified premises and search for a child and may include another child in the order if it believes there might be another child on the premises.[58]

The order gives the applicant parental responsibility for the child,[59] but this is limited: the power to remove or to prevent removal can only be exercised to safeguard and

---

[48] As defined by s 8(3), (4), discussed in Ch 14.

[49] Children Act 1989 s 44(6), discussed at The power to add directions, p 587.

[50] Per Munby J in *Re M (Care Proceedings: Judicial Review)* [2003] EWHC 850 (Admin) [2003] 2 FLR 171 at [44] point (iv).

[51] [2004] EWHC 2015 (Fam) [2005] 1 FLR 341 at [57] points (viii) and (ix). See also *Re X (Emergency Protection Orders)* [2006] EWHC 510 (Fam) [2006] 2 FLR 510, at [101] per McFarlane J.

[52] Vol 1 *Court Orders* (2008) para 4.2.

[53] Per Munby J in *X Council v B (Emergency Protection Orders)* [2004] EWHC 2015 (Fam) [2005] 1 FLR 341 at [57] point (vii) repeating what he said in *Re M* at [44] point (iii).

[54] Children Act 1989 s 45(7).

[55] According to Munby J in *X Council v B* at [57] point (xii) even after it has obtained an order the local authority is still under an obligation to consider less drastic alternatives to emergency removal.

[56] Section 44(4)(b).   [57] Section 44(4)(a).

[58] Section 48(3), (4). This does not give the power to make a forced entry. If the applicant is refused or likely to be refused entry, the court may issue a warrant authorising a constable to assist in the execution of the order using reasonable force if necessary: s 48(9).   [59] Section 44(4)(c).

promote the child's welfare.[60] Hence, for example, if the applicant gains access and finds that the child is neither harmed nor likely to be harmed, he may not remove the child.[61] In any event, an applicant can exercise responsibility only insofar as it is reasonably required to safeguard or promote the child's welfare, having regard in particular to the duration of the order.[62] In other words, an emergency protection order only gives authority to the applicant to make the necessary day-to-day decisions whilst taking care of the child.

(e) The power to add directions

In the absence of a court direction the applicant must, during the subsistence of the order, allow the child reasonable contact with his parents, any other person with parental responsibility, any person with whom he was living immediately before the order, any person named in a child arrangements order as a person with whom the child is to spend time or otherwise have contact and any person acting on behalf of those persons.[63] The court, however, may give such directions as it considers appropriate about contact and may impose conditions.[64]

Medical evidence is likely to be of importance in any future care proceedings, so that early decisions or directions about examinations are crucial. For this reason, although the parental responsibility acquired on the making of the order would permit the applicant to consent to the child's examination or assessment, it might be preferable to seek directions on the issue. Section 44(6)(b) empowers the court to make directions as to a medical or psychiatric examination or other assessment of the child, and under s 44(8) the court may direct that there be no such examination or assessment. Although s 44(7) expressly provides that, notwithstanding a court order, the child can, if of sufficient understanding to make an informed decision, refuse to submit to an examination or other assessment, as we discuss in relation to the equivalent provision in relation to interim care,[65] it has been controversially held[66] that the High Court has an inherent power to override that refusal.

(f) The power to add an exclusion requirement

Following amendments introduced by the Family Law Act 1996 courts can add an exclusion requirement[67] to any emergency protection order.[68] Such an order requires the person named in the order to leave the child's home or defined area where the home is situated and prohibits him from re-entering the home or defined area.[69] This power, conferred by s 44A of the 1989 Act, is subject to the court being satisfied of three conditions:

(1) there is reasonable cause to believe that the child will consequently not be likely to suffer significant harm or that the enquiries will cease to be frustrated;

---

[60] Section 44(5)(a). Removals should normally be at an agreed time following consultation with appropriate professionals. A proper explanation must be given to the child: Department of Health *Guidance and Regulations*, Vol 1, para 4.58.

[61] Similarly, if a return appears safe, the child should be returned: s 44(10). In each case this might occur where the alleged abuser vacates the home. [62] Section 44(5)(b).

[63] Section 44(13), as amended by the Children and Families Act 2014 Sch2 para 35. This presumption of reasonable contact is in line with the general policy of the Act: see the discussion in Ch 18.

[64] Section 44(6) and (8).

[65] Viz. s 38(6), discussed in Ch 17, Making directions on interim applications, pp 645ff.

[66] Per Douglas Brown J in *South Glamorgan County Council v W and B* [1993] 1 FLR 574.

[67] For the background to this provision, see the Law Commission report, Law Com No 207 *Domestic Violence and the Occupation of the Family Home* (1992) paras 6.15ff.

[68] Separate statements of evidence in support of exclusions, which must be served personally on the relevant person, are required: FPR 2010 r 12.28(1), (2) and *Re W (Exclusion: Statement of Evidence)* [2000] 2 FLR 666. [69] Section 44A(3).

(2) there is someone (whether a parent or some other person) living in the home who is able and willing 'to give to the child the care which it would be reasonable to expect a parent to give to him'; and

(3) that that other person consents[70] to the exclusion requirement.

The exclusion requirement may last no longer than the emergency protection order, though it can be made for a shorter period.[71] In any event, the exclusion ceases to be enforceable if the applicant removes the child from the dwelling place for more than 24 hours.[72] A power of arrest may be attached to the requirement.[73]

Instead of making the exclusion requirement, the court is empowered to accept undertakings in similar terms.[74] However, although such undertakings are enforceable through contempt proceedings, no power of arrest can be attached.[75]

(g) Duration of the order

In the first instance an emergency protection order may be granted for up to eight days.[76] Save where the applicant is an individual,[77] the court can, upon application, grant one period of extension[78] for a further seven days.[79] It has been said[80] that no order should be made for 'any longer than is absolutely necessary to protect the child' and that where an application is made ex parte very careful consideration should be given to making the order for the 'shortest possible period commensurate with the preservation of the child's immediate safety'.

There is no appeal against the making or refusal to make an emergency protection order.[81] However, an application to discharge the order may be made by the child, parent, any other person with parental responsibility or any person with whom the child was living before the order was made,[82] except where the person was given notice of and was present at the original hearing.[83] The former embargo against hearing an application for the discharge of an order before the expiry of 72 hours after the making of the order was repealed by the Children and Young Persons Act 2008.[84]

The inability to appeal a *refusal*[85] to make or extend an order has been criticised on more than one occasion. A striking example was *Re P (Emergency Protection Order)*,[86] in which justices refused to extend an order notwithstanding firm medical evidence pointing to a risk of life-threatening abuse (the mother having being diagnosed as suffering from fabricated illness syndrome by proxy). The inability to challenge that refusal prompted Johnson J to comment[87] that consideration should be given to providing a mechanism for review, though he added that such a mechanism would have to be one which could operate very quickly.

---

[70] The consent must either be written or given orally to the court: FPR 2010 r 12.29(1)(b).

[71] Section 44A(4).   [72] Section 44A(10).   [73] Section 44A(5).

[74] Section 44B.   [75] Section 44B(2).   [76] Section 45(1).

[77] Section 45(4) only permits applications for extensions by those entitled to apply for a care order, viz. a local authority or 'authorised person'.

[78] Section 45(6).   [79] Section 45(5).

[80] Per Munby J in *X Council v B (Emergency Protection Orders)* [2004] EWHC 2015 (Fam) [2005] 1 FLR 341 at [57] point (v).

[81] Section 45(10).   [82] Section 45(8).   [83] Section 45(11).

[84] Section 30, which repealed s 45(9) of the 1989 Act. As the Explanatory Notes to the 2008 Act explains (see paras 128-9) the reason for the repeal was to ensure the discharge provisions are compatible with Arts 6 and 8 of the European Convention on Human Rights.

[85] Technically it might be possible to challenge an unreasonable refusal by judicial review.

[86] [1996] 1 FLR 482. See also *Essex County Council v F* [1993] 1 FLR 847, per Douglas Brown J.

[87] [1996] 1 FLR 482 at 484–5.

(h) The use of emergency protection orders

Compared with the annual numbers of place of safety orders made before the 1989 Act (about 5,000) the number of emergency protection orders since the Act has been dramatically low. Indeed, under half that number, 2,300 were made in 1993 and, although this rose to 3,100 in 1994, they had dropped back again to about 2,565 by 1996.[88] Since then they declined further to 2,390 in 2004[89] and only 1,181 in 2011.[90] Given that the new powers were not intended to be used as a routine way of starting care proceedings, some reduction in numbers was to be expected. However, given the subsequent sharp fall in the number of emergency protection orders (as against a general rise in care orders) it is clear some other explanation needs to be sought. It has been suggested[91] that against a general background of local authorities being less interventionist, they are in fact more prepared to make alternative arrangements, and in particular to accommodate a child without prejudicing the possibility of later seeking a care order after a further investigation. In short, while emergency protection orders provide an important and, on occasion, essential means of protecting children from immediate threats of harm, they are more in the nature of back-up powers should other means of protection not be sufficient. Indeed one of the aims of good social work practice is to avoid emergencies arising wherever possible.

3. CHILD ASSESSMENT ORDERS

Described as 'a multi-disciplinary assessment in non-emergency situations',[92] a child assessment order[93] had no parallel in the pre-1989 Act law. It was first proposed in the report into the death of Kimberley Carlile[94] (in which, prior to her death, social workers had been frustrated by her carers on numerous occasions in their attempts to see Kimberley) but the order was only included in the 1989 Act as a late amendment in response to a demand for a power to be able to see, examine and assess a child where there is concern as to his welfare, in the face of lack of co-operation from those responsible for him. As the *Statutory Guidance on court orders and pre-proceedings* explains:[95]

> A child assessment order enables an assessment of the child's health or development, or of the way in which s/he has been treated, to be carried out where significant harm is suspected. Its use is most relevant in circumstances where the child is not thought to be at immediate risk, to the extent that removal from his/her parents' care is required, but where parents have refused to cooperate with attempts to assess the child. This may be where the suspected harm to the child appears to be longer-term and cumulative rather than sudden and severe.

Examples of where an assessment order might be appropriate, have been said to include:[96]

---

[88] These at times inexact statistics can be found in the CAAC Reports of 1997, 1994/5 and 1993/4. See in particular Table 2C of the 1997 Report (note that the graph is based on a six-month period). See J Masson 'Emergency Intervention to Protect Children: Using and Avoiding Legal Controls' [2005] CFLQ 75.

[89] See *Judicial Statistics* for 2004, Table 5.2.   [90] *Civil Judicial Statistics* for 2011, Table 2.4.

[91] R White, P Carr and N Lowe *Children Act in Practice* (2002, 3rd edn) 7.51.

[92] By David Mellor 158 HC Official Report, col 596.

[93] See generally R Lavery 'The Child Assessment Order—A Re-Assessment' [1996] CFLQ 41 and J Dickens 'Assessment and the Control of Social Work: An Analysis of Reasons for the Non-Use of the Child Assessment Order' [1993] JSWFL 88.

[94] *A Child in Mind—The Report of an Inquiry into the Death of Kimberley Carlile* (1987).

[95] DfE (2014) ch 4 para 5.   [96] See DCSF *Guidance and Regulations* (2008) para 4.12.

A persistent concern about a child who appears to be failing to thrive;

Parents who are ignorant of or unwilling to face up to possible harm to their child arising from his state of health or development; or

The existence of some evidence that the child may be subject to continuing or periodic
abuse and/or where there is an urgent need to gather particular forensic evidence which
would not otherwise be available.

In all cases the local authority should always make enquiries into the child's circumstances, details of which the court will expect to be given.[97]

(a) Application and criteria

As with applications for care and supervision orders, but unlike emergency protection
orders, only the local authority and the NSPCC (as the only authorised person)[98] may
apply for a child assessment order.

Under s 43(1) the court may make an order if it is satisfied that:

(a) the applicant has reasonable cause to suspect that the child is suffering or is likely to
suffer significant harm;

(b) an assessment of the state of the child's health or development, or of the way in which
he has been treated, is required to enable the applicant to determine whether or not
the child is suffering, or is likely to suffer, significant harm; and

(c) it is unlikely that such an assessment will be made, or be satisfactory, in the absence of
a child assessment order.

It has been said[99] that if the real purpose of an application is to have the child assessed then
consideration should be given as to whether that objective 'cannot equally effectively, and
more proportionately' be achieved by a child assessment order rather than emergency protection order. Nevertheless it is to be emphasised that this order is not intended to be in any
sense a substitute for an emergency protection order. Indeed s 43(4) specifically enjoins the
court *not* to make an assessment order if there are grounds for making an emergency protection order and the court thinks it ought to make such an order. The court is empowered
to treat an application for an assessment order as an application for an emergency protection order.[100] The fact that applications are made on notice[101] and the hearing is *inter partes*
further emphasises that these orders are not designed to deal with emergencies.

Even if the court is satisfied as to the existence of the conditions, it is not bound to make
the order. As with other orders under the 1989 Act, the court must, pursuant to s 1(1) and
(5), have regard to the paramountcy of the child's welfare and be satisfied that making the
order would be better for the child than making no order at all. However, because these
proceedings do *not* rank as 'family proceedings',[102] the court *cannot* make a s 8 order.

A child assessment order cannot be made where an emergency protection or care order
is made, but in principle there is no reason why it cannot be made in respect of an accommodated child, and it can co-exist with a s 8 order. It is thought, however, that there is

---

[97] Ibid at para 4.14.   [98] Children Act 1989 s 31(9) and s 43(13).

[99] Per Munby J in *X Council v B (Emergency Protection Orders)* [2004] EWHC 2015 (Fam) [2005] 1 FLR
341 at [49] and [57] point (iv). See also *Re X (Emergency Protection Orders)* [2006] EWHC 510 (Fam) [2006]
2 FLR 701.

[100] Section 43(3).   [101] Section 43(11).

[102] See s 8(3), (4), discussed in Ch 14, Family proceedings, p 535. Nor need the checklist under s 1(3) be
applied: *Re R (Recovery Orders)* [1998] 2 FLR 401.

no power to treat an application for an emergency protection order as one for a child assessment order, even if the court believes that the less interventionist order is all that is required.[103]

(b) Effect, commencement and duration of the order

A child assessment order has the twofold effect of placing a duty on any person, who is in a position to do so, to produce the child to the person named in the order and to comply with such directions relating to his assessment as may be specified,[104] and of authorising any person carrying out the assessment, or any part of it, to do so in accordance with the order.[105]

To give time to make suitable arrangements to set up the assessment, the maximum period of the order is seven days, but this period runs from the date specified in the order and not from the date on which the order was made.[106]

Section 43(6) empowers the court to make directions on any matter relating to the assessment, including directions as to the kind of assessment which is to take place and with what aim, by whom and where it will be carried out, and whether it will be subject to conditions, such as that the assessment should be a joint one involving experts appointed by the child's parents or the children's guardian as well as by the local authority. If an intrusive examination is to take place, such as a biopsy or genital examination, specific direction should be given. The order should include a direction as to whom the result of the assessment should be given.

Directions may also be made about whether and, if so, for how long, a child may be kept away from home.[107] Indeed, since an assessment order does not confer parental responsibility, the child may only be kept away from home in accordance with court directions. If the child is to be kept away from home, the order must contain such directions as the courts thinks fit as to the contact the child is to be allowed to have with other persons.[108]

Notwithstanding any court directions, if the child is of sufficient understanding to make an informed decision he may refuse to submit to a medical or psychiatric examination or other assessment.[109]

(c) The use of child assessment orders

The expectation[110] that child assessment orders would not be made frequently has been borne out by experience. For example, in the year ending 30 September 1992 (that is the first year in which the 1989 Act operated) only 105 applications were made,[111] but their use has declined even from this. In 2011 only 18 applications were made, of which 8 were withdrawn, 1 refused and 9 orders made.[112] One reason for the lack of use of assessment orders is the seven-day time limit; indeed one researcher found[113] this to be one of the key

---

[103] See Butterworths *Family Law Service* at 3A [3738.2].   [104] Section 43(6).

[105] Section 43(7).

[106] Section 43(5). It is thought that the period must run continuously rather than eg one day a week for seven weeks: see Clarke Hall and Morrison, on *Children*, 8 [63].   [107] Section 43(9).

[108] Section 43(10).

[109] Section 43(8). There is a similar provision (s 44(7)) in relation to emergency protection orders, upon which note *South Glamorgan County Council v W and B* [1993] 1 FLR 574, discussed at The power to add directions, p 587.

[110] The Department of Health's *Guidance*, (1991) Vol 1, para 4.23 advised 'The child assessment order should be used sparingly'.   [111] Children Act Report 1992 (HMSO).

[112] *Civil Judicial Statistics for 2011*, Table 2.4.

[113] J Dickens 'Assessment and the Control of Social Work: An Analysis of Reasons for the Non-Use of the Child Assessment Order' [1993] JSWFL 88 at 97.

reasons for not seeking to use the powers. Clearly, given the limited length of the order, any assessment of the child will be little more than an initial one (and for this reason arrangements for the assessment need to be carefully planned). Although it has been suggested[114] that it was misconceived to apply any time limit to the order, it is important to bear in mind that the whole purpose of the order is to obtain sufficient evidence either to allay fears about the child's well-being or to justify further action. Seven days should therefore give enough time to achieve this limited purpose. It has also been said[115] that the technical requirements of s 43 make it difficult to operate such that local authorities prefer instead to persist with efforts to obtain the co-operation of those caring for the child.

There had been some speculation that Munby J's comments in *X Council v B (Emergency Protection Orders)*[116] that the 1989 Act provides a 'carefully calibrated hierarchy of means' to respond to a child's needs and that any order 'must provide for the least interventionist solution consistent with the preservation of the child's immediate safety', might have led to assessment orders being used more often but the statistics show that they have not.

Given the paucity of orders one may wonder whether child assessment orders are really necessary but in theory, at any rate, the s 43 powers remain of some use, particularly where parents are ignorant or resistant to thinking about the possible harm to their child because of the state of his health or development.

4. POLICE PROTECTION

The police have limited but important powers to protect children.[117] Indeed, in some areas out of hours protection is arranged through the use of police protection.[118] Section 46(1) of the 1989 Act enables a constable who has reasonable cause to believe that a child would otherwise be likely to suffer significant harm either to remove him to suitable accommodation and keep him there, or to 'take such steps as are reasonable to ensure that the child's removal from any hospital, or other place, in which he is then being accommodated, is prevented'. Although there is no power to enter premises to search for a child under s 46,[119] where search and entry is required, other powers may be used as, for example, obtaining a warrant under s 48 of the Police and Criminal Evidence Act 1984.[120] No child may be kept in police protection for more than 72 hours.[121]

Commonly, the power has been used to hold children such as runaways or glue sniffers or those whose parents have abandoned them. It may also be used where an officer attends a domestic dispute and finds a child living in unhygienic conditions. *Langley v Liverpool City Council*[122] establishes that although the s 46 power to remove a child can be exercised even where an emergency protection order is in force, a police officer who knows that such an order is in force should not exercise the s 46 power unless there are compelling reasons

---

[114] R Lavery 'The Child Assessment Order—A Re-Assessment' [1996] CFLQ 41 at 55.

[115] R White, P Carr and N Lowe *Children Act in Practice* (2008, 4th edn) para 7.62.

[116] [2004] EWHC 2015 (Fam) [2005] 1 FLR 341 at [49].

[117] Note: we are not discussing a police protection *order* as is commonly supposed. See generally DfE *Statutory Guidance on court orders and pre-proceedings* (2014) ch 4 paras 30-38; the Department for Schools, Children and Families' *Guidance and Regulations*, Vol 1 (2008), paras 4.64 – 4.71; C Cobley *Child Abuse and The Law* (1995) pp 51ff; C Cobley 'Child Abuse, Child Protection and the Criminal Law' (1992) 4 *Journal of Child Law* 78; and A Borkowski 'Police Protection and Section 46' [1995] Fam Law 204.

[118] See J Masson 'Emergency intervention to protect children: using and avoiding legal controls' [2005] CFLQ 75 at 78-79, and M Booth *Delay in Public Children Act Cases Second Report* (1996) para 8.15.

[119] The statement to the contrary in *Working Together* (2013) at ch 2 para 16 is wrong.

[120] Section 17(1)(e): See the revised *Guidance and Regulations* (2008) para 4.64.

[121] Children Act 1989 s 46(6).   [122] [2005] EWCA Civ 1173 [2006] 1 WLR 375.

to do so. In other words, removal of children should usually be effected pursuant to an emergency protection order and s 46 invoked only where it is not practical to do so. As *Working Together* states:[123]

> Police emergency powers can help in an emergency situation but should be used only where necessary. Wherever possible, the decision to remove a child from a parent or carer should be made by a court.

This advice echoes Hedley J's comment in *A v East Sussex County Council and Chief Constable of Sussex Police*[124] that where practicable an order of the court should be sought in preference to the use of the s 46 power. The *East Sussex* case is also authority for saying that where a removal is made under s 46, an *inter partes* court hearing should normally be arranged within two days.[125]

Section 46(4) requires a constable taking a child into police protection to inform, as soon as is reasonably practicable, relevant local authorities, the child, his parents and other specified persons about the steps that have been taken in relation to the child.

He must secure that the case is inquired into by a 'designated officer'. That officer on completing his enquiries must release the child, unless he considers that there is still reasonable cause for believing that the child would be likely to suffer significant harm if released.[126] Where the child remains at risk the designated officer may seek an emergency protection order on behalf of the local authority,[127] if necessary, without consultation.[128]

The police do not acquire parental responsibility, but must do what is reasonable in all the circumstances of the case for the purpose of safeguarding or promoting the child's welfare, having regard, in particular, to the length of the period during which the child will be in police protection.[129]

---

[123] Ch 2 para 16. The need to use s 46 sparingly is re-iterated in *Statutory guidance on court orders and pre-proceedings* (2014) ch 4 para 30.   [124] [2010] EWCA Civ 743 [2010] 2 FLR 1596 at [23].

[125] See also *A (A Child) v Chief Constable of Dorset Police)* [2010] EWHC 1748 (Admin) [2011] 1 FLR 11 in which a 16 year old was compulsorily taken to and detained for 90 minutes in a safe centre in connection with alcohol and drugs under s 46, in which it was held that the parents were entitled to know the broad kind of harm from which the boy was thought to be at risk.

[126] Section 46(5).   [127] Section 46(7).

[128] Section 46(8). It is normally expected that there will be consultation: see Borkowski, op cit, at 205.

[129] Section 46(9).

17

CHILDREN AND LOCAL AUTHORITIES: CARE AND SUPERVISION PROCEEDINGS

A. INTRODUCTION

The Children Act 1989 places considerable importance on local authorities working in partnership with families and the avoidance wherever possible of court proceedings. Furthermore, as Lord Clyde observed in *Lancashire County Council v B*,[1] even the making of a care application is a step not lightly to be embarked upon since the:

> stress which care proceedings may well impose on the parents may . . . itself be damaging to the child. If the parents are themselves in fact innocent of any harm to the child the proceedings may simply be defeating the basic purpose and the policy of the Act. The initiating of proceedings may in some cases be readily and immediately a matter of obvious necessity. But in other cases it may be something not to be embarked upon without careful deliberation and a professional objectivity.

As Lord Clyde said,[2] the need for caution and restraint is underlined by Art 8 of the European Convention on Human Rights, which by conferring a right to respect for private and family life, protects both child and parents from arbitrary interference by the State. The expectation[3] is that voluntary arrangements through the provision of services to the child and his family should always be fully explored before compulsory powers are sought from the courts. As *Statutory guidance on court orders and pre-proceedings* (hereinafter *Statutory guidance*) says,[4] '[e]arly parental engagement in the child protection process is key to avoiding the creation of barriers between the local authority and the family.' In this connection use may be made of independent specialist advice and advocacy which can help parents to participate in the local authority planning process from an informed position. Another process that can be useful is a family group conference which is a voluntary process led by family members, though chaired by an independent co-ordinator, to plan and make decisions for a child who is at risk of harm.[5] As one commentary explains,[6] the conference offers a way of valuing the expertise and commitment of families while ensuring that planning about children is informed by professionals' knowledge and skills. They have been encouraged in England and Wales (having first

---

[1] [2000] 2 AC 147 at 170.   [2] Ibid.

[3] See the Department for Children, Schools and Families *Guidance and Regulations*, Vol 1, *Court Orders* (2008) para 3.7.   [4] DfE, 2014, para 20.

[5] See DfE, *Statutory guidance on court order and pre-proceedings* (2014), p 15.

[6] E Isaacs and C Shepherd *Social Work Decision–Making A Guide for Childcare Lawyers* (2012, 2nd edn) 2.51–2.52.

been developed in New Zealand) as means of avoiding court proceedings. Their aim is to develop a plan for the child that involves wider family members.

Nevertheless, restraint is not always justified and voluntary arrangements will not solve all problems and the 1989 Act makes provision, in the form of care and supervision orders, for compulsory measures to be taken to safeguard and promote children's welfare. But before these measures can be sought, as clearly explained by *Statutory guidance*,[7] the local authority needs, first of all, to hold a legal planning meeting to obtain legal advice. Such meetings should be attended by the child's social worker, work managers and the local authority lawyer. At this meeting a decision needs to be taken on whether the threshold criteria (discussed shortly) have been met in principle. The local authority then has to decide whether it is in the child's best interests to provide further support or to initiate care proceedings.

If the authority decides on more formal action it will send to the parents or anyone else with parental responsibility either a *pre-proceedings letter*, which explains that proceedings are being contemplated or a *letter of issue*, stating that proceedings have been initiated. The former letter (commonly referred to as a 'Letter before proceedings' or 'LBP') should set out a summary of the local authority's concerns, the issues that need to be addressed and what support will be provided and provide information on how to obtain legal advice and advocacy. The letter should also invite the parents or others with parental responsibility to a pre-proceedings meeting. The LBP together with the pre-proceedings meeting provides a final opportunity, ahead of any court proceedings, for the local authority to work with the family and to explore all options. Importantly, as the *Statutory guidance* states,[8] upon the receipt of either letter, the parents or others with parental responsibility are entitled to non-means tested publicly funded legal advice.

The *Statutory guidance* places on a formal footing the former practice for some, but not all,[9] local authorities to send Letters Before Proceedings and reflects the support for and encouragement of the practice by the *Family Justice Review*.

By way of final introduction it needs to be said that no child may be taken into care without a court order. There is only one route into care,[10] ie as a result of a care order being made under s 31. Courts cannot make care or supervision orders on their own motion nor can they require a local authority to take proceedings.[11] Instead such orders can only be made upon an application by a local authority or authorised person.[12] On the other hand, once proceedings have been started they can only be withdrawn with leave of the court which means that the court[13] is thereafter in final control of the ultimate disposal of the application.[14]

---

[7] See ch 2, paras 25 ff.   [8] At para 35.

[9] See the research by J Masson *Families on the edge of care proceedings* (interim report, 2011), see the *Family Justice Review*, Final Report (2011) at para 3.108. For the full report on the research see J Masson and J Dickens *Care proceedings reform, the future of the pre-proceedings process* (2013). See also E Isaacs and C Shepherd *Social Work Decision-Making* (2012, 2nd edn) 4.84 ff.

[10] Under the former law there were at least 12 different routes into compulsory care: see eg the *Review of Child Care Law*, Discussion Paper No 3

[11] See *Nottingham County Council v P* [1994] Fam 18, CA.

[12] The only 'authorised person' is the NSPCC.

[13] Accordingly, a care order can be made even though a local authority no longer wishes to pursue its application. For an example, see *Re M (A Minor) (Care Order: Threshold Conditions)* [1994] 2 AC 424, HL, discussed at Is suffering, p 604.

[14] Family Procedure Rules (FPR) 2010, r 29.4(2). In deciding whether to grant leave the child's welfare is the paramount consideration: *London Borough of Southwark v B* [1993] 2 FLR 559, CA (in which leave was granted). It is a decision that needs to be considered as carefully as any other decision and opportunity should be given to the guardian to express his or her views: *Re F (A Minor) (Care Order: Withdrawal*

B. INITIATING PROCEEDINGS

1. APPLICANTS

Under s 31(1) of the 1989 Act only a local authority or authorised person may apply for a care or supervision order. An 'authorised person' is defined by s 31(9) as the NSPCC and any of its officers or any other person authorised by the Secretary of State (of which there are none, as yet). Where an authorised person proposes to make an application, he must, if it is reasonably practicable to do so and before making the application, consult the authority where the child is ordinarily resident.[15]

The police and local education authorities cannot apply for care or supervision orders, though the latter may apply for an education supervision order.[16] Parents or guardians have no right to initiate proceedings themselves and the 1989 Act has no procedure equivalent to that under the former law[17] which enabled parents to force a local authority to take action in relation to a child beyond their control.[18]

2. IN RESPECT OF WHOM APPLICATIONS MAY BE MADE

No care or supervision orders may be made with respect to a child who has reached the age of 17 (or 16 if he is married).[19] This means, unlike the former law, that compulsory measures cannot be taken in respect of such adolescents,[20] although such persons may themselves approach the authority with a view to being provided with accommodation.[21]

3. PARTIES

The child and any person with parental responsibility are all automatically parties in care proceedings.[22] It is open to any other person to apply to be joined as a party and within the court's powers to direct that they be joined. Although fathers without parental responsibility are not automatically parties they should nevertheless be served with notice of the proceedings and as a general rule, unless there is some justifiable reason for not doing so, they should be permitted to participate in the proceedings as a party where they wish to do so.[23]

---

of Application) [1993] 2 FLR 9 (leave refused). See also *Re N (Leave to Withdraw Care Proceedings)* [2000] 1 FLR 134 (leave refused); *X Council v B (Emergency Protection Orders)* [2004] EWHC 2015 Fam [2005] 1 FLR 341 (leave granted); *Redbridge London Borough Council v B and C and A ('Through His Children's Guardian)* [2011] EWHC 517 (Fam) [2011] 2 FLR 117 (leave granted); and *Re K (Children With Disabilities: Wardship)* [2011] EWHC 4031 (Fam) [2012] 2 FLR 745 (leave granted).

[15] Section 31(6). Note also the restrictions under s 31(7).

[16] Under s 36, discussed in Ch 10 Enforcing the duty, p 349.

[17] Under the Children and Young Persons Act 1963 s 3 (as amended).

[18] As J Masson and M Morris *Children Act Manual* (1992) say (at p 97) 'A parent who is unable to control his child can only request assistance from the local authority and make a complaint under s 26(3)(b) [discussed in Ch 18] if it is refused.'

[19] Children Act 1989 s 31(3). Orders can still be made if the child is under 16 and validly married according to the laws of another country: cf *Alhaji Mohamed v Knott* [1969] 1 QB 1.

[20] See *Re SW (A Minor) (Wardship: Jurisdiction)* [1986] 1 FLR 24 where the High Court acting under its inherent jurisdiction committed a 17-year-old into care (which power was specifically abolished by s 100(2)(a)).

[21] See Ch 15.   [22] FPR 2010, r 12.3(1).

[23] See *Re B (Care Proceedings: Notification of Father Without Parental Responsibility)* [1999] 2 FLR 408. Cf *Re P (Care Proceedings: Father's Application To Be Joined As Party)* [2001] 1 FLR 781, where because of delay, leave was refused, the father having previously chosen not to participate in the proceedings. Art 6 of the Human Rights Convention was held not to be thereby breached.

C. THE THRESHOLD CRITERIA

1. SOME PRELIMINARY OBSERVATIONS

(a) The rationale of the criteria

No care or supervision order may be made unless the conditions set out by s 31(2) have been satisfied.[24] These conditions have come to be known as the 'threshold criteria'[25] to emphasise the point that they are not in themselves grounds or reasons for making a care or supervision order, but rather the minimum preconditions for obtaining such orders. As Lord Mackay LC said in his Joseph Jackson Memorial Lecture:[26]

> Those conditions are the minimum circumstances which the government considers should always be found to exist before it can ever be justified for a court even to begin to contemplate whether the State should be enabled to intervene compulsorily in family life.

Echoing this comment Lord Nicholls said in *Re O and another (Minors) (Care: Preliminary Hearing); Re B (A Minor)*:[27]

> The purpose of this threshold requirement is to protect families, both adults and children, from inappropriate interference in their lives by public authorities through the making of care and supervision orders.

By requiring the State to justify its interference beyond purely welfare considerations[28] the threshold conditions help to ensure that domestic law is human rights compliant.[29] There is, however, a basic dilemma, for as Baroness Hale said in *Re J (Children) (Care Proceedings: Threshold Criteria)*:[30]

> In a free society, it is a serious thing indeed for the state compulsorily to remove a child from his family of birth. Interference with the right to respect for family life, protected by article 8 of the European Convention for the Protection of Human Rights and Fundamental Freedoms, can only be justified by a pressing social need. Yet it is also a serious thing for the state to fail to safeguard its children from the neglect and ill-treatment which they may suffer in their own homes. This may even amount to a violation of their right not to be subjected to inhuman or degrading treatment, protected by article 3 of the Convention. How then is the law to protect the family from unwarranted intrusion while at the same time protecting children from harm?

---

[24] But note: failure to satisfy the conditions does not necessarily mean that the child will be returned to his or her parents since the court can still make a s 8 order, see Where the threshold criteria cannot be satisfied, p 632.

[25] See generally M Freeman 'Care After 1991' and S Cretney 'Defining the Limits of State Intervention: The Child and the Courts', both in D Freestone (ed) *Children and the Law* (1990) pp 130 *et seq* and pp 58 at 68–71 respectively.   [26] (1989) 139 NLJ 505 at 506.

[27] [2003] UKHL 18 [2004] 1 AC 523 at para [14].

[28] The DHSS *Review of Child Care* (1985) para 15.10 expressly rejected compulsory State intervention being based on the welfare principle.

[29] The European Court of Human Rights has repeatedly stressed the gravity of removing children from their families particularly where this results in terminating contact, see eg *P, C and S v United Kingdom* [2002] 2 FLR 631 (removal of a child at birth held not to be justifiable in the particular circumstances). Human rights considerations remain equally relevant at the 'welfare stage', see *Re B (Care: Interference With Family Life)* [2003] EWCA Civ 876 [2003] 2 FLR 813.   [30] [2013] UKSC 9 [2013] 1 AC 680 at [1].

She goes on to point out that the 1989 Act tries to balance these two objectives by setting a threshold which must be crossed before consideration can be given to what order, if any, should be made to enable local authorities to protect a child.

Satisfaction of the threshold criteria permits the court to proceed to the second stage, commonly referred to as the 'welfare stage', in which the court must decide what, if any, order to make.[31] At this stage, but not before, the child's welfare is paramount, and the court must have regard to the welfare checklist set out in s 1(3) including any harm the child has suffered or is at risk of suffering and how capable each of his parents is of meeting his needs and, having regard to s 1(5), whether making any order is better for the child than making no order.

(b) The Burden and Standard of Proof

Two further important points need to be adverted to, namely, the burden and standard of proof. Both issues were considered by the House of Lords in *Re H (Minors) (Sexual Abuse: Standard of Proof).*[32]

With regard to the former, it was held that the legal burden of establishing the threshold criteria falls upon the applicant, normally the local authority. The burden of proof has particular relevance to the establishment of the likelihood of the child suffering significant harm and to the issue of uncertain perpetrators (that is, where harm to the child can be established, but the perpetrator cannot, a typical example being that the child must have been harmed by one of the parents but each deny responsibility) which we discuss later.

With regard to the standard of proof their Lordships rejected the assertion that there is a standard higher than the preponderance of probability but below the criminal standard, holding that the only standard of proof in child protection proceedings is the balance of probabilities. Although Lord Nicholls expressly rejected the idea that the standard of proof should be commensurate with the gravity of the allegation and the seriousness of the consequences, he continued:[33]

> When assessing the probabilities the court will have in mind as a factor, to whatever extent is appropriate in the particular case, that the more serious the allegation the less likely it is that the event occurred and, hence, the stronger should be the evidence before the court concludes that the allegation is established on the balance of probability.

This seemed to involve a higher standard of proof, particularly when combined with his statement that:

> this approach also provides a means by which the balance of probability standard can accommodate one's instinctive feeling that even in civil proceedings a court should be more sure before finding serious allegations proved than when deciding less serious or trivial matters.

Lord Lloyd (who dissented) preferred a simple balance of probabilities test. As he pointed out, Lord Nicholls' test leads to the 'bizarre' result that the more serious the anticipated

---

[31] The 'welfare stage' is discussed at The welfare stage, pp 625ff.
[32] [1996] AC 563. Discussed further at The two stage test, p 609.   [33] [1996] AC 563 at 587.

injury the more difficult it becomes for the local authority to satisfy the standard of proof. Moreover he commented:[34]

> there is a danger that the repeated use of the words will harden into a formula, which, like other formulae (especially those based on a metaphor), may lead to misunderstanding.

This proved to be prophetic. As Baroness Hale explained in *Re B (Children) (Care Proceedings: Standard of Proof) (Cafcass intervening)* ('*Re B*'):[35]

> Lord Nicholls' nuanced explanation left room for the nostrum 'the more serious the allegation, the more cogent the evidence needed to prove it' to take hold and be repeated time and time again in fact-finding hearings in care proceedings.

Re B laid this approach to rest, Baroness Hale announcing 'loud and clear' that:[36]

> the standard of proof in finding the facts necessary to establish the threshold under s 31(2) or the welfare considerations in section 1 of the 1989 Act is the simple balance of probabilities, neither more nor less. Neither the seriousness of the allegation nor the seriousness of the consequences should make any difference to the standard of proof to be applied in determining the facts. The inherent probabilities are simply something to be taken into account, where relevant, in deciding where the truth lies.

While this was a welcome clarifying decision, *Re B* by no means ended the debate about the standard of proof, at least in the context of uncertain perpetrators, and in any event needs to be contrasted with what has to be proved to satisfy the 'likelihood' of harm test.[37]

2. THE CRITERIA

Section 31(2) provides that a court may only make a care or supervision order if it is satisfied:[38]

    (a) the child concerned is suffering significant harm, or is likely to suffer significant harm; and

    (b) the harm or likelihood of harm is attributable to—

        (i) the care given to the child, or likely to be given to him if the order were not made, not being what it would be reasonable to expect a parent to give to him; or

        (ii) the child's being beyond parental control.

This wording reflects the recommendations of the Child Care Review.[39] The criteria comprise two separate limbs, each of which has to be satisfied. The first, sometimes referred to as the 'significant harm' condition, focuses on present or anticipated harm. The second,

---

[34] Ibid at 577–78.
[35] [2008] UKHL 35 [2009] 1 AC 11 at [64]. For a commentary on this case, see C Cobley and N Lowe 'Interpreting the Threshold Criteria under section 31(2) of the Children Act 1989 – the House of Lords decision in *Re B*' (2009) 72 MLR 463.   [36] [2008] UKHL 35 [2009] 1 AC 11 at [70].
[37] See Is likely to suffer, pp 608ff.
[38] Because the *court* must be satisfied that the criteria exist, it is not relieved of that duty because the parties agree: see *Re G (A Minor) (Care Proceedings)* [1995] Fam 16.
[39] DHSS *Review of Child Care Law* (1985) paras 15.12–15.27.

sometimes referred to as the 'attributable' or 'attributability' condition, is that the harm or likelihood of harm is attributable to the lack of reasonable parenting of the child or to the child being beyond parental control. In determining whether the threshold criteria are satisfied the child's welfare is *not* the court's paramount consideration.[40]

Soon after implementation, in *Newham London Borough v AG*,[41] Sir Stephen Brown P commented:

> I very much hope that in approaching cases under the Children Act 1989 the court will not be invited to perform in every case a strict legalistic analysis of s 31. Of course, the words of the statute must be considered, but I do not believe that Parliament intended them to be unduly restrictive when the evidence clearly indicates that a certain course should be taken in order to protect the child.

One can readily sympathise with the notion that legalistic arguments should not be allowed to obscure the purpose of the provisions, namely to protect the welfare of children. Nevertheless, given that s 31 is the benchmark against which State intervention into the family is or is not justified, it seems perfectly proper that its meaning should be fully tested in court. In the event, s 31 has generated considerable case-law including a large number of Senior Court decisions.

(a) The significant harm condition

'Harm'

'Harm' is defined by s 31(9) as meaning 'ill-treatment or the impairment of health or development *including, for example, impairment suffered from seeing or hearing the ill-treatment of another*'.[42] Ill-treatment and impairment are to be regarded as alternatives, so that satisfaction of either is sufficient.[43] According to the Department of Health's 1991 *Guidance and Regulations*[44] ill-treatment is sufficient proof of harm in itself and it is not necessary to show that impairment of health or development has resulted or even is likely to result (though that will be relevant to the welfare stage).[45] As Baroness Hale pointed out in *Re B (A Child) (Care Proceedings: Threshold Criteria)*,[46] ill-treatment 'will generally involve some active conduct, whether physical or sexual abuse, bullying or other forms of active emotional abuse. Impairment may also be the result of active conduct towards the child, but it could also be the result of neglecting the child's needs, for food, for warmth, for shelter, for love, for education, for health care.' Another difference between ill-treatment and impairment is that in judging whether the harm is significant, courts are directed[47] in the case of impairment but not ill-treatment,[48] to compare the position of a similar child (discussed shortly).

---

[40] See *Humberside County Council v B* [1993] 1 FLR 257.   [41] [1993] 1 FLR 281 at 289, CA.

[42] The italicised words were inserted by s 120 of the Adoption and Children Act 2002 to reflect the growing understanding of the deleterious effect that domestic violence perpetrated on another member of the family can have upon children.

[43] See the Department of Health's *Guidance and Regulations*, Vol 1, *Court Orders* (1991), para 3.19. This comment is not repeated in the revised 2008 *Guidance and Regulations*, Vol 1 *Court Orders* (DCSF, 2008).

[44] Vol 1, *Court Orders*, para 3.19. This comment is not repeated in the 2008 Guidance.

[45] Consequently a child who is injured but who has made a complete recovery can still be demonstrated to have suffered 'harm' for the purposes of s 31.

[46] [2013] UKSC 33 [2013] 1 WLR 1911 at [192]. For a commentary on this decision, see J Doughty 'Re B (A Child) (Care Order)' (2013) 35 JSWFL 491.

[47] By s 31(10), discussed at Comparison with 'similar child', p 603.

[48] The 1991 Guidance, wrongly it is submitted, assumed s 31(10) applies to all types of 'harm'—see para 3.20. The 2008 Guidance at para 3.39, however, simply repeats the wording of the sub-section.

Although distinguishing ill-treatment and impairment can be justified inasmuch as the former poses a greater immediate danger than the latter, it also puts a premium upon being able to distinguish the two types of harm. In this respect the definition of 'ill-treatment' in s 31(9) as 'including sexual abuse and forms of ill-treatment which are not physical' is not helpful. While it is clear that both physical and sexual abuse rank as ill-treatment (though even in these cases there can be debate as to what amounts to 'abuse'),[49] it remains unclear as to what amounts to 'forms of ill-treatment which are not physical'. Does it include emotional abuse,[50] verbal abuse or unfairness,[51] or witnessing or hearing violence perpetrated upon someone else? In this latter respect the amendment to the s 31(9) seems to classify it as impairment. But in *Re M (A Minor) (Care Order: Threshold Conditions)*[52] Bracewell J held that a child suffered ill-treatment by being permanently deprived of the love and care of his mother when she was murdered by the father. However, while it could hardly be doubted that the child suffered harm, it is surely stretching language to consider it as ill-treatment *of the child*.[53] It was ill-treatment of the mother not the child.[54]

Section 31(9) defines development as 'physical, intellectual, emotional, social or behavioural development' and health as 'physical or mental health'. This seems, as one commentary has said,[55] 'wide enough to cover any case of neglect—poor nutrition, low standards of hygiene, poor emotional care or . . . failure to seek treatment for an illness or condition'. It has been held that truancy (formerly a specific ground for a care order) can cause a child 'harm' by the consequential impairment of intellectual or social development.[56] 'Harm' is also wide enough to embrace 'moral danger', which was formerly a specific ground for making a care order.[57] The extension of the meaning of 'harm' to include 'impairment suffered from seeing or hearing the ill-treatment of another' is intended to emphasise the potential harm that a child can suffer having witnessed violence perpetuated by one parent on another.

---

[49] See, for example, *Re MA (Care Threshold)* [2009] EWCA Civ 853 [2010] 1 FLR 431, in which a child who had been kicked by her mother at least three times and hit on the side of her face by her father was found to have suffered harm but not 'significant' harm, and *Re W (Minors) (Residence Order)* [1998] 1 FCR 75, CA which involved an uninhibited attitude towards nudity which in itself was not thought to be abusive. On this whole issue see the discussion by M Freeman 'Care After 1991' in D Freestone (ed) *Children and the Law* (1990) pp 140–2.

[50] In this respect, note Baroness Hale's reference in *Re B (A Child) (Care Proceedings: Threshold Criteria)*, earlier, at [192] to 'active emotional abuse'. See also the pre-Children Act decision in *F v Suffolk County Council* (1981) 2 FLR 208.

[51] Lord Mackay indicated during debates on the Bill that it does: 503 HL Official Report, col 342.

[52] [1994] Fam 95.

[53] Though see the defence of Bracewell J's view in R White, P Carr and N Lowe *Children Act in Practice* (2002, 3rd edn) at 8.72 who argued that it *is* ill-treatment of the child to deprive him permanently of his mother.

[54] See J Whybrow 'Re M—past, present, and future significant harm' [1994] *Journal of Child Law* 88 at 89.

[55] J Masson and M Morris *Children Act Manual* (1992) p 99.

[56] *Re O (A Minor) (Care Proceedings: Education)* [1992] 1 WLR 912 per Ewbank J. See also *Re V (Care or Supervision Order)* [1996] 1 FLR 776, CA—a mother's resistance to allowing her 17-year-old son, who suffered from cerebral palsy, to attend a special school by keeping him at home instead was held likely to cause the boy 'significant harm', though, in most such cases an education supervision order under s 36 (discussed in Ch 10 Enforcing the duty, p 349) is more likely to be sought.

[57] See eg Freeman, op cit, pp 154–5 and 161, who, referring to a pre-Children Act decision, *Alhaji Mohamed v Knott* [1969] 1 QB 1, involving a 13-year-old Nigerian child who was validly married under her country's law, thought that the child would now be considered to be suffering or likely to suffer significant harm by having intercourse with her husband, a man twice her age and who had venereal disease.

In short, the impairment part of 'harm' is extremely wide[58] which is important given that as the Cleveland Inquiry observed,[59] the categories of abuse are not closed and that s 31 provides the only route into public care. On the other hand, it needs to be applied with appropriate caution,[60] particularly bearing in mind the human rights requirement for the State response (including local authority investigation) to be proportionate to the alleged harm.[61] However, in this respect the additional safeguard is the requirement that any harm is 'significant'.

Is the harm 'significant'?

Whatever the nature of the harm, the court has to consider whether it is 'significant'.[62] Vital though this is to the application of the condition, 'significant' is not defined in the Act. In the absence of a statutory definition, the early commentaries[63] turned to the dictionary definition, that is, 'noteworthy, of considerable amount or effect or importance'. The 1991 *Guidance*[64] suggested that 'significant' excludes 'minor shortcomings in health care or minor deficits in physical, psychological or social development…unless cumulatively they are having or are likely to have, serious and lasting effects upon the child'. In *Humberside County Council v B*[65] Booth J accepted that the dictionary definition was the right test such that, to be 'significant', the harm should be considered either 'considerable or noteworthy or important'. However, she also accepted the submission that it was 'harm which the court should take into account in considering a child's future'. Although this approach has generally been accepted not least by Baroness Hale in *Re B (A Child) (Care Proceedings; The Threshold Criteria)*, who considered the dictionary definition helpful,[66] Wilson LJ commented in *Re MA (Care Threshold)*,[67] 'On any view the description by Booth J of significant harm as being harm which the court should take into account in relation to the child's future is extremely broad'. He added that he would not have expressed himself in quite such broad terms, but tantalisingly did not say in what terms he would have put it.

Although one might question whether Booth J intended her 'definition' of 'significant' regarding the child's future to be read independently of the notions of noteworthy etc harm, it raises the question whether the statute should have given at least some indication of its meaning. Notwithstanding Hedley J's caution in *Re L (Care: Threshold Criteria)*[68] against attempting an all embracing definition, it has been suggested[69] that a combination of the dictionary definition and the 1991 Guidance would have been helpful.

In *Re B (A Child) (Care Proceedings: Threshold Criteria)* the Supreme Court disapproved of Ward LJ's suggestion in *Re MA (Care Threshold)*,[70] that Article 8 of the European Human Rights Convention informs 'the meaning of "significant" and serves to

---

[58] Which is perhaps why the 2008 Guidance, Vol 1, *Court Orders* at para 3.39 says that 'in most cases the impairment of health or development is likely to provide the evidence of "harm".'

[59] *Report of the Inquiry into Child Abuse in Cleveland* (1988, Cmnd 412) p 4.

[60] It would be all too easy, for example, to consider parental conduct such as shouting at a child as leading to emotional abuse.

[61] On which see *Re B (A Child) (Care Proceedings: Threshold Criteria)* [2013] UKSC 33 [2013] 1 WLR 1911, discussed further at The welfare stage, p 625.

[62] See generally M Adcock, R White and A Hollows (eds) *Significant Harm* (1998, 2nd edn).

[63] See e.g. R White, P Carr and N Lowe *A Guide To The Children Act* (1990, 1st edn) at 6.11 and R White 'Examining the threshold criteria' in *Significant Harm*, op cit, 3 at 6.

[64] At para 3.21. The 2008 Guidance avoids making any comment, see para 3.39.

[65] [1993] 1 FLR 257 at 263.   [66] [2013] UKSC 33 [2013] 1 WLR 1911 at [185].

[67] [2009] EWCA Civ 853 [2010] 1 FLR 431 at [29].   [68] [2007] 1 FLR 2050 at [51].

[69] C Cobley and N Lowe 'The Statutory "Threshold" under Section 31 of the Children Act 1989 – Time to Take Stock' (2011) 127 LQR 396.   [70] [2009] EWCA Civ 853 [2010] 1 FLR 431 at [54].

emphasise that there must be a "relevant and sufficient" reason for crossing the threshold.' Quite apart from, in Lord Wilson's view, adding 'an inappropriate layer of complexity to the inquiry whether harm is significant', the general consensus was that the decision as to whether or not the threshold is crossed does not engage Article 8 rights since *at that stage* there is no interference with family life.[71]

Whether 'harm' is 'significant' is an issue of fact to be decided in each case, but it must be remembered that it is the harm that must be significant, not the incident that caused it. So, for example, while a broken leg is a serious injury, the implications of a small cigarette burn might be more significant. Similarly, behaviour such as shaking that might be innocuous to an older child might be very significant for a baby. In *Re O (A Minor) (Care Proceedings: Education)*[72] Ewbank J took the view that lack of suitable education leading to the impairment of the child's intellectual development was of itself 'significant harm'.

Comparison with 'similar child'

Where the harm is due to ill-treatment, no further guidance is given, but in the case of impairment of health or development, reference must be made to s 31(10), which provides:

> Where the question of whether harm suffered by a child is significant turns on the child's health or development, his health or development shall be compared with that which could reasonably be expected of a similar child.

This is a problematic provision for although its general drift is understandable, enabling, for example, the intellectual development of a Down's Syndrome child to be compared with that of another such child rather than against children in general,[73] its precise meaning defies easy interpretation. For example, is a deaf child of deaf parents a 'similar child' to a deaf child of hearing parents?[74] To what extent should regard be had to the child's background and in particular is it open to the courts to apply different standards to children from different ethnic backgrounds?[75]

Case-law is inconclusive on whether the child's circumstances and background including cultural background should be taken into account when applying the 'similar child' test. In *Re D (Care: Threshold Criteria: Significant Harm)*[76] Wilson J doubted whether the cultural context of a family should be taken into account, but in *Re K; A Local Authority v N and Others*,[77] Munby J considered that the court must always be sensitive to the cultural, social and religious circumstances of the particular child and family. In *Re O (A Minor) (Care Proceedings: Education)*[78] Ewbank J held that in the case of a 15-year-old truant of average intelligence:

> . . . 'similar child' meant a child of equivalent intellectual and social development, who has gone to school and not merely an average child who may or may not be at school.

---

[71] See Lord Wilson at [29], Lord Neuberger at [62] and Baroness Hale at [186].

[72] [1992] 1 WLR 912.

[73] This example is taken from G. Douglas *An Introduction to Family Law* (2004, 2nd edn) p 147.

[74] This is but one of the many examples that Freeman 'Care After 1991' in D Freestone (ed) *Children and the Law* (1990) 130 at 147–149, uses to highlight the difficulties of this test.

[75] Similar issues arise when determining the appropriate standard of care required to satisfy the attributable criteria, discussed at The attributable condition, p 613.   [76] [1998] Fam Law 656.

[77] [2005] EWHC 2956 (Fam) [2007] 1 FLR 399 at [26]. This view was expressed in the general context of s 31 and not specifically in relation to s 31(10).

[78] [1992] 1 WLR 912. For valuable comments on *Re O* see J Fortin 'Significant harm revisited' (1993) 5 *Journal of Child Law* 151.

In other words, his Lordship was not prepared to compare the child with someone who was not properly attending school.

Is suffering

The original Bill contained the words 'has suffered' rather than 'is suffering' but was changed to prevent an order being made 'on the basis of significant harm suffered several years previously and which is not likely to be repeated'.[79] In other words, Parliament intended that past harm should not in itself be sufficient to satisfy the criteria, though it might be relevant to establishing future likelihood of harm. On the other hand, while the present tense implies an existing condition, it is clear that that does not necessarily mean that the condition should exist *at the date of the hearing*. The leading decision is *Re M (A Minor) (Care Order: Threshold Conditions)*.[80] In that case, following the murder, in the children's presence, of the mother by the father, a baby together with his half-siblings were accommodated by the local authority. Subsequently, the siblings went to live with a cousin of the mother, but she felt unable to look after the baby as well and he was fostered. Whilst in his foster placement the boy thrived and had regular contact with the mother's cousin and his siblings. However, because he could not remain with his foster mother indefinitely, seven months later the local authority brought care proceedings. By that time the cousin had changed her mind and sought what was then a residence order in respect of the boy. The care proceedings were heard some 16 months after the murder, at a time when the father had received a life sentence. The local authority supported the cousin and no longer actively sought a care order. However, both the father and the guardian[81] supported the making of a care order with a view to the boy being adopted outside the birth family.

At first instance Bracewell J held that the threshold criteria were satisfied. In her view the relevant date for determining 'is suffering' was 'the period immediately before the process of protecting the child is first put into motion'. The Court of Appeal disagreed,[82] holding that the threshold criteria had to be satisfied at the date of the hearing. While this did not require the court to be satisfied that the child is suffering significant harm at the precise moment when the court is considering the application—it being sufficient if there is a continuum in existence at that time—nevertheless, as Balcombe LJ said:

> . . . it is not enough that something happened in the past which caused the child to suffer harm of the relevant kind if before the hearing the child has ceased to suffer such harm.

What this seems to have meant was that a continuum of harm was required, rather than a continuum of protection following the harm. In the Court of Appeal's view since the boy was thriving in foster care he could not be said to be suffering harm at the date of the hearing.[83] Accordingly, the local authority failed to establish the threshold criteria.

---

[79] Per David Mellor MP, HC Official Report, Standing Committee B 23 May 1989, col 221. See also *Re G (Care Proceedings: Threshold Conditions)* [2001] EWCA Civ 968 [2001] 2 FLR 1111 at [16]—father found guilty of actual bodily harm for inflicting a cigarette burn on a child. No care proceedings brought as father and mother had separated (father subsequently died) and she was not implicated. This incident was properly ruled irrelevant in care proceedings subsequently brought in respect of the mother's upbringing of the child.

[80] [1994] 2 AC 424, HL. Note also *Re G (Care Proceedings: Threshold Conditions)* [2001] EWCA Civ 968 [2001] 2 FLR 1111 in which it was held that a local authority is entitled to rely upon information acquired after its intervention and even upon later events provided those later events are capable of proving the state of affairs at the time of the intervention.   [81] Guardianship is discussed in Ch 8.

[82] [1994] Fam 95.

[83] Furthermore, there was held to be no likelihood of future harm as the cousin was willing to look after the child and the father, being in prison, could not interfere.

The House of Lords, however, held that provided it can be shown that there was significant harm at the time of the local authority intervention and what Lord Mackay referred to as 'protective arrangements' have thereafter been continuously kept in place, the fact that the child had been removed from harm at the date of the hearing will not defeat the plea that the child 'is suffering significant harm'.

Lord Templeman, having acknowledged the 'tyranny of language', nevertheless pointed to the Court of Appeal's 'preoccupation with the present tense' leading to a proposition that he could not accept, namely, 'that if a child suffers harm and is rescued by a local authority, a care order cannot be made in favour of the local authority because it cannot be said that the child is suffering harm and if the parent who caused the child harm is dead or in prison or disclaims any further interest it cannot be said that the child is likely to suffer harm'.[84] Lord Nolan, agreeing, said:[85]

> The focal point of the inquiry must be the situation which resulted in the temporary measures taken, and which has led to the application for a care or supervision order.

Although as a matter of interpretation it is perfectly tenable to decide, as the Court of Appeal did, that 'is' refers to the continuum of harm, the Lords were surely right to overturn this view. The compelling argument is that, as Lord Mackay said, the Court of Appeal approach effectively deprives the first limb of s 31(2)(a) of effect, since in many cases the harm will have abated or it will be, as one commentator pointed out,[86] simply random as to whether or not it has abated. Given that Parliament provided for both present *and* anticipated harm it cannot have been its intention to squeeze out the former.

Having ruled that the s 31 threshold was satisfied, the House of Lords made a care order notwithstanding that it was accepted that the mother's cousin, with whom the boy had by now spent seven months, had perfectly satisfactorily looked after him.[87] Although their Lordships made it clear that they expected the boy to continue to live with her, they nevertheless held that 'having regard to the history and circumstances it was highly desirable that the local authority should exercise a watching brief on his behalf'.[88]

Although the final disposal is questionable, it is submitted that the House of Lords were right to overrule the Court of Appeal. Notwithstanding the criticism that *Re M* weakens the position of the family,[89] the decision preserves flexibility which is crucial to child protection. In any event, if the local authority's initial intervention is justified, it seems right that the subsequent application for a care order should be determined according to the broader considerations at the welfare stage and not simply upon the more technical requirements of the threshold condition.

While *Re M* may have settled the 'is' debate it did not, as we now discuss, eliminate all problems associated with the first limb.

What are protective arrangements?

An important element in Lord Mackay LC's judgment in *Re M* is that, although the court is permitted to examine the position at the point of intervention in determining

---

[84] [1994] 2 AC 424 at 440.   [85] Ibid at 441.

[86] J Whybrow '*Re M*—past, present and future significant harm' (1994) 6 *Journal of Child Law* 88 at 90.

[87] This is one of the ironies of the case, since at first instance Bracewell J had hesitantly concluded that the cousin might not be able to give the boy the quality of emotional care that he was likely to require. See the comments on this by S Cretney [1994] Fam Law at 503.

[88] [1994] 2 AC 424 at 440, per Lord Templeman.

[89] See J Masson 'Social Engineering in the House of Lords—*Re M*' [1994] *Journal of Child Law* 170.

whether the child is suffering the requisite harm, it can only do so where 'there are in place arrangements for the protection of the child by the local authority on an interim basis which protection has been continuously in place for some time'. But what are 'arrangements' for these purposes? While there has never been any doubt that they include court-sanctioned arrangements such as interim care orders and emergency protection orders, there was initial speculation as to whether they also embrace accommodation provided under s 20. However, by expressly approving[90] *Northamptonshire County Council v S*[91] in which Ewbank J stated that in judging the criterion of 'is suffering' the court:[92]

> ... had to consider the position immediately before an emergency protection order, if there was one, or an interim care order, if that was the initiation of protection, or *as in this case, when the child went into voluntary care*. (Emphasis added)

Lord Mackay himself seemed to envisage accommodation as coming within the concept of protective arrangements. This interpretation of *Re M* commended itself to Charles J in *Southwark London Borough Council v B*[93] and was applied in *Re SH (Care Order: Orphan)*[94] and *Re M (Care Order: Parental Responsibility)*.[95] Accordingly, there seems little doubt that accommodation is within the concept of protective arrangements though whether there are any limits regarding the length of time that the child has been accommodated has yet to be decided (see later).

Whether other types of 'interventions', for example where there is an ongoing investigation following an adjournment of a child protection conference,[96] can also be classified as 'protective arrangements' remains to be decided, but to hold that they do seems a big step to take.

When does harm cease after a justifiable intervention?

Although local authority intervention cannot be justified by purely past harm there remains the unresolved question of when harm ceases after justifiable intervention. In this respect there are two issues, namely, a temporal one and what may be described as a causative one. With regard to the former, does there come a point where intervention was so far in the past that it cannot sensibly be said that the child 'is' suffering harm? The issue arises particularly in connection with accommodation which can itself be in place for years. It remains to be seen how far into the past the courts will be prepared to enquire, though it may be noted that in the *Northamptonshire* case the children had been in (what would now be called) accommodation for six months before the care application and 10 months before the hearing.[97]

The causative issue arises if the raison d'être for intervention ceases before the making of a care order as, for example, in the situation posed by one commentary[98] where the child is removed from home because of suspected child abuse and the abuser subsequently dies.

---

[90] [1994] 2 AC 424 at 437.   [91] [1993] Fam 136 at 140.

[92] 'Voluntary care' was the forerunner of what became local authority accommodation: see Ch 15.

[93] [1998] 2 FLR 1095 at 1109.

[94] [1995] 1 FLR 746, discussed at The application of the threshold criteria to orphaned and abandoned children, p 607.

[95] [1996] 2 FLR 84, discussed at The application of the threshold criteria to orphaned and abandoned children, p 607.

[96] This is one of the questions posed by J Masson [1994] *Journal of Child Law* 170.

[97] In *Re SH (Care Order: Orphan)* [1995] 1 FLR 746 the child had been accommodated for seven months before the care application and for 13 months by the time of the hearing.

[98] G Douglas *An Introduction to Family Law* (2004, 2nd edn) 148.

While no-one could doubt that provided the remaining carer is capable of looking after the child a care order should not be made; is that because the 'harm' has ceased or because it is not in the child's interests to make the order? In other words in such a situation does the application fail at the threshold or at the welfare stage? A pointer that it fails at the threshold stage is Lord Mackay's comment in *Re M*:

> If after a local authority had initiated protective arrangements the need for these had terminated, because the child's welfare had been satisfactorily provided for otherwise, in any subsequent proceedings, it would not be possible to found jurisdiction on the situation at the time of initiation of these arrangements.[99]

The application of the threshold criteria to orphans and abandoned children

One of Balcombe LJ's concerns in *Re M* was that if the prospective harm test could be satisfied without regard to potential carers that would mean that where a child's parents had both been killed in an accident then, even if:

> . . . there was an aunt or uncle willing to take him into his or her family and bring him up with his siblings and cousins, it would nevertheless be open to the court to say that the second threshold condition was satisfied and make a care order. This would amount to a form of social engineering which we are satisfied is wholly outside the intention of the 1989 Act.[100]

In line with this approach Thorpe J held in *Birmingham City Council v D, Birmingham City Council v M*[101] that it would be a plain distortion of the threshold test to find some theoretical risk of significant harm in the case of orphans who, at the time of the application for a care order, were being accommodated by the local authority and leading well-settled lives. In his Lordship's view the local authority had adequate powers to look after and safeguard and promote the children's interests.[102] The *Birmingham* decision, however, predated the House of Lords' decision in *Re M*. Furthermore, arguments were solely directed towards the issue of prospective harm. In contrast, *Re SH (Care Order: Orphan)*,[103] attention was focused on the first limb of s 31(2)(a) for, as Hollis J put it, the House of Lords in *Re M* had held:

> that the word 'is' in fact means 'was' in the sense that the child was suffering significant harm when the rescue operation was instigated, provided the care of the child concerned was continued until the final hearing.

In *Re SH* the child was already being accommodated at the time of his parents' death, the father having being suspected of perpetrating, and the mother of being implicated in, the sexual abuse of the boy. Hollis J held that, as the boy had been continuously accommodated since then, he could properly be considered at the date of the initial intervention to be suffering significant harm, thereby satisfying the first limb of s 31(2)(a). In other words, the passing of the threshold was due to the alleged sexual abuse rather than the death of the parents. However, in subsequently making the care order, Hollis J, in contrast

---

[99] [1994] 2 AC 424 at 433–4. On this logic, however, the House of Lords were surely wrong to have held the threshold to have been satisfied.
[100] [1994] Fam 95 at 105.   [101] [1994] 2 FLR 502.
[102] Viz. under s 22(3), s 23(1) and s 24 of the 1989 Act.   [103] [1995] 1 FLR 746.

to Thorpe J,[104] held that without having parental responsibility the local authority would have difficulties in convincing whoever was concerned that they had authority to decide what to do with the boy. Accordingly, he held that it was in the child's interests for the care order to be made.

The second post-House of Lords' decision, *Re M (Care Order: Parental Responsibility)*,[105] involved a baby found abandoned on the steps of a health centre who was discovered to have a number of medical problems likely to require medical intervention. In Cazalet J's view, the very fact of abandonment was enough to satisfy the existing harm limb of s 31(2)(a), since it amounted to a complete dereliction of parental responsibility and as such constituted 'ill-treatment'. His Lordship further held that as a result of the abandonment the baby was also likely to suffer significant harm, thus satisfying the second limb of s 31(2)(a). Like Hollis J, Cazalet J thought that, quite apart from the baby's particular problems, it was essential that some proper person or body have parental responsibility for the baby and that in this case it was vital for the local authority to have full powers of decision-making. He therefore made a care order.

Although this latter decision is authority for saying abandonment per se satisfies the threshold test, it is not yet beyond argument whether the death of both parents *ipso facto* satisfies the criteria. It is submitted, however, that, given that the first limb of s 31(2)(a) can be satisfied as at the date of intervention,[106] the *Birmingham* decision cannot be relied upon and indeed should have been decided the other way. Consequently the death of the parents ought to be regarded as falling within the existing harm criterion if, at the time of local authority intervention (be it through accommodation or emergency protection), there is no other family member able and willing to look after the child.[107] On this basis there is no need to enquire whether the prospective harm test would also be satisfied. Satisfaction of the threshold criteria, however, does not necessarily mean that a care order should be made. That issue, which is governed by the welfare principle,[108] must depend on all the circumstances, though (unless there are other individuals in whose favour a child arrangements order should be made) the court may well, as *Re SH* and *Re M* illustrate, be predisposed to make a care order to ensure that some person or body has parental responsibility for the child. However, if subsequent to the local authority intervention another family member does emerge as able and willing to look after the child, then no doubt the courts will, mindful of the general policy under the Children Act to maintain a child's links with his birth family, be predisposed to make an order in that person's favour. In this way it is submitted that Balcombe LJ's fears about social engineering were exaggerated.

Is likely to suffer

The two-stage test

The inclusion of the future element was an important innovation of the 1989 Act and was introduced to provide a remedy where harm had not occurred but there were considerable

---

[104] This apparent difference of view can be explained on the basis that each judge was considering different questions: Thorpe J deciding whether the absence of responsibility *ipso facto* satisfied the prospective harm test—Hollis J determining whether it was in the child's interests, *the threshold test having been satisfied*, to vest parental responsibility via a care order in the local authority.

[105] [1996] 2 FLR 84.

[106] Viz. by the House of Lords in *Re M (A Minor) (Care Order: Threshold Conditions)*,

[107] If, following the parents' deaths, the child is being looked after by a relative, then to justify intervention the local authority would have to prove that the child is suffering or likely to suffer significant harm notwithstanding that relative's care of the child.   [108] See The welfare stage, pp 625ff.

future risks for the child. Not surprisingly, given its speculative nature, the prospective test has been the subject of intense argument. Not least of the disputes has been the one concerning the correctness of the House of Lords' decision, *Re H (Minors) (Sexual Abuse: Standard of Proof)*.[109] In that case a mother had four daughters, two by her husband and two by her subsequent partner. Her eldest daughter alleged that she had been sexually abused by the partner. She was subsequently accommodated by the local authority and the partner was charged but acquitted of rape. Notwithstanding this acquittal the local authority sought care orders in respect of the three younger children. They argued that, because of the lower standard of proof in civil cases, the court could still be satisfied that the partner had sexually abused the eldest daughter or at least find that there was a substantial likelihood of his having done so and from this hold that the other three girls were likely to suffer significant harm.

At first instance, the judge, though more than a little suspicious that the partner had abused the eldest daughter as she alleged, nevertheless held that he could not be sure 'to the requisite high standard of proof' that the girl's allegations were true. He accordingly dismissed the care order applications. His decision was subsequently upheld by a majority in the Court of Appeal and by a bare majority in the House of Lords. The closeness of the result bears testimony to the difficulties and anxieties raised by the case.

The key issue was how the assessment of future harm should be conducted and, in particular, from what is a court permitted to infer a risk or likelihood of harm? The majority view was that s 31(2)(a) obliged the court to apply a two-stage test: first, to make a finding on the balance of probabilities, as to the alleged facts giving rise to the application, and secondly, based on that finding, to assess the likelihood of future harm. According to this view, 'unresolved judicial doubts and suspicions can no more form the basis of a conclusion that the second threshold condition in s 31(2)(a) has been established than they can form the basis that the first has been established'.[110] It therefore followed that, given the trial judge's finding that sexual abuse had not been proved, there was nothing from which a risk of future harm could be inferred.

The minority view was that the two-stage approach was wrong and over-complicated. As Lord Lloyd said:[111]

> Parliament has asked a simple question: Is the court satisfied that there is a serious risk of significant harm in the future? The question should be capable of being answered without too much over-analysis.

Furthermore, in Lord Browne-Wilkinson's view:

> To be satisfied of the existence of risk does not require proof of the occurrence of past historical events but proof of facts which are relevant to the making of a prognosis.[112]

In the minority view there were sufficient worrying findings[113] to justify the finding of a likelihood of harm.

---

[109] [1996] AC 563, HL, on which see the thoughtful analyses by M Hayes 'Reconciling protection of children with justice for parents in cases of alleged child abuse' [1997] *Legal Studies* 1 and C Keating 'Shifting standards in the House of Lords—*Re H and Others (Minors) (Sexual Abuse: Standard of Proof)*' [1996] CFLQ 157.   [110] [1996] AC 563 per Lord Nicholls at 589.
[111] [1996] AC 563 at 581.   [112] Ibid at 572.
[113] The so-called micro facts such as the consistency of the eldest child's story, the wrongful denial of the cohabitant that he had even been alone with the child, the mother's suspicion that something had been going on and her attempt to dissuade one of the other children from speaking to social workers.

Although the minority view has its attractions, there nevertheless seem good arguments for applying the two-stage test. First, unlike for earlier stages concerned with preliminary or interim steps or orders, s 31(2)(a) uses the language of proof, not suspicion, which makes sense given what is at stake at the final hearing. Second, if as must be the case, satisfying the first limb of s 31(2)(a) is dependent upon proof of significant harm, it would be odd, as Lord Nicholls put it, 'if, in respect of the self-same non-proven allegations, the self-same insufficient evidence would none the less be regarded as sufficient factual basis for satisfying the court there is a real possibility of harm to the child in the future'. Third, basing the likelihood of harm upon suspicion would effectively reverse the burden of proof since, in Lord Nicholls' words: 'It would mean that once apparently credible evidence of misconduct has been given, those against whom the allegations are made must disprove them'.

Lord Nicholls' overall conclusion also seems compelling:[114]

> But as I read the Act, Parliament decided that the threshold for a care order should be that the child is suffering significant harm, or there is a real possibility that he will do so. In the latter regard the threshold is comparatively low. Therein lies the protection for children. But, as I read the Act, Parliament also decided that proof of the relevant facts is needed if this threshold is to be surmounted. Before the s 1 welfare test and the welfare 'checklist' can be applied, the threshold has to be crossed. Therein lies the protection for parents. They are not to be at risk of having their child taken from them and removed into the care of the local authority on the basis only of suspicions, whether of the judge or of the local authority or anyone else. A conclusion that the child is suffering or is likely to suffer harm must be based on facts, not just suspicion.

To this must be added that care orders based on suspicions cannot be human rights compliant.[115]

Despite these arguments Re H has been criticised for setting the threshold bar too high thereby swinging the law too heavily in favour of parents. As Hayes has eloquently written, the decision raises in an acute form the question:[116]

> . . . how can the law and the court strike the correct balance before dispensing dispassionate justice to parents and safeguarding children from actual or likely significant harm? Parents should not be at risk of having children taken from them on the basis of false allegations of child abuse. This is unjust, it is a violation of the rights of the parents, and it is a violation of the rights and interests of children. Yet if local authorities are required to produce very powerful evidence that children are being abused, or are at risk of abuse, before courts can intervene, this may lead to some vulnerable children being subjected to horrific forms of undetected ill-treatment within the privacy of the family home. This outcome too is unjust, and it is a violation of the rights of children to be protected by the civil law. The dilemma to be resolved is how the legal framework, and the legal process, can best reconcile safeguarding children from suffering significant harm with the obligation to respect parental autonomy and family privacy.

---

[114] [1996] AC 563 at 592.

[115] As Baroness Hale convincingly put it in Re B (Children) (Care Proceedings: Standard of Proof) [2008] UKHL 35 [2009] 1 AC 11 at [78], relying upon K & T v Finland (2001) 31 EHRR 18; Scozzari and Giunta v Italy (2002) 35 EHRR 12; and Kutzner v Germany (2002) 35 EHRR 25: Given the need for 'relevant and sufficient' reasons to justify interfering with the child's Article 8 rights, '[i]t is difficult to see how the reasons for taking a child away from her family for the indefinite future can be 'relevant and sufficient' if they rely upon unproven allegations as the only basis for inferring that the child is at risk of harm.'

[116] M Hayes 'Reconciling Protection of Children with Justice for Parents in Cases of Alleged Abuse' (1997) 17 Legal Studies 1 at 1–2.

Against this it can be argued that some of these fears have been allayed by the Lords' clarification of the balance of probabilities test in *Re B*. Furthermore, some of the fears are arguably misplaced. *Re H* was unusual in being a single issue case and in such cases it cannot be denied that the two-stage test creates consequent difficulties as the court is faced with the stark dilemma of only being able to protect a child who alleges that they have been abused if the one allegation can be proved. Yet in the majority of cases there will usually be many facts from which an inference of risk of harm can be drawn.[117]

Without gainsaying some of the difficulties that undoubtedly flow from *Re H*, not least that in certain profoundly worrying situations (for example, where an older child has died in suspicious circumstances but non-accidental injury cannot be proved)[118] the court will be powerless to act, it is nevertheless submitted that *on the facts as found* the majority decision was right, for it does seem in principle to be wrong to justify local authority intervention into family life because of a risk of harm based on a mere suspicion. However, the propriety of the initial finding seems doubtful. Lord Lloyd was surely right when he said that the first instance judge was in fact applying the now discredited higher than ordinary standard of proof.[119] The case should have been remitted back for re-hearing.

Whatever one's views about the appropriateness of the two-stage test it is clearly settled law. In *Re B*[120] the House of Lords emphatically rejected the invitation to depart from *Re H* and any remaining doubts that the newly created Supreme Court might have taken a different line were scotched by *Re S-B (Children) (Care Proceedings: Standard of Proof)*.[121]

The meaning of 'likely'

Although divided on the need for a two-stage test, in *Re H* the House of Lords unanimously held that 'likely' did not require the court to find that the harm was 'more likely than not': it was sufficient that such harm was a real possibility—'a possibility that cannot sensibly be ignored'. As Lord Nicholls subsequently observed in *Re O, Re B*,[122] this is a comparatively low level of risk. Given the inherent uncertainty of predicting the future, balanced against the need to protect children, this lower threshold makes sense. As Baroness Hale observed in *Re S-B*:[123]

---

[117] See, for example, the comments of Lord Nicholls in *Re H*, earlier, at 591–592 and Baroness Hale in *Re B* at [55]. This is not to say, however, that reliance on a number of allegations does not raise its own difficulties, see *Re R (Care: Disclosure: Nature of Proceedings)* [2002] 1 FLR 755 (in which guidance is given as to how to conduct proceedings in cases of multiple allegations).

[118] As in *Re P (A Minor) (Care: Evidence)* [1994] 2 FLR 751 (though in that case a higher standard of proof was applied).See also *Lancashire County Council v B* [2002] 2 WLR 346, CA, (discussed at *Lancashire County Council v B ('Lancashire')*, p 617) in which a care order application in respect of a child-minder's child was dismissed upon the failure to establish whether the child-minder was responsible for the injuries to another child she was employed to look after. Cf *Re B (Non Accidental Injury)* [2002] EWCA Civ 752 [2002] 2 FLR 1133 in which the Court of Appeal upheld a first instance ruling that the threshold had been established even though the medical evidence did not positively establish but was consistent with non-accidental injury and that there was no more probable explanation (the judge had concluded that the child's subdural haemorrhages had been caused by shaking by one or other of the parents); and *Re P (Emergency Protection Order)* [1996] 1 FLR 482 in which Johnson J was satisfied that, because medical evidence had eliminated any medical cause for the child nearly suffocating, the mother must have been responsible.

[119] He was also surely right in saying (at 578) that the Court of Appeal (and, it might be,added, Lord Nicholls who accepted the Court of Appeal's assessment, see earlier at 587) had been over generous to the trial judge in holding that in fact he had applied the right test—he clearly did not.

[120] *Re B (Children) (Care Proceedings: Standard of Proof) (Cafcass intervening)* [2008] UKHL 35 [2009] 1 AC 11.   [121] [2009] UKSC 17 [2010] 1 AC 678.

[122] *Re O and Another (Minors) (Care: Preliminary Hearing); Re B (A Minor)* [2003] UKHL 18 [2004] 1 AC 523 at [16].   [123] [2009] UKSC 17 [2010] 1 AC 678 at [9].

> the law has drawn a clear distinction between probability as it applies to past facts and probability as it applies to future predictions. Past facts must be proved to have happened on the balance of probabilities, that is, that it is more likely than not that they did happen. Predictions about future facts need only be based upon a degree of likelihood that they will happen which is sufficient to justify preventative action.

But even this aspect of the threshold is not problem free. One issue, raised in *Re MA (Care Threshold)*,[124] is whether having shown a likelihood, it is still necessary to prove that the risk is of *significant* harm. In other words, is the low threshold applied simply to the existence of the *risk*, or is it to be applied to establishing *a risk of significant harm*? In *Re MA*, Ward LJ considered it was the former so that the low threshold applied only to the existence of the risk but that it is still necessary to prove, presumably on the balance of probabilities, that the risk is of significant harm. Referring to *Re H*, he observed[125] that when Lord Nicholls:

> spoke of the threshold being comparatively low, it was having to show no more than *a real possibility* of harm (as opposed to proving a balance of probability) that made the threshold a low one. But it still has to be a real possibility of *significant* harm. Lord Nicholls was not saying that the threshold for establishing the *significance* of the harm was comparatively low. He was not dealing with the meaning and weight to be given to the word 'significant' at all. After all the harm has to be significant whether one is dealing with harm which has been suffered as well as or where one is dealing only with the likelihood of it being suffered.

It was upon this basis that Ward LJ felt he could not interfere with the first instance judge's finding that notwithstanding the appalling treatment of a non-biological child being looked after by a couple in mysterious circumstances combined with evidence of slapping and kicking of the elder of the couple's two natural children (which itself was not acceptable behaviour), while there was a risk of future harm to the two children it was not of 'significant' harm. He pointed out that no mark was found on the elder child and that both she and her sibling were well nourished, well cared for and had a close attachment to their parents.

Hallett LJ agreed with Ward LJ though not specifically on the point of interpretation of the 1989 Act, but rather upon the case being a classic example of 'trusting the judgment of the trial judge'.

Wilson LJ dissented. For him 'the conclusion inexorably driven by the combination of the gross ill-treatment of [the non-biological child] and of the ill-treatment of [the elder daughter] is that all three children were *likely* to suffer significant emotional and physical harm'. In his view, given the history and in particular the lack of explanation for why the parents behaved so appallingly towards the non-biological child gave the trial judge 'no platform for a conclusion that it would not be likely to be replicated[126] towards their own three children'.

While many will sympathise with Wilson LJ's view, his approach masks a difference in principle, for he seems to be saying[127] that once a likelihood of harm has been established

---

[124] [2009] EWCA Civ 853 [2010] 1 FLR 431, on which see H Keeting '*Re MA*: the significance of harm' [2011] CFLQ 115.   [125] [2009] EWCA Civ 853 [2010] 1 FLR 431 at [52].

[126] As Wilson LJ pointed out the conduct had already to some extent begun to be replicated in respect of the eldest of the biological children.

[127] See para [29] in which Wilson LJ refers to Lord Nicholls' view that 'in relation to a likelihood of significant harm, the threshold is set at a comparatively low level'.

upon the basis of the parents' ill-treatment of other children in the family, there is in effect a rebuttable presumption that other children are likely to suffer significant harm. Ergo, the comparatively low threshold applies to establishing a risk of significant harm and not just to establishing the risk.

Wilson LJ is not alone in taking this line. In *Re K (Care: Threshold Criteria)*[128] the trial judge found that a child had been deliberately injured by one or other of the parents, but concluded that there was no risk of significant harm to another child of the family who had not been injured. Allowing the local authority's appeal, Wall LJ commented:[129]

> if the court is not to find the threshold criteria met in relation to the uninjured child, there have either to be highly unusual circumstances in the case, alternatively the judge must give a full and reasoned explanation of why it is he takes the view that the child is not likely to suffer significant harm in those circumstances.

While neither Wilson nor Wall LJJ are saying that what we have called a presumption of likelihood of significant harm cannot be rebutted,[130] the concern is that their approach could be seen as effectively reversing the legal burden of proof which clearly lies on the local authority.

A second problem associated with likelihood is whether the test of possibility varies according to the nature of the harm. This seems to be the implication of Baroness Hale's statement in *Re S-B*:[131]

> Predictions about the future need only be based upon a degree of likelihood that they will happen which is sufficient to justify preventive action. This will depend upon the nature and gravity of the harm: *a lesser degree of likelihood that the child will be killed will justify immediate preventive action than degree of likelihood that the child will not be sent to school.* (Emphasis added)

While the sentiment of this statement is clear enough—take fewer risks where the child's life as opposed to his education is at stake—precisely how does the degree of likelihood differ? Will this herald debate on the degree of likelihood of future events just at a time when arguments about the degree of probability of past events have been settled?

(b) The attributable condition

Once the existence of significant harm (or a risk thereof) has been proved, s 31(2)(b) requires the court to be satisfied that the harm or likelihood of harm is attributable to (i) the lack of care given or likely to be given if the order were not made, or (ii) the child's being beyond parental control.

The application of these criteria is crucial to maintaining the balance between the protection of children and the right of families to be free from unjustified state intervention. As Baroness Hale stated in *Re S-B*,[132] the object of these criteria is 'to limit intervention to certain kinds of harm – harm which should not happen if a child is being looked after properly'.

---

[128] [2005] EWCA Civ 1226 [2006] 2 FLR 868.   [129] At [40].

[130] A good example is *AP v Vale of Glamorgan* [2007] EWCA Civ 1265, sub nom *Re P (Split Hearing)* [2007] All ER (D) 475 (Nov) in which an isolated act of violence by the father on his nephew was held not to establish a likelihood of significant harm to his own children about whom there had been no previous concerns.

[131] [2009] UKSC 17 [2010] 1 AC 678 at [9].   [132] Ibid at [20].

Is the harm attributable to the care given or likely to be given?

The meaning of 'care'

The Act is silent on what is meant by 'care' in this context. Although 'care' could simply be interpreted as referring to the physical day-to-day care given to the child by the person with whom the child is living, it is clear that it means more than this. As the 2008 *Guidance* puts it:[133]

> 'Care' is not defined but in the context is interpreted as including responsibility for making proper provision for the child's health and welfare (including promoting his physical, intellectual, emotional, social and behavioural development) and not just meeting basic survival needs.

Hence, in a case of a child being accommodated by a local authority but living with foster parents, the threshold criteria might still be satisfied notwithstanding that the parents are now able to look after their child, if they have not been visiting or keeping in touch.[134] On the other hand, if the parent has shown all the care and concern that a reasonable parent would show to a child living away from home for a time, then on either interpretation the criteria would not be satisfied. In such cases, however, the court would have to consider whether it would be preferable to make a child arrangements order in favour of the foster parents.[135]

Care by whom?

When the care given by the parents is in issue no problems of interpretation arise. However the phrase 'care given' would be seriously deficient if it were restricted to *parental* care[136] and the question arises as to who, other than parents, may be responsible for the care given for the purposes of satisfying the threshold. The courts' approach is that, in the normal case, parents or other primary carers are within the scope of the provision whereas third parties are not. But this distinction is not clear cut. It seems that the phrase 'other primary carers' is intended to encompass those who are in the position of parents, such as partners or close relatives who are involved in the day-to-day care of the child within the family home. However, the precise ambit of the term is unclear and as Lord Clyde commented in *Lancashire County Council v B*:[137]

> ... [W]hile in practice the term [primary carer] may be conveniently adopted as a term of reference, there may well be problems of definition in determining for the purpose of the statutory provision the precise persons who would qualify as a 'primary carer'.

The term 'third parties' clearly applies to those who have access to a child outside the family home, such as doctors and teachers. As Baroness Hale said in *Re S-B*,[138] '[i]t cannot have been intended that a parent whose child has been harmed as a result of a lack of proper care in a hospital or school should be at risk of losing her child.'

---

[133] Vol 1 *Court Orders* (DCSF, 2008) at para 3.40.

[134] Hence, in a case like *M v Wigan Metropolitan Borough Council* [1979] Fam 36, where children were repeatedly looked after by the authority during the mother's difficult pregnancies but where the parents were reluctant to take responsibility for them, the criteria would be satisfied.

[135] See further Section 8 orders, p 631.

[136] See, for example, Lord Clyde in *Lancashire County Council v B* [2000] 2 AC 147 at 169.

[137] Ibid at 169–170.   [138] [2009] UKSC 17 [2010] 1 AC 678 at [21].

Failure to protect as an alternative ground for intervention

Commonly, the parents will be directly responsible for the harm or risk of harm to the child and, provided only that they have fallen below the standard of care expected, the causal link will be readily established. If the child has been harmed by a third party, an alternative approach would be to establish the causal link on the basis of the parents' failure to protect the child. As Lord Nicholls explained in *Lancashire*:[139]

> ...if a parent entrusts a child to a third party without taking the precautionary steps a reasonable parent would take to check the suitability of the third party, and subsequently the third party injures or sexually abuses the child, the harm suffered by the child may be regarded as attributable to the inadequate care of the parent as well as the third party.

Failure to protect may also be a useful device to avoid some of the difficulties encountered in uncertain perpetrator cases (discussed shortly). However, whilst a failure to protect a child may be sufficient to satisfy the threshold, the House of Lords has rejected[140] suggestions that cases should proceed to the welfare stage simply on this basis and in particular not in cases where a child has been harmed by one parent but the parent responsible cannot be identified.

Not being what it would be reasonable to expect a parent to give to him

This rather inelegant phrase imports an objective test. In other words, to satisfy s 31(2)(b)(i) the care given or likely to be given must fall below an objectively acceptable level. As Lord Nicholls pointed out in *Lancashire County Council v B*,[141] '[t]hat level is the care a reasonable parent would provide for the child concerned.' In other words the objective test is applicable to a hypothetical parent and not to the child, who must treated as he or she actually is.[142] In this regard, it is no answer to say that the care given was to the best of the parents' limited abilities. Parents cannot argue that they have particular problems, that they are unintelligent, irresponsible, alcoholic, drug abusers, poor or otherwise disadvantaged, and are thus justified in providing a lower standard of care. It is no answer either that the care given was no different from that given by others in the same street or neighbourhood.[143] Nevertheless identifying the level of care expected of a reasonable parent can be problematic.

Although Munby J has indicated[144] that the social, cultural and religious background of the child and the family should be considered in determining the standard of care expected, this would arguably open up an unacceptably wide range of enquiries which might be more appropriately considered at the welfare stage. Without gainsaying the difficulties of identifying the standard of care expected, once a child's individual needs have been identified, in determining whether the threshold has been met the courts should strive to apply a consistent, objective standard of care which reflects generally accepted norms of parenting.

---

[139] [2000] 2 AC 147 at 162.

[140] *Re O and Another (Minors) (Care: Preliminary Hearing); Re B (A Minor)* [2003] UKHL 18 [2004] 1 AC 523 at [30].   [141] [2000] 2 AC 147 at 162.

[142] This was made clear by Lord Mackay during the passage of the Bill. HL Deb, 8 November 1989, Vol 512, col 756.

[143] These matters may, however, be relevant to the question whether an order should be made, that is, at the welfare stage, discussed at The welfare stage, pp 625ff.

[144] *Re K; A Local Authority v N and Others* [2005] EWHC 2956 (Fam) [2007] 1 FLR 399 at [26].

The focus of attention is on the care given or likely to be given to the child in question, not to an average child. If, for example, the child has particular difficulties in relation to his behaviour or impairment, the court will have to consider what a reasonable parent would provide for him. In *Re V (Care or Supervision)*,[145] for example, a mother, who was protective of her son who suffered from cerebral palsy, sought to keep him at home rather than sending him to a specialist school. It was held that whilst the mother's care was beyond criticism on the grounds of devotion and affection it nevertheless fell short of the standard of care which was reasonably expected of her in the circumstances.

The child's being beyond parental control

As the 2008 *Guidance* states,[146] this alternative causal condition:

> requires the court to determine whether as a matter of fact, the child is beyond control: it is immaterial whether who, if anyone is to blame. In such cases, the local authority will need to demonstrate how the child's situation will improve if the court makes an order – how his behaviour can be brought under control, and why an order is necessary to achieve this.

In *Re O (A Minor) (Care Order: Education: Procedure)*,[147] Ewbank J commented that in respect of a 15-year-old truant:

> . . . where a child is suffering harm in not going to school and is living at home it will follow that either the child is beyond her parents' control or that they are not giving the child the care that it would be reasonable to expect a parent to give.

According to *M v Birmingham City Council*,[148] the phrase 'being beyond parental control' imports no time element and is therefore 'plainly a substantial expression capable of describing a state of affairs in the past, in the present or in the future according to the context in which it falls to be applied'. It was also held that while 'parental control' refers to the parent of the child in question and not to parents, or reasonable parents, in general, regard can properly be had to the control exercised by that parent in conjunction with a partner even if that partner is not the parent of the child.

Applying the attributable condition where the perpetrator of the harm is uncertain

Where it is sought to satisfy the threshold on the basis of injury caused to a child, a problematic aspect of the attributable condition has been identifying the perpetrator. It is generally accepted that it is in the public interest for those who cause serious non-accidental injuries to children to be identified[149] and it is clear that, if the perpetrator can be identified, then it is the judge's duty to do so.[150] Furthermore, *Re B* established that, in identifying the perpetrator, the simple balance of probabilities test should be applied[151] and the Supreme Court in *Re S-B* has confirmed this.[152] However, although the clarification of the standard of proof to be applied ameliorated some of the problems in dealing

[145] [1996] 1 FLR 776, CA.   [146] Vol 1 *Court Orders* (DCSF, 2008) para 3.41.
[147] [1992] 1 WLR 912 at 917–18.   [148] [1994] 2 FLR 141 at 147.
[149] *Re K (Non-Accidental Injuries: Perpetrator: New Evidence)* [2005] 1 FLR 285 at [55], per Wall LJ.
[150] Per Wall LJ in *Re D (Care Proceedings: Preliminary hearings)* [2009] EWCA Civ 472 [2009] 2 FLR 668 at [12]. See *Re S-B* [2009] UKSC 17 [2010] 1 AC 678, at [36]–[38].
[151] [2008] UKHL 35 [2009] 1 AC 11 at [73].   [152] [2009] UKSC 17 [2010] 1 AC 678 at [34]

with uncertain perpetrators, as the following discussion shows, the issue has not thereby been fully resolved.

Lancashire County Council v B ('Lancashire')

Lancashire[153] was the first of a series of senior court decisions dealing with the position of where it cannot be proved who is responsible for the child's injuries. In that case a young child sustained serious non-accidental injuries but the unresolved question was who was responsible. There were three possible perpetrators, namely, either of the parents or the paid child-minder. The House of Lords ruled that where actual harm or risk of harm can be proved then, in the case of 'shared care arrangements', provided the harm can be shown to have been inflicted by one of the carers, there is no need to identify the actual perpetrator of the harm to satisfy s 31(2)(b)(i). As Lord Clyde said,[154] '[w]hat the subsection requires is the identification of the incidence of harm, not the hand which caused, or may be likely to cause it.'

In Lord Nicholls' view, the phrase 'the care given to the child' is not confined to the care given to the child by parents or other primary carers but in the case of shared care arrangements extends to the care given by any of the carers. Further, although he accepted that 'attributable to' connotes a causal connection between the harm and the care, in his view, that 'connection need not be that of a sole or dominant or direct cause and effect; a contributory causal connection suffices'.[155] A more restrictive interpretation, said Lord Nicholls, would mean that notwithstanding that a child has repeatedly sustained non-accidental injuries, the court would be powerless to intervene to protect the child unless it could be shown who was responsible. That, in his view, could not have been Parliament's intention and given that Parliament seems not to have foreseen this particular problem, the court had to 'apply the statutory language to the unforeseen situation in the manner which best gives effect to the purposes the legislation was enacted to achieve'.[156]

Whilst this approach avoids some of the difficulties encountered in the uncertain perpetrator cases, it nevertheless raises the matter of principle as to whether interpretation of a statutory provision should so vary. It also raises the question as to what amount to 'shared care' arrangements. It clearly embraces all forms of multi-care arrangements, including those who look after the child during the day whilst the parents are at work and presumably also those who look after the child whilst the parents are out socially. However, it arguably would not extend to those who merely have unsupervised access to the child, such as a teacher who comes to the home to give a child private tuition.[157]

Although the overall outcome of *Lancashire* is generally regarded as correct since it ensures that the local authority can take appropriate protective action in cases involving uncertain perpetrators,[158] the Lords' approach to arriving at this outcome has been criticised. Hayes[159] has suggested that a preferable approach would be to base the decision

---

[153] [2000] 2 AC 147, on which see A Bainham 'Attributing Harm: Child Abuse and the Unknown Perpetrator' (2000) 59 CLJ 458; J Herring 'The Suffering Children of Blameless Parents' (2000) 116 LQR 116 and A Perry '*Lancashire County Council v B* Section 31—Threshold or Barrier?' [2000] CFLQ 301.

[154] [2000] 2 AC 147 at 169C.   [155] Ibid at 162A–B.   [156] Ibid at 166E.

[157] Note *North Yorkshire County Council v SA* [2003] EWCA Civ 839 [2003] 2 FLR 849 at [25] in which Butler-Sloss P seemed to imply that those who merely have 'fleeting contact' will not rank as 'carers' for these purposes.

[158] *Lancashire* was cited with approval by Baroness Hale in *Re B* [2008] UKHL 35 at [61] and in *Re S-B* [2009] UKSC 17 at [21].

[159] M Hayes 'Uncertain Evidence and Risk-Taking in Child Protection Cases' [2004] CFLQ 63.

on the risk of future harm which would more fairly reflect the position in *Lancashire*: ie that attribution to the parents of the harm might be entirely wrong, but that the level of risk to the child if the parents were, indeed, the perpetrators of that harm demands that the court has power to intervene. However, given that *Re H* and *Re S-B* establish that the risk of future harm must be based on proved facts, were this suggestion to be followed, then in any case where the perpetrator cannot be identified, the threshold could only be met if all the possible perpetrators are likely be involved in the future care of the child. In *Lancashire*, for example, as the child-minder presumably would not have been so involved, the threshold would not have been met.

As Lord Nicholls himself recognised, the *Lancashire* decision means that the attributable condition may be satisfied when there is no more than a possibility that the parents were responsible for inflicting the injuries and that consequently parents who may be wholly innocent and whose care may not have fallen below that of a reasonable parent will face the possibility of losing their child with all the pain and distress that that involves.[160] What persuaded him to adopt this stance was 'the prospect that an unidentified, and unidentifiable, carer may inflict further injury on a child he or she has already severely damaged'. Without gainsaying the difficulties, it is submitted that *Lancashire* was right and goes some way to mitigating the consequences of the earlier ruling in *Re H*. Were it to be necessary to prove who the actual perpetrator of harm is in every case it would, as one judge has observed,[161] render the statutory provisions ineffective to deal with a commonplace aspect of child protection. As Lord Nicholls said in the later decision, *Re O and another (Minors) (Care: Preliminary Hearing; Re B (A Minor))*,[162] the interpretation adopted by *Lancashire* 'is necessary to avoid the unacceptable consequence that, otherwise, if the court cannot identify which of the child's carers is responsible for inflicting the injuries the child will remain wholly unprotected'.

It is important to appreciate that *Lancashire* did not decide that a care order should be made but only that the threshold had been satisfied, thus permitting the court then to consider at the so-called welfare stage what, if any, order it should make.[163] But again, as Lord Nicholls acknowledged, the decision in *Lancashire* poses considerable problems for determining what order, if any, should be made inasmuch as it will not be known which individual was responsible for inflicting the injuries. We discuss these problems further when considering the welfare stage.[164]

Re S-B (Children) (Care Proceedings: Standard of Proof)('Re S-B')

In *Re S-B*[165] the local authority applied for care orders in respect of two children. The elder, born in 2007, was found to have suffered non-accidental injury in the form of bruising at the age of four weeks. The bruising was caused by the mother or the father, but the judge was unable to decide who was responsible.[166] The younger child was born in 2008. By this time the parents had separated and the father played no further part in the proceedings. The younger child had not been injured and the case for removing

---

[160] The dilemma in *Lancashire* was even greater since if the child-minder was responsible for the injuries not only was the child removed from innocent parents, but the child-minder's own child was left unprotected.

[161] Wall J in *Re B (Minors) (Care Proceedings: Practice)* [1999] 1 WLR 238 at 248.

[162] [2003] UKHL 18 [2004] 1 AC 523 at [19].

[163] Indeed, it was for this very reason that Lord Clyde considered it justifiable to allow a degree of latitude in the scope of the threshold.   [164] See Uncertain perpetrators, p 626.

[165] [2009] UKSC 17 [2010] 1 AC 678.

[166] The bruising was not such that the non-abusing parent must have known that the child was being harmed.

him from his mother rested on the likelihood of his being harmed in the future if he were to stay with her.

At the fact-finding hearing the judge found that, although she could not identify the perpetrator, the threshold had been crossed in relation to both children. Nevertheless, following Lord Nicholls' encouragement in Re O, Re B[167] to judges to express a view on the comparative likelihood as between the possible perpetrators, the judge explained in a written Adjunct to Judgment, '[i]nvidious though it is to be too specific, but to help further assessment, I am prepared to say that I feel it 60% likely that the father injured the child and 40% likely that it was the mother.'

The mother appealed, contending that as the judge had been 60% satisfied as to the father's responsibility for the injuries, it followed that there had to be a finding on the balance of probabilities that the father was the perpetrator, with a consequential finding that she was absolved of all responsibility. The Court of Appeal dismissed the appeal, holding that the Adjunct to Judgment had not been intended by the judge to amount to a finding of fact. The Supreme Court, however, allowed the mother's appeal and remitted the case for a rehearing before a different judge. The principal reason for this decision was that, as the trial judge had misdirected herself on the standard of proof,[168] the court could not know what finding she would have made in relation to the identification of the perpetrator had she directed herself correctly in the first place.[169]

Having confirmed that the relevant standard of proof in identifying the perpetrator was the simple balance of probabilities, the court then considered the proper approach to cases where the perpetrator cannot be identified to this standard.

The key to understanding the Supreme Court decision is to appreciate the facts ('the primary facts') which must be proved on the balance of probabilities in order to satisfy the threshold. In a case where a child has been harmed but an individual perpetrator cannot be identified, the primary facts are that the child is suffering significant harm and that the perpetrator is either a parent or primary carer or, in the case of shared care arrangements, a carer. In relation to an unharmed child, the primary facts are that harm has been caused to another child such that this harm gives rise to an inference of the likelihood of future significant harm, *and* that all possible perpetrators of that harm will be involved in the future care of the child. In other words, if an individual perpetrator cannot be identified on the balance of probabilities, before the threshold can be satisfied, it is necessary to identify the whole pool of possible perpetrators.

Identifying possible perpetrators

In determining the pool of possible perpetrators the first question is whether the approach to filling the pool should be an exculpatory (that is, determining who falls outside the possible pool) or an inculpatory one (that is, determining who falls within the pool). In the past the courts have tended to adopt the former—as Baroness Hale commented,[170] '[t]he

---

[167] [2003] UKHL 18 [2004] 1 AC 523 at [32]. This practice is now discredited, see Baroness Hale's comments in Re S-B at [44].

[168] She had said that the appropriate standard of proof had to be based on evidence of reliability and cogency equivalent to the gravity of the allegations, ie she applied the test discredited by Re B(Children) (Care Proceedings: Standard of Proof) (Cafcass intervening) [2008] UKHL 35 [2009] 1 AC 11, discussed at The burden and standard of proof, p 598.

[169] A further reason to remit was that the judge had been wrong to find the threshold satisfied in relation to the younger child on the basis that there was a real possibility that the mother had injured the elder child.

[170] In Re S-B, see earlier, at [43].

cases are littered with references to a "finding of exculpation" or to "ruling out" a particular person as responsible for the harm suffered.' However, as the local authority bears the burden of proving the threshold criteria, the appropriate approach should logically be an inculpatory one and in *Re S-B*, the Supreme Court made it clear that this is the correct approach.

A second issue—identifying the correct test for inclusion in the pool—is more controversial. As the pool only has to be considered if the perpetrator cannot be identified on the balance of probabilities, such identification must necessarily involve a lower level of probability than the balance of probabilities, but where the line is to be drawn is a matter of some dispute. In *North Yorkshire County Council v SA*[171] a child had been injured on two occasions and according to the trial judge the possible perpetrators included the parents, the grandmother and a nanny. The issue on appeal was to determine the correct test for identifying the possible perpetrators. The trial judge held that he should only exclude an individual as a possible perpetrator if there was 'no possibility' that he or she could have inflicted the injuries upon the child. The Court of Appeal held this to be the wrong test as it was 'patently too wide and might encompass anyone who had even a fleeting contact with the child in circumstances in which there was no opportunity to cause the injuries'.[172] Butler-Sloss P preferred the test of 'real possibility' which had been adopted by Lord Nicholls in *Re O, Re B*[173] when he held that, in uncertain perpetrator cases, the court should proceed to the welfare stage on the footing that each of the possible perpetrators is, indeed, just that: a possible perpetrator. As Butler-Sloss P explained:[174]

> Although Lord Nicholls was focusing on the welfare or disposal stage of the hearing, [his comments] relate equally directly to the task of the judge trying the first, section 31(2) part of the case. In his observations about the likelihood of future risk and the likelihood that carers were possible perpetrators of past injuries to children he was, in my judgment, applying the same test of real possibility.

The correct test was therefore held to be whether there is a real possibility or likelihood that one or more of a number of people with access to the child might have caused the injury to the child.[175]

Criticising this test, counsel for the local authority in *Re S-B* argued that the 'real possibility' test had been adopted in *Re H* in relation to the prediction of likelihood of future harm and it was not intended as a test for identification of possible perpetrators in the past.[176] Whilst Baroness Hale accepted that this may be so, she claimed that there were real advantages in adopting the approach and continued:[177]

> If the evidence is not such as to establish responsibility on the balance of probabilities it should nevertheless be such as to establish whether there is a real possibility that a particular person was involved.

---

[171] [2003] EWCA Civ 839 [2003] 2 FLR 849.   [172] Ibid at [25].

[173] *Re O and Another (Minors) (Care: Preliminary Hearing); Re B (A Minor)* [2003] UKHL 18 [2004] 1 AC 523 at [28].   [174] [2003] EWCA Civ 839 [2003] 2 FLR 849 at [21].

[175] Ibid at [26]. Butler Sloss P also made it clear that for this purpose, real possibility and likelihood can be treated as the same test.   [176] [2009] UKSC 17 [2010] 1 AC 678 at [42].

[177] Ibid at [43]. Although this might be an oblique way of doing so, Baroness Hale is generally taken to be upholding the decision of *North Yorkshire*. See, for example, the headnote of the case at [2010] 2 WLR 238 at 239. In *Re J (Children) (Care Proceedings: Threshold Criteria)* [2013] UKSC 9, [2013] 1 AC 680, at [34], Baroness Hale makes it clear that she was approving *North Yorkshire* in *Re S-B*.

However, she also held that the trial judge had been wrong to find the threshold had been satisfied in relation to the younger child on the basis that there was a real possibility that the mother had injured the elder child, saying:[178]

> It was established in *Re H* and confirmed in *Re O* that a prediction of future harm has to be based upon findings of actual fact made on the balance of probabilities. It is only once those facts have been found that the degree of likelihood of future events becomes the 'real possibility' test adopted in *Re H*.

At first sight, it is difficult to square this apparent acceptance of the 'real possibility' test for determining the pool of possible perpetrators with her conclusion that the trial judge had been wrong to find the threshold satisfied in relation to the younger child. One explanation is that the identification of perpetrators is not a *primary* fact which has to be proved in order to satisfy the threshold. In *Re S-B*, in relation to the *injured* child, it was sufficient that the mother was a possible perpetrator (the only other possible perpetrator being the father).The threshold would also have been satisfied in relation to the unharmed younger child if the father had continued to be involved in the future care of the children; the proved facts being that one or other of the parents was responsible for the injuries to the elder child and that since both would be involved in the future care of the younger child, this was sufficient to give rise to the required 'real possibility' of future harm.

The trial judge had been wrong to find the threshold crossed in relation to the younger child, not because the wrong test had been applied in identifying the mother as a possible perpetrator, but because the father was no longer involved with the care of that child and it was thus not established *on the balance of probabilities* that the likelihood of harm was attributable to the care likely to be given to the child.

On this analysis, Baroness Hale's judgment endorses (a) an inculpatory approach and (b) the application of the 'real possibility' test for determining who is in the pool of possible perpetrators. One consequence of this is that the real possibility test now fulfils two functions—one prospective and one retrospective: first, following *Re H*, it is used to quantify the risk of future harm; and secondly following *Re S-B*, it is used to establish the likelihood that an individual was responsible for the harm caused to a child where that cannot be proved on the balance of probabilities. However, determining the likelihood of past facts having occurred (when they either did or did not, in fact, happen) is a very different exercise from predicting the future (which is inherently uncertain). Furthermore, it is clear that different considerations will be relevant in each case—in quantifying the risk of future harm, the gravity of the feared harm will clearly be relevant[179] whereas in determining past events, the gravity of the harm suffered and the inherent improbability of an event having taken place will presumably not be relevant. As Baroness Hale said in *Re B* '... once the evidence is clear that [the child has been injured]... the inherent improbability of the event has no relevance to deciding who [injured the child]'.[180] Courts will need to keep a clear distinction between the prospective and retrospective applications of the real possibility test if confusion is not to creep in.

---

[178] [2009] UKSC 17 [2010] 1 AC 678 at [49].
[179] See, for example, Baroness Hale in *Re S-B* at [9].
[180] [2009] UKSC 17 [2010] 1 AC 678 at [73].

The 'mixed pool' dilemma

In cases based on a single issue, if no individual perpetrator can be identified and the pool of possible perpetrators contains both parents or other primary carers[181] *and* third parties, the threshold will not be met in relation to the injured child on the basis of actual harm. Furthermore, unless all in the pool are involved in the future care of the child, neither will the threshold be satisfied on the basis of a risk of future harm. It will also be an inevitable consequence that the threshold will not be met in relation to any other children in the family. We refer to this as the 'mixed pool' dilemma.

This dilemma arose in *Lancashire*. As previously discussed, the House of Lords adopted a purposive approach to the interpretation of the phrase 'care given' which brought the child-minder within the phrase and thus satisfied the threshold in relation to the injured child. In the same case, however, the local authority also sought a care order in relation to the child-minder's own child, who had not suffered any injury. The trial judge, having found that the threshold criteria could not be established in relation to the injured child, inevitably concluded that they could not be established on the basis of future harm in relation to the child-minder's child. The Court of Appeal upheld this decision, stating that the risk of future harm could only be established on the basis of proven facts and, as it had not been established that the child-minder was responsible for shaking the injured child, there was nothing on which to establish the risk of future harm to her own child. No further appeal was taken on this point. Questioning the reasoning of the Court of Appeal, it has been argued that the 'fact' which must be proved in order to establish that a child is likely to suffer significant harm is the fact of significant harm having been suffered, rather than the precise identity of the perpetrator of that harm and that confusion between the importance of proof of the fact of harm itself and the identity of the perpetrator of the harm led the Court of Appeal to reach the wrong conclusion on this point.[182] The fallacy of this argument is its failure to consider the need to satisfy the attributable condition. As Baroness Hale clearly said in *Re S-B*[183] a likelihood of future harm cannot be based upon the premise that there is a real possibility that the future likely carer (in that case, the mother) had injured another child.

The uncomfortable consequence of this reasoning, however, is that whenever there is a pool of possible perpetrators, but not all are involved with the future care of another child, the threshold can never be satisfied. In other words the mixed pool dilemma is insoluble, leaving children unprotected who may well be at risk. This is well illustrated by yet another Supreme Court decision, *Re J (Children) (Care Proceedings: Threshold Criteria)* ('*Re J*').[184]

Re J

In *Re J* the mother's first child died of asphyxia when 3 weeks old, having sustained serious injuries. When her second child was born the local authority immediately began care proceedings. The threshold was found to be satisfied but at the fact-finding hearing it was

---

[181] Or, in the cases case of shared care, those within the shared care arrangements.

[182] See A Perry. 'Section 31 – threshold or barrier?' [2000] CFLQ 301 at 309. See also J Hayes 'The threshold test and the unknown perpetrator' [2000] Fam Law 260.

[183] [2009] UKSC 17 [2010] 1 AC 678 at [49].

[184] [2013] UKSC 9 [2013] 1 AC 680, on which see the thought-provoking article by M Hayes 'The Supreme Court's failure to protect vulnerable children: *Re J (Children)*' [2013] Fam Law 1015. See also S Gilmore '*Re J (Care Proceedings: Past Possible Perpetrators in a New Family Unit)* [2013] UKSC 9: Bulwarks and logic – the blood which runs through the veins of the law – but how much blood will be spilled in the future?' [2013] CFLQ 215 and J Hayes 'The Judge's Dilemma' [2014] Fam Law 91.

found that the injuries had been caused by the mother or father or both but that it was impossible to say on the balance of probabilities who the perpetrator was. The mother later separated from the father, moved areas, and began a relationship with a new partner who had two children of his own. Subsequently, the mother had a third child and, having discovered the facts about the mother's first child, the local authority brought care proceedings in respect of all three children living with the mother and her partner on the basis that they were 'likely to suffer significant harm'. The issue before the Supreme Court was confined to the narrow single issue[185] of whether the previous court finding that the mother was a possible perpetrator of harm caused to her first child could support a finding that the three unharmed children living with her and her new partner were at risk of suffering significant harm for the purpose of crossing the threshold. It was unanimously held that it could not.

In reaching this conclusion reliance was placed on *Re H, Lancashire* (including the Court of Appeal decision) and *Re S-B*, in particular, that the consignment of a carer (in this case the mother) to the pool of possible perpetrators is insufficient to establish that unharmed children in another household (albeit one including that carer) are thereby at risk of significant harm. There was, however, disagreement as to whether that consignment was relevant at all to the question of future risk of harm. The majority view was that it could be relevant, at any rate, when coupled with other facts or circumstances. In Lord Hope's words, it 'may have a bearing on the weight of evidence when looked at as a whole, including an assessment of the balance of probabilities.'[186] The minority view[187] was that it was simply irrelevant. Whether this disagreement will lead to yet further litigation at the highest level remains to be seen but the concern of Lord Wilson[188] is that the majority view, might lead to the minority view in *Re H* gaining ascendancy by the back door. Lord Wilson emphasised that it remained his view 'that the need for the local authority to prove the facts which give rise to a real possibility of significant harm in the future is the bulwark against too ready an interference with family life on the part of the state.'[189]

(c) Commentary

The basic dilemma

The threshold stage is crucial in determining whether or not State intervention into family life is justified. The critical question is to how rigorous the threshold test should be. On the one hand protecting children thought to be at risk of harm argues for a less rigorous test. While on the other, protecting the family against undue State intervention argues for a more rigorous approach. Although some members of the judiciary have favoured a flexible approach,[190] the corpus of case-law has favoured a more rigorous interpretation of the threshold. This is clearly demonstrated by the majority view in *Re H* which has been fully endorsed by the House of Lords in *Re B* and the Supreme Court in *Re S-B* and *Re J*.

---

[185] Reflecting the concerns of the Court of Appeal, particularly those of Lord Judge LCJ (see [2012] 2 FLR 842, at [139], Baroness Hale (at [5]) was critical of the artificiality of restricting the issue, but Lord Wilson (at [69]) and Lord Hope (at [82]) thought it right and helpful to confine the issue so that it could be determined once and for all.

[186] [2013] UKSC 9 [2013] 2 WLR 69 at [87]. See also Baroness Hale at [50] and [54] and Lord Reed (with whom Lords Clarke and Carnworth agreed) at [95], [96] and [98].

[187] Ie Lord Wilson at [78]–[80] and Lord Sumption at [92].

[188] [2013] UKSC 9 [2013] 2 WLR 69 at [80].

[189] [2013] UKSC 9 [2013] 1 AC 680 at [75].

[190] See, for example, comments by Sir Stephen Brown P in *Newham London Borough v AG* [1993] 1 FLR 281 at 289, cited at The criteria, p 600. See also the comments by Lord Clyde in *Lancashire* [2000] 2 AC 147, at 170.

One notable and long-standing critic of this rigorous approach, Mary Hayes, has described as 'startling and depressing' the Supreme Court's 'lack of deep reflection on what policies should underpin decisions in complex child protection cases'.[191] She says of *Re J*,[192] in particular, that the Supreme Court concentrated on:

> black-letter, judge-made 'rules' relating to proven facts. The Justices did not investigate the potential outcomes of their inflexible approach to the law. Their judgment virtually ignores the impact these rules will have on unharmed children living with possible perpetrators of significant harm to another child. They give rise to the real possibility that a child's Art 3 right 'not to be subjected to torture or inhuman or degrading treatment or punishment' may be in jeopardy.

Lastly, she points to what she maintains is the inconsistency of the approach of the Senior Courts, pointing in particular to the more purposive approach of Lord Nicholls in *Re O and another (Minors) (Care: Preliminary Hearing); Re B (A Minor)*,[193] as against that adopted in *Re S-B* and *Re J*.

Powerful though these arguments may be, they are not themselves beyond criticism and there are those who support the rigorous standpoint at any rate in relation to uncertain perpetrators.[194] In response to the so-called 'black letter law' criticism, one may point to the fact that many of the leading decisions were made in the context of a single issue being brought before them which (a) is far from typical (as Baroness Hale said in *Re J*[195] '[m]ost cases are not "one-off whodunit" cases. They come with a multitude of facts'), and (b) raised an important point of principle which should not lightly be glossed over. The apparent inconsistency of the Senior Courts is explained, as the Supreme Court said in *Re J*, by the fact that the courts were dealing with different issues. Without gainsaying Hayes' Article 3 point, the need to comply with Article 8 of the European Convention on Human Rights so as to protect both children and parents from undue State interference, also needs to be taken into account.

Whatever one's standpoint on the basic dilemma, it seems imperative that the governing law should be as clear and comprehensible as possible such that judges at all levels can apply it. In this regard, while the law has been clarified in some important respects, in particular as to the requisite standard of proof to be applied, it is undoubtedly complicated and at times hard to follow.[196]

The way forward—should s 31 be reformed?

The price of having a rigorously applied threshold test is to leave some children potentially at risk of harm. This problem arises particularly in cases where not all possible perpetrators of harm to one child are involved in the future care of any unharmed children. The classic example put to the court in *Re F (Interim Care Order)*[197] is where two parents are consigned to a pool of possible perpetrators of non-accidental injuries

---

[191] 'The Supreme Court's failure to protect vulnerable children: *Re J (Children)*' [2013] Fam Law 1015, at 1029. It should also be said that *Re SB* has been said to have caused consternation among local authorities and among other professionals working in the rea of public law. See the arguments both in *Re F (Interim Care Order)* [2011] EWCA Civ 258 [2011] 2 FLR 856 at [15] and repeated in the *Re J* litigation.

[192] At 1030.   [193] [2003] UKHL 18 [2004] 1 AC 523.

[194] See C Cobley and N Lowe 'The Statutory "Threshold" under Section 31 of the Children Act 1989—Time to Take Stock' (2011) 127 LQR 396.   [195] [2013] UKSC 9 [2013] 1 AC 680 at [5].

[196] See the comments on *Re S-B* by Cobley and Lowe, op cit, at 419.

[197] [2011] EWCA Civ 258 [2011] 2 FLR 856 at [15].

to their child; and who then separate; and who each, with other partners, produce a further child, and together become the subject of conjoined care proceedings. Counsel then asked 'Are both applications for care orders required to be dismissed even though before the court is, on any view, a perpetrator of injuries to that older child?' To which the answer is, on the present law, yes. To many this seems to be an unacceptable gap in our child protection law, but the question remains how, if at all, that gap can be bridged.

An unsuccessful attempt, was made, at the instigation of Mary Hayes and Stephen Gilmore, to add an amendment to what was then the Children and Families Bill designed to reverse *Re S-B* and *Re J* by expressly permitting a court 'to infer that a child is likely to suffer significant harm from the sole fact that the child is, or will be, living with a person who is a possible perpetrator of significant harm to another child'.[198] Another possibility suggested by Hayes[199] is that there should be a lower threshold for supervision orders. But one objection to this is that it could increase the number of interventions by local authorities which in itself can be damaging to family life. Others have suggested[200] that the solution lies in empowering courts to take some action to safeguard children possibly at risk notwithstanding that the threshold cannot be satisfied, the suggestion being to permit courts to make 'watching brief' orders requiring short term periodic review with a view to bringing the case back before the court if the circumstances justify it. But this, too, seems to have fallen on deaf ears.

D. THE WELFARE STAGE

Crossing the threshold is not a reason for making a care order[201] but merely opens the way to the possibility that such an order may be made.[202] This is because, having considered the threshold criteria, it is incumbent upon the court, in deciding what order, if any, to make to apply the general principles under s 1. This is known as the 'welfare stage'.[203]

At the welfare stage the court must, pursuant to s 1(1), regard the welfare of the child as the paramount consideration.[204] It is also *bound*[205] to have regard to the statutory check list contained in s 1(3),[206] and, pursuant to s 1(5), to consider whether it is better for the child to make any order than to make no order at all. Another important consideration, stressed by the Supreme Court in *Re B (A Child) (Care Proceedings: Threshold Criteria)*,[207] in determining what order to make is that of human rights, it being recognised that the level of intervention must be proportionate to the nature and gravity of the harm established or feared. In *Re B* Lord Neuberger said[208] that it is inherent in s 1(1) that a care order should be the last resort, that is, where nothing else will do.

---

[198] See [2014] Fam Law 7.

[199] M. Hayes 'Reconciling Protection of Children with Justice for Parents in Cases of Alleged Child Abuse' [1997] *Legal Studies* 1, 20–21.

[200] Cobley and Lowe, op cit, at 421. See also their suggested re-draft of s 31.

[201] Per Lord Nicholls in *Re O and Another (Minors) (Care: Preliminary Hearing); Re B (A Minor)* [2003] UKHL 18 [2004] 1 AC 523 at [23].

[202] Per Lord Clyde in *Lancashire County Council v B* [2000] 2 AC 147 at 170.

[203] See Butler Sloss LJ in *Re M and R (Child Abuse: Evidence)* [1996] 2 FLR 195, at 202 CA.

[204] Discussed in Ch 10.   [205] See s 1(4)(b).   [206] Discussed in Ch 10.

[207] [2013] UKSC 33 [2013] 1 WLR 1911. See also *Re G (Care Proceedings: Welfare Evaluation)* [2013] EWCA Civ 965 [2014] 1 FLR 670, discussed at Court orders, p 629.

[208] At [77].

In considering which course is in the child's best interests the court will have regard to all the circumstances of the case. It has also been said[209] that it is at the welfare stage that the non-adversarial or inquisitorial nature of the proceedings comes to the fore.

1. HAVING REGARD TO PAST EVENTS

Applying the welfare principle, as Lord Nicholls has observed,[210] involves both looking at the past and also looking into the future. We begin this part of the discussion of the welfare stage by examining issues with regard to past events.

(a) Uncertain perpetrators

The leading case is *Re O and another (Minors) (Care: Preliminary Hearing); Re B (A Minor)*,[211] in which the House of Lords heard appeals in respect of two conflicting decisions of the Court of Appeal. In *Re B* the Court of Appeal held that since it had not been proved that the mother had been responsible for any of the child's injuries, the court should proceed at the welfare stage on the footing that she did *not* pose a risk to the child. In *Re O*, however, where again it could not be proved whether the mother or her partner had caused the injuries (from which the child died), it was held that the mother should *not* be disregarded as a risk to the elder sibling in the future. The House of Lords ruled that in these 'uncertain perpetrator' cases the court should proceed at the welfare stage 'on the footing that each of the possible perpetrators is indeed, just that: a possible perpetrator'.[212] As Lord Nicholls said,[213] it would be grotesque that because neither parent considered individually has been proved to be the perpetrator the court should proceed at the welfare stage on the footing that neither represents a risk. Accordingly, the correct approach is to 'have regard', to whatever extent is appropriate', to the facts found by the judge at the preliminary hearing'.[214]

Although it is difficult to see what other solution the House of Lords could have reached, it does put a premium on the precise findings at the preliminary stage.[215] Moreover the effect of the decision, namely, as the mothers would see it in *Re O* etc, that their children would be removed from them on the basis of suspicions,[216] stands in contrast to the raison d'être of Lord Nicholls' approach in *Re H*.[217] However, the crucial difference is that harm to the children concerned had been proved in *Re O* whereas it had not in *Re H*. In any event, the subsequent ruling in *North Yorkshire County Council v SA*[218] that possible perpetrators can be excluded from the pool if there is no real possibility that they are involved, does at least reduce the potential number of possible perpetrators in any particular case.

---

[209] Per Charles J in *Re R (Care: Disclosure: Nature of Proceedings)* [2002] 1 FLR 755 at 772.

[210] *Re O* [2003] UKHL 18 [2004] 1 AC 523 at [23].

[211] [2003] UKHL 18 [2004] 1 AC 523, on which see M Hayes '*Re O and R; Re B*—Uncertain Evidence and Risk Taking in Child Protection Cases' [2004] CFLQ 63.

[212] [2003] UKHL 18 [2004] 1 AC 523 at [28].   [213] Ibid at [26].   [214] Ibid at [31].

[215] As Lord Nicholls said (see [35]) the views and indications of the judge at the preliminary hearing can be of great assistance at the welfare stage and for these reasons judges should be astute to express such views as they can at the earlier hearing.

[216] See A Bainham 'Children Law at the Millennium' in S Cretney (ed) *Essays for the new Millennium* (2000) 113 at 124 that suspicions should be relevant to the making of supervision but not care orders. But this suggestion would surely be too restrictive to protect children adequately.

[217] *Re H (Minors) (Sexual Abuse: Standard of Proof)* [1996] AC 563, discussed at The two-stage test, p 608.

[218] [2003] EWCA Civ 839 [2003] 2 FLR 849, discussed at Identifying possible perpetrators, p 619.

(b) Unproved allegations of harm

In *Re O* Lord Nicholls made some obiter observations[219] about 'the type of case where the threshold criteria are satisfied on one ground, such as neglect or failure to protect, but not on another ground, such as physical harm'. In such a case the question arises as to what extent the court can, at the welfare stage, 'take into account the possibility that the non-proven allegation might, after all, be true'. Since having regard at the welfare stage to allegations of harm rejected at the threshold stage would effectively deprive both the child and family of the protection intended to be afforded by the threshold conditions, Lord Nicholls concluded that at the welfare stage 'the court should proceed on the footing that the unproven allegations are no more than that'.[220]

This conclusion was said to be in accord with *Re M and R (Child Abuse: Evidence)*,[221] in which the threshold criteria were met on the basis of emotional harm but allegations of sexual abuse were not found proved. The Court of Appeal rejected the argument based on the paramountcy test, that at the welfare stage the court could when assessing the risk of harm under s 1(3)(e) act on possibilities rather than proof on the preponderance of probabilities. As Butler-Sloss LJ said, '[i]t would be extraordinary if Parliament intended that evidence which is insufficient to establish that a child is likely to suffer significant harm for the purposes of s 31 should nevertheless be treated as sufficient to establish that a child is at risk of suffering harm for the purposes for s 1.' The trial judge's decision to ignore the allegations of sexual abuse at the welfare stage was thus upheld.

2. HAVING REGARD TO THE FUTURE—CARE PLANS

In deciding what order, if any, it should make at the welfare stage, regard must be had to s 1(5) which, as we discussed in Chapter 10, requires the court to consider whether it is better for the child to make any order than to make no order at all. To answer this question in the context of care proceedings the court will have to consider the plans which the authority is proposing for the child should a care order be made. These plans are known as 'care plans'.[222]

The requirement to submit a care plan was first put on a statutory footing by amendments to the 1989 Act introduced by the Adoption and Children Act 2002,[223] though in fact it had long been the established practice.

Section 31A requires the appropriate local authority[224] in an application where a care order might be made[225] to prepare a care plan within a timescale set by the court. Furthermore, while such an application is pending the authority must keep the plan under review and 'if they are of the opinion some change is required, revise the plan, or make a new plan, accordingly'.[226]

Following the recommendations made by the *Family Justice Review*,[227] s 31(3A) has been rewritten by s 15 of the Children and Families Act 2014 so as to *require* a court, when deciding whether or not to make a care order, to consider the permanence provisions

---

[219] [2003] UKHL 18, [2004] 1 AC 523 at [37].

[220] A similar position obtains where unproved allegations are abandoned, see *Re R (Care: Disclosure: Nature of Proceedings)* [2002] 1 FLR 755, approved by Lord Nicholls at [41].   [221] [1996] 2 FLR 195.

[222] For care planning generally see HM Government *Guidance and Regulations* Vol 2 *Care Planning, Placement and Case Review* (2010) ch 2.

[223] Section 121, which inserted s 31(3A) and 31A into the 1989 Act.

[224] Where more than one authority is involved, the care plan needs to be prepared in co-operation between them: *L v London Borough of Bexley* [1996] 2 FLR 595.

[225] But not an interim care order: s 31A(5).   [226] Section 31A(2).

[227] November 2011, paras 3.12–3.44, and the 'Final Recommendation' set out on p 101.

(ie those that set out the long-term plan for the child's upbringing)[228] of the s 31A plan but not those parts dealing with contact arrangements. The purpose of this amendment is to encourage courts to focus on the core or essential components the plan. However, as Explanatory Notes point out,[229] courts can still choose to look at these other plans.

When scrutinising care plans the court should consider whether they are the best available plans for the child and, if so, why an order is necessary to implement them. Although there are limits to this scrutiny process—it does not mean, for example, that there should be an over-zealous investigation into matters that are properly within administrative discretion[230]—nevertheless, even where a care order is the inevitable eventual outcome, the court should not be deflected from using the litigation process to maximum effect such that all parties are properly listened to.[231]

If the court is not satisfied that the plan is in the child's interests it can suggest[232] changes and, if these are not accepted, it can refuse to make an order.[233] However, as we discuss later in this chapter, what the court cannot do is to keep the local authority plans under review inter alia by making a conditional care order although there is a mechanism (also discussed later in this chapter) in appropriate cases for getting the plan back before the court.

E. TACKLING DELAY IN CARE PROCEEDINGS

When the Children Act 1989 was first implemented it was expected that public law cases would be disposed of within 12 weeks. This expectation proved wildly optimistic and by 2003 the average care case lasted for almost a year.[234]

As the *Family Justice Review*[235] observed, delay really matters: long proceedings may deny children a chance of a permanent home; they can damage a child's development; they may put maltreated and neglected children at risk if they remain at home during the proceedings and they can cause already damaged children distress and harm.

Over the years there have been a number of initiatives to tackle what has often been described as an endemic problem of delay. In 2003 a *Protocol for Judicial Case Management in Public Law Children Act Cases*[236] was devised. Its overall object was 'to improve the completion of all cases within an overall timetable of not more than 40 weeks, save in exceptional and unforeseen circumstances.'[237] To that end the Protocol provided detailed guidance on the management of applications at all the vital stages (viz. the issue of the application; the first hearing in the Family Proceedings Court; the Allocation hearing

---

[228] Specifically, whether the plan is for the child to live with a parent or any member or friend of the child's family, or whether the child is to be adopted or placed in other long term care: s 31(3B).

[229] At para 147.

[230] See Wall J in *Re J*, earlier, at 262. This was also a concern expressed by the *Family Justice Review*.

[231] Per Thorpe LJ in *Re CH (Care or Interim Care Order)* [1998] 1 FLR 402, CA—the judge was wrong to refuse to hear evidence at the behest of the guardian, having reached a consensus which was acceptable to all the parties save for the guardian. Note also *Re H (Care: Change in Care Plan)* [1998] 1 FLR 193, CA—a parent was entitled to have an order based on a flawed care plan reconsidered, even if that order remained in force.

[232] But it cannot force changes. Note also that, while the court can make non-binding observations upon what it had in mind about the order, even these can cause difficulties: see *L v London Borough of Bromley* [1998] 1 FLR 709.

[233] Though in Nourse LJ's view, at any rate, such circumstances where a refusal will be justified will be rare: *Re T (A Minor) (Care Order: Conditions)* [1994] 2 FLR 423 at 429.

[234] See the Foreword to the 2003 Protocol, referred to shortly.   [235] Final Report (2011), para 3.5.

[236] [2003] 2 FLR 719. The Protocol came into force on 1 November 2003.

[237] *Court Business* Family Special Edition, October 2003.

and directions; the case management conference; the pre-hearing review and the final hearing) and provided a target timetable for each stage.

The *Protocol* was only partially successful and was replaced in 2008 by the *Public Law Outline* ('PLO'),[238] the basic aim of which was to streamline the *Protocol*, placing greater emphasis on pre-proceedings preparation such that applications would only be made to court where the circumstances justify and that they would reach the court properly prepared. Each key stage had a time target and the overall disposal target was 26 weeks.

Despite these initiatives and in part due to the increasing volume of cases,[239] care and supervision proceedings continued to lengthen. Between January and June 2011 they took an average of 61 weeks in care centres and 48 weeks before magistrates.[240] In its response to the *Family Justice Review*[241] the Government promised that it would introduce a *statutory* time limit of 26 weeks and would act on recommendations to make the system resolutely more focused on reducing the 'current unacceptable delays'. Consistent with this promise the Children and Families Act 2014, s 14 amended s 32 of the 1989 Act to make express provision for an overall disposal of care or supervision applications within 26 weeks from being issued, subject to tightly drawn exceptions. Section 14 also requires the court to have particular regard when drawing up a timetable for a case and to any subsequent revision of it, to the impact of the timetable on the child's welfare. Meanwhile the *Protocol* has been further revised and refined.[242] Whether these initiatives prove any more successful than their predecessors remains to be seen but there are early signs that disposals are getting quicker—in July to September 2013 the average time had dropped to 35.8 weeks.[243]

F. COURT ORDERS

1. INTRODUCTION

At the welfare stage of care proceedings the court must, pursuant to s 1(1) regard the welfare of the child as the paramount consideration; have regard to the statutory checklist contained in s 1(3) and in particular to s 1(3)(g) which directs the court to consider all its options before deciding which order to make; and pursuant to s 1(5) only make orders where that is considered better for the child than making no order. The import of s 1(3)(g) is that since Part IV proceedings rank as 'family proceedings' for the purposes of s 8,[244] the court must, even if the threshold criteria are satisfied, consider whether it should make a s 8 order. This power to make a s 8 order can be exercised whether or not an application has been made for it.[245] Further, as s 31(5) makes clear, supervision orders can be made upon applications for care orders and care orders upon applications

---

[238] See MoJ *Public Law Outline—Guide to Case Management of Public Law Proceedings* (2008). For the background to the PLO see DCA/DfE *Review of the Child Care Proceedings System in England and Wales* (2006) and J Masson 'Reforming care proceedings—Time for Review' [2007] CFLQ 421.

[239] According to statistics quoted by the *Family Justice Review* (Final Report, 2011, at para 3.2, n 38) there was a 3% increase in the number of children involved in public law applications in the 12 months ending 30 June 2011 over the previous year.

[240] See the statistics quoted by the *Family Justice Review* (Final Report, 2011) at para 3.2.

[241] See *The Government Response to the Family Justice Review: A system with children at its heart* (Cm 8273, 2012), paras 52–55.

[242] 'PLO 2014', having been piloted in 2013, came into effect at the end of April 2014.

[243] See *Court Statistics Quarterly July to September 2013*, referred to in [2014] Fam Law at 239.

[244] Section 8(3), (4).

[245] Viz. pursuant to its powers under s 10(1)(b), discussed in Ch 14, Upon application or upon the court's own motion, p 537.

for supervision orders. It is also clear that care or supervision orders can be made even though the local authority no longer wish to pursue that option.[246] However, as Hale J observed in *Oxfordshire County Council v L (Care or Supervision Order)*,[247] 'there must in general be urgent and strong reasons to force upon the local authority a more draconian order than that for which they have asked'. Furthermore, if the court is minded to make an order which has not been sought, it must give the parties an opportunity to address the court on the desirability of making that order.[248]

In summary, at the welfare stage the court, guided by the welfare principle, but not necessarily constrained by what the parties have themselves sought, has, if the threshold criteria have been satisfied, a wide range of powers to make no order at all, a s 8 order (with or without a supervision order), a supervision order, or a care order. Where the threshold criteria have not been satisfied, the court still retains its powers to make s 8 orders and is not bound to return the child to his or her parents.

Even where the threshold criteria have been satisfied, as Hale J has pointed out,[249] the court should not overlook the local authorities' preventive duties to children in need under Part III of the Act[250] and 'should begin with a preference for the less intervention-ist rather than the more interventionist approach'.[251] This latter point is now further underscored by human rights considerations, it being well established[252] that whatever action is to be taken must be a proportionate response to the nature and gravity of the feared harm. However, as the McFarlane LJ said in *Re G (Care Proceedings: Welfare Evaluation)*:[253]

> The judicial exercise should not be a linear process whereby each option, other than the most draconian, is looked at in isolation and then rejected because of internal deficits that may be identified, with the result that, at the end of the line, the only option left standing is the most draconian and that is therefore chosen without any particular consideration of whether there are internal deficits within that option... What is required is a balancing exercise in which each option is evaluated to the degree of detail necessary to analyse and weigh its own internal positives and negatives and each option is then compared, side by side against the competing option or options.

A key consideration in determining what, if any, order should be made is how much public control (as exercised by the local authority) is thought to be needed to protect the child in question. Where most control is needed, a care order will be appropriate. Where least control is required, then a s 8 order might be sufficient. Supervision orders come somewhere between those two options and may be appropriate where there is a concern about the parental care but not sufficient to warrant the removal of the child and the mak-ing of a full care order.[254]

---

[246] See eg *Re M (A Minor) (Care Order: Threshold Conditions)* [1994] 2 AC 424, HL, discussed at Is suf-fering, p 630, in which a care order was made notwithstanding that the local authority wanted to withdraw their application; and *Re K (Care Order or Residence Order)* [1995] 1 FLR 675, discussed at The effects of a care order, p 636, where a care order was made contrary to the authority's wishes.

[247] [1998] 1 FLR 70 at 73. See also *Re T (Care Order)* [2009] EWCA Civ 121 [2009] 2 FLR 574, discussed at Supervision orders, p 632.   [248] *Croydon London Borough Council v A* [1992] Fam 169.

[249] See *Re O (Care or Supervision Order)* [1996] 2 FLR 755 at 759 and *Oxfordshire County Council v L (Care or Supervision Order)* [1998] 1 FLR 70 at 74.   [250] Discussed in Ch 15.   [251] In *Re O* at 760.

[252] See *Re B (A Child) (Care Proceedings: Threshold Criteria)* [2013] UKSC 33 [2013] 1 WLR 1911

[253] [2013] EWCA Civ 965 [2014] 1 FLR 670 at [49] and [54].

[254] On rare occasions it might be appropriate to grant care and control to individuals under a ward-ship regime with legal control vested in the court, see eg *Re RJ (Wardship)* [1999] 1 FLR 618 or to make a combination of s 8 orders and a supervision order under the overall umbrella of wardship, see *Re M and J*

If the court is not in a position to make a final order it can make interim orders, that is, an interim care or supervision order, or a limited duration s 8 order. The philosophy of the Act is that those in whom parental responsibility is vested should be able so far as possible to exercise that responsibility without interference by the court. However, at the interim stage the court retains significantly more control over the child than when it makes a final order. This is equally true whether responsibility vests in individuals or in the local authority.

It remains to consider these options in more detail.

2. SECTION 8 ORDERS

(a) Where the threshold criteria are satisfied

Given the preference for the least interventionist approach, in those cases where the threshold criteria have been satisfied and some order is thought necessary, some consideration should be given to the appropriateness of a s 8 order.

One example may be where it is felt that, though parental care had been inadequate in the past, given sufficient support in the future a parent could cope. A court could for instance name that parent as a person with whom the child is to live in a child arrangements order coupled with a condition that she live at a mother and baby unit for some specified time.[255] In this type of case, although it is outside the court's power to make a specific issue order forcing the local authority to provide a particular service,[256] it is a legitimate expectation that a service will be provided, since notwithstanding the child arrangements order the child may still qualify for services as a child in need.[257]

Another example where a care order might not be thought appropriate is where abuse has been proved but the perpetrator has since left, or is prepared to leave the home.[258] In such a case the remaining parent may be named as a person with whom the child is to live in a child arrangements order coupled, perhaps, with a prohibited steps order forbidding the perpetrator from having contact with the child.[259]

A further example is where a parent has been proved inadequate, for example through alcohol or drug dependence, but there is a relative who is already looking after or who could look after the child. In these circumstances a child arrangements order naming the

---

(Wardship, Supervision and Residence Orders) [2003] EWHC 1585 (Fam) [2003] 2 FLR 541 and Re W and X (Wardship: Relatives Rejected As Foster Carers) [2003] EWHC 2206 (Fam) [2004] 1 FLR 415, discussed further in Ch 20.

[255] But note that further conditions, such as having to hand over the child to the care of staff if so requested, cannot be added, as that would be inconsistent with a child arrangements order relating to the child's living arrangements: see Birmingham City Council v H [1992] 2 FLR 323, cf C v Solihull Metropolitan Borough Council [1993] 1 FLR 290 in which Ward J made what was then a residence order conditional upon the parents undertaking a programme of assessment and co-operating with all reasonable requests by the local authority to participate in that programme.

[256] See Re J (Specific Issue Order: Leave to Apply) [1995] 1 FLR 669.

[257] Accordingly the local authority will be obliged to continue so to treat the child pursuant to the duties under s 17(1) and (10): see Ch 15.

[258] For the powers to include an 'exclusion requirement' in interim care and emergency protection orders see Attaching an exclusion order to an interim care order, p 648 and Ch 16 The power to add an exclusion requirement, p 587. For the powers to make longer term exclusion orders under the Family Law Act 1996 Part IV see Ch 6. Note also that under Sch 2 para 5 to the Children Act 1989, the local authority may give assistance, including cash, to enable that other person to obtain alternative accommodation.

[259] But it seems that what cannot be done is to make it a condition of the child arrangements order that the parent does not invite the other parent, or named person, back into the home: see Re D (Residence: Imposition of Conditions) [1996] 2 FLR 281, CA, discussed in Ch 14, No power to order a parent's removal from the family home, p 502.

relative as a person with whom the child is to live, might be thought preferable to a care order.[260]

Provided the threshold criteria have been satisfied, it is open to the court to make both a s 8 and a supervision order.[261] The advantage of coupling a s 8 order with a supervision order is that the child's upbringing can be closely supervised, and it may be that where it is thought right to make conditional child arrangements orders it will generally also be appropriate to make a supervision order.[262]

It is to be emphasised that the court cannot make both a s 8 order and a care order. The two are inconsistent.[263]

(b) Where the threshold criteria cannot be satisfied

If the threshold criteria under s 31 cannot be satisfied then, although the court cannot make a care or supervision order, it can still make a s 8 order.[264] One example might be where a child accommodated by a local authority has been happily fostered for some time, and the parent wishes to resume care.[265]

3. SUPERVISION ORDERS

Supervision orders can only be made provided the threshold criteria under s 31(2) have been satisfied. However, pursuant to s 31(5)(a), which allows the court to make a supervision order in care proceedings, they are frequently made where the application is for a care order.[266] As the Court of Appeal stressed in *Re T (Care Order)*,[267] the court is not bound by the parties' agreement upon the type of order that should be made but instead has a duty to consider for itself what the appropriate order should be. At the same time, as Potter P said,[268] 'there must in general be cogent and strong reasons to force upon a local authority a more draconian order than that for which it has asked. All the more is that the case when the children's guardian supports the making of a less draconian order as appropriate to the child's needs.'

(a) The nature and purpose of supervision orders

Supervision orders[269] are designed for cases where an element of child protection is involved.[270] On the other hand, they do not give local authorities the same degree of control over parents as do care orders, from which they are thus clearly distinguishable.[271]

---

[260] See eg *Re H (A Minor) (Care or Residence Order)* [1994] 2 FLR 80, but cf *Re M (A Minor) (Care Order: Threshold Conditions)* [1994] 2 AC 424, HL (discussed at Is suffering, p 630), in which a care order was made notwithstanding that the child was happily living with his mother's cousin, and *Re K (Care Order or Residence Order)* [1995] 1 FLR 675 (discussed at The effects of a care order, p 636), in which the grandparents did not want the responsibility of what was then a residence order. Furthermore, it seems unlikely that a court would wish to make an order in favour of the relative without first seeing that person.

[261] For an example, see *Re S (Parenting Skills: Personality Tests)* [2004] EWCA Civ 1029 [2005] 2 FLR 658.

[262] Compare the position on making an interim order under s 38(3) discussed at Alternative orders under s 8, p 649.   [263] Sections 9 and 91.

[264] It can also make a family assistance order under s 16, discussed in Ch 14.

[265] Cf *Re P (A Minor) (Residence Order: Child's Welfare)* [2000] Fam 15, CA in which in private law proceedings what was then a residence order was made in favour of the applicant foster parents.

[266] Section 31(5)(a).   [267] [2009] EWCA Civ 121 [2009] 2 FLR 574.

[268] At [64]. In *Re T* the local authority supported the guardian and the parents and decided not to pursue its application for a care order seeking instead the child's phased return to the parents under a supervision order. The Court of Appeal reversed the trial judge's decision to make a care order.

[269] See generally DCSF *Guidance and Regulations*, Vol 1, *Court Orders* (2008), paras 3.80–3.84.

[270] Per Wall J in *Re DH (A Minor) (Child Abuse)* [1994] 1 FLR 679 at 702.

[271] See further Supervision and care orders compared, p 634.

A supervision order puts the child under the supervision of a designated local authority or a probation officer.[272] It does *not* vest parental responsibility in the local authority, nor does it fix them with the duty under s 22 to safeguard or promote the child's welfare.[273] The court cannot make both a care order and a supervision order, though it may make both a s 8 order and a supervision order.[274]

The person, under whose supervision the child is or is to be, is known as the supervisor,[275] and for the duration of the order it is his or her duty:

(a) to advise, assist and befriend the supervised child;[276]
(b) to take such steps as are reasonably necessary to give effect to the order; and
(c) where—
(i) the order is not wholly complied with; or
(ii) the supervisor considers that the order may no longer be necessary,
to consider whether or not to apply to the court for its variation or discharge.[277]

These basic duties are substantially expanded by Sch 3 to the 1989 Act, which also empowers the court to make orders inter alia for the child's psychiatric or medical examination.

(b) Duration of a supervision order

A supervision order is a short-term order and initially lasts for one year,[278] though it can be made for a shorter period.[279] It can, however, be extended upon an application by the supervisor for up to a maximum of three years from the date when the order was made.[280] Although acknowledging that these provisions lacked 'comprehensive clarity', the Court of Appeal held in *Wakefield Metropolitan District Council v T*[281] that a court cannot make an initial order for more than one year. Nevertheless it pointed to the illogicality of only permitting an initial one year order yet allowing extensions for up to two years. The Court doubted the need for making any application to extend a one year order before the last quarter of its life but at the same time stressed that neither should an application be delayed so as to imperil the local authority's imperative need for a determination before the expiry of the initial order so as to avoid the requirement to re-establish the threshold criteria.

An application to extend the period of a supervision order is governed by the welfare principle, so that further proof of the threshold criteria is not required.[282]

(c) Requirements imposed under a supervision order

The essence of a supervision order is to subject the supervised child (regardless of whether the child consents) to certain directions by the supervisor. Schedule 3 para 2 provides that an order may require the supervised child to comply with any directions

---

[272] Section 31(1)(b). See also Sch 3 para 9 with regard to the selection of a supervisor.
[273] Section 22 is discussed in Ch 18.
[274] See eg *Re B (Care: Expert Witness)* [1996] 1 FLR 667, CA and *Re DH (A Minor) (Child Abuse)* [1994] 1 FLR 679.
[275] Section 105(1).   [276] Note that there is no duty owed to the parent.
[277] Section 35(1).   [278] Sch 3 para 6(1).
[279] *M v Warwickshire County Council* [1994] 2 FLR 593.   [280] Sch 3 para 6(3), (4).
[281] [2008] EWCA Civ 199 [2008] 1 FLR 1569.
[282] *Re A (Supervision Order: Extension)* [1995] 1 FLR 335, CA.

given from time to time by the supervisor which require him to do all or any of the following:

> (a) live at a place or places specified in the directions for a specified period or periods;
> (b) present himself to a specified person at a place and on a day specified;
> (c) participate in specified activities, such as education or training.

The precise directions are a matter for the supervisor and not the court,[283] though in no event is the supervisor empowered to give directions as to the child's medical or psychiatric treatment.[284] Although the supervisor is not empowered to give directions as to the child's medical or psychiatric examination or treatment, they can be made the subject of specific direction by the court.[285] In each case, however, the power is, in the case of a child of sufficient understanding to make an informed decision, subject to that child's consent.[286]

As well as empowering supervisors to make directions, a supervision order may also include a requirement that, with his or her consent, a 'responsible person'[287] take all reasonable steps to ensure that the child complies with any direction given by the supervisor.[288]

The fact that the responsible person must consent to the requirement being imposed is crucial to the operation of a supervision order, since there are no direct means of enforcing any of the directions or requirements,[289] and it has been held that the court has no power either to make such agreement a condition of the order[290] or to accept an undertaking to agree.[291]

(d) Supervision and care orders compared

Notwithstanding that before either order may be made the threshold conditions under s 31 have to be satisfied, care orders and supervision orders are fundamentally different in that the former but not the latter (a) vests parental responsibility in the local authority and (b) places the local authority under an obligation, pursuant to s 22, to look after and to safeguard and promote the child's welfare. As Judge Coningsby QC put it in *Re S (J) (A Minor) (Care or Supervision Order):*[292]

> We tend to look at supervision orders and care orders under the same umbrella because the threshold criteria for the coming into operation of the two is the same. But when we actually look at the content of the two orders we find they are wholly and utterly different.

---

[283] Sch 3 para 2(2).   [284] Sch 3 paras 2(3) and 5.

[285] See Sch 3 paras 4 and 5. In the case of examinations the court can either require the supervised child to submit to a medical or psychiatric examination or to submit to any such examination from time to time as directed by the supervisor: Sch 3 para 4(1).

[286] Sch 3 para 4(4)(a) and para 5(5)(a). This wording is stronger than the equivalent provisions in s 38(6) (interim orders), s 43(8) (child assessment orders) and s 44(7) (emergency protection orders), so that even if the decision in *South Glamorgan County Council v W and B* [1993] 1 FLR 574 (discussed at Making directions on interim applications, p 645) that the High Court has inherent jurisdiction to override a child's refusal is thought right, it may nevertheless be thought inapplicable here, given the nature of the provision.

[287] Any person who has parental responsibility for the child and any other person with whom the child is living: Sch 3 para 1.   [288] Sch 3 para 3.

[289] The only sanction is for the supervisor to return to court and ultimately for the local authority to make a fresh application for a care order. See *Re V (Care or Supervision Order)* [1996] 1 FLR 776 at 785 per Waite LJ.

[290] *Re V* [1996] 1 FLR 776.

[291] *Re B (Supervision Order: Parental Undertaking)* [1996] 1 FLR 676, CA.

[292] [1993] 2 FLR 919 at 950 and cited with approval by Dillon LJ in *Re V* at 788.

This is because of s 22 and because of the passing of parental responsibility. *Supervision should not in any sense be seen as a sort of watered down version of care. It is wholly different.* (Emphasis added)

The effect of these differences is, as Bracewell J observed in *Re T (A Minor) (Care or Supervision Order)*,[293] that whereas the nature of a supervision order is to help and assist a child whilst leaving full responsibility with the parents, a care order places a positive duty on the local authority to promote the child's welfare and to protect him or her from inadequate parenting. Moreover, as Hale J pointed out in *Re O (Care or Supervision Order)*,[294] whereas under a care order, contact apart, the court cedes all control over what is to happen to the children to the local authority, under a supervision order the local authority has to return to the court either for an extension, or for a care order if things do not go well. In this limited sense the court retains a greater control under a supervision order than under a care order.

In summary the two orders are different and the temptation to regard supervision simply as a less invasive form of care order should be resisted.[295] Nevertheless human rights considerations need to be borne in mind and as Potter P said in *Re T (Care Order)*[296] 'the necessity to consider proportionality means that in any case where there is a fine balance to be struck as to which order is appropriate, the reasoning behind the order made should be clearly spelt out'. The courts are likely to be acutely aware of the need for proportionality following the Supreme Court decision in *Re B (A Child) (Care Proceedings: Threshold Criteria)*.[297]

(e) Supervision or 'no order'

Although more attention has been paid to comparing supervision orders with care orders, as Wall J said in *Re K (Supervision Orders)*,[298] it is also important to consider the choice between making a supervision order and no order at all. Indeed it is incumbent upon the court, pursuant to s 1(5), to be satisfied that it is in the child's interests to make any order rather than none at all. In this regard the decisive issue is whether the children need more protection than can be given without a court order. It would be an inappropriate, for example, to make a supervision order simply to persuade a reluctant local authority to fulfil its duties to the child concerned under Part III. In *Re K* itself a supervision order was held appropriate since that was the best means of promoting co-operation between the mother and the local authority would allocate greater resources to monitoring the family.

(f) The use of supervision orders

Supervision orders are made less frequently than care orders. In 2011, for example, 5,119 supervision orders were made as against 11,411 care orders.[299] As one commentary has observed[300] applications are rarely made for supervision orders, but may be made by the courts as an alternative to what may be seen as a draconian care order. Indeed as Hale J pointed out in *Re O (Care or Supervision Order)*,[301] courts can properly begin with a preference for the less rather than the more interventionist approach. This, as has just

---

[293] [1994] 1 FLR 103 at 106–7, CA.
[294] [1996] 2 FLR 755 at 760.   [295] See *Re V.*
[296] [2009] EWCA Civ 121 [2009] 2 FLR 574 at [33].
[297] [2013] UKSC 33 [2013] 1 WLR 1911, discussed in this respect at Court orders, p 630.
[298] [1999] 2 FLR 303 at 317-318.   [299] *Civil Judicial Statistics 2011*, Table 2.4.
[300] R White, P Carr and N Lowe *Children Act in Practice* (2008, 4th edn) 8.190.
[301] [1996] 2 FLR 755 at 759–60.

been discussed, is further underscored by human rights considerations, namely, that any intervention into family life must be proportionate to the risks to the children. In *Re O (Supervision Order)*,[302] for example, it was evident that the local authority's care plan contemplated a high level of service delivery but without great interference in the family's life nor was there a high risk of matters deteriorating (the mother had mental health problems). In these circumstances it was 'absolutely right' to make a supervision order.

Typically, a supervision order is a realistic option where the plan is for the child to remain at home with the parents and those parents are likely to co-operate with the local authority if the order was made. Supervision orders are not, however, appropriate if there is evidence of immediate harm and it is sought to remove the child from the family, nor should they be used to control an otherwise obdurate or inadequate parent.[303]

The general need for parents to be co-operative does not mean that a supervision order is without legal effect. Indeed, one judge[304] has described it as part of a strong package, given that it provides for instant access into the home by a social worker. The ability to direct a treatment programme for the child combined with a finding that the threshold criteria are satisfied has been described as a 'powerful tool',[305] and there seems no doubt that, where parents are prepared to co-operate, a supervision order has a useful role to play. In *Re B (Care or Supervision Order)*[306] Holman J held that a supervision rather than a care order was more appropriate in a case where the pressing needs of the children were for them to be closely monitored within their home and to undertake work with professionals away from home to teach them how to protect themselves. A supervision rather than a care order was also made in *Oxfordshire County Council v L (Care or Supervision Order)*,[307] where, although there were concerns about the standards of parenting, the parents themselves had responded well to help in the past and there was no evidence to suggest that they would not continue to be responsive in the future.

4. CARE ORDERS

(a) The effects of a care order

A care order places the child in the care of the designated local authority.[308] The making of a care order discharges any s 8 order,[309] supervision order, and a school attendance order. It also brings wardship to an end.[310]

As far as the designated authority is concerned, care orders have the twofold effect of:

(i) requiring them 'to receive the child into their care and to keep him in their care while the order remains in force';[311] and

(ii) vesting parental responsibility in the authority.[312]

Whilst in their care local authorities are charged with the duty of safeguarding and promoting the child's welfare.[313]

---

[302] [2001] EWCA Civ 16 [2001] 1 FLR 923.

[303] See eg *Re T (A Minor) (Care or Supervision Order)*, earlier, *and Re S(J) (A Minor) (Care or Supervision Order)*, earlier.   [304] Judge Coningsby in *Re S (J) (A Minor) (Care or Supervision)*, above, at 947.

[305] See White, Carr and Lowe, op cit, at 8.190.   [306] [1996] 2 FLR 693.

[307] [1998] 1 FLR 70.   [308] Section 31(1)(a).

[309] It also discharges any *applications* for a s 8 order, which application should therefore be considered before a care order is made: *Hounslow London Borough Council v A* [1993] 1 WLR 291.

[310] Section 91(2)–(5).   [311] Section 33(1).   [312] Section 33(3)(a).

[313] Under s 22, discussed in Ch 18.

Placing the child 'in the care' of the designated authority

Although it might be supposed that the effect of a care order is to remove the child from his family home and to place him in institutional or foster care, in fact the phrase 'placing the child in the care of' the authority is properly understood as placing the child under the *control* of the authority. Accordingly, it is consistent with a care order to plan for the child to remain at home with his or her parents.[314] However, where this is the plan, the court should consider why a care order is preferable to the less draconian alternatives of a supervision order or even a child arrangements order. As Hale J said in *Oxfordshire County Council v L (Care or Supervision Order)*,[315] there are three broad reasons why a care order might be preferred to a supervision order where the child is to stay at home. First, it allows the authority to remove the child in cases of emergency and to place him or her elsewhere on a long-term basis—in each case without judicial sanction. But this, in her view, would only be appropriate where the parents' behaviour merits serious criticism. Secondly, it enables the local authority to share responsibility with the parents, which is an appropriate consideration where the parents are or are likely to be unco-operative. Thirdly, it gives the local authority specific duties in relation to the child which may be thought to go beyond the general duties imposed by Part III of the 1989 Act, but this should not be used as an excuse to encourage the local authority to perform statutory duties which they already owe to a child in need.

Care orders might also be appropriate notwithstanding that the child will continue to live with relatives, though again there needs to be good reason for vesting control in the local authority. In *Re K (Care Order or Residence Order)*[316] care proceedings were brought in respect of two children aged five and six following an unexplained injury to the younger child and the accompanying disturbed and bizarre behaviour of the mother (who was subsequently found to be suffering from schizophrenia). Immediately after the incident the children went to live with their grandparents. Subsequently, both children were diagnosed as suffering from a muscle-wasting disease which would confine them to wheelchairs from about the age of 10. There was general agreement that the grandparents had responded magnificently to their grandchildren's needs and there was no question of removing them from their care. Indeed, the local authority, given the level of care by the grandparents, no longer wanted a care order. On the other hand, the grandparents considered that a care order would give them the support that they needed, not least when approaching their old age. It was held that in these unusual circumstances a care order should be made notwithstanding both that the children would continue to live with their grandparents and the local authority's opposition. It was thought right to vest parental responsibility in the authority, and to impose upon them the duty to look after the children, not least when they were older and more difficult to manage. Another consideration was the consequential financial support that would be given by the local authority if a care order was made, namely, a weekly boarding out allowance and a capital allowance to modify the current or any future home of the grandparents to accommodate

---

[314] As at 31 March 2012 there were 3,600 children 'looked after' who were placed with parents, representing 5% of all children looked after: DfE *Children Looked After by Local Authorities* (2012) Table A3. This proportion has declined from 8% in 2008 and 10% in 2004.

[315] [1998] 1 FLR 70—a care order was not made because, notwithstanding the parents' past lapses, they were not unco-operative and seemed to have the capacity to work with and learn from the local authority social worker. See also *Manchester City Council v B* [1996] 1 FLR 324; cf *Re T (A Minor) (Care or Supervision Order)* [1994] 1 FLR 103, CA, in which a care order was made, the parents' previous four children having been removed on the basis of 'massive neglect'. *Re C (Care or Supervision Order)* [1999] 2 FLR 621—care order made notwithstanding that the local authority, supported by the parents, sought a supervision order.

[316] [1995] 1 FLR 675.

the children's growing disabilities. As Stuart-White J said, while it would be wholly inappropriate to make a care order *solely* for the purpose of conferring a financial benefit on the carers, such a factor could nevertheless be properly taken into account and weighed in the balance with other factors.

The acquisition of parental responsibility by the designated authority

Notwithstanding the acquisition of parental responsibility by the local authority, parents do not lose their responsibility upon the making of a care order.[317] However, despite this notion of shared responsibility, control very much rests with the local authority, as is emphasised by s 33(3)(b) which provides that the authority has the power to determine the extent to which a parent, guardian, special guardian or a step-parent who has parental responsibility by virtue of s 4A order or agreement may meet his parental responsibility insofar as it is necessary to do so to safeguard or promote the child's welfare.[318] Nevertheless, those mentioned in s 33(3)(b) who have care of the child are still entitled to do what is reasonable in all the circumstances of the case for the purpose of safeguarding or promoting the child's welfare[319] and still retain any right, duty, power, responsibility or authority in relation to the child and its property under any other enactment.[320] It is also established[321] that notwithstanding a care order there is nothing to prevent unmarried parents from making a parental responsibility agreement since that is a self-contained facility which does not depend upon the exercise of parental responsibility.[322]

Limitations on the exercise of local authority responsibility

The parental responsibility acquired by a local authority has some specific limitations. They are not allowed to cause the child to be brought up in any religious persuasion other than that in which he would have been brought up if no order had been made.[323] This embargo has been interpreted[324] to mean the religious upbringing followed by the parents prior to the care order. Any subsequent change of religion by either of both parents should be taken into account but not necessarily followed since the court's duty in this respect is subject to the overriding duties under ss 17(1) and 22(3) to safeguard and protect the child's welfare.

Local authorities do not have the right to consent, or to refuse to consent, to an adoption order or a proposed foreign adoption order, nor to appoint a guardian.[325] Furthermore,

---

[317] Section 2(6). It will be noted, however, that those who have parental responsibility by virtue of a child arrangements order, will lose it because a care order discharges all s 8 orders.

[318] See eg *Re P (Children Act 1989, ss 22 and 26: Local Authority Compliance)* [2000] 2 FLR 910—in appropriate circumstances s 33(3)(b) permits the local authority to exclude a parent (here an unmarried father without parental responsibility) from information concerning, or participation in, decision making in relation to the child. Note also *Re P (Care Orders: Injunctive Relief)* [2000] 2 FLR 385 in which an injunction requiring the parents to allow their child to attend college without interference and permitting the local authority to monitor the family, was granted ancillary to the care order to support the rights conferred by s 33(3)(b). According to Judge Batterbury in *Re B (A Minor) (Child in Care: Blood Test)* [1992] Fam Law 533, since it is an incident of parental responsibility to take reasonable steps to ascertain who else shares that responsibility, the local authority should pay for what are now scientific tests to determine paternity.

[319] Section 33(5).

[320] Section 33(9). As, for example, the right to consent to the child's marriage. See Ch 2.

[321] *Re X (Parental Responsibility Agreement: Children in Care)* [2000] 1 FLR 517.

[322] This ruling must also apply to parents making a parental responsibility agreement with a step-parent.

[323] Section 33(6)(a).

[324] *Re A and D (Local Authority: Religious Upbringing)* [2010] EWHC 2503 (Fam), [2011] 1 FLR 615.

[325] Section 33(6)(b).

while a care order is in force no person[326] may cause the child to be known by a new surname without the written consent of every person with parental responsibility or by leave of the court.[327] The same consents are required before a child may be removed from the United Kingdom.[328]

(b) Duration of a care order

A care order lasts until the child is 18[329] unless it is brought to an end earlier. An application to discharge the care order may be made by any person with parental responsibility, the child himself, or the designated authority.[330] A person who does not otherwise have parental responsibility can, with court leave, apply for a child arrangements order naming them as a person with whom the child is to live, which, if granted, ends a care order.[331] The making of an adoption also ends any order made under the Children Act 1989.[332] The making of a placement order only suspends the care order.[333]

(c) Controlling the local authority after a care order

The general scheme

The fundamental idea of the 1989 Act is that, once a care order has been made, responsibility for looking after the child is vested in the authority and that therefore the court has no general power to keep the case under review. As Lord Nicholls explained in *Re S (Minors) (Care Order: Implementation of Care Plan; Re W (Minors) (Care Order: Adequacy of Care Plan)*,[334] this was a deliberate departure from the previous position under the wardship jurisdiction of the High Court, where the court retained power to give directions to the local authority. In line with this philosophy, as the Court of Appeal confirmed in *Re T (A Minor) (Care Order: Conditions)*,[335] the court cannot fetter local authority control over a child in care by imposing any conditions on a care order. As Nourse LJ put it,[336] 'it is clear beyond peradventure that the court has no power under s 31 to impose any conditions on a care order'. In so holding, the court rejected the argument[337] that 'if the welfare principle is truly paramount, the court must have the power, when initiating the placement into care, to make an order which reflected the full scope of its perception of the child's welfare'. In the court's view[338] the scheme of the Act is clear: the welfare test applies when considering whether to make a care order, but there are no provisions which allow the court to rely on the welfare principle to superimpose conditions on the care order.

---

[326] This does not include the Secretary of State in the case of removals: *Re L (Care Order: Immigration Powers To Remove)* [2007] EWHC 158 (Fam) [2007] 2 FLR 789.

[327] Section 33(7). Exceptionally (eg where all contact has been lost) an order can be granted without notice: *Re J (A Minor) (Change of Name)* [1993] 1 FLR 699.

[328] Section 33(7) and (8)(a). If the local authority wish to arrange for a child in care to live outside England and Wales then, pursuant to Sch 2 para 19(1), the court's approval is required. Compare the position where the child is being accommodated, when the approval of everyone with parental responsibility is required: Sch 2 para 19(2).

[329] Section 91(12).   [330] Section 39(1), discussed at Discharge of a care order, p 651.

[331] Section 91(1).   [332] Adoption and Children Act 2002 s 46(2)(b).

[333] Adoption and Children Act 2002 s 29(2). Placement orders are discussed in Ch 19.

[334] [2002] UKHL 10 [2002] 2 AC 291 at [27].

[335] [1994] 2 FLR 423 applying *Re B (Minors) (Termination of Contact: Paramount Consideration)* [1993] Fam 301, CA and approving *Kent County Council v C* [1993] Fam 57, in which Ewbank J held there was no power on a care order to direct that a guardian ad litem remain involved to oversee a rehabilitation programme. See also *Re B (A Minor) (Care Order: Review)* [1993] 1 FLR 421 and *Re S (A Minor) (Care: Contact Order)* [1994] 2 FLR 222, CA, discussed in Ch 18, The court's powers, p 657.

[336] [1994] 2 FLR 423 at 428–9.   [337] Raised by counsel for the guardian [1994] 2 FLR 423 at 427.

[338] [1994] 2 FLR 423 at 429 per Nourse LJ.

The court is not divested of *all* powers of control over a child in care, since it retains jurisdiction to consider issues of contact[339] and the power to grant a discharge[340] and to decide whether or not to make an adoption placement order and, ultimately, an adoption order.[341] But the making of a care order effectively gives the local authority control over most of the future arrangements for the child including, crucially, determining where and with whom the child is to live and whether or not he should be rehabilitated with his family. Of course, as we discuss shortly,[342] in deciding whether to make the care order in the first place the court will have regard to the local authority's care plan, but while it can suggest changes to the plan it cannot force the authority to alter its plan and is ultimately faced with the stark choice of whether to accept it or reject it.

Reviewing the care plan—the former position

Under the original scheme of the 1989 Act, once the court had made the care order it had no control over whether that plan was implemented. However, as Baroness Hale explained in *Re G (A Minor) (Interim Care Order: Residential Assessment)*[343] the 1997 President's inter-disciplinary Conference revealed general judicial disquiet about the lack of control over the implementation of the care plan once a care order had been made. This issue was subsequently brought into sharp relief in two cases; one involving Bedfordshire *(Re W)* and the other, Torbay *(Re S)*.

In the former case, Bedfordshire instituted care proceedings in respect of two children, the care plan being that they should be placed with the maternal grandparents with continuing contact with the parents. The grandparents lived in the United States but agreed to move to England to care for the children. At first instance, the judge concluded that the children were unable in the immediate future to return safely to their parents. All the parties agreed that the grandparents would be suitable carers but the evidence that they would be able to come to England was 'exiguous in the extreme'. Although the judge described the care plan as inchoate because of all the uncertainties involved, he nonetheless made care orders.

In the second case, Torbay sought care orders for three children. The care plan for the eldest was that he should remain in foster care which was agreed. But the plan for the two younger children was that an attempt should be made to rehabilitate them with their mother. The mother argued that a care order should not be made because she was sceptical about whether Torbay would carry out the plan. She contended that interim orders should be made instead. The judge made the care orders expressing confidence that Torbay would implement the care plan. In fact, however, the plan was not implemented in part because of a financial crisis within Torbay leading to substantial cuts in the social services budget.

The Court of Appeal heard appeals in both these unrelated cases together in a decision reported as *Re W and B; Re W (Care Plan)*.[344] They reversed the Bedfordshire decision on the basis that the plan was too uncertain but declined to disturb the decision in the Torbay case. However, in reaching these decisions, as Lord Nicholls summarised it on appeal to

---

[339] Under s 34, discussed in Ch 18. The boundary between controlling contact under s 34 and attempting to fetter the local authority powers by making a conditional care order can be difficult to draw: see eg *Kent County Council v C* [1993] Fam 57 but cf *Re B (A Minor) (Care Order)* and compare *Re S (A Minor) (Care: Contact Order)* with *Re E (A Minor) (Care Order: Contact)* [1994] 1 FLR 146, CA, discussed in Ch 18, The court's powers, p 657.   [340] Under s 39, discussed at Discharge of a care order, pp 651ff.

[341] Viz. under the Adoption and Children Act 2002, discussed in Ch 19.

[342] See Having regard to the future – care plans, p 627.

[343] [2005] UKHL 68 [2005] 3 WLR 1166 at [53].   [344] [2001] EWCA Civ 757 [2001] 2 FLR 582.

the House of Lords,[345] the Court of Appeal fashioned two innovations, namely, enunciating guidelines intended to give a wider discretion to make interim care orders[346] and
more radically a new procedure:

> by which at the trial the essential milestones of a care plan would be identified and ele-
> vated to a 'starred status'. If a starred milestone was not achieved within a reasonable time
> after the date set at trial, the local authority was obliged to 'reactivate the interdisciplinary
> process that contributed to the creation of the care plan'. At least the local authority must
> inform the child's guardian of the position. Either the guardian or the local authority
> would then have the right to apply to the court for further directions.

Subsequent to the Court of Appeal decision, application was successfully made to the trial
judge in the Torbay case to 'star' various items in the care plan. This starred plan appeared
to be working well.

The principal reason that the Court of Appeal, and Thorpe LJ in particular, felt able
to make such a radical decision was that without such a system it was their belief that
the 1989 Act was incompatible with human rights and that they were consequently
mandated by s 3 of the Human Rights Act to interpret the Act in a way to make it
compatible.

The House of Lords comprehensively rejected the Court of Appeal's decision. Lord
Nicholls reiterated that the:[347]

> cardinal principal of the Children Act is that when the court makes a care order it becomes
> the duty of the local authority designated by the order to receive the child into its care
> while the order remains in force. So long as the care order is in force the authority has
> parental responsibility for the child. The authority also has power to decide the extent to
> which a parent of the child may meet his responsibility for him . . . The Children Act 1989
> delineated the boundary with complete clarity. Where a care order is made the responsi-
> bility for the child's care is with the authority rather than the court. The court retains no
> supervisory role, monitoring the authority's discharge of its responsibilities. That was the
> intention of Parliament.

In his view, this clear transgression of the cardinal principle by the Court of Appeal was
not justified on human rights grounds since the basic scheme of the Act was not incompatible with Art 8. He considered that it was not the Act that was incompatible; but the
subsequent local authority action or inaction, if any. In any event, the judicial innovation
of 'starred milestones' went well beyond the bounds of interpretation as required by s 3
of the Human Rights Act 1998 and was tantamount to legislation. He did, however, recognise that while parents might have effective remedies via judicial review[348] or under
s 7 of the 1998 Act, such remedies might not always in practice be available to a child
without a parent to act for him but that in itself was a breach of Art 13 which was not
enacted in the 1998 Act.[349] He similarly acknowledged that a local authority's failure to
provide proper access to court as required by Art 6 would be a breach in an individual
case but that in itself did not make the Act incompatible, though it might signify a lacuna
in the Act.

---

[345] Reported as *Re S (Minors) (Care Order: Implementation of Care Plan; Re W (Minors) (Care Order: Adequacy of Care Plan)* [2002] UKHL 10 [2002] 2 AC 291.
[346] Interim care orders are discussed at Interim orders, pp 642ff.
[347] At [23] and [25].   [348] Judicial review is discussed in Ch 18.
[349] See further Ch 18, Taking the case to the European Court of Human Rights, p 677.

Reviewing the care plan—the current position

Notwithstanding the rejection of the Court of Appeal approach, both Lords Nicholls and Mackay stressed[350] that the decision should 'not obscure the pressing need for the Government to attend to the serious and practical problems identified by the Court of Appeal . . .'.

In response to this plea, s 118 of the Adoption and Children Act 2002, amended s 26 of the Children Act 1989, so as to require local authorities to keep care plans under review or make a new one where necessary *and* to appoint a person (an independent reviewing officer)[351] whose task it is to participate in the review, monitor the authority's functions, and, where appropriate refer the care plan to a Cafcass officer who then has the power to refer the matter back to the court.[352]

Although this scheme is similar to that proposed by the Court of Appeal, it has been pointed out[353] that since it relies on the willingness of the independent reviewing officer working within the local authority to refer the matter to Cafcass and on the expeditious work on the part of Cafcass, rather than on a *requirement* to bring the matter back before the court, it might not necessarily solve all the problems. Another concern, reflected by the *Family Justice Review*,[354] is how independent such officers are.

Whether the law should go further and require court sanction for making *any* subsequent changes to a rehabilitation plan can be debated.

5. INTERIM ORDERS

(a) The court's powers to make interim care or supervision orders

Power to make either an interim care or interim supervision order is conferred by s 38.[355] Such orders may be made, either following a s 37 direction by the court to a local authority to investigate the child's circumstances, or on an adjournment in care proceedings.[356] Under s 38(2) such orders cannot be made unless the court 'is satisfied that there are reasonable grounds for believing that the circumstances with respect to the child are as mentioned in section 31(2).' In other words, the court only has to be satisfied that there are reasonable grounds for believing that the so-called threshold conditions exist, rather than having to be satisfied as to their existence. In *Re B (A Minor) (Care Order: Criteria)*,[357] there was evidence before the court to satisfy the test that a girl was likely to suffer significant harm (arising from allegations of sexual abuse), but difficulties arose over the attribution of that harm. However, as Douglas Brown J said, it was enough that he had reasonable grounds for believing that the s 31 threshold was satisfied. As he put it 'I have not got to be satisfied that they

---

[350] At [106] and [112] respectively.

[351] The position of the independent reviewing officer was put on a more secure statutory footing by the Children and Young Persons Act 2008 s 10, which added ss 25A–C to the 1989 Act.

[352] Detailed provisions are now contained in the Review of Children's Cases (Amendment) (England) Regulations 2004 (SI 2004/1419). See also HM Government *Guidance and Regulations* Vol 2 *Care Planning, Placement and Case Review* (2010) paras 2.94–2.107.

[353] By R White, P Carr, N Lowe *Children Act in Practice* (2005, 3rd edn) at 8.112.

[354] See the Final Report (2011) at paras 3.112 ff. For a further critical assessment of Independent Reviewing Officers, se H Jelicic et al *The Role of Independent Reviewing Officers (IROs) in England* (2014).

[355] See DCSF *Guidance and Regulations,* Vol 1, *Court Orders* (2008) paras 3.44–3.56.

[356] Children Act 1989 s 38(1). When considering adjourning the case the court should be mindful of the general principle that under s 1(2) delay is prima facie prejudicial to the child's welfare. Proceedings should not be adjourned because criminal proceedings are pending against the alleged abuser: *Re TB (Care Proceedings: Criminal Trial)* [1995] 2 FLR 801, CA, contradicting *Re S (Care Order: Criminal Proceedings)* [1995] 1 FLR 151, CA.

[357] [1993] 1 FLR 815. Cf *Re M (Interim Care Order: Removal)* [2005] EWCA Civ 1594 [2006] 1 FLR 1043 in which the evidence was too speculative to give grounds even for a reasonable belief that the threshold criteria were met.

exist in fact.' In that case an assessment was crucial to attributing blame and an interim care order was made which ensured that an investigation could properly be carried out.

Notwithstanding these decisions it is important to emphasise that interim orders are not routine matters and even where the application is unopposed it is important that the court is satisfied both as to the existence of the criteria and that the removal of a child from his or her parents even on a temporary basis is fully justified. Failure to do so may be in breach of the parents' human rights.[358] In any event, even where the threshold criteria for making an interim order have been satisfied, careful consideration needs to be given as to whether it is nevertheless justified to order the removal of the child from the parents. As Wall P said in *Re G (Interim Care Order)*[359] in deciding whether to order a child's removal the question to be asked is whether the child's safety (including both psychological and physical elements) required immediate removal and whether the removal is proportionate in the light of the risks posed by leaving the child where he or she was. One example of where there was insufficient justification for immediate removal is *Re F (Care Proceedings: Interim Care Order)* in which the judge's elevation of emotional harm to justify the children's removal from their parents was said not to begin to meet the high threshold established by the authorities.[360] The judge was held to have fallen in to the classic trap of focussing on issues that fall to be addressed at the final hearing. In this case the parents were competent to deliver good enough care in the interim. On the other hand, the bar is not so high as to require 'an imminent risk of serious harm' and deteriorating chronic neglect placing the children's welfare in jeopardy will justify a removal.[361]

(b) The nature of interim orders

As Lord Nicholls emphasised in *Re S (Minors) (Care Order: Implementation of Care Plan); Re W (Minors) (Care Order: Adequacy of Care Plan)*,[362] the purpose of an interim care order:

> is to enable the court to safeguard the welfare of a child until such time as the court is in a position to decide whether or not it is in the best interests of the child to make a care order. When that time arrives depends on the circumstances of the case and is a matter for the judgement of the trial judge. That is the general, guiding principle.

They are, in short, temporary holding measures. Moreover, it is also important to appreciate, as Waite LJ emphasised in *Re G (Minors) (Interim Care Order)*,[363] that:

> The regime of interim care orders laid down by s 38 is designed to leave the court with the ability to maintain strict control of any steps taken or proposed by a local authority in the exercise of powers that are by their nature temporary and subject to continual review. *The making of an interim care order is an essentially impartial step, favouring neither one side nor the other, and affording no one, least of all the local authority in whose favour it is made, an opportunity for tactical or adventitious advantage.* (Emphasis added)

---

[358] See *Re H (A Child) (Interim Care Order)* [2002] EWCA Civ 1932 [2003] 1 FCR 350.
[359] [2011] EWCA Civ 745 [2011] 2 FLR 955 at [22]. See also to similar effect *Re GR (Care Order)* [2010] EWCA Civ 871 [2011] 1 FLR 669; *Re B (Interim Care Order)* [2009] EWCA Civ 324 [2010] 2 FLR 283; and *Re B (Care Proceedings: Interim Care Order)* [2009] EWCA Civ 1254 [2010] 1 FLR 1211.
[360] [2010] EWCA Civ 826 [2010] 2 FLR 1455 at [23] per Thorpe LJ. See also *Re NL (Appeal: Interim Care Order: Facts and Reasons)* [2014] EWHC 270 (Fam) [2014] 1 FLR 1384.
[361] See, for example, *Re LA (Care: Chronic Neglect)* [2009] EWCA Civ 822 [2010] 1 FLR 80.
[362] [2002] UKHL 10 [2002] 2 AC 291 at [90].   [363] [1993] 2 FLR 839 at 845.

Further, as Cazalet J observed in *Hampshire County Council v S*:[364]

> Justices should bear in mind that they are not, at an interim hearing, required to make a final conclusion; indeed it is because they are unable to reach a final conclusion that they are empowered to make an interim order. An interim order or decision will usually be required so as to establish a holding position, after weighing all the relevant risks, pending the final hearing. Nevertheless, justices must always ensure that the substantive issue is tried and determined at the earliest possible date. Any delay in determining the question before the court is likely to prejudice the welfare of the child [see s 1(2) of the Act].

In short, any decision taken by the court must necessarily be limited to issues that cannot await the substantive hearing and must not extend to issues that are being prepared for determination at that hearing.[365]

(c) Deciding whether to make a final or interim care order

In principle a final care order should not be made if important evidence remains outstanding or unresolved, eg where assessments are still being made and their outcome awaited. In *Hounslow London Borough Council v A*[366] magistrates were held to be wrong to make a final care order at a time when the assessment of the father as a full-time carer had not been completed. Similarly, in *C v Solihull Metropolitan Borough Council*,[367] children, the younger of whom had suffered serious non-accidental injuries whilst with the parent, were placed with their grandparents who had what was then a residence order. Ward J held that, pending the outcome of an assessment of the parents to see whether it was safe to return the children to them, the proper order was an interim care order. Such an order kept control of events in the court, which in these circumstances was preferable both to returning the children to the parents subject to a supervision order and to making a full care order which effectively would have abdicated the court's responsibility to the local authority.

However, merely because some issues remain uncertain it does not necessarily mean that an interim care order has to be made. For example, in *Re L (Sexual Abuse: Standard of Proof)*[368] the judge found that two children had been sexually abused. He also found that there was some prospect of rehabilitation with the mother but little such prospect with the father. The authority's care plan was based on removing the children from the family and placing them permanently for adoption. Although the judge expressed the hope that the local authority would be sympathetic to his views regarding rehabilitation, he nevertheless made a full care order in respect of each child based on the belief that an interim order should not be used to control what the local authority was doing. The Court of Appeal refused to interfere. After pointing out that once a care order is made, then—other than by control over contact—the court has no further part to play in the future welfare of the child, Butler-Sloss LJ commented:[369]

> The Children Act provides for many of the most important decisions, including whether to place a child for adoption, to be made by the local authority and therefore there is nothing untoward in the judge leaving the ultimate decision in the hands of the local authority with whom the child is placed.

---

[364] [1993] Fam 158 at 165.

[365] Per Thorpe LJ in *Re L (Care: Chronic Neglect)* [2009] EWCA Civ 822 [2010] 1 FLR 80 at [7], in turn referring to *Re K and H* [2006] EWCA Civ 1898 [2007] 1 FLR 2043.

[366] [1993] 1 FLR 702.   [367] [1993] 1 FLR 290.

[368] [1996] 1 FLR 116. See also *Re R (Care Proceedings: Adjournment)* [1998] 2 FLR 390, CA.

[369] [1996] 1 FLR 116 at 124–125.

She continued by pointing out that interim care orders should not be used to provide continuing control over the activities of the local authority and quoted with approval Wall J's earlier comments in *Re J (Minors) (Care: Care Plan)*:[370]

> . . . there are cases (of which this is one) in which the action which requires to be taken in the interest of children necessarily involves steps into the unknown and that provided the court is satisfied that the local authority is alert to the difficulties which may arise in the execution of the care plan, the function of the court is not to seek to oversee the plan but to entrust its execution to the local authority.

It has been said[371] that, once all the facts are known, it can seldom if ever be right for the court to continue adjourning the case, and certainly not just to enable the court to monitor the situation. But in a challenge to this approach Thorpe LJ said, in *Re W and B; Re W (Care Plan)*,[372] that trial judges should have a 'wider discretion' to make an interim care order 'where the care plans seem inchoate or where the passage of a relatively brief period seems bound to see the fulfilment of some event or process vital to planning and deciding the future'. But this view was rejected by the House of Lords.[373] Lord Nicholls emphasised[374] that 'an interim care order is not intended to be used as a means by which the court may continue to exercise a supervisory role over the local authority in cases where it is in the best interests of a child that a care order should be made'. However, he also said[375] that when deciding whether to make a care order 'the court should normally have before it a care plan which is sufficiently firm and particularised for all concerned to have a reasonably clear picture of the likely way ahead for the child for the foreseeable future'. In the subsequent House of Lords' decision, *Re G (A Minor) (Interim Care Order: Residential Assessment)*,[376] it was again emphasised that the court should resist the temptation to postpone making its final decision until any uncertainties have been resolved.

(d) Making directions on interim applications

One of the key differences between a full and interim order is that in the latter case the court may give certain directions.[377] This power is conferred by s 38(6), which states:

> Where the court makes an interim care order, or interim supervision order, it may give such direction (if any) as it considers appropriate with regard to the medical or psychiatric examination or other assessment of the child; but if the child is of sufficient understanding to make an informed decision he may refuse to submit to the examination or other assessment.

---

[370] [1994] 1 FLR 253.

[371] *Re P (Minors) (Interim Care)* [1993] 2 FLR 742, CA. In overruling Hollings J's decision to make a succession of interim care orders until the placement of two young girls with their mother and her cohabitant who were proposing to move to Northern Ireland was settled, Waite LJ said: 'It can never be right for the court, in granting an interim care order at one sitting, to attempt to lay down a policy which would or might fetter the discretion of any future sitting to grant or refuse a further interim order.'

[372] [2001] EWCA Civ 757 [2001] 2 FLR 582 at [29].

[373] The appealed case is reported as *Re S (Minors) (Care Order: Implementation of Care Plan); Re W (Minors) (Care Order: Adequacy of Care Plan)* [2002] UKHL 10 [2002] 2 AC 291. [374] At [90].

[375] At [99]. [376] [2005] UKHL 68 [2005] 3 WLR 1166 at [57] per Baroness Hale.

[377] For a review of the legislative history see the analysis by Baroness Hale in *Re G* [2005] UKHL 68 [2005] 3 WLR 1166 at [63]–[64].

Although clearly empowering courts to make directions as to medical or psychiatric examinations of children,[378] the precise ambit of this provision has been the subject of considerable litigation. The matter was authoritatively resolved by the House of Lords in *Re C (A Minor) (Interim Care Order: Residential Assessment)*.[379] In that case, the child suffered unexplained injuries while in the care of his parents. An expert considered the injuries to be non-accidental and the local authority social workers themselves recommended (supported by the guardian and the clinical psychologist) an in-depth assessment involving both parents and the child at a residential unit. The local authority, however, resisted the recommendation inter alia because of the lack of explanation for the injuries by the parents and because of their unstable relationship. They considered that rehabilitation could expose the children to an unacceptable level of risk and accordingly were not prepared to pay the considerable sum of £18,000–£24,000 for the residential placement, which in any event, in their view, had little chance of success. Could they be ordered to carry out the assessment? The House of Lords ruled that both s 38(6) and s 38(7) (which empowers the court to direct there be no such examination or assessment) should be broadly construed to confer jurisdiction on the court to order or prohibit any assessment which involves the participation of the child and which is directed to providing the court with material which is necessary to enable it to reach a proper decision at the final hearing. They rejected the argument based on the *ejusdem generis* principle that (a) 'assessments' had to be of the same type as medical or psychiatric; and (b) the powers were confined to assessments 'of the child' and not of the parents. With regard to the latter, Lord Browne-Wilkinson pointed out that it was impossible to assess a young child divorced from his environment or his parents.[380]

The House also rejected the argument that the local authority are better qualified than the court to decide whether expenditure on such a scale is a sensible allocation of their limited resources. Lord Browne-Wilkinson noted that such an argument could not be made in respect of directed medical treatment under s 38(6), so why should it be for other assessments? In any event, to hold otherwise would be tantamount to allowing:

> . . . the local authority to decide what evidence is to go before the court at the final hearing—to allow the local authority by administrative decision to pre-empt the court's judicial decision.

The ambit of s 38(6) was further considered by the House of Lords in *Re G (A Minor) (Interim Care Order: Residential Assessment)*.[381] The child in question had become the subject of care proceedings almost immediately upon her birth because of concerns about the mother's ability to care for her following the death of her second child resulting from non-accidental injuries. (Her first child was placed in her father's care.) The local authority agreed to a six to eight week residential placement for the parents and child

[378] But it is not confined to such directions, see *Re B (Interim Care Order: Directions)* [2002] EWCA Civ 25 [2002] 1 FLR 547 in which the court directed the mother and child to live at a particular home. But note the criticism of this decision by Lord Scott in *Re G (A Minor) (Interim Care Order: Residential Assessment)* [2005] UKHL 68 [2005] 3 WLR 1166 at [12] that the order strayed beyond an 'assessment'.

[379] [1997] AC 489. See also *Re M (Residential Assessment Directions)* [1998] 2 FLR 371, in which it was held that the child's welfare was not the paramount consideration when deciding whether to make directions under s 38(6).

[380] Though note that there is apparently no power of the court to order *parents* to take part in any assessment against their wishes—see Lord Browne-Wilkinson in *Re C* [1997] AC 489.

[381] [2005] UKHL 68 [2005] 3 WLR 1166, for comments on which, see J Cohen and C Hale 'Treatment or Therapy: The House of Lords Decision in *Re G (Interim Care Order: Residential Assessment)*' [2006] Fam Law 294.

at a hospital specialising in the assessment and treatment of severely disturbed adults and their families. This period was later extended for a further four weeks specifically to assess the risk that the mother posed to the child. At the end of this period the hospital and an expert instructed by the local authority agreed that there was a significant shift in the mother's ability to address her involvement in the second child's death, and further that with appropriate therapeutic intervention the mother was likely to respond sufficiently well so as to be able to safely parent her child. The local health authority were not, however, willing to fund this further treatment. The question was whether the court had the power under s 38(6) to direct the local authority to fund the treatment. The House of Lords held there was no power to make the direction since in effect it amounted to treatment of the mother rather than an assessment of the child's position.

A succinct summary of the decision was given by Lord Mance who said:[382]

any assessment order by s 38(6) . . . by a court when making an interim care order, is intended to take place and be completed over a relatively short period, focussing on the current position of the child in that period; . . . What is not permissible under s 38(6) is the giving of directions for a longer process aiming at bringing about long-term change. Secondly, . . . directions under s 38(6) can only be made if they can properly be described as being with regard to the medical or psychiatric examination or other assessment 'of the child', rather than if they involve, as here, a programme focussed in substance on the child's parent and the improvement of her parenting skills.

Baroness Hale concluded her judgment by saying:[383]

what is directed under s 38(6) must clearly be an examination or assessment of the child, including where appropriate her relationship with her parents, the risk that her parents may present to her, and the ways in which those risks may be avoided or managed, all with a view to enabling the court to make the decisions which it has to make under the 1989 Act with the minimum of delay. Any services which are provided for the child and the family must be ancillary to that end. They must not be an end in themselves.

Arguments about the parents' Art 8 rights were dealt with robustly. As Lord Scott said,[384] 'There is no Art 8 right to be made a better parent at public expense.'

While no doubt there will remain cases where it is hard to distinguish assessment from treatment there can be few quibbles with the overall thrust of Re G. To have held otherwise would have, as Baroness Hale pointed out,[385] conflicted with the cardinal principle,[386] namely, that it is for the court to decide (without undue delay) whether or not to make a care order and for the local authority to decide how the child should be cared for once an order has been made.

Subsequent to these decisions there were a number of Court of Appeal decisions[387] that some had taken to suggest that a parent facing the permanent removal of his or her

---

[382] [2005] UKHL 68 [2005] 3 WLR 1166 at [73].
[383] Ibid at [69].   [384] Ibid at [24].   [385] Ibid at [57].
[386] Following Lord Nicholls in Re S (Minors) (Care Order: Implementation of Care Plan); Re W (Minors) (Care Order: Adequacy of Care Plan) [2002] UKHL 10 [2002] 2 AC 291 at [28] and discussed at Controlling the local authority after a care order, p 639.
[387] See eg Re L and H (Residential Assessment) [2007] EWCA Civ 213 [2007] 1 FLR 1370; Re B (Care Proceedings: Expert Witness) [2007] EWCA Civ 556 [2007] 2 FLR 979; Re K (Care Order) [2007] EWCA Civ 697 [2007] 2 FLR 1066; and Re J (Residential Assessment: Rights Of Audience [2009] EWCA Civ 1210 [2010] 1 FLR 1290.

child had a right to assessment of their choice rather than an assessment undertaken by the local authority, but this notion was firmly dismissed by the Court of Appeal in *Re T (Residential Parenting Assessment)*.[388] That case reaffirmed the general principle that an assessment under s 38(6) should only be authorised by the court where such an assessment will bring something important to the case which neither the local authority nor the children's guardian could provide.

Notwithstanding that s 38(6) expressly says that a child of sufficient understanding to make an informed decision may refuse to submit to an examination or assessment Douglas Brown J held in *South Glamorgan County Council v W and B*[389] that he had an inherent power to override a competent child's refusal to submit to an examination. In doing so he purported to follow *Re W (A Minor) (Medical Treatment: Court's Jurisdiction)*,[390] in which the Court of Appeal overruled a 16-year-old anorexic child's refusal of treatment. However, with respect to Douglas Brown J, it is one thing to interpret a statute—in the case of *Re W*, s 8 of the Family Law Reform Act 1969, which permits 16- and 17-year-olds to give valid consent to medical treatment—restrictively, but quite another flatly to contradict it. It is suggested that the *South Glamorgan* decision is bad law and ought not to be followed.

(e) Attaching an exclusion requirement to an interim care order

Implementing the Law Commission's recommendation,[391] the Children Act was amended to empower the courts to add, either upon application or its own motion, an exclusion requirement to an interim care order.[392] This power, which is conferred by s 38A, enables a court to exclude a suspected abuser from the family so as to protect a child without having to remove him or her from the home.[393]

Under s 38A(1) an exclusion requirement may only be added to an interim care order and not therefore to an interim supervision order; nor, in the former case, may it be added to an order based on the child being beyond parental control. In any event, before an exclusion requirement may be made the court must be satisfied of three conditions:[394]

(1) there is reasonable cause to believe that if a relevant person is excluded from the child's home the child will cease to suffer or cease to be likely to suffer significant harm;

(2) there is another person (whether a parent or someone else) living in the home who is able to give the child the care which it would be reasonable to expect a parent to give; and

(3) that other person consents[395] to the inclusion of the exclusion requirement.

The exclusion requirement requires[396] the relevant person to leave the dwelling house in which he is living with the child, and prohibits him from re-entering. It may also exclude

---

[388] [2011] EWCA Civ 812 [2012] 2 FLR 308.

[389] [1993] 1 FLR 574.

[390] [1993] Fam 64, CA, discussed in Ch 9, *Gillick* – a false dawn?, p 322.

[391] Law Com No 207, *Domestic Violence and the Occupation of the Family Home* (1992).The amendments were made by the Family Law Act 1996.

[392] For a similar power to add an exclusion requirement to an emergency protection order see Ch 16, The power to add an exclusion requirement, p 587. The Law Commission, at Law Com No 207 para 6.17, found no support for long-term exclusion as an alternative to a care order. For the power generally to exclude a person from his or her own home, see Ch 6.

[393] See DCSF *Guidance and Regulations,* Vol 1, *Court Orders* (2008) paras 3.53–3.57.

[394] Section 38A(2).

[395] This consent must be in writing or given orally to the court: FPR 2010 r 12.29.

[396] Section 38A(3).

him from a defined area in which the dwelling house is situated. The requirement cannot last longer than the interim order though it can be made for a shorter period.[397] When seeking an exclusion requirement applicants must prepare a separate statement of the evidence in support and that statement together with a copy of the order must be served on the relevant person.[398] The statement should set out in concise form the factual material relied upon, the relevant statutory requirements and to make it clear that the particular person is required to leave the dwelling house.[399]

The court can attach a power of arrest to the exclusion requirement,[400] which entitles a police constable to arrest without a warrant any person whom he has reasonable cause to believe is in breach of the requirement.[401] Instead of formally making an exclusion requirement courts can accept undertakings in similar terms,[402] but in these cases no power of arrest can be attached.[403]

If, while the exclusion requirement is in force, the local authority remove the child from the dwelling house for more than 24 hours, then the requirement or undertaking ceases to have effect.[404]

(f) Duration and renewal of interim orders

The duration of interim orders is governed by s 38(4), as amended by the Children and Families Act 2014.[405] The amendments made by the 2014 Act remove the former limit on the length of interim orders (eight weeks for an initial order and four weeks for subsequent orders) and allow the judge to make an order for a period which is considered appropriate in all the circumstances. As the Explanatory Notes to the Act state,[406] the expectation is that interim orders will be aligned with the timetable for the care proceedings so as to avoid the need to make multiple orders within the proceedings. Nevertheless if an order does expire before the proceedings have been resolved, the court is able to make a further order.

(g) Alternative orders under s 8

As an alternative to making an interim care order the court may make a s 8 order for a limited period. The combination of s 11(3) and s 11(7) allows the court to make an order for a specified period and subject to conditions, even though it is not yet in a position finally to dispose of the case. For example, the court could make a child arrangements order until the next hearing naming a relative as a person with whom the child is to live and a parent as a person with whom the child is to have contact. Under s 38(3), as amended by the 2014 Act, if, upon an application for care or supervision, the court makes a child arrangements order with respect to the child's living arrangements, it *must* make an interim supervision order unless it is satisfied that the child's welfare will be satisfactorily safeguarded without it. In other words, there is a rebuttable presumption that if such a child arrangements order is made, so should an interim supervision order. The power to make s 8 orders the court is governed by the paramountcy of the child's welfare under s 1(1) and by the enjoinder under s 1(5) not to make any order unless it considers that doing so would be better for the child than making no order.

---

[397] Section 38A(4).   [398] FPR 2010 r 12.29.

[399] *Re W (Exclusion: Statement of Evidence)* [2000] 2 FLR 666.

[400] Section 38A(5). See also *Practice Direction 12K – Practice Direction Children Act Exclusion Requirement*.   [401] Section 38A(8).

[402] Section 38B and see Sch 2 para 5—power to assist suspected perpetrator to obtain alternative accommodation, discussed in Ch 15, Provision of accommodation by third party to protect children, p 563.

[403] Section 38B(2).   [404] Section 38A(10), s 38B(2).   [405] Section 14(4).

[406] See para 144.

G. APPEALS

Before the Children Act 1989 the law governing appeals in public law cases was complicated and anomalous. Some, but not all, parties could appeal against the making of a care or supervision order, but there was no general right of appeal against the refusal to make such orders. Where appeals did lie from magistrates' decisions, they lay before the Crown Court and were by way of a full rehearing.[407] Under the 1989 Act the position is straightforward: any party in the original proceedings may appeal against the making of, or refusal to, make a care or supervision order (including an interim order).[408] This means that, like any other party, local authorities have full rights of appeal.[409]

As we discussed in Chapter 14, apart from appeals from magistrates' decisions and those against the making of a committal order or a secure accommodation order, permission to appeal is required.[410]

Public law appeals are governed by the general principles laid down in *Re B (A Child)(Care Proceedings: Threshold Criteria)*.[411] *Re B* establishes that for a successful appeal against evaluative decisions such as whether or not the statutory threshold has been crossed or whether a care order is a proportionate response to the harm or risk of harm found the lower court decision has to be shown to be wrong or 'unjust because of a serious procedural or other irregularity in the proceedings of the lower court.'[412] It is not enough that the appellate court would have reached a different decision. In *Re B* there was a division of opinion as to the proper function of an appellate court with regard to the decisions about the proportionality of care orders in relation to the harm or risk of harm found. The majority view[413] was that neither human rights jurisprudence nor s 6 of the Human Rights Act 1998 requires the appellate court to depart from its normal appellate function of secondary review. In other words the court does not have to make a fresh evaluation of proportionality. The dissenting view[414] was that because the appellate court is itself a public body for these purposes it follows that has the obligation to make its own assessment of proportionality.

The significance of *Re B* is that it establishes that in appeals against evaluative decisions the former test established by the House of Lords in *G v G (Minors: Custody Appeal)*[415] does not apply with the consequence that it is sufficient that lower court decision is 'wrong' as opposed to having to show that it was 'plainly wrong'. In *Re B* Lord Neuberger helpfully set out[416] a scale of possible findings by an appellate court, namely, that the trial judge's view was (i) the only possible view, (ii) a view which is considered right, (iii) a view on which there are doubts but on balance is considered right, (iv) a view which cannot be considered right or wrong, (v) a view on which there are doubts but on balance is considered wrong, (vi) a view which is considered wrong, and (vii) a view which is insupportable. In the case of findings (i) to (iv) the appeal must be dismissed. In the case of findings (vi) and (vii) the appeal should be allowed.

According to Lord Neuberger, so far as finding (iv) is concerned, there will be number of cases where an appellate court may think that there is no right or wrong answer but an appellate court is much less likely to conclude that this category applies where the trial judge's decision was not based on an assessment of the witnesses' reliability or likely

---

[407] See generally, H Bevan *Child Law* (1989) paras 14.114–14.116.
[408] Including a direction made under s 38(6): see *Re O (Minors) (Medical Examination)* [1993] 1 FLR 860.
[409] See inter alia, s 94 (1) of the Children Act 1989.   [410] FPR 2010 r 30.3. CPR 1998 r 52.3.
[411] [2013] UKSC 33 [2013] 1 WLR 1911. Discussed in Chs 12 and 14.
[412] As per FPR 2010 r 30.12(3) and CPR 1998 r 52.11(3).
[413] See Lords Wilson, Neuberger and Clarke.   [414] See Lord Kerr and Baroness Hale.
[415] [1985] 1 WLR 647, HL, discussed in Ch 14.   [416] At [93]–[94].

future conduct. As to category (v) the appellate court should think very carefully about the benefit the trial judge had in seeing the witnesses and hearing the evidence.

H. DISCHARGE OF CARE ORDERS AND DISCHARGE AND VARIATION OF SUPERVISION ORDERS

Section 39 of the Children Act makes provision for the discharge[417] (but not a variation, since that would interfere with the general principle that management of compulsory care is the local authority's responsibility)[418] of care orders and for the variation and discharge of supervision orders.[419] Additionally, it should be noted, the making of a child arrangements order dealing with the child's living arrangements and a special guardianship order automatically discharges a care order.[420] A care order is suspended, though not discharged, upon the making of an adoption placement order.[421]

1. DISCHARGE OF A CARE ORDER

Under s 39(1) application for discharge of a care order may be made by any person who has parental responsibility, the child himself or the local authority. The requirement to have parental responsibility means that, since the making of a care order discharges any s 8 order,[422] including a child arrangements order relating to the child's living arrangements, only mothers, married fathers, unmarried fathers and second female parents having parental responsibility by virtue of registration, a s 4 order or agreement,[423] guardians, special guardians and step-parents with responsibility by virtue of an order or agreement under s 4A may apply under s 39. Unmarried fathers without parental responsibility, relatives and foster parents cannot therefore apply under s 39, but they can seek to apply for a child arrangements order under s 8 naming them as a person with whom the child is to live which, if granted, operates to discharge a care order.[424] Unmarried fathers and second female parents can apply as of right for a child arrangements order, but others will need first to apply for leave.[425] There is nothing to prevent those with parental responsibility from applying for a child arrangements order rather than for a discharge under s 39, though unless there is a dispute between the applicants there would be little advantage in doing so.

So far as the child is concerned, s 39(1)(b) has been interpreted[426] as giving a right to apply, so that unlike the private law there is no requirement to obtain the leave of the court. In practice, most applications for discharge of care orders are made by local authorities, who are required by the Review of Children's Cases Regulations 1991[427] to consider at least at every statutory review of a case of a child in their care whether to apply for a discharge.[428] Furthermore, as part of each review the child has to be informed, inter

---

[417] See generally the DfE *Statutory guidance on court orders and pre-proceedings. For local* authorities (2014) paras 36 ff, and the revised DCSF *Guidance and Regulations*, Vol 1, *Court Orders* (2008) paras 3.65 *et seq.*

[418] Department of Health's *Guidance and Regulations*, Vol 1 *Court Orders* (1991) para 3.54, a comment not made in the 2008 Guidance.

[419] For the background to the provision, see the DHSS *Review of Child Care Law* (1985) ch 20.

[420] Sections 91(1) (as amended by the Children and Families Act 2014) and 91(5A).

[421] Adoption and Children Act 2002 s 29 (1). Placement orders are discussed in Ch 19.

[422] Children Act 1989 s 91(2).   [423] Discussed in Ch 11.

[424] Children Act 1989 s 91(1), as amended by the Children and Families Act 2014 Sch 2 para 37.

[425] See Ch 14, Persons entitled to apply with leave, p 515, for discussion of foster parents' use of this provision.   [426] *Re A (Care: Discharge Application by Child)* [1995] 1 FLR 599, per Thorpe J.

[427] Sch 2 para 1.   [428] Sch 1 para 5 to the 1991 Regulations.

alia, of steps he may take himself for the discharge of the order. These reviews are chaired by independent reviewing officers who must ensure that the child's wishes and feeling are understood and taken into account.[429]

Rather than grant the discharge the court is empowered to substitute a supervision order.[430] In doing this there is no requirement that the threshold provisions under s 31(2) be proved again.[431] Indeed, the controlling principle in all such applications is the paramountcy of the child's welfare,[432] and in reaching its decision the court is required to have regard to the statutory checklist under s 1(3).[433] This means, as the Court of Appeal held in *Re S (Discharge of Care Order)*,[434] that the jurisdiction under s 39 is entirely discretionary; there is, for example, no obligation upon the applicant to satisfy the court that the threshold requirements under s 31 no longer apply. Instead, in deciding what, if any, order to make, the primary focus must be on the child's welfare as it appears to be at the date of the discharge hearing. In assessing the child's welfare, an important consideration is, as s 1(3)(e) directs the court to consider, any harm that the child has suffered or is at risk of suffering. In the vast majority of cases the court is only likely to be concerned with evidence of recent harm and appraisal of current risk. However, it was also accepted in *Re S* that on very limited occasions the court might properly be concerned with the soundness of the original findings in the earlier care proceedings. In so ruling, however, it was emphasised that judges should be alert to see that this theoretical power should not be abused by allowing issues that have already been determined to be litigated afresh. Parents (or the child) may have difficulty in establishing that a discharge is in the child's interests, especially where there has been little contact.[435] On the other hand, the court is entitled to take into account the effect or lack of effect of the care order. It is also a relevant consideration to take into account the benefits of the leaving care provisions if the care order is continued.[436]

Contrary to the recommendation of the *Review of Child Care Law*,[437] the 1989 Act makes no express provision to postpone the discharge of a care order to allow for a gradual or phased return of the child to his family. How far this can be done by other means is debatable. The best option would seem to be to make a supervision order allowing a gradual return.[438] Alternatively, the court could control rehabilitation through its powers under s 34 to make care contact orders (see further, later), though technically such orders can only be made upon express application.[439] Whether it is possible to grant a child arrangements order to the parents but to provide under s 11(7) or, as part of the 'arrangements' that the child remains with the foster parents with increasing contact to the parents prior to living with them, remains to be determined.

---

[429] See the 2008 *Guidance* para 3.67.

[430] Children Act 1989 s 39(4). But it has no power to substitute an interim care order: *NP v South Gloucestershire County Council* (2005) 7 November, CA, cited by Clarke Hall and Morrison at 9 [196].

[431] Section 39(5).   [432] Section 1(1).

[433] Discussed in Ch 10.   [434] [1995] 2 FLR 639, CA.

[435] See *Re S and P (Discharge of Care Order)* [1995] 2 FLR 782 in which Singer J upheld a magistrates' decision, that having heard the mother's oral evidence, they should proceed no further with the case since it was clearly hopeless. But note FPR 2010 r 12.14 (4) which requires the court to give the guardian, the solicitor for the child and the child himself, if of sufficient understanding, the opportunity to make representations.

[436] *Re C (Care: Discharge Of Care Order)* [2009] EWCA Civ 955 [2010] 1 FLR 774, in which a discharge order was upheld in the case of a 15 year old boy who had a history of repeated absconding and returning home.   [437] At para 20.26.

[438] See *Re T (Care Order)* [2009] EWCA Civ 121 [2009] 2 FLR 574.

[439] Note the power under s 40(3) to postpone the effect of a discharge order or to subject a care order to conditions only arises where an appeal is pending.

Once an application has been disposed of, no further application without leave can be made within six months.[440]

2. DISCHARGE AND VARIATION OF SUPERVISION ORDERS

Under s 39(2) applications for discharge or variation of a supervision order may be made by any person who has parental responsibility for the child, the child himself or the supervisor. In addition, under s 39(3), a person who is not entitled to apply for a discharge but is a person with whom the child is living, can apply to vary a requirement made upon him under the supervision order.[441]

As with applications for the discharge of care orders, in deciding what order to make the court must apply the principle of the paramountcy of the child's welfare. The court has no power to vary the order to a care order.[442] Instead, if that is what is required, the local authority must make a fresh application under s 31.[443]

No application may be made without leave of the court within six months of the disposal of a previous application.[444]

---

[440] Children Act 1989 s 91(15).

[441] A requirement made under Sch 3 to the 1989 Act: see Duration of a supervision order, p 633.

[442] There is no similar provision to that substituting a supervision order for a care order under s 39(5).

[443] Consequently, the s 31 threshold will have to be re-established as at the date of the hearing: *Re A*, earlier.   [444] Section 91(15).

18

CHILDREN AND LOCAL AUTHORITIES: THE POSITION OF CHILDREN IN CARE

A. INTRODUCTION

In this chapter we discuss the position of children in local authority care. We begin by discussing the issue of contact with children in care. We then consider more broadly local authorities' duties to all children looked after by them which includes those who are accommodated as well as those who are subject to care orders. Finally, we discuss the various means by which local authority decisions with respect to children being looked after by them can be challenged.

B. CONTACT WITH CHILDREN IN CARE

1. INTRODUCTION

The Children Act 1989 places considerable importance on the active promotion by local authorities of contact between children being looked after by them and their families,[1] even to the extent of helping with the costs incurred in the visit.[2] As the *Guidance and Regulations* puts it:[3]

> The interests of the majority of looked after children are best served by sustaining or creating links with their birth families including wider family members. Consideration of contact is an essential element in the planning process.

This duty continues after a care order has been made and is underscored by the general provision under s 34(1) that there be reasonable contact between the child and inter alia his parents, which can only be departed from by agreement or by court order.

(a) The position before the 1989 Act

Before the 1989 Act, although emphasis was placed on the importance of maintaining contact between the child and his family, the arrangements were mainly within the exclusive control of the local authorities. Only if contact was refused or terminated (but not

---

[1] See generally the DCSF *Guidance and Regulations*, Vol 1, *Court Orders* (2008) paras 3.71–3.79 and HM Government *Guidance and Regulations*, Vol 2 *Care Planning, Placement and Case Review* (2010) paras 2.78–2.92.
[2] Children Act 1989 Sch 2 para 16.   [3] HM Government (2010) at para 2.78.

if restricted) was it possible for parents, guardians or others to challenge the decision in court.[4] Even this was an inadequate remedy, since no application could be made until well after the termination or refusal, so that by the time the issue got to court, there was often little choice but to uphold the local authority's decision.[5]

(b) The 1989 Act reforms

Implementing the recommendations of the *Review of Child Care Law*,[6] and anticipating that the continued inability to challenge restrictions of contact with children in care would be contrary to the European Convention on Human Rights,[7] s 34 effectively turned the previous law on its head by requiring the local authority to seek a court order *before* terminating or restricting reasonable contact. This fundamental change, arguably among the most significant changes introduced by the 1989 Act,[8] means that parents and others have a more realistic chance of opposing local authority contact plans. Furthermore according to Wall J in *Re F (care: termination of contact)*,[9] the scheme under s 34 is fully human rights compliant. In this latter respect it will be noted that the European Court of Human Rights has said on numerous occasions[10] that while States enjoy a wide margin of appreciation to remove a child into care stricter scrutiny is required of any limitations on the ability to have contact.

2. THE SCHEME UNDER SECTION 34

(a) The presumption of reasonable contact

The basic position, set out by s 34(1), is that local authorities must normally allow the child reasonable contact with his or her parents (including the unmarried father or second female parent regardless of whether they have parental responsibility), guardians, special guardians, step-parents who have parental responsibility by virtue of s 4A,[11] any person named in a child arrangements order as a person with whom the child is to live immediately before the making of the care order[12] and a person who had the care of the child by virtue of an order under the High Court's inherent jurisdiction. This duty is subject to the local authority's obligation to safeguard and promote the welfare of any child they are looking after.[13] Accordingly, if allowing contact with any of those persons just mentioned would not safeguard and promote the welfare of the child, the local authority should not allow the contact.[14] Furthermore, following an amendment by the Children and Families

---

[4] Child Care Act 1980 ss 12A–F,

[5] In a study carried out by S Millham, R Bullock, K Hosie and M Little *Access Disputes in Child Care* (1989) p 53, of 309 terminations notice only nine parents (3%) re-established contact through legal proceedings.

[6] Ch 21; cf the Second Report of the House of Commons Social Services Committee 1983–1984 (the 'Short Report') HC 360, paras 73 and 324 which expressed concern that local authority power had already been eroded too far by the access provisions under the Child Care Act 1980.

[7] See eg *R v United Kingdom* [1988] 2 FLR 445, ECtHR; *O v United Kingdom* (1987) 10 EHRR 82, ECtHR; *W v United Kingdom* (1987) 10 EHRR 29, ECtHR; and *B v United Kingdom* (1987) 10 EHRR 87, ECtHR.

[8] According to research by H Cleaver (see *Fostering family contact* (2000)) four times as many children in foster care had weekly contact with their parents after implementation of the Act as before.

[9] [2000] 2 FCR 481.

[10] See eg *HK v Finland* [2007] 1 FLR 632, ECtHR (Grand Chamber); *Kosmopoulou v Greece* [2004] 1 FLR 800, ECtHR; and *Scott v United Kingdom* [2000] 1 FLR 958, ECtHR.

[11] Ie by a parental responsibility order or agreement, discussed in Ch 11.

[12] See the amendment made to s 34 by the Children and Families Act 2014 Sch 2 para 31.

[13] Section 34(1), as amended by s 8(2) of the Children and Families Act 2014.

[14] See para 82 of the Explanatory Notes to the 2014 Act.

Act 2014,[15] where contact has been refused by the local authority acting under s 34(6) or by a court order under s 34(4) (both discussed shortly) there is no duty to promote contact with the person with whom contact has been refused.

The local authority, the child and any person concerned are expected, as far as possible, to agree upon reasonable arrangements before the care order is made.[16] Section 34(11) requires the court, before making a care order,[17] to consider any contact arrangements that the authority have made or propose to make and to invite the parties to the proceedings to comment on those arrangements. As Ewbank J observed,[18] 'reasonable contact' is not the same as contact at the discretion of the local authority: rather it implies either that which is agreed between the local authority and the parties, or, in the absence of such an agreement, contact which is objectively reasonable.

Important though contact is, it was held in *Re K (Care Proceedings: Care Plan)*,[19] that if a court considers that a care order should be made, it should not refuse to do so because of concerns about contact (in *Re K* the issue was about post adoption contact, the plan being to place the child for adoption after the making of the care order); rather the proper course is for the court itself to consider how best the contact issue should be handled.

(b) Departing from the general presumption

As an exception to the presumption of reasonable contact, s 34(6) permits a local authority in matters of urgency to refuse contact for up to seven days provided 'they are satisfied that it is necessary to do so in order to safeguard or promote the child's welfare'. As the *Regulation and Guidance* says,[20] a 'decision to refuse contact under s 34(6)... should not be undertaken lightly.' Where contact is so refused, the local authority are required to give written notice explaining the decision to the child, if he is of sufficient understanding, to any person with whom there is a presumption of reasonable contact and (in England) to the Independent Reviewing Officer.[21]

Apart from this limited power it is incumbent upon the local authority to seek a court order restricting or denying contact,[22] if they wish to depart from the general presumption.[23]

(c) The position of the child and other interested persons

A child in care has the right[24] to make an application both for defined contact to be allowed with a named person and for an order authorising the authority to refuse to allow

---

[15] Section 8 inserting s 34(6A) into the 1989 Act.

[16] See the DCSF Vol 1 *Court Orders* (2008) para 3.71.

[17] Including an interim care order: see s 33(11). Similar considerations also apply when the court is considering making, varying or discharging an order made under s 34 itself: s 34(11), as amended by s 8(5) of the Children and Families Act 2014.

[18] In *Re P (Minors) (Contact with Children in Care)* [1993] 2 FLR 156 at 161; cf *L v London Borough of Bromley* [1998] 1 FLR 709 in which Wilson J held that a magistrates' order that contact be at the local authority's discretion could not be interpreted as absolving them of their duty to afford reasonable contact.

[19] [2007] EWHC 393 (Fam) [2008] 1 FLR 1 per Munby J.

[20] DCSF Vol 1 *Court Orders* (2008) at para 3.76.

[21] Care Planning, Placement and Case (Review (England) Regulations 2010 (SI 2010/959), reg 8(2) (England). Contact with Children Regulations 1991 (SI 1991/891) reg 2 (Wales) (which now only applies in Wales).

[22] As they are entitled to do respectively under s 34(2) and (4).

[23] Once an order has been made it can be departed from by agreement: see Departing from a s 34 order by agreement, p 660.

[24] Note, therefore, that unlike when seeking s 8 orders the child does not need leave of the court, nor, consequently, need such an application be heard in the High Court; cf *Re A (Care: Discharge: Application by Child)* [1995] 1 FLR 599, discussed in Ch 17, Discharge of a care order, p 651.

contact with any named person.[25] No doubt in most cases the authority will take the proceedings, but where, for example, the authority are thought to be obstructive, the child may wish to take the initiative. It has been held,[26] however, that the court has no power to force the person named in the order, or, if that person was a minor, the person with whom he or she lived, to have or permit the contact provided for.

It is also open to a person to whom the Act's presumption of reasonable contact applies,[27] and any other person who has obtained leave of the court,[28] to apply for an order about contact at any time if he is dissatisfied with the arrangements made or proposed for contact between the child and himself.[29] The ability of anyone to seek leave means that relatives and former foster parents, for example, may take steps to seek orders.

In deciding whether to grant leave it has been held[30] that the court should take account of the criteria set out in s 10(9),[31] which means[32] that the court should have particular regard at least to:

(a) the nature of the contact being sought;

(b) the connection of the applicant to the child (the more meaningful and important the connection to the child, the greater is the weight to be given to this factor);

(c) any disruption to the child's stability or security; and

(d) the wishes of the parents and local authority, which are important but not determinative.

(d) The court's powers

The court is empowered both on making a care order and subsequently, either upon application or acting upon its own motion,[33] to make such order as it considers appropriate either as to the contact to be allowed[34] or to refuse contact with a named person.[35] In each case it can impose such conditions (for example, to restrict contact to specific periods or places) as are considered appropriate.[36] The wording of these provisions is wide enough to permit the court to make interim orders, including an interim order for no contact.[37] Although not defined, it is thought that 'contact' under s 34 includes visiting, staying or other forms of contact, for example by e-mail, text, skype, telephone or letter.[38] Before making any order under s 34(4) the court must consider any contact arrangements that the authority have made or propose to make and invite the parties to the proceedings to comment on those arrangements.[39]

---

[25] Children Act 1989 s 34(2) and (4).

[26] Per Wilson J in *Re F (Contact: Child in Care)* [1995] 1 FLR 510.

[27] Viz. those persons mentioned in s 34(1).   [28] Section 34(3)(b).   [29] Section 34(3).

[30] *Re M (Care: Contact: Grandmother's Application For Leave)* [1995] 2 FLR 86, CA.

[31] Discussed in Ch 14, The application of s 10(9), p 516.

[32] Per Ward LJ in *Re M,*[1995] 2 FLR 86 at 95–9 but note that Ward LJ's suggestion that the applicant should also have a good arguable case was said to be inappropriate, per Thorpe LJ in *Re J (Leave to Issue Application for Residence Order)* [1993] 1 FLR 114 at [18]–[19], discussed in Ch 14, The application of s 10(9), p 518.

[33] Children Act 1989 s 34(5). For an example of a contact order made (in favour the child's uncle) on the court's own initiative, see *Tower Hamlets London Borough Council v MK and Others* [2012] EWHC 426 (Fam) [2012] 2 FLR 762.   [34] Section 34(2).

[35] Section 34(4). For an example of a short-term total denial of contact with a young mother, see *Re K (Contact)* [2008] EWHC 540 (Fam) [2008] 2 FLR 581.   [36] Section 34(7).

[37] See *West Glamorgan County Council v P* [1992] 2 FLR 369.

[38] See eg *Clarke Hall and Morrison on Children* at 9 [216].

[39] Section 34(11) as amended by s 8(5) of the Children and Families Act 2014.

Wide though the powers are, the court is not entitled to make a contact order with a direction that the matter be brought back before the judge at a later date to enable him 'to keep an eye on the case',[40] nor that a guardian should have contact with the child after the care order,[41] in each case because that was simply an attempt to keep the care order under review. It has also been said that in view of the statutory presumption of reasonable contact there should be no need to make such an order *imposing* it.[42] There is no power under s 34 for courts to prohibit local authorities from permitting contact with children in their care.[43]

In deciding what, if any, order to make the court must apply the general principles set out by s 1, that is, to regard the child's welfare as the paramount consideration, to consider the statutory checklist and to make an order only where it is in the child's interests to do so.[44]

The application of the welfare principle where more than one child is involved can be problematic. In *Birmingham City Council v H (A Minor)*,[45] where both mother and child were in care, the mother (who was herself a 15-year-old child) sought contact with her baby. The House of Lords ruled that, as s 34(4) made it clear that the subject matter of the application is the child in care in respect of whom an order is sought, it was the baby's welfare and not the mother's that was paramount. Lord Slynn also said that[46] if a child in care sought contact with a named person, then that applicant's welfare would still be paramount even if contact was being sought with another child. It seems apparent, however, from the subsequent decision, *Re F (Contact: Child in Care)*,[47] that that analysis depends on the precise nature of the action. In *Re F* a child in care sought contact with her four younger siblings who were not in care. The parents were opposed to such contact and Wilson J held that the application under s 34(2) was misplaced because it could not oblige the parents to permit contact, since the compulsory effect of the sub-section only runs against the local authority.[48] It was accepted that the appropriate action would have been to have sought an order under s 8[49] which, since it concerned the children not in care, was not caught by the embargo against making s 8 orders with respect to child who is in care, under s 9(1).[50]

Notwithstanding this dismissal Wilson J observed[51] that where under s 34(2) an applicant child is seeking contact with other children who are not in care and who are willing to see him, then it is the interests of the applicant child that are paramount. However, if an order is sought under s 8, then it would be the interests of the other children that would be paramount. Where the other children are also in care, some commentators,[52] following the above analysis, have taken the view that it is the children in respect of whom the order

---

[40] *Re S (A Minor) (Care: Contact Order)* [1994] 2 FLR 222, CA.

[41] *Kent County Council v C* [1993] Fam 57.   [42] *Re S*, [1994] 2 FLR 222.

[43] *Re W (Section 34(2) Orders)* [2000] 1 FLR 502, CA.

[44] See *Re A and D (Local Authority: Religious Upbringing)* [2010] EWHC 2503 (Fam) [2011] 1 FLR 615 at [47] per Baker J.

[45] [1994] 2 AC 212, HL discussed also in Ch 12, Child-parents and babies, p 428.

[46] Ibid at 222.   [47] [1995] 1 FLR 510.

[48] Though, note, it is possible to attach a penal notice to a s 34 order so as to enforce it against a local authority (see *Re P-B (Contact: Committal)* [2009] EWCA Civ 143 [2009] 2 FLR 6, 6) and to prevent contact being frustrated by foster parents.

[49] Ie what would now be a child arrangements order naming a person with whom the child is to spend time or otherwise have contact. In fact it emerged during the hearing in *Re F* that none of the children wanted contact and the s 8 application was dismissed by consent.

[50] Section 9(1) is discussed in detail in Ch 14, Children in local authority care, at p 510.

[51] In *Re F (Contact: Child in Care)* [1995] 1 FLR 510 at 514.

[52] See R White, P Carr and N Lowe *Children Act in Practice* (2008, 4th edn) at 8.206.

is sought whose welfare is paramount. Assuming this analysis to be correct[53] it may be questioned whether it is right that the issue of paramountcy should be determined simply by the accident of who brought the action.[54]

Section 34 gives the court wide power to control the future direction of the case and, although the court must always be mindful of what the local authority considers practicable, it is not limited by what the authority thinks is reasonable. As Butler-Sloss LJ put it in *Re B (Minors) (Termination of Contact: Paramount Consideration):*[55]

> The presumption of contact, which has to be for the benefit of the child, has always to be balanced against the long-term welfare of the child and particularly, where he will live in the future. Contact must not be allowed to destabilise or endanger the arrangements for the child and in many cases the plans for the child will be decisive of the contact application . . . *The proposals of the local authority, based on their appreciation of the best interests of the child, must command the greatest respect and consideration from the court, but Parliament has given to the court, and not to the local authority, the duty to decide on contact between the child and those named in section 34(1).* Consequently, the court may have the task of requiring the local authority to justify their long term plans to the extent only that those plans exclude contact between parent and child. (Emphasis added)

Agreeing with this Simon Brown LJ subsequently observed:[56]

> . . . if on a s 34(4) application the judge concludes that the benefits of contact outweigh the disadvantages of disrupting any of the local authority's long term plans which are inconsistent with such contact then . . . he must give effect to it by refusing the local authority's application to terminate this contact.

It has been observed[57] that contact should not be refused under s 34(4) whilst there remains a realistic possibility of rehabilitation of the child with the person in question. At all events, a denial of contact is a draconian order which should not be made lightly.

(e) Variation and discharge

Upon application by the local authority, child or any person named in the order, the court can vary or discharge any previous order made under s 34.[58] However, under s 91(17) where an applicant has been refused contact he may not make another such application

---

[53] Charles J agreed with Wilson J's analysis in *Re S (Contact: Application by Sibling)* [1998] 2 FLR 897 at 908.

[54] See criticism of the *Birmingham* decision by G Douglas 'In Whose Best Interests?' (1994) 110 LQR 379, who argues that ultimately each child's welfare has to be balanced against the other's.

[55] [1993] Fam 301 at 311, CA.

[56] *Re E (A Minor) (Care Order: Contact)* [1994] 1 FLR 146, CA. See also *Berkshire County Council v B* [1997] 1 FLR 171—since the child's welfare was paramount, contact should be ordered if it was in the child's interests, notwithstanding that the long-term plan of the local authority envisaged termination of parental contact; cf *Re D and H (Termination of Contact)* [1997] 1 FLR 841, CA where it was held on the facts to be wrong to phase out contact contrary to the local authority's recommendations.

[57] Per Simon Brown LJ in *Re T (Minors) (Termination of Contact: Discharge of Order)* [1997] 1 All ER 65, CA.

[58] Section 34(9). Although the Act is not specific on the point, the making of a child arrangements order determining with whom the child is to live under s 8 must discharge a s 34 order, since this is dependent upon the existence of a care order, which is itself discharged by virtue of s 91(1).

within six months without leave of the court. Before varying or discharging any order under s 34(4) the court must consider any contact arrangements that the authority have made or propose to make and invite the parties to the proceedings to comment on those arrangements.[59]

In deciding whether or not to discharge a s 34 order the court must treat the child's welfare as its paramount consideration.[60] Upon such an application it is not normally appropriate to reinvestigate whether the original order was made appropriately and the court should be astute to screen out disguised appeals. Instead the court should have two main interlocking considerations in mind, namely, the extent to which circumstances have changed since the making of the order and, in the light of such changes, whether it remains in the child's interests for the original order to stay in place.

(f) Departing from a s 34 order by agreement

Local authorities do not always require court sanction to depart from the terms of a s 34 order, since the Regulations[61] allow this to be done by agreement between the authority and the person in relation to whom the order is made, subject inter alia to the agreement of the child if he is of sufficient understanding. The idea behind this provision is to allow for flexibility and partnership in contact arrangements and to obviate the need to go back to court when all concerned agree to this arrangement.[62] The existence of this remarkable power effectively to override a court order by consent has led one judge to say[63] that in cases where the court takes the view that there should be no contact to a child in care it would normally be better to make no order at all rather than an order authorising refusal under s 34(4). The problem, however, with making no order is that the local authority would then continue to be under an obligation to afford reasonable contact.[64]

C. LOCAL AUTHORITY DUTIES TOWARDS 'LOOKED AFTER CHILDREN'

The 1989 Act places a number of duties on the local authority in respect of children 'looked after' by them.[65] The phrase 'looked after' refers both to children who are provided with accommodation (which is defined as accommodation for a continuous period of more than 24 hours)[66] and to those who are in care as a result of a care order.[67]

---

[59] Section 34(11) as amended by s 8(5) of the Children and Families Act 2014.

[60] *Re T (Minors) (Termination of Contact: Discharge of Order)* [1997] 1 All ER 65, CA. Aliter where an application is made under s 91(17) for leave to apply—see *Re T* at 74, per Simon Brown LJ; cf the similar stance in relation to applications for leave under s 91(14) taken by Wilson J in *Re R (Residence: Contact: Restricting Applications)* [1998] 1 FLR 749, CA.

[61] Viz. reg 8 (4) of the Care Planning, Placement and Case (Review (England) Regulations 2010 (England) and reg 3 of the Contact with Children Regulations 1991 (Wales) (which now only applies in Wales).

[62] See the Department of Health's *Guidance and Regulations*, Vol 3 (2001) para 6.31. Note also *Re W (Section 34(2) Orders)* [2000] 1 FLR 502, CA which establishes that courts cannot prohibit local authorities from agreeing to contact to a child in care.

[63] Ewbank J in *Kent County Council v C* [1993] Fam 57.

[64] See the comment at [1993] Fam Law 134.

[65] See generally HM Government, *Guidance and Regulations*, Vol 2 *Care Planning, Placement and Care Review* (2010), paras 1.20ff and E Isaacs and C Shepherd *Social Work Decision-Making: A Guide for Childcare Lawyers* (2012, 2nd edn) ch 7.

[66] Children Act 1989 s 22(2).   [67] Section 22(1).

In relation to such a child, the authority have a duty to:

(a) safeguard and promote his welfare (including in particular to promote the child's educational achievement)[68] and to make such use of services available for children cared for by their own parents as appears to the authority reasonable in the case of a particular child;[69]

(b) ascertain as far as practicable the wishes and feelings of the child, his parents, any other person who has parental responsibility and any other person the authority consider to be relevant, before making any decision with respect to a child they look after or propose to look after;[70]

(c) give due consideration, having regard to his age and understanding, to such wishes and feelings of the child as the authority have been able to ascertain, to his religious persuasion, racial origin and cultural and linguistic background and to the wishes and feelings of any person as mentioned in (b).[71]

Where an authority is 'looking after' a child, it must provide him with accommodation while he is in their care and must maintain him.[72] However, underscoring the general duty to consider rehabilitation with the family, s 22C[73] provides that, unless to do so would not be consistent with the child's welfare or reasonably practicable, the authority should make arrangements for the child to live with his or her parent, a person who has parental responsibility or, where the child is in care and there was a child arrangements order in force immediately before the care order was made, a person named as a person with whom the child was to live.[74] Where a local authority is unable to place the child with a parent etc, it may, as a matter of priority,[75] place the child with a relative, friend or other person connected with the child or, failing that, a local authority foster parent not connected to the child, in a registered children's home or by such other arrangements as seem appropriate to the authority.[76] At all events, under s 22C(8) the local authority must, so far as is reasonably practicable and consistent with the child's welfare, secure that the accommodation is near his home and that siblings are accommodated together.

With regard to placements with the child's own family, a distinction needs to be made between accommodated children and those in care. In the former case, as there are no formal restrictions on removal, he may simply be returned home, in which case the child ceases to be accommodated.[77]

A key duty owed to looked after children is both to make and review the care plan.[78] As the *Guidance and Regulations* comments:[79]

The responsibility of local authorities in improving outcomes and actively promoting the life chances of children they look after has become known as 'corporate parenting' in recognition of the task must be shared by the whole local authority and partner agencies.

[68] Section 22 (3A), added by the Children Act 2004 s 52.   [69] Section 22(3).
[70] Section 22(4).   [71] Section 22(5).   [72] Sections 22A and 22B, respectively.
[73] Added by the Children and Young Persons Act 2008, s 8.
[74] Section 22C(3), as amended by the Children and Families Act 2014 Sch 2 para 29.
[75] Section 22C(7)(a).   [76] Section 23C(6).
[77] Outside this circumstance, however, it is by no means clear when accommodation ceases, in particular with regard to placements with relatives or friends.
[78] See the Care Planning, Placement and Case Review (England) Regulations 2010 (SI 2010/959), Part 3 (England) and the Review of Children's Cases Regulations 1991 (SI 1991/895) (Wales) (which now only applies in Wales).
[79] HM Government Vol 2 *Care Planning, Placement and Care Review* (2010) para 1.14.

The role of the corporate parent is to act as the best possible parent of each child they look after and to advocate on his/her behalf to secure the best possible outcomes.

The plan for each looked after child must first be kept under review.[80] The authority must ensure that there are regular visits by their representatives to monitor the placement.[81] Furthermore, each responsible authority must appoint an Independent Reviewing Officer to carry out the review.[82] Local authorities also have duties to make provision of advocacy services for children or young persons wishing to make complaints.[83]

There are extensive duties towards children, known as 'former relevant children', leaving care.[84]

D. DISPUTING LOCAL AUTHORITY DECISIONS

1. INTRODUCTION

Although, as the Department of Health's 1991 *Guidance* says,[85] the Children Act 1989 'envisages a high degree of co-operation between parents and authorities in negotiating and agreeing what form of action will best meet a child's needs and promote his welfare', nevertheless the required co-operation will not always be achieved or will break down.[86] In any event, other members of the family may also be in dispute with the local authority: grandparents, for instance, may feel that they should be able to take over the care of the child. Disputes can also arise between foster parents and the authority. The former, for example, may wish to resist the latter's decision to remove a child from their care.

In some cases the objection may be unfounded, while in others the complaint will be of a relatively minor nature. Many such disputes can be and are resolved informally, often by patient counselling by social workers. However, not all disputes will thereby be solved and, while no doubt every effort is made to promote each child's welfare, serious mistakes are sometimes made by local authorities in their management of the child. There is little doubt too that the interests of parents, of the wider family, or of foster parents are, on occasion, unjustly ignored. The question therefore arises to what extent, and to whom, local authorities are or should be accountable for their management of children in care.

Apart from applying for a discharge of a care order under s 39 or challenging a decision about contact under s 34, which we have already discussed,[87] there are a number of other ways in which a local authority decision may be challenged. Use can be made of local authorities' formal complaints or representation procedures. A complaint can also be made to the 'local ombudsman'. In the case of Wales recourse can sometimes be had to

---

[80] See Part 6 of the 2010 Regulations (England); the Review of Children Cases Regulations 1991, reg 7 (Wales) (which now only applies in Wales).

[81] Sections 23ZA and 23ZB, added by the Children and Young Persons Act 2008 s 15. For a critical assessment of the operation and effectiveness of Independent Reviewing Officers see H Jelicic et al *The Role of Independent Reviewing Officers (IROs) in England* (2014) and the *Family Justice Review* (Final Report, 2011) paras 3.112 ff.

[82] See Part 8 of the 2010 Regulations (England); the Review of Children Cases Regulations 1991, reg 2A (Wales).   [83] Children Act 1989 s 24D. The complaints procedure is discussed at pp XXXff.

[84] See s 23C, added by the Children (Leaving Care) Act 2000 s 2 and the Children and Young Persons Act 2008 s 21. See generally E Isaacs and C Shepherd *Social Work Decision-Making: A Guide for Childcare Lawyers* (2012, 2nd edn) ch 13.   [85] Vol 3 *Family Placements* (1991) para 10.3.

[86] See generally E Isaacs, J Weston, L Meyer and C Shepherd *Challenging and Defending Local Authority Care Decisions* (2013).

[87] In Ch 17, Discharge of a care order, p 651 and Variation and discharge, p 659 (contact under s 34).

the Commissioner for Children. Actions can be brought under the High Court's inherent jurisdiction or by seeking leave to apply for a child arrangements order or for judicial review. It may be possible to sue the local authority for negligence or for violating a human right under the European Convention on Human Rights.

We discuss each of these options in turn, but in the ensuing discussion it should be borne in mind that the issue of reviewing local authorities' action is not simple. Although ideally one would wish to safeguard both the child's and the parents' (or other interested adults') interests it must be remembered that, ultimately, priority must be given to the child's welfare. A local authority may, for example, have acted improperly, yet a court may nevertheless be forced to uphold their decision, because it has become in the child's interests to do so. On the other hand, while court scrutiny might be more effective if action had to be sanctioned by the court before it is carried out by the authority, such control might so fetter local authority action that the inevitable consequential delay would be to the general prejudice of children in care.

2. THE COMPLAINTS PROCEDURE

Under s 26(3) of the Children Act 1989 it is mandatory for all local authorities to have a formal representation or complaints procedure[88] in relation to their Part III powers and functions.[89] To ensure that there is an independent element, s 26(4) provides that at least one person who is not a member or officer of the authority concerned must take part in the consideration of the complaint or representation and in any discussions held by the authority about the action to be taken. Equally importantly, under s 26(8) there is an obligation to publicise the complaints procedure.[90] Rules governing the scope and procedure of the complaints scheme are provided by, in England, the Children Act 1989 Representation Procedure (England) Regulations 2006 (SI 2006/1738) (hereafter the 2006 Regulations) and, for Wales, by the Representations Procedure (Children) (Wales) Regulations 2005 (SI 2005/3365) (W. 262) (hereafter 'the 2005 Regulations).

To meet what had been identified as a priority need,[91] s 26A[92] makes provision for advocacy support for children seeking to make representations or complaints. Section 26A(1) imposes a duty on every local authority to make arrangements for the provision of assistance (including assistance by way of representation)[93] for children who make or intend to make representations under s 26 and for care-leavers complaining under s 24D. There is an obligation both to publicise these arrangements and to monitor their compliance with the Regulations.[94]

---

[88] See generally C Oliver, A Knight and M Candappa *Advocacy for looked after children and children in need: achievements and challenges* (2006); C Williams 'The practical operation of the Children Act complaints procedure' [2002] CFLQ 25; C Williams and H Jordan 'Factors relating to publicity surrounding the complaints procedure under the Children Act 1989' [1996] CFLQ 337; C Williams and H Jordan *The Children Act 1989 Complaints Procedure: A Study of Six Local Authority Areas* (1996); and for the background, DHSS *Review of Child Care Law* (1985) paras 220 *et seq*.

[89] Failure to have a procedure or having one that fails to comply with the regulations (set out shortly) can be remedied by invoking the Secretary of State's default powers under s 84; per Auld LJ in *R v London Borough of Barnet, ex p B* [1994] 1 FLR 592 at 598.

[90] As Williams and Jordan 'Factors relating to publicity surrounding the complaints procedure under the Children Act 1989' at 338 observe, a complaints procedure is 'otiose, if those most in need of such a procedure are unaware of its existence and operation'. In fact they were of the view that publicity for such schemes is generally disappointing.

[91] Ie in the response to Department of Health *Listening to People* (2000).

[92] Inserted into the CA 1989 by s 119 of the Adoption and Children Act 2002. Note also the Department of Health's *National Standards for the Provision of Children's Advocacy Services* (2002).

[93] Section 26A(2).   [94] See s 26A(5) and (4) respectively.

(a) Who can complain?

Under s 26(3) complaints may be made by:

(a) a child whom the local authority are looking after or who is not being looked after but is in need. This is intended both to ensure that children are consulted on decisions taken about them and to establish the system of complaints procedures for children the authorities are looking after. It may also assist a child who believes he should be accommodated where the authority are refusing to offer the service;[95]

(b) a parent;[96]

(c) any person (other than a parent) with parental responsibility;

(d) any local authority foster parent; or

(e) such other person as the authority considers has a sufficient interest in the child's welfare to warrant representations being considered by them.

In addition young people can complain if they consider that the local authority has not given them adequate preparation for leaving care or adequate after-care.[97]

Although s 26(3) permits a wide range of people, including foster parents, to use the procedure, those falling into category (e) as listed may only be heard at the local authority's discretion. Nevertheless while an authority may decide who it considers has a sufficient interest in the child's welfare, it would be difficult to deny that professionals in other agencies providing a service to the child would qualify.

(b) What may be complained about?

The statutory complaints procedure originally only catered for complaints about local authority support for families and their children under Part III of the 1989 Act. However, the scope was widened[98] to include Parts IV and V of the 1989 Act as well as adoption and special guardianship services.[99] Complaints may be made in respect of an individual child or about matters affecting a group of children.

(c) Procedure and outcome

The complaints procedure is separately governed by the 2006 Regulations in the case of England and by the 2005 Regulations in the case of Wales. Although their broad thrust is similar, the two Regulations differ in detail and emphasis. However in broad terms, they both provide a two-stage process for handling complaints (which can be made at any time): a relatively informal stage and, if that does not resolve matters, a formal stage before a review panel comprising three independent persons.[100]

Although a panel decision is not strictly binding upon the local authority,[101] as Peter Gibson LJ said in *R v London Borough of Brent, ex p S*,[102] it would be 'an unusual case when a local authority acted otherwise than in accord with the panel's recommendations

---

[95] See also Ward J in *R v Royal Borough of Kingston-upon-Thames, ex p T* [1994] 1 FLR 798 at 812.

[96] Including the unmarried father or second female parent.

[97] Children Act 1989 s 24(D), added by the Children (Leaving Care) Act 2000.

[98] By s 26(3A) and (3B), inserted by the Adoption and Children Act 2002 s 117.

[99] Adoption and special guardianship are discussed in Ch 19.

[100] Regs 18 and 19 of the 2006 Regulations (England). Under the 2005 Regulations, in Wales the independent panel is appointed by the Welsh Assembly.

[101] This is implicit in s 26(7) which requires the authority, having had due regard to the findings, to 'take such steps *as are reasonably practicable*' (emphasis added).   [102] [1994] 1 FLR 203 at 211.

and the independent person's views'. Furthermore, simply to ignore or fail reasonably to consider the recommendations will lay the authority open to judicial review.[103]

Local authorities are required to monitor the operation and effectiveness of the procedure. To this end they are required to keep a record of each complaint received, its outcome and whether there was compliance with the time limits. They must also produce an annual report.[104]

(d) Impact of the complaints procedure

One impact of the complaints procedure has been to reduce the need and indeed the ability successfully to invoke the court's powers under judicial review (discussed later in this chapter). In *R v Birmingham City Council, ex p A*[105] judicial review was sought to challenge a local authority's apparent inability speedily to place a child with special needs with an appropriate specialist foster parent. Sir Stephen Brown P commented that in cases such as those where neither fact nor law was in dispute but instead the ground of complaint was the way the authority was carrying out its duty, the appropriate remedy was a complaint under s 26. It has been similarly held[106] that the complaints procedure would in ordinary circumstances provide a suitable alternative remedy to judicial review to question a local authority decision not to apply for a care order. But in *R v Royal Borough of Kingston-upon-Thames, ex p T*[107] Ward J went further, holding that it was the clear broad legislative purpose that the complaints procedure should be invoked in preference to judicial review in respect of matters within the remit of s 26. He pointed out that the remedy was quicker[108] and more convenient and he specifically rejected both the argument that because the panel was dominated by local authority membership it was likely to be biased, and that it was ineffective. In relation to the first he was satisfied that professional integrity would ensure fairness and in relation to the second he pointed to the availability of judicial review should any recommendation simply be ignored.

The effectiveness of the system is an important issue, particularly as the existence of the complaints system was used as one of the justifications for not imposing a general duty of care in tort upon local authorities.[109] Relatively little is known about the actual use made of the procedure,[110] though there is evidence that children themselves are reluctant to complain because of fear of victimisation or retaliation.[111] Research in other contexts[112] has found that people are generally reluctant to complain, either because they are tired of battling the system or cannot see the point in doing so, the damage already having been done.

---

[103] Per Ward J in *R v Royal Borough of Kingston-upon-Thames, ex p T* [1994] 1 FLR 798 at 814. For examples, of where judicial review was successfully invoked see *Re T (Accommodation by Local Authority)* [1995] 1 FLR 159, discussed in Ch 15, Challenging a refusal to accommodate, p 570, and *R v Avon County Council, ex p M* [1994] 2 FCR 259. Judicial review is discussed further later in this chapter.

[104] Regulation 13 of the 2006 Regulations (England) and Reg 19 of the 2005 Regulations (Wales).

[105] [1997] 2 FLR 841.

[106] Per Scott Baker J in *R v East Sussex County Council, ex p W* [1998] 2 FLR 1082. See also *R (BG) v Medway Council* [2005] EWHC 1932 (Admin) [2006] 1 FLR 663.   [107] [1994] 1 FLR 798.

[108] But note *R (B) v Merton London Borough Council* [2003] EWHC 1689 (Admin) [2003] 2 FLR 888 in which it was held that the lack of immediate relief under the complaints scheme did justify the use of judicial review to determine the age of an asylum seeker who had no means of support in the United Kingdom.

[109] See *X v Bedfordshire County Council* [1995] 2 AC 633, HL (discussed at The Bedfordshire decision, p 673).

[110] Though see C Williams and H Jordan *The Children Act 1989 Complaints Procedure: A Study of Six Local Authority Areas* (1996).

[111] See C Williams and H Jordan 'Factors relating to publicity surrounding the complaints procedure under the Children Act' (1996) 8 CFLQ 337.

[112] See eg M Murch, N Lowe, V Beckford, M Borkowski and A Weaver *Supporting Adoption—Reframing the Approach* (1999) 251–2.

3. APPLYING TO THE 'LOCAL GOVERNMENT OMBUDSMAN'

Another procedure for questioning local authority decisions over children is to complain (in England) to the commissioner for local administration ('the local government ombudsman') or (in Wales) to the Public Services Ombudsman in Wales.[113] Under this procedure a local commissioner may investigate written complaints of 'maladministration'. Before a complaint is made, the local authority must first be given an opportunity to address it[114] but if this approach does not produce a satisfactory result, a complaint can be made. Complaints can be made directly to the commissioner or through a councillor. The commissioner cannot normally investigate complaints concerning proceedings or events that occurred more than 12 months previously.[115] To find the complaint justified the local commissioner must find that the authority has been guilty of 'maladministration'. At the conclusion of his investigation the commissioner issues a report and, if he has found maladministration and injustice, he may recommend an *ex gratia* payment.[116] Although the local authority must consider these recommendations it is not *bound* to follow them and indeed, given the passage of time, may not be able to do so if that would be inconsistent with the child's welfare.

As a general mechanism for scrutinising administrative action, the procedure obviously has its merits, but like judicial review it is of questionable use in the context of local authority decisions in respect of children in care. The main drawbacks are that the central concern is with procedural propriety and not the child's welfare; the commissioner may have no expertise in child matters; the investigation is itself a long process[117] and will probably result in delaying implementation of plans for the child's long-term future;[118] and, even if 'maladministration' is established, there is no power to interfere with the decision taken by the authority.[119]

4. CHILDREN'S COMMISSIONERS

Unlike the Children's Commissioner for England,[120] the Children's Commissioner for Wales[121] has limited powers to examine cases of individual children coming within his jurisdiction. This power, however, is confined to cases where the Commissioner considers

---

[113] See N Lowe and H Rawlings 'The Local Ombudsman and Children in Care' (1979) 42 MLR 447 and 'The Child and the local Ombudsman' (1979) 2 *Adoption and Fostering* 38, and D Oliver 'Challenging local authority decisions in relation to children in care—Part 2' (1989) 1 *Journal of Child Law* 58 at 61.

[114] Local Government Act 1974 s 26(5).   [115] Section 26(4).

[116] Awards of £1,000 have been recommended where a local authority failed to follow a case conference's recommendation, and of £2,000 where children were inappropriately interviewed about allegations of sexual abuse. See respectively Complaint 91/A/1176 and 90/C/2717.

[117] Though in this respect it is to be noted that in *Re A Subpoena (Adoption: Comr for Local Administration)* [1996] 2 FLR 629 it was held that the Commissioner was entitled to subpoena a local authority to produce adoption documents.

[118] In *R v Local Commissioner for the North and East Area of England, ex p Bradford* [1979] QB 287, for example, where the claim of maladministration failed, the children were eventually adopted: see *Re SMH and RAH* [1990] FCR 966n (decided in 1979), though their placement was delayed pending the outcome of the Commission's investigations; cf *Re BA (Wardship and Adoption)* [1985] FLR 1008.

[119] In *Z and others v United Kingdom* [2001] 2 FLR 612, ECtHR, the Government accepted (see [107]) that in the particular circumstances of the case complaining to the Local Government Ombudsman and/or under the complaints procedure was insufficient to satisfy the requirements of Art 13 of the European Convention on Human Rights. See further Suing the local authority for breach of human rights, p 673.

[120] This post was created by Part I of the Children Act 2004, see Ch 13.

[121] The post was created by s 74 of the Care Standards Act 2000 (as amended by the Children's Commissioner for Wales Act 2001), see Ch 13.

that the case raises matters of principle which have a more general application or relevance to the rights or welfare of children than those in the particular case.[122] He must also take into account whether the case has been, or is being, considered by any other person.[123]

5. WARDSHIP AND THE INHERENT JURISDICTION

(a) The position before the Children Act 1989

Before the Children Act 1989,[124] local authorities, encouraged by the courts, frequently turned to wardship as a means of committing children to their care.[125] In stark contrast, although it was accepted that the wardship jurisdiction had not been abrogated by the comprehensive statutory scheme governing local authority care,[126] the courts refused to allow their prerogative jurisdiction to be used as a means of challenging authorities' decisions over children in care. The basic rationale for what became known as the 'Liverpool principle' was that as Parliament had vouchsafed a wide discretion to local authorities over the management of children in care, it was not for the courts to subvert that policy by allowing parents and others a right of challenge through wardship and therefore outside the statutory system. As Lord Wilberforce said in A v Liverpool City Council:[127]

> In my opinion the court has no . . . reviewing power. Parliament has by statute entrusted to the local authority the power and duty to make decisions as to the welfare of children without any reservation of a reviewing power to the court.

In Liverpool itself, the House of Lords refused to interfere with a local authority's decision to restrict a mother's contact with her child in care to a monthly supervised visit limited to one hour at a day nursery.[128]

Following Liverpool, decisions successively barred the use of wardship as a means of challenge from foster parents, natural parents, relatives and unmarried fathers[129] and there was little doubt that the 'Liverpool principle' would equally have applied to any potential applicant, including a 'Gillick competent' child. Not only was it established that the principle applied regardless of the applicant, but it had also been held to apply both in relation to a child in care and where the local authority were actively contemplating taking proceedings.[130] Furthermore, in Re W (A Minor) (Wardship: Jurisdiction)[131] the House of Lords denied the existence of a residual category for intervention even in 'exceptional circumstances', while in Re DM (A Minor) (Wardship: Jurisdiction)[132] the Court of

---

[122] See the Children's Commissioner for Wales Regulations 2001 (SI 2001/2787) (W 237), as amended, reg 5.   [123] Regulation 6.

[124] See generally D Oliver 'Challenging Local Authority Decisions in Relation to Children in Care—Part I' (1988) 1 Journal of Child Law 26.   [125] See Ch 20.

[126] See eg Re M (An Infant) [1961] Ch 328 at 345, CA per Lord Evershed MR; Re B (Infants) [1962] Ch 201 at 223, CA per Pearson LJ; and A v Liverpool City Council [1982] AC 363 at 373, HL per Lord Wilberforce.

[127] [1982] AC 363 at 372.

[128] Under the law as it then stood, local authorities had complete discretion over the amount of contact with a child in care.

[129] See eg Re W (A Minor) (Wardship: Jurisdiction) [1985] AC 791, HL and Re M and H (Minors) (Local Authorities: Parental Rights) [1990] 1 AC 686, HL.

[130] See Re E (Minors) (Wardship: Jurisdiction) [1984] 1 All ER 21, CA; W v Shropshire County Council [1986] 1 FLR 359, CA; and W v Nottingham County Council [1986] 1 FLR 565, CA.

[131] [1985] AC 791, see particularly Lord Scarman at 797.   [132] [1986] 2 FLR 122, CA.

Appeal ruled that, even if a local authority could be shown to have acted improperly, the proper action was judicial review and not wardship.

Effectively, therefore, by the time the Children Act 1989 was implemented wardship could not be used as a means of challenging local authority decisions unless the authority itself chose to submit to the jurisdiction.[133]

(b) The position after the Children Act 1989

Under the Children Act 1989 wardship and local authority care are incompatible in the sense that a child cannot both be in care and a ward of court.[134] Accordingly, it is clear that individuals seeking to challenge a local authority's decision in respect of a child in care cannot attempt to do so by wardship and that consequently there can be no question of the local authority submitting to the jurisdiction. It is, however, possible for a challenge to be mounted under the High Court's inherent jurisdiction (which is discussed in Chapter 20). Although the point has yet to be directly tested, it seems clear that the 'Liverpool principle' will operate in this situation.[135] A fortiori the 'Liverpool' principle' will apply in cases where a wardship application can still properly be made, ie where the child is not subject to a care order. A foster parent looking after a child accommodated by a local authority can still in theory ward a child, but if it is intended to challenge the authority's decision, eg to remove the child, then the 'Liverpool' principle' will surely be applied.[136]

6. SEEKING LEAVE TO APPLY FOR A CHILD ARRANGEMENTS ORDER

In Chapter 17,[137] mention was made of the ability of parents and guardians to apply to be named as a person with whom the child is to live in a child arrangements order as an alternative means of seeking a discharge of a care order. However, it is open to *any* interested party to seek the court's leave to apply for such a child arrangements order, pursuant to s 10 of the Children Act 1989. This possible means of challenging a local authority decision was explored in *Re A (Minors) (Residence Orders: Leave to Apply)*,[138] in which a foster mother sought to challenge a local authority's decision that she should no longer be permitted to foster four children in their care. In the course of an action for judicial review, the applicant applied for leave to apply for what was then a residence order. In refusing leave the Court of Appeal accepted the ability of the court, pursuant to s 9(1), to make the order sought notwithstanding that the child is in care. However, that did not mean that on the application for leave the court should give no weight to the local authority's views. On the contrary, s 10(9)(d)(i) expressly provides that the court is to have particular regard to the authority's plans for the future. Furthermore, given that under s 22(3) it is the authority's duty to safeguard and promote the welfare of any child in its care, it was held that the court should approach the application on the basis that the authority's plans for the child's future were designed for his welfare and that any departure from such plans might well be harmful to the child. In other words the court should, in these circumstances, be slow to grant leave.

---

[133]   See eg *A v B and Hereford and Worcester County Council* [1986] 1 FLR 289.
[134]   Children Act 1989 s 100(2)(c) and s 91(4), discussed in Ch 20.
[135]   This was Balcombe LJ's view in *Re A (Minors) (Residence Orders: Leave to Apply)* [1992] Fam 182, CA, discussed shortly.
[136]   As extended inter alia by *Re E (Minors) (Wardship: Jurisdiction)* [1984] 1 All ER 21.
[137]   At Discharge of a care order, p 651.   [138]   [1992] Fam 182.

7. JUDICIAL REVIEW

(a) Nature of the remedy

Judicial review is the standard administrative law remedy for correcting decisions taken by inferior courts, tribunals and other bodies including local authorities. Applications are made to the Administrative Court. As the Civil Procedure Rules 1998 r 54.1(2)(a) states:

> a 'claim for judicial review' means a claim to review the lawfulness of
> (i) an enactment; or
> (ii) a decision, action or failure to act in relation to the exercise of a public function.

No special rules apply in children cases.[139] The function of the court, as Scott Baker J neatly expressed it, is 'to consider in each case not whether the decision itself is right or fair but whether the manner in which the decision is made is fair'.[140] The child's welfare is not the paramount consideration in judicial review proceedings.[141]

There are the following remedies:

(1) *mandatory orders* (formerly *mandamus*), that is, where a body is ordered to comply with statutory duty, for example, that the local authority provide some specific support service as set out in Part III of Sch 2 to the Children Act,[142] or to set up a complaints procedure that complies with the regulations issued under s 26.[143]

(2) *quashing orders* (formerly *certiorari*), that is, that the original decision be quashed as, for example, a Director of Social Services' decision not to ratify a complaints panel decision that a 17-year-old be accommodated;[144]

(3) *prohibiting orders* (formerly prohibition), that is, restraining a body from acting unlawfully; and

(4) *declarations* that an action or policy is unlawful[145] and/or an *injunction* to prevent an unlawful act taking place or an unlawful policy from continuing.[146]

---

[139] But this is not to say that in judging the reasonableness of a local authority's action in respect of children in their care attention should not be paid to the authority's duty to safeguard the child's interests; cf *R v Harrow London Borough Council, ex p D* [1990] Fam 133, CA, per Butler-Sloss LJ cited at Circumstances in which judicial review has been sought, p 672.

[140] *R v Hereford and Worcester County Council, ex p D* [1992] 1 FLR 448 at 457. See also Munby J's comment in *Re M (Care Proceedings: Judicial Review)* [2003] EWHC 850 (Admin) [2003] 2 FLR 171 at [25] that in judicial review proceedings 'the focus of the court's investigation... is not with the *merits* of the local authority's case but rather with the more limited question of the *legality* of the local authority's decision-making process'.

[141] *R (on the application of O) v London Borough of Hammersmith and Fulham* [2011] EWCA Civ 925 [2012] 1 WLR 1057.

[142] See eg *R (on the Application of S) v London Borough of Wandsworth, London Borough of Hammersmith and Fulham, London Borough of Lambeth* [2001] EWHC Admin 709 [2002] 1 FLR 469 in which Lambeth and Wandsworth were ordered to make an assessment of whether the children concerned were in 'need'.

[143] See *R v London Borough of Barnet, ex p B* [1994] 1 FLR 592, 598 per Auld LJ. The complaints procedure is discussed earlier in this chapter.

[144] *Re T (Accommodation by Local Authority)* [1995] 1 FLR 159. If a quashing order is made the court may remit the matter to the decision-maker and direct it to reconsider the matter, but if it feels there is no purpose in remitting the court can make the decision itself: CPR 1998 r 54.19.

[145] See eg *R (Howard League for Penal Reform) v Secretary of State for the Home Department* [2002] EWHC 2497 (Admin) [2003] 1 FLR 484 and *R v Cornwall County Council, ex p LH* [2000] 1 FLR 236.

[146] When seeking declarations or injunctions it is not *mandatory* to use the judicial review procedure laid down in the CPR 1998 Pt 54, see r 54.3.

It is also possible to include a claim for damages in a claim for judicial review but not to seek damages alone.[147] The court may at any time during the course of judicial review proceedings grant interim relief.[148]

(b) The requirements for judicial review

A prerequisite for a claim for judicial review is that there must be a reviewable 'decision'. Even if there is a reviewable 'decision', to guard against frivolous, vexatious, or merely hopeless actions, applicants must first obtain permission to proceed.[149] Claims must be filed promptly and in any event not later than three months after the grounds to make the claim first arose.[150] Claims must, inter alia, state any remedy (including any interim remedy) being sought, and provide a detailed statement of the grounds for bringing the claim and be accompanied by any written evidence in support.[151]

Leave is not a formality. As Balcombe LJ said in *R v Lancashire County Council, ex p M*,[152] there must be a reasonable prospect of the court coming to the decision that the local authority's conclusion was so unreasonable that no reasonable local authority could ever have come to it. Bearing in mind that as far as individuals are concerned some information will be confidential,[153] having to establish even a prima facie case may be difficult. Yet it is only if the applicant can first negotiate this hurdle that the matter will then be heard. Furthermore, in some cases it is likely to be held that an alternative remedy is preferable. Indeed, as we discussed earlier, where neither fact nor law is in dispute but rather the way the local authority has carried out their duty, it is established[154] that the proper remedy is under the complaints procedure rather than judicial review. Challenges to proposed local authority care plans should generally be made in care proceedings rather than by judicial review.[155] Nevertheless, as a matter of principle, the availability of an alternative remedy does not mean that there cannot be a judicial review.[156]

To substantiate a claim for judicial review, the applicant must be able to bring himself within the so-called *Wednesbury* principle[157] as interpreted by the House of Lords in *Council of Civil Service Unions v Minister for the Civil Service*.[158] According to Lord

---

[147] CPR 1998 r 54.3(2)

[148] CPR 1998 Pt 25. It may also adjourn proceedings, for example to invite the local authority to reconsider its position: *Re S and W (Care Proceedings)* [2007] EWCA Civ 232 [2007] 2 FLR 275

[149] CPR 1998 r 54.4. Applications for permission are generally considered on the papers alone. A claimant does not have the right to have the permission determined at an oral hearing, though there is a right to request that a decision to refuse or limit the grant of permission be reconsidered at an oral hearing: CPR 1998 r 54.12(3) and *Practice Direction—Judicial Review* para 8.4.

[150] CPR 1998 r 54.5. See *Re S (Application for Judicial Review)* [1998] 1 FLR 790, CA where permission was refused, the application being made four months after the expiration of the time limit. See also *R (H) v Essex County Council* [2009] EWCA Civ 1504 [2010] 1 FLR 1781.

[151] CPR 1998 Pts 8.2 and 54.2 and the accompanying *Practice Direction—Judicial Review* paras 5.1, 5.6 and 5.7.   [152] [1992] 1 FLR 109 at 113, CA.

[153] Such as records compiled in relation to foster carers, see the Fostering Services (England) Regulations 2011 (SI 2011/581), reg 32, and Fostering Service (Wales) Regulations 2003 (SI 2003/237) (W. 35), reg 32.

[154] *R v Birmingham City Council, ex p A* [1997] 2 FLR 841, per Stephen Brown P.

[155] See eg *Re M (Care Proceedings: Judicial Review)* [2003] EWHC 850 (Admin) [2003] 2 FLR 171, in which it was sought to challenge a local authority decision to apply for an emergency protection order in respect of a baby as soon as it was born; and *Re C (Adoption: Religious Observance)* [2002] 1 FLR 1119 where a guardian sought to challenge a local authority care plan.

[156] *R v High Peak Magistrates' Court, ex p* [1995] 1 FLR 568, per Cazalet J.

[157] Following *Associated Provincial Picture Houses Ltd v Wednesday Corporation* [1948] 1 KB 223, CA.

[158] [1985] AC 374, HL.

Diplock in that case,[159] there are three main heads under which court intervention may be justified:

'illegality' (where there was an error of law in reaching the relevant decision);

'procedural impropriety' (where the relevant rules have not been complied with); and

'irrationality' (where a decision 'is so outrageous in its defiance of logic or of accepted moral standards that no sensible person who had applied his mind to the question to be decided could have arrived at it').

(c) Circumstances in which judicial review has been sought

In the context of disputing local authority decisions,[160] claimants are commonly parents, grandparents, foster parents, prospective adopters, the children themselves and guardians.[161] Complaints have been made about a variety of decisions: including refusing to accommodate the claimant on the basis that he was an adult;[162] treating the provision of services as if under s 17 rather than s 20;[163] rejecting a recommendation for a specialist residential placement of an accommodated child;[164] a local authority assessment that the imminent release of a man (with whom the mother had had a relationship) convicted of a sexual assault of a 10 year old son of a friend posed no particular risk to three children who now lived with their maternal grandmother;[165] deciding not to place the child at home on trial with the parents;[166] removing a child from foster parents;[167] removing a person from the list of approved adopters;[168] placing a local authority employee on an index of individuals considered unsuitable to work with children;[169] and disclosing to others allegations of child abuse by a named person.[170] Challenges have also been made in respect of local authorities paying related foster carers at a lower rate than non-related foster carers.[171]

---

[159] Ibid at 410.

[160] Of course claims concerning children can be made against bodies other than local authorities, as for example, Cafcass, see *R and Others v Cafcass* [2012] EWCA Civ 853 [2012] 2 FLR 1432 (in which the Official Solicitor unsuccessfully argued that Cafcass had breached its duty by failing promptly to appoint a guardian in care proceedings), the police, see eg *A (A Child) v Chief Constable of Dorset Police* [2010] EWHC 1748 (Admin) [2011] 1 FLR 11 (which concerned the police use of emergency protection measures) and prison authorities, see eg *R (P) v Secretary of State for the Home Department; R (Q) v Secretary of State for the Home Department* [2001] EWCA Civ 1151 [2001] 1 WLR 2002.

[161] For a useful chart of a summary of reported judicial review decisions, see Clarke Hall and Morrison at 11[184].

[162] See *R (A) v Croydon London Borough Council; R (M) v Lambeth London Borough Council* [2009] UKSC 8 [2009] 1 WLR 2557, discussed in Ch 15.

[163] See eg *R (A) v Coventry City Council* [2009] EWHC 34 (Admin) [2009] 1 FLR 1202.

[164] See eg *R (on the application of O) v London Borough of Hammersmith and Fulham* [2011] EWCA Civ 925 [2012] 1 WLR 1057; *R (L) v Merton London Borough Council* [2008] EWHC 1628 (Admin) [2008] 2 FLR 1481; and *Re T (Judicial Review: Local Authority Decisions Concerning Child In Need)* [2003] EWHC 2515 (Admin) [2004] 1 FLR 601.

[165] *R (ET) v Islington Borough Council* [2012] EWHC 3228 (Admin) [2013] 2 FLR 347.

[166] *R v Bedfordshire County Council, ex p C* [1987] 1 FLR 239; cf *R v Hertfordshire County Council, ex p B* [1987] 1 FLR 239 (child removed after being placed at home on trial).

[167] *R (CD) v Isle of Anglesey County Council* [2004] EWHC 1635 (Admin) [2005] 1 FLR 59; *R v Hereford and Worcester County Council, ex p D* [1992] 1 FLR 448 and *R v Lancashire County Council, ex p M* [1992] 1 FLR 109, CA. [168] *R v London Borough of Wandsworth, ex p P* [1989] 1 FLR 387.

[169] *R (M) v London Borough of Bromley* [2002] EWCA Civ 1113 [2002] 2 FLR 802. See also *Re S (Sexual Abuse Allegations: Local Authority Response)* [2001] EWHC Admin 334 [2001] 2 FLR 776.

[170] *R v Devon County Council, ex p L* [1991] 2 FLR 541 and *R v Lewisham London Borough Council, ex p P* [1991] 1 WLR 308.

[171] *R (X) v London Borough of Tower Hamlets* [2013] EWHC 480 (Admin) [2013] 2 FLR 199. See also *R (on the Application of L) and Others v Manchester City Council; R (on the Application of R) v Manchester City Council* [2002] EWHC Admin 707 [2002] 1 FLR 43.

By no means all of the above applications were successful, but of those that were, an important factor was the failure of the local authority to allow the claimant to put his or her side of the case or otherwise to explain their own reasoning. For example, in *R v Devon County Council, ex p O (Adoption)*,[172] which involved the removal of a child placed for adoption with the applicants, judicial review succeeded because the local authority failed to consult or give the claimants an opportunity to be heard. Another striking example is *R v Norfolk County Council, ex p M*,[173] which concerned a plumber working in a house where a teenage girl made allegations that she was sexually abused by him. She had twice previously been the victim of sexual abuse and a few days later made similar allegations against another man. After a case conference (what is now a child protection conference) the plumber's name was entered on (what was then called) the Child Abuse Register as an abuser. His employers were informed and they suspended him pending a full enquiry. The plumber first learned of these allegations through a letter informing him of the decision to place his name on the register. Waite J held that, given the serious consequences of registration for the plumber, the local authority had a duty to act fairly, which they had manifestly failed to do by not giving him an opportunity to meet the allegations.

The *Norfolk* case was exceptional. In *R v Harrow London Borough Council, ex p D*,[174] it was said that the courts should not encourage applications to review what would now be child protection conference decisions or recommendations, because, in Butler-Sloss LJ's words, it was important for those involved in this difficult area to 'be allowed to perform their task without having to look over their shoulder all the time for the possible intervention of the court'. Furthermore, she pointed out that in 'balancing adequate protection for the child and the fairness to an adult, the interest of an adult may have to take second place to the needs of the child'.[175] Notwithstanding these observations, there may still be occasions when judicial review is appropriate. In *R v Cornwall County Council, ex p LH*,[176] for example, an action for judicial review succeeded against the Council in respect of their policy (a) not to permit solicitors to attend child protection case conferences on behalf of parents, other than to read out a prepared statement, and (b) not to provide parents attending such conferences with a copy of the minutes.

Other examples of where judicial review has succeeded include *B v Lewisham Borough Council*[177] in which a local authority fixed, contrary to a sensible interpretation of the Special Guardianship Guidance, special guardianship allowances by reference to adoption rather than to the higher level of fostering allowances and *R (CD) v Isle of Anglesey County Council*[178] in which the local authority's care plan (to terminate a successful foster placement) had been fixed without giving due consideration to the child's consistently

---

[172] [1997] 2 FLR 388. Cf *R v Avon County Council, ex p Crabtree* [1996] 1 FLR 502, CA where the de-registration of an approved foster carer was only made after careful consideration and consultation. Consequently the action failed.

[173] [1989] QB 619. See also *R v Bedfordshire County Council, ex p C*, earlier; *R v Hereford and Worcester City Council, ex p D*, earlier; and *R v London of Wandsworth, ex p P*, earlier.

[174] [1990] Fam 133, CA.

[175] Ibid at 138. See also *R v London Borough of Wandsworth, ex p P*, earlier, at 308 in which Ewbank J said: 'Foster-parents have to accept that their interests may have to be subordinated to the children they care for. Accordingly, provided the rules of fairness are complied with, the decision as to whether there is a risk or not, is one that has to be taken by the local authority. In the ordinary way, provided the rules of natural justice are complied with the foster-parents have no redress.' See also *R v Birmingham City Council, ex p A* [1997] 2 FLR 841.

[176] [2000] 1 FLR 236. As Scott Baker J commented (at 243) what was complained about in this case was not 'the decision of the conference but the manner in which its deliberations were conducted'.

[177] [2008] EWHC 738 (Admin) [2008] 2 FLR 523.

[178] [2004] EWHC 1635 (Admin) [2005] 1 FLR 59.

expressed views and the mother's capability to care for the child who suffered from quadriplegic cerebral palsy.

Although Butler-Sloss LJ's remarks in *R v Harrow London Borough Council, ex p D* specifically concerned what were then case conference decisions and recommendations, her observations about the need to balance considerations have general application.[179] Indeed, it can be said that, given the local authority's duty to safeguard the interests of children, in the absence of procedural irregularity it is hard to impugn a local authority decision. It is certainly not enough to question the wisdom of a decision. The applicant must discharge the heavy onus of showing that no reasonable local authority could have reached the particular decision complained of. In *R (on the application of O) v London Borough of Hammersmith and Fulham*,[180] for instance, in which there was a dispute as to how best to accommodate an autistic 13 year old with complex needs, it was observed that where a local authority chose one way of meeting a child's needs rather than another (52 weeks per year accommodation but with residential care at one school and education at another, rather than at a single school as the parents had argued) that could not be said to justify making a mandatory order (nor did it violate Art 8). In *R v Hertfordshire County Council, ex p B*[181] a mother's action for judicial review failed. In that case a child in care was allowed home on trial with the mother, but after three months was removed on the ground that rehabilitation had failed. A neighbour had asserted that the mother had come home late one night and being drunk lay in the snow for some time with her child running about. In fact it was found that the authority had been concerned with wider considerations, including the child's weight loss, his disruptive behaviour and hyperactivity. In dismissing the application Ewbank J observed that there were many cases where children were allowed home on trial and where the local authority had later to decide that it was not a success. Such a decision was well within the local authority's parental power and was not amenable to judicial review.

8. SUING THE LOCAL AUTHORITY FOR NEGLIGENCE

(a) The *Bedfordshire* decision

At one time, English law set its face against superimposing a common law duty of care on local authorities in relation to performance of their duties to protect children. The leading case was *X (Minors) v Bedfordshire County Council*,[182] which comprised five test cases, two of which concerned the way local authorities had dealt with child abuse. In the *Bedfordshire* case, five children claimed damages for personal injury based either on breach of statutory duty or common law negligence by the local authority. The claims alleged that by failing properly to investigate reports suggesting that the children had been abused, the local authority had failed adequately to protect them. In contrast, in *M v Newham London Borough Council*[183] a child and her mother claimed damages for personal injury against the local authority, area health authority, and a psychiatrist on

---

[179] See also *R v East Sussex County Council, ex p R; R v Devon County Council, ex p L*; and *R v Lewisham London Borough Council, ex p P*.   [180] [2011] EWCA Civ 925 [2012] 1 WLR 1057.

[181] [1987] 1 FLR 239. See also *R (W) v Leicestershire County Council* [2003] EWHC 704 (Admin) [2003] 2 FLR 185; *R v East Sussex County Council, ex p R; R v Devon County Council, ex p L*; and *R v Lewisham London Borough Council, ex p P*.

[182] [1995] 2 AC 633, HL, on which see C Cane 'Suing public authorities in tort' (1996) 112 LQR 13, K Oliphant 'Tort' (1996) 49 *Current Legal Problems* 29 and 31 and R Bailey-Harris and M Harris 'The Immunity of local authorities in child protection functions—Is the door now ajar?' [1998] CFLQ 227.

[183] Dealt with in the same judgment.

the basis of the child wrongfully being taken into care following a mistaken diagnosis identifying the mother's cohabitant as the abuser.

In both instances the House of Lords held that the actions failed, since breach of a statutory duty did not, by itself, give rise to any private law cause of action.

Although *Bedfordshire* did not establish a blanket immunity for any action taken by a local authority in respect of children, it seemed to limit the possibilities of action. However, a number of decisions subsequently widened the scope for actions for negligence. Moreover, the House of Lords' decision was itself later ruled in breach of the European Convention on Human Rights, and as we discuss at the end of this chapter, an alternative to suing a local authority for negligence is to sue for breach of human rights.

(b) The retreat from *Bedfordshire*

The first significant post-*Bedfordshire* change was the House of Lords refusal in *Barrett v Enfield London Borough Council*,[184] to strike out a claim for negligence against the local authority for their alleged catalogue of errors during the 17 years that the claimant had been in their care and which resulted in him leaving care with deep-seated psychological and psychiatric problems. Their Lordships drew a distinction between deciding to take a child into care pursuant to a statutory duty, which, unless it was wholly unreasonable so as not to be a real exercise of the discretion, was not normally justiciable, and looking after a child in care, when it might be easier to establish a breach of duty. However, while their Lordships were not prepared to strike out the claim,[185] the decision by no means indicated that the claim would in fact succeed. Indeed Lord Slynn expressly said that many of the allegations would be difficult to establish and were likely to fail.

Barrett was subsequently applied in *S v Gloucestershire County Council, L v Tower Hamlets London Borough Council*[186] in which claims for negligence were brought against the local authorities by children who alleged that the foster-fathers with whom they had been placed had abused them sexually and as a result they had suffered long-term damage. In each case the foster-fathers had eventually been convicted of sexual offences with children. According to May LJ[187] the relevant law derived from *Barrett* can be summarised as follows:

(a) depending upon the particular facts of the case, a claim in common-law negligence may be available to a person who claims to have been damaged by failings of a local authority which was responsible under statutory powers for his care and upbringing . . .;

(b) the claim will not succeed if the failings alleged comprise actions or decisions by the local authority of a kind which are not justiciable. These may include, but will not necessarily be limited to, policy decisions and decisions about allocating public funds;

(c) the border line between what is justiciable and what is not may in a particular case be unclear. Its demarcation may require a more extensive investigation than is capable of being made from material in traditional pleadings alone;

---

[184] [1995] 2 AC 633.

[185] Their Lordships were mindful of the obligation under Art 6 of the European Convention on Human Rights to allow everyone to have a fair and public hearing and referred expressly to the decision in *Osman v United Kingdom* (1999) 29 EHRR 345, [1999] 1 FLR 193, ECtHR, on which see J Miles 'Human rights and child protection' [2001] CFLQ 431 and C Gearty '*Osman* unravels' (2002) 65 MLR 87.

[186] [2000] 1 FLR 825, CA.   [187] Ibid at 848–849.

(d) there may be circumstances in which it will not be just and reasonable to impose a duty of care of the kind contended for. It may often be necessary to conduct a detailed investigation of the facts to determine this question; and

(e) in considering whether a discretionary decision was negligent, the court will not substitute its view for that of the local authority upon which the state has placed the power to exercise discretion, unless the discretionary decision was plainly wrong. But decisions of, for example, social workers, are capable of being held to have been negligent by analogy with decisions of other professional people. Here again, it may well be necessary to conduct a detailed factual enquiry.

Applying these principles it was held that the allegation that Gloucestershire County Council had failed to deal with the abuse by the foster carer after being informed of it, was actionable. However, in the case of Tower Hamlets there was held to be no real prospect of establishing negligence in their approval of the foster parents nor in their subsequent placement of the child with them and the action was struck out.

In *W v Essex County Council*[188] a foster child, known by the social worker to be an active sexual abuser, sexually abused the birth children of the foster carers. The Court of Appeal held that while the foster parents' claim for negligence against the local authority should be struck out, the children's should not. The majority held that a social worker placing a child with foster parents had a duty of care to the foster parents' children to provide their parents, before and during the placement, with such information about the placed child as a reasonable social worker would provide in all circumstances, and a local authority was vicariously liable for the conduct of its social worker relating to that. Although appeals were lodged on both counts, that relating to the children was not pursued but in relation to the action by the parents, the House of Lords held that that too should not be struck out on the basis that it could not be said that such a claim was unarguable. Indeed in a separate action against Essex County Council, adoptive parents succeeded in obtaining damages in respect of injury, loss and damage sustained during the placement (but not after the adoption) of two siblings, the local authority being liable in negligence for not disclosing the boy's serious behavioural problems, including severe violence on his sister, which required constant adult supervision.[189]

(c) The *East Berkshire* limits

Although in *D v East Berkshire Community Health NHS Trust*[190] Lord Nicholls accepted[191] that the law had moved on since the *Bedfordshire* decision (the Court of Appeal had unequivocally said that that decision did not survive the Human Rights Act 1998),[192] the House of Lords nevertheless restrained the seemingly relentless widening of the duty of care owed by professionals when dealing with a child. In that case the Lords upheld the dismissal of claims by parents that medical professionals had negligently misdiagnosed

---

[188] [1999] Fam 90, CA, reversed in part by House of Lords at [2001] 2 AC 592.

[189] See *A v Essex County Council* [2003] EWCA Civ 1848 [2004] 1 FLR 749, CA upholding the first instance decision, reported as *A and B v Essex County Council* [2002] EWHC 2707 (QB) [2003] 1 FLR 615. If negligence is established, the Court of Appeal in *C v Flintshire County Council* [2001] 2 FLR 33 doubted whether the Judicial Studies Board guidelines on damages for psychiatric harm applied to cases of abuse of children in care by their carers. In *NXS v Camden London Borough Council* [2009] EWHC 1786 (QB) [2010] 1 FLR 100, in which damages of £60,000 were awarded against a local authority for failing in their duty to protect a child from her mother's emotional abuse when they had know of the risk posed by the mother for several years but had done nothing about it.

[190] [2005] UKHL 23 [2005] 2 WLR 993.   [191] Ibid at [82].

[192] [2003] EWCA Civ 1151 [2003] 2 FLR 1166 at [83]–[85] per Lord Phillips MR.

child abuse. In so ruling, the Lords upheld the Court of Appeal's ruling that a distinction had to be made between the children's position and the parents' position. While in the former there can now be said to be a duty of care towards the child in relation to the investigation of suspected child abuse and the institution and pursuit of care proceedings, the same cannot be said of the parents. All that is owed to the parent is that clinical and other investigations must be conducted in good faith.[193]

Since *East Berkshire* there have been attempts to argue that a local authority's common law duty of care should extend to parents. In *Lawrence v Pembrokeshire County Council*[194] the argument principally rested upon human rights considerations. It was submitted that 'the advent of Art 8 to our law' since the facts giving rise to the House of Lords decision called 'for an evolutionary change in our law of negligence' inter alia in recognition of the Strasbourg jurisprudence that duties of care in cases of suspected child abuse may be owed both to children and to parents suspected of abusing them. The Court of Appeal rejected the human rights argument, pointing out that Art 8(2) requires the public body interfering with family life to justify its conduct. Put in terms of a common duty of care, it would mean that a local authority would have to prove, by reference to their concern for the child's welfare that they were not in breach. Such a development, it was said, would amount to a plain distortion of the common law action in negligence. In any event the argument overlooked the whole point of the *East Berkshire* solution, which was to forestall by robust and timely intervention, if at all possible, the greater possible harm when a local authority suspected parental abuse of children in the context of family life. In the court's view, the 1998 Act did not undermine or weaken as a matter of public policy the primary need to protect children from abuse, or the risk of abuse from inter alia parents. In other words, the reasoning in *East Berkshire* was entirely compatible with human rights. In any event, the absence of a duty of care does not preclude an action under the Human Rights Act (discussed at the end of this chapter).

A further challenge to *East Berkshire* was rejected in *B v Reading Borough Council and Another*.[195] There, it was contended that the majority's reasoning in the House of Lords case was intended to be confined to cases of vicarious responsibility for breach of duty on the part of the doctor or social worker. In other words it did not apply to direct liability. In the Court of Appeal's view the House of Lords' reasoning applied both to vicarious and direct liability and there was no room to distinguish the two.

In stark contrast to the decisions just discussed, in *Merthyr Tydfil Borough Council v C* it was held that *East Berkshire* 'did not lay down any general principle that, where an authority owe a duty of care to a child (even where there is a suspicion that that child has been abused), it cannot as a matter of law at the same time owe a duty of care to parents of that child.'[196] In that case the court refused to strike out a mother's claim against the local authority in respect of psychiatric symptoms suffered when her children had been sexually abused by her neighbour's child, about whom the local authority had taken no action, notwithstanding that the mother had reported the abuse to the authority. Whether this decision will prove to be a catalyst for a further re-think remains to be seen.

---

[193] See Lord Nicholls at [2005] UKHL 23 [2005] 2 WLR 993 at [90]. Lord Bingham dissented. This ruling was followed in *D v Bury Metropolitan Borough Council* [2006] EWCA Civ 1 [2006] 1 WLR 917, in which it was held that the local authority did not owe a duty of care to the parents of a child who was the subject of a child abuse investigation.   [194] [2007] EWCA Civ 446 [2007] 1 WLR 2991.

[195] [2007] EWCA Civ 1313 [2008] 1 FLR 797.

[196] [2010] EWHC 62 (QB) [2010] 1 FLR 1640 at [29], per Hickinbottom J.

9. SUING THE LOCAL AUTHORITY FOR BREACH OF HUMAN RIGHTS

A local authority decision can be challenged as being in breach of the European Convention on Human Rights. To succeed, the applicant must show that his Convention right(s) have been violated, the most relevant of which are, in this context Art 8, under which there is 'the right to respect for . . . private and family life' and Art 6, under which there is a right to determine one's civil rights and obligations in a fair trial.

(a) Taking the case to the European Court of Human Rights

Until the implementation of the Human Rights Act 1998 the only way of mounting a direct action was to take the case to the European Court of Human Rights at Strasbourg, which meant exhausting domestic remedies first. Notwithstanding this impediment there were a number of successful challenges, for example, in respect of the former inability of parents to question local authority decisions concerning contact with children in care[197] and an authority's refusal to give access to the case records of a child in their care.[198] More recently the four children denied relief by the House of Lords[199] in the *Bedfordshire* case and both the mother and child involved in the *Newham* decision, subsequently took their claims before the European Court of Human Rights. In both cases, respectively reported as *Z v United Kingdom*[200] and *TP and KM v United Kingdom*,[201] the claim that the striking out of the negligence claims by the House of Lords amounted to a breach of Art 6 of the Convention was rejected on the basis that while that Article generally safeguards a right of access to the courts in respect of complaints of unlawful interference with civil rights, it does not guarantee a particular content of these civil rights or obligations. In other words, States can properly restrict those rights provided they do so for legitimate reasons and 'there is a reasonable relationship of proportionality between the means employed and the aim sought to be achieved'. In the Court's view the UK had legitimately restricted the application of negligence. Nevertheless despite this ruling the Court found other reasons for holding the UK to be in breach of the Convention in each of the two cases.

In *Z v United Kingdom* the European Court upheld the children's claim that there had been a breach of Art 3. The local authority were found to be aware of the appalling treatment and neglect suffered over a period of years by the applicants at the hands of their parents (the UK Government did not contest the Commission's finding that the treatment suffered by the children had reached the level of severity prohibited by Art 3, ie that it amounted to inhuman and degrading treatment) but had failed, despite the powers available to them, to take effective measures to bring it to an end. Accordingly, the State too had failed in its positive obligation under Art 3 to provide the applicants with adequate protection against inhuman and degrading treatment. The Court further held that notwithstanding the propriety of striking out the negligence claim, the absence of an effective remedy for the breach itself amounted to a breach of Art 13 (under which everyone should have an effective remedy for a violation of a Convention right). The court awarded £32,000 compensation to each applicant.

Since Art 3 was found to have been broken the Court in *Z* found it unnecessary to consider whether Art 8 had also been breached in that case. In *TP and KM v United Kingdom*,

---

[197] See eg *R v United Kingdom* [1988] 2 FLR 445, ECtHR and *O v UK* (1987) 10 EHRR 82, ECtHR.

[198] *Gaskin v United Kingdom* (1990) 12 EHRR 36, ECtHR.

[199] [1995] 2 AC 633, discussed at The Bedfordshire decision p 673.

[200] [2001] 2 FLR 612, ECtHR, on which see the excellent analysis by R Bailey-Harris [2001] 2 FLR 549, ECtHR.   [201] [2001] 2 FLR 549, ECtHR.

however, the Court upheld the mother's and daughter's complaint that because the child had unjustifiably been taken into care and separated from her mother, both claimants' Art 8 rights had been breached. What constituted the violation in the Court's view was the local authority's failure to disclosure to the mother a video of the child's disclosure interview which in turn deprived the mother of an effective opportunity to deal with allegations that the child could not be safely returned to her. As in Z the absence of an effective domestic remedy was found to be a breach of Art 13 and each applicant was awarded £10,000.

In *MAK and RK v United Kingdom*[202] a father took his daughter to hospital in respect of marks on her legs. Unknown to him the girl had hurt herself in the genital area while riding her bicycle. The girl was admitted for further examination and, contrary to the father's request that there be no further examination without her mother's consent, the girl was subjected to further tests and photographs. When the mother arrived at the hospital she was told that her daughter had been sexually abused. The hospital prevented the father from seeing his daughter. Subsequently, the girl was diagnosed with a rare skin condition and discharged from hospital. Notwithstanding a NHS Independent Review Panel's conclusion that the hospital had acted improperly by not consulting a dermatologist as a matter of urgency, the father's negligence claims (but not the daughter's) were struck out. The European Court of Human Rights ruled that while there had been sufficient reasons for the authorities to suspect child abuse when the girl was first admitted to hospital, the delay in consulting a dermatologist extended the interference with both the father's and the daughter's Art 8 rights and was not proportionate to the legitimate aim of protecting the girl. The girl's Art 8 rights were also found to be violated by the medical examination of her without her parents' consent. The father's Art 13 rights were also found to be violated since at the time (that is, before the implementation of the Human Rights Act 1998) he had no enforceable domestic remedy. The father was awarded €2,000 damages and the girl €4,500.

Following the implementation of the Human Rights Act 1998 such challenges have first to be made domestically, though if they fail it is still possible to take the case to Strasbourg.[203] It remains to discuss the domestic remedy.

(b) Actions under ss 7 and 8 of the Human Rights Act 1998

Section 7 of the Human Rights Act 1998 enables victims to bring proceedings against public authorities (which includes both local authorities and the courts)[204] in respect of acts claimed to be incompatible with a Convention right and if successful, s 8 empowers the court to grant 'such relief or remedy, or make such order, within its powers as it considers just and appropriate'. These latter powers include making declarations that a local authority has acted incompatibly with the claimant's Convention rights,[205] restraining a local authority from taking a particular course of action,[206] and awarding damages. As Lord Nicholls observed in *Re S (Minors) (Care Order: Implementation of Care Plan); Re W (Minors) (Care Order: Adequacy of Care Plan)*,[207] '[t]he object of these sections is

---

[202] [2010] 2 FLR 451, ECtHR.

[203] For guidance on how to bring such actions see L Clements, N Mole and A Simmons *European Human Rights—Taking a Case under the Convention* (1999, 2nd edn).   [204] See s 6(3).

[205] See eg *A and S v Lancashire County Council* [2012] EWHC 1689 (Fam) [2013] 2 FLR 803.

[206] See eg *Re H (Care Plan: Human Rights)* [2011] EWCA Civ 1009 [2012] 1 FLR 191, local authority prevented from separating a mother and child until the case could return to court.

[207] [2002] UKHL 10 [2002] 2 AC 291 at [61]. As Lord Nicholls said, unlike Art 13, which makes it a 'right' to have an effective remedy, ss 7 and 8 simply provide a remedy for enforcing a Convention right. Note: the United Kingdom has *not* incorporated Art 13 into domestic law.

to provide in English law the very remedy Art 13 declares is the entitlement of everyone whose rights are violated.'

There are important limits on the ability to invoke ss 7 and 8. First, the claimant has to show that he or she is a 'victim', that is, a person who is directly affected by the act or omission.[208] It is therefore insufficient to be a secondary victim, which would have meant, for example, that the foster carers in *W v Essex County Council* would have had no action.[209] Secondly, the action must be brought within one year of the act complained of, although claims after that can be admitted at the court's discretion.[210] Thirdly, there must be no other appropriate remedy. Indeed, in *Re S (Minors) (Care Order: Implementation of Care Plan), Re W (Minors) (Care Order: Adequacy of Care Plan)*[211] Lord Nicholls considered actions generally under s 7 to be a 'longstop remedy'. He commented: 'One would not expect proceedings to be launched under s 7 until any other appropriate remedial routes have first been explored'. His Lordship did not explain why s 7 actions should be of 'last resort', but it has been said[212] that the judges should be 'vigilant to guard against the misuse of litigation, and opportunity for mischief-making, which the Human Rights Act sometimes allows.' It would be an abuse of process, for example, to deploy arguments under the 1998 Act that have already been considered and rejected in previous litigation.

So far as the quantum of damages is concerned, s 8(4) of the 1998 Act directs the court to 'take into account the principles applied by the European Court of Human Rights in relation to the award of compensation under Art 41 of the Convention'. According to Lord Woolf CJ in *Anufrijeva v Southwark London Borough Council*[213] the critical message is that the remedy has to be 'just and appropriate', the approach being an equitable one. This also means that establishing a breach does not *entitle* the claimant to damages.[214]

There have not been many actions under ss 7 and 8 but one example is *Re M (Care: Challenging Decisions By Local Authority)*[215] in which, following a review of their care plan for a child in their care, the local authority finally ruled out any further prospect of the child returning to live with her mother or of ever going to live with her father. In reaching this decision, however, the authority was held to have acted unfairly and therefore in breach of Art 8 by not involving the parents to a degree sufficient to provide their interests with the requisite protection. Exercising his powers under s 8 of the 1998 Act upon an application by the parents under s 7, Holman J set the local authority decision aside. He also gave directions for a full hearing of the review issues and of applications for the discharge of the care orders. Holman J's decision was specifically endorsed by Lord Nicholls in *Re S (Minors) (Care Order: Implementation of Care Plan)*.[216] At the same time his Lordship emphasised that wide though the powers are under s 8 they are nevertheless confined to acts or proposed acts which the court finds are or would be unlawful. The Act does not confer a power to give relief in respect of acts by public authorities who have not and are not proposing to act in breach of a Convention right.

---

[208] Section 7(7) applying Art 34 of ECHR.

[209] Cf *A and B v United Kingdom* [1998] 1 EHRLR 82 in which the father of a son who was beaten by his stepfather was not considered to be a 'victim'.   [210] Section 7(5).

[211] [2002] UKHL 10 [2002] 2 AC 291 at [62].

[212] Per Baker J in *Re A and D (Local Authority: Religious Upbringing)* [2010] EWHC 2503 (Fam) [2011] 1 FLR 615 at [59].   [213] [2003] EWCA Civ 1406 [2004] QB 124

[214] See also *Re C (Breach of Human Rights: Damages)* [2007] EWCA Civ 2 [2007] 1 FLR 1957.

[215] [2001] 2 FLR 1300. Cf *R (TG) v Lambeth London Borough Council (Shelter Intervening)* [2011] EWCA Civ 26 [2011] 2 FLR 1024 where damages were refused notwithstanding the decision that the claimant should have been accommodated by the local authority and declaring him to be a 'former relevant child' so as to be entitled to support on leaving care (discussed in Ch 15, The duty to accommodate, p 564).

[216] [2002] UKHL 10 [2002] 2 AC 291 at [46].

In *Re C (Breach of Human Rights: Damages)*[217] the claimant established a breach of her Art 8 rights inasmuch as although the decision was taken in her absence and the subsequent removal of her baby was lawful[218] the local authority were in breach for deciding, at the removal meeting, to abandon the care plan, namely, that the mother was to have six months to demonstrate that she had the capacity to parent her child, and which was the basis upon which the care order was made.[219] However, the Court of Appeal considered the breach to have been purely procedural and at the low end of the spectrum of seriousness and upheld the decision of Holman J not to award damages. There was no evidence that her exclusion from the meeting was the cause of any additional injury and in any event the local authority had mitigated the breach by going to considerable lengths to keep her lawyer informed.

E. SOME CONCLUDING REMARKS

The issue of how best to look after children following their removal (whether voluntarily or compulsorily) from their parents is as important as it is difficult. One key question from the outset is what the local authority plan is for the child. Indeed, as we discussed in Chapter 17, local authorities are required to prepare a care plan whenever they are seeking a care order. In many cases the child's removal will be intended to be temporary in which case it will be important for the authority to work towards rehabilitation with the family as soon as possible and consistent with the child's welfare in any particular case. In part this is underlined by s 34 of the 1989 Act which, as we discussed at the beginning of this chapter, provides that there be reasonable contact between a child in care and his or her family subject only to a court order or clear agreement to the contrary. Human rights considerations dictate that a child's permanent removal from his or her family requires special justification particularly where the plan is for the child to be adopted. We discuss this issue further in Chapter 19.

A second issue is how to ensure that local authorities offer the best possible care to those children who are being looked after. Of course law can only do so much. Nevertheless considerable legislative effort has been invested in re-casting local authority duties over looked-after children not least with regard to their educational attainment and towards children leaving care.

Despite these legislative developments there is, as the *Family Justice Review* put it,[220] 'an undercurrent of deep scepticism about the ability of local authorities to deliver adequate care for children.' But while it cannot be denied that local authorities do sometimes fail in their responsibilities in providing and planning care for children, there is, again in the words of the *Review*,[221] 'a tendency to overlook the successes of the care system'. The *Review* pointed to research[222] which showed that the majority of maltreated or neglected

---

[217] [2007] EWCA Civ 2 [2007] 1 FLR 1957.

[218] The mother had made threats of serious harm to others and possibly towards herself and the baby.

[219] Originally there had been a concurrent care plan giving the mother six months to demonstrate her parenting capacity but at the same time preparatory steps towards adoption were taken if removal was necessary. The plan recorded that if the baby was removed the mother would be kept fully informed.

[220] Final Report (2011) para 3.21.   [221] At para 3.24.

[222] Eg J Wade, N Biehal, N Ferally and I Sinclair *Maltreated Children in the looked after system: a comparison of the outcomes for those who go home and those who do not* (DfE, 2010) and E Farmer and E Lutman *Case management and outcomes for neglected children returned to their parents: a five year follow-up study* (DSF, 2010).

children who stay in care or who are adopted do better in terms of well-being and stability than those who remain at home. The deep concern of the *Review*, however, was that the relationship between local authorities and the courts could, at times, verge on the dysfunctional[223] based on mutual distrust. Yet, as the *Review* put it[224] 'it cannot be right to allow the legal system to function on a starting assumption that local authorities are incompetent.'

Whether the *Review*'s concerns were exaggerated can be debated, but what cannot be denied is that it is important for the courts not to encroach upon the role of the local authorities in looking after children. That said, however, it is also important that there are mechanisms by which local authority decisions can be challenged. As a substantial part of this chapter shows, there is indeed a variety of mechanisms, both informal and formal, by which local authority decisions can be challenged but the essential characteristic of these procedures is that they are designed to provide a remedy only where the local authority can be shown to have acted wrongly rather than unwisely. In this way it is sought allow local authorities to do their job without undue interference yet to provide protection where they have failed to discharge their obligations.

[223] See para 3.47.

[224] See para 3.27. Consequent upon the *Review*'s concern that the respective responsibilities of courts and local authorities be restored, it recommended that courts should focus only on the core issues of whether the child should live with parents and not with all aspects of the care plan, see the discussion in Ch 17, Reviewing the care plan—the current position, p 642. It also recommended that there be a dialogue both nationally and locally between the judiciary and local authorities.

19

ADOPTION AND SPECIAL GUARDIANSHIP

A. INTRODUCTION

1. THE NATURE OF ADOPTION AND BACKGROUND TO THE LEGISLATION

In English law adoption[1] refers to the process by which a child's legal parentage is entirely and irrevocably transferred from one set of adults, usually the birth parents, and vested in other adults, namely the adoptive parents.[2] As the Houghton Committee's report[3] put it, adoption involves: 'the complete severance of the legal relationship between parents and child and the establishment of a new one between the child and the adoptive parent'. Apart from parental orders under s 54 of the Human Fertilisation and Embryology Act 2008[4] adoption is the only child-related order under English law that lasts throughout adulthood (an adoption is truly for life) and it is the only means by which parents can lose their parental responsibility for their child whilst a minor.

Adoption can only be effected through a court process, and the jurisdiction is entirely statutory. This is because at common law parental rights and duties were held to be inalienable.[5] Hence, no change of status comparable to the *adoptio* or *adrogatio* of Roman law could be recognised. The absence of such a mechanism generated considerable dissatisfaction both from couples who were childless and anxious to bring up another's child as their own, but who hesitated to do so because of the lack of legal safeguards, and from those who had effected a de facto adoption but who

---

[1] For general reference see C Bridge and H Swindells *Adoption The Modern Law* (2003) and its sister work H Swindells and C Heaton *Adoption The Modern Procedure* (2006).

[2] In lay terms 'adoption' can have a wider meaning. For example, it is sometimes said that a person, particularly a stranger in blood, who looks after a child in the event of parental death or abandonment, has 'adopted' him. This relationship is described as foster parenthood in this book, and its legal consequences are referred to in Ch 8, Distinguishing guardians from private foster parents, p 294 and in Ch 14, Persons entitled to apply with leave, p 515. For the meaning of 'adoption' for the purposes of the Immigration Rules see *R v Immigration Appeal Tribunal, ex p Tohur Ali* [1988] 2 FLR 523, CA. Unlike French law, for example, which makes provision for two types of adoption, ie 'full adoption' which involves the transfer of parentage, and 'simple adoption' which does not break all links with the birth family, English law has but the one form.

[3] Cmnd 5107, 1972, at para 14. See also *Review of Adoption Law*, 'The Nature and Effect of Adoption' (No 1, 1990) at para 2, which describes adoption as the process by which the legal relationship between a child and his or her birth parents is severed and an analogous relationship between the child and the adoptive parents is established.   [4] Discussed in Ch 8.

[5] *Vansittart v Vansittart* (1858) 2 De G & J 249; *Walrond v Walrond* (1858) John 18; *Humphrys v Polak* [1901] 2 KB 385, CA; and *Brooks v Blount* [1923] 1 KB 257.

felt vulnerable to the very real risk of the parents later turning up and taking the child back.[6]

Although there were a variety of factors[7] that contributed to the increased pressures for reform, the main catalyst was the substantial increase in the number of orphans following the First World War, which in turn led to a large increase in de facto adoptions. The resulting demand for reform led to the passing of the Adoption of Children Act 1926.[8]

The 1926 Act was extensively amended in the light of subsequent experience and criticisms,[9] and all earlier legislation was repealed and consolidated by the Adoption Act 1958.[10] Further dissatisfaction with various aspects of the law and procedure led to the appointment of a Departmental Committee, the 'Houghton Committee', whose report was published in 1972.[11] Most of their recommendations (some of them in modified form) were accepted and incorporated into the Children Act 1975 which was eventually consolidated by the Adoption Act 1976.

Adoption was the one area of child law not to be reviewed during the 1980s. However, after the enactment of the Children Act 1989[12] a full scale review of adoption law was undertaken. This review,[13] eventually led to publication in 1996 of a Government White Paper, *Adoption—A Service for Children* which included a proposed 'Adoption Bill—A Consultative Document'.[14] Apart from the passing of the Adoption (Intercountry Aspects) Act 1999 which paved the way for the United Kingdom's ratification in 2003 of the 1993 Hague Convention on Intercountry Adoption,[15] no action was taken on the 1996 'Bill'. However, a new initiative was launched in 2000 to review in particular the adoption of children being 'looked after' by local authorities.[16] This led to the publication of the Prime Minister's Review of Adoption[17] and of another Government White Paper, *Adoption: a new approach*.[18] That in turn led to the Adoption and Children Act 2002. The 2002 Act was amended by the Children and Families Act 2014 giving effect to proposals made by the Department for Education in their papers *An Action Plan for Adoption:*

---

[6] The Report of the Committee on Child Adoption ('The Hopkinson Report') (1921) Cmnd 1254, para 13 commented that it was not unknown for parents who had previously rejected the child to reclaim him once he had reached the age when he could work and earn wages.

[7] See S Cretney *Family Law in the Twentieth Century* (2003) ch 17. See also N Lowe 'English Adoption Law: Past, Present and Future' in S Katz, J Eekelaar and M Maclean (eds) *Cross Currents—Family Law and Policy in the US and England* (2000) 307.

[8] Passed following the 'Hopkinson Report' and two Reports (the 'Tomlin Reports') of the Child Adoption Committee, Cmnd 2401 and 2469 (1925).

[9] Following eg the Horsburgh Committee's Report on Adoption Societies and Agencies Cmd 5499 (1937), by the Adoption of Children (Regulation) Act 1939 and by the Adoption of Children Act 1949 which for the first time treated the child as that of the adopters for the purpose of inheritance.

[10] Which was based on the Hurst Committee's Report on the Adoption of Children Cmd 9248 (1954).

[11] Cmnd 5107. In fact after Sir William Houghton's death the chair was taken by Judge Stockdale.

[12] Sch 10 to which, amended the 1976 Act inter alia to bring adoption into line with the changes of concepts, terminology and philosophy introduced by the 1989 Act.

[13] This review was conducted by an Inter-Departmental Committee under the aegis of the Department of Health. It produced four Discussion Papers (*The Nature and Effect of Adoption* (No 1, 1990), *Agreement and Freeing* (No 2, 1991), *The Adoption Process* (No 3, 1991) and *Intercountry Adoption* (No 4, 1992)) and three Background Papers ((*International Perspectives* (No 1, 1990), *Review of Research Relating to Adoption* (No 2, 1990) and *Intercountry Adoption* (No 3, 1992)), and culminated in the publication of 'Adoption Law Review: Consultation Document' in 1992. Following this document a Government White Paper 'Adoption—the Future' Cm 2288 was published in 1993. Separate consultation papers 'Placement for Adoption' and 'The Future of Adoption Panels' were published in 1994.

[14] Published by the Department of Health and Welsh Office.   [15] Discussed in Ch 26.

[16] Ie children accommodated by local authorities or subject to care orders. See Ch 14.

[17] A Performance and Innovation Unit Report (2000).   [18] Cm 5017 (2000).

Tackling Delay[19] and *Further Action on Adoption*[20] to speed up the adoption process, to give prospective adopters a more active role in identifying possible matches with children, to improve adoption support by placing new duties on local authorities to provide personal budgets, and to make changes to contact arrangements between birth parents and adopted children with the aim of reducing the disruption that inappropriate contact can cause to adoptive placements.[21]

2. A COMPARISON OF ADOPTION WITH OTHER LEGAL RELATIONSHIPS AND ORDERS

As already said, an adoption order completely severs the legal relationship between the child and his birth parents and vests full parental responsibility exclusively in the adopters.[22] Consequently for all legal purposes, the adopters step into the shoes of the child's birth parents: by 'parents', in other words, is now meant not the child's birth parents, but his adoptive parents.[23]

An adoption order is distinguishable both from a child arrangements order dealing with the child's living arrangements under s 8 of the Children Act 1989 and a special guardianship order under s 14A because it severs the legal ties between the child and his birth parent, whereas the latter orders do not. Furthermore, whereas an adoption order is permanent (ie the child remains a member of the adoptive family even after he attains his majority) and is not variable,[24] the latter can subsequently be varied and, in any event, cease to have effect once the child reaches the age of 18.

3. ADOPTION AND HUMAN RIGHTS

In broad terms adoption raises two human rights issues: the extent, if any, of a right to adopt and the extent to which the granting of adoptions can be regarded as a justified interference with the right to respect for private and family life conferred by Art 8.

With regard to the first issue it is established that the Convention does not guarantee the right to adopt as such. It was held in *Fretté v France*[25] that because the right to respect for family life presupposes the existence of a family and does not safeguard the mere desire to found a family,[26] the denial of an application by a single homosexual man of authorisation to adopt, did not in itself violate any Convention right. However, where national law gives a right to apply to adopt it is incumbent upon the authorities not to discriminate against an applicant on grounds inter alia of sexual orientation, unless such discrimination can be justified. In *Fretté* it was held that, given the lack of uniformity among Contracting States regarding the acceptability of adoption by homosexuals, and because the national authorities were legitimately and reasonably entitled to consider that the right to adopt was limited by the interests of children eligible to be adopted, the decision to deny the applicant authorisation to adopt on the basis of his homosexuality, fell within the State's margin of appreciation.[27] *Fretté* may be contrasted with *EB v France*[28] in

---

[19] DfE, 2012.   [20] DfE, 2013.   [21] See the Explanatory Notes to Part 1 of the 2014 Act.

[22] See the Adoption and Children Act 2002 s 46.

[23] The effects of an adoption order are discussed more fully at The effects of an adoption, pp 722ff.

[24] But for a limited power to set an adoption order aside, see Setting adoption aside, p 723.

[25] [2003] 2 FLR 9 at [32], ECtHR relying inter alia upon *X v Belgium and Netherlands* (1975) D & R 75.

[26] See *Marckx v Belgium* (1979–80) 2 EHRR 330, ECtHR.

[27] But note the Court did find a breach of Art 6 on the facts.

[28] [2008] 1 FLR 850, ECtHR (Grand Chamber), on which, see I Curry-Sumner '*EB v France* – a missed opportunity?' [2009] CFLQ 356. Cf *Gas and Dubois v France* (App No 25951/07, 15 March 2012) in which the

which a woman living in a stable relationship with another woman sought authorisation to adopt a child.[29] Having failed to obtain the necessary authorisation from the French authorities, she argued before the European Court of Human Rights, that because the decision had been based on her sexual orientation she had been discriminated against contrary to Art 14 taken in conjunction with Art 8. She succeeded. The Grand Chamber ruled that although Art 8 neither guarantees the right to found a family nor the right to adopt, the applicant's Art 8 rights were engaged since such rights encompassed the right to establish and develop relationships with other human beings. Further, since French law permitted adoption by a single person, to deny the applicant the right to seek adoption because of her sexual orientation amounted to discrimination and thus violated Art 14 taken in conjunction with Art 8.

The human rights aspect of granting adoption orders has assumed great prominence in English law following, first, the Supreme Court decision, *Re B (A Child) (Care Proceedings: Threshold Criteria)*,[30] but which was primarily concerned with the granting of a care order, and the Court of Appeal decision, *Re B-S (Children) (Adoption Order: Leave to Oppose)*,[31] which was concerned with giving parents leave to oppose the making of an adoption order. But even before these decisions the human rights position had been well explained by Hale LJ in *Re B (Adoption By One Natural Parent to Exclusion Of Other)*.[32] As she said:

> an adoption order is undoubtedly an interference by a public authority, in the shape of the court that makes it, with the exercise of the right to respect for family life, whether by the child . . . or by anyone else with whom [the child] enjoys 'family life'. Indeed it is the most drastic interference with the right which is permitted by the law.

Accordingly, to be compliant with Art 8 the interference must fall within Art 8(2) being in accordance with the law and necessary in a democratic society, inter alia to protect the rights and freedom of others. Again, as Hale LJ put it in *Re B*,[33] to be necessary in a democratic society the interference 'must meet a pressing social need and be proportionate to that need. The more drastic the interference, the greater must be the need to do it'. On the other side of the coin, as her Ladyship said, in the 'right circumstances' adoption 'is a most valuable way of supplying a child with the "family for life" to which everyone ought to be entitled and of which some children are so tragically deprived'.

In *Re B-S* Sir James Munby P referred[34] to the following comment of Hale LJ in *Re C and B (Care Order: Future Harm)*,[35] which he described as being the overarching principle, namely:

> Intervention in the family may be appropriate, but the aim should be to reunite the family when circumstances enable that, and the effort should be devoted towards that end. Cutting off all contact and the relationship between the child or children and their family is only justified by the overriding necessity of the interests of the child.

---

discrimination argument was rejected and on which decision see P Johnson 'Adoption, Homosexuality and the European Convention on Human Rights' (2012) 75 MLR 1136.

[29] Note: she only sought authorisation for herself as her partner did not feel committed to the adoption application.   [30] [2013] UKSC 33 [2013] 1 WLR 1911.

[31] [2014] 1 WLR 563.

[32] [2001] 1 FLR 589 at (37), CA. For further discussion of this case, which went on appeal to the House of Lords, see Adoptions by one person or a couple, p 707.   [33] [2001] 1 FLR 589 at (37).

[34] [2013] EWCA Civ 1146 [2014] 1 WLR 563, at [18].   [35] [2001] 1 FLR 611 at [34].

Sir James also referred to the European Court of Human Rights' observation in *YC v United Kingdom*:[36]

> family ties may only be severed in very exceptional circumstances and ... everything must be done to preserve personal relations and, where appropriate, to 'rebuild' the family. It is not enough to show that a child could be placed in a more beneficial environment for his upbringing.

Very much reinforcing this standpoint, Sir James referred to what he described as a stringent and demanding test as set out by *Re B*. As he put it:[37]

> The language used in *Re B* is striking. Different words and phrases are used, but the message is clear. Orders contemplating non-consensual adoption – care orders with a plan for adoption, placement orders and adoption orders – are 'a very extreme thing, a last resort', only to be made where 'nothing else will do', where 'no other course [is] possible in [the child's] interests, they are "the most extreme option", a "last resort" – when all else fails', to be made 'only in exceptional circumstances and where motivated by overriding requirements pertaining to the child's welfare, in short, where nothing else will do'.

Although *Re B* and *Re B-S* clearly signal that non-consensual adoption requires special justification (and to that end local authorities and guardians are expected to address all the realistic alternative options), it remains to be seen what impact these decisions will have on the number of applications and orders, particularly as most adoptions are uncontested[38] and given current Government policy[39] to maximise the number of adoptions. It should also be borne in mind that correctly applied English adoption law satisfies human rights requirements. Indeed in *YC v United Kingdom*[40] the European Court of Human Rights observed that the considerations listed in s 1 of the 2002 Act 'broadly reflect the various elements inherent in assessing the necessity under Art 8 of a measure placing a child for adoption.' Relying on that decision the Court of Appeal has said[41] that a judge who properly applies s 1 will thereby normally be complying with the requirement of Art 8. It might also be observed that, so far, none of the challenges made to the European Court of Human Rights against the United Kingdom about adoption decisions has been successful.[42]

What has yet to be tested is whether the adopted child and possibly other members of the birth family, particularly siblings and grandparents, can claim a breach of their Art 8 rights by the severance of the legal ties with the whole family resulting from the adoption. It is certainly not beyond argument that the complete severance of legal ties with the whole family is a disproportionate effect of adoption.[43]

---

[36] [2012] 2 FLR 332 at para 134.   [37] [2014] 1 WLR 563 at [22].

[38] As Lord Nicholls pointed out in *Re B (Adoption: Natural Parent)* [2001] UKHL 70 [2002] 1 WLR 258 at [29] a parent who unconditionally consents to the adoption cannot complain that his or her Art 8 rights have been violated.

[39] See eg *Children and Families Bill 2013: Contextual Information and Responses to Pre-Legislative Scrutiny* Cm 854 (2013) para 11.   [40] [2012] 2 FLR 332 at [35].

[41] Per Sir James Munby P in *Re C (a child) (Adoption: leave to oppose)* [2013] EWCA Civ 431 [2014] 1 FCR 50 at [41].

[42] See *RP v United Kingdom* [2013] 1 FLR 774; *YC v United Kingdom* [2012] 2 FLR 332; *R and H v United Kingdom* [2011] 2 FLR 1236; and *Scott v United Kingdom* [2000] 1 FLR 958.

[43] See N Lowe 'English Adoption Law: Past, Present and Future', op cit, at 337–8.

4. THE CHANGING PATTERN OF ADOPTION

Since the 1960s[44] there has been a dramatic reduction in the number of adoptions: from a peak of 24,831 orders made in England and Wales in 1968 there were 5,206 orders in 2012.[45] One of the main reasons for this decline is the reduction in the number of babies available for adoption. In 1970, for instance, out of a total of 22,373 adoptions 8,833 (or 39%) were of babies, that is, of children under the age of 12 months. Figures since then show a continuous drop in the overall total of adoptions of babies, declining from eg 4,548 in 1975 and 1,115 in 1989 to just 213 (4%) in 2003[46] and 115 (2.2%) in 2012.[47] The decline in the number of babies available for adoption was noted in 1972 by the Houghton Committee[48] and was then thought to be accounted for by the reduction in the number of unwanted babies because of the increased availability of contraception and abortion. Furthermore, unmarried mothers tend to keep their children because of the changing attitude to illegitimacy and the availability of state benefits and reasonable employment prospects and day care provision. Today one would add that an increasing number of children are born to unmarried couples living together in a stable union.

Although attention has perhaps understandably been focused on the reduction in the number of baby adoptions, in fact there have also been large reductions in the number of adoptions of children in most age groups.[49] A possible explanation for this overall reduction is that, as it became increasingly accepted that unmarried mothers would keep their babies, so there developed a more general culture of families being reluctant to give up their children. Eventually, however,[50] a further major reason for the decline in adoption numbers was a change in the law consequent upon the Houghton Committee's recommendation[51] aimed at discouraging joint adoptions by birth parents and step-parents.[52] In 1971, for instance, 10,751 step-parent adoption orders were made and even in the late 1970s there were still over 7,000 a year, representing 70% of all adoptions. However, by 1983 there were 2,872 such orders, which represented 31.8% of the total number of orders made, while in 2004 there were just 1,107 such orders representing 23% of the overall number of adoptions.[53] In 2013 only 7% of adoptions were by step-parents.[54]

The obvious corollary of the decline in baby adoption is the rising proportion of older child adoptions. In 1970, for example, 20% of the children adopted were aged between five and nine with a further 10% aged 10 or over. By 1995 these proportions had risen to 37% and 31% respectively but in 2003 the proportions had dropped to 31% and 18% respectively[55] and to 24% and 11% in 2012.[56]

---

[44] See generally S Cretney 'From Status to Contract?' in F Rose (ed) *Consensus Ad Idem* (1996) 251, N Lowe 'Adoption Law; Past, Present and Future' op cit, and N Lowe 'The Changing face of adoption—the gift/donation model versus the contract/services model' [1997] CFLQ 371.

[45] ONS *Adoptions in England and Wales* (2013). The 2012 figure was 9% higher than in 2011, when there were 4,740 adoptions.   [46] *Marriage, Divorce and Adoption Statistics* Table 6.26.

[47] ONS *Adoptions in England and Wales* (2013) Table 2 b. This was an increase from 2011.

[48] At para 20.

[49] In 1975, for example, 5,523 children aged between one and four were adopted, 7,278 between five and nine, and 3,316 between 10 and 14, whereas in 2012 the comparable figures were 3,266, 1,221 and 435 respectively (with a further 166 aged between 15 and 17): ONS *Adoptions in England and Wales* (2013) Table 2 b.

[50] But note that the significant drop of adoptions between 1975, when there were 21,299 adoptions, 1976 when there were 17,621 and 1977 when there were 12,748, cannot be attributed to a decline of step-parent adoptions.   [51] At para 115.

[52] Discussed at Step-parent adoptions, p 707.   [53] *Judicial Statistics 2004* Annual Report Table 5.4.

[54] See MOJ *Court Statistics Quarterly January to March 2013, April-June 2013 and July–September* (2013) Figures 2.18, 2.8 and 2.15 respectively.

[55] See Table 6.2a of the *Marriage, Divorce and Adoption Statistics*.

[56] See *Adoptions in England and Wales* (ONS, 2013), Table 2b.

(a) The practice of adoption

Adoption of 'looked after' children

A key change in adoption practice occurred when local authorities came to see adoption as a means by which they could secure the long-term welfare not just of babies but also of older children (including those who were physically or mentally disabled) in their care.[57] This change of practice in turn sprang from the childcare policy which, in the 1970s, began in the United Kingdom to be termed permanency planning.[58] It was stimulated by the seminal work of Goldstein, Freud and Solnit, *Beyond the Best Interests of the Child*, published in 1973, in which they challenged the prevailing traditional mode of thought that biological and legal parenthood should take precedence over psychological parenthood. Their thesis was intended to reinforce the security of the adoptive, psychological parent–child relationship. Many of their—at the time revolutionary—notions subsequently came to be accepted by social work and legal practitioners working in the child care and adoption fields. They strengthened the view[59] that children from neglectful, disrupted and severely disordered families might often do much better if placed permanently with loving, secure and more stable families. Other research, particularly Rowe and Lambert's *Children Who Wait*, also published in 1973,[60] which emphasised the need for long term planning for children in care, together with Report of the Inquiry into the Death of Maria Colwell[61] (who had been killed by her stepfather after having been removed from foster parents), reinforced the view that for certain abused or neglected children long-term care away from their families was in their best interests and that adoption was a key means of achieving this even where the birth parents were opposed to it.

Although not everyone was swayed by this permanency movement (and in any event it was not infrequently bad social work practice rather than parental failure that had led to many children languishing in care) and indeed there was something of a backlash in the mid to late 1980s, there were nevertheless lasting significant changes in adoption practice. First, local authorities made and continue to make determined efforts to secure adoption placements for so-called hard to place children to the extent of having extensive publicity campaigns, one of the best known being the 'Be My Parent' scheme organised by the British Agencies for Adoption and Fostering.[62] Second, there was a consequential increase in the number of adoptions in which parental consent was dispensed with.[63] Third, there was an overall rise in the age of children adopted out of care. For example, at a time when the overall numbers of adoptions were falling, the number of children adopted from care rose from 1,488 in 1979 to 2,605 in 1990.[64] In the late 1990s the Labour

---

[57] Ie children subject to a care order or who are being accommodated by a local authority. See Ch 18.

[58] See particularly R Parker *Planning for Deprived Children*. See also M Ryburn 'In whose best interests?—post adoption contact with the birth family' [1998] CFLQ 53 at 55–6.

[59] It might be pointed out that the Curtis Report, op cit, at para 448 had espoused similar views and even the Hopkinson Report, op cit, at para 11 was strongly of the view that adoption was preferable to institutional care.   [60] See also M Adcock, R White and O Rowlands *The Administrative Parent* (1983).

[61] HMSO *Report of the Committee of Inquiry into the Care and Supervision provided in relation to Maria Colwell* (1974).

[62] Under which written profiles with photographs, or video profiles of individual (but unidentified) children are widely circulated. There have also been television campaigns from time to time.

[63] This was noted first by the House of Commons' Second Report on the Children Act 1975, HMSO, 1984, see Table B when 11% of applications involved dispensing with agreement. A later study by M Murch, et al *Pathways to Adoption—Reframing the Approach* (1999), found, in a sample of applications made between 1986 and 1988, 19% involved dispensing with agreement.

[64] See Adoption Review, *Discussion Paper No 3*, op cit, para 9. Of children who left care in the year ending March 1985, 5.8% were adopted: (1988) *Adoption and Fostering*, Vol 12, No 2 at 55. This proportion for the year end March 1988 rose to 7.4%: see Adoption Law Review, *Discussion Paper No 1*, para 56.

Government took a strong line on the value of local authorities planning for the adoption of those children whose long term interests are that they should not be returned to their birth families. Following concerns about the variable quality of adoption services which emerged from Social Service Inspectorate reports in 1996 and 1997[65] a Local Authority Circular, *Adoption—Achieving The Right Balance*,[66] emphasised that where:

> children cannot live with their families, for whatever reason, society has a duty to provide them with a fresh start and where appropriate a permanent alternative home. Adoption is the means of giving children an opportunity to start again; for many children, adoption may be their only chance of experiencing family life.

This positive message about adoption was underscored by the Government's *Quality Protects* Programme, one of the aims of which was to 'maximise the contribution that adoption can make to provide permanent families for children in appropriate cases'.[67] Further pressure to increase adoptions has been placed on local authorities by making the number of adoptions a performance indicator of good practice.[68] The Government's declared intention when introducing the 2002 Act was to achieve a 40% and, if possible, a 50% increase in the number of looked-after children who are adopted. It continues to be Government policy to maximise the number of adoptions of children in long-term care[69] who cannot be rehabilitated with their family. To this end reforms contained in Part 1 of the Children and Families Act 2014 are designed[70] to encourage local authorities to place children for whom they are considering adoption with their potential adopters more quickly; to reduce delay by removing the explicit wording around the child's ethnicity so that black and minority children are not left waiting in care longer than necessary because a perfect or partial ethnic match is being sought; to enable the Secretary of State to require local authorities to commission adopter recruitment services from other adoption agencies, and to give approved prospective adopters a more active role in identifying possible matches with children for whom the local authority are considering adoption by having access to the Adoption and Children Register.[71]

Not surprisingly, these developments and initiatives have had an impact on both the number and proportion of public law adoptions. In 2012 there were 3,695 adoptions of 'looked after' children.[72] These constituted 71% of all adoptions.

In short, public law adoptions, which were almost unimaginable when adoption was first introduced in 1927, now form the majority of all adoptions.

Before leaving the issue of public law adoptions, attention also needs to be drawn to related developing practices in this sphere. Conscious of the need to keep the number

---

[65] Viz. Department of Health *For Children's Sake: An SSI Inspection of Local Authority Adoption Services* (1996) and Department of Health *For Children's Sake—Part II: An Inspection of Local Authority Adoption Services* (1997). One suspects that the Government was also influenced by P Morgan's thesis that all children who have been in local authority care for 12 months ought to be adopted, see *Adoption and the Care of Children* (IEA, 1998).

[66] LAC (98) 20. A national survey of implementation of this Circular was carried out in 1999.

[67] Department of Health *The Government's Objectives for Children's Social Services* (1999) paras 1–3.

[68] See Performance Indicator C23, at para 1.3.

[69] See DfE *Further Action on Adoption: Finding More Loving Homes* (2013) and *Children and Families Bill 2013: Contextual Information and Responses to Pre-Legislative Scrutiny* Cm 854 (2013) para 11.

[70] See the Explanatory Notes to the 2014 Act, para 8 and see in particular ss 4, 6 and 7 of the 2014 Act.

[71] This Register was established by s 125 of the 2002 Act and contains details of children suitable for adoption and prospective adopters who are suitable to adopt, to which s 7 of the 2014 Act adds s 125A.

[72] See the statistics published by BAAF.

of placements of the child to a minimum and at the same time come to speedier decisions concerning the child's long-term placement a number of different schemes have been developing. One is so-called 'concurrent planning', which has been defined as 'the process of working towards family reunification, while at the same time establishing an alternative permanent plan'.[73] In other words, it involves the social worker working both with the child's foster carers as potential adopters should rehabilitation fail, *and* with the birth parents to secure rehabilitation. Less dramatic is so-called 'twin tracking' in which the social worker works with the birth parents on rehabilitation while the child is in a foster placement but at the same time preparing the ground for a care order or a long-term fostering or adoptive placement elsewhere. Slightly different is so-called 'contingency planning' whereby a plan has been made and is being moved forward but at the same time a fall-back position has been thought about and decided upon should the first plan fail.[74]

Adoption and contact

Traditionally, adoption had been a secretive process[75] designed not simply to facilitate the irrevocable transfer of parentage, but to protect unmarried mothers and their children from excessive stigma and to enable childless couples to avoid the oppressive taint of infertility.[76] Law and practice were designed so that the birth parents would have nothing to do with the process of selecting adopters: on the contrary they would generally have no knowledge of the adopters and of course they would have no further contact with their child. Similarly, adopters would not know the birth parents' identity. One result of this secrecy was that adopters were generally reluctant to tell their children that they were adopted which is now regarded as bad practice.[77] Studies in the 1960s and 1970s had demonstrated the deleterious effect upon adopted children of not knowing their own identities,[78] and the law was eventually[79] changed permitting adults who had been adopted to obtain their original birth certificate and to pursue the possibility of establishing contact with their birth family.[80] Following the introduction of this right, an Adoption Contact Register was also created[81] which provides 'a safe and confidential way for birth parents

---

[73] By L Katz, Programme Director of the Seattle Concurrent Planning Project, where the idea was pioneered. Pilot schemes have been running in England and Wales see L Katz and B Clatworthy 'Innovation in Care Planning for Children' [1999] Fam Law 108 and 'The Goodman Team—Concurrent Planning' [2001] Fam Law 301.

[74] N Lowe and M Murch, K Bader, M Borkowski, R Copner and J Shearman *The Plan for the Child, Adoption or Long-term Fostering* (2001) found that social workers were often confused by these different policies.

[75] See generally M Ryburn 'In whose best interests?—post adoption contact with the birth family' [1998] CFLQ 53.

[76] See J Triseliotis 'Open adoption' in *Open Adoption—The Philosophy and the Practice* (1970) p 19.

[77] This is not an enforceable obligation: see eg *Re S (A Minor) (Adoption by Step-parents)* [1988] 1 FLR 418, CA. Such an attitude would, however, if known, militate against that person's approval as an adopter in the first place: see Lowe 'The Changing Face of Adoption', op cit, at pp 375–6.

[78] See A McWhinnie *Adopted Children: How They Grow Up* (1967) and J Triseliotis *In Search of Origins* (1973).

[79] With effect from November 1975 (upon the recommendation of the Houghton Committee, at 303) though controversially it was introduced with retrospective effect. In fact the Hurst Committee, op cit, at para 150, had recommended in 1954 that all adopters should be required to give a formal undertaking to tell the child about his or her adoption.

[80] By 1990 it was estimated that 33,000 children had taken advantage of the facility: *Adoption Law Review*, Discussion Paper No 1, note 140. For details of the current law see The adopted children register, p 721.

[81] Originally by s 51 A of the 1976 Act. See now s 80 of the Adoption and Children Act 2002, discussed at The adoption contact register, p 722.

and other relatives to assure an adopted person that contact would be welcome and to give a contact address.'[82]

This change of law only enables adopted children to consider contacting their family after they have attained adulthood, but another important change in practice has been to permit on-going contact with the birth family throughout the adoption. Commonly referred to as 'open adoption',[83] this change came about when it became realised that the automatic termination of contact between the child and his natural family was not necessarily in the child's interests.[84] In turn, following the ground-breaking decision in *Re J (A Minor) (Adoption Order: Conditions)*,[85] the courts began to accept that it is not inconsistent with adoption for the child to have continued contact with his family. *Re J* was authoritatively confirmed by the House of Lords in *Re C (A Minor) (Adoption Order: Conditions)*,[86] in which contact was preserved between a child who was in long-term care and a sibling. Although, as we shall see,[87] the courts remain reluctant to *impose* a formal contact order on adopters, in practice some form of continuing contact (whether direct or indirect) is not uncommon in agency adoptions.[88] Post-adoption contact can take many different forms, for example, the exchange of information, reports and photographs most likely through a confidential adoption agency 'letter box' service. It can also include face-to-face meetings or take the form of indirect contact via telephone calls, texting and e-mails.[89]

A further stage of 'open adoption' is to involve the birth parents in the process of selecting adopters and there are some agencies that actively encourage this.

Post-adoption support

The conventional view of adoption was that it was an end in itself and that, having achieved a legal transfer of the child from one family to another, the adoptive family were thereafter left to their own devices and resources to bring up the child on their own. This model, which has been labelled the 'gift/donation' model, sits uneasily with the adoption of older children and the growing practice of open adoption.[90] It has become increasingly recognised that adoption is not the end of the process but merely a part of an ongoing and often complex process of family development and that in many, if not most, cases the adoptive family will need ongoing support.[91]

[82] Department of Health *The Children Act 1989, Guidance and Regulations* (1991), Vol 9 *Adoption Issues* para 3.2.

[83] See generally: Ryburn, op cit; A Mullender (ed) *Open Adoption—The Philosophy and the Practice* (1991); 'Openness in Adoption' (1991) 15(4) *Adoption and Fostering* at 81–115; and the *Adoption Law Review*, Discussion Paper No 1, op cit, Part C and paras 98–109 and the Consultative Document (1992) pp 9–14.

[84] See eg J Triseliotis 'Adoption with Contact' (1985) 9(4) *Adoption and Fostering* at 19 and J Fratter *Family Placement and Access* (1989).

[85] [1973] Fam 106.   [86] [1989] AC 1, HL.   [87] See Contact considerations, p 719.

[88] See eg E Neil 'Post-adoption contact and openness in adoptive parents' minds: consequences for children's development' (2009) 39 *British Journal of Social Work* 5.

[89] For a detailed discussion of contact see M Murch et al *Supporting Adoption*, op cit, ch 15. But note difficulties are frequently encountered in recruiting would-be adopters to accept ongoing contact. Research has also found that ongoing contact with the birth family was one of the key factors in local authorities choosing to place a child for long-term fostering rather than adoption, see N Lowe and M Murch et al *The Plan for the Child* (2002).

[90] See N Lowe 'The Changing Face of Adoption—the gift/donation model versus the contract/services model' [1997] CFLQ 371.

[91] Interestingly, wide though the Houghton Committee (op cit) envisaged a comprehensive adoption service should be, it made no mention of post-adoption support. For discussion about what a post-adoption service should provide see the Review of Adoption Law, Discussion Paper No 3 *The Adoption Process*, para 88, the Consultative Document 1992 (op cit) Part VII; the Government White Paper *Adoption: The Future* Cm 2288 (1993) 4.25.

The provision of post-adoption support is an express obligation of adoption agencies under the 2002 Act. It can take many forms, ranging from the provision of allowances, the organisation of post-adoption contact, payment for the provision of therapy for the child, ongoing counselling for the adoptive (and birth) family including the child, the provision of updating information and the organisation of support groups.[92]

So far as adoption allowances are concerned, their initial introduction was not without controversy. They were first recommended by the Houghton Committee[93] on the basis that more adoptive homes might be found for children in need if adopters were financially supported to adopt. The issue was hotly contested in Parliament and indeed in Standing Committee it was only the chairman's casting vote that saved the provision.[94] Nevertheless, a provision permitting adoption agencies to submit a scheme for the payment of an adoption allowance for approval by the Secretary of State was introduced in 1982.[95] In fact by the 1990s virtually all statutory agencies and some voluntary agencies had successfully applied for approval of a scheme.[96] Reflecting this development, the law was changed first by the Children Act 1989[97] and then by the 2002 Act[98] so as to empower *all* agencies to pay an adoption allowance. Further changes have been made by the Children and Families Act 2014 so as to provide for personal budgets for adopters (or adopted children) in England (but not Wales).[99]

5. RESPONSIBILITY FOR PLACING CHILDREN FOR ADOPTION

(a) Prohibition of private placements

When first introduced into England and Wales, adoption was remarkably unregulated. The Adoption of Children Act 1926 essentially provided, as one commentator put it, 'a process whereby, under minimal safeguards supervised by the court, a civil contract was registered and recognised'.[100] In particular, there were no provisions regulating who could arrange adoptions. In 1939, however, it became an offence for a body of persons other than a registered adoption society or a local authority to make any arrangements for the adoption of children.[101] But until 1982 there was no restriction on *individuals* placing children for adoption. Although commonly such private arrangements were made through doctors or even solicitors, there was, as the Houghton Committee pointed out,[102] nothing to prevent a mother making a placement with a casual acquaintance she had met at the launderette. This lack of control had obvious dangers: if the potential adopters were unsuitable (a not unlikely consequence, given the inexperience of the placers) the placement could be disastrous for the child; it could also lead to improper pressure being brought upon the mother. Following the Houghton Committee's recommendation[103] it became unlawful for a person other than an adoption agency to

---

[92] For a detailed study of those services offered during the adoption process see M Murch et al *Supporting Adoption*, op cit.

[93] At Recommendation 17. But see the discussion by N Lowe, 'The Changing Face of Adoption', op cit, at 379.   [94] Standing Committee A (Ninth Sitting), cols 447–80.

[95] Viz. Children Act 1975 s 32, subsequently re-enacted by s 56(4)–(7) of the Adoption Act 1976.

[96] See L Lambert and J Seglow *Adoption Allowances in England and Wales: The Early Years* (1988).

[97] Substituting s 57A for s 56 (4)–(7) of the Adoption Act 1976.

[98] The obligation to provide support including financial support is provided by s 4 as supplemented by the Adoption Support Services Regulations 2005 (SI 2005/691) discussed at The Current position, p 697.

[99] See s 5 inserting s 4A into the 2002 Act, see further The Current position, p 698.

[100] S Cretney 'From Status to Contract?' in *Consensus Ad Idem*, op cit, at p 252.

[101] By the Adoption of Children (Regulation) Act 1939 s 1, which implemented the recommendation of the Horsburgh Committee's Report on Adoption Societies and Agencies Cmd 5499 (1937).

[102] Cmnd 5107 at para 81.   [103] Ibid at para 92.

place a child for adoption unless the proposed adopter was a relative of the child or was acting pursuant to a High Court order.[104] From that moment, as one commentary put it,[105] the process of the 'professionalisation of adoption work' was completed. So far as individuals seeking to adopt non-relatives are concerned, adoption is fully regulated and they require agency approval before they can even begin the adoption process.

(b) Adoption agencies

The task of selecting potential adopters and placing children for adoption outside their families rests with adoption agencies, that is, registered adoption societies (otherwise known as voluntary agencies) and local authorities, (otherwise known as statutory agencies).[106] In 2014, there were 30 voluntary organisations[107] so that together with statutory agencies there are in all in over 150 adoption agencies in England and Wales.[108] Voluntary societies have long helped to facilitate adoptions. Indeed, at one time they dealt with the majority of agency adoptions[109] but now most agency work is done by statutory agencies.

The functions and duties of adoption agencies are tightly controlled by the Adoption Agency Regulations 2005 (SI 2005/389) in England and by the Adoption Agency (Wales) Regulations 2005 (SI 2005/1313) (W.95) in Wales. Under these Regulations the agency is obliged to set up an adoption panel,[110] whose function with regard to every child referred to it is to consider and make recommendations as to whether the child should be placed for adoption[111] and whether the prospective adopter is a suitable person to adopt the child.[112] The agency itself has extensive duties whenever it is considering adoption to provide a counselling service for the child and to explain to the child in an appropriate manner the procedure and legal implications of adoption to the child.[113] A similar duty is owed to the parents, guardians or any other person the agency considers relevant,[114] and to the prospective adopters.[115] The agency also has a duty to collect and collate information about the child and his parents, to make arrangements for medical examinations, to provide background information about the child to the prospective adopters, to visit the child after placement, and generally to provide advice and assistance.[116]

As a result of these provisions, which have steadily become more extensive, children are only placed for adoption with applicants who have been carefully screened by professional and experienced bodies.

---

[104] Originally by s 28 of the Children Act 1975. Private placements are now prohibited by s 92 of the Adoption and Children Act 2002, discussed at Illegal placements, p 728.

[105] N Lowe 'English Adoption Law—Past, Present and Future', op cit, at 325.

[106] Adoption and Children Act 2002 s 2(1), (2).   [107] See Clarke Hall and Morrison at 11[20].

[108] A full list and location of agencies is published in BAAF *Adopting a Child* (2013, 10th edn).

[109] See N Lowe 'The changing face of adoption—the gift/donation model versus the contract/services model' [1997] CFLQ 371 at 374.   [110] Regulation 3–5 (England), reg 3 of the Welsh Regulations.

[111] Regulation 18 (England), reg 18 of the Welsh Regulations. In making this recommendation the panel must have regard inter alia to the child's permanence report that agencies must prepare about the child's background, health and wishes and feelings as set out in reg 17 (England), reg 17 of the Welsh Regulations.

[112] Regulation 26 (England), reg 25 of the Welsh Regulations.

[113] Regulation 13(England), reg 13 of the Welsh Regulations.

[114] Regulation 14(England), reg 14 of the Welsh Regulations.

[115] Regulation 22(England), reg 21 of the Welsh Regulations.

[116] For further details see Butterworths *Family Law Service* Vol 3 (1), Ch 22.

B. GENERAL PRINCIPLES WHEN REACHING DECISIONS ABOUT ADOPTION

1. THE WEIGHTING OF THE CHILD'S WELFARE

(a) The former position

Although the courts have always had to be satisfied that an adoption order is for the child's benefit, until the implementation of the Children Act 1975 there was no specific guidance on the weighting to be accorded to the child's welfare during the various stages of the adoption process. However, when it was introduced, the guiding principle, eventually provided by the Adoption Act 1976 s 6, directed courts and adoption agencies to give *first* rather than paramount 'consideration to the need to safeguard and promote the welfare of the child throughout his childhood when reaching any decision relating to adoption'.

Although, given the irrevocable severance of family ties, there is some justification for not treating the child's welfare as the paramount consideration, there are powerful counter-arguments. First, even supposing it is right to protect the parents' interests, there is little justification in applying the lesser weighting to issues that do not involve the parents. Accordingly, it may be thought right to have the paramountcy principle govern all adoption issues save that of dispensing with parental consent. That indeed was the proposal made in the Consultative Document in 1992.[117] Secondly, looked at from the child's point of view, his welfare ought to be considered paramount in all cases, including adoption, where his future upbringing is directly in issue. It was this argument that ultimately prevailed.

(b) The position under the 2002 Act

Section 1(1) and (2) of the 2002 Act state that 'whenever a court or adoption agency is coming to a decision relating to the adoption of a child', the 'paramount consideration of the court or adoption agency must be the child's welfare, throughout his life'.

The requirement to consider the child's welfare 'throughout his life' is to be noted and marks a further distinction between adoption orders, which have life-long effects, and orders made under the Children Act 1989 which do not.[118] However, as Wall LJ observed in *Re P (Placement Orders: Parental Consent)*,[119] this does not mean that there is some enhanced welfare test to be applied in cases of adoption in contrast to a so-called simple welfare test under the 1989 Act. Nevertheless the 2002 Act requires the court or adoption agency to focus on the child's welfare throughout his life thereby emphasising that adoption, unlike other forms of order made under the 1989 Act, is something with life-long implications. The test is clearly child centred and does not, for instance, privilege the birth family over the adoptive parents.[120]

---

[117] Op cit at paras 7.1ff.

[118] In fact the Act did not break new ground in this respect but put in statutory form the position established by pre-2002 Act case law. See eg *Re B (Adoption Order: Nationality)* [1999] 2 AC 136, HL and *Re D (A Minor) (Adoption Order: Validity)* [1991] Fam 137, CA.

[119] [2008] EWCA Civ 535 [2008] 2 FLR 625 at [127]–[128]. See also *Re Q (Adoption)* [2011] EWCA Civ 1610 [2012] 1 FLR 1228 at [58] per Munby LJ.

[120] See *Re C (A Child) (Adoption: Duty of Local Authority)* [2007] EWCA Civ 1206 [2008] Fam 54 at [15] per Arden LJ.

In determining the child's welfare, the court or adoption agency must have regard to a statutory checklist set out in s 1(4) of the 2002 Act Although similar to the welfare checklist under the 1989 Act[121] inasmuch as regard must be had to the child's wishes and feelings, needs, age, sex, background and any harm which the child has suffered or is likely to suffer, the 2002 checklist is significantly more extensive.[122] By s 1(4)(c) regard must be had to:

> the likely effect on the child (throughout his life) of having ceased to be a member of the original family and become and adopted person.

While s 1(4)(f) directs that regard is to be had to:

> the relationship[123] which the child has with relatives,[124] and with any other person in relation to whom the court or agency considers the question to be relevant, including—
> (i) the likelihood of any such relationship continuing and value to the child of its doing so,
> (ii) the ability and willingness of any of the child's relatives, or of any such person, to provide the child with a secure environment in which the child can develop, and otherwise to meet the child's needs, and
> (iii) the wishes and feelings of any of the child's relatives, or of any such person, about the child.

Section 1(4)(c), as Wall LJ has observed,[125] directs attention to the consequences for the child throughout his life. Section 1(4)(f), on the other hand, requires the court or adoption agency to consider the child's existing relationships and the value of such relationships continuing. Having to consider the parents' views is a reminder that while the focus must be on the child, the parents' interests cannot simply be ignored.

In *YC v United Kingdom*[126] the European Court of Human Rights observed that the considerations listed in s 1 of the 2002 Act 'broadly reflect the various elements inherent in assessing the necessity under Art 8 of a measure placing a child for adoption.' Relying on that decision the Court of Appeal has said[127] that a judge who properly applies s 1 will thereby normally be complying with the requirement of Art 8.

Although 'welfare' is a sufficiently wide term to include material benefits conferred by adoption, it is important not to confuse the purpose of adoption with the benefits of rights of abode and citizenship of this country.[128] There must be a genuine intention that the applicants should stand in loco parentis to the child. An order will be refused where it is clear, for example, that the real motive for the application is to enable the child (particularly, if he has nearly attained his majority) to acquire British citizenship rather than to promote his welfare.[129]

---

[121] Children Act 1989 s 1(3), discussed in Ch 12.
[122] A point emphasised by Wall LJ in *Re P* [2008] EWCA Civ 535 [2008] 2 FLR 625 at [128].
[123] Relationships are not confined to legal relationships: s 1(8)(a).
[124] Which for these purposes would include the birth parents: see s 1(8)(b).
[125] In *Re P* [2008] EWCA Civ 535 [2008] 2 FLR 625 at [128].   [126] [2012] 2 FLR 332 at [135].
[127] Per Sir James Munby P in *Re C (a child) (Adoption: leave to oppose)* [2013] EWCA Civ 431 [2014] 1 FCR 50 at [41].
[128] See *Re B (Adoption Order: Nationality)* [1999] 2 AC 136, HL. See also *Re S and J (Adoption: Non-Patrials)* [1994] 2 FLR 111. It was confirmed that a similar position obtained post the 2002 Act, see *ASB v MQS (Secretary of State for the Home Department)* [2009] EWHC 2491 (Fam) [2010] 1 FLR 748.
[129] See eg *Re IH (A Child) (Permission To Apply For Adoption)* [2013] EWHC 1235 (Fam) [2014] 1 FLR 70.

(c) Religious, racial, cultural and linguistic considerations

At one time consent to adoption could be conditional on the child being brought up in a particular religion but this was changed by the Adoption Act 1976 s 7 which required agencies only to have regard so far as practical to parental wishes about the child's religious upbringing. This was modified and extended by s 1(5) of the 2002 Act to require agencies, when placing a child for adoption, to 'give due consideration to the child's religious persuasion, racial origin and cultural and linguistic background'. However, following amendments made by s 3 of the Children and Families Act 2014, s 1(5) no longer applies to local authorities in, or registered adoption societies whose principal office is in, England, though it continues to apply in Wales. The disapplication of s 1(5) in England is to avoid any suggestion that the legislation places a child's religious persuasion, racial origin and cultural and linguistic background above the other factors mentioned in s 1(2)–(4).[130]

(d) Delay

Section 1(3) directs both the court and adoption agency at all times to 'bear in mind that, in general, any delay in coming to the decision [relating to adoption] is likely to prejudice the child's welfare'. As under the Children Act 1989, to reinforce this general principle, s 109 obliges the court to draw up a timetable to determine the question of whether an adoption order or placement order should be made without delay and to give appropriate directions to ensure that the timetable is adhered to.

(e) Making an order only where it is better for the child than not doing so

Again, mirroring the Children Act principles, s 1(6) of the 2002 Act directs the court to consider the whole range of powers available to it either under the 2002 Act or the Children Act 1989 and in any event 'not to make any order under this Act unless it considers that making the order would be better for the child than not doing so'.

Proceedings under the Adoption and Children Act 2002 are designated 'family proceedings' for the purposes of the Children Act 1989.[131] Consequently, in adoption proceedings, courts are empowered, either upon application, or upon their own motion, to make s 8 orders including child arrangements orders dealing with the child's living arrangements.[132] They are also empowered, either upon application, or upon their own motion, to make a special guardianship order.[133]

As we discuss elsewhere in this chapter, the obligation to consider all other options is important particularly from the human rights perspective.[134]

C. ADOPTION SERVICE

1. THE DEVELOPMENT OF AN ADOPTION SERVICE

The first attempt to regulate adoption practice was by the Adoption of Children (Regulation) Act 1939. However while that Act could be said to have created the

---

[130] See the Explanatory Notes to the 2014 Act, at para 57.
[131] Children Act 1989 s 8(4)(d), as amended.
[132] Children Act 1989 s 10(1)(b) discussed in Ch 14.
[133] Children Act 1989 s 14A(6). See further Applying for an order, p 731.
[134] See *Re B-S (Children) (Adoption Order: Leave to Oppose)* [2014] 1 WLR 563, discussed at Placement orders, p 701.

rudimentary foundations of what might now be called an adoption service, it was only concerned with the placement of children and only controlled the activities of registered adoption agencies. Some changes were subsequently made to this system, not least in clarifying the role of local authorities in arranging adoptions. But it was not until the reforms prompted by the Houghton Committee's report that an adoption *service* could truly be said to have been created. The Houghton Committee recommended that *all* local authorities should have a statutory duty to provide an adoption service as part of their general child care and family casework provision.[135] Further, recognising that voluntary adoption societies had a valuable role to play, not least in providing a choice of service, the Committee recommended[136] that local authorities have a statutory duty 'to ensure, in co-operation with voluntary societies, that a comprehensive adoption service is available throughout their area'.

The Houghton Committee's recommendations were accepted and subsequently enacted by s 1 of the Adoption Act 1976 under which it became the duty of *every* local authority to establish and maintain an adoption service. This duty is now provided for and expanded upon by the Adoption and Children Act 2002, which has since been amended by the Children and Families Act 2014.

2. THE CURRENT POSITION

By s 3 of the 2002 Act:

> Each local authority must continue to maintain within their area a service designed to meet the needs, in relation to adoption, of—
>   (a) children who may be adopted, their parents and guardians,
>   (b) persons wishing to adopt a child,
>   (c) adopted persons, their parents, natural parents and former guardians;
> and for that purpose must provide the requisite facilities.

'Requisite facilities' must include making and participating in arrangements both for the adoption of the child and, importantly, for the provision of adoption support services.[137] In other words, this duty covers all aspects of a local authority's activities in relation to adoption and applies to all types of adoption (ie whether domestic, or intercountry, relative, step-parent, foster carer or stranger adoption). Local authorities may meet their obligations to provide these services by ensuring that they are provided by a registered adoption society or any other person as prescribed by regulation.[138] Each local authority is required to publish their plan of the services that they maintain.[139]

The 2002 Act imposed for the first time the *clear* obligation to provide adoption support both pre- *and* post-adoption. Such support services are defined as 'counselling, advice and information, and any other services prescribed by regulations'.[140] Under s 4 a whole range of people affected by adoption or prospective adoption (including not just the child, his or her parents and prospective and adoptive parents but also the child's natural sibling(s), other children of the adoptive parents and adopted adults, their parents,

---

[135] Paras 42 and 44 and Recommendation 2.   [136] Para 41 and Recommendation 3.
[137] Section 3(2).   [138] Section 3(4).
[139] Section 5. Such plans are required to be kept under review, see the Adoption Support Services (England) Regulations and Adoption Agencies (Miscellaneous Amendments) Regulations 2005 (SI 2005/2720), reg 6 and the Adoption Support Services (Wales) Regulations 2005 (SI 2005/1514), reg 4
[140] Section 2(6) and the Adoption Support Services (England) Regulations 2005, reg 3 and the Adoption Support Services (Wales) Regulations 2005, reg 2.

natural parents and former guardians) may request an assessment of their need for adoption support services. This right to an assessment does not mean that any such person has a right to receive services. That remains a matter for the local authority. Nevertheless it is incumbent upon authorities to act reasonably.[141] If the local authority decides to provide any adoption support service to a person they must prepare a plan and keep that plan under review.[142]

Following amendments made by the Children and Families Act 2014, provision is made in England for personal budgets, being an amount to be made available to secure particular adoption support services.[143] As the Explanatory Notes to the 2014 Act explain:[144]

> Personal budgets may take the form of direct payments, where families can purchase for themselves, notional personal budgets, which families can prepare with the local authority and which the local authority can spend on their behalf at their direction, or a combination of both.

The 2014 Act also imposes a new duty on local authorities in England to provide a range of information about adoption support services and other prescribed information to any person who has contacted a local authority to request information about adopting a child, or who has informed the authority that they wish to adopt a child.[145]

D. PLACEMENT FOR ADOPTION

1. INTRODUCTION

An important change made by the 2002 Act was to introduce a new regime for the placement of children for adoption. As John Hutton (the then Health Minister) said during the debates on the earlier Bill:[146]

> The new system is intended to provide greater certainty and stability for children by dealing as far as possible with parental consent *before* they have been placed with the prospective new family; to reduce the uncertainty for the prospective adopters, who possibly face a contested hearing at the adoption order stage; and to reduce the extent to which birth families are faced with a fait accompli at the final adoption hearing, if the child has been placed with prospective adopters for some time.

The placement scheme under the 2002 Act replaced the former procedure known as 'freeing the child for adoption'. Freeing was a procedure whereby adoption agencies could seek a formal court order freeing the child for adoption, which could only be granted if the court was satisfied either that those whose consent was required (primarily parents) had unconditionally agreed to the making of the order or that their agreement should be dispensed with. An important prerequisite was that the court had to be satisfied that adoption was in the child's interests and that the agency's plans for placement were realistic. The effect of the freeing order was to transfer parental responsibility from the parent to

---

[141] See Bridge and Swindells, op cit, at 13.24.   [142] Section 4(5).
[143] See s 5 of the 2014 Act, inserting s 4A into the 2002 Act.   [144] At para 62.
[145] See s 6 of the 2014 Act, inserting s 4B into the 2002 Act.
[146] HC Debs Vol 365, no 59, col 708 (26 March 2001).

the agency.[147] The agency could then place the child for adoption knowing that, provided the placement was satisfactory, the final adoption would be made. In simple terms a freeing order amounted to a 'mini adoption' in favour of the adoption agency.

Despite its apparent simplicity freeing was judged to be a failure.[148] Among the reasons for this conclusion was its inconsistent use (there being no compulsion upon agencies to use freeing) with some agencies using the process to free children already placed with prospective adopters.[149] But a major problem was that instead of being the speedy process that it was intended to be, it was in practice a lengthy process riddled with delay. Finally, there was the unsatisfactory result that upon a freeing order being made the child was placed in 'adoption limbo' and became a 'statutory orphan' which on occasion still causes problems where the child has not been adopted.[150]

The shortcomings of freeing led the Adoption Law Review[151] to conclude that the process should be replaced by an entirely new procedure that better safeguarded the interests of all parties. Devising a suitable alternative, however, proved problematic. Initial proposals made by the *Consultative Document on Adoption Law*[152] were rejected in favour of a more flexible scheme proposed by a 1994 Consultation Paper.[153] This dealt more appropriately with, on the one hand, babies whose birth parents had requested adoption and, on the other, older children removed or kept from their parents against the latter's wishes. It was these later proposals that were essentially enacted by the 2002 Act.

2. THE PLACEMENT SCHEME UNDER THE 2002 ACT

(a) The general scheme

The general scheme for adoption placements is set out by s 18. There are only two routes: placements with parental consent and those authorised by court order. By s 18(1), except in the case of a child who is less than six weeks old, an adoption agency (that is, both a local authority or a registered adoption society)[154] may only place a child for adoption with prospective adopters where each parent or guardian[155] has consented to the placement or, if the agency is a local authority, where it has obtained a placement order. 'Placement' in this context includes not just the initial placement but also leaving a child in an existing placement with prospective adopters. This last point covers the situation where a child is initially fostered but the agency later plan for the child's adoption by those foster carers.

Before any placement for adoption may be made the agency must be satisfied that the child ought to be placed for adoption.[156]

---

[147] There were provisions to revoke a freeing order upon the parent's application, following notification that the child had not been placed for adoption within 12 months of the making of the freeing order.

[148] See the Adoption Law Review Discussion Paper No 2 at para 76, N Lowe and M Murch et al *Report of the Research into the Use and Practice of the Freeing for Adoption Provisions* (1993) and in Scotland, Lambert, Buist, Triseliotis and Hall *Freeing Children for Adoption* summarised in (1990) 14 *Adoption and Fostering* 36.

[149] The agencies' motive for doing this was to shield the would-be adopters from the stress of taking on the contest with the birth parents. But not everyone agreed that this was a legitimate use of freeing.

[150] See eg *A City Council v C* [2013] EWHC 8 (Fam) [2013] 1 WLR 3009.

[151] Adoption Law Review, Discussion Paper No 2, *Agreeing and Freeing*, (1991) para 180.

[152] (1992) Recommendations 16–18.

[153] *Placement for Adoption—a consultation document* (1994).

[154] Adoption and Children Act 2002, s 2(1), discussed at Adoption agencies, p 693.

[155] Including special guardian, see s 144(1). Special guardianship is discussed at Special guardianship, pp 730ff.   [156] Section 18(2).

Where a child is placed or authorised to be placed for adoption by a local authority, the child is a 'looked after child'.[157]

The birth parent(s) retain parental responsibility notwithstanding a placement, an authorisation to place or a placement order until the final adoption order is made, though it is shared with the adoption agency *and* prospective adopters with whom the child is placed.[158]

(b) Placing children with parental consent

Section 19 allows[159] an adoption agency to place a child for adoption where it is satisfied that each parent[160] or guardian[161] has consented[162] to the child being placed for adoption and that that consent has not been withdrawn. The consent may be to placements with identified[163] prospective adopters or with any prospective adopters who may be chosen by the agency.[164] Consent may be withdrawn at any point before an application for an adoption order has been made.[165]

Special provision is made for the consensual placement of babies under six weeks old. The mother's consent is ineffective if given less than six weeks after the child's birth (this is to allow her time to recover from the birth)[166] but placements are permitted, unless the child is subject to care proceedings, with her informal consent.[167] However, before an adoption order can be made, her formal consent is required.[168] It has been held[169] to be good practice for agencies to obtain formal consent when the child reaches the age of six weeks.

By s 20, a parent may consent to the making of a future adoption order at the same time as consenting to the placement. This consent may be to adoption by identified prospective adopters or to any prospective adopters chosen by the agency. This 'advance consent' can be withdrawn before any application to adopt is made but such withdrawal must be by notice in writing to the agency or in the form prescribed.[170] In addition to giving advance consent the parent can give notice to the agency that he or she does not wish to be informed when an application for an adoption order is made, and to withdraw any such

---

[157] Section 18(3). For the consequences of being 'looked after', see Ch 18.

[158] Section 25, see further The legal effects of placement, p 703.

[159] Save where care proceedings are pending or a care order or placement order was made after the consent was given: s 19(3).   [160] Ie a parent with parental responsibility: s 52(6).

[161] Including any special guardian: s 144(1).

[162] For the meaning of 'consent' see s 52, discussed at Form of consent, p 712. Where a child has been placed for adoption with the mother's consent, and the father or second female parent (for the meaning of which, see Ch 8) later acquires parental responsibility, he or she will be deemed to have given consent in the same terms as the mother: s 52(9), (10). Such consent may subsequently be withdrawn.

[163] As Bridge and Swindells, op cit, at 9.16 point out, 'identified' was deliberately chosen to enable parents to consent to a placement with specific adopters whose name they did not know but with whose characteristics and details they might be familiar with through, for example, an anonymous profile passed on by the agency.

[164] Alternatively, a specific consent can be combined with a general one if the initial placement breaks down: s 19(2). Presumably, if the consent is to a specific placement only, fresh consent or a court order is required to place the child elsewhere.

[165] Section 52(4). If consent is withdrawn before placement the child must be returned within one week: s 31. If withdrawn after placement but before an application for adoption is made, the child must be returned within 14 days: s 32. This is, however, subject to a local authority not having a duty to apply for a placement order under s 22(1), see When placement orders should be sought, p 701.   [166] Section 52(3).

[167] Section 18(1) and Adoption Agencies Regulations 2005, reg 35(4) (England), Adoption Agencies (Wales) Regulations 2005, reg 36(7). See also DfE *Adoption Guidance: Adoption and Children Act 2002* (2011) ch 2 paras 87–92.   [168] Section 47(4)(b)(i).

[169] See *A Local Authority v GC* [2008] EWHC 2555 (Fam) [2009] 1 FLR 299.

[170] Sections 20(3) and 52(4), (8).

notice.[171] In this way provision is made for a parent to relinquish their child for adoption and have no further involvement in the proceedings.

We discuss the legal effects of children being placed by agreement or order shortly, but suffice to say here that it affects the allocation of parental responsibility, ends the ability to apply for a child arrangements order, puts contact in issue and substantially restricts the parent's ability to oppose the making of the final adoption order. In other words, consenting to a child's placement for adoption has serious legal consequences and, given that no court is involved at this stage, puts a premium on the agency being satisfied that there is real and genuine agreement. In this respect it will be noted that the signing of the consent to placement form must be witnessed by a Cafcass officer (or in Wales, a Welsh family proceedings officer) who has the responsibility for deciding that consent is freely and unconditionally given with a full understanding of the consequences.[172]

(c) Placement orders

When placement orders should be sought

By s 21(1) a placement order is one made by a court authorising a *local authority* to place a child with any prospective adopters who may be chosen by the authority. It will be noted that only local authorities (and not, therefore, registered adoption agencies) are able to apply for a placement order.[173]

By s 22 local authorities *must* apply for a placement order if:

(a) the child is placed for adoption by them or is being provided with accommodation by them;

(b) no adoption agency is authorised to place the child for adoption (ie there is no formal parental consent);

(c) the child has no parent or guardian or the authority consider that the conditions in s 31(2) of the Children Act (the so-called threshold conditions)[174] are met; *and*

(d) the authority are satisfied that the child ought to be placed for adoption.

Local authorities *must* also apply if they are satisfied that the child ought to be placed for adoption and either care proceedings are pending or a care order has been made and the authority are not authorised to place the child for adoption. Local authorities *may* also apply for an order notwithstanding that the child is subject to a care order and the authority is authorised to place the child for adoption with parental consent.

The overall effect of this scheme is that whenever a local authority are seeking a care order with adoption as the care plan or where their existing placement or plan changes to adoption, they must have that plan or placement authorised by a court order. It will not infrequently be the case that local authorities will seek a care order and a placement order at the same time.

Deciding whether to make a placement order

The court may only make a placement order if (a) the child is subject to a care order, or (b) it is satisfied that the statutory threshold criteria for making a care order are satisfied,

---

[171] Section 20(4). Formerly, under the 1976 Act, this non-involvement could be achieved by making a s 18(6) declaration, but in practice such declarations were made only in minority of cases, see Lowe et al *Report of the Research into the Use and Practice of the Freeing for Adoption Provisions*, op cit, Table 3.45.

[172] See the Family Procedure Rules 2010 r 14.10 and *Practice Direction 5A*.

[173] As Bridge and Swindells, op cit, at 9.27 point out, it was eventually considered inappropriate to permit voluntary agencies to have a child compulsorily placed for adoption against the parents' wishes.

[174] These are the conditions that must be satisfied before a care order may be made, see Ch 18.

or (c) the child has no parent or guardian. Section 21(3) further provides that a court may only make a placement order if it is satisfied that each parent or guardian has consented to the placement for the child with any prospective adopters chosen by the authority and have not withdrawn that consent, or that their consent should be dispensed with.[175]

It is established[176] that before consent can dispensed with the court must be satisfied that the child's welfare throughout his life requires adoption rather than something short of adoption. If, at the time of the placement order application, the child's position is uncertain such that it cannot yet be said whether or not adoption is the right option, the placement order application must be refused. In *Re F (a child) (placement order best interests)*,[177] for example, the placement order was discharged because the child was found not to be ready for adoption since she needed to undergo a programme of therapeutic training designed to strengthen the bond between her and her main carer. According to expert evidence a judgment would have to be made later as to whether the potential benefits of adoption would outweigh the potential problems that severing the child's ties with her foster parents might cause her. On the other hand, if it is established that adoption would be in the child's best interests, it is no objection that the search for adoptive parents might prove unsuccessful and that the local authority's alternative plan is for the child's long term fostering.[178]

In determining the application the court is bound by the general principles set out in s 1 of the 2002 Act and in particular must, having regard to the welfare checklist, treat the child's welfare throughout his or her life as the paramount consideration and be satisfied, having considered the whole range of its powers, that making the placement order is better for the child than not doing so. In this regard, judges should apply the guidelines set out by the Court of Appeal in *Re B-S (Children) (Adoption Order: Leave to Oppose)*,[179] namely that there be (a) proper evidence from the local authority and guardian addressing all the realistic options including an analysis of the pros and cons of each option, and (b) an adequately reasoned judgment evaluating all the options. In this latter regard the judicial task has been said to be[180] to undertake a global, holistic and multi-faceted evaluation of the child's welfare which takes into account all the negatives and the positives of each option. The *B-S* guidelines are designed to be human rights compliant as articulated in particular by the Supreme Court in *Re B (A Child) (Care Proceedings: Threshold Criteria)*.[181] Only if, after exercising this discipline, it is considered that adoption is the right option for the child should a placement order be made. A placement order cannot be made subject to condition, for example, that the 'right' adopters be found.[182]

---

[175] The powers to dispense with consent are discussed at Dispensing with consent, pp 713ff.

[176] See *Re P (Placement Orders: Parental Consent)* [2008] EWCA Civ 535 [2008] 2 FLR 625.

[177] [2013] EWCA Civ 1277 [2014] 1 FCR 415. See also *Re T (Placement Order)* [2008] EWCA Civ 248 [2008] 1 FLR 1721. See also *NS-H v Kingston Upon Hull City Council and MC* [2008] EWCA Civ 493 [2008] 2 FLR 918, in which because of the child's failure to thrive whilst in foster care the immediate plan for adoption had been shelved. The mother was given leave to apply to revoke the placement order because there was a real prospect that she could show that the child was not in a condition to be adopted and that therefore the placement order should not have been made.

[178] See *Re P (Placement Orders: Parental Consent)* [2008] EWCA Civ 535 [2008] 2 FLR 625 at [37] per Wall LJ.

[179] [2014] 1 WLR 563. For a case where these criteria were not met, see *Re S (a child)(care and placement orders; proportionality)* [2013] EWCA Civ 1073 [2014] 2 FCR 139. See also *Re S (Appeal from Care and Placement orders)* [2014] EWCA Civ 135, [2014] Fam Law 774.

[180] Per Sir James Munby P in *Re B-S* [2013] EWCA Civ 1146 [2014] 1 WLR 563 at [44], adapting McFarlane LJ's judgment in *Re G (Care Proceedings: Welfare Evaluation)* [2013] EWCA Civ 965 [2014] 1 FLR 670.

[181] [2013] UKSC 33 [2013] 1 WLR 1911.

[182] See *Re A (children) (placement orders: conditions)* [2013] EWCA Civ 1611 [2014] 2 FCR 123.

Duration and revocation of placement orders

A placement order remains in force until an adoption order is made or until the child marries, forms a civil partnership or reaches 18 or until it is revoked.[183] Revocation is governed by s 24. It may be sought at any time by the child or local authority or by anyone else, including a parent, provided they have court leave *and* the child has not yet been placed with prospective adopters. By 'placement' is meant where the child begins to live with the prospective adopters or, if already living with them in their capacity of foster parents, when the adoption agency formally allows the child to continue to live with them in their fresh capacity as prospective adopters.[184] Unless or until it is revoked the parents or guardians have no right to have their child returned.[185]

By s 24(3) leave to apply to revoke a placement order may only be given if there has been a change in circumstances since the order was made. It is established[186] that granting leave is a two-stage process, namely, first, determining whether there has been a change of circumstances and, if so, secondly, determining whether leave should be given. The change of circumstances does not have to be significant but does need to be of a nature and degree sufficient to open the door to a consideration of whether leave should be given.[187] If there has been no change of circumstances then leave cannot be given, but even if there has, that in itself does not justify leave being given: that remains a matter of judicial discretion, which is the second stage. At this stage the question for the court is whether in all the circumstances, including the applicant's prospects of success in securing the revocation of the placement order and the child's interests, leave should be given.[188] It is accepted that in determining the leave question the child's welfare, though relevant, is *not* paramount.[189]

Once leave has been given and an appeal for revocation is pending then, if the child has not already been placed, he or she may not be placed without court leave.[190]

(d) The legal effects of placement

Placements or authorisations to place under s 19 and placement orders, give parental responsibility to the agency concerned and, where placed, to the prospective adopters. Although parents do not thereby lose parental responsibility, at all times the agency may determine that the parents' parental responsibility or that of the prospective adopters be restricted.[191] This latter power, however, is fettered to the extent that without court leave or the parents' or guardians' written consent, no-one can cause the child to be known by a new surname or remove the child from the United Kingdom for any period

---

[183] Section 21(4).

[184] See *Coventry City Council v O (Adoption)* [2011] EWCA Civ 729 [2011] 2 FLR 936. Introductory visits do not amount to a 'placement', see *Re S (Placement Order: Revocation)* [2008] EWCA Civ 1333 [2009] 1 FLR 503. [185] Section 34.

[186] See *Re B-S* [2014] 1 WLR 563 at [7] per Sir James Munby P.

[187] See *Re P (A Child) (Adoption Proceedings)* [2007] EWCA Civ 616 [2007] 1 WLR 2556. Note in *NS-H v Kingston Upon Hull City Council and MC* [2008] EWCA Civ 493 [2008] 2 FLR 918, the local authority were said to be wise to withdraw their submission that the change of circumstances related to those of the placement rather than with regard to the child.

[188] See *NS-H v Kingston Upon Hull City Council and MC* [2008] EWCA Civ 493 [2008] 2 FLR 918 at [27] per Wilson LJ.

[189] See *M v Warwickshire County Council (M intervening)* [2007] EWCA Civ 1084 [2008] 1WLR 991. This view is based on the wording of s 1(7) of the 2002 Act, see Wilson LJ's reluctant conclusion at [22]. This conclusion was accepted in *Re B-S*.

[190] Section 24(5), but note this provision is not triggered by an application for leave to revoke: *Re F (Placement Order)* [2008] EWCA Civ 339 [2008] 2 FLR 550. [191] Section 25.

of a month or more.[192] Subject to these latter restrictions, though, the local authority is in overall control.[193]

Placements or authorisations to place under s 19 prevent the parent or guardian from applying for a child arrangements order regulating the child's living arrangements and a guardian from applying for a special guardianship order without court leave.[194] Upon the making of a placement order, any existing s 8 order under the Children Act 1989 and any supervision order cease to have any effect and while in force no prohibited steps order, specific issue order, supervision order or child assessment order may be made.[195]

Separate provision is made for contact by s 26. Any contact provision in an existing s 8 child arrangements orders and any related activity direction and any s 34 order providing for parental contact with a child in care cease to have effect upon s 19 placements or authorisations to place and placement orders;[196] applications can nevertheless be made for a new contact order under s 26.[197] In this respect note should be taken of the requirement under the Adoption Agencies Regulations 2005, reg 46 (reg 47 of the Adoption Agencies (Wales) Regulations 2005) that agencies should consider when deciding that a child be placed for adoption what arrangements they should make for contact. Deciding whether to make a s 26 order is deemed by s 1(7) to be a decision relating to adoption. Consequently the governing welfare principle is that governed by s 1 of the 2002 Act rather than that by the s 1 of the 1989 Act. Contact orders under s 26 can be made between siblings.[198] Even where a s 26 contact order is made, an agency can nevertheless refuse contact in cases of urgency for up to seven days.[199]

A further extremely important consequence of a s 19 placement or placement order is that the parent may only oppose the making of an adoption order with court leave which can only be given if the court is satisfied that there has been a change in circumstances since the consent was given or the placement order was made.[200]

E. THE MAKING OF ADOPTION ORDERS

1. WHO MAY BE ADOPTED

Unlike some systems which provide for the adoption of adults, English law had, until the 2002 Act, been strictly confined to the adoption of children. However, while it remains the case that *applications* may only be made in respect of a person who is under the age of 18,[201]

---

[192] Section 28(2)–(4).

[193] This is not dissimilar to the local authority's position upon the making of a care order, see s 33(3)(b) of the 1989 Act 1989, discussed in Ch 17, The acquisition of parental responsibility by the designated local authoritiy, p 638.

[194] Section 28(1), as amended by the Children and Families Act 2014 Sch 2 para 61.

[195] Section 29, as amended by the Children and Families Act 2014 Sch 2 para 62. However, with court leave a child arrangements order with respect to the child's living arrangements or special guardianship order may be sought in any subsequent adoption application: s 29(4), (5), as amended.

[196] Section 26(1) as amended by the Children and Families Act 2014, Sch 2 para 60(2).

[197] But not for a child arrangements order dealing with contact or under 34, see s 26(2)(a), as amended by the Children and Families Act 2014, Sch 2 para 60(3).

[198] See *Re P (Placement Orders: Parental Consent)* [2008] EWCA Civ 535 [2008] 2 FLR 625.

[199] Section 27(2).

[200] Section 47(4), (5) and (7). A similar restriction applies to advance consent give under s 20, see s 47(2) (b), (3) and (7). Discussed further at Placing children with parental consent, p 700.

[201] Section 49(4).

orders can be made until the person has reached the age of 19.[202] The child must be single and never been married or entered a civil partnership.[203] An adopted child may be re-adopted.[204]

2. WHO MAY APPLY FOR ADOPTION

(a) Age, health, and domicile of applicant

Although the law has always prescribed a minimum age for adoptive applicants it has had different policies as to what that age should be. When it was first introduced the applicant had to be 25 or not less than 21 years older than the child to be adopted.[205] Twenty-five remained the minimum age for some time but it was eventually lowered to a uniform requirement of 21.[206] Currently, reflecting changes originally made by the Children Act 1989, applicants must be 21, save where the application is made by a couple[207] where it is sufficient if one is the mother or father of the child and aged at least 18 and the other is at least 21.[208] Although there is no prescribed maximum age, it should be appreciated that in practice adoption agencies will take age into account particularly as regards potential adopters for healthy babies.[209] Obviously age, for example in the case of grandparent applicants, can be a factor that the court may take into account when deciding whether an adoption order would be for the child's benefit. Whether upper age limits should be made more explicit either in legislation or guidance was raised by the Adoption Law Review,[210] but no action was taken.

Although there are no statutory requirements in respect of the health of adopters, as the Adoption Law Review pointed out,[211] adoption agencies are required by the regulations to obtain a report on the prospective adopters' health.[212]

A sole applicant, or, in the case of an application by a couple, one of the applicants, must be domiciled and habitually resident for at least one year in a part of the British Islands.[213]

(b) Adoptions by one person or a couple

An application for an adoption order may be made by a couple or by one person.[214] Reversing the former rule that only married couples were allowed to make a joint adoption application,[215] the 2002 Act permits joint applications by spouses (including same sex spouses), civil partners and by 'two people (whether of different sexes or the same

---

[202] Section 47(9). Apparently this change was made to ensure that applications for adoption would not be thwarted immediately upon the child becoming 18.

[203] Section 47(8) and (8A) added by the Civil Partnership Act 2004 s 79(3). The child's domicile does not affect jurisdiction: *Re B (S) (Infant)* [1968] Ch 201.   [204] Section 46(5).

[205] Adoption of Children Act 1926 s 2. At that time the age of majority was 21.

[206] Adoption Act 1976 s 14(1) and s 15(1).   [207] As defined by s 144(4).

[208] Adoption and Children Act 2002 ss 50 and 51.

[209] See the discussion in the Adoption Law Review, Discussion Paper No 3, at paras 40 *et seq.* These conditions may be relaxed where approval is sought to adopt older children or those with disabilities: see para 43.

[210] Ibid at para 44.   [211] Ibid at para 46.

[212] Adoption Agencies Regulations 2005, reg 25(3)(a) (England), reg 26(3)(a) of the. Adoption Agencies (Wales) Regulations 2005 These matters include personal and family history and the current state of health, including consumption of tobacco and alcohol.

[213] Section 49(2), (3). 'British Islands' means the United Kingdom (ie England and Wales, Scotland and Northern Ireland), Channel Islands and the Isle of Man.

[214] Adoption and Children Act 2002 s 49(1). According to statistics published by BAAF, 10% (420) of children adopted out of care in the year ending 31 March 2013 were by single adopters.

[215] According to pre-2002 Act law if it later emerged that the joint applicants were not married to each other, the order was voidable and not void: *Re F (Infants) (Adoption Order: Validity)* [1977] Fam 165, CA, cf *Re RA* (1974) 4 Fam Law 182.

sex) living in an enduring family relationship'.[216] In other words, spouses, civil partners and unmarried couples (whether of different sexes or the same sex) may all apply for joint adoptions though the latter have to prove that they are living 'in an enduring family relationship'.[217] Given that under the former law one member of an unmarried couple had been allowed to adopt,[218] the 2002 Act reform was arguably long overdue.[219] In any event, as Dr Harris MP put it:[220]

> Children must grow up in the real world. They must grow up in the 21st century in which 40% of children are born outside marriage and in which many people who are committed to one another choose not to marry. That applies to 15% of households and the figure is expected to rise to 30%.

Notwithstanding this observation, the key motivation for the fundamental change was the widening of the pool of potential applicants for adoption to meet the overall object of 'giving a child the chance to live in a stable living family rather than being left in care'.[221]

Save in the case of a step-parent application (which we discuss next) an order may not be made on the sole application of a married person or civil partner unless his spouse or partner cannot be found or is by reason of ill health, whether physical or mental, incapable of making an application for an adoption order or, alternatively, if the spouses or partners have separated and are living apart and the separation is likely to be permanent.[222] This embargo is designed to avoid the situation of a child being adopted by one of two spouses or civil partners living together, the other of whom refuses to apply for an order.

If the sole applicant is the mother or father of the child, by s 51(4), no order may be made unless the court is satisfied that the other natural parent is dead or cannot be found or by virtue of the Human Fertilisation and Embryology Act 2008 legislation[223] there is no other parent, or there is some other reason justifying the child being adopted by the applicant alone. The court must record that it is satisfied as to either of the first two mentioned facts or, in the latter case, record its reason. Section 51(4) has the potential for severing the ties with the other birth parent rather than to promote the child's welfare,[224]

---

[216] See the definition of 'couple' in s 144(4) of the 2002 Act, as amended by the Civil Partnership Act 2004 s 79.

[217] Nevertheless, when approving adopters, adoption agencies must in the case of *any* couple have proper regard to the need for stability and permanence in their relationship: Suitability of Adopters Regulations 2005 (SI 2005/1712). But note the pre-2002 Act decision in *Re WM (Adoption: Non-Patrial)* [1997] 1 FLR 132 where an adoption order was made despite the married couple separating *after* the making of the application.

[218] See eg *Re AB (Adoption: Joint Residence)* [1996] 1 FLR 27 and *Re W (Adoption: Homosexual Partner)* [1997] 2 FLR 406.

[219] Note also the House of Lords' ruling that regulations in Northern Ireland prohibiting unmarried couples from adopting were contrary to Art 14 taken in conjunction with Art 8 of the European Convention of Human Rights: *Re G (Adoption: Unmarried Couple)* [2008] UKHL 38 [2009] AC 173, on which see U Kilkelly 'In *Re P*: adoption, discrimination and the best interest of the child' [2010] CFLQ 115 and D Feldman 'Adoption and Discrimination: What Are Convention Rights?' [2008] CLJ 481.

[220] HC Deb Vol 385, col 969 (16 May 2002).

[221] C Bridge and H Swindells *Adoption: The Modern Law* (2003) 10.12, citing Dr Harris MP in HL Deb vol 388, cols 970–1. According to MOJ *Court Statistics Quarterly January to March 2013* (2013) Figure 2.18, 6% of adoptions were made in favour of same-sex couples. A similar proportion were made in April–June 2013 and July–September 2013, see respectively Figure 2.8 and 2.15 of the quarterly statistics.

[222] Adoption and Children Act 2002 s 51(3) and (3A) (added by the Civil Partnership Act 2004 s 79(4)).

[223] Discussed in Ch 8.

[224] This was precisely the concern of the Houghton Committee, op cit, paras 98–102 on whose recommendations the provision is originally based.

which was the issue in *Re B (Adoption: Natural Parent)*.[225] There, a baby had been put up for adoption by an unmarried mother who had informed the father neither of her pregnancy nor the birth. By chance the local authority discovered the father's whereabouts and he, when contacted, expressed the desire to care for the child himself. The child was placed with him, and the father gave up work to look after her. Notwithstanding that he had parental responsibility for the child by reason of a parental responsibility agreement, he nevertheless sought adoption. Though she had reservations, the mother did not oppose the adoption and maintained that she had no desire to interfere in the child's life. The question raised was whether it was in the *child*'s interest for the mother to be excluded. At first instance[226] Bracewell J thought that it was, on the basis that (a) the father's anxiety about the mother's continuing status as a parent with parental responsibility would perpetuate insecurity for him and potentially affect the child's stability and (b) the mother had consented and had no general wish to interfere. The Court of Appeal[227] set the adoption aside, holding that because of the general importance of having two parents adoption was, within the terms of Art 8 of the European Convention on Human Rights, a disproportionate response. The House of Lords, however, while agreeing that the circumstances in which it was in the best interests of the child to be adopted by one parent to the exclusion of the other were likely to be exceptional, could not fault Bracewell J's decision, which was accordingly reinstated.

(c) Step-parent adoptions

An important change introduced by the 2002 Act was ending the necessity of the birth parent and new partner having jointly to adopt. The former requirement meant that to effect a step-parent adoption the birth parent had to adopt their own child which was described[228] during the debates on the Bill as a 'ridiculous anomaly'. This change results, somewhat obscurely, from s 51(2) which provides that 'an adoption order may be made on the application of one person who has attained the age of 21 if the court is satisfied that the person is the partner of a parent of the person to be adopted' and s 46(3)(b) which says that in such cases the adoption by the partner 'does not affect the parental responsibility of that parent . . .'. These provisions apply equally to the birth parent's spouse, civil partner or anyone else with whom he or she has an 'enduring relationship'.[229] One curious effect of this change is that the child becomes 'half adopted', which poses interesting questions about access to birth records, for example, and the consequences for succession purposes.

Whether the law should permit step-parent adoptions and, if so, to what extent, is a long-standing issue. Until the Children Act 1975 there were no formal restrictions on any type of step-parent adoption applications. The Houghton Committee, however, was concerned[230] about the growing number of such adoptions which by 1970 exceeded 10,000 per annum. They were particularly concerned with 'post-divorce' step-parent adoptions which they felt were an inappropriate use of the jurisdiction and, given the consequential extinguishment of the legal links with half his family, potentially damaging to the child. The Committee felt that the preferable alternative was to extend the provisions enabling

---

[225] [2001] UKHL 70 [2002] 1 WLR 258, on which see A Bainham 'Unintentional Parenthood: the Case of the Reluctant Mother' [2002] CLJ 288 and S Harris-Short 'Putting the Child at the Heart of Adoption' [2002] CFLQ 325.   [226] See *B v P (Adoption by Unmarried Father)* [2000] 2 FLR 717.

[227] See *Re B (Adoption By One Natural Parent To Exclusion of Other)* [2001] 1 FLR 589.

[228] By John Hutton MP, HC Debs Vol 365, Col 709 (26 March 2001).

[229] See s 144(4) on the definition of 'partner'.

[230] At paras 103–110. As N Lowe pointed out in 'English Adoption Law—Past, Present and Future' op cit, unlike adoptions overall, step-parent adoptions continued to rise after the overall peak of 1968. In the case

a step-parent to apply to become a guardian. Following these concerns, the law was changed, with the courts being directed to dismiss 'post-divorce' step-parent adoption applications if they considered the matter would be better dealt with by an application to the divorce court for what was then a custody order.[231] The provisions were repealed by the Children Act 1989.[232]

The issue of step-parent adoption was again raised during the Adoption Law Review, but although concern was expressed that some applications 'appear to be made without full consideration of the needs of the child', it was nevertheless felt inappropriate to prohibit such adoptions.[233] Instead, the 2002 Act, as we discussed in Chapter 11, extended the ability to acquire parental responsibility either by agreement or court order to those married to (or in a civil partnership with) the parent. In 2013, 7% of all adoptions were made in favour of step-parents.[234]

(d) Adoption by relatives

Although there are no formal restrictions against relatives applying to adopt, the courts have long had reservations about granting adoption to such applicants not least because it distorts the natural relationship, particularly in the case of adoption by grandparents.[235] It is also felt that the severance of legal ties with the birth parents fits uneasily with an adoption within the family. Another concern in the case of grandparent applicants can be their age.[236]

The Houghton Committee reiterated concern about such adoptions, fearing the consequential dangers of hiding the real circumstances from the child.[237] They considered that an application for guardianship would normally be preferable. Following this recommendation a new order, custodianship, was created, by which applicants could seek orders vesting in them parental rights and duties but which did not extinguish the legal relationship between the child and his birth parents. It was hoped and expected that relatives would use this option rather than adoption, but in the event the take-up was thought to be disappointing and it was abolished by the Children Act 1989.[238] However, as we discuss at the end of this chapter, the 2002 Act introduced an order, not dissimilar to custodianship, namely, special guardianship. This order can be made on application or by the court of its own motion in any family proceedings including, therefore, adoption proceedings.

---

of legitimate children the numbers more than doubled from 4,038 in 1968 to 9,262 in 1975, while in the case of 'illegitimate' children, numbers rose from 4,479 in 1968 to 5,691 in 1974.

[231] Adoption Act 1976 s 14(3), in cases where the application was made jointly by a parent and step-parent, and s 15(4) where the application was by the step-parent alone.

[232] Adoption Act 1976 s 14(3) and s 15(4) and the Children Act 1975 were repealed by the Children Act 1989 Sch 15.   [233] Consultative Document 1992, para 19.

[234] See MOJ *Court Statistics Quarterly January to March 2013, April–June 2013 and July–September* (2013) Figure 2.18, 2.8 and 2.15 respectively.

[235] As Vaisey J said in *Re DX (An Infant)* [1949] Ch 320 at 321, 'The ostensible relationship of sisters between those who are in fact mother and child is unnatural and its creation might sow the seeds of grievous unhappiness for them both . . .'. Although in *Re C (A Minor) (Adoption Order: Conditions)* [1989] AC 1, Lord Ackner dismissed the contention that an adoption order should be refused because the child would be devastated to learn that her natural brother would no longer be in law her brother as being 'quite unreal', the concern about the distortion of relationships continue to be expressed, see in particular *Re S (Adoption Order or Special Guardianship Order* [2007] EWCA Civ 54 [2007] 1 FLR 819 at [51],per Wall LJ.

[236] See eg *Re W (A Minor) (Adoption by Grandparents)* (1980) 2 FLR 161, CA.   [237] At para 111.

[238] In fact, the evidence showed that grandparents were beginning to apply for custodianship. see, E Bullard, E Malos and R Parker who found that more than half of custodianship applications were by grandparents: HMSO *Custodianship: Caring for other people's children* (1991) Tables 24–8. On the other hand the court's power to make a custodianship order upon an adoption application was rarely exercised. Only two such cases were found in the *Pathways to Adoption* study, op cit, Table 2.10.

Special guardianship in particular, but also a child arrangements order dealing with the child's living arrangements, offer very real alternatives to adoption by relatives, especially so since the clear message of *Re B-S (Children) (Adoption Order: Leave to Oppose)*[239] that alternative options need to be considered before making an adoption order, they nevertheless do not always rule out the appropriateness of adoption for such applicants. The Adoption Law Review[240] saw no reason to rule out the possibility of adoption by relatives, which they envisaged to be appropriate where the child's parents are dead, or living in another country and unlikely ever to be able to make parental decisions in respect of the child's upbringing. It is difficult to disagree with this conclusion and indeed the case for prohibiting adoption by relatives seems weaker than that for step-parents. A good example is *N v B and Others (Adoption by Grandmother)*[241] in which adoption orders in respect of two children were granted to the maternal grandmother following the murder of the mother by the father (for which he was serving a life sentence). As Theis J observed, the children needed a secure home and it was undesirable for the grandmother to share parental responsibility with the father.

3. CONSENT TO THE MAKING OF AN ORDER

By s 47(2) it is one of the fundamental conditions for the making of an adoption order that:

> in the case of each parent or guardian of the child, the court is satisfied—
> (a) that the parent or guardian consents to the making of the adoption order,
> (b) that the parent or guardian has consented under section 20 (and has not withdrawn the consent) and does not oppose the making of the adoption order, or
> (c) that the parent's or guardian's consent should be dispensed with.

It is by this means that the law recognises and seeks to protect the parental interest. Indeed, so important is the right to refuse to consent, that it is not lost even if others, including a local authority, acquire parental responsibility.[242]

(a) Whose consent is required?

The Act requires the consent of each parent or guardian. By 'parent' is meant a parent with parental responsibility.[243] It does not therefore include the unmarried father,[244] unless he has parental responsibility through registration, court order or agreement. However, if the mother has already consented to the child's placement for adoption before the father acquires parental responsibility, he will be deemed to have given consent.[245] This is to prevent the father from frustrating or obstructing an arrangement which the mother has already entered into with an adoption agency, and indeed without this provision

---

[239] [2014] 1 WLR 563 discussed at Adoption and human rights, p 684.
[240] See the Consultative Document, op cit, at para 20.4.
[241] [2013] EWHC 820 (Fam) [2014] 1 FLR 369. For examples of where adoption was held preferable to special guardianship see *Re AJ (Adoption Order or Special Guardianship Order)* [2007] EWCA Civ 55 [2007] 1 FLR 507, adoption made in favour of a paternal aunt and *Re M-J (Adoption Order or Special Guardianship Order)* [2007] EWCA Civ 56 [2007] 1 FLR 691, adoption made in favour of an uncle and aunt.
[242] See Children Act 1989 s 12(3) and s 33(6)(b). For the position where a special guardianship order is made, see The effects of special guardianship orders, p 735.
[243] Adoption and Children Act 2002 s 52(6).
[244] See *Re M (An Infant)* [1955] 2 QB 479, CA; and *Re C (Adoption: Parties)* [1995] 2 FLR 483, CA. It similarly excludes a 's 43 second female parent', for the meaning of which see Ch 8.
[245] Adoption and Children Act 2002 s 52(9), (10).

authority for the placement would lapse immediately. Nevertheless it has been queried[246] whether this provision is in breach of Art 8 in terms of the father's right to respect for family life. 'Parent' does not include 'step-parent', even if they have parental responsibility. In the case of an adopted child, 'parent' refers to each adoptive parent.[247] 'Guardian' refers to any person formally appointed by an individual or by a court[248] and, by s 144(4), a special guardian.[249]

The parents' position where their child has been placed by an adoption agency

By s 47(5) a parent may not, without court leave, oppose the making of an adoption order if a child has been placed by an adoption agency with parental consent or under a placement order. Leave cannot be given unless the court is 'satisfied that there has been a change of circumstances since the consent of the parent was given or, as the case may be, the placement order was made.'[250]

As established by *Re P (A Child) (Adoption Proceedings)*[251] and subsequently endorsed by *Re B-S (Children) (Adoption: Leave to Oppose)*,[252] obtaining leave involves a two-stage process: determining whether there has been a change of circumstances and, if so, determining whether leave should be given. If no change can be established, leave must be refused, but establishing a change is not in itself sufficient as the court must then exercise its discretion in deciding whether leave should be given. At this second stage the child's welfare throughout his life is paramount since the leave decision falls within the definition of 'coming to a decision in relation to the adoption of the child' within the meaning of s 1(7), thus triggering the application of s 1(2) of the 2002 Act.[253]

Section 47(7) does not qualify 'change of circumstances' in any way. It is therefore wrong to require that the change be 'significant' but as Wall LJ said in *Re P* it must be of a nature and degree sufficient to open the door to the exercise of the judicial discretion. Nevertheless the test should not be set too high because parents 'should not be discouraged from bettering themselves or from seeking to prevent the adoption of their child by the imposition of a test which is unachievable.'[254]

---

[246] See Clarke Hall and Morrison on *Children* at 10 [235] n 1.

[247] But if the adoption order in question is a foreign order which is not recognised by the English court, then the birth parents' consent will still be required: *Re G (Foreign Adoption: Consent)* [1995] 2 FLR 534. But note Charles J's reservations in *Re A (Adoption of a Russian Child)* [2000] 1 FLR 539 at 543.

[248] Under the pre-2002 Act law there was a dispute as to whether to qualify as a guardian for these purposes, the appointment had to be made under s 5 of the Children Act 1989 and not therefore under foreign legislation. This narrow construction was favoured by Holman J in *Re D (Adoption: Foreign Guardianship)* [1999] 2 FLR 865 but the predominant view since then is that that approach was too narrow, see eg *Re J (Adoption: Consent of Foreign Public Authority)* [2002] EWHC 766 (Fam) [2002] 2 FLR 618 per Charles J and *Re AGN (Adoption: Foreign Adoption)* [2000] 2 FLR 431 per Cazalet J. See further N Lowe 'Do Foreign Appointed Guardians Qualify as 'Guardians' for the purposes of the Adoption and Children Act 2002?' [2008] Fam Law 163.

[249] This latter right of consent, however, is said by s 14C(2)(b) of the 1989 Act, not to affect 'any rights which a parent of the child has in relation to the child's adoption or placement for adoption.' This presumably means that notwithstanding that s 52(6) requires the consent of each parent *or* (in this case) special guardian, in fact the consent of both is required.

[250] Section 44(7). Similarly if advance consent has been given under s 20, leave is required to oppose the making of an adoption order: s 44(3), which can only be given if s 44(7) is satisfied.

[251] [2007] EWCA Civ 616 [2007] 1 WLR 2556. [252] [2013] EWCA Civ 1146 [2014] 1 WLR 563.

[253] See the discussion in *Re P* at [19]–[24]. Cf the position when determining whether to give leave to apply to revoke a placement order under s 24(2), on which see *M v* Warwickshire *County Council (M intervening)* [2007] EWCA Civ 1084 [2008] 1 WLR 991, discussed at Duration and revocation of placement orders, p 703. See also *Re W (A Child) (Adoption Order: Leave to Oppose) (Practice Note)* [2013] EWCA Civ 1177 [2014] 1 WLR 1993. [254] [2007] EWCA Civ 616 [2007] 1 WLR 2556 at [30]–[32].

According to Sir James Munby P in *Re B-S*, at the second stage the court has to consider all the circumstances but in particular the parent's ultimate prospect of success in resisting the making of the adoption order and the impact on the child of its decision always bearing mind that the child's welfare throughout his life is paramount. He added that as a general proposition 'the greater the change of circumstances (assuming, of course, that the change is positive) and the more solid the parent's grounds for seeking leave to oppose, the more cogent and compelling the arguments based on the child's welfare must be if leave to oppose is to be refused.'[255]

The position of the unmarried father without parental responsibility

An unmarried father without parental responsibility is not automatically a party to the proceedings[256] nor is his consent required. The court however, has a discretion to make him a party.[257] Furthermore, under s 1(4)(f) of the 2002 Act both the court and adoption agency have to consider the wishes and feelings of the child's relatives including both the mother and father.[258] In any event, it well established[259] that there is a very high bar on excluding a father from adoption proceedings and, indeed, where he has a meaningful relationship with the child, applications to exclude him will very rarely succeed. Nevertheless, as Thorpe LJ accepted in *Re G (Adoption Order)*,[260] there can be a wide spectrum of circumstances: 'There will be cases in which the father will have very little merit, and accordingly, very little entitlement to consideration. At the other end of the scale, there will be cases in which the natural father should be given what will be something akin to the statutory right [of consent].' *Re H, Re G (Adoption: Consultation of Unmarried Fathers)*[261] well illustrates this spectrum. In *Re H* the parents had had a relationship, including cohabitation, that had lasted several years and the father had shown a continuing commitment to the elder child. He was therefore entitled to respect for his family life with the child under Art 8 of the European Convention on Human Rights and it was held that to place the child for adoption without notice to him would breach this right. In contrast, in *Re G* the parents had never cohabited and their relationship did not have the constancy to show de facto family ties. Consequently the father had no Art 8 right and it was not necessary for him to be notified of the proceedings. In *C v XYZ County Council*[262] a young mother, who only realised at a late stage that she was pregnant after a one night stand, concealed the pregnancy and birth from her family, did not identify the father and left the child in hospital after she was born with a view to her being adopted. It was held that in these circumstances it was not in the child's interests for the local authority to disclose the child's existence to the maternal family, nor to the father if he could be identified. In cases such as this, provided no proceedings have started, adoption agencies or local authorities can ask for court directions on the need to give a father without parental responsibility notice of the intention to place child for adoption.[263]

---

[255] [2013] EWCA Civ 1146 [2014] 1 WLR 563 at [74].   [256] See the FPR 2010, r 14.3(1).
[257] FPR 2010, r 14.3(3)(a).   [258] Adoption and Children Act 2002 s 1(8).
[259] See *Re A (Father: Knowledge of Child's Birth)* [2011] EWCA Civ 273 [2011] 2 FLR 123.
[260] [1999] 1 FLR 400 at 403, CA.   [261] [2001] 1 FLR 646, per Butler-Sloss P.
[262] [2007] EWCA Civ 1206 [2008] Fam 54, on which see B Sloan 'Adoption, Welfare and the Procreative One-Night Stand' [2008] CLJ 33. See also *A & B and P Council and M (A Child by his Children's Guardian)* [2014] EWHC 1128 (Fam) [2014] All ER (D) 181 (Apr) and *Re L (Adoption: Contacting Natural Father)* [2007] EWHC 1771 (Fam) [2008] 1 FLR 1079 for other examples in which it was held that the father need not be contacted.   [263] FPR 2010 r 14.21.

The position of the child

In deciding whether an adoption order will be for the child's welfare, the court and adoption agency are bound[264] to have regard to 'the child's ascertainable wishes and feelings regarding the [adoption] decision (considered in the light of the child's understanding)'. The child's *consent* is not, however, required.[265]

The Adoption Law Review's recommendation[266] that an adoption order should not be made in relation to a child aged 12 or over unless the court was satisfied either that the child had consented or that he was incapable of doing so, was not included in the 2002 Act. That recommendation was open to the objection that it seemed to place on the child the responsibility for making the decision[267] and that in any event 12 was a particularly young age to choose and out of line with other provisions,[268] notably the Family Law Reform Act 1969 s 8, under which those aged 16 or over can give a valid consent to medical treatment.[269] Notwithstanding that formal consent is not required, it is clearly bad practice to plan for an older child's adoption against their wishes.[270]

(b) Form of consent

By s 52(5), 'consent' means:

> consent given unconditionally and with a full understanding of what is involved;[271] but a person may consent to adoption without knowing the identity of the person in whose favour the order will be made.

Although it has long ceased to be possible to make consent conditional on the child being brought up in a particular religion,[272] when placing a child for adoption, the court or adoption agencies in Wales must give 'due consideration to the child's religious persuasion,

---

[264] Adoption and Children Act 2002 s 1(4)(a).

[265] In some other jurisdictions such as Scotland, the older child's consent is required: see eg Adoption Law Review, *Background Paper No 1*, paras 116–20. Note also Art 5 of the 2008 European Convention on the Adoption of Children (Revised) which requires the consent of a child considered in law to have sufficient understanding (by Article 5(1)(b) the minimum age for these purposes is 14), though States are permitted to take a reservation on this, see Art 27(1), a right which is likely to be taken advantage of by England and Wales.

[266] See the Consultative Document, op cit, at 9.5 and cl 41(7) of the proposed Adoption Bill.

[267] Particularly if the child were to be required formally to sign a consent form.

[268] Ironically, according to some research (see J Fratter, J Rowe, I Sapsford and J Thoburn *Permanent Family Placement: a decade of experience* (1991)), adoption placements at 12 are most likely to break down.

[269] Discussed in Ch 9. Though in this respect it must be acknowledged that the courts have effectively lowered this age by accepting the validity of consent by '*Gillick* competent children' under the age of 16.

[270] See *Re M (Adoption or Residence Order)* [1998] 1 FLR 570, in which what was then a residence order rather than an adoption order was made in view of the 11-year-old child's objection to being adopted.

[271] See *Re A (Adoption: Agreement: Procedure)* [2001] 2 FLR 455 in which it failed to be established that the consent of a 14 year old mother who was a refugee from the Kosova conflict was sufficiently informed, unequivocal, mature or stable. There is some support for saying that a parent must know all the material facts before his consent should be regarded as having been given: cf *Re M (Minors) (Adoption)* [1991] 1 FLR 458, CA (order set aside where father consented to adoption by mother and step-father in ignorance that his wife, who died three months later, was terminally ill), discussed further at Setting adoptions aside, p 723, and *Re An Adoption Application* [1992] 1 FLR 341 (mother's consent, given in ignorance that male applicant was involved in criminal proceedings, not to be relied upon).

[272] This right was ended by the Adoption Act 1976.

racial origin and cultural and linguistic background'.[273] This reflects the importance attached to the maintenance of the Welsh language and culture.

The mother cannot give an effective agreement until the child is six weeks old.[274]

Where the parent is prepared to consent to a placement under s 19 or to give advance consent to adoption under s 20 the adoption agency must request the appointment of a Cafcass officer or a Welsh family proceedings officer to witness the signing of the consent form.[275]

So far as court proceedings (both for a placement order and for adoption) are concerned, wherever it appears that a parent is willing to consent, the court will appoint a reporting officer. That officer has to witness the signing of consent, having ensured so far as reasonably practical that the parent is giving consent unconditionally and with full understanding of what is involved, and having investigated all the circumstances relevant to that consent. The officer must then submit a confidential report to the court.[276]

4. DISPENSING WITH CONSENT

Section 52 of the 2002 Act permits the court to make placement for adoption orders or adoption orders having dispensed with parental consent which, as Baroness Hale observed in *Down Lisburn Health and Social Services Trust*,[277] makes the UK unusual among Council of Europe States in permitting the total severance of family ties without parental consent.

The power to dispense with consent is not new, but as we now discuss, the 2002 Act substantially re-drew the balance in favour of securing the child's welfare. Nevertheless, it is worth remembering that even under the former law applications were rarely refused.[278]

(a) The pre-2002 Act position

Under the Adoption Act 1976, before parental 'agreement' to adoption could be dispensed with, the court had to be satisfied as to the existence of one of six grounds. The first of these grounds was that the parent 'cannot be found or is incapable of giving agreement' which is preserved by the 2002 Act. The other grounds, which have all been swept away by the 2002 Act, were that the parent or guardian:

(b) is withholding his agreement unreasonably;
(c) has persistently failed without reasonable cause to discharge his parental responsibility for the child;
(d) has abandoned or neglected the child;
(e) has persistently ill-treated the child;
(f) has seriously ill-treated the child . . .

---

[273] Adoption and Children Act 2002 s 1(5). Note this provision no longer applies in England: s 3 of the Children and Families Act 2014, discussed at Religious, racial, cultural and linguistic considerations, p 696.

[274] Section 52(3). This condition is designed to prevent the mother from being persuaded to give her agreement before she has recovered from the child's birth.

[275] Adoption Agencies Regulations 2005 reg 20 (England); Adoption Agencies (Wales) Regulations 2005 reg 20 (Wales).   [276] See the FPR 2010 r 16.30.

[277] [2006] UKHL (NI) 36 [2007] 1 FLR 121 at [34] and cited by Sir James Munby P in *Re B-S (Children) (Adoption Order) (Leave to Oppose)* [2014] 1 WLR 563 at [19].

[278] In the *Pathways to Adoption Study*, op cit, at para 2.1, less than 1% of the applications in the sample were refused.

The hallmark of grounds (c) to (f) was parental culpability. On the other hand, ground (b) was clearly the catch-all ground and potentially quite wide. It was established by *Re W (An Infant)*[279] that under this ground:

> . . . the test is reasonableness and not anything else. It is not culpability. It is not indifference. It is not failure to discharge parental duties. It is reasonableness in the context of the totality of the circumstances. But, although welfare *per se* is not the test, the fact that a reasonable parent does pay regard to the welfare of his child must enter into the question of reasonableness as a relevant factor. It is relevant in all cases if and to the extent that a reasonable parent would take it into account. It is decisive in those cases where a reasonable parent must so regard it . . .

These dispensing grounds operated in a framework in which, when deciding whether or not to make an adoption order, the child's welfare was the first and not the paramount consideration. It was therefore not the case that an adoption would be made simply because it was for the child's welfare. Indeed it became established[280] that in cases where agreement was withheld the courts were required to apply a two-stage process, namely to determine first whether it was for the child's welfare to be adopted and then, if it was, to determine whether parental agreement should be dispensed with.

The Adoption Law Review considered the position to be 'clearly unsatisfactory', pointing out[281] that the fault-based dispensation grounds were objectionable both because faults or shortcomings of parental care do not *ipso facto* justify adoption as a suitable option for the child nor, where adoption is thought right, should they imply that parents are necessarily at fault. The Review also considered[282] the unreasonable withholding ground unsatisfactory, since it was problematic as to how much weight a reasonable parent should place on the child's welfare; and in any event it seemed wrong to fix a parent with the stigma of being an 'unreasonable parent'.

(b) The position under the 2002 Act

The 2002 Act replaced the previous six grounds with just two. In applying these grounds the court is bound by s 1(2) to treat the child's welfare, throughout his life, as the paramount consideration and in assessing this, the court must have regard to the 'welfare' checklist in s 1(4).

Cannot be found or lacks capacity within the meaning of the Mental Capacity Act 2005 to give consent

As originally enacted the 2002 Act exactly mirrored the former law, but s 52(1)(a) was amended by the Mental Capacity Act 2005[283] in relation to the lack of capacity to consent.

So far as 'cannot be found' is concerned, it is well established that consent will not lightly be dispensed with on this ground. In *Re F (R) (An Infant)*[284] it was held that before the court could be satisfied that the parent 'could not be found' it had to be shown that all reasonable and proper steps had been taken. In that case it was held that all such steps had not been taken since in their search for the birth mother the applicants had failed to get in touch with the maternal grandfather with whom the mother was still in contact.

---

[279] [1971] AC 682 at 700, per Lord Hailsham LC.
[280] *Re C (A Minor) (Adoption: Parental Agreement: Contact)* [1993] 2 FLR 260, CA
[281] See para 12.5.   [282] See para 12.4.   [283] See s 67 and Sch 6.
[284] [1970] 1 QB 385, CA. A similar test applies in Scotland, see *Re S (Adoption)* [1999] 2 FLR 374, Ct of Session.

For these purposes reasonable steps will include making enquiries at the last known address, asking questions of relatives and seeking the assistance of Government bodies.

Occasionally, where the parents live abroad, circumstances or even the law may mean that there are no practical means of communicating with them and consent has consequently been dispensed with on the basis that they cannot be found.[285]

To establish incapacity to consent within the meaning of the Mental Capacity Act 2005 it must be shown that the parent is unable at that time (ie incapacity does not have to be permanent) inter alia to understand the information relevant to the decision; retain that information; use or weigh that information as part of the process of making the decision or communicating that decision. This lack of capacity may be because of an impairment of, or disturbance in, the functioning of the mind or brain.[286] Although this definition is wide enough to cover mental disability and physical disability as, for example, by being in a coma,[287] it is not as wide as the former law which had been held to include incapacity due to ignorance.[288]

As one commentary says,[289] if the parent has a disability but expressly withholds consent, the court may have to consider whether to dispose with that consent either on the basis of incapacity or the welfare ground. In any event if the parent is or may be under a disability, the court will have to consider appointing a Litigation Friend.[290]

The welfare of the child requires the consent to be dispensed with

As already mentioned, the welfare ground provided by s 52(1)(b) upon which consent can be dispensed with, replaced the former culpability and reasonableness grounds. When coupled with the change made in s 1 of the 2002 Act to apply the paramountcy principle in coming to any decision relating to the adoption of a child, it is clearly a wide ground. Indeed, as Wall LJ put it in *Re S (Adoption Order or Special Guardianship Order)*, at 'first blush it would appear likely to be the case that once the court has reached the conclusion that adoption is in the best interests of the child, it will follow that his or her welfare will require the court to dispense with parental consent to adoption.'[291]

Re P

The Court of Appeal had its first opportunity to give detailed consideration to s 52(1)(b) in *Re P (Placement Order: Parental Consent)*.[292] *Re P* confirmed that it is incumbent upon the court, when applying 'welfare' in this context, to apply s 1 of the 2002 Act. That provision requires the court to treat the child's welfare, *throughout his life*, as its paramount consideration taking into account the welfare checklist set out in s 1(4) which, as Wall LJ pointed

---

[285] See *Re R (Adoption)* [1966] 3 All ER 613 (dangerous to contact parents living under a totalitarian regime) and *Re A (Adoption of a Russian Child)* [2000] 1 FLR 539 (contrary to Russian law to make contact with the mother). Cf *Re J (Adoption: Consent of Foreign Public Authority)* [2002] EWHC 766 (Fam) [2002] 2 FLR 618, in which, on the assumption that it was the child's 'guardian', it was held, obiter, that the Jordanian public authority's consent could have been dispensed with on the ground that, since public duties prevented it from giving consent, it was 'incapable of doing so'.   [286] See ss 1 and 2.

[287] See Clarke Hall and Morrison at 10 [305].   [288] See *Re R (Adoption)* [1966] 3 All ER 613.

[289] Clarke Hall and Morrison, above, at 10 [305].

[290] See the Family Procedure Rules 2010, r 14.9 (4). Appointments of litigation friends are governed by Chapter 5 of the FPR. For an example of a litigation friend being appointed, see *RP v Nottingham City Council and the Official Solicitor (Mental Capacity of Parent)* [2008] EWCA Civ 462, [2008] 2 FLR 1516, a decision subsequently ruled to be human rights compliant in *RP and Others v UK* [2013] 1 FLR 744, ECtHR.

[291] [2007] EWCA Civ 54 [2007] 1 FLR 819 at [71]. Interestingly, Wall LJ declined to express a final decision on this point, see [72].   [292] [2008] EWCA Civ 535 [2008] 2 FLR 625.

out, is far wider than that provided by the Children Act 1989.[293] We discussed s 1(4) earlier in this chapter.[294] Suffice to say here, that the courts are specifically directed to consider 'the likely effect on the child (throughout his life) of having ceased to be a member of the original family and become an adopted person' and the continued value to the child of any existing relationship, which the court considers to be relevant.[295]

In *Re P* Wall J emphasised[296] that in applying the welfare test it is not sufficient simply to use the words of ss 52(1)(b) and 1(4) as a mantra, rather their application needs careful analysis to justify the conclusion that the child's welfare *requires* the consent to be dispensed with. 'Requires' in this context has the Strasbourg meaning of 'necessary'; in Wall LJ's words, it has 'the connotation of the imperative, what is demanded rather than what is merely optional or reasonable or desirable.'[297] Put in the context of s 51(2)(b), what has to be shown is that the child's welfare 'requires' adoption as opposed to something short of adoption. To be able properly to reach such a conclusion, a court must, as required by s 1(6) of the 2002 Act, explore all the options and, bearing in mind human rights considerations for the need for proportionality,[298] be satisfied that adoption is proportionate to the legitimate aim of protecting the welfare and interests of the child. In short, as Wall LJ explained:[299]

> what therefore has to be shown is that the child's welfare 'requires' *adoption* as opposed to something short of adoption. A child's circumstances may 'require' statutory intervention, perhaps even 'require' the indefinite or long-term removal of the child from the family and his or her placement with strangers, but that is not to say that the same circumstances will necessarily 'require' that the child be adopted. They may or they may not. The question, at the end of the day, is whether what is 'required' is adoption.

Re B-S

Wall LJ's analysis was endorsed by the Court of Appeal in the leading decision, *Re B-S (Children) (Adoption Order: Leave to Oppose)*.[300] This in turn was concerned to apply the general principles set out by the Supreme Court in *Re B (A Child) (Care Proceedings: Threshold Criteria)*,[301] which had emphasised that making a non-consensual placement order or adoption order was a most extreme option to be made only as last resort where nothing else will do.

Giving the judgment of the court, Sir James Munby P emphasised that the court should apply the 'least interventionist' approach and drew attention to Hale J's comment in *Re O (Care or Supervision Order)*[302] that 'the court should begin with a preference for the less interventionist rather than the most interventionist approach. This should be considered to be in the better interests of children...unless there cogent reasons to the contrary.'

---

[293] [2008] EWCA Civ 535 [2008] 2 FLR 625 at [115]. Note: when an application is made both for a care order and a placement order, the court has to apply the 1989 Act checklist and that under the 2002 Act respectively and it is important not to muddle the two.

[294] See The position under the 2002 Act, p 694. 　　　[295] See s 1(4)(c) and (f).

[296] [2008] EWCA Civ 535 [2008] 2 FLR 625 at [131].

[297] [2008] EWCA Civ 535 [2008] 2 FLR 625 at [125] and repeated by Sir James Munby P in *Re B-S (Children) (Adoption Order: Leave to Oppose)* [2013] EWCA Civ 1146 [2014] 1 WLR 563 at [20].

[298] Emphasised inter alia by Hale LJ in *Re C and B (Care Order: Future Harm)* [2001] 1 FLR 611 at [33] and *Haase v Germany* [2004] 2 FLR 39, at [93], ECtHR.

[299] [2008] EWCA Civ 535 [2008] 2 FLR 535 at [126].

[300] [2014] 1 WLR 563.

[301] [2013] UKSC 33 [2013] 1 WLR 1911, discussed in this context, at Adoption and human rights, p 684.

[302] [1996] 2 FLR 755 at 760.

Bearing in mind the Supreme Court's decision in *Re B* and Lord Neuberger's judgment in particular, Sir James Munby P set out the following three points that need to be applied when deciding whether to dispense with consent under s 52 (1)(b). First, as he put it:[303]

Re BS

> although the child's interests in adoption case are paramount, the court must never lose sight of the fact that those interests include being brought up by the natural family, ideally by the natural parents, or at least one of them, unless the overriding requirements of the child's welfare make that not possible.

Secondly, the court must consider all the options before coming to a decision. What those options might be will depend upon the individual circumstances of the case, but at their widest they can range from making no order to making the adoption order or placement order. In between these extremes there can be an order for the return of the child to the parents' care with the support of a family assistance, care or supervision order, or for the child to be placed with relatives or someone else under a child arrangements order or special guardianship order. To help it arrive at its decision the expectation is that the local authority and the children's guardian will present the court with a fully argued analysis of the advantages and disadvantages of all the realistic options.

Thirdly, in Munby P's words:[304]

> the court's assessment of the parents' ability to discharge their responsibilities towards the child must take into account the assistance and support which the authorities would offer... It is the obligation of the local authority to make the order which the court has determined is proportionate work. The local authority cannot press for a more drastic form of order, least of all, press for adoption, because it is unable or unwilling to support a less interventionist form of order. Judges must be alert to the point and must be rigorous in exploring and probing the local authority thinking in cases where there is any reason to suspect that resource issues may be affecting the local authority's thinking.

(c) Commentary

There can be little quarrel with the first dispensation ground under s 52(1)(a) since it is clearly necessary to make provision for cases where the parents cannot be found or are incapable of giving consent. At the time of the Act, however, although few, if any, supported the retention of the unreasonably withholding test, nor opposed the ending of the fault-based grounds, there was concern at the potential width of the welfare ground under s 52(1)(b). As one commentator tellingly asked,[305] if a simple welfare test is considered inadequate to justify the compulsory removal of children into care, how could it be right to justify the complete and irrevocable transfer of parentage? One response to these fears was to point to the adoption welfare checklist under s 1(4) which was both expected and intended to strike the balance between the child's and the parents' interest.[306] But the problem was that the Act left it to the court's discretion as to how the welfare ground should be interpreted and it was for that reason that in the previous edition[307] we

---

[303] [2014] 1 WLR 563 at [26].

[304] [2014] 1 WLR 563 at [28]–[29].

[305] See eg E Cooke 'Dispensing with parental consent to adoption—a choice of welfare tests' [1997] CFLQ 259 at 263.

[306] See J Paton 'Adoption' in M Thorpe and C Cowton (eds) *Delight and Dole* (2003) 55 and John Hutton MP in HC Deb Vol 365, col 703 (26 March 2001). [307] At p 859.

supported the Adoption Law Review's recommendation[308] that the 'test should require the court to be satisfied that the advantages to the child of becoming part of a new family are so significantly greater than the advantages of any alternative option as to justify overriding the wishes of a parent or guardian.'

Although by emphasising the 'requirement' element of s 51(2)(b), the Court of Appeal in *Re P* and *Re B-S*, perhaps took a different approach to that predicted at the time of the 2002 Act, the two decisions have allayed fears that the dispensing ground would be set too high for parents. Indeed, it is suggested that the Court of Appeal have applied a stricter version of the test recommended by the Adoption Law Review.

F. PROCEDURE FOR THE MAKING
OF ADOPTION ORDERS

1. THE CHILD MUST LIVE WITH THE APPLICANTS BEFORE THE MAKING OF AN ORDER

Before any adoption order may be made there has to have been a 'settling in' period so as to be able to assess whether such a placement would be in the child's interests.[309] The required period is governed by s 42. This provides that in the case of agency placements,[310] placements made in pursuance of a High Court order or where the applicant is a parent of the child, no application may be made unless the child has had his home with the applicant or, in the case of an application by a couple, with one or both of them at all times during the period of 10 weeks before the application. In the case of step-parents the period is six months, in the case of a non-agency application by local authority foster parents the period is one year;[311] and in any other case[312] the period is 'not less than three years (whether continuous or not) during the period of five years preceding the application'.

The former provision[313] that in determining with whom the child has his home, any absence at a hospital or boarding school and any other temporary absence, was to be disregarded, is not repeated by the 2002 Act. It was felt to be too restrictive (for example, it made no allowance for temporary absences by other parties) and that it was therefore better to leave the whole issue to the court's discretion.[314] However, the possibility that the whole period could be spent away from the applicants' home is guarded against by the further provision that the agency placing him, or the local authority in non-agency placements, must have sufficient opportunities to see the child with the applicant or, in the case of a joint application, both applicants together, in the home environment.[315]

---

[308] See the Consultative Document, R 13.

[309] Note that under s 35(2) an agency may, having served due notice, end the placement by that agency. See further Duration and revocation of placement orders, p 703.

[310] For the meaning of 'placements', see the discussion at Duration and revocation of placement orders, p 703.

[311] Applications can be made earlier with court leave: s 42(6).

[312] Eg private foster parents or relatives. As Bridge and Swindells, op cit, at 10.54 point out, this cumulative probationary period of three years where relatives concerned has been extended from the former requirement of 13 weeks, but this is a deliberate policy to discourage such applications and to encourage the use of other options.   [313] Viz. Adoption Act 1976 s 72(1A).

[314] See Jacquie Smith MP in HC Deb Vol 386, no 150, col 191 (20 May 2002).

[315] Adoption and Children Act 2002 s 42(7). Note that for theses purpose the 'home' does not have to be within the jurisdiction: *Re A (Adoption: Removal)* [2009] EWCA Civ 141 [2009] 2 FLR 597.

'Home' is not defined in the Act but pre-2002 Act case law[316] considered that, though difficult to define with precision, it must comprise some element of regular occupation (whether past, present, or intended for the future, even if intermittent) with some degree of permanency, based on some right of occupation whenever it is required: it is where you find the fixed comforts of a home; the fixed residence of a family or household. While ultimately a question of fact to be determined in each case, a house that is merely visited by members of the family is unlikely to constitute a 'home' for these purposes.[317]

2. NOTICE TO LOCAL AUTHORITY MUST BE GIVEN IN NON-AGENCY PLACEMENTS

In all cases where the child has not been placed for adoption by an adoption agency the applicant must, not more than two years or fewer than three months before the order, give written[318] notice to the local authority within whose area the child has his home of the intention to apply for an adoption order.[319]

Upon receipt of such notice the local authority must investigate the matter, in particular the suitability of the applicants, and any other matter relevant to the child's long-term welfare and submit a report to the court.[320]

G. CONTACT CONSIDERATIONS

1. SECTION 46(6)

By s 46(6), before making an adoption order:

the court must consider whether there should be arrangements for allowing any person contact with the child; and for that purpose the court must consider any existing or proposed arrangements and obtain the views of the parties to the proceedings.

Although, as discussed earlier,[321] it has long been accepted that in principle the court may make an order for post-adoption contact this was the first *statutory* recognition of such a power.

Notwithstanding s 46(6) and certain judicial statements identifying the value of post-adoption contact,[322] the general reluctance to impose a contact order against the wishes of adopters that was evident before the 2002 Act,[323] remains the case after the Act. The

---

[316] *Re Y (Minors) (Adoption: Jurisdiction)* [1985] Fam 136.

[317] But note *Re KT (A Minor: Adoption)* [1993] Fam Law 567 where 'home' was held to have been established by weekend visits.

[318] See the definition of 'notice' in the Adoption and Children Act 2002 s 144(1).

[319] Adoption and Children Act 2002 s 44. Where a person needs court leave to make an application pursuant to 42(4) and (5) notice to adopt may only be given if that leave has been given: s 44(4).

[320] Section 42(5)–(6). Adoption agencies are under a similar obligation in respect of agency placements: s 43.

[321] See Adoption and contact, p 690. See in particular *Re C (A Minor) (Adoption Order: Conditions)* [1989] AC 1.

[322] See in particular Ward LJ in *Re G (Adoption: Contact)* [2002] EWCA Civ 761 [2003] 1 FLR 270 and the dissenting speech of Baroness Hale in *Down Lisburn Health and Social Services Trust v H* [2006] UKHL 36 [2007] 1 FLR 121.

[323] See *Re C* [1989] AC 1. at 17-18, per Lord Ackner, and *Re T (Adoption: Consent)* [1995] 2 FLR 251 at 257, per Butler-Sloss LJ.

tone was set by Wall LJ in *Re R (Adoption: Contact)*, who said[324] 'under the jurisprudence which has developed, contact orders in adoption proceedings are of themselves unusual, and that both the practice of the court and the courts approaching them have regarded such orders as unusual.' In that case the Court of Appeal dismissed an appeal refusing a half-sister leave to apply for contact. *Re R* was quoted with approval by the Court of Appeal both in *Oxfordshire County Council v X, Y and J*,[325] in which an application by the birth parents that the adopters provide them annually with a photograph of the child, was refused, and in *Re T (Adoption: Contact)*,[326] in which a grandmother's application for contact was dismissed.

As well as making provision for contact under what would now be a child arrangements order at the same time as an adoption order it is possible for a free-standing application to be sought subsequently. However, applications by birth parents (who, post-adoption are no longer the child's legal parents) or relatives, including a sibling will require court leave, which will not be easily granted.[327]

2. SECTION 51A ORDERS

Although s 46(6) directs the court to consider contact it does not itself confer a power to make an order. Instead an order must be sought and made, if at all, either under the 1989 Act in the case of non-agency adoptions (which means that the welfare principle and checklist under that Act rather than the 2002 Act and, as just discussed, the leave provisions under the 1989 Act apply) or by virtue of a new 's 51A order' in the case of agency adoptions (that is, where an agency has placed or was authorised to place a child for adoption)

A s 51A order, which may be made by the court when making an adoption order or at any time afterwards, is one either:

(a) requiring the person in whose favour the adoption order is or has been made to allow the child to visit or stay with the person named in the order ... or for the person named in that order to have contact with each other, or

(b) prohibiting the person named in the order ... from having contact with the child.[328]

It is expressly provided[329] that orders prohibiting contact can be made by the court on its own initiative, the implication being therefore that contact orders can only be made upon application.

Those that can be named in the order include former relatives or guardians of the child, any person who had parental responsibility for the child immediately before the adoption order was made and any person with whom the child has lived for at least one year.[330] The child, adoptive applicant(s) and adopter(s) are entitled without court leave to apply for a s 51A order. Everyone else, including former relatives, need court leave to make an

---

[324] [2005] EWCA Civ 1128 [2006] 1 FLR 373 at [45].

[325] [2011] EWCA Civ 581 [2011] 1 FLR 272, on which, see the thoughtful analysis by K Hughes and B Sloan 'Post-adoption photographs: welfare, rights and judicial reasoning' [2011] CFLQ 393.

[326] [2010] EWCA Civ 1527 [2011] 1FLR 1805.

[327] See eg *Re R* [2005] EWCA Civ 1128 [2006] 1 FLR 373.   [328] Section 51A(2).

[329] Section 51A(6).

[330] Section 51A(3). The period of one year mentioned in the last category need not be continuous but must not have started more than five years before the application was made: s 51A(7). Those entitled to apply for a s 26 order (discussed at The legal effects of placement, p 704) may also be named.

application.[331] In determining whether to grant leave s 51A(5) directs the court to consider the possible risk of harm that might be caused to the child by the proposed application, the applicant's connection to the child and any representations made to the court by the child, the adoptive applicant(s) or the adopter(s).

A s 51A order may contain directions on how it will be carried into effect and be made subject to appropriate conditions. It can be subsequently varied or revoked upon an application by the child, the adoptive applicant(s) or the adopter(s) and lasts until the child becomes 18.[332]

Determining applications under s 51A is deemed to be 'coming to a decision relating to the adoption of a child' within the meaning of s 1(7).[333] Consequently, in contrast to an application made under the 1989 Act in relation to non-agency adoption, the welfare principles and checklist under s 1 of the 2002 Act apply.

The s 51A powers, where applicable, supersede those under a child arrangements order and a specific issue or prohibited steps order may not be made when the same result could be achieved by a s 51A order.[334]

Given the recent jurisprudence, discussed in the previous section, it seems unlikely that this new provision will lead to more contact orders being made, but one can envisage orders being made to prohibit contact, which would be in line with one of the intentions of Part 1 of the 2014 legislation, namely, to reduce the disruption that inappropriate contact can cause to adoptive placements.[335]

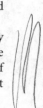

H. REGISTRATION OF ADOPTION AND THE ADOPTION CONTACT REGISTER

1. THE ADOPTED CHILDREN REGISTER

The Registrar General is obliged to maintain a separate register of adoptions known as the Adopted Children Register.[336] This register is not open to public inspection or search.[337] The Registrar General is also obliged to maintain an index of the Adopted Children Register.[338] Although s 78(2) states that any person may search the index and have a certified copy of any entry in the Register, this is subject to the embargo[339] that a person is not entitled to a copy of an entry in the Register relating to an adopted person who is under 18, save where the applicant has provided the Registrar General with the full name and date of birth of the adopted person who is under 18, and the full name of the adoptive parent(s).[340] As one commentary[341] says, this is a security measure intended to prevent the tracing of children without recourse to the proper channels.

By s 79 the Registrar General is required to make traceable the connection between any entry in the registers of live births or other records which has been marked 'Adopted' and any corresponding entry in the Adoption Children Register. The disclosure of this

---

[331] Section 51A(4).   [332] Section 51B(1).
[333] Section 51B(2) but note the error of numbering, this reference is to the second subsection 2
[334] See respectively ss 51A(8) and 51B(7).
[335] See the comments in the Explanatory Notes to the 2014 Act at para 8.
[336] Section 77(1).   [337] Section 77(2).
[338] Section 78(1).   [339] Section 78(3).
[340] Adopted Children and Adoption Contact Registers Regulations 2005 (SI 2005/924) reg 10.
[341] Clarke Hall and Morrison on *Children* at 10 [468].

information is subject to the conditions set out in s 79 and the Regulations and is also dependent upon when the adoption order was made.[342]

The pre-2002 Act 'right' of an adopted adult upon reaching the age of 18 to apply for and receive copies of their birth certificate and thus to be able to trace their parents is preserved by s 60 and Sch 2. The mechanisms for doing this, however, are different according to when the adoption order was made. For those adults adopted before 30 December 2005 (ie when the 2002 Act came into force) the information may be sought directly from the Registrar-General. Pre-2002 Act case law established that this is not an absolute right. In *R v Registrar-General, ex p Smith*[343] the Registrar-General's refusal to give details was upheld upon the basis that there was a real fear for the mother's life if identifying information were disclosed to the adopted adult applicant. For those adults adopted after 30 December 2005 the system is different inasmuch as applications are made to the adoption agency rather than to the Registrar-General. Moreover, the right is expressly made subject, by s 60(2), to the High Court's power to order otherwise. Under either method, before information is given, applicants should be informed that counselling services are available and where they may be obtained.[344]

2. THE ADOPTION CONTACT REGISTER

The ability to trace and make contact with birth parents is one thing but it is quite another as to whether that contact is welcome. In this regard the Adoption Contact Register is important. This was first created in the 1990s[345] and is now provided for by s 80 of the 2002 Act. The purpose of the register is 'to put adopted people and their birth parents or other relatives in touch with each other where this is what they both want. The register provides a safe and confidential way for birth parents and other relatives to assure an adopted person that contact would be welcome and give a contact address.'[346] The register comprises two Parts: Part I, in which are maintained the name and address of any adopted person who is over 18 and has a copy of his birth certificate and who wishes to contact a relative; and Part II, in which are entered, subject to certain prescribed conditions,[347] the current address and identifying details of a relative[348] who wishes to contact an adopted person. Surprisingly, there is no requirement for counselling, nor is there a facility for exchanging limited information, such as medical information, in using the register.

I. THE EFFECTS OF AN ADOPTION ORDER

1. COMPLETE AND PERMANENT TRANSFER OF LEGAL PARENTAGE

By s 46(1) of the 2002 Act, an adoption order gives parental responsibility for the child to the adopter(s), while s 46(2) provides that the making of such an order operates to

---

[342] For detailed discussion see Bridge and Swindells, op cit, ch 12.   [343] [1991] 2 QB 393, CA.

[344] See s 63.

[345] See the Adoption Act 1976 s 51A (added by the Children Act 1989 Sch 10 para 21).

[346] Department of Health's *Guidance and Regulations*, Vol 9, para 32.

[347] Ie that the applicant is aged 18 or over that the Registrar General has either the record of the applicant's birth or that the applicant is a relative: s 80(5).

[348] Ie 'any person who (but for his adoption) would be related to [the adopted person] by blood (including half-blood) or marriage': s 80(2).

'extinguish' the parental responsibility which any person (other than the adopter(s) or the parent in the case of step-parent adoptions)[349] had for the child immediately before the making of the order, though it does not affect parental responsibility so far as it relates to any period before the making of an order.[350] Although expressed in terms of parental responsibility, s 46(1) effectively means that an adoption order effects a complete and permanent transfer of legal parentage.

An adoption order also operates to 'extinguish' any previous order, including a care order, made under the Children Act 1989.[351]

(a) Revocation of adoption orders

Notwithstanding the general irrevocability of adoption orders, there is one circumstance where express provision is made to revoke an order, namely, where a person adopted by the mother or father alone has subsequently become legitimated by his parents' marriage. In such a case, s 55 permits 'any of the parties concerned' to apply for a revocation.

(b) Setting adoptions aside

Apart from the statutory power of revocation, there is a right of appeal both against making and the refusal to make an adoption order.[352] In exceptional cases leave to appeal may be granted out of time. In *Re M (Minors) (Adoption)*[353] a father agreed to his children being adopted by his former wife and her new husband in ignorance of the fact that she was terminally ill. It was held in this 'very exceptional case' that in the children's interests the time for appeal would be extended and the adoption orders set aside on the ground that the father's ignorance of his wife's condition vitiated his consent. Similarly, leave to appeal out of time was granted and the adoption set aside in *Re K (Adoption and Wardship)*,[354] which was an horrific case involving a Bosnian 'orphan' who originally had been found beneath the corpses of persons thought to be her parents. The child had been allowed to come to England for medical treatment, and an English couple began to foster her after she left hospital. This couple then applied to adopt her at a time when they knew that the child's grandfather and aunt had been traced and wanted the child back and that the Bosnian Government had stopped all adoptions from that country. In the original adoption proceedings the judge had not deemed it necessary to appoint a guardian, nor was any attempt made to contact the child's guardian in Bosnia. In these extraordinary circumstances, amounting to a fundamental breach of natural justice, the Court of Appeal set the order aside.[355]

Re M and *Re K* are best looked upon as exceptional cases and not as precedents laying down a general power to set orders aside. As Sir James Munby P said in *Re C (a child) (adoption: leave to oppose)*,[356] 'The law sets a very high bar against any challenge to an adoption order. An adoption order once lawfully and properly made can be set aside only

---

[349] Adoption and Children Act 2002 s 46(3)(b). For one effect of extinguishment see *Secretary of State for Social Services v S* [1983] 3 All ER 173, CA (the mother who took her birth son to live with her after his adoptive mother's death was not his 'parent' and was therefore entitled to a guardian's allowance).

[350] Section 46(3)(a).   [351] Section 46(2)(b).

[352] See generally the FPR 2010, Part 30. As a matter of practice, when appealing against an adoption order the applicant should immediately seek a stay and expedited hearing: *Re PJ (Adoption: Practice on Appeal)* [1998] 2 FLR 252, CA.

[353] [1991] 1 FLR 458, CA.   [354] [1997] 2 FLR 221, CA.

[355] In the subsequent re-hearing (see [1997] 1 FLR 230) Sir Stephen Brown P held that although the adoption application should be refused, nevertheless care and control should be granted to the foster parents together with substantial contact to the child's birth family, with the child herself remaining a ward of court.

[356] [2013] EWCA Civ 431 [2014] 1 FCR 50 at [44].

in highly exceptional and very particular circumstances.' This is well illustrated first by *Re B (Adoption: Jurisdiction To Set Aside)*,[357] in which the applicant, whose origins were Arabic, unsuccessfully applied some 35 years after the order was made to set aside his adoption by a Jewish couple. As the Court of Appeal made clear, there is no general inherent power to set an adoption aside and, in the absence of procedural irregularities or mistakes, no power exists to revoke an order. To hold otherwise would be, in Swinton Thomas LJ's words, to 'undermine the whole basis upon which adoption orders are made, namely that they are final and for life as regards the adopters, the natural parents and the child'. *Re B* was subsequently applied in an equally striking decision, *Webster v Norfolk County Council and the Children (By Their Children's Guardian)*.[358] In that case care orders had been made in respect of three children on the basis that the eldest had been physically abused by one or both of the parents. All three children were subsequently adopted. Care proceedings were later brought in relation to a fourth child but the parents produced fresh expert evidence strongly suggesting that the older child's injuries had been caused by scurvy (a diagnosis subsequently confirmed by other experts) and not by abuse. The care proceedings were discontinued and the fourth child remained with the parents. A year later and three years after the adoption orders had been made, the parents sought to leave to appeal the adoption orders out of time. Leave was refused, it being held that even though the biological parents had suffered a serious injustice the public policy considerations relating to the permanence of adoption made it impossible to set aside the orders. In reaching this conclusion, the Court of Appeal, relying on the European Court of Human Rights decisions, *Pini and Bertani; Manera and Atripaldi v Romania*[359] and *Görgülü v Germany*,[360] rejected the argument that refusing leave violated Arts 6 and 8 of the European Convention on Human Rights. In a third case, *Re W (a child) (revocation of adoption: inherent jurisdiction)*, a local authority sought leave to invoke the inherent jurisdiction[361] to set aside an adoption order made some nine years earlier but which had broken down with the child being taken back into care. The application was refused. As Bodey J put it,[362] granting permission in these circumstances would have opened a 'Pandora's box and the court should only go there . . . if it seems proportionate, necessary and reasonably likely to be ultimately successful.' In the judge's view the application failed to satisfy all of the prerequisites.

The only other way the adoption status may be changed is by a second adoption,[363] but this is not to say that even former parents have no other remedies, since the making of an adoption order does not prevent the normal application of private and public law in relation to the adoptive family. Former parents, like anyone else, may, with court leave, seek to apply for s 8 orders in respect of the adopted child. However, leave will not normally be given and in any event would require, in Thorpe J's words,[364] 'some fundamental change of circumstances' before permitting the re-opening of crucial issues such as contact and a fortiori, the child's living arrangements. Nevertheless there is at least one reported example of a birth parent subsequently obtaining an order that the adopted child should live with her.[365]

---

[357] [1995] Fam 239, CA.
[358] [2009] EWCA Civ 59 [2009] 1 FLR 1378, on which see A Bainham 'The Peculiar Finality of Adoption' [2009] CLJ 283. [359] [2005] 2 FLR 596.
[360] [2004] 1 FLR 894. [361] The inherent jurisdiction is discussed in Ch 20.
[362] [2013] EWHC 1957 (Fam) [2013] 3 FCR 336 at [12].
[363] Which is expressly permitted by s 46(5).
[364] *Re C (A Minor) (Adopted Child: Contact)* [1993] Fam 210.
[365] See *Re O (A Minor) (Wardship: Adopted Child)* [1978] 2 All ER 27, CA.

2. THE CHILD'S CHANGE OF STATUS

The corollary of transferring parental responsibility is that the child's status is also changed. This is governed by s 67 which declares that from the date of adoption:

(1) An adopted person is to be treated as if born as the child of the adopters or adopter.

(2) An adopted person is the legitimate child of the adopters or adopter[366] and, if adopted by

(a) a couple, or

(b) one of a couple under section 51(2),

is to be treated as the child of the relationship of the couple in question.

(3) An adopted person—

(a) if adopted by one of a couple under section 51(2),[367] is to be treated in law as not being the child of any person other than the adopter and the other one of the couple, and

(b) in any other case, is to be treated in law, subject to subsection (4), as not being the child of any person other than the adopters or adopter;

but this subsection does not affect any reference in this Act to a person's natural parent or to any other natural relationship.

(4) In the case of a person adopted by one of the person's natural parents as sole adoptive parent, subsection (3)(b) has no effect as respects entitlement to property depending on relationship to that parent, or as respects anything else depending on that relationship.

3. CONSEQUENCES OF THE CHANGE OF STATUS AND TRANSFER OF PARENTAGE

(a) Citizenship

Consistent with the change of status, a child (of whatever nationality) adopted by an order made by a court in the United Kingdom will become a British citizen if one of the adopters is a British citizen.[368] On the other hand, adoption cannot deprive a child of British citizenship if he or she already has it.[369]

(b) Peerages, dignities and titles

An adoption does *not* affect the descent of any peerage or dignity or title of honour.[370] Similarly, it does not, in the absence of any contrary indication, 'affect the declaration of any property (expressly or not) to devolve (as nearly as the law permits) along with any peerage, dignity or title of honour.'[371]

---

[366] But note that adoption of a child born outside marriage by a birth parent as sole adoptive parent will not prevent his legitimation if the adopter later marries the other parent: Legitimacy Act 1976, s 4. See Ch 9 Legitimation, at p 302.

[367] Note: in *Re N (Recognition of Foreign Adoption Order)* [2009] EWHC 29 (Fam) [2010] 1 FLR 1102 it was held that s 67(3)(a) should be treated as applying to equivalent orders made abroad and recognised in England and Wales.

[368] British Nationality Act 1981 s 1(5). In the case of a joint adoption the child will acquire British citizenship if one of the adopters possesses it. He will retain British citizenship even if the order ceases to have effect for any reason: ibid, s 1(6). But note *Re K (A Minor) (Adoption Order: Nationality)* [1995] Fam 38, CA, in which it was held that s 1(6) does not apply to appeals: hence citizenship can be lost if an appeal against the making of an order succeeds.   [369] Adoption and Children Act 2002 s 74(2).

[370] Section 71(1).   [371] Section 71(2)(3).

(c) Change of surname

Although normally the child's surname is changed to that of the adopters on the making of the adoption,[372] technically, the power to change the name becomes vested in the adopter(s) who can therefore choose not to do so. Once registered, however, an adopter cannot thereafter in the case of a joint adoption, unilaterally change the name.[373]

(d) Prohibited degrees and incest

The adoptive child and his adoptive parents are deemed to come within the prohibited degrees of consanguinity, so that they may not intermarry or enter into a civil partnership.[374] This continues to apply if a subsequent adoption order is made; hence the child may not marry a former adoptive parent.[375] Adoption, however, does not prevent a marriage or civil partnership between the child and his adoptive sibling or with any other adoptive relative. Conversely, as the modern law takes some account of genetics, the child may not marry nor enter a civil partnership with any person who would have come within the prohibited degrees if no adoption order had been made.[376] For the purpose of incest the crime continues to relate to the child's birth relationships but, curiously, not to adoptive relatives.[377]

(e) Maintenance

Any duty to make payments for the child's maintenance by virtue of an order or agreement ceases upon the making of an adoption order unless the agreement constitutes a trust or expressly provides to the contrary.[378] One consequence of this is that after the adoption no application for maintenance may be made against the child's father even if the adoption is by the mother alone. Liability for maintenance of an adopted child lies exclusively upon the adoptive parents.[379]

(f) Claims under the Inheritance (Provision for Family and Dependants) Act 1975 and the Fatal Accidents Act 1976

Since an adopted child is regarded as the child of his adopter or adopters, he or she may claim under the Fatal Accidents Act 1976 as a dependant of his adoptive parent or other adoptive relative, but not of his birth parent.[380] Similarly adoption bars the child's inheritance claims against the birth parents' estate under the Inheritance (Provision for Family and Dependants) Act 1975.[381]

(g) Pensions

An adoption order does *not* affect entitlement to a pension which is payable to or for the child's benefit provided it is in payment at the time of the order.[382]

---

[372] The application form expressly provides for the new names to be identified.

[373] Ie adoptive parents are subject to the same law on names as the birth parents, see the discussion in Ch 10, Naming the child, p 356.

[374] Marriage Act 1949 Sch 1, Part I and the Civil Partnership Act 2004 Sch 1.

[375] Adoption and Children Act 2002, s 74(1).

[376] Section 74(1)(a), applying the Marriage Act 1949 Sch 1, Part 1 and the Civil Partnership Act 2004 Sch 1.

[377] Section 74(1)(b) and (c) applying the Sexual Offences Act 2003 ss 64 and 65.

[378] Section 46(2)(d) and (4). These provisions do not affect liability for arrears existing at the time of the adoption order.

[379] Child Support Act 1991 ss 1 and 54 and Social Security Administration Act 1992 ss 78(6) and 105(3).

[380] See *Watson v Willmot* [1991] 1 QB 140.   [381] See *Re Collins* [1990] Fam 56.

[382] Adoption and Children Act 2002 s 75.

(h) Insurance

The rights and liabilities of an insurance policy taken out by the birth parents for payment of funeral expenses upon the child's death transfer to the adoptive parents.[383]

(i) Property

When first introduced by the Adoption of Children Act 1926 adoption did not affect the devolution of property; the child remained the child of his birth parents. That position was changed by the Adoption of Children Act 1949. Ever since, as regards interests in property, the general principle is that from the date of the adoption order an adopted child is deemed to become the child of the adopter or adopters and ceases to be regarded as the child of his birth parents or, if he has been previously adopted, of his former adopters, and therefore is no longer considered as related to any other person through his birth or former adoptive parents.

In the case of instruments made on or after 1 January 1976 or wills of testators dying on or after that date and subject to any contrary indication, an adopted child may claim in such cases whether the disposition takes effect before or after the adoption. A disposition depending on the date of birth of a child of the adoptive parent or parents is to be construed as though the adopted child was born on the date of his adoption and two or more children adopted on the same day rank inter se in the order of their actual births. This provision, however, does not affect the operation of any condition depending on the child's reaching an actual age.[384] Thus, if there is a bequest to K's eldest child at 18 and K adopts a child A and subsequently has a natural child B, A can claim when he reaches the age of 18 whether his adoption preceded or followed the testator's death.[385]

Notwithstanding the general rule there are various provisions designed to ensure that a child adopted by one of his unmarried parents as the sole adoptive parent is not thereby deprived of an interest he could otherwise have taken. First, such an adoption does not affect the child's entitlement to any property depending on his relationship to the adoptive parent.[386] Secondly, if a disposition depends on the date of birth of the child, neither his adoption by one of his parents as sole adopter nor his legitimation if he has been adopted will affect his entitlement.[387]

Trustees and personal representatives are not liable if they distribute property in ignorance of the making or revocation of an adoption order, but beneficiaries may trace property into the hands of anyone other than a purchaser.[388]

---

[383] Section 76.

[384] Section 69(2)(a). A disposition includes a power of appointment and any other disposition of an interest in or right over property: s 73(2).

[385] Note also s 69(4), which deals with contingent interests.

[386] Adoption and Children Act 2002, s 70.

[387] Section 70; Legitimacy Act 1976 s 6(2). Similarly, the revocation of an adoption order following the marriage of a child's parents will not affect any claim he could have made to property had the order remained in force: Legitimacy Act 1976 s 4(2). If the child has been adopted and dies before his parents' marriage, he is deemed to be legitimate on that date for the purpose of preserving interests to be taken by or in succession to his spouse, children and remoter issue: Legitimacy Act 1976 s 5(6). For the effect of an adoption by a woman over 55 and the operation of the presumption that she is incapable of bearing children, see Adoption and Children Act 2002 s 69(5).   [388] Adoption and Children Act 2002 s 45.

J. OFFENCES

1. ILLEGAL PLACEMENTS

As previously discussed, since 1982 it has been an offence for an individual, other than an adoption agency, to place or make arrangements for the child's adoption, unless the proposed adopter is a relative or he is acting in pursuance of a High Court order. This restriction was strengthened by s 92 of the 2002 Act, whereby any person who is not an adoption agency or acting in pursuance of a High Court order commits on offence by:

(a) asking a person other than an adoption agency to provide a child for adoption;
(b) asking a person other than an adoption agency to provide prospective adopters for a child;
(c) offering to find a child for adoption;
(d) offering a child for adoption to a person other than an adoption agency;
(e) handing over a child to any person other than an adoption agency, with a view to the child's adoption by that or another person;
(f) receiving a child handed over to him in contravention of paragraph (a);
(g) entering into an agreement with any person for the adoption of a child or for the purpose of facilitating the adoption of a child, where no adoption agency is acting on behalf of the child in the adoption;
(h) initiating or taking part in negotiations of which the purpose is the conclusion of an agreement within paragraph (g);
(i) causing another person to take any of the steps mentioned in paragraphs (a) to (h).

No offence is committed under paras (d), (e), (g), (h), or (i) if the prospective adopters are parents, relatives[389] or guardians or a partner of the parent of the child.[390]

The offences just listed are punishable on summary conviction by imprisonment of up to six months and/or a fine of £10,000.[391] Prosecutions may be brought up to six years after the commission of the offence.[392]

The wide scope of the offences, combined with tough penalties, provide a powerful deterrent to illicit adopters. It may be noted, however, that s 92 does not prevent private *fostering* placements being made nor is there anything to prevent such foster parents from subsequently applying to adopt. However, if it is clear that the foster arrangement is a mere subterfuge, an offence will be committed.[393]

According to the pre–2002 Act decision, *Re G (Adoption: Illegal Placement)*,[394] while there is no power retrospectively to authorise an illegal placement, the High Court

---

[389] Defined by s 144(1) as 'grandparent, brother, sister, uncle or aunt, whether of the full blood or half-blood or by marriage or civil partnership'. Pre–2002 Act cases, *Re S (Arrangements for Adoption)* [1985] FLR 579, CA and *Re C (Minors) (Wardship: Adoption)* [1989] 1 All ER 395, CA establish that great aunts and uncles are not 'relatives' for these purposes nor is a 'commissioning non-genetic partner' in a surrogacy arrangement: *Re MW (Adoption: Surrogacy)* [1995] 2 FLR 759.

[390] Section 92(3), (4). For other 'defences' see s 93(2)–(4).   [391] Section 93(5).

[392] Section 138. This is considerably longer than the usual time limit of six months for summary offences under s 127(1) of the Magistrates' Courts Act 1980.

[393] As in *Gatehouse v Robinson* [1986] 1 WLR 18.

[394] [1995] 1 FLR 403, CA. See I Sandland 'Problems in the Criminal Law of Adoption' [1995] JSWFL 149. See also *Re A (Placement of Child in Contravention of the Adoption Act 1976, s 11)* [2005] 2 FLR 727.

nevertheless retained the power to grant the adoption. It remains to be established whether this remains the case.[395]

2. ILLEGAL PAYMENTS

It has always been regarded as wrong for people to buy and sell children for adoption and the 2002 Act continues the policy of making it an offence to do so. However, unlike previously,[396] there is no express prohibition in the 2002 Act on making an adoption order where illegal payments have been made, nor conversely, is there power retrospectively to authorise payments.[397]

Illegal payments are governed by s 95 under which it is an offence for a person to make[398] or receive any payment or reward[399] (other than an 'excepted payment') for the adoption of a child, giving any consent for a child's adoption, removing from the United Kingdom a child who is a Commonwealth citizen or is habitually resident in the United Kingdom to a place outside the British Isles for the purpose of adoption, for making arrangements for illegal placements for adoption[400] and for the commissioning or preparing of prohibited reports.[401] As with illegal placements, those guilty of an offence under s 95 are liable on summary conviction to imprisonment of up to six months and/or a fine of up to £10,000.[402]

'Excepted payments' are those for reasonable expenses such as legal and medical expenses in relation to adoption, payments to a local authority or registered adoption society for expenses incurred for arranging the adoption of a child whose country of origin is outside the United Kingdom and those for reasonably incurred travel and accommodation expenses where a child is being taken out of the United Kingdom.[403]

3. ADVERTISEMENTS

By s 123 it is an offence to publish or distribute an advertisement or information or to cause such an advertisement or information to be published or distributed (including advertisements or information being distributed via any electronic means, for example, by means of the internet)[404] indicating that a parent or guardian wants a child to be adopted, that a person wants to adopt a child, that a person other than adoption agencies is willing to make arrangements for the adoption or that a person is willing to remove a child from the United Kingdom for the purposes of adoption. The offence itself, however, is confined to the United Kingdom and the provisions do not apply to publications or distributions by or on behalf of an adoption agency.[405]

---

[395] Bridge and Swindells, op cit, at 16.41, cautiously thought the same position would be applied. Cf Butterworths *Family Law Service* at 3A [4374.1].

[396] See s 24(2) of the Adoption Act 1976.

[397] This was formerly provided for by s 57(3) of the 1976 Act, which had been interpreted as permitting the court retrospectively to authorise payments and thus to make an adoption order, see *Re G (Adoption: Illegal Placement)*, earlier, at 405, per Balcombe LJ (obiter), *Re WM (Adoption: Non Patrial)* [1997] 1 FLR 132 and *Re Adoption Application (Payment for Adoption)* [1987] Fam 81. Compare the position with regard to making parental orders under s 54 of the Human Fertilisation and Embryology Act 2008, discussed in Ch 8.

[398] Including agreeing or offering to make such payments: s 95(3)(b).

[399] By s 97(b) 'payment' includes reward.   [400] Ie those made in contravention of s 92.

[401] Ie those made in contravention of s 94 which prohibits reports being carried out by non-professionally qualified staff, see the Restriction on the Preparation of Adoption Reports Regulations 2005 (SI 2005/1711).

[402] Section 95(4).   [403] Section 96.

[404] Section 123(4)(a). This provision was added in the light of a case involving a North Wales couple who, wishing to adopt, had contacted American organisations via the internet.

[405] At any rate, provided the authority has obtained the necessary recommendation from its adoption panel, see *Re K (Adoption) (Permission To Advertise)* [2007] EWHC 544 (Fam) [2007] 2 FLR 326.

The penalty for a s 123 offence is a term of imprisonment of up to three months and/or a fine not exceeding level 5 on the standard scale.[406]

K. SPECIAL GUARDIANSHIP

1. INTRODUCTION

A key part of the strategy to offer alternative legal options to adoption introduced by the Adoption and Children Act 2002 was the creation of special guardianship. The proposal to have a new form of guardianship was first made in the Consultative Document on Adoption Law in 1992.[407] At that stage it was proposed that there should be a power to appoint what was to be called 'the child's *inter vivos* guardian' (hardly an attractive title). Such guardians were to have all the rights, duties and powers of a guardian under s 5 of the 1989 Act[408] save for the power to agree to the child's adoption. This proposal was not, however, included in the draft Adoption Bill 1996[409] but eventually re-emerged in the 2002 Act.

The provisions governing special guardianship are contained in ss 14A–G of the Children Act 1989[410] and came into force at the end of 2005.

Special guardianship orders are intended to provide a more permanent status for non-parents than that provided by being named in a child arrangements order as a person with whom the child is to live but, unlike adoption,[411] they do not extinguish the legal relationship between the child and his or her birth family. In other words special guardianship orders are intended to meet the needs of children for whom adoption is not appropriate (eg older children who do not wish to be adopted) but who cannot return to their birth parents and who 'would benefit from the permanence provided by a legally secure family placement'.[412] Special guardians are distinguishable from guardians since unlike the latter, who replace the deceased parents, [413] they take office during the parents' life-time. Furthermore unlike guardians, special guardians can only be appointed by a court. There is no power to make private appointments. Special guardians are in a similar position to those non-parents named in a child arrangements order as a person with whom the child is to live inasmuch as they have parental responsibility for the child for the duration of the order which they share with the parents (though in this respect the power to act without consulting parents is expressed in rather more clear terms).[414] However, as we discuss shortly, special guardians are in a stronger position than the

---

[406] Section 124(3). Note the requirement under s 124 to prove that the accused knew or had reason to suspect that s 123 applied to the advertisement or information.

[407] Department of Health 1992, para 6.5. See also *Re S (Adoption Order or Special Guardianship Order)* [2007] EWCA Civ 54 [2007] 1 FLR 819 at [5]–[13] per Wall LJ. [408] Discussed in Ch 8.

[409] Attached to the Government White Paper 'Adoption—A Service for Children' (1996).

[410] Inserted by s 115 of the 2002 Act and slightly amended by the Children and Families Act 2014 Sch 2 paras 24–26.

[411] See Adoption and Children Act 2002 s 46(2), discussed at Complete and permanent transfer of legal parentage, p 722.

[412] See the Explanatory Notes to the 2002 Act, para 18 and the Explanatory Memorandum to the Special Guardianship Regulations 2005, (SI 2005/1109) para 7.2. See also the chart annexed to *Re AJ (Adoption Order or Special Guardianship Order)* [2007] EWCA Civ 55 [2007] 1 FLR 507 [413] See Ch 8.

[414] Compare s 14C(1)(b), which states that a special guardian 'is entitled to exercise parental responsibility to the exclusion of any other person with parental responsibility for the child (apart from another special guardian)', with s 2(7) which permits, in the case of multiple holders of parental responsibility, that each 'may act alone without the other (or others) in meeting that responsibility'.

latter in that they are entitled to appoint a guardian, to remove a child from the United Kingdom for up to three months and are more likely to obtain court leave to change the child's surname. Another crucial difference, and importantly from the point of view of security and stability, it is more difficult for parents to apply to vary or discharge a special guardianship order than a child arrangements order.[415] A further difference, and evidence of the hybrid nature of the order, is that unlike those named in a child arrangements order as a person with whom the child is to live, special guardians are *entitled* to local authority support services.

2. THE POWER TO MAKE SPECIAL GUARDIANSHIP ORDERS

(a) Who can be appointed

A special guardianship order is an order appointing one or more individuals to be a child's special guardian, or special guardians.[416] Only non-parents can be appointed.[417] By confining the power to appoint 'individuals' it is clear that the court cannot appoint a body such as a local authority nor what has been described as an 'artificial individual' such as a director of children's services.[418] On the other hand, orders may be granted to a single individual or a couple, whether married or not. Individuals must be aged 18 or over.[419]

(b) Applying for an order

The court may make a special guardianship order either upon application or upon its own motion in any 'family proceedings'.[420] Guardians; those named in a child arrangements order as a person with whom the child is to live; those with whom the child has lived for a period of at least three years,[421] and any person having the consent of (i) each of the persons in named in a child arrangements order which is in force as a person with whom the child is to live, (ii) the local authority if the child is subject to a care order, or (iii) in any other case, each of the persons who have parental responsibility for the child, are *entitled* to apply for a special guardianship order.[422] Anyone else, for example, grandparents who have not provided a home for the child for the requisite period and the child himself, must obtain court leave.[423] In deciding whether to grant leave the court must have regard to the same criteria as for deciding whether to grant leave to apply for a s 8 order.[424] Local authority foster parents (unless relatives) will additionally need the consent of the local authority, if the child has not lived with them for one year.[425]

---

[415] See s 14D(3) and (5) which provides that inter alia parents require court leave to apply to vary or discharge a special guardianship order which cannot be given 'unless there has been a significant change in circumstances since the making of the . . . order'. Parents are entitled without court leave to apply to vary or discharge a child arrangements order.

[416] Section 14A(1).   [417] Section 14A(2)(b).

[418] See the similar restriction in appointing guardians under s 5 of the 1989 Act and applied in *Re SH (Care Order: Orphan)* [1995] 1 FLR 746, discussed in Ch 8, When the power may be exercised, p 290.

[419] Section 14A(2)(a).

[420] Section 14A(6)(b). 'Family proceedings' are defined by s 8(3), (4), see Ch 14, Family proceedings, p 535. Inter alia this means that the court has power to make special guardianship orders in adoption proceedings. Conversely, the court can make a s 8 order in a special guardianship application.

[421] The period of three years need not be continuous but must not have begun more than five years before nor ended three months before the making of the application: s 14A(5)(c) applying s 10(10).

[422] Section 14A(5), read in conjunction with s 10(5)(b), (c) and (10).   [423] Section 14A(3)(b).

[424] Section 14A(12) applying s 10(8) and (9) discussed in Ch 14. The leave criteria, p 515.

[425] Section 14A(4) applying s 9(3) (as amended).

It was pointed out in *Re S (Adoption Order or Special Guardianship Order)*[426] that it is implicit in the power to make a special guardianship order upon its own motion that the court can impose such an order on unwilling parties. This is most likely to arise in cases where, as in *Re S* itself, the applicant is seeking to adopt the child but the court thinks that a special guardianship would better serve the child's interests. As Wall LJ said:[427]

> The jurisdictional position is very clear: the court has the power to impose a special guardianship order on an unwilling party to the proceedings. Whether or not it should do so will depend upon the facts of the individual case, including the nature of the refuser's case and its interrelationship with the welfare of the particular child. What seems to us clear is that if the court comes to the view on all the facts and applying the welfare checklist under the 1989 Act (including the potential consequences to the child of the refuser implementing the threat to refuse to be appointed a special guardian) that a special guardianship order will best serve the welfare interests of the child in question, that is the order which the court should make.

However, when making special guardianship orders in such circumstances regard must still be had to the requirement under s 14A(8) for there to be a local authority report on the suitability of such an order.[428]

(c) Local authority involvement in making applications

A prerequisite of applying is for applicants to give three months' written notice to the local authority of their intention to apply for such an order.[429] The local authority[430] must then investigate the matter and prepare a report for the court about the suitability of the applicant and any other relevant matters.[431] The court, too, has power to direct a local authority to make such an investigation and report[432] and must do so if it wishes to make such an order.[433] In other words, in no circumstances can a special guardianship order be made without a local authority report.[434] According to *Re S (Adoption Order or Special Guardianship Order) (No 2)*,[435] where a court is minded to make a special guardianship order rather than an adoption order for which application has been made and for which a local authority report has been filed, a s 14A(8) report has still to be filed before a special guardianship order can be made. Nevertheless, such a report need not be entirely new. It will be sufficient for the court to ask the local authority to provide the missing information required under s 14A(8).

The interaction of these provisions can be complicated. In *Birmingham City Council v R*[436] the local authority sought a care order (it was common ground that the threshold

---

[426] [2007] EWCA Civ 54 [2007] 1 FLR 819. See also *Re L (Special Guardianship: Surname)* [2007] EWCA Civ 196, [2007] 2 FLR 50.   [427] At [77].

[428] See *Re S (Adoption Order or Special Guardianship Order) (No 2)* [2007] EWCA Civ 90 [2007] 1 FLR 853.

[429] Section 14A(7). But note this three month period does not apply where a person has leave to make a competing application for a special guardianship order at a final adoption hearing: Adoption and Children Act 2002, s 29(6). As C Bridge and H Swindells *Adoption The Modern Law* (2003) point out at 7.118, this prevents the competing application delaying the adoption hearing.

[430] But they can arrange for someone else to carry out the investigation: s 14A(10).

[431] Section 14A(8). The matters to be dealt with in the report are specified in the Schedule to the Special Guardianship Regulations 2005 (SI 2005/1109) (note that separate Regulations, viz. the Special Guardianship (Wales) Regulations 2005 (SI 2005/1513) apply to Wales). They include a detailed assessment of the child and the child's family (including in each case their wishes and feelings), of the prospective special guardian(s) and details of the local authority including details of any past involvement with the applicant, a summary of support services available and where the authority has decided not to provide any, the reasons why, their overall recommendations on whether or not a special guardianship order should be made and what arrangements there should be for contact between the child and his relatives.   [432] Section 14A(9).

[433] Section 14A(11).   [434] See *A Local Authority v Y, Z and Others* [2006] 2 FLR 41.

[435] [2007] EWCA Civ 90 [2007] 1 FLR 853.   [436] [2006] EWCA Civ 1748 [2007] Fam 41.

criteria under s 31 were satisfied and that neither of the child's parents was capable of caring for the child) but the mother and maternal grandparents (who had party status in the care proceedings) wanted the child to live with the grandparents under a special guardianship order. Notwithstanding that the grandparents had not sought leave to apply for such an order, the judge, pursuant to s 14A(9), directed the local authority to prepare a s 14A(8) report. It was held that he had been wrong to do so since he had no power to order a report at the behest of a person who requires but has not obtained leave to apply for a special guardianship order. Consequently this meant that he could only do so provided, pursuant to s 14A(6)(b), he was satisfied that such an order should be made. However, when he ordered the report he could not be so satisfied and hence he had no power under s 14A(9) to make the direction.

3. PRINCIPLES UPON WHICH ORDERS ARE MADE

In deciding whether or not to make a special guardianship order the court must regard the child's welfare as the paramount consideration and be satisfied that making an order is better than making no order at all.[437] It must also apply the welfare checklist under s 1(3).[438] It is also obliged to be mindful of the general principle[439] that delay is likely to prejudice the child's welfare and to that end courts are empowered to set timescales for proceedings involving special guardianship applications.[440] However, as Wall LJ observed in *Re S (Adoption Order or Special Guardianship Order)*,[441] where the court is considering whether to make a special guardianship *or an adoption order* it must apply both the welfare checklist under s 1(3) of 1989 Act in relation to special guardianship and s 1(4) of the Adoption and Children Act 2002 in relation to adoption. As previously discussed,[442] the welfare test under the two Acts is not identical.

4. POWERS WHEN MAKING A SPECIAL GUARDIANSHIP ORDER

Before making an order the court must consider whether a child arrangements order containing contact provision should be made at the same time.[443] Although this latter power seems to signal that unlike adoption orders, special guardianship with contact is not to be regarded as unusual, it is clear that this should not be an a priori position but instead is to be regarded as an issue which is dependent upon what is thought to be for the child's welfare.[444]

---

[437] Section 1(1) and (5) of the 1989 Act discussed in Ch 10. These provisions apply by reason of the fact that the special guardianship provisions are inserted into Part II of the 1989 Act.

[438] See the specific amendment by the Adoption and Children Act 2002, s 115(3) to s 1(4)(b) of the Children Act 1989. The checklist provisions apply by reason of the fact that the special guardianship provisions are inserted into Part II of the 1989 Act.

[439] Under s 1(2), discussed in Ch 12, Delay prima facie prejudicial to the child's welfare, pp 436ff.

[440] See s 14E.   [441] [2007] EWCA Civ 54 [2007] 1 FLR 819 at [48].

[442] See The weighting of the child's welfare, p 694.

[443] Section 14B(1)(a), as amended by the Children and Families Act 2014 Sch 2 para 25. By 'contact provision' is meant provision regulating with whom and when a child is to spend time or otherwise have contact with any person. The reference to spending time or otherwise having contact is 'doing that otherwise as a result of living with the person', s 14B(1A) added by Sch 2 para 25(3) to the 2014 Act.

[444] See particularly *Re S (Adoption Order or Special Guardianship Order)* [2007] EWCA Civ 54 [2007] 1 FLR 819 and *Re L (Special Guardianship: Surname)* [2007] EWCA Civ 196 [2007] 2 FLR 50 in which the Court of Appeal upheld an order granting supervised contact with the mother and indirect contact to the father (with details of the number of cards and letters and presents). See also *A Local Authority v Y, Z and Others* [2006] 2 FLR 41 in which contact was left to the special guardians to determine.

More generally, the court must consider whether *any* s 8 order in force with respect to the child should be varied or discharged.[445] While it is easy to contemplate an existing order dealing with contact arrangements (whether or not modified) running alongside a special guardianship order, the making of a special guardianship order is surely normally[446] incompatible with the continuation of an existing order dealing with child's living arrangements.[447] It is therefore surprising that a special guardianship order does not *automatically* discharge such orders.[448] However, given that it does not, courts need to be aware of the need to make an express discharge order.

There is no restriction comparable to that under s 9(6) with respect to s 8 orders, that orders relating to 16 or 17-year-olds should only be made in exceptional circumstances. However, no special guardianship order may be made where an adoption placement order is in force unless an application for a final adoption order has been made *and* the applicant has obtained leave to make the application or is the guardian of the child.[449]

On making a special guardianship order the court may also give leave for the child to be known by a new surname.[450] This power signals a difference between these orders and adoption, where a new surname is automatic, and a child arrangements order where a change of name is not encouraged.[451] This is not to say, however, that such orders should always be made. Indeed, as *Re L (Special Guardianship: Surname)*[452] shows, such an order should not be made where it would interfere with the child's identity needs. In that case the Court of Appeal upheld a decision to grant special guardianship[453] to 'devoted excellent grandparents' (with whom the three year old child had lived from the age of three months) but refusing their application for the child's surname to be changed, on the basis that it would interfere with her emotional identity needs. In so ruling, the court rejected the grandparents' contention that there was an inconsistency between the granting of a special guardianship order on the one hand and, on the other, the restrictive effect of the orders under attack upon the free exercise of the overriding parental responsibility conferred on them by the order. As Ward LJ put it:[454]

> Links with the natural family are not severed as in adoption but the purpose undoubtedly is to give freedom to the special guardians to exercise parental responsibility in the best interests of the child. That, however, does not mean that the special guardians are free from the exercise of judicial oversight.

---

[445] Section 14B(1)(b).

[446] Perhaps one exception is where the person named in a child arrangements order as someone with whom the child is to live is the spouse or civil partner living with the applicant for a special guardianship order though even in this circumstance one would expect the couple to make a joint application for special guardianship.

[447] Note Wall LJ's comment in *Re S (Adoption Order or Special Guardianship Order)* [2007] EWCA Civ 54 [2007] 1 FLR 819 at [30] that 'it is plain that a special guardianship order...has the effect of discharging [what was then] any residence order in relation to the same child.'

[448] Likewise the *subsequent* making of a child arrangements order does not automatically discharge a special guardianship order although the person named in a child arrangements order as a person with whom the child is to live can then apply for a discharge: s 14D(1)(c), as amended by the Children and Families Act 2014 Sch 2 para 26.

[449] Adoption and Children Act 2002 s 29 (5). Adoption placement orders are discussed at Placement orders, pp 701ff.

[450] Section 14B(2)(a). Leave was given in *S v B and Newport City Council; Re K* [2007] 1 FLR 1116.

[451] See Ch 14, Change of child's surname, pp 520ff.

[452] [2007] EWCA Civ 196 [2007] 2 FLR 50.

[453] In fact the grandparents had applied for adoption.   [454] At [33].

The court can give permission for the child to be taken outside the United Kingdom for more than three months.[455] As with s 8 orders the court is empowered to add directions and conditions to any special guardianship order,[456] and to make provisions which have effect for a specified period.[457] The court can also make other supporting orders such as a prohibited steps or a specific issue order or a s 91(14) order.[458]

5. THE EFFECTS OF SPECIAL GUARDIANSHIP ORDERS

Special guardians have, for the duration of the order, parental responsibility for the child which, for the most part, they can exercise to the exclusion of anyone else, apart from another special guardian.[459] The power to act to the *exclusion* of anyone else is stronger than under s 2(7), which generally permits co-holders of parental responsibility to 'act alone and without the other (or others)'. Put in other terms,[460] whereas a child arrangements order dealing with whom the child is to live is based upon the concurrent exercise of parental responsibility, special guardianship is based upon its exclusive exercise. However, whether this makes any practical difference seems doubtful since even a person named in a child arrangements order as a person with whom the child is to live is in a stronger position than others with parental responsibility. Moreover, like a person with whom the child is to live, a special guardian is not empowered to exercise responsibility independently in circumstances where the law requires the consent of *all* parties with parental responsibility,[461] for example, sterilisation,[462] ritual circumcision,[463] immunisation,[464] and to consult about changes in the child's education.[465] Special guardians are not stated to be able to act to the 'exclusion' of another special guardian but presumably the normal rule under s 2(7) that a co-holder of responsibility can act alone applies to joint special guardians.

Special guardians are entitled to remove the child from the United Kingdom for a period of less than *three* months.[466] On the other hand, neither they nor anyone else can (a) cause the child to be known by a new surname or (b) remove a child from the United Kingdom for a period of more than three months, while a special guardianship order is in force.[467] Special guardians can appoint a guardian to take their place upon their death.[468]

---

[455] Section 14B(2)(b).   [456] Section 14E(4).

[457] Section 14E(5), applying s 11(7) (see Ch 14, Additional directions and conditions, pp 504ff), save s 11(7)(c) under which there is a general power to make an order for a specified time.

[458] See *S v B and Newport City Council; Re K* [2007] 1 FLR 1116, and *Re S (Adoption Order or Special Guardianship Order)* [2007] EWCA Civ 54 [2007] 1 FLR 819 at [59]. For further discussion of the use of s 91(14), see Ch 14, Restricting further applications under s 91(14), p 508.   [459] Section 14C(1).

[460] See Butterworths *Family Law Service* 3A [4485].   [461] Section 14C(2)(a).

[462] This example is given in the Explanatory Notes to the Act at para 277.

[463] *Re J (Specific Issue Orders: Muslim Upbringing and Circumcision)* [2000] 1 FLR 571, CA, discussed in Ch 11 Sharing parental responsibility for a child, p 394.

[464] *Re C (Welfare of Child: Immunisation)* [2003] EWCA Civ 1148 [2003] 2 FLR 1095, discussed in Ch 11, Sharing parental responsibility for a child, p 394.

[465] Cf *Re G (Parental Responsibility: Education)* [1994] 2 FLR 964, CA, discussed in Ch 11, Sharing parental responsibility for a child, p 393.

[466] Section 14C(4). Cf child arrangements orders which entitle those named in the order as a person with whom the child is to live to remove a child from the United Kingdom for a period of less than *one* month, see Ch 14, Removal of the child from the United Kingdom – 'External relocation', p 525. Note: the entitlement to remove does not apply if an adoption placement order is in force: Adoption and Children Act 2002 s 29(7)(b).   [467] Section 14C(3).

[468] Section 5(4) of the Children Act 1989 as amended by the Adoption and Children Act 2002 s 115(4)(b).

They also have an obligation to take reasonable steps to inform parents with parental responsibility and guardians that the child has died.[469] They are also empowered to consent to the child's adoption[470] but not to the prejudice of the parents' right to consent or withhold consent.[471]

If a care order is subsequently made, the local authority has the power to determine the extent to which a special guardian may meet his parental responsibility.[472] Similarly, if an adoption placement order is in force the special guardian's exercise of parental responsibility may be restricted by the adoption agency.[473]

A special guardianship order automatically discharges any existing care order and related s 34 contact order[474] but, as we have seen, does not automatically discharge *any* existing s 8 order. Nor does an order prevent a subsequent application being made for a child arrangements order naming the applicant as a person with whom the child is to live, though leave of the court will be required.[475] As was pointed out in *Re S (Adoption Order or Special Guardianship Order)*[476] there are no leave requirements for parents to apply for any other s 8 order either. The only apparent way to restrict the parents exercising their right is to make a s 91(14) order with indefinite duration.[477]

A subsequent child arrangements order does not automatically discharge a special guardianship order but the person named in such an order as a person with whom the child is to live can apply for its discharge.[478]

In summary, as the Explanatory Notes to the Act explain:[479]

> The intention is that the special guardian has a clear responsibility for all the day to day decisions about caring for the child or young person and for taking decisions about his upbringing. But the order retains the basic link with the birth parents, unlike adoption. They remain legally the child's parents, though their ability to exercise their parental responsibility is limited. They retain the right to consent or not to the child's adoption or placement for adoption.

6. VARIATION AND DISCHARGE

Unlike adoption orders, special guardianship orders may be varied or discharged either upon application or upon the court's own motion.[480]

Under the scheme provided by s 14D, those who can apply without leave are: the special guardian(s), an individual (*other* than a parent or guardian) named in a child arrangements order as a person with whom the child is to live and, if a care order is subsequently made, the designated local authority.[481] Those who can apply with leave are: any parent

---

[469] Section 14C(5).

[470] This is because by s 144(1) of the Adoption and Children Act 2002 'guardians' include 'special guardians' and by s 47(2) guardians can consent or withhold consent to adoption.

[471] Section 14C(2)(b).

[472] Section 33(3)(b), as amended by the Adoption and Children Act 2002 Sch 3 para 63(a)(i).

[473] Adoption and Children Act 2002 s 29(7)(a) applying s 25(4).

[474] Section 91(5A) added by Sch 3 to the 2002 Act. Section 34 orders are discussed in Ch 19.

[475] Section 10(7A) added by Sch 3 para 56(d) to the 2002 Act.

[476] [2007] EWCA Civ 54 [2007] 1 FLR 819 at [64]ff, per Wall LJ.

[477] Even then, as Wall LJ pointed out, the test for overcoming the leave restriction has historically been seen as relatively low.

[478] Section 14D(1)(c), as amended by the Children and Families Act 2014 Sch 2 para 26.

[479] See para 278.   [480] Section 14D(1) and (2) respectively.

[481] Section 14D(1), as amended by the Children and Families Act 2014 Sch 2 para 26.

or guardian, anyone else other than a special guardian, parent or guardian or a person named in a child arrangements order as a person with whom the child is to live who had parental responsibility immediately before the making of the special guardianship order, and the child him- or herself.[482]

So far as the child is concerned, leave may only be granted if the court is satisfied that the child has sufficient understanding to make the application.[483] In the case of parents, guardians and step-parents who have parental responsibility by virtue of a s 4A parental responsibility order or agreement, leave may be granted provided the court 'is satisfied that there has been a significant change in circumstances since the making of the special guardianship order'.[484] This latter restriction is important and is designed to provide additional security for special guardians. Nevertheless its scope has not yet been authoritatively determined. The better view seems to be[485] that (a) the criteria set out in s 10(9)[486] are not applicable and (b) the phrase 'significant change of circumstances' should be interpreted in line with the simple 'change of circumstances' test in s 24 (3) of the 2002 Act.[487] It has been said[488] that a change of circumstances is a necessary but not sufficient condition of leave to apply for the discharge of a special guardianship order.

Although the Act is silent on this, presumably when considering whether to grant a variation or discharge the court must apply the paramountcy of the child's welfare principle.

7. DURATION OF ORDER

No specific provision is made for the duration of a special guardianship order but in accordance with general principles it must come to an end upon the child attaining 18[489] or upon the death of the child or special guardian (or surviving special guardian in the case of a joint appointment).[490] It remains a moot point whether it ends upon the child's marriage.

8. SPECIAL GUARDIANSHIP SUPPORT SERVICES

Section 14F makes important provision requiring local authorities to make arrangements within their area of special guardianship support services, namely, to provide counselling, advice and information and any other services, including financial support, as prescribed by regulation.[491] The intention[492] is to ensure that local authorities put in place a range of support services, including financial support, to be available where appropriate for special guardians and their children. To this end local authorities are obliged, upon

---

[482] Section 14D(3).   [483] Section 14D(4).   [484] Section 14D(5).

[485] See *Re G (Special Guardianship Order)* [2010] EWCA Civ [2010] 2 FLR 696, but in which the point was not fully argued.   [486] Discussed in Ch 14, The application of s 10(9), p 516.

[487] Discussed at Duration and revocation of placement orders, p 713. In other words noting turns on circumstances having to be 'significant'.

[488] Per Wilson LJ in *Re G (Special Guardianship Order)* [2010] EWCA Civ [2010] 2 FLR 696 at [13].

[489] References to a 'child' in the Children Act 1989 generally refer to a child under 18, see s 105(1). It is also the underlying assumption in the provision of financial support, see reg 9 of the Special Guardianship Regulations 2005.

[490] This would be in line with the position in guardianship, see Ch 8, Termination of guardianship, p 291.

[491] Viz. the Special Guardianship Regulations 2005 (England) (SI 2005/1109), Special Guardianship (Wales) Regulations 2005 (SI 2005/1513)(W.117). For an interesting discussion of the policy behind the introduction of these Regulations, see the Explanatory Memorandum to each of the Regulations. See also *Special Guardianship Guidance* (DfES, 2005) (England) and *Special Guardianship (Wales) Regulations 2005 Guidance* (National Assembly for Wales, 2006).   [492] See the Explanatory Notes to the 2002 Act, para 282.

the request of a relevant child[493] looked after by them (or previously looked after before the making of a special guardianship order), a special guardian or prospective special guardian or a parent of such a child, to carry out an assessment of that person's needs (including the need for financial support) for special guardianship support services.[494] In other cases the local authority may carry out such an assessment upon the written request inter alia of the child or a special guardian or any person whom the local authority consider to have a significant and ongoing relationship with a relevant child[495] but if they are minded not to, they must give the person 'notice of the proposed decision (including the reasons for it) and must allow the applicant a reasonable opportunity to make representations in relation to that decision'.[496] Where the local authority do decide to provide support services (other than advice or information) on more than one occasion they must provide a plan[497] and keep that plan under review.[498] These provisions are given additional teeth by s 14G which requires local authorities to establish a procedure for considering representations (including complaints) made to them in respect of these support services by either special guardians or their children.

Under the Special Guardianship Regulations both for England and Wales the prescribed services (in addition to counselling advice and information) comprise those to enable relevant children, the special guardians or prospective special guardians and the parents of relevant children to discuss matters relating to special guardianship; assistance, including mediation services in relation to contact arrangements; services in relation to a relevant child's therapeutic needs; and, assistance to ensure the continuance of the relationship between a relevant child and a special guardian, or prospective special guardian.[499] In each of these cases the services may include giving assistance in cash.[500]

A key part of the special guardianship support services is financial support. Such support is only payable in the circumstances provided for under reg 6 of the 2005 Special Guardianship Regulations (England) and reg 4 of the Welsh Regulations and is only payable to the special guardian or prospective special guardian where the local authority consider it is necessary to ensure that the special guardian or prospective special guardian can look after the child; that the child needs special care which requires a greater expenditure of resources than would otherwise be the case because of his illness, disability, emotional or behavioural difficulties or the consequences of his past abuse or neglect; it is appropriate to contribute to any legal costs; it is appropriate to contribute to the expenditure necessary for the purposes of accommodating and maintaining the child, including the provision of furniture and domestic equipment, alternations to and adaptations of the home, provision of meals, of transport and of clothing and toys and other items necessary for the purpose of looking after the child.

Support may also include a remuneration element in cases where it was paid to the former local authority foster parent of a child who has now become the special guardian or prospective special guardian.[501] Payments may be paid periodically or as a single

[493] Viz. a child subject to a special guardianship order, or to an application for such an order or in respect of whom the court is considering such an order and has asked the local authority to investigate and report: Special Guardianship Regulations 2005, reg 2(1) (England), reg 1(3) of the Welsh Regulations.

[494] Section 14F(4) and reg 11(1) of the 2005 Regulations (England). Cf reg 5 of the Welsh Regulations.

[495] Section 14F(3) and reg 11(2) of the 2005 Regulations (England). Cf reg 4 of the Welsh Regulations.

[496] Reg 11(3) of the 2005 Regulations (England).

[497] Section 14F(6) and reg 14 of the 2005 Regulations (England).

[498] Ch 4 of the 2005 Regulations (England); reg 12 of the Welsh Regulations.

[499] Reg 3(1)(a)–(d) of the 2005 Regulations (England), reg 3 of the Welsh Regulations.

[500] Reg 3(2) of the 2005 Regulations (England). The Welsh Regulations are silent on this issue.

[501] Reg 7. The Welsh Regulations are silent on this issue.

sum.[502] Support ceases to be payable if the child ceases to have a home with the special guardian or prospective special guardian; ceases full-time education or training and commences employment; qualifies for income support or jobseekers allowance in his own right; or attains the age of 18 unless he continues in full-time education or training, when it may continue until the end of the course of training he is then undertaking.[503]

Financial support is reviewable upon any relevant change of circumstances and, in any event, annually.[504] In *R (TT) v London Borough of Merton*[505] it was held wrong for a local authority to ignore the *Special Guardianship Guidance*'s recommendation[506] to consider the National Fostering Network's minimum allowance and to use that as a starting point, when determining the allowance for a special guardian.

9. THE USE MADE OF SPECIAL GUARDIANSHIP

Since its introduction by the 2002 Act (at the end of 2005), special guardianship has become established as an important and increasingly used order.[507] Even in its first full year of operation (2006) just over 900 orders were made[508] and by 2011 the number had increased to 4,261.[509] The majority of orders (2,973, 70% in 2011)[510] are made in public law proceedings. The numbers are likely to continue to rise in the light of the ruling in *Re B-S (Children) (Adoption Order: Leave to Oppose).*[511]

The expectation that the main users would be relatives, particularly grandparents, and long-term foster parents, particularly of older children (who may not wish to be *legally* separated from their birth families), who feel they can take over parental responsibility from the local authority, seems to have been borne out by experience. Other contexts in which special guardianship might be appropriate include sibling groups where the older child is the carer and the sibling relationship is more important to a younger child than the need for adoption; children in some minority ethnic communities, who have religious and cultural difficulties with adoption as it is set out in law; and unaccompanied asylum-seeking children who need secure, permanent homes, but who have strong attachments to their families abroad.[512]

In the case of familial carers who are not parents, the advantage of special guardianship, as Hedley J pointed out in *A v B and Newport City Council: Re K,*[513] is that it permits them to have all the practical authority and standing of parents, while leaving intact relationships within the family. Another general advantage of the order is the consequential support provisions (though, in the private law context, the requirement to notify and be investigated by local authority might act as a deterrent to some possible applicants).

---

[502] Reg 8. Note also no support is payable until the conditions set out in reg 10 have been complied with. There are no comparable provisions in the Welsh Regulations.

[503] Reg 9 (England), reg 4(2) of the Welsh Regulations.

[504] Reg 18 (England), reg 12(2) of the Welsh Regulations.

[505] [2012] EWHC 2055 (Admin) [2013] 2 FLR 773. See also *B v Lewisham Borough Council* [2008] EWHC 738 (Admin) [2008] 2 FLR 523 in which it was held wrong for a local authority when fixing the appropriate rate for special guardianship allowances to ignore fostering allowances and ally them instead to adoption allowances. [506] DfES, 2005 at para 65.

[507] See A Bainham 'Permanence for children: special guardianship or adoption?' [2007] CLJ 520 and A Hall 'Special Guardianship: A missed opportunity – Findings from Research' [2008] Fam Law 148 and 'Special Guardianship – Themes emerging from case law' [2008] Fam Law 244.

[508] *Judicial and Court Statistics* Cm 7273 (2007),Table 5.4. [509] Table 2.4.

[510] This compares with 80% in 2006.

[511] [2014] 1 WLR 563, discussed at Adoption and human rights, p 684.

[512] See the Explanatory Memorandum to the Special Guardianship Regulations 2005 (both the English and Welsh versions). [513] [2007] 1 FLR 1116.

It is established that each case has to be determined according to its own facts. As Wall LJ said in *Re S (Adoption Order or Special Guardianship Order)*[514] 'There can be no routine solutions... Each case needs to be decided on the application of the statutory provisions to the best interests of the particular child or children concerned.' This means that there are no paradigm situations and no a priori assumptions can be made as, for example, grandparents looking after grandchildren being granted special guardianship rather adoption.

Nevertheless Wall LJ commented:[515]

> A particular concern is that an adoption order has, as a matter of law, the effect of making the adopted child the child of the adopters for all purposes. Accordingly, where a child is adopted by a member of his wider family, the familial relationships are inevitably changed. This is frequently referred to as the 'skewing' or 'distorting' effect of adoption, and is a factor which the court must take into account when considering whether or not to make an adoption order in such a case.

On the other hand, he also observed:[516]

> It must be accepted that special guardianship does not always provide the same permanency of protection as adoption. In our judgment this is a factor, which, in a finely balanced case could well tip the scales in favour of adoption.

In *Re S* itself, the mother having dramatically changed her lifestyle since the making of care order, had a good relationship with the foster mother and enjoyed regular contact with her child, the Court of Appeal upheld a decision to grant the foster mother special guardianship rather than the adoption she applied for. In contrast, in *N v B and Others (Adoption by Grandmother)*,[517] adoption orders in respect of two children in favour of a maternal grandmother were thought preferable to a special guardianship order in a case in which she had become the carer following the murder of the mother by the father. *N v B* may in turn be contrasted with *Surrey County Council v Al Hilli and Others*,[518] in which a special guardianship order was made in respect of two orphaned children being looked after by their maternal aunt and uncle following the murder of their parents and grandparents. In that case it was felt it was in the children's interests to retain their existing family links and their identity as the children of their tragically deceased parents.

---

[514] [2007] EWCA Civ 54 [2007] 1 FLR 819 at [43] and [61].   [515] At [51].   [516] At [68].

[517] [2013] EWHC 820 (Fam) [2014] 1 FLR 369 For other examples of adoption being preferred to special guardianship, see *Re AJ (Adoption Order or Special Guardianship Order)* [2007] EWCA Civ 55 [2007] 1 FLR 507—adoption made in favour of a paternal aunt and *Re M-J (Adoption Order or Special Guardianship Order)* [2007] EWCA Civ 56 [2007] 1 FLR 691—adoption made in favour of an uncle and aunt.

[518] [2013] EWHC 3404 (Fam) [2014] 2 FLR 217.

20

THE HIGH COURT'S INHERENT POWERS IN RESPECT OF CHILDREN

A. INTRODUCTION

No discussion of child law would be complete without having regard to the High Court's inherent powers in respect of children. The development of these powers, principally under the aegis of the wardship jurisdiction, was highly influential in the modern development of law and practice concerning children, and the Children Act 1989 incorporates many of its features. Even now, long after the implementation of the 1989 Act, the residual inherent powers remain useful, particularly when the statutory system offers no suitable remedy.

Before the 1989 Act, discussion of these inherent powers would have focused solely on the wardship jurisdiction which, as will be seen, is not based on any statute but is an ancient jurisdiction derived from the sovereign's obligation as *parens patriae* to protect the person and property of those of his subjects, such as children, who are unable to look after themselves. However, in the light of the changes made by the 1989 Act (discussed later in this chapter) it is important to distinguish the well-established wardship jurisdiction from the inherent jurisdiction of the High Court.

Although the existence of a *parens patriae* power to protect children independent of wardship had been acknowledged by the court[1] before the 1989 Act, there had been little cause to develop it, given the wide-ranging nature of the wardship jurisdiction. However, in his Joseph Jackson Memorial Lecture,[2] Lord Mackay LC commented:

> . . . in the government's view wardship is only one use of the High Court's inherent *parens patriae* jurisdiction. We believe, therefore, that it is open to the High Court to make orders under its inherent jurisdiction in respect of children other than through wardship.

The Children Act 1989 is predicated on this view. Indeed, as will be seen, if a local authority wishes to obtain a High Court order in respect of a child already in care, they must seek to use the inherent rather than the wardship jurisdiction.

Although it is clear that the High Court's inherent jurisdiction is equally exercisable whether the child is or is not a ward of court,[3] there are important conceptual differences

---

[1] See eg *Re N (Infants)* [1967] Ch 512; *Re L (An Infant)* [1968] P 119, CA; and *S v McC; W v W* [1972] AC 24 at 47–50, per Lord MacDermott.

[2] (1989) 139 NLJ 505 at 507. See also *Practice Direction 12D Inherent Jurisdiction (including Wardship proceedings)*, para 1.3.

[3] See eg *MA v DB (Inherent Jurisdiction)* [2010] EWHC 1697 (Fam) [2011] 1 FLR 724 and *Re W (A Minor) (Medical Treatment: Court's Jurisdiction)* [1993] Fam 64, CA, per Lord Donaldson MR.

between the two jurisdictions. In particular, unlike wardship, the exercise of the inherent jurisdiction does not place the child under the ultimate responsibility of the court. This means that at no point will the child be subject to the rule obtaining in wardship that all important steps in the child's life have to be sanctioned by the court.[4] In other words, the inherent jurisdiction empowers the High Court to make orders dealing with particular aspects of the child's welfare, whereas wardship additionally vests in the court a continuing supervisory function over the child. Accordingly, notwithstanding the commonality of the powers and the 1989 Act's and the Family Procedure Rules 2010's tendency to obscure the distinction by using the term 'inherent jurisdiction' to refer to both wardship and the residual jurisdiction,[5] wardship is best regarded as one distinct manifestation of the inherent jurisdiction.[6] As *Practice Direction 12D—Inherent Jurisdiction (Including Wardship) Proceedings*[7] puts it:

> The court's wardship jurisdiction is part of and not separate from the court's inherent jurisdiction.

B. WARDSHIP

1. HISTORICAL DEVELOPMENT

Wardship[8] has a fascinating history. Its origins[9] lie in feudal times, when it was an incident of tenure by which, upon a tenant's death, the lord became guardian of the surviving infant heir's land and body. Although there was a protective element in the guardianship in that the lord was supposed to look after his ward, maintaining and educating him according to his station, the right was a valuable one since, inter alia, the lord was entitled to keep the profits of the land until the heir reached his majority. No one benefited more

---

[4] *Re W (A Minor) (Medical Treatment: Court's Jurisdiction)* [1993] Fam 64 at 73F–G, per Lord Donaldson MR.

[5] Section 100 is headed, 'Restriction on use of wardship jurisdiction', but the substance of the section relates to the inherent jurisdiction as much as to wardship. In contrast, FPR 2010 Part 12 ch 5 is entitled 'Special Provisions about the inherent Jurisdiction Proceedings' but most of the consequent rules only apply to wardship. Rule 2.3 defines 'inherent jurisdiction' as meaning 'the High Court's power to make any order or determine any issue in respect of a child, including in wardship proceedings, where it would be just to do so unless restricted by legislation or case law.' Note also that s 8(3) includes the 'inherent jurisdiction' in the definition of 'family proceedings', which is intended to cover wardship.

[6] Note Ward LJ's comment in *Re Z (A Minor) (Identification: Restrictions on Publication)* [1997] Fam 1 at 14, CA that 'For all practical purposes the jurisdiction in wardship and the inherent jurisdiction over children is one and the same . . .'.   [7] At para 1.3.

[8] For a detailed analysis of the jurisdiction before the Children Act 1989 see N Lowe and R White *Wards of Court* (1986, 2nd edn); L Custer 'The Origins of the Doctrine of *Parens Patriae*' (1978) 27 Emory LJ 195; J Seymour '*Parens Patriae* and Wardship Powers: Their Nature and Origins' (1994) 14 *Oxford Journal of Legal Studies* 159; S Abramowicz 'English Child Custody Law 1660–1839: the Origins of Judicial Intervention in Parental Custody' (1999) 99 Columbia LR 1344; and Law Com Working Paper No 101 *Wards of Court*. For valuable accounts by (then) High Court judges, see Cross J 'Wards of Court' (1967) 83 LQR 200 and Balcombe J 'Wardship' (1981–2) Lit 223. For post-Children Act discussion see N Lowe 'Inherently Disposed to Protect Children—The continuing Role of Wardship' in R Probert and C Barton (eds) *50 Years in Family Law—Essays for Stephen Cretney* (2012) 161 and HHJ Mitchell 'Whatever Happened to Wardship?' [2001] Fam Law 130 and 212.

[9] For a more detailed historical account see Lowe and White *Wards of Court*, op cit, at paras 1.1 *et seq* and the references there cited. See also *Re Eve* (1986) 31 DLR (4th) 1, Canadian Supreme Court.

than the Crown (whose rights arose upon the death of a tenant-in-chief) and in 1540 the Court of Wards was created to enforce the sovereign's rights and the execution of his duties in connection with wardship. These rights, together with the Court of Wards, were abolished in 1660.[10] The wardship jurisdiction, however, survived in the hands of the Court of Chancery.

Jurisdiction was claimed upon the basis that the sovereign, as *parens patriae*, had a duty to protect his subjects, particularly those, such as infants,[11] who were unable to protect themselves, and that this duty had been delegated to the Lord Chancellor and through him to the Court of Chancery. Although there is some doubt about the historical validity of this claim, by the end of the nineteenth century (by which time jurisdiction had become vested in the Chancery Division of the High Court), it had become the authoritatively accepted basis of the jurisdiction.[12] Furthermore, it became established that the jurisdiction was not dependent upon the existence of property belonging to the infant.[13]

Although by the turn of the twentieth century wardship had acquired most of the characteristics of the modern jurisdiction,[14] it needed two further reforms to make the jurisdiction more accessible, namely that in 1949,[15] enabling children to be made wards solely to protect them and that in 1971 transferring the jurisdiction to the newly created Family Division of the High Court[16] and permitting wardship proceedings to be brought in the provinces (through the district registries) as well as in London (in the principal registry).

Until 1986 wardship had been an exclusively High Court jurisdiction, but since then it has been possible, at any rate after the main issues have been resolved, to transfer cases to the Family Court (formerly transfers were made to the county court).[17]

2. CHARACTERISTICS OF THE WARDSHIP JURISDICTION

(a) Control vested in the court

A unique and fundamental characteristic of the jurisdiction is that throughout the wardship legal control over both the child's person and property is vested in the court. As Lord Scarman put it,[18] once a party persuades the court that it should make the child its ward 'the court takes over ultimate responsibility for the child'. Although, in the past at any rate, wardship was quite frequently referred to as a 'parental jurisdiction', the court is not

---

[10] By the Tenures Abolition Act 1660.

[11] And, originally, lunatics. Although it seemed to be established that there is no longer a *parens patriae* jurisdiction with regard to incapacitated adults: *Re F (Mental Patient: Sterilisation)* [1990] 2 AC 1, HL, a quasi-wardship protective jurisdiction has been developed, principally by Munby J, as he then was, see for example, *Re PS (Incapacitated or Vulnerable Adult)* [2007] EWHC 2689 (Fam) [2009] 1 FLR 487. Furthermore this jurisdiction has been held to continue notwithstanding the Mental Capacity Act 2005 and the Mental Health Acts of 1983 and 2007, see *DL v Local Authority* [2012] EWCA Civ 253.

[12] *Johnstone v Beattie* (1843) 10 Cl & Fin 42 at 120 per Lord Eldon LC, and *Hope v Hope* (1854) 4 De GM & G 328 at 344–5 per Lord Cranworth LC.

[13] See *Re Spence* (1847) 2 Ph 247 at 251 per Lord Cottenham LC. In fact, until 1949 it was common practice to begin wardship by making a nominal settlement upon the child and then commencing an action to administer the trusts of the settlement: see *Re D* [1943] Ch 305 at 306 and *Re X's Settlement* [1945] Ch 44 at 45.

[14] See eg *R v Gyngall* [1893] 2 QB 232 at 248, CA per Kay LJ.

[15] By the Law Reform (Miscellaneous Provisions) Act 1949.

[16] Under the Administration of Justice Act 1970 s 1(2) and Sch 1.

[17] Pursuant to s 38(2)(b) of the Matrimonial and Family Proceedings Act 1984, as amended by the Courts and Crimes Act 2013, s 17 and Sch 11. See also FPR 2010 r 12.36.

[18] In *Re E (SA) (A Minor) (Wardship)* [1984] 1 All ER 289 at 290, HL.

in the same position as a parent or other persons with parental responsibility in any strict sense. As Lord Donaldson MR said, it is clear that:

> . . . the practical jurisdiction of the court is wider than that of parents. . . . It is also clear that this jurisdiction is not derivative from the parents' rights and responsibilities, but derives from, or is, the delegated performance of the duties of the Crown to protect its subjects . . .[19]

Notwithstanding this observation, in Children Act terms it must also be the case that wardship vests parental responsibility for the child in the court.[20]

The effects of the court's control

Being under the court's protection does not mean that the ward is physically in the court's or judge's care, but rather that the child and those with parental responsibility or otherwise having de facto care and control are subject to the court's control. This control is both an immediate and automatic consequence of wardship.[21] As Cross J put it,[22] once the child has been made a ward, 'no important step in the child's life can be taken without the court's consent'. Failure to obtain the court's consent constitutes a contempt of court, for which the ultimate sanction is imprisonment and a fine.[23]

Extent of control

Despite the potential draconian sanction it is not easy to say precisely what constitutes an 'important step'.[24] It is well established that no-one may marry a ward[25] nor take the ward outside the jurisdiction without the court's consent. Formerly, the latter embargo meant that leave was required before a ward could travel outside England and Wales. However, under the Family Law Act 1986 s 38 the automatic[26] embargo does not prevent the child's removal to another part of the United Kingdom in which divorce or other matrimonial proceedings (in respect of the ward's parents) are continuing or in which the child is habitually resident.

Other 'steps' requiring prior court consent include: applying to adopt or to place such a child for adoption with parental consent or to start proceedings for a placement order in relation to such a child;[27] moving a ward to new care-givers, as for example, seeking

---

[19] In *Re R (A Minor) (Wardship: Consent to Medical Treatment)* [1992] Fam 11 at 24, CA. See also *Re W (A Minor) (Medical Treatment: Court's Jurisdiction)* earlier.

[20] That was clearly Hedley J's view in *T v S (Wardship)* [2011] EWHC 1608 (Fam) [2012] 1 FLR 230 at [22] (1). According to *Practice Direction 12D–Inherent Jurisdiction (Including Wardship) Proceedings* para 1.3(a), wardship vests *custody* of the child in the court. However, this reference to 'custody' seems dated. For jurisdictional purposes wardship has been regarded as a form of guardianship thereby falling within the scope of the revised Brussels II Regulation, see *A v A (Children: Habitual Residence) (Reunite International Child Abduction Centre intervening)* [2013] UKSC 60 [2014] AC 1 at [29] per Baroness Hale.

[21] The control begins as soon as the wardship application is issued and without any specific court order. It ends when the wardship ends. Whether such immediate and automatic wide-ranging protection can be justified has been questioned by the Law Commission: Law Com Working Paper No 101 paras 4.3 and 4.13.

[22] In *Re S (Infants)* [1967] 1 WLR 396 at 407. The same comment is made in *Practice Direction 12D*, para 1.3 (b).

[23] See *Re B (JA) (An Infant)* [1965] Ch 1112 at 117, per Cross J and see more generally N Lowe and R White *Wards of Court* (1986, 2nd edn) ch 8.

[24] For a detailed discussion see Clarke Hall & Morrison *On Children*, Division 6 at [66] ff.

[25] Marriage Act 1949 s 3(6), which, following the Marriage (Same Sex Couples) 2013 equally forbids entering into a same sex marriage with a ward. It is implicit in the Civil Partnership Act 2004, s 4(4) that there is a similar embargo against entering into a civil partnership with a ward.

[26] But the court can still make an express order prohibiting the ward's removal from England and Wales.

[27] FPR 2010 r 12.42.

compulsory admission to hospital of a mentally ill ward;[28] changing the ward's whereabouts;[29] making material changes in a ward's education;[30] and, performing major medical treatment on a ward.[31]

Warding a child does not *in itself* impose a complete ban on publicity about the child[32] but, because court proceedings are confidential (unless judgment is given in open court), it is a contempt to publish any information relating to those proceedings.[33] The interrelationship between wardship and the criminal law is not straightforward but in summary,[34] while leave is not required for the police to interview a child who has been arrested merely because he happens to be a ward,[35] nor to call a ward as a witness in criminal proceedings, it is required to interview a ward on behalf of a defendant in a criminal trial[36] and for the Crown Prosecution Service to administer a caution to a ward.[37] Leave is also required to apply on a ward's behalf for compensation from the Criminal Injuries Compensation Authority.[38]

(b) The special nature of the jurisdiction

Because legal control of the child vests in the court, wardship proceedings have always been regarded as special. In *Re E (SA) (A Minor) (Wardship)*[39] Lord Scarman commented that when exercising its wardship jurisdiction a court:

> . . . must never lose sight of a fundamental feature of the jurisdiction, namely, that it is exercising a wardship, not an adversarial jurisdiction. Its duty is not limited to the dispute between the parties: on the contrary, its duty is to act in the way best suited in its judgment to serve the true interest and welfare of the ward. In exercising wardship jurisdiction, the court is a true family court. Its paramount concern is the welfare of its ward.

---

[28] Mental Health Act 1983 s 33. See also *Re CB (A Minor) (Wardship: Local Authority)* [1981] 1 All ER 16 at 24, CA, per Ormrod LJ. But there is no requirement to obtain leave to apply for an emergency protection order: cf *Re B (Wardship: Place of Safety Order)* (1979) 2 FLR 307.

[29] FPR 2010 r 12.39(2). If this is a simple change of residence it is sufficient to give the Registry written notice.   [30] See the Notice of Wardship issued with the application.

[31] Eg. abortion, according to *Re G-U (A Minor) (Wardship)* [1984] FLR 811 and sterilisation, according to Lord Templeman in *Re B (A Minor) (Wardship: Sterilisation)* [1988] AC 199 at 205.Cf *Re E (A Minor) (Medical Treatment)* [1991] 2 FLR 585 in which it was held that the court's consent was not required to perform an operation for therapeutic purposes even though a side effect was to sterilise the child. Leave is probably required to conduct tests to establish parentage: see Lowe and White, op cit, at paras 5–24.

[32] *Re L (A Minor: Freedom of Publication)* [1988] 1 All ER 418 and *Re W (Minors) (Wardship: Contempt)* [1989] 1 FLR 246. But note *Re S (A Child) (Identification: Restrictions on Publicity)* [2004] UKHL 47 [2005] 1 AC 593 which establishes that jurisdiction to restrain publicity is properly to be regarded as being founded upon the European Convention on Human Rights rather than on any inherent powers.

[33] Administration of Justice Act 1960 s 12. The embargo covers not just the actual proceedings but also statements of evidence, reports, accounts of interviews and such like which are prepared for use in court once the wardship proceedings have started: see *Re F (Otherwise A) (A Minor)* [1977] Fam 58.

[34] See more generally, *Practice Direction 12D*, paras 5.1 ff.

[35] *Re R, Re G (Minors)* [1990] 2 All ER 633, though those having care and control should inform the wardship court at the earliest opportunity. See also *Re K (Minors) (Wardship: Criminal Proceedings)* [1988] Fam 1.

[36] *Re R (Minors) (Wardship: Criminal Proceedings)* [1991] Fam 56, CA.

[37] *Re A (A Minor) (Wardship: Police Caution)* [1989] Fam 103.

[38] *Practice Direction* [1988] 1 All ER 182 and *Re G (A Minor) (Ward: Criminal Injuries Compensation)* [1990] 3 All ER 102, CA.

[39] [1984] 1 All ER 289 at 290, HL. For similar comments see eg Viscount Haldane in *Scott v Scott* [1913] AC 417 at 437, HL and Cross J in *Re B (JA) (An Infant)* [1965] Ch 1112 at 1117.

Before the Children Act the uniqueness of wardship was both especially marked and useful, since it could often be invoked to overcome other statutory jurisdictions or gaps in the law.[40] However, it was the policy of that Act, in the words of Butler-Sloss LJ:[41]

> ... to incorporate the best of the wardship jurisdiction within the statutory framework without any of the perceived disadvantages of judicial monitoring of administrative plans.

Hence, wardship now shares many of its characteristics with other child law jurisdictions. For example, in all family proceedings hearsay evidence is admissible[42] and the court can make s 8 orders whether or not they have been applied for.[43] The paramountcy principle applies in all proceedings concerning a child's upbringing and, following the Children Act, there has been a general move away from an adversarial approach in all children cases. Nonetheless wardship remains unique in that control over the child is vested in the court. Furthermore, that control arises immediately the child becomes a ward and only ceases when the wardship itself ceases.

3. WHO CAN BE WARDED

(a) Must be a child under the age of 18

Only children, that is, persons under the age of 18,[44] may be warded.[45] There is some doubt whether a married child can be warded.[46] Although once a matter of speculation, it is settled that an unborn child cannot be made a ward of court.[47]

(b) The child must be subject to the jurisdiction

Historically, jurisdiction to ward a child was based upon the child's allegiance to the Crown.[48] This meant that in theory any child who was a British subject could be warded regardless of his place of birth, domicile or residence.[49] So far as alien children were concerned, their physical presence, however, fleeting,[50] was sufficient to found

---

[40] Particularly in the context of committing children into local authority care: see Rising number of wardships, p 753.

[41] In *Re B (Minors) (Termination of Contact: Paramount Consideration)* [1993] Fam 301 at 310, CA.

[42] See the Children (Admissibility of Hearsay Evidence) Order 1993 (SI 1993/621). In wardship hearsay evidence has always been admissible: *Re W (Minors) (Wardship: Evidence)* [1990] 1 FLR 203, CA.

[43] Children Act 1989 s 10(1)(b), discussed in Ch 14, Upon application or upon the court's own motion p 537; cf *Re E (SA)*, earlier.

[44] Family Law Reform Act 1969 s 1. On occasion, the court may need to determine the age of the alleged 'child' as a preliminary issue of jurisdiction, see *E (By her Litigation Friend, PW) v London Borough of X* [2005] EWHC 2811 (Fam), [2006] 1 FLR 730.

[45] See generally N Lowe 'Who can be made a ward of court?' (1989) 1 *Journal of Child Law* 6.

[46] *Re Elwes (No 2), The Times*, 30 July 1958 suggests there is jurisdiction, whereas cases on guardianship, eg *Mendes v Mendes* (1747) 1 Ves Sen 89 at 91 per Lord Hardwicke LC; *R v Wilmington Inhabitants* (1822) 5 B & Ald 525 at 526 per Abbot CJ and *Hewer v Bryant* [1970] 1 QB 357 at 373 per Sachs LJ, suggest there is not. See Lowe and White, op cit, at paras 2.1 and 2.2.

[47] *Re F (In Utero)* [1988] Fam 122, CA; J Fortin 'Legal Protection of the Unborn Child' (1988) 51 MLR 54; and A Grubb and D Pearl (1987) 103 LQR 340. For a similar position taken in Canada, see *Winnipeg Child and Family Services (Northwest Area) v G* (1997) 152 DLR (4th) 193, Can Sup Ct but for the contrary view in New Zealand see *Re An Unborn Child* High Court, Hamilton M171/02, 11 October 2002. The inability to ward a foetus does not prevent anticipatory relief being granted, see *Re D (Unborn Baby)* [2009] EWHC 2811 (Fam) [2009] 2 FLR 313.   [48] See *Re P (GE) (An Infant)* [1965] Ch 568 at 587 per Pearson LJ.

[49] See *Harben v Harben* [1957] 1 All ER 379 at 381 per Sachs LJ and *Re P (GE) (An Infant)* [1965] Ch 568, per Lord Denning (at 582) and per Pearson LJ (at 587).

[50] See eg *Re C (an Infant)* (1956) *Times* December 14, child en route from the USA to the USSR.

jurisdiction.[51] At one stage, it seemed that this historical position had been abandoned. In *H v H (Jurisdiction To Grant Wardship)*,[52] for example, Thorpe LJ said that there is no jurisdiction to ward a child who is neither habitually resident nor present in England and Wales. However, at best, that position could only be regarded as a self denying stance since, as Baroness Hale subsequently observed in *A v A (Children: Habitual Residence) (Reunite International Child Abduction Centre intervening)*,[53] the jurisdiction continues to exist insofar as it has not expressly been removed by statute.

The Supreme Court decision in A v A

In *A v A* the Supreme Court held that jurisdiction to make a child a ward of court could exceptionally be based upon a child's British nationality. In summary,[54] the basis of the decision was as follows: jurisdiction to ward a child is governed by the revised Brussels II Regulation as it is an order relating to parental responsibility but it is not governed by the Family Law Act 1986 as it is not a 'Part 1 order' for the purposes of that Act.[55] The application of Art 8 of the Regulation normally requires that, regardless of nationality, the child must be habitually resident in England and Wales. However, Art 14 of the Regulation provides that in cases where *no* Member State has jurisdiction under the terms of the Regulation, a Member State is free to apply its own rules. This means, so the Supreme Court ruled, that because the 1986 Act does not apply to making of the wardship order, exceptionally, where the child is not habitually resident nor present in England and Wales[56] nor in any other Member State but has British nationality, jurisdiction can be taken according to the common law basis of allegiance through nationality.

The Supreme Court only determined whether jurisdiction *could* be taken upon the basis of nationality. It did not determine whether that jurisdiction should be exercised. That issue was remitted back to the first instance judge (discussed shortly). However, it is clear that it is by no means an automatic consequence of the ruling that the jurisdiction should be exercised. Baroness Hale acknowledged that there were arguments against its exercise not least of which was that it was inconsistent with and potentially disruptive of the scheme under the Family Law Act 1986 inasmuch as the child could be ordered to come to England and upon arrival the courts were empowered to make a whole range of orders on the basis of the child's presence. In so doing, as Wilson J (as he then was) once said,[57] 'in effect the whole architecture of the 1986 Act would collapse'. These considerations led Baroness Hale to agree with Thorpe LJ's observation in *Al Habtoor v Fotheringham*[58] that the jurisdiction should be exercised with 'extreme circumspection', that is, to use phrases from earlier decisions referred to by the Supreme Court, where the circumstances are 'sufficiently dire and exceptional'[59] or 'at the very extreme end of the spectrum'.[60]

---

[51] Unless the child was a member of the household of a parent entitled to diplomatic immunity, see *Re C (An Infant)* [1959] Ch 363 and *Re P (Children Act: Diplomatic Immunity)* [1998] 1 FLR 624.

[52] [2011] EWCA Civ 796 [2012] 1 FLR 23 at [52].   [53] [2013] UKSC 60 [2014] AC 1 at [63].

[54] For a more detailed analysis see Clarke Hall & Morrison on *Children* at 6 [22] ff.

[55] Both the revised Brussels II Regulation and the Family Act 1986 are discussed in more detail in Ch 26.

[56] The majority held (Lord Hughes dissenting) that because the child in question had spent his whole life in Pakistan and had never set foot in England he could not be said to be habitually resident either here or elsewhere within the EU. 'Habitual residence' is discussed further in Ch 26.

[57] In *Re V (Jurisdiction: Habitual Residence)* [2001] 1 FLR 253 at 264, not referred to by the Supreme Court.   [58] [2001] EWCA Civ 186 [2001] 1 FLR 951 at [42].

[59] Per Hogg J in *Re B: RB v FB and MA (Forced Marriage: Wardship Jurisdiction)* [2008] EWHC 1436 (Fam) [2008] 2 FLR 1624 at [10].

[60] Per McFarlane LJ in *Re N (Abduction: Appeal)* [2012] EWCA Civ 1086 [2013] 1 FLR 57 at [29].

The remitted decision in A v A

In the subsequent remitted hearing Parker J did exercise jurisdiction. She accepted that it was only in the rarest possible cases that the exercise of jurisdiction based on nationality would be justified. *A v A*, however, was such a case and indeed the facts are striking. The mother and father married in Pakistan but settled in England where they had three children. The father and the three children had dual British and Pakistani nationality and the mother had indefinite leave to remain in England. The marriage broke down and the father returned alone to Pakistan. Later the mother went with the children to visit her family in Pakistan but was forced to resume living with her husband in Pakistan. She subsequently became pregnant and gave birth to their fourth child. Eventually the mother managed to return alone to England where she subsequently sought the return of all four children. From the point of view of jurisdiction there was no issue about the three elder children since they were considered to habitually resident in England but, as the Supreme Court had ruled, the same could not be said of the youngest child since he had never set foot here. However, Parker J determined that she should exercise the wardship jurisdiction in relation to the fourth child on the basis that (a) the three elder children had their closest connection with England, (b) the mother had been subject to coercion whilst in Pakistan and (c) it would be much easier for the father to return to the country which in reality was his home and where the family property was situated. Accordingly, Parker J ordered the return of all four children.[61]

Wardship based on nationality has also been exercised to protect a 15 year old child, born and raised in Pakistan but who had British nationality through her father, from a forced marriage arranged by her mother following the father's death.[62] On the other side of the coin, jurisdiction was declined in case where the Bangladeshi court was already seised of the case.[63]

4. THE DISCRETION TO EXERCISE JURISDICTION

Even if it has jurisdiction, the court is not bound to exercise it. The court generally refuses to exercise jurisdiction to review the exercise of discretionary powers vested in other bodies or tribunals such as local authorities[64] or the immigration service,[65] or to interfere with the normal operation of criminal proceedings[66] or military law.[67] The court is reluctant to exercise jurisdiction where the child's presence is merely a fleeting one, and in cases where the child has been abducted into this country it is established, in cases not governed by the abduction Conventions (see Chapter 26), that the court must decide

---

[61] *A v A (Return Order on the Basis of British Nationality)* [2013] EWHC 3298 (Fam). In a further sequel, see *A v A* [2013] EWHC 3554 (Fam), [2014] Fam Law 157, the father in fact returned with the three elder children who were made the subject of interim care orders. The youngest child was left with relatives in Pakistan because of alleged difficulties of obtaining a passport for him. A further order for his return was made.

[62] See *Re B: RB v FB and MA (Forced Marriage: Wardship Jurisdiction)*, earlier. This seems a very borderline decision.

[63] *H (Father) v B (Mother)* [2013] EWHC 2950 (Fam). See also *Re N (Abduction: Appeal)*, earlier, in which jurisdiction was declined in respect of a child who had been in Lebanon for 18 months.

[64] *A v Liverpool City Council* [1982] AC 363, HL, discussed in Ch 18, Wardship and the inherent jurisdiction, p 667.

[65] *Re Mohamed Arif (An Infant), Re Nirbhai Singh (An Infant)* [1968] Ch 643, CA, *Re F (A Minor) (Immigration: Wardship)* [1990] Fam 125, and *R (Anton) v Secretary of State For The Home Department, Re Anton* [2004] EWHC 2730/2731 (Admin/Fam) [2005] 2 FLR 818, CA. See further The de facto limits, p 767.

[66] *Re K (Minors) (Wardship: Criminal Proceedings)* [1988] Fam 1.

[67] *Re JS (A Minor) (Wardship: Boy Soldier)* [1990] Fam 182.

whether it is in the child's best interests to be returned immediately or to have the full merits of the case heard by the English court.[68] The court has a statutory power[69] to refuse to make orders or to stay proceedings if the matter has been or is being dealt with in proceedings outside England and Wales.

5. WHO CAN APPLY TO WARD A CHILD?

Any person with a genuine interest may apply to make a child a ward of court. Applications may also be made by the child and, with the court's permission, a local authority.[70] What ranks as a 'genuine interest' for this purpose is left open, though it seems clear that those having a blood tie with or parental responsibility for the child or who are the child's de facto carers are likely to be regarded as having such an interest. But applicants are not restricted to such persons. In *Re D (A Minor) (Wardship: Sterilisation)*,[71] for example, an educational psychologist attached to a local authority warded a child to prevent her being sterilised.

Unlike applying for section 8 orders under the 1989 Act there is no leave requirement for making wardship applications. However, applicants are required, when making their application, to state their relationship to the child and the reason for the application[72] and the particulars are then sent for recording in the register of wards.[73] If there is any doubt about the propriety of the application, the recording officer will immediately refer the matter to the appropriate district judge who can dismiss the application if it is considered to be an abuse of process,[74] or refer the application to a judge.

In the past there has been some doubt as to whether a court could make a child a ward on its own motion[75] but there are now numerous instances in which this has been done, at any rate, in the context of other ongoing proceedings.[76]

6. RESPONDENTS

The rules are equally flexible as to who can be made respondents to wardship proceedings. According to FPR 2010 r 12.3 the respondents to an application for an order relating to the exercise of the court's inherent jurisdiction, including wardship proceedings, are

---

[68] *Re J (A Child) (Custody Rights: Jurisdiction)* [2005] UKHL 40 [2006] 1 AC 80, discussed in Ch 26, The law as settled by *re J*, p 1026.   [69] Under the Family Law Act 1986 s 5.

[70] FPR 2010 r 12.3. Query whether by referring to 'person' the Rule is intended to exclude 'bodies'? In the past, clinics have brought wardship proceedings to authorise abortions. For an example of where a child made herself a ward, see *Re E (By her Litigation Friend, PW) v London Borough of X* [2005] EWHC 2811 (Fam) [2006] 1 FLR 730.

[71] [1976] Fam 185. See also the case referred to in *The Times* on 21 May 1985 where the Brook Advisory Centre warded a child to authorise an abortion.

[72] FPR 2010 r 5 and *Practice Direction 5A Forms* para 3.1.   [73] FPR 2010 r 12.38.

[74] A classic example of such an abuse is *Re Dunhill* (1967) 111 Sol Jo 113, where a nightclub owner made one of his models a ward for publicity purposes. Where an application is judged to be an abuse of process, the applicant will at least be liable for costs and may be held to have committed contempt.

[75] See See *Re AW Adoption Application)* [1993] 1 FLR 62 at 78-79, per Bracewell J.

[76] See eg *Re K (Children With Disabilities: Wardship)* [2012] 2 FLR 745 at [39], in which, upon granting the local authority permission to withdraw care proceedings, the court made the children wards; *Re S (Wardship: Peremptory Return)* [2010] EWCA Civ 465 [2010] 2 FLR 1960, in which it was considered that given that the 1980 Hague Abduction Convention did not apply to the particular circumstances of the case, wardship provided the only means of securing the child's return to England and Wales. See also *Re A (Custody Decision After Maltese Non-Return Order)* [2006] EWHC 3397 (Fam) [2007] 1 FLR 1923 and *Re S (Brussels II Revised: Enforcement of Contact Order)* [2008] 2 FLR 1358 at [47].

the parent or guardian of the child, any other person who has an interest in or relationship to the child and, in the case of wardship and with the court's permission, the child (but see further later). To protect a ward, it has been the long standing practice that where a child is warded to prevent an undesirable association with another person, that that person should not be made a respondent.[77]

Surprisingly, perhaps, the child who is the subject of wardship proceedings is not automatically a party and indeed must not be made a respondent to those proceedings unless the court gives permission.[78]

Examples of cases in which it may be appropriate to make the child a party are:

(a) where a teenage ward is in dispute with his or her parents;

(b) where the ward is old enough (usually aged eight or over) to express a view and that view is likely to be of particular importance, for example, if in cases where it is alleged that child has been 'brain-washed' against one parent;

(c) where a specific task has to be carried out by an independent party, such as the psychiatric examination of a ward;

(d) where there are difficult issues on law or facts, such as international problems or questions affecting the life or death of the ward, disputed medical evidence or where there are special or exceptional points of law;[79]

(e) in a residence dispute between local authority foster parents on the one hand and the local authority and father who sought residence on the other hand.[80]

7. DURATION OF WARDSHIP

(a) Wardship taking effect upon the making of an application

Section 41(1) of the Senior Courts Act 1981[81] states that, subject to the provisions of that Act, no child can be made a ward of court except by an order to that effect made by the High Court. Section 41(2) provides that a child (other than a child who is subject to a care order)[82] becomes a ward *immediately* an application for wardship is made.

(b) When wardship ends

A child who automatically becomes a ward of court on the making of an application ceases to be a ward on the determination of the application unless the court orders that the child be made a ward.[83] After the making of such an order the court can subsequently order that any child ceases to be a ward.[84] Wardship automatically ends upon the making of a care order[85] or upon the child attaining the age of 18.[86]

---

[77] See *Practice Direction 12D* para 3.1.1.   [78] FPR 2010 r 12.37(1).

[79] See *Re B (A Minor) (Wardship: Medical Treatment)* [1981] 1 WLR 1421.

[80] *A Local Authority v D* [2006] EWHC 295 (Fam) [2006] All ER (D) 392 (Feb).

[81] Formerly known as the Supreme Court Act 1981.

[82] Supreme Court Act 1981 s 41(2A), added by the Children Act 1989 Sch 13 para 45(2).

[83] FPR 2010 r 12.41(1).

[84] Senior Courts Act 1981 s 41 (3). Applications can also be made to withdraw wardship proceedings (under FPR 2010 r 29.4), the effect of which, if granted, is that child ceases to be a ward. Applicants for withdrawal can be ordered to pay costs: *R and another v A (Costs in Children Proceedings)* [2011] EWHC 1158 (Fam) [2011] 2 FLR 672.   [85] Children Act 1989 s 91(4).

[86] Family Law Reform Act 1969 Sch 3 para 3.

8. THE COURT'S POWERS

(a) Confirming or discharging the wardship

At the initial hearing the judge must first decide whether or not to continue the wardship. It is at this stage that issues of jurisdiction should be taken.[87] The wardship may be discharged if the court declines to exercise its jurisdiction, for example, because it considers the application spurious, because it declines to interfere with a decision of another body or tribunal (in which case, it will be noted, the child's welfare is not the paramount consideration), or because it decides that wardship is of no further benefit to the child. It should be discharged where there is no significant evidence on which to exercise the jurisdiction.[88] It is established[89] that the wardship should not be continued unless it offers advantages to the child concerned which cannot be secured by the use of the orders available under the 1989 Act or, presumably, under the residual inherent jurisdiction. Once the wardship has been continued, its subsequent discharge is governed by the paramountcy principle.

(b) Orders that can be made

In this and the following section consideration is given to the powers that the court has on the assumption that the wardship will be continued. In this respect the issue is not just what powers are available to the court but whether the exercise of them is consistent with the court's continuing overall control of its ward.

The statutory powers

Since wardship proceedings rank as 'family proceedings',[90] the court is empowered in those proceedings to make any s 8 order whether or not they have been applied for. It can therefore make any form of a child arrangements order (formerly residence and contact orders), a prohibited steps order and specific issue order. As a general principle while these powers do not oust the court's inherent powers, whenever there is a choice, the former should be exercised.[91]

Although it is likely that upon making an order determining with whom the child is to live, the court will discharge the wardship,[92] it is accepted that it is not inconsistent with the court's control over its ward to make such an order and continue the wardship.[93] Where the wardship is ordered to continue, the parents and those named in a child arrangements order as a person with whom the child is to live [formerly residence order holders], if different, have parental responsibility subject to the general requirement to obtain the court's consent with regard to any important steps in the child's life.

---

[87] Particularly where the issue is one of discretion: see eg *Re D (A Minor)* (1978) 76 LGR 653.

[88] *Re F (Minors) (Wardship: Jurisdiction)* [1988] 2 FLR 123, CA. See also *Re Z (Minors) (Child Abuse: Evidence)* [1989] 2 FLR 3.

[89] See *Re T (A Minor) (Wardship: Representation)* [1994] Fam 49, CA, *Re M and J (Wardship: Supervision and Residence Orders)* [2003] EWHC 1585 (Fam) [2003] 2 FLR 541 and *Re W (Wardship: Discharge: Publicity)* [1995] 2 FLR 466, CA.

[90] Children Act 1989 s 8(3), discussed in Ch 14, Family proceedings, p 535.

[91] *Re T (A Minor) (Wardship: Representation)* [1994] Fam 49.

[92] *Re T (A Minor) (Wardship: Representation)* earlier. See also *B v B (Residence: Condition Limiting Geographic Area)* [2004] 2 FLR 979—wardship discharged; residence order made with condition attached.

[93] See eg *Re P (Surrogacy: Residence)* [2008] 1 FLR 177, *Re M and J (Wardship: Supervision and Residence Orders)* [2003] EWHC 1585 (Fam) [2003] 2 FLR 541, *Re R-J (Minors) (Fostering: Person disqualified)* [1999] 2 FLR 60. Note also *Re M (Child's Upbringing)* [1996] 2 FLR 441, in which the court ordered the child to return to live with his birth family in South Africa but maintained the wardship. It is submitted that a similar position obtains with regard to making special guardianship orders.

It is within the court's powers to make a child arrangements order determining with whom the child will have contact and to continue the wardship.[94] A similar position obtains with regard to making of prohibited steps and specific issue orders, though the availability of such orders will commonly make the continuation of wardship unnecessary.[95] One consequence of the ability to make a prohibited steps order has been to eliminate the necessity to invoke wardship to prevent a child's association with or prospective marriage to a particular person, or to prevent a person associating or communicating with or harbouring a child, which were former classic instances of the use of the jurisdiction.

There is pre-Children Act authority that it is inconsistent with the continuation of wardship to appoint an individual to be the child's guardian.[96] There is, however, nothing to prevent the court making a guardianship appointment under the 1989 Act and de-warding the child.[97]

The non-statutory powers

Notwithstanding the availability of s 8 orders, the court retains its inherent powers to protect its wards, at any rate, provided there is no statutorily available remedy. This may occur where the desired remedy falls outside the terms of s 8 or in circumstances where the protection sought falls outside the statutory scheme altogether.

Although at one time it had been doubted whether the concept of 'care and control' had survived the 1989 Act,[98] care and control orders have been made in wardship proceedings.[99] The advantage of such an order is that it allows an individual or individuals to have day-to-day care of the child without having parental responsibility which on occasion can be a useful way of defusing the tension between the parties or preserving the status quo.

We discuss later in this chapter the current ambit of the inherent powers in the context of the High Court's general inherent jurisdiction. Suffice to say here that while s 8 orders must directly relate to children and, in the case of prohibited steps and specific issue orders, must concern an aspect of parental responsibility, the inherent powers are not so restricted. Orders, for example, can be directed against *adult* parties as in *Re J (A Minor) (Wardship)*,[100] in which the mother was prevented from leaving the jurisdiction to provide time for a blood sample to be taken to establish paternity. It is equally established that the inherent powers are not restricted to aspects of parental responsibility.

9. THE PRINCIPLES ON WHICH THE COURT ACTS

In the past, statements have been made which suggest that the welfare of a ward is always the paramount consideration.[101] It is clear, however, that the individual ward's

---

[94] See, for example, *T v T (Child Abduction: Non Convention Country)* [1998] 2 FLR 1110.

[95] See, for example, *Re R (A Minor) (Blood Transfusion)* [1993] 2 FLR 757.

[96] *Re C (Minors) (Wardship: Adoption)* [1989] 1 WLR 61.

[97] The former statutory power under the Family Law Reform Act 1969 s 6 to make maintenance orders was repealed by the Courts and Legal Services Act 1990,Sch 20, and insofar as the court has any power (in view of the Child Support Act 1991) to make financial provision for its ward, its jurisdiction to do so is governed by Sch 1 to the Children Act 1989, which is discussed in Ch 21.

[98] See *R v R (Private Law Proceedings: Residential Assessment)* [2002] 2 FLR 953 at 960, per Holman J.

[99] See eg *T v S (Wardship)* [2011] EWHC 1608 (Fam) [2012] 1 FLR 230 and *Re RJ (Fostering: Person Disqualified)* [1999] 1 WLR 581.   [100] [1988] 1 FLR 65.

[101] In *Re D (A Minor) (Justices' Decision: Review)* [1977] Fam 158 at 163, Dunn J memorably referred to the 'golden thread' running through the wardship jurisdiction, namely the welfare of the child 'which is considered in this court first, last and all the time'.

interests are not always overriding.[102] In historical terms this is because the para-mountcy principle only applies where the court is called upon to exercise its custodial jurisdiction. That jurisdiction is now encapsulated by the Children Act 1989 s 1(1),[103] which is as binding on the wardship court as it is on any other court when dealing with issues relating to children. Section 1(1) applies whenever the court is called upon to determine any question in which the child's upbringing or the administration of his property is in issue.

The application of s 1(1) means that in the vast majority of cases the court will be bound to treat the ward's welfare as its paramount consideration. However, as discussed in Chapter 12, s 1(1) only applies where the child's upbringing etc is *directly* in issue. Where the court is called upon to exercise a purely protective jurisdiction (ie where the issue falls outside the scope of s 1(1) of the 1989 Act and is not governed by other statutes), the ward's welfare is not accorded any special weight, though it will remain an impor-tant consideration. Whether the court will protect a ward will depend on how seriously and how directly the child's interests may be harmed and how important any competing interests are.

As well as the paramountcy principle, the wardship court is also bound to have regard to the 'delay principle' as set out in the 1989 Act, s 1(2) whenever the ward's upbringing or property is directly in issue. On the other hand, it is only *bound* to apply the welfare checklist, pursuant to s 1(3) of the 1989 Act, and to consider whether any order is justified as provided by s 1(5) of that Act, when considering whether to make a contested s 8 order.

10. THE USE OF THE JURISDICTION

(a) The position before the Children Act 1989

Rising numbers of wardships

Before the Children Act 1989[104] the many and often unique characteristics of wardship proved useful to disparate applicants, although the high costs[105] and lengthy delays in obtaining a court hearing militated against an even greater use. Nevertheless, there had been, particularly during the 20 years preceding the 1989 Act, a steep rise in the number of wardships from 74 in 1951, 622 in 1971 to a peak of 4,961 in 1991.[106]

The key reason for this growth was the use of wardship by local authorities, which found that the jurisdiction offered a way round the restrictions and difficulties presented by the then child care legislation both as a means of committing children into their care and of keeping them there. By the late 1980s over half of all wardship applications were made by local authorities. But there were other uses of the jurisdiction too, namely, by relatives, who, until 1985, had no other means of initiating court proceedings either to seek to look after the child or to have contact, and particularly by parents in relation to international child abduction. Finally, there were always the novel cases where the avail-ability of High Court expertise, as well as the jurisdiction's wide powers and the court's

---

[102] See, for example, *Re M and N (Minors) (Wardship: Publication of Information)* [1990] Fam 211 at 223, where Butler-Sloss LJ expressly said that in cases where restraint of publicity is sought 'the welfare of the ward is not the paramount consideration'. [103] Discussed in Ch 12.

[104] See generally Law Com Working Paper No 101 (1987) *Wards of Court*, Part III.

[105] The DHSS Child Care Review Costings Working Party (1986, para 5.21) estimated the average cost of an order confirming wardship to have been £5,960 in an uncontested case and £7,970 in a contested case.

[106] The 1951 and 1971 figures can be found in S Cretney *Principles of Family Law* (1974, 1st edn) p 289. The 1991 figure was published in the 1991 *Judicial Statistics* (CM 1991), Table 5.8.

supervisory control, were clearly an advantage, as for example for dealing with the future of the UK's first and much publicised commercially arranged surrogate child.[107]

The moves to restrict the use of wardship

In many ways the growth of wardship was an indicator of the inadequacies of the family justice system and in particular of its public law provisions. There was concern, too, at the escalating costs of wardship and indeed of the basic unfairness of some but not all children being given a Rolls Royce service through wardship. In the mid 1980s the Social Services Committee considered[108] that in the local authority context the expansion had gone far enough and called upon the Family Division judges to exercise restraint in accepting wardship applications. The *Review of Child Care Law*[109] subsequently made proposals for overhauling the public law provisions, the effect of which was estimated[110] potentially to halve the number of wardship applications. This *Review* was followed by the Law Commission's review of the private law[111] and the eventual radical overhaul of English child law through the Children Act 1989.

(b) The position after the Children Act 1989

Restrictions in public law cases

With a view to curbing or, at any rate, significantly restricting the public law use of wardship the Act[112] makes wardship and local authority care incompatible.[113] If a care order is made under s 31 in respect of a ward of court, the wardship ceases[114] and while in care a child cannot be made a ward of court.[115] Furthermore, both the former statutory and inherent powers to commit wards of court into local authority care and to make supervision orders were respectively repealed and revoked by s 100(1) and (2)(a). In support of these provisions it has been commented[116] that by restricting the availability of wardship the 1989 Act emphasises that the function of the courts is to decide issues and that it is no part of the court's business to take a child into care and decide how it is to be brought up.

Notwithstanding these restrictions, like any other court in 'family proceedings',[117] in cases where it appears that a care or supervision order may be appropriate, the High Court can, in wardship proceedings, direct a local authority to investigate the child's circumstances with a view to the authority making an application for a care order under s 31[118] and to make an interim care order pending the outcome of the authority's decision.[119] Furthermore the restrictions imposed under the 1989 Act do not prevent the High

---

[107] *Re C (A Minor)(Wardship: Surrogacy)* [1985] FLR 846.

[108] See their Second report for the Session 1983–4 *Children in Care* Vol 1, HC 360–1, para 82.

[109] HMSO, 1985. [110] See the Costings Working Party Report (1986) para 5.12.

[111] *Review of Child Law, Guardianship and Custody*, Law Com No 172 (1988).

[112] See generally R White, P Carr and N Lowe *Children Act in Practice* (2008, 4th edn) paras 12.4ff; M Parry 'The Children Act 1989: Local Authorities, Wardship and the Revival of the Inherent Jurisdiction' [1992] JSWFL 212; and A Bainham 'The Children Act 1989—The Future of Wardship' [1990] Fam Law 270.

[113] See the Department of Health's *Guidance and Regulations*, Vol 1, *Court Orders* (1991), para 3.99. The revised Guidance issue in 2008 by the Department for Children, Schools and Families does not repeat this comment, see para 3.85.   [114] Children Act 1989 s 91(4).

[115] Section 100(2)(c) and the Senior Courts Act 1981 s 41(2A).

[116] S Cretney 'Defining the Limits in State Intervention' in *Children and the Law—Essays in Honour of Professor HK Bevan* (ed D Freestone, 1991) 58 at 68–69.

[117] Wardship proceedings are 'family proceedings' by reason of s 8(3)(a).

[118] Children Act 1989, s 37, discussed in Ch 14. Section 37 Directions, p 550. See eg *E (By Her Litigation Friend, PW) v London Borough of X* [2005] EWHC 2811 (Fam) [2006] 1 FLR 730.

[119] Children Act 1989 s 38.

Court from exercising its *inherent* jurisdiction to decide a specific question in relation to a child in local authority care.[120]

Restrictions in private law cases—the ruling in Re T

Although the 1989 Act is silent on the use of wardship in the private law context, its clear policy was to reduce the need to resort to wardship in *both* the public and private law arenas.[121] The full import of this was made clear in *Re T (A Minor) (Child: Representation)* in which Waite LJ referred to wardship being 'an exceptional status under the modern law as it must now be applied'.[122] In that case the issue was whether a child could bring proceedings on her own behalf without the need for a guardian ad litem. It was found that the Rule[123] providing that she could, applied equally whether or not the child was a ward. Accordingly, there was no justification for continuing the wardship.

In discontinuing the wardship, Waite LJ observed that while it survives as an independent jurisdiction the 'courts' undoubted discretion to allow wardship to go forward in a suitable case is subject to their clear duty, in loyalty to the scheme and purpose of the Children Act legislation, to permit recourse to wardship only when it becomes apparent' that the child's welfare demands it and there is no other available remedy.

(c) The current use of wardship

The impact of the 1989 Act on the use of wardship was both immediate and predictably dramatic. Whereas in 1991 there were 4,961 wardship applications, in 1992 there just 492 but interestingly, there were similar numbers in 1998 (431) and in 1999 (418).[124] Applications further declined to 268 in 2010 but rose to 420 in 2011,[125] 450 in 2012 and 358 in the first ten months of 2013.[126] In this final section consideration is given to this continued use.[127]

Use in public law cases

Given the restrictions imposed by the 1989 Act it might have been thought that the use of wardship in public law cases had effectively been ended but it is clear that it has not. In fact the Act does not prohibit the use of wardship in public law cases *per se* but only as means of obtaining a care order (or compulsory accommodation) or a supervision order, maintaining court control over children in local authority care or as a means of keeping children in their care. Where the child is already subject to a care order the use of wardship is prohibited;[128] and instead, in such cases, where the High Court's wider powers are thought appropriate recourse must be had to the *inherent* jurisdiction rather than the wardship jurisdiction. In summary, there is no embargo on the use of wardship where the child is not in care provided the protection put in place does not have the effect of placing the child under the care of the local authority.

---

[120] Discussed at Circumstances in which the criteria for giving leave might be satisfied, p 769.

[121] See *The Children Act 1989 Guidance and Regulations* Vol 1 *Court Orders* (1991) para 3.98, which commented 'By incorporating many of the beneficial aspects of wardship, such as the "open door" policy, and a flexible range of orders, the Act will subsequently reduce the need to have recourse to the High Court.'

[122] [1994] Fam 49 at 65C.   [123] Then FPR 1991 r 9(2A), now FPR 2010 r 16.6.

[124] See the figures cited by HHJ John Mitchell 'Whatever Happened to Wardship?' [2001] Fam Law 130 and 212.

[125] See the figures cited by N Lowe 'Inherently Disposed to Protect Children—The Continuing Role of Wardship' in R Probert and C Barton (eds) *50 Years in Family Law – Essays for Stephen Cretney* (2012) 161 at 167.

[126] Figures obtained from the Court Service.

[127] See generally Lowe 'Inherently Disposed to Protect Children – The continuing Role of Wardship', op cit, at 167 and HHJ Mitchell 'Whatever Happened to Wardship?', op cit, at 130.   [128] See s 100(2)(c).

Before discussing the use of wardship in public law cases it should be appreciated that its use can be sought upon an application by a local authority or by the High Court acting upon its own motion. In the former case local authorities are required to obtain court leave,[129] which may only be given upon the court being satisfied that: (a) the remedy sought to be achieved cannot be achieved by the making of a s 8 order (it must be remembered that local authorities can with court leave apply for a prohibited steps or specific issue order); and (b) the child is likely to suffer significant harm if the jurisdiction is not exercised.[130] Of course, the leave criteria do not apply where the court is acting upon its own motion but it is a nice point as to whether nevertheless regard should be had to them. In practice, while there is little evidence that the courts expressly have regard to the 'significant harm' point, it is clear that regard is paid to the existence of alternative statutory remedies. In any event regardless of the context in which consideration of the use of wardship arises, s 100(2)(d)[131] prevents the courts from making orders the effect of which is to confer upon authorities aspects of parental responsibility that they do not already have. Furthermore the general embargoes against making s 8 orders under s 9 of the 1989 Act also equally apply.[132]

The principal alternative statutory remedies are s 8 orders but since such orders do not cover every situation, in cases where the local authority are not themselves seeking care but are nevertheless concerned about a child's well-being as, for example in connection with medical treatment,[133] wardship might still be the right solution, at any rate, where there is thought to be a need for the court's continuing control.

Wardship remains an option where the child is *not* in care, including where the child is being accommodated under s 20 of the 1989 Act. Although wardship cannot be used to bring about such an arrangement,[134] unlike care, accommodation is not itself incompatible with wardship. Illustrative of the use of wardship in this context is *Re E (Wardship Order: Child In Voluntary Accommodation)*,[135] which concerned a child who was being voluntarily accommodated. The local authority sought a care order but in the 'difficult and exceptional' circumstances of the case the first instance judge's preferred choice was to make a wardship order since it had more to offer than a care order inasmuch as it would make both the local authority and the parents accountable to the court. It would enable the court to oblige the local authority to keep the court and the parents informed about its progress in arranging therapy and about the progress of therapy once begun. It would also enable the court to ensure that the parents received the information proposed by the care plan. Were it necessary to do, it would enable the court to regulate the parents' contact with the child and the school.

Despite these advantages the judge felt constrained to make a care order since he considered that s 100(2) prevented him from making a wardship order. On appeal, however, the Court of Appeal held that there was 'nothing in s 100 that either explicitly or implicitly precludes a court from making an order in wardship where the child is not required to be accommodated, but is voluntarily accommodated.'[136] It accordingly set aside the care order and replaced it with a wardship order. It observed, however, that the wardship order was contingent on the s 20 placement remaining in place. Once the accommodation agreement came to an end the court would not then be in a position to require the local authority to accommodate or supervise the child.

---

[129] Pursuant to s 100(3), discussed further at The need to obtain leave, p 768.
[130] See s 100(4).   [131] Discussed at Limitations imposed by the Children Act 1989, p 764.
[132] Discussed in Ch 14 General restrictions on making section 8 orders. p 510.
[133] See the discussion later in this section, at p 759.   [134] See s 100(2)(b).
[135] [2011] EWCA Civ 1173 [2013] 2 FLR 63.   [136] Ibid at [16], per Thorpe LJ.

Re E is one of a growing number of cases in which, in the context of public law proceedings, the court has found it advantageous to make a wardship order. In *Re K (Children With Disabilities Wardship)*[137] the court permitted a local authority to withdraw its care applications (the proceedings had been ongoing for over two years) but warded the three children with disabilities to provide for some legal structure to remain in place and thereby preserve equality between the parents (who both suffered from mental and physical ill-health as a result of the demands of caring for their children) and the local authority whilst also reminding all that they remained accountable to the court for making the necessary arrangements for the children's care, education and nurturing. In this particular context, that is where the court was satisfied that it was not in the children's interests to require a trial on the statutory threshold and where the withdrawal of care proceedings would positively benefit the children, wardship provided the best solution.

An earlier example of court intervention in care proceedings resulting in wardship is *Re RJ (Fostering: Person Disqualified)*.[138] *Re RJ* concerned children who, though happily placed with foster carers, could not, according to Regulations then in place,[139] remain there since the foster-father had previously been formally cautioned for actual bodily harm to another foster child (subsequently adopted by him and his wife). Following the foster parents' intervention in care proceedings at which the mother was still seeking her children's return,[140] it was held that although the Regulations did not prevent the court from making what was then a residence order, in this case the preferable course was to discharge the interim care orders, ward the children and grant interim care and control to the foster parents. In this way the status quo could be preserved as nearly as possible pending the full hearing and, by not granting even interim residence orders which would have vested parental responsibility in the foster parent, any perception of prejudice by the mother could be avoided. At the subsequent hearing,[141] it was held that, given the exceptional circumstances, the appropriate long-term solution was to continue the wardship and to grant care and control to the foster carers. This solution was considered advantageous, inter alia because (a) giving ultimate control to the court would be reassuring to the foster carer (who would otherwise have shared parental responsibility with the mother had they been granted residence orders); (b) it was only by this means that the local authority could remain involved in what had become a private law case; and, (c) it would allow the children's guardian to continue to be involved.

Not dissimilar to *Re RJ* is *Re W and X (Wardship: Relatives Rejected As Foster Carers)*,[142] in which care proceedings had been brought in respect of children living with their maternal grandparents after the death of a sibling. It was common ground that the threshold criteria had been satisfied but the local authority's preferred option was to leave the

---

[137] [2012] 2 FLR 745. Cf *A Local Authority v SB, AB and MB* [2010] EWHC 1744 [2010] 2 FLR 1203, in which it was held that upon giving the local authority permission to withdraw their care application there was no outstanding issue for the court to decide and it declined to make any further order.

[138] [1999] 1 WLR 581.

[139] Viz. the Children (Protection From Offenders) (Miscellaneous Amendments) Regulations 1997 (SI 1997/2308), which aimed to prevent paedophiles from becoming foster parents.

[140] After the local authority's unsuccessful attempt to challenge the application of the Regulations to this case, see *Lincolnshire County Council v RJ, X Intervening* [1998] 2 FLR 110, they encouraged the parents to apply for a residence order. As Chadwick LJ pointed out in *Re RJ*, the local authority could not itself apply for what was then a residence order, nor could the court make an order requiring the children to be accommodated by on behalf of the local authority by reason of 1989 Act, ss 9(2), 100(2) and (5).

[141] *Re J (Fostering: Wardship)* [1999] 1 FLR 618.

[142] [2003] EWHC 2206 (Fam) [2004] 1 FLR 415.

children with the grandparents but under a care order. However, because the authority had previously rejected the grandparents as foster parents, Regulations[143] meant that this option could not be adopted since the children would have to be removed from them immediately the care order was made. It was held that the inability to pursue what was perceived to be the best option was a lacuna in the legislation which wardship could properly remedy since it neither infringed the letter nor the spirit of s 100 given that the court were not seeking to control the local authority. Moreover, the children's placement warranted long-term external control, profitably by the court, which could not be achieved by a care order but only through wardship. The children were accordingly warded with what were then residence orders made in favour of the grandparents and supervision orders to the local authority.[144]

The cases just discussed demonstrate the court's willingness to use wardship to overcome restrictions imposed by Regulations on local authorities' freedom to put children in foster placements which would otherwise operate to the detriment of the particular children concerned. But two further cases are illustrative of a potentially wider use. In *Re M and J (Wardship: Supervision and Residence Orders)*[145] a mother and stepfather conceded the threshold criteria in care proceedings and agreed to the psychologist's recommendation that one boy should live with his father and the other with his maternal grandmother. The local authority did not agree with this recommendation but did not seek alternative orders. Charles J took the 'exceptional course' of making a residence order and a supervision order coupled with wardship orders in respect of each child, and an order for contact. The justification for wardship was to manage the inevitable future tensions that would arise within the family which he felt that by themselves the authority may not have been able to handle.

In *E v London Borough of X*,[146] E, who had come to England from Ghana, was being temporarily accommodated following the breakdown of E's relationship with a woman she believed to be her mother. E made herself a ward of court but after a s 37 investigation, the other woman denied she was the mother and alleged that E was aged 20. The local authority was asked to make an age assessment which found E to be 'at least 20'. E then sought an order in wardship that she was 17. The court acceded to her request, ruling it was not prevented from doing so by s 100(2); found her to be 17 and continued the wardship until E's majority 'in the light of the uncertainty as to her present circumstances should she be obliged to leave her present lodging', it appearing to the court to be 'desirable' for it to 'retain oversight of her welfare for the 10 months or so of her minority'.

An example of the use of wardship in a different public law context is *Re F (Mental Health Act: Guardianship)*[147] in which a 17-year-old with a mental age of between 5 and 8 had been accommodated by a local authority because of chronic neglect (her seven siblings were taken into interim care for the same reason). Her parents sought her return. Care proceedings were not possible because of the child's age[148] and the local authority instead obtained a guardianship order under the Mental Health Act 1983. It was held that wardship was the more appropriate remedy because the 1983 Act was not a child centred jurisdiction and the child lacked the benefit of independent representation. Furthermore,

---

[143] Viz what were then, the Fostering Services Regulations 2002, SI 2002/57 since replaced by the Fostering Services (England) Regulations 2011, SI 2011/581. In Wales the governing regulations are the Fostering Services (Wales) Regulations 2003, SI 2003/ 237.

[144] Presumably the supervision order was made under its statutory powers since s 100(2)(a) prevents the High Court from exercising its inherent jurisdiction to put a child under local authority supervision.

[145] [2003] EWHC 1585 (Fam) [2003] 2 FLR 541.

[146] [2005] EWHC 811 (Fam) [2006] 1 FLR 731.   [147] [2000] 1 FLR 192.

[148] A care order cannot be made in respect of 17 year olds: s 31(3) of the 1989 Act.

on the particular facts wardship enabled a single judge to consider the interests both of the child in question and her seven siblings.

The decisions just mentioned are examples of where, in the context of public law proceedings, the *court* has taken the initiative in warding children but there are cases where the wardship order has directly resulted from a local authority initiative, that is, in cases where the authority is not itself seeking care but is nevertheless concerned about the child's well-being.

An early post-Children Act 1989 example, is *Re R (A Minor) (Contempt)*,[149] where a local authority warded a 14 year-old child accommodated by them to protect her from a relationship with a 33 year-old man. Other instances of wardship being used have been where the local authority was concerned about the medical treatment for a child. Past examples have included concerns about a child's sterilisation and contested cases involving emergency medical treatment of children in care.[150]

But the problem with these examples is that a prohibited steps or specific issue order would have provided an effective remedy. Indeed it is hard to justify the use of wardship to resolve a one-off issue unless there is no statutory remedy or where there are ongoing concerns about the child's welfare which are felt best managed by the court under its prerogative jurisdiction. An example is *Re S (Wardship: Peremptory Return)*,[151] in which the local authority, having initiated care proceedings, successfully invoked wardship to ensure the child's return to the jurisdiction in circumstances where the 1980 Hague Abduction Convention was inapplicable because the removal had been lawful and, as a result, no other remedy was available.

Whether these cases should be regarded as a series of 'one-off' decisions or as a core of law defining or beginning to set out the parameters within which wardship can continue to operate in what may be considered to be quasi-public law remains to be seen. But what they undoubtedly illustrate is that it is premature to think wardship has no role to play in cases involving local authorities.

Use in private law cases

Notwithstanding the strictures of *Re T (A Minor) (Child: Representation)*[152] against invoking wardship save where it is the only legitimate means of securing a child's welfare, the immediacy of protection, the width of the court's powers and the continuing court protection have proved useful in diverse situations. One important remaining advantage of the wardship jurisdiction is that as soon as the application is made, the child becomes a ward and no important step may then be taken without prior court sanction.[153] In effect the issuing of the application provides a unique quasi-administrative mechanism by which the child's legal position can be immediately frozen, which is useful when dealing with emergencies, such as threatened child abduction, particularly when an international element is involved. Invoking wardship can also be an effective way of halting a proposed medical operation on the child and can provide a usefully speedy means by which non-parents who would otherwise have to seek leave to apply for a s 8 order can safeguard their

---

[149] [1994] 2 FLR 185.

[150] See respectively *Re B (A Minor) (Wardship: Medical Treatment)* [1981] 1 WLR 1421 and *Re O (A Minor) (Medical Treatment)* [1993] 2 FLR 149 and *Re R (A Minor) (Blood Transfusion)* [1993] 2 FLR 757.

[151] [2010] EWCA Civ 465 [2010] 2 FLR 1960. Though note that while in that case the court continued the wardship order, it set aside the peremptory return order, staying the return pending the outcome of the local authority's application for interim care. See also *R (T) and Legal Aid Agency v London Borough of Ealing* [2013] EWHC 960 (Admin). Cf *Islington London Borough Council v E* [2010] EWHC 3240 (Fam) [2011] 1 FLR 1681, where because there was an alternative remedy the wardship was dismissed.

[152] [1994] Fam 49 at 65.   [153] Discussed at Control vested in the court, p 743.

position, for example, by preventing parents from removing the child from their care pending a court hearing.

The most common private law use of wardship is in cases where there is an international element and especially in connection with international child abduction. Because of the automatic embargo against the child's removal from England and Wales without court leave arising immediately upon warding the child, and the consequent triggering of mechanisms both to impose port alerts and to trace children, the jurisdiction is a useful device to prevent abduction and to deal with children who have been abducted into the country. It can also sometimes be advantageous to use wardship to obtain the return of children wrongfully taken abroad or to secure their return where permission to leave the jurisdiction has been given.[154]

Useful though wardship is as a means of preventing a child's removal, as Munby J warned in *S v S*,[155] it should not be used for an impermissible purpose, such as warding a child in order that the Family Division judge might direct the Secretary of State to release the dependant of a failed asylum seeker from administrative detention, or by the court putting pressure on the Secretary of State by making a declaration about the child's health. Such action would be regarded as an abuse of the wardship process, and could be penalised in costs. Note should also be taken of Thorpe LJ's comment in *Re H (Abduction: Habitual Residence: Agreement)*[156] that while wardship is an important remedy that survives the 1980 Hague Abduction Convention in those cases where the jurisdiction to which the child has been removed, or within which the child is retained, is not a party to the Convention it has 'no useful purpose…in any case where the two countries involved are both signatories to the Convention and the Convention proceedings are still live.'

There has been a raft of cases involving children being taken to the Indian sub-continent for arranged or sometimes forced marriages. We have already discussed two extreme examples where jurisdiction was exercised on the basis of the child's nationality.[157] Further examples include *Re KR (Abduction: Forcible Removal By Parents)*,[158] in which a 16 year-old Sikh girl living in England was taken to the Punjab by her parents for an arranged marriage. Her elder sister issued wardship proceedings and, following what has been described[159] as 'an imaginative order, replete with recitals' which secured the co-operation of the Indian authorities, the ward was returned. In *B v A and B*[160] a child was warded in a dispute between a mother and the paternal grandmother over allegations that the grandmother had removed the child from her in Pakistan at a time when the mother had no visa to return to England. The court ordered Cafcass to investigate the circumstances. In *Re S (Wardship: Stranded Spouses)*[161] in concluding that

---

[154] See eg *Re S (Leave To Remove From Jurisdiction: Securing Return From Holiday)* [2001] 2 FLR 507—children warded as one safeguard, among others, to secure their return to the jurisdiction, upon giving leave to remove for a holiday.   [155] [2008] EWHC 2288 (Fam) [2009] 1 FLR 241 at [17].

[156] [2013] EWCA Civ 148 [2013] 2 FLR 1426 at [8].

[157] Namely *A v A (Return Order on the Basis of British Nationality)*[2013] EWHC 3298 (Fam), [2014] Fam Law 157 and *Re B; RB v FB and MA (Forced Marriage: Wardship Jurisdiction)* [2008] EWHC 1436 (Fam) [2008] 2 FLR 1624, discussed at The remitted decision in *A v A*, p 748.

[158] [1999] 2 FLR 542. See also *SB v RB (Residence: Forced Marriage: Child's Best Interests)* [2008] EWHC 938 (Fam) [2008] 2 FLR 1588, an 11 year old girl was made a ward of court after her mother agreed to marry her to a 20-year old in Bangladesh. Cf *RB v FB & MA* [2008] EWHC 1669 (Fam) [2008] 2 FLR 1588, a 15 year old Pakistani girl with British nationality who had never been to the UK but was due to arrive for an arranged marriage was warded. Note also *P v P* [2006] EWHC 2410 (Fam) [2007] 2 FLR 439, wards returned from Nepal in compliance with the order.

[159] HHJ J Mitchell 'Whatever Happened to Wardship?' [2001] Fam Law 212 at 215.

[160] [2005] EWHC 1291 (Fam).

[161] [2010] EWHC 1669 (Fam) [2011] 1 FLR 305.

a mother had been forcibly separated from her child and removed and abandoned in another jurisdiction, the court made an urgent plea to the immigration authorities that consideration be given as to what arrangements could be put in place to assist mothers to return to this jurisdiction in similar circumstances. Following this plea guidance has now been issued[162] including the advice that the best vehicle for these types of cases is wardship, the proceedings of which should be managed, if possible, and heard by a judge of the Family Division.

Wardship has been found useful in other international situations. In *Re M (Child's Upbringing)*,[163] for example, a boy of Zulu origin born in South Africa was brought, with the parents' consent, to England by a white woman who later applied to adopt him. The parents objected to the adoption and the child was warded. The adoption application was refused and the child was ordered to be returned to his parents but the wardship was continued. The boy's return proved unsuccessful and he returned to England living with the applicant under a wardship order. In *Re K (Adoption and Wardship)*[164] a Bosnian Muslim orphan baby was brought to England by an English couple initially to receive medical treatment. The couple were later granted an adoption order. However, because they had failed to reveal to the court that the child had relatives who wished to look after her, the adoption was set aside. Nevertheless the court felt that she should remain with the couple because of her psychological bond with them. The wardship was therefore continued with the couple being granted care and control and contact granted to the relatives.

Wardship continues to have a role in domestic cases, particularly in the context of ongoing protracted familial disputes where the court's overall control of its wards has been thought advantageous. In *T v S (Wardship)*,[165] for example, faced with unabated and continuing disputation between the parents, the court continued the wardship so as to manage the disputes at least in the short term and by granting care and control rather than making residence orders a more neutral status could be created thereby lowering the tension between the parents. In *Re P (Surrogacy: Residence)*[166] in the context of a dispute over a surrogacy agreement (the mother concealing the birth) it was held appropriate, when making a residence order in favour of the biological and commissioning father and his wife with contact to the surrogate mother and her husband, that the child and his surrogate sibling be made wards of court to enable there to be a level of court supervision of the situation in the absence of any input by the local authority. Such an arrangement also enabled the children's guardian who had played a vital role in the contact arrangements to remain involved in the case. Wardship also proved useful in *JP v LP and Others (Surrogacy Arrangements: Wardship)*,[167] in which a married couple arranged with a friend (a partial surrogate) for the insemination of the surrogate's egg with the husband's sperm. The parties entered into a surrogacy agreement drawn up by solicitors[168] and the hospital allowed the couple to take the baby home. The child was registered with the husband as the father and the surrogate as the mother. The couple separated but were granted what was then a shared residence order upon an undertaking that they would seek a parental order under s 54 of the Human Fertilisation and Embryology Act 2008 to regularise the

---

[162] *Re S (Wardship) Guidance in cases of Stranded Spouses* [2011] 1 FLR 319.

[163] [1996] 2 FLR 441.

[164] [1997] 2 FLR 221. See also *Re R (Inter-Country Adoption)* [1999] 1 FLR 1014.

[165] [2011] EWHC 1608 (Fam), [2012] 1 FLR 230.

[166] [2008] 1 FLR 177. Note also *Re T (Wardship: Review of Police Protection Decision)(No 1)* [2010] 1 FLR 1017; *Re W (Wardship: Discharge: Publicity)* [1995] 2 FLR 466; and *Nottinghamshire County Council v October Films Ltd* [1999] 2 FCR 529.   [167] [2014] EWHC 595 (Fam) [2014] Fam Law 813.

[168] Who thereby committed an offence under the Surrogacy Arrangements Act 1985 s 2, discussed in Ch 8.

child's status. However, the application was not made within six months of the child's birth which meant that it was not possible to make a parental order. It was held that, in what were described as wholly exceptional circumstances, the appropriate solution was for the child to remain a ward of court until further notice, with the shared residence order being continued but with parental responsibility being delegated to the 'parents' and the surrogate being prohibited from exercising any parental responsibility without prior court leave.

The continuing overall control could also be thought to be advantageous, for example, in the case of an abandoned child, where no-one looking after him has parental responsibility or, as in *Re C (A Baby)*, in which Sir Stephen Brown P said that the courts were ready to assist with taking responsibility in cases of grave anxiety. In that case the child developed meningitis which left her brain damaged and unable to survive without artificial ventilation and who would suffer increasing pain and distress with no hope of recovery. Sir Stephen Brown P commented:

> It appeared appropriate that the courts should take responsibility for this child and relieve the parents in some measure of the grave responsibility which they have borne since her birth.[169]

C. THE INHERENT JURISDICTION

1. JURISDICTION AND PROCEDURE

Only the High Court has inherent[170] powers to protect children.[171] The inherent jurisdiction can be invoked either upon specific application or by the High Court itself in cases where it is already seized of proceedings.[172] Applications for declarations may also be made under the inherent jurisdiction.[173]

---

[169] [1996] 2 FLR 43 at 44D–E.

[170] For a scholarly treatise on the whole topic of inherent powers see J Jacob 'The Inherent Jurisdiction of the Court' (1970) 23 *Current Legal Problems* 23.

[171] *D v D (County Court Jurisdiction: Injunctions)* [1993] 2 FLR 802, CA, in which it was held that the county court had no inherent power to grant injunctions. See also *Devon County Council v B* [1997] 1 FLR 591, CA and *Re S and D (Children: Powers of Court)* [1995] 2 FLR 456, CA. A fortiori magistrates' courts have no inherent jurisdiction. Note, however, that where proceedings relating to the exercise of the inherent jurisdiction has been transferred from the High Court to the county court, pursuant to s 38(2)(b) of the Matrimonial and Family Proceedings Act 1984, the court can, pursuant to s 38(5), exercise the same powers as the High Court.

[172] See, for example, in the context of adoption proceedings *Re J (Recognition of Foreign Adoption Orders)* [2012] EWHC 3353 (Fam) [2013] 2 FLR 298, in which a declaration recognising the validity of a foreign adoption order was made under the inherent jurisdiction; *A City Council v C* [2013] EWHC 8 (Fam) [2013] 1 WLR 3009, in which the use of the inherent jurisdiction in connection with revocation of a freeing order is discussed; and *Re W (a child) (revocation of adoption:inherent jurisdiction)* [2013] EWHC 1957 (Fam) [2013] 3 FCR 336, in which leave to invoke the inherent jurisdiction to set aside an adoption order was refused because it was not in the child's best interests to do so. For other examples, see *Re R (A Minor) (Blood Test: Constraint)* [1998] Fam 66, in which Hale J held there to be power under the inherent jurisdiction to order a child to provide a blood sample for the purposes of establishing paternity; and *Re X (A Minor) (Adoption Details: Disclosure)* [1994] Fam 174, in which it was held to be an appropriate use of the inherent jurisdiction by the High Court hearing an adoption application to order that during the minority of the child in question the Registrar General should not disclose to any person without leave of the court the details of the adoption entered in the Adopted Children Register.

[173] CPR 1998 r 40.20. It is also possible to obtain interim declarations: CPR 1998 r 25.1(9).

Applications to invoke the inherent jurisdiction must be made to the High Court.[174] Local authorities wishing to invoke the jurisdiction must first obtain leave of the court.[175] The procedure for making applications to invoke the inherent jurisdiction is the same as for wardship and is governed by the Family Procedure Rules 2010 and the accompanying *Practice Direction 12D Inherent Jurisdiction (Including Wardship) Proceedings*.

Since wardship is properly regarded as being part of rather than separate from the High Court's inherent jurisdiction[176] it must follow that there must be co-extensive jurisdiction to make orders under it. Consequently for the reason already discussed[177] jurisdiction will normally be governed by the revised Brussels II Regulation which normally requires the child to be habitually resident in England and Wales.[178]

2. THE EFFECT OF INVOKING THE INHERENT JURISDICTION

Unlike wardship, the exercise of the inherent jurisdiction does not place the child under the ultimate responsibility of the court. This means that at no point will the child be subject to the rule obtaining in wardship that all important steps in the child's life have to be sanctioned by the court.[179]

3. THE COURT'S POWERS

(a) The general extent of the inherent powers

Proceedings under the inherent jurisdiction rank as 'family proceedings' for the purposes of the Children Act 1989,[180] so that in general terms the court is empowered either upon application or its own motion to make any s 8 order. Although these statutory powers should be used whenever possible,[181] there will be occasions when either the courts are barred from using them, as where children are already in local authority care,[182] or where what is being sought lies outside their scope. On these occasions recourse can properly be had to the court's inherent powers.

These inherent powers are the same as those under the wardship jurisdiction. As Lord Donaldson MR put it in *Re W (A Minor) (Medical Treatment: Court's Jurisdiction)*:[183]

> it should be made clear that the High Court's inherent jurisdiction in relation to children—the *parens patriae* jurisdiction—is equally exercisable whether the child is or is not a ward of court . . .

---

[174] FPR 2010 r 12.36 (1).

[175] Children Act 1989 s 100(3), discussed at The need to obtain leave, p 768.

[176] See *Practice Direction 12D* at para 1.3.

[177] See The Supreme Court decision in *A v A*, p 747.   [178] See Ch 26.

[179] *Practice Direction 12D*, para 1.3 and *Re W (A Minor) (Medical Treatment: Court's Jurisdiction)* [1993] Fam 64 at 73F-G, per Lord Donaldson MR. Note that this accords with Lord Mackay LC's comments in his Joseph Jackson Memorial Lecture (1989) 139 NLJ 505 at 508 that it was not thought 'appropriate or practicable for the responsibility for a child in the care of a public authority which is statutorily charged with looking after him to be subject to the detailed directions of another public authority, namely the courts.'

[180] Children Act 1989 s 8(3)(a).

[181] See *Practice Direction 12D* para 1.1 and *Re T (A Minor) (Child: Representation)* [1994] Fam 49, CA; and *Re R (A Minor) (Blood Transfusion)* [1993] 2 FLR 757.

[182] See s 9(1)–(2) of the Children Act 1989, discussed in Ch 14, Children in local authority care, p 510.

[183] [1993] Fam 64 at 73F. See also Balcombe LJ at 85. See also *MA v DB (Inherent Jurisdiction)* [2010] EWHC 1697 (Fam) [2011] 1 FLR 724.

(b) Limitations imposed by the Children Act 1989

The Children Act 1989 s 100(2) limits the exercise of the High Court's inherent jurisdiction by preventing (a) a child being placed in the care or put under the supervision of a local authority and (b) a child from being accommodated by or on behalf of a local authority. These embargoes are in line with the general policy of the Act to prevent the courts from making care or supervision orders other than under s 31. Section 100(2)(d) also prevents the High Court from exercising its inherent jurisdiction:

> . . . for the purpose of conferring on any local authority power to determine any question which has arisen, or which may arise, in connection with any aspect of parental responsibility for the child.

In other words, while the High Court may make orders under its inherent jurisdiction in respect of a child, in doing so it may not confer on the local authority any degree of parental responsibility that it does not already have.[184] This is less likely to cause problems where the child is in care, since the local authority will already be vested with parental responsibility. Hence, the determination of a particular question by the court, for example, obtaining a return order against abducting parents, will not be contrary to s 100(2)(d).[185] Similarly, the court is free to determine the scope and extent of parental responsibility and can, for instance, make orders giving leave for a child in care to be interviewed by the father's solicitor to prepare a defence to criminal charges.[186] If the local authority do not have parental responsibility for the child, the High Court may not under its inherent jurisdiction make orders which in any way confer parental responsibility upon the authority. Hence, for example, while the court can sanction named persons to look after the child[187] it could not authorise a local authority to place the child. It is not altogether clear whether a bare injunction preventing the removal of an accommodated child from fosters carers infringes the restriction.[188]

It has, however, been held wrong that s 100 be restrictively interpreted and that it is perfectly proper for a local authority to invite the court to exercise its inherent jurisdiction to protect children even if the exercise of that power would be an invasion of a person's parental responsibility, for example, by restricting a non-family member from contacting or communicating with the children in question.[189]

(c) Other restrictions on the exercise of the inherent powers

Courts have traditionally declined to define the limits[190] of their inherent powers to protect children and these have been habitually described as theoretically unlimited.[191]

---

[184] See the revised DSCF *Children Act 1989 Guidance and Regulations* Vol 1 *Court Orders* (2008) para 3.88.   [185] See *Southwark London Borough v B* [1993] 2 FLR 559 at 571 per Waite LJ.

[186] Per Hale J in *Re M (Care: Leave to Interview Child)* [1995] 1 FLR 825.

[187] As in *Re RJ (Wardship)* [1999] 1 FLR 618, *Re M and J (Wardship: Supervision and Residence Orders)* [2003] EWHC 1585 (Fam) [2003] 2 FLR 541 and *Re W and X (Wardship: Relatives Rejected as Foster Carers)* [2003] EWHC 2206 (Fam) [2004] 1 FLR 415.

[188] See *Re MA (Care Threshold)* [2009] EWCA Civ 853 [2010] 1 FLR 431 at [6]–[7] and note also *Re E (Wardship Order: Child In Voluntary Accommodation)* [2011] EWCA Civ 1173 [2013] 2 FLR 63.

[189] Per Thorpe J in *Devon County Council v S* [1994] Fam 169, accepting the argument that the local authority were not seeking leave to apply to the court to confer any power upon themselves, but were asking the court to exercise its own powers.

[190] See generally N Lowe 'The Limits of the Wardship Jurisdiction, Part 2: The extent of the court's powers over a ward' (1989) 1 *Journal of Child Law* 44.

[191] See eg *Re W (A Minor) (Medical Treatment: Court's Jurisdiction)* [1993] Fam 64, at 81 per Lord Donaldson MR; *Re R (A Minor) (Wardship: Restrictions on Publication)* [1994] Fam 254 at 271, per Millett

Nevertheless, although it is accepted that the High Court's inherent power to protect children is wider than that of a parent,[192] it is equally well established that, whatever may be the theoretical position, there are 'far-reaching limitations in principle' on the exercise of that jurisdiction.[193] As Ward LJ put it in *Re Z (A Minor) (Identification: Restrictions on Publication)*:[194]

> The wardship or inherent jurisdiction of the court to cast its cloak of protection over minors whose interests are at risk of harm is unlimited in theory though in practice the judges who exercise the jurisdiction have created classes of cases in which the court will not exercise its powers.

However, because of the court's tendency to approach the issue on a case-by-case basis rather than by laying down general guidance, the precise limits, even to the extent of determining whether there are, as Ward LJ suggests, necessarily de facto rather than de jure limits, are still far from clear.

The de jure *limits*

Notwithstanding that the established limits have developed more as a result of practice than of strict legal restraint, there are clearly some *de jure* as well as de facto limits to protecting the child in question. They cannot be used, for instance, to protect the parent qua parent.[195] Secondly, there is no inherent power to make orders that are prohibited by statute. As we have seen, the inherent power to commit children into local authority care or to make supervision orders was expressly revoked by s 100(2)(a) of the Children Act.[196] As a general proposition, however, it would seem that the courts should be slow to hold that an inherent power has been abrogated or restricted by Parliament, and they should only do so where it is clear that Parliament so intended.[197] Moreover, it can be a matter

---

LJ; and *Re B (Child Abduction: Wardship Power to Detain)* [1994] 2 FLR 479 at 483, per Butler-Sloss LJ and at 487, per Hobhouse LJ, CA.

[192] See *Re R (A Minor) (Wardship: Consent to Medical Treatment)* [1992] Fam 11 at 25B and 28G and *Re W (A Minor) (Medical Treatment: Court's Jurisdiction)*, above. Note also that a similar standpoint has been taken by the Australian High Court in *Department of Health and Community Services v JWB and SMB* (1992) 66 ALJR 300.

[193] Per Balcombe LJ in *Re W* [1993] Fam 64, at 85, citing Sir John Pennycuick in *Re X (A Minor) (Wardship: Jurisdiction)* [1975] Fam 47 at 61, CA.   [194] [1997] Fam 1 at 23.

[195] See *Re V (A Minor) (Wardship)* (1979) 123 Sol Jo 201, where the court refused to hear a father's cross-application for an ouster order against his wife.

[196] See Limitations imposed by the Children Act 1989, p 764. It is on this ground that Douglas Brown J's decision in *South Glamorgan County Council v W and B* [1993] 1 FLR 574 (discussed in Ch 17, Making directions on interim applications, p 648) that the High Court has an inherent power to override a child's refusal to submit to an examination when placed inter alia in interim care can be criticised, since there is clear statutory power (see eg s 38(6)) to do so. Note also *Re O (A Minor) (Blood Tests: Constraint)* [2000] Fam 139 in which Wall J refused to exercise the inherent jurisdiction to override the refusal of a parent with care and control to consent to a blood sample being taken from her child since the then s 21 of the Family Law Reform Act 1969 entitled her to do so. Section 21 has since been amended by the Child Support, Pensions and Social Security Act 2000 s 82, discussed in Ch 8, The need for consent, p 267).

[197] It was for this reason that it had been held before the Children Act that, despite the then statutory scheme dealing with children in local authority care, the wardship jurisdiction had not thereby been ousted or abrogated, since the prerogative jurisdiction was neither expressly nor by necessary implication so restricted: see *Re M (An Infant)* [1961] Ch 328 at 345, CA, per Lord Evershed MR and accepted by the House of Lords in *A v Liverpool City Council* [1982] AC 363. Query whether Douglas Brown J's ruling in *South Glamorgan* can be justified on the ground that ss 38(6), 43(8) and 44(7) are properly regarded as not having abrogated the inherent power to override those wishes?

of fine judgment to determine what the legislative intention is.[198] A further complication is that it is accepted that the inherent powers can be used to fill unintended lacunae in legislative schemes.[199]

A third possible limitation is that there is no inherent power to make orders that are purely statutory in origin, as, for example, to attach a power of arrest to a non-molestation order[200] or to make a declaration of paternity.[201] Whether there is an inherent power to make so-called ouster orders[202] is problematic following the House of Lords ruling in *Richards v Richards*,[203] which seemed to put an end to its existence, and the Court of Appeal decision in *Pearson v Franklin*[204] in which it held that in the case of former spouses whose marriage has been dissolved by decree absolute there remained an inherent power to make ouster orders. However, in *Re S (Minors) (Inherent Jurisdiction: Ouster)*[205] Connell J granted a local authority's request under s 100 for leave to pursue an application to exclude a father from the matrimonial home, while in the second, *C v K (Inherent Powers: Exclusion Order)*[206] Wall J also concluded that there remained an inherent power to protect children by means of an ouster order.

It has been argued[207] that a further limit to the jurisdiction is that there is no power to restrain the activities of those who are not in a family or personal relationship with the child in question. This argument was based on *Re X (A Minor) (Wardship: Jurisdiction)*,[208] in which the applicant sought in wardship to prevent the publication of a book containing details about the ward's dead father's alleged sexual predilections, on the basis that its publication would be grossly damaging to his 'highly strung' 14-year-old stepdaughter. The application failed, not because it was held that there was no such power, but because in this instance it was felt that freedom of speech was more important than the ward's welfare, which was in any event only indirectly at risk. The implications of reaching a contrary decision would have been enormous, since it would have meant that any activity that could be considered even indirectly harmful to a child might have been restrained by way of the wardship jurisdiction. Nevertheless, *Re X* is not authority for

---

[198] Compare, for example, *Re RJ (Foster Placement)* [1998] 2 FLR 110 in which Sir Stephen Brown P considered granting care and control to disqualified foster parents would subvert the policy behind the Children (Protection From Offenders) Miscellaneous Amendments Regulations 1997, with that of the Court of Appeal at [1999] 1 WLR 581 (discussed at Use in public law cases, p 757) which was content to say that the Regulations were not directed at the courts.

[199] See eg *Re W and X (Wardship: Relatives Rejected as Foster Carers)* [2003] EWHC 2206 (Fam) [2004] 1 FLR 415, discussed at Use in public law cases, p 757 and *Re C (A Minor) (Adoption: Freeing Orders)* [1999] Fam 43, in which, relying on *Re J (A Minor) (Wardship: Jurisdiction)* [1984] 1 WLR 81 (which in turn relied upon dicta by Lord Wilberforce in *A v Liverpool City Council* [1982] AC 363, at 372–3), Wall J held remedying a lacuna under the then adoption law, that he had inherent power to revoke a freeing order notwithstanding the mother's declaration that she no longer wished to be involved with her child.

[200] See *Re G (Wardship) (Jurisdiction: Power of Arrest)* (1982) 4 FLR 538, discussed by N Lowe 'The Limits of the Wardship Jurisdiction, Part 2: The extent of the court's powers over a ward' (1989) 1 *Journal of Child Law* 44, at 45–6. An alternative explanation of this case is that a distinction needs to be made between the power to make orders and the power to *enforce* them, the latter not being specially developed under the inherent jurisdiction—see also *Re B (Child Abduction: Wardship: Power to Detain)* [1994] 2 FLR 479, CA (no power to detain a person under the inherent jurisdiction in the absence of a finding of contempt). It is a nice point whether the power to make maintenance orders is a purely statutory power; cf the Report of the Committee on the Age of Majority (the Latey Committee) Cmnd 2342 (1967) para 250, which thought there was no inherent power and *Calderdale Borough Council v H and P* [1991] 1 FLR 461 and *W v Avon County Council* (1979) 9 Fam Law 33 in which it was held that there was an inherent power to make maintenance orders.

[201] See *Re J S (A Minor)* [1981] Fam 22, CA. Cf *T v Child Support Agency* [1997] 2 FLR 875.

[202] An ouster order excludes another person from a particular property.

[203] [1984] AC 174, HL, discussed in Ch 6.   [204] [1994] 1 WLR 370, discussed in Ch 6.

[205] [1994] 1 FLR 623.   [206] [1996] 2 FLR 506.

[207] R Everton 'High Tide in Wardship' (1975) 125 NLJ 930.   [208] [1975] Fam 47, CA.

saying that the independent activities of others can never be restrained to protect a ward, or even that freedom of speech can never be curbed. Indeed, in *X County Council v A*,[209] for example, it was held that the press ought to be restrained from publishing details that could lead to the identity and whereabouts of the ward, who was the child of a woman (Mary Bell) who attracted notoriety upon her conviction of manslaughter when a child. After the mother's release from prison she was given a new identity. In this latter case the restraint was on publicity directly referring to the ward and which would have been directly harmful.

Not all the cases seeking to control the activities of those unconnected with the ward have concerned publicity. In the extraordinary case of *Re C (A Minor) (Wardship: Jurisdiction)*[210] an independent day school run by a charity on orthodox Jewish principles admitted the son of Jewish parents on stringent conditions (including that the child should not live with his parents), but then indicated that the boy would be required to leave at the end of his first term. The local authority, concerned for the child's future, issued wardship proceedings seeking a mandatory injunction against the school requiring it to educate the boy. The application was refused. As Sir Stephen Brown P put it:

> If theoretically [the court] possesses such a power, I am clearly of the view that it is beyond the practical boundary of its wardship jurisdiction. This jurisdiction is not appropriate for use as an alternative to, or a cloak for, what appears, in fact, to be a claim for breach of contract by the parents against the school.

What these cases in general, and *Re C* in particular, show is that, whilst the courts are reluctant to hold that there is no power to control the activities of those unconnected with a ward, they will only exercise that power where it is essential to do so to protect the ward from direct harm. In other words, such a limitation is de facto rather than *de jure*.

The de facto limits

As Ward LJ said in *Re Z (A Minor) (Identification: Restrictions on Publication)*[211] the most obvious and well established of the de facto limits of the exercise of the inherent powers is where Parliament has entrusted the exercise of a competing discretion to another body or court. It has thus been long established that the court will not use its inherent powers to interfere with the exercise of discretion by local authorities over the children in their care,[212] the immigration service,[213] the prison service,[214] or by another court of

---

[209] [1985] 1 All ER 53. Note the House of Lords' subsequent ruling in *Re S (A Child) (Identification: Restrictions on Publication)* [2004] UKHL 47 [2005] 1 AC 593 that the foundation of jurisdiction to restrain publicity is now properly regarded as deriving from the European Convention on Human Rights rather than the inherent jurisdiction.   [210] [1991] 2 FLR 168, CA.

[211] [1997] Fam 1 at 23.

[212] See *A v Liverpool City Council*, [1982] AC 363, HL and *E (By her Litigation Friend, PW) v London Borough of X* [2005] EWHC 2811 (Fam), discussed in Ch 18, Wardship and the inherent jurisdiction, p 667.

[213] See *Re Mohamed Arif (An Infant), Re Nirbhai Singh (An Infant)* [1968] Ch 643, CA; *Re F (A Minor) (Immigration: Wardship)* [1990] Fam 125, CA; *Re A (A Minor) (Wardship: Immigration)* [1992] 1 FLR 427, CA and *R (Anton) v Secretary of State For The Home Department, Re Anton* [2004] EWHC 2730/2731 (Admin/Fam), [2005] 2 FLR 818. However, the wardship might be continued to safeguard the children where that would not interfere with the immigration service's functions: *Re F*, above and *Re K and S (Minors) (Wardship: Immigration)* [1992] 1 FLR 432.

[214] *CF v Secretary Of State For The Home Department* [2004] EWHC 111 (Fam), [2004] 2 FLR 517, *London Borough of Islington v TM* [2004] EWHC 2050 (Fam) and *R (Howard League for Penal Reform) v Secretary of State for the Home Department)* [2002] EWHC 2497 (Admin), [2003] 1 FLR 484.

competent jurisdiction.[215] By analogy it is also well established that there is no inherent power to order a doctor directly or indirectly to treat a child contrary to his or her clinical judgment.[216]

Quite apart from those limits, the courts also seem to be moving to a position of saying that the inherent jurisdiction should not be exercised so as to exempt the child from the general law, or to obtain rights and privileges for a specific child that are not generally available to all children.[217] It is established that the inherent powers cannot be used to interfere with the normal criminal process,[218] nor with the normal operation of military law.[219] At one time the courts were greatly exercised by the extent of the inherent power to shield a child from adverse publicity. However, in *Re S (A Child) (Identification: Restrictions on Publication)*[220] the House of Lords ruled that the foundation of jurisdiction to restrain publicity is now properly regarded as being derived from the European Convention on Human Rights (and therefore involves balancing the right to respect for private and family life under Art 8 and the right to freedom of expression under Art 10) and not upon the inherent jurisdiction.

4. LOCAL AUTHORITY USE OF THE JURISDICTION

(a) The need to obtain leave

Although local authorities cannot look to the inherent jurisdiction as a means of putting them in charge of the child's living arrangements,[221] they can nevertheless seek to use it to resolve specific questions about the child's future. Indeed, because of the unavailability of wardship[222] and of s 8 orders (by reason of the embargoes in s 9(1) and (2)),[223] they must do so if the child is in their care. Nevertheless, this avenue is fettered because under s 100(3) of the 1989 Act local authorities must first obtain the court's leave to apply for any exercise of the High Court's inherent jurisdiction.[224]

(b) Criteria for granting leave

Under s 100(4)(a) the court must be satisfied that the result being sought cannot be achieved under any statutory jurisdiction. This bar applies even where the statutory remedy is contingent upon the local authority having first to obtain leave before being

---

[215] See eg *Re A-H (Infants)* [1963] Ch 232; *Re K (KJS) (An Infant)* [1966] 3 All ER 154; and *Re PJ (An Infant)* [1968] 1 WLR 1976. Note also *Re G (A Minor) (Witness Summons)* [1988] 2 FLR 396—no power to set aside a witness summons issued by the US authorities in connection with a Court Martial to be held in England since, under the terms of the Visiting Forces Act 1952, the court martial was a sovereign court vested with exclusive powers.

[216] *Re J (A Minor) (Child in Care: Medical Treatment)* [1993] Fam 15, CA, and *Re C (Medical Treatment)* [1998] 1 FLR 384.

[217] See eg *Re R (A Minor) (Wardship: Restrictions on Publication)* [1994] Fam 254 at 271, per Millett LJ and *R v Central Independent Television plc* [1994] Fam 192, CA.

[218] See eg *Re K (Minors) (Wardship: Criminal Proceedings)* [1988] Fam 1.

[219] See *Re JS (A Minor) (Wardship: Boy Soldier)* [1990] Fam 182.

[220] [2004] UKHL 47 [2005] 1 AC 593. Query whether in drawing the balance between Arts 8 and 10 it is relevant whether the child is under the court's protective wing as suggested in *Re Z (A Minor) (Identification: Restrictions on Publication)* [1997] Fam 1.

[221] Children Act 1989 s 100(2).   [222] See Restrictions in public law cases, p 754.

[223] Discussed in Ch 14, Children in local authority care, p 510.

[224] See *Devon County Council v B* [1997] 1 FLR 591, CA. But note that according to Charles J in *Re P (Care Orders: Injunctive Relief)* [2000] 2 FLR 385 insofar as powers are sought under s 37 of the Senior Courts Act 1981 (viz. injunctive relief to support rights conferred by the Children Act 1989) leave is not required.

able to seek an order.[225] Furthermore, the bar applies where alternative relief is available under *any* statutory jurisdiction. It is not confined, for example, to the availability of s 8 orders.[226]

This restriction makes it particularly difficult for an authority to obtain leave for the exercise of the inherent jurisdiction in respect of a child *not* in their care, since in those circumstances they could seek to obtain a prohibited steps or specific issue order under s 8[227] or possibly injunctive relief under s 37 of the Senior Courts Act 1981.[228] In *Re R (A Minor) (Blood Transfusion)*[229] a local authority, wishing to obtain sanction for a blood transfusion for a child contrary to his parents' (who were Jehovah's Witnesses) wishes, were refused leave because, as the child was not in care, an appropriate remedy could have been obtained under s 8.

Even if there is no alternative statutory remedy, s 100(4)(b) still requires the court to be satisfied that: 'there is reasonable cause to believe that if the court's inherent jurisdiction is not exercised with respect to the child he is likely to suffer significant harm'. It has been accepted that cases determining the meaning of 'likely to suffer significant harm' for the purposes of s 31 are also relevant to its meaning under s 100(4)(b).[230] However, unlike seeking a care order, the court need only be satisfied that there is 'reasonable cause to believe that if the inherent jurisdiction is not exercised the child is likely to suffer significant harm', a test akin to that required when making interim care orders.[231] Notwithstanding this latter point the need for this potentially stringent requirement may be questioned.[232] Since a local authority must of necessity not be seeking to acquire parental responsibility but to have some specific matter of upbringing determined, a less onerous welfare test would surely have been appropriate.

(c) Circumstances in which the criteria for *giving* leave might be satisfied

Local authorities are not often justified in having recourse to the inherent jurisdiction. The expectation is that where a child is in care the local authority will have parental responsibility and should normally make decisions themselves and in cases where the

---

[225] Section 100(5)(b).

[226] Cf *Islington London Borough Council v E* [2010] EWHC 3240 (Fam) [2011] 1 FLR 1681 in which, on the facts, because it was found that Sch 2 para 19 of the Children Act 1989 (which permits, with court approval, local authorities to arrange placements abroad) did provide an alternative remedy, albeit not the preferred solution, the hurdle posed by s 100(4)(a) could not be overcome.

[227] See eg *Re C (HIV Test)* [1999] 2 FLR 1004 in which a local authority successfully applied for a specific issue order to have a baby tested for HIV. But note the difficulties of doing so, see *Langley v Liverpool City Council* [2005] EWCA Civ 1181 [2005] 3 FCR 303 at [73]–[78] per Thorpe LJ and *Nottingham County Council v P* [1994] Fam 18, discussed in Ch 14, Restrictions in the case of local authorities, pp 511–512.

[228] See *Re P (Care Orders: Injunctive Relief)* earlier—injunction granted under the Children Act 1989 to require parents to allow the child (who was being fostered) to attend school without interference.

[229] [1993] 2 FLR 757, per Booth J. This point was apparently overlooked by Thorpe J in *Re S (A Minor) (Medical Treatment)* [1993] 1 FLR 376; cf *Re O (A Minor) (Medical Treatment)* [1993] 2 FLR 149. Note also *A Local Authority v SB, AB and MB* [2010] EWHC 1744 (Fam) [2010] 2 FLR 1203 in which Wall P held that where there is no dispute between the parents and the hospital over proposed medical treatment there is no scope for court intervention.

[230] Per Connell J in *Essex County Council v Mirror Group Newspapers Ltd* [1996] 1 FLR 585, in which leave was refused.

[231] See *Re A and C (Equality and Human Rights Commission Intervening)* [2010] EWHC 978 (Fam) [2010] 2 FLR 1363, at [92] per Munby LJ and in which a local authority was granted a declaration there was no deprivation of liberty, contrary to Art 5 of the European Convention on Human Rights, in the case of a child suffering from Smith-Magenis Syndrome and cared for at home, of the carers looking the child in the bedroom overnight.

[232] By J Eekelaar and R Dingwall (1989) 139 NLJ 217. See also N Lowe (1989) 139 NLJ 8.

child is not in care, specific issue or prohibited steps orders under s 8 will normally provide an appropriate remedy.[233] Nevertheless, there will be occasions when recourse to the High Court will be appropriate. Lord Mackay LC instanced[234] the exercise of the inherent power to sanction an abortion being carried out on a child in care, where there are no other statutory means of seeking a court order and the decision, if wrong, is clearly likely to cause significant harm. In *Re W (A Minor) (Medical Treatment: Court's Jurisdiction)*[235] it was thought right to invoke the inherent jurisdiction to override a refusal of a 16-year-old anorexic child in care to consent to medical treatment. Other examples of medical treatment where leave is likely to be given include sterilisation,[236] contested cases involving emergency medical treatment of a child in care,[237] or where life saving treatment is in issue.[238]

The listed medical problems are extreme examples of situations when High Court intervention might be justified, but circumstances do not always have to be so extraordinary. In *Southwark London Borough v B*[239] leave was granted to a local authority first to seek a return order of a child in care and then to enforce that order. Similarly, it has been held[240] permissible for a local authority to invoke the inherent jurisdiction (via wardship) to seek the return of a child (about which the authority had concerns) to the jurisdiction in circumstances where, because the 1980 Hague Abduction Convention was inapplicable, there was no alternative remedy. In other cases, for example, where a local authority seeks an injunction to prevent a violent father from discovering his child's whereabouts,[241] or from molesting the child[242] or, possibly, to restrain harmful publicity about the child,[243] then the inherent jurisdiction is the *only* means of obtaining the remedy and it should not be too difficult to satisfy the criteria for granting leave.

In *Devon County Council v S*[244] it was held appropriate to exercise the inherent jurisdiction to prevent a family friend (a Sch 1 offender and a paedophile) from having contact with the children and to prevent the mother from allowing the children to have contact with him, since there was no other means of obtaining such a remedy. In *Re M (Care: Leave To Interview Child)*[245] the jurisdiction was successfully invoked to permit a child in care to be interviewed by the father's solicitor with a view to preparing evidence in the father's defence in furthering criminal proceedings against him.

Although in theory the granting of leave does not automatically mean that the court must exercise its jurisdiction, given that it must be satisfied that the child is likely to suffer

---

[233] See the revised *Guidance and Regulations*, Vol 1, *Court Orders* (2008) paras 3.86 and 88.

[234] (1989) 139 NLJ 505 at 507.

[235] [1993] Fam 64, CA, discussed at Gillick – a false dawn?, pp 323ff. See also *Re C (Detention: Medical Treatment)* [1997] 2 FLR 180.

[236] This is one of the examples given by the revised *Guidance and Regulations*, op cit, at para 3.87. It also instances restraining harmful publicity about a child, though this example must now be regarded as subject to the. House of Lords' ruling in *Re S (A Child) (Identification: Restrictions on Publication)* [2004] UKHL 47 [2005] 1 AC 593 that the foundation of jurisdiction to restrain publicity is now properly regarded as being derived from the European Convention on Human Rights rather than the inherent jurisdiction.

[237] See *Re O (A Minor) (Medical Treatment)* [1993] 2 FLR 149.

[238] See eg *Re C (Medical Treatment)* [1998] 1 FLR 384; *Re T (a minor) (wardship: medical treatment)* [1997] 1 All ER 906, CA; and *Re C (A Baby)* [1996] 2 FLR 43.   [239] [1993] 2 FLR 559, CA.

[240] *Re S (Wardship: Peremptory Return)* [2010] EWCA Civ 465 [2010] 2 FLR 1960.

[241] See *Re JT (A Minor) (Wardship: Committal to Care)* [1986] 2 FLR 107.

[242] See *Re B (A Minor) (Wardship: Child in Care)* [1975] Fam 36.

[243] See eg *Re Jane (Publicity)* [2010] EWHC 3221 (Fam) [2011] 1 FLR 1261.   [244] [1994] Fam 169.

[245] [1995] 1 FLR 825.

significant harm if the jurisdiction is not exercised[246] it would be an unusual case where leave was given and the jurisdiction not subsequently exercised.[247]

5. PRIVATE LAW USE OF THE JURISDICTION

Although individuals can invoke the inherent jurisdiction there is normally little advantage in doing so, not least because of the continued availability of wardship. Nevertheless it can be usefully invoked in abduction proceedings as, for example, where the child is 16 or over so that the 1980 Hague Abduction Convention cannot apply.[248] It has been invoked by the court itself following its refusal to order the child's return in a Hague application in cases not covered by the revised Brussels II Regulation.[249]

Where the child is in local authority care then, since wardship cannot be used, the High Court's inherent powers can only be invoked, if at all, under the wider inherent jurisdiction. However, the well-established embargo against using wardship to challenge local authority decisions[250] applies equally to that use of the inherent jurisdiction.[251]

Despite the restrictions just discussed on local authorities and even individuals in accessing the inherent jurisdiction (though the courts are not so constrained in being able to exercise their powers), strikingly innovative use has been made of the inherent powers when dealing with unusual situations. It has been well said that the inherent jurisdiction is 'a sufficiently flexible remedy to evolve with social needs and values'. In *Re SK (an adult) (forced marriage: appropriate relief)*,[252] for example, a solicitor, at the request of the Foreign and Commonwealth Office, successfully applied under the inherent jurisdiction on behalf of a child who was a British citizen at risk of a forced marriage in Bangladesh, for orders against members of her family, to ascertain her whereabouts and whether she was exercising her free will, and an injunction preventing them from arranging any marriage.

In *Chief Constable of Greater Manchester v KI and KW (by their Children's Guardian, CAFCASS Legal), and NP*,[253] it was held that the court had jurisdiction to give (or refuse) consent to a police interview of children (who had witnessed their sister being shot with a gun fired by their brother) for the purpose of the criminal investigation. The court could control this aspect of parental responsibility by the use of a specific issue order or, in any event, under the inherent jurisdiction. The test was the balance of rights and interests, in which the child's welfare was not the paramount consideration. While in *Re M (children) (interviewing children)*[254] an order was made under the inherent jurisdiction in a case resulting from evidence in care proceedings leading to criminal charges being brought

[246] It is submitted that this requirement distinguishes s 100 from granting leave under s 10 to apply for a s 8 order, where it is established that there is no presumption that an order be made following the granting of leave: see Ch 14, The application of s 10(9), p 516.

[247] For an example where leave was refused see *Essex County Council v Mirror Group Newspapers Ltd* [1996] 1 FLR 585, in which on the facts Connell J held the potential harm had not been established.

[248] See, for example, *Re C (Abduction: Separate Representation of Children)* [2008] EWHC 517 (Fam) [2008] 2 FLR 6 in which there were several siblings, the eldest being 16; and *Re H (Abduction: Child of 16)* [2000] 2 FLR 51 in which the child became 16 during Hague proceedings.

[249] See eg *D v S (Abduction: Acquiescence)* [2008] EWHC 363 (Fam) [2008] 2 FLR 293. The 1980 Hague Abduction Convention and the revised Brussels II Regulation are discussed in Ch 26.

[250] See *A v Liverpool City Council* [1982] AC 363, discussed in Ch 18, Wardship and the inherent jurisdiction, p 667.

[251] See *Re B (Minors) (Termination of Contact: Paramount Consideration)* [1993] Fam 301 at 309.

[252] [2004] EWHC 3202 (Fam) [2005 3 ALL ER 421.

[253] [2007] EWHC 1837 (Fam) [2008] 1 FLR 504 in which the court ordered that the children should be interviewed. [254] [2007] EWCA Civ 1150 [2008] 1 FCR 787.

against both parents; the order allowed the daughter to be interviewed in relation to the criminal proceedings.

In *Hartshorne v Gardner*[255] the inherent jurisdiction was used (with the parties' agreement) to decide a dispute between divorced parents over whether their adult child's body should be cremated or as to the place of funeral or cremation.

In *Re G (Abduction: Withdrawal of Proceedings, Acquiescence, Habitual Residence)*[256] a father applied under both the 1980 Hague Abduction Convention and the inherent jurisdiction for the return of his two children who had been retained in Canada by their mother. The alternative bases for jurisdiction were necessary since on the facts it was found that the Hague Convention did not actually apply. In *W and W v H (Child Abduction: Surrogacy) (No 2)*[257] an order for the summary return of twin children born as a result of a commercial surrogacy arrangement to California was made under the inherent jurisdiction for those courts to determine the merits of the future care of the children.

D. COMMENTARY

Although the continued existence of both wardship and the general or residual inherent jurisdiction is undoubtedly a peculiarity of the current legal system for dealing with children and does not easily stand with a comprehensive statutory scheme, it is evident that the High Court's inherent powers still have a useful, if small, role to play. There is no evidence that the judiciary are using their inherent powers to subvert the statutory scheme. On the contrary, they have shown restraint and only used them where no other remedy is available. In short, the inherent jurisdiction (including wardship) continues to provide an invaluable additional means of securing certain children's interests who would otherwise not be protected.

---

[255] [2008] EWHC B3 (Ch) [2008] 2 FLR 1681. See also *Burrows v Coroner for Preston* [2008] EWHC 1387 (QB) [2008] 2 FLR 1235 in which the court ordered that a child who committed suicide should be cremated in accordance with the wishes of the paternal uncle who had cared for him, rather than buried as the mother wanted.

[256] [2007] EWHC 1837 (Fam) [2008] 2 FLR 351. See also *B v D (Abduction: Inherent Jurisdiction)* [2008] EWHC 1246 (Fam) [2009] 1 FLR 1015 and *D v S (Abduction: Acquiescence)* [2008] EWHC 363 (Fam) [2008] 2 FLR 293.   [257] [2002] 2 FLR 252.

21

FINANCIAL OBLIGATIONS TO MEMBERS OF THE FAMILY

A. INTRODUCTION

A legal obligation to provide financial support for another member of the family, often referred to as 'family solidarity' in civil law systems, may be seen as the most tangible recognition of the moral ties created by family relationships.[1] Where such an obligation is imposed, it also sheds light on social conceptions of the appropriate scope of those ties.[2] Different societies at different times may impose the obligation upon different degrees of relationship.[3] Under the Poor Law, there was an obligation (albeit enforceable only by the Poor Law authorities) to provide financial support for one's grandchildren.[4] Until the nineteenth century, a child born outside wedlock was not entitled to support from either parent,[5] and an unqualified liability on the father of such a child has existed only since 1987.[6] There is still no direct liability to support an unmarried partner, although, through support for the child, there may be an indirect imposition of a requirement to do so.[7]

The view of the proper extent to which the State, rather than the family, should bear the 'burden' of support has shifted over time, with the high point of the 'welfare state' in the latter part of the twentieth century giving way to a reassertion of private duty, but ultimately it is still recognised that the State will have to provide residual support for those who have no one else to turn to when they are unable to support themselves. This chapter begins with a brief résumé of the historical development of the law, including the role of the welfare state;[8] then we consider mechanisms whereby family members can seek

---

[1] J Finch *Family Obligations and Social Change* (1989). But for a thought-provoking consideration of precisely how the imposition of a legal duty of support can be justified, see S Altman 'A Theory of Child Support' (2003) 17 Int Jo of Law, Policy and the Fam 173.

[2] For discussion of the nature of commitment and obligation (not limited to the financial) in personal relationships: see in particular, J Eekelaar and M Maclean *The Parental Obligation* (1997) and 'Marriage and the Moral Bases of Personal Relationships' (2004) 31 JLS 510; J Lewis *Marriage, Cohabitation and the Law: Individualism and Obligation* (1999) and *The End of Marriage: Individualism and Intimate Relationships* (2001).

[3] See J Millar and A Warman *Family Obligations in Europe* (1996): southern European states are more likely to impose obligations upon the wider family; some northern European states impose obligations upwards from children to parents, as well as downwards; Scandinavian states are less likely to impose any support obligations at all.

[4] Poor Relief Act 1601 s 6. For a discussion of the history of the 'liable relative' rule under the poor law and the welfare state, see N Wikeley 'The strange death of the liable relative rule' (2008) 30(4) *Journal of Social Welfare and Family Law* 339.

[5] See later, Support obligations outside marriage or civil partnership, p 775.

[6] Family Law Reform Act 1987 s 17.

[7] See later, Proceedings under Schedule 1 to the Children Act 1989, Exercising the powers, p 796.

[8] For detailed consideration of the State's role, see M Partington and M Fletcher *Social Security Law in the United Kingdom* (2012).

support from each other, namely through private agreements, court orders and finally under the child support scheme. Recognition of the ties of affection, regardless of marriage bonds, has in some respects been more readily granted where a party has died, and the general question of how the moral support obligations of a deceased person are legally recognised is dealt with in Chapter 25.

1. THE DUTY TO MAINTAIN A SPOUSE OR CIVIL PARTNER

(a) At common law

The common law rules relating to spousal maintenance were the inevitable consequence of the doctrine of unity of legal personality.[9] The wife, lacking the capacity to hold property and to contract, could neither own even the necessities of life nor enter into a binding contract to buy them. Two principles followed: First, one of the essential obligations imposed upon a married man was to provide his wife with at least necessities; and secondly, a married woman could in no circumstances be held liable to maintain her husband. The common law rule that neither spouse could sue the other precluded her from enforcing her right by action if her husband failed to fulfil his duty to maintain her: this difficulty was overcome by giving the wife a power to pledge her husband's credit for the purchase of necessities if he did not supply her with them himself.

Scope of the husband's duty

The husband's common law duty to provide his wife with the necessities of life was prima facie complied with if he provided a home for her.[10] She had no right to separate maintenance in a separate home unless she could justify living apart from him. The fact of marriage raised a presumption that the husband was under a duty to maintain his wife. But her right to maintenance, generally speaking, was co-extensive with her right to her husband's consortium, and if her conduct released him from the duty to cohabit with her, he automatically ceased to be under a duty to maintain her.[11] A single act of adultery could automatically deprive her of her right, and if she deserted him her right was suspended until her desertion came to an end.[12]

The agency of necessity

The power to pledge the husband's credit, termed the wife's agency of necessity,[13] extended to the purchase of necessaries both for herself and for the spouses' minor children. The term 'necessaries' in this context included not only necessary goods such as food and clothing, but also necessary services such as lodging, medical attention and education. Although the wife could divest herself of the right to be maintained by her own conduct, the husband could not revoke the authority by his unilateral act.

The agency of necessity was of great importance so long as the wife was generally incompetent to contract and own property at common law. Both these disabilities were removed by the Married Women's Property Act 1882, and by the end of the nineteenth century she could obtain maintenance from her husband not only in the High Court but also much more speedily in the magistrates' court. When it also became possible

---

[9] See Ch 4, The doctrine of unity, p 90.   [10] See *Price v Price* [1951] P 413, at 420–1, CA.

[11] *Chilton v Chilton* [1952] P 196 at 202.

[12] *Jones v Newtown and Llanidloes Guardians* [1920] 3 KB 381.

[13] For examples of the tactical use of this power, see L Stone *Broken Lives: Separation and Divorce in England 1660–1857* (1993) passim.

for the wife to obtain immediate assistance through the social security system, and to claim the benefits of the National Health Service and the legal aid scheme, the doctrine became an anachronism and was eventually abolished by the Matrimonial Proceedings and Property Act 1970.[14]

(b) The current position

The common law duty on the husband to maintain his wife has been prospectively abolished.[15] The means by which maintenance can be claimed by a spouse are now governed entirely by statute. Unlike the common law it is open to either spouse to claim maintenance from the other, and since claims for maintenance no longer depend upon the duty to cohabit, the commission of adultery or desertion is no longer a bar. The two statutes governing maintenance between separated spouses are the Domestic Proceedings and Magistrates' Courts Act 1978 and the Matrimonial Causes Act 1973 s 27. For civil partners the equivalent provision is contained in the Civil Partnership Act 2004 Schs 5 (Part 9) and 6. However, in practice, actions are rarely brought under this legislation: a spouse needing support either turns to the social security system or seeks comprehensive provision under the divorce jurisdiction, which is discussed in Chapter 22.

2. PARENTS' DUTY TO MAINTAIN CHILDREN

At common law a father was under a duty to maintain only his legitimate minor children and to provide them with food, clothing, lodging and other necessities.[16] But the duty was wholly unenforceable. A child has never had an agency of necessity[17] and a father was under no legal obligation to reimburse a person who supplied his child with necessaries. Unless he constituted the child his agent, the only way in which he could be compelled to fulfil his obligation was through the wife's agency of necessity, which extended to the purchase of necessities for the children of the marriage as well as for herself.[18]

As with maintaining spouses and civil partners, the means by which financial provision can be claimed for children is governed by statute. Where it is sought to obtain financial provision for children alone, strong encouragement is given to making private maintenance agreements with the other parent, now known as 'family-based arrangements',[19] but where these are inappropriate, recourse may be had to the Child Support Act 1991, or, where this Act does not apply,[20] to the courts' matrimonial jurisdictions, or to Sch 1 to the Children Act 1989 which provides an alternative jurisdiction.

3. SUPPORT OBLIGATIONS OUTSIDE MARRIAGE OR CIVIL PARTNERSHIP

Reflecting the common law position, it remains the case that even between cohabiting adults there is no duty to maintain, although, as we shall see, in assessing the level of

---

[14] Section 41. This followed the recommendations of the Law Commission: see Law Com No 25, paras 108–109 and Appendix II, paras 41–52 and 108.   [15] By the Equality Act 2010 s 198.
[16] This common law obligation has not been abolished: see Baroness Hale of Richmond in *R (Kehoe) v Secretary of State for Work and Pensions* [2005] UKHL 48 [2006] 1 AC 42 at [69].
[17] *Mortimore v Wright* (1840) 6 M & W 482.   [18] *Bazeley v Forder* (1868) LR 3 QB 559.
[19] http://www.cmoptions.org/en/family/ [online] (accessed 3 May 2014). See later, The child support scheme: Mark 3, p 803.   [20] See later, The residual role of the courts, p 820.

maintenance to be paid by an unmarried parent for any child, an element to cover the costs of the carer may be included by the court.[21]

With regard to children born outside marriage, at common law neither the father nor the mother was liable for maintenance.[22] Although the Poor Law legislation cast upon the mother the obligation of maintaining her illegitimate child, she could still not recover the expenses of maintenance from the father in the absence of any contract to that effect between them.[23] A statute of 1576 empowered justices to make an order against the unmarried father for the maintenance of an illegitimate child charged on the parish,[24] but it was not until the Poor Law Amendment Act 1844 that the mother was given the power to apply for an order for maintenance to be paid to herself. The law was amended and consolidated in the Bastardy Laws Amendment Act 1872 and again in the Affiliation Proceedings Act 1957. Under this legislation the right of unmarried mothers to claim from alleged fathers was circumscribed. For example, applications could only be made to magistrates' courts, applicants had to be 'single' mothers, claims had to be brought within three years of the child's birth,[25] and the mother's evidence had to be corroborated. These limitations were removed by the Family Law Reform Act 1987, and the relevant provisions are now contained in the Children Act 1989. As we shall discuss, the Child Support Act 1991 has gone still further in equalising the law governing the support of children born inside and outside marriage.

B. STATE SUPPORT

1. TAX ALLOWANCES AND CREDITS

The State may provide support to individuals and families to maintain themselves through two main mechanisms. On the one hand, it may provide tax allowances (or 'credits') so that the beneficiary pays less tax than would otherwise be the case, and hence retains more of their income for expenditure on their own and their family's wants.[26] Entitlement to the allowance or credit depends upon earning, or having, an income of a size at which tax is payable and upon meeting the particular criteria (such as marital or parental status) laid down. On the other hand, the state may establish a social security system, whereby 'benefits' are paid to eligible applicants as a cash sum to meet their particular needs. Entitlement to such benefits may depend upon past contributions (the 'national insurance' approach), or simply upon fulfilment of criteria based on the particular needs to be met, such as disability or poverty.

Tax allowances and credits have the psychological and political advantages of presenting state support of those in need as if it were a mechanism which costs the state nothing (because what is done is to leave the recipient with more take-home pay) rather than as a direct expense for the state (because, although the amount of benefit paid to the recipient may be calculated according to his wages, it comes directly from the state). In reality, the state 'pays' under either system. However, allowances and credits carry less stigma to

---

[21] See later, Proceedings under Schedule 1 to the Children Act 1989, Exercising the powers, p 796.
[22] *Ruttinger v Temple* (1863) 4 B & S 491.
[23] As to agreements to pay maintenance, see later, Private agreements, Between parents, pp 784 et seq.
[24] 18 Eliz 1 c 3.   [25] Unless the father was voluntarily paying money for the child.
[26] For a discussion of the use of the tax system to meet welfare needs, see J Kvist and A Sinfield 'Comparing Tax Welfare States' in M May, E Brunsdon and G Craig (eds) *Social Policy Review 9* (1997).

recipients and 'reinforce the distinction between the rewards of work and remaining on welfare'.[27]

The best known family tax allowance is the married couple's allowance, originally the married *man's* allowance, based on the assumption, at one time well-founded, that a married man would be expected to meet the bulk, if not all, of the financial needs of his wife and family out of his own income. The allowance was introduced in 1918, enabling the husband to start to pay tax at a higher threshold than a single person. In 1990, in a belated acknowledgement of women's financial contributions to the living standards of their families, all married women became separately taxed from their husbands, and the allowance became a 'married couple's' allowance, payable to either spouse (although paid to the husband unless the couple requested its transfer to the wife, or apportionment between both of them).[28] The allowance is now only payable where one of the couple[29] was born before 6 April 1935 and its value has been steadily eroded, being payable at only 10% compared with the basic rate of tax at 20%. However, the symbolism attached to the allowance as a means of representing the state's 'support' for the institution of marriage means that the Conservative party continues to pledge to reintroduce an allowance (albeit of token amount) for all married couples[30] and was able to include a limited measure to be implemented in 2015, under which basic rate taxpayers could benefit by up to £200 per year. by one spouse transferring up to £1,000 of their personal tax allowance to the other spouse.[31]

2. WELFARE BENEFITS

The present social security system derives in part from the Beveridge reforms enacted in the National Assistance Act 1948 which abolished the Poor Law.[32] Since then, however, there have been huge changes. Both under the Labour Government of 1997 to 2010[33] and the Coalition,[34] the focus has been predominantly on encouraging more people into work and out of dependence upon state benefits. One of the key elements in this strategy was to provide tax credits, rather than social security payments, as the bridge between total dependence upon benefits and take-up of full-time employment.[35] A more recent emphasis has been on 'fairness' to the tax-payer and 'working families', using the argument (which echoes the concept of 'less eligibility'[36] at the time of the Poor Law reforms in the nineteenth century) that those on benefits should not enjoy a standard of living higher than that being experienced by those who are paying taxes to cover those benefits.[37]

Broadly speaking, anyone over the age of 18 whose income falls below the relevant sum laid down by the legislation is currently entitled to apply for tax credits if in work, or welfare benefits (including income support or jobseeker's allowance) if not in work or,

---

[27] HM Treasury, *Work Incentives* (1998) para 3.19.

[28] Finance Act 1988, which came into effect on 6 April 1990.   [29] Including civil partners.

[30] Conservative Party, *Invitation to Join the Government of Britain* (2010) p 35.

[31] HM Treasury, 'Marriage Transferable Tax Allowance announced by government' 30 September 2013. The allowance will, of course, apply to same-sex married couples and civil partners.

[32] For a full discussion of the historical context, see N Harris (ed) *Social Security Law in Context* (2000) chs 3–7.

[33] Department of Social Security *New Ambitions for Our Country: A New Contract for Welfare* Cm 3805 (1998).   [34] DWP *Universal Credit: welfare that works* Cm 7957 (2010).

[35] HM Treasury, *Work Incentives* (1998) ch 3.

[36] The principle of less eligibility meant that those receiving poor law relief should experience a lifestyle worse than that which they would enjoy if supporting themselves: hence, for example, they should be forced to live in workhouses rather than receive 'outdoor relief' in their homes.

[37] *Daily Telegraph*, 'Iain Duncan Smith: We've brought back fairness to welfare', 30 December 2012.

in respect of children, child tax credits.[38] The Welfare Reform Act 2012[39] prospectively abolishes these 'benefits' and 'credits' and replaces them with 'Universal Credit' which will pay an allowance to those both in and out of work to meet their needs and those of their children, as now, but which will, it is intended, provide a simplified system which facilitates the transition into paid work for claimants.[40]

Support may also be provided for the payment of rent through housing benefit which is administered by local authorities. Regulations made under the Welfare Reform Act 2012 s 69[41] impose a limit on the amount of housing benefit that can be claimed, through the determination of how many bedrooms the claimant's family 'needs'—officially called the 'spare room subsidy' but known as the 'bedroom tax'. Where it is concluded that there are surplus bedrooms for the size of family (for example, each child has their own bed-room, whilst the Regulations provide that two children under 10 or of the same sex should share), such that the rent being charged is too high, the amount of benefit payable will be reduced. This risks breaking up families who may have to move to other accommodation, or move in with relatives, thus disrupting children's schooling and parents' ability to take work. It may also affect the ability of separated or divorced parents to 'share' care of their children as the appropriate number of bedrooms is determined by which parent receives child benefit (see next section).

Where means-tested welfare benefits have been provided to a party to a marriage or civil partnership, then in line with the poor law philosophy, the sums paid were always recoverable from that person's spouse or civil partner,[42] although in practice, such recovery does not appear to have been pursued for several years.[43] Ironically, while the political focus and rhetoric since 1990 has been on seeking to ensure that parents support their children, the *public law* liability to do so was abolished by the Child Maintenance and Other Payments Act 2008[44] so that the State could no longer pursue the parent to recover social security payments made for the child. Extraordinarily, there is a *criminal* liability to support one's spouse or civil partner,[45] and this has been retained, presumably for primarily symbolic purposes, but the civil liability of a spouse or civil partner has been prospectively repealed,[46] suggesting that in reality, the state no longer takes an interest in recouping its direct costs of support from another family member. Instead, its attention lies in getting the beneficiary into paid work.

---

[38] Determination of which benefit or credit is appropriate in different circumstances, and at what level of payment, is dependent upon the relevant legislation, discussed fully in CPAG *Welfare Benefits and Tax Credits Handbook* (2012, 14th edn). Payment of child tax credit to the person with 'main responsibility' for the child where care is shared between both parents when they are separated is not discriminatory towards fathers even though they generally care for children for less time, as the intention of the policy behind the credit payment is to reduce child poverty and splitting the payment between both parents would be less effective in achieving that: *Humphreys v Revenue and Customs Commissioners* [2012] UKSC 18 [2012] 4 All ER 27.   [39] Part 1 and s 33.

[40] DWP *Universal Credit: welfare that works* Cm 7957 (2010) paras 4 *et seq.*

[41] Housing Benefit (Amendment) Regulations 2012 (SI 2012/3040).

[42] Liability terminated on divorce or dissolution.

[43] See N Wikeley 'The strange death of the liable relative rule' (2008) 30(4) *Journal of Social Welfare and Family Law* 339.

[44] Section 45. Parents remain liable to support their children under the Child Support Act 1991 and private law; see further Obtaining financial relief for children, p 791 and Maintenance under the Child Support Act 1991, p 800 ff. Child tax credits were never recoverable.

[45] Social Security Administration Act 1992 s 105 as amended. The offence is punishable by fine or imprisonment for up to three months but the power to imprison has been prospectively repealed by the Criminal Justice Act 2003 Sch 37 Part 9.

[46] Social Security Administration Act 1992 s 106 prospectively repealed by the Welfare Reform Act 2009 Sch 7 Part 1.

3. CHILD BENEFIT

Direct financial aid to assist families bringing up children was proposed as long ago as 1796 by William Pitt. However, it was not until the Family Allowance Act 1945 that such a scheme was put into practice. Under that Act family allowance was paid to the mother, but only to families with at least two children. The amount hardly changed in 20 years. Tax allowances for all children were also available to set against income tax. Since married women were then less likely to be in paid employment than is now the case, such allowances generally enhanced the take-home pay of the father, and it was argued that the children did not always receive the benefit of them. Integration and reform of the two schemes were called for in the late 1960s, and finally achieved under the Child Benefit Act 1975, after which child tax allowances were phased out. Child benefit was originally a tax-free benefit payable to all eligible parents or carers regardless of their income, but it was made subject to the 'high income child benefit charge' in 2012 so that where a parent in receipt of the benefit earns more than £50,000 net p.a. the benefit is taxed, at a rate increasing to 100% at the point when the parent earns more than £60,000.[47]

Section 141 of the Social Security Contributions and Benefits Act 1992[48] provides:

> A person who is responsible for one or more children or qualifying young persons in any week shall be entitled . . . to a benefit . . . for that week in respect of the child or qualifying young person, or each of the children or qualifying young person for whom he is responsible.[49]

Under s 143 a person is treated as responsible for a child (or young person) if he or she has the child living with him or her or is contributing to the cost of providing for the child at a weekly rate not less than the child benefit payable for that child. Where care of a child is split between parents, for example where there is shared residence or extensive staying contact, they may agree between themselves who is to receive the benefit, or, in default of agreement, the Secretary of State may decide.[50] The recipient need not be a parent of the child, or even a relative, and there may be many cases where there are competing claims. Schedule 10 sets out an order of priority, so that a person having the child living with him or her has priority over a person contributing to the cost of providing for the child; a wife has priority over her husband where they are residing together; a parent takes priority over a non-parent; and a mother takes priority over an unmarried father where they are residing together.

C. PRIVATE AGREEMENTS

1. BETWEEN SPOUSES AND CIVIL PARTNERS

Financial agreements between the spouses[51] made at different stages in their relationship have been treated differently by the law. As Baroness Hale explained in *Granatino*

---

[47] Finance Act 2012 s 8 and Sch 1, inserting s 681B *et seq* into Income Tax (Earnings and Pensions) Act 2003.　　　　　　　　　　　　　　　　　　[48] As amended by the Child Benefit Act 2005 s 1(1).

[49] A child is defined by s 142 as a person under the age of 16; and a qualifying young person includes people under the age of 20 and receiving full-time non-advanced education or approved training.

[50] Social Security Contributions and Benefits Act 1992 Sch 10 para 5. As with child tax credit, child benefit may not be split but *Humphreys v Revenue and Customs Commissioners* [2012] UKSC 18 [2012] 4 All ER 27 would seem to apply to render this not discriminatory against fathers.

[51] References to spouses in the discussion include civil partners.

v Radmacher (Formerly Granatino)[52] one can identify three different types. The first is made while the spouses are living together and the courts were traditionally reluctant to enforce these agreements where they related to financial or housekeeping allowances on the ground that it is presumed that the couple had no intention to enter into legal relations.[53] The second type is an agreement made on the point of or after separation. Such 'separation agreements' were important when divorce was difficult to obtain, in determining financial arrangements that would last for possibly several years between the spouses whilst they were living apart. The third is an agreement to compromise their claims under the courts' matrimonial jurisdiction on divorce (or annulment).

A Type 1 agreement (or even more so one made before the wedding—a 'pre-nup') which sets out what financial arrangements would apply if the spouses were to separate at some point in the future, was traditionally regarded as contrary to public policy as being likely to encourage the parties to end their marriage.[54] But in *Granatino v Radmacher* the Supreme Court ruled that both pre- and post-nuptial agreements of this kind can be given effect unless it would not be fair to do so,[55] in part because there is no longer, in their view, a duty upon spouses to cohabit.[56]

A Type 2 agreement, made at or after the point of separation, did not infringe the first principle of public policy (since the couple had already split up),[57] but might fall foul of another. In *Hyman v Hyman*,[58] the House of Lords held that an agreement which included a provision purporting to prevent a spouse from subsequently applying for financial relief in divorce proceedings would be void. The reason for this decision is that the court's power to order the husband to maintain his former wife after divorce is intended to protect not only her but also any person dealing with her and, indirectly, the State, in view of the possibility of her having to apply for what are now known as social security benefits. Consequently, it would be contrary to public policy to permit the parties to oust the court's jurisdiction by agreement.[59]

To be legally enforceable, an agreement of either of these types must constitute a contract between the parties. Consequently, if it is not by deed,[60] the party seeking to enforce a promise to pay maintenance must show that she (or he) has furnished consideration. Basically the parties' rights and duties are determined by the general law of contract,[61] but as we shall see, the law imposes certain extra requirements in the case of spouses or civil partners, as a protection to them and the State.

A Type 3 agreement is now the predominant form of agreement made by separating spouses, because divorce has become much more readily available and the parties can now achieve a final 'clean break' in relation to all of their financial assets and obligations.[62]

---

[52] [2010] UKSC 42 [2011] 1 AC 534 at [141]–[150]. The case is usually known as the *Radmacher* case.

[53] *Balfour v Balfour* [1919] 2 KB 571; *Gould v Gould* [1970] 1 QB 275; *Re Windle* [1975] 3 All ER 987. See the discussion in Ch 4, Contracts, p XXX.

[54] *Cocksedge v Cocksedge* (1844) 14 Sim 244; *H v W* (1857) 3 K & J 382.

[55] *Granatino v Radmacher* [2011] UKSC 42 [2011] 1 AC 534, and see Ch 22, Pre- and post-nuptial agreements, *Granatino v Radmacher* p 856.

[56] *MacLeod v MacLeod* [2008] UKPC 64; [2010] 1 AC 298 at [38] and *Granatino v Radmacher* [2011] UKSC 42 [2011] 1 AC 534 at [152], [157]. See Ch 4, Consortium, p 94.

[57] *Merritt v Merritt* [1970] 2 All ER 760, CA.   [58] [1929] AC 601, HL.

[59] [1929] AC 601, HL at 608 and 629.

[60] For the meaning of which see the Law of Property (Miscellaneous Provisions) Act 1989 s 1.

[61] It may therefore be set aside on the basis of undue influence, frustration or mistake etc; see *NA v MA* [2006] EWHC 1227 (Fam) [2007] 1 FLR 1760: wife's will overborne when she signed an agreement in order to dissuade the husband from divorcing her for adultery.

[62] See Ch 23, Placing greater emphasis on the parties becoming self-sufficient, p 876.

However, such an agreement it is not binding as a contract, and becomes enforceable only when it has been embodied in a court order after the court has scrutinised its terms to ensure they are conformable with the court's own jurisdiction.[63] This does not mean that the court will ignore the agreement (or a Type 2 'separation agreement') in subsequent matrimonial proceedings, and the wife may well be held to its terms.[64] A striking example is *T v T (Agreement not embodied in Consent Order).*[65] The spouses made a 'separation agreement' (i.e. a Type 2 agreement) in 1991. They divorced in 1995 and carried out its terms but no claim for financial remedies was made and so it was not turned into a consent order. The husband prospered but the wife got into financial difficulties. She brought an application over 20 years after making the agreement but the court held that it was of 'magnetic importance' justifying holding her to its terms by way of a consent order. But the uncertainty of not knowing whether the court will, or will not, uphold the terms of such an agreement has been criticised. In *Pounds v Pounds*[66] Hoffmann LJ characterised the position as the worst of all worlds and commented that:

> In our attempt to achieve finely ground justice by attributing weight but not too much weight to the agreement of the parties, we have created uncertainty and, in this case and no doubt others, added to the cost and pain of litigation.[67]

(a) Maintenance agreements

The parties' agreement may constitute a 'maintenance agreement' for the purposes of s 34 of the Matrimonial Causes Act 1973.[68] This provision and the succeeding section have been described as 'dead letters for more than thirty years'[69] because, as we have noted, separating couples usually go on to divorce and seek a final resolution of their financial and property relationship through the courts so that this provision and its relationship with the courts wider divorce powers have rarely been considered. Nonetheless, given the trend away from legal proceedings towards 'private ordering' and the loss of legal aid from most family proceedings, it is conceivable that these sections may become more important in the future as couples seek to avoid court proceedings entirely but draw up (possibly by themselves) written agreements purporting to determine their financial affairs after divorce.[70] The provision has come under some scrutiny recently, as part of the courts' broader consideration of whether a pre- or post-nuptial agreement should be given legal effect, but as we shall see, their reflections on the matter have not been entirely helpful.

To come within s 34 of the Matrimonial Causes Act 1973,[71] an agreement must be *in writing* and made 'between the parties to a marriage'. It must also be:

> (a) an agreement containing financial arrangements, whether made during the continuance or after the dissolution or annulment of the marriage; or
> (b) a separation agreement which contains no financial arrangements in a case where no other agreement in writing between the same parties contains such arrangements.

---

[63] *Xydhias v Xydhias* [1999] 1 FLR 683, *Granatino v Radmacher (Formerly Granatino)* [2010] UKSC 42 [2011] 1 AC 534 discussed in Ch 22, Consent orders, p XXX ff.

[64] See *Edgar v Edgar* [1980] 3 All ER 887, Ch 22, The weight attached to the parties' agreement, p 851.

[65] [2013] EWHC B3 (Fam) [2013] Fam Law 801.   [66] [1994] 1 FLR 775.

[67] At p 791G.   [68] Or Sch 5 paras 67, 68 to the Civil Partnership Act 2004.

[69] *Granatino v Radmacher* [2009] EWCA Civ 649 [2009] 2 FLR 1181 at [134] per Wilson LJ.

[70] Cf Baroness Hale in *Granatino v Radmacher* [2011] UKSC 42 [2011] 1 AC 534 at [169] that people should not be obliged to go to the divorce courts to get an enforceable arrangement.

[71] Or para 67 of Sch 5 to the Civil Partnership Act 2004, substituting a reference to civil partners for that of spouses.

From this it will be seen that an agreement entered into after a divorce or nullity decree absolute can come within the statute provided it contains financial arrangements. An agreement containing no such arrangements can come within the statute only if it is a separation agreement made whilst the parties are still married to each other. Unfortunately, a 'separation agreement' is not defined.

Financial arrangements are defined as:

> ... provisions governing the rights and liabilities towards one another when living separately of the parties to a marriage (including a marriage which has been dissolved or annulled) in respect of the making or securing of payments or the disposition or use of any property, including such rights and liabilities with respect to the maintenance or education of any child, whether or not a child of the family.[72]

In *MacLeod v MacLeod*[73] the Privy Council held that agreements within this section are not limited to those where the couple have already separated, but extend to those contemplating future separation (i.e. they would also include Baroness Hale's first type of agreement made while the spouses are living together). However, they considered, obiter, that *pre*-nuptial agreements could not fall within the section. The power to vary an agreement in s 35 is governed by the definition of a maintenance agreement in s 34 which, as can be seen, is one which is made *between the parties to a marriage.*[74] They concluded therefore that s 35 could not apply to a pre-nup and they did not consider it fair to hold an agreement to be *enforceable* if it was not also *variable*.[75] But in *Granatino v Radmacher (Formerly Granatino)*[76] the majority of the Supreme Court ruled that the correct distinction to draw is rather between 'separation' agreements, which they saw as making financial arrangements for the parties' *present* separation, and agreements (pre- or post-nuptial) made in contemplation of a possible future separation. They argued that, at the time the legislation was originally enacted, the latter would have been regarded as contrary to public policy and therefore void anyway. They did not therefore consider that the general contractual enforceability of pre- or post-nuptial agreements should depend upon whether they come within s 34 and nor did they think that the power to vary under s 35 should be a pre-condition of such enforceability. Their interpretation suggests that section 34 (and the following sections 35 and 36) applies only to agreements made when the parties are separating or have separated. With respect, this is not what the section appears to say; one would expect to see a specific reference to a 'separation agreement' in paragraph (a) as well as (b) if the section is meant to be limited to such types of agreement. As their comments were obiter, the matter remains to be resolved.[77]

(b) Void provisions in maintenance agreements

The original ruling in *Hyman v Hyman* meant that the whole agreement would be void, rather than just the provision 'ousting' the court's jurisdiction, which could cause the

---

[72] Matrimonial Causes Act 1973 s 34(2). See to like effect, Sch 5 para 67(2) to the Civil Partnership Act 2004. It has been held that this does not include the making of a lump sum payment: *Furneaux v Furneaux* (1973) 118 Sol Jo 204. Sed quaere? A lump sum is a 'payment'. The point was left open in *Pace v Doe* [1977] Fam 18 at 23, but the decision in *Furneaux* is consistent with the approach taken to the court's powers on variation of a court order under s 31 of the Act: *Boylan v Boylan* [1988] 1 FLR 282.

[73] [2008] UKPC 64 [2010] 1 AC 298 at [37].

[74] See Baroness Hale's explanation in *Granatino v Radmacher (Formerly Granatino)* [2010] UKSC 42 [2011] 1 AC 534 at [157].

[75] *MacLeod* at [35] and see later.   [76] [2010] UKSC 42 [2011] 1 AC 534 at [54]–[56].

[77] In *F v F (Financial Remedies: Premarital Wealth)* [2012] EWHC 438 (Fam) [2012] 2 FLR 1212 at [24]–[26] it was held that a shareholders' agreement between the spouses and trustees of a family trust which gave the wife access to a joint bank account was inconsistent with the idea of them separating and therefore

beneficiary hardship as she could no longer rely on any of its terms. Section 34 accordingly provides that any term in the 'maintenance agreement' purporting to restrict any right to apply to a court for an order containing financial agreements shall be void but that any other financial arrangements in the agreement shall not *thereby* be rendered void or unenforceable and shall be binding on the parties unless void or unenforceable for any other reason. The precise effect of this section is uncertain. Clearly the inclusion of the offensive term does not make the whole agreement illegal: consequently, even if the wife's undertaking not to apply for an order is the sole consideration, the husband can be sued if his covenant to pay her maintenance is made by deed. If it is not made by deed, however, it seems that the husband's promise is still not actionable if the sole consideration is the wife's undertaking not to institute other proceedings for the further reason that, as her promise is void, his promise is supported by no valuable consideration at all.[78]

(c) Alteration of maintenance agreements

Although any sum agreed on by the parties by way of maintenance might well have been reasonable at the time the agreement was made, as Baroness Hale pointed out in *Granatino v Radmacher (Formerly Granatino)*[79] it is obvious that in some cases an adherence to this in the light of subsequent events could work hardship. The husband's earning capacity may be reduced, which will make reasonable a reduction in the sum he has undertaken to pay the wife; alternatively, the wife's illness or increases in the cost of living may well make the sum absurdly small, particularly if it was agreed on some years ago. To overcome difficulties such as these, s 35 of the Matrimonial Causes Act 1973[80] empowers the court to alter any agreement which is a maintenance agreement for the purpose of s 34 provided that it is satisfied either:

(a) that by reason of a change in the circumstances in the light of which any financial arrangements contained in the agreement were made or, as the case may be, financial arrangements were omitted from it (including a change foreseen by the parties when making the agreement), the agreement should be altered so as to make different, or, as the case may be, so as to contain, financial arrangements, or

(b) that the agreement does not contain proper financial arrangements with respect to any child of the family.

In *MacLeod v MacLeod* the Privy Council held that the court should look for a change in the circumstances in the light of which the financial arrangements were made, which would make those arrangements 'manifestly unjust'.[81] In *Radmacher* the Supreme Court did not consider that this test would be appropriate when deciding whether to hold the

---

not a 'maintenance agreement' within s 34. Macur J held that the definition should be construed 'to cover only those agreements made with the expressed or clearly implied purpose of governing the parties' financial affairs including in the event of separation and not those that could do so only if certain terms of the agreement were reconstituted' and so she did not deal with the question whether the agreement, since it had been made before the parties separated, was outside the definition according to the Supreme Court's interpretation. However, she certainly seems to have assumed she was following the Supreme Court: see [21].

[78] *Sutton v Sutton* [1984] Ch 184, where an oral agreement was held void, since there was no other consideration. The Privy Council in *MacLeod v MacLeod* [2008] UKPC 64 [2010] 1 AC 298 and the Supreme Court in *Granatino v Radmacher* [2011] UKSC 42 [2011] 1 AC 534 appear to have assumed that the statutory formulation had resolved the problem of lack of other consideration but did not address the precise point (and the agreement in question in *MacLeod* had been made by deed so the need for consideration did not arise).

[79] [2010] UKSC 42 [2011] 1 AC 534 at [145].

[80] Or Sch 5 paras 69–73 to the Civil Partnership Act 2004.

[81] [2008] UKPC 64 [2010] 1 AC 298 at [41].

parties to a post-nuptial, as distinct from a separation, agreement. They noted that there is a difference between the latter, which is contemplating the parties' requirements in the light of their current as well as future circumstances so that 'it makes sense to look for a significant change of circumstances as the criterion justifying a departure from the agreement', and the former, which might have been made many years earlier so that circumstances are bound to have changed anyway and wider considerations might be relevant.[82] Given that the majority considered that s 34 (and s 35) only applies to 'separation agreements', it would seem that they would therefore regard the 'manifestly unjust' or 'significant' change of circumstances as the correct test to apply to these. Baroness Hale agreed that there is a difference between the two types of agreement—but now considered that the *MacLeod* test would be too strict to apply to s 35 and is unwarranted given that this is not the test set out in the section itself. Once more, then, there is room for doubt as to how the section should be applied. In the absence of legislative reform, it would obviously be sensible for the courts definitively to determine what should be the correct relationship between these sections—and between Baroness Hale's three different types of agreements—and the wider matrimonial jurisdiction.

2. BETWEEN PARENTS

(a) Validity

Binding agreements made between spouses or civil partners can include provision for their children, as we have just seen, but they can also make binding agreements solely for the benefit of their children. Indeed, as early as 1842 it was recognised that an agreement between the mother and father of an illegitimate child that the latter should pay the former maintenance for the child was actionable.[83]

The Children Act 1989 Sch 1 para 10 now defines a 'maintenance agreement' as:

> any agreement in writing made with respect to a child, ... which—
>
> (a) is or was made between the father and mother[84] of the child; and
> (b) contains provision with respect to the making or securing of payments, or the disposition or use of any property, for the maintenance or education of the child, and any such provisions are in this paragraph, and paragraph 11, referred to as "financial arrangements".

By contrast, the Child Support Act 1991 s 9(1) defines a 'maintenance agreement' as 'any agreement for the making, or for securing the making, of periodical payments by way of maintenance, ... to or for the benefit of any child.' It will be seen that the Children Act definition is broader, in that it is not limited to agreements for periodical payments, but could include other forms of disposition, such as capital sums or items of property. On the other hand, the Child Support Act definition is not limited to agreements in writing (although proof of the terms of an oral agreement may be problematic if disputed by one party); nor need it be between the parents of the child (but could presumably be between a mother and the father's own parents, or between a parent and a private foster carer).

---

[82] [2011] UKSC 42 [2011] 1 AC 534 at [65] and [168].
[83] *Jennings v Brown* (1842) 9 M & W 496; cf *Tanner v Tanner* [1975] 3 All ER 776, CA.
[84] Or a second female parent under s 43 or 43 of the Human Fertilisation and Embryology Act 2008: Sch 1 para 10(8).

Section 9(2) of the Child Support Act 1991 provides that maintenance agreements—as defined under that Act—are not restricted by that Act.[85] However, s 9(3) and (4) state that the existence of such an agreement cannot prevent a party, or any other person, from seeking a maintenance calculation under the Act, and any provision in the agreement purporting to restrict the right of any person to apply for a calculation shall be void. Nonetheless, private agreements are now the preferred means of settling the support that a non-resident parent will make for his or her children when parents separate or divorce since they are regarded as more likely to be complied with, and agreements are strongly encouraged as promoting a more harmonious (or at least less acrimonious) relationship between the parents, which is beneficial for the child.[86] Thus, s 9(2A) provides that the Secretary of State may, in order to reduce the need for applications to be made under the Act, take steps to encourage the making and keeping of maintenance agreements, and 'in particular, before accepting an application… invite the applicant to consider… whether it is possible to make such an agreement.'[87] A parent may also apply for an indica-tion of what level of child support would be calculated if there were to be an application under the Child Support Act, so that they can use this in negotiating an agreement.[88] So while the *Hyman* principle of preventing the parties from contracting to rule out recourse to the State remains in the statute, there is a strong conflicting message that the State does not actually wish to see the parties using its machinery for sorting out child maintenance.

(b) Alteration of agreements

Powers to alter maintenance agreements within the Children Act definition are contained in paras 10 and 11 of Schedule 1 to the Children Act 1989. As in the case of agreements for spousal maintenance, the court must be satisfied either:[89]

(a) that, by reason of a change in the circumstances in the light of which any financial arrangements contained in the agreement were made (including a change foreseen by the parties when making the agreement) the agreement should be altered so as to make different financial arrangements; or

(b) that the agreement does not contain proper financial arrangements with respect to the child.

Provided it is satisfied, the court may vary or revoke any financial arrangements when it may appear just to do so.[90] The Supreme Court's apparent view in *Granatino v Radmacher (Formerly Granatino)*,[91] discussed earlier, in relation to *separation* agree-ments, that there should be a significant change of circumstances for the court to be so satisfied appears inapplicable here, given that agreements for child maintenance may last throughout the child's minority and are thus closer to the Supreme Court's concep-tion of post-nuptial agreements instead.

However, s 9(5) of the Child Support Act 1991 restricts the use of these powers if the court would not have jurisdiction to make a maintenance order by virtue of s 8 of that

---

[85] Which does, as we shall see later, The residual role of the courts, p 820, restrict recourse to the *courts* for orders for child maintenance.   [86] See The child support scheme: Mark 3, p 803.

[87] Inserted by the Welfare Reform Act 2012 s 136(1), as amended.

[88] Child Support Act 1991 s 9A, inserted by Welfare Reform Act 2012 s 138.

[89] Sch 1 para 10(3).

[90] Any altered periodical payment provision should not in the first instance extend beyond the child's seventeenth birthday, save where the child is or will be receiving instruction at an educational establishment or undergoing training for a trade or profession, or where there are special circumstances: Sch 1 para 10(5).

[91] [2010] UKSC 42 [2011] 1 AC 534.

Act. That section limits the court's jurisdiction to make an order for *periodical payments* (but not other forms of provision) except where the parties have reached an agreement and are seeking a consent order in its terms. Once the consent order has been made, the court may then exercise its jurisdiction to vary it. The courts have held that this provision can be satisfied where, although the parties disagree as to the quantum of maintenance, they nonetheless agree at the start of the proceedings to a nominal order, and then ask the court to adjudicate on how to vary the amount. It would appear, therefore, that the parties would need at the outset of the proceedings for variation of their maintenance agreement to *agree* to the court making the variation. But if the payer were reluctant to do so, then the applicant would be forced instead to use the child support jurisdiction.[92]

D. THE COURTS' JURISDICTION TO MAKE ORDERS FOR FINANCIAL SUPPORT

1. ORDERS FOR SPOUSES OR CIVIL PARTNERS

(a) Introduction

Until 1878 only the ecclesiastical courts or their successors, the Divorce Court and the High Court, could make orders for maintenance. The Matrimonial Causes Act 1878 enabled a criminal court, before which a married man had been convicted of an aggravated assault upon his wife, to make an order that she should no longer be bound to cohabit with him if it felt that her future safety was in peril.[93] The court could also order a husband to pay maintenance to a wife in whose favour such a separation order was made, and vest in her the legal custody of any children of the marriage under the age of 10. The powers of the magistrates' courts were gradually extended, although limits on the amount of maintenance which could be ordered to be paid each week remained until 1968 (£7.50 for a spouse and £3.50 for a child). After the divorce law was reformed in 1970, removing the emphasis upon marital misconduct and extending the court's powers to deal with the spouses' finances and property, the jurisdiction to order maintenance was also reformed to bring it into line with that approach.[94]

There are two statutes providing powers to the courts to order financial support outside of divorce in respect of spouses: the Domestic Proceedings and Magistrates' Courts Act 1978,[95] and the Matrimonial Causes Act 1973 s 27.[96] There is equivalent provision for civil partners made under s 72 and Sch 6, and Sch 5 Part 9, to the Civil Partnership Act 2004.

The courts' jurisdiction to make such orders has declined in popularity and no separate statistics are now published on their use. This decline is probably due to four main reasons. First, the availability of social security means that women who are unable to work due to child care responsibilities may be supported by the state and need not seek maintenance from their spouse or partner when the marriage breaks down. In many ways the

---

[92] See *V v V (Child Maintenance)* [2001] 2 FLR 799.

[93] See AJ Hammerton *Cruelty and Companionship: Conflict in Nineteenth-Century Married Life* (1992) pp 52–67.

[94] See Law Com No 77, *Report on Matrimonial Proceedings in Magistrates' Courts* and the Domestic Proceedings and Magistrates' Courts Act 1978.

[95] Confined to magistrates, who are now part of the Family Court under the Crime and Courts Act 2013 s 17 and Sch 10.

[96] Which applies to the county or High Court as now incorporated into the Family Court under the Crime and Courts Act 2013 s 17 and Sch 10.

job centre has become the 'marital casualty clearing station' which the Law Commission had considered the function of the magistrates' courts when reviewing their jurisdiction in 1976.[97] Indeed, it was this preference for state support, with the consequent drain on public resources, which, as we will see, lay, in part, behind the enactment of the Child Support Act 1991.[98] Secondly, with the liberalisation of divorce by the Divorce Reform Act 1969, couples found that their marriages could be dissolved relatively quickly and easily,[99] and there was a less pressing need to seek a maintenance order in the meantime. Where such maintenance was required, it could be sought, once a petition had been filed for a divorce, via provision under the Matrimonial Causes Act 1973[100] or by agreement. Thirdly, as more women have remained in or returned to the work place notwithstanding marriage and having children, they have become more likely to favour a clean break from their husbands, involving no ongoing financial support for themselves and, provided that their children's needs are met, they may be reluctant to seek orders for their own benefit. Finally, a further reason for reluctance to resort to law may have been the unpopularity of the magistrates' court as a forum for hearing matrimonial disputes because of its association with criminal matters. The provisions have become, in Wilson LJ's words, 'dead letters',[101] so only a brief outline is given of them here.

(b) Orders under the Domestic Proceedings and Magistrates' Courts Act 1978

Orders for financial provision

Application for financial provision may be made in one of three different sets of circumstances.[102] First, there is what one might term the 'normal' application, when the applicant must establish one of the grounds set out in s 1 of the Act. Secondly, if the spouses have agreed what financial provision should be made, either may apply to have the terms of the agreement embodied in a court order. Thirdly, the court may make an order if the spouses are living apart by agreement and the respondent has been making periodical payments to the applicant.

Applications under s 1

Either party to a marriage may apply for an order on the ground that the respondent spouse has failed to provide reasonable maintenance for the applicant,[103] or has behaved in such a way that the applicant cannot reasonably be expected to live with the respondent, or has deserted the applicant. The latter two grounds are interpreted in the same way as on divorce, but there is no need to establish irretrievable breakdown, nor any minimum period of desertion. The ground must exist when the application is made and also at the time of adjudication.

---

[97] Law Com No 77, *Report on Matrimonial Proceedings in Magistrates' Courts* para 2.4.

[98] See Maintenance under the Child Support Act 1991, Background, p 800.

[99] But see G Davis et al *Simple Quarrels* (1994) who demonstrate that this speed and ease are only relative; negotiations concerning divorce settlements can still take a number of years to conclude.

[100] Matrimonial Causes Act 1973 s 22, see Ch 22, Maintenance pending suit and Legal Services Orders, p 836.   [101] *Granatino v Radmacher* [2009] EWCA Civ 649 [2009] 2 FLR 1181 at [134].

[102] For the background to the legislation see generally O McGregor, L Blom-Cooper and C Gibson *Separated Spouses; Report of the Committee on One-Parent Families*, Cmnd 5629, passim; Law Com No 77, *Matrimonial Proceedings in Magistrates' Courts*, Pt II. The equivalent provisions for civil partners are contained in Sch 6 to the Civil Partnership Act 2004. The magistrates' jurisdiction is now part of the Family Court under the Crime and Courts Act 2013 s 17 and Sch 10.

[103] There is also a ground relating to failure to provide reasonable maintenance for any child of the family: s 1(b). See further Obtaining financial relief for children, Matrimonial and civil partnership jurisdictions, pp 791 *et seq*.

Whether the respondent has provided reasonable maintenance for the applicant or any child of the family is clearly a question of fact. To answer it the court must ask itself a hypothetical question: assuming that a ground for applying for an order existed, what order should we make? If the provision in fact being made by the respondent is lower—or at least significantly lower—than this, then he must be failing to provide reasonable maintenance. The word 'failure' implies culpability only insofar as it suggests that the respondent has the means to make the provision; and as his resources must be taken into account in deciding what sum to order, the court must be satisfied that he has the capacity to make the payments.

When hearing an application under s 1, the court is required to consider whether there is any possibility of a reconciliation between the parties and if, either then or later, it appears that there is a reasonable possibility, it may adjourn the proceedings and, if it sees fit, request a CAFCASS officer or other person to attempt to effect one.[104]

Orders that may be made

The court may order the respondent to do one or more of the following:[105]

(a) to make periodical payments to the applicant;[106]

(b) to pay a lump sum not exceeding £1,000 for the applicant.[107]

It may allow the respondent to pay a lump sum or may order him to pay it by instalments.[108] The order may be made for a fixed term, for example pending the applicant's return to employment.[109] The order will terminate on the remarriage or formation of a civil partnership (but not divorce)[110] or death of the recipient or on the death of the person liable to make the payments.[111]

Consent orders

The Family Court is able to make a consent order without the applicant having to establish any ground. Under s 6, upon either party's application and provided the court is satisfied that either the applicant or the respondent has agreed to make the financial provision[112] specified in the application, it may make an order giving effect to the agreement.[113] The order may contain precisely the same terms as an order made following an application under s 1 except that, as the respondent has agreed to it, a lump sum may be for *any amount* and is not limited to £1,000. The court may not make the order proposed if

---

[104] Domestic Proceedings and Magistrates' Courts Act 1978 s 26, as amended.

[105] Domestic Proceedings and Magistrates' Courts Act 1978 s 2.

[106] Such orders may subsequently be varied or revoked on the application of either spouse: s 20.

[107] A lump sum order may not be varied, although if it is payable by instalments, the amount of these, and the dates of their payment, may be varied: s 22. For orders for children of the family, see Obtaining financial relief for children, Matrimonial and civil partnership jurisdictions, p 791.

[108] Magistrates' Courts Act 1980 s 75.

[109] Domestic Proceedings and Magistrates' Courts Act 1978 s 2(1)(a) and (c), s 4(1) and s 5(2). Interim orders may also be made pending a final order or dismissal of the application: s 19.

[110] Section 4(2) as amended by Civil Partnership Act 2004 Sch 27 para 57; Civil Partnership Act Sch 6 para 26(2).

[111] Section 4(1); Civil Partnership Act Sch 6 para 26(1)(b). An order ceases to have effect if the parties continue, or resume, living together for a continuous period exceeding six months: s 25(1), s 88(2); Civil Partnership Act Sch 6 para 29(2).   [112] Periodical payments or lump sum payments: s 6(2).

[113] If proceedings are begun for an order under s 2 and the respondent then agrees to the order, the applicant may apply for an order under s 6: s 6(4).

COURTS' JURISDICTION TO MAKE ORDERS

it considers that it would be contrary to the interests of justice to do so.[114] This seems most likely to occur if the amount specified in the application looks too low, or if it appears that undue pressure has been put on either party. In such cases, however, it is open to the parties to come forward with a fresh agreement. Alternatively, the court itself might take the initiative and suggest what order would be appropriate: if the parties both agree, this may be embodied in an order.[115]

Orders following separation

In cases where the parties have separated and one party is actually providing the other with reasonable maintenance, the recipient may be concerned that, without the security of an order, he may choose to stop at any time. To secure her position, she may apply to the court under s 7 for an order embodying the de facto terms of the arrangement.[116] The parties must have lived apart, without either being in desertion, for a continuous period exceeding three months, and one must have been making periodical payments for the benefit of the other or a child of the family.[117] 'Living apart' is not defined, but it presumably bears the same meaning as under the law of divorce.[118] If the court considers that the sums paid fail to provide reasonable maintenance for the applicant, the ground under s 1 must necessarily be made out; the court may therefore treat the application as though made under that section and will then have full powers to make such orders for periodical payments and lump sum payments as it thinks fit.[119]

Assessment

The Act sets out a checklist of the matters which a magistrates' court is to take into account when making an order. The court must 'have regard to all the circumstances of the case, first consideration being given to the welfare while a minor of any child of the family who has not attained the age of 18'.[120] The other factors to be considered are, with minor exceptions,[121] identical to those on divorce. As the law has been much more fully worked out in connection with divorce, detailed examination of these matters will be deferred until Chapter 23, but some general principles and certain points of dissimilarity should be mentioned here.

Absence of power to adjust property rights

The main difference between the powers under this Act and those applying on divorce is that magistrates cannot make property adjustment orders. This is because the making of property adjustment orders is inconsistent with the principle that magistrates should regulate the parties' financial position during a period of marital breakdown which is not necessarily permanent or irretrievable. It is to be assumed that whichever spouse or civil partner is in the family home will stay there for the time being: if either of them wishes to bring about a change, he or she must invoke the jurisdiction of the courts in some other way.

---

[114] Section 6(1)(b).   [115] Section 6(5).

[116] Or Civil Partnership Act 2004 Sch 6 Part 3.

[117] Section 7(1); Civil Partnership Act 2004 Sch 6 para 15(1). The payments need not have been made to the applicant. Hence, for example, the payment of rent could amount to periodical payments for this purpose.

[118] Under which spouses living under the same roof may be regarded as living apart provided that they are living in two separate households: *Mouncer v Mouncer* [1972] 1 All ER 289; see Ch 7, Two years separation and the respondent's consent to the decree, p 220.

[119] Section 7(4); Civil Partnership Act 2004 Sch 6 para 18.

[120] Section 3(1): Civil Partnership Act 2004 Sch 6 para 3.

[121] Para (c) of s 25(1) of the Matrimonial Causes Act 1973 refers to 'the standard of living enjoyed by the family before the breakdown of the marriage'. The divorce court is additionally required to consider the loss, inter alia, of pension rights. See Ch 23, Loss of benefit, p 903.

No requirement to consider 'self-sufficiency'

Another important difference between the magistrates' powers and those applicable on divorce is that the former are not directed to consider whether the parties could become self-sufficient. Magistrates have no powers to make a 'clean break' order settling financial liability in a once-and-for-all order.

Remarriage and cohabitation

The payer's remarriage will not normally be relevant in magistrates' proceedings, but it may become so if the order continues in force after a later divorce. In this case it may be proper to reduce the order because of the payer's increased financial responsibilities; the same result will follow if he lives with another woman, particularly if they have children whom he has to support.[122] Likewise, the wife's living with another man may lead the court make a reduced order, or none at all, not because she is committing adultery, but because the man will be, or may be expected to be, supporting her.

(c) Orders for financial provision under s 27 of the Matrimonial Causes Act 1973

Section 27 of the Matrimonial Causes Act 1973 provides that either party to a marriage may apply to the court[123] for an order on the ground that the other has failed to provide reasonable maintenance for the applicant.[124]

The ground upon which an application may be made is the same as the first on which a spouse may apply for an order under the Domestic Proceedings and Magistrates' Courts Act 1978 s 1, ie that the respondent has failed to provide reasonable maintenance for the applicant. However, in determining whether this ground is made out and, if so, what order to make, the court is also required to take into account the matters set out in s 25(2) of the Matrimonial Causes Act 1973.[125] The welfare of a child of the family is to be regarded as the court's first consideration only where an application is made in respect of such a child, and not where maintenance for the applicant alone is sought, but it is doubtful whether this change of emphasis makes any difference in practice.

The court may make an interim order for periodical payments to the applicant if it appears that the latter is in immediate need of financial assistance.[126] If the ground is made out, the court may make one or more financial provision orders[127] against the respondent.

The question of assessment of orders is essentially the same as that of orders made under the 1978 Act, except that periodical payments may be secured and there is an unlimited power to order lump sum payments. Both these matters will be dealt with more fully when we consider financial provision after divorce;[128] in the case of lump sum payments, however, it should be borne in mind that the court has no power to make property adjustment orders under s 27, and consequently a lump sum order should not be used as a

---

[122] See *Delaney v Delaney* [1990] 2 FLR 457, CA.

[123] The divorce court, now part of the Family Court.

[124] There is equivalent provision for civil partners in Sch 5 Part 9 to the Civil Partnership Act 2004.

[125] Section 27(3). See Ch 23, Factors to be taken into account when assessing what orders should be made for a spouse, pp 882–903. These matters, which apply also in relation to divorce and dissolution of civil partnerships, are to be read as if they referred to a failure to provide reasonable maintenance instead of the breakdown of the marriage or civil partnership: s 27(3B): Civil Partnership Act 2004 Sch 5 para 43(4).

[126] Section 27(5); Civil Partnership Act 2004 Sch 5 para 40.

[127] Section 27(6); Civil Partnership Act 2004 Sch 5 para 41. Financial provision orders are orders for periodical payments (secured or unsecured) or for lump sums. A lump sum may be made payable in instalments and the instalments may be secured.

[128] See Ch 22, Periodical payments, Orders in favour of spouses, p 839 and Lump sum payments p 840.

means of circumventing this restriction. Section 27(7)[129] specifically provides that a lump sum may be ordered to enable the applicant to meet any liabilities or expenses already incurred in maintaining herself (or himself); in addition, it may properly be ordered (as on divorce) whenever a capital sum is more valuable to the applicant than periodical payments.[130] Orders are payable and enforceable in the same way as orders for periodical payments on divorce.[131]

2. OBTAINING FINANCIAL RELIEF FOR CHILDREN

(a) Matrimonial and civil partnership jurisdictions

Where the Child Support Act does not apply,[132] it will be possible to utilise any of the jurisdictions discussed so far to obtain an order for a child, as orders under the Domestic Proceedings and Magistrates' Courts Act 1978, the Matrimonial Causes Act 1973 and the Civil Partnership Act 2004 may be made payable both to the applicant and to, or for the benefit of, any 'child of the family'. The court may make an order for financial provision for a child whether or not it makes any other order relating to the child.

Factors to be considered

In deciding what, if any, orders should be made in addition to those considerations applicable to orders for spouses, the court must also have regard to:

(a) the financial needs of the child;

(b) the income, earning capacity (if any), property and other financial resources of the child;

(c) any physical or mental disability of the child;

(d) the standard of living enjoyed by the family before the occurrence of the conduct which is alleged as the ground of the application (or before the parties to the marriage lived apart); and

(e) the manner in which the child was being and in which the parties expected him to be educated or trained.[133]

We have already considered the meaning of 'child of the family',[134] but it should be emphasised that just because a child is found to be a child of the family does not mean that the respondent will be ordered to make financial provision for him.[135] When deciding whether to make an order against a party to the marriage in favour of a child who is not his own natural or adopted child and, if so, how much to award, the court must further have regard:[136]

(a) to whether he has assumed any responsibility for the child's maintenance and, if he did, to the extent to which, and the basis on which, he assumed that responsibility and to the length of time during which he disregarded that responsibility;

---

[129] Civil Partnership Act 2004 Sch 5 para 42(1). [130] See Ch 22, Lump sum payments, p 840.
[131] See Ch 23, Enforcement of orders, p 916. [132] See later, The residual role of the courts, p 820.
[133] Domestic Proceedings and Magistrates' Courts Act 1978 s 3(4), s 7(5). A court hearing an application under s 27 of the Matrimonial Causes Act must consider a similar list of factors: s 27(3A) and s 25(3).
[134] Ch 9, The meaning of 'child of the family', p 296.
[135] Compare liability under the Child Support Act 1991 (discussed later, Qualifying child, p 806), which depends upon legal parenthood.
[136] Domestic Proceedings and Magistrates' Courts Act 1978 s 3(3), s 7(5); Matrimonial Causes Act 1973 ss 27(3A), s 25(4).

(b) to whether in assuming and discharging that responsibility he did so knowing that the child was not his own child; and

(c) to the liability of any other person to maintain the child.

Whether a party assumed responsibility for a child must be judged objectively, and, in the absence of a clear contrary indication, the payment of the expenses of a family unit including the child implies an assumption of responsibility, even though other resources may be available for his maintenance.[137] In para (a), the word 'extent' refers to the amount of the spouse's contribution in contradistinction to the length of time during which he made it.[138] The reference in para (c) to the liability of any other person to maintain the child covers any liability enforceable at law, and thus embraces the potential liability of a parent or of a party to another marriage who has treated the child as a child of the family.[139] It will be seen that the need to take all these matters into account means that the court might well conclude, for example, that no order should be made against a husband who had married the wife in the mistaken belief that he was the father of her child, or who had made it clear at the time of the marriage that he was undertaking no financial responsibility for her children by a previous marriage if their own father was quite capable of providing for them.[140]

In determining what is reasonable maintenance for a child, as Bagnall J said in a comment approved by the Court of Appeal in *Lilford v Glynn*:[141]

> In the vast majority of cases the financial position of a child of a subsisting marriage is simply to be afforded shelter, food and education, according to the means of his parents.

Courts are encouraged to have regard to the level of support which would be assessed under the Child Support Act in deciding on an appropriate amount of maintenance for the child, including a nil amount.[142] Lump sum orders may be useful to meet particular expenses for a child, for example, to buy a uniform or other clothes for a new school, or to pay for fees and other incidental expenses on starting a course of training.

Duration of orders

Since some children will start earning when they reach the upper limit of the compulsory school age, no order for periodical payments is to extend in the first instance beyond the date of the child's birthday next following his attaining that age, unless the court thinks it right to specify a later date (as it obviously must if he is already older). No order may be made at all, however, if the child is over the age of 18, and an existing order may not continue after his eighteenth birthday. To both limbs of this rule there are two exceptions: there is no age limit on the making or continuation of orders so long as the child is (or, if an order were made, would be) receiving instruction at an educational establishment or undergoing training for a trade, profession or vocation (whether or not he is also gainfully employed) or, in any event, if there are special circumstances justifying this.[143]

---

[137] *Snow v Snow* [1972] Fam 74 at 111–12, CA.

[138] *Roberts v Roberts* [1962] P 212.   [139] *Snow v Snow* at 112.

[140] See *Bowlas v Bowlas* [1965] P 450, CA.

[141] [1979] 1 All ER 441 at 447, referring to *Harnett v Harnett* [1973] Fam 156 at 161. See also *Kiely v Kiely* [1988] 1 FLR 248.

[142] *E v C (Child Maintenance)* [1996] 1 FLR 472.

[143] Domestic Proceedings and Magistrates' Courts Act 1978 s 5(1)–(3), s 6(7) and s 7(7); Matrimonial Causes Act 1973 s 29; *G v G (Periodical Payments: Jurisdiction)* [1997] 1 FLR 368, CA; *B v B (Adult Student: Liability to Support)* [1998] 1 FLR 373, CA.

Periodical payments could therefore continue indefinitely, if, for example, the child were incapable of earning his own living owing to some physical or mental disability. The order terminates on the death of the child or of the person liable to make the payments.[144]

Variation on the child's application

The child himself may apply for a variation if he has attained the age of 16. He may also, once he has attained the age of 16 but before he reaches 18, apply for an order to be revived.[145] He may well wish to take advantage of this provision if he decides to undergo further education or training at some stage after leaving school and beginning to earn his own living.

In practice, very few such applications are brought under these jurisdictions, since arrangements for the child will usually be made under the divorce (or dissolution of civil partnership) jurisdiction discussed in Chapter 22, or the Child Support Act. Of greater practical importance is the following jurisdiction, Sch 1 to the Children Act 1989.

(b) Proceedings under Schedule 1 to the Children Act 1989

The courts are empowered by the Children Act 1989 s 15 and Sch 1 to make financial provision solely for the benefit of children in circumstances where the Child Support Act does not apply. The 1989 Act also permits children over the age of 18 to seek financial orders against their parents in certain circumstances. Usually, this jurisdiction is invoked when the parents have not been married to each other, although it is in fact available to married parents (or civil partners). As just noted, parents who have been married to each other would usually use the divorce jurisdiction and/or Child Support Act. However, this is not invariably the case: for example, in *Re S (Child: Financial Provision)*[146] the parents divorced abroad and the mother remarried soon after, and was thus unable to seek an order under the divorce jurisdiction[147] but she was held entitled to apply for an order under Sch 1.

When orders may be made

The court may make financial provision for children either upon application[148] or upon its own motion when making, varying or discharging a child arrangements or special guardianship order,[149] or where the child is a ward of court.[150]

Who can apply

Applications may be made by parents, guardians, special guardians and any person in whose favour a child arrangements order is in force.[151] For these purposes 'parents'

---

[144] Domestic Proceedings and Magistrates' Courts Act 1978 s 5(4), s 6(7) and s 7(7); the order ceases to have effect once the spouses have resumed living together for six months: s 25(1), but where payments are ordered to be made *to the child himself*, neither the continuation nor the resumption of cohabitation by the spouses will have any effect on the order unless the court otherwise directs: s 25(2); Matrimonial Causes Act 1973 s 29(4); Civil Partnership Act 2004 Sch 5 para 49(6); Sch 6 para 27(6).

[145] Domestic Proceedings and Magistrates' Courts Act 1978 s 20(12)(b), s 20A(1); Matrimonial Causes Act 1973 s 27(6B); Civil Partnership Act 2004 Sch 5 para 55; Sch 6 para 39(b).

[146] [2004] EWCA Civ 1685 [2005] 2 FLR 94. Discussed further Who can apply, p 794. See also *B v B (Transfer of Tenancy)* [1994] Fam Law 250.

[147] See further Ch 23, Financial relief after foreign divorce, dissolution, annulment or legal separation, pp 920–925 for jurisdiction to make financial orders after an overseas divorce.

[148] Children Act 1989 Sch 1, para 1(1).   [149] Sch 1 para 1(6) as amended.

[150] Sch 1 para 1(7). Wardship is discussed in Ch 20, Wardship, p 742.

[151] Previously a residence order: Sch 1, para 1(1) as amended.

includes both married and unmarried parents (including the unmarried father) and second female parent under the Human Fertilisation and Embryology Act 2008 and any party to a marriage (whether or not subsisting), or any civil partner in a civil partnership (whether or not subsisting) in relation to whom the child concerned is a child of the family, eg a step-parent.[152] The parent need not be the person caring for the child: in *Re S (Child: Financial Provision)*[153] the child had been wrongfully retained in the Sudan after a contact visit, and the mother was granted an order to cover the costs of travelling to the Sudan and pursuing legal proceedings to recover the child.

Although guardians are entitled to apply, they are unlikely to do so very often, since they can only take office during the lifetime of the surviving spouse when the deceased appointing parent had a residence order or child arrangements order in his favour at the time of death.[154]

Against whom orders can be made

Orders may be made against either or both parents of the child.

As with applicants, 'parents' for these purposes includes unmarried fathers, second female parents and step-parents of 'children of the family'. However, only those who have been married to, or in a civil partnership with, a parent of the child are within the definition of step-parent in Sch 1 para 16(2).[155]

Although there is power to order step-parents of 'children of the family' to make financial provision, the Law Commission envisaged that applications are more likely to be made *by* them.[156] No orders may be made against a guardian or special guardian. This is in line with the general policy of not making such persons liable to make financial provision or property transfers in the same way as a parent.[157] Similarly, no orders can be made against those, other than parents, who have child arrangements orders in their favour.[158]

Powers

All levels of the Family Court may order the making of unsecured periodical payments either to the applicant for the benefit of the child or to the child himself, or partly to both, for such term as may be specified in the order.[159] Similarly, they can order lump sum payments,[160] although in the case of magistrates' orders there is a prescribed maximum limit of £1,000 or such larger amount as the Secretary of State shall fix.[161] Lump sum orders may provide for payment to be made by instalments,[162] and more than one such order may be made.[163] An order for periodical payments or lump sums may be made,

---

[152] Sch 1 para 16(2) as amended. See also *Re A (Child of the Family)* [1998] 1 FLR 347 (grandfather who had brought up grandchild as part of his own family).   [153] [2004] EWCA Civ 1685 [2005] 2 FLR 94.

[154] See Ch 8, Guardianship, When the appointment takes effect, p 288.

[155] Hence, a non-married step-parent cannot apply for, or be required to meet, an order under the Schedule: *J v J (A Minor: Property Transfer)* [1993] 2 FLR 56. The Supreme Court of Canada has held that a married step-parent 'standing in the place of a parent' ie performing the social role of parent, may be obliged to support the child: *Chartier v Chartier* [1999] 1 SCR 242.

[156] Law Com No 172, para 4.63.   [157] Law Com No 172, para 2.25.

[158] See *S v X and X (Interveners)* [1990] 2 FLR 187 (third party interveners who had been granted custody were held not liable to maintain the child). Sch 1 para 15 provides that a local authority may make contributions to a person (other than a parent or step-parent of the child) with a child arrangements (formerly residence) order, towards the cost of the accommodation and maintenance of the child, but it is unclear how this could be enforced: see *Re K and A (Local Authority: Child Maintenance)* [1995] 1 FLR 688.

[159] Sch 1 para 1(1)(a), (b) and 1(2)(a).   [160] Sch 1 para 1(1)(a), (b) and 1(2)(c).

[161] Sch 1 para 5(2).   [162] Sch 1 para 5(5).

[163] Sch 1 para 1(5)(a): see *H v C* [2009] 2 FLR 1540.

notwithstanding that the child is living outside England and Wales.[164] 'Benefit' has a wide meaning, and the benefit for the child need not be direct: orders to cover the applicant's legal expenses in the Sch 1 proceedings themselves may be awarded, if the proceedings are to benefit the child and not just to 'satisfy the applicant's taste for litigation'.[165] In *Re S (Child: Financial Provision)*,[166] noted earlier, it was held that the payments to enable the mother to travel to the Sudan and take proceedings there for the return of the child to her care, were capable of being for the child's benefit. By contrast, in *N v C (Financial Provision: Schedule 1 Claims Dismissed)*[167] the parents had informally agreed that the mother and child could occupy a property owned by the father until the child reached 18 or completed her secondary education. The parents fell out and the child went to live with her father when she was 12. The mother sought an order, inter alia, allowing her to remain in the property until their daughter was 18, but the court rejected her claim as focused on her own, rather than the child's benefit.

Judges of the High Court and Family Court may additionally order the making of secured periodical payments, settlements of property and property transfers.[168] A similarly broad view of 'benefit' for the child to that taken in *Re S* was applied in relation to a transfer of property in *K v K (Minors: Property Transfer)*.[169] There, it was held that the words 'the benefit of the child' are not confined to *financial* benefit for the child. Accordingly, it was held that there was power to order an unmarried father to transfer to the mother for the benefit of the children his interest in the family home, namely a joint council tenancy.

In recommending the power to order transfers of property, the Law Commission thought[170] that the provisions could be useful to enable the court to make a once-and-for-all settlement in cases where the father did not intend to have anything to do with the child (although this stance looks outmoded given the importance now attached to joint parenting and the value to the child of having a meaningful relationship with the non-resident parent). They noted that few commentators thought it a valid objection that a transfer was tantamount to giving the unmarried mother a right to support for her own benefit.[171] However, they did not envisage the power being used at all frequently, relying on the practice of the divorce courts to lean against making such orders, and especially the reluctance to award a child provision beyond dependency.[172] That practice has indeed been followed by courts when considering their powers under this jurisdiction. They prefer to make a limited transfer (not dissimilar to *Mesher* orders in the divorce context)[173] until the child has grown up.[174]

---

[164] Sch 1 para 14. The paragraph does not preclude an application for provision by the parent living within the jurisdiction where the other parent has taken the child abroad: *Re S (Child: Financial Provision)* [2004] EWCA Civ 1685 [2005] 2 FLR 94 at [21].

[165] *M-T v T* [2006] EWHC 2494 (Fam) [2007] 2 FLR 925 at [18] per Charles J. For further discussion of such orders, see Ch 22, Orders for payment in respect of legal services, p 838.

[166] [2004] EWCA Civ 1685 [2005] 2 FLR 94.   [167] [2013] EWHC 399 (Fam) [2013] Fam Law 799.

[168] Sch 1 paras 1(1)(a) and respectively 1(2)(b), (d) and (e). Settlements and transfers may only be made once: Sch 1 para 1(5)(b). A lump sum may not be ordered where it is intended as a device akin to a settlement order as a means of avoiding the effect of sub-para (5): *Phillips v Peace* [2004] EWHC 3180 (Fam) [2005] 2 FLR 1212.

[169] [1992] 2 All ER 727, CA. This case was brought under the Guardianship of Minors Act 1971, but it was accepted (at 733 per Nourse LJ) that the provisions of the Children Act 1989 were not materially different in this respect.

[170] Law Com No 118, para 6.6.   [171] Law Com No 118, para 6.7.

[172] See *Chamberlain v Chamberlain* [1974] 1 All ER 33, CA at 38 per Scarman LJ and *Draskovic v Draskovic* (1980) 11 Fam Law 87.   [173] See Ch 23, *Mesher* orders, p 905.

[174] See *T v S (Financial Provision for Children)* [1994] 2 FLR 883, *A v A (A Minor: Financial Provision)* [1994] 1 FLR 657, discussed later, Exercising the powers, p 798; but cf *Pearson v Franklin* [1994] 1 WLR 370

Exercising the powers

In assessing what, if any, order to make and what amount will be appropriate, the court is directed[175] to have regard to all the circumstances of the case including the following matters:

(a) The income, earning capacity, property and other financial resources which [any parent, the applicant and any other person in whose favour the court proposes to make the order][176] has or is likely to have in the foreseeable future.

(b) The financial needs, obligations and responsibilities which [any parent, the applicant and any other person in whose favour the court proposes to make the order] has or is likely to have in the foreseeable future.

(c) The financial needs of the child.

(d) The income, earning capacity (if any), property and other financial resources of the child.

(e) Any physical or mental disability of the child.

(f) The manner in which the child was being, or was expected to be, educated or trained.

These guidelines are virtually the same as under the other jurisdictions save that the court is not specifically enjoined to have regard to the family's standard of living, and no weighting of the child's welfare is specified.[177] The child's welfare is, however, one of the relevant circumstances to be taken into account[178] and has been said to be a constant influence on the discretionary outcome of any claim.[179] It has also been held that courts should have information as to the level of any child support assessment that might otherwise be made, so that they can take this into account when exercising their discretion.[180]

The absence of an express direction concerning standard of living leaves open the question of whose standard of living an order should reflect. This is likely to be a particularly difficult issue where an unmarried couple have never lived together. Where, for example, the mother is a woman who is never likely to enjoy a high income and the father earns a high salary, it is tempting to say that the child (for whose benefit the order is being made) ought not to be prejudiced by his mother's position, and this is the view of the courts.[181] In *J v C (Child: Financial Provision)*,[182] for example, where the father won the lottery after the parents' relationship (which had not included cohabitation) had ended, Hale J held that

at 250B–C per Nourse LJ. But where the parents were joints owners of the property while they were cohabiting, an order may provide that the mother is to retain a share in the property after the child's minority: *Re B (Child: Property Transfer)* 1999] 2 FLR 418, CA. See E Cooke, 'Children and Real Property—Trusts, Interests and Considerations' [1998] Fam Law 349, who notes also that it is appropriate in the case of jointly owned property to bring proceedings under both this Act and the Trusts of Land and Appointment of Trustees Act 1996. In *W v W (Joinder of Trusts of Land Act and Children Act Applications)* [2003] EWCA Civ 924 [2004] 2 FLR 321, the Court of Appeal held that such joint applications *should* be made, and must be heard together, the Sch 1 application having leading status since the powers under this jurisdiction are more extensive.

[175] Sch 1 para 4(1).   [176] Sch 1 para 4(4).

[177] The child's welfare is not the paramount consideration, because s 105(1) expressly excludes maintenance from the definition of upbringing, and unlike the other Acts there is no direction in Sch 1 to treat the child's welfare as the first consideration. See also *K v H (Child Maintenance)* [1993] 2 FLR 61 at 64G.

[178] *J v C (Child: Financial Provision)* [1999] 1 FLR 152.

[179] *Re P (Child: Financial Provision)* [2003] EWCA Civ 837 [2003] 2 FLR 865.

[180] *E v C (Child Maintenance)* [1996] 1 FLR 472.

[181] See also *H v P (Illegitimate Child: Capital Provision)* [1993] Fam Law 515; *A v A (A Minor: Financial Provision)* [1994] 1 FLR 657—*Haroutunian v Jennings* (1980) 1 FLR 62, followed.

[182] [1999] 1 FLR 152.

since parents are responsible for the children throughout their dependency, the fact that the father had become wealthy after the break-up did not affect the child's entitlement to be brought up in circumstances bearing some relationship with his current resources and standard of living. She also noted that the nature and duration of the parents' relationship were not matters of great weight—a child should not suffer because the pregnancy might have been unplanned.

However, if a child is to be brought up in living conditions closer to the payer's standard of living than those of the carer, the latter will clearly benefit, yet if she was not married to the payer, she is owed no duty of support for herself. The courts have been prepared nonetheless to recognise that the child must be looked after and that the child's primary carer must therefore receive an allowance sufficient to enable her to do this at the level appropriate to the other aspects of the standard of living (such as housing, private schooling, private health insurance, etc) that the child is to enjoy. This is well-illustrated by *Re P (Child: Financial Provision)*,[183] the leading authority on this issue. There, the parents had an intermittent sexual relationship resulting in the birth of their child. The father was an immensely wealthy businessman; the mother came from an affluent family background, had no career and was dependent upon her parents for her own standard of living. The Court of Appeal held that in a case where 'one or both of the parents lie somewhere on the spectrum from affluent to fabulously rich'[184] the court should first decide the kind of home that the respondent should provide for the child. Secondly, the judge should assess the cost of furnishing and equipping the home, and the cost of a family car. Then, the court must determine what the carer would reasonably require to fund her expenditure in maintaining the home and its contents and meeting her other living costs, such as travel, holidays, outings, etc. Finally, the court must assess the allowance to be made for the mother's care of the child and in so doing, must:

> recognise the responsibility, and often the sacrifice, of the unmarried parent (generally the mother) who is to be the primary carer for the child, perhaps the exclusive carer if the absent parent disassociates from the child. In order to discharge this responsibility the carer must have control of a budget that reflects her position and the position of the father both social and financial.[185]

Applying this approach, the father was ordered to pay a sum of £1 million to purchase a house, a further sum of £100,000 for furnishings etc and periodical payments[186] of £70,000 per annum. Similarly, in *N v D*[187] the judge considered that a teenage child's financial need for a carer can be just as burdensome as a smaller child and that the carer's allowance was justified where the child was 14. In *PG v TW (No 2) (Child: Financial Provision)* however, the judge considered that the 'device' of a carer's allowance was created in order to enable a mother to obtain a more realistic sum than had previously been the practice of the old magistrates' affiliation jurisdiction. He took the view that the concept is now 'past its utility' and that the 'reality is a single household and my task is to fix an appropriate level of

---

[183] [2003] EWCA Civ 837 [2003] 2 FLR 865 on which see S Gilmore 'Re P (Child) (Financial Provision)—Shoeboxes and comical shopping trips—child support from the affluent to the fabulously rich' [2004] CFLQ 103.   [184] *Re P (Child: Financial Provision)* per Thorpe LJ at para 45.

[185] *Re P (Child: Financial Provision)* per Thorpe LJ at paras 48, 49. Note that the fact that the mother will be working full-time does not mean she should receive a lower allowance as the child's primary carer since it is a matter for her whether she chooses to work: *F v G (Child: Financial Provision)* [2004] EWHC 1848 (Fam) [2005] 1 FLR 261.

[186] These were for 'top up' maintenance over and above a child support assessment.

[187] [2008] 1 FLR 1629.

support within it sufficient to reflect in some degree the father's circumstances without a profit element for mother.'[188] Avoidance of a possible 'profit element' may explain, in part, the court's decision in *DE v AB (Financial Provision for Child)*[189] where the father (who had not wanted the mother to continue the pregnancy after a short relationship) had been ordered to pay a lump sum of £85,000 to help clear the mother's debts on top of a housing fund of £250,000. Both parties wanted to live lavish lifestyles, and the mother was living in a house with a £600,000 mortgage even though she was now unemployed and dependent on social security. Baron J sought to bring home to *both* that they had to make financial sacrifices for the child they had brought into the world and reduced the lump sum to £40,000. Similarly, Charles J has emphasised that the order must be fair to both parties, and consideration must be given to what opportunities the mother has to resume employment and ensure the order is affordable by the payer.[190]

As already noted, the courts regard their function under Sch 1 as being to seek to secure the child's financial position during dependency, and capital windfalls in adulthood are not to be made. Thorpe LJ in *Re P (Child: Financial Provision)* considered that the appropriate legal mechanism to apply, where circumstances permit, to the question of providing the child with a home, is to make a settlement of property order, and '[s]ince the respondent is entitled to the reversion, which in certain circumstances may fall in before the child's majority, the respondent must have some right to veto an unsuitable investment.'[191] In *T v S (Financial Provision for Children)*,[192] it was ordered at first instance that a property be bought from the father's resources, to be held on trust with sale postponed until the youngest of the five children of the parents reached the age of 21 or all had ceased full-time education, the equity then to pass to the children in equal shares. On appeal, Johnson J held that the property should revert to the father.[193] Similarly, in *A v A (A Minor: Financial Provision)*,[194] a house was settled upon trust for A for a term expiring six months after she reached the age of 18 or ceased full-time education.

Since, in most circumstances, the Child Support Act 1991 has removed the jurisdiction to order periodical payments for a child, it has been held that it is not right to award a lump sum to the child instead, as a form of capitalised maintenance. The purpose of a lump sum, according to Johnson J in *Phillips v Peace*[195] should be to meet the child's need with respect to a particular item of capital expenditure, such as to provide a home or, for instance, to modify a home for a child with disabilities. There, the mother, having failed to obtain child support from the apparently wealthy father because he was assessed by the Child Support Agency as having a nil net income, was successful in obtaining an order under Sch 1 to require him to settle property for the mother and child to live in, with reversion to him when the child reached adulthood, and a lump sum for the cost of furnishings for the home.[196] It was later held, in renewed litigation between these parents,[197] that a court may not make more than one settlement or transfer or property order against a parent, and if an order of one type has been made, the court cannot later make an order of the other type. Thus, the mother could not come back to court seeking various orders so that she could now acquire a larger property for her and the child to live in. Nor could

---

[188] [2014] 1 FLR 940 at [104]–[106] and citing *Haroutunian v Jennings* (1980) 1 FLR 62.

[189] [2011] EWHC 3792 (Fam) [2012] 2 FLR 1396.

[190] *FG v MBW (Financial Remedy for Child)* [2011] EWHC 1729 (Fam) [2012] 1 FLR 152.

[191] [2003] EWCA Civ 837 [2003] 2 FLR 865 at [45].   [192] [1994] 2 FLR 883.

[193] At 888–9.   [194] [1994] 1 FLR 657   [195] [1996] 2 FLR 230.

[196] Lump sum orders may also be made to enable the applicant to meet any liabilities or expenses incurred in connection with the birth of the child or in maintaining the child or reasonably incurred before the making of the order: Sch 1 para 5.   [197] *Phillips v Peace* [2004] EWHC 3180 (Fam) [2005] 2 FLR 1212.

she seek an additional lump sum to achieve the same result, even though the legislation permits further lump sum orders to be made,[198] since this would be a device intended to circumvent the prohibition on further property orders.

Where an order against a step-parent of a child of the family is contemplated, then, as under the other jurisdictions, the court is directed[199] to have regard to:

(a) Whether that person had assumed responsibility for the maintenance of the child and, if so, the extent to which and the basis on which he assumed that responsibility and the length of the period during which he met that responsibility.
(b) Whether he did so knowing that the child was not his child.
(c) The liability of any other person to maintain the child.

If the court makes an order against a person who is not the father of the child, it must record in the order that it is made on that basis.[200]

Duration, variation and enforcement

Orders for periodical payments may begin with the date of the making of the application and shall not in the first instance extend beyond the child's seventeenth birthday, and in any event shall not extend beyond his eighteenth birthday, save where the child is receiving instruction at an educational institution or undergoing training for a trade, profession or vocation 'whether or not he also is, will be or would be in gainful employment' or where there are other special circumstances.[201] Such circumstances will usually relate to the child, rather than, for example, the unwillingness of the respondent to provide full details of his present and future finances.[202] Unsecured orders cease upon the death of the payer.[203]

The usual point at which periodical payments cease should also be the point at which a settlement of property should revert to the payer, unless, as with periodical payments, there are special or exceptional circumstances.[204] In *Re N (Payments for Benefit of Child)*[205] Munby J held that the order should usually terminate at age 18 or completion of tertiary education and disagreed with the view of Hale J in *J v C (Child: Financial Provision)*,[206] where she ordered that the reversion was not to take effect until the child reached the age

---

[198] Sch 1 para 1(5)(a). See also *PK v BC (Financial Remedies: Schedule 1)* [2012] EWHC 1382 (Fam) [2012] 2 FLR 1426: parents had been divorced and a clean break settlement had been reached. Mother could not now return to court using Sch 1 to obtain more capital as the settlement had dealt fully with the needs of the child cf *MB v KB* [2007] EWHC 789 (Fam) [2007] 2 FLR 586, where the mother had not compromised her child's future claims through the consent order made on divorce.   [199] Sch 1 para 4(2).

[200] Sch 1 para 4(3).

[201] Sch 1 para 3(1), (2). The jurisdiction exists even though the Child Support Act 1991 provides that a child support calculation (which may also be in force in respect of the same child) cannot continue after the child's nineteenth birthday: *C v F (Disabled Child: Maintenance Order)* [1998] 2 FLR 1, CA. A child over 18 has an independent right to apply for periodical payments or a lump sum from either parent where the child is in education or training, or there are other exceptional circumstances justifying the order, but this will not apply if there was a periodical payments order in force immediately before the applicant reached the age of 16, nor where the parents are living together: Sch 1 para 2.

[202] *T v S (Financial Provision for Children)* [1994] 2 FLR 883 at 889C.

[203] Sch 1 para 3(3). Periodical payment orders may be made notwithstanding that the parents are living together but, as under the 1978 Act, cease to have effect if they continue to live together or subsequently resume living together for a continuous period of more than six months: Sch 1 para 3(4).

[204] *Re N (Payments for Benefit of Child)* [2009] EWHC 11 (Fam) [2009] 1 FLR 1442.

[205] [2009] EWHC 11 (Fam) [2009] 1 FLR 1442.   [206] [1999] 1 FLR 152.

of 21 (or ended her full-time education), on the basis that increasingly, children are not fully independent until at least that age. In Munby J's view:

> it is not enough, as it seems to me, simply to have regard to the fact, if fact it be, that increasing numbers of legally emancipated adults are continuing to live at home rent free with their parents, or that, absent such special circumstances as disability – no doubt widely defined for this purpose – the particular child in question is likely, for whatever reason, to go on living after majority with one or other parent. It is not for the courts to impose legally binding obligations on unwilling parents merely because some parents choose, for whatever reason, voluntarily to assume a financial burden which the law of England does not, generally speaking, impose upon the parent of an adult child with legal capacity.[207]

Nonetheless, he, and other judges, recognised that the completion of university education will justify postponement of the reversion in the same way that it would justify extension of the periodical payments.

There is a general power to vary, suspend, revive and revoke orders for periodical payments, and the court may order the payment of a lump sum on an application for a variation.[208]

E. MAINTENANCE UNDER THE CHILD SUPPORT ACT 1991

1. BACKGROUND

(a) History

During the 1980s increasing attention was paid to the question of whether the existing provision for the assessment and collection of child maintenance through the private law mechanisms discussed so far was satisfactory.[209] The law was amended in 1984 to require that, in deciding what orders for financial provision should be made on divorce or matrimonial breakdown, the court should give first consideration to the welfare whilst a minor of any child of the family,[210] and attempts were made to increase the awareness of the courts as to the real costs of raising children, by circulating them with information on current Income Support rates, and the National Foster Care Association's recommended rate for paying foster-parents. Notwithstanding the availability of such information, the Government found that the 'going rate' for maintenance for one child, of any age up to 18, was £18 per week in 1990,[211] at a time when the National Foster Care Association was recommending a payment of £34.02 per week for a child under the age of five. Such disparity is hardly surprising, given the finding by Eekelaar that, in his survey of 38 registrars (now district judges) handling financial provision, 14 rejected the National Foster Care Association rates as irrelevant because they were regarded as unrealistically high.[212] The Government found that maintenance awards represented only about 11% of total net

---

[207] [2009] EWHC 11 (Fam) [2009] 1 FLR 1442 at [79].

[208] For enforcement of orders, see Family Procedure Rules 2010 Parts 32, 33.

[209] For a lively account of the development and changes to the Scheme, and an analysis of why its history has been so troubled, see A King and I Crewe, *The Blunders of our Governments* (2013) Ch 6 and passim.

[210] See Ch 22, Development of the courts' powers, Subsequent legislative change, p 829.

[211] White Paper, *Children Come First*, Cm 1264, Vol 1, para 1.5.

[212] J Eekelaar *Regulating Divorce* (1991) p 95.

incomes of absent parents on above average incomes.[213] It further found wide variations in the amounts of maintenance being awarded, one example being of two fathers, each earning £150 per week net. One was required to pay £5 per week in maintenance, and the other £50 per week.[214]

Not only was there concern that the amounts of maintenance awarded might be too low, but also that awards were neither being complied with nor adequately enforced.[215] Where maintenance awards are low, there is little incentive to seek their enforcement, especially where the recipient is in any event dependent upon social security benefits. Yet even where what was then the Department of Social Security had the power to seek enforcement against liable relatives, in only 23% of cases was the full amount of arrears of maintenance recovered.[216]

While low levels of maintenance and high proportions of orders in arrears were not particularly new, a further element which led to a determination to alter the law was the impact of these factors on the social security budget. The Government found that about 770,000 single parents, or around two-thirds of the total number at that time, were dependent upon income support in 1989, up from 330,000 such families in 1980.[217] Fewer than one-quarter of these were receiving any maintenance, while the cost to the Treasury of their benefits was £3.2 billion in 1988/89. The cost of supporting lone parent families appeared incompatible with the renewed emphasis upon asserting and strengthening parental responsibility for children under the Children Act 1989.

(b) The child support scheme: Mark 1

The desire to do something more fundamental about parental obligations to support children resulted in the Government's White Paper, *Children Come First*, published in 1990, and the Child Support Act 1991.[218] The scheme set up by the Act drew, to some extent, upon similar initiatives in both the United States of America and Australia.[219] It sought to calibrate the level of child maintenance to be paid by reference to both the income of the non-resident parent and the parent with care, and in the light of social security rates which set a benchmark for the amount of money that the State regards as acceptable for families to live on. The result was a fearsomely complicated formula underpinned by Regulations of mind-numbing detail. The scheme lived down to the expectations of those who criticised it as a futile attempt to re-impose 'traditional family values' on a society which has moved increasingly away from the normative typical family of married parents living with their dependent children. Reception of the new ideology promoted

---

[213]   *Children Come First*, Cm 1264.

[214]   *Children Come First*, Cm 1264.

[215]   S Edwards, C Gould and A Halpern 'The Continuing Saga of Maintaining the Family after Divorce' [1990] Fam Law 31.

[216]   White Paper Vol 2, para 5.1.2, and see C Gibson 'The Future for Maintenance' [1991] CJQ 330.

[217]   White Paper Vol 2 p i.

[218]   See J Eekelaar 'A Child Support Scheme for the United Kingdom' [1991] Fam Law 15; M Maclean 'The Making of the Child Support Act 1991: Policy Making at the Intersection of Law and Social Policy' (1994) 21 *Journal of Law and Society* 505.

[219]   See L Weitzman and M Maclean (eds) *Economic Consequences of Divorce: The International Perspective* Part Four; S Parker 'Child Support in Australia: Children's Rights or Public Interest?' (1991) 5 *International Journal of Law and the Family* 24. For more recent discussions, see B Fehlberg and M Maclean, 'Child support policy in Australia and the United Kingdom: changing priorities but a similar tough deal for children?' (2009) 23(1) Int Jo of Law Policy and the Family 1; and K Cook and K Natalier, 'The gendered framing of Australia's child support reforms' (2013) 27(1) Int Jo of Law Policy and the Family 28, and for comparison of child maintenance systems in the UK, the US, Iceland, Finland and the Netherlands, see C Skinner et al, 'A comparative analysis of child support schemes in five countries' (2012) Eur Jo of Social Security 330.

by the legislation was not helped by unacceptably high levels of error and inefficiency in the Child Support Agency (also known as the CSA). Many parents 'with care' were concerned that the activity of the Child Support Agency had disrupted their relationship with the non-resident parent. Those who claimed out of work benefits were required to authorise the Child Support Agency to pursue the other parent for maintenance under the scheme, at the risk of suffering a significant reduction in the benefits they received if they unreasonably declined to co-operate with the Agency in pursuing him. Where they did co-operate, they found that they saw none of the maintenance collected, as it was off-set pound for pound against their benefits anyway, since a primary motivation for the new scheme was to reduce the amount expended by the State on financial support for families. Children too seem to have suffered from the deterioration in the parents' relationships.[220] But it was the unprecedented level of anger expressed by those, mainly fathers, who were required to meet their obligations under the new scheme[221] that forced Parliamentarians to press, and Government to act, to change the system.[222]

(c) The child support scheme: Mark 2

Throughout the 1990s, a number of changes were made both to the primary legislation and to the horrendously detailed regulations underpinning it in various attempts to ame-liorate the system.[223] Eventually, the incoming Labour Government in 1997 undertook a more thorough-going reform,[224] enacting the Child Support, Pensions and Social Security Act 2000, which substantially amended the 1991 Act. This introduced a fundamentally different way of approaching the calculation of child support (the 'new rules'), seeking greatly to simplify the formula on which this is based. It came into force for new applica-tions on 3 March 2003. However, existing cases remained subject to the 'old rules'[225] until computerisation would permit their transfer onto the new scheme—this has never been fully achieved and there were still nearly 250,000 (out of a total of 1.11 million) such cases in 2013.[226]

The new rules[227] focused on the non-resident parent's net income and deducting a fixed proportion of that, rather than seeking to tailor-make the amount levied by (very complicated) reference to the incomes of both parents and the actual needs of the child. This means that amounts payable may often be token rather than substantively directed towards the support of the child. In 2005, it was reported that the average weekly amount assessed as payable for one qualifying child under the new rules was £24, compared to £40 under the old rules.[228]

[220] G Gillespie 'Child Support—The Hand that Rocks the Cradle' [1996] Fam Law 162.

[221] See R Collier 'The Campaign against the Child Support Act: "errant fathers" and "family men" ' [1994] Fam Law 384; J Wallbank 'The Campaign for Change of the Child Support Act 1991: Reconstructing the "Absent Father" ' (1997) 6 *Social & Legal Studies* 191.

[222] The most thorough-going study of the system was carried out by G Davis et al, *Child Support in Action* (1998).

[223] See White Paper *Improving Child Support* Cm 2745 (1995), the Child Support Act 1995 and the last edition of this work especially pp 737–42.

[224] Department of Social Security, *Children First: A New Approach to Child Support* Cm 3992 (1998), *A New Contract for Welfare: Children's Rights and Parents' Responsibilities* Cm 4349 (1999).

[225] Details of the 'old rules' scheme may be found in the 9th edition of this work, pp 734–746.

[226] DWP, *Child Support Agency Quarterly Summary of Statistics for Great Britain* (June 2013) [online] https://www.gov.uk/government/uploads/system/uploads/attachment_data/file/232316/csa-qtr-summ-stats-jun13.pdf (accessed 3 May 2014) p 10.

[227] Details may be found in the 10th edition of this work, pp 931–47.

[228] HC Select Committee on Work and Pensions, *The Performance of the Child Support Agency* (2005) HC 44 para 87.

(d) The child support scheme: Mark 3

In 2006, the Government commissioned an independent review of the child support scheme, by Sir David Henshaw.[229] He concluded that parents should be encouraged to reach private agreements or obtain consent orders for maintenance, with a State-provided service operating as a back-up rather than first port of call. Yet a study in 2007 found that 6 out of 10 parents with care who were not using the child support system had no maintenance arrangement at all.[230] While half of these felt confident about making a private arrangement, nearly two thirds of those using the CSA were not confident they could do so. Both groups cited fears over conflict, lack of trust, and the unwillingness of the non-resident parent to pay up without being forced to do so, as primary reasons for their reluctance to contemplate private ordering.[231]

Henshaw also recommended that parents with care who were in receipt of benefits should no longer be required to authorise the making of a child support calculation and should be allowed to keep any maintenance without it affecting their benefits. At first, a £10 'disregard' was introduced, later raised to £20, but a full disregard was implemented in 2010. This had a significant effect. Research found that the average weekly amount of maintenance being received by single parents dependent on welfare benefits rose from £11.71 in 2007 to £23.01 in 2012, and enabling parents to keep all of the maintenance rather than lose it from their benefits enabled 62% of single parents on benefit receiving maintenance to live above the poverty line, compared with 43% previously.[232]

He further recommended abolishing the Child Support Agency, establishing instead a new body focused on enforcement in a smaller number of difficult cases, and implementing a more simplified method of calculating the amount of maintenance due. The Government accepted the thrust of the proposals and enacted the Child Maintenance and Other Payments Act 2008 (CMOPA) to implement them. This Act laid down yet another set of rules to govern the calculation of the maintenance payable, moving from *net* to *gross* income. It also created the Child Maintenance and Enforcement Commission (CMEC) to oversee the work of the Child Support Agency.

When the Coalition Government was formed it reviewed the issues again.[233] It found that it cost the Child Support Agency £460m to run the scheme which delivered £1.1bn in maintenance—a cost of 40p in the pound, which it regarded as delivering poor value to the taxpayer.[234] And it took the view, in line with Henshaw, that:

> families themselves are best placed to determine what arrangements will work best for them. Underlying our approach is the assumption that government should use mechanisms to encourage and support parents to:
>
> - fulfil their responsibilities as parents in terms of continuing involvement in their children's lives and through the payment of child maintenance; and
> - make family-based arrangements concerning these issues wherever possible, which is better for children, rather than relying on government services to step in and administer these arrangements on parents' behalf.[235]

[229] Sir David Henshaw, *Report to the Secretary of State for Work and Pensions: Recovering Child Support: Rates to Responsibility* (2006) Cm 6894 and Government response at (2006) Cm 6895.

[230] N Wikeley et al, *Relationship separation and child support study* (2008) DWP Research Report No 503 para 4.2.1.   [231] DWP Research Report No 503 (2008) Table 7.20.

[232] C Bryson et al, *Kids aren't free: the child maintenance arrangements of single parents on benefit in 2012* (2013) p 9.

[233] DWP, *Strengthening families, promoting parental responsibility: the future of child maintenance* (2011) Cm 7990.

[234] Cm 7990 p 17.   [235] Cm 7990 p 6.

It defined a 'family-based arrangement' as 'one in which both parents agree on how to provide child maintenance for their child, how much and when, independently of the CSA or the courts. It is more flexible than other types of arrangement, emphasises collaboration between parents rather than conflict and helps to keep both parents involved in their child's life after separation.' It can be seen that this definition is both descriptive and normative, sending a message about the superior value of such an arrangement and in line with the ideological significance attached to shared parenting. There is some support for this view. A study conducted in 2000,[236] in which nearly 2,500 parents with care and non-resident parents were interviewed about their views on the 'old rules' system, concluded that non-resident parents' perceptions of the fairness of the system, and their willingness to comply with it, reflected the degree to which their lives remained intertwined with those of their children, and they saw their obligations to their children as negotiable, not subject to the rigid fixed rules of the State scheme.

The Coalition adopted the reforms started under Labour, but abolished CMEC in 2012, transferring its powers to the Department for Work and Pensions, and it proceeded just as slowly as the previous Government in introducing reforms to the system, so that the change from net to gross income was only in place for new claims from November 2013.[237] Consistent with its focus on 'family-based arrangements' it proposed a 'new child maintenance landscape' in which anyone wishing to make use of the 'statutory Child Maintenance Services' must first go through a 'gateway conversation' in which private agreements and alternatives are discussed first.[238] A further incentive to make a private arrangement will be driven by the introduction of a £20 charge to make an application, and an ongoing charge on each parent if they make use of the statutory collection and enforcement system, of 20% on the payer, and 4% on the payee.[239] Charges were a proposed feature of the original system, but it was never efficient enough to warrant their being levied. It remains to be seen whether it can deliver at a level of competence to justify charging under the new system, and whether parents who cannot arrive at family-based arrangements will be willing—or able—to incur the costs of using the statutory system. The following discussion sets out the key features of the scheme, focusing on how it is intended to operate under the Mark 3 model, and then considers how the Government's promotion of private ordering can sit alongside the statutory jurisdiction and the likelihood of its success.

2. THE KEY FEATURES OF THE CHILD SUPPORT SCHEME

The two key characteristics of the child support scheme are first, that it lays down a *formula* to be applied to calculate the amount of maintenance needed by the child and to be met by the absent parent. The original aim of the formula was to ensure that adequate

---

[236] N Wikeley et al, *National Survey of Child Support Agency Clients* (2001) DWP Research Report No 152, summarised by G Davis and N Wikeley, 'National Survey of Child Support Agency Clients—The Relationship Dimension' [2002] Fam Law 522.

[237] Child Maintenance and Other Payments Act 2008 (Commencement No. 11 and Transitional Provisions) Order 2013 (SI 2013/1860).

[238] There is a clear parallel with the MIAM—mediation information and assessment meeting—that applicants in family proceedings must attend. See Ch 1, Private Ordering and the Withdrawal of Legal Aid, p 10. The creation of the 'gateway' is part of the steps to be taken to promote private ordering which is legislatively underpinned by s 9(2A) of the Child Support Act 1991 as inserted by s 136 of the Welfare Reform Act 2012.

[239] DWP, *Supporting separated families: securing children's futures* (2012) Cm 8399. No charge will be levied if the applicant has declared they are a victim of family violence, or both parents are under 18: p 6. The original intended fee for payees was 7% but the Government announced a reduction to 4% in its *Response* to the consultation (2013) Cm 8742 p 8. Child Support Fees Regulations 2014 SI 2014/612.

amounts of maintenance are awarded, and to achieve consistency, so that families in similar circumstances will be assessed for similar amounts of maintenance. However, as is explained later, the Mark 2 and Mark 3 rules pay less attention to the adequacy of the maintenance and more to achieving a rough and ready 'fairness' or balance between the needs of payer and child alike. Secondly, the assessment, collection and enforcement of maintenance are carried out, not by the courts, but, for Mark 1 and 2 cases, by the Child Support Agency and, for Mark 3 cases, the Child Maintenance Service, operating within the Department for Work and Pensions.

(a) The role of the Agency or Service

Neither of the terms 'Child Support Agency' nor 'Child Maintenance Service' appear in the legislation,[240] which instead refers to the Secretary of State, whose actions and decisions, of course, must be carried out in practice by officers, who are referred to in this section as child support or child maintenance officers.

Where the exercise of any discretionary power[241] conferred by the Act is to be considered, the Secretary of State shall, under s 2, 'have regard to the welfare of any child likely to be affected by his decision'. This requirement is both narrower and wider than similar conditions in other legislation. Since welfare is not made the first consideration, still less the paramount consideration, s 2 is narrower than s 25(1) of the Matrimonial Causes Act 1973, or s 1 of the Children Act 1989. On the other hand, the duty to consider welfare lies in respect of *any* child who may be affected by the decision, and not just the child directly in issue. The Act gives no guidance on how welfare is to be taken into account, nor on how a balance should be struck between different children who may be affected and has been characterised by one judge as 'hollow indeed'.[242] In *Brookes v Secretary of State for Work and Pensions*[243] Hughes LJ considered that:

> What s 2 of the 1991 Act requires is that any impact on children's welfare be taken into account as a factor in deciding whether or not to do something discretionary under the Act. Clearly, the greater the likely negative impact on welfare, the greater the case against making the decision. But the welfare considerations must still be balanced against all other relevant considerations. Those will include, but are not limited to: the welfare of other children with different interests, the duty of the paying parent to support his/her children, the general public interest in a parent meeting that duty and the particular interest of the public, qua taxpayer, in that duty being enforced rather than the support of the children being left to fall on the state.

Thus, the Court of Appeal held that CMEC had been entitled to take enforcement action against Mr Brookes, including the potential use of bailiffs to seize his property, despite the possible negative impact on the children of his current household.[244] At the time of writing, there is no reported case where 'welfare' has overridden the decision of a child support officer to take some form of action against a parent although no doubt it may well do so in 'street-level' decision-making which never reaches the attention of the law reports.

---

[240] Although CMEC was established by CMOPA 2008 s 1, but was in turn abolished by the Public Bodies (Child Maintenance and Enforcement Commission: Abolition and Transfer of Functions) Order 2012 (SI 2012/2007).

[241] This excludes the calculation of the assessment under the formula, since this is not discretionary.

[242] Per Thorpe J in *R v Secretary of State for Social Security ex p Biggin* [1995] 1 FLR 851 at 855E–F.

[243] [2010] EWCA Civ 420 [2010] 2 FLR 1038 at [14].

[244] See also *R (Joplin) v Child Maintenance and Enforcement Commission* [2010] EWHC 1623 (Admin) [2010] 2 FLR 1510.

(b) The relevant parties

Qualifying child

Section 1(1) provides that 'each parent of a qualifying child is responsible for maintaining him'.[245] A child is defined in s 55 as a person under the age of 16, or under the age of 20 who is in full time education and for whom child benefit is payable,[246] and who has not been married. Such a child is a 'qualifying child' within s 3(1) if:

> (a) one of his parents is, in relation to him, a non-resident[247] parent; or
> (b) both of his parents are, in relation to him, non-resident parents.

Non-resident parent

A parent is a non-resident parent under s 3(2) if:

> (a) that parent is not living in the same household with the child; and
> (b) the child has his home with a person who is, in relation to him, a person with care.

A parent is defined in s 54 as 'any person who is in law the mother or father of the child'. This definition covers birth parents,[248] parents by virtue of adoption, and parents by virtue of the Human Fertilisation and Embryology Acts 1990 and 2008. There is no concept of 'child of the family' which underpins private maintenance obligations.[249] The approach of the Act is to attach liability only to those with the legal status of parents.

Person with care

A 'person with care' is defined in s 3(3) as a person:

> (a) with whom the child has his home;
> (b) who usually provides day to day care for the child (whether exclusively or in conjunction with any other person); and
> (c) who does not fall within a prescribed category of person.[250]

More than one person may be a person with care in relation to the child under s 3(5).

The question of what is meant by a person having the 'care' of a child arose in *GR v CMEC (CSM)*.[251] The child's mother died when she was four years old and the maternal grandparents became her guardians and were given a residence order. Because she suffered from severe dyslexia, it was agreed when she was about 10 that she should live with family friends in the United States where she could attend a special school. The

---

[245] As we saw earlier, Welfare Benefits, p 778, this is now the only public law duty to maintain imposed upon a parent, as parents are no longer included within the definition of a 'liable relative'.

[246] Section 55 amended by CMOPA 2008 s 42 and SI 2012/2785. Compare the ages set down under the matrimonial jurisdictions and Schedule 1 to the Children Act 1989, discussed earlier, Obtaining financial relief for children, matrimonial and civil partnership jurisdictions at p 792 and Proceedings under Schedule 1 to the Children Act 1989, p 799.

[247] The original term was 'absent' parent, but this was criticised by the House of Commons Social Security Committee as offensive: *The Performance and Operation of the Child Support Agency* 2nd Report of the House of Commons Social Security Committee, Session 1995–96, para 54 and was duly changed.

[248] Excluding, of course, gamete and embryo donors in licensed clinics, since they are not regarded as 'parents' of the child.

[249] See Ch 9, The meaning of 'child of the family', p 296.

[250] The Secretary of State shall not so prescribe parents, guardians, persons with a child arrangements order in their favour, under s 8 of the Children Act 1989: s 3(4) (as amended).

[251] [2011] UKUT 101 (AAC) [2011] 2 FLR 962.

non-resident father, who had never had contact, had been paying child support which the grandmother had remitted to the friends in the USA, together with child benefit. He queried the assessment and on appeal it was held that 'care' does not mean 'responsibility'. The fact that the grandmother had parental responsibility for the child was not the key factor in determining whether she had 'care'; rather, the focus should have been on:

> who was providing the hands-on care or the 'immediate, short-term and mundane aspects of care' . . . bearing in mind that 'child support law is concerned with maintenance and the costs of bringing up a child are more related to the aspects of day-to-day care as I have analysed it than to the longer-term decisions about upbringing' . . . it is about who puts food on the table, washes the child's clothes, deals with the letters from school and reads a bedtime story.[252]

Where care of a child is shared, disputes may arise as to which of them is the 'parent (or person) with care' and which the 'non-resident parent'. For Mark 3 cases, where the parents share care *equally*, there will be no 'non-resident parent' and thus no ability to seek child support.[253] For unequal shared care, where the child spends, or is to spend, on average at least one night a week with the non-resident parent, a deduction in the amount of child support will be made.[254] A 'night' 'will count where the non-resident parent has the care of the qualifying child overnight and the child stays at the same address as the non-resident parent'. 'Has the care of' means 'when the non-resident parent is looking after the child'.[255] One can envisage rather difficult disputes concerning situations where the child stays with the grandparents and the non-resident parent visits at the same time and stays over with the child—who, in such circumstances, 'has the care of' the child?

The officer must consider the terms of any agreement between the parties, or any court order[256] providing for 'contact' between the non-resident parent and qualifying child. The omission of a reference to shared care arrangements through residence and child arrangements orders seems to be an oversight as they must surely be highly relevant. Where there is no such agreement or court order, the officer may consider whether a 'pattern' of shared care has been established, and where the parties disagree as to the quantum of nights of shared care, the officer can *assume* a pattern of one night per week.[257]

Application for a maintenance calculation

Under s 4(1) the person with care or a non-resident parent may apply for a maintenance calculation to be made with respect to the qualifying child.[258] The person with care may apply by phone or face-to-face interview, or by completing a form which can be downloaded from the internet. A non-resident parent who applies will either complete a form or be sent one to check the information that the Agency has recorded by phone.

The scheme as originally enacted required that, where a parent with care was receiving means-tested benefits she or he had to authorise the Child Support Agency to take action

[252] [2011] UKUT 101 (AAC) [2011] 2 FLR 962 per Upper Tribunal Judge Wikeley at [48].
[253] Child Support Maintenance Calculation Regulations 2012 (SI 2012/2677) reg 50. The parents could, however, use the courts' jurisdictions, such as the Children Act 1989 Sch 1.
[254] Child Support Act 1991 Sch 1 paras 7, 8 (as amended).
[255] Child Support Maintenance Calculation Regulations 2012 (SI 2012/2677) reg 46(5).
[256] The terms of the order were held relevant although not decisive under the earlier Regulations: *C v Secretary of State for Work and Pensions* [2002] EWCA Civ 1854 [2003] 1 FLR 829.
[257] Child Support Maintenance Calculation Regulations 2012 (SI 2012/2677) regs 46, 47.
[258] Unless s 4(10) applies, see later, Where there is no jurisdiction under the Child Support Act, p 821.

under the Act to recover child support maintenance from the non-resident parent,[259] with a penalty of a reduction of benefits for unreasonable non-cooperation.[260] As we have seen, Sir David Henshaw recommended that this requirement be lifted, and the change was made in 2008, but despite the removal of compulsion, researchers found that a CSA (rather than family-based) arrangement still accounted for two thirds of all maintenance arrangements which single parents on benefit reported as having in 2012.[261]

(c) Providing information to make the assessment

The applicant must, so far as she reasonably can, supply information to the Agency to enable the non-resident parent to be traced (if necessary), and the maintenance calculation made and collected.[262]

Information will also be needed from the non-resident parent in order to discover his means and liabilities. Non-resident parents and their current or recent employers are required to provide information, and an offence may be committed if false information is knowingly supplied or the request to provide the information is not complied with.[263] Information will also be obtained from HM Revenue and Customs, with Mark 3 cases requiring such information from PAYE or self assessment tax returns for self-employed parents to discover their gross income.[264] Inspectors may be appointed to exercise powers of entry and enquiry with a view to obtaining information required under the Act,[265] although there is no evidence that in practice use has been made of this power. In its early years, the Agency was described as a 'toothless dragon' which was ill-equipped, and reluctant, to challenge assertions by non-resident parents about their financial circumstances, and hence was incapable of determining the true situation from which a reliable and fair assessment could be made.[266] However the Agency does seem more ready actively to pursue information nowadays, and can seek it from banks and building societies, credit reference agencies and utility suppliers.[267]

Default maintenance decision

Under s 12 the officer may make a default maintenance decision where it appears to him that he does not have sufficient information to form a final judgment. The original aim of this provision was to set a higher assessment than might otherwise have been expected, in order to prompt the non-resident parent to provide the additional information needed so that the final figure could be reduced. In 1997, the average interim maintenance assessment was around £89 per week.[268] But the Mark 3 system provides that a default decision imposes a flat rate figure depending upon the number of qualifying children—£39 for

---

[259]   Child Support Act 1991 s 6.   [260]   Section 46(5).

[261]   C Bryson et al, *Kids aren't free: the child maintenance arrangements of single parents on benefit in 2012* (2013) p 10.

[262]   Section 4(4).

[263]   Section 14A. It is not a defence under s 14A(4) of 'reasonable excuse for failing to comply' that the parent is helping the other to avoid incriminating herself: *CMEC v Forrest* [2010] EWHC 264 (Admin) [2010] 2 FLR 1805 (parent with care alleged to have misled the social security authorities as to the extent to which the children lived with her in order to obtain welfare benefits).

[264]   Child Support Maintenance Calculation Regulations (SI 2012/2677) Part 4. See further, Determining gross income, p 812.   [265]   Section 15.

[266]   G Davis et al, *Child Support in Action* (1998) p 97.

[267]   See CSA, *How does the Child Support Agency Use and Store Information?* (2011) [online] (accessed 4 May 2014) https://www.gov.uk/government/uploads/system/uploads/attachment_data/file/222555/dg_198856.pdf.   [268]   *Quarterly Summary of Statistics* (covering period to February 1997).

one, £51 for two and £64 for three or more—resulting in a less punitive outcome for the non-cooperating parent.[269]

(d) Disputes about parentage

A question may arise whether the non-resident parent is in fact the father (or mother or second female parent) of the qualifying child. Under s 26, if the alleged parent denies parentage, the child support officer shall not make a maintenance assessment unless the case falls within one of a number of categories. These are where:

Case A1:   the child is habitually resident in England and Wales; the Secretary of State is satisfied that the alleged parent was married to the child's mother at some time in the period beginning with the conception and ending with the birth of the child; and the child has not been adopted;

Case A2:   the child is habitually resident in England and Wales; the alleged parent has been registered as the child's father under the relevant legislation for England and Wales, Scotland or Northern Ireland; and the child has not subsequently been adopted;

Case A3:   the result of a scientific test (within the meaning of s 27A)[270] taken by the alleged parent would be relevant to determining the child's parentage; and the alleged parent (a) refuses to take the test; or (b) has submitted to such a test and it shows that there is no reasonable doubt that the alleged parent is a parent of the child;

Case A: the parent has adopted the child;

Case B: the parent has a parental order under the Human Fertilisation and Embryology Act 1990 or 2008;

Case B1:   the Secretary of State is satisfied that the alleged parent is a parent of the child by virtue of the Human Fertilisation and Embryology Act 1990 or 2008;

Case C: a declaration that the alleged parent is the parent is in force under ss 55A or 56 of the Family Law Act 1986[271] and the child has not subsequently been adopted;

Case D: a declaration is in force under s 27 of the Act[272] and the child has not subsequently been adopted; [. . .][273]

Case F: the alleged parent has been found or adjudged to be the father of the child in relevant proceedings[274] in England and Wales . . . , the finding still subsists and the child has not subsequently been adopted.[275]

Interestingly, as originally enacted, the Act did not provide that the marital presumption or the prima facie evidence of registration as the child's father would justify an

---

[269] SI 2012/2677 reg 49. Albeit that the level of payment is higher than for Mark 2 cases, which levy £30 for one, £40 for two and £50 for three or more children: Child Support (Maintenance Calculation Procedure) Regulations 2001 reg 7.

[270] Discussed later in this section.

[271] Or under the equivalent legislation in Scotland or Northern Ireland.

[272] See later in this section.   [273] Case E applies to Scotland only.

[274] Within s 12 of the Civil Evidence Act 1968, as amended.

[275] The making of a parental responsibility order under s 4 of the Children Act 1989 necessarily incorporates a 'finding' of paternity for the purposes of Case F, even if the s 4 order is subsequently discharged on its merits: *R v Secretary of State for Social Security ex p West* [1999] 1 FLR 1233, CA and (on the substantive issue) *R v Secretary of State for Social Security ex p W* [1999] 2 FLR 604.

assumption of parentage, perhaps because it was not contemplated that men would dispute their paternity when they had been married to the parent with care or had their name on the birth register. The change was made by the Child Support, Pensions and Social Security Act 2000,[276] when the opportunity was also taken to treat a refusal to take a DNA test which would determine the matter one way or the other in the same way as the courts would so treat it—ie by regarding that as evidence of parentage in itself.[277]

Where the alleged parent denies parentage and falls outside these categories, then the Agency will ask the relevant parties to undergo a DNA test at a reduced cost to the alleged non-resident parent. This includes testing the child. In *L v P (Paternity Test: Child's Objection)*[278] the man (who had been married to the mother and was named on the child's birth certificate as the father) sought a declaration that he was *not* the father of the child, in relation to whom he owed £20,000 arrears in child support maintenance. The child, now aged 15, refused to give a DNA sample and her refusal was upheld by the court, leaving the man liable to meet the arrears.[279] If the man is found not to be the parent, the fee is refunded. Under s 27 of the Child Support Act, the Agency or the person with care may also apply to the court for a declaration under s 55A of the Family Law Act 1986[280] that a person is, or is not, a parent of the child.

(e) Making the child support calculation

The formula for calculating the amount of child support maintenance which the non-resident parent must pay for the qualifying child is set out in Sch 1 to the Act. Details for the scheme in its Mark 1 and 2 modes are to be found in previous editions to this work.[281] Discussion here relates to Mark 3.

The rate of child support payable depends upon the income of the non-resident parent. The 'general rule' is that the 'basic rate' applies, but a reduced, flat or nil rate may be applicable instead,[282] as explained later.

The basic rate

The non-resident parent pays 12% of his gross weekly income for one qualifying child, 16% for two, and 19% where there are three or more such children, up to an income of £800 per week. On any income above this amount, he will pay 9% for one child, 12% for two, and 15% for three or more.[283] Where the parent has other 'relevant children' (that is, children for whom he or his partner receives child benefit—effectively, children in his current relationship, be they his own, or step-children),[284] a reduction of 11, 14 or 16% depending on the number of children, is to be made to his gross income *before* it is applied in favour of his qualifying children.[285] This means that the income available for

---

[276] Section 15(1). See N Wikeley 'Child Support, Paternity and Parentage' [2001] Fam Law 125.

[277] See Ch 8, The use of blood and DNA tests to establish parentage, p 263.

[278] [2010] EWCA Civ 1145 [2011] 1 FLR 708. See also *Law v Inostroza Ahumuda and Others* [2010] EWCA Civ 1145 [2011] 1 FLR 708 where, similarly, the child had refused to be tested and the court had found the man to be the father.

[279] Where the test is carried out other than by direction, and shows that the alleged parent cannot be excluded from being one of the child's parents, the Agency can recover the costs of the test from the non-resident parent if he accepts parentage or has been declared a parent: s 27A of the Child Support Act 1991.

[280] See Ch 8, Declarations of Parentage, p 270. In such proceedings, the child should be made a party and represented: *Re L (Family Proceedings Court) (Appeal: Jurisdiction)* [2003] EWHC 1682 (Fam) [2005] 1 FLR 210.   [281] See respectively, pp 734–737 of the 9th edition and pp 937–944 of the 10th edition.

[282] Child Support Act 1991 Sch 1 para 1, as amended.

[283] Child Support Act 1991 Sch 1 paras 2(1), (2).

[284] Child Support Act 1991 Sch 1 para 10C(2).   [285] Child Support Act 1991 Sch 1 para 2(2).

child support is correspondingly reduced, thus benefiting the children of his second family. This is contrary to the original scheme, which sought to prioritise the financial needs of the first family rather than the second, and it appears to be an attempt to encourage non-resident parents to pay at least something by way of child support in the knowledge that at least their current family's needs are not being squeezed.[286] It should also be noted that, unlike the original formula, which linked the amount payable to the 'needs' of the qualifying child (as assessed according to the relevant income support benefit rates then payable for such a child), the Mark 2 and 3 rules make no attempt to determine what the qualifying child's financial needs might actually be. The focus is on getting the non-resident parent to pay a proportion of his income in recognition of his liability, regardless of how far this may or may not actually relieve the child's needs. It can be seen that the rationale is therefore different from that operating in the courts' jurisdictions which focus on meeting the ascertained needs of the child from the available resources of the parent. Both systems, however, recognise the legal and moral obligation of the payer to his second family as reducing what he can be expected to pay for his first.

Reduced rate

If the non-resident parent's gross income is above £100 per week, but below £200, he pays a 'reduced rate' or a minimum amount of £5 per week.[287] The reduced rate is calculated by reference to a percentage of the gross income between £100 and £200, depending upon the number of qualifying and relevant other children, and adding this to the minimum £5. For example, if the non-resident parent has a gross income of £150 per week, one qualifying child and no relevant children, he pays 19% of £50 (= £9.50) + £5 = £14.50 per week in child support. For two qualifying children, the percentage is 27% and for three or more, it is 33%. The percentage of income taken in child support reduces where he has relevant children, so that, for example, if he had three such children, it would reduce from 19% to 15.2% for one qualifying child (so that he would pay 15.2% of £50 (= £7.60) + £5 = £12.60 per week).[288]

Flat rate

A flat rate of £5 per week is payable where the non-resident parent's gross income is £100 per week or less, or he is in receipt of certain welfare benefits. The rate is halved if he or his partner is in receipt of an income-related benefit and the partner is also a non-resident parent for whom a child support application is in force.[289] The minimum has been prospectively raised to £7, and the intention is to raise it to £10 when all cases are subject to the Mark 3 system.

Nil rate

No child support is payable if the non-resident parent has gross income of below £5 per week, or is of a prescribed description, such as a child, prisoner, or person living in a care home.[290]

---

[286] Non-resident parents may indeed be likely to put the children of their current relationship before their 'own' children, according to a survey commissioned by the DWP: A Atkinson and S McKay *Investigating the compliance of Child Support Agency clients*, Research Report no 285 (2005).

[287] Child Support Act 1991 Sch 1 para 3.

[288] The relevant percentages are specified in SI 2012/2677 reg 43. A reduction is also made where the non-resident parent is liable to make payments under a qualifying maintenance arrangement (order or agreement) in relation to another child who is habitually resident in the UK: Child Support Act 1991 Sch 1 para 5A.   [289] Child Support Act 1991 Sch 1 para 4 and SI 2012/2677 reg 44.

[290] Child Support Act 1991 Sch 1 para 5 and SI 2012/2677 reg 45. The amount has been prospectively raised to £7.

Determining gross income

It will be seen that the amount of child support payable depends upon the gross income of the non-resident parent. Unlike for Mark 1 cases, no account is now taken of the income of the parent with care, the previous Government taking the view (which was strongly criticised by some)[291] that since the child shares that parent's standard of living anyway, a contribution by the carer to the support of the child is already being made.[292] To avoid a wealthy non-resident parent from having income taken from him far in excess of his child's needs, a ceiling is placed on the amount of gross income that can be included in the calculation, of £3,000 per week.[293] This means that the maximum amount of child support that could be paid will be £482 per week. However, in this situation, were it felt appropriate, an application for 'top up maintenance' could be made to the courts.[294]

Much therefore hinges on determining how much gross income the non-resident parent has. As we have noted, this is now to be determined by reference to information held by HMRC, taken either from the most recent PAYE or self-assessment tax return (the 'historic income') for the latest available tax year, or where this is not available (perhaps because the parent has only recently become employed), or differs by more than 25% from 'current income', then it can be derived from current information as to earnings and profits.[295] This is intended to simplify the process of calculation, not only for the Child Maintenance Service but also for parents seeking to arrive at their own agreements using the child support figure as a basis for negotiation. But it is problematic. Under the scheme Mark 1 and 2, child support officers (or more usually tribunals hearing appeals from parents with care who considered the CSA's calculation of support to be too low) could— and on occasions, did[296]—go behind tax returns to consider wider evidence relating to income and resources. As Judge Howell argued, 'what is required . . . is the true and full amount of [the parent's profits] defined as taxable by law, not any lesser amount a person may happen to get away with as a result of that law being evaded, avoided or imperfectly administered.'[297] But the mandatory use of HMRC returns or other tax records to determine income means that it will be very difficult in future to dispute what the non-resident parent asserts, with a potential loss to the child of a level of support that the parent could in fact well afford.[298]

(f) Variations

A formula-based approach to calculating how much child support should be made will always lead to some decisions that do not fit individual circumstances. Fairness may be sacrificed for consistency. The original formula was criticised so heavily by both parents

---

[291] See, eg N Mostyn 'The Green Paper on Child Support—Children First: a new approach to child support' [1999] Fam Law 95.

[292] *Children First: a new approach to child support* Cm 3992 (1998) p 31.

[293] Child Support Act 1991 Sch 1 para 10(3) as amended.

[294] See later, Orders instead of or in addition to child support, p 822.

[295] SI 2012/2677 regs 4, 34–42. Query whether monthly sums paid by a company as repayments of a loan back to the non-resident parent constitute such income, as was held in *Chapman v Secretary of State for Work and Pensions* [2007] EWCA Civ 1211 [2008] 1 FLR 638.

[296] See *Gray v Secretary of State for Work and Pensions* [2012] EWCA Civ 1412 [2013] 2 FLR 424.

[297] In *DB v CMEC* [2011] UKUT 202 (AAC) at [31]. See *Smith v Secretary of State for Work and Pensions* [2006] UKHL 35 [2006] 1 WLR 2024 for an example of how the vagaries of tax allowances and returns can distort the true picture of the parent's income: profit of £169,000 reduced by 'capital allowances' of £148,000 resulting in an 'income' assessed as only £21,000 for the year until the House of Lords ruled that no such deduction should have been made under the Regulations then governing the case.

[298] Note the comments by Lord Walker in *Smith v Secretary of State for Work and Pensions* at [64] and Baroness Hale at [78].

with care and non-resident parents that one might say that it led to virtually no fair out-comes. Eventually, in response to lobbying, the Government was forced to enact fur-ther primary legislation, the Child Support Act 1995, amending the 1991 Act, which fundamentally struck at the objective of ensuring consistency by introducing an ele-ment of discretion into the process. Again, the legislation drew on the Australian model. However, whereas in Australia, it is for the courts to determine whether to give a 'depar-ture order' diverting from the formula, in the United Kingdom, the discretion is vested in the Secretary of State.[299] Under ss 28A(1) of the 1991 Act, where an application for a maintenance calculation is made, or a calculation is in force, the person with care or the non-resident parent may apply for the rules by which the calculation is made to be varied in accordance with the terms of the Act.[300]

The Secretary of State may agree to a variation if he is satisfied that the case falls within one or more of the cases set out in Sch 4B to the Act, or the Regulations thereto, and it is his opinion that, in all the circumstances of the case, it would be just and equitable to agree.[301]

Special expenses

The first category of case for which a variation can be made concerns special expenses which ought to be deducted from the income of the non-resident parent so as to reduce his liability. Many complaints about the original formula related to the narrow range of items allowed to the non-resident parent as part of the income which was 'exempt' from liability, and the Mark 2 rules narrowed these still further by limiting income basically to take-home pay. Yet a parent may have many financial commitments which are a part of everyday life and which people are required, or certainly encouraged, to take on. On the other hand, the fundamental philosophy of the legislation is to require parents to meet their obligations to their children before incurring further expenditure and to pre-vent them from claiming that, because of such expenditure, they are less able to support their children. Thus, the Government sought to extend, but only to a degree, the types of expenditure which absent parents would be able to claim as having a higher priority on their resources than the cost of maintaining their first family.

The items which may be claimed as special expenses[302] are as follows. First, there are costs incurred in maintaining contact with the qualifying child[303] (many non-resident parents having complained that it was nonsensical to require them to pay so much

---

[299] There is provision for an application to be referred direct to an Appeal Tribunal where it is particularly novel or contentious: s 28D(1)(b).

[300] Pending the outcome of such an application, the Secretary of State may give an 'interim maintenance decision' under s 12 of the Child Support Act 1991, applying the formula in Sch 1.

[301] Section 28F as amended. The Act makes provision for certain property or capital transfers which occurred before 5 April 1993 and which were intended to reduce the non-resident parent's liability to maintain the child. They are not discussed here since they are now redundant (other than in cases of long-standing arrears). There are now no children under the age of 20 who are qualifying children under the Act who could be affected by such a transfer having taken place. Details are provided in the 10th edi-tion at pp 941–942.

[302] Child Support Act 1991 Sch 4B para 2, as amended. The expenses must be over £10 per week except in relation to costs due to the illness or disability of a relevant child: Child Support Maintenance Calculation Regulations (SI 2012/2677) reg 68.

[303] In *CMEC v NC* [2009] UKUT 106 (AAC) [2010] 2 FLR 1812, it was held that the non-resident parent could not claim expenses incurred in having contact with another child of his living in France as the provi-sion applies only to a 'qualifying child'. However, if the parent is supporting that child, the maintenance calculation will be correspondingly reduced as if the child were the subject of a qualifying maintenance arrangement: Child Support Maintenance Calculation Regulations (SI 2012/2677) reg 52.

maintenance that they could no longer actually afford to see their children);[304] and costs attributable to the long-term illness or disability of a relevant child.

These items will have usually arisen after the breakdown of the relationship. The next group of items relates to financial obligations incurred before the breakdown which continue to have to be met. Thus, a variation may be given for certain debts incurred before the breakdown in the relationship, and which were incurred for the parties' joint benefit or for the benefit of the person with care (if the non-resident parent is liable for the payments), or for the child (or a child who lived with them during their relationship). Many types of debt are excluded from consideration, such as credit card debts, legal costs of the separation or divorce, and debts taken over as part of a financial settlement of the divorce or separation.[305] The types of expenditure which would be covered include the purchase by credit agreement or hire purchase of furniture, home improvements, private medical or dental treatment, or taking out a loan to help an older child through university. Express provision is also made for the payment of the qualifying child's boarding-school fees, although the Regulations provide that only the maintenance element of these may be allowed.[306]

An important addition made in 2000 was to allow for payments being kept up by the non-resident parent, for a mortgage on the home that the parties had shared, if the non-resident parent no longer has an interest in it, and the parent with care and qualifying child still live there.[307]

Additional cases

Although the main clamour for reform of the system came from non-resident parents seeking reductions in their child support liability, concern was also expressed at the limited efforts apparently made by the Child Support Agency to establish the true financial situation of many non-resident parents who are self-employed or who appear to have complicated business affairs. Since one of the original motives for introducing the scheme was to tackle the situation of lone parents and their children living on subsistence benefits while the other parent enjoys a much more affluent standard of living, it is hardly surprising if many parents with care might resent the apparent disparity in lifestyle and seek to argue that the non-resident parent can afford to pay far more than he ostensibly appears to do. Accordingly, provision was made to give a variation, inter alia, where the non-resident parent had a lifestyle inconsistent with his income. However, the Coalition Government considered that such cases were difficult to administer and they may no longer be brought in relation to Mark 3 cases. It will still be possible to seek a variation based on the non-resident parent having unearned income of £2,500 per annum or more; or weekly income of £100 or more which has not been taken into account in the calculation (eg because the non-resident parent is a child but has a part-time job); or where he has diverted income (eg paying his new partner a company director's salary in his own business and drawing a small salary himself).[308] But it will no longer be possible to

[304] For example, *B v M (Child Support: Revocation of Order)* [1994] 1 FLR 342. The Secretary of State may decide to allow a sum lower than the cost claimed if he regards this as unreasonably high, but he cannot set a figure so low as to make it impossible, in his opinion, for contact to be maintained at the frequency specified in any court order, so long as the contact is taking place: reg 68(4). The pattern of contact need not be 'set in stone' and consideration should be given to the realities and practicalities of post-separation parenting arrangements: *PB v CMEC* [2009] UKUT 262 (AAC) [2010] 2 FLR 956.
[305] SI 2012/2677 reg 65.   [306] SI 2012/2677 reg 66.
[307] Child Support Act 1991 Sch 4B para 2(3)(e).
[308] Child Support Maintenance Calculation Regulations (SI 2012/2677) regs 69–71. But if he receives income in a form outside the Regulations, he can no longer be subject to a variation application: cf *Secretary*

point to a standard of living seemingly incompatible with the parent's declared income because his financial standing will be determined only by his tax return. The loss of the 'lifestyle' category is a further indicator of the Government's preference for a rough and ready method of fixing child support maintenance over precision or—in some cases, one might argue—basic fairness.[309]

Determining what is just and equitable

It is ironic, therefore, that once the application is found to come within one or more of the cases in Sch 4B, the Secretary of State must then determine whether it would be just and equitable[310] to give a variation. Section 28E and s 28F provide guidance on how this is to be determined. Section 28E sets out two 'general principles':

(a) parents should be responsible for maintaining their children whenever they can afford to do so;
(b) where a parent has more than one child, his obligation to maintain any one of them should be no less of an obligation than his obligation to maintain any other of them.

These provisions were apparently intended to remind parents of their obligation and also to reassert that duties to the first family should not be superseded by those taken on towards the second. But they can equally be read the other way—that the children of the second family should not be subordinated to those of the first. On this basis, the needs of all of a parent's children ought to be ranked and met equally.

Section 28F requires the Secretary of State to have regard to any representations made by the parties and to the welfare of any child likely to be affected by the decision to give a variation—this could obviously impact both on the qualifying child and children living with the non-resident parent. The Regulations also set out factors to which he is *not* to have regard.[311] These include the fact that the child's conception was unplanned; that a party may have been responsible for the breakdown in the relationship; that a new relationship has been formed; and that contact arrangements have, or have not, been made and are, or are not, being adhered to.

The effects of a decision

The Secretary of State may agree or refuse the application and then revise, supersede, or make, a child support calculation in the light of his decision.[312] The extent of the difference in the calculated figure will depend upon the type of case. Where special expenses are allowed, these reduce the applicant's gross income. Where the direction is given on the basis of unearned income or diversion of income, the quantified amount of extra income is added to the non-resident parent's gross income.

---

of State for Work and Pensions v Wincott [2009] EWCA Civ 113 [2009] 1 FLR 1222—non-resident parent received £27,000 dividend from his company; held, could be treated as income spread over a year and divided by 52.

[309] See for example, *Phillips v Peace* [1996] 2 FLR 230, where an absent parent lived in a house worth £2.6 million and owned cars worth £190,000, but was assessed by the Child Support Agency as having no income from his share-dealing business and was given a nil calculation.

[310] It is hard to see what is added to the word 'just' by the word 'equitable'. The phrase appears to have been borrowed from the Australian legislation: Child Support (Assessment) Act 1989 s 98C(1)(b)(ii) and s 117(1)(b)(ii).   [311] SI 2012/2677 reg 60.

[312] SI 2012/2677 regs 72, 73. A variation will not be given where the amount of maintenance will be reduced to less than £7, and the maximum amount of gross income which may be taken into account remains the ceiling amount of £3,000: reg 57.

(g) Termination and alteration of calculations

Under Sch 1 para 16 the calculation ceases to have effect on the death of the non-resident parent or person with care, or on the non-resident parent ceasing to be the child's parent (that is, if the child is adopted or made the subject of a parental order), or on there no longer being a qualifying child with respect to whom it would have effect. In *Brough v Law*,[313] it was held that the focus is on the child ceasing to be a 'child' for the purposes of the Act, such as by leaving school or getting married. Thus, the fact that the parents had briefly reconciled after the original calculation had been made, did not render the child no longer 'qualifying'. The Court noted that the Regulations applying to the specific case were later altered and that those currently in force (and now for Mark 3 cases) have omitted a reference to the parents resuming cohabitation for at least six months. It considered that this omission might well produce a different outcome. However, it is submitted that the reasoning of the Court applies just as much regardless of the omission in the Regulations, and should be followed.[314]

Mark 3 cases are subject to a *periodic case check* annually, to see if circumstances have changed and a revision is needed.[315] Under s 16 the Agency can *revise* a decision on the application of either party or of its own motion, within 30 days of notification of the decision or outside that period if, for example, the decision was made in error.[316] Under s 17, a decision may be *superseded* due to a change of circumstances, or where an error of law or ignorance of some material fact is discovered.[317] The usual reason will be a change of circumstances, for example, where the non-resident parent becomes unemployed, or has another child with a new partner and therefore seeks a downward revision of his maintenance calculation. Equally, the person with care might seek an increase if the non-resident parent is known to have obtained a higher paid employment.

The problem of keeping up to date with the numerous changes of circumstance in people's lives proved particularly difficult for the Child Support Agency. It would not be unusual in the course of a year for a non-resident parent to be joined by a new partner and her children, to become a father of a child of his new relationship, to change jobs or become unemployed, to cease earning overtime or to gain a profit-related bonus of pay. Each change could be the subject of an application for the former calculation to be superseded. To attempt to limit the resulting workload, Mark 3 cases are accordingly subject to a 25% 'tolerance' for any changes outside of the annual review (or where an error of law has been made); in other words, no change will be made to the calculation unless the amount of the non-resident parent's gross income has changed by at least 25%.[318]

(h) Appeals

Under s 20 a 'qualifying person', ie a person with care or non-resident parent, may appeal to the First-tier Tribunal against a decision of the Secretary of State regarding a child support calculation (including a decision regarding a revision or supersession). Parentage issues must be appealed to the Family Court.[319] If the appeal succeeds, the Tribunal may make such decision as it considers appropriate, or remit the case to the Secretary of State for reconsideration in the light of its ruling. The former option is preferable as it enables the issue to be resolved and any change implemented at once, rather than requiring it to go back for yet more consideration and consequent delay. Further appeals on questions of law may be made to the Upper Tribunal and then to the Court of Appeal.[320]

---

[313] [2011] EWCA Civ 1183 [2012] 1 FLR 375.

[314] Additionally, a calculation must be cancelled at the request of a person who applied for it: Child Support Act 1991 s 4(5).   [315] SI 2012/2677 regs 19–22.

[316] SI 2012/2677 reg 14.   [317] SI 2012/2677 reg 17.   [318] SI 2012/2677 reg 23.

[319] Section 45.   [320] Section 24 and Tribunals, Courts and Enforcement Act 2007 s 13.

(i) Collection and enforcement

Collection

One of the main objectives of the 1991 Act was to improve the collection and enforcement of maintenance. Section 29 empowers the Secretary of State to carry out the collection and enforcement of calculations where this is requested by those applying for a calculation under s 4, but for Mark 3 cases the Secretary of State will only be able to do so with the non-resident parent's agreement or where he considers that otherwise, the maintenance is unlikely to be paid.[321] The original intention was that all forms of periodical payments, including those ordered by the courts or settled by agreement would be collected via the Child Support Agency,[322] but this never proved attainable, and the policy now, as we have noted, is to *discourage* use of the 'statutory' child maintenance services as far as possible in favour of family-based arrangements. Even where the service is used to *calculate* the amount of child maintenance, there is still encouragement to make a private arrangement for its collection whereby the service provides the parties with a payment schedule, but the non-resident parent makes direct payments to the parent with care, rather than to the service which then forwards them on. This is known as 'Maintenance Direct' or 'Direct Pay'. It makes sense from the service's point of view, now that no deductions are made from the child support payment to help recoup the cost of the recipient's social welfare benefits, but of course, it depends upon the ability of the couple to agree on such payment and trust in the willingness of the payer to keep paying.[323] A study of single parents on benefit found that of those with a child support calculation, 51% used the CSA (known as its 'Collect and Pay' service) and 49% 'Maintenance Direct' for collection, but 22% of the total group had never received any maintenance.[324] However, the study also found that in the main, where maintenance *was* paid, it was usually paid at the set level with 80% of respondents reporting that they received it in full.[325]

Where the non-resident parent appears to be resistant to paying, s 31 empowers the Secretary of State to make a 'deduction from earnings' order, directed to the non-resident parent's employer, instructing him to make deductions from earnings and pay them to the Secretary of State.[326] Such an order is only suitable for those in regular employment. Powers added by the CMOPA 2008 increased the armoury available to the Secretary of State, however, by enabling him to make similar 'deduction orders' in relation to bank, building society or Post Office accounts, providing for payments to be made either periodically or by lump sum,[327] and these measures may reach more self-employed non-resident parents for whom deduction from earnings orders are inappropriate. Perhaps the most interesting new measure provided is the ability under s 43A to recover sums from the non-resident parent's estate after his death.[328]

---

[321] Section 4(2A) inserted by the Welfare Reform Act 2012 s 137.   [322] See s 30.

[323] Unsurprisingly perhaps, 'Maintenance Direct' is more popular with non-resident parents than parents with care: A Bell, A Kazimirski and I La Valle *An Investigation of CSA Maintenance Direct Payments: Qualitative study* (2006).

[324] C Bryson et al *Kids aren't free: The Child maintenance arrangements of single parents on benefit in 2012* (2012) p 10.

[325] Bryson et al *Kids aren't free* p 71. 46% of maintenance arrangements were set at the flat rate only, reflecting the low incomes of many non-resident parents whose former partners are on benefit. Nonetheless, 'every little helps' and such payments are worth collecting in helping to raise the children's living standards.

[326] Section 32(5).

[327] Child Support Act 1991 ss 32A–32K, inserted by CMOPA 2008 ss22 *et seq.* Failure to take all reasonable steps to comply with an order is an offence: ss 33D, 32K.

[328] There were 110 cases resulting in recovery from the deceased's estate in 2013–14, yielding £419,615: DWP, *Child Support Agency Quarterly Summary of Statistics for Great Britain* (March 2014) Table 16.

From April 2013 to February 2014, 62,280 deduction from earnings orders were made, with a further (mere) 1,500 deduction orders (regular and lump sum payments from accounts) made. The compliance level for deduction from earnings orders was 88% and they secured £303m in child support payments. Deduction orders secured £2.08m, showing how much harder it is to get payments from unwilling non-resident parents who are not in regular employment.[329]

Enforcement

Where payment has been missed, the Secretary of State may currently apply to a magistrates' court for a liability order against the liable person under s 33. In future, it will be possible for him to make the order himself.[330] The resort to action for a liability order is not an interference with the non-resident parent's rights under Art 8 or Protocol 1, Art 1 of the European Convention on Human Rights, or, if it is an interference, it is proportionate as a means of seeking to ensure that parents fulfil their responsibilities to support their children.[331] The order enables the Secretary of State to take enforcement action by applying to the courts for a variety of orders. For example, he may seek to use bailiffs to take control of the parent's goods to the value of 'the appropriate amount' (the amount of maintenance unpaid together with charges connected with the proceedings).[332] Alternatively, he can apply for a charging order as if the amount unpaid were payable under a county court order[333] or for an order preventing or setting aside a transfer or disposition of property made by the non-resident parent with the intention of avoiding payment.[334] There is also power under s 49D (not in force at time of writing), to pass on prescribed information about the non-resident parent to credit reference agencies, which could be a very potent measure likely to persuade him into compliance for fear of damaging his credit score.

If such means prove unsuccessful, the Secretary of State may apply to the magistrates' court to disqualify the non-resident parent from driving or from holding a passport for 12 months in the first instance, and up to a maximum of two years[335] or to commit him to prison for a maximum period of six weeks,[336] but only if the court is of the opinion that there has been wilful refusal or culpable neglect to pay. In future, he will also be able to seek a curfew order requiring the person to remain at home for between two and 12 hours per day, for a maximum period of six months.[337] Where such action is contemplated, the agency (or service) must ensure they act in accordance with the parent's human rights by actually having tried the less drastic means of enforcement by way of seizure of property or a charging order first. They must also ensure that imprisonment is the order of last resort.[338]

---

[329] DWP, *Child Support Agency Quarterly Summary of Statistics for Great Britain* (March 2014) Table 16.
[330] Section 32M.
[331] *R (Denson) v Child Support Agency* [2002] EWHC 154 (Admin) [2002] 1 FLR 938.
[332] Section 35.
[333] Section 36. Where the money is paid under the charging order, it will retrospectively affect the payee's entitlement to benefits which may result in her having been overpaid: *KW v Lancaster City Council and Secretary of State for Work and Pensions* [2011] UKUT 266 (AAC) [2012] 1 FLR 282 (parent with care liable for overpayments of housing benefit which would have been reduced had the non-resident parent paid child support regularly).
[334] Section 32L. Note also that where the non-resident parent makes himself bankrupt voluntarily and enters into an IVA (individual voluntary arrangement) to clear part of his debts, the full amount of child support remains outstanding and the CSA cannot vote at the creditors' meeting as it has no power to compromise that sum. The IVA will usually prejudice the interests of the CSA and may be set aside: *CMEC v Beesley and Whyman* [2010] EWCA Civ 1344 [2011] 1 FLR 1547.
[335] Child Support Act 1991 ss 39A *et seq.*   [336] Child Support Act 1991 s 40.
[337] Child Support Act 1991 ss 39H, 39I.
[338] *Karoonian v CMEC; Gibbons v CMEC* [2012] EWCA Civ 1379 [2013] 1 FLR 1121.

Whenever any application is made to a court, the court may not question the liability order under which the application is made, or the maintenance calculation in respect of which the action is being taken.[339] Thus, a defendant may not argue that he refuses to pay because the amount is wrong—the correct action to take in such circumstances is to appeal or seek a supersession of the calculation decision.[340] Similarly, an alleged failure to consider the welfare of a child affected by the assessment is not a ground for granting an appeal against a deduction from earnings order (or other measure taken for enforcement).[341] However, the parent can argue that he made the due payment by an alternative means, as in *Bird v Secretary of State for Work and Pensions*,[342] where, instead of paying the child support payments, the father paid the mortgage instalments on the former family home as he and the mother had previously agreed.

These measures have been described as intended 'to pressurise the parent who is wilfully refusing or culpably neglecting either to meet his financial obligations or to suffer a distasteful alternative... essentially a stick and carrot provision rather than one that permits "proceedings" to recover a sum of money.'[343] It follows that even where the penalty is imposed, the money may remain unpaid.

Enforcement action of these more drastic kinds is rarely taken. From April 2013 to March 2014, 11,785 liability orders were granted by courts, and 8,520 referrals to bailiffs for seizure of goods and 1,395 charging orders were made in England and Wales. Still fewer of the punitive measures are sought—only 245 sentences of suspended committal to prison were made in 2012–2013, with 10 actual committals; 55 disqualifications from driving were suspended, and five actual disqualifications made.[344]

Arrears

This array of powers should mean that, once a non-resident parent has been tracked down and assessed, there should be little scope for avoiding compliance, but this has not proved to be the case. The Child Support Agency reported in 2013 that while the proportion of non-resident parents making payments had risen from just over 45% in 1995/96 to around 80% in 2011/12, there was outstanding debt of £3.8 billion in arrears, of which £1.2 billion was effectively uncollectable.[345] 59.6% of arrears at March 2014 were for under £1,000, but this made up only 5.8% of the total[346] showing that there are many parents who have built up many thousands of pounds in non-payment.

---

[339] Section 33(4); *Farley v Secretary of State for Work and Pensions* [2006] UKHL 31 [2006] 3 All ER 935; *Child Support Agency v Learad; Child Support Agency v Buddles* [2008] EWHC 2193 (Admin) [2009] 1 FLR 31.   [340] *Secretary of State for Social Security v Shotton* [1996] 2 FLR 241.

[341] *R v Secretary of State for Social Security, ex p Biggin* [1995] 1 FLR 851. See also *Brookes v Secretary of State for Work and Pensions* [2010] EWCA Civ 420 [2010] 2 FLR 1038 and *R (Joplin) v Child Maintenance and Enforcement Commission* [2010] EWHC 1623 (Admin) [2010] 2 FLR 1510.

[342] [2008] EWHC 3159 [2009] 2 FLR 660. See also *R (Green) v Secretary of State for the Department for Work and Pensions* [2010] EWHC 1278 (Admin) (father paid school fees which should have been offset by the CSA against the child support he owed).

[343] *CMEC v Mitchell* [2010] EWCA Civ 333 [2010] 2 FLR 622. But it also means that the measure is not an action to recover any sum recoverable by virtue of an enactment, and thus not caught by the Limitation Act 1980 s 9, so that the agency were entitled to seek a disqualification order seven years after the liability order had been obtained.

[344] DWP, *Child Support Agency Quarterly Summary of Statistics for Great Britain* (March 2014) Table 16. These figures are lower than the average over the previous five years, but very similar to those reported for 2001–2005 to the HC Select Committee on Work and Pensions, *The Performance of the Child Support Agency* HC 44 (2005) para 168. Figures not available for 2013–2014 at time of writing.

[345] DWP, *Preparing for the future: tackling the past: Child maintenance—Arrears and Compliance Strategy 2012–2017* (2013) p 25.

[346] DWP, *Child Support Agency Quarterly Summary of Statistics for Great Britain* (March 2014), p 39.

A survey of non-resident parents' attitudes to child support helps explain this situation. The researchers found that many such parents resented the Child Support Agency and regarded it as aimed at 'errant fathers', a label they did not apply to themselves. They were often unaware of the true cost of bringing up children, and regarded child support payments as an additional 'burden' on top of what were often high living costs (such as large mortgages) which they had incurred after separating from the parent with care.[347] A more empathetic account argues that stigmatising non-resident parents for failing to meet their responsibilities misunderstands the complexity of their feelings and the importance they may attach to reciprocity, expressed most obviously in the argument that contact with the child and payment of maintenance are—and should be—linked.[348] It is argued that such views stem from regarding child support as a private obligation, whilst the State has sought—at least until recently—to conceive it as a public good. [349]

Yet the House of Lords held in *R (Kehoe) v Secretary of State for Work and Pensions*[350] that a parent with care has no right under Art 6 of the European Convention on Human Rights to challenge how the Child Support Agency chooses, or does not choose, to enforce a calculation, as the Act, in their view, has replaced any pre-existing rights of either a child[351] or a parent to periodical payments for the maintenance of that child. It has also been held that the *children* whose non-resident parent fails to support them cannot claim a breach of the right to respect for private and family life under Art 8 against the agency, for its failure to recover the maintenance owed.[352] The decision in *Kehoe* was upheld by the European Court of Human Rights, which considered that access to judicial review is a sufficient remedy for a parent aggrieved by the agency's failure or inefficiency in pursuing enforcement.[353] However, the Court did not rule on whether the House of Lords were correct in holding that there is no 'civil right' to maintenance protected under Art 6. It is submitted that this question still requires resolution, especially now that the mandatory use of the child support system by benefit claimants has been abolished. This would appear to hand back to all parents the decision whether or not to invoke the child support scheme to collect maintenance. It must be arguable that such a change reinstates (if one accepts that the right had been abolished) the 'right' of a parent—or perhaps the child—to seek to recover support from the liable parent by giving her a choice of mechanisms by which to do this.

3. THE RESIDUAL ROLE OF THE COURTS

Given the difficulties that have beset the child support scheme and the encouragement to avoid using it, it is not surprising that family lawyers will seek to advise their clients on means of avoiding the scheme wherever possible. However, parents are *prevented* from using the courts' jurisdictions except in certain circumstances. The original rationale for

---

[347] A Atkinson and S McKay *Investigating the compliance of Child Support Agency clients* Research Report No 285 (DWP 2005).

[348] For an opposing view, see G Douglas et al 'Contact is not a commodity to be bartered for money' [2011] Fam Law 491.

[349] C Skinner 'Child Maintenance Reforms: Understanding Fathers' Expressive Agency and the Power of Reciprocity' (2013) 27(2) Int Jo of Law, Policy and the Family 242.

[350] [2005] UKHL 48 [2006] 1 AC 42. For a powerful critique of this decision, see N Wikeley 'A Duty but not a right: Child support after *R (Kehoe) v Secretary of State for Work and Pensions*' [2006] CFLQ 287. There is no duty of care which can form the subject of a negligence claim either: *R (Rowley) v Secretary of State for Work and Pensions* [2007] EWCA Civ 598 [2007] 2 FLR 945.

[351] Baroness Hale dissented: [2005] UKHL 48 [2006] 1 AC 42, [68]–[77].

[352] *Treharne v Secretary of State for Work and Pensions* [2008] EWHC 3222 (QB) [2009] 1 FLR 853 (arrears of £42,000).   [353] (Application no 2010/06) [2008] 2 FLR 1014.

the restriction was to ensure that what was regarded as the ineffectual court-based system of maintenance would be superseded by what was intended to be the default regime of child support. As we have seen, things did not work out quite in the way that was hoped. But the failings of the child support scheme coincided with the growing disenchantment with the use of the family justice system to resolve disputes and with the strong imperative to cut funding for litigation. Thus, the response was not to hand everything back to the courts but to encourage parents to make family-based arrangements, as we have discussed earlier. We consider the implications and difficulties of this approach at the end of this chapter; here, we consider when the courts *will* be available to parents seeking maintenance for their children, which depends upon the jurisdictional rules of the Child Support Act 1991.

(a) Where there is no jurisdiction under the Child Support Act

Section 8(1) and (3) of the Child Support Act provides that:

> . . . in any case where the Secretary of State would have jurisdiction to make a maintenance calculation with respect to a qualifying child and a non-resident parent of his on an application duly made by a person entitled to apply for such a calculation with respect to that child . . . no court shall exercise any power which it would otherwise have to make, vary or revive any maintenance order in relation to the child and non-resident parent concerned.[354]

Under s 44 the Secretary of State only has jurisdiction if the person with care, the non-resident parent and the qualifying child are habitually resident in the United Kingdom.[355] Where any of these persons is not so resident, the jurisdiction of the agency is excluded and the court may make an order.

Secondly, a child support assessment may only be made against a non-resident parent who is the legal parent of the qualifying child. Where maintenance is sought for a step-child, the jurisdiction of the courts, which is based on the concept of the 'child of the family',[356] will be the only applicable jurisdiction and the Act will not apply.

Thirdly, where a child is over the age of 16, or is not a qualifying child within s 3(1), the court may still have jurisdiction (for example, if the child is not in full-time non-advanced education but still needs financial support).[357]

Fourthly, and in practice, most importantly, the court may make a maintenance order *by consent*[358] and once such an order has been made, the courts have jurisdiction to vary it.[359] The Act also provides that no child support application may be made where there is a maintenance order which was made before 3 March 2003 or one made on or after that date, but which has been in force for less than one year. (In the latter situation, the child support system *may* be used after the expiry of one year, in order to prevent a permanent

---

[354] Section 10 brings a court order to an end on the making of a child support calculation. See *PK v BC (Financial Remedies: Schedule 1)* [2012] EWHC 1382 (Fam) [2012] 2 FLR 1426, later, Orders instead of or in addition to child support, p 823.

[355] There is jurisdiction where the non-resident parent is not habitually resident in the United Kingdom, but is employed in the civil service of the Crown or is a member of the armed forces, or employed by a company or body of a prescribed description: s 44(2A).

[356] See Ch 9, The meaning of 'child of the family', p 296.

[357] Since the scheme of the Act imposes liability to pay child support maintenance only on a non-resident parent, where maintenance is sought from the person with care instead, the courts may continue to be used: s 8(10).

[358] Section 8(5).   [359] Section 8(3A).

opting out of the scheme where one party might subsequently wish to utilise its provisions).[360] These provisions enable parents to avoid the child support scheme, so long as they can agree with each other on the terms of any maintenance for their children.[361] The courts have facilitated this avoidance of the child support scheme by upholding various devices intended to enable the parties to get the benefit of the court's adjudication whilst apparently remaining within the terms of the statute. First, where the parties do not agree on the quantum of maintenance, the court may make a nominal order at the start of proceedings, by consent, and then vary it to the amount the court sees fit.[362] Secondly, the court may make an order (known as a 'Segal order')[363] for spousal maintenance pending suit[364] which includes an amount for the costs of the children, such amount to be reduced pro tanto by any sums payable under a child support calculation (when subsequently made).[365] The child support scheme thus became a scheme used in two sorts of situations. First, by parents with care on benefits, who, until the requirement to authorise a child support application to be made was abolished, had no choice in the matter and secondly, by those parents with care whose relationship with their ex-partner was particularly bad. This in part helps explain the extremely adverse criticism it has suffered ever since its inception.

(b) Orders instead of or in addition to child support

In some situations, notwithstanding the fact that a maintenance calculation may be carried out, it will remain possible to utilise the courts' jurisdiction. First, under s 8(6), where there is a maintenance calculation in force, which was set at the ceiling fixed by Sch 1, and 'the court is satisfied that the circumstances of the case make it appropriate for the non-resident parent to make or secure the making of periodical payments under a maintenance order in addition to the child support maintenance' the court may continue to exercise its powers to award maintenance, known as 'top up' maintenance. In the case of a wealthy non-resident parent it will therefore still be possible to increase the amount of maintenance to be paid by recourse to the court. Similar powers exist in s 8(7) and (8) to enable the court to make a maintenance order where this is solely to meet costs incurred in receiving education or training, or to cover expenses attributable to the child's disability. School fees, support for a student, and special expenses connected with a child's disability may therefore be met through the court system.[366]

The 1991 Act defines a maintenance order as 'an order which requires the making or securing of periodical payments' and so does not affect the court's powers to make an order for the payment of a lump sum or property adjustment.[367] Although traditionally the courts have not approved of such orders as being appropriate for children, the jurisdiction to make them is unaffected by the Act, and, as discussed already, there may be

---

[360] Section 4(10)(aa).

[361] Compare *B v M (Child Support: Revocation of Order)* [1994] 1 FLR 342: s 8(4) permits the court to revoke a maintenance order, but it was held that it is not appropriate to do so simply to bring the applicant within the jurisdiction of the child support scheme.

[362] *V v V (Child Maintenance)* [2001] 2 FLR 799.

[363] Named after District Judge Segal of the Principal Registry who developed the practice.

[364] See Ch 22, Maintenance pending suit and Legal Services Orders, Maintenance for ongoing support, p 837.   [365] *Dorney-Kingdom v Dorney-Kingdom* [2000] 2 FLR 855, CA.

[366] In *C v F (Disabled Child: Maintenance Order)* [1998] 2 FLR 1, the Court of Appeal held that the court may require that such an order continue in effect after the child reaches the age of 19, since its jurisdiction to do so derives inter alia from the Children Act and not from the Child Support Act, and Sch 1 para 3(2) permits an order to extend beyond the child's nineteenth birthday.

[367] Section 8(11).

situations where they will be suitable.[368] But, in contrast to the courts' willingness to assist parents to avoid the child support jurisdiction entirely, they are more reluctant to see them using their jurisdiction to attempt to get a second bite at the cherry where child support does not yield an adequate result. In *PK v BC (Financial Remedies: Schedule 1)*[369] for example, the court had made a consent order in divorce proceedings under which the father paid £15,000 per year and school fees for the child. He lost his job and applied to the CSA (the order having been in force for over one year) which made a lower calculation of child support. The mother brought proceedings under Sch 1 to the Children Act 1989 to make up the lost maintenance, but it was held that the court had no jurisdiction to grant periodical payments since his income was now below the child support ceiling and a lump sum order was deemed inappropriate as she had already received a capital settlement for housing and living costs for herself and the child at the time of the divorce.

F. EVALUATION

In the early days of the child support scheme, it was argued that the system should be abolished and its work returned to the family justice system. However, the workload of the Child Support Agency is enormous and vastly outstrips the capacity of the civil courts. In June 2013, it was handling around 1.39 million cases; by contrast, the courts handled around 80,000 applications for all kinds of financial remedies in matrimonial proceedings in 2011.[370] The gendered and fraught nature of child support is reflected by the fact that 95% of non-resident parents are male[371] and the debate over the shortcomings of the system has been very bound up with the debates over shared parenting and increased father contact which are the prime feature of developments in private child law over the past decade.[372] It has also become linked to the need to reduce expenditure on the justice system.

As we have seen, both the current and former Government accepted the Henshaw view that private agreements, now known as family-based arrangements, should be the default mode of sorting out maintenance for children. In line with the recommendations of the Family Justice Review,[373] the Government has sought to provide information and encouragement to make such arrangements via web-based provision. Its Child Maintenance Options service[374] and the 'Sorting Out Separation' (SOS) 'hub',[375] contain advice and information to parents, including a pro-forma to draw up an agreement for maintenance and a calculator to determine the amount. Their decision to introduce charges for applying for child support and for use of the collection service is intended to add a further spur to parents to make their own arrangements. Research suggests that there is willingness to do so, and potential for more such arrangements, with an increase from 4% to 20% of single parents on benefit having a private agreement, between 2007 and 2012.[376] It also

---

[368] See earlier, Proceedings under Schedule 1 to the Children Act 1989, Powers, p 794.

[369] [2012] EWHC 1382 (Fam) [2012] 2 FLR 1426.

[370] DWP, *Quarterly Summary of Statistics for Great Britain* (March 2014) p 9; MoJ, *Judicial and Court Statistics 2011* (2012) Table 2.6. [371] DWP, op cit, p 10.

[372] See Ch 14, Changes made by the Children and Families Act 2014, p 481.

[373] Sir D Norgrove, *Family Justice Review Final Report* (2011) paras 4.74–4.79.

[374] http://www.cmoptions.org/index.asp (accesed 4 May 2014).

[375] http://www.sortingoutseparation.org.uk/en/hub/ (accessed 4 May 2014).

[376] C Bryson et al *Kids aren't free: the child maintenance arrangements of single parents on benefit in 2012* (2013) p 10.

found that private arrangements appear to be more productive of maintenance actually being paid (although the researchers warn that parents whose private arrangement has failed to deliver any payments may have responded that they had no such arrangement). However, the study also found that private arrangements are most likely to be made soon after the parents first separate, and unlikely to be chosen after other arrangements have been tried and broken down. They are also prone to be unsustainable over time, with half of the parents who reported that they had tried a private arrangement saying that it had broken down.[377] Factors associated with a private arrangement continuing included having a good relationship between the parents, the non-resident parent having some overnight contact with the child, absence of fear of domestic violence and the non-resident parent being employed. Single parents worried that a change in circumstances, including the other parent re-partnering, and the children growing older and wanting less contact with him, might jeopardise the arrangement.[378] Unsurprisingly, all of these factors chime with what is known about the sustainability of shared care and contact arrangements and they show that those who are already best able to cope and co-operate will do best for their children, both emotionally and financially.

The Government has recognised that the promotion of private arrangements means that those non-resident parents who are the most resistant to paying maintenance will form a larger proportion of their future clientele.[379] It is for this reason that they have sought to increase the range of enforcement measures available in the event of non-compliance. The result is a rather confused picture. Would-be applicants are told to avoid using the statutory services and rely on the willingness of the non-resident parent to abide by a voluntary agreement to support the child. Yet the relevant websites are silent as to the legal enforceability of family-based arrangements and, as we discussed earlier, their validity and the extent to which recourse may be had to a court to vary them if circumstances change, are unclear. On the other hand—in theory at least[380]—if parents do use the statutory service, there is a reasonable chance that they will get their money because the powers to extract it are now extensive. It becomes all the more difficult for a parent with care who cannot get the non-resident parent to agree to a voluntary arrangement to decide what action to take. Will the risk of damaging an already fragile relationship with him if an application is made be outweighed by the benefit of obtaining a possibly more secure form of support which, research also shows, could make a decisive difference to her children's living standards?[381]

In *Kehoe v United Kingdom*,[382] the European Court of Human Rights stated that:

> The provision of a State enforcement scheme for maintenance payments inter alia benefits the many parents with care of children who do not have the time, energy, resources or inclination to be embroiled in ongoing litigation with the absent parent and allows the State to pursue those absent parents who default on their obligations leaving their families on the charge of the social security system and the taxpayer. The mere fact that it is possible to envisage a different scheme which might also allow individual enforcement action by parents in the particular situation of the applicant is not sufficient to disclose a failure by the state in its obligations under Art 6.

---

[377] Bryson et al *Kids aren't free* p 97.   [378] Bryson et al, *Kids aren't free* p 98.

[379] DWP, *Preparing for the future: tackling the past: Child maintenance—Arrears and Compliance Strategy 2012–2017* (2013) p 9.

[380] Bryson et al *Kids aren't free* pp 71–73 found that 23% of single parents on benefit with a CSA calculation never received anything, and a further 27% received something only intermittently.

[381] Bryson et al *Kids aren't free* pp 117–118.

[382] (Application no 2010/06) [2008] 2 FLR 1014 at [49].

One could argue that recent developments show that the issue now is not whether the State acts on behalf of parents lacking the time, energy, resources or inclination to pursue a parent for maintenance, but how far the State puts obstacles in the way of those who need support and assistance to do so. Public opinion seems to run counter to the thrust of recent trends—the majority of the public think that the State *should* be involved financially in enforcing non-resident parents' obligations to support their children, and they would require parents to pay considerably more by way of maintenance than the child support formula produces.[383] Yet, as this chapter has outlined, the current law leaves the status of parents' private agreements uncertain, particularly in relation to whether they can be subject to variation by a court when circumstances change. It also prevents most parents from using the courts other than to obtain a consent order, yet simultaneously deters them from using the child support system. This itself has shifted from being expected to be the default position to becoming the option of last resort. The conclusion seems to be that the State has shown itself unable and unwilling to make the system work properly on the scale necessary to meet the needs of separating families, in the hope that leaving it up to the parents themselves will somehow produce a more positive outcome.

[383] C Bryson et al, 'Child maintenance: how much should the state require fathers to pay when families separate?' [2013] Fam Law 1296, 1309.

22

FINANCIAL REMEDIES ON DIVORCE, DISSOLUTION, NULLITY AND SEPARATION: THE COURT'S POWERS

A. INTRODUCTION

The growth of divorce in modern times has inevitably led to much greater significance being attached to the financial consequences of marriage breakdown, both for the parties and their children, and for the State. Research studies in this country, the United States and Australia, all confirm that, for mothers with children to care for, divorce is likely to have a major detrimental effect on their standard of living, while divorced men are likely to see no major decline in theirs.[1] The reason for the difference is primarily that the earning capacity of divorced women is less than that of men—they are more likely to have interrupted their careers to have children and hence earn lower amounts than men, and they are less likely to be able to resume (or remain in) full-time employment to make up the shortfall when their marriage breaks down. Even after their children have grown up, they are likely to remain less well off because they are unable to build up sufficient funds for an adequate pension when they retire.[2] The policy dilemma for Government is to decide whether, and to what extent, it should attempt to meet the resulting shortfall by either making the former husband maintain, or compensate, the wife, or by taking on the burden through the social security system. As we saw in Chapter 21, attempting to make non-resident *parents* support their children and thus relieve public expenditure, at least in part, has been a consistent policy objective, though with limited success. As regards

---

[1] For research into the system and its effects in England and Wales, see J Eekelaar and M Maclean *Maintenance After Divorce* (1986); G Davis, S Cretney and J Collins *Simple Quarrels: Negotiating Money and Property Disputes on Divorce* (1994); M Maclean and J Eekelaar *The Parental Obligation* (1997) ch 7; A Perry et al *How Parents Cope Financially on Marriage Breakdown* (2000); J Eekelaar, M Maclean and S Beinart *Family Lawyers: The Divorce Work of Solicitors* (2000); G Davis et al 'Ancillary relief outcomes' [2000] CFLQ 43, S Arthur et al *Settling Up: Making Financial Arrangements After Divorce or Separation* (2002); E Hitchings 'Everyday Cases in the Post-White Era' [2008] Fam Law 873; 'The impact of recent ancillary relief jurisprudence in the "everyday" ancillary relief case' [2010] CFLQ 93. For international perspectives see L Weitzman and M Maclean (eds) *Economic Consequences of Divorce* (1992) and the collection of articles contained in (2005) 19(2) Int J of Law, Pol and Fam. For consideration of the relationship between debt and relationship breakdown, see S Bridges and R Disney 'Household indebtedness and separation in Britain: evidence from the Families and Children Survey' [2012] CFLQ 24.

[2] See J Ginn and D Price 'Do divorced women catch up in pension building?' [2002] CFLQ 157.

the termination of marriage (most usually by divorce),[3] the law again seeks to regard the financial consequences as a matter to be dealt with as far as possible by adjusting the spouses' assets and earnings between them, with state support providing a safety net. But while there is a legal logic to attaching liability to a parent, or a spouse, in recognition of a *continuing* legal relationship between payer and recipient, the argument is more complicated once the legal tie between spouses has been ended.

In this chapter, for convenience, we discuss the law in the context of a divorce (but refer to dissolution of a civil partnership, nullity and separation where relevant), and we refer to the husband as the payer and the wife as recipient, unless otherwise specified. However, it should be noted that the obligations of the spouses (including, of course, same-sex spouses) and civil partners are equal and reciprocal. We deal with the court's powers and the procedures under which these are exercised in this chapter, and we consider in Chapter 23 how the courts exercise these powers.

1. THE SETTLEMENT CULTURE

We saw in Chapter 1 that family justice, like civil justice in general, is characterised by high rates of settlement between the parties occurring either before any legal proceedings are begun, or before the point of trial. This position is no different when it comes to determining the parties' financial positions after a divorce or dissolution.[4] There is a considerable shortfall between the number of orders made by the courts (either by consent or after adjudication) and the number of divorces (or dissolutions) pronounced. In 2011, for example, while 115,189 divorces were finalised, there were only 33,497 cases disposed of.[5] The reasons for the shortfall are not known, but suggestions have included a move away from reliance upon continuing financial support between the ex-spouses obviating the need for an order requiring such support to be made; short, childless marriages which have generated no financial dependency between the parties and which have accumulated little by way of capital marital assets to be shared between them;[6] minimal assets and income available to be shared in any event; the need to sort things out in advance of the time taken in bringing legal proceedings; a wish to avoid the costs; and a wish to avoid the perceived 'adversarial' approach taken by some family lawyers.[7] Whatever the reasons, as many as four in 10 divorcing couples apparently make no use of legal advice,[8] and of those who do, over a third may not use their solicitor to negotiate the settlement with the other spouse, but merely to draw up the terms of the agreement they have reached.[9]

---

[3] And now, dissolution for civil partnership.

[4] The development of the so-called 'settlement culture' is not without its critics: see generally G Davis, S Cretney and J Collins *Simple Quarrels: Negotiating Money and Property Disputes on Divorce* (1994) and especially at pp 260–3. For further consideration of the place of settlement in family justice and its promotion by solicitors, barristers and judges, see J Eekelaar, M Maclean and S Beinart *Family Lawyers: The Divorce Work of Solicitors* (2000); M Maclean and J Eekelaar *Family Law Advocacy: How Barristers Help the Victims of Family Failure* (2009) and *Family Justice: The Work of Family Judges in Uncertain Times* (2013).

[5] Ministry of Justice, *Court Statistics (quarterly) January to March 2014* (2014) Table 2.6. It is unclear if this includes orders connected with civil partnership dissolutions.

[6] C Barton and A Bissett-Johnson 'The declining number of ancillary financial relief orders' [2000] Fam Law 94.

[7] G Douglas and A Perry 'How parents cope financially on separation and divorce—implications for the future of ancillary relief' [2001] CFLQ 67.

[8] A Barlow et al 'Mapping Paths to Family Justice: a national picture of findings on out of court family dispute resolution' [2013] Fam Law 306 at 307.   [9] Douglas and Perry [2001] CFLQ 67 at p 77.

The legal enforceability of a private agreement (whether reached with the benefit of legal advice or not) may be problematic if the parties later dispute what was agreed or how it was to be implemented. It is therefore beneficial to obtain a binding court order even where there has been a settlement, so that the parties can then take advantage of the court's enforcement powers. As we will see later,[10] the parties may submit the terms of their agreement to the court to be embodied in a 'consent order'. These make up the vast majority of court orders for financial remedies: in 2013, 28,926 cases were disposed of completely uncontested, 10,619 began as contested proceedings but settled before trial, and only 3,737 disposals were the results of court adjudication—just 8.6% of the total.[11]

It can therefore be seen that the elaborate and complex processes, legislation and jurisprudence which underpin the financial outcomes of divorce constitute only the backdrop against which most couples arrive at some sort of settlement or resolution of their financial positions. Many couples may never go near the court; relatively few will see the inside of the court room, and very few will have the merits of their case determined by a judge. This does not mean that the law we are about to discuss is irrelevant or unimportant; on the contrary, the principles and dispositions laid down by statute and case-law enable us to evaluate whether the law provides adequate protection for the rights of each spouse and their children, and whether they can bargain effectively 'in the shadow of the law'[12] to enforce those rights. Settlement, rather than adjudication, of claims, is strongly promoted by the family justice system.

2. DEVELOPMENT OF THE COURT'S POWERS

The ecclesiastical courts were able to give financial protection to a wife by ordering the husband to pay her alimony (periodical maintenance). After 1857 this power was vested in the Divorce Court, which was also empowered on granting a decree of divorce to order the husband to secure maintenance for the wife's life. If the husband had no capital on which the payments of maintenance could be secured, hardship was likely to be caused to the wife; this was cured in 1866, when the court was given the power to order the husband to pay unsecured maintenance to the wife. As this would have to come out of his income, however, the maximum term for which it could be ordered was the spouses' joint lives. After 1937 a wife petitioning for divorce or judicial separation on the ground of her husband's insanity could be ordered to pay him maintenance. In 1963 the courts were given a power to order the payment of a lump sum in addition to or instead of maintenance on divorce, nullity and judicial separation.

Where a husband obtained a divorce or judicial separation on the ground of his wife's adultery the 1857 Act gave the court power to order that any property settled to her own use be settled for the benefit of the husband or children. This power was later extended to the property of wives who were divorced for cruelty or desertion. On divorce or nullity, either party could benefit from the exercise of the court's jurisdiction, going back to 1859, to vary ante-nuptial and post-nuptial settlements.[13]

(a) The Matrimonial Causes Act 1973

Piecemeal modifications of the law spread over more than a century produced confusing anomalies, and pressure for wholesale reform increased after the passing of the Divorce

---

[10] At Consent orders, p 849.

[11] Ministry of Justice, *Court Statistics (quarterly) January to March 2014* (2014) Table 2.6.

[12] R Mnookin and L Kornhauser 'Bargaining in the Shadow of the Law: The Case of Divorce' (1979) 88 *Yale Law Journal* 950.   [13] See S Cretney *Family Law in the Twentieth Century: A History* (2003) ch 10.

Reform Act 1969, when the fear was expressed that many innocent wives, divorced against their will, would be left with inadequate provision. The result was the passing of the Matrimonial Proceedings and Property Act 1970, which was based upon the recommendations of the Law Commission.[14] Most of its provisions were repealed and re-enacted in Part II of the Matrimonial Causes Act 1973, which, in its amended form, governs the award of financial orders in the family court. The Act abolished the confusing variations in types of order for maintenance, and described all as 'financial provision', which may take the form of periodical payments or a lump sum payment. The court was given equal powers to order either spouse to make financial provision for the other, regardless of who is seeking the divorce. The Act also widened the court's powers in two important respects. First, the court's redistributive powers extend to all the assets that either or both the spouses own, irrespective of when and from whom they acquired them.[15] Secondly, in making orders in respect of the spouses' property, the court is not bound to enforce existing rights and can, for instance, order the transfer of ownership from one spouse to another. This latter power was vested in the court partly in response to the decisions in *Pettitt v Pettitt*[16] and *Gissing v Gissing*,[17] which, as we have seen,[18] established that the powers under the Married Women's Property Act 1882 s 17 are declaratory only and that therefore the courts had no power to transfer ownership of property between spouses. These wider redistributive powers represent one of the key remaining distinctions between the ending of a marriage and the ending of cohabitation.

(b) Subsequent legislative change

The 1973 Act was amended by the Matrimonial Homes and Property Act 1981, which gave the divorce courts the express statutory power to order the sale of any of the spouses' property.[19] More importantly, the Matrimonial and Family Proceedings Act 1984[20] both extended the court's powers by enabling it to *impose* a clean break (ie a once-and-for-all settlement between the spouses with no continuing financial ties) upon a spouse,[21] and altered the way that the powers are to be exercised. Two of the most important changes were: (1) to require the court, when deciding what orders should be made, to give first consideration to the welfare, whilst a minor, of any child of the family under 18;[22] and (2) to impose a duty upon the court to consider whether it is appropriate so to exercise its powers that the financial obligations of each party terminate immediately or as soon

---

[14] Law Com No 25, *Report on Financial Provision in Matrimonial Proceedings* (1969) on which see S Cretney 'The Maintenance Quagmire' (1970) 33 MLR 662.

[15] But see Ch 23, Matrimonial and non-matrimonial property, pp 882–886 for how the courts exercise their powers in relation to 'non-matrimonial' property.   [16] [1970] AC 777, HL.

[17] [1971] AC 886, HL. See also Law Com No 25, paras 64–75.

[18] Ch 4, Proceedings under s 17 of the Married Women's Property Act 1882, p 117.

[19] By s 7 which added s 24A to the 1973 Act.

[20] This Act is based on the Law Commission's recommendations: see Law Com No 112 *The Financial Consequences of Divorce* (1981). See also their earlier paper, Law Com No 103 *The Financial Consequences of Divorce: The Basic Policy* (1980). For an interesting account of the background and reasons for the Law Commission recommending changes, see S Cretney 'Money After Divorce—The Mistakes We Have Made?' in M Freeman (ed) *Essays in Family Law* (1985) pp 34 *et seq*, particularly at pp 36–42. See also G Douglas 'Simple Quarrels? Autonomy vs. Vulnerability' in R Probert and C Barton (eds) *Fifty Years in Family Law: Essays for Stephen Cretney* (2012) p 217.

[21] Under the Matrimonial Causes Act 1973 s 25A(3), which was originally added by s 3(4) of the Matrimonial and Family Proceedings Act 1984, and amended by the Welfare Reform and Pensions Act 1999 s 19 and Sch 3 paras 1, 6.

[22] Section 25(1) as substituted by s 3 of the 1984 Act. For 'child of the family', see Ch 9, The meaning of 'child of the family', p 296.

as possible.[23] The 1984 Act also ended the obligation of the court to attempt to place the parties in the position that they would have been had the marriage not broken down. Subsequently, the Pensions Act 1995[24] and the Welfare Reform and Pensions Act 1999[25] extended the court's powers in relation to the parties' pensions and pension rights.

(c) Dissolution of civil partnerships

We saw in Chapter 7 that there are provisions based on those applicable to divorce for the dissolution of a civil partnership. The Civil Partnership Act 2004 accordingly provides similar financial relief, in Sch 5, for civil partners who separate, or terminate their partnership, to that available to spouses.[26] The provisions are not discussed separately in the following text, but the table at the end of this chapter sets out the equivalent provisions in the two Acts.

3. POWERS OF THE COURT

The court has statutory power[27] to make an order against *either spouse* with respect to any one or more of the following:[28]

    (1) Unsecured periodical payments to the other spouse.

    (2) Secured periodical payments to the other spouse.

    (3) Lump sum payments to the other spouse.

    (4) Unsecured periodical payments for any child of the family.

    (5) Secured periodical payments for any child of the family.

    (6) A lump sum payment for any child of the family.

    (7) Transfer of property to the other spouse or for the benefit of any child of the family.

    (8) Settlement of property for the benefit of the other spouse or any child of the family.

    (9) Variation of any marriage settlement.

    (10) A 'pension sharing order' reallocating part or all of a spouse's accrued pension rights to the other on nullity or divorce.[29]

Orders coming within (1)–(6) are collectively known as financial provision orders and those coming within (7)–(9) as property adjustment orders. A financial provision order may also direct that a share of a spouse's pension be 'attached' or 'earmarked' and paid to the other on retirement.[30]

    Where a court makes a secured periodical payments order, a lump sum order or a property transfer order, it can further order a sale of property belonging to either or both spouses.[31] Orders for the sale of property are neither classified as financial provision nor property adjustment.[32]

---

[23] Section 25A(1), (2) as substituted by s 3(4) of the 1984 Act.

[24] Pensions Act 1995 s 166(1) which inserted ss 25B–25D (subsequently amended by the Welfare Reform and Pensions Act 1999 s 21 and Sch 4) into the Matrimonial Causes Act 1973.

[25] Welfare Reform and Pensions Act 1999 Schs 3 and 4, inserting ss 21A, 24B–D into the 1973 Act.

[26] See s 72 (1) and Sch 5.

[27] But the court can accept a party's undertaking to accept other obligations: see later, The effects of a consent order, p 853.   [28] Under the Matrimonial Causes Act 1973 ss 21, 23 and 24.

[29] As inserted by the Welfare Reform and Pensions Act 1999 Sch 3.

[30] Under the Matrimonial Causes Act 1973 ss 25B–25D as inserted by the Pensions Act 1995 s 166(1).

[31] Matrimonial Causes Act 1973 s 24A as added by the Matrimonial Homes and Property Act 1981 s 7.

[32] *Omielan v Omielan* [1996] 2 FLR 306, CA.

Although, as we shall see, there are statutory guidelines on the matters to be taken into account when exercising these powers, it should be appreciated at the outset that considerable discretion is left to the judge in deciding what order should be made in any individual case.[33] This discretion applies equally to determining what order should be made with regard to the spouses' property and with regard to their income. This vesting of wide discretion in the courts is in contrast to the position taken even in some other common law jurisdictions.[34] In New Zealand, for instance, the matrimonial home and family chattels must generally be divided equally, although there is discretion to adjust these shares to compensate for economic disparity between the separated parties,[35] while in Scotland there is a statutory presumption in favour of equal division unless special circumstances exist which justify a departure from this principle.[36] Discussion has long continued regarding whether the breadth of discretion is desirable, with concern voiced by the courts that it encourages forum shopping such that 'London is regularly described by the press as the divorce capital of the world',[37] and we consider this further in Chapter 23.[38]

4. APPLICATION FOR ORDERS

An order for financial provision, property adjustment or pension attachment may be made on or after the grant of decree of nullity,[39] divorce or judicial separation, but shall not take effect unless (in the case of the former two) the decree has been made absolute.[40] A pension sharing order may only be made on or after a decree of nullity or divorce.[41]

It is a general principle of the Matrimonial Causes Act 1973 that, if the former spouse remarries, she (or he) must look to the new partner for financial provision for herself, and not to the old one. Consequently, a party who has remarried cannot apply for an order at

[33] For judicial acknowledgement of this discretion and that it should be exercised with restraint, see Waite J in *Thomas v Thomas* [1995] 2 FLR 668 at 670, CA. For criticism of the operation of the discretionary approach see G Davis, S Cretney and J Collins *Simple Quarrels: Negotiating Money and Property Disputes on Divorce* (1994) especially at ch 11.

[34] In most continental legal systems there is some form of community of property which severely restricts or even precludes the court from being able to redistribute the parties' property; moreover, parties may usually contract out of the default regime to limit still further any scope for sharing of property after divorce. For an account of various community of property regimes, see E Cooke, A Barlow and T Callus *Community of Property: A regime for England and Wales?* (2006); K Boele-Woelki et al *Principles of European Family Law Regarding Property Relations Between Spouses* (2013). Marital property agreements are discussed later, Pre- and post-nuptial agreements pp XXX and Ch 23, Reform, Marital property agreements, p 927.

[35] Under the Property (Relationships) Act 1976 (as amended), save in certain defined circumstances, eg where the marriage has been of short duration. See B Atkin 'The rights of married and unmarried couples in New Zealand—radical new laws on property and succession' [2003] CFLQ 173.

[36] Family Law (Scotland) Act 1985 s 9(1) and s 10(1). See *Lightbody (or Jacques) v Jacques* 1997 SC (HL) 20.

[37] See the summary of legal developments and the need for reform expressed by Sir Mark Potter P in his 'Postscript' to the judgment in *Charman v Charman (No 4)* [2007] EWCA Civ 503 [2007] 1 FLR 1246 at [106]–[126]. The jurisdictional rules laid down in 'Brussels II' in relation to divorce and hence ancillary relief (see Ch 1, The European Union and the Brussels Regulations, p 28) are intended to try to limit such forum shopping at least amongst EU residents, although they may arguably have the opposite effect.

[38] Reform, pp 925–933.

[39] Thus, even though the marriage is void, financial orders can be made, which may be important for those who undergo a flawed marriage ceremony. See also *Whiston v Whiston* [1995] Fam 198, CA, *Rampal v Rampal (No 2)* [2001] EWCA Civ 989 [2001] 2 FLR 1179, *J v S-T (Formerly J) (Transsexual: Ancillary Relief)* [1997] 1 FLR 402, CA. A fortiori there is power to order financial relief if the marriage is voidable: see *Johnston v Johnston* (1976) 6 Fam Law 17, CA. But there is no such power in the case of a 'non-marriage': see Ch 3, A void marriage—or no marriage at all? pp 67–70.

[40] Matrimonial Causes Act 1973 ss 23(1)(5), 24(1)(3), 24B(1)(2).

[41] Matrimonial Causes Act 1973 s 24B(1)(2).

all, except in relation to a child of the family,[42] although an application already made can be entertained notwithstanding the remarriage.[43] This rule applies even though the second marriage is void or voidable:[44] the party's remedy lies in seeking financial provision in the nullity proceedings. Even where the applicant has not remarried, he or she cannot expect the former spouse to act as 'insurer against life's eventualities'.[45] In *Vince v Wyatt* the parties, who had lived a 'New Age' lifestyle, divorced in 1992 but no papers remained about the proceedings and no financial provision orders were apparently made at that time. Each formed later partnerships. The husband subsequently became very wealthy and the wife applied in 2011 for financial remedies. The Court of Appeal held that her claim should have been struck out. As Thorpe LJ noted, the facts were extreme:

> Impecuniosity has been the experience of all the wife's adult life. Both the men with whom she has entered into family life were seemingly equally impecunious. Her husband was the most improbable candidate for affluence. The wife no doubt can appeal to his sense of charity but in my judgment he is not to be compelled to boost the wife's income by the exercise of the jurisdiction under the Matrimonial Clauses Act 1973 the existence of which cannot now be plainly established and can only be presumed.[46]

Furthermore, a financial remedies claim is not a cause of action which survives against the other party's estate, so that no order can be made after the death of either of them.[47] Where the order was sought by the surviving spouse, the effect of this is mitigated by the extensive powers given to the court by the Inheritance (Provision for Family and Dependants) Act 1975[48] but in *McMinn v McMinn (Ancillary Relief: Death of Party to Proceedings)*[49] the husband killed the wife before the court had granted decree absolute. The financial order that the district judge had made after decree nisi had not, therefore, taken effect, and the wife's executors were not able to take over her claim.

5. FINANCIAL REMEDIES PROCEDURE

(a) Procedure

The cost of family proceedings, particularly for financial remedies, is notorious and has frequently been the subject of adverse comment by the courts.[50] Parties are encouraged, through the facts that (absenting violence) there is no legal aid to support their litigation and each must usually bear their own legal costs, to avoid protracted proceedings, and ideally any court hearings at all. As we noted earlier, negotiations between themselves, or with the assistance of lawyers, are the primary way in which settlements have always

---

[42] Matrimonial Causes Act 1973 s 28(3); *E v E* [2008] 1 FLR 220. If the embargo applies and the former spouse wishes to dispute ownership of any matrimonial property, he or she can, within three years after the divorce, seek a declaration under the Married Women's Property Act 1882 s 17.

[43] *Jackson v Jackson* [1973] Fam 99. This does not apply to an application for periodical payments for the spouse which will in any case cease on remarriage: see later, Periodical payments, Orders in favour of spouses, p 839.   [44] Matrimonial Causes Act 1973 s 52(3).

[45] Per Thorpe LJ in *Vince v Wyatt* [2013] EWCA Civ 495 [2014] 1 FLR 246 at [35].

[46] *Vince v Wyatt* [2013] EWCA Civ 495 [2014] 1 FLR 246.

[47] *Dipple v Dipple* [1942] P 65; *McMinn v McMinn (Ancillary Relief: Death of Party to Proceedings)* [2002] EWHC 1194 (Fam) [2003] 2 FLR 823.

[48] See Ch 25, Reasonable provision, For a surviving spouse or civil partner, p 983.

[49] [2002] EWHC 1194 (Fam) [2003] 2 FLR 823.

[50] See eg *Evans v Evans* [1990] 2 All ER 147; *Piglowska v Piglowski* [1999] 1 WLR 1360; *White v White* [2001] 1 AC 596. In *Sekhi v Ray* [2013] EWHC 2290 (Fam) [2014] 1 FLR 612 Holman J described as a 'human

been reached. Mediation, collaborative law, and family arbitration,[51] are other initiatives designed to help the parties keep their costs down. A Pre-Application Protocol[52] expects the parties to exchange information and engage in negotiation from the outset. However, litigation cannot always be avoided, and the judiciary and practitioners therefore sought to streamline the court procedure, resulting in a revised system introduced in 2000,[53] and subsequently updated by the more comprehensive Family Procedure Rules 2010.[54] As we saw in Chapter 1, the overriding objective of the Rules and accompanying Practice Directions is to enable the court to deal with cases justly and proportionately and the process and procedure governing financial claims are designed to deliver these aims.

An application for financial remedies is begun by filing a 'Form A' which should detail every order that the applicant is seeking. Both parties must then complete a 'Form E' which is intended (together with prescribed documents which must be attached to it, such as property valuations) to contain sufficient information about their circumstances to enable the case to be disposed of, without either overwhelming the parties (or the court) with a surfeit of documentation, or concealing matters relevant to achieving a fair outcome. Both spouses are under a duty to make full, frank and up-to-date disclosure of their assets and circumstances.[55] A former practice, known as the 'millionaire's defence',[56] whereby wealthy respondents (almost always men) could decline to disclose their assets (in detail at least) on the basis that these were sufficient to meet any order that the court might make against them, was firmly disapproved by the Court of Appeal in *McFarlane v McFarlane; Parlour v Parlour*.[57] The court pointed out that it was both discriminatory to wives to require them to document their needs and resources, whilst permitting their husbands to conceal theirs, and unfair in preventing the court from obtaining a true picture of what such husbands could in fact afford.[58] However, it may be preferable to compromise on precision and detail in order to reduce costs, particularly where complex corporate dealings are involved[59] or the value of the disputed items is minimal in comparison to the overall size of the marital pot.[60]

The progress of the case is actively managed by the court, with a fixed timetable, which can be varied only by judicial order. A first appointment is scheduled to enable the judge to define the issues and issue directions, and also, if possible, to turn the appointment into a financial dispute resolution appointment ('FDR'). This is a privileged (ie confidential) meeting at which the judge (who will not hear the case if it fails to settle) assists the parties, and their legal advisers, in exploring common ground and narrowing the issues in dispute with a view to reaching agreement. This can include giving the parties an 'indication' or 'early neutral

---

tragedy' a case where the couple, whose combined wealth was £4 million, had run up costs of £600,000 simply in litigation to determine in which jurisdiction their divorce should be dealt with.

[51] See Ch 1, Private ordering and the withdrawal of legal aid, p 10.   [52] [2000] 1 FLR 997.

[53] Family Proceedings (Amendment No 2) Rules 1999 (SI 1999/3491).

[54] SI 2010/2955 (L17). See Ch 1, A more managerial approach, p 19.

[55] *Livesey (formerly Jenkins) v Jenkins* [1985] AC 424, HL; *Clibbery v Allan and Another* [2002] EWCA Civ 45 [2002] Fam 261, discussed later, The information before the court, p 849. Deliberate deception may result in conviction for perjury: see T Paskins 'Family Relief Disclosure—Beware of Perjury' [2004] Fam Law 57. Complex cases where disclosure is often pivotal should be managed by an allocated High Court judge: *K v K (Financial Relief: Management of Difficult Cases)* [2005] EWHC 1070 (Fam) [2005] 2 FLR 1137.

[56] *Thyssen-Bornemisza v Thyssen-Bornemisza (No 2)* [1985] FLR 1069, CA.

[57] [2004] EWCA (Civ) 872 [2005] Fam 171 per Thorpe LJ at para 83.

[58] [2004] EWCA (Civ) 872 [2005] Fam 171. See dicta by Thorpe LJ at paras 78, 82 and Latham LJ at para 117. A solicitor may be ordered to produce documentation that may assist a wife in quantifying or locating the husband's assets or indeed his whereabouts: *Kimber v Brookman Solicitors* [2004] 2 FLR 221.

[59] *J v V (Disclosure: Offshore Corporations)* [2003] EWHC 3110 (Fam) [2004] 1 FLR 1042: wife's costs £700,000.

[60] *B v B (Financial Orders: Proportionality)* [2013] EWHC 1232 (Fam) [2013] Fam Law 1374.

evaluation' of what the judge thinks would be the likely outcome of the case if no settlement were reached. Where the parties are not ready for this at the first appointment, the FDR will be timetabled for a future date.

If the case settles, the court will make a consent order. The parties are warned about the costs and time implications of not settling.[61] A final hearing may require more information to be before the court than was assembled for the FDR, which will add to the costs.[62]

(b) Disclosure

The court possesses extensive powers to enable one party to obtain additional information from the other, and may make orders for discovery where financial and other documents and records are required to be produced.[63] Those who attempt to deceive the court by failing to make full disclosure will forfeit its sympathy,[64] and it is open to the court to draw the adverse inference that beneath a false presentation there are undisclosed assets, provided that there is a sound evidential base for doing so.[65] In *Young v Young*[66] for example, the litigation took six and a half years to come to trial, involved 65 separate hearings, resulted in the husband being imprisoned for six months for contempt of court and cost the wife £6.4 million in legal costs, largely caused by the husband's reluctance to make full disclosure, and resulted in the wife securing an award of £20 million after the judge concluded—with difficulty—that the husband's assets were some £45 million (but not the £779 million at which the wife's expert pitched the husband's maximum wealth). The court may, in its discretion, penalise a reluctance or refusal to make proper disclosure in its order for costs.[67]

One major potential drawback to full and frank disclosure is the risk that the information revealed will be passed on to the authorities. Both the HMRC and the police may be interested in discovering material which might reveal evidence of tax evasion or criminal activity. In *S v S (Inland Revenue: Tax Evasion)*,[68] Wilson J refused an application by the Inland Revenue for disclosure of documents in a case in which he had made general and inferential findings of tax evasion, and required them to return the copy of his judgment they had received. In *R v R (Inland Revenue: Tax Evasion)*,[69] by contrast, he ruled that the Inland Revenue should be permitted to keep a copy of a judgment which had been passed to them, in which he had made a finding of tax evasion on explicit evidence, because there, the public interest in reducing tax evasion outweighed that of candour in the proceedings.[70] The public interest in law enforcement was also predominant in the view of Charles J in *A v A; B v B*[71] who considered that the court should itself report relevant material to the appropriate authority where this comes to light in the proceedings. However, in *HMRC v Charman and Charman*[72] Coleridge J emphasised that the general rule is that documents and evidence produced in financial remedy proceedings are only disclosable by order of the court to a third party with very good reason. The tax authorities had issued

---

[61] The parties are encouraged to try out of court mediation as well as the FDR process, no matter how conflicted their positions: see the views of the Court of Appeal in *Al-Khatib v Masry* [2004] EWCA Civ 1353 [2005] 1 FLR 381.   [62] See *W v W (Ancillary Relief: Procedure)* [2000] Fam Law 473.

[63] This includes the use of detailed questionnaires, and oral discovery: see *OS v DS (Oral Disclosure: Preliminary Hearing)* [2004] EWHC 2376 (Fam) [2005] 1 FLR 675. For an order made against beneficiaries of an offshore trust, see *Tchenguiz-Imerman v Imerman* [2013] EWHC 3627 (Fam) [2014] Fam Law 451.   [64] See *C v C (Financial Relief: Short Marriage)* [1997] 2 FLR 26, CA.

[65] *NG v SG (Appeal: Non-Disclosure)* [2011] EWHC 3270 (Fam) [2012] 1 FLR 1211.

[66] [2013] EWHC 3637 (Fam) [2014] Fam Law 291.

[67] For discussion of costs see later, Costs, p 863.   [68] [1997] 2 FLR 774.

[69] [1998] 1 FLR 922.

[70] In *S v S (Inland Revenue: Tax Evasion)*, he considered that the balance lay in the public interest in ensuring full disclosure in the financial proceedings.   [71] [2000] 1 FLR 701.

[72] [2012] EWHC 1448 (Fam) [2012] 2 FLR 1119.

an assessment of £11.5m in unpaid tax against the husband, who was appealing to the First Tier Tax Chamber. They applied for disclosure of the documents and other evidence filed in his financial relief proceedings. But the application was refused on the basis that the HMRC had advanced no compelling reason why the general rule should be relaxed for what was a routine tax assessment in which there was no suggestion that the husband had been guilty of tax evasion or criminal conduct.

Proceeds of Crime Act 2002

Parties in such situations should be warned of their privilege against self-incrimination, but there is clearly a risk that material will then be concealed from their legal advisers (or mediators) and hence the court.[73] There was a danger that this risk had been compounded by the enactment of the Proceeds of Crime Act 2002. This Act, intended to clamp down on money laundering, imposes criminal liability on a person who becomes 'concerned in an arrangement which he knows or suspects facilitates the acquisition, retention, use or control of criminal property by or on behalf of another person'.[74] Such liability may be avoided if the person makes an 'authorised disclosure' to, now, the National Crime Agency and obtains their consent to continue with the transaction. The question arose whether, in financial remedy (or other proceedings), a lawyer (or mediator) was obliged by these provisions to inform the authorities of any suspicions he or she might have regarding the activities of the client. In *Bowman v Fels*[75] the Court of Appeal overturned a decision by the President of the Family Division[76] that such was indeed the position. They held that the Act is not intended to cover or affect the ordinary conduct of litigation by legal professionals, including any step taken by them in litigation from the issue of proceedings up to its final disposal by judgment. Relying on Art 6 of the European Convention on Human Rights, they noted that:

> legal proceedings are a state-provided mechanism for the resolution of issues according to law . . . Parliament cannot have intended that proceedings or steps taken by lawyers in order to determine or secure legal rights and remedies for their clients should involve them in 'becoming concerned in an arrangement which . . . facilitates the acquisition, retention, use or control of criminal property', even if they suspected that the outcome of such proceedings might have such an effect.[77]

The court went on to hold that the Act could not be interpreted as overriding the defence of legal professional privilege or require a lawyer to breach his duty to the court by disclosing to a third party outside the litigation documents revealed to him through the disclosure processes. Finally, the court rejected the argument that facilitating a settlement in proceedings could be construed as 'an arrangement' within the terms of the Act: such an interpretation would undermine the need to encourage consensual settlement of legal disputes.

---

[73] See the discussion by B Molyneux 'The Privilege against Self-Incrimination in Ancillary Relief Proceedings' [2001] Fam Law 603.   [74] Proceeds of Crime Act 2002 s 328(1).
[75] [2005] EWCA Civ 226 [2005] 2 FLR 247. See E Powles 'All that Glisters is not Gold: Laundering the UK Money Laundering Regime' (2006) 65 CLJ 43; A Chandler 'POCA and NCIS: *Bowman v Fels*' [2005] Fam Law 359; D Burrows '*Bowman v Fels*: Privilege Revived' [2005] Fam Law 386. See also guidance from the Law Society at http://www.lawsociety.org.uk/advice/practice-notes/aml/money-laundering-offences/ (accessed 11 May 2014).
[76] *P v P (Ancillary Relief: Proceeds of Crime)* [2003] EWHC Fam 2260 [2004] 1 FLR 193.
[77] At para 84.

This judgment importantly reassured lawyers (and other professionals involved with separating couples) that they can safely advise and assist their clients without fear of, in the words of one commentator, presenting 'an image to the client that the solicitor is a fully paid-up member of the police'[78] and should assist in encouraging clients to make proper disclosure (whilst not obviating the solicitor's duty to avoid becoming embroiled in potentially criminal evasion).

'Self-help'

What if a spouse has strong suspicions, or even knows that the other has not made—or is unlikely to make—full disclosure? The question arose as to whether such a spouse could lawfully employ 'self help' techniques, such as copying the contents of the other's computer files, or making photocopies of documents, to inform his or her own legal team in formulating their negotiating strategy or arguments in court. A practice, based on what were known as the 'Hildebrand Rules',[79] had arisen in the Family Division whereby parties who had obtained material in this way would be permitted to use it in the litigation provided that they disclosed the fact to the other side. In Imerman v Tchenguiz and Others[80] the wife's brother, who was in business with her husband, obtained access to his computer and copied many documents which were forwarded to the solicitors handling her divorce. When the husband discovered this, he sought an injunction requiring the return of all the documents. The Court of Appeal ruled that the brother's action was a breach of confidence, and a likely breach of Art 8 of the ECHR. It rejected the Hildebrand approach as not justifiable on any basis, be it lawful excuse, 'self-help' or public interest. It considered that the proper action for a spouse to take when concerned about non-disclosure is to seek the appropriate orders for discovery, or freezing of assets.[81] It also considered that while the spouse who had wrongly obtained the evidence could seek to rely on their knowledge in court, the court has a discretion whether to admit this, depending upon fairness to both parties.[82] The ruling has undoubtedly made life harder for applicants who suspect, but find it hard to obtain proof, that their spouse has hidden assets, but the Court's view that the previous practice was ethically dubious is hard to dispute.

B. ORDERS THAT MAY BE MADE

1. MAINTENANCE PENDING SUIT AND LEGAL SERVICES ORDERS

The power to order the husband to pay maintenance pending suit goes back to the ecclesiastical courts.[83] It was based on the idea that a wife was entitled to be maintained by her husband

---

[78] P Wylie 'P v P (Ancillary Relief: Proceeds of Crime)—Disclosure under the Proceeds of Crime Act 2002 of suspicions of tax evasion gained during ancillary relief negotiations' [2004] CFLQ 203 at 209.

[79] Hildebrand v Hildebrand [1992] 1 FLR 244. In fact, the case provided no authority for this course of action, the trial judge, Waite J, declining to rule on its legality or legitimacy.

[80] [2010] EWCA Civ 908 [2010] 2 FLR 814. The wife subsequently obtained an order requiring disclosure of information (other than that which was privileged) held by a Jersey offshore trust in which most of the husband's wealth was placed, despite the misgivings of the Royal Court of Jersey: Tchenguiz-Imerman v Imerman [2013] EWHC 3627 (Fam) [2014] Fam Law 451.

[81] For guidance on the issue of freezing orders, see UL v BK (Freezing Orders: Safeguards: Standard Examples) [2013] EWHC 1735 (Fam) [2013] Fam Law 1379.

[82] An action may lie against the spouse's solicitors for wrongly holding the documents: White v Withers LLP and Dearle [2009] EWCA Civ 1122 [2010] 1 FLR 859.

[83] See C Vernier and J Hurlbut 'The Historical Background of Alimony Law and Its Present Statutory Structure' (1939) 6 Law and Contemporary Problems 197 at 200–201.

so long as the marriage remained in existence; the purpose of interim orders was to ensure that she and any children of the marriage living with her obtained a sufficient allowance until the outcome of the proceedings.

(a) Maintenance for ongoing support

The Matrimonial Causes Act 1973 gives the courts power, on an application for divorce, nullity or judicial separation, to order either spouse to make such periodical payments to the other pending suit as it thinks reasonable.[84] The court has no power to deal with the parties' *capital assets* by way of interim order.[85] Separated spouses of average means are unlikely to apply for such maintenance, and payments would be unfeasible where a spouse has a low income. Instead, a separated spouse is more likely to depend on a voluntary arrangement with the other (perhaps to keep up the mortgage payments on the home) or on their own earnings, savings, loans (from family and friends) or social security payments.[86]

In *F v F (Ancillary Relief: Substantial Assets)*[87] Thorpe J said that even in 'big money' cases disputes about the amount of interim awards were 'almost unknown'. No guidelines are laid down governing the exercise of the court's discretion under s 22,[88] and in *TL v ML and Others (Ancillary Relief: Claim against Assets of Extended Family)* it was said that 'the sole criterion to be applied in determining the application is "reasonableness" . . . which, to my mind, is synonymous with "fairness"'.[89] So far as possible, all the circumstances are to be taken into account, with the most attention being paid to the spouses' immediate financial position and the needs of the children of the family.[90] The parties' standard of living will be highly relevant to determining what will be a 'reasonable' order, but other factors may be relevant: thus, in *M v M (Maintenance Pending Suit)*[91] the fact that the husband's lifestyle had been funded by his father, who no longer wished to do so in light of the divorce proceedings, needed to be taken into account in determining what award to make to the wife pending the final order. In *BN v MA*[92] in making an order in the same terms as the parties had reached

---

[84] Matrimonial Causes Act 1973 s 22. An order under s 22 cannot be categorised as a protective or provisional measure within Art 12 of the Brussels II Convention (Council Regulation (EC) 1347/2000 on Jurisdiction and the Recognition and Enforcement of Judgments in Matrimonial Matters and in matters of Parental Responsibility for Children of Both Spouses (2000) OJ L 160/19) so as to give jurisdiction after a court elsewhere has been seized: *Wermuth v Wermuth (No 2)* [2002] EWCA Civ 50 [2003] 1 WLR 942. However, the court has jurisdiction to make an order under s 22 where there is a preliminary issue as to whether there is jurisdiction to hear the divorce suit: *Moses-Taiga v Taiga* [2005] EWCA Civ 1013 [2006] 1 FLR 1074 although the court should be very cautious in so ordering: *Z v Z* [1992] 2 FLR 291 and *MET v HAT (Interim Maintenance)* [2013] EWHC 4247 (Fam) [2014] Fam Law 447.

[85] *Wicks v Wicks* [1998] 1 FLR 470, CA. However, it may be possible to obtain such sums under other jurisdictions, including the Children Act 1989 Sch 1: see *Re G (Maintenance Pending Suit)* [2006] EWHC 1834 (Fam) [2007] 1 FLR 1674. For a full survey, see D Burrows, 'Costs allowances in Family Proceedings' [2013] Fam Law 457.

[86] See A Perry et al *How Parents Cope Financially on Marriage Breakdown* (2000).

[87] [1995] 2 FLR 45.

[88] The guidelines laid down under Matrimonial Causes Act 1973 s 25 (see Ch 23, Factors to be taken into account when assessing what orders should be made for a spouse, pp 882–903) do not apply to orders made under s 22.

[89] [2006] 1 FLR 1263 per N Mostyn QC sitting as a Deputy High Court Judge at [124].

[90] See eg *Peacock v Peacock* [1984] 1 All ER 1069. While it is neither essential nor appropriate to conduct an exhaustive financial enquiry, enough evidence must be available to allow the court to carry out the balancing exercise between the payer's resources and the applicant's needs: *S v M (Maintenance Pending Suit)* [2012] EWHC 4109 (Fam) [2013] 1 FLR 1173.   [91] [2002] EWHC 317 (Fam) [2002] 2 FLR 123.

[92] [2013] EWHC 4250 (Fam) [2014] Fam Law 443 at [33].

in a pre-nuptial agreement[93] made not much more than 18 months earlier, Mostyn J also held that:

> when adjudicating a question of interim maintenance, where there has been a prenuptial agreement, the court should seek to apply the terms of the prenuptial agreement as closely and as practically as it can, unless the evidence of the wife in support of her application demonstrates, to a convincing standard, that she has a likely prospect of satisfying the court that this agreement should not be upheld.

(b) Maintenance to cover legal expenses—'costs allowances'

One potentially major expense of getting divorced is, of course, the costs of the legal proceedings themselves. It was held, in *A v A (Maintenance Pending Suit: Provision of Legal Fees)*[94] that 'maintenance', which is not statutorily defined, was not restricted to the costs of 'daily living' but could include legal costs, where these are a pressing need and expense. Holman J considered that such an order was also justified by Art 6 of the European Convention on Human Rights which requires the parties to legal proceedings to have 'equality of arms'—ie that each party must be afforded a reasonable opportunity to present his case under conditions that do not place him at a substantial disadvantage vis-à-vis his opponent.[95] The Court of Appeal confirmed this approach in *Currey v Currey (No 2)*.[96] There, the wealthy wife challenged an order requiring her to pay £10,000 per month to the husband to fund his legal costs in protracted financial proceedings between them. Wilson LJ ruled that the applicant for such support must show that they cannot reasonably procure legal advice and representation by any other means (for example, selling existing assets to raise funds, or taking a loan). The court then has a discretion to order payments taking into account the subject-matter of the proceedings, the reasonableness of the applicant's litigation stance and fairness to the respondent.

(c) Orders for payment in respect of legal services

With the withdrawal of most legal aid from family proceedings, there is an even greater possibility of a spouse being unable to afford legal representation for litigation against the other on divorce and hence an inequality of arms.[97] The Legal Aid, Sentencing and Punishment of Offenders Act 2012 (LASPO) codified the jurisprudence[98] on 'costs allowances' in financial proceedings, and amended s 22 to provide that it would no longer be possible to order a spouse to make payments to the other under that section. Instead, it inserted s 22ZA, under which a new 'legal services order' may be made requiring the spouse to pay 'an amount for the purpose of enabling the applicant to obtain legal services for the purposes of the proceedings',[99] and set out the grounds on which such an order may be made. The court must

---

[93] See later, Pre- and post-nuptial agreements, p 853.   [94] [2001] 1 FLR 377.

[95] *Dombo Beheer BV v Netherlands* (1993) 18 EHRR 213; *Airey v Ireland* (1979) 2 EHRR 305.

[96] [2006] EWCA Civ 1338 [2007] 1 FLR 946.

[97] Various mechanisms have been developed to try to assist in such circumstances, including the assignment to the spouse's solicitors of the right to part of a future lump sum (or property adjustment order) obtained in the proceedings, known as a 'Sears Tooth' charge, after *Sears Tooth (a firm) v Payne Hicks Beach (a firm)* [1997] 2 FLR 116. For the range of ways in which a litigant might obtain funding to help with legal costs, see *Young v Young* [2013] EWHC 3637 (Fam) [2014] Fam Law 291 [4]–[14], where the wife's costs amounted to around £6.4 million.

[98] See the view of Mostyn J in *BN v MA* [2013] EWHC 4250 (Fam) [2014] Fam Law 443 at [36].

[99] Section 22ZA(1)(2). 'Proceedings' means divorce, nullity or judicial separation, or financial relief in connection with such proceedings. See A Commins 'The costs allowance "revolution" in proceedings for financial relief' [2012] Fam Law 1491.

be satisfied that, without the amount ordered, 'the applicant would not reasonably be able to obtain appropriate legal services for the purposes of the proceedings or any part of the proceedings'.[100] Legal services means the following types of services:

(a) providing advice as to how the law applies in the particular circumstances,
(b) providing advice and assistance in relation to the proceedings,
(c) providing other advice and assistance in relation to the settlement or other resolution of the dispute that is the subject of the proceedings, and
(d) providing advice and assistance in relation to the enforcement of decisions in the proceedings or as part of the settlement or resolution of the dispute,
    and they include, in particular, advice and assistance in the form of representation and any form of dispute resolution, including mediation.[101]

This represents the partial 'privatisation' of the provision of legal aid for a spouse taking—or defending—financial relief proceedings (in the absence of violence), by transferring the liability from the State to the other spouse. It will be noted that an order may be made in respect of any form of dispute resolution including mediation—yet legal aid *is* still available (subject to means) in relation to mediation, so presumably an order would only be made where the applicant is above the legal aid eligibility limits.

2. PERIODICAL PAYMENTS

(a) Orders in favour of spouses

The court may order either spouse to make unsecured periodical payments to the other or to 'secure' periodical payments to the other, ie require an item of property or capital to be designated as security for the payments, to be realised if the payer defaults.[102] Any order for periodical payments may be backdated to the date on which the application for the order was first made.[103]

As periodical payments are generally intended for the payee's maintenance,[104] they must in any event terminate on her (or his) death. Unsecured periodical payments will normally come out of the payer's income and an order for their payment cannot extend beyond the payer's death.[105] There is, however, no reason why *secured* payments should not continue after the payer's death, as the capital will always have been charged; consequently in this case the order can last for the payee's life.[106] Furthermore, (whether the payments are secured or not) the order must also provide for their termination on the payee's marriage.[107] She (or he) must thereafter look to the new spouse for support.

---

[100] Section 22ZA(3). Under subsection (4), 'the court must be satisfied, in particular, that—(a) the applicant is not reasonably able to secure a loan to pay for the services, and (b) the applicant is unlikely to be able to obtain the services by granting a charge over any assets recovered in the proceedings.' In *BN v MA* [2013] EWHC 4250 (Fam) [2014] Fam Law 443 it was held that the wife could secure a loan, albeit at a 'fairly steep' rate of interest, and, coupled with her attempt to evade the consequences of a recently-made pre-nuptial agreement, she had not therefore satisfied the court that a costs allowance should be given.

[101] Section 22ZA(10).   [102] Matrimonial Causes Act 1973 s 23(1)(a), (b).

[103] Matrimonial Causes Act 1973 s 28(1)(a)(b).

[104] But not always: see *Miller v Miller: McFarlane v McFarlane* [2006] UKHL 24 [2006] 2 AC 618, Ch 23, *Miller v Miller: McFarlane v McFarlane*, p 870.   [105] Matrimonial Causes Act 1973 s 28(1)(a).

[106] Matrimonial Causes Act 1973 s 28(1)(b).

[107] Matrimonial Causes Act 1973 s 28(1)(a)(b). It is immaterial that the second marriage is void or voidable: Matrimonial Causes Act 1973 s 52(3).

The very fact of security obviously makes secured payments more attractive to the payee, for there is no problem of enforcement. By tying up the payer's capital, it also prevents him from trying to frustrate the order by disposing of his assets, and the payee will be protected even though the payer becomes bankrupt. We have also seen that the payee can continue to benefit from a secured order after the other's death. Whether periodical payments can be secured, however, must depend on the capital or secured income which the other has available, and the number of spouses against whom such an order can be made is small. Thorpe LJ has commented that secured orders 'have been virtually relegated to the legal history books',[108] being replaced in practice by a commuted capital payment.[109]

(b) Orders in favour of children of the family

As well as having power to make orders in favour of a spouse the court may, in proceedings for divorce, nullity and judicial separation, provided that the provisions of the Child Support Act 1991 are inapplicable,[110] make periodical payments orders (which may be secured or unsecured) in favour of a 'child of the family'.[111] The court may make an order for a child over the age of 18 so long as the child is (or, if an order were made, would be) receiving education or training, or there are special circumstances justifying support. Periodical payments could therefore continue indefinitely if, for example, the child is incapable of earning his or her own living owing to a disability. The order terminates on the death of the child or the payer.[112] Normally the sums will be payable by one spouse (or former spouse) to the other, but either (or presumably both)[113] of them may be ordered to make payments to a third person, if the child is living with that person, or to the child him- or herself.

3. LUMP SUM PAYMENTS

The court may order either party to pay a lump sum or lump sums to the other.[114] It can also order a lump sum to be paid to a specified person for the benefit of any child of the family or to the child himself.[115] In practice, lump sum orders in favour of children are rare.[116] However, in *V v V (Child Maintenance)*[117] they were used where a father declined to consent to the court's fixing periodical payments for the children (the common means of avoiding the potential jurisdiction of the child support scheme)[118] above the amount which he was prepared to pay, and which the court deemed inadequate. In order to ensure that the children were left with adequate support during their dependency, Wilson J,

---

[108] *AMS v Child Support Officer* [1998] 1 FLR 955 at 964A.
[109] Discussed in Ch 23, Variation of orders, Capitalisation of periodical payments, p 914.
[110] See Ch 21, The residual role of the courts, p 820.
[111] See Ch 9, The meaning of 'child of the family', p 296.
[112] Even if secured: s 29(4); see *B v B (Adult Student: Liability to Support)* [1998] 1 FLR 373, CA.
[113] The court had power under previous legislation to make an order against both spouses: *Freckleton v Freckleton* [1966] CLY 3938.
[114] Matrimonial Causes Act 1973 s 23(1)(c).   [115] Matrimonial Causes Act 1973 s 23(1)(d).
[116] Per Booth J in *Kiely v Kiely* [1988] 1 FLR 248 at 251, CA.   [117] [2001] 2 FLR 799.
[118] See Ch 21, Where there is no jurisdiction under the Child Support Act, p 821.

having made the periodical payments orders at the agreed level, also made lump sum orders in their favour to meet the shortfall.[119]

A lump sum may be ordered to enable the payee to meet any liabilities or expenses already incurred in maintaining herself or himself or any child of the family before an application is made.[120] It may also be made payable by instalments.[121] Care must be taken to be clear in the order as to whether what is intended is a lump sum, payable in instalments—which may be varied (both as to quantum and timing) in the future—or a series of staged lump sums over a period of time, which may not.[122]

The court may *in the same order* direct the payment of more than one lump sum. These may be payable at different dates (eg one may be payable immediately to enable a wife to put down a deposit on a home and another payable when the husband sells the matrimonial home); one may be payable by instalments and the other not. There is no power to make a second or subsequent order for a lump sum in favour of a spouse.[123]

However, the most important use of this statutory power is to adjust the parties' capital assets. If, for example, the husband owns shares, the court may wish the benefit of a proportion of these to be given to the wife. It may do this directly by ordering them to be transferred to her, but it may alternatively order him to make a lump sum payment to her. This will leave the husband free to sell some of his shares or to raise the money in some other way if he prefers to do so. When the matrimonial home is the only capital asset and it is sold or the wife leaves and the husband remains,[124] the court will commonly make an order for the payment of a lump sum representing the value of that part of the assets of which the other party is to be given the benefit.

Lump sums will be commonly ordered where one party has substantial means, but such an order might also be the best solution if the husband has a little capital (for example, the proceeds of sale of the matrimonial home) but little or no income: the capital may be of real value to the wife, because it will give her some financial base, whilst the husband will be relieved of the obligation of finding continuing support for her out of meagre earnings. A lump sum payment with consequent reduction in periodical payments may also be ordered if the wife (or husband) has particular need of capital, eg to enable her to purchase a house, furniture,[125] or the goodwill of a business,[126] or to clear off a mortgage with which she is buying a new house so that she can make a fresh start.[127] A further use is to protect the payee against probable default on the other's part, eg if it appears that the party against whom financial provision is being sought is likely to remove his assets from the jurisdiction.[128] Another advantage of a lump sum is that (assuming the sum is paid) the payment is final and there are no continuing problems of enforcement, which may be of particular importance if the parties' relationship is particularly bitter.[129]

---

[119] He distinguished *Phillips v Peace* [1996] 2 FLR 230 (discussed in Ch 21, Proceedings under Schedule 1 to the Children Act 1989, Exercising the powers, p 798) because there, the mother had originally invoked the child support jurisdiction and her application for a lump sum was intended to side-step the Child Support Agency's arrival at a nil assessment against the father, whereas in *V v V*, the mother had not applied to the CSA, and, in light of the court's having made the periodical payments order at the level the father was prepared to countenance, now could not do so.

[120] Matrimonial Causes Act 1973 s 23(3): see *Askew-Page v Page* [2001] Fam Law 794 (county court) for an example of a lump sum order made to meet debts referable to the children.   [121] Section 23(3)(c).

[122] *Hamilton v Hamilton* [2013] EWCA Civ 13 [2014] 1 FLR 55.

[123] *Coleman v Coleman* [1973] Fam 10.

[124] See Lord Denning MR in *Wachtel v Wachtel* [1973] Fam 72 at 96.

[125] *S v S* [1977] Fam 127, CA.

[126] *Gojkovic v Gojkovic (No 2)* [1992] Fam 40, CA (lump sum order of £1 million to wife to buy hotel).

[127] *Harnett v Harnett* [1974] 1 All ER 764, CA.   [128] *Brett v Brett* [1969] 1 All ER 1007, CA.

[129] See *Griffiths v Griffiths* [1974] 1 All ER 932 at 942, CA.

Lump sum applications should ordinarily be disposed of once and for all, but there is jurisdiction to adjourn the application where there is a *real* possibility of capital from a specific source becoming available in the near future.[130]

4. ORDERS IN RELATION TO PENSIONS

The court has power to make two kinds of orders in relation to pensions[131]—pension attachment (formerly known as earmarking) orders, which are forms of financial provision order made under s 23, and pension sharing orders which are a separate type of order made under s 24B.

By s 25B(1) of the Matrimonial Causes Act 1973 the court is placed under a duty to have regard to the spouses' pension entitlements, being:

(a) any benefits under a pension arrangement which a party to the marriage has or is likely to have; and

(b) any benefits under a pension arrangement which, by reason of the dissolution or annulment of the marriage, a party will lose the chance of acquiring.[132]

For this purpose, a pension arrangement is defined as an occupational pension scheme or personal pension scheme, a retirement annuity contract, an annuity or insurance policy purchased, or transferred, for the purpose of giving effect to rights under an occupational or personal pension scheme, and an annuity purchased or entered into for the purpose of discharging liability in respect of a pension credit.[133]

(a) Pension attachment

The court has powers to order the person responsible for the pension arrangement[134] to make payments (including lump sums) for the benefit of a pensioner's spouse as and when such payments fall due on retirement.[135] The order must express the amount of the payment as a percentage of the payment due to the pensioner.[136] If a pensioner enjoys the appropriate rights under the terms of the arrangement, the court may also order him to

---

[130] *Davies v Davies* [1986] 1 FLR 497, CA; *D v D (Lump Sum Order: Adjournment of Application)* [2001] 1 FLR 633, where Connell J upheld the trial judge's decision to adjourn the wife's lump sum application until the size of the husband's cash bonus under his employer's incentive scheme was known; cf *Burgess v Burgess* [1996] 2 FLR 34, CA, where the husband's prospects of obtaining substantial assets from his business were not taken into account, since there was no real likelihood of a sale. In *Michael v Michael* [1986] 2 FLR 389, CA, a spouse's inheritance expectancy was held too remote, while in *MT v MT (Financial Provision: Lump Sum)* [1992] 1 FLR 362 the wife's application was adjourned until the death of her 83-year-old German father-in-law. Under German law the husband would automatically inherit one-eighth of his father's estate.

[131] See H Woodward with M Sefton *Pensions on Divorce: An Empirical Study* (2014) and 'Pensions on divorce: a study on when and how they are taken into account' [2014] Fam Law 509; B Morris and G Mathieson 'Pensions on marital breakdown' Parts I, II, III, IV [2012] Fam Law 705, 856, 968, 1234; A Dnes *The Division of Marital Assets following Divorce with Particular Reference to Pensions*, Lord Chancellor's Department Research Series 7/97.

[132] Including any 'Pension Protection Fund' (PPF) compensation payable under Chapter 3 of Part 2 of the Pensions Act 2004: Matrimonial Causes Act 1973 s 25E inserted by Sch 12 para 3 of the Pensions Act 2004. For discussion, see D Salter 'Pensions Law Simplification and the Family Lawyer' [2004] Fam Law 795.

[133] Matrimonial Causes Act 1973 s 25D(3).

[134] Meaning the trustees or managers of the pension scheme, the annuity provider or the insurer: s 25D(4).

[135] Matrimonial Causes Act 1973 s 25B(4) and s 25C(2)(a).

[136] Matrimonial Causes Act 1973 s 25B(5).

commute the whole or any part of the payments due,[137] or to nominate his spouse as the beneficiary of any lump sum payment which he may receive.[138] These provisions enable a court to 'earmark' (as it used to be called) some or all of a spouse's future pension in favour of the other. It has been held,[139] however, that their enactment does not *require* the court to compensate a spouse for actual or potential loss of pension benefits. All that they do is to provide a further option available to the court, as a form of financial provision order under s 23, to deal with the parties' assets in a way best suited to the circumstances of the case—and it will not always be appropriate to make an order of this kind. Such orders have been unpopular, and have now been largely superseded by pension sharing orders, discussed shortly. The difficulty with attachment is that first, there is the problem of uncertainty inherent in attempting to assess future income and capital provision from a pension, which might not fall due for many years; secondly, the order only takes effect when the pension becomes payable. As Wilson J put it:

> It is relevant to the present claim for me to stress the limitations of an attachment order as a vehicle for making provision for a wife out of the husband's pension rights. It does not carve out of his rights pension rights for her, bespoke to her needs and in particular to the length of her life. It merely impresses upon whatever may be payable to the husband under a pension scheme a compulsory redirection to the wife in satisfaction of his obligations under court orders. Thus no part of his pension is payable to the wife, whatever her age and however great her need, until, within the limits open to him under the scheme, the husband chooses to retire. Even more significantly, no further payment falls to be made to her in the event that following his retirement he predeceases her. In a sentence, the problem is that, notwithstanding divorce, the wife who has the benefit only of an attachment order remains hitched to the husband's wagon.[140]

(b) Pension sharing

A better solution is to make a pension sharing order instead.[141] This re-adjusts the spouses' pension entitlements and enables each party to make future pension arrangements independently of the other. The spouse in whose favour the order is made can either become a member of the other's pension scheme in her own right, or she can transfer the value of the ordered share into her own pension arrangement. The advantage of this approach over that of attachment is that, by allocating the pension *rights* at the time of the divorce, the intended recipient knows that she can take the benefit of those rights regardless of whether the other spouse dies before retirement.

Initial provision for pension sharing was made in the Family Law Act 1996[142] but was not brought into force. Instead, following consultation,[143] the Welfare Reform and Pensions

---

[137] Matrimonial Causes Act 1973 s 25B(7).

[138] Matrimonial Causes Act 1973 s 25C(2)(b).

[139] In *T v T (Financial Relief: Pensions)* [1998] 1 FLR 1072.

[140] *R (Smith) v Secretary of State for Defence and Secretary of State for Work and Pensions* [2004] EWHC 1797 (Admin) [2005] 1 FLR 97 at para 15.

[141] But such an order may only be made after divorce or annulment, not judicial separation: Matrimonial Causes Act 1973, s 24B(1). See B Morris and G Mathieson 'Pensions on marital breakdown' Parts I, II, III, IV [2012] Fam Law 705, 856, 968, 1234. Note also that pension sharing must be *ordered*: a private agreement to share is ineffective. This means that a settlement reached by the parties which involves pension sharing must be embodied in a court order.

[142] Section 16.

[143] Department of Social Security, *Pension Sharing on Divorce: reforming pensions for a fairer future* Cm 3345 (1998).

Act 1999 was passed, and amended Part II of the Matrimonial Causes Act 1973. A pension sharing order is an order which:

(a) provides that one party's shareable rights under a specified pension arrangement, or shareable state scheme rights, be subject to pension sharing for the benefit of the other party, and

(b) specifies the percentage value to be transferred.[144]

The basic state pension cannot be shared (since it already enables a divorced spouse to substitute the contribution record of their former spouse for their own) but the additional state pension may be.[145] The court may make one or more such orders, but cannot do so where the arrangement is already the subject of such an order, or a pension attachment order, between the parties.[146]

To settle pension rights, the couple have to obtain a valuation of these from any pension arrangement to which either or both belongs or has belonged in the past. The valuation will be based on a cash equivalent value of the accrued benefits,[147] but as Singer J noted, in *T v T (Financial Relief: Pensions)*:[148]

I should perhaps emphasise that these values are at best a guide, and that their apparent precision (down to the nearest pound) is illusory, and the product of mathematical rather than predictive accuracy. For they necessarily incorporate various assumptions (as to the rate of future inflation before and after the pension commences in payment; an appropriate discount rate reflecting the tax-exempt environment (currently) enjoyed by the pension fund; and of course that ultimately unpredictable factor, mortality) . . . the only fact which can be predicted with absolute accuracy is that the prediction will turn out to be inaccurate. These figures are therefore, at best and when it is appropriate to have regard to them at all, a guide rather than a rule.

Depending upon the type of pension arrangement in question, recipients of a pension sharing order are able to become members of the scheme, or transfer the accrued rights to another. The pension arrangement is notified by the court of the order which it has made, and has four months to implement it.[149] The order is in the form of a percentage share of the member's rights,[150] and the scheme will recover, from the parties, the reasonable administrative costs involved, either in cash, or by deduction from the pension rights.[151] The recipient of the order acquires 'pension credits' in the original pension arrangement or that to which the rights are transferred.[152] Her eventual pension will depend on the rules of that arrangement and her own circumstances when the pension becomes due, and not those of the former spouse from whom the rights have been transferred. In particular, this means that normally, the pension credit member cannot receive the pension under an occupational pension scheme until she reaches statutory retirement age, even if her ex-spouse is permitted to draw the pension early.[153]

[144] Matrimonial Causes Act 1973 s 21A(1).   [145] Welfare Reform and Pensions Act 1999 s 47(2).
[146] Matrimonial Causes Act 1973 s 24B(3),(5).
[147] See the explanation in B Morris and G Mathieson [2012] Fam Law, Part III at 971 and Part IV at 1235.
[148] [1998] 1 FLR 1072 at 1079.   [149] Welfare Reform and Pensions Act 1999 s 34(1).
[150] Matrimonial Causes Act 1973 s 21A(1)(b).   [151] Matrimonial Causes Act 1973 s 24D.
[152] Welfare Reform and Pensions Act 1999 s 29.
[153] *R (Smith) v Secretary of State for Defence and Secretary of State for Work and Pensions* [2004] EWHC 1797 (Admin) [2005] 1 FLR 97. See ss 101C(1) and 101B of the Pension Schemes Act 1993. Ways round this

Although pensions are an increasingly important financial asset, the only detailed study of their treatment in divorce cases found that while they were referred to in 80% of the 369 court files sampled, pension orders (all sharing, and never attachment) were made in only 17% of cases, overwhelmingly in favour of wives (which reflects the generally stronger financial position of husbands) amongst better-off couples (which reflects their greater financial resources) and where the marriage had lasted a long time (the median length being 25 years). The researchers concluded that they are an under-used remedy, with practitioners put off by complex legal provisions, a lack of judicial guidance and difficulties in valuing the pension pot.[154]

5. TRANSFER AND SETTLEMENT OF PROPERTY

The court may order either party to the marriage to transfer such property as may be specified to the other party or to, or for the benefit of, a child of the family. The court may also order either of them to settle any property for the benefit of the other party or any child of the family although settlements are no longer commonly made.[155] The court's power to transfer (but not to settle) property to a child over the age of 18 is limited to where the child is receiving instruction at an educational establishment or is undergoing training for a trade, profession or vocation, or where there are other special circumstances (eg the child is suffering from some physical or mental disability).[156] The court can order an absolute transfer of the whole of the party's interest in the property specified or any part of it. It has equally wide powers when ordering a settlement.[157] The transfer order effects a disposition creating an equitable interest in favour of the transferee at the moment it is made and vesting beneficial ownership in the transferee.[158]

The transfer power is of particular importance to enable the court to make appropriate orders with respect to the matrimonial home and similar assets (eg furniture or the family car), but it may also be ordered as an alternative to the payment of a lump sum when it is more sensible to order one spouse to transfer investments than to compel him to sell them to raise the necessary capital.

(a) Property that may be the subject of an order

The Act empowers the court to make an order with respect to any property to which the spouse in question is entitled either in possession or in reversion.[159] The established view

---

limitation are either, where possible, to transfer her rights to a personal pension scheme or to order the pension member to make periodical payments to the ex-wife to meet the payment gap: see D Salter 'Pensions Law Simplification and the Family Lawyer' [2004] Fam Law 795 at 804.

[154] H Woodward with M Sefton *Pensions on Divorce: An Empirical Study* (2014).

[155] Matrimonial Causes Act 1973 s 24(1)(a)(b). For an example of settlement of property on children, see *H v H (Financial Provision: Conduct)* [1998] 1 FLR 971 (lump sum settled on trusts for husband to enable him to buy suitable home in which children could have contact with him; reversion to the children). See also *Tavoulareas v Tavoulareas* [1998] 2 FLR 418, CA. However, substantial capital orders in favour of children are rare: see *Kiely v Kiely* [1988] 1 FLR 248, CA; *Chamberlain v Chamberlain* [1974] 1 All ER 33, CA; *Lilford v Glynn* [1979] 1 All ER 441, CA.   [156] Section 29(1)–(3).

[157] As in *Compton v Compton* [1960] P 201 where property was settled on children for life with remainder to grandchildren. Quaere whether the remainder to the grandchildren was not ultra vires, as this does not benefit *children of the family*; *Style v Style* [1954] P 209, CA (settlement on husband for life).

[158] *Mountney v Treharne* [2002] EWCA Civ 1174 [2002] 2 FLR 930.

[159] For an illustration of the breadth of the courts' powers in this regard see *Harwood v Harwood* [1991] 2 FLR 274, CA (husband ordered to transfer to wife his interest in assets of a dissolved partnership with a third party). No transfer or settlement will be ordered if the property is outside the jurisdiction and effective control of the court: *Hamlin v Hamlin* [1986] Fam 11, CA.

is that there is no power to order a transfer or settlement that the party could not make voluntarily: eg of a protected life interest (which is determinable on the occurrence of any event which will deprive the beneficiary of the right to receive any part of the income), or of a lease containing a covenant against assignment.[160] The latter limitation may be of particular importance when the court is dealing with rights in the matrimonial home. Similarly it was accepted that the party must be able to claim the property *as of right*; hence, if he is a beneficiary under a discretionary trust, the court apparently has no power to order the settlement of any income which the trustees *may* in their discretion pay him,[161] nor presumably could it order the settlement of any property which *might* come to him as the result of the exercise of a power of appointment vested in another. In *Thomas v Thomas*,[162] however, the Court of Appeal suggested that the court should look at the reality of the situation; it ought not to disregard the potential availability of wealth from sources owned or administered by others. In appropriate circumstances a judge may frame his order to afford 'judicious encouragement' to third parties to provide a spouse with the means to comply with the court's view of the justice of the case. In *Charman v Charman*,[163] Wilson LJ said that the appropriate question to ask is whether the trustees would be likely to advance the capital immediately or in the foreseeable future. The court is not bound to accept the say-so of the trustees, and it may draw robust—but realistic—conclusions as to the likelihood of future benefit for the payer.[164]

An order may also be made in respect of property which is the subject of a separate application to enforce a criminal confiscation order under the Drug Trafficking Act 1994 or Criminal Justice Act 1988: these Acts do not take priority over the Matrimonial Causes Act so that where the court considers it appropriate, it may transfer the property (in this case the matrimonial home) to the ex-spouse even though this may prevent the authorities from realising the full amount of the confiscation order.[165]

(b) Company assets

While trusts and offshore accounts may be one form of attempted 'shelter' for one party's property from the reach of the other spouse, another important vehicle is that of a private company controlled by the payer. The general principle in law is that the 'corporate veil' of

---

[160] See *Hale v Hale* [1975] 2 All ER 1090, CA. The question was left open by Lord Penzance in *Milne v Milne* (1871) LR 2 P & D 295, but cf *Loraine v Loraine* [1912] P 222, CA.

[161] *Milne v Milne*. Nevertheless, the existence of the interest can be taken into account: cf *Browne v Browne* [1989] 1 FLR 291, CA.

[162] [1995] 2 FLR 668, CA where the court applied the principles to a private family company (rather than a discretionary trust) where the shareholders were the husband, his brother, his mother and a family trust; *Rye v Rye* [2002] EWHC 956 (Fam), [2002] 2 FLR 981—complex accounting arrangements masked husband's true wealth but did not prevent substantial orders being made in favour of wife and children. But cf *Scheeres v Scheeres* [1999] 1 FLR 241, where the Court of Appeal held that an order should not be founded on speculative assessment as to the likelihood of a business recovering from difficult trading conditions; and *George v George* [2003] EWCA Civ 202 [2004] 1 FLR 421—court should have adjourned to await outcome of proceedings in Queen's Bench Division against husband for recovery of a debt and not assumed that the transactions between the husband and the debtor were a sham.

[163] [2005] EWCA Civ 1606 [2006] 2 FLR 422 at [13].

[164] *BJ v MJ (Financial Order: Overseas Trust)* [2011] EWHC 2708 (Fam) [2012] 1 FLR 667. See also *TL v ML and Others (Ancillary Relief: Claim against Assets of Extended Family)* 1 FLR 1263; *Whaley v Whaley* [2011] EWCA Civ 617 [2012] 1 FLR 735; *RK v RK (Financial Resources: Trust Assets)* [2011] EWHC 3910 (Fam) [2013] 1 FLR 329.

[165] Neither Act has priority: see *Re MCA: HM Customs and Excise Commissioners and Long v A and A; A v A (Long Intervening)* [2002] EWCA Civ 1039 [2003] 1 FLR 164. In *X v X (Crown Prosecution Service Intervening)* [2005] EWHC 296 (Fam) [2005] 2 FLR 487 it was held that it would be wrong to effect a financial settlement in such as way as to reduce the husband's liability under a confiscation order. The spouse must not have been complicit in the illegal activity: *Stodgell v Stodgell* [2009] 2 FLR 244.

a company may only be 'pierced' so as to attach some liability to the individuals controlling or owning it where 'the company was used as a device or facade to conceal the true facts, thereby avoiding or concealing any liability of those individual(s).'[166] However, courts in the family jurisdiction considered that, in order to ensure the matrimonial jurisdiction was effective in providing appropriate provision for a spouse on marital breakdown, they could, if necessary, make orders awarding assets vested in companies of which one spouse was the sole shareholder to the other.[167] In *Ben Hashem v Al Shayif*[168] Munby J echoed his own earlier caution at this approach[169] and sought to remind the family courts of the general rule and to stress that the corporate veil could only be pierced where necessary to provide a remedy for impropriety, that is (mis)use of the company as a device or facade to conceal wrongdoing. The matter was eventually resolved in *Prest v Petrodel Resources Ltd and Others*.[170] The husband was found to own and control a number of limited companies registered in the Isle of Man, which held the title to various residential properties in England and Wales. The wife sought the transfer of these to her in divorce proceedings. At first instance, Moylan J considered that the husband had not acted with impropriety in relation to the spouses' divorce proceedings so that he could not 'pierce the corporate veil'. Any improper behaviour the husband might have engaged in regarding his control of the companies had nothing to do with seeking to evade his liabilities to the wife but was more to do with tax avoidance and wealth maximisation. The Supreme Court agreed. But while Moylan J considered that s 24 *did* give him the power to treat the husband as effectively 'entitled' to the wealth of the companies, the Supreme Court held that the social purpose of the Matrimonial Causes Act could not be utilised to 'indicate that the legislature intended to authorise the transfer by one party to the marriage to the other of property which was not his to transfer.'[171] As Lord Sumption put it, 'Courts exercising family jurisdiction do not occupy a desert island in which general legal concepts are suspended or mean something different. If a right of property exists, it exists in every division of the High Court and in every jurisdiction of the county courts. If it does not exist, it does not exist anywhere.'[172] Although the Court recognised that the husband might have acted without regard for the requirements and obligations of company law, it noted that, if the family courts' approach was correct, it would apply to even the most conscientious of shareholders and even where the company had 'vigorously opposed' the spouse's actions, to the detriment of the company and its creditors. Thus a strong pro-business approach was adopted by the Supreme Court to the general issue. However, Moylan J had also found that the husband had deliberately sought to conceal the extent of his assets and had failed to meet his disclosure obligations. The Supreme Court therefore went on to hold that adverse inferences could be drawn against him to the effect that had proper disclosure taken place, it would have revealed that the companies held the properties on resulting trust for the benefit of the husband and he was thus beneficially entitled to them. The potential of *Prest* as a means of exposing a spouse who is seeking to hide assets is thus limited: the other spouse may need to take specific proceedings to challenge the disposition of assets intended to defeat a financial relief claim.[173]

---

[166] *Trustor AB v Smallbone (No 2)* [2001] 1 WLR 1177 per Sir Andrew Morritt VC at [23].

[167] See eg *Green v Green* [1993] 1 FLR 326; *Mubarak v Mubarak* [2001] 1 FLR 673; *Kremen v Agrest (No 2)* [2011] 2 FLR 490.

[168] [2009] 1 FLR 115. [169] In *A v A* [2007] 2 FLR 467.

[170] [2013] UKSC 34 [2013] 2 AC 415. [171] [2013] UKSC 34 [2013] 2 FLR 732 at [40].

[172] [2013] UKSC 34 [2013] 2 FLR 732 at [37].

[173] See Ch 23, Attempts to defeat claims for financial relief, at p 918. See also *M v M and Others* [2013] EWHC 2534 (Fam) [2014] 1 FLR 439 where the husband put various properties into the names of various companies that he controlled in order to defeat the wife's claims—held, he retained beneficial ownership and

6. VARIATION OF MARRIAGE OR RELEVANT SETTLEMENTS

The court may make an order varying any marriage settlement for the benefit of the parties to a marriage and the children of the family or either or any of them,[174] other than one in the form of a pension arrangement.[175] The court may also make an order extinguishing or reducing the interest of either of the parties under any marriage settlement (again, other than a pension arrangement).[176] These powers are complementary to those already discussed and are used less in view of the wider powers to order transfers of property. However, they may be useful where complex family trusts have been set up, including those utilising offshore arrangements.[177]

For this purpose, a marriage settlement means an ante-nuptial or post-nuptial settlement made on the parties, including one made by will[178] and it must be one made on the footing that the marriage should continue.[179] It should thus not be confused with pre- or post-nuptial agreements which are (generally) concerned with determining the parties' financial rights and obligations in the event of the marriage being terminated, and which we discuss later.

The terms 'ante-nuptial and post-nuptial settlements' are used in a sense much wider than that usually given to them by conveyancers, the essential condition being that the benefit must be conferred on either or both of the spouses *in the character of spouse or spouses*.[180] It was even taken to extend to a personal pension scheme established by a business man under which he and his spouse were beneficiaries.[181] This construction was used as a means of making adequate pension provision for the ex-wife at a time before pension attachment and pension sharing had been enacted. It is no longer possible to use the power to deal with pensions in this way[182] but the House of Lords' view in *Brooks v Brooks*[183] that a wide interpretation should be given to the term 'nuptial settlement' remains good law. The same broad approach would be taken regarding a 'relevant settlement' in relation to civil partners—'a settlement made, during its subsistence or in anticipation of its formation, on the civil partners including one made by will or codicil, but not including one in the form of a pension arrangement'.[184]

7. ORDERS FOR THE SALE OF PROPERTY

As originally enacted, the Matrimonial Causes Act 1973 conferred no *express* power to order a sale of spouses' property. However, following a Law Commission

---

the properties were therefore capable of being transferred to the wife. Cf *Smith v Bottomley* [2013] EWCA Civ 953 [2014] 1 FLR 626 where the evidence did not establish that the company was not the bona fide owner of the property in dispute.

[174] Sch 5 para 7(3) to the Civil Partnership Act 2004 refers to a 'relevant settlement'.

[175] Matrimonial Causes Act 1973 s 24(1)(c) as amended by the Welfare Reform and Pensions Act 1999 Sch 3 para 3.

[176] Matrimonial Causes Act 1973 s 24(1)(d) as amended by the Welfare Reform and Pensions Act 1999 Sch 3 para 3.

[177] See eg *BJ v MJ (Financial Order: Overseas Trust)* [2011] EWHC 2708 (Fam) [2012] 1 FLR 667; *Hope v Krejci and Others* [2012] EWHC 1780 (Fam) [2013] 1 FLR 182; *Tchenguiz-Imerman v Imerman* [2013] EWHC 3627 (Fam) [2014] Fam Law 451.

[178] Section 24(1)(c).   [179] *Young v Young* [1962] P 27, CA.

[180] Per Hill J in *Prinsep v Prinsep* [1929] P 225 at 232.

[181] *Brooks v Brooks* [1986] AC 375, HL. See also *C v C (Variation of Post-Nuptial Settlement: Company Shares)* [2003] EWHC 1222 (Fam), [2003] 2 FLR 493, where the husband's shareholding in his company was transferred into a settlement in the Cayman Islands, with the wife as a beneficiary.

[182] See s 24(1)(c) as amended.   [183] [1986] AC 375, HL.   [184] Sch 5 para 7(3).

recommendation,[185] it is now expressly provided by s 24A[186] that where the court makes an order under s 22ZA, or, under sections 22A to 24, a secured periodical payments order, a lump sum order, or a property adjustment order, then it may make:

> ... a further order for the sale of such property as may be specified in the order, being property in which or in the proceeds of sale of which either or both of the parties to the marriage has or have a beneficial interest, either in possession or reversion.

The power to order a sale is a consequential or ancillary power and not an independent one. In other words, it can only be made where an order relating to the parties' capital has already been made; it does not confer a jurisdiction to order a sale 'in the air'. [187]

In the case of property belonging to one spouse and a third party the court is directed that, before it decides whether to order a sale, the third party must be given the opportunity to make representations, and any such representations are then to be included in the circumstances to which the court must have regard under s 25 of the 1973 Act.[188]

8. CONSENT ORDERS

(a) Encouraging agreement

There is nothing to prevent the parties themselves from agreeing to the terms of the financial provision and property adjustment orders to be made, or to turn to a private family arbitrator to seek an award, under the terms of the Institute of Family Law Arbitrators (IFLA) Scheme noted in Chapter 1. Indeed, the whole trend in recent years has been to encourage them to do so. We have already noted the emphasis placed on the promotion of settlements. Negotiated settlements may work to reduce hostility and acrimony between the parties;[189] furthermore, it makes obvious sense for the parties to reach agreement to save the costs of a full court hearing, which can be extremely heavy.[190] With the withdrawal of legal aid, many more couples may be expected to reach agreements without the benefit of advice or assistance from a lawyer or mediator and which do not receive any scrutiny by a court. There is an obvious risk of couples making poor arrangements in consequence.

(b) The information before the court

When the parties have come to terms, it is commonly sought to have their agreement incorporated into a court order[191] (but as we have just noted, this may be less likely if the couple have had no legal or other assistance). The court may make an order on the agreed

---

[185] Law Com No 99, *Orders for Sale of Property under the Matrimonial Causes Act 1973*.

[186] Added by the Matrimonial Homes and Property Act 1981 s 7 and amended by the LASPO Act 2012, s 51.

[187] *Omielan v Omielan* [1996] 2 FLR 306, CA.

[188] Matrimonial Causes Act 1973 s 24A(6), added by the Matrimonial and Family Proceedings Act 1984 Sch 1 para 11.

[189] See eg Lord Scarman in *Minton v Minton* [1979] AC 593 at 608, HL: 'The law now encourages spouses to avoid bitterness after family breakdown and to settle their money and property problems.'

[190] See eg *F v F (Ancillary Relief: Substantial Assets)* [1995] 2 FLR 45, where the parties' total costs approached £1.5 million; *Piglowska v Piglowski* [1999] 1 WLR 1360, where the costs of £128,000 exceeded the parties' assets of £127,400; *Young v Young* [2013] EWHC 3637 (Fam) [2014] Fam Law 291, where the wife's costs were £6.4 million and she was awarded £20 million. See further Costs, p 862.

[191] See E Hitchings, J Miles and H Woodward *Assembling the jigsaw puzzle: Understanding financial settlement on divorce* (2013), which explores the processual aspects of achieving a settlement which is embodied in a consent order by the court.

terms on the basis only of prescribed information furnished with the application.[192] The court retains the power, and indeed the duty, to scrutinise the proposed arrangements: in particular it must still have regard to the considerations set out in s 25 of the 1973 Act.[193] The realities of life in the family courts, however, mean that district judges have only limited time to examine the terms of proposed consent orders put up to them and '. . . whilst the court is no rubber stamp nor is it some kind of forensic ferret'.[194] The function of the court when approving financial consent orders is confined to a broad appraisal of the parties' financial circumstances, without descent into the valley of detail.[195] The fact that the parties have arrived at a settlement will itself be prima facie evidence that its terms are reasonable, at least if they were at arms length and were both legally advised:

> The statutory duty [ie to consider the proposed arrangements in the context of s 25 of the 1973 Act] cannot be ducked, but the court is entitled to assume that parties who are *sui juris* and who are represented by solicitors know what they want.[196]

Consequently, the court will normally approve the terms of the agreement which is proposed by the parties, provided it is not contrary to public policy, and will incorporate it in an order.[197] But where one or both spouses are litigants in person, as will be more common in the future, the court may have to adopt a more inquisitorial approach to try to ensure that they understand the implications of their bargain and that its terms are broadly fair.

In *Livesey (formerly Jenkins) v Jenkins*[198] the House of Lords held that, because the court cannot properly discharge its function under s 25 without complete and up-to-date information, the parties owe a duty to the court to make full and frank disclosure of material facts to each other, not simply up to the time of the agreement, but right up until the time of the court order. Failure to make such disclosure can lead to the order being set aside. In *Livesey v Jenkins* the wife agreed to relinquish all claims for maintenance in return for the husband's agreeing to transfer to her his half-share in the matrimonial home. After the agreement had been reached, but before it had been embodied in a court order, the wife became engaged to be married, but this was not disclosed to the husband or the court. It was held that this failure to disclose was so important[199] that the order should be set aside. Lord Brandon, however, emphasised[200] that not every failure of disclosure would justify setting a consent order aside. On the contrary, to justify setting an order aside the absence of disclosure must have led the court to make a substantially different order from that which it would have made had there been full disclosure.[201] This

---

[192] Matrimonial Causes Act 1973 s 33A added by the Matrimonial and Family Proceedings Act 1984 s 7 as amended by Welfare Reform and Pensions Act 1999 Sch 3 paras 1, 8. For the prescribed information and procedure, see the Family Procedure Rules 2010 r 9.26 and Practice Direction 5A.

[193] Discussed in Ch 23, Factors to be taken into account when assessing what orders should be made for a spouse, pp 882–903.   [194] *Harris v Manahan* [1997] 1 FLR 205 at 213, CA per Ward LJ.

[195] *Pounds v Pounds* [1994] 1 FLR 775 at 779, CA per Waite LJ.

[196] *Harris v Manahan* at 213 per Ward LJ. For a contrary view, see M Maclean and J Eekelaar *Family Justice: The Work of Family Judges in Uncertain Times* (2013) at pp 15–17.

[197] *Dean v Dean* [1978] Fam 161, following *Brockwell v Brockwell* (1975) 6 Fam Law 46, CA.

[198] [1985] AC 424, HL approving *de Lasala v de Lasala* [1980] AC 546, PC and disapproving on this point *Wales v Wadham* [1977] 2 All ER 125.

[199] It will be appreciated that once the wife had remarried she would no longer be entitled to receive periodical payments, so she was not relinquishing very much.

[200] [1985] AC 424, HL at 445.

[201] See also *Sharland v Sharland* [2014] EWCA Civ 95 [2014] 2 FLR 89: husband had been fraudulent but this would have made no difference to the order the court made by consent.

test has been strictly applied, no doubt to prevent a flood of applications to set aside on the basis of material non-disclosure. For the same reason the Court of Appeal has sought to restrict the development of an earlier judicial suggestion[202] that the poor quality of legal advice which a spouse receives prior to entering into an agreement may enable him (or her) subsequently to resile from it. In *Harris v Manahan*,[203] the court recognised that, while bad legal advice may have a part to play in deciding whether a spouse should be held to a bargain, the need for finality in litigation requires that 'only in the most exceptional case of cruellest injustice' should it be a ground for the court interfering with a consent order. The remedy for a badly advised spouse lies in an action in negligence against his (or her) solicitors in the appropriate case.

(c) The weight attached to the parties' agreement

A further problem arises if one of the parties wishes to go back on an agreement before the court approves it and embodies it in an order. We have already seen that the agreement cannot preclude an application to the court[204] and obviously a party will not be bound if the agreement was made under duress or undue influence, but the question is how far the court should give effect to the agreement if it appears to leave one party disadvantaged as compared with how the court would have exercised its discretion in an adjudication.

In *Edgar v Edgar*[205] a multi-millionaire and his wife entered into a separation deed in which the husband made capital provision for her amounting to some £100,000 and undertook to make periodical payments to her of £16,000 a year together with periodical payments for the children. In return she covenanted not to seek financial relief in any divorce proceedings that might take place in the future. She executed the deed after being warned by her legal advisers that she would probably obtain a much better order from the court. When divorce proceedings were launched, she attempted to resile from the agreement and claimed a lump sum payment. Dismissing her application, the Court of Appeal held that, although the husband's financial position put him in a much stronger bargaining position, there was no evidence that he had exploited it, and consequently the wife must be held to her agreement. They held that 'formal agreements, properly and fairly arrived at with competent legal advice, should not be displaced unless there are good and substantial grounds for concluding that an injustice will be done by holding the parties to the terms of their agreement'.[206]

Edgar concerned a separation agreement, made by deed.[207] Its validity was not in doubt but since the jurisdiction of the court cannot be ousted, the question for the court was whether any different provision should be made for the wife. It is more common these days for the parties to negotiate and agree terms during the divorce proceedings, and then submit the agreement to the court for embodiment as a consent order.[208] The legal basis underpinning

---

[202] *Camm v Camm* (1982) 4 FLR 577 at 580, CA per Ormrod LJ (referring to his earlier judgment: *Edgar v Edgar* [1980] 3 All ER 887, CA). His Lordship made it clear that it was not necessarily negligent legal advice which was required: *B v B (Consent Order: Variation)* [1995] 1 FLR 9.

[203] [1997] 1 FLR 205. While recognising that on the facts the wife had suffered injustice, Ward LJ accepted, with regret, that 'a wronged individual is to be sacrificed on the high altar of policy'. He added (at 224): 'To deny justice to the wife is hard—and to that extent justice is imperfect; but justice must be done to the husband; to do justice to children is paramount; to do justice to the system into which these disputes are fed is essential.'

[204] Above, p 783.   [205] [1980] 1 WLR 1410, CA.

[206] [1980] 1 WLR 1410, CA at 1417. For a striking application of the principle, see *T v T (Agreement not embodied in Consent Order)* [2013] EWHC B3 (Fam) [2013] Fam Law 801: ('separation agreement' made in 1991 and acted upon but never embodied in consent order. Wife's application over 20 years later for provision from ex-husband dismissed).

[207] A 'Type 2' agreement: see Ch 21, Private agreements, Between spouses and civil partners, p 780.

[208] A 'Type 3' agreement: see Ch 21, Private agreements, Between spouses and civil partners, ibid.

this situation was spelled out by the Court of Appeal in *Xydhias v Xydhias*.[209] There, the parties reached an agreement and draft consent orders were produced by counsel. The husband then sought to withdraw his consent and have the case fully tried. The wife applied for an order in the terms of the agreement that had been reached. In upholding her successful application, the Court nonetheless made clear that the normal rules of contract do not apply in the matrimonial jurisdiction, and until the terms of an agreement intended to determine the couple's claims under the Act have been embodied in a court order, they are not binding in law.[210] The purpose of the parties' negotiations is only to reduce the length and complexity of the proceedings and if the parties dispute whether an agreement was reached, it is for the court to determine this: good practice will usually ensure that heads of agreement signed by the parties, or a clear exchange of solicitors' letters, will establish the necessary consensus. If the court concludes that the parties did reach an agreement, it then has to consider whether its terms are vitiated by a factor such as non-disclosure, and the broader question of whether they should be upheld in the light of the court's duty under s 25.

Endorsement of out of court settlement reached through family *arbitration* suggests that it will be very difficult to persuade the court to reject a package arrived at either by agreement or by arbitration, so long as its terms are in line with English law. As the President put it in *S v S (Financial Remedies: Arbitral Award)*, 'Where the parties have bound themselves . . . to accept an arbitral award of the kind provided for by the IFLA Scheme, this generates, as it seems to me, a single magnetic factor of determinative importance.'[211] He went on to note that:

> Where the consent order which the judge is being asked to approve is founded on an arbitral award under the IFLA Scheme or something similar (and the judge will, of course, need to check that the order does indeed give effect to the arbitral award and is workable) the judge's role will be simple. The judge will not need to play the detective unless something leaps off the page to indicate that something has gone so seriously wrong in the arbitral process as fundamentally to vitiate the arbitral award. Although recognising that the judge is not a rubber stamp, the combination of (a) the fact that the parties have agreed to be bound by the arbitral award, (b) the fact of the arbitral award (which the judge will of course be able to study) and (c) the fact that the parties are putting the matter before the court *by consent*, means that it can only be in the rarest of cases that it will be appropriate for the judge to do other than approve the order. With a process as sophisticated as that embodied in the IFLA Scheme it is difficult to contemplate such a case.[212]

However, he cautioned that different considerations might apply where the arbitral process is based on a different system of law 'or, in particular, where there is reason to believe that, whatever system of law is purportedly being applied, there may have been gender-based discrimination.'[213]

---

[209] [1999] 1 FLR 683. See also *TW v PL (Agreement)* [2013] EWHC 3078 (Fam) [2014] 2 FLR 106 where the mother gave an interview to a magazine describing the father in unflattering terms and he sought to argue that the agreement that they had just reached for provision for their child under Sch 1 to the Children Act 1989 should not be embodied in a consent order. Held, while the mother had been unwise, her actions did not vitiate the terms of the agreement so as to justify not giving effect to it, but that she should understand that undertakings she had given in the agreement to avoid publicity would henceforth be binding on her.

[210] Thus, a determination reached by an arbitrator under the IFLA scheme (noted earlier, Ch 1, Private ordering and the withdrawal of legal aid, p 12) will need to be embodied in a consent order to make it enforceable.

[211] [2014] EWHC 7 (Fam) [2014] 1 FLR 1257 at [19].

[212] [2014] EWHC 7 (Fam) [2014] 1 FLR 1257 at [21].

[213] [2014] EWHC 7 (Fam) [2014] 1 FLR 1257 at [27]. For consideration of the role of religious tribunals in purporting to arbitrate or determine ancillary matters relating to the ending of a marriage, see G Douglas

(d) The effects of a consent order

It should be appreciated that, once the parties' agreement is incorporated into a court order, it derives its authority from the order and not from the agreement.[214] This has two important consequences. First, the court is no more entitled to make orders outside the terms of the 1973 Act than it is in respect of contested orders.[215] Secondly, the rules against reopening 'clean break' orders[216] and varying property adjustment orders[217] apply equally to consent orders as they do to a contested order.[218] The courts have warned of the need for legal representatives to be especially careful in drafting the terms of proposed consent orders and to advise their clients on precisely what impact their agreement will have.[219] The failure by a legal adviser to protect his client's interests in respect of a consent order may constitute professional negligence, for which substantial damages may be awarded.[220]

It will not infrequently be the case that the parties will have reached an agreement which is perfectly proper in itself but which is outside the terms of the Matrimonial Causes Act 1973, as in *Livesey v Jenkins*,[221] where, after the transfer of the husband's share in the matrimonial home, the wife agreed to be solely responsible for the mortgage and all other outgoings on the house and to be solely responsible for certain specific bank overdrafts. The court has no power to incorporate such agreements in a consent order. However, it is possible to make such agreements binding by including them in an undertaking to the court.[222]

(e) Pre- and post-nuptial agreements

What if the spouses do not wait until their marriage ends to reach a settlement on their financial obligations towards each other, but seek to allow for the eventuality in advance even before the wedding itself?[223] A wealthy person who has inherited property, or built up a business, might wish to shield his or her assets from the other or ensure they are ring-fenced for the benefit of children from a former relationship, and may be unwilling to risk a court subsequently transferring a substantial part of them if the marriage ends in divorce. The incentive to do so has grown since the House of Lords ruled, in *White v White* that assets should usually be shared, using a 'yardstick of equality' so that even fabulously wealthy spouses may lose half of their wealth.[224]

---

et al, who found, in a case study of three well-established tribunals (Roman Catholic, Jewish and Muslim) that they were wary of exercising such a 'jurisdiction' and were clear to advise those using their services that only the family courts may make binding rulings: 'The role of religious tribunals in regulating marriage and divorce' [2012] CFLQ 139.

[214] *de Lasala v de Lasala* [1980] AC 546, HL; *Masefield v Alexander* [1995] 1 FLR 100, CA.

[215] See Lord Brandon in *Livesey v Jenkins* [1985] AC 424 at 444, and see *Belcher v Belcher* [1995] 1 FLR 916.

[216] Discussed in Ch 23, Appeal out of time, p 909. The most common form of consent order provides for a clean break. [217] See Ch 23, Orders that may be varied, pp 912 *et seq.*

[218] See *Minton v Minton* [1979] AC 593, HL.

[219] See eg *Pounds v Pounds* [1994] 1 FLR 775 at 790 per Waite LJ.

[220] *Dickinson v Jones Alexander & Co* [1993] 2 FLR 521 (decided in 1989).

[221] [1985] AC 424, HL.

[222] [1985] AC 424, HL per Lord Brandon at 444. See also *TW v PL (Agreement)* [2013] EWHC 3078 (Fam) [2014] 2 FLR 106 earlier.

[223] See J Scherpe (ed) *Marital Agreements and Private Autonomy in Comparative Perspective* (2012) which collates information on the approach taken in a number of jurisdictions, both common law and civil law-based. For discussion of the case law leading up to the current position, see N Lowe and R Kay 'The Status of Prenuptial Agreement in English Law—Eccentricity or sensible pragmatism?' in B Verschraegen (ed) *Family Finances* (2009) and J Miles 'Marital Agreements: "The More Radical' Solution"' in R Probert and C Barton (eds) *Fifty Years in Family Law: Essays for Stephen Cretney* (2012).

[224] See Ch 23, Fairness, pp 869–874.

It was long thought that an agreement of this kind[225] was null and void as being contrary to public policy. However, the courts drew a distinction between a 'separation agreement' reached when the parties were on the point of separation or had already separated[226]—which could be upheld—and one which provided for future separation.[227] The latter, whether reached before or after the marriage had taken place, would be regarded as agreeing to release the parties from their common law duty to cohabit and thus unacceptable.[228]

In *F v F (Ancillary Relief: Substantial Assets)*,[229] Thorpe J considered that such 'pre-nuptial agreements' 'must be of very limited significance' in this jurisdiction. Indeed, as we have just seen, *Xydhias v Xhydias*[230] establishes that only the court can finally dispose of the parties' claims against each other, so that all that a family court exercising the matrimonial jurisdiction can do is to take the terms of the agreement into account, either as part of all the circumstances of the case, or as 'conduct' under s 25(2)(g) of the Matrimonial Causes Act 1973[231] and then consider how far it wishes to hold the parties to their arrangement.

But as 'separation agreements' became subsumed within the settlement approach taken to dealing with the financial consequences of divorce, under which agreements were to be encouraged rather than condemned, the courts began to revisit their stance and attach more weight to the fact of an agreement even if made before the marriage, particularly where the spouses had entered into the agreement in another jurisdiction where it would be given full legal effect. Thus, in *N v N (Foreign Divorce: Financial Relief)*[232] where the parties were Swedish nationals, Cazalet J considered that, while their pre-nuptial agreement would not be conclusive in England (as it was in Sweden), it was nonetheless a material consideration, to which the court should have regard in applying the criteria in s 25 of the 1973 Act. In *S v S (Divorce: Staying Proceedings)* Wilson J said that there was a danger that the words of Thorpe J in *F v F* might be taken out of context. Looking to the future, his Lordship added:

> There will come a case . . . where the circumstances surrounding the pre-nuptial agreement and the provision therein contained might, when viewed in the context of other circumstances of the case prove influential or even crucial . . . I can find nothing in s 25 to compel a conclusion . . . at odds with personal freedoms to make agreements for ourselves . . . carefully struck by informed adults. It all depends.[233]

One such case was *Crossley v Crossley* where a couple who had both been married before (the wife, three times, the husband once) and who were independently wealthy, made a pre-nuptial agreement that neither would seek any financial provision against the other. The marriage lasted barely a year and the wife applied for divorce, including a claim for financial remedies. In dismissing an appeal by the wife concerning directions the trial judge had given for handling the claim, Thorpe LJ (having moved on from his opinion in *F v F*) commented that:

---

[225] A 'Type 1' agreement: see Ch 21, Private agreements, Between spouses and civil partners, p 780.
[226] A 'Type 2' agreement: see Ch 21, Private agreements, Between spouses and civil partners, p 780.
[227] *Marquis of Westmeath v Marchioness of Westmeath* (1830) 1 Dow & Cl 519.
[228] *Cocksedge v Cocksedge* (1844) 14 Sim 244; *Cartwright v Cartwright* (1853) 3 De GM & G 982; *H v W* (1857) 3 K & J 382. It was applied to a pre-nuptial agreement to live apart which was re-signed immediately after marriage in *Brodie v Brodie* [1917] P 271.   [229] [1995] 2 FLR 45 at 66.
[230] [1999] 1 FLR 683, CA.   [231] Discussed in Ch 23, Conduct, pp 899–903.
[232] [1997] 1 FLR 900.   [233] [1997] 2 FLR 100 at 102.

> if ever there is to be a paradigm case in which the court will look to the prenuptial agreement as not simply one of the peripheral factors in the case but as a factor of magnetic importance, it seems to me that this is just such a case.[234]

The matter came up for consideration at the highest level in two subsequent cases, one dealt with by the Privy Council and the other by the Supreme Court.

MacLeod v MacLeod

In *MacLeod v MacLeod*[235] the spouses, American citizens, made a pre-nuptial agreement on the day of their wedding in Florida which limited the wife's claims against the (much wealthier and older) husband but also set out what the husband would provide for her *during* the marriage. They renegotiated the terms twice after they were married including at the point when the marriage was in difficulties. At each stage, each had legal advice. They spent most of their married life in the Isle of Man, and the husband petitioned for divorce there. The wife argued that the agreement should be ignored in determining what financial provision should be made for her (and the spouses' children). The Privy Council followed the earlier judicial distinction between a pre-nuptial and post-nuptial agreement. Baroness Hale, giving the judgment of the Board, considered that

> There is an enormous difference in principle and in practice between an agreement providing for a present state of affairs which has developed between a married couple and an agreement made before the parties have committed themselves to the rights and responsibilities of the married state purporting to govern what may happen in an uncertain and unhoped for future ... Post-nuptial agreements ... are very different from pre-nuptial agreements. The couple are now married. They have undertaken towards one another the obligations and responsibilities of the married state. A pre-nuptial agreement is no longer the price which one party may extract for his or her willingness to marry. There is nothing to stop a couple entering into contractual financial arrangements governing their life together, as this couple did [when they amended the agreement after they were married]....[236]

Not only was Baroness Hale influenced by the lesser inequality of bargaining power that might be assumed to arise once the parties are married as compared to before the wedding, but she also considered that the old public policy objection could not apply to a post-nuptial agreement since the duty to cohabit was no longer enforceable once the decree of 'restitution of conjugal rights' had been abolished[237] and thus the rationale for the rule had gone.[238] The Board took the view that the spouses' agreement was therefore valid and enforceable as a contract, but subject to the provisions in the Matrimonial Causes Act 1973 s 34 (that the court's jurisdiction could not be ousted) and s 35 (that the terms could be varied in the event of a change in circumstances or to make proper arrangements for any child of the family). It followed that in determining whether to uphold the agreement, a court should have regard to evidence of a change in circumstances, whether it would be contrary to public policy, in the sense of leaving a spouse dependent upon the State for support, and whether the circumstances concerning the

---

[234] [2007] EWCA Civ 1491 [2008] 1 FLR 1467 at [15].
[235] [2008] UKPC 64 [2010] 1 AC 298.   [236] [2008] UKPC 64 [2010] 1 AC 298 at [31], [36].
[237] See Ch 4, Consortium, p 94.   [238] At [39].

making of the agreement rendered it unfair.[239] However, they also considered, obiter, that sections 34 and 35 do not apply to an agreement made prior to marriage, and it would be unfair to make a pre-nuptial agreement *enforceable* but not *variable*.[240]

The Privy Council were clear that if greater recognition of pre- as opposed to post-nuptial agreements were to be given, this should be determined by Parliament, which could then consider the ramifications and any necessary supporting requirements (such as the extent to which agreements should be subject to particular formalities to ensure they had been entered into fairly). The matter was referred to the Law Commission so that they could examine the issue in the round and do precisely that, and we consider their proposals in Chapter 23.[241] But in the meantime, the Board's ruling, which of course, whilst highly persuasive authority was not binding on courts in England and Wales, left pre- and post-nuptial agreements in different positions regarding both their status (contract or not?) and how far a court should be willing to be bound by their terms when exercising its s 25 discretion in financial remedies proceedings, and the whole issue was revisited in *Granatino v Radmacher (Formerly Granatino)*.[242]

Granatino v Radmacher

Here, the German wife came from a hugely wealthy family. Her French husband was also wealthy and worked as a banker. Before they married, they signed a notarised agreement in Germany, to be governed by German law, providing that neither spouse would derive any interest in or benefit from the property of the other, either during the marriage or on its termination. The agreement made no provision for what should happen if they had any children. It was written in German, and although—as is common in civil law systems—the notary advised both parties as to the terms, there was no full disclosure of the parties' (especially the wife's) wealth and the husband did not take independent legal advice nor seek a translation into French. The couple moved to London where they had two children. Subsequently, the husband decided to go into academic scientific research, thus losing his substantial earnings in the financial sector, and when the marriage broke down, he sought financial provision from the wife despite the terms of the agreement.

The Supreme Court, by a majority (Baroness Hale dissenting), held that the rule of public policy regarding post-nuptial agreements as void was indeed obsolete as the Privy Council had held in *MacLeod*, but they went on to say (obiter) that the objection to pre-nuptial agreements was equally obsolete.[243] They rejected the distinction that had been drawn between the two on the basis of sections 34 and 35 of the 1973 Act, instead suggesting that there is rather a difference between a *separation* agreement and a post-nuptial agreement insofar as the former relates to the circumstances applying at the point when the parties are about to, or have already separated, whilst the latter may be made, as *MacLeod* made clear, at any point during the marriage. They were not convinced that the power to vary a maintenance agreement under s 35 should apply to the court's consideration of all post-nuptial agreements, as distinct from *separation* agreements, as

---

[239] At [40]–[42]. The Board upheld the terms of the agreement as satisfying the criteria laid down by the Isle of Man statute (which was equivalent to the Matrimonial Causes Act 1973 s 25) so that the wife should not be given any additional provision, but they remitted the case for reconsideration of the provision to be made for the children.

[240] At [35].   [241] See Marital property agreements, p 927.

[242] [2010] UKSC 42 [2011] 1 AC 534. See J Miles 'Marriage and Divorce in the Supreme Court and the Law Commission: for Love or Money?' (2011) 74 MLR 430; J Scherpe 'Fairness, freedom and foreign elements—marital agreements in England and Wales after *Granatino v Radmacher*' [2011] CFLQ 513; N Lowe 'Prenuptial Agreements: The Developing English Position' in A-L Verbeke et al (eds) *Confronting the Frontiers of Family and Succession Law: Liber Amicorum Walter Pintens* Vol 1 (2012).

[243] [2010] UKSC 42 [2011] 1 AC 534 at [52].

the Privy Council had held. They accordingly did not consider that the power to vary under s 35 should be seen as a precondition to holding that a nuptial agreement can take effect as a contract.[244]

Secondly, they rejected the view that there is necessarily a material difference between pre- and post-nuptial agreements—the equivalence of the parties' bargaining positions will vary according to the facts.[245] Indeed, noting that the court's jurisdiction under the Matrimonial Causes Act 1973 cannot be ousted by agreement and the court must always exercise its discretion under s 25, they considered that the question whether a (pre- or post-) nuptial agreement is a contract is a 'red herring' and the court should apply the same principles to the exercise of its discretion regardless of when the agreement was made.[246]

In setting out the factors the court must consider in determining this question, the majority identified three issues of principle. First, were there circumstances attending the making of the agreement which would detract from the weight that it should be accorded? They noted that both spouses must enter into the agreement of their own free will, without undue influence or pressure, and informed of its implications.[247] A Government consultation document published in 1998 had set out suggested criteria designed to ensure this, including a 21 day cooling-off period before the wedding and the importance of independent legal advice.[248] But the majority considered that such black and white rules are not necessary under the current law; the real focus should be on whether there was any *material* lack of disclosure, information or advice. A court should first consider whether any of the standard vitiating factors—duress, fraud or misrepresentation—was present. It should then take into account any 'unworthy conduct, such as exploitation of a dominant position to secure an unfair advantage', a party's emotional state and any pressures he or she was under to agree. This will vary depending upon the age, maturity and marital experience of the couple. Here, the Supreme Court agreed with the Court of Appeal that the husband had well understood the effect of the agreement and the extent, if not the detail, of the wife's wealth, so that the agreement should not be vitiated on those grounds.[249]

Secondly, the court must consider whether there were any circumstances attending the making of the agreement that *enhance* the weight it should be accorded. It had been argued that the fact that the agreement was drawn up in a jurisdiction where these are the norm should be accorded additional weight. But the majority considered that the 'foreign element' was no longer of significance in the light of their ruling that such agreements may be given effect.[250]

Thirdly, and most importantly, the court must consider whether the circumstances prevailing at the time of the proceedings make it fair or just to depart from the agreement. One of the key objections to enforcing such agreements is that couples cannot foresee how their lives will turn out and may fail to cater for the circumstances which transpire. On the other hand, the very fact of having made an agreement has a bearing on what should be regarded as fair as between the parties. The majority accordingly formulated the test to be applied as follows:

> The court should give effect to a nuptial agreement that is freely entered into by each party with a full appreciation of its implications unless in the circumstances prevailing it would not be fair to hold the parties to their agreement.[251]

---

[244] [2010] UKSC 42 [2011] 1 AC 534 at [56].   [245] See [57]–[61].

[246] At [63]. However, by dismissing the distinction between pre- and post-nuptial agreements made in *MacLeod* they in fact ruled that a pre-nuptial agreement *can* be given effect as a valid contract, see [56]–[63] although—as Baroness Hale and Lord Mance pointed out—this was strictly obiter: [127], [161].

[247] At [68].   [248] Home Office, *Supporting Families* (1998) para 4.23.

[249] [69]–[73] and [114]–[117].   [250] [74].   [251] [75].

In deciding the 'difficult question' of when it would not be fair, the court indicated that the following factors are relevant.[252] First, since the court exercising its discretion under s 25 must give first consideration to the welfare of any child of the family under the age of 18,[253] a nuptial agreement cannot be allowed to prejudice the reasonable requirements of such a child. Secondly, the court should give due respect to the parties' individual autonomy as to how their financial affairs should be regulated, especially where the agreement addresses their actual circumstances. Thirdly, an agreement to exclude 'non-matrimonial' property[254] from any claim by the other spouse may be objectively justified. Fourthly, the court should consider how far an agreement that fails to meet the needs, and the requirement to compensate for loss generated by the marital relationship,[255] should be upheld.

> The parties are unlikely to have intended that their ante-nuptial agreement should result . . . in one partner being left in a predicament of real need, while the other enjoys a sufficiency or more, and such a result is likely to render it unfair to hold the parties to their agreement.[256]

By contrast, if each party is able to meet his or her own needs, but the parties had contracted not to share the matrimonial assets it might well be fair to hold them to their agreement even though the courts have adopted the general principle of such sharing.[257] The court did not elaborate on what it meant by a 'predicament of real need'; in particular it is unclear how far this suggests an absolute standard or the much more nuanced interpretation of 'needs' as applied generally in the matrimonial jurisdiction.[258]

On the facts, the majority considered that on the basis of giving 'decisive' weight to the agreement, the husband should not have been granted provision from the wife in his capacity as her husband, but only, as the Court of Appeal had ruled, in his role as a father and homemaker for the children. Thus, a capital sum to enable him to buy a house in which he could have the children to stay should not be his absolutely but should revert to the wife, and an income fund should be capitalised to cover his needs, only until the children were grown-up.

While the majority was overwhelmingly in favour of giving effect to pre-nuptial agreements unless this would not be fair, Baroness Hale delivered an extremely powerful dissenting judgment which draws out the opposing arguments of principle. It is perhaps unsurprising, given that she gave the sole judgment in *MacLeod v MacLeod*, that Baroness Hale did not agree with the majority's approach. First, she reiterated the Privy Council's view that the question of whether, and how, to give effect to pre-nuptial agreements is much better left to the Law Commission and the legislature than the courts deciding individual cases on their facts.[259] But more importantly, she pointed out that 'unlike a separation agreement, the object of an ante-nuptial agreement is to deny the economically weaker spouse the provision to which she – it is usually although by no means invariably she[260] – would otherwise be entitled.' And she noted 'there is a gender dimension to the issue which some may think ill-suited to decision by a court consisting of eight men and one woman.'[261] The point that a pre-nuptial agreement may be deliberately designed to disadvantage one spouse in the event of a divorce underscored her view (also spelled out

---

[252] [74]–[82].
[253] See Ch 23, Treating the welfare of any child of the family as the first consideration, p 874.
[254] See Ch 23, Matrimonial and non-matrimonial property, p 882.
[255] See Ch 23, Compensation, p 871.   [256] [81].   [257] See Ch 23, Sharing, p 873.
[258] See Ch 23, Needs, obligations and responsibilities, pp 888–891.
[259] [133]–[136].   [260] Of course, in *Radmacher* itself, the wife was wealthier than the husband.
[261] [137].

in *MacLeod*) that such an agreement should certainly not be regarded as binding unless, as with a post-nuptial agreement, it is subject to variation under s 35—and she reiterated her interpretation of the definition of a 'maintenance agreement' in s 34 as *not* applying to couples who have not yet married.[262]

Baroness Hale also criticised the majority's formulation of the test to be applied by the court as introducing a presumption that the agreement should be upheld which would be both an 'inadmissible judicial gloss' on the statute, and inapplicable to the discretionary exercise the court has to carry out.[263] She considered that the guiding principle laid down in the case-law[264] of fairness 'is fairness in the light of the actual and foreseeable circumstances at the time when the court comes to make its order.' Thus, for her, the test should be formulated as

> Did each party freely enter into an agreement, intending it to have legal effect and with a full appreciation of its implications? If so, in the circumstances as they are now, would it be fair to hold them to their agreement?[265]

In her view, this formulation would avoid imposing a presumption in favour of upholding the agreement while allowing the court to give full effect to the agreement if fair to do so. In her application of this approach, she agreed with the majority that the husband had freely entered into the agreement and had understood its implications, but she parted company from them and the Court of Appeal in regarding the husband as entitled to financial provision only in his role as father and carer of their children. As she put it, the Court of Appeal 'decided to treat these parents as if they had never been married'[266] and she would have awarded him a life interest in the home.

The aftermath of Radmacher

The strong ruling by the majority in *Radmacher* made clear that both a pre- and post-nuptial agreement may be upheld and given effect by a court hearing a financial remedies claim, with the onus on the party seeking to avoid its terms to establish that it would be unfair to hold her or him to them.[267] Although the majority did not consider the husband to have been disadvantaged by what might be regarded, in this jurisdiction but not others in civil law systems, as procedural failings in the making of the agreement, some subsequent decisions have emphasised the need for adequate protection of the vulnerable party at the point of entering into the agreement. Moreover, the majority's indication that it will be easier to regard an agreement as *unfair* where it fails to cater for a spouse's needs or entitlement to be compensated for loss caused by the marriage, has been followed in subsequent cases.

Given that it is only since *Radmacher* that legal advisers have been able to give clear guidance as to how an agreement would be viewed by the English courts, it is not surprising that many of the cases have involved couples who married abroad. In *Kremen v Agrest (Financial Remedy: Non-Disclosure: Post-Nuptial Agreement)*[268] where the parties had

---

[262] [157]. See Ch 21, Maintenance agreements, p 781. [263] [166].

[264] *White v White* [2001] 1 AC 596; *Miller v Miller; McFarlane v McFarlane* [2006] UKHL 24 [2006] 2 WLR 1283, discussed in Ch 23, Fairness, pp 869–874. [265] [169]. [266] [192].

[267] For consideration of the public acceptability of pre-nuptial agreements, and the propensity of couples to make them, see A Barlow and J Smithson 'Is modern marriage a bargain? Exploring perceptions of pre-nuptial agreements in England and Wales' [2012] CFLQ 304, who find that there is increasing acceptance of the idea of making them, though recognition of the potential for exploitation of the weaker partner and for the weakening of trust between the parties.

[268] [2012] EWHC 45 (Fam) [2012] 2 FLR 414.

entered into a post-nuptial agreement later made into an order by an Israeli court, it was held that 'it will only be in an unusual case where it can be said that absent independent legal advice and full disclosure, a party can be taken to have freely entered into a marital agreement with a full appreciation of its implications.' A spouse would have to be shown to have a 'high degree of financial and legal sophistication' (which the Supreme Court attributed to Mr Granatino) in order to have a full appreciation of what legal rights he or she is signing away.[269]

In that case, the court was dealing with a 'serious and serial non-discloser who is determined to do down his wife by "foul means"',[270] and who was hiding several million pounds-worth of assets, so the court was hardly disposed to be particularly willing to give him the benefit of the *Radmacher* presumption. But the same judge, Mostyn J, showed even more caution in *B v S (Financial Remedy: Marital Property Regime)*.[271] There, he held that, to uphold the terms of an agreement in this jurisdiction, a 'full appreciation' of its implications does not require that the party received specific legal advice on its effect in English law: as he pointed out, such a requirement would vitiate every agreement made prior to *Radmacher*. But he went on to hold that the parties must have intended—and received legal advice to this effect—that the agreement would be effective in a jurisdiction operating a discretionary equitable distribution (such as applies in England and Wales). But one must doubt how commonly such advice is given to the myriad of couples around the world entering into nuptial agreements who might, one day, perhaps, end up living in this (or another discretionary) jurisdiction.

A more accommodating approach was taken in *V v V (Prenuptial Agreement)*.[272] The Swedish couple entered into a pre-nuptial agreement drawn up by a lawyer known to the wife's family, under which the husband would keep property he had acquired before the marriage (worth about £1m). The wife had no legal advice and full disclosure was not made, but the court held that as intelligent people, the couple would have understood the effect of the agreement, and the wife's evidence showed that she would have still will-ingly entered into it had she been expressly told of it. Similarly, in *Z v Z (No 2) (Financial Remedy: Marriage Contract)*[273] where the French couple made an agreement witnessed by two notaries but there had been no independent legal advice, the judge noted the similar-ity with *Radmacher* and considered that the wife had known exactly what the agreement entailed and both parties knew enough about each other's financial positions without needing the full detail.[274]

There is thus some division of opinion between the judiciary as to what will constitute adequate knowledge and understanding of the effects of a pre-nuptial agreement. There is more agreement on the importance of ensuring that a spouse (and of course any children) would not be left in hardship as a result of the agreement, although as we have noted, the Supreme Court did not give guidance on how such 'need' is to be assessed.[275] It is worth

---

[269] At [73].   [270] [35].   [271] [2012] EWHC 265 (Fam) [2012] 2 FLR 502.

[272] [2011] EWHC 3230 (Fam) [2012] 1 FLR 1315.

[273] [2011] EWHC 2878 (Fam) [2012] 1 FLR 1100. Compare *GS v L (Financial Remedies: Pre-Acquired Assets: Needs)* [2011] EWHC 1759 (Fam) [2013] 1 FLR 300 where Eleanor King J attached no weight to a post-nuptial agreement made by the parties in Spain, where they resided. The Spanish legal experts could not agree upon its implications and thus she inferred that the parties could not have had a full appreciation of them either.

[274] Mostyn J took a robust view himself in *SA v PA (Pre-marital Agreement: Compensation)* [2014] EWHC 392 (Fam) [2014] Fam Law 799, where he held that an agreement made in the Netherlands drawn up by a single notary was binding on the wife as to capital division, rejecting her claim that she had not seen all the drafts nor attended the notarising of the final version.

[275] For the Law Commission's consideration of this issue, see *Matrimonial Property, Needs and Agreements* Law Com No 343 (2014) Ch 3, discussed in Ch 23, p 927–931.

noting that civil law systems treat 'maintenance' separately from property division and nuptial agreements are not binding in relation to the former. In *Z v Z (No 2)*, for example, the agreement made no provision for maintenance of the wife and children. The court was therefore able to make an award to the wife based on their 'needs', which resulted in her receiving 40% of the assets, despite the terms of the agreement, which excluded the sharing of marital property, being upheld. In *V v V*, the court similarly considered that although the agreement was an important factor in determining the outcome, an award which met the housing needs of the wife and child was required, although, to reflect the fact of the agreement, this should be satisfied by giving the husband a charge-back on the house to be realised when the children reached adulthood (as in *Radmacher*). In a purely domestic case, *Luckwell v Limata*,[276] the wife came from a very wealthy family. The husband had little earning capacity. She (and her father) insisted on a pre-nuptial agreement being made, and on subsequent agreements when substantial gifts were made to her by the father. No provision was made for the husband in the event of a divorce. Holman J held that although the husband had understood the terms of the agreement and had had legal advice, its failure to provide him with any means at all with which to house himself and accommodate his children when they came to visit was unfair, and he ordered the wife to provide a capital sum to enable the husband to obtain accommodation, eventually reverting to the wife on his death.

Clearly, the ramifications of *Radmacher* have still to be fully tested in case-law, and the position will change when legislation is enacted to give effect to the recommendations of the Law Commission, who were asked to review the law.[277] One of the difficulties involved in assessing the value of nuptial agreements is that there is little empirical evidence on the extent to which people might enter into them, or the kinds of terms they might wish to include in them. Anecdotal evidence from practitioners specialising in cases involving 'high net worth' clients is not an adequate evidence base on which to make policy. Qualitative research of the experience of a study of 39 experienced family practitioners does provide some more reliable data, albeit small-scale.[278] The study found that few of the sample had advised on more than a handful of cases per year and very few were familiar with drafting *post*-nuptial as distinct from pre-nuptial agreements. Those practising in London were more likely to have experience. It also found that clients seeking 'pre-nups' were more likely to have an international background, and be seeking to protect family wealth (as in *Radmacher*) or self-generated wealth: the suggestion that a pre-nup might be utilised by a person wishing to protect assets for children from a former relationship was not borne out by the sample. A worrying finding was the suggestion that independent legal advice might be prevented by the wealthier party paying for the advice for the prospective spouse and being unwilling to sanction the cost of a more expert opinion.[279]

Practitioner evidence cannot demonstrate the views of the wider public. However, there is some research into public attitudes to marital agreements.[280] This found that overall, 58% of a nationally representative sample of 2,827 people were in favour of couples being able to make pre-nuptial agreements. However, it also found that 65% thought that they might be a bad idea because of the difficulty of predicting what will happen in the future

---

[276] [2014] EWHC 502 (Fam) [2014] 2 FLR 168.

[277] Law Commission, *Marital Property Agreements* Consultation Paper No 198 (2010); *Matrimonial Property, Needs and Agreements* Law Com No 343 (2014).

[278] E Hitchings 'From pre-nups to post-nups: dealing with marital property agreements' [2009] Fam Law 1056. [279] Ibid at p 1062.

[280] A Barlow and J Smithson 'Is modern marriage a bargain? Exploring perceptions of pre-nuptial agreements in England and Wales' [2012] CFLQ 304.

and regarded them as carrying less weight the longer the marriage continues. A follow-up study was able to probe 26 of the participants' views in more depth, and found that people were mainly concerned to ensure fairness at the time of the divorce and were worried about potential power imbalances between couples. Thus, 94% considered that it was important for both parties to take legal advice before making an agreement. When the 1,550 who had been or were married were asked the key question of whether they would themselves have made a pre-nuptial agreement had the law permitted it when they got married, 80% said they would *not* have done so and many of those interviewed in depth said they would have felt suspicious or offended had their partner asked them to enter into one. It is generally assumed that making a marital agreement is a rational act entered into by those seeking to think calmly about how best to arrange their finances (and safeguard their financial interests)—indeed, one of the criticisms of pre-nuptial agreements is that they take the romance out of marriage—but the researchers found respondents who had made agreements in order to demonstrate their love and commitment to their spouse, and they concluded that they were 'left wondering whether in circumstances where the motives for entering the agreement blind one to its consequences, paternalism leading to court-imposed fairness might not be the preferable option.'[281] We consider the proposals of the Law Commission on the issue in Chapter 23 after we have discussed the application of the court's powers in detail.

9. COSTS AND THE LEGAL AID STATUTORY CHARGE

(a) Costs

In civil cases generally, the loser must usually pay the winner's costs, and this was also the starting point in family cases,[282] but the courts in all cases have discretion not so to order. However, it became the common practice in financial proceedings (strongly encouraged as an incentive to earlier settlement) to make written offers of settlement, known as '*Calderbank* offers'.[283] These resembled a payment into court,[284] with one party making an offer to the other 'without prejudice as to costs'. If the offer was rejected, no reference was made to it until after the court had made its order. If the order was more favourable to the offeree than the terms of the *Calderbank* offer, the court would usually award the offeree his or her costs; if not, the court might order the offeree to pay the costs of both sides from the date on which the *Calderbank* offer was made.[285] In *H v H (Financial Relief: Costs)*,[286] Holman J criticised the tactical 'poker' of *Calderbank* exchanges, and suggested that the time was fast approaching when it should be removed altogether. In *Norris v Norris; Haskins v Haskins*,[287] the Court of Appeal reminded courts of their discretion to depart from the normal costs rule where appropriate, but called for the rules to be amended. In so doing, they took on board the serious criticisms that the existing regime promoted uncertainty as to the outcome of cases, and a sense of grievance amongst litigants. New

---

[281] Barlow and Smithson [2012] CFLQ 304 at p 317.

[282] *Gojkovc v Gojkovic (No 2)* [1992] Fam 40, CA.

[283] *Calderbank v Calderbank* [1976] Fam 93, CA.

[284] *Gojkovic v Gojkovic (No 2)* at 237 (per Butler-Sloss LJ at 239).

[285] For a case where the court's order 'beat' the husband's '*Calderbank* offer' so the wife received her costs see *Thompson v Thompson* [1993] 2 FLR 464, CA.

[286] [1997] 2 FLR 57. See too *P v P (Financial Relief: Non Disclosure)* [1994] 2 FLR 381, although the court's order 'beat' the terms of the husband's *Calderbank* offer, the court declined to make a costs order in the wife's favour, to reflect the wife's serious misconduct, and culpability within the litigation.

[287] [2003] EWCA Civ 1084 [2003] 2 FLR 1124 at [28]–[29], [64].

rules were passed in 2006[288] and now appear in the Family Procedure Rules 2010 r 28, which provides that:

(5) Subject to paragraph (6), the general rule in financial remedy proceedings is that the court will not make an order requiring one party to pay the costs of another party.

(6) The court may make an order requiring one party to pay the costs of another party at any stage of the proceedings where it considers it appropriate to do so because of the conduct of a party in relation to the proceedings (whether before or during them).

(7) In deciding what order (if any) to make under paragraph (6), the court must have regard to –

   (a) any failure by a party to comply with these rules, any order of the court or any practice direction which the court considers relevant;

   (b) any open offer to settle made by a party;

   (c) whether it was reasonable for a party to raise, pursue or contest a particular allegation or issue;

   (d) the manner in which a party has pursued or responded to the application or a particular allegation or issue;

   (e) any other aspect of a party's conduct in relation to proceedings which the court considers relevant; and

   (f) the financial effect on the parties of any costs order.

Thus, only where there is litigation misconduct should a court consider awarding costs against a party to financial proceedings, and even where such misconduct is established, the court must consider the financial effect on the parties of making any order.[289] Nonetheless, the judge has a wide discretion whether to penalise misconduct in costs[290] but will bear in mind that ultimately, costs come from the parties' assets, so a costs order may simply diminish the size of the 'pot' from which the other party's award must be met.[291] The aim of this approach is to deny either party the opportunity of running up costs in an 'arms race' seeking to pressure the other into settlement, but equally to encourage *both* to settle as they see their own costs rising whilst proceedings continue.

(b) Statutory charge

The same impetus to settle and to hold down costs of course applies to those – now few – proceedings which are supported by legal aid since the Legal Aid, Sentencing and Punishment of Offenders Act 2012 (LASPO) came into force in April 2013. It is important to note that where legal aid *is* received for the purposes of legal representation (as distinct from mediation), s 25(1) of LASPO provides that the cost of providing such 'legal services'[292] is a first charge on any 'property recovered[293] or preserved by the individual in proceedings, or in

---

[288] Family Proceedings Rules 2006 (SI 2006/352) (L.1) in force in respect of applications made on or after 3 April 2006. See also *Practice Direction (Ancillary Relief: Costs)* 20 February 2006.

[289] The costs awarded must be properly justified: see *Ezair v Ezair* [2012] EWCA Civ 893 [2013] 1 FLR 281.

[290] *Malialis v Malialis* [2012] EWCA Civ 1748 [2013] 2 FLR 1216.

[291] See M Harrop 'Costs orders in financial proceedings: The holistic approach' [2011] Fam Law 608.

[292] LASPO 2012 s 8(1); The Civil Legal Aid (Statutory Charge) Regulations 2013, SI 2013/503 reg 4.

[293] See *Parkes v Legal Aid Board* [1997] 1 FLR 77, CA where the Court of Appeal held that the charge applied to property co-owned by two unmarried parents. A compromise was reached whereby the female cohabitant would remain in the house with her child until certain events occurred, whereupon it would be sold and the proceeds divided between the parties. The Court of Appeal upheld the decision of the lower court that the obtaining, by the female cohabitant, of an exclusive right of occupation against her former cohabitant amounted to a 'recovery', so that the charge attached to her interest in the property.

any compromise or settlement of a dispute, in connection with which the services were provided.' Periodical payments and pension attachment periodical payments or lump sums are expressly exempted from this charge,[294] but the Legal Aid Agency is entitled to recover its costs out of lump sums, property adjustment orders or proceeds of sale insofar as they can be regarded as property 'recovered or preserved'. Given the high costs of proceedings, this charge can be substantial. In *Hanlon v Hanlon*,[295] for example, where the matrimonial home with an equity worth £10,000 was transferred to the wife, the wife's legal aid costs amounted to £8,025. In cases where the money or property recovered or transferred is to be used either to fund the purchase of a new home or as the funded party's home, then enforcement of the charge may be postponed (with interest).[296] In *Scallon v Scallon*[297] it was held that a court may assume that the discretion will be exercised to defer enforcement of the charge, so as not to frustrate the purpose of the court order.

The ambit of the statutory charge is both wide and at times bizarre. It has been held to apply, for example, to a lump sum payment in commutation and in full and final settlement of a spouse's rights to claim and receive periodical payments even though, as we have noted, periodical payments are exempt.[298] In another case,[299] where both parties were legally aided and an order was made dividing the proceeds of the matrimonial home equally, the charge only attached to the husband's share because he had successfully resisted his wife's claim for a larger share, whereas it did not attach to the wife's share since the husband had made no claim to it.

Although it is clear that the existence of the charge can materially alter the effect or even destroy the intention of orders, it seems established that the court is not allowed to compensate for this (even where the higher costs are attributable to one side's intransigence) by making a larger award than would be the case had the parties' needs been considered without reference to the charge.[300] On the other hand, it would seem proper to make a different *type* of order if that would be a more efficient use of the parties' resources, such as a property transfer order rather than a lump sum order.[301]

10. THE LIMITS OF THE COURT'S POWERS

Although the powers to redistribute spouses' property upon divorce etc are extremely wide, they are not unlimited. One obvious limitation is that the court has no power over property that does not belong to either of the spouses.[302] It cannot order the sale of the matrimonial home which is owned by someone else as, for example, where the parties live in tied accommodation.

The court also has no power to make an order against a third party, so no order should be made which will effectively have to be paid out of a spouse's new partner's capital or income, though that partner's assets are relevant to the extent that they relieve the spouse's needs.[303]

A further limitation of the court's powers is that the relief granted must come within the terms of the Matrimonial Causes Act 1973. In *Milne v Milne*,[304] for instance, it was

---

[294] Civil Legal Aid (Statutory Charge) Regulations 2013 (SI 2013/503) reg 5.
[295] [1978] 2 All ER 889, CA.   [296] SI 2013/503 reg 22.   [297] [1990] 1 FLR 194, CA.
[298] *Stewart v Law Society* [1987] 1 FLR 223; *Watkinson v Legal Aid Board* [1991] 2 All ER 953, CA.
[299] *Parry v Parry* [1986] 2 FLR 96, CA.
[300] *Parry v Parry* and *Collins v Collins* [1987] 1 FLR 226, CA.
[301] Or a periodical payments order instead of a lump sum order—see eg *Anthony v Anthony* [1986] 2 FLR 353, CA.   [302] *Gowers v Gowers* [2011] EWHC 3485 (Fam) [2012] 1 FLR 1040.
[303] *Macey v Macey* (1981) 3 FLR 7 and *Brown v Brown* (1981) 3 FLR 161. See further Ch 23, Needs, obligations and responsibilities, p 888.   [304] (1981) 2 FLR 286, CA.

held that there was no power to order a husband to take out an insurance policy to make capital provision for his wife because the Act only empowers payments to be made to a spouse or child of the family and not to a third party. It has been similarly held that there is no power to order one party to pay out of the proceeds of sale of the matrimonial home the debts of either party which were unconnected to the interest in the property.[305]

At first sight these latter limitations may seem an unfortunate gap in the court's powers, particularly as in some cases, in order to do justice between the parties, a complete restructuring of their financial affairs may be required. However, as we have seen,[306] in practice this type of restructuring can be achieved by the parties giving undertakings to the court.

C. FINANCIAL PROVISION AFTER DIVORCE ETC OR DISSOLUTION: COMPARABLE PROVISIONS UNDER THE MATRIMONIAL CAUSES ACT 1973 AND CIVIL PARTNERSHIP ACT 2004

Note that not all the provisions listed are discussed in this chapter.

Matrimonial Causes Act 1973 Part II	Civil Partnership Act 2004 Schedule 5
S 22 maintenance pending suit	Part 8, para 38
S 22ZA orders for payment in respect of legal services	Part 8, para 38A
S 23 financial provision orders	Part 1, paras 1, 2, 3, 4, 5
S 24 property adjustment orders	Part 2, paras 6, 7, 8, 9
S 24A orders for sale	Part 3, paras 10, 11, 12, 13, 14
S 24B pension sharing orders	Part 4, para 15
S 21A, S 25D	Para 16
S 24D	Para 17
S 24B	Paras 18, 19(1)
S 24C	Para 19
S 25 matters to which court is to have regard	Part 5, paras 20, 21, 22
S 25A terminating financial obligations	Para 23

---

[305] *Burton v Burton* [1986] 2 FLR 419 and *Mullard v Mullard* (1981) 3 FLR 330. See also *Livesey (formerly Jenkins) v Jenkins)* [1985] AC 424, HL (wife agreeing to be solely responsible for discharging a bank overdraft and for mortgage repayments—held to be outside the court's powers to order). There appears to be no power to order a spouse to use money or property for a *designated purpose*. Similarly, there is no express statutory power to require a spouse to execute a charge over the former matrimonial home, although such orders appear to be frequently made in practice. See eg *Barber v Barber* [1993] 1 FLR 476, CA and *M v M (Property Adjustment: Impaired Life Expectancy)* [1993] 2 FLR 723, CA.

[306] Earlier, The effects of a consent order, p 853.

S 25B pensions	Part 6, paras 24, 25
S 25C pensions: lump sums	Para 26
S 25D pensions: supplementary	Paras 27, 28, 29
S 25E Pension Protection Fund	Part 7, paras 30, 31, 32, 33, 34, 35, 36, 37
S 26 commencement of proceedings	Part 10, para 46
S 27 failure to maintain	Part 9, paras 39, 40, 41, 42, 43, 44, 45
S 27(6A), (6B) variation of order for child	Part 11, para 55
S 28 duration of continuing financial provision orders for spouse	Paras 47, 48
S 28(1A)direction preventing application for extension	Para 47(5)
S 29 duration of continuing financial provision orders for children	Para 49
S 31 variation or discharge	Part 11, paras 50, 51, 52, 56, 57, 58, 60, 61, 62
S 31(7) matters to which court is to have regard	Para 59
S 31(7A)–(7G) power to make supplemental provision on variation	Paras 53, 54
S 32 payment of arrears unenforceable without leave	Part 12, para 63
S 33 orders for repayment	Para 64
S 38 orders for repayment after cessation of order by reason of remarriage	Para 65
S 33A consent orders	Part 13, para 66
S 34 maintenance agreements	Paras 67, 68
S 35 alteration of agreement by court	Para 69, 70, 71, 72
S 36 alteration of agreement after death of party	Para 73
S 37 avoidance of transactions intended to prevent or reduce financial relief	Part 14, paras 74, 75
S 30 settlement of instrument for securing payment or effecting property adjustment	Para 76
S 39 avoidance of settlement on bankruptcy	Para 77
S 40 payments in favour of person suffering from mental disorder	Para 78
S 40A appeals relating to pension sharing order which have taken effect	Para 79
S 21, 52 interpretation (inc 'child of the family')	Para 80

23

FINANCIAL REMEDIES: PRINCIPLES AND ASSESSMENT

A. INTRODUCTION

As we saw in Chapter 22, most of the legislation governing the financial arrangements on the ending of a marriage dates back over 40 years, when attitudes and economic and social factors affecting marriage were very different. How are the courts to exercise the wide powers to make orders that we discussed in a world where most married women now work but child care must be paid for, when job security is vanishing so that future income cannot be guaranteed but social security is also increasingly conditional and temporary, where the family home may be an important financial asset but one subject to severe house price fluctuations and when a person may experience divorce and re-partnering several times in their life-time?

Although there were some minor, though significant, statutory amendments made to the jurisdiction in the 1980s, which we will discuss, it has been left to the courts to attempt to keep the law in step with societal changes through case-law and their pronouncements form the substance of the material dealt with in the first half of this chapter. We then consider in brief outline how the orders made by the courts are enforced or altered in the light of subsequent events and what provision can be made for spouses who are divorced abroad and may have been unable to receive appropriate financial protection in those proceedings. We conclude by discussing proposals for thoroughgoing reform of this area of law.

B. GENERAL PRINCIPLES

1. THE OBJECTIVE OF THE JURISDICTION

Following the 1971 reforms, the general principles to be applied when the court is making an order for financial provision or the adjustment of property rights on divorce, nullity or judicial separation were contained in s 5 of the Matrimonial Proceedings and Property Act 1970 and re-enacted in s 25 of the Matrimonial Causes Act 1973.[1] Under s 25, as originally enacted, the court was directed, as its overall object, to have regard to all the

---

[1] Equivalent provisions are contained in Sch 5 Part 5 to the Civil Partnership Act 2004, and the court applies the same approach to civil partnership as it would to a marriage: *Lawrence v Gallagher* [2012] EWCA Civ 394 [2012] 2 FLR 643.

circumstances of the case and so to exercise its powers 'as to place the parties, so far as it is practicable and, having regard to their conduct, just to do so, in the financial position in which they would have been if the marriage had not broken down and each had properly discharged his or her financial obligations and responsibilities towards the other'. In most cases this objective or target (variously referred to as the status quo ideal or the minimal loss principle) was impossible to achieve, since few can afford to support two households at the same standard as the former one. One judge[2] described it as 'an elusive concept based on a difficult hypothesis', while one commentator[3] criticised it as being 'the mandate of restitution . . . misconceived [and]. . . almost always incapable of fulfilment'.

Criticism regarding the unworkability of the law became compounded with anger felt by many divorced men at the idea that, under the concept of irretrievable breakdown of the marriage, they might be divorced for no 'fault' of their own yet nonetheless be required to support their ex-wife potentially for life, since it was implicit in the status quo principle that a spouse had a right to life-long support from the other spouse even after divorce. The matter was referred to the Law Commission, and responses received by them to their original discussion paper were overwhelmingly of the view that the status quo directive was no longer appropriate.[4] Accordingly, in their final report, the Commission felt able to recommend its removal, and the legislation was amended by the Matrimonial and Family Proceedings Act 1984. However, no alternative primary objective was substituted. Instead, greater priority was to be given to the welfare of any child of the family and greater emphasis was to be placed on the parties becoming self-sufficient and financially independent from each other.

The lack of statutory guidance on the basic objective for the redistribution of resources after divorce has long been criticised.[5] The basic objection is that there is no clear theoretical basis for the claim against the other spouse—if the parties are no longer legally bound to each other and no longer subject to the duty to maintain,[6] how can one be required to continue to support the other? On what basis should property owned by one spouse—perhaps acquired through their considerable hard work over many years, or perhaps inherited—be subject to a transfer order in favour of the other spouse? The courts have had to provide some of the answers to these important questions, which

---

[2] Bagnall J in *Harnett v Harnett* [1973] Fam 156 at 161.

[3] K Gray *Reallocation of Property on Divorce* (1977) at p 319.

[4] Law Commission, Law Com No 103 *The Financial Consequences of Divorce: the Basic Policy*; Law Com No 112 *The Financial Consequences of Divorce, The Response to the Discussion Paper*. For an interesting account of the Law Commission's role in promoting reform, see S Cretney 'Money After Divorce—The Mistakes We Have Made?' in M Freeman (ed) *Essays In Family Law* (1985) pp 34–42 and for discussion of Dr Cretney's own contribution to these reforms see G Douglas 'Simple Quarrels? Autonomy vs. Vulnerability' in R Probert and C Barton (eds) *Fifty Years in Family Law: Essays for Stephen Cretney* (2012). The Law Commission were concerned at the general absence of empirical information about the working of divorce law and recommended (Law Com No 112 at para 46) that provision be made for monitoring any amending legislation. This recommendation was not implemented. For empirical research on the financial consequences of divorce, see J Eekelaar and M Maclean *Maintenance after Divorce* (1986); M Maclean and J Eekelaar *The Parental Obligation* (1997) ch 7; A Perry et al *How Parents Cope Financially on Marriage Breakdown* (2000); G Davis et al 'Ancillary relief outcomes' [2000] CFLQ 43; S Arthur et al *Settling Up: Making Financial Arrangements After Divorce or Separation* (2002).

[5] Contrast Scottish law: see the Family Law (Scotland) Act 1985 ss 9 and 10. See Lord Chancellor's Advisory Group on Ancillary Relief Report 1998; Home Office, *Supporting Families* (1998) ch 4. For a 'law and economics' perspective which argues that the current law may create perverse incentives to divorce, see A Dnes 'The Division of Marital Assets Following Divorce' (1998) 25 *Journal of Law and Society* 336. The question of whether further statutory guidance would be desirable is discussed later, Reform, pp 925–933.

[6] Discussed in Ch 21, The duty to maintain a spouse or civil partner, p 774.

they have done by clarifying the principles, if not the objectives, under which the juris-diction must operate.

2. FAIRNESS

(a) *White v White*

The starting-point for the modern approach to the law derives from a House of Lords judgment in 2000. *White v White*[7] concerned a couple who had been married for over 30 years, and ran a farming business in which both were partners. At the time of the divorce, their combined assets were valued at some £4.6 million, of which £1.5 million was in the wife's name. The first instance judge awarded her an additional lump sum of £800,000, based on her 'reasonable requirements' for housing, continuing to run a business, and income.[8] On appeal, the Court of Appeal raised the award to £1.5 million, taking account of the farming partnership and her contribution to the family as wife and mother. This gave her a share of the combined assets of some 40%. Both parties appealed to the House of Lords, which upheld the Court of Appeal's award, but took the opportu-nity, in the words of Lord Nicholls of Birkenhead, to spell out what the courts should be seeking to achieve in the financial relief jurisdiction:

> Everyone would accept that the outcome on these matters, whether by agreement or court order, should be fair. More realistically, the outcome ought to be as fair as is possible in all the circumstances. But everyone's life is different. Features which are important when assessing fairness differ in each case. And, sometimes, different minds can reach different conclusions on what fairness requires. Then fairness, like beauty, lies in the eye of the beholder . . . In consequence, the legislation does not state explicitly what is to be the aim of the courts when exercising these wide powers. Implicitly, the objective must be to achieve a fair outcome . . . there is one principle of universal application which can be stated with confidence. In seeking to achieve a fair outcome, there is no place for dis-crimination between husband and wife and their respective roles . . . If, in their different spheres, each contributed equally to the family, then in principle it matters not which of them earned the money and built up the assets. There should be no bias in favour of the money-earner and against the home-maker and the child-carer.[9]

The impact of this reasoning, which might appear to be stating the obvious, has been profound in producing a shift in the exercise of the courts' discretion, most importantly in requiring courts to 'value' what husbands and wives do in a marriage as of equal worth, and thus in emphasising a conception of marriage as an equal partnership.[10] This may (but need not—as the decision in *White v White* itself demonstrates) result in the parties receiving equal shares in the family assets; an outcome which, whilst possibly reflecting

---

[7] [2001] 1 AC 596.

[8] The significance of 'reasonable requirements' is discussed later, 'Big money' cases, p 889.

[9] [2001] 1 AC 596 at 599 *et seq.*

[10] For discussion, including critical comment, on the reasoning of the House of Lords and the implica-tions of the judgment, see R Bailey-Harris 'Fairness in Financial Settlements on Divorce' [2001] LQR 199; E Cooke '*White v White*: A new yardstick for the marriage partnership' [2001] CFLQ 81; A Diduck 'Fairness and Justice for All? The House of Lords in *White v White*' (2001) 9 Fem LS 173. For an interesting perspective considering fairness in the context of the circumstances of minority ethnic families, see S Edwards 'Division of Assets and Fairness—"Brick Lane"—Gender, Culture and Ancillary Relief on Divorce' [2004] Fam Law 809.

popular expectation of what spouses *should* receive on divorce, was almost never ordered by courts prior to this decision. But his Lordship went on to state:

> A practical consideration follows from this. Sometimes, having carried out the statutory exercise, the judge's conclusion involves a more or less equal division of the available assets. More often, this is not so. More often, having looked at all the circumstances, the judge's decision means that one party will receive a bigger share than the other. Before reaching a firm conclusion and making an order along these lines, a judge would always be well-advised to check his tentative views against the yardstick of equality of division. As a general guide, equality should be departed from only if, and to the extent that, there is good reason for doing so. The need to consider and articulate reasons for departing from equality would help the parties and the court to focus on the need to ensure the absence of discrimination.[11]

Lord Nicholls considered that the introduction of a 'yardstick of equality' was not meant to be the same as a 'presumption' of equality, or even a 'starting point'[12] since this would be to go beyond the permissible bounds of interpretation of s 25. Nonetheless, it gradually became elevated in priority both in the reasoning of the courts and the negotiating positions of legal advisers, thus bearing out the view of Lord Cooke of Thorndon who doubted 'whether the labels "yardstick" or "check" will produce any result different from "guidelines" or "starting point".'[13] Indeed, in *Miller v Miller; McFarlane v McFarlane*,[14] Lord Nicholls himself referred to an 'equal sharing principle' and 'sharing entitlement'. Subsequently, in *Charman v Charman (No 4)* the Court of Appeal held that the idea of equal sharing had clearly become more than a yardstick; it is a principle and as such, should not be postponed to the end of the court's deliberations. Rather, they concluded, 'we take "the sharing principle" to mean that property should be shared in equal proportions unless there is good reason to depart from such proportions.'[15]

(b) *Miller v Miller; McFarlane v McFarlane*

The House of Lords decision in *Miller; McFarlane* elaborated on the meaning of fairness not only by elucidating the principle of sharing but identifying two other key principles which underpin it. In so doing, the House further refined and updated the legal conception of marriage as one characterised by *interdependence* rather than, as the legislation had originally envisaged, *dependence* by one spouse, the wife, on the other, the husband. As Lord Nicholls put it: 'The parties share the roles of money-earner, home-maker and child-carer. Mutual dependence begets mutual obligations of support.'[16]

(c) *Needs*

To reflect this mutual dependence, Lord Nicholls considered that 'fairness requires that the assets of the parties should be divided primarily so as to make provision for the parties' housing and financial needs, taking into account a wide range of matters such as the parties' ages, their future earning capacity, the family's standard of living, and any disability of either party. Most of these needs will have been generated by the marriage,

---

[11] [2001] 1 AC 596 at 05F–G.   [12] [2001] 1 AC 596 at 606E.   [13] [2001] 1 AC 596 615D–E.

[14] [2006] UKHL 24 [2006] 2 AC 618 at [20], [29].

[15] [2007] EWCA Civ 503 [2007] 1 FLR 1246 at [65]. But for the view that the courts have gone into 'reverse gear' in their application of the sharing principle, see A Murray 'Are our higher courts prejudiced against the role of married women? The need for reform' [2013] Fam Law 66.

[16] [2006] UKHL 24 [2006] 2 AC 618 at [11].

but not all of them. Needs arising from age or disability are instances of the latter.'[17] As he pointed out, for most couples, this is as far as fairness can go, since there will usually be insufficient wealth to do anything more than meet their needs and those of their children.[18] However, it will be noted that he included needs *not* created by the marriage, such as age or disability, and considered that these too should be met, if possible. By contrast, Baroness Hale proposed a slightly different approach. For her, only the needs which are *generated by the marriage* should be met, for example, needs created by the presence of children, or having to care for elderly parents,[19] since these may affect the spouse's ability to earn and thus achieve self-sufficiency. Moreover, she considered that current need may have been created by having had to care for children or other family members in the past:

> Many parents have seriously compromised their ability to attain self-sufficiency as a result of past family responsibilities. Even if they do their best to re-enter the employment market, it will often be at a lesser level than before, and they will hardly ever be able to make up what they have lost in pension entitlements. A further source of need may be the way in which the parties chose to run their life together. Even dual career families are difficult to manage with completely equal opportunity for both. Compromises often have to be made by one so that the other can get ahead. All couples throughout their lives together have to make choices about who will do what, sometimes forced upon them by circumstances such as redundancy or low pay, sometimes freely made in the interests of them both. The needs generated by such choices are a perfectly sound rationale for adjusting the parties' respective resources in compensation.[20]

It will be seen that this slight difference of opinion between Lord Nicholls and Baroness Hale leaves unresolved the question of whether, and if so why, a person no longer married to a spouse should be expected to meet their needs after divorce. Baroness Hale appears to hold that this is only justifiable where the needs are caused by the marriage, but her reference to caring for parents does not square with that position, and the statute clearly requires a court to have regard to factors such as age, and disability,[21] which cannot be causally connected to the marriage. The question is not addressed by most courts, or most parties settling their financial arrangements between themselves, at present. It is expected and assumed that a party's needs, regardless of what has caused them, may be met by the other spouse where possible albeit, as we shall see, this will usually be done (where financially feasible) by an appropriate transfer of capital at the time of the divorce rather than by ongoing periodical payments. But the Law Commission have addressed the issue, and their views are discussed later.[22]

(d) *Compensation*

In alluding to compensation, Baroness Hale identified another, related, principle which the House considered as an aspect of fairness. She referred to 'compensation for relationship-generated disadvantage.'[23] In her view, this is distinct from meeting the *needs* generated by the marriage, since due 'compensation' may require payment going

---

[17] [2006] UKHL 24 [2006] 2 AC 618 at [11].

[18] For empirical evidence, see E Hitchings 'Everyday Cases in the Post-*White* Era' [2008] Fam Law 873; 'The impact of recent ancillary relief jurisprudence in the "everyday" ancillary relief case' [2010] CFLQ 93.

[19] But the latter is not a consequence of the marriage, unless the parents are one's in-laws.

[20] [2006] UKHL 24 [2006] 2 AC 618 at [138].

[21] Matrimonial Causes Act 1973 s 25(2)(d)(e), discussed later, Age and duration of marriage, p 892 and Disability, p 896.   [22] See Reform, Needs and non-matrimonial property, p 930.

[23] [2006] UKHL 24 [2006] 2 AC 618 at [140]. Emphasis added.

beyond the relief of the spouse's need. The prime example arose in *McFarlane* itself. The wife and husband married when each was beginning their careers, she as a solicitor in a city firm, he as an accountant. When they had children, they decided that it would make sense for her to give up work to care for them while he concentrated on his career. As a result, when they divorced after a 16 year marriage, he had an income of around £750,000 net per annum while the wife had no prospect of returning to a lucrative legal career. Baroness Hale considered that 'If [the husband], who has been the beneficiary of the choices made during the marriage, is a high earner with a substantial surplus over what is required to meet both parties' needs, then a premium above needs can reflect that relationship-generated disadvantage.' Lord Nicholls agreed. In his view, where the couple have arranged their affairs so as to advantage one spouse financially over the other, then 'the wife suffers a double loss: a diminution in her earning capacity and the loss of a share in her husband's enhanced income.' Despite increased levels of married women working, they are still overwhelmingly more likely to lose financially by leaving the job market for at least a period of time to care for children and when this is the case, 'fairness requires that this feature should be taken into account by the court when exercising its statutory powers'[24] and although 'double-counting' is to be avoided, he agreed that compensation may, where appropriate, meet the financial loss incurred in excess of the spouse's needs, for even if the spouse could support herself, she may still have been disadvantaged by the sacrifice she made for the sake of the family.

Some judges subsequently have shown a distinct lack of enthusiasm for the compensation principle,[25] which was described by Mostyn J in *SA v PA (Pre-Marital Agreement: Compensation)*[26] as 'extremely problematic and challenging both conceptually and legally'. He suggested the following requirements must be met before it could be applied:

i) It will only be in a very rare and exceptional case where the principle will be capable of being successfully invoked.
ii) Such a case will be one where the court can say without any speculation, i.e. with almost near certainty, that the claimant gave up a very high earning career which had it not been foregone would have led to earnings at least equivalent to that presently enjoyed by the respondent.
iii) Such a high earning career will have been practised by the claimant over an appreciable period during the marriage. Proof of this track-record is key.
iv) Once these findings have been made compensation will be reflected by fixing the periodical payments award . . . towards the top end of the discretionary bracket applicable for a needs assessment on the facts of the case. Compensation ought not to be reflected by a premium or additional element on top of the needs based award.

These constraints would appear to limit the principle to circumstances effectively the same as those pertaining in *McFarlane v McFarlane*; however, it has been applied, albeit more as a background factor than as a decisive element in an award, in other cases,[27] and a clear appellate ruling on its scope would be beneficial.

---

[24] [2006] UKHL 24 [2006] 2 AC 618 at [13].
[25] See, for example, *VB v JP* [2008] EWHC 112 (Fam) [2008] 1 FLR 742 and *RP v RP* [2006] EWHC 3409 (Fam) [2007] 1 FLR 2105.   [26] [2014] EWHC 392 (Fam) [2014] Fam Law 799 at [24] and [36].
[27] See eg *Lauder v Lauder* [2007] EWHC 1227 (Fam) [2007] 2 FLR 802; *H v H* [2007] EWHC 459 (Fam) [2007] 2 FLR 548.

(e) *Sharing*

The third principle, as we have seen, is sharing. This stems from the view of marriage, first endorsed in *White v White,* as a partnership of equals in which the parties commit themselves to sharing their lives. For Lord Nicholls, this provides the justification, when the partnership ends, for each to be entitled to an equal share of the assets of the partnership, unless there is a good reason to the contrary. 'Fairness requires no less'.[28] As Baroness Hale pointed out, this reflects a general public assumption, and preference, for equal division of marital assets. But as both emphasised, the automatic division of the assets in this way may not be 'fair' in the actual circumstances of the case—a spouse whose future earning capacity will be limited by ongoing child care responsibilities may require a larger share of the assets to meet her, and any children's needs, for a secure home, while the other, who may have a considerable earning capacity (like Mr McFarlane) may be much more able to make up any capital loss and recover his financial position in the future.

The House of Lords did not rank the three principles in order of priority, but it will be recalled that in the later case of *Charman v Charman (No 4)*[29] the Court of Appeal considered that equal sharing should be the presumption and hence (once the parties' financial positions have been assessed) the court's 'starting point'. However, this can create difficulties. Is one to calculate the parties' respective needs, see if an equal division of assets will satisfy these, and if so, simply divide them accordingly? Or does one meet the parties' respective needs first from the total pool of assets, and then divide any surplus left over? While the courts are clear that needs must in fact always be satisfied first[30]—and in many if not most cases, there will be no surplus to dispute—the outcome where there is a surplus could be significantly different depending upon which approach is taken. For example, suppose the marital assets are valued at £1m, and the wife's needs are for £400,000 (home and capital to live on pending her return to full-time work when the children are grown up) while the husband's needs are for £100,000 (to provide a substantial deposit and part-purchase of a home he can then afford to buy with a mortgage). Compare the following:

a) Equal division sufficient to meet needs:

    W receives £500,000; H receives £500,000. W has £100,000 in excess of her needs; H has £400,000 in excess of his needs.

b) Meet needs and then share surplus equally:

    W receives £400,000; H receives £100,000. Surplus of £500,000, divided equally so that W has an additional £250,000 and H has £250,000, leaving W with a total of £650,000 and H with £350,000.

In *Charman* the Court of Appeal considered that the former approach is appropriate. This was because, first, having adopted equal sharing as a starting point, the Court then went on to consider that any departure from it should operate 'within' rather than outside that principle. Secondly, they were concerned that the latter approach could encourage the spouses to inflate their claimed needs in order to secure a larger share and thus lead to greater dispute and forensic effort in examining the minutiae of each spouse's 'budget'.[31] It has also been argued that the latter provides W with an unnecessary windfall at the expense of H.[32] But given that the surplus is property which is regarded as a product of

---

[28] *Miller v Miller; McFarlane v McFarlane* [2006] UKHL 24 [2006] 2 AC 618 at [16].
[29] [2007] EWCA Civ 503 [2007] 1 FLR 1246.
[30] *Miller; McFarlane* at [142]; *Charman (No 4)* at [73].   [31] *Charman (No 4)* at [77].
[32] See J Miles '*Charman v Charman (No 4)*—making sense of need, compensation and equal sharing after *Miller/McFarlane*' [2008] CFLQ 378 at 388–389.

their marriage and thus to be shared between them,[33] and that one spouse's needs have been assessed objectively as greater than the other's, it is not that obvious why H should be able to enjoy most of his share as a 'windfall' which he does not require to meet his needs, whilst W has to devote most of hers to securing her needs alone. It seems that practice varies across the country as to which approach is adopted.[34]

The principles of need, compensation and sharing do not appear in the Matrimonial Causes Act 1973, although they are implicit in the factors set out in s 25(2) that the court must consider, as we will see. Judges have from time to time reminded practitioners that it is inappropriate to construe and seek to apply the principles *as if* they did appear in the statute,[35] and this should be borne in mind in assessing the case-law. It also means that, whichever approach is under consideration, a court should always ultimately have regard to the terms of the statute and the imperative of arriving at what will be the *fair* outcome in the particular case, and that may well depend, as Lord Nicholls and Baroness Hale noted in *Miller;McFarlane*[36] on other factors including the parties' earning power and future prospects. However, insofar as the abolition of the status quo principle has been replaced by anything, in her view the 'ultimate objective is to give each party an equal start on the road to independent living'[37]—which can be seen as the polar opposite of the original objective of the jurisdiction and a reflection on how far attitudes to divorce and its consequences have changed since the 1970s.

3. TREATING THE WELFARE OF ANY CHILD OF THE FAMILY AS THE FIRST CONSIDERATION

When the status quo objective was removed in 1984, s 25(1) of the Matrimonial Causes Act 1973[38] was amended to direct the court, when considering whether to exercise its powers and, if so, in what manner:

> ... to have regard to all the circumstances of the case, first consideration being given to the welfare while a minor of any child of the family who has not attained the age of eighteen.

This was done because evidence suggested that provision for children tended to be 'tacked on', almost as an afterthought, to the arrangements for the spouse and with little reference made to the actual economic realities of bringing up children.[39]

It will be observed that the court is required to give first and not paramount consideration to the welfare of any child of the family. This means, as was emphasised in *Suter v Suter and Jones*,[40] that the child's welfare is not the overriding consideration, though of

---

[33] On which, see later, Matrimonial and non-matrimonial property, p 882.

[34] Law Commission, Consultation Paper No 208 *Matrimonial Property: Needs and Agreements, A Supplementary Consultation Paper* (2012) para 4.102 and note their discussion of this issue at paras 4.96–4.104.

[35] See eg *RP v RP* [2006] EWHC 3409 (Fam) [2007] 1 FLR 2105; *VB v JP* [2008] EWHC 112 (Fam) [2008] 1 FLR 742; *R v R (Financial Remedies: Needs and Practicalities)* [2011] EWHC 3093 (Fam) [2013] 1 FLR 120.

[36] At [29] 'no invariable rule on this' and [144] rejecting a 'hard and fast rule'.   [37] At [144].

[38] As amended by the Matrimonial and Family Proceedings Act 1984 s 3 and further by the Welfare Reform and Pensions Act 1999 Sch 3 para 5.

[39] See Law Commission, Law Com No 103 *The Financial Consequences of Divorce: the Basic Policy*; Law Com No 112 *The Financial Consequences of Divorce, The Response to the Discussion Paper*.

[40] [1987] Fam 111, CA; cf *Anthony v Anthony* [1986] 2 FLR 353, CA, where not all the children's interests were necessarily identical.

course it is an important one. Thus, in *B v B (Financial Provision: Welfare of Child and Conduct)*[41] where the father had abducted the child from the mother, had failed to disclose assets and was unlikely to pay maintenance, it was fair to order that the whole of the proceeds of sale of the former matrimonial home should be transferred to the wife so that she could use them to re-house herself and the child. The child's need for security for the future was regarded (in addition to other factors relevant under s 25(2)) as an important consideration.

Priority is only accorded to children of the family[42] and not, for example, to any children of the spouses' second families, though a spouse's obligation to the second family is a relevant consideration in deciding what order to make.[43] It might be added that not even all children of the family are necessarily accorded priority. Where, for example, the child is not that of the husband, then even if he has 'treated' the child as one of the family he is not for that reason alone liable to maintain him. In determining this, the court is directed by s 25(4) of the Matrimonial Causes Act to have regard:

(a) to whether that party assumed any responsibility for the child's maintenance, and, if so, to the extent to which, and the basis upon which, that party assumed such responsibility and to the length of time for which that party discharged such responsibility;

(b) to whether in assuming and discharging such responsibility that party did so knowing that the child was not his or her own;

(c) to the liability of any other person to maintain the child.

If the court decides that the husband is not liable[44] to maintain the child at all, then of course that child's welfare ceases to be of any relevance in that case.

Priority is only to be given to the child's welfare during his or her minority. This reflects the well established principle that orders for children should be related to their dependency and should not, in the absence of special needs such as physical or learning disabilities, provide for continuing support during adulthood.[45] In fact the cases show that the court is prepared to take a broader view, and (if not necessarily according priority) at least recognise that children's needs, and the period of dependency, do not necessarily come to an end on one's eighteenth birthday, but may continue, for example, until the child completes university education or professional training. In *Richardson v Richardson (No 2)*[46] the Court of Appeal upheld the decision of Thorpe J,[47] who had set aside a consent order, and extended a periodical payment order in favour of the wife, so she could complete her responsibility for bringing up her two daughters whilst they were at college. As Thorpe J added:[48]

In my judgment, the fact the children of the family are no longer minors is not decisive. What is decisive is that they are still dependent.[49]

---

[41] [2002] 1 FLR 555.

[42] For a detailed discussion of the meaning of 'child of the family', see Ch 9, The meaning of 'child of the family', p 296.

[43] See eg *Fisher v Fisher* [1989] 1 FLR 423, CA where the wife's responsibility to a child born after the marriage was dissolved was taken into account to increase a periodical payments order.

[44] As in *W v W (Child of the Family)* [1984] FLR 796, CA and *Leadbeater v Leadbeater* [1985] FLR 789.

[45] See eg *Lilford v Glynn* [1979] 1 All ER 441, CA. It is on this basis that capital orders for children are not common: see *Kiely v Kiely* [1988] 1 FLR 248, CA; *Chamberlain v Chamberlain* [1974] 1 All ER 33, CA; cf *Griffiths v Griffiths* [1984] Fam 70, CA; *A v A (A Minor: Financial Provision)* [1994] 1 FLR 657.

[46] [1996] 2 FLR 617, CA.   [47] [1994] 2 FLR 1051.   [48] [1994] 2 FLR 1051 at 1054.

[49] See also *B v B (Adult Student: Liability to Support)* [1998] 1 FLR 373, CA, where the father's argument that he should not be expected to support his daughter since she was receiving a student grant was rejected

4. PLACING GREATER EMPHASIS ON THE PARTIES BECOMING SELF-SUFFICIENT

Inextricably bound up with the idea that it is no longer appropriate to have a right to life-long support from a former spouse is that of expecting the former spouses to become financially independent of each other wherever, and as soon as, possible after the divorce. The idea of a 'clean break' from each other after divorce first came to prominence in *Minton v Minton* where Lord Scarman said:[50]

> There are two principles which inform the modern legislation. One is the public interest that spouses, to the extent that their means permit, should provide for themselves and their children. But the other—of equal importance—is the principle of "the clean-break". The law now encourages spouses to avoid bitterness after family break-down and to settle their money and property problems. An object of the modern law is to encourage each to put the past behind them and to begin a new life which is not overshadowed by the relationship which has broken down.

The Law Commission found that there was widespread support for this view and that the courts should be more clearly directed to the desirability of 'promoting the severance of financial obligations between the parties at the time of divorce' and to give greater weight to the view that periodical payments in favour of one spouse 'should be primarily directed to secure wherever possible a smooth transition from marriage to the status of independence'.[51]

Following the Law Commission's recommendations, the courts are, pursuant to s 25A(1) of the Matrimonial Causes Act 1973,[52] under a *duty* in all cases (other than in relation to maintenance pending suit) to consider:

> . . . whether it would be appropriate so to exercise those powers that the financial obligations of each party towards the other will be terminated as soon after the grant of the decree as the court considers just and reasonable.[53]

If a periodical payments order is thought appropriate, the court is directed by s 25A(2) to consider:

> . . . whether it would be appropriate to require those payments to be made or secured only for such term as would in the opinion of the court be sufficient to enable the party in whose favour the order is made to adjust without undue hardship to the termination of his or her financial dependence on the other party.

In effect, under s 25A(1) the court is directed to consider whether it can make an immediate clean break order, ie an order which will settle once and for all the parties' financial liability to each other. If this is not thought possible, then under s 25A(2) the court is directed to consider whether it can nevertheless make a periodical payments order for a

---

in the light of the clear statutory recognition that support could be ordered under s 29 (see Ch 22, Periodical payments, Orders in favour of children of the family, p 840).

[50] [1979] AC 593 at 608, HL.   [51] Law Com No 112, para 30.

[52] Added by the Matrimonial and Family Proceedings Act 1984 s 3, as further amended by Welfare Reform and Pensions Act 1999 Sch 3 para 6.

[53] It will be noted that the statutory duty does not apply to judicial separation, since the marriage is not terminated.

limited term rather than for an indefinite period. In order to achieve these objectives the court has the power under s 25A(3) to impose a clean break order upon the parties[54] and under s 28(1A) the court may direct that a party is not entitled to apply for an extension of a fixed term periodical payments order.[55]

In its most extended form, either type of clean break order will also incorporate a declaration that neither party may make any further application for a lump sum or property adjustment order,[56] nor be entitled to apply for financial provision out of the other's estate under the Inheritance (Provision for Family and Dependants) Act 1975.[57]

(a) Imposing an immediate clean break

While a clean break may be inappropriate where a dependent spouse is caring for young children, or is past retirement age with very limited pension rights, empirical evidence shows that it has become the preferred outcome and spousal maintenance is increasingly unusual.[58] Tomlinson LJ stated in *Matthews v Matthews*[59] that 'Parliament has indicated that there should be a clear presumption in favour of making a clean break'. This runs counter to earlier rulings[60] and he immediately went on to qualify what he said by adding,

---

[54] It is unusual to see cases reported where a court has exercised this power (perhaps because most cases settle and most spouses desire a clean break anyway), but see *Seaton v Seaton* [1986] 2 FLR 398, CA for an unusual example where the husband had no earning capacity but the court dismissed his claim against the wife in part because she had borne the financial burden of the marriage due to his drink problem. Note that there is no comparable power to dismiss an application for periodical payments to or for the benefit of any child of the family. There is no provision for a 'clean break' between parent and child: see *Crozier v Crozier* [1994] 1 FLR 126.

[55] Further, under ss 31(7A)–(7G), where the court discharges a periodical payments order, or varies it to a fixed term, it may also make a lump sum, property adjustment or pension sharing order and direct that the recipient is not entitled to make any further application for periodical payments, or further extension of their duration. The power extends only to dissolution of the marriage, not nullity: s 31(7A). See also s 25(2)(a), discussed later, Income and earning capacity, p 886, under which the court is directed to consider whether there is any increase in earning capacity which it is reasonable to expect a party to take steps to acquire.

[56] The court may make such a declaration despite the absence of express statutory authority: *H v H (Financial Provision)* [1988] 2 FLR 114.

[57] Inheritance (Provision for Family and Dependants) Act 1975 s 15 as amended by Matrimonial and Family Proceedings Act 1984, discussed in Ch 25, Relationship to existing agreements and orders, p 992. The court will only make this order if it considers it just to do so. It must therefore have evidence as to the likely size of the spouse's estate and an indication of those who are likely to have claims upon it: *Whiting v Whiting* [1988] 2 All ER 275, CA. Note also *Cameron v Treasury Solicitor* [1996] 2 FLR 716, CA where it was suggested (in the context of a consent order) that a clean break order which did not bar claims under the 1975 Act would be so irregular as to suggest a fundamental drafting error.

[58] See A Perry et al, op cit; S Arthur et al, op cit. In 2011. 3472 orders for periodical payments were made, out of a total of 77,129 orders for financial relief: *Judicial and Court Statistics 2011* Table 2.6.

[59] [2013] EWCA Civ 1874 [2014] Fam Law 962 at [15] per Tomlinson LJ.

[60] *SRJ v DWJ (Financial Provision)* [1999] 2 FLR 176, CA: wife still caring for youngest child and had given up her place in the world of work during a long marriage—clean break inappropriate even though husband could not afford more than nominal periodical payments in present circumstances; *Phippen v Palmers (a firm)* [2002] 2 FLR 415: elderly wife should not have been advised to accept a clean break leaving her with a shortfall in meeting her income requirements. Although cf *Suter v Suter and Jones* [1987] Fam 111, CA, where, although a nominal order was eventually made, the Court of Appeal held that the trial judge should have considered whether the wife could become financially independent, even though she was caring for dependent children. See also *Whiting v Whiting* [1988] 2 All ER 275, CA, where, although the majority refused to overrule the trial judge, they stressed that declining to make a clean break order because of concern for the future and a wish to preserve a 'backstop' of support for the wife, may be the easy, but is not always the right solution.

'in the sense that that is something which the court is mandated to consider.' This suggests that there is actually no *presumption* in the strict legal sense. The court's overriding duty to achieve fairness may require an ongoing financial tie (if only for a fixed term), where, for example, there is inadequate capital to achieve a fair split, or where fairness cannot be achieved at present because of illiquid assets.[61] But a clean break has advantages where the payer is unreliable so that periodical payments cannot be awarded with confidence.[62] Similarly, where the parties are very bitter towards each other, a clean break will be desirable.[63]

(b) Making deferred clean break orders

The *requirement* to consider whether to limit a periodical payments order to a fixed term was introduced in 1984, along with the *power* under s 28(1A) to direct that no application can be made to extend the term provided for in the order. It should be understood, however, that unless the court expressly adds a s 28(1A) direction, there is nothing to stop a spouse from returning to the court prior to the expiry of the term to ask that the term be extended.[64]

The desirability of a deferred clean break was considered by the Court of Appeal in *McFarlane v McFarlane; Parlour v Parlour*.[65] The facts of these conjoined appeals were highly unusual. In each, the husband had extremely high earnings (in the former case, the accountant husband earned some £750,000 per annum, and in the latter the husband was a Premier League footballer earning £1.19 million per annum), but the available capital assets were insufficient to achieve an appropriately fair clean break between the spouses. The dispute between the parties concerned what periodical payments order should accordingly be made in favour of the wife. In each case, a joint lives order was made, with no limit of time, but both wives disputed the level at which the payments were set (in the former case, at £180,000 per annum,[66] and in the latter at £212,500 per annum), arguing that they should receive amounts significantly above what they 'needed' to maintain a comfortable lifestyle. The Court allowed the appeals, but substituted limited term orders (of five years and four years respectively),[67] focusing on what it saw as the duty to seek where possible to achieve a clean break within a reasonable time.[68]

---

[61]　See eg *McFarlane v McFarlane; Parlour v Parlour* [2004] EWCA Civ 872 [2005] Fam 171 discussed further shortly; *R v R (Lump Sum Repayments)* [2003] EWHC 3197 (Fam) [2004] 1 FLR 928.

[62]　*Fournier v Fournier* [1998] 2 FLR 990, CA.

[63]　See eg *Clifton-Brown v Clifton-Brown (orse CB v CB)* [1988] Fam Law 471.

[64]　*Richardson v Richardson* [1994] 1 FLR 286. So long as the application to extend the term is made before its expiry, the court has jurisdiction so to order, even though that order is made after the term has expired: *Jones v Jones* [2000] 2 FLR 307. In *Fleming v Fleming* [2003] EWCA Civ 1841 [2004] 1 FLR 667 the court considered that there must be some exceptional justification for the extension of a fixed term order, and in *Yates v Yates* [2012] EWCA Civ 532 [2013] 2 FLR 1070 the court followed this approach in doubting (but not altering) the decision of a first instance judge to extend an initial 3 year term for a further *twelve* years.　　　　　　　　　　　　　　　　　　　　[65]　[2004] EWCA Civ 872 [2005] Fam 171.

[66]　Having been reduced on initial appeal from £250,000.

[67]　Although without a s 28(1A) direction. In the *Parlour* case, the husband's high income was expected to reduce as his playing career wound down and then ended, making the current level of periodical payments impossible to sustain in the long term.

[68]　See Thorpe LJ at [66] and Wall LJ at [133]. It also increased the level of periodical payments that the husbands would have to make during the limited term of the orders (to £250,000 p.a. in *McFarlane* and to £444,000 p.a. in *Parlour*), rejecting the view that the level of periodical payments awarded should be confined to satisfying the recipient's 'needs' (however generously interpreted)—see further 'Big money' cases, p 889.

Mrs McFarlane appealed to the House of Lords for restoration of the joint lives order and we have discussed the general principles the House laid down in her case already.[69] They upheld her claim. Their reasoning for doing so was two-fold. First, they considered that, having established 'compensation' as a basis for achieving *fairness* between the parties, it could not be right to limit the level of periodical payments to what would satisfy the wife's 'needs'.[70] Secondly, however, the House considered that a five-year term was 'most unlikely to be sufficient to achieve a fair outcome'.[71] The onus should be on the husband, rather than the wife, to seek a variation as future circumstances changed.[72] As Baroness Hale put it, 'A clean break is not to be achieved at the expense of a fair result.'[73] Indeed, the wife successfully applied subsequently for an increase in the amount of periodical payments in light of the husband's increased earnings.[74]

In so deciding, the House recognised that, as women have advanced in the work-place and in forging careers, the loss that they incur if they give this up to raise a family 'comes at a price which in most cases is irrecoverable.'[75] When the clean break principle was first introduced in the 1980s, this was not appreciated. The realisation of the importance of non-discrimination between the spouses elucidated in *White v White* has therefore prompted a reconsideration of the correct balance to be drawn between the desirability of a clean break, and ongoing support to redress the financial disadvantage created by the marriage—and usually suffered by the wife rather than the husband. It is said, anecdotally, that orders for periodical payments are more readily ordered in the London area (where income levels are highest) than in other parts of the country, although this may have less to do with seeking to compensate wives who have given up high-flying careers than to ensure that wives who have enjoyed a wealthy lifestyle while married are given a commensurate 'cushion' on divorce.

In considering whether to make a limited term order, the court is directed under s 25A(2) to consider whether the party in whose favour an order is made can adjust *without undue hardship* to the termination of financial dependence on the other party. As was stressed in *Morris v Morris*,[76] this is a mandatory requirement needing specific evidence. It is unclear precisely what is meant by 'undue hardship' (though it is implicit that a party can expect some hardship), but it is evident that a limited term order and, a fortiori, a s 28(1A) direction should not be made upon some vague expectation that the dependent spouse will be able to obtain a job, nor should that spouse's potential earning capacity be unrealistically viewed. However, the assumption that a wife can, and should, become financially independent, has become more common over the years, with less willingness to preserve periodical payments 'just in case' things turn out badly. In *Flavell v Flavell*[77] in 1997, Ward LJ considered that:

---

[69] *Miller v Miller; McFarlane v McFarlane* [2006] UKHL 24, [2006] 2 AC 618. The *Miller* case was an appeal from *Miller v Miller* [2005] EWCA Civ 984 [2006] 1 FLR 151.

[70] But see *B v S (Financial Remedy: Marital Property Regime)* [2012] EWHC 265 (Fam) [2012] 2 FLR 502 where Mostyn J considered that other than in an exceptional case like *McFarlane,* periodical payments should be fixed by reference to the principle of need alone. Query, given that the rationale for the use of such payments was that there was inadequate capital to achieve a clean break which would give due recognition to the wife's claim for 'compensation'. Why should this not be equally true in a case of 'sharing'?

[71] Per Lord Nicholls at [26]. Lord Hope of Craighead noted that Scots law does not permit recognition of 'compensation' through continuing periodical payments beyond three years, and may work injustice in consequence. He urged that the matter be re-examined.

[72] Lord Nicholls at [97], Baroness Hale at [155].   [73] At [134].

[74] *McFarlane v McFarlane* [2009] EWHC 891 (Fam) [2009] 2 FLR 1322.

[75] Lord Hope at [118].   [76] [1985] FLR 1176, CA.   [77] [1997] 1 FLR 353, CA at 358.

> There is, in my judgment, often a tendency for these [ie finite term] orders to be made more in hope than in serious expectation. Especially in judging the case of ladies in their middle years, the judicial looking into the crystal ball rarely finds enough of substance to justify a finding that adjustment can be made without undue hardship. All too often, these orders are made without evidence to support them.

But in *D v D (Financial Provision: Periodical Payments)*[78] in 2004, Coleridge J allowed the husband's appeal against a joint lives order and limited its term to 10 years where he considered that otherwise, the attempt to achieve equality between the spouses in the capital award would be frustrated. He left the door open to the wife, should her circumstances deteriorate, however, by refusing to attach a s 28(1A) direction.[79] And in 2011, in *L v L (Financial Remedies: Deferred Clean Break)*[80] Eleanor King J substituted a 2 year 5 months non-extendable fixed term order for a joint lives order where the wife had 'never left the workplace' but simply needed time to refocus her fashion business and had a farm as a capital asset to fall back on—there was no difficulty in her 'adjusting' to financial independence.

5. THE CURRENT APPROACH

The discussion we have just outlined seeks to explain how the courts have arrived at their current approach. The 1984 Act established that the desirable goal of the jurisdiction (albeit not expressed as a statutory aim) is to enable the parties to achieve financial independence after divorce, rather than to impose continuing liability to keep the dependent spouse as far as possible in the manner to which he or (more usually) she had become accustomed. The implicit question that then arose was on what basis the parties' assets should be divided in order to achieve that independence? In the majority of divorces, which are not 'big money' cases of the type discussed in most of the reported cases, the court continues to have to seek to meet the parties' basic needs (and those of their children) as they adjust to living in two households rather than one.[81] The most important of these is for accommodation and the major task will be to deploy the available powers so as to provide a home, first for the children (if any) and whoever is their primary carer, and secondly, if possible and appropriate, for the other spouse.[82] The support needs of

---

[78] [2004] EWHC 445 (Fam), [2004] 1 FLR 988.

[79] Compare *N v N (Consent Order: Variation)* [1993] 2 FLR 868, CA, where the parties, who had a son, divorced after a seven-year marriage. An agreement was reached whereby (against legal advice) the wife accepted periodical payments for a five-year term, and entered into a 'side letter' whereby she agreed not to apply for an extension except 'for the protection of the child in a case of quite unforeseen circumstances of serious illness or disability'. The wife realised that she would not be successful as an opera singer, and decided to train as a barrister. She applied for an extension of the specified term. The Court of Appeal rejected her application. While questioning the appropriateness of a side letter in child cases, and whilst itself unenforceable, it was nonetheless 'highly relevant'. On the principles of *Edgar v Edgar* [1980] 3 All ER 887, CA, the court considered it should uphold an agreement freely entered into after legal advice.

[80] [2011] EWHC 2207 (Fam) [2012] 1 FLR 898.

[81] The following is derived from the 'principles' for ancillary relief suggested by the Government in its Consultation Paper, Home Office, *Supporting Families* (1998) Ch 4, as based on, in particular, the views of the Association of District Judges, enunciating what they saw as the current practice in England and Wales, in their Memorandum to the Lord Chancellor's Ancillary Relief Advisory Group, *Possible Reforms to the Substantive Law on Ancillary Relief Reform* (1998). See also J Eekelaar, M Maclean and S Beinart *Family Lawyers: The Divorce Work of Solicitors* (2000) pp 125–8.

[82] But, as in *B v B (Financial Provision: Welfare of Child and Conduct)* [2002] 1 FLR 555, this may not be achievable or desirable in every case.

the children should then be met. If there is continuing need for support for a dependent spouse (ideally only until she can achieve self-sufficiency), this may then be met if possible, either from a capital transfer which the recipient could then invest[83] or use to boost her available income (such as by taking a smaller mortgage on a new home and thus reducing her outgoings), or, if the spouse can afford them, by means of periodical payments. If any surplus assets remain, they may be used to redress financial disadvantage or shared out as the fruits of the marriage.

In bringing 'equality' into the court's calculations, *White v White* can be seen as bringing a 'contribution' *or* 'recognition/compensation' approach to the assessment of the spouses' claims rather than one based primarily on dependency, at least where the parties' assets allow. A spouse's contributions—in *White v White* as a full business partner in the farming enterprise, as well as a 'wife and mother'—should be recognised as giving her a claim to her due share. As will be seen, however, the contribution approach can give rise to disputes and competitions as to how much of a contribution one spouse has made compared to the other. It may be seen as stemming from a 'partnership of equals' view of marriage under which each spouse is seen as capable of making a contribution to the success of the family and therefore entitled to whatever value is put on that contribution—an 'equality of opportunity' model, one might say.[84] By contrast, as *Miller v Miller; McFarlane v McFarlane* demonstrates, a recognition/compensation approach can give allowance to the fact that one spouse (currently usually the wife) may give up the opportunity to make a full *financial* contribution to the family through her career or employment, by concentrating on child care and home-making. Or a spouse may simply be unable to contribute as much financially as the other, because of lesser earning ability, pay differentials in the labour market, or a poorer family background so that she or he cannot bring an inheritance into the family. This does not mean that this spouse's contribution is 'worth' any less than that of the bread-winning or wealthier spouse. On this view, marriage is a 'joint enterprise' in which both spouses make equal, but different, contributions to the welfare of the family and 'equality of outcome' will require that the economic balance between the spouses may accordingly need to be redressed to ensure that one is not unfairly disadvantaged after the marriage ends.[85] Structural inequalities in the labour market and wider society may mean it is impossible to remove all of the disadvantages faced by the economically weaker spouse. The goal must be only to achieve *fairness* as between the two parties to the marriage. The trend of recent cases suggests that the courts are trying to move towards such an equality of outcome model.

An added impetus towards applying an equality of outcome approach is the implementation of Sch 5 to the Civil Partnership Act 2004 in relation to the dissolution of civil partnerships,[86] and in future, the divorces of same sex married couples. The traditional bread-winner/house-wife model may be even less applicable to such unions than it is to modern marriage. Valuing the 'contributions' of civil partners or same-sex spouses without the straightjacket of stereotyped thinking about the nature of the roles played by each partner may prove liberating for heterosexual spouses too.[87]

---

[83] See The *Duxbury* calculation, p 890.

[84] See R Bailey-Harris 'Dividing the Assets on Family Breakdown: The Content of Fairness' (2001) *Current Legal Problems* 533. For a critique of a 'formal equality' outcome, see A Scully '*Parra v Parra*—Big money cases, judicial discretion and equality of division' [2003] CFLQ 205.

[85] For discussion of the 'partnership of equals' and 'joint enterprise' models of marriage, see G Douglas *An Introduction to Family Law* (2004, 2nd edn) p 11 and passim. The Scottish law attempts to achieve this redress too: see Family Law (Scotland) Act 1985 ss 9, 10.

[86] As pointed out by M Harper et al *Civil Partnership: The New Law* (2005) at para 5.19.

[87] For consideration of the difference between same-sex and heterosexual partnerships in terms of the power dynamics (albeit in another context), see R Auchmuty 'When Equality is not Equity: Homosexual Inclusion in Undue Influence Law' (2003) 11 Fem LS 163.

The question to discuss next is how the courts exercise their discretion in order to try to achieve fair outcomes.

C. FACTORS TO BE TAKEN INTO ACCOUNT WHEN ASSESSING WHAT ORDERS SHOULD BE MADE FOR A SPOUSE

Reference has already been made to the fact that, whilst the court must have regard to all the circumstances of the case, it must also take into account certain specific factors. Some of these are relevant to calculating the parties' resources and needs; others will lead the court to make a greater or smaller award than it otherwise would have done. Although the list is not intended to be exhaustive, it covers almost all the matters to which the court had always had regard in the past. However, it is important to note that the factors are not ranked in any kind of hierarchy and the weight given to any of them depends upon the facts in the individual case.[88] It is proposed to consider the facts in the order in which they are set out in s 25(2) of the Matrimonial Causes Act.[89]

1. INCOME, EARNING CAPACITY, PROPERTY AND RESOURCES

> (a) The income, earning capacity, property and other financial resources which each of the parties to the marriage has or is likely to have in the foreseeable future, including in the case of earning capacity any increase in that capacity which it would in the opinion of the court be reasonable to expect a party to the marriage to take steps to acquire

(a) Matrimonial and non-matrimonial property

The court must have regard to all the income and capital belonging to the spouses.[90] So far as capital is concerned, provided it belongs to one of the spouses, it had been assumed that it must be taken into account and it is irrelevant how the spouse came to own it. However, once the yardstick of equality laid down in *White v White* became an important measure of arriving at a fair settlement, the question arose whether assets brought into the marriage, or not generated by the parties' joint efforts, such as a gift or inheritance or wealth produced by one earner's efforts, should be subject to sharing.[91] In *Miller v Miller; McFarlane v McFarlane*[92] Lord Nicholls and Baroness Hale agreed that the source of an asset is a relevant issue in determining how it is to be allocated or shared, but differed in

---

[88] *Piglowska v Piglowski* [1999] 1 WLR 1360, HL.

[89] As amended by the Matrimonial and Family Proceedings Act 1984 and Welfare Reform and Pensions Act 1999.

[90] Where the spouses live with their extended family, it may be difficult to determine who owns what, with scope to claim that other family members in fact have a beneficial interest: *G v G (Matrimonial Property: Rights of Extended Family)* [2005] EWHC 1560 (Admin) [2006] 1 FLR 62 (claim rejected).

[91] In *White v White* [2001] AC 596 itself, the House of Lords upheld an unequal share of the parties' property because some of it had been acquired with financial help from the husband's father. In community property systems, such assets may be excluded: see K Boele-Wolki et al (eds) *European Family Law in Action Volume IV: Property Relations between Spouses* (2009).

[92] [2006] UKHL 24 [2006] 2 AC 618.

their view of what forms of asset might be distinguished. The issue was important because Mr Miller, a highly successful fund manager, had come into the marriage with some £13m cash derived from his employment. During the marriage, which lasted less than three years, his wealth grew to £17m. He also bought shares in the new company—'New Star'—which he joined after the wedding, which were valued at between £12m and £18m by the time of the divorce hearing. At first instance, upheld by the Court of Appeal, Singer J awarded the wife, who had been earning £85,000 per annum before she was married, and had assets worth about £100,000, capital of £5m, comprising the former matrimonial home and a lump sum and other assets.

Lord Nicholls distinguished between property acquired during the marriage, otherwise than by inheritance or gift—the 'marital acquest' or 'matrimonial property'—which is the financial product of the parties' common endeavour, and other property which is not. The former should be subject to sharing, regardless of the length of the marriage. The matrimonial home, even if brought into the marriage by one spouse, should normally be treated as matrimonial property because it 'has a central place in any marriage'. But non-matrimonial property which the parties bring into the marriage, or receive by gift or inheritance may be treated differently. In a short marriage, fairness may require that this should not be shared, reflecting 'the instinctive feeling that parties generally have less call upon each other on the breakdown of a short marriage.'[93] In longer marriages, such property may, by contrast, represent a contribution made to the marriage by one of the parties. On his reasoning, the shares that Mr Miller owned were 'matrimonial property' because their value had grown during the marriage thanks in part to the husband's efforts in working for New Star. They were therefore relevant to determining the award to the wife, and he dismissed Mr Miller's appeal.

Baroness Hale categorised assets rather differently. She identified, on the one hand, *family assets* of a 'capital nature' such as the family home and its contents and of a 'revenue nature' such as earning capacity, plus other assets acquired for the benefit of the family such as furniture, holiday homes, insurance policies and family savings, and family businesses or joint ventures in which both parties work.[94] On the other hand, there may be *'business or investment assets which have been generated solely or mainly by the efforts of one party'* and in respect of which it cannot be demonstrated that the spouse's domestic contribution has contributed to their acquisition.[95] In a very small number of cases where there are such assets, of which *Miller* might be one, the short duration of the marriage may justify a departure from the yardstick of equality of division. On this basis, the husband's shares were business assets generated solely by him and this, coupled with the shortness of the marriage, justified the departure from equal sharing which would otherwise have left Mrs Miller with very substantially more capital than the £5m she was awarded. Baroness Hale therefore also upheld that award.

It will be seen that their Lordships accordingly differed in deciding whether wealth generated by one spouse, which no real contribution of a domestic nature could be regarded as helping to acquire (Mr Miller could have paid a housekeeper for the wife's home-making services, after all) is a form of matrimonial 'acquest' or not, Lord Nicholls regarding it as such and Baroness Hale excluding it. Lords Hoffmann and Mance agreed with Baroness Hale's

---

[93] At [22]–[24]. See further Short marriages, p 892. Compare *G v B (Financial Remedies: Asset Beneficiaries)* [2013] EWHC 3414 (Fam) [2014] Fam Law 290 where all of the wealth came from the husband's father and was held in a Liechtenstein foundation. The trial judge gave some, but not great, weight to this, but took more account of the fact that the foundation had been intended to benefit the father's grandchildren as well as his son. [94] [2006] UKHL 24 [2006] 2 AC 618 at [149].

[95] [2006] UKHL 24 [2006] 2 AC 618 at [150].

opinion[96] so that has formed the guidance which has subsequently been followed. The issue is related to the question of whether a spouse's earning capacity itself can be regarded as a matrimonial asset. In her application of her approach to the facts in *McFarlane*, Baroness Hale considered that the main family asset in that case was indeed the husband's 'very substantial earning power, generated over a lengthy marriage in which the couple deliberately chose that the wife should devote herself to home and family and the husband to work and career.'[97] However, in *Charman v Charman (No 4)* the Court of Appeal were doubtful whether this could be subject to the 'sharing principle' and viewed it as an area of 'complexity and potential confusion'.[98] Part of the complexity lies in the attempt to 'value' this 'asset' (over what period of time, and taking into account what features?). Part of the confusion lies in cases where the husband was already successful and 'fledged' ie already launched on his career, which he thus claims as an asset brought into the marriage and hence to be treated as 'non-matrimonial' property.[99] In *Jones v Jones*[100] the Court of Appeal held that earning capacity should not be valued or 'capitalised' as an asset, but, as the paragraph requires the court to do, taken into account as a factor relevant to the court's overall decision.

While it is easier to understand the distinction between matrimonial and non-matrimonial assets when applied to inherited property or gifts, or wealth clearly brought into the marriage,[101] it does not follow that determining what to do as a result is equally straightforward. The most important point to bear in mind is that non-matrimonial property can only be 'quarantined' or justify a 'departure from equality' where it is not required to meet the parties' needs or claim for compensation. While Lord Nicholls suggested in *White v White*[102] that the spouse to whom the property was given should, where possible, be allowed to keep it, even ancestral property handed down the generations may have to be taken into account, although the court may seek to avoid its transfer or sale by satisfying the spouse's claims from other property first.[103]

A second issue concerns whether the non-matrimonial property is to be deducted from the total 'pool' of assets ('quarantined') which is then to be shared equally, or whether it should be included within the pool but the pool itself is then divided unequally (possibly so that none of the non-matrimonial property is shared at all).[104] The Court of Appeal in *Charman v Charman (No 4)*[105] adopted the latter approach, and this has been followed subsequently. For example, in *Robson v Robson* Ward LJ said that '[s]ince inherited wealth forms part of the property and financial resources which a party has, it must be taken into account pursuant to' the statute, and 'no formula and no resort to percentages will provide the right answer. Weighing the various factors and striking the balance of fairness is, after all, an art not a science.'[106] But in *Jones v Jones*[107] Wilson LJ advocated the

---

[96] Lord Hope agreed with both her and Lord Nicholls.

[97] [2006] UKHL 24 [2006] 2 AC 618 at [154].   [98] [2007] EWCA Civ 503 [2007] 1 FLR 1246 at [67].

[99] See for example, the critical comments of this approach, which stemmed from *GW v RW (Financial Provision: Departure from Equality)* [2003] EWHC 611 [2003] 2 FLR 108 made by the Court of Appeal in *Jones v Jones* [2011] EWCA Civ 41[2011] 1 FLR 1723.

[100] [2011] EWCA Civ 41[2011] 1 FLR 1723.

[101] See, for example, *McCartney v Mills McCartney* [2008] EWHC 401 (Fam) [2008] 1 FLR 1508: husband's wealth very largely generated before the parties had even met.

[102] [2001] 1 AC 596 at 994E–F.

[103] *Y v Y (Financial Orders: Inherited Wealth)* [2012] EWHC 2063 (Fam) [2013] 2 FLR 924.

[104] *K v L (Non-Matrimonial Property: Special Contribution)* [2011] EWCA Civ 550 [2011] 2 FLR 980.

[105] [2007] EWCA Civ 503 [2007] 1 FLR 1246 at [66].

[106] [2010] EWCA Civ 1171 [2011] 1 FLR 751 at [43]. Followed in *J v J (Financial Orders: Wife's Long-term Needs)* [2011] EWHC 1010 (Fam) [2011] 2 FLR 1280; *AR v AR (Treatment of Inherited Wealth)* [2011] EWHC 2717 (Fam) [2012] 2 FLR 1 (both Moylan J).

[107] [2011] EWCA Civ 41 [2011] 1 FLR 1723 at [33]–[35]. Followed in *N v F (Financial Orders: Pre-Acquired Wealth)* [2011] EWHC 586 (Fam) [2011] 2 FLR 533 and *B v B (Assessment of Assets: Pre-Marital Property)* [2012] EWHC 314 (Fam) [2012] 2 FLR 22.

former, more 'formulaic' approach, while recognising that either is equally arbitrary and subject to the overall search for a fair outcome. The formula approach is certainly easier for a court seeking to rationalise its decision and for parties trying to reach a negotiated agreement, as recognised by the Law Commission in their review of marital property in 2014.[108]

A third problem concerns the length of time during which the property is held during the marriage. In *Miller; McFarlane* it was recognised that the longer the marriage, the less justification there may be for giving weight to the source of the asset.[109] However, it does not automatically follow that the passage of time will of itself move an asset from one side of the line to the other. In *K v L (Non-Matrimonial Property: Special Contribution)*[110] the wife had inherited a major shareholding before she met the husband. They were married for 21 years and had three children. They lived off the income generated by the shares, but kept a very frugal lifestyle. At the time of the divorce the shares were worth around £57m and the husband sought a lump sum of £18m. He was awarded £5m, based on a very generous assessment of his needs and he appealed, arguing in part that the length of the marriage reduced the weight to be given to the fact that the shares had been inherited. Wilson LJ giving the judgment of the Court of Appeal considered that three different situations may arise:

(a) Over time matrimonial property of such value has been acquired as to diminish the significance of the initial contribution by one spouse of non-matrimonial property.

(b) Over time the non-matrimonial property initially contributed has been mixed with matrimonial property in circumstances in which the contributor may be said to have accepted that it should be treated as matrimonial property or in which, at any rate, the task of identifying its current value is too difficult.

(c) The contributor of non-matrimonial property has chosen to invest it in the purchase of a matrimonial home which, although vested in his or her sole name, has – as in most cases one would expect – come over time to be treated by the parties as a central item of matrimonial property.[111]

The fact that the couple had not lived off the capital, but that the shares had always been 'ring-fenced' to grow in value, indicated that they remained to be regarded as 'non-matrimonial' assets. Once the husband's needs had been met, there was no authority he could rely on to support his claim that such assets should be subject to the sharing principle.

Even damages recovered for loss of earnings, damage to property or personal injuries form part of the recipient's assets and are thus potentially available to meet the claim of the other spouse. However, in *Daubney v Daubney*[112] Scarman LJ was careful to point out that it would not be a correct exercise of the court's discretion to make an order which would in effect deprive the spouse of all benefit of the compensation: the court must decide in each case what would be a fair sum to bring into account. The fact that an injured spouse may have special needs, or an impaired future earning capacity must be considered by the court in the

---

[108] Law Commission, *Matrimonial Property, Needs and Agreements* Law Com No 343 (2014) at para 8.81.

[109] [2006] UKHL 24 [2006] 2 AC 618 at [25] and [152].

[110] [2011] EWCA Civ 550 [2011] 2 FLR 980.   [111] [2011] EWCA Civ 550 [2011] 2 FLR 980 at [18].

[112] *Daubney v Daubney* [1976] Fam 267, CA at 277; cf *Jones v Jones* [1976] Fam 8, CA; *Wagstaff v Wagstaff* [1992] 1 All ER 275, CA.

exercise of its discretion.[113] In *Mansfield v Mansfield*[114] the husband received £500,000 in damages before he met the wife, which he invested partly in a specially adapted bungalow in which he lived and partly in a buy-to-let property. The Court of Appeal upheld a lump sum of £285,000 awarded to the wife to enable her to rehouse herself and the children after divorce but granted the husband a charge-back of a third of the equity upon sale when the children had grown up (known as a *Mesher* order)[115] to reflect the fact that the lump sum had to be raised from his damages investment and to enable funds to be available to meet his increasing physical needs as he aged.

Assets may derive from many sources; the prospect of a large sum resulting from a lottery win is the kind of factual scenario beloved of examination-setters, but it fell for consideration in *S v AG (Financial Orders: Lottery Prize)*.[116] The marriage was unhappy. The wife bought a lottery ticket with a friend and they shared a £1m win. She used part of her winnings to buy a new matrimonial home in her sole name where the spouses lived until they separated three years later. The husband claimed a share. The court held that whether a lottery prize is to be treated as matrimonial or non-matrimonial property must be fact-specific and could not be determined by the source of the trivial amount of money used to buy the ticket. Here, the fact that the wife had unilaterally bought the ticket in a syndicate with a friend, and that the marriage was in trouble at that stage, pointed to viewing the win as non-matrimonial. However, part of the money had been used to acquire the matrimonial home, and had thus been converted into matrimonial property. It did not follow that the husband should receive an equal share in the circumstances—he had not contributed to the purchase and had lived in the home only for a relatively short period—but on a needs basis, he should receive a lump sum of £85,000. The decision illustrates both how property which is categorised as non-matrimonial can be converted into a marital asset but also that even where that is the case, the starting-point of an equal share may be readily rebutted by the circumstances.

(b) Income and earning capacity

In appropriate cases regard must be had to the husband's ability to earn higher wages by working overtime,[117] to raise money by overdrafts,[118] or loans secured on his property[119] or, if he is unemployed, to obtain work if he wishes.[120] Increases in either spouse's income or capital after their separation must also be considered, as these are properly to be regarded as part of their resources.[121] In the case of a very rich spouse, who may well live largely on capital and capital profits, his capital assets will be of particular importance,[122] and such a person's standard of living may be the best guide to the level of his real income.[123]

The specific requirement to consider whether a spouse could increase his or her earning capacity results from an amendment introduced in 1984 and is used primarily to focus attention to the potential earning capacity of a wife who has been out of the labour market

---

[113] See s 25(2)(e) discussed later, Disability p 896 and see *C v C (Financial Provision: Personal Damages)* [1995] 2 FLR 171, in which the husband received a structured settlement damages award after a car accident of about £950,000, but potentially worth up to £5m if he achieved his estimated life expectancy. The court declined to award the wife a lump sum which would frustrate the husband's reasonable expectation of obtaining a suitable house and long-term care.   [114] [2011] EWCA Civ 1056 [2012] 1 FLR 117.

[115] *Mesher v Mesher and Hall* (1973) [1980] 1 All ER 126n, CA discussed later, *Mesher* orders, p 905.

[116] [2011] EWHC 2637 (Fam) [2012] 1 FLR 651.   [117] *Klucinski v Klucinski* [1953] 1 All ER 683.

[118] *J-PC v J-AF* [1955] P 215, CA.   [119] *Newton v Newton* [1990] 1 FLR 33, CA.

[120] *McEwan v McEwan* [1972] 2 All ER 708.

[121] *Schuller v Schuller* [1990] 2 FLR 193: wife's property inheritance after a decree absolute was taken into account to reduce her lump sum.

[122] *Brett v Brett* [1969] 1 All ER 1007, CA.   [123] See *W v W (No 3)* [1962] P 124.

caring for children. The provision is clearly related to the general requirement to consider whether the spouses can become self-sufficient.

It is to be noted that the court should only pay regard to any increase in earning capacity that it is 'reasonable' to expect the spouse to take steps to acquire. Obviously, in deciding this, the court must take into account all the circumstances of the case, but particularly relevant will be any commitments to look after any children;[124] the age, health and qualifications of the spouse; and the length of time since the spouse last worked. The courts must also have in mind the state of the job market and the difficulties faced by older workers—particularly women—in obtaining suitable employment.[125] In *Leadbeater v Leadbeater*,[126] for example, it was held to be unreasonable to expect a 47-year-old woman with no particular skills (she was, at the time of the marriage, the secretary to her former husband) to adapt to new technology used in offices. However, it was thought that she could increase the number of hours that she was currently working as a receptionist. One might think that the court's approach was rather patronising to women and the decision looks rather outmoded on its facts. By contrast, in *Mitchell v Mitchell*[127] it was held that a wife who was an experienced secretary but who had taken a part-time job in a canteen could, when the children had left school (the younger child was 13), reasonably be expected to increase her earning capacity, and the resulting lump sum awarded to her reflected this.

(c) Other resources

The court must have regard not only to the resources which each party has at the time of the hearing,[128] but also to those which they are likely to have in the foreseeable future.[129] If the benefit is one to which a party may be contingently entitled in the future, the court may take it into account by ordering him to pay an appropriate lump sum if and when he acquires the interest[130] or by imposing a charge on the property.[131] Where the value of a future asset will be known reasonably shortly, the application may be adjourned.[132] Where it is known that the party will receive the asset, but not its value (such as a bonus based on performance in his employment), a cap should be set on the amount that he is to pay from that asset to the other spouse.[133] On the other hand, if the contingency is too uncertain or remote, it may be left out of account altogether.[134]

---

[124] This may include a child who is *not* the husband's, and who was born after the breakdown of the marriage: see *Fisher v Fisher* [1989] 1 FLR 423, CA.

[125] See also the discussion earlier, Making deferred clean break orders, p 878.

[126] [1985] FLR 789.   [127] [1984] FLR 387, CA.

[128] The court may 'add back' assets recklessly dissipated in calculating the total sum by assuming the party still has them: *Vaughan v Vaughan* [2007] EWCA Civ 1085 [2008] 1 FLR 1108; *AC v DC and Others (No 2)* [2012] EWHC 2420 (Fam) [2013] 2 FLR 1499.

[129] One particular difficulty may concern whether assets can be realised in order to pay a lump sum or effect a transfer to the recipient spouse. In *N v N (Financial Provision: Sale of Company)* [2001] 2 FLR 69, the court justified a departure from equal division of the surplus assets because of the illiquidity of the husband's assets; the wife received only 39%.

[130] *Calder v Calder* (1975) 6 Fam Law 242, CA (interest contingent on husband surviving his mother).

[131] *Parra v Parra* [2002] EWCA Civ 1886 [2003] 1 FLR 942.

[132] *MT v MT (Financial Provision: Lump Sum)* [1992] 1 FLR 362: wife's application adjourned pending the death of her 83-year-old German father-in-law: under German law, husband entitled to a fixed portion of his father's substantial estate. For an example of dealing with an adjourned application, notwithstanding the wife's remarriage in the interim, see *Re G (Financial Provision: Liberty to Restore Application for Lump Sum)* [2004] EWHC 88 (Fam) [2004] 1 FLR 997.

[133] *H v W (Cap on Wife's Share of Bonus Payments)* [2013] EWHC 4105 (Fam) [2014] Fam Law 445.

[134] See eg *Michael v Michael* [1986] 2 FLR 389 where, because of the uncertainty whether and when the wife would receive an interest under her mother's will, it was left out of account. See also *Priest v Priest* (1987)

Another issue is the presence of a new partner. It is established that the financial means of the husband's second wife are relevant (though there can be difficulties in discovering them),[135] but only to the extent that they diminish the needs of the husband, thereby extending his resources to support his first family. An order cannot be made which has the effect of making the new partner pay out of her income or capital.[136]

The fact that the wife has remarried or is about to remarry or is living with another man who is supporting her clearly affects her financial position. Remarriage automatically terminates periodical payments[137] and although, for this purpose, cohabitation is not necessarily to be equated with remarriage,[138] it may nonetheless lead the court to conclude that the wife no longer needs the husband's support;[139] but leaving aside the question of the matrimonial home, all these facts should generally be disregarded in dividing capital assets unless a lump sum award represents the capitalisation of periodical payments.[140] The wife is withdrawing her part of the capital from the former family partnership, and the amount she receives should not depend on what she proposes to do with it.[141] The mere chance that the wife may remarry at some time in the future should be ignored when dividing capital assets.[142]

2. NEEDS, OBLIGATIONS AND RESPONSIBILITIES

(b) The financial needs, obligations and responsibilities which each of the parties to the marriage has or is likely to have in the foreseeable future

The most obvious examples of factors to be considered under this head are the parties' need to maintain themselves and their responsibility to provide for their dependants. It is important to consider the needs of *both* parties: in *A v L (Departure from Equality: Needs)*[143] Moor J held that an order requiring the husband, who had limited earning capacity, to pay £500 per month to the wife, who had even less, had failed to give due regard to his needs, although the disparity in the parties' incomes did justify the wife receiving 70% of the equity in the matrimonial home in an immediate clean break.

Usually, it will be desirable to ensure that the need of both parties for a suitable home is met, especially if they have children who will be spending time with each parent.[144] However, there is no principle or presumption that the available assets must be split to enable each spouse to acquire accommodation. In *Piglowska v Piglowski*[145] the first

1 FLR 189, CA where a gratuity that could arise 15 years after the hearing was thought to be too far in the future to be taken into account. For consideration of trusts and the willingness of trustees to advance capital to enable a spouse to pay a lump sum, see *Charman v Charman (No 4)* [2007] EWCA Civ 503 [2007] 1 FLR 1246 [47]–[58]; *Whaley v Whaley* [2011] EWCA Civ 617 [2012] 1 FLR 735.

[135] See *Wynne v Wynne and Jeffers* [1980] 3 All ER 659, CA; *W v W* (1981) 2 FLR 291.

[136] *Macey v Macey* (1981) 3 FLR 7 and *Brown v Brown* (1981) 3 FLR 161.

[137] See Ch 22, Periodical payments, Orders in favour of spouses, p 839.

[138] *Atkinson v Atkinson* [1988] Fam 93, CA.

[139] See *Atkinson v Atkinson* [1995] 2 FLR 356; *Fleming v Fleming* [2003] EWCA Civ 1841 [2004] 1 FLR 667: a fixed-term periodical payments order should not be extended where the means of the wife and her cohabiting partner sufficed to discharge their living expenses.

[140] See eg *Duxbury v Duxbury* [1992] Fam 62n, CA.

[141] *Duxbury v Duxbury* (it was irrelevant that the wife would spend part of a lump sum award to benefit her cohabitant).   [142] *S v S* [1976] Fam 18n at 23.

[143] [2011] EWHC 3150 (Fam) [2012] 1 FLR 985.

[144] *M v B (Ancillary Proceedings: Lump Sum)* [1998] 1 FLR 53; *Calderbank v Calderbank* [1976] Fam 93.

[145] [1999] 1 WLR 1360.

instance judge ordered that the wife was to receive the former matrimonial home in return for transferring a flat in Spain to the husband, who had remarried in Poland but wished to return to England. This was not worth enough to enable him to rehouse himself and his second wife and step-children in England but the House of Lords upheld the order as within the trial judge's discretion.

In supporting dependants, the maintenance of children must come first but in addition one must take into account the needs of a second spouse,[146] infirm parents, brothers and sisters unable to work, and any other person whom it is reasonable to expect either party to look after in the circumstances. It will be seen that not all these obligations are legally enforceable: in this context a moral obligation and the voluntary assumption of a responsibility (provided that it is reasonable) may be as relevant as a legal obligation. For example, a father's moral duty to make voluntary payments for the upkeep of his stepchild is indistinguishable for this purpose from his legal liability to comply with a court order.[147] But if the liability has been assumed in a purely voluntary way, the court can obviously take it into account only if it is reasonable. Thus a wife could not look to the husband to help her meet payments on a mortgage of the matrimonial home, when she had been given a lump sum to pay it off, but had chosen to invest this (unwisely) because she was hoping to sell the property later.[148]

As in the case of the parties' resources, the court must have regard to the needs, obligations and liabilities that they are likely to have in the foreseeable future as well as those already incurred at the time of the order. In all cases the spouses are entitled to have only their *reasonable* needs taken into account but, of course, what is 'reasonable' very much depends upon the circumstances of each case. In *Leadbeater v Leadbeater*,[149] for example, where the husband's assets amounted to some £250,000, it was held that while the wife could reasonably justify the purchase of a two bedroom house, given that she would live in it by herself, she could not justify the need for a three bedroom property.

(a) 'Big money' cases

Pre-*White v White*

At the wealthiest end of the spectrum it has been said that it is impossible to lay down guidelines to help calculate the appropriate levels of lump sum payments,[150] though in *Preston v Preston*[151] Ormrod LJ considered that the word 'needs' in s 25(2)(b) was equivalent to 'reasonable requirements', and seemed to hint there might be some ceiling to awards that might be made where the parties' available resources are very large. On the facts, the husband, who had capital assets estimated at £2.3 million, was ordered to pay a lump sum of £600,000 to produce an annual income of £20,000 after tax. In a number of

---

[146] *Barnes v Barnes* [1972] 3 All ER 872, CA. But this does not justify postponing the interests of the first family (and a fortiori any child of the family) to those of the second family: *Roberts v Roberts* [1970] P 1. In *S v S (Financial Provision: Departing from Equality)* [2001] 2 FLR 246, the liability of the husband to support his second family was held to justify the wife receiving only 46% of the assets, but in *H-J v H-J (Financial Provision: Equality)* [2002] 1 FLR 415 and *Norris v Norris* [2002] EWHC 2996 (Fam) [2003] 1 FLR 1142 this was regarded as inappropriate in a case where there are surplus assets: the husband assumes the liability of a second family by his own choice.

[147] *Blower v Blower* [1986] 1 FLR 292; cf *Fisher v Fisher* [1989] 1 FLR 423, CA, for a mother's responsibility towards a child born outside the marriage. Note also *Vicary v Vicary* [1992] 2 FLR 271, CA (where there are plentiful resources, the financial provision made for a wife may include prospective payments which she might make to adult daughters and grandchildren, if such payments had been made during the marriage, and the husband had contributed to them or, at least, had not objected to the payments having been made).

[148] See *Yates v Yates* [2012] EWCA Civ 532 [2013] 2 FLR 1070.   [149] [1985] FLR 789.

[150] *Gojkovic v Gojkovic (No 2)* [1992] Fam 40 at 50, CA, per Russell LJ.   [151] [1982] Fam 17.

similar 'big money' cases the 'reasonable requirements' approach, with its ceiling on the award made to the wife, was adopted and followed.[152]

Unease at the inequality of outcome which such an approach could produce led to some tentative attempts to escape in some cases, where, at least, the facts enabled the court to focus on some factor other than 'needs' or requirements as of significance. Thus, in *Gojkovic v Gojkovic*[153] the husband and wife had, by dint of their efforts, built up a hotel and property business worth over £4 million. The Court of Appeal held that the wife's substantial contribution to the development of the family business should be recognised and upheld the award of a lump sum of £1 million to the wife, which she intended to use to acquire and run her own hotel. In the later case of *Conran v Conran*,[154] Wilson J described as 'in every sense outstanding' the wife's contributions over 30 years in helping to develop the husband's 'Habitat' furniture stores and restaurants, her work and reputation as a nationally recognised cookery writer and journalist and her other family contributions. The judge considered the correct approach would be to assess the wife's reasonable requirements without reference to her contributions, and then to bring the latter into the balance. From the husband's total wealth of some £85 million, the wife was awarded £8.4 million for her 'reasonable requirements' and a further £2.1 million for her 'contributions'.[155]

Post-*White v White*

Butler-Sloss LJ acknowledged in *Dart v Dart*[156] that the courts may have given too much weight to an assessment of a spouse's 'reasonable requirements' over and above the other criteria set out in s 25 of the Matrimonial Causes Act 1973, with the result, in 'big money' cases, that awards may have been 'over-modest'. She suggested that any change should be a matter for the legislature, but the House of Lords took the initiative in *White v White*.[157] Noting that the term 'reasonable requirements' does not appear in the statute itself, the House firmly rejected this approach as discriminatory, since, by limiting the wife's share to her 'reasonable requirements' (however generously interpreted) it enabled the husband to keep all of the surplus assets, regardless of the contributions that the wife might have made during the marriage.[158] Since this decision, it has been accepted that an award should not be limited to the dependent spouse's reasonable requirements, if there are surplus assets available to be shared.

It does not follow that a spouse will therefore receive an award based on the sharing principle, however. In *McCartney v Mills McCartney*[159] for example, the parties' marriage lasted only four years. It was held that the wife's needs were 'a factor of magnetic importance'[160] in determining a fair outcome, given that the husband's fortune had been largely accumulated before they had met and the short duration of the marriage.[161] While 'reasonable requirements' have thus ceased to be a ceiling to an award, they may still determine the outcome, and 'needs, generously assessed' has become a phrase regularly used to convey the same idea. Here, the husband was ordered to pay a lump sum to the wife of £16.5m, against his total wealth of around £400m.

(b) The Duxbury calculation

One common feature of 'big-money' cases first made its appearance in *Duxbury v Duxbury*,[162] where a capital sum was ordered which would produce an annual income

---

[152] See eg *O'D v O'D* [1976] Fam 83; *Page v Page* (1981) 2 FLR 198; *Dart v Dart* [1996] 2 FLR 286, CA.
[153] *(No 2)* [1992] Fam 40, CA.   [154] [1997] 2 FLR 615.   [155] See further, Contribution, p 896.
[156] [1996] 2 FLR 286, CA at 305F–G.   [157] [2001] 1 AC 596.
[158] [2001] 1 AC 596 at 608F–G. See further Contribution, p 896.
[159] [2008] EWHC 401 (Fam) [2008] 1 FLR 1508.   [160] At [311].
[161] See further. Short marriages, p 892.   [162] [1992] Fam 62n, CA.

thought to be a reasonable sum to preserve a luxurious standard of living. The advantage of using this kind of device is that it provides a continuing income stream for the payee whilst achieving a clean break through the payment of a lump sum or transfer of an investment. The firm of accountants who acted for the wife devised a sophisticated computer program, designed to take account of a number of financial and other variables, including life expectancy, inflation, tax, investment return and capital growth to produce an estimate of the lump sum required to meet the recipient's needs for life. This so-called 'Duxbury calculation' has been used as a helpful guide to the assessment of the requirements of a wife whose husband is wealthy and thus to assist in determining whether an equal division of assets will meet her 'needs'.[163] However, as Butler-Sloss LJ explained in Gojkovic v Gojkovic,[164] it ought not to be elevated to a rigid arithmetical calculation; each case must be decided upon its own facts, and in accordance with the principles set out in s 25 of the Matrimonial Causes Act. Moreover, it may produce the 'Duxbury paradox', whereby 'the longer the marriage and hence the older the wife, the less the capital sum required for a Duxbury type fund'.[165] As Lord Nicholls noted in White v White:[166]

financial needs are only one of the factors to be taken into account in arriving at the amount of an award. The amount of capital required to provide for an older wife's financial needs may well be less than the amount required to provide for a younger wife's financial needs. It by no means follows that, in a case where resources exceed the parties' financial needs, the older wife's award will be less than the younger wife's. Indeed, the older wife's award may be substantially larger.

And he added that although a wish to leave money to one's children is not a financial 'need' within s 25(2)(b), the judge is entitled to have it in mind when arriving at a final figure, should the parties' assets permit. Similarly, in AR v AR (Treatment of Inherited Wealth), the court considered that the lump sum arrived at should be such as to enable the wife to 'spend money on additional, discretionary, items which will vary from year to year and which are not reflected in her annual budget'[167] such as holidays or the provision of a new kitchen.

3. STANDARD OF LIVING

(c) The standard of living enjoyed by the family before the breakdown of the marriage

This factor overlaps with consideration of the parties' needs. It is particularly important when substantial assets are available and one of the spouses has been living at a much higher level than he or she did before the marriage.[168] In Calderbank v Calderbank[169] the

---

[163] A simplified version of the Duxbury tables is published in a booklet produced annually by the Family Law Bar Association entitled 'At a Glance'.   [164] (No 2) [1994] Fam 40 at 48, CA.
[165] Per Holman J in White v White at first instance, cited by Lord Nicholls of Birkenhead at [2001] 1 AC 596 at 609C.   [166] [2001] 1 AC 596 at 609.
[167] [2011] EWHC 2717 (Fam) [2012] 2 FLR 1 at [71].
[168] See eg Dart v Dart [1996] 2 FLR 286; McFarlane v McFarlane; Parlour v Parlour [2004] EWCA Civ 872 [2005] Fam 171.
[169] [1976] Fam 93, CA. See also H v H (Financial Provision: Conduct) [1998] 1 FLR 971, in which the children's welfare required that the husband—the family's 'poor relation'—should have a home they could regard as belonging to him.

wife, a relatively rich woman, was ordered to pay a lump sum to the husband (who had no capital and had remarried) so that he might buy a house suitable to the former spouses' way of life in which he might see his children. But neither party's standard of living should be raised above what it otherwise would have been, for this would in effect mean that the order was being used as a means of punishing the other.[170] Equally, where a modest lifestyle was enjoyed during the marriage, as in *K v L (Non-Matrimonial Property: Special Contribution)* the fact that a spouse could afford a much more lavish standard of living does not justify making an award at the higher level.[171]

4. AGE AND DURATION OF MARRIAGE

(d) The age of each party and the duration of the marriage

(a) Short marriages

This must be looked at in conjunction with the contribution made by each of them to the welfare of the family (considered later). Before *White v White*,[172] a spouse seeking provision after a short marriage could generally expect much less favourable terms than one who was divorcing after years of married life: she would have made less of a contribution to the family than a wife of long-standing.[173] However, even then, the particular needs and circumstances of the spouses had, of course, to be taken into account. If the breakdown of the marriage had caused a spouse financial loss or other hardship, she could expect a substantial order in her favour.[174] In *C v C (Financial Relief: Short Marriage)*,[175] for example, the Court of Appeal upheld an award 'at the very top of the bracket' where a marriage had broken down after just nine months, but there was a small child and the wife's fragile health had been seriously impaired by the marriage breakdown, and her prospects of successful medical treatment and her future earning capacity were uncertain.

However, since the House of Lords' decision in *White v White*, with its emphasis on non-discrimination and the yardstick of equality, there has been some uncertainty in how to assess the significance of the length of the marriage. In *GW v RW (Financial Provision: Departure from Equality)*[176] the judge found it 'fundamentally unfair to be required to find that a party who has made domestic contributions during a marriage of 12 years should be awarded the same proportion of the assets as a party who has made the

---

[170] See *Attwood v Attwood* [1968] P 591 at 595.
[171] [2011] EWCA Civ 550 [2011] 2 FLR 980; cf *A v A (Financial Provision)* [1998] 2 FLR 180, where the family's past relatively simple lifestyle was not regarded as determining entirely the wife's future standard of living, which should reflect the reality of the husband's substantial wealth.   [172] [2001] 1 AC 596.
[173] In *Browne v Pritchard* [1975] 3 All ER 721, CA, the wife's half-share in the matrimonial home (to the purchase of which she had contributed nothing) was reduced to a third after a marriage which lasted only three years. In *Hobhouse v Hobhouse* [1999] 1 FLR 961, the marriage lasted four years and was childless. Both parties had inherited the bulk of their wealth: the husband had assets of around £8.5 million and the wife £500,000 with the prospect of a further £1.5 million on her mother's death. The wife was awarded a lump sum of £175,000 to enable her to re-establish her financial independence and return to her home in Australia.
[174] *Whyte-Smith v Whyte-Smith* (1974) 5 Fam Law 20 (separation after three months; breakdown caused wife illness and loss of job); *Abdureman v Abdureman* (1978) 122 Sol Jo 663 (separation after 12 weeks; wife had given up job and lost pension on marriage).   [175] [1997] 2 FLR 26, CA.
[176] [2003] EWHC 611 (Fam) [2003] 2 FLR 108.

domestic contributions for a period in excess of 20 years.'[177] He accordingly awarded the wife 40% of the assets. The judge was influenced by John Eekelaar's argument that the:

> length of the marriage is relevant, in and of itself . . . to the amount allocated because it is defensible to hold that parties who share their lives together *earn a share in one another's assets relative to the length of time they have shared their lives*.[178]

One of the difficulties with this approach is in determining at what point the claimant spouse has 'earned' a full share of the available assets. In *GW v RW* the judge adopted the period of 20 years drawing on apparent practice in the United States.[179] But it is unclear why 20 years is a better target figure than 10, or 25, or any other. In any event, it does not follow that an equal share is necessarily inappropriate after a short marriage. In *Foster v Foster*[180] the parties were married for four years, and both had contributed what they could from their incomes to buying up properties for development and resale. The wife earned twice as much as the husband and had put much more capital into acquiring the properties than he had. She argued that this should be reflected in her share of the assets on divorce. The Court of Appeal held that where the capital surplus had been generated by the parties' joint efforts, it should not matter whether it had taken them a short or long time to build this up, and its division should be based on what was fair.[181] The court stressed that spouses may earn unequal amounts, but that these should not be *valued* as of unequal worth, just as non-financial contributions to welfare, through home-making and child care, should not be valued as of less worth than financial contributions.[182] This is a crucial point. If the reason for not valuing domestic contributions as inherently of less value than those of a financial nature is to avoid gender discrimination, then giving weight to the durational element is arguably as discriminatory to women as the previous 'reasonable requirements' approach, since it will usually be the wife who is seeking a share of the assets generated or owned by the husband and who therefore has to prove she has 'earned' her share. Moreover, it would surely be wrong, given the clear lack of priorities in s 25(2), to regard duration of the marriage as of greater significance than other factors, just as it was wrong to focus on a party's 'reasonable requirements' as setting a ceiling on her fair share of the assets.

In *Miller v Miller*,[183] the marriage had lasted less than three years. The House of Lords agreed with the Court of Appeal that older cases which had focused on arriving at awards that enabled the wife to 'get back on her feet'[184] after a short marriage should no longer be followed, and that the approach taken in *Foster* is correct. As Lord Nicholls put it, 'A short marriage is no less a partnership of equals than a long marriage.'[185] Nonetheless,

---

[177] [2003] EWHC 611 (Fam) [2003] 2 FLR 108 at para 43. See also *Leadbeater v Leadbeater* [1985] FLR 789: 25% should be discounted from the sum that was thought appropriate to meet the wife's reasonable needs since the marriage had been short, lasting only four years.

[178] J Eekelaar 'Asset Distribution on Divorce—The Durational Element' (2001) 117 LQR 552 at 556. See also J Eekelaar 'Asset Distribution on Divorce—Time and Property' [2003] Fam Law 828.

[179] [2003] EWHC 611 (Fam) [2003] 2 FLR 108 at [28] and [37].

[180] [2003] EWCA Civ 565 [2003] 2 FLR 299.

[181] [2003] EWCA Civ 565 [2003] 2 FLR 299 at para 19.

[182] [2003] EWCA Civ 565 [2003] 2 FLR 299 at para 18. See Contribution, p 896. However, the court did not in fact award the spouses equal shares, but reinstated the trial judge's division of 61% to the wife and 39% to the husband.

[183] Heard with *McFarlane v McFarlane* [2006] UKHL 24 [2006] All ER 1. Discussed earlier, Matrimonial and non-matrimonial property, p 882.

[184] *Robertson v Robertson* (1982) 4 FLR 387 at 392 per Balcombe J.   [185] At [17].

both he and Baroness Hale recognised that there is an 'instinctive feeling'[186] or 'perception'[187] that the parties have less of a claim upon each other after a short marriage and one might therefore expect that equal shares may be less appropriate as the outcome and they upheld the award to Mrs Miller which represented either one third or one sixth of the husband's wealth, depending upon how that was calculated. *McCartney v Mills McCartney*,[188] already discussed, is a further illustration of this view.

By contrast, as we have also seen, a long marriage (bearing in mind the difficulty of determining what is 'long' or 'short' in this context), may help demonstrate that 'non-matrimonial' property has become 'matrimonial' and therefore amenable to the sharing principle.

An additional problem with focusing on the duration of the marriage is that this ignores the parties' future lives. In *B v B (Mesher Order)*,[189] Munby J upheld a lump sum payment of £175,000 to the wife and periodical payments of unlimited duration, after a marriage lasting just 10 months. The marriage had produced a child, whom the wife would have the burden of caring for in the future, and this would accordingly impede her ability to accumulate capital and income for years to come. The husband had argued that the wife's periodical payments should cease on the child's fifth birthday and that he should have a charge on the house to be realised when the child had ceased education[190] but the uncertainty of the wife's future circumstances led the judge to conclude that such limitations would result in a settlement unfair to the wife. One could also argue that the wife's *future* contribution to the welfare of the child created by the marriage would be of greater significance than the time she had spent with the husband during that marriage.[191]

(b) Measuring duration

This leads to another issue—what *is* the duration of the marriage? The court will take notice of the de facto, rather than de jure, length of the marriage, ie the length of time the parties lived together up to the point of separation.[192] However, given the prevalence of *pre-marital* cohabitation the question has arisen whether this should be taken into account as well. Earlier case-law which rejected this view[193] has become outmoded.

It might be thought that it would not be possible for the court to include such a period under this factor, which states clearly that it refers to the length of the *marriage*. But in *GW v RW*[194] the judge considered that:

> where a relationship moves seamlessly from cohabitation to marriage without any major alteration in the way the couple live, it is unreal and artificial to treat the periods differently. On the other hand, if it is found that the pre-marital cohabitation was on the basis of a trial period to see if there is any basis for later marriage then I would be of the view that it would not be right to include it as part of the "duration of the marriage".[195]

---

[186] Per Lord Nicholls at [24].   [187] Per Baroness Hale at [147].

[188] [2008] EWHC 401 (Fam) [2008] 1 FLR 1508 at [240], [311].

[189] [2002] EWHC 3106 (Fam) [2003] 2 FLR 285.   [190] See *Mesher* orders, p 905.

[191] See also *McFarlane v McFarlane; Parlour v Parlour* [2004] EWCA Civ 872 [2005] Fam 171 and *Re G (Financial Provision: Liberty to Restore Application for Lump Sum)* [2004] EWHC 88 (Fam) [2004] 1 FLR 997 for a similar approach.

[192] See *Krystman v Krystman* [1973] 3 All ER 247, CA: no order made when the parties had cohabited for only a fortnight at the beginning of a marriage which had taken place 26 years earlier.

[193] See *Campbell v Campbell* [1976] Fam 347; *Foley v Foley* [1981] Fam 160; but cf *Kokosinski v Kokosinski* [1980] Fam 72.

[194] [2003] EWHC 611 (Fam) [2003] 2 FLR 108. For a critique, see S Gilmore 'Duration of Marriage *and* Seamless Preceding Cohabitation?' [2004] Fam Law 205. See also the useful survey of the case-law by J Edwards 'Duration of Marriage: From "I Do", "I Promise" or "I May"?' [2004] Fam Law 726.

[195] [2003] EWHC 611 (Fam) [2003] 2 FLR 108 at [33].

He accordingly included the parties' 18 months of pre-marital cohabitation in his calculation of the duration of the marriage.[196] Notwithstanding the clear words of the statute,
this approach has been adopted subsequently. Indeed, in *Miller v Miller*, where the parties
did not cohabit before the wedding, the House of Lords took note of the parties' engagement (although, given the shortness of the actual 'marriage' it did not make a perceptible
difference to the outcome).

There is a better justification for considering the whole length of the parties' relationship in the requirement in s 25(1) for the court to take account of 'all the circumstances of the case', or as relevant to weighing a party's contribution to the welfare of
the family under s 25(2)(f), or as 'conduct' under s 25(2)(g). For example, in *Kokosinski v
Kokosinski*[197] the husband was a Polish refugee who had lived in this country since the
Second World War. He started to live with the petitioner in 1947 and a son was born in
1950. He could not marry her until his first wife (who was still living in Poland) divorced
him, which she did not do until 1969. In the meantime the petitioner had been loving,
faithful and hardworking, had brought up their child and had played a substantial part
in building up the husband's business. The parties married in 1971 but separated in the
following year. Wood J was of the opinion that in these circumstances it would offend a
reasonable person's sense of justice to ignore this long period of cohabitation and took it
into account in deciding what order to make, either as part of all the circumstances, or
as 'conduct'.[198] In *Co v Co (Ancillary Relief: Pre-marital Cohabitation)*[199] Coleridge J took
account of eight years' cohabitation prior to a four-year marriage, commenting that:

> Committed, settled relationships which often endure for years in the context of
> cohabitation (often but not always with children) outside marriage must, I think, be
> regarded as every bit as valid as those where parties have made the same degree of
> commitment but recorded it publicly by civil registration, ie by marriage. This has
> nothing to do with morality or religious belief and everything to do with striving
> to achieve financial fairness as between a couple at a particular stage in society's
> development . . . Section 25 is concerned with taking into account the reality of a
> couple's circumstances and situation during their relationship. It is concerned with
> establishing fact not fiction in all areas including the financial. To ignore such a factor
> as cohabitation would lead the court to be considering the case on an untrue basis and
> almost inevitably lead to unfairness.[200]

He therefore regarded it as part of the circumstances of the case or, if it were necessary to
fit it within one of the specific factors, as part of 'contribution' or 'conduct'.

This issue may arise in particular in relation to civil partnerships. Just as was
the case in *Kokosinski v Kokosinksi*[201] civil partners will have been prevented from

---

[196] In fact, he regarded it as cancelled out by the 18 months that followed from the issue of the divorce
petition until the decree: [34].

[197] [1980] Fam 72. The facts are not dissimilar from those which would entitle a cohabitant to an order
under the Inheritance (Provision for Family and Dependants) Act 1975 after the man's death. See Ch 25,
Factors relevant to applications by cohabitants, p 987.

[198] See also *Gojkovic v Gojkovic (No 2)* [1992] Fam 40, CA, where the substantial award to the wife was in
large part based upon her outstanding contribution to the family business and much of her effort was made
during pre-marital cohabitation.   [199] [2004] EWHC 287 (Fam) [2004] 1 FLR 1095.

[200] [2004] EWHC 287 (Fam) [2004] 1 FLR 1095 at [44]–[46]. See also *M v M (Financial Relief: Substantial
Earning Capacity)* [2004] EWHC 688 (Fam) [2004] 2 FLR 236: 'in modern society it is a couple's commitment to each other by cohabiting that is the relevant start date for consideration in most cases' per Baron J
at [55].   [201] [1980] Fam 72.

obtaining legal recognition of their relationships and thus cannot build up a long duration post-registration for several years to come, but many may have lived together for a
long time. One would expect the courts to adopt Coleridge J's approach to ensure that a
fair settlement is nonetheless achieved.

A different problem arose *Hill v Hill*.[202] The Court of Appeal allowed a 'wife' to seek
further financial relief, over 25 years after the parties had divorced, and during which
period they had reconciled and cohabited. Just as the court could take pre-marital cohabitation into account in the appropriate circumstances, so too could it consider a period of
post-divorce cohabitation in arriving at a reasonable and just solution.

5. DISABILITY

(e) Any physical or mental disability of either of the parties to the marriage

In practice, these issues are subsumed under the other heads in s 25, especially, of course,
that which refers to the parties' needs. For example, as already noted, in *C v C (Financial
Provision: Personal Damages)*,[203] a husband who was rendered paraplegic in a car accident was deemed to need all of the damages awarded to him in a structured settlement,
and thus his wife and child received nothing, notwithstanding their dependence upon
social security benefits, and in *Mansfield v Mansfield*[204] the husband was awarded a
charge-back on property so that his future needs could be met when the couple's children
were no longer dependent.

6. CONTRIBUTION

(f) The contributions which each of the parties has made or is likely in the foreseeable
    future to make to the welfare of the family, including any contribution by looking after
    the home or caring for the family

It is expressly provided that this is to include any contribution made by looking after the
home or caring for the family, but it includes a financial contribution, such as the contribution of a spouse to the family business,[205] as well as by means of an inheritance.[206] Thus,
in *K v L (Non-Matrimonial Property: Special Contribution)*,[207] which we noted earlier,
the husband's claim that it would be discriminatory, in the light of *White v White*,[208] to
regard the wife's *financial* contribution to supporting the family through her inherited

---

[202] [1998] 1 FLR 198, CA. While noting 'as a matter of policy' that a cohabitant should not have the
equivalent rights of a wife, or former wife, the court pointed to another policy issue—that of encouraging
reconciliation—which (in this case) meant that the parties' children had been brought up by them both, in
a settled home.

[203] [1995] 2 FLR 171. See earlier, Matrimonial and non-matrimonial property, p 886 n 113.

[204] [2011] EWCA Civ 1056 [2012] 1 FLR 117.

[205] *Gojkovic v Gojkovic (No 2)* [1992] Fam 40, CA; *Conran v Conran* [1997] 2 FLR 615 discussed earlier,
'Big money' cases, p 890; *R v R (Financial Orders: Contributions)* [2013] Fam Law 28.

[206] So held by Ormrod LJ in *P v P* [1978] 3 All ER 70 at 74, CA.

[207] [2011] EWCA Civ 550 [2011] 2 FLR 980. See also, *B v B (Ancillary Relief)* [2008] EWCA Civ 284 [2008]
2 FLR 1627.   [208] [2001] 1 AC 596.

share income, as carrying more weight than his *non-financial* contribution in caring for the family, was rejected. Wilson LJ held:

> what is unacceptable is discrimination in the division of *labour* within the family, in particular between the party who earns the income and the party whose work is in the home, unpaid . . . But the law does not abjure *all* discrimination. On the contrary it is of the essence of the judicial function to discriminate between different sets of facts and thus between different claims. What is outlawed is discrimination on the ground of superficial differences which, on analysis, do not reflect substantive differences . . . To find that, on top of the efforts of equal value made by each party in the home, the wife made a financial contribution to the marriage of great importance is not to discriminate between the parties in any unacceptable way: on the contrary it correctly recognises a substantive difference.[209]

But the principle was primarily introduced to give the wife credit for her contribution in kind as housekeeper, wife and mother[210] and it has been exceptionally important in this regard. This is first because it marks out a different approach to how provision should be made for a spouse as compared with the more rigid rules governing property law[211] and secondly because, since *White v White*[212] the evaluation of 'contributions' has become steadily more non-discriminatory towards women. It is important to trace this development.

Initially, after the House of Lords' decision, there was an attempt, at first by respondents, to justify a departure from the 'yardstick of equality' on the basis that one spouse had made a bigger contribution to the welfare of the family than the other. This might be shown by, for example, bringing money into the marriage, from which the family business was built up[213] or by the particular business acumen displayed by the husband. In *Cowan v Cowan*[214] for example, the husband spotted the potential of plastic bin liners in revolutionising waste collection and disposal and set up companies to supply and market these to local authorities and supermarkets. The Court of Appeal awarded the wife 38% of the combined assets, justifying their departure from equality by virtue of the husband's special business talent, described by his counsel as a 'stellar' contribution. This ruling led to a number of cases where the spouses argued over whether or not the husband could be said to have been exceptionally gifted in business.[215] In *L v L (Financial Provision: Contributions)*[216] the wife was awarded only 37% of the assets, the husband being characterised as having made a special or exceptional contribution through his business, although 'he was not a genius'. By contrast, in *H-J v H-J (Financial Provision: Equality)*[217] and *G v G (Financial Provision: Equal Division)*[218] Coleridge J declined to regard one

---

[209] [2011] EWCA Civ 550 [2011] 2 FLR 980 at [15]. Query, however: would a wife have been treated in this way had the husband inherited the shares? See M Hatwood and L Hewitt 'Do family courts in England and Wales discriminate against husbands?' [2012] Fam Law 674.

[210] See eg *Duxbury v Duxbury* [1992] Fam 62n, CA (a wife who had done 'everything expected of her as a wife and mother' was entitled to have her contribution recognised by the court). See also *Vicary v Vicary* [1992] 2 FLR 271, CA, where the wife's lump sum was assessed by reference to her acting as an 'unimpeachable wife and mother', enabling the husband to concentrate on his business activities.

[211] See Ch 5, Ownership, pp 123–144.   [212] [2001] 1 AC 596.

[213] As in *White v White* itself, where the husband's father lent the couple money to help acquire the first of their farms. See also *Dharamshi v Dharamshi* [2001] 1 FLR 736 (husband's business success aided by his family).   [214] [2001] EWCA Civ 679 [2002] Fam 97.

[215] Or, in *Norris v Norris* [2002] EWHC 2996 (Fam), [2003] 1 FLR 1142, whether the contribution of the wife, both in lending her inherited wealth to the husband's business and looking after the child of the marriage, could be regarded as exceptional.   [216] [2002] 1 FLR 642.   [217] [2002] 1 FLR 415.

[218] [2002] EWHC 1339 (Fam) [2002] 2 FLR 1143.

spouse's contribution as greater than the other, regarding attempts to distinguish between the spouses as contrary to the principles underlying *White v White* and as opening 'a forensic Pandora's box'.[219] The matter was resolved when *L v L* went on appeal as *Lambert v Lambert*.[220] The Court of Appeal firmly attempted to close Pandora's box to forestall further attempts to distinguish, apart from in the most exceptional of cases, between the different contributions of the spouses. Thorpe LJ commented:

> the danger of gender discrimination resulting from a finding of special financial contribution is plain. If all that is regarded is the scale of the breadwinner's success then discrimination is almost bound to follow since there is no equal opportunity for the homemaker to demonstrate the scale of her comparable success. Examples cited of the mother who cares for a handicapped child seem to me both theoretical and distasteful. Such sacrifices and achievements are the product of love and commitment and are not to be counted in cash. The more driven the breadwinner the less available will he be physically and emotionally both as a husband and a father.[221]

In awarding the wife 50% of the combined assets, the court held that, once the trial judge had rejected the argument that the husband was a business genius, and had accepted that the wife could not have done any more to contribute to the welfare of the family, he should not have elevated the husband's contribution above that of the wife. As previously noted, when civil partnerships and same-sex marriages are dissolved, it may be even harder to distinguish between the parties' respective contributions.

Since *Lambert*, it may be said that the spouses' contributions are more likely to be regarded as being of equal worth, regardless of the form they have taken, and an equal division of surplus assets has become more common.[222] In *Miller v Miller; McFarlane v McFarlane*[223] their Lordships agreed that the correct approach is to regard contribution as a factor pointing away from equality of division only when it would be inequitable to do otherwise. In so holding, they drew, as will be seen, on the approach taken to 'conduct' under s 25(2)(g).

However, there remains significant scope for the claim to be made and in *Charman v Charman (No 4)*[224] the Court of Appeal pointed out that, given the express reference to contribution in the statute, it could not be made subject to a blanket rule that all contributions must be treated equally. In that case, the parties had agreed that all of the wealth enjoyed by the family, valued at £131m, all of which was 'matrimonial property', came from the husband's 'special contribution' as a successful businessman who had started the marriage (which had lasted 28 years) with nothing. The Court upheld Coleridge J's award to the wife of £40m (36.5% of the total including £8m in her own name) as appropriately recognising the husband's contribution, and suggested that where such a 'special'

---

[219] [2002] EWHC 1339 (Fam) [2002] 2 FLR 1143 at [34].

[220] [2002] EWCA Civ 1685 [2003] 1 FLR 139. See R Bailey-Harris, '*Lambert v Lambert*—Towards the recognition of marriage as a partnership of equals' [2003] CFLQ 417. See also *Parlour v Parlour* [2004] 2 FLR 904 at [40]: the husband was a premier league footballer whose talent enabled him to command a very high salary but the wife had made a significant contribution in promoting his career by encouraging him to curb his heavy drinking.   [221] [2002] EWCA Civ 1685 [2003] 1 FLR 139 at [45].

[222] See eg *Norris v Norris; C v C (Variation of Post-Nuptial Settlement: Company Shares)* [2003] EWHC 1222 (Fam) [2003] 2 FLR 493. One would certainly expect a wife such as Lady Conran to obtain a significantly higher proportion of the assets than she did in *Conran v Conran* [1997] 2 FLR 615, discussed earlier, 'Big money' cases, p 890.

[223] [2006] UKHL 24 [2006] 3 All ER 1. See Lord Nicholls at [68] and Baroness Hale at [146].

[224] [2007] EWCA Civ 503 [2007] 1 FLR 1246.

contribution is established, it should be acknowledged by an unequal division of the relevant assets in a range between 66.6% and 33.3% at the most, and 45%–55% at the least.[225]

The Court recognised that the 'notion of a special contribution to the welfare of the family will not successfully have been purged of inherent gender discrimination unless it is accepted that such a contribution can, in principle, take a number of forms; that it can be non-financial as well as financial; and that it can thus be made by a party whose role has been exclusively that of a home-maker.' But it went on to note that 'Nevertheless in practice, . . . the claim to have made a special contribution seems so far to have arisen only in cases of substantial wealth generated by a party's success in business during the marriage. The self-evident reason is that in such cases there is substantial property over the distribution of which it is worthwhile to argue.'[226]

Wilson LJ used this dictum to argue in *K v L (Non-Matrimonial Property: Special Contribution)*[227] that a 'special contribution' is 'now a term of art in the law of ancillary relief which is used to describe a contribution entirely different from that of non-matrimonial property.' He considered that it arises in circumstances in which a spouse's contribution, direct or indirect, to the creation of *matrimonial* property has been so *extraordinary* as to dictate a departure within the sharing principle from the *ordinary* consequence of its equal division.' But while the Court apparently pays lip service to the need to recognise the home-maker and non-financial role, if a 'special contribution' which is going to justify the unequal division of assets can actually only be made through the creation of 'property', i.e. wealth, then it takes us right back to the trap of gender discrimination identified by Thorpe LJ in *Lambert v Lambert*.

What of the case, however, where one spouse has *not* made a contribution (or any sufficient contribution) to the welfare of the family? Should he or she be penalised by being awarded a reduced settlement? In *H v H*[228] a wife who had left her husband for another man after 15 years of married life and bringing up four children was given a smaller award on the ground that she had 'left the job unfinished' and in *E v E (Financial Provision)*[229] it was said that the wife, who had committed adultery, had made a negative, or minimal, contribution. But in *W v W*[230] Wilson J held that such terms are unhelpful when weighing each spouse's contribution under s 25(2)(f) and should be raised, if at all, as 'conduct' under s 25(2)(g). He accordingly attached no weight to the husband's allegation that the wife, who was a recovering alcoholic, had made a 'negative contribution' during her years of drinking.

7. CONDUCT

(g) The conduct of each of the parties, if that conduct is such that it would in the opinion of the court be inequitable to disregard it

The extent to which the court should take a spouse's conduct during the marriage into account when assessing what order should be made is understandably an emotionally charged issue. Yet even before 1971, when the substantive law was based upon the concept

---

[225] [2007] EWCA Civ 503 [2007] 1 FLR 1246 at [90]. See also *Sorrell v Sorrell* [2005] EWHC 1717 (Fam), [2006] 1 FLR 497: husband who had built up a business from a small base to a worldwide enterprise worth over £7 billion had talent amounting to genius justifying a departure from equality; wife received 40% of assets worth £75m after a marriage of 32 years.

[226] [2007] EWCA Civ 503 [2007] 1 FLR 1246 at [80].

[227] [2011] EWCA Civ 550 [2011] 2 FLR 980 at [20], [21].

[228] [1975] Fam 9; cf *West v West* [1978] Fam 1, CA.   [229] [1990] 2 FLR 233.

[230] [2001] Fam Law 656.

of matrimonial fault, there had been a tendency by the courts, when hearing undefended cases, to place much less stress on the technical finding of innocence or guilt. When irretrievable breakdown became the sole ground for divorce in 1971, conduct arguably became of much less significance. The law was subject to further change in 1984 and again in 1996, but the latter amendment, contained in the Family Law Act, was never implemented.[231]

(a) The law before the 1984 reform

Under s 25 as originally enacted, the court was directed, inter alia, to exercise its powers so:

> . . . to place the parties, so far as it is practicable and, *having regard to their conduct just to do so*, in the financial position in which they would have been if the marriage had not broken down and each had properly discharged his or her financial obligation and responsibilities towards the other.[232]

It soon became apparent that 'conduct' should not often be taken into account. The basic principle was established in the leading case, *Wachtel v Wachtel*,[233] in which Lord Denning MR, delivering the judgment of the court, said:[234]

> It has been suggested that there should be a 'discount' or 'reduction' in what the wife is to receive because of her supposed misconduct, guilt or blame (whatever word is used). We cannot accept this argument. In the vast majority of cases it is repugnant to the principles underlying the new legislation . . . There will be many cases in which a wife (though once considered guilty or blameworthy) will have cared for the home and looked after the family for many years. Is she to be deprived of the benefit otherwise to be accorded to her by s 25(1)(f) because she may share responsibility for the breakdown with her husband? There will no doubt be a residue of cases where the conduct of one of the parties is . . . 'both obvious and gross', so much so that to order one party to support another whose conduct falls into this category is repugnant to anyone's sense of justice. In such a case the court remains free to decline to afford financial support or to reduce the support which it would otherwise have ordered. But, short of cases falling into this category, the court should not reduce its order for financial provision merely because of what was formerly regarded as guilt or blame. To do so would be to impose a fine for supposed misbehaviour in the course of an unhappy married life . . . In the financial adjustments consequent upon the dissolution of a marriage which has irretrievably broken down, the imposition of financial penalties ought seldom to find a place.

In brief, conduct would not affect the order made unless it would be offensive to one's sense of justice to ignore it.[235]

In view of this discussion, it is hardly surprising that conduct was rarely taken into account. Matrimonial misconduct such as adultery was usually ignored,[236] as were 'brief periods of callous unkindness or brutality'.[237] But of course there were some cases where

---

[231] Family Law Act 1996 s 66(1) and Sch 8 Pt I para 9(2) repealed by Children and Families Act 2014 s 18(2)(e).
[232] Emphasis added.
[233] [1973] Fam 72, CA. For discussion, see G Douglas 'Bringing an end to the matrimonial post mortem: *Wachtel v Wachtel* and its enduring significance for ancillary relief' in S Gilmore, J Herring and R Probert (eds) *Landmark Cases in Family Law* (2011).   [234] At 90.
[235] Per Orr LJ in *Jones v Jones* [1976] Fam 8 at 15, CA.
[236] See eg *Trippas v Trippas* [1973] Fam 134, CA and *Harnett v Harnett* [1974] 1 All ER 764, CA.
[237] *Griffiths v Griffiths* [1974] 1 All ER 932.

conduct was held to be relevant.[238] Amongst reported cases, the wife's share was reduced where she had accepted a half-share of the matrimonial home whilst carrying on an adulterous affair,[239] where she had fired a shotgun at her husband,[240] and where she had twice wounded her husband and damaged his career by her behaviour.[241]

(b) The law after the 1984 reform

Although the courts sought to disregard conduct except in extreme cases, Parliament regarded it as a matter that ought more regularly to be taken into account. In 1984, with the removal of the status quo ideal or minimal loss principle, conduct was reintroduced as a new s 25(2)(g) of the Matrimonial Causes Act 1973.[242] The court was directed to have regard to 'the conduct of each of the parties, if that conduct is such that it would in the opinion of the court be inequitable to disregard it'. It could have been said that, since conduct now stood as a separate circumstance to which the court had 'in particular' to have regard, it had been given greater statutory emphasis. In the event, however, there was no change in practice: the courts continued to restrict recognition of 'conduct' to grave and exceptional instances. In one reported case, *Anthony v Anthony*,[243] where the trial judge took conduct into account because, in his view, the wife 'broke up the marriage', the Court of Appeal held that there was nothing in her conduct of such a serious nature as to justify any reliance upon it. In *Leadbeater v Leadbeater*,[244] conduct was again dismissed as an issue, in part because each spouse's conduct cancelled the other's out, but mainly because the judge did not think it inequitable to ignore it. On the other side of the line is *Kyte v Kyte*,[245] where the husband suffered from manic depression, which caused the wife suffering and unhappiness. On several occasions the husband tried, unsuccessfully, to commit suicide. The registrar found that on one of these occasions the wife (who knew she stood to inherit on the husband's death) did nothing to stop him. On another she provided drugs and alcohol to facilitate the attempt. The wife had also formed 'a deceitful relationship' with another man. In the Court of Appeal, Purchas LJ (giving the judgment of the court) said[246] that a spouse should only be penalised where the imbalance of conduct, one way or the other, would make it inequitable to ignore the comparative conduct of the parties. On this basis, the wife's behaviour (even when considered in the context of the husband's) was gross and obvious and so her lump sum award was reduced from £14,000 to just £5,000.

Where one spouse commits a criminal offence against the other, conduct, unsurprisingly, will be taken into account. In *Evans v Evans*,[247] for example, the Court of Appeal upheld the discharge of a periodical payments order in favour of a wife when she was convicted of inciting others to kill her husband. In *H v H (Financial Relief: Attempted Murder as Conduct)*[248] the husband stabbed the wife so severely that the trial judge regarded her

---

[238] See also *Kokosinski v Kokosinski* [1980] Fam 72 where 'good' conduct was taken into account.

[239] *Cuzner v Underdown* [1974] 2 All ER 351, CA (wife ordered to transfer the half-share to husband).

[240] *Armstrong v Armstrong* (1974) 4 Fam Law 156, CA (wife's share reduced to a quarter). A comparison of this case with the last suggests that the courts looked more leniently on a wife who intended to inflict serious injury on a husband than on one who was unfaithful!   [241] *Bateman v Bateman* [1979] Fam 25.

[242] As a result of an amendment made under the Matrimonial and Family Proceedings Act 1984 s 3.

[243] [1986] 2 FLR 353, CA.

[244] [1985] FLR 789; cf *Suter v Suter and Jones* [1987] Fam 111, CA, where there is some suggestion that introducing a lover into the former matrimonial home could be taken into account under s 25(2)(g); but contrast *Duxbury v Duxbury* [1992] Fam 62n, CA where Ackner LJ said that applying s 25 is essentially a 'financial not a moral exercise'.   [245] [1988] Fam 145, CA.

[246] At 155.

[247] [1989] 1 FLR 351, CA. See also *H v H (Financial Provision: Conduct)* [1994] 2 FLR 801 (husband's conduct in brutally assaulting wife taken into account) and *A v A (Financial Provision: Conduct)* [1995] 1 FLR 345 (husband's assault upon wife was conduct which was taken into account but not so as to deprive the husband of all his capital).   [248] [2005] EWHC 2911 (Fam) [2006] 1 FLR 990.

survival as miraculous. She was granted the entire equity in the former matrimonial home and the rest of the parties' assets, apart from the husband's personal belongings, in exchange for his receiving a lump sum of £30,000, so that she could have a secure future free from financial worry or pressure.

A perhaps unduly merciful approach was taken, however, in *Clark v Clark*.[249] The wife, in her forties and in debt, married the husband, a wealthy man aged nearly 80. During the six-year marriage, which was never consummated, she induced the husband to purchase properties which were put in her name, introduced her lover into the house and confined the husband to a caravan in the grounds, and then a part of the house. The trial judge considered that, although the wife's conduct was inequitable to disregard, it would be unduly harsh to leave her with nothing and he also noted the husband's generosity to her during the marriage. He awarded her a lump sum of around £500,000 out of the husband's worth of £2.5 million. The Court of Appeal commented that it would be hard to conceive of a case of graver marital misconduct and noted that to have left the wife with nothing would not have exceeded the wide ambit of judicial discretion. They nonetheless awarded the wife £175,000, to which the husband had been prepared to agree.

The misconduct may be aimed at the spouse in his or her capacity as a parent of the children of the marriage, rather than directly against him or her. For example, abduction of the children of the marriage has also been held to be conduct that it would be inequitable to disregard. In *Al-Khatib v Masry*[250] Munby J held that the husband's conduct in abducting the children and 'depriving them and the wife of that most basic human right, their mutual society, falls squarely within the class of case contemplated by Parliament when enacting s 25(2)(g) of the 1973 Act.'[251]

It should be noted that the conduct to which the court may have regard is not restricted to that in relation to the breakdown of the marriage: it also embraces conduct in the context of the proceedings themselves. Whilst misconduct in the proceedings is usually reflected in the court's order for costs,[252] on occasion it influences the amount of the award the court makes. For example, in *Al Khatib v Masry*[253] the husband also refused to file a Form E or any other formal evidence, would not answer questions and refused to attend court. Transactions purporting to transfer shares in properties were found to be shams. When he finally did file a Form E, the wife was able to identify a number of specific instances of non-disclosure and inconsistency. The husband's wealth was therefore estimated at comfortably in excess of £50 million, of which the wife was awarded £23 million.

On numerous occasions in the debates on the Family Law Bill in 1996 the concern was expressed that the courts were reluctant to take into account conduct in relation to the making of financial and property orders. An amendment to s 25(2)(g) was passed, in an attempt '. . . to emphasise that conduct of the parties of whatever nature, should it be inequitable for the court to disregard it, has to be considered and that it is not only conduct in the course of ancillary relief proceedings that is to be considered.'[254] It inserted the additional wording '. . . whatever the nature of the conduct and whether it occurred

---

[249] [1999] 2 FLR 498, CA.   [250] [2002] EWHC 108 (Fam) [2002] 1 FLR 1053.

[251] [2002] EWHC 108 (Fam) [2002] 1 FLR 1053 at para 103. See also *B v B (Financial Provision: Welfare of Child and Conduct)* [2002] 1 FLR 555: husband had abducted child to Italy and been imprisoned for the offence.

[252] See eg *Tavoulareas v Tavoulareas* [1998] 2 FLR 418, CA; *Young v Young* [1998] 2 FLR 1131, CA. See also *FZ v SZ and Others (Ancillary Relief: Conduct: Valuations)* [2010] EWHC 1630 (Fam) [2011] 1 FLR 64 where each party's conduct was taken into account—thus, in effect, cancelling out the other's. Mostyn J warned that he might choose to penalise them appropriately in costs.

[253] [2002] EWHC 108 (Fam) [2002] 1 FLR 1053.

[254] Standing Committee E, Official Report, 16 May 1996, Col 370.

during the marriage or after the separation of the parties or (as the case may be) dissolution or annulment of the marriage'. The potential impact of this provision was difficult to assess. It sat uneasily with the greater emphasis in the Family Law Act on irretrievable breakdown as the sole criterion of the failure of the marriage, and on mediated settlements and compromise. With the decision not to implement Part II of the 1996 Act, such speculation has become irrelevant.

However, it seemed for a while that the courts themselves were recognising that 'conduct' might be a relevant factor, even if not 'obvious and gross'. In *Miller v Miller*[255] the Court of Appeal agreed with the trial judge that the husband's conduct in leaving the wife for another woman entitled the trial judge to attach less weight to the short duration of the marriage than he would have done otherwise.[256] The House of Lords firmly rejected this[257] and endorsed the long-standing principle that only 'obvious and gross' conduct should be regarded as affecting the outcome.

8. LOSS OF BENEFIT

(h) In the case of proceedings for divorce or nullity of marriage, the value to each of the parties to the marriage of any benefit (for example, a pension) which, by reason of the dissolution or annulment of the marriage, that party will lose the chance of acquiring[258]

As we have seen, the court has power to make financial provision and pension sharing orders in relation to pensions. But even where a pension sharing or attachment order is not made, the loss of the pension may still be 'offset' in determining the share of the available assets that the parties are to receive. It is common for the wife to receive the matrimonial home in return for not seeking a share of the husband's pension, for example.[259]

One additional right that a divorced wife loses is that of claiming certain social security benefits by virtue of her husband's contributions; another is the loss of an entitlement on the husband's intestacy. A further example of a lost benefit is to be seen in *Trippas v Trippas*.[260] After the parties had separated, the husband received a considerable sum from the sale of a family business. The court awarded the wife a lump sum of £10,000 on the ground that, had the marriage still been on foot, she would have received such a benefit either directly in cash or indirectly in kind; furthermore, the husband could have been expected to leave her a large sum if he had predeceased her, so that she had lost something analogous to a pension.

D. THE MATRIMONIAL HOME

The matrimonial home presents particular problems which require separate discussion. In many cases (perhaps apart from accrued pension rights) it will be the only

---

[255] [2005] EWCA Civ 984 [2006] 1 FLR 151.

[256] See also *G v G (Financial Provision: Separation Agreement)* [2004] 1 FLR 1011.

[257] *Miller v Miller; McFarlane v McFarlane* [2006] UKHL 24 [2006] 2 AC 618 at [65], [145].

[258] As amended by Pensions Act 1995 s 166(2).

[259] See H Woodward with M Sefton, 'Pensions on divorce: a study on when and how they are taken into account' [2014] Fam Law 509 at 511.

[260] [1973] Fam 134, CA but was not the loss to the wife caused by the breakdown of the marriage, rather than by its dissolution? See also *Kokosinski v Kokosinski* [1980] Fam 72.

asset of any value owned by either spouse. It may be the only means of giving one of the spouses (whom, for the sake of argument, we shall assume to be the wife) the security of a home with the children in the future. Consequently the parties' interests will often be in direct conflict: the wife will wish to be given the right to occupy the house, whilst the husband will want an immediate sale so as to realise his capital, without which he may be unable to buy another home (perhaps for his second family). Faced with this, and given that the court's first consideration must be the welfare of the children, it must seek to ensure that the children (and therefore the spouse with whom the children are living) have a home.[261]

We now consider the various ways in which the court may use the wide range of powers that it has at its disposal.

(a) Transfer of share to the other spouse in return for compensation

The court may require one spouse to transfer his or her share to the other and order the other to pay a lump sum equal to its value or of a reduced amount.[262] This is often a good solution because the spouse—often the wife—retains a roof over her head and the other gets the immediate use of his money. Obviously, however, such an order can be made only if the spouse has sufficient capital or, alternatively, a large enough income to pay the sum in instalments, or to raise it by borrowing (usually secured by mortgage on the property).[263] If, however, the husband does not need the capital immediately, the payment can be deferred until the house is sold.[264]

(b) Outright transfer of share to other spouse with no compensation

The court can order the husband to transfer his share of the home to the wife without any compensating payment on her part. There are a number of quite dissimilar situations in which this may offer the best solution. If the house forms only part of the capital assets which have to be apportioned, it may be transferred to the wife in part or complete satisfaction of her claim for a lump sum or other capital settlement. Again, if the husband is wealthy, the wife might take the house as representing the capitalisation of part, or all of her claim for periodical payments which will be proportionately reduced or, in a suitable case, discharged altogether, thereby achieving an 'immediate' clean break. It might also be felt desirable to capitalise periodical payments if the husband's past behaviour indicated that any other order might prove to be ineffective.[265] At the other end of the economic scale, if the husband's earnings are so small that it will be impossible for him to make an adequate contribution towards the support of the wife and children of the family, the only possible solution might be to transfer the matrimonial home to her unconditionally and make no order, or only a minimal order, against him for periodical payments.[266] Even if the parties are not at either extreme of the economic spectrum, the particular circumstances may make it necessary to order a transfer of the matrimonial home without payment, but with a compensating reduction or forgoing of periodical payments, as the only way of ensuring that either of them has a home[267] and it is common for

---

[261] *Browne v Pritchard* [1975] 3 All ER 721 at 724, CA; *Scott v Scott* [1978] 3 All ER 65, CA. See E Hitchings 'Everyday cases in this post-*White* era' [2008] Fam Law 873 at 874.
[262] *Mortimer v Mortimer-Griffin* [1986] 2 FLR 315, CA.
[263] *Wachtel v Wachtel* [1973] Fam 72 at 96.
[264] *Mesher v Mesher and Hall* (1973) reported [1980] 1 All ER 126n, CA. See later, *Mesher* orders p 905.
[265] As in *Bryant v Bryant* (1976) 6 Fam Law 108, CA.   [266] *S v S* [1976] Fam 18n.
[267] *Hanlon v Hanlon* [1978] 2 All ER 889, CA.

a spouse to offset a claim to a share of the husband's pension by receiving a larger part, or all, of the equity in the home.

(c) Postponing sale of the home until a specified event

Mesher orders

The order may provide that both spouses shall keep or acquire an interest in the house as equitable tenants in common (with shares which may or may not be equal, depending upon the circumstances), which will involve settling it on them on trust (if it is not already so held), with sale of the home to take place at some specified time in the future. In the meantime the wife will be given exclusive possession. Such an order enables both spouses to keep their interest in the capital, but also resolves the immediate problem of accommodation for the wife and the children. The commonest type of this order is referred to as a *Mesher* order.[268] This provides that the sale of the property should not take place until the youngest child reaches a specified age or, now more likely, until all the children have completed their (university) education, or until further order.[269]

Mesher orders have a number of complications and have been criticised by the courts.[270] In the first place, the husband and wife will have to act together to effect the sale, perhaps many years after the divorce, and this may cause difficulties, particularly if their relationship is bitter.[271] Secondly, children often do not leave home until long after they have completed their education and may therefore still need the house as their home. Thirdly, being 'property transfer orders' they are not variable even if, for example, the husband reneges on his obligation to make periodical payments.[272] Finally, and perhaps most significantly, a *Mesher* order may lead to a wife being thrown on the housing market in later life, after her children have left home, without the capital or income to secure adequate alternative accommodation for herself. There is evidence that the *McFarlane* case may have prompted some reconsideration of the merits of *Mesher* orders where there is sufficient wealth to ensure these pitfalls can be avoided,[273] but, given the emphasis on the yardstick of equality in *White v White*,[274] if such an order will produce significant inequality of outcome between the parties as to their eventual capital positions when the sale takes place, or there is doubt as to whether the wife will be able to re-house herself, then it should not be made.[275]

Martin orders

A different order, in effect, if not in form, is a *Martin* order. As with the *Mesher* order, the matrimonial home is settled upon the spouses on trust for themselves as beneficial

---

[268] From the name of the case in which such an order was made, *Mesher v Mesher and Hall* (1973) reported [1980] 1 All ER 126n, CA.

[269] It is important that the court should retain the option of ordering an earlier sale in case the wife remarries or some unforeseen event occurs.

[270] See eg *Hanlon v Hanlon* [1978] 2 All ER 889 at 892–3, CA, per Ormrod LJ; *Carson v Carson* [1983] 1 All ER 478 at 482–3, CA per Ormrod LJ; and *Harman v Glencross* [1986] 1 All ER 545 at 556, CA per Balcombe LJ; *Mortimer v Mortimer-Griffin* [1986] 2 FLR 315 at 319, CA per Parker LJ.

[271] For problems relating to the need for repairs to the house: see *Harvey v Harvey* [1987] 1 FLR 67. See also *S v B (Ancillary Relief: Costs)* [2004] EWHC 2089 (Fam) [2005] 1 FLR 474 [2005] 1 FLR 474; *Tattersall v Tattersall* [2013] EWCA Civ 774 [2014] 1 FLR 997.

[272] As in *Carson v Carson*. See also *Dinch v Dinch* [1987] 1 All ER 818, HL.

[273] See eg *Dorney-Kingdom v Dorney-Kingdom* [2000] 2 FLR 855, CA; E Hitchings 'Everyday Cases in the Post-*White* Era' [2008] Fam Law 873 at p 876. [274] [2001] 1 AC 596, HL.

[275] *B v B (Mesher Order)* [2002] EWHC 3106 (Fam) [2003] 2 FLR 285.

tenants in common. However, the contingent events specified in the order as triggering a sale are designed to ensure that the wife remains in occupation of the house for as long as she needs a roof over her head. In *Martin v Martin*[276] the husband had left to live with another woman in a council house of which the latter was the tenant and which would apparently be transferred to them both jointly. The wife was left alone in the former matrimonial home which belonged to both spouses beneficially in equal shares. The Court of Appeal affirmed the judge's order that the house should be held on trust for the wife during her life, or until her remarriage or such earlier date as she should cease to live there and thereafter on trust for them both in equal shares. The husband was already provided with another home and consequently had no need of the capital; the wife, on the other hand, would have been unable to purchase alternative accommodation with her half-share of the capital and so an immediate sale would have deprived her of the modest comfortable home that she had before the marriage broke down.[277]

(d) Transfer with charge on the home

The court may order the husband to transfer his interest to the wife and give him a charge on the house equal to the value of his share (or for some other proportion).[278] The charge should not be realised until the wife no longer needs to live in the house and it can be sold. This solution is to be preferred because the husband will not have to concur in the sale and the spouses can make a clean break.[279] His charge should represent a given fraction of the value of the house at the time of the sale;[280] if it is fixed by reference to its present value, the sum which the husband will eventually receive will not have increased to take account of inflation.

(e) Immediate sale and division of proceeds

The court could order the house to be sold[281] and the proceeds to be divided in such proportions as it thinks fit. This might be the best way of dealing with the situation if there were no children living at home, or it is necessary for both spouses to 'downsize' to stretch their limited capital further. The money should be sufficient to give at least one of them (and preferably both) enough to put down as a deposit on the purchase of a new house or flat.

---

[276] *Martin v Martin* [1978] Fam 12, CA, cf *Eshak v Nowojewski* (1980) 11 Fam Law 115, CA: sale deferred until death of husband who had custody of children and was unable to work; wife had remarried and her second husband was catering for her needs. See also *Clutton v Clutton* [1991] 1 All ER 340, CA: sale to take place on death, remarriage or cohabitation of wife, whereupon proceeds to be divided two-thirds to wife and one-third to husband. For criticism of the *Clutton* Order, see M Hayes 'Cohabitation Clauses in Financial Provision and Property Adjustment Orders—Law, Policy and Justice' (1994) 110 LQR 124.

[277] The implications for legally aided parties of the statutory charge (discussed in Ch 22, Statutory charge, p 863) must not be overlooked.

[278] There is no express statutory power in the Matrimonial Causes Act 1973, Pt II to *order* a spouse to execute a charge over the former matrimonial home, or *impose* a charge on property ordered to be transferred from one spouse to another. However, it appears such orders can be effected by imposing conditions on the exercise of the express powers in Pt II (eg H can be ordered to *transfer* Whiteacre to W *upon condition* W executes a charge in favour of H) or, alternatively, they can be incorporated into consent orders formulated as undertakings given to the court following *Livesey (formerly Jenkins) v Jenkins* [1985] AC 424, HL.

[279] See *Schuller v Schuller* [1990] 2 FLR 193, CA.

[280] As in *Browne v Pritchard* [1975] 3 All ER 721, CA.

[281] Under s 24A of the Matrimonial Causes Act 1973.

(f) Transfer of tenancy

In respect of rented property, the court may make an order transferring a protected statutory, secure or assured tenancy[282] from one spouse to the other.[283] If the spouses are joint tenants, the court has a similar power to extinguish the interest of one of them and vest the tenancy exclusively in the other.[284]

The Family Law Act 1996 sets out guidelines to which the court must have regard when deciding whether to order a transfer.[285] The court must consider the circumstances in which the tenancy was granted to either or both parties, or the circumstances in which either or both became a tenant under the tenancy. It must also take into account the respective housing needs and resources of the parties and any relevant child,[286] the parties' financial resources, the likely effect of transferring or not transferring the tenancy on the health, safety or well-being of the parties and any relevant child, and the suitability of the parties as tenants.[287] The Law Commission, on whose recommendations these provisions are based,[288] drew an analogy with the case-law governing orders for sale of property under what is now the Trusts of Land and Appointment of Trustees Act 1996 ss 14–15.[289] In exercising its powers, the court is entitled to have regard to the local authority's housing policy, and its likely impact on the parties, and their separate prospects of re-housing.[290]

A transfer takes effect as a compulsory assignment, and the transferee takes subject to all the benefits and burdens of the covenants and the transferor ceases to be liable under them,[291] in the absence of a court order directing otherwise.[292] The Family Law Act also gave an additional power to the court to order the applicant to pay either immediate, or deferred, compensation to the transferor of the tenancy, by lump sum or instalments. In deciding whether to exercise the power to make an order for compensation, the court must have regard to all the circumstances, including the financial loss that would otherwise be suffered by the transferor, the financial needs and resources of the parties, and their present and future financial obligations to each other and any relevant child.[293] The

---

[282] See C Hunter and S Blandy 'Relationship breakdown, women and tenants' rights—choice or paternalism' [2004] CFLQ 165; M Davis and D Hughes 'An End of the Affair—Social Housing, Relationship Breakdown, and the Human Rights Act 1998' [2004] Conv 19.

[283] Family Law Act 1996 s 53 and Sch 7 as amended by the Civil Partnership Act 2004 Sch 9. The landlord must be given an opportunity to be heard: 1996 Act Sch 7 para 14(1). Orders for transfer of tenancies other than *statutory* tenancies may be made under s 24 of the Matrimonial Causes Act 1973 (see eg *Jones v Jones* [1997] 1 FLR 27, CA) but Sch 7 is the preferred route due to its more detailed provisions.

[284] Family Law Act 1996 Sch 7 para 8(1)–(2). The transfer order may not take effect before the decree of nullity or divorce is made absolute or the order is made final, in the case of nullity or dissolution of a civil partnership: Family Law Act 1996 Sch 7 para 12(a)(b) as amended by the Civil Partnership Act 2004 Sch 9 para 17. An application may not be made if the applicant has remarried or formed a(nother) civil partnership: Sch 7 para 13 as amended by the 2004 Act Sch 9 para 18.   [285] Sch 7 para 5.

[286] Defined by s 63(2) as a child who is living with, or who might reasonably be expected to live with either party to the proceedings; or whose welfare is in question in Children Act or Adoption and Children Act proceedings, or whose interests the court considers relevant.

[287] Section 33(6)(a)–(c) and Sch 7 para 5(c). Conduct may also be considered: *Lake v Lake* [2006] EWCA Civ 1250 [2007] 1 FLR 427.

[288] Law Com No 207, *Domestic Violence and Occupation of the Family Home* (1992) paras 6.3–6.9.

[289] Discussed in Ch 5, The court's powers under s 14 of the Trusts of Land and Appointment of Trustees Act 1996, p 144.

[290] *Jones v Jones* [1997] 1 FLR 27, CA.

[291] Family Law Act 1996 Sch 7 para 7(1)–(2).   [292] Family Law Act 1996 Sch 7 para 11.

[293] Sch 7 para 10(4).

matters which might be relevant could range from the payment of removal expenses, to the transferor's loss of his right to buy in respect of a secure tenancy.

E. APPEALS

1. APPEAL

Given the breadth of the court's powers and the width of its discretion, every case will turn on its particular facts, and there will frequently be a variety of outcomes that might be arrived at. The costs of matrimonial litigation may be extremely high and an appeal may do little to improve an outcome for a disappointed party, even if he or she 'wins'. The courts therefore take a restrictive approach to permitting appeals. The Family Procedure Rules 2010 r 30.3(7) provides that permission may only be given where the court considers that the appeal would have a real prospect of success; or there is some other compelling reason why the appeal should be heard. A real prospect of success means a realistic, rather than fanciful, one.[294]

Even if permission is granted, the test for allowing the appeal is a narrow one. In *Piglowska v Piglowski*,[295] the parties' costs equalled the value of the assets they were fighting over. The House of Lords applied its earlier ruling in *G v G*[296] to the effect that it is 'only where a lower court's decision exceeds the generous ambit within which reasonable disagreement is possible, and is, in fact, plainly wrong, that an appellate body is entitled to interfere.'[297] Lord Hoffmann noted that the parties' case had been heard by five differently constituted tribunals, and he commented:

> This cannot be right. To allow successive appeals in the hope of producing an answer which accords with perfect justice is to kill the parties with kindness.[298]

In *Re B (Care Proceedings: Appeal)*[299] in the same context as *G v G* of determining care proceedings, the Supreme Court ruled that the test for allowing an appeal should be whether the lower court had been 'wrong', not 'plainly wrong'. The Court addressed its discussion only to the particular context so that it is not clear whether this approach was intended to apply to other proceedings, including financial proceedings, but in fact, it was foreshadowed in the Family Procedure Rules 2010 r 30.12(3) which states that

> The appeal court will allow an appeal where the decision of the lower court was –
>
> (a) wrong; or
> (b) unjust because of a serious procedural or other irregularity in the proceedings in the lower court.

The appeal is limited to a review of the decision or order of the district judge, unless the judge considers that in the circumstances of the case it would be in the interests of justice to hold a rehearing.[300]

---

[294] *CR v SR (Financial Remedies: Permission to Appeal)* [2013] EWHC 1155 (Fam) [2014] 1 FLR 186 applying *Tanfern Limited v Cameron MacDonald and Another* [2000] 1 WLR 1311; *AV v RM* [2012] EWHC 1173 (Fam) [2012] 2 FLR 709; cf *NLW v ARC* [2012] EWHC 55 (Fam) [2012] 2 FLR 129 where Mostyn J considered that the appellant must show it is more likely than not that the appeal would be allowed.

[295] [1999] 1 WLR 1360, HL.   [296] [1985] 1 WLR 647, HL.

[297] [1985] 1 WLR 647, HL at 228, per Lord Fraser of Tullybelton, quoting Asquith LJ in *Bellenden (formerly Satterthwaite) v Satterthwaite* [1948] 1 All ER 343 at 345.   [298] [1999] 1 WLR 1360, HL at 1373.

[299] [2013] UKSC 33 [2013] 2 FLR 1075.   [300] Family Procedure Rules 2010 Part 30.

2. APPEAL OUT OF TIME

In exceptional circumstances it is possible to obtain leave to appeal out of time. This may be the only option in cases where, whether upon a consent order or a contested one, a clean break order has been made. Of course, the whole point of a clean break order or a property adjustment order is that there should be a final settlement between the parties. Nevertheless, circumstances may subsequently occur that so fundamentally change the position that in all justice the order should be reopened. It seems established, however, that, in the absence of fraud, misrepresentation or material non-disclosure,[301] or a fundamental mistake common to both parties, events occurring after the making of an order only give grounds for appeal in exceptional circumstances. The leading case is *Barder v Caluori*.[302] Here, in a full and final settlement made with a consent order the husband agreed to transfer to his wife his half-interest in the matrimonial home subject to her taking responsibility for two outstanding mortgages. The order specified that the transfer should take place within 28 days. Neither party gave notice of appeal, but before the order was executed the wife killed both the children and committed suicide. It was held by the House of Lords that because the fundamental assumption on which the order had been made, namely that the wife and children would require a suitable home for a substantial period, had been totally invalidated within so short a time of the original order being made, leave to appeal should be granted. It was further held that the original order should be set aside.

The House of Lords laid down four conditions which must be satisfied if leave to appeal out of time is to be granted from an order for financial provision or property adjustment (whether or not made by consent):

(1) new events must have occurred since the making of the order which have invalidated the basis or assumption upon which the order was made so that the appeal would be certain, or very likely, to succeed;

(2) the new events should have occurred within a relatively short time of the order being made;

(3) the application for leave should be made reasonably promptly;

(4) the grant of leave should not prejudice third parties who have acquired interests in good faith and for value in the property which is the subject of the order.

In Lord Brandon's view, these conditions sought to reconcile two conflicting principles: on the one hand, that there should be finality in litigation and, on the other, that justice requires that cases be decided on their true facts rather than on assumptions or estimates which turn out to be erroneous.[303]

Where the court does grant leave to appeal out of time, it should reassess the order for financial provision or property adjustment afresh, and consider the criteria in s 25(2) of the Matrimonial Causes Act 1973 having regard to all the facts as they are known at the time of the appeal hearing.[304]

Cases applying the *Barder* criteria may be categorised into three groups.

---

[301] In such cases, as in those concerning supervening events, the application to appeal must be made promptly: *Shaw v Shaw* [2002] EWCA Civ 1298 [2002] 2 FLR 1204. [302] [1988] AC 20, HL.

[303] [1988] AC 20, HL at 41. But see Z Saunders,'FPR 2010; In Defence of *Barder*' [2011] Fam Law 1356, who plausibly argues that FPR 2010 r 30.12(3) appears to preclude a *Barder*-type appeal since the first court's decision cannot be regarded as having been 'unjust' or 'wrong' at the time it was made.

[304] *Smith v Smith (Smith Intervening)* [1992] Fam 69, CA; *Garner v Garner* [1992] 1 FLR 573, CA.

(a) Change in the personal circumstances of the spouses

Something highly significant may take place concerning one of the spouses themselves, as in *Barder v Caluori* itself, where the supervening event was the unexpected death of one of the spouses. In *Smith v Smith (Smith Intervening)*,[305] for example, the wife committed suicide six months after the making of a clean break consent order, and the Court of Appeal set the original order aside. By contrast, in *Benson v Benson*[306] the court held that the wife's death 15 months after the making of the order was an event entitling the court to intervene but nonetheless dismissed the husband's application. The husband had delayed his application for over a year, and so had not proceeded with reasonable promptness. In deciding whether application for leave to appeal has been made reasonably promptly, account should be taken of the situation in which the individual finds himself; there should be no unreasonably inflexible rule of thumb.[307]

Less dramatically, there are cases where a spouse has sought leave to appeal out of time where, subsequent to the making of the original order, the other spouse has remarried and vacated the former matrimonial home. In *Wells v Wells*[308] (a case which pre-dated *Barder*), just six months after the husband had been ordered to make a property transfer to provide a home for the wife and children, the wife remarried and began living with her second husband. The Court of Appeal held that these new events had invalidated the basis of the original order, and substituted an order for the sale of the property and the division of the proceeds of sale. In *Dixon v Marchant*[309] by contrast, although the husband had suspected his ex-wife of cohabiting when negotiating with her to capitalise her periodical payments, the majority of the Court of Appeal held that her remarriage, seven months after a consent order was made, did not invalidate the order since its purpose was to achieve a clean break between the parties, as to which the wife's cohabitation was not the crucial factor.

In *S v S (Financial Provision) (Post Divorce Cohabitation)*,[310] the unforeseen event was the reconciliation of the spouses after their divorce, and their subsequent cohabitation. In that case, a consent order was set aside, some 15 years after it was made, where the divorced couple had cohabited in the meanwhile. The judge considered that, in the highly unusual circumstances of the case, the wife had satisfied the *Barder* criteria, since she had applied to set aside the order with reasonable promptness when she realised the relationship had finally broken down. However, in *Hewitson v Hewitson*,[311] the Court of Appeal later doubted whether post-divorce cohabitation could amount to relevant circumstances entitling the court to set aside an order: 'There has to be finality and an end to litigation . . . the umbrella of the dissolved marriage which covers the post-divorce period cannot remain open for ever.'[312]

(b) Change in the law

A further basis upon which it has been argued that the *Barder* criteria apply to justify the setting aside of an earlier order is a change in the law. In *Crozier v Crozier*[313] this argument

---

[305] [1992] Fam 69, CA.   [306] [1996] 1 FLR 692.

[307] Cf *Reid v Reid* [2003] EWHC 2878 (Fam) [2004] 1 FLR 736: wife dying two months after consent order was not reasonably foreseeable and had it been foreseen, a different settlement would have been reached which gave more weight to the husband's needs rather than the wife's contributions after a long marriage.

[308] [1992] 2 FLR 66, CA (decided in 1980). See also *Williams v Lindley* [2005] EWCA Civ 103 [2005] 2 FLR 710: wife became engaged one month after order. Order set aside.

[309] [2008] EWCA Civ 11 [2008] 1 FLR 655, Wall LJ dissented.

[310] [1994] 2 FLR 228.   [311] [1995] 1 FLR 241, CA.

[312] [1995] 1 FLR 241, CA at 244 (per Butler-Sloss LJ). Cf *Hill v Hill* [1998] 1 FLR 198, CA (discussed earlier, Measuring duration, p 894).   [313] [1994] 1 FLR 126.

was rejected. A consent order had been made whereby the husband had transferred his interest in the former matrimonial home to the wife who, in return, had accepted nominal maintenance payments for herself and her child. Following the implementation of the Child Support Act 1991, the husband's maintenance payments for the child, as an absent parent, were substantially increased. Booth J rejected the husband's argument that the 1991 Act, and its new administrative machinery for the assessment and collection of child maintenance, constituted a 'new event' which invalidated the fundamental basis upon which the earlier consent order and capital settlement had been made. The 1991 Act did not alter the position which had existed previously—that parents could not, by agreement or otherwise, throw off their continuing legal liability to support their children. However, in *S v S (Ancillary Relief: Consent Order)*[314] Bracewell J held that the ruling in *White v White*[315] *was* capable of constituting a *Barder* event, because its effect on the outcome in 'big money' cases was very significant and the wife would very likely have received more capital after a long marriage than she had done under the consent order. Nonetheless, the wife failed because, by the time the consent order was made, argument had been heard and judgment reserved in *White v White* and it had been, or should have been, known to her advisers that the House of Lords was due to rule shortly. They could have suspended negotiations pending the House of Lords' judgment. Her Ladyship concluded that the ruling was thus 'foreseeable and the impact avoidable.'[316]

(c) Change in valuation of property

In a large group of cases, it has been argued that a property valuation, which was used by the court in making its original order, has turned out to be inaccurate and unreliable, thus invalidating the basis upon which the order was made. However, whilst some cases have upheld such a claim, the courts have been fearful of 'opening the floodgates' particularly in times of high price volatility, and have thus taken an increasingly robust line in rejecting the argument. An early example of the supportive stance is *Hope-Smith v Hope-Smith*[317] where the husband was ordered to pay to the wife £32,000 out of the proceeds of sale of the former matrimonial home, then valued at £116,000. As a result of the husband's 'wilful conduct and dilatory tactics' the house remained unsold some two years later when it was worth over £200,000. The Court of Appeal held that the *Barder* conditions were satisfied through no fault of the wife.[318] It substituted an order that the wife was to receive 40% of the ultimate net sale proceeds, which would be sufficient to enable her to re-house herself. In contrast, in *Rooker v Rooker*,[319] on broadly similar facts, the court dismissed the wife's appeal because, although the husband had delayed the sale, the wife had not taken proper steps to enforce the original order.

In subsequent cases the courts have adopted a restrictive approach, particularly where the substance of an application is based on little more than that property has turned out to be worth more, or less, than at the date of the court's order. In *Cornick v Cornick*,[320]

---

[314] [2002] EWHC 223 (Fam) [2003] Fam 1.   [315] [2001] 1 AC 596, HL.

[316] [2002] EWHC 223 (Fam) [2003] Fam 1 at [54]. In *Williams v Thompson Leatherdale and Francis* [2008] EWHC 2574 (QB) [2009] 2 FLR 730, it was held that whilst failure to advise of the potential impact of *White v White* on a financial settlement was negligent, the spouse would not have reached a different settlement in the circumstances anyway and so had suffered no loss.   [317] [1989] 2 FLR 56, CA.

[318] See also *Middleton v Middleton* [1998] 2 FLR 821, CA: value of premises used for sub-post office business dropped from around £54,000 to virtually nothing after husband transferred the business to other premises. Consent order set aside because entire basis upon which it had been made had been deliberately frustrated by the husband's actions. Cf *McGladdery v McGladdery* [1999] 2 FLR 1102: wife's refusal to comply with orders 'nowhere near the *Barder* territory'.   [319] [1988] 1 FLR 219, CA.

[320] [1994] 2 FLR 530.

for example, there was a dramatic increase in the value of the husband's shareholdings, the effect of which was to reduce the wife's share of the family wealth from some 51%, at the date of the court order, to just 20% 18 months later. Hale J reviewed earlier authorities, and considered that for the *Barder* principles to apply, something unforeseen and unforeseeable[321] must have happened which dramatically affected the value of assets so as to bring about a substantial change in the balance of assets effected by the court order. This was not such a case, and the sharp increase in the value of the husband's shares was not a 'new event' within the scope of the *Barder* principles. The husband's shares had been properly valued at the date of the hearing and the case-law showed that the property price fluctuations, however dramatic, did not of themselves entitle the court to intervene.

Similarly, in *Myerson v Myerson (No 2)*[322] the husband had wished to retain control over his business rather than release a share in it to his wife, and it was held that he could not complain that the global downturn had caused it to lose significant value such that his share of the matrimonial assets had dropped from 57% to 14%. In an even more striking example, in *S v S (No 2) (Ancillary Relief: Application to Set Aside Order)*[323] the husband 'grew' the business himself but at the time of the divorce, its value was speculative and the trial judge concluded that the wife was not entitled to share in its value going forward. She was awarded around £1.1m including the matrimonial home and part of the husband's pension. The company was sold a year later and the husband received £137m, but it was held that since the judge would not have awarded the wife a share in the business in any event, there was no reason to set aside the order. As has been well said, in summarising these cases, 'It can therefore be said with confidence that the obstacles to any application to set aside on the grounds of an enhanced (or reduced) valuation of an asset are now virtually insurmountable.'[324]

F. VARIATION OF ORDERS

1. ORDERS THAT MAY BE VARIED

The court has power to vary, discharge or suspend any of the following orders and to revive any term suspended:[325]

— maintenance pending suit and any interim order for maintenance;
— periodical payments (secured and unsecured);
— an order relating to instalments in the case of lump sum payments;
— a deferred order made in relation to pensions;
— an order for the settlement (but not the transfer) of property made on or after the grant of a decree of judicial separation;

---

[321] For another judgment focusing on foreseeability, see *Maskell v Maskell* [2001] EWCA Civ 858 [2003] 1 FLR 1138: husband's redundancy not unforeseeable: 'There is nothing permanent about employment of the sort that Mr Maskell held at the date of judgment before the district judge. There are hundreds of thousands of breadwinners who have to face the challenge of the loss of what seems to be secure employment as a result of all sorts of events' per Thorpe LJ at [4].   [322] [2009] EWCA Civ 282 [2009] 2 FLR 147.

[323] [2009] EWHC 2377 (Fam) [2010] 1 FLR 993.

[324] P Moor 'Where Did Our Love Go: Recent Developments in Ancillary Relief' [2011] Fam Law 34.

[325] Matrimonial Causes Act 1973 s 31(1), (2), as amended by the Pensions Act 1995 s 166(3)(a) and the Welfare Reform and Pensions Act 1999 Sch 3 para 7(2). The court may also order any instrument to be varied etc: s 31(3).

— an order for the variation of a marriage settlement made on or after the grant of a decree of judicial separation;

— any order for the sale of property;

— a pension sharing order made at a time before the decree has been made absolute.

Periodical payments are normally variable because if either party's needs or resources change, justice may demand a corresponding change in the amount payable. Accordingly, unless the fixed term for which the court may have ordered periodical payments to continue has expired,[326] an application may be made to vary an order. The principal exception is where the court has expressly added a s 28(1A) direction, ie that the period fixed for the order cannot be extended. As we have already seen, such orders are intended to provide for a 'deferred clean break' between the parties where it is thought that the parties can become financially independent of one another.

On the other hand, once a lump sum has been paid, it cannot be discharged or varied; it would therefore be unfair to the payee if her right to a sum not yet paid could be prejudiced because the court had made things easier for the payer by providing that he could pay the sum in question over a period of time. The same objection cannot be raised, however, to a change in the period or manner in which the instalments are paid, and consequently these can be varied by an alteration of their size or frequency.[327] In *Hamilton v Hamilton*[328] the question arose whether a series of lump sum payments should be regarded as payment of the total sum by instalments ordered under s 23(3)(c)—which would be variable under s 31—or a series of separate lump sums made under s 23(1)(c), which would not. The court had made a consent order whereby the wife would pay the husband five lump sums totalling £450,000 over a four year period. She paid £240,000 but her business got into difficulties and she was unable to pay the rest. The husband brought enforcement proceedings and the wife applied for a variation of the original order arguing that it was a lump sum payable by instalments. Parker J accepted the argument and, finding that if the wife was held to the original order there was a very real risk of bankruptcy, varied the order requiring the wife to pay the sums due in instalments by 2016. The Court of Appeal dismissed the husband's argument that in fact what had been intended was a series of separate lump sums which were not open to variation, because this was not how the order made by the court had been expressed. They recommended that in such situations, the order should include a recital clarifying what the parties intended.

In *Westbury v Sampson* (a claim for professional negligence by the husband's solicitor) Bodey J, with whom the other judges in the Court of Appeal agreed, held that the court may also vary, suspend or discharge the principal sum itself and the Court of Appeal agreed with this point in *Hamilton*.[329] However, he made clear that the goal of finality means that courts should apply a similar approach to this question as when determining whether to re-open an order following supervening events, and that such power must be used 'particularly sparingly'.[330]

---

[326] In *T v T (Financial Provision)* [1988] 1 FLR 480 a periodical payments order in favour of a wife was expressed to take effect until the wife remarried, or the husband retired or until further order. It was held that the wife could not apply for a variation after the husband retired. The words 'or further order' could be relied on for an earlier variation, ie before the happening of the specified event, but not afterwards. The same approach was adopted in *Richardson v Richardson* [1994] 1 FLR 286 and approved by the Court of Appeal in *G v G (Periodical Payments: Jurisdiction)* [1997] 1 FLR 368, CA. Here Ward LJ suggested that one way around the problem would be for a court to make a substantial periodical payments order for a fixed term followed by a nominal order. This, at least, would 'give a peg on which to hang a late variation application'.

[327] *Penrose v Penrose* [1994] 2 FLR 621, CA.   [328] [2013] EWCA Civ 13 [2014] 1 FLR 55.

[329] At [43]. The point did not arise since Parker J did not alter the total quantum to be paid but only the time-scale for payment.   [330] [2001] EWCA Civ 407 [2002] 1 FLR 166 at para 18.

By contrast, the reason that, generally speaking, orders relating to property cannot be varied is that they are designed to make a final adjustment of the spouses' rights, so that any subsequent change in their needs and resources is irrelevant. A *Mesher* order, being a property adjustment order, cannot therefore be varied.[331]

2. FACTORS TO BE TAKEN INTO CONSIDERATION

The Act provides that, on hearing an application for variation, the court shall have regard to all the circumstances of the case, first consideration being given to the welfare, while a minor, of any child of the family who has not attained the age of 18, and the circumstances of the case shall include any change in the matters to which it was required to have regard when making the order in the first place.[332] It should be noted that while it is important not to allow variation applications to be used as a disguised appeal against the terms of the original order, the court's discretion is generally unfettered.[333] However, the obligation to consider whether a clean break can be achieved between the parties will be 'much enhanced' where the periodical payments order was term-limited and the parties had expected that the payer's obligations were to terminate absolutely on the expiry of the term. 'In such circumstances, the exercise of a power to extend obligations requires some exceptional justification.'[334]

In *Flavell v Flavell*[335] the Court of Appeal held that jurisdiction to vary an order does not depend upon an exceptional or material change of circumstance, although the absence of such change may affect the exercise of the court's discretion. The court is not required to proceed from the starting point of the original order, but will consider the matter afresh.

Two judicial limitations have been placed on the court's power, however. First, the parties are still estopped *per rem judicatem* from raising matters inconsistent with a previous decree or order, and neither party may adduce evidence which could have been put before the court when the original order was made.[336] Secondly, a party who has led the other to act to his or her detriment on the assumption that he will continue to honour the order may not later apply to have it reduced or discharged.[337]

If the change of circumstances on which the application is based is not likely to be permanent (eg the husband's temporary unemployment), the order should be suspended rather than discharged, so that it can be revived later if necessary.[338]

(a) Capitalisation of periodical payments

Section 31(7)(a) of the 1973 Act 1973[339] places the court's duty to consider making a 'clean break' on a variation application on the same footing as in relation to original orders.

---

[331] *Carson v Carson* [1983] 1 All ER 478. See also *Norman v Norman* [1983] 1 All ER 486; *Omielan v Omielan* [1996] 2 FLR 306, CA (order for sale could not be deferred when triggering event occurred). Compare *Thompson v Thompson* [1986] Fam 38, CA where the sale was deferred inter alia 'until further order': held there was power to order an earlier sale under s 24A, at any rate on the application of the party in occupation, since in the court's view this would be to work out the terms of the original order rather than to amount to a substantive variation of its terms.   [332] Matrimonial Causes Act 1973 s 31(7)(a).

[333] *Lewis v Lewis* [1977] 3 All ER 992, CA; *Garner v Garner* [1992] 1 FLR 573, CA (a case concerning child maintenance); *Cornick v Cornick (No 2)* [1995] 2 FLR 490, CA. In *Pearce v Pearce* [2003] EWCA Civ 1054 [2004] 1 WLR 68 at para 25, Thorpe LJ considered that this line of authority does not apply to the orders defined in s 31(7B)(a) and (b), which are orders that the court has no power to vary.

[334] Per Thorpe LJ in *Fleming v Fleming* [2003] EWCA Civ 1841 [2004] 1 FLR 667 at [13], followed in *Yates v Yates* [2012] EWCA Civ 532 [2013] 2 FLR 1070 (but decision by trial judge upheld as an exercise of discretion on the facts).   [335] [1997] 1 FLR 353, CA.   [336] *Hall v Hall* (1914) 111 LT 403, CA.

[337] *B (MAL) v B (NE)* [1968] 1 WLR 1109.   [338] See *Mills v Mills* [1940] P 124, CA.

[339] As amended by Family Law Act 1996 Sch 8 para 16.

The court has power[340] to direct that an order for variation or discharge of a periodical payments order shall not take effect until the expiry of a specified period, thus enabling the payee to adjust, in the interim, to a termination of the payments in her favour or a reduction in their amount. Where, on a variation application, the court imposes a clean break (by either discharging a periodical payments order or directing it continues only for a fixed period), it also has power[341] to order a 'compensating' lump sum,[342] property adjustment order[343] or pension sharing order.[344] The court may also order that the payee under the original periodical payments order shall not be entitled to apply for a further order, or for an extension of its term.[345]

The court is not given any statutory guidance on calculating a fair level of capital commutation, but in *Vaughan v Vaughan*[346] the Court of Appeal held that the first enquiry is to identify the level of periodical payments which should in principle continue to be made, including whether they should continue to be made at all and thus whether the payee could adjust without undue hardship to their termination. If the conclusion is that periodical payments at a specified level should in principle continue to be made, the second enquiry is to calculate their capital equivalent according to the *Duxbury* formula. The court must finally survey whether it is fair to both parties to capitalise the payments, and in particular whether it is reasonably practicable for the payer to pay the capital sum rather than to continue making the periodical payments.

3. VARIATION OF CONSENT ORDERS

The fact that a party has consented to an order being made against him cannot act as an estoppel or give the other party a contractual right to have the order kept in force indefinitely, and a consent order may generally be varied in the same circumstances as any other order.[347] Usually, however, the court should be slower to accede to an application to vary consent orders, because otherwise parties and their solicitors might be deterred from negotiating them altogether. Hence a variation sought on the ground that the applicant's consent was given as a result of a mistake (eg about the other party's income) should be made only if justice demands it and a substantially different order would be made.[348] The court might also exercise its power if the applicant had not been independently and competently advised[349] (although the Court of Appeal subsequently held[350] that only in the most exceptional case will bad legal advice be a ground for interfering with a consent order) or if, for whatever reason, the order was grossly unjust.[351] In any case, it is doubtful whether the court can vary or

---

[340] Matrimonial Causes Act 1973 s 31(10).

[341] Matrimonial Causes Act 1973 s 31(7A) and (7B) as inserted by Family Law Act 1996 Sch 8 para 16.

[342] Where a lump sum is ordered in these circumstances, it may be ordered to be paid by instalments, which may be secured: Matrimonial Causes Act 1973 s 31(7C).

[343] Where the court makes more than one property adjustment order in favour of the same party, it may only make a single order of each type: Matrimonial Causes Act 1973 s 31(7E).

[344] Matrimonial Causes Act 1973 s 31(7B)(ba) inserted by Welfare Reform and Pensions Act 1999 Sch 3 para 7(5).   [345] Matrimonial Causes Act 1973 s 31(7B)(c).

[346] [2010] EWCA Civ 349 [2010] 2 FLR 242, applying *Pearce v Pearce* [2003] EWCA Civ 1054, [2004] 1 WLR 68.

[347] *B (GC) v B (BA)* [1970] 1 All ER 913.   [348] *B (GC) v B (BA)* [1970] 1 All ER 913.

[349] Per Baker P in *Wilkins v Wilkins* [1969] 2 All ER 463; *Peacock v Peacock* [1991] 1 FLR 324 where Thorpe J said (at 328) that he would not hold the parties to any agreement that they may have concluded, since the area of negotiation was complicated, neither spouse had had the benefit of legal advice, and both were 'way out of their depth'.   [350] *Harris v Manahan* [1997] 1 FLR 205, CA.

[351] As in *Smethurst v Smethurst* [1978] Fam 52, where, for reasons which were not apparent, the sum originally ordered was about twice that which the husband could reasonably afford to pay.

discharge an order which it has no power to make in the first place, eg an order for unsecured periodical payments for the payee's life.[352]

G. ENFORCEMENT OF ORDERS

1. METHODS OF ENFORCEMENT

(a) Periodical payments

One of the major reasons for seeking a clean break (or a secured order) is to avoid the problem of ensuring that ongoing payments are actually made to the recipient, on time and in full. Various mechanisms do exist to enforce an order, but they are complex and not always effective.

If periodical payments are secured, there is of course no question of enforcement. When arrears[353] of unsecured periodical payments accrue, the payee's position is basically different from that of a successful claimant in an action for damages for tort or breach of contract, for the order is not a final judgment and he or she does not have the full rights of a judgment creditor.[354]

If the party in default applies to have the order varied or discharged, the court in effect has a discretion to remit the arrears in part or even entirely by making a retrospective order.[355] In order to prevent large sums from mounting up, arrears which have been due for twelve months or more may not be enforced without the leave of the court: this gives some protection to a party who has stopped paying the full sum ordered and has been mistakenly led to believe by the other's acquiescence that she will not enforce the rest.[356] The court can also give the debtor time to pay and, in particular, may order payment by instalments. Because of this discretion, the arrears do not constitute a legal debt and cannot be sued for as such,[357] nor may the payee institute bankruptcy proceedings as a means of execution or prove in the other party's bankruptcy for arrears.[358] But with these

---

[352] See *Mills v Mills* [1940] P 124, CA and *Hinde v Hinde* [1953] 1 All ER 171, CA. But they probably can be varied, etc, by consent, and an undertaking given to the court may be discharged: *Russell v Russell* [1956] P 283, CA.

[353] The court also has power to order the recovery of overpayments: see Matrimonial Causes Act 1973 s 33 and s 38.

[354] The order may be registered in a different court to that which originally made it, in order to take advantage of the enforcement mechanisms available therein: Maintenance Orders Act 1958 as amended. Orders made abroad may also be registered for enforcement in this jurisdiction: Maintenance Orders (Reciprocal Enforcement) Act 1972 as amended by Crime and Courts Act 2013 Sch 11. Note that Council Regulation (EC) No 4/2009 on Jurisdiction, applicable law, recognition and enforcement of decisions and cooperation in matters relating to maintenance obligations and Schedule 6 to the Civil Jurisdiction and Judgments (Maintenance) Regulations 2011 (SI 2011/1484) apply in relation to orders made in jurisdictions within the EU. Maintenance (in the context of divorce) has been defined by the European Court as any 'financial obligations between former spouses after divorce which are fixed on the basis of their respective needs and resources'. The Regulation does not, however, apply to 'rights in property arising out of a matrimonial relationship,' In *Van Den Boogaard v Laumen* [1997] QB 759, the European Court of Justice held that orders other than for periodical payments may be classed as 'maintenance' and hence enforceable in another Contracting State if the purpose of making the order was to ensure the former spouse's maintenance. In *Al-Khatib v Masry* [2002] EWHC 108 (Fam) [2002] 1 FLR 1053 Munby J held that a *Duxbury* fund may constitute 'maintenance' for this purpose. See generally, M Barnes and D Hammond *International Child Maintenance and Family Obligations: A Practical Guide* (2013).

[355] *MacDonald v MacDonald* [1964] P 1CA.   [356] Matrimonial Causes Act 1973 s 32.

[357] *Bailey v Bailey* (1884) 13 QBD 855, CA; *Robins v Robins* [1907] 2 KB 13.

[358] *Cartwright v Cartwright (No 2)* [2002] EWCA Civ 931 [2002] 1 FLR 919. Consequently the arrears are not affected by bankruptcy and may be enforced by other methods: *Linton v Linton* (1885) 15 QBD 239;

important exceptions she has available all the usual means of execution open to a judgment creditor.[359]

One way of enforcing the payment of arrears is by issuing a judgment summons under s 5 of the Debtors Act 1869,[360] when the court can make an order for the payment by instalments and commit the debtor spouse to prison for contempt if he 'refuses or neglects' to pay them. Because the process subjects the debtor to the risk of imprisonment, it must comply with the rights conferred by Art 6 of the European Convention on Human Rights, including a presumption of innocence, precise articulation of the charge, adequate time to prepare a defence and examination of supporting evidence.[361] The test is whether the debtor has the means to pay, not whether he has the earning potential to raise the sums owing.[362] The judge should consider whether the order might have been varied or suspended if the debtor had applied for that purpose, and if so, may make a new order for payment of the amount due together with the costs of the summons.[363] In *Constantinides v Constantinides*,[364] Holman J drew attention to the complexity of the law, the fact that much of it dates back to the Victorian era and to the increasing likelihood that it will be applied by courts dealing with litigants in person and urged that the rules should be reformed and simplified.

Alternatively, the payee may apply for an attachment of earnings order requiring payments owed to be deducted from the payer's salary by the employer and paid direct to the payee, and in order to make this effective, the court may order payment by standing order or other means, which in turn may require the payer to open a bank account.[365] Unfortunately, statistical data on the use of these procedures[366] does not distinguish between applications made in relation to family proceedings and under the general civil law so it is not possible to assess how often they are resorted to, nor their effectiveness in securing payment in matrimonial cases.

(b) Other orders

An order for the payment of a lump sum is more in the nature of a judgment for damages and generally may be enforced in the same way. A lump sum (or costs) order is provable on the bankruptcy of the payer spouse.[367] The payee may issue a judgment summons or apply for

---

Re Henderson (1888) 20 QBD 509, CA. For bankruptcy proceedings as a means of enforcing payment of a lump sum, see Attempts to defeat claims for financial relief, p 918.

[359] An undertaking to make payments given to the court may be enforced in the same way as an order (at least if the court would have had jurisdiction to make a similar order): *Gandolfo v Gandolfo* [1981] QB 359, CA.   [360] Or Magistrates' Courts Act 1980 ss 76 and 93.

[361] *Mubarak v Mubarak* [2001] 1 FLR 698, CA; *Karoonian v CMEC; Gibbons v CMEC* [2012] EWCA Civ 1379 [2013] 1 FLR 1121 (the same procedure applies to committal both under the Child Support legislation and the Debtors Act); *Bhura v Bhura* [2012] EWHC 3633 (Fam) [2013] 2 FLR 44.

[362] *Constantinides v Constantinides* [2013] EWHC 3688 (Fam) [2014] Fam Law 440.

[363] Family Procedure Rules 2010 r 33.16(1); *Zuk v Zuk* [2012] EWCA Civ 1871 [2013] 2 FLR 1466.

[364] [2013] EWHC 3688 (Fam) [2014] Fam Law 440 at [37].

[365] Attachment of Earnings Act 1971 as amended, prospectively, by the Tribunals, Courts and Enforcement Act 2007 and Maintenance Enforcement Act 1991 s 1.

[366] Ministry of Justice, *Judicial and Court Statistics 2011* (2012) Table 1.18.

[367] Insolvency Rules 1986 (SI 1986/1925) r 12.3. The bankrupt will be released from his obligation under the order when discharged. Cf *Woodley v Woodley (No 2)* [1993] 2 FLR 477, CA, where Balcombe LJ suggested the rules be changed to allow a lump sum order to be provable on a payer's bankruptcy and yet not to be released on his discharge. Note that the court has power to make a lump sum order against a bankrupt spouse, although it should have a clear picture of the assets and liabilities of the bankrupt and consider the effect the bankruptcy has on the debtor spouse's ability to pay: *Woodley v Woodley* [1992] 2 FLR 417, CA and *Hellyer v Hellyer* [1996] 2 FLR 579, CA.

an attachment of earnings order. As in the case of periodical payments, a lump sum payment (or any part payable by instalment) cannot be enforced more than 12 months after it falls due without the leave of the court.[368]

Once a property adjustment order in financial relief proceedings has taken effect (on decree absolute), it confers on the beneficiary an equitable interest in the property which may then be enforced, including in situations where the property has since vested in the payer's trustee in bankruptcy. Thus, in a case where the husband was made bankrupt before the order could be executed, his trustee took subject to the wife's interest in the husband's share in the matrimonial home, which he had been ordered to transfer to her.[369]

2. ATTEMPTS TO DEFEAT CLAIMS FOR FINANCIAL RELIEF

A spouse might well try to defeat an application for financial relief by disposing of his property or transferring it out of the jurisdiction. He might do this beforehand in anticipation of an application or order or, alternatively, after an order has been made in order to reduce the property available to meet it. To prevent fraudulent dispositions of this kind, a measure of protection is given by the Matrimonial Causes Act 1973 s 37.[370]

If the court is satisfied that the husband[371] is about to make any disposition or to transfer out of the jurisdiction or otherwise deal with any property with the intention of defeating the wife's claim, it may make such an order as it thinks fit to restrain him from doing so and to protect the claim.[372] It cannot, however, issue a mandatory injunction to require him to take steps in relation to assets in order to release these to the payee. In *Field v Field*,[373] for example, it was held that the court could not order the husband to elect to take the maximum lump sum from his pension in order to pay the second instalment of a lump sum order to the wife.

In *Crittenden v Crittenden*[374] the Court of Appeal held that, for the purpose of s 37, 'property' means property in which either or both spouses has or had a beneficial interest, in possession or reversion, while 'dealing with' refers to some *positive* dealing with property, and not to anything which is purely negative, such as failing to deal with property.[375] It followed that the court had no power, under s 37, to make orders relating to assets owned by a *company* in which the husband held the issued shares.

---

[368] Matrimonial Causes Act 1973 s 32.

[369] *Mountney v Treharne* [2002] EWCA Civ 1174 [2002] 2 FLR 930. Other methods of seeking enforcement include freezing orders (for guidance on which see *UL v BK (Freezing Orders: Safeguards: Standard Examples)* [2013] EWHC 1735 (Fam) [2013] Fam Law 1379), oral examination, production appointments, sequestration and injunctions preventing the payer from leaving the jurisdiction: see, for example, the continuing litigation in *Young v Young* [2012] EWHC 138 (Fam) [2012] 2 FLR 470 and that in *Kremen v Agrest* [2013] EWCA Civ 41 [2013] 2 FLR 187, *Kremen v Agrest (Committal Under Debtors Act)* [2011] EWCA Civ 1482 [2012] 1 FLR 894, which show that all such methods ultimately depend upon the willingness of the payer to comply.

[370] There is similar power under s 423 of the Insolvency Act 1986, and applications may be made under both Acts. For a useful comparison of these powers, see *Trowbridge v Trowbridge* [2003] 2 FLR 231 [49]–[61].

[371] The position is of course the same where the wife is the payer, and in the case of civil partners.

[372] It has been held that this power extends to restraining dispositions of property already situated abroad: *Hamlin v Hamlin* [1986] Fam 11, CA. However, the court will only make an order if it can be enforced.

[373] [2003] 1 FLR 376: furthermore, the husband's pension rights did not give him a beneficial interest in the fund which could amount to 'property' for the purposes of s 37.   [374] [1990] 2 FLR 361, CA.

[375] The extent to which the company might be regarded as subject to the control of the husband will be governed by the Supreme Court ruling in *Prest v Petrodel Resources Ltd and Others* [2013] UKSC 34 [2013] 2 AC 415 discussed in Ch 22, Transfer and settlement of property, Company assets, p 847.

If the court is satisfied that the husband has already made a disposition with the intention of defeating the wife's claim, it may make an order setting the disposition aside.[376] In this case, however, a wife who has not yet obtained an order for financial relief must also show that, if the disposition were set aside, the court would make a different order from that which it would otherwise make.[377]Defeating the wife's claim may take the form of preventing her from obtaining an order at all, reducing the amount that might be ordered, or impeding or frustrating the enforcement of any order that might be made or has been made. It seems, despite an earlier judicial suggestion to the contrary,[378] that where a husband declares himself bankrupt to avoid a claim for ancillary relief, the bankruptcy itself is not a reviewable disposition entitling the court to intervene under s 37. The correct procedure is for application to be made under s 282(1)(a) of the Insolvency Act 1986 to annul the bankruptcy order on the basis it ought not to have been made.[379]

In many cases it may be difficult to establish what the husband's intention was when he made a disposition. Consequently the Act introduced a compromise designed to protect the interests of the wife, the husband and the transferee. If the husband made the disposition three years or more before the application to set it aside, the wife must prove affirmatively that he had the intention to defeat her claim. If he made it less than three years before or is about to make it, this intention will be presumed if the effect of the transaction would be to defeat her claim or, where the disposition has already taken place and an order is in force, if it has had this effect: the burden then shifts on to him to prove that this was not his intention. In *Kemmis v Kemmis (Welland Intervening)*[380] it was held that the husband's intention to defeat the wife's claim has to be a subjective intention, but does not have to be the husband's sole or even dominant intention. It suffices if it plays a *substantial* part in the husband's intention as a whole.

The disposition is voidable and not void, and consequently, even if it is set aside, this cannot affect any subsequent dealings with the property in good faith.[381] Hence, if the husband's immediate transferee is not protected but disposes of the property to a bona fide purchaser for value without notice, the latter's title cannot be upset by the order.[382]

Certain transactions may not be upset at all. No order may be made after the husband's death with respect to any disposition made by him by will or codicil. A disposition inter vivos *already* made may not be set aside if it was made for valuable consideration (other than marriage) to a third party acting in good faith and without notice of the husband's intention to defeat the wife's claim.[383] Where a third party had *actual* knowledge of the husband's intention, it is difficult to see how he could claim to act in good faith, and so the transaction will be

---

[376] But it may be unnecessary to go to these lengths where it is clear that the husband retains control over the assets: the court may simply deal with the case on the basis that the property remains his: *Purba v Purba* [2000] 1 FLR 444, CA: husband transferred funds to accounts in names of relatives who were bare trustees.

[377] In *Muema v Muema* [2013] EWHC 3864 (Fam) the husband, as a joint tenant of rented property, applied under s 37 to set aside the wife's notice to quit to the local authority. It was held that even if her unilateral action had been in breach of his human rights (which it was not) the court would not have set the transaction aside since it would have been to the disadvantage of the wife and their children.

[378] *Woodley v Woodley* [1992] 2 FLR 417 at 423F (per Ewbank J).

[379] *F v F (Divorce: Insolvency: Annulment of Bankruptcy Order)* [1994] 1 FLR 359; the bankruptcy proceedings may be transferred to the Family Division: see *Couvaras v Wolf* [2002] 2 FLR 107 where Wilson J had thoroughly investigated the husband's finances in the financial relief proceedings and determined that the bankruptcy petition was a sham and the proceedings an abuse of the process of the court.

[380] [1988] 1 WLR 1307, CA. See also *Kremen v Agrest* [2010] EWHC 2571 [2011] 2 FLR 478.

[381] *AC v DC and Others (Financial Remedy: Effect of s 37 Avoidance Order)* [2012] EWHC 2032 (Fam) [2013] 2 FLR 1483.

[382] *National Provincial Bank Ltd v Hastings Car Mart Ltd (No 3)* [1964] Ch 665, CA.

[383] Section 37(4): *Ansari v Ansari (Miah intervening)* [2008] EWCA Civ 1456 [2010] Fam 1.

set aside. However, in *Kemmis v Kemmis (Welland Intervening)*[384] the Court of Appeal held the defence is also not available to a third party who has *constructive* notice of the husband's intentions.

H. FINANCIAL RELIEF AFTER FOREIGN DIVORCE, DISSOLUTION, ANNULMENT OR LEGAL SEPARATION

1. BACKGROUND TO THE LEGISLATION

Formerly, the court could only make financial orders under the Matrimonial Causes Act 1973 in the course of matrimonial proceedings instituted in England and Wales. This meant that spouses who had been divorced, or whose marriage had been annulled abroad could not seek such relief from the English divorce courts.[385] Though logical, this rule could nevertheless cause hardship, particularly to those who were habitually resident in England and Wales and who, having been divorced abroad, sometimes without their knowledge,[386] had no other means of redress.[387] Responding to calls for reform,[388] the Law Commission[389] recommended widening the jurisdiction of the divorce courts to give redress to such applicants. These recommendations were enacted in the Matrimonial and Family Proceedings Act 1984, Part III.[390]

2. WHEN RELIEF MAY BE SOUGHT

Under s 12(1) of the 1984 Act, where a marriage has been dissolved or annulled, or the parties to the marriage are legally separated, by means of judicial or other proceedings in an overseas country, and the divorce, annulment or legal separation is entitled to be recognised as valid in England and Wales,[391] then either party may apply to the court for financial relief. It will be noted that under this provision:

(1) The divorce etc must have been granted in an 'overseas country', which means a country or territory outside the British Islands.[392] Hence, for example, a spouse who has been divorced in Scotland cannot, under these provisions, subsequently seek financial relief in the English court.

---

[384] [1988] 1 WLR 1307, CA.

[385] Similarly, since they were no longer married, they could not seek maintenance under the Matrimonial Causes Act 1973 s 27, or under the Domestic Proceedings and Magistrates' Courts Act 1978.

[386] As could happen, for example, where divorce by talaq is permitted. See also *Lamagni v Lamagni* [1995] 2 FLR 452, CA where an English wife obtained a divorce decree in England without knowledge that her Italian husband had earlier obtained a divorce in proceedings in Belgium.

[387] See eg *Torok v Torok* [1973] 3 All ER 101 and *Quazi v Quazi* [1980] AC 744, HL.

[388] Not least by the Law Lords in *Quazi v Quazi*.

[389] Law Com No 117 *Financial Relief after Foreign Divorce* (1982).

[390] The Civil Partnership Act 2004 s 72(4) and Sch 7 Part 1 make equivalent provision for civil partnerships dissolved abroad.

[391] For a discussion of the rules of recognition see eg J Fawcett and J Carruthers *Cheshire, North and Fawcett, Private International Law* (2008, 14th edn).

[392] Matrimonial and Family Proceedings Act 1984 s 27. British Islands means the United Kingdom, the Channel Islands and the Isle of Man: Interpretation Act 1978 Sch 1.

(2) The divorce etc must have been by means of 'judicial or other proceedings'. The phrase 'other proceedings' is intended to cover cases where the marriage has been terminated extra-judicially, for example by talaq.[393]

(3) Provided the first two criteria are satisfied, *either* party may apply for relief.

(4) A party who has been legally separated abroad can apply for relief even though he or she may be able to apply for divorce etc in an English court.

(5) A party who forms a subsequent marriage or civil partnership (but not the other party) loses the right to apply for relief.[394]

3. APPLICANTS ARE REQUIRED TO OBTAIN LEAVE

(a) Procedure

Before any substantive claim may be made, applicants must first obtain the court's leave to make an application for a financial order. The court cannot grant leave unless it considers that there is a substantial ground for making the application and that there is jurisdiction to make the order.[395] Applications for leave are made without notice and should be accompanied by a statement stating the facts relied upon and the grounds upon which it is alleged the court has jurisdiction.[396] The requirement to obtain leave is intended to filter applications whilst at the same time providing maximum protection for all those concerned. The idea is to save the potential respondent the time and expense of being involved in the case before the bona fides of the application have been tested.

Leave may be granted notwithstanding that an order has been made by a court outside England and Wales requiring the respondent to make financial provision for, or to transfer property to, the applicant or a child of the family.[397] The courts formerly took a restrictive approach to this requirement, holding that the jurisdiction should only be exercised in 'exceptional circumstances'. In *Agbaje v Agbaje*,[398] for example, the spouses were born in Nigeria and had joint Nigerian-British citizenship. They were married for 38 years and there were five children of the family, all born in the UK. The wife had lived continuously in England since 1999 when the marriage broke down. The husband obtained a divorce in Nigeria in 2005, when the Nigerian court awarded the wife a life interest in a property in Nigeria, worth about £86,000 and a lump sum worth about £21,000. The parties' combined assets were worth around £700,000, of which £530,000 represented two houses in London in the husband's name. The Court of Appeal allowed the husband's appeal against the grant of leave to the wife to pursue a Part III application, holding that

---

[393] For the complexities that may arise, see eg *A v L (Overseas Divorce)* [2010] EWHC 460 (Fam) [2010] 2 FLR 1418 (Egypt); *H v S (Recognition of Overseas Divorce)* [2012] 2 FLR 157 (Saudi Arabia). See also, for a 'panchayat' Hindu divorce, *NP v KRP (Recognition of Foreign Divorce)* [2013] EWHC 694 (Fam) [2013] Fam Law 1385. In *MET v HAT (Interim Maintenance)* [2013] EWHC 4247 (Fam) [2014] Fam Law 447 it was held that a pure talaq involving no state authorities was a 'non-proceedings' divorce excluding resort to the Part III jurisdiction. Subsequently, however, expert evidence established the contrary: *MET v HAT (Interim Maintenance) (No 2)* [2014] EWHC 717 (Fam).

[394] Matrimonial and Family Proceedings Act 1984 s 12(2). The right is lost even if the subsequent marriage or civil partnership is void or voidable: s 12(3).

[395] Matrimonial and Family Proceedings Act 1984 s 13(1) and s 15.

[396] Family Procedure Rules 2010 rr 8.24–8.25.

[397] Matrimonial and Family Proceedings Act 1984 s 13(2), though this is a factor to be taken into account in deciding whether to make an order: s 16(2), discussed later, Applying for an order, p 923. The reference to a court outside England and Wales means that there is jurisdiction even if a court in another part of the United Kingdom has made an order. This could happen, for example, where the divorce takes place abroad, the applicant is domiciled in Scotland and the matrimonial home is in England.

[398] [2010] UKSC 13 [2010] 1 AC 628.

the purpose of Part III is to remit hardship in the exceptional case where serious injustice would otherwise be done.[399] However, the Supreme Court fundamentally disagreed.[400] Lord Collins, giving the judgment of the Supreme Court, pointed out that there is no such requirement, nor any pre-condition that an applicant must otherwise suffer 'real hardship' before leave can be given, although hardship will be relevant to the exercise of the court's discretion.[401] Rather, the 'threshold is not high, but is higher than the "serious issue to be tried" or "good arguable case" found in other contexts. It is perhaps best expressed by saying that in this context "substantial" means "solid".'[402] However, where leave is granted, it may be followed by an application to set aside, which can add to the costs and duplicate proceedings.[403] His Lordship therefore added that, 'unless it is clear that the respondent can deliver a knockout blow, the court should use its case management powers to adjourn an application to set aside to be heard with the substantive application.'[404]

(b) Jurisdiction

Before leave may be granted, the court must be satisfied that there is jurisdiction to make the order.[405] Subject to the provisions governing EU Member States,[406] the court has jurisdiction if:

(a) either party to the marriage was domiciled in England and Wales on the date of the application for leave or when the divorce, nullity or legal separation took effect; or

(b) either party was habitually resident there throughout the period of one year ending on the date of the application for leave or when the divorce etc took effect; or

(c) either or both parties had at the date of the application for leave a beneficial interest in possession[407] in a dwelling house[408] situated in England and Wales which was at some time during the marriage a matrimonial home of the parties to the marriage.[409]

If jurisdiction is taken on the last basis, the court's powers are more limited.[410]

(c) Interim orders

Once leave has been granted, then, save where jurisdiction has been taken solely upon the matrimonial home basis, and provided that it appears to the court that the applicant or

---

[399] [2009] EWCA Civ 1 [2009] 1 FLR 987.

[400] [2010] UKSC 13 [2010] 1 AC 628 at [59]–[61]; *Holmes v Holmes* [1989] Fam 47 and *Hewitson v Hewitson* [1995] Fam 100 disapproved; followed in *Traversa v Freddi* [2011] EWCA Civ 81 [2011] 2 FLR 272.

[401] [2010] UKSC 13 [2010] 1 AC 628 at [61]. See further, Orders that may be made, p 923.

[402] [2010] UKSC 13 [2010] 1 AC 628 at [33].   [403] *Jordan v Jordan* [1999] 2 FLR 1069.

[404] [2010] UKSC 13 [2010] 1 AC 628 at [33]. For consideration of how leave can be tempered by conditions to prevent over-expansive claims, see *Z v A (Financial Remedies: Overseas Divorce)* [2012] EWHC 467 (Fam) [2012] 2 FLR 667 where Coleridge J rejected the husband's claim of an oral pre-nuptial agreement which would potentially have delivered such a 'knockout blow'. See also *Golubovich v Golubovich* [2011] EWCA Civ 479 [2011] 2 FLR 1193 where Moylan J dealt with the leave application, the husband's application to adjourn and the substantive application all together.

[405] Pursuant to s 15(1) of the 1984 Act.

[406] Council Regulation (EC) No 4/2009 on jurisdiction, applicable law, recognition and enforcement of decisions and cooperation in matters relating to maintenance obligations. See further, n 413, p 923.

[407] This includes the receipt of or the right to receive rent or profits: s 27.

[408] This includes any building or part thereof which is occupied as a dwelling, and any yard, garden, garage or outhouse belonging to the dwelling-house and occupied therewith: s 27.

[409] This latter requirement implies that the married parties must have lived together in the property in question.   [410] Under s 20: see Orders that may be made, p 923.

any child of the family is in need of immediate financial assistance, the court may make an interim order for maintenance.[411] As the provisions regarding costs allowance orders do not apply to applications under the 1984 Act, it appears that the court would be able to make an order under this section requiring the respondent to meet the applicant's legal costs.[412]

4. APPLYING FOR AN ORDER

Once leave has been granted, application may be made for financial relief. Before an order will be made the court must consider whether in all the circumstances it is appropriate for an English court to do so.[413] In deciding that issue the court is directed[414] to have regard to a number of matters which include the connection the parties have to England and Wales, and to the country where the marriage was dissolved; any financial benefit the applicant has received under the law of that country; and the extent to which any financial relief order made in that country has been or would be likely to be complied with. In *Agbaje v Agbaje*,[415] the Court of Appeal allowed the husband's appeal against the grant of leave to the wife to pursue a Part III application, holding that the purpose of Part III is to remit hardship in the exceptional case where serious injustice would otherwise be done, and the criteria in s 16(2) should be construed accordingly. They considered that it would be wrong to compare what the applicant received in the foreign jurisdiction with what an English court would have awarded her as otherwise comity would be undermined and London's reputation as the 'divorce capital of the world' would be reinforced.[416] But, the Supreme Court took a different view. They reminded the courts that the question is not whether it is appropriate for an order to be made, nor whether England and Wales is the *only* appropriate forum, but whether England and Wales is an appropriate venue for the application.[417]

5. ORDERS THAT MAY BE MADE

Provided it is satisfied that it should make an order, the court has the same powers (save where jurisdiction is taken on the matrimonial home basis) as under the Matrimonial

---

[411] Section 14 of the 1984 Act. Under this provision the court may order the respondent to make periodical payments to the applicant or any child of the family for such term as the court thinks fit but beginning no earlier than the date of the grant of leave and ending with the date of the determination of the application for the order. [412] *M v M (Financial Provision)* [2010] EWHC 2817 (Fam) [2011] 1 FLR 1773.

[413] Section 16(1) of the 1984 Act. If the court has jurisdiction in relation to the application or part of it by virtue of Council Regulation (EC) No 4/2009 on Jurisdiction, applicable law, recognition and enforcement of decisions and cooperation in matters relating to maintenance obligations and Schedule 6 to the Civil Jurisdiction and Judgments (Maintenance) Regulations 2011 (SI 2011/1484), the court may not dismiss the application or that part of it on the ground mentioned in subsection (1) if to do so would be inconsistent with the jurisdictional requirements of that Regulation and that Schedule: s 16(3). See the comments by Lord Collins in *Agbaje v Agbaje* [2010] UKSC 13 [2010] 1 AC 628 at [55]–[57] regarding the jurisdiction in relation to 'maintenance' governed by the Regulation, as compared to applications governing 'rights in property' which are not so governed. In *CG v IF (Inter-Relationship of Part III Matrimonial and Family Proceedings Act 1984 and Lugano Convention)* [2010] EWHC 1062 (Fam) [2010] 2 FLR 1790, Mostyn J held that if the husband's claim for provision under Part III included meeting his 'needs', then a request for a property adjustment order might amount to a claim for maintenance which would be barred by a Swiss consent order dismissing such claims. For consideration of its application to pension sharing orders, see A Heenan 'Scuppering *Schofield*? The impact of the EU Maintenance Regulation on claims for pension sharing' [2012] Fam Law 191, referring to *Schofield v Schofield* [2011] EWCA Civ 174 [2011] 1 FLR 2129.

[414] By s 16(2). [415] [2010] UKSC 13 [2010] 1 AC 628. [416] At [52].

[417] *Agbaje v Agbaje* [2010] UKSC 13 [2010] 1 AC 628 at [41], [49], [71].

Causes Act 1973, Part II.[418] In deciding what orders to make the court must have regard to the same considerations as it would when dealing with a domestic application,[419] though in addition it must consider the extent to which any overseas order has been or is likely to be complied with.[420]

Decisions at first instance held that the court should limit awards to 'the minimum extent necessary so as to remedy the injustice perceived to exist without intervention'.[421] However the Supreme Court in *Agbaje v Agbaje*[422] again considered that the lower courts had misinterpreted the 1984 legislation. Lord Collins noted that the Act contains no such limitation and that it would be contrary to principle. At the same time, he compared the English legislation with that applying in Scotland, which had clearly expressed that, once the (more onerous) jurisdictional hurdle had been surmounted there, the Scottish court should apply exactly the same criteria as to a domestic case. He considered that it was not the intention of Parliament to enable the court to 'top up' the foreign award to give the applicant exactly what she would have received if the divorce had been granted in England and Wales. Rather, he held that the jurisdiction is 'flexible'—where a case has a

> strong English connection . . . it will be appropriate to ask what provision would have been made had the divorce been granted in England. There will be other cases where the connection is not strong and a spouse has received adequate provision from the foreign court. Then it will not be appropriate for Part III to be used simply as a tool to 'top-up' that provision to that which she would have received in an English divorce.[423]

Thus the Supreme Court concluded that the duties of the court under sections 16 and 18 are interrelated with the factors that the court must consider having a bearing at both the 'appropriate venue' stage and the 'what order to make' stages. While the applicant need not establish exceptional circumstances justifying an order, mere disparity between the award in the foreign jurisdiction and here will not suffice. The English court will not lightly describe the foreign law, or a foreign order as 'unjust' but if hardship or injustice is present, that may well affect the decision whether to make an order, and if so, of what kind. The following general principles apply: first, the welfare of the children of the marriage must be given primary consideration; secondly, 'it will never be appropriate to make an order which gives the claimant more than she or he would have been awarded had all proceedings taken place within this jurisdiction.'[424] Thirdly, where possible the order should provide for the reasonable needs of each spouse. But subject to these principles, the court has a broad discretion. 'Where the English connections of the case are very strong there may be no reason why the application should not be treated as if it were made in purely English proceedings.'[425]

In *Agbaje* itself, the first instance judge had awarded the wife the equivalent of 39% of the joint assets, from the proceeds of sale of one of the London properties in which she had been living, on the basis that the award should be limited to what was required to overcome injustice. As the wife did not appeal against quantum, the Supreme Court restored the award, commenting that the total provision that the wife achieved from both

---

[418] Section 17, and under Sch 7 to the Family Law Act 1996 (transfer of tenancies). Where jurisdiction is assumed on the matrimonial home basis, the court's powers are confined to making orders concerning that property or to making lump sum orders not exceeding the paying party's interest in it: s 20. There are also provisions similar to those in domestic proceedings for dealing with consent orders: s 19; variation and discharge: s 21, as amended; and restriction and setting aside of transactions intended to defeat claims: s 23.

[419] Section 18(1)–(5) as amended.   [420] Section 18(6).

[421] See eg *A v S (Financial Relief after Overseas US Divorce)* [2002] EWHC 1157 (Fam) [2003] 1 FLR 431.

[422] [2010] UKSC 13 [2010] 1 AC 628.

[423] At [64]–[65].   [424] At [73].   [425] Ibid.

jurisdictions did not in fact fall markedly short of what she would have received in a purely domestic proceeding.[426] They concluded:

> It was not so much that there was a very large disparity between what the wife received in Nigeria and what she would have received in England, but that there was also a very large disparity between what the husband received and what the wife received such as to create real hardship and a serious injustice.[427]

Rather unhelpfully, this appears to re-introduce the requirements of 'hardship' and 'injustice' which the judgment had previously rejected, and the statement of general principles does not clarify whether an award based on 'sharing' or 'compensation' would be appropriate. In *Z v A (Financial Remedy after Overseas Divorce)*[428] Coleridge J linked the extent of the parties' connections to the jurisdiction with the scale of the award to be made, finding that the parties were a truly international family with connections to several different jurisdictions. He awarded the wife a sum of £3m in a clean break settlement based on fair and reasonable provision for her and their child's needs, after a marriage lasting four and a half years in which much of the husband's £34m wealth had been generated. One must conclude that, as with the discretion under the Matrimonial Causes Act 1973, the Part III discretion is similarly broad and fact-dependent.

I. REFORM

The legislation, case-law and practice which we have discussed in this and Chapter 22 are so immensely complex and important that, inevitably, the whole topic remains the subject of continuing calls and proposals for reform.[429] The high level of divorce and increasing dissolutions of civil partnerships in England and Wales mean that substantial numbers of couples are caught up in the web of negotiation, settlement and litigation over finance and property each year. The costs, for the parties themselves and the State through such legal aid as remains and the provision of the courts themselves, are high and it might be argued that greater certainty of outcome would reduce disputes and hence help cut costs further. But the unpredictability of court decisions and variability between different courts militates against helping the parties to negotiate or reach a mediated settlement: they cannot be sure whether the bargain they are striking is a fair or appropriate one.[430]

In the 1990s the Government established an Ancillary Relief Advisory Group, composed of legal practitioners, the judiciary, and academics, to advise the Lord Chancellor on all aspects of financial remedies, and to consider ways of reforming the law. In particular, the Group was invited to consider whether the Scottish system (which applies a presumption of equal sharing of family assets) might be applied in England and Wales and

---

[426] At [74].   [427] At [76].

[428] [2012] EWHC 1434 (Fam) [2013] Fam Law 393.

[429] See J Eekelaar 'Should Section 25 be Reformed?' [1998] Fam Law 469; R Bailey-Harris 'Dividing the Assets on Family Breakdown' (2001) 54 *Current Legal Problems* 533.

[430] See R Mnookin and L Kornhauser 'Bargaining in the Shadow of the Law: The Case of Divorce' (1979) 88 *Yale Law Journal* 950; G Davis et al 'Ancillary relief outcomes' [2000] CFLQ 43; G Douglas and A Perry 'How parents cope financially on separation and divorce—implications for the future of ancillary relief' [2001] CFLQ 67; S Arthur et al *Settling Up: Making Financial Arrangements After Divorce or Separation* (2002); Law Society, *Financial Provision on Divorce: Clarity and Fairness—Proposals for Reform* (2003); E Hitchings 'Everyday Cases in the Post–White Era' [2008] Fam Law 873; 'The impact of recent ancillary relief jurisprudence in the "everyday" ancillary relief case' [2010] CFLQ 93.

whether pre-nuptial agreements should be given greater weight.[431] The group was unanimously against the introduction of a system of presumptive equal division, considering
it inappropriate for the jurisdiction in England and Wales. Whilst agreeing that there is a
strong case in principle for codification of the principles that are currently applied in the
courts, the group was divided on whether it would be desirable to enact a fresh statutory
objective. In sum, the group was unenthusiastic about any major reform in the absence of
much more evidence as to its need and as to what would represent an improvement over
the current position. The members rightly noted that they were drawn only from the legal
community and that social and public policy issues required a wider research base and
consultative forum for debate.[432]

The Government accepted the group's recommendation not to introduce a presumption of equal division of assets[433] but they produced a Green Paper, *Supporting Families*[434]
in which they did suggest that pre-nuptial agreements should be binding in certain circumstances,[435] and that 'an over-arching objective and a set of guiding principles' might
provide greater certainty and clarity in the law. While no legislation resulted from the
Green Paper the impetus for reform was strengthened by the House of Lords' ruling in
White v White[436] which, as we have seen, brought the 'yardstick of equality'—in effect,
equal shares—to the forefront of attention when parties are negotiating, in small as well
as (if not more than) in 'big money' cases. The subsequent working through of the implications of that judgment, and the increasingly complex elaboration of the principles
underlying 'fairness' set out in *Miller; McFarlane*[437] and later case-law, have continued to
add momentum to the calls for re-examination of the law. These were demonstrated most
powerfully, perhaps, by Potter P in *Charman v Charman (No 4)*[438] whose 20 paragraph
'postscript' to the judgment of the Court provided a précis of the developing law since
1970 which noted that 'it has been said by many that London has become the divorce
capital of the world for aspiring wives' and echoed calls for the Law Commission to review
the whole matter. Government resisted such calls, but growing demands for recognition of pre- (and post-) nuptial agreements in the light of the Supreme Court's decision
in *Granatino v Radmacher (Formerly Granatino)*[439] did result in the Law Commission
undertaking a review of the particular question of whether these should be legally
enforceable as contracts, and if so, subject to what, if any, conditions and safeguards.[440]
In carrying out that review, they concluded that they would have to examine two broader

---

[431] [1998] Fam Law 381.
[432] Lord Chancellor's Ancillary Relief Advisory Group, *Report to the Lord Chancellor* (1998).
[433] See [1998] Fam Law 654.   [434] Home Office (1998) Ch 4.
[435] Home Office (1998) para 4.23, including independent legal advice, full disclosure, and making the
agreement not less than 21 days before the wedding. The agreement would not have been binding if there
was a child of the family (born before or after the agreement was made) nor if it would cause 'significant
injustice' to a party or child.
[436] [2001] 1 AC 596.   [437] [2006] UKHL 24 [2006] 2 AC 618.
[438] [2007] EWCA Civ 503 [2007] 1 FLR 1246, [106]–[126].
[439] [2010] UKSC 42 [2011] 1 AC 534. See J Miles 'Marriage and Divorce in the Supreme Court and the Law
Commission: for Love or Money?' (2011) 74 MLR 430; J Scherpe, 'Fairness, freedom and foreign elements—
marital agreements in England and Wales after *Granatino v Radmacher*' [2011] CFLQ 513.
[440] Law Commission, Consultation Paper No 198 *Marital Property Agreements* (2010) and *Matrimonial
Property, Needs and Agreements* Law Com No 343 (2014). See N Lowe and R Kay 'The Status of Prenuptial
Agreement in English Law—Eccentricity or sensible pragmatism?' in B Verschraegen (ed) *Family Finances*
(2009); J Miles 'Marital Agreements: "The More Radical' Solution"' in R Probert and C Barton (eds) *Fifty
Years in Family Law: Essays for Stephen Cretney* (2012); N Lowe 'Prenuptial Agreements: The Developing
English Position' in A-L Verbeke et al (eds) *Confronting the Frontiers of Family and Succession Law: Liber
Amicorum Walter Pintens* Vol 1 (2012). For consideration of the case-law and of European approaches, see
J Scherpe (ed) *Marital Agreements and Private Autonomy in Comparative Perspective* (2012); for a common

issues which have emerged as central in the *Miller; McFarlane* line of cases—the concepts of 'needs' and of non-matrimonial property, since these impinge directly on how far the law should give effect to private agreements which might seek to exclude them from consideration at the end of a marriage.[441]

(a) Marital property agreements

The Law Commission set out the arguments for and against upholding nuptial agreements (which, as we have seen, may be made before or after the wedding).[442] They noted that both those for, and those against, making agreements enforceable argue that this would 'support' marriage, the former on the basis that it would enable those loath to put their assets at risk of 'sharing' to marry (rather than merely cohabit), confident that they could protect their wealth and the latter that encouraging couples to contemplate the possibility of their marriage 'failing' would devalue the institution. They also pointed out that the argument most frequently made in support of recognition is that it would promote the value of autonomy by respecting the right of adults to make their own agreements, whilst denial of recognition is patronising and paternalistic. However, pressure can be put on the more vulnerable party to agree to unfavourable terms even in the context of a loving relationship, and as they noted:

> the autonomy that is prayed in aid of binding marital property agreements is not simply the freedom to make an agreement, nor simply the freedom to do as one wishes. It is the freedom to force one's partner to abide by an agreement when he or she no longer wishes to do so. It is freedom of contract, but it is therefore freedom to use a contract to restrict one's partner's choices.[443]

They recognised the advantage of certainty of outcome that a nuptial agreement would provide, but added that for the majority of couples whose assets do not exceed their 'needs', the law is already 'certain', at least as to the objective that must be satisfied. Nor did they attach weight to the argument that English law should come into line with that operating in most other first world jurisdictions, especially other EU Member States, which recognise nuptial agreements, for, as they noted, other jurisdictions usually limit or prohibit the contracting-out from liability for maintenance and agreements operate as opt-outs to a default sharing or community of property regime in the first place. The starting-point and context for their recognition is thus quite different. Moreover, experience in common law jurisdictions, notably Australia, suggests that lawyers are reluctant to advise clients to enter into *pre-nuptial* as opposed to separation agreements, precisely because of their binding nature.

The Law Commission set out a variety of options for consultation. They defined a 'qualifying nuptial agreement' as one which would be contractually valid, and satisfy certain further tests relating to its form and the circumstances in which it is made.[444] They sought opinions on whether such an agreement should be a 'broad model', unlimited in the scope of its financial terms, or a 'narrow model' which could encompass *only* property

European model, see K Boele-Woelki et al *Principles of European Family Law Regarding Property Relations Between Spouses* (2013) ch II.

[441] Law Commission, Consultation Paper No 208 *Matrimonial Property: Needs and Agreements, A Supplementary Consultation Paper* (2012) repeated in *Matrimonial Property, Needs and Agreements* Law Com No 343 (2014) at para 5.33.

[442] Law Commission, Consultation Paper No 198 *Marital Property Agreements* (2010) ch 5 and *Matrimonial Property, Needs and Agreements* Law Com No 343 (2014) paras 5.28–5.39.

[443] Law Com No 343 at para 5.31.   [444] Law Com Consultation Paper No 198 (2010) at para 5.7.

acquired before the marriage (or civil partnership); property inherited before or during the marriage; and property given to either party before or during the marriage.[445] More importantly, perhaps, they also outlined the issues governing the substance of a qualifying agreement. They were clear that it should not be possible to make a binding agreement which failed to make sufficient provision for the children of the family, or which would leave a party dependent upon social security benefits which could be avoided if an order for financial remedies were made. In so doing, they were endorsing—hardly surprisingly—the stance taken in the law since *Hyman v Hyman*[446] and agreed by the Supreme Court in *Radmacher*.[447] But they also raised for consideration the further matters of whether there should be any other safeguards against hardship, possibly by requiring that the agreement cease to have effect after a certain period of time, or cease to be binding if it failed to provide for a particular event (such as the birth of a child), or, more broadly, a proviso that an agreement could not be enforced if it would create unfairness, or 'manifest' or 'significant' injustice—but they were concerned about the difficulty of defining such terms and the risk of creating litigation over their ambit. They also asked whether an agreement should be unenforceable if it failed to provide for a party's 'needs' and if so, how these should be defined.

Qualifying nuptial agreements

In their Report, they recommended first, that statutory effect should be given to the ruling in *Radmacher* that an agreement should not be regarded as void or contrary to public policy only by virtue of the fact that it provides for the financial consequences of a later separation, divorce or dissolution.[448] From there, they went on to recommend that it should be possible to make a nuptial agreement which would be binding as a contract, to be known as a 'qualifying nuptial agreement'.

However, they considered that it should not be possible to contract out of meeting a spouse's financial needs, nor deprive a child of financial support.[449] 'Needs' would be as understood under the general law of financial remedies, and not a more limited form of 'real needs' as suggested in *Radmacher*, since this has not been the subject of subsequent judicial consideration and its meaning is unclear.[450] Moreover, given the likelihood that it is wealthier couples who will be making qualifying agreements, the fact that their wealth will generally exceed their needs 'increases the relevance of the marital lifestyle to the quantification of those needs as there is more than enough "to go around".'[451]

The effect of the qualifying nuptial agreement would be to limit the court's powers to make financial orders under the Matrimonial Causes Act 1973 inconsistent with its terms, except in order to meet a party's needs or in the interests of a child of the family.[452] Such interests are not defined, and presumably, could require the wealthier spouse to enable the caring parent to remain in the former matrimonial home if that would enhance the child's welfare, rather than provide capital from other assets to purchase another property.[453] The agreement would take effect as a binding contract, but the Law Commission suggested that any dispute regarding it should be heard by a family judge with appropriate

---

[445] Law Com Consultation Paper No 198 (2010) at para 5.56.
[446] [1929] AC 601, discussed in Ch 21, Private agreements, Between spouses and civil partners, p 780.
[447] [2010] UKSC 42 [2011] 1 AC 534.
[448] Law Com No 343 para 4.29.   [449] Law Com No 343 para 5.68.
[450] Law Com No 343 para 5.82. See below for discussion of their consideration of the more general issue of determining a party's needs under the Matrimonial Causes Act 1973.
[451] Law Com No 343 para 5.83.   [452] Law Com No 343 para 5.87.
[453] The same limitations on the court's powers would apply to variation under s 35 of the 1973 Act.

experience of financial remedies.[454] An agreement which does not 'qualify' for recognition would still be subject to the *Radmacher* test, so that a court could uphold the agreement unless it would be unfair to do so. Moreover, they considered that even in the case of a qualifying agreement, the parties might still seek a consent order to give effect to its terms, rather than rely on it as a contract alone, in order to prevent any later challenge to its validity or the provision it might make for meeting the family's needs.[455]

To render a nuptial agreement 'qualifying', it would have to satisfy certain formal requirements.[456] Most importantly, they concluded that the agreement must be made by deed, that is, in writing, signed by each party and witnessed.[457] This would help ensure the parties understand the significance of their agreement, and avoid any complication of having to find consideration for the contract to take effect. To bolster the parties' understanding, they also recommended that the parties additionally sign a statement that they understand that the agreement removes the court's discretion to make financial orders (other than to meet needs).[458] Moreover, they were persuaded (contrary to their view in their Consultation Paper) that, in the case of a *pre*-nuptial agreement, there should be a cooling-off period of 28 days before the wedding if the agreement is to qualify,[459] in order to help mitigate problems in the worst cases, such as where the agreement is presented as an ultimatum on the eve of the ceremony. However, they did not consider that such a period is required in the case of a post-nuptial agreement, because the risk of pressure on a party is less, thus lending some weight to the distinction drawn between the two by Baroness Hale in *MacLeod v MacLeod*,[460] and later rejected by the majority in *Radmacher*.

The parties would be required to make 'material' disclosure, that is, regarding such 'circumstances as would reasonably be considered to be material to a decision by the other party to enter into the nuptial agreement on the relevant terms contained within it'[461] and both would be required to take independent legal advice.[462] It would be possible to revoke an agreement, but only by an agreement in writing, and signed by or on behalf of each party.[463] It is suggested that it would be preferable to require the agreement to be witnessed, just as the original agreement would have to be, given the importance of such revocation to the parties' future positions.

Would the enactment of the Law Commission's draft Nuptial Agreements Bill, which would give effect to these recommendations, make much difference to divorcing couples? The Commission considered that such an agreement might be useful for couples who wish to control the financial consequences of an eventual divorce and to preserve individual property, or an inheritance from having to be shared, or to ensure that the financial position of children from a former relationship is safeguarded.[464] The very wealthy, and those coming from jurisdictions where such agreements are commonplace, would certainly benefit from a regime which finally clarifies the status and effect of their agreement. However, since most couples lack the financial resources to do more than meet their needs and those of their children, it is likely that many, perhaps most, will continue not to bother. For them, the 'default' regime contained in the Matrimonial Causes Act will remain more important, and it is to the Law Commission's other reform proposals that we now turn.

---

[454] Law Com No 343 para 5.90–5.92.   [455] Law Com No 343 para 7.64.   [456] Ch 6.
[457] Law Com No 343 para 6.36. See Law Reform (Miscellaneous Provisions) Act 1989 s 1(3).
[458] Law Com No 343 para 6.40.   [459] Law Com No 343 para 6.63.
[460] [2008] UKPC 64 [2010] 1 AC 298 at [31], [36] discussed in Ch 22, *MacLeod v MacLeod*, p 855.
[461] Law Com No 343 at para 6.93.
[462] Law Com No 343 paras 6.125, 6.159. The same requirements would apply to variation of an agreement: para 6.186.
[463] Law Com No 343 para 6.190.   [464] Law Com No 343 para 7.3.

(b) Needs and non-matrimonial property

As the Law Commission's work on marital property agreements demonstrated, one cannot determine the ambit of such agreements without considering their impact on other aspects of the financial remedies regime and in particular, on the concepts of 'needs' and 'non-matrimonial property' as these have been developed by the courts. They accordingly issued a supplementary consultation document[465] seeking further views on how these should be formulated and made recommendations in the light of responses in their 2014 Report.[466] Criticism of 'needs' as a basis for post-divorce provision goes back to the introduction of irretrievable breakdown as the ground for divorce in 1969, and abolition of the 'minimal loss' principle in 1984—if the spouse is no longer to be 'punished' for his or her guilt through a financial penalty, and the objective is no longer to seek to put the payee in the position she would have been in if the marriage had not ended, then on what basis can an *ex*-spouse expect to have her needs met by her former spouse into the indefinite future? The Commission accepted that the financial consequences of the ending of the marriage are likely to bear unequally on one party, and so the other should, as a matter of justice, be required to redress that so far as possible, but for how long, and at what level? And what of needs that arise independently of the marriage, but affect the party's ability to be financially self-sufficient? They examined approaches in the USA, New Zealand and Canada which are based on a 'compensation' or a 'merger over time' model.[467] The former seeks to limit payment to quantified loss due to the marriage[468] but this involves speculation as to what the spouse might have done if she had not married (and given up work, for example) and appears harsh if the answer is that the spouse has 'lost' nothing because she would not have prospered in a career anyway. Under this model, needs caused other than by the marriage would not be compensable at all. The second model assumes that as the marriage continues, the couple's human capital becomes merged so that over time, it becomes harder to distinguish what each has 'brought' into the marriage from what both have created within it. It is suggested that payment or allocation of property can then be fixed according to the duration of the marriage, taking account of the marital standard of living and how the spouses shared their responsibilities for children or other dependants.[469]

Responses presented a mixed picture: while there was little support for the compensation model, there was more in favour (albeit not unqualified) of the merger over time approach.[470] The Law Commission accordingly recommended that 'the objective of financial orders made to meet a party's needs should be to enable a transition to independence', whilst recognising that the parties might have made choices during the marriage which render this more difficult or impossible to achieve.[471] They accepted that the broad concept of needs as elucidated by the courts remains apposite and rejected any rigid time limit for periodical payments, although they did recommend that a fixed term order should not last for more than 10 years.[472] However, they did not propose amending s 25 to incorporate the objective into the statute, since it would be difficult to assess the impact

---

[465] Law Commission, Consultation Paper No 208 *Matrimonial Property: Needs and Agreements, A Supplementary Consultation Paper* (2012).   [466] Law Com No 343 Ch 3.

[467] Law Commission, Consultation Paper No 208 *Matrimonial Property: Needs and Agreements, A Supplementary Consultation Paper* (2012), Ch 4.

[468] I Ellman 'The Theory of Alimony' (1989) 77(1) *California Law Review* 1 discussed by the Law Commission in Consultation Paper No 208, paras 4.34–4.51.

[469] S Sugarman 'Dividing Financial Interests on Divorce' in S Sugarman and H Kay (eds) *Divorce Reform at the Crossroads* (1990) discussed by the Law Commission in Consultation Paper No 208 at paras 4.52–4.61.

[470] Law Com No 343 paras 3.27–3.39.   [471] Law Com No 343 para 3.67.

[472] Law Com No 343 para 3.110; where payments are required for longer than 10 years, they considered that a joint lives order should be made instead.

of such a provision on the rest of the factors contained within the section, which they had not been asked to review. Rather, they saw this as a clarification and recognition of what the courts seek to do already, and—mindful of the increasing number of divorcing couples who have little or no legal assistance—recommended that the message be transmitted via 'authoritative guidance' to be drafted and issued by the Family Justice Council[473] which should contain information regarding what 'needs' are, at what level they should be met and for how long. This, with respect, is a rather weak, though undoubtedly pragmatic, suggestion, but the status of such guidance and the effectiveness of attempts to transmit it to members of the public may be open to question.[474]

A 'merger over time' model invites, and, in other jurisdictions, has utilised, a formula to calculate the sum owed,[475] but experience of the formula used for child support has made both Government and law reformers wary of going down that path, and so the Law Commission made clear that further research and consideration would have to be devoted to the issue and proposed the establishment of a working group to work on the issue.[476]

In the second part of their Consultation Paper, the Law Commission considered the issues raised by the developing concept of non-matrimonial property. They provisionally proposed that this should be defined as 'property held in the sole name of one party . . . and (1) received as a gift or inheritance; or (2) acquired before the marriage or civil partnership took place' and 'should no longer be subject to the sharing principle on divorce or dissolution, save where it is required to meet the other party's needs.'[477] They also sought views on whether items of property initially classed as 'non-matrimonial' should continue to be capable of becoming matrimonial and provisionally proposed that the mere fact of use by the family of the asset should not result in a change of status, but that where non-matrimonial property is sold and substitute property bought which *is* used for the family, or where the proceeds are invested in matrimonial property, it should be classed as matrimonial.[478] As they acknowledged, there are fine distinctions being drawn in such cases, and their conclusion that it would always be possible to make a nuptial agreement to deal with the matter may be evidence of the difficulty they felt in grappling with the issue. This ambivalence and uncertainty was reflected in the range of responses they received, and they concluded that they could not express a view on how the case-law should develop on the issue, beyond indicating their preference for the *Jones v Jones*[479] approach to dividing up property by excluding non-matrimonial assets from the pool first.[480]

(c) Wider questions

One obstacle to assessing reform proposals and their likely impact, as the Law Commission recognised, is a continuing lack of adequate, robust data on how the current system operates. We have noted how the reported cases are dominated by 'big money' cases and 'big money' concerns of minimal relevance to the mass of the divorcing population. We have little knowledge of how far the jurisprudence developed in such cases 'trickles down' the

---

[473] Law Com No 343 paras 3.69–3.78.

[474] As several respondents indicated: see Law Com No 343 paras 3.79–3.85.

[475] See the US and Canadian examples outlined at Law Com No 343 paras 4.62–4.68 and 4.69–4.73.

[476] Law Com No 343 para 4.1 and see Wider questions.

[477] Law Com No 343 para 6.41. See also J Scherpe (ed) *Marital Agreements and Private Autonomy in Comparative Perspective* (2012) and 'Towards a Matrimonial Property Regime for England and Wales?' in R Probert and C Barton (eds) *Fifty Years in Family Law: Essays for Stephen Cretney* (2012) and K Boele-Woelki et al *Principles of European Family Law Regarding Property Relations Between Spouses* 2013, pp 214 and 337.

[478] Law Com No 343 para 6.77, 6.87, 6.88.   [479] [2011] EWCA Civ 41 [2011] 1 FLR 1723.

[480] Law Com No 343 Ch 8 and para 8.81.

wealth scale[481] although one study[482] found that, as one might expect, 'needs' dominate solicitors' advice and guidance to their clients, with practical and pragmatic solutions being sought to the particular circumstances of the case. Where there were sufficient assets, 'sharing' could provide a theoretical backdrop to the way in which settlements were arrived at, and the possibility of *Mesher* orders or periodical payments rather than a straightforward clean break might be mooted as a more nuanced way of achieving 'equality'.[483] This kind of information is crucial because otherwise, regardless of the extent of consultation and advice taken into account by the Law Commission (or other reformers) the choice of reform will have to be based on theoretical arguments which, however elegant and logical, may not withstand the brutal reality of implementation particularly well.

The recommendations emanating from the Law Commission's Government-circumscribed review of the law should be able to tackle some of the most pressing issues arising from recent developments in the case law, but cannot address the more fundamental criticism that the wide discretion conferred on the courts without a clear objective governing its exercise is both unprincipled and unhelpful. It might be said that the 1970 reforms which bestowed such wide powers on the courts reflected a view of the spouses which is now out-dated: a housewife/mother dependent upon a breadwinner husband and a view of the developing case-law as being 'generous' to the wife. Such 'generosity' appeared particularly striking when the House of Lords introduced the concept of equal sharing in *White v White*[484] and the lower courts took them at their word in cases such as *Lambert v Lambert*.[485] To a great extent, the subsequent jurisprudence has been directed towards seeking to limit and row back on such 'generosity'. This has been done by seeking to get round the implications of equality through first, the idea of a 'special' or 'stellar' contribution, then by the innovation of seeking to ring-fence certain property as 'non-matrimonial' and finally, by the recognition and endorsement of marital property agreements.[486]

All such developments, and the stance taken by the Law Commission in their work on the issue, assume that, as Baroness Hale put it in *Miller; McFarlane* the 'ultimate objective [of the jurisdiction] is to give each party an equal start on the road to independent living'.[487] Most would agree with this view, but it requires a more fundamental examination of what we mean by 'equal' before it can be categorically adopted in legislation. This may in turn depend upon our modern view of marriage. The underlying rationale for proposals such as the 'merger over time' formula employed in the US and Canadian guidelines is that entitlement to share in property held by a spouse must be 'earned' by the claimant, through her (or his) contributions and effort put into the marriage. For example, John Eekelaar[488] has suggested that 'parties who share their lives together earn a share in one another's assets relative to the length of time they have shared their lives' and this view

---

[481] L Fisher 'The Unexpected Impact of *White*—Taking "Equality" Too Far?' [2002] Fam Law 108 conducted a small-scale study based on interviews with ten solicitors a year after *White* was decided. She reported that it had influenced settlements both at the big money and poor end of the scale, with a greater tendency toward 'equality' albeit falling short of a 50/50 split.

[482] E Hitchings 'Everyday Cases in the Post-White Era' [2008] Fam Law 873; 'The impact of recent ancillary relief jurisprudence in the "everyday" ancillary relief case' [2010] CFLQ 93.

[483] See also H Woodward with M Sefton *Pensions on Divorce: An Empirical Study* (2013) Ch 6 and E Hitchings, J Miles and H Woodward *Assembling the jigsaw puzzle: Understanding financial settlement on divorce* (2013).

[484] [2000] UKHL 54 [2001] 1 AC 596.   [485] [2002] EWCA Civ 1685 [2003] 1 FLR 139.

[486] See G Douglas 'Women in English Family Law: When is Equality Equity?' [2011] Sing JLS 18.

[487] [2006] UKHL 24 [2006] 2 AC 618 at [144].

[488] J Eekelaar 'Asset Distribution on Divorce—The Durational Element' (2001) 117 LQR 552 at 556.

has been echoed in the case-law.[489] It is the reason why the decision in *Miller* v *Miller*,[490] where the wife received £5 million after a marriage lasting less than three years, was so heavily criticised in the media, even though the House of Lords, in upholding this award, nonetheless agreed that 'parties will generally have less call upon each other on the break-down of a short marriage'[491] and that it may be appropriate to make 'a reduction [from equal shares] to reflect the period of time over which the domestic contribution has or will continue.'[492]

The problem with this view is that, even today, assets tend to be concentrated in the hands, and obtainable through the earning power, of men rather than women; as we have seen, the courts find it difficult to conceive of a 'stellar' contribution made in a non-financial way. But on that basis, any system based on 'contributions' will inevitably advantage men. On the other hand, if wives are then to be 'compensated' for their disad-vantage, should this be confined to such loss generated as a result of decisions made dur-ing the marriage, or must there be recognition of the structural inequality that they face? But how could that be 'fair' to the husband?

A different question arises in trying to determine whether, and if so how, the law should promote consistency and predictability of outcome. The lack of a primary objective in the statute at present has been likened to giving a bus driver advice on how to drive the bus, but no indication of where the bus is supposed to get to.[493] But even with a clear objective set, if the court has a discretion as to how to get there, there will be room for uncertainty and diversity of outcome. That could be a very valuable strength of discretion itself, but it could also be seen as increasing the difficulty of reaching a settlement and giving too much scope for inconsistency. As the Law Commission have recognised,[494] there is also therefore a need to consider whether a more structured, or limited, discretion or even a more formulaic approach such as is common in other jurisdictions, would be beneficial in helping contain costs and create predictability. In an age of diminishing access to legal advice and support and an increasing expectation that couples will sort everything out for themselves (with some mediation perhaps to nudge them to agreement), a Ford model T which does a rough and ready job of dividing the couple's assets and spelling out any future obligations between them may be a more desirable and democratic legal vehicle than a Rolls Royce model which hardly anyone can afford to buy. It may well be that the general public assumption that you split property 50/50 on divorce will (and does) deter-mine most couple's settlements anyway, regardless of the esoteric deliberations going on in the higher courts, while for some who do not wish such an outcome, a qualifying nup-tial agreement may eventually become a feature of planning the wedding. The ultimate objective for law reformers, made all the more urgent as we move to a post-legal aid world, is to create a body of law which will enable couples to negotiate and settle with a clear and accurate appreciation of their rights and obligations, to reach an outcome which truly delivers fairness to both parties and their children.

---

[489] See, in particular, *GW* v *RW (Financial Provision: Departure from Equality)* [2003] EWHC 611 (Fam) [2003] 2 FLR 108.   [490] [2006] UKHL 24 [2006] 2 AC 618.

[491] [2006] UKHL 24 [2006] 2 AC 618 per Lord Nicholls at [24].

[492] [2006] UKHL 24 [2006] 2 AC 618 per Baroness Hale of Richmond at [152].

[493] P Parkinson 'The Diminishing Significance of Initial Contributions to Property' (1999) 13 Australian J Fam Law 52, quoted by the Law Commission in Consultation Paper No 208 *Matrimonial Property: Needs and Agreements, A Supplementary Consultation Paper* (2012) at para 3.3.

[494] Law Com No 343 (2014) Ch 3.

24

COHABITATION

A. INTRODUCTION

As noted at various points in this book, one of the most significant developments in recent decades has been the growth in the number of couples, both heterosexual and same-sex, living together outside marriage (or civil partnership). There is a continuing and long-standing debate concerning how far such couples should be given a recognised legal status, akin, if not equal, to marriage and this debate has prompted a variety of policy responses in different parts of the developed world.[1] In England and Wales, the pattern has been to give ad hoc recognition as a response to particular needs in particular contexts, and we have discussed these as they have arisen throughout this work. It is now apposite to focus more directly upon the particular phenomenon of cohabitation and to consider the legal response to it. We begin by considering the demographic and sociological picture concerning its growth and extent. We next consider how it has been defined and recognised in the law, in particular noting how far cohabitation is required to mimic marriage in order to be given such recognition. Cohabitation becomes most problematic for the law when the couple separate. We therefore consider how the law currently addresses this issue, and then review proposed reforms and evaluate whether these, which the previous and present Government have both declined to implement, should be adopted. We conclude by considering whether the example of cohabitation sheds light on other alternative forms of family organisation and what implications a shift from a focus on formal status to functional and practical family arrangements has for the body of law called 'family' law.

Whilst extra-marital cohabitation might be assumed to be a modern phenomenon, it is clear that what has changed in the past half-century has been a decline in the social stigma that attaches to it, and hence its degree of visibility and acceptability. There have always been some couples who have lived together without benefit of marriage although recent historical research suggests that cohabitation was rare—at certain periods, 'vanishingly rare'—until the modern era,[2] but the attitude towards them has changed from, as Probert has put it,[3] treating them as 'fornicators' to be punished, to begrudging recognition of the reality of the phenomenon.[4] Legal recognition has often been in response to what has become seen as a pressing social problem, as, for example, in the extension of remedies for domestic violence to those who cohabit and not just those who marry.[5] The

---

[1] See (2001) 15(1) *Int Jo of Law, Policy and the Family* 'Special Issue: Unmarried Cohabitation in Europe'; Baroness Hale of Richmond 'Unmarried Couples in Family Law' [2004] Fam Law 419; and (2004) 26 *Law and Policy* special issue edited by A Barlow and R Probert.

[2] R Probert, *The changing legal regulation of cohabitation: from fornicators to family 1600-2010* (2012) pp 14-20, 35, 278 and passim cf S Parker, *Informal Marriage, Cohabitation and the Law 1753–1989* (1990).

[3] R Probert *The changing legal regulation of cohabitation: from fornicators to family 1600-2010* (2012).

[4] R Probert '"Unmarried wives" in war and peace' [2005] CFLQ 1.

[5] See Ch 6, Historical developments, p 166.

purpose of such extension was to ensure that victims could be protected, regardless of the structure of their family arrangements. It has also reflected a (sometimes rather resigned) acceptance of changing social mores, rather than a whole-hearted embrace of diversity in family form, as, for example, in the context of the rules on eligibility for welfare benefits and tax credits, which treat unmarried couples living in the same household as if they were married. The purpose here is not protective, but limiting. The State seeks to confine its exposure to having to give financial support to families, by assuming that those who live together are mutually dependent, even though there is no legal obligation on one cohabitant to support the other. But as cohabitation has come to be seen more as a 'life-style choice' and particularly as attitudes towards children born outside marriage have become more liberal, new debates over how far it should be *accepted* rather than simply tolerated, have exercised policy makers, and there is as yet no clear conclusion on where, as a society, the UK stands on the issue.

B. THE EXTENT OF COHABITATION

1. INCIDENCE

There has been a very significant growth in the number of people cohabiting outside marriage in the past 40 years. 'In 2012, there were 5.9 million people cohabiting in the United Kingdom, double the 1996 figure. Over the same period, the percentage of people aged 16 or over who were cohabiting steadily increased, from 6.5 per cent in 1996 to 11.7 per cent in 2012.'[6] The rise in cohabitation is a phenomenon not confined to Britain but is apparent in Europe and North America as well. European countries can be divided into three groupings, according to its incidence: the Nordic countries, where it is very common; the Benelux countries, France, Britain, Ireland, Germany and Austria where it is increasingly common; and Southern European countries where rates are lower. The United States would fall into the 'intermediate' category as well.[7]

Cohabitation is related to age, with more people in the younger age cohorts cohabiting than those in the oldest, but the greatest increase over the same time period was amongst those over 65, reflecting both a growth in divorce in the higher age groups, but also the growing social acceptance of cohabitation outside marriage. One can distinguish different types or purposes of cohabitation—pre-marital cohabitation, where the couple may be trying out living together as a prelude to marriage; cohabitation where the couple *cannot* marry, perhaps because one or both is already in a marriage or civil partnership (which might have been the predominant form of cohabitation when marriage was near-universal but divorce was difficult);[8] and cohabitation as an alternative to marriage, where the couple (or one of them) has no wish to formalise the union. Although cohabitation has increased across all such types, the most striking social change has been in the growth of the first of these. One survey published in 2011 summarises the trend as follows:

---

[6] ONS, *Short Report: Cohabitation in the UK, 2012* (2012) p 1.
[7] K Kiernan 'Unmarried Cohabitation and Parenthood in Britain and Europe' (2004) 26 *Law and Policy* 33 at p 39.
[8] K Kiernan 'Unmarried Cohabitation and Parenthood in Britain and Europe' at p 34. It will be recalled (see Ch 7) that one of the arguments in favour of liberalising the ground for divorce in 1969 was that it would enable those in 'illicit stable unions' to divorce and then marry their cohabitant partners.

In the 1960s, living with a prospective marital partner before marriage was relatively rare, with just three per cent of those marrying at ages below 30 doing so. By the 1970s a quarter of men and women marrying at ages under 50 cohabited with their partner prior to marriage ... it is since the late 1980s that more than half of all couples marrying have lived together beforehand, and so premarital cohabitation has been a majority practice for a quarter of a century. In recent years, the vast majority of people marrying at ages under 50 - close to four in five - have lived together prior to marriage. Indeed, marriage without first living together is now as unusual as premarital cohabitation was in the 1970s.[9]

2. DURATION AND STABILITY

The duration of cohabitation has implications for legal policy, for if cohabitation is primarily a short-term experience, the expectations and obligations imposed on the partners may be less than and different from those placed upon spouses whose lives become significantly more intertwined and interdependent. It could be argued that, if most cohabiting couples split up relatively quickly or eventually marry, the detrimental impact of the cohabitation on their economic circumstances is limited or mitigated.[10] This reduces the need to provide a remedial policy response, or at any rate, weakens any argument that cohabitation should be treated as *equal* to marriage. The demographic evidence in fact shows that the duration of cohabitation is increasing, although it is difficult to calculate this authoritatively. Surveys asking respondents how long their cohabiting relationship has lasted can only indicate its duration up to the time of interview, and not, of course, how much longer it will last. Nonetheless, Haskey reported that the median duration of cohabitation increased between 1986 and 1998, for single men from just under two years to just over three years, and for single women from roughly 18 months to over three years. Divorced men and women's cohabiting relationships lasted about one third longer.[11] Later research confirmed these data and found that by the tenth anniversary of moving in together, half of cohabiting couples had married each other, four in ten had separated and only one in ten were still cohabiting.[12] By comparison, nearly three quarters of marriages were still in existence at this point. It has been argued that cohabitation is assuming a greater significance in people's life cycles,[13] but it may still be premature to assert that it should be regarded as functionally equivalent to marriage.

But it is also important to note, from a legal policy perspective, that an increasing number of cohabiting couples are having children within that relationship (rather than marrying when the child comes along). About 60 per cent of all British families, in both 1986 and 1998, contained dependent children but the proportion of these which were formed by cohabiting partners grew from one in 30 to one in 12 (although it appears that cohabiting couples have fewer children than married couples).[14] By 2007, just under three

[9] E Beaujouan and M Ni Bhrolchain 'Cohabitation and marriage in Britain since the 1970s' *Population Trends No 145* (2011) pp 8–9.

[10] For an argument along these lines, see R Probert 'Trusts and the modern woman—establishing an interest in the family home' [2001] CFLQ 275 at p 277.

[11] J Haskey 'Cohabitation in Great Britain: past, present and future trends—and attitudes' (2001) *Population Trends No 103* 4 at p 13.

[12] E Beaujouan and M Ni Bhrolchain 'Cohabitation and marriage in Britain since the 1970s' *Population Trends No 145* (2011) p 19.

[13] A Barlow and G James 'Regulating Marriage and Cohabitation in 21st Century Britain' (2004) 62 MLR 143 at p 154.

[14] J Haskey 'Cohabitation in Great Britain: past, present and future trends—and attitudes' (2001) *Population Trends 103* 4.

in ten women having their first birth were cohabiting, nearly five times the figure of 6% in 1980–84.[15] While it might be argued that autonomy should be respected and that adults do not require protection if they choose to cohabit, the same argument cannot be applied to their children—there may need to be a policy response if it appears that the children of cohabiting parents are at particular risk of insecurity and vulnerability. And indeed, the evidence suggests that there are higher rates of breakdown amongst cohabiting unions than marriages, with cohabitants being three times more likely to separate by the time their child is aged five, than married couples.[16] It does not follow that marriage itself is more stable than cohabitation, since couples who cohabit tend to be younger, poorer and less well-educated, but it equally does not follow from this that they should not therefore receive legal protection—one could argue the reverse.

3. ATTITUDES TO COHABITATION

(a) General social attitudes

Politicians and lobby groups have often expressed the view that improving the legal position of cohabitants would 'undermine' marriage by reducing the incentive to marry and that this would be detrimental to society since—as we have seen—cohabitation appears less stable than marriage.[17] Even though there is no evidence that cohabitation in itself *causes* insta-bility, the argument might still have merit if there were high proportions of the population who regard cohabitation as 'wrong'.[18] However, statistical surveys over several years have collected data on social attitudes in Britain, and have revealed a very marked reduction in disapproval of extra-marital cohabitation, although this is age-related, with hostility higher amongst the older generation. In 1993/94, over 60% of British men and women over 60 said they would advise a young person to marry without living together first: the corresponding proportions amongst the younger generations were 40% for those aged 40 to 59, and under 20% for those aged 20 to 39. By 2000, the overall proportion of the population surveyed, who agreed that it is alright to live together without intending to get married, was 67%, and only 27% believed that married parents make better parents than unmarried ones.[19]

(b) The attitudes of cohabitants and spouses compared

A number of qualitative research studies have explored the attitudes of cohabitants in order to determine whether the nature of their commitment to each other is different

---

[15] E Beaujouan and M Ni Bhrolchain 'Cohabitation and marriage in Britain since the 1970s' *Population Trends No 145* (2011) p 10.

[16] A Goodman and E Greaves *Cohabitation, marriage and relationship stability* IFS Briefing Note BN 107 (2010) pp 2–4.

[17] See for example, Centre for Social Justice *Forgotten Families: The vanishing agenda* (2012) pp 8–9; The Marriage Foundation,*The case for marriage* http://www.marriagefoundation.org.uk/Web/Content/Default. aspx?Content=395 (accessed 5 May 2014).

[18] One might argue that this would appear logically unlikely since one would not expect to find high numbers of couples cohabiting if there were strong social pressure not to do so—but logic does not always govern personal behaviour, and Haskey reported ((2001) *Population Trends 103* at p 6) that over 80% of the population surveyed continue to regard adultery as always or mostly wrong, yet adultery is a frequently cited fact relied upon for divorce.

[19] A Barlow, S Duncan, G James and A Park 'Just a Piece of Paper? Marriage and Cohabitation in Britain' in A Park, J Curtice, K Thomson, I Jarvis and C Bromley (eds) *British Social Attitudes: The 18th Report* (2000). But note that there is a difference in the questions asked–the former asks the respondent to advise on a course of action to a given person, whilst the latter asks if the respondent thinks it is 'alright' for others to cohabit— see Haskey (2001) *Population Trends 103* at p 7.

from that of spouses and would thus explain the higher breakdown rate of cohabitation. The 'nature of commitment' has been an issue used by politicians to deny cohabitants equal treatment with spouses. For example, the Family Law Act 1996 s 41(2), provided that where a court was considering whether to make an order excluding a cohabitant partner from the family home in order to protect a cohabitant at risk of domestic abuse, if the applicant had no legal right to remain in the home then the court was required to 'have regard to the fact that they have not given each other the commitment involved in marriage'. This provision was repealed but the court must still consider 'the level of commitment involved in' the parties' relationship.[20] The *assertion* that cohabitation of itself involves a lesser commitment (and the inference that it is therefore less deserving of protection) has been tested by the empirical evidence.

Smart and Stevens,[21] for example, found that cohabitants could be categorised according to their position on a continuum of commitment from *mutual* to *contingent*. By relationships based on mutual commitment, they meant those in which the couples had reflected on the reasons for cohabiting, who sought jointly to define the nature of their relationship, monitored its progress and put in place contingency plans to deal with changes. By contingent commitment, they meant those 'based on taking a chance... or seizing an opportunity... when faced with significant life events.'[22] In their sample of 20 women and 20 men, 15 of the women were regarded as clustered toward the contingent end of the continuum and only five toward the other but only five of the women were opposed to the institution of marriage and had thus deliberately *preferred* cohabitation. By contrast, 12 of the 20 men were opposed to marriage per se. On the commitment continuum, half (10) were at the contingent end, six at the mutual end, and four were found to have had no commitment to the relationship at all.[23]

Further studies[24] have confirmed the contingent nature of cohabitation, in terms of how couples come to cohabit, although it does not follow that the respondents do not feel committed to the relationship. Studies have found that marriage may be regarded negatively as reinforcing traditional values, whilst cohabitation is seen as permitting a sense of individual freedom, greater gender equality and as a more 'honest' relationship. More prosaically, another common view expressed by respondents was that until the parties could afford an appropriately lavish wedding, they would instead cohabit—but often, the expenditure required for such a wedding is put towards other spending priorities and the wedding is postponed indefinitely.

These studies did not include a comparison with married partners, so the question whether spouses are likely to have a 'stronger' commitment to each other than cohabitants could not be explored. Other studies find different and complex patterns, however. Lewis, for example, found[25] that in a survey of cohabitants and married couples, the vast majority (over 90%) of both types of partners agreed that 'a relationship is about making a long-term commitment to each other'. Yet there *was* a difference in the *nature* of their commitment to each other, both by form of relationship, and age. The married couples

---

[20] Repealed by s 2 of the Domestic Violence, Crime and Victims Act 2004; now see Family Law Act 1996 s 36(6)(e). See Ch 6, Non-entitled applicants where the respondent has property rights, p 189.

[21] C Smart and P Stevens *Cohabitation breakdown* (2000).

[22] C Smart and P Stevens *Cohabitation breakdown* (2000) at p 24.

[23] C Smart and P Stevens *Cohabitation breakdown* (2000) at p 30.

[24] C Lewis, A Papacosta and J Warin *Cohabitation, separation and fatherhood* (2002); A Barlow and G James 'Regulating Marriage and Cohabitation in 21st Century Britain' (2004) 67 MLR 143.

[25] J Lewis 'Relationship Breakdown, Obligations and Contracts' (1999) *Family Law* 149 at p 150. A full discussion of the research may be found in J Lewis *The End of Marriage? Individualism and Intimate Relationships* (2001).

often spoke of making a *public* commitment to each other. But the younger couples felt they had made an *active* choice to marry whilst the older spouses had not felt they had had a choice about whether to marry if they wanted to live together and have children. The cohabitants saw themselves as having a *private* commitment to each other, unshaped, and unsanctioned, by any State, religious or community expectations.

A later study by Eekelaar and Maclean[26] found, when they examined whether individuals tended to view their relationships in terms of a focus on the couple themselves, on the couple as embedded within their wider families, or as part of a wider kin network, that those in the first of these categories tended to be the cohabitants.[27] This suggests that there may still be some difference between the married and unmarried as to how they view the nature of their partnership, with the former perhaps recognising more overtly that they are now part of a wider 'family'. However, all of the studies suggest that there may be more in common between young cohabitants and young spouses than between the latter and older married people; there may be more in common between spouses and cohabitants with children, than between the latter and cohabitants engaged in pre-marital cohabitation, and there may be a need for caution in combining evidence of the views of those who are still within cohabiting relationships with those who have separated, since perceptions can change with experience.

C. DEFINING COHABITATION

Although case law has inevitably developed to interpret the meaning of statutory language used to define cohabitation, it has not been possible for the courts themselves to develop a concept of cohabitation which might attract legal rights and obligations. In the property sphere, for example, which we discussed in Chapters 4 and 5, the focus of attention has been on property and financial ties arising because of the parties' conduct towards each other, usually regardless of the nature of the personal relationship between the parties. It has been for Parliament to enact provisions expressly identifying cohabitants as included within their scope. We therefore turn to consider the varying definitions utilised by Parliament and consider how the courts have interpreted them.

The 1970s saw the first real recognition of cohabitants as a class for whom legal provision should be made. The Domestic Violence and Matrimonial Proceedings Act 1976, for example, which enabled an applicant to obtain an injunction to control a spouse's behaviour and even to exclude him or her from the matrimonial home, also applied to 'a man and a woman who are living with each other in the same household as husband and wife'.[28] The subsequent case law illustrates the difficulties that can arise in interpretation of this kind of definition.

1 'ARE LIVING WITH EACH OTHER'

First, taken literally, it could imply that, once a partner had left the home because of the other's violence, he or she was no longer 'living with' the other so as to come within the

---

[26] J Eekelaar and M Maclean 'Marriage and the Moral Bases of Personal Relationships' (2004) 31 *Journal of Law and Society* 510; M Maclean and J Eekelaar 'The Obligations and Expectations of Couples within Families: Three Modes of Interaction' (2004) 26 *Journal of Social Welfare and Family Law* 117.

[27] Maclean and Eekelaar (2004) 26 *Journal of Social Welfare and Family Law* 117 at p 128.

[28] Section 1(2).

statute and claim its protection. The courts therefore interpreted it to mean that the parties must have been living together at the time of the incident which led the applicant to leave the home.[29] But if the applicant failed to take action until some time after he or she had left, the court might conclude that it could no longer be said that the couple were living together.[30]

2. 'IN THE SAME HOUSEHOLD'

Secondly, it will be noted that the provision required the couple to be living 'in the same household'. This too could cause problems if the couple's relationship had deteriorated but they were still living under the same roof. In *Adeoso v Adeoso*[31] the couple lived in a two bedroomed flat. They slept in separate rooms and communicated only by notes. They continued to share the living expenses. Ormrod LJ described their situation as:

> exactly comparable to a marriage which is in the last stages of break-up. . . . In practical terms you cannot live in a two-room flat with another person without living in the same household. You have to share the lavatory, share the kitchen, share the bathroom and take great care not to fall over one another in most of these cases; and it would be quite artificial to suggest that two people living at arm's length in such a situation, from which they cannot escape by reason of the housing difficulties, are to be said to be living in two separate households.[32]

Difficulty may arise at the start of a relationship too. Many couples 'drift' into living together, gradually spending more time under the same roof, with one partner gradually moving his or her belongings into the other's property. At what point can it be said that the couple are now living in the same household with each other? This may be relevant both to provisions of the type included within the domestic violence legislation, where it is sufficient that the parties are currently (albeit expansively defined) living together, and to those where they must have been living together for a certain period of time before they come within their scope. For example, the Inheritance (Provision for Family and Dependants) Act 1975 and the Fatal Accidents Act 1976 both include a cohabitant who had lived with the deceased for at least two years within the list of those who may make a claim. In *Kotke v Saffarini*[33] the partners each had their own home. The deceased had worked away from both during the week, but kept a change of clothes and spent most weekends at the claimant's house. He used his own home as his postal address, and when their child was born, he gave it as his address on the birth certificate. Later, he began to use his partner's address as his for official purposes. The Court of Appeal upheld the trial judge in distinguishing between wanting to live in the same household, planning to do so, and actually doing so, and agreed with his conclusion that the deceased's 'centre of gravity' had not shifted until after the couple discovered that the claimant was pregnant. She thus failed to satisfy the two-year threshold for making a claim under the Act. But 'living apart together'[34] in this way is recognised as a growing phenomenon and if the 'functional' basis of family relationships is regarded as of greater significance than the

---

[29]   *O'Neill v Williams* [1984] FLR 1, CA.
[30]   See eg *Harrison v Lewis* [1988] 2 FLR 339, CA where there was a nine-month delay in taking proceedings and the court held it had no jurisdiction.   [31]   [1980] 1 WLR 1535, CA.
[32]   At 1537D–E, 1539A–B.   [33]   [2005] EWCA Civ 221 [2005] 2 FLR 517.
[34]   S Duncan et al *Living apart together: uncoupling intimacy and co-residence* (2013).

'form' of those relationships, which we discuss at the end of this chapter, there may be no good reason to exclude such arrangements from the legal protection given to those who happen to live under the same roof for more of the time.

3. 'A MAN AND A WOMAN'

Thirdly, the Domestic Violence and Matrimonial Proceedings Act referred to 'a man and a woman' living with each other. Its successor section, contained in the Family Law Act 1996 s 62(1), also defined cohabitants as 'a man and a woman who, although not married to each other, are living together as husband and wife'. It has been convincingly argued that such a definition could not be interpreted so as to include same-sex partners because the language is too clear and unambiguous.[35] By contrast, the House of Lords were able to rule that a similar provision in the Rent Act 1977 *could* be re-interpreted so as to be non-discriminatory and hence ECHR-compliant. Schedule 1 para 2(2) to that Act provided that '*a person*[36] who was living with the original tenant as his or her wife or husband shall be treated as the spouse of the original tenant' so as to be able to take over a protected tenancy on the tenant's death. In *Fitzpatrick v Sterling Housing Association Ltd*,[37] before the Human Rights Act 1998 came into force, the House had considered that these words were gender-specific and could not be extended to cover couples of the same sex. However, the issue arose before them again in *Ghaidan v Godin-Mendoza*.[38] This time, they ruled that restricting the ambit of the provision to heterosexual couples was discriminatory towards those of the same sex, and that such discrimination infringed Art 14 of the European Convention on Human Rights taken with the right to respect for one's home under Art 8. Finding no objective or reasonable justification for such discrimination,[39] the House held that the provision should be interpreted so as to give effect to the surviving partner's Convention rights. They thus held, agreeing with the Court of Appeal, that the words 'as his or her wife or husband' should be read as stating 'as *if they were* his or her wife or husband'.

It is most unlikely that the different wording used in the two Acts was anything other than accidental, yet it would have deprived same-sex partners of a remedy in what is certainly no less serious a situation—domestic violence—than being required to leave one's home because the landlord will not accept a person as their tenant. Clearly, also, same-sex partners may require the same protection from domestic violence as heterosexuals, just as it was recognised in the 1970s that cohabitants might deserve the same protection as spouses. Section 62 as originally enacted would therefore probably be regarded as incompatible with the European Convention on Human Rights. To prevent such a ruling, it was first amended to:

> two persons who, although not married to each other, are living together as husband and wife or (if of the same sex) in an equivalent relationship.[40]

[35] R Bailey-Harris and J Wilson '*Mendoza v Ghaidan* and the Rights of De Facto Spouses' [2003] Fam Law 575. [36] Emphasis added.
[37] [2001] 1 AC 27, HL. See A Diduck 'A Family by any other Name . . . Or Starbucks Comes to England' (2001) 28 *Journal of Law and Society* 290.
[38] [2004] UKHL 30 [2004] 2 AC 557. Lord Millett dissented. See R Probert 'Same-Sex Couples and the Marriage Model' (2005) 13 Fem LS 135.
[39] See also the same conclusion reached by the European Court of Human Rights in *Karner v Austria* [2003] 2 FLR 623 in relation to the phrase 'life companion' used in the equivalent Austrian legislation.
[40] By the Domestic Violence, Crime and Victims Act 2004 s 3.

This definition was further amended by the Civil Partnership Act 2004[41] and now reads:

> two persons who are neither married to each other nor civil partners of each other but are living together as husband and wife or as if they were civil partners.

4. 'AS HUSBAND AND WIFE'

These changing definitions identify another potential problem for those seeking to apply them to different factual situations. To live together 'as husband and wife'[42] implies some *quality* in the arrangement which differs from, say, that of landlord and lodger, or flat-sharing friends, or even family members of different generations. It goes to the essence of the relationship, but what does it entail? The various authorities[43] on this point were fully reviewed in *Kimber v Kimber*.[44] There, the ex-husband was required to pay maintenance to his former wife until she remarried or cohabited. He claimed that her fiancé was cohabiting with her, and stopped payments. She then sued for the arrears. The fiancé had been a lodger in the ex-wife's bed and breakfast establishment, but he moved out and rented a flat elsewhere. However, he spent much of his time with her, often staying the night, and he helped her run the business. In concluding that the couple were cohabiting, the judge considered the following factors, or 'signposts', as material:

(1) Living together in the same household
    Generally this means that the parties live under the same roof, illness, holidays, work and other periodical absences apart. . . .
(2) A sharing of daily life
    Living together seems to me to inevitably involve a mutuality in the daily round: a sharing of tasks and duties. . . .
(3) Stability and a degree of permanence in the relationship; that it is not a temporary infatuation or passing relationship such as a holiday romance. . . .
(4) Finances
    Is the way in which financial matters are being handled an indication of the relationship? . . .
(5) A sexual relationship
    It is enough for me to state that this is admitted and is ongoing. . . .
(6) Children
(7) Intention and motivation
(8) The opinion of the reasonable person with normal perceptions.[45]

By contrast, in *Butterworth v Supplementary Benefits Commission*,[46] the female applicant was refused welfare benefits on the basis that she was cohabiting. In fact, she was being cared for in her own home after a serious accident by her former partner. On appeal, the court found that he was doing this out of loyalty and friendship. He had his own bedroom

---

[41] Sch 9 para 13.

[42] Cf the criterion used in the Immigration Rules (HC 395) para 295A: a 'relationship akin to marriage'.

[43] See *Atkinson v Atkinson* [1988] 2 FLR 353; *Crake v Supplementary Benefits Commission*; *Butterworth v Supplementary Benefits Commission* (1981) FLR 264; *Re J (Income Support: Cohabitation)* [1995] 1 FLR 660; *Re Watson (Deceased)* [1999] 1 FLR 878.   [44] [2000] 1 FLR 383.

[45] At pp 391–3. Compare the Family Law (Scotland) Act 2006 s 25(2), which provides: 'In determining whether a person is a cohabitant of another person the court shall have regard to—(a) the length of the period during which A and B have been living together (or lived together); (b) the nature of their relationship during that period; and (c) the nature and extent of any financial arrangements subsisting, or which subsisted, during that period.'   [46] (1981) FLR 264.

and they did not have a sexual relationship. He did cook and perform household tasks that she was unable to carry out because of her injuries. Both regarded the arrangement as temporary until the applicant had recovered. The court concluded that the couple were not living together as husband and wife, because it was not their intention to do so.

Hitherto, and as such cases indicate, the courts have tended to focus on the degree to which the parties' lives are intertwined. But in *Nutting v Southern Housing Group Ltd*[47] the court looked instead at the degree of permanent commitment in the relationship. The claimant had had a tempestuous same-sex relationship with his partner, at one time being ordered from the flat (of which the partner was sole tenant) and imprisoned for breach of a non-molestation order. The partner had now died. The claimant sought to succeed him as tenant under the Housing Act 1988 (a provision equivalent to that in issue in the *Fitzpatrick* and *Ghaidan* cases discussed earlier). The court accepted that the ruling in *Ghaidan* meant that the provision should be interpreted as extending to same-sex couples but rejected the claim. On appeal it was held that the couple had not been living together as if they were husband and wife. Evans-Lombe J upheld the first instance judge, who had emphasised the need to establish that the relationship was an emotional one of 'mutual lifetime commitment rather than simply one of convenience, friendship, companionship or the living together of lovers'.[48] Further, he considered that the relationship must also be one which has been presented to the outside world 'openly and unequivocally so that society considers it to be of permanent intent—the words "till death us do part" being apposite'.

In emphasising these criteria, the court confronted the question of what is meant by the expression, living 'as husband and wife', as distinct from 'as lovers'. It demonstrated that the statutory language in such provisions does indeed apply marriage-likeness, or marriage-equivalence, as the key criterion for eligibility, and as we saw earlier, one of the fundamental features of marriage is that it is intended to last for life. As we have seen, circumstances may well arise where a couple who 'cohabit' would find it difficult honestly to say that they intended or even hoped to do so for the rest of their lives.[49] It is submitted that in some statutory contexts, despite the requirement of the relationship having to be 'marriage-like', such a strict test should not be imposed. For example, we have noted that under the Family Law Act 1996, a court deciding whether to make an occupation order in favour of a cohabitant must in any event have regard to the 'level of commitment' in the couple's relationship:[50] whatever one thinks of the motivation of Parliament in imposing such a test on cohabitants, it recognises that one may be 'living as husband and wife', without making exactly the same kind of commitment to each other as spouses do and without it following that the applicant must necessarily be deprived of the remedy being sought.

Evans-Lombe J also appeared to regard it as essential that the parties' relationship was 'openly and unequivocally' presented to the outside world. But here again, he may have gone too far. In reaching this view, he referred in particular to the speech of Lord Millett in *Ghaidan v Godin-Mendoza*.[51] His Lordship (who actually dissented in that case) certainly emphasised the importance of 'outward appearances'[52] but with respect, both Evans-Lombe J and the court in *Nutting* may have been confusing the requirement to satisfy an objective test of whether a couple can be said to be living as husband and wife, with a necessity to *present* themselves as so living. The two are different things. One might imagine that some couples, especially same-sex couples in some communities, would seek to keep the nature of their relationship private from their neighbours,

---

[47] [2004] EWHC 2982 (Ch) [2005] 1 FLR 1066.   [48] At para 9.

[49] See the discussion earlier, The attitudes of cohabitants and spouses compared, pp 937–939.

[50] Section 36(6)(e) as amended by Domestic Violence, Crime and Victims Act 2004 s 2(2).

[51] [2004] UKHL 30 [2004] 2 AC 557.   [52] Para 92.

employers and family. It should not follow that the life they share together cannot be classed as 'marriage-like'. Indeed, it would be ironic if, just because it used to be more common for cohabiting women to take their partner's name and refer to themselves as 'Mrs', in order to avoid the stigma of being known to 'live in sin', a couple who now choose not to demonstrate the intimacy of their relationship to the outside world should be regarded as not cohabiting. Moreover, the original 'cohabitation rule', from which the criteria in *Kimber v Kimber*[53] were drawn, was developed precisely because benefit claimants hid the fact that they were cohabiting from the outside world in general and the authorities in particular.

As already mentioned, the Civil Partnership Act amended the law to import into the relevant legislation a new definition of cohabitation for same-sex partners of 'living as if civil partners'. This concept has yet to be unpacked. What does this phrase mean? How does it differ from living together as if married, or as 'husband and wife'? Is the nature of a civil partnership in some way different from marriage? Now that the Marriage (Same Sex Couples) Act 2013 requires the terms 'marriage', 'married couple' etc to be construed as including a reference to same-sex couples, does it follow that civil partnership should be interpreted differently? Schedule 3 para 2 to the Act provides that:

(1) In existing England and Wales legislation—
  (a) a reference to persons who are not married but are living together as a married couple is to be read as including a reference to a same sex couple who are not married but are living together as a married couple;
  (b) a reference to a person who is living with another person as if they were married is to be read as including a reference to a person who is living with another person of the same sex as if they were married.
  ...

3 (1) This paragraph applies to existing England and Wales legislation which deals differently with—
  (a) a man and a woman living together as if married, and
  (b) two men, or two women, living together as if civil partners.

(2) If two men, or two women, are living together as if married, that legislation applies to them in the way that it would apply to them if they were living together as civil partners.

It is unclear which pieces of legislation do in fact 'deal differently' with heterosexual and same-sex cohabiting couples, since the objective of such legislative language has been to ensure they are dealt with in the same way. Nevertheless, it could be argued that this provision does suggest that there is now expected to be some qualitative difference in the relationship between spouses and civil partners, so one is taken back to the question of what that difference might be, on which judicial guidance is awaited.

5. A GENERAL DEFINITION?

Such issues demonstrate some of the sensitivities and difficulties in arriving at a workable general definition of cohabitation. They indicate why the extension of legal protections has been ad hoc, and why the definitions have not been uniform. Context is of paramount importance in this area of the law. For example, we have noted that a claimant must demonstrate having lived for two years with the deceased when claiming under the

---

[53] [2000] 1 FLR 383.

Fatal Accidents Act 1976 or Inheritance (Provision for Family and Dependants) Act 1975. Other jurisdictions adopt different qualifying periods, such as, in New Zealand, where a three-year qualifying period, or the birth of a child, is required for a claim under the Property (Relationships) Act 1976.[54] Any such periods are bound to be arbitrary and can work injustice: a woman who has been living with a man for 18 months may be as much in need of compensation if he is killed as if she had been living with him for two years. For this reason, the Family Law (Scotland) Act 2006 adopts no minimum qualifying period at all for those seeking financial remedies on cohabitation breakdown, but requires the court to consider the duration of the parties' living together in deciding whether they were actually cohabiting.[55]

Whether it would be possible or desirable to produce a uniform definition to apply to all contexts is a debatable point and not one which governments have seemed keen to tackle. However, a private member's bill, the Cohabitation Rights Bill, was introduced into Parliament in 2013 to make provision for cohabitants in relation to their financial position on separation or death. It would have defined cohabitants as:

any two people (whether of the same sex or the opposite sex) who—
  (a) live together as a couple, and
  (b) meet the first and second conditions specified in subsections (2) and (3).

(2) The first condition is that any of the following apply to the two people ("A" and "B") who live together as a couple—
  (a) A and B are each treated in law as being mother, father or parent of the same minor child,
  (b) a joint residence order in favour of A and B is in force in respect of a minor child,
  (c) A and B are the natural parents of a child *en ventre sa mere* at the date when A and B cease to live together as a couple (whether or not that child is subsequently born alive), or
  (d) A and B have lived together as a couple for a continuous period of two years or more.

(3) The second condition is that A and B—
  (a) are neither married to each other nor civil partners of each other, and
  (b) are not within prohibited degrees of relationship in relation to each other.

The Bill did not define what was meant by living 'together as a couple' and thus did not address the problems adverted to in this section. Whether it would make sense for yet a further model of cohabitation to appear in a statute may be open to question.

D. LEGAL PROVISION FOR SEPARATING COHABITANTS

The position of cohabitants affected by particular areas of the law, where they are already given express recognition under the relevant statutes, such as remedies for domestic abuse, or on the death of a partner, are discussed in this book in the chapters dealing

---

[54] See B Atkin 'The rights of married and unmarried couples in New Zealand—radical new laws on property and succession' [2003] CFLQ 173.   [55] Section 25.

with those issues.[56] We also consider the application of the law where it makes *no* special provision at all for cohabitants and uses general rules and principles, such as determining the ownership of property, in Chapter 5.[57] But cohabitants face greatest difficulty under the law when the relationship ends through separation as it is then that they are likely to dispute the legal consequences of their relationship and may be most in need of financial protection. In order to determine whether the law should be reformed to improve their position, we need to consider what recognition has been given to this problem.

1. COHABITANTS' PROPERTY ARRANGEMENTS

It is first necessary to consider the nature of cohabitants' property interests, since the extent to which the law may need to be amended to protect cohabitants depends upon whether they are likely to incur significant disadvantage under the current property rules. The available data relates to the family home, since this is the largest and most significant asset for most couples. Haskey[58] reported in 2001 that about one quarter of cohabitants responding to a large statistical survey stated that they had moved into their partner's existing accommodation when cohabitation began, and the rest acquired new accommodation, either having previously lived in their own home or with their parents. Whilst roughly the same proportions of never married men and women moved into their partner's home, amongst the separated and divorced it was much more common for men than women to do so, probably because many separated and divorced women have retained the former family home as part of a settlement in which they have primary care of the children and the home has been preserved for them to be brought up in it until they reach adulthood.[59] In general, cohabiting couples were slightly more likely to rent their home than married couples, who were more likely to be buying their property with the aid of a mortgage. For example, 46% of cohabiting men and women were renting and about 40% buying, compared with 41% of married men and women renting and 45% buying.[60] Clearly, although financially vulnerable cohabitants whose relationship ends may face hardship if they lose their home, if the couple were renting, they will not run the risk of losing out on the investment in the capital value of the property which might have increased in value during the cohabitation.

As we saw in Chapter 5, whether the property is held in joint names or by one partner only is an important aspect of legal entitlement. Haskey found very little difference between men and women regarding this question. About a third each of cohabiting men and women reported that their home was in their name, in their partner's name, and in joint names.[61] But cohabiting women were disadvantaged as compared with married women in this regard since 43% of married women lived in homes held in joint names. However, age made a difference, with younger cohabitants more likely to hold in joint names. Since cohabitation is concentrated amongst the younger age groups, this may suggest that the vulnerability of some cohabitants, especially women, because of lack of legal entitlement to occupy may diminish over time as a higher proportion of cohabitants acquire homes jointly in the future. Moreover, Haskey found that the length of time a couple had been cohabiting was generally shortest amongst those where the home was in the man's name and longest when it was not.[62] This may reflect couples acquiring a new

---

[56] See Chs 6 and 25.   [57] Ch 6.

[58] J Haskey 'Cohabiting couples in Great Britain: accommodation sharing, tenure and property owner-ship' (2001) *Population Trends 103* 26.   [59] Haskey (2001) *Population Trends 103* at p. 32.

[60] Haskey (2001) *Population Trends 103* Table 1.   [61] Haskey (2001) *Population Trends 103* Table 2.

[62] Haskey (2001) *Population Trends 103* at p 34.

home after living together for a while, and putting it in joint names. In any case, in the event of the relationship breaking down, the woman will have been proportionately less disadvantaged because of the shortness of the partnership.

2. COHABITANTS' KNOWLEDGE OF THEIR LEGAL POSITION

One might argue that where a couple choose to cohabit outside marriage, they can easily protect themselves by reaching an agreement on what legal consequences should flow if they separate. The major difficulty with this is that it appears that many cohabitants assume their relationship carries the same legal consequences as marriage.[63] In one national survey in 2006, 51% of people believed that cohabitation for a period of time gives the same legal rights as marriage—the 'myth' of the 'common law marriage', and 53% of cohabiting couples believed this.[64] In fact, marriage ceased to be governed by the common law in England and Wales in 1753,[65] when marriage law was codified. However, the persistence of the belief that the concept of 'common law marriage' still exists is unsurprising: although it should be noted that a 'common law marriage' was a valid *marriage*, whilst those couples who refer to themselves as 'common law' husbands or wives today know that they are not, in fact, married, but are claiming instead that they have the same rights *as if* they were.[66] First, social security rules generally treat married and unmarried couples alike, so that many couples who have had experience of these will assume that the rest of the law does too. Secondly, as just noted, in areas of the law such as inheritance and domestic violence, the position of cohabitants has been largely assimilated with that of spouses through legislative reform. So cohabitants may perhaps be forgiven for assuming, or hoping, that the law treats them the same in all circumstances. Moreover, cohabitants may have different—very often gendered—expectations of their relationship and the legal consequences that would or should flow from it and what appear to be 'irrational' decisions (leaving the person legally unprotected) may make sense within the context of the relationship as they see it.[67]

It may well be that since a significant proportion of couples separate after relatively short periods of cohabitation, perhaps when a 'trial marriage' has proved unsuccessful, their finances and property may have had little time to become enmeshed, and complex issues are less likely to have arisen by the time of separation. Moreover, as other researchers have noted,[68] few 'ordinary people... have a clear and accurate understanding of their legal position and the legal consequences of everyday actions.' Even on relationship breakdown, however, when those involved might be thought to recognise the need

---

[63] A Barlow and S Duncan 'Supporting families? New Labour's communitarianism and the "rationality mistake" Parts I and 2' (2000) 22 JSWFL 23 and 129; A Barlow et al 'Just a Piece of Paper? Marriage and Cohabitation in Britain' in A Park et al (eds) *British Social Attitudes: The 18th Report* (2000).

[64] A Barlow et al 'Cohabitation and the law: myths, money and the media' in A Park et al (eds) *British Social Attitudes: The 24th Report* (2008). This represented a small decline, from 56% in 2000, but the proportion of people who positively *knew* there is no such thing had barely changed, despite a major Government publicity campaign—see later in this section.

[65] See Ch 2, Formalities of marriage, Reform of the common law, p 48.

[66] See further, R Probert 'Common-law marriage: myths and misunderstandings' [2008] CFLQ 1; *The changing legal regulation of cohabitation: from fornicators to family 1600-2010* (2012) ch 7.

[67] A Barlow and J Smithson 'Legal assumptions, cohabitants' talk and the rocky road to reform' [2010] CFLQ 328.

[68] C Smart and P Stevens *Cohabitation breakdown* (2000) at p 41. See also G Douglas et al *A Failure of Trust: Resolving Property Issues on Cohabitation Breakdown* (2007) p 48.

for legal advice and help, it seems that fewer cohabitants turn to lawyers than is the case amongst the divorcing population.[69] This is likely to be exacerbated by the withdrawal of legal aid from most family litigation.

In the light of the evidence of this level of ignorance, a considerable amount of very useful information was made available on the internet through the Government's 'Living Together' campaign.[70] Researchers[71] found that users of the site found it helpful, with the proportion reporting that they felt they were very well informed about the legal position of cohabitants increasing from 19% before they had visited the site to 61% after. Over a third said that they would now discuss matters with their partner, and nearly 30% said they would make a will or seek legal advice. Yet by the end of the study, few had actually acted on these intentions, with one of the main reasons being that there was no suitable action that they could take to improve their position. For example, whilst in theory they felt that cohabitation agreements were a good idea, in practice they were not likely to be useful because respondents were uncertain about their enforceability. Others were reluctant to face the costs of taking legal measures which might be unnecessary, and others did not want to contemplate their relationships ending. Some had difficulty in persuading their partners to do anything.

3. CONTRACTS

Some better-informed cohabitants will nonetheless seek to contract with each other regarding the financial and property implications of their relationship. But a refusal to find an intention to enter into legal relations has been demonstrated in cases concerning unmarried partners, just as it has in relation to spouses.[72] In *Horrocks v Forray*[73] the executors of a man's will sought possession of a house in his name, occupied by the defendant and her two children. She had been the man's mistress for some 17 years and claimed that she had a contractual licence[74] to remain in the house. But the Court of Appeal held that although the man may have intended to make some provision for her financial security, this did not amount to an intention to enter into a binding agreement to do so, still less to relate specifically to her being permitted to occupy the house. As Scarman LJ put it:

> whatever relationship did exist between these two, it could as well be referable to the con-tinuance of natural love and affection as to an intention to enter into an agreement which they intended to have legal effect.[75]

In the absence of the agreement being made by deed, it may be equally difficult to establish that there was any consideration for it. In the context of occupation of the family home, it has been held that if one partner has given up some existing right or suffered some other detriment to go and live with the other, it may be possible to regard this as consideration and thus give rise to a contractual licence. In *Tanner v Tanner*,[76] for example, the plaintiff

---

[69] M Maclean and J Eekelaar *The Parental Obligation* (1997); S Arthur, J Lewis, M Maclean, S Finch and R Fitzgerald, *Settling Up: making financial arrangements after divorce or separation* (2002); R Moorhead, M Sefton and G Douglas *The Advice Needs of Lone Parents* (2004).

[70] http://www.advicenow.org.uk/livingtogether (accessed 5 May 2014).

[71] A Barlow, C Burgoyne and J Smithson *The Living Together Campaign—An investigation of its impact on legally aware cohabitants* (2006).   [72] See Ch 4, Contracts, Between the spouses, p 98.

[73] [1976] 1 All ER 737, CA.

[74] Relying on the decision of the Court of Appeal in *Tanner v Tanner* [1975] 3 All ER 776, CA.

[75] At 547; See, to like effect, *Layton v Martin* [1986] 2 FLR 227.

[76] [1975] 3 All ER 776, CA, discussed further in Ch 5, Other forms of protected occupation, Contractual licence, p 156.

bought a house for the defendant and their twin daughters and the defendant surrendered a rent-controlled tenancy to move into it. When the plaintiff later claimed possession of the house, it was held that, as the defendant had furnished consideration by giving up the security of her flat, the licence was a contractual one. But in *Horrocks v Forray*, Megaw LJ, whilst not basing his decision on the point, was satisfied that the woman had made no equivalent sacrifice sufficient to found consideration for the man's alleged offer to look after her.[77]

A complicating factor in establishing consideration in the case of agreements between unmarried partners has been the role of public policy. At one time, an agreement between cohabitants might have been struck down as based on 'immoral consideration' because of its promoting a sexual relationship outside marriage.[78] As Lord Wright stated in *Fender v St John Mildmay*:

> The law will not enforce an immoral promise, such as a promise between a man and a woman to live together without being married or to pay a sum of money or to give some other consideration in return for an immoral association.[79]

But such a view was refined in *Sutton v Mishcon De Reya and Gawor and Co*,[80] at least in relation to the question of whether partners may contract with each other as regards their financial and property rights. The claimant formed a sado-masochistic relationship with a wealthy businessman, in which the claimant was the 'master' and the businessman his 'slave'. They jointly instructed the first defendants to draft a deed designed to 'create legally binding arrangements as to financial and other matters'[81] and which documented that the slave would give all his financial assets to the master. The couple were advised that the agreement might be regarded as unenforceable. The relationship broke down, and the claimant sued the solicitors and another firm which had advised him about the terms of a separation for negligence. Hart J, striking out the claim, held that whilst a property contract between two people who were cohabiting *could* be valid, the agreement in issue was primarily a contract for sexual relations outside marriage[82] and therefore unlawful. He considered that the agreement sprang directly from and was intended to give meaning to the sexual master/slave fantasy that the couple were enacting.[83] The distinction between an agreement concerning sexual relations on the one hand, and property rights arising from a relationship which involves sexual relations on the other, thus appears still to exist in English law, but at least it is clear that the latter should not now be struck down, without more, simply because the parties are in a sexual relationship.[84] Indeed, precedents for cohabitation contracts[85] are readily available, and as *marital* property agreements

---

[77] [1976] 1 All ER 737, CA at 745a.

[78] See the discussion by R Probert *The changing legal regulation of cohabitation: from fornicators to family 1600-2010* (2012) pp 46–49, 92–95.   [79] [1938] AC 1 at 42.

[80] [2003] EWHC 3166 (Ch) [2004] 1 FLR 837. See M Pawlowski 'Cohabitation Contracts: The *Sutton* Case' [2004] Fam Law 199; R Prober, '*Sutton v Mischon de Reya and Gawor & Co*—Cohabitation contracts and Swedish sex slaves' [2004] CFLQ 453.   [81] At para 11.

[82] It has been argued that categorising non-marital sexual relations as 'unlawful' is contrary to Art 8 of the ECHR and that marital status is irrelevant—the court will not, even within a marriage, enforce sexual relations: see G Wilson '*Sutton* in Practice' [2004] Fam Law 202.

[83] At para 23.

[84] His Lordship considered that the agreement would in any case have been unenforceable either because of actual undue influence by the claimant over his partner, or because there was no intent to enter into legal relations, but the latter ground appears dubious given the care taken by both parties to have the agreement drawn up by solicitors in the first place. See the comment by R Bailey-Harris at [2004] Fam Law 247.

[85] See C Barton *Cohabitation Contracts* (1985); A Barlow *Cohabitants and the Law* (2001, 3rd edn), E Kingdom 'Cohabitation Contracts and the Democratization of Personal Relations' (2000) 8 Fem LS 5.

become more common in the wake of their recognition in *Granatino v Radmacher*[86] one would expect them to be readily accepted by the courts provided they conform to the usual contractual requirements and are focused on the financial and property aspects of the relationship.

4. TRANSFER OF TENANCIES

Oddly, notwithstanding concerns amongst politicians regarding the extension of legal protection to cohabitants, Parliament did in fact take a highly significant *symbolic* step on the way towards equalising the position of married and unmarried couples by enacting Schedule 7 to the Family Law Act 1996 when reforming the law on the grant of non-molestation and occupation orders. The power given in that Schedule to transfer tenancies applies to cohabitants (and former cohabitants)[87] as well as to spouses and former spouses, civil partners and former civil partners.

Cohabitants are defined, by s 62(1),[88] as:

> two persons who are neither married to each other nor civil partners of each other but are living together as husband and wife or as if they were civil partners.

The court may make an order to transfer the tenancy of the dwelling-house in which the couple cohabited, when they have ceased living together.[89] When deciding whether to make an order, the court must have regard, where only one of the cohabitants was entitled to occupy the property, in addition to matters in respect of spouses or civil partners,[90] to the following factors:

— the nature of the parties' relationship, and in particular the level of commitment involved in it;

— the length of time they cohabited;

— whether they have had any children together, or have had parental responsibility for any children; and

— the length of time since they ceased to cohabit.[91]

The court may also exercise powers to adjust the parties' liabilities in respect of the tenancy and to order the transferee to compensate the transferring tenant. Unlike former spouses, a former cohabitant may apply even after he or she has married or begun to cohabit with someone else, although this will clearly be a factor the court will take into account when determining whether to make the order.

---

[86] [2010] UKSC 42 [2011] 1 AC 534.   [87] Sch 7 para 1.

[88] As amended by Civil Partnership Act 2004 Sch 9 para 13. Prior to that Act entering into force, the relevant definition was 'two persons who, although not married to each other, are living together as husband and wife or (if of the same sex) in an equivalent relationship;' as inserted by s 3 of the Domestic Violence, Crime and Victims Act 2004.

[89] Sch 7 paras 3(2), 4(b). A transfer cannot be made where the tenancy is held jointly by the entitled cohabitant and a third party: *Gay v Sheeran* [1999] 2 FLR 519, CA.

[90] See Ch 23, Transfer of tenancy, p 907. The matters include the parties' financial resources, their needs and those of any relevant child, the effect of transferring, or not transferring, the tenancy on their health, safety and well-being, and their suitability as tenants.

[91] Section 36(6)(e)–(h), as amended, discussed in Ch 6, Non-entitled applicants where the respondent has property rights, p 189.

There are no reported decisions relating to such transfers in respect of cohabitants, so how far the courts are prepared to make these orders is not known. If they do show a willingness to do so in appropriate cases (presumably where the couple lived together for a long time, and perhaps more likely where they were joint tenants), it may well be asked why there is no equivalent power to make a transfer order in respect of owner-occupied property.[92]

E. REFORM OF THE LAW

1. COHABITANTS' SEPARATION ARRANGEMENTS

The lack of a discretionary jurisdiction to allow the court to divide cohabitants' property, or to order periodical payments, as it can do on a divorce, and the existence of highly complex case-law on establishing an entitlement to share in the beneficial interest in property through the device of a constructive trust, *might* appear to be productive of injustice for cohabitants, but only empirical research can help to determine whether this is in fact the case. One study of 62 former cohabitants in the year 2000 found that cohabitants' settlements of their property after separating were characterised by each retaining the assets seen as 'theirs'—both in relation to assets they had brought into the relationship and those acquired during it.[93] They were much less likely than divorcees to reach a settlement based on the parties' respective needs, unless there were children of the relationship, and less likely to divide the assets equally. Instead, the researchers found that 'entitlement' was the dominant model, although understandings of such entitlement were not straightforward: cohabitants might base their view of legal entitlement on what they believed or assumed was the position (which could range from believing the law followed strict title, to believing it required equal shares), or on a view that a larger contribution to the acquisition of an asset should be reflected in a larger share. They conducted a further study in 2006[94] and found similar outcomes: homes owned by one partner were always retained by him or her, jointly-owned homes were either retained by one partner or sold. They found that, as before, the most important influence on settlement was ownership, with contributions or the needs of the children or adults carrying little weight except in relation to what happened to jointly-owned property or household goods.

Another study also found similar outcomes, and noted the difficulty practitioners acting for cohabitants had in predicting the terms of the settlement reached because of the uncertainty of the case-law on constructive trusts. The researchers considered that many cohabitant applicants would have fared better under the divorce jurisdiction, especially women with children who had no interest in the family home, and cohabitants of either sex who were trying to obtain compensation for contributions they had made to property held in their former partner's sole name.[95]

---

[92] See the comment by M Hayes in her written evidence to the House of Lords Special Public Bill Committee, Session 1994–95 HL 55, p 37.

[93] S Arthur et al *Settling Up: making financial arrangements after divorce or separation* (National Centre for Social Research, 2002).

[94] R Tennant, J Taylor and J Lewis *Separating from cohabitation: making arrangements for finances and parenting* DCA Research Series 7/06 (2006).

[95] G Douglas et al 'Cohabitants, Property and the Law: A Study of Injustice' (2009) 27 MLR 24, pp 34–36.

2. REFORM PROPOSALS BY THE LAW COMMISSION

Such findings lend support to the argument that the existing law requires reform. Many other jurisdictions,[96] including Australia[97] and New Zealand[98] have introduced legislative schemes dealing with these points. Some, such as New Zealand, simply equate cohabitants with spouses (after the couple have lived together for a certain length of time) and enable them to apply under the same jurisdiction. Others, such as Scotland, provide a discrete jurisdiction which provides remedies for cohabitants albeit on a more limited basis than would apply to spouses. For example, there, the Family Law (Scotland) Act 2006 provides a discretionary regime enabling cohabitants to apply for a capital sum to compensate for having suffered an economic disadvantage in the interests of the other party or a child, or where that other party has derived an economic advantage from the applicant's contributions.[99] In Ireland, the Civil Partnership and Certain Rights and Obligations of Cohabitants Act 2010 enables a cohabitant who has lived with a partner for five years, or two years where they have had a child together, to obtain compensatory maintenance or a property adjustment order where he or she is 'financially dependent' on the other as a result of the cohabitation.[100]

Although the Law Commission had earlier failed to come up with recommendations for a scheme relating to the general law relating to 'Sharing Homes',[101] the more precise issue of whether special provision should be made for cohabitants was referred to them and they reported in 2007.[102] Their initial consultation paper had summed up the problems with the current law as follows:

> [the rules are] . . . relatively rigid and extremely difficult to apply, and their application can lead to what many would regard as unfairness between the parties. The formulation of a claim based on these rules is time consuming and expensive, and the nature of the inquiry before the court into the history of the relationship results in a protracted hearing for those disputes that are not compromised. The inherent uncertainty of the underlying principles makes effective bargaining difficult to achieve as parties will find it hard to predict the outcome of contested litigation.[103]

(a) Rationale for provision to be made

The Law Commission accordingly proposed a new statutory discretionary scheme to cater for eligible cohabitants, from which they could opt out if they chose, but which would not

[96] See Law Commission, Law Com No 278 *Sharing Homes: A Discussion Paper* (2002) Part IV; L Fox 'Reforming property law—comparisons, compromises and common dimensions' [2003] CFLQ 1.

[97] See M Pawlowski 'Property rights of home-sharers: recent legislation in Australia and New Zealand' (2001) 10 Nottingham LJ 20.

[98] See B Atkin 'The rights of married and unmarried couples in New Zealand—radical new laws on property and succession' [2003] CFLQ 173.

[99] Indeed, the Scots proposals pre-dated the Law Commission: see Scot Law Com No 135 *Report on Famiily Law* (1992) Part XVI, para 16.23 and Scottish Executive, *Family Matters: Improving Family Law in Scotland* (2004) Section 4. For discussion of the early working of the Scottish law, see F McCarthy 'Cohabitation: lessons from north of the border?' [2011] CFLQ 277; J Miles et al 'Cohabitation: lessons from research north of the border?' [2011] CFLQ 302.

[100] See J Mee 'Cohabitation law reform in Ireland' [2011] CFLQ 323.

[101] See Law Commission, Law Com No 278 *Sharing Homes: A Discussion Paper* (2002), see Ch 5, Reform, p 162.

[102] See Law Commission, Law Com No 179 *Cohabitation: The Financial Consequences of Relationship Breakdown* (2006) and Law Com No 307 (2007). The project included examination of cohabitants' position where the partner dies. See Ch 25, Intestate succession, Updating the legislation, p 967 and The position of cohabitants, p 973 for discussion.

[103] Law Com No 179 para 1.28.

be a simple extension of the Matrimonial Causes Act 1973 to couples living together. They rejected this latter approach because they considered it a 'strong argument' that cohabitants 'have not given each other the legal commitment, or accepted the status, of marriage or civil partnership'[104] and they were mindful that the yardstick of equality used in the financial remedies jurisdiction on divorce, may not be acceptable to the general public when applied to cohabitants who might have lived together for a relatively short time.[105] They also noted the criticisms that have been made of the divorce jurisdiction, particularly its lack of predictability, but considered that any formulaic scheme would be too inflexible. They therefore proposed 'a principled discretion, whereby the court would be given distinct objectives and some leeway in how they were to be achieved. Outcomes would be predictable within a range of possibilities and settlement would thereby be facilitated.'[106]

To ensure due predictability, they proposed that the discretion given to the courts would be 'weaker' than that applying under the 1973 Act, in that the statute would determine the pre-conditions for relief and its objectives.[107] They next had to decide what those objectives should be. Unlike during marriage, there is no statutory duty on cohabitants to maintain each other during the relationship, and they therefore did not consider that the relief of 'needs' could offer a principled justification.[108] This did not mean that needs are irrelevant. Rather, they concluded that the rationale for the jurisdiction lies in relieving the loss or hardship suffered by a cohabitant, which has been generated by the cohabiting relationship itself. This might well consist of meeting their resulting needs, but it might not be *limited* to this.[109] Such relief of relationship-generated disadvantage has been recognised as one of the principles underpinning the exercise of the divorce jurisdiction,[110] and as we have noted earlier, it also forms the basis of the Scottish scheme for cohabitants. They recommended that the applicant would therefore have to prove that:

(1) the respondent has a retained benefit; or
(2) the applicant has an economic disadvantage;

as a result of qualifying contributions the applicant has made . . .

A **qualifying contribution** is any contribution arising from the cohabiting relationship which is made to the parties' shared lives or to the welfare of members of their families. Contributions are not limited to financial contributions, and include future contributions, in particular to the care of the parties' children following separation.

A **retained benefit** may take the form of capital, income or earning capacity that has been acquired, retained or enhanced.

An **economic disadvantage** is a present or future loss. It may include a diminution in current savings as a result of expenditure or of earnings lost during the relationship, lost future earnings, or the future cost of paid childcare.[111]

It will be seen that this scheme would recognise the non-financial contributions (including caring for the couple's children, or for other family members, or taking on more child care so that the other can work longer hours to meet the costs of the household)[112] both past and future,[113] that the partner makes, which are currently not taken into account

---

[104] Law Com No 307 at para 4.2.
[105] Law Com No 307 para 4.9.   [106] Law Com No 307 para 4.15.
[107] Law Com No 307 para 4.16.   [108] Law Com No 307 paras 4.20–4.21.
[109] Law Com No 307 paras 4.24 *et seq*. Cf the Irish scheme, critiqued by Mee in [2011] CFLQ 323, which focuses on financial dependence.   [110] As discussed in Ch 23.
[111] Law Com No 307 paras 4.33–4.36, emphasis added.   [112] Law Com No 307 para 4.44.
[113] Law Com No 307 para 4.49.

when determining whether a constructive trust has arisen but which are so important in the divorce jurisdiction. It would thus meet one of the major limitations of current property law in remedying unfairness to financially vulnerable cohabitants. It also enables due focus to be given not just to how far that vulnerable party has lost out, but also how the partner may have *gained* from the cohabitation. However, it insists on a causal connection between the financial impact and the cohabiting relationship[114] although the Commission were at pains to seek to reassure that the kinds of evidential difficulties which bedevil constructive trust claims should be minimised by a regime which is seeking to provide a discretionary solution rather than the precise quantification of loss or gain.[115]

A retained benefit would be found where, for example, the property is held in one partner's sole name, but the other has contributed to its acquisition, or the other had increased the value of the property through improvements.[116] The aim of the jurisdiction would be to 'reverse' that retained benefit by requiring the title holder to recompense the other for the cost incurred—subject to discretionary factors which we note later. One might expect that more commonly, the claim would be brought based on the economic disadvantage suffered by the applicant, particularly through loss of future earnings or failure to secure adequate pension provision through having given up work to undertake caring responsibilities, but also possibly failing to make savings or investments that it could be proved would otherwise have been undertaken.[117]

(b) Eligibility to make a claim

We earlier discussed the difficulties of defining cohabitation, and in particular, the problematic nature of the marital analogy whereby couples applying for certain remedies (such as non-molestation orders) must show that they are living with each other as husband and wife (or even more awkwardly, as civil partners). The Law Commission regarded such analogies as confusing but, since they did not attach a draft Bill to their report, they did not feel it incumbent upon them to produce their own definition instead. Rather, they proposed that 'the essential type of relationship that should be covered by any new scheme is that of a couple who share a household' but who are not married to each other nor civil partners.[118] They rejected the idea of a checklist of factors to guide the court but in fact, they used the same kinds of 'signposts' that we have outlined[119] as being 'helpful' to a court determining if the relationship was the requisite one.

We also saw that legal remedies for cohabitants may impose further requirements, relating to the duration of the relationship and the presence of children, since these seem to reflect public understandings of the commitment that they consider is required to justify eligibility for the remedy. The Law Commission recommended that if the couple have a child together, the duration of their cohabitation should be irrelevant, but that childless couples should have to have lived together for a minimum period. However, they did not feel it appropriate to propose what that period should be, other than within the range of two to five years. Inevitably, any time period will be arbitrary but these lengths reflect both existing law (such as the two-year minimum for claims under the Inheritance (Provision for Family and Dependants) Act 1975) and the upper limits applying in other

---

[114] Law Com No 307 at para 4.43.
[115] Law Com No 307 at para 4.28.   [116] Law Com No 307 at paras 4.52–4.55.
[117] Law Com No 307 at para 4.60.
[118] Law Com No 307 at paras 3.11–3.13. Indeed, they suggested that areas of the law utilising the marital analogy should be amended along such lines.   [119] Earlier, 'As Husband and Wife', p 942.

jurisdictions.[120] They did recommend that if a longer minimum than two years were fixed, then consideration should be given to allowing the court to dispense with it to alleviate hardship particularly where, for example, the couple might have had a child living with them who is not a child of both parties.[121]

(c) Orders the court could make

In line with the matrimonial jurisdiction, the Law Commission recommended that the court should be able to make both financial provision and property adjustment and pension orders,[122] but that periodical payments should be limited to meeting the costs of child care.[123] They reasoned that the clean break principle carries greater weight in relation to cohabitants given that they have not made a legal commitment to support each other during the relationship and that it is important for the payer to know exactly where he or she stands financially once and for all.[124] Their scheme would clearly be wider than the Scottish one, but the exclusion of periodical payments appears unnecessary and illogical given the recognition by the House of Lords in *McFarlane v McFarlane*[125] that relationship-generated disadvantage—the very rationale for the Law Commission's scheme—might need to be recompensed by means of such payments if the payer lacks sufficient capital with which to do so.

(d) Factors the court would take into account

As a discretionary regime, albeit one with a clearer objective than applies to orders made on divorce, the Law Commission's scheme would require the court to consider a number of factors in order to decide the amount of relief and the form of order that might be made.[126] These factors are similar—but not identical—to the divorce jurisdiction:

(1) the welfare while a minor of any child of both parties who has not attained the age of eighteen [[to which first consideration would be given];

(2) the financial needs and obligations of both parties;

(3) the extent and nature of the financial resources which each party has or is likely to have in the foreseeable future;

(4) the welfare of any children who live with, or might reasonably be expected to live with, either party; and

(5) the conduct of each party, defined restrictively [as on divorce] but so as to include cases where a qualifying contribution can be shown to have been made despite the express disagreement of the other party.[127]

It may be noted that first consideration would not be given to a 'child of the family' as applies when making financial orders on divorce, but only to the children of the relationship, although the welfare of children who live or might live with either party would be relevant. The main reason for the limitation appears to be the Commission's wish to focus on the scheme as a remedial jurisdiction for the adult partners—liability to support children may be the subject of applications under Schedule 1 to the Children Act 1989 where the partner was a married step-parent.[128] The Commission also considered that, while

---

[120] Such as the five year period (for claims on intestacy) in South Australia: para 3.47 n 58.
[121] Law Com No 307 para 3.58.   [122] Law Com No 307 para 4.40.
[123] Law Com No 307 para 4.99.   [124] Law Com No 307 para 4.98.
[125] [2006] UKHL 24 [2006] 2 AC 618. See Ch 23, Compensation, p 872.
[126] Law Com No 307 para 4.82.   [127] Law Com No 307 para 4.38.
[128] See Ch 21, Proceedings under Schedule 1 to the Children Act 1989, p 794.

'conduct' should rarely be relevant (as with the divorce jurisdiction), the fact that a quali-fying contribution had been made *against the wishes* of the other party, might be taken into account. This sounds a little odd, but the Commission reasoned that the essence of the scheme is that the consequences of the joint decision-making and life-choices of the couple are shared fairly between them.[129] Where this was not the case, then in their view, the court should take this into account in deciding what, if any, order to make. It should also be noted that whilst the objective of the proposed scheme is not, as we noted earlier, to meet the partner's needs, the needs and obligations of both would clearly be relevant in determining what orders to make.

In compensating for economic disadvantage, the Law Commission considered that this:

> is a continuing cost of the relationship... for which there may be no corresponding retained benefit that could form the subject of a claim in itself and which should be shared rather than borne by one party alone. We are not here addressing losses that have been caused by the wrongdoing of one party against the other. By contrast, economic disad-vantage encompasses losses which have been borne exclusively by one party when they should be shared. It would therefore be clearly inappropriate to find that the applicant had suffered a loss and then to reverse it, simply transferring the burden to the shoulders of the other party.[130]

This reasoning is difficult to follow: why should a partner who has foregone career oppor-tunities only be compensated for half his or her loss, whilst had he or she put an equivalent 'investment' in the shape of cash into the other's property, the other would be required—so far as they were able—to 'reverse' their benefit completely?

More understandable is the Commission's view that when making an order to share the economic disadvantage, the court should not thereby place the applicant in the longer-term in a *stronger* economic position than the respondent, which they called the 'economic equality ceiling'. This would prevent the financially stronger party from mak-ing a claim based on disadvantage that they might also have incurred as a result of the relationship (such as themselves foregoing a lucrative career move for the sake of the partnership).[131]

(e) Evaluation

The Law Commission's recommendations did not find favour with the Government. The Labour Government proposed to wait until the results of research into the operation of the new Scottish scheme were available before deciding whether to implement the pro-posals, an admirable nod to the importance of evidence-based policy-making which was unfortunately revealed as a sham by its own failure to fund such research. When the research was eventually undertaken,[132] it suggested that the wider powers and clearer objectives of the Law Commission's proposals had the potential to deliver a more effec-tive scheme than that legislated in Scotland, although problems of comprehensibility to laypeople and establishing proof of disadvantage would be equally challenging. There was no opening of the floodgates when the scheme was introduced in Scotland, indeed, there were fewer claims made than might have been expected, so it is unlikely that either

---

[129] Law Com No 307 paras 4.50, 4.95.
[130] Law Com No 307 para 4.70. The Commission's explanation is at para 4.71, but with respect, is unconvincing.   [131] Law Com No 307 paras 4.77–4.78.
[132] J Miles, F Wasoff and E Mordaunt 'Cohabitation: lessons from research north of the border?' [2011] CFLQ 302.

lawyers or courts would be swamped with claims in England and Wales. But by that time, the Coalition had formed the Government and the Conservatives were not prepared to do anything to appear to 'promote' cohabitation rather than marriage and they announced that they would not bring forward any reforms in the current Parliament.

Of course, with the loss of legal aid, the potential under-use of the scheme would now be accentuated. However, one might speculate that the introduction of a discretionary jurisdiction might well alter cohabitants' expectations when they separate and reduce the proportion of those who simply opt for the default of strict legal ownership governing their claims against each other, which as we noted earlier, is currently the position. Whether the possibility of opting-out of the statutory scheme by making a cohabitation contract would be taken up in large numbers is open to doubt, but perhaps the publicity attached to 'pre-nups' governing celebrity divorces may raise public awareness of the possibility anyway. The lack of political enthusiasm for any reform[133] rendered the proposals largely academic when they first emerged, but as cohabitation continues to develop as at least a normal stage in the family life-cycle, it will become increasingly impossible to ignore amending the law in the longer term.

3. STATUS OR FUNCTION?

That raises a final question to consider. The Law Commission were clear that their terms of reference were not directed towards developing any proposals regarding a general 'status' of 'cohabitant'.[134] Even if their proposals were enacted, we would therefore still have a patchwork of laws of greater or lesser consistency of definition and applicability covering legal issues on an ad hoc basis. But equally, if it were to be resolved instead to undertake a wholesale reform of the law,[135] the resultant creation of effectively a new 'status' of cohabitant would not address the broader issue of whether it is right for the law to focus on such status, when the ways in which people live their lives are becoming increasingly diverse and episodic. Many scholars have argued that the law should rather concentrate on identifying the functions and practices that people engage in which ought to give rise to legal consequences such as rights and obligations, regardless of the form in which they do them, with the rationale for imposing such consequences flowing from their mutual interdependence.[136] Thus, those who 'live apart together' but do not live in the same household, or those, such as elderly siblings, who live together but do not have sexual relationships, might face similar problems of financial dependency and loss, which could be addressed without worrying that they do not 'conform' to more common family forms.

The problem for the law, however, is that lines ultimately have to be drawn. If spouses, cohabitants, and siblings or three-generation families all require some forms of legal redress if their relationships turn sour or end in death, one might say the same for lodgers and student flat-mates. While the latter *might* incur lesser financial hardships because

---

[133] But Lord Lester of Herne Hill did introduce a Private Member's Bill along similar (but wider) lines into the House of Lords in 2008 and Lord Marks of Henley-on-Thames introduced a measure seeking to enact the Law Commission's proposals both for separating cohabitants and those where one partner dies intestate through his Cohabitation Rights Bill in 2013.   [134] Law Com No 307 at paras 1.2 and 1.24.

[135] Lord Marks' Bill, see earlier, would not represent a 'wholesale' reform being limited to separation and intestacy.

[136] See eg A Barlow and G James 'Regulating Marriage and Cohabitation in 21st Century Britain' (2004) 62 MLR 143; A Diduck, 'Shifting Familiarity' (2005) 58 *Current Legal Problems* 235; L Glennon 'The limitations of equality discourses on the contours of intimate obligations' in J Wallbank, S Choudhry and J Herring (eds) *Rights, Gender and Family Law* (2010) 197; S Wong 'Shared commitment, interdependency and property relations: a socio-legal project for cohabitation' [2012] CFLQ 60. For a critical comparative review, see R Leckey, 'Cohabitation and Comparative Method' (2009) 72 MLR 48.

of the more contingent and short-term nature of their relationships, this will not always be the case. In their *Sharing Homes* discussion paper in 2002, the Law Commission concluded that they were unable to produce reform which could adequately respond to the myriad ways in which people share homes. It is no more likely that they, or other legal policy-makers, could do so in determining duties of support or duties of care. Ultimately, a 'family law' has to be a law for and about families, and such families have to be defined and delineated according to shared values and understandings. The result may be frustrating as social mores change in advance of legal norms, but legal reformers are, it is submitted, rightly cautious about either creating new legal statuses (or forms) of recognised family such as cohabitants, or widening legal obligations beyond what public opinion will regard as 'appropriate' ties of intimacy or blood.

25

INHERITANCE AND INTESTACY

When a person dies, there are various legal consequences, the most important of which will concern the status of any partner, if the deceased was married or had a civil partnership, and the distribution of any property the deceased owned. In this chapter we consider first the rare situation where a person's death must be legally presumed so that a spouse or civil partner can regard her or himself as free to remarry, and relatives can deal with his or her estate. We then consider the law concerning succession.

A. PRESUMPTION OF DEATH

The death of either party brings a marriage (or civil partnership) to an end. The Matrimonial Causes Act 1973 s 19[1] permitted the court to make a decree[2] of presumption of death and of dissolution of the marriage if satisfied that there were reasonable grounds for supposing that the applicant's spouse is dead and s 55 of the Civil Partnership Act 2004 made equivalent provision for a 'presumption of death order'.[3] These provisions are superseded from 1 October 2014,[4] under the Presumption of Death Act 2013 by a new, general process for obtaining a declaration that a person is presumed to be dead. Section 1 of the Act provides that where a person who is missing is thought to have died, or has not been known to be alive for a period of at least seven years, any person may apply to the High Court for a declaration that the missing person is presumed to be dead.[5] The court must refuse to hear the application if it is brought by someone other than the missing person's spouse, civil partner, parent, child or sibling and the court considers that the applicant does not have a sufficient interest in the determination of the application. Under s 2, the court must make the declaration if it is satisfied that the person has died or has not been known to be alive for a period of at

---

[1] The power was originally given by the Matrimonial Causes Act 1937.

[2] Note that, as with nullity and divorce, a decree nisi and decree absolute were granted. A decree nisi had to be rescinded if the other spouse was found to be still alive: *Manser v Manser* [1940] P 224. Once it had been made absolute, however, it dissolved the marriage irrevocably even though the other subsequently reappeared, but in that case the court had power to make orders for financial relief: *Deacock v Deacock* [1958] P 230, CA

[3] Rather than a decree.

[4] Section 16. Civil Partnership Act 2004 s 55 is not repealed by the 2013 Act, but Sch 2 para 3 to that Act amends s 222 of the 2004 Act to provide that the court may only make an order under that Act if the High Court would not have jurisdiction to make a declaration under the 2013 legislation.

[5] The missing person must have been domiciled in England and Wales when they went missing, have been habitually resident in England and Wales for at least one year ending on that day, or the applicant for the declaration must him- or herself be domiciled, or habitually resident for one year, in the jurisdiction: s 1(3), (4).

least seven years—a time period in line with the former common law presumption of death, and that contained in s 19 of the 1973 Act.[6]

A copy of the declaration must be sent to the Registrar General and, once any possible appeal has been exhausted, the declaration will be conclusive of the person's presumed death and effective against all persons and for all purposes, including for the purposes of the acquisition of an interest in any property and the ending of a marriage or civil partnership to which the missing person was a party.[7] The court may make such orders as it considers reasonable relating to any interest in property acquired as a result of the declaration,[8] which should facilitate the transfer and transmission of title, for example, a Register of Presumed Deaths will record the declaration and a certified copy will act as a death certificate to be used by those left behind to deal with the person's estate and affairs.[9] Should the missing person be discovered alive, the declaration can be revoked, or, if, for example, the date of their death is discovered to be different from that previously thought, it can be varied.[10]

Under s 19(3) of the Matrimonial Causes Act 1973, the decree might be granted based on 'the fact that for a period of seven years or more the other party to the marriage has been continually absent from the petitioner and the petitioner has no reason to believe that the other party has been living within that time', which would constitute evidence that the other party was dead until the contrary was proved. This placed an emphasis on the applicant's belief and in *Thompson v Thompson*[11] Sachs J held that nothing must have happened during the period of seven years from which the applicant, as a reasonable person, would conclude that the other spouse was still alive. Under the 2013 Act, the declaration must be made if the court is satisfied that the missing person has died or has not been *known* to be alive for at least seven years. This appears to apply a more obviously objective test, although even under the matrimonial jurisdiction, a court would hardly be likely to accept that the petitioner's belief was reasonably held unless satisfied that they had made all appropriate enquiries.

B. SUCCESSION

The law of succession[12] in England and Wales is based on the principle of freedom of testation. A person who makes a valid will may choose to whom they leave their property without restriction (although, in limited circumstances, this may be subject to challenge later

---

[6] *Chard v Chard* [1956] P 259. See G Treitel 'Presumption of Death' (1954) 17 MLR 530; *Tweney v Tweney* [1946] P 180; *Re Watkins* [1953] 2 All ER 1113; *Bullock v Bullock* [1960] 2 All ER 307.   [7] Section 3.

[8] Section 4.   [9] Section 15.   [10] Section 5.

[11] [1956] P 414. A pure speculation was insufficient. The petitioner must give evidence: *Parkinson v Parkinson* [1939] P 346.

[12] See R Kerridge with A Brierley, *Parry and Kerridge: The Law of Succession* (2009, 12th edn). For an empirical study of family wills, see J Finch et al *Wills, Inheritance and Families* (1996) and J Finch and J Mason *Passing On: Kinship and Inheritance in England* (2000) and for evidence of public attitudes to inheritance and the law, see C Williams et al 'Cohabitation and intestacy: public opinion and law reform' [2008] CFLQ 449; A Humphrey et al *Inheritance and the family: attitudes to will-making and intestacy* (2010); G Douglas et al 'Inheritance and the Family: Public Attitudes' [2010] Fam Law 1308; G Douglas et al 'Enduring Love? Attitudes to Family and Inheritance Law in England and Wales' (2011) 38 *Journal of Law and Society* 245. For consideration of inheritance tax levied on an estate, and attempts to avoid—and repeal—it, see A Mumford 'Inheritance in Socio-Political Context: The Case for Reviving the Sociological Discourse of Inheritance Tax Law' (2007) 34 *Journal of Law and Society* 567; N Lee 'Inheritance tax—an equitable tax no longer: time for abolition?' (2007) *Legal Studies* 678.

under the provisions of the Inheritance (Provision for Family and Dependants) Act 1975, discussed in Section C). This position is in contrast to most civil law regimes (including, to some extent, Scotland)[13] where the testator's freedom is circumscribed and fixed (or 'forced') shares are allocated to particular relatives.[14]

However, only around one-third of adults in England and Wales have made a will.[15] Although this proportion increases with age[16] and death rates are much higher for those over pension age,[17] it appears that nearly one-third of people aged 65 or over have not made a will.[18] As the Law Commission have noted, it is difficult to obtain precise statistics for the number of people dying without leaving a will, as it is less likely that those with small estates will bother to do so, and there is no requirement to obtain a grant of representation to distribute the estate in these cases or where property passes automatically to a survivor (such as on a joint tenancy). The numbers are likely to be well over 100,000 per annum.[19] The rules governing the position when someone dies without making a will—the intestacy rules—therefore play an important part in determining the orderly transmission of property on a death.

We discuss the rules governing the disposition of property in three different contexts. First, we examine the position where the deceased dies leaving a will. Secondly, we consider the intestacy rules applying where no will (or valid will) has been made. Thirdly, we discuss the opportunities to challenge the disposition of property where a person considers that they have not been adequately provided for under either the will which was made, or under the intestacy rules. In all of these contexts, it will be seen that the rules make assumptions about what constitute family relationships and the appropriateness of recognising these through devolution on death.

1. TESTATE SUCCESSION

The law relating to wills and testate succession[20] generally presents few problems peculiar to family law. Until the beginning of the last century the most important question was the testamentary capacity of a married woman. At common law she had virtually no power to make a will, although she could always devise and bequeath property held to her separate use in equity even if it were subject to a restraint upon anticipation.[21] When the equitable concept of separate property was extended to legal separate property by the Married

---

[13] Scottish Law Commission, *Discussion Paper on Succession* Discussion Paper No 136 (2007) and *Succession* Scots Law Com No 215 (2009). For commentary on their proposals, see D Reid 'From the Cradle to the Grave: Politics, families and inheritance law' (2008) 12 *Edinburgh Law Review* 391 and D Reid 'Inheritance Rights of Children' (2010) 14 *Edinburgh Law Review* 318. For a study of Scottish social attitudes to inheritance law, see Scottish Executive *Attitudes Towards Succession Law: Findings of a Scottish Omnibus Survey* (Scottish Executive Social Research, 2005).

[14] See European Commission *Green Paper, Succession and Wills* COM (2005) 65 Final; C Castelain, R Foqué and A Verbeke *Imperative Inheritance Law in a Late-Modern Society* (2009).

[15] National Consumer Council *Finding the will: a report on will writing behaviour in England and Wales* (2007) p 3; K Rowlingson and S McKay *Attitudes to Inheritance in Britain* (2005) p 71, Humphrey et al op cit n 12, ch 3.   [16] K Rowlingson and S McKay op cit p 85.

[17] ONS *Mortality Statistics: Deaths Registered in 2007* (2008) Table 4, DR_07.

[18] S Brooker *Finding the will: a report on will-writing behaviour in England and Wales* (2007) 3.

[19] The figure is extrapolated from the Law Commission, who note that of around 500,000 deaths each year, there are about 280,000 grants of representation of which about a third concern intestate estates; added to these there will be substantial numbers of very small estates: Consultation Paper 191, *Intestacy and family provision claims on death* (2009) para 1.6.

[20] See C Sherrin et al (eds) *Williams on Wills* (2008, 9th edn and supplements).

[21] See Ch 5, The restraint upon anticipation, p 106.

Women's Property Act 1882, her power to dispose of it by will was likewise extended, so that her testamentary incapacity remained only with respect to property acquired by her before 1883. Under the Law Reform (Married Women and Tortfeasors) Act 1935 she was given full power to dispose of all her property as if she were a feme sole.[22]

There are, however, still certain matters of particular importance to family members which we must note.

(a) Revocation of wills by marriage or civil partnership

By s 18 of the Wills Act 1837 every will made by a man or woman is revoked by his or her marriage (including now, of course, a same-sex marriage).[23] The section does not apply if the marriage is void,[24] but does in the case of voidable marriages.[25] Equivalent provisions apply to civil partnerships[26] and one would expect these to be interpreted in the same way as they have been in relation to marriage.

There are a number of exceptions to the general rule. First, a will is not to be revoked by marriage, insofar as it is made in exercise of a power of appointment, if the property thereby appointed would not pass in default of appointment to the testator's personal representatives.[27] This is because the marriage cannot possibly affect the devolution of the property involved.

The other exceptions are designed to fulfil the intention of a testator who makes his will on the eve of his wedding. If it appears from a will that at the time it was made the testator was expecting to be married to a particular person and that he or she intended that the will should not be revoked by the marriage, the marriage to that person is not to revoke it. The same rule applies if it appears that the testator intended that a particular disposition should not be revoked by the marriage: in that case the disposition is to take effect, as are all other dispositions in the will, unless it appears that the testator intended that a particular disposition was to be revoked.[28]

These exceptions relating to wills made in contemplation of marriage which have been inserted into the Wills Act 1837 replace an exception (couched in significantly different terms) contained in s 177 of the Law of Property Act 1925. This section was liberally construed. For example, in *In the Estate of Langston*[29] a will by which the testator left his whole estate to 'my fiancée MEB' was held not to have been revoked by his marriage to her two months later. Similarly, a will would now be saved if the testator made a bequest 'to my fiancée ABC' but gave the residue of his estate to others.[30] Difficulty arises because it is frequently impossible to tell whether, by making a gift to his fiancée, a testator was

---

[22] For an interesting empirical perspective on the modern position of women as will-makers, see E Hasson, ' "Where there's a Will There's a Woman": Exploring the Gendered Nature of Will-Making' (2013) 21 *Feminist Legal Studies* 21.

[23] As substituted by s 18 of the Administration of Justice Act 1982, implementing the recommendations of the 22nd Report of the Law Reform Committee (*The Making and Revocation of Wills*) 1980 (Cmnd 7902). The changes made by the Administration of Justice Act do not apply to wills *made* before 1 January 1983: s 73(7).

[24] *Mette v Mette* (1859) 1 Sw & Tr 416.   [25] *Re Roberts* [1978] 3 All ER 225, CA.

[26] Section 18B inserted by s 71 and Sch 4 para 2 to the Civil Partnership Act 2004.

[27] Section 18(2). Hence the will may be revoked in part but not insofar as the power is exercised: *In the Goods of Russell* (1890) 15 PD 111. See also *In the Goods of Gilligan* [1950] P 32.

[28] Section 18(3), (4). This provision does not apply to wills made before 1 January 1983 (Administration of Justice Act 1982 s 73(7) and s 76(11)) which are still governed by s 177 of the Law of Property Act 1925.

[29] [1953] P 100. See also *Pilot v Gainfort* [1931] P 103, where the testator made a will by which he bequeathed his personalty to 'DFP my wife'. Although he was living with her at the time, he did not marry her until 18 months later. It was held that the will was not revoked by the marriage. Contrast *In the Estate of Gray* (1963) 107 Sol Jo 156.   [30] Thus reversing *Re Coleman* [1976] Ch 1.

intending to provide for his future wife or was merely making a temporary arrangement in case he should die before the proposed marriage took place. In many cases this problem may be resolved by s 21 of the Administration of Justice Act 1982, which permits extrinsic evidence to be admitted to resolve ambiguities in the wording of a will.[31] But in *Court and Others v Despallieres*[32] the judge held that a will leaving the whole of an estate worth some £7 million to the deceased's same-sex partner, with whom he shortly afterwards entered into a civil partnership, was revoked by the partnership notwithstanding a clause directing that the will not be revoked by 'subsequent marriage, Civil Union Partnership nor adoption', because it did not show clearly enough that he expected to form any civil partnership, still less with that particular person.

(b) Revocation of wills by dissolution or annulment

Whereas the entry into a marriage or civil partnership automatically revokes a will (unless one of the exceptions just considered applies), its dissolution used not to do so. Consequently, if the testator did not make another will, his or her estate might pass to a former spouse from whom he or she had long been divorced and who might have remarried. To overcome this difficulty, s 18A of the Wills Act[33] was added to provide that:

(a) provisions of the will appointing executors or trustees or conferring a power of appointment, if they appoint or confer the power on the former spouse, shall take effect as if the former spouse had died on the date on which the marriage is dissolved[34] or annulled, and

(b) any property which, or an interest in which, is devised or bequeathed to the former spouse shall pass as if the former spouse had died on that date,

except in so far as a contrary intention appears by the will.[35]

The section operates if the marriage was dissolved or annulled by a court of civil jurisdiction in England and Wales or by a divorce or annulment obtained elsewhere and entitled

---

[31] In any case, the surviving spouse now needs less protection because of the substantial sums that she (or he) takes on intestacy and the court's wide powers to make financial provision for a dependant under the Inheritance (Provision for Family and Dependants) Act 1975 (see later, Who may apply for an order, p 976ff and Reasonable provision, For a surviving spouse or civil partner, p 983 *et seq*). Cf *Anthony and Another v Donges and Another* [1998] 2 FLR 775: testator provided that if wife survived him, she was to have 'such minimal part of my estate . . . as she may be entitled to under English law for maintenance purposes'. Held, the clause was void for uncertainty, there being no such entitlement, and the testator could not provide jurisdiction to the court to apply the 1975 Act in modified form. But other beneficiaries, with no alternative claim, may be deprived of their gifts by revocation. See J Tiley 'Wills and Revocation—Marriage and Contemplation' (1975) 34 CLJ 205.

[32] [2009] EWHC 3340 (Ch) [2011] 2 All ER 451. See D Monk 'Sexuality and Succession Law: Beyond Formal Equality' (2011) *Feminist Legal Studies* 231 at pp 243–247, who argues that the revocation rule should not apply to civil partnerships because, inter alia, many couples will form the partnership as a 'belt and braces' measure intended to complement, not weaken, the will in favour of the surviving partner.

[33] Added by the Administration of Justice Act 1982 s 18(2). The section was amended by s 3 of the Law Reform (Succession) Act 1995 to reverse the decision in *Re Sinclair* [1985] Ch 446, where the Court of Appeal held that, on a proper construction of the words in the section as it then stood, the testator's property would pass on intestacy and not, as he had intended, to charity, because the former spouse had not predeceased him. The Law Commission reviewed the decision (Law Com No 217, *Family Law, The Effect of Divorce on Wills* (1993); see R Kerridge 'The Effect of Divorce on Wills' (1995) 59 Conv 12) and recommended that it should be replaced to provide that, in the event of a divorce or annulment, property should pass as if the former spouse had predeceased the testator.   [34] The relevant date is the date of decree absolute.

[35] This formulation applies where the testator dies on or after 1 January 1996, regardless of the date of the will or of the divorce or annulment. See C Barton and R Wells 'A Matter of Life and Death—the Law Reform (Succession) Act 1995' [1996] Fam Law 172; G Miller 'Intestacy, divorce and wills' (1995) 145 NLJ 1693.

to recognition in this country. It will not operate, however, if no proceedings are taken for the annulment of a void marriage. Section 18C[36] makes equivalent provision in relation to civil partnerships.

The Law Reform (Succession) Act 1995 also amended the law to provide that, where the spouse (and now civil partner) of the testator is appointed in the will as a guardian, the appointment is revoked if the marriage (or civil partnership) is subsequently dissolved or annulled.[37]

(c) Mutual wills

Although mutual wills are rare, they are still made occasionally, and they are of particular interest in family law as mutual testators are usually (although not invariably) spouses. The essence of mutual wills is that the parties agree to make wills in similar terms and to be bound to dispose of their estate in a specified manner. It is not sufficient that the testators agree to make identical wills: it must also be established that there is a contract enforceable at law to the effect that each party will give effect to the agreement between them and will not exercise his testamentary freedom to make a will with different provisions.[38] Although English law knows of no such thing as an irrevocable will, equity takes the view that it would be inequitable to permit the survivor to take the benefits under the other's will[39] without giving effect to the agreement him- or herself and it protects the other beneficiaries by attaching a trust to the property on the first testator's death.

Let us suppose that a husband, H, and wife, W, agree to make mutual wills in the following form: 'I devise and bequeath the whole of my estate to trustees on trust for my wife W (or my husband H) for life and then on trust for my son S absolutely' or alternatively '—to W (or H) provided that she (or he) survives me, and if she (or he) does not, to S'. The following illustrations will show how the equitable principle operates:

(1) H and W agree that they will no longer be bound by their agreement. Both are free to revoke their wills and no trust is created on the death of either.

(2) H revokes his will and tells W that he has done so. W is free to revoke her will and no trust is created.[40]

(3) H revokes his will without telling W. H dies first and W discovers the revocation. As she is still free to make other testamentary dispositions, she may do so and no trust is created.[41]

(4) W dies first without having revoked her will. As it would be unconscionable to permit H to take the interest given by W's will without adhering to the agreement which effectively gave it to him, equity imposes an obligation on him to observe it and regards him as holding both estates on trust to carry out its terms.

---

[36] Inserted by s 71 and Sch 4 para 2 to the Civil Partnership Act 2004.

[37] Children Act 1989 s 6(3A) inserted by s 4 of the 1995 Act, and s 6(3B) inserted by s 76 of the Civil Partnership Act 2004. See further, Ch 8, Revoking an appointment, p 287.

[38] For a case where it was held that there was insufficient evidence to prove an agreement, see *Birch v Curtis* [2002] EWHC 1158 (Ch) [2002] 2 FLR 847. Note that in *Re Dale* [1994] Ch 31, it was held that the mutual wills doctrine applied to parents who had made wills in favour of their children, even though they had left no property to each other.

[39] *Re Cleaver* [1981] 2 All ER 1018; *Re Oldham* [1925] Ch 75; *Gray v Perpetual Trustee Co Ltd* [1928] AC 391, PC; *Re Goodchild (Deceased)* [1997] 1 WLR 1216, CA.

[40] *Birmingham v Renfrew* (1936) 57 CLR 666 at 682 (Aust) cited with approval in *Re Cleaver* at 1023.

[41] *Stone v Hoskins* [1905] P 194; a minor alteration will be sufficient to revoke the agreement: *Re Hobley* [2006] WTLR 467.

Consequently, if he later revokes his will[42] (or revoked it before W's death without informing her), his personal representatives are bound to give effect to the agreement and take his estate with a trust impressed on it for the benefit of S.[43] There are conflicting dicta on whether H would still be bound by the agreement if he repudiated it by disclaiming the gift to himself, but since the trust arises from the prior agreement, the better view is that it is automatically impressed on the property on the first party's death and the survivor's accepting the gift is therefore immaterial.[44]

If these conditions are satisfied, the trust takes effect from the moment the first testator dies.[45] Consequently those beneficiaries entitled to the remainder have a vested interest from this time.[46] However, they may face a number of difficulties in seeking to enforce the gift, not the least of which may be in determining what property is subject to the trust.[47]

(d) Gifts to the testator's wife or husband

In a home-made will it is not uncommon for a testator to make a bequest in the form: 'I give my whole estate to my wife, W, and after her death to my children'. His probable intention was that she should have full power to dispose of capital and income but that anything that was left at her death should go to the children.[48] The effect, however, was to give her only a life interest, because an absolute interest would be incompatible with the gift over. To remedy this, the Administration of Justice Act 1982 s 22[49] provides that, if a testator makes a gift to his or her spouse in terms which in themselves would confer an absolute interest and by the same instrument gives an interest in the same property to his or her issue, the gift to the spouse takes effect absolutely unless a contrary intention is shown. The section is not well drafted. The absolute gift to the spouse presumably destroys the gift to the issue: if, therefore, the wife predeceases the testator, the gift will fall into residue and may not pass to the issue, which will again defeat the testator's intention. Hart J has doubted the wisdom of the approach adopted in the section and in *Re Harrison (Deceased)*[50] held that the court should look at the words used by the testator in the context of the will as a whole to determine his true intention. In this case, the husband stated in his will 'The Bungalow I leave in trust to my wife . . . On

---

[42] Query if the will is revoked by operation of law if H remarries. In *Re Marsland* [1939] Ch 820, CA, it was held that this did not amount to a breach of an express covenant not to revoke a will. It is submitted that this principle should not be applied to mutual wills, because the trusts attach on the death of the first testator and, if it were applied, they would frequently fail; and see *Re Goodchild (Deceased)* [1996] 1 FLR 591 (upheld on appeal, [1997] 1 WLR 1216, CA) where it was held (obiter) that effect should be given to the original intention, and that it was immaterial that revocation was by operation of law. See Grattan 'Mutual wills and remarriage' (1997) 61 Conv 153. Kerridge with Brierley (op cit, at p 117 n 166) suggest that this may be harsh where the surviving spouse was widowed at an early age.

[43] *Dufour v Pereira* (1769) 1 Dick 419.

[44] See the different interpretations placed on Lord Camden's judgment in *Dufour v Pereira* by Lord Hailsham LC in *Gray v Perpetual Trustee Co Ltd* at 399, and by Clauson J in *Re Hagger* [1930] 2 Ch 190 at 195. If this were not so and the survivor were the widow or widower of the other, he or she might disclaim the legacy and take the estate on intestacy, thus obtaining the benefit whilst going back on the agreement. *Re Dale* supports this view: since neither testator was to benefit under the other's will, the trust could not be conditional upon acceptance of the gift.   [45] *Re Hagger; Re Green* [1951] Ch 148; *Re Goodchild*.

[46] *Re Hagger.*   [47] See Kerridge with Brierley (op cit) paras 6.39–6.41.

[48] See the 19th Report of the Law Reform Committee (*Interpretation of Wills*) 1973 (Cmnd 5301), para 60.

[49] Implementing the recommendations of the Law Reform Committee: ibid, para 62. An equivalent provision applies to civil partners: Civil Partnership Act 2004 Sch 4 para 5.

[50] [2005] EWHC 2957 (Ch) [2006] 1 WLR 1212.

her death the Bungalow is to be sold and cash raised is to be equally divided between [his four children].' Hart J concluded that the words 'in trust', coupled with the other provisions in the will relating to the children's interests, led to the conclusion that an absolute gift had not been intended.

It will also be observed that the section does not apply to a gift to an unmarried cohabitant, or if the gift over is to someone other than the testator's issue (as might be the case if he were childless).

Provided it was obviously the testator's intention, a gift to the testator's 'wife' (or 'husband') will take effect in favour of a woman (or man) with whom he (or she) is living as husband and wife, even though they are not legally married.[51] Such a gift will even be valid if it is directed to be held on trust during widowhood: in this case it will be construed as being determinable upon the other's contracting a valid marriage after the testator's death.[52]

Unlike the position on intestacy,[53] the surviving spouse cannot demand that the matrimonial home or personal chattels should be appropriated as part of a gift (eg a residuary bequest). If they have not been specifically disposed of by the will, the only thing a widow or widower wishing to retain such property can do is to ask the personal representatives to exercise their power of appropriation in this way.[54]

(e) Gifts to children

The common law presumption that the term 'children' in a will applied only to legitimate children was reversed by the Family Law Reform Act 1969 s 15.[55] The Legitimacy Act 1926, which enabled legitimated children to take under a disposition after their legitimation, was extended by the Children Act 1975 to wills taking effect after 1 January 1976, even where they came into operation before the parents' marriage.[56] An adopted child, however, is treated as the legitimate child of the adoptive parents,[57] and not of his or her birth parents, so that, unless a will specifies that the child is still to take as a beneficiary, he or she would be excluded from succeeding to property from the birth parents (or other birth relatives).[58] Equally, the adopted child will succeed to property bequeathed by the adoptive parents to their 'child' or by a testator who has left property to descendants whose own birth child has adopted the child.[59]

---

[51] *Re Brown* (1910) 26 TLR 257. A fortiori if he names her (eg 'to my wife EAS'): *Re Smalley* [1929] 2 Ch 112, CA.

[52] Even though the 'wife' was in fact married to another man while cohabiting with the testator: *Re Wagstaff* [1908] 1 Ch 162, CA; *Re Hammond* [1911] 2 Ch 342; cf *Re Lynch* [1943] 1 All ER 168.

[53] See later, Intestate succession, Rights with respect to the family home, p 971.

[54] For the personal representatives' powers of appropriation, see the Administration of Estates Act 1925 s 41.   [55] In respect of any disposition made on or after 1 January 1970.

[56] Schedule 1 Pt III re-enacted in Legitimacy Act 1976 s 5(3).

[57] Adoption and Children Act 2002 s 67.

[58] Adoption and Children Act 2002 s 69(4) provides that the child would succeed if the interest were already vested in possession at the date of the adoption, reversing *Staffordshire County Council v B* [1998] 1 FLR 261, discussed at Ch 19, Consequences of the Change of Status and Transfer of Parentage, p 727 and this provision has now been extended by s 4(1) Inheritance and Trustees' Powers Act 2014 to apply to a contingent interest in the estate of the birth parent (but no other relative), on the recommendation of the Law Commission in Report No 331, *Intestacy and Family Provision Claims on Death* HC 1674 (2011) para 4.51.

[59] Adoption and Children Act 2002 s 69. It was held, in *Re Erskine Trust* [2012] EWHC 732 (Ch) [2012] 2 FLR 725, that it may be possible to construe references to 'children' in dispositions drafted prior to the inclusion of such children in the construction of wills and other instruments, by the Adoption of Children Act 1949, where no clear contrary intention by the testator is shown, in order to avoid unlawful discrimination within Art 14 ECHR.

2. INTESTATE SUCCESSION

(a) Intestate succession before 1926

Before the Administration of Estates Act 1925 came into force, there was a considerable difference between the descent of real and personal property.[60] All inheritable estates of freehold descended to the heir at law subject to the husband's curtesy and the wife's dower.[61] The husband took all his wife's personal property (including her separate estate if she had not disposed of it by will). On the death of a married man his widow took one-third of his personal property if he left issue and one-half if he did not; the remainder of his estate was divided among his issue or, in default of issue, among his next-of-kin as defined by the Statutes of Distribution of 1670 and 1685. Under the Intestates' Estates Act 1890, which was passed to give a widow a larger provision if the estate was small and the intestate left no issue, she took the whole of the real and personal estate if the total value did not exceed £500; if it exceeded this sum, the estate was to stand charged with the payment to her of £500.

(b) Administration of Estates Act 1925

This Act radically overhauled the law relating to intestate succession in two respects. First, the law relating to real and personal property was put on the same footing; and secondly the distribution of estates was completely changed. The principal effect of this Act, and subsequent amendments, was to give the surviving widow a much greater interest than she had before 1926 and to give the surviving widower the same rights as the surviving widow. The Civil Partnership Act 2004 further amended the Act to extend the rights of the surviving spouse to surviving civil partners[62] and it now of course applies to same-sex spouses.

(c) Updating the legislation

Despite these largely consequential amendments, the 1925 Act has continued to govern the position, despite dating back to a time when family life and social conditions were far removed from what they are today. In 1989, the Law Commission reviewed the law and recommended that a surviving spouse should receive the whole estate on intestacy as the best means of ensuring her or him adequate provision and in order to simplify the rules.[63] It also appeared to be in line with public opinion.[64] However, their view was criticised as failing adequately to consider the needs of a deceased person's minor children, and of unduly benefiting second or subsequent spouses.[65] The Government rejected it when enacting other reforms to the intestacy rules in the Law Reform (Succession) Act 1995.

---

[60] See C Sherrin and R Bonehill *The Law and Practice of Intestate Succession* (2004, 3rd edn); Law Commission *Distribution on Intestacy* Report No 186 (1989); Law Commission, *Intestacy and Family Provision Claims on Death* Consultation Paper No 191 (2009) and Report No 331, HC 1674 (2011). For an attempt to provide a statistical estimate of the number of people dying who leave different categories of kin (eg surviving spouse, descendant, parent or sibling), see J Haskey 'Intestacy and Surviving Kin: Law Commission Research' [2010] Fam Law 964.

[61] See Ch 4, Property consequences of marriage and civil partnership, Common law, p 104.

[62] Civil Partnership Act 2004 s 71 and Sch 4 paras 7–12.

[63] Law Com No 187 *Distribution on Intestacy* paras 25, 29.

[64] Law Com No 187 *Distribution on Intestacy* paras 25, 29.

[65] S Cretney 'Reform of Intestacy: The Best We Can Do?' (1995) 111 LQR 77; R Kerridge 'Distribution on Intestacy: The Law Commission's Report' (1990) 54 Conv 358; J Finch et al *Wills, Inheritance and Families* (1996) ch 7. The same criticism was levelled at the original scheme: see G Keeton and L Gower 'Freedom of Testation in English Law' (1935) 20 *Iowa Law Rev* 326 at 330.

The Law Commission also considered, but rejected, the view that a surviving unmarried cohabitant should be treated like a surviving spouse, on the grounds that this would increase the complexity and cost of administration, and special rules would be needed to deal with the situation where both a spouse and a cohabitant survived. They considered that any hardship done to a cohabitant, or to a relative or dependant of the deceased by the intestacy rules could be adequately remedied by a claim under the Inheritance (Provision for Family and Dependants) Act 1975 (hereafter the Inheritance Act),[66] and they proposed strengthening the claim of a cohabitant under that Act.[67] It is also always open to all the beneficiaries under a will or an intestacy, if of full age and capacity, to agree to distribute the estate in any way they wish so as to remedy any injustice that they might feel would otherwise be caused to the partner (or other relative or loved one) of the deceased.[68]

However, further subsequent growth in cohabitation prompted a review by the Law Commission of the position of cohabitants on the breakdown of a relationship, with some consequential recommendations regarding their position under the Inheritance Act.[69] In that review, they recommended that the position of cohabitants on the death of their partner needed to be considered as part of a wider re-examination of the law of intestacy. They therefore undertook a further review of both intestacy and family provision and produced their final recommendations in 2011.[70] In doing so, they took account, inter alia, of empirical research, which found[71] that the intestacy rules favouring close kin, especially the surviving spouse and children, are reflected in the provisions testators make in their own wills. Moreover, the researchers found a similar preference for close family in a representative survey of public opinion, when respondents were asked to consider how the intestacy rules should prioritise potential beneficiaries; strong support for the inclusion of cohabitants within the rules;[72] and concern to ensure that children of the deceased are recognised in some way, particularly where they are the children of a former relationship and the deceased has remarried.[73] The Law Commission recommended reform but recognising the political sensitivity of legislating to improve the position of cohabitants, they presented their recommendations in two parts, such that those relating to cohabitants could be hived off from their less controversial proposals which could be the subject of early legislative action. As was expected, the Coalition declined to adopt the reforms for cohabitants but introduced the non-controversial recommendations in the Inheritance and Trustees' Powers Act 2014 and the discussion which follows takes account of the changes this has made to the 1925 Act.

(d) The rights of a surviving spouse or civil partner

The spouse (or civil partner) must survive the intestate by 28 days.[74] This requirement is to prevent 'the assets of both spouses going to the parents or relatives of the second to

---

[66] See later, Provision for members of the family and other dependants, pp 974–993.

[67] As was done by the Law Reform (Succession) Act 1995, discussed later, A person who was cohabiting with the deceased when he or she died, p 978.

[68] Known as the rule in *Saunders v Vautier* (1841) Cr & Ph 240.

[69] Law Commission, *Cohabitation: The Financial Consequences of Relationship Breakdown* Law Com No 307 (2007) paras 6.11–6.49. See further, Ch 24.

[70] Law Commission, *Intestacy and family provision claims on death* Consultation Paper No 191 (2009) and Report No 331, Cm 1674 (2011).

[71] A Humphrey et al *Inheritance and the family: attitudes to will-making and intestacy* (2010) ch 7.

[72] Echoing findings made by C Williams et al 'Cohabitation and intestacy: public opinion and law reform' [2008] CFLQ 449.

[73] A Humphrey et al *Inheritance and the family: attitudes to will-making and intestacy* (2010) chs 4, 5.

[74] Administration of Estates Act 1925 s 46(2A), inserted by Law Reform (Succession) Act 1995 s 1(1) as amended by the Civil Partnership Act 2004 Sch 4 para 7. The Law Commission pointed out in their Report

die, in cases of not quite simultaneous death, usually in accidents'[75] and echoes survivorship clauses usually inserted into wills. Where the deceased was lawfully married polygamously, his surviving polygamous wives together constitute the 'spouse' for the purposes
of the intestacy rules.[76]

The surviving spouse or civil partner takes the following interests.[77]

Personal chattels

The surviving spouse or civil partner is always entitled to the personal chattels (provided
that the estate is solvent). The 1925 Act set out a detailed list of such chattels:[78]

> Carriages, horses, stable furniture and effects (not used for business purposes), motor
> cars and accessories (not used for business purposes), garden effects, domestic animals,
> plate, plated articles, linen, china, glass, books, pictures, prints, furniture, jewellery,[79]
> articles of household or personal use or ornament, musical and scientific instruments
> and apparatus, wines, liquors and consumable stores, but [they] do not include any
> chattels used at the death of the intestate for business purposes[80] nor money or securi-
> ties for money.

This list was clearly outdated, and the Law Commission recommended it be simplified
and modernised. However, they recognised that any new list of items would also fall out
of date and they therefore proposed an alternative approach focusing on the nature rather
than type of property to be included.[81] They suggested that the surviving spouse/civil
partner 'should receive all of the deceased's tangible movable property *other than* property consisting of money or securities for money, or which was used at the death of the
deceased solely or mainly for business purposes, or was held solely as an investment. This
would enable a valuable painting, bought both as an investment and as something to be
enjoyed, to be included, whilst a chattel purchased solely for investment would fall into
the residual estate.[82] The section was amended accordingly by s 3(1) of the Inheritance and
Trustees' Powers Act 2014.

(b) Statutory legacy and residuary interests

The interest which the surviving spouse or civil partner takes over and above the personal
chattels depends upon what other relatives the intestate leaves surviving. The provisions
are set out in s 46 of the Administration of Estates Act 1925 as amended by the Inheritance
and Trustees' Powers Act 2014.

No 331 para A.94 that this provision rendered redundant the subsequent sub-section (3) which, in the case of
an intestate, disapplied the usual rule that the younger of two persons survives the other, and it was repealed
by the Inheritance and Trustees' Powers Act 2014 Sch 4 para 1(2).

[75] Law Com No 187 para 57.
[76] *Official Solicitor to the Senior Courts v Yemoh and Others* [2010] EWHC 3727 (Ch) [2011] 4 All ER 200.
[77] Administration of Estates Act 1925 s 46 as amended; Family Provision (Intestate Succession) Order (SI
1993/2906). See DCA, *Administration of Estates: Review of the Statutory Legacy* (2005).
[78] Administration of Estates Act 1925 s 55(1)(x). This section was widely construed and was held to
include a 60-foot motor yacht (*Re Chaplin* [1950] Ch 507) and a collection of clocks and watches (*Re Crispin's
Will Trusts* [1975] Ch 245, CA). The mere fact that the property might be regarded as an investment did not
prevent it from being a personal chattel too: *Re Reynold's Will Trusts* [1965] 3 All ER 686 (valuable stamp
collection, which was deceased's principal hobby, held to be an article of personal use); express statutory
provision is now made for such an asset.
[79] Including cut but unmounted jewels: *Re Whitby* [1944] Ch 210, CA.
[80] See *Re Ogilby* [1942] Ch 288.   [81] Law Com No 331 para 2.111.
[82] Quite which category fine wines might fall into could be a difficult decision, however.

If the intestate leaves any children or remoter issue,[83] the spouse[84] takes what is usually termed a 'statutory legacy', currently of £250,000 together with part of any sum left over. Prior to the 2014 Act, this was a *life* interest[85] in half the residue. If the deceased leaves no issue but a parent or a brother or sister of the whole blood or issue of such a brother or sister, then before the 2014 Act the surviving spouse or civil partner took a statutory legacy of £450,000 and an *absolute* interest in half the residue. If the deceased leaves neither issue nor any of the above relations, the surviving spouse or civil partner takes the whole of the residue absolutely.

The Law Commission noted[86] that when the statutory legacy for the surviving spouse was first introduced in 1925, it was set (at £1,000) so as to ensure that most estates would pass in their entirety to the widow. The current statutory legacy limits operate so that at least 90% of surviving spouses inherit the whole estate where the lower level of £250,000 applies, and at least 98% where the upper level of £450,000 applies.[87] This should operate, in most cases, to preserve the former matrimonial home for the surviving spouse (where it was not jointly owned) and thus avoid forcing him or her to move out.[88] However, they also noted the countervailing concern expressed in social attitude research[89] to ensure that any children of the deceased are not cut out from a share. They therefore recommended first, that where the deceased leaves a spouse or civil partner but no children or other descendants, the surviving spouse/civil partner should receive the whole estate rather than a portion of it,[90] and s 1(2) of the 2014 Act amends s 46 of the Administration of Estates Act 1925 accordingly.

Where there are children, they concluded that strong public support for giving priority—but not the whole of the estate—to the surviving spouse should be weighed against ensuring that any change in the law would not reduce that spouse's current entitlement under the rules.[91] Responses to their consultation paper had also shown strong criticism of the current use of a life interest for the surviving spouse's share in the estate above the statutory legacy due to its complexity, the expense of administering the trust and the inability to produce a clean break.[92] They accordingly proposed a simplification of the law through the grant of a fixed absolute share (rather than a life interest) of half of the balance of the estate above the statutory legacy[93] and this again is achieved by s 1(2) amending the 1925 Act.

Empirical research has shown that there is less public support for prioritising a second spouse where the deceased had children from a former relationship.[94] This appears to

---

[83] 'Issue' means the lineal descendants of the deceased.

[84] Polygamous wives hold an equal share in the statutory legacy and (prior to the 2014 Act coming into effect) hold the life interest until the last of them to die: *Official Solicitor to the Senior Courts v Yemoh and Others* [2010] EWHC 3727 (Ch) [2011] 4 All ER 200.

[85] The survivor could require the personal representatives to redeem the life interest by paying the capital value to him or her: Administration of Estates Act 1925 s 47A as amended by Civil Partnership Act 2004 Sch 4 para 9.   [86] Law Com No 331 paras 2.5–2.6.

[87] The statutory legacy has frequently been outstripped by inflation. The Law Commission accordingly recommended that it should be reviewed at least every five years: para 2.128. Sch 1A para 4 to the Administration of Estates Act 1925, inserted by Sch 1 to the Inheritance and Trustees' Powers Act 2014, places the Lord Chancellor under a duty to do so.

[88] We discuss later the power to require the personal representatives to appropriate the matrimonial home to meet the surviving spouse's interest.

[89] A Humphrey et al *Inheritance and the family: attitudes to will-making and intestacy* (2010) chs 4, 5.

[90] Law Com No 331 para 2.25.   [91] Ibid para 2.38.   [92] Ibid para 2.42.

[93] Ibid para 2.62. The surviving spouse/civil partner would continue to receive the personal chattels.

[94] A Humphrey et al *Inheritance and the family: attitudes to will-making and intestacy* (2010) ch 4, section 4.5.

provide some support for 'conduit theory'—the premise that a surviving spouse is less likely to pass on the deceased's property to children who are not also her own offspring.[95] However, the Law Commission were sceptical as to the extent or cogency of this theory, and noted conflicting views amongst practitioners and experts. They concluded that it would be impractical and wrong in principle to draw such a distinction between spouses in this situation.[96] There is always the possibility of a child seeking provision under the Inheritance (Provision for Family and Dependants) Act 1975 if it is felt that they have not been adequately provided for.[97]

Rights with respect to the family home

The Intestates' Estates Act 1952 gives the surviving spouse or civil partner a right, within certain limits,[98] to retain the matrimonial or civil partnership home.[99] Where the intestate's estate comprises an interest in a dwelling-house in which the surviving spouse or civil partner was resident at the time of the intestate's death, the survivor may require the personal representatives to appropriate the house in or towards satisfaction of any absolute interest that the survivor has in the estate,[100] and if the value of the house exceeds the value of the survivor's interest, this option may be exercised so long as the excess value is paid to the representatives.[101] The survivor must exercise this option within 12 months of representation being taken out, but this period may be extended by the court.[102] Consequently the personal representatives are forbidden to sell the house within this period without the written consent of the surviving spouse or civil partner unless this is necessary for the payment of expenses or debts.[103]

Judicial separation or separation order in relation to a civil partnership

By s 18(2) of the Matrimonial Causes Act 1973, if either spouse dies intestate as respects any real or personal property whilst a judicial separation is in force and the parties remain separated, his or her property is to devolve as though the other were dead. A similar provision is contained in s 57 of the Civil Partnership Act 2004 in relation to civil partners who are subject to a separation order under that Act. The reason for these provisions is

---

[95] Advanced by L Waggoner 'The Multiple-Marriage Society and Spousal Rights Under the Revised Uniform Probate Code' (1990-91) 76 *Iowa Law Rev* 223. Discussed in the Law Commission's Consultation Paper No 191 paras 3.98–3.111 and Report No 331 paras 2.67–2.82.

[96] Law Com No 331 para 2.82.

[97] See later, Reasonable provision, Factors relevant to applications by a child, or child of the family, of the deceased, p 988 and *Re Callaghan* [1985] Fam 1.

[98] In particular, these provisions normally do not apply if the house is held upon a lease which had less than two years to run from the date of the intestate's death or which could be determined by the landlord within this period: Intestates' Estates Act 1952 Sch 2 para 1(2); and the survivor cannot require the personal representatives to appropriate the house in certain specified instances except on an order of the court, which must be satisfied that the appropriation is not likely to diminish the value of assets in the residuary estate (other than the interest in the house) or make these assets more difficult to dispose of: Sch 2 para 2.

[99] Section 5 and Sch 2 as amended by Civil Partnership Act 2004 Sch 4 para 13.

[100] Intestates' Estates Act 1952 Sch 2 para 1(1). 'Dwelling-house' includes part of a building occupied as a separate dwelling and an absolute interest includes a redeemed life interest: ibid, para 1(4)–(5).

[101] Intestates' Estates Act 1952 Sch 2 para 5(2); *Re Phelps* [1980] Ch 275, CA. The value is to be assessed at the date of appropriation: *Robinson v Collins* [1975] 1 All ER 321.

[102] Intestates' Estates Act 1952 Sch 2 para 3 as amended by Sch 4 para 2 of the Inheritance and Trustees' Powers Act 2014. It cannot be exercised after the surviving spouse's death by his or her personal representatives: ibid, para 3(1)(b).

[103] Intestates' Estates Act 1952 Sch 2 para 4. But if they fail to observe this provision, the spouse has no right to claim the house from the purchaser: ibid, para 4(5).

that the rules of intestate succession are intended to reflect the testamentary dispositions the deceased might reasonably be expected to have made, and as separation almost always marks the de facto end of the relationship, it is highly unlikely that either would have left anything to the other.

(d) Interests taken by the intestate's children and remoter issue

If the intestate leaves a surviving spouse or civil partner, the personal representatives must hold one-half of the residue (after taking out the personal chattels and the £250,000 due to the survivor) on the statutory trusts for the intestate's issue and the other half on trust for the surviving spouse.[104] If the intestate leaves no surviving spouse or civil partner, the personal representatives must hold the whole of the residue on the statutory trusts for the issue.[105]

The property is to be held on trust in equal shares for all the children alive at the intestate's death who reach the age of 18 or marry or form a civil partnership under that age.[106] But if any of his children has predeceased him, that child's share is held upon the same trusts for his own children or remoter issue (if any) under the *per stirpes* rule. This means that they share between them the amount that would have gone to their parent. For example, if the intestate left two children, one of whom had previously died, herself leaving two children, the surviving child will receive a half share, and the other child's children share between them the other half share.[107]

(e) Children of unmarried parents

Originally, in accordance with the general rule at common law, only legitimate persons and those claiming a relationship through legitimate persons, could participate in intestate succession. Those who had been legitimated could claim after the passing of the Legitimacy Act 1926,[108] and the Family Law Reform Act 1969 permitted illegitimate children and their parents to succeed to each other.[109] In pursuance of the policy of removing the disadvantages flowing from birth outside marriage, s 18 of the Family Law Reform Act 1987 provides that, for the purposes of the distribution of the estate of an intestate, any relationship shall be construed without regard to whether the parents of the deceased, the claimant or any person through whom the claimant is related to the deceased were married to each other.[110] But because of the difficulty in tracing some fathers, whose identity might not be known, a person whose parents were not married to each other is to be presumed not to have been survived by his father or by anyone related to him through

---

[104] Administration of Estates Act 1925 s 46(1) as amended by Inheritance and Trustees' Powers Act 2014 s 1(2). Before the 2014 Act, the second half would have been held on the same trusts subject to the surviving spouse's life interest.

[105] Administration of Estates Act 1925 s 46(1) as amended by Civil Partnership Act 2004 Sch 4 para 7.

[106] Administration of Estates Act 1925 s 47(1) as amended by Civil Partnership Act 2004 Sch 4 para 8.

[107] Administration of Estates Act 1925 s 47(1)(i) Family Law Reform Act 1969 s 3(2). Under the forfeiture rule, a person is not to profit from his crime; thus, if the deceased were unlawfully killed by his or her child, the child could not inherit the deceased's property (under either a will or an intestacy): *Re DWS (Deceased)* [2001] Ch 568, CA, and neither could the child's (innocent) descendants. The Law Commission (Law Com No 295) *The Forfeiture Rule and the Law of Succession* (2005) recommended that the effect of *Re DWS* should be reversed so that in such circumstances the child should be treated as if himself dead, enabling the next closest in the list of those entitled to succeed to take. This was duly done by the Estates of Deceased Persons (Forfeiture Rule and Law of Succession) Act 2011, inserting s 46A into the Administration of Estates Act 1925.   [108] Now see the Legitimacy Act 1976 s 5.   [109] Section 14.

[110] Applying s 1 of the 1987 Act (see Ch 9, The Family Law Reform Act 1987, p 306). Any reference to statutory next of kin in an instrument taking effect on or after this date is to be construed likewise: s 18(3).

his father unless the contrary is shown.[111] The Law Commission noted that this concern carried much less weight where, as is now by far the prevailing norm, the father is named on the child's birth certificate, and recommended that the provision should not apply in such cases.[112] This change has been effected by the Inheritance and Trustees' Powers Act 2014.[113]

(f) Adopted children

An adopted child is treated as though he were the child of his adopters and of no other person.[114] If adopted by a couple, he or she will be in the position of a brother (or sister) of the whole blood of any other child or adopted child of both the adopters and a brother of the half blood of any child or adopted child of one of them; if adopted by one person only, he or she will be in the position of a brother or sister of the half blood of any child or adopted child of his adopter. The child has no claims on the death of his or her birth parents or anyone related to them.[115]

(g) Interests taken by other members of the family

If the intestate dies leaving no surviving spouse or civil partner and no issue, the whole estate must be held on trust for the persons coming into the first of the following classes that can be satisfied: the intestate's parents; his brothers and sisters of the whole blood (or their issue); his brothers and sisters of the half blood (or their issue); surviving grandparents; uncles and aunts of the whole blood (or their issue) and uncles and aunts of the half blood (or their issue). If none of these classes is filled, the whole estate will go to the Crown as bona vacantia.[116]

The statutory trusts are exactly the same in the cases just discussed as the statutory trusts for the intestate's children and issue. All the interests are contingent upon the beneficiary's attaining his majority or marrying, and if no member of any class takes a vested interest, the members of the next class will take.[117]

(h) The position of cohabitants

We discussed the growth in extra-marital cohabitation in Chapter 24, and considered its implications for family law, including the difficulties of defining cohabitation and arguments concerning how far a lifestyle and demonstrable 'commitment' to the relationship equivalent to that of marriage or civil partnership should be conditions for improved or

---

[111] Family Law Reform Act 1987 s 18(2). Equivalent provision is made where a person has a second female parent (not in a civil partnership with the mother) by virtue of s 43 of the Human Fertilisation and Embryology Act 2008: s 18(2A) inserted by s 56 and Sch 6 Pt 1 para 25(1)(2) of the 2008 Act.
[112] Law Com No 331 para 5.29.　　[113] Section 5.
[114] Adoption and Children Act 2002 s 67(1). The position is the same for a child who is the subject of a parental order made under s 54 of the Human Fertilisation and Embryology Act 2008. A child adopted by one of his birth parents cannot claim on the death of the other: s 67(4).
[115] Compare the position where the child has a contingent interest in a bequest, considered earlier at Testate succession, Gifts to children, p 966. The Law Commission recommended no change to the position on intestacy: Law Com No 331 para 4.33.
[116] For details, including discretionary payments to dependants of the deceased and 'other persons for whom the intestate might reasonably have been expected to make provision' under the Administration of Estates Act 1925 s 46(1)(vi), see Law Com No 191 paras 6.69–6.77.
[117] If all the members of a particular class (apart from parents or grandparents) are dead, but one or more have left issue, the issue will take in preference to the members of a more remote class: Re Lockwood [1958] Ch 231. For example, issue of a brother or sister of the whole blood will take before a brother and sister of the half blood.

equal protection under the law. The Law Commission found 'no overwhelming consensus in favour of reform'[118] (to include cohabitants in the intestacy rules) but in the light of the responses to their consultation paper and the empirical evidence of public attitudes noted earlier, they maintained their provisional view that certain cohabitants should have an entitlement on intestacy. They proposed that a 'qualifying cohabitant', should be defined as the survivor of a cohabiting relationship who was, immediately before the death of the deceased, living in the same household as the deceased as his or her spouse.[119]

Evidence of public opinion considers the duration of a cohabiting relationship to be a significant factor in determining the (level of) entitlement of a surviving partner, since the longer the relationship the more 'marriage-like' or 'committed' it appears to be. The fact that a couple have had a child together is also regarded as an important marker, or 'proxy' of commitment.[120] In order to demonstrate sufficient commitment and interdependence to justify inclusion within the intestacy rules, the Law Commission therefore recommended that where a cohabiting couple had no children, the surviving partner should have lived with the deceased for the whole of the period of five years immediately before his or her death,[121] or, if they had children, for the whole of the period of two years before that death.[122] But they dropped their provisional suggestion that where the couple had lived together for more than two but less than five years and had not had a child, the surviving partner should have a reduced share in the estate.[123] Their consultation responses and further reflection led them to conclude that a 'graduated entitlement' would be complex and unnecessary, and ultimately unprincipled.[124] Finally, they recommended that if the deceased was married or in a civil partnership immediately before the death, the cohabitant would not be regarded as eligible and the surviving spouse/civil partner should have primacy.[125]

As already noted, the Law Commission recognised that extending entitlement on intestacy to cohabitants would be a highly controversial and politicised issue, and legislative reform was not taken forward by the Coalition. It would perhaps make sense for reform of the intestacy (and family provision) rules as they apply to cohabitants to await the more thorough-going reform which has been proposed for such couples who separate.[126] On the other hand, the fact that the Inheritance (Provision for Family and Dependants) Act 1975 was extended to cohabitants in 1995 suggests that politicians may be more sympathetic to cohabitants whose partners have died than to those who have separated from them, so it is not inconceivable that statutory reform will come sooner in relation to provision on death, than to provision on separation. It is to the 1975 Act and the 'family provision' jurisdiction that we now turn.

C. PROVISION FOR MEMBERS OF THE FAMILY AND OTHER DEPENDANTS

The Dower Act 1833 permitted a husband to extinguish his wife's right to dower, and in so doing, abolished the last vestige of family provision in English law.[127] After that there

---

[118] Law Com No 331 at para 8.36.   [119] Ibid para 8.61.

[120] A Humphrey et al *Inheritance and the family: attitudes to will-making and intestacy* (2010) ch 4, section 4.3; C Williams et al 'Cohabitation and intestacy: public opinion and law reform' [2008] CFLQ 449.

[121] Law Com No 331, para 8.87.   [122] Ibid para 8.102.   [123] Law Com No 191 para 4.85.

[124] Law Com No 331 paras 8.117–8.118.   [125] Ibid paras 8.67–8.68.

[126] As the Cohabitation Rights Bill, a private member's Bill introduced into the House of Lords in 2013, attempted to do.

[127] See J Unger 'The Inheritance Act and the Family' (1943) 6 MLR 215.

was nothing to stop a man (or a woman with respect to her separate property) from devising and bequeathing his whole estate to a charity or a complete stranger and leaving his widow and children penniless. To prevent this evil, the Inheritance (Family Provision) Act 1938 was passed.[128] It did not cast upon a testator any positive duty to make reasonable provision for his dependants but enacted that, if he failed to do so, the court might order such reasonable provision as it thought fit to be made out of his estate for the benefit of the surviving spouse and certain classes of children.[129] In 1952 the principle underlying this Act was applied to cases of intestacy.[130] It is easy to see that the law of intestate succession might leave a child without adequate support: the whole estate might go to a widow who refused to make any provision for the children of a previous marriage or might be divided between a daughter married to a rich man and a minor son whose education was incomplete. In 1958 a similar power to apply for provision was given to a former spouse, that is, one whose marriage to the deceased had been dissolved or annulled and who had not remarried.[131]

Notwithstanding these extensions, there were still many gaps and deficiencies in the law. The term 'dependant' was so narrowly defined that it excluded many who had been supported by another during his lifetime and who had a moral, if not a legal, claim on his estate. No application could be made, for example, by a parent, brother or sister, another's children who had been treated as members of the deceased's family, or a person with whom he had been cohabiting outside marriage. Provision could be ordered only out of property which the deceased had power to dispose of by will, so that he could defeat the operation of the Act altogether by settling his property during his lifetime or by contracting to leave it to a third person after his death.[132] Furthermore, the court was limited to ordering reasonable provision for the dependant's maintenance and had no power to divide capital assets: the result was that a surviving wife could be in a worse position than a divorced wife who obtained a property adjustment order. When the Law Commission examined the whole question of family property law, they rejected the proposal that a surviving spouse should have a right to inherit a fixed proportion of the deceased's estate, as is the norm in civil law jurisdictions, in favour of the more flexible approach of family provision. They added, however, that this would need strengthening, and in particular 'the surviving partner of a marriage should have a claim upon the family assets at least equivalent to that of a divorced person'.[133] Their detailed recommendations[134] led to the enactment of the Inheritance (Provision for Family and Dependants) Act 1975,[135]

---

[128] See J Dainow 'Limitations on Testamentary Freedom in England' (1940) 25 Cornell LQ 337, who also traces the attempts to introduce a family provision law prior to the 1938 Act.

[129] See R Oughton *Tyler's Family Provision* (1998, 3rd edn); K Green 'The Englishwoman's Castle: Inheritance and Private Property Today' (1988) 51 MLR 187; G Douglas 'Family provision and family practices: the discretionary regime of the Inheritance Act of England and Wales' (2014) *Onati Socio-Legal Series* [online] 4(2), 222.   [130] Intestates' Estates Act 1952.

[131] Matrimonial Causes (Property and Maintenance) Act 1958, subsequently re-enacted in the Matrimonial Causes Act 1965 ss 26–8. This was of particular value to a divorced wife who had obtained an order for unsecured periodical payments which would cease on her former husband's death, but see later, Who may apply for an order, A former spouse or civil partner of the deceased, who has not formed a subsequent marriage or civil partnership, p 977.

[132] *Schaefer v Schuhmann* [1972] AC 572, PC. But the disposition might possibly have been set aside had it been fraudulent: see later, Property available for financial provision, p 989.

[133] Law Com No 52 *First Report on Family Property: a New Approach* (1973) paras 31–45.

[134] Law Com No 61 *Second Report on Family Property: Family Provision on Death* (1974).

[135] For an interesting analysis of the apparently different approaches taken to claims under the Act in the Family Division and Chancery Division, see F Cownie and A Bradney 'Divided Justice, Different Voices: inheritance and family provision' (2003) 23 LS 566 and for a recognition of the difficulties of applying

which replaced the existing relevant legislation with a new code. This, in turn, was further amended in the light of the Law Commission's recommendation that cohabitants should be given additional rights to claim family provision[136] and by the Civil Partnership Act 2004 to enable same-sex partners to have equivalent rights to spouses after a partner's death.[137] In their most recent review of the law,[138] the Law Commission proposed further reforms, and these are discussed after we have considered the current provisions.

The Act originally applied only if the person against whose estate the claim was being made died domiciled in England and Wales.[139] This was so even if he left considerable property in this jurisdiction, as in *Cyganik v Agulian* where the deceased left property worth £6.5 million and a will admitted to probate here but was regarded as having retained his domicile of origin in Cyprus.[140] The Law Commission proposed providing an alternative basis of jurisdiction where the deceased left assets governed by English succession law (i.e. that he or she owned immovable property here, or choice of law rules in private international law would apply English domestic succession law to part of the estate).[141] However, the Inheritance and Trustees' Powers Act 2014[142] adopted an easier alternative approach by amending s 1(1) of the 1975 Act to provide that a claim may also be made where the claimant is habitually resident in England and Wales.

1. WHO MAY APPLY FOR AN ORDER

The following may make an application for provision under s 1(1ZA) of the Act:[143]

- the spouse or civil partner of the deceased;
- a former spouse or civil partner (provided they have not formed a subsequent marriage or civil partnership);
- a person who, during the whole of the period of two years immediately before the death of the deceased, was living in the same household as the deceased as his or her husband or wife, or civil partner;
- a child of the deceased;
- any person (not being a child of the deceased) who, in the case of any marriage or civil partnership to which the deceased was at any time a party, or otherwise in

---

principles developed in one jurisdiction to another, see the dicta of Briggs J in *Lilleyman v Lilleyman* [2012] EWHC 821 (Ch) [2013] 1 FLR 47 at [45].

[136] Law Com No 187 *Distribution on Intestacy* (1989) paras 58–60. The recommendation was enacted by s 2 of the Law Reform (Succession) Act 1995, discussed later, A person who was cohabiting with the deceased when he or she died, p 978.   [137] Civil Partnership Act 2004 s 71 and Sch 4 paras 15–27.

[138] Law Com No 331 *Intestacy and Family Provision Claims on Death* HC 1674 (2011).

[139] Section 1(1).

[140] [2006] EWCA Civ 129 [2006] 1 FCR 406. Compare *Holliday v Musa* [2010] EWCA Civ 335 [2010] 2 FLR 702, where the deceased (again a native of Cyprus), was found to have an English domicile on his death and thus the claim was admissible.   [141] Law Com No 331 paras 7.37–7.38.

[142] Sch 2 para (2)(2)(b) and (3).

[143] Inserted by Sch 2 para 2 to the Inheritance and Trustees' Powers Act 2014. An application may not be made more than six months after the date on which representation is first taken out without the permission of the court: ss 4 and 23. The personal representatives will not be personally liable for distribution after this time if no application is then pending, but property may be recovered from the beneficiaries to whom it has been transferred if it is needed to make provision for a dependant to whom the court gives leave to make a late application: s 20(1). An application may be made before a grant of representation is taken out, s 4 amended by Inheritance and Trustees' Powers Act 2014 Sch 2 para 7, reversing *Re McBroom* [1992] 2 FLR 49, on the recommendation of Law Com No 331, para 7.51.

relation to any family in which the deceased at any time stood in the role of a parent, was treated by the deceased as a child of the family;[144]

- any person who, immediately before the death of the deceased, was being maintained, either wholly or partly, by the deceased.

(a) Deceased's spouse or civil partner

This category includes a person who had in good faith entered into a void marriage or civil partnership with the deceased.[145] The reason is that such a person is de facto in the position of a surviving spouse or civil partner and may not discover that the union is void until after the other party's death, when it will be too late to apply for financial relief in nullity proceedings. Consequently, the survivor may not make an application under this head if during the deceased's lifetime the marriage or civil partnership has been dissolved or annulled by a decree recognised in England and Wales or he or she has entered into a later union and thus in effect treated the first as at an end.[146]

(b) A former spouse or civil partner of the deceased, who has not formed a subsequent marriage or civil partnership

A former spouse or civil partner of the deceased, whose union with the deceased was dissolved or annulled during his lifetime under the law of any part of the British Islands[147] or recognised as valid in England and Wales and who, in either case, has not formed a subsequent marriage or civil partnership, may apply.[148] This enables the court to make or continue financial provision for those to whom it could award financial relief under the Matrimonial Causes Act 1973 or Civil Partnership Act 2004. An application by a former spouse or civil partner will, as the Court of Appeal pointed out in *Re Fullard*,[149] rarely be successful. In that case it refused to make an order in favour of the applicant who had accepted a half-share of the matrimonial home (the parties' only asset) only a few months before her former husband's death. Normally, the court said, it would be appropriate to make an award in such circumstances only if the sole order made in previous proceedings had been for periodical payments, which had been running for a long time, and the deceased's estate could support their continuation,[150] or if the death had released a substantial capital sum, such as the payment of an insurance policy, of which the deceased was aware and which therefore should be taken into account in deciding whether he had made reasonable provision for the applicant.[151] Where a clean break settlement is made at the time of the divorce, it will include a provision made by virtue of s 15 of the 1975 Act that a party may not be entitled to apply for provision, so claims by former spouses are rare.

---

[144] Amended by Sch 2 para 2 to the Inheritance and Trustees' Powers Act 2014. The reference to a family in which the deceased stood in the role of a parent includes a family of which the deceased was the only member (apart from the applicant) (ie a single parent family): s 1(2A) of the 1975 Act inserted by Sch 2 para 2(3) of the 2014 Act.

[145] A party to a polygamous marriage is a spouse for the purposes of the Act: *Re Sehota* [1978] 3 All ER 385.

[146] Section 25(4), (4A) as amended. A later marriage or civil partnership includes one which is void or voidable (because the person in question would have a claim against the other party to it): s 25(5), (5A) as amended.

[147] The United Kingdom, Channel Islands and Isle of Man: Interpretation Act 1978, Sch 1.

[148] Section 25(1), as amended. Formation of a subsequent marriage or civil partnership includes one which is void or voidable: s 25(5) as amended. [149] [1982] Fam 42, CA.

[150] As in *Re Crawford* (1982) 4 FLR 273.

[151] But not other accretions of wealth since the divorce: *Re Fullard* at 52.

(c) A person who was cohabiting with the deceased when he or she died

The Law Reform (Succession) Act 1995 s 2 added to the list of applicants a person who has lived as husband and wife with the deceased in the same household, for the whole of the period of two years ending immediately before the date of his death.[152] The aim of this reform, recommended by the Law Commission,[153] was to give greater recognition to the position of cohabitants who, previously, had to show dependence upon the deceased if they were to succeed in a claim.[154] The Civil Partnership Act 2004 further amended the list to provide similarly for a person who lived with the deceased as his or her civil partner.[155]

The courts have adopted a broad view of what constitutes living together as husband and wife for the purposes of this provision. In *Re Watson (Deceased)*[156] the applicant and the deceased had known each other for 30 years, initially intimately, but had not married, each having to care for their elderly parents. After these died, the applicant moved in with the deceased but did not have a sexual relationship with him. On his death the question arose whether she had a claim on his estate which would otherwise go to the Crown as bona vacantia. It was held that:

> the court should ask itself whether, in the opinion of a reasonable person with normal perceptions, it could be said that the two people in question were living together as husband and wife; but, when considering that question, one should not ignore the multifarious nature of marital relationships.[157]

On this basis, the court concluded that the applicant satisfied the test, noting that:

> It cannot be doubted but that it is not unusual for a happily married husband and wife in their mid-fifties (which was the age of the parties when they started living together in the present case) not merely to have separate bedrooms, but to abstain from sexual relations. [The parties] lived alone together for over 10 years in a house where they shared the bathroom and the living rooms. He went out to work and earnt the bulk of the household's income, while she did the housekeeping (save three hours a week cleaning in the first four or five years), the shopping, the washing, the cooking and the gardening. No doubt, they ate together every day and that they enjoyed the living rooms jointly.[158]

---

[152] See C Harrap 'Provision for Cohabitants on Death' [1997] Fam Law 422; B Sloan 'The Concept of Coupledom in Succession Law' (2011) 70 CLJ 623 for a comparative critique of the limitations of the eligibility criteria and the definition of cohabitation in the case-law.

[153] Law Com No 187 paras 58–61.

[154] See further, Any other person who as being maintained, either wholly or in part, by the deceased immediately before his death, p 1110.

[155] Civil Partnership Act 2004 Sch 4 para 15(5). In *Saunders v Garett* (2005) NLJ 1486, it was held, before the 2004 Act came into force, that the 1975 Act should be read as including same-sex cohabiting partners, although the applicant failed on the basis that reasonable provision had in fact been made for him in the deceased's will.

[156] [1999] 1 FLR 878.   [157] At p 883G.

[158] At p 884B. See Ch 24 for discussion of how cohabitation has been or should be defined. In particular, the question of whether, in order to qualify, the couple must have held themselves out 'as if married' or 'living as if civil partners' is a difficult one. In *Baynes v Hedger* [2008] EWHC 1587 (Ch) [2008] 3 FCR 151, Lewison J held that this was an essential requirement, following Evans-Lombe J in *Southern Housing Group Ltd v Nutting* [2004] EWHC 2982 (Ch) [2005] 1 FLR 1066. The point was not raised in the appeal ([2009] EWCA Civ 374 [2009] 2 FLR 767) which was brought in relation to eligibility under s 1(1)(e), discussed below. For discussion, see D Monk 'Sexuality and Succession Law: Beyond Formal Equality' (2011) *Feminist Legal Studies* 231 at pp 241–243.

In *Re Watson* the deceased went into hospital about three weeks before he died, and the court was clear that no argument could be put that the couple were not living together 'immediately before the date of the death' on this account. However, in *Gully v Dix*[159] the claimant, who had cohabited with the deceased (who was alcoholic, incontinent and eventually diagnosed as suffering from Huntingdon's Chorea) for some 17 years, left him and moved in with her daughter three months before he died because she could not cope with his medical condition. She had left him on previous occasions and returned, and he phoned her frequently while she was away asking her to come back, but her daughter did not pass on his messages. The Court of Appeal upheld the trial judge's view that he should look at 'the settled state of affairs during the relationship between these parties and not the immediate de facto situation prevailing before the deceased's death'.[160] The couple's cohabitation was, in his view, only 'suspended' and had not been terminated, so that the claimant could proceed with her claim.

In *Kotke v Saffarini*[161] the issue was not whether the parties' cohabitation had come to an end, but whether it had ever begun. The claim was brought under the Fatal Accidents Act 1976 but is equally relevant to this provision. The parties had a sexual relationship but each owned a house. The deceased worked away from both his own house, which he rented out, and that of the applicant, staying with her at weekends. She became pregnant and their child was born shortly before the deceased was killed in a road accident. The Court of Appeal held that the trial judge had correctly determined that the relevant question was whether, at the requisite time (two years before the death) it could be demonstrated that, albeit retaining a separate domestic establishment in the house in which he had lived for some years, the deceased had effectively 'moved' to live under the same roof as the claimant, 'illness, holidays, work and other periodical absences' apart. The judge's view that there is a difference between wanting and intending to live in the same household, planning to do so, and actually doing so, was correct and his view that, on the evidence, the parties had not crossed the statutory threshold into the final stage could not be challenged.[162]

We noted earlier that the Law Commission recommended the inclusion of certain cohabitants in the intestacy rules, provided that they either lived with the deceased for at least two years immediately before the death, and were the parent of a child of the deceased; or lived with the deceased for a period of five years. In relation to a family provision claim, however, they considered that there could well be 'deserving cases' where the claimant had not lived together with the deceased for the requisite period.[163] They therefore recommended that provided the claimant had a child with the deceased and was living with him or her at the time of the death, the claimant should be entitled to apply for provision; the current two-year qualifying period would remain for claimants who had not had a child with the deceased.[164]

(d) A child of the deceased

This includes a child whose parents were not married to each other, an adopted child, a child made the subject of a parental order under the Human Fertilisation and Embryology

[159] [2004] EWCA Civ 139 [2004] 1 WLR 1399.　　[160] Ibid para 15.
[161] [2005] EWCA Civ 221 [2005] 2 FLR 517.
[162] Compare *Lindop v Agus, Bass and Hedley* [2009] EWHC 1795 (Ch) [2010] 1 FLR 631: applicant maintained her postal address at her father's residence, but was held to have cohabited with the deceased in his property.　　　　　　　　　　　　　　　　　　　　　　[163] Law Com No 331 para 8.152.
[164] Ibid para 8.158. A claimant could always try to bring him or herself within the category of a person who was being maintained by the deceased, under s 1(1)(e) in a suitable case—see Any other person who as being maintained, either wholly or in part, by the deceased immediately before his death, p 980.

Act 2008 and a child *en ventre sa mère* at the time of the death.[165] The age and marital status of the child are irrelevant.[166]

(e) Any other person whom the deceased treated as a child of the family

This corresponds to the court's power to award financial relief to a child of the family under the Matrimonial Causes Act or Civil Partnership Act. Obviously anyone who is a child of the family for the purpose of those Acts[167] will qualify as an applicant under the Inheritance Act. However, the category of persons able to apply for provision after death is wider, for only the deceased (and not his or her spouse or civil partner) need have treated the applicant as a child of the family, and children placed as foster children are not automatically excluded.[168] The Law Commission considered that the ambit of this provision as originally drafted was nevertheless too narrow, as it omitted situations where the deceased acted towards a child as a parent outside the context of a marriage (or civil partnership). They recommended that the reference to treatment as a child of the family be widened to refer to any family in which the deceased 'stood in the role of a parent', thus including cohabiting relationships and situations where the deceased acted as if a 'single parent' to the child[169] and the change was made by the 2014 Act.[170]

(f) Any other person who was being maintained, either wholly or in part, by the deceased immediately before his death

This provision gives an applicant a legal claim after the deceased's death whereas she (or he) may have had no claim at all during his lifetime. However anomalous this may be, it can be justified on the ground that the deceased would presumably have continued to provide for the applicant had he or she survived. In many cases there will be a clear moral claim, and the deceased's failure to provide for her after his death may be due to oversight or accident, eg the failure to make a will in time or the revocation of an earlier will by marriage.[171] Although in some cases the applicant and the deceased will have been members of the same family—eg two sisters who lived together—it is not necessary to establish such a relationship. What is essential is a de facto dependence. Pending enactment of the Law Commission's recommendations to include qualifying cohabitants within the intestacy rules, and notwithstanding the specific inclusion of cohabitants within the category of eligible applicants made by the 1995 Act, the commonest example is still likely to be that of a cohabitant.

'Maintained'

For the purpose of this provision, the applicant will be regarded as having been maintained by the deceased provided that the latter 'was making a substantial contribution in money or money's worth towards the reasonable needs of that person, other than a contribution made for full valuable consideration pursuant to an arrangement of a commercial nature.'[172]

---

[165] Section 25(1); Adoption and Children Act 2002 s 67; Human Fertilisation and Embryology Act 2008 s 54. Conversely, if the deceased's natural child is adopted after the deceased's death, he cannot subsequently apply for an order under the Act as the deceased's child: *Re Collins (Deceased)* [1990] Fam 56. The Law Commission (Law Com No 331) considered this issue but decided there was insufficient evidence that this position causes injustice to require a change: para 4.54.   [166] *Re Callaghan* [1985] Fam 1.

[167] See Ch 9, The meaning of 'child of the family', p 296.   [168] See *Re Leach* [1986] Ch 226, CA.

[169] Law Com No 331 para 6.42.   [170] Sch 2 para 2.   [171] See Law Com No 61 paras 85–94.

[172] Section 1(3) as amended by Inheritance and Trustees' Powers Act 2014 Sch 2 para 3; *Jelley v Iliffe* [1981] Fam 128, CA; *Bishop v Plumley* [1991] 1 All ER 236, CA.

In *Re Beaumont*,[173] it was held by Megarry V-C that a claimant must establish not only that he or she was being maintained, but in addition that the deceased had assumed responsibility for doing so, since s 3(4) of the Act, which applies when the court is considering what provision to make for the claimant, required a court to 'have regard to the extent to which and the basis upon which the deceased assumed responsibility for the maintenance of the applicant and to the length of time for which the deceased discharged that responsibility.' In *Jelley v Iliffe*[174] the Court of Appeal held that it is not necessary to establish such assumption of responsibility as a separate matter; rather, it may be *presumed* from the fact of the deceased having made the substantial contribution.[175] However, the suggestion that assumption of responsibility creates an additional threshold to surmount in order to bring a claim was the subject of criticism and the Law Commission recommended that it be made clear that it need not be established in order to be eligible to claim, although it should continue to be a relevant factor in assessing whether there was a failure to make reasonable provision and if so, what provision should be made.[176] Section 3(4) was accordingly amended to clarify the position.[177] It now provides that the court shall have regard:

(a) to the length of time for which and basis on which the deceased maintained the applicant, and to the extent of the contribution made by way of maintenance;
(b) to whether and, if so, to what extent the deceased assumed responsibility for the maintenance of the applicant.

This enables the court, in the exercise of its discretion, to make an order even if the deceased had not assumed responsibility for the applicant's maintenance if it nonetheless finds that he or she was in fact maintaining them and considers it appropriate to make provision.

It can be seen that two classes of possible claimants are still outside this definition. The first are those who have not been in receipt of a *substantial* contribution. This means that the deceased's mistress may have a claim if he set her up in her own home and paid all her domestic bills,[178] but not if he did no more than make her casual payments and gifts. Secondly, the requirement that the contribution must have been made otherwise than for full valuable consideration clearly excludes claims by, for example, a housekeeper or companion who worked for an economic salary. This focus on an exchange relationship led the courts to adopt what was known as the 'balance sheet approach' to assessing eligibility. According to Stephenson LJ in *Jelley v Iliffe*:[179]

The court has to balance what [the deceased] was contributing against what [the applicant] was contributing, and if there is any doubt about the balance tipping in favour of [the deceased's] being the greater contribution, the matter must go to trial. If, however, the balance is bound to come down in favour of [the applicant's] being the greater contribution, or if the contributions are clearly equal, there is no dependency.

---

[173] [1980] Ch 444.

[174] *Jelley v Iliffe* [1981] Fam 128 at138. See also *Graham v Murphy* [1997] 1 FLR 860 (male cohabitant living in deceased's house at her expense); *Rees v Newbery and the Institute of Cancer Research* [1998] 1 FLR 1041 (applicant living in flat owned by the deceased at substantially below the market rent).

[175] For an example of the rebuttal of the presumption, see *Baynes v Hedger* [2009] EWCA Civ 374 [2009] 2 FLR 767 at para 46: support through gifts and 'soft loans' to a god-daughter did not amount to the deceased assuming responsibility to support her.   [176] Law Com No 331 para 6.59.

[177] By Inheritance and Trustees' Powers Act 2014 Sch 2 para 5(4).

[178] As in *Malone v Harrison* [1979] 1 WLR 1353.

[179] [1981] Fam 128 at 138.

But as Griffiths LJ stressed,[180] it is essential to use common sense and ask whether the applicant could fairly be called a dependant: it would not be right to deprive a woman, with whom a man had been living as his wife, of a claim by arguing that she had been performing the duties of a housekeeper whom it would have cost him more to employ.[181] Similarly, in *Bouette v Rose*[182] the Court of Appeal allowed a mother's claim to go forward after the death at the age of 14 of her daughter, who had been the beneficiary of a substantial damages award administered by the Court of Protection. The award had been used to purchase a home for the mother and daughter to live in and to provide income for the mother to see to the daughter's care. It was held that the daughter had made a substantial contribution, through the payments made by the Court, to the mother's financial and material needs.

The 'balance sheet approach' was criticised as it required the applicant's contribution to be less than that of the deceased and it failed to recognise interdependency: as Kerridge and Brierley have put it, 'It does seem odd that an applicant who claims to have been a dependant will benefit from demonstrating that he or she was slothful and uncaring'.[183] The Law Commission recommended dropping the requirement for cases other than where there was a commercial relationship between the deceased and applicant[184] and the wording of s 1(3) set out earlier is intended to achieve this by expressly excluding from eligibility only 'a contribution made for full valuable consideration pursuant to an arrangement of a commercial nature'.[185]

'Immediately before the death of the deceased'

The applicant must also prove that the deceased was maintaining him (or her) immediately before his death. This requirement was subject to a detailed examination by the Court of Appeal in *Jelley v Iliffe*.[186] As Stephenson LJ said:[187]

> In considering whether a person is being maintained 'immediately before the death of the deceased' it is the settled basis or general arrangement between the parties as regards maintenance during the lifetime of the deceased which has to be looked at, not the actual, perhaps fluctuating, variation of it which exists immediately before his or her death. It is, I think, not disputed that a relationship of dependence which has persisted for years will not be defeated by its termination during a few weeks of mortal sickness.

On the other hand, if the deceased had clearly abandoned responsibility for the applicant's maintenance before his death, the latter will have no claim.[188] Nor will the applicant have one if he was being maintained on a purely temporary basis or by chance at the

---

[180] At 141. Applied in *Bishop v Plumley*.
[181] See also *Churchill v Roach* [2004] 2 FLR 989: deceased bought property adjoining claimant's which was knocked through into hers. They lived together and he paid the bulk of the living expenses. He died before the titles to the two properties could be amalgamated as had been planned. Held, he had partially maintained her. [182] [2000] 1 FLR 363, CA.
[183] Kerridge with Brierley, op cit at para 8.79 and see *Bishop v Plumley* at 242.
[184] Law Com No 331 paras 6.66–6.80.
[185] Section 1(3) as amended by Inheritance and Trustees' Powers Act 2014 Sch 2 para 3.
[186] [1981] Fam 128, CA.
[187] At 136 following *Re Beaumont* [1980] Ch 444 at 456. Griffiths LJ expressed the same view at 141. Cumming-Bruce LJ agreed with both judgments. See also *Witkowska v Kaminski* [2006] EWHC 1940 (Ch) [2006] 3 FCR 250: deceased was maintaining applicant through occasional payments made to her whilst she was living in Poland and last payment made three months before his death.
[188] *Kourkgy v Lusher* (1981) 4 FLR 65: claimant unsuccessful when deceased had stopped cohabiting with her and returned to his wife three weeks before his death.

time of the death, eg if he was a friend whom the deceased had taken in for a few days whilst he recovered from an illness.

2. REASONABLE PROVISION

Having established eligibility to bring a claim, the court must then carry out a two-stage exercise.[189] The first issue to be determined is whether the provisions of the deceased's will or the law relating to intestacy (or the combination of both if there is a partial intestacy) made reasonable financial provision for the applicant.[190] This is a question of fact, but if the applicant cannot discharge the burden of proof, he or she has no claim at all. It is not the purpose of the Act merely to enable the court to provide legacies or rewards for meritorious conduct.[191] If it is found that reasonable provision was not made, the court will then go on to decide what, if any, orders to make.

(a) For a surviving spouse or civil partner

In defining reasonable provision, the Act draws a significant distinction between surviving spouses or civil partners[192] and all other applicants. If the application is made by a surviving spouse or civil partner,[193] reasonable financial provision means such financial provision as it would be reasonable in all the circumstances of the case for a husband or wife (or civil partner) to receive, *whether or not that provision is required for his or her maintenance*.[194] The reason for this is that a surviving spouse or civil partner would normally expect to receive a share of the deceased spouse's estate and it would be anomalous if the court could give her (or him) less after the other's death than it could on divorce or dissolution.

(b) Maintenance for any other applicant

In all other cases, the financial provision to be considered is that which it would be reasonable in all the circumstances of the case for the applicant to receive *for his maintenance*. When considering the provision of maintenance, the court is not limited to assessing the amount needed for bare necessities, nor must it take into account everything which the applicant might regard as reasonably desirable for his benefit or welfare. One must ask whether the applicant will be able to maintain him or herself in a manner suitable to the circumstances.[195]

'Maintenance' means:

> . . . payments which, directly or indirectly, enable the applicant in the future to discharge the cost of his daily living. . . The provision that is to be made is to meet recurring expenses, being expenses of living of an income nature.[196]

---

[189] *Re Krubert (decd)* [1997] Ch 97.

[190] Sections 1(1) and 2(1). For a clear example of failure to make *reasonable* provision, see *Hanbury v Hanbury* [1999] 2 FLR 255 (county court) where the deceased bequeathed his seriously disabled daughter by his first marriage only £10,000 as compared with his second wife who held assets worth over £260,000.

[191] *Re Coventry* [1980] Ch 461 at 486 and 495; *Re Abram (Deceased)* [1996] 2 FLR 379 at 388H; cf *Re Christie* [1979] Ch 168, doubted in *Re Coventry* at 490.

[192] See J Miller 'Provision for a Surviving Spouse' (1997) 61 Conv 442.

[193] Except where a decree of judicial separation or separation order was in force and the separation was continuing at the deceased's death.

[194] Section 1(2) as amended by the Civil Partnership Act 2004 Sch 4 para 14(6).

[195] *Re Coventry* [1980] Ch 461, CA, at 485 (per Goff LJ), and 494 (per Buckley LJ) respectively. As it was put per Roach JA in *Re Duranceau* [1952] 3 DLR 714 (Canada) at 720, is 'the provision sufficient to enable the dependant to live neither luxuriously nor miserably but decently and comfortably according to his or her station in life?' cited by Goff LJ in *Re Coventry* at 485 and Slade LJ in *Re Leach* [1986] Ch 226 at 240.

[196] Per Browne-Wilkinson J in *Re Dennis (Deceased)* [1981] 2 All ER 140 at 145–6.

3. FACTORS TO BE TAKEN INTO ACCOUNT

The Act specifically requires the court to have regard to the following matters when determining whether reasonable financial provision has been made for the applicant, and, if not, what orders it should make.[197]

(a) Factors relevant to all applications

> (a) the financial resources and financial needs which the applicant has or is likely to have in the foreseeable future;
> (b) the financial resources and financial needs which any other applicant for an order. . . has or is likely to have in the foreseeable future;
> (c) the financial resources and financial needs which any beneficiary of the estate of the deceased has or is likely to have in the foreseeable future;
> (d) any obligations and responsibilities which the deceased had towards any applicant for an order. . . or towards any beneficiary of the estate of the deceased;
> (e) the size and nature of the net estate of the deceased;
> (f) any physical or mental disability of any applicant. . . or any beneficiary of the estate of the deceased;
> (g) any other matter, including the conduct of the applicant or any other person, which in the circumstances of the case the court may consider relevant.[198]

Financial resources and financial needs

The financial resources and needs[199] of the applicant, any other applicant for an order, and any beneficiary of the estate,[200] and any physical or mental disability from which any of them suffers, must be considered.

In this connection the court must take into account the individual's earning capacity, any resources and needs which he is likely to have in the foreseeable future, and his financial obligations and responsibilities.[201] It is necessary to consider the position of other applicants and beneficiaries, because any order made will limit the property available for them; consequently an applicant may be more likely to succeed if an order in his or her favour can be made at the expense of a beneficiary towards whom the deceased had no obligations.[202]

Obligations and responsibilities of the deceased

Both legal and moral obligations are included, but they must have been in existence immediately before the deceased's death. Thus, a failure to support a child after the deceased's marriage broke down (45 years earlier when the child was aged 2) did not justify an award to the now adult child.[203]

---

[197] Section 3.   [198] Section 3(1).

[199] For a needs-based award, see in particular, *Barron v Woodhead* [2008] EWHC 810 (Ch) [2009] 1 FLR 747, where the elderly widower's imminent homelessness justified an award from the wife's estate, despite his having dissipated family assets, allegedly attempted to defeat creditors and been adjudicated bankrupt.

[200] Beneficiary includes not only a person claiming under the deceased's will or on his intestacy, but also anyone nominated by him to receive money or property after his death and any recipient of a *donatio mortis causa* (gift in contemplation of death), because all this property forms part of the net estate: s 25(1).

[201] Including his debts: *Re Goodchild (Deceased)* [1996] 1 All ER 670.

[202] As in *Re Besterman* [1984] Ch 458, CA; *Re Bunning* [1984] Ch 480; *Rees v Newbery and the Institute of Cancer Research* [1998] 1 FLR 1041. In each of these cases the residuary legatees were charities.

[203] *Re Jennings (Deceased)* [1994] Ch 286, CA.

The early cases on this issue seemed to establish that an adult child would have to show either that the deceased owed him a moral obligation, going beyond the mere fact of a blood relationship, to make provision for him out of his estate, or some other reason why, in the circumstances, it was unreasonable that no, or no more, provision had been made.[204] However, this approach has been held to be wrong,[205] and in *Ilott v Mitson and Others* the Court of Appeal confirmed that the Act imposes no express requirement to establish a moral obligation or special circumstances.[206] The daughter and her mother were estranged for 20 years. The mother died in 2004 leaving an estate of about £486,000, the bulk of which was left to three animal charities, with nothing to the daughter, who had five children and lived mainly on welfare benefits. The Court of Appeal upheld the first instance judge's decision that the daughter should receive an award (ultimately set at £50,000), holding that the question whether reasonable financial provision had been made is a 'value judgment' with which an appellate court should be slow to interfere.[207]

The size and nature of the estate

The size and nature of the estate[208] are relevant to the question of whether any provision should be made, and if so, how much. If, for example, the deceased had a large income but little capital, it might be reasonable for him to leave the whole of his estate to his widow to the total exclusion of others whom he had supported during his lifetime, or to provide an absolute, rather than life, interest in the available property.[209] Likewise the source of the deceased's capital may be relevant; for example, if it came largely from a former spouse, the children of that spouse may have a stronger claim than the deceased's spouse or relations.[210] If the estate is small, the courts discourage applications altogether because of the danger that it will be entirely swallowed up by the costs of the action.[211]

Any other relevant matter, including the conduct of the applicant or any other person

In the case of a former spouse the test should be the same whether the application is made on divorce or after the other party's death.[212] The same should now be true for a (former)

---

[204] *Re Coventry* [1980] Ch 461; *Williams v Johns* [1988] 2 FLR 475.

[205] *Re Hancock (Deceased)* [1998] 2 FLR 346, CA; *Re Pearce (Deceased)* [1998] 2 FLR 705, CA; *Espinosa v Bourke* [1999] 1 FLR 747. See also *Garland v Morris* [2007] EWHC 2 (Ch) [2007] 2 FLR 528 para 29 and *Ilott v Mitson* [2011] EWCA Civ 346 [2012] 2 FLR 172 paras 23, 24 which both point out that the Court of Appeal in *Re Coventry* did not accept that the relevant dictum of Oliver J at first instance imposed a requirement to show some moral obligation in any case.

[206] [2011] EWCA Civ 346 [2012] 2 FLR 172; and see [2014] EWHC 542 (Fam) [2014] Fam Law 789.

[207] But see K Green 'The Englishwoman's Castle: Inheritance and Private Property Today' (1988) 51 MLR 187 pp 199–205 for the argument that the courts are engaged in a moral exercise in determining whose claims should succeed.

[208] Including property forming part of an unsevered joint tenancy or a transaction or contract intended to defeat an application under the Act: *Kourkgy v Lusher* (1981) 4 FLR 65; *Hanbury v Hanbury* [1999] 2 FLR 255.

[209] *Iqbal v Ahmed* [2011] EWCA Civ 900 [2012] 1 FLR 31: a life interest in the former matrimonial home would not of itself make adequate provision for the widow given the cost of repairs needed to renovate the property; she was awarded a half-share and the residuary estate. On the other hand, where a childless couple had deliberately severed their joint tenancy to limit the risk of the value of the matrimonial home being swallowed up in meeting the care needs of the disabled wife, it was held that reasonable provision for her would be met by a life interest enabling her to live in the property as long as she was able, with the residue going to a family friend, niece and nephew: *Moore v Holdsworth* [2010] EWHC 683 (Ch) [2010] 2 FLR 1501.

[210] *Re Callaghan* [1985] Fam 1. See the discussion earlier, Statutory legacy and residuary interests at p 971 regarding 'conduit theory'.

[211] See *Re Coventry* at 486 (per Goff LJ); *Re Fullard* [1982] Fam 42 at 46 (per Ormrod LJ).

[212] *Re Snoek* (1983) 13 Fam Law 18.

civil partner. It is accepted that the court should take into account the fact that a child has given up work to look after a parent,[213] but, on the other hand, it is not easy to see what weight should be given to a child's uncaring conduct. It is suggested that the test should be this: bearing in mind the deceased's treatment of the applicant, was the latter's conduct towards him such that a reasonable parent would have considered that he had forfeited any further claim to financial provision?[214]

(b) Factors relevant to applications by spouses or civil partners

If the applicant is a surviving or former spouse or civil partner, the court must also have regard to the duration of the marriage/ partnership, the applicant's age, and the contribution he or she made to the welfare of the deceased's family, including any contribution by looking after the home or caring for the family.[215] If the couple have been living apart, the length of their separation will also be relevant.[216] Again, the similarity with the law of divorce will be seen. Moreover (except when a decree of judicial separation or separation order was in force and the separation was continuing at the deceased's death), the court must also consider what provision the applicant might reasonably have expected to receive had the marriage or civil partnership been terminated by divorce or dissolution instead of death,[217] on the ground that it would be anomalous if the latter could expect less on death than she would have got on divorce or dissolution.

This 'divorce cross-check' was considered in the leading case, *Fielden and Another v Cunliffe*.[218] There, the wife worked as the deceased's housekeeper before marrying him a year before he died. At first instance, she was awarded a lump sum of £800,000 out of the estate valued at some £1.4 million. In reducing the award to £600,000, the Court of Appeal held that the correct approach for the court to adopt, following the House of Lords decision in *White v White*,[219] is to apply the statutory provisions to the facts of the individual case with the objective of achieving a result which is fair, and non-discriminatory. This does not mean that an equal share may result, for the situation is not identical to that of a divorce. As Wall LJ put it:

> A marriage dissolved by divorce involves a conscious decision by one or both of the spouses to bring the marriage to an end. That process leaves two living former spouses, each of whom has resources, needs and responsibilities. In such a case the length of the marriage and the parties' respective contributions to it assume a particular importance when the court is striving to reach a fair financial outcome. However, where the marriage, as here, is dissolved by death, a widow is entitled to say that she entered into it on the basis that it would be of indefinite duration, and in the expectation that she would devote the remainder of the parties' joint lives to being his wife and caring for him. The fact that the marriage has been prematurely terminated by death after a short period may therefore render the length of the marriage a less critical factor than it would be in the case of a divorce.[220]

---

[213] See *Re Coventry* [1980] Ch 461 at 489–90.

[214] See *Williams v Johns* [1988] 2 FLR 475.

[215] Section 3(2) as amended by Civil Partnership Act 2004 Sch 4 para 17.

[216] *Re Rowlands* [1984] FLR 813, CA.

[217] Section 3(2) as amended by Civil Partnership Act 2004 Sch 4 para 17(5). See *Re Besterman; Re Bunning; Jessop v Jessop* [1992] 1 FLR 591, CA at 597.

[218] [2005] EWCA Civ 1508 [2006] Ch 361 at para [30]. For consideration of the principles set out in *Miller v Miller; McFarlane v McFarlane* [2006] UKHL 24 [2006] 2 AC 618, see *Lilleyman v Lilleyman* [2012] EWHC 821 (Ch) [2013] 1 FLR 47.

[219] [2001] 1 AC 596.   [220] *Fielden v Cunliffe* [2005] EWCA Civ 1508 [2006] Ch 361 at [30].

However, the deceased is entitled to bequeath his estate to whoever he likes, and is only subject to the statutory obligation to make *reasonable* financial provision for the surviving spouse (or civil partner). In the context of securing such 'reasonable financial provision', the Court of Appeal concluded that the brevity of the marriage and the fact that the widow had made only a very small contribution to the family wealth were factors against equality of division in ensuring a *fair* outcome to the case. The duration of the marriage will therefore be an important consideration and by contrast with the decision in this case, a long marriage may be expected to produce more generous provision.[221] But ultimately, the court must bear in mind that the comparison with divorce is only a 'cross-check', which constitutes neither a floor nor a ceiling to the award.[222] The Law Commission recommended that the legislation should make clear that the divorce analogy should not be treated as setting either an upper or lower limit on the award.[223] This has been done by the Inheritance and Trustees' Powers Act 2014 which amends s 3(2) accordingly.[224] Should the Commission's Nuptial Agreements Bill be enacted, it would provide that the terms (including those contemplating the death of a spouse) of a qualifying nuptial agreement could be taken into account in deciding what, if any, provision should be made.[225]

(c) Factors relevant to applications by cohabitants

In the case of applications by cohabitants,[226] the court must additionally have regard to the age of the applicant, the length of the period of cohabitation,[227] and the contribution made by the applicant to the welfare of the family or of the deceased, including any contribution made by looking after the home or caring for the family.[228]

The courts have also taken account of the lifestyle that the couple enjoyed together.[229] In their Consultation Paper, the Law Commission argued that this is correct in that it recognises that a cohabiting relationship goes beyond one of mere dependency, includes mutual contributions and gives due regard to its duration,[230] but they also pointed out that it is inconsistent with the requirement that provision be limited strictly to 'maintenance'. They accordingly recommended that a cohabitant's claim should not be limited to maintenance but should instead be defined as 'such financial provision as it would be reasonable in all the circumstances of the case for the applicant to receive, whether or not that provision is required for the applicant's maintenance.'[231] However, after consulting, they withdrew their recommendation. As we have just seen, provision for a spouse or civil partner requires comparison with what they would have received on a divorce or dissolution, but pending implementation of the Law Commission's (or other) proposals for reform of the law governing property allocation when a cohabiting couple separate, there is no 'cross-check' which can be applied to determine how to calibrate a family provision award for a cohabitant. They did, however, suggest that, should financial remedies be

---

[221] *Iqbal v Ahmed* [2011] EWCA Civ 900 [2012] 1 FLR 31.

[222] *P v G, P and P (Family Provision: Relevance of Divorce Provision)* [2004] EWHC 2944 (Fam) [2006] 1 FLR 431; *Lilleyman v Lilleyman* [2012] EWHC 821 (Ch) [2013] 1 FLR 47.

[223] Law Com No 331 para 2.146.   [224] Sch 2 para 5(2).

[225] Law Commission *Matrimonial Property, Needs and Agreements* Law Com No 343 (2014) paras 5.106, 5.124. See Ch 23.   [226] Section 3(2A) as amended by Civil Partnership Act 2004 Sch 4 para 18.

[227] See e.g. *Webster v Webster* [2008] EWHC 31 (Ch) [2009] 1 FLR 1240 at [39], 'longer . . . than many marriages' (36 years); *Cattle v Evans* [2011] EWHC 945 (Ch) [2011] 2 FLR 843 [53] (17 years, with 2 year interruption).

[228] Section 3(2A) as amended by Civil Partnership Act 2004 Sch 4 para 18.

[229] *Negus v Bahouse* [2007] EWHC 2628 (Ch) [2008] 1 FCR 768 followed in *Webster v Webster*.

[230] Law Com No 191 para 4.130.   [231] Ibid para 4.134.

introduced for cohabitants who separate, then the position regarding the maintenance standard should be reviewed.[232]

(d) Factors relevant to applications by a child, or child of the family, of the deceased

If the applicant is a child of the deceased or a person whom he treated as a child of the family, the court must also have regard to the manner in which he was being or might expect to be educated or trained. If he is a child of the family but not the deceased's own child, the court must also consider whether the deceased maintained the applicant and, if so, the length of time for which and basis on which he or she did so; the extent of the contribution made by way of maintenance; and whether and, if so, to what extent the deceased assumed responsibility for the maintenance of the applicant.[233]

In line with the position on divorce, the general view of the courts is that adult children should not generally expect to receive financial support from their parents and thus it may be difficult for such a child who is financially independent to obtain an award *for their maintenance*.[234] The Law Commission considered whether this is fair, especially where the applicant is not the child of the surviving spouse or partner, who might, under the 'conduit theory' noted earlier,[235] choose to leave (or die intestate and leave) all their property to their own children. However, they rejected the argument that such a child should be able to receive more than his or her 'maintenance', on grounds of both consistency with the principle of testamentary freedom, and complexity.[236]

(e) Factors relevant to applications by dependants

If the applicant is relying on a de facto dependence during the deceased's lifetime, the court must specifically have regard to the extent of the length of time for which and basis on which the deceased maintained the applicant; to the extent of the contribution made by way of maintenance; and to whether and, if so, to what extent the deceased assumed responsibility for the maintenance of the applicant.[237] These are three of the matters which the court has to take into account when considering applications from persons who have been treated as children of the family and the similarity of their position is obvious.

---

[232] Law Com No 331 paras 8.164–8.165.

[233] Section 3(3) as amended by Inheritance and Trustees' Powers Act 2014 Sch 2 para 5(3).

[234] *Re Coventry* [1980] Ch 461, CA. See JG Miller 'Provision for Adult Children under the Inheritance (Provision for Family and Dependants) Act 1975' (1995) 59 Conv 22 and N Peart and A Borkowski 'Provision for adult children on death—the lesson from New Zealand' [2000] CFLQ 333. Kerridge and Brierley (op cit) paras 8-57–8-62, categorise potentially successful claimants based upon whether the child worked for the parent on an understanding that he would inherit (*Re Abram (Deceased)* [1996] 2 FLR 379; *Re Pearce (Deceased)* [1998] 2 FLR 705); the estate having come from the other parent on the understanding that the surviving parent would leave it to the claimant (*Re Goodchild* [1997] 1 WLR 1216); and the 'lame duck' child who is in financial difficulties (*Re Hancock (Deceased)* 1998] 2 FLR 346; *Espinosa v Bourke* [1999] 1 FLR 747). Compare *Garland v Morris* [2007] EWHC 2 (Ch) [2007] 2 FLR 528, where the 'lame duck' daughter had already inherited from her mother (whose estate came in large part from her divorce settlement with the father, now the deceased), and whose failure to keep in touch with her father following the mother's death was regarded as another important factor in concluding that she had not established that he should have made reasonable provision for her in his will.

[235] See Statutory legacy and residuary interests, p 971.   [236] Law Com No 331 paras 6.2–6.26.

[237] Section 3(4) as amended by Inheritance and Trustees' Powers Act 2014 Sch 2 para 5(4). See *Graham v Murphy* [1997] 1 FLR 860; *Rees v Newbery and the Institute of Cancer Research* [1998] 1 FLR 1041.

4. PROPERTY AVAILABLE FOR FINANCIAL PROVISION

Except for the power to order the variation of an ante-nuptial or post-nuptial settlement or the equivalent in relation to a civil partnership, the court can only make orders for the payment of money out of the deceased's net estate or affecting property comprised in that estate.[238] Basically, this means such property[239] as the deceased had power to dispose of by will,[240] less the amount of funeral, testamentary and administration expenses and any liabilities.[241] The court may also order the severance of a joint tenancy or joint interest (eg in a bank account) or any part of a joint tenancy or interest to which the deceased was entitled immediately before his death and which would therefore otherwise pass to the other joint tenants, on the basis that he could have effected a severance himself and thus brought the property into his estate.[242] The undivided share will then form part of the net estate.[243]

Finally, the estate includes any money or property ordered to be restored or provided if a disposition or contract is set aside. One of the weaknesses of earlier legislation was that the deceased could defeat an application by settling or disposing of his property during his lifetime so that it never formed part of his estate at all or, alternatively, could contract to leave it to a third person after his death.[244] The 1975 Act contains provisions designed to frustrate such transactions.[245]

5. ORDERS THAT MAY BE MADE

(a) Interim orders

If a dependant is in immediate need of financial assistance,[246] and property forming part of the net estate can be made available to meet his needs but it is not yet possible to make a final order, the court may make an interim order. This may take the form of one payment or of periodical payments, and the court may later direct that any sum paid under an interim order shall be treated as having been paid on account of the final order. As far

---

[238] Section 2(1) (as amended by Civil Partnership Act 2004 Sch 4 para 16) and s 8(1).

[239] Including property situated abroad: *Bheekhun v Williams* [1999] 2 FLR 229.

[240] Otherwise than by virtue of a special power of appointment.   [241] Section 25(1), (2).

[242] Section 9. See *Jessop v Jessop* [1992] 1 FLR 591, CA; *Hanbury v Hanbury* [1999] 2 FLR 255. The previous time limit which prevented the court exercising this power unless the application for an order for financial provision was made within six months from the date on which representation was first taken out was removed by Sch 2 para 7(2) of the 2014 Act. Any person dealing with the property before an order for severance is protected: s 9(3).

[243] See *Dingmar v Dingmar* [2006] EWCA Civ 942 [2007] Ch 109 where the court ordered transfer of the deceased's half share in the beneficial interest (which has passed by the right of survivorship under a joint tenancy to his son) to the widow. Cf *Lim (An Infant) v Walia* [2014] EWCA Civ 1076—terminal illness benefit was a severable interest but had nil value as no claim made before death.

[244] See eg *Hanbury v Hanbury* [1999] 2 FLR 255 where the father sought (unsuccessfully) to prevent his estate being vulnerable to a claim by his adult (handicapped) daughter. If the transaction was effected fraudulently with intent to defeat the dependant's claim, it is arguable that it could be set aside under the court's general power to upset fraudulent transactions, or perhaps under s 423 of the Insolvency Act 1986: see *Cadogan v Cadogan* [1977] 3 All ER 831, CA. This might still be relevant eg if the transaction was made more than six years before the deceased's death.

[245] See ss 10 and 11 and *B v IB (Order to set aside disposition under Insolvency Act)* [2013] EWHC 3755 (Fam) [2014] Fam Law 287 which confirmed that an application could also be brought under the Insolvency Act 1986 s 423 in the alternative.

[246] See *Smith v Smith* [2011] EWHC 2133 (Ch) [2012] 2 FLR 230: estranged wife living in Moscow had not proved that she was in immediate need of living in the former matrimonial home in England pending determination of her claim, nor that she lacked sufficient income and assets to cover her needs.

as possible, the same matters should be taken into account in making an interim order as in making a final order.[247]

(b) Final orders

If the court is satisfied that reasonable financial provision has not been made for the applicant, it may make a final order containing one or more of the provisions set out in this section.[248] In determining what order (if any) to make, the court must have regard to the same matters as it has when deciding whether reasonable provision has been made.[249]

Periodical payments

These may be for a specified amount or for an amount equal to the whole or any part of the income of the net estate or of such part of the estate as the court directs to be set aside or appropriated for this purpose, or it may be determined in any other way the court thinks fit.[250] The order may last for such term and be subject to such conditions as the court directs. Formation of a subsequent marriage or civil partnership of the deceased's spouse or civil partner will not automatically discharge the order (although it may be a ground for an application to have it discharged by the court). It would be anomalous, however, to give former and separated spouses or civil partners greater rights on the deceased's death than they had before, and consequently an order for periodical payments made in their favour will terminate automatically on remarriage or new civil partnership.[251] In other cases it would normally be reasonable to direct that payment to a child should terminate on his ceasing to receive education or training, or that payment to an applicant who is temporarily unable to work owing to illness should terminate on her ceasing to be under a disability.

An order may be varied, suspended or discharged on the application of anyone who has already applied for an order or would be entitled to apply if not time-barred.[252] The variation can take the form of a lump sum or the transfer of the property, as well as the provision of further periodical payments.

Lump sum

A lump sum order would be particularly valuable if the estate is so small that any periodical payments would be valueless. It could also enable, say, a claimant to purchase the goodwill of a business. If the estate is large enough, it is submitted that this will normally be the proper order to make in favour of a surviving spouse or civil partner. If the order is made at the expense of beneficiaries towards whom the deceased had no obligations, a spouse or civil partner will probably obtain more under the Inheritance Act than she (or he) would have obtained in divorce or dissolution proceedings, because the estate is no longer needed for the deceased's support and it may be reasonable to give the applicant a cushion to provide against future contingencies.[253] In *Fielden v Cunliffe*[254] Wall LJ suggested that the view that such a 'cushion' should be given must be regarded with

---

[247] Section 5. For the protection of personal representatives, see s 20(2).

[248] Section 2(1). See generally Law Com No 61 paras 109–26.   [249] Section 3(1).

[250] Section 2(2), (3).

[251] Section 19(2) as amended by Civil Partnership Act Sch 4 para 26. This applies to separated spouses or civil partners only if the decree or order was in force and the separation continuing at the time of the deceased's death.   [252] Section 6.

[253] See *Re Besterman* [1984] Ch 458; *Re Bunning* [1984] Ch 480; J Miller 'Provision for a Surviving Spouse' (1986) 102 LQR 445; T Prime 'Family Provision—The Spouse's Application' [1986] Fam Law 95.

[254] [2005] EWCA Civ 1508 [2006] Ch 361 at [77].

caution, since it pre-dated *White v White*. However, he saw it as still being 'authority for the proposition that the blameless widow of a wealthy man is entitled to look forward to financial security throughout her remaining life-time, and that "reasonable financial provision", which is not limited to maintenance, must be viewed accordingly'. In *Lilleyman v Lilleyman*[255] it was also noted that the principles of sharing and compensation might be a valuable part of the divorce cross-check in identifying what would be 'reasonable' provision for the surviving spouse (or civil partner) and one might expect these to be particularly relevant to consideration of a lump sum award.

A lump sum may be valuable if relationships in a family are so bitter that a clean break is desirable,[256] or to avoid embarrassment, or to achieve finality in the interests of the other beneficiaries.[257] The disadvantage of such an order is that it cannot be varied to take account of unforeseen changes in the circumstances of the applicant or a beneficiary and, if it represents the capitalisation of periodical payments, events may prove the estimate to have been wildly inaccurate. Consequently, the courts have been reluctant to order the payment of a lump sum to an applicant who is elderly or in poor health, because premature death would often result in the deceased's assets being vested in someone outside the family.[258]

As on divorce, the court may order that a lump sum be paid by instalments.[259]

The transfer or settlement of property comprised in the net estate

The court might order that the former family home be transferred or settled for the benefit of a surviving partner[260] particularly if he or she has to bring up young children. In other cases it may be more convenient, as on divorce, to order the transfer of property than the payment of a lump sum.

The transfer or settlement of property to be acquired out of the estate

This has no counterpart in the Matrimonial Causes Act 1973 and is designed particularly to enable a home to be bought for the applicant.[261]

The variation of any ante-nuptial or post-nuptial settlement or settlement in relation to a civil partnership

This is strictly equivalent to the court's powers on divorce or dissolution and the variation may be made only for the benefit of the surviving party to the marriage or civil partnership or a child of the family in relation to that marriage or civil partnership.[262]

---

[255] [2012] EWHC 821 (Ch) [2013] 1 FLR 47.

[256] See *Re Collins (Deceased)* [1990] Fam 56: need to achieve finality where defendant was violent man and applicant, his daughter, had been fostered; *Iqbal v Ahmed* [2011] EWCA Civ 900 [2012] 1 FLR 31: equal share in matrimonial home and residuary estate awarded to widow, in part because of deeply hostile relationship between her and the deceased's son by an earlier marriage.

[257] *Graham v Murphy* [1997] 1 FLR 860; *Rees v Newbery and the Institute of Cancer Research* [1998] 1 FLR 1041.

[258] See *Re Debenham* [1986] 1 FLR 404: daughter aged 58, epileptic, given small lump sum and annuity. In *Stead v Stead* [1985] FLR 16, CA: the lump sum awarded to a widow, aged 82, was limited to the amount needed to cover certain eventualities, apparently on the ground that, if she were given more, she would merely save it. But this is not an invariable rule and a lump sum may be ordered in other circumstances: *Kusminow v Barclays Bank Trust Co Ltd* [1989] Fam Law 66, *Re Pearce (Deceased)* [1998] 2 FLR 705, CA.

[259] Section 7. The court may subsequently vary the number and amount of instalments and the dates on which they are to be paid, but not the total sum payable.

[260] As in *Harrington v Gill* (1983) 4 FLR 265, CA. See also *Musa v Holliday* [2012] EWCA Civ 1268 [2013] 1 FLR 806 where relations were so bitter between the surviving partner and the deceased's children that the court upheld the transfer of the former family home and shares in order to achieve a clean break.

[261] See Law Com No 61 para 116.

[262] Section 2(1)(f), (g) inserted by Civil Partnership Act 2004 Sch 4 para 16.

The variation of any trust on which the deceased's estate is held

The Inheritance and Trustees' Powers Act 2014 added a new power,[263] on the recommendation of the Law Commission, to enable the court to vary any trust forming part of the deceased's estate for the applicant's benefit. Prior to this addition, although a trust could be varied in order to satisfy an order (eg 'by resettling on new trusts property that is held on existing trusts'),[264] it was not possible to order a variation of the trust itself.

6. RELATIONSHIP TO EXISTING AGREEMENTS AND ORDERS

It must not be forgotten that other liabilities to support a dependant may survive the deceased's death. An order for secured periodical payments may have been made in his or her favour during previous proceedings or he or she may be a party to a maintenance agreement under which payments continue. Not only will the existence of the continuing right affect any order that may be made if financial relief is sought under the Act but also, in the changed circumstances brought about by the death, it may make unfairly generous provision for him or her compared with the amount left for other applicants. To prevent the unnecessary duplication of proceedings, the court may vary existing orders and agreements in proceedings under the Inheritance Act.[265]

The definition of a maintenance agreement is the same as that contained in s 34 of the Matrimonial Causes Act 1973[266] except, importantly, that it need not be in writing.[267] The court has no power to reduce the sums payable if, in proceedings brought by another applicant under the Act, it concludes that they are too large. This can be done only if the personal representatives themselves take proceedings to have the order or agreement varied under the Matrimonial Causes Act or Civil Partnership Act, which they may be unwilling to do.

Conversely, if the personal representatives, the recipient of secured periodical payments or a party to a maintenance agreement applies for a variation of the order or agreement under those Acts,[268] the court may deem the application to have been accompanied by an application for an order under the Inheritance Act and exercise all the powers it has under that Act.[269] This may be of particular importance to a party to an agreement, because under the other Acts there is no power to set aside a disposition intended to defeat an application for a variation of a maintenance agreement after the payer's death. By invoking this jurisdiction, the court can exercise its power to set aside dispositions and contracts under ss 10 and 11.

Whether as part of an agreed financial settlement, or in pursuance of the principle that a clean break should be made wherever possible, the court dealing with financial provision on divorce, dissolution, nullity or separation may wish to exclude the possibility of a future application under the Inheritance Act. Accordingly it may make an order having this effect on the application of either party to the marriage or civil partnership if it is satisfied that it is just to do so.[270] However, the fact that such a clause has not been included

---

[263] Inheritance and Trustees' Powers Act 2014 Sch 2 para 4 inserting s 2(1)(h) into the 1975 Act.
[264] Law Com No 331 para 7.124.   [265] See further Law Com No 61 Part VII.
[266] And Sch 5 para 67 to the Civil Partnership Act 2004. See Ch 21, Maintenance agreements, p 781.
[267] Section 17(4).
[268] In such a case, the agreement must be a maintenance agreement within the meaning of those Acts.
[269] Inheritance (Provision for Family and Dependants) Act 1975 ss 18 and 18A (inserted by Civil Partnership Act 2004 Sch 4 para 25).
[270] Sections 15, 15ZA as inserted by the Civil Partnership Act 2004 Sch 4 para 21.

does not, of itself, strengthen a claim.[271] The order will take effect only when a decree of nullity or divorce is made absolute or the nullity or dissolution order is made final or, in the case of a separation, if the decree or order is in force and the separation is continuing on the death of one of the parties. The court has the same power if it makes an order for financial relief following a foreign dissolution, annulment or legal separation granted in an overseas country and recognised here.[272]

By analogy with applications for financial relief in matrimonial proceedings, a party presumably cannot contract out of his or her power to apply under the Inheritance Act except by way of a consent order[273] or marital property agreement upheld by the court.[274]

D. CONCLUSION

In many ways the issues arising on a death in the family, the dispositions made by people in their wills, the obligations that they recognise to their loved ones, and the expectations that society may have of what it is 'reasonable' to leave to one's family, are at the front line of changes in how we define families and how we live together in family relationships. Questions concerning how far the law does and should take account of and accommodate cohabiting relationships, serial relationships and 'blended families' and how it should prioritise the claims of competing family members caught up in these lifestyles, have formed the substance of this book, at each stage in the family life course, from formation of adult relationships to their termination by separation or death.

The certainties of definition which could be applied a century ago by a society confident of its values have given way to a more questioning attitude as to which relationships in what circumstances should be given legal recognition, and what forms that recognition should take. Family law will continue to be shaped by the efforts of policy makers and legal practitioners to keep abreast of the social revolution which has so profoundly transformed family life. It will do so in the understanding that, while the form or structure of the 'family' may change, its essential characteristics will remain, in the words of Lord Slynn in *Fitzpatrick v Sterling Housing Association Ltd* 'a degree of mutual inter-dependence, of the sharing of lives, of caring and love, of commitment and support.'[275] How these new policy dilemmas are to be accommodated in a world where families are increasingly 'globalised' forms the subject of the final chapter.

[271] *Cameron v Treasury Solicitor* [1996] 2 FLR 716, CA (but note that there the divorce had taken place at a time when such a clause could only be added by consent and was not routine); cf *T v T (Financial Relief: Pensions)* [1998] 1 FLR 1072 where Singer J thought that such an application might be fairer than attempting to attach the husband's pension many years before he might be expected to die.

[272] Section 15A, inserted by the Matrimonial and Family Proceedings Act 1984 s 25(3) and s 15B, inserted by the Civil Partnership Act 2004 Sch 4 para 22. [273] See *Re M (Deceased)* [1968] P 174.

[274] Under the principles in *Granatino v Radmacher (Formerly Granatino)* [2010] UKSC 42 [2011] 1 AC 534 (see Ch 22, *Granatino v Radmacher*, p 857).

[275] [2001] 1 AC 27, HL at 38C–D.

26

INTERNATIONAL ASPECTS OF CHILD LAW

A. INTRODUCTION

In Chapter 1 we adverted to what we describe as the 'internationalisation of family law' resulting from the growing phenomenon of cross-border families. We noted, too, the different types of international instruments to which national law has to conform, namely, those such as UN Convention on the Rights of the Child and the European Convention on Human Rights that set internationally agreed standards or norms, and those more operational instruments that seek to provide common solutions to what are perceived as being international problems. In this final chapter we concentrate on the latter as they affect some aspects of the law relating to children.

We begin by discussing the revised Brussels II Regulation since that is now the pre-eminent instrument within the EU and provides the basic rules of jurisdiction for hearing cases concerning children. It also provides a system of recognition and enforcement of decisions concerning parental responsibility. We then examine the international aspects of adoption and, in that context, the 1993 Hague Convention on Intercountry Adoption. We next turn our attention to what is the most developed area of international child law, namely international parental child abduction, and in respect of which a number of international instruments come into play. Finally, we discuss the international protection of children as governed by the 1996 Hague Convention on the Protection of Children which the UK ratified in 2012.

B. THE REVISED BRUSSELS II REGULATION

1. BACKGROUND

As we discussed in Chapter 1,[1] the EU's previous hands-off family law approach was radically changed by the conclusion of Council Regulation (EC) No 1347/2000 of 29 May 2000 on jurisdiction and the recognition and enforcement of judgments in matrimonial matters and in matters of parental responsibility for children of both spouses which was popularly known as 'Brussels II'.[2] That Regulation came into force in March 2001. It was, however, relatively limited in its scope applying only to matters of parental responsibility for children of both spouses involved in matrimonial proceedings; provided complex and

---

[1] At The European Union and the Brussels Regulations, p 28.
[2] See generally N Lowe, M Everall and M Nicholls *The New Brussels II Regulation A Supplement to International Movement of Children* (2005) and N Lowe 'Negotiating the Revised Brussels II Regulation' [2004] IFL 205.

inappropriate rules of jurisdiction; and, made no provision for an administrative body to help litigants.[3] Most, if not all, of these shortcomings were addressed by the revised Brussels II Regulation[4] (sometimes referred to as Brussels IIA but commonly abbreviated to BIIR), which came into force in March 2005 and which repealed the original Regulation.[5] Being an EU Regulation the instrument is directly binding on the UK. Consequently there is no implementing legislation but domestic regulations have been made under s 2(2) of the European Communities Act 1972 to make domestic law consistent with BIIR.[6] BIIR binds all Member States of the European Union except Denmark.[7]

The final arbiter on the application of BIIR is the Court of Justice of the European Union (CJEU). National courts can make references to the CJEU whenever they are uncertain as to application of the Regulation and, indeed should do so, unless its meaning is clear (*acte claire*).[8]

2. THE GENERAL SCOPE OF BIIR

BIIR has a wide scope. By Art I(1)(b) and Recital (5) it applies to *all* 'civil matters relating to . . . the attribution, exercise, delegation, restriction or termination of parental responsibility'.[9] It applies not merely to court judgments but also (see Art 46) to: (a) any decision pronounced by an authority (eg local authorities) having jurisdiction in matters of parental responsibility; (b) documents formally drawn up (for example, by notaries) or registered as 'authentic documents' that are enforceable in the Member State in which they are drawn up or registered; and (c) agreements concluded between the parties to the extent that they are enforceable in the Member State in which they are concluded.

Parental responsibility for these purposes specifically includes rights of custody and rights of access and also encompasses guardianship and the placement of a child in a foster family or in institutional care.[10] It expressly excludes establishing or contesting the parent–child relationship, adoption, names, emancipation, maintenance obligations, trusts and succession, and measures taken as a result of criminal offences committed by children.[11] The holder of parental responsibility may be a natural person or a legal person.[12]

The concept of 'civil matters' is broadly defined for the purposes of the Regulation and covers *all* matters listed in Art 1(2). Even if a specific matter of parental responsibility is

---

[3] For a critique of the limitations of the original Regulation, see N Lowe 'New International Conventions Affecting the Law Relating to Children—a Cause for Concern?' [2001] IFL 171 and 'The Growing Influence of the European Union on International Family Law—A View From The Boundary' (2003) 56 *Current Legal Problems* 440, 457–64 and the authorities there cited.

[4] Council Regulation (EC) No 2201/2003 of 27 November 2003 concerning jurisdiction and the recognition and enforcement of judgments in matrimonial matters and the matters of parental responsibility, repealing Regulation (EC) No 1347/2000.

[5] A useful guide to the Regulation has been produced by the European Commission, see 'Parental Responsibility in the European Union—Practice Guide for to the Application of the Brussels II Regulation' (2005).

[6] See (for England and Wales) the European Communities (Jurisdiction and Judgments in Matrimonial and Parental Responsibility) Regulations 2005 (SI 2005/265).   [7] See Art 2(3) of BIIR.

[8] See Art 267 (TFEU). For a discussion of making references, see Lord Justice Thorpe and E Sharpston 'References to the Court of Justice of the European Union in Family Proceedings' [2010] Fam Law 601. The first reference under this provision from the UK was made by the CA in *Mercredi v Chaffe* (Case C-497/PPU) [2012] Fam 27.

[9] Art 1(1)(b). By Art 1(1)(a) the Regulation also applies to civil proceedings relating to divorce, legal separation and annulment.

[10] Arts 1(2) and 2(7).   [11] Art 1(3).   [12] Art 2(7).

a 'public law' measure according to national law, for example, the placement of a child in a foster family or in institutional care, it shall nevertheless be considered as a 'civil matter' for the purposes of BIIR.[13] Indeed it seems accepted that BIIR provides the general jurisdictional basis for the institution of public law orders.[14] Applications inter alia for parental responsibility orders are clearly governed by the Regulation.[15]

'Child' is not defined and as the BIIR Practice Guide says,[16] the Regulation does not therefore prescribe a maximum age. That is left to national law. This therefore preserves the Scottish practice of dealing with children up to the age of 16 rather than 18 as in England and Wales and Northern Ireland. In this latter respect it will be noted that the Regulation has a wider scope than either the Hague or European Conventions which only apply to children under the age of 16. What the Practice Guide does not deal with is whether the Regulation can have any application to unborn children.[17]

BIIR binds all Member States of the European Union except Denmark[18] and, for recognition and enforcement purposes, applies as between Member States and not *within* a Member State. Accordingly, BIIR does not govern the recognition and enforcement of orders within the UK.[19]

3. THE JURISDICTIONAL RULES

(a) Jurisdiction based on the child's habitual residence

The basic rule of jurisdiction under BIIR is provided by Art 8(1), namely:

> The courts of a Member State shall have jurisdiction in matters of parental responsibility over a child who is habitually resident in that Member State at the time the court is seised.

'Habitual residence' is not defined by BIIR but the ECJ/CJEU has ruled[20] that it:

> must be interpreted as meaning that it corresponds to the place which reflects some degree of integration by the child in a social and family environment. To that end, in particular the duration, regularity, conditions and reasons for the stay on the territory of a Member State and the family's move to that State, the child's nationality, the place and conditions of attendance at school, linguistic knowledge and the family and social relationships of

---

[13] See *Re C* (Case C-435/06) [2008] 1 FLR 490, ECJ. See also, to the same effect, *Re A (Area of Freedom, Security and Justice)* (C-523/07) [2009] 2 FLR 1, ECJ. For an application of this by an English court, see *Re T (A Child: Art 15, BIIR)* [2013] EWHC 521 (Fam) [2013] 2 FLR 909.

[14] See *Bridgend County Council v GM and Another* [2012] EWHC 3118 (Fam) [2013] 1 FLR 987 at [24] per Moor J.

[15] *A v B (Jurisdiction)* [2011] EWHC 2752 (Fam) [2012] 1 FLR 768. Query whether, on the basis of these decisions, education supervision orders made under s 36 of the Children Act 1989 are governed by BIIR?

[16] 'Parental Responsibility in the European Union—Practice Guide for the Application of the new Brussels II Regulation' para 2.1.

[17] Compare *B v H (Habitual Residence: Wardship)* [2002] 1 FLR 388, in which it was tentatively suggested that it might be possible for a father who does not have parental responsibility to issue proceedings to give him rights of custody in respect of his unborn child. Although, as a matter of English law (see eg *C v S* [1988] QB 135, discussed in Ch 11, In respect of whom is there responsibility? p 390) such a suggestion seems untenable, it might have been better had BIIR specifically dealt with the matter.   [18] See Art 2(3)

[19] These issues are governed by the Family Law Act 1986.

[20] *Re A (Area of Freedom, Security and Justice)* (Case C-523/07) [2009] 2 FLR 1 and *Mercredi v Chaffe* (Case C-497/10 PPU) [2012] Fam 27, CJEU (on which, note the comments of Baroness Hale and Lord Hughes in *A v A (Children: Habitual Residence) (Reunite International Child Abduction Centre intervening)* [2013] UKSC 60 [2014] AC 1 at [54] and [80], respectively, discussed further at Habitual residence, p 1040).

the child in that State must be taken into consideration. It is for the national court to establish the habitual residence of the child, taking account of all the circumstances specific to each individual case.

We discuss the meaning of habitual residence more fully in the context of child abduction.[21]

(b) Exceptions to the basic rule—the position where the child lawfully relocates—special provisions for dealing with cross-border access

Notwithstanding the basic rule under Art 8, in the case of a child's *lawful* movement to another Member State, Art 9 provides that even where a new habitual residence is acquired (but, note, until it is acquired, Art 8 continues to apply), the court that made an *access* order retains jurisdiction to modify it for *three months* following the removal (unless the holder of the access rights accepts jurisdiction of the new court by participating in proceedings there) provided the holder of access rights by the judgment continues to be habitually resident in the State of Origin.

This is a useful provision to review the access rights, or other contact arrangements, to adapt them to the new circumstances. But it is a limited provision. It only comes into play upon the acquisition of the new habitual residence. Furthermore, as the BIIR Practice Guide points out,[22] there must be a pre-existing court decision;[23] the provision only applies to lawful moves; it only applies for the three-month period dating from the child's physical move; the holder of access rights must still be habitually resident in the State of Origin and must not have accepted the new jurisdiction; and it does not prevent the new court from dealing with other issues. It should also be noted that the State of Origin only has jurisdiction to 'modify' the order which presumably does not include the power to end contact. The time period is particularly short and if Art 9 is to be interpreted strictly in the sense that even if seised of the case jurisdiction to modify ends immediately three months have elapsed from the child's move (as the BIIR Practice Guide suggests it must be), then national courts will need a fast track procedure to deal with such applications.

(c) Exceptions to the basic rule—the position where the child is wrongfully removed to or retained in another jurisdiction

In the case of *wrongful* removals or retentions, Art 10 provides that the courts of the child's former habitual residence retain jurisdiction until the child acquires a new habitual residence in another Member State *and* either:

(a) *each* person, institution or other body having rights of custody has acquiesced in the removal or retention; or

(b) the child has resided in the second Member State for at least one year after the holders of rights of custody have or should have had knowledge of the child's whereabouts[24] *and* the child is settled in his or her new environment *and* either no request

---

[21] See Habitual residence, pp 1040ff.

[22] At II 2(a). For some discussion of the application of Art 9, see *B v B (Brussels II Revised: Jurisdiction)* [2010] EWHC 1989 (Fam) [2011] 1 FLR 54.

[23] Note there is no modifying power over access *agreements*. Art 46 is confined to recognition and enforcement.

[24] For an example of where an Art 10 argument was unsuccessful because on the facts it was found that the father did not know of his child's whereabouts, see *M v M (Abduction: Settlement)* [2008] EWHC 2049 (Fam) [2008] 2 FLR 1884, at [48].

for a return has been lodged (or has been withdrawn) in that period, or the case has been closed pursuant to Art 11(7)[25] or a custody judgment not entailing the child's return has been made in the State of the former habitual residence.

'Wrongful removal or retention' is defined by Art 2(11) to mean:

> a child's removal or retention where: (*a*) it is in breach of custody acquired by judgment or by operation of law or by an agreement having legal effect under the law of the Member State where the child was habitually resident immediately before the removal or retention; and (*b*) provided that, at the time of removal or retention, the rights of custody were actually exercised, either jointly or alone, or would have been so exercised but for the removal or retention. Custody shall be considered to be exercised jointly when, pursuant to a decision or by operation of law, one holder of parental responsibility cannot decide on the child's place of residence without the consent of another holder of parental responsibility.

In *Re SH v MM and RM (Prohibited Steps Order: Abduction)*[26] it was held that a removal of a child by an unmarried mother contrary to a prohibited steps order was a 'wrongful removal' under BIIR.

Article 10 is aimed at preventing jurisdiction being changed by abduction. Terms such as 'acquiescence' and 'settled in his or her new environment' are not defined. Although national courts will have regard to the jurisprudence developed respectively under Arts 13(a) and 12(2) of the 1980 Hague Abduction Convention,[27] under BIIR, the ultimate arbiter of their meaning is the ECJ/CJEU.

In *Povse v Alpago*[28] the ECJ held that given the general policy of deterring child abduction such that the unlawful removal of a child should not in principle have the effect of transferring jurisdiction even if following the abduction the child has acquired an habitual residence in the Member State to which he or she has been taken, Art 10(b)(iv) in particular should be strictly interpreted. It was therefore held that Art 10(b)(iv) only applies if 'a judgment on custody that does not entail the return of the child' is a final one. It does not apply to an interim order.[29] In *Re A, HA v MB (Brussels II Revised: Article 11(7) Application)*,[30] Singer J held that where jurisdiction is retained until, in the terms of Art 10(b)(iv) 'a judgment on custody that does not entail the return of the child has been issued', the court keeps that jurisdiction until the formal issuance of the document containing the terms of the court order. Consequently, the court can make a contact order notwithstanding that in the final analysis it will have made a judgment not entailing the return of the child.[31]

(d) Prorogation of jurisdiction

Under Art 12(1) courts having jurisdiction to deal with divorce, legal separation or annulment will also have jurisdiction 'in any matter relating to parental responsibility

---

[25] Discussed at The position following a refusal to return—Art 11(6)–(8), p 1077.

[26] [2011] EWHC 3314 (Fam) [2012] 1 FLR 837.

[27] From which Convention they are ultimately borrowed, though the Article itself is modelled on Art 7 of the 1996 Hague Protection Convention.

[28] (Case C-211/10 PPU) [2011] Fam 199. Note: the mother and child's claims that the enforcement of the order as per the CJEU's ruling violated their Art 8 rights, were dismissed by the ECtHR: *Povse v Austria* [2014] 1 FLR 944, discussed further at Compatibility with the European Convention on Human Rights, p 1036.

[29] For an example of the application of this ruling by an English court, see *Re AJ (Brussels II Revised)* [2011] EWHC 3450 (Fam) [2012] 2 FLR 689 and *Re AJ (Contact: Brussels II Revised)* [2012] EWHC 931 (Fam) [2012] 2 FLR 1065.   [30] [2007] EWHC 2016 (Fam) [2008] 1 FLR 289.

[31] Singer J rejected the argument that a contact order constituted a judgment which requires the return of the child, discussed further at The English decisions, p 1079.

connected with that application' where at least one of the spouses has parental responsibility in relation to that child *and* jurisdiction has been accepted 'expressly or otherwise in an unequivocal manner' by the spouses and by other holders of parental responsibility at the time the court is seised *and* 'is in the superior interests of the child'.

Jurisdiction under Art 12(1) is dependent upon both the spouses *and* any other holder of parental responsibility's consent *and* a finding that it is in the child's 'superior' interests. These conditions are strict. There has to be unequivocal consent from both parents to the exercise of jurisdiction specifically in relation to matters of parental responsibility. Furthermore election for the court seised with divorce proceedings to hear the child case has to be consistent with the best interests of the child.[32] The use of the word 'superior' here is a mistake and no difference is intended between this term and the reference to the 'best' interests of the child elsewhere in BIIR.[33] Indeed other language versions use the same expression throughout. Article 12(1) applies to all children involved in matrimonial proceedings and not just those of both spouses.

By Art 12(2) jurisdiction conferred under Art 12(1) ceases when (a) the judgment allowing or refusing the application for divorce etc. becomes final; (b) in those cases where proceedings in relation to parental responsibility are still pending on that date referred to in (a), a judgment in those proceedings has become final; and (c) the proceedings referred to in (a) and (b) have come to an end for some other reason.[34]

Article 12(3) further provides that courts of a Member State shall have jurisdiction if the child has a substantial connection with that State (viz. because of one of the parents' habitual residence or the child's nationality in that State) *and* jurisdiction has been accepted 'expressly or otherwise in an unequivocal manner by all parties to the proceedings at the time the court is seised and is in the best interests of the child'. To trigger the prorogation powers it is essential that *all* the relevant parties, that is, those who are parties to the proceedings at the time when the court is seised, accept the jurisdiction of the other State in matters of parental responsibility. Jurisdiction is also subject to it being in the child's best interests.[35]

Jurisdiction acquired by one State by virtue of Art 12 cannot be terminated by a court decision in another State. Further while the test of the child's superior/best interests applies to the acquisition of jurisdiction under Art 12 it does not do so when considering whether to retain jurisdiction though it will be relevant to a subsequent Art 15 application (discussed shortly).[36]

Article 12(4) adds that where the child's habitual residence is in a third State (that is not a Contracting Party to the 1996 Hague Convention on the Protection of Children) then jurisdiction under Art 12 'shall be deemed to be in the child's interest, in particular if it is found impossible to hold proceedings in the third State in question'. As the BIIR Practice Guide points out,[37] this provision provides a prorogation option for a party to choose to seise a court of a Member State in which the child is not habitually resident but with which

---

[32] See *Bush v Bush* [2008] EWCA Civ 865 [2008] 2 FLR 1437. For a discussion of the best interests test in this context, see *Re I (A Child) (Contact Application: Jurisdiction) (Centre for Family Law and Practice Intervening)* [2009] UKSC 10 [2010] 1 AC 319 per Baroness Hale at [36]–[40], who makes it clear that for the purposes of Art 12 'welfare' requires consideration of *forum conveniens* and not an in-depth investigation of the child's circumstances.   [33] See eg *Re I (A Child)* at [50], per Lord Collins.

[34] Art 12(2) has been held to be of general application and equally applies to jurisdiction taken on the basis of Art 12(3) or Art 15, see *Re S (Brussels IIR: Prorogation)* [2013] EWHC 647 (Fam) [2013] 2 FLR 1584, per Cobb J.

[35] *See eg B v B (Brussels II Revised: Jurisdiction)* [2011] EWHC 1989 (Fam) [2010] 1 FLR 54—not in child's interests for English court to take jurisdiction.

[36] *Re S-R (Jurisdiction: Contact)* [2008] 2 FLR 1741.   [37] At Chapter XI.

the child has a substantial connection. In *Re I (A Child) (Contact Application: Jurisdiction)*[38] the Supreme Court held that Art 12(4) applies even where the child is not habitually *resident* in any Member State other than in a Contracting State to the 1996 Convention (to which that Convention will apply). In that case the child concerned was in Pakistan, the father having been given leave to take the child there to live with his mother and sister on an undertaking that he would return to the child if asked to do so. Interim contact was granted in favour of the mother who lived in England. In a subsequent action brought by the mother to enforce and vary the contact, it was held that, given the father's acceptance of jurisdiction and the child's clear connection with England and Wales, there was jurisdiction to hear the case on the basis of Art 12(3) and (4).

(e) Position where habitual cannot be established and for refugee and internationally displaced children

Article 13(1) of BIIR provides that if a child's habitual residence cannot be established[39] *and* jurisdiction cannot be determined upon the basis of Art 12 then the child's presence will be sufficient to found jurisdiction.[40] A similar rule applies, by reason of Art 13(2) to refugee children and to those internationally displaced because of disturbances occurring in their country. The phrase 'internationally displaced children' will help to offset any restricted meaning that may otherwise be placed on the term 'refugee'.

(f) Position where no Member State has jurisdiction pursuant to Arts 8–13

Where no court of a Member State has jurisdiction pursuant to Arts 8–13,[41] then, by Art 14, jurisdiction is determined in each Member State by the laws of that State. This provision was relied upon by the Supreme Court in *A v A (Children: Habitual Residence) (Reunite International Child Abduction Centre intervening)*,[42] in which it was held in relation to a young child born in Pakistan and who had never been outside that country that notwithstanding the extreme circumstances (in that the mother was involuntarily in Pakistan when she gave birth) that it would be hard to say that the child was habitually resident in England and Wales or in any other Member State and that therefore Art 14 permitted the English court to apply its domestic law which in this case meant that because the child had British nationality there was jurisdiction to make the child a ward of court.[43]

(g) Transferring jurisdiction

Article 15(1) permits a transfer of a case in whole or in part from the court having jurisdiction according to the preceding Articles, either upon request by a party or on the court's own motion or upon an application from a court of another Member State with which the child has particular connection, to a court of another Member State with which the child

---

[38] [2009] UKSC 10 [2010] 1 AC 319. See also *AP v TD (Relocation: Retention of Jurisdiction)* [2010] EWHC 2040 (Fam) [2011] 1 FLR 1851—a case involving Canada.

[39] Though note: it is generally accepted that the courts should be slow to find that a child has no habitual residence but. for a recent example of where jurisdiction was taken on this basis, see *Re T (A Child: Art 15, BIIR)* [2013] EWHC 521 (Fam) [2013] 2 FLR 909, not overturned on this point on appeal, see [2013] EWCA Civ 895 [2014] 1 FLR 749.

[40] For examples, see *Re T* and *Bridgend County Council v GM and another* [2012] EWHC 3118 (Fam) [2013] 1 FLR 987.

[41] This provision will be strictly interpreted, cf *Sundelind Lopez v Lopez Lizazo* (Case C-68/07) [2008] Fam 21, CJEU, applying Art 7(1) in relation to divorce, ruling that because France had jurisdiction, the Swedish court could not apply their own rules of jurisdiction.

[42] [2013] UKSC 60 [2014] AC 1.   [43] Discussed in Ch 20.

has a particular connection and which would be better placed to hear the case or specified part thereof and that it is in the best interests of the child. For these purposes, Art 15(3) provides that a child shall be considered to have particular connection with a Member State if that State:

(a) has become the habitual residence of the child after the court referred to in paragraph 1 was seised, or
(b) is the former habitual residence or the child, or
(c) is the place of the child's nationality, or
(d) is the habitual residence of a holder of parental responsibility, or
(e) is the place where property of the child is located and the case concerns measures for the protection of the child relating to the administration, conversation or disposal of this property.

Article 15 only governs transfers of jurisdiction between Member States. It therefore has no application to transferring jurisdiction within a Member State and in particular to transfers within the UK and the Isle of Man.[44]

Only the court having jurisdiction as to the substance of the matter can make the substantive decision under Art 15(1).[45] To guard against delay, the court making the transfer must set a time limit within which the second court should become seised. In any event, the second court must accept jurisdiction within six weeks of their seizure. Only one transfer is permitted under this scheme, though there is nothing to prevent fresh applications being made to ask the court with jurisdiction to reconsider a refusal to transfer. As the BIIR Practice Guide says, proceedings cannot be transferred to a third court (see Recital 13).

As Munby J observed in *AB v JLB (Brussels II Revised: Article 15)*,[46] the application of Art 15 requires three cardinal questions to be considered, namely the determination of (i) whether the child has a 'particular connection' with a relevant Member State, (ii) whether the court of that other Member State 'would be better placed to hear the case, or a specific part thereof', and (iii) whether a transfer to that other court 'is in the child's best interests'. In an attempt to distil the applicable principles when considering a transfer application under Art 15, in *Re T (A Child: Art 15, BIIR)*,[47] Mostyn J sought to pull the threads together not just of *AB v JLB* but of other case-law, including *M v M (Stay of Proceedings: Return of Children)*.[48] On appeal,[49] however, Mostyn J was held to have erred insofar as he relied upon *M v M* since that determined the domestic law approach in cases brought under the domestic jurisdiction, whereas the construction of Art 15 has to be uniform throughout the courts of the Member States. However, the Court of Appeal did not disapprove of all of Mostyn J's distilled principles but only those derived from *M v M*. Using this analysis but taking into account the Court of Appeal decision, the following principles can be said to be applicable, namely:

(1) Article 15 applies to public law as well as private law proceedings.

---

[44] *Re PC, YC and KM (Brussels IIR: Jurisdiction Within the UK)* [2013] EWHC 2336 (Fam) [2014] 1 FLR 605.
[45] See *AB v JLB (Brussels II Revised: Article 15)* [2008] EWHC 2965 (Fam) [2009] 1 FLR 517, per Munby J. For another example of the exercise of this power, see *J v J (Relinquishment Of Jurisdiction)* [2011] EWHC 3255 (Fam), [2012] 1 FLR 1259.   [46] [2008] EWHC 2965 (Fam) [2009] 1 FLR 517.
[47] [2013] EWHC 521 (Fam) [2013] 2 FLR 909 at [24].
[48] [2005] EWHC 1159 (Fam) [2006] 1 FLR 138.
[49] *Re T (Brussels II Revised: Art 15)* [2013] EWCA Civ 895 [2014] 1 FLR 749.

(2) As a precondition the court must be satisfied within the meaning of Article 15(3) that the child has 'a particular connection' with the other relevant Member State.

(3) The applicant must satisfy the court that the other court would be better placed to hear the case (or a specific part thereof). In making this evaluation the applicant must show that the other court is clearly the more appropriate forum.

(4) In assessing the appropriateness of each forum, the court must discern the forum with which the case has the more real and substantial connection in terms of convenience, expense and availability of witnesses.

(5) In the exercise conducted at (3) and (4) the court must consider the child's best interests. BUT

(6) In making the best interests analysis at (5) the court will not embark on a profound investigation of the child's situation and upbringing but will dwell in an attenuated inquiry upon the sort of considerations which will come into play when deciding upon the most appropriate forum.

Note might also be taken of *Re L-M (Transfer of Irish Proceedings)*,[50] in which Cobb J, having held that a transfer request must be considered judicially rather than administratively, commented that the 'the "best interests" evaluation will necessarily not be as profound as on a full hearing of an application for substantive relief with the benefit of the full evidence'.

(g) The position in cases of urgency

As Art 20(1) makes clear, in urgent cases none of the foregoing rules prevents courts of a Member State 'from taking such provisional, including protective measures in respect of persons or assets in that State as may be available under the law of that Member State, even if the court of another Member State has jurisdiction under BIIR over the substance of the matter. It has been observed[51] that Art 20 does not confer jurisdiction but simply permits the exercise of already existing powers in urgent cases. Any measures taken are temporary only and by Art 20(2) cease to have effect when the competent court has taken the measures appropriately'. Interim measures taken under Art 20 are not enforceable extra-territorially.[52]

Article 20 neither states the basis upon which provisional measures may be taken (though the assumption is that the power should only be exercised where the child is physically present or that his or her property is situated in the jurisdiction), nor defines 'urgency'. In *Re A (Area of Freedom, Security and Justice)*[53] the ECJ emphasised that the powers under Art 20 are conditional on (a) the measure being urgent, (b) that it is taken in respect of persons in the Member State concerned and (c) it must be provisional.[54] It was further held that although there is no requirement upon the national court having taken the protective measure to transfer the case to the court of another Member State having jurisdiction, it should, insofar as the protection of the child's best interests require,

---

[50] [2013] EWHC 646 (Fam) [2013] 2 FLR 708 and approved by Munby P in *Re HJ (Transfer of Proceedings)* [2013] EWHC 1867 (Fam) [2014] 1 FLR 430. For an example of a refusal of a transfer request, see *Walsall Metropolitan Borough Council v K* [2013] EWHC 3192 (Fam) [2014] 2 FLR 227.

[51] *Parrrucker v Vallés Pérez* (Case C-256/09) [2011] Fam 254, CJEU.   [52] Ibid.

[53] (Case C-523/07) [2009] 2 FLR 1.

[54] Ie there is no jurisdiction to make a final as opposed to an interim care order—a point adverted to in *Re S (Care: Jurisdiction)* [2008] EWHC 3013 (Fam) [2009] 2 FLR 550.

inform, directly or through its central authority, the court having jurisdiction that it has taken such protective measures.

Article 20 empowers courts to take wide ranging measures, including making an interim order placing a child in a residential unit[55] or an interim care order,[56] but not to grant custody to one parent where a court of another Member State which has jurisdiction over the substance of the dispute has already provisionally granted custody of the child to the other parent and that judgment has been declared enforceable in the State purporting to act under Art 20.[57]

(h) The position where a court is second seised etc, the application of Art 19

Where proceedings relating to parental responsibility are brought in different Member States involving the same child and the same cause of action[58] then, by Art 19(2) and (3), it is the court first (properly) seised that has priority. The court second seised is required of its own motion to stay any proceedings until the first court decides whether it has jurisdiction.[59] There is no power to impose a stay and then lift it for a period to make provisional arrangements for the case to be heard in London should the foreign court decline jurisdiction.[60] If the court first seised decides it has jurisdiction then the second court must dismiss the application.

By Art 17 where a court of a Member State is seised of a case over which it has no jurisdiction and over which a court of another Member State does have jurisdiction under BIIR, then it must declare of its motion that it has no jurisdiction. However, as the ECJ ruled in *Re A (Area of Freedom, Security and Justice)*,[61] while Art 17 does not impose a consequential requirement to transfer the case to another court, the national court, should, insofar as the protection of the best interests of the child so require, directly or through its central authority inform the court of the Member State having jurisdiction.

'Seised' is defined in Art 16 as lodging the document that institutes the proceedings 'provided the applicant has not subsequently failed to take the steps he was required to take to have service effected on the respondent'. In *Mercredi v Chaffe*,[62] the CJEU held that to be 'seised' the document instituting the proceedings must be lodged with the court. Telephone applications are not sufficient. It has also been held that Art 19(2) does not apply where the national court is seised only for the purpose of the granting of provisional matters within Art 20.[63]

---

[55] See *Health Service Executive v SC and AC* (Case C-29/12 PPU) [2012] 2 FLR 1040, CJEU and *HSE Ireland v SF* [2012] EWHC 1640 (Fam) [2012] 2 FLR 1131.

[56] As in *Re A (Area of Freedom, Security and Justice)* (Case C-523/07) [2009] 2 FLR 1.

[57] *Detiček v Sgueglia* (Case C-403/09 PPU) [2010] 1 FLR 1381, ECJ, on which see L Walker 'The Relationship between BIIR and the Hague Convention: *Detiček v Sgueglia*' [2010] IFL 203.

[58] The phrase 'same cause of action' must be given an 'independent European meaning' see the ECJ decision in *Gubisch Maschinenfabrik v Palumbo* (Case 144/86) [1987] ECR 4861.

[59] If a foreign court rules that it is second seised then notwithstanding any appeal in that State, the courts of *both* countries should operate on the basis of that ruling: *L-K v K (Brussels II Revised: Maintenance Pending Suit)* [2006] EWHC 153 (Fam) [2006] 2 FLR 1113. Cf *Re EC (Child Abduction) (Stayed Proceedings)* [2006] EWCA Civ 1115 [2007] 1 FLR 57.

[60] Applications for a stay are governed by FPR 2010 r 12.68.

[61] (Case C-523/07) [2009] 2 FLR 1.

[62] (Case C 497/10 PPU) [2012] Fam 27, on which see D Williams 'Wednesday's Child is Full of Woe—*Mercredi v Chaffe*: To the CJEU and Back Again' [2011] IFL 196.

[63] *Parrucker Vallés Pérez (No 2)* (Case C-296/10) [2012] 1 FLR 925, CJEU.

4. RECOGNITION AND ENFORCEMENT

(a) Recognition

Orders and agreements (if they are enforceable in the Member State of Origin)[64] relating to parental responsibility made under BIIR are automatically recognised by all other BIIR States without the need to invoke any special procedure.[65] A foreign custody order is still recognisable even if subsequent proceedings have been taken under the 1980 Hague Abduction Convention.[66] Nevertheless any interested party[67] can apply for a judgment or agreement to be or not to be recognised.[68]

Limited grounds for non-recognition are provided for by Art 23,[69] namely:

that the judgment is manifestly contrary to the public policy of the Member State in which recognition is sought;[70]

taking into account the best interests of the child, it was given (except in the case of urgency) without the child being given an opportunity to be heard, in violation of the fundamental principles of procedure in that Member State;[71]

it is irreconcilable with a later judgment given in that state or another Member State or the state of the child's habitual residence;

it was given in default of appearance and the person in default was not served;

or without giving an opportunity for a holder of parental responsibility to be heard.

These are the *only* grounds for refusing recognition. Moreover, Arts 26 and 24 respectively forbid the courts to review either the jurisdiction of the court of origin or a judgment as to its substance.

Potentially the widest of these exceptions is the first but following *Re S (Brussels II: Recognition: Best Interests of the Child) (No 1)*[72] it is evident that it is hard to establish. In *Re S* it was argued that the exception should have prevented recognition of a Belgian access order because (a) the father had untruthfully represented to the Antwerp first instance court that the mother had brought the child concerned to England without his consent and (b) were the order to be enforced there would be the danger that the father would unlawfully keep the child in Belgium. The argument was rejected, for as Holman J said:

---

[64] See Art 46.   [65] Art 21(1).

[66] See *Re T and J (Abduction: Recognition of Foreign Judgment)* [2006] EWHC 1472 (Fam) [2006] 2 FLR 1290.

[67] According to the Borras Report (the Explanatory Report on what was then the Brussels II Convention) [1988] OJ C221/27, paras 65 and 80 the concept of an 'interested party' should be broadly interpreted so it may include not only the parents and children but also 'the public prosecutor or other similar bodies' where permitted in the State addressed.

[68] Art 21(3). Recognition proceedings may be stayed if the judgment is under appeal: Art 27.

[69] These grounds replicate those provided for by Art 15(2) of the original Regulation. According to Recital 21 'the grounds for non-recognition should be kept to the minimum required'.

[70] Under the analogous provision in the Brussels I Regulation (viz. Council Regulation (EC) No 44/2001 on Jurisdiction and the Recognition of Judgments in Civil and Commercial Matters) the public policy defence has been narrowly construed by the ECJ, according to which even fraud is insufficient: *Societé d'Information Service Realisation v Ampersand Software BV, The Times*, 29 July 1993, CA.

[71] As the Borras Report, at para 73, points out, while this exception is confined to the relevant rules of the Member State in question, nevertheless those rules must take account of Art 12 of the UN Convention on the Rights of the Child (see Ch 13, UN Convention on the Rights of the Child, p 448).

[72] [2003] EWHC 2115 (Fam) [2004] 1 FLR 571—a decision on the identically worded Art 15(a) of the original Brussels II Regulation.

To say something is contrary to public policy is a high hurdle, to which the Article adds the word 'manifestly'.

Neither of the arguments were thought to come close to crossing the hurdle.

In short, as Munby LJ put it in *Re L (A Child) (Recognition of Foreign Order)*,[73] 'the test is stringent' and the bar is set high. It has been held[74] that the passage of time without more is not sufficient to avoid recognition. In fact, as Thorpe LJ observed in *Re L*,[75] there is no reported example of a refusal to recognise an apparently valid judgment on the grounds of public policy.

(b) Enforcement

There are two routes to enforcement under BIIR,[76] the ordinary route and the 'fast track' for enforcing access orders for the return of a child under Art 11(8). Under the ordinary procedure it is necessary to obtain a declaration of enforceability before enforcement. In contrast under the 'fast track' procedure the order can be enforced directly, provided that the appropriate certificate has been issued by the court of origin.

The ordinary procedure

According to Art 28(1), in general an enforceable judgment on the exercise of parental responsibility made in one Member State can be declared enforceable in another Member State upon the application of any interested party. However, under Art 28(2) judgments only become enforceable within the UK when, upon application of any interested party, they have been registered for enforcement.[77] The national law of the enforcing State governs both the procedure for applying to enforce[78] (though applicants who are holders of parental responsibility are entitled to information and assistance from the central authority)[79] and the enforcement procedure itself.[80] Nevertheless as the BIIR Practice Guide says,[81] 'it is of the essence that national authorities apply rules which secure efficient and speedy enforcement of decisions issued under the Regulation so as not to undermine its objectives'. In any event, Art 31(1) states that the court applied to 'shall give its decision without delay'.

Although in no event at any stage of the enforcement process can a judgment be reviewed as to its substance,[82] Art 31(2) permits a refusal to enforce upon the same limited grounds upon which a refusal to recognise a judgment can be based.[83] Indeed according to *Re S (Brussels II: Recognition: Best Interests of Child) (No 2)*,[84] while there is an overriding duty to enforce an order previously 'recognised', what is now Art 31(2)

---

[73] [2012] EWCA Civ 1157 [2013] Fam 94.

[74] *LAB v KB (Abduction: Brussels II Revised)* [2009] 2243 (Fam) [2010] 2 FLR 1664. See also *Re N (Abduction: Brussels II Revised)* [2014] EWHC 749 (Fam) [2014] Fam Law 947.   [75] At [86].

[76] See N Lowe 'The Enforcement of Custody and Access decisions under the Revised Brussels II Regulation' [2011] IFL 121.   [77] Query the advantage of having this registration requirement?

[78] Art 30. For the procedure in England and Wales, see FPR 2010 Part 31 and *Practice Direction 31A*, for details of which, see Clarke Hall and Morrison on *Children* at 5 [159] ff.

[79] Art 55(b). Note: unlike the 1980 Hague Abduction and European Conventions applicants do not qualify for legal representation at public expense save to the extent that applicants who benefited from complete or partial legal aid are entitled 'to benefit from the most favourable legal aid . . . provided by the law of the Member State addressed': Art 50.   [80] Art 47(1).

[81] *Practice Guide for the application of the new Brussels II Regulation* (drawn up by the European Commission 2005) p 43.   [82] Art 31(3).

[83] See in particular Art 23, discussed at Recognition, p 1004.

[84] [2003] EWHC 2974 (Fam) [2004] 1 FLR 582 per Holman J.

nevertheless permits a refusal even in these circumstances. However, it has been said[85] that a refusal to enforce a previously recognised judgment should be regarded as 'wholly exceptional'. Enforcement was, however, refused in *Re S (Brussels II Revised: Enforcement of Contact Order)*,[86] in which it was found that the mother only consented to an order giving extensive contact between the father and the daughter so as afford the opportunity of fleeing the country with the daughter. Furthermore, given the mother's increasing hostility, the child's new circumstances required a completely fresh approach and assessment.

Under Art 36 provision is made for partial enforcement, with Art 36(1) permitting the court not to enforce the whole order and Art 36(2) permitting the applicant only to request a partial enforcement. In the latter case, as Holman J observed in *Re S*,[87] the court need not enforce an order save in those respects requested but in the former case the power is strictly limited, namely, to relieve a court from seeking to enforce that which is impossible, it being incumbent upon the court to enforce the rest. No provision is made to *vary* an order but according to *Re S* there is a power to 'phase in' an order.[88]

Re S also establishes that in determining an enforcement application the court is *not* bound to treat the child's welfare as its paramount consideration.[89] Any decision made on an enforcement application may be appealed.[90]

The fast-track procedure

Judgments concerning rights of access and orders made under Art 11(8)[91] are *directly* enforceable (that is, without the need for declaration of enforceability nor with the possibility of opposing recognition) in another Member State provided the appropriate certificate has been issued by the court of the Member State of Origin.[92] As the CJEU has emphasised,[93] the issue of a certificate in the Member State of Origin is to be recognised and automatically enforced in another Member State, there being no possibility of opposing its recognition.

'Rights of access' for enforcement purposes: 'include in particular the right to take a child to a place other than his or her habitual residence for a limited period'.[94] Although there is no authority on its meaning in this context, 'habitual residence' is best understood as referring to the child's home rather than the country of residence. Were it otherwise, English orders, namely a child arrangements orders naming a person with whom the child is to spend time or otherwise have contact, would normally fall outside these provisions as they do not confer a unilateral right to take the child abroad. It has been held[95] that it is not open to a party to choose to extract 'rights of access' from an agreement (or, presumably, an order) involving the exercise of parental responsibility so as to take advantage of the fast-track enforcement provisions.

---

[85] Per Roderick Wood J in *LAB v KB* [2009] EWHC 2243 (Fam) [2010] 2 FLR 1664 at [36].

[86] [2008] 2 FLR 1358.   [87] Ibid at [11].   [88] Ibid at [14].

[89] Ibid. Though in *Re D (Brussels II Revised: Contact)* [2007] EWHC 822 (Fam) [2008] 1 FLR 516, Black J was a liitle more circumspect. However, his position is clearly in line with that generally taken in enforcement decisions, see eg *Re LW (children) (contact order: committal)* [2010] EWCA Civ 1253 [2011] 1 FLR 1095, discussed in Ch 14, Determining whether to impose a penalty, p 539.   [90] Art 33.

[91] Viz. orders requiring the child's return made in proceedings in the requesting State following a refusal to return under the 1980 Hague Abduction Convention by the requested State—discussed at The position following a refusal to return—Art 11(6)–(8), p 1077.   [92] See respectively Arts 11(8) and 41(1).

[93] In *Aguirre Zarraga* (Case C-491/10 PPU) and *Health Service Executive v SC and AC* (Case C-92/12 PPU) [2012] 2 FLR 1040, on which see P McEleavy 'The movement of children in Europe: mutual trust, distrust and human rights' [2013] IFL 172.   [94] Art 2(10).

[95] *Re L (A Child) (Recognition of Foreign Order)* [2012] EWCA Civ 1157 [2013] Fam 94.

The judge of origin should only issue a certificate where all the parties including the child (unless it was considered inappropriate having regard to his or her age or degree of maturity) have been given the opportunity to be heard. In the case of a judgment given in default, the person defaulting must have been served with the document instituting proceedings in due time to arrange for his or her defence, or, if not, it is nevertheless established that he or she accepted the decision unequivocally. In access cases, where the rights of access involve a cross border situation at the time that the judgment is given, the certificate must be issued *ex officio* when the judgment becomes enforceable, even if only provisionally, or a certificate may be issued subsequently.[96] The certificate itself must be issued in the standard form provided for in Annex III to BIIR.[97]

In the case of an Art 11(8) order the certificate is issued by the judge of origin[98] of his or her own motion using the standard form in Annex IV to BIIR.

The party seeking enforcement must produce both a copy of the judgment and the certificate.[99] No appeal lies against the issuing of the certificate (though in cases of error it is possible to seek ratification before the judge of origin).[100] The actual enforcement procedure is a matter for the domestic law of each Member State.[101]

Although the court of enforcement cannot review an access judgment or agreement nor change its substance, it may, by Art 48, 'make practical arrangements for organising the exercise of rights of access, if the necessary arrangements have or have not sufficiently been made in the judgment delivered by the courts of the Member State having jurisdiction as to the substance of the matter *and provided the essential elements of this judgment are respected*' (emphasis added).

The extent of the modifying power is uncertain. Does it preclude, for example, altering the place and frequency of access?[102] As the BIIR Practice Guide points out, Art 48 is *not* a jurisdictional rule and does not confer jurisdiction as to the substance on the court of enforcement.

5. CENTRAL AUTHORITIES

Adopting the standard approach of the modern Hague and European Conventions dealing with children, Art 53 obliges each Member State to establish a central authority (with a discretion to establish separate authorities for each territorial court). However, although it is mandatory to establish such a body neither its location nor its structure is dictated by BIIR. So far as the England and Wales is concerned the International Child Abduction and Contact Unit (ICACU), acts as the central authority as it does for the 1980 Hague Abduction Convention and the 1980 European Custody Convention.[103]

So far as specific cases are concerned, holders of parental responsibility can submit requests for assistance either to their own central authority or to that of the child's habitual residence or presence.[104] 'Assistance' includes, pursuant to Art 55, the collection and exchange of information inter alia on the child's situation, facilitating communication between the courts, and facilitating agreements between the parties through mediation (the importance of which is stressed by the BIIR Practice Guide) or other means.

---

[96] Art 41(3).   [97] Art 41(2).   [98] Ie a judge in the court that made the original order.

[99] Art 45.   [100] Art 43.   [101] Art 47.

[102] The interpretation of Art 11(2) of the 1980 European Custody Convention is discussed at Applying for access, p 1087. If the approach of Thorpe LJ in *Re G (Foreign Contact Order: Enforcement)* [2004] 1 WLR 521 is followed, there would be a wide latitude to modify orders.

[103] Discussed at The 1980 European Custody Convention, p 1083. But note that for the purposes of BIIR, it is known as the 'Domestic Central Authority': FPR 2010 r 12.58(1)(a) as amended by SI 2012/2046.

[104] Art 57(1).

Central authorities must also 'provide information and assistance to holders of parental responsibility seeking recognition and enforcement of decisions on their territory, in particular concerning rights of access and the return of the child'. All these duties may be discharged either directly or through public authorities or other bodies. Importantly, central authorities must bear their own costs in discharging their duties and offer their services free of charge.[105]

C. INTERNATIONAL ASPECTS OF ADOPTION

1. INTRODUCTION

A developing area of adoption is so-called 'intercountry adoption'.[106] That is a general term referring to the adoption of a child from one country, commonly a developing nation, by adopters living in another country, commonly a developed nation. Intercountry adoption raises a number of fundamental issues such as the obvious dangers of exploiting vulnerable birth parents, the possible undesirability of transracial adoptions and the difficulty of international control.[107] Against these are the need of the adopters themselves, who are often desperate to have children but who are too old to be considered by adoption agencies, at any rate to adopt babies and, not least, the desperate plight of some of the children involved. It is by no means easy to balance these considerations, though practicality suggests that attempting to control intercountry adoption is probably better than attempting to outlaw it and, as we are about to discuss, a bold attempt at global control is provided for by the 1993 Hague Convention on Intercountry Adoption to which the UK is a Contracting State.

Although compared with a number of other jurisdictions there are still relatively few intercountry adoptions in England and Wales,[108] the issue came into prominence in the 1990s in the wake particularly of the sad plight of Romanian and later Bosnian orphans which in turn led to more general media coverage and public interest in the horrifying conditions suffered by children in South American countries. In point of fact, however, many of the British intercountry adoptions are of children from China or from countries of the former Soviet Union.

As we discuss shortly, after an earlier less successful attempt, through the 1965 Hague Convention on Jurisdiction, Applicable Law and Recognition of Decrees relating to Adoptions, to provide a uniform law and jurisdiction,[109] a more comprehensive attempt to provide international regulation of intercountry adoption was successfully introduced by the 1993 Hague Convention on Protection of Children and Co-operation in Respect of Intercountry Adoption (hereafter 'the 1993 Hague Convention on Intercountry Adoption').

---

[105] Art 57(4) and (3).

[106] See generally D Hodson *International Family Law Practice 2013-2014* (2013, 3rd edn) ch 16; 'International Adoption' by H Blackburn in C Bridge and H Swindells *Adoption: The Modern Law* (2003), chs 14 and 15 and N Angel 'Inter country adoption and the court process in England and Wales' [2012] IFL 422.

[107] See P Hayes 'The Legality and Ethics of Independent Intercountry Adoption under the Hague Convention' (2011) IJLPF 288.

[108] According to statistics prepared by Professor Selman for the Permanent Bureau of the Hague Conference (2014) there were 369 cases in 2005, declining to just 200 in 2009 in which England was the receiving State for intercountry adoptions and 4 in 2009 in which England was the State of Origin.

[109] That Convention was only ratified by Austria, Switzerland and the UK, all of which denounced it upon ratifying the 2003 Convention.

Following the UK's ratification of the 1993 Convention, there may be said to be three basic 'types' of intercountry adoptions namely (1) Convention adoptions, (2) overseas adoptions falling outside the Convention and (3) children whose carers or prospective carers wish to bring the child to the UK for adoption here. Each of these issues will be discussed in turn.

2. THE 1993 HAGUE CONVENTION ON INTERCOUNTRY ADOPTION

The UK ratified the 1993 Hague Convention on Intercountry Adoption[110] in June 2003 through the Adoption (Intercountry Aspects) Act 1999 and consequential Regulations. Schedule 1 to the 1999 Act contains the text of the 1993 Convention as implemented by the UK. However, most of the legislation governing intercountry adoption, as it operates in England and Wales, is contained in the Adoption and Children Act 2002 and the Adoptions with a Foreign Element Regulations 2005 (SI 2005/392).

Local authorities have responsibility for providing services in relation to the Convention as part of the Adoption Service. In practice much of the work is delegated to a small number of adoption societies approved by the Secretary of State to provide Convention adoption services.

The 1993 Convention has three basic objects:

(1) to establish safeguards to ensure that intercountry adoptions only take place after the best interests of the child have been properly assessed and in circumstances which protect his or her fundamental rights;

(2) to establish a system of co-operation amongst Contracting States to ensure that these safeguards are respected; and

(3) to secure the recognition in Contracting States of adoptions made in accordance with the Convention.[111]

To achieve these broad objectives the Convention makes a distinction between 'States of Origin' from which children are sent for adoption and 'Receiving States' in which the adopted child will live. It is the responsibility of a State of Origin, via its 'competent authorities' (discussed shortly) to establish that the child is adoptable and that intercountry adoption as opposed to placement within the country of origin is in the child's best interests.[112] States of Origin are also obliged to have ensured that the requisite consents to the child's adoption (it will be noted that the Convention makes no attempt to prescribe what the internal laws on consent should be) have, after due counselling, been freely given with a full understanding of what is involved and without financial inducement.[113] Such States are similarly expected to ensure that, 'having regard to the age and maturity of the child', such a child has been counselled and duly informed about the effects of adoption and, where required, freely consented to the adoption without financial inducement.[114]

---

[110] See generally The Explanatory Report on the 1993 Convention by G Parra-Aranguren (1994) and by the same author 'An Overview of the 1993 Hague Inter-Country Adoption Convention' in N Lowe and G Douglas (eds) *Families Across Frontiers* (1996) at 565; W Duncan 'Conflict and Co-operation: The Approach to Conflicts of Law in the 1993 Hague Convention on Intercountry Adoption' in *Families Across Frontiers* at 577, and D Watkins 'Intercountry adoption and the Hague Convention: Article 22 and limitations upon safeguarding' [2012] CFLQ 389.
[111] See Art 1 and see the explanation in the Government White Paper *Adoption: The Future* Cm 2288 (1994) para 6.19ff.
[112] Art 4(a) and (b).   [113] Art 4(c).   [114] Art 4(d).

In contrast, the responsibility of Receiving States is to determine that the prospective adoptive parents are eligible and suited to adopt and to ensure that they have been counselled as may be necessary and, importantly, to have determined that the child is or will be authorised to enter and reside permanently in that State.[115]

The administrative mechanism through which the Convention operates is primarily through the tried and tested system of central authorities. Each Contracting State is obliged to set up a central authority.[116] Under the Adoption (Intercountry Aspects) Act 1999 s 2(1) the UK set up separate central authorities for England, Scotland and Wales. This was the first time that Wales had a separate central authority to operate an international convention. In each of the former jurisdictions the central authorities are to be discharged by the Secretary of State and in Wales by the National Assembly for Wales. There is also a separate central authority for Northern Ireland. Central authorities are generally charged to co-operate with one another,[117] to take all appropriate measures to prevent improper financial or other gain in connection with an adoption and to deter all parties from acting contrary to the rights of the Convention.[118] Under Art 9 central authorities are under a duty to collate, preserve and exchange information about the situation of the child and the prospective adopters, to facilitate and expedite proceedings, to promote development of adoption counselling and post-adoption services, and to respond to requests from other central authorities for information about a particular adoption situation.

These Art 9 duties may be discharged either by the central authority itself or by, or with, 'accredited bodies'. Accredited bodies should be authorised bodies capable of preparing and arranging adoptions.[119] In the UK a registered adoption society is an accredited body.[120]

The procedure for facilitating a Convention adoption is as follows. Persons who are habitually resident in one Contracting State, who wish to apply to adopt a child habitually resident in another Contracting State, should apply to their own central authority.[121] If the central authority of the Receiving State is satisfied as to the applicants' eligibility and suitability to adopt, it should prepare and transmit the request to the central authority of the State of Origin.[122] There is a reciprocal duty on the State of Origin to prepare and transmit a report on the child that is considered adoptable and in that connection to ensure that the requisite consents have been given.[123]

Under Art 17 any decision in the State of Origin that a child should be entrusted to prospective adopters[124] may only be made if the central authorities of *both* States agree that the adoption may proceed, the central authority of the State of Origin having ensured that the prospective adopters agree and the central authority of the Receiving State has approved such a decision, having considered the prospective adopters suitable and having determined that the child is or will be authorised to enter and reside permanently in that State. The adoption order is then made in the Receiving State.

Chapter V of the Convention deals with the important issue of the recognition and effects of a Convention adoption. The basic provision is Art 23, which provides that an

---

[115] Art 5.   [116] Art 6.

[117] Art 7(1). Under Art 7(2) they must also provide information about the law, keep one another informed about the operation of the Convention and, as far as possible, eliminate any obstacles to its application.

[118] Art 8.   [119] Arts 10 and 11.   [120] Adoption (Intercountry Aspects) Act 1999 s 2(2A).

[121] Art 14.   [122] Art 15.   [123] Art 16.

[124] 'Entrusted to prospective adopters' has been held to equate to making of a parental responsibility order under s 84 of the 2002 Act (discussed at Removing a child from the British Islands for adoption, p 1015); *Haringey London Borough Council v MA, JN and IA* [2008] EWHC 722 (Fam) [2008] 2 FLR 1857.

adoption certified by the competent authority of the State of the adoption as having been made in accordance with the Convention shall be recognised by operation of law in the other Contracting States. Under Art 24 recognition may, however, be refused in a Contracting State if the adoption 'is manifestly contrary to its public policy, taking into account the best interests of the child'. So far as England and Wales are concerned the High Court may annul a Convention adoption or a Convention adoption order on the ground that the adoption is contrary to public policy.[125] But subject to this, the validity of a Convention adoption or Convention adoption order cannot be challenged in any court in England and Wales.[126]

Article 26(1) provides that recognition includes recognition of:

(a) the legal parent-child relationship between the child and his or her adoptive parents;
(b) parental responsibility of the adoptive parents for the child;
(c) the termination of a pre-existing legal relationship between the child and his or her mother and father, if the adoption has that effect in the Contracting State where it was made.

This, as one commentator has pointed out,[127] is not a comprehensive enumeration of the effects of recognition, but rather a list of the minimal consequences of recognition. Article 26(2) further provides that where the adoption has the effect of terminating a pre-existing legal parent–child relationship (in other words a 'full' adoption), the child is to enjoy in all States where the adoption is recognised as well as the Receiving State, rights equivalent to those resulting from full adoption in such States.[128] The recognition issue is further complicated by Art 27 which provides:

Where an adoption granted in the State of Origin does not have the effect of terminating a pre-existing legal parent-child relationship, it may, in the Receiving State which recognises the adoption under the Convention, be converted into an adoption having such an effect—

(a) if the law of the receiving State so permits; and
(b) if the consents referred to Article 4 paragraphs (c) and (d) have been or are given for the purpose of such an adoption.

Section 88 of the Adoption and Children Act 2002 attempts to deal with the problem of handling simple adoptions.[129] It provides that where a child has been adopted under a Convention order and the High Court is satisfied:

(a) that under the law of the country in which the adoption was effected the adoption was not a full adoption;

---

[125] Adoption and Children Act 2002 s 89(1). A 'Convention adoption' is an order effected under the law of a Convention country outside the British Islands, s 66(1)(c); a 'Convention adoption order' is an order made under the Convention within the British Islands, s 144(1).   [126] Section 89(4).

[127] Duncan, op cit, at 586.

[128] There is considerable doubt as to how this should be interpreted: see eg, R Frank 'The Recognition of Intercountry Adoption in the Light of the 1993 Hague Convention on Intercountry Adoptions' in *Families Across Frontiers* at 591; and M Brennan et al 'Intercountry Adoption—the recognition of foreign adoptions in the simple and full terms' in the *Report on the Cross Border Movement of Children* (1999, Society for Advanced Legal Studies). The *Explanatory Report* to the 1993 Convention, at para 439, emphasises that Art 26 was the result of compromise and that it reflects the minimum consensus that could be reached.

[129] Ie adoptions which do not sever the legal relationship of the child with his birth family.

(b) that the consents referred to in Article 4(c) and (d) of the Convention have not been given for a full adoption, or that the United Kingdom is not the receiving State (within the meaning of Article 2 of the Convention); and

(c) that it would be more favourable to the adopted child for a direction to be given under this subsection . . .

the court may direct that the order shall not be treated as a full adoption, or not to the extent as may be specified in the direction. This provides a mechanism for the High Court to give a direction whether and to what extent a child adopted under a simple adoption under the Convention should be treated as if he were not the child of any person other than the adopter or adopters. It will be available only if the adoption was not a full adoption, if the consents to a full adoption were not given or if the UK is not the Receiving State. It must be more favourable to the adopted child for the direction to be given.

An order made under the 1993 Convention, whether by a UK court or outside the British Islands automatically confers British citizenship upon a child if he does not already have it, provided the adopter(s) are habitually resident in the UK and at least one of the adoptive parents is a British citizen.[130] Convention orders must also be entered on the Adopted Children Register.[131]

Although the 1993 Convention is a bold attempt to provide global control of inter-country adoption it generally seems to be working. Certainly in terms of Contracting States the Convention is highly successful. As at June 2014, there were 93 Contracting States to the 1993 Convention, including the UK and, critically, the USA. After the UN Convention on the Rights of the Child, there are more Contracting States to the 1993 Convention than any international child law instrument. Perhaps one of the reasons for the Convention's success is that it is noticeably non-prescriptive, providing only for mini-mum safeguards, and avoids extensive use of traditional conflicts of laws rules. Instead the Convention provides a framework based on trust and co-operation. However, one important test of the Convention's success is whether Receiving States have confidence in the ability of the State of Origin to ensure that the adoption process has been properly car-ried out and that in particular, both the child's and the birth family's interests have been properly safeguarded. It is important, too, that the central authorities are able to work and co-operate with one another. In this regard note will be taken of s 9 of the Children and Adoption Act 2006 which allows the Secretary of State to suspend intercountry adoptions from countries (including Convention countries) where the Secretary determines that it would be contrary to public policy to further the bringing of children into the UK by British residents from that State.[132]

3. OVERSEAS ADOPTIONS

Convention adoptions are not the only foreign adoptions recognised by English law. Recognition is also accorded to 'overseas adoption', by which is meant a non-Convention

---

[130] British Nationality Act 1981 s 1(5), as amended.

[131] See now the Adopted Children and Adoption Contact Register Regulations 2005 (SI 2005/924) regs 3–5.

[132] The Government has in the past imposed a temporary suspension on adoptions from Cambodia, see P Cordery 'Suspension by the UK of Intercountry Adoptions' [2005] Fam Law 925 and the note to *R (Charlton Thomson and Others) v Secretary of State for Education and Skills* [2005] EWHC 1378 (Admin) at [2005] Fam Law 861.

adoption 'of a description specified in an order made by the Secretary of State, being a description of adoptions effected under the law of any country or territory outside the British Islands'.[133] In short this means an adoption order made in a country or territory on the 'designated list'.[134]

Since they are expressly included in the definition of adoption in s 66(1)(d) of the 2002 Act, overseas adoptions are automatically recognised as an adoption order in England and Wales. Consequently, there is no need to re-adopt domestically nor does its status need to be established in court proceedings. Indeed, to the contrary, the validity of an overseas order cannot be impugned in proceedings in any court in England and Wales,[135] save where the High Court orders it to cease as being contrary to public policy or that the authority that purported to authorise it was not competent to do so.[136] Although children of an overseas adoption are treated as children of their adopted parents (as in any other adoption) they do not necessarily acquire British citizenship, and they may be subject to immigration rules. However, where an overseas order has been obtained by UK citizens, the child does have a right of entry and may apply for British citizenship.[137]

Where an adoption order is made outside the British Islands but is neither a Convention nor an overseas adoption it may still be recognised according to the common law principles. *Re Valentine's Settlement*,[138] which first established the possibility or common law recognition, held that a minimum requirement for recognition was that the applicants were domiciled in the country in which the order was made and that the child must have been resident there. In *Re R (Recognition of Indian Adoption)*,[139] however, a foreign adoption order was recognised even though only one of the applicants was habitually resident in India. As Hedley J observed, the ratio of *Re Valentine* was that an adoption order would be recognised if, but only if, the conditions that existed in the foreign jurisdiction were such that would permit an adoption in this jurisdiction. He pointed out that since *Re Valentine* English domestic law had been changed by s 49 of the Adoption and Children Act 2002 which requires only one of the adoptive applicants to be habitually resident in the UK. Consequently *Re Valentine* had to be interpreted in that light.

While agreeing with Hedley J's analysis, Peter Jackson J held in *A County Council v M and Others (No 4) (Foreign Adoption: Refusal of Recognition)*,[140] after a thorough review of the relevant post-*Valentine* case-law, that it is now established that before a foreign adoption will be recognised at common law, it must satisfy the following criteria:

(1) The order must have been lawfully obtained in the foreign country.

(2) The concept of adoption in that jurisdiction must substantially conform to that in England.

(3) The adoption process that was undertaken must have been substantially the same as would have applied in England at the time.

---

[133] Adoption and Children Act 2002 s 87.

[134] Currently contained in the Adoption (Designation of Overseas Adoptions) Order 1973, as amended in 1993. The list comprises 39 Commonwealth countries (excluding inter alia India and Bangladesh) and 22 other countries including China, USA, South Africa, and Western European countries. This list is currently under review. Anyone habitually resident in the UK wishing to adopt from a country on the designated list will still have to comply with entry requirements: see Adoptions with a Foreign Element Regulations 2005.

[135] Adoption and Children Act 2002 s 89(4).   [136] Ibid s 89(2).

[137] British Nationality Act 1981 s 3(1).   [138] [1965] Ch 831.

[139] [2012] EWHC 2956 (Fam) [2013] 1 FLR 1487.

[140] [2013] EWHC 151 (Fam) [2014] 1 FLR 881 at [61].

(4) There must be no public policy considerations militating against recognition.

(5) Recognition must be in the best interests of the child.

In this case, recognition of an adoption order lawfully made in Kazakhstan was refused as it failed to satisfy criterion 3 and, crucially, criterion 5.

4. DOMESTIC ADOPTIONS OF FOREIGN CHILDREN

Before the UK's ratification of the 1993 Hague Intercountry Adoption Convention, couples seeking to adopt a foreign child would commonly bring the child into this country to be adopted according to English law.[141] Although restrictions and control have since been considerably tightened it is still possible to do so lawfully, namely by obtaining formal Home Office clearance[142] and being approved as adopters following a home study.

Even if the rules are broken and an offence committed, an English court is not barred from making an adoption order though obviously regard must be had to all the circumstances.[143] It is established[144] that in determining whether adoption is in the child's interests benefits accruing from a change of immigration status can be taken into account but an order will not be made where the adopters do not intend to exercise any parental responsibility in what are termed as 'accommodation' adoptions. Applications should be made to an intercountry adoption centre in the Family Court or to the High Court.

5. RESTRICTIONS ON BRINGING CHILDREN INTO THE UK FOR ADOPTION

An important part of the control on bringing children into the UK for adoption is provided by s 83 of the 2002 Act, which provides regulatory power to restrict entry. This section applies to any British resident[145] who, save where the child is intended to be adopted under a Convention adoption order:[146]

(a) brings, or causes another to bring, a child who is habitually resident outside the British Islands into the United Kingdom for the purpose of adoption by the British resident, or

(b) at any time brings, or causes another to bring, into the United Kingdom a child adopted by the British resident under an external adoption effected within the period of twelve months ending with that time.[147]

An 'external adoption' means an adoption of a child, other than a Convention adoption, effected under the law of any country or territory outside the British Islands whether or

---

[141] N Angel 'Inter country adoption and the court process in England and Wales' [2012] IFL 422 at 428ff.

[142] The requirements for which are strict. They include being satisfied about the child's position and that there is written permission both from the birth parents and the authorities responsible for the child's care in his or her country of origin. Note also the guidance given by Bracewell J in *Re R (Intercountry Adoptions: Practice)* [1999] 1 FLR 1042.

[143] See, for example, *Re WM (Adoption: Non-Patrial)* [1997] 1 FLR 132: a child was adopted abroad, and notwithstanding concerns as to the adopters' suitability (having been rejected by an adoption agency in this country), there was no option other than to make an adoption order in the child's interests. Cf *Re IH (A Child) (Permission to Apply for Adoption)* [2013] EWHC 1235 (Fam) [2014] 1 FLR 70—permission to apply for adoption was refused in respect of a 14 year old who had been brought from Pakistan without immigration clearance.   [144] *Re B (Adoption Order: Nationality)* [1999] 2 AC 136, HL.

[145] Ie those who are habitually resident in the British Islands: s 83(1).   [146] Section 83(2).

[147] Section 83(1). Note the period mentioned in s 83(1)(b) was extended from six months to 12 months by the Children and Adoption Act 2006 s 14.

not the adoption is an adoption within the meaning of Chapter 4 of the 2002 Act or a full adoption.[148]

Pursuant to the Adoption with a Foreign Element Regulations 2005 issued under s 83(4), prospective adopters have in effect to be assessed and approved as suitable to adopt by an adoption agency and to have obtained a certificate of approval by the Secretary of State (for which services the Secretary of State can charge).[149] Where these conditions are complied with the child must have lived with the applicant(s) for six months before an application to adopt can be made. Where they have not, the requisite period is three years.[150]

Non-compliance with these provisions is an offence punishable upon summary conviction to imprisonment for a maximum of six months and/or a fine not exceeding the statutory maximum or, upon conviction on indictment, imprisonment for up to 12 months and/or a fine of unlimited amount.[151] There is no time limit in respect of this offence.

6. REMOVING A CHILD FROM THE BRITISH ISLANDS FOR ADOPTION

A child who is a Commonwealth citizen or is habitually resident in the UK must not be removed from the UK to a place outside the British Islands for the purpose of adoption unless with the authority of a High Court order under s 84.[152] Any person who does so is guilty of an offence,[153] for which the penalty on summary conviction is imprisonment for up to six months and/or a fine not exceeding the statutory maximum and on indictment is imprisonment of up to 12 months and/or a fine not exceeding the statutory maximum.[154]

An order under s 84 confers parental responsibility on the applicant and extinguishes the parental responsibility of any other person. An application may only be made if the child has had his home, with both applicant(s) at all times during the preceding 10 weeks, though this does not mean that both applicants must be physically present throughout this period.[155] An order cannot be made unless the court is satisfied that the adoption agency has had sufficient opportunity to see the child and the applicant in the home environment and that the requirements prescribed by the Adoption with Foreign Element Regulations 2005 have been met.[156]

---

[148] Section 83(3).

[149] Section 91A of the Adoption and Children Act 2002 (added by the Children and Adoption Act 2006 s 13).

[150] Adoptions with a Foreign Element Regulations 2005 reg 9.   [151] Section 83(7), (8).

[152] Section 85(1). But note: a court can nevertheless give leave under s 28(2) of the 2002 Act for a local authority to place a child abroad for a time-limited period: *Re A (A Child) (Adoption: Placement outside Jurisdiction* [2013] EWHC 578 (Fam) [2013] 3 WLR 1454, relying in part upon *Re M (A Child) (Adoption: Placement outside Jurisdiction)* [2010] EWHC 1694 (Fam) [2011] Fam 110, which established that the statutory period requiring the child to live with adoptive applicants before an order maybe made can be spent outside the jurisdiction.

[153] Section 85(4).   [154] Section 85(6).

[155] See *Re G (Adoption: Placement Outside the Jurisdiction)* [2008] EWCA Civ 105 [2008] 1 FLR 1484. Note also the sequel to this decision: *Re G (Adoption: Placement Outside the Jurisdiction) (No 2)* [2008] EWCA Civ 1052 [2008] 1 FLR 1497.

[156] For an example of a s 84 being made, see *Re G (Surrogacy: Foreign Domicile)* [2007] EWHC 2814 (Fam) [2008] 1 FLR 1047.

D. INTERNATIONAL PARENTAL CHILD ABDUCTION

1. INTRODUCTION

The subject of the next part of this chapter is international parental child abduction, that is, the unilateral removal of children across jurisdictional boundaries or the unilateral retention of children in another jurisdiction by one parent without the other's consent. The factual background of abductions varies enormously: at one end of the scale is the situation where one parent, usually the mother, decides unilaterally to return with her children to her home country following a break-down of the relationship with her husband or partner or where one parent takes the children on holiday with the other's consent but then decides not to return; at the other end of the scale is where the abduction itself is violent, as for example in a German case,[157] in which a French mother was ambushed in country woods by men acting for her estranged husband, dragged from her car, and then watched helplessly as the men drove away with her two terrified children (aged seven and three) screaming in the back of the car. In between is where the abduction is a deliberate attempt to frustrate an unfavourable court order. Post-abduction conduct should not be overlooked for while some parents will live relatively settled lives, others will be constantly covering their tracks hiding from the authorities.

No matter how the abduction is perpetrated, its effects on the children can be devastating. It is likely to be traumatic in the short term and potentially permanently damaging in the long term. As the International Forum on Parental Child Abduction[158] put it:

> Children who are abducted will have already suffered from their parents' separation but, in addition, they will experience the trauma of being suddenly cut off from their familiar environment—a parent, grandparents, school and friends. This experience is devastating enough, but many children do not understand what is happening or why the abducting parent is hiding from the police or taking precautions against re-abduction. Such a 'state of war' between parents catches the children in a horrible cross-fire.

Statistical surveys of the 1980 Hague Abduction Convention[159] estimate that globally, up to 1,280 applications either for return of or access to children abducted across international borders were made under that Convention in 1999 rising to 1,540 in 2003 and to 2,321 in 2008. The increase from 2003 to 2008 was striking and on direct comparison

---

[157] *Tiemann* BVerfGE 99, 145 (FRG). See also *Re K (A Child) (Reunite International Child Abduction Centre Intervening)* [2014] UKSC 29 [2014] 2 WLR 1304, in which the child was snatched from a grandmother when on their way home from school and bundled into a back of a van, injuring the grandmother in the process.

[158] 1999, National Center for Missing and Exploited Children, USA.

[159] See respectively N Lowe, S Armstrong and A Mathias 'A Statistical Analysis of Applications made in 1999 under the Hague Convention of 25 October 1980 on the Civil Aspects of International Child Abduction', Prel. Doc. No. 3 (Revised Version, November 2001) ('the 1999 Statistical Survey'); N Lowe, E Atkinson and K Horosova 'A Statistical Analysis of Applications made in 2003 under the Hague Convention of 25 October 1980 on the Civil Aspects of International Child Abduction', presented to the 5th meeting of the Special Commission in September/October 2006 ('the 2003 Statistical Survey') and N Lowe and V Stephens 'A Statistical Analysis of Applications made in 2003 under the Hague Convention of 25 October 1980 on the Civil Aspects of International Child Abduction', presented to the 6th meeting of the Special Commission in June 2011('the 2008 Statistical Survey'). For an overall analysis of these surveys, see N Lowe and V Stephens 'Global trends in the Operation of the 1980 Hague Abduction Convention' (2012) 46 Fam LQ 41 and N Lowe with K Horosova 'The Operation of the 1980 Hague Abduction Convention—A Global view (2007) 41 Fam LQ 59.

amounted to a 45% increase in return applications and 40% in access applications. According to the 2008 Statistical Survey, the English central authority (which was second busiest authority under the Convention—only the USA handled more applications) made 238 applications and received 228.[160] None of the statistics just mentioned include abductions to and from countries that are not parties to the Conventions but according to statistics provided by the Foreign and Commonwealth Office, they handled in excess of 122 such cases in 2012/2013.[161] In addition to the cases just mentioned there are also those in which the children have been wrongfully taken or retained in other parts of the UK.

Until the 1980s there was little international co-operation on parental child abduction and court orders made in one jurisdiction were generally neither recognised nor enforceable in another. This state of international 'anarchy' operated as an encouragement to would-be abductors who, by appropriate forum shopping, could hope to take their children from one jurisdiction to another and there obtain judgment in their favour. However, following negotiations during the 1970s, two quite different international conventions were concluded. The first in time was the European Convention on the Recognition and Enforcement of Custody of Children and on Restoration of Custody of Children ('the 1980 European Convention') which was signed in May 1980. The second was the Hague Convention on the Civil Aspects of International Child Abduction ('the 1980 Hague Abduction Convention') which was formally adopted in October 1980. The UK ratified both Conventions in August 1986.

For some time these were the only international instruments dealing with child abduction but now there are others, including the revised Brussels II Regulation or 'BIIR' discussed earlier in this chapter, and the 1996 Hague Protection of Children Convention,[162] which the UK ratified in November 2012.

As if these instruments are not enough there is, in addition, the Family Law Act 1986 under which certain orders relating to children made in one part of the UK or the Isle of Man can be enforced in another part of the UK or the Isle of Man.

As a result of these developments there are different laws dealing with abduction depending on the country to or from which the child has been taken or brought. Thus, while the chances of foiling an attempted abduction and of recovering a child wrongfully taken have improved, the resulting law is complex.

2. PREVENTING CHILDREN FROM BEING ABDUCTED OUT OF THE UNITED KINGDOM

The best chance of recovery is to prevent the child from leaving the jurisdiction in the first place.[163] To this end both the criminal and the civil law may be invoked.

---

[160] See the national report in Part 2 of the Survey and the summary by N Lowe and V Stephens 'Operating The 1980 Hague Abduction Convention: The 2008 Statistics' [2011] Fam Law 1216. In a follow-up study, funded by the Nuffield Foundation, Lowe and Stephens found that applications rose again in 2011 with the central authority handling a total of 448 applications.

[161] See FCO Press Release, 12 December 2013.

[162] The 1996 Hague Convention on Jurisdiction, Applicable Law, Recognition, Enforcement and Co-operation in Respect of Parental Responsibility and Measures for the Protection of Children.

[163] See generally Law Commission Consultation Paper No 200 *Simplification of Criminal Law: Kidnapping* (2011) and Clarke Hall and Morrison on *Children* 5[37] ff. Note also the Guide to Good Practice under the Hague Convention of 25 October 1980 on the Civil Aspects of International Child Abduction—*Part III—Preventive Measures.*

(a) Criminal sanctions

Child Abduction Act 1984

Under the Child Abduction Act 1984 s 1(1)[164] it is an offence for a parent to take his own child (under the age of 16) out of the UK[165] without the consent (which need not be in writing) of the other parent, anyone else[166] with parental responsibility or leave of the court.[167] The only exception to this is where a person is named in a child arrangements order as a person with whom the child is to live or is a special guardian, in which case he or she is permitted to remove the child outside the UK for a period respectively of less than one month or three months without anyone's consent, unless this is in breach of a prohibited steps order.[168] Where a parent has sole parental responsibility, as for example the unmarried mother where the father has not acquired parental responsibility by registration as the father or by a court order or agreement,[169] or where the married parent is the sole living parent, then no consent for the child's removal from the jurisdiction is required.

Although the principal object of the Act is to deter parents from abducting their children out of the country, it also provides the means by which abduction may be prevented. As it is an offence to *attempt* to take a child out of the UK, the police can arrest anyone they reasonably suspect of attempting to take a child out of the country contrary to the provisions of the 1984 Act.[170] Furthermore, if the police decide to act they can, through their 'all ports warning system', activate a port stop, or port alert as it is sometimes known.

The all ports warning system

The police can, through their own 'all ports warning system', make a port stop which means that immigration officers at the ports will hold the name of a child at risk of unlawful removal on an index and try to assist the police by identifying the child if removal is attempted. To effect a port stop the particulars of the child at risk are circulated by way of the police national computer broadcast facility.[171] As this is the only means of activating a port alert, any parent fearing that his child might be taken out of the country and wishing to take advantage of this facility must inform the police, who maintain a 24-hour service in this regard.[172]

Before instituting a port alert the police must be convinced that the complaint is bona fide and the danger of removal real and imminent.[173] Although it is not necessary to have

---

[164] Exceptionally the common law offences of child kidnapping (see *R v D* [1984] AC 778, HL), discussed in Ch 10, Bringing up the child, p 339, or unlawful imprisonment (see *R v Rahman* (1985) 81 Cr App Rep 349) might be relevant, see in particular *R v Kayani; R v Solliman* [2011] EWCA Crim 2871 [2012] 1 WLR 1927 and *R (Nicolaou) v Redbridge Magistrates' Court* [2012] EWHC 1647 (Admin) [2012] 2 Cr App R 23.

[165] Viz. England and Wales, Scotland and Northern Ireland. But *not* including the Channel Islands or the Isle of Man. It is *not* therefore an offence under this Act to remove a child to another part of the UK.

[166] Ie guardians, special guardians and those named in a child arrangements order as a person with whom the child is to live (but not an emergency protection order) in their favour.

[167] Child Abduction Act 1984 s 1(3), amended by the Children and Families Act 2014 Sch 2 para 47(3). But note: where the child is a ward of court (discussed in Ch 20), court leave will always be required.

[168] Section 1(4) and (4A).

[169] As emphasised by Hale J in *Re W; Re B (Abduction: Father's Rights)* [1999] Fam 1 at 6.

[170] For a successful prosecution for an *attempted* abduction, see *R v Griffin* [1993] Crim LR 515, CA.

[171] See Family Procedure Rules 2010 *Practice Direction 12F—International Child Abduction* Part 4.

[172] See *Practice Direction 12F* paras 4.4 and 4.5.

[173] Within 24–48 hours: *Practice Direction 12F* para 4.6.

obtained a court order beforehand,[174] the existence of an order will be good evidence of the seriousness of the request for action from the police. Parties seeking police assistance should furnish as much information as possible, and in particular furnish the following details:[175]

(a) name, sex, date of birth, description and passport number of child;

(b) name, sex, description, nationality and passport number of abductor;

(c) their relationship;

(d) whether the child will assist in the removal;

(e) name, relationship, nationality and telephone number of applicant;

(f) solicitor's name and telephone number;

(g) likely time of travel, port of embarkation and port of arrival.

Upon application, the court can request a port alert and, on rare occasions where no one else is able to institute an alert, the court itself may direct the National Ports Office to institute a port alert.[176] Once the alert is activated, the child's name will remain on the stop list for four weeks.[177] The effectiveness of the alert is dependent on liaison between the police at individual air and sea ports and the security staff at those ports.

(b) Court prohibitions against removal

The advantages of court orders

Although, in view of the Child Abduction Act 1984 there is no requirement to obtain a court order to obtain a port alert, there are advantages in having an order:

(1) It establishes the applicant's bona fides, which may help to convince the police of the need for action.

(2) An order prohibiting the child's removal can act as a deterrent in itself.

(3) It enables the applicant to enlist the aid of Government agencies to trace the child.[178]

(4) The High Court can specifically order publicity to trace the child.[179]

(5) Where there is inadequate information as to the child's whereabouts the court can order any person who is believed to have that information to disclose it to the courts.[180]

(6) Upon obtaining a prohibition against removal, steps can be taken to prevent the issue of a UK passport,[181] or, if one has already been issued, to ask the court to order its surrender.[182] To prevent the reissue of a passport the court will notify HM Passport Office in every case in which a surrender of a passport has been ordered.[183] It has been held[184] that the High Court's inherent jurisdiction extends

---

[174] Though note in the case of children aged 16 or 17 a court order *is* required, since the Child Abduction Act 1984 does not apply. In practice abduction of such older children is unusual.

[175] *Practice Direction 12F* para 4.7.

[176] See N Lowe, M Everall and M Nicholls *International Movement of Children, Law Practice and Procedure* (2004) at 9.57.   [177] *Practice Direction 12F* para 4.8.

[178] FPR 2010 *Practice Direction 6C Practice Direction (Disclosure of Addresses by Government Departments)*.   [179] *Practice Direction 12F* para 4.15.

[180] Family Law Act 1986 s 33. For the case of wardship see FPR 2010 r 12.39.

[181] See the guidance issued by the Passport Agency at [1994] Fam Law 651.

[182] Family Law Act 1986 s 37.   [183] *Practice Direction 12F*, para 4.10.

[184] *Re A-K (Foreign Passport: Jurisdiction)* [1997] 2 FLR 569, CA. Note also that if a solicitor agrees to hold a foreign passport he owes a duty of care to the other parent not to let it out of his possession: *Al-Kandari v JR Brown & Co* [1988] QB 665, CA.

to ordering the surrender of a *foreign* national's passport where to do so is in the child's best interests.

(7) An order will be required if it becomes necessary to invoke the 1980 European Custody Convention or to recover the child from another part of the UK or the Isle of Man. Orders may be enforced under BIIR and/or the 1996 Hague Convention on the Protection of Children.

(8) It will enable outstanding disputes to be resolved upon the child's return, or sanctions to be imposed if the child is not returned.

Orders that may be obtained

An applicant may obtain a prohibited steps order forbidding a child's removal from the UK or any specified part of the UK under s 8 of the Children Act 1989.[185] Furthermore, an embargo against removal from the UK for any period in excess of one month is automatically included in a child arrangements order dealing with the child's living arrangements.[186]

An embargo against the child's removal from the jurisdiction can also be obtained by making the child a ward of court.[187] The unique advantage of wardship is that the embargo automatically arises immediately the child is warded,[188] and no other relief need be sought. It is this immediate effect that makes it advantageous to invoke wardship if no other proceedings are already on foot.

Whatever means are used, speed is of the essence if an attempted abduction is to be foiled, but even if all preventive measures have been taken in good time there is no guarantee that the child's removal will be stopped.

Where the court gives leave for the child's removal from the jurisdiction, measures can be taken to secure the child's return. One option is to obtain an order in the foreign country to a similar effect to that made by the English court. These are known as 'mirror orders'.[189] There is also a power in wardship proceedings and presumably in the High Court generally to require the person given leave to enter into a bond to ensure that the child will be duly returned.[190] Subsequently, if the order is broken the court can order the bond to be forfeited and assigned to the aggrieved party. Other actions that can be taken following the breaking of a court order are fining or committing the contemnor (ie the person breaking the order) to prison or, more potently in some cases, sequestering the contemnor's assets.[191] This latter remedy can be a useful lever against the abducting parent who has left property in this country, particularly as the court has power to order

---

[185] See, for example, *Re D (A Minor) (Child Removal From Jurisdiction)* [1992] 1 WLR 315, CA, according to which such orders can be applied for ex parte and, in appropriate cases, can be enforced without notice. NB, however, even if a prohibited steps or specific issue order is obtained, the port alert procedure must still be activated by the applicant.

[186] Section 13(1)(b) and s 13(2) as amended by the Children and Families Act 2014 Sch 2 para 22, discussed in Ch 14.

[187] Wardship is discussed in Ch 20. NB the embargo normally prohibits the ward's removal from England and Wales without the court's leave. However, under the Family Law Act 1986 s 38, unless the court has directed otherwise, leave is not required to take the child to another part of the UK or the Isle of Man if matrimonial proceedings are continuing, or if the child is habitually resident there.

[188] See Ch 20.   [189] See Lowe, Everall and Nicholls, op cit, at 9.38.

[190] For details of which, see Clarke Hall and Morrison on *Children* 5[21]. It is the normal practice for there to be consent to the giving of the bond and it is not appropriate to impose it on a party who was not responsible for the child's removal: see *Re H (Minors) (Wardship: Surety)* [1991] 1 FLR 40, CA.

[191] The effect of a sequestration order is to freeze the contemnor's assets: see Ch 14, The Family Court's general enforcement powers for contempt of court, p 538.

the sale of sequestered assets and can direct that the money raised by the sequestrators be used to pay the costs of tracing the child and instituting proceedings abroad for the return of the child etc.[192] A further option is for the person given leave to remove the child to give an undertaking to return the child, which may be enforceable abroad where the 1996 Hague Protection of Children Convention applies.[193]

3. DEALING WITH CHILDREN TAKEN TO OR BROUGHT FROM ANOTHER PART OF THE UNITED KINGDOM AND ISLE OF MAN

(a) Introduction

Before implementation of the Family Law Act 1986, orders made in another part of the UK were treated no differently from an order made in any other part of the world: they were neither recognised nor enforceable. Moreover, as different parts of the UK had different jurisdictional rules there could be, and were, cases where competing orders were made in respect of the same child. A notorious example was *Babington v Babington*[194] in which the mother, who was domiciled in Scotland, left the matrimonial home in Scotland to live in England. She made her 11-year-old daughter, who attended a boarding school in England but who spent her holidays with her parents in Scotland, a ward of court.[195] The effect of wardship was to prevent the child going to Scotland without the court's consent.[196] Meanwhile the father, also a Scottish domiciliary, petitioned in Scotland for what was then custody and access. The Scottish Court of Session held that as the court of domicile it had pre-eminent jurisdiction, and granted access to the husband. The father then applied to the English court for leave to take the child out of the jurisdiction, which the mother opposed and sought leave herself to take the child to Switzerland for a holiday. Notwithstanding the Scottish order the English court refused the husband's application and granted the wife's instead. In effect, as the English and Scottish Law Commissions subsequently commented,[197] each court disregarded the order of the other.

Clearly, this state of affairs was unsatisfactory[198] and, after protracted discussions,[199] the English and Scottish Law Commissions made recommendations[200] upon which the Family Law Act 1986 is based. This Act applies to England and Wales, Scotland and Northern Ireland,[201] and, by subsequent extension, to the Isle of Man.[202]

(b) The Family Law Act 1986

The 1986 Act essentially does two things. First it provides for common rules of jurisdiction throughout the UK and the Isle of Man (hereinafter simply referred to as the

---

[192] See respectively *Mir v Mir* [1992] Fam 79 and *Richardson v Richardson* [1989] Fam 95.

[193] See *Re Y (Abduction: Undertakings Given for Return of Child)* [2013] EWCA Civ 129 [2013] 2 FLR 649.   [194] 1955 SC 115.

[195] Jurisdiction being taken on the basis of the child's presence in England and Wales.

[196] The full effects of wardship are discussed in Ch 20.

[197] Law Com Working Paper No 68 and Scot Law Com Memorandum No 23, *Custody of Children—Jurisdiction and Enforcement within the UK* (1976) para 3.12.

[198] Although *Babington* caused deep resentment in Scotland, where it was dubbed 'legal kidnapping', the Scottish courts could be equally unco-operative: see eg *Hoy v Hoy* 1968 SLT 413.

[199] It took nine years to produce the final report following the working paper.

[200] Viz. *Custody of Children: Jurisdiction and Enforcement within the UK* Law Com No 138 and Scot Law Com No 91, 1985.   [201] See s 42 of the 1986 Act.

[202] Family Law Act 1986 (Dependent Territories) Order 1991 (SI 1991/1773) Sch 3.

UK). Secondly, it provides a system for the recognition and enforcement throughout the UK of orders made in any one part of the kingdom or dependent territory.

Common jurisdictional rules

It is established[203] that BIIR has no application to jurisdictional conflicts *within* the UK and Isle of Man since it is not concerned with conflicts within a single Member State. Such conflicts therefore continue to be exclusively governed by the 1986 Act, the aim of which is to ensure that only one court in the UK has jurisdiction to make a 'Part 1 order' over a child, except in emergencies. 'Part 1 orders' are defined by s 1(1)(a) and (d) to mean, so far as England and Wales is concerned, s 8 orders under the Children Act 1989 (excluding variations or discharges) and orders made under the High Court's inherent jurisdiction giving care of the child to any individual or providing for contact with or the education of the child, but excluding variations or discharges of such orders.

The basic scheme is:[204]

(1) to vest primary jurisdiction in the UK court in which divorce, nullity or separation proceedings and the equivalent proceedings in connection with civil partnerships are continuing;

(2) where there are no such proceedings continuing, primary jurisdiction vests in the UK court in which the child is habitually resident;

(3) where the child is not habitually resident in any part of the UK, jurisdiction vests in the UK court in which the child is physically present.

With regard to point (2) reference needs to be made to s 41, which provides that a child under the age of 16, who has been wrongfully removed or retained outside a part of the UK in which he has been habitually resident, will be deemed to continue to be habitually resident in that part for one year after the removal.[205] 'Wrongfully' is defined by s 41(2) as being a removal to or a retention in another jurisdiction either without the consent of all persons having the right to determine where the child is to reside or in contravention of a court order.[206] By s 41(3) such deemed habitual residence ceases if the child becomes 16 or habitually resident in another part of the UK with the consent[207] of all those having the right to determine where the child is to reside and not in contravention of a court order. In any event once the year has elapsed jurisdiction passes to the part of the UK in which the child has become habitually resident.[208]

Section 41 is designed to prevent any jurisdictional advantage being gained by abducting a child from one part of the UK to another (the provision has no extra-territorial effect

---

[203] *Re W-B (Family Proceedings: Appropriate Jurisdiction Within UK)* [2012] EWCA Civ 592 [2013] 1 FLR 394, per McFarlane LJ at [10] and followed in *Re PC, YC and KM (Brussels IIR: Jurisdiction Within United Kingdom)* [2013] EWHC 2336 (Fam) [2014] 1 FLR 605, in which it was held that the transfer provisions under BIIR Art 15 have no application to transfers *within* the UK.

[204] Family Law Act 1986 s 2, s 2A and s 3.

[205] Section 41(1). For a case where this was applied, see *D v D (Custody: Jurisdiction)* [1996] 1 FLR 574. It has been questioned where a year is too long, see N Lowe and R White *Wards of Court* (1986, 2nd edn) at 17–59.

[206] But such an order must still be in force: see *Re M (Minors) (Residence Order: Jurisdiction)* [1993] 1 FLR 495, CA.

[207] But it seems that it must be proved that the consent is to the child becoming 'habitually' resident, ie it is not enough to show consent to a temporary removal: see *D v D (Custody: Jurisdiction)* at 580.

[208] *Re B (Court's Jurisdiction)* [2004] EWCA Civ 681 [2004] 2 FLR 741.

and does not therefore apply to children wrongfully removed to or from a jurisdiction outside the UK).[209]

Recognition and enforcement

Under s 25 of the 1986 Act any Part I order[210] made by a court in any part of the UK and in force in respect of a child under the age of 16 is to be recognised in any other part of the UK.[211] This means, for example, that a prohibition against the child's removal from any part of the UK will be effective throughout the UK.[212]

Recognition does not itself mean that the order will be enforced.[213] Instead, application must be made to the court that made the original order for it to be registered in another part of the UK. Under s 27(1) any person on whom rights have been conferred by a Part 1 order may apply for that order to be registered in another part of the UK.[214] There is no scrutiny as to why it is sought to register the order, ie there is no need to show that a removal is imminent. It can therefore be invoked as an insurance, for example, where the parties come from different jurisdictions and it is felt that the one might be tempted to return home. The court will then forward to the 'appropriate court'[215] a copy of the order and an appropriate officer will cause the order to registered.[216]

Once the order is registered, the registering court has the same enforcement powers as it would have had, had it made the original order which is the subject of the application for enforcement.[217] Even so, an application to enforce the order is still required.[218] At the enforcement hearing, objections may be made by any interested party, for example upon the grounds that the original order was made without jurisdiction or, because of changed circumstances, the original order should be varied. The court has power either to enforce the order or to stay or to dismiss the application.[219]

Pending the outcome of the application the court may give such interim directions as it sees fit.[220] When considering an enforcement application the English court must not purport to act as a court of appeal from the court having jurisdiction in another part of the UK. Consequently, the judge should not question the correctness of the procedures and orders of the other UK court.[221]

It has been suggested[222] that the whole enforcement process under the 1986 Act needs to be rethought. In particular it has been questioned whether it is sensible to have a two stage process, namely, registration and then enforcement. Why not simply have a straightforward mandatory scheme of automatic mutual recognition and enforcement?

---

[209] *Re S (A Child: Abduction)* [2002] EWCA Civ 1941 [2003] 1 FLR 1008—no application of s 41 in respect of a child brought from Germany and retained in Wales.

[210] Except those in relation to a child in local authority care. It might be noted that the courts can only enforce Part I orders and not, for example, injunctions: see *Re K (Wardship: Jurisdiction: Interim Order)* [1991] 2 FLR 104, CA. [211] See generally Lowe, Everall and Nicholls, op cit, at 11.3 *et seq.*

[212] Section 36. [213] Section 25(3).

[214] The registration procedure is governed by FPR 2010 Part 32 Chapter 4.

[215] Ie the Supreme Court of the jurisdiction to which the child has been taken: s 32(1) and FPR 2010 r 32.23.

[216] Section 27(3) and FPR 2010 r 32.26. [217] Section 29(1). [218] Ibid.

[219] Sections 30–31. The power to order a stay may be appropriate, for example, where the original order was made without jurisdiction: see Law Com 138 and Scot Law Com No 91 at para 5.33.

[220] Section 29(2).

[221] Per Stephen Brown P in *Re M (Minors) (Custody: Jurisdiction)* [1992] 2 FLR 382 at 386–7. A similar position obtains in Scotland: see *Cook v Blackley* 1997 SLT 853.

[222] By Lowe, Everall and Nicholls, op cit, at 11.32–11.35.

4. DEALING WITH CHILDREN ABDUCTED TO OR BROUGHT FROM A 'NON-CONVENTION COUNTRY' OUTSIDE THE UNITED KINGDOM

(a) Dealing with children abducted to a 'non-Convention State'

Once a child is removed outside the UK or the Isle of Man to a country that is not party to an international instrument[223] dealing with abduction to which the UK is also a party (which, for convenience, we will call 'non-convention countries'), the chances of recovering the child may be slim. Unless the abducting spouse returns voluntarily, the only legal means[224] is to institute proceedings in the country to which the child has been taken, if that is known, or, if the country in question has an extradition treaty with the UK, to try to have the abductor extradited for abduction and the child returned.[225] The Foreign and Commonwealth Office (FCO) Consular Department can offer practical (but not legal) advice to individuals[226] while the domestic courts exercising family jurisdiction can seek diplomatic assistance from the FCO in London and from the relevant British Embassies and High Commissions abroad.[227]

(b) Dealing with children abducted from a 'non-Convention State'

Children brought to England and Wales from a non-convention country[228] are subject to the common law. Such cases are commonly litigated under the wardship jurisdiction[229] but they can be the subject of s 8 proceedings under the Children Act 1989.[230] Provided the jurisdictional rules are satisfied,[231] a child may be made a ward of court after he has been brought to this country even if the removal from another jurisdiction was unauthorised.[232] Regardless of which proceedings are brought the substantive law to be applied is the same.

The basic issue and dilemma

It is well established[233] that the English courts are not bound by foreign custody orders[234] and instead must, applying the principle of the paramountcy of the child's welfare, make

---

[223] Ie the 1980 Hague Abduction Convention, the 1980 European Custody Convention, BIIR, the 1996 Hague Protection of Children Convention or the UK-Pakistan Protocol.

[224] As opposed to re-abducting the child.

[225] Apart from the length of time involved in obtaining extradition, an important drawback of the procedure is that only the 'wrongdoer' is extradited, so that there is no guarantee that the child will be returned.

[226] *Practice Note (Minor: Removal from Jurisdiction)* [1984] 1 WLR 1216. Help can also usefully be sought from REUNITE.

[227] Liaison Between Courts in England and Wales and British Embassies and High Commissions Abroad [2004] Fam Law 68. Assistance can include: locating the child, conducting interviews and facilitating travel arrangements but *not* retaining passports or paying for the child's repatriation.

[228] See generally Lowe, Everall and Nicholls, op cit, 457ff, Clarke Hall and Morrison on *Children* 5[106]ff.

[229] Wardship is discussed in Ch 20.

[230] In *Re J (A Child) (Custody Rights: Jurisdiction)* [2005] UKHL 40 [2005] 3 WLR 14, for example, an application was made for a specific issue order for the child's return.

[231] Viz. those under ss 1–3 of the Family Law Act 1986.

[232] In fact a child who has been taken from a *Convention* country may also be warded, but the wardship is liable to be overridden by a subsequent Convention application. Should the Convention application fail, however, then any earlier wardship proceedings are revived and may be determined upon their merits: see *Re M (A Minor) (Abduction: Child's Objections)* [1994] 2 FLR 126. A similar position applies to s 8 proceedings.

[233] *Re B's Settlement* [1940] Ch 54 and *McKee v McKee* [1951] AC 352, PC. Historically, a distinction was made between children who were British subjects and those that were not. In the former case a foreign court order was not regarded as binding: *Dawson v Jay* (1854) 3 De G, M & G 764; in the latter the foreign order was binding save in exceptional cases: *Nugent v Vetzera* (1866) LR 2 Eq 704.

[234] Not even (before the implementation of the Family Law Act 1986) an order made in Scotland. For a notorious example see *Babington v Babington* 1955 SC 115, discussed at Introduction, p 1021.

their own independent judgment of the appropriate course of action. A fortiori they must make their own assessment where there is no foreign court order. The basic decision of course is whether or not to order the child's return to the place whence he or she was taken but in determining that question the court must first decide whether it should investigate the full merits of the case or simply make a summary order for the child's return. This decision is further complicated by the question of how far, if at all, the foreign law in question should be investigated, in order for the court to be satisfied that if returned, the child's welfare will continue to be treated as the paramount consideration.

Deciding whether or not to make a return order presents the court with a dilemma. If it refuses to make a return order that will be seen as giving an advantage to the wrongdoer (ie the abducting parent, who may, though not necessarily, have deliberately flouted a foreign court order), yet while a court can hardly condone abduction both in the interests of justice and comity, a refusal may well be justified in the interests of the child, which interests the court is statutorily obliged to secure. In short, the court has to balance the individual child's welfare and the twin needs of policy of not encouraging abduction and not antagonising foreign regimes lest they in turn adopt a policy of non-return of children habitually resident in England and Wales.

The developing response to child abduction

At one time, the practice was to make a 'summary' order for the child's return (ie there would be no full investigation into the merits of the case) unless a return could be shown to be harmful to the child.[235] In this way it was felt that the child's welfare was reasonably protected whilst the abduction was discouraged. That approach, however, was held to be inconsistent with the welfare principle as applied by the House of Lords in *J v C*,[236] and it became established that the decision whether to make a summary order or to hear the full merits of the application had to be determined according to the child's welfare.[237] But this welfare approach became diluted when the courts began to treat non-Convention cases as quasi Hague Abduction Convention cases. In *Re F (A Minor) (Abduction: Jurisdiction)*[238] the Court of Appeal, emphasising that it was normally in the child's interests not to be abducted and that any decision about his upbringing was best decided by the court in the State in which he had hitherto been habitually resident, held that a return should be ordered provided the English court was satisfied that (a) the foreign court in question would apply principles acceptable to the English court and (b) there were no contra-indications such as those referred to in Art 13 of the Hague Convention.[239]

The problem with applying the Hague Abduction Convention even by analogy was, as Ward LJ pointed out in *Re JA (Child Abduction: Non Convention Country)*,[240] that when applying the Convention, the *individual* child's welfare is *not* the paramount consideration whereas it is in non-Convention cases. Moreover, whereas in non-Convention cases evidence has to be adduced to *justify* the return, in Hague cases evidence needs to be adduced to *prevent* a return.

---

[235] See *Re H (Infants)* [1966] 1 All ER 886, CA and *Re E (D) (An Infant)* [1967] Ch 287, CA.

[236] [1970] AC 668, HL, discussed in Ch 9 *J v C*, at p 314.

[237] *Re L (Minors) (Wardship: Jurisdiction)* [1974] 1 WLR 250, CA.

[238] [1991] Fam 25, CA. See also *G v G (Minors) (Abduction)* [1991] 2 FLR 506, CA (decided in 1989) upon which the court relied in *Re F*. For a thoughtful review of this and other decisions, see D McClean and K Beevers 'International child abduction—back to common law principles' [1995] CFLQ 128.

[239] Art 13 of the Hague Convention is discussed at The exceptions to the duty to return, pp 1054ff.

[240] [1998] 1 FLR 231 at 234.

The other proposition espoused by *Re F*, that a return should not be ordered unless the foreign court in question would apply principles acceptable to English law, proved problematic.[241] It raised two issues, namely (a) the extent to which evidence had to be led as to the principles and procedure the foreign court will apply, and (b) how tolerant the English court should be towards legal systems that have different notions of child welfare.

With regard to the former there was a dispute as to whether any evidence needed to be led at all. In a trilogy of decisions culminating in *Re M (Minors) (Abduction: Peremptory Return)*[242] and *Osman v Elasha*,[243] it was held that unless evidence is led to the contrary it should be presumed that judges in other countries will apply principles acceptable to English law. However, in *Re JA (Abduction: Non-Convention Country)*[244] Ward LJ (with whom Lord Woolf and Mummery LJ agreed) castigated this approach on the basis that not to make enquiries was an abdication of the court's duty to the child.

The second issue concerning the English courts' tolerance of other systems that do not espouse similar notions of child welfare similarly did not admit of simple solutions but there was a clear trend, based upon notions of comity,[245] to order a return. This trend was evidenced by a further trilogy of Court of Appeal decisions, the effect of which was, at any rate where the parents had a close connection with the foreign State in question, to justify a refusal to return, strong evidence was required to show that the foreign law's principles was repugnant and not merely different to the English notion of welfare principles. The problem with that approach was that it was questionable whether the individual child's welfare was really being treated as the court's paramount consideration.

It was this uncertain state of the law that the House of Lords was called upon to resolve in *Re J (A Child) (Custody Rights: Jurisdiction)*.[246]

The law as settled by Re J

At issue in *Re J* was whether a young boy (who himself had US, UK and Saudi Arabian citizenship) who had been retained in England by his mother (who had dual UK and Saudi citizenship) without his Saudi Arabian father's consent should be summarily returned to Saudi Arabia. The House of Lords upheld the decision not to make the summary return order sought by the father. In so ruling, the House of Lords settled the principles to be applied in non-Convention cases, explained how those principles are to be applied in such cases, and discussed the relevance of human rights.

The principle

The House of Lords held that in non-Convention cases the child's welfare is paramount and that the specialist rules and concepts contained in the 1980 Hague Abduction Convention are not applicable. Baroness Hale pointed out[247] that s 1 of the Children Act 1989 is of general application and there is 'no warrant, either in statute or authority, for the principles of the Hague Convention to be extended to countries which are not parties to it'. Furthermore there was ample authority[248] for the application of the paramountcy

---

[241] See generally the analysis by U Khaliq and J Young 'Cultural diversity, human rights and inconsistency in the English courts' (2001) 21 LS 192.
[242] [1996] 1 FLR 478. See also *Re M (Abduction: Non-Convention Country)* [1995] 1 FLR 89, and *Re M (Jurisdiction: Forum Conveniens)* [1995] 1 FLR 224.   [243] [2000] Fam 62, per Thorpe and Pill LJJ.
[244] [1998] 1 FLR 231. In that case the court refused to order a child's return to the United Arab Emirates, the evidence being that that State's court powers were limited and that the child's welfare was not the test.
[245] But for a convincing critique on this reliance on comity see Khaliq and Young, op cit.
[246] [2005] UKHL 40 [2005] 3 WLR 14.   [247] Ibid at [22].
[248] Viz. *Re B's Settlement* [1940] Ch 54, *McKee v McKee* [1951] AC 352 expressly approved by the House of Lords in *J v C* [1970] AC 668.

principle even in a case where a friendly foreign State has made orders about the child's future. However, it was consistent with the welfare principle to order the child's return to a foreign jurisdiction without conducting a full investigation of the merits if that was in the child's best interests. In that respect Baroness Hale approvingly referred to[249] the *locus classicus*, namely Buckley LJ's comments in *Re L (Minors) (Wardship: Jurisdiction)*:[250]

> To take a child from his native land, to remove him to another country where, maybe, his native tongue is not spoken, to divorce him from the social customs and contacts to which he has been accustomed, to interrupt his education in his native land and subject him to a foreign system of education, are all acts (offered here as examples and of course not as a complete catalogue of possible relevant factors) which are likely to be psychologically disturbing to the child, particularly at a time when his family life is also interrupted. If such a case is promptly brought to the attention of a court in this country, the judge may feel that it is in the best interests of the infant that these disturbing factors should be eliminated from his life as speedily as possible. A full investigation of the merits of the case in an English court may be incompatible with achieving this. The judge may well be persuaded that it would be better for the child that those merits should be investigated in a court in his native country.

Baroness Hale concluded[251] that the application of the principles just mentioned means:

> that there is always a choice to be made. Summary return should not be the automatic reaction to any and every unauthorised taking or keeping a child from his home country. On the other hand, summary return may very well be in the best interests of the individual child.

Deciding whether or not to make a summary return order

Observing[252] that the focus must be on the individual child in the particular circumstances of the case, Baroness Hale rejected the contention that there should be 'a strong presumption' that it is 'highly likely' to be in the best interests of a child subject to unauthorised removal or retention to be returned to the country of habitual residence so that any issues which remain can be decided there. As her Ladyship said, such an approach would come so close to applying Hague Convention principles by analogy that it would be indistinguishable from it in practice. Furthermore such a presumption is incapable of taking into account the huge variety of circumstances which can arise in these cases. In Baroness Hale's view,[253] the most one can say is:

> that the judge may find it convenient to start from the proposition that it is better for a child to return to his home country for any disputes about his future to be decided there. A case against his doing so, has to be made. But the weight to be given to that proposition will vary enormously from case to case. What may be best for him in the short run may be different from what will be best for him in the long run. It should not be assumed . . . that allowing a child to remain here while his future is decided here inevitably means that he will remain here forever.

Baroness Hale identified a number of factors that are important in determining what decision should be made:[254]

---

[249] [2005] UKHL 40 [2005] 3 WLR 14 at [26].   [250] [1974] 1 WLR 250 at 264.
[251] [2005] UKHL 40 [2005] 3 WLR 14 at [28].   [252] Ibid at [29].   [253] Ibid at [32].
[254] Ibid at [33]–[40], of which the following is a summary.

(1) *The degree of the child's connection with each country*—ie with which country does the child have the closer connection; what is his 'home' country? In this respect factors such as nationality, where the child has mostly lived, first language, race or ethnicity, religion, culture and education are all relevant.

(2) *The length of time the child has spent in each country*—uprooting a child from one environment and bringing him to a completely unfamiliar one, especially if done clandestinely, may well not be in his best interests, but if he is already familiar with this country and has been here for some time without objection, it may be less disruptive to remain a little longer while his medium and longer term future is decided than it would be to return.

(3) *The difference of approach of the other foreign legal system*—the extent to which the difference of approach of the legal system of the country to which it is sought to return the child is relevant depends on the particular facts. English law does not start from any prior assumptions about what is best for any individual child and it would be wrong to say that the future of every child within the jurisdiction of the courts of England and Wales must be decided according to their conception of child welfare. Nevertheless differences between the legal systems are relevant and, depending upon the facts may be decisive. For example, where there is a genuine issue between the parents as to which country it is best for the child to live, it must be relevant whether that issue is capable of being tried in the courts of the country to which the return is being sought. If those courts have no choice but to do as the father wishes so that the mother cannot ask them to decide with an open mind which country is best for the child then the English court must ask itself whether it is in the child's best interests to enable that dispute to be heard.[255] The absence of a relocation jurisdiction may be a decisive factor[256] but not if the mother could not in any event make a good case for relocation. It may also be that the connection of the child and all the family with the other country is so strong that any difference between the legal systems should carry little weight.

(4) *The effect of the decision upon the child's primary carer* is relevant but not decisive. A child cared for by nannies or sent away to boarding school may move between countries much more readily than a child who has been looked after by a single primary carer. On the other hand, there is an understandable reluctance to allow a primary carer to profit from her own wrongdoing by refusing to return with the child if the child is ordered to return. Consequently it is often entirely reasonable to expect the carer to return with the child. Equally, however, there are occasions where it is necessary to consider whether it is indeed reasonable to expect the carer to return, the sincerity of the declared refusal to do so and what is to happen to the child if the carer does not also return.

One circumstance not mentioned in *Re J* is the significance of the family being involved in asylum proceedings. In that respect it should be noted that when

---

[255] In *Re J* itself, at first instance, Hughes J refused to make a return order on the basis that were the father to make allegations about the mother's association with another man (an allegation he made but withdrew in the proceedings before Hughes J) in any subsequent hearing before the Sharia Court in Saudi Arabia, the latter court was bound to find in favour of the father.

[256] Baroness Hale, considered that Hughes J had underplayed the importance of this factor and had been wrong to leave it out of account, see [46].

exercising its jurisdiction the court is *not* precluded from ordering the child's return (if that is in the child's best interests) merely because of the family's involvement in such proceedings.[257]

The relevance of human rights

Deciding whether or not to return a child abroad necessarily engages human rights[258] and in particular those conferred by Art 6 (right to a fair trial), Art 8 (right to respect for private and family life) and Art 14 (prohibition against discrimination taken in conjunction with, for these purposes, Arts 6 and 8) of the European Convention on Human Rights. In *Re J*[259] the Court of Appeal considered that those rights had limited territorial effect. Consequently the fact that the mother might experience in Saudi Arabia what in England would be breaches of those rights did not render the English court in breach if it returned the child there. However, on appeal, Baroness Hale pointed out[260] that the House of Lords had since held[261] that 'our obligations may be engaged where there is a real risk of particularly flagrant breaches . . . in the foreign country'. In *Re J* itself there was no such risk. She also pointed out that in relation to Art 8 there is a distinction between 'domestic' cases where family life here may be disrupted by a forced return to another country and 'foreign' cases where the only breach would take place abroad. However, in her Ladyship's view, this distinction added nothing to the welfare inquiry since the strength of the child's connection with this country and the effect upon his parent here are in any event relevant to whether a summary return is in the child's best interests. However, Baroness Hale appeared to consider[262] that human rights considerations might be relevant if, akin to Art 20 of the Hague Abduction Convention,[263] the return 'would not be permitted by the fundamental principles of the requested State relating to the protection of human rights and fundamental freedoms'. In other words any discrimination in the foreign country which was contrary to Art 14 of the European Convention on Human Rights would permit, but not require, the court to refuse to return the child.

The need to act urgently

It is of the essence in these cases that the judge should act urgently.[264] This means, as Waite LJ observed in *Re M (Abduction: Non-Convention Country)*,[265] that 'the court has no time to go into matters of detail. The case has to be viewed from the perspective of a quick appraisal of its essential features.' The general aim is, as with cases brought under

---

[257] See *Re S (Child Abduction: Asylum Appeal)* [2002] EWCA Civ 843 [2002] 2 FLR 465, in which it was held that s 15 of the Immigration and Asylum Act 1999 was not intended to circumscribe the duty and discretion of a judge exercising the wardship jurisdiction, but was instead directed to the immigration authorities. See also *Re H (Child Abduction: Mother's Asylum)* [2003] EWHC 1820 (Fam), [2003] 2 FLR 1105 in which it was held to be in the child's best interests to be returned to his habitual residence in Pakistan notwithstanding that the mother (who had lawfully kept her son in the UK) had been granted asylum on the basis of a well-founded fear of persecution.

[258] For further discussion of human rights issues in abduction cases, see Compatibility with the European Convention on Human Rights, p 1035.

[259] Reported as *Re J (Child Returned Abroad: Human Rights)* [2004] 2 FLR 85.   [260] At [42].

[261] See *R (Ullah) v Special Adjudicator; Do v Immigration Appeal Tribunal* [2004] UKHL 26 [2004] 2 AC 323.

[262] [2005] UKHL 40 [2005] 3 WLR 14 at [43]–[45].

[263] In fact Art 20 of the 1980 Hague Abduction Convention has not been incorporated by UK, see further The court's role, p 1038.

[264] As Baroness Hale commented, at [41], the considerations to be taken into account in determining what order to make 'should not stand in the way of a swift and unsentimental decision to return the child to his home country' if that is what his interests require.   [265] [1995] 1 FLR 89, at 90, CA.

the 1980 Hague Abduction Convention and BIIR, that court proceedings should be completed within six weeks.[266]

The special case of Pakistan

In 2003, the President of the Family Division and the Honourable Chief Justice of Pakistan, in consultation with senior members of the family judiciary of the UK and the Islamic Republic of Pakistan, signed a record of 'consensus' which has since become known as the UK–Pakistan Protocol.[267] The kernel of the Protocol lies in paragraphs 1 and 2[268] which state:

1. In normal circumstances the welfare of a child is best determined by the courts of the country of the child's habitual/ordinary residence.
2. If a child is removed from the UK to Pakistan, or from Pakistan to the UK, without the consent of the parent and with a custody/residence order or a restraint/interdict order from the court of the child's habitual/ordinary residence, the judge of the court of the country to which the child has been removed shall not ordinarily exercise jurisdiction over the child, save insofar as it is necessary for the court to order the return of the child to the country of the child's habitual/ordinary residence.

In short, under the Protocol each State is normally expected to respect each other's custody or what, in England and Wales, are now child arrangements orders naming a person with whom the child is to live. Whilst this Protocol can only operate as guidance, it is intended nevertheless to have a strong influence on the way judges exercise their discretion in UK–Pakistan cases and it has since been held that English judges should have regard to it even in cases (commonly, those where there is no existing order or in so-called holiday cases in which permission is sought to visit Pakistan for a holiday) falling outside the Protocol.[269]

Although it seems more helpful than not in promoting the interests of children in having this mutual understanding, and indeed the Protocol seems to be working well especially in the UK[270] the propriety of having a Protocol negotiated by the judiciary

---

[266] See *Practice Direction 12F* para 3.5.

[267] On which see Rt Hon Lord Justice Thorpe 'The Pakistan Protocol' [2012] IFL 167; M Bashir 'The UK-Pakistan Judicial Protocol: A Need for Greater Judicial Understanding' [2010] IFL 266; M Freeman 'When the 1980 Hague Child Abduction Convention Does Not Apply: The UK-Pakistan Protocol" [2009] IFL 181.

[268] Para 3 deals with visitation rights. The full text of the Protocol is set out in Lowe, Everall and Nicholls, op cit, at 23.6. Guidance on the operation of the Protocol was issued by the President: see 'Implementation of the UK-Pakistan Judicial Protocol on Child Contact and Abduction: Guidance from the President's Office' [2004] IFL 191 and see *Practice Direction 12F* Part 6.

[269] See *Re H (Child Abduction: Mother's Asylum)* [2003] EWHC 1820 (Fam) [2003] 2 FLR 1105— child ordered to be returned notwithstanding the fact that the mother had been granted asylum in the UK on the grounds of her husband's violence. The return was subject to undertakings by the husband inter alia to divorce his wife, to allow her to continue to care for the child until the court ordered otherwise, non-molestation and not to seek disclosure of her address in Pakistan until the court directed otherwise.

[270] As of December 2011 there have been at least 17 applications (in which 15 return orders were made) that have been dealt with by the English courts under the strict terms of the Protocol, with 81 (of which, 61 return orders were made) under the spirit and 85 holiday cases (with 80 return orders being made) in which the Protocol has been cited. In contrast, in Pakistan, 5 applications (in which 1 return order was made) were dealt with under the strict terms of the Protocol, with 13 (in which 1 return order was made) under the spirit of the Protocol: see the statistics produced in the Annual Report of the Head of International Family Justice, reproduced at [2012] IFL 166.

has been questioned both in the UK and Pakistan.[271] It may be argued that, in any event, the Protocol is incompatible with the House of Lords' ruling in *Re J (A Child) (Custody Rights: Jurisdiction).*[272] In this respect it may be noted that in *Re Z (A Child)*[273] a 13-year-old child was ordered to be returned to Pakistan, contrary to her wishes, on the basis of the application of the welfare principle rather than of the Protocol. The Court of Appeal could not fault (and therefore refused permission to appeal against) a first instance decision holding inter alia that the existence of Pakistani residence and contact orders did not oust the application of the welfare principle.

E. DEALING WITH CHILDREN ABDUCTED TO OR BROUGHT FROM A 'CONVENTION COUNTRY'

1. THE RELEVANT INTERNATIONAL INSTRUMENTS

The UK is party to four international instruments dealing with or having relevance to international parental child abduction, namely, the 1980 Hague Abduction Convention, the 1980 European Convention (or Luxembourg Convention, as it is sometimes called), BIIR and the 1996 Hague Protection of Children Convention ('the 1996 Convention').

The UK implemented the two 1980 Conventions through the Child Abduction and Custody Act 1985.[274] Both Conventions apply to children (under the age of 16) taken from the UK to another country that has implemented that Convention (known as a 'Contracting State') and vice versa. As of June 2014 there were 92 Contracting States to the 1980 Hague Abduction Convention and 37 to the 1980 European Convention.[275] Unlike the European Custody Convention, which is confined to Europe, the Contracting States to the 1980 Hague Convention include countries from the Americas, parts of Africa, Asia and Australasia as well as from Europe. It was the first international instrument governing family matters which the USA ratified.

BIIR, as we discussed earlier in this chapter, came into force on 1 March 2005. It binds all Member States of the EU except Denmark.

We discuss the 1996 Convention in more detail at the end of this chapter. Suffice to say here that UK implemented it in November 2012.

---

[271] See J Young 'The Constitutional Limits of Judicial Activism' (2003) 66 MLR 823; M Bashir 'The UK-Pakistan Judicial Protocol: A Need for Greater Judicial Understanding', op cit, at 267–268 and A Darr 'Abduction: Legal remedies in Pakistan' [2010] IFL 269 at 270.

[272] Discussed at The law as settled by *Re J*, p 1026.

[273] [2006] EWCA Civ 1219. See also *Z v Z (Removal of Child: Consent)* [2012] EWHC 3954 (Fam) [2013] 2 FLR 500, in which a return order to Pakistan was made in wardship proceedings. The Protocol did not apply as at the time of the child's removal there was no existing custody order.

[274] For a helpful explanation of the objectives of this Act see Lord Hailsham LC in 460 HL Official Report (5th series) cols 1248 *et seq*, 1985. The 1985 Act contains in its Schedules the texts of the two conventions as implemented by the UK. The full text together with explanation can be found in Cmnd 8155 (1981) (the European Convention) and in Cmnd 8281 (1981) (the Hague Convention). For general contemporary discussion of the Hague Convention see the Explanatory report by E Pérez-Vera (1982) and A E Anton 'The Hague Convention on International Child Abduction' (1981) 30 ICLQ 537, and of the European Convention see R L Jones 'Council of Europe Convention on Recognition and Enforcement of Decisions Relating to the Custody of Children' (1981) 30 ICLQ 467.

[275] A full list of Contracting States (as they affect the UK) can be found in Clarke Hall and Morrison on *Children*, Vol 3 D-16-17. Liechtenstein is the only State to have ratified the 1980 European Custody Convention but not the 1980 Hague Abduction Convention.

2. THE STRATEGY AND AIMS OF THE INTERNATIONAL INSTRUMENTS

A key difference between the two 1980 Conventions is that whereas the Hague Abduction Convention is concerned with the return of children wrongfully removed in breach of rights of custody or in breach of rights of access, the European Convention is concerned with the recognition and enforcement of custody orders and decisions relating to access. In other words, whereas it is a prerequisite for applicants to have a court order in their favour to invoke the European Convention, it is not necessary to have such orders to invoke the Hague Abduction Convention. Nevertheless, although their strategy is different, both Conventions have the same basic aims, namely to trace abducted children, to secure their prompt return and to organise or secure effective rights of access.

Insofar as it applies to child abduction,[276] BIIR governs jurisdiction and, akin to that of the European Convention, provides for a system of recognition and enforcement of custody and access orders. However, unlike the European Convention, BIIR also applies to legally binding *agreements*.[277] In addition, it makes provision for how the courts should apply the 1980 Hague Abduction Convention when considering return applications made by one Member State to another and governs what is to happen if a court refuses to return a child under that Convention.

Like BIIR, the 1996 Convention is a recognition and enforcement instrument and is not specifically concerned with child abduction. However, when BIIR does not apply, it provides an independent means of enforcing custody and access orders and it contains some provisions that are of general application in child abduction cases.[278]

As between Member States of the European Union (except Denmark) BIIR takes precedence over both the 1980 Conventions and the 1996 Convention.[279] Where the Regulation does not apply then, so far as the UK is concerned, the 1980 Hague Abduction Convention takes precedence over the 1980 European Convention.[280] There are, however, no rules governing order of precedence between the 1980 Conventions and the 1996 Convention.

Operationally, the working instrument for dealing with abductions is the 1980 Hague Abduction Convention, though if the case is between two EU Member States (other than Denmark), the Convention's operation will also be governed by BIIR. The scope for invoking the European Convention is severely restricted by BIIR and can effectively only be used where the other state is Denmark or a non-EU state that is party to the 1980 Convention.[281]

3. CENTRAL AUTHORITIES

Under each of the 1980 Conventions, Contracting States are bound to designate an administrative body known as the 'central authority' which has the duty of tracing the child and taking steps, if necessary by court proceedings, to secure the child's return or to secure access. These tasks are carried out mainly at the expense of each authority. To secure the prompt return of children and to achieve the other obligations under the

---

[276] The Regulation has a wider ambit than governing abduction, see The general scope of BIIR, p 995.
[277] See Art 46 discussed at The general scope of BIIR, p 995.   [278] See Commentary, p 1100.
[279] See BIIR, Arts 60(d) and (e) and 61.
[280] See s 16(4)(c) of the Child Abduction and Custody Act 1985.
[281] Viz Andorra, Liechtenstein, Macedonia, Moldova, Norway, Serbia, Switzerland, Turkey and Ukraine.

Conventions[282] central authorities are expected to co-operate with each other. In practice, this administrative system has proved highly successful.[283]

Article 53 of BIIR also requires Member States to designate a central authority. It was envisaged that the same bodies that exercise that function under the 1980 Conventions would also operate the Regulation. Authorities must provide information and assistance to holders of parental responsibility seeking recognition and enforcement of decisions in their territory, in particular concerning rights of access and the return of the child.[284] Central authorities must bear their own costs in discharging their duties and offer their services free of charge.[285]

Contracting States are similarly obliged to designate a central authority under the 1996 Convention.[286] Authorities have mandatory duties to co-operate with other central authorities and to provide information about their law and services, and among their specific duties are to provide assistance in discovering the whereabouts of the child and to facilitate by mediation, conciliation or similar means, agreed solutions for the protection of children.[287]

In England and Wales the Central Authority for the 1980 Conventions and BIIR is the Lord Chancellor,[288] who has delegated the day-to-day operational functions to the International Child Abduction and Contact Unit (ICACU), which is based in London. In England there is a similar arrangement under the 1996 Convention[289] but there is a separate central authority for Wales, namely, the Welsh ministers,[290] who have delegated the operational functions to the Welsh Government Child Social Services.

4. HOW ABDUCTION APPLICATIONS ARE HANDLED

In the case of children taken from England and Wales the transmission of applications overseas will normally be handled by the ICACU. In the case of children wrongfully brought to this country the practice is that, upon receiving an application which it is satisfied is in correct form, the ICACU allocates (usually within 24 hours) the case to a specialist firm of solicitors drawn from a national panel of 41 firms. The ICACU does not 'instruct' the panel solicitor and the applicant is the solicitor's not the ICACU's client.

Immediately upon the receipt of the application, the panel solicitor will apply for public funding which, in the case of applications made under the 1980 Convention, will be granted regardless of the applicant's means and will not be subject to a merits test.[291] In other words, an important advantage for a foreign citizen in using a Convention rather than a domestic jurisdiction such as wardship is that they will be able to obtain free legal representation.[292] Once legal aid is granted (normally within 48 hours), the solicitor has sole responsibility for the conduct of the case and will seek to resolve the case as quickly as possible.

---

[282] Viz. those set out in Art 7 of the Hague Convention and Art 5 of the European Convention.

[283] See C Bruch 'The Central Authority's role under the Hague Abduction conventions—A friend indeed' (1994) 28 FLQ 34.

[284] See Art 55.   [285] See Art 57.   [286] By Art 29.   [287] See Arts 30 and 31.

[288] Child Abduction and Custody Act 1985 ss 3 and 14, in the case of the 1980 Conventions, and FPR 2010 r 12.58, for BIIR.   [289] See FPR 2010 r 12.58(1)(b), as amended.

[290] See FPR 2010 r 12.58(1)(c), as amended.

[291] Legal Aid, Sentencing and Punishment of Offenders Act 2012 Part I of Sch 1 para 18(3) and Civil Legal Aid (Financial Resources and Payments of Services) Regulations 2013 (SI 2013/480) Pert 2 Chapter 1 reg 5(1)(h).

[292] Such arrangements, however, are not reciprocated in every other Convention country, notably the USA.

5. THE 1980 HAGUE ABDUCTION CONVENTION

(a) What the Convention is trying to do

Securing prompt returns and respect for rights of access

A feature of the 1980 Hague Abduction Convention[293] is the simplicity of its objectives which are set out in Art 1:

> (a) to secure the prompt return of children wrongfully removed to or retained in any Contracting State; and
> (b) to ensure that rights of custody and access under the law of one Contracting State are respected in other Contracting States.

These objectives are based, as the Preamble explains, upon the firm conviction 'that the interests of children are of paramount importance in matters relating to their custody' and upon the desire 'to protect children internationally from the harmful effects of their wrongful removal or retention and to establish procedures to ensure their prompt return to the State of their habitual residence, as well as to secure protection for rights of access'.

Although there is no formal hierarchy of objectives under the Convention,[294] the vast majority of applications (84% according to the 2008 Statistical Survey) are for return.

The relevance of the child's welfare

The Preamble refers to the 'paramount' importance of the interests of the children in matters relating to their custody but this does not mean that an *individual* child's welfare is paramount in a Hague return application. As the Canadian Supreme Court pointed out,[295] the Preamble 'speaks of the "interests of children" generally, not the interest of the particular child before the court'. In *Re E (Children) (Abduction: Custody Appeal)*[296] the English Supreme Court rejected the argument that Hague proceedings are governed by s 1 of the Children Act 1989. As Baroness Hale and Lord Wilson said,[297] Hague applications 'are not proceedings in which the upbringing of the child is in issue. They are proceedings about where the child should be when that issue is decided.' In any event, Art 16 expressly forbids the court of the requested State from deciding on the merits of the rights of custody until it has been determined that the child is not to be returned under the Convention.[298]

---

[293] See generally R Schuz *The Hague Child Abduction Convention – A Critical Analysis* (2013); K Trimmings *Child Abduction Within The European Union* (2013); D Hodson *The International Family Law Practice 2013-2014* (2013, 3rd edn) ch 15; S Vigers *Mediating International Child Abduction Cases* (2012); N Lowe, M Everall and M Nicholls *International Movement of Children, Law Practice and Procedure* (2004); P Beaumont and P McEleavy *The Hague Convention on International Child Abduction* (1999); and M Weiner 'Uprooting Children in the Name of Equity' (2101) Fordham Int Law Jo 409.

[294] See the Pérez-Vera Report at para 18 but cf *Thomson v Thomson* [1994] 3 SCR 551, Can Sup Ct, in which La Forest J commented that it was clear 'that the primary object of the Convention is the enforcement of custody rights'.   [295] Per La Forest J in *Thomson v Thomson*.

[296] [2011] UKSC 27 [2012] 1 AC 144, on which see V Stephens and N Lowe 'Children's welfare and human rights under the 1980 Hague Abduction Convention—the ruling in *Re E*' (2012) 34 JSWFL 125.

[297] [2011] UKSC 27 [2012] 1 AC 144 at [13]. Baroness Hale and Lord Wilson gave the joint decision of the Court.

[298] See also Art 19 which provides that a decision to return the child under the Convention 'shall not be taken to be a determination on the merits of any custody issue'.

Compatibility with the UN Convention on the Rights of the Child

Not treating an individual child's interests as the paramount consideration when determining a return application raises the issue of the 1980 Convention's compatibility with Art 3 of the UN Convention on the Rights of the Child 1989 (UNCRC) which provides that in all actions concerning children 'whether undertaken by public or private social welfare institutions, courts of law, administrative authorities or legislative bodies, *the best interests of the child shall be a primary consideration*'. Addressing this question, and having noted the Supreme Court's earlier observation[299] that '*a* primary consideration' is not the same as '*the* primary consideration' still less as 'the paramount consideration', the Supreme Court in *Re E* held that a court's faithful application of the 1980 Convention is compliant with Art 3 of UNCRC. It observed that the fact that the return mechanism under the 1980 Convention does not expressly consider the best interests of the child 'does not mean that they are not at the forefront of the whole exercise.'[300] To the contrary, the Convention does aim to serve the best interests of the individual child by making certain rebuttable assumptions about what will best achieve this. As the Court put it:[301]

> The premise is that there is a left-behind person who also has a legitimate interest in the future welfare of the child: without the existence of such a person the removal is not wrongful. The assumption then is that if there is a dispute about any aspect of the future upbringing of the child the interests of the child should be of paramount importance in resolving that dispute. Unilateral action should not be permitted to pre-empt or delay that resolution. Hence the next assumption is that the best interests of the child will be served by a prompt return to the country where she is habitually resident. Restoring a child to her familiar surroundings is likely to be a good thing in its own right.

On this analysis the 1980 Convention was said to be[302] 'devised with the best interests of children generally, and of the individual children involved in such proceedings, as a primary consideration'.

Another pointer to compatibility is Art 11 of UNCRC, which entreats States 'to take measures to combat the illicit transfer and non-return of children abroad',[303] and Art 35 which requires States Parties to 'take all appropriate national, bilateral and multilateral measures to prevent the abduction of, the sale of or traffic in children for any purpose or in any form.'

Compatibility with the European Convention on Human Rights

English courts have long taken the view that as between the parents and the child sought to be returned a return order will rarely be thought to be in breach of Art 8 of the European Convention on Human Rights as interfering with the right to respect for family life.[304] Even with regard to a sibling who is not the subject of the application, though a return

---

[299] In *ZH (Tanzania) v Secretary of State for the Home Department* [2011] UKSC 4 [2011] 2 AC 166 at [25].
[300] [2011] UKSC 4 [2011] 2 AC 166 at [14].   [301] Ibid at [15].
[302] Ibid at [18]. For authoritative rulings on the compatibility of the 1980 Convention and UNCRC in other jurisdictions, see eg *DP v Commonwealth Central Authority* [2001] HCA 39 (Australia), *W v O*, 14 June 1995 (INCADAT cite: HC/E/AR 362) (Argentina) and *G and G v Decision of OLG Hamm* 18 January 1995, 35 ILM 529 (1996) (Germany).
[303] It was on the basis of Art 11 that the Full Court of the Family Court of Australia, rejected the charge of incompatibility in *In the Marriage of Murray and Tam* (1993) 16 Fam LR 982.
[304] See *Re F (Abduction: Child's Right to Family Life)* [1999] Fam Law 806 in which custody of two girls had been shared between the unmarried Portuguese parents. However, the mother, who had subsequently come

INTERNATIONAL ASPECTS OF CHILD LAW

order necessarily engages his Art 8 rights, pressure on his or her private life cannot be avoided if the protection and freedoms of the other family members are accorded the precedence required by the Hague Convention.[305] In other words, interference with a sibling's Art 8 rights by making a return order in respect of the child who is the subject of proceedings is justified if it is in accordance with the law, in pursuit of a legitimate aim and necessary and proportionate in a democratic society. It has been held by the European Court of Human Rights (ECtHR) that the enforcement of an order in conformity with a CJEU ruling will not be considered to violate human rights.[306]

Nevertheless, as Baroness Hale pointed out in *Re D (Abduction: Rights of Custody)*,[307] this does not mean that human rights arguments are irrelevant to Hague cases since in some cases it might be appropriate to argue that a return or non-return would be a disproportionate interference with the right to respect for the family life of a particular parent with the child or as between siblings. Furthermore, it is well established that the failure *expeditiously* to enforce a return order under the Hague Convention can be a breach of Art 8 on the basis of a failure to meet the positive obligation on States to ensure effective respect for family life by taking measures to enforce a parent's right to be reunited with his or her child.[308] It has also been held[309] that the failure to inform the divorce courts of the existence of Hague Convention proceedings deprived the Convention of its very purpose, namely, to prevent a decision on the merits of the right to custody being taken in the State of refuge, and had thus been in breach of Art 8.

The ECtHR (Grand Chamber) ruling in *Neulinger and Shuruk v Switzerland*[310] that on the facts the enforcement of a return order made some four years earlier would violate both the abducting parent's and the child's Art 8 rights since it would amount to a disproportionate interference with their right to respect private and family life, caused the question of the application of human rights considerations to Hague applications to be revisited. However, in *Re E (Children) (Abduction: Custody Appeal)*,[311] the Supreme Court essentially re-stated the previously accepted position. As Baroness Hale and Lord Wilson observed,[312] the most that can be said was that *Neulinger* (and an earlier decision, *Maumousseau and Washington v France*)[313] acknowledges:

---

to England with one daughter and wrongfully detained the other, unsuccessfully argued that by splitting the two siblings a return order would be in breach of Art 8 ECHR. As Cazalet J pointed out, the mother's own actions had disrupted the previous settled arrangements sanctioned by the Portuguese court.

[305] See *S v B (Abduction: Human Rights)* [2005] EWHC 733 (Fam),[2005] 2 FLR 878.

[306] *Povse v Austria* [2014] 1 FLR 944.   [307] [2006] UKHL 51 [2007] 1 AC 619 at [65].

[308] See eg *Shaw v Hungary* [2012] 2 FLR 1314, discussed further at The timing obligation under Art 11(3), p 1076, *Ignaccolo-Zenide v Romania* (Application No. 31679/96) (2001) 31 EHRR 7, ECtHR; *Sylvester v Austria* (Application Nos 36812/97 and 40104/98) [2003] 2 FLR 211, ECtHR on which see W Duncan *The Judges' Newsletter* Vol VI, Autumn 2003, 53–54 and *Maire v Portugal* (Application No. 48206/99) [2004] 2 FLR 653, ECtHR. See also the excellent analysis by A Schulz 'The 1980 Hague Child Abduction Convention and the European Convention on Human Rights' in (2002) 12 *Transnational Law and Contemporary Problems* 355.

[309] *Iosub Caras v Romania* [2007] 1 FLR 660.

[310] [2011] 1 FLR 122, on which see Judge J Costa 'The Best Interests. Of the Child: Recent Case-law from the European Court of Human Rights' [2011] IFL 183, in which the then President of the Court sought to draw back from some of the implications of *Neulinger*. See also N Lowe 'A supra-national approach to interpreting the 1980 Hague Abduction Convention – a tale of two European courts. Part 2 the substantive impact of the two European Courts' ruling upon the application of the 1980 Convention' [2012] IFL 170.

[311] [2011] UKSC 27 [2012] 1 AC 144, on which see D Wheeler '*Re E (Children)*: Understanding the implications of *Neulinger* and *Maumousseau*' [2011] IFL 224. Note also *Re S (A Child) (Abduction: Rights of Custody)* [2012] UKSC 10 [2012] 2 AC 257.

[312] [2011] UKSC 27 [2012] 1 AC 144 at [26].   [313] [2007] 51 EHRR 822.

that the guarantees in article 8 have to be interpreted and applied in the light of both the Hague Convention and the UNCRC: that all are designed with the best interests of the child as a primary consideration; that in every Hague Convention case where the question is raised, the national court does not order return automatically and mechanically but examines the particular child in order to ascertain whether a return would be in accordance with the Convention; but that is not the same as a full blown examination of the child's future; and that it is, to say the least, unlikely that if the Hague Convention is properly applied, with whatever outcome, there will be a violation of the article 8 rights of the child or of either of the parents.

The Supreme Court did not rule out highly unusual cases where a return order could violate Art 8,[314] but as was said 'that is a far cry from the suggestion that article 8 "trumps" the Hague Convention: in virtually all cases, as the Strasbourg court has shown, they march hand in hand'.

Enjoinders repeatedly made by the ECtHR[315] that to be human rights compliant when making decisions under the 1980 Convention, courts should conduct an 'in-depth examination of the whole family situation' seemed to run counter to the embargo against investigating the merits or at least came perilously close to doing so and were in any event resisted by the English Supreme Court.[316] However, in the Grand Chamber decision in *X v Latvia*,[317] the ECtHR Grand Chamber helpfully clarified the position, commenting[318] that:

The court considers that a harmonious interpretation of the European Convention and the Hague Convention…can be achieved provided that the following two conditions are observed. First, the factors capable of constituting an exception to the child's immediate return under Arts 12, 13 and 20 of the said Convention, particularly where they are raised by one of parties to the proceedings, must genuinely be taken into account by the requested court. The court must then make a decision that is sufficiently reasoned on this point in order to enable the court to verify that those questions have been effectively examined Secondly, these factors must be evaluated in the light of Art 8 of the European Convention.

It remains to be seen how the jurisprudence develops. It is worth pointing out, however, that there is no indication as to what is meant by an 'in-depth examination' and while court hearings can often last days in common law systems, in civil systems they tend to be measured in terms of hours.

Commentary

Whether the Hague Convention strikes the right balance can be legitimately debated. There are those who argue that generally too little attention is paid to the interests of the

---

[314] As, for example, by exposing an abducting parent returning to face a real risk of torture or degrading treatment and where a child cannot be safely returned without that parent. Cf human rights issues arising in the context of the court of the child's habitual residence ordering a child's return pursuant to Art 11 (7) of BIIR following an initial refusal to return by the 'abduction court' (discussed at The position following a refusal to return—Art 11(6)–(8), p 1077), see *Šneersone and Kampanella v Italy* [2011] 2 FLR 1232, ECHR.

[315] See in particular *Neulinger and Shuruk v Switzerland* [2011] 1 FLR 122 (Grand Chamber); *Raban v Israel* [2010] ECHR 1625 and, at first instance, *X v Latvia* [2012] 1 FLR 860.

[316] See *Re E* and *Re S*, earlier   [317] [2014] 1 FLR 1135.

[318] At 106. It may nevertheless be noted that notwithstanding this softening of approach Latvia was still found by a majority of 9 to 8, to have violated Art 8 by not considering a psychiatrist's report that the mother wished to put into evidence.

children,[319] while, on the other, there are those who will say too great a latitude is given, principally through the exceptions provided by Art 13, to courts to refuse a return. Nevertheless, it is to be observed that not only is the 1980 Convention thought to be basically compatible with the two major so-called 'Rights Conventions', but also that its fundamental premise that the court of the State of the child's habitual residence is best able to hear the merits of a custody case, forms the basis of the 1996 Hague Convention on the Protection of Children[320] and underpins BIIR, under which, as between Member States of the European Union, even if the requested State refuses to make a return order under the Hague Convention, the child's home court still retains jurisdiction to hear the merits of a custody dispute.[321]

Seeking a child's return

The general procedure

A person claiming that a child has been taken to or detained in another Contracting State, and who wishes to secure the child's return, can seek assistance from the central authority of the child's habitual residence or from the authority of the State to which the child has been taken. Although by Art 29, direct application may be made to the judicial or administrative authorities of a Contracting State, applicants are normally best advised to apply via their own central authority.

Upon receiving the relevant documents the central authority will transmit the application to the appropriate central authority (Art 9) in another Contracting State which must then take steps to discover the child's whereabouts and seek the child's return. The authorities must act expeditiously. If no decision has been reached within six weeks of the commencement of proceedings, the requesting central authority or the applicant has the right to request a statement of the reasons for delay (Art 11).[322] The central authority may refuse an application where it is manifest that the requirements of the Convention are not fulfilled or that the application is not well founded (Art 27).[323]

The court's role

To facilitate the child's return, application may be made to a judicial or administrative authority of the requested State. Article 16 forbids a court from investigating the merits of the rights to custody until it has been determined that the child is not to be returned under the Convention or unless the application has not been lodged within a reasonable time following receipt of the notice.[324] Equally, a decision to return the child is not to be taken to be a determination on the merits of any custody issue (Art 19). So far as England and Wales is concerned all Convention applications are dealt with by the High Court.[325]

Under the Child Abduction and Custody Act 1985 s 5, upon an application being made, the court may give such interim directions as it thinks fit 'for the purpose of securing the

---

[319] For a critical examination of the application of the welfare principle under the Convention, see R. Schuz 'The Hague Child Abduction Convention: Family Law and Private International Law' (1995) 44 ICLQ 771. [320] Discussed at The jurisdictional rules, p 1093.

[321] See The position following a refusal to return—Art 11(6)–(8), p 1077.

[322] It will be noted that this provision stops short of directing States to resolve return applications within six weeks. However, there *is* a six week *obligation* imposed by Art 11(3) of the revised Brussels II Regulations, see further The timing obligation under Art 11(3), p 1076.

[323] According to the 2008 Statistical Survey, op cit, the ICACU rejected 2% of applications as against a global average of 5%.

[324] Effectively this freezes any prior applications, including, in England and Wales, any child arrangements order concerning the child's living arrangements or wardship applications: s 9 and s 27 of the Child Abduction and Custody Act 1985.

[325] Child Abduction and Custody Act 1985 s 4; by contrast, in a number of other jurisdictions (eg Germany and USA) jurisdiction is vested in courts at the lowest level.

welfare of the child concerned or of preventing changes in the circumstances relevant to the determination of the application'. Exercising this power, it has been held appropriate to authorise the Tipstaff to collect the child and return him to the applicant, even before the child's arrival in the jurisdiction[326] and, when all other alternative arrangements have been considered and found wanting, and notwithstanding the statutory scheme under the Children Act 1989, to make arrangements to place the child with a local authority.[327] Interim directions may also include orders for electronic tagging[328] and for direct or indirect contact.

If the application is brought within one year of the wrongful removal or retention, Art 12 directs the court to 'order the return of the child forthwith'. If more than a year has elapsed, the child should still be returned 'unless it is demonstrated that the child is now settled in its new environment'. Article 12, however, is subject to Art 13, which provides for exceptional circumstances in which a return may be refused. The burden of establishing these exceptions lies on the respondent. The Convention provides, via Art 20, an additional ground for refusing a return where to do so 'would not be permitted by the fundamental principles of the requested State relating to the protection of human rights and fundamental freedoms'. However, the UK has not implemented Art 20 in part because its meaning and scope 'would at least be uncertain', in part because it could not 'be easily accommodated in a UK legal text' and in part because in any event situations triggering Art 20 would probably be covered by Arts 12 and 13.[329] In fact, global use of this exception is limited.[330]

The normal expectation is that the court will order the child's return. Furthermore, even if an exception is established, the court still has a discretion to order a return under Art 18.[331] It is conceivable that a child's return might be successfully opposed on grounds *outside* the terms of Art 12 or Art 13, but the court is likely to be reluctant to undermine the spirit of the Convention.[332]

We discuss the exceptions to the duty to return later in the chapter.

(b) When the Convention applies

By Art 4, the 1980 Convention applies to any child, under the age of 16 and habitually resident in one Contracting State, who has been wrongfully removed or retained in another Contracting State.[333] To appreciate the scope of Art 4 it is necessary to explore the meaning of 'child', 'habitual residence' and 'wrongful removal or retention'.

---

[326] *Re N (Child Abduction: Jurisdiction)* [1995] Fam 95.

[327] *Re A (Children) (Abduction: Interim Powers)* [2010] EWCA Civ 586 [2011] Fam 179.

[328] See *Re A (Family Proceedings: Electronic Tagging)* [2009] EWHC 210 (Fam) [2009] 2 FLR 891.

[329] See Lord Hailsham LC in the debate on the Child Abduction and Custody Bill in Hansard HL Deb Vol 461 at col 1175. But had the 1985 Act followed rather than preceded the Human Rights Act 1998, there would have been no reason not to incorporate Art 20, see *Re J (A Child) (Custody Rights: Jurisdiction)* [2005] UKHL 40 [2005] 3 WLR 14 at [44] per Baroness Hale. For a detailed discussion of Art 20 see Lowe, Everall and Nicholls, op cit, at 17.86 *et seq.*

[330] According to the 1999 statistical survey no application was refused on this ground but there were four such refusals (all in Chile) found in the 2003 survey. The 2008 recorded no refusal solely based on Art 20 but two partially relying upon it. For an argument that it should be used more often see M Weiner 'Strengthening Article 20' (2004) 38 Univ of San Francisco Law Review 701, summarised at [2005] IFL 209.

[331] See The residual discretion to return, p 1068.

[332] In *Re B (Minors) (Abduction) (No 1)* [1993] 1 FLR 988, for example, the court rejected an application to have proceedings stayed or dismissed because of the applicant's active participation in the respondent's English family proceedings.

[333] But for the purposes of access it has been held sufficient for the child to be habitually resident in *a* Contracting State at the time of breach: *Re G (A Minor) (Enforcement of Access Abroad)* [1993] Fam 216, discussed further at Securing rights of access, p 1081. In the case of a re-abduction, the court may refuse to hear the case: *Re O (Child Abduction: Re-Abduction)* [1997] 2 FLR 712 (child abducted to Sweden and then to England).

Child

The 1980 Convention does not apply to unborn children. As Hedley J said in *Re F (Abduction: Unborn Child)*,[334] 'it is not possible in law to abduct a foetus so as to constitute a wrongful removal within the terms of Art 3 of the Convention'. Furthermore, the provision in Art 4 that the Convention ceases to apply when the child attains the age of 16 has been strictly interpreted such that even where the application was properly brought in the first place there is no power *under the* Convention[335] to continue with proceedings once the child becomes 16 notwithstanding that it would continue to apply to a younger sibling.[336]

Habitual residence

Before a wrongful removal or retention can be established under the Convention it has to be shown that the child has been removed from or retained out of the State of his or her habitual residence.[337] In other words, it is the residence immediately before the wrongful removal or retention that is relevant.[338] Since it is a requirement to be habitually resident in a *Contracting State*, it follows that the Convention is not retrospective in the sense that the wrongful act must have taken place after the Contracting State has implemented the Convention.[339]

It is well established that for these purposes it is not possible for a child to have two habitual residences simultaneously,[340] although, in principle, it might be possible to establish alternating habitual residences.

The general meaning

Habitual residence is not defined by the Convention. Nevertheless while it is accepted that it is for the requested State to determine habitual residence and notwithstanding that the lack of a Convention definition, the concept is properly considered to have an autonomous rather than a domestic law meaning.[341]

Given its significance in establishing 'abduction' coupled with the lack of definition, it is hardly surprising that the concept of 'habitual residence' has generated considerable jurisprudence, particularly by the English courts when applying the 1980 Convention but also by the CJEU when applying various Regulations. Happily, some of this jurisprudence has been rendered of historic interest by the Supreme Court ruling in *A v A (Children: Habitual Residence) (Reunite International Child Abduction Centre intervening)*[342] and

---

[334] [2006] EWHC 2199 (Fam), [2007] 1 FLR 626 at [5]. However, as that case shows, that does not prevent arguments being raised about wrongful retention *subsequent* to the child's birth.

[335] Though there is power to deal with a child, whilst still a minor, under the High Court's inherent jurisdiction, see eg *Re C (Abduction: Separate Representation of Children)* [2008] EWHC 517 (Fam) [2008] 2 FLR 6.   [336] *Re H (Abduction: Child of 16)* [2000] 2 FLR 51.

[337] See generally Clarke Hall and Morrison on *Children*, 5[231]ff.

[338] *Re S (A Minor) (Abduction)* [1991] 2 FLR 1, CA. See also *Re F (A Minor) (Child Abduction)* [1992] 1 FLR 548, CA.

[339] *Re H (Minors) (Abduction: Custody Rights), Re S (Minors) (Abduction: Custody Rights)* [1991] 2 AC 476, HL. A similar conclusion had been reached in Scotland in *Kilgour v Kilgour* 1987 SLT 568. For this reason the implementation dates (for which see Clarke Hall and Morrison Vol 3, at D [2104]) are important.

[340] *Re L (Recognition of Foreign Order)* [2012] EWCA Civ 1157 [2013] Fam 94 at [67], per Munby LJ and *Re V (Abduction: Habitual Residence)* [1995] 2 FLR 992.

[341] Per Lord Hughes in *A v A (Children: Habitual Residence) (Reunite Child International Abduction Centre intervening)* [2013] UKSC 60 [2014] AC 1, at [80 i)] relying on *Proceedings brought by A* (Case C-523/07) [2010] Fam 42.   [342] [2013] UKSC 60 [2014] AC 1.

by the CJEU decision in *Proceedings brought by A*.[343] Nevertheless there is running tension between insisting that the concept is a factual one, which has been the long-standing 'English' position, and the relevance of intention, which is perhaps more of an element in the 'European' definition. [344] The English courts have also been insistent that no legal gloss should be placed on the factual concept. It was for this reason that the Supreme Court rejected the argument that a child cannot acquire a new habitual residence pending the outcome of an appeal.[345]

In *A v A* Baroness Hale, giving the majority judgment, felt able draw the following threads together:[346]

(i)   ...habitual residence is a question of fact and not a legal concept such as domicile. There is no legal rule akin to that whereby a child automatically takes the domicile of his parents.

(ii) It was the purpose of the [Family Law] 1986 Act to adopt a concept which was the same as that adopted in the Hague and European Conventions. The [revised Brussels II] Regulation must also be interpreted consistently with those Conventions.

(iii) The test adopted by the European court is 'the place which reflects some degree of integration by the child in a social and family environment' in the country concerned. This depends on numerous factors, including the reasons for the family's stay in the country in question.

(iv) It is now unlikely that that test would produce any different results from that hitherto adopted by the English courts under the 1986 Act and the Hague Child Abduction Convention.

(v)   In my view, the test adopted by the European court is preferable to that earlier adopted by the English courts, being more focussed on the situation of the child, with the purposes and intentions of the parents being merely one of the relevant factors. The test derived from *R v Barnet London Borough Council, Ex p Shah*[347] should be abandoned when deciding the habitual residence of a child.

(vi) The social and family environment of an infant or young child is shared with those (whether parents or others) on whom he is dependent. Hence it is necessary to assess the integration of that person or persons in the social and family environment of the country concerned.

(vii) The essentially factual and individual nature of the inquiry should not be glossed with legal concepts which would produce a different result from that which the factual inquiry would produce.

(viii) As the Advocate General pointed out in opinion, para 45 and the court confirmed in judgment, para 43 of *Proceedings brought by A*, it is possible that child may have no country of habitual residence at a particular point in time.

---

[343] (Case C-523/07) [2010] Fam 42.

[344] Ironically, one of the reasons for using it is to avoid the concept of 'domicile', which is even more difficult to apply, since it depends upon the party's intention where he or she is *permanently* to reside. Habitual residence is also thought less artificial than 'nationality'. For discussion of the merits of the various connecting factors see H Thue 'Connecting Factors in International Law' in N Lowe and G Douglas (eds) *Families Across Frontiers* (1996) 53.

[345] See *Re L (A Child) (Custody: Habitual Residence) (Reunite International Child Abduction Centre intervening)* [2013] UKSC 75 [2013] 3 WLR 1597, in which a mother brought a child to England pursuant to a return order made by a court in Texas which was subsequently overturned on appeal.

[346] [2013] UKSC 60 [2014] AC 1 at [54]. Although Lord Hughes dissented in part, he agreed with this summary, see [81].   [347] [1983] 2 AC 309.

A v A helpfully establishes that the concept of habitual residence should be interpreted as having the same meaning under the 1980 Hague Abduction Convention as under the BIIR and that that test is the one laid down by the European Court in *Proceedings brought by A*, namely:[348]

> as meaning that it corresponds to the place which reflects some degree of integration by the child in a social and family environment. To that end, in particular the duration, regularity, conditions and reasons for the stay on the territory of a Member State and the family's move to that State, the child's nationality, the place and conditions of attendance at school, linguistic knowledge and the family and social relationships of the child in that State must be taken into consideration. It is for the national court to establish the habitual residence of the child, taking account of all the circumstances specific to each individual case.

A was followed by *Mercredi v Chaffe*[349] in which the CJEU re-emphasised that habitual residence must be distinguished from mere temporary residence and, as a general rule, must have a certain duration to reflect an adequate degree of permanence. Nevertheless BIIR does not lay down a minimum period of residence. The Court added:[350]

> Before habitual residence can be transferred to the host State, it is of paramount importance that the person concerned has it in mind to establish there the permanent or habitual centre of his interests, with the intention that it should be of a lasting character. Accordingly, the duration of a stay can serve only as an indicator in the assessment of the permanence of the residence, and the assessment must be carried out in the light of all circumstances of fact specific to the individual case.

The Court repeated its point made in *Re A* that it is for the national court to determine the habitual residence in all the particular circumstances of the case.

The reference to 'permanence' in *Mercredi*, which was not made in *Re A*, led to some concern being expressed in the English courts. However, following Sir Peter Singer's analysis in *DL v EL (Hague Abduction Convention: Effect of Reversal of Return Order on Appeal)*[351] at first instance and endorsed by the Court of Appeal[352] in which he compared the French and English texts of the judgment in *Mercredi*, it is accepted that the reference to 'permanence' was not being used by the CJEU in the sense of forever or even necessarily indefinite, the contrast is with the idea of 'temporary' or stability. This view has also been endorsed by the Supreme Court in *A v A*.[353]

In the course of emphasising the factual nature of habitual residence the Supreme Court in *A v A* considered the effect of Lord Brandon's dictum in *Re J (A Minor) (Abduction: Custody Rights)*:[354]

---

[348]   [2010] Fam 4, at para 44. It was applied by the Supreme Court in *Re LC (Children) (Reunite International Child Abduction Centre intervening)* [2014] UKSC 1 [2014] 2 WLR 124.

[349]   (Case C-497/10 PPU) [2012] Fam 27—the first BIIR reference from a UK court (see further Background, p 995), on which see D Williams 'Wednesday's Child is Full of Woe—*Mercredi v Chaffe*: To the CJEU and Back Again' [2011] IFL 196. For the domestic sequel to this decision, see *Mercredi v Chaffe* [2011] EWCA Civ 272 [2011] 3 WLR 1229.   [350]   At para [51].

[351]   [2013] EWHC 49 (Fam) [2013] 2 FLR 163 at [74]ff.

[352]   *DL v EL (Reunite International Child Abduction Centre intervening)* [2013] EWCA Civ 865 [2013] 3 FCR 69, not commented upon on appeal to the Supreme Court, *Re L (A Child) (Custody: Habitual Residence) (Reunite International Child Abduction Centre intervening)* [2013] UKSC 75 [2013] 3 WLR 1597.

[353]   [2013] UKSC 60 [2014] AC 1 at [51], per Baroness Hale and at [80 vii], per Lord Hughes.

[354]   [1990] 2 AC 562, at 578.

The third point is that there is a significant difference between a person ceasing to be habitually resident in country A, and his subsequently becoming habitually resident in country B. A person may cease to be habitually resident in country A in a single day if he or she leaves it with a settled intention not to return to it but to take up long-term residence in Country B instead. Such a person cannot, however become habitually resident in Country B in a single day. An appreciable period of time and a settled intention will be necessary to enable him or her to become so. During that appreciable period of time the person will have ceased to be habitually resident in country A but not yet have become habitually resident in country B. The fourth point is that where the habitual residence of a young child is in question, the element of volition will usually be that of the person or persons who has or have the parental responsibility for that child.

As Lord Hughes said in *A v A*,[355] the cited passage:

offers at least three generally stated propositions, many of which have since been treated in some quarters as amounting to propositions of law. One is that habitual residence in country A may be abandoned in a single day. A second is that habitual residence in country B cannot be established (or, as English lawyers are prone to say, 'acquired') in a single day, and a third is that an infant who is in the sole lawful custody of his mother will necessarily have the same habitual residence as she has (or, as English lawyers are prone to say, will 'derive' his habitual residence from hers).

Both Lord Hughes and Baroness Hale considered[356] that Lord Brandon's propositions are best regarded as helpful generalisations of fact rather than propositions of law. Indeed, Baroness Hale expressly rejected the proposition that it is impossible to become habitually resident in a single day but she did accept that 'one may cease to be habitually resident in one country without yet having become habitually resident in another.'

The issue in *A v A* itself was whether it is ever possible to be considered habitually resident in a State in which one has never set foot. This has exercised the courts on more than one occasion, particularly in relation to new born children.[357] In *A v A* the facts were stark since the mother, who was undoubtedly habitually resident in England as were her three elder children, had been effectively kept in Pakistan against her will and had the baby there. She managed to retrieve her passport and returned to England but without her children. Although the majority held that had jurisdiction depended on answering this question[358] they would have had to make a reference to the CJEU as the matter could not be said to be *acte claire*,[359] it was clear that they took the view that a factum of residence is required in order to establish habitual residence.[360] Lord Hughes dissented on

---

[355] [2013] UKSC 60 [2014] AC 1 at [72].   [356] See [73] and [44] respectively.

[357] See eg *B v H (Habitual Residence: Wardship)* [2002] 1 FLR 388, in which Charles J held that 'generally a baby born of a married couple (who are habitually resident in England at the time of the birth of the child) will also at birth generally be habitually resident in England, notwithstanding that he (or she) is born abroad.' Cf *Re F (Abduction: Unborn Child)* [2006] EWHC 2199 (Fam) [2007] 1 FLR 626 in which Hedley J commented that while habitual residence might exceptionally be possible notwithstanding physical absence the usual approach is to look for some physical presence. In that case the court refused to make a declaration concerning the habitual residence of a mother and child, the mother having travelled to Israel during her pregnancy with the father's consent and who remained there with the baby after the birth.

[358] It was held that jurisdiction to ward the baby could be taken on the basis of his British nationality, see Ch 20.   [359] For the meaning of which, see Background, p 995.

[360] Indeed it was necessary consequence of the decision to apply Art 14 of BIIR (discussed at Position where no Member State has jurisdiction pursuant to Arts 8–13, p 1000) that the child was not habitually resident in England and Wales.

this point and it is noticeable that unlike the Court of Appeal,[361] the Supreme Court has not overruled *B v H*.[362] It seems implicit in *Mercredi v Chaffe*[363] that a factum of residence is required.

As Lord Hughes observed in *A v A*,[364] simple physical presence is not by itself sufficient to establish habitual residence and it will be a matter for the court in any particular case to decide whether the established residence has matured in habitual residence. The key enquiry, in line with the CJEU test, is to determine whether the child has become integrated in the social and family environment.[365] It remains the case that there is no fixed period by which this can be established. As Lord Slynn said in *Nessa v Chief Adjudication Officer*,[366] 'the requisite period is not a fixed period. It may be longer where there are doubts.' Alternatively, where there are no doubts it may be short. In *Re F (A Minor) (Child Abduction)*,[367] for example, the Court of Appeal approved a judicial finding that a family had acquired a fresh habitual residence only one month after arrival in a new country. In that case Butler-Sloss LJ observed[368] that a court 'should not strain to find a lack of habitual residence where, on a broad canvas, the child has settled in a particular country' since without such an habitual residence the child cannot be protected under the Convention. In *Re S (Habitual Residence)*,[369] a period of seven–eight weeks was held sufficient to establish habitual residence.

In *Re P-J (Children) (Abduction: Consent)*[370] habitual residence was established by the children spending an academic year (as the parties had agreed) in Wales. *Re P-J* was followed in *Re H-K (Habitual Residence)*,[371] in which children were found to be habitually resident in the UK following the family's relocation from Australia which was initially planned to last one year. In fact, after ten months, the mother informed the father that she would not return and it was agreed that she and the children would stay for a further four months.

Although it was accepted in *A v A* that it will normally be the case that while the parents are living together their young child will be regarded as having the same habitual residence as the parents, it is not an invariable rule. Indeed, in *Re M (Abduction: Habitual Residence)*[372] the Court of Appeal rejected the suggestion that it was a proposition of law that a 'child's habitual residence is that of the parents unless they agree that it shall have some other habitual residence and so long as that agreement continues'. Accordingly,

---

[361] [2012] EWCA Civ 1396 [2013] 2 WLR 1061.   [362] Referred to at n 357.

[363] (Case C-497/10 PPU) [2012] Fam 27, CJEU.

[364] [2013] UKSC 60 [2014] AC 1 at [80 (iv)].

[365] Cf in the divorce context, *Mark v Mark* [2005] UKHL 42 [2006] 1 AC 98, in which the House of Lords ruled that habitual residence can be established by a person whose presence in the jurisdiction is illegal. In *Re H (A Child) (Abduction: Habitual Residence: Agreement)* [2012] EWCA Civ 148 [2013] 2 FLR 1426, it was held that the mere signature of an agreement between the parents cannot legitimate a long period of residence that clearly was not habitual because it was based on deceit and wrongful conduct.   [366] [1999] 2 FLR 1116 at 1121, HL.

[367] [1992] 1 FLR 548, CA. Cf *Re A (Abduction: Habitual Residence)* [2007] EWHC 779 (Fam), [2007] 2 FLR 129 where 7 or 8 days' residence was insufficient to establish habitual residence albeit that on their arrival in the USA both parents had a settled intention to remain there, though so far as the mother was concerned that evaporated within a day or two.

[368] [1992] 1 FLR 548, at 555–556. Cf *Re A (Abduction: Habitual Residence)* [1998] 1 FLR 497 in which a stay of three weeks of an intended six-week visit was held not to establish an habitual residence.

[369] [2009] EWCA Civ 1021 [2010] 1 FLR 1146.   [370] [2009] EWCA Civ 588 [2010] 1 WLR 1237.

[371] [2011] EWCA Civ 1100 [2012] 1 FLR 436. See also *FVS v MGS (Habitual Residence)* [2011] EWHC 3139 (Fam) [2012] 2 FLR 1184, Cf *Re H (A Child) (Abduction: Habitual Residence: Agreement)* [2012] EWCA Civ 148 [2013] Fam Law 783—passage of two days from the signing of an agreement between the parents that their child was legitimately residing in Mexico did not elevate presence to habitual residence.

[372] [1996] 1 FLR 887 at 895.

while parents can expressly or impliedly agree that their child should live apart from them and thus either retain[373] or acquire[374] an habitual residence different from their own, it by no means automatically follows that upon the ending of that agreement the child's habitual residence reverts to that of the parents.[375]

The relevance of an older child's standpoint in determining his or her habitual residence was considered by the Supreme Court in *Re LC (Children) (Reunite International Child Abduction Centre intervening).*[376] That case establishes that in determining whether a child has achieved a sufficient degree of integration into a social and family environment in a country in which he or she was living, a relevant factor, at any rate, in the case of an adolescent or a child with the maturity of an adolescent, is the child's state of mind. In *Re LC*, after their marriage broke down the mother, with the father's agreement, moved with their four children to Spain. The children returned some five months later to England for a holiday with their father and made it clear that they wished to stay. The mother immediately issued Hague proceedings for the children's return, which in turn raised the question of where the children were habitually resident. At the Supreme Court the focus was on the eldest child, a 12 year old girl, since she was one of the appellants. She was found to be confident and intelligent and had a maturity beyond her years. She said that she hated it Spain and that it had never been home. It was held that her state of mind should have been considered in determining her habitual residence. Although the case of all four children's habitual residence was remitted for a re-hearing, there was difference of opinion as to the relevance of the younger children's state of mind, with the majority confining their decision to adolescents or those having the maturity of an adolescent[377] and the minority not restricting their decision to adolescents etc but extending it to younger children.[378] In short, the decision in *Re LC* is not clear cut and is likely to produce further litigation.[379]

'Wrongful' removal or retention

Although the applicant is not required to have a court order in his favour, to invoke the 1980 Convention it must be shown[380] that the removal or retention is 'wrongful' within the meaning of Art 3. For these purposes the act is 'wrongful' if (a) it is in breach of rights of custody accorded to a person or institution or other body, either jointly or alone, by the law of the Contracting State in which the child is habitually resident, and (b) if at the time of removal or retention those rights were actually exercised either jointly or alone, or would have been so exercised but for the removal or retention.

---

[373] See the example given in *Re M (Abduction: Habitual Residence)* at 894 of a child born in India and who had spent the whole of his or her life there with grandparents, while the parents came to this country and acquired a habitual residence in England.

[374] As, for example, where parents agree to send their child to live with relatives abroad, as in *Re M (Abduction: Habitual Residence).*

[375] *Re M (Abduction: Habitual Residence)*, where, pursuant to parental agreement, the child was sent to and remained living with his grandparents in India and in which it was held that, upon the mother's withdrawal from that agreement, the child's habitual residence could not revert to that of his mother in England, since there was no current factum of residence there. Indeed, without finally deciding the point Sir John Balcombe commented that 'in all probability' the child was still habitually resident in India.

[376] [2014] UKSC 1 [2014] 2 WLR 124, on which see H Blackburn 'Habitual residence – *Re LC*' [2014] IFL 8 and D Williams 'The Supreme Court trilogy: a new habitual residence arises!' [2014] IFL 84.

[377] See Lord Wilson at [43] with whom Lords Toulson and Hodge agreed.

[378] See Baroness Hale at [58], with whom Lord Sumption agreed.

[379] See the note on this decision by G Douglas at [2014] Fam Law 410.

[380] Failure to discharge this burden is fatal to the application: see *Re M (A Minor) (Abduction)* [1996] 1 FLR 315, where experts disagreed on whether under Greek law an interim custody order vested exclusive rights to determine the child's place of residence. Accordingly, the application failed.

Article 3 refers both to wrongful *removal* and wrongful *retention* and in *Re H, Re S*[381] the House of Lords held that these are separate and mutually exclusive events, both of which occur once and for all on a specific occasion. *Removal* occurs 'when a child, which has previously been in the State of its habitual residence, is taken away across the frontier of that State, whereas *retention* occurs where a child, which has previously been for a limited period of time outside the State of its habitual residence, is not returned on the expiry of such limited period'.[382]

A retention can subsequently become 'wrongful' if, following the removal, the court of the child's habitual residence makes a valid order giving interim care and control to the applicant and for the return of the child which is not obeyed.[383] In *Re B (Minors) (Abduction) (No 2)*[384] Waite J held that because the Convention should be construed purposively rather than semantically, proper effect could only be given to the term 'retention' if it was construed as being wide enough to comprise not only acts of physical restraint on the part of the retaining parent, but also judicial orders obtained on his initiative. However, as Wall J has pointed out in *Re S (Minors) (Abduction: Wrongful Retention)*,[385] it is only where such applications provide clear evidence of a party's intention to break the agreement that such acts can be considered wrongful. It would not, for example, be wrongful to seek court orders solely to protect the child's presence within the jurisdiction in accordance with the agreement. As against this, it is established[386] that a lawful removal pursuant to a return order made under the 1980 Hague Abduction Convention does not *retrospectively* become 'wrongful' because that order is subsequently overturned on appeal and whether it subsequently becomes a wrongful retention will depend on where the child is habitually resident.[387]

Since 'wrongful removal' is not a continuing state of affairs, it follows that a subsequent removal after a temporary return of the child to the state of habitual residence constitutes a new 'wrongful removal' within the meaning of Art 3.[388] Accordingly, the time limits under the Convention[389] run from the date of the second removal.

In each case removal or retention refers to removal or retention out of the jurisdiction of the courts of the State of the child's habitual residence. Wrongful removal or retention within the borders of the State of the child's habitual residence falls outside the scope of the Convention.[390]

Rights of custody

Central to the notion of 'wrongful' removal or retention is that the act must be in breach of rights of custody. As Baroness Hale observed in *Re K (A Child) (Reunite International*

---

[381] *Re H (Minors) (Abduction: Custody Rights), Re S (Minors) (Abduction: Custody Rights)* [1991] 2 AC 476, HL. [382] Per Lord Brandon ibid at 500.

[383] *Re S (A Minor) (Custody: Habitual Residence)* [1998] AC 750, HL.

[384] [1993] 1 FLR 993. See also *Re AZ (A Minor) (Abduction: Acquiescence)* [1993] 1 FLR 682 at 689 per Sir Michael Kerr. [385] [1994] Fam 70.

[386] See *DL v EL (Reunite International Child Abduction Centre intervening)* [2013] EWCA Civ 865 [2013] 3 FCR 69 at [52] per Thorpe LJ and on which point permission to appeal to the Supreme Court was refused, see *Re L (A Child) (Custody: Habitual Residence) (Reunite International Child Abduction Centre intervening)* [2013] UKSC 75 [2013] 3 WLR 1597 at [12].

[387] In *Re L* [2013] UKSC 75 [2013] 3 WLR 1597 the child's habitual residence was held to be in England so that a wrongful retention had not been established but it was held nevertheless that there was an inherent power to order the child's return (see further The extent of the discretion, p 1069).

[388] See *Re S (Child Abduction: Delay)* [1998] 1 FLR 651, per Wall J but he left open whether mere physical presence, however transient, can form the basis of a fresh wrongful removal under Art 3.

[389] Viz. 12 months under Art 12: see The exceptions to the duty to return, p 1054.

[390] See *Re H, Re S* above at 498, per Lord Brandon, and *Re V (Abduction: Habitual Residence)* [1995] 2 FLR 992.

Child Abduction Centre intervening),[391] 'rights of custody' have two functions, namely, first to identify those removals that are presumptively so harmful to the child's welfare that the authorities must take swift action to return the child to his place of habitual residence, and secondly, to secure that long-term decisions about the child's future are taken in his habitual residence.

The general approach in determining this issue has been well summarised by Dyson LJ in *Hunter v Murrow (Abduction: Rights of Custody)*.[392] The first task, the so-called 'domestic law question', is to establish what rights, if any, the applicant had under the law of the State in which the child was habitually resident immediately before his or her removal or retention.[393] This question is determined in accordance with the domestic law of that State[394] and involves deciding what rights are recognised by that law and how these rights are characterised.[395] The second task, the so-called 'Convention question', is to determine whether those rights are properly to be categorised as 'rights of custody'. This is a matter of international law and depends upon the application of the autonomous meaning of the phrase 'rights of custody'.

As Art 5(a) states, ' "rights of custody" includes rights relating to the care of the person of the child, and, in particular the right to determine the child's place of residence'. Such rights, as Art 3 says, may arise by 'operation of law or by reason of a judicial or administrative decision, or by reason of an agreement having legal effect under the law of that State'. These rights may be vested in an individual, institution or a body, including the court.

Rights of custody vested in individuals

In broad terms, so far as English law is concerned, 'rights of custody' should be understood in the context of the Children Act 1989 to refer to holders of parental responsibility, whether that responsibility is vested automatically, as in the case of married parents and unmarried mothers, or, in the case of unmarried fathers and unmarried second female parents, by virtue of being registered as the father or parent, a parental responsibility agreement or order.[396] It has been held[397] that an unmarried father who had been granted interim care and control in wardship proceedings after the child's removal (but while the child still remained habitually resident in the jurisdiction from where he was taken) did have 'rights of custody' notwithstanding that they were on an interim basis and that he shared them with the High Court.

Similarly, again in broad terms, so far as foreign jurisdictions are concerned, those who have automatic parental rights or have custody orders in their favour will generally be regarded as having rights of custody. In this latter respect it has been held[398] that it is

---

[391] [2014] UKSC 29 [2014] 2 WLR 1304, at [2].

[392] [2005] EWCA Civ 976 [2005] 2 FLR 1119 at [46]–[47].

[393] Note: the applicable law provisions in the 1996 Hague Convention on the Protection of Children (discussed at Applicable law, p 1097) might be of relevance in this determination.

[394] Including, according to Munby J in *Re JB (Child Abduction) (Rights of Custody: Spain)* [2003] EWHC 2130 (Fam) [2004] 1 FLR 796 its private international law. In that case it was found that notwithstanding their habitual residence in Spain, because all the parties were British nationals, their personal law (in that case English law) would be applied.

[395] In *Hunter v Murrow* itself, it was held that the English court was not bound by a New Zealand Court's declaration (under Art 15, discussed at Declarations, p 1053) that a father's rights of access were sufficient to amount to rights of custody).

[396] Presumably, those named in a child arrangements order as a person with whom the child is to spend time but who also have been granted parental responsibility must also be regarded as having 'rights of custody'.   [397] *Re S (A Minor) (Custody: Habitual Residence)* [1998] AC 750, HL.

[398] See *Re E (Abduction: Rights of Custody)* [2005] EWHC 848 (Fam) [2005] 2 FLR 759 per Potter P.

inappropriate for an English court to go behind a decision of a competent court of another Contracting State dealing with custody. It has been held[399] in a case where the mother belatedly alleged that the applicant was not the father and therefore had no 'rights of custody', that DNA testing should only be 'ordered' in Hague proceedings, if at all, as a last resort, that is, where it is clear that the question of 'rights of custody' is dependent upon a finding of biological fatherhood.

In *Re J (A Minor) (Abduction: Custody Rights)*[400] the House of Lords held that the Convention only protected established legal rights and not de facto custody. Accordingly, notwithstanding that the child in question was living with both the unmarried parents at the time of removal, it was held that the father (who, under the then Western Australian law, had no formal rights) had no 'rights of custody'.

Re J, however, was decided before the second meeting of the Special Commission held in 1993 to review the operation of the Convention at which it was concluded that 'rights of custody' should have an autonomous Convention meaning. Reflecting this, Waite LJ said in *Re B (A Minor) (Abduction)*:[401]

> . . . the Convention is to be construed broadly as an international agreement according to its general tenor and purpose, without attributing to any of its terms a specialist meaning which the word or words in question may have acquired under the domestic 'law of England' and that 'rights of custody' is a term which, when so construed, enlarges upon, and is not necessarily synonymous with the simple connotations of 'custody' when that word is used alone . . .

In his view,[402] provided the aggrieved parent was, at the time of the wrongful removal or retention, exercising functions in the requesting State of a parental or custodial nature, he could be regarded as having 'rights of custody' without the benefit of any court order or official custodial status. *Re B* was followed in *Re O (Abduction: Custody Rights)*[403] in which German grandparents, who had been exclusively looking after the child in question for over 12 months before the mother took the child to England, were held to have 'rights of custody'. However, as Hale J observed in *Re W; Re B (Child Abduction: Unmarried Father)*,[404] the recognition of these so-called 'inchoate rights' as being within Arts 3 and 5 is hard to reconcile with the House of Lords' decision in *Re J*.

A distinguishing factor of *Re B* and *Re O* was that, unlike *Re J*, the applicant was exercising responsibility either alone or with someone who did not have custodial rights. In *Re C (Child Abduction) (Unmarried Father: Rights of Custody)*,[405] Munby J concluded that the authorities show that there can be circumstances in which an unmarried father will acquire rights of custody even if he is not the sole primary carer of the child and even if he is sharing care with another person *other* than the mother. But that is as far as the authorities go and to go any further would be inconsistent with *Re J*. In *Re G (Abduction: Rights of Custody)*[406] a paternal grandmother was held to have acquired rights of custody by virtue of a long-term placement (which had lasted for over a year before the child's removal)

---

[399] *Re M (Abduction: Paternity: DNA Testing)* [2013] EWCA Civ 1131 [2014] 1 FLR 695.

[400] [1990] 2 AC 562.

[401] [1994] 2 FLR 249, CA. See also *Re F (A Minor) (Abduction: Custody Rights Abroad)* [1995] Fam 224, CA.

[402] Peter Gibson LJ dissented on this point, while Staughton LJ appeared to hold that the applicant's 'right of custody' arose out of an agreement made with the mother.   [403] [1997] 2 FLR 702.

[404] [1998] 2 FLR 146 at 155.

[405] [2002] EWHC 2219 (Fam) [2003] 1 FLR 252. See also *Re F (Abduction: Unmarried Father: Sole Carer)* [2002] EWHC 2896 (Fam) [2003] 1 FLR 839, and *Re H (Child Abduction) (Unmarried Father: Rights of Custody)* [2003] EWHC 492 (Fam) [2003] 2 FLR 153.   [406] [2002] 2 FLR 703.

coupled with a right to make decisions for the child. In the same case the unmarried father was held to share those rights by virtue of living with his mother (the grandmother) and the child for four months. However, it can be a matter of fine judgment as to whether even a sole de facto carer will necessarily have rights of custody. In *Re J (Abduction: Acquiring Custody Rights By Caring For Child)*[407] it was held that a father's short-term care of a child in Greece while the mother was working in England in an effort to rescue the family's financial position did not give him rights of custody, since on the facts the mother had neither abandoned her child nor delegated her role as the primary carer while she was of necessity abroad solely to sort out the family's finances.

It seemed inevitable that in the light of the development of inchoate rights *Re J* would at some point have to be revisited not least to make it child centred rather than adult centred.[408] That opportunity arose in *Re K (A Child) (Reunite International Child Abduction Centre intervening)*,[409] in which a child had been looked after by his maternal grandparents for seven years before being removed by the mother in harrowing circumstances and shortly after she had withdrawn the parental authority that had been given to the grandparents. After a thorough review of the relevant national and international authorities, the Supreme Court confirmed the application of the notion of inchoate rights and by a majority held that the grandmother did have 'rights of custody' on the day of the child's removal. In so holding the Court held[410] that before persons can be held to have inchoate rights of custody they must establish that (a) they are undertaking the responsibilities, and thus enjoying the concomitant rights and power, entailed in the primary care of the child; (b) they are not sharing these responsibilities with the person having a legally recognised right to determine where the child shall live and how he shall be brought up; (c) that that person must have either abandoned the child or delegated his primary care to them; (d) there must be some form of legal or official recognition of their position in the country and of habitual residence; and (e) there must be every reason to believe that, were they to seek the protection of the courts of that country, the status quo would be preserved for the time being so that the long-term future of the child could be determined in those courts in accordance with his best interests and not by the pre-emptive strike of abduction. Dissenting, Lord Wilson, though agreeing that 'rights of custody' can be satisfied by the establishment of inchoate rights, thought that criterion (d) was unnecessary and that (e) 'set the bar too low'. On the facts he thought that the grandmother had failed to establish that she had rights of custody following the mother's withdrawal of parent authority.

Rights of access are not rights of custody

As Hale J observed in *S v H (Abduction: Access Rights)*,[411] the Convention draws a distinction between 'rights of custody' and 'rights of access' and the court should be reluctant to allow the latter to metamorphose into the former. In that case an unmarried mother with sole custody of her son who came lawfully to England was held not to have acted in breach of the father's 'rights of custody', since he had no parental authority and the

---

[407] [2005] 2 FLR 791.

[408] In this respect note might be taken of Judge Pinto de Albuquerque's view expressed in *X v Latvia* [2014] 1 FLR 1135, at n 18 of his judgment that inchoate custody rights cannot be reconciled with the European Court of Human Rights', the European Court of Justice's and the House of Lords' case-law.

[409] [2014] UKSC 29, [2014] 2 WLR 1304.

[410] See [59], per Baroness Hale, giving the majority judgment.

[411] [1998] Fam 49 [1997] 3 WLR 1086. In the domestic law context this means that a person named in a child arrangements order as a person with whom the child is to spend time or otherwise have contact will not have rights of custody unless they also be granted parental responsibility.

access order in his favour did not entitle him to prevent the mother taking the child out of the jurisdiction. Similarly it was held in *Re V-B (Abduction: Custody Rights)*[412] that an access order coupled with a right to be consulted on where the child should reside but without a power of veto was insufficient to vest the father with rights of custody. In contrast, in *Re P (A Child) (Abduction: Custody Rights)*[413] it was held that a *ne exeat* clause (ie a clause forbidding removal from the jurisdiction) in a New York order was sufficient to give the father (who otherwise only had visitation rights) a 'right to custody' regardless of whether the New York State or Federal Law so regarded it. Subsequently, in *Re D (A Child) (Abduction: Rights of Custody)*,[414] the House of Lords clearly stated that a right of veto does amount to a right of custody. However, Baroness Hale at least, drew the line at a parent's *potential* right of veto (ie the right to go to court inter alia to seek an order on relocation abroad) conferring rights of custody. As her Ladyship pointed out,[415] to hold otherwise would remove the distinction between 'rights of custody' and 'rights of access' altogether.

Rights of custody vested in a court

It is well established that for the purposes of Arts 3 and 5, 'rights of custody' can be vested in a court.[416] The leading English case is *Re H (A Minor) (Abduction: Rights of Custody)*[417] which involved a child's removal from Ireland to England by her mother during her father's application to be appointed as the child's guardian and for defined access. That application was adjourned by consent with access to the father being agreed but the mother subsequently took the child to England without the father's consent. The House of Lords, agreeing with the Court of Appeal, held that on the facts of this case the removal was in breach of rights of custody vested in the court, since the application for guardianship raised the issue of custody within the meaning of the Convention. What *Re H* establishes, at any rate in general terms, is that before a court can have rights of custody the application before it must itself raise a question of custody within the meaning of the Convention. Conversely, an application that in substance only seeks the determination of contact is not sufficient to vest 'rights of custody'.[418] Even then, the mere issue of proceedings is insufficient; they must at least be served (this is perhaps open to argument in the case of wardship proceedings)[419] and possibly be actively pursued.

---

[412] [1999] 2 FLR 192, CA. Note also *Hunter v Murrow (Abduction: Rights of Custody)* [2005] EWCA Civ 976 [2005] 2 FLR 1119 in which regular access constituting substantial intermittent possession and care, was not enough to constitute 'rights of custody'.   [413] [2004] EWCA Civ 971 [2005] Fam 293.

[414] [2006] UKHL 51 [2007] 1 AC 619 at [19] per Lord Hope, at [37] per Baroness Hale. Lord Carswell at [74] reserved his position on the issue. For a similar ruling by the US Supreme Court, see *Abbott v Abbott* 560 US (2010) (No 08-65).

[415] At [38]. In *Re D* itself, under Romanian Law as it then stood, the divorced father essentially only had a right of access since he had no right of veto against the child's removal from Romania. Cf *Re F (Children) (Abduction: Rights of Custody)* [2008] EWHC 272 (Fam), [2008] 3 WLR 527, in which applying *Re D*, it was held that a father given a right of co-decision over 'vital problems' in connection with his children's upbringing, education and medical treatment, had 'rights of custody'.

[416] It is also possible for rights of custody to be vested in other bodies, for example, a licensed adoption agency, see *Re JS (Private International Adoption)* [2000] 2 FLR 638.   [417] [2000] 2 AC 291, HL.

[418] See *Re V-B (Abduction: Custody Rights)*.

[419] It is long established jurisprudence (see Ch 20) that once a child becomes a ward of court no important step can be taken in the child's life, including taking the child out of the jurisdiction, without the court's consent, which would on the face of it seem to vest rights of custody in the court. But in the Court of Appeal in *Re H* (see [2000] 1 FLR 201 at 211) Thorpe LJ clearly signalled that mere issue of wardship proceedings was insufficient and Lord Mackay in the House of Lords seemed to agree.

Actual exercise of rights of custody

Article 3(b) requires that at the time of the removal or retention, the rights of custody 'were actually exercised either jointly or alone or would have been but for the removal or retention'. In *Re H; Re S (Abduction: Custody Rights)*[420] Lord Brandon considered that the provision should be construed widely meaning the custodial parent in maintaining the stance and attitude of such a parent. Consequently a parent who consents to his child travelling or living abroad for a period is not only exercising rights of custody when giving that permission but is still doing so while the child is away.[421]

A similarly wide and purposive approach is evident from the decisions that imprisonment or hospitalisation does not in itself suspend rights of custody or their actual exercise.[422]

A potential problem is the relationship between Art 3(b) and Art 13(a) under which a return may be refused if the applicant 'is not actually exercising custody rights at the time of removal or retention'.[423] As we discuss later in this chapter, there is a similar problem about whether to deal with consent under Art 3 or Art 13(a) and in that context it is now settled that it should generally be dealt with under Art 13. It is suggested that a similar resolution be applied to the Art 3(b)/Art 13(a) conundrum.

When removals or retentions are wrongful

Normally, a wrongful removal or retention will be in breach of someone else's rights, but it has been accepted by the English courts that a removal or retention is 'wrongful' if it is in breach of custody rights vested in a court,[424] or even of the child's own rights.[425]

While it is clearly 'wrongful' if the removal is contrary to an express court order,[426] it is also 'wrongful' if the removal is prohibited according to the general law of the jurisdiction from where the child was taken.[427] Similarly, it is 'wrongful' to retain a child beyond the time allowed by a court or beyond the period agreed by the parties. In *Re S (Minors) (Abduction: Wrongful Retention)*[428] it was held that retention of a child *before* the expiry of the agreed period was wrongful when the mother had announced her intention never to return the child. According to Wall J in *Re S*, a retention becomes wrongful from the time the parent abandons the intention to honour the agreement.[429] This analysis, however, has been questioned[430] and Macur J declined to apply it in *RS v KS (Abduction: Wrongful Retention)*,[431] holding instead that the relevant date for determining when a retention

[420] [1991] 2 AC 476 at 500–501.
[421] See eg *W v W (Child Abduction: Acquiescence)* [1993] 2 FLR 211.
[422] *Re L (A Child)* [2005] EWHC 1237 (Fam) [2006] 1 FLR 843 and *Re A (Abduction: Rights of Custody Imprisonment)* [2004] 1 FLR 1, (imprisonment) and in Scotland, *JS v SS* 2003 SLT 344 (hospitalisation).
[423] Discussed further at Non-exercise of rights of custody, p 1056.
[424] See Rights of custody vested in a court, p 1050.
[425] *Re H (A Minor) (Abduction)* [1990] 2 FLR 439 ('wrongful' for a parent with interim custody in her favour to remove the child from the jurisdiction).
[426] *Re C (A Minor) (Abduction)* [1989] 1 FLR 403, CA.
[427] *C v C (Minors) (Child Abduction)* [1992] 1 FLR 163.
[428] [1994] Fam 70, per Wall J. See also *H v H (Child Abduction: Stay of Domestic Proceedings)* [1994] 1 FLR 530 in which Thorpe J held that a similar position obtained from the unilateral abandonment of an agreement to be in England for an unspecified period.
[429] Contrast the view of Sir Michael Kerr in *Re AZ (A Minor) (Abduction: Acquiescence)* [1993] 1 FLR 682 at 689D who doubted whether an uncommunicated decision to abandon an agreement could constitute a wrongful retention.
[430] See *D v S (Abduction: Acquiescence)* [2008] EWHC 363 (Fam) [2008] 2 FLR 293 at [179] per Charles J.
[431] [2009] EWHC 1494 (Fam) [2009] 2 FLR 1231 and note also Sir Michael Kerr in *Re AZ (A Minor) (Abduction: Acquiescence)* [1993] 1 FLR 682 at 689D who doubted whether an uncommunicated decision to abandon an agreement could constitute a wrongful retention.

occurs is that on which the child should have returned. In her view an uncommunicated decision not to return a child is not sufficient to constitute a 'wrongful retention' under the Convention

'Wrongful' removal and state immunity

It has been held[432] that the return of a Government diplomat and his family in compliance with a direct order of his employing Government was 'an act of a governmental nature and therefore subject to state immunity from legal process.' Accordingly, such a removal could not be considered 'wrongful' for the purposes of the Hague Convention.

'Wrongful' removal and the issue of consent

Having observed in *Re C (Abduction Consent)*[433] that it can plausibly be said that a removal or retention cannot be 'wrongful' if done with the consent of the other party, Holman J nevertheless considered that such an argument cannot be made under the Hague Convention, since the issue of consent is specifically dealt with under Art 13(a) as providing an exception to the obligation to order the child's return. In *Re O (Abduction: Consent and Acquiescence)*[434] Bennett J disagreed with Holman J insofar as he was implying that the issue of consent must always be dealt with under Art 13(a). In his view, a distinction can be drawn between challenges to the validity of consent which come within Art 3 and those concerning whether consent was given at all, which come within Art 13(a).

In *Re P (A Child) (Abduction: Custody Rights)*[435] however, the Court of Appeal upheld Holman J's view. As Ward LJ put it:

> If the giving of consent prior to the removal had the effect that the removal could never be classified as wrongful or in breach of the right of custody then there would be no need for Art 13 at all . . . The policy of the Convention is to protect children internationally from the harmful effects of their wrongful removal or retention. If a child is removed in prima facie breach of a right of custody, then it makes better sense to require the removing parent to justify the removal and establish that the removal was with consent rather than require the claimant, asserting the wrongfulness of the removal, to prove that he or she did not consent.

(c) Declarations

Article 15 permits the judicial or administrative authorities of a Contracting State to request from the authorities of the State of the child's habitual residence a declaration that the removal or retention was 'wrongful' within the meaning of Art 3.

Although on its face Art 15 is restricted to obtaining decisions or determinations as to whether removals or retentions are wrongful, the Child Abduction and Custody Act 1985 s 8 widens its scope to allow the High Court to make an Art 15 declaration upon the application by 'any person appearing to the court to have an interest in the matter' to make a declaration that a removal of any child from, or his retention outside the UK is 'wrongful' within the meaning of Art 3.[436] In other words, Art 15 can also be used to obtain a ruling as to what domestic law rights were enjoyed by the applicant before removal or

---

[432] *Re P (Diplomatic Immunity: Jurisdiction)* [1998] 1 FLR 1026.   [433] [1996] 1 FLR 414 at 417.
[434] [1997] 1 FLR 924.
[435] [2004] EWCA Civ 971 [2005] Fam 293 at [33]. For the implications of this ruling with regard to the application of Art 11 of BIIR, see The basic scheme, p 1077.
[436] See the explanation in *K v L (Child Abduction)* [2012] EWHC 1234 (Fam), [2013] 1 FLR 998.

retention. Such an action could be useful to those such as unmarried fathers who might not have rights of custody. In *Re J (Abduction: Declaration of Wrongful Removal)*,[437] for example, an unmarried father, fearing that his cohabitant would remove their child to South Africa, sought a without notice order for parental responsibility and to prohibit the child's removal. The application was adjourned so that it could be heard on notice but on that very day the mother removed the child. Being advised that because of his lack of parental responsibility it was unlikely that he would be regarded as having 'rights of custody' for the purposes of the Convention, the father successfully sought a declaration of wrongful removal under s 8.[438]

In *Hunter v Murrow (Abduction: Rights of Custody)*,[439] the Court of Appeal cautioned against making such requests particularly if they are solely for determinations of so-called Convention questions, namely, whether removals or retentions are 'wrongful'. In *Re D (A Child) (Abduction: Rights of Custody)*,[440] however, unable to resolve a difference of opinion between experts as to the effect of orders made in Romania concerning a child, the court requested the father to obtain a determination from a Romanian court as to the legal effect of the order pursuant to Art 15. Although because of the inevitable delay involved[441] both Lords Hope and Carswell[442] cautioned against too ready a resort to Art 15, Lord Carswell at least thought the reference in that case was 'fully justified'.

Applications for declarations may be made during the pendency of other proceedings in another Contracting State determining the child's habitual residence, provided it would serve some useful purpose and not simply delay proceedings.[443] It is no objection that the person seeking the declaration is no longer living in England and Wales.[444] In *A v B (Abduction: Declaration)*[445] an unmarried father successfully sought a s 8 declaration following the dismissal of a Hague return application by a French court based on what the English court considered to be an erroneous Opinion that under English law the father had no rights of custody. An appeal against the French court's ruling was pending and the English court took the view that while it did not wish to trespass upon the functions of the French court, it would be helpful to correct the Opinion on which the first instance decision was based, though it was for the French appeal court to determine what weight should be attached to the English declaration.

Declarations are discretionary remedies and may be refused if they can make no contribution towards, or might delay or otherwise impede, the application for a return order.[446] Although, not strictly binding, it is apparent, following the House of Lords' ruling in *Re D (A Child) (Abduction: Rights of Custody)*,[447] that at the very least the court of the requesting State should attach considerable weight to an Art 15 determination made

---

[437] [1999] 2 FLR 653.
[438] On the basis that by refusing to return the child as ordered by the court, the mother was in breach of the *court's* rights of custody.   [439] [2005] EWCA Civ 976 [2005] 2 FLR 1119.
[440] [2006] UKHL 51 [2007] 1 AC 619.
[441] In *Re D* itself it took over two years to obtain the determination. This delay was held by the ECtHR to be a breach of Art 6 of the Human Rights Convention by the Romanian authorities. Note that the UK was not found to be in breach and indeed the Art 8 complaints against both countries were dismissed: *Deak v Romania and the United Kingdom* [2008] 2 FLR 994.   [442] See [6] and [70], respectively.
[443] *Re P (Abduction: Declaration)* [1995] 1 FLR 831.
[444] *Re L (Children) (Abduction: Declaration)* [2001] 2 FCR 1.
[445] [2008] EWHC 2524 (Fam) [2009] 1 FLR 1253.
[446] See eg *Re P (Diplomatic Immunity: Jurisdiction)* [1998] 1 FLR 1026—declaration refused when it could make no contribution to proceedings in the USA in which the issue was whether the children should live with their American father or in Germany with their German mother.
[447] [2006] UKHL 51 [2007] 1 AC 619, disapproving the approach of the Court of Appeal in *Hunter v Murrow* [2005] EWCA Civ 976 [2005] 2 FLR 1119 at [27].

by the requested State. It is impermissible to adduce fresh expert evidence to question the determination of the domestic law position. In Lord Brown's view there would need to be 'some compelling reason to reject [an Art 15 determination] such as a flagrant breach of the rules of natural justice in the foreign judicial process or a manifest misdirection as to the autonomous meaning of the Convention terms "rights of custody"'.[448]

(d) Who can invoke the Convention

Article 8 provides that '*any* person, institution or other body claiming that a child has been removed or retained in breach of custody rights' (emphasis added) may apply for the child's return. Hence, although commonly applicants are individuals having 'rights of custody' or 'rights of access', it would seem that *any* person (including possibly the child himself, if old enough), institution or body (eg local authorities or courts) may seek assistance provided it can be shown that the child's removal or retention is 'wrongful' within the meaning of Art 3.

(e) The exceptions to the duty to return

As discussed earlier, under Art 12 courts are under a general duty to order the child's return in cases of wrongful removal or retention. This duty, however, is subject to a number of exceptions, which understandably have been the subject of voluminous case law, though it is worth bearing in mind that globally, judicial refusals to return are comparatively unusual. According to the 2008 Statistical Survey,[449] only 15% of return applications ended in a judicial refusal to return.[450]

If a return is ordered,[451] then any other custody order ceases to have effect, but if a return is refused then, unless the BIIR applies, the court can hear any other application upon its merits.[452] Although return orders are, subject to any appeal, normally final, there is nevertheless is a residual power to set the order aside, though only in truly exceptional circumstances.[453]

It remains now to consider the application of the exceptions to the duty to order the child's return under Art 12 and Art 13.

The application of Article 12 where the commencement of proceedings is more than 12 months after the wrongful removal or retention

If proceedings are brought more than 12 months after the wrongful removal or retention, Art 12 provides that a return should still be ordered 'unless it is demonstrated that the child is now settled in its new environment'.[454] The deliberate concealment of a child does not stop the year's time running. As Thorpe LJ said in *Cannon v Cannon*:[455]

---

[448] At [81]. The decision to reject the Art 15 determination in *Hunter v Murrow*, may, however, have been justified upon the basis that the New Zealand court ruling was out of line with the international understanding of the Convention's terms, see Baroness Hale in *Re D* at [44].   [449] Op cit.

[450] Of the cases determined by a court, 61% concluded with a return order being made.

[451] The practice of the English courts is to return the child to the state of his habitual residence and not to the person: *B v K (Child Abduction)* [1993] 1 FCR 382, per Johnson J and *Re A (A Minor) (Abduction)* [1988] 1 FLR 365 at 373 per Nourse J. Cf *O v O (Child Abduction: Return to Third Country)* [2013] EWHC 2970 (Fam) [2014] 2 WLR 1213—child returned to where mother was now living and not to the State of habitual residence.

[452] Child Abduction and Custody Act 1985 s 25 and Art 16. 'Custody orders' include s 8 orders under the Children Act 1989: Child Abduction and Custody Act 1985 Sch 3. The application of BIIR following refusal to return is discussed at The position following a refusal to return—Art 11(6)–(8), p 1077.

[453] See *Re C (Abduction: Application to Set Aside Return Order: Remission)* [2012] EWCA Civ 1144 [2013] 1 FLR 403.

[454] This exception is commonly referred to as Art 12(2), though in fact no such numbering is to be found in the Article.   [455] [2004] EWCA Civ 1330 [2005] 1 WLR 32 at [51].

> I would not support a tolling rule that the period gained by concealment should be disregarded and therefore subtracted from the total period of delay in order to ascertain whether or not the 12-month mark has been exceeded. That seems to me to be too crude an approach.

If the child returns to the state of habitual residence only to be removed again then, for the purposes of Art 12, time begins to run from the date of the second removal.[456]

In *Re N (Minors) (Abduction)*[457] Bracewell J held that 'now' refers to the date of the commencement of proceedings and not the date of the hearing; that 'settled' involves both a physical element in the sense of relating to or being established in a community and an emotional constituent denoting security; and that 'new environment' encompasses place, home, school, people, friends, activities and opportunities but not, per se, the relationship with the parent. With regard to the meaning of 'settled' Bracewell J's view was endorsed by the Court of Appeal in *Cannon v Cannon*[458] in which Thorpe LJ concluded, after a thorough review of both domestic and international authority, that 'it is not enough to regard only the physical characteristics of settlement. Equal regard must be paid to the emotional and psychological elements'. It has been held[459] that being unsettled in a personal, emotional or psychological state (such as, as a result of being bullied at school) did not preclude a finding of being settled for the purposes of Art 12. Similarly, Art 12 settlement is not legally impaired by a mother and child's uncertain immigration status.[460]

Although deliberate concealment and subterfuge by the abductor cannot, *ipso facto*, prevent there being 'settlement', as Thorpe LJ said in *Cannon*:[461] 'the burden of demonstrating the necessary elements of emotional and psychological settlement is much increased. The judges in the Family Division . . . should look critically at any alleged settlement that is built on concealment and deceit especially if the defendant is a fugitive from criminal justice.' Indeed in Thorpe LJ's view 'it will be very difficult indeed for a parent who has hidden the child away to demonstrate that it is settled in its new environment'. However, at the remitted hearing[462] Kirkwood J found the girl in question to be 'settled'.

Cannon also establishes that even if 'settlement' is established the court retains a discretion nevertheless to order the child's return.[463] However, at the remitted hearing, Kirkwood J, having accepted that the greater the degree of turpitude the more unwilling the court should be to decline to order a return, nevertheless in the light of evidence painting 'a clear and compelling picture' of a happy, successful, stable, settled and flourishing child who was settled in every sense, declined to order her return.

---

[456] *Re S (Child Abduction: Delay)* [1998] 1 FLR 651.   [457] [1991] 1 FLR 413.

[458] [2004] EWCA Civ 1330 [2005] 1 WLR 32 at [61]. For a review of some Commonwealth jurisdictions' decisions see J Caldwell 'Child welfare defences in child abduction cases—some recent developments' [2001] CLFQ 121 at 133–4.

[459] *Re C (Child Abduction: Settlement)* [2006] EWHC 1229 (Fam) [2006] 2 FLR 797.

[460] *Re C.* In that case, however, it was thought that the parties' deportation was unlikely to take place in the near future. See also *F v M and N (Abduction: Acquiescence: Settlement)* [2008] EWHC 1525 (Fam) [2008] 2 FLR 1270—child found to be 'settled' notwithstanding deprivation of her relationship with her father. Cf *M v M (Abduction: Settlement)* [2008] EWHC 2049 (Fam) [2008] 2 FLR 1884, notwithstanding that it was accepted that a child could be 'settled' notwithstanding a parent's vulnerable and watchful state of mind, the children were not found to be 'settled'.   [461] [2004] EWCA Civ 1330 [2005] 1 WLR 32 at [61].

[462] Reported as *Re C (Abduction: Settlement) (No 2)* [2005] 1 FLR 938.

[463] See further The residual discretion to return, p 1068.

Failure to conduct Convention proceedings with proper diligence and speed may entitle the court to strike the application out.[464]

Globally, 11% of refusals to return are based upon Art 12.[465]

The application of Article 13(a)

Under Art 13(a) the authority may refuse to order the child's return if it is shown that the person, institution or other body having the care of the person of the child was not actually exercising the custody rights at the time of removal or retention, or has consented to or subsequently acquiesced in the removal or retention.

Non-exercise of rights of custody

Refusals based on the non-exercise of custody rights are relatively unusual.[466] Indeed, there is no reported English example of a refusal being so based. It has been held that being imprisoned[467] or hospitalised[468] does not mean that for these purposes the left-behind parent is not exercising rights of custody.

In practice the two most common applications of Art 13(a) are in relation to consent and acquiescence. Even so, according to the 2008 survey globally, there were only five refusals *solely* based on consent (although a further 18 refusals relied upon this ground in conjunction with another) and only four refusals relying solely on acquiescence (with a further 11 relying on this ground in conjunction with another).[469]

Although often pleaded in the alternative, consent and acquiescence are mutually exclusive. As Lord Donaldson MR said in *Re A (Minors) (Abduction: Custody Rights)*,[470] the difference between the two 'is simply one of timing. Consent, if it occurs, precedes the wrongful taking or retention. Acquiescence, if it occurs, follows it.'

Consent

The leading case on consent is *Re P-J (Children) (Abduction: Consent)*[471] in which the overall current position was authoritatively summarised by Ward LJ as follows:

(1) Consent to the removal of the child must be clear and unequivocal.

(2) Consent can be given to the removal at some future but unspecified time or upon the happening of some future event.

(3) Such advance consent must, however, still be operative and in force at the time of the actual removal.

(4) The happening of the future event must be reasonably capable of ascertainment. The condition must not have been expressed in terms which are too vague or uncertain for both parties to know whether the condition will be fulfilled. Fulfilment of the condition must not depend on the subjective determination of one party, for example, 'Whatever you may think, I have concluded that the marriage has

---

[464] See eg *Re G (Abduction: Striking Out Application)* [1995] 2 FLR 410, per Connell J. Alternatively, the court can exercise its discretion not to return the child provided, at any rate, an exception under Art 13 can first be established: *Re S*, earlier.   [465] See the 2008 Statistical Survey, op cit.

[466] According to the 2008 Statistical Survey, op cit, globally, only 4% of refusals were solely based on this ground, but rising to 7% when relying on this ground in conjunction with another.

[467] See *Re A (Abduction: Rights of Custody: Imprisonment)* [2004] 1 FLR 1 and *Re L (A Child)* [2005] EWHC 1237 (Fam) [2006] 1 FLR 843.   [468] See the Scottish decision, *JS v SS*, 2003 SLT 344.

[469] In England and Wales one application made in 2003 was refused on the basis of consent and one on acquiescence.   [470] [1992] Fam 106 at 123.

[471] [2009] EWCA 588 [2010] 1 WLR 1237 at [48].

broken down and so I am free to leave with the child'. The event must be objectively verifiable.

(5) Consent, or the lack of it, must be viewed in the context of the realities of family life, or more precisely, in the context of the disintegration of family life. It is not to be viewed in the context of nor governed by the law of contract.

(6) Consequently consent can be withdrawn at any time before actual removal. If it is, the proper course is for any dispute about removal to be resolved by the courts of the country of habitual residence before the child is removed.

(7) The burden of proving consent rests on him or her who asserts it.

(8) The inquiry is inevitably fact specific and the facts and circumstances will vary infinitely from case to case.

(9) The ultimate question is a simple one even if a multitude of facts bear upon the answer. It is simply this: had the other parent clearly and unequivocally consented to the removal?

It is established that the consent to the child's removal must be real, positive and unequivocal. It can neither be inferred from an overlap of intentions[472] nor (unlike acquiescence) can it be passive.[473] Consent or the lack of it must be viewed in the context of the realities of family life, or more precisely, 'in the context of the realities of the disintegration of family life. It is not to be viewed in the context of nor governed by the law of contract'.[474] Statements made in anger in the heat of an argument which were neither intended nor understood as giving permission to remove or retain a child, cannot be regarded as 'consent'.[475] A fortiori, 'consent' obtained by fraud will not be considered valid. Indeed, as Waite LJ commented in *Re B (A Minor) (Abduction)*:[476]

> ... the only starting-point that can be stated with reasonable certainty is that the courts of the requested State are unlikely to regard as valid a consent that has been obtained through a calculated and deliberate fraud on the part of the absconding parent.

It is accepted that consent need not be in writing nor need it be express.[477] Although it is commonly said that to establish consent the evidence needs to be 'clear and compelling', it has been suggested[478] that to be consistent with the House of Lords' decision in *Re B (Children) (Care Proceedings: Standard of Proof)*[479] the burden is more accurately stated as being to establish on a simple balance of probability that there has been a 'positive and unequivocal giving of consent' to the child's removal.

The consent must be operative at the time of removal though it does not have to be to the specific removal.[480] An earlier consent can be withdrawn before the child's

---

[472] See *D v S (Abduction: Acquiescence)* [2008] EWHC 363 (Fam) [2008] 2 FLR 293.

[473] *Re W (Abduction: Procedure)* [1995] 1 FLR 878.

[474] Per Ward LJ in *Re P-J (Children) (Abduction: Consent)* [2009] EWCA 588 [2010] 1 WLR 1237 at [48].

[475] *JPC v SLW and SMW (Abduction)* [2007] EWHC 1349 (Fam) [2007] 2 FLR 900.

[476] [1994] 2 FLR 249 at 261, CA.

[477] See *Re C (Abduction: Consent)* [1995] 1 FLR 878, per Holman J and *Re K (Abduction: Consent)* [1996] 1 FLR 414 at 418 and 419, per Hale J and *Re M (Abduction) (Consent: Acquiescence)* [1999] 1 FLR 171, per Wall J. Note, however, Munby J's view in *C v H (Abduction: Consent)* [2009] EWHC 2660 (Fam) [2010] 1 FLR 225, that the evidence will normally need to be in writing or evidenced by documentary material.

[478] Per Munby J in *C v H (Abduction: Consent)*.

[479] [2008] UKHL 35 [2009] 1 AC 11, discussed in Ch 17.

[480] See *Re L (Abduction: Future Consent)* [2007] EWHC 2181 (Fam) [2008] 1 FLR 914 and *Zennel v Haddow* 1993 SLT 975, both cited with approval in *Re P-J*.

removal but to be effective the withdrawal must be objectively plain to the party who would otherwise seek to rely upon it.[481] However, once consent has been acted upon it cannot then be withdrawn by the parent giving it subsequently thinking better of it.[482]

Acquiescence

In the leading case on 'acquiescence', *Re H (Minors) (Abduction: Acquiescence)*,[483] the House of Lords abandoned previous attempts to distinguish between active and passive acquiescence,[484] holding that instead a common approach was to be applied in all cases. That approach was summarised by Lord Browne-Wilkinson to be as follows:[485]

> (1) For the purposes of Article 13 of the convention, the question whether the wronged parent has "acquiesced" in the removal or retention of the child depends upon his actual state of mind. As Neill LJ said in *Re S (Minors) (Abduction: Acquiescence)* [1994] 1 FLR 819 at 838: ". . . the court is primarily concerned, not with the question of the other parent's perception of the applicant's conduct, but with the question whether the applicant acquiesced in fact."
> (2) The subjective intention of the wronged parent is a question of fact for the trial judge to determine in all the circumstances of the case, the burden of proof being on the abducting parent.
> (3) The trial judge, in reaching his decision on that question of fact, will no doubt be inclined to attach more weight to the contemporaneous words and actions of the wronged parent than to the bare assertions in evidence of his intention. But that is a question of the weight to be attached to evidence and is not a question of law.
> (4) There is only one exception. Where the words or actions of the wronged parent clearly and unequivocally show and have led the other parent to believe that the wronged parent is not asserting or going to assert his right to the summary return of the child and are inconsistent with such return, justice requires that the wronged parent be held to have acquiesced.

In other words, unless the can prove to the court's satisfaction that the applicant clearly acquiesced, the defence can succeed only if it can be brought within the 'exceptional' category.

Following *Re H* the first question a court must settle is whether looking at the subjective mind of the applicant after the child's removal he or she had in fact acquiesced or 'gone along' with that removal. A good example is *Re M (Abduction) (Consent: Acquiescence)*[486] in which a father, knowing his wife intended a permanent removal, took the line that she

---

[481] Per Macur J in *Re Z (Abduction)* [2008] EWHC 3473 (Fam) [2009] 2 FLR 298 at [34]—the plea of withdrawal failed in that case. Cf *VK v JV (Abduction: Consent)* [2012] EWHC 403 (Fam) [2013] 2 FLR 237, in which the contention that consent had been withdrawn in relation to one of the children concerned was successful.

[482] Per Hale J in *Re K (Abduction:Consent)* [1997] 2 FLR 212. See also *VK v JV (Abduction: Consent)* in which it was held that in relation to one of the children concerned the withdrawal of consent was too late since the mother and that child had, acting on an agreement, already moved to the UK.

[483] [1998] AC 72, HL. See R Bailey Harris 'Acquiescence under the Hague Convention on International Child Abduction' (1997) 113 LQR 529 and D McClean 'International child abduction—some recent trends' (1997) 9 CFLQ 387 at 395–8.

[484] First established in *Re A (Minors) (Abduction: Custody Rights)* [1992] Fam 106, CA and inter alia in *Re AZ (A Minor) (Abduction: Acquiescence)* [1993] 1 FLR 682, CA and *Re S (Minors) (Abduction: Acquiescence)* [1994] 1 FLR 819.

[485] Ibid at 90.   [486] [1999] 1 FLR 171

would do as she wished (he assumed that she would not manage on her own in England and would therefore return to Greece) and did not change his attitude after the removal in July until the following February. He was held to have acquiesced. Similarly, in *Re D (Abduction: Acquiescence)*,[487] acquiescence was established in a case where the applicant had genuinely agreed to the making of what was then a residence order in favour of the abducting parent and intended to return (in this case to Wales) to live near the children.

Re D was notable in that the father was found to have acquiesced even though he mistakenly thought that the Hague Convention did not apply to his case. This case raises the general issue of the extent to which knowledge of the wrongfulness of the act is relevant to the issue of acquiescence. According to Butler-Sloss LJ in *Re S (Abduction: Acquiescence)*[488] while knowledge of the facts and that the act of removal or retention is wrongful will normally be necessary, to expect the applicant necessarily to have knowledge of the rights which can be enforced under the Convention is to set too high a standard. In that case, seeking contact and not a summary return of the child after being given adequate and realistic advice, but not being fully informed of his rights under the Convention, was held to amount to acquiescence.[489]

Each case has to be assessed on its own facts but absence of court action does not necessarily indicate acquiescence,[490] though delay in taking any action can be so indicative.[491] In *Re H* itself, it was held that the father, who was an Orthodox Jew, had not acquiesced in the children's removal from Israel to England merely by obeying the instruction of his local Beth Din to ignore English proceedings brought by the mother.

The fact that the applicant has applied for custody in the State of the child's habitual residence is a strong indication that there has been no acquiescence,[492] though there is nothing necessarily inconsistent with acquiescing in a current state of affairs and applying for the child's care and control at a later date.[493]

Although in principle acquiescence can be evidenced by written statements, it is well established that they must be written in clear and unambiguous terms.[494] Extracting a single and ambiguous sentence from a four page letter, for example, will not be enough to establish acquiescence.[495] Furthermore, in Lord Browne-Wilkinson's view, the clear and unequivocal conduct that brings the case within the exception is not normally to be found in passing remarks or letters written by a parent who has recently suffered the trauma of the removal of his children.

---

[487] [1998] 2 FLR 335, CA. Cf *Re B (Minors) (Abduction) (No 2)* [1993] 1 FLR 993—merely entering an appearance in the abductor's court application is not in itself acquiescence.

[488] [1998] 2 FLR 115 at 122, CA.

[489] See also *B-G v B-G* [2008] EWHC 688 (Fam) [2008] 2 FLR 965 in which acquiescence was established (evidenced by the father's intention to return to England to be near his children) notwithstanding that three different French lawyers failed to advise him about the Convention; and *D v S (Abduction: Acquiescence)* [2008] EWHC 363 (Fam) [2008] 2 FLR 293 reliance on erroneous legal advice that the left-behind parent would fail in Hague proceedings for the child's return, was held to be acquiescence.

[490] *Re F (A Minor) (Child Abduction)* [1992] 1 FLR 548, CA. See also *Re R (Minors) (Abduction)* [1994] 1 FLR 190 (delay inter alia because of legal advice to await the outcome of domestic proceedings in France and because of the subsequent 'deplorable' delay in the French Central Authority's communication with the English Central Authority) and *Re S (Minors) (Abduction: Acquiescence)* [1994] 1 FLR 819, CA (delay due to erroneous legal advice).

[491] See eg *W v W (Child Abduction: Acquiescence)* [1993] 2 FLR 211 (father's inactivity for some 10 months after learning of his wife's decision not to return held to amount to acquiescence).

[492] *Re A (Minors) Abduction* [1991] 2 FLR 241, CA.

[493] *Re AZ (A Minor) (Abduction: Acquiescence)* [1993] 1 FLR 682.

[494] See eg *Re A (Minors) (Abduction: Custody Rights)*. Indeed, such clear statements can come within Lord Browne-Wilkinson's 'exceptional category'.

[495] Per Millett LJ in *Re R (Child Abduction: Acquiescence)* [1995] 1 FLR 716 at 733.

Clearly, the most difficult part of *Re H* is that relating to the 'exception'. According to Lord Browne-Wilkinson, one example is *Re AZ (A Minor) (Abduction: Acquiescence)*,[496] in which a mother, with the father's consent, took their child from Germany (where the father was stationed with the US Air Force) to England to stay with her family. Once there the mother decided not to return. She left her son with her sister and the father asked her to look after him until he could come to England a little later. However, before his arrival the aunt applied for what was then a residence and prohibited steps order. The father was served with the papers after his arrival in England but he indicated that he would not contest the application. However, some three months later he told the family for the first time that he intended to take the boy back to Germany, though it was not for another six weeks that he finally initiated Convention proceedings. It was held that the father had 'acquiesced'. In Lord Browne-Wilkinson's view[497] *Re AZ* was a rare example of a case falling into the exceptional category where the wronged parent's conduct is so clear as not to require proof of his subjective intention, ie it was a case 'in which the wronged parent, knowing of his rights, has so conducted himself vis-à-vis the other parent and the children that he cannot be heard to go back on what he has done and seek to persuade the judge that all along he has secretly intended to claim the summary return of the children'. Other examples falling into this exceptional category mentioned by Lord Browne-Wilkinson were[498] the signing of a formal agreement that the child is to remain in the country to which he has been abducted and the active participation in proceedings in the country to which the child has been abducted to determine the child's long-term future. Another example is *Re B (Abduction: Acquiescence)*[499] where, following his wife's removal of their child to England, the father at first negotiated with her suggesting that he would not oppose her move if the reconciliation he was proposing failed and subsequently deciding to settle in England and seek contact in the English court. It was held notwithstanding his ignorance of the Convention (neither his American nor English lawyers apparently mentioned it to him) that his conduct overall amounted to acquiescence.

On the other hand, as was held in *P v P (Abduction: Acquiescence)*,[500] merely seeking to compromise a situation by allowing the abducting parent to remain in the country to which he or she has gone, provided that the wronged parent is satisfied as to other matters in issue between them, will not, in the absence of any concluded agreement, be regarded as falling into the 'exceptional category'.

In this case, after the mother had taken the child to England from Cyprus, the father sought through his lawyer to negotiate a settlement whereby the child would reside with his mother in England but have extensive staying contact with him in Cyprus. When these negotiations failed, the father issued Hague proceedings. It was held that in the absence of a concluded agreement the father could not be said to have 'acquiesced' within the meaning of Lord Browne-Wilkinson's 'clear and unequivocal' conduct category. Indeed Ward LJ agreed with Hale J's first instance comment:[501]

> . . . it would be most unfortunate if parents were deterred from seeking to make sensible arrangements, in consequence of what is usually an acknowledged breakdown in the relationship between them, for fear that the mere fact that they are able to contemplate that the child should remain where he has been taken will count against them in these proceedings. Such negotiations are, if anything, to be encouraged.

---

[496] [1993] 1 FLR 682.   [497] [1998] AC 72 at 89F.   [498] Ibid at 89D–E.
[499] [1999] 2 FLR 818.   [500] [1998] 2 FLR 835, CA.   [501] At 840.

It is established that acquiescence cannot subsequently be withdrawn.[502]

The application of Article 13(b)

Under Art 13(b) the court may refuse to order the child's return if it is shown that 'there is a grave risk that his or her return would expose the child to physical or psychological harm or otherwise place the child in an intolerable situation'. As the Pérez-Vera Report comments,[503] whereas the Art 13(a) exceptions are based on the wronged parent's conduct, Art 13(b) clearly derives from the consideration of the child's interests inasmuch as 'the interest of the child in not being removed from its habitual residence . . . gives way before the primary interest of any person in not being exposed to physical or psychological danger or being placed in an intolerable position'.

Article 13(b) is the most litigated of all the exceptions and, notwithstanding a generally strict interpretation adopted in most jurisdictions (discussed shortly) it is the one most often successfully invoked. According to the 2008 Statistical Survey, globally over a fifth (21%) of all judicial refusals were based solely on this ground.[504]

As we discuss later, if the proceedings are governed by BIIR a return order cannot be refused under Art 13(b) if it established that 'adequate arrangements have been made to secure the protection of the child after his or her return'.[505] According to the 2008 Statistical Survey, however, a greater proportion of refusals were based on this ground as between Brussels II States than in cases not governed by the Regulation.[506]

The basic test

The risk of physical or psychological harm must be more than an ordinary one, but weighty, substantial and not trivial.[507] In principle it is possible for a number of factors only when taken together as opposed to being considered separately to satisfy the 'otherwise intolerable' situation.[508] Although it is well established that the burden, which is upon the applicant to establish, is a stringent one, as the Supreme Court explained in *Re E (Children) (Abduction: Custody Appeal)*,[509] that is because of the very terms of Art 13(b) and not because that provision should be narrowly construed. As Baroness Hale and Lord Wilson put it,[510] 'The words of article 13 are quite plain and need no further elaboration or "gloss"'. In particular there is:

> nothing to indicate that the standard of proof is other than the ordinary balance of probabilities. But in evaluating the evidence the court will of course be mindful of the limitations involved in the summary nature of the Hague Convention process. It will rarely

---

[502] *Re A (Minors) (Abduction: Custody Rights)* [1992] Fam 106, CA, not commented upon on this point by the House of Lords in *Re H* and followed in *Re S (Abduction: Acquiescence)* [1998] 2 FLR 115 at 122, CA, per Butler-Sloss LJ.   [503] Op cit, at para 29 and see also para 116.

[504] Op cit. In fact 27% of all refusals were based solely *or in part* on Art 13(b). There were six Art 13(b) refusals in England and Wales.

[505] BIIR, Art 11(4), discussed at Applying Article 13(b) of the Hague Convention in compliance with BIIR, p 1075.   [506] Ie 34% as against 20%.

[507] See eg *Re A (A Minor) (Abduction)* [1988] 1 FLR 365, CA.

[508] Per Hughes J in *E v E (Child Abduction: Intolerable Situation)* [1998] 2 FLR 980, though on the facts the defence failed.

[509] [2011] UKSC 27 [2012] 1 AC 144, on which see V Stephens and N Lowe 'Children's welfare and human rights under the 1980 Hague Abduction Convention – the ruling in *Re E'* (2012) 34 JSWFL 125.

[510] At [31]–[32]. In this respect the Supreme Court 'shared the view' of the High Court of Australia in *DP v Community Central Authority; JLM v Director-General NSW Department of Community Services* (2001) 180 ALR 402, a position previously resiled from by the CA in *Re S (Abduction: Custody Rights)* [2002] EWCA Civ 908 [2002] 2 FLR 815.

be appropriate to hear oral evidence of the allegations made under article 13 (b) and so neither those allegations nor their rebuttal are usually tested in cross-examination.

The ruling in *Re E* was intended to end debate that the Strasbourg decision in *Neulinger and Shuruk v Switzerland*[511] meant that Art 13 in general and, Art 13(b) in particular, has to be interpreted in the light of the child's best interests. Though that does not negate the argument accepted by Baker J in *WF v FJ, BF and RF (Abduction: Child's Objections)*,[512] that Art 13(b) has to be interpreted within the Human Rights framework.

Although there can be legitimate debate as to the precise effect of *Re E*, the better view is that it did not fundamentally change the approach to establishing an Art 13(b) 'defence', though, as the Supreme Court later put it in *Re S (A Child) (Abduction: Rights of Custody)*,[513] 'it was primarily an exercise in the removal from it of disfiguring excrescence'.

Subject to this caveat, in general terms it is wrong to allow the abducting parent to rely upon adverse conditions brought about by a situation which he or she has created by his or her own conduct for as was famously said[514] that would 'drive a coach and four through the Convention . . .'. But as Potter P has pointed out[515] that 'is not a principle articulated in the Convention or the [Child Abduction and Custody Act 1985] and should not be applied to the effective exclusion of the very defence itself which is in terms directed to the questions of risk of harm to the child and not the wrongful conduct of the abducting parent'.

Examples of failed Art 13(b) applications

Case law abounds with examples of failed Art 13(b) pleas. In *N v N (Abduction: Article 13 Defence)*,[516] for example, an allegation of sexual abuse by the applicant was held insufficient to justify a refusal to return. Similarly in *Re S (Abduction: Return into Care)*[517] the defence failed notwithstanding that there were serious allegations of sexual abuse against the mother's cohabitant because the court accepted that the matter would be adequately dealt with and the child protected by the Swedish authorities upon the child's return. In *Re M (Abduction: Intolerable Situation)*[518] the defence failed, notwithstanding the mother's genuine fear of physical harm by her husband who, having been imprisoned for murdering someone whom he believed to be having an affair with the mother, was due to be released, since the court again believed that the mother would be adequately protected by the Norwegian authorities to whom mirror undertakings had been given. In *Re K (Abduction: Psychological Harm)*[519] a mother, who contended that as she had no immigration status she would be unable to support herself and would not therefore exercise any possession rights as defined by a Texan court, failed to convince the court that the child would be placed in an intolerable position if ordered to be returned to the USA. In *Re L (Abduction: Pending Criminal Proceedings)*[520] it was held that neither the possibility of criminal proceedings being brought nor even the possibility of the mother being arrested at the airport on her return was enough to establish a grave risk of harm to the children.

---

[511] [2011] 1 FLR 122, discussed at Compatibility with the European Convention on Human Rights, p 1035.   [512] [2010] EWHC 2909 (Fam) [2011] 1 FLR 1153.

[513] [2012] UKSC 10 [2012] 2 AC 257 at [31].

[514] Per Butler-Sloss LJ in *C v C (Minor: Abduction: Rights of Custody Abroad)* [1989] 1 WLR 645.

[515] In *S v B (Abduction: Human Rights)* [2005] EWHC 733 (Fam) [2005] 2 FLR 878 at [49].

[516] [1995] 1 FLR 107.   [517] [1999] 1 FLR 843.

[518] [2000] 1 FLR 930.   [519] [1995] 2 FLR 550, CA.

[520] [1999] 1 FLR 433 (but note that the US rules have since been eased through the use of 'Significant Public Benefit Parole'). See also *Re C (Abduction: Grave Risk of Psychological Harm)* [1999] 1 FLR 1145, CA.

In *Re S (Abduction: Intolerable Situation: Beth Din)*[521] the court rejected a mother's defence that it was not possible for her to get justice from the religious court in Israel, the Beth Din, and that as a woman she would be discriminated against in Israel since she would be unable to obtain a 'get' without the positive assistance and consent of the father. It has also been held[522] to be wrong to place too much weight on the interests of a child who was not the subject of the Convention.

A harsh example of not allowing a respondent to rely upon her own wrongdoing is *Re C (Abduction: Grave Risk of Physical or Psychological Harm)*[523] in which a mother wrongfully removed her six-year-old son together with his 16-year-old half-sister (who was not the subject of the proceedings) from Cyprus. The evidence was that the girl had not been happy in Cyprus, was well settled in England and would refuse to return. The mother pleaded that returning the boy to Cyprus would mean splitting the family, forcing her to choose whether to stay in England with her daughter or to go to Cyprus with her son. Notwithstanding this terrible dilemma, the mother's pleas fell on deaf ears.

Another issue of major concern[524] is the operation of Art 13(b) in the context of domestic violence. A leading example is *TB v JB (Abduction: Grave Risk of Harm)*.[525] This case was unusual in that the source of the alleged risk to the children in question was not their father, the mother's first husband, but the mother's second husband, the father of her youngest child who was not the subject of the proceedings. The mother, who indisputably had wrongfully removed the three children by her first husband (plus her child by her second husband) from New Zealand to England, claimed that her primary motivation for leaving was to get away from her second husband (against whom there were allegations of maltreatment both of the mother and of the children and of bizarre behaviour) and that she was too frightened to return. The first husband applied for the return of the three elder children but at first instance this was refused under Art 13(b) on the basis of expert evidence that the mother was seriously vulnerable to the anxieties created by the second husband and that she was suffering from mild to moderate depression which would be exacerbated by a return. Accordingly, the children (who were each found to be troubled and upset) would be exposed to harm because the mother would face the same risks as previously and might cease to cope with the pressure that could be placed on her. On appeal, however, by a majority this decision was overruled. In Laws LJ's view, Art 13(b) could only be satisfied in truly exceptional cases of which this was not one. Arden LJ accepted that deterioration of the mother's condition and consequently in her ability to care for her children could be sufficient to satisfy Art 13(b) but she considered that in evaluating such a risk the court was entitled to expect that the mother would make all appropriate use of orders of the New Zealand courts for her and her children's protection. In her Ladyship's view, given the New Zealand court's powers to protect the mother and her children, a 'grave risk' could not be said to have been made out. Dissenting, Hale LJ recognised the vulnerability of victims of domestic abuse and did not believe that on

---

[521] [2000] 1 FLR 454.

[522] *Re C (Abduction: Grave Risk of Physical or Psychological Harm)*.

[523] [1999] Fam 478. For a case involving not a dissimilar dilemma and in which the Art 13(b) plea failed see *S v B (Abduction: Human Rights)* [2005] EWHC 733 (Fam), [2005] 2 FLR 878.

[524] See M Weiner 'International Child Abduction and the Escape from Domestic Violence' (2000) 69 *Fordham Law Review* 593, M Kaye 'The Hague Convention and the Flight from Domestic Violence: How Women and Children are being Returned by a Coach and Four' (1999) 13 Int Jo of Law, Policy and the Family 191 and C Bruch 'The Unmet Needs of Domestic Violence and Their Children in Hague Abduction Cases' (2004) 38 Fam LQ 529.

[525] [2001] 2 FLR 515, CA. See also *Re H (Abduction: Grave Risk)* [2003] EWCA Civ 355 [2003] 2 FLR 141 in which the Court of Appeal did not consider that in that case the Belgian authorities' previous failure to protect children from their dominating and violent father, per se, justified a refusal to make a return order.

these facts the New Zealand courts could protect the mother and therefore the children and thus an Art 13(b) defence had been made out.[526] Many might agree with this latter standpoint. Furthermore, as we discuss shortly, there have been refusals based on violence.

A further example of the difficulty of succeeding under Art 13(b) is *Re S (Abduction: Custody Rights)*[527] in which a mother claimed that because of the worsening situation in Israel (which was for all intents and purposes at war) she was paralysed with fear at the very thought of returning there and that therefore because she would be unable to provide day-to-day care her child would suffer grave harm. The Court of Appeal, however, refused to interfere with a decision to return the child. Whilst acknowledging that there was a *risk* of harm because of the worsening situation it was not felt to be so great as to amount to a grave risk within the contemplation of Art 13(b), nor did they accept the argument that because of her anxieties and concern (which were considerable) the child was at grave risk from the breakdown of the mother's health. The court accepted that the *mother* would find a return to Israel 'intolerable' but that was not the test under Art 13(b). In *Re M (Children) (Abduction: Rights of Custody)*[528] the House of Lords refused to disturb the rejection at first instance of an Art 13(b) defence based on Zimbabwe being a 'failed state'.

Examples of successful Art 13(b) applications

Despite the difficulty of discharging the burden there are examples of where the 'defence' succeeded. In *Re F (A Minor) (Abduction: Custody Rights Abroad)*[529] a return order was refused because, accepting the respondent's uncontroverted evidence, the applicant had been shown to be violent towards the child and had been engaged in a campaign of intimidation and harassment against the mother, which had adversely affected the child. Another example is *Re D (Article 13B: Non-Return)*[530] in which a mother was shot in the head and shoulder allegedly at the behest of her husband with whom she was involved in an acrimonious and protracted custody dispute over their two children aged seven and five. The children were anxious for their own safety and in the exceptional circumstances of the case, it was accepted that their psychological welfare was put at 'grave risk beyond the normal disruption of an enforced return'. Accordingly, a return order was refused.

In *Re S (A Child) (Abduction: Rights of Custody)*[531] a refusal to return was based inter alia on incontrovertible evidence of the father's substantial descent into alcohol and drug abuse, his contemplation of suicide and of serious violence against the mother coupled with the mother's consequential fragile psychological health and that she would suffer crippling anxiety and depression were she to be required to return. In that case the Supreme Court confirmed that a respondent's subjective perception of the risks of a return leading to an intolerable situation for the child can be sufficient to establish an Art 13(b) 'defence'. The 'defence' also succeeded in *X v Y and Z Police Force, A, B and C (By Their Children's Guardian)*[532] in which because of the abducting father's work as an

---

[526] Subsequent to this decision the mother sought to set the order aside on the twin basis of fresh evidence as to her emotional state and the impracticality of enforcing the order, but this attempt failed: *Re B (Children) (Abduction: New Evidence)* [2001] EWCA Civ 625 [2001] 2 FCR 531. However, the children strongly resisted being taken to the airport and a stay was placed on the return order.

[527] [2002] EWCA Civ 908 [2002] 2 FLR 815.

[528] [2007] UKHL 55 [2007] 3 WLR 975. On the facts it was felt that the father would be able to provide properly for his children, though a return was refused under Art 12(2).

[529] [1995] Fam 224. This was the first time the Court of Appeal had refused a return on this ground. See also *Re M (Minors) (Abduction: Psychological Harm)* [1998] 2 FCR 488, CA.

[530] [2006] EWCA Civ 146.   [531] [2012] UKSC 10 [2012] 2 AC 257.

[532] [2012] EWHC 2838 (Fam) [2013] 1 FLR 1277.

undercover police officer it was not safe for the family to return to Australia where he had been relocated.

In *Re W (Abduction: Domestic Violence)*[533] Wall LJ rejected the suggestion made at first instance in that case[534] that there is no realistic chance of an Art 13(b) defence ever being established unless there has been violence or other specific abuse to the child, him- or herself. In this respect reference may be made to *Re G (Abduction: Psychological Harm)*.[535] A return was refused on the basis that if the mother were to return with the children, as she would have done had the order been made, there was a grave risk that the children would have been exposed to psychological harm because their mother's mental health would seriously deteriorate. This seems an extreme decision and some caution needs to be exercised when applying it. It is to be noted that the court was satisfied that the mother was not someone who was seeking to manipulate the court in order to get her own way. Ewbank J also observed that, notwithstanding the children's habitual residence was in Texas, all the parties were English. The defence might also be established if it can be shown in relation to the law of the requesting State that there is some fixed embargo on allowing the removal of children or precluding the removal of children by a parent who had once wrongly removed them, or where the length of time that the requesting State might take to decide issues concerning the children is excessive.[536]

Another example is *B v K (Child Abduction)*,[537] in which, having held that two older siblings should not be returned because of their objections (see further later), Johnson J ruled that a return order should also be refused in respect of a third child since, if he were returned and his two siblings were not, he would be exposed to psychological harm and placed in an intolerable position within the meaning of Art 13(b). A similar conclusion was reached, albeit reluctantly, in *Re T (Abduction: Child's Objections to Return)*[538] in relation to a six year-old (who was too young and immature for his views to be taken into account) whose 11 year-old sister on whom he was dependent (at times she was his 'little mother') had successfully objected to being returned to her mother in Spain, notwithstanding a Spanish court's assessment that whatever the mother's past failing she was currently capable of discharging her responsibilities properly.

Commentary

The generally strict interpretation of Art 13(b) has not escaped criticism. One argument is that the courts too readily assume that children will be adequately protected on their return. Cases like *TB v JB (Abduction: Grave Risk of Harm)* highlight this issue. One solution is that central authorities should accept a wider responsibility to protect children upon their return.[539] A second more fundamental criticism[540] is that whereas

---

[533] [2004] EWCA Civ 1366 [2005] 1 FLR 727 at [49].

[534] See *Re W (Abduction: Domestic Violence)* [2004] EWHC 1247 (Fam), [2004] 2 FLR 499, per Baron J.

[535] [1995] 1 FLR 64, per Ewbank J.

[536] Per Singer J in *Re O (Child Abduction: Undertakings)* [1994] 2 FLR 349, though in that case the defence was not made out.

[537] [1993] 1 FCR 382. Note also *Ontario Court v M and M (Abduction: Children's Objections)* [1997] 1 FLR 475 (child's fears that she would have to live with her grandmother and lose her father held to amount to placing her in an 'intolerable position').

[538] [2000] 2 FLR 192, CA. But cf *LCG v RL (Abduction: Habitual Residence and Child's Objections)* [2013] EWHC 1383 (Fam), [2014] 1 FLR 307, in which such a 'defence' was rejected.

[539] This was discussed extensively at the third and fourth meeting of the Special Commission to review the Convention, see Lowe, Everall and Nicholls, op cit, 17.137–138.

[540] See in particular M Freeman 'In the Best Interests of Internationally Abducted Children?—Plural, Singular, Neither or Both?' [2002] IFL 77 and R Schuz 'The Hague Child Abduction Convention: Family Law and Private International Law' (1995) 44 ICLQ 771.

the Convention was predicated upon abductors being non-carers it is now clear that the majority are in fact the primary carers[541] and that in turn begs the question whether it is in children's interests generally to be returned to their home jurisdiction. In reply it has been said[542] that this alleged shift in the pattern of abduction does not necessarily mean that the Convention has become increasingly flawed for there remains the argument that it is basically wrong for children to be uprooted from their home by unilateral act of either parent and taken to a foreign jurisdiction and thus to be separated from the other parent. However, whether Art 13(b), as it currently operates, properly draws the balance can and, no doubt, will continue to be debated. In 2013 a Hague Conference Working Party was appointed to examine the operation of Art 13(b).

Undertakings

An additional reason for the difficulty of establishing an Art 13(b) defence is the English practice of accepting undertakings, since they can alleviate what might otherwise be regarded as an intolerable situation.[543] As Butler-Sloss LJ explained in *Re M (Minors) (Abduction: Undertakings)*,[544] undertakings are accepted to make the return of children easier and to provide for their necessities such as a roof over their heads and adequate maintenance. They are intended to have a short life, ie until the court of the child's habitual residence becomes seized of the proceedings. Accordingly, the court should be careful not in any way to usurp or be thought to usurp the functions of the court of habitual residence. Furthermore, undertakings must not be so elaborate that their implementation might become bogged down in protracted hearings and investigations.

Undertakings have been held[545] to be 'protective measures' for the purposes of the 1996 Hague Convention on the Protection of Children (discussed later in this chapter) and are therefore recognisable and enforceable under that instrument. Although on the one hand this ruling could lead to an increased use of undertakings, it may be that measures will be taken under the 1996 Convention itself to ensure a child's safe return.[546]

The child's objections

Article 13 permits a refusal to make a return order if the judicial or administrative authority 'finds that the child objects to being returned and has attained an age and degree of maturity at which it is appropriate to take account of its views'. According to the 2008 Statistical Survey, globally, the child's objections were relied upon in whole or in part in 17% of all refusals. It was the second most relied upon ground after Art 13(b).[547]

To bring the case within this exception requires the judge to make findings of fact both as to whether the child objects (which means more than a mere expression of wishes and feelings but indicates a strength, a conviction and rationality of view against being

---

[541] According to the 2008 Statistical Survey, op cit, 72% of abductors were either the primary or joint primary carer (though the information on this was by no means complete).

[542] N Lowe with K Horosova 'The Operation of the 1980 Hague Abduction Convention – A Global View' (2007) 41 Fam LQ 59, at 70–71.

[543] Per Singer J in *Re O (Child Abduction: Undertakings)*. Note also *Re K (Abduction: Child's Objections)* [1995] 1 FLR 977 (court entitled to have regard to whether any risk of harm can be reduced or extinguished by undertakings). For the practice on undertakings, so called safe harbour orders and mirror orders see Lowe, Everall and Nicholls, op cit, at 17.123 *et seq* and D McClean 'International child abduction–some recent trends' (1997) 9 CFLQ 387 at 392–5.   [544] [1995] 1 FLR 1021, CA.

[545] *Re Y (Abduction: Undertakings Given for Return of Child)* [2013] EWCA Civ 129 [2013] 2 FLR 649.

[546] Under Art 11 in particular, see Powers conferred by Arts 11 and 12, p 1094.

[547] Op cit. In England and Wales there were four refusals based on the child's objections.

returned)[548] and whether the child has attained an age and degree of maturity at which it is appropriate to take account of the child's views. These findings are sometimes referred to as the 'gateway findings'.[549] According to *Re S (A Minor) (Abduction: Custody Rights)*,[550] this part of Art 13 is independent of the rest of it. Consequently, there is no additional requirement to establish that there is a grave risk that a return order would expose the child to psychological harm etc. *Re S* also establishes that for these purposes the return to which the child objects is that which would otherwise be ordered under Art 12. The court is not required to consider whether the child objects to returning in any circumstances, eg to see the other parent on an access visit. On the other hand, as established by *Re M (A Minor) (Child Abduction)*,[551] under Art 13 the court is entitled to take into account the child's objection to returning to the person and not simply to the country. It has been held that in the case of siblings, it is unnecessary to make 'gateway' findings for each child, it being sufficient to look at the sibling group in the round.[552]

There is no chronological threshold below which a child's view will not be taken into account, though in general the younger the child the less likely that he will have the maturity to make it appropriate to take his views into account.[553] Practice varies between Contracting States though in general the age at which refusals have been based have steadily reduced. According to the 2008 Statistical Survey while the average age of 'an objecting child' was 10.7 years, 14% of refusals were based on the objections of children less than eight years, compared with none in the 2003 survey and just one case in the 1999 survey. This experience has been reflected in England and Wales with the objections of children as young as eight and six being held to justify a refusal to return.[554] These, however, are relatively unusual cases, and children below the age of 10 or 11 are not normally considered sufficiently mature.

In *Re S* the Court of Appeal refused to lay down general guidance to be adopted in ascertaining the child's view and degree of maturity. Instead, each issue was thought to be a question of fact 'peculiarly within the province of the trial judge'. Similarly in *Re T (Abduction: Child's Objection to Return)* Ward LJ commented[555] that he 'would not wish to venture any definition of maturity. Clearly the child has to know what has happened to her and to understand that there is a range of choice. A child may be mature enough for it to be appropriate for her views to be taken into account even though she may not have gained the level of maturity that she is fully emancipated from parental dependence and can claim autonomy of decision-making'.

To help the court evaluate the child's views it is permissible for a child to be questioned by a suitably skilled independent person (eg a Cafcass officer) with a view to discovering how far the child is capable of understanding, and does actually understand, the implications of objecting to being returned.[556] In exceptional cases the child can be made a party

---

[548] Per Thorpe LJ in *Re K (Abduction: Case Management)* [2010] EWCA Civ 1546 [2011] 1 FLR 1268 at [24].
[549] Per Waite LJ in *Re S (Minors) (Abduction: Acquiescence)* [1994] 1 FLR 819 at 826.
[550] [1993] Fam 242, CA.   [551] [1994] 1 FLR 390, CA.
[552] *WF v FJ, BF and RF (Abduction: Child's Objections)* [2010] EWHC 2909 (Fam) [2011] 1 FLR 1153 at [37]–[41] per Baker J.
[553] Per Balcombe LJ in *Re R (Child Abduction: Acquiescence)* [1995] 1 FLR 716 at 730.
[554] See *Re W (Abduction: Acquiescence: Children's Objections)* [201] EWHC 332 (Fam) [2010] 2 FLR 1150, unsuccessfully appealed, see *Re W (Abduction: Appeal) (Minors)* [2010] EWCA 520 [2010] 2 FLR 1165. See also *B v K (Child Abduction)* [1993] 1 FCR 382 in which the objection of an 8 and 7 year were held to justify a refusal to return, and *Re S (A Minor) (Abduction: Custody Rights)* [1993] Fam 242, CA; and *Ontario Court v M and M (Abduction: Children's Objections)* [1997] 1 FLR 475 in which the objections of 9 year old children were relied upon.   [555] [2000] 2 FLR 192, at 203.
[556] Per Waite LJ in *Re S (Minors) (Abduction: Acquiescence)* [1994] 1 FLR 819 at 827.

to the proceedings.[557] Even where it is appropriate to take account of the child's views, as Wilson J said in *Re J and K (Abduction: Objections of Child)*,[558] that does not relieve the court of the task of deciding, in the discretionary analysis, what weight should be afforded to the objection. Among the reported cases of where a return has been refused on the basis of the child's objections are *Re R (A Minor: Abduction)*[559] in which a 14-year-old was threatening suicide if returned; *B v B (Abduction: Child With Learning Difficulties)*,[560] a case involving a 14 year old child with Asperger's Syndrome; *Re J (Abduction: Child's Objections To Return)*[561] in which the 11-year-old girl's objections related to her mother's alcoholism; *Re B (abduction: views of children)*,[562] in which the refusal was based on the objections of children aged 12 and seven who had become well and truly settled after being in England for more than two years; *Re J (Abduction: Child's Objections to Return)*,[563] in which the objections of a 13-year-old were based on his father's obsessive and frightening control and his strong dislike of his school in Croatia); *Re M (Abduction: Child's Objections)*,[564] in which there were strong objections of a 'bright' 8 year old to returning to Serbia in a case where her father was bent upon planting drugs upon the mother inter alia to secure her arrest, prosecution and imprisonment; and *Re F (Children) (Abduction: Rights of Custody)*,[565] in which the objections were expressed by intelligent and articulate 11 and 13 year old siblings who after 11 months in England were making excellent progress at school and who were both happy and secure in their English environment.

The residual discretion to return

The extent of the discretion

Even if an exception is established under Arts 12 or 13, there nevertheless remains a discretion[566] in the court to order the child's return. There has never been a doubt about this in relation to the Art 13 exceptions since the Article itself is clearly phrased to confer such a discretion. But there had been uncertainty about the position where an exception is established under Art 12(2) since it not clearly phrased in permissive form. However, this issue has now been resolved, following a thorough review, both of academic opinion (which took the view that there was no discretion) and of international jurisprudence, (which was more equivocal), first by the Court of Appeal in *Cannon v Cannon*[567] and

---

[557] See *Re M (A Minor) (Abduction: Child's Objections)* [1994] 2 FLR 126, CA and *Re HB (Abduction: Children's Objections)* [1998] 1 FLR 422, CA.

[558] [2004] EWHC 1985 (Fam) [2005] 1 FLR 273   [559] [1992] 1 FLR 105.

[560] [2011] EWHC 2909 (Fam) [2012] 1 FLR 881.

[561] [2004] 2 FLR 64. See also *Re L (Abduction: Child's Objections To Return)* [2002] EWHC 1864 (Fam) [2002] 2 FLR 1042—objections of a 14-year-old based on his anxiety and distress caused by his poor relationship with his father and the effects of being exposed to the disharmony between his parents.

[562] [1998] 3 FCR 260. For other examples see *Re (A Minor) (Abduction: Custody Rights)* [1993] Fam 242—(nine-year-old's views respected); *B v K (Child Abduction)* (objections of a girl aged eight and boy aged seven held to justify a refusal to return); *Re M (A Minor) (Abduction: Child's Objections)* [1994] 2 FLR 416 (objection of a boy aged 13 held to justify a refusal to return); *Ontario Court v M and M (Abduction: Child's Objections)* [1997] 1 FLR 457 (a nine-year-old girl's objections to being returned to her grandmother taken into account); *Re S (Child Abduction: Delay)* [1998] 1 FLR 651 (refusal to return based upon a 10-year-old girl's objections to being returned to her father in Germany).

[563] [2004] 2 FLR 64.   [564] [2007] EWCA Civ 260 [2007] 2 FLR 72.

[565] [2008] EWHC 272 (Fam) [2008] 3 WLR 527. See also *WF v FJ, BF and RF (Abduction: Child's Objections)* [2010] EWHC 2909 (Fam) [2011] 1 FLR 1153—strong objection by a 13 year old but with more ambivalence by a 12 year old sibling and *CB v CB (Abduction: Child's Objections)* [2013] EWHC 2092 (Fam) [2014] 1 FLR 663—refusal based on a 14 year old's rational objections.

[566] See R Schuz 'In search of a settled interpretation of Article 12 (2) of the Hague Child Abduction Convention' [2008] CFLQ 64.   [567] [2004] EWCA Civ 1330 [2005] 1 WLR 32.

then by the House of Lords in *Re M (Children) (Abduction: Rights of Custody).*[568] These decisions establish that there is a general discretion to order the child's return though the basis for holding is differed. In *Cannon* it was held that this discretion is specifically conferred by Art 18 which provides:

> The provisions of this Chapter do not limit the power of a judicial or administrative authority to order the return of the child at any time.

However, notwithstanding this conclusion Thorpe LJ said that but for Art 18 he would 'have been inclined to infer the existence of a discretion under Art 12'.[569] In *Re M* the House of Lords, however, based the discretion upon Art 12 rather than Art 18. Baroness Hale concluded 'not without considerable hesitation' that Art 12 itself envisaged that a settled child might nevertheless be returned within the Convention procedures, observing that the 'words "shall . . . unless" leave the matter open'. She further pointed out that such an interpretation 'would be consistent with all the other exceptions to the rule of return. It would avoid the separate and perhaps unfunded need for proceedings in the unusual event that summary return would be appropriate in a settlement case. It recognises the flexibility in the concept of settlement, which may arise in a wide variety of circumstances and to very different degrees. It acknowledges that the late application may be the result of active concealment of where the child has gone. It leaves the court with all options open.'[570]

On the *Re M* view, which of course is the pre-eminent authority, the discretion to return even where a child is settled within the meaning of Art 12(2) is implicit in the wording in the provision itself and not because of the application of Art 18. That Article is accordingly best regarded as a provision simply designed to preserve the application of any domestic powers outside the Convention to order a return rather than to confer any Convention power. But that is not without significance as the Supreme Court decision, *Re L (A Child) (Custody: Habitual Residence) (Reunite International Child Abduction Centre intervening),*[571] illustrates. In that case a US District Court made an order under the Hague Convention that a child be returned to the UK. The father appealed but did not seek to stay the order and, pending the appeal, the mother brought the child here. Subsequently, the US Court of Appeals allowed the appeal and subsequently the US District Court ordered the child's return to the US. The father now sought the child's return before the English courts. The Supreme Court held that although the father's application under the Hague Convention could not succeed as the child had become habitually resident here, there was nevertheless an inherent discretion,[572] preserved by Art 18, to order the child's return. On the facts a return order was made.

How the discretion should be exercised

With regard as to how the court should exercise its discretion to order a return following the establishment of an exception under Arts 12(2) or 13, *Re M (Abduction: Rights of Custody)* establishes that it is wrong to import at this stage any notion of 'exceptionality'. As Baroness Hale put it,[573] where a discretion arises from the terms of the Convention itself, that discretion is at large. Nevertheless the court is entitled to take into account the

---

[568] [2007] UKHL 55 [2008] AC 1288.   [569] *Cannon v* Cannon, above at [62].

[570] [2007] UKHL 55 [2008] AC 1288, at [31].

[571] [2013] UKSC 75 [2013] 3 WLR 1597, on which see D Williams 'The Supreme Court trilogy: a new habitual residence arises!' [2014] IFL 84.

[572] For the discussion of which, in the context of non-Convention cases, see The law as settled by *Re J*, p 1026.   [573] [2007] UKHL 55 [2008] 1 AC 1288 at [42]–[44].

various aspects of the Convention policy (ie the swift return of abducted children, com-ity between Contracting States, respect for one another's judicial processes and to deter abduction in the first place, the message going out to potential abductors that there are no safe havens among the Contracting States) alongside the circumstances which gave the court a discretion in the first place and the wider considerations of the child's rights and welfare. She added:

> The Convention itself has defined when a child must be returned and when she need not be. Thereafter the weight to be given to Convention considerations and to the interests of the child will vary enormously. The extent to which it will be appropriate to investigate these welfare considerations will also vary. But the further away one gets from the speedy return envisaged by the Convention, the less weighty those general Convention considerations must be.

Although *Re M* was concerned with a non-European Hague Convention case it has been held[574] that the principles set out by it apply equally to Hague Convention cases which are subject to BIIR.

Without gainsaying the need to exercise each case on its facts, Baroness Hale neverthe-less considered 'by way of illustration only' how the discretion might operate according to which exception has been established.[575] She referred to her comment in *Re D (A Child) (Abduction: Rights of Custody)*[576] that in effect, having established an Art 13(b) exception, it was 'inconceivable' that the court would nevertheless return a child to face his fate, add-ing that it 'was not the policy of the Convention that children should be put at serious risk of harm or placed in intolerable situations.'

With regard to consent or acquiescence cases, she considered that general considerations relating to the speed of legal proceedings and approach to relocation in the home country and individual considerations relating to the particular child might point to a speedy return so that the child's future can be decided in his home country. Notwithstanding *Re M*, when considering the exercise of discretion following the establishment of the consent exception, one might have regard to Sumner J's comment in *M v M*[577] that it might not be appropriate to do so very often since it 'amounts to the consenting party being given the option to change their mind after the other party has acted in reliance on the consent'. Nevertheless note may be taken of *Re D (Abduction: Discretionary Return)*[578] in which Wilson J ordered the children's return to France notwithstanding that the father had established that the mother had consented to the children living with him in England, principally on the basis that were he to do otherwise the children might never have been able to visit France to see their mother because of the father's fear that the French custody order to the mother would then be enforced.

With regard to child's objections Baroness Hale observed that once the discretion comes into play:

> the court may have to consider the nature and strength of the child's objections, the extent to which they are "authentically her own" or the product of the influence of the abducting parent, the extent to which they coincide or are at odds with other considerations which are relevant to her welfare, as well as the general Convention considerations . . . The older the child, the greater the weight that her objections are likely to carry.

---

[574] *Re F (Children) (Abduction: Rights of Custody)* [2008] EWHC 272 (Fam) [2008] 3 WLR 527 per Potter P.
[575] [2007] UKHL 55 [2008] 1 AC 1288 at [45]–[48].   [576] [2006] UKHL 51 [2007] 1 AC 619, at [45].
[577] [2007] EWHC 1404 (Fam) [2007] 2 FLR 1010.   [578] [2000] 1 FLR 24.

Re M must have laid to rest the dispute over the basis of the discretion following the establishment of the child objection exception, namely, as to whether it is simply the trigger for the discretion which was the majority view in *Re R (Child Abduction: Acquiescence)*,[579] or whether Millett LJ was right when he said in the same case that if the child 'is of sufficient age and maturity for his views to be taken into account, the Convention clearly envisages that he will not be returned against his wishes unless there are countervailing factors which require his wishes to be overridden'. This latter view simply cannot be squared with *Re M*.[580] It has been held[581] that once the child objection exception has been established parental behaviour, such as a parent's clandestine removal, does not disqualify that parent from relying upon it for, were it otherwise, the child's voice would effectively be neutered.

With regard to settlement cases 'it must be borne in mind that the major objective of the Convention cannot be achieved. These are no longer "hot pursuit" cases . . . The object of securing a swift return to the country of origin cannot be met'. Consequently it cannot be assumed that the country of origin is the better forum for the resolution of the parental dispute and in such cases the policy of the Convention would not necessarily point towards a return.

What these 'illustrations' seem to demonstrate is that it will be extremely difficult to justify a return where an Art 13(b) exception is established nor will it be easy to do so in Art 12(2) settlement cases.[582] In *Re M* itself the court refused to order the children's return saying that they 'should not be made to suffer for the sake of the general deterrence of the evil of child abduction world-wide'.

(g) Handling international child abduction within the BIIR States

Introduction and background

In contrast to the original Brussels II Regulation, which did not affect the operation of the 1980 Hague Abduction Convention,[583] Art 60(e) of the revised Regulation (BIIR)[584] provides that in relations between Member States of the European Union[585] BIIR 'takes precedence over the 1980 Convention insofar as they concern matters governed by this Regulation.'[586]

The background to this radical change is interesting.[587] It began with a French proposal aimed at facilitating the exercise of cross-border rights of access[588] which was followed

---

[579] [1995] 1 FLR 716, per Balcombe LJ, with whom Sir Ralph Gibson agreed.

[580] In fact, even before *Re M*, the majority view had been preferred, see *Zaffino v Zaffino (Abduction: Child's View)* [2005] EWCA 1012 [2006] 1 FLR 410. For an example of a return order being made notwithstanding the establishment of the child objections 'defence', see *LCG v RL (Abduction: Habitual Residence and Child's Objections)* [2013] EWHC 1383 (Fam) [2014] 1 FLR 307.

[581] *Re H (A Child: Summary Return: Child's Objections)* [2012] EWHC B32 (Fam) [2013] 2 FLR 1163.

[582] Though for an example see *F v M and N (Abduction: Acquiescence: Settlement)* [2008] EWHC 1525 (Fam) [2008] 2 FLR 1270, though in that case Black J 'suspended' the return order to allow the mother to seek permission from the Polish court to bring the child to England.

[583] Council Regulation (EC) No 1347/2000 of 28 May 2000. Art 4 in fact required Member States to exercise jurisdiction 'in conformity' with the 1980 Convention.

[584] Council Regulation (EC) No 2201/2003 of 27 November 2003.

[585] Except Denmark, see Art 2(3).

[586] See generally Lowe, Everall and Nicholls *The New Brussels II Regulation* (2005) ch 6; N Lowe 'Regulating International Child Abduction—Brussels Style' (2002/3) 6 *Contemporary Issues in Law* 315 and 'Negotiating the Revised Brussels II Regulation' [2004] IFL 205.

[587] See eg N Lowe 'The Growing Influence of the European Union on International Family Law—A View from the Boundary' (2003) 56 *Current Legal Problems* 439 at 470 *et seq*.

[588] Initiative of the French Republic with a view to adopting a Council Regulation on the mutual enforcement of judgments on rights of access to children, OJ 2000 C234/7.

by the European Commission's own proposal[589] designed to improve the original Regulation but which controversially addressed the problem of child abduction through provisions on jurisdiction and on the return of the child. Eventually, the two proposals were amalgamated into a new Commission proposal.[590] This proposal would have effectively disapplied the 1980 Convention within the Community in favour of allowing courts of the State to which the child had been abducted at best only to make provisional holding orders and even then only provided the exceptions akin to those set out in Art 13 of the 1980 Convention applied, with the courts of the child's habitual residence free to make custody orders according to the merits. The proposal attracted passionate and protracted debate[591] and Member States were split. However, just when the Commission appeared to be giving up on getting agreement the Danes (who ironically are not party to BIIR) brokered a compromise. That compromise was broadly that applications for return of children wrongfully removed or retained would continue to be dealt with under the 1980 Hague Convention but in the event of a refusal to return the court then had to notify the court of the requesting State which in turn had to notify the parties giving them the opportunity to pursue the custody claim which would be decided upon the merits. If that court then required the child's return, that order would be enforceable without further question.

This compromise seemed to satisfy all parties and negotiations were eventually completed in November 2003. In fact, however, the impact of BIIR on the operation of the 1980 Hague Convention is, as we shall now see, rather more intrusive than might have been contemplated at the time of the compromise.

The impact of BIIR on the 1980 Hague Abduction Convention

The basic scheme of BIIR is to:

(a) preserve the pre-eminence of the 1980 Convention for dealing with applications for the return of abducted children but nevertheless to give some direction on how that Convention should be applied as between Member States; and

(b) govern the position in cases where a court refuses to make a return order under the Convention.

The crucial provision is Art 11.[592]

Article 11(1) directs the authorities of Member States when dealing with applications for the return of a child 'wrongfully removed in a Member State other than the Member State where the child was habitually resident immediately before the wrongful removal or retention' to apply paragraphs 2 to 8. Paragraphs 2–5 comprise directions on how return applications should be handled under the 1980 Hague Convention; paragraphs 6–8 govern what is to happen if a return order is refused.

---

[589] Proposal for a Council Regulation on jurisdiction and the recognition and enforcement of judgments in matters of parental responsibility OJ No C332 of 27.11.2001, 269.

[590] Proposal for a Council Regulation concerning jurisdiction and the recognition and enforcement of judgments in matrimonial matters and in matters of parental responsibility repealing Regulation (EC) No 1347/2000 and amending Regulation (EC) No 44/2001 in matters relating to maintenance, Brussels 3.5.2002 Com (2002) 222 Final.

[591] See the debate between N Lowe 'Article 5(3) of the Draft EU Regulation on Parental Responsibility—Dealing with Child Abduction' [2002] IFL 36 and I Karsten 'Article 5(3) of the Draft EU Regulation on Parental Responsibility—A Reply' [2002] IFL 42.

[592] See N Lowe 'A Review of the Application of Article 11 of the Revised Brussels II Regulation' [2009] IFL 27.

According to the BIIR Practice Guide[593] the judge must first determine whether a 'wrongful removal or retention' has taken place *in the sense of the Regulation*. It points out that the definition in Art 2(11)(b) is similar but not identical to that under Art 3 of the 1980 Hague Abduction Convention.

Applying Articles 12 and 13 of the Hague Convention in compliance with BIIR

Article 11(2) of BIIR provides:

> When applying Articles 12 and 13 of the 1980 Hague Convention, it shall be ensured that the child is given the opportunity to be heard during the proceedings unless this appears inappropriate having regard to his or her age or degree of maturity.

As well as Art 11(2) regard might also be had to Recital (19) which states that while the hearing of the child plays an important role in the application of the Regulation the instrument 'is not intended to modify national procedures' and the advice by the Practice Guide that it is not necessary for the child's view to be heard at the actual court hearing.

Although mechanisms had long been available to hear children's views in abduction cases principally via an enquiry and report by a Cafcass officer or less frequently by joining the child as a party, in *Re D (A Minor) (Abduction: Rights of Custody)* Baroness Hale considered that Art 11(2) required a fresh look at the question of hearing children's views. She made the following comment:[594]

> Rather than the issue coming up at a late stage in the proceedings, as has tended to take place up to now, European cases require the court to address at the outset whether and how the child is to be given the opportunity of being heard. If the options are canvassed then and there and appropriate directions given, this should not be an instrument of delay. CAFCASS officers and, in the few cases where this is appropriate, children's representatives are just as capable of moving quickly if they have to as anyone else. The vice has been when children's views have been raised very late in the day and seen as a 'last ditch stand' on the part of the abducting parent. This is not the place they should take in proceedings.

Following *Re D*, the Court of Appeal in *Re F (Abduction: Child's Wishes)*[595] held, in a case concerning a seven year old brought to England from Spain, that the failure to consider the obligations under Art 11(2), was a fundamental deficiency in the judge's decision which could not be papered over. The case was accordingly remitted so that the child's views could be heard through the preparation of a Cafcass report. In so ruling it was said to be necessary for the question of how and whether the court will hear the child in discharge of its obligation under Art 11(2) to be considered at its first directions appointment and at any subsequent directions appointment to ensure that the essential ingredient of the obligation is never out of the spotlight.

Unlike formerly there are now clear provisions for making a child a party to the proceedings and, indeed the court is obliged as soon as practicable after the application has been made to give directions as to whether the child should be made a party.[596] In *Re M (Children) (Abduction: Rights of Custody)*[597] Baroness Hale commented:

---

[593] Viz. 'Parental Responsibility in the European Union—Practice Guide for the Application of the New Brussels Regulation' drawn up by the European Commission (2005).

[594] [2006] UKHL 51, [2007] 1 AC 619 at [61].

[595] [2006] EWCA, Civ 468, [2007] 2 FLR 697. Cf *K v K* [2006] EWHC 2685 (Fam), [2007] 1 FCR 355, in which Sumner J was satisfied in the case of a 9 year old that Art 11(2) had been complied with, the child having been twice seen by experienced Cafcass reporters.   [596] FPR 2010 r 12.48(1)(c).

[597] [2007] UKHL 55 [2008] 1 AC 1288 at [57].

> To order separate representation in all cases, even in all child's objection cases, might be
> to send them the wrong messages. But it would not send the wrong messages in the very
> small number of cases where settlement is argued under the second paragraph of Article
> 12. These are the cases in which the separate point of view of the children is particularly
> important and should not be lost in the competing claims of the adults. If this were to
> become routine there would be no additional delay. In all other cases the question for the
> directions judge is whether separate representation of the child will add enough to the
> court's understanding of the issues that arise under the Hague Convention to justify the
> intrusion, the expense and the delay that might result. I have no difficulty in predicting
> that in the general run of cases it will not. But I would hesitate to use the word 'excep-
> tional'. The substance is what counts, not the label.

Applying *Re M*, Ryder J held in *Re C (Abduction: Separate Representation of Children)*[598]
that following *Re M*, the proper test for the court in considering an application for the
child's separate representation in Convention cases is whether such representation
'will add enough to the court's understanding of the issues that arise under the Hague
Convention to justify the intrusion and the expense and delay that may result'. A grant of
party status to a child leaves the court with a wide discretion to determine the extent of
the role which the child should play in the proceedings.[599]

In short, Art 11(2) quickly led to the key change that the court must always consider
as early in the process as possible, whether and, if so, how to hear the child's views.
Furthermore this change of practice is applied to all Hague cases regardless of whether
they are governed by BIIR.

As well as requiring the child to be heard, Art 11(5) also provides that:

> A court cannot refuse to return a child unless the person who requested the return of the
> child has been given an opportunity to be heard.

This obligation remains to be fully considered by the courts but is not without its
problems since the general practice (designed to facilitate speedy disposals) is not to
hear oral evidence when determining Hague applications and leave to do so tends
to be exercised sparingly. However, regard also needs to be had to Regulation (EC)
No 1206/2001 on co-operation between courts of the Member States in taking of
evidence in civil and commercial matters. By this Regulation a party can be heard
in their home State and, as the Practice Guide says, the use of video and 'conference
call' proposed by the Regulation could be useful. However, helpful though this latter
Regulation is, the requirement to hear the applicant is bound to slow down the proceedings and it is not clear how much will normally be gained over and above written
submissions.

The application of Arts 2 and 5 is not without relevance to the debate referred to earlier
in this chapter, about the need for an 'in-depth' examination of Hague applications, from
a human rights perspective.

---

[598] [2008] EWHC 517 (Fam) [2008] 2 FLR 6 at [31]–[33]. Note Baker J's comment in *WF v FJ, BF and RF
(Abduction: Child's Objections)* [2010] EWHC 2909 (Fam) [2010] 1 FLR 1153 at [25] that it is clearly preferable, time and resources permitting, for a child to be seen by the Cafcass High Court team before any decision is taken as to the child's party status.

[599] Per Lord Wilson in *Re LC (Children) (Reunite International Child Abduction Centre intervening)*
[2014] UKSC 1 [2014] 2 WLR 124 at [55].

Applying Article 13(b) of the Hague Convention in compliance with BIIR

According to Art 11(4):

> A court cannot refuse to return a child on the basis of Article 13b of the 1980 Hague Convention if it is established that adequate arrangements have been made to secure the protection of the child after his or her return.

Art 11(4) is intended to reinforce the principle of immediate return by restricting the exception allowed for under Art 13(b) of the 1980 Convention to a strict minimum. What Art 11(4) essentially does, as the *Guide* explains, is to extend the obligation to return even if the requisite Art 13(b) harm can be proved if it is established that the authorities in the Member State of Origin have made arrangements to secure the child's protection after the return. According to the Practice Guide it is not enough just to establish that procedures exist but instead it must be shown that the authorities in the Member State of Origin have taken concrete measures to protect the child in question. As Baroness Hale and Lord Wilson observed in *Re E (Children) (Abduction: Custody Appeal)*,[600] 'Article 11(4) clearly contemplates that adequate measures actually be in force.'

Given that it is now established that a judge cannot refuse a return unless satisfied that adequate arrangements are not available to protect the child in question,[601] it seems to follow that it is for the applicant to show adequate means of protection are in place. According to *Practice Direction 12F*,[602] in return applications made in England and Wales, the applicant must provide 'any details of measures taken by courts or authorities to ensure the protection of the child after its return to the Member State of habitual residence'.

Article 11(4) only applies to refusals to return under Art 13(b) of the Hague Convention and does not, for instance, apply to refusals to return based upon the child's objections.[603] It has also been said[604] to be 'near impossible to assert without a specific and detailed case that a Brussels' signatory's legal process is such that it, of itself, produces intolerability: in other words the actual circumstances of intolerability must be pleaded'.

Although the clear intention of Art 11(4) was to make reliance upon Art 13(b) more difficult, according to the 2008 Statistical Survey, a higher proportion (45%) of refused applications between BIIR States were based solely or in part on the article compared with 37% of applications received by such States from non-BIIR States. This was also the case in 2003 when 27% of refusals between what would now be BIIR States were based on Art 13(b) compared with 18% from non-BIIR States.[605] Why this should be so can only be speculated upon but a possible explanation is that BIIR has had the opposite effect to that intended, resulting in a more liberal application of the exception because as we discuss shortly, Art 11(8) provides that even if the court refuses to return the child, 'any subsequent judgment which requires the return of the child issued by a court having jurisdiction under this Regulation shall be enforceable . . . in order to secure the return of the child' and so the court of habitual residence may still override any decision and demand a return. In other words, the 'abduction court' does not have the final say and may be more relaxed about a refusal.

---

[600] [2011] UKSC 27 [2012] 1 AC 144 at [37].

[601] See eg Baroness Hale's comments in *Re D (A Minor) (Abduction: Rights of Custody)* [2006] UKHL 51 [2007] 1 AC 619 at [52].   [602] Para 2.11 (b).

[603] *Vigreux v Michel* [2006] EWCA Civ 630 [2006] 2 FLR 1181. See also the comments of Potter P in *Re F (Children) (Abduction: Rights of Custody)* [2008] EWHC (Fam) [2008] 3 WLR 527 and *M v T (Abduction)* [2008] EWHC 1383 (Fam) [2009] 1 FLR 1309.

[604] Per Ryder J in *F v M (Abduction: Grave Risk of Harm)* [2008] 1467 (Fam) [2008] 2 FLR 1263 at [18].

[605] See the analysis by N Lowe and V Stephens in 'Global Trends in the Operation of the 1980 Hague Abduction Convention' (2012) 46 Fam LQ 41 at 62.

The timing obligation under Art 11(3)

The basic premise of the 1980 Convention is that return applications should be dealt with 'promptly'. Indeed it has been well said that Hague Convention applications are 'intended to be a hot pursuit remedy'.[606] The accepted yardstick of promptness is six weeks. This is based on the second paragraph of Art 11 of the 1980 Convention which states:

> If the judicial or administrative authority concerned has not reached a decision within six weeks from the date of commencement of the proceedings, the applicant or the Central Authority of the requested State, on its own initiative or if asked by the Central Authority of the requesting State, shall have the right to request a statement of the reasons for the delay. If a reply is received by the Central Authority of the requested State, that Authority shall transmit the reply to the Central Authority of the requesting State, or the applicant as the case may be.

This provision has received little, if any, judicial analysis and it is perhaps an open question as to whether it should be construed as applying from the time of receipt of the application by the requested central authority rather than from the commencement of court proceedings. But however it is construed it stops short of directing Contracting States to resolve applications within six weeks, though, arguably at least, it provides a target time frame. BIIR, Art 11 (3), however, is intended to translate this 'target' into a more specific 'obligation'.

Article 11(3) provides:

> A court to which an application for return of a child is made as mentioned in paragraph 1 shall act expeditiously in proceedings on the application, using the most expeditious procedures available in national law. Without prejudice to the first subparagraph, the court shall, except where exceptional circumstances make this impossible, issue its judgment no later than six weeks after the application is lodged.

Although it is clearly the spirit of BIIR that Member States should at least have in place procedures that ensure that court hearings will normally be completed within six weeks, Member States are not obliged to introduce *new* procedures so as to meet the six week deadline.

As with Art 11 of the 1980 Convention, the scope of BIIR Art 11(3) is not beyond argument. The BIIR Practice Guide[607] suggests that the six week time limit covers court proceedings, including an appeal. In practice, the generally accepted view is that it applies to first instance proceedings only. This means that there are no time limits for issuing court proceedings in the first place.

Although Art 11(3) is mandatory in form, realistically there is no effective EU sanction.[608] However, in an important ruling by the European Court of Human Rights in *Shaw*

---

[606] Per Thorpe LJ in *Re C (Abduction: Grave Risk of Physical or Psychological Harm)* [1999] Fam 478 at 488.

[607] See para 2.4.

[608] Under EC law there are sanctions against States for failing to meet their Community obligations: By Art 10 of the EC Treaty Member States must take all appropriate measures to ensure the fulfilment of their Treaty obligations (including obligations resulting from actions taken by the Community institutions, such as this Regulation). In the event of a Member State's failure to do so the Commission may take the defaulting State before the ECJ pursuant to the procedure laid down in Art 226 EC. The obligation imposed on Member States by Art 10 extends to national courts in respect of matters within their jurisdiction (Case 14/83 *Von Colson v Kamann v Land Nordrhein-Westfalen* [1984] ECR 1891, [1986] 4 CMLR 430) although hitherto the Commission has not taken a Member State before the ECJ under Art 226 because of the actions (or failure to act) of its judiciary. Furthermore, individuals who suffer damage as a consequence of a Member State's

v Hungary,[609] Hungary was held to have violated Art 8 of the Human Rights Convention for failing to act expeditiously in hearing a return application *inter alia* because of the time taken both to hear a first appeal (13 weeks from the first decision) and a second appeal (a further 11 weeks). So far as England and Wales is concerned, the Court of Appeal[610] has made it clear that it expects Art 11(3) to be complied with. As Wall LJ put it:[611]

> Failure to adhere to the timetables proposed will not only result in the English court being in breach of its international obligations, it will represent an unacceptable abnegation of the court's responsibility to address cases of international child abduction—a matter in which, in the past, we have taken legitimate pride.

The global statistical surveys have repeatedly pointed up how difficult it is to meet a deadline of six weeks even when confined to first instance court proceedings. As the 2008 Survey highlighted, Hague applications are generally taking longer. Furthermore, Art 11(3) has made little or no difference as between Member States. The Survey found that only 26% of applications between BIIR States were resolved by a court within six weeks and in some States no application was resolved in this time.[612] In England and Wales (which is generally acknowledged to be a model Convention jurisdiction) only 28% met the deadline.[613] In a follow-up study[614] looking at applications received by England and Wales in 2011, the proportion of BIIR cases meeting the six deadline rose to 31% and application were generally disposed marginally faster than non-BIIR applications.

Although in principle Art 11(3), is to be welcomed, for speed of disposal is key to the successful operation of the Hague Convention, it has to be questioned first whether the provision is clear or comprehensive enough and secondly whether the six-week deadline is realistic. It has been suggested that there should be separate time targets of six weeks for each stage of the process, namely, the time between the receipt of the application by the central authority and the issue of court proceedings, the first instance proceedings and any appeal. It may be noted that that new Dutch system allows for six weeks for each of these stages. No doubt timing will be an important issue in the review of BIIR, expected to be completed in 2015.

The position following a refusal to return—Art 11(6)–(8)

The basic scheme

BIIR broke new ground by dealing with the position following a refusal to return. According to Art 11(6) once a court has refused to order a return under Art 13 of the Hague Convention (but note *not* under the other provisions),[615] it:

failure to fulfil its Community obligations may sue that State for damages in the national court (Cases C-46, 48/93 *Brasserie du Pêcheur SA v Germany, R v Secretary of State for Transport ex p Factortame Ltd and others* [1996] ECR I-I1029, [1996] 1 CMLR 889).

609   [2012] 2 FLR 1314.   610   In *Re M (A Child)* [2006] EWCA Civ 360.   611   At [88].

612   See Part II of the Overall Report, 'Regional Trends: 1. Brussels II a Regulation'.

613   See the National Report on England and Wales in 2008 Statistical Survey, op cit.

614   N Lowe and V Stephens 'The Timing of 1980 Hague Abduction Convention Applications: The 2001 Findings' (2013) and summarised by N Lowe, 'Timing Issues in Settling Applications under the 1980 Hague Abduction Convention' in N Witzleb et al (eds) *Festschrift Für Dieter Martiny Zum 70 Geburtstag* (2014) 107.

615   Eg Art 12(2) see *RD (Child Abduction) (Brussels) II Revised: Articles 11(7) and (19)* [2009] 1 FLR 586, Art 20 (not implemented by the UK but is in other Member States). Nor does it apply to rejections of an application under the 1980 Convention because the case does not comply with the requirements under Arts 3 or 5, see *Re SJ (a child) (Habitual Residence: Application to Set Aside)* [2014] EWHC 58 (Fam) and *Re RC and BC (Child abduction) (Brussels II Revised: Article 11(7)* [2009] 1 FLR 574.

> must immediately either directly or through its central authority transmit a copy of the court order on non-return and of the relevant documents, in particular a transcript of the hearings before the court, to the court with jurisdiction or central authority in the Member State where the child was habitually resident immediately before the wrongful removal or retention, as determined by national law. The court shall receive all the mentioned documents within one month of the date of the non-return order.

Unless the court of habitual residence is already seised by one of the parties, then, according to Art 11(7):

> the court or central authority that receives the information mentioned in paragraph 6 must notify it to the parties and invite them to make submissions to the court, in accordance with national law, within three months of the date of notification so that the court can examine the question of custody of the child.

If no submissions are received by the court within this three-month time limit, the case must be closed.

These provisions aim to (a) prevent the court of the requested State from assuming jurisdiction following a refusal to return the child; and (b) give the parties the opportunity of having determined a 'custody application' on its merits in the child's 'home court'.

If, following that adjudication (for which no time limit is prescribed), the court order requires the child to be returned, then by Arts 11(8), 40(1)(b) and 42, such an order is automatically enforceable, that is, 'without the need for a declaration of enforceability and without any possibility of opposing its recognition' simply upon the issue of a certificate by the judge of origin.[616]

Scrutiny of the scheme by the ECJ/CJEU

The scheme was scrutinised by the ECJ in *Re Rinau*[617] in which, during the pendency of divorce proceedings in Germany, where the couple had lived throughout their marriage, the mother and child failed to return from a holiday in Lithuania. The German court subsequently provisionally awarded custody of the child to the father, who then brought Hague Convention proceedings for the child's return. This application was refused by the Lithuanian court and the refusal was transmitted to the German central authority which passed it onto the court. In fact the refusal to return was later overturned on appeal and the children were ordered to be returned to Germany. However, enforcement of that decision was repeatedly suspended. Later the German court granted the divorce, awarded full custody to the father and ordered the mother to return the child and at the same time annexed to its decision an Art 42 certificate. The mother then brought proceedings in Lithuania for non-recognition of the Germany custody and return order. These proceedings came before the Supreme Court which made a reference to the ECJ, seeking a ruling on whether, given that the refusal to return had been overturned, the German court had correctly invoked Art 11(8) and attached a Art 42 certificate to its return order.

It was held that it had. The ECJ accepted that it was a *sine qua non* that an Art 11(8) judgment backed by an Art 42 certificate could only be made *following* a decision not to return the child made by the requested State. However, once such a decision *had been made and communicated to the court of origin* then because of the need for speed, it was irrelevant

---

[616] For details of this so-called 'fast track' enforcement procedure, see The fast-track procedure, p 1006.
[617] (Case C-195/08 PPU) [2008] 2 FLR 1495. This was the first reference made and dealt with under the urgent procedure. Judgment was delivered two months after the reference was received.

for the purposes of issuing a certificate that the non-return decision had been 'suspended, overturned, set aside or, in any event, has not become *res judicata* or has been replaced by a decision ordering return, insofar as the return of the child has not actually taken place.' Furthermore, given that the responsibility for properly issuing the certificate lies with the court of origin (viz. that the child and the parties had been given the opportunity to be heard and the court had taken into account the requested court's reasons for and evidence underlined its non-return decision) once the authenticity of the certificate is not in doubt, opposing its recognition is not permitted and the requested court must therefore declare the enforceability of the certified decision and allow the child's immediate return.[618]

In another reference, *Povse v Alpago*,[619] the ECJ was asked to rule on the application of Art 11(8) to return orders made in the context of interim custody orders. In this case, after the separation of an unmarried couple and contrary to an interim order of an Italian court, the mother and her daughter went to Austria. The father brought Hague abduction proceedings seeking a return of the daughter but this was refused by the Austrian courts. There followed a series of legal proceedings both in Italy and Austria culminating in the Italian court making a certified order requiring the mother to return the child to Italy and the Austrian court granting custody to the mother. Before that custody became final, the father sought to enforce the Italian return order. That issue came before the Austrian Supreme Court which made the reference to the ECJ.

The ECJ ruled that a decision of a Member State with jurisdiction requiring the child's return falls within Art 11(8) even though that State's court has not made a final decision on custody. Furthermore, a subsequent judgment granting provisional custody rights made by a court in the Member State of Enforcement and deemed enforceable under the law of that State, does not preclude the enforcement of a certified order requiring the child's return. It was also held that the enforcement of a certified judgment cannot be refused in the Member State of Enforcement because, as a result of a subsequent change of circumstances, it might be seriously detrimental to the best interests of the child. Such a change must be pleaded before the court which has jurisdiction in the Member State of Origin, which should also hear any application to suspend enforcement of its judgment.

The English decisions

In the first English decision on Art 11(6)–(8), *Re A (Custody Decision after Maltese Non-Return Order)*,[620] a mother invoked Hague proceedings for the return of her youngest son following his failure to return from a holiday in Malta. The Maltese court refused to make a return order on the basis of Art 13(b) of the Hague Convention and the mother, exercising her right under Art 11(7) of BIIR, issued proceedings effectively seeking a review of the Maltese decision and that her son be ordered to return to England forthwith. The child was made a party to the proceedings and the intention was that the guardian appointed to represent the child would travel to Malta to meet the father and the child and any other

---

[618] The inviolability of an Art 42 certificate was similarly emphasised in *Aguirre Zarraga* (Case C-491/10 PPU) unreported, and *Health Service Executive v SC and AC* (Case C-92/12 PPU) [2012] 2 FLR 1040, on which see P McEleavy 'The movement of children in Europe: mutual trust, distrust and human rights' [2013] IFL 172.

[619] (Case C-211/10 PPU) [2011] Fam 199. Note the dismissal of the mother and child's subsequent complaint that the enforcement of the Italian order by the Austrian authorities violated their Art 8 rights: *Povse v Austria* [2014] 1 FLR 944, ECtHR, discussed at Compatibility with the European Convention on Human Rights, p 1035.

[620] [2006] EWHC 3397 (Fam) [2007] 1 FLR 1923. For the first reported example of an English non-return order being 'trumped' by an overseas order (in this case by a Polish court) see *Re F (Abduction: Refusal To Return)* [2009] EWCA Civ 416 [2009] 2 FLR 1023.

relevant individuals and to investigate the child's circumstances living with the father. This plan was, however, frustrated by the father who failed to respond to all attempts to involve him.

Although the requirements under Art 42(2) to give both the child and the parties the opportunity to be heard were noted, Singer J held that neither requirement meant that nothing could be done until they had in fact been heard. Were it to be otherwise then by simple non co-operation the Regulation could be frustrated. Singer J also rejected, relying inter alia on the BIIR Practice Guide, the argument that the mother should first have exhausted her domestic remedies by going to the Court of Appeal in Malta. Having satisfied himself that it was proper to do so, Singer J investigated the merits of the mother's case and, applying the paramountcy principle of the child's welfare and the welfare checklist under the Children Act 1989, concluded that the child should be returned to England. He then issued a certificate to that effect under Art 42(1). In a postscript to the judgment it is explained that a week after the certificate was issued the Maltese Court of Appeal dismissed the father's appeal and confirmed that it was bound to recognise and enforce Singer J's judgment. The child subsequently returned to England a fortnight later.

A second case, Re A, HA v MB (Brussels II Revised: Article 11(7) Application),[621] also decided by Singer J, concerned the deceptively simple issue of how the scheme operates if the 'home' court decides to make a 'contact order' rather than a 'custody order'. In that context Singer J held that a contact order did not 'require the child's return' and, as such, fell outside Art 11(8). As Singer said, to 'elevate an order for contact ... to an Art 11(8) judgment requiring the child's return ... would render the scheme BIIR unworkable' since it would mean that the 'home court' would retain jurisdiction indefinitely, thus overriding the jurisdictional priority accorded under Art 8 to the court of the child's habitual residence (which was now France).

In M v T (Abduction: Brussels II Revised, Art 11 (7)),[622] following a Lithuanian court's decision to refuse to return a child on the basis of Art 13(b) the father promptly applied to the English court for the return of the child under BIIR, Art 11(7). Having found that it would not be in the child's best interests to be permanently returned to England but that it was important to promote and nurture the relationship between the child and his father in England, Charles J made a return order under Art 11(7) together with a contact regime and also making an order granting the mother permission to remove the child permanently from the jurisdiction.

In reaching his decision Charles J observed[623] that the Art 11(7) jurisdiction is not an appeal process in respect of a foreign court decision, but a welfare jurisdiction under Art 10. Accordingly a welfare approach has to be applied. In exercising this welfare jurisdiction the court has power to order the child's summary return which does not involve a full welfare inquiry. He also considered that the requirement to act expeditiously laid down by Art 11(3) also informs the way Art 11(7) applications should be dealt with. These points were reiterated in a helpful summary of the current position by Theis J in D v N and D (By the Guardian Ad Litem) (Brussels II Revised: Art 11 (7)),[624] and in which it was held that any summary order for return is directly enforceable under BIIR.

---

[621] [2007] EWHC 2016 (Fam) [2008] 1 FLR 289. See also Re H (Abduction: Jurisdiction) [2009] EWHC 2280 (Fam) [2010] 1 FLR 598.

[622] [2010 EWHC 1479 (Fam) [2010] 2 FLR 1685. See also AF v T and Another (Brussels II Revised: Art 11 (7) Application) [2011] EWHC 1315 (Fam) [2011] 2 FLR 891, in which return was refused but a contact order being made instead.   [623] At [17].

[624] [2011] EWHC 471 (Fam) [2011] 2 FLR 464 at [29] and cited by Peter Jackson J in AF v T and Another (Brussels II revised: Art 11 (7) Application) [2011] EWHC 1315 (Fam) [2011] 2 FLR 891 and by Baker J in Re AJ (Brussels II Revised) [2011] EWHC 3450 (Fam) [2012] 2 FLR 689.

Commentary

Although some have said that this scheme enables the court of habitual residence to 'trump' a no return order, it seems a reasonable compromise in itself. The 1980 Hague Abduction Convention does not deal with jurisdiction after a refusal to return and it is not unreasonable to vest that jurisdiction in the court of the child's habitual residence. The clear problems of doing so, though, are that the child and the abductor will not be present in that jurisdiction (though as Recital (20) and the BIIR Practice Guide point out, it is possible to hear both the child and abducting parent in the State in which they are staying by using the arrangements laid down in Regulation (EC) No 1206/2001 on cooperation between the courts of the Member States in taking evidence in civil or commercial matters) and that there is a danger of delay in disposing of the custody application. In this latter respect it might have been better if provision had also been made for the expeditious disposal of the merits hearing.

The English experience, as shown through reported cases, is interesting in that, contrary to early speculation, an order for the child's return to this jurisdiction notwithstanding a refusal to return by an 'abduction' court has not been the norm, rather the predominant concern has been the issue of contact. Whether this is the common experience among BIIR States is unknown and needs to be investigated. There is a pressing need to have empirical evidence on how Art 11(6)–(8) is working and, in its absence, it is suggested that no radical action should be taken in the current review of BIIR and certainly not, as has been suggested,[625] to abandon the Convention altogether within EU States, leaving the court of habitual residence to determine disputes on their merits.

(g) Securing rights of access

Under the 1980 Hague Abduction Convention applications for organising or securing the effective exercise of rights of access[626] can be presented to a central authority in the same way as an application for the child's return. However, the ability to make such applications is limited by the application of the BIIR which as between EU Member States (except Denmark) takes precedence, and which must be used for the recognition and enforcement of access orders or agreements.[627] Only a minority (16%, in the 2008 Statistical Survey) of applications made under the 1980 Convention are for access, though, surprisingly, in view of the Convention's limited application, the Survey recorded a 40% increase in such applications compared with 2003.

By Art 7 central authorities have a duty to co-operate with each other and to promote co-operation amongst the competent authorities in their respective States to achieve the Convention's obligations including, therefore, to ensure that rights of access are 'effectively respected' in compliance with Art 1(b). They are particularly directed 'either directly or through any intermediary' to take all appropriate measures; '(f) to initiate or facilitate the institution of judicial or administrative proceedings with a view . . . in a proper case, to make arrangements for organising or securing the effective exercise of rights of access'.

---

[625] M Hat'apka 'Article 11 of the Brussels IIa Regulation: is there justification for return proceedings in the area of harmonised rules of jurisdiction and mutual recognition of decisions?' [2014] IFL 182.

[626] See generally N Lowe 'Regulating Cross-Border Access to Children' in S Hofer, D Klippel and U Walter (eds) *Perspektivan Des Familienrechts—Festschrift Für Dieter Schwab* (2005) 1153 at 1159–65; L Silberman 'Patching Up the Abduction Convention: A Call for a New International Protocol and a suggestion for Amendments to ICARA' (2003) 38 Texas Int LJ 41; 'Transfrontier Access/Contact and the Hague Convention of 25 October 1980 on the Civil Aspects of International Child Abduction'—Final Report, Preliminary Document No 5 of July 2002 for Special Commission of September/October 2002 (hereafter the 'Duncan Report'); Lowe, Everall and Nicholls, op cit, at 25.2 *et seq*.

[627] For the application of which, see The fast-track procedure, p 1006.

The key provision is Art 21, by which central authorities are required to promote the peaceful enjoyment of access rights and to take steps to remove, as far as possible, all obstacles to the exercise of access, and may initiate or assist in the initiation of proceedings to organise or protect access. For the purposes of English domestic law a decision relating to access means a child arrangements order naming a person with whom the child is to spend time or otherwise have contact.[628]

According to *Re G (A Minor) (Enforcement of Access Abroad)*,[629] Art 21 continues to apply even where the child is habitually resident in England and Wales at the time of the application.[630] However, *Re G* also establishes that whilst it may impose duties upon the central authority, Art 21 imposes no duties whatever upon judicial authorities. Indeed Hoffmann LJ queried whether Art 21 was so vague or permissive as to create no rights at all, but insofar as it might, those rights were in public law and enforceable only against the central authority. Accordingly, applicants who are seeking contact rather than a return of the child should apply for a child arrangements order naming them as a person with whom the child is to spend time under the Children Act 1989 s 8, which will be heard on the merits. It was held in *Re T (Minors) (Hague Convention: Access)*[631] that upon receiving an application under Art 21 the central authority's only duty is to make appropriate arrangements for providing English solicitors to act on the applicant's behalf to institute proceedings under the 1989 Act. It has no mandate to institute proceedings itself. Furthermore, the advantageous provision for legal aid does not apply to applications under the 1989 Act nor may a legal representation certificate issued under the Convention be extended to these proceedings.

In view of these restrictions, as Hoffmann LJ observed in *Re G*, in appropriate cases applicants might be better advised to apply to enforce access under the 1980 European Convention.[632] However, it will rarely be possible to use this Convention to enforce access orders since actions involving other EU States (except Denmark) must be brought under BIIR.[633]

Interestingly, in *Hunter v Murrow (Abduction: Rights of Custody)*[634] Thorpe LJ signalled that the decision in *Re G* may have to be revisited. His reasoning was that the Convention is a living instrument but as revisions of the text are 'simply impracticable . . . evolutions necessary to keep pace with social and other trends must be achieved by evolutions in interpretation and construction'. He maintained that this is permitted by reason of Art 31(3)(b) of the Vienna Convention on the Law of Treaties 1969, which allows a construction that reflects 'any subsequent practice in the application of the treaty which establishes agreement of the parties regarding its interpretation'.

There is in fact no consistent approach even among common law jurisdictions on how Art 21 should be interpreted. The *Re G* approach is taken in the USA with decisions such

---

[628] Child Abduction and Custody Act 1985 s 27(4), as amended by the Children and Families Act 2014.

[629] [1993] Fam 216, CA. See also *Practice Note* [1993] 1 FLR 804.

[630] It is sufficient for the application of Art 21 that the child is habitually resident in *a* Contracting State before any breach of a right of access: Art 4.

[631] [1993] 2 FLR 617. For a shorter report of this case see *Re T (Minors) (International Child Abduction: Access)* [1993] 3 All ER 127n.   [632] Discussed at Applying for access, p 1087.

[633] See *Re G (Foreign Contact Order: Enforcement)* [2003] EWCA Civ 1607 [2004] 1 WLR 521, applying the original Regulation. The consequence of this is that the European Convention can only be invoked to enforce access orders made in Denmark, Iceland, Liechtenstein, Montenegro, Norway, Serbia, Switzerland, the former Yugoslav Republic of Macedonia, Turkey and Ukraine.

[634] [2005] EWCA Civ 976 [2005] 2 FLR 1119 at [30]–[31].

as *Bromley v Bromley*[635] and *Tejeiro Fernandez v Yeagar*[636] establishing that Art 21 does not give the courts any independent authority to enforce rights of access in respect of children. Ireland, too, deals with access under its domestic legislation.[637] Other common law jurisdictions take a less rigid line. In New Zealand, for example, it has been held[638] that while the relevant legislation implementing the Hague Convention[639] did not of itself specify a right to apply to court it had clearly to remove the right before it could be inferred that there is no right of application for access to a court. In Australia courts deal with access under the implementing Regulations[640] rather than under domestic legislation. In Scotland, following *Donofrio v Burrell*[641] and the amended Rule 70.5(2) of the Rules of the Court of Session applications to enforce 'rights of access granted by any court of a Contracting party to the Hague Convention' can be made to the court 'under the Convention'.[642] But like England and Wales it is accepted that Art 21 does not confer upon individuals private rights or remedies attributable to the Convention nor does it place any obligation on the judicial authorities of the requested State.

The position in civil law jurisdictions is similarly varied with some such as Italy, Spain and Mexico regarding Art 21 as binding on the courts while others such as Sweden and France do not. Other States, for example, the Netherlands have interpreted Art 21 as empowering the Central Authority to bring a court action with the application being determined upon domestic law principles. Yet a further variation is that applying in Slovakia which regards Art 21 as binding upon the courts where a court order is sought to be enforced but applying domestic law to the enforcement of 'rights of access' falling short of a court order.[643]

In short, even if *Re G* is revisited, it is not at all certain how Art 21 should be interpreted. We discuss later,[644] whether in the light of the varied interpretation, Art 21 should be reformed.

6. THE 1980 EUROPEAN CUSTODY CONVENTION

Although of historic importance, this Convention[645] now operates very much as a residual instrument given the precedence accorded to BIIR and the preference to use the 1980 Hague Abduction Convention when BIIR is not applicable.

[635] 30 F Supp 2d 857 (ED Pa 1998), US District Ct for the Eastern District of Pennsylvania.
[636] 121 F Supp 2d 1118 (WD Mich 2000), US District Ct for the Western District of Michigan. See also *Janzik v Shand* No. 99C 6515, 2000 WL 1745203 (DN111. Nov. 27, 2000).
[637] See N Lowe and S Armstrong *Country Report: Ireland* (NCMEC 2002) 4.2. For the more complicated position in Canada see eg N Lowe, S Armstrong and A Mathias: *Country Report: Canada* (NCMEC 2002) 4.1–4.2.
[638] See *Secretary for Justice v Sigg* (1992) 10 FRNZ 164 and *Gumbrell v Jones* [2001] NZFLR 593.
[639] New Zealand has chosen not simply to directly incorporate the Convention into its domestic law but also to re-enact it in its own terms. See now the Care of Children Act 2004 Part 2, sub-part 4 on which see N Lowe and K Hollingsworth *Country Report: New Zealand* (NCMEC 2005).
[640] Like New Zealand, Australia has re-enacted the Convention in its own terms under the Family Law (Child Abduction Conventions) Regulations 1986, as amended.
[641] 2000 SLT 1051, extensively discussed by Lowe, Everall and Nicholls, op cit, at 25.27 *et seq.*
[642] Consequently applicants will have the benefit of free legal aid. A not dissimilar position operates in Israel, see N Lowe and R Schuz *Country Report: Israel* (NCMEC, 2005) 4.1/4.2.
[643] For a review of the different positions, see the Duncan Report, op cit, at 397.
[644] See Evaluating the use and effect of the 1980 Conventions, p 1088.
[645] See generally R Jones 'Council of Europe Convention on Recognition and Enforcement of Decisions Relating to the Custody of Children' (1981) 30 ICLQ 46,7; Lowe, Everall and Nicholls, op cit, ch 19 and Clarke Hall and Morrison on *Children* 5[555]ff.

(a) When the Convention applies

This Convention applies to the 'improper removal' of any person of any nationality who is under the age of 16 and who does not have the right to decide his own place of residence.[646] Under Art 1(d), 'improper removal' means:

> the removal of a child across an international frontier in breach of a decision relating to his custody which has been given in a Contracting State and which is enforceable in such a State; "improper removal" also includes:
>
> (i) the failure to return a child across an international frontier at the end of a period of the exercise of the right of access to this child or at the end of any other temporary stay in a territory other than that where the custody is exercised;
>
> (ii) a removal which is subsequently declared unlawful within the meaning of Article 12.

As 'improper removal' has to be across 'an international frontier' the Convention has no application to abductions *within* the UK. It a prerequisite under this Convention that an applicant has a court order in his favour, although under Art 12, if there is no enforceable decision at the time of the removal, an application may subsequently be made by any interested person for a declaration that the removal is 'improper'.[647] In *Re S (A Minor) (Custody: Habitual Residence)*[648] the House of Lords held that Art 12 and s 23(2) of the 1985 Act effectively empower courts to make orders which can *subsequently* make the child's continuing retention in another country an 'improper removal' within the meaning of Art 1(d).

Under Art 1(c) 'a decision relating to custody' means a decision of a judicial or administrative authority insofar as it relates to the care of the person of the child including the right to decide on the place of his residence, or to the right of access to him. It is clear that any type of child arrangements order under s 8 of the Children Act 1989 will satisfy this requirement. Whether it includes a foreign court making a return order under the 1980 Hague Abduction Convention has yet to be determined, though sensible arguments can be raised either way.[649]

(b) Recognition and enforcement

Under Art 7 decisions relating to custody made and enforceable in one Contracting State are recognised and enforceable in every other Contracting State. But to secure that recognition and enforcement, an application has to be made for those purposes in the other Contracting State.

(c) Applying for the child's return

To secure the child's return, an application may be made through a central authority.[650] Upon receiving the application the central authority in the State addressed must, without

---

[646] By analogy with *Re H (Abduction: Child of 16)* [2000] 2 FLR 51 the Convention will cease to apply to a child upon his attaining the age of 16 even if the application was made before he was 16. There remains, however, the power to deal with the child whilst a minor under the High Court's inherent jurisdiction.

[647] In England and Wales such a declaration can be made in any 'custody proceedings': Child Abduction and Custody Act 1985 s 23(2). 'Custody proceedings' are defined in Sch 3, as amended by the Children and Families Act 2014 Sch 2 para 48 and refer principally to child arrangements orders relating to the child's living arrangements.   [648] [1998] AC 750, HL.

[649] See *Re L (Abduction: Pending Criminal Proceedings)* [1999] 1 FLR 433 at 442, per Wilson J.

[650] Art 4(2).

delay, take appropriate steps, inter alia, to secure the recognition and enforcement of the custody order.[651] Recognition and enforcement are achieved by registering the court order in a court of the Contracting State to which the child has been taken. In England and Wales applications to register must be made in the High Court.[652] Once the order is registered the court has the same powers of enforcement as if it had made the original order,[653] and in this way the child's return can be ordered.

In *Re H (A Minor) (Foreign Custody Order: Enforcement)*[654] it was held that whilst registration is a *sine qua non* condition of enforcement, enforcement does not automatically follow recognition, since there is a discretion to apply the exceptions (under Arts 9 and 10) to the issue of enforcement notwithstanding a previous registration.

(d) Refusing recognition or enforcement

Where an application has been made promptly after an improper removal, recognition and enforcement of the order and restoration of the child must normally follow unless an exception, provided by Arts 9 and 10, can be established. The burden of proving an exception lies on the person opposing the recognition or enforcement and the court is expected to recognise and register the order unless it *expressly* finds one of the exceptions proved.[655] In no event is the court entitled to review a foreign decision as to its substance.[656]

The latitude for refusal depends upon whether the Contracting State has implemented Art 8. If it has, then provided the application is made within six months of the child's removal, registration is virtually mandatory, since Art 8 permits only the narrow exceptions under Art 9 to be raised. However, most Contracting States, including the UK,[657] have not implemented Art 8.[658] In these States, registration may, in all cases, be refused within the terms of either Art 9 or Art 10.[659]

The Art 9 exceptions are narrow and may best be thought of as comprising procedural defects in the making of the order sought to be enforced. Under Art 9 registration or enforcement may be refused where:

(a) through no fault of the respondent, he or she was not served with notice of the relevant proceedings in the state of origin;

(b) the court of origin lacked competence to make the order in question since it was not founded on the habitual residence of any of the parties; or

---

[651] Art 5.
[652] Child Abduction and Custody Act 1985 s 16. For the procedure see FPR 2010 rr 12.44–12.57.
[653] Child Abduction and Custody Act 1985 s 18 and Art 7.   [654] [1994] Fam 105, CA.
[655] *Re A (Foreign Access Order: Enforcement)* [1996] 1 FLR 561, CA.   [656] Art 9(3).
[657] The UK did not implement Art 8 because it was felt to be too draconian and contrary to the provisions of the Hague Convention: see Lord Hailsham LC in 460 HL Official Report (5th series) col 1253, 1985. For the list of other states making a similar reservation, see Lowe, Everall and Nicholls, op cit, at 19.14, n 21.
[658] Art 17 permits states to take a reservation on Art 8. Art 17 was the compromise arrived at to accommodate two opposing views, namely that the return of recently abducted children should be virtually automatic as against the view that the requested State should retain an ultimate discretion to refuse a return where this would be manifestly contrary to the child's view. See Jones, op cit, at 472–473, where he fully articulates the debate.
[659] Note: under Art 17(2) where a child is removed from a State that has made a reservation on Art 8, to a State that has not, the latter State can nevertheless apply Art 10. In other words, in the spirit of reciprocity no advantage can be taken of the one State entering and the other not entering a reservation.

(c) there was already a prior decision in the state addressed which became enforceable before the improper removal.

By contrast, the Art 10 exceptions are considerably wider, particularly Art 10(1)(b),[660] which permits refusal:

> where it is found that by reason of a change of circumstances, including the passage of time but not including a mere change in the residence of the child after an improper removal, the effects of the original decision are manifestly no longer in accordance with the welfare of the child.

Before making any decision under Art 10(1)(b) the court is required by Art 15 to ascertain the child's views 'unless this is impracticable having regard in particular to his age and understanding'. Unlike the Hague Abduction Convention, however, a refusal is not permitted because of the child's objections per se.

Article 10(1)(b) has been interpreted strictly by the English courts. It has been emphasised that for the exception to operate at all there must be a change of circumstances,[661] and that there is a heavy burden to discharge to show that the original order is 'manifestly no longer in accordance with the child's welfare'. It has been held,[662] for instance, that it is not enough to show that the child has settled well and is happy. Nevertheless there have been cases where registration and enforcement have been refused. In *F v F (Minors) (Custody: Custody Order)*[663] it was held that a foreign order for custody should not be enforced where the children had been in England for 21 months, and 12 months had elapsed between the making of the foreign order and the enforcement hearing. Similarly, in *Re R (Abduction: European and Hague Conventions)*[664] recognition and enforcement of a Swiss order in favour of grandparents were refused on the basis that the mother had since remarried and the emotional and financial support that her new spouse provided had transformed the situation, with the child in question now thriving and happy and emphatically not wishing to return to Switzerland. Article 10(1)(b) was also found to be satisfied in *T v R (Abduction: Forum Conveniens)*[665] in which a return to a father in Sweden after living for four years with the mother in England, was held to be manifestly not in the child's short-term interests.

---

[660] Art 10(1)(a) refers to the effect of the decision being 'manifestly incompatible with the fundamental principles' of the law in the State addressed (on which note the failed applications in *Re G (A Minor) (Child Abduction: Enforcement)* [1990] 2 FLR 325 and *T v R (Abduction: Forum Conveniens)* [2002] 2 FLR 544, discussed by Lowe, Everall and Nicholls, op cit, at 19.110); Art 10(1)(c) refers to children who are nationals or habitual residents in the State addressed and who have no such connection with the State of Origin; and Art 10(1)(d) refers to the incompatibility of the decision with a decision given in the State addressed or enforceable in that State after being given in a third State. For a refusal on this ground see *Re M (Child Abduction: European Convention)* [1994] 1 FLR 551 where enforcement proceedings began after an English court had made an interim residence order and it was not thought to be in the children's welfare to be returned pending the outcome of the English decision since they had lived in England for the last 18 months.

[661] Per Leggatt LJ in *Re A (Foreign Access Order: Enforcement)* [1996] 1 FLR 561, at 564.

[662] Per Booth J in *Re G (A Minor) (Abduction: Enforcement)* [1990] 2 FLR 325. See also *Re L (Child Abduction: European Conventions)* [1992] 2 FLR 178 and *Re K (A Minor) (Abduction)* [1990] 1 FLR 387.

[663] [1989] Fam 1.

[664] [1997] 1 FLR 663, CA. Enforcement was also refused in *Re H (A Minor) (Foreign Custody Order: Enforcement)* [1994] Fam 105, in which a 13-year-old girl, who had been in the UK for about five years, was adamant that she did not wish to have any further contact with her father.

[665] [2002] 2 FLR 544. But note this application was adjourned, see later.

(e) Adjourning recognition and enforcement

Article 10(2) permits postponing recognition and/or enforcement:

(a) if an ordinary form of review of the original decision has been commenced;
(b) if proceedings relating to the custody of the child, commenced before the proceedings in the State or origin were instituted, are pending in the State addressed;
(c) if another decision concerning the custody of the child is the subject of proceedings for enforcement or of any other proceedings concerning the recognition of the decision.

It may be observed that the pendency of other proceedings relating to the child is a ground for adjournment even though it is not a ground for refusing recognition or enforcement. In *T v R (Abduction: Forum Conveniens)*[666] it was held that if the court refuses to recognise the original order under Art 10(1), it can nevertheless adjourn the application rather than dismiss it.

(f) Applying for access

Under Art 11(1) access decisions[667] are recognised and enforceable in the same way as custody decisions. According to *Re A (Foreign Access Order: Enforcement)*[668] the scheme of the Convention is plain and the judge's task is clear, namely to recognise and register the foreign access order unless an exception under Arts 9 or 10 is established. The burden for establishing a defence lies on the party opposing registration.

Successfully opposing the enforcement of an access order is as hard as opposing the enforcement of custody. In *Re A*, in which a father sought to enforce a French access order by which there was to be staying access in France every August, it was held that the 'hardening' of the children's objections to going to France came nowhere near the change of circumstances rendering the original decision 'manifestly no longer in accordance with the child's welfare', envisaged by the Convention. In *Re G (Foreign Contact Order: Enforcement)*[669] Thorpe LJ commented:

The European Convention would be rendered impotent and its policy frustrated were primary carers able to avoid enforcement by asserting circumstances and developments that cry out for profound investigation by the courts of the jurisdiction primarily seised.

In *Re L (Abduction: European Convention: Access)*,[670] however, the enforcement of a French access order in favour of grandparents was refused because it was predicated on the basis that the children were living in France close to the grandparents, whereas they were now living in England with their parents. It was held that in these circumstances, given that the French order would have required the children (aged seven and three) to travel to France twice a month for contact, it was neither practical nor in the children's interest to enforce it. Accordingly, the defence under Art 10(1)(b) that enforcement was 'manifestly no longer in accordance with the welfare of the [children]' was made out.

Notwithstanding the general scheme to register or to refuse to register an access order, Art 11(2) empowers the competent authority addressed to 'fix the conditions for implementation and exercise of the right of access taking into account, in particular,

---

[666] Ibid.
[667] See further Lowe, Everall and Nicholls, op cit, at 25.42ff and N Lowe 'Regulating Cross Border Access to Children' in S Hofer, D Klippel and U Walter (eds) *Perspektivan Des Familienrechts Festschrift für Dieter Schwab* (2005) 1153, 1154–8.   [668] [1996] 1 FLR 561, CA.
[669] [2004] 1 WLR 521.   [670] [1999] 2 FLR 1089.

undertakings given by the parties on this matter'. In effect, Art 11(2) enables the State addressed to modify decisions of other Contracting States to make them consistent with local practice. However, as emphasised in *Re A (Foreign Access Order: Enforcement)*,[671] this modifying power is still subject to the embargo under Art 9(3) against reviewing orders as to their substance. Accordingly, it was held to be a misuse of Art 11(2) to modify a French order that the father have annual contact in France by granting him staying access in England instead when it was known that the father could only afford staying access in France.

In contrast to *Re A* a more liberal approach was signalled by Thorpe LJ's comment in *Re G (Foreign Contact Order: Enforcement)*:[672]

> Access orders can seldom be written on stone tablets. The orders are peculiarly vulnerable to change of circumstance, the maturation of children, and the dynamics within sometimes the old family and sometimes a newly constituted family. In consequence enforcement, not only after lapse of time but after relocation and in a foreign court, is always likely to be problematic. *These realities, in my judgment, demand a liberal construction of Art 11(2) in order to achieve the overriding objectives of the European Convention, one of which is to ensure that the act of relocation does not avoid the orders for contact made by the court that granted permission.* (Emphasis added.)

One can only agree. Unless it is thought right to limit Art 11(2) to being a purely supplementary power (for example, to give some definition to open ended orders such as defining school holidays or 'reasonable' access) then some flexibility has surely to be permitted. Even so where the line is to be drawn in a particular case is problematic.

The flexibility provided for by Art 11(2), particularly as interpreted by Thorpe LJ in *Re G*, makes these provisions superior not just to those of the 1980 Hague Abduction Convention but also to the powers provided by BIIR and the 1996 Hague Convention on the Protection of Children. Furthermore, because it is a Convention obligation *upon the court* to enforce orders, unlike under the 1980 Abduction Convention, applicants are entitled to free legal representation regardless of means or merits, when seeking to enforce access orders.

Yet despite these advantages, the scope for invoking the Convention is severely limited since it has been superseded within Member States of the European Union (other than Denmark) by BIIR, under which, in any event, the enforcement procedure is quicker.

7. EVALUATING THE USE AND EFFECT OF THE 1980 CONVENTIONS

Although both the 1980 Conventions have attracted growing numbers of Contracting States, it is evident that the Hague Abduction Convention has proved far more useful than the European Custody Convention. In practice even before the coming into force of the BIIR, the European Convention was little used. In part this is because the need for a custody or access order limits its scope, but it seems its restricted use also stems from its alleged complexity.[673] In contrast, there is general agreement that the Hague Convention is generally working well. However, whether this view is over-sanguine can be debated. The 2008 Statistical Survey found that overall, 46% of return applications ended either in the child's voluntary return or in a return order made by the court as against 51%

---

[671] [1996] 1 FLR 561.   [672] [2004] 1 WLR 521.
[673] See N Lowe and A Perry 'International Child Abduction—the English Experience' (1998) 47 ICLQ 127.

recorded in the 2003 Survey and 50% as found in the 1999 Survey. However, while this might seem a relatively low proportion it needs to be appreciated that a relatively high proportion (18% in 2008)[674] of applications were withdrawn[675] and a further 5% were rejected by central authorities as not being well founded in Convention terms.[676] In fact a relatively small, though rising, proportion (18% in 2008, as against 12% in 2003 and 11% in 1999) ended in a judicial refusal to return. Put another way, of the applications that went to court 39% of applications were refused in 2008 as against 28% in 2003 and 26% in 1999. In that sense the Convention is broadly working as it was intended to, though there is a noticeable higher trend of refusals.

So far as speed is concerned, as we discussed earlier in this chapter, the accepted target under the Hague Convention is six weeks for courts to dispose of proceedings, a target which has been made an obligation by BIIR. It is evident, however, that return applications are disposed of rather more slowly than this (though still, one suspects, considerably quicker than domestic applications would generally be determined). More depressingly, the three surveys show that applications are taking longer to complete, though this is against as exponential rise (45% over the 2003 Survey) in the number of applications. BIIR seems to have made little difference to timing. This is a matter of real concern since speed is of the essence if the Convention is to work in children's interests. In this respect one suggestion that might be worth pursuing is limiting appeals. It was a striking finding of the 2008 Survey that 80% of appeals upheld the original decision.

Of course, some Contracting States perform worse than others, but even here international pressure can be brought to bear on countries that are thought to be falling below the accepted Convention standards. In this regard the periodic reviews conducted by the Permanent Bureau of the Hague Conference are enormously helpful and influential. It may also be supposed that the current review of BIIR will lead to further insights into practice and, hopefully, some beneficial reforms.

One area where the Hague Convention is acknowledged not to be working well is in relation to access.[677] Not only do they form a minority of applications but in terms of outcome and speed they are markedly less successful than return applications. According to the 2008 Statistical Survey, only 21% of access applications ended in access being gained as a result of a voluntary agreement or court order, a considerable decline from 34% in the 2003 Survey and 43% in 1999. In the 2008 Survey, 73% of applications resolved judicially and 74% resolved voluntarily took over six months to do so.

There has been much discussion in the Special Meetings of the Commissions reviewing the Hague Convention as to what, if anything, to do about access, though in the EU context, the issue has become arguably less pressing given the provision in BIIR for fast-track enforcement.[678] At the 2002 Meeting it was agreed that the Bureau draw up a Good Practice Guide and that was published in 2008.[679] Note might be taken of other international instruments that can make a contribution in this area, in particular, the 1996 Hague Convention on the Protection of Children which does have useful provisions on access, and which we discuss\ at the end of this chapter.

---

[674] As against 15% in 2003 and 14% in 1999.

[675] The 1999 survey found a variety of reasons for withdrawals including lack of finance, on the one hand, and parties reaching a private agreement on the other.

[676] As against 6% in 2003 and 11% in 1999. Examples include where the child is too old (ie 16 or over) or where the child could not be found or was found in another State.

[677] The issue was acknowledged and extensively discussed at the Second Special Commission Meeting of the Review of the Hague Convention held in 1993.   [678] Discussed at The fast-track procedure, p 1006.

[679] *Transfrontier Contact Concerning Children.*

Yet another international instrument of potential relevance is the Council of Europe's 2003 Convention on Contact Concerning Children.[680] The Convention usefully sets out general principles which domestic courts should observe when dealing with contact issues and contains some provisions directly concerned with the recognition and enforcement of transfrontier contact cases including the novel provision of providing a procedure for advance recognition and enforcement of contact orders and provision for the prompt return of children at the end of a period of transfrontier contact.

While these latter two Conventions are useful they undoubtedly make the legal landscape more complicated and indeed there is a real danger that the proliferation of international instruments will in themselves defeat the very object of improving the law regulating the cross border movement of children.

Access is not the only issue of concern. Other debates concern the lack of legal aid (particularly in the USA) and whether there should be concentrated jurisdiction when dealing inter alia with Hague cases (in this respect there is a clear trend for States to reduce the number courts able to hear Hague cases). But perhaps the acid test of success is whether the Conventions deter would-be abductors. This is much harder to assess. The statistical studies have long shown the majority of abductions are by mothers (69% according to the 2008 Survey) who are normally the child's sole or joint primary carer (88% of abducting mothers and 32% of abducting fathers fell into this category in so far as information was available to the 2008 Survey) and commonly (60% according to the 2008 Survey) tended to be returning to their jurisdiction of nationality (ie 'going home'). In other words, the abductions were generally not aimed, as another study[681] termed it, at 'throwing off pursuers by escaping abroad', but instead abductors were 'returning to a culturally familiar country where family and legal support may be available'.

One theory about the changing pattern of abduction is that the Conventions deter would-be abductors in the popular sense of the word, ie men (or non-primary carers) 'kidnapping' their children. On the other hand, the deterrent effect of the Convention has not been so strong among women because, it is argued, their motivation is likely to be to escape violent or abusive relationships.[682] Whether this is so has yet to be definitely established but there is undoubted concern that there is no real mechanism under the Conventions for ensuring the child's safety after being returned, nor indeed for ensuring that any steps are subsequently taken. This in turn led to the suggestion at the third review of the Hague Convention[683] that central authorities ought to be obliged to take responsibility for children returned under the Convention. Although this suggestion drew substantial support, no formal action has yet been taken because of the extra commitment and costs involved. In practice, however, there is considerable liaison both between the judiciary and the central authorities, and in cases of real concern it is possible to make informal arrangements and, as we discuss shortly, depending on how it is interpreted, the 1996 Protection of Children Convention does have provisions that can help in this respect.

The fact that 'abductors' tend to be primary caring mothers returning home has led some[684] to query the very appropriateness of the Hague Abduction Convention.

---

[680] The UK has not ratified this Convention. For a detailed discussion of the 2003 Convention see Lowe, Everall and Nicholls, op cit, 25.83 et seq.

[681] G Greif and R Hager *When Parents Kidnap* (1993).

[682] See the discussion by Lowe and Perry, op cit.   [683] By the Australian delegation.

[684] See eg M Freeman 'In the Best Interests of Internationally Abducted Children?—Plural, Singular, Neither or Both?' [2002] IFL 77 and R Schuz 'The Hague Child Abduction Convention: Family Law and Private International Law' (1995) 44 ICLQ 771. Cf N Lowe with K Horosova 'The Operation of the 1980 Hague Abduction Convention—A Global View' (2007) 41 Fam LQ 59, at 70–71.

One further challenge is in respect of Islamic countries which with the outstanding exceptions of Morocco and Iraq (whose accession only took effect in June 2014) have so far not acceded to the Convention. The dilemma here is that while it is desirable to have as many nations as possible within the 'Convention fold', not all nations hold to the same basic values and, in particular, they may not treat all parents equally, having different concepts of what is in children's interests.[685]

F. INTERNATIONAL PROTECTION OF CHILDREN: THE 1996 HAGUE CONVENTION ON THE PROTECTION OF CHILDREN

1. INTRODUCTION

We conclude this chapter by examining the third of the modern trilogy of Hague Conventions[686] concerned with children, namely, the 1996 Hague Convention on the Protection of Children.[687] This Convention provides for the recognition and enforcement within all Contracting States of measures directed to the protection of children's person and property and to establish the necessary co-operation between the authorities of Contracting States in order to achieve this basic purpose.[688] Its overall aim is to (a) provide better protection of children involved in cross border civil (but not criminal) disputes; (b) improve international co-operation for the protection of vulnerable children up to the age of 18; and (c) avoid conflicts in decisions concerning child placements. Essentially, it is a jurisdiction, recognition and enforcement instrument. Although it bears a striking similarity to BIIR, which is hardly surprising as the latter was modelled on the former, there are important differences relating in particular to its scope, some of its jurisdictional rules, and its applicable law provisions.

The 1996 Convention formally came into force in 2002,[689] Since then the number of ratifications and accessions has gradually increased such that as of July 2014 there were 41 Contracting States including all EU Member States except Italy.

The UK's ratification came into force in November 2012. Remarkably, for ratification purposes it was felt appropriate[690] to implement the 1996 Convention by using the European Communities Act 1972 s 2(2).[691] As a result, the 1996 Convention was treated

---

[685] In this respect there have been long running meetings (commonly known as 'the Malta process') to discuss how to accommodate Islamic nations.

[686] See generally The Explanatory Report on the 1996 Convention by Paul Lagarde Proceedings of the Eighteenth Session, Tome 11, Permanent Bureau (1998) ('the Lagarde Report'), *Practical Handbook on the operation of the 1996 Hague Child Protection Convention* (2014); N Lowe and M Nicholls *The 1996 Hague Convention on the Protection of Children* (2012) and K Siehr 'The 1996 Hague Convention of Children and its application in the EU and the World' [2012] IFL 74.

[687] Its full title is Convention of 19 October 1996 on Jurisdiction, Applicable Law, Recognition, Enforcement and Co-operation in Respect of Parental Responsibility and Measures for the Protection of Children.   [688] See Art 1.

[689] Ie following Slovakia's ratification, thereby providing the third ratification (Monaco and the Czech Republic having previously ratified) necessary for its coming into force under Art 61(1).

[690] This was because ratification was subject to EU rules on Sate competence, on which see N Lowe and M Nicholls *The 1996 Hague Convention on the Protection of Children*, op cit, at 1.22 ff.

[691] This route was formally invoked by specifying that the 1996 Convention is to be regarded as one of the EU treaties as defined by the European Communities Act 1972 s 1(2): see the European Communities (Definition of Treaties) (1996 Hague Convention on Protection of Children etc) Order 2010 (SI 2010/232).

as being an EU Regulation such that it became directly effective. Consequently there was no need formally to incorporate it into domestic legislation (in contrast to the 1980 Conventions). Instead all the necessary changes, including amendments to primary legislation (principally the Family Law Act 1986), were achieved through secondary legislation.[692] An unfortunate result of that process is that, like other EU Regulations, the text of the 1996 Convention is not available in UK legislation.[693]

2. SCOPE OF THE CONVENTION

(a) The meaning of 'child'

In contrast to BIIR, which does not define 'child', Art 2 states that the 1996 Convention applies to 'children from the moment of their birth until they reach the age of 18 years'. It will be noted that the Convention (a) does not apply to unborn children;[694] (b) applies until the child reaches the age of 18 and not 16, as in the case of the 1980 Hague Abduction Convention; and (c) notwithstanding its application until the age of 18, does not thereby determine the age of majority for any Contracting State.[695]

(b) The meaning of 'protection'

In general terms, 'protection' refers to both private and public law measures taken by judicial or administrative bodies to safeguard children. In the first English decision on the Convention, *Re Y (Abduction: Undertakings Given for Return of Child)*,[696] it was held that undertakings given as part of a return order 'package' in accordance with Art 11(4) of BIIR[697] amounted to 'protective measures' for the purpose of the Convention.

The types of matters covered by the Convention are set out, but not exhaustively defined, by Art 3, namely: the attribution, exercise, termination and delegation of parental responsibility; rights of custody and access;[698] guardianship, curatorship and analogous institutions; the designation and functions of any person or body having charge of the child's person or property, representing or assisting the child; placing a child in foster or institutional care or the provision of care by *Kafala* or an analogous institution; public authority supervision of the care of a child by any person having charge of the child; and, finally, the administration, conservation or disposal of the child's property. The inclusion of *Kafala* is important because it represents a real attempt to engage with Islamic nations. Both *Kafala* and fostering fall outside the scope of the 1993 Intercountry Adoption Convention and BIIR.

---

[692] Viz. the Parental Responsibility and Measures for the Protection of Children (International Obligations (England and Wales and Northern Ireland) Regulations 2010 (SI 2010/1898) and the Parental Responsibility and Measures for the Protection of Children (International Obligations (Scotland) Regulations 2010 (SI 2010/213).

[693] Instead an official version was laid before Parliament in the form of a Command Paper: Cm 7727 (2009).

[694] A proposal to extend the Convention to unborn children was decisively rejected: see the Lagarde Report, para 15.

[695] See the Lagarde Report, at para 16. Emancipation is expressly excluded from the Convention by Art 4(d).

[696] [2013] EWCA Civ 129 [2013] 2 FLR 649. See also the reference to *Re Y* in *C v D (Abduction: Grave Risk of Harm)* [2014] Fam Law 404.

[697] Discussed at Applying Article 13(b) of the Hague Convention in compliance with BIIR, p 1075.

[698] By Art 3(b), rights of custody are defined as 'including rights relating to the care of the person of the child and, in particular, the right to determine the child's place of residence, as well as rights of access including the right to take a child for a limited period of time to a place other than the child's habitual residence', which is similar to the definition in Art 5 of the 1980 Hague Abduction Convention, discussed at Rights of custody, p 1046.

In contrast to Art 3, Art 4 provides an exhaustive list of what the 1996 Convention does *not* cover, namely: establishing or contesting a parent–child relationship; adoption; names; emancipation; maintenance obligations; trusts or succession; social security, general public measures on health or education; measures taken as a result of penal offences committed by children; and the right of asylum and immigration decisions. The rationale for these exclusions is that they are matters already covered by other Conventions.

Although taken together, Arts 3 and 4, give a good idea of what is and what is not covered by the Convention,[699] in detail, their application can be difficult. For example, in the English context, while all s 8 orders under the Children Act 1989 seem to fall within the ambit of Art 3, specific issue and prohibited steps orders fall outside the scope of the Convention if they are orders in respect of children's names by reason of Art 4. Article 4 might also be thought to exclude contact orders made under ss 26 and 51A of the Adoption and Children Act 2002. There may be doubts, too, as to whether education supervision orders made under s 35 of the 1989 Act fall within the scope of the 1996 Convention.

3. THE JURISDICTIONAL RULES

(a) The basic scheme

In line with other modern child Conventions, primary jurisdiction, as provided for by Art 5,[700] is vested in the authorities of the Contracting State in which the child is habitually resident. 'Habitual residence' is not defined but should be regarded as having the same meaning as under the 1980 Hague Abduction Convention and BIIR. Indeed, in *A v A (Children: Habitual Residence) (Reunite International Child Abduction Centre intervening)*,[701] the English Supreme Court has said that it expects the concept as explained by the CJEU in, for example, *Mercredi v Chaffe*[702] to be applied under the 1996 Convention.

Article 5(2) provides that where the child's habitual residence changes to another Contracting State it is the authorities of this latter State that have pre-eminent jurisdiction. However, this is subject first to Art 7 which (akin to BIIR Art 10)[703] provides, in cases of wrongful removal or retention,[704] that jurisdiction remains in the State of the child's former habitual residence unless either there has been acquiescence or the child has resided in the new Contracting State for at least one year after those having rights of custody have or should have had knowledge of the child's whereabouts and 'no request for return lodged within that period is still pending and the child is settled in his or her new environment'. Neither 'acquiescence' nor 'settled in his or her new environment' are defined in the 1996 Convention, but regard will no doubt be had to the jurisprudence on those concepts developed under the 1980 Hague Abduction Convention.

---

[699] But note: certain other issues are *implicitly* excluded, eg *general* legal remedies such as damages for tort or contract, notwithstanding that they might in certain instances protect the child.

[700] For a useful comparative chart of the jurisdictional rules under 1996 Convention and BIIR, see Clarke Hall and Morrison on *Children* at 1[984].   [701] [2013] UKSC 60 [2014] AC 1 at [35].

[702] (Case C-497/PPU) [2012] Fam 27 discussed at The general meaning, p 1040.

[703] Discussed at Exceptions to the basic rule – the position where the child is wrongfully removed to or retained in another jurisdiction, p 997.

[704] Defined by Art 7(2) as where '(a) it is in breach of rights of custody attributed to a person, an institution or any other body, either jointly or alone, under the law of the State in which the child was habitually resident immediately before the removal or retention; and (b) at the time of removal or retention those rights were actually exercised, either jointly or alone, or would have been so exercised but for the removal of retention'. This definition is in the same terms as Art 3 of the 1980 Hague Abduction Convention, discussed at 'Wrongful' removal or retention, p 1045.

The second proviso to authorities of the child's new habitual residence acquiring pre-eminent jurisdiction is by Art 13, which provides that authorities of a Contracting State must abstain from exercising jurisdiction (other than emergency or temporary jurisdiction) if, at the time of the commencement of proceedings, corresponding measures have been requested from the authorities of another Contracting State having jurisdiction according to Arts 5 to 10, and those proceedings are still pending. The only exception to this embargo is where the authority first seised declines jurisdiction.[705]

An exception the habitual residence rule is with regard to refugee children, those who 'due to disturbances occurring in their country, are internationally displaced'; and children whose habitual residence cannot be established, in which cases jurisdiction can be based on the child's presence.[706] Jurisdiction can also be based on presence in cases of urgency and to make provisional measures, which we discuss shortly.

Similar to BIIR, Art 10 permits a court already exercising jurisdiction over divorce etc, to take measures to protect children, if their domestic law so permits, providing that, at the commencement of proceedings: (a) one of the child's parents is habitually resident in that State and one of them (but not necessarily the parent just referred to) has parental responsibility; *and* (b) the parents and anyone else with parental responsibility agree to such jurisdiction being so exercised *and* that it is in the child's best interests to do so. However, jurisdiction to take protective measures ceases as soon as the decision allowing or refusing the application for divorce, etc has become final or when the proceedings have come to an end for another reason.

Again, similar to BIIR, Arts 8 and 9 make provision for the transfer of proceedings (in whole or in part) between *Contracting* States (ie not to a non-Contracting State) upon the basis that the other court is better placed to determine the best interests of the child.

(b) Powers conferred by Arts 11 and 12

As already mentioned, there are special rules dealing with cases of urgency and to make provisional measures. As these provisions are different to other instruments they merit a little more discussion.

By Art 11 jurisdiction to take measures can, in cases of urgency, be taken upon the basis of either the child's presence or that of his property. Such measures have *extra-territorial effect* though they lapse as soon as a Contracting State otherwise with jurisdiction under the Convention takes its own protective measures. In non-urgent situations jurisdiction to take measures 'of a provisional character' can be based on the presence of the child or his property under Art 12, but such measures only have effect *within* the territory making the order and lapse once a Contracting State otherwise with jurisdiction takes protective measures. It will be noted that the power to act under either Art 11 or 12 can be based upon the child's presence *or* that of his or her property. According to the Lagarde Report,[707] jurisdiction taken on the property basis does not prevent measures being taken to protect the child, since it is possible:

> to conceive that the urgency requires the sale in one country of the property of the child in order to furnish him or her in the country where he or she is present, the resources which are immediately necessary.

---

[705] Art 13(2).   [706] Art 6.
[707] At para 69. According to para 70 of the Report, jurisdiction may even be taken even if the property rights are in dispute.

There are four key differences between Arts 11 and 12. First, orders made under Art 11 have extra-territorial as well as domestic effect. Art 12 orders only have domestic effect. Secondly, unlike Art 11, Art 12 cannot be relied upon in cases of wrongful removal.[708] Thirdly, unlike Art 11, Art 12 orders cannot be incompatible with measures already taken by an authority of competent jurisdiction. Fourthly, measures can only be taken under Art 11 in cases of urgency whereas Art 12 permits measures 'of a provisional character' to be taken at large save to the extent of not being incompatible with existing measures.

While it is easy to appreciate the need for Art 11, which, its extra-territorial effect apart, is a fairly standard provision akin to BIIR Art 20,[709] Art 12 is more unusual. It is designed to permit provisional and territorially limited measures to protect children on a temporary visit to a foreign jurisdiction as, for example, a holiday, an educational exchange visit or even an access visit, in cases where, strictly, there is no urgency. The example given in the Lagarde Report[710] is where a family receiving the child is overburdened such that it may be desirable to place the child with another family or in a shelter under the supervision of a local social authority.

So far as Art 11 is concerned, a key question is what amounts to 'a case of urgency', which is not defined in the Convention. The Lagarde Report instances[711] a child's need for urgent medical treatment or the need for the rapid sale of perishable goods belonging to the child but it clearly covers more ground than that. It is tempting to draw an analogy with the application of BIIR Art 20, particularly in the light of the ECJ's ruling in *Re A (Area of Freedom, Security and Justice)*,[712] such that measures taken under Art 11 must truly be urgent. However, such an analogy may not be apt, for as the CJEU remarked in *Parrucker v Vallés Pérez*,[713] whereas Art 11 of the 1996 Convention clearly confers *jurisdiction* and is subject to provisions permitting limited powers to refuse recognition and/or enforcement, Art 20 of BIIR only confers a *power* to act and is not subject to review. On this basis, BIIR Art 20 might well be interpreted more strictly than Art 11 of the 1996 Convention. The *Practical Handbook*[714] suggests that 'a useful approach ... may be to consider whether the child is likely to suffer irreparable harm or ... have his/her protection or interests compromised if a measure is not taken to protect the child in the period likely to elapse before the authorities with general jurisdiction ... can take the necessary measures of protection.'

The meaning of 'urgency' has been debated in the context of child abduction. It had been widely assumed that Art 11 could be usefully invoked to make orders for the child's safe return following the making of a return order. However, the legitimacy of using Art 11 in this way was discussed at the 6th Special Commission held at The Hague in 2011, it being queried whether the need to ensure a child's safe return could be said to qualify as a case of 'urgency'. But even on a strict interpretation, short-term measures to ensure a child's safe return must surely rank as 'urgent'.[715]

Another issue of some practical importance is the scope of the orders that can be made under Art 11 and in particular whether they have to *directly* relate to the child. While in general terms the measures of protection that can be taken under Art 11 have the same material scope as the measures that can be taken under Arts 5 to 10, that is, 'they are measures directed to the protection of the person or property of the child' as defined in Arts 3

---

[708] Art 7(3).   [709] Discussed at The court's role, p 1038.
[710] At para 7.4.   [711] See para 68.
[712] (Case C-523/07) [2009] 2 FLR 1, discussed at The general meaning, p 1040.
[713] (Case C-256/09) [2011] Fam 254 at [89]–[90].
[714] *Practical Handbook on the operation of the 1996 Hague Child Protection Convention* (2014), at para 6.2.
[715] See also the discussion in *Practical Handbook*, at para 6.4, n 189. Art 11 was used to facilitate a safe return by Mostyn J in *B v B* [2014] EWHC 1804 (Fam).

and 4, the Convention provides no definition of what are 'necessary measures of 'protection'. According to the Lagarde Report[716] this was a deliberate omission. The Report itself describes such measures as a 'functional concept, the urgency dictating in each situation.' While clearly there have to be some limits on the type of measures that can be taken (for example, they must surely be broadly confined to protecting the child), that still begs the question whether they have directly to do so. This is an issue of some moment in the context of international child abduction where the 'abduction court' might wish to put in place a raft of protective measures to ensure the child's safety on being returned to his or her home jurisdiction. Measures could include directing the left-behind parent to provide accommodation and financial support for the abducting parent (usually, the mother) and the child upon their return and perhaps also to prevent the applicant harassing or molesting the defendant parent.

However Art 11 may be interpreted, it is clear measures taken under it can only be temporary so, for example, while an interim care order might be possible it would not be possible to make a final care order.[717]

4. APPLICABLE LAW

A novelty of the 1996 Convention is its applicable law provisions contained in Arts 15–19. These have particular relevance to parental responsibility.[718]

(a) The general position

The basic principle, provided for by Art 15(1), is that, in exercising their jurisdiction, the authorities of the Contracting State apply their own internal law.[719] Article 15(3) deals with the situation where there has been a change of the child's habitual residence. Although, by Art 14, measures previously taken by other authorities remain in effect, by Art 15(3), the conditions by which those measures operate is governed by the law of the new habitual residence. The Lagarde Report instances[720] the example of a guardian who, by the law of the State of original habitual residence needs court permission to take certain actions. If, however, the law of the State of the new habitual residence does not impose such a requirement, Art 15(3) operates to allow that guardian to act alone.

An overall rider to all the applicable law provisions is Art 22 which provides that the application of the law of habitual residence may only be refused if its application would be manifestly contrary to the public policy of the forum taking into account the best interests of the child.[721]

(b) The position with regard to parental responsibility

Articles 16–18 provide specific rules dealing with parental responsibility. Art 16 (1) and (2) respectively provide that the attribution (that is, determining who is a holder of

---

[716] See para 70 of the Report.

[717] Cf *Re S (Care: Jurisdiction)* [2008] EWHC 3013 (Fam) [2009] 2 FLR 550 and see the Parental Responsibility and Measures for the Protection of Children (International Obligations) (England and Wales and Northern Ireland) Regulations 2010 (SI 2010/1898) reg 5.

[718] On which see the extensive discussion in Lowe and Nicholls, above, in Ch 4 and the *Practical Handbook*, op cit, in Ch 9.

[719] See N Lowe 'The Applicable Law Provisions of the 1996 Convention on the Protection of Children and the Impact of the Convention on International Child Abduction' [2010] IFL 51.   [720] At para 91.

[721] Art 22 corresponds to Art 20 of the 1980 Hague Abduction Convention which the UK has not implemented (see The court's role, p 1038). A reservation on Art 22 is not permitted by the 1996 Convention (Art 60(1)) but then neither was an Art 20 reservation provided for by the 1980 Convention.

parental responsibility) or extinguishment of parental responsibility conferred either by operation of law[722] or by agreement or unilateral act,[723] is governed by the law of the child's habitual residence (whether or not that is the law of a non-Contracting State).[724] In cases where parental responsibility is conferred by a court order, Art 15 operates and the courts apply their own law. These provisions are straightforward. The difficulty arises where the child's habitual residence changes.

Article 16(3) and (4) respectively provide that the parental responsibility which exists under the law of the State of the child's habitual residence will continue to exist notwithstanding a change of that residence to another State (thereby ensuring continuity and stability and avoiding the need to take fresh steps in the new country), but where the law of the State of the child's new habitual residence automatically confers parental responsibility on a person who does not already have it, it is the latter law that will prevail. In other words, while a change of habitual residence cannot extinguish parental responsibility, it can confer it. Effectively, this means that the 1996 Convention gives a preference for a substantive rule imposing parental responsibility whenever possible.

This position, however, is tempered first by Art 17 which provides that the *exercise* of parental responsibility is governed by the law of the State of the child's habitual residence including, where that habitual residence changes, the law of the State of that new residence. Secondly, by Art 18, which provides that the authorities of the State of the current habitual residence of the child, can subsequently terminate or modify parental responsibility. Thirdly, by Art 22 which provides a general release from applying these provisions where to do so would be manifestly contrary to public policy taking into account the child's best interests.

What all this means in a purely domestic case is that the attribution and exercise of parental responsibility is governed by the relevant UK domestic law (ie English, Northern Irish or Scottish law). Similarly, a court exercising jurisdiction regarding a child, say, in England and Wales, will apply English law. However, in the case of a child becoming habitually resident in England and Wales, Art 16 becomes relevant with regard to the attribution of parental responsibility. The classic example is where the child's parents are not married to each other—as a result of Art 16 (3) a child's unmarried father will continue to have automatic parental responsibility if he had it under the law of the child's previous habitual residence regardless of whether he is registered as the father. Conversely, unmarried fathers, step-parents and female parents or anyone else who has acquired parental responsibility under English law will continue to have it, subject to the application of Art 22 of the grounds of public policy, in any other Contracting State in which the child becomes habitually resident, regardless of the law of that State.

5. RECOGNITION AND ENFORCEMENT

Recognition and enforcement is governed by Chapter IV of the 1996 Convention. The basic rule of the Convention is, pursuant to Art 23(1), that measures taken by the authorities of a Contracting State must be recognised by operation of law in all other Contracting States. Limited exceptions to this basic obligation are provided for by Art 23(2). Separate provision is also made under Art 24 for advance recognition.

Under Art 26(1), measures entitled to recognition taken in one Contracting State and enforceable there must, at the request of an interested party, be declared enforceable

---

[722] Ie without the intervention of a judicial or administrative authority.

[723] Ie without intervention by the courts, as where the parents make a formal agreement or appoint someone to be a guardian.   [724] See Art 20.

or registered for enforcement in another Contracting State. Such a request can only be refused on one of the grounds under Art 23(2) on which recognition may be refused.[725] Under Art 26(2), Contracting States are obliged to apply 'a simple and rapid' procedure for enforcement and, under Art 27, they are forbidden to review the merits of the measure taken. Once declared enforceable or registered for enforcement, the measure can be enforced as if it had been made by the second State. According to Art 28, enforcement takes place 'in accordance with the law of the requested State to the extent provided by such law, taking into consideration the best interests of the child'. There is no equivalent to the fast-track procedure under BIIR.[726]

An important provision for what, in effect, is advance recognition, is provided by Art 24, which states:

> any interested person may request from the competent authorities of a Contracting State that they decide on the recognition or non recognition of a measure taken in another Contracting State. The procedure is governed by the law of the requested State.

One drawback of recognition by operation of law is that it is only when the measure is invoked that a possible dispute over its recognition may be subject to a ruling. Having to wait for such a ruling may cause inconvenience, hardship or insecurity. A classic instance is international relocation, where, for example, a father agrees to the mother moving to another State on condition that he continues to have contact with the children. To allay his concern that following the move the mother may not obey any contact order made in the child's home State, Art 24 enables him to seek a ruling from the State to which the mother is moving as to whether or not the contact order will be recognised.

Limited exceptions to the basic enjoinder both to recognise and enforce measures taken by other Contracting States are provided by Art 23(2). There are six grounds, namely:

(a) jurisdiction was not based on a Convention ground;

(b) the child was not given the opportunity to be heard in violation of fundamental principles of procedure of the requested State;

(c) a person claiming parental responsibility has not been given the opportunity to be heard;

(d) recognition would be 'manifestly contrary to public policy of the requested State, taking into account the best interests of the child';

(e) the measure is incompatible with a later measure taken in the non-Convention State of the child's habitual residence; and

(f) Art 33 has not been complied with.

These are the only grounds for refusal. They are the equivalent to those provided by BIIR, which, as we have discussed,[727] are hard to establish.

6. CO-OPERATION

As with other modern child Conventions, the crucial vehicle for co-operation is the central authority which, under Art 29, all Contracting States are obliged to create. Under Art 30, central authorities must co-operate with one another to achieve the purposes of the

---

[725] Art 26(3).   [726] Discussed at The fast-track procedure, p 1006.
[727] At Recognition, p 1004.

Convention and to this end take appropriate steps to provide information as to the laws of, and services available in, their States relating to the protection of children. Under Art 31, they must either themselves or through public authorities or other bodies take all reasonable steps to (a) facilitate communication between authorities where this is needed under Arts 8 and 9 (the transfer of jurisdiction provisions); (b) facilitate by mediation, conciliation or similar means, agreed solutions for the protection of children; and (c) provide assistance in discovering the whereabouts of the child.

Under Art 32, a central authority of the place where the child is habitually resident and present may, at the request of another central authority with which the child has a substantial connection, provide a report on the circumstances of the child and/or request the competent authority of its State to consider the need to take measures to protect the child. So far as England and Wales is concerned, where a central authority considers that it would be appropriate to provide a report, it is specifically empowered[728] to request specified public bodies to provide a report on the child's situation, with which request the body must comply unless to do so would endanger the child or his family or would constitute contempt of court or a criminal offence. An Art 32 report can be useful in the context of child abduction where the court after ordering the child's return might wish to ensure that the child will be protected in the foreign State upon his or her return. This protection is further augmented by Art 36, which provides that if the child is exposed to serious danger, the competent authorities of the State where measures for protection for that child have been taken must inform the authorities of the child's residence or presence of the dangers involved and the measures taken, unless this would place the child or a member of his or her family in serious danger.[729]

In addition to the duties expressly imposed upon central authorities, further provisions designed to promote co-operation are provided by Art 35. Article 35(1) in particular provides:

> The competent authorities of a Contracting State may request the authorities of another Contracting State to assist in the implementation of measures of protection taken under this Convention, especially in securing the effective exercise of rights of access as well as of the right to maintain direct contacts on a regular basis.

Another useful provision is Art 35(2) which permits a parent who is seeking to obtain or maintain access but who is living in one Contracting State while the child is habitually resident in another Contracting State to request the competent authorities of the State in which the child is residing to 'gather information or evidence and may make a finding on the suitability of that parent to exercise access and on the conditions under which access is to be exercised'.[730] This information is then admissible evidence in proceedings in the child's habitual residence and indeed, under Art 35(3), the court may adjourn proceedings pending the outcome of such a request.

7. COMMENTARY

The 1996 Convention has been described[731] as something of a sleeping giant in the sense that it has only gradually attracted Contracting States and even now, since most of the

---

[728] By reg 12 of SI 2010/1898.   [729] Art 37.

[730] For the first reported use of this provision, see *F v Y (Abduction: Acquiescence)* [2014] Fam Law 406.

[731] By N Lowe 'The Applicable Laws Provisions of the 1996 Hague Convention on the Protection of Children and the Impact of the Convention on International Child Abduction' [2010] IFL 51.

41 Contracting States are EU States, its application is restricted by BIIR, which takes precedence over it.[732] Nevertheless, the Convention has many advantages not least of which is
providing for a *global* system, and one which might be attractive to and appropriate to the
Islamic world, of recognition and enforcement of custody, access and guardianship orders
as well as of public law orders, which is further backed up by useful co-operative duties.[733]
Moreover, its access provisions might go some way to alleviate the generally acknowledged failings of the 1980 Hague Abduction Convention in that regard while Art 11,
which confers temporary jurisdiction to make protective orders with extra-territorial
effect in cases of urgency, offers a potentially neat solution to the problem posed by
the 1980 Convention of how to safeguard and protect abducted children ordered to be
returned. But the Convention is not problem-free: it is complex in itself and many find
the applicable law provisions in particular hard to understand. But perhaps the greatest
problem is the 1996 Convention's inter-relationship with the other existing international
instruments particularly the 1980 Hague Abduction Convention and, though to a lesser
extent, BIIR. Time will tell whether it will begin to be more used but for that to happen
there needs to be more ratifications and in that respect the position of the USA, which has
signed but not ratified the Convention, is critical.

[732] See BIIR Art 60(e).
[733] See J Pirrung 'Improvements to international child protection as a result of the 1996 Hague Child
Protection Convention' [2012] IFL 70. See also Ch 13 of the *The Practical Handbook* which explores diverse
potential uses of the Convention.

INDEX

abduction *see* **international child abduction**
abuse *see* **child abuse**
access *see* **child arrangements orders**
accommodation of children in need
see also **secure accommodation**
agreements 569–70
appeals against refusal 570–1
background 564
discretionary powers 567
duty to accommodate 564–7
effect of being accommodated 571
limitations 568–9
operation in practice 571
statutory provisions 563
wishes of the child 567–8
activity conditions
contents 497
directions distinguished 498
monitoring compliance 498
requirements 497
requirements for making order 496
activity directions
activity conditions distinguished 498
contents 497
decision to make direction 497
meaning 496–7
monitoring compliance 498
requirements for making order 496
adoption
see also **adoption orders**
advertisements 729–30
applicants 705–9
background 682–4
changing patterns
age of adoptees 687
contact arrangements 690–1
looked after children 688–90
number of adoptions 687
post-adoption support 691–2

comparisons with other relationships and orders 684
consent
dispensing with consent 713–18
guardians 709–11
parents 709–11
unmarried fathers without parental responsibility 711
contact
arrangements 690–1
changing patterns 690–1
post-adoption contact 719–20
section 51A orders 720–1
criminal offences
advertisements 729–30
illegal payments 729
illegal placements 728–9
delay 696
domestic adoptions of foreign children 1014
fatal accidents 726
general principles
background of child 696
delay 696
'no order' alternative 696
welfare principle 694–6
Hague Convention on Intercountry Adoption 1993 1009–12
human rights
compliance 684–6
illegal payments 729
illegal placements 728–9
international issues
domestic adoptions of foreign children 1014
Hague Convention on Intercountry Adoption 1993 1009–12
overseas adoptions 1012–14
overview 1008–9
removing a child from the British Islands for adoption 1015
restrictions on brining children into UK for adoption 1014–15
jurisdiction 16

looked after children 688–90
nature 682–4
'no order' alternative 696
overseas adoptions 1012–14
participation of children in decision-making 446
placement
adoption agencies 692–3
background 698–9
private placements 692–3
reform proposals 698–9
statutory scheme
consent to adoption 700–1
general principles 699–700
legal effect 703–704
orders 701–3
post-adoption
contact 719–20
procedure
notice to local authority 719
settling in period 718–19
registration
Adopted Children Register 721–2
Adoption Contact Register 722
revocation 723
rights on intestacy 973
section 51A orders 720–1
setting aside 723–4
settling in period 718–19
statutory scheme 700–3
statutory service 696–8
transfer of parentage 722–4
who may apply
age of applicant 705
couples 705–7
domicile of applicant 705
health of applicant 705
relatives 708–9
single persons 705–7
step-parents 707–8
who may be adopted 704–5
adoption orders
see also **adoption**
Adopted Children Register 721–2
Adoption Contact Register 722

adoption orders (*Cont.*)
　change of status
　　citizenship 725
　　financial support 726
　　insurance 727, 871
　　peerages and titles 725
　　pensions 726
　　prohibited degrees of
　　　marriage 726
　　property 727
　　provision for
　　　dependants 726
　　statutory provisions 725
　　surname 726
　complete and permanent
　　transfer of legal
　　parentage 722–4
　consent
　　dispensing with
　　　consent 713–18
　　form of consent 712–13
　　guardians 709–11
　　parents 709–11
　　unmarried fathers
　　　without parental
　　　responsibility 711
　effect 722–4
　procedure
　　notice to local authority 719
　　settling in period 718–19
　revocation 723
　setting aside 723–4
　statutory scheme 701–3
　transfer of parentage 722–4
　who may apply
　　age of applicant 705
　　couples 705–7
　　domicile of applicant 705
　　health of applicant 705
　　single persons 705–7
　　step-parents 707–8
　who may be adopted 704–5
adultery
　bars to relief 215
　divorce 214–15
advertisements
　adoption 729–30
affinity
　prohibited degrees of
　　marriage 45–7
age
　adoption
　　adoptees 687
　　applicants 705
　capacity to marry 44–5
　cohabitants 935
　marriage 44–5
　parental responsibility and
　　age of child 337
agency of necessity 774–5

agreements
　accommodation of children
　　in need 569–70
　civil partnerships 40
　financial remedies
　　disclosure of
　　　information 849–52
　　effects of order 853
　　pre-nuptial
　　　agreements 853–62
　　revoking agreement before
　　　order made 851–2
　　weight attached to
　　　agreement 851–2
　maintenance
　　parents, between 784–6
　　spouses/civil
　　　partners 779–84
　marriage
　　breach of promise 39
　　civil partnerships 40
　　engagements 39
　　generally 39–40
　　meaning 39
　　proof of engagement 40
　parental responsibility
　　372–3, 379–86
　pre-nuptial agreements
　　financial support 780
　　significance 853–62
　provision for
　　dependants 993
all ports warnings
　international child
　　abduction 1018–19
allowances
　costs 838
　expenses 111–12
　housekeeping 111–12
alternative dispute resolution
　arbitration 12
　collaborative law 12, 833
　conciliation
　　appeals out of time 910
　　civil partnerships 241
　　divorce 229–30
　　maintenance orders in
　　　magistrates' court 788
　mediation 12–13
　trend in family law 12–13
**American Convention on
Human Rights**
　protection for the family 21
　rights of individuals in
　　family 21–2
ancillary relief *see* **financial
remedies**
annulment
　see also **void marriages;
voidable marriages**

　civil partnerships 87
　decree 63–70
　jurisdiction 16
　relevance of current law 86
appeals
　assessment of financial
　　remedies 908–12
　care and supervision
　　orders 650–1
　child support scheme 816
　financial remedies
　　out of time
　　　change in
　　　　circumstances 910
　　　change in law 910–11
　　　change in valuations
　　　　911–12
　　　generally 909
　　reconciliation 910
　　remarriage of spouse 910
　refusal to accommodate
　　children in need 570–1
　section 8 orders
　　appellate court
　　　powers 544–6
　　position pending
　　　appeal 544
　　procedure 543–4
　　routes of appeal 543–4
　secure accommodation
　　orders 577
applications without notice
　domestic violence and
　　abuse 194–5
approved premises
　solemnisation of
　　marriage 54
arbitration
　Institute of Family Law
　　Arbitrators 12
arranged marriages 51
arrest
　forced marriage protection
　　order 199
　limitations on inherent
　　jurisdiction 764
　non-molestation and
　　occupation orders
　　192–4
　undertakings 195
artificial insemination
　meaning 245
　non-genetic
　　fatherhood 250–6
assisted reproduction
　meaning 245–6
　non-genetic
　　fatherhood 250–6
Australia
　Family Court 17

autonomy
   growing trend in family
      law 9–10

bank accounts 110–11
bankruptcy
   family home 159–62
   family protection 159–62
   mortgages and
      charges 158–9
   voidable transactions 116–17,
      159
behaviour
   bars to relief on divorce 217
   basis for dissolution of civil
      partnership 241
   basis for divorce 215–218
benefits *see* **welfare benefits**
birth certificates
   acquisition of parental
      responsibility 371
   proof of parentage 271–2
blood tests
   consent 267–9
   court directions 263–9
   nature 263–4
Brussels Convention 28
Brussels II Regulation (BIIR)
   background 994–5
   central authorities 1007–8
   conflict of laws 1071–81
   enforcement of orders and
      agreements
      fast-track
         procedure 1006–7
      ordinary
         procedure 1005–6
      overview 1005
   habitual residence of
      child 996–7
   international child
      abduction 1071–81
   international issues 28–9
   internationally displaced
      children 1000
   jurisdiction
      cross-border access 997
      exceptions to the basic
         rule 997–8
      generally 16
      habitual residence of
         child 996–7
      internationally displaced
         children 1000
      no Member State
         has jurisdiction,
         where 1000
      prorogation of
         jurisdiction 998–1000
      refugees 1000

   relocation of child 997
   second seised, where
      court 1003
   transferring
      jurisdiction 1000–2
   urgent cases 1002–3
   wrongful removal of
      child 997–8
   overview 28–9
   recognition of orders and
      agreements 1004–5
   refugees 1000
   scope 995–6
burden of proof
   care and supervision
      local authorities 598–9
      threshold criteria 598–9
   child abuse 598–9
   welfare principle 440

Cafcass
   background 452–3
   children and family court
      reporters 453
   consent to adoption 713
   creation 14
   criticisms 454
   current system 453–4
   family assistance orders 546
   functions 453–4
   High Court team 453
   national standards 454
   origins 452–3
   reform 453
canon law
   divorce 262–3
   legitimation 302
   power to grant alimony 828
capacity
   civil partnerships 59–60
   consent to adoption 714–15
   marriage 41–4
      age 44–5
      conditions 40–1
      inter-sex persons 41–2
      sex 41–4
      transsexuals 41–4
      unsoundness of
         mind 79–81
      void marriages 71
   void marriages 71
care orders
   discharge 651–3
   duration 639
   effects 636–9
   limitations 638–9
   parental responsibility 638
   placing child in care
      of designated
         authority 637–8

   subsequent control of local
      authority 639–40
care proceedings
   accommodation of children
      in need 567
   contact arrangements
      court orders 657–9
      historical
         background 654–5
      importance 654
      other interested
         parties 656–7
      presumption of reasonable
         contact 655–6
      refusal of contact 656
   disputing decisions
      Children's Commissioners
         666–7
      Commissioner for Local
         Administration 666
      complaints
         procedure 663–5
      human rights
         claims 677–80
      judicial review 669–73
      negligence claims 673–6
      overview 662–3
      wardship 667–8
   initiation of proceedings 596
   limitations on inherent
      jurisdiction 764
   looked after children 660–2
   orders
      appeals 650–1
      care orders 636–42
      discharge 651–3
      interim orders 642–9
      section 8 orders 631–2
      supervision orders 632–6
   overview 594–5
   parental responsibility 395–6
   parties 596
   procedure
      protocol 628–9
   threshold criteria
      attributable to care
         given 613–19
      burden of proof 598–9
      likely to suffer 608–13
      mixed pool dilemma 622–5
      overview 599–600
      rationale 597–8
      significant harm 600–8
      standard of proof 598–9
      statutory provisions
         597–8
   welfare principle
      future plans 627–8
      past events 626–7
      statutory provisions 625–6

carers
  guardianship
    distinguished 294
central authorities
  international child
    abduction 1032–3
child abuse
  see also care proceedings;
    domestic violence and abuse
  burden of proof 598–9
  delay 628–9
  diagnosis 14
  emergency protection orders
    additional directions 587
    denial of access to the
      child 584–6
    duration 588
    effects of order 586–7
    exclusion requirements
      587–8
    grounds 584–6
    likely to suffer harm 584
    procedure 586
    purpose 583–4
    use 589
  expert witnesses 14
  investigation by local
    authority
    co-operation with other
      agencies 580–2
    requirement 579–80
  local authority
    support 562–3
  short-term protection by
    local authorities LAs
    child assessment orders
      application 590–1
      criteria 590–1
      effects 591
      use 592
    emergency protection orders
      additional directions 587
      denial of access to the
        child 584–6
      duration 588
      effects of order 586–7
      exclusion requirements
        587–8
      frequency of use 589
      grounds 584–6
      likely to suffer
        harm 584
      procedure 586
      purpose 583–4
      use 589
    examples of use 589–90
    overview 582–3
    police protection 592–3
    purpose 589
  treatment 14

child arrangements orders
  additional directions and
    conditions 504–8
  conditions concerning
    contact 507–8
  deciding what order to
    make 491–6
  effects
    parental responsibility
      520
    removal of child from the
      UK 525–35
    surname of child 520–5
  meaning 485
  naming a person with whom
    the child is to live 486–8
  naming a person with whom
    the child is to spend
    time or otherwise have
    contact 489–91
  parental responsibility
    379–80, 389–90
  prohibiting a child from
    spending time or having
    contact with named
    person 491
  purpose 485
  siblings 489–90
child assessment orders
  application 590–1
  criteria 590–1
  effects 591
  examples of use 589–90
  purpose 589
  use 589–92
child protection see child
  abuse; local authorities
child maintenance see child
  support scheme; family
  based arrangements;
  maintenance
Child Support Agency 13
child support scheme
  alteration of calculations 816
  appeals 816
  application for a maintenance
    calculation 807–8
  background 800–4
  calculations 810–12
  collection 817–18
  family based
    arrangements 803, 804
  generally 13
  key features of
    scheme 805–20
  non-resident parent 806
  parentage 809–10
  parties 806–8
  qualifying child 806
  residual role of courts 820–3

role of Agency or Service 805
statutory provisions 805–20
variation of orders 812–16
children
  see also child arrangements
    orders; orders in family
    proceedings; parental
    responsibility; welfare
    principle
  care of parents 2–3
  carers without legal
    responsibility 395
  child of the family 296–8
  Cobb Report 475
  Commissioners for
    Children 475–8
  direct participation in
    proceedings
    human rights 469–70
    judicial interviews 465–6
    law reform 474–5
    parties, as 467–9
    public law
      proceedings 470
    research 472–4
  domestic violence 13
  financial remedies
    lump sum
      payments 840–2
    periodical payments
      orders 840–2
    statutory powers 830
  financial support
    child benefit 779
    child support scheme
      alteration of
        calculations 816
      appeals 816
      application for a
        maintenance
        calculation 807–8
      background 800–4
      calculations 810–12
      collection 817–18
      enforcement 818–20
      evaluation of
        effectiveness 823–5
      information
        provision 808–9
      key features of
        scheme 805–20
      non-resident parent
        806
      parentage 809–10
      parties 806–8
      qualifying child 806
      residual role of
        courts 820–3
      role of Agency or
        Service 805

statutory provisions
805–20
variation of orders 812–16
duty to maintain 775
jurisdiction to make
orders 791–800
maintenance agreements
between parents 784–6
person with care 806–7
High Court jurisdiction
inherent jurisdiction
court powers 763–8
effect 763
individuals, use by 771
local authorities, use
by 768–71
procedure 762–3
overview 741–2
wardship
characteristics 743–6
court powers 751–2
discretion to exercise
jurisdiction 748–9
general principles 752–3
historical background
742–3
scope 746–8
uses 753–62
investigation of children's
views
Cafcass 452–4
children's
guardian 459–64
law reform 474–5
methods 451–64
research 472–4
welfare reports 455–9
jurisdiction 16
litigants, as
procedure 471–2
substantive law 470–1
meaning of child 296
non-molestation orders 181
Norgrove Review 474–5
orders
appeals against s 8
orders 543–6
application of welfare
principle
statutory checklist 401–8
substantive law 581–3
Children and Adoption
Act 2006 480–1
Children and Families Act
2014 481–5, 551
discharge 543
enforcement orders 541–2
enforcement of s 8 orders
compensation for
financial loss 542–3

contempt of court 538–40
handing over of
children 538
warning notices 540–1
family assistance
orders 546–50
general restrictions
child applicants 513
children in local authority
care 510–11
children over 16 510
local authorities 511–13
jurisdiction under s 8
any child 536–7
applications on court's
own motion 537
family proceedings
535–6
local authority care or
supervision 550–1
original scheme 479–80
persons entitled to apply
applications on
behalf of someone
else 519–20
child applicants 520
criteria for leave 515–19
with leave 515
without leave 513–15
physical, emotional
and educational
needs 403–8
prohibited steps
orders 498–500
restrictions on further
applications without
leave 508–9
section 8 orders
additional directions and
conditions 504–8
limits on jurisdiction
501–4
meaning 485
specific issue
orders 500–1
special guardianship
directions and
conditions 733–4
discharge 736–7
duration 737
effects 735–6
policy objectives 730–1
statutory powers 731–3
support services 737–9
use of orders 739–40
variation 736–7
welfare principle 733
surnames 520–5
variation 543
paramountcy principle

appeals 426–7
application to more than
one child 428–30
historical background
397–8
human rights
compliance 415–18
meaning of paramount
414–15
UN Convention
compared 418–19
when applicable 401–3
when not applicable 420–30
parentage
assisted reproduction
245–6
birth certificates 271–2
breaking exclusivity of
genetic link 257–8
changing nature of
relationships
development of welfare
principle 312–18
fatherhood 308–11
international
law 325–9
motherhood 311–12
overview 307–8
self-decision
making 318–25
comparative law 269–70
declarations 270–1
fatherhood
genetic fathers 248–50
non-genetic fathers
250–6
female parenthood 256–7
law reform 259
more than two legal
parents 259
motherhood 246–8
proof
exclusivity of genetic
link 257–8
fatherhood 260–9
motherhood 260
right to know 272–3
significance
citizenship 274
residence in UK 274
parental responsibility
acquisition after birth
step-parents 385–9
third parties 389–90,
395
unmarried fathers
369
age of child 337
agreement of the
parties 336

children (*Cont.*)
  child arrangements
    order 379–80
  civil partners 369
  contractual liability 63–4
  criminal liability
    child's crimes 364–5
    interference with rights
      366
  definitions 333–6
  delegation 395
  duration 391–2
  female partners 369
  female spouses 369
  foetuses 391
  gender change 369
  relevance 331–3
  rights 336
  scope
    administration of
      property 360
    bringing-up of
      child 338–9
    contact with
      child 339–40
    criminal liability 341–2
    discipline 344–7
    disposal of corpse
      359–60
    domestic services 360
    education 347–50
    emigration 355–6
    foreign travel 355–6
    information about
      child 361–3
    legal representation
      358–9
    list 337–8
    medical treatment
      350–4
    names 356–9
    passports 354–5
    protection 340–4
    religious upbringing
      350
    tortious liability 342–4
  scope of responsibility
    337
  shared obligations 392–4
  terminology 330
  tortious liability
    child's wrongful
      acts 364
    interference with
      rights 366–7
  unborn children 391
  unmarried mothers 369
  participation in
    decision-making
  adoption 446

Commissioners for
  Children 446
European Convention
  on the Exercise of
  Children's Rights 451
human rights 448
international law 448–51
Norgrove Review 445
private law proceedings
  446–7
public law proceedings
  448
periodical payments 840
proposed arrangements
  after divorce 225–6
provision for
  dependants 979–80
rights on intestacy 972–3
status
  declarations 303–4
  legitimacy 299–303
  significance 304–5
  statutory reform 306–7
supporting elderly
  parents 2–3
trend of shift from adults to
  children 6
welfare principle
  critical analysis 430–2
  delay 436–8
  development 312–18
  form 443
  meaning of welfare
    application of checklist
      401–3
    case law 398–9
    statutory checklist
      499–03
  ongoing relationship
    with both parents,
    importance of 432–5
  orders only when
    appropriate
    application of principle
      440–3
    burden of proof 440
    form 443
    interrelationship
      with paramountcy
      principle 443–4
    scope 439–40
    statutory provisions
      438–9
  scope 439–40
  statutory provisions 438–9
Children and Family Court
  Advisory and Support
  Service *see* **Cafcass**
Children's Commissioners *see*
  Commissioners for Children

children's guardians
  appointment 460–1
  discharge of duties 462–4
  duties 461–2
  effect of appointment 464
  family court reporters
    distinguished 459–60
Church of England
  marriage 51–2
  solemnisation of
    marriage 52–4
citizenship
  adoption 725
  consequences of
    marriage 101–4
  deportation 104
  doctrine of unity 101–2
  effect of adoption 725
  immigration 274
  parentage 274
  significance of parentage
    274, 305
civil liability
  contractual liability
    between the parties 98–9
    disputes between partners 117
    mutual wills 964–5
    parental responsibility
      363–4
  disputes between
    partners 117
  interference with domestic
    services 360
  local authorities 673–6
  parental responsibility
    342–4, 363–4
  interference with
    rights 366–7
  personal consequences of
    marriage 99–100
civil marriages
  solemnisation
    register offices 53–4
civil partnerships
  adoption rights 705
  advantages 32
  agreements 40
  annulment 87
  background 32
  capacity 59–60
  conversion into marriage 61
  declarations 87
  definition 3
  dissolution 211–12
  entry into civil
    partnership 58–61
  female parenthood 256–7
  financial support
    duty to maintain
      child 775

duty to maintain spouse/
 civil partner 774–5
jurisdiction to make
 orders
 children 791–800
 spouses/partners 786–800
formalities
 registration 60–1
 under 18's 60
home rights 152
improvements to family
 home 143–4
introduction 31–3
jurisdiction 16
legal background 32–3
legal effect 32–3
legislation 32
maintenance agreements
 children 784–6
 partners 779–84
meaning 32
nature of partnership 58–9
non-molestation orders 180
ownership of family
 home 125
personal consequences
 deportation 104
 disputes between
  partners 117–19
 disputes with
  strangers 119
 immigration rules 101–4
 law reform 119–21
 legal testimony 96–8
 property acquired by
  partners 108–14
 transactions between
  partners 114–17
 use of surname 94–5
provision for dependants
 reasonable provision 983
 relevant factors 986–7
 who may apply 976–83
religious ceremonies 59, 61
revocation of wills 962–3
rights on intestacy 968–72
separation orders 243
sibling relationships 59–60
statistics 31
validity
 annulment 87
 declarations 87
 void civil partnerships 87
 voidable civil
  partnerships 88
void civil partnerships 87
voidable civil
 partnerships 88
clean breaks
 appeals out of time 909

change in circumstances
 910
change in law 910–11
change in valuations
 911–12
reconciliation 910
remarriage of spouse 910
deferral 878–80
general principle 876–7
immediate clean
 breaks 877–8
cohabitation
adoption rights 705
age of cohabitants 935
arguments for and against 8
attitudes to cohabitation
 cohabitants 937–9
 social attitudes 937
 spouses 937–9
children of cohabitees 936–7
contracts 948–50
definition
 'a man and a woman'
  941–2
 'are living with each
  other' 939–40
 'as husband and
  wife' 942–4
 generally 939
 'in the same household'
  940–1
duration 936–7
duty to maintain
 partner 775–6
extent of cohabitation
 935–9
family 2
fatal accidents 7, 945
growth 6–8, 31, 934–6
historical background
 934–5
immorality 7
intestacy 973–4
knowledge of legal
 position 947–8
law reform
 assessment of
  proposals 957–8
 Law Commission 952–7
 separation 951
legal context 944–5
legal effect 7
legal recognition 6–8, 934–5
names 94–5
non-molestation
 orders 180–1
normative role of family
 law 4
occupation orders
 entitled applicants 183–7

non-entitled
 applicants 187–91
ownership of family
 home 125
parental responsibility 369
personal consequences
 contractual obligations
  between the
  parties 98–9
 disputes between
  partners 117–18
 disputes with
  strangers 119
 law reform 119–21
 legal testimony 96–8
 property acquired by
  partners 108–14
 transactions between
  partners 114–17
 use of surname 94–5
property arrangements
 946–7
provision for dependants
 generally 7
 reasonable provision 983
 relevant factors 987–8
 who may apply 978–9
public policy 7
purposes 935
reasons for cohabiting 6–7
rights 7–8
separation
 contracts 948–50
 knowledge of legal
  position 947–8
 law reform 951
 legal provision 945–51
 property
  arrangements 946–7
 transfer of
  tenancies 950–1
stability 936–7
statistics 2, 6
surnames 94–5
tenanted property 7
transfer of tenancies 950–1
types 935
unmarried fathers 2
welfare benefits 7
Commissioners for Children
background 475–6
care and supervision,
 disputing decisions
 relating to 666–7
England
 discharge of functions 478
 Dunford Review 477–8
 function 477–8
 law reform 478
 role 476–8

common intention
  constructive trusts 129–34
'common law marriage' 56
compellability as witnesses
  spouses 97–8
competence
  spouses 96–7
conciliation
  appeals out of time 910
  civil partnerships 241
  divorce 229–30
  maintenance orders in
    magistrates' court 788
conduct
  assessment of financial
    remedies 899–903
  divorce
    behaviour 215–18
  financial remedies 899–903
  provision for
    dependants 985–6
  voidable marriages 84–5
consanguinity
  prohibited degrees of
    marriage 45–6
consent
  adoption
    dispensing with
      consent 713–18
    form of consent
      712–13
    parents 709–11
    statutory scheme 700–1
    unmarried fathers
      without parental
      responsibility 711
  blood and DNA tests 267–9
  family home
    transactions 150–1
  financial remedies orders
    disclosure of
      information 849–51
    effects of order 853
    encouraging agreement
      849
    pre-nuptial agreements
      853–62
    revoking agreement before
      order made 851–2
    weight attached to
      agreement 851–2
  medical treatment of
    children 350–4
  variation of financial
    remedies 915–16
conspiracy
  spouses 101
constructive trusts
  common intention
    constructive trusts 129–34

establishing a beneficial
  interest 127–9
  quantification of shares 135–7
consummation of marriage
  background 73–4
  canon law 73
  inability to consummate 75
  meaning 74–5
  voidable marriage 73–6
  wilful refusal to
    consummate 75–6
contact
  see also **activity conditions;**
    activity directions; child
    arrangements orders
  adoption
    arrangements 690–1
    changing patterns 690–1
    post-adoption
      contact 719–20
    section 51A orders
      720–1
  children in care
    court orders 657–9
    historical
      background 654–5
    importance 654
    other interested
      parties 656–7
    presumption of reasonable
      contact 655–6
    refusal of contact 656
  international arrangements
    European Custody
      Convention 1083–8
    Hague Convention
      1073–83, 1088–91
  parental
    responsibility 339–40
  special guardianship
    orders 733
contempt of court
  section 8 orders
    Family Court's
      powers 538–40
contractual liability
  between the parties 98–9
  disputes between
    partners 117
  mutual wills 964–5
  parental responsibility 63–4
costs
  '*Calderbank*' offers 862
  disclosure in
    financial remedies
      proceedings 832–3
  financial remedies 862–3
  statutory charge 863–4
Council of Europe
  international issues 26

county courts
  jurisdiction 15
  staff 15
Court of Justice of the
  European Union
  role 29
criminal liability
  adoption offences
    advertisements 729–30
    illegal payments 729
    illegal placements 728–9
  domestic violence and abuse
    criminal justice
      system 169–73
    Crown Prosecution
      Service 169–70
    harassment 173–8
    police policy 169–70
    victim reluctance to
      prosecute 171–2
  parental responsibility
    child's crimes 364–5
    interference with
      rights 366
    scope 341–2
  personal consequences of
    marriage 100–1
Crown Prosecution Service
  domestic violence and abuse
    policy 170–1

day care
  local authorities, duty of 563
death in the family
  appeals out of time 910
  appointment of child's
    guardian 286
  mutual wills 964–5
  parental responsibility
    administration of
      property 360
    disposal of corpse 359–60
  presumption of
    death 959–60
  provision for dependants
    available property 989
    orders
      final orders 990–3
      interim orders 989–90
      other agreements and
        orders 992–3
    reasonable provision 983
    relevant factors
      all applicants 984–8
      spouses and civil
        partners 986–7
    statutory provisions
      974–7
    who may apply 976–83
  revocation of wills

divorce 963–4
    marriage 962–3
succession
    intestacy
        children 972–3
        cohabitants 973–4
        other family members 973
        statutory provisions
            967–8
    surviving spouses 968–72
termination of
    guardianship 291–3
testamentary gifts
    children 966
    spouses 965–6
declarations
    marital status 62–3
    parentage 270–1
decrees of divorce
    law reform 230–1
    procedure 226–9
    protection of respondent
        postponement 224–5
        refusal 222–4
    statutory reform 234–8
decrees of nullity *see*
    annulment; void marriages;
    voidable marriages
delay
    adoption 696
    child abuse 628–929
    family justice system 20–1
    local authorities 628–9
    welfare principle 436–8
deportation
    consequences of
        marriage 104
desertion
    basis for divorce 218–19
detained persons
    solemnisation of
        marriage 54–5
directions
    see also **activity directions**
    blood and DNA tests 264–7
    emergency protection
        orders 587
    interim care and supervision
        orders 645–8
    orders relating to children
        additional directions and
            conditions 504–8
        local authority care or
            supervision 550–1
        special guardianship
            orders 733–4
discharge of orders
    care and supervision
        orders 651–3
    child support scheme 816

contact with children in
    care 659–60
financial remedies 912–15
section 8 orders 543
special guardianship
    orders 736–7
wardship 751
discipline of children
    parental
        responsibility 344–7
disclosure of information
    financial remedies by
        consent 849–52
    Form E 833
    HMRC inquiries 834–5
    proceeds of crime 835–6
    welfare reports 457–8
discrimination
    human rights 4
    same sex couples 4
dispute resolution
    appointments
    financial remedies 833–4
dissolution of civil
    partnerships
    financial remedies 830
    generally 240–1
    provision for
        dependants 977
    revocation of wills 963–4
District Judges
    magistrates' courts 15
divorce
    see also **financial remedies**
    adultery 214–15
    bar to divorce 214
    desertion 218–19
    five years' separation 221
    ground for divorce 214
    historical background
        Divorce Reform Act
            1969 213–14
        doctrine of insolubility
            212
        equalisation of men and
            women 212–13
        extension of grounds for
            divorce 212–13
        full divorce by judicial
            process 212
        Matrimonial Causes Act
            1857 212
        Morton Commission
            213
    information meeting 235–7
    irretrievable breakdown
        adultery 214–15
        behaviour of
            respondent 215–18
        desertion 218–19

    five facts for proving
        irretrievable
        breakdown 214–21
    five years' separation 221
    ground for divorce 214
    two-years' separation
        and consent of
        respondent 219–21
    jurisdiction 16
    law reform
        Booth Committee 230–1
        government response 233–4
        Law Commission 231–4
    parental responsibility 394
    period for reflection and
        consideration 237–8
    procedure
        decrees 226–9, 228–9
        law reform 233
        special procedure 226–8
    proof of breakdown
        adultery 214–15
        behaviour of
            respondent 215–18
        desertion 218–19
        five years' separation 221
        separation and
            consent 219–20
        two-years' separation
            and consent of
            respondent 219–21
    protection of children 225–6
    protection of respondent
        postponement of
            decree 224–5
        refusal of decree 222–4
        religious marriages 225
    provision for
        dependants 977–8
    reconciliation 229–30
    reform 107–8
    revocation of wills 963–4
    significance 211
    statement of marital
        breakdown 236–7
    statistics 211–12
    status of children 304–5
    statutory reform
        Family Law Act
            1996 234–8
        future reforms 238–40
        general principles 235
        procedure 234–8
    time limits 214
    two-years' separation
        and consent of
        respondent 219–21
divorce *a mensa et thoro* 241
divorcees
    remarriage 30

DNA tests
consent 267–9
court directions 264–7
nature 263–4
doctrine of unity
citizenship 101–2
criminal liability 100–1
domestic violence and abuse
see also **child abuse**
children 13
civil law remedies
additional provisions 191–2
applications without
notice 194–5
enforcement 192–5
harassment 195–6
injunctions
inherent jurisdiction
196–7
non-molestation
orders 179–83
occupation orders
balance of harm
test 185–6
discretionary test 186
duration of order 187
entitled applicants
183–187
non-entitled applicants
187–91
payment of outgoings
191–2
payment of rent or
mortgage 191
repair and maintenance
obligations 191
undertakings 195
Clare's Law 168
controlling behaviour 164
criminal sanctions
criminal justice
system 169–73
Crown Prosecution
Service 170–1
harassment 173–8
police policy 169–70
sentencing 172–3
victim reluctance to
prosecute 171–2
definition 13, 164–5
disclosure regime 168
domestic homicide
reviews 168
domestic violence protection
notices
associated person 202
authorising officer 202
background 201–2
contents of notice 202
duration 202

human rights 203
power to issue notice 202
domestic violence protection
orders
background 201–2
conditions 203
hearing 203
human rights 203
power to issue 202
education and
prevention 210
female genital
mutilation 165
forced marriages 165
protection orders 197–201
gender-based abuse 168–9
historical background
166–7
homelessness legislation
intentional
homelessness 208
local connection 209
meaning of
homelessness 205–7
priority need 207–8
'honour' based violence 165
housing law remedies
eviction 204
tenanted property 203–5
termination of
tenancy 204–5
human rights 168–9
jurisdiction 16
legal aid 13
legal response 209–10
multi-agency
approach 167–8
parental responsibility
orders 373–9
reform
Government strategy
167–8
Safety and Justice White
Paper 167
repair and maintenance
obligations 191
scale 165
sentencing 172–3
domicile
adoption applicants 705
capacity to marry 40
declarations of status 303
decrees of nullity 63
financial remedies 922
international child
abduction 1021, 1041
legitimacy of children 300, 302
parentage 254, 270
parental orders 278
presumption of death 959

provision for family and
dependants 975
wardship 746
duress
voidable marriages 76–9

education
parental responsibility
347–50
egg donation
meaning 246
non-genetic fatherhood
250–6
embryo donation
meaning 246
non-genetic
fatherhood 250–6
emergency protection orders
additional directions 587
denial of access to the
child 584–6
duration 588
effects of order 586–7
exclusion
requirements 587–8
frequency of use 589
grounds 584–6
likely to suffer harm 584
procedure 586
purpose 583–4
use 589
emigration
parental responsibility
355–6
enforcement
Brussels II Regulation
(BIIR)
fast-track procedure
1006–7
ordinary procedure
1005–6
overview 1005
child support scheme 818–20
financial remedies
attempts to defeat
claim 918–20
lump sum
payments 917–18
periodical
payments 916–17
international child abduction
European Custody
Convention
1980 1083–8
monitoring compliance
with family proceedings
orders 498
section 8 orders
compensation for financial
loss 542–3

contempt of court 538–40
enforcement
    notices 541–2
    Family Law Act 1986, s
        34 538
    general principles 537–8
    handing over of children
        538
    warning notices 540–1
engaged couples
    agreement to marry 39
    disputes between
        partners 118–19
    disputes with strangers 119
    gifts between couples 109
    improvements to family
        home 144
    non-molestation orders 180
    proof of engagement 40
enticement, tort of 93
**equalisation of men and
    women**
    consortium 92–4
    divorce 212–13
    family law 4–5
equitable interests
    family home
        common intention
            constructive trusts
                129–34
        constructive trusts
            127–34
        establishing a beneficial
            interest 127
        improvements 143–4
        proprietary estoppel
            139–42
        protection of beneficial
            interests
        consent to transactions
            150–1
        registered land 147–50
        unregistered land 150
        quantification of
            shares 135–9
        resulting trusts 127–9
        trusts of land
            court powers 144–6
    historical overview
        105–6
    meaning
        establishing a beneficial
            interest 127
        family home
            common intention
                constructive trusts
                    129–34
            constructive trusts
                127–34
            improvements 143–4

estoppel
    licences by estoppel 157
EU law
    parentage 328–9
**European Convention on
    Human Rights**
    see also **right to respect for
        private and family life**
    discrimination 23–4
    family, meaning of 1–2
    impact 24
    inhuman or degrading
        treatment or
        punishment 23
    right to liberty and
        security 23
    right to marry 23, 35–7
    role 23
**European Custody
    Convention 1980**
    applicability 1083
    application for access 1087–8
    enforcement 1084–5
    evaluation of use 1088–91
    recognition 1084–5
    refusing recognition or
        enforcement 1085–6
European Union
    international issues 28–9
eviction
    see also **homelessness**
    remedies for domestic
        violence and abuse 204
evidence in legal proceedings
    compellability 97–8
    competence 96–7
ex parte **applications**
    domestic violence and
        abuse 194–5
exclusion requirements
    interim care orders 648
expense allowances 111–12
expert witnesses
    child abuse 14

family
    ancestors 1
    blood ties 1
    care of parents by
        children 2–3
    categories 2
    cohabitation 2
    defined 1–3
    European Convention on
        Human Rights 1–2
    marriage 2
    meaning
        definition 1–3
        European Convention on
            Human Rights 1–2

    right to respect for private
        and family life
        cohabitation 1
        fathers 1
        meaning 1–2
        mother and child 1
        spouses 1–2
        status ties 1
family assistance orders
    background 547
    circumstances of
        order 547–8
    duration 548
    effect of order 548
    jurisdiction 547–8
    practical operation 548–50
    statistics 548–9
    statutory powers 547–8
family based arrangements
    child support scheme 803,
        804
    encouragement to use 817,
        821
    enforcement 824
    maintenance
        agreements 775, 803, 823
    private ordering 803
family breakdown see
    relationship breakdown
Family Court
    background 17–18
    composition 18
    contempt of court 538–40
    Designated Family Judge
        19
    enforcement
        section 8 orders 538–40
    Family Justice Review 17–18
    judiciary 18
    jurisdiction 17–18
    law reform 17–18
    local Family Court 19
    other jurisdictions 17
    proposals 17–19
    recommendations 18
    single Family Court 18
    structure 18
    unified Family Court 18
family home
    home rights
        background 152–3
        defined 153–5
        duration 155–6
        effect 154–5
        registration 155
    insolvency
        bankruptcy 159–62
        mortgages and
            charges 158–9
        law reform 162–3

family home (*Cont.*)
  occupation
    contractual licences 156–7
    home rights
      background 152–3
        defined 153–5
          duration 155–6
          scope 152
        effect 154–5
        registration 155
    licences by estoppel 157
    third party rights 157–8
  overview 122–3
  ownership
    application of ordinary
      principles 125–6
    common intention
      constructive
        trusts 129–34
    constructive
      trusts 127–34
    establishing a beneficial
      interest 127
    history and
      background 123–5
    improvements 143–4
    proprietary
      estoppel 139–42
    protection of beneficial
      interests
      consent to
        transactions 150–1
      registered land 147–50
      unregistered land 150
    quantification of
      shares 135–9
    resulting trusts 127–9
    title documents 125–6
    trusts of land
      court powers 144–6
  property adjustment orders
    buying out another's
      share 904
    immediate sale
      and division of
      proceeds 906
    importance 903–4
    outright transfer without
      compensation 904–5
    postponement of
      sale 905–6
    Martin orders 905–6
    Mesher orders 905
    transfer with charge 906
    transfer of share to
      spouse in return for
      compensation 904
  rights on intestacy 971
Family Justice Board
  composition 19

  establishment 19
  local boards 19
  national board 19
Family Justice Review 17–20,
  438, 445, 449, 454, 464,
  474–75, 557
Family Justice Service
  establishment 19
family law
  discrimination 4
  dispute resolution 4
  equalisation of men and
    women 4–5
  Family Court
    proposals 17–19
  family justice system
    Child Arrangements
      Programme 21
    delay 20–1
    Family Court
      proposals 17–19
    Family Court
      system 15–19
    Family Justice Board 19
    jurisdiction 15–17
    managerial
      approach 19–21
    Private Law
      Programme 20
    procedure 20
    Public Law Outline 20
    single Family Court 15,
      18–19
  functions 3–4
  internationalisation 21–9
  judicial discretion 4
  meaning 1–3
  multi-disciplinary
    approaches 14
  non-legal professionals 14
  normative role 3–4
  remedial role 4
  role 3–4
  same sex couples 4
  specialist approaches 14
  status 3
  traditional approach 10
  trends
    adults to children, shift
      from 6
    autonomy 9–10
    cohabitation 6–8
    equalisation of men and
      women 4–5
    legal aid 10–14
    multi-disciplinary
      approaches 14
    private ordering 10–14
    same sex relationships
      8–9

    shift away from fault to
      needs 5–6
    specialist approaches 14
family proceedings courts
  meaning 15
fatal accidents
  adopted children 726
  children, financial support
    for 304
  cohabitation 7, 945
  dependants 367
  financial losses 93–4
fatherhood
  changing nature of
    relationship 308–11
  meaning
    genetic fathers 248–50
    non-genetic fathers 250–6
  presumptions 260–3
  proof
    blood and DNA
      tests 264–9
fault
  see also **conduct**
  dispensing with consent to
    adoption 714
  divorce
    irretrievable
      breakdown 214–15
    reform proposals 231–2
  trends in family law 5–6
financial remedies
  appeals out of time 909
    change in
      circumstances 910
    change in law 910–11
    change in
      valuations 911–12
    reconciliation 910
    remarriage of spouse
      910
  application for orders 831–2
  assessment of provision
    appeals 908–12
    big money cases 889–90
    general principles
      compensation 871–2
      current
        approach 880–2
      fairness 869–74
      needs 870–1
      objective of
        jurisdiction 867–9
      self-sufficiency 876–7
      sharing 873–4
      welfare principle
        874–5
    matrimonial home
      buying out another's
        share 904

immediate sale and
   division of proceeds
   906
importance 903–4
postponement of
   sale 905–6
transfer with
   charge 906
transfer without
   compensation 904–5
relevant factors
age and duration of
   marriage 892–6
conduct 899–903
contributions 896–9
disability 896
earning capacity 886–7
financial
   resources 882–6
income 886–7
loss of benefit 903
needs and
   obligations 888–91
other resources 887–8
standard of
   living 891–2
bars to relief 831–2
civil partnerships 830
consent orders
benefits
disclosure of
   information 849–51
effects of order 853
pre-nuptial
   agreements 853–62
revoking agreement
   before order
   made 851–2
encouraging
   agreement 849
costs allowances 838
court's powers,
   development 828–30
disability 896
dissolution of civil
   partnerships 830
financial provision orders
costs allowances 838
legal services orders 838–9
lump sum
   payments 840–2
maintenance for ongoing
   support 837–8
maintenance pending
   suit 836–9
periodical payments
   children 840
   spouses 839–40
foreign proceedings, after
   applicability 920–1

background 920
interim orders 922–3
jurisdiction 922
orders 923–5
permission 921–3
procedure 921–3
growing importance 826–7
historical background
   828–30
jurisdiction 16
law reform 925–32
legal services orders 838–9
lump sum payments 840–2
maintenance for ongoing
   support 837–8
maintenance pending
   suit 836–9
orders
enforcement
   attempts to defeat
      claim 918–20
   lump sum
      payments 917–18
   periodical payments
      916–17
   statutory charge 863–4
marriage and civil
   partnerships
   compared 865–6
periodical payments
   children 840
   spouses 839–40
procedure
application for
   orders 831–2
disclosure 834–6
dispute resolution
   appointments 833–4
Form A 833
Form E 833
self-help 836
property adjustment orders
pensions
   attachment
      orders 842–3
   overview 842
sale of property 848–9
sharing orders 843–5
transfer and settlement
   of property 845–7
variation of marriage
   settlements 848
reform 925–33
self-help 836
settlement culture 827–8
statutory powers 830–1
variation orders
consent 915–16
relevant factors 914–15
scope 912–14

financial support
   see also financial remedies
adoption 726
child support scheme
   alteration of calculations
      816
   appeals 816
   application for a
      maintenance
      calculation 807–8
   background 800–4
   calculations 810–12
   collection 817–18
   enforcement 818–20
   evaluation of
      effectiveness 823–5
   information
      provision 808–9
   key features of
      scheme 805–20
   non-resident parent 806
   parentage 809–10
   parties 806–8
   person with care 806–7
   qualifying child 806
   residual role of
      courts 820–3
   role of Agency or
      Service 805
   statutory provisions
      805–20
   variation of orders 812–16
cohabitants 775–6
duty to maintain child 775
duty to maintain spouse/civil
   partner 774–5
   agency of necessity 774
jurisdiction to make orders
   children 791–800
   spouses/partners 786–800
maintenance agreements
   parents, between 784–6
   spouses/civil
      partners 779–84
overview 773–4
postponement of
   decree 224–5
refusal of decree 222–4
state benefits
   child benefit 779
   tax allowances and
      credits 776–7
   welfare benefits 777–8
Finer Report 17
forced marriages 51
   protection orders
      applicants 199
      arrest 199
      background 197–8
      effectiveness 200–1

forced marriages (*Cont.*)
  introduction 197–8
  order 198–9
foreign travel
  parental responsibility 355–6
formalities
  civil partnerships 47–55
    registration 60
    under 18's 60
  marriage
    arranged marriages 51
    authorisation to marry 51
    Church of England 51–2
    forced marriage 51
    historical
      background 47–50
    non-Church of England
      marriages 52
    notice 51
    persons under the age of
      18 50–1
    reform 55–6
    solemnisation 52–5
foster parents
  guardianship
    distinguished 294–5
France
  same sex relationships 33
freeing orders *see* **placement
  orders**

gender reassignment
  marriage 41–4
  voidable marriages 83–4
gifts
  between engaged
    couples 109
  between partners
    chattels 114
    loans
      distinguished 116–17
    undue influence 114–15
    voidable transactions
      116–17
  third parties 113–14
  wills
    children 966
    spouses 965–6
guardianship
  acquisition of parental
    responsibility 371,
    389–90, 394
  appointment
    commencement of
      appointment 288–9
    court powers 290–1
    disclaimer 289
    private arrangements
      287–9
    revocation 287–8

carers distinguished 294
consent to adoption 709–11
current law 286–93
evaluation of law 292–3
foster parents
  distinguished 294–5
historical background
  284–5
law reform 285
non-parents in child
  arrangement orders
    distinguished from 294
parents distinguished 293
pre-Children Act 1989
  position 284–5
special guardianship orders
  directions and
    conditions 733–4
  distinguished from
    guardianship 294
  duration 737
  effects 735–6
  policy objectives 730–1
  statutory powers 731–3
  support services 737–9
  variation and
    discharge 736–7
  welfare principle 733
statutory provisions 286
termination
  automatic termination 291
  removal of guardian by
    court 291–2

habitual residence of child
  Brussels II Regulation
    (BIIR) 996–7
  international child
    abduction 1040–5
Hague Conference
  international issues 26–8
harassment
  civil law remedy 195–6
  criminal liability 173–8
  definition 174
  putting in fear of
    violence 176
  stalking
    definition 173
    offences 173, 175–6
  statistics 178
hardship
  postponement of decree 224
  refusal of decree 222–4
High Court
  Family Division 15
  jurisdiction 15
  jurisdiction over children
    inherent jurisdiction
      court powers 763–8

    effect 763
    individuals, use by 771
    local authorities, use
      by 768–71
    procedure 762–3
  overview 741–2
  wardship
    characteristics 743–6
    court powers 751–2
    discretion 748–9
    general principles 752–3
    historical
      background 742–3
    scope 746–8
    uses 753–62
  staff 15
  transfer of jurisdiction 18
home *see* **family home**
homelessness
  intentional
    homelessness 208
  local connection 209
  meaning of
    homelessness 205–7
  priority need 207–8
homosexuality
  see also **civil partnerships;
    same sex relationships**
  adoption 2
  unmarried fathers 2
house-bound persons
  solemnisation of
    marriage 54–5
**housekeeping
  allowances** 111–12
human rights
  see also **right to respect for
    private and family life**
  adoption 684–6
  children's participation in
    decision-making 448
  deportation 104
  direct participation
    of children in
      proceedings 469–70
  discrimination 4
  domestic violence and
    abuse 168–9
  domestic violence protection
    notices 203
  domestic violence protection
    orders 203
  family home 122–3
  immigration rules 103
  local authorities, claims
    against 677–80
  marital rape 96
  parentage 327–8
  right to marry 23,
    35–7

secure accommodation
577–8
welfare principle
exceptions 423–5
paramountcy 415–18
Human Rights Act 1998
basic scheme 24
compatibility
requirements 24
declaration of
invalidity 24–5
enforcement of Convention
rights 25
functions of the Act 24–5
requirements 2
violation of Convention
rights 24

illegitimacy
changing nature of
fatherhood 311
common law position 299–300
declarations of status 303–4
legitimation 302–3
re-labelling 305–7
significance of status 304–5
statutory reform 306–7
void marriages 300–1
voidable marriages 301–2
immigration
consequences of
marriage 101–4
sham marriages 81–2
significance of parentage
citizenship 274
residence in UK 274
status of children 305
improvements to family home
equitable interests 143–4
in vitro fertilisation
meaning 245
non-genetic fatherhood
250–6
income
financial remedies 886–7
investments 110–11
personal property 110–11
savings 110–11
information meeting
divorce 235–7
inhuman or degrading
treatment or punishment
European Convention on
Human Rights 23
injunctions
disputes between
partners 117
domestic violence and abuse
historical background
166–7

inherent jurisdiction
196–7
restraining orders 176–7
insolvency
bankruptcy 159–62
family protection 194–6
mortgages and
charges 158–9
voidable transactions
116–17, 159
inter-sex persons
marriage 41–2
interim orders
care and supervision
alternative s 8 orders 649
court powers 642–3
directions 645–8
duration 649
exclusion requirements
648
final orders
compared 644–5
nature of order 643–4
financial remedies 922–3
maintenance pending
suit 836–9
provision for
dependants 989–90
international child abduction
all ports warnings 1018–19
another part of the UK/Isle
of Man, children taken to
or brought from
enforcement of
orders 1023
Family Law Act
1986 1021–3
generally 1021
jurisdiction 1022–3
recognition of orders 1023
summary return
orders 1021–31
bars to relief 1066–8
central authorities 1032–3
convention countries
aims of international
instruments 1032
central authorities 1032–3
European Custody
Convention 1980
applicability 1083–8,
1084
evaluation of
use 1088–91
recognition and
enforcement 1084–5
refusing recognition or
enforcement 1085–8
evaluation of
effectiveness 1088–91

handling of abduction
applications 1033
implementation of
conventions 1031
relevant international
instruments 1031
strategy of international
instruments 1032
European Custody
Convention 1980
applicability 1083–8
generally 1016–17
habitual residence 1040–5
Hague Convention 1980
access arrangements
1073–83
conflict of laws 1071–81
exercise of discretion
1069–71
residual discretion
1068–9
access rights 1049–50
actual exercise of custody
rights 1051
aims 1034–5
applicability 1039–40
assessment of
convention 1065–6
child, meaning of 1040
custody rights 1046–50
declarations 1052–4
evaluation of use 1088–91
exceptions to duty to
return
acquiescence 1058–61
basic test 1061–2
consent 1056–8
failed applications,
examples of 1062–4
generally 1054
non-exercise of custody
rights 1056
successful applications,
examples of 1064–5
time limits 1054–6
failed applications,
examples of 1062–4
habitual residence
1040–5
human rights
compatibility 1035–7
objections from
child 1066–8
seeking return of
child 1038–9
standing 1054
successful applications,
examples of
1064–4065
undertakings 1066

international child
  abduction (*Cont.*)
    wrongful removal or
      retention 1045–6,
      1051–2
    Hague Convention 1996
      applicable law
        general position 1096
        parental responsibility
        1096–7
      assessment of
        Convention 1099–100
      background 1091–2
      child, meaning of 1092
      co-operation 1098–9
      jurisdictional
        rules 1093–6
      protection, meaning
        of 1092–3
      recognition and
        enforcement 1097–8
      scope 1092–3
    jurisdiction 16
    non-Convention countries
      abduction of children
        from non-Convention
        State 1024–31
      abduction of children
        to non-Convention
        State 1024
    prevention of abduction
      from the UK
      all ports warnings
        1018–19
      court prohibition against
        removal 1019–21
      criminal sanctions
      all ports
        warnings 1018–19
      Child Abduction Act
        1984 1018
      generally 1017–18
    statistics 1016–17
    time limits 1054–6
international issues
  see also **Brussels II**
    Regulation (BIIR);
    European Convention
    on Human Rights;
    international child
    abduction
  adoption
    domestic adoptions of
      foreign children 1014
    Hague Convention on
      Intercountry Adoption
      1993 1009–12
    overseas
      adoptions 1012–14
    overview 1008–9

removing a child from
  the British Islands for
  adoption 1015
restrictions on brining
  children into UK for
  adoption 1014–15
Brussels Regulation 28–9
Council of Europe 26
European Union 28–9
financial remedies
  applicability 920–1
  background 920
  interim orders 922–3
  jurisdiction 922
  orders 923–5
  permission 921–3
  procedure 921–3
growing importance of
  international law 21–2
Hague Conference 26–8
internationalisation 21–9
norm-setting 21–2
parentage 325–9
parental responsibility
  330–1
participation of children in
  decision-making 448–51
sources of conventions
  Brussels Regulation 28–9
  Council of Europe 26
  European Union 28–9
  Hague Conference 26–8
  overview 25
  United Nations Convention
    on the Rights of the
    Child 22–3
  Universal Declaration of
    Human Rights 21
intestacy
  children 972–3
  cohabitants 973–4
  other family members 973
  statutory provisions 967–8
  surviving spouses 968–72
investments
  income 110–11

Jewish marriages
  religious divorce 225
  solemnisation of
    marriage 53
joint residence orders *see*
  shared residence orders
judicial review
  nature of remedy 669–70
  requirements 670–1
  scope 671–3
judicial separation
  advantages 242
  basis 242

divorce *a mensa et thoro* 241
effect of decree 242
historical background 241–2
jurisdiction 16
rights on intestacy 971–2
uses 242
judiciary
  managerial approach 19–20
jurisdiction
  adoption 16, 682
  appointment of
    guardians 287–91
  Brussels II Regulation (BIIR)
    cross-border access 997
    exceptions to the basic
      rule 997–8
    generally 16
    habitual residence of
      child 996–7
    internationally displaced
      children 1000
    no Member State
      has jurisdiction,
      where 1000
    prorogation of
      jurisdiction 998–1000
    refugees 1000
    relocation of child 997
    second seised, where
      court 1003
    transferring
      jurisdiction 1000–2
    urgent cases 1002–3
    wrongful removal of
      child 997–8
  care and supervision
    proceedings 596
  children 16
  civil partnerships 16
  county courts 15
  disputes between
    partners 117–18
  dissolution of civil
    partnerships 241
  divorce 16
    Act of Parliament 212
    full divorce by judicial
      process 212
  domestic violence and abuse
    injunctions
    inherent jurisdiction
      196–7
  domestic violence
    applications 16
  family assistance
    orders 547–8
  Family Court 17–18
  family court system 15–16
  Family Division 15
  female parenthood 256–7

financial remedies 16
financial remedies foreign
  proceedings, after 922
High Court 15
High Court powers in
  respect of children
  inherent jurisdiction
    court powers 763–8
    individuals, use by 771
    local authorities, use
      by 768–71
    procedure 762–3
  overview 741–2
  wardship
    applicants 749
    characteristics 743–6
    court powers 751–2
    general principles 752–3
    procedure 748–9
    respondents 749–50
    scope 746–8
    uses 752–3
international child
  abduction 16
  convention
    countries 1071–81
judicial separation 16
magistrates' courts 15–16
medical treatment of
  children 353–4
nullity 16
orders for financial support
  children 791–800
  spouses/partners 786–800
ownership of family
  home 124–5
public law 16
section 8 orders
  any child 536–7
  applications on court's
    own motion 536–7
  family proceedings 535–6
transfer of
  proceedings 16–17

law reform
  adoption placement 698–9
  children's orders 479–80
  cohabitation
    assessment of
      proposals 957–8
    Law Commission 952–7
    separation 951
  discipline of children 345–7
  divorce
    Booth Committee 230–1
    future reform 238–40
    government
      response 233–4
    Law Commission 231–4

divorce reform 107–8
domestic violence and abuse
  Government
    strategy 167–8
  family home 162–3
  financial remedies 925–33
  guardianship 285
  married women's
    property 106–8
  parentage 259
  property consequences of
    marriage 119–21
  status of children 305–7
legal aid
  domestic violence 13
  LASPO (Legal Aid,
    Sentencing and
    Punishment of Offenders
    Act 2012) 13, 210, 838, 863
  mediation 12–13
  withdrawal 12–14
legal representation
  children's guardians
    appointment 460–1
    discharge of duties
      462–4
    duties 461–2, 464–2
    family court reporters
      distinguished 459–60
    parental responsibility
      358–9
legal services orders
  financial orders 838–9
legitimacy
  changing nature of
    fatherhood 308–11
  common law
    position 299–300
  declarations of status 303–4
  legitimation 302–3
  re-labelling 305–7
  revocation of
    adoption 722–3
  second female parent,
    children with 302
  significance of status 304–5
  statutory reform 306–7
  void marriages 300–1
  voidable marriages 301–2
licences
  to occupy
    contractual
      licences 156–7
    licences by estoppel 157
litigation friends
  parental responsibility 359
  procedure 471–2
local authorities
  acquisition of parental
    responsibility 390

care and supervision
  assessment of
    provisions 680–1
  contact arrangements
    court orders 657–9
    historical background
      654–5
    importance 654
    other interested
      parties 656–7
    presumption of
      reasonable
        contact 655–6
    refusal of contact 656
  delay 628–9
  disputing decisions
    Commissioner for Local
      Administration 666
    complaints procedure
      663–5
    human rights claims
      677–80
    judicial review 669–73
    negligence
      claims 673–6
    overview 662–3
    wardship 667–8
  initiation of
    proceedings 596
  'looked after
    children' 660–2
  orders
    appeals 650–1
    care orders 636–42
    discharge 651–3
    interim orders 642–9
    section 8 orders 631–2
    supervision
      orders 632–6
    welfare
      principle 629–31
  overview 594–5
  parties 596
  protocol 628–9
  threshold criteria
    attributable to care
      given 613–19
    burden of proof 598–9
    likely to suffer 608–13
    mixed pool
      dilemma 622–5
    overview 599–600
    rationale 597–8
    significant harm 600–8
    standard of
      proof 598–9
    statutory
      provisions 597–8
  welfare principle
    future plans 627–8

local authorities (*Cont.*)
    past events 626–7
    statutory provisions 625–6
  child protection
    basic dilemmas 552–3
    development of
      powers 553–7
    good social work
      practice 559
    High Court powers in
      respect of children
      use of inherent
        jurisdiction 768–71
    investigation of child abuse
      co-operation with other
        agencies 580–2
      requirement 579–80
    key legal principles 557–9
    maintenance of links
      between child and his
      family 558
    non-intervention
      principle 557
    partnerships with
      parents 557–8
    pre-1989 developments
      553–5
    role of courts 553
  directions under s 37 550–1
  emergency protection orders
    additional directions 587
    denial of access to the
      child 584–6
    duration 588
    effects of order 586–7
    exclusion
      requirements 587–8
    grounds 584–6
    likely to suffer harm 584
    police protection 592–3
    procedure 586
    purpose 583–4
    use 589
  restrictions on s 8
    orders 511–13
  secure accommodation
    appeals 577
    basic scheme 573
    court orders 575–7
    criteria 574–5
    historical background 572–3
    human rights compliance
      577–8
    meaning 573
    persons subject to secure
      accommodation 574
  short-term child protection
    child assessment orders
      application 590–1
      criteria 590–1

    effects 591
    use 592
  special guardianship
    orders 732–3
  special guardianship support
    services 737–9
  support for children and
    families
    accommodation of
      children in need
      agreements 569–70
      appeals against
        refusal 570–1
      background 564
      discretionary
        powers 567
      duty to accommodate
        564–7
      effect of being
        accommodated 571
      limitations 568–9
      operation in
        practice 571
      wishes of the
        child 567–8
    background 559–60
    duty towards children
      in need
      advice on upbringing 562
      day care 563
      discharge of duty 561
      general duty 560–2
      identification of
        children in need 562
      in need, meaning of
        560–1
      prevention of
        abuse 562–3
      provision of third party
        accommodation 563
      racial groups 563
      statutory provisions
        560–2
      types of services
        provided 561–2
looked after children
  adoption 688–90
  care and supervision 660–2
  child abuse 660–2
lump sum payments
  enforcement 917–18
  pensions
    attachment orders 842–3
    overview 842
    sharing orders 843–5
  provision for
    dependants 990–1

magistrates' courts
  district judges 15

  jurisdiction 15–16
  justices' clerk 15
  lay magistrates 15
  magistrates 15
  maintenance orders
    spouses/partners 786–800
  transfer of proceedings 18
maintenance
  agreements
    parents, between 784–6
    separation 780
    spouses/civil
      partners 779–84
  cohabitants 775–6
  duty to maintain child 775
  duty to maintain spouse/civil
    partner 774–5
  family based arrangements
    775, 803, 823
maintenance for ongoing
support
  financial provision
    orders 837–8
maintenance pending suit
  financial remedies 836–9
marital coercion
  criminal offences by married
    woman 100–1
marital property
  agreement 927–9
  autonomy 10
  financial remedies 38, 932
  inheritance 993
  needs 930
  qualifying nuptial
    agreements 928–9
  use 949–50
marriage
  see also **annulment; civil**
    partnerships; void
    marriages; voidable
    marriages
  acquisition of parental
    responsibility 368–9
  affinity 45–7
  age 44–5
  agreements to marry
    breach of promise 39
    civil partnership
      agreements 40
    engagement 39
    generally 39–40
    meaning 39
    proof of engagement 40
  approved premises 54
  arranged marriages 51
  capacity
    age 44–5
    conditions 40–1
    gender reassignment 41–4

inter-sex persons 41–2
prohibited degrees 45–7
sex 41–4
transsexuals 41–4
Church of England 51–2
'common law marriage' 56
conditions of marriage
38–9
consanguinity 45–6
consortium 92–4
contract, as 37
contractual nature 37
conversion of civil
partnership 61
current debates 30
declaration as to marital
status 62–3
decline in marriage 31
definition 38–9
diversity and 30–1
doctrine of unity 90–2
engagements 39
family 2
financial support
duty to maintain child 775
duty to maintain
spouse 774–5
jurisdiction to make
orders
children 784–5,
791–800
spouses/partners
786–800
spouses 779–84
forced marriage 51
formalities
arranged marriages 51
authorisation to marry 51
Church of England 51–2
forced marriage 51
non-Church of England
marriages 52
notice 51
persons under the age of
18 50–1
reform 55–6
sham marriages 55
solemnisation 52–5
gender reassignment 41–4
historical background 30–1
inter-sex persons 41–2
life, for 38
monogamy 38, 47
nature of marriage
contractual nature 37
status 37–8
non-Church of England
marriages 52
normative role of family
law 3–4

personal consequences
citizenship 101–4
consortium 92–4
contractual obligations
between the parties
98–9
third parties 98–9
criminal liability 100–1
doctrine of unity 90–2
legal testimony 96–8
overview 89–90
same sex marriages 89–90
sexual intercourse 95–6
tortious liability 99–100
use of surname 94–5
polygamous marriages 30
preliminaries 50-2
presumption of
marriage 56–8
prohibited degrees 45–7
property consequences
disputes between
partners 117–19
disputes with strangers
119
history and background
104–8
law reform 119–21
overview 89–90
property acquired by
partners 108–14
transactions between
partners 114–17
provision for dependants
relevant factors 986–7
who may apply 977–8
transactions between
partners
reasonable provision
983
remarriage
divorcees 30
revocation of wills 962–3
right to marry 23, 35–7
same sex relationships 4, 9,
33–4, 50
sham marriages 55
solemnisation
Church of England 52
civil marriages 53–4
detained persons 54–5
house-bound
persons 54–5
Jewish marriages 53
other religious rites 52
Quaker marriages 53
registered buildings 53
state control 30–1
statistics 31, 89
status, creating 37–8, 89–90

third persons, effect on 38
transsexuals 41–2
unity, doctrine of 90–2
validity
declaration as to marital
status 62–3
variation of marriage
settlements 848
voluntariness 38
Martin orders 905–6
mediation
attendance 12–13
legal aid 12–13
mediation information
and assessment
meeting 12
mediation information and
assessment meeting 12
medical treatment
parental
responsibility 350–4
mental disorder
voidable marriages 82
Mesher orders 905
MIAM (mediation
information and
assessment meeting) 12
monogamy
marriage 38, 47
mortgages
insolvency 158–9
statutory charge 863–4
transfer of matrimonial
home 906
motherhood
changing nature of
relationship 311–12
female parenthood 256–7
meaning 246–8
proof 260
mutual wills
succession 964–5

names
adoption 703–4, 726
child arrangements
orders 520–5
cohabitation 94–5
parental responsibility
356–9
rights to use 94–5
special guardianship
orders 734
needs
assessment of financial
remedies 888–91
move towards focus on
5–6
provision for dependants
984–8

New Zealand
    Family Court 17
no order principle
    adoption 696
non-molestation
    orders
    arrest powers 192–5
    breach as criminal
        offence 192–3
    criteria 182–3
    historical background 166
    limitations on inherent
        jurisdiction 764
    procedure 182
    standing to apply 180–2
    statutory remedy 179–83
    terms 183
    undertakings 195
Norgrove Review see Family
    Justice Review
nullity *see* annulment

occupation orders
    arrest powers 192–5
    balance of harm test
        185–6
    criteria
        entitled applicants 183–7
        non-entitled applicants
            188–90
    discretionary test 186
    duration 187, 190
    standing to apply
        entitled applicants 183–7
        non-entitled
            applicants 187–8
    terms 188
    types of order 184–5
    undertakings 195
occupation rights
    contractual licences 156–7
    home rights
        background 152–3
        defined 153–5
        duration 155–6
        effect 154–5
        registration 155
        scope 152
    licences by estoppel 157
    third parties 157–8
old age
    statistics 2
ombudsmen
    complaints about children in
        care 666
orders
    see also adoption orders;
        child arrangements
        orders; financial
        remedies; orders in family

proceedings; prohibited
    steps orders; specific issue
    orders
care and supervision
    appeals 650–1
    care orders 636–42
    discharge 651–3
    interim orders 642–9
    section 8 orders 631–2
    supervision orders 632–6
    welfare principle 629–31
child support scheme 820–3
children
    application of welfare
        principle
        physical, emotional
            and educational
            needs 403–8
        relevant characteristics
            of child 410–14
        risk of harm 412–13
    change in circumstances
        409–10
    parental responsibility
        373–86
    residency 379–86
    special guardianship
        directions and
            conditions 733–435
        duration 737
        effects 735–6
        policy objectives 730–1
        statutory powers 731–3
        support services 737–9
        variation and
            discharge 736–7
        welfare principle 733
financial provision orders
    legal services orders
        838–9
    lump sum payments
        840–2
    maintenance pending
        suit 836–9
    periodical payments
        children 840
        spouses 839–40
financial remedies
    by consent
        disclosure of
            information 849–51
        effects of order 853
        pre-nuptial
            agreements 853–62
        revoking agreement
            before order
            made 851–2
    enforcement
        attempts to defeat
            claim 918–20

lump sum payments
    917–18
periodical
    payments 916–17
foreign proceedings,
    after 923–5
limitations on court
    powers 864–5
marriage and civil
    partnerships
    compared 865–6
statutory charge 863–4
jurisdiction for financial
    support
    children 791–800
    spouses/partners 786–800
local authorities
    child assessment orders
        application 590–1
        criteria 590–1
        effects 591
        use 592
    emergency protection
        orders
        additional directions
            587
        denial of access to the
            child 584–6
        duration 588
        effects of order 586–7
        exclusion
            requirements 587–8
        grounds 584–6
        likely to suffer
            harm 584
        procedure 586
        purpose 583–4
        use 589
    secure accommodation
        575–7
ouster orders
    historical background
        166–7
    limitations on inherent
        jurisdiction 764
property adjustment orders
    pensions
        attachment
            orders 842–3
        overview 842
        sharing orders 843–5
    sale of property 848–9
    transfer and settlement of
        property 845–7
    variation of marriage
        settlements 848
provision for dependants
    final orders 990–3
    interim orders
        989–90

relationship to other
  agreements and
  orders 993
wardship 751–2
welfare principle
  burden of proof 440
  form 443
  scope 439–40
  statutory provisions
    438–9
orders in family proceedings
  see also **child arrangements
    orders; prohibited steps
    orders; specific issue
    orders**
  activity conditions 497–8
  activity directions 496–7
  appeals against s 8
    orders 543–6
  application of welfare
    principle
    statutory checklist 401–8
  Children and Adoption Act
    2006 480–1
  Children and Families Act
    2014 4810–485
  enforcement of s 8 orders
    compensation for family
      loss 542–3
    contempt of court 538–40
    enforcement orders 541–2
    handing over of
      children 538
    warning notices 540–1
    enforcement orders 541–2
  family assistance
    orders 546–50
  general restrictions
    child applicants 513
    children in local authority
      care 510–11
    children over 16 510
    local authorities 511–13
  jurisdiction under s 8
    any child 536–7
    applications on court's
      own motion 537
    family proceedings 535–6
  local authority care or
    supervision 550–1
  overview 479–80
  persons entitled to apply
    child applicants 520
    criteria for leave 515–19
    with leave 515
    without leave 513–15
  prohibited steps
    orders 498–500
  removal from UK 525–35
  restrictions on further

applications without
  leave 508–9
section 8 orders
  see also **child
    arrangements orders;
    prohibited steps orders;
    specific issue orders**
  additional directions and
    conditions 504–8
  discharge 543
  prohibited steps
    orders 498–500
  specific issue
    orders 500–1
  variation 543
ouster orders
  historical background 166–7
  limitations on inherent
    jurisdiction 764
overriding interests
  protection of beneficial
    interests 147–50
overseas adoptions 1012–14

paramountcy principle *see*
  welfare principle
parentage
  adoption, effect of 722–3
  assisted reproduction 245–6
  birth certificates 271–2
  breaking exclusivity of
    genetic link 257–8
  changing nature of
    relationships
    development of welfare
      principle 312–18
    fatherhood 308–11
    international law 325–9
    motherhood 311–12
    overview 307–8
    self-decision making 318–25
  child support scheme,
    liability under 809–10
  common law 244
  comparative law 269–70
  declarations 270–1
  fatherhood
    genetic fathers 248–50
    non-genetic fathers 250–6
  guardianship
    distinguished 293
  law reform 259
  legal parentage 244–5
  motherhood 246–8
  proof
    fatherhood
      blood and DNA
        tests 264–9
      presumptions 260–3
    motherhood 260

right to know 272–3
significance
  citizenship 274
  residence in UK 274
status of children
  declarations 303–4
  legitimacy 299–303
  re-labelling of
    illegitimacy 305–7
  significance 304–5
  statutory reform 306–7
parental orders
  applicants 278
  assessment of law 282–4
  conditions 278–80
  determination of
    applications 280–1
  effect 277, 281–2
  governing principles 280–1
  standing 278
  surrogacy 276–84
  uses 282
parental responsibility
  acquisition after
    birth 368–85
    step-parents 385–9
    third parties 389–90, 394
  adoption
    compared 684
    consent 709
    legal effect 703–4
  age of child 337
  agreement of the parties 336
  care orders 638
  carers without legal
    responsibility 395
  child arrangements
    orders 379–80, 389–90, 520
  civil partners 369
  contractual liability 363–4
  criminal liability
    child's crimes 364–5
    interference with
      rights 366
  definitions 333–6
  delegation 395
  duration 391–2
  female spouses 369
  guardianship 286
  international acceptance
    of concept 330–1
  ongoing relationship with
    both parents, importance
    of 432–5
  prohibited steps
    orders 498–500
  relevance 331–3
  scope
    administration of
      property 360

parental responsibility (*Cont.*)
    bringing-up of child 338–9
    contact with child 339–40
    criminal liability 341–2
    discipline 344–7
    disposal of corpse 359–60
    domestic services 360
    education 347–50
    information about
      child 361–3
    legal representation 358–9
    medical treatment 350–4
    names 356–9
    passports 354–5
    protection 340–4
    religious upbringing
      350
    responsibility 337
    tortious liability 342–4
  section 8 orders
    additional directions and
      conditions 504–8
    limits on jurisdiction
      501–4
    prohibited steps
      orders 498–500
    specific issue
      orders 500–1
  shared obligations 392–4
  terminology 330
  tortious liability
    child's wrongful acts
      364
    interference with
      rights 366–7
    unborn children 391
  unmarried mothers and
    fathers 369
  unmarried mothers and
    female partners 369
  gender change 369
passports
  parental responsibility
    355–6
pensions
  adoption 726
  attachment orders 842–3
  property adjustment orders
    overview 842
    sharing orders 843–5
period for reflection and
  consideration
  divorce 237–8
periodical payments
  children 840
  enforcement 916–17
  provision for
    dependants 990
  spouses 839–40

perjury
  void marriages 71
permission
  applications for section 8
    orders
    criteria for leave 515–19
    persons entitled to apply
      with leave 515
    persons entitled to apply
      without leave 513–15
    successive applications
      508–9
  financial remedies
    foreign proceedings,
      after 921–3
  inherent jurisdiction local
    authorities 768–71
personal property
  gifts between partners 114
  gifts of chattels 115–16
  historical overview 105
  income and investments
    110–11
  law reform 119–21
  presumption of
    ownership 108, 112–13
  statutory reform 106–8
police protection
  child protection 592–3
polygamous marriages
  recognition 30
post-nuptial agreements
  see also **marital property**
    agreements
  financial remedies 853–62
  financial support 780
pre-nuptial agreements
  financial remedies 853–62
  financial support 780
  traditional approach 10
pregnancy
  voidable marriage where
    pregnancy by another 83
presumptions
  advancement 110–11
  challenging presumption of
    marriage 56–8
  contact with children in
    care 655–6
  death 959–60
  fatherhood 260–3
  loans between
    partners 116–17
  marriage 56-8
  parentage 251
  resulting trusts 127
  undue influence 114–15
prisoners
  right to marry 54–5

privacy
  care and supervision
    information about
      children 361–3
  welfare principle 423–5
private ordering
  child support 803
  encouragement to use 804
  family based
    arrangements 803
  maintenance agreements 781
  'settlement culture' 10
  withdrawal of legal aid 10–14
privileged communications
  self-incrimination 835–6
procedure
  adoption orders
    settling in period 718–19
  appeals
    section 8 orders 543–4
  care and supervision
    protocol 628–9
  children as litigants 471–2
  complaints about children in
    care 664–5
  dissolution of civil
    partnerships 241
  divorce
    decrees 226–9, 228–9
    reform proposals 233–4
    special procedure 226–8
    statutory reform 234–8
  emergency protection
    orders 586
  exceptions to welfare
    principle 425–7
  Family Procedure Rules
    overriding objective 20
  financial remedies
    application for
      orders 831–2
    disclosure 834–6
    dispute resolution
      appointments 833–4
    foreign proceedings,
      after 921–3
    proceeds of crime 835–6
    self-help 836
  non-molestation orders 182
  special guardianship
    orders 731–3
  streamlining 20
proceeds of crime
  financial remedies 835–6
prohibited degrees of
  marriage
  adoption 726
  affinity 45–7
  consanguinity 45–6

prohibited steps orders
applicants 499–500
disguised child arrangement
orders 503
examples of use 499
inherent jurisdiction of High
Court 503–4
limits on courts' powers to
make order 501–4
limits on jurisdiction 501–4
meaning 498–9
parental responsibility
501–2
persons against whom order
may be made 499–500
publicity 502
removal of parent from
family home 502
uses 499
property
see also **property adjustment
orders**
adoption 727
consequences of relationship
disputes between
partners 117–19
disputes with
strangers 119
history and
background 104–8
law reform 119–21
property acquired by
partners 108–14
transactions between
partners 114–17
family home
insolvency 158–62
occupation 151–8
overview 122–3
ownership 122–51
title documents 125–6
property adjustment orders
matrimonial home
transfer with charge 906
buying out another's
share 904
immediate sale
and division of
proceeds 906
importance 903–4
transfer of tenancy 907–8
pensions 842–5
postponement of sale
Martin orders 905–6
Mesher orders 905
provision for
dependants 991
sale of property 848–9
statutory powers 830

transfer and settlement
orders 845–7
transfer without
compensation 904–5
variation of marriage
settlements 848
proprietary estoppel
ownership of family home
common intention
constructive trusts
129–34
constructive trusts
139–40
detrimental reliance 141–2
quantification 142
representation 140–1
quantification of
shares 139–44
provision for dependants
adoption 726
available property 989
cohabitation 7, 987–8
orders
final orders 990–3
interim orders 989–90
relationship to other
agreements and
orders 992–3
persons maintained by
deceased immediately
before death 980–2
reasonable provision 983
relevant factors 984–8
statutory provisions 974–7
public funding
statutory charge 863–4
public law
Children Act cases 20
jurisdiction 16
time limits 20
public law proceedings
children's guardians 464
direct participation of
children 448, 470
public policy
cohabitation 7
void marriages 71
publicity
prohibited steps orders 502
specific issue orders 502

Quaker marriages
solemnisation of
marriage 53

rape
marriage, within 96
reconciliation
appeals out of time 910

civil partnerships 241
divorce 229–30
reform *see* **law reform**
refugees
Brussels II Regulation
(BIIR) 1000
register offices
marriage 53–4
registered buildings
solemnisation of
marriage 53
registration
adoption orders
Adopted Children
Register 721–2
Adoption Contact
Register 722
birth certificates
acquisition of parental
responsibility 371
proof of parentage 271–2
home rights 155
**religious upbringing of
children**
parental responsibility 350
remarriage
divorcees 30
statistics 31
removal of children from UK
see also **child abduction;
international child
abduction**
child arrangements orders
external relocation
525–35
internal relocations
compared 535
removals for less than one
month 526
removals for more than
one month 526–35
special guardianship
orders 734
repossession
remedies for domestic
violence and abuse 204
residence orders *see* **child
arrangements orders**
resolution
code of practice 12
restraining orders 176–7
resulting trusts
establishing a beneficial
interest 127–9
quantification of shares
135
revocation of wills
divorce 963–4
marriage 962–3

right to liberty and security
European Convention on
Human Rights 23
right to marry
prisoners 54–5
role 23
**right to respect for private and
family life**
family
cohabitation 1
fathers 1
meaning 1–2
mother and child 1
spouses 1–2
meaning of family 1–2
role 23
unmarried fathers 1–2
Rosset tests 130–4

sale of property orders
financial remedies 848–9
matrimonial home
immediate sale
and division of
proceeds 906
Martin orders 905–6
Mesher orders 905
same sex relationships
see also **civil partnerships**
adoption rights 705
consent by religious
authority 72–3
discrimination 4
family law 4
France 33
greater recognition 8–9
marriage
background to legislation
9, 33–4
consent by religious
authority 72–3
Marriage (Same Sex
Couples) Act 2013
33–4, 41
religious ceremonies
59
religious objections 50
right to marry 36–7
void marriages 72–3
tenanted property 9
trends in family law 8–9
savings
income 110–11
secure accommodation
appeals 577
basic scheme 573
court orders 575–7
criteria 574–5
historical background
572–3

human rights
compliance 577–8
meaning 573
persons subject to secure
accommodation 574
self-help
financial remedies 836
sentencing
domestic violence and
abuse 172–3
separation
agreement 780
civil partnerships 243
cohabitation
contracts 948–50
knowledge of legal
position 947–8
legal provision 945–51
property
arrangements 946–7
transfer of
tenancies 950–1
grounds for divorce
five years' separation 221
reform proposals 231–2
two years' separation and
consent 219–20
judicial separation
basis 242
effect of decree 242
historical
background 241–2
uses 242
rights on intestacy 971–2
settlements *see also*
agreements; maintenance
encouragement 13–14
legal aid 10–14
private ordering 10–14
'settlement culture' 10
variation of marriage
settlements 848
sexual intercourse
see also **consummation of
marriage**
within marriage 95–6
sham marriages
consent 81
immigration law 81–2
meaning 55, 81
voidable marriages 81–2
short marriages
financial remedies 892–4
siblings
paramountcy of welfare
principle 428–30
social security benefits *see*
welfare benefits
solemnisation of marriage
approved premises 54

Church of England 52
civil marriages 53–4
detained persons 54–5
house-bound persons 54–5
Jewish marriages 53
other religious rites 52
Quaker marriages 53
registered buildings 53
special guardianship orders
directions and
conditions 733–5
duration 737
effects 735–6
guardianship
distinguished 294
policy objectives 730–1
statutory powers 731–3
support services 737–9
variation and
discharge 736–7
welfare principle 733
specific issue orders
disguised child arrangements
orders 503
examples of use 500–1
inherent jurisdiction of High
Court 503–4
limits on courts' powers to
make order 501–4
limits on jurisdiction 501–4
meaning 500
parental responsibility 501–2
publicity 502
sperm donation
licensed clinics 249–50
meaning 249–50
non-genetic fatherhood
251–6
posthumous use of
sperm 250
stalking *see* **harassment**
standing
care and supervision
proceedings 596
complaints about children in
care 663–5
forced marriage protection
order 199
Hague Convention
1980 1054
non-molestation
orders 180–2
occupation orders
entitled applicants 183–7
non-entitled
applicants 187–8
parental orders 278
provision for
dependants 976–83
wardship 748–9

state benefits *see* welfare
  benefits
statement of marital
  breakdown 236–7
status
  adoption
    citizenship 725
    financial support 726
    insurance 727
    peerages and titles 725
    pensions 726
    prohibited degrees of
      marriage 726
    property 727
    provision for
      dependants 726
    statutory provisions
      725
    surname 726
  alteration 3
  children
    declarations 303–4
    direct participation in
      proceedings 465–70
    legitimacy 299–303
    re-labelling of
      illegitimacy 305–7
    significance 304–5
    statutory reform 306–7
  definition 3
  family law 3
  marriage 37–8
statutory charges
  legal aid charge 863–4
step-parents
  acquisition of parental
    responsibility 385–9
  adoption 707–8
succession
  intestacy
    children 972–3
    cohabitants 973–4
    other family members 973
    statutory
      provisions 967–8
    surviving spouses 968–72
  mutual wills 964–5
  overview of law 960–1
  revocation of wills
    divorce 963–4
  testamentary gifts
    children 966
    spouses 965–6
  testate succession 961–6
supervision orders
  care orders compared
    634–5
  care and supervision
    proceedings 632–6
  discharge 653

  duration 633
  nature of orders 632–3
  no order as alternative 635
  purpose 632–3
  requirements imposed under
    order 633–4
  use 635–6
surnames
  adoption 703–4, 726
  child arrangements
    orders 520–5
  cohabitation 94–5
  parental
    responsibility 356–9
  rights to use 94–5
  special guardianship
    orders 734
surrogacy
  agreements 274–7
  defined 246
  disputes 276–7
  meaning 274–5
  offences 275–6
  parental orders 276–84

tenanted property
  cohabitation 7
  property adjustment
    orders 907–8
  remedies for domestic
    violence and abuse
    eviction 204
    termination of
      tenancy 204–5
    transfer of tenancy 203–4
  same sex relationships 9
theft
  spouses 101
time limits
  dissolution of civil
    partnerships 240
  divorce 214
  international child
    abduction and return of
    child 1054–6
  public law 20
titles of honour 304–5
  adoption, effect of 725
transfer of property
  orders 845–7
transfer of tenancies
  cohabitation 950–1
  financial remedies 907
  remedy for domestic violence
    and abuse 203–4
transsexuals
  marriage 41–4
trusts
  trusts of land
    court powers 144–6

unborn children
  parental responsibility
    391
undertakings
  domestic violence and
    abuse 195
undue influence 114–15
United Nations
  parentage 325–7
  participation of children in
    decision-making 448–51
  welfare principle 418–19
United Nations Convention on
  the Rights of the Child 22–3
United States
  Family Court 17
unity doctrine
  citizenship 101–2
  criminal liability 100–1
  generally 90–2
Universal Declaration of
  Human Rights
  protection for the family
    21
unmarried fathers
  acquisition of parental
    responsibility 369
  cohabitation 2
  consent to adoption 711
  homosexuality 2
  right to respect for private
    and family life 1–2
  rights of children on
    intestacy 972–3
  trans-gender 2
unsoundness of mind
  voidable marriages 79–81

validity of marriage *see*
  annulment; void marriages;
  voidable marriages
variation orders
  child support scheme 812–16
  contact with children in
    care 659–60
  financial remedies
    consent 915–16
    relevant factors 914–15
    scope 912–14
  maintenance agreements
    children 783–4
    partners 781–4
  marriage settlements 848
  provision for
    dependants 991–2
  section 8 orders 543
  special guardianship
    orders 736–7
venereal disease
  voidable marriages 83

void marriages
  formal defects
    defects which may
      invalidate a marriage
      72–3
    defects which will
      never invalidate a
      marriage 72
    failure to comply
      with Marriage Act
      provisions 72
    grounds for void
      marriage 71–3
    law of the place where
      the ceremony was
      performed 71
    perjury 71
    public policy 71
    reform proposals 73
    same sex couples 72–3
    technical defects 71
  grounds
    capacity 71
    formalities 71–3
    generally 70–1
    law of the place where
      the ceremony was
      performed 71
    reform proposals 73
    same sex couples 72–3
    technical defects 71
  perjury 71
  public policy 71
  reform proposals 73
  relevance of current law 86
  status of children 300–1
  technical defects 71
voidable marriages
  bars to relief
    lapse of time 85
    petitioner's conduct
      84–5
    petitioner's knowledge 85
  duress 76–9
  effects of decree 85–6
  gender reassignment 83–4
  generally 73
  lack of consent
    duress 76–9
    overview 76
    sham marriages 81–2
    unsoundness of
      mind 79–81
  mental disorder 82
  pregnancy by another 83
  relevance of current law 86
  sham marriages 81–2
  status of children 301–2
  unconsummated marriage
    background 73–4

    canon law 73
    grounds 73–6
    inability to
      consummate 75
    meaning of
      consummation 74–5
    same sex marriages 74
    wilful refusal to
      consummate 75–6
  unsoundness of mind 79–81
  venereal disease 83

wardship
  characteristics
    control vested in
      court 743–5
    special nature 745–6
  court powers 751–2
  general principles 752–3
  historical background 742–3
  local authority disputes 668
  procedure
    applicants 749
    parties 749–50
    respondents 749–50
  scope
    children in
      jurisdiction 746–8
    minors 746
  uses
    assessment of use 772
    current use 755–62
    post-1989 754–5
    pre-1989 753–4
warning notices
  enforcement of s 8
    orders 540–1
welfare benefits
  child benefit 779
  cohabitation 7
    treatment of cohabiting
      couples 947
    scope 777–8
welfare principle
  adoption 694–6
  application
    capability of
      parents 413–14
    change in circumstances
      409–10
    physical, emotional
      and educational
      needs 403–8
    relevant characteristics
      of child 410–14
    risk of harm 412–13
    statutory checklist 401–8
  assessment of financial
    remedies 874–5
  capability of parents 413–14

care and supervision
  future plans 627–8
  making of orders 629–31
  past events 626–7
  statutory provisions
    625–6
consent to adoption 715–17
criteria for leave to apply
  under s 8 515–19
critical analysis 430–2
delay 436–8
development 312–18
meaning of welfare
  application of
    checklist 401–3
  case law 398–9
  statutory checklist
    401–4703
ongoing relationship with
  both parents, importance
  of 432–5
orders
  capability of parents
    413–14
  change in circumstances
    409–10
  physical, emotional
    and educational
    needs 403–8
  relevant characteristics of
    child 410–14
  risk of harm 412–13
orders only when
  appropriate
    application of principle
      440–3
    burden of proof 440
    form 443
    interrelationship
      with paramount
      principle 443–4
    scope 439–40
    statutory
      provisions 438–9
paramountcy principle
  appeals 426–7
  historical
    background 397–8
  human rights
    compliance 415–18
  interrelationship no order
    principle 443–4
  meaning of paramount
    414–15
  UN Convention
    compared 418–19
  when applicable 401–3,
    419–20
  when not applicable
    day-to-day life 421

indirect concerns with upbringing 422–6
statutory provisions 427–8
physical, emotional and educational needs 410–14
relevant characteristics of child 410–14
risk of harm 412–13

special guardianship orders 733
wardship 752–3
welfare reports
applicability 456–7
content 457–8
disclosure 457–8
form 457–8
form of order 457
statutory powers 455–6

wills
mutual wills 964–5
revocation
divorce 963–4
marriage 962–3
testamentary gifts
children 966
spouses 965–6

Youth courts 15